P9-AEU-960

A DICTIONARY OF MODERN LEGAL USAGE

A DICTIONARY OF MODERN LEGAL USAGE

SECOND EDITION

Bryan A. Garner

New York Oxford
OXFORD UNIVERSITY PRESS
1995

OXFORD UNIVERSITY PRESS

Oxford New York
Athens Auckland Bangkok Bogota Bombay
Buenos Aires Calcutta Cape Town Dar es Salaam
Delhi Florence Hong Kong Istanbul Karachi
Kuala Lumpur Madras Madrid Melbourne
Mexico City Nairobi Paris Singapore
Taipei Tokyo Toronto

and associated companies in
Berlin Ibadan

Published by Oxford University Press, Inc.,
198 Madison Avenue, New York, New York 10016

Library of Congress Cataloging-in-Publication Data

Garner, Bryan A.
A dictionary of modern legal usage / Bryan A. Garner. — 2nd ed.
p. cm.
Includes bibliographical references.
1. Law—United States—Terminology. 2. Law—United States—Language. 3. Legal composition. 4. English language—Usage.
I. Title.
KF156.G367 1995 340'.03—dc20 95–3863
ISBN 0–19–507769–5

Acknowledgments of permission to quote from previously published works are made in a special section on page 953.

Printing (last digit): 9 8 7 6 5 4 3 2

Printed in the United States of America
on acid-free paper

For Teo
and our children,
Caroline and Alexandra

CONTENTS

PREFACE TO THE SECOND EDITION

Although there is much new material in this second edition, little need be said by way of introduction. I therefore confine this space to a word about citations and a listing of my literary debts.

Readers familiar with the first edition will note that I have added several thousand new illustrative quotations, with full citations. This represents a significant change in approach.

When writing the first edition, I omitted citations for four reasons. First, I was following the model of H.W. Fowler's *Modern English Usage* (1926), which simply quotes sentences from anonymous sources. (His earlier work, *The King's English* (1906), which he cowrote with his brother, F.G., named sources such as *The Times* but gave no detailed citation.) Second, because the quotations merely reflected what I was reading at the time, they came predominantly from judicial opinions issued by Texas courts and the U.S. Court of Appeals for the Fifth Circuit; having just completed a Fifth Circuit clerkship as I finished the manuscript in 1985, I thought it would not be particularly gracious of me, in a work of this kind, to cite a disproportionately high percentage of Fifth Circuit opinions. Third, as I had begun practicing law in Texas, it seemed imprudent to cite the work of judges before whom I might appear. Finally, the lawyers' briefs from which I drew quotations did not lend themselves to citation.

Although I still quote briefs without citing them, other sources are now fully cited. Why? I now think it helpful to show sources—helpful both legally and lexicographically—so I reject Fowler's approach. Further, the citations in this second edition represent a breadth that was unattainable for the first edition, so I am satisfied that the sources from Texas and surrounding states are only slightly overrepresented, if at all. Finally, I am satisfied that the lexicographic value of citations outweighs the risk of offending someone who has written something that might offend against the language.

I have tried to be dispassionate in my approach to citations. This means, for example, that I have unfavorably cited my own work (see **bequest**), the work of my grandfather (see **feoff** (C)), and the work of my mentor, Charles Alan Wright (see **disinterested**). Of course, in Wright's case, there must be 100 other instances in which I quote him favorably.

One more thing about citations. I collected many of them before 1991, when the *Bluebook* began to require first names for authors of books and articles. This caused me no end of needless work, but there were finally a few elusive citations for which neither I nor my research assistants—nor, indeed, my allies in law libraries—could fill in the blanks. In those few instances, I made concessions to the shortness of life and followed the pre-1991 *Bluebook* form.

Readers will find that this edition is much enriched with quotations not only from cases, but also from books and other sources. The shame is that it is not more enriched than it is, for in January 1991 a small lexicographic catastrophe occurred—an event that will no doubt bedevil me for as long as I care about lexicography. That month, I arranged to ship some 40 lawbooks from my office at the University of Texas to the American office of the Oxford Dictionary Department. These books had been thoroughly marked up for excerpting thousands of illustrative quotations, and they represented several years of work. Mysteriously these books—which were to be returned to me for use in preparing this edition—disappeared. They have never been accounted for. And the work that went into marking them can probably never be duplicated.

That loss, though, has been greatly outweighed by the tremendous help I have received from dozens of friends and colleagues. My debts are vast. I must merely list them as an insolvent debtor might do, in schedule form. Some of these friends have simply sent me comments and suggestions without my ever having met them face to face. Others I have known for many years, and I merely prevailed upon them to look over several entries within their areas of expertise; luckily for me, no one ever *seemed* prevailed upon—in fact, quite the opposite. They have all helped in splendid ways:

David Anderson
Michèle M. Asprey
Hans W. Baade
J.H. Baker
Griffin B. Bell
John A. Bell
Vicki V. Bonnington
A.W. Bradley
Jeffrey B. Brawner
John Browning
Robert W. Burchfield
Jenny Burg
Beverly Ray Burlingame
Peter Butt
Thomas Cable
Lauren Chadwick
Neil H. Cogan
Charles Dewey Cole, Jr.
Kirsten L. Concha
Edward H. Cooper
Daniel R. Coquillette
Sir Brian Cubbon
Robert O. Dawson
A. Darby Dickerson
Lance E. Dickson
Robert Eagleson
Frank H. Easterbrook
Eric B. Easton
David Elliott
Stephen F. Fink
Betty S. Flowers
Caroline B. Garner
Gary T. Garner
Teo Garner
(the late) Thomas Gibbs Gee
Lord Goff of Chieveley
Erwin N. Griswold
R.J. Grogan, Jr.
Alan Gunn
(the late) Alan M.F. Gunn
David Gunn
Robert W. Hamilton
Trevor C. Hartley
John L. Hauer
Geoffrey C. Hazard, Jr.
Nathan L. Hecht
Dewey R. Hicks, Jr.
William B. Hilgers
Nancy Hoagland
Wm. Terrell Hodges
Peter W. Hogg
Steve Holmes
Tony Honoré
Hadley Huchton
Lynn N. Hughes
Laird Hunter
Stanley Johanson
Robert H. Johnston III
Michael E. Keasler
Robert E. Keeton
William Keffer
Elizabeth S. Kerr
Joseph Kimble
N. Stephan Kinsella
Kenneth S. Klein
Karen Larsen
Douglas Laycock
Clyde Leland
Thomas B. Lemann
Sanford Levinson
David J. Luban
Joseph R. Lundy
Peter G. McCabe
Neil MacCormick
Becky R. McDaniel
Thomas O. McGarity
Lord Mackenzie-Stuart
Joseph McKnight
Nanneska N. Magee
Karen Magnuson
John Mann
Thomas Mayo
Sir Robert E. Megarry
Roy M. Mersky
Ernest Metzger
Richard H. Miller
Fred Misko, Jr.
B. Prater Monning
James E. Moore
Frederick Moss
Ron Moss
R. Eric Nielsen
John T. Noonan, Jr.
James A. Parker
David Peeples
Kenneth L. Penegar
Richard W. Pogue
Rick Prahl
George C. Pratt
Jonathan Pratter

Jack Ratliff
Alan Rau
Hal R. Ray, Jr.
Thomas M. Reavley
Charles Rembar
Christopher Ricks
Kenneth F. Ripple
Marlyn Robinson
Kimberly Rogaliner
C. Paul Rogers III
David Schultz
Fred Shapiro
David J. Sharpe
Christopher Simoni
A.W.B. Simpson
Katherine Smith
David Simon Sokolow
Bruce S. Sostek
Joseph F. Spaniol
Martin Stanford
Mark E. Steiner
Alicemarie Stotler
Michael Sturley
Pat Sullivan
Barbara M. Tearle
Linda Thomas
Randall M. Tietjen
Michael Tigar
John R. Trimble
John W. Velz
Richard S. Walinski
David M. Walker
Patricia H. Webb
Russell J. Weintraub
Carla Wheeler
Julie J. White
Sir David G.T. Williams
William R. Wilson
Sir Harry Woolf
Charles Alan Wright
Custis Wright
Suzanne F. Young
Mark G. Yudof

If I've omitted anyone, as I must have, my apologies.

Perhaps my vastest debts are to David M. Walker, of Glasgow, and Beverly Ray Burlingame, of Dallas. These fine scholars read the whole of my first draft and gave detailed comments in the margins. I doubt that there is a page in the book that hasn't been improved by their work.

Law librarians have repeatedly come to my aid. I've received the most help from Roy M. Mersky and his staff at the Tarlton Law Library in Austin. David Gunn in particular has generously run down countless sources for me, with uncommon skill and verve. Likewise, the Southern Methodist University Law Library has been extremely helpful. I cannot overstate how important it was to my research when the director, Gail Daly, gave me two card catalogues for storing lexicographic cards. (That may sound quaint in the age of computers, but index cards remain indispensable to lexicographers everywhere.) Finally, Barbara Tearle and R.G. Logan of the Bodleian Law Library, in Oxford, kindly helped me track down some sources that were otherwise inaccessible. As you might guess, I have never met a law librarian I didn't like.

I'm grateful to Dean Paul Rogers of S.M.U. Law School for allocating research-assistant funds that made it possible for me to have all quotations and citations verified. I don't know another dean who would extend this courtesy to a *former* faculty member, but S.M.U. is a special place.

I've benefited enormously from the teaching I've done in continuing legal education, primarily through LawProse, Inc. From my LawProse colleagues—Betty S. Flowers and John R. Trimble, both English professors at the University of Texas at Austin—I have learned a great deal. Many of the new entries show the influence they have had on me: from Betty I have learned more about the writing process, and from John I have learned more about effective editing. John has also contributed useful terminology, such as "miscues," and is largely responsible for my about-face on the subject of contractions.

I've also learned from the thousands of lawyers who have participated in LawProse workshops on legal writing and legal drafting. Through questions and comments, many of these participants have given me a deeper understanding of specific legal-linguistic issues.

The members of the H.W. Fowler Society—a loose organization I founded in order to monitor modern usage—have contributed dozens of examples and ideas for headwords. Most notably, John W. Velz, a great Shakespearean scholar and professor emeritus of English at the University of Texas at Austin, has faithfully sent me hundreds of so-called gleanings. I would not have entries such as the ones on **wile away** and **wreckless** if it weren't for him.

This edition owes much to Claude Conyers and Nancy Hoagland of Oxford University Press. Time and again, Claude approved my requests for extraordinary assistance of one kind or another. And Nancy is the author's dream of what a production editor should be: perfectionist and highly proprietary in her approach to the book, but respectful on those rare occasions when I perversely resisted her improvements.

I am much indebted to my wife, Teo, for all her support while I've labored over this book. During my first week of law school in 1981, I told her of my plan to write it—I even told her the name of it—and she didn't laugh. Indeed, she encouraged me. We also became engaged that week, and she saw me beginning the work on 3-by-5 cards, which in the coming years accumulated in mountainous piles. Between 1981 and 1987, she supportively watched the book materialize, and many entries have benefited—both in the first edition and in this one—from her fine scholarly judgment.

When *DMLU* came out in 1987, my daughter Caroline had just been born some six months earlier. There is a funny photograph of her sitting beside the one-foot-tall pile of manuscript. Now she is eight, and her sister, Alexandra, is three; meanwhile, the manuscript pile has doubled in size. As my girls continue to grow, I'm rather hoping that *DMLU* has reached its full maturity. But I somehow doubt it.

PREFACE TO THE FIRST EDITION

In 1921, an article in the *American Bar Association Journal* called for a book on "writing legal English."[1] The author of that article, Urban A. Lavery, pointed out that lawyers rarely consult a book on grammar or composition even once to the hundred of times they consult lawbooks; and yet, as he observed, when convincing argument is to the fore, or clearness of expression is desired, the elements of good writing are often more important than piled up citations of cases.[2] Since Lavery proclaimed his judgment, many books on "writing legal English" have been published, but none with the broad scope or easy accessibility that might allow readers to resolve at a glance the many grammatical and stylistic questions that arise in legal writing. Filling that gap is the goal of this book.

Anglo-American law has a language of its own, consisting in a vocabulary with an unusually large number of foreign phrases, archaic words and expressions, terms of art, and argot words. Its formal style reflects the dignity and solemnity with which the profession views its mission. These distinctive qualities of legal language—evident alike in the speech and the writing of lawyers—are well enough documented. What has remained uncollected and unscrutinized in any systematic way is the vast body of legal usage.

For a specialist language, the language of law remains remarkably variable, largely because it has been incompletely recorded and mapped. In this respect it is analogous to English before 18th-century grammarians attempted to reduce its variability and make logical its many quiddities. This is not to say, of course, that the language of the law has the malleable capacity of Elizabethan English, which, in the hands of a creative genius like Shakespeare, could be supremely expressive and evocative. Quite the opposite. Stare decisis remains at the core of our system of law—so much so that the continual search for precedents often discourages legal writers from straying beyond precisely how things have been said before. As a result, many locutions have become fossilized in legal language over generations. And the inheritors of that language cannot always distinguish mere form from necessary substance, to the extent that form and substance are ever separable.

Legal traditionalists may be justified in not wanting to throw over too readily what has long served well. Yet tradition alone is not sufficient reason for retaining outmoded forms of language. Modern legal writers must strike a difficult balance in the quest to simplify legal English. They should not cling perversely to archaic language, which becomes less comprehensible year by year, for its own sake. Nor should they seek to jettison every word or phrase that bears the stamp of legal tradition.

As for students of law, they learn the technical language that they will need—the quirks of legal jargon, the peculiar idiomatic expressions, the

[1]Lavery, *The Language of the Law,* 7 A.B.A. J. 277 (1921).
[2]*Id.* at 280.

grammatical idiosyncrasies, the neologisms that cannot be found even in the most current unabridged dictionaries—largely by osmosis. These linguistic matters are, for the most part, seldom discussed by lawyers or law professors; rather, they are part of the spoken and written legal discourse that neophyte lawyers absorb every day and learn to use unconsciously. This casualness in acquiring the language frequently leads to variable and contradictory linguistic habits that need explicating, codifying, and, in some instances, taming.

Granted these basic facts of legal language—the course of its growth, the challenge of its use, the pattern of its acquisition—this book aims at serving three primary functions. First, it helps lawyers chart their way safely through the bogs of legal language. In the past, anyone wanting such a guide has had to make do with general writing manuals. Though this dictionary lays no claim to comprehensiveness, it offers the legal writer guidance on hundreds of specific points of usage. The advice it gives is generally on the conservative side of usage and grammar, for the simple reason that lawyers generally write in a relatively formal context. Lapses from what has come to be accepted as correct irritate and distract the educated reader, and this makes the writing less persuasive. Yet the conservative approach exemplified in these pages aspires to be an *informed* conservatism, one that neither battles hopelessly against linguistic faits accomplis nor remains blind to the inevitable growth and change that occur in language.

Second, the dictionary addresses a great many usage problems that do not ordinarily arise in the writing of persons untrained in the law, and therefore that are not addressed in standard writing guides. Certainly it covers territory common to general guides, as inevitably it must. But one of its chief uses should be in pointing out divergences between legal and lay usage, many of which have remained heretofore unrecorded. To this end, the dictionary serves lawyers and nonlawyers alike, for it can help both groups bridge the linguistic gulf that separates them, to the degree that is possible. The greater effort here needs to be made by lawyers, who in recent years have become increasingly aware of the importance of using legal language that is simple and direct. Indeed, simplicity and directness, two of the touchstones of good writing, are advocated throughout this dictionary in an effort to tag and to discard legalese and highfalutin jargon.

Third, this work may serve, to some extent, as an instrument of reform. Where lawyers and judges use terms imprecisely or ambiguously (or, indeed, incorrectly), this dictionary often presents standards that will enhance rather than destroy valuable nuances. If ever a prescriptive approach to language is justified, it is in law, where linguistic precision is often of paramount concern, and where ambiguity and vagueness (except when purposeful) are quite intolerable. Within its compass, the dictionary thus seeks to preserve the rich differentiation in our legal vocabulary, to set out some of the important grammatical usages and traditional idioms, and to oppose slipshod usages that blur well-developed distinctions. Of course, no work of this kind can be a panacea for the problems that occur in legal writing. But such a work can realistically seek to make legal writers sensitive to the aesthetic possibilities of their prose, to goad them into thinking more acutely about what works in a given context, and what does not.

Modern Legal Usage is arranged so that the legal writer, unsure of or puzzled by a particular word or point of grammar, can consult a specific entry addressing the problem at hand. Virtually all the sentences quoted to illustrate legal usage, including linguistic pitfalls, originated in judicial opinions. A few come from statutes, fewer still from lawyers' briefs and other sources. The authors of the quoted specimens generally remain anonymous, because ordinarily it is unimportant *who* made a particular mistake. Attention should be focused on the mistake itself, and how to remedy it. Where stare decisis is the ruling principle, citations are necessary; in a dictionary of usage they are not, except of course when documenting usages that are lexicographically noteworthy. Whenever specimens do receive attribution, the importance of that fact lies in documenting the source, not in giving context to the quoted matter; hence subsequent histories of cases cited are not given.

Undertaking to write a dictionary of this kind is a precarious task. For by setting oneself up as an arbiter of usage, one also sets one's prose before the magnifying glasses of readers, who are certain to find blemishes of one sort or another. Such was H.W. Fowler's fate in his *Dictionary of Modern English Usage* (1926), a work that has served me as both exemplar and caution. For whatever may be amiss or at fault in this dictionary, I readily acknowledge full responsibility in advance.

As my manuscript swelled, any number of friends and colleagues looked on with far more than a polite interest. Several have actively contributed to whatever merit the final product has. Randall K. Glover of Austin and Kelly Bowers of Seattle called problematical words to my attention almost daily during the year we worked side by side for Judge Thomas M. Reavley. The Judge himself, whose approach to life and law cannot but inspire, gave me advice and encouragement that emboldened me to persevere.

Several fellow lawyers undertook to read large portions of the manuscript and made expert comments throughout. My learned friends Dr. Betty S. Flowers, David Radunsky, Michelle D. Monse, Roy J. Grogan, Jr., Hal Roberts Ray, Jr., Joe W. Pitts III, Alfredo Estrada, Roger Arnold, Lindsay H. Lew, Kenneth S. Klein, Lisa M. Black, Laura Cale, Sim Israeloff, and Jeffrey B. Brawner have all left the work sharper than they found it. I am indebted also to the late John N. Jackson, whose comments reflected years of thought on the subject of legal writing style.

The Honorable Robert W. Calvert, formerly Chief Justice of the Supreme Court of Texas, generously read and marked up a prototypical draft of the work; he kept me on the reader's path and gave me a number of useful ideas. I am grateful to Justice Sandra Day O'Connor for corresponding with me on some of the stylistic practices of the United States Supreme Court.

Edmund S.C. Weiner, the accomplished Oxford lexicographer, and Martin S. Stanford, an extremely knowledgeable and thoughtful editor in New York, minutely read the full manuscript and made innumerable improvements. To these two scholars I am especially beholden, as I am to my father, Dr. Gary T. Garner, who spent many hours reading galleys.

Finally, I cannot adequately express my gratitude to my dear wife, to whom this book is dedicated, for her keen insights and unfaltering support in the face of what must have seemed at the outset to be a grossly overambitious task.

CLASSIFIED GUIDE TO ESSAY ENTRIES

This guide lists essay entries that may be grouped according to (1) style; (2) grammar and usage; (3) legal lexicology and special conventions; (4) word formation, inflection, spelling, and pronunciation; and (5) punctuation and typography. The guide does not include any entries that are concerned only with the meaning or idiomatic use of title words, or with their spelling, pronunciation, etymology, or inflections.

Style

SEXISM
- A. The Pronoun Problem
- B. Words in *man-* and *-man*
- C. Feminine Forms in *-ess* and *-trix*
- D. Equivalences
- E. Statute of Limitations

SIMILES

SLIPSHOD EXTENSION

SOUND OF PROSE, THE
- A. Undue Alliteration or Rhyme
- B. Unwieldy or Illogical Imagery
- C. Unnecessary or Awkward Repetition
- D. Arrhythmic Plodding
- E. Jarring Contrasts
- F. Misleading Parts of Speech

SUPERFLUITIES

SUPERSTITIONS
- A. Never End a Sentence with a Preposition
- B. Never Split an Infinitive
- C. Never Split a Verb Phrase
- D. Never Begin a Sentence with *and* or *but*
- E. Never Write a One-Sentence Paragraph
- F. Never Begin a Sentence with *because*
- G. Never Use *since* to mean *because*
- H. Never Use *between* with More Than Two Objects
- I. Never Use the First-Person Pronouns *I* and *me*
- J. Never Use Contractions
- K. Never Use *you* in Referring to Your Reader

SYNONYMY

TAUTOLOGY

TERMS OF ART

TITULAR TOMFOOLERY

VERBAL AWARENESS

VERBOSITY

VOGUE WORDS

WEASEL WORDS

WOOLLINESS

WORD-PATRONAGE

WORDS OF AUTHORITY
- A. *Shall*
- B. *Shall not*
- C. *Must*
- D. *Will*
- E. *May*
- F. *Must not; may not*
- G. *Is entitled to*
- H. Using a Consistent Glossary

Grammar and Usage

ABSOLUTE CONSTRUCTIONS

ADJECTIVES
- A. What One Is
- B. Uncomparable Adjectives
- C. Adjectives as Nouns
- D. Adjectives as Verbs
- E. Coordinate Adjectives
- F. Proper Nouns as Adjectives
- G. Pronominal Indefinite Adjectives
- H. Past-Participial Adjectives

ADVERBS, PROBLEMS WITH
- A. Placement of Adverbs
- B. Awkward Adverbs
- C. Adjectives or Adverbs After Linking Verbs
- D. Redundantly Formed Adverbs

ANTECEDENTS, FALSE
- A. Ghostly Antecedents
- B. False Attraction
- C. With Possessives

ANTICIPATORY REFERENCE
- A. *As do*
- B. Noun References
- C. Pronouns

APPOSITIVES
- A. With Possessives
- B. Punctuation

ARTICLES
- A. Omitted Before Party Denominations
- B. Wrongly Omitted
- C. Wrongly Inserted
- D. Repeated

BE-VERBS
- A. Wrongly Omitted in Nonfinite Uses
- B. Circumlocutions
- C. Used Unidiomatically in Place of Action Verbs

CENTURY DESCRIPTIONS

COLLECTIVE NOUNS

COMPARATIVES AND SUPERLATIVES
- A. Choice Between Comparative and Superlative
- B. Which to Use—Suffixes, or *more* and *most?*
- C. Swapping Horses
- D. *Be*-Verbs Repeated After Comparatives

CONCORD
- A. Subject-Verb Disagreement
- B. Noun-Pronoun Disagreement
- C. One Result Wrongly Attributed to Two or More Subjects

CORRELATIVE CONJUNCTIONS
- A. *Neither . . . nor*
- B. *Either . . . or*
- C. *Both . . . and*
- D. *Although . . . yet*
- E. *Notwithstanding . . . yet*
- F. Other Correlatives

COUNT NOUNS AND MASS NOUNS
- A. *Fewer* and *less*
- B. Treating a Mass Noun as a Count Noun

DANGLERS
- A. Danglers Ending in *-ing*
- B. Past-Participial Danglers
- C. Dangling Gerunds

Legal Lexicology and Special Conventions

Word Formation, Inflection, Spelling, and Pronunciation

MUTE E
NEEDLESS VARIANTS
NEGATIVES
NON-
- A. As a Separable Prefix
- B. With Nouns
- C. With Adjectives
- D. With Verbs

-OR, -OUR
PER-
PLURALS
- A. Borrowed Words
- B. Mass (Noncount) Nouns
- C. Words Ending in *-o*
- D. Nouns Formed from Past-Participial Adjectives
- E. Compound Nouns
- F. Proper Names

PORTMANTEAU WORDS
POSSESSIVES
- A. Singular Possessives
- B. Plural Possessives
- C. Units of Time or Value and the Genitive Adjective
- D. Of Inanimate Things
- E. Incorrect Omission of Apostrophe
- F. Past-Participial Adjectives as Attributive Nouns
- G. Phrasal Possessives
- H. Followed by Relative Pronouns
- I. Attributive Possessives

POST-
PRE- [+ NOUN]
PRONUNCIATION
- A. General Principles
- B. Commonly Mispronounced Lawyers' Words
- C. Latin Terms
- D. Law French
- E. BrE Idiosyncrasies

RE- PAIRS
SEXISM (B), (C)
SUB-
VOWEL CLUSTERS
-WARD(S)
-WISE
-WORTHY

Punctuation and Typography

CAPITALIZATION
- A. All Capitals
- B. Initial Capitals
- C. Rules of Law
- D. Vessel Names
- E. Judges' Names
- F. Trademarks
- G. Party Names

DOCUMENT DESIGN
- A. A Readable Typeface
- B. White Space
- C. Headings and Subheadings
- D. Avoiding All Caps
- E. Avoiding Underlines
- F. Listing
- G. Bullets
- H. Hanging Indents
- I. A Ragged Right Margin
- J. Citations in Footnotes
- K. Characters Per Line

ENUMERATIONS
- A. *First(ly), second(ly), third(ly); one, two, three*
- B. Comma Before the Last Member

INITIALESE
ITALICS
- A. Generally
- B. Foreign Phrases
- C. Of Latin Phrases Beginning with *in*

NUMERALS
- A. General Guidance in Using
- B. Coupling Numerals with Words
- C. Not Beginning Sentences with Numerals
- D. Round Numbers
- E. Decades
- F. Judicial Votes

PARENTHESES
- A. Syntactically
- B. Overuse of

PUNCTUATION
- A. The Apostrophe
- B. The Colon
- C. The Comma
- D. The Dash
- E. The Exclamation Mark
- F. The Hyphen
- G. Parentheses
- H. The Period or Full Stop
- I. The Question Mark
- J. Quotation Marks
- K. The Semicolon
- L. Square Brackets

PRONUNCIATION GUIDE

Pronunciations are shown within virgules. Syllables are separated by hyphens in pronunciations, and syllables spoken with the greatest stress are shown in boldface type.

ə	*for all vowel sounds in* turbid, among, journal, trust, monk
a	*as in* pact, democrat, drafting
ah	*as in* alms, father, calm
ahr	*as in* bargain, argue, pardon
air	*as in* care, lair, aware
aw	*as in* law, cause, flaw
ay	*as in* litigate, delay
b	*as in* brief, bankruptcy, bench
ch	*as in* chambers, chance, chief
d	*as in* deposition, divorce, disclose
e	*as in* evidence, appellate, rescue
ee	*as in* freedom, appeal, pleading
eer	*as in* peer, gear, weird
f	*as in* forensic, bailiff, iffy
g	*as in* guilt, flog, grieve
h	*as in* hang, holiday, hornbook
hw	*as in* which, while, whether
i	*as in* civil, innocent, condition
ɪ	*as in* trial, right, file
j	*as in* juror, jail, justice
k	*as in* clerk, check, county
l	*as in* law, liberty, legislate
m	*as in* marshal, matrimony, methods
n	*as in* none, end, run
ng	*as in* gang, rank, hung
o	*as in* modern, confidential, conscience
oh	*as in* over, parole, quote
ohr	*as in* lore, floor, bore
oi	*as in* moist, oyster, toy
oo	*as in* too, boon, flute
oor	*as in* poor, boor, tour
ow	*as in* power, our, flower
p	*as in* primary, plenary, prison
r	*as in* reporter, reprieve, rules
s	*as in* sue, swear, sentence
sh	*as in* shoe, shoulder, push
t	*as in* term, transact, testify
th	*as in* thief, theory, ethics
th	*as in* that, whether, either
uu	*as in* book, full, woman
v	*as in* venire, relevant, device
w	*as in* win, wordy, work
y	*as in* yes, year, yellow
z	*as in* zap, dizzy, busy
zh	*as in* pleasure, vision, leisure

LIST OF ABBREVIATIONS

adj. = adjective
adv. = adverb
AHD = *American Heritage Dictionary* (3d ed. 1992)
Am. = American
AmE = American English
Aus. = Australia
Black's = *Black's Law Dictionary* (6th ed. 1990)
Br. = British
BrE = British English
c. = century
ca. = circa
Can. = Canada; Canadian
CDL = *A Concise Dictionary of Law* (2d ed. 1990)
cf. = compare with
C.J. = Chief Justice
COD = *The Concise Oxford Dictionary* (8th ed. 1990)
colloq. = colloquial
ed. = edition; editor
e.g. = (*exempli gratia*) for example
Eng. = England; English
esp. = especially
ex. = example
fr. = from; derived from; found in
Fr. = France; French
G.B. = Great Britain (i.e., England, Scotland, and Wales)
Gk. = Greek
id. = (*idem*) in the same work
i.e. = (*id est*) that is
Ir. = Ireland; Irish
Ital. = Italy; Italian
J. = Justice; Judge
JJ. = Justices; Judges
J.P. = Justice of the Peace
K.B. = King's Bench
L. = Latin
La. = Louisiana
L.F. = Law French
lit. = literally
L.L. = Law Latin
MEU1 = H. W. Fowler's *A Dictionary of Modern English Usage* (1926)
MEU2 = H. W. Fowler's *A Dictionary of Modern English Usage* (Ernest Gowers ed., 2d ed. 1965)
M.R. = Master of the Rolls
n. = noun
N.B. = (*nota bene*) note well
N.Z. = New Zealand
OAD = *Oxford American Dictionary* (1980)
obs. = obsolete
OCL = David M. Walker's *The Oxford Companion to the Law* (1980)
OED = *The Oxford English Dictionary* (2d ed. 1989)
OED Supp. = *A Supplement to the Oxford English Dictionary* (4 vols., 1972–1986)
O.F. = Old French
orig. = originally
Oxford Guide = *The Oxford Guide to English Usage* (1983)
par. = paragraph
P.C. = Privy Council
phr. = phrase
P.J. = Presiding Judge
pl. = plural
pmbl. = preamble
pp. = pages
p. pl. = past participle
prep. = preposition
Q.B. = Queen's Bench
q.v. = (*quod vide*) which see
qq.v. = pl. form of *q.v.*
quot. = quotation
repr. = reprinted
rev. = revised by; revision
RHD = *The Random House Dictionary of the English Language* (2d ed. 1987)

Rhod. = Rhodesia (before the name change to Zimbabwe)

S. Afr. = South Africa

Scot. = Scotland

Sp. = Spain; Spanish

specif. = specifically

TLS = Times Literary Supplement

U.C.C. = Uniform Commercial Code

U.K. = United Kingdom (i.e., G.B. and—since 1922—Northern Ireland)

U.S. = United States

U.S.C. = United States Code

usu. = usually

vb. = verb

v.i. = intransitive verb

v.t. = transitive verb

W2 = *Webster's New International Dictionary* (2d ed. 1939)

W3 = *Webster's Third New International Dictionary* (1961)

W10 = *Merriam Webster's Collegiate Dictionary* (10th ed. 1993)

Abbreviations within case names follow the conventions established in the *Bluebook* (15th ed. 1991), § T.6, at 264–65.

As for symbols within the work, a virgule (/) separates different illustrative quotations that are not part of a bulleted list. A parenthetical geographic reference following such a quotation, such as (Eng.) or (Aus.), indicates the national origin of the quotation. (Illustrative quotations not having a geographic reference are American in origin.) Small capitals refer the reader to the named article for further information.

MODERN LEGAL USAGE

A

a; an. This entry treats two common problems with the indefinite articles; for advice on using definite and indefinite articles generally, see ARTICLES.

A. Choice Between *a* and *an*. The indefinite article *a* is used before words beginning with a consonant sound, including *-y-* and *-w-* sounds. The other form, *an,* is used before words beginning with a vowel sound. Hence *a European country, an LL.B. degree, a heuristic device, a uniform, an F.B.I. agent, an SEC subpoena.* And, for those who have been wondering, the correct form is *a usufruct* in Louisiana law and *a hypothec* in Scots law.

The distinction between *a* and *an* was not solidified until the 19th century. Before that time *an* preceded most words beginning with a vowel, regardless of how the first syllable sounded. The U.S. Constitution reads: "The Congress shall have Power . . . To establish *an uniform* Rule of Naturalization . . . ." U.S. Const. art. I, § 8. But that is no excuse for a 20th-century writer: "[T]hus retaining *an unique* [read *a unique*] and personal quality style creates nevertheless an essential value in all written expression." Perlie P. Fallon, *The Relation Between Analysis and Style in American Legal Prose,* 28 Neb. L. Rev. 80, 80 (1949).

Writers on usage formerly disputed whether the correct article is *a* or *an* with *historian, historical,* and a few other words. The traditional rule is that if the *-h-* is sounded, *a* is the proper form. If we follow that rule in the U.S. today, most people would say *a historian.* Even Fowler, in the England of 1926, advocated *a* before *historic(al)* and *humble.*

The theory behind using *an* in such a context, however, is that the *-h-* is very weak when the accent is on the second rather than the first syllable (giving rise, by analogy, to *an habitual offender, an humanitarian, an hallucinatory image,* and *an harassed schoolteacher*). Thus no authority countenances *an history,* though several older ones prefer *an historian* and *an historical.* Cardozo wrote: "What we hand down in our judgments is *an hypothesis.* It is no longer a divine command." *Law and Literature,* 52 Harv. L. Rev. 472, 478 (1939). Earlier Holmes used the same phrase.

Today, however, *an hypothesis* and *an historical* are likely to strike readers and listeners as affectations. As Mark Twain once wrote, referring to *humble, heroic,* and *historical:* "Correct writers of the American language do not put *an* before those words." *The Stolen White Elephant* 220 (1882) (as quoted in C.M. Babcock, *The Ordeal of American English* 1, 2 (1961)). Anyone who sounds the *-h-* in such words should avoid pretense and use *a.* Thus *a hypothecation, a hereditament, a hallucinatory image, a harassed schoolteacher.* An humanitarian is, judged even by the most tolerant standards, a pretentious humanitarian. See **humble.**

B. In the Distributive Sense. *A,* the distributive sense <ten hours a day>, is preferable to *per,* which originated in commercialese and LEGALESE. It is wrong to consider *a* informal or colloquial in this context. The natural idiom is *sixty hours a week* and *ten dollars a pair,* not *sixty hours per week* and *ten dollars per pair.* E.g., "At oral argument, St. Genevieve suggested that nominal damages be awarded at one dollar *per* [read *an*] acre."/ "These employees were paid less than the minimum hourly wage and they regularly worked more than forty hours *per* [read *a*] week without receiving overtime pay."

Nonetheless, *per* is at least minimally acceptable, except in the phrase *as per,* q.v. And in a few contexts, especially when used attributively, *per* is the only idiomatic word. E.g., "The case asks whether the same *per-unit* lease term amounts to a tax on imports in violation of the Import-Export Clause of the Constitution."

A.B. See **able-bodied seaman.**

abalienate. See **alien,** v.t.

abandon = (1) to give up property or some right with the intent of never claiming it again; or (2) in family law, to leave children or a spouse willfully and without an intent to return. In sense (1), a person's losing a billfold (say) and then giving up an unsuccessful search does not mean that the person *abandons* the lost billfold: to *abandon* it, the person would have to take some purposeful action such as throwing it away.

abandoned property. See **lost property.**

abandonee means, not "one who is abandoned," as the suffix *-ee* might suggest, but "one to whom property rights [in a thing] are relinquished." As in *advancee* (= one to whom money is advanced) and *patentee* (= one to whom a patent has been issued), the suffix *-ee* carries a dative sense. Leff writes that "there are numerous circumstances in which abandonment of something by one person will have the practical or even legal effect of vesting that thing in a particular other person, who thus may usefully be called an *abandonee.*" Arthur A. Leff, *The Leff Dictionary of Law,* 94 Yale L.J. 1855, 1856 (1985). See -EE (A).

abandum; abandonum. The former is the correct spelling of this word, which means "anything prohibited or ordered to be cast away." *Abandonum* is a misspelling.

abate is a FORMAL WORD common in legal contexts, meaning (1) *v.t.,* "to nullify; quash; demolish" <to abate a legal action>; (2) *v.t.,* "to diminish" <to abate a debt>; or (3) *v.t.,* to remove physically <to abate a nuisance>; or (4) *v.i.,* "to come to an end" <all suits abate upon the death of the plaintiff>. There is, additionally, a technical legal sense that is rarely if ever used today: "to thrust oneself tortiously into real estate after the owner dies and before the legal heir enters" <abatement of freehold>.

Today *abate* is used most often in senses (2) and (3). Sense (2): "If the noise remains audible to lessee's tenants for more than five consecutive days, the lessor shall *abate* the rental payments in proportion to the square footage affected by the noise." Sense (3): "A person who suffers from a nuisance may *abate* it, i.e. remove it, even without giving notice, if he can do so without going on to another's land . . . ." William Geldart, *Introduction to English Law* 144 (D.C.M. Yardley ed., 9th ed. 1984).

The adjective is *abatable,* as in, "Appellants further contend that, where a nuisance is *abatable,* the damages assessed must be limited to the rental value of the property."

abator. So spelled.

ABBREVIATIONS. See ACRONYMS AND INITIALISMS & INITIALESE.

abbuttals. See **abutment.**

abdicate may mean (1) "to disown"; (2) "to discard"; or (3) "to renounce." In legal writing it usually takes on sense (3)—e.g.: "We did not . . . imply that we had *abdicated* our equitable powers to prevent an unjust forfeiture." *Foundation Dev. Corp. v. Loehmann's, Inc.,* 788 P.2d 1189, 1195 (Ariz. 1990)./ "The majority, as I see it, has *abdicated* its responsibility to enforce federal constitutional norms." *Clemons v. Mississippi,* 494 U.S. 738, 774 (1990) (Blackmun, J., concurring in part & dissenting in part).

abduct; abduce. These words overlap in meaning, but are not interchangeable. Both may mean "to draw away (a limb, etc.) from its natural position" (*OED*). Yet the more common meaning of *abduct* is "to lead away by force." (For a fuller definition, see **abduction.**) Although the *OED* contains a notation that *abduce* is archaic, *W3* does not label it so; in any event, it is certainly rare.

abductee. See -EE (C).

abducter. See **abductor (B).**

abduction; kidnap(p)ing; child-stealing. *Abduction* = the act of leading (someone) away by force or fraudulent persuasion. It constitutes a statutory offense in many states; for example, *abduct* is statutorily defined in one state as "to restrain a person with intent to prevent his liberation by: (A) secreting or holding him in a place where he is not likely to be found; or (B) using or threatening to use deadly force." Tex. Penal Code Ann. § 20.01 (Vernon 1989).

In England, *abduction* is generally given a narrower sense: "the offence of taking an unmarried girl under the age of 16 from the possession of her parents or guardian against her will" (*CDL*). The *OCL* additionally defines *abduction* in English law as taking "a girl under 18 or a defective woman of any age from the possession of her parent or guardian for the purpose of unlawful sexual intercourse, or a girl under 21 with property or expectations of property from such possession to marry or have unlawful sexual intercourse, or . . . taking away and detaining any woman with the intention that she shall marry or have unlawful sexual intercourse with a person, by force or for the sake of her property or expectations of property."

In current AmE, *abduction* has virtually no connotations relating to the victim's sex. But in British legal writing—and at common law—the victim is almost invariably a woman. Abduction of voters, a criminal offense in G.B., is one usage in which the abductee's sex is irrelevant.

Kidnapping = the act or an instance of stealing, abducting, or carrying away a person by force or fraud, often with a demand for ransom (*W3*). *Kidnapping* (the *-pp-* spelling is preferred) is not restricted in application to children as victims, though the etymology suggests it. *Child-stealing* is the technical statutory term for the abduction of children. See **kidnapping (B).**

abductor. A. Plural Form. *Abductor* forms two plurals: *-tors* and *-tores.* The English plural, *abductors,* is preferable to the Latin plural, *abductores.*

B. And *abducter*. This alternative spelling,

which is etymologically inferior, is not as widespread as *abductor.*

aberration; aberrance; aberrancy; aberrant, n. *Aberration* means (1) "a deviation or departure from what is normal or correct," or (2) "a mental derangement." *Aberrance* and *aberrancy* are NEEDLESS VARIANTS.

Although the word *aberration* is not limited to persons, *aberrant* almost always is. As a noun, it means "a deviant; one deviating from established norms."

aberrational; aberrant, adj.; **aberrative.** *Aberrational* = of or pertaining to an aberration (see the preceding entry). E.g., "It is our duty to allow a decision to be made by the Attorney General's delegate, as long as it is not so *aberrational* that it is arbitrary rather than the result of any perceptible rational approach." *Aberrant* = deviating from behavioral or social norms. *Aberrative* = tending to be aberrational.

abet. See **aid and abet.**

abetment (= the act of abetting) is sometimes erroneously made *abettance* or *abettal,* both NEEDLESS VARIANTS.

abettor. A. And *abetter*. In both BrE and AmE, *abettor* is the more usual spelling; the *OED* states that it "is the constant form of the word as a legal term." *Abettator* is the defunct LAW LATIN term from old English law. Cf. **bettor.** See -ER (A) & **perpetrator.**

B. And *accessory*. An *abettor,* as distinguished from an *accessory,* is usually one who is present at the scene of a crime and gives aid or encouragement.

abeyance has a general sense ("a state of suspension, temporary nonexistence, or inactivity" [*OED*]) and a technical legal sense ("expectation or contemplation of law; the position of waiting for or being without a claimant or owner" [*OED*]). Even in legal contexts, however, the general lay sense is commonly used, as in, "Texas would not consider his claim if this action were held in *abeyance.*"

abhorrent, meaning literally "shrinking from in abhorrence" or "strongly opposed to," frequently refers to things in legal contexts in the sense "so far removed from (a thing) as to be repugnant or inconsistent." E.g., "The very nature of a partnership is such that joint tenancy between one of the partners and a stranger to the partnership would be *abhorrent* to the Act."

abide. A. General Senses. *Abide* = (1) to stay <the right of entering and abiding in any state in the Union>; (2) to tolerate, withstand; (3) to obey; (4) to await; or (5) to perform or execute (in reference to orders or judgments). The last is the strictly legal meaning: "Since we do not doubt that the court will promptly proceed to *abide* our judgment and certify our decision before proceeding to trial, we decline to issue a peremptory order at this time."

Abide also commonly takes on the sense "to await," as in the following legal construction: "The judgment should be reversed, and a new trial granted, with costs to *abide* the event."

Abide by is a PHRASAL VERB meaning "to acquiesce in or conform to"—e.g.: "Jurors must *abide by* the oath with respect to both sentencing and determining guilt or innocence."/ "Eastman indicated his intention to *abide by* the plea agreement, clearly hoping that this would be a consideration in favor of leniency."

Abiding = lasting, enduring. E.g., "The two gifts are both of a kind that indicates an *abiding* and unconditioned intent—one to a church, the other to a person whom she called her adopted son."

B. Past-Tense and Past-Participial Forms. With the meanings most probably to be found in legal texts ("await" and "execute"), *abided* is the preferred past tense and past participle. In the archaic sense "to stay, dwell," *abode* is the preferred past tense, and either *abode* or *abided* as the past participle. For most ordinary purposes, *abided* serves well without seeming stilted.

ability; capacity. Whereas *ability* is qualitative, *capacity* is quantitative. *Ability* refers to a person's power of body or mind <a lawyer of great ability>; *capacity,* meaning literally "roomy, spacious," refers figuratively to a person's physical or mental power to receive <her memory has an extraordinary capacity for details>.

***ab initio*; *in initio*.** The former means "from the beginning" <an act beyond one's legal competence is void *ab initio*>; the latter means, as its prefix suggests, "in the beginning." Neither LATINISM seems quite justified in ordinary contexts, although *ab initio,* which in legal writing is used commonly in the phrase *void ab initio,* is common enough not to be particularly objectionable—e.g.: "Smith secured from an equity court, *ab initio,* an injunction against Jones." Leff notes that the phrase is sometimes used in the sense "thoroughly," roughly equivalent to "from first to last." Arthur A. Leff, *The Leff Dictionary of Law,* 94 Yale L.J. 1855, 1863 (1985). E.g., "We find respondent's argument that the decision in that case is controlling here unpersuasive *ab initio,* because the relevant language of the two statutes differs materially."

abjudge; adjudge. These words are antithetical in one sense. *Abjudge* is a rare term (not in most abridged dictionaries) meaning "to take away by judicial decision" (*OED*). *Adjudge,* in contrast, means "to award, grant, or impose judicially" (*id.*). One *abjudges from* and *adjudges to.* For the latter term's other senses, see **adjudge.**

abjudicate is synonymous with *abjudge,* q.v.

abjure; adjure. The former may mean either (1) "to renounce" <Germany abjured the use of force>, or (2) "to avoid" <her evaluation abjured excessive praise>. The latter means "to charge or entreat solemnly" <Reagan adjured the Soviets to join him in this noble goal>.

The noun forms are *abjuration* (or *abjurement*—now defunct) and *adjuration.* The adjectival forms end in *-tory.* The agent nouns are *abjurer* and *adjurer.*

abjurer; abjuror. The *-er* spelling is preferred. See -ER (A).

able. For the meaning of this word in the phrase *ready, willing, and able,* see **ready, willing, and able.**

-ABLE. A. Choice of *-able* or *-ible.* Many adjectives have competing forms ending in *-able* and *-ible.* Some of these have undergone DIFFERENTIATION in meaning; the less commonly used forms in some pairs are merely NEEDLESS VARIANTS of the predominant forms. The lists that follow contain the most troublesome words of this class.

Unlike *-ible, -able* is a living suffix that may be added to virtually any verb without an established suffix in either *-able* or *-ible.* Following are some of the adjectives preferably spelled *-able:*

actionable	circumscribable	diagnosable
addable	commensurable	diffusable
advisable	committable	discussable
affectable	condensable	endorsable
allegeable	conductable	enforceable
analyzable	connectable	excisable
annexable	contestable	excludable
arrestable	contractable	expandable
assessable	conversable	extendable
averageable	convictable	garnishable
bailable	correctable	ignitable
blamable	definable	immovable
changeable	demurrable	improvable
chargeable	detectable	includable
inferable	ratable	suspendable
movable	redressable	tractable
noticeable	retractable	transferable
patentable	salable	willable
persuadable		

The following words, limited in number because *-ible* is dead as a combining form in English, are spelled with the *-i-:*

accessible	dismissible	perceptible
adducible	divisible	perfectible
admissible	edible	permissible
audible	educible	plausible
avertible	eligible	possible
collapsible	erodible	producible
collectible	exhaustible	protectible
combustible	expressible	reducible
commiscible	extendible	remissible
compactible	fallible	reprehensible
compatible	feasible	repressible
comprehensible	flexible	resistible
compressible	forcible	responsible
concussible	fusible	reversible
contemptible	horrible	revertible
controvertible	impressible	risible
convertible	incorrigible	seducible
corrodible	indelible	sensible
corruptible	intelligible	submersible (*or*
credible	interfusible	submergible)
deducible	inventible	suggestible
deductible	invincible	suppressible
defeasible	irascible	susceptible
defensible	irresistible	terrible
descendible	legible	transfusible
destructible	negligible	uncollectible
digestible	omissible	vendible
discernible	ostensible	visible

Some adjectives with these variant suffixes have different meanings. Thus *impassable* means "closed, incapable of being traversed"; its twin, *impassible,* means "unable to feel pain," or, less distinctively, "impassive, emotionless." *Passable* and *passible* have correspondingly positive meanings. (These pairs are formed from different Latin roots, L. *passus* "having suffered" and L. *passare* "to step.") Similarly, *impartible* means "not subject to partition" and *impartable* "capable of being imparted." *Conversable* means "oral," whereas *conversible* is a NEEDLESS VARIANT of *convertible.* *Forcible* means either "effected by means of force" <forcible entry> or "characterized by force"; *forceable,* much less frequently encountered, would be the better term to describe a door that is "capable of being forced open." See **forcible.**

Other variant adjectives, though, are merely duplicative. Typical examples are *extendable, extendible,* and *extensible.* The first of these is now prevalent in AmE (though labeled obsolete in the *OED*). *Extensible* was, through the mid-20th century, the most common form, but today it trails *extendable* by a substantial margin, while *extendible* continues to appear infrequently. Writers and editors ought to settle on the most firmly established form—*extendable,* which is as well formed as the variants—and trouble their minds with weightier matters. See NEEDLESS VARIANTS, DIFFERENTIATION & MUTE E.

B. Appended to Nouns. This suffix is usually appended as a passive suffix to verbs (e.g., *forgettable, avoidable, reproachable*). Sometimes, however, it has been joined with nouns (e.g., *objectionable, actionable, dutiable, marriageable, salable*—even *clergyable* and *reversionable,* qq.v.). These do not mean "able to be objectioned," "able to be actioned," and so on. *Objectable* would perhaps have been the more logical formation, though time, idiom, and usage have made many such forms as *actionable* both ineradicable and unobjectionable.

C. Converting *-ate* Verbs into *-able* Adjectives. When the suffix *-able* is added to a transitive polysyllabic word ending in *-ate,* that suffix is dropped. Hence, *accumulable, calculable, estimable,* etc. (See -ATABLE.) Exceptions, however, occur with the two-syllable words (e.g., *rebatable, debatable*).

D. Dropping or Retaining the Medial *-e-*. This question arises in words such as *movables,* q.v., which sometimes takes the form *moveables.* Maine used such forms as *irreconcileable* and *resumeable*—forms that are now archaic. See Henry S. Maine, *Ancient Law* 85, 241 (17th ed. 1901; repr. [New Universal Lib.] 1905, 1910). Generally today, both AmE and BrE drop such a medial *-e-,* except in words with a soft *-c- (traceable)* or a soft *-g- (chargeable).* See MUTE E.

able-bodied seaman; able seaman. The former, though much more recent, seems to be the usual term in admiralty law, meaning "a merchant seaman certified for all seaman's duties" (*AHD*). It is abbreviated *A.B.* The phrase *able seaman* is used in the United States Shipping Code, 46 U.S.C. § 7307 (1988). It also appears in Herman Melville's *Billy Budd* (1891). It would be difficult and footless to categorize either as a NEEDLESS VARIANT of the other. See **seaman & mariner.**

aboard. Usually restricted to ships in BrE, this word is used broadly in AmE—e.g.: "Two of the passengers *aboard* the bus were killed." *State Farm Fire & Casualty Co. v. Tashire,* 386 U.S. 523, 525 (1967).

abode, as past tense of *abide.* See **abide (B).**

abode, place of. This phrase is a pretentious way of referring to someone's home or house.

abolishment; admonishment. These nouns are inferior to—and much rarer than—the organically derived *abolition* and *admonition;* no longer is there any difference in meaning between the *-ment* and the *-tion* forms. The *-ment* forms waywardly persist in much legal writing. E.g., "The Securities Industry Association issued a 'legal alert' that refers to the NYSE memo and its strongly worded *admonishment* [read *admonition*] to have securities loan arrangements covered by written agreement."/ "The Legislature must be given a fair opportunity to take whatever action it should deem advisable before the *abolishment* [read *abolition*] of the long-accepted immunity."

aborigine was long considered to be correct only in the plural form, *aboriginal* being the singular noun. Today, however, *aborigine* has entered standard English as a singular noun. But in Australia, *Aboriginal* with the initial capital is the only correct form in formal usage.

abort = (1) (of a pregnancy) to end prematurely; (2) (of a fetus) to cause to be expelled before full development; or (3) (of a pregnant woman) to cause to have an abortion. Senses (1) and (2) are more usual than sense (3), which, as an example of HYPALLAGE, strikes many readers as odd. E.g., "In a case of 1949, the trial judge sentenced a husband who had tried to *abort* his wife and killed her to five years' penal servitude . . . ." Glanville Williams, *The Sanctity of Life and the Criminal Law* 155 (1957).

abortee. Logically, one might expect this word to refer to the fetus (one who is aborted)—but by convention, and based on sense (3) of *abort,* the word *abortee* refers to the woman whose miscarriage has been produced. See Rollin M. Perkins, *Criminal Law* 100 (1957). Today the word is little used even in legal contexts, perhaps because it seems callous. See -EE.

aborticide. See **abortion.**

abortifacient; contraceptive. The former is anything intended to produce an abortion. The latter is anything designed to prevent conception. *Abortifacient* should not be used to include *contraceptive.*

abortion; aborticide; feticide. The word *abortion,* strictly speaking, means no more than "the expulsion of a nonviable fetus" (*W3*). In this sense it is synonymous with *miscarriage.* But today it more commonly applies specifically to an intentionally induced miscarriage—not one that results naturally or accidentally. Though *abortion* was once used interchangeably with *criminal abortion,* that is no longer so with the advent of *legalized abortion.* In the criminal context, then, it is necessary to use the full phrase *criminal abortion* or *crime of abortion.*

Aborticide = the act of destroying a live fetus. It appears to be a NEEDLESS VARIANT of *abortion*—and a tendentious one. In any event, though, *aborticide* is an ill-formed equivalent of *feticide.* If, as the dictionaries suggest, it is formed on the verb *abort,* then ironically it is what Fowler called an "abortion," but here is termed a MORPHOLOGICAL DEFORMITY. If it is formed on the noun *abortus* (= an aborted fetus), then it is illogical, for an abortionist does not—except in the grossest imaginable circumstances—"kill" (*-cide*) a fetus that has already been aborted. *Aborticide* is to be avoided in favor of the superior alternative, *feticide* (BrE *fœticide*).

The term *feticide* is often used to describe the death of a fetus caused by an assault and battery against the mother.

The current euphemism for *abortion*—a highly charged term since the Supreme Court handed down *Roe v. Wade,* 410 U.S. 113 (1973)—is *pregnancy termination.* See EUPHEMISMS.

ABORTIONS, LINGUISTIC. See MORPHOLOGICAL DEFORMITIES.

abortive; aborted. *Abortive* may mean (1) "unsuccessful," or (2) "inchoate." With sense (1), it takes on the figurative sense of *aborted* (= cut short), as *an abortive trial,* i.e., one cut short before the verdict by, e.g., settlement of the dispute. (Note that *-ive,* an active suffix, here has a passive sense.) E.g., "A jury convicted appellants of various offenses arising out of an *abortive* scheme to import a large quantity of marijuana into the United States from Mexico." In the following sentence, *abortive* has the sense "unsuccessful" without the connotations of "cut short": "More cross-examinations with well-chosen objectives are rendered *abortive* by the pursuit of 'will o' the wisp' decoys than by any other single factor."

Abortive is archaic in reference to abortions of fetuses, except in the sense "causing an abortion"; and in that sense, it is a NEEDLESS VARIANT of *abortifacient,* q.v.

abound. See **many (B).**

about; approximately. *Approximately* is a FORMAL WORD; *about* is the ordinary, perfectly good equivalent. *About* should not be used, as it often is, with other terms of approximation such as *estimate* or *guess,* because it means "roughly" or "approximately." Hence, "roughly about $10,000" is redundant.

above. A. Meaning "more than" or "longer than." This usage is to be restricted to informal contexts. "*Above* [read *More than*] six-hundred lawsuits have been filed since the tragedy."/ "Should the piano remain, by mutual consent, *above* [read *longer than*] the term of four months, it is understood that the company is to pay Stieff interest at the rate of six percent per annum."

B. For *above-mentioned.* *Above* is an acceptable ellipsis for *above-mentioned* if clear in context; and it is much less inelegant—e.g.: "The *above* arguments apply only to judicial disqualification under section 455(a)."

It was long thought that *above* could not properly act as an adjective; but the word has been so used in legal writing throughout the 20th century, even by the best legal writers. E.g., "[I]f the *above* sections were the only law bearing on the matter, [we assume] that they created a civil liability to make reparation to any one whose rights were infringed." *Slater v. Mexican Nat'l R.R.,* 194 U.S. 120, 126 (1904)./ "Yet in the middle of the *above* passage from Lord Lindley's opinion there is a sudden and question-begging shift in the use of terms." (Hohfeld) The *OED* records this use from 1873 and states: "By ellipsis of a pple. as *said, written, mentioned, above* stands attributively, as 'the above explanation.'"

Some critics have suggested that *above* in this sense should refer only to something mentioned previously on the same page, but this restriction seems unduly narrow. Nevertheless, it is generally better to make the reference exact by giving a page or paragraph number, rather than the vague reference made possible by *above.* Idiom will not, however, allow *above* to modify all nouns: *above vehicle* is unidiomatic for *above-mentioned vehicle.* Better yet would be *the vehicle,* if we know from the context which one we are talking about.

A less than common and NEEDLESS VARIANT of *above-mentioned* is *before-mentioned.* See **above-mentioned, afore & aforesaid.**

C. As an Attributive Noun. This casualism, which has appeared even in Supreme Court opinions, derives from the uses discussed in section (B). E.g., "Do not hesitate to call me if the *above* is not the agreement we have made."

above-captioned. See **above-mentioned.**

above-made is an unnecessary word, and an ugly one. E.g., "The following decisions of this court fully sustain the *above-made statements* [read *these statements* or *the above statements*]."

above-mentioned; above-quoted; above-styled; above-captioned. All such compounds should be hyphenated; one sees the tendency nowadays to spell *above-quoted* and *above-mentioned* as single words. Actually, it is best to avoid these compounds altogether by using more specific references; that is, instead of writing *the above-mentioned court,* one should name the court (or, if it has just been named, write *the court, that court,* or some similar identifying phrase). Then again, any of these options may simply be a sign of OVERPARTICULARIZATION, the cure for which would be simply to omit the reference altogether. See **above (B), aforesaid** & **captioned.**

above-referenced. See **reference,** v.t.

above-stated. See **above (B)** & **aforesaid.**

abridgable. See **abridgeable.**

abridge; violate. Constitutional and other rights are often said to be *abridged* or *violated.* A connotative distinction is possible, however. *Violate* is the stronger word: when rights are *abridged,* they are merely diminished; when rights are *violated,* they are flouted outright. Following are examples of the milder term: "The provision of a new and sanitary building does not ensure that it will be operated in a constitutional way; the first amendment can be *abridged* in the cleanest quarters."/ "A statute denying nonresidents the privilege of serving as trustees of living trusts might be unconstitutional as *abridging* the privileges and immunities of citizens of the United States."

abridg(e)able. *Abridgeable* is more common in AmE, *abridgable* in BrE.

abridg(e)ment. The British usually spell it with the *-e-,* and the Americans always without it. Armed with this knowledge, an American writer should not defend his "misspelling" on grounds that he prefers the BrE form. Cf. **acknowledg(e)ment** & **judg(e)ment.**

abrogate; obrogate; arrogate. *Abrogate,* far more common than *obrogate,* means "to abolish (a law or established usage) by authoritative or formal action; annul; repeal." *Abrogate* is occasionally confused with *arrogate* (= to usurp). The proper use of *abrogate* is illustrated here: "Texas courts will *abrogate* school district policies only when they clearly violate statutory provisions."

Obrogate is a civil-law term meaning "to repeal (a law) by passing a new one" (*OED*).

Arrogate (= to usurp) is properly used in the following sentence: "Courts may *arrogate* the authority of deciding what the individual may say and may not say, and there may be readily brought about the very condition against which the constitutional guaranty was intended as a permanent protection." See **arrogate.**

abscond is both transitive ("to hide away, conceal [something]") and intransitive ("to depart secretly or suddenly; to hide oneself"). The latter is more common in modern contexts—e.g.: "He sold the cottages, called in the mortgage, and *absconded* with the proceeds . . . ." Rupert Cross & J.W. Harris, *Precedent in English Law* 46 (4th ed. 1991).

abscondee (= one who absconds) is, like *escapee,* q.v., illogically formed, and it is rarer than the better-formed *absconder,* the usual agent-noun: "Evidently, because of loose security safeguards, the *abscondees* [read *absconders*] just walked out of the hotel." *Ledesma-Valdes v. Sava,* 604 F. Supp. 675, 677 (S.D.N.Y. 1985)./ "Appellant, age 15, was an *abscondee* [read *absconder*] from a youth development center . . . ." *Commonwealth v. Thomas,* 392 A.2d 820, 821 (Pa. Super. 1978). See -EE.

abscondence; abscondment; absconsion. The second and third are NEEDLESS VARIANTS rarely found; *abscondence* is the preferred and much more common noun corresponding to the verb *abscond,* q.v. E.g., "[D]efendant demonstrated a command of the English language not likely to have been acquired during his period of abscondence . . . ." *People v. Ferrer,* 551 N.Y.S.2d 201, 201-02 (N.Y. App. Div. 1990). *Abscondance* is an infrequent misspelling.

absconder. See **abscondee.**

absent (= in the absence of; without) is commonly used as a preposition in legal writing. It can be effective if sparingly used. E.g., "The statute, in permitting a verdict of guilty *absent* a finding of a design to effect death, allows the imputation of intent from one defendant to another."/ "*Absent* a clear manifestation of a contrary intent, it is presumed that the settlor intended the trustee to take a fee simple so that in selling he could pass title as owner rather than as donee of a power." For an interesting discussion of how this American LEGALISM has spread into nonlegal contexts, see two pieces by Alan R. Slotkin: Absent *"Without": Adjective, Participle, or Preposition,* 60 Am. Speech 222 (1985); *Prepositional* Absent*: An Afterword,* 64 Am. Speech 167 (1989).

absentee, used as an adverb, is a new and useful linguistic development. E.g., "Our inquiry as to [read *into*] why the defendants took Alaniz and her son and daughter to vote *absentee* has to begin with whether the request came from Alaniz herself." It would be cumbersome in that context to have to write, "to vote as absentees." *W3* records *absentee* as a noun only, but the adverbial usage is increasingly widespread. The word may also function as an adjective, as in *absentee* landlord.

ABSOLUTE CONSTRUCTIONS. Nominative absolutes, increasingly rare in modern prose, allow writers to vary their syntax while concisely subordinating incidental matter. Such phrases do not bear an ordinary grammatical relation to the rest of the sentence, since the noun or noun phrase does not perform any of the usual functions (subject, object, apposition, etc.) that grammatically attach nouns to other words in the sentence. Yet the whole absolute phrase adverbially modifies some verb. E.g., *"The court adjourning* [i.e., *When the court adjourned*], we left the courtroom."

This construction often has an antique literary flavor. Few modern writers would use the nominative absolute in the way Herman Melville did: "[A] drumhead court was summarily convened, *he electing* the individuals composing it . . . ." *Billy Budd* 63 (1891; repr. Signet ed. 1979). (The pronoun *he* is modified by the participle *electing*; *the individuals composing it* is the object of *electing.* The whole phrase *he electing the individuals composing it* is a nominative absolute, for it has no grammatical function in the statement *A drumhead court was summarily convened.*)

But most modern examples don't strike readers as being so stuffy, as the following examples of the nominative absolute show:

- "In *Martin v. Texas, Harlan writing* again for a unanimous Court, the defendant's allegations of discrimination were unsupported by any evidence whatever and were denied." (If a pronoun were to be used instead of *Harlan,* the absolute phrase would read "he writing again for the court.")
- "For the purposes of this proceeding, at least, it is conceded that the collision was solely the result of Holeman's negligence, *he apparently having been intoxicated* at the time."
- *"The husband being about to sail,* the alleged parol agreement sued upon was made." (Eng.)
- *"This court having found that* the two types of uses under the trademark maintenance program were not sufficient uses to avoid prima facie proof of abandonment, the district court must specifically address Exxon's intent to resume use of the HUMBLE trademark."

In the following example, the writer attempted a nominative absolute, but incorrectly used the possessive rather than the nominative case: "The trial court concluded [that] Vance was not a good candidate for non-state prison sanction, *his* [read *he*] having 'manipulated the system before.'" *Vance v. State,* 475 So. 2d 1362, 1363 (Fla. Dist. Ct. App. 1985).

absolute, decree. See **decree absolute.**

absolute liability. See **strict liability.**

absolute, rule. See **decree absolute.**

absolve, depending on the context, takes either *of* or *from.* One is absolved *of* financial liability, and absolved *from* wrongdoing—assuming the courts treat one kindly. In the following sentence, *from* appears wrongly for *of:* "If the mother contributed nothing to his support because she was absolved *therefrom* [read, if we must, *thereof*] under the act, no expectation of pecuniary advantage exists."

Here the opposite error appears: "Cnudde considered that Hardgrave's letter completely *absolved* her *of* [read *from*] any charges of improper behavior in her teaching methods or in the context of her course."

absolvitor. See **assoil.**

absorb; adsorb; sorb. *Absorb* is the common term meaning "to soak up"; *adsorb* is a scientific term used in referring to condensing gas. *Sorb* is a relatively obscure term comprehending both of its prefixed siblings.

abstract, n. American lawyers often use *abstract* as a shortened form of the phrase *abstract of title* (= the history of a particular tract of land, consisting of a written summary of the material parts of every recorded instrument affecting title).

abstract, v.t.**; abstractify.** *Abstract* is the CHAMELEON-HUED verb meaning (1) "to separate"; (2) "to summarize" <to abstract a judgment or title>; (3) "to divert"; (4) "to steal"; or (5) "to make (something concrete) abstract."

The *OED* labels sense (4) a EUPHEMISM. In that sense—"to take away secretly, slyly, or dishonestly"—*abstract* is a FORMAL WORD that really beclouds the act it describes. E.g., "Universal's funds were surreptitiously *abstracted* and deposited in Richfield's account." A more common word, such as *removed* or *withdrawn,* would be preferable.

Abstractify is not listed in the dictionaries, though it has appeared in legal texts. It serves as a pejorative alternative for sense (5) of *abstract.* Perhaps it is a useful invention, for there is no reason for *abstract* to undergo any further degeneration of meaning.

abstracter. See **abstractor.**

abstractify. See **abstract.**

abstraction means, to nonlawyers, (1) (rarely) "the act of removing"; (2) "an abstract idea"; (3) "abstractedness"; or (4) "an example of abstract art" (*OAD*). In law, however, *abstraction* = the act of taking, usu. wrongfully or fraudulently, as in *abstraction of funds.* But in the phrase *abstraction of water* (= the taking of water from a river or other source of supply [*CDL*]), the word connotes no wrongdoing, for in England one may obtain a license. See **abstract,** v.t.

ABSTRACTITIS. "How vile a thing . . . is the abstract noun! It wraps a man's thoughts round like cotton wool." Arthur Quiller-Couch, *On the Art of Writing* 109 (1916). *Abstractitis* is Ernest Gowers's term for writing that is so abstract and obtuse (hence abstruse) that the writer does not even know what he or she is trying to say—far be it from the reader, then, to give such writing a coherent meaning.

One sympathizes with a keen reader like Judge Learned Hand, who wrestled with the Internal Revenue Code: "[T]he words . . . dance before my eyes in a meaningless procession: cross-reference to cross-reference, exception upon exception—couched in abstract terms that offer no handle to seize hold of—leave in my mind only a confused sense of some vitally important, but successfully concealed, purport, which it is my duty to extract, but which is within my power, if at all, only after the most inordinate expenditure of time." Learned Hand, *Thomas Walter Swan,* 57 Yale L.J. 167, 169 (1947).

Perhaps the best antidote to this malady—which in some degree afflicts most sophisticated writers—is an active empathy for one's readers. Rigorous thought about concrete meaning, together with careful revision, can eliminate abstractitis.

Three short examples suffice to illustrate the malady:

- "This Note, therefore, structures its analysis around a consideration of definitional methodology and proposes a constitutional definition of religion on the basis of that consideration." Timothy L. Hall, *The Sacred and the Profane,* 61 Tex. L. Rev. 139, 140 (1982). What? The sentence states that the note proposes a definition of religion on the basis of a consideration of methodology, which makes little sense. See OBSCURITY.
- "[A]s used within the context of this book . . . , demonstrative evidence is evidence *which* [read *that*] has, in some form or fashion, been processed." Mark A. Dombroff, *Dombroff on Demonstrative Evidence* 2 (1983). One reads that sentence with mounting expectations of a punch word at the end—yet all we get is the vague word *processed.* What is evidence that has, in some form or fashion, been processed? Been processed by the brain? Unfortunately, even the fuller context of that quotation provides little help.
- "Win or lose, the County Committee is a focal force of substantiality within the electoral process, whether it be for federal, state or local purposes." *Doherty v. Meisser,* 321 N.Y.S.2d 32, 41 (N.Y. Sup. 1971). What is a *focal force of substantiality?*

The first and third examples contain the archetypal abstract words, here termed BURIED VERBS—that is, words ending usually with these suffixes: *-tion, -sion, -ity, -ence, -ance, -ment.* Writers are well advised to take these longish nouns and turn them back into verbs if possible—that is, write *to state,* not *to make a statement*; *to submit,* not *to make a submission*; *to rely on,* not *to evidence a reliance on*; and so on.

The Fowlers quote the following sentence—laden with buried verbs—in *The King's English* (1906): "One of the most important reforms mentioned in the rescript is the unification of the organization of judicial institutions and the guarantee for all the tribunals of the independence necessary for securing to all classes of the community equality before the law." The following revision eliminates the buried verbs: "One of the most important reforms is that of the courts, which need to be independent within a uniform structure. In this way only can people be assured that all are equal before the law." Arthur Quiller-Couch, *The Art of Writing* at 109–10.

The newest vogue in legal theorizing, Critical Legal Studies (q.v.), is characterized by abstractitis and jargonmongering, the favored words in the field being *purposivist, constitutive, coopting, demobilizing, structuralism, deconstruction, formalism,* and *praxis,* among others. See

Louis B. Schwartz, *With Gun and Camera Through Darkest CLS-Land,* 36 Stan. L. Rev. 413, 440 (1984). Some CLS writing reads on this order: "In the reciprocity of roles that are artificial, you think people are more alienated in that bank than I think they are. I think there's more intersubjective zap and unalienated relatedness among tellers." Peter Gabel & Duncan Kennedy, *Roll Over Beethoven,* 36 Stan. L. Rev. 1, 25 (1984). The phrase *intersubjective zap,* by the way, has become a buzz-phrase among CLSers, having now appeared in well over 20 law-review articles.

By some accounts, abstractitis leads to far worse things. "If concepts are not clear," wrote Confucius, "words do not fit." But he did not stop there: "If words do not fit, the day's work cannot be accomplished, morals and art do not flourish. If morals and art do not flourish, punishments are not just. If punishments are not just, the people do not know where to put hand or foot." Confucius, *Analects* XIII, 3. It is no frivolous assertion to say that, when we descend into abstractitis, more than just our language is afflicted.

Fred Rodell—the Yale law professor, realist, and semanticist who frequently criticized lawyers' language—issued his own inimitable warning about abstractitis: "Dealing in words is a dangerous business, and it cannot be too often stressed that what The Law deals in is words. Dealing in long, vague, fuzzy-meaning words is even more dangerous business, and most of the words The Law deals in are long and vague and fuzzy. Making a habit of applying long, vague, fuzzy, general words to specific things and facts is perhaps the most dangerous of all, and The Law does that, too." Fred Rodell, *Woe Unto You, Lawyers!* 39 (1939; repr. 1980).

ABSTRACT NOUNS, PLURALS OF. See PLURALS (B).

abstract of title. See **abstract & title.**

abstractor; abstracter. The *OED* notes that *-or* is "analogically the more regular form"; it is the more usual as well. See -ER (A).

abuse of discretion, the phrase denoting a lenient standard of reviewing a lower court's judgment, signifies "no single level of deference or scrutiny." 1 Steven A. Childress & Martha S. Davis, *Standards of Review* § 4.21, at 287 (1986). The "variability [of the phrase] is not hopeless. It just means that generalizations about the standard may not be helpful." *Id.* at 288.

Abuse in this context is not pejorative; the word here is "wholly unrelated to the meaning of the . . . term when used in common parlance." *Beck v. Wings Field, Inc.,* 122 F.2d 114, 116 (3d Cir. 1941). Thus some writers have proposed substituting *misuse* in place of *abuse.* See, e.g., *Pearson v. Dennison,* 353 F.2d 24, 28 n.6 (9th Cir. 1965). The phrase *abuse of discretion* is unlikely, however, to be changed.

abuse of process. See **malicious prosecution.**

abutment; abuttals. An *abutment* is the place at which two or more things touch. *Abuttals*—a term used only in the plural—means "land boundaries." *Abuttals* usually refers to abstract boundaries, and *abutments* usually to physical structures (e.g., the walls of bridges adjoining land). *Abbuttals* is a variant spelling to be avoided.

abutter; abuttor. *Abutter* is the accepted spelling. The word means either (1) "the owner of adjoining land"; or (2) "land that adjoins the land in question." Sense (1) is far more common.

abysm(al); abyss(al). The nouns are synonymous in signifying "a bottomless gulf." *Abyss* is the more current form, and is therefore to be preferred. Though *abysm* is obsolescent, *abysmal* thrives (indeed, has become trite) as a figurative term for "deep" or "immeasurably great" (*W3*) <abysmal benightedness>. *Abyssal* is a technical oceanographic term <the geology of the abyssal deep>.

accede; exceed. *Accede* = (1) "to agree or consent"; (2) "to come into office or a position of stature"; or (3) "to enter a treaty or accord." It is an intransitive verb that takes the preposition *to. Exceed,* a transitive verb, means (1) "to surpass"; or (2) "to go beyond the proper limits." The first syllable of *accede* should be pronounced with a short *-a-*, so as to differentiate its sound from *exceed.*

accent, v.t.; **accentuate.** These synonyms have a latent distinction that might usefully be observed. Fowler notes that *accent* is more common in literal, and *accentuate* in figurative, senses. Hence one properly *accents* the third syllable of *appellee,* and *accentuates* the weaknesses in an opponent's legal arguments. E.g., "These elements, although *accentuating* the wrong, are not the essence of it."

acceptance; acceptancy; acceptation. The first corresponds to the active sense of the verb (to accept), and the second the passive sense (to be accepted). *Acceptance* = the act of accepting; specif., the final and unqualified expression of assent to the terms of a contractual offer. *Acceptation* = the state of being accepted <widespread acceptation of the doctrine of strict liability in tort

was long in coming>. *Acceptancy* is a NEEDLESS VARIANT of *acceptance,* just as *acception* is for *acceptation.*

Following are examples of *acceptation*—the less common word—used correctly: "In actions of slander, words are to be taken in their common *acceptation.*"/ "That there is no right of property in a dead body in the ordinary *acceptation* of that term [Which term: *property* or *dead body?*] is undoubtedly true when limited to a property right in the commercial sense."

acceptance for honor; acceptance supra protest. Both terms mean "a form of acceptance of a bill of exchange to save the good name of the drawer or an endorser" (*CDL*). Both are TERMS OF ART, *acceptance for honor* perhaps being the more generally comprehensible of the two. *Acceptance supra protest* ought to be avoided.

acceptancy; acceptation. See **acceptance.**

accepter; acceptor. "The first form is now generally used for one who accepts. The second (earlier) form is the legal term, one who accepts, or undertakes the payment of, a bill of exchange." Margaret Nicholson, *A Dictionary of American-English Usage* 6 (1957). *Acceptor* is also regularly used in law, however, of one who accepts an offer to enter into a contract—e.g.: "From the point of view of the offeror it seems immaterial whether the *acceptor* knew of the offer or not." P.S. Atiyah, *An Introduction to the Law of Contract* 52 (3d ed. 1981).

access, as a verb, has its origins in COMPUTERESE. Like a number of nouns turned into verbs (e.g., *contact*), it now seems increasingly well ensconced in the language. As Fowler notes with regard to *contact,* it is an ancient and valuable right for English-speaking peoples to turn their nouns into verbs when they are so minded. *Gain access to* or some other such equivalent is admittedly ungainly alongside *access,* though the latter still jars sensitive ears. "Other electrical units do not *access* the electric energy source through the plug."

accession /*ak-**se**-shən*/ = (1) a coming into possession of an office or right; (2) acquisition of (something connected to one's property) by growth, labor, or the like; or (3) a secondary or subordinate thing that is connected with another thing. Sense (1) is the most common in legal and nonlegal contexts alike <Rehnquist's accession to the Chiefship>; senses (2) and (3) are largely peculiar to legal contexts. Sense (1): "The right [of acquisition] is obtained without an act of possession by: . . . *'Accession,'* when the owner of the principal object becomes also owner of its accessory." Thomas E. Holland, *The Elements of Jurisprudence* 218 (13th ed. 1924)./ Sense (2): "It often happened, however, that of the two things united, one was a mere *accession* to the other, a mere secondary or subordinate part . . . ." James Hadley, *Introduction to Roman Law* 170 (N.Y., D. Appleton & Co. 1881)./ Sense (3): "[W]e held that tires and tubes added to a car did not become a part of it by *accession.*" *Bank of America v. J. & S. Auto Repairs,* 694 P.2d 246, 251 (Ariz. 1985) (en banc).

accessorial (= [1] of or relating to an accessory; or [2] collateral) appears most commonly in sense (1)—e.g.: "We now come to another set of cases in which the English courts have departed from, or at least modified, the derivative theory of *accessorial* liability." Andrew Ashworth, *Principles of Criminal Law* 386 (1991).

Sense (2) has been largely superseded by either *accessory* <accessory promise> or *collateral* <collateral obligation>. See **collateral obligation.**

accessorial obligation. See **collateral obligation.**

accessory, n. **A. And *accessary,*** n. *Accessory* now predominates in AmE and BrE in meaning both "abettor" and "a thing of lesser importance." Though Fowler believed a distinction existed between *accessory* and *accessary* (the first applying primarily to things, the second to persons), the second is now merely a NEEDLESS VARIANT and should be avoided.

B. Pronunciation. Both words discussed in (A) should be pronounced with the first *-c-* as a hard *-k-* sound—hence /*ak-**ses**-ə-ree*/. A common mispronunciation is /*ə-**ses**-ə-ree*/.

C. And *accomplice.* See **accomplice & principal (B).**

accident. A. And *mistake.* In law, the usual distinction is that an *accident* occurs without the willful purpose of the person who causes it. A *mistake,* by contrast, presupposes the operation of a person's will in producing the event, even though the person has been misled by erroneous impressions.

B. And *incident.* "Available statistics establish that flight engineers have rarely been a contributing cause or factor in commercial aircraft *accidents* or *incidents.*" Here *incident* apparently means "near-accident," and for the purposes of one-time differentiation may be justified. *Incident* should be avoided, however, as a EUPHEMISM for *accident.*

accidentally. So spelled; *accidently* is a solecism. The confusion may arise from the form of *evidently* and *patently.* Cf. **incidentally.**

acclimate, -ation; acclimatize, -ization. H.W. Fowler and other authorities prefer the *-ize* forms. Similarly, *W10* includes the primary definitions under *acclimatize* and *acclimatization,* the better forms. In the noun, using *acclimatization* keeps listeners from confusing the homophones *acclimation* and *acclamation.*

accommodable. The word is so formed—not *accommodatable,* as it is sometimes erroneously written. E.g., "[E]qual treatment of inmates is not a legitimate interest when it is accomplished at the expense of denying the exercise of an otherwise *accommodatable* [read *accommodable*] constitutional right." *Goodwin v. Turner,* 908 F.2d 1395, 1405 (8th Cir. 1990) (en banc). See -ATABLE.

accommodation. So spelled. The word is commonly misspelled with one *-m-*.

accommodatum. See **commodatum.**

accomplice; accessory. American writers tend to use *accomplice* to include all principals and accessories before the fact, but to exclude accessories after the fact. Thus, the word embraces all perpetrators, abettors, and inciters. See Rollin M. Perkins & Ronald N. Boyce, *Criminal Law* 727 (3d ed. 1982).

Other writers use *accomplice* to include all principals and *accessories.* The *CDL,* for example, defines *accomplice* as "one who is a party to a crime, either as a perpetrator or as an accessory." And it defines *accessory* as "one who is a party to a crime that is actually committed by someone else (the perpetrator)." This usage appears to be primarily BrE—e.g.: "[W]e are concerned with the first topic—the parties in different degrees of complicity to a crime, who are termed '*accomplices.*' Accomplices consist of the perpetrator and the accessories." Glanville Williams, *Textbook of Criminal Law* 285 (1978).

Still other writers, however, use *accomplice* and *accessory* as synonyms—e.g.: "[A] *principal* is a person whose acts fall within the legal definition of the crime, whereas an *accomplice* (sometimes called an '*accessory*' or '*secondary party*') is anyone who aids, abets, counsels, or procures a principal." Andrew Ashworth, *Principles of Criminal Law* 363–64 (1991). See **accessory.**

accomptant general. See **accountant general.**

accord; accordance. To be *in accord* is to be in agreement. E.g., "This holding was in *accord* with the overwhelming weight of authority in the state courts as reflected in Wigmore's classic treatise on the law of evidence."

This phrasing should not be used in place of a more direct statement—e.g.: "The adoption of this method was based on the premise that the order in point of time of deposits and withdrawals was essential to proof, and that the burden was upon claimant; we are not *in accord with* [read *we reject* (or *disagree with*)] that view."

To be *in accordance* is to be in conformity or compliance. *In accordance* is sometimes cumbersome, but often useful. E.g., "The search was conducted *in accordance* with FCI regulations and without excessive use of force." *Out of accordance* = not in conformity.

Accord is wrongly used for *accordance* in the following sentences: "The agency disbursed funds in *accord* [read *accordance*] with the plan."/ "In *accord* [read *accordance*] with the approach taken by this court in these decisions, we hold that the presentation of an administrative claim in excess of $100,000 is a sum certain under 28 C.F.R. § 14.2."

accord, v.t.; **afford,** v.t. These are CHAMELEON-HUED words that share the meaning "to furnish or grant," as commonly used in legal texts <accorded (or afforded) all the rights due him under due process>. Yet some DIFFERENTIATION is possible: *accord* has the nuance of granting something because it is suitable or proper <accord litigants a stay of costs pending appeal>. E.g., "The children were not *accorded* procedural due process before school officials reached the conclusion that they could not continue to attend school." *Accord* in this sense should usu. take a personal object, not an inanimate one; this error most commonly occurs when *accord* is used as high-sounding substitute for *give:* "I cannot subscribe to the court's sweeping refusal to *accord* [read *give*] the equal protection clause any role in this entire area of the law."/ "Courts generally *accord* [read *give*] statutory language its commonsense meaning." The origin of the correct use of *accord* lies in the historical (and still current) sense "to grant (a thing asked) *to* (a person), to give with full consent, to award" (*OED*).

Intransitively, *accord* takes the prepositions *in, to,* or *with,* depending on the context <we accord in our opinions> <we accord to plaintiff his due> <this accords with the prevailing view>.

Afford is the more general term, meaning "to furnish (something) as an essential concomitant" <afford to the indigent defendant legal representation>. E.g., "The Sixth Amendment guarantees that a person brought to trial in any federal court must be *afforded* the right to assistance of counsel before he can be validly convicted."/"If we *afford* relief *to* this town, will we have to do likewise as each unincorporated village decides to incorporate?"

accord, n.; **concord,** n. Both mean "an amicable arrangement between parties, esp. between peoples or nations; compact; treaty." *Accord* is perhaps the less formal word, and the more frequently used today. See **concord (A).**

accord, used as a signal in citations, ordinarily indicates that the authority cited directly supports the proposition, but in a way slightly different from previously cited authorities. One should include a parenthetical explanation of what that difference is, rather than leaving the reader to search for it. Sometimes it introduces like cases from other jurisdictions. See CITATION OF CASES.

accordance. See **accord.**

accord and satisfaction; compromise and settlement. The former appears usually in contractual contexts. Though the two phrases may overlap to some extent, *compromise and settlement* is used in the context of a dispute more probably giving rise to litigation. It applies to all disputes, not just to those arising from contracts. The two substantive words in *compromise and settlement* are broader than those in *accord and satisfaction,* but *compromise* is roughly analogous to *accord,* and *settlement* to *satisfaction.*

An *accord* is an agreement to substitute for an existing debt or obligation some alternative form of discharging that debt; a *satisfaction* is the actual discharge of the debt by the substituted means. Stated otherwise, an *accord* is the agreement to perform (in an alternative way), and the *satisfaction* is the actual performance. Any claim (if disputed, unliquidated, or undisputed and liquidated) may be discharged by an *accord and satisfaction.*

But only a disputed or unliquidated claim may be the basis for a *compromise and settlement.* Though the two words in this phrase have been used with a variety of meanings and even synonymously, at base *compromise* means "an agreement between two or more persons to settle matters in dispute between them"; *settlement* means "the performance of promises made in a compromise agreement."

according. A. *According to.* This is a weak form of attribution <according to Corbin, . . .>; a text sprinkled with *according to*'s gives the appearance of having little originality. Legal writers should avoid the phrase when attributing an idea.

B. *According as.* This phrase means "in a manner corresponding to the way in which; just as." E.g., "The special law is either favorable or unfavorable *according as* it enlarges or restricts, in opposition to the common rule, the rights of those for whom it is established." (See the quotation from Blackstone under **misdemeanor.**)

C. *According to; accordingly to.* *According to* = (1) depending on; (2) as explained or reported by (a person); or (3) in accordance with. Sense (1): "The Courts exercise what, *according to* our prepossessions, we call a moderating or an obstructive influence." W.W. Buckland, *Some Reflections on Jurisprudence* 43 (1945).

D. As a Dangler. For *according* as an acceptable dangling modifier, see DANGLERS (D).

accordingly. See **according (C).**

accost (= to approach and usu. to speak to in an abrupt or challenging manner) has historically had no connotations of physical contact. Hence it would traditionally be considered inappropriate in the following sentence: "One lady leaving the shop was grabbed by the arm and in a threatening manner told that she had better not go in the place again because it was a 'scab' shop; another lady was likewise *accosted* and told that she ought to be shot for going into that 'scab' shop." *Accost* is not a strong enough word for that context; *assault* (in the nonlawyer's sense) might have served better.

In the following sentence, the author might not have contemplated physical contact as part of the "initial contact," so the meaning is unclear: "[W]here the two were strangers and the circumstances of the initial contact were involuntary—*accosted* in parking lots, house break-ins—nearly everyone was certain that a rape had occurred." Susan Estrich, *Real Rape* 13 (1987). Cf. **altercation & assault.**

account, n. = (1) a detailed statement of the debits and credits between parties to a contract or to a fiduciary relationship; (2) a statement of monetary transactions; (3) at common law, a legal action used by a lord of a manor to order his bailiff to account for the profits of the manor; (4) more modernly, a legal action commenced by one who has given another person money to be applied in a particular way, the action being designed to compel the receiver of the money to provide details of the debts owed to the plaintiff. For one variety of sense (4), see **account stated.**

accountable takes *for* or *to,* not *from.* E.g., "A factor or commission merchant is to be held strictly accountable *from* [read *for*] any deviation from instructions received from his principal."

accountancy. See **generally accepted accounting principles.**

accountant is a POPULARIZED LEGAL TECHNICALITY that originally, in the 15th century, denoted "the defendant in an action of account." (See **account,** n.) By extension, in the 16th century, the word came to mean "one whose occupation is the keeping of accounts."

accountant general; accomptant general. The latter spelling—originating in the Renaissance habit of respelling French loanwords on the Latin model—is archaic. Cf. **comptroller.**

accounting. See **bookkeeping** & **generally accepted accounting principles.**

account stated. This phrase bears two distinct meanings: (1) an agreed balance between parties settling an action for debt; (2) a defendant's plea, in response to a bill for an accounting, in which the defendant states that the balance found due on the statement of the account has been discharged and that the defendant holds the plaintiff's release. See **account.**

accouter(ments); accoutre(ments). As with many other words having this suffix, the *-er* form is AmE, the *-re* BrE.

accreditate, a BACK-FORMATION from *accreditation,* is a NEEDLESS VARIANT of *accredit.*

accrual; accruer. *Accruer,* like *accruement,* is an obsolete form of *accrual,* the general noun corresponding to the verb *accrue. Accruer* survives only in the phrase *clause of accruer.* Yet *accrual* has made substantial inroads even into this phrase, so that *accrual* and *accruer* now coexist needlessly. It is time to reject the archaic, and to establish firmly the modern form. Hence we should write *clause of accrual.*

accrue. A. Restriction to Financial Context. At least two critics have recommended that this word be restricted to monetary contexts, quite unaware of its most common meaning in legal contexts. Interest *accrues,* we may be certain, but so do causes of action—at least in jurisdictions in which they do not *arise.* (See (B).) E.g., "Plaintiff's cause of action for silicosis did not *accrue* until the plaintiff either knew of or had reason to know of the disease."

This use should not be extended further to mean "to inure to the benefit of," however, as here: "The appellate issue turns on whether the tax attributes associated with operations of certain commercial real estate properly *accrued to* [read *inured to the benefit of*] the corporation that held legal title."

B. *Accrue* and *arise.* In reference to causes of action, some courts have held that *accrue* and *arise* are synonymous, others that they can be distinguished. *Arise* may refer to the onset of the underlying wrong (e.g., exposure to asbestos), whereas *accrue* may refer to the ripeness of the claim (e.g., contraction of asbestosis or discovery of the disease). We need not set down a rule of usage so much as beware of the ambiguities of these terms in this particular context.

accruement. See **accrual.**

accruer. See **accrual.**

accumulate, -tive; cumulate, -tive. The former is far more common as the verb; the latter is current only in the adjective it yields *(cumulative). Accumulate* and *cumulate* both mean "to pile up; collect." *Cumulate,* however, should generally be avoided as a NEEDLESS VARIANT. *Accumulate* has the additional intransitive sense "to increase."

The adjectives demonstrate more palpable DIFFERENTIATION. In one sense they are synonymous: "increasing by successive addition," in which meaning *cumulative* is the usual and therefore the preferred term. *Cumulative* also means: (1) "relating to interest or a dividend paid to the corpus if not disbursed when due"; or (2) in law, "increasing in force as a result of additional or supporting evidence." In Scots law, *cumulative* is used also to mean "concurrent" <to serve cumulative sentences>.

Accumulative = acquisitive; inclined to amass. In addition, it has the meanings ascribed to *cumulative.* Yet it would be salutary to strengthen the distinction and restrict *accumulative* to the sense "acquisitive."

accusation; accusal. The first, of course, is current; the second is an obsolete word now classifiable as a NEEDLESS VARIANT. E.g., "Even families who limit themselves to superficial conversations . . . will recognize the dynamics at work here—the mother-son thing, the mother-daughter thing, the sister-brother thing, the brother-brother thing, the whole stew of tensions and attractions, *accusals* [read *accusations*] and denials." Dan Sullivan, *"Total Blame,"* L.A. Times, 2 Dec. 1989, at F9. Cf. **recusal.**

accusative. See **accusatory.**

accusatorial; inquisitorial. *Accusatorial* = (1) of or pertaining to an accuser; or (2) indicating the form of criminal prosecution in which the alleged criminal is publicly accused of the crime and is tried in public by a judge who does not act as the prosecutor" <accusatorial procedure>. Sense (2) grew directly out of sense (1), for, in the accusatorial system of criminal trial, the victim (i.e., accuser) made complaint against the offender.

Today, of course, *accusatorial* denotes the common-law system of criminal procedure. It is commonly contrasted with the civil-law term *inquisitorial,* which describes "a system of criminal justice . . . in which the truth is revealed by an inquiry into the facts conducted by the judge" (*CDL*).

Despite its neutral sense in civil law, *inquisitorial* often appears in common-law contexts as a pejorative word—e.g.: "The interrogation described in *Miranda* illustrated the extreme importance that American society placed on criminal prosecution, allowing tricks, cajolery, and even coercion to secure evidence from the suspect; the distinction between the *inquisitorial* and the *accusatorial* systems had become blurred."

A variant term for *accusatorial procedure* is *adversary procedure,* although the latter term may suggest civil as well as criminal proceedings.

accusatory; accusative; accusatorial. *Accusatory* (= accusing; of the nature of an accusation) is occasionally confused with *accusatorial,* q.v.

Accusative, although sometimes used in the place of *accusatory,* should be restricted to its grammatical sense relating to the objective case of nouns. E.g., "The feelings, attitudes and relations of the parents of the five-year-old child are strained, *accusative* [read *accusatory*] and acrimonious." *Rodgers v. Hill,* 453 So. 2d 1057, 1058 (Ala. Civ. App. 1984)./ "There is no contention herein that the witness was emotional, condemnatory, *accusative* [read *accusatory*] or demanding vindication." *McQueen v. Commonwealth,* 669 S.W.2d 519, 523 (Ky. 1984).

accuse may be used transitively or, less commonly, intransitively. Here it is intransitive: "It is conceivable that the Court has overstepped its boundaries as the dissenting Justices *accuse.*" See **charge (A).**

Usually a word for criminal-law contexts, *accuse* has also been used to introduce allegations of noncriminal conduct (as in the preceding quotation). E.g., "The teams stand *accused,* essentially, of refusing to grant plaintiff's cablecast rights in furtherance of a conspiracy with Cablevision to monopolize cable television trade in Huntington."

accuse; charge. One is *accused of,* but *charged with,* a misfeasance.

accused, n., (= the defendant in a criminal case) was once said to be "more appropriate than either *prisoner* or *defendant.*" Archibald Brown, *A New Law Dictionary* 10 (1874; repr. 1988). Its superiority to *prisoner*—a word that can prejudice juries (and perhaps even judges)—is unquestionable. But why it should have been considered "more appropriate" than *defendant* is a mystery. Today it is certainly less common in American and British courts than *defendant,* a colorless term: "[I]f you were on trial for a crime, would you rather be called 'the *accused*' or 'the *defendant*'? It seems to me that the latter expression is preferable, as the more neutral." Glanville Williams, *Textbook of Criminal Law* 93 n.3 (1978).

From a stylistic point of view, *accused* becomes awkward in the possessive case or as a plural: "The *accused's* silence may generate a reasonable inference that the accused believed the statement to be true." Usually this awkwardness can be remedied by use of the genitive: "The *silence* (or *statement*) of the accused . . ."; or, "The *accused person's silence* (or *statement*) . . . ." Cf. **deceased.** See POSSESSIVES (F) & PLURALS (D).

accusee is a NEEDLESS VARIANT of *accused,* q.v. E.g., "Later, [Judge Oren R. Lewis] turned to James S. Augus, the senior Justice Department trial lawyer, and accused him of 'shifting the burden of proof from the accuser [the Justice Department] to the *accusee* [read *accused*] . . . .'" Robert Meyers, *Courtroom Becomes Classroom,* Washington Post, 17 March 1979, at C3./ "This would, of course, suggest Nicholas Daniloff, U.S. News' Moscow correspondent, as the actual *accusee* [read *accused*]." Rance Crain, *Spying Inside the Inside Story,* Advertising Age, 29 Sept. 1986, at 46. See -EE.

accuser; accusor. The *-er* form is standard. See -ER (A).

accustomed. Formerly, the idiom was *accustomed to do*—e.g.: "[F]rom the beginning of our legal studies we are *accustomed to think* of law and equity as sharply divided." Carleton K. Allen, *Law in the Making* 413 (7th ed. 1964). But in the mid-20th century, the idiom shifted to *accustomed to doing, accustomed to thinking,* etc. Today the older usage sounds strange to many ears, but some traditionalists stick to it.

acerbic, in AmE, is sometimes considered inferior to *acerb,* but the latter is so rare—and the former so common—that the criticism is misplaced. *Acerbic* is standard in BrE, in which *acerb* is virtually unknown. The noun is *acerbity.*

acknowledg(e)ment. A. Spelling. As with *judgment* and *abridgment,* the spelling without the *-e-* is preferable in AmE, *acknowledgement* being more common in BrE.

B. And *verification.* An *acknowledgment* is a formal declaration made in the presence of an authorized officer, such as a notary public, by someone who signs a document and swears to the authenticity of the signature. E.g., "It is sufficient if the testator states to the witnesses that the signature is his signature. This is known as *ackowledgment* of the signature." Robert Kratovil, *Real Estate Law* 245 (1946).

A *verification,* by contrast, is such a formal declaration by which one swears to the truth of the statements in the document. E.g., "After making demand for judgment for $955, defendants appended a *verification,* notarized and sealed, in which they swore that the facts stated in the [answer were] . . . 'true and correct.'" *Miller v. Master Home Builders, Inc.,* 239 A.2d 696, 697 (Del. Super. Ct. 1968).

a consiliis. See **of counsel.**

acquaintanceship is a NEEDLESS VARIANT of *acquaintance*; it adds nothing to the language except another syllable, which we scarcely need. E.g., "The trial judge's *acquaintanceship* [read *acquaintance*] with the witness was not unusual in that it is to be expected that he would have contacts with other members of his bar in the normal practice of law."

acquiesce takes *in* or *to.* Some authorities have suggested that *in* is the only proper preposition. Yet the *OED* shows age-old examples with the construction *acquiesce to,* and its labeling that construction obsolete must be deemed a premature judgment, for it is fairly common in legal texts. E.g., "[T]he defense requested, or at least *acquiesced to,* the inclusion of a voluntary manslaughter instruction in the jury charge." Clara Tuma, *Appeal of Self-Made Error Denied,* Tex. Law., 7 Oct. 1991, at 9. *Acquiesce with* is not, however, in good use. The verb has three distinct syllables: /*ak-wee-**es***/.

acquiescence. See **permission.**

acquirement; acquisition. "The former denotes the power or faculty of acquiring; the latter, the thing acquired." Eric Partridge, *Usage and Abusage* 17 (1973). E.g., "His *acquirements* in law surpass his *acquisition* of wealth." Both also mean "the act of acquiring," though *acquisition* is more usual.

acquirer. So spelled—not *acquiror,* as it is sometimes misspelled: "[T]he *acquiror* [read *acquirer*] gained a substantial position in the target company's stock." *Gearhart Indus., Inc. v. Smith Int'l, Inc.,* 592 F. Supp. 203, 218 (N.D. Tex. 1984).

acquisition. See **acquirement.**

acquit. A. Civil and Criminal Contexts. Leff writes: "One might loosely refer to a party '*acquitted*' in a civil action, though one would ordinarily be tempted to use the terminology only if the cause were quasi-criminal, e.g., an action charging actual fraud, or an intentional physical tort like battery." Arthur A. Leff, *The Leff Dictionary of Law,* 94 Yale L.J. 1855, 1905 (1985).

B. Preposition with. The verb *acquit* takes *of,* not *from*—e.g.: "In the end James was induced to withdraw a letter resigning from the Society, after the Council had passed a resolution *acquitting* him *from* [read *of*] any unfairness." K.M. Elisabeth Murray, *Caught in the Web of Words* 286 (1977).

C. Past Tense. As a past-tense verb or a past-participial adjective, the form *acquit* is obsolete. It lives only in the LAW FRENCH phrase *autrefois acquit* (= heretofore acquitted). The accepted form today is *acquitted.*

acquittal; acquittance; acquitment. The first is the usual term, meaning both (1) "a release or discharge from debt or other liability" (*W3*); and (2) "a setting free or deliverance from the charge of an offense by verdict of a jury, sentence of a court, or other legal process" (*W3*). *Acquitment,* a NEEDLESS VARIANT, is obsolete.

Acquittance is obsolete in all senses except "a written release showing that a debtor has been discharged of an obligation." Perhaps it would be advantageous to allow *acquittance* this commercial meaning, and to leave *acquittal* to the criminal law. E.g., "There are suggestions in the case that if Mrs. Beer on receipt of the last installment had given Dr. Foakes an '*acquittance*'—that is, an acknowledgment of payment in full—that would have been binding on her." Grant Gilmore, *The Death of Contract* 31 (1974).

acquittal-prone. See **guilt-prone.**

acquittee (= one acquitted of a crime) is an ugly NEOLOGISM; the phrase *acquitted defendant* is ordinarily the better choice. E.g., "The Code also provides that the *acquittee* [read *acquitted defendant*] is entitled to a judicial hearing every six months." *Jones v. U.S.*, 463 U.S. 354, 354 (1983)./ "He is, therefore, not an 'insanity *acquittee*' but a 'criminally insane committee.'" *Glatz v. Kort,* 650 F. Supp. 191, 195 (D. Colo. 1984). [Read *He is therefore not a defendant acquitted by reason of insanity, but one committed to a guardian as criminally insane.*] See **committee** & -EE.

ACRONYMS AND INITIALISMS. Four points merit our attention here. First, we should be aware of the traditional distinction between the two types of abbreviated names. An *acronym* is made from the initial letters or parts of a phrase or compound term. One ordinarily reads or speaks it as a single word, not letter by letter (e.g., *radar* = radio detection and ranging). An *initialism,* by contrast, is made from the initial letters or parts of a phrase or compound term, but is usually pronounced letter by letter, not as a single word (e.g., *r.p.m.* = revolutions per minute).

Second, the question often arises whether to place periods after each letter in an acronym or initialism. Search for consistency on this point is futile. The trend nowadays is to omit the periods; including them is the more traditional approach. Yet surely if an acronym is spoken as a single word (e.g., ERISA, ERTA), periods are meaningless. If an initialism is made up of lowercase letters, periods are preferable: *rpm* looks odd as compared with *r.p.m.*, and *am* looks like the verb (as opposed to *a.m.*). One method of determining whether to omit or include periods is to follow the form of the organization one names (e.g., IRS, HUD), although inconsistencies are common.

Third, the best practice is to give the reader some forewarning of uncommon acronyms by spelling out the words and enclosing the acronym in parentheses when the term is first used. A reference to *CARPE Rules* may confuse a reader who does not at first realize that three or four lines above this acronym the writer has referred to a Committee on Academic Rights, Privileges, and Ethics.

Finally, as illustrated under the entry entitled INITIALESE, the use in a single text of a number of these abbreviated forms leads to dense and frustrating prose.

act. **A. And *action*.** These are important words in law; yet they are often used indiscriminately. To be sure, the words overlap a great deal, and it is difficult to delineate the distinctions accurately. *Act* is the more concrete, *action* the more abstract word. But even *act* is a vague word, "being used in various senses of different degrees of generality. When it is said, however, that an act is one of the essential conditions of liability, we use the term in the widest sense of which it is capable. We mean by it any event [that] is subject to the control of the human will." M.G. Paulsen & S.H. Kadish, *Criminal Law and Its Processes* 212 (1962).

Generally, *act* denotes the thing done, *action* the doing of it. Crabb approaches a workable demarcation:

> When these words are taken in the sense of the thing done, they admit of a . . . distinction. An *act* is the single thing done, or what is done by a single effort, as that is your *act* or his *act*; an *action* may consist of more *acts* than one, or embrace the causes or the consequences of the action, as a bold *action,* to judge of *actions,* etc.
>
> Hence it is that the term *act* is more proper than *action* where it is so defined as to imply what is single and simple, as an *act* of authority, an *act* of government, an *act* of folly, and the like; but otherwise the word *action* is to be preferred where the moral conduct or character is in question. We may enumerate particular *acts* of a man's life, as illustrative of certain traits of his character, or certain circumstances of his life; but to speak at large of his *actions* would be to describe his character.
>
> George Crabb, *Crabb's English Synonymes* 24–25 (1917).

As a further gloss, *action* suggests a process—the many discrete events that make up a bit of behavior—whereas *act* is unitary.

B. *Act of omission.* Is it proper to speak of an *act of omission,* or does *act* invariably denote a positive act, i.e., an act of commission? Usage differs: in the phrase *act or omission,* the word *act* denotes an act of commission, as opposed to a forbearance; but at other times the word appears to include a forbearance as well as an act of commission. Thus, the phrase *act of omission* may be proper; at the same time, though, some readers are likely to sense a MISCUE by wondering whether *of* is a typographical error for *or.*

C. And *enactment.* *Act* has many meanings, but, when used as a synonym for *statute,* it is usually clear from the context. Strictly, *enactment* should refer to the passing or enacting of a law (i.e., its enactment), but not to the law once enacted. E.g., "[T]he purpose of an *enactment* [read *act*] is embedded in its words even though it is not always pedantically expressed in words." *U.S. v. Shirey,* 359 U.S. 255, 261 (1959) (per Frankfurter, J.)./ "Several states that have patterned their surveillance statutes on the federal model have simply incorporated this exception into their *enactments* [read *acts*; see INELEGANT VARIATION], and other states have adopted consent surveillance statutes." *Enaction* is a NEEDLESS VARIANT of *enactment.* To sum up, courts pass on the constitutionality of *acts,* not *enactments;* one witnesses the *enactment* of a bill.

In BrE, *Act* (= statute) is usually capitalized so as to prevent MISCUES—e.g.: "[W]hen an *Act* was repealed, and the repealing statute itself was subsequently repealed, the first *Act* was revived as from the original time of its commencement." Carleton K. Allen, *Law in the Making* 472 (7th ed. 1964). See **treaty.**

actio(n). In phrases such as *actio(n) ex contractu* and *actio(n) ex delictu, action* is better than *actio.* Better yet is *contract action* or *tort action.*

action. A. And *suit.* *Action* = a mode of proceeding in court to enforce a private right, to redress or prevent a private wrong, or to punish a public offense. As the latter part of that definition suggests, it is possible to speak of criminal actions. Originally, *action* referred exclusively to proceedings in a court of law; *suit* referred to proceedings in chancery (or equity), as well as to prosecutions at law. When the jurisdictional distinction existed, an *action* ended at judgment, but a *suit* in equity ended after judgment and execution. Today, since virtually all jurisdictions have merged the administration of law and equity, the terms *action* and *suit* are interchangeable. See **suit.**

B. And *act.* See **act** (A).

C. In Phrases Such as *action in trespass, action in detinue.* Often such phrases are shortened to *trespass, detinue,* etc., and the result is often a MISCUE. In the following sentence, for example, the trespasser and the complainant seem to be transposed: "*Trespass* by Rollin A. Richmond [the plaintiff] against James W. Fiske [the trespasser]." *Richmond v. Fiske,* 35 N.E. 103, 103 (Mass. 1893).

actionable has two important senses: (1) "furnishing grounds for a lawsuit"; and (2) "liable to a lawsuit." Sense (1) is the most usual in legal contexts—e.g.: "One of the general rules governing this action is that words are *actionable* when spoken of one in an office of profit which may probably occasion the loss of his office."/ "Plaintiff Banks states no *actionable* claim of constitutional deprivations."

The word has recently taken on a third sense: "giving rise to an act or action; act-on-able"—e.g.: "He had an *actionable* intent—that is, he would act on it."/ "Many are ambitious visions of a utopian business state—nebulous feel-good credos designed to inspire employees but lacking any *actionable* component." William B. Yanes, *Mission Statements Can Be Inspiring but Impractical,* Investor's Daily, 10 Dec. 1990, at 8./ "Only [a marketing professional] who understands the real world of lawyering can utilize the data to make recommendations that are precise and *actionable.*" Mercy Jimenez, *The Group,* A.B.A. J., Jan. 1991, at 86. But most dictionaries do not record any definition consistent with this usage, which is predicated upon a misunderstanding of *action* (= lawsuit) as used in the term (i.e., "giving rise to a lawsuit").

action, form of. See **form of action.**

action for money had and received. See **money had and received, action for.**

action for money paid. See **money had and received, action for.**

action on the case, a LOAN TRANSLATION of the LAW FRENCH *action sur le case,* is the common-law term for a personal tort action. E.g., "This is an *action on the case* by husband for the alienation of affections of his wife by her parents, the defendants."

Trespass on the case and *case* alone are variant forms. None of these phrases is used much in modern legal prose, except in historical contexts—e.g.: "The modern torts, for the most part, are the offspring of that prolific '*action on the case*' which began to be developed in the later years of the fourteenth century." C.H.S. Fifoot, *History and Sources of the Common Law* 3 (1949). See **trespass on the case.**

activable. So formed—not *activatable,* as some writers mistakenly write: "Perry does not assert that film coatings *activatable* [read *activable*] to adhesiveness by head were new in the art." *S.D. Warren Co. v. Nashua Gummed & Coated Paper Co.,* 205 F.2d 602, 604 (1st Cir. 1953). See -ATABLE.

activate. See **actuate.**

ACTIVE VOICE. See PASSIVE VOICE.

act of God is a vague, frequently vilified shorthand expression that does not lend itself to clear legal thinking. It is narrower than *vis major* or *force majeure* in that it denotes an unusual and uncontrollable action of nature, whereas *vis major* and *force majeure* also include the results of human action. See **force majeure & vis major.**

actual; constructive. These words are opposed in a variety of legal phrases, for example, *constructive* as against *actual fraud, constructive* as against *actual possession.* When *actual* is used in such a phrase, the extrinsic facts merit the legal conclusion that, e.g., fraud or possession exists. When *constructive* is used, the extrinsic facts do not fall within the strict definition of, say, fraud or possession, but the court finds (or is requested to find), usu. on equitable grounds, that the legal conclusion of fraud or possession should apply. Lon Fuller considered the adjective *constructive* a "badge of shame," saying that expressions such as those just mentioned "stand out like ugly scars in the language of the law, the linguistic wounds of discarded make-believes." Lon L. Fuller, *Legal Fictions* 22–23 (1967; repr. 1977). See **constructive.**

actual fact, in. A redundancy: all facts are actual, just as they are all true. When one is uncertain of the truth of allegations, then there might be "alleged facts." *In actual fact* is a pomposity for *actually.*

actuality is frequently a turgid substitute for *reality* or *fact.* E.g., "The existence of a fiduciary relationship is to be determined from the *actualities* [read *facts*] of the relationship between the persons involved."/ "The great divide in the equal-protection decisions lies in the difference between emphasizing *actualities* [read *realities*] and the abstractions of legislation." *In actuality* is always inferior to *actually.*

actuate; activate. The Evanses wrote that *actuate* means "to move (mechanical things) to action" and that *activate* means "to make active." Bergen Evans & Cornelia Evans, *Contemporary American Usage* 10 (1957). The distinction is a fine one not generally followed by dictionaries. Here *actuation* is correctly used: "A blade brake control device would stop the blade less than one second after *actuation.*"

More often, however, *actuate* and *actuation* appear in legal prose as fancy substitutes for *motivate* and *motivation* in a variety of contexts. This usage should generally be avoided on stylistic grounds, but it is not strictly incorrect—e.g.: "To prevent imposition of a constructive trust, the wife would have to establish by a preponderance of the evidence that the conveyance was *actuated* [read *motivated*] by fraud."/ "The wrong was *actuated* [read *motivated*] by a positive design to injure the third person to whom the duty was due."

The temptation to use *actuate* rather than *motivate* is much greater where the noun *motive* appears, so that one avoids REDUNDANCY. But a simple rewording usually obviates the need for *actuate*—e.g.: "When one exercises a legal right, *the motive that actuates him is immaterial* [read *one's motives are immaterial*]."/ "Counsel had the absolute privilege of making such deductions, even though they were false and he *was actuated by improper motives* [read *had improper motives*]."/ "The showing of invidiousness is made if a defendant demonstrates that *the government's selective prosecution is actuated by constitutionally impermissible motives* [read *the government, in its selective prosecution, was acting on constitutionally impermissible motives*]." See **animate.**

actus non facit reum nisi mens sit rea. This MAXIM, phrased in LAW LATIN, is pronounced /***ak***-*təs-non-**fas**-ət-**ree**-əm-nɪ-sɪ-men-sit-**ree**-ə*/. Meaning "an act does not make a person guilty unless his or her mind is guilty," the maxim expresses the criminal-law requirement of *mens rea* in addition to an *actus reus.* Traceable to the early 12th century, the brocard (q.v.) appears much more commonly in British than in American legal writing—e.g.: "Intent becomes the chief, though not the only, test; and the general rule is formed: *actus non facit reum nisi mens sit rea,* i.e., an act does not make the doer guilty unless his mind is guilty . . . ." O. Hood Phillips, *A First Book of English Law* 196 (3d ed. 1955).

actus reus. See ***mens rea* & overt act.**

A.D. This abbreviation (for *Anno Domini,* not *after death*) is unnecessary after dates in legal documents. In fact, it is absurd to use it with a modern date.

ad for *advertisement* is acceptable only in very informal contexts.

adapt and *adopt* are occasionally confounded. To *adapt* something is to modify it for one's own purposes; to *adopt* something is to accept it wholesale and use it.

adapt(at)ion, -(at)ive. The longer form is preferred in the noun (*adaptation*), the shorter in the adjective (*adaptive*).

a dato; a datu. Both LEGALISMS mean "from the date," and both are anachronistic. *A dato* is the better Latin form.

addable; addible. The former is preferred. See -ABLE (A).

ad damnum [L. "to the damage"] = (1) *adj.,* of, relating to, or constituting the clause stating—in a declaration, writ, or pleading—what damages the plaintiff demands; (2) *n.,* a prayer for relief that names the amount of damages claimed; or (3) *n.,* the amount of damages that a plaintiff claims in any given case.

Generally, it is possible for legal writers to use clearer phrasing without this LATINISM—e.g.: "Thus, even if the statute were retroactively applicable . . . it refers only to the *ad damnum plead-*

ing [read *pleading demanding damages*] and not to the closing argument." *Gumbs v. Pueblo Int'l, Inc.,* 823 F.2d 768, 771 n.1 (3d Cir. 1987)./ "[A] plaintiff may file a lawsuit *with an ad damnum* [read *claiming damages*] in excess of the amount in the notice of claim." *McFarlane by McFarlane v. U.S.,* 684 F. Supp. 780, 782 (E.D.N.Y. 1988)./ "Counsel reasoned that each of the original plaintiffs claimed an amount far in excess of $10,000 in the *ad damnum clause of* [read *in the prayer for relief in*] their amended complaint." *Sterling v. Velsicol Chem. Corp.,* 855 F.2d 1188, 1195 (6th Cir. 1988).

added to. See **together with.**

addicted; dependent. In the realm of human reaction to drugs, the distinction between these terms can be an important one. One who is *addicted* to a habit-forming drug has a compulsive physiological need for it. One who is *dependent* on a drug has a strong psychological reliance on it after having used it for some time. *Addiction,* then, is primarily physical, whereas *dependency* (also known as *habituation*) is primarily psychological.

additament is a NEEDLESS VARIANT of *addition.*

additur; increscitur. Neither synonym is as common as the correlative term—*remittitur* (for which see **remitter**)—but *additur* is the more usual of the two, as Traynor explained: "*Additur,* sometimes called *increscitur,* is used . . . to describe an order by which a plaintiff's motion for a new trial on the ground of inadequate damages is denied on the condition that the defendant consent to a specified increase of the award." *Dorsey v. Barba,* 240 P.2d 604, 610 n.1 (Cal. 1952) (en banc) (Traynor, J., concurring & dissenting).

The term *additur* is an American NEOLOGISM of the early 20th century; it does not occur in English cases, and the first contextual use by an American court suggests its newness: "[T]he order made in this case, might perhaps be termed an '*additur.*'" *Schiedt v. Dimick,* 70 F.2d 558, 563 (1st Cir. 1934). For an interesting but erroneous account of the word—erroneous because it attributes the word first to a *Yale Law Journal* article commenting on the case just cited—see Michael H. Cardozo, *A Word Is Born: "Additur," 1934–____,* 2 Scribes J. Legal Writing 143 (1991).

address, v.t., = (1) to call attention to for discussion or consideration; or (2) to state (a question) (to someone). In sense (1) it is a FORMAL WORD that is sometimes used inappropriately—e.g.: "That portion of the trial court's decree is not, therefore, assailed by Maria Rosa, as clearly her discontent *addresses* [read *centers on* or *arises out of*] the denial of a jury trial on the only factual issues raised having to do with proper division of the estate." That sentence exemplifies HYPALLAGE run amok; generally, *address* should take personal subjects, although by legitimate transference one might say that arguments or pleas *address* certain points. But *discontent* is not a proper subject for the verb. Following is a correct use of the term: "These points of error all relate to events after the making of the contract and fail to *address* the issue of fraud in the inducement."

Address should be accented on the second syllable both as a verb and as a noun.

addressable is listed in *RH2* as a NEOLOGISM dating from 1950–1955, but much earlier examples exist in law—e.g.: "[I]nasmuch as counsel themselves say that [the objections] are made not so much to impeach the validity of the act as to show its injustice, a consideration *addressable* to the Legislature, but not to us, no discussion of them is required." *Riley v. Chambers,* 185 P. 855, 859 (Cal. 1919).

addressee. See -EE.

adduce; educe; deduce. All are useful in reference to evidence. To *adduce* is to put forward for consideration something by way of evidence or arguments. E.g., "In the original panel opinion we held that Rushing's live testimony at trial would have had only a cumulative effect on this issue, because Wells had access to and did *adduce* testimony concerning the town's supervision and training of Rushing."

To *educe* is to draw out or evoke or elicit. E.g., "That divorce judgment, after the filing of this suit, was reversed and remanded for retrial by a Texas intermediate court on October 27, 1983, as was *educed* on further showings made in the federal trial court before that court's judgment of dismissal now before us on appeal."

To *deduce* is to infer—e.g.: "The jury could reasonably have *deduced* that defendant intended such a result." See **deduce & educe.**

adducible. So spelled—not *adduceable.* (See -ABLE (A).) Occasionally, *adducible* (or its misspelled variant) is misused for *deducible*—e.g.: "Thus, if . . . we determine that the residue of facts is so devoid of evidence of probative value and reasonable inferences *adduceable* [read *deducible*] therefrom, as to preclude guilt beyond a reasonable doubt, we should so declare." *Liston v. State,* 250 N.E.2d 739, 743 (Ind. 1969)./ "On appeal, after . . . presuming the existence of every fact reasonably *adduceable* [read *deducible*] from the evidence, the court must determine whether substantial evidence supports the finding of premeditation and deliberation." *People v. Mitchell,* 183 Cal. Rptr. 166, 171 (Cal. Ct. App. 1982).

adduction, n., corresponds to the verb *adduce* but is not nearly as common as that verb. E.g., "His only reply to Scrope's *adduction* of a named case is, 'Never will you see such an avowry received.'" Carleton K. Allen, *Law in the Making* 194 (7th ed. 1964).

adeem is the verb form of *ademption.* The pair is analogous to *redeem / redemption.*

ademption. A. And *lapse*. Whereas *lapse* occurs when a beneficiary does not survive to receive property given in a will, *ademption* occurs when the testator otherwise disposes of the property: "Lapse was a matter of no-Henry. *Ademption* is a matter of no-car. To raise the question is usually to answer it. If the testator has no car at his death, what if anything does he want Henry to have? The will should say. If it does not say, the dispute will turn on whether the bequest is specific—in which case it is adeemed by extinction and Henry gets nothing—or general, in which case the executor will have to get a car for Henry." Thomas L. Shaffer, *The Planning and Drafting of Wills and Trusts* 180 (2d ed. 1979).

B. Two Types. The two types of *ademption* are usefully distinguished. *Ademption by extinction* is the forfeiture of a legacy, bequest, or devise by the beneficiary because the property specifically described in the will is not in the estate at the testator's death. *Ademption by satisfaction* occurs when the testator, while alive, gives property to a donee named in the will, with the intention of rendering the testamentary gift inoperative.

adequate; sufficient. Though originally both words were used in reference to quantity, today there is a trend toward using *adequate* qualitatively, and *sufficient* quantitatively. Hence *adequate* means "suitable to the occasion or circumstances," and *sufficient* means "enough for a particular need or purpose."

In contracts, with respect to *consideration,* q.v., a special distinction applies. One rule of consideration is that it need not be *adequate* but it must be *sufficient.* Here, *adequate* consideration means a realistic economic equivalent of the promise it buys, whereas *sufficient* consideration means something having economic value and not stemming from a preexisting legal duty.

ad fin(em) = to the end. One would be hard-pressed to justify the Latin phrase in place of the English equivalent. (See LATINISMS.) The phrase is sometimes used in citations in a sense similar to *et seq.,* q.v., but the better practice is to cite specific pages, that is, to give an ending as well as a starting point. If, however, *ad fin.* is to be used, a period should follow the abbreviated form (as just given).

adherence. A. And *adhesion*. Both words derive from the verb *to adhere,* but *adhesion* is generally literal and *adherence* generally figurative. One should write of *adherence* to tenets or beliefs, and of *adhesion* of bubble gum to the sole of one's shoe. The word more frequently called upon in legal contexts is *adherence:* "There are also authorities to the contrary and we might make mention of a retreat by the Supreme Court of Nebraska from *adherence* to the rule."/ "Can conspirators signify their *adhesion* [read *adherence*] at different times?" Glanville Williams, *Textbook of Criminal Law* 353 (1978).

Yet the standard rules of usage relating to these words find exceptions in the law. One exception to the foregoing advice is the phrase *adhesion contract* or *contract of adhesion.* Said to have been introduced into legal nomenclature by Edwin W. Patterson in *The Delivery of a Life Insurance Policy,* 33 Harv. L. Rev. 198, 222 (1919), the term refers to a standard printed contract prepared by one party, to be signed by the party in a weaker position, usu. a consumer, who has little choice about the terms of the contract. The metaphor suggested is that the consumer must *adhere* to the contract as presented, or reject it completely. (Such a contract is also known, more familiarly to nonlawyers, as a *take-it-or-leave-it contract.*) *Adhesion,* then, has a figurative rather than a literal sense in this legal phrase. See **leonine contract.**

Another exception, not so frequently encountered, involves treaties. When a government enters into some but not all of the provisions of a treaty already existing between two other governments, *adhesion* is the term to describe the third government's entrance into the treaty.

B. Preposition with. *Adherence,* like *adhesion,* takes the preposition *to.* "This holding mandates close adherence *from* [read *to*] the letter of the law."

adhibit, v.t., and its noun equivalent *adhibition* are pompous LEGALISMS. To *adhibit* is to apply; an *adhibition* is an application (of something to something else). E.g., "We are importuned by the Dayton Newspapers, Inc., in this original action in this court to *adhibit* [read *apply*] the extraordinary writ of prohibition . . . ." *State ex rel. Dayton Newspapers, Inc. v. Phillips,* 351 N.E.2d 127,

139 (Ohio 1976) (Corrigan, J., dissenting)./ "[A]ppellants' *adhibition* [read *application*] of mortality tables and their presentation and argument in the second trial . . . were predicated . . . on the metachronism that Sally was born nineteen years before the accident [that] took her life in 1970 . . . ." *Hines v. Sweet,* 567 S.W.2d 435, 438 (Mo. Ct. App. 1978)./ "A threshold requirement for the *adhibition* [read *application*] of Title VI to a federal grantee's employment practices appears in § 604." *Guardians Ass'n v. Civil Serv. Comm'n,* 466 F. Supp. 1273, 1281 (S.D.N.Y. 1979).

ad hoc, adv. & adj., is a widespread and useful term meaning "for this specific purpose." Though some witch-hunting Latin-haters have questioned its justification in English (see, e.g., Vigilans [Eric Partridge], *Chamber of Horrors* 26 (1952)), it is firmly established and serves legal language well when used correctly <ad hoc committee>.

By extension—some would say SLIPSHOD EXTENSION—the term has come to mean "without any underlying principle that can be consistently applied"—e.g.: "The majority opinion insufficiently considers the basic substantive rules of law invoked by plaintiff's complaint; it is an *ad hoc* opinion that grants desired relief to needy persons but its effects on established law could be serious." Sometimes the phrase appears to mean "improvised from whatever is at hand," as here: "This procedure is carried out on a very *ad hoc* [read *haphazard?*] basis."/ "Lawyers and judges apparently devise voir dire questions in a fairly *ad hoc* [read *haphazard* or *desultory*] way; sometimes prosecutors inadvertently pose questions that work to the advantage of the defense, and vice-versa."

Generally speaking, the phrases *on an ad hoc basis* and *in an ad hoc way* are verbose for the adverb *ad hoc.* (See **basis (B).**) Likewise, *ad hoc* should rarely if ever be qualified by *very* or *fairly.* Finally, attempts to coalesce the phrase into one word have failed, and should be forgotten. Cf. **pro hac vice (A).**

ad hominem [L. "to the man"] is shortened from the LATINISM *argumentum ad hominem* (= an argument directed not to the merits of an opponent's argument but to the personality or character of the opponent).

The word is sometimes misspelled *ad hominum*—e.g.: "The Petitioners object to the conclusion that it is permissible to challenge an expert witness through an *ad hominum* [read *ad hominem*] argument . . . ." *U.S. v. Ellingsworth,* 692 F. Supp. 356, 369 (D. Del. 1988)./ "[T]he Commonwealth has chosen to couch its appeal in language characterized by an *ad hominum* [read *ad hominem*] attack on the trial judge." *Commonwealth v. Rosario,* 583 A.2d 1229, 1233 (Pa. Super. Ct. 1990) (Cavanaugh, J., dissenting).

ad idem = to the same point or matter; in agreement. E.g., "That being so, there was no consensus *ad idem,* and therefore no binding contract."/ "At the end of the short trial I felt constrained to find that the plaintiff and defendant *were never ad idem* [read *never had the same understanding*] on the purported sale of land by the defendant to the plaintiff." (Eng.) An English equivalent, such as *of the same mind* or *to that effect,* is generally more comprehensible than this Latin phrase, and even more elegant. See FORBIDDEN WORDS. For *consensus ad idem,* see **meeting of the minds.**

adjacent; contiguous. These words should be distinguished. *Adjacent* = lying near. *Contiguous* = directly abutting or bordering on. See **adjoin.**

adjective law is not a set of rules governing words that modify nouns, but rather the aggregate of rules on procedure. In law as in language, the adjective affects the substantive. E.g., "The *adjective law* of workmen's compensation, like the substantive, takes its tone from the beneficent and remedial character of the legislation." 3 Arthur Larson, *Workmen's Compensation Law* § 77A.10, at 15-1 (1986).

Adjectival law is a little-used variant—e.g.: "[A] constructive trust frequently is classified as a division of *adjectival* rather than substantive law." 76 Am. Jur. 2d *Trusts* § 222, at 448 (1975)./ "*Adjectival law* relates to the enforcement of rights and duties: in particular, it concerns procedure and evidence." Glanville Williams, *Learning the Law* 19 (11th ed. 1982).

ADJECTIVES. **A. What One Is.** An adjective is a word that modifies a noun. The word is sometimes used sloppily as if it meant "noun"—e.g.: "'Excellence' is an *adjective* [read *noun*] that describes something which is of the highest quality." *Their Work Stands Out,* Barrister, Summer 1989, at 5.

B. Uncomparable Adjectives. A number of adjectives describe absolute states or conditions and therefore cannot take comparative degrees in *most* or *more, less* or *least,* or intensives such as *very* or *quite* or *largely.* The illogic of such combinations is illustrated in this sentence: "It is possible that this idea too has outlived its usefulness and soon will be *largely discarded.*" The literal meaning of *discard* impinges on the metaphor here: it is hard to imagine a single idea being halfway discarded, though certainly it could be halfway discredited.

The best-known uncomparable adjective is *unique* (= being the one and only of a kind). Because something is either unique or not unique, there can be no degrees of uniqueness. Hence *more unique* and *very unique* are incorrect. Yet something may be *almost unique* or *not quite unique*—if, for example, there were two such things extant. (See **unique.**) Many other words belong to this class, such as *preferable:* "We think that, while perhaps the denial did not follow *the most preferable* [read *the preferable*] course, it was adequate."

Following is a short list of uncomparable adjectives:

absolute	fundamental	possible
adequate	ideal	preferable
basic	impossible	principal
certain	inevitable	stationary
chief	irrevocable	sufficient
complete	main	true
devoid	major	unavoidable
entire	manifest	unbroken
essential	minor	uniform
false	necessary	unique
fatal	only	universal
final	perfect	void
first	perpetuity	whole

The general prohibition against using these words in comparative senses should be tempered with reason; it has exceptions. For example, Thomas Jefferson used the phrase *more perfect* in the Declaration of Independence, and the phrase then made its way into the U.S. Constitution: "We the People of the United States, in order to form a *more perfect* Union, establish Justice, insure domestic Tranquility, provide for the common defence, promote the general Welfare, and secure the Blessings of Liberty to ourselves and our Posterity, do ordain and establish this Constitution for the United States of America." U.S. Const. pmbl. One writer criticizes this phrase and suggests that it "should read 'to form a *more nearly perfect* Union.'" George J. Miller, *On Legal Style,* 43 Ky. L.J. 235, 246 (1955). Although the Constitution is not without stylistic blemishes, this surely is not one of them, and the suggested edit is pedantic. See **more perfect.**

In short, good writers occasionally depart from the rule, but knowingly and purposefully. Poor writers use uncomparable adjectives indiscriminately, and in the end weaken their writing through hyperbolic qualification. See WEASEL WORDS.

C. Adjectives as Nouns. Words in the English language frequently have the ability to change parts of speech. Thus nouns may act as adjectives (*deposition testimony, court protocol*) and adjectives as nouns (*corporeals* [BrE] = corporeal things). Legal writers refer to *innocents* (= innocent persons), *immovables, movables,* and *necessaries* (= necessary things). *Indigent* was originally an adjective (15th c.), but it came to be used as a noun (16th c.).

The same process occurred with *hypothetical, postmortem, principal* (= principal investment), *ignitables, potential, explosives,* and *recitative.* More modern examples are *finals* (= final examinations) and *classifieds* (= classified advertisements). Similarly, we refer to *the poor, the homeless, the rich, the religious,* and *the destitute.*

Though recent semantic shifts remain unsuitable for formal contexts, we should resist the benighted temptation to condemn all such shifts in parts of speech. Cf. NOUNS AS ADJECTIVES.

D. Adjectives as Verbs. Though noun-to-adjective, adjective-to-noun, and even noun-to-verb transformations are common in English, adjective-to-verb transformations have never been common. They usually have a jargonistic quality (as in the first example below) or a trendy quality (as in the second). Careful writers avoid them or, when quoting someone else, distance themselves by using telltale quotation marks (as Gilmore and Black did): "The New York City Fire Commissioner directed that her cargo tanks be *'inerted'* through the introduction of carbon dioxide into the tanks." Grant Gilmore & Charles L. Black, Jr., *The Law of Admiralty* 925 (2d ed. 1975)./ "Clinton would be well-advised to *low-key* the task force before it announces anything embarrassing . . . ." Joe Klein, *Time to Step Back,* Newsweek, 17 May 1993, at 40. Cf. NOUNS AS VERBS.

E. Coordinate Adjectives. When two adjectives, both modifying the same noun, are related in sense, they should be separated by *and* or by a comma—e.g.: "[T]he purpose of Rule 11 as a whole is to bring home to the individual signer his *personal, non-delegable responsibility.*" Jeffrey N. Cole, *Rule 11 Now,* 17 Litigation 10, 12 (Spring 1991).

But when the consecutive adjectives are unrelated, they should have no intervening comma or conjunction—e.g.: "An interesting contrast in judicial philosophy as to the scope of an employee's ethical duty is revealed in a *similar and Texas case* [read *similar Texas case*]."

Some consecutive adjectives present close questions—e.g.: "The *brief, unsigned Supreme Court opinion* said that the lawyers for Ms. Benten had failed to show a substantial likelihood that the case would be won if it were argued before the United States Court of Appeals for the Second Circuit . . . ." Phillip J. Hilts, *Justices Refuse to Order Return of Abortion Pill,* N.Y. Times, 18 July 1992, at 1. Is the fact that the opinion is brief related to the fact that it is unsigned (i.e., per curiam)? If so, the comma is proper; if not, the comma is improper. Because signed opinions tend to be longer than unsigned opinions, the comma is probably justified.

For more on the punctuation of successive adjectives, see PUNCTUATION (C)(1).

F. Proper Names as Adjectives. When a proper name is used attributively as an adjective, the writer should capitalize only that portion used in attribution. In *Southmark Properties v. The Charles House Corp.,* 742 F.2d 862 (5th Cir. 1984), the opinion is scattered with references to "The Charles House property." *The,* however, should be lowercased, for the skeletal phrase is "the property," and only *Charles House* is being used attributively. The definite article, then, derives from the skeletal phrase and not from the name of the party, even though the name of the party is *The Charles House Corporation.*

The practice of using place-names as adjectives is generally to be resisted, although it is increasingly common. Using a city plus the state as an adjective disrupts the flow of the sentence—e.g.: "Farmland's president, Marc Goldman, sent out sleuths who traced the missing containers to an *Elizabeth, N.J., warehouse* he says is filled with discarded bottles of designer water." Edward Felsenthal, *Nobody's Crying Yet, But There Must Be Spilled Milk Somewhere,* Wall St. J., 20 June 1990, at B1. Such constructions contribute to NOUN PLAGUE, lessen readability, and offend sensitive, literate readers.

The disruption does not occur when the city's name occurs without the state—e.g.: "An Austin jury returned a verdict in the court of Judge Walter Smith of Waco." *Accountant Found Guilty,* Austin American-Statesman, 21 July 1990, at B6.

G. Pronominal Indefinite Adjectives. Adjectives such as *each, any, every, all, no,* and *some* should be used only when they serve some demonstrable purpose. When a subject is plural, such an adjective is usually unnecessary—e.g.: "*All corporate officers* [read *Corporate officers*] shall . . . ."

A few conventions with these words are useful in the realm of DRAFTING. First, if a right, privilege, or power is extended, the drafter should use *each* or *a* <each director may>. Second, if a duty is imposed, the drafter should use *each* or *a* <each director must>. And third, if a proscription is set out, the drafter should use *no* <no director may>. See STATUTE DRAFTING & WORDS OF AUTHORITY.

H. Past-Participial Adjectives. Some past participles work perfectly well as adjectives, and others do not. There can be a *tired* or *irritated* person, but not a *disappeared* person: "Because of the nonaccess between C.W. and her *disappeared husband* [read *husband who has disappeared*], such a presumption should fail." The reason is that *disappeared* has not been accepted idiomatically as a prepositive adjective, whereas other past participles (such as *tired* and *irritated*) have been. Some legal phrases can be framed either way: thus, *cases decided* and *cases cited,* or *decided cases* and *cited cases.*

I. Phrasal or Compound Adjectives. See PHRASAL ADJECTIVES.

J. Modification of Adjectives Ending in *-ed.* See **very (B).**

K. Adjectives Ending in *-ly.* See ADVERBS, PROBLEMS WITH (B).

L. Adjectives That Follow the Noun. See POSTPOSITIVE ADJECTIVES.

M. Dates as Adjectives. See DATES (C).

adjoin means both "to join" and "to lie adjacent to." In the latter sense, it is transitive and should take a direct object: "The park was likened to a garden that traditionally (as an appurtenance) *adjoined to a residence* [read *adjoined a residence*]." Etymologically, *adjoining* means "directly abutting; contiguous," as opposed to *adjacent,* q.v.

adjourn [fr. F. *à jour* "to a day"] means literally "to put off to another day or place." E.g., "But the case was *adjourned* to the court of Exchequer Chamber, where all the judges of England considered difficult cases . . . ." Alan Harding, *A Social History of English Law* 105 (1966)./ "[M]agistrates have very wide powers to grant or refuse bail when a person is first brought before them, and the case has to be *adjourned* to a later date." P.S. Atiyah, *Law and Modern Society* 25 (1983).

adjournment; adjournal. Except in Scotland, the latter is a NEEDLESS VARIANT. In Scotland, the *Books of Adjournal* are the records of the Justiciary Court.

adjudge; adjudicate; dijudicate; judge. *Adjudge* = (1) to consider judicially; to rule upon; (2) to deem or pronounce to be; or (3) to award judicially. *Adjudicate* shares all three meanings of *adjudge* and is more common than *adjudge* in sense (1). In senses (2) and (3), *adjudge* is the more usual term: "Nor can a court of equity adjudge [sense (2)] the decree of any other court binding or punish the violation of any decrees but its own."/ "Costs are adjudged [sense (3)] to appellant." For examples of *adjudicate* in sense (2), see **adjudicate (B).**

Dijudicate (= to decide between; adjudicate) is a rare term without justification in modern prose.

Judge is the general term meaning "to try a

person or case as a judge does." Additionally, it has the lay meaning "to form a critical estimate of." *Judge* should not be used in sense (2) of *adjudge,* as here: "Plaintiff argues that the society must declare a winner of the contest or be *judged* [read *adjudged*] to have breached an implicit agreement with the contestants."

The Evanses wrote that *adjudicate* was more common than *judge* in reference to disputes outside the courts. Bergen Evans & Cornelia Evans, *Contemporary American Usage* 261 (1957). Lawyers, however, restrict *adjudicate* to contexts involving courts or other resolvers of disputes, whereas they may use *judge* in nonlegal senses. See **adjudicate.**

Adjudge is best used with the object immediately following: "The court found him guilty of the charge and *adjudged* him in contempt." There is a tendency (to be avoided) to insert *as* after *adjudge*—e.g.: "adjudge as bankrupt" for "adjudge bankrupt." Cf. **abjudge.**

adjudg(e)ment. See **judg(e)ment.**

adjudicataire. See **adjudicator.**

adjudicate. A. Proper Object with. Disputes and controversies are adjudicated, or "settled judicially"; *property* cannot be adjudicated, although conflicting rights in it can be. E.g., "The supersedeas bond must be in the amount of the judgment or the value of *property adjudicated* [read *property in dispute,* or *property subject to adjudication*]."/ "We reverse the judgment of the Supreme Court of Kansas insofar as it held that Kansas law was applicable to all the *transactions that it sought to adjudicate* [read *transactions giving rise to this controversy* (or *adjudication*)]." See **adjudication.** Cf. **litigate.**

B. Meaning "to deem." *Adjudicate* frequently means "to deem or pronounce judicially," sense (2) of *adjudge,* q.v. "Neither dolomite nor granite has been *adjudicated* a 'mineral.'"/ "Once laws are validly enacted it is not for the courts to *adjudicate* upon their wisdom, their appropriateness, or the necessity for their existence." (Eng.)/ "Associates continued to deteriorate financially and in 1975, it was placed in liquidation and, in separate proceedings, *adjudicated* a bankrupt." (Most legal texts written in BrE say that an insolvent entity is "adjudicated bankrupt," not "adjudicated a bankrupt," as in AmE.) For other senses of *adjudicate,* see **adjudge.**

adjudicated has come into use as an adjective. Thus instead of writing, "The ward *was adjudicated* an incompetent," some legists have begun to write, "The ward is *an adjudicated* bankrupt." The adjectival usage purports to give the statement more authority, for it focuses on what the subject *is,* as opposed to what someone *has done to it.*

adjudication; adjudicature. *Adjudication* = (1) the process of judging; (2) a court's pronouncement of a judgment or decree; or (3) the judgment so given. *Adjudicature* is a NEEDLESS VARIANT. (See **judicature.**) On the plural use of *adjudication,* see PLURALS (B).

Leff writes that, in modern usage, "*adjudication* can . . . be used as a rough synonym for *litigation*—e.g.: 'the matter is in *adjudication* now.'" Arthur A. Leff, *The Leff Dictionary of Law* 1855, 1934 (1985). This SLIPSHOD EXTENSION should be avoided unless, of course, the writer intends to refer to the deliberative process of judges and not to the courtroom proceedings in which lawyers take part. See **adjudicate (A)** & **litigate.**

adjudicative; adjudicatory; judicative; judicatory; judicatorial. As between *adjudicative* and *adjudicatory,* both meaning "having the character or attribute of adjudicating," the former is standard, easier to pronounce, and better sounding. Yet the latter appears with some frequency. Thus, even though we have *adjudicative facts* and *adjudicative hearings,* our legal texts reveal *adjudicatory proceedings* and *an adjudicatory action.* There is no need for the two to coexist, for no workable DIFFERENTIATION now appears to be possible. One is best advised to use *adjudicative* in all contexts.

Judicative is a NEEDLESS VARIANT of *adjudicative.* Likewise, *judicatorial* is a NEEDLESS VARIANT of *judicial.* For *judicatory,* see **judicature.** See also **judicative.**

adjudicative facts. See **legislative facts.**

adjudicator; adjudicataire; judicator. *Adjudicator* = one who adjudicates. If used merely for *judge,* it is a pomposity. But in some contexts it is quite defensible—e.g.: "We find nothing in the history or constitutional treatment of military tribunals that entitles them to rank along with Article III courts as *adjudicators* of the guilt or innocence of people charged with offenses for which they can be deprived of their life, liberty, or property." *Adjudicataire,* a term from Canadian law, means "a purchaser at a judicial sale" (*W3*). *Judicator* is a NEEDLESS VARIANT of *adjudicator.*

adjudicature for *adjudication.* See **judicature** & **adjudication.**

adjure (= to urge earnestly) for *require* is an odd error: "Arizona law *adjures* [read *requires*] that statutes should be construed to effect their objects . . . ." *Knapp v. Cardwell,* 667 F.2d 1253, 1261 (9th Cir. 1982)./ "Assaying the quality of defendant's acts and omissions . . . *adjures* [read *requires*] just such a judgment call." *Swift v. U.S.,* 866 F.2d 507, 511 (1st Cir. 1989). See **abjure.**

But *adjure* for *abhor* is even odder: "Most of us don't dislike lawyers individually; we *adjure* [read *abhor?*] them as a group." *Our Legal System's Put Us in a Box,* Chicago Tribune, 23 Aug. 1988, at C19.

adjurer; adjuror. The *-er* spelling is preferred. See -ER (A).

adjuster; adjustor. *Adjuster* (= one who seeks to determine the amount of loss suffered when an insurance claim is submitted and who attempts to settle the claim) is the preferred spelling. See -ER (A).

ad litem [L. "for the suit"]. Formerly—and still in English law—a guardian *ad litem* represented only an underage defendant (a next friend or *prochein ami* representing an underage plaintiff). BrE retains this restrictive sense—e.g.: "For purposes of litigation . . . an infant can and must be represented by an adult, who will be called 'the next friend' of an infant plaintiff, the 'guardian *ad litem*' of an infant defendant . . . ." William Geldart, *Introduction to English Law* 45 (D.C.M. Yardley ed., 9th ed. 1984). But in modern AmE, underage plaintiffs (as well as defendants) are afforded guardians *ad litem.*

In AmE, the phrase *guardian ad litem* is often shortened to *ad litem.* E.g., "As you requested, I called the *ad litem* [i.e., the guardian *ad litem*] today." See **guardian *ad litem.***

adminicular(y). *Adminicular* (= corroborative), seen usu. in the phrase *adminicular evidence,* is the standard adjectival form of the noun *adminicle,* meaning "supporting or corroborative evidence" (*OED*). In Scots law, *adminicle* has the more specific sense "a writing that tends to establish the existence and terms of a lost document."

administer; minister. *Administer* suffices in most legal contexts. It is a transitive verb and, in its most common legal sense, means "to manage and dispose of the estate of a deceased person, either under a will or under letters of administration" (*OED*). E.g., "Generally speaking, a natural person has the same capacity to take, to hold, and to *administer* property under a trust as he has to take, to hold, and to *administer* property for his own benefit." *Administer* may also mean (1) "to dispense (as justice or as punishment); or (2) "to give (an oath)."

The verb *minister,* now primarily intransitive, shares these last two meanings, albeit only rarely. *Minister* is most commonly used in the sense of attending to others' needs, or, in religious contexts, of administering sacraments. Persons in need are *ministered to.* E.g., "A testator's favor expressed in a will may be won by devoted attachment, self-sacrificing kindness, and *ministering to* him through friendship and love."

administerial. See **administrative.**

administrable; administratable; administerable. The first form is correct; the others are near-abominations, and NEEDLESS VARIANTS to boot. E.g., "This court did in fact find a more *administratable* [read *administrable*] way to evaluate the property—the trial de novo." *U.S. v. 2,175.86 Acres of Land,* 687 F. Supp. 1079, 1081 (E.D. Tex. 1988). See -ATABLE.

administrate is an objectionable BACK-FORMATION from *administration;* it should be avoided as a NEEDLESS VARIANT of *administer.* E.g., "By the same reasoning, the legislature could delegate the power to promulgate regulations having the force of law to *administrate* [read *administer*] organs of the government." John H. Merryman, *The Civil Law Tradition* 24 (1969).

administrative; administerial; administrational. *Administrative* is the general, all-purpose term meaning "of or pertaining to administration or *an* administration." *Administerial* and *administrational* are NEEDLESS VARIANTS.

administrative law = the law governing the organization and operation of the administrative branch of government and the relations of the administration with the legislature, the judiciary, and the public. "Administrative law . . . has suffered a long gestation and a difficult birth in our [Anglo-American] legal system. It is still a delicate child, with an uncertain future, but it is beginning to take the shape of manhood. It has been forced upon us, against much blind prejudice, by irresistible circumstances. It is now taught in our law schools as a branch of law [that] is essential to an understanding of our whole legal system, though with all its growing complexities it is difficult to fit into a legal education." Carleton K. Allen, *Law in the Making* 605 (7th ed. 1964).

administrative-law judge; hearing officer. In U.S. federal law, so-called *hearing officers* had their titles changed in 1978 to *administrative-law* *judges.* The U.S. Supreme Court has said that they are "functionally comparable" to U.S. District Judges. See **ALJ.**

administrator; executor. Both terms refer to the personal representative who administers the estate of a decedent. An *executor* is named in a will, whereas an *administrator* (usu. someone close to the decedent) is court appointed. There are two kinds of the latter: the first is an *administrator cum testamento annexo* (or *c.t.a.*)—i.e., with the will annexed; the second is an *administrator de bonis non* (or *d.b.n.*), an elliptical phrase for *administrator de bonis non administratis* (= administrator of goods not administered). An *administrator c.t.a.* is appointed if the testator does not name an executor or if the named executor for any reason does not act; an *administrator d.b.n.* is appointed if a prior administrator has begun to act but later dies or is removed.

The phrase *administrator c.t.a.* is often translated *administrator with the will annexed,* a healthy practice that helps minimize the LATINISMS associated with this area of the law.

administratrix. Pl. *administratrixes,* preferably not *administratrices.* See SEXISM (C).

admiralty. A. And *maritime law; law of the sea.* *Black's* states that the first two terms are "virtually synonymous" in referring to the law of marine commerce and navigation, the transportation at sea of persons and property, and marine affairs in general. Today the words are used interchangeably.

Yet Article III, section 2 of the U.S. Constitution is not redundant in providing, "The judicial power shall extend . . . to all Cases involving admiralty and maritime Jurisdiction." One commentator notes that *admiralty* (dated from ca. 1327 in the *OED*) was the better-known term when the Constitution was drafted, and that *maritime* (*OED:* ca. 1550) was used in conjunction with *admiralty* for two reasons: "(1) to exclude that jurisdiction which the English Admiralty anciently exercised or attempted to exercise over nonmaritime cases arising ashore, and (2) to preclude a resort to those English instances in which common law courts encroached upon the jurisdiction of admiralty . . . ." Elijah Jhirad et al., 1 *Benedict on Admiralty* § 101, at 7-3 (7th ed. 1983).

Law of the sea carries a distinct meaning: "the rules governing the relationships between states regarding the use and control of the sea and its resources." Thomas J. Schoenbaum, *Admiralty and Maritime Law* § 2-1, at 20 (1987). Thus, the law of the sea falls within public international law, whereas admiralty or maritime law is a division of private law.

B. *The admiralty.* The phrase *the admiralty* refers to the office of an admiral (fr. Arabic *amir-al-bahr* "chief of the sea") or other person entrusted by the crown with command of the seas and of royal ships. Because the admirals came to have jurisdiction over maritime matters, the phrase by extension came to refer to that jurisdiction. E.g., "The theory of the case, according to the summary of argument in the Supreme Court report, was that Chelentis, in a common law action outside *the admiralty,* could recover damages on common law tort principles without regard to the maritime law." Grant Gilmore & Charles L. Black, Jr., *The Law of Admiralty* 325 (2d ed. 1975).

admissible; admissable; admittable. *Admissible* (the standard word) = (1) allowable; or (2) worthy of admittance (i.e., gaining entry). The other two forms are NEEDLESS VARIANTS to be avoided.

admission. A. And *admittance.* The distinction between these terms is old and useful, but it has a history of being ignored. The latter term is purely physical, as in signs that read "No admittance." E.g.,"Plaintiff instituted an action to enjoin defendant from refusing her *admittance* to its amusement park because of her race or color, or for any other reason not applicable alike to other citizens."

Admission is used in figurative and nonphysical senses, such as: "His *admission* to the bar in 1948 began a career that would be long and noteworthy." *Admission* is also used, however, in physical senses when rights or privileges are attached to gaining entry: "The *admission* of aliens into the United States is considerably more restricted in this century than it was in the last."

B. And *confession.* In criminal law, a distinction has traditionally existed between these words: an *admission* is a concession that an allegation or factual assertion is true without any acknowledgment of guilt with respect to the criminal charges, whereas a *confession* involves an acknowledgment of guilt as well as of the truth of predicate factual allegations.

C. In Civil Litigation. Although nonlawyers tend to associate *admission* with criminal law (see B), it has broad uses in noncriminal evidentiary contexts: "An *admission* is a statement oral or written, suggesting any inference as to any fact in issue or relevant fact, unfavourable to the conclusion contended for by the person by whom or on whose behalf the statement is made." James F. Stephen, *The Law of Evidence* 23 (1876).

admit. **A. *Admit to.*** In the sense of "confess," *admit to* is generally much inferior to *admit.* E.g., "In 1978, appellant admitted *to* [omit *to*] killing his wife and daughter and pleaded guilty to two charges of first-degree murder." See **confess (to).**

B. ***Admit of.*** *Admit of* = to allow; to be susceptible of. E.g.,"This clause in the contract *admits of* two interpretations."/ "The former construction should be adopted if the language used will *admit of* such a construction."

C. ***Admitted to the bar; called to the bar.*** The former is the American phrase for qualifying to practice—e.g.: "I was *admitted to the bar* at Chattanooga." William G. McAdoo, *Crowded Years* 40 (1931). The phrase *called to the Bar* is the British phrase for qualifying to practice as a barrister (as distinguished from a solicitor, who is *called to the roll*). *Called to the bar,* q.v., appears infrequently in AmE.

admittable. See **admissable.**

admittance. See **admission (A).**

admonish; monish. See **admonition.**

admonishment. See **abolishment.**

admonition; monition. In general usage, both mean "a warning; caution." *Admonition* is the more common, less technical term: "We must follow the Supreme Court's *admonition* that courts ought not to impose constitutional restraints that would inhibit the ability of the political branches to respond through immigration policy to changing world conditions." *Admonition* has the additional sense "a mild reprimand."

Monition is the more specialized legal term; it may mean (1) in admiralty and civil-law contexts, "a summons to appear and answer in court as a defendant or to contempt charges"; (2) in ecclesiastical contexts, "a formal notice from a bishop mandating that an offense within the clergy be corrected." The object of a monition is a *person monished.*

admonitory; admonitorial; monitory; monitorial. The *-ory* forms predominate.

adopt. See **adapt.**

adopted. See **adoptive.**

adoption; ratification; novation. In contractual contexts, these three words have deceptively similar meanings. *Adoption* of a contract is accepting it as one's own, or consenting to be bound by it, though it was entered into by someone else acting on one's behalf. A *ratification* is the confirmation of a contract performed or entered into on one's behalf by another who at the time assumed without authority to act as an agent. These two words are near-synonyms. *Novation* has two important meanings: (1) "the substitution of a new contract between parties in place of an existing contract"; and (2) "the substitution of a new party in an existing contract." Sense (1) predominates in American law. See **novation.**

In corporate law, the distinctions have relevance, and are somewhat different, when a promoter enters into a contract that purports to bind a newly formed corporation, or one soon to be formed. If a promoter contracts with a third person when it is understood that the corporation will be formed, the corporation is later properly said to *adopt* the contract. *Ratify,* in contrast, is the proper word when the corporation already existed when the contract was signed. If, after a corporation *adopts* or *ratifies* the contract, the promoter is expressly relieved from liability, the *adoption* or *ratification* becomes a *novation.*

adoptive; adopted. *Adoptive* = (1) related by adoption <an adoptive son>; or (2) tending to adopt <adoptive admissions under Fed. R. Evid. 801(d)(2)(b)>. The phrase *adopted father* is an example of HYPALLAGE, to be avoided in favor of *adoptive father.* The original Latin word, *adoptivus,* applied both to the adopting parent and to the adopted child.

Here the correct usages are observed: "If an *adopted* child can inherit from or through his natural or *adoptive* parents, the child of an *adopted* child can claim through him in an appropriate case."/ "The controlling statute provides that an *adopted* child inherits through his *adoptive* parent."

adpromissor (= surety, bail) has two plural forms in *adpromissors* and *adpromissores,* the latter being unEnglish and therefore inferior. (See PLURALS (A).) The dilemma of choosing between plural forms is easily remedied by writing *sureties.*

ADR. See **alternative dispute resolution.**

adsorb. See **absorb.**

adulter. See **adulterer.**

adulterant. See **adulterous.**

adulterate. See **adulterous.**

adulteration; adultery. *Adulteration* = (1) the act of debasing, corrupting, or making impure; (2) a corrupted or debased state; or (3) something corrupted or debased. *Adultery* = sexual intercourse engaged in voluntarily by a married person with someone who is not the person's lawful spouse. The Latin verb *adulterare,* from which both English words derive, encompasses all these senses. See **adulterine bastard.**

adulterer; adulter; adulteress; adultera; adulterator. *Adulterer* is the usual form meaning "one who commits adultery." *Adulter* is an obsolete variant of *adulterer* that also had the meaning of *adulterator* (= counterfeiter).

Adulteress is the feminine form, now disfavored because of the growing awareness of SEXISM—likewise with *adultera,* the term from the civil law. *Adulterator,* as suggested above, derives from the noun *adulteration,* and not from *adultery,* like the other personal nouns discussed in this entry.

adulterine bastard. Leff defines this phrase as "the child of a married woman by a man other than her husband," and comments: "As 'adultery' has come to include sexual relations by a married man with a woman not his wife, whether she is married or not, the term *adulterine bastard* has sometimes come to include a child born to an unmarried woman by a married man. This makes no difference, as no legal consequences presently attach to adulterine bastardy that do not attach to plain old bastardy." Arthur A. Leff, *The Leff Dictionary of Law,* 94 Yale L.J. 1855, 1951 (1985). The form *adulterine bastard* is preferable to *adulterous bastard,* the latter suggesting an unfaithful spouse rather than a child produced by adultery.

The very term *bastard* is now being displaced by euphemistic terms in legal contexts. See **bastard, illegitimate child** & EUPHEMISMS.

adulterous; adulterine; adulterant; adulterate, adj.; **adulterated.** *Adulterous* and *adulterate* both mean "of, characterized by, or pertaining to adultery," the former term being the more common. E.g., "We think there was evidence that his conduct and that of the defendant had a legitimate tendency to prove *adulterous* inclination, although insufficient to establish criminal conversation." *Adulterate,* adj., more common in Shakespeare's day than in ours, has been relegated to the status of a NEEDLESS VARIANT.

Adulterine = (1) spurious; (2) illegal; or (3) born of adultery <adulterine bastard>. (See **adulterine bastard.**) *Adulterant* = tending to adulterate. *Adulterated* = (1) corrupted or debased, or (2) vitiated or made spurious.

adultery; fornication. The latter implies that neither party is married; if either participant is married, *adultery* is the proper term. See **adulteration.**

adumbrate (= [1] to foreshadow, or [2] to outline) is a FORMAL WORD that has been called an affectation. But legal writers have considered it serviceable in formal contexts. "The contours of the action for indemnity among tortfeasors were *adumbrated* by the Louisiana Supreme Court."/ "The majority's holding and reasoning in *Alvarez-Gonzalez II* tended to expand the concept of functional equivalency as *adumbrated* by the Supreme Court fourteen years earlier in *Almeida-Sanchez.*"

advance; advancement. Generally, the former refers to progress, the latter to promotion. Hence, one might get an occupational *advancement,* but one speaks of the *advance* of civilization. E.g., "The *advancement* [i.e., promotion] of religion has ever been held to be one of the principal divisions of charitable trusts."/ "These actions, according to the complaint, violated the plaintiff's rights under the first and fourteenth amendments to associate for the *advancement* of their common interests in dealings with the college."/ "Any one of these considerations might tend toward the *advancement* of the employees."

In senses suggesting the action of moving up or bringing forth, *advancement* is the proper word. "Considering the backlog of cases in most jurisdictions and the absence of any further right to *advancement* on the court calendar, the significance of victory or defeat at this stage is readily apparent."/ "The *advancement* of a prosecutorial-vindictiveness claim brings into conflict two antithetical interests."

The distinction gets fuzzier in financial contexts. Although we speak (properly) of *cash advances* and *advances on royalties,* in law *advancement* takes on a sense similar to that which *advance* has in these phrases. Leff defines *advancement* in this sense as "a gift, i.e., an expenditure not legally required, made by a parent to or on behalf of a child, with intention that the value thereof be deducted from the amount that the child would otherwise receive if the parent died intestate." Arthur A. Leff, *The Leff Dictionary of Law,* 94 Yale L.J. 1855, 1952 (1985). E.g., "The father had made numerous *advancements* to the son by way of establishing him in life with a college education, by setting him up in business, and by buying him an automobile and other items of personal property."

This legal usage is too well entrenched to allow a precisian's attempted "correction" of it: "This use led in turn to the 'hotchpot clause' in deeds and wills, similarly designed to ensure that an *advance* [read *advancement*] inter vivos to one of the class entitled to share in the estate should be brought to account."

advance directive. See **living will.**

advancee is an inaesthetic and unnecessary NEOLOGISM. E.g., "The Code does not state in detail what the writing must contain, although as applied to a writing by the intestate, a statement of an 'intent to advance' would seem necessary and presumably also a description of the property and the name of the *advancee* [read *recipient of the advancement*]." See -EE (A).

advancement. See **advance.**

advance sheet. See **slip opinion.**

adventitious; adventitial. *Adventitious* means "added extrinsically" or "accidental." It was formerly a legal term meaning "befalling a person by fortune," and was opposed to *profectitious* (= deriving from a parent or ancestor). These terms are now archaic except in the civil law. *Adventitious* is used today, however, in nonlegal senses—e.g.: "Her obtaining a law degree had the *adventitious* effect of nearly doubling her starting salary when she entered the business world."

Adventitial is a medical term that means "of or pertaining to a membrane that covers an organ."

ADVERBS, PROBLEMS WITH. A. Placement of Adverbs. A fairly well-known manual on legal style long cautioned its readers to avoid splitting verb phrases with adverbs—e.g.: "He *had quickly gone* to the scene of the crime," recommending instead, "He *quickly had gone* to the scene of the crime." This nonsense apparently derives from a phobia of anything resembling a SPLIT INFINITIVE. Here a phobic writer fell into the awkward phrasing: "The task of questioning veniremen and evaluating their answers is more difficult *than anything that heretofore has been attempted* [read *than anything that has heretofore been attempted* or, better yet, *than anything that has been attempted before*] in the process of jury selection." See HYPERCORRECTION (H) & SUPERSTITIONS (C).

In fact, as all reputable authorities agree, frequently the most proper and natural placement of an adverb is in the midst of the verb phrase. E.g., "The corporation *was virtually bankrupted* by the massive tort liability."

B. Awkward Adverbs. Adjectives ending in *-ly* often make slightly cumbersome adverbs, e.g., *sillily, friendlily, uglily,* and so on. One need not be timid in writing or pronouncing such adverbs when they are called for; but if they seem unnatural, one can easily rephrase the sentence, e.g., *in a silly manner.* Words such as *timely* and *stately,* however, act as both adjectives and adverbs.

In any event, unusual adverbs are to be used sparingly. Some writers display an overfondness for them. One judicial opinion, for example, contains the adverbs *corollarily, consideredly,* and the spurious *widespreadedly,* q.v. See *United Medical Labs. v. Columbia Broadcasting Sys., Inc.,* 404 F.2d 706 (9th Cir. 1968).

C. Adjectives or Adverbs After Linking Verbs. English contains a number of linking verbs (or copulas) apart from *to be,* for example, *appear, seem, become, look, smell, taste.* These verbs connect a descriptive word with the subject; hence the descriptive word following the linking verb describes the subject and not the verb. We say *He turned professional,* not *He turned professionally.*

Legal writers frequently fall into error when they use linking verbs. One must analyze the sentence, rather than memorize a list of common linking verbs, much as this may help. Often an unexpected verb of this kind appears—e.g.: "No other testimonial privilege sweeps so *broadly* [read *sweeps so broad*]." The writer is not describing a manner of sweeping, but instead is saying that the privilege *is* broad.

D. Redundantly Formed Adverbs. Some adverbial forms are incorrectly formed by adding *-ly* to words that already function as adverbs. See HYPERCORRECTION (D), **doubtless(ly), much(ly), over(ly) & thus (B).**

E. No Hyphens with Adverbs Ending in *-ly*. See PHRASAL ADJECTIVES (A).

adversary, adj.; **adversarial; adversarious; adversative; adversive; adverse.** *Adversary,* which can act as both noun and adjective, is the legal term used in phrases such as *an adversary relationship.* E.g., "The need to develop all relevant facts in the *adversary* system is both fundamental and comprehensive."

Adversarial is not listed in most dictionaries, though it is fairly common as a near-equivalent of the adjective *adversary.* E.g., "Rarely does this type of *adversarial* [read *adversary*] relationship exist between school authorities and pupils." *New Jersey v. T.L.O.,* 469 U.S. 325, 349-50 (1985) (Powell, J., concurring)./ "The evolution of this area of the law has been and will remain a product of the interaction of two *adversarial* forces—prosecutors who seek to exclude all scrupled jurors, and defense counsel eager to retain them." In fact, *adversarial* and *adversary* have begun to undergo DIFFERENTIATION: *adversarial* connotes animosity <adversarial conferences>, whereas *adversary* is a neutral, clinical word.

Adversarious (= hostile), though listed in the *OED,* has dropped from the language. *Adversative* is a term of grammar and logic meaning "expressing an antithesis or opposition" <adversative conjunction>. *Adversive* is an anatomical term for "opposite." See **adverse.**

adversary procedure. See **accusatorial.**

adverse; averse. Both may take the preposition *to; adverse* also takes *from.* To be *averse to* something is to have feelings against it. To be *adverse to* something—the phrase is usually used of things and not of people—is to be turned in opposition against it.

Adverse is used as an adjective in the phrase *adverse party* (= opposing party) in reference to persons, but seldom elsewhere. In reference to circumstances, *adverse* means "potentially afflictive or calamitous," but most great triumphs come in the face of adverse conditions.

Adverse(ly) to for *against* is a slight pomposity. E.g., "The court rendered a judgment *adverse to* [read *against*] the plaintiff."/ "Most of the questions raised by this appeal have been disposed of *adversely to* [read *against*] the appellants in the companion case decided this day."

adversive. See **adversary.**

advert; avert. To *advert to* something is to refer to it, to bring it up in speech or writing. It is a word best reserved for contexts that are especially formal, except in BrE, where it is more common. "Finally, I must *advert to* the pain suffered and to be suffered by the appellant as a result of the car accident." (Eng.) (See **allude (A).**) The word should not be used in its etymological sense "to turn to," as here: "*Before adverting to* [read *Before turning to*] the factual setting, we briefly outline the legal context in which the issue of fraudulent transfer arises."

To *avert* is to ward off, turn away, or avoid. Thus a national leader who has failed to *avert* a political scandal might *avert* his or her eyes. E.g., "The rule *averts* potential diplomatic embarrassment from the courts of one sovereign sitting in judgment over the public acts of another." See **avert.**

advertise; advertize. The former spelling is standard (AmE, BrE).

advice. See **advisement.**

advisatory. See **advisory.**

advise. A. In Commercial Contexts. Here *advise* takes on a meaning with which nonlawyers are generally unfamiliar. It means "to announce; give formal notice of." E.g., "The letter of credit was *advised* through the Bank of America in Quito, Ecuador." In such contexts, *advise* has very nearly taken on the meaning "to negotiate."

B. For *tell* or *say.* This is a pomposity to be avoided. "*I was advised by him* [read *He told me*] that the deadline had not yet elapsed."/ "The dispatcher returned their call in several minutes but *advised* [read *told*] them that the computer had broken down, and that he could not check the registration."

C. And *instruct.* In G.B., barristers are said to *advise* solicitors (or clients through solicitors), whereas solicitors *instruct* barristers. See **attorney (A).**

advisedly means, not "intentionally," but "after careful consideration."

advisement; advice. Judges frequently take matters *under advisement,* meaning that they will consider and deliberate on a particular question before the court. E.g., "Punishment for contempt is hereby taken *under advisement* by the court." *Advisement* is best not used outside the legal idiom for *advice* or *advising* <the advising of entry-level officers>.

adviser; advisor. The *-er* spelling is sanctioned over the *-or* spelling in the dictionaries. Note, however, that the adjectival form is *advisory.* See -ER (A).

advisory; advisatory. The latter is a NEEDLESS VARIANT of *advisory,* which commonly appears in phrases such as *advisory opinion, advisory capacity,* and *advisory council.*

advocacy; advocation. The first is the art or work of an advocate; the second was formerly the term in Scots law for an appellate court's review of lower-court decisions. *Advocation* should not be used, although occasionally it is, where *advocacy* would suffice.

advocate; advocator. The latter is a NEEDLESS VARIANT.

advocation. See **advocacy.**

advocatory = of or pertaining to an advocate. Hence it corresponds to *advocacy,* q.v., not *advocation.*

advocatus diaboli, the Latin term for *Devil's advocate,* is an example of highfalutin humor and should be used cautiously if at all. Its opposite is *advocatus dei.*

advowson. This archaic legal term, though suggestive of a type of person, refers to a property right in an ecclesiastical office. The right is transferable and inheritable in perpetuity.

AE is a remnant of the Latin digraph, formerly ligatured (æ), appearing in such words as *aegis, aesthetic,* and *praetor.* In most Latinate words in which this digraph once appeared, the initial vowel has been dropped. One sees this tendency still at work in *(a)esthetic, (a)eon,* and *(a)ether.* Compare the retention of the digraphs in BrE (e.g., *anaesthetic* and *foetus*) with the shortened forms *anesthetic* and *fetus,* which are prevalent in AmE. See **pr(a)edial.**

aegis was originally a mythological term meaning "protective shield" or "defensive armor." The word is now used exclusively in figurative senses. One must be careful not to confuse *aegis* with *auspices* (= sponsorship; support). E.g., "Generally, it is required that what has been done regularly under the *aegis* [correct] of the law will be considered valid and will remain so even after a change in legislation." Idiom requires *under the aegis,* not *with the aegis.*

aesthetic; esthetic. Although the Merriam-Webster dictionaries have long recorded *esthetic* as the primary form in AmE, the form *aesthetic* remains more common in AmE and BrE alike.

aetiology. See **etiology.**

affect; effect. In ordinary usage, *affect* is always a verb; it means "to influence; to have an effect on." *Effect,* as suggested by its use in that definition, is a noun meaning "result" or "consequence." To *affect* something is to have an *effect* on it. (See **impact.**) As a verb, *effect* means "to bring about; produce" <they could not effect a coup>.

In the following sentences, *affect* is wrongly used for the noun *effect:* "[T]he laws of New Jersey shall control the *affect* [read *effect*] of the agreement." *Developers Small Business Inv. Corp. v. Hoeckle,* 395 F.2d 80, 84 (9th Cir. 1968) (quoting a contract)./ "The participants must be afforded maximal protection against harmful side *affects* [read *effects*]."

Likewise, *effect* is sometimes misused for *affect.* See **effect.**

affectable; affectible. The former spelling is preferred. See -ABLE (A).

AFFECTATION, LITERARY. See PURPLE PROSE & LITERARY ALLUSION (B).

affected, adj.**; affective; affectional; affectionate.** *Affected,* as an adjective, means "assumed artificially; pretended" (*OED*); *affective* = emotional; *affectional* = pertaining to affection; and *affectionate* = loving, fond.

Just as *affect,* q.v., is sometimes misused for *effect, affective* is sometimes wrongly placed where *effective* belongs: "The parties to the contract would have had to stipulate an *affective* [read *effective*] date." We might prefer to call this a typographical error rather than an ignorant bungle.

affection; affectation. The former means "love, fondness"; the latter, "pretentious, artificial behavior." In Elizabethan English, these words were used more or less interchangeably, but now each has acquired its own distinct sense—which is good for the language.

Affectation doctrine is sometimes seen for *affects doctrine* in the context of American constitutional law, specifically of the commerce clause. E.g., "For the essence of the *affectation doctrine* [read *"affects" doctrine* or *effects doctrine*] was that the exact location of this line made no difference, if the forbidden effects flowed across it to the injury of interstate commerce . . . ." *Mandeville Island Farms, Inc. v. American Crystal Sugar Co.,* 334 U.S. 219, 232 (1948). *Affects* is the correct word because the test is whether the activity "affects" commerce. Because the noun corresponding to *affect* (= to influence) is *effect*—not *affectation*—a better phrasing would be *effects doctrine* (i.e., "that has effects"), but it has not gained currency. See **affect & effect.**

affectional; affectionate. See **affected.**

affective. See **affected.**

affeer; amerce. Both words mean generally "to fine." Specifically, *affeer* = to fix the amount of [a fine] (*W3*). The variant spellings *affeere* and *affere* should be avoided. *Amerce* = to fine arbitrarily (*OED*), meaning that the amount of the fine is not prescribed by statute, but rather is lodged in the discretion of the court. Etymologically speaking, when being *amerced,* one is "at the mercy" of the court.

The nominal forms are *affeerment* and *amercement*—*amerciament* having gone the way that all NEEDLESS VARIANTS should. *Amerce* has no recorded personal nominal form. *Affeeror* and *affeerer* are competing forms, the *-or* spelling perhaps the better one because it is more distinctly pronounceable.

affianced. See **affined.**

affiant /ə-*fī*-ənt/, a term that began as an Americanism in the mid-19th century, ordinarily means "one who gives an affidavit." More broadly, and less accurately, it refers to any deponent. See **further affiant . . . .**

affidavit [L. "he swore"] is ordinarily a noun referring to a voluntary declaration of facts written down and sworn to by the declarant before an officer authorized to administer oaths.

Occasionally, however, lawyers have used the word as a verb. But a better choice is invariably available—e.g.: "This counsel later testified that the reason for filing the Notice of Change of Judge was 'personal to us and the plaintiff, [and that] we *affidavited or noticed* [read *filed an affidavit and notice of*] that change of judge, on Judge Patterson . . . .'" *Hickox v. Superior Court,* 505 P.2d 1086, 1087 (Ariz. Ct. App. 1973) (quoting counsel)./ "Noteworthily missing from this record, however, is any *affidavited* [read *sworn*] assertion by a representative of the banks . . . ." *In re Drexel Burnham Lambert Group Inc.,* 113 B.R. 830, 840 (S.D.N.Y. 1990).

The phonetic misspelling *affidavid* is not uncommon.

For a redundancy involving this word, see **sworn affidavit.**

affiliation, in BrE, refers to a father's maintenance of illegitimate children. E.g., "The mother has the right to the custody of her illegitimate children, and is bound to maintain them. She may obtain an *affiliation* order against the father from the local police court, either before the child is born or within twelve months after the birth . . . ." Anon., *The Home Counsellor* 172 ([London: Odhams Press] ca. 1940–1945)./ "[T]here is the rule [that] requires the testimony of the plaintiff in an action for breach of promise of marriage, and the applicant in an *affiliation* case, to be corroborated by independent evidence." Edward Jenks, *The Book of English Law* 77 (P.B. Fairest ed., 6th ed. 1967).

affined; affianced. *Affined* = closely related; connected. Archaically, *affined* means "obligated." *Affianced* = engaged, betrothed.

affinity; consanguinity. The former refers to relationship by marriage, the latter to relationship by blood. The distinction is usually carefully observed in legal writing. E.g., "The statutes prescribe the classes of persons entitled to appointment as administrator and indicate an order of precedence based on kinship by *consanguinity* or *affinity with* the decedent."

Affinity takes the preposition *between* or *with,* not *to* or *for.*

affirm. Usually only judgments are *affirmed* by appellate courts; cases are *remanded;* and opinions or decisions are *approved* or *disapproved.* (See JUDGMENTS, APPELLATE-COURT.) The practice of writing "The trial court was *affirmed*" is informally an acceptable ellipsis for "The trial court's judgment was *affirmed,*" but such phrasing should not appear in formal legal writing. E.g., "Had the trial judge followed his initial decision and overruled the motion for new trial without expressing any desire for leniency, *he would be affirmed* [read *his judgment would be affirmed*]."

affirmance; affirmation. There is, unfortunately, some overlap of these terms. Yet a useful rule might be formulated: When an appellate court affirms a lower court's judgment, there is an *affirmance.*

In all other contexts, *affirmation* is the preferable term. E.g., "Finally, we refer to the restatement and *affirmation* of the doctrine in *Hood v. Francis.*" In the following sentences, *affirmance* is used where *affirmation* would be better: "The long-established recognition in Massachusetts of the doctrine of independent significance makes unnecessary statutory *affirmance* [read *affirmation*] of its application to pour-over trusts."/ "The court held that the instrument was a conveyance and a recognition, acceptance, and *affirmance* [read *affirmation*] of the devise, and not a renunciation."

Here the opposite error appears, *affirmation* for *affirmance:* "After the final decision in *Finney* and the appellate court's *affirmation* [read *affirmance*] of the judgment, the district court determined that the petitioner was not entitled to any relief other than injunctive relief already granted to class members." Cf. **disaffirmation.**

Quite apart from its ordinary meaning, *affirmation* has a specialized legal sense: "a formal and solemn declaration, having the same weight and invested with the same responsibilities as an oath, by one who conscientiously declines to take an oath" (*OED*). Many American jurisdictions now have statutes permitting *affirmations* under circumstances in which obtaining a notary public's acknowledgment would be inconvenient. The person *affirming* is termed an *affirmant.* See **affirmant & oath.**

affirmant; deponent. One who testifies by deposition and swears to the truth of the testimony is termed a *deponent.* One who, instead of swearing or taking an oath, affirms or solemnly states that the testimony is true, is termed an *affirmant.*

affirmation. See **affirmance.**

affirmative action. The phrase is sometimes used generically to denote "a positive step taken," as well as more specifically to denote "an attempt to reverse or mitigate past racial discrimination." Compare 15 U.S.C. § 2622(2)(b) (1988) ("the Secretary shall order . . . the person who committed such violation to take *affirmative action* to abate the violation") with 29 U.S.C. § 791(b) (1988) ("each department . . . shall . . . submit . . . an *affirmative action* program for the hiring, placement and advancement of individuals with handicaps").

affirmative, in the; negative, in the. These phrases have been criticized as jargonistic and pompous. (See, e.g., Quiller-Couch's statement quoted under JARGON (B).) They appear frequently in legal writing and in other types of formal prose. E.g., "The sole question raised on this appeal is whether the Texas rule that a defendant must prove duress by a preponderance of the evidence violates the due process clause of the fourteenth amendment; answering *in the negative,* we affirm."/ "The Sixth Circuit, when confronted with the identical question, answered *in the affirmative* and permitted the use of this same deposition against asbestos companies not represented in *DeRocco.*"

This phrasing is probably better than the closest alternative: "Reversing the judgment of the bankruptcy court, we answer both questions presented 'No.'" In the formal context of judicial opinions, *in the affirmative* and *in the negative* should be allowed to exist peacefully. But when these phrases are used of mundane questions in mundane situations, they look foolish.

affirmative pregnant. See **negative pregnant.**

affixture; affixation; affixion. *Affixture* = the state of being affixed; *affixation* = the act of affixing or the use of an affix. *Affixion* = *affixation* or *affixture,* but it adds nothing to either; it should be avoided as a NEEDLESS VARIANT.

afflatus; afflation; inflatus. For the sense "inspiration," or "supernatural impulse," *afflatus* is the standard term. E.g., "The decisions under the revenue acts have little weight as against legislation under the *afflatus* of the Eighteenth Amendment." (Holmes, J.) *Inflatus* and *afflation* are secondary variants. The plural of *afflatus* is *afflatuses,* not *afflati.* See PLURALS (A).

afflict. See **inflict.**

affluent and *affluence* are accented on the first rather than the second syllable.

afford. See **accord.**

affranchise. See **franchise.**

affray; fray. Both terms, though somewhat quaint, are still used in legal opinions. *Affray* is classically defined as "unpremeditated fighting in a public place that tends to disturb the public peace." E.g., "To some extent, crimes such as riot, violent disorder, and *affray* appear as inchoate offences of violence or even actual offences of violence." Andrew Ashworth, *Principles of Criminal Law* 35 (1991).

There is some dispute over whether an affray must be in public. From the late 18th century onward, legal writers discussing *affray* said—mistakenly, it seems—that the fighting must occur in public. The germ of the error began with Blackstone's definition of *affray* in 1769 as "the fighting of two or more persons in some public place, to the terror of His Majesty's subjects: for, if the fighting be in private, it is no *affray* but an assault." 4 Blackstone, *Commentaries* 145 (1769). In 1822, the first edition of Archbold's *Pleading and Evidence in Criminal Cases* (p. 337) asserted, without support, that the allegation "in a public street or highway" should be charged in the indictment and proved. But the House of Lords has held that Archbold incorrectly grafted this requirement onto the law of affray—that an affray need not be in a public place. See *Button v. Director of Public Prosecutions,* [1966] A.C. 591, 608, 627 (H.L.).

The idea that an affray must be public still holds sway, however, in most American jurisdictions. Thus, a leading criminal-law text states: "At common law an *affray* is a mutual fight in a public place to the terror or alarm of the people." Rollin M. Perkins & Ronald N. Boyce, *Criminal Law* 479 (3d ed. 1982).

affreighter. See **charterer.**

affreightment; affretement. Meaning "the hiring of a ship to carry cargo," *affreightment* is standard in common-law countries and in Louisiana (a civil-law jurisdiction). E.g., "Owners will be more likely to permit their charterers to enter freely into contracts of *affreightment* if owners know that no 'secret liens' will arise from obscure provisions in subagreements." (La.) *Affretement* is the spelling used in French civil law.

affront. See **effrontery.**

aficionado is often misspelled *afficionado,* as in *Butts v. National Collegiate Athletic Ass'n,* 751 F.2d 609, 613 (3d Cir. 1984).

afore (= before) is a dead ARCHAISM except in the phrases *aforesaid* and *aforementioned.* Words like *aforedescribed* need not be rescued from oblivion. See **above (B), aforesaid & above-mentioned.**

aforesaid; aforementioned. These LEGALISMS have little or no justification in modern writing. They often appear in spoofs and complaints—e.g.: "Individual laws . . . may be complicated and forbiddingly so, with the endless paragraphs, their *aforesaids* and *provided howevers.*" Lon L. Fuller, *Anatomy of the Law* 14–15 (1968).

Aforesaid or *aforementioned* is unnecessary when the reference to what has already been named is clear. E.g., "Plaintiff, in the normal routine of his employment, was exposed to various toxic materials and irritants. Exposure *to the aforementioned* [read *to these*] substances and irritants caused him to contract pneumoconiosis, and finally he died of lung cancer caused by his occupational exposure *to the aforementioned* [read *to these*] toxic substances." See **above-mentioned.**

Worse yet, *aforesaid* is a word of imprecision: it sometimes refers to what immediately preceded, to what came just before that, or to everything that has come before. When the reference is intended to be vague, it would be better to use *abovestated* or some other equivalent that is less stilted and legalistic. See FORBIDDEN WORDS (A) & **said (E).**

The word *aforesaid* is, of course, a past-participial combination (*afore* + *said*) that is almost always used adjectivally <aforesaid land>. Occasionally, however, it appears as the past participle of a verb: "The association secretly and with intent to deprive appellant of the opportunity of purchasing said property, and with the intent to profit through the information obtained as *aforesaid,* immediately began to negotiate with the owner for the purchase of said property." The literary quality of that sentence speaks for quality of the participial use of *aforesaid.* Cf. **said (A).**

aforethought (= thought of in advance) is now used only in the phrase *malice aforethought.* It is essentially synonymous with *premeditated* or *prepense.* See **malice aforethought,** POSTPOSITIVE ADJECTIVES, **prepense & willfulness.**

a fortiori /***ah***-*fohr-shee-****ohr****-ee*/ is an argumentative term meaning "by even greater force of logic; so much the more." The phrase is often used effectively—e.g.: "If an act is not a civil wrong, it cannot, *a fortiori,* be criminal." (Eng.)

The emphatic form of the term is *a multo fortiori* (= by far the stronger reason).

Legal writers sometimes use *a fortiori* as an adjective, a usage to be resisted—e.g.: "We have set forth the other two lines of possible proof only to suggest the *a fortiori* [read *even stronger*] position presented in the instant case."/ "Clearly, if laws depend so heavily on public acquiescence, the case of conventions is an *a fortiori* [read *even more compelling*] one." P.S. Atiyah, *Law and Modern Society* 59 (1983).

after-acquired = obtained after a certain (specified) time. The term is ordinarily placed before the noun it modifies: "The agreement to hold the proceeds of the sale in trust is, in effect, an agreement to hold *after-acquired* personal property in trust."

afterborn, adj., = born after (a certain event, such as the father's death or the birth of a sibling) <an afterborn child>. The word is also used as a noun in pretermitted-child statutes; it means "a child born after the execution of a will."

aftereffect should be spelled as one word.

after having [+ past participle]. This construction is ordinarily incorrect for *after* [+ *present participle*]—e.g.: "*After having passed* [read *After passing*] a general educational test and given evidence of good character, the candidate must procure himself to be admitted as a student at one of the four Inns of Court above named." Edward Jenks, *The Book of English Law* 66 (P.B. Fairest ed., 6th ed. 1967)./ "The flurry of laches litigation, *after having gone* [read *after going*] on for the better part of ten years, began to subside after the mid-1960's." Grant Gilmore & Charles L. Black, Jr., *The Law of Admiralty* 774 (2d ed. 1975)./ "*After having survived* [read *After surviving* or *Having survived*] eight years of attacks during the Reagan administration, the Legal Services Corp. . . . still faces challenges." Nat'l L.J., 14 Oct. 1991, at 1.

afterward(s). See -WARD(S).

against. See **contra, versus & as against.**

against conscience is a primarily BrE equivalent of *unconscionable,* q.v. "It is clear that any civilized system of law is bound to provide remedies for cases of what has been called unjust enrichment, that is, to prevent a man from retaining the money of or some benefit derived from another which it is *against conscience* that he should keep." (Eng.)

against nature. See EUPHEMISMS & **unnatural.**

against the peace. This phrase was traditionally used in a charging instrument for a misdemeanor, just as *feloniously* (q.v.) was used in a felony indictment. Sometimes the phrase is elaborated to *against the peace of the king* (or *against the king's peace*) or *against the peace and dignity of the state.*

ag(e)ing. See MUTE E.

agency, as a TERM OF ART, refers to any relationship in which one person (called an *agent*) acts for another (called a *principal*) in commercial or business transactions. Nonlawyers are largely unfamiliar with *agency* used in this way, although they understand the personal noun *agent* as meaning "representative."

agenda is (1) the plural form of the Latin noun *agendum,* which means "something to be done" (another, less proper plural of *agendum* being *agendums*); and, more commonly, (2) a singular noun meaning "a list of things to be done" or "a program." The plural of *agenda* in sense (2) is *agendas;* decrying *agendas* as a double plural is bootless.

Yet all careful writers should avoid the erroneous form *agendae,* the result of HYPERCORRECTION—e.g.: "Mr. Douglas . . . prepared *agendae* [read *agendas*] for meetings with the trustee and his attorneys . . . ." *In re New England Fish Co.,* 33 B.R. 413, 416 (Bankr. W.D. Wash. 1983).

agent; servant. "The words *agent* and *servant* are not synonyms; nevertheless they both relate to voluntary action under employment." *Lemmon v. State,* 3 A.2d 299, 300 (N.J. 1938). An *agent* is a business representative who handles contractual arrangements between the principal and third persons. A *servant,* by contrast, is an employee whose function is to render service, not to create contractual obligations. In the modern legal idiom, *servant* has been almost entirely displaced by *employee.* See **agency & employer and employee.**

AGENT NOUNS, FALSE. See -ER (B).

age of capacity; age of consent; age of majority; age of reason. All these terms share the general sense "the age at which a person is legally capable (of doing something)." But, over time, each term has assumed a specific sense in a particular context. In the following discussion, the numerical ages listed are established by statute and may vary from jurisdiction to jurisdiction.

Age of capacity, usu. 18, denotes the age when one is legally capable of agreeing to a contract, executing a will, maintaining a lawsuit, and the like.

Age of majority, usu. 18, includes the rights attained at the age of capacity, but is broader because it also includes civil and political rights, esp. the right to vote. See **majority (D).**

Age of consent, usu. 16, denotes the age when one is legally capable of agreeing to marriage (without parental consent) or to sexual intercourse so that, regarding the latter, intercourse with someone under the age of consent is statutory rape. See **statutory rape.**

Age of reason denotes the age when one is able to distinguish right from wrong and is thus legally capable of committing a crime or tort. It varies from 7 to 14: 7 years is usu. the age below which a child is conclusively presumed not to have committed a crime or tort, while 14 years is usu. the age below which a rebuttable presumption applies. For related terms, see **child, infant, minority (A) & nonage.**

aggrandize; engrandize; ingrandize. The last two are NEEDLESS VARIANTS of the first.

aggravate for *annoy* or *irritate,* though documented as existing since the 1600s, has never gained the cachet of stylists and should be avoided in formal writing. Properly, *aggravate* means "to make worse; exacerbate." This meaning obtains in many legal phrases, such as *aggravated assault.* In its proper sense, *aggravate* is opposed to *mitigate* or *extenuate*—e.g.: "Here the indignity was of an *aggravated* sort; it occurred at a public place and in the presence of a large number of people."/ "It is clear that a state cannot explicitly make the murder of a white victim an *aggravating* circumstance in capital sentencing."

Even the brilliant Justice Holmes nodded once, using *aggravate* for *irritate* in a letter to Sir Frederick Pollock in 1895: "[O]ur two countries *aggravate* each other from time to time. . . ." 1 *Holmes-Pollock Letters* 66 (1941).

aggravated damages. See **punitive damages.**

aggregable is the preferred form, not *aggregatable*—e.g.: "[T]he Commission notified defendants that their trading activities were *aggregatable* [read *aggregable*]." *Commodity Futures Trading Comm'n v. Hunt,* 591 F.2d 1211, 1227 n.5 (7th Cir. 1979). See -ATABLE.

aggregate, n.; **aggregation.** Both may mean "a mass of discrete things or individuals taken as a whole," *aggregate* being the more usual term. *Aggregate* stresses the notion "taken as a whole" (as in the phrase *in the aggregate*), and *aggregation* more "a mass of discrete things." Here the former term is used: "The price, while of trifling moment to each reader of the newspaper, is sufficient in the *aggregate* to afford compensation for the cost of gathering and distributing the news."

For "the act of aggregating," only *aggregation* will suffice. E.g., "There should not be *aggregation* of two or more obtainings of credit for the purpose of one offense."/ "It is a mass that has grown by *aggregation,* with very little intervention from legislation."

aggregate, vb. **A. Sense.** *Aggregate* = to bring together a mass of discrete things or individuals into a whole. The verb is sometimes misused for *total* in reference to sums: "Before us, appellant argues that the fines imposed, *aggregating almost $15,000* [read *totaling almost $15,000* or *in the aggregate almost $15,000*] were excessive.

B. *Aggregate together.* This phrase is a REDUNDANCY—e.g.: "For the purpose of establishing the rate at which capital transfer tax is payable, all property (with certain exceptions) passing on the death is *aggregated together* [read *aggregated*]." William Geldart, *Introduction to English Law* 90 (D.C.M. Yardley ed., 9th ed. 1984).

aggrievance. See **grievance.**

aggrievant. See **grievant.**

aggrieve (= to bring grief to; to treat unfairly) is now used almost exclusively in legal contexts, and almost always in the form of a past participle. E.g., "An *aggrieved* spouse is not compelled to seek the courts of another state for the protection of her marital status."/ "Suppression of the product of a Fourth Amendment violation can be successfully urged only by those whose rights have been violated by the search itself, not by those who are *aggrieved* solely by the introduction of damaging evidence."

aggrievement (= an act or instance of causing grief to a person) is illustrated in the *OED* with but one citation, but it appears with some frequency in law—e.g.: "[The exceptions do not] offer[ ] reason for *aggrievement,* and signify nothing except general dissatisfaction with the entire report." *Kowalsky v. American Employers Ins. Co.,* 90 F.2d 476, 480 (6th Cir. 1937).

The word should not be used as a variant of *grievance*—e.g.: "Another of MacDonald's *aggrievements* [read *grievances*] centers on the deterioration of a bloody footprint, which he was no longer able to distinguish adequately at trial." *U.S. v. MacDonald,* 632 F.2d 258, 270 (4th Cir. 1980).

agnate; cognate. In Roman law, an *agnate* is a relative through one's father; a *cognate* is any relative, through one's father or mother. The corresponding adjectives are *agnatic* and *cognatic.*

a gratia. See ***ex gratia.***

agréation; agrément. The first is a process, and the second is the usual result of the process. *Agréation* = a diplomatic procedure by which a receiving state makes a prior determination whether a proposed envoy will be acceptable; *agrément* = the approval of a diplomatic representative by the receiving state.

agree. A. And *concur.* In G.B., appellate judges who join in an opinion are said to *agree,* whereas in the U.S. they *concur.*

B. *Agreed to* and *agreed upon.* These are slightly awkward as PHRASAL ADJECTIVES, but when used before a noun, they should be hyphenated. E.g., "This clause refers to our previously *agreed-to* verbal contract." (See **verbals.**) / "To the extent that the nonoccurrence of a condition would cause disproportionate forfeiture, a court may excuse the nonoccurrence of that condition unless its occurrence was a material part of the *agreed-upon* exchange."

In a few phrases, *agreed* suffices as an idiomatic ellipsis for *agreed-upon,* as in *agreed verdict,* q.v., and *agreed judgment.* Generally, though, the entire phrase should appear: "As shown by the charge in the *agreed* [read *agreed-upon*] statement, Jan, at the time of the distribution, is the only child of an only child of a child of Hastings."/ "It cannot be said as a matter of law that their delay for an hour and a quarter was reasonable; the facts as to this are not *agreed* [read *agreed upon*]."

A similar ellipsis occurs with *agreed to* and *agreed on,* seemingly on the mistaken notion that one should avoid ending a sentence with a preposition—e.g.: "[I]n America there is a famous decision holding that a negotiating party who strings another party along with prolonged negotiations, constantly changing his terms, may be held liable to the other party for actual loss suffered if no contract eventually is *agreed* [read *agreed to*]." P.S. Atiyah, *An Introduction to the Law of Contract* 62 (3d ed. 1981)./ "However, Mr Dlouhy said the essentials had been *agreed* [read *agreed on*]." Leslie Colitt & John Lloyd, *Comecon Takes First*

Steps to Dismantle Itself, Fin. Times, 28 March 1990, at 1. See PREPOSITIONS (C).

agree and covenant. See **covenant and agree.**

agreed verdict (BrE) = *consent decree* (AmE).

agreement; contract. The former may refer either to an informal arrangement with no consideration (e.g., a "gentlemen's agreement") or to a formal legal arrangement supported by consideration. *Contract* is used only in this second sense. The distinction applies also with the verbs *agree* and *contract.* The intended sense of *agree(ment)* is usually clear from the context.

Although every contract is an agreement, not every agreement is a contract. For example, one may agree to meet a friend at 7:00 p.m. for dinner, and the result is properly called an *agreement*—but not a *contract,* to which a legal obligation attaches. See **bargain.**

AGREEMENT, GRAMMATICAL. See CONCORD (A).

agrees and covenants. See **covenant and agree.**

agree with; agree to; agree on. *Agree with* means "to be in accord with (another)"; *agree to,* "to acquiesce in (usu. the performance or specifications of something)." *Agree on* refers to the subject of the agreement: one agrees *with* someone *on* a certain settlement. E.g., "Plaintiff *agreed with* defendant *on* the contractual provisions relating to time of delivery."

agrément. See ***agréation.***

ahold and its variant *aholt* are dialectal. They might perhaps be justified in bizarre contexts such as this: "Plaintiff, driving her car, suddenly becomes convinced that God is taking *ahold* of the steering wheel."

-AHOLIC, -AHOLISM. Speakers and writers should avoid indiscriminately appending these newfangled "suffixes" to words to indicate various addictions. Each time this is done, a MORPHOLOGICAL DEFORMITY is created.

aid and abet = "to assist the perpetrator of the crime while sharing in the requisite intent." *U.S. v. Martinez,* 555 F.2d 1269, 1271 (5th Cir. 1977). This phrase is a well-known legal DOUBLET that, like most doublets, has come down to us from the Middle Ages and Renaissance, when it was common to embellish terms with synonyms. Singly, *aid* is the more general term, *abet* generally appearing only in contexts involving criminal intent.

Aid and abet is sometimes called a TERM OF ART, but in fact it is, in the words of the chief American and British criminal-law commentators, "unnecessarily verbose" and "antiquated." See Rollin M. Perkins & Ronald N. Boyce, *Criminal Law* 724–25 (3d ed. 1982); Glanville Williams, *Textbook of Criminal Law* 288 (1978). It is still used in both AmE and BrE, although in the 1970s England's Law Commission Working Party proposed replacing the phrase with *help*—a proposal that was not accepted. Perkins and Boyce recommend *abet,* which can stand alone unaided.

The agent noun is *aider and abettor*—e.g.: "The appellant now makes the further claim that the complaint charged the defendant as an original instigator only, and that he cannot be held liable thereunder as an *aider and abettor.*"/ "The court stated that it had found no other case discussing whether a nonparty *aider and abettor* is subject to the court's jurisdiction." See **abettor.**

Sometimes the phrase is made even wordier: "The further contention of the appellant is that defendant's acts are insufficient to support the trial court's conclusions that he knowingly *aided, abetted, and assisted* [read *abetted*] in the prosecution of false charges against defendant, and adopted them as his own." See DOUBLETS, TRIPLETS, AND SYNONYM-STRINGS.

aid(e)-de-camp (= military aide) is borrowed from the French and should retain the Gallicized spelling—*aide*—especially considering that *aide* is itself now an English word (meaning "a staff member under one's authority"). The plural is *aides-de-camp.*

In BrE, the phrase is often abbreviated *A.D.C.* <he was A.D.C. to General Montgomery in 1943>.

aim to [+ present infinitive]; aim at [+ gerund]. The idiom *aim to establish* is typical of AmE, *aim at establishing* typical of BrE.

airworthy is used in reference to aircraft and means "fit for operation in the air" (*W3*). The word, surprisingly enough first used in 1829, was analogized from *seaworthy,* q.v.

aitiology. See **etiology.**

alas; alack. *Alas* should express woe caused by a lamentable state of affairs. Here, in a quotation from a journal entitled *Ethnicity,* it is nonsensical: "There have been a number of meetings around the land about ethnicity (the phenomenon, *alas,* not this journal)." The writer would hardly bemoan the increasing attention given to ethnicity as an academic subject, even if the writer were editor of the journal. If one were to guess at the intended meaning in that quotation, *alas* might be a MALAPROPISM for some phrase such as *to be sure.*

Alack is archaic; *alas and alack* is a tiresome CLICHÉ.

al barre. See **at (the) bar.**

albeit. This conjunction, though termed "archaic" by Eric Partridge (the British lexicographer), thrives in AmE, both legal and nonlegal. And it still appears in BrE, esp. in legal writing. Labeled "literary" in the *COD,* the word *albeit* means "though" and introduces concessive phrases and sometimes subordinate clauses. The even more literary *howbeit,* by contrast, means "nevertheless" and begins principal clauses.

A. Introducing Phrases. The predominant modern use is for *albeit* to introduce concessive phrases: "The parties addressed the issue, *albeit* in fairly leisurely fashion."/ "Petitioner located employment in 1978, *albeit* at a lower wage than he earned working for the respondents."

B. Introducing Clauses. *Albeit* may begin a clause, albeit *although* is more common in this context: "The fifty-five mile-an-hour speed limit has its benefits; it also has its costs, *albeit* they may not seem apparent because a majority is willing to pay them."/ "When the relevant credit extends to £10, that is the moment at which the offense is committed, *albeit* it may be by aggregating a series of smaller sums." (Eng.)/ "We think that we have for review a decision on a stipulated record, *albeit* the matter was styled as a determination on motions for summary judgment."

C. For *even if*. Archaically, *albeit* is sometimes used for *even if* in beginning a clause: "Separate and distinct false declarations that require different factual proof of falsity may properly be charged in separate counts, *albeit* [read *even if*] they are all related and arise out of the same transaction or subject matter." This use of the term is to be discouraged.

aleatory; stochastic; fortuitous. These words have similar but distinct meanings. *Aleatory* = depending on uncertain contingencies <contingent remainders are aleatory>. E.g., "We will respect the *aleatory* nature of the settlement process, whether any of the parties are ultimately found to have made a favorable settlement."

Stochastic = random. *Fortuitous* = accidental, occurring by chance. See **fortuitous.** Cf. **adventitious.**

alegal, adj. This late-20th-century NEOLOGISM—lit. "without law"—recognizes the increasingly common view that we should not put every action or event on the plane of legality and illegality. In the view of some scholars, if an action is neither mandated nor prohibited by law, then it should be characterized as *alegal*—e.g.:

- "Think of the many human beings in pre-industrial society related through their dependence on territorial magnates, or guilds, or church organizations. They were not *alegal* institutions." Joseph Vining, *Legal Identity: The Coming of Age of Public Law* 49 (1978).
- "At the free, *alegal* end of the spectrum, realism views judges as charging their own individual courses unencumbered by law in all respects but form . . . ." Lewis A. Kornhauser & Lawrence G. Sager, *Unpacking the Court,* 96 Yale L.J. 82, 93 (1986).
- "[Treating] the promises of unmmarried cohabitors as contractual words rather than *alegal* words of commitment puts public force behind what is otherwise legally vacuous." Mark Kelman, *A Guide to Critical Legal Studies* 105 (1987).

In using this term, of course, one must respect the boundaries between *alegal* and *illegal.* Otherwise, the same confusion might arise as exists between *amoral* and *immoral.* See **immoral.**

For related terms, see **extralegal & nonlegal.**

alias is both adverb (= otherwise [called or named]), as an elliptical form of *alias dictus,* and noun (= an assumed name), today usually the latter. *Alias* refers only to names, and should not be used synonymously with *guise* (= assumed appearance, pretense). See POPULARIZED LEGAL TECHNICALITIES.

alibi. A. As a Noun for *excuse*. The words are not synonymous, although the confusion that has grown out of their meanings is understandable. *Alibi* is a specific legal term referring to the defense of having been at a place other than the scene of a crime. By SLIPSHOD EXTENSION it has come to be used for any excuse or explanation for misconduct, usually that shifts blame to someone else.

The Evanses wrote of this term:

> Cynicism and the common man's distrust of the law have tinged *alibi* with a suggestion of improbability and even of dishonesty. Purists insist that it should be restricted to its legal meaning, and those who wish to be formally correct will so restrict it. In so doing, however, they will lose the connotation of cunning and dishonesty which distinguishes it from *excuse.*
>
> Bergen Evans & Cornelia Evans, *Contemporary American Usage* 24 (1957).

Lawyers perhaps more than others ought to "wish to be formally correct."

B. As an Adverb. In recent years *alibi* has been used as an adverb (meaning "elsewhere" <she proved herself alibi>), but this usage should be eschewed. Although "elsewhere" is the original Latin meaning of alibi (originally a locative of L. *alius* "other"), in English it has long served only as a noun, and it is an affectation to hark back to the classical sense.

C. As a Verb. Nor should *alibi* be used as a verb, as it is in the following sentences. The first sentence is doubly bad, for the misbegotten verb is based on the misused noun (see A): "The party cannot *alibi* [i.e., excuse] losses in the election."/ "The defendants *alibied themselves* [i.e., exculpated themselves by proving that they were not at the scene of the crime] and accused other men."/ "The conspirators attempted to *alibi* [i.e., provide alibis for] one another." The *OED* records this usage from 1909 and labels it colloquial.

alien, adj., takes the preposition *from* or, more commonly, *to*. For purposes of DIFFERENTIATION, "there is perhaps a slight preference for *from* where mere separation is meant (*We are entangling ourselves in matters alien from our subject*), and for *to* when repugnance is suggested (*Cruelty is alien to his nature*)" (*MEU2* 17).

alien, v.t.; **alienate; abalienate.** When we talk about property changing hands, the best choice of verb is *convey* or *transfer* rather than any of these legalistic words. But if some form of *alien* must be used, the most common and therefore the best word in all senses is *alienate,* whether one writes about alienation of property or of affections. Nonlawyers may understand that in certain contexts *alienate* means "to transfer (as property)"; they have little chance of understanding *alien* in such a context—much less *abalienate* (a NEEDLESS VARIANT from the civil law). E.g., "Since property owned by tenants by the entireties is not subject to the debts of either spouse, they may *alien* [read *alienate*] it without infringing the rights of their individual creditors."/ "The rule of common law is that a man cannot attach to a grant or transfer of property, otherwise absolute, the condition that it shall not be *alienated.*" *Aliene* is an archaic variant spelling of the verb *alien.*

Alienate frequently takes on the lay sense in legal writing, as in the phrase *alienation of affections,* or as here: "This false statement was designed to *alienate* supporters of plaintiff and to affiliate them with the other candidate."

alienee (= one to whom ownership of property is transferred) is an unnecessary, and unnecessarily obscure, equivalent of *grantee.* See the quotation in the following entry.

alienor; alienist. *Alienor* (= one who transfers property) is equivalent to *grantor;* it should be avoided where *grantor* or *transferor* will serve: "Conveying lands by means of a fictitious or collusive suit, commenced by arrangement by the intended *alienee* [read *grantee* or *recipient*] against the *alienor* [read *grantor*]" (quoted in *OED*).

Alienist is an obsolescent term for *psychiatrist.* E.g., "The only witness testifying that the testator was incompetent was an *alienist* who had never seen him and the testator's divorced wife who had not seen him in two years."

alimony. See **palimony.**

alio intuitu is not a justified LATINISM, when there are so many more precise alternatives such as *from a different point of view* or *with respect to another case (or condition).* E.g., "Counsel urges us to reject all observations to the contrary in the other authorities as made *alio intuitu* [read *under different circumstances*] on the strength of admissions." (Eng.).

aliquot; aliquant. *Aliquant* = being a part of a number or quantity but not dividing it without leaving a remainder <4 is an aliquant part of 17> (*W3*); *aliquot* = contained an exact number of times in something else <4 is an aliquot part of 16> (*id.*).

These are technical terms generally best left to technical contexts. *Aliquot* adds nothing to the following sentence: "Compromises are contracts of settlement, and the compromise of one *aliquot* part of a single liability and payment of the balance in full is a settlement of all parts of such single liability."

One justified technical use of these terms occurs in the field of trusts, where payment of an *aliquot* or *aliquant* part of the consideration for transfer of legal title may determine whether the presumption of a resulting trust will arise. When a payor's contributions for the purchase of property in another's name are *aliquot* parts of the purchase price, some courts presume the contributions to be a gift or loan; when, however, these contributions are *aliquant* parts of the purchase price, the presumption does not arise. See *Restatement (Second) of Trusts* § 454 comment c (1959). This distinction may be obsolescent; the *Restatement* rejects it in comment b to section 454.

The term *aliquot* is also used in determining whether a gift of property in a will is a specific or a general legacy: "[B]equests of all testator's property, an *aliquot* part thereof, or all property except certain things . . . have been held to amount to general legacies." Thomas E. Atkinson, *Handbook of the Law of Wills* 733–34 (2d ed. 1953). See **legacy.**

aliunde (= from another source, from elsewhere) is a LATINISM with little justification in place of an English equivalent. The phrase *evidence aliunde,* for example, means "evidence from outside (an instrument, for example); extrinsic evidence." E.g., "Thereupon . . . counsel would present their respective reviews of the nature and effect of the state of the record with respect to the existence of *sufficient evidence aliunde* [read *enough other evidence*] to justify admission of the testimony." *U.S. v. Azzarelli Constr. Co.,* 612 F.2d 292, 297 (7th Cir. 1979).

ALJ; A.L.J.; a.l.j. The usual abbreviation for *administrative-law judge* is *ALJ* (without periods)—an abbreviation first used in 1973 and now commonplace. For the first recorded use, see *Hawkins v. Weinberger,* 368 F. Supp. 896, 897 (D. Kan. 1973). The plural is *ALJs.* See **administrative-law judge.**

The uses of *A.L.J.* in late-19th-century American opinions generally meant either *additional law judge* or *associate law judge.*

all. A. *All (of).* The more formal construction is to omit *of* and write, when possible, "*All* the arguments foundered." E.g., "Appellant was to guarantee unconditionally appellee's performance under the purchase agreement, including *all* appellee's obligations and liabilities." When the phrase is followed by a pronoun, *all of* is the only idiomatic choice (*all of them,* not *all them*), except when the pronoun is possessive <all my personal property>.

Before general nouns, *all of* is more common in AmE than in BrE; nevertheless, it should generally be avoided in formal writing. Rarely, *all of* reads better than *all* even where a pronoun does not follow—e.g.: "*All of* John's property was therefore subject to the IRS lien."

B. With Negatives. *Not all*—as opposed to *all . . . not*—is usually the correct sequence in negative constructions. "It seems that *all* things were *not* going well in Wheeler's own unit." (This expanded version of the idiomatic "All is not well" does not work. [Read either *It seems that not all things were going well* or, better, *It seems that all was not well.*])/ "However, *all* American courts *did not* reject it." Roscoe Pound, *The Formative Era of American Law* 89 (1938). [Read: *But not all American courts rejected it.*]/ "Students rightfully protest; and while *all of their complaints do not* [read *not all their complaints*] have merit, they too should be heard . . . ." William O. Douglas, *Points of Rebellion* 14 (1970). Cf. **every (C)** & **everyone . . . not.**

C. And *any.* *All* follows a superlative adjective <most of all>; *any* follows a comparative adjective <more than any other>. Constructions such as *more . . . than all* are illogical—e.g.: "Thompson & Knight [a Dallas law firm] spent more time doing pro bono work *than all* Dallas law firms." [Read *Thompson & Knight spent more time doing pro bono work than any other Dallas law firm.*] See OVERSTATEMENT.

For *any and all,* see **any and all.**

all and singular is a collective equivalent of *each and every.* It is almost always unnecessary—e.g.: "Defendant denies *each and every, all and singular, the allegations* [read *all the allegations*] contained in the plaintiff's original petition." See DOUBLETS, TRIPLETS, AND SYNONYM-STRINGS.

all deliberate speed. See **with all deliberate speed.**

allegation; allegement; *allegatum.* The second and third forms are NEEDLESS VARIANTS.

allegator = one who alleges. It is not often used, even in legal writing, perhaps because of its jocular suggestiveness of *alligator.*

allegatum. See **allegation.**

allege; contend. To *allege* is formally to state a matter of fact as being true or provable, without yet having proved it. The word once denoted stating under oath, but this meaning no longer applies. To *contend,* in the advocatory sense, means "to state one's position in a polemical way, to submit." (In its popular sense, *contend* means "to strive against.")

Allege should not be used as a synonym of *assert, maintain, declare,* or *claim. Allege* has peculiarly accusatory connotations. One need not allege only the commission of crimes; but certainly the acts alleged must concern misfeasances or negligence.

allegeable; allegible. *Allegeable* is the only recognized form of the word.

allegedly does not mean "in an alleged manner," as it would if the adverb had been formed as English adverbs generally are. Follett considered adverbs like this one ugly and unjustified (esp. *reportedly*). See Wilson Follett, *Modern American Usage* 279 (1966). Yet *allegedly* is a convenient space- and time-saver for *it is alleged that* or *according to the allegations.* Though not logically formed, *allegedly* is well established and unobjectionable, if used in moderation. See **reportedly.**

allegement. See **allegation.**

allegible. See **allegeable.**

Allen charge. See CASE REFERENCES (C) & **dynamite charge.**

aller sans jour. See LOAN TRANSLATIONS.

all fours. See **on all fours.**

allide; collide. The former is used only in a special context in reference to ships in admiralty law. When two ships *allide,* one of them is stationary; ships *collide* when both are moving before impact. *Black's* notes that the distinction is not carefully observed. See **collision.**

allision. See **collision.**

ALLITERATION. **A. Rhetorically Effective Examples.** "The primary appeal of the language," wrote Jerome Frank, "is to the ear." The SOUND OF PROSE is therefore a critical concern. And writers frequently harness sounds for any of several effects. When they repeat sounds, the result is called *alliteration.*

Sometimes alliteration creates a sarcastic tone, as when Vice President Spiro Agnew referred to the *nattering nabobs of negativism.* E.g., "And what is implied by that lovely limpid legalism, 'due process of law' ? " Fred Rodell, *Woe Unto You, Lawyers!* 51 (1939; repr. 1980)./ "Unblinded by the tweedledum-tweedledee twaddle of much that passes for learned legal argument, . . . he seems essentially a direct, plain-spoken politician . . . ." Fred Rodell, *Nine Men* 331 (1955).

At other times it merely creates a memorable phrase—e.g.: "[J]udges do and must legislate but they can do so only interstitially; they are confined from molar to molecular motions." *Southern Pac. Co. v. Jensen,* 244 U.S. 205, 221 (1917) (Holmes, J., dissenting).

B. Unconscious Examples. The unconscious repetition of sounds, especially excessive sibilance (too many *-s-* sounds, as in the phrase *especially excessive sibilance*), can easily distract readers: "[W]hen used by accident it falls on the ear very disagreeably." W. Somerset Maugham, "Lucidity, Simplicity, Euphony," in *The Summing Up* 321, 325 (1938).

Though alliteration is quite common with *-s-* sounds, other unconscious repetitions can occur. In the following sentence (Uniform Probate Code 2-104), three words in a five-word phrase rhyme: "This section is not to be applied where its application would result in a taking of *intestate estate by the state.*" [A possible revision: *This section does not apply when its application would result in the escheat of an intestate estate.*] Although one can avoid the use of *state, intestate estate* is well-nigh unavoidable. (The English Parliament enacted the Intestates' Estate Act, 15 & 16 Geo. VI & 1 Eliz. II, c. 64 (1952).) Sometimes one wishes that we could use the terms *willed* and *unwilled* rather than *testate* and *intestate:* "It is familiar law that the will is the source of the beneficiaries' title in the case of *testate estates,* while in *intestate estates* the source of title is the statute."

One good way to avoid the infelicity of undue alliteration is to read one's prose aloud when editing. See SOUND OF PROSE, THE.

all . . . not. See **all (B).**

allocable is the proper form, not *allocatable*—e.g.: "The division . . . held that the portion of increased tax expense attributable to facilities actually providing intrastate service was properly *allocatable* [read *allocable*] to Narragansett's intrastate operations." *Nepco Mun. Rate Comm. v. FERC,* 668 F.2d 1327, 1346 (D.C. Cir. 1981). See -ATABLE.

allocatee. See -EE.

allocator; allocatur. *Allocator* = one who allocates. *Allocatur* (lit., "it is allowed") in former practice meant "a certificate duly given at the end of an action, allowing costs" (*OED*).

allocute (= to deliver in court a formal, exhortatory address, i.e., an allocution) is a BACK-FORMATION from the noun *allocution,* q.v. Although some years ago the verb might have been viewed as a barbarous MORPHOLOGICAL DEFORMITY, just as *electrocute* once was, we should accept *allocute* as a useful addition to legal language. E.g., "The appellants assert that the district court erroneously found that it had no cause to *allocute.*"

Because *allocution* most properly refers to the court's and not to the criminal defendant's address, it is the court that *allocutes*; this distinction has given way to SLIPSHOD EXTENSION, however: "The trial judge denied the defendant the opportunity *to allocute.*"

allocution; *allocutus.* *Allocution* is inadequately defined by the major dictionaries (usu. some variation on "a formal address"). In modern legal usage, the word refers to a trial judge's asking a criminal defendant to speak in mitigation of the sentence to be imposed. By SLIPSHOD EXTENSION, the word has come to denote the accused person's speech in mitigation of the sentence, rather than the judge's address asking the accused to speak. E.g., "The contention of this federal habeas corpus petitioner that he was not accorded his right of *allocution* in state court fails to raise a federal question." *Allocutus* is a NEEDLESS VARIANT and an unnecessary LATINISM. See **elocution.**

The phrase *victim allocution*—a popular phrase since the 1980s—refers to a crime victim's addressing the court with the objective usu. of persuading the sentencer to impose a harsher sentence. Arguably the result of SLIPSHOD EXTENSION, the phrase is now established in American law.

allocutory is the adjective corresponding to the noun *allocution,* q.v.—e.g.: "[T]he right to make *allocutory* and other legal claims should be made effective by a right to counsel at sentencing." Note, *Procedural Due Process at Judicial Sentencing for Felony,* 81 Harv. L. Rev. 821, 833 (1968)./ "[*A*]*llocutory* pleas for mercy would have been unavailing and were not allowed." *Harris v. State,* 509 A.2d 120, 125 (Md. Ct. App. 1986).

allodial is the proper adjective, *alodian* being an erroneous form.

al(l)odium, -ial. *Black's* and the *OED* list *allodium* (= land held in fee simple absolute) as standard, *alodium* as a variant; *W3*'s listing is the opposite. Both forms may lay claim to etymological precedent. *Allodium* seems to be the more common and, because unanimity is desirable on this point, should be used to the exclusion of its single-elled counterpart. The plural is generally *allodia.*

The adjective form is *allodial*—e.g.: "There remained scattered tracts of '*allodial*' land (literally, land 'without a lord') which were not incorporated into the system of feudal tenure and whose owners did not even in theory become tenants." Peter Butt, *Land Law* 38 (2d ed. 1988).

all of. See **all** (A).

allograph; autograph. An *allograph* is an agent's writing or signature for the principal. An *autograph,* of course, is one's own signature.

allonge (= a piece of paper attached to a note or other negotiable instrument, usu. to make room for further indorsements) derives from the French verb *allonger* (= to lengthen). Anglo-American lawyers borrowed the word from French law in the mid-19th century. Although *Ballentine's Law Dictionary* (3d ed. 1969) suggests that the word is pronounced /*a-lə**nj***/, the better and more common pronunciation is /ə-***lonj***/.

allow. A. Senses. *Allow* = (1) to give or grant (something) as a right or privilege <she allowed her neighbor an easement>; (2) to approve by not objecting <the court allowed appellee's counsel to reply to the rebuttal>; (3) to make provision for <the rules allow depositions upon written questions>; or (4) in BrE, to sustain (a judgment, claim, or appeal) <the appeal should be allowed>.

B. And *permit*. The words *allow* and *permit* have an important connotative difference. *Allow,* as in sense (2), suggests merely the absence of opposition, or refraining from a proscription. In contrast, *permit* suggests affirmative sanction or approval.

allowable, though structurally an adjective, often functions as a noun in legal contexts. As a noun it refers to the amount of oil or gas that an operator is allowed to extract from a well or field in one day, under proration orders of a state regulatory commission. E.g., "A well bottomed in this sand had an *allowable* that would enable it to recover an amount of oil and gas in excess of the tract's fair share of production from both reservoirs." See ADJECTIVES (B).

all ready. See **already.**

all right; alright. *Alright* for *all right* has never been accepted as standard and probably never will be. Although the phrase is considered unitary, the one-word spelling has not been recognized "perhaps because the expression remains largely an informal one" (*Oxford Guide*).

all the; all these. See **all** (A).

all together. See **altogether.**

allude. A. And *advert; refer*. To *allude* is to refer to (something) indirectly or by suggestion only. To *advert* or *refer* is to bring up directly, *advert,* q.v., being the more FORMAL WORD. *Allude* is commonly misused for *refer;* the indirect nature of *allusion* is an important element of the word's sense. E.g., "In a work purporting to discuss the ethical side of practice, a passing *allusion* [read *reference*] to the subject seems eminently proper if not necessary."/ "As the above notice contained an *allusion* to the plaintiff, and also statements that he considered were calculated to damage his character and the credit of his firm, a solicitor was consulted, and a letter was written by him to the defendants, protesting against the plaintiff's name being used as intended in the advertisement." (Eng.) (Here the final phrase reveals that the name was actually mentioned: that the publication contained a *reference,* not an *allusion,* to the plaintiff.) In the following sentence the writer creates an OXYMORON: "There being no words *expressly alluding* [read *referring*] to that contingency, the court is to cure the defect by implication."

B. And *illude; elude.* To *illude* is to deceive with an illusion; to *elude* is to avoid or escape. Here *elude* is misused for *allude,* a startling blunder: "That is the reason for the problem the dean was *eluding to* [read *alluding to*]."

C. For *suggest.* This is an attenuated use of *allude* to be avoided. "Appellants attempt to *allude* [read *suggest*] that their assistance in evading Iranian currency controls and that rebating money to appellee in American money was a major service that takes the contract outside the purview of the U.C.C."

allusion; illusion. The first is an indirect reference <literary allusion>, the second a deception or misapprehension <optical illusion>. For the difference between *illusion* and *delusion,* see **illusion.**

ALLUSION. See LITERARY ALLUSION (A).

allusive; allusury. *Allusive* is standard.

alluvio(n); alluvium. In the strictest sense, *alluvion* means "the flow or wash of water against a riverbank," and *alluvium* "a deposit of soil, clay, or the lack of such a deposit caused by an alluvion." *Alluvion* has come, however, to be used for *alluvium*—a regrettable development, for the DIFFERENTIATION is worth preserving. *Alluvio* is the Roman-law term for *alluvion.*

The plural forms of the English terms are *alluvions* and *alluviums* (or, less good, *alluvia*). See PLURALS (A). The adjective for *alluvium* is *alluvial,* the forms *alluvious* and *alluvian* being NEEDLESS VARIANTS. *Alluvion* has no clear-cut adjective; it should act as its own adjective.

ally. As a noun, the accent is on the first syllable /***al***-ɪ/; as a verb, on the second /ə-***lɪ***/.

almoi(g)n. See **frankalmoi(g)n(e).**

alodian. See **al(l)odium.**

alongside (of). The word *alongside,* as a preposition, means "at the side of." Hence, one car is parked *alongside* another, and logs are stacked *alongside* one another. It is unnecessary to write *alongside of.*

already; all ready. *Already* has to do with time <finished already>, and *all ready* with preparation <we are all ready>.

alright. See **all right.**

also. See **too** (A).

also not is usually inferior to *nor*—e.g.: "*The cases are also not* [read *Nor are the cases*] in accord as to the effect of an accidental killing of another during an attempt to commit suicide." Rollin M. Perkins & Ronald N. Boyce, *Criminal Law* 122 (3d ed. 1982)./ "My motion pictures were *also not* very good." [Read: *Nor were my motion pictures very good.*] Stephen White, *The Written Word* x (1984).

alterative; alterant. Both words may act as noun and adjective. As adjectives, they both mean "causing alteration." As nouns, however, the meanings diverge. An *alterant* is "anything that alters or modifies." *Alterative* is a term used in medical contexts—though rarely now by physicians—meaning "a medicine that gradually changes unhealthy bodily conditions into healthy ones."

altercation. This word refers to "a noisy brawl or dispute," not rising to the seriousness of physical violence. Here the word is almost certainly misused for *fight* in the physical sense: "While serving a term of imprisonment in a North Carolina penitentiary, the respondent Perry became involved in an *altercation* with another inmate; a warrant issued, charging Perry with the misdemeanor of assault with a deadly weapon." Leff ill-advisedly wrote that "coming to . . . blows is not totally excluded from the ambit of this term," and used it for a physical affray in his entry on *aggressor.* Arthur A. Leff, *The Leff Dictionary of Law,* 94 Yale L.J. 1855, 2003, 1981 (1985). For authority limiting the term to the sense "wordy strife," see the *OED, W2, W3,* and Partridge, *Usage and Abusage* 27 (1973).

alter ego (lit., "other I") = a second self. To nonlawyers, it means "a kindred spirit" or "a constant companion." To American lawyers it has a special meaning in the corporate context: "a corporation used by an individual in conducting personal business, such that a court may impose personal liability (by piercing the corporate veil) when fraud has been perpetrated on third persons dealing with the corporation." The phrase should not be hyphenated unless it functions as a PHRASAL ADJECTIVE <alter-ego theory>.

alternate; alternative. **A. As Nouns.** An *alternative* is a choice or option—usually one of two choices, but not necessarily. It has been argued by etymological purists that the word (fr. L. *alter* "the other of two") should be confined to contexts involving but two choices; Fowler termed this contention a fetish, and it has little or no support among other stylistic experts or in actual usage. E.g., "None of the *three alternatives* pretends to show the sequence of transactions."/ "The defendant is directed to provide to the court within fourteen days in affidavit form information concerning *three alternatives.*"

Indeed, *alternative* carries with it two nuances absent from the near-synonym *choice.* First, *alternative* may suggest adequacy for some purpose <ample alternative channels>; and second, it may suggest compulsion to choose <the alternatives are liberty and death>.

Alternate, n., means: (1) "something that proceeds by turns with another"; and (2) "one who substitutes for another." It is helpful to understand that *alternative* is called upon for use far more frequently than *alternate.*

B. As Adjectives. *Alternative* = mutually exclusive; available in place of another (*COD*). E.g., "Nevertheless, if he has failed to show an unlawful conspiracy and monopoly, he has under his *alternative* demand shown a cause of action to recover damages from either or both of the defendants."

Alternate = (1) coming each after one of the other kind, every second one; or (2) substitute. This sentence illustrates sense (1) of *alternate:* "The examination may be made either by one person reading both the original and the copy, or by two persons, one reading the original and the other the copy, and it is not necessary (except in peerage cases) that each should *alternately* read both." (Eng.) Here sense (2) of *alternate* applies: "Statutes providing for *alternate* jurors to sit on a case so that they can substitute for jurors ceasing to sit on the case sometimes provide for additional peremptory challenges with respect to such jurors."/ "Thereafter, the testator decided he did not wish to nominate this *alternate* executor."

In the following sentences, *alternate* is misused for *alternative*—a common mistake, perhaps understandable because of the close sense (2) of *alternate:* "Nor does it appear likely that further conversations would have convinced counsel to pursue *alternate* [read *alternative*] defenses [i.e., defenses available in place of the primary defense pleaded]."/ "Appellant based his claim on *alternate* [read *alternative*] theories."/ "The court permitted a damage action there despite the existence of the *alternate* [read *alternative*] remedy."

The notion that an *alternative* is one of two choices is strongly enough rooted that *two alternatives* usually seems redundant: "Where a trust instrument contains *two alternative conditions* [read *contains alternative conditions*], of which the first might be too remote and the second, which actually occurs, is not too remote, the rule is not violated." In any event, because *alternative* suggests mutual exclusivity when referring to two objects, *either* is redundant when used in proximity: "A search of the record in this case establishes a likely absence of complete diversity between the parties *on either of two alternative theories* [read *on either of two theories* or *on alternative theories*]."

alternative dispute resolution; alternate dispute resolution. The proper form is *alternative dispute resolution.* The phrase is commonly abbreviated *ADR.* See **alternate (B).**

although; though. As conjunctions, the words are virtually interchangeable. The only distinction is that *although* is more formal and dignified, *though* more usual in speech and familiar writing. In certain formal contexts, however, *though* reads better. *Though* serves also as an adverb <He stated as much, though>.

Tho and *altho* are old-fashioned truncated spellings that were at one time very common but failed to become standard. They should be avoided.

although . . . yet was formerly a common construction; these two words were once considered CORRELATIVE CONJUNCTIONS. Today the construction is seen only in the most formal contexts: "*Although* the relation of parent and child subsists, *yet* if the child is incapable of performing any services, the foundation of the action fails." (Eng.) In most modern contexts, either conjunction will suffice to give the same meaning as if both were used.

altogether; all together. *Altogether* = completely; wholly. "Such appeals are *altogether* frivolous." *All together* = at one place or at the same time. "The defendants were tried all together."

alumnus. **A. Sense.** This term is obsolete as a LEGALISM for *foster-child;* today it means only "a male former student (of a particular school, esp. an institution of higher learning)." Strictly speaking, one need not be a graduate to be an *alumnus.* One who abandons a course of study is still an *alumnus.*

B. The Plural Forms *alumni* and *alumnae*. The first, strictly speaking, refers to former students who are male; the singular form is *alumnus.* The second refers to former students who are female; the singular is *alumna.* Nowadays, however, *alumni* refers to males and females alike. The same is not true, however, of *alumnae,* which can refer only to women. "Throughout its history, the Securities and Exchange Commission has attracted lawyers of the highest quality; among its *alumnae* [read *alumni*], for example, are Mr. Justice William Douglas, Judge Gerhard Gesell, Professor Louis Loss, and Professor Homer Kripke." This statement might come as a surprise to the persons mentioned.

A more common mistake than confusing the gender of these words is confusing their NUMBER, as by using *alumni* or *alumnae* as a singular. That these are plural forms of *alumnus* and *alumna* should be apparent to anyone with even the faintest familiarity with Latin.

C. And *alumnor*. An *alumnor* is one employed to work with or at an ex-students' association. The word is a MORPHOLOGICAL DEFORMITY, because the *-or* suffix should generally be appended to a verb, and *alumn* is no verb.

a.m., A.M.; p.m., P.M. It does not matter whether capitals or lowercase letters are used, as long as a document is consistent throughout. The lowercase letters are now more common. The phrases for which these abbreviations stand are *ante meridiem* and *post meridiem,* not *meridian.* Periods are preferred in these abbreviations.

amalgam; amalgamation. Some DIFFERENTIATION is possible. *Amalgam,* the older term, means "a combination" <a perfect amalgam of virtuosity and elegance>. *Amalgamation* means primarily "the act of combining or uniting; consolidation" <effecting an amalgamation of the companies>. *Amalgamation* is best avoided in the sense given to *amalgam.*

amatory. See **amorous.**

ambassador; embassador. The former is the preferred spelling. See **embassy.**

ambiance. See **ambience.**

ambidexter = a solicitor who, retained by one party to litigation, abandons that party for the adversary. E.g., "He is a d——d rascal, and an immoral and base man, and unless ignorance of the law makes a lawyer he is no lawyer—he is an *ambidexter* and a disgrace to his profession." *Goodenow v. Tappan,* 1 Ohio 60, 61 (1823) (quoting a declaration). See LAWYERS, DEROGATORY NAMES FOR (A).

ambience; ambiance. The first form, the English form, is preferable. The latter is a Frenchified affectation that has become a VOGUE WORD. See **ambit.**

AMBIGUITY, despite what many lawyers seem to believe, inheres in all writing. Even the most tediously detailed documents that attempt to dispel all uncertainties contain ambiguities; indeed, usually the more voluminous the writing, the more voluminous the ambiguities. (See MYTH OF PRECISION.) Nevertheless, we must strive to rid our writing of ambiguities that might give rise to misreadings. DRAFTING especially is a constant battle against ambiguity—a battle that no one can entirely win: "Ambiguity is inherent in any language more complex than grunts, and even a grunt can be ambiguous." Philip Howard, *At the Double, and Be Rather Sharp About It,* The Times, 8 Feb. 1991, at 92.

The war against ambiguity should not be waged by overwriting and attempts at hyperprecision through exhaustive specificity. Rather, the legal writer should work on developing a concise, lean, and straightforward writing style, along with a sensitivity to words and their meanings. Once a writer has acquired such a style, ambiguities tend to become more noticeable, and therefore easier to correct. (See PLAIN LANGUAGE (D).) At the same time, an increased linguistic sensitivity allows one to see ambiguities in what might previously have seemed a model of clarity.

What exactly *is* an ambiguity? William Empson, the greatest expounder of ambiguity, has defined it as "any verbal nuance, however slight, which gives room for alternative reactions to the same piece of language." William Empson, *Seven Types of Ambiguity* 19 (1930; Penguin ed. 1977). Courts tend to define ambiguity more narrowly: "An 'ambiguous' word or phrase is one capable of more than one meaning when viewed objectively by a reasonably intelligent person who has examined the context of the entire integrated agreement and who is cognizant of the customs, practices, usages and terminology as generally understood in the particular trade or business." *Walk-In Medical Ctrs., Inc. v. Breuer Capital Corp.,* 818 F.2d 260, 263 (2d Cir. 1987).

Ambiguity should be distinguished from *vagueness:*

> It is unfortunate that many lawyers persist in using the word *ambiguity* to include vagueness. To subsume both concepts under the same name tends to imply that there is no difference between them or that their differences are legally unimportant. Ambiguity is a disease

> of language, whereas vagueness, which is sometimes a disease, is often a positive benefit. . . . Whereas *ambiguity* in its classical sense refers to equivocation, *vagueness* refers to the degree to which, independently of equivocation, language is uncertain in its respective applications to a number of particulars. Whereas the uncertainty of ambiguity is central, with an 'either-or' challenge, the uncertainty of vagueness lies in marginal questions of degree.
>
> Reed Dickerson, *The Interpretation of Statutes* 48–49 (1975).

Of course, even highly reputed legal writers confuse the two terms—e.g.: "[A] written constitution must be enormously *ambiguous* [read *vague*] in its general provisions." Edward H. Levi, *An Introduction to Legal Reasoning* 59 (1949; repr. 1972)./ "A wise draftsman, when he is dealing with novel issues in course of uncertain development, will deliberately retreat into *ambiguity* [read *vagueness*—there being no such thing as "purposeful ambiguity"]." Grant Gilmore, *The Death of Contracts* 76 (1974).

Dickerson, of course, discusses ambiguity from the vantage of the legal drafter rather than that of the poet; for the latter, ambiguity is hardly "a disease of language." As Empson has so well demonstrated, in literature it is often "a positive benefit."

Following are some examples of the more common types of ambiguity in legal writing. Some of these are equivocal only in a technical (or stickler's) sense (i.e., are patent ambiguities); others create real dilemmas in meaning (i.e., are latent ambiguities); either way, these ambiguities detract from the context in which they appear.

A. Uncertain Stress. "Even if a merchant sells a product, if he was not engaged in selling that particular product in the normal course of business, he may not be held liable." Read the sentence once stressing *may,* the next time stressing *not* in the final clause. Rewording the sentence eliminates the ambiguity. Assuming the writer meant to say that the merchant is immune from liability (and not that he *might* or *may* be immune), he might better have written: *he cannot be held liable* (see **can**) or *he is not subject to liability.* See **may.**

B. Syntax. The ordering of sentence-parts is basic to clarity. When phrases are arranged with little reflection, ambiguities are certain to arise.

1. Verbal Correspondence

- "The parties shall make every reasonable effort to agree on and have prepared as quickly as possible a contract . . . ." Should the sentence read "to have prepared"? Does *have* correspond syntactically to *shall,* to *make,* or to *agree?* The three possible meanings vary substantially.
- "The artificial entity may sue or be sued as though it were a person, it pays taxes, it may apply for business licenses in its own name, it may have its own bank account, it may have its own seal, and so forth." All the *its* in this sentence have the antecedent *entity.* Yet, because of the placement of the first *it,* one is led to believe that the later ones will have a parallel structure ("as though it were a person, as though it pays taxes, as though it may apply . . ."). Thus the reader is syntactically sidetracked for a moment.

2. Poorly Placed Modifiers

- "No well shall be drilled within 200 feet of any residence or barn now on said land *without lessor's consent.*" No well may be drilled without the lessor's consent? (This, obviously, is the intended meaning.) Or is it that the barn must be on the land without the lessor's consent?
- "The court concluded that literacy tests had abridged the right to vote *on account of race or color.*" The right to vote on account of race or color was abridged? No: the right to vote was abridged on account of race or color.
- "Fear that a jury will wrongly convict an innocent man of rape because it believes a woman who is ambivalent or deceitful after the fact *historically* has pervaded the law of rape." Leslie J. Harris, Book Review, 66 Tex. L. Rev. 905, 905 (1988). Ambivalent or deceitful historically? No: *historically* is a squinting modifier that should be placed in the midst of the verb phrase: *has historically pervaded.* See ADVERBS, PROBLEMS WITH (A).
- "As such, the court would be correct in ordering a partial distribution of the amounts of the fund *that has been sought in the motion.*" Does the relative pronoun *that* refer to *fund, amounts,* or *distribution?* Seemingly the last of these, because the verb (*has*) is singular—and *fund* is not logically the right word. *Amounts* is the right word logically, but it does not fit with *has.*
- "This chilling tale, told in a 13-page report released today by Edward F. Stancik, the Special Commissioner of schools, raised serious questions about the detection and reporting of child abuse *by school officials.*" Josh Barbanel, *Girl Writes About Rape by Father but School Ignores Plight,* N.Y. Times, 5 Feb. 1993, at B1. Readers may infer that the story is about *child abuse by school officials*; in fact, however, it is about *detection and reporting by school officials.*
- "Israeli police officers pulled tires away from a burning fire lit in response to the slayings *by Jewish protesters* Tuesday." *2 Israeli Police Gunned Down,* Daily Texan, 31 Mar. 1993, at 3 (adding that "[p]olice blamed militant Arabs for the pre-dawn slayings"). Is it *slayings by Jewish*

protesters or *fires lit by Jewish protesters?* Though the latter interpretation seems more far-fetched, that is what the writer intended.

NOUN PLAGUE exemplifies one type of poorly placed modifiers. For example, *alimentary canal smuggling* was intended by the U.S. Supreme Court to mean "smuggling contraband goods by concealing them temporarily in one's gut." But the phrase suggests "the smuggling of alimentary canals." E.g., "A divided panel . . . reversed [defendant's] convictions, holding that her detention violated the Fourth Amendment . . . because the customs inspectors did not have a 'clear indication' of *alimentary canal smuggling* at the time she was detained." *U.S. v. Montoya de Hernandez,* 473 U.S. 531, 533 (1985).

C. Poor Word Choice. "No one has ever told them how to edit syntactic confusion into clear prose." Joseph Williams, *Style: Ten Lessons in Clarity and Grace* 4–5 (1981). To get at the author's true sense, read *transform* for *edit.* Otherwise, *edit . . . into* can read as if it were *insert . . . into.*

These problems are remedied easily enough by thoughtful attention to one's prose, and by editing and revising with the realization that legal writers harm only themselves when they burden readers with these dilemmas in meaning. Drafters who commit these sins do their clients a disservice, unless, of course, the clients enjoy litigation for the sake of litigation. Cf. MISCUES.

ambit; ambience. The former means "scope," the latter "the immediate environment; atmosphere." Here the former is correctly used: "Yet this very narrow *ambit* of judicial review does not release us from our responsibility to scrutinize the record in its entirety to determine whether substantial evidence does support the Secretary's findings." See **ambience.**

ambulance chaser = (1) a lawyer who approaches victims of street accidents in hopes of persuading them to sue for damages; (2) a lawyer's agent who engages in this activity; (3) *by extension,* one who solicits personal-injury cases for a lawyer, usu. in return for a percentage of the recovery (today an illegal activity in most jurisdictions); or (4) *by further extension,* one who seeks to profit from the misfortunes of others <that politician is nothing more than a foreign-policy ambulance-chaser>.

The first so-called *ambulance chaser*—and the reputed coiner of the term—was Abraham Gatner, who in 1907 persuaded a New York law firm to let him sign up accident victims on retainer agreements for the law firm. Actually, though, the term was a misnomer from the beginning because Gatner would not reach the injured person until hours later—and often the next day. See Murray T. Bloom, *The Trouble with Lawyers* 118–19 (1970). See LAWYERS, DEROGATORY NAMES FOR (A).

ambulatory (lit., "able to walk") has a special sense in the law of wills: "taking effect not from when [the will] was made but from the death of the testator" (*CDL*), or "capable of being revised." A will is *ambulatory* because it is revocable until the testator's death. E.g., "The holding of the chancery court was based on the proposition that a will is *ambulatory,* speaks only at the death of the maker, and the 1955 will having been destroyed in the lifetime of the testatrix, it never had the effect of revoking the 1954 will."

ameliorate; meliorate. *Ameliorate* is the standard term meaning "to make or become better." E.g., "These anomalies appear sufficiently enmeshed in the current tangled web of jurisprudence on this subject to be beyond *amelioration* by a panel of this court."/ "Society's view of land as a commercial asset plays an important part in the law of *ameliorative* waste." *Meliorate* is a NEEDLESS VARIANT.

It is incorrect to use *ameliorate* as if it meant "to lessen": "The First, Second, and Eleventh Circuits found that any resort to Iranian courts to recover the movants' monetary losses, should the preliminary injunction be denied, would be futile and that the Iran–United States Claims Tribunal did not *ameliorate* [read *lessen*] the likelihood of irreparable injury."

ameliorating waste. See **waste.**

amenability; amenity. These words, of unrelated origin, are occasionally confused. *Amenability* = legal answerability; liability to being brought to judgment <amenability to the jurisdiction of the foreign forum>.

Amenity = (1) agreeableness; (2) something that is comfortable or convenient; or (3) a convenient social convention. Here the word is almost certainly misused: "Fiat moved to dismiss the action against it for lack of personal jurisdiction, arguing that it was . . . *not susceptible to the amenities of a Massachusetts forum* [read *not amenable to the Massachusetts forum*]."

amenable takes the preposition *to* <amenable to process>.

amend; emend. Both derive from the Latin verb *emendare* (= to free from fault). *Amend* = (1) to put right, change; or (2) to add to, supplement. This is the general word; the other is more specialized. *Emend* = to correct (as a text).

Amend out has been used to mean "to excise." E.g., "This provision, essentially the same as that in the Senate bill, was *amended out* on the House floor." *Taken out, cut out,* or *excised* would have been more felicitous. See PARTICLES, UNNECESSARY & **out (A).**

The nominal forms of *amend* and *emend* are *amendment* and *emendation.*

amendatory; amendable. *Amendatory* = effecting an amendment; *amendable* = capable of being amended.

amended pleading. See **supplemental pleading.**

amendment = (1) a legislative change in a statute or constitution, usu. by adding provisions not in the original; or (2) the correction of an error or the supplying of an omission in process or pleadings. This noun may take either *to* or *of,* usually the former—e.g.: "The continuing episodes of protest and dissent in the United States have their basis in the First *Amendment to* the Constitution, a great safety valve that is lacking in most other nations of the world." William O. Douglas, *Points of Rebellion* 3 (1970).

amenity. See **amenability.**

a mensa et thoro (lit., "from board and bed") is a standard phrase in canon law denoting a decree of divorce—now generally outmoded because it does not permit remarriage—that was the forerunner of modern judicial separation. (Such a divorce is distinct from the later divorce *a vinculo matrimonii,* which does allow remarriage.) The LATINISM seems little justified today. "This was only a divorce *a mensa et thoro,* equivalent to the modern judicial separation and infrequent at that." (Eng.)/ "In *Barber v. Barber,* the Supreme Court held that a wife could sue in federal court in Wisconsin on the basis of diversity of citizenship to enforce a New York state court decree granting her a divorce *a mensa et thoro.*" The phrase *divorce from board and bed* is sometimes used instead. See **divorce.**

amerce = (1) to fine; (2) to punish; or (3) to hold liable. Today, it is little more than a pretentious LEGALISM—e.g.: "To treat that clause as though it were a redundant or an insubstantial part of the agreement is to flout familiar experience of the readiness of juries to *amerce insurance companies* [read *hold insurance companies liable*]." *Watson v. Employers Liab. Assurance Corp.,* 348 U.S. 66, 75–76 (1954)./ "When we provided . . . that costs were to be awarded to defendants and intervenors, we did not intend to *amerce the plaintiffs with* [read *hold the plaintiffs liable for*] all of the costs of the litigation since its inception." *Environmental Defense Fund, Inc. v. Froehlke,* 368 F. Supp. 231, 254 (W.D. Mo. 1973). See **affeer.**

amercement; amerciament; merciament. *Amercement* [fr. F. *estre à merci* "to be at [one's] mercy"] = (1) the imposition of a fine; or (2) the fine so imposed. Usually *fining* (sense 1) or *fine* (sense 2) suffices in place of this little-known word. Sometimes, though, an appropriate edit is not at all apparent—e.g.: "It appears that an *amercement* proceeding may properly be initiated by motion in the principal action." *Vitale v. Hotel California, Inc.,* 446 A.2d 880, 882 n.1 (N.J. Super. Ct. 1982).

Amerciament and *merciament* are archaic variants. See **affeer.**

AMERICANISMS AND BRITISHISMS. Throughout this book Americanisms are labeled "AmE" and Britishisms are labeled "BrE." For guidance on distinctions not covered here, see Norman W. Schur, *English English* (1980); Norman Moss, *British/American Language Dictionary* (1984); and Martin S. Allwood, *American and British* (1964). For differences in editorial style, compare *The Chicago Manual of Style* (14th ed. 1993) with Judith Butcher, *Copy-Editing: The Cambridge Handbook* (2d ed. 1981).

amicable; amiable. The former we borrowed from Latin, the latter from French; but the two forms are at base the same word. Useful DIFFERENTIATION has emerged to set these words apart, however. *Amiable* applies to persons <an amiable judge>, *amicable* to relations between persons <an amicable settlement>.

amicable action. See **friendly suit.**

amicus brief. One *amicus brief,* two *amicus briefs*—not *amici briefs.* E.g., "An aberration of the norm occurred in *Chadha:* both petitioner Chadha and the respondent Justice Department were allowed to reply to the *amici briefs* [read *amicus briefs*]." Barbara H. Craig, *Chadha: The Story of an Epic Constitutional Struggle* 104 (1988). See **amicus curiae.**

amicus curiae; friend of the court. The Latin phrase is well established, and is not likely to be replaced in legal writing by its LOAN TRANSLA-

TION, *friend of the court.* At times lawyers have forgotten the role of the *amicus curiae*—"one who, not as [a party], but, just as any stranger might, for the assistance of the court gives information of some matter of law in regard to which the court is doubtful or mistaken, rather than one who gives a highly partisan account of facts." *New England Patriots Football Club, Inc. v. University of Colorado,* 592 F.2d 1196, 1198 n.3 (1st Cir. 1979) (ellipses omitted).

Amicus-curiae practice is less restricted in the U.S. than in England, where "it is customary to invite the Attorney General to attend, either in person or by counsel instructed on his behalf, to represent the public interest, [although] counsel have been permitted to act as *amicus curiae* [read *amici curiae?*] on behalf of professional bodies (e.g., the Law Society)" (*CDL*). In the U.S., virtually anyone with interests affected by the litigation, or indeed with political interest in it, may, when represented by counsel, be approved as an *amicus curiae.*

Amicus is frequently used as an elliptical form of *amicus curiae.* E.g., "This *amicus* believes in an absolute prohibition of the practice."/ "The court also rejected the state's contention that since the United States is only an *amicus,* it cannot ask for affirmative relief." *Amicus* also serves as an elliptical adjective: "Texas also failed to seek intervention or file an *amicus* brief in a Second Circuit case directly reviewing the contract rates."

Amicus is sometimes even used as an ellipsis for *amicus brief:* "In its *amicus,* El Salvador explains its interest in securing the ultimate relocation of the pilot station of what it views as its national carrier." *Airline Pilots Ass'n Int'l, AFL-CIO v. TACA Int'l Airlines, S.A.,* 748 F.2d 965, 971 (5th Cir. 1984). This ellipsis is perhaps too elliptical, because *amicus* does not readily suggest itself as a shortened form of *amicus curiae brief* or *amicus brief,* either of which should have appeared in the quoted sentence. See **amicus brief.**

Although the modern trend is to place the phrase before the noun it modifies, *amicus curiae* is often used as a POSTPOSITIVE ADJECTIVE—e.g.: "The conclusion of the Administrator, as expressed in the brief *amicus curiae,* is that the general tests point to the exclusion of sleeping and eating time of these employees from the workweek and the inclusion of all other on-call time."/ "When he represents no new questions, a third party can contribute usually most effectively and always most expeditiously by a brief *amicus curiae* and not by intervention." See POSTPOSITIVE ADJECTIVES.

Friend of the court, as an equivalent of *amicus curiae,* is primarily journalistic; it appears in many newspapers and journals with a general appeal. E.g., "In a *friend-of-the-court* brief, the home builders say that permitting lawsuits for damages would show that the Supreme Court recognized 'limits on local regulatory powers that destroy private property rights.'" Wall St. J., 9 Jan. 1985, § 2, at 25. Even this translated phrase, however, must baffle the lay reader not familiar with court practice. The translation is therefore of limited value. See LOAN TRANSLATIONS.

The plural of *amicus curiae* is *amici curiae.* Frequently the singular is wrongly used for the plural: "The practice is particularly used in the U.S. Supreme Court, where organizations deeply interested in an area of constitutional law . . . will frequently petition for and be granted permission to participate as *amicus curiae* [read *amici curiae*]." Arthur A. Leff, *The Leff Dictionary of Law,* 94 Yale L.J. 1855, 2012 (1985)./ "The utilities may seek to present their views as *amicus curiae* [read *amici curiae*], and leave to do so is here granted."/ "Counsel for respondents, as *amicus curiae* [read *amici curiae*], assert that conclusion as their principal argument before this court."

The singular is pronounced /*ə-**mee**-kəs-**kyoor**-ee-ɪ*/ and the plural /*ə-**mee**-kee-**kyoor**-ee-ɪ*/ or /*ə-**mee**-see*/. Another acceptable pronunciation of the first word—a common pronunciation in AmE—is /***am**-ə-kəs*/.

amid(st); in the midst of; mid; 'mid. *Amid* and *amidst* are somewhat learned, to the degree that they have been branded bookish or quaint. The charge may be unjust, for *amid(st)* has its uses (see **among** (B)). AmE prefers *amid,* and BrE *amidst*; in AmE, *amidst* is considered a literary word. *In the midst of* is an informal and wordy equivalent. The preposition *mid* is poetic in all but traditional phrases (e.g., *midnight, midstream*) or scientific uses; if the word is appropriate, however, *mid* is better than *'mid.*

amok; amuck. Usage authorities once held firmly to the idea that *amuck* is preferable to *amok*—solely on the mistaken notion that *amuck* is older in English and *amok* (though a better transliteration of the Malaysian word) was a latecoming "didacticism." In fact, both forms date from the 17th century. And, in any event, *amok* is by far the more common spelling today—e.g.: "[T]here are important exceptions—exceptions that ought sufficiently to demonstrate the possibility that the linguistic sense of a profession can run *amok.*" Lon L. Fuller, *Legal Fictions* 22 (1967)./ "RICO is a statute run *amok* and no one is beyond its reach." Rick Boucher, *Trying to Fix a Statute Run Amok,* N.Y. Times, 12 March 1989, at 2F.

among. A. And *amongst*. Forms in *-st,* such as *whilst* and *amidst,* are generally ARCHAISMS. *Amongst* is no exception: in AmE it is pretentious at best. E.g., "Schools that have offered special composition courses for pre-law students (Illinois, Utah, Wayne State, Loyola of Chicago, *amongst* [read *among*] several others) have generally found them well received and oversubscribed." George D. Gopen, *The State of Legal Writing,* 86 Mich. L. Rev. 333, 355 (1987).

Amongst seems more common and more tolerable in BrE, where it carries no hint of affectation: "The first count of the declaration stated that plaintiff had contracted to perform in the theatre for a certain time, with a condition, *amongst* others, that she would not sing or use her talents elsewhere during the term without plaintiff's consent in writing." (Eng.)

Elmer A. Driedger wrote: "To divide *amongst* seems to be a little clearer than to divide *among;* in all other cases *among* is probably to be preferred." *The Composition of Legislation* 78 (1957). His first statement is unfounded: *divide amongst* provides no gain in clarity, and no difference in connotation or denotation.

B. With Mass Nouns. *Among* is used with count nouns and *amid* with mass nouns. Thus one is *among* people but *amid* a furor. (See COUNT NOUNS AND MASS NOUNS & **amid(st).**) In the following sentences, *among* is misused for other prepositions:

- "The DEA agents discovered large quantities of marijuana *among the shipment* [read *amid the shipment*]."
- "Incompetence in writing English is widespread *among* [read *in*] the legal profession." Robert W. Benson, *The End of Legalese,* 13 N.Y.U. Rev. L. & Soc. Change 519, 570 (1984–1985).
- "*Among* [read *With*] the president's contingent are Mr Robert Mosbacher, commerce secretary, and around 20 top US executives." Stefan Wagstyl, *Japan Promises to Boost US Imports,* Fin. Times, 8 Jan. 1992, at 1.
- "*Among the evidence* [read *A part of the evidence*] cited in support of the theory is Brawner's denial of any concrete knowledge of plaintiff's intentions."

C. And ***between*.** See **between (A).**

amoral. See **immoral.**

amorous; amatory; amative. *Amorous* = (1) strongly moved by love and sex; (2) enamored; or (3) indicative of love. *Amative* is a NEEDLESS VARIANT. *Amatory* = of, relating to, or expressing sexual love (*W10*).

amortise. See **amortize.**

amortization; amortizement. The first is the regular and preferred form.

amortize; amortise. The *-ize* form is preferred in both AmE and BrE.

amortizement. See **amortization.**

amount; number. The former is used of mass nouns, the latter of count nouns. Thus we say "an increase in the *amount* of litigation" but "an increase in the *number* of lawsuits." See COUNT NOUNS AND MASS NOUNS.

amount of, an. See SYNESIS.

amphibious, adj., is frequently used in reference to mariners who work both ashore and on ship. E.g., "Our past decisions have enunciated several factors to be evaluated in determining whether an *amphibious* employee becomes the 'borrowed' employee of other than his payroll employer."/ "The cases all involve the delicate question whether the federal interest in an *amphibious* worker's personal injury claims is sufficiently strong to justify federal courts' supplanting state law with federal common law of admiralty." This extended sense of *amphibious* probably had its origin in the phrase of World War II vintage, *amphibious forces.*

amphibology; amphiboly. The form *amphibology* (= quibble; ambiguous wording) predominates. E.g., "The term 'and/or' as ordinarily used is a deliberate *amphibology.*" The other form is a NEEDLESS VARIANT.

The corresponding adjective is *amphibological.*

amuck. See **amok.**

amuse. See **bemuse.**

an. See **a.**

anachronism; parachronism; prochronism; archaism. All these words indicate that, in some respect, the time is out of joint. An *anachronism* is any error in chronology, or something that is chronologically out of place. "We rejected the longstanding but *anachronistic* rule of *Lincoln.*"/ "Professor Wigmore termed the privilege against adverse spousal testimony 'the merest *anachronism* in legal theory and an indefensible obstruction to truth in practice.'" *Parachronism* is a NEEDLESS VARIANT of *anachronism.*

A *prochronism* is a reference to an event at an earlier date than the true date. An *archaism* is something archaic, outmoded, or old-fashioned. E.g., "Death statutes have their roots in dissatisfaction with the *archaisms* of the law that have been traced to their origin in the course of this opinion." See ARCHAISMS.

anachronistic; anachronous; anachronic. The last two are NEEDLESS VARIANTS.

anaconda clause. See **Mother Hubbard clause.**

analects; analecta. In both AmE and BrE, the English plural (*analects*) is preferred to the Greek (*analecta*).

analog. See **analogy.**

analogism. See **analogy.**

analogous; analogical. These words mean different things. *Analogous /ə-**nal**-ə-gəs/* = similar in certain respects. The word should be avoided where *similar* suffices; the two are not perfectly synonymous.

*Analogical /an-ə-**loj**-i-kəl/* = of, by, or expressing an analogy. E.g., "In Anglo-American law we do not think of *analogical* development of the traditional materials of the legal system as interpretation." Roscoe Pound, *An Introduction to the Philosophy of Law* 51 (1922; repr. 1975).

analogy; analog(ue); analogism. An *analogy* is a corresponding similarity or likeness; in logic, *analogy* means "an inference that, if two or more things are similar in some respects, they must be alike in others."

An *analogue* is a thing that is analogous to something else. E.g., "The *Esso* decision suggests that *analogues* to such traditional equity doctrines as laches, election of remedies, and estoppel may justify a finding of peculiar circumstances." (The spelling *analog* should be confined to technical contexts involving physics or computers.)

Analogism is a term meaning "reasoning by analogy."

analyse. See **analyze.**

analysis. See **analyzation** & **in the final analysis.**

analyst; analyzer; analyzist. The last two are NEEDLESS VARIANTS.

analytic(al). No DIFFERENTIATION has surfaced between the two forms. The shorter generally serves better, although occasionally the longer form may be more euphonious, as where another *-al* adjective is proximate: "In most cases, the court treats the validity of a particular allegedly charitable trust as a legal issue to be decided largely by *analytical* and historical methods."/ "But the use of civilian treatises by English and American *analytical* and historical jurists had led to attempts to force common-law institutions and doctrines into civilian molds which retarded their effective development" (Roscoe Pound).

analytical jurisprudence = a method of legal study that examines law purely in its existing structure (without resort to its history), classifies its terms and concepts, and denies the law any validity unless it derives from or is sanctioned by a determinate sovereign. E.g., "Austin, the father of English *analytical jurisprudence,* viewed all law as essentially a command of the sovereign power." H.G. Hanbury, *English Courts of Law* 15 (2d ed. 1953).

An adherent to this view of the law is typically referred to as an *analytical jurist*—e.g.: "Early in this century English and American *analytical jurists* produced a good deal of scholarship that resembles the work of legal science in a number of ways, and a revival of analytical jurisprudence is now going on in the common law world." John H. Merryman, *The Civil Law Tradition* 85 (1969). See **jurist.** Cf. **sociological jurisprudence.**

analyzation, a pseudo-learned variant of *analysis,* has no place in the language—e.g.: "Defense counsel was then provided with ample opportunity to cross-examine to expose any weaknesses in Wagenhofer's credentials or process of *analyzation* [read *analysis*]." *U.S. v. Bartley,* 855 F.2d 547, 552 (8th Cir. 1988).

analyze; analyse. The former is AmE, the latter BrE. *Analyse* does not merit a bracketed *sic* when quoted in an American publication, as here: "The dust jacket tells us: 'In this book, the author brings to bear empirical evidence and legal theory in a critical comparison of English and American discovery, and *analyses* [*sic*] and evaluates the differences between the two systems." Book Review, 61 Tex. L. Rev. 929, 929 (1983). See ***sic*** **(A).**

analyzer; analyzist. See **analyst.**

ananym. See **anonym.**

anarchy, -ic(al), -ial; anarchism, -ist(ic). *Anarchism* is a political theory antithetical to any form of government; *anarchy* is a state or quality of society. Only *anarchy* (= lawlessness, disorder) has pejorative connotations. Here *anarchism* is misused for *anarchy:* "Unless we find a better way of working together, sheer *anarchism* [read *anarchy*] will result." The preferred adjectival forms are *anarchic* and *anarchist.*

ancestor. Only in legal writing does the term *ancestors* include parents as well as grandparents and others more remote. Nonlawyers do not generally think of their fathers and mothers as *ancestors.* See **ascendant (B).**

ancillarity = the quality of being ancillary or of maintaining ancillary jurisdiction (in the U.S., jurisdiction assumed by the federal courts for purposes of convenience to the parties, although the reach of the jurisdiction exercised extends beyond the constitutional or congressional grant). *Ancillarity* is not recorded in any dictionary, but is gaining ground as a legal term—e.g.:

- "Hence it seems quite clear that as concerns venue there are what may be termed 'degrees of *ancillarity.*'" *Lesnik v. Public Indus. Corp.,* 144 F.2d 968, 976 (2d Cir. 1944).
- "Many early decisions seem to go beyond this limited concept of *ancillarity.*" *Chicago & North W. Transp. Co. v. Atchison, Topeka & Santa Fe Ry.,* 367 F. Supp. 801, 805 n.1 (N.D. Ill. 1973).
- "[T]here may be three possible bases for the exercise of federal subject-matter jurisdiction over these third-party claims: admiralty, diversity, or *ancillarity.*" *Joiner v. Diamond M Drilling Co.,* 677 F.2d 1035, 1038 (5th Cir. 1982).
- "The concept of *ancillarity* may explain decisions which hold that actions to enforce an alimony or custody decree are outside the diversity jurisdiction if the decree remains subject to modification by the court that entered it." *Lloyd v. Loeffler,* 694 F.2d 489, 492 (7th Cir. 1982).

and. A. Beginning Sentences. It is rank superstition that this coordinating conjunction cannot properly begin a sentence. And for that matter, the same superstition has plagued *but,* q.v. But this transitional artifice, though quite acceptable, should be sparingly used; otherwise the prose acquires an undesirable staccato effect.

The very best legal writers find occasion to begin sentences with *and*—e.g.:

- "There are certain emergencies of nations in which expedients that in the ordinary state of things ought to be forborne become essential to the public weal. *And* the government, from the possibility of such emergencies, ought ever to have the option of making use of them." *The Federalist* No. 36, at 223 (Alexander Hamilton) (Clinton Rossiter ed., 1961).
- "This period gave rise to what came to be called the law merchant, and saw the hesitant but unmistakable beginnings of the law of intellectual and industrial property. *And* it is to these times that we may trace in recognizable form the patterns of modern shipping and its associated law." Grant Gilmore & Charles L. Black, Jr., *The Law of Admiralty* 5 (2d ed. 1975).
- "Acts of Parliament after all are very real laws, as lawyers would unhesitatingly agree. *And* Acts of Parliament have a very tangible 'existence.'" P.S. Atiyah, *Law and Modern Society* 1–2 (1983).
- "Despite errors and failings, Blackstone did manage to put in brief order the rank weeds of English law. But even his picture was partial and defective, like a dictionary that omitted all slang, all dialect, all colloquial and technical words. *And* even this imperfect guide was not available to colonials before the 1750s." Lawrence M. Friedman, *A History of American Law* 21 (2d ed. 1985).
- "The judges allowed shifting uses; that is, where a fee was to pass from one person to another upon a contingency. And they allowed springing uses . . . ." J.H. Baker, *An Introduction to English Legal History* 326 (3d ed. 1990).

See SUPERSTITIONS (D).

B. For *or*. Oddly, *and* is frequently misused for *or* where a singular noun, or one of two nouns, is called for. E.g., "Prisoners' cases are usually heard before federal magistrates *and* district judges." This construction wrongly implies that magistrates and district judges go together—that is, that they hear such cases at the same time. The true sense of the sentence is "magistrates *or* district judges."

Sloppy drafting sometimes leads courts to recognize that *and* in a given context means *or,* much to the chagrin of some judges—e.g.: "We give our language, and our language-dependent legal system, a body blow when we hold that it is reasonable to read *'or'* for *'and.'*" *MacDonald v. Pan Am. World Airways, Inc.,* 859 F.2d 742, 746 (9th Cir. 1988) (Kozinski, J., dissenting).

For the opposite mistake—*or* for *and*—see the third bulleted quotation under **ancillarity.** For a fuller discussion of the ambiguities caused by these words, see **or (A).**

C. In Enumerations. Legal writers have a tendency, especially in long enumerations, to omit *and* before the final element. To do so in legal writing is often infelicitous: the reader is jarred by the abrupt period ending the sentence and may even wonder whether a part of the enumeration has been inadvertently omitted. One may occasionally omit *and* before the final element in an enumeration with a particular nuance in mind: without *and* the implication is that the series is incomplete—rhetoricians call this construction "asyndeton"; with *and* the implication is that the series is complete. This shade in meaning is increasingly subtle in modern prose. For examples drawn from the writings of Benjamin N. Cardozo, Karl Llewellyn, and Gerald Gunther, see Bryan A. Garner, *The Elements of Legal Style* 159–60 (1991).

Finally, on the question of punctuating enumerations, the best practice is to place a comma before the *and* introducing the final element. See PUNCTUATION (C)(2).

and etc. See **etc.**

and his children; and her children. This phrase ought to be avoided in wills because it gives rise to an interpretative dilemma: is the phrase one of limitation, i.e., does it indicate the size of the estate given? Or is it one of purchase, i.e., does it indicate a gift also to the afterborn children themselves? See **words of purchase.**

and his heirs; and her heirs. These phrases are quintessential pre-20th-century TERMS OF ART—pieces of magical language—formerly necessary to create a fee-simple interest. They are no longer necessary, as it is now possible to say, "I convey to you Blackacre in fee simple," and the words will have that very effect.

and/or. A. General Recommendation. A legal and business expression dating from the mid-19th century, *and/or* has been vilified for most of its life—and rightly so. The upshot is that "the only safe rule to follow is not to use the expression in any legal writing, document or proceeding, under any circumstances." Dwight G. McCarty, *That Hybrid "and/or,"* 39 Mich. State B.J. 9, 17 (1960). Many lawyers would be surprised at how easy and workable this solution is. See **either (D).**

B. A Little History. Lawyers have been among *and/or*'s most ardent haters, though many continue to use it. The term has been referred to as "that befuddling, nameless thing, that Janus-faced verbal monstrosity, neither word nor phrase, the child of a brain of someone too lazy or too dull to express his precise meaning, or too dull to know what he did mean, now commonly used by lawyers in drafting legal documents, through carelessness or ignorance or as a cunning device to conceal rather than express meaning." *Employers' Mut. Liab. Ins. Co. v. Tollefsen,* 263 N.W. 376, 377 (Wis. 1935) (per Fowler, J.). Another court has stated: "[T]o our way of thinking the abominable invention *and/or* is as devoid of meaning as it is incapable of classification by the rules of grammar and syntax." *American Gen. Ins. Co. v. Webster,* 118 S.W.2d 1082, 1084 (Tex. Civ. App.—Beaumont 1938) (per Combs, J.).

These views, in retrospect, are more amusing than insightful. *And/or,* though undeniably clumsy, does have a specific meaning (*x and/or y = x or y or both*). But, though the phrase saves a few words, it "lends itself . . . as much to ambiguity as to brevity . . . it cannot intelligibly be used to fix the occurrence of past events." *Ex parte Bell,* 122 P.2d 22, 29 (Cal. 1942). *And/or* "commonly mean[s] 'the one or the other or both.'" *Amalgamated Transit Union v. Massachusetts,* 666 F.2d 618, 627 (1st Cir. 1981). (See the quotation under **amphibology.**) This definition suggests the handiest rewording: a good way to avoid the term is to write *unlawful arrest or malicious prosecution, or both,* instead of *unlawful arrest and/or malicious prosecution.*

Sometimes *and/or* is inappropriate substantively as well as stylistically. Many types of legal documents have been spoiled by the indecisiveness of *and/or:*

- a finding of fact ("associate and/or employ");
- a pleading ("office and/or agent");
- an affidavit ("fraud and/or other wrongful act");
- a will ("to Ann and/or John");
- an indictment ("cards, dice, and/or dominoes");
- a judgment (in an action that described the plaintiff by the formula *Jones and/or Jones, Inc.*).

Courts have not been kind to the word—e.g.: [T]he highly objectionable phrase *and/or* . . . has no place in pleadings, findings of fact, conclusions of law, judgments or decrees, and least of all in instructions to a jury. Instructions are intended to assist jurors in applying the law to the facts, and trial judges should put them in as simple language as possible, and not confuse them with this linguistic abomination." *State v. Smith,* 184 P.2d 301, 303 (N.M. 1947).

Moreover, the term gives a false sense of precision when used in enumerations: "In an enumeration of duties or powers, either conjunction is generally adequate. If *or* is used, no one would seriously urge that if one enumerated duty or power is performed or exercised, the remainder vanish; and if *and* is used, no one would say that an enumerated duty or power cannot be exercised or performed except simultaneously with all the others." Elmer A. Driedger, *The Composition of Legislation* 79 (1957).

C. Editing the Hieroglyph. Sometimes *and/or* ought to be replaced by *and* itself—e.g.: "There is usually a blackboard, on which issues *and/or* [read *and*] votes may be recorded." Robin T. Lakoff, *Talking Power: The Politics of Language in Our Lives* 122 (1990). (No one would seriously suggest that both issues and votes must be recorded on such a blackboard in a jury room.)/ "Mr Pearce *and/or* [read *and*] his publisher are to be congratulated for working so fast." Joe Rogaly, *Behind the Man from Nowhere,* Fin. Times (Weekend), 27–28 April 1991, at xviii. (If the book has come out promptly, then both the author and the publisher must have worked fast.)

At other times, *and/or* ought to be replaced by *or*—e.g.: "The legal disadvantages of illegitimacy can mostly be avoided by making a will *and/or* [read *or*] adopting the child . . . ." Glanville Williams, *The Sanctity of Life and the Criminal Law* 121 (1957). (No one would seriously suggest that one could be put to an election between making a will and adopting a child—i.e., that one could not do both.) For dealing with the construction *either . . . and/or,* see **either (E).**

D. *Or/and.* This reversal of the words is a rare variant of *and/or* with none of the latter's virtues, and all its vices. Rather than hopelessly confuse readers by resorting to its pretended nuance, one should abstain from it completely.

and other good and valuable consideration. This phrase, used in consideration clauses of contracts, is sometimes false, as when all the legal consideration for the contract given is mentioned explicitly. The phrase should be avoided unless it serves a real function; that is, unless the rest of the items of consideration are too numerous and individually trifling to merit specific inclusion, or unless the parties to the contract do not wish to recite the true price in a publicly recorded document. The drafter of a contract should have some purpose in mind in using this phrase. For the distinction between *good consideration* and *valuable consideration,* see **consideration (D).**

and which. See **which (C).**

anecdotal; anecdotic(al). The first is standard; the other forms are NEEDLESS VARIANTS. In reference to evidence, *anecdotal* refers not to anecdotes, but to personal experiences of the witness testifying. Leff trenchantly calls *anecdotal evidence* "a term of abuse in assessing a social science argument." Arthur A. Leff, *The Leff Dictionary of Law,* 94 Yale L.J. 1855, 2023 (1985). E.g., "In probing discriminatory intent, the trial court may examine the history of the employer's practices, *anecdotal* evidence of class members, and the degree of opportunity to treat employees unfairly in the appraisal process."

anent. Bernstein writes, "Except in legal usage, *anent* [= about] is archaic and semiprecious." Theodore M. Bernstein, *More Language That Needs Watching* 24 (1962). He could have omitted *except in legal usage* and *semi-*.

Another usage critic (following Fowler) has given somewhat narrower guidelines, for the term is still sometimes used in Scotland: "[A]part from its use in Scotch law courts, [*anent*] is archaic." Margaret Nicholson, *A Dictionary of American-English Usage* 25 (1957). Perhaps the best statement is that *anent* "is a pompous word and nearly always entirely useless." Percy Marks, *The Craft of Writing* 47 (1932).

The term was not uncommon through the first half of the 20th century. E.g., "*Anent* [read *With regard to*] the dismissal, the bank's attorney testified that . . . the memorial company had advertised the property for sale on December 7." *Gandy v. Cameron State Bank,* 2 S.W.2d 971, 973 (Tex. Civ. App.—Austin 1927). Today it occurs only infrequently in legal writing, but examples of it can still be found: "The district court denied Fiat's motion to dismiss . . . and ordered the parties to resolve any dispute *anent* [read *about* or *over*] service on that basis." *Boreri v. Fiat S.P.A.,* 763 F.2d 17, 19 (1st Cir. 1985).

anesthetic, n.; **anesthesia.** An *anesthetic* (e.g., ether) causes *anesthesia* (= loss of sensation). AmE prefers these spellings, BrE *anaesthetic, anaesthesia.*

anesthetist; anesthesiologist. Generally, *anesthetist* will serve for "one who administers an anesthetic." The term dates from the late 19th century. *Anesthesiologist,* of World War II vintage, refers specifically to a physician specializing in anesthesia and anesthetics.

ANFRACTUOSITY, or syntactic twisting and turning and winding, has been one of the historical banes of legal prose. It was more common in the late 19th and early 20th centuries than it is today. Let us trace our gradual liberation from anfractuosity, while noting some modern throwbacks. The following is a classic 19th-century example:

> Unless the code, by abolishing the distinction between actions at law and suits in equity, and the forms of such actions and suits, and of pleadings theretofore existing, intended to initiate, and has initiated new principles of

> law, by which a class of rights and of wrongs, not before the proper subjects of judicial investigation and remedy, can now be judicially investigated and remedied, the facts stated in the plaintiff's complaint in this action, do not constitute a cause of action, and the demurrer of the defendant to that complaint is well taken.
>
> *Cropsey v. Sweeney,* 27 Barb. 310 (N.Y. App. Div. 1858).

Here, from 1919, is perhaps the quintessential example of what *not* to do syntactically:

> Upon the petition of Armour & Co. of New Jersey, Armour & Co. of Texas, a foreign and domestic corporation, respectively, and F.M. Etheridge and J.M. McCormick, of Dallas, Tex., having for its purpose the cancellation of a contract between the city of Dallas, the Texas & Pacific Railway Company, and the Wholesale District Trackage Company, on the ground that it was void, because illegal, and for temporary injunction restraining all parties thereto from performing said contract or any portion thereof pendente lite, and alleging that the petitioners were taxpayers of the city of Dallas, and sued for themselves and all other taxpayers in said city of Dallas, Hon. Horton B. Porter, judge of the Sixty-Sixth district court in Hill county, upon the sworn allegation that the proceeding was a class suit, by fiat indorsed upon the petition in Hillsboro, directed the clerk of the district court of Dallas county to file the petition and docket the cause in the Fourteenth district court in Dallas county, and upon the petitioners entering into a bond in the sum of $10,000, conditioned as required by law, to forthwith issue the temporary injunction.
>
> *City of Dallas v. Armour & Co.,* 216 S.W. 222, 223 (Tex. Civ. App.—Dallas 1919).

Perish the thought of one idea to a sentence!

This phenomenon frequently occurs when one tries to sum up the entire case—the facts and the law—in one sentence. From 1984: "Here, the hazard—the scaffolding which was unsafe to work on until its guardrail was installed as planned—was a temporary structure, not a part of the ship itself, its gear, or equipment, which was created and used entirely by the independent contractor, who both owned and controlled it." And here, from 1985:

> Also of importance, without Ms. Stanlin's testimony that lawn mowers were actually missing from the Four Seasons store, it is doubtful that the evidence would have proved beyond a reasonable doubt that the delivery by the driver (even if he was Marshall) of two boxes, of unknown content, showed that two lawn mowers, or any, were dropped off at Frederick Street, even though one of the (perhaps previously discarded) boxes indicated that, at least at one time, a lawn mower had been contained within it.
>
> *U.S. v. Marshall,* 762 F.2d 419, 422–23 (5th Cir. 1985).

Frequently, anfractuosity leads to grammatical and syntactic blunders. E.g., "We further hold it was reversible error to deprive the jury of the opportunity to consider the opinions of those who best knew the person whose fate *they* were to determine, and with it, the opportunity to reject, accept, and assign weight to evidence concededly relevant, *which,* as the exclusive arbiters of fact, *was* the jury's sole function." In that sentence, *which* has no clear antecedent, and therefore *was* has no clear subject; *they* refers (loosely) to the jury.

When the syntax becomes so convoluted that it is unwieldy, or when the subject has become so far removed from the verb that readers no longer remember the subject when they reach the verb, it is time to break the sentence up into two or more tractable sentences. As Cardozo once wrote, "the sentence may be so overloaded with all its possible qualifications that it will tumble down of its own weight." Benjamin N. Cardozo, *Law and Literature,* 52 Harv. L. Rev. 472, 474 (1939).

Chief Justice Rehnquist offers a solution that will still allow the occasional long sentence: "If a sentence takes up more than six lines of type on an ordinary page, it is probably too long. This rule is truly stark in its simplicity, but every draft I review is subjected to it." William H. Rehnquist, *The Supreme Court: How It Was, How It Is* 299 (1987). See SENTENCE LENGTH.

angry takes the preposition *at* or *with.* The phrase *angry at* is used in reference to things <she was angry at the judge's denial of the injunction>, and *angry with* in reference to persons <he was angry with the opposing counsel>. See **mad.**

anguishment is a NEEDLESS VARIANT of *anguish*—e.g.: "The trial court award represented special damages for medical, surgical, and hospital and nursing expenses ($1,825.30), property damage ($425.00), . . . and general damages . . . for mental *anguishment* [read *anguish*], humiliation, and embarrassment." *Pierrotti v. Louisiana Dep't of Highways,* 146 So. 2d 455, 460 (La. Ct. App. 1962).

animadversion was once a legal term meaning "the act of taking judicial cognizance [q.v.] or notice of." Today it means "harsh criticism," as here: "In an Alabama case of 1948, a mother who was convicted of murdering her newly born child received a sentence of twenty years' imprisonment; happily, the conviction was reversed on appeal for lack of evidence, but there was no *animadversion* upon the terrible sentence that the trial court had thought fit to impose." Glanville Williams, *The Sanctity of Life and the Criminal Law* 31 (1957).

animate (= to move to action) has been used as a substitute for *actuate*—e.g.: "While the evidence may have shown that the action was *animated* by malice, in the ordinary acceptation of the term, the proof fails to show any legal malice." Like *motivate, animate* is a serviceable replacement for *actuate,* the ready LEGALISM. See **actuate.**

animo. See **animus (B).**

animus. A. Generally. *Animus* is a double-edged term. At times it is neutral, meaning "intention; disposition"—particularly the mental element in some conduct. This is the generally accepted legal meaning in legal contexts in G.B. and occasionally in the U.S. E.g., "This doctrine was overruled by statute in England, and the jury is now permitted to judge the whole case, and to decide not merely upon the responsibility of the publication, but upon the *animus* with which it was made."

More often in AmE *animus* denotes ill will, as if it were synonymous with *animosity:* "Appellant's lower salary was based on impermissible gender *animus.*"/ "None of these houses were hooked up to city water and sewage lines until 1981; Campbell claims that this was due to racial *animus* on the part of city officials."/ "Thomas won [the Senate's] approval by 52–48 and said it was 'a time for healing, not a time for anger or for *animus* or animosity.'" Aaron Epstein, *Bush Nominee Carries Closest Vote Since 1888,* Philadelphia Inquirer, 16 Oct. 1991, at 1-A.

B. Latinisms. The malevolent sense just mentioned stems perhaps from the several Latin phrases denoting malicious intentions: "In my opinion all the circumstances prove that the words were spoken without *animus injuriandi* [= intent to injure]—even if they had the defamatory meaning ascribed to them." (S. Afr.) Similar phrases are *animus furandi* (= the intention to steal), *animo felonico* (= with felonious intent), and *animus defamandi* (= the intent to defame). These phrases are, happily, obsolescent if not obsolete.

Several neutral *animus* phrases have persisted, especially in the law of wills, yet these LATINISMS generally add nothing to analysis and muddy the waters. We know something is amiss when lawyers begin grammatically misusing Latin terms. For example, *animo revocandi* = with the intent to revoke (a will). In Latin, it is in the ablative case (equivalent to adverbial uses in English), here properly used: "It was generally held in common-law courts that by the destruction, *animo revocandi,* of a will containing a revocatory clause, a former preserved uncanceled will was thereby revived." In the following sentence, however, *animo revocandi* is wrongly used as a noun phrase: "To effect revocation of a duly executed will, by any of the methods prescribed by statute, two things are necessary: (1) the doing of one of the acts specified; and (2) the intent to revoke—the *animo revocandi* [read *animus revocandi*]." Just the opposite mistake appears here, the nominative being used where the ablative belongs: "There can be no conflict between these ambulatory instruments—these wills—until death, and as the latter were destroyed *animus revocandi* [read *animo revocandi*], they thus never constituted wills under § 64–59, and never revoked the 1938 and 1939 wills."

The same sorts of errors occur with other phrases, such as *animus testandi* (= testamentary intent) and *animo testandi* (= with testamentary intent). "The admissibility of such evidence for the purpose of establishing the *animo testandi* [read *animus testandi*] when offered for the purpose of supporting the writing as a testamentary disposition, is, in our opinion, the most serious question involved in this case." We can avoid these embarrassments by sticking to what we all know: English.

Of course, the British seem to know their Latin better, and only rarely misuse *animo* for *animus,* or vice versa. But they are apt to go off the deep end in their proclivity for Latinisms: "The *animus vicino nocendi* may enter into or affect the conception of a personal wrong." (Eng.)

annex, n.; **annexation; annexment; annexion.** *Annex* = something annexed or attached, as an appendix or a wing of a building. *Annexation* = the act of annexing or the state of having been annexed. In the parlance of property law, *annexation* refers to the point at which a fixture becomes a part of the realty to which it is attached. *Annexment* and *annexion* are NEEDLESS VARIANTS of *annexation.*

annex (= to attach) appears more frequently in BrE than in AmE, and in both far more frequently in legal than in nonlegal writing. "The facts are stated in the case, to which are *annexed* four representative contracts." (Eng.)

Annex is more physical in connotation than *attach,* and probably should not be used figuratively: "The courts do, nevertheless, at times deny validity to a condition *annexed* [read *attached*] to a testamentary gift where the condition is calculated to influence the future conduct of the beneficiary in a manner contrary to the established policy of the state."

Attach or annex is an unnecessary DOUBLET: "The officer's certificate, under official seal, *must be attached or annexed* [read *must be attached*] *to the will* in form and content substantially as follows."

annexable. So spelled.

annexation; annexment; annexion. See **annex.**

annihilate is rather too strong a term for *nullify* in legal contexts. "Where no execution issues within the prescribed time, the judgment is *annihilated* [read *nullified*]." See **annul.**

annotation; note; lawnote; casenote. An *annotation* is a note that explains or criticizes (usu. a case), esp. to give, in condensed form, some indication of the law as deduced from cases and statutes, as well as to point out where similar cases can be found. In law, *annotations* appear in the *Lawyers' Edition of the United States Reports* and in *American Law Reports* (ALR). *Annotations* usually follow the text of a reported case.

A *note* or *lawnote* is a scholarly legal essay shorter than an article and restricted in scope, usually written by a student for publication in a law review. In this sense *note* and *lawnote* are synonymous, the latter being slightly more specific. A *casenote* is so restricted in scope that it deals only with a single case; *lawnotes,* in contrast, tend to treat many cases in a general area of the law.

announce; annunciate; enounce; enunciate. *Announce,* the best known of these terms, may mean (1) "to proclaim"; (2) "to give notice of"; or (3) "to serve as announcer of." *Annunciate* is a NEEDLESS VARIANT, except in religious contexts. *Enunciate* =(1) to formulate systematically; (2) to announce, proclaim; or (3) to articulate clearly. *Enounce* is a NEEDLESS VARIANT in sense (1) of *enunciate.*

In reference to judicial opinions, *announce* means "to write for the majority." E.g., "Mr. Justice Douglas *announced* the judgment of the Court and delivered the following opinion, in which the Chief Justice, Mr. Justice Black and Mr. Justice Reed concur." *Screws v. U.S.,* 325 U.S. 91, 92 (1945).

annoy. See **aggravate.**

annuitant; pensioner. *Annuitant* = a beneficiary of an annuity. E.g., "[A] contract to buy an annuity was void where, at the time of the contract, the *annuitant* had died, so that the annuity no longer existed." G.H. Treitel, *The Law of Contract* 249 (8th ed. 1991).

Pensioner = a person receiving a pension. For some purposes the terms are interchangeable. Yet *annuitant* has less disparaging connotations, perhaps because the person it denotes has usually established the annuity, whereas a *pensioner* is generally the beneficiary of a pension provided by a third party, such as the government or an employer. *Pensioner* sometimes suggests one who lives off a very limited fixed income.

annul; nullify. These words have much the same meaning ("to counteract the force, effectiveness, or existence of"). *Annul* more strongly suggests abolishing or making nonexistent by legal action <to annul a marriage>. E.g., "If at any time the seisin happens to be without a home it immediately returns to the transferor (or to his heirs if he is dead), and all subsequent interests are *annulled* and destroyed." *Annul* frequently appears in the verbose phrase *annul and set aside;* the last three words of that phrase are unnecessary. See DOUBLETS, TRIPLETS, AND SYNONYM-STRINGS.

Nullify has the broader meaning, and generally carries no necessary implication of legal action. "The Eighth Circuit *nullified* a breach-of-contract judgment obtained against the corporation in an Iranian court."/ "The senator's vote was not *nullified,* but rather cast in the absence of certain information." See **set aside (A).**

annulment. So spelled—not *annullment* (a common misspelling). See **divorce (A).**

annunciate. See **announce.**

anoint is sometimes misspelled *annoint,* as in *Gulf States Tel. Co. v. Local 1692, AFL-CIO,* 416 F.2d 198, 201 (5th Cir. 1969).

anomalous; anomalistic. *Anomalous* is the general adjective corresponding to the noun *anomaly. Anomalistic* should refer only to astronomical anomalies. But legal writers occasionally misuse *anomalistic* for *anamalous*—e.g.: "This kind of reasoning would inject into waiver proceedings the *anomalistic* [read *anomalous*] proposition that waiver should be granted because the child is 'too good' for placement in the youth correctional facility." *In re Doe,* 604 P.2d 276, 279 (Haw. 1979).

anomie; anomy. The former spelling is preferred; the adjective is *anomic.*

anonym(e); ananym. An *anonym* (preferably spelled without the final *-e*) is an anonymous person. (See **pseudonym.**) An *ananym* is a pseudonym arrived at by spelling the author's name backward (as, hypothetically, *Renrag* for *Garner*).

answer. To nonlawyers, this word denotes a reply to a question or a solution to a problem. In U.S. law, it usually refers to the first pleading of a defendant addressing the merits of the case. In G.B., however, *answer* = (1) a reply to an interrogatory; or (2) a response to a divorce petition.

ANTE-, ANTI-. The prefix *ante-* means "before," and *anti-* "against." Thus *antecedent* (= something that goes before) and *antipathy* (= feelings against, dislike). In but one word, *anticipate* (= to consider or use *before* the due or natural time), *ante-* has been changed to *anti-*. In compound words, the prefix *anti-* may cause ambiguities. See **antimarital-facts privilege & antinuclear protester.**

ANTE-, PRE-. See PRE-.

ante; supra; ubi supra; infra; post. Literally *ante* means "before," and *supra* "above." Some literalists therefore use *supra* for something higher up on the same page and *ante* for something further afield, with corresponding conventions for *infra* and *post.* That practice now has few adherents, at least in the U.S.

Both *ante* and *supra* are today used to refer to a preceding part of the text—however far afield—as in "*supra* at 11." *Ubi supra* was formerly used where *supra* now appears. It means "where above," and really has no place in modern legal writing.

Because *supra* is the more usual term, and because it is desirable that we achieve uniformity on this point, the recommendation here is to use *supra* for general purposes, not *ante.* An additional advantage of *supra* is that it translates directly into English. "See note 5 above" is English; "See note 5 before" is not.

The U.S. Supreme Court is one of few courts that distinguish between the signals *supra* and *ante* in usage; it also makes a distinction between *infra* and *post.* The term *ante* is used to cite a previous opinion published in the same volume of the U.S. Reports, whether or not that opinion is in the same case as that in which the citation appears. For example, *ante* is used in a dissent to cite a page in the majority opinion. *Supra* is used to refer either to earlier pages within the same opinion or to a previously cited authority. The Supreme Court uses *post* correlatively with *ante,* and *infra* with *supra.*

The phrases *ut infra* (= as below) and *ut supra* (= as above) are not current in legal writing, although they were common up to the mid-20th century. See ***ex ante*** & ***infra.***

All these Latin words—*supra, ante, infra, post*—should be used only as signals; they should not replace ordinary English terms in prose. E.g., "We discuss this argument *infra* [read *below*] and remand for the appropriate findings." Even in their use as signals, these terms are often vague without some specification of the reference; they are generally best avoided in CITATION OF CASES.

antecede, v.t., has become nothing more than an inflated and NEEDLESS VARIANT of *precede,* though the adjectives *antecedent* and *precedent* have distinct uses. In exalted prose, such as the passage following, it may be justified. "Language survives everything—corruption, misuse, ignorance, ineptitude. Linking man to man in the dark, it brought man out of the dark. It is the human glory which *antecedes* all others. It merits not only our homage but our constant and intelligent study." (Anthony Burgess)

antecedent; prior. Used as adjectives—e.g., to qualify the term *debt*—these words are generally inferior to *earlier* or *preexisting.* Like *previous, prior* may occasionally be justified; *antecedent* may on rare occasions be forgivable, but not here: "Until the bonds mature, a purchaser for value, without notice of their invalidity as between *antecedent parties* [read *previous parties* or *predecessors in interest*], would take them discharged from all infirmities."/ "An allegation of special damages as a matter of aggravation is a substantive allegation of fact, and not an inference of law resulting from facts *antecedently* [read *previously*] stated."

The phrase *antecedent to* (= *before*) is a ludicrous pomposity. "If the defendant has the right, when did it accrue to him? If at all, it must have been *antecedent to* [read *before*] the finding by the plaintiff, for that finding could not give the defendant any right."/ "An alien in America, *antecedent to* [read *before*] the revolution, was entitled to all the rights and privileges of an alien in England, and many more." Cf. **anterior to, previous to & prior to.**

But if the phrase is to be used, it should not lose the particle *to,* as here: "*Antecedent* [insert *to*] this assigned Justice['s—see FUSED PARTICIPLES] joining the Court, facets of this controversy were here in *In re Powers's Estate.*" *In re Estate of Powers,* 134 N.W.2d 148, 150 (Mich. 1965).

antecedents (= background; record) is broader in AmE than in BrE, where it means "an accused or convicted person's background, esp. any previous criminal record or evidence of bad character." In legal writing in the U.S., this term may be used in reference to a witness as well as to an accused: "Where the litigation is important the character, reputation and *antecedents* of the main witnesses of the adverse party should be investigated thoroughly." Asher L. Cornelius, *The Cross-Examination of Witnesses* 11 (1929). In such contexts, however, *background* would be a better term.

A 19th-century usage critic stung this word with a venom that has not lost its power: "This use of the word . . . is not defensible . . . [f]or in meaning it is an awkward perversion, and in convenience it has no advantage. . . . [I]t is a needless absurdity. For if, instead of, What do you know of his *antecedents?* it is asked, What do you know of his previous life? or, better, What do you know of his past? there is sense instead of nonsense, and the purpose of the questions is fully conveyed." Richard G. White, *Words and Their Uses, Past and Present* 91–92 (2d ed. 1872).

ANTECEDENTS, AGREEMENT OF NOUNS WITH. See CONCORD (B).

ANTECEDENTS, FALSE. An antecedent is a noun or noun phrase that is referred to by a pronoun. When used correctly and effectively, antecedents are explicitly mentioned, are prominent, and are not far removed from the pronouns that substitute for them. A variety of problems can occur, however, and some of them are here discussed.

A. Ghostly Antecedents. The problem of nonexistent antecedents occurs frequently when a word such as *this* or *it* (see DEICTIC TERMS) is intended to refer, not as it should to a preceding noun, but to the action accomplished in the verb phrase. E.g., "They are also told that X., a doctor employed by defendant, will vaccinate anyone who wishes to have this done." (What is the noun that acts as antecedent of *this?* We may supply the antecedent *vaccination,* but the sentence itself should supply the antecedent.)/ "To some degree, though not quantified, defendant's sales have declined; but quantification is not required because plaintiff is not seeking damages therefor [for what?]." (The writer intended—but failed—to say that plaintiff is not seeking damages for the decline in sales.)/ "The foregoing sufficiently answers, *if any be necessary* [read *if any answer be* (or *is*) *necessary*], the suggestion that the statute is unconstitutional." See ANTICIPATORY REFERENCE (C).

B. False Attraction. In the context of problems with antecedents, false attraction occurs when, instead of referring to the subject, a pronoun such as *this* or *it* refers to a noun appearing between the subject and the pronoun. E.g., "Harrelson nonetheless contends now that the admission of this testimony was reversible error because it had been hypnotically induced." What had been *hypnotically induced?* The writer intended to convey that the *testimony,* not its *admission,* had been induced by hypnosis. See SUBJECT-VERB AGREEMENT.

C. With Possessives. A noun in the possessive case is not a suitable antecedent for a pronoun, because the possessive makes the noun functionally an adjective. The parts of speech of an antecedent and its referent must match. "Indeed, the Court's reading of the plain language of the Fourth Amendment *is* incapable of explaining even *its* own holding in this case." What is the subject of *is,* the antecedent of *its?* The intended antecedent is *court,* but the possessive *court's* is merely an adjective modifying *reading,* and is incapable of acting as the antecedent of *it,* or as the subject of *is.* [Read *Indeed, the Court in its reading* . . . .]/ "There may have been inimical voices raised among the jury, *such as the foreman's, who* [read *such as that of the foreman, who*] had just had an unpleasant brush with the bailiff." See APPOSITIVES (A), DEICTIC TERMS, POSSESSIVES (H) & **it.**

D. Remote Antecedents. See MISCUES (C) & REMOTE RELATIVES.

antecedent to. See **antecedent.**

antedate; predate. Both words are so commonly used that it would be presumptuous to label either a NEEDLESS VARIANT. One sees a tendency to use *antedate* in reference to documentary materials, and *predate* in reference to physical things and historical facts. E.g., "The origin of the rule *predates* our dual federal-state court system." The DIFFERENTIATION is worth enhancing.

antemortem; antemortal; premortal; premortem; premortuary. *Antemortem* corresponds to *postmortem,* q.v. *Premortal* = (1) occurring before the time when human mortality was assumed (i.e., quite ancient); (2) occurring immediately before death. *Premortem* is a NEEDLESS VARIANT of *antemortem* and *premortal. Premortuary* = occurring before the funeral. The distinction between *antemortal* and *premortal* (in sense (2)) is that *antemortal* refers to any time before death, whereas *premortal* refers to the time immediately preceding death.

antenuptial; prenuptial. The latter is far more common in AmE today; *antenuptial* is the usual term in BrE, however. It is bootless, then, to label either a NEEDLESS VARIANT. Oddly, *antenuptial* does not appear in most English-language dictionaries. But it appears regularly in British legal writing—e.g.: "[T]he husband was liable for her *antenuptial* debts." O. Hood Phillips, *A First Book of English Law* 270 (3d ed. 1955). See **postnuptial.**

antepenultimate. See **penultimate.**

anterior to for *before* is, like its various bombastic competitors, almost risible. It would be, alas, if some lawyers did not use it with a straight face. E.g., "The authorities petitioner cites to the effect that an express contract made *anterior to* [read *before*] his entering upon his duties is essential to a claim by an officer of a corporation for compensation, are against rather than for him." Cf. **antecedent to, prior to & previous to.**

ANTHROPOMORPHISM, the attribution of human qualities or characteristics to things, is not uncommon in the language of the law. One common manifestation of this phenomenon occurs in phrases referring to what a statute does or does not *contemplate*—e.g.: "The statutory provision *contemplates* a result contrary to the statute as a whole." Or this, a form of HYPALLAGE: "A *concerned jurisdiction* is one that in view either of *its thinking* about the particular substantive issue raised or of its more general legal policies, can be taken to have *expressed some interest* in regulating an aspect of the multistate transaction in question."

Occasionally, anthropomorphism reflects poor style, as when a writer refers to the mindfulness of pellucidity: "Notwithstanding the fact that it is centered chiefly in construction, *pellucidity* in legal writing is not *unmindful* of discriminating diction and choice figures of speech." There are no choice figures of speech in that sentence.

antiaircraft. See VOWEL CLUSTERS.

anticipatable (= that can be expected or anticipated) is listed in the *OED,* with one citation from 1872, but appears in neither *W2* nor *W3.* "Stone's statement . . . was elicited to dispel the *anticipatable* suggestion that the government might be using threats of prosecution to induce Schbley to testify favorably." *U.S. v. Fusco,* 748 F.2d 996, 998 (5th Cir. 1984). The quoted sentence illustrates the loose usage of *anticipate,* q.v.; *foreseeable* would have been the better word. See -ATABLE.

anticipate = (1) to take care of beforehand; to preclude by prior action; forestall; or (2) to expect. Sense (2) has long been considered a SLIPSHOD EXTENSION; it should be avoided in formal legal writing. Lord Evershed, M.R., once addressed this question, saying: "[T]he liking [that] many persons appear to have for the use of words having twice as many syllables as the more natural and proper word to use has, in fairly recent times, undoubtedly led to the use of the word *anticipate* when the correct word is *expect.*" *Jarman v. Lambert & Cooke Contractors,* [1951] 2 K.B. 937, 942.

The poor usage is now seemingly ubiquitous—e.g.: "Generally the measure of damages for a tort is the amount that will compensate for all the detriment proximately caused thereby, whether it could have been *anticipated* [read *foreseen*] or not."/ "It is clear that the parties and the court still *anticipated* [read *expected*] that further remedial proceedings would take place before the court approved any proposal."/ "It is not clear that the defendant might reasonably have *anticipated* [read *foreseen*] being haled into court in Louisiana."

The use of *anticipated* in the sense "eagerly awaited" constitutes still further corruption of the word. E.g., "The Supreme Court decided nearly twenty cases during its 1983–84 term relating to the Fourth Amendment; among these, the 'good-faith exception' cases were perhaps the most *anticipated* and controversial."

The following sentences illustrate the correct use of the word: "The trailer court was not built, nor was the sewage plant, at the time the action was started, and thus the injunction was sought against an *anticipated* nuisance." (Here *anticipated* = considered before the appropriate time.)/ "A spendthrift clause restrains the power of a beneficiary to *anticipate* his right to income or perhaps to principal." (Here *anticipate* = to preclude by prior action.)

anticipatory; anticipative. The former is standard in phrases such as *anticipatory breach.*

ANTICIPATORY REFERENCE is the vice of referring to something that is yet to be mentioned. Thus a sentence will be leading up to the all-important predicate, but before reaching it will refer to what is contained in the predicate. The reader is temporarily mystified. E.g., "Conflict of laws is the study of whether or not, *and if so, in what way,* the answer to a legal problem will be affected because the elements of the problem have contacts with more than one jurisdiction." This sentence would better read: "Conflict of laws is the study of whether *the answer* to a legal problem will be affected because the elements of the problem have contacts with more than one jurisdiction; *and, if so, how the answer* will be affected."

Only rarely can anticipatory reference be used in a way that does not disturb the reader—e.g.: "We think it is clear—*and no party disputes this point*—that the statutory commitment of review of FCC action to the Court of Appeals affords this court jurisdiction over claims of unreasonable delay." For innocuous examples with personal pronouns, see the second paragraph in (C) below.

The vexatious examples, which are far more common, occur in a variety of forms.

A. *As do.* "Texas, *as do* most jurisdictions, recognizes three general theories of recovery under which a manufacturer of a defective product may be held liable under strict liability principles." (One must either put *as do most jurisdictions* after the verb, or change the *as do* to *like.*)/ "Law professors, *as do* [read *like*] state court judges, produce a body of writing that can be analyzed to discern their political philosophies." See **like (A).**

A related error occurs with *have:* "The court, *as have* [read *like*] the parties, construes this motion as one for judgment notwithstanding the verdict."

B. Noun References. "Kramer made, among others, the following untrue and misleading statements of material fact." [Read *Kramer made the following untrue and misleading statements of fact, among others.*]/ "*In an action, inter alia, to recover* [read *In an action to recover, inter alia,*] moneys allegedly due, plaintiff appeals."/ "Mr Hytner is a director who knows how to keep the pot on the boil; whether you agree with *them* or not, he makes *his points* with boldness and panache." John Gross, *A Badly Brought-Up Bunch of Girls,* Sunday Telegraph, 15 July 1990, at ix. (Reverse the positions of *them* and *his points.*)

C. Pronouns. "The defense *of itself* is without a doubt one of the foremost concerns of any nation." [Read *A nation's self-defense is without doubt one of its foremost concerns.*]/ "The formidable difficulty involved in *its* definition and measurement is partially responsible for the lack of attention to quality." (*Its* has no clearly identifiable antecedent in the sentence just quoted; only at the end of the sentence do we realize that *quality* is the referent.)/ "Even if *he* construed the evidence most favorably to the state, *a reasonable juror* should have doubted that the left side of the safe was within the building." (Reverse the positions of *he* and *a reasonable juror;* and consider making the reference nonsexist. See SEXISM (A).)/ (Opening sentence of an opinion:) "After a hearing at which *he* and *his* office manager testified, appellant Reehlman, an orthopedic surgeon, was adjudged in contempt for disobeying a subpoena." (Recast the sentence so that *he* and *his* follow *Reehlman.*)/ "Assuming *it* applies to claims based on injunctive relief, *the doctrine of res judicata* would not bar a suit based on acts of the defendant that have occurred subsequent to the final judgment asserted as a bar." (Reverse *it* and the italicized noun phrase.) See ANTECEDENTS, FALSE (A).

Occasionally an anticipatory reference by pronoun is acceptable, but only where the "antecedent" follows the reference closely: "Making *himself* understood is *the writer's* first task."/ "Independently of the scope of *his* response to the auditor's request for information, *the lawyer* may have as part of his professional responsibility an obligation to advise the client concerning the need for public disclosure."

ANTICIPATORY SUBJECTS. See EXPLETIVES.

anticlimactic is the correct form; *anticlimatic* is a solecism. See **climactic.**

anticompete, like *noncompete,* is a NEEDLESS VARIANT of *noncompetition*—e.g.: "Defendants Kentile . . . by adopting . . . the *anticompete* [read *noncompetition*] provision . . . have participated . . . in a contract . . . in violation of 15 U.S.C. § 1." *Golden v. Kentile Floors, Inc.,* 475 F.2d 288, 290 (5th Cir. 1973)./ "Berkeley argues that it would be a disservice to the shopping center to allow Drug Fair to obtain the benefit of the *anticompete* [read *noncompetition*] clause." *Berkeley Dev. Co. v. Great Atlantic & Pac. Tea Co.,* 518 A.2d 790, 796 (N.J. Super. Ct. 1986).

antilapse statute. See **lapse statute.**

antimarital-facts privilege. This is an obtuse name for the evidentiary privilege allowing a spouse not to testify about "marital facts," i.e., intimate facts relating to the marriage. The phrase *antimarital facts* = facts whose disclosure tends to harm the marriage. The prefix *anti-* causes the problem, for the privilege is not "antimarital." Yet the disclosure of the facts *is* thought to be "antimarital." The ambiguity caused by the prefix disappears when an alternative name for the privilege is used (e.g., *privilege against adverse spousal testimony, spousal privilege,* or *marital privilege*). The first of these alternative versions is used by the Supreme Court in *Trammel v. U.S.,* 445 U.S. 40 (1980).

antinomy; antimony. These words are not to be confused. *Antinomy* = a contradiction in law or logic; a conflict of authority. This is the word used in legal contexts—e.g.: "The law was taken to be complete and self-sufficient, without *antinomies* and without gaps, wanting only arrangement, logical development of the implications of its several rules and conceptions, and systematic exposition of its several parts." Roscoe Pound, *An Introduction to the Philosophy of Law* 19 (1922; repr. 1975)./ "[H]e has even more difficulty in absorbing the notion that *antinomies* among the principles of legal morality may be encountered in the design of legal institutions." Lon L. Fuller, *The Morality of Law* 240 (rev. ed. 1969).

Antimony is rather arcane, meaning "a brittle

silvery-white metallic element, used esp. in alloys" (*COD*).

antinuclear protester is technically ambiguous, though everyone should know what is intended. For the literally minded, however, it might refer to "a protester *denouncing* the antinuclear cause," instead of "a protester *espousing* the antinuclear position." Thus it might be preferable to write *nuclear-energy* (or *-weapon*) *protester* or *antinuclear advocate.* See **protest.**

antipathy takes *against, to, toward,* or *for.* The writer of the following sentence haplessly inserted one of the few unidiomatic prepositions: "J.W. has focused on the 'terrible plight of the American Indian' as a stratagem to publicize his *antipathy of* [read *antipathy toward*] government in general and, ludicrously, socialism in particular."

antisuit (= of or relating to a court order prohibiting the filing of another lawsuit against the same party or making the same claim) is a mid-20th-century legal NEOLOGISM that remains unrecorded in most English-language dictionaries. E.g., "Where the two courts involved are a state and a federal court, special attention should be given to such an *antisuit* injunction." *Blanchard v. Commonwealth Oil Co.,* 294 F.2d 834, 839 (5th Cir. 1961)./ "Ordinarily *antisuit* injunctions are not properly invoked to preempt parallel proceedings on the same in personam claim in foreign tribunals." *Laker Airways Ltd. v. Sabena, Belgian World Airlines,* 731 F.2d 909, 915 (D.C. Cir. 1984).

antithetic(al). The longer form has become established in the phrase *antithetical to* and in most other contexts. The shorter form should be avoided as a NEEDLESS VARIANT. *Antithetical* = exhibiting direct opposition. E.g., "We believe that requiring domestic litigants to resort to the Hague Convention to compel discovery against their foreign adversaries encourages the concealment of information—a result directly *antithetical* to the express goals of the Federal Rules and of the Hague Convention." (*Directly antithetical* verges on REDUNDANCY.) The phrase should not be used as a mere synonym of *opposed,* a slightly broader word.

antitrust. So written—without a hyphen.

Anton Piller order. See CASE REFERENCES (C).

anxious. This word most properly means "uneasy; disquieted; worried." To use the word as a synonym for *eager* is to give in to SLIPSHOD EXTENSION—e.g.: "The wife seeks the court's directions as to the validity of the decree absolute and is *anxious* [read *eager*] to know what her present status is." (Eng.)/ "Defense counsel in death cases are *anxious* [read *eager*] to retain the scrupled jurors that prosecutors seek to exclude."

any. A. Singular or Plural. *Any* may be either singular or plural. Here is an example of the (rarer) singular use: "Consider whether any of the presidential statements is inconsistent with the modern Court's claims." In such contexts *any* is elliptical for *anyone,* q.v.

B. In Legislation. *Any* is greatly overworked in statutes <if any person shall commit any action upon any other person>. Usually, replacing *any* with the indefinite article *a* or *an* results in heightened readability with no change in meaning.

C. And *all*. See **all** (C).

any and all. The word *all* precisely captures the sense 99 out of 100 times. The one other time, it merely captures the sense. See DOUBLETS, TRIPLETS, AND SYNONYM-STRINGS.

anyhow (= in any way; in any manner) is, in AmE, considered colloquial—almost dialectal—for *anyway* or *nevertheless.* E.g., "He understood the right to remain silent, but decided to talk *anyhow* [read *anyway*]."

In BrE, however, the word does not seem to strike readers as such a casualism—e.g.: "[I]n many cases it is not for one moment expected that a contracting party will actually perform in person, and when the contracting party is a corporation this would *anyhow* be a physical impossibility." P.S. Atiyah, *An Introduction to the Law of Contract* 283 (3d ed. 1981).

anymore. Unless it appears in a negative statement <the courts have no such requirement anymore>, this word is dialectal in the sense "nowadays"—e.g.: "*Anymore,* [read *Nowadays* or *These days*] the price of housing is outrageous."

anyone. A. And *any one*. In reference to persons, *anyone* should be spelled as one word. Formerly it was written as two words; now, however, the unification of the phrase is complete.

Yet sometimes the phrase is wrongly made one word when, not meaning "anybody," it should be two: "A question might arise as to *anyone* [read *any one*] or all of these legitimate 'conceivables.'" *Any one* = any single person or thing (of a number).

B. *Anyone . . . they*. See CONCORD (B) & SEXISM (A).

C. *Anyone else's*. See **else's** & POSSESSIVES (G).

anyplace (= anywhere) is not in good use. The word is vastly inferior to *anywhere.*

Any place (= any location) should always be two words <at any place>.

anything; any thing. The distinction is sometimes important in legislative DRAFTING. *Any thing* implies an opposition to *any person. Anything* is the far more general word meaning "whatever thing."

anything to the contrary contained herein notwithstanding. See **notwithstanding anything to the contrary contained herein.**

anytime, adv., = at any time; whenever. E.g., "*Anytime* a seller rents back from a buyer, an interim occupancy agreement should be completed." Dian Hymer, *Seller Rent-Back Can Benefit Both Sides,* San Francisco Examiner, 25 Oct. 1992, at F-1. Some writers consider this term a casualism, but it is highly convenient and has—for whatever reason—gained more widespread acceptance than *anymore* (in positive contexts) and *anyplace.* Cf. **anymore & anyplace.**

apanage. See **ap(p)anage.**

apart from. See **aside from.**

apex forms the plurals *apexes* and *apices.* The English plural—*apexes*—is preferred.

apology; apolog(ue); apologia. *Apology,* in its general sense, applies to an expression of regret for a mistake, usually with the implication of guilt. It may also refer to a defense of one's position, a sense shared with *apologia.* The latter should preempt this meaning for purposes of DIFFERENTIATION. An *apologue* is an allegory that conveys a moral. (*Apolog* is not recorded in the dictionaries and should be avoided. For analogous forms, see **analogy** (for *analog*) & **catalog(ue).**)

apostasy; apostacy. The latter spelling is mistaken, the original Gk. word being *apostasia.* E.g., "Would he then have embraced and defended the *Donovan apostacy* [read *apostasy*] with the same generosity with which he yielded to the *Camara* majority in *Barlow?*" Maurice Kelman, *The Forked Path of Dissent,* 1985 Sup. Ct. Rev. 227, 245.

a posteriori. See **a priori.**

APOSTROPHES. See PUNCTUATION (A).

appal(l). The standard spelling is *appall.*

ap(p)anage. Though in today's French this term is spelled *apanage,* in the French of the 16th century it was spelled with two *-p*-s. We borrowed the word from the French early in the 17th century, and the *OED* notes that the spellings have been "equally common" in English. The *OED* favors *apanage,* whereas *W3* favors *appanage.* The latter certainly *appears* more English, and on that basis alone might be deemed preferable.

In its literal and historical sense, *appanage* /***ap**-ə-nij*/ means "a grant (as of lands or money) made by a sovereign or a legislative body for the support of dependent members of the royal family" (*W3*). Because Americans are not saddled with such burdens, the term is purely figurative in AmE, meaning "a customary or rightful endowment" (*W3*).

apparatus has the plural forms *apparatus* and *apparatuses.* The former is a Latin plural and the latter an English plural. When referring to more than one apparatus in Latin, write *apparatus.* When using English, however, use *apparatuses.* See PLURALS (A).

Apparati is an example of HYPERCORRECTION—e.g.: "Her testimony indicates that she had definite ideas as to where and how these *apparati* [read *apparatuses*] were to be used . . . ." *Clarke v. O'Connor,* 435 F.2d 104, 107 (D.C. Cir. 1970)./"The court attempted to establish a procedure for determining whether a doctor could disconnect life-sustaining *apparati* [read *apparatuses*] from other patients." Linda F. Gould, *Right to Die Legislation,* 39 Mercer L. Rev. 517, 523 (1988).

apparent is frequently misused in the press, and sometimes in legal writing, in reference to fatal maladies. "Cardinal Cody died this morning of an *apparent* heart attack." One does not die of an "apparent" heart attack. [Read *Cardinal Cody died this morning, apparently of a heart attack.*]

For the sense of *apparent* in *heir apparent,* see **heir** (B).

apparent authority; ostensible authority. Both refer to the authority that an agent appears to have by virtue of the principal's conduct—and that third parties might reasonably assume that the agent actually has. The usual phrase today, in BrE and AmE alike, is *apparent authority.*

appeal, n. **A. Idioms.** In AmE, cases are said to go *on appeal*; in BrE, the idiom *under appeal* is common. E.g., "Their Lordships are of opinion that the decision *under appeal* is not in accordance with that principle." (Eng.) The British phrase *appeal allowed* is equivalent to the American *reversed.* See **appeal allowed, allow & on appeal.**

Where American writers would refer to an *appeal from* a judgment, British writers typically refer to an *appeal against* a judgment—e.g.: "Again, in the case of *Harris* in 1952, the speeches were postponed until after the House had intimated that his appeal against conviction for larceny would be allowed." H.G. Hanbury, *English Courts of Law* 78–79 (2d ed. 1953).

B. And *certiorari; review.* In referring to consideration by the U.S. Supreme Court of lower-court and state-court judgments, many American lawyers make the mistake of calling the genus by the name of one species; that is, they refer to *appeal* when they mean to include *certiorari* as well. In fact, though, *appeal* is rare in the U.S. Supreme Court. See Charles A. Wright, *The Law of Federal Courts* 775–76 (5th ed. 1994). The more accurate term for the genus—the word that includes *certiorari* as well as *appeal*—is *review.* See **review (A).**

appeal, adj. See **appellate & appeals,** adj.

appeal, vb. Depending on the context, *appeal* may be either intransitive or transitive in AmE. Usually one *appeals from* a judgment—e.g.: "Defendant *appeals from* a verdict and judgment against him in an action for libel."/ "We find no error in the decree *appealed from.*"/ "Plaintiff *appealed from* an order sustaining separate demurrers of the defendants on the ground that the complaint does not state a cause of action."

Nearly as often, however, *appeal* is used transitively in AmE—e.g.: "Appellant *appeals* his conviction of possessing a firearm after having been convicted of a felony."/ "The United States *appeals* the suppression of evidence obtained during a warranted search."/ "Nolen *appeals* the award of an injunction against him."

In BrE—in which the transitive use has been obsolete since the late 16th century—one *appeals against* a lower court's decree. E.g., "The architect *appealed against* the master's order to Chapman J., who allowed his appeal and set aside the master's order." (Eng.)/ "An erroneous judgment may stand, and acquire an undeserved authority, merely because the losing party does not *appeal against* it . . . ." Carleton K. Allen, *Law in the Making* 313 (7th ed. 1964).

appeal allowed; appeal dismissed. These British phrases are equivalent to the American phrases *judgment reversed* and *judgment affirmed.* See JUDGMENTS, APPELLATE-COURT.

appealer. See **appellant.**

appeals, adj. In jurisdictions that have a *court of appeals*—as opposed to a *court of appeal*—the alternative wording is *appeals court,* not *appeal court.* E.g., "[A] federal *appeals court* in Philadelphia ruled last August that the OMB officials didn't have the authority to do so." Stephen Wermiel, *Supreme Court Will Review OMB's Powers,* Wall St. J., 16 May 1989, at B7. Even so, the term *appellate* is usually more natural-sounding in AmE.

Of course, where, as in England, the name of the intermediate appellate court is the *Court of Appeal,* the phrase *appeal court* is entirely proper—e.g.: "Within a week, the High Court decided that Lord Young, the trade secretary, should publish and refer to the Monopolies and Mergers Commission an inspectors' report on the takeover; then a unanimous three-judge *appeal court* decided he need do no such thing." *Curbed in the Courts,* Economist, 28 Jan.–3 Feb. 1989, at 56.

appear. The phrase *it would appear* is invariably inferior to *it appears* or *it seems.* There is no need for the modal verb *would* in this construction, unless a hypothetical subjunctive is intended. "As of the middle of this century, *it would appear* [read *it appears,* or, depending on the sense, *appeared*] that the extent of present development along these lines has [or *had*] been somewhat overstated." See **would** & SUBJUNCTIVES.

On the difference between *appear* and *make an appearance,* see **appearance, make an.**

appearance, make an; appear, v.i. The phrase *make an appearance* contains a BURIED VERB (*appear*), but uncovering the verb may shift the connotation slightly. Many American lawyers believe that a party *makes an appearance* by filing a paper in court or by having a lawyer present, but that to *appear* means to show up personally in court. Some have used this rationale to avoid changing *make an appearance* to *appear* in court rules.

Even so, actual usage supports the idea that *appear* is equivalent to *make an appearance*—e.g.: "In most cases, the husband and wife both desire divorce. If the husband gets his divorce in Nevada and the wife *appears* there—which means that an arrangement is made to have a lawyer in Nevada represent her—there will be no trouble." Max Radin, *The Law and You* 68 (1948).

appellant; appealer; appellor. Perhaps few readers have seen or heard any term other than the first. *Appealer* has not gained currency and should not be introduced as a fancy variant of *appellant,* properly pronounced /ə-**pel**-ənt/.

Appellor is an archaic term from English law

meaning "one who accuses of crime, demands proof of innocence by wager of battle, or informs against an accomplice [by *approvement,* q.v.]" (*OED*). E.g., "Appeals of felony continued in use as a means of recovering stolen goods, or of achieving the execution of an aggressor; but the *appellor* ran the risk of having to fight a battle, or of being severely punished if the appeal failed." J.H. Baker, *An Introduction to English Legal History* 71 (3d ed. 1990).

appellate; appellant, adj.**; appeal,** adj.**; appellative.** *W3* records *appellant* as having been used adjectivally in phrases such as *appellant jurisdiction,* perhaps mainly by nonlawyers. In legal writing, however, the adjective corresponding to the noun *appeal* is invariably *appellate.*

Appellate is defined by Johnson (1755) as "the person appealed against," the meaning now given *appellee.* But today the word is used only as an adjective.

In BrE especially, *appeal* itself functions as an adjective in contexts in which Americans would write *appellate*—e.g.: "The judges (at least in England) are not elected by the people, nor are they accountable to anybody (other than *appeal* courts) for their decisions." P.S. Atiyah, *Law and Modern Society* 14 (1983). See **court of appeal(s).**

Appellative, adj., is a specialized grammatical term. *Appellative interrogation* is a variant (and fairly pompous) name for *rhetorical question,* q.v. As a noun, *appellative* = term, name. E.g., "It is a matter of common knowledge that the *appellative* 'revenue laws' is never applied to the statutes involved in these classes of cases."

appellee is pronounced /*ap-ə-**lee***/, not /*ə-**pel**-ee*/.

appellor. See **appellant.**

appendixes; appendices. Both are correct plural forms for *appendix,* but *appendixes* is preferable in nontechnical contexts.

appertain; pertain. Some DIFFERENTIATION is possible. Both take the preposition *to,* but *appertain* usually means "to belong to rightfully" <the privileges appertaining to this degree>, whereas *pertain* usually means "to relate to; concern" <the appeal pertains to defendant's Fifth Amendment rights>.

Here *appertain* is correctly used: "The general principle seems to be that jurisdiction over an inchoate crime *appertains* to the state that would have had jurisdiction had the crime been consummated." (Eng.)/ "The ancient remedy of a bill of peace originated in and *appertained* to the jurisdiction of the court of chancery."

In the following sentence, however, it appears to have been used merely as a fancy variant of the more usual *pertain:* "There is a compelling reason why district courts should not be divested of jurisdiction over matters 'incident to or *appertaining* [read *pertaining*] to an estate' regarding pending probate proceedings."

appetite; appetence; appetency. In all but scientific contexts, *appetence* and *appetency* are NEEDLESS VARIANTS of *appetite.*

applicable. A. And *appliable; applyable.* These two variants are incorrect forms. *Applicable,* the correct form, is properly accented on the first, not on the second, syllable.

B. And *applicative; applicatory.* The last two forms are NEEDLESS VARIANTS of *applicable. Applicative* is also a NEEDLESS VARIANT of *applied,* as in the phrase *applicative psychology.*

C. *Is applicable to.* This construction is almost always inferior to the simple verb *applies*—e.g.: "The doctrine *is not applicable* [read *does not apply*] here."

applicant; applicator; applier. An *applicant* is "one who applies for something (as a position in a firm)." *Applicator* = (1) a device for applying a substance, or (2) one who applies a substance. *Applier* is a NEEDLESS VARIANT of *applicator.*

When *applicant* is used merely for *movant* (as in American federal courts), the latter term is preferable. (See **application.**) In G.B., one who seeks a writ of habeas corpus or judicial review by means of mandamus, prohibition, or certiorari is termed an *applicant.*

application. In some jurisdictions, this term is merely a variant name for *motion.* Where that is so, *motion* is the better term.

apply. See **follow.**

applyable. See **applicable (A).**

appointor, despite its odd appearance, is the accepted spelling of the legal correlative of *appointee.*

apposite. See **apt.**

APPOSITIVES point out the same persons or things by different names, usually in the form of explanatory phrases that narrow in on the precise meaning of a prior more general phrase. Thus, in the sentence "My brother Brad is a musician," *Brad* is the appositive of *brother.* Usually, in phrases less succinct than *my brother Brad* (in which *Brad* is restrictive), the appositive is set off by commas or parentheses: "Plaintiff's decedent, John Doe, was killed in a plane accident," or, "The appellee in this case (XYZ, Inc.) has counterclaimed against the appellant." In these hypothetical sentences, *John Doe* is an appositive of *decedent,* and *XYZ, Inc.* is an appositive of *appellee.* Two problems crop up with appositives.

A. With Possessives. An appositive should match its antecedent syntactically. Here is the correct use of an appositive with a possessive antecedent: "A cannot confer on C *his, A's,* right to possess and deal with the chattel for a partnership purpose." (The appositive is unnecessary, however; see MYTH OF PRECISION.)

Having either an antecedent or an appositive that is possessive (and therefore adjectival) matched up with a nominal mate creates awkwardness, as in the following sentences: "In this case, appellant challenges the district court's grant of T.J. Stevenson & Co.'s *(Stevenson) motion* [read *(Stevenson's) motion*] for summary judgment."/ "In his petition, Wagner misrepresented to the court that federal jurisdiction became apparent during *plaintiff's, Davis,* [read *plaintiff Davis's*] closing argument."/ "We hold that the Appeals Council had the power to reopen the Administrative Law Judge's *(ALJ)* [read *(ALJ's)*] decision . . . ." *Cieutat v. Bowen,* 824 F.2d 348, 350 (5th Cir. 1987).

Here are two other examples of appositives that are needlessly awkward: "Appellee-plaintiffs Donald and Doris Taylor's property was damaged by floods in the summer of 1975." [Read *The property of the appellee-plaintiffs, Donald and Doris Taylor, was damaged* . . . .]/ "The scope of your brief should not be affected *by the scope of your opponent, the appellant's brief* [read *by the scope of that of your opponent, the appellant*]." See POSSESSIVES (G).

B. Punctuation. This problem has been touched on earlier in this entry. Generally, commas (or, less frequently, parentheses) must frame appositives except when the appositive is restrictive. Thus a person might write *my brother Blair* to distinguish Blair from another brother (say, Brad). But if one had only one brother, the reference would be to *my brother, Blair.*

One telltale signal that the appositive is restrictive is the definite article *the* preceding the noun (e.g., *the maxim* nulla poena sine lege *is one generally respected by civilized nations*).

When commas are omitted in nonpossessive phrases, the effect is that of a RUN-ON SENTENCE: "Plaintiffs offered the testimony of Jesus Leon an airport mechanic." (A comma should appear after the name *Jesus Leon.*)

An emphatic appositive is never set off by commas—e.g.: "He *himself* [no commas before or after] testified that the hiring requirement of a college degree was unrelated to performance on the job."

appraisal; appraisement. *W3* treats these as variants; the *OED* definitions suggest some divergence in meaning. Both may mean "the act of appraising, the setting of a price, valuation." But *appraisement,* when connoting the acts of an official appraiser, is the term usually used in reference to valuation of estates; it appears far more frequently in legal than in nonlegal texts.

The more broadly applicable term *appraisal* is also frequent in legal texts, in figurative as well as literal senses. E.g., "The order, in my view, is too strong, too broad, and not fine-tuned enough in its *appraisal* of the statutory language, the legislative history, and the congressional purposes."/ "The court's *appraisal* of appellant's claim of prosecutorial vindictiveness must adhere to the principles established by the Supreme Court in *Blackledge v. Perry.*"

Appraisal commonly appears in the writing of lawyers but is more a part of the everyday language. Ironically, however, Fowler classified it among those words "that have failed to become really familiar and remained in the stage in which the average man cannot say with confidence offhand that they exist" (*MEU1* 14). Since he wrote that, however, *appraisal* has become the standard term in BrE as well as in AmE, largely because of the American influence. *Appraisal* is now preferred in all ordinary contexts, unless the connotative distinction frequently given to *appraisement* is desired.

As with many other pairs of variant word terms, here the vice of INELEGANT VARIATION may tempt the writer. E.g., "The inventory and *appraisement* will then be filed by the attorney in the executor's name with the clerk of court, who will record them. The purpose of the inventory and *appraisal* [read *appraisement*] is to serve as the basis upon which the executor makes his accounts and furnishes information concerning the estate to interested persons; however, the *appraisal* [read *appraisement*] is conclusive upon no one."

appraisal valuation, though fairly common in corporate-law contexts in AmE, is illogical and redundant.

appraise; apprise. The first means "to valuate," the second "to inform." In these sentences *appraise* is used for *apprise:* "Doctors have an obligation to keep their patients *appraised* [read *apprised*] of their condition [*conditions* makes better sense, because not all patients' conditions will be the same]."/ "The objection nowhere *appraised* [read *apprised*] the trial court that Ford Motor was complaining that the inquiry be limited."/ "Cementation were fully *appraised* [read *apprised*] of the requirements and responsibilities of the main contract." *Greater Nottingham Cooperative Society Ltd v. Cementation Piling & Foundations Ltd,* [1989] 1 Q.B. 71, 95, [1988] 2 All Eng. Rep. 971, 981.

A rarer mistake is for *apprise* to be misused for *appraise:* "The discussion thus far should indicate the limited value of superficial observation in *apprising* [read *appraising*] the effects of appellant's mental illness." Here *apprise* is correctly used: "It does not follow that because an officer may lawfully arrest a person only when he is *apprised* of facts sufficient to warrant a belief that the person has committed or is committing a crime, the officer is equally unjustified, absent that kind of evidence, in making any intrusions short of an arrest."

appraisement. See **appraisal.**

appreciate = (1) to fully understand; (2) to increase in value; or (3) to be grateful for. The last meaning began as a SLIPSHOD EXTENSION but is now established.

apprehend; comprehend. *Apprehend* = (1) to seize in the name of the law; to arrest <to apprehend a criminal>; or (2) to lay hold of with the intellect (*OED*). It should not be used as a supposed FORMAL WORD for *believe,* as here: "We *apprehend* [read *believe*] that it is unnecessary at this time to cite authority in support of the right in equity to maintain class suits." *Comprehend* = (1) to understand, grasp with the mind, or (2) to include, comprise, contain.

apprehension does not always mean "fear," its common lay meaning. It frequently takes on nominal senses corresponding to the verb *apprehend*—e.g.: "In the law of torts, one of the necessary ingredients of an assault is *apprehension* by the plaintiff of the imminent contact." Here *apprehension* refers merely to perception, not to fear or anxiety. See **apprehend.**

apprise; apprize. See **appraise.**

appro is an abbreviated form of *approval,* in phrases such as *goods on appro.* It is appropriate for telegrams but not for legal prose.

approbate and reprobate (= to accept and reject), used in the context that one may not accept the benefits of a legal document while challenging some of its conditions, is an unjustified LATINISM that Leff aptly calls "insufferably fancy." Arthur A. Leff, *The Leff Dictionary of Law,* 94 Yale L.J. 1855, 2046 (1985). The simpler words used in the definition are preferable.

approbation; approval; approvement. There is no generally accepted distinction between the first two words, apart from the observation that the first is more unusual and dignified. Follett suggests that we restrict *approbation* to a favorable response on a particular occasion and use *approval* for a general favorable attitude. Wilson Follett, *Modern American Usage* 72 (1966). E.g., "Again expressing our *approbation* of this doctrine, we conclude that the proof tendered should have been admitted." Follett's distinction would suggest that *approval* be used here: "This extreme view has never met the *approbation* [read *approval*] of the bar, either in England or in America, and is repudiated by the great majority of reputable practitioners." See **disapprobation.**

Rarely does *approbate* justifiably supersede *approve*—e.g.: "It must follow that all arranged or Sikh marriages are a priori void, unless the parties knew each other beforehand or *approbated* [read *approved*] the marriage afterwards." (Eng.) For a legal nuance of the verb *approbate,* see **approbate and reprobate.**

Approvement is an old term with two quite distinct meanings at common law: (1) "the practice of criminal prosecution by which a person accused of treason or felony was permitted to exonerate himself by accusing others and escaping prosecution himself" (*Black's*); and (2) "the conversion to his own profit, by the lord of the manor, of waste or common land by enclosure and appropriation" (*OED*).

approbatory; approbative. *Approbatory* is the standard form.

appropriable is the adjective corresponding to *appropriate,* v.t.—not *appropriatable.* E.g., "[T]he Preissers have argued lack of standing on the part of the objectors and have contended that they are entitled to decrees, irrespective of the question of availability of *appropriatable* [read *appropriable*] water." *In re Application for Water Rights of Preisser,* 545 P.2d 711, 712 (Colo. 1976) (en banc). See -ATABLE.

appropriate, v.t.; **expropriate.** The verb *appropriate* may mean (1) "to give to a particular person or organization for a specific purpose" <government-appropriated moneys>; or (2) "to take from a particular person or organization for a specific purpose." The first sense is the more usual in AmE (and better known to the nonlawyer), perhaps because it is better to give than to receive. Following are examples of sense (2), the lawyer's sense: "Under this authorization she withdrew from the bank various sums of money, a considerable amount of which she evidently *appropriated* to her own use without any accounting to him."/ "The only matter that has been urged before us is whether defendant may lawfully be restrained from *appropriating* news taken from bulletins issued by complainant, for the purpose of selling it to defendant's client."

Expropriate means (1) "to exercise eminent domain over; to take, by legal action, private land for public use"; or (2) "to transfer title to another's property to oneself." See **misappropriate.**

In sense (2), *appropriate* is distinguished from *expropriate* because a private or semipublic entity does the former, whereas a public governmental entity does the latter. The difference between the terms is carefully observed by the courts. E.g., "[I]t makes no difference in determining the amount to be awarded that the property was *appropriated* and not formally *expropriated.*" *Gray v. State Through Dep't of Highways,* 202 So. 2d 24, 30 (La. 1967).

appropriation = (1) the exercise of control over property; (2) the bringing about of a transfer of title or of a nonpossessory interest in the property; (3) a public body's act of voting a sum of money for any of various public purposes; or (4) the sum of money so voted.

In the following passage, a court has overstated the traditional significance of the term (sense 1): "Implicit in the meaning of the word *appropriation,* when it comes to competing and equal possessory interests in property, is that the accused person must have exercised 'unauthorized' control over the property." *Freeman v. State,* 707 S.W.2d 597, 605 (Tex. Crim. App. 1986). See **misappropriate.**

approval. See **approbation.**

approve. A. *Approve (of).* *Approve* may be either transitive or intransitive, but in legal usage is usually the former (i.e., it usually takes no *of*). "In our system evidentiary rulings provide the context in which the judicial process of inclusion and exclusion *approves* some conduct as comporting with constitutional guarantees and *disapproves* other actions by state agents."

B. And *endorse.* The two should be distinguished. To *approve,* apart from the legal sense of giving official sanction, is to consider right or to have a favorable attitude toward. The verb conveys an attitude or thought. To *endorse* is to support actively and explicitly. The word connotes action as well as attitude.

approvement. See **approbation.**

approvingly cited is awkward for *cited with approval.* "Judge Rubin found that neither of two kinds of contracts met the *Howey* test for an investment contract, a finding *approvingly cited* [read *cited with approval*] in *Moody v. Bache & Co.*" Other awkward variations have appeared: "This suggestion, as illustrated by the *Rogers* decision, was *approvingly used* [omit *approvingly*] in the Commerce Clearing House Rewrite Bulletin of June 8, 1983." The implication here is that, by *using* a suggested legal theory, the user implicitly *approves* that theory.

approximate; approximal; proximate. *Approximate* = (1) closely resembling; (2) nearly accurate; or (3) close together. *Approximal* = contiguous. *Proximate* = (1) very near; or (2) directly related. See **proximate.**

approximately is almost never as good as about—e.g.: "These prior costs will be *approximately* [read *about*] $9,600." See **about.**

approximately about is a REDUNDANCY. See **about.**

à prendre. See **profits à prendre.**

a priori; a posteriori. These terms are best left to philosophical contexts. Very simply, *a priori,* the more common term, means "deductively; reasoning from the general to the particular," and *a posteriori* means "inductively; reasoning from the particular to the general, or from known effects to their inferred causes." Here *a priori* is used correctly, although the writer might better have written *deductive:* "*Witherspoon's* teaching is not limited to that particular inference; it counsels against any *a priori* judicial assumptions about the views of veniremen."

A priori becomes vague and confusing when it is used to mean "presumably" or "without detailed consideration," as here: "But we cannot say, *a priori,* without evidence, that there is not a sufficient rational distinction between such restaurants and other commercial establishments to warrant a study." This usage is a SLIPSHOD EXTENSION.

Nonlawyers frequently misuse *a priori* for *prima facie.*

apropos (of). The two variations of this phrase are generally inappropriate in legal writing in the place of some English equivalent; they may prove serviceable in informal letters. *Apropos of* (suggested by the French phrase, *à propos de*) is well established in English and is correct. Yet *apropos* may be used as a preposition to mean "concerning, apropos of." Hence there is generally no reason to include *of.* The preposition *to* is always incorrect with *apropos.*

apt; apposite. Both words mean "fit; suitable"; *apposite,* common in legal writing, is a FORMAL WORD.

Apt for *likely* is a loose usage. As Fowler explains, however, "in British usage *apt* always implies a general tendency; for a probability arising from particular circumstances, *likely* is the word" (*MEU2* 34).

The same distinction applies in the best American usage. In the following sentences, *apt* is correctly used of general or habitual tendencies, rather than a likelihood in a particular instance—e.g.: "The restaurant is extremely popular and generally *apt* to be crowded."/ "Psychiatrists are more *apt* to see people face to face, sitting up and once a week rather than the traditional five times." (Note the MISPLACED MODIFIER and the lack of PARALLELISM in the final clause. A less awkward structure, and one easier to take in at a first reading, would be: "Psychiatrists are more *apt* to see people face to face, to see them sitting up, and to see them once rather than five times a week.")

For a similarly problematic word, see **liable.**

a quo; a qua. *A quo* = from which. A court *a quo* is a court from which a case has been removed or appealed. E.g., "If the court *a quo* has no jurisdiction, then a court *ad quem* gains none by appeal . . . ." Eugene A. Jones, *Manual of Equity Pleading and Practice* 12 n.24 (1916).

A qua was originally a solecism for *a quo.* It has gained some degree of currency in legal prose, although *a quo* remains the preferred term. Because *a quo,* the correct form, has persisted alongside the bastardized version, it is not overreaching to say that we should stick with what is correct. It is the only form given, for example, by Leff in his *Dictionary of Law,* 94 Yale L.J. 1855, 2050 (1985). "On March 30, 1984 the district court *a qua* [read *a quo*] stayed the scheduled execution, dismissed with prejudice the foregoing enumerated claims 2, 4, and 5 and docketed an evidentiary hearing on claims 1 and 3."/ "The sole question posed on appeal is whether the federal court *a qua* [read *a quo*] had personal jurisdiction over the nonresident defendant." Cf. **terminus a quo.**

arbiter. See **arbitrator.**

arbitrable (= subject to or appropriate for arbitration) is the correct form, not *arbitratable.* Hence the corresponding noun is *arbitrability*—e.g.: "The appeals-court panel said, 'Since RICO claims are *arbitratable* [read *arbitrable*], we see no reason here for limiting *arbitratability* [read *arbitrability*] . . . .'" Wall St. J., 31 Jan. 1991, at B4. See -ATABLE.

arbitrage; arbitration. For the sense of *arbitration,* see the entry under that word. *Arbitrage* = the simultaneous buying and selling of currencies or securities at different values in order to profit by price discrepancies.

arbitrage(u)r. Though English-language dictionaries generally put their entries under the Frenchified *arbitrageur,* most journalists and courts now seem to prefer the naturalized form, *arbitrager*—e.g.: "The profit to the *arbitragers* was the difference between the price paid by them for the preferred [stock] and the amount received by them upon the sale of the common [stock]." *Austrian v. Williams,* 103 F. Supp. 64, 92–93 (S.D.N.Y. 1952)./ "The *arbitragers* who were indicted yesterday were D. Ronald Yogada . . . ." Kurt Eichenwald, *Two Firms Are Charged as Insiders,* N.Y. Times, 3 Nov. 1988, at 29./ "Robert Freeman, 46, of Goldman, Sachs & Co., was one of the country's most powerful takeover-stock speculators, or *arbitragers* . . . ." Steve Swartz & James B. Stewart, *Kidder's Mr. Wigton, Charged as "Insider," Ends His Long Ordeal,* Wall St. J., 21 Aug. 1989, at 1.

arbitral. A. And *arbitrary.* *Arbitral* = relating to arbiters or arbitration; *arbitrary* usually may be equated with "capricious, randomly chosen." (See **arbitrary.**) It also has a more and more disused legal meaning: determinable by the decision of a judge or tribunal rather than defined by statute. This, take note, was the *original* meaning of *arbitrary.* Could it be that its other, more modern meanings have grown out of this first one?

Arbitral may correspond to either *arbitrator* or *arbiter.* In legal language, it is almost invariably the adjectival form of *arbitrator,* q.v. <arbitral discretion>. It also sometimes corresponds to the noun *arbitration,* as in the phrase *arbitral tribunal.* See *Graphic Communications Union v. Chicago Tribune Co.,* 779 F.2d 13, 15 (7th Cir. 1985).

B. And *arbitrational; arbitrative.* Both *arbitrational* and *arbitrative* are NEEDLESS VARIANTS of *arbitral.* E.g., "The witness privilege applies in any judicial, official, investigatory, legislative, or *arbitrational* [read *arbitral*] proceeding . . . ." Phillip J. Kolczynski, *The Criminal Liability of Aviators,* 51 J. Air L. & Com. 1, 42 (1985)./ "[Every

Kansas corporation can sue and be sued] in all courts and participate . . . in any judicial, administrative, *arbitrative* [read *arbitral*] or other proceeding, in its corporate name . . . ." Kan. Stat. Ann. § 17-6102(2) (1992).

arbitrament; arbitrement. The first spelling is standard for this word, meaning (1) "the power to decide for others," or (2) "a decision or sentence." When first imported into English from French in the late 16th century, the word was spelled with *-e-* in the penultimate syllable. Thereafter the spelling was Latinized to *arbitrament,* which the *OED* notes has been the accepted spelling since about 1830. Following is an illustration of sense (1): "The court may not leave both the questions of law and of fact to the *arbitrament* of the jury."

In sense (2), the word was once common in arbitration contexts; it referred to the arbitrators' decision or award. This particular use is labeled obsolete in Katharine Seide, *A Dictionary of Arbitration* 24 (1970).

arbitrary; unreasonable. These words are extremely complex in law, their senses not readily encapsulated; but their most elemental senses are worth noting. *Arbitrary* = with no purpose or objective. (See **arbitral (A).**) *Unreasonable* = with a purpose that is excessively imposed.

arbitrate = (1) (of one or more parties) to settle by, or submit to, arbitration; or (2) (of an arbitral tribunal) to decide a dispute being arbitrated. Though surprisingly common, references to courts "arbitrating" disputes reflect poor usage—e.g.: "The plaintiff's lawyers would simply tell the plaintiff what he would net if he instructed them to accept the offer; if the plaintiff thought the lawyers were taking too much, he could ask the court to *arbitrate* [read *decide*] the dispute . . . ." *Chesny v. Marek,* 720 F.2d 474, 478 (7th Cir. 1983).

arbitration. **A. And *mediation*.** Both terms refer to methods of dispute resolution involving a neutral third party. The results of *arbitration* are binding—that is, the parties to the arbitrator's decision are bound by it. In *mediation,* to the contrary, the mediator merely tries to help two disputing parties reach a mutually agreeable solution; the parties are not, however, bound by a mediator's decisions. See **mediation.**

B. "Trying" an Arbitration. To say that an arbitration is *tried* is to betray an ignorance of idiom, as well as the process involved, by treating it as if it were litigation in a public tribunal. And, in any event, *arbitration* refers to a process: a *case* may be tried (or arbitrated), but a so-called litigation cannot be tried.

The standard idiom would be to say that an arbitration is *heard* or *conducted.* But legal writers increasingly get it wrong—e.g.: "[T]his would be prejudicial to the Hideca-Nereus arbitration which, it was claimed by Hideca, should logically be *tried* [read *heard*] first." *Compania Espanola de Petroleos, S.A. v. Nereus Shipping, S.A.,* 527 F.2d 966, 971 (2d Cir. 1975)./ "[T]he court vacated the arbitration award since the arbitration had been *tried* [read *conducted*] on a totally different theory than the one on which arbitration had been ordered." *Metropolitan Property & Liab. Ins. Co. v. Streets,* 856 F.2d 526, 529 (3d Cir. 1988).

arbitrator; arbiter. An *arbitrator* is a person chosen to settle differences between two parties embroiled in a controversy. *Arbiter,* by contrast, is more general, meaning "anyone with power to decide disputes, as a judge." E.g., "As long as the pleas of both employer and employee are lawful, the courts have not been constituted *arbiters* of the fairness, justice, or wisdom of the terms demanded by either the employer or the employee."

The terms do, however, overlap considerably, and they cause confusion on both sides of the Atlantic. Yet when referring to legal arbitration, one should term the resolver of disputes the *arbitrator.* "To order arbitration is not to approve in advance of all or everything that the *arbiter* [read *arbitrator*] does." (Scots law presents an exception: one appoints an *arbiter* to hold an arbitration.)

Leff rightly rejects a distinction of a different nature: "Sometimes a distinction is sought to be made between an *arbiter,* who decides according to rules, and an *arbitrator,* who is free to settle matters in his own sound discretion. But the distinction doesn't hold; *arbiters* often have huge moments of discretionary power, and more important, most *arbitrators* today proceed according to elaborate rules, both procedural and substantive." Arthur A. Leff, *The Leff Dictionary of Law,* 94 Yale L.J. 1855, 2050 (1985). That distinction, in fact, goes back to Roman law, but it has no validity today.

The phrase is always *final* or *ultimate arbiter,* not *arbitrator.* E.g., "The judicial system is regarded as the *ultimate arbitrator* [read *ultimate arbiter*] of disputes."/ "In an earlier and ruder age the appeal was to arms, and force was the final *arbiter.*"

Arbitor is a misspelling—e.g.: "As the chief *arbitor* [read *arbiter*] in disputes between producers and the screenwriters' and directors' guilds, it is Dern's role to settle disputes ranging from payment schedules and credits to working conditions." Black, *Dixon Q. Dern, Esq.: Hollywood Law,* M Mag., May 1989, at 48, 53. See **arbitral.**

arbitrement. See **arbitrament.**

archaism. See **anachronism.**

ARCHAISMS, outmoded words or expressions that are not yet obsolete, abound in the language of the law. This work attempts to treat them individually under specific entries. A great many are collected under the entries FORBIDDEN WORDS, LAWYERISMS & LATINISMS.

Among the archaisms especially to be avoided are the following:

alack	haply	to wit
anent	howbeit	verily
anon	maugre	whilom
belike	methinks	withal
divers	perchance	wot
fain	shew (for *show*)	wroth

One writer aptly says of a similar list: "These are easily avoided by anyone of the least literary sensibility . . . ." Herbert Read, *English Prose Style* 9 (1952). See **nay.**

archetype; prototype. These words are close in meaning, but their DIFFERENTIATION should be encouraged. As commonly used, *archetype* means "a standard or typical example," whereas *prototype* means "the original type that has served as a model for successors." In the sentence following, *prototype* is misused for *archetype:* "The *prototype* [read *archetype*] of a personal benefit requiring heightened judicial scrutiny is cash flowing directly to the union officer from the union treasury."

archetypic; archetypical; prototypic; prototypical. Inconsistently enough, the preferred adjectival forms are *archetypal* and *prototypical.*

architectural; architectonic. *Architectural* is usually the literal, and *architectonic* the figurative, term. Whereas *architectural* relates to the design of physical structures, *architectonic* relates to rational organization or to the abstract structure of a thing or idea. Although *architectonic* is sometimes used like *architectural,* it should be confined to figurative or abstract senses to make the DIFFERENTIATION complete.

Arden, Enoch. See **Enoch Arden law.**

ARGOT. See JARGON.

arguendo. In AmE, *arguendo* is unnecessary in place of *for the sake of argument.* Although brevity would commend it, its obscurity to nonlawyers is a distinct liability. E.g., "Assuming *arguendo* that her answers establish that she actually attempted to warn appellant, the court of appeals erred in inferring that her having done so established that she was acting as a state agent." *Arguendo* is one of those LATINISMS that neophyte lawyers often adopt as pet words to advertise their lawyerliness.

In BrE, the word means something else entirely: "during the course of argument." E.g., "'This air is too pure for a slave to breathe in,' was already ancient when Serjeant Davy uttered it *arguendo* in 1772 . . . ." R.E. Megarry, *A Second Miscellany-at-Law* 198 (1973).

argufy = to dispute, wrangle. Krapp calls this term "illiterate or, in cultivated speech, a humorous and contemptuous form of *argue.*" G.P. Krapp, *A Comprehensive Guide to Good English* 50 (1927). Lawyers could use a good sarcastic term for *argue,* and *argufy* fills the bill. Cf. **speechify.**

argument(ation). *Argumentation* refers to the act or process of arguing, or the art of persuading. *Argument* should be reserved for all other contexts.

argument(at)ive. The longer form is preferred as an adjectival form of *argumentation.*

ARGUMENT, MODES OF. The Romans categorized and gave names to several different modes of argument, all of which (both names and modes) are still used today. Although it might be somewhat precious to use some of the more recondite Latin phrases in ordinary contexts (e.g., *argumentum ad crumenam*), they are at least as useful as most things that appear in legal footnotes. Following are some of these phrases, each of which is preceded by *argumentum:*

ab auctoritate	=	from authority (of a statute or case)
ab impossibili	=	from impossibility
ab inconvenienti	=	from inconvenience
a contrario	=	for contrary treatment
ad baculum	=	dependent on physical force to back it up
ad captandum	=	appealing to the emotions of a crowd
ad crumenam	=	appealing to the purse or self-interest
ad hominem	=	based on disparagement or praise of another in a way that obscures the real issue

ad ignorantiam = based on an adversary's ignorance
ad invidium = appealing to hatred or prejudice
ad misericordiam = appealing to pity
ad populum = appealing to the crowd
ad rem = on the point at issue (what every good judge likes to hear)
ad verecundiam = appealing to one's modesty
a fortiori = from the stronger case
a simili = by analogy or similarity; from a like case
ex silentio = out of silence (based on the absence of solid evidence)

arise. See **accrue (B).**

arm's-length; arms-length. In phrases such as *arm's-length transaction,* the correct form is to make *arm* possessive; the phrase is usually and best hyphenated when it appears before the noun it modifies—e.g.: "The stock was sold in an *arm's-length* transaction."/ "The renewal did not result from independent, *arms-length* [read *arm's-length*] negotiations." See PHRASAL ADJECTIVES (A).

An inferior method of signaling the adjectival quality of the phrase is to place quotation marks around it (by referring, for example, to *an "arm's length" position.*) This method, to be avoided, appears repeatedly in Geoffrey Hazard, *Triangular Lawyer Relationships,* 1 Geo. J. Legal Ethics 15, 33–34 (1987).

In the phrase *at arm's length* (= not having a confidential relationship), the second two words are not hyphenated.

around is informal for *about* or *approximately,* and should be avoided in favor of either of those substitutes.

around; round. In AmE *around* is preferred where in BrE *round* is.

arraignment; indictment. The meanings of these terms vary, depending on the jurisdiction. An *indictment* is the usual instrument charging a person with a felony. It also refers, loosely, to the act of charging someone with a crime. An *arraignment,* within the federal system of the U.S., is the "reading [of] the indictment or information to the defendant or stating to him the substance of the charge and calling on him to plead thereto." Fed. R. Crim. P. 10. See **indictment.**

arrant; errant. The original word was *errant,* which means "traveling, wandering" <knight errant>. By extension it has come to mean "straying out of bounds" and "erring, fallible." (See **errant.**) *Arrant* began as an alteration of *errant,* and originally had the same sense ("wandering"), but now usually appears as a term of contempt in the phrase *arrant knave.* It means "utter; extreme" or "egregious; outstandingly bad."

array; arrayal; arrayment. The three terms differ. *Array* is the most common, meaning (1) "order or arrangement"; (2) "venire; a panel of potential jurors, or a list of impaneled jurors" <after challenges for cause to the first array of jurors in the box>; (3) "clothing"; (4) "militia"; (5) "a large number" <an array of setbacks>; or (6) "a series of statistics or a group of elements." The specific meaning is usually apparent from the context. (See CHAMELEON-HUED WORDS.) By the definition under sense (2), *array* may refer either to a roster of jurors or to the body of jurors collectively.

Arrayal = the act of arraying or ordering. *Arrayment* shares this meaning, but more commonly means "clothing, attire." *Arrayment* developed into another form that is now more generally used in this archaic and learned sense, *raiment.*

Array as a verb has the special legal senses (1) "to impanel a jury for trial" <the jurors have been arrayed on the panel>; or (2) "to call out the names of the jurors one by one" <the defense lawyers scrutinized the jurors as they were arrayed>.

arrear(s); arrearage(s). The most common use of either of the terms is the phrase *in arrear(s)* (= behind in the discharge of a debt or other obligation). Current AmE idiom calls predominantly for *in arrears,* whereas a common BrE and older AmE idiom is *in arrear. In arrearages* is obsolete.

Arrearage, a LEGALISM, legitimately remains only in the sense "the condition of being in arrears." In all other meanings *arrears* serves: (1) "unfinished duties" <arrears of work that have accumulated>; and (2) "unpaid or overdue debts" <the creditor has reached an agreement with the debtor on settling the arrears>. E.g., "Earned income credits constitute 'refunds of federal taxes paid' and 'overpayment to be refunded' subject to withholding to satisfy child-support *arrears.*"

Yet legal writers frequently use *arrearage* (not even listed in the *COD*) where *arrears* would be preferable. E.g., "In *Fanchier v. Gammill,* a Nevada court had awarded a wife alimony that, because of *arrearages* [read *arrears*], she was forced to reduce to a judgment in Mississippi."

In the singular, *arrearage* is common enough in legal texts to be perhaps forgivable, *arrear* being an unnatural-sounding singular. E.g., "This order recites findings that appellant paid $1000 of the $4000 *arrearage* found to exist by the 1982 order, leaving an *arrearage* of $3000 denominated in the order as 'amended *arrearage.*'" The *OED* records an incorrect American use of *arrears* as a singular: "They constitute a large *arrears* [read *arrear* or *arrearage*], which should be dealt with speedily."

arrestable. So spelled. See -ABLE (A).

arrestee. See -EE.

arrester; arrestor. The former is the preferred spelling.

arrivee. See -EE.

arrogate, a transitive verb, should not be used reflexively, as here: "Should a justice court attempt to grant a divorce, its decision would be invalid as if the reader were to *arrogate himself to do so* [read *to arrogate to himself this power* or *to appoint himself to do so*]." The following sentence illustrates the correct idiom: "John had allowed sheriffs to *arrogate* to themselves once more the power of hearing pleas of the Crown . . . ." H.G. Hanbury, *English Courts of Law* 51 (2d ed. 1953). See **abrogate.**

arse; ass. *Arse* is the spelling (in the anatomical sense, not in horse-sense) in formal English.

arsen(i)ous. The spelling with the *-i-* is standard, the other form being a NEEDLESS VARIANT. *Arsenious* /ahr-**sen**-ee-əs/ (= of or pertaining to arsenic) should not be confused as being an adjectival form of *arson.* See **arsonable.**

arson; houseburning. *Arson* = (1) *at common law,* the malicious burning of someone else's dwelling house; or (2) *under any of various statutes,* the malicious burning of someone else's or one's own dwelling house or of anyone's commercial or industrial property.

The word *houseburning* denotes the common-law misdemeanor of intentionally burning one's own house that is within the city limits or that is close enough to other houses that they might be in danger of catching fire. The term applies only when no one else is actually damaged by the fire.

arsonable; arsonous. Both terms are omitted from most English-language dictionaries, including the *OED, W2, W3,* and *AHD.* But they are serviceable. *Arsonable* = (of property) of such a nature as to give rise to a charge of arson if maliciously burned. E.g., "It is sometimes said that the explanation of this rule is that a chattel is (with certain exceptions) *non-arsonable* property, while a building is *arsonable,* and it is therefore not possible to transfer the malice between the two legal species of property." Glanville Williams, *Criminal Law* 130 (2d ed. 1961).

Arsonous = of or relating to arson. E.g., "After they poured ten gallons of gasoline about the inside of the home in preparation for their *arsonous* act, an unexpected explosion occurred which trapped Frank Owen in the home and resulted in his death." *Smith v. Moran,* 209 N.E.2d 18, 19 (Ill. App. Ct. 1965)./ "[T]he relatively few firebugs could not buy out the orphans for an amount remotely near the costs of their *arsonous* conduct." Mayer G. Freed & Daniel D. Polsby, *Just Cause for Termination Rules and Economic Efficiency,* 38 Emory L.J. 1097, 1112 (1989)./ "[S]tatement . . . not hearsay when offered as false exculpatory statement intended to conceal *arsonous* purpose for being in alley." Roger C. Park, *"I Didn't Tell Them Anything About You": Implied Assertions as Hearsay Under the Federal Rules of Evidence,* 74 Minn. L. Rev. 783, 816 n.180 (1990).

artefact. See **artifact.**

artful pleading. See **well-pleaded complaint.**

article, v.t., means "to bind by articles," and is conjugated *articled, articling.* An *articled clerk* (who is said to "take articles"), for instance, was formerly the term for an apprentice bound to serve in a solicitor's office in return for learning the trade. The verb is invariably used in reference to apprenticeships. E.g., "[Among the necessary qualifications for becoming a solicitor is an apprenticeship] or service under articles of clerkship to a practising solicitor for a period varying from two and a half to five years, according to the previous attainments of the clerk. This service is exclusive; and, unlike the Bar student, the *articled clerk* cannot devote any part of his attention to matters other than the study and practice of the law." Edward Jenks, *The Book of English Law* 70 (P.B. Fairest ed., 6th ed. 1967).

ARTICLES. A. Omitted Before Party Denominations. It is a convention in legal writing to omit both definite and indefinite articles before words such as *plaintiff, defendant, petitioner, respondent, appellant,* and *appellee.* It is almost as if these designations in legal writing become names, or proper nouns, that denote the person or persons referred to. The convention is a useful one because cutting even such slight words can lead to leaner, more readable sentences. Perhaps the most important aspect of one's preference, though, is to be consistent within a piece of writing. The convention of omitting articles should not spread beyond these few standard party designations, for beyond these standard party-names the convention may seem unidiomatic. E.g., "If *decedent* [read *the decedent*] disposes of his estate by will, he devises property and the takers are devisees, even though the subject is personal property."/ "*Intervenors*' [read *The intervenors*'] opposition to plaintiff's motion has two bases." (See the examples under (B) of this entry in which *taxpayer* appears without an article.)

To some, the practice of omitting these articles may seem symptomatic of LEGALESE. They are entitled to their point of view. The rest of us can enjoy not having to write, "The plaintiff, now *the appellant,* sued *the defendant,* now *the appellee.*" (In fairness, though, "*Plaintiff,* now *appellant,* sued *defendant,* now *appellee*" is not much better reading.)

B. Wrongly Omitted. There is a contagious tendency in legal writing to omit articles before nouns, perhaps on the analogy of the special legal convention for party-names (see A). E.g., "*Distinction* [read *A distinction*] must be recognized between the review proceeding here involved and those which . . . are allowed only . . . through a 'civil action commenced . . . in the district court.'" *White v. U.S.,* 342 F.2d 481, 484 (8th Cir. 1965). In our quest for concision through CUTTING OUT THE CHAFF, however, our writing should not become so abbreviated that we omit necessary articles; articles are more than mere chaff: they are signposts for the reader, who may become temporarily lost without them. There is a tendency, for example, in tax cases, to refer to *taxpayer* without an article, as if it were a proper name. E.g., "Federal law also required that *taxpayer* [read *the taxpayer*] make contributions under the Federal Insurance Contributions Act."/ "*Taxpayers*' [read *The taxpayers*'] request for compensatory and punitive damages is barred by the doctrine of sovereign immunity." These usages offend a sensitive ear, whether it is the mind's ear or one's actual ear.

Here are a few similar examples: "In approaching *solution* [read *a solution*] to this problem, we must look beyond the immediate consequences of the decision of this case."/ "The award as remitted by *trial judge* [read *the trial judge*] was not so gross as to be contrary to right reason."/ "If a sale is necessary, the representative can sue to set aside a fraudulent conveyance made by decedent during *lifetime* [read *his lifetime*]." For exceptions to the general rule, see (A) above.

C. Wrongly Inserted. Writers sometimes unidiomatically insert articles where they have no business; this phenomenon is inexplicable, except insofar as we can identify the writer's failure to distinguish between COUNT NOUNS AND MASS NOUNS. E.g., "The nature of the agency relationship is such that the principal would be subject to *a* vicarious liability [omit *a*] as a defendant to another who may have been injured by the agent's negligence."/ "The Commission has taken the position that it may by its order allow *an* overproduction [omit *an*] for a period of time to meet the market demand."

D. Repeated. When two or more nouns are connected by a conjunction, it is usually best to repeat the article before each noun. When the article is not repeated, the sense conveyed is that the nouns are identical or synonymous. "The committee elected a secretary and treasurer" (one person); "The committee elected a secretary and a treasurer" (two persons).

The article should not be repeated in a second, parallel adjectival phrase. "Appellant testified and the United States admitted that P.A.L. was a validly formed and *an* existing corporation [omit *an*]."

E. Indefinite. See **a.**

articulable, not *articulatable,* is the correct form—e.g.: "The government argues that the stop of the car was either part of an 'extended border search' or a '*Terry* stop' based on *articulatable* [read *articulable*] suspicion." *U.S. v. Weston,* 519 F. Supp. 565, 569 (W.D.N.Y. 1981). See -ATABLE.

artifact; artefact. The former spelling is standard in AmE, the latter in BrE.

artifice is sometimes misspelled *artiface,* as in "a scheme and *artiface* [read *artifice*] to defraud." *U.S. v. Edwards,* 716 F.2d 822, 823 (11th Cir. 1983).

artificial person. See **juristic person.**

artisan; artizan. The former spelling is standard.

as. A. Causal words: *as; because; since; for.* In the causal sense *as* should generally be avoided, because (not *as!*) it may be misunderstood as having its more usual meaning "while," especially when it is placed anywhere but at the beginning of the sentence. Fowler states: "To causal or explanatory *as*-clauses, if they are placed before the main sentence . . . there is no objection." E.g., "But *as* the case has been discussed here and below without much regard to the pleadings, we proceed to consider the other grounds upon which it has been thought that a recovery could be maintained." *Robins Dry Dock & Repair Co. v. Flint,* 275 U.S. 303, 308 (1927) (per Holmes, J.)/ "*As* I read the court's opinion to be entirely consistent with the basic principles which I believe control this case, I join in it." The reverse order is infelicitous, however, unless the reader necessarily knows what is to be introduced by the *as*-clause: "We do not explore the problem further, *as* [read *since*] the issue of damages was not litigated below."

The causal *as* becomes troublesome even at the beginning of a sentence when a temporal *as* appears in the same sentence. "*As* Nelda returned to her occupation *as* soon *as* appellant drove her from Newark to New York, and *as* he knew full well that she would do this, one might suppose that the violation of the Mann Act was clearly established." The first and last occurrences of *as* in that sentence are causal, the second and third temporal; the causal words should be changed to *since* or *because.*

Because of the syntactic restrictions on *as,* we are left with three general-purpose causal conjunctions. *Because* is the strongest and most logically oriented of these. *Since* is less demonstratively causal and frequently has temporal connotations. But using *since* without reference to time is not, despite the popular canard, incorrect. (See SUPERSTITIONS (G).) *For* is the most subjective of the three, and the least used. If *because* points out a direct cause-effect relationship, *for* signals a less direct relationship, adding independent explanation or substantiation. Moreover, *for* is a coordinating conjunction, and not, like *because* and *since,* a subordinating conjunction; hence it can properly begin sentences.

B. In Anticipatory Reference. When coupled with *do*-words, *as* can cause mischief of the kind outlined under ANTICIPATORY REFERENCE (A). E.g., "Texas, *as do* [read *like*] most jurisdictions, recognizes three general theories of recovery in products liability." See **like (C).**

C. And *like*. See **like** & HYPERCORRECTION (E).

as against means "toward; with respect to; in regard to," but with the implication of adversity or conflict—e.g.: "Every admission is deemed to be a relevant fact *as against* the person by or on whose behalf it is made." (Eng.)/ "[I]f a stick of timber comes ashore on a man's land, he thereby acquires a 'right of possession' *as against* an actual finder who enters for the purpose of removing it." Oliver W. Holmes, *The Common Law* 176 (1881; repr. 1963).

But the phrase is sometimes misused for *against:* "Defendant was allowed, however, to testify *as against* [read *against*] the plaintiff [if the defendant gave adverse testimony]."/ "In a trial for felony the prisoner can make no admissions so as to dispense with proof, though a confession may be proved *as against* [read *against*] him." (Eng.)

Because *as against* is an idiom with a fairly set meaning in English, it should not be used in unfamiliar ways, such as in an ellipsis of *as being against:* "The policy is void *as against public policy* [read *as being against public policy*] because it opens a wide door by which a constant temptation is created to commit for profit the most atrocious of crimes."

as and when. This is a redundant expression; either *as* or *when* will suffice. "The bill provides that the balances shall be met by the Exchequer *as and when* [read *as*] they mature for payment." (Eng.—ex. fr. V. H. Collins, *Right Word, Wrong Word* 19 (1956)).

The variant *when and as* is equally bad: "A court of equity acts *only when and as* [read *only when*] conscience commands."

as . . . as. A. And *so . . . as*. In positive statements, the *as . . . as* construction is preferred. "If the guard had thrown [the packaged explosive] down knowingly and willfully, he would not have threatened the plaintiff's safety, *so far as* [read *as far as*] appearances could warn him." *Palsgraf v. Long Island R.R.,* 162 N.E. 99, 101 (N.Y. 1928) (per Cardozo, J.)/ "*So long as* [read *As long as*] the courts fail to come to grips with that fact, *so long as* [read *as long as*] they persist in assuming that every juror has a precise and firmly held position, the process of jury selection will be unpredictable, arbitrary, and ultimately lawless."

Twenty years ago it was commonly believed that *so . . . as* is preferable to *as . . . as* in negative statements such as, "The limitations period was *not so* long *as* I had thought." But *as . . . as* generally serves equally well in such negative statements. Following is a construction in which *not so . . . as* does not read as well as *not as . . . as:* "Back at Bennie's Corners, affairs were not going so happily as they were at McGill University." On first reading this sentence, the reader may be temporarily misled into thinking that *so* means "very," in its colloquial sense, as it would if the sentence ended after *happily.* See **as long as; equally as (B)** & **so as.**

B. Repetition of Verb After. Often, when the second *as* in this construction is far removed from the first *as,* the verb is repeated for clarity: "Perhaps no area of corporate law is *as* beset with conflicting judicial opinions, variations among statutes, and confusion and uncertainty concerning the likely outcome of litigation *as is* the duty of loyalty."

as at (= as of) is characteristic chiefly of BrE and of financial contexts in AmE. E.g., "This book reflects the law *as at* August 1986." Stanley Berwin, *The Economist Pocket Lawyer* i (1986)./ "The common law took the coldly logical view that bastardy was judged *as at* the date of birth and was indelible . . . ." J.H. Baker, *An Introduction to English Legal History* 558 (3d ed. 1990).

as a whole. See **in whole.**

as between (= in a comparison of [usu. two things]) is much more common in legal than in nonlegal writing. In fact, most general English-language dictionaries neglect the phrase. E.g., "The controversy as to the type of law, whether custom or common law or tradition, on the one hand, or legislation, on the other, the controversy as to the relation of law to morals, the discussion *as between* adjudication and administration, *as between* law and equity, *as between* strict and free procedure, all run back to this problem of stability and change." Roscoe Pound, *The Formative Era of American Law* 18 (1938)./ "A judgment gives rights and obligations to litigants *as between* themselves." 1 E.W. Chance, *Principles of Mercantile Law* 10 (P.W. French ed., 13th ed. 1950)./ "This does not mean that in the English courts of the thirteenth century justice was no more than 'justice *as between* man and man.'" Carleton K. Allen, *Law in the Making* 401 (7th ed. 1964).

ascendant. A. Spelling. Both as a noun and as an adjective, the spelling *ascendant* is preferred over *ascendent.*

B. And *ancestor; collateral; descendant.* In the language of decedents' estates, both *ascendant* and *ancestor* mean "a person related to an intestate or to one who claims an intestate share in the descending lineal line (e.g., parents and grandparents)." *Ancestor* is the more universally comprehensible word but has two severe disadvantages: first, it is less likely to be understood as referring to a parent; second, it lacks the *-ant* suffix, which makes *ascendant* parallel with *descendant.* See **ancestor.**

Descendant denotes one who is descended from an ancestor—i.e., offspring in any degree, near or remote. E.g., "No one will deny that a marriage between an *ascendant* and *descendant* in the same line is properly within the forbidden degrees." Max Radin, *The Law and You* 41 (1948). See **descendant.**

A *collateral* is a relative who traces relationship to the intestate through an ancestor in common, but who is not in the lineal line of ascent or descent.

C. *In the ascendant.* This phrase is sometimes misconstrued to mean "ascending"; actually, it means "dominating, supreme." The phrase has been handed down to us from medieval astrology.

ascension; ascent. Both mean "the act of ascending." *Ascent,* however, has these additional senses: (1) "the act of rising in station or rank, or in natural chronological succession" <the ascent of man>; (2) "a method of ascending" <an unorthodox ascent>; and (3) "the degree of slope or acclivity" <a steep ascent>.

as concerns. See **as regards.**

ascribe (= to attribute to a specified cause) is sometimes misused for *subscribe* in the sense "to think of favorably"—e.g.: "We *ascribe* [read *subscribe*] to the notion that judges should limit the evidence in criminal trials to what is relevant."

as do. See **as (B)** & ANTICIPATORY REFERENCE (A).

as equally. See **equally as (D).**

as far as. This phrase must be followed by *is concerned* or *goes,* or else idiom is severely violated—e.g.: "*As far as* damages [add *are concerned*], the case does not seem to be promising."

Idiom aside, however, this construction usually signals VERBOSITY. In the sentence just quoted, for example, the writer might have said: "We expect the damages to be insignificant."

as follow(s). *As follows* is always the correct form, even for a long enumeration.

as from, a formal way of dating the onset of something, is more common in BrE than in AmE. E.g., "Eventually it was decided that *as from* 1979 criminal causes in the House of Lords should be reported under the same title as in the court below." Glanville Williams, *Learning the Law* 17–18 (11th ed. 1982)./ "Most building societies credit accounts with monies [q.v.] paid-in by cheque *as from* the date of deposit." *Council Had No Choice,* Fin. Times, 27 Jan. 1990, at 5.

aside from was once considered inferior to *apart from.* It has become standard, though it is confined primarily to AmE.

as, if, and when. This phrase, which commonly appears in real estate contracts, could almost always be made *when* with no loss in meaning. See **as and when, if and when** & DOUBLETS, TRIPLETS, AND SYNONYM-STRINGS.

as if; as though. Attempts to distinguish between these idioms have proved futile. Euphony should govern the choice of phrase.

as is; as was. "He bought the company '*as is.*'" Although a martinet of logic might insist on *as was* in the preceding sentence, that phrase is jarringly unidiomatic. *As is,* in the context of that sentence, is really an elliptical form of *on an "as is" basis,* and is infinitely better than that paraphrase. The purpose of the phrase *as is,* of course, is for a seller to disclaim warranties and representations.

as long as; so long as. These phrases are not purely temporal constructions; more often than not, they express a condition rather than a time limit <as long as the transferees abide by these restrictions, they may enjoy possession of the land>. See **as . . . as (A).**

as much as or more. When *than* follows these words, the second *as* must appear <as much as or more than>. A common error is to write *as much or more than.*

In the following sentences, however, *as much or more* (not followed by *than*) is correct: "A legatee or devisee can witness a will if he takes *as much or more* as heir if the testator dies intestate."/ "Was she not *as much or more* a victim of the system as the astonishingly bright and collected Gregory?" Neil MacCormick, *With Due Respect,* TLS, 22 Jan. 1993, at 3. Cf. **as well as or better than.** See ILLOGIC (A).

as of. A. Generally. *As of* should be used with caution. Originally an Americanism, the phrase frequently signifies the effective legal date of a document, as when the document is backdated or when the parties sign at different times. When such a nuance is not intended, *as of* is the wrong phrase. E.g., it is often inferior to *on:* "The plaintiff's employment with the defendant ended *as of* [read *on*] September 30." Cf. **as at.**

B. Used Unnecessarily. Sometimes the phrase needlessly displaces a more direct word—e.g.: "It is also important to note that Arizona had itself not suffered any direct harm *as of the time that* [read *when*] it moved for leave to file a complaint . . . ." *Maryland v. Louisiana,* 451 U.S. 725, 743 (1981).

C. *As of now.* This phrase, along with *as of* itself, has been criticized as a barbarism. Lord Conesford wrote that "an illiteracy is introduced when the words *as of* precede not a date, but the adverb *now. As of now* is a barbarism which only a love of illiteracy for its own sake can explain. What is generally meant is *at present.*" Lord Conesford, "You Americans Are Murdering the Language," in *Advanced Composition* 374, 383 (J.E. Warriner et al. eds., 1968).

But *as of now* does not mean "at present"; rather, it means "up to the present time." Follett also disapproved of the phrase, recommending instead *up to now* or *for the present,* but *as of now* is today unobjectionable in AmE.

Still, like its shorter sibling, it sometimes appears needlessly—e.g.: "Norman Mailer is a practiced writer. I am among those who are not convinced that he knows *what* to write, but it is clear he knows *how* to write. His most recent novel, *as of just now,* [delete *as of just now* and surrounding commas] contains the following sentence . . . ." Stephen White, *The Written Word* 81 (1984).

as of course. The phrase *as of course,* as opposed to *as a matter of course,* strikes nonlawyer readers as unidiomatic. But in law the idiom is common—e.g.: "It does hold that if such transfers are allowed *as of course,* the same right of transfer must be extended to every other child regardless of the dissimilarities of his circumstances." *Dillard v. School Bd. of Charlottesville,* 308 F.2d 920, 929 (4th Cir. 1962) (Haynsworth, J., dissenting)./ "A motion is not a 'responsive pleading,' within the meaning of rule 15(a), and thus the right to amend *as of course* is not defeated because the other party has filed a motion attacking the pleading." Charles A. Wright, *The Law of Federal Courts* 428 (4th ed. 1983)./ "[C]osts shall be allowed *as of course* to the prevailing party . . . ." Fed. R. Civ. P. 54(d). See **of course.**

as of now. See **as of (C).**

as of right is acceptable legal shorthand for *as a matter of right*; the phrase means "by virtue of a legal entitlement"—e.g.: "Writs of error to the state courts have never been allowed *as of right.*"/ "The action for damages is always available, *as of right,* when a contract has been broken." G.H. Treitel, *The Law of Contract* 824 (8th ed. 1991).

as of yet. See **as yet.**

as per is commonly understood to mean "in accordance with" or "in accordance with the terms of." *In re Impel Mfg. Co.,* 108 F. Supp. 469, 473 (E.D. Mich. 1952). It should, however, be commonly eschewed as an unrefined locution.

Originating in commercialese, *as per* is almost always redundant for *per.* Yet even *per* is a LAT-

INISM in place of which many everyday equivalents will suffice (e.g., *according to* or *in accordance with*). E.g., "The memorandum noted that the release between Avondale and Bean *as per* [read *in accordance with*] clause 6 thereof indicated an intent to allow third-party claims and was not a full release."/ "The secretary distributed the residual assets *as per* [read *in accordance with*] the judgment of the Louisiana court."

aspersions, to cast is a prolix CLICHÉ for *to asperse*—but the verb is little known.

asphyxia; asphyxiation. The former refers to the condition of having insufficient oxygen, resulting in suffocation. The latter is the action of producing suffocation.

asportable (= capable of being asported) is a lexicographic oversight, omitted from most English-language dictionaries, including the *OED, W2,* and *W3.* E.g., "[I]t was a reasonable inference . . . that once inside the department store warehouse the intruders would have access to a whole range of valuable, readily *asportable* consumer goods." *State v. S.G.,* 438 A.2d 256, 260 (Me. 1981).

asport(ate), v.t. *Asport* (the better form) = to carry away or remove feloniously. E.g., "[T]he crime of larceny entails not only the act of taking property but also of *asporting* it." *People v. Hammon,* 236 Cal. Rptr. 822, 829 (Ct. App. 1987).

Though usually appearing in the context of larceny—hence of personal property—the verb can refer to the illegal carrying away of persons. E.g., "Between that act and the completion of the kidnapping is the drive into the District to the club where Ms. Allwine allegedly worked, finding her there, luring her outside to the car, and effectively restraining and *asporting* her." *Frye v. State,* 489 A.2d 71, 75 (Md. 1985).

Asportate is a poorly formed BACK-FORMATION and a NEEDLESS VARIANT—e.g.: "On this venue issue, the trial court interpreted the stipulation between the parties as sufficient to show the truck was *asportated* [read *asported*] from Day County, South Dakota." *State v. Graycek,* 335 N.W.2d 572, 574 (S.D. 1983)./ "[T]he prosecutor . . . add[ed] the value of the pistol first removed from the display case and secreted in the thief's waistband to the value of the second pistol *asportated* [read *asported*] a few minutes later in the same manner." *Sendejo v. State,* 676 S.W.2d 454, 455 (Tex. App.—Fort Worth 1984).

asportation is a historical TERM OF ART meaning "the act of carrying off." The word denotes a necessary element of larceny. E.g., "The writ of trespass on the case might be joined with trespass quare clausum fregit or trespass for the *asportation* of chattels." (Eng.)

This old word has been adapted in modern contexts to mean "the act of driving (a vehicle) away": "Thereafter, by convoluted reasoning, it is held that under the facts of this case the *asportation* [= *the driving away*] of the automobile is a continuing process." See **larceny, burglary** & **stole, took, and carried away.**

asporter is the agent noun corresponding to *asport,* v.t. E.g., "The evidence did not identify any particular person as the actual *asporter* of the property from the room in which it was stored." *State v. Hollis,* 113 So. 159, 159 (La. 1927).

as regards; as respects; as concerns. *As regards* is a much maligned phrase; it is usually inferior to *regarding* or *concerning,* but it is not a solecism. E.g., "That service when finally effected was technically improper *as regards* the newspaper and two of the individual defendants."/ "It is true that Lady Dufferin's interest was a protected life interest, but she was left free *as regards* dealing with it in one particular way: surrender in favor of persons entitled in remainder." (Eng.) The phrase was a favorite of the great legal scholar Wesley N. Hohfeld, who used it frequently in his *Fundamental Legal Conceptions* (1919).

Though *as regards* is no more objectionable than *with regard to,* the whole lot of such phrases is suspect: "Train your suspicions to bristle up whenever you come upon *as regards, with regard to, in respect of, in connection with, according as to whether,* and the like. They are all dodges of JARGON, circumlocution for evading this or that simple statement." Arthur Quiller-Couch, *On the Art of Writing* 114 (1916; repr. 1961). Cf. **regard (A).**

As respects and *as concerns* are equivalent phrases not commonly found outside legal writing. E.g., "This obligation may be limited by the certificates so that the insurance applies only to an injury *as respects* [better: *to*] ASI's operations."/ "Presentments as a method of instituting prosecutions are obsolete, at least *as concerns* [better: *in*] the federal courts."

ass. See **arse** & **pompous ass.**

assail (= to attack) is usually used figuratively in both legal and nonlegal contexts. Both *attack* and *assail* are used of findings and holdings of lower courts with which an appellant is displeased: "Appellants *assail* particularly these findings by the district court."/ "The writ of habeas corpus involves a collateral attack, while in certiorari the judgment is directly *assailed.*"/ "In my opinion, the county court judge's finding cannot be *assailed* and the appeal must be dismissed with costs." (Eng.)

assassin; assassinator. The latter is a NEEDLESS VARIANT. "The first amendment is not a shelter for the character *assassinator* [read *assassin*]."

assault; battery. These terms have distinct meanings in criminal and in tort law. Essentially, an *assault* is the use or threat of force upon another that causes that person to have a well-founded fear of physical injury or offensive touching. A *battery* is the use of force or violence on another (in the criminal sense), or any repugnant intentional contact with another (in the tortious sense). Cf. **accost.**

Shooting a gun just to the side of someone, if that person reasonably fears physical injury, or shooting a blank gun directly at someone would be an *assault.* Hitting someone with a bullet makes the act a *battery,* even if the person never knew of the hit. In the tort sense, an uninvited kiss by a stranger would be considered a *battery.* See **battery.**

Leff notes that the distinction is observed only by lawyers, and even by them not consistently: "[I]n ordinary language, and even to some extent in legal talk, the two are conflated, and one speaks of an *assault* frequently in referring to the whole incident, from the threat through its consummation. Indeed, at least in ordinary understanding, use of the word *assault* most likely requires the actual *battery*; most people would not use 'He got angry and *assaulted* her' to describe an incident in which no physical contact was made." Arthur A. Leff, *The Leff Dictionary of Law,* 94 Yale L.J. 1855, 2069 (1985).

assaultee (= one who is assaulted) is a mid-20th-century legal NEOLOGISM omitted from most English-language dictionaries. E.g., "The appellant denied that he assaulted the *assaultee* for any purpose other than getting her money . . . ." *McKee v. State,* 33 So. 2d 50, 53 (Fla. 1947) (en banc) (Chapman, J., dissenting)./ "The intent to kill may be established by a number of circumstances, such as, the fact that the weapon is directed at some vital spot on the *assaultee's* body . . . ." *Caraker v. State,* 84 So. 2d 50, 51 (Fla. 1955)./ "Self-defense is relative. It is available as an exculpation, or an excuse for assault, to an *assaultee,* not an assailant." *State v. Brent,* 347 So. 2d 1112, 1116 (La. 1977). See -EE.

assaulter. So spelled.

assaultive is the only adjective corresponding to *assault.* E.g., "The prior conviction here was for rape—an *assaultive* crime."

assault with intent to commit rape; assault to rape. Both forms occur in criminal cases, the former being somewhat more common. See **rape (C).**

assay; essay. These words, related etymologically, have distinct meanings. *Assay* = to test, to analyze. E.g., "The degree of harm must be *assayed* in light of the entire charge, the state of the evidence, the arguments of counsel, and any other relevant information revealed by the record of the trial as a whole."/ "Tenuous theories of liability are better *assayed* in the light of facts than in a pleader's suppositions."

Essay, though sometimes used synonymously as a verb with *assay,* most frequently takes on the meaning "to attempt; to try to accomplish." E.g., "The supreme court of the state has decided, in a case definitely involving the point, that the legislature has not *essayed* to interfere with the constitutional liberty of citizens to organize a party and to determine the qualifications of its members."/ "Lawyers' language *essays* precision by choice of particular words and phrases, and by devices of composition such as numbering, lettering, indexing, and even symbolic logic." *Essay* thus used is quite formal and somewhat archaic; *attempt* or *try* serves better in ordinary contexts. Cf. **endeavor.**

assemblage; assembly. An *assemblage* is a disorganized group of persons or things. An *assembly* is a group of persons that is organized and united for some common purpose.

assembly, unlawful. See **riot.**

assent; consent. These words are very close in meaning, yet "there is some implication that *assent* is more active and enthusiastic than *consent,* the meaning of which sometimes slides over almost to 'acquiescence.'" Arthur A. Leff, *The Leff Dictionary of Law,* 94 Yale L.J. 1855, 2069 (1985).

assenter; assentor. For "one who assents," *assenter* is standard. *Assentor* has the specialized legal meaning in England of "one who, in addition to the proposer and seconder of a candidate's nomination in an election, signs the nomination paper of that candidate." It should not be used in other senses.

assertedly. See **reportedly, allegedly & confessedly.**

assertive; assertory. The former is the word for ordinary purposes; the latter was at one time used by grammarians in reference to sentences or constructions in the form of affirmations. *Assertory* is used in but one legal phrase, *assertory oath,* which denotes a statement of facts under oath.

assertor, not *asserter,* is the usual agent noun corresponding to the verb *assert.* See -ER (A).

assessment. See **tax.**

asseverate. See **aver.**

assign, v.t., is frequently merely an inflated synonym of *give.* E.g., "We dismiss for reasons expressed above and those *assigned* by the district court." The verb is a less inflated LEGALISM when used in the sense "to transfer," as in "He *assigned* his right in the property to his son."

assign, n.; **assignee.** Both words mean "one to whom property rights or powers are transferred by another." *Assignee* is more understandable to nonlawyers, who know *assign* as a verb only. The DOUBLET *heirs and assigns* is unlikely to disappear, however; *assign* as a noun almost always appears, as in the phrase just adduced, in the plural.

assignability. See **negotiability.**

assignee. See **assign,** n.

assigner. See **assignor.**

assignment; assignation. *Assignment* = (1) the transfer of property, or the property so transferred; (2) the instrument of transfer; or (3) a task or job. See **negotiability.**

Assignation = (1) assignment; (2) tryst; or (3) assign (meaning "one to whom property rights or powers are transferred"). *Assignation* is a NEEDLESS VARIANT in senses (1) and (3), and should be confined to sense (2), in which it is truly useful. In sense (1), however, *assignation* is the usual and proper term in Scots law.

assignment of error = a specification of errors made at trial and contained in an application for writ of error directed to an appellate court. On appeal one *assigns error* to certain alleged prejudicial mistakes at trial. (See **error (A).**) E.g., "By proper *assignments of error* and cross-errors, the correctness of each of the trial court's conclusions of law and that part of the temporary injunction undertaking to prescribe a form of permissible picketing is challenged."

assignor; assigner. In all legal senses, *assignor* is preferred; it is the correlative of *assignee. Assigner* has appeared in nonlegal contexts, and there it should remain. See -ER (A).

assise. See **assize.**

assist, n., has come into the language through basketball lingo <with an assist from counsel>. It should be avoided as a newfangled variant of *assistance.*

assist, v.t., is usually inferior to *help.*

assistance. The phrases *to provide assistance* and *to be of assistance*—containing the BURIED VERB *assistance*—are generally much inferior to *help.*

assize, n., = (1) a session of a court or council; (2) a law enacted by such a body, usu. one setting the measure, weight, or price of a thing; (3) the procedure provided for by such an enactment; (4) the court that hears cases involving that procedure; (5) a jury trial; or (6) the jury's finding in such a trial. In short, this word is, historically speaking, a CHAMELEON-HUED WORD.

In the plural (*assizes*), the term refers to the sessions or sittings of a court, especially of a superior court in England or Wales, held twice a year, at which cases were tried by a judge and jury. The *assizes* ceased to exist in Great Britain after the Courts Act 1971. *Assise* is a variant spelling generally best avoided.

associate together is a REDUNDANCY; *associate together in groups* is even worse: "The first amendment protects the right of all persons to *associate together in groups to further* [read *to associate in furtherance of*] their lawful interests."

associational; associative. The *OED* defines these words as virtual synonyms ("of, pertaining to, or characterized by association"). It suggests, however, that *associational* refers to particular associations <his associational loyalties>, whereas *associative* refers to association generally. But *W3* suggests that *associative* is now largely confined to contexts involving psychology and mathematics.

Certainly the usual term in legal contexts is *associational:* "Further, it is extremely doubtful that the rights to visitation asserted by the Thornes are the sorts of *associational* rights protected by the first amendment."/ "Any thought that due process puts beyond the reach of the criminal law all individual *associational* relationships, unless accompanied by the commission of specific acts of criminality, is dispelled by familiar concepts of the law of conspiracy and complicity." *Scales v. U.S.,* 367 U.S. 203, 225 (1961).

assoil; assoilzie; absolvitor. *Assoil* (= to pardon, release, acquit) is an obsolete ecclesiastical term for the reversal of an excommunication. *Assoilzie,* a Scottish dialectal variant, is still used in civil and criminal Scottish cases in the sense "to free of liability by order of court." The Scottish decree is called *absolvitor.*

ASSONANCE. See ALLITERATION (A).

assort(at)ive. The longer form is preferred.

assume; presume. The connotative distinction between these words is that *presumptions* are more strongly inferential and more probably authoritative than mere *assumptions,* which are usually more hypothetical. E.g., "Defendants rely upon the ancient legal *presumption* that a woman is considered legally capable of bearing children at any age."/ "Where any document purporting to be thirty years old is produced from any custody that the judge considers proper, it is *presumed* that the signature and every other part of such document is in that person's handwriting." (Eng.)

Presumptions lead to decisions, whereas *assumptions* do not: "We *assume,* without deciding, that except for the provisions of section 18 of the Decedent Estate Law the trust would be valid." The phrase *we assume, without deciding,* is a favorite of common-law courts.

Where adverbs are concerned, one should always use the common forms derived from *presume;* that is, *presumably* (= I presume, it is to be presumed) or *presumptively* (= there is a presumption at law that). Here the writer seems to have been trying to avoid the simple term in favor of an outlandish one: "However, the life tenant is *assumedly* [read *presumably*] entitled to $5,760 per year."

Assumptive is pretentious for either *assumed* <assumptive beliefs> or *assuming* or *presumptuous* <an assumptive character>. For the sense of *presumptive* in *heir presumptive,* see **heir (B).**

assuming. See DANGLERS (D).

assumpsit, a LAW LATIN term, means literally "he undertook" or "he promised." "Of the terms used in connection with the subject of restitution, *assumpsit* is one of the oldest and also perhaps one of the most troublesome." Peter W. Davis, Comment, *Restitution: Concept and Terms,* 19 Hastings L.J. 1167, 1182 (1968). The term originally applied to an action for breach of a simple contract, then was extended (after *Slade's Case* [1602]) to cases in which no independent agreement to pay could be proved, and finally to implied contracts and quasi-contracts. This CHAMELEON-HUED WORD is no longer widely used by common-law courts; in England the cause of action was abolished by the Judicature Acts of 1873–1875.

assumption, in lay writing, most commonly means "a supposition"; in legal contexts it frequently takes on the older sense "the action of taking for or upon oneself" (*OED*). E.g., "It is not clear whether ITT consented to an *assumption* of indebtedness." See **assume.**

assumption of the risk; contributory negligence. Originally these two were separate doctrines, but *assumption of the risk* has been, in most jurisdictions, subsumed by the doctrine of *contributory* (or *comparative*) *negligence. Assumption of the risk* = the principle that a party who has taken on the risk of loss, injury, or damage consequently cannot maintain an action against the party having caused the loss. An example of assumed risk is the man who volunteers his profile to a friend who wants to practice sword-throwing.

Perhaps because *assumption of the risk* as applied by the courts came to bar otherwise meritorious claims, legal scholars began to point out that *contributory negligence* could be applied to any case involving *assumption of the risk.* And with the rise of *comparative negligence,* q.v., the doctrine of *assumption of the risk* became especially unjust if applied to bar a claim. See ***volenti non fit injuria.***

assumptive; presumptive. See **assume.**

assurance; insurance. The nouns follow from the verbs; hence the reader might first consult the next entry. Since *ensurance* is no longer with us, *insurance* is the nominal form of both *insure* and *ensure.* Usually, *insurance* refers to indemnification against loss (from the verb *insure*); in BrE, *assurance* is sometimes given this meaning, although Partridge notes its decline; its one surviving use in this sense is in reference to life policies. Generally, however, *assurance* = that which gives confidence. See **insurance (B).**

In AmE, *assurance* chiefly means "pledge" or "guaranty." E.g., "*To give further assurance* [better: *To further ensure*] that these rules will not be breached, the states may wish to add 'safeguard' provisions." (See SPLIT INFINITIVES (C).)/ "The reviewing court may inquire whether there is adequate *assurance* that the respondent will be protected against the loss of proprietary information."/ "The heirs would have no *assurance* that the question of the personal fault of the executor would be properly tried."/ "Respondents received *assurance* that the customers would be willing to give them their laundry work."

Assurance also has the specialized, rather rare legal meaning "the act of transferring real property." *Assure* formerly had the corresponding meaning "to convey by deed."

assure; ensure; insure. A. *Assure* for *ensure*. One person *assures* (makes promises to, convinces) other persons, and *ensures* (makes certain) that things occur or that events take place. Any object beginning with *that* should be introduced by the verb *ensure,* if the verb is in the active voice. Here *assure,* which always takes a personal object, is properly used: "If Mr. Lucy's promise to pay for the Zehmer's farm becomes enforceable merely on the Zehmers' making their promise in return, how is Lucy *assured* [correct, because passive voice] that he will not have to pay the price unless he gets the farm?"/ "Although the court's instruction did petitioner no harm, it was thought that petitioner was *assured* a new trial if counsel had complained."

In the following sentences, *assure* is misused for *ensure:* "This course will be more likely to *assure* [read *ensure*] that the police officer will not be exposed to personal liability."/ "The State's strong interests in *assuring* [read *ensuring*] the marketability of property within its borders would also support jurisdiction."/ "Filing of a solicitation letter *assures* [read *ensures*] the public's ample protection."

Ensure is properly used in the following sentences: "Changes were made to *ensure* against overexpenditures in the program."/ "The verdict *ensured* that he would spend a long time in jail."/ "The requirement of minimum contacts *ensures* that the states, through their courts, do not reach beyond the limits imposed on them by the status as coequal sovereigns in the federal system."

B. *Insure* and *ensure*. *Insure* should be restricted to financial contexts involving indemnification; it should refer to what insurance companies do; *ensure* should be used in all other senses of the word. Intransitively, *insure* is commonly followed by the preposition *against* <insure against loss>; it may also be used transitively <insure one's valuables>. Following is a commonplace peccadillo: "Care must be taken to *insure* [read *ensure*] that the return of the loser does not become the guideline of the judgment."

C. Noun Forms. See **assurance.**

assurer; assuror. The *-er* spelling is preferred. See -ER (A) & **underwriter.**

as the case may be. See **case** (A).

as though. See **as if.**

as to is a vague, all-purpose preposition that should be avoided whenever a more specific preposition will fit the context. *As to* does not clearly establish syntactic or conceptual relationships; it hampers the comprehensibility of texts in which it appears. Were it not a phrase, it might justifiably be classed among FORBIDDEN WORDS.

A. Indefensible Uses. To illustrate the slippery variability of *as to,* a list of problematic usages follows; in each example, another preposition would more directly and forcefully express the thought.

1. For *of.* "Registration in the Patent and Trademark Office creates presumptions *as to* [read *of*] ownership and the exclusive right to use."/ "A contract in a lease giving an option of purchase might be good, provided it did not infringe the law *as to* [read *of*] perpetuities."/ "The jury was also instructed that if it believed appellant was guilty of either murder or involuntary manslaughter, but was unsure *as to* [read *of*] which, it was to find him guilty of the lesser offense."

2. For *on.* "The UCC is silent *as to* [read *on* or *about*] the reconciliation of different terms."/ "The will violates the common-law rule *as to* [read *on*] contingent remainders."/ "But the question really must be regarded as an open one, *as to* [read *on*] which commentators disagree."/ "We find no authority for the contention that the rule *as to* [read *on*] the destruction of contingent remainders should be applied to a case in which the estate is vested in quality but contingent in quantity."/ "Because the State produced no evidence *as to* [read *on*] this essential element, it is impossible to say that a rational trier of fact could have found beyond a reasonable doubt the facts necessary to support the life sentence."

3. For *with.* "In the business of life insurance, the value of a man's life is measured in dollars and cents according to his life expectancy, the soundness of his body, and his ability to pay premiums; the same is true *as to* [read *with,* or perhaps *of*] health and accident insurance."

4. For *for.* "The rule is the same *as to* [read *for*] specialists."

5. For *to.* "Offeree must wait until he gets an *answer as to* [read *answer to*] his counter-offer."/

"Was the option provision too uncertain to be enforced, so that parol evidence should not have been *admitted as to* [read *admitted to*] clarify its meaning?"/ "He was entirely *indifferent as to* [read *indifferent to*] the results."

6. For *by*. "Counsel was continually surprised at trial *as to* [read *by*] the evidence presented by his opponent."

7. For *in* or *into*. "When the petition is correct *as to* [read *in*] form, a notification shall be prepared."/ "The court submitted issues to the jury inquiring *as to* [read *into*] what was a reasonable attorney's fee."

8. For *applicable to*. "That is a fundamental doctrine *as to* [read *applicable to*] fiduciaries of all sorts, that it is somewhat surprising to find it questioned."

9. Completely Superfluous. "The trial court failed to *specify as to what* [read *specify what*] predicate under the statute plaintiff relied upon."/ "The Court does not *say here as to how* [read *say here how*] carefully the survey was conducted."/ "The only *real issue* in the case *is as to* [read *real issue . . . is*] the question of insanity." / "The *question is as to* [read *question is*] the validity of the twenty-eighth clause of the will of Mary C. Durbow, a childless widow." See **as to whether** & **question as to whether.**

10. Used Twice in One Sentence, with Differing Meanings. "The defense moved for a judgment of acquittal *as to* [read *on*] all counts, arguing, *as to* [read *with respect to*] the tax evasion count, that an affirmative act of concealment had to be found to convict the defendant."/ "The question *as to* [superfluous] whether information *as to* [read *about*] particular processes or other matters was 'confidential' or 'secret' is outside the scope of this annotation."/ "Petitioner's right to a salary before it was voted to him was so indefinite *as to* [read *in*] both amount and obligation *as to be* [read *that it was*] unenforceable."/ "It is the contention of the contestant that the residuary legatees under the will *so* unduly and improperly influenced the testator to make the will in their favor *as to* [read *with regard to*] the residue of this estate *as to render* [read *that they rendered*] the will of no legal effect." In each of the last two sentences quoted, the final *as to* is a part of the phrase *so . . . as to,* q.v. The suggested changes of those phrases to clauses beginning with *that* are for the purpose merely of enhancing clarity; apart from the confusion caused by using *as to* twice in different senses, the phrase *so . . . as to* is used in those sentences in a technically proper way.

B. Defensible Uses. The phrase is most justifiable when introducing the discussion of a matter previously mentioned only cursorily in the text: "*As to* these nine plaintiffs who failed to apply for re-appointment, the ruling in *McBee v. Jim Hogg County* requires rejection of their section 1983 claims."/ "*As to* whether the object that this bill discloses was sought to be attained [see PASSIVE VOICE (F)] by the members of the union was a lawful one, the authorities of this country are clearly in conflict." In beginning sentences in this way, *as to* is equivalent to the more colloquial *as for*.

The phrase is defensible when used for *about*. Nevertheless, it is stylistically inferior to *about* in most contexts, as in the following sentences: "The buyer was silent *as to* [better: *about*] the disclaimer."/ "Any doubt *as to* [better: *about*] the existence of a material fact is to be resolved against the moving party."/ "Complaints *as to* [better: *about*] procedural irregularities in a condemnation case must be preserved at the trial court level by motion, exception, objection, plea in abatement, or some other vehicle."

The phrase is sometimes a passable shorthand form of "with regard to" or "on the question of," a meaning it properly carries when beginning a sentence. E.g., "California has done what we think should here be done; it has made its solution *as to* life insurance proceeds consonant with its other community property laws."/ "The trial court entered judgment of nonsuit *as to* all defendants, from which plaintiff appeals."/ "The document is silent *as to* beneficial title." (Eng.)/ "The district court erred in denying the new trial sought *as to* the dismissal." In each of these sentences the *as to* phrase can be used to start the sentence and link it more firmly with a topic mentioned previously.

as to whether. The Fowlers describe it as "seldom necessary" in *The King's English* 344 (3d ed. 1930). That judgment has withstood the test of time. See **as to (A)(9)** & **question as to whether.**

as was. See **as is.**

as well. When used at the beginning of a sentence, this phrase is a casualism at best—e.g.: "*As well,* [read *Also,*] people are questioning how well the legal system really does protect people's rights." Alan Reid, *Seeing Law Differently* 4 (1992).

as well as. See **together with** & SUBJECT-VERB AGREEMENT (G).

as well as or better than. Some writers illogically leave out *as* after well—e.g.: "Women would write in detail why they were working *as well* [*as*] *or better than* their male counterparts." Simon

Hoggart, *All Present and Incorrect,* Observer Sunday, 15 Dec. 1991, at 37, 38. Cf. **as much as or more.** See ILLOGIC (A).

as yet is invariably inferior to *yet* alone, *thus far,* or some other equivalent phrase. "The judge has not decided as yet." [Read *The judge has not yet decided.*]/ "One must question whether the stipulation automatically extended to the *not-as-yet-filed claim* [read *yet-unfiled* or *yet-to-be-filed claim*]." (See PHRASAL ADJECTIVES.)/ "No court *has as yet* [read *has yet*] held that such an injunction is entitled to full faith and credit in the sense that the action toward which the injunction is directed must be abated."/ "Plaintiff has *as yet* [read *thus far*] had no opportunity to testify about this matter." *As of yet* is illiterate. Cf. **as of now.**

asylee, a late-20th-century legal NEOLOGISM, is becoming a standard word in the language of the law for "a refugee applying for asylum." It has not yet made its way into most English-language dictionaries. Like many personal nouns ending in *-ee,* it is illogically formed. But illogical morphology has not presented an obstacle to many other forms ending in *-ee.* "This portion of the complaint as amended alleges . . . that plaintiffs as a class are *'asylees.'*" *Fernandez-Roque v. Smith,* 539 F. Supp. 925, 932 (N.D. Ga. 1982). / "[T]he severity of harm to the erroneously excluded *asylee* outweighs the administrative burden of providing an asylum hearing." *Chun v. Sava,* 708 F.2d 869, 877 (2d Cir. 1983). See -EE.

The popular press tends to use the phrase *asylum-seeker* (a phrase best hyphenated)—e.g.: "More than 10,440 Haitians are in custody at Guantanamo, and more *asylum-seekers* are on cutters offshore." Barbara Crossette, *U.S. Starts Return of Haiti Refugees After Justices Act,* N.Y. Times, 2 Feb. 1992, at 1./ "*Asylum seekers* poured into Germany last month at the rate of more than one a minute . . . ." Christopher Parkes, *Asylum Seekers Flood Germany,* Fin. Times, 5 Aug. 1992, at 1.

at is incorrect when used with any locative such as *where*—e.g.: "Where is it at?" A curious example appears in the writing of Llewellyn: "[I]ts central notice-filing provisions make it cheap and easy for the prospective seller to find out just *where* he is *at.*" Karl N. Llewellyn, *Why We Need the Uniform Commercial Code,* 10 U. Fla. L. Rev. 367, 379 (1957). U.S. District Judge William Terrell of Florida reports that, as an editor of the law review in 1957, he tried unsuccessfully to persuade Llewellyn to omit the *at.* See PREPOSITIONS (A).

-ATABLE does not generally appear other than in *-able* adjectives derived from two-syllable verbs (e.g., *create, vacate*), because in those short words the adjective would become unrecognizable. Fowler notes some long exceptions to the general rule (*inculcatable, inculpatable, incubatable*) and states his standard: "The practice should be to use *-atable* where the shorter form is felt to be out of the question." (*MEU2* 41) Other examples with which the shorter form is impracticable are *anticipatable, translatable,* and *infiltratable* (so that *infiltrable* not be thought to be derived from *infilter* [= to sift or filter in] rather than from *infiltrate*).

The following words, which occur with some frequency in legal prose, are better formed with *-able:*

abbreviable	confiscable	manipulable
abdicable	cultivable	mitigable
abrogable	delegable	navigable
accommodable	delineable	obligable
accumulable	demonstrable	obviable
activable	detonable	operable
administrable	differentiable	originable
adulterable	educable	participable
affiliable	expropriable	penetrable
aggregable	generable	perpetrable
agitable	indicable	perpetuable
alienable	inebriable	predicable
allocable	inextirpable	propagable
annihilable	inextricable	regulable
appreciable	infatuable	replicable
appropriable	infuriable	repudiable
arbitrable	integrable	segregable
articulable	invalidable	subjugable
calculable	investigable	vindicable
communicable	isolable	violable
compensable	litigable	vitiable

at all events; in any event. These phrases are perfectly synonymous. The former is more common in BrE, the latter in AmE. Yet *at all events* does appear infrequently in American texts as well: "*At all events,* from an early date, if not in Glanville's time, the necessity of a formal delivery of devised land to the executor was got rid of in England as Beseler says that it was on the continent." (Holmes)/ "When the option to purchase is given to Clarkson, it prima facie *at all events* means to include Clarkson's assigns."

In legal writing these phrases are preferable to *in any case* when used in the same sense, because *in any case* contains the confusingly ambiguous word *case,* q.v., which usually refers to a lawsuit in legal contexts.

at arm's length. See **arm's-length.**

at bar. See **at (the) bar.**

at bench. See **case at bench.**

at circuit. See **circuit, to ride.**

at common law, a LOAN TRANSLATION of the LAW FRENCH *al common ley,* is the legal idiom used to introduce statements of common-law doctrine. E.g., "*At common law,* the death of the injured person or of the tortfeasor, at any time before verdict, abated the action."/ "'*At common law,*' says Sir W. Erle, 'every person has individually, and the public also have collectively, a right to require that the course of trade be kept free from unreasonable obstruction.'" (Eng.) The preposition *at* is not used, however, in references to either equity or civil law.

As in the two examples quoted, some writers use the past tense when introducing a statement with the phrase *at common law.* Others use the present tense. Neither method can be recommended for all cases, but it is possible to formulate a rule: when referring to a rule that is long since defunct, use the past tense; but when referring to a rule that has some continuing validity, use the present tense.

at fault; in fault. An American critic once wrote that "hunting dogs [that] lose the scent are said to be *at fault.* Hence the phrase means perplexed, puzzled." He added that *in fault* means "in error, mistaken," with this example: "No certified public accountant should be *in fault.*" Clarence Stratton, *Handbook of English* 24, 158 (1940). Today, however, *in fault* is seldom used in that way.

The phrase *at fault* is now standard in the sense "responsible for a wrong committed; blameworthy." E.g., "Apportionment of the percentages of fault among the parties found to be *at fault* cannot be accepted." The phrase is virtually never used synonymously with *perplexed* or *puzzled.*

at first blush. This phrase, common in legal writing, occurs in BrE as well as in AmE. *At first blush* is a home-grown equivalent of the LATINISM *prima facie,* q.v., but the two have distinct uses. Rather than serving as a simple adjective or adverb like *prima facie,* the phrase *at first blush* conveys the sense "upon an initial consideration or cursory examination." *Blush* here carries an otherwise obsolete sense: "a glance, glimpse, blink, or look." E.g., "*At first blush,* a reading of the rule would countenance joinder of the United States as a defendant along with another defendant in a situation such as is present here."/ "*At first blush* this punishment does not seem very severe." *At first blush* is becoming a grossly overworked CLICHÉ. The variant phrase *on first blush* is not idiomatic. See **prima facie.**

at hand; in hand. In the U.S., the former has ousted the latter in figurative senses, because *in hand* is most frequently used literally, as in "I have the contract *in hand.*" One still occasionally sees the figurative *in hand,* but this is not the current idiom: "When justice in the cause *in hand* [read *at hand*] has been attained as near as may be and has been attained on grounds and in a manner prescribed by law, the duty of the judge under the civil law has been performed."/ "In their briefs in connection with Smith's motion, counsel on both sides state that they have been unable to find any case dealing with the specific problem *in hand* [read *at hand*]."

In G.B., however, *in hand* is frequently used in the metaphorical sense: "The court might have reached the same decision on the simple ground that the rule in Clayton's case was irrelevant to the issue *in hand.*" (Eng.)

at issue. See **issue (A).**

at law. See **under law.**

at present. See **at the present time.**

attach. See **annex.**

attached hereto, a REDUNDANCY for *attached,* is a LEGALISM to be avoided.

attachment = (1) the taking into custody of a person to hold that person as security for the payment of a judgment; or (2) the taking into custody of a person's property to secure a judgment or to be sold in satisfaction of a judgment. Sense (1): "[Courts of equity] may order a writ of *attachment* for the arrest and detention of the body of the contumacious party until obedience to the decree has been secured." Eugene A. Jones, *Manual of Equity Pleading and Practice* 139 (1916). / Sense (2): "The disputed residence was important because a writ of *attachment*—briefly, an order freezing cash or other assets—cannot be obtained against a person unless the person has a foreign address." Joseph Goulden, *The Million Dollar Lawyers* 52–53 (1978). See **sequestration.**

attain, v.t.; **obtain.** The two are sometimes confused. *Attain* = to achieve, accomplish. E.g., "Another's business may be attacked only to *attain* some purpose in the eye of the law." *Obtain* = to get, acquire <obtain a license>. It is a FORMAL WORD.

Attain, in another sense, is also a FORMAL WORD

for "to reach (an age)". E.g., "In *Saunders v. Vautier,* the English Chancery Court granted a petition by the sole beneficiary to terminate a trust upon his *attaining* the age of majority."

attainder; attaint, n. Both nouns derive from the (originally French) verb *attaint* (= to accuse, convict). As legal terms they are primarily of historical interest. *Attainder* usually appears in the phrase *bill of attainder* or *act of attainder,* and means "the act of extinguishing someone's civil rights by sentencing the person to death or declaring the person to be an outlaw, usu. in punishment for treason or a felony."

Attaint was formerly used to mean "the conviction of a jury for giving a false verdict" *(OED).* E.g., "An action called *'attaint'* could be brought against jurors for giving a false verdict, and if it was successful the verdict would be quashed." J.H. Baker, *An Introduction to English Legal History* 156 (3d ed. 1990).

attaint; taint. These terms were originally unrelated, but the senses of the former came to be heavily tainted by erroneous association with the latter. *Attaint* = (1) to subject to attainder, to condemn; (2) to touch or affect; or (3) [obs.] to accuse. *Attaint* is justified today only in sense (1); *taint* is otherwise the better word. E.g., "In trials for high treason, or misprision of treason, no one can be indicted, tried, or *attainted* (unless he pleads guilty) except upon the oath of two lawful witnesses." (Eng.)

Taint = (1) to imbue with a noxious quality or principle; (2) to contaminate or corrupt; or (3) to tinge or become tinged. *Taint* is by far the more common word in modern writing: "The Court found that the initial illegal entry did not *taint* the discovery of the evidence subsequently seized under the valid warrant."/ "It is urged that if evidence is inadmissible against one defendant or conspirator, because *tainted* by electronic surveillance illegal as to him, it is also inadmissible against his codefendant or co-conspirator."

Taint is just as frequently used as a noun: "The practice is not shown to be such as to fix upon complainant the *taint* of unclean hands."

attempt. **A. *Criminal attempt.*** In criminal law, *attempt* refers to the crime of intending to commit a crime, along with taking a step to carry out the crime. E.g., "Mallory thereupon pleaded guilty to the crime of *attempt* to commit burglary of the second degree and was given a short county jail term." *People v. Eastman,* 154 P.2d 37, 37 (Cal. Ct. App. 1944)./ "In England, indeed, the abortion legislation is worded only in terms of *attempt,* it being immaterial for the purpose of the offence whether the abortion itself is effected or not." Glanville Williams, *The Sanctity of Life and the Criminal Law* 180 (1957).

B. And *endeavor; assay.* See **endeavor & assay.**

attestant. See **attester.**

attestation clause; testimonium clause. Both appear at the end of a will. The *testimonium clause* is signed by the testator, the *attestation clause* by the witnesses to the will. A typical *testimonium clause* reads: "This will was signed by me on the 14th day of October, 1985, at Wilmington, Virginia." *Testimonium clauses* have traditionally begun with the phrase *in witness whereof,* q.v. See **testimonium clause.**

The *attestation clause* recites the formalities required by the jurisdiction in which the will might be admitted to probate. It raises a presumption that the formalities recited have been performed and thus aids the proponent of the will at probate. A typical *attestation clause* reads: "The foregoing instrument, consisting of four typewritten pages, was signed and declared by the testator to be her last will in the presence of us, who, at her request, and in her presence and the presence of one another, have subscribed our names as witnesses."

In Scots law, the *attestation clause* is called a *testing-clause.*

attest(at)ive; attestational. *Attestative* is the best adjective corresponding to *attestation;* it means "of or relating to attestation." *Attestational* is a NEEDLESS VARIANT. *Attestive* is a NEEDLESS VARIANT of *attesting.*

attester; attestor; attestator; attestant. *Attester* is standard in legal contexts. The others are NEEDLESS VARIANTS.

at (the) bar (= now before the court) derives from the LAW FRENCH phrase *al barre. At the bar,* which appears in early decisions such as *Marbury v. Madison* and *McCulloch v. Maryland,* has gradually been displaced in the U.S. by *at bar* in phrases such as *in the case at bar.* E.g., "In the case *at bar* there was no necessity of proving spite or ill will toward the plaintiff."/ "We think that no more was covered than situations substantially similar to those then *at bar.*"

The British still use *at the bar,* "Until the present argument *at the bar* it may be doubted whether shipowners or merchants were ever deemed to be bound by law to conform to some imaginary 'normal' standard of freights or prices." (Eng.)

One writer states that *at bar* is used, esp. in law school, to refer to a case already decided and at the time under discussion by professor and students. Arthur A. Leff, *The Leff Dictionary of Law,* 94 Yale L.J. 1855, 2088 (1985). This usage is probably peculiar to certain law schools; to those unfamiliar with it, it smacks of the judge-manqué. Cf. **at (the) trial.** See ***sub judice.***

at the present day is inferior to *today*—e.g.: "Criminal proceedings *at the present day* [read *today*] do not result only in death, imprisonment or fine . . . ." O. Hood Phillips, *A First Book of English Law* 192 (3d ed. 1955).

at the present time; at this time; at present. These are inferior to *now, nowadays,* or *today.*

at the time that; at the time when. These phrases are invariably verbose for *when.*

at (the) trial. The shorter form is the more usual and the more idiomatic in AmE. "*At the trial* [read *at trial*], a nonsuit was denied." In the U.S. *at the trial* is outmoded except as an adverbial of place <he was seen at the trial>. Cf. **at (the) bar.**

In BrE, however, judges still write *at the trial:* "The practice has been, wherever possible, to adduce *at the trial,* before pronouncement of decree nisi, evidence of the proposed arrangements for the children." (Eng.)

Still another vanishing idiom is *on (or upon) the trial:* "*On the trial* plaintiff was nonsuited."/ "No such evidence was produced *upon the trial.*" Today both phrases would be *at trial* in American legal writing. See **trial, at.**

at this time. See **at the present time.**

attorn, vb., is pronounced /ə-**tərn**/. See **attornment.**

attorney. A. And Its Near Synonyms. Lawyers, like those in other walks of life, have long sought to improve their descriptive titles. Boswell relates: "The Society of Procurators, or Attornies, had obtained a royal charter, in which they had taken care to have their ancient designation *Procurators* changed into that of *Solicitors,* from a notion, as they supposed, that it was more genteel." 4 *Life of Johnson* 128 (1791).

The connotations of *attorney* and its near synonyms have historically been quite different in BrE and AmE. Originally, *attorney* denoted a practitioner in common-law courts, *solicitor* one in equity courts, and *proctor* one in ecclesiastical courts; all instructed barristers to appear and argue. *Attorney,* it seems, soon developed an unpleasant smell about it: one commentator writes that the 18th-century efforts "to deodorize the word *attorney* [were] later abandoned, and in the nineteenth century it was supplanted in England by *solicitor.* There *solicitor* lacks the offensive American connotation, as in 'No peddlers or solicitors.' In England, *attorney,* for a lawyer, survives only as *the attorney* (the attorney general), while in America the chief respectable lawyer-solicitor is the *solicitor-general.*" David Mellinkoff, *The Language of the Law* 198 (1963).

The two most common terms in AmE, *lawyer* and *attorney,* are not generally distinguished even by members of the profession. In the U.S., *attorney, attorney-at-law,* and *lawyer* are generally viewed as synonyms. Today there seems to be a notion afoot, however, that *attorney* is a more formal (and less disparaging) term than *lawyer.*

Technically, *lawyer* is the more general term, referring to one who practices law. *Attorney* literally means "one who is designated to transact business for another." An *attorney,* technically and archaically (except in the phrase *attorney in fact* [see (B) below]), may or may not be a lawyer. Thus Samuel Johnson's statement that *attorney* "was anciently used for those who did any business for another; now only in law." *A Dictionary of the English Language* (1755) (s.v. *attorney*).

From the fact that an *attorney* is really an agent, Bernstein deduces that "a *lawyer* is an *attorney* only when he has a client. It may be that the desire of *lawyers* to appear to be making a go of their profession has accounted for their leaning toward the designation *attorney.*" Theodore M. Bernstein, *The Careful Writer* 60 (1965). Yet this distinction between *lawyer* and *attorney* is rarely, if ever, observed in practice.

In the U.S., those licensed to practice law are admitted to practice as "attorneys and counselors." (The *-l-* spelling of *counselor* is preferred in AmE, the *-ll-* spelling in BrE. See DOUBLING OF FINAL CONSONANTS.) This combination of names is unknown in English law, in which *attorney* = solicitor, and *counsellor* = barrister. Yet "in the United States, the term *attorney* has come to have a generic significance that embraces all branches of legal practice." G.W. Warvelle, *Essays in Legal Ethics* 53 (1902).

In G.B., a *solicitor* or *attorney* does all sorts of legal work for clients but generally appears only in inferior courts; a *barrister* is a trial lawyer or litigator.

In AmE, *counsel* and *counselor* are both, in one sense, general terms meaning "one who gives (legal) advice," the latter being the more formal term. *Counsel* may refer to but one lawyer <opposing counsel contends> or, as a plural, to more than one lawyer <opposing counsel contend>. See **counsel (B) & postman.**

B. Kinds of Attorneys (*attorney in fact; attorney at law*). The former means "one with power of attorney to act for another; legal agent." E.g., "It is held in *Tynan v. Paschal* that a letter of a decedent to his *attorney in fact* directing him to destroy his will does not operate ipso facto as a revocation of it." The latter means "a licensed lawyer." The plural forms are *attorneys in fact* and *attorneys at law.* See (D).

C. As a Verb. *Attorney,* like *lawyer,* has come to be used as a verb. E.g., "Among a number of mock trials that lawyers have liked to write is a *Trial of Sir John Falstaff,* wherein the Fat Knight is permitted to answer for himself concerning the charges against him, and *to attorney* his own case." (Eng.) See **lawyering.**

D. Plural. *Attornies* is an obsolete plural of the word (see the quotation from Boswell under (A) of this article); *attorneys* is now the universally accepted plural. Cf. **monies,** which is inferior to *moneys.*

attorney-client privilege should be hyphenated.

attorneydom. See **lawyerdom.**

attorney general, made plural, forms *attorneys general* in AmE, *attorney-generals* in BrE. See PLURALS (E).

attorneying. See **attorney (C) & lawyer,** v.i.

attorney's fees; attorneys' fees; attorney fees; counsel fees. The first of these now appears to be prevalent. See Attorney's Fee Act, 42 U.S.C. § 1988 (1988). The plural possessive *attorneys' fees* is just as good, and some may even prefer that term in contexts in which there is clearly more than one attorney referred to. *Attorney fees* is inelegant but increasingly common. It might be considered a means to avoid having to get the apostrophe right. (But cf. the phrase *expert-witness fees.*) *Counsel fees* is another, less-than-common variant.

The only form to avoid at all costs is *attorneys fees,* in which the first word is a genitive adjective with the apostrophe wrongly omitted. This form appears in Arthur A. Leff, *The Leff Dictionary of Law,* 94 Yale L.J. 1855, 1969 (1985), under "affirmative relief." See POSSESSIVES (E).

attornies. See **attorney (D).**

attornment has two analogous senses, the first relating to personal property and the second relating to land. It may mean either (1) "an act by a bailee in possession of goods on behalf of one person acknowledging that he will hold the goods on behalf of someone else" (*CDL*); or (2) "a person's agreement to hold land as the tenant of someone else." Both senses are used in BrE and AmE.

An English court has stated that the *attornment* clause in mortgages "is entirely obsolete and at the present time performs no useful purpose." *Steyning & Littlehampton Bldg. Society v. Wilson,* [1951] Ch. 1018, 1020.

attractive nuisance (= a dangerous condition that may attract children onto a property owner's land, thereby causing a risk to their safety) is a seeming OXYMORON. Statements such as the following illustrate the irony of the phrase: "We have no hesitation in affirming the jury's conclusion that the filthy, polluted, weed-choked, garbage plagued drainage canal located near a school . . . constituted an *attractive nuisance.*" *Orange County v. Gipson,* 539 So. 2d 526, 529 (Fla. Dist. Ct. App. 1989). See **nuisance.**

at trial. See **at (the) trial.**

attribute, n.; **attribution.** Although these terms overlap to a great extent, a distinction might advantageously be observed: *attribution* = the act or an instance of ascribing a characteristic or quality; *attribute* = a characteristic or quality so ascribed.

attributive; attributory. The former is the standard term.

at variance. See **variance.**

at which time is invariably prolix for *when.*

at will. *Employee at will* is an ellipsis for *employee at* [*the employer's*] *will. At will* is slowly changing from its position after the noun into a position before the noun it modifies <an at-will employee>. See POSTPOSITIVE ADJECTIVES. Cf. **tenant at will.**

atypical; untypical. The preferred term is *atypical.*

auctorial. See **authorial.**

aught (= [1] anything; [2] all) is an ARCHAISM to be avoided. E.g., "*For aught that appears* [read *For all that appears*], the essence of what petitioner seeks either has been revealed to him already through the interrogatories or is readily available to him." *Hickman v. Taylor,* 329 U.S.

495, 509 (1947)./ "*For aught appearing* [read *For all that appears*], Patel has not sought legal entry." *Patel v. Sumani Corp.*, 660 F. Supp. 1528, 1535 (N.D. Ala. 1987). Cf. **naught.**

auspices. *Under the auspices* is frequently misconstrued as meaning "in the form of" or "in accordance with." Actually, it means "with the sponsorship or support of." The term is properly used in this sentence: "The contest was determinable *under the auspices* of the newspaper company."

Here are examples of the all-too-frequent misusage: "The issue on appeal is the extent to which the Federal Savings and Loan Insurance Corporation, *under the auspices of* [read *in the form of*] a receivership or conservatorship, can preclude judicial review of a state claim."/ "After rendition of the circuit court's opinion and order, plaintiffs filed a motion for new trial with the court of appeals *under the auspices of* [read *under* or *in accordance with*] Fed. R. Civ. P.50(d)." See **aegis.**

autarchy; autarky. *Autarchy* = absolute rule or sovereignty, autocracy. *Autarky* = national economic self-sufficiency; isolationism.

authentication—so spelled—is occasionally misrendered *authentification.* E.g., "[N]either the statutory authority nor the case law require[s] *authentification* [read *authentication*] of signatures." *Commonwealth v. Gordon,* 633 A.2d 1199, 1204 (Pa. Super. Ct. 1993).

author is becoming standard as a verb, though fastidious writers still avoid it. Generally it is a highfalutin substitute for *write, compose,* or *create.* E.g., "*Shelley v. Kraemer* stands at least for the proposition that, where parties of different races are willing to deal with one another, a state court cannot keep them from doing so by enforcing a privately *authored* [read *created*] racial restriction."/ "The orderly administration of an injunctive decree must be carried through by the court that *authored* [read *composed* or *originated*] and is administering that decree."

Nor is attribution to a collective body among the legitimate uses of this word: "Congress adopted an inclusionary approach when it *authored* [read *drafted* or *framed*] this rule." *Coauthor* has been considered more acceptable as a verb, perhaps because *co-write* seems deadpan. See NOUNS AS VERBS.

With reference to *the author* (= I), see FIRST PERSON (B).

authoress. See SEXISM (C).

authorial; auctorial. The latter is a stuffy NEEDLESS VARIANT of the former.

autograph. See **allograph.**

autopsy; postmortem, n. These equivalents are each current in AmE and BrE. *Autopsy* is slightly more common in AmE, *postmortem* in BrE.

autopsy, v.t., was not until recently recorded in the dictionaries. It means "to perform a postmortem examination on." E.g., "Their testimony should be rejected as a matter of law because it ignored pathological studies of *autopsied* tissues of the bronchi and lungs that did not reveal the presence of chromates."

autrefois /*oh*-tər-foyz/ is a LAW FRENCH term, meaning "on another occasion, formerly," used in the phrases *autrefois acquit* (= a plea in bar of arraignment that the defendant has been acquitted of the offense by a jury) and *autrefois convict* (= a plea in bar of arraignment that the defendant has been convicted of the offense by a jury). These phrases are much more common in G.B. than in the U.S.

autre vie, pur. See ***pur autre vie.***

auxillary is a bastard formation probably having arisen from confusion of *auxiliary* with *ancillary.*

avail, vb., because it is most properly a reflexive verb only <he availed himself of the opportunity>, does not work in the PASSIVE VOICE. E.g., "Congress meant that damages from or by floods should not afford any basis of liability against the United States regardless of *whether the sovereign immunity was availed of or not* [read *whether the government availed itself of sovereign immunity*]."/ "Sovereign immunity could not at that time be *availed of* by them for their participation in such wrongful conduct." *Barrett v. U.S.,* 798 F.2d 565, 574 (2d Cir. 1986). [Read: *They could not then avail themselves of sovereign immunity because they had participated in such wrongful conduct.*]

The verb is best not used as a nonreflexive transitive or intransitive verb. In each of the following examples, *help, profit,* or *benefit* should replace *avail:* "The defence of fair dealing may *avail* a defendant who cites passages from the plaintiff's work in order to criticise the underlying doctrine or philosophy." (Eng.)/ "Plaintiff has not brought this action under any of the civil-rights statutes, and it would not have *availed* him if he had."/ "Plaintiff testified that the contract of employment was for life; even if it were, however, the contract would *avail* him nothing, for an employment contract for life is prohibited under our law."

availment (= the act of availing oneself of something) has scant support in the *OED* and is omitted from most other English-language dictionaries, but the word is now widely used in American legal writing. E.g., "[T]he employment of the known pure electron discharge above ionization voltages in tubes of the DeForest type was but the *availment* of those skilled in the art of the store of knowledge that had been accumulated and lay ready at hand . . . ." *General Elec. Co. v. DeForest Radio Co.,* 23 F.2d 698, 707 (D. Del. Cir. 1928)./ "The conditions necessary for *availment* of this provision are not present in the instant suit." *Henderson v. Prudential Ins. Co.,* 238 F. Supp. 862, 866 (E.D. Mich. 1965)./ "If on remand the plaintiffs amend their pleadings accordingly, they will have established a case on the purposeful *availment* issue sufficient to resist dismissal on the face of the pleadings." *Thompson v. Chrysler Motors Corp.,* 755 F.2d 1162, 1173 (5th Cir. 1985).

avails, n., (= profits or proceeds esp. from a sale of property) is correctly labeled "archaic" in *W3* and in the *SOED.* Legal writers—fond as they are of ARCHAISMS—still occasionally use it. E.g., "[N]o particular items are selected as representing the *avails* of the trust fund." George G. Bogert & George T. Bogert, *The Law of Trusts and Trustees* § 923, at 390 (2d ed. 1982).

Avail, the singular form, is frequently used—e.g.: "The evidence in this regard, to have *avail,* should be of the most satisfactory kind."/ "We know that the admonition to the children would be wholly impotent and of no *avail.*" Cf. **availment.**

avenge; revenge. To *avenge* is to visit fitting retribution upon another, usu. on behalf of a relative, friend, or the like. To *revenge* is to inflict suffering or harm upon another out of personal resentment. *Avenge* and *vengeance* have to do with justice and the legal process, *revenge* with getting even. *Revenge* is both intransitive and transitive; *avenge* is transitive only. Moreover, *revenge* can act as a noun, whereas *avenge* cannot.

aver; asseverate. These terms are popular with lawyers as substitutes for *say* or *state. Aver* has its place in solemn contexts—it should not be lightly used. *Asseverate,* an even weightier word, is seldom justified. Both refer to affirmations of fact, usually with no implication that an oath has been taken.

average is a word that assumes a broad sample of subjects. The word does not mix well with *each:* "Each Houston partner *averages* ten years of Houston experience." [Read *Partners in Houston have an average of ten years' experience.*] See **each (B).**

averageable. So spelled.

averment; averral. *Averment* is the preferred noun corresponding to *aver* in both AmE and BrE. E.g., "One plea on which the respondents' case depends is the relevancy of *averments.*" (Eng.)/ "Upon review of a dismissal for failure to state a claim, we must accept all well-pleaded *averments* as true and view them in the light most favorable to the plaintiff." *Averral* is a NEEDLESS VARIANT.

averse. See **adverse.**

avert (= to turn away, prevent), when used for *advert,* is a MALAPROPISM if it is not merely a typographical error—e.g.: "Appellee correctly *averts* [read *adverts*] to the delineation in *Brown Shoe Co. v. U.S.,* in which the Supreme Court stated that 'the outer boundaries of a product market are determined by the reasonable interchangeability of use.'" For a correct use of *avert,* see **advert.**

avertible; avertable. The *-ible* form is preferable. See -ABLE (A).

aviate; avigate. No distinction was originally intended with the introduction of *avigate,* although some DIFFERENTIATION in emphasis has emerged. *Aviate,* a BACK-FORMATION of *aviation* first used in the late 19th century, means "to operate an aircraft."

Avigate, a PORTMANTEAU WORD formed from *aviate* and *navigate,* means "to handle and guide (i.e., navigate) an aircraft in the air"—e.g.: "An occasional statute has made it a misdemeanor to operate a train, navigate a vessel, or *avigate* an airplane, while in an intoxicated condition." Rollin M. Perkins & Ronald N. Boyce, *Criminal Law* 999 (3d ed. 1982). *W3* records *avigation* but not *avigate*; the *OED* neglects both words.

In the American law of easements, the usual phrase is *avigational* or *avigation easement.* E.g., "An *avigational* easement . . . permits free flights over the land in question." *U.S. v. Brondum,* 272 F.2d 642, 645 (5th Cir. 1959)./ "We see no reason why an *avigation* easement may not be acquired by prescription in this state." *Drennen v. County of Ventura,* 112 Cal. Rptr. 907, 909 n. 2 (Cal. Ct. App. 1974)./ "[O]verflights of aircraft flying into and out of the airport had occurred with such frequency and intensity as to have ripened into the taking of an *avigational* easement." *Fields v. Sarasota-Manatee Airport Auth.,* 512 So. 2d 961, 962 (Fla. Dist. Ct. App. 1987). See **easement (A).**

avocation; vocation. These words are almost opposites, although many writers misuse *avocation* for *vocation.* The former means "hobby," whereas the latter means "a calling or profession." Here is the common mistake: "We defer to the opinions of our legal advisers, physicians, tradesmen, and artisans in all matters relating to their respective *avocations.*" Did the writer of that sentence have in mind golf, gardening, and numismatics?

avoid, void, v.t.**; avoidance, voidance.** In legal writing these verb and noun pairs are perfectly synonymous. *Avoid,* in law, often means "to make void or to cancel," although in the language of nonlawyers it invariably means "to refrain from" or "to escape or evade." Here is an example of *avoid* in the old-fashioned legal sense: "We are next to consider, how a deed may be *avoided,* or rendered of no effect." (Blackstone)/ "Strictly, the word 'voidable' means valid until *avoided.*" *Void* can act as noun, verb, or adjective. The noun *voidance* denotes "the act of voiding."

The legal senses of *avoid* and *avoidance* invariably confuse nonlawyers, who are accustomed to the ordinary meanings of these words. It might therefore be advisable to prefer *void* and *voidance.* E.g., "If the wife has inchoate dower in land transferred in living trust and does not release her dower, her dower claim is not *avoided* [read *voided*]." / "The Wills Act of 1837 added a provision *avoiding* [read *voiding*] the interest of a party whose spouse was a witness, but went on to declare that no will should fail because the witnesses thereto were incompetent." The archaic sense of *avoid* is ensconced in a number of statutes—e.g.: "[T]he trustee may *avoid* any transfer of an interest of the debtor in property." 11 U.S.C. § 547(b) (1988).

Here the popular meaning of *avoid* appears in a legal context in such a way that a lawyer might at first wonder whether the legal meaning was intended: "The affidavit contains nothing more than a recital of unsupported allegations, conclusory in nature; as such, it is insufficient to *avoid* summary judgment."

In its lay sense "to evade or escape," *avoid* is sometimes misused for *prevent* or *circumvent:* "Wide public participation *avoids* [read *prevents*] the problem of unfairness."

avoidable-consequences doctrine. See **mitigation-of-damages doctrine.**

avoidance. See **confession and avoidance.**

avowal; avowry, avowtry. The noun corresponding to *avow* in its common meaning ("to declare openly") is *avowal.* Its sibling, *avowry,* serves as the noun form corresponding to the specialized common-law meaning of *avow* ("to acknowledge, in an answer, that one has taken something, and to justify the act"). *Avowry* is the equivalent in actions of replevin to the general common-law doctrine of confession and avoidance. E.g., "The reply of a plaintiff to an *avowry* by a defendant in a replevin action might take one of several forms." F.A. Enever, *History of the Law of Distress* 199 (1931). *Avowtry* is an obsolete synonym of *adultery.*

avulsion. Lawyers may run across the medical as well as the legal use of this word; hence it may be useful to understand the common thread in meaning. Generally, *avulsion* denotes the action of pulling off, plucking out, or tearing away; forcible separation (*OED*).

In land law, *avulsion* refers to the sudden removal of land, by change in a river's course or by the action of flood, to another person's estate; in which event, contrary to the rule of *alluvion* (q.v.) or gradual accretion of soil, it remains the property of the original owner (*OED*). Medically, however, the term has come to denote "a tearing away of a structure or part accidentally or surgically" (*W3*) <avulsion of the diseased limb>.

await; wait. *Await* is always transitive (i.e., it takes a direct object), and *wait* is always intransitive. One *awaits* something, but one *waits for* or *on* something. If no object is supplied, *wait* is the proper term: "Then she brought the dishes in to where the family *awaited* [read *waited*], sitting at the low table."

awake(n). See **wake.**

award over is verbose for *award.* E.g., "What is at stake, as far as the charity is concerned, is the cost of reasonable protection and the amount of the insurance premium, not the *awarding over* [read *awarding*] of its entire assets in damages." See PARTICLES, UNNECESSARY & **over (A).**

aw(e)less. The spelling with the *-e-* is standard.

awful originally meant "inspiring or filled with awe." E.g., "No tribunal can approach such a question without a deep sense of its importance, and of the *awful* responsibility involved in its decision." *McCulloch v. Maryland,* 17 U.S. (4 Wheat.) 316,

400 (1819) (per Marshall, C.J.). Its meaning has now degenerated to "horrible, terrible."

awhile; a while. Generally, one should use this term adverbially, without the preposition, and spell it as one word <he rested awhile>. Whenever the term is introduced by a preposition, however, it should be spelled as two words <he rested for a while>.

axiom = an established principle that is universally accepted within a given framework of reasoning or thinking. The term should not be used of propositions argued for by advocates; if the issue is the subject of controversy, it is not an *axiom,* unless the question is the applicability of an axiom to a given situation.

B

baby-snatching. See **kidnapping (B).**

baby, splitting the. See **splitting the baby.**

backadation. See **backwardation.**

backberend; backberand; backverinde; backbearing. This Anglo-Saxon term means "having stolen goods in one's possession when apprehended" and refers to a person carrying off stolen property (lit., "bearing it on one's back"). Now confined to historical contexts, the word is most often spelled *backberend.* The other forms are variants.

Some writers prefer *backbearing* (often hyphenated in BrE) because it is the most modern form—e.g.: "The first dealt with the criminal taken in the act, and for him there was short shrift. Many local custumals relate the various deaths assigned to the hand-having and *back-bearing* thief." Theodore F.T. Plucknett, *A Concise History of the Common Law* 427 (5th ed. 1956).

BACK-FORMATIONS, or clippings, are words formed by removing an affix from longer words that are mistakenly assumed to be derivatives. This process occurs most commonly when a *-tion* noun is erroneously shortened to make a verb ending in *-te*—e.g., from *emotion* comes *emote.*

Such back-formations are objectionable when they stand merely as NEEDLESS VARIANTS of already extant verbs:

Back-Formation	*Usual Word*
accreditate	accreditation
administrate	administer
asportate	asport
cohabitate	cohabit
delimitate	delimit
evolute	evolve
indemnificate	indemnify
interpretate	interpret
orientate	orient
registrate	register
remediate	remedy
solicitate	solicit
subornate	suborn

Sculpt, arguably a NEEDLESS VARIANT of *sculpture,* v.t., is now actually the more common verb.

Many back-formations never gain real legitimacy (e.g., *enthuse*), some are aborted early in their existence (e.g., *ebullit, frivol*), and still others are of questionable vigor (e.g., *aggress, attrit, effulge, elocute, evanesce*). *Burgle,* q.v., (back-formed from *burglar*) continues to have a jocular effect (in AmE), as do *effuse, emote,* and *laze.* Three 20th-century back-formed words, *choate, liaise,* and *surveil,* have come to be used with some frequency in legal contexts.

Many examples have survived respectably, among them *diagnose, donate, orate, resurrect,* and *spectate. Enthuse* may one day be among these respectable words, although it has not gained approval since it first appeared in the early 19th century. But many have become accepted as legitimate because they have filled gaps in the language and won acceptance through their usefulness. The best rule of thumb is to avoid newborn back-formations that appear newfangled, but not, like a prig, to eschew common back-formations that are useful. Only philologists today recognize as back-formations *beg* (from *beggar*), *jell* (from *jelly*), *peddle* (from *peddler*), *rove* (from *rover*), and *type* (from *typewriter*).

For specific discussions of legal examples, see **asport(ate), novate, registrate, remediate, solicitate, subinfeudate & subornate.**

back of; in back of. These Americanisms strike a more casual tone than their equivalent *behind,* the word that good editors tend to substitute. E.g., "An original writ was an order issuing from the Chancery, 'as a matter of course.' . . . *Back of* [read *Behind*] the writ lay the authority of the king." C. Gordon Post, *An Introduction to the Law* 30 (1963)./ "The notion *back of* [read *behind*] these quotations is essentially the same as that of the familiar saying, 'The king can do no wrong.'" Lon L. Fuller, *Anatomy of the Law* 24 (1968).

backpay is commonly spelled as one word in AmE. The British tend to spell it as two words.

backverinde. See **backberend.**

backwardation; backadation. Leff defines this term (having two forms) as, "in stock market parlance, a fee paid by a seller for the privilege of delaying the delivery of securities past their normal delivery date," and puts his main entry under *backadation.* See Arthur A. Leff, *The Leff Dictionary of Law,* 94 Yale L.J. 1855, 2113 (1985). Most dictionaries, however, spell the term *backwardation.* Fowler included the term in his "ill-favored list" of HYBRID derivatives (*MEU2* at 253), but it has become standard.

bad, in law, may mean "not valid"—e.g.: "As though thumbing their noses at a starving woman while self-righteously wrapping themselves in the flag, the Four Horsemen [q.v.] and Roberts held the law *bad.*" Fred Rodell, *Nine Men* 241 (1955). The *OED* attests this legal usage from the late 19th century.

bad; badly. See ADVERBS (C).

bade. See **bid.**

bad(-)faith. *Bad faith* is the noun phrase <in bad faith>, *bad-faith* the adjectival phrase <bad-faith promises>. See ***mala fide(s).***

bad law. See **bad.**

bad-man theory. "But if we take the view of our friend, the *bad man,* we shall find that he does not care two straws for the axioms or deductions, but that he does want to know what the Massachusetts or English courts are likely to do in fact. I am much of his mind. The prophecies of what the courts will do in fact, and nothing more pretentious, are what I mean by the law." Oliver Wendell Holmes, "The Path of the Law," in *Collected Legal Papers* 172–73 (1920; repr. 1952). This famous passage gave a substantial impetus to the realist movement among legal theorists—that one must study the actual behavior of courts and lawyers as well as, or even instead of, theorizing about ultimate sources of law and deductions from those sources. In fact, Holmes did not hold this iconoclastic view but wished to point to the fact that, for the parties, what matters about law is what happens, what the court decides or orders.

The passage gave rise to what theorists now customarily call the *bad-man theory of law.* Karl Llewellyn took the idea a step beyond Holmes's formulation: "[T]he people who have the doing in charge, whether they be judges or sheriffs or clerks or jailers or lawyers, are officials of the law. *What these officials do about disputes is, to my mind, the law itself.*" Karl N. Llewellyn, *The Bramble Bush* 3 (1930; repr. 1981) (emphasis in orig.).

Later writers repeated the name often enough that it has become a basic idea in modern law, especially as framed originally by Holmes—e.g.: "Holmes returned to this idea (which he sometimes referred to as his *'bad man' theory of law*) over and over throughout his career." Grant Gilmore, *The Death of Contract* 126–27 n.124 (1974).

bail is a CHAMELEON-HUED legal term. As a noun, it means (1) "the person who acts as a surety for a debt"; (2) "the security or guaranty agreed upon"; or (3) "release on surety of a person in custody." In sense (3), modern idiom requires *release on bail,* although formerly *in bail* was not uncommon—e.g.: "Mr. Bartletta was then taken before the recorder and released *in bail* to await the act of the grand jury."

As a verb, *bail* means (1) "to set (a person) free for security on the person's own recognizance for appearance on another day" <the prisoner was not bailed but committed>; (2) "to become a surety for"; (3) "to guarantee"; or (4) to place (personal property) in someone else's charge.

bailable (= admitting of or entitled to bail) may refer either to persons or to offenses. E.g., "Furthermore, the record shows that Dovalina's attempted murder charge was not *bailable.*" (One might as naturally have written that Dovalina himself was not *bailable,* because he had been charged with attempted murder.)/ "Even if Congress is free to define *nonbailable* offenses, certainly the allowable justifications are limited and cannot include punishing a defendant before the final determination of his guilt." See -ABLE.

bail bondsman. See **bailor.**

bailee; bailie. *Bailee* = one to whom personal property is delivered (or *bailed*) without any change in ownership. E.g., "At common law a *bailee* (i.e., a person to whom the possession of goods is entrusted by the owner) who acted dishonestly had some immunity, since he was considered to be in lawful possession of the goods." L.B. Curzon, *English Legal History* 244 (2d ed. 1979).

Bailie is a term for a Scottish magistrate; it is also a dialectal variant of *bailiff,* q.v. See also **bailment.**

bailer. See **bailor.**

bailie. See **bailee.**

bailiery; bailiary. The former is the preferred form of this word, meaning "the jurisdiction of a bailie."

bailiff, n., = (1) in England, a sheriff's officer employed to serve writs, make arrests, and execute process (see **bumbailiff**); (2) in the U.S., a court officer who keeps order with the parties, attorneys, and jurors during court proceedings.

bailiff, v.i. Primarily in law-school mock trials and moot court, the age-old noun *bailiff* has come to be used as a verb meaning "to act as bailiff." That being so, the newfangled verb will perforce soon infiltrate the speech of the profession. It is an American casualism that should not appear in serious contexts. See NOUNS AS VERBS.

bailiwick; sheriffwick; sheriffdom. *Bailiwick* = the office, jurisdiction, or district of a bailiff. Figuratively, it has become synonymous with *domain. Sheriffwick* = the office, jurisdiction, or district of a sheriff.

Because in one sense *bailiff* and *sheriff* are synonymous, the derivatives in *-wick* (lit. "village") have become synonyms. *Bailiwick* is the more common of the two: "A bailiff was popularly referred to as a 'bailie,' and before long a bailie's wick [i.e., village] was expressed as his *'bailiwick.'* And in time this word came to be used to indicate the special territory over which a peace officer exercises his authority as such." Rollin M. Perkins & Ronald N. Boyce, *Criminal Law* 1096 (3d ed. 1982). *Bailiffry* is a NEEDLESS VARIANT, and *bailivia* is an obsolete variant, of *bailiwick.*

In the sense "the office of the sheriff," *sheriffwick* is less common than *sheriffdom,* which was originally a Scotticism. E.g., "The history of the *sheriffdom* is one of the most important departments of the constitutional history of England." *Grifenhagen v. Ordway,* 113 N.E. 516, 517 (N.Y. 1916). See **sheriffalty.**

bail jump, n., = the act of defaulting on [i.e., "jumping"] one's bail. Though seemingly slang, state and federal courts in the U.S. regularly use the term—e.g.: "[T]he presiding judge made the following statement: . . . 'I intend to hold Mr. Lupo for the Grand Jury on the felony *bail jump* in that the warrant has been outstanding since 1970 . . . .'" *People v. Lupo,* 345 N.Y.S.2d 348, 350 (N.Y. City Crim. Ct. 1973)./ "McLennan timely moved to dismiss the indictment prior to trial arguing that it was fatally defective because it did not specifically allege that Chagra's *bail jump,* to which McLennan was allegedly an accessory, was willful." *U.S. v. McLennan,* 672 F.2d 239, 242 (1st Cir. 1982).

Whereas a specific instance is referred to as a *bail jump* (or sometimes *bail-jump*), the crime itself is known as *bail-jumping* (an older phrase)—e.g.: "On February 10, 1938, a short affidavit was filed in the Magistrates' Court charging the defendant with the crime of *bail jumping.*" *People v. Davis,* 5 N.Y.S.2d 411, 412 (N.Y. Gen. Sess. 1938). Often the expression serves as a PHRASAL ADJECTIVE—e.g.: "It appears that he was not convicted on the *bail-jumping* charge but did plead guilty to a different misdemeanor charge . . . ." *People ex rel. Lobell v. McDonnell,* 71 N.E.2d 423, 425 (N.Y. App. Div. 1947). See **jump bail.**

bailment = (1) a delivery of personal property by a person (a *bailor*) to another (a *bailee*) who holds it under an express or implied-in-fact contract; (2) the personal property delivered to a bailee; (3) the action of posting bail for a criminal defendant; or (4) the record of one's posting bail for a criminal defendant. The definitions appear in order of decreasing frequency. Sense (1) is by far the most common—e.g.: "Another kind of situation [that] has traditionally been treated as contractual . . . is the relationship created by what is known as a gratuitous *bailment,* i.e., a transaction in which goods are loaned to, or deposited with, another party without payment." P.S. Atiyah, *An Introduction to the Law of Contract* 120–21 (3d ed. 1981).

bailor; bailer; bailee; bail bondsman. *Bailor* and *-er* are not at all clearly distinguished in actual legal usage, although they might easily and usefully be given clear DIFFERENTIATION. *Bailor* and *bailee* (i.e., the persons on the giving and receiving ends of a bailment [sense (1)]) are correlative personal nouns. E.g., "No *bailee* is permitted to deny that the *bailor* by whom any goods were entrusted to him was entitled to those goods at the time when they were so entrusted." (Eng.) See **bailee** & -ER (A).

Bailer (or *bail bondsman*) should be reserved for the sense "one who attaches bail (the surety in criminal law)." Nevertheless, the spelling *bailor* is often used in that sense, and *bailer* appears occasionally in civil contexts. Given the inevitable objections to *bail bondsman* on grounds of SEXISM, we ought to encourage wider use of *bailer* in this sense.

balance of probability; beyond a reasonable doubt. These phrases express two different burdens of proof. In a civil trial, once both sides have presented evidence, the jury is instructed to find for the party that, on the whole, has the stronger case, i.e., the party whose evidence tips the *balance of probability*—however slight the edge may be. But in a criminal trial, the proof necessary for a conviction must be *beyond a reasonable doubt,* because of the presumption of innocence. See **burden of proof & preponderance of the evidence.**

ballot. See **vote.**

banc. See **en banc (A).**

bandit has two plural forms, *bandits* and *banditti.* The native English form (*bandits*) is preferred. See PLURALS (A).

banish, v.t., generally takes the preposition *from* <he was banished from the country>. Krapp cites the use "The king *banishes* you his presence," with two objects, but this use is archaic. George Philip Krapp, *A Comprehensive Guide to Good English* 68 (1927).

banknote is one word in both AmE and BrE.

bankrupt, adj.; **bankrout.** The latter is an obsolete form of the word. In the English Renaissance, scholars respelled French borrowings such as *bankrout* on the Latin model, hence *bankrupt.* Many of these respellings did not survive (e.g., *accompt* for *account*); *bankrupt* is one of the few that did. See **comptroller.**

bankrupt, n. Although in popular speech and writing it is common to refer to a *bankrupt*—a usage dating from at least the early 16th century—most modern bankruptcy statutes use the term *debtor* instead. Thus, one treatise states: "Nobody is a *bankrupt.* There is no such person under the Bankruptcy Code." David G. Epstein et al., *Bankruptcy* 6 (1993).

bankruptcy [fr. L. *bancus* "table" + *ruptus* "broken"] = (1) the fact of being financially unable to pursue one's business and meet one's engagements, esp. of being unable to pay one's debts; (2) the fact of having declared bankruptcy under a bankruptcy statute; or (3) the field of law dealing with those who are unable or unwilling to pay their debts. See **insolvency.**

Bankruptcy is often misspelled *bankruptsy.*

Bankruptcy Act; Bankruptcy Code. In the U.S., the phrase *Bankruptcy Act* refers to the Bankruptcy Act of 1898; it governed bankruptcy cases filed before 1 October 1979. The phrase *Bankruptcy Code* refers to the Bankruptcy Reform Act of 1978 (frequently amended since then), which governs all cases filed since 1 October 1979.

bankrupt(cy) law. The normal idiom today is *bankruptcy law(s),* although *bankrupt law* was once fairly common—e.g.: "Under the *bankrupt law* [read, in more modern terms, *bankruptcy law*] the defendant had the same right to prove up the note for payment in the bankruptcy proceedings that the plaintiffs had, and . . . they were under no obligation to go into the *bankrupt court* [read, in more modern terms, *bankruptcy court*] and prove the claim for the benefit of the surety." *Levy v. Wagner,* 69 S.W. 112, 114 (Tex. Civ. App. 1902).

bankruptee, n., is an unnecessary NEOLOGISM equivalent to the well-established noun *bankrupt* (= one that has declared bankruptcy). E.g., "[A] judge sets a payback plan on the unsecured debt [that] he thinks the *bankruptee* [read *bankrupt*] can meet in good faith." Lisa J. McCue, *Bankruptcy Changes Called Possible,* Am. Banker, 29 Jan. 1981, at 3./ "The second method allows *bankruptees* [read *bankrupts*] to propose to the court a 'good faith' repayment program . . . ." Phil Battey, *Bankruptcy Reform Drive Hits Lawmakers at Home,* Am. Banker, 31 Aug. 1981, at 1./ "For legal purposes, the family homestead can include up to 200 acres (100 for a single adult) of real property that aren't located within city, town, or village limits, and/or one acre of land, plus any temporary residence if the *bankruptee* [read *bankrupt*] has not acquired another home." Shropshire, *The Nouveau Broke,* D Magazine, Nov. 1986, at 89 (inset). See **bankrupt,** n.

bankruptsy. See **bankruptcy.**

bar, n. In the U.S., all lawyers are members of a bar, whether they are litigators or office practitioners. In G.B., only barristers (in Eng.) and advocates (in Scot.), as opposed to solicitors, make up the *Bar* (the word is customarily capitalized in BrE). See **called to the bar & attorney (A).**

Unified bar and *integrated bar* are interchangeable terms referring to bar associations in which membership is a statutory requisite for the practice of law in a given geographic area.

For the sense of relating to a defendant's judgment on the merits, see **merger (B).**

bar; debar; disbar. The first two have closely related meanings. *Bar* means "to prevent (often by legal obstacle)." E.g., "The English Statute of Westminster II *barred* dower of a wife who deserted her husband and committed adultery; and some states have statutes *barring* an elective share on a similar principle."/ "The court concluded that these warranty disclaimers did not necessarily *bar* a breach of contract claim."/ "Legislative immunity does not, of course, *bar* all judicial review of legislative acts." *Bar* serves also as a noun <a bar to all claims>.

Debar, a somewhat archaic FORMAL WORD, means "to preclude from having or doing." E.g., "It would require very persuasive circumstances enveloping congressional silence to *debar* this Court from re-examining its own doctrines."/ "There is no reason why the plaintiff should be confined to his action on the special agreement, and be *debarred* his remedy on the assumpsit implied by law." (Eng.) *Disbar* means "to expel from the legal profession." The corresponding nouns are *debarment* and *disbarment.*

bar entails. See **entail.**

bargain, n.; **agreement; contract.** Williston sorted these terms out with admirable clarity: "A *bargain* is an agreement of two or more persons to exchange promises, or to exchange a promise for a performance. Thus defined, *bargain* is at once narrower than *agreement* in that it is not applicable to all agreements, and broader than *contract,* since it includes a promise given in exchange for an insufficient consideration. It also covers transactions [that] the law refuses to recognize as contracts because of illegality." 1 Samuel Williston & W.H.E. Jaeger, *A Treatise on the Law of Contracts* § 2A, at 7 (3d ed. 1957).

bargain, v.t. In law, an otherwise obsolete sense persists: "to agree to buy and sell; to contract for." See **grant, bargain, sell, and convey.**

bargained-for exchange. This phrase is sometimes erroneously rendered *bargain for exchange.* Here variations of it are correctly used: "The doing of the act constitutes acceptance, the *bargained-for* consideration, and the offeree's performance."/ "If the termination of obligations were an immediate *bargained-for* right of consequence, he would presumably have taken advantage of his freedom from testamentary obligation to make a new will."

The origin of the phrase *bargained-for exchange* may be seen from this sentence: "Consideration is something bargained for and given in exchange."

bargainee (= the purchaser in a bargained-for exchange) is more obscure than *purchaser,* but the word is perhaps a useful correlative of *bargainor.* E.g., "The Statute itself operated to vest the seisin of the bargainor in the *bargainee.*" Cornelius J. Moynihan, *Introduction to the Law of Real Property* 183 (2d ed. 1988). See -EE & **bargainer.**

bargainer; bargainor. Though one might suspect that the two forms are synonymous, they are not. *Bargainer* means "one who bargains." *Bargainor* has a more specific legal meaning: "the seller in a bargained-for exchange." See **bargainee.**

bargee. Though illogically formed with the *-ee* suffix, the established form *bargee* (17th c.) is a variant of *bargeman* (14th c.), without the infelicity of SEXISM. E.g., "The story of the Elmhurst's *bargee* was that off Bedloe's Island a third tug of the railroad . . . came alongside, struck the barge a heavy blow on her port quarter, nearly capsizing her, driving her forward against the barge ahead, and breaking some planks forward." *Sinram v. Pennsylvania R.R.,* 61 F.2d 767, 768 (2d Cir. 1932) (per L. Hand, J.). See -EE (A).

barrator. See **champertor.**

barratrous is the adjective corresponding to the noun *barratry* (q.v.)—e.g.: "The statute is clear that *barratrous* conduct is to be treated as a criminal offense." *Galinski v. Kessler,* 480 N.E.2d 1176, 1179 (Ill. App. Ct. 1985)./ "They simply state that the Master sailed away with the cargo and conclude that this conduct was *barratrous.*" *Tradewinds Marketing, Inc. v. General Accident Ins. Co.,* 665 F. Supp. 104, 105 (D.P.R. 1987).

barratry; simony. Why these terms are sometimes confused is not at all apparent. *Barratry* = (1) in criminal law, vexatious persistence in, or incitement to, litigation; (2) in admiralty, (of a master or crew) fraudulent or grossly negligent conduct that is prejudicial to a shipowner; (3) in older Eng. and Scots law, the act of going abroad to purchase a benefice from Rome; or (4) in Scots law, the accepting of a bribe by a judge. The adjective is *barratrous* (q.v.) and the agent noun *barrator.*

Simony = the purchase or sale of an ecclesiastical promotion. The adjective is *simoniac(al),* the agent noun either *simonist* or *simoniac.*

barrister = a specialist consultant and pleader belonging to a class of lawyers that is given predominant (formerly exclusive) rights of audience in superior courts. Ordinarily, the word applies to an English or Northern Irish pleader (the Scottish counterpart being an *advocate*). When used in reference to an American lawyer, the word smacks of highfalutin journalese—e.g.: "The prestige and importance of the federal circuit bench [in the U.S.] attracts high-caliber *barristers* [read *lawyers*]." Donald D. Jackson, *Judges* 312 (1974). See **attorney (A), counsel (A), Queen's Counsel** & **solicitor.**

barristerial = of or pertaining to a barrister; lawyerly. The term is, naturally, more common in BrE than in AmE, but it appears in the latter as well—e.g.: "Since the 12(e) motion is prone for implementation of *barristerial* shadow boxing, its exercise should be cast in the mold of strictest necessity." *Lincoln Labs. v. Savage Labs.,* 26 F.R.D. 141, 142 (D. Del. 1960)./ "Having taken this position, plaintiffs, in the exercise of commendable *barristerial* caution, have nevertheless submitted documents indicating that . . . Dr. Newman directed the formation of a university-wide Salary Review Committee . . . ." *Chang v. University of Rhode Island,* 554 F. Supp. 1203, 1205 (D.R.I. 1983).

base fee. See **fee simple (D).**

basis. A. For *reason.* *Basis* is sometimes used unidiomatically for *reason*—e.g.: "The court, after a full review of the authorities, concluded that there was now no sound *basis* [read *reason*] why the value of life insurance coverage, as well as the cash surrender value, might not be considered in a property division between parties to a divorce action." *Basis* is properly followed by *for* <the basis for the decision>. *Reason,* by contrast, fits with either *for* <the reason for the decision> or *why* (as in the example quoted above). Writers who use *basis why* are probably driven to it by the SUPERSTITION that *reason why* is an error. See **reason why.**

B. *On a . . . basis.* This long-winded phrase often ousts a simpler, more legitimate adverb—e.g.:

- "The commission was set up *on a provisional basis* [read *provisionally*]."
- "Those issues must be *determined on a case-by-case basis* [read *determined case by case*]."
- "The attorney represented his clients *on a contingent-fee basis* [read *for a contingent fee*]."
- "In *Usery v. Brandel,* nine migrant farm laborers working *on a sharecropper basis* [read *as sharecroppers*] sought to intervene in a suit brought by the Secretary of Labor to enforce the . . . Fair Labor Standards Act."

See FLOTSAM PHRASES.

C. Plural Form. The plural of *basis,* as well as *base,* is *bases;* the pronunciations differ, however: for *basis,* the plural is pronounced /***bay**-seez*/, for *base* /**bays**-*ez*/.

bastard, a term of abuse generally, is still used neutrally in the law, in either of two senses: (1) "a child born out of wedlock"; or (2) "a child born to a married woman whose husband, for some provable reason, could not possibly be the father." Sense (1) has always been more common—e.g.: "Although a *bastard* cannot inherit from his parents or other ancestors at common law, statutes or judicial decisions permit a *bastard* to inherit from his mother and the mother to inherit from her *bastard.*"

Today, however, the law's technical neutrality is not without comic overtones. See **adulterine bastard, illegitimate child, natural child** & EUPHEMISMS.

bastardy = (1) the condition of a bastard; illegitimate birth; or (2) the begetting of bastards; fornication (*OED*). Today in sense (1), *illegitimacy* is the more usual term, and the preferable one for avoiding unduly derogatory connotations. Sense (2) is not common.

bathos; pathos. These two words sometimes cause confusion. *Bathos* means "a sudden descent from the exalted to the trite, or from the sublime to the ridiculous." *Pathos* means "sympathetic pity" and is useful, e.g., in reference to juries.

battery. To nonlawyers, *battery* connotes physical violence. The legal meaning, however, is "the intentional or negligent application of physical force to, or the offensive contact with, someone without consent." Thus, offensive contact is enough—for example, an unwelcome kiss or caress. E.g., "[T]he *battery* here was a technical one, and was accompanied by neither physical injury nor violence. It was a mere touching of the person of the plaintiff, a mere incident of the restraint, the false imprisonment." *Fisher v. Rumler,* 214 N.W. 310, 311 (Mich. 1927). As a tort, *battery* is a civil wrong giving rise to a cause of action for damages; as a crime, it is a social harm punished by the state. See **assault.**

bawdy house; house of ill fame; disorderly house. These phrases are three of the EUPHEMISMS by which lawyers have traditionally referred to a brothel or house of prostitution. The quaint phrase *disorderly house* is the broadest of the three, denoting a house where people carry on activities that constitute a nuisance to the neighborhood; these activities might include gambling and drug-dealing as well as prostitution.

beak is a BrE slang term for a magistrate or justice of the peace. E.g., "In the cities a lone example was set by Henry Fielding (1707–54), the novelist, sitting at Bow Street as the self-styled 'principal Westminster magistrate,' and his brother and successor, Sir John Fielding, 'the Blink *Beak*.' Unpaid, like other magistrates, they spurned the bribes . . . ." Alan Harding, *A Social History of English Law* 270–71 (1966). The *OED* quotes many examples from the 16th to the 19th century, including one from Dickens's *Oliver Twist* (1837–1838), and notes that the precise etymology is unknown.

bear the relation. See **relation (B).**

because. A. Punctuation with. Generally, the word *because* should not follow a comma. E.g., "This court should remand the *case, because* the defendants have created federal jurisdiction pretextually." (Delete the comma after *case.*)

B. Causing Ambiguity After a Negative. When a causal phrase follows a negative, the resulting expression is usually ambiguous—though sometimes only technically so. E.g., "A proposition is not false because it is a truism darkly expressed." W.W. Buckland, *Some Reflections on Jurisprudence* 109 (1945).

In fact, putting a purpose clause or phrase after a negative often causes ambiguities, attested by a priest's unintentionally humorous statement: "I wear no clothes to distinguish myself from the congregation."

C. Coupled with *reason*. *Because* creates a REDUNDANCY when used as a conjunction after *reason.* E.g., "Clearly, one *reason why* this argument no longer appeals is *because* [read *that*] it rests upon an élitist assumption . . . ." P.S. Atiyah, *Law and Modern Society* 93 (1983). (On still another question raised by that sentence, see **reason why.**)

In the following sentence, the construction is inverted: "*Because* [read *That*] the lessor accepted the first payment is no reason to conclude that the corporation existed by estoppel." See **reason . . . is because.**

D. Beginning Sentences with. An odd superstition holds that beginning a sentence with *because* is a mistake. There is nothing to it. See SUPERSTITIONS (F).

E. Wordy Substitutes for. *Because* is often needlessly replaced by verbose phrases such as *for the reason that, due to the fact that, on the ground that,* and the like. E.g., "It is still thought that many magistrates are too disinclined to reject police evidence, however implausible, perhaps *for the reason that* [read *because*] they feel the police should always be supported as a matter of principle." P.S. Atiyah, *Law and Modern Society* 26 (1983).

F. As a Causal Word Generally. See **as (A).**

before for *by.* Cases come *before* courts and are then *reviewed by* those courts. But some writers mar these idioms—e.g.: "We note that such a determination is a matter placed within the sound discretion of the district judge, and review *before* [read *by*] us is very limited." Cf. **anterior to.** See **previously.**

before-mentioned. See **above-mentioned** & **aforesaid.**

beg is occasionally used in dissenting opinions in the phrases *beg to differ* and *beg to advise.* These are ARCHAISMS to be eschewed.

For the phrase *beg the question,* see **begging the question.**

begat; begot. See BIBLICAL AFFECTATION.

beget is today used only figuratively. E.g., "The services and gifts must have been rendered with a frequency that *begets* an anticipation of their continuance." In its literal sense, *beget* is an ARCHAISM. E.g., "When proof has been given of the non-access of the husband at any time when his wife's child could have been *begotten,* the wife may give evidence as to the person by whom it was *begotten.*" (Eng.) The more usual term today is *to conceive* or *to father.*

begging the question does not mean "evading the issue" or "inviting the obvious questions," as some mistakenly believe. The proper meaning of *begging the question* is "basing a conclusion on an assumption that is as much in need of proof or demonstration as the conclusion itself." The formal name for this logical fallacy is *petitio principii.* Following are two classic examples: "Reasonable men are those who think and reason intelligently." *Patterson v. Nutter,* 7 A. 273, 275 (Me. 1886). (This statement begs the question, "What does it mean to think and reason intelligently?")/ "Life begins at conception! [Fn.: 'Conception is defined as the beginning of life.']" *Davis v. Davis,* unreported opinion (Cir. Tenn. Eq. 1989). (The "proof"—or the definition—is circular.)

In the following sentence, the writer mangled the SET PHRASE *to beg the question* and misapprehended its meaning (by using *begs* for *ignores*): "Blaming Congress and the Democrats for 'criminalizing of policy differences with the executive branch' *begs* a much larger *issue* here: Should members of the executive branch be allowed to withhold vital information from those members of Congress charged by law to monitor specific actions of the president?" Letter of John M. Burns, Wall St. J., 16 May 1990, at A17.

begin. **A. *To begin.*** As an introductory phrase used to enumerate reasons, the idiomatic phrase is *to begin with,* not *to begin.* In the following sentence, the lack of the preposition *with* makes *to begin* sound narrowly chronological, as if *A* actually began something and then, at some indeterminate point, stopped: "To begin [add *with*], A played a substantial role in negotiating both agreements."/ "*To begin* [add *with*], it was clear that Dixon suffered a permanent injury and that he died of an unrelated disease."

B. And *commence & start.* *Begin* is the usual word, to be preferred nine times out of ten. *Commence* is a FORMAL WORD; ceremonies and exercises are likely to *commence,* as are legal proceedings. *Start* is usually used of physical movement <to start running>. Both *begin* and *start*—but not *commence*—may be followed by an infinitive. See **commence.**

behalf. A distinction exists between the phrases *in behalf of* and *on behalf of.* The former means "in the interest or in defense of" <he fought in behalf of a just man's reputation>; the latter, *on behalf of,* means "as the agent of, as representative of" <on behalf of the corporation, I would like to thank . . . > <she appeared on behalf of her client>.

Upon behalf of is now considered much inferior to *on behalf of.* "We conclude that the public interest involved in this dispute compels us to look beyond the immediate interests of the named litigants and to consider the situation of the natural gas consumers *upon* [read *on*] whose behalf the Mississippi Power Service Commission has intervened." See **upon.**

behavior. See COUNT NOUNS AND MASS NOUNS (B) & PLURALS (B).

behavior(al)ism. The correct name for the doctrine that human behavior provides the only significant psychological data is *behaviorism.*

behest is a stronger word than *request;* it means (1) "a command," or (2) "a strong urging." *Bequest* is sometimes misused for *behest,* as here: "It is enough that a writing defamatory in content has been read and understood at the *bequest* [read *behest*] of the defamer."/ "At his *bequest* [read *behest*], I undertook this onerous task, but have been thankful to him for so urging me." See MALAPROPISMS.

behoof is the noun, *behoove* (AmE) or *behove* (BrE) the verb. Both noun and verb have an archaic flavor. Historically, the verb in BrE was pronounced, as it now is in AmE, to rhyme with *move* and *prove.* In BrE today "it is generally made to rime with *rove, grove,* by those who know it only in books" (*OED*).

belabor; labor, v.t., (= to beat severely). Modern dictionaries suggest that in practice the words are interchangeable. Historically, however, in the best usage *belabor* is not to be used figuratively in phrases such as to *belabor* an argument; the preferred expression is to *labor* an argument—e.g.: "I need not *labor* the point that the four elements of the positivist creed just outlined are interdependent . . . ." Lon L. Fuller, *The Morality of Law* 193 (rev. ed. 1969).

The popular grammarian Edwin Newman has chided a justice of the U.S. Supreme Court for writing "to say more would belabor the obvious," stating: "To *belabor* the obvious is to hit it, which hardly seems judicial conduct." Edwin Newman, Foreword to Morton S. Freeman, *A Treasury for Word Lovers* viii (1983). Examples of this usage are legion—e.g.: "Without *belaboring* [read *laboring*] the point, we observe that the separation agreement in this case will be at least partly performed in Texas because the payor resides in that state."/ "Brawner conceded his right against Pendarvis without undue *belaboring* [read *laboring*]."

belated has made its way into legal language as a synonym of *untimely.* E.g., "We must decline to entertain appellant's *belated* cross-points." Its use in this context is perfectly acceptable.

belie = (1) to disguise, give a false idea of; (2) to leave unfulfilled; or (3) to contradict or prove the falsity of. Sense (3) is by far the most common in legal contexts. E.g., "The Court suggests that the search for valuables in the closed glove compartment might be justified as a measure to protect the police against lost property claims; again, this suggestion is *belied* [i.e., *contradicted*] by the record."/ "Appellant contends that his lawyer's failure to put on evidence at the penalty stage prejudiced his ability to avoid the death sentence; but the nature of the evidence appellant asserts his attorney should have presented *belies* [i.e., *proves the falsity of*] the argument." See **vitiate.**

belief. Lawyers frequently speak of a *genuine belief,* a *bona fide belief,* or an *honest belief.* In fact, all such phrases are REDUNDANCIES, since it is quite impossible to believe something ungenuinely, in bad faith, or dishonestly.

belligerence; belligerency. *Belligerence* refers to a person's truculent attitude. *Belligerency* has traditionally, in international law, been the preferred term in referring to the status of a state that is at war—e.g.: "[O]ther states are within their rights in declaring themselves neutral in the struggle, and since there can be no neutrals unless there are two belligerents, such a declaration is equivalent to a recognition of the *belligerency* of both parties." J.L. Brierly, *The Law of Nations* 134 (5th ed. 1955).

bellwether (= one who takes the lead or initiative; a trendsetter) is sometimes mistakenly written *bellweather*—e.g.: "The sheriff conducted me to one of the two vacant jury rooms, then the jury, *bell-weathered* [read *bellwethered*] by Callahan, the court officer, filed out and retired into the other directly opposite." Ephraim Tutt, *Yankee Lawyer* 226 (1943). (The verbal use illustrated in the quoted sentence is unusual—see NOUNS AS VERBS.)

below is often used by appellate courts to mean "at the trial-court stage." E.g., "As the district court noted *below,* this litigation involves only that portion of the contract relating to the actual construction of the platform." Some appellate courts—especially American ones—avoid this term because it may seem to slight trial judges. See **inferior (B).**

below-mentioned; under-mentioned. The former is AmE or BrE; the latter is BrE only. *Below,* like *above,* q.v., is frequently used as an ellipsis for *below-mentioned.*

bemean. See **demean.**

bemuse; amuse. The former is frequently taken to be a fancy variant of the latter; the meanings differ significantly, however. *Bemuse* = (1) to plunge into thought, preoccupy; or (2) to muddle (one's mind); bewilder. Here sense (2) of *bemuse* applies: "It is easy to see why an equity court, *bemused* by the expression 'Equity acts in personam and not in rem,' would be tempted to say that an equity court has no 'power' to affect directly land titles in another state." *Amuse* needs no definition here.

bench = (1) the court considered in its official capacity <remarks from the bench>; (2) judges collectively <bench and bar>; or (3) the judges of a particular court <the Queen's Bench>. Cf. **court.**

Renaissance lawbooks, in referring to *the Bench,* invariably meant the Court of Common Pleas, not the King's Bench.

bencher, in England, means generally "one who sits on a bench" (*OED*), but particularly refers to a member of the governing body of one of the Inns of Court. E.g., "In Pennsylvania, Andrew Hamilton, a barrister and *bencher* of Gray's Inn, came to Philadelphia in 1682." Roscoe Pound, *The Development of Constitutional Guaranties of Liberty* 59 (1957)./ "There was thus little occasion for controversies as to discipline to be brought before the judges, unless the *benchers* failed in the performance of their duties." *People ex rel. Karlin v. Culkin,* 162 N.E. 487, 490 (N.Y. 1928) (per Cardozo, C.J.). *Benchers* are known formally as *Masters of the Bench.*

Archaically, the term was used more generally in reference to magistrates, judges, assessors, and senators.

benchmark (= a point of reference from which to make measurements) is best spelled as one word.

bench memo (AmE) = (1) a short brief submitted by a lawyer to a trial judge, often at the judge's request; or (2) a legal memorandum prepared by an appellate judge's law clerk to help the judge prepare for and participate in oral argument.

bench trial has become—mostly in southern parts of the U.S.—a common equivalent of *trial to the bench* (= a nonjury trial). See **nonjury.**

bench warrant, n., = process that a court issues for the attachment or arrest of a person who has been held in contempt, has been indicted, or has disobeyed a subpoena.

Some legal writers, esp. in Texas, have transformed this noun phrase into a PHRASAL VERB—e.g.: "Having been *bench warranted* from the Texas Department of Corrections where he is serving time for two prior convictions, appellant is hardly a fit candidate for probation." *Roberts v. State,* 587 S.W.2d 724, 725 n.1 (Tex. Crim. App. 1979)./ "Appellant sought the continuance so that Mr. Babineaux could either be *bench warranted* back to testify or deposed." *Babineaux v. Babineaux,* 761 S.W.2d 102, 103 (Tex. App.—Beaumont 1988). If the phrase is to be used as a verb, it should be hyphenated: hence *bench-warranted* would have been the better form in both quotations. See NOUNS AS VERBS.

benefic(ent); beneficial; benevolent. The etymological difference between *beneficent* and *benevolent* is the difference between deeds and sentiments. *Beneficent* = doing good, charitable (*benefic* now being merely a NEEDLESS VARIANT). *Benevolent* = well-wishing, supportive, (emotionally) charitable. The DIFFERENTIATION should be cultivated; we should reserve *beneficent* for "doing good," and *benevolent* for "inclined or disposed to do good." In the following sentences, *benevolence* is used for *beneficence:* "The beneficiary of a charity (e.g., one who uses a charitable hospital) has impliedly [q.v.] waived his right to sue in tort, by virtue of having accepted its *benevolence* [read *beneficence*]."/ "The will and the entire record reveal that the decedent was a very *benevolent man* [read *beneficent man*] who was in the habit of making charitable gifts all over the world."

Beneficial has the general meaning "favorable, producing benefits," and the specialized legal meaning "consisting in a right that derives from something (as a contract or an expectancy) other than legal title" <beneficial interest>. That specialized sense comes from the older legal meaning "of or pertaining to usufruct" (*OED*). E.g., "It is well established that the settlor (creator) may revoke the trust with the consent of all persons beneficially interested therein." Cornelius J. Moynihan, *Introduction to the Law of Real Property* 157 (2d ed. 1988)./ "The supervised administration embraces a determination of the persons *beneficially* entitled to the estate after debts, expenses, and taxes are paid." See **malevolent.**

beneficiary. See ***cestui que trust*** & **devisee.**

benefit. Invariably the passive form of this verb can be advantageously made into an active construction: "Defendant has an adverse interest because he would *have been benefited by* [read *have benefited from*] a ruling in favor of the insurance company." See BE-VERBS (B).

benefit(t)ed; benefit(t)ing. These words should be spelled with one *-t-*, not two. See DOUBLING OF FINAL CONSONANTS.

benefitee. Though it has not yet made its way into most general English-language dictionaries, this word has appeared frequently in American legal prose since the 1950s. The earliest known use is a 1958 case styled (in full) *Liberty Mut. Ins. Co., a Corporation, Individually and as Use* Benefitee *of The Howell Co., v. Hartford Accident & Indem. Co.,* 251 F.2d 761 (1958). Soon it had spread—e.g.: "This provision, without undermining the liberal scope of interrogatory discovery, places the burden of discovery upon its potential *benefitee.*" David W. Louisell, *Modern California Discovery* 124–25 (1963).

The spelling *benefittee* is incorrect (cf. *benefited*) because the accent falls not on the penultimate syllable but on the last syllable. But the word is almost certainly unnecessary for *beneficiary.* See -EE.

benefit of clergy = (1) at common law (12th c.–19th c.), the right of a clergyman not to be tried for a felony in the King's Court; or (2) by SLIPSHOD EXTENSION, religious approval as solemnized in a church ritual. By invoking the benefit of clergy—usu. by reading the so-called *neck verse* (q.v.)—a defendant could have the case transferred from the King's Court (which imposed the death penalty for a felony) to the Ecclesiastical Court (which dispensed far milder punishments).

In sense (2), the phrase is not only a slipshod extension but also a POPULARIZED LEGAL TECHNICALITY, appearing most often in reference to children out of wedlock—e.g.: "With her, and *without benefit of clergy,* he had five children, and it was his boast that, as each arrived, he dispatched it promptly to a foundling home." René A. Wormser, *The Story of the Law* 215 (1962)./ "Wakefield's generation, twenty years on, didn't just engage in sex *without benefit of clergy,* they talked about it." Rhoda Koenig, *Talkin' 'Bout Their Generation,* New York (Mag.), 1 June 1992, at 57.

benevolent. See **benefic(ent).**

benign; benignant. The latter is a NEEDLESS VARIANT. The antonym of *benign,* however, is *malignant.*

bequeath. A. And *devise; devolve.* *Bequeath* = (1) to give (an estate or effect) *to* a person by will <she bequeathed the diadem to her daughter>; or (2) to give (a person) an estate or effect by will <she bequeathed her daughter the diadem>. Lawyers and nonlawyers alike use this term metaphorically: "While its origins are somewhat obscure, we know that the marital privilege is *bequeathed* to us by the long evolution of the common law, not by constitutional adjudication." See **legate.**

Devise = to give property (usu. real property) by will. As a noun, *devise* refers to the realty so given—the analogue for personal property is *bequest.* The Uniform Probate Code uses only the term *devise* to describe giving property by will whether the property is real or personal; it would be bootless to call this well-ensconced terminological shift incorrect. See **devise** & **give, devise, and bequeath.**

Devolve = to pass on (an estate, right, liability, or office) from one person to another. In the context of estates, *devolve* usually takes the preposition *upon,* and sometimes *to.* See **devolve.**

B. For *give.* Using *bequeath* as a fancy equivalent of *give* or *present* is an ignorant pretension—e.g.: "Apparently Mayor Annette Strauss plans to *bequeath* [read *present*] the gift personally to Her Majesty—something rarely done, according to protocol experts. Usually, a gift is *bequeathed* [read *presented*] to the queen's secretary, who then *bequeaths* [read *gives*] it to the queen . . . ." Helen Bryant, *Names & Faces,* Dallas Times Herald, 5 April 1991, at A2.

bequest, n.; **bequeathal; bequeathment.** *Bequest* = (1) the act of bequeathing; or (2) personal property (usu. other than money) disposed of in a will. (Cf. **legacy.**) *Bequest* is sometimes confused with *behest,* q.v. See **devise.**

Bequeathal and *bequeathment* are NEEDLESS VARIANTS of sense (1) of *bequest*—e.g.: "We agree that [the statute] is not applicable, since the trust was demonstrative and not a *bequeathal* [read *bequest*] of specific property." *Estate of Naulin v. Clancy,* 201 N.W.2d 599, 603 (Wis. 1972)./ "The testator's preference for his relatives, it is claimed, was evident from . . . the *bequeathment* [read *bequest*] in Article VI . . . ." *Estate of Fleer v. Elmhurst College,* 315 N.E.2d 260, 261 (Ill. App. Ct. 1974).

bequest, v.t., is a silly error that has appeared in a would-be Shakespearean scholar's writing: "And by so felicitously using the words newly *bequested* [read *bequeathed*] to English, [Shakespeare], more than any other writer of the English Renaissance, validated the efforts of earlier and contemporary neologists." Bryan A. Garner, *Shakespeare's Latinate Neologisms,* 15 Shakespeare Stud. 149, 151 (1982).

bereave, v.t., yields past-tense forms *bereft* or *bereaved,* and the same forms as past participles. *Bereaved* is used in reference to loss of relatives by death. *Bereft* is used in reference to loss of incorporeal possessions or qualities.

To be *bereft of* something is not just to lack it but to have had it taken away. Hence the following uses are incorrect: "The Mann Act was not designed to cover voluntary actions *bereft of* [read *lacking*] sexual commercialism."/ "Because the certification was *bereft of* [read *without*] any clue as to the district judge's reasoning, we could merely vacate the order and remand for a fuller evaluation." *Spiegel v. Trustees of Tufts College,* 843 F.2d 38, 44 (1st Cir. 1988).

beside (= [1] alongside; or [2] in comparison with) is surprisingly often misused for *besides* (= [1] other than; except; or [2] in addition)—e.g.: "When we speak of a unilateral contract, we mean a promise in exchange for which an act or something *beside* [read *besides*] another promise has been given as consideration." Clarence D. Ashley, *What Is a Promise in Law?* 16 Harv. L. Rev. 319, 319 (1903)./ "Hill is the only man *beside* [read *besides*] Trevino to win on the Senior Tour this year . . . ." Jaime Diaz, *At Tradition, Duel Falls Short of Hope,* N.Y. Times, 31 March 1990, at 30.

bestowal; bestowment. *Bestowal* is the usual form, *bestowment* being a NEEDLESS VARIANT.

bet > bet > bet. *Bet* is the preferred (and the far more frequent form) of the past tense and the past participle. E.g., "Thus, if a person *betted* [read *bet*] on Salisbury Plain there would be no place within the Act." Hugh P. Macmillan, *Law and Other Things* 158 (1938)./ "The defendant, Portner, answered that the consideration for his check to Caldwell was small pieces of celluloid called 'checks' representing money *betted* [read *bet*] and lost by him in a game of chance." *Scolaro v. Bellitto,* 184 N.E.2d 604, 606 (Ohio Ct. App. 1962).

betrothal; betrothment. The latter is a NEEDLESS VARIANT.

bettor is the standard spelling for "one who bets or wagers." *Better* has also been used in this sense, but is liable to confusion with the comparative form of *good.* Cf. **abettor.**

between. A. And *among*. *Between* is commonly said to be better with two, and *among* with more than two, things. Sir Ernest Gowers calls this a "superstition" and quotes the *OED:* "In all senses *between* has been, from its earliest appearance, extended to more than two. . . . It is still the only word available to express the relation of a thing to many surrounding and individually; *among* expresses a relation to them collectively and vaguely: we should not say *the space lying among the three points* or *a treaty among three Powers*" (*MEU2* at 57).

The rule as generally enunciated, then, is merely simplistic. Although it is an accurate guide for the verb *divide* (*between* with two objects, *among* with more than two), the only ironclad distinction is that stated by the *OED. Between* expresses one-to-one relations of many things, and *among* expresses collective and undefined relations.

Thus, Article VII of the U.S. Constitution uses *between* seemingly to express reciprocal relations: "The Ratification of the Conventions of nine States, shall be sufficient for the Establishment of this Constitution *between* the States so ratifying the Same."

Yet even the more valid distinction is a relatively new one, not observed by the English courts in 1607: "All the Justices, viz., POPHAM, Chief Justice of England, COKE, Chief Justice of the

Common Pleas, FLEMING, Chief Baron, FENNER, SEARL, YELVERTON, WILLIAMS, and TANFIELD, JJ., were assembled at Sergeants-Inn, to consult what prerogative the King had in digging and taking of saltpetre to make gunpowder by the law of the realm; and upon conference *between* them, these points were resolved by them all, una voce." *The Case of the King's Prerogative in Saltpetre,* 12 Co. 12 (1607).

In the same case in which Justice Marshall several times writes, "*among* the defendant, the forum, and the litigation," Justice Brennan, in his concurring and dissenting opinion, writes: "*between* the controversy, the parties, and the forum state." See *Shaffer v. Heitner,* 433 U.S. 186, 225 (1977). The latter phrasing might be said to express a more specific individual relation between each of the named things, the former phrasing (perhaps consciously) expressing a vaguer relation.

B. *Between* and Numbers. The word *between* may cause problems when used with numbers, particularly if the numbers at either end of the spectrum are intended to be included. E.g., "If three petitioners and one respondent advance to Round Three from a bracket, then those four teams' names will be placed in a hat, and *between one and three* [read *from one to three*] teams will be chosen to switch sides." (Two is the only whole number between one and three.)/ "Saleh met with several other defendants in a Queens garage *between June 23 and June 24* [read *on June 23 and June 24*] to discuss getting cars for the conspiracy." Peg Tyre & Kevin McCoy, *Busted at Beach,* Newsday, 24 July 1993, at 3. (There is no time "between" June 23 and June 24.)

C. *Between you and I.* One commentator has pointedly termed this locution "a grammatical error of unsurpassable grossness." Little can be added to that judgment. See HYPERCORRECTION (B).

D. *Between; as between.* Sometimes *as between* (= comparing; in comparison of) is misused for the straightforward preposition. E.g., "The contractual *provisions as between* [read *provisions between*] the parties are as follows." Cf. **as against.**

E. Fewer Than Two Objects. This construction is a peculiar brand of ILLOGIC, as in *between each house* or *between each speech* (instead of, properly, *between every two houses* and *between speeches*). Another manifestation of this error is *between . . . or,* with two prepositional objects, rather than *between . . . and:* the misuse results from confusion between *either . . . or* and *between . . . and.*

betwixt is an ARCHAISM.

BE-VERBS. A. Wrongly Omitted in Nonfinite Uses. *Be*-verbs, usually in the infinitive or participial form, are often omitted from sentences in which they would add clarity. One explanation is that they are intended to be "understood." (See UNDERSTOOD WORDS.) But this explanation does not excuse the ambiguities and awkwardnesses often caused by such omissions. The bracketed verbs in the sentences following were originally omitted:

- "These devices can be used to intercept a wire or oral communication; specifically designated as not [*being*] such devices are telephone or telegraph equipment furnished to a user and used in the ordinary course of business, and hearing aids."
- "The annotation necessarily starts with the assumption that the process or information involved was regarded as [*being*] of a secret or confidential nature."
- "If the western film offer were found [*to be*] different [*from*] or inferior to the musical film offer, it makes no difference whether Parker reasonably or unreasonably refused the second offer."
- "Because this instruction was substantially similar to the willfulness instruction at the end of the trial, which we have previously held [*to be*] proper, the instruction was not erroneous."
- "If I thought those two cases [*to be*] in point, I should have to consider them very carefully, but I do not." (Eng.)

B. Circumlocutions. Verb phrases containing *be*-verbs are often merely roundabout ways of saying something better said with a simple verb. Thus *be determinative of* for *determine* is verbose. But *be determinative* is all right where there is no object, as in Judge Learned Hand's statement: "All such attempts are illusory, and, if serviceable at all, are so only to center attention upon which one of the factors may *be determinative* in a given situation."

The following circumlocutory uses of *be*-verbs are common in legal writing; the simple verb is ordinarily to be preferred:

be abusive of *(abuse)*
be amendatory of *(amend)*
be applicable to *(apply to)*
be benefited by *(benefit from)*
be conducive to *(conduce to)*
be decisive of *(decide)*
be derived from *(derive from)*
be desirous of *(desire* or *want)*
be determinative of *(determine)*
be dispositive of *(dispose of)*
be in agreement *(agree)*
be in attendance *(attend)*

be indicative of *(indicate)*	be operative *(operate)*
be in dispute *(dispute or disagree)*	be persuasive of *(persuade)*
be in error *(err)*	be possessed of *(possess)*
be in exercise of due care *(exercise due care)*	be productive of *(produce)*
be in existence *(exist)*	be probative of *(prove)*
be influential on *(influence)*	be promotive of *(promote)*
be in receipt of *(have received)*	be violative of *(violate)*

Many such wordy constructions are more naturally phrased in the present tense singular: *is able to* (can), *is authorized to* (may), *is binding upon* (binds), *is empowered to* (may), *is unable to* (cannot).

C. Used Unidiomatically in Place of Action Verbs. One should always use the specific verb that conveys the idea of the action described, rather than an unspecific *be*-verb: "Some agencies adopt procedures that permit some public participation; understandable pressures from interested outsiders *are* [read *require*] that more agencies should or (in some cases) must do so."

beyond a reasonable doubt. See **balance of probability.**

beyond cavil. See **cavil, beyond.**

beyond the pale. See **pale, beyond the.**

BFP = bona fide purchaser. Though the abbreviation is an initialism and not an acronym, the periods are customarily omitted—e.g.: "Having thus failed to comply with federal law, the Bank is hardly in a position to claim the advantageous status of a *BFP* without notice . . . ." *First Nat'l Bank v. Lewco Secs. Corp.,* 860 F.2d 1407, 1414 (7th Cir. 1988).

BI-, SEMI-. One can remember the proper prefix in a given context by noting that *bi-* means "two," and *semi-* "half." Hence *bimonthly* = every two months (not "twice a month") and *semimonthly* = every half-month, or twice a month. *Biweekly* and *semiweekly* work similarly.

Still, *bi-* has been used to mean "occurring twice in a (specified span of time)" so often (and legitimately, e.g., in *biennial*) that, for the sake of clarity, it may be better to avoid the prefix altogether when possible. See the next entry.

biannual; biennial; semiannual. *Biannual* and *semiannual* both mean "occurring twice a year." *Biennial* means "occurring once every two years." The distinction between these words becomes important, for example, when employment contracts provide for "*biannual* meetings of the committee to dispose of accident and bonus questions, and any other agreements." It is imprudent, however, to rely on a word like *biannual* for such a contractual provision. See BI-.

BIBLICAL AFFECTATION. In many respects the language of the law resembles the language of the King James Version (1611) or of Shakespeare. It is full of the ARCHAISMS we associate either with the Bible or, less commonly, with Shakespeare. Thus, as late as the 1980s, the Supreme Court of Mississippi published a sentence containing *doth,* q.v., which many readers have encountered only in traditional versions of the Bible. Likewise, *hath* and *hast* appear occasionally in DRAFTING (of a mediocre kind). Courts still occasionally use the Elizabethan *burthen,* q.v., as a variant of *burden,* though it has not been current for several centuries. And much of the syntax of legal prose is biblical: "A lawyer may never give unsolicited advice to a layman that he retain a client." See **that (C).**

Even today one can open up law reports and read of a *bounden duty,* as in the line from the *Book of Common Prayer* ("We beseech thee to accept this our *bounden duty* and service.")—e.g.: "It is enough for this purpose that valiant efforts were made to persuade the district to do voluntarily what the United States Supreme Court and the California Supreme Court had held was its *bounden duty.*" *Los Angeles Branch NAACP v. Los Angeles Unified Sch. Dist.,* 750 F.2d 731, 752 (9th Cir. 1984) (Pregerson, J., concurring). The origins of the phrase were legal and not religious, but today "when we say *bounden duty* we do not call in any way to mind the bond [that] tied the feudal underling to his lord or the apprentice to his master." Jocelyn Simon, *English Idioms from the Law* (pt. 1), 76 Law Q. Rev. 283, 285 (1960).

Though traditions die hard, these linguistic anachronisms ought not to be perpetuated. They needlessly widen the rift between what is legal and what is lay and unwholesomely lend the air of priestly sanctity to the legal profession. Even the terms *lay* and *legal* used as opposites, much like *lay* and *ecclesiastical,* conjure up this notion; but they are not easily avoided.

It is worth adding to this discussion that citation to the Bible as legal precedent is not an admirable practice. Cardozo once wrote, "In days not far remote, judges were not unwilling to embellish their deliverances with quotations from the poets. I shall observe toward such a practice the tone of decent civility that is due those departed." *Law and Literature,* 52 Harv. L. Rev. 471, 484 (1939). Yet, even in as religiously diverse a society as the U.S., the practice of quoting from the Bible has persisted. For example:

> [As] far as money buried or secreted on privately owned realty is concerned, the old distinction between treasure-trove, lost property, and mislaid property seems to be of little value and not worth preserving. The principal point of distinction seems to be the intent of the true owner who necessarily is not known and not available. Therefore the evidence on his intent will usually be scant and uncontroverted. . . . I would guess his motivation often to be that of the one-talent servant in the parable in the 25th Chapter of Matthew: "And I was afraid, and went and hid thy talent in the earth. . . ." We should hold that the owner of the land has possession of all property secreted in, on and under his land and continues to hold possession for the true owner, who, incidentally, may not always be the person doing any burying. Matthew 13:44—"Again, the kingdom of heaven is like unto treasure hid in a field; the which when a man hath found, he hideth, and for joy thereof goeth and selleth all that he hath, and buyeth that field." What reason is there for transferring possession to the individual who happens to dig up the property? Or for guessing about the intent or the memory of the person doing the burying? A simple solution for all of these problems is to maintain the continuity of possession of the landowner until the true owner establishes his title.
>
> *Schley v. Couch,* 284 S.W.2d 333, 339–40 (1955) (Wilson, J., concurring).

The thing speaks for itself.

bicentennial; bicentenary. See **centennial.**

bid (= to offer a bid) forms *bid* in the past tense. E.g., "[T]he defendant *bid* for the wrong property at an auction sale . . . ." William F. Walsh, *A Treatise on Equity* 479 (1930)./ "The tax is computed on the amount *bid* for the property . . . ." Robert Kratovil, *Real Estate Law* 48 (1946).

In the sense of *bid farewell* (= to wish someone well upon parting), the past tense is *bade,* rhyming with *glad,* and the past participle is *bidden.* "She did as she was *bid* [read *bidden*]."

But which past tense is correct in the phrase *to bid fair* (= to seem likely)—is it *bid fair* or *bade fair?* Writers have used both—e.g.: "[J]udicial decision as an agency of legal growth *bade fair* to become sterile . . . ." Roscoe Pound, *The Formative Era of American Law* 70 (1938)./ "[C]ertainly the action of *indebitatis assumpsit bid fair* to overtake, at one time or another, most of the other forms of action." J.H. Baker, *An Introduction to English Legal History* 420 (3d ed. 1990). The *OED* records only *bade fair,* the better form.

bid, n.; **tender,** n. In AmE, both terms are used, whereas in BrE only the latter would appear, in the sense "a submitted price at which one will perform work or supply goods."

biennial = every two years. If we scale the numerical summit, we have *triennial* (3), *quadrennial* (4), *quinquennial* (5), *sexennial* (6), *septennial* (7), *octennial* (8), *novennial* (9), *decennial* (10), *vicennial* (20), *centennial* (100), *millennial* (1,000). See BI- & **biannual.**

bigamy; polygamy; digamy; deuterogamy. *Bigamy* = going through a marriage ceremony with someone when one is already lawfully married to someone else (*CDL*). It may be committed knowingly or unknowingly; if knowing, *bigamy* is a criminal offense.

Digamy and *deuterogamy* both mean "a legal second marriage occurring after an annulment or a divorce from or the death of the first spouse." *Deuterogamy* is the more common term (to the extent that either might be called common!) and is not, like *digamy,* liable to confusion with *bigamy.* Hence *digamy* should be considered a NEEDLESS VARIANT.

Polygamy is the generic term for "multiple marriages," and encompasses *bigamy*; it is much used by anthropologists, describing both *polygyny* (the practice of having several wives) and *polyandry* (the practice of having several husbands).

big-gun lawyer. See LAWYERS, DEROGATORY NAMES FOR (A).

bilateral contract; unilateral contract. A *unilateral contract* is one in which a promise is given by one party in exchange for the actual performance by the other party. A *bilateral contract* is one in which each party promises a performance, so that each party is an obligor on his own promise and an obligee on the other's promise.

It is a legal solecism to use *unilateral contract* to mean a promise for which no consideration was requested, or for which no sufficient consideration was given. Instead, the phrase "should be reserved for cases in which a legal obligation has been created, but only one party to the obligation has made a promise." 1 Samuel Williston & W.H.E. Jaeger, *A Treatise on the Law of Contracts* § 13, at 26 (3d ed. 1957). If the transaction does not result in a legal obligation, *unilateral offer* or *unilateral promise* may describe the transaction, but not *unilateral contract. Id.*

bill = (1) a formal written complaint, such as a court paper requesting some specific action for reasons alleged; (2) a pleading or court paper in equity, such as a *bill of certiorari,* a *bill of discovery,* a *bill in interpleader,* a *bill of peace,* or a *bill of review;* (3) a legislative proposal offered for debate before its enactment; (4) loosely, an enacted statute; (5) an invoice; or (6) a bill of exchange, i.e., an unconditional order in writing, addressed by one person to another, signed by the person giving it, requiring the addressee to pay on demand, or at a particular future time, a sum certain in money to or to the order of a specified person or to bearer. With such an array of meanings, *bill* is classifiable as a CHAMELEON-HUED WORD. See **suit.**

billa vera. See **true bill.**

bill in chancery; bill in equity. See **chancery.**

billion. In the U.S. and France, *billion* means "one thousand millions" (= 1,000,000,000); but in G.B., Canada, and Germany, it means "one million millions" (= 1,000,000,000,000). An American *trillion,* q.v., equals the British *billion.* In BrE, however, the AmE meaning is gaining ground esp. in journalism, technical writing, and even in government statements about finance.

bill of indictment. See **indictment.**

bill of lading. See **lading, bill of.**

bill of particulars; motion for more definite statement. In 1948, the Federal Rules of Civil Procedure were amended to abolish the *bill of particulars,* which was superseded by the *motion for more definite statement.* The latter allows a party who must respond to a pleading to ask the court to require the other party to refile a vague or ambiguous pleading. In several jurisdictions, though, the *bill of particulars* remains in current practice.

bill of rights = a section or addendum, usu. in a constitution, that defines the situations in which a politically organized society will permit free, spontaneous, and individual activity, and that assures members of the society that government powers will not be used in certain ways. The most famous such document is the *Bill of Rights* (conventionally capitalized) of the U.S. Constitution. But England also had a *Bill of Rights of 1689,* which established that the government could not raise revenue without parliamentary authorization.

bimonthly; semimonthly. See BI-.

bind = to impose a legal duty on (a person or institution). Thus, courts are said to be *bound* by precedent and persons who have signed contracts are said to be contractually *bound.*

binder = (1) in property law, a document in which the seller and the buyer of real property declare their common intention to bring about a transfer of ownership, usu. accompanied by the buyer's initial payment; (2) loosely, the buyer's initial payment in the sale of real property; or (3) *in insurance,* an insurer's memorandum giving the insured temporary coverage while the application for an insurance policy is being processed.

binding precedent. See **precedent (B).**

birth, v.i., was used with some frequency in the Middle Ages as a verb. It fell into disuse, however, and only recently has been revived in AmE <the birthing of babies>. Some dictionaries label it dialectal. Given its usefulness and its long standing in the language, there can be no substantial objections to it.

bite > bit > bitten. Writers occasionally fall into dialectal usage by using *bit,* the past-tense form, as a past participle—e.g.: "In a Texas case the court said hypothetically that if defendant had *bit* [read *bitten*] off such a portion of the victim's under lip as to deprive him of the lip, and the piece had been put back and made to grow 'it would still be maiming under the law.'" Rollin M. Perkins & Ronald N. Boyce, *Criminal Law* 242 n.38 (3d ed. 1982).

bite at the apple, one. See **one bite at the apple.**

bite at the cherry, one. See **one bite at the apple.**

biweekly; semiweekly. See BI-.

Blackacre is the proverbial example of real estate in hypothetical property problems. Abutting tracts are usually called *Whiteacre, Brownacre,* or some other colorized denomination. These terms have long been a part of the common-law tradition: "Where a devise is of *blackacre* to A., and of *whiteacre* to B. in tail, and, if they both die without issue, then to C., in fee, here A. and B. have cross remainders by implication." (Blackstone)/ "The world of bar law is a peculiar place. Every house has a name, usually *Blackacre* or *Whiteacre.*" Stephen Labaton, *At the Bar,* 18 Aug. 1989, at 20.

blackletter law. *Black-letter* is a term that describes Gothic or Old English type in antiquated books <black-letter type>. (The word is usu. hyphenated in nonlegal contexts relating to typography—but see the final paragraph.) From 1482 to 1679, the medieval Year Books were printed in so-called *Black Letter editions,* which were printed in a heavy Gothic type (and which contain many errors).

By extension the term came to be applied to legal principles that are fundamental and well settled, or statements of such principles in a quasi-mathematical form, because such principles were traditionally printed in boldface type in lawbooks. Law students frequently distinguish between professors with a predilection for *blackletter law* (what the law is) and those whose interest lies more in public policy (why the law is or what it ought to be). See **Blackstone lawyer** & **hornbook law.**

Formerly hyphenated, legal writers have conveniently merged the phrase into a solid word—e.g.: "Robinson correctly stated the general understanding as of 1939 in *blackletter* text . . . ." Grant Gilmore & Charles L. Black, Jr., *The Law of Admiralty* 342 (2d ed. 1975)./ "The format of *blackletter* rule and explanatory comment, familiar from real Restatements, is well suited to its purpose." Douglas Laycock, *The Death of the Irreparable Injury Rule* 266 (1991).

blackmail referred originally to rent payable in cattle, labor, or coin other than silver (i.e., *white money*). Then it came to denote, esp. in Scotland, a kind of protection money: payment that robbers extorted from landowners for exemption from their raids. Today the word applies to any menacing demand made without justification—i.e., to illegal extortion generally.

Since at least the late 19th century, the word has been a verb as well as a noun—e.g.: "Thus often arises secret intimidation, enforced confessions, and *blackmailed* pleas of guilty. These sinister dangers were extinguished from the Common Law of England more than six centuries ago." 1 Winston Churchill, *A History of the English Speaking Peoples* 223 (1956).

Blackstonean. The adjective is preferably so spelled. Some writers ill-advisedly make it *Blackstonian.*

Blackstone lawyer = (1) a lawyer with a broad knowledge of black-letter principles; (2) a self-educated lawyer, esp. in antebellum America, whose legal training consists primarily of reading Blackstone's *Commentaries.* Sense (2) usu. appears in historical contexts—e.g.: "For every Jefferson devoting five full years to legal training, scores of *'Blackstone lawyers'* entered the profession after a few months of study, self-proclaimed masters of one text." Robert A. Ferguson, *Law and Letters in American Culture* 29 (1984). For an example from the writings of Thomas Jefferson, see LAWYERS, DEROGATORY NAMES FOR (A).

blamable. See **blameworthy (B).**

blamableness. See **blameworthiness.**

blame, v.t. In the best usage, one *blames* a person; one does not, in the traditional idiom, *blame* a thing *on* a person. E.g., "I *blame the fires* on him." [Read I *blame him* for the fires.]

blameworthiness; blamableness. The latter is a NEEDLESS VARIANT—e.g.: "The only rational basis for allowing recovery in tort seems to be *blamableness* [read *blameworthiness*]." C.B. Whittier, *Mistake in the Law of Torts,* 15 Harv. L. Rev. 335, 335 (1902).

blameworthy. A. And *culpable.* Though the two words are etymologically equivalent, in 20th-century usage the Anglo-Saxon *blameworthy* has tended to be used in noncriminal, the Latinate *culpable* in criminal contexts. Hence *blameworthy* in civil contexts: "The indemnitee's conduct is sufficiently *blameworthy* to preclude indemnity."/ "Plaintiff is not *blameworthy* in failing to bring suit earlier; thus laches does not apply."/ "We also consider whether there was trickery or *blameworthy* action by the police."

And *culpable* in criminal contexts: "The court's focus must be on the defendant's *culpability,* not on those who committed the robbery and shot the victims."/ "The defense of mistake of fact was not available as a defense to negate the *culpable* mental state of criminal negligence."/ "It is reasonable to presume that the sentencing judge who revokes probation takes a fresh look at the defendant's *culpability* and circumstances and considers at that point the amount of time the defendant should be required to serve." See **guilty.**

Occasionally, however, *culpability* creeps into civil contexts, as here in the context of punitive damages, a hybrid remedy: "Exemplary damages are awarded only in cases of extreme *culpability* and are limited to the plaintiff's demonstrable litigation expenses." Nevertheless, the writer of that sentence was describing egregious conduct, and *blameworthiness* today hardly seems appropriate for flagrant conduct.

B. And *blameful; blamable.* *Blameworthy* and *blamable* both mean "deserving to be blamed," the latter being a NEEDLESS VARIANT. *Blameful* (= imputing blame; blaming) has been mistakenly used for *blameworthy.* We need not use up more words for the meaning replicated by *blameworthy* and *blamable.* Cf. **certworthy** & **enbancworthy.**

blandish; brandish. The former means "to cajole; to persuade by flattery or coaxing." The latter means "to wave or shake in a menacing or threatening way."

blatant; flagrant. There is a well-defined distinction, but each word is frequently misused for the other. What is *blatant* stands out as glaring and repugnant; what is *flagrant* is shocking and deplorable; this latter term connotes outrage. A perjurer might tell *blatant* lies to the grand jury to cover up for his *flagrant* breach of trust. Egregious criminal acts are *flagrant* <flagrant arson>, not *blatant.* E.g., "For any *flagrant* dereliction or disregard of professional duty on the part of the attorney, the license by which he was admitted to practice may be revoked."/ "The court could have properly determined, as it did, that Batson's conduct was so *flagrant* as to justify severe sanctions."

Blatant is correctly used in this sentence: "The question concerning the blinding of the Libyan in the Colorado shooting was *blatantly* improper." Here *flagrant* is misused for *blatant:* "The constitutional violation is *flagrantly* [read *blatantly*] apparent in a case involving the imposition of a maximum sentence after reconviction."/ "No matter how infrequently the special counsel has brought Hatch Act charges in the past, federal employees can hardly be faulted for concluding that registering voters in *flagrant* [read *blatant*] disregard of the special counsel's advice is not worth the grave risk to their livelihoods."

Black's defines *flagrant necessity* as "a case of urgency rendering lawful an otherwise illegal act," and *flagrantly against the evidence* as "so much against the weight of the evidence as to shock the conscience and clearly indicate passion and prejudice of the jury." *Flagrant* is the wrong choice of word in the first phrase, though arguably correct in the second because of the element of shock. *Blatant necessity* would be the better wording for the first phrase, *blatant* here taking on its nonpejorative meaning "completely obvious or strikingly conspicuous"; a *blatant necessity* would allow one, e.g., to commit battery upon another by shoving him out of the way of an oncoming bus.

The phrase *blatantly obvious* is a REDUNDANCY. E.g., "The reasons for the dropping pass rate on the bar exam *are blatantly obvious* [read *are obvious*]."

BLENDS. See PORTMANTEAU WORDS.

bloc; block. Political groups or alignments are *blocs. Block* serves in all other senses.

blot on title. See **cloud on title.**

blow hot and cold = to take mutually contradictory positions or put forward contradictory views.

- "The plaintiff is *blowing hot and cold* in this case; if we follow him in this latter position, why then he loses the case on the merits." *Hall v. Keller,* 80 F. Supp. 763, 774 (W.D. La. 1948).
- "Inconsistent allegations can be made in separate claims or defenses under F.R.C.P. 8(e)(2); but no authority is known to the undersigned which permits *blowing hot and cold* in the same cause of action, as attempted by the proposed amendment." *Steiner v. Twentieth Century-Fox Film Corp.,* 140 F. Supp. 906, 908 (S.D. Cal. 1953).
- "Allen had not only earlier taken a directly contrary position . . . he had taken the same contrary position in one state administrative proceeding where that also suited his purpose . . . . [N]o further judicial aid should be given this particular enterprise of *blowing hot and cold* as the occasion demands." *Allen v. Zurich Ins. Co.,* 667 F.2d 1162, 1167 n.3 (4th Cir. 1982).
- "The theory of attack by prior inconsistent statements is not based on the assumption that the present testimony is false and the former statement is true, but rather upon the notion that talking one way on the stand and another way previously is *blowing hot and cold,* and raises a doubt as to the truthfulness of both statements." Charles T. McCormick et al., *Evidence* § 34, at 74 (3d ed. 1984).

For an amusing example of blowing hot and cold, see **Codd's Puzzle.**

Blue Book = (1) in G.B., a printed report (as of a Royal Commission) presented to Parliament and traditionally softbound in blue covers; (2) in some American states, a compilation of session laws; (3) a volume formerly published to give parallel citation tables for a volume in the National Reporter System; or (4) the formal name for the citation guide, formerly called *A Uniform System of Citation* (usu. written *Bluebook*).

For more terms connected with sense (1), see **Green Paper & White Paper.**

blue-pencil test = a judicial standard sometimes applied by a court considering an illegal contractual provision and deciding whether to invalidate the entire contract or only the offending words, the standard consisting in whether it would be possible to sever the offending words simply by running a blue pencil through them, as opposed to changing, adding, or rearranging words. E.g., "Despite such criticisms, numerous jurisdictions have presented meritorious justifications for requiring a strict application of the *'blue pencil' test*." *Holloway v. Faw, Casson & Co.,* 552 A.2d 1311, 1325 (Md. Ct. Spec. App. 1989). "It used to be thought that promises could be severed merely because the *'blue pencil' test* was satisfied; but this view no longer prevails. The test may restrict, but it does not determine, the scope of the doctrine of severance." G.H. Treitel, *The Law of Contract* 449 (8th ed. 1991).

blue-sky laws. In the early 20th century, *blue sky* meant "an unsound investment, esp. in fake securities." Hence laws designed to protect gullible investors in securities have been given the name *blue-sky laws.* The phrase is used in BrE as well as in AmE—in the latter, usually in reference to state laws.

As casual JARGON, *blue-sky* (usu. hyphenated) has been transformed into a verb meaning "to approve (the sale of securities) in accordance with *blue-sky* laws." The form of the verb is almost always past tense or past participle—e.g.: "This solicitation and purchase was unlawful under California law because it had not been *blueskyed.*" *Hecht v. Harris, Upham & Co.,* 283 F. Supp. 417, 443 (N.D. Cal. 1968). Less commonly, the past-participial adjective means "having blue-sky laws" <blue-skyed states>. See NOUNS AS VERBS.

blunderbuss (= an obsolete firearm that scatters shot and is intended for close-range shooting) is often used figuratively in legal contexts. E.g., "This claim—on which every serious constitutional question turns—was pleaded in *blunderbuss* fashion in each of the complaints."/ "Many of the discovery requests are specific, many are *blunderbuss,* and many seek discovery previously refused by the court."/ "Since double payments can be prevented by a letter or a telephone call, it is unreasonable to accomplish this objective by the *blunderbuss* method of denying assistance to all indigent newcomers for an entire year." The more recent sense of *blunderbuss* (= a blundering person) has nothing to do with this sense. The term is infrequently misspelled *blunderbus.*

Sometimes the equivalent *shotgun* or *scatter-gun* is used: "'Fraud, deceit, negligence, or estoppel' is a *scatter-gun* blast that could hardly miss winging the intended quarry."

blush, at first. See **at first blush.**

bodily heirs; heirs of the body; body heirs. The first and second are the classic formulations of the phrase, both unobjectionable. *Body heirs* is much inferior to *bodily heirs* for two reasons: first, generally we should not use a noun adjectivally when we have a serviceable adjective; and second, *body heirs* is so little used that it grates on the legally trained ear.

body corporate is a variant of *corporation* that emphasizes the entity and the members that make it up rather than the abstract notion (*corporation*); *body corporate* is now used more commonly in BrE than in AmE. E.g., "A *body corporate* cannot be appointed receiver . . . ." J. Charlesworth, *The Principles of Company Law* 175 (4th ed. 1945).

body heirs. See **bodily heirs** & **heir.**

bogus check. See **check, worthless.**

boilerplate [fr. the newspaper business, in which it originally referred to syndicated material in mat or plate form] = (1) ready-made or all-purpose language that will fit in a variety of documents; or (2) fixed or standardized language that is not subject to modification. Sense (1) expresses the lawyer's usual understanding; sense (2) expresses the nonlawyer's common understanding.

The term first entered American legal usage in the 1950s and is today commonly used either as a noun or as an adjective (in phrases such as *boilerplate clause* or *boilerplate language*). The earliest known legal example appeared in Ohio: "After what appears to be the ordinary *'boilerplate'* reference to payment of debts, taxes and costs of administration, the testatrix in the case at bar gave more than usual attention to arrangements in connection with her last rites." *In re Estate of Carrington,* 136 N.E.2d 182, 185 (Ohio Prob. Ct. 1956).

The word is best spelled as one word in AmE. In BrE, it is commonly hyphenated (*boiler-plate*). For an example of boilerplate language, see **attestation clause.**

bolster = (of a courtroom lawyer) to build up a witness's credibility in anticipation of impeachment—a practice generally disallowed by American evidentiary rules. E.g., "[T]he prosecutor may not, among other things, make explicit personal assurances that a witness is trustworthy or implicitly *bolster* the witness by indicating that information not presented to the jury supports the testimony." *U.S. v. Lewis,* 10 F.3d 1086, 1089 (4th Cir. 1993)./ "Attempts to *bolster* a witness by vouching for his credibility are normally improper and an error." *U.S. v. Baptista-Rodriguez,* 17 F.3d 1354, 1372 (11th Cir. 1994).

bombastic is sometimes misconstrued to mean "strident" or "violent." Properly, *bombastic* (lit., "full of stuffing or padding") means "pompous; highfalutin; overblown." Here is a journalistic example of the error: "'If there is any change in the mood of the kids, it is for the worse,' says the Brixton police superintendent. 'They are more *bombastic,* they are cocky, they threaten riot as an answer if they don't get what they want.'" (Eng.) This confusion may arise from the suggestiveness of *bomb* in *bombastic.*

bona et catalla is the archaic LATINISM from which, by LOAN TRANSLATION, derives the DOUBLET *goods and chattels.*

bona fide. A. And *good-faith,* adj. *Bona fide,* adj., is understood by educated speakers of English; as a legal term, it is unlikely to give way completely to *good-faith.* Cf. ***bona fides.***

B. Adjective or Adverb. *Bona fide* was originally adverbial, meaning "in good faith" <the suit was brought bona fide>. The phrase is still used in this way, most often in BrE—e.g.: "[T]he undertaking was given *bona fide,* i.e., without any knowledge that the claim was not a good one." 1 E.W. Chance, *Principles of Mercantile Law* 25 (P.W. French ed., 13th ed. 1950).

Today it is more commonly used as an adjective <it was a bona fide suit>. None of the forms of this term should be hyphenated or written as one word, as *bona fide* sometimes is when functioning as a PHRASAL ADJECTIVE. The opposite of *bona fide* is *mala fide,* q.v.; the opposite of *bona fides* is *mala fides.*

C. Meaning "sincere, genuine." In legal contexts, the adjective *bona fide* should be avoided in the lay sense arrived at through SLIPSHOD EXTENSION, namely "genuine; not fake." E.g., "Even within the 50-mile area, containers that go directly to the owner of the cargo or to *bona fide warehouses* [read *genuine warehouses*] are exempted from the rule."/ "Ms. Rebhun argued successfully that Michael's alcoholism was a *bona fide illness* [read *genuine illness*] that prevented him from taking responsibility for filing his taxes." *For Special Cases, a "Tax Therapist,"* N.Y. Times, 8 Dec. 1989, at 27.

One court has justifiably criticized the phrase *bona fide doubt* in reference to a judge's doubt, saying that the phrase "appears to be a faulty construction of words . . . . [U]nfortunately, it has reached a level of being standard legal idiom in mental competency cases . . . . For purposes of determining whether an evidentiary hearing should be held, . . . *'bona fide doubt'* is a misnomer. It does not convey the correct sense of the test: the question whether an evidentiary hearing is required does not depend on the sincerity, genuineness, etc. of the judge's doubt—we can assume any judge's doubt has these qualities." *Griffin v. Lockhart,* 935 F.2d 926, 929 n.2 (8th Cir. 1991) (citing *DMLU* and recommending instead *sufficient doubt*).

bona fides, **n.; good faith; *bonne foi.*** Though the adjective *bona fide* has been fully anglicized, the noun phrase *bona fides* has lost much ground—esp. in AmE—to *good faith,* n., which is generally preferable. The pronunciation of *bona fides, /boh-nə-***fɪ***-deez/,* unlike that of its adjectival sibling, sounds foreign and bombastic. *Bonne foi,* a Frenchified variant, sounds still more so; fortunately, it is rarely encountered.

Typically, one writes, "He executed the contract in *good faith,*" not really thinking of *bona fides* as an alternative wording, although admittedly it is sometimes used: "[T]heir *bona fides* was manifest on the record." *Patterson v. American Tobacco Co.,* 634 F.2d 744, 748 (4th Cir. 1980).

As in the example just quoted, the noun phrase *bona fides* is singular: *this bona fides,* not *these bona fides.* But writers sometimes mistakenly make it plural—e.g.: "Southwest asserts that it was denied the opportunity to be present and to present evidence when Lowe's *bona fides were* [read *bona fides was*] examined by the Land Office Manager." *Southwestern Petroleum Corp. v. Udall,* 361 F.2d 650, 657 (10th Cir. 1966)./ "[H]e was neither advised at trial that his *bona fides were* [read *bona fides was*] in issue nor given an opportunity to disprove . . . the inference drawn by the court." *Sledge v. J.P. Stevens & Co.,* 585 F.2d 625, 641 (4th Cir. 1978).

bona vacantia (lit. "vacant goods") is a TERM OF ART meaning "property not disposed of by a decedent's will and to which no relative is entitled upon intestacy." E.g., "The Crown sought to interpose a claim to *bona vacantia* between creditors and former members." (Eng.) The phrase should not be used when *unclaimed property* or *ownerless goods* will suffice. Cf. **escheat.**

bond = (1) a written promise to pay a debt or to do some act (e.g., an appeal bond); (2) an interest-bearing certificate of debt that is issued by a corporation or governmental entity usu. to provide for a particular financial need (e.g., a municipal bond); or (3) an insurance agreement whereby a person or corporation becomes a surety to pay, within defined limits, for a financial loss suffered by a second person under certain circumstances (e.g., a bail bond, delivery bond, indemnity bond, or judicial bond). See **debenture.**

In criminal law, *bail bond* (= security for a

released prisoner's return for trial) is archaic in BrE but current in AmE. See **bond out.**

bond out (= to post a bail bond and thereby obtain release from [jail]) is an American casualism. E.g., "Loretta Lynn's son Ernie has *bonded out* of a Tennessee jail . . . ." Helen Bryant, *Names & Faces,* Dallas Times Herald, 5 April 1991, at A2.

book, bring to. See **bring to book.**

bookkeeping; accounting. *Bookkeeping* (so spelled, being the only word in the English language with three consecutive sets of doubled letters) is the mechanical recording of debits and credits, or the summarizing of financial information, usu. about a business enterprise. *Accounting* differs from bookkeeping because it is not mechanical: it requires judgment about such issues as when a specified type of transaction should be recorded, how the amount of the transaction should be calculated, and how a balance sheet and income statement should be presented.

bootstrap(ping). The original expression was one among several variants of *to pull oneself up by one's bootstraps* (a futile effort)—e.g.: "[I]t would be as impossible for the directors, in undertaking to contract with themselves, to accomplish any result as it would be for them to undertake to *lift themselves over a fence by their bootstraps.*" *In re State Exch. Bank,* 159 N.E. 839, 840 (Ohio Ct. App. 1927)./ "That would be equivalent to *pulling one's self out of the mire by his own bootstraps.*" *McCarthy v. State ex rel. Harless,* 101 P.2d 449, 453 (Ariz. 1940)./ "To support the doctrine of precedent by reference to precedent would be to try to *pull itself up by its own bootstraps.*" Glanville Williams, *Learning the Law* 88 (11th ed. 1982).

The idea has now been telescoped into the gerund *bootstrapping*—e.g.: "It is only by deciding on appeal and on the merits that the claim of foreclosure is insubstantial that this court can [reach its own conclusion]. . . . This appellate *bootstrapping* is the more improper because the question of the adequacy of the foreclosure is in fact not concluded by this appeal." *Pettit v. Olean Indus., Inc.,* 266 F.2d 833, 839 (2d Cir. 1959) (Lumbard, J., dissenting)./ "This argument, too, does not warm us and indeed strikes us as a *bootstrapping* approach." *Hudson v. John Hancock Mut. Life Ins.,* 314 F.2d 16, 23 (8th Cir. 1963). The term is now often used, esp. in law, in the sense "making a success out of one's meager resources."

bordereau (= [1] a note of account or, more commonly, [2] a description of reinsured risks) is the singular, *-reaux* the plural.

The word has recently come to be used as a verb—e.g.: "American and Southeastern Fire Insurance Co., to which the policy had been *'bordereauxed,'* refused payment." *Merchants Nat'l Bank v. Southeastern Fire Ins. Co.,* 751 F.2d 771, 773 (5th Cir. 1985). The proper verb form, however, would be *bordereau* (singular), not *-reaux.* Hence, in the above quotation the word should be *bordereaued.*

bork, v.t., an eponym of Robert Bork, President Reagan's unsuccessful nominee for the U.S. Supreme Court, means (1) "(of the U.S. Senate) to reject a nominee for the U.S. Supreme Court because of his or her untraditional political and legal philosophy"; or (2) "(of political and legal activists) to embark on a media campaign that helps pressure U.S. Senators into rejecting a president's nominee for the U.S. Supreme Court." Originally, the word was usually capitalized, but no longer. It most often appears in sense (2)—e.g.: "One of the legacies of the Bork nomination is, I think, a contribution to the political dictionary. I'm referring to the verb, *to bork,* which is what Sen. Edward Kennedy, D-Mass., did to Robert Bork. The passive, to be *borked,* is what happened to Bork. Now, what does it mean to be *borked?* Simply this: Your opponents take a matter involving a law and criticize you in terms of policy outcome. You defend yourself by discussing the issue in legal jargon." Terry Eastland, *Reagan's Legacy at Justice Poses Challenge to New President,* Manhattan Law., 1 Nov. 1988, at 12./ "After they persuaded Ms. Hill to submit an unsworn statement by fax, members of the Senate trio—probably in cahoots with a team of high-powered Washington lawyers, lobbyists and public relations specialists out to *'bork'* the nominee—caused the sensational Hill statement to be leaked to a couple of reputable reporters." William Safire, *The Plumbers' Return,* 17 Feb. 1992, at A11.

born; borne. Both are past participles of *bear. Borne* is for general purposes <she has borne a child> <he has borne that burden for a long time>. *Born* is used either as an adjective <a born swindler> <their firstborn son> or as the fixed passive verb in *to be born* <she was born last June in London>.

Bear in mind yields *borne in mind:* "It should be *born in mind* [read *borne in mind*] that while the *McAlester* factors will often plainly indicate that immunity is available, there are situations in which immunity must be afforded even though one or more of the factors does not obtain."

both. A. *Both . . . and.* This construction comprises a pair of CORRELATIVE CONJUNCTIONS that must frame syntactically analogous parts of a sentence. E.g., "The Chancellor decided all questions *both of law and fact* [read *both of law and of fact* or *of both law and fact*]."

B. *Both . . . as well as.* This construction is incorrect for *both . . . and.* E.g., "Attorney's fees are expressly authorized *both under* section 1983, 42 U.S.C. § 1988, *as well as under* [read *both under . . . and under* or *under . . . as well as under*] the Rehabilitation Act, 29 U.S.C. § 794a(b)."/ "*Both Norton as well as the judges* [read *Norton as well as the judges* or *Both Norton and the judges*] conceded that Moses had a cause of action for special assumpsit on the agreement to indemnify him against the consequences of his agreement."

C. Redundancies with. Several wordings with *both* cause redundancies. One is *both . . . each other*—e.g.: "*Both* Signad and Sugar Land are seeking in personam, rather than in rem, judgments against *each other.*" The sentence would bear either *both* or *each other,* but it cannot take them together.

Another is *both alike*—e.g.: "The statutes of these states *are both alike* [read are *alike*]."

Yet another is *both concurrently*—e.g.: "Happily now, as we shall see, every judge has both a Common Law and an Equity mind, and applies them *both concurrently* [read *concurrently*]." Edward Jenks, *The Book of English Law* 36 (P.B. Fairest ed., 6th ed. 1967).

D. *Both (of) the.* Though the idiom is falling into disuse, *both the* (or *both these*) has a fine pedigree and continues in formal English—e.g.: "The hazard, in *both these* respects, could only be avoided, if at all, by rendering that tribunal more numerous . . . ." *The Federalist,* No. 65, at 398 (Alexander Hamilton) (Clinton Rossiter ed., 1961)./ "The Commission is to promote *both these* purposes." J.L. Brierly, *The Law of Nations* 82 (5th ed. 1955)./ "For *both these* reasons, over reliance on foreign authorities diminished . . . ." Grant Gilmore & Charles L. Black, Jr., *The Law of Admiralty* 46 (2d ed. 1975). The alternative phrasing, *both of the* (or *both of these*), is increasingly common in AmE.

E. *Both . . . equally as.* See **equally as (C).**

bottleneck is accepted as standard in the dictionaries. Certainly it has legitimate figurative uses—e.g.: "Our *bottleneck* in housing is particularly far-reaching and decisive." Oddly, the word may never have been used in a literal sense (i.e., "the neck of a bottle").

bottom, v.i. & v.t., may be used literally: "The well was *bottomed* in sand A." Or it may be used figuratively, as it more frequently is in legal contexts: "The district court properly dismissed plaintiff's section 1983 claim, *bottomed* on her assertion of an illegal arrest."/ "This contention is unsound, and the argument predicated thereon is *bottomed* wholly upon a false premise." *Ford v. Moody,* 276 S.W. 595, 597 (Ark. 1925). This peculiar legal idiom was originally nonlegal, dating in the *OED* from 1637. From a modern stylistic point of view, *base* might be preferable to *bottom* in figurative senses.

The transference to a nominal sense of *bottom* is likely to provoke laughter: "Title VI on its own *bottom* [read *foundation*] reaches no further than the Constitution." *Guardians Ass'n v. Civil Serv. Comm'n,* 463 U.S. 582, 589–90 (1983)./ "The decisions demonstrate that the due process approach considers each case on its own *bottom* [read *basis*]."

bottomry; bottomage. *Bottomry,* denoting a special type of commercial-insurance contract in admiralty, may be used as both n. & v.t. *Bottomage* is a NEEDLESS VARIANT from LAW FRENCH.

bound bailiff. See **bumbailiff.**

bounden. See BIBLICAL AFFECTATION.

bountiful; bounteous. *Bounteous* is poetic or literary for *bountiful,* which is preferred in legal contexts.

bounty, which is becoming an ARCHAISM, is current in the context of wills and estates, although little used elsewhere. It means "munificence; liberality in giving; gift" (*COD*). E.g., "The court will distribute the testator's *bounty* equally among all persons belonging to the class designated in the will, wherever the person."/ "Spendthrift trusts allow the donor to control his *bounty,* through the creation of the trust, so that it may be exempt from liability for the donee's debts."/ "The testator may, if he chooses, fail to make provision in his will for his children, though they are the natural objects of his *bounty.*"

b(o)urgeois. The spelling with the *-o-* is preferred.

boutique. Since the mid-1980s, *boutique* has, in AmE, denoted a small law firm specializing in one particular aspect of law practice. E.g., "Davis, Everby & Feinberg is a small, *boutique* law firm specializing in litigation." Mark H. Epstein & Brandon Wisoff, *Winding Up Dissolved Law Part-*

nerships, 73 Calif. L. Rev. 1597, 1625 (1985)./ "Samuel Sterrett . . . resigned Oct. 31 with partner Michael Durney to launch a tax *boutique.*" Jennifer Frey, *Myerson & Kuhn Loses Cabot and Office in D.C.,* Manhattan Law., 7–13 Nov. 1989, at 4.

bracery. See **embracery.**

BRACKETS, USE OF. See PUNCTUATION (L).

Bracton. This proper name commonly refers both to the 13th-century judge (Henry of Bratton, who sat on the Court of King's Bench and of Assize in the reign of Henry III) and to the book he is thought to have written (*De Legibus et Consuetudinibus Angliae,* c. 1250). Some historians doubt that Bracton was the author of *Bracton* (italicized when referring to the book)—e.g.: "The author of *Bracton* appreciated this point . . . ." J.H. Baker, *An Introduction to English Legal History* 300 (3d ed. 1990).

Brandeis brief. In *Muller v. Oregon,* 208 U.S. 412 (1908), Louis Brandeis persuaded the Court that minimum-hours legislation for women was reasonable—and not unconstitutional—with an unconventional brief that consisted primarily of statistical, sociological, economic, and physiological information. Such a brief has come to be known, since the 1940s, as a *Brandeis brief,* the main characteristics of which are: (1) reliance on extrarecord facts, esp. economic and sociological materials, that can be judicially noticed; (2) lengthiness. E.g., "The brief submitted on the law was . . . five pages, six pages, and on the facts whatever it was, 150 pages . . . . This kind of brief has ever since then been called 'a *Brandeis brief.*'" Felix Frankfurter, *Felix Frankfurter Reminisces* 97 (Harlan B. Phillips ed., 1960)./ "Plaintiff offered no evidence, nothing even in the way of a *Brandeis brief,* from which we might compare factually the problems private tortfeasors and governmental subdivisions have in dealing with stale claims, investigation of claims, and the budget process." *Miller v. Boone County Hosp.,* 394 N.W.2d 776, 783 (Iowa 1986).

brandish. See **blandish.**

breach can be a troublesome word. Its most frequent legal use is in the phrase *breach of contract.* The word *breach* always suggests its more common cognate, *break.* One can either *breach* or *break* a contract; and another may refer to one's *breach* or *breaking* of it. That much is simple.

In general usage, *breach* is confused with two other words, *breech,* n. (= [1] buttocks; or [2] the lower or back part of something, as a gun bore) and *broach,* v.t. (= [1] to make a hole in to let out liquid; or [2] to bring up for discussion). The confusion of *breach* with *breech* consists in writers' mistakenly using the latter where *breach* belongs <breach of a treaty>. The lapse with *broach* occurs when someone writes of *breaching* (read *broaching*) a topic.

The meanings of *breach* and *broach* become close only in reference to dikes or levees and walls (*breach* = to break open; *broach* = to make a hole in). E.g., "Less than three months ago—in the immediate aftermath of the *breaching* of the Berlin Wall—the Chancellor's closest aides were predicting that five to eight years might still be needed before unity became a reality." David Marsh, *Kohl Takes the Burden of Unity on His Shoulders,* Fin. Times, 22 Feb. 1990, at 3.

breachee is objectionable as an obtuse word meaning "one whose contract has been breached by the other contracting party." E.g., "The *breachor's* initial failure to comply establishes the inadequacy of the *breachee's* remedy at law." *Stewart v. Stewart,* 300 S.E.2d 263, 266 (N.C. Ct. App. 1983)./ "The breacher will offer the *breachee's* expectancy values plus some portion of the surplus." Michael L. Zigler, *Takings Law and the Contracts Clause,* 36 Stan. L. Rev. 1447, 1463 n.83 (1984)./ "[S]ince there is the incentive for the *breachee* to induce breach when circumstances change, the defendant should be allowed to raise the induced breach in mitigation." Thomas S. Ulen, *The Efficiency of Specific Performance,* 83 Mich. L. Rev. 341, 354–55 (1984).

The word is also an illogically formed word because it means not "one who is breached (by another)," but rather "one whose contract has been breached." *Breachee* is not, like *refugee,* an established exception. See -EE.

breacher (= a party in breach). So spelled—not *breachor.* See **contract-breaker.**

breach, more honored in the. Strictly speaking, this phrase refers to an unjust rule that is better broken than obeyed. Often, though, through SLIPSHOD EXTENSION, writers use the phrase to refer to a just rule that, in practice, is often broken. E.g., "Although the obligation of lawyers to cooperate with one another long has been considered a significant professional obligation, it, too, has been more and more *honored in the breach* [read *frequently breached*]." Roger J. Miner, *Lawyers Owe One Another,* Nat'l L.J., 19 Dec. 1988, at 13./ "[I]t is an American custom (perhaps *more honored in the breach*) as well as a Chinese one to show respect for one's elders."

Judith Martin, *Ingenuity Can Overcome This Language Barrier,* Chicago Tribune, 8 Oct. 1989, at 6C./ "The code of professional responsibility requires reporting an unethical colleague—a requirement more honored in the breach than observance." Raoul L. Felder, *A Degree Isn't a License to Steal,* Newsday, 19 March 1991, at 98.

break, v.t. **A. In Contract Law.** *Break* is frequently a casual equivalent of *breach,* v.t.—e.g.: "The power but not the right to *break* a contract exists, like the power to commit a crime or tort, but the breach is a wrong in either case." William F. Walsh, *A Treatise on Equity* 301–02 (1930)./ "[I]t is a crime to *break* such a contract, if the probable consequence will be to cause injury or danger or grave inconvenience to the community." William Geldart, *Introduction to English Law* 162 (D.C.M. Yardley ed., 9th ed. 1984).

B. As an Element of the Crime of Burglary. In the law of burglary, the word *break* is used in a peculiar sense. It does not require damage to property, yet it is more than crossing an imaginary line when we speak of "breaking into a house." Entering through an open door or window is not breaking; all that is needed is opening a door or window, even if not locked or latched.

breakdown = (1) failure; or (2) subdivision. The former meaning is much older (ca. 1832); the latter has been considered OFFICIALESE since it first appeared in the mid-20th century.

break-in, n. So hyphenated.

breaking and entering. See **housebreaking.**

breast (of the court), in the. See LOAN TRANSLATIONS.

breath; breathe. The first is the noun, the second the verb. How one might mistake *breath* for *breathe* is almost inexplicable: "The complainant began screaming and appellant again covered her nose and mouth with his hand; the complainant began gagging and could not *breath* [read *breathe*]."

breathable. See **breath(e)able.**

breathalyzer; intoxilyzer; drunkometer; alcoholometer. *Breathalyzer* is a PORTMANTEAU WORD for *breath-analyzer.* The nominal form is *breath-analysis.* In BrE the word is *breathalyser* (standard) or *breathaliser;* in AmE it is sometimes spelled *breathalizer,* although *-lyzer* is more common: "The taking of a *breathalyzer* test with the consent of a defendant accused of driving while intoxicated violates none of his rights."

Intoxilyzer, likewise a PORTMANTEAU WORD (for *intoxication-analyzer*), is an increasingly popular term for the device that measures blood-alcohol content. See, e.g., *State ex rel. Collins v. Seidel,* 691 P.2d 678, 679 (Ariz. 1984) (en banc). *Intoxilyzer* is new enough, however, that it is not included in the dictionaries. *Drunkometer,* a HYBRID, was widespread when the device was still new (in the 1930s), but has fallen into disuse, perhaps because of its jocular effect. The term *alcoholometer* is likewise little used today.

In referring to the test performed rather than to the device performing it, *breath test* is the most succinct phraseology, used often by the U.S. Supreme Court and by British courts as well. *Breathalyzer test,* a somewhat inferior variant, is also commonly used. See, e.g., *Simpson v. State,* 707 P.2d 43, 45 (Okla. Crim. App. 1985).

breath(e)able. The parenthesized *-e-* should be omitted: *breathable.* See MUTE E.

breech. See **breach.**

brethren. Where persons are not brothers by birth, the plural form *brethren* has survived only in religious and legal contexts. E.g., "In this case I have the misfortune to differ in opinion from a majority of my *brethren.*" *Smith v. Richards,* 38 U.S. (13 Pet.) 26, 43 (1839) (Story, J., dissenting)./ "In *Rookes v. Barnard* Lord Devlin, with the unanimous approval of his *brethren,* had laid down that exemplary damages could only be awarded in three types of circumstances." Michael Zander, *The Law-Making Process* 167 (2d ed. 1985).

Courts have considered the word generic in testamentary contexts (i.e., as referring both to males and to females). But most readers are unlikely to see it as gender-neutral: one commentator writes that this EUPHEMISM "gives a not wholly misleading indication of the frequency with which women are appointed as judges." David Pannick, *Judges* 157 (1987). The word is unlikely to flourish in AmE because of its perceived SEXISM. Nor does *brethren and sistren* seem likely to catch on, *sistren* being the analogous archaic plural of *sister.* That plural, unlike its brother, is now chiefly dialectal. See **brother & sistren.**

Brothers is sometimes used where *brethren* would normally appear—e.g.: "[W]hile I see more ambiguity than do my dissenting *brothers,* it is of no matter because we do not write on a clean slate." *James v. U.S.,* 760 F.2d 590, 606 (5th Cir. 1985) (Higginbotham, J., dissenting).

breve [fr. *brevis* "short"] is the LAW LATIN equivalent of *writ*. Hence, in older texts, *breve originale* means "original writ" and *breve de recto* means "writ of right." E.g., "A writ (*breve* in Latin, *brief* in French) was a thin strip of parchment containing a letter in the name of the king, usually written in Latin, and sealed with the great seal." J.H. Baker, *An Introduction to English Legal History* 67 (3d ed. 1990)./ "Furthermore, novel disseisin only lies in the Royal courts; there is no form of writ corresponding to the *breve de recto.*" A.W.B. Simpson, *An Introduction to the History of the Land Law* 28 (1961). (See **writ of right.**) Pl. *brevia.*

briber; bribee; bribe-giver; bribe-taker. A *bribe* is a reward or favor given or promised to a person in a position of trust in order that that person's judgment will be skewed or conduct corrupted in one's favor. The one who gives the bribe is termed the *briber,* the one who receives it the *bribee.* E.g., "Made when the allegedly extorted bribe money was being paid, the tape recording in this case is of the actual voices of the *briber* and the *bribee.*" *U.S. v. Sopher,* 362 F.2d 523, 525 (7th Cir. 1966)./ "This section does not reach a simple breach of fiduciary duty; it covers only corrupt breaches that involve a bribe. *Briber* and *bribee* are then equally guilty." Tex. Penal Code § 32.43, *Practice Commentary* at 667 (West 1974).

Some writers use the terms *bribe-giver* and *bribe-taker,* which are undoubtedly clearer to more readers. E.g., "The usual pleas of the *bribe-giver* or *-taker* is that he only followed the example he saw everywhere about him, that he only did directly and candidly what others were doing indirectly and hypocritically." Lon L. Fuller, *Anatomy of the Law* 49 (1968)./ "The starting point in the law of bribery seems to have been when a judge, for doing his office or acting under color of his office, took a reward or fee from some person who had occasion to come before him,—and apparently guilt attached only to the judge himself and not to the *bribe-giver.*" Rollin M. Perkins & Ronald N. Boyce, *Criminal Law* 527 (3d ed. 1982).

bribery (= the corrupt payment, receipt, or solicitation of a private favor for official action) generally refers to the bribe-giver's actions as well as to the bribe-taker's. (Some jurisdictions restrict *bribe* to the act of the bribe-giver and refer to the bribe-taker's offense as *receiving a bribe.*) A misdemeanor at common law, the offense has been made a statutory felony in most English-speaking jurisdictions.

In the phrase *commercial bribery,* the term has been extended beyond its traditional reference to the act of a government official. *Commercial bribery* refers to the advantage that one competitor secures over other competitors by surreptitious, corrupt dealing with the agents and employees of prospective buyers. See **extortion.**

brief, n. = (1) in AmE, the written arguments of counsel for consultation by the court; (2) in BrE, a document by which a solicitor instructs a barrister with an abstract of the pleadings and facts as the barrister prepares to appear as an advocate in court; (3) in BrE, a barrister's authority to appear; or (4) in AmE and BrE, an abstract of all the documents affecting the title to real property (known also as *abstract of title,* q.v.).

For the LAW FRENCH *brief* (= writ), see ***breve.***

brief, v.t., occurs primarily in legal, military, diplomatic, and business contexts. In American legal writing, the term refers to preparing a written brief—e.g.: "Both the statutory and constitutional issues have been fully *briefed* and argued here." In British legal writing—as in American business, diplomatic, and military contexts—the term refers to preparing, informing, or authorizing a person. E.g., "The company *briefed* counsel to oppose the claim." (Eng.) See also **debriefing.**

briefcase gets its name from the legal profession, being originally "a case in which lawyers carry their briefs." *Briefcase* and *attaché (case)* are the only terms current in AmE. In BrE, *brief-bag* (for barristers), *deed-case* or *briefcase* (for solicitors), and *attaché case* are used.

brief, hold a. See **hold a brief for.**

briefing attorney. See **clerk.**

briefly = (1) soon; or (2) not for long. Thus it may cause ambiguities in some contexts <he will deliver his speech briefly>. Cf. **presently.**

BRIEF-WRITING. Except on technical points touched on throughout, brief-writing as a discipline is largely beyond the purview of this book. Still, a few points deserve mention here.

First, a hardly disputable point: American judges find most briefs that they read tough going. As one federal appellate judge chastely puts it, "[I]n my experience it is the rare brief-writer who seizes the opportunity to employ the clarity, simplicity, and directness of expression necessary to endow a brief with maximum persuasive force." Roger J. Miner, *Confronting the Communication Crisis in the Legal Profession,* 34 N.Y.L. Sch. L. Rev. 1, 9 (1989). Other federal appellate judges have called most briefs "execrable" and have estimated the number of "truly helpful" briefs at somewhere between 5% and 10%. Though elected judges are generally more forgiving in their assessment, anyone concerned with the literary aspects of practicing law must be troubled by these evaluations.

Second, even though most briefs fall short of most judges' standards, those standards probably ought to be higher than they are. Consider the standard suggested by Karl Llewellyn in a brilliant lecture just a few days before he died: "[Y]ou need to interest them [the judges] in that brief. You've got to make them feel that when they come to the brief, 'Oh, baby; is it going to be hot.' And they've got to approach the brief with that favorable atmosphere you need." *A Lecture on Appellate Advocacy,* 29 U. Chi. L. Rev. 627, 639 (1962). In the hands of the right brief-writer, of course, virtually any brief can be "hot." But few are.

Third, the most important—and frequently the most neglected—aspect of any brief is the statement of the issues. Framing issues well has become an all but lost art among modern lawyers. For an explanation of how to frame issues effectively, see ISSUE-FRAMING.

For helpful discussions of the subject, see John W. Cooley, *Callaghan's Appellate Advocacy Manual* (looseleaf); *Appellate Practice Manual* (Priscilla A. Schwab ed., 1992) (pt. 3); Ruggero J. Aldisert, *Winning on Appeal* (1992); Edward D. Re, *Brief Writing and Oral Argument* (6th ed. 1987); Girvan Peck, *Writing Persuasive Briefs* (1984); and Jean Appleman's *Persuasion in Brief Writing* (1968). For a discussion of the most common sin in briefs, see OVERPARTICULARIZATION.

bright-line rule = a judicial rule of decision that is simple and straightforward and that avoids or ignores the ambiguities or difficulties of the problems at hand. The phrase dates from the mid-20th century. The metaphor of a bright line is somewhat older than the phrase *bright-line rule*—e.g.: "The difficult part of this case comes with regard to . . . the activity of the Board of Temperance . . . . A *bright line* between that which brings conviction to one person and its influence on the body politic cannot be drawn." *Girard Trust Co. v. I.R.C.,* 122 F.2d 108, 110 (3d Cir. 1941)./ "[T]he *McCambridge* majority opinion . . . agrees that the *Kirby bright-line-rule* is but a mere formalism . . . ." J.G. Trichter, *Bright-Lining Away the Right to Counsel,* Tex. Law., 6 Nov. 1989, at 26. Cf. **hard and fast rule.**

brilliance; brilliancy. *Brilliance* is preferred in describing a quality or state. *Brilliancy,* not quite a NEEDLESS VARIANT, may be called on to mean "something brilliant" <the brilliancies in Justice Holmes's writings are legion>.

bring; take. "*Bring* is confused with *take* only by the illiterate or the unthinking." E. Partridge, *Usage and Abusage* 61 (1957). The *OED* notes that *bring* "implies motion towards the place where the speaker or auditor is, or is supposed to be, being in sense the causal of *come;* motion in the opposite direction is expressed by *take* [being in sense the causal of *go*]." The distinction would seem to be too elementary for elaboration here, but: "One of plaintiff's duties was to pick up old tie plates from around the railroad tracks and *bring* [read *take*] them to a central location."

bring an action against is verbose for *sue*—e.g.: "Hynes' mother *brought an action for damages against the company* [read *sued the company for damages*]." C. Gordon Post, *An Introduction to the Law* 86 (1963).

bring error = bring an appeal. See **error (A).**

bring in (a verdict). Juries are traditionally said to *bring in* a verdict—that is, to bring it back into the courtroom. E.g., "The Judge's summing-up was brief but thorough, and after a short retirement the jury *brought in* a verdict of guilty." Stanley Jackson, *The Life and Cases of Mr. Justice Humphreys* 175 (n.d. [1951])./ "The jury *brought in* a $4.9 million verdict for the Coliseum . . . ." Douglas Laycock, *The Death of the Irreparable Injury Rule* 115 (1991).

bring to book = to arrest and try (an offender). E.g., "The genuinely unfortunate aspect of today's ruling is not that fewer fugitives will be *brought to book.*" *Steagald v. U.S.,* 451 U.S. 204, 231 (1981) (Rehnquist, J., dissenting)./ "Since then, however, both Reagan and Bush have been frustrated in their attempts to *bring terrorists to book* and to end the saga of US hostages in Beirut." Simon O'Dwyer-Russell, *£2.5m Reward to Find Lockerbie Bombers,* Sunday Telegraph, 29 April 1990, at 2./ "[I]t is not the aim of the EC to *bring governments to book* before the European Court of Justice." *Tories Accused of Trying to Subvert Brussels Directive,* The Times, 2 June 1990, at 3.

BRITISHISMS. See AMERICANISMS AND BRITISHISMS.

broach. See **breach.**

broad. See **wide.**

broad brush is a legal METAPHOR signifying a general or sweeping effect. E.g., "We are aware that exemption is a *broad brush*; the club that loses its exemption becomes taxable on income from all sources, including dues, assessments, and membership fees."/ "Congress is much more comfortable painting with a *broad brush*—'discrimination is forbidden'—than in filling in the details." Linda Greenhouse, *A Changed Court Revises Rules on Civil Rights,* N.Y. Times, 18 June 1989, at E1.

broadcast; telecast; cablecast; radiocast. These are the correct forms for the past as well as for the present tense. Adding *-ed,* though fairly common, is incorrect.

Broadcast sometimes acts as an illusory intransitive. "There are no doubt substantially more individuals who want to *broadcast* than there are frequencies to allocate." Though it has no object in this sentence, *broadcast* is not really used intransitively, for the object is understood. Obviously one broadcasts *programs,* and there is no need to specify what would be broadcast if it is plainly understood. See **forecast.**

brocard /***broh**-kard*/ = an elementary legal principle or maxim, esp. one deriving from Roman law or ancient custom. The word is omitted from most abridged English-language dictionaries, such as *W10* and *AHD.* E.g., "That important and novel legal questions should not be decided in a vacuum is a *brocard.*" *U.S. v. Birrell,* 262 F. Supp. 97, 99 (S.D.N.Y. 1967)./ "[T]he *brocard* that a patent is a legally conferred monopoly ordinarily carries precious little value . . . ." Edward H. Cooper, *Attempts and Monopolization,* 72 Mich. L. Rev. 373, 416 (1974)./ "Mindful of these precepts, and of the *brocard* that summary judgments should be granted only sparingly in Title VII cases, . . . we find the district court's summary disposition improvident." *Price v. Southwestern Bell Telephone Co.,* 687 F.2d 74, 78 (5th Cir. 1982).

brokerage; brokage. *Brokerage* = (1) the business or office of a broker <real-estate brokerage is a profession requiring knowledge and experience>; or (2) a broker's fee <brokerage differs from an underwriting commission>.

The archaic *brokage* (or, alternatively, *brocage*) means "the corrupt jobbing of offices; the bribe unlawfully paid for any office" (*OED*). In this sense, *brokage* is the lay equivalent of *simony.* See **barratry.**

Brokage is also an archaic NEEDLESS VARIANT of *brokerage,* but it remains the standard form in a single phrase, *marriage brokage*—e.g.: "[T]he law of England will not enforce a contract of 'marriage *brokage*' . . . ." Thomas E. Holland, *The Elements of Jurisprudence* 277 (13th ed. 1924)./ "So, also, marriage-*brokage* contracts have long been held to be void . . . ." P.S. Atiyah, *An Introduction to the Law of Contract* 242 (3d ed. 1981)./ "A marriage *brokage* contract is one by which a person promises in return for a money consideration to procure the marriage of another." G.H. Treitel, *The Law of Contract* 390 (8th ed. 1991).

brother. This term is often used, by judges, of a male associate on the bench. E.g., "Our trial *brother* [i.e., the trial court judge] fell into error of law in his analysis by his implicit assumption that the appellant's 'substantial disability' provided the postal service legally sufficient grounds for rejecting appellant's bid for the clerk/carrier position." See **brethren.**

A substitute for *brother* in this context, perhaps useful in avoiding SEXISM or in referring to a fellow judge who is a woman, is *colleague:* "I disagree with my *colleagues* because I believe the stipulation signed by the two attorneys was at best ambiguous."

brother-in-law. Pl. *brothers-in-law.*

brush, broad. See **broad brush.**

brusque; brusk. The former spelling is preferred.

brutum fulmen (= an empty noise; an empty threat) is no TERM OF ART; it is the worst type of LATINISM in the law, expressing a commonplace notion for which a variety of English phrases suffice. E.g., "A court of equity cannot lawfully enjoin the world at large, no matter how broadly it words its decree; if it assumes to do so, the decree is pro tanto *brutum fulmen* [read *ineffectual*] and the persons enjoined are free to ignore it."

budget, vb., forms *budgeted* and *budgeting* in AmE, *budgetted* and *budgetting* in BrE. See DOUBLING OF FINAL CONSONANTS.

budget-making is best hyphenated. See **decision-making.**

buggery is a legal term usually meaning "sodomy," but sometimes also "bestiality." *Bugger* (= sodomite) was originally a respectable legal term, though now it is a dialectal term of playful abuse, not necessarily implying sodomy. As the *SOED* chastely notes, *bugger* is "vulgar exc. in law." Here the original meaning obtains, though with contemptuous overtones: "The middle age of *buggers* is not to be contemplated without horror" (Virginia Woolf).

In BrE, *buggery* is the more usual legal term than *sodomy.* It means "anal intercourse by a man with another man or a woman or bestiality by a man or a woman" (*CDL*). E.g., "*Buggery*[:] One of the circumstances constituting this offence is where the penis penetrates the anus of a male or female, and the maximum penalty is life imprisonment." Andrew Ashworth, *Principles of Criminal Law* 310 (1991). The active bugger is guilty as the *agent,* whereas the receiving bugger is called (and is guilty as) the *patient.* See EUPHEMISM.

bulk, n., sometimes causes writers to doubt which form of the verb to use, singular or plural—e.g.: "The vast *bulk* of recorded crimes *falls* [read *fall?*] into the category of property offences." Andrew Ashworth, *Principles of Criminal Law* 39 (1991). Some writers, finding support in the principle of SYNESIS, would write *fall* in that sentence. And they have the better position: when the phrase *bulk of the* is followed by a plural COUNT NOUN, the verb should be plural—a form attested from the early 19th century in historical dictionaries. Hence, *the bulk of the people are* is better than *the bulk of the people is* (a dehumanizing formulation).

bulk large is an acceptable variant of *loom large.* E.g., "Transferability of interests should not ordinarily *bulk large* in the decision whether or not to incorporate."/ "It *bulks* very *large,* for instance, in every census of India." Both *loom large* and *bulk large* have become CLICHÉS.

bumbailiff is a BrE slang term for "a bailiff or sheriff's officer who collects debts." *Bum* (= buttocks) was aptly coupled with *bailiff* in this term—actually a corruption of *bound bailiff*—because of the debt-collectors' habit of catching debtors from behind. This humorous word is now obsolescent. See **bailiwick.**

buncombe; bunkum. This term (meaning "political talk that is empty or insincere") derives from Buncombe County, North Carolina, because the congressman from the district embracing that county early in the 19th century felt compelled, despite interruptions, to "make a speech for Buncombe." *Buncombe* has remained the standard spelling, and is to be preferred because it recalls the interesting origin of the word. E.g., "Or would we dig deeply into our stories of neighborliness and *buncombe* and cobble together something almost great?" Thomas Hine, *Don't Blame Mrs. O'Leary,* N.Y. Times, 15 July 1990, § 7, at 13.

burden of proof. A. Senses. This ambiguous term refers to two distinct concepts, as James Bradley Thayer was the first to observe in the late 19th century. See 1 James B. Thayer, *Evidence* 355–64 (1898). Many judicial decisions that ignore the distinction contain muddled reasoning.

The first concept is known more particularly—and unambiguously—as the *risk of nonpersuasion,* the *burden of persuasion,* and the *persuasion burden.* A party meets this burden by convincing the fact-finder to view the facts in a way that favors that party. Today the phrase *burden of proof* most often bears this meaning.

The second concept is known more particularly—and unambiguously—as the *duty of producing evidence,* the *burden of going forward with evidence,* the *production burden,* or the *burden of evidence.* A party meets this burden by introducing enough evidence to have a given issue considered in the case.

One writer explains what has emerged as the modern scholarly consensus: "[I]t is now commonplace that the term *burden of proof* is used in a double sense," adding: "Much confusion would be eliminated if . . . the ambiguous word *proof* [were] entirely discarded." Roy R. Ray, *Texas Law of Evidence* § 41, at 48 (3d ed. 1980).

B. And *onus of proof.* The phrase *burden of proof* is usual in American legal writing; both phrases are used in British legal writing. E.g., "The judge next directed the jury as to the *onus of proof* upon the issue of provocation." (Eng.) See **onus** & LOAN TRANSLATIONS.

bureau. The better plural form is *bureaus*; the Frenchified plural, *bureaux,* should be avoided as a pretension.

burgeon literally means "to put forth buds; sprout." Although some usage experts have considered it objectionable in meaning "to flourish, grow," no good reason exists to avoid *burgeon* in these figurative senses: but it should be used of growth at its incipient stages, not of full-blown expansion. Here it seems inappropriate: "The creation of 35 new circuit judgeships in 1978 was not intended as a long-term solution to the problem, but was simply one response to *burgeoning* caseloads."/ "Unsanitary and unsafe, many of our overflowing prisons no longer have the capacity to legally hold the *burgeoning* inmate populations created by our ever-increasing war on crime."

burglarious = of, relating to, or inclined to burglary. E.g., "The completion of the *burglarious* intent is not essential to guilt . . . ." Rollin M. Perkins, *Criminal Law* 169 (1957)./ "Although primarily aimed against the carrying of *burglarious* tools, it applies also to the possession of a large variety of other objects with the requisite intent . . . ." Glanville Williams, *Textbook of Criminal Law* 819–20 (1978).

Burglariously (L. *burglariter*) was formerly obligatory in indictments for burglary at common law. The word still occasionally appears in more modern contexts—e.g.: "[T]he state argued . . . that . . . he had *burglariously* and feloniously remained in the women's home." *State v. Thomson,* 861 P.2d 492, 495 (Wash. Ct. App. 1993).

burglarize; burgle. *Burglarize* is an American coinage from the late 19th century meaning "to rob burglariously" (*OED*). It is still largely confined to AmE. *Burgle,* a BACK-FORMATION of comparable vintage, has the same meaning; in AmE, *burgle* is usually facetious or jocular, whereas in BrE it is standard and colorless—e.g.: "If you think it is a good idea that the prime minister's house should be *burgled,* it is just as well not to express the thought to a cracksman . . . ." Glanville Williams, *Textbook of Criminal Law* 31 (1978).

In American judicial opinions, *burglarize* appears about 30 times as frequently as *burgle.* E.g., "He readily spoke about burglaries, . . . but attributed them to someone named 'George,' a person of bad influence who forced Heirens to search out places for him to *burglarize.*" *People v. Heirens,* 122 N.E.2d 231, 234 (Ill. 1954)./ "While he was away both apartments were *burglarized* and damaged." *U.S. v. Doby,* 684 F. Supp. 558, 560 (N.D. Ind. 1988). See **rob.**

burglary. **A. And *robbery; theft; larceny.*** These four terms may overlap to a degree, but no two are perfectly synonymous. *Burglary* = (1) (in the classic sense) the act of breaking and entering another's house at night with intent to commit a felony (e.g., murder) or—in jurisdictions with statutes making petit larceny a misdemeanor—possibly petit larceny as well; (2) (in the modern AmE sense) the act of breaking and entering a building with the intent to commit a felony (dropping the requirements that it be [a] a house, and [b] at night); or (3) (in the modern BrE sense) the offense either of entering a building, ship, or inhabited vehicle (e.g., a caravan) as a trespasser with the intention of committing one of four specified crimes in it (*burglary with intent*) or of entering it as a trespasser but subsequently committing one of two specified crimes in it (*burglary without intent*) (*CDL*). The specified offenses in G.B. are, for *burglary with intent:* (1) stealing; (2) inflicting grievous bodily harm; (3) causing criminal damage; and (4) rape. And for *burglary without intent:* (1) stealing or attempting to steal; and (2) inflicting or attempting to inflict grievous bodily harm.

Robbery = feloniously taking personal property by force or threat of force from the immediate presence of the victim. *Theft* is a statutory wrong that is broader than *robbery,* although nonlawyers often consider the words synonymous; *robbery* means "the taking of personal property belonging to another without his consent, and with the intent to deprive the owner of its value." *Theft* is also broader than *larceny* (= the felonious stealing of personal property, the fraudulent taking and carrying away [*asportation,* q.v.] of a thing without claim of right), for it includes the lawful acquisition and subsequent appropriation of the personalty. In England, the common-law felony of larceny was superseded by the Theft Act of 1968.

The exact definitions of these terms may vary from jurisdiction to jurisdiction. But it is universal that *people* are the objects of *robbery; places* are the objects of *burglary;* and *things* are the objects of *larceny* and *theft.*

In American legal writing, when *of* follows *burglary,* some infelicity or other is almost certain to follow; *burglary of an automobile* would traditionally have been considered a legal blunder, though several states now have statutes that incorporate this phrase; *burglary of a building* is a REDUNDANCY, unless the reference is to a particular building, as *burglary of the Stokes Building.*

B. And *housebreaking.* Whereas a *burglary* traditionally occurred at night, a *housebreaking* (q.v.) might occur at any time of day. In Scots law, either offense has historically been called *housebreaking.*

burgle. See **burglarize.**

BURIED VERBS. Jargonmongers call them "nominalizations," i.e., verbs that have been changed into nouns. Without the jargon, one might say that the verbs have been buried in a longer noun—usually a noun ending in one of the following suffixes: *-tion, -sion, -ment, -ence, -ance, -ity.* It is hardly an exaggeration—no, one hardly exaggerates—to say that, whenever the verb will work in context, the better choice is to use it instead of a buried verb. Thus:

The Verb Buried	*The Verb Uncovered*
arbitration	arbitrate
compulsion	compel
computerization	computerize
conformity, -ance	conform

contravention	contravene
dependence	depend
enablement	enable
enforcement	enforce
hospitalization	hospitalize
identity	identify
incorporation	incorporate
indemnification	indemnify
litigation	litigate
mediation	mediate
knowledge	know
maximization	maximize
minimization	minimize
obligation	obligate, oblige
opposition	oppose
penalization	penalize
perpetration	perpetrate
perpetuation	perpetuate
reduction	reduce
utilization	utilize, use (vb.)
violation	violate

Naturally, you will sometimes need to refer to arbitration or litigation or mediation as a procedure, and when that is so you must say *arbitration* or *litigation* or *mediation.* But if a first draft refers to *the mediation of the claims by the parties,* you might well consider having the second draft refer to *the parties' mediating the claims* or to *the time when the parties will mediate their claims.*

Why uncover buried verbs? Three reasons are detectable to the naked eye: first, you generally eliminate prepositions in the process; second, you often eliminate be-verbs by replacing them with so-called "action" verbs; and third, you humanize the text by saying who does what (an idea often obscured by buried verbs).

The fourth reason is not detectable to the naked eye: in fact, it is the sum of the three reasons already mentioned. By uncovering buried verbs, you make your writing much less abstract—it becomes much easier for readers to visualize what you're talking about. (Compare: "After the transformation of nominalizations, the text has fewer abstractions; readers' visualization of the discussion is enhanced.") Writing that is laden with buried verbs tends to numb the mind: "In our day, long English words of Latin origin—sometimes in the form of sociological or pseudo-scientific gobbledygook—often have hypnotic or sleep-inducing effects." *Sperbeck v. A.L. Burbank & Co.,* 190 F.2d 449, 450 n.8 (2d Cir. 1951). See ABSTRACTITIS.

Though long neglected in books about writing, buried verbs ought to be a sworn enemy of every serious writer. In legal writing, they constitute a more serious problem even than PASSIVE VOICE—whether in analytical writing, persuasive writing, or drafting.

burthen is an ARCHAISM and a NEEDLESS VARIANT of *burden* that still occasionally burdens legal writing. Shakespeare used it frequently, but it has little place in 20th-century prose. E.g., "That the title of the land, when acquired by the community, was taken in the name of the wife, imposes no additional *burthen* [read *burden*] upon the purchaser of inquiring into the equities of the husband and wife in respect to it."

bus, n. & v.t. The plural form of the noun (meaning a large vehicle that holds many passengers) is *buses.* The verb (meaning "to transport by bus") is inflected *bus* > *bused* > *bused*; the present participle is *busing.* When the *-s-* is doubled, the sense is different: *bussed* means "kissed," and *bussing* means "kissing."

Arthur A. Leff knowingly uses *bussing* for *busing* in *The Leff Dictionary of Law,* 94 Yale L.J. 1855, 1967 (1985). In his entry under *busing,* Leff takes the position that the word is "also properly spelled *bussing.*" Accepting that dictum would destroy the DIFFERENTIATION that has evolved between the forms, and therefore it is to be taken as unsound. *Busing* is preferred even in BrE in nonosculatory senses. See *Oxford Guide* 9.

bush lawyer is an Australian term meaning "a person pretending to have considerable legal knowledge" (*W3*). This term might deserve universal adoption, for we *need* such a name. See LAWYERS, DEROGATORY NAMES FOR (B).

bussing. See **bus.**

but. A. Beginning Sentences with. It is a gross canard that beginning a sentence with *but* is stylistically slipshod. In fact, doing so is highly desirable in any number of contexts, and most style books that squarely discuss the question say that *but* is better than *however* at the beginning of a sentence. See Garner, *On Beginning Sentences with "But,"* 3 Scribes J. Legal Writing 87 (1992). For combinations with *and* and *but* starting sentences, see **and (A).** See also SUPERSTITIONS.

Good writers frequently begin sentences with *but,* and have always done so—e.g.:

- "*But* let it be admitted, for argument's sake, that mere wantonness and lust of domination would be sufficient to beget that disposition . . . ." *The Federalist* No. 17, at 119 (Alexander Hamilton) (Clinton Rossiter ed., 1961).
- "When a vessel at sea begins to founder there comes a time when it must be given up as lost. *But* we do not give the order to abandon ship

as soon as, let us say, a fuel pump begins to function erratically." Lon L. Fuller, *Anatomy of the Law* 21 (1968).

- "It is not beyond the bounds of possibility that such a husband might be convicted either of manslaughter or of abetting suicide. *But* he ought not to be." Glanville Williams, *Textbook of Criminal Law* 531 (1978).
- "[T]he strongest case for imposing legal liability arises where there are both benefit and detrimental reliance. *But* it is not necessary that both detriment and benefit should be present in order that the consideration should be good." P.S. Atiyah, *An Introduction to the Law of Contract* 101 (3d ed. 1981).
- "Despite errors and failings, Blackstone did manage to put in brief order the rank weeds of English law. *But* even his picture was partial and defective, like a dictionary that omitted all slang, all dialect, all colloquial and technical words." Lawrence M. Friedman, *A History of American Law* 21 (2d ed. 1985).

B. More Than One in a Sentence. Putting this coordinating conjunction (also called a "coordinator") twice in one sentence invariably makes the sentence unwieldy and less than easily readable. E.g., "There is authority for damages when the employment denied would have enhanced the employee's reputation, as a motion-picture credit would, *but* this has been applied only once in the United States, *but is* [read *though it is*] common in England." See the following subsection.

C. For *and*. This is a common mistake. In the following sentences, the second clause follows naturally from the first—it does not state an exception to or qualification of the first—hence *and* is the appropriate conjunction. E.g., "Summary judgment is a potent weapon, *but* [read *and*] courts must be mindful of its aims and targets and beware of overkill in its use."/ "This action was brought by the administrator of Katherine Veach against the Louisville & Interurban Railway Company, to recover damages for [Miss Veach's] death in the sum of $25,000, *but* [read *and*] a trial resulted in a verdict and judgment in favor of the administrator." *Veach's Adm'r v. Louisville & Interurban Ry.*, 228 S.W. 35, 35 (Ky. 1921).

D. Preposition or Conjunction. The use of *but* in a negative sense after a pronoun ("No one *but she* or *her*") has long caused confusion. If we take *but* to be a preposition (meaning "except"), the objective *her* (or *him*) follows. But if we take *but* as a conjunction, the nominative *she* (or *he*) would be proper.

The correct form depends on the structure of the sentence. If the verb precedes the *but*-phrase, the objective case should be used—e.g.: "None of the defendants were convicted *but him.*"

If, however, the *but*-phrase precedes the verb, the nominative case is proper: "None of the defendants *but he* were convicted." This sentence is considered equivalent to "None of the defendants were convicted, *but he was convicted.*" *But* thus acts as a conjunction when it precedes the verb in a sentence such as this, from Thomas Jefferson: "You, however, can easily correct this bill to the taste of my brother lawyers, by making every other word a 'said' or 'aforesaid,' and saying everything two or three times, so that nobody *but we* of the craft *can understand* the diction, and find out what it means."

but for (= if not for, except for) has become a useful LEGALISM, as in the following sentences: "I also think that the statute is constitutional, and *but for* the decision of my brethren I should have felt pretty clear about it." *Adair v. U.S.*, 208 U.S. 161, 190 (1908) (Holmes, J., dissenting)./ "The evidence also showed that, *but for* the negligence of Lee-Vac, the socket would never have failed."/ "It is therefore quite plain that *but for* the constitutional prohibition on the operation of segregated public parks, the City of Macon would continue to own and maintain Baconsfield."/ "A bad motive will render a conveyance or transfer of property void which, *but for* the bad motive, would have been valid."

In American legal writing, the phrase is frequently used attributively as an adjective, as in *but-for test* or *but-for relationship.* In such phrases, it is better to hyphenate than to use quotation marks around the phrasal adjective. See PHRASAL ADJECTIVES. For *but-for causation,* see CAUSATION (A).

One should avoid using this phrase in two different senses in close proximity, as here (in the third appearance of the phrase): "[T]here is no pretense that the Coliseum would ever be restored to the position it would have occupied *but for* [i.e., were it not for] the wrong. *But for* [i.e., were it not for] the NFL's antitrust violation, the Coliseum would have had college football plus the Raiders, and it would have had the Raiders immediately instead of later. It is true that these losses were short-term, *but for* [i.e., except that for] that period they were irreplaceable, and therefore irreparable." Douglas Laycock, *The Death of the Irreparable Injury Rule* 114 (1991).

but rather is usually unnecessary, either word singly doing the work that both purport to do. E.g., "The court does not mean to suggest by this opinion that all former sufferers of mental illness should be permitted to own firearms; *but, rather,* [read *rather,*] if Congress has determined that there are circumstances under which former criminals can own and possess weapons and a means is provided to establish such an entitlement, former mental patients are entitled to no less."

but yet is always a REDUNDANCY for *yet.* E.g., "This report focuses on three *disparate but yet related* [read *disparate yet related*] areas of broker-dealer compliance." Cf. **as yet.**

buy; purchase. As a verb, *buy* is the ordinary word, *purchase* the more FORMAL WORD. Generally, *buy* is the better stylistic choice. As one commentator says, "Only a very pompous person indeed would say he was going to *purchase* an ice-cream cone or a bar of candy." Robert Hendrickson, *Business Talk* 61 (1984). Traditionally, however, *purchase* has been the proper word for real property. See **descent.**

Purchase, may also act as a noun; *buy* is informal and colloquial as a noun <a good buy>. See **purchase.**

buyback, n. One word.

buydown, n. One word.

buyer; purchaser. In most contexts, *buyer* is the better term because it is plainer.

buyout. One word.

by and between. Though this is a hallowed expression at the outset of contracts, it is unnecessary: *between* alone suffices. E.g., "This is an agreement *by and between* [read *between*] Grand Force, Inc. and William Shipley." See DOUBLETS, TRIPLETS, AND SYNONYM-STRINGS.

by and through, typical LEGALESE, can be replaced by either *by* or *through.* E.g., "On March 12, 1987, Defendant Caterpillar, *by and through* [read *through*] its counsel, Stephen Schoettmer, responded to Plaintiff's first amended interrogatories." See DOUBLETS, TRIPLETS, AND SYNONYM-STRINGS.

by and with is a classic legal REDUNDANCY with but one legitimate use: "For appointments to constitutional offices the phrase *by and with the advice of the Senate* is a TERM OF ART and should not be changed." Reed Dickerson, *Legislative Drafting* 75 n.4 (1954). See DOUBLETS, TRIPLETS, AND SYNONYM-STRINGS.

by(e)-election. *By-election* is preferred in both AmE and BrE.

byelaw. See **bylaw.**

by its four corners. See **four corners of the instrument.**

bylaw; byelaw. Not only the spelling but also the sense differs in AmE from that in BrE. In G.B., *byelaws* are regulations made by a local authority or corporation, such as a town or a railway. In the U.S., *bylaws* are most commonly the administrative provisions of a corporation that are either attached to the articles of incorporation or kept privately.

The spelling without the *-e-* is preferred in AmE. Though etymologically inferior, *byelaw* (sometimes hyphenated) is standard in British legal texts. E.g., "Clause four requires the contractor to comply with Acts of Parliament and *byelaws.*" (Eng.)/ "It would surprise me if the courts of England would hold that when the English Parliament gave the Birmingham Municipality the authority to make *bye-laws* for the good government of the city, it intended also to give the municipality the authority to segregate West Indians from Europeans in the use of public conveniences." (Rhod.) For British publications, the house style of Oxford University Press, however, is *by-law.* See **ordinance.**

by law. See **under law.**

by means of is usually verbose for *by.*

by-product is usually hyphenated, though there is a tendency to make it one word.

by reason of is wordy for *because of*—e.g.: "[*B*]*y reason of* [read *Because of*] the injuries aforesaid, the plaintiff has been put to great expense for care and medical treatment . . . ." Max Radin, *The Law and You* 102 (1948) (quoting a pleading).

by the court; per curiam. *By the court* is merely an English translation of *per curiam* (see LOAN TRANSLATIONS), a term that appears in opinions not attributed to any one member of the court. Contrary to the notion that some lawyers have, *per curiam* opinions usually deal with routine matters that are seen by the judges as having little precedential value; they often dispose of such cases summarily. *Per curiam* opinions should not be construed as exhibiting greater unanimity among members of the court than a signed opinion without a dissent.

Some courts variously use both *per curiam* and *by the court,* of course without differentiation. (Though the practice is now rare, some courts have used merely *the court* for *per curiam* opinions.) It might be best to stick with a single phrase, lest readers of the opinions come to think there must be a distinction. On the one hand, *per curiam* is unambiguous and can be used attributively (*per curiam opinion*), whereas *by the court* may create ambiguities in speech and in writing. Though it is a LATINISM, *per curiam* is a useful and well-established one: it is not likely to be discarded any time soon. On the other hand, *by the court* is at least a comprehensible phrase to all speakers of English, even if they do not all understand its import. Certainly this is the better phrase for popular journalism.

by the later of [date] and [date]; by the later of [date] or [date]. See **later of [date] or [date].**

by virtue of. See **virtue of, in & by.**

byword (= a proverb or saying) is best spelled as one word and not hyphenated. "We are not harking back to Latin *bywords* (*Nemo debet esse judex in propria causa* [i.e., "No man ought to be a judge in his own case"]) without sanction of our highest court."

C

cab(b)ala(h) (= an esoteric or secret doctrine) is preferably spelled *cabala* in AmE, *cabbala* in BrE.

cablecast. See **broadcast.**

cab-rank rule = the rule (in G.B.) that a barrister or advocate, if not already engaged, must accept any case in his or her area of practice, however unpopular or disreputable the cause may be. The rule dates back to the 13th century, when the serjeants-at-law were sworn to represent all comers. The metaphor, of course, refers to how cabdrivers must line up to accept each fare in turn, without turning away any potential customer in favor of others. Nowadays, in English law practice, the rule is "more celebrated for the way in which it has been ignored." Robert Rice, *Amendment to Cab-Rank Clause Is Welcomed,* Fin. Times, 14 May 1990, at I-12.

caducary; caduciary; caducous. Most often rendered *caducary,* the word means (of a bequest or estate) "subject to, relating to, or by way of escheat, lapse, or forfeiture." Labeled "Old Law" in the *OED,* it has nevertheless persisted from Blackstone's day to 20th-century AmE—usu. in the phrase *caducary succession*—esp. in New York practice. See, e.g., *In re Peer's Estate,* 245 N.Y.S. 298, 301 (Surr. Ct. 1930) (noting that the amendments "were apparently intended to waive the rights of the State to claim escheat, or rights of '*caducary* successions,' where there were no blood relatives").

The *SOED* entry appears under *caduciary,* which is the "nonetymological form" that, according to the *OED,* received the superfluous *-i-* by confusion with *fiduciary.* Perhaps because of its spurious origins, *caduciary* has not appeared in recent American or English caselaw. But Scottish texts predominantly use this spelling. One, for example, posits the question "whether the rights of the Crown in England are to be regarded as *caduciary* or successoral." A.E. Anton, *Private International Law* 679 (2d ed. 1990). Like *caducous,* the form *caduciary* is—outside Scotland—best considered a NEEDLESS VARIANT.

caduce, v.t. = to take by escheat or lapse. Derived as a BACK-FORMATION from *caducary,* q.v., this NEOLOGISM has achieved a surprising degree of currency. E.g., "As it is clear that the Government of Ecuador would not assume the obligation to pay the royalties, and that the contract provided that the companies would pay royalties only on oil they sold, the Government, in effect, *caduced* the plaintiff's royalty rights." *Norsul Oil & Mining Co. v. Texaco, Inc.,* 703 F. Supp. 1520, 1542 (S.D. Fla. 1988)./ "The next day, the Government delivered a formal notice that Gulf Ecuador would be *caduced* unless it delivered all funds owed within 30 days." *Phoenix Canada Oil Co. v. Texaco, Inc.,* 658 F. Supp. 1061, 1076 (D. Del. 1987).

caduciary. See **caducary.**

caducity (= lapse of a testamentary gift) is current mostly in jurisdictions with strong civil-law ties, such as Louisiana and Puerto Rico. E.g., "In a civil-law context, time-for-suit provisions are of two kinds: prescription and *caducity.* The first can be tolled under some circumstances. The second cannot be tolled." *Edelmann v. Chase Manhattan Bank,* 668 F. Supp. 99, 102 n.5 (D.P.R. 1987)./ "The testatrix has not expressed any contingency for the *caducity* of the legacy . . . ." *In re Vance,* 2 So. 54, 56 (La. 1887).

caducous. See **caducary.**

Cain, mark of. See **scarlet-letter.**

calculatable, which has appeared in several reported cases, is incorrect in place of *calculable.*

calculated = (1) deliberately taken or made <a calculated risk>; or (2) likely <no prospectus may be calculated to deceive>. Sense (2) represents a debasement in meaning that, particularly in criminal-law contexts, damages the utility of the word even in sense (1). See SLIPSHOD EXTENSION.

calculate out is verbose for *calculate.* E.g., "I need her to *calculate out* [read *calculate*] her lost profits." Cf. **distribute out.** See PARTICLES, UNNECESSARY.

calculus is best confined to mean "a method of calculation," and not "calculation" itself. Here it is properly used: "One factor that weighs heavily in this *calculus* [i.e., *method of calculation*] is Louisiana's interest in providing effective means of redress for its residents."

In the following sentence, *calculus* should probably be replaced by *calculation:* "It is no answer to say that chance would have been of little value even if seasonably offered; such a *calculus* [read *calculation*] of probabilities is beyond the science of the chancery."

By SLIPSHOD EXTENSION of its proper sense ("a method of calculation") *calculus* has come to mean "a method of analysis" or even "analysis," an imprecise usage: "Many of the questions that are posed by the contemporary due process *calculus* [read *analysis*] cannot be answered with confidence."

calendar is used in BrE for *docket* or *cause-list* in criminal cases only; in the U.S. it is used for both civil and criminal cases. See **docket.**

American lawyers often use the word as a verb <the case was calendared for May 23, 1994>—a centuries-old and unexceptionable use of the word.

caliber; calibre. The preferred spelling in AmE is *-er,* in BrE *-re.*

call. See **put.**

called to the bar = (1) in BrE, admitted to practice as a barrister or advocate; (2) in AmE, admitted to law practice of any kind. Though primarily a BrE locution—limited strictly to barristers and advocates—the phrase has achieved some currency among American lawyers. E.g., "When I was first *called to the bar,* I received a very large certificate bearing the Governor's signature evidencing my appointment as Attorney at Law and Solicitor in Chancery." Letter of S.B. Rounds, *quoted in* William Safire, *I Stand Corrected* 417 (1984).

In BrE, to be *called within the bar,* as opposed to merely *to* the bar, is to be appointed King's or Queen's Counsel.

The noun phrase is *call to the bar*—e.g.: "Timothy, my former pupil, being by some two or three years the senior in *call to the Bar,* is detained more often than not by the claims of his profession." Sarah Caudwell, *Thus Was Adonis Murdered* 10 (1981; repr. 1983). Sometimes the phrase is shortened to *call:* "[H]e almost invariably became a member of the Serjeants' Inn, and ceremonially departed from his Inn of call . . . ." R.E. Megarry, *A Second Miscellany-at-Law* 25–26 (1973). See **admit (C).**

callous; callus. The former is the adjective ("hardened, unfeeling"), the latter the noun ("hardened skin"). Unfortunately, during the early 1990s Dr. Scholl's—the firm specializing in foot products—mistakenly advertised *callous removers* instead of *callus removers,* encouraging further confusion.

calumny is a somewhat old-fashioned equivalent of *defamation. Calumny* may refer to either (1) the act of falsely and maliciously misrepresenting the words or actions of others, calculated to injure their reputations (*OED*), or (2) the false charges or imputations themselves. Although this term was used at common law as a technical legal word, today it is more literary than legal. The phrase *breath of calumny* is an old CLICHÉ.

The verb is *calumniate*—e.g.: "I suppose this woman to be completely innocent of the offence laid to her charge; but she has not been wantonly or maliciously *calumniated.*" (Eng.) *Calumnize* is a NEEDLESS VARIANT that appears here as a purple flourish: "The second string to the defendant's bench trial bow *calumnizes* [read *criticizes?*] the granting of the motion." *Moores v. Greenberg,* 834 F.2d 1105, 1109 (1st Cir. 1987). See PURPLE PROSE.

The adjective is *calumnious* (*calumniatory* being a NEEDLESS VARIANT), and the agent noun is *calumniator.*

came on for hearing; coming on for hearing. These INVERSIONS begin legalistically worded court orders—e.g.: "*Came on for hearing* this 5th day of July 1994 the plaintiff's motion for summary judgment . . . ." Such a sentence is best reworded—e.g.: "On July 5, 1994, *the court heard* the plaintiff's motion for summary judgment."

camera (lit., "chamber"—i.e., the judge's private room) is used in the phrase *in camera,* q.v. See also **chambers.**

can; may. The distinction between these words has been much discussed. Generally, *can* expresses physical ability <he can lift 500 pounds>; *may* expresses permission or authorization <the defense may now close>, and sometimes possibility <the trial may end on Friday>. Although only an insufferable precisian would insist on observing the distinction in speech or informal writing (esp. in questions such as, "Can I wait until August?"), writers are best advised to distinguish between these words in formal contexts.

cancel (out). See PARTICLES, UNNECESSARY.

cancel(l)ed. Because the primary accent falls on the first syllable, in AmE the *-l-* should not be doubled in the second syllable. The *-ll-* spelling often mistakenly crops up in American writing, as in this passage: "Unless *cancelled* [read *canceled*] as provided in the agreement, the option could be exercised by giving written notice thereof no later than April 1, 1968." Note, however, that in *cancellation* the ells are doubled (*-ll-*). See DOUBLING OF FINAL CONSONANTS.

candidacy; candidature. The former is the regular term in AmE, the latter in BrE.

cannon. See **canon.**

cannot should not appear as two words, except in rare instances such as, "With the principles of good English and literary composition to guide the author, legal writing *can not* only be literature, but also be good literature of obvious excellence and enduring value," in which *not* is part of the phrase *not only . . . but also.* (See **not only . . . but also.**) *Cannot* is preferable to *can't* in formal writing. See CONTRACTIONS.

cannot be heard to say is a trite LEGALISM that expresses the notion of estoppel. E.g., "Certainly if the conduct is eventually found by the National Labor Relations Board to be protected by the Taft–Hartley Act, the State *cannot be heard to say* that it is enjoining that conduct for reasons other than those having to do with labor relations." *Weber v. Anheuser-Busch, Inc.,* 348 U.S. 468, 480 (1955)./ "All parties were familiar with the custom of the industry regarding liability of pilots and mooring masters and *cannot be heard to say* that they were ignorant of the practice of attributing mooring masters' negligence to the shipowner." *Kane v. Hawaiian Indep. Refinery, Inc.,* 690 F.2d 722, 724 (9th Cir. 1982).

cannot help but be; cannot help being; cannot but be. In formal contexts, the last two phrases have traditionally been preferred. Still, because *cannot help being* and (esp.) *cannot but be* are increasingly rare in AmE and BrE alike, they strike modern readers as stilted and perhaps even alien. *Cannot help but be* is becoming an accepted idiom that should no longer be stigmatized—e.g.: "Experts say Thomas' court performance *cannot help but be* affected by the traumatic Senate confirmation hearings." Aaron Epstein, *Thomas Survives Controversy, Wins Senate Confirmation, 52–48,* Philadelphia Inquirer, 16 Oct. 1991, at 1-A./ "[I]t does not seem that any such argument was ever advanced . . . ; if it had been, I *cannot help but think* that it would have been given very short shrift indeed." *National Employers' Mut. Gen. Ins. Ass'n Ltd v. Jones,* [1990] 1 A.C. 24, 59, [1988] 2 All E.R. 425 (H.L.).

canon; cannon. *Canon* = (1) a corpus of writings <the Holmes canon>; (2) an accepted notion or principle <canons of descent>; (3) a rule of ecclesiastical law (either of the Roman Catholic canon law, or of the Anglican Church); or (4) a cathedral dignitary.

Cannon = (1) a big gun; or (2) the ear of a bell, by which the bell hangs. *Cannon* incorrectly displaces *canon* surprisingly often: "[T]he district court focused in part on the sections of the Indiana Code that make bailiffs 'at will' employees and [on] the *Cannons* [read *Canons*] of Professional Ethics." *Meeks v. Grimes,* 779 F.2d 417, 420 n.2 (7th Cir. 1985)./ "He was found to be guilty of violation of the *cannons* [read *canons*] of professional ethics by neglecting a legal matter entrusted to him by a client . . . ." *Kentucky Bar Ass'n v. Lester,* 781 S.W.2d 517, 517 (Ky. 1989).

canon law; church law. These synonymous phrases refer to the codified law governing a church. Traditionally, the word refers specifically to the ecclesiastical law governing the Roman Catholic church, consisting largely of papal bulls, other official decrees, and writings by personages within the church.

The adjectival form corresponding to *canons* (= the laws or rules of the church) is *canonical,* which has long been a secularized synonym of *axiomatic:* "This court has so repeatedly held that complete dominion and authority over the property imports a fee simple title in the devisee that the rule is *canonical.*" See **axiom.**

canon-law method. See **civil-law method.**

canonist = a specialist in ecclesiastical law, esp. in medieval times. Maine states that the English common law "borrows far the greatest number of its fundamental principles from the jurisprudence of the *Canonists.*" Henry S. Maine, *Ancient Law* 132 (17th ed. 1901; repr. [New Universal Lib.] 1905, 1910). Scholars frequently refer to canonists' opinions in discussing moral questions: "[A]ccording to many of the early *canonists,* the soul was not infused into the infant's body until some time after conception." Glanville Williams, *The Sanctity of Life and the Criminal Law* 196 (1957; repr. 1972). Cf. **civilian.**

canvas; canvass. *Canvas,* almost always a noun, is a heavy cloth. In its rare verbal sense, it means "to cover with such a cloth."

Canvass, n. & v.t., means, as a verb, (1) "to examine (usu. votes) in detail"; (2) "to discuss or debate"; (3) "to solicit orders or political support"; or (4) "to take stock of public opinion." Here sense (4) applies: "An alderman stated that he had *canvassed* the board of aldermen, and that 23 would oppose the measure." Sense (1) is also common in legal contexts: "It was contended for the husband that there must be some evidence called or some substantial opening of the case or some *canvassing* of the issues." (Eng.)/ "Having determined that our rules on prosecutorial vindictiveness govern the instant case, we must *canvass* the competing policies, beginning with the defendant's interest in minimizing the apprehension of prosecutorial vindictiveness." The noun *canvass* means "the act of canvassing."

capability. See **capacity.**

capable of = (1) able to be affected by; of a nature, or in a condition, to allow or admit of; admitting; susceptible (*OED*); (2) having the needful capacity, power, or fitness for (some specified purpose or activity) (*id.*); or (3) having capacity, ability, or intelligence. Sense (1) is far more common today in legal than in lay writing: "Allegations of perjured testimony must be supported by substantial factual assertions *capable of* resolution by an evidentiary hearing."/ "'Submission to arbitration' is *capable of* more than one meaning." (Eng.)

Sense (2) appears widely in lay and legal writing, but is not used in quite the same way; whereas nonlawyers usually connect a participial phrase to *capable of,* lawyers frequently follow it with a simple noun. E.g., "Appellees argue that the purchase of automobiles in New York would not occur but for the fact that the automobiles are *capable of use* in distant states like Oklahoma." Most modern writers would make it *capable of being used.*

capacitas rationalis is a LATINISM whose perpetration in non-Roman contexts is unforgivable, what with English phrases like *rational capacity, rational faculties, reason,* and *rationality* to do the work. In the following sentence the phrase arguably refers to the Roman-law doctrine: "The principle of *capacitas rationalis* embodies the free-will retributive idea that man is a rational being with the capacity to understand his actions intelligently and control them accordingly." (Eng.)

capacitate = to qualify; to make legally competent. This term is a fancy LEGALISM, in place of which *qualify* or *make competent* is more widely comprehensible.

capacity; capability. These words overlap, but there are nuances. *Capacity* = the power to receive, hold, or contain. Figuratively, it refers to mental faculties in the sense "the power to take in knowledge." In law, it is frequently used in the sense "legal competency or qualification" <capacity to contract>.

Capability = (1) power or ability in general, whether physical or mental; or (2) the quality of being susceptible of.

capacity; competency. *Capacity* refers to legal ability or qualification, as to sue, to make contracts, or to commit crimes. *Competency* is a closely analogous word used in evidentiary contexts, as in *competency to testify.*

capias (L. "that you take," a general term used of writs of attachment or arrest) is generally the shortened form of *capias ad respondendum,* which is a writ to enforce attendance at court. In AmE, the phrase *arrest warrant* is gradually displacing this use of *capias.*

There are also some less well-known species of *capias,* including:

- *capias ad satisfaciendum,* which was formerly used after judgment to imprison the defendant until the plaintiff's claim was satisfied. This phrase is often abbreviated *ca. sa.,* as here: "Another basis for amercement exists where a writ of *ca. sa.* has issued to the sheriff who makes a return that the defendant cannot be found in the county." *Poultrymen's Serv. Corp. v. Winter,* 244 A.2d 308, 309-10 (N.J. Super. 1968). In England, this writ was available in rare cases until 1981.
- *capias ad respondendum,* which authorizes the sheriff to arrest a defendant.

- *capias in withernam,* which authorizes the sheriff to seize the cattle or goods of a wrongful distrainor.
- *capias utlagatum,* which commands the arrest of an outlawed person.

The word *capias*—as the shortened and anglicized form of *capias ad respondendum*—is a singular noun with the plural form *capiases.* Yet *capias* is occasionally misapprehended as being plural as well as singular. E.g., "On behalf of himself and others similarly situated, Stephen Crane brought an action complaining that Dallas County regularly issued *capias* [read *capiases*] without a finding of probable cause by a neutral and detached magistrate."

capital, n.; **capitol.** The former is a city, the seat of government; the latter is a building in which the state or national legislature meets (fr. L. *capitoleum,* the Roman temple of Jupiter). Until October 1698, when the Virginia governor specified that *Capitol* would be the name of the planned statehouse in a village then known as Middle Plantation, the word *capitol* had been used only as the name of the great Roman temple at Rome. See Mitford M. Mathews, *American Words* 62–63 (1959; repr. 1976).

Capital, whether as a noun or as an adjective (see the following entry), is called on far more frequently than *capitol.*

capital, adj. Lawyers use this word in two closely allied senses: (1) "punishable by death" <capital crimes>; and (2) "involving capital punishment" <capital cases>. The first example illustrates sense (1), the second and third sense (2): "No person shall be held to answer for a *capital,* or otherwise infamous crime, unless on presentment or indictment of a Grand Jury . . . ." U.S. Const. amend. V./ "[I]t's the rare court-appointed lawyer who is skilled in the complexities of *capital* cases." Sally B. Donnelly, *You Don't Always Get Perry Mason,* Time, 1 June 1988, at 38, 39./ "A lawyer whose practice is primarily civil may initially face some trepidation in taking on criminal appellate or postconviction *capital* work." Paul J. Bschorr, *Challenges for the Decade,* 17 Litigation 1, 2 (Summer 1991). The *OED* traces these senses to the late 15th and early 16th centuries and lists a lesser-included sense in Roman law, in which *capital* = involving the loss of civil rights.

Additionally, *capital* can refer to the money used by an organization, as distinct from income.

capitalist(ic). *Capitalist* is the general adjective; the *-istic* form, a favorite of Marxists, is pejorative.

CAPITALIZATION. Conventions of capitalization abound in legal writing; several of the more important ones are here discussed. They vary, to be sure, as practices in capitalizing are governed as much by personal taste as by a set of rules. Sections (A), (B), and (C) below prescribe what might be called "rules" of capitalization, while sections (D), (E), (F), and (G) explain and describe common practices.

A. All Capitals. Avoid them. They impair readability because the eye cannot easily distinguish among characters that are all of a uniform size. Try reading these passages, which are ordered by increasing readability:

> EXCEPT AS MAY BE OTHERWISE SPECIFICALLY PROVIDED IN THIS AGREEMENT, ALL NOTICES SHALL BE IN WRITING AND SHALL BE DEEMED TO BE DELIVERED WHEN DEPOSITED IN THE UNITED STATES MAIL, POSTAGE PREPAID, REGISTERED OR CERTIFIED MAIL, RETURN RECEIPT REQUESTED, ADDRESSED TO THE PARTIES AT THE RESPECTIVE ADDRESSES SET FORTH ON EXHIBIT B OR AT SUCH OTHER ADDRESSES AS EITHER PARTY MAY SPECIFY BY WRITTEN NOTICE.

vs.

> Except as May Be Otherwise Specifically Provided in This Agreement, All Notices Shall Be in Writing and Shall Be Deemed to Be Delivered When Deposited in the United States Mail, Postage Prepaid, Registered or Certified Mail, Return Receipt Requested, Addressed to the Parties at the Respective Addresses Set Forth on Exhibit B or at Such Other Addresses as Either Party May Specify by Written Notice.

vs.

> Except as may be otherwise specifically provided in this Agreement, all notices shall be in writing and shall be deemed to be delivered when deposited in the United States mail, postage prepaid, registered or certified mail, return receipt requested, addressed to the parties at the respective addresses set forth on Exhibit B or at such other addresses as either party may specify by written notice.

What an odd phenomenon it is that lawyers—whenever they want to draw special attention to passages, such as main issues in a brief or warnings in drafted documents—make them typographically impenetrable. Using all caps is bad enough; underlining them is even worse. If you feel impelled to use all caps, make sure that they do not run for more than one line.

Writers should avoid using all caps even for the conventions discussed in sections (D)–(G) below. Large and small caps, as in the titles of essay entries in this book, are preferable to all caps because they provide greater typographic variety and are therefore easier on the eye. See DOCUMENT DESIGN.

B. Initial Capitals. When capitalizing only the initial letters of words—as in headings or titles—follow these conventions:

1. Capitalize the first letter of every important word, such as a noun, pronoun, verb, adjective, and adverb, no matter how short the word. Thus, words such as *pi, it,* and *be* should be capitalized in headings that use initial caps.
2. Capitalize the initial letter of the first and last word, no matter what part of speech either may be; also, capitalize the first letter of any word that follows a colon or a dash.
3. Put articles (*the, a, an*), as well as conjunctions (*and, or*) and prepositions having four or fewer letters (*of, by, with*) in lowercase.

C. Rules of Law. These are variously written with initial letters either capitalized (as if they were titles) or lowercased. Even when we capitalize, however, the extent of capitalization is not settled; thus we have *the rule in Shelley's case, the Rule in Shelley's case, the Rule in Shelley's Case,* and *The Rule in Shelley's Case.* The first of these is a mere description; the second is not quite logical, for its last noun (*case*) is presented as a descriptive term while its first noun (*Rule*) is treated as a proper noun; the third is the best form, and the most usual; and the fourth makes *the* a part of the name or title, which makes sense for a book or article bearing that name, but not for general references to the rule.

Other rules of law have just as many variations. (See, e.g., **Rule against Perpetuities.**) In questionable instances, the best policy is to determine to what extent general legal usage has sanctioned a certain phrase as being a rule of law, and then to capitalize those words essential to the name of the doctrine or rule. Hence *the doctrine of the Destructibility of Contingent Remainders* but *the Rule in Shelley's Case; Destructibility of Contingent Remainders* frequently appears without *the doctrine* or *the rule,* which is not really a part of the name of the rule, but *Shelley's Case* almost never occurs without *the Rule in* preceding it. Likewise *the Rule Forbidding a Remainder to the Grantor's Heirs* and *the Doctrine of Worthier Title.*

D. Vessel Names. These are now more commonly capitalized than not. But the habit of using all capitals is apparently of fairly recent origin. In a typical 19th-century case, *The Harrisburg,* 119 U.S. 199 (1886), the name of the ship had only the first letter capitalized; yet modern cases often write *THE HARRISBURG* when referring to the ship in that case. The older, more conservative convention might seem preferable, since words in all capitals are often distracting and difficult to read. See (A) in this entry. Cf. INITIALESE.

E. Judges' Names. It has long been a tradition, both in English and in American courts, to spell judges' names in all capitals when the names are referred to in opinions—though not elsewhere. (For an older English example, see the quotation under **between (A).**) The U.S. Supreme Court regularly follows this practice. E.g., "This view garnered three votes in *Arnett,* but was specifically rejected by the other six Justices. See [*Arnett v. Kennedy,* 416 U.S. 134, 166–67 (1974)] (POWELL, J., joined by BLACKMUN, J.); *id.* at 177–78, 185 (WHITE, J.); *id.* at 211 (MARSHALL, J., joined by DOUGLAS and BRENNAN, JJ.)." *Cleveland Bd. of Educ. v. Loudermill,* 470 U.S. 532, 540 (1985).

F. Trademarks. Some judges prefer to use all capitals in spelling out trademarks. See, e.g., *Conan Properties, Inc. v. Conans Pizza, Inc.,* 752 F.2d 145 (5th Cir. 1985). This convention has the advantage of distinguishing between the mark and the party, as here: "In addition, starting from the time of the changeover to *EXXON* as its primary mark, *Exxon* developed plans for extended use of the *HUMBLE* mark, as reflected in numerous internal memoranda." Again, however, using all capitals can be immensely distracting to readers.

G. Party Names. Some people ill-advisedly use all caps for party names: "It is conventional although not essential to put short forms in quotation marks when they are established: JOHN DOE ('DOE'). The quotation marks are dropped for all subsequent references. It is archaic and uselessly wordy to recite 'JOHN DOE (hereinafter referred to as 'DOE')." Barbara Child, *Drafting Legal Documents* 123 (2d ed. 1992). For an example of how distracting it is to use all capitals for party names, see *Schneider v. Indian River Community College Found., Inc.,* 684 F. Supp. 283 (S.D. Fla. 1987).

capitalize (= to provide with capital, i.e., money) is a late 19th-century American NEOLOGISM that has gained universal acceptance. E.g., "Plaintiffs *capitalized* the project at $3 million." *Sodima v. International Yogurt Co.,* 662 F. Supp. 839, 842 (D. Or. 1987).

capital punishment, whether one is for or against what it denotes, is a legal EUPHEMISM for state-imposed death. See **death penalty.**

capitol. See **capital.**

capitulatory, not *capitulative,* is the adjective corresponding to *capitulation.* E.g., "A defendant might moot the suit by taking unilateral *capitulatory* action."

caption. The sense "arrest or seizure by legal process" is the oldest for this word; now archaic, that sense has surfaced in several opinions that are, by the law's standards, within living memory. E.g., "That the debt was attachable in confiscation proceedings was held by this court in *Miller v. The United States,* and it was ruled that attachment or seizure could be made without manual *caption* of the visible evidences of the credit." *Brown v. Kennedy,* 82 U.S. (15 Wall.) 591, 599 (1872).

The usual sense in modern writing—that of a heading—derives ultimately from that legal sense. *Caption* came to be used in the 17th century as a shortened form of *certificate of caption* or *taking;* such a certificate appeared at the top of a legal process to show where, when, and by what authority it was to be served or executed. Lawyers then pressed *caption* into service in a variety of contexts, such as to describe the heading on an abstract of title (where the land is described).

American journalists in turn extended this LEGALISM further by making it refer, in the mid-19th century, to headings of newspaper articles and the like, where the English would have said *title, head,* or *heading.* See **head.**

captioned, as a short form of *above-captioned* <the captioned cause>, is, like the longer form, unnecessary JARGON. It is preferable to write *this case, that case, the Smith case,* or the like. See **above-mentioned.**

captor; capturer. The latter is a NEEDLESS VARIANT.

Cardozo is not only widely mispronounced */kahr-**doh**-zə/* instead of */kahr-**doh**-zoh/*; it is misspelled *Cardoza* in more than 50 reported cases, such as *State v. Saia,* 302 So. 2d 869, 879 (La. 1974) (Summers, J., dissenting); *Brubaker v. Glenrock Lodge Int'l Order of Odd Fellows,* 526 P.2d 52, 59 (Wyo. 1974).

The better adjectival form is *Cardozan*—e.g.: "*Cardozan* prose is not of consistent quality, but it should not be judged by its worst examples, as it is by his detractors." Richard A. Posner, *Cardozo: A Study in Reputation* 23 (1990). A variant form is *Cardozoean*—e.g.: "Corbin . . . proposed to the Restaters what might be called a *Cardozoean* [read *Cardozan*] definition of consideration . . . ." Grant Gilmore, *The Death of Contract* 63 (1974).

careen, v.t.; **career,** v.t. *Careen* = (1) v.i., to tip or tilt <the sailboat careened and then sank>; or (2) v.t., to cause to tip or tilt <the wind careened the sailboat>. *Career,* v.i., = to move wildly at high speed. E.g., "[H]is car overturned yesterday after *careering* out of control across three lanes of the motorway." *M4 Driver Drowns,* Sunday Telegraph, 11 Feb. 1990, at 2.

Since the early 20th century, AmE has tried to make *careen* do the job of *career,* as by saying that a car *careened* down the street. On September 7, 1992, in a campaign speech in Wisconsin, President George Bush said that "product liability has *careened* out of control." Despite the increasing currency of this use, however, careful writers reserve the verb *career* to signify something moving wildly at high speed.

carelessness, in law, can be a misleading word because it suggests that a person's actually caring negates carelessness. In the context of criminal and tort law, though, *carelessness* generally states an objective—not a subjective—standard. So, regardless of how careful a bicyclist might *try* to be, consciously assessing the risks, that bicyclist still might not reach the objective standard. In short, even those who care deeply can commit legal carelessness. Cf. **recklessness.**

cargo. The pl. *cargoes* is preferable to *cargos.* See PLURALS (C).

carnal knowledge. This is an old legal EUPHEMISM for sexual intercourse—dating back at least to the 17th century. The phrase is often paired, in references to rape, with *ravish,* q.v., a word that today strikes many readers as romanticizing a horrible criminal act. Generally, the phrase *carnal knowledge* might be advantageously replaced with a more direct phrase such as *sexual intercourse.*

carrier. See **underwriter.**

carrying-away, n. See **asportation.**

carte blanche; carta blanca. The French form, *carte blanche* (= free permission), is the usual one in English contexts—not the Italian form (*carta blanca*), which is a NEEDLESS VARIANT. The phrase, meaning literally "a white card," does not take an article. "Codefendants conspired with the securities swindler and gave him *a carte blanche* [read *carte blanche;* no article] to conceive and carry out a securities fraud."/ "It is almost meaningless to contemplate a 'regulatory' policy that gives every regulated entity *carte blanche* to excuse itself from the consequences of the regulation."

cartelize = to organize into a cartel. (See -IZE (A).) Yet *cartel* has three quite different meanings: (1) "an agreement between hostile nations"; (2)

"an anticompetitive combination, usu. that fixes commercial prices"; and (3) "a combination of political groups that work toward common goals." Modern usage favors sense (2).

carve out (an exception or the like) is a hackneyed METAPHOR in legal writing. E.g., "[W]e decline to *carve out an exception* to this principle in criminal negligence cases." *State v. Tranby,* 437 N.W.2d 817, 821 (N.D. 1989). See CLICHÉS.

ca. sa. = *capias ad satisfaciendum.* See **capias.**

case. A. Generally. *"In the case of John Doe deceased, etc.,* is the sort of jargon which disfigures almost all legal writing." Percy Marks, *The Craft of Writing* 52 (1932). "It is permissible, of course, to write of a law case, a medical case, or a case of linen, but it certainly is not advisable to use *case* in any other way." *Id.* at 53. Quiller-Couch condemned this word as "Jargon's dearest child," esp. in the phrase *in the case of,* in his essay "Jargon," in *On the Art of Writing* (1916; repr. 1961). *In the case of* is, to be sure, generally an obnoxious phrase; it has its legitimate uses, but not generally in legal writing, in which *case* so frequently refers to a lawsuit, not an instance.

Even in the sense synonymous with *cause,* the word *case,* in a phrase such as *in the case of Monroe v. Pape,* is inferior to the case name itself: *in Monroe v. Pape.* E.g., *"The case of Blair v. Commissioner* [read *Blair v. Commissioner*] is to be distinguished from the present case in that there the corpus of the trust was in existence."

The worst offenders are the phrases *in any case* [read *in any event*], *in case* [read *if*], *in the case of* [usu. best deleted or reduced to *in*], *in every case* [read *always* or *in every instance*], and *as the case may be* [a phrase that is not easily circumvented]. "There is perhaps no single word so freely resorted to as a trouble-saver, and consequently responsible for so much flabby writing." (Fowler, *MEU2* 76.) Especially does *case* lead to flabbiness when it is used in a sentence twice with different meanings, as in the two examples following: "The popular image of a divorce *case* has long been that of a private detective skulking through the bushes outside a window with a telephoto lens, seeking a candid snapshot of the wife *in flagrante delicto* with a lover. Such is not exactly the *case.*" J. Goulden, *The Million Dollar Lawyers* 41 (1978)./ "I shall read in extenso the passage of general importance in *case* the instant *case* (or part of it) is reported." (Eng.)

B. Meaning "argument." This meaning, seen in the phrase *the case for the defendant,* is commonplace and immune from the objections lodged against the various phrases discussed in section (A). E.g., "Lincoln repeated his *case* from town to town in the seven debates with Douglas." Alfred Kazin, *A Forever Amazing Writer,* N.Y. Times, 10 Dec. 1989, § 7 (Book Rev.), at 3./ "The bank's *case* was that Tesam had not crossed the threshold which must be cleared before an English court had jurisdiction under the Convention to hear the claims." *English Court Can Hear Shoe Case,* Fin. Times, 27 Oct. 1989, at 12.

C. As Ellipsis for *trespass on the case* or *action on the case.* See the entries under those phrases.

D. And *cause.* See **cause (A).**

case at bar. This is the most usual expression in which *at bar* is used, but legal and evidentiary issues may be *at bar,* as well as cases. E.g., *"National Union* involved a termination clause similar to the one *at bar."* See **at (the) bar.**

case at bench is a variant of *case at bar,* q.v., cast from the judge's rather than the advocate's point of view. E.g., "And in this country, Mr. Justice Story felt so strongly on the point that although the *case at bench* was robbery on the high seas . . . ." Rollin M. Perkins & Ronald N. Boyce, *Criminal Law* 144 (3d ed. 1982). Even so, most judges use *case at bar,* not *case at bench.*

casebook. Preferably one word in both AmE and BrE, though it occasionally appears in the latter as two words or as a hyphenated phrase.

casebook method; hornbook method; lecture method. These are the names of different pedagogical techniques in law. The *casebook method* (known also as the *case method, casebook system,* or *case system*) was devised in the 1870s at Harvard Law School by Professor Christopher Columbus Langdell. Instead of learning the law from lectures and textbooks, Langdell's students read law cases and then were questioned about them through the Socratic method. They were thus led to induce principles of law instead of receiving them as predigested deductions. Langdell's *Selection of Cases on the Law of Contracts* (1871) was the first such book of its kind.

The *hornbook* or *lecture method,* by contrast, involves a straightforward presentation of legal doctrine, sometimes interspersed with questions and problems. This method predominates in certain fields of law, such as procedure and evidence, and in civil-law countries.

Scholars continue to debate the merits of one system over the other. These comments from the literature help define the contours of the terms: "Under the *casebook method* the student, when confronted with a decision, is expected to analyze it in terms of a knowledgeable separation of superfluous facts from those issues impregnated with legal significance." Arthur D. Austin, *Is the Casebook Method Obsolete?* 6 Wm. & Mary L. Rev. 157, 161 (1965)./ "The *'casebook method'* of teaching Law is still the vogue in the law schools . . . . In many ways, the old fashioned *hornbook method* of legal education made more sense. It was more direct and more straightforward and you could learn more principles faster." Fred Rodell, *Woe Unto You, Lawyers!* 140–41 (1939; repr. 1980).

case-by-case. When used as a PHRASAL ADJECTIVE before the noun <on a case-by-case basis>, the phrase should be hyphenated—but not when it follows what it modifies <the court will draw those lines case by case>.

The phrase *case-to-case* is a variant of *case-by-case:* "Typically federal courts, either by rule or by *case-to-case* determination, follow the forum state's practice." 10 Charles A. Wright et al., *Federal Practice and Procedure* § 2671, at 228–29 (1983).

caseflow. This NEOLOGISM is commonly written as one word. E.g., Sallman, *Observations on Judicial Participation in Caseflow Management,* 8 Civ. Just. Q. 129 (1989).

case-in-chief. This term is useful legal JARGON. It means "that part of a trial in which the party with the initial burden of proof presents his evidence, after which he rests" (*Black's*). E.g., "In numerous cases this court has held that mention of the fact of defendant's silence following arrest by the prosecutor in his *case-in-chief* is a violation of constitutional dimensions."/ "The issue was raised by the offer of the gun as a part of the state's *case-in-chief.*" The phrase should be hyphenated. See **in chief.**

case(-)law. This term appears in modern texts in three ways: as a single word, as two words, and hyphenated. Although all three forms can be found in abundance, the phrase is increasingly written as a single solid word. E.g., "That kind of surveillance does not, under the *caselaw,* constitute an actionable invasion of privacy." *Pemberton v. Bethlehem Steel Corp.,* 502 A.2d 1101, 1117 (Md. App. 1986). See **decision(al) law, jurisprudence (B), & common law (B)(6).** Cf. **organic law.**

Caselaw is usually opposed to *statutory law* (or *statute law*): "The law derived wholly or partially from adjudication and the law derived from ancient customs through the medium of judicial decisions together make up the *Case Law,* as distinguished from the Statute Law." William M. Lile et al., *Brief Making and the Use of Law Books* 7 (3d ed. 1914). Oddly, caselaw is often referred to as the *unwritten law,* q.v., though it is certainly written.

case, law of the. See **law of the case.**

case lawyer = a lawyer who has something approaching an encyclopedic knowledge of the caselaw within his or her jurisdiction. E.g., "These were still the days of the *case lawyer,* who knew his reports and found his way about them partly by use and wont . . . partly with the help of the *Digests* . . . ." Lord Wright, *The Study of Law,* 54 Law Q. Rev. 185, 185 (1938)./ "Since Cardozo was one of the best *case lawyers* who ever lived, the proof was invariably marshalled [q.v.] with a masterly elegance." Grant Gilmore, *The Ages of American Law* 75 (1977). Cf. **cause lawyer.**

caseload. Listed as two words in *W3,* this term is usually spelled as one word in American legal writing. E.g., "Cases are then grouped to mix the *caseload* (some civil, some criminal, some agency-administrative) and to spread the work load." Barbara H. Craig, *Chadha: The Story of an Epic Constitutional Struggle* 174 (1988). Cf. **case(-) law.**

case method. See **casebook method.**

casenote. See **annotation.**

case of first impression = a legal situation that the courts in a given jurisdiction have never before addressed. E.g., "Let us suppose that this was a *case of first impression,* that is, a situation [that] is before an American court for the first time." C. Gordon Post, *An Introduction to the Law* 81 (1963). Cf. the inferior LATINISM *res nova,* q.v.

case of, in the. See **case (A).**

case or controversy. This phrase is the buzzword for the rule that federal courts in the U.S. do not decide hypothetical cases, or legal questions presented in a vacuum. Instead, the questions must arise in a genuine *case or controversy.*

The phrase, interestingly, has its origins in poor constitutional drafting—that is, drafting that violates the Golden Rule by engaging in INELEGANT VARIATION. Article III, § 2 of the U.S. Constitution describes nine categories of matters that are within the judicial power of the U.S. The first three categories speak of "all Cases" and the next six refer simply to "Controversies." It is because of this that we join the two and say that a federal court can decide only a "case or controversy." State courts have no such inherent limitation—indeed, many state courts are free to decide matters that would not be a "case or controversy" as federal courts understand the phrase.

Historical considerations aside, the first word swallows the second in this DOUBLET: "a *'controversy,'* if distinguishable at all from a *'case,'* is distinguishable only in that it is a less comprehensive term, and includes only suits of a civil nature." Charles A. Wright, *The Law of Federal Courts* 53 (4th ed. 1983). See **justiciability.**

CASE REFERENCES. A. Short-Form References. For shorthand reference to a case already mentioned, the usual practice is to use the first name in the case style, or the more distinctive name if the first is fairly common or is a place-name (e.g., *Board of Education,* a state's name, *United States,* etc.). Hence *Erie R.R. v. Tompkins,* when shortened, is *Erie,* not *Tompkins;* but *Marshall v. Mulrenin* usually becomes *Mulrenin,* and *National Mut. Ins. Co. v. Tidewater Transfer Co.* is shortened to *Tidewater.* Case names are not usually abbreviated when the parties' names are short; e.g., *Roe v. Wade* is rarely shortened to *Roe.*

It is a good idea to avoid using a shortened name attributively when it might seem to ridicule the court. Thus, one would not want to write *the Seven Elves court* or *the Wolfish court* when referring to the courts that decided *Seven Elves, Inc. v. Eskenazi,* 635 F.2d 396 (5th Cir. 1981), and *Bell v. Wolfish,* 441 U.S. 520 (1979). One judge, referring to *the Petty court,* felt obliged to write, "no pun intended." *Welch v. State Dep't of Highways & Pub. Transp.,* 739 F.2d 1034, 1038 (5th Cir. 1984) (per Gee, J.). See (C) below.

B. Locatives with. *In which,* not *where,* is the better way of referring to what the facts were or what the court said in a given case. E.g., "Second, we rely . . . on this Court's decision in *Lewis, where* [read *in which*] Lewis, an employee of Timco, sued Atwood Oceanics, the vessel owner." See **where (B).**

C. As Attributive Adjectives. Some cases have become so well known to the courts that routinely apply them as precedents that these courts have come to use the shortened case names as adjectives. There is no harm in this habit, although case citations might be helpful to less well-informed readers. Rarely, for example, is *Erie R.R. v. Tompkins* cited with the phrase *Erie-bound,* q.v. Other adjectivally used case names appear in phrases such as these:

- *Terry stop* or *Terry frisk* (fr. *Terry v. Ohio,* 392 U.S. 1 (1968)). See ***Terry* stop.**
- *Miranda warning* (fr. *Miranda v. Arizona,* 384 U.S. 436 (1966)). See **Mirandize.**
- *Allen charge* (fr. *Allen v. United States,* 164 U.S. 492 (1896)). See **dynamite charge.**
- *Anton Piller order,* referring to an order by a court in a civil case allowing a party to inspect and remove a defendant's documents, esp. when the defendant might destroy evidence (fr. *Anton Piller K.G. v. Manufacturing Processes Ltd.* [1976] Ch. 55; [1976] 1 All E.R. 779).
- *Mareva injunction,* referring to an interlocutory injunction to restrain a person from removing assets outside the jurisdiction in an attempt to frustrate litigation in England (fr. *Mareva Compania Naviera S.A. v. International Bulk Carriers* [1980] 1 All E.R. 213).

Citation to the full case is especially important when lesser-known cases are used as adjectival phrases, a practice not to be engaged in without restraint. E.g., "Langa contends that his counsel failed to move for a mistrial when the government elicited co-conspirator hearsay testimony without first securing a *James* ruling." The adjective *James,* which will draw a blank for most readers, refers to *U.S. v. James,* 590 F.2d 575 (5th Cir.) (en banc), *cert. denied,* 442 U.S. 917 (1979).

In some instances, the precedent itself is unimportant to the phrase, and the case name has merely been adopted to denote certain types of factual situations, as with *Totten trust* (fr. *In re Totten,* 71 N.E. 748 (N.Y. 1904)) and *Mary Carter agreement* (fr. *Booth v. Mary Carter Paint Co.,* 202 So. 2d 8 (Fla. Dist. Ct. App. 1967)). When, as in these phrases, the case name is used not to refer to precedent but to describe certain facts or denote types of transactions, citing the case is virtually always unnecessary. See CITATION OF CASES.

D. Hypallage with. It is unobjectionable to write that a certain case *held* something, rather than to say that the court, in that case, held such and such. This practice is an innocuous form of HYPALLAGE. E.g., "*National Carbide* held that the Tax Court had improperly failed to distinguish between 'agency' and 'practical identity' when it ruled the subsidiaries were true agents." But there is a fine line between this type of hypallage and the fallacious personification of cases discussed in (E): cases might *hold* something or other, but they probably do not *cite* or *reason* or *argue.*

E. Personification of Cases. This type of ANTHROPOMORPHISM characterizes hack-writing about judicial opinions—e.g.: "*INS v. Lopez-Mendoza,* in declining to apply the exclusionary rule to deportation proceedings, cited approvingly cases finding that the absence of *Miranda* warnings did not render otherwise voluntary statements inadmissible in deportation proceedings." The way to correct the problem, of course, is to write *The court in* INS v. Lopez-Mendoza, etc.

case-specific = patterned after or adjusted to the facts of a given case <case-specific instructions>. E.g., Johns, *How the Zauderer Decision Impacted* (q.v.) *Case-Specific Solicitation in Lawyer Advertising,* 26 Comp. Jurid. Rev. 107 (1989).

case stated = (1) historically, a procedure by which the Court of Chancery referred difficult legal questions to a common-law court—abolished in 1852; (2) in G.B., a criminal procedure in which the prosecution and the defendant, usu. in a test case, request that a magistrates' court prepare findings along with its decision, so that the parties may then obtain appellate review of a point of law by a three-judge Divisional Court of the Queen's Bench Division; (3) in G.B., a similar procedure in which the parties obtain review of a decision by a lands tribunal or (until 1979) an arbitrator; (4) in the U.S., a civil procedure in which the parties submit an agreed statement of the facts to a trial court so that they can obtain a decision on a point of law; or (5) the factual statement submitted for review under any of the procedures just described.

Fairly uncommon in the U.S., the procedure is used most frequently today in Massachusetts and Pennsylvania. The usual idiom is *upon a case stated*—e.g.:

- "Upon a *case stated,* a decree was entered confirming a former ruling of the Attorney General that the executors would be entitled to a refund of any overpayment." *Comptroller of the Treasury v. Davidson,* 199 A.2d 360, 360 (Md. Ct. App. 1964). (The Maryland court rule providing for this procedure—Rule 329—was abolished in 1984.)
- "Upon this bill in equity . . . , the facts were agreed. A Superior Court judge properly treated the matter as presented upon a *case stated." Moore v. Zoning Bd. of Appeals,* 276 N.E.2d 712, 714 (Mass. 1971).
- "A judgment based upon a *case stated* is not appealable unless the parties expressly have reserved the right to appeal in the *case-stated* submission." *McSwain v. City of Farrell,* 624 A.2d 256, 257 n.2 (Pa. Commw. Ct. 1993).

As the last quoted example shows, when the phrase appears as a PHRASAL ADJECTIVE, it should be hyphenated <case-stated procedure>.

case system. See **casebook method.**

case, trespass on the. See **trespass on the case.**

case where is inferior to *case in which,* but the locution is hardly new: "The books are full of *cases where* [better: *cases in which*] a party has gone into equity only to find that he has mistaken the true theory of his case and must sue at law." William M. Lile et al., *Brief Making and the Use of Law Books* 356 (3d ed. 1914). See **where (B)** & CASE REFERENCES (B). Cf. **example where.**

cash damages. See **damages (A).**

cast is the correct past tense and past participle, *casted* being an incorrect variant. See **broadcast.**

casting vote = the deciding vote cast by the presiding officer of a deliberative body when the votes of those deliberating are equal. The U.S. Constitution gives the vice-president the casting vote in the Senate. See U.S. Const. art. I, § 3.

cast in stone. See **stone, etched in.**

castle doctrine; my home is my castle; every man's house is his castle. The first of these is the legal incarnation of the latter two, which are popular bywords in legal contexts. The so-called *castle doctrine* is an exception to the *retreat rule,* q.v. Under that rule, even the innocent victim of a murderous assault must retreat safely, if possible, instead of resorting to deadly violence unless the victim is in his or her "castle" at the time. See Rollin M. Perkins & Ronald N. Boyce, *Criminal Law* 1133–35 (3d ed. 1982). "That every man's house is 'his *castle*' is a concept that has been echoed down through the ages and the social interest in the security of his '*castle*' has its origin in antiquity; for just as an animal or a bird resents any intrusion into its place of abode, so no doubt did primitive man." *Id.*

As for the longer phrases, using the first person forestalls any objections on grounds of sexism, as one writer did in referring to the Fourth Amendment as "the '*my home is my castle*' Amendment." René A. Wormser, *The Story of the Law* 347 (1962). See SEXISM (A) & MAXIMS.

casual. Because it is occasionally mistaken for *causal* (and vice versa), *casual* may at first seem wrong in certain contexts even when it is properly intended: "It was precisely this sort of *casual* evidentiary inference that *Witherspoon* expressly condemned: 'It cannot be assumed that a juror who describes himself as having conscientious or religious scruples against the infliction of the death penalty . . . thereby affirms that he could never vote in favor of it.'" The meaning apparently intended in that sentence is "offhand, cursory." But inferences are often *causal* in nature, hence the reader's initial expectation that *causal* would have been the right word; if the writer had chosen *careless* or *desultory* (or some other word) rather than *casual,* the careful reader's expectations would not be undercut. See SOUND OF PROSE, THE.

casualty; casuality. *Casuality* is an obsolete NEEDLESS VARIANT of *casualty,* the usual word.

casus belli; casus fœderis. *Casus belli* (= an event that provokes war) is both a legal and a literary word—here the latter: "Sherry vomited in the defendant's taxicab on their way home, and this became the *casus belli* of this litigation." *Noble v. Louisville Taxicab & Transfer Co.,* 255 S.W.2d 493, 494 (Ky. 1952). As a term in international law, it refers to a provocative act that, in the opinion of an offended power, justifies it in making or declaring war.

A *casus fœderis,* by contrast, is a provocative act by one state toward another, entitling the latter to call upon an ally to fulfill the undertakings of the alliance. See Ernest M. Satow, *Guide to Diplomatic Practice* app. 1 at 16 (5th ed. 1979), which notes that the two phrases are sometimes confused.

casus male inclusus denotes the all-too-common occurrence when legislation is overbroad and, unfortunately, covers a "case wrongly included." Like *casus omissus,* q.v., the LATINISM does not have a ready English substitute—nor, however, is the phrase very common in American legal writing. Here is a BrE example: "To extend a statute to a regrettably omitted case looks like legislation, whereas refusing to extend it to a *casus male inclusus* is more like imposing a provisional fetter on legislation." Glanville Williams, *Learning the Law* 110 (11th ed. 1982).

casus omissus = a circumstance omitted or not provided for, as by a statute (and therefore governed by the common law) (*W2*). Since this LATINISM has a specific meaning not readily conveyed by a simpler phrase, one might be tempted to hail it as a useful addition to the legal vocabulary. It is common in British legal writing—e.g.: "The appellant, however, contends that the section does not apply because it provides that the disponer (i.e., the wife) shall 'be liable to be taxed': the wife, it is said, is not a taxable person and so this provision does not operate; there is a *casus omissus.*" (Eng.)

Though unfamiliar to most American lawyers, the phrase does appear occasionally in American law reports—e.g.: "The federal courts have treated this as a *casus omissus,* and have divided on the question whether traditional rules of evidence require the exclusion of hearsay offered on direct examination of an expert as the basis of his opinion . . . ." *McMunn v. Tatum,* 379 S.E.2d 908, 912 (Va. 1989).

The plural form is *casus omissi.*

cataclysm; cataclasm. The meanings of these words are fairly close, esp. in figurative senses. A *cataclysm* is a tremendous flood or violent disaster. A *cataclasm* is a tearing down or disruption.

catalog(ue). Though librarians have come to use *catalog* with regularity, *catalogue* is still the better form. *Cataloging* makes about as much sense as *plaging.* "If the professionals decline to restore the *-u-* to the inflected forms," wrote Follett, "let them simply double the *-g-*." Wilson Follett, *Modern American Usage* 97 (1966). The U.S. Supreme Court has used the more conservative form: "The cases we have reviewed show . . . the impossibility of resolution by any semantic *cataloguing.*" *Baker v. Carr,* 369 U.S. 186, 217 (1962).

catapult, in keeping with the metaphor, is best a transitive and not an intransitive verb. The correct use of this verb in the active voice demands an agent and an object, as in "The men *catapulted* stones over the wall." If an agent is omitted, the verb must appear in the passive voice: "He was *catapulted* to fame."/ "The victim was *catapulted* through the windshield." With such a construction, the means is implied. Yet a common blunder today is: "He *catapulted* to fame." This verb, even when used figuratively, so inevitably calls to mind its literal sense that, used intransitively, it is illogical. See METAPHORS.

catchword (BrE) = *keynote* (AmE). E.g., "At the head [of a case in the law reports] are what are called catchwords, indicating briefly what the case is about." Glanville Williams, *Learning the Law* 38 (11th ed. 1982).

categorical question. See **leading question.**

categorically = without qualification. E.g., "Testimony of appellant and of appellant's witnesses of the agreement was by the respondent *categorically* denied." For a MALAPROPISM involving this word, see **uncategorically.**

causa causans. See CAUSATION (B).

causal; causative. These words have, unfortunately, been muddled by legal writers. The meanings should be kept distinct. *Causal* is the more common word, meaning "of or relating to causes; involving causation; arising from a cause." *Causative* = operating as a cause; effective as a cause. These two words share the sense "expressing or indicating cause," although *causal* is preferred for that sense.

In the following sentences, the words are correctly used: "A plaintiff may still recover attorneys' fees if he can show both a *causal connection* between the filing of the suit and the defendant's actions and that the defendant's conduct was required by law." (*Causal connection* and *causal link* are SET PHRASES.)/ "Plaintiffs are unable to show how any additional discovery could supply an inference of conspiratorial or *causative* conduct any stronger than that provided by the contracts themselves."/ "In *Sohyde* we found relevant to the jurisdictional analysis that all the *causative* factors could have as easily occurred on land and that the injury and damages were indistinguishable from those arising from land-based blowouts."

Here, *causal* is misused for *causative:* "Appellant's argument is that appellee was asked to pay only for those damages resulting from its defective product and thus was not charged with any injury attributable to other *causal* [read *causative*] faults [i.e., faults that would tend to cause the injury]."

In the following sentences, the opposite mistake appears: "The court's use of the words 'produced by' clearly reflects the *causative* [read *causal*] element of the *Christie* test."/ "The final type of cancer and mesothelioma evidence—Comstock's expert testimony on the *causative* [read *causal*] relationship between asbestos exposure and those diseases—is relevant to the issue of liability." See **casual.**

causal challenge = *challenge for cause,* q.v. The two-word phrasing allows legal writers a nice parallel for the other type of challenge, the *peremptory challenge.* E.g., "[T]he liberal allowance of *causal challenges* frequently exhausts the array or reduces it to the point where the trial cannot proceed until additional jurors have been summoned." 1 Burton R. Laub, *Pennsylvania Trial Guide* § 34.4, at 81 (1959)./ "[I]f the Kennedy affidavit is correct, appellant was prevented from intelligently exercising his peremptory and *causal challenges* because of the juror's intentional nondisclosure." *U.S. v. Colombo,* 869 F.2d 149, 151 (2d Cir. 1989). The phrase *cause challenge* sometimes appears, but *causal challenge* is preferable because it puts the adjective in the true adjectival form.

causality; causation. These words have a fine distinction. *Causality* = the principle of causal relationship; the relation of cause and effect. *Causation* = the causing or producing of an effect. In law, *causation* has long been given the additional sense "the relation of cause and effect," a sense best reserved to *causality* in nonlegal contexts.

Causation should not be used for *cause,* as here: "Under the facts of *Kubrick,* the plaintiff had actual knowledge of his injury and its *causation* [read *cause*]."

causa mortis (= in contemplation of one's death) is a LATINISM and TERM OF ART used primarily in the phrase *gift causa mortis* (or the thoroughly Latinate phrase *donatio causa mortis*). E.g., "The power of a donor, in a gift *causa mortis,* to revoke the gift and divest title of the donee is another clear example of the legal quantities now being considered."/ "A gift *causa mortis* must be made when the donor is in imminent peril of death and under such circumstances that the gift would not be made were it not for the peril." In BrE, the phrase is often written *mortis causa.*

causation. See **causality.**

CAUSATION is one of the subjects that have inspired legal writers to don their philosophers' caps and to work out any number of systems of analysis. The general principles of analysis have proved to be more or less universal in Anglo-American jurisdictions, but the terminology of that analysis does vary—hence the explanations in this entry.

As one writer aptly put it, "There are few words in the English vocabulary that have given rise to more legal problems than the words *cause* and *causing.*" Note, 88 Law Q. Rev. 451, 451 (1972). Technically speaking, everything that contributes to a given result is, as a matter of fact, a cause of that result. Consider this illustration:

> In homicide by shooting, for example, while the mind turns first to the man who pulled the trigger, it was obviously impossible for him to have committed that homicide (by shooting) without a loaded weapon. As he did not, in all probability, make the gun himself, it is necessary to consider others, such as those who made and sold the weapon, and even the inventor of that particular kind of firearm. Others perhaps were connected with the result because they made the shell or the bullet or the powder, or assembled the finished cartridge. The mind gets lost in the labyrinth of contributory factors long before the possibilities are exhausted. As only a portion of the factors [that] actually contribute to such a result will receive

juridical consideration, it is neither necessary nor useful to exhaust the philosophical possibilities of actual causation.

Rollin M. Perkins & Ronald N. Boyce, *Criminal Law* 771–72 (3d ed. 1982).

By contrast, though it would be desirable to exhaust the legal terminology of causation, this entry can do no more than discuss the very most common terms. The terminology illustrates the truth of Glanville Williams's observation: "The lawyer is interested in the causal parentage of events, not in their causal ancestry." Glanville Williams, *Textbook of Criminal Law* 328 (1978).

In the end, legal terminology reflects the fact that courts are concerned with determining "cause" from the standpoint of attaching liability, not of ascertaining physical or medical cause. For example, a lawyer might say that A's death was caused by B's negligent driving while a doctor would say it was caused by shock and loss of blood.

A. *Proximate cause; legal cause; direct cause.* All three terms are used synonymously. The term *proximate cause* has become an indispensable term in American tort law; it means simply "a cause that directly produces an effect; that which in natural and continuous sequence, unbroken by any new independent cause, produces an event, and without which the injury would not have occurred." (See **but for.**) The following definition—perhaps more direct—signals just how fuzzy the phrase is: "a cause of which the law will take notice." The Latin equivalent is *causa proxima.*

The *CDL* does not include an entry on *proximate cause,* since the term *legal cause* is more usual in BrE. That is likewise the term preferred by the American Law Institute. See *Restatement (Second) of Torts* § 9 (1965). *Direct cause* is now increasingly rare.

B. *Immediate cause; effective cause; causa causans.* These terms are used to denote the last link in the chain of causation (as, e.g., a *supervening cause). Causa causans* is little used except in BrE.

C. *Producing cause; procuring cause.* These terms are virtually synonymous with *proximate cause* but in some jurisdictions are used in particular contexts such as workers' compensation (*producing cause*) and real-estate brokerage (*procuring cause* [of a sale]). The choice of term is usually statutorily prescribed.

D. *Intervening cause; supervening cause.* These denote a cause that comes into active operation *after* a defendant's negligence, even if that cause does not break the chain of causation. The point is that *intervening* and *supervening* are used, then, in a purely temporal sense in reference to the chain of causation. *Intervening* is the better choice of term, for *supervening cause* is sometimes confused with *superseding cause.* See (E).

In BrE, the equivalent Latinisms *novus actus interveniens* and *nova causa interveniens* are commonly used. See LATINISMS.

E. *Superseding cause; sole cause.* These phrases denote an *intervening cause* that breaks the chain of causation. Thus if X shoots Y, who is then stabilized and recovering nicely but soon dies after poor medical treatment, that medical negligence will be held to be a *superseding cause* (a phrase more common than *sole cause*). The phrase *supervening cause* is also sometimes used in this sense, but it should be avoided because of its use also for *intervening cause.* See (D).

causative. See **causal.**

cause. A. And *case.* Both terms are used to describe litigated actions, despite some published nonsense to the contrary: "The legal theory of the party may be a cause of action. However, the lawsuit itself is not a 'cause.'" Irwin Alterman, *Plain and Accurate Style in Court Papers* 172 (1987). *Case* is more commonly used, to be sure, but *cause* (= lawsuit) has long been current in the speech and writing of lawyers. E.g., "Eventually it was decided that as from 1979 criminal causes in the House of Lords should be reported under the same title as in the court below." Glanville Williams, *Learning the Law* 17–18 (11th ed. 1982). Indeed, the word *cause* has extended beyond law into popular writing: "It is not necessary here to plead the cause of truffles and sauteed mushrooms." P.J. Wingate, *The Fungus Is Still Among Us,* Wall St. J., 3 April 1989, at A12.

The peaceful coexistence of these terms need not be threatened by branding either one a NEEDLESS VARIANT. When writing or speaking for nonlawyers, however, *case* is the clearer term.

Black's notes that DIFFERENTIATION is possible between these terms, although if it does exist at all it is little heeded: "*case* not infrequently has a more limited signification, importing a collection of facts, with the conclusion of law thereon," whereas "*cause* imports a judicial proceeding entire, and is nearly synonymous with *lis* in Latin, or *suit* in English."

B. And *action.* Although *cause* and *action* are nearly synonymous, the legal idioms in which the phrases are used differ. Thus an *action* or *suit* is said to be 'commenced,' but a *cause* is not. Similarly, a *cause* but not an *action* is said to be 'tried.' Any substantive distinction between the words is subtle: broadly, *action* connotes legal procedure and *cause* denotes the merits of the dispute.

C. Disposition by Courts. *Causes* (or *cases*) are *on dockets*; they may be *remanded* (by an appellate court) or *disposed of* (by any court). But they may not be *reversed* or *affirmed.* E.g., "This is the keystone of the opinion below: If it is in error, the *cause must be reversed* [read *judgment must be reversed*]." See JUDGMENTS, APPELLATE-COURT.

cause challenge. See **causal challenge.**

cause lawyer = a lawyer who is so deeply committed to a (usu. social) cause that he or she cannot objectively consider issues relating to that cause. E.g., " *'Cause' lawyers,* they say, often lack an adequate understanding of their adversaries' positions, forcing the parties into rancorous, costly lawsuits when more amicable resolutions might be possible." Felsenthal, *Lawyers Who Switch Sides Draw Ire with Big Checks,* Wall St. J., 19 July 1990, at B1, B5. Cf. **case lawyer.**

cause-list is the BrE term corresponding to *docket* or *calendar,* qq.v., in AmE.

cause of action; right of action; ground of action. These terms "should not be confused . . . . They are not interchangeable." *Swankowski v. Diethelm,* 129 N.E.2d 182, 184 (Ohio App. 1953). *Cause of action* = (1) a group of operative facts, such as a harmful act, giving rise to one or more rights of action; or (2) a legal theory of a lawsuit. Writers on civil procedure prefer that the term be confined to sense (1). The acceptance of sense (2) by some courts actually caused the drafters of the Federal Rules of Civil Procedure to avoid the term altogether. See Fleming James, *Civil Procedure* § 2.11, at 87 (1965).

Sometimes *cause of action* is misused for *prima facie case,* q.v., as here: "Plaintiff failed to make out his *cause of action* [read *prima facie case*], and therefore his claim must fail."

Right of action has two senses: (1) "the right to take a particular case to court" *(CDL);* and (2) "a chose in action." Here sense (1) obtains: "The foundation of the *right of action* was a family relationship with the deceased." For *chose in action,* see **chose.**

Ground of action is an infrequent variant of *cause of action*—e.g.: "As a child so young was incapable of performing acts of service, the *ground of action* failed."

cause to be. A cartoon some years ago depicted a lawyer at a cocktail party talking with a friend and saying, "I met Joan in law school, where certain sparks were caused to be made." And certain idioms were caused to be learned as well, alas.

This one—*cause to be*—was born of a fear of not sufficiently expressing the idea that an agent may, as opposed to the principal, carry out an act. E.g., "The directors must *cause books to be kept* . . . ." J. Charlesworth, *The Principles of Company Law* 247 (4th ed. 1945). If the sentence said, *The directors must keep books* . . . , the result is not to disallow any delegation of bookkeeping matters. In most contexts, this phrase is noxious. See **effect (A).**

caution */**kay**-shən/*, in civil (and esp. Scots) law, means "security." *Cautionry /**kay**-shən-ree/* = a surety obligation. *Cautioner /**kay**-shən-ər/* = a surety.

cautionary; cautious. *Cautionary /**kaw**-shən-ar-ee/* = encouraging or advising caution. E.g., "This time we do not award damages but sound a *cautionary* note to those who would persistently raise arguments against the income tax that have been put to rest for years." *Cautious* = exercising caution.

In Scots law, a *cautionary /**kay**-shən-ar-ee /* obligation is one of suretyship. See **caution.**

caveat */**ka**-vee-aht/* (lit., "let him [or her] beware") means, in nonlegal speech and writing, merely "a warning," from the common phrase *caveat emptor* (= let the buyer beware). E.g., "The expression *caveat emptor* . . . still applies, and so long as the vendor does not actually mislead the purchaser, the purchaser has only himself to blame if he finds that the house is by no means what he thought it was." Anon., *The Home Counsellor* 207 (n.d. [London: Odhams Press, ca. 1940–1945]).

In legal prose, however, *caveat* often signifies a notice, usually in the form of an entry in a register, to the effect that no action of a certain kind—e.g., probate of a will—may be taken without first informing the person who gave the notice (the *caveator,* q.v.). E.g, "In the probate practice of many states, a will contest commences with the filing of a *caveat* or written objection setting forth the facts upon which the contest is based."/ "The question on this appeal is whether a judgment creditor of an heir may file and prosecute a *caveat* to a will of the ancestor of that heir, by which real property is devised to other persons."

caveat, v.t., is an AmE extension of the noun use described in the preceding entry. E.g., "The petition has no right or interest in the property or estate of the testator necessary to maintain a suit to *caveat* the last will and testament of the testator." The verb is inflected *caveated /**ka**-vee-ə-təd/*, *caveating /**ka**-vee-ə-ting/.*

caveatee. See **caveator.**

caveator; contestant. A *caveator* is not one who warns, but one who has entered a caveat, i.e., one who challenges the validity of a will. The person whose interest is challenged is termed the *caveatee.* E.g., "The district court did require the defendant-*caveatee* to proceed first in order of proof with evidence of due execution. However, the ultimate burden of persuasion was put on the plaintiff-*caveator.*" *Curtis v. Curtis,* 481 F.2d 549, 550 (D.C. Cir. 1973). *Caveatrix* is an obsolete form (see SEXISM (C)). See **caveat.**

Contestant is used in jurisdictions in which the procedure of filing a *caveat* is not used. E.g., "We now return to the statute that the *contestant* says was disregarded when George and the Gillises subscribed their signatures to the questioned instrument." See **contestant.**

cavil, beyond (= beyond even the most trivial objection) is a favorite expression of judges. E.g., "The fact of damage was established *beyond cavil.*"

cease is a FORMAL WORD for *stop* or *end.* E.g., "In a jurisdiction that bases the imposition of exemplary damages on general deterrence, the fact that the defendant has *ceased* the offending conduct is irrelevant, as the exemplary damages may be used as a future deterrent to others." Cf. **desist.**

cease-and-desist order (= an order from a governmental authority directing a person violating the law to stop doing so) should be hyphenated thus. (See PHRASAL ADJECTIVES (A).) Usually used in reference to administrative orders, this DOUBLET (*cease-and-desist order*) performs a useful function. Where the doublet functions as a verb phrase and not as an adjective (*We order you to cease and desist*), of course, the hyphens should not appear. The simpler expression *stop order* is confined to securities law.

The phrase *cease-and-desist letter* refers to an analogous demand letter, having no governmental authority behind it but threatening legal action. E.g., "Last November, Thoroughbred Racing sent *cease-and-desist letters* to several artists who had depicted Easy Goer, winner of last year's Travers Stakes at Saratoga." David Margolick, *At the Bar,* N.Y. Times, 23 Feb. 1990, at B11. See **desist.**

ceasefire. One word in both AmE and BrE.

cede; secede; concede. The distinctions are as follows. *Cede* = to give up, grant, admit, or surrender. "By the Treaty of October 4, 1864, the Klamath Indian Tribe *ceded* approximately twenty million acres of aboriginal land to the government of the United States." *Secede* = to withdraw formally from membership or participation in. *Concede* = (1) to admit to be true; (2) to grant (as a right or a privilege); or (3) to admit defeat in (as an election).

ceiling, used in the sense of "maximum," is in itself unobjectionable but can sometimes lead to unfortunate mixed metaphors. E.g., "The task force recommended a general *increase* in the *ceilings.*" One *raises* a ceiling rather than *increases* it. An English writer on usage quotes a preposterous example about "a ceiling price on carpets." In using words figuratively, one must keep in mind their literal meanings. See METAPHORS. Cf. **catapult.**

celui qui trust. See ***cestui que trust.***

censor; censure. To *censor* is to scrutinize and revise, to suppress or edit selectively. E.g., "The right of the superintendent in the exercise of a reasonable discretion to *censor* the ordinary mail written by a patient who has been adjudged insane is not challenged."

As a noun, *censor* = one who inspects publications before they are published to ensure that they contain nothing heretical, libelous, or offensive to the government. It would be nice to pronounce this use of the term obsolete, but in some countries the censors remain prominent.

To *censure* is to criticize severely, to castigate. E.g., "In 1978, the Alabama Court of the Judiciary *censured* a judge for merely associating with a former convict."/ "The SEC may remove from office or *censure* any officer or director of a self-regulatory organization if it finds that he has willfully violated the rules or abused his position." The noun *censure* means "an official reprimand" or "severe criticism."

censor, n.; **sensor.** The first is one who suppresses; the second is something that detects.

censorious (= severely critical) is the adjective corresponding to the verb *censure,* not *censor.* E.g., "As to the manner in which Messrs. Wigmore and Kocourek have executed their task, it is very easy to be *censorious* . . . ." Morris R. Cohen, *Reason and Law* 197 (1961).

censorship (= the institution or practice of suppressing ideas thought to be uncongenial to those in power), whose mention immediately implicates the First Amendment, is one of those politically charged VOGUE WORDS that people use irresponsibly: "[E]ver since the controversy over federal funding for exhibitions of Robert Mapplethorpe's brutalizing photographs of sadomasochistic behavior erupted a couple of years ago, little cries of 'censorship' have filled the air like the buzz of locusts wherever politically correct intellectuals congregate. Moreover, it soon became clear that this chorus was determined to construe *'censorship'* so broadly that anyone denied government largesse could claim to be a victim of oppression." *The PC Line on Censorship,* New Criterion, Dec. 1991, at 2.

censure. See **censor.**

centennial; centenary. In all the anniversary designations (*bi-*, *sesqui-*, etc.), whether used as adjectives or as nouns, the *-ial* forms are preferred in AmE, the *-ary* forms in BrE.

center around for *center on* or *in.* Something can *center on* (avoid *upon*) or *revolve around* something else, but it cannot *center around,* as the center is technically a single point. The error is common—e.g.: "Bracton's discussion *centres around* [read *centres on*] the word 'heirs.'" Theodore F.T. Plucknett, *A Concise History of the Common Law* 559 (5th ed. 1956)./ "Almost all of his [i.e., Puccini's] works *center around* [read *center on* or *revolve around*] the heroine." J.M. Balkin, *Turandot's Victory,* 2 Yale J. Law & Humanities 299, 315 (1990).

The PHRASAL VERB is frequently used when a straightforward BE-VERB would be preferable: "Perhaps the greatest concern to issuers considering junior stock *centers around* [read *is*] the accounting treatment of junior stock."

Center has been used of late as a transitive verb, perhaps to avoid the prepositional dilemma: "Computation of pecuniary damages recoverable for a barge's injury in a maritime collision *centers* [i.e., *is at the center of*] this cause." This phrasing is unidiomatic, however.

CENTURY DESCRIPTIONS. Some of us, apparently, forget from time to time that *20th century* describes the 1900s, that *19th century* describes the 1800s, and so on. Thus R.B. Collins's article entitled *Can an Indian Tribe Recover Land Illegally Taken in the Seventeenth Century?* 1984–1985 Preview of United States Supreme Court Cases no. 8, p. 179 (Jan. 18, 1985), which discusses land acquired by New York from the Oneida Indians in 1795. The title should refer to the *18th century,* not the *17th.*

What particular years make up the course of a century has also caused confusion. The *Oxford Guide to English Usage* points out that

> strictly, since the first century ran from the year 1 to the year 100, the first year of a given century should be that ending in the digits 01, and the last year of the preceding century should be the year before, ending in two noughts. In popular usage, understandably, the reference of these terms has been moved back one year, so that one will expect the twenty-first century to run from 2000 to 2099.
> *Oxford Guide* 95 (1983).

One other point merits our attention. As compound adjectives, the phrases denoting centuries are hyphenated; but they are not hyphenated as nouns. Hence, "The 12th-century records were discovered in the 19th century." See ADJECTIVES (C).

ceremonial; ceremonious. The DIFFERENTIATION between these words lies more in application than in meaning; both suggest a punctilio in following the customs and trappings of ceremony. *Ceremonial* is the general word; it relates to all manner of ceremonies, and is used only of things. E.g., "Doubtless many divorced men disinherit their wives, some even with *ceremonial* bonfires and whoops of joy; what we are considering, however, is the probable intent of those divorced men who do not destroy their wills." *Ceremonious,* lightly disparaging, suggests an overdone formality, and is used of both persons and things.

cert, in AmE, is frequently used as a colloquial shortening of *certiorari,* q.v.: "As a result of this newfound determination to forge ahead with my *'cert'* memos, I managed to finish several more that afternoon." William H. Rehnquist, *The Supreme Court: How It Was, How It Is* 38 (1987).

In nonlegal contexts, of course, *cert* can be a shortened form of *certificate, certainty,* or *certify.* In BrE, it appears frequently in the phrase *dead cert* (a complete certainty): "I found some of my American colleagues surprised that their reports of the visit, on a normal day *dead certs* for the front page, had been pushed aside by news of 'Maggie' and her departure." Christopher Hitchens, *In Each Other's Pockets,* Independent, 16 Dec. 1990, at 27.

certain can cloy as readily as almost any other word; *said,* q.v., surpasses it, but not by much: "[The plaintiff] was lawfully possessed of a *certain* donkey, which said donkey of the plaintiff was then lawfully in a *certain* highway, and the defendant was then possessed of a *certain* waggon and *certain* horses drawing the same." *Davies v. Mann,* (1842) 10 M. & W. 546, 546, 152 Eng. Rep. 588, 588. The *OED* labels this use of *certain,* as well as the phrase *certain of* <certain of his possessions> "somewhat archaic." The phrase *certain of* is here used: "She brought suit under section 1983 in the United States District Court against Rotramel and the city, alleging that their actions had deprived Tuttle of *certain of* his constitutional rights."

certainly. See **clearly & obviously.**

certainty; certitude. *Certainty* = (1) an undoubted fact; or (2) absolute conviction. Sense (2) is very close to that reserved for *certitude,* which means "the quality of feeling certain or convinced." E.g., "The only thing that gives us slight pause is the question how much *certitude* the agents must have that the premises they are entering, though not listed on the dealer's license as his place of business, really are such." Holmes stated, rather memorably, "*Certitude* is not the test of *certainty.* We have been cock-sure of many things that were not so." Oliver W. Holmes, "Natural Law," in *Collected Legal Papers* 311 (1920).

Occasionally, writers misuse *certitude* for sense (1) of *certainty*—e.g.: "History is a matter of probability, not *certitude* [read *certainty*]." C. Gordon Post, *An Introduction to the Law* 130 (1963).

certificate = (1) a document in which a fact is formally attested; (2) a document certifying the status or authorization of the bearer to act in a specified way; (3) a writing made in one court, by which notice of its proceedings is given to another court, usu. by transcript.

A variation of sense (3) denotes one of the three methods of taking a federal case from the court of appeals to the U.S. Supreme Court: "The court of appeals may certify at any time any question of law in any civil or criminal case for which instructions are desired. The power is that of the court of appeals, and it has been said to be improper for the parties to move for certification. Certification is limited to questions of law, and the questions must be distinct and definite. The Court will dismiss a *certificate* in which the questions are so broad that in effect they bring up the whole case, although when a case has been certified the Court may itself require that the entire record be sent up for decision of the entire matter in controversy." Charles A. Wright, *The Law of Federal Courts* 776 (5th ed. 1994).

certificate of acknowledgment. See **acknowledgment (B).**

certificate of title. This AmE phrase denotes one of the four types of evidence of title, the other three being abstract and opinion, title insurance, and a Torrens certificate. The *certificate of title*—issued by a lawyer who has examined the public records—is used extensively in the eastern and southern parts of the U.S.

certification. See **certificate.**

certiorari (L. "to be more fully informed") refers to a writ or order by which an appellate court comes to review cases of a certain type. The most troublesome aspect of the word is its pronunciation: /*sərsh-ee-ə-**rar**-ee*/ or /*sərsh-ee-ə-**rahr**-ee*/ or /*sərsh-ee-ə-**rar**-I*/. See **appeal (B) & review (A).**

certitude. See **certainty.**

certworthy; certworthiness. These AmE legal NEOLOGISMS are used as JARGON by those who practice before, closely follow, or sit on the U.S. Supreme Court. *Certworthy* = (of a case) meriting Supreme Court review by grant of a writ of certiorari. E.g., "Accordingly, while I believe the case is not '*certworthy,*' I would affirm the judgment below." *Tipton v. Socony Mobil Oil Co.,* 375 U.S. 34, 38 (1963) (Harlan, J., dissenting)./ "From these circumstances emerges the '*certworthy*' question whether the Fourth Circuit's *Erie* duty obliged it to certify the false imprisonment issue to the Florida Supreme Court." Robert L. Stern et al., *Supreme Court Practice* 843 (6th ed. 1986)./ "Scholars and the Court generally deem a case '*certworthy*' when the underlying issue on which the lower courts disagree is, in some abstract sense, sufficiently important." Michael F. Sturley, *Observations on the Supreme Court's Certiorari Jurisdiction in Intercircuit Conflict Cases,* 67 Tex. L. Rev. 1251, 1252 (1989). For an insightful discussion of the term, see David J. Sharpe, *The Maritime Origin of the Word "Certworthiness,"* J. Maritime Law & Comm. 667 (1993). Cf. **enbancworthy.**

cesser is a LEGALISM meaning "the premature termination of some right or interest" (*CDL*). It usually appears in the phrase *cesser clause* or *cesser provision.* E.g., "The oldest method of protecting the beneficiary from his own indiscretions is the *cesser* provision or forfeiture clause, which provides that the interest of the beneficiary ceases if he assigns or his creditors attempt to reach his interest by legal process." See -ER (B).

cession; session. *Cession* = a giving up, granting; the act of ceding. E.g., Michael J. Powell, *Professional Divestiture: The Cession of Responsibility for Lawyer Discipline,* 1986 Am. B. Found. Res. J. 31. It is used often of nations or peoples who *cede* land. *Session* = a meeting or gathering, and is used of deliberative bodies <court is in session>.

cestui */**sed**-ee/* (= beneficiary) commonly appears as an elliptical form of *cestui que trust,* q.v. For example, "The only person who can object to the disposition of the trust property is the one having some definite interest in the property—he must be a trustee, or a *cestui,* or have some reversionary interest in the trust property."/ "If the *cestui* has the transaction with the trustee set aside, of course he must return any consideration paid by the trustee to him." As with the full phrase, *beneficiary* is a preferable term.

cestui que trust */**sed**-ee-kee-**trəst**/* (originally, in Law French, *cestui à que trust,* lit., "that person for whose benefit" or "he who trusts") is a legal ARCHAISM that persists in AmE (in legal contexts only), but is obsolescent in BrE and unknown in Scotland. The phrase is inferior to the simple word *beneficiary,* which is far more widely understood. E.g., "No trustee can be compelled to produce (except for the purpose of identification) documents in his possession as such, which his client, *the cestui que trust* [read *the beneficiary*], would be entitled to refuse to produce if they were in his possession." (Eng.)

Other forms of the phrase, such as *celui qui trust* and *cettui que trust,* have appeared—see Sidney S. Alderman, *The French Language in English and American Law,* 7 La. B.J. 33, 37 (1959) (preferring *celui qui trust*)—but they are fairly obscure. The phonetic form *settiki* is more than just fairly obscure. See Theodore F.T. Plucknett, *A Concise History of the Common Law* 576 n.2 (5th ed. 1956).

The plural has been variously formed *cestuis que trust, cestuis que trusts,* and *cestuis que trustent.* The last of these has aptly been called "hopelessly wrong." Note, 26 Law Q. Rev. 196, 196 (1910). Another writer has sorrowfully remarked: "[F]rom time to time, it must be regretfully admitted, the Law Reports have ascribed this deplorable version to one of His Majesty's judges." R.E. Megarry, *Miscellany-at-Law* 33 (1955). Scott and Fratcher explain the trouble: "It is not uncommon to say *cestuis que usent* or *cestuis que trustent* on the theory that the last word in each case is a verb that requires the ending of the French third person plural. Professor Maitland has shown, however, that these words are nouns, not verbs, that the term *cestui que use* is an ellipsis, [and] that the full expression is perhaps *cestui a qui oes la terre est tenue,* or something of that sort. If this is true, it is of course absurd to add the plural verb ending." 1 Austin W. Scott & William F. Fratcher, *The Law of Trusts* § 3.2, at 52–53 (4th ed. 1987). The Latin ending in *-ent,* then, is a "hypercorrect" form. See HYPERCORRECTION (A).

The best plural form, in short, is *cestuis que trust.* On elliptical use of the phrase, see **cestui.**

cestui que use */**sed**-ee-kee-**yoos**/* (originally, in Law French, *cestui à que use,* lit., "that person for whose use") refers to the beneficiary of a use, q.v. Today the term appears primarily in historical contexts, inasmuch as uses have been abolished in England. E.g., "The *cestui que use* of a freehold estate had no action at common law to enforce his claim against the feoffee."/ "The person who enjoyed a use was known as the *cestui que use;* the feoffor to use and the *cestui que use* might be the same person or different persons." Some American jurisdictions retain the term, however; as with *cestui que trust, beneficiary* is a preferable term in modern contexts.

On the plural form *cestuis que usent,* see ***cestui que trust.*** Oddly, Plucknett more or less acknowledges that *cestuis que use* is the better form, and then five pages later writes *cestuis que usent.* See Theodore F.T. Plucknett, *A Concise History of the Common Law* 576 n.2, 579 [*cestuis que use*], 586 [*cestuis que usent*] (5th ed. 1956). Brian Simpson, another legal historian, calls *cestuis que usent* "an expression calculated to give a grammarian bad dreams." A.W.B. Simpson, *An Introduction to the History of the Land Law* 164 (1961; repr. 1964). See HYPERCORRECTION (A).

Still other historians, such as J.H. Baker, prefer the spelling *cestuy que use,* presumably because it was the more frequent spelling among medieval lawyers. See J.H. Baker, *An Introduction to English Legal History* 285–86, 329 (3d ed. 1990).

ceteris paribus */**kay**-tər-əs-**par**-ə-bəs/* (= other things being equal or the same) is an unnecessary LATINISM, since we have the common English phrase. E.g., "[T]he fact is, they don't knowingly take losers. *Ceteris paribus* [read *Other things being equal*], the trial lawyer spends his time on the winners. And if a client has a promising case, the lawyer will stake him to it out of sheer self-interest." John A. Jenkins, *The Litigators* xii (1989). Cf. **mutatis mutandis.**

chain of title = the recorded history of the title to a piece of realty—including all conveyances and encumbrances—from the time of the earliest records of ownership. The phrase draws upon the metaphor of links (i.e., successive periods of ownership) forming, through time, a connected chain.

chairman; chairwoman; chairperson; chair. Sensitivity to SEXISM impels many writers to use *chair* rather than *chairman,* on the theory that doing so avoids gender-bias. E.g., "Governor

James Thompson, *co-chair* of the task force, urged that most of the recommendations to combat violent crime would be of no avail for a nation left with no place to put violent offenders because of a lack of safe, humane prison facilities." Certainly *chair* is better than *chairperson,* an ugly and trendy word.

Many readers and writers continue to believe, however, that there is nothing incongruous in having a female *chairman,* inasmuch as *-man* has historically been sexually colorless. In the federal judicial opinions issued in 1990, *chairman* outnumbered *chairperson* by more than ten to one.

Even so, the nonsexist forms are quickly gaining ground and are likely to prevail entirely within the next couple of decades. If we are to adopt a substitute wording, we ought to ensure that *chair* (which goes back to the mid-17th c.) and not *chairperson* becomes the standard term: "In so ruling, he ignored the uncontradicted testimony of Ms. Connie Mooney, coordinator and *chairperson* [read *chair*] of the Charleston Woman's Health Group . . . ." *Doe v. Charleston Area Medical Ctr., Inc.,* 529 F.2d 638, 645 (4th Cir. 1975). See SEXISM (B).

One caveat: if we adopt a term such as *chair,* it must be used in reference to males and females alike. During the 1970s, 1980s, and 1990s, there has been a lamentable tendency to have female *chairs* and male *chairmen.* That is no better than having *chairwomen* and *chairmen;* after all, in most circumstances in which people lead committees and the like, the sex of the leader is irrelevant. See SEXISM (B).

challenge for cause (= a lawyer's striking of a veniremember on grounds of bias) is, in AmE, often collapsed into *cause challenge* or *causal challenge,* q.v. Of these two shortened forms, *causal challenge* is preferable: "When the judge has concluded the *cause challenges* [read *causal challenges* or *challenges for cause*], the lawyers have the right to exercise a given number of *peremptory challenges*—dismissals for no stated reason." Robin T. Lakoff, *Talking Power: The Politics of Language in Our Lives* 110 (1990). The shorter form (*causal challenge*) corresponds more neatly than the longer form (*challenge for cause*) to the two-word phrase *peremptory challenge.*

challenged. See EUPHEMISMS.

chambers. This word refers to a judge's or magistrate's private office. In BrE, it additionally has the sense "the offices occupied by a barrister or group of barristers" (*CDL*). The word is always plural in form, regardless of the number of rooms denoted. Nonlawyers sometimes wrongly make the word singular, as in *judge's chamber.* See, e.g., Margaret Nicholson, *A Dictionary of American-English Usage* (1957), under *camera.*

The one use in which the singular *chamber* is correct is as an adjective: "During this period, however, other events not formally reflected in the record took place; these include *chambers conferences* [read *chamber conferences* or *conferences in chambers*], which were, of course, known to the district court."

CHAMELEON-HUED WORDS. "In any closely reasoned problem, whether legal or nonlegal, chameleon-hued words are a peril both to clear thought and to lucid expression." Wesley N. Hohfeld, *Fundamental Legal Conceptions* 35 (1919; repr. 1966). More than one great legal mind has made this observation: "When things are called by the same name it is easy for the mind to slide into an assumption that the verbal identity is accompanied in all its sequence by identity of meaning." *Lowden v. Northwestern Bank & Trust Co.,* 298 U.S. 160, 165 (1936) (per Cardozo, J.). "A word is not a crystal, transparent and unchanged, it is the skin of a living thought and may vary greatly in color and content according to the circumstances and the time in which it is used." *Towne v. Eisner,* 245 U.S. 418, 425 (1918) (per Holmes, J.).

The English language, and therefore the language of the law, teems with words that have many different—sometimes strikingly different—meanings. There are at least two types of chameleon-hued words. The first type consists in words such as *temporal,* which has several distinct meanings: (1) of or relating to time <temporal relations of events>; (2) secular, not spiritual <temporal pastimes>; (3) chronological <temporal sequence>; or (4) of or relating to the temples on the side of one's skull <temporal lobes>.

Similar words abound in the language, and often they are the most important ones. For example, Frankfurter wrote, "I do not use the term *jurisdiction* because it is a verbal coat of too many colors." *United States v. L.A. Tucker Truck Lines, Inc.,* 344 U.S. 33, 39 (1952) (Frankfurter, J., dissenting). An English judge has said much the same thing about *condition* in contractual contexts. See *The Varenna* [1984] Q.B. 599, 618 (calling it "a chameleon-like word [that] takes on its meanings from its surroundings").

The second type consists essentially in words, usually adjectives, that are empty vessels, to be filled with meaning by the reader. Lawyers delight in such terms as *reasonable, substantial, meaningful,* and *satisfactory.* These terms are often usefully vague, allowing drafters to provide a standard for performance in unforeseen circumstances. It is worth the warning, however, to note that "a competent draftsman would not deliberately pick a word which instead of controlling the context is easily colored by it." *In re Coe's Estate,* 201 A.2d 571, 577 (N.J. 1964).

champertor; maintainer; barrator; embracer. The differences are concisely set forth in the following passage: "If a *maintainer* is one who stirs up vexatious suits to which he is not a party, if a *barrator* is one who makes a profession of doing so, if a *champertor* is one who does so for pecuniary gain and if an *embracer* is one who in the course of such proceedings seeks to influence or intimidate judge or jury, it must be admitted that in the minds of the lay public, the chief *maintainers, barrators, champertors,* and *embracers* of today are the members of the legal profession." Max Radin, *Maintenance by Champerty,* 24 Calif. L. Rev. 48, 66–67 (1935). The word *champertor* is mislabeled obsolete in the *OED.* See **champerty, barratry & embracery.**

champertous. See **champerty (C).**

champerty. A. And *maintenance.* These words denote related but distinct offenses. *Champerty*—a subspecies of *maintenance*—is "an illegal proceeding in which a person (often a lawyer) not naturally concerned in a lawsuit engages to help the plaintiff or defendant to prosecute it, on condition that, if it is successful, that person will receive a share of the property in dispute." *Maintenance* is "the action of wrongfully aiding and abetting litigation; the act of sustaining a suit or litigant by a party who has no interest in the proceedings or who acts from an improper motive."

The element of pecuniary return is absent from the notion of *maintenance.* Pollock noted in the late 19th century that "[a]ctions for maintenance are in modern times rare though possible." Frederick B. Pollock, *The Law of Torts* 211 (1887). The same might now be said of *champerty.* Contingent fees, which fit within the traditional definition of *champerty,* are now common in the U.S.; they have been excepted from the prohibition of *champerty* and in most cases are proper under American ethical canons. See **contingent fee.**

Misconduct under either name—*champerty* or *maintenance*—is more likely to surface today as a defense to a civil action rather than as a criminal offense. See Rollin M. Perkins & Ronald N. Boyce, *Criminal Law* 585 (3d ed. 1982). For an insightful discussion of the status of champerty and maintenance in American law, see Susan L. Martin, *Syndicated Lawsuits: Illegal Champerty or New Business Opportunity?* 30 Am. Bus. L.J. 485 (1992).

B. Pronunciation. The *Law Student's Pronouncing Dictionary* (1948) gives the pronunciation of *champerty* as /**sham**-pərty/. In AmE, however, the word usually has a hard *-ch-* sound, not an *-sh-* sound.

C. Adjectival Form. The adjective corresponding to *champerty* is *champertous.* E.g., "For an agreement to be *champertous,* the financier must have no [proper] interest in the litigation to be financed." *U.S. ex rel. Balboa Ins. Co. v. Algernon Blair, Inc.,* 795 F.2d 404, 409 (5th Cir. 1986).

chancellor = (1) in England, the nominal head of the Court of Chancery and of the whole judiciary who is also Speaker of the House of Lords and a member of the Cabinet—properly called the Lord High Chancellor of Great Britain; (2) in G.B., the single judge of the consistory court of a diocese; (3) the titular head of a university; (4) in the U.S., a judge in equity, or on any court denominated "chancery."

The title is not nearly as exalted in the U.S. as it is in G.B. Here are some examples of the term's use: "Plaintiff finally invokes the rule that findings of the *chancellor* on conflicting evidence will not be disturbed unless clearly and palpably against the weight of the evidence."/ "There is no claim of fraud or overreaching and the *chancellor* found that the agreement was not unfair or inequitable under the circumstances." See **chancery, Keeper of the King's Conscience & Lord Chancellor.**

chancellor's foot. John Selden, the 17th-century barrister and scholar, said, "Equity is a roguish thing. For law we have a measure, know what to trust to: equity is according to the conscience of him that is Chancellor, and as that is larger or narrower, so is equity. 'Tis all one as if they should make the standard for the measure, a *Chancellor's foot.* What an uncertain measure would this be! One Chancellor has a long foot, another a short foot, a third an indifferent foot; 'tis the same thing in the Chancellor's conscience." John Selden, *Table Talk* (1689) (as quoted in Thomas E. Holland, *The Elements of Jurisprudence* 74 (13th ed. 1924)).

The phrase has continued to stand for inequitable variability in court rulings. E.g., "[T]he defense of entrapment enunciated in these opinions was not intended to give the federal judiciary a *'chancellor's foot'* veto over law enforcement practices of which it did not approve." *U.S. v. Russell,* 411 U.S. 423, 435 (1973). American courts, alas, have sometimes got the reference wrong: "Hundreds of years ago, likewise, equity ceased to be the measure of the *'King's foot.'*" *U.S. v. Parkinson,* 240 F.2d 918, 921 (9th Cir. 1956).

chance-medley. One criminal-law text defines this quaint legal phrase as "an ordinary fistfight or other nondeadly encounter," suggesting that it would be a loose usage to speak of a homicide resulting from a *chance-medley.* See Rollin M. Perkins & Ronald N. Boyce, *Criminal Law* 1121 (3d ed. 1982). But ever since it was first used in the 15th century, the phrase has referred primarily to deadly encounters—esp. in the longer phrase *manslaughter by chance-medley.* A *chance-medley* was excusable as opposed to justifiable homicide. See Barry, *The Defence of Provocation,* 4 Res Judicatae 129, 129 (1949).

There are two views on the etymology of the phrase. One traces the phrase from the Fr. *chance medlée,* meaning "mixed or mingled chance or casualty." In this view, *medley* is a POSTPOSITIVE ADJECTIVE, *chance* being the noun. As the *OED* notes, however, the phrase has been misused by those who took *medley* to be the noun and *chance* to be an adjective—as if the phrase meant "fortuitous medley." It does not. But in an alternative view, *chance* is in fact an adjective, the original having been *chaude,* indicating hot blood. Those who take this view trace the word from *chaude mêlée* (= a killing in the course of a spontaneous, heated quarrel). In support of this latter view, see J.H. Baker, *An Introduction to English Legal History* 601 & n.40 (3d ed. 1990).

chancery; equity. *Chancery* = (1) the office of the Chancellor; (2) a court of equity; or (3) equity. Sense (1) is most usual in England, primarily as a historical usage: "The *Chancery,* in fact, readily abandoned any legal topic as soon as the common law mended its ways and provided a more adequate treatment." (Eng.) Sense (3) is today almost purely an American extension <principles of chancery>. E.g., "The general rule in Virginia is that a cestui que trust is not bound by a decree rendered against his trustees in a *chancery* suit to which he is not a party."/ "Before probating the second will it was not necessary to file a bill in *chancery* under the statute to set aside the probate of the former will."

Since the 19th century in AmE, *chancery* has also been synonymous with *bankruptcy* in some states. Thus Thoreau wrote about *going into chancery,* meaning "going bankrupt," in the middle of that century. Such locutions are no doubt restricted to states in which the state bankruptcy courts are called chancery courts. Formerly, American legists used *bill in equity* and *bill in chancery* interchangeably. Today in Delaware, the *Court of Chancery* has jurisdiction over insolvency and receiverships of corporations.

Equity has three basic senses that are relevant in comparison to *chancery:* (1) evenness, fairness, justice; (2) the application to particular circumstances of what seems naturally just and right, as contrasted with the application of a legal rule; and (3) the body of principles and rules developed since medieval times and applied by the Chancellors of England and the Courts of Chancery. Sense (1) is the general sense used by nonlawyers and lawyers alike; sense (2) is the commonest meaning in legal contexts; and sense (3), in the narrow definition given, is historical and generally British. Senses (2) and (3) are the senses in which *chancery* is sometimes used for *equity,* q.v.

chancy is colloquial for *uncertain* or *risky.* E.g., "Each party recognizes that it must make some response to the demands of the other party, for issues left unresolved will be submitted to the court, a recourse *that is always chancy* [read *that always has risks*]."

channelize; channel, v.t. The *COD* suggests some DIFFERENTIATION between these terms. *Channel* = (1) to form channels in, to groove; or (2) to guide. *Channelize* = to convey (as if) in a channel; to guide. *Channel* is the common term, to be used unless the connotations suggested by the definition of *channelize* are peculiarly appropriate.

channel(l)ed; channel(l)ing. These words take one *-l-* in AmE, two in BrE. See DOUBLING OF FINAL CONSONANTS.

chapter = (1) in G.B., an act of Parliament, each of which is a numbered chapter of the total legislation of the year; (2) a subdivision of a legislative act, comprising a number of sections; (3) the dean and clergy of a cathedral.

Chapter 11, in AmE, has become synonymous with corporate reorganization for the purpose of handling debts in a structured way, under the protection of a federal bankruptcy court. The phrase is often used attributively—e.g.: "The purpose of a *Chapter 11 filing* is to give a chief executive an opportunity to reorganize a financially troubled business by putting its creditors on hold. When the money problems have been straightened out and the company restored to health, it emerges from the protection of the bankruptcy courts and picks up where it left off." John Taylor, *Bankruptcy Was a Disappointment,* N.Y. Times, 10 Dec. 1989, § 7, at 11.

A common colloquialism nowadays is *to go*

Chapter 11: "Of course, Campeau's badly overextended retailing Empire would soon *go Chapter 11* anyway, throwing thousands out of work and rippling damage through the U.S. economy." Book Note, American Way, Jan. 1992, at 78 (reviewing John Rothchild, *Going for Broke* (1991)).

character; reputation. These words are frequently used in the law of defamation and of evidence. Very simply, the semantic distinction is that *character* is what one is, whereas *reputation* is what one is thought by others to be.

charge, n. & v.t. **A. In the Sense "accusation."** To write that someone has been *accused* of a *charge* is a REDUNDANCY. E.g., "In announcing Mr. X's suspension, the [newspaper] management pointed out that 'Mr. X *had neither been accused nor convicted of any charge* (read *had neither been charged nor convicted*).'" (Ex. fr. Wilson Follett, *Modern American Usage* 47 (1966).) See **accuse.**

B. Active and Passive Use. *In charge of,* Nicholson writes, may be used both actively and passively—e.g.: "The livestock were left *in charge of* the foreman; the foreman was left *in charge of* the livestock." The usual passive wording is *in the charge of,* which prevents any possible ambiguities. E.g., "The truck was *in charge of* [read *in the charge of*] Mack Free, who was instructed not to permit any person to ride upon or drive it." To one not accustomed to *in charge of* in the passive construction, subject and object appear to have been confused, i.e., the sentence seems to say that the truck had control of or authority over Mack Free. One more example: "It had been the practice in Texas to assign a Pullman conductor to trains with two or more sleeping cars, while in trains with only one sleeping car that car was *in charge of* [read *in the charge of*] a porter."

C. *That*-phrase Objects. It is permissible to write, "He charged that the prosecutorial misconduct was of constitutional dimensions," although in BrE *charge* generally takes a simple noun, either a person or a thing. E.g., "Count one *charged* the defendant that on or about October 27, 1969, being an undischarged bankrupt he had obtained credit to the extent of £451 13s. 9d. from Lloyds Bank Ltd without informing the said bank that he was then an undischarged bankrupt." *Regina v. Hartley,* [1972] 2 Q.B. 1.

Both simple nouns and *that*-phrase objects are common in AmE. Here is another example of the latter type: "The complainant further *charged* that the above-mentioned book was printed by defendant."

D. *Charge the jury.* When a trial judge *charges* the jury, or gives the jury its *charge,* the judge tells the jurors what the law is and explains that, if they believe one version of the facts, they must render their verdict for the plaintiff—but if they believe the other version of the facts, they must render their verdict for the defendant. E.g., "The trial judge, in *charging the jury,* required no less than this." The noun phrase is *jury charge* (= the judge's instructions).

E. And *accuse.* See **accuse.**

chargé d'affaires. Pl. *chargés d'affaires.* Pluralizing often begets error—e.g.: "Washington is full of *chargé d'affaires* [read *chargés d'affaires*]." Sidney S. Alderman, *The French Language in English and American Law,* 7 La. B.J. 33, 37 (1959).

chargee = (1) the holder of a charge upon property, or of a security over a contract (*OED*); or (2) one charged with a crime. Sense (1), though unrecorded in American dictionaries (apart from *W2*), appears more frequently in AmE than in BrE. E.g., "I prefer to regard the gift over as a charge coupled with an ancillary power of sale. The objections are that it is not formally such, and that it gives the trustee greater rights than a *chargee* would have." *Boal v. Metropolitan Museum of Art,* 292 F. 303, 305 (S.D.N.Y. 1923) (per L. Hand, J.)./ "[T]he critical distinction between trusts and charges for the purposes of resolution of the issues posed in this case is the absence of any fiduciary element in the *chargee's* duty toward the beneficiary of the charge." *Gadekar v. Phillips,* 375 A.2d 248, 255 (Md. Ct. Spec. App. 1977).

Sense (2), which most dictionaries do not record, appears infrequently. E.g., "She says that a charge of a crime in the vague language of the questioned statute does not apprise the *chargee* with notice of prohibited conduct . . . ." *State v. Grinstead,* 206 S.E.2d 912, 918 (W. Va. 1974)./ "An indictment performs the office of advising the *chargee* of the charge . . . ." *People v. Addison,* 220 N.E.2d 511, 513 (Ill. App. 1966).

Charta, Magna. See **Magna C(h)arta.**

charterer; affreighter. Both mean "a person to whom a vessel is chartered in a charterparty." *Charterer* is more usual. See the quotation under **affreightment.**

charterparty [fr. L. *charta partita* or *carta partita* "a writing divided"]. American dictionaries spell the phrase as two words (the *CDL* spells it as one), but American and English courts increasingly make it one. See, e.g., *Scrutton on Charterparties and Bills of Lading* (A. Mocatta et al. eds., 18th ed. 1974) (an English work). Of course, "[d]ictionaries lag behind linguistic realities," *Security Center, Ltd. v. First Nat'l Sec. Ctrs.,* 750 F.2d 1295, 1298 n.4 (5th Cir. 1985); no doubt most dictionaries will soon correctly list *charterparty* as a single word.

Charter should be avoided as an elliptical form of *charterparty,* because *charter* has so many other meanings that using it in this way may give rise to uncertainties, even if it may sometimes be unambiguous. The tendency to use *charter* is understandable if we view *charterparty* as two words; the solution is to spell it as one.

chary (= cautious), a FORMAL WORD close in meaning to *wary,* is a favorite word of some judges. "We have been extremely *chary* about extending the 'commercial speech' doctrine beyond this narrowly circumscribed category." The word sometimes implies "sparing, ungenerous" <chary of praise>.

chaser. See LAWYERS, DEROGATORY NAMES FOR (A).

chasm is pronounced /***kaz***-əm/.

chaste (= pure from unlawful sexual intercourse; virtuous, continent) is a word that applies to men and women alike. Unfortunately, however, a bias pervades its usual applications so that it almost always refers to women and girls. E.g., "One view is that a fallen woman who has fully reformed is *chaste,* while another is that chastity before marriage means physical virginity—a woman can be seduced only once. There is nothing unchaste about marital intercourse and hence, under either view, a widow or divorcee may be an unmarried female of previously-*chaste* character." Rollin M. Perkins & Ronald N. Boyce, *Criminal Law* 463–64 (3d ed. 1982).

chasten; chastise. These words are close in meaning, but distinct. *Chasten* = to discipline, punish, or subdue. *Chastise* = to punish, thrash. In the U.S., *chastise* has also the dialectal sense "to castigate, criticize."

Chastise is so spelled; *chastize,* an incorrect spelling, is not uncommon. See -IZE (B).

chattelize (= to treat as a chattel) began as a nonlegal word in the 19th century to describe human degradation, as in the phrase *chattelized humanity.* The word has since migrated into legal contexts, as here: "This would plainly be true as to ordinary chattels, and *'chattelized'* property like securities should go by the same rule." *Boston Safe Deposit & Trust Co. v. Paris,* 447 N.E.2d 1268, 1271 n.3 (Mass. App. Ct. 1983)./ "[W]hen the intangible is *chattelized* in a document, the analogies to property predominate." Eugene F. Scoles & Peter May, *Conflict of Laws* § 19.27, at 758 (1982). See **chattels.**

chattel mortgage; conditional sales contract. The distinction between these two concepts is important when a buyer of goods cannot pay the entire purchase price at once. In such cases, the buyer makes a down payment, and the rest of the purchase price is payable in installments. Under a *chattel mortgage,* the seller transfers title to the buyer, who gives the seller a mortgage to secure the unpaid balance. Under a *conditional sales contract,* the buyer takes delivery, but the title remains in the seller until the entire purchase price is paid. The latter method, naturally, is more common in installment sales, which usually involve adhesion contracts. See **mortgage.**

In the context of real property, a *conditional sales contract* is often called a *contract for deed.*

chattels is commonly defined as "personal property," but this definition misleads. The proper definition is "any property other than freehold land"; a leasehold interest in land, having characteristics of both real and personal property, is termed a *chattel real.* E.g., "American courts have been much more liberal than the courts of England in recognizing future interests in *chattels real.*"

Tangible goods or intangible rights, as in patents, stocks, or shares, are termed *chattels personal.* E.g., "*Chattels personal* may be consumable or nonconsumable, tangible or intangible." The distinction is best observed fastidiously; nevertheless, this terminology is falling into disuse. *Chattel personal* = *chose,* q.v.

cheat = a common-law misdemeanor involving a swindle perpetrated by means of a false token. This wrong—which thrived from the 17th to the 19th centuries—falls today under the rubric of *false pretenses,* q.v.

The origin of the word *cheat* is interesting. It derives from *escheat,* q.v. In the Middle Ages, the *escheator* was an officer who assessed the value of an escheat—that is, property reverting to the public treasury upon the death of the King's tenant-in-chief for lack of an heir. So corrupt and greedy were the *escheators,* however, that, by the 15th century, the modern sense of *cheat* and *cheater* had developed. Meanwhile, a century later, thieves began to refer to their stolen goods as *cheat,* as if the goods were escheated or confiscated. These two uses of the word coalesced into the modern sense.

cheatee. See -EE (A).

check = an order for payment of money on demand, drawn on a banker, and expressed as being payable either to bearer or to (the order of) a named person. *Cheque* is the BrE spelling.

check, worthless; bogus check; cold check; false check; rubber check. What should we call an unaltered check that bears the drawer's genuine signature but is drawn on a bank in which the drawer has either no account or insufficient funds? *Rubber check,* which is slang, derives from the idea that the check "bounces"; the phrase suggests that the drawer's account has insufficient funds but not that the drawer has no account, so it is not as broad as the other phrases. *False check* and *bogus check* inappropriately suggest a forgery, which is a different idea altogether. *Cold check,* like *rubber check,* is slang. *Worthless check* is the least objectionable phrase, though it is slightly misleading because the check may finally have some value; despite that shortcoming, criminal-law scholars commonly use *worthless check* (which is not to say that they ever use worthless checks). See, e.g., Rollin M. Perkins & Ronald N. Boyce, *Criminal Law* 385 (3d ed. 1982).

cherry-picking is AmE legal slang for the modern law firm's practice of luring select lawyers from other firms with special inducements. E.g., "[T]heir lawyers will be easy prey in this age of *cherry-picking* and big-firm branching." Steven Brill, *The End of Partnership?* American Law., Dec. 1989, at 3./ "It's been an incredible decade marked by law firm collapses, mergers and *cherry-picking.*" Rita H. Jensen, *Firms Face the New Decade,* Nat'l L.J., 25 Dec. 1989–1 Jan. 1990, at 1. The verb *cherry-pick* is a BACK-FORMATION: "Dell downplays the effect his attempts to *cherry-pick* will have on San Francisco's legal market." Audrey Duff, *S.F. v. L.A.: Battling for Talent,* American Law., May 1990, at 16.

chicane. See **chicane(ry).**

chicanerous (= engaging in or exhibiting chicanery) is a useful NEOLOGISM perhaps invented by Professor Arthur Miller of Harvard, the first known user: "[I]t was believed that a pleading containing inconsistent allegations indicated falsehood on its face and was a sign of a *chicanerous* litigant seeking to subvert the judicial process." 5 Charles A. Wright & Arthur R. Miller, *Federal Practice and Procedure* § 1283, at 372 (1969) (section acknowledged as Miller's). Other uses swiftly followed—e.g.: "The trial judge grounded his dismissal on a finding that 'the United States Attorney's office actions in juggling this case back and forth . . . is [*sic*] vexatious, oppressive, *chicanerous* . . . .'" *U.S. v. Jefferson,* 257 A.2d 225, 226 (D.C. 1969).

chicane(ry). In contexts other than those involving horse racing and card games, *chicane* is a NEEDLESS VARIANT of *chicanery* (= trickery). "The lack of business ethics displayed by defendant invites and receives the condemnation of all who love fair play and scorn *chicane* [read *chicanery*] and deceit."/ "The ancient complaint about the attorney's *chicane* [read *chicanery*] was reinforced in the 16th century with the addition to the English language of the opprobrious 'pettifogger.'"

chide > chided > chided are the preferred inflections in AmE and BrE alike. *Chid* is an AmE variant past tense and past participle. The variant past participle *chidden* should be avoided.

The gerund *chiding* acts as the noun <perhaps this chiding will have some effect>. With *chidance,* Rodell was surely punning on *guidance:* "But the thirty-year story of the Court under Holmes's *chidance* [read *chiding*] can best be told neither in strict chronological sequence nor in the specific records of specific Justices (other than Holmes) . . . ." Fred Rodell, *Nine Men* 191 (1955).

chief judge; presiding judge. On each U.S. Court of Appeals (since 1948), the *chief judge* is the active judge (i.e., not having taken senior status, that is, gone into semiretirement) with the longest service on the court. The chief judge generally hears almost as many cases as other judges, acts as the circuit's administrative head, and schedules all court sittings. Before 1948, what we now know as the *chief judge* was called the *senior circuit judge.*

A *presiding judge* is the senior active judge on a three-member panel that hears and decides cases. One may be a presiding judge one month and the most junior member on a panel the next month. Unlike *chief judge,* then, *presiding judge* is not a permanent title—it is a situational title.

Chief Justice of the United States. Though usage has varied over time, this is now the generally preferred title—not *Chief Justice of the United States Supreme Court* or *Chief Justice of the Supreme Court of the United States.* But that was not always so, as Charles Warren explains with abundant historical evidence:

> The official title of the Chief Justice seems to have varied at different periods of the Court's history. Jay was commissioned under the title of "Chief justice of the Supreme Court of the United States," as were Rutledge, Ellsworth,

> Marshall, Taney, Chase and White. Fuller was commissioned as "Chief Justice of the United States." The Constitution mentions the office of Chief Justice only once; in Article One, Section three, relative to impeachments in which it is provided—"When the President of the United States is tried, the Chief Justice shall preside." The Judiciary Act of Sept. 24, 1789, provided that the Supreme Court "shall consist of a chief justice and five associate justices." The Act of July 13, 1866, c. 210, for the first time officially used the term "Chief Justice of the United States" providing that "thereafter the Supreme Court shall consist of a Chief Justice of the United States and six associate justices." The Act of April 10, 1869, c. 22, provided that the Court shall "hereafter consist of the Chief Justice of the United States and eight associate justices." The Revised Statutes, Section 673, and the Act of March 3, 1911, c. 231, codifying the laws relating to the judiciary, Section 215, refer to "a Chief Justice of the United States." On the other hand, the statutes relating to the salaries of the Court, viz.: the Act of March 3, 1873, c. 226, the Act of Feb. 12, 1902, c. 547, and the Act of March 3, 1911, c. 231, Section 218, all refer to "the Chief Justice of the Supreme Court of the United States." *New England Historical and Genealogical Register* (1895), XLIX, 275.
>
> Charles Warren, *The Supreme Court in United States History* 11–12 n.2 (rev. ed. 1928).

Both popular and legal writers use variations on the title—e.g.: "[T]he chief justice of the United States Supreme Court [capitalize *Chief Justice*], Mr. Rehnquist, has said that no rational person could equate a request for aid of counsel with a guilty mind." J. Gary Trichter, *The Civil Law and DWI,* 50 Tex. B.J. 1093, 1096 (1987)./ "*The Chief Justice of the Supreme Court of the United States,* several years ago, was elucidating in the course of the Court's opinion a little point of law." Fred Rodell, *Woe Unto You, Lawyers!* 119 (1939; repr. 1980).

Chief Justiceship; Chiefship. The former is more common, but the latter is admirably succinct: "But both Wilson, who had literally applied for the *Chiefship,* and Rutledge, whose friends had campaigned for him, were named Associate Justices." Fred Rodell, *Nine Men* 47 (1955).

child *en ventre sa mere.* See ***en ventre sa mere.***

child (of tender age or years); young person; juvenile; minor; pupil. In American law, a *child of tender age* or *years* has generally not reached his or her 14th birthday. In English law, *child* itself usually means one who is not yet 14, though some English lawyers, up to the mid-20th century, used *child* to refer to someone under 21.

In most American states, a *juvenile*—a 20th-century statutory word—is one who has not reached the age of 18. See Juvenile Delinquency Act, 18 U.S.C. § 5031 (1988). In England, *juvenile* denotes one who has not reached 17—i.e., either a *child* (as defined above) or a *young person* (meaning someone who has reached 14 but is not yet 17).

While *minor* (like *infant*) covers all these categories in most English-speaking jurisdictions, that is not so in Scotland, where *minor* has a more restrictive sense. In Scots law, *minors* are those 16 to 18 years old. Younger persons are called *pupils.* Scots lawyers typically use the word *nonage* to denote the status of pupils and minors.

Only lawyers could construct a system in which an *infant* can be older than *child.* See **age of capacity, infant, infancy, minority & nonage.**

childlike; childish. *Childlike* connotes simplicity, innocence, and truthfulness. *Childish* connotes puerility, peevishness, and silliness.

child-kidnap. See **kidnapping (B).**

child-slaying. See **infanticide.**

child-stealing. See **abduction & kidnapping (B).**

chill (= to inhibit, discourage <to chill a person's rights>) is now a common term in American legal JARGON. The standard phrase is *chilling effect*—e.g.: "The majority held that the waiting-period requirement is unconstitutional because it has a *chilling effect* on the right to travel."

The origin of this usage lies in the word's figurative sense, recorded by both the *OED* and *W3,* "to affect as with cold; to check, depress, or lower (warmth, ardour, etc.); to damp, deject, dispirit" (*OED*). All the examples quoted in the *OED* to illustrate this sense involve the chilling of something, usually an emotion, that is figuratively warm (enthusiasm, courage, admiration, zeal, etc.).

American lawyers have extended *chill* by applying it to rights and freedoms, to the exercise of rights and freedoms, and even to the persons exercising them. E.g., "The opinions emphasized that such thoughtlessly broad statutes affected not only the immediate litigants but the atmosphere of freedom generally, because they may '*chill* that free play of the spirit which all teachers ought especially to cultivate and practice.'" Robert G. McCloskey, *The American Supreme Court* 204 (1960)./ "Courts have said that the danger that the mere pendency of the action will *chill* the exercise of First Amendment rights requires more specific allegations than would otherwise be required."

The basic phrase *chilling effect* is sometimes jargonistically elaborated: "The purpose of this limitation is to prevent juries from giving excessive awards, and thereby imposing a pecuniary *chill factor* on the media." (See SET PHRASES.) Now used indiscriminately, *chill(ing)* and *chilling effect* have become legal CLICHÉS.

chimera. Pl. *-as.*

Chinese Wall = a screening mechanism that protects client confidences by preventing one or more lawyers within an organization from participating in any matter involving that client. A principal purpose of this mechanism is to allow a lawyer to move to a new law firm without the fear of vicariously disqualifying that firm from representing certain clients. Typically, the procedures used in erecting a Chinese Wall include prohibiting the lawyer in question from any contact with the case—no access to files, no share in any fees derived from the case, and sometimes even sequestration from those handling the case. See M. Peter Moser, *Chinese Walls: A Means of Avoiding Law Firm Disqualification When a Personally Disqualified Lawyer Joins the Firm,* 3 Geo. J. Legal Ethics 399, 400 (1990).

The metaphor derives, of course, from the Great Wall of China—not from any ethnic bias. Even so, some lawyers worry that the phrase might be understood in a derogatory sense; those who do tend to use a phrase such as *ethical wall.*

In conflict-of-interest cases, the phrase dates from about 1977. But earlier references appear in other legal contexts to evoke the idea of artificial insularity. E.g., "[S]ome of them had said the Corn Products Refining Company had built a *Chinese wall* against competitors and kept them in chains." *U.S. v. Corn Prods. Refining Co.,* 234 F. 964, 979 (S.D.N.Y. 1916) (per L. Hand, J.)./ "But we do not think that the state may erect a *Chinese Wall* around itself by adopting regulations . . . ." *Barnwell Bros., Inc. v. South Carolina State Highway Dep't,* 17 F. Supp. 803, 815 (E.D.S.C. 1937). Today, however, the phrase almost invariably concerns legal ethics or complex financial transactions.

The phrase is sometimes written *Chinese wall,* but today the second word is usually capitalized.

Chip Smith charge. See **dynamite charge.**

chirograph = (1) a written deed, subscribed and witnessed; (2) such a deed in two parts, written head to head, divided by the word "chirographum" in capitals, and the two parts separated by an indented line through the word "chirographum," each party retaining one part. See **party of the first part.**

chit [fr. Anglo-Indian *chitty* letter, note certificate (c. 1673), borrowed from Hindi *chitthī*] = (1) a signed voucher for money received or owed, usu. for food, drink, etc.; or (2) a slip of paper with writing on it. Both meanings are common. Sense (1): "After each meal the Club member is presented with a *chit* upon which he subscribes his name. All chits signed during a month are consolidated and monthly statements are rendered . . . ." *Baltimore Country Club, Inc. v. Comptroller of Treasury,* 321 A.2d 308, 310 (Md. 1974)./ Sense (2): "[S]he was to make memoranda incident to her acts of prostitution, and . . . [w]ould transcribe thereon the amount of money collected from each customer, the time at which she started and finished each transaction, along with her professional identification as 'Pam.' These *chits* . . . were placed . . . in a bag . . . ." *Schweinefuss v. Commonwealth,* 395 S.W.2d 370, 373 (Ky. 1965).

choate. Holmes wrote Pollock in 1878 that he had read in a legal text from California that "the wife on marriage acquires an *inchoate* right of dower which by the death of her husband becomes *choate.*" *Holmes–Pollock Letters* 11 (Howe ed., 2d ed. 1961). *Choate,* a BACK-FORMATION from *inchoate,* is a misbegotten word, for the prefix in *inchoate* is intensive and not negative. (See EN- & NEGATIVES (B).) The word derives from the Latin verb *inchoare* "to hitch with; to begin." Yet, because it was misunderstood as being a negative (meaning "incomplete"), someone invented a positive form for it, namely *choate* (meaning "complete").

In AmE, the word has become more or less standard in the phrase *choate lien,* corresponding to *inchoate lien.* Justice Minton used the word in *U.S. v. City of New Britain,* 347 U.S. 81, 84 (1954): "The liens may also be perfected in the sense that there is nothing more to be done to have a *choate* lien—when the identity of the lienor, the property subject to the lien, and the amount of the lien are established." The three requirements mentioned in that quotation make up what has come to be known in the U.S. as the *choateness doctrine,* which means that "where a security interest arising under state law . . . comes into conflict with a federal tax lien, the state law security interest 'attaches' only when it becomes *choate.*" *J.D. Court, Inc. v. United States,* 712 F.2d 258, 261 (7th Cir. 1983).

Although the word is etymologically misbegotten, it is now fairly well ensconced in the legal vocabulary. It has supplied a name for a fairly arcane legal doctrine, which is unlikely to be renamed. *Choate* is recognized in legal literature as "an illegitimate back formation" (William T. Plumb, *Federal Liens and Priorities,* 77 Yale L.J.

228, 230 (1967), but it is used even by those who deprecate its origins.

Pollock heard of the word from Holmes, but otherwise the *choate* is virtually unknown in G.B. See **inchoate.**

choice of law; choice of jurisdiction. These terms, used in conflicts of law, are occasionally confused. *Choice of law* = the question of which jurisdiction's law applies. *Choice of jurisdiction* = the choice of the country that should exercise jurisdiction over a case. When either phrase is used attributively as a PHRASAL ADJECTIVE, it should be hyphenated <Delaware's choice-of-law rules>. See **conflict of laws.**

choreograph and *orchestrate,* q.v., have become CLICHÉS when used figuratively. In the most jejune modern language, careers are *choreographed* and events are *orchestrated.* See VOGUE WORDS.

chose, n., is a Law French word meaning literally "a thing." In modern legal writing, *chose* = chattel personal, q.v. E.g., "There were four reasons why equity could not simply allow the assignee of a legal *chose* to sue the debtor in the Court of Chancery." G.H. Treitel, *The Law of Contract* 578 (8th ed. 1991).

Traditionally, *choses* are of two kinds. *Choses in possession* are tangible goods capable of being actually possessed and enjoyed (e.g., books and clothes); *choses in action* are rights that can be enforced by legal action (e.g., debts or causes of action in tort). E.g., "If the *chose in action* is not embodied in a writing or evidenced thereby, delivery must be by a written assignment."/ "No particular formalities are required for a gift of a *chose in action* not represented by a so-called indispensable account." The phrase *chose in action* is sometimes anglicized *thing in action.* Cf. **chattels.**

chose jugée = a matter already settled, and therefore not open to further consideration. This phrase is an unnecessary French equivalent of *res judicata,* q.v.

Christian name; christian name. The phrase refers, of course, to one's forename or given name, as opposed to the *surname,* q.v. The first word is usu. capitalized—though Chief Justice Charles Evans Hughes made it lowercase in *George A. Ohl & Co. v. Smith Iron Works,* 288 U.S. 170, 177 (1933).

chrysalis. Pl. *chrysalides.*

church law. See **canon law.**

chuse, an archaic spelling of *choose,* appears in Article I, Section 2 of the U.S. Constitution, and indeed throughout the document. The archaic spelling was commonly used in British opinions of the period: "[S]he did not *chuse* to expose herself to contempt again. The action then is to depend entirely on the nerves of the actress; if she *chuses* to appear on the stage again, no action can be maintained . . . ." *Ashley v. Harrison,* (1793) Peake 256, 258 (K.B.) (spelling modernized at 170 Eng. Rep. 148, 149).

chutzpah /***huut**-spə*/ is a curious word, having both positive and negative connotations in AmE. On the one hand, it is said:

> Alan Dershowitz, the white knight of religious correctness, should have been a tad more judicious in his choice of a title for his book *Chutzpah.* Leo Rosten's book *Hooray for Yiddish!* defines *chutzpah* as "ultra-brazenness, shamelessness, hard-to-believe effrontery, presumption or gall"—traits that many Jews and Gentiles would hardly classify as desirable.
>
> Letter of Chloë Ross, *New York,* 16 Dec. 1991, at 6.

On the other hand—and perhaps this says something about American culture—many consider *chutzpah* something desirable. *W10* defines it first as "supreme self-confidence," but then unnerves us with "nerve, gall." The word sits uneasily on the fence that divides praise and scorn.

-CIDE. This suffix denotes either the act of slaying [fr. L. *-cīdium* "cutting, killing"] or one who slays [fr. L. *-cīda* "cutter, killer"]. Thus *fratricide* is either the killing of one's brother or someone who kills his or her brother. The more common words ending in this suffix are these:

homicide	= the act of killing a person
	= the killer of another person
infanticide	= the act of killing a newborn
	= one who kills a newborn
matricide	= the act of killing one's mother
	= the killer of one's own mother
parricide	= the act of killing one's father
	= the killer of one's own father
patricide	See the entry at **parricide.**
regicide	= the act of killing the king or queen
	= the killer of the king or queen
suicide	= the act of killing oneself
	= one who kills oneself

Though a few others, such as *fratricide* and *sororicide,* are generally known, we also have many less common words ending in *-cide.* For example, *famicide* (= the destroyer of someone's reputation) was once used as a synonym for *slanderer. Prolicide* (= the act of killing offspring either before or soon after birth) is broad enough to subsume both *feticide* (see **abortion**) and *infanticide.* The coinages with this suffix, naturally, are no more sex-neutral than in any other corner of the language: the *OED* records *uxoricide* (= the slayer of one's wife), but *mariticide* (= the slayer of one's husband) is not recorded: it can only be deduced from the adjective *mariticidal* (= of or relating to one who murders her husband).

Scientists have developed *algicides, fungicides, germicides,* and *insecticides* (known also as *pesticides,* though this word can be used more broadly than *insecticides*).

To disinfect their combs and other utensils, American barbers commonly use a trademarked product ominously called "Barbicide." Hence this suffix, like -EE, is perhaps losing its literal force.

Naturally, wags have seized on this suffix for jocular purposes to make such words as *suitorcide* (a nonce-word meaning "fatal to suitors") and *prenticecide* (= the killing of an apprentice). Justice Holmes's father, the poet Oliver Wendell Holmes, invented a word that some dictionaries label jocular. Perhaps, however, this word ought to be taken seriously: *verbicide*—"that is," Holmes wrote, "violent treatment of a word with fatal results to its legitimate meaning, which is its life." Both "[h]omicide and verbicide . . . are alike forbidden." Oliver W. Holmes [Sr.], *An Autocrat at the Breakfast-Table* 10 (1859). One mission of this dictionary is to prevent verbicide in the legal context.

For entries related to this one, see **murder** (A) & **parricide.**

C.I.F. See **cost, insurance, and freight** & **F.O.B.**

c.i.p. = continuation in part. In American patent practice, a *c.i.p. application* is a patent application filed during the lifetime of an earlier application by the same applicant, repeating a substantial part of the earlier application but adding to or subtracting from it. See Louis B. Applebaum et al., *Glossary of United States Patent Practice* 24 (1969).

Circuit Judge, U.S. This is the proper title for a federal appellate judge who sits on a U.S. Court of Appeals (not *Circuit Court of Appeals*). Journalists often incorrectly give the title as *Judge of the Court of Appeals.*

In England, by contrast, a *circuit judge* sits in a county court and hears civil matters.

circuit, to ride; to go on circuit; on circuit; at circuit. These phrases refer to the practice of having itinerant courts, similar in some ways to the *Curia Regis* of early common law. State and federal judges in the U.S. commonly *rode circuit* or *went on circuit* through the beginning of the 20th century. Various idioms have emerged from the practice—e.g.: "In contrast to the system in England, where judges *went on circuit,* most courts in the United States came to be permanently and locally fixed." René A. Wormser, *The Story of the Law* 427 (1962)./ "For English judges, [having judgments given in Welsh] can hardly have added to the attractions of *going circuit* in Wales . . . ." R.E. Megarry, *A Second Miscellany-at-Law* 169 (1973)./ "[W]hile the justices of the Supreme Court were not relieved directly of the burden of *circuit riding,* the pressure of their other duties was such that increasingly the circuit court was held by a single district judge." Charles A. Wright, *The Law of Federal Courts* 38 (4th ed. 1983). For an interesting account of an English judge on circuit, see Frank Douglas MacKinnon, *On Circuit: 1924–1937* (1941).

Lawyers, too, frequently rode circuit: "One of [Abraham Lincoln's] nominees was David Davis, a friend from Lincoln's days as a *circuit-riding* lawyer in Illinois." Donald Dale Jackson, *Judges* 333 (1974).

circumlocution is roundabout speech or language, or using many words where one or two would suffice. It is not the nominal form corresponding to *circuitous,* which means "winding, tortuous, anfractuous"—the noun for *circuitous* being *circuity,* and the adjective corresponding to *circumlocution* being *circumlocutory.*

CIRCUMLOCUTION. See BE-VERBS (B) & PERIPHRASIS.

circumscribable; circumscriptable; circumscriptible. The first of these three forms is preferred. See -ABLE (A).

circumspection = cautiousness; watchfulness; prudence <the judge exercised circumspection in disbelieving the interested witnesses>. This word is sometimes misunderstood as meaning "examination." E.g., "The circumstances surrounding the removal are far from typical and present what the court ascertains as a novel question, requiring almost a complete *circumspection* [read *examination*] of the removal provisions for its resolution."

circumstances. Some writers prefer *in the circumstances* to *under the circumstances.* The latter is unobjectionable, however, and is much more common. E.g., "*Under the circumstances,* we are of the opinion that the sole purpose for which the trust was created has become impossible of accomplishment and has been terminated." Fowler wrote that the insistence on *in the circumstances* as the only right form is "puerile."

circumstantial evidence; indirect evidence. The former is the more common phrase in both AmE and BrE for evidence from which the factfinder may infer the existence of a fact in issue, but which does not directly prove the existence of the fact. E.g., "Susman told the jurors his case was going to involve mainly *circumstantial evidence,* a perfectly acceptable way for him to prove his case." John A. Jenkins, *The Litigators* 279 (1989). See **direct evidence.**

circumvent; undermine. *Circumvent* may mean "to undermine"—e.g.: "Resort to judicial injunction to *circumvent* the decision of Board 2901 would subvert the purpose of the Railway Labor Act." But *circumvent* is connotatively a somewhat more neutral word than *undermine.* See **obviate.**

citation = (1) an official summons directing a person to appear before a court; or (2) an oral or written reference to a legal authority, usu. a case or statute. The term is used primarily in American and Scottish courts, as opposed to the English courts.

Perhaps that explains why the English authorities cannot agree about to whom a citation in sense (1) must be directed. Several say that it must go to a nonparty. See *OCL;* W.A. Jowitt, *The Dictionary of English Law* 376 (2d ed. 1959); Roger Bird, *Osborn's Concise Law Dictionary* 73 (7th ed. 1983). Another authority of repute, however, defines the word as "a summons to a party to appear." E.R. Hardy Ivamy, *Mozley & Whiteley's Law Dictionary* 80 (10th ed. 1988). Still others define the word as broadly as it is in AmE—so that it may be directed either to parties or to nonparties. See *CDL*; P.H. Collin, *English Law Dictionary* 44 (1986); Gavin McFarlane, *The Layman's Dictionary of English Law* 46 (1984). Because usage varies, the narrower definitions are really too narrow to describe BrE accurately.

CITATION OF CASES. The standard work in the field is *The Bluebook: A Uniform System of Citation* (15th ed. 1991). It has weathered recent competition from *The Maroonbook* (1989) better than might be expected, esp. since every new edition of the *Bluebook* seems much longer than the previous one. Still, it provides reliable guidance on hundreds of tricky citational problems, and the editors have tried to make it easy to use.

American writers have produced a number of ancillary aids for citing cases. Among the useful ones are these: Mary Miles Prince, *Bieber's Dictionary of Legal Citations* (3d ed. 1988); C.E. Good, *Citing and Typing the Law: A Course on Legal Citation and Style* (3d ed. 1992). For identifying obscure citations, esp. in historical materials, Marion D. Powers's *Legal Citation Directory* (1971) is useful.

For British form, there are no up-to-date counterparts to the *Bluebook*; for the nearest equivalent, see *Manual of Legal Citations* (1959) (in two parts); Sweet & Maxwell, *Guide to Law Reports and Statutes* (4th ed. 1962); Donald Raistrick, *Index to Legal Citations and Abbreviations* (1981). For Canadian legal writers, the *Canadian Guide to Uniform Legal Citation* (2d ed. 1988) and Chin-Shin Tang's *Guide to Legal Citation and Sources of Citation Aid: A Canadian Perspective* (2d ed. 1988) are serviceable guides.

A few points not within the purview of those works merit our attention here, the most important being the last.

A. Beginning Sentences with Citations. It is stylistically poor to begin a sentence with a citation—e.g.: "26 U.S.C. § 7213 provides that it is unlawful for any officer or employee of the United States to willfully disclose to any person . . . tax returns or return information." A better method is to state the proposition and to place the citation at the sentence's end.

B. Mid-Sentence Citations. The legal writer's general preference should be not to cite cases in mid-sentence, for it is distracting to the reader, especially if that citation is longer than fifteen or so characters (as an appeals court case that was denied certiorari). Only occasionally does it seem appropriate—e.g.: "Our holding in *Harrington v. Bush,* 553 F.2d 190 (D.C. Cir. 1977), requires us to reject Senator Helms's arguments and to deny him standing."

Courts formerly tried setting off these mid-sentence citations in parentheses, but the results are little better than any other mid-sentence citations, and doing so does not conform to the general rules of legal citation. Here is an egregious example:

> The doctrine of incorporation by reference, even if applicable at all where an intent to incorporate in the usual sense is negatived (*In re Estate of York,* 95 N.H. 435, 437, 65 A.2d 282, 8 A.L.R.2d 611; Lauritzen, *Can a Revocable Trust Be Incorporated by Reference,* 45 Ill. L. Rev. 583, 600; Polasky, *"Pourover" Wills and the Statutory Blessing,* 98 Trusts & Estates 949, 954–955; compare *Old Colony Trust Co. v. Cleveland,* 291 Mass. 380, 196 N.E. 920; *Bolles v. Toledo Trust Co.,* 144 Ohio St. 195, 58 N.E.2d 381, 157 A.L.R. 1164; Restatement [2d]: Trusts, § 54, comments e–j, 1), could not import the nonexistent amendment.
>
> *Second Bank-State Street Trust Co. v. Pinion,* 170 N.E.2d 350, 352 (Mass. 1960).

C. Incidental Use of Case Names. See CASE REFERENCES.

D. Citations in Text. Only the hardiest of stylists will own up to this difficult fact: in many types of legal writing—in briefs and memos, for example—the only sensible place for citations is in footnotes. Putting them in the body clutters the text, slows the reader, and hampers the writer's ability to construct a coherent paragraph. Few writing reforms would benefit the legal world more than adopting the following rules: (1) put all citations in footnotes; and (2) ban footnotes for all purposes other than providing citations.

citator, n., refers, in LEGALESE, not to a person, but to a book that helps lawyers determine the treatment of cases by courts subsequently considering them—whether on appeal or as precedents. By a system of code signs, citators show whether the later cases overrule, follow, limit, or distinguish a given case. Now that much of this information has been converted to electronic formats, citators have become somewhat outmoded.

cite, n. Using *cite* as a noun—in place of *citation*—is a casualism. Some excellent legal writers have used it in this way—e.g.: "[T]he *see's* and *cfs.* far outnumber the points that rest on a simple *cite.*" Karl Llewellyn, *The Common Law Tradition: Deciding Appeals* 491 (1960)./ "String *cites* are out of style among academic lawyers; for some legal theorists, reading cases is out of style." Douglas Laycock, *The Death of the Irreparable Injury Rule* viii (1991). Even so, in certain phrases, such as *cite omitted,* the shorter form looks very lax. See, e.g., *U.S. v. David,* 662 F. Supp. 244, 245 (N.D. Ga. 1987) (twice using *cite omitted*). Cf. **quote.**

cite, v.t. **A. General Senses and Use.** *Cite,* v.t. = (1) to commend <the mayor cited him for his commendable pro bono work>; (2) to adduce as precedent or as binding law <counsel then cited the appropriate statutory provision>; or (3) to summon before a court of law <he was cited for contempt>.

In sense (2), the object of *cite* should be the precedent or statute cited, not the person to whom it is cited. The following loose usage is not uncommon in AmE: "A law dictionary such as this, . . . which *cites the reader to leading treatises* [read *cites leading treatises*] such as Wigmore on *Evidence,* . . . can easily instill the suspicion in a diligent patron of law that he has the makings of an advocate." E.J. Bander, *Dictionary of Selected Legal Terms and Maxims* v (2d ed. 1979)./ "*We are cited to the case of* [read *We are asked to consider* or *The defense cites*] Lovelady v. State . . . ." *Smith v. State,* 180 S.W.2d 622, 625 (Tex. Crim. App. 1944). See OBJECT-SHUFFLING.

A related problem is using *cite* as an intransitive rather than as a transitive verb—that is, saying that the writer is *citing to a case* rather than *citing a case.* This looseness results perhaps from the noun form, *citation to,* as in: "Citations to both the U.S. Reports and the Supreme Court Reporter are included for ease of research."

B. And *quote*. Lawyers commonly differentiate between these words. To *cite* an authority is to give its substance and to indicate where it can be found. To *quote* is to repeat someone else's exact words and to enclose them in quotation marks. In legal writing, citations routinely follow quotations.

citizen. A. And *resident*. With U.S. citizens, the terms *citizen* and *resident* are generally viewed as being interchangeable in reference to state residency or citizenship. See Charles A. Wright, *The Law of Federal Courts* 243–44 (4th ed. 1983) (noting that at least two circuit courts have held otherwise—that the terms are related but "not necessarily one and the same thing").

The words are not interchangeable when other political entities (e.g., cities) are the frame of reference, for *citizen* implies political allegiance and a corresponding protection by the state, whereas *resident* denotes merely that one lives in a certain place. E.g., "Plaintiff, a *citizen* of the State of Washington, seeks a declaratory judgment pursuant to 28 U.S.C. § 400." (He is a *citizen* of Washington merely by virtue of being a U.S. citizen and residing in that state; yet he would be able to avail himself of the protections of state law—hence *citizen* is appropriate.) It is possible to be a *citizen* of the United States while being neither a *citizen* nor a *resident* of any particular state.

A corporation is not a citizen of any state—though it is treated as if it were for jurisdictional purposes. See Charles A. Wright, *The Law of Federal Courts* 449 (4th ed. 1983).

With foreign citizens, the distinction between *resident* and *citizen* becomes acute, inasmuch as an alien remains a *citizen* of a foreign country but may be a *resident* of a state. For purposes of American diversity jurisdiction in federal courts, the alien's *citizenship,* rather than *residency,* controls, under the principle first laid down in *Breedlove v. Nicolet,* 32 U.S. (7 Pet.) 413, 431–32 (1833). See **citizenship & domicil(e).**

B. And *subject*. *Subject* (= a person subject to political rule; any member of a state except the sovereign [*COD*]) is not merely the BrE equivalent of the American *citizen.* A *citizen* is a person from a country in which sovereignty is believed or supposed to belong to the collective body of the people, whereas a *subject* is one who owes allegiance to a sovereign monarch.

citizenry; citizens. Both are acceptable plurals of *citizen, -s* being the more general. Two aspects of *citizenry* distinguish it: first, it is a COLLECTIVE NOUN (although it frequently takes a plural verb), emphasizing the mass or body of citizens; and second, *citizenry* is, as *W2* notes, frequently used by way of contrast to soldiery, officialdom, or the intelligentsia. Here it is opposed to one part of officialdom (some might say *intelligentsia*): "The written Constitution lies at the core of the American 'civil religion'; not only judges but also the *citizenry* at large habitually invoke the Constitution."

citizen's arrest; private arrest. The former phrase is current in both AmE and BrE. The latter phrase is a primarily British variant.

citizenship; domicile; residence. "For purposes of federal diversity jurisdiction, *citizenship* and *domicile* are synonymous." *Hendry v. Masonite Corp.,* 455 F.2d 955, 955 (5th Cir. 1972). For other purposes, however, the words are quite different. *Citizenship* denotes the status of being a citizen, with its attendant rights and privileges. In other words, *citizenship* "carries with it the idea of identification with the state and a participation in its functions. As a citizen, one sustains social, political, and moral obligation to the state and possesses social and political rights under the Constitution and laws thereof." *Baker v. Keck,* 13 F. Supp. 486, 487 (E.D. Ill. 1936). See **citizen (A).**

Domicile = residency at a particular place accompanied with positive or presumptive proof that the person intends to remain there for an unlimited time. *Mitchell v. U.S.,* 88 U.S. (21 Wall.) 350, 352 (1874).

Residence is, for legal purposes, usable in place of *domicile,* but is broader, inasmuch as in one sense it is a FORMAL WORD for "house, home." See **domicil(e) & residence.**

citizenship, diversity of. See **diversity.**

city lawyer. See LAWYERS, DEROGATORY NAMES FOR (A).

city part = (in the language of New York state courts) a trial court created to hear trip-and-fall and other personal-injury claims against the City of New York. The proliferation of such suits prompted the creation of a special division composed of various "parts" to dispose of them. See David B. Saxe, *An Afternoon in a City Part,* 17 Litigation 1, 1 (Winter 1991).

civic rights. See **civil rights.**

civil action. In so-called code states, this phrase replaced *action at law* and *suit in equity* upon the merger of law and equity in American courts. See 1 G.W. Field, *Field's Lawyers' Briefs* 1 (1884). Rule 2 of the Federal Rules of Civil Procedure (1938) established the *civil action* as the "one form of action" in federal courts in the U.S.

Civil Code. See **Napoleonic Code.**

civil death, a LOAN TRANSLATION of *mors civilis,* was formerly opposed to *natural death.* At common law, a person who (1) was banished or outlawed, (2) was attainted of felony, or (3) had entered a monastery, was said to have suffered a *civil death:* "In one large department of law the fiction [of civil death] is elegantly maintained. A monk or nun can not acquire or have any proprietary rights. When a man becomes 'professed in religion,' his heir at once inherits from him any land that he has, and, if he has made a will, it takes effect at once as though he were naturally dead." 1 Frederick B. Pollock & Frederic W. Maitland, *History of English Law* 434 (2d ed. 1899).

Now obsolete in England, this FICTION is still applied in some American states in reference to prisoners. One commentator argues convincingly that the fiction is unnecessary and confusing in the modern world:

> For the sake of preserving the fiction of *civil death,* which satisfied the logic and rules of an earlier day, words are robbed of all ordinary meaning, yet nothing of technical sharpness results. As it is now, the rules that govern the civil rights of prisoners must still be spelled out in statute and case law. In the confusion over the metaphysics of *civil death* even earnest men find themselves wandering. Much simpler to drop the whole *civil death* business.
> David Mellinkoff, *The Language of the Law* 328 (1963).

The antonym, *natural life,* q.v., is a legal ARCHAISM that lives with us still, although its usefulness too is largely gone.

civil disobedience (= the refusal to obey laws as part of a political protest) originated in Henry David Thoreau's retitled essay of that name (1866), in which he wrote: "Under a government which imprisons any unjustly, the true place for a just man is also a prison." The idea behind *civil disobedience* was refined by Gandhi and Martin Luther King, Jr. The latter wrote: "I submit that an individual who breaks a law that conscience tells him is unjust, and who willingly accepts the penalty of imprisonment in order to arouse the conscience of the community over its injustice, has in reality the highest respect for the law." Martin Luther King, Jr., *Why We Can't Wait* 86 (1964).

civilian, n., = a lawyer in a civil-law, as opposed to common-law, jurisdiction. As an adj., *civilian* = *civil-law.* In the three sentences that follow, the first two uses of the word exemplify the noun, the last two the adjective. "'Jura realia' and 'personalia' are expressions occasionally used by modern *civilians* as adjectival forms of 'jura in rem' and 'in personam.'"/ "Albert Tate, Jr., a *civilian* scholar, then an intermediate appellate court judge, later a justice of the Louisiana Supreme Court, and now a member of this court, expressed the view that the 1912 Legislature amended 456, vastly expanding the items specifically covered."

Even in legal writing, of course, *civilian* (n. & adj.) appears also in its nonlegal sense (= [of or relating to] a nonmilitary person)—e.g.: "A *civilian* trial, in other words, is held in an atmosphere conducive to the protection of individual rights, while the military trial is marked by the age-old manifest destiny of retributive justice."/ "The Articles of War were revised to provide for military trial, even in peacetime, of certain specific *civilian* crimes committed by persons 'subject to military law.'"

civil law. A. As Noun. The term *civil law* is ambiguous; legal writers should be careful to specify which meaning they attribute to the term. *Civil law* = (1) (to a common-law practitioner) private law, as opposed to criminal law, administrative law, military law, or ecclesiastical law <civil litigation>; (2) (to a legal historian) the civil law of Rome; (3) (to a comparative-law specialist within the common-law system) the civil-law tradition in civil-code countries; the entire legal system in nations falling within the civil-law tradition; (4) (to a civil-law practitioner) the fundamental content of the legal system (as opposed to public and commercial law)—of persons, of things, of obligations; and (5) (to an ethicist) the law imposed by the state; temporal as opposed to moral law.

Sense (5) is perhaps the rarest one—hence most in need of illustration: "A favorite theory with many of the philosophers is that ethics is an exposition of the moral law as distinguished from the *civil law*; the former being imposed by the conscience, the latter by the power of the state." George W. Warvelle, *Essays in Legal Ethics* 4 (1902).

B. Form of Adjective. Like its sibling *common law,* q.v., this term should be hyphenated when it is used as an adjective <civil-law jurisdiction>, and written as two words when used as a noun <the civil law of Louisiana>. See PHRASAL ADJECTIVES (A).

civil-law method; canon-law method. These refer to methods of determining degrees of blood relationship. Under the *civil-law method,* commonly used in the U.S., you ascertain how closely related a person is to a decedent by counting up or back from the decedent to the nearest ancestor who is common to both the decedent and the relative in question. Then you count down from the ancestor to the relative in question, counting one degree for each generation.

Under the *canon-law method,* you count similarly in each line and the longer line to the common ancestor determines the degree.

civil lawyer (= civilian, q.v., as defined above) is the usu. form, not *civil-law lawyer*—e.g.: "Common lawyers tend to be much less rigorous about such matters than *civil lawyers.*" John H. Merryman, *The Civil Law Tradition* 26 (1969). But cf. **common-law lawyer.**

civil liberties. See **civil rights.**

civil offense. This phrase is a misnomer, *offense* properly referring to a criminal act. The better phrase is *civil wrong.* See **offense.**

civil remedy. See **remedy.**

civil rights; civil liberties; civic rights. *Civil rights,* an Americanism, refers generally to the individual rights guaranteed by the Bill of Rights and by the Thirteenth, Fourteenth, Fifteenth, and Nineteenth Amendments, as well as by legislation such as the Voting Rights Act. These rights include especially the right to vote; freedom from involuntary servitude; the enjoyment of life, liberty, and property; privacy; due process; and equal protection of the law. Some of these rights, such as the right to vote, are restricted to citizens; others, such as the rights of due process and equal protection, apply equally to anyone within a jurisdiction.

Some writers distinguish *civil rights* from *political rights,* contending that the latter phrase embraces participation "in the management of government through such practices as voting." Jack Plano & Milton Greenberg, *The American Political Dictionary* 266 (8th ed. 1989). By this definition, then, the right to vote is not a civil right. But this discrepancy merely shows that the phrase *civil rights* is fuzzy at the edges.

The phrase *civil liberties* is more widely used than *civil rights*—that is, not just in AmE—to refer generally to the liberties guaranteed to all persons by law or custom against undue governmental interference. *Civil rights* is also sometimes used in this broader sense: "The subject was *'civil rights,'* that is, the liberties of man as man and not primarily as an economic animal." Robert G. McCloskey, *The American Supreme Court* 170 (1960).

Civic rights is a much less common phrase. It sounds at once less weighty than the other two phrases and less idiomatic. But it has appeared, probably generally as a NEEDLESS VARIANT of *civil rights*—e.g.: "Lincoln, unwilling to alienate a public opinion that everywhere in the North was implacably, savagely opposed to giving slaves movement or *civic rights,* was, on one occasion in the debates, not above snarling 'nigger.'" Alfred Kazin, *A Forever Amazing Writer,* N.Y. Times, 10 Dec. 1989, § 7 (Book Rev.), at 3.

civil suit. Does this phrase exclude all cases involving the government? Rodell suggests so: "Thus the two sides in what The Law would call a *'civil suit'*—an ordinary case not involving the government—might be required to pick their own expert or experts to settle their dispute for them . . . ." Fred Rodell, *Woe Unto You, Lawyers!* 175 (1939; repr. 1980). That parenthetical definition is puzzlingly wrong: government lawyers frequently refer to their involvement in *civil suits* or *civil actions*—indeed, the Federal Rules of Civil Procedure provide expressly for *civil actions* in which the government is a party.

civil wrong is broader than *tort* or *delict,* embracing also breaches of contract and of trust, breaches of statutory duty, and defects in performing public duties. See **civil offense & offense.**

claim. A. Transitive Verb. *Claim* = (1) to take or demand as one's right; (2) to assert emphatically (something of questionable or questioned credibility). Sense (1) of *claim* often appears without an explicit object (i.e., with the object as an UNDERSTOOD WORD). E.g., "Plaintiffs are sisters of Mrs. Girard and *claim* as her heirs [i.e., *claim her estate as her heirs*]."

Sense (2), primarily an Americanism, is subject to SLIPSHOD EXTENSION when writers use *claim* to mean merely "to say," as in, "He *claims* [read *states* or *says*] the Supreme Court has never ruled on the point." But it is groundless to insist that this verb can properly mean only "lay claim to" or "demand as one's due," and not "assert, allege." *Claim* has long been used in the latter as well as in the former sense. E.g., "The police officer *claimed* that he had heard a rumor months earlier that the defendant would meet a drug buyer at some restaurant."/ "The defendant also *claimed* that there could be no rescission as *restitutio in integrum* was not possible, the plaintiffs having at a clearing sale disposed of the plant, machinery, and stock." (Aus.)

B. Noun. From sense (2) of the verb has grown the nominal sense "assertion, contention" <her claim that the immunity applies here>, in addition to the older sense "a right to something." To be avoided at all costs is the use of the term in different senses in a single context: "The government *claims* [read *argues*] that Sherlock's *claim* [read *assertion*] of fifth amendment privilege is moot." Either substitution eliminates the problem.

claimant. Ordinarily, the word refers to one who asserts a property right or makes a demand, but recently it has been extended to refer also to one who posits a legal claim such as a constitutional privilege, or even one who claims in the sense of "argues." E.g., "A person whose conduct is clearly within the constitutional scope of a statute may not successfully challenge it for vagueness . . . . The burden is on the claimant to show that in its operation the statute is unconstitutional to her in her situation . . . ." *Lear v. State,* 753 S.W.2d 737, 740 (Tex. App.—Austin 1988).

claim preclusion; issue preclusion. The first phrase is synonymous with *res judicata* (q.v.) in its strict sense, without being susceptible to the ambiguities of the LATINISM. The second phrase is synonymous with *collateral estoppel* (q.v.) in its strict sense. Professor Allan Vestal long argued—with considerable success—that courts should use the terms *claim preclusion* and *issue preclusion;* the *Restatement (Second) of Judgments* follows that usage. "[T]he principal distinction," explains Professor Wright, is that *claim preclusion* "forecloses litigation of matters that have never been litigated. This makes it important to know the dimensions of the 'claim' that is foreclosed by bringing the first action, but unfortunately no precise definition is possible." Charles A. Wright, *The Law of Federal Courts* 681 (4th ed. 1983).

claim quit. See **quitclaim.**

claim(s) agent; claim(s) adjuster. *Claims* is the standard form. See **adjuster.**

class is not interchangeable with *kind* or *type.* We may have a type or kind of *thing,* but a class of *things.* E.g., "In this *class of case* [read *type of case* or *class of cases*], the contract is executed by the promoter and the third party when both are aware that the corporation has not been formed."

class action = a lawsuit instituted by one or more parties on behalf not only of themselves but also of many other parties, when common questions of law and fact are involved. "The *class action* was an invention of equity . . . mothered by the practical necessity of providing a procedural device so that mere numbers would not disable large groups of individuals, united in interest, from enforcing their equitable rights nor grant them immunity from their equitable wrongs." *Montgomery Ward & Co. v. Langer,* 168 F.2d 182, 187 (8th Cir. 1948).

The phrase *class-action suit* is wordy for *class action.*

classic(al). *Classical* refers to anything relating to "the classics" (whether in Greek or Latin literature, English literature, or music); *classic* may also serve in this sense, although not in phrases such as *classical education* or *classical allusions. Classic,* an easily overworked word, has the additional sense "outstandingly authoritative or important."

class of, a. See SYNESIS.

clause. In grammar, of course, this word refers to any group of words that contains a subject and a verb. In law, *clause* generally refers vaguely to some unit of a legal instrument or statute—often a paragraph, subdivision, or section. It need not be restricted, in its application, to a single sentence, as some lawyers mistakenly believe.

In G.B., a *clause* in a bill before Parliament becomes a section when the bill is given Royal Assent.

clause of accrual (or **accruer**). See **accrual.**

claw back, v.t.; **clawback,** n. As a transitive PHRASAL VERB, *claw back* = (1) to take back money that has already been allocated; (2) (of a taxing authority) to take back previously granted tax relief. E.g., in sense (1): "Taxpayers' inability to *claw back* money if property declines in value does not persuade us that there is a problem in the logic of *Pyle.*" *Grimes v. I.R.C.,* 851 F.2d 1005, 1009 (7th Cir. 1988).

The noun *clawback* = (1) money taken back; or (2) the loss of previously granted tax relief.

Clawback provision = a penalty in the nature of a tax. E.g., "It could make it easier to sue for libel, by granting legal aid for litigants but with stiff *clawback provisions* to discourage frivolous writs." The Economist, 28 Jan.–3 Feb. 1989, at 18./ "A blocking statute is a law passed by the foreign government imposing a penalty upon a national for complying with a foreign court's discovery request. France and Britain have passed blocking laws aimed at discovery in American antitrust suits. These statutes are also known by the descriptive moniker: *clawback provisions." In re Anschuetz & Co.,* 754 F.2d 602, 614 n.29 (5th Cir. 1985).

clean, v.t.; **cleanse.** *Clean* is literal, *cleanse* figurative. Hence *cleanse* is often used in religious or moral contexts, or, as here, in law: "[T]he court can take ex post facto measures to *cleanse* the error." *Marine Coatings of Alabama, Inc. v. U.S.,* 792 F.2d 1565, 1568 (11th Cir. 1986).

clean hands is a metaphor from equity, derived from the maxim *He who comes to equity must come with clean hands,* i.e., must be free from taint of fraud. E.g., "The maxim that he who comes into equity must come with *clean hands* is far more than a mere banality."/ "The nature of the *unclean-hands* defense in patent and unfair competition litigation has not been clearly established." A memorable statement of the principle is: "He that hath committed Iniquity, shall not have equity." Richard Francis, *Maxims of Equity* 5 (1727).

cleanliness; cleanness. *Cleanliness* is used in reference to persons and their habits, *cleanness* in reference to things and places.

cleanse. See **clean.**

clear (= to exonerate) is a casualism common in JOURNALESE: "On Monday the jury *cleared* the defendants of charges that they tried to overthrow the Government by force . . . ." *U.S. Won't Retry 3 in Bombings,* N.Y. Times, 2 Dec. 1989, at 9.

clear and convincing clarity. Several state and federal courts have announced *clear and convincing clarity* as the standard for proving actual malice in defamation cases. The phrase is an unfortunate amalgamation of the two phrases *clear and convincing* and *convincing clarity.* See Thomas A. Woxland, *Clear Clarity,* 1 Scribes J. Legal Writing 143–44 (1990). Need it be said that the phrase is a redundant and wordy redundancy?

clear and convincing evidence. See **preponderance of the evidence.**

clear and present danger. This is the phrase Holmes coined to express his test of whether certain speech is protected by the First Amendment. See *Schenck v. U.S.,* 249 U.S. 47, 52 (1919). Rodell calls this famous formula Holmes's "greatest, and only major, judicial error. The pat phrase was first used in a case where an anti-war extremist, who had urged that young men dodge the draft, was jailed for thus committing a federal crime . . . . Little more than a year later, Holmes himself had cause to regret the *'clear and present danger'* excuse for letting Congress curb freedom of speech, which he had handed his colleagues on the platter of his eloquence." Fred Rodell, *Nine Men* 210 (1955). The Supreme Court later widened the meaning of the phrase, giving, in Rodell's words, its "free-speech-sapping operations the protective cover of the words of Holmes." *Id.*

clear(-)cut, adj., should be hyphenated. "The testator, thus indicating a *clearcut* [read *clear-cut*] intention to postpone vesting until the termination of each trust, created a remainder contingent upon survival of the life beneficiary."

clearly. "[I]t seems to be a familiar joke among some ironic observers that when a judge (some other judge) begins a sentence with a term of utter conviction (*Clearly, Undeniably, It is plain that* . . .), the sentence that follows is likely to be dubious, unreasonable, and fraught with difficulties." Walker Gibson, *Literary Minds and Judicial Style,* 36 N.Y.U. L. Rev. 915, 925 (1961). This skepticism has grown from an abuse of these terms to express certainty. Where they are used merely to buttress arguments, they become WEASEL WORDS and weaken those arguments. They should be used only where one's bitterest opponent could not object.

Just how much *clearly* can weaken a statement is evident here: "*Clearly,* I am not to be convinced that this is a small matter . . . ." Stephen White, *The Written Word* 3 (1984). See **obviously** & **doubtless(ly).**

clearly erroneous. This phrase expresses the standard of review that, in many jurisdictions (such as the U.S. federal courts), an appellate court applies in judging a trial court's treatment of factual issues. A judgment is reversible if it resolves issues in a clearly erroneous manner.

cleave, v.t., has the opposite meanings (1) "to divide or separate" and (2) "to adhere to firmly." In sense (1), *cleave* yields the past tense *cleft* (or, less good, *clove*) and the past participle *cleft* (or *cleaved,* again not preferred). The past-participial adjective is *cloven.* Hence, "He cleft the Devil's cloven hoof with a cleaver."

In sense (2), the verb is inflected *cleave* > *cleaved* > *cleaved.* The *COD* sanctions, for BrE usage, *cleave* > *clove* > *cloven* for all senses, though *cleft* is used adjectivally in set phrases such as *cleft palate* or *cleft stick.* Luckily, the term is a literary one, so that generally only literary scholars must trouble themselves with these inflections.

clench. See **clinch.**

clergyable; nonclergyable. *Clergyable* = (of an offense) susceptible to benefit of clergy. *Nonclergyable* = (of an offense) punishable without benefit of clergy. E.g., "Although originally those entitled to benefit of clergy were simply delivered to the bishop for ecclesiastical proceedings, with the possibility of degradation from orders, incarceration, and corporal punishment for those found guilty, during the 15th and 16th centuries the maximum penalty for *clergyable* offenses became branding on the thumb, imprisonment for not more than one year, and forfeiture of goods." *McGautha v. California,* 402 U.S. 183, 197–98 (1971). See **benefit of clergy** & **neck verse.**

The spelling *clergiable,* though listed as the primary spelling in the *OED* and in most law dictionaries, occurs less frequently than *clergyable* in legal texts.

clerk; law clerk; summer associate; extern; briefing attorney. The rather undignified term *clerk* is used in reference to an American law student who works for a law firm before receiving a law degree and passing the bar exam. In response to the meniality connoted by this term, some lawyers have borrowed *extern* from the medical profession, but its use is not widespread. For clerks who work with a firm during the summer months, lawyers have hit upon *summer associate,* which has gained currency throughout the U.S. among firms that recruit heavily.

Law clerk is used both as a synonym of *summer associate* and as a term describing a select graduate who spends a year or two as a judge's apprentice. Unlike law firms' law clerks, judges' law clerks have usu. already passed the bar exam and accepted a permanent position for the following year. Hence, although they are already *lawyers,* the apparent meniality of *law clerk* is especially ironic. Some courts therefore call their clerks *briefing attorneys,* but to one accustomed to the unpretentiousness of *law clerk,* this term seems inflated.

The best advice is to follow the practice of a particular firm or judge: at a firm that hires *law clerks,* they should not call themselves *summer associates* (though the reverse practice is unobjectionable); if a judge hires *law clerks,* they should not parade the name *briefing attorney.* The understated title *law clerk* is to be worn as a badge of honor.

clew. See **clue.**

Clichés. Why is it that, in legal prose, common sense always *dictates* certain actions? That precedents are never to be *lightly overruled?* That to look at something a second time is invariably to *revisit* it? Why are trial judges whom appellate courts agree with always *learned,* but never wise or perspicacious or erudite? Why is any significant evidentiary hearing always termed *full-blown?* Too often in legal writing, parties *strenuously object;* judges write *vigorous dissents;* legal principles are never settled but that they are *well-settled;* trial judges always have *sound discretion* rather than mere discretion; exceptions are never created—instead, they are *carved out;* bad statutes are inevitably *constitutionally infirm* rather than invalid or, better yet, unconstitutional; opinions we agree with are invariably *well reasoned,* but almost never cogent or compelling.

Meanwhile, statutory words are *not talismanic;* we don't want to turn rules into *paper tigers* while wending our way through a *statutory mosaic;* as we examine the *parade of horrors* before us we fear that our opponents have a *private agenda;* going too far, they want to *throw the baby out with the bathwater.* So we respond, naturally: *"If it ain't broke, don't fix it."*

Clichés should generally be used sparingly in any writing, but especially in legal writing. Yet we are beset with hackneyed phrases inappositely employed in legal briefs and judicial opinions. To begin with, good writers have sensitized themselves to what a cliché is. Acquiring this sensitivity requires some literary taste, but mostly a background that includes wide reading. One need not read very many American judicial opinions to find, e.g., that *We do not write on a clean slate* (or *on a tabula rasa*) is a commonplace often repeated.

General English clichés are also common in legal writing. E.g., *"It all started* on a *fateful day* in December of 1981, when the Equity Shipping Corporation chartered its vessel to the GHR Energy Corporation."/ "In the *hallowed days of yore,* parties seeking to stay their proceedings in an action at law had to *cross the street* into a court of equity for an injunction." (The main clause manages to *sound* like a cliché without actually being one.) It would be easy to list hundreds of English-language clichés such as *time is of the essence, crystal clear, proverbial snowball in hell, dire need,* and *flatly refused;* but no purpose would be served. If one finds oneself writing or talking in ready-made phrases, it is time to draw back and frame the thought anew. The occasional cliché may be justifiable, to be sure; it is the habitual use of clichés that is stylistically objectionable. For a fuller discussion, see Eric Partridge, *Dictionary of Clichés* (1963) and James Rogers, *Dictionary of Clichés* (1985).

Finally, if one must use a cliché, do it straightforwardly. Slight variations on clichés are neither clever nor cute. E.g., "He wore his heresy on his sleeve." (Figuratively, only one's heart (or feelings) can be worn on one's sleeve.) Likewise, one should not change *madding crowd* to *maddening crowd.* See SET PHRASES.

One lawyer has written wittily about the dissolution of his partnership, citing in part "an occupational nervous affliction" that causes lawyers to spout clichés. The culminating altercation, this lawyer recalled, sounded like this:

> "You're being arbitrary and capricious!"
> "Well you're being willful and wanton!"
> "I'm going to seek affirmative relief."
> "Are you suggesting that in futuro we do business separate and apart?"
> "I'm telling you that you have been guilty of cruel treatment of me and have inflicted personal indignities upon me, rendering my life burdensome so that it is no longer possible for me to remain your partner!"
> "Does this mean that our agreement is null and void?"
> "It means that it's of no further force and effect."
> "In that event I will no longer be responsible for your debt, default or misdoings," he rejoined. "And I'll want the library for myself, free and clear of any encumbrances."
> Edward H. McKinlay, *Legal Cliché Experts,* 49 Fla. B.J. 444 (1975).

client; customer. The line of demarcation between these two words has shifted considerably in recent years. By the 1980s, Massachusetts bureaucrats had begun calling welfare recipients their "clients." See Keller, *Massachusetts's Strange Protest Vote,* Wall St. J., 20 Sept. 1990, at A14. Things have gotten worse in the 1990s. For example, *The Sunday Times* writes of two prostitutes: "Both women took *clients* to their flats." Davison & Durham, *Prostitutes Go in Fear of London 'Ripper',* Sunday Times, 18 Aug. 1991, at 1-5.

clientage. See **clientele.**

cliental = of or relating to a client. The *OED* labels this word "rare," but the Merriam-Webster dictionaries contain no such notation. Still, lawyers have little occasion to use it.

clientele; clientelage; clientage; clientry; clients. The last is the best: the least pretentious and most common. *Clientele* has degenerated somewhat in meaning, having been widely used in nonprofessional contexts. E.g., "The complaint alleges that the plaintiffs are engaged in business as high-grade dressmakers under the name 'Boue Soeurs,' with the most exclusive *clientele*." Often when *clientele* appears in professional contexts, it is used in reference to the oldest profession. See **client.**

Clientage, clientelage, and *clientry* are NEEDLESS VARIANTS of *clientele.*

climactic; climacteric; climatic. *Climactic* is now established as the adjective of *climax,* though formerly it was thought to be inferior to *climacteric,* which, having lost the battle, is now to be avoided as a NEEDLESS VARIANT. *Climatic* is the adjective corresponding to *climate*; occasionally it becomes a MALAPROPISM for *climactic.*

clinch; clench. Similar in meaning, these words are used differently. *Clench* is applied to physical matters, and *clinch* is used figuratively. Hence one *clenches* one's jaw or one's fist, but *clinches* an argument or debate. E.g., "It was the good fortune of Professor W.H. Dunham to *clinch* the argument by discovering, and printing, two such slips." Theodore F.T. Plucknett, *A Concise History of the Common Law* 270 (5th ed. 1956).

The exceptions to this distinction occur in boxing, carpentry, and metalworking: clutching one's opponent in boxing is *clinching,* and fastening with a screw or a rivet is likewise *clinching.* Apart from these specialized meanings, *clinch* should be reserved for nonphysical contexts. Here it is used ill-advisedly: "After their speeches, Mr. Bentsen and Mr. Clinton *clinched* [read *clenched*] hands together with Gov. Ann Richards on the stage of the party's state convention as *Deep in the Heart of Texas* played over the loudspeakers." Sam Attlesey & Wayne Slater, *Bentsen Strongly Endorses Clinton,* Dallas Morning News, 6 June 1992, at 1A.

CLIPPING. See BACK-FORMATIONS.

clog on the equity (of redemption). See **cloud on title.**

closely held corporation; close(d) corporation. These phrases are generally synonymous in denoting a company whose stock is not freely traded and is held by only a few people (often within the same family). *Closely held corporation* is perhaps the phrase that lawyers most commonly use, but *close corporation* is most common statutory phrase in AmE. In BrE, the term is generally *closed corporation.*

close of the evidence is the legal idiom denoting the end of the presentation of testimony in a trial. E.g., "At the *close of all the evidence,* the district court granted an instructed verdict in favor of appellee on nearly all the issues."

close proximity is a common REDUNDANCY.

closing = the completion of a sales contract. On the *closing date,* the seller delivers the deed and the buyer pays the balance of the purchase price.

closing statement; settlement sheet. Both phrases are used in AmE to denote a statement, approved by both buyer and seller, listing all the credits and charges attributable to each one. The credits and charges listed are used to adjust or prorate items in the sales contract and result in a net amount due by the buyer and a different amount due to the seller (other parties, typically, being involved in the transaction).

closure; cloture. The general noun corresponding to the verb *to close* is *closure.* E.g., "The court held that *closure* of a trial must be necessitated by a compelling governmental interest." In AmE, *cloture* is preferred in but one narrow sense: "the procedure of ending debate in a legislative body and calling for an immediate vote." *Closure* is usual in BrE in this parliamentary sense.

clothe. In law, persons are frequently described metaphorically as being *clothed* with certain powers or privileges. E.g., "He was *clothed* with the apparent authority to enter into contracts for the corporation."/ "The will imposed no duties upon the trustee; it *clothed* her with no discretionary powers."/ "Mrs. Sterdahl, her innocence of wrongdoing established, stands before us *clothed* with the protection equity provides in favor of all bona fide purchasers of interests in property."/ "The Supreme Court under the Constitution and statutes of this state is *clothed* with the power to exercise both appellate and original jurisdiction." If sparingly used, this legal CLICHÉ might be tolerable; but it is sufficient to say merely that a person *has* the powers or privileges in question.

The noun *clothing,* too, was once common as a legal metaphor—e.g.: "He is an Emptor Familiæ, and inherits the legal *clothing* of the person whose place he begins to fill." Henry S. Maine, *Ancient Law* 220 (17th ed. 1901; repr. [New Universal Lib.] 1905, 1910).

cloture. See **closure.**

cloud on title; clog on the equity (of redemption). A *cloud on title* is a defect or potential defect in the owner's title to a piece of land arising, e.g., from a lien, an easement, or a court order. The phrase is generally an American one.

E.g., "[H]ave your contracts signed in the presence of a notary public, notarized and then recorded at your county courthouse. The reason for doing this is to create your own *'cloud on the title'* of the property you have contracted to buy or option." Lucier, *How to Make Money from Sale of Purchase Option Contracts,* Daily Legal News [Cleveland], 17 Aug. 1989, at 1./ "Flint and others brought a bill to restrain appellee from proceeding further and for a declaration freeing their title from the *cloud* cast upon it by appellee's judgment."/ "The historical equity suit to remove a *cloud on title* suffered from some self-imposed handicaps; it could not be used to cancel an instrument constituting a *cloud* that was void on its face."

A *clog on the equity* (often written *clog on the equity of redemption*) is any condition or agreement that prevents a mortgagor from getting back the property free from encumbrance upon paying the debt or performing the obligation for which the security was given. The phrase is common in both BrE and AmE. E.g., "[T]he doctrine against the *clog on the equity of redemption* seems one of the striking examples of the great truth that the ethical standard of our law is often higher than the average morality of the commercial community." Bruce Wyman, *The Clog on the Equity of Redemption,* 21 Harv. L. Rev. 459, 475 (1908).

The metaphor is an old one in law: Richard W. Turner, in *The Equity of Redemption* 29 (1931), quotes a court that wrote, in 1639: "[I]n some cases . . . the mortgagee will suddenly bestow unnecessary costs upon the mortgaged lands, of purpose to *clogg* the lands, to prevent the mortgager's redemption" (quoting *Bacon v. Bacon,* Tot. 133). See METAPHORS (B).

clue; clew. *Clue* is the only current spelling for the sense "a hint; a bit of evidence." The spelling *clew* survives as a nautical term ("the lower corner of a sail") and as a sewing term ("a ball of thread").

CO-. A. Hyphenation with. Generally, this prefix—which means "together with" or "joint"—does not take a hyphen. Only when the hyphenated form is established (e.g., *co-respondent, co-relation*), when the unhyphenated form may lead the reader to mistake the syllables (e.g., *co-citation, co-heir*), or when the writer believes he is creating a new form (e.g., *co-secretary*) should the hyphen appear.

B. Attaching to Noun Phrase. This creates an awkward construction but is sometimes all but unavoidable, as in *copersonal representative.*

co-appellant; co-appellee. These terms are used to denote the relation of joint parties on appeal. E.g., "The appellant was a policeman in the City of Newport, and had executed a bond as required by law, with his codefendant and *co-appellant,* National Surety Co., as surety thereon."

co-citation is best hyphenated. This word, not uncommon in legal writing, is not listed in the *OED* or in *W3.* See CO- (A).

co(-)conspirator. Hyphenating the word indicates immediately to the reader what the primary word (*conspirator*) is. As the term becomes more common, though, *coconspirator* is likely to become established. See CO- (A).

Notably, a *conspirator* is one who plots with another; a "sole conspirator" is impossible. This point has led to some confusion about whether *co-conspirator* is redundant. William Safire writes: "[T]o me, a *co-conspirator* is as redundant as a *co-equal.*" *Let's Kill All the Copy Editors,* N.Y. Times (Mag.), 6 Oct. 1991, § 6 at 16.

But like *coequal,* the word *co-conspirator* suggests a point of comparison—it is used only where we would otherwise say *fellow conspirator,* as in *his co-conspirator* (where we would not, indeed could not, say *his conspirator*).

For analogous examples, see **codefendant, coequal** & **coplaintiff.** For a similar word with an important difference, see **copartner** (in which *partner* itself suggests the point of comparison, so that *copartner* is unnecessary).

cocounsel. So written—without a hyphen. E.g., "He turned the task over to students hired by S.C. Godha, the Indian *cocounsel* whom the Bhopal mayor had set up with the day before . . . ." John A. Jenkins, *The Litigators* 71 (1989). See CO- (A).

C.O.D. = (1) cash on delivery (*COD* & *W3*); (2) collect on delivery (*COD* & *W3*); (3) cash on demand (*Black's*); or (4) costs on delivery (*OED*). Whatever the abbreviation stands for, its effect is the same.

codal (= of or relating to a code), dating from the late 19th century, is an adjective used in some civil-law jurisdictions to refer to the civil code. E.g., "The Judge found that the broker's conduct was violative of two *codal* Articles of the Louisiana Law of Mandate." *McCurnin v. Kohlmeyer & Co.,* 477 F.2d 113, 115 (5th Cir. 1973)./ "Professor Malone suggested that enterprise liability should be founded directly upon the basic *codal* language, 'Every act whatever of a man that causes damage to another obliges him by whose fault it happened to repair it.' La. Civ. Code art. 2315(A) (West Supp. 1985)."

The word is sometimes (unnecessarily) capitalized: "[T]he *Codal* [read *codal*] provisions taken from the French . . . established the rights of the good faith parties in putative marriages." *Cortes v. Fleming,* 307 So. 2d 611, 615 (La. 1973).

The only adjectival form of *code* recognized by the dictionaries, however, is *codical* (= pertaining to, or of the nature of, a codex or code). It is not used by civilians in Louisiana.

Codd's Puzzle is the classic parody of inconsistent pleading. Codd, counsel for a defendant charged with stealing a duck, pleaded:

1. that his client had bought the bird;
2. that he had found it;
3. that it had flown into his garden;
4. that its owner had given it to him;
5. that some unknown person or persons had stuffed it into his pocket while he was asleep;
6. that the duck had not existed at any material time; and
7. that his client would if necessary make a full confession.

The lay jury is reported to have acquitted Codd's client. See Theo Ruoff, 30 Austral. L.J. 512 (1957).

code; codification. The word *code,* derived from Justinian's *Codex* of 534 A.D. (a collection of legislation), has been applied in several ways in Anglo-American law: (1) to a compilation of existing statutes; (2) to a systematic consolidation of statutory law; (3) to a revision of the whole law, both statutory and case law, reducing its principles to a clear and compact statement. Senses (1) and (2) are better termed *consolidation.*

Citing sense (3) as the primary one, Glanville Williams comments: "[F]or reasons that it would not be flattering to examine in detail English lawyers have always been hostile (or, at best, indifferent) to this." Glanville Williams, *Learning the Law* 44 (11th ed. 1982).

Specialist lawyers frequently refer elliptically to "the Code" to mean whatever code they deal with most frequently, such as the Civil Code, the Bankruptcy Code, the Uniform Commercial Code, the Family Code, or the Code of Judicial Conduct. Depending on the jurisdiction, these codes may fit any one of the three senses of *code* just enumerated.

Codification, one of Jeremy Bentham's NEOLOGISMS, most properly refers to the process of codifying—e.g.: "Although his major aims—codification and complete simplification—have not been achieved, yet to him we owe numerous important legal reforms." Jerome Frank, Introduction to Fred Rodell, *Woe Unto You, Lawyers!* xii (1939; repr. 1980). But the word often refers, in a transferred sense, to the finished product—the code itself.

Code Civil. See **Napoleonic Code.**

codefendant. This word, meaning "a joint or fellow defendant," is common; oddly, however, *coplaintiff* (q.v.) is comparatively rare. See CO- (A).

code law, a more specific term than *statutory law,* is sometimes contrasted, as here, with *case-law:* "It is written *case-law,* and only different from *code-law* because it is written in a different way." Henry S. Maine, *Ancient Law* 11 (17th Ed. 1901; repr. [New Universal Lib.] 1905, 1910). Today, *code law* is preferably two words. Cf. **case(-)law.**

Code Napoléon. See **Napoleonic Code.**

code pleading; fact pleading; notice pleading; general pleading. The first two are synonymous phrases referring to the requirement, in some post-common-law pleading, that one allege merely the facts giving rise to the claim, not the conclusions of law necessary to sustain the claim. See Charles E. Clark, *Handbook of the Law of Code Pleading* 1–2 (2d ed. 1947). *Code pleading* (as it is usually known) developed originally in New York in the late 1840s, under the influence of David Dudley Field.

The idea of code pleading was to move beyond the formulary technicalities of common-law and equity pleading. The term first appeared in the late 19th century: "The only case arising under the modern *code pleadings* and bearing upon this question . . . is Fosgate v. Herkimer Mfg. & Hydraulic Co. . . . ." *Gibbons v. Martin,* 10 F. Cas. 292, 293 (C.C.D. Or. 1877) (No. 5,381)./ "[U]nder the system of *code pleading,* a technical variance between the allegations and the proof is not deemed material unless the adverse party is prejudiced thereby . . . ." *Wilson v. Haley Live-Stock Co.,* 153 U.S. 39, 47 (1894).

In the late 19th and early 20th centuries, code pleading led to gross overpleading. And lawyers came to realize the futility of the endeavor: "'The facts as they actually existed or occurred,' 'the dry, naked, actual facts'—these and these only are to be stated. Can it be done? I think not; it has never been done and never will be done, either by a pleader or by anyone else. Philosophically, logically, it is an impossibility." Walter W. Cook, "The Utility of Jurisprudence in the Solution of

Legal Problems," in 5 *Lectures on Legal Topics* 337, 369 (1928).

So, in 1938, the drafters of the Federal Rules of Civil Procedure modified the pleading requirements still further so as to allow *notice pleading* or *general pleading,* which requires merely a "short and plain statement of the claim showing that the pleader is entitled to relief." Fed. R. Civ. P. 8(a). Up to that time, judicial glosses on code pleading had resulted in overpleading that caused "frightful expense, endless delay and an enormous loss of motion." Thomas E. Skinner, *Pre-Trial and Discovery Under the Alabama Rules of Civil Procedure,* 9 Ala. L. Rev. 202, 204 (1957).

code state; noncode state. These terms—current primarily in the early to mid-20th century—distinguished between states that had merged law and equity, and those that had not. E.g., "[I]n any *code state* in which law and equity have been merged in the same court and in which every action is both legal and equitable in that all rights of the parties, legal and equitable, must be adjudicated therein, the court has full power to give relief . . . [that] the nature of the case calls for, irrespective of whether it would have been classed as a case in equity or a case at law under the old order." William F. Walsh, *A Treatise on Equity* 367 (1930) (referring at pp. 102–03 to "*non-code states* in which equity is still administered as a separate system").

This terminology can be confusing because many readers would think of a *code state* as one having a Civil Code—i.e., Louisiana.

codex is a NEEDLESS VARIANT of *code*—and a pompous one—unless the writer is referring to one of the ancient European codes (e.g., *Codex Theodosianus* of 438 A.D.), a *codex rescriptus* (= a palimpsest, or written-over manuscript), or the like. Pl. *codices.*

codicil; will. *Codicil* = a testamentary supplement that varies or revokes provisions in a will. *Will* = a written or oral expression of one's intention regarding the disposition of one's property at death. See **last will and testament** & **will.**

codification. See **code.**

codifier; codist. Whereas a *codifier* is one who makes a code, a *codist* is one learned in legal codes, esp. in the civil codes of different nations.

codify is best pronounced /***kod**-i-fī*/, not /***kohd**-i-fī*/. This word, like *codification,* was one of Jeremy Bentham's NEOLOGISMS; it dates from ca. 1800.

codifying statute. See **consolidating statute.**

codist. See **codifier.**

co-employee is a NEEDLESS VARIANT of *coworker.* See CO- (A).

coequal, n. & adj., often means nothing that *equal* does not also mean; it should be rejected in such contexts. E.g., "All constitutional rights are *co-equal* [read *equal*] and must be harmonized with each other, no one such right being permitted to override or submerge another."

The word is useful only in implying the standard of comparison; for example, in a snippet quoted in the *OED,* "the co-eternal and *co-equal* Son," if only *equal* had been used, the reader would wonder, Equal with what? *Co-equal* implies the second and third things with which the Son is said to be equal. This nuance is rare, however; for most purposes, *equal* suffices. Still, it is simplistic to say, as William Safire does, that "[t]oday's usage frowns on *co-equal* as redundant." *Send in Sovereign for Socialist,* N.Y. Times, 6 Jan. 1991, § 6, at 8, 10. For a mini-tirade on the subject, see Robert C. Cumbow, *The Subverting of the Goeduck,* 14 Univ. Puget Sound L. Rev. 755 (1991) ("Not only does A equal B, and B equal A, but A and B equal *each other!* Imagine! They're *both* equal *together!*" [etc.]). Cf. **copartner** & **co(-)conspirator.**

On the issue of writing *coequal* as a solid word, see CO- (A).

coercible. So spelled. See -ABLE (A).

coercion, though originally applicable only to physical force, is now commonly used of moral and economic pressures. E.g., "It has never been held by this court that a labor union is without justification in fairly setting forth its claims by newspaper advertisements as a legitimate means of economic *coercion.*" Such uses are a natural extension of the original sense ("the control by force of a voluntary agent or action").

In criminal law, *coercion* has historically had a more limited sense—*compulsion* being reserved for any action or restraint imposed upon one by another. In this context, *coercion* ordinarily refers specifically to such an action or restraint imposed by a husband on his wife. E.g., "Under the English 'rule of *coercion,*' the bare command of the husband was a complete defense to the wife, with a few exceptions such as treason or murder." Rollin

M. Perkins & Ronald N. Boyce, *Criminal Law* 1062 (3d ed. 1982).

cofelon (= a felon involved in the same crime as another felon) need not be hyphenated. See CO- (A).

cofiduciary = joint fiduciary. The word is best made solid, without a hyphen. See CO- (A).

cognate. See **agnate.**

cognation; cognition. *Cognition* = thinking; use of the intellect. *Cognation* = a cognate relationship. In Roman law, *cognation* (specif., natural relationship by descent from a common ancestor, whether through males or females) was opposed to *agnation* (relationship through males only). See **agnate.**

cognisance. See **cognizance.**

cognisant. See **cognizant.**

cognition. See **cognation.**

cognitive; cognitional. The latter is a NEEDLESS VARIANT. *Cognitive* = of or pertaining to cognition, or to the action or process of knowing. It should be avoided in its use as a jargonistic filler, as here: "The totality of the relevant facts supports the finding that the City of Apopka has engaged in a systematic pattern of *cognitive* acts and omissions, selecting and reaffirming a particular course of municipal services that inescapably evidences discriminatory intent." What the word means in that sentence is a minor mystery.

cognitor is an archaic word for *attorney* that derives from Roman law and existed in English only briefly.

cognizable; cognoscible. *Cognizable /**kog**-ni-zə-bel/* = (1) capable of being known; perceptible; (2) capable of being, or liable to be, judicially examined or tried; within the jurisdiction of a court of law (*OED*). Sense (2) is common in the phrase *cognizable claims:* "Nor do I believe that a criminal suspect who is shot while trying to avoid apprehension has a *cognizable claim* of a deprivation of his sixth amendment right to trial by jury."

Cognoscible is a NEEDLESS VARIANT that appears in many older texts—e.g. (fr. 17th c.): "No external act can pass upon a man for a crime that is not *cognoscible.*" 2 Jeremy Taylor, *Works* 313 (1835).

cognizance. A. And *recognizance.* Though superficially similar, these words have unrelated meanings. *Cognizance* = (1) knowledge, esp. as attained by observation or information; or (2) the action of taking judicial notice. Sense (2) is rarer now than it once was. See **judicial notice.**

Recognizance = (1) the bond by which a person engages before a court or magistrate to observe some condition, e.g., to keep the peace, pay a debt, or appear when summoned (*COD*); or (2) the sum pledged as a surety of this bond. See **recognizance.**

B. Pronunciation. Glanville Williams writes of *cognizance, recognizance,* and *cognizable:* "we refuse to 'take cognisance of' the intrusive 'g' in speaking, though we do in writing." *Learning the Law* 64 (11th ed. 1982). That may be so in the best speech of English lawyers */**kon**-i-zəns/* (etc.), but not in BrE generally or in AmE—in which the pronunciations are */**kog**-ni-zəns/*, */ri-**kog**-ni-zəns/*, and */**kog**-ni-zə-bəl/*. Cf. **cognoscente.**

cognizant; cognisant. The *-z-* spelling is preferred in AmE and in BrE.

cognoscente, sing.; **cognoscenti,** pl. This word, almost always used in the plural (*-ti*), is misspelled only a little less frequently than it is used. E.g., "The criminal *cogniscenti* [read *cognoscenti*] will quickly learn that, when this judge's proffer is rejected, the defendant, if convicted, will pay a higher price; it is a denial of due process for the judge thus to stain his robes." That example illustrates an ironic use of the term; generally, *experts* or *authorities* will suffice, either one being easier to spell—not to mention to pronounce */kon-yə-**shent**-ee/* or */kog-nə-**shent**-ee/*.

cognoscible. See **cognizable.**

COGSA; C.O.G.S.A.; Cogsa. This acronym, for the Carriage of Goods by Sea Act, is generally rendered *COGSA,* though at least one well-written treatise makes it *Cogsa.* See Grant Gilmore & Charles L. Black, *The Law of Admiralty* 93–192 (2d ed. 1975).

cohabit, the verb for *cohabitation,* is analogous to *inhabit.* "To *cohabit* is to dwell together," says one treatise, "so that matrimonial cohabitation is the living together of a man and woman ostensibly as husband and wife." 1 Joel P. Bishop, *Marriage, Divorce, and Separation* § 1669, at 694 (1891).

Cohabitate is a misbegotten BACK-FORMATION: "As more couples adopt this lifestyle, our courts will be called upon with increasing frequency to settle disputes over the legal rights of *cohabitating* [read *cohabiting*] couples."

cohabitant; cohabitor; cohabitee. *Cohabitee,* though increasingly common (esp. in BrE) for a person living with another as if married, is etymologically the poorest form. (See -EE.) It ought to be avoided—e.g.: "The issue in the case was whether section 1 of the Domestic Violence and Matrimonial Proceedings Act 1976 conferred jurisdiction on a County court judge to order a man who was joint tenant of a council flat to vacate the premises on the application of the female *cohabitee* [read *cohabitant*] who had suffered horrifying violence at his hands." Rupert Cross & J.W. Harris, *Precedent in English Law* 112 (4th ed. 1991).

Cohabitant, derived from the present participle of the Latin verb, is etymologically preferable. (See *OED 2*.) *Cohabitor* is a NEEDLESS VARIANT. For still another variant, see **CUPOS.**

cohabit(at)ive. The general rule is that, in Latinate nouns of this type, the adjectival form derives from the nominal form. Thus *cohabitative* is the correct form, following from the noun *cohabitation.*

cohabitee; cohabitor. See **cohabitant.**

co-heir (= a joint heir) is generally hyphenated thus, though the estimable *Century Dictionary* (1895) makes it *coheir.* (See CO- (A).) E.g., "A group of persons considered in law as a single unit, might succeed as *co-heirs* to the Inheritance." Henry S. Maine, *Ancient Law* 150 (17th ed. 1901; repr. [New Universal Lib.] 1905, 1910).

cohort(s). AmE legal usage, traditional and formal though it is, has given in to the modern sense (some would say corruption) of this word—e.g.: "Respondent and two *cohorts* were indicted for robbing a savings and loan." Traditionally, *cohort* has been a mass noun denoting "a band of warriors." "The extension of *cohort* to nonmilitary uses is natural enough," Follett writes,

> but if the word is to retain its force it should observe two requirements: (1) it should designate members, too numerous to be conveniently counted, of some sort of united group, and (2) it should imply some sort of struggle or contest. *No one of the candidates succeeded in completely marshaling his cohorts before the first ballot / To the legion of the lost ones, to the cohort of the damned*—in such uses the sense of the word is preserved.
>
> Wilson Follett, *Modern American Usage* 99 (1966).

This is a very conservative view of the word, especially given the fact that the sense "colleague, associate, companion" has been by far the most common in the last quarter century. E.g., "Senator Biden and his *cohorts* didn't hear, but it appears that thousands of others did." *Mr. Bork's Book,* Wall St. J., 8 Dec. 1989, at A10. Nevertheless, this newer meaning has remained a rather informal one for this respectable word, which in formal writing should retain its older sense.

Follett's sense (1) is common in phrases such as *baby-boom cohort* and *birth cohort,* the latter being defined as a "group, born in the same year, selected for study as the individuals march through time so that researchers can assess the nature and influence of factors affecting their behavior." See Dermot Walsh & Adrian Poole, *A Dictionary of Criminology* 22 (1983).

coif. The Order of the Coif is an organization of great distinction among those who excel in studying law in American universities. The name comes from the title given to *serjeants-at-law* or *serjeants of the coif,* the barristers of high standing in common-law courts. They took their name, through the linguistic process known as metonymy, from the linen headpieces they wore: "The coif (a close-fitting cap of white lawn) which the judges wore they wore as serjeants, and neither judge nor serjeant ever doffed his coif 'even in he presence of the king, even though he is talking to His Highness.'" Alan Harding, *A Social History of English Law* 174 (1966). See **Order of the Coif.**

coin a phrase. To *coin* is to mint afresh, to invent, or to make current; it does not mean "to employ," as persons who commit the following error apparently think: "*To coin an old phrase,* we are guardedly optimistic." One cannot coin an *old* phrase.

Here something is truly coined: "It will be the age of, to coin a rather clumsy neologism, countrycules." Edwin M. Yoder, Jr., *Strange New World: The Rise of the Modern Micro-State,* Wash. Post, 24 June 1990, at C2.

Coke, Lord. The name is pronounced as if it were *Cook.* Getting it wrong is the mark of a legal novice.

cold blood. The metaphor derives from long-outmoded physiological theories about how human blood can boil or become very cold depending on one's passion, physical exertion, or excitement. It signifies what is done "coolly," with time for decision or even reflection.

Though the phrase is part of everyday speech, criminal-law commentators find it useful: "While it is true, to take a test from the homicide cases, that one may incite in the heat of passion what another carries out in *cold blood,* it is also true that one, acting with malicious premeditation, may instigate that which is perpetrated by another at once in the heat of passion." Rollin M. Perkins & Ronald N. Boyce, *Criminal Law* 763 (3d ed. 1982).

cold check. See **check, worthless.**

coliseum; colosseum; Colosseum. For the amphitheater of Vespasian at Rome, *Colosseum* is the correct name. For any other large building or assembly hall, the word is *coliseum* (AmE) or *colosseum* (BrE).

collaborate. See **corroborate (C).**

collapsible. So spelled. See -ABLE (A).

collate. See **collocate.**

collateral, n., = (1) a person collaterally related to a decedent; or (2) security for a loan. See **collateral kinship**; see also **ascendant (B)** & **collateralize** (sense 2).

collateral estoppel. A. And *issue preclusion; res judicata; claim preclusion.* The lines of demarcation in meaning are distinct; yet these terms have long caused confusion among judges and advocates. *Collateral estoppel* and *issue preclusion* (= BrE *issue estoppel*) are synonymous; the latter phrase has sprung perhaps from a desire to be more descriptive in naming this legal doctrine. *Collateral estoppel* is the doctrine that prevents the relitigation of an issue that was actually litigated and was a critical and necessary part of the earlier judgment. The judgment on the issues litigated in the first action, then, is binding upon the parties in all later litigation in which those issues arise.

Res judicata—also called *claim preclusion*—is the same principle, but broader: when a matter has been finally adjudicated by a court of competent jurisdiction, none of the original parties may reopen or challenge that previous determination. *Res judicata* implies, then, that no further issues exist relating to the dispute, whereas with *collateral estoppel* there may be other adjudicable issues. The best way of remembering these doctrines clearly is to view *collateral estoppel* as a miniature of *res judicata:* the former applies to issues, the latter to entire claims or lawsuits.

One might cite any number of instances in which judges have written *collateral estoppel* when they meant *res judicata* and vice versa. E.g., "Although the court of appeals in our present case speaks in terms of *res judicata* . . . , the court actually applies principles of *collateral estoppel* in affirming the award of indemnity. . . . *Collateral estoppel* is narrower than *res judicata.* It is frequently [termed] *issue preclusion* because it bars relitigation of any ultimate issue of fact actually litigated and essential to the judgment in a prior suit." *Bonniwell v. Beech Aircraft Corp.,* 663 S.W.2d 816, 818 (Tex. 1984). See Fleming James, *Civil Procedure* 549–50 (1965) (noting that *res judicata* "has been given a good many different meanings" and suggesting, further, that *res judicata* is the genus of which *collateral estoppel* is one species).

B. And *direct estoppel.* The *Restatement of Judgments* distinguishes between these two phrases in this way: *collateral estoppel* applies to later controversies involving some of the same facts but a different cause of action, whereas *direct estoppel* applies to later controversies involving the same cause of action (where the plaintiff's cause of action is not extinguished by the rules of merger and bar). See *Restatement of Judgments* 176 (1942). See **merger (B).**

collateralize = (1) to serve as collateral for; (2) to make (a loan) secure with collateral. This word looks newfangled, and it is, having been recorded only as far back as 1931: "'[H]e found he did not have sufficient paper to *collateralize* the note . . . .'" *Dealer's Finance Co. v. Coulter,* 3 F. Supp. 114, 115 (W.D. Ark. 1931) (quoting testimony) (antedating *W10*'s earliest citation by 10 years).

For real-estate lawyers (*conveyancers,* q.v.) and bankers, however, this Americanism is a useful word for summing up what otherwise would take several words. Both senses are common—e.g.: (Sense 1) "The property purchased *collateralized* the notes."/ (Sense 2) "It is significant that the bank realized that the loan was *collateralized.*"

collateral kinship; lineal kinship. These phrases denote the two types of kinship. *Lineal kinship* exists between persons connected in a direct line of descent—such as father and son, grandmother and granddaughter, and the like. *Collateral kinship* exists among those who descend from the same common ancestor but not from one another—such as sister and sister, or cousin and cousin.

collateral obligation; accessorial obligation. Both terms refer to the liability of a person, such as a guarantor, bound on another's debt. *Collateral obligation* has, in modern usage, supplanted *accessorial obligation.* Small wonder.

collateral order = an interlocutory order that is an offshoot from the principal litigation in which it is issued, and that is generally immediately appealable as a "final decision" without regard to whether the principal litigation is final. See Charles A. Wright, *The Law of Federal Courts* 701 (4th ed. 1983).

collateral-order doctrine (= the doctrine, first laid down in *Cohen v. Beneficial Finance Corp.,* 337 U.S. 541 (1949), that made some collateral orders appealable) is best hyphenated thus. See PHRASAL ADJECTIVES (A).

collect is a verb sometimes used loosely, especially in the press. As every lawyer knows, being awarded damages is quite a different thing from collecting them: "Under Thursday's ruling, plaintiffs could *collect* [read *seek* or *receive*] damages from local governments only if they proved that discrimination resulted not from the act of an individual but from an official policy." Choyke, *High Court Backs DISD in Rights Suit,* Dallas Morning News, 23 June 1989, at 1A. Perhaps most local governments would be good for most judgments, but to use *collect* in this way is sloppy thinking about the law. *Receive,* which sounds closely akin to *collect,* is actually quite different because it connotes a giver (the jury).

The mistake is surprising when it occurs in the prose of model legal writers—e.g.: "If an action *in personam* against the shipowner has been joined to the action *in rem* against the ship, there is no difficulty in *collecting* [read *being awarded*] the deficiency *from* [read *against*] the defendant in the *in personam* action." Grant Gilmore & Charles L. Black, Jr., *The Law of Admiralty* 801 (2d ed. 1975).

collectible; collectable. The *-ible* spelling is preferred. See -ABLE (A).

COLLECTIVE NOUNS. Consistency in the use of singular or plural is the main consideration in the skillful handling of collective nouns. A judge who in the beginning of an opinion writes *the jury was* should refer to *jury* as a singular noun throughout. A judge who wishes to emphasize the individual persons more than the body of persons may decide to write *the jury were.*

But switching back and forth between a singular and a plural verb is lamentably common: "Mark Pattison's *Memoirs* is not strictly speaking an autobiography . . . . His *Memoirs* do not so much tell the story of his life . . . . Mark's father, as the *Memoirs* make plain, dominated his son's early years . . . . The *Memoirs* describes clearly . . . ." V.H.H. Green, Introduction, Mark Pattison, *Memoirs of an Oxford Don* 1, 6 (1988).

Apart from the desire for consistency, there is little "right" and "wrong" on this subject: collective nouns take sometimes a singular and sometimes a plural verb. The trend in the U.S. is to regard the collective noun as expressing a unit; hence, the singular is the usual form. When the individuals in the collection or group receive the emphasis, the plural verb is acceptable. E.g., "[T]he law-of-nature school were not wholly in error . . . ." Roscoe Pound, *The Formative Era in American Law* 63 (1938). But generally in AmE writing collective nouns take singular verbs, as in *the jury finds, the panel is, the faculty demands, the board has decided, the Supreme Court is,* and so on.

Just the opposite habit generally obtains in G.B., where collective nouns tend to take plural verbs. A text in BrE on statute-drafting has even attempted to enshrine this habit, though without giving reasons: "Though the practice varies, in legislative DRAFTING it is advisable to treat collective nouns as plural: that is, such nouns as *authority* or *Board* should be followed by a verb in the plural." Alison Russell, *Legislative Drafting and Forms* 86 (1938). The British tend to write, for example, "The *board have* considered the views of the judges of the appellate division." (Eng.)

BrE has gone so far in some contexts that many Americans would suspect a typographical error: "Oxford were the winners of the 136th University Boat Race, but many will say that Cambridge were the heroes." Richard Burnell, *Oxford Hold Off Brave Light Blues,* Sunday Times, 1 April 1990, at B1.

In the days soon after the American Revolution, not surprisingly, the American practice was closer to the prevailing British practice. E.g., "The House of Representatives shall chuse *their* [modernly, *its*] Speaker and other Officers; and shall have the sole Power of Impeachment." U.S. Const. art. I, § 2./ "The Senate shall chuse *their* other Officers . . . ." U.S. Const. art. I, § 3.

The reversal in practice has become so firmly established in the U.S. that it is hardly wrong to say that, with certain collective nouns, singular verbs are *preferred.* One cannot be doctrinaire on this point of usage, however. The dilemma frequently occurs with nouns such as *majority* and *press* and *faculty.* E.g., "The press *have* [read (in U.S.) *has*] the same rights that the rest of the community *have* [read (in U.S.) *has*]."/ "Constitutionalizing basic welfare benefits for the poor will not happen as long as the middle class *remain* [read (in U.S.) *remains*] so conservative, so numerous, and so prosperous." (For examples with *jury,* see the entry under that word.)

These are questions more of local idiom than of correct or incorrect grammar. *Majority* can be especially troublesome for those seeking consistency. "The majority in *their* [read (in U.S.) *its*] footnote 6 *allude* [read *alludes*] to the testimony of Hinojosa." This preference for singular verbs with *majority* leads us down unidiomatic paths in sentences such as this, however, in which the noun best takes the plural verb: "A majority of the members of the committee *are* [rather than *is*] satisfied that the applicant is qualified for membership. See COUNT NOUNS AND MASS NOUNS.

On the question whether to use a singular or a plural verb after constructions such as *a number of people* and *a host of problems,* see SYNESIS.

collectively termed. Lawyers frequently use, in definitions, a phrase such as *herein collectively termed* "———." A question that sometimes arises is whether that last word can be plural, as when the writer enumerates a number of specific railroads and then writes *collectively termed Railroads.* Grammar and common sense alike allow that phrasing. But common sense disallows *herein,* q.v.

collegial; collegiate. It would serve the purposes of DIFFERENTIATION, and would not run counter to educated usage, to reserve *collegial* as the adjective corresponding to *colleague,* and *collegiate* as the adjective for *college.*

collide. See **allide.**

collision; allision. Both are used, in the U.S. law of admiralty, in reference to vessels that meet each other unexpectedly. In an *allision,* one of the vessels is stationary. In a *collision,* usually both are moving, although *collision* does not necessarily imply force from each of the clashing objects.

Since we have this DIFFERENTIATION in the terminology of admiralty, however, we should observe the distinction, if only in this limited context. E.g., "The litigation before us arises out of a series of four *collisions* by ships over a two-month period." In the following sentence, *allision* would have been the better word: "This case arises out of a *collision* [read *allision*] that allegedly occurred between a tug owned by Dow and a boat docked alongside the plaintiff's shrimp boat." (The docked boat was stationary, presumably.) Even specialized authorities have used *collision* in this way, however: "The anchored vessel is almost, and usually quite, helpless to avoid *collision,* and moving vessels must keep clear of her." John W. Griffin, *The American Law of Collision* § 145, at 348 (1949). See **allide.**

Allision is most properly used only of two ships, and not, e.g., of a ship and a bridge or dock: "This case arises out of an *allision* [read *collision* or *accident*] that occurred after midnight in early 1982, when the Tug Beth, with two barges in tow, struck the closed lift span of the Galveston Railway Causeway Bridge."/ "The dock, on the bank of the Calcasieu River near Lake Charles, was struck by the barge on July 4; at some point before the *allision* [read *collision* or *mishap*], a socket had failed."

collocate; collate. *Collocate* = (v.t.) to arrange in place; to set side by side; (v.i.) to occur in tandem with something else. *Collate* = (1) to compare minutely and critically; (2) to collect and compare for the purpose of arranging accurately; or (3) to assemble in proper order <he collated the appendixes to the brief>.

Both terms are useful in legal analysis, *collocate* being perhaps more common, especially in the form of the noun *collocation* (= a distinct arrangement, esp. of words). E.g., "The element in intellectual productions that secures copyright protection is not the knowledge, truths, ideas, or emotions that the composition expresses, but the *collocation* of visible or audible points—of lines, colors, sounds, or words."/ "In considering the general question of property in news matter, it is necessary to distinguish between the substance of the information and the particular form or *collocation* of words in which the writer has communicated it."

collogue; colloque. Both are informal words meaning "to confer in private." Krapp labeled *collogue*—the more common word—"colloquial for *talk confidentially.*" George P. Krapp, *A Comprehensive Guide to Good English* 152 (1927). Either would be useful as a verb corresponding to the noun *colloquy,* q.v., which is frequently found in legal prose. Because it is already more common, *collogue* is more likely to gain wide acceptance.

COLLOQUIALITY, within the bounds of modesty and naturalness, is to be encouraged in legal writing as a counterbalance to the frequent use of rigid and pompous formalities. Many people misunderstand the meaning of *colloquiality,* however. The term is not a label for substandard usages; rather, it means "a conversational style." The writer of this sentence demonstrates an understanding of the term's meaning: "The Federal Securities Act of 1933 and state statutes *colloquially* called 'blue sky laws' require corporations to register issues of securities with the SEC or state security commissions before they are sold publicly."

The best legal minds look kindly upon colloquiality: "[A]lthough there are no certain guides [in the interpretation of a statute], the *colloquial* meaning of the words of the statute is itself one of the best tests of purpose." *Brooklyn Nat'l Corp. v. C.I.R.,* 157 F.2d 450, 451 (2d Cir. 1946) (per L. Hand, J.). "The courts will not be astute to discover fine distinctions in words, nor scholastic differentiations in phrases, so long as they are sufficiently in touch with affairs to understand the meaning which the man on the street attributes to ordinary English." *Vitagraph Co. v. Ford,* 241 F. 681, 686 (S.D.N.Y. 1917).

All this is to say that colloquiality is fine in its place. In formal legal writing, occasional colloquialisms may serve to give the prose more variety and texture; they may even be appropriate in judicial opinions in moderation. Still, the colloquial tone should not overshadow the generally serious tone of legal writing, and should never descend into slang.

Good writers would not always agree on where to draw that line. Some judges feel perfectly comfortable using a picturesque verb such as *squirrel away:* "This sufficed, in the absence of any record-backed hint that the prosecution . . . *squirrelled* [read *squirreled*] the new transcript *away.*" *U.S. v. Chaudhry,* 850 F.2d 851, 859 (1st Cir. 1988). Others would disapprove. A stylist like Justice Jackson writes forcefully of *blasting* a party's marriage where nonstylists would probably refer to *terminating the matrimonial relationship.* See *Rice v. Rice,* 336 U.S. 674, 680 (1949) (Jackson, J., dissenting). Some, like Justice Douglas, would use *pell mell:* "The circuits are in conflict; and the Court goes *pell mell* for an escape for this conglomerate from a real test under existing antitrust law." *Missouri Portland Cement Co. v. Cargill, Inc.,* 418 U.S. 919, 923 (1974) (Douglas, J., dissenting). Others would invariably choose a word like *indiscriminately* instead. Some, like Chief Justice Rehnquist, would use the phrase *Monday-morning quarterbacking.* See *Vermont Yankee Nuclear Power Corp. v. Natural Resources Defense Council, Inc.,* 435 U.S. 519, 547 (1978). Or *double-whammy.* See *American Bankers Ass'n v. SEC,* 804 F.2d 739, 749 (D.C. Cir. 1986).

For my part, I side with the colloquialists. In a profession whose writing suffers from verbal arteriosclerosis, some relaxation—and perhaps even some thinning of the blood—is in order. But progress comes slowly. The battle that Oliver Wendell Holmes fought in 1924 is repeated every day in law offices and judicial chambers throughout this country. Remember that Holmes wanted to say, in an opinion, that amplifications in a statute would "stop rat holes" in it. Chief Justice Taft criticized, predictably, and Holmes answered that law reports are dull because we believe "that judicial dignity require[s] solemn fluffy speech, as, when I grew up, everybody wore black frock coats and black cravats." 2 *Holmes–Pollock Letters* 132 (M. Howe ed. 1941). Too many lawyers still write as if they habitually wore black frock coats and black cravats.

colloquy; colloquium. The plural form of *colloquy* (= a formal discussion, as between a judge and counsel) is *colloquies.* Following is a typical use of the word: "The record from the state court contains no *colloquy* between appellant and the court with respect to this issue." (The old word in this sense was *interview,* common in the 19th c.) The verb corresponding to *colloquy* is *collogue,* q.v.

Colloquium (= an academic conference or seminar) is frequently misspelled *colloquim. W10* prefers the plural *-quiums,* the (British) *COD -quia.* Many academicians seem to use *colloquia* (and even *auditoria*) merely to avoid possible criticism by colleagues, however unwarranted.

collude. Occasionally this word is misunderstood, primarily by nonlawyers, to mean "to collaborate," rather than (properly) "to collaborate in wrongdoing."

collusion = (1) an agreement between two or more persons to defraud another; (2) an agreement by which the defendant allows the plaintiff to sue so as to confer jurisdiction on the court; (3) in divorce proceedings (in the days before no-fault divorces), an agreement between husband and wife for one or the other to commit (or appear to commit) adultery or another marital breach in order to obtain a divorce. *Collusion* always has the flavor of fraud.

The mistake cited under *collude*—i.e., using *collusion* for *collaboration*—is fairly common: Fowler cites the example, "The two authors, both professors at Innsbruck, appear to be working in *collusion* [read *collaboration*]" (*MEU2* 95).

collusive; collusory. *Collusive* (= of, relating to, or involving a secret agreement or understanding for illegal or deceitful ends) is preferred; *collusory* is a NEEDLESS VARIANT.

color. In the phrase *under color of state law,* the word *color* = appearance, semblance, guise. The development of this bit of legal JARGON is instructive:

> Sometimes a party put in a plea designed to make what was really a point of fact appear to be a point of law, so as to transfer the decision from the jury to the judge: this was called *colour.* The expression was in due course applied to the title . . . in question. "If the defendant," wrote Blackstone, "in assise or action of trespass, be desirous to refer

the validity of his title to the court rather than to the jury, he may state his title specially, and at the same time *give colour* to the plaintiff, bad indeed in point of law, but of which the jury are not competent judges." Blackstone, *Commentaries* 309 (emphasis in original).

Jocelyn Simon, *English Idioms from the Law,* 76 Law Q. Rev. 429, 440 (1960) (Part 2).

Alongside this sense of an apparent or prima facie title or right there has developed the modern expressions *no color of title, no color of right,* and *no color of law,* meaning without any sort of title or right.

colorable is used in law in the sense "having at least a prima facie aspect of justice or validity" (*OED*) <a colorable claim to property>.

The word has been extended to a broader sense, as if it were synonymous with *ostensible* or *apparent:* "Of the documents prepared by the attorneys themselves, none were even colorably prepared in anticipation of this or any other litigation." *U.S. v. Davis,* 636 F.2d 1028, 1040 (5th Cir. 1981). One might be tempted at first to brand this usage a SLIPSHOD EXTENSION, but it is old—Justice Story used *colorable* in this way in charging a jury in 1814. See *Odiorne v. Winkley,* 18 F. Cas. 581, 582 (C.C.D. Mass. 1814) (No. 10,432) ("Mere *colorable* alterations of a machine are not enough . . . "). See **color.**

colore officii (= by or under color of office) is a LATINISM without redeeming value. "As a general rule, the corporation is not responsible for the unauthorized and unlawful acts of its officers, though done *colore officii.*"

The English equivalent serves better, and most readers will not pass it over uncomprehendingly, as they will the Latinism. Further, the English phrase is common—e.g.: "Common-law extortion is the corrupt collection of an unlawful fee by an officer *under color of office* . . . ." Rollin M. Perkins & Ronald N. Boyce, *Criminal Law* 443 (3d ed. 1982).

color of office. See ***colore officii.***

colosseum. See **coliseum.**

combination; confederacy; conspiracy. The first two are more neutral than the third. E.g., "Appellants announce their willingness to accept this definition of the boycott, substituting the word *confederacy* or *combination* for *conspiracy.*" *Combination* = the banding together or union of persons for the pursuance of some common goal. The *OED* notes that it was formerly used synonymously with *conspiracy,* but it has appreciated in meaning. E.g., "A strike is one of the legal means to which parties have a right to resort to enforce a legal *combination.*" Today *combination* is often used in antitrust contexts. *Confederacy* = a union by league or contract between persons, bodies of men, or states, for mutual support or joint action; a league, alliance, compact (*OED*). The *OED* states that in law this word has traditionally been given a bad sense, as if synonymous with *conspiracy*; no longer is such a meaning predominantly given to the word.

Both *confederacy* and *combination* may refer to an agreement by two or more persons to do an illegal act, but this sense is best reserved for a third word. *Conspiracy* = an agreement between two or more people to behave in a manner that will automatically constitute an offense by at least one of them (e.g., two people agree that one of them shall steal while the other waits in a getaway car) (*CDL*).

combine, n., is an American business colloquialism synonymous with *combination,* usually implying fraudulent or anticompetitive ends. Krapp disapproved of this use of the word in 1927, and Bernstein approved of it in 1965, but only as a casualism. So it remains. See **combination.**

come down is the intransitive PHRASAL VERB used of judicial decisions. E.g.,"When the decision finally *came down* in October it was based upon more study than a case ordinarily receives in our court or in any other with an equally heavy docket." Cf. its counterparts in the active voice, **hand down a decision.**

come(s) now; now comes. Traditionally the standard commencements in pleadings, these phrases are falling into long-overdue disuse. During the late 1980s and early 1990s, judges in four American states (Florida, Louisiana, Michigan, and Texas) were polled on whether they preferred the legalistic opener (*Now comes the plaintiff, John Jones, by and through his attorneys of record, and would show unto the court the following*) as opposed to a plain-language version (*Plaintiff complains of defendant and says*). Not surprisingly, more than 80 percent of them preferred the shorter, more direct version. Yet many lawyers—most in Texas and probably elsewhere—stick to the tired old wordy forms.

The phrasing *comes now* is an example of archaic INVERSION. *Comes now* is the form for a singular, *come now* for a plural subject. It is not uncommon for modern pleaders to bungle SUBJECT-VERB AGREEMENT with inverted phrases of this kind, as in "*Comes now the plaintiffs, Russ and Leslie Blanchard* [read *Come now the plaintiffs* . . .]." The wording in a judicial order analogous to this phrase is "*Came on* for consideration the defendant's motion."

Comes now the plaintiff is occasionally mispunctuated—e.g.: "*Comes, now, the plaintiff* . . . ." The first comma in the phrase should follow *plaintiff,* after which the person's name acts as an APPOSITIVE. Placing a comma after the verb betrays the writer's misunderstanding of the inversion of subject and verb. This antiquated wording is sometimes modernized *now comes.*

come to court is the BrE equivalent of *go to trial,* q.v. E.g., "Among critics of the existing system is the woman at the centre of last week's trial, an American who waited a year for the case to *come to court.*" *Judges' Old Boy Network Under Fire After Rape Trial,* Sunday Times, 15 April 1990, at A5. An American journalist writing that sentence would have phrased it *go to trial, reach trial,* or *get to court.*/ "It took 12 years for the Jack Bernardent case to *come to court.*" Melcher, *Leuvre Accused Over "Theft" of Tapestries,* The European, 13–15 July 1990, at 2.

comic(al); comedic. These words are confusingly similar. *Comic* and *comical* both mean "funny" or "humorous." *Comic* is generally used, however, of what is intentionally funny, and *comical* of what is unintentionally funny. Hence the latter term may mean "laughable" in a derisive sense. *Comedic* = of or pertaining to the form or nature of a dramatic comedy (as the opposite of *tragic*).

comingle. See **com(m)ingle.**

coming on for hearing. See **came on for hearing.**

comity = courtesy among political entities (as nations or courts of different jurisdictions). The term is often defined as if it were wholly a matter of international law, as here: "*Comity,* in the legal sense, is neither a matter of absolute obligation, on the one hand, nor of mere courtesy and good will, upon the other. But it is the recognition which one nation allows within its territory to the legislative, executive or judicial acts of another nation, having due regard both to international duty and convenience, and to the rights of its own citizens, or of other persons who are under the protection of its laws." *Hilton v. Guyot,* 159 U.S. 113, 163-64 (1895). (On the lack of PARALLELISM between *neither* and *nor* in that sentence, see CORRELATIVE CONJUNCTIONS (A).)

But *comity* applies also to political entities within a given country. E.g., "[T]he decision to extradite is a matter of *comity* between sister states." *State v. Robbins,* 590 A.2d 1133, 1138 (N.J. 1991)./ "While our research has not uncovered a reported case involving an attempt by a state or local government to prohibit its employees from contributing to partisan campaigns in other states, we suspect any such attempt would offend the principle of interstate *comity* . . . ." *City of Cincinnati v. Ohio Council 8,* 576 N.E.2d 745, 756 (Ohio 1991).

The word is sometimes—esp. in BrE—mistaken as meaning "league" or "federation," esp. in the phrase *comity of nations.* For example, Bertrand Russell spoke out in 1915 against World War I and said: "A month ago Europe was a peaceful *comity* of nations . . . " (as quoted in *Differences of Opinion,* Sunday Times, 8 Dec. 1991). Nearly 80 years later the usage persists, but primarily in British writing—e.g.: "What with . . . South Africa's readmission to the *comity* of nations . . . , this is far from fanciful." Ivo Tennant, *Gatting Lobby Holds Out for Change of Heart,* The Times (London), 18 April 1992 (sport section).

commander-in-chief. Pl. *commanders-in-chief.*

COMMAS. See PUNCTUATION (C).

COMMA SPLICES. See RUN-ON SENTENCES.

commemorative; commemoratory. The usual form is *-tive; -tory* is a NEEDLESS VARIANT.

commence; begin; start. Except in describing formal ceremonies or exercises, or legal actions, *commence* is usually unnecessarily stilted for *begin,* with which it is denotatively equivalent. The *OED* notes that "*begin* is preferred in ordinary use; *commence* has more formal associations with law and procedure, combat, divine service, and ceremon[y]." *Commence* is justified in the following sentences: "This action was *commenced* against the defendants under these circumstances, the father having died before the *commencement* of the action."/ "It is settled that a prevailing party may recover fees for time spent before the formal *commencement* of the litigation on such matters as attorney-client interviews."

Following are examples of the stilted *commence:* "Early in the year 1922 some newcomers *commenced* [read *began*] selling papers in a London area which, in the opinion of the London district council of the retail federation, was already sufficiently equipped with retail newsagents." (Eng.)/ "When the plane failed to return, a search was *commenced* [read *started* or *begun*]."/ "Ilsa then *commenced* [read *began*] living in California with her mother during the school year and spending vacations with her father." (One does not, idiomatically, *commence* to live somewhere.) See **begin (B).**

Commence has long been criticized by stylists when introducing an infinitive; *begin* is here preferable: "In most cases, the Mississippi statute *commences* [read *begins*] to run on the date of the wrongful act."

Definite nuances exist with *start* as opposed to *begin* or *commence.* Usually used of physical movement, *start* suggests an abruptness not present in *begin;* one *starts* to do something or engage in some activity (e.g., to run).

commencement. See **introductory clause.**

commendable; commendatory. The former means "praiseworthy, laudable," and the latter means "expressing commendation; laudatory." Like other differentiated pairs ending in the *-able* and *-atory* suffixes, these words are sometimes confused: "It is reprehensible . . . to write a brief primarily to express an uncomplimentary opinion of one's adversary; it is *commendatory* [read *commendable*] to write a brief for the purpose of advising the court; it is neither reprehensible nor *commendatory* [read *commendable*] to write a brief because the client insists—merely good business." Mortimer Levitan, *Confidential Chat on the Art of Briefing,* 1957 Wis. L. Rev. 59, 60.

commensurate; commensurable. In all but mathematical contexts, *commensurable* is a NEEDLESS VARIANT of *commensurate. Commensurable* legitimately means "having, or reducible to, a common measure; divisible without remainder by the same quantity" (*OED*). *Commensurate* means: (1) "coextensive"; or (2) "proportionate." Here the rarer term, *commensurable,* is used where its sibling should appear: "The policy initially issued must be read to cover all the expenses arising from Gina's mental disability, *commensurably* [read *commensurately* (i.e., coextensively)] with coverage from other illnesses."

comment(ate). Although the longer form is a BACK-FORMATION from *commentator,* it is an established one dating from the late 18th century. If *commentate* were only a NEEDLESS VARIANT of *comment,* its existence would be unjustified. But it has undergone DIFFERENTIATION, and today means "to give a commentary on" or "to expound persuasively or interpretatively." Meanwhile, *comment* implies brevity. Hence legal commentators typically *commentate* rather than *comment* when expounding the law. The word *commentate* is, of course, grandiose when used of television journalists who cover sporting events, though it is too late to object to their being called *commentators.*

commentator; commenter. In law, these ordinary words have special senses. *Commentators* are usually scholars who write within a particular field; *commenters,* in AmE, are those who send comments to an agency about a proposed administrative rule.

commerce. Formerly, *commerce* was usable in all the senses of *intercourse;* hence the phrase *sexual commerce* (= sexual intercourse) in many older legal writings (not necessarily involving prostitution). See **intercourse.**

commercial bribery. See **bribery.**

commercial domicile. See **domicil(e) (C).**

commercial law = (1) traditionally, the law merchant, i.e., a system of justice that merchants created to govern their affairs separately from the systems of civil, criminal, and ecclesiastical justice; or (2) *in AmE,* the substantive law dealing with the sale and distribution of goods, negotiable instruments, and the financing of credit transactions on the security of the goods sold. Sense (2), now the primary sense, has spread beyond AmE: "Today the term '*commercial law*' has assumed a new meaning, a meaning [that] is new at least to Europe, but not so to the United States or to Louisiana. I refer, of course, to the meaning in which the term is used to describe a certain area of expertise in legal practice or learning, or that branch of the law . . . of special interest to business people. It is in this sense that the term is used in the United States in the title of the Uniform Commercial Code . . . ." Max Rheinstein, "Problems and Challenges of Contemporary Civil Law of Obligations," in *Essays on the Civil Law of Obligations* 10–11 (Joseph Dainow ed., 1969).

commercial paper. See **negotiable instruments.**

comminate; comminute. The former means "to denounce," the latter "to pulverize."

com(m)ingle. *Commingle* (= to mingle together) is now the accepted spelling. *Comingle,* though slightly older, has failed to become standard. "There has been a tendency to *comingle* [read *commingle*] the Full Faith and Credit Clause of the Constitution with the doctrine of comity by cross-citing various cases between the two principles." *Mingle* has also been used in reference to combining funds, but *commingle* is the more usual term. "The situation is analogous to one where a wrongdoer *mingles* his own funds with other funds he has misappropriated." *Commingles* would ordinarily appear in such a context.

comminute. See **comminate.**

commission. See **commitment.**

commissionee. See -EE.

commissioner; commissionor. The former spelling is standard.

commitment; committal; commission. *Commitment* and *commission* are common words that will here be discussed only to the extent that they are confusable with *committal,* which is in all but two specific senses a NEEDLESS VARIANT. In England, a *committal* in civil proceedings is a method of enforcing judgment by obtaining an order that a person be imprisoned. E.g., "The mode of enforcing decrees in the time of Henry VI down to the end of the reign of Charles I., where the party was taken, appears to have been by *committal* to the Fleet prison; for the Chancellor could not bind the right, he could only coerce the person." 1 George Spence, *Equitable Jurisprudence* 390 (1846)./ "The judge had inherent jurisdiction to make a *committal* order ex parte [committing a delinquent party to jail]." (Eng.) See **committer.**

Committal also has the sense "the action of committing the body to the grave at burial" (*OED*). E.g., "A decent *committal* of the body to the deep in accordance with the custom in such matters ordinarily discharges the duty which the law imposes."

In the sense "the action of committing an insane or mentally retarded person to the charge of another," *commitment* is the usual and the preferred term: "The broad rule generally prevails that a valid proceeding to commit a person to an insane asylum requires an opportunity for the incompetent to be heard before the order of *commitment* is issued."/ "At a proceeding before the Circuit Court of Albemarle County it was adjudged that the infirmities of Mary Thomas did not require the *committal* [read *commitment*] of her person to a guardian." *Commitment* is also the preferred term in the broad sense of "the action of entrusting, giving in charge": "Few men retain their money in their own custody but commit its care to others, both for the feeling of security that such *committal* [read *commitment*] engenders and the facility with which it may be transferred and paid out by means of checks."

Commission is preferred in the sense "the action of doing or perpetrating (as a crime)." The *OED* records examples of *committal* and even of *commitment* in this sense, but these are anomalous.

committable; committible. The first is preferred. See -ABLE (A).

committal. See **commitment.**

committee (= a person who is civilly committed, usu. to a psychiatric hospital) is a splendid example of how lawyers take an ordinary English word and give it an alien sense and pronunciation /*com-i-**tee***/. The usage invites double-takes from both lawyers and nonlawyers: "The civil commitment hearing does not address whether the *committee* has engaged in conduct that constitutes the elements of a crime; rather, that hearing focuses on whether a *committee* is mentally ill or dangerous . . . ." *Benham v. Edwards,* 678 F.2d 511, 538 (5th Cir. 1982). See *Hickey v. Morris,* 722 F.2d 543, 547 (9th Cir. 1983) (referring to the "differences between insanity acquittees and civil *committees*"). Of course, those who have had the privilege of serving on more than a few committees (in the usual sense) may see this usage as a logical extension of meaning. See **acquittee.**

Some writers have used the spelling *commitee* to differentiate the legal from the ordinary use of the word. That spelling, however, violates the principles of DOUBLING OF FINAL CONSONANTS and merely suggests that the writer possesses neither an ear for the language nor a computer with a spelling-checker.

Confusingly, *committee* has still another legal sense—esp. common in BrE—referring not to the psychiatric patient but to the guardian for the patient. E.g., "The appointment of a guardian or *committee* for the person and property of another is not conclusive evidence as to the mental capacity of such person to execute a deed."/ "[T]he '*committee*' of a person of unsound mind was a single person to whom the care of such person was entrusted by the court, the stress being on the last syllable. *Committees* are no longer appointed." Glanville Williams, *Learning the Law* 64 (11th ed. 1982).

committer; committor. These words constitute one of the few pairs with a clear-cut DIFFERENTIATION arising from these variable suffixes. *Committer* is the general word meaning "one who commits (e.g., a crime)." *Committor* is an uncommon legal term for "a judge who commits an insane or mentally retarded person to the charge of another." See -ER (A).

commodatum; accommodatum. The usual spelling of this term from Roman law, meaning "a gratuitous loan (of something) for use without compensation" is *commodatum.*

common. A. And *several.* What is *common* is shared in some way; what is *several* (q.v.) is separate in some way. But the terms are vague enough that they cause problems when used in several common legal tests: "[T]he distinction between a common undivided interest and several and distinct claims is something less than clear. This is to be expected. Except in property law contexts, such terms as *'common'* and 'several' are poor words for a test of jurisdiction—or anything else—since they 'have little or no clear and ascertainable meaning.'" Charles A. Wright, *The Law of Federal Courts* 198 (4th ed. 1983) (quoting Benjamin Kaplan, *Continuing Work of the Civil Committee,* 81 Harv. L. Rev. 356, 380 (1967)).

B. And *mutual.* See **mutual.**

commonality; commonness; commonalty; commonage; commonty. The common character of these words may cause confusion. The ordinary words are *commonality* and *commonness;* although historically the two have overlapped, they are best kept separate, in accordance with the following definitions. *Commonness,* the general noun corresponding to *common,* may mean: (1) "the state or quality of being common" <the commonness today of fax machines>; (2) "the quality of being public or generally used" <the commonness of the thoroughfare>; (3) "the having of run-of-the-mill qualities" <the commonness of his writing>; or (4) "vulgarity" <the commonness of a sot>. *Commonality* = the possession of an attribute in common with another. The term is usual in class-action suits. E.g., "The district court denied class certification because it found that the petitioner had not satisfied the *commonality* and typicality prerequisite of Federal Rule of Civil Procedure 23 [i.e., the class members having claims with factual and legal issues *in common* with one another]."

The remaining words are more easily distinguished. *Commonalty* = (1) commoners; the general body of the community (excluding nobility); (2) a municipal corporation (a sense to be avoided with this word, as *corporation* is the ordinary word); or (3) a general group or body. In the following sentence, by contrast, the writer may be using *commonalty* in sense (3)—a redundancy—or may have intended *commonality:* "The Alabama code stood as a statement of the rules of the game that a family of professionals . . . adhered to in recognition of their *commonalty* [read *commonality?*] and because it might, by forcing an affiliation, help keep them out of trouble." Jethro K. Lieberman, *Crisis at the Bar* 56 (1978).

Commonage = (1) the right of pasturing animals on common land; (2) the condition of land held in common; or (3) an estate or property held in common (*OED*). *Commonty,* in its existing uses, is a NEEDLESS VARIANT of *commonage.*

commonhold (BrE), referring to condominium ownership, is a new system of tenure in G.B., allowing flats to be sold in freehold. E.g., "*Commonhold,* a new form of flat ownership, has been proposed in a Law Commission report published yesterday. *Commonhold,* another name for the US condominium, would provide an alternative to freehold and leasehold ownership, combining their advantages and removing some of the disadvantages." A.H. Hermann, *Alternative to Leasehold of Flats Proposed,* Fin. Times, 23 July 1987, at I-6./ "The system of *commonhold,* announced by the Government last month, could deal with many of the problems which long leasehold tenants and their landlords are experiencing, says a report published yesterday." *New Lease of Life for Victims of Landlords,* Daily Telegraph, 14 Aug. 1991, at 6.

common law. A. As Noun—in Broad Contrasts. In modern usage, *common law* is contrasted with a number of other terms. First, in denoting the body of judge-made law based on that developed originally in England, *common law* is contrasted by comparative jurists to *civil law,* q.v. Second, "with the development of equity and equitable rights and remedies, *common law* and equitable courts, procedure, rights, remedies, etc., are frequently contrasted, and in this sense *common law* is distinguished from *equity*" (*OCL*). Third, the term is similarly distinguished from *ecclesiastical law.* Fourth, it is occasionally used to denote the law common to the country as a whole—as distinguished from law that has only local applications. Finally, and perhaps most commonly within Anglo-American jurisdictions, *common law* is contrasted with *statutory law* <statutes in derogation of the common law are to be strictly construed>.

B. As Noun—Its Specific Senses. The phrase has at least seven senses—and "the precise shade of meaning in which this chameleon phrase is used depends upon the particular context, and upon the contrast that is being made." Glanville Williams, *Learning the Law* 25 n.1 (11th ed. 1982). Among its senses are:

1. in historical England, the "immemorial slow-growing custom declared by juries of free men who gave their verdicts case by case in open

court" (1 Winston Churchill, *A History of the English Speaking Peoples* 225 (1956; repr. 1983));

2. general law as distinguished from special law such as royal decrees and the local customary law of any district (see James Hadley, *Introduction to Roman Law* 43 (N.Y., D. Appleton & Co. 1881) (discussing English common law as "common . . . to all parts of the kingdom, in distinction from the local usages"));—in this sense the phrase is analogous to Fr. *droit commun* & Ger. *Gemeinrecht;*
3. in comparative law, a body of law based on the English legal system, as distinct from a civil-law system;
4. "the set of rules that lawyers use to settle any dispute or problem to which no constitution or statute applies" (Fred Rodell, *Woe Unto You, Lawyers!* 20 (1939; repr. 1980);
5. the power of judges to create new law under the guise of interpreting it (Glanville Williams, *Learning the Law* 29–30 (11th ed. 1982);
6. modern judge-made law (see, e.g., *Bernard Johnson, Inc. v. Continental Constructors, Inc.,* 630 S.W.2d 365, 370 n.4 (Tex. App.—Austin 1982) ("The defense of 'privity of contract' having been established by the common law, it obviously may be abolished by statute or by the common law."));
7. a widely adopted statute (e.g., "Carl Zeitz . . . said the judge's ruling appears to be a 'logical extension' of the common laws [dramshop statutes] that hold taverns partly responsible for damages incurred if they serve alcohol to a visibly intoxicated person." R.B. Smith, *Casinos May Be Held Liable for Drunken Patrons [sic] Losses,* Wall St. J., 23 June 1989, at B1).

Sense (7) is the nonlawyer's unfortunate MISCUE—nothing more. Sense (6) is arguably loose; one book, supporting this sense, states that *common law* is "[s]ometimes referred to as *case law.*" Stephen Foster, *Business Law Terms* 17 (1988). But *common law* really encompasses much more than *caselaw,* q.v., which usually refers to a limited number of cases within a field. Still, drawing the line between *caselaw* and *common law*—esp. as used in a phrase such as *federal common law*—is a difficult, if not impossible, task.

In the U.S.—contrary to popular belief—the common law includes many early English statutes. For example, the crime known as *false pretenses* (q.v.), unknown to English common law, was made a misdemeanor by an English statute old enough to have been incorporated into the common law of American states. Of course, once adopted in the various American states, the common law has grown in a variety of directions, and only rarely does a question of modern American law depend on English common law. As Holmes once acutely observed, "The common law so far as it is enforced in a State, whether called common law or not, is not the common law generally but the law of that State existing by the authority of that State without regard to what it may have been in England or anywhere else." *Black & White Taxicab & Transfer Co. v. Brown & Yellow Taxicab & Transfer Co.,* 276 U.S. 518, 533–34 (1928) (Holmes, J., dissenting). See generally Morris L. Cohen, *The Common Law in the American Legal System,* 81 Law Lib. J. 13, 18 (1989).

C. *At common law.* A LOAN TRANSLATION of the LAW FRENCH *al common ley,* this phrase is the legal idiom used to introduce statements of common-law doctrine—that is, in sense (1) outlined under (B) above. E.g., "*At common law,* the death of the injured person or of the tortfeasor, at any time before verdict, abated the action."/ " '*At common law,*' says Sir W. Erle, 'every person has individually, and the public also have collectively, a right to require that the course of trade be kept free from unreasonable obstruction.' " (Eng.)

Writers and editors occasionally puzzle over whether to use the present or the past tense after this phrase. In the previous paragraph we see an example of each. The distinction lies here: If the doctrinal statement of immemorial law continues to hold true, the present tense is called for; if the statement is of historical interest and the doctrine long since obsolete, the past tense is appropriate.

Oddly, the preposition *at* is not used in any parallel idiom for civil law.

D. As Adjective. The phrase is hyphenated when it serves as a PHRASAL ADJECTIVE but not when it serves as a noun. Both uses are illustrated in this sentence: "But these are all *common-law* cases, and the *common law* has its peculiar rules in relation to this subject." Cf. **civil(-)law (B).**

common-law cheat. See **cheat.**

common-law lawyer; common lawyer. The better form is *common-law lawyer*; the repetition of *law* is no cause for anxieties about REDUNDANCY—e.g.: "But there the court of appeal, the Privy Council, has been largely composed of *common-law lawyers.*" Oliver W. Holmes, *The Common Law* 27–28 (1881; repr. 1946). Several learned writers such as John Chipman Gray, Roscoe Pound, and Lawrence Friedman have used *common-law lawyer.*

But many others—mostly British—have used *common lawyer,* as in the title of Frederick H. Lawson's book, *A Common Lawyer Looks at the Civil Law* (1953). Consider: "On the whole the *common lawyers* used the device well, understanding the purpose for which the fiction was created . . . ." George W. Paton, *A Textbook of Jurisprudence* 58 (4th ed. 1972)./ "The *common lawyer* is pious and platitudinous about the insularity of English law." Samuel J. Stoljar, *A Common Lawyer's French,* 47 Law Lib. J. 119, 119 (1954). The *OED,* interestingly, contains examples of the phrase *common lawyer* dating from as early as 1588.

As if to avoid a MISCUE—as by reading *common lawyer* to be analogous to *common strumpet*—at least two eminent writers have taken to hyphenating the phrase: "Under either view, the *common-lawyers* seem significantly prominent in the creative days of early equity." Theodore F.T. Plucknett, *A Concise History of the Common Law* 180 n.4 (5th ed. 1956)./ "But the *common-lawyers* . . . were forced into the position of saying that the seisin . . . was in the lord . . . ." A.W.B. Simpson, *An Introduction to the History of the Land Law* 150 (1961; repr. 1964).

That urge to hyphenate is understandable, but the hyphen belongs in *common-law lawyer* and not in *common lawyer.*

common-law marriage has one meaning in the U.S., another in Scotland, and still another in England. In the U.S., it generally denotes an agreement to marry, followed by cohabitation and a public recognition of the marriage. Common-law marriages are valid in many states, such as Texas, though others have abolished the institution, as New York did in 1932.

In Scotland, the phrase denotes cohabitation for a substantial period with the acquisition of the reputation of being married (an agreement to marry not being necessary).

And in England, *common-law marriage* is now used only of a marriage celebrated according to a common-law form in a place where the local forms of marriage cannot be used (e.g., a desert island) or are morally unacceptable to the parties (e.g., a Muslim country) or where no cleric is available (*OCL*). Additionally—and more commonly in BrE—the phrase refers to an illicit union of some duration. As Sir Robert Megarry writes, "The so-called *common-law marriage,* little known in England save as a polite verbal cloak for fornication or adultery of the less ephemeral type, has a respectable ancestry in America." *A Second Miscellany-at-Law* 210 (1973).

In none of these jurisdictions is the phrase to be confused with its near-homophone *common-law mortgage.*

COMMON-LAW PLEADINGS. Until the Judicature Act of 1873, the pleadings allowed in English courts were as follows:

Plaintiff	*statement of claim* or *declaration*
Defendant	*defence* (BrE sp.) or *answer*
Plaintiff	*reply* or *replication*
Defendant	*rejoinder*
Plaintiff	*surrejoinder*
Defendant	*rebutter*
Plaintiff	*surrebutter*

Modern practice has been greatly simplified. In English practice today, the pleadings are generally the plaintiff's *statement of claim,* the defendant's *defence,* and (sometimes) the plaintiff's *reply.* In American federal practice, the pleadings are generally the plaintiff's *complaint* and the defendant's *answer,* both of which are commonly amended repeatedly. See **pleading (C),** EQUITY PLEADINGS & WORLD COURT PLEADINGS.

common-law wife is a misnomer of sorts: "No such woman was known to the common law, but [the phrase] means a woman who is living with a man in the same household as if she were his wife. She is to be distinguished from a *mistress,* where the relationship may be casual, impermanent, and secret." *Davis v. Johnson,* [1979] A.C. 264, 270 (per Lord Denning, M.R.). The *OCL* states that "the term *common-law wife* is sometimes applied [no doubt as a EUPHEMISM] to a concubine or mistress where the relationship is of some duration or stability." In AmE, this use of the term is properly considered a corrupt one. See **common-law marriage.**

common lawyer. See **common-law lawyer.**

commonness. See **commonality.**

common pleas, court of. At early common law, common pleas were actions over which the crown did not claim exclusive jurisdiction—as distinguished from *pleas of the crown.* Later, the phrase *common pleas* referred more specifically to civil actions between private citizens.

Through metonymy (as early as the 13th century), *common pleas* came to refer to the court hearing civil actions—a court that lasted in England until 1875, when it was merged into the newly established High Court. Several North American jurisdictions still have courts of common pleas, including the states of Connecticut, Ohio, Pennsylvania, South Carolina, and the province of Ontario.

commonsense, adj.; **commonsensical; commonsensible.** All three forms date from the 19th century. *Commonsense* should generally be preferred over *commonsensical* or *commonsensible* <a commonsense approach>—though *commonsense* may cause a MISCUE if it does not immediately precede the noun it modifies. For example, if Rodell had used *commonsense* here instead of *commonsensible,* some readers might have hesitated: "Ten of the men under whom I took courses were sufficiently skeptical and *common-sensible* about the branches of law they were teaching so that, unwittingly of course, they served together to fortify my hunch about the phoniness of the whole legal process." Fred Rodell, *Woe Unto You, Lawyers!* xx (1939; repr. 1980).

The noun is two words: *common sense.*

commonty. See **commonality.**

commonweal; commonwealth. *Commonweal* = the general welfare or common good. E.g., "Testamentary conditions in general restraint of marriage are regarded as contrary to public policy and to the *commonweal.*"/ "The sixteenth-century ideal of the '*commonweal*'—what would now be called 'public policy'—is an originally Roman principle still invoked in the courts." Alan Harding, *A Social History of English Law* 236 (1966).

Commonwealth = a nation, state, or other political unit <the British Commonwealth>. For the distinction between this term and *dependency* and *territory,* see **territory.**

commorientes = persons who die at the same time, such as spouses who die in an accident. Although this LATINISM would seem to be useful in the context of simultaneous-death statutes, it is little used in the U.S. outside Louisiana. But it does occasionally surface in general American caselaw: "All of that evidence showed prima facie that husband and wife perished in a common disaster as *commorientes* . . . ." *Cruson's Estate v. Long,* 221 P.2d 892, 900 (Or. 1950)./ "Let me next refer for a moment to the general law governing successions from *commorientes* who perish in a common disaster." *In re Fowles' Will,* 158 N.Y.S. 456, 459 (Surr. Ct. 1916). See **simultaneous death.**

Presumably the term is more common in BrE, for it is included in the compendious *CDL.* And it appears in the work of respected British legists—e.g.: "By reason of the English rule relating to *commorientes* the husband was deemed to have died intestate . . . ." R.H. Graveson, *Conflict of Laws* 384 (7th ed. 1974).

In Louisiana usage, *commorientes* has undergone SLIPSHOD EXTENSION to refer not to the persons who die simultaneously, but to the rule of succession regarding such persons. Thus, one occasionally sees references to the *doctrine of commorientes*—e.g.: "Plaintiff suggests that the *doctrine of commorientes* . . . might have applied but for the assumption by the heirs that the deaths were simultaneous." *Morelock v. Aetna Life Ins. Co.,* 63 So. 2d 612, 614 (La. 1953)./ "I do not think it necessary to cope with the difficult problem of whether the doctrine of *commorientes* . . . is applicable to a wrongful death action." *Chateau v. Smith,* 297 So. 2d 268, 271 (La. Ct. App. 1974) (Schott, J., concurring).

communication is often used as a COUNT NOUN in the law of evidence. It refers to any writing or conversation from one person to another or between persons.

Partridge states, in reference to *communicate* and *communication,* that if all you mean by *communicate* is *write* or *tell,* or by *communication* a *note* or a *letter,* then say so. Eric Partridge, *Usage and Abusage* 77 (1973). As a general rule, that advice is well taken; but if the lawyer particularly wishes to emphasize the applicability of a rule of evidence relating to *communications,* use of the longer, broader word is certainly justified.

communicative; communicatory. The latter is a NEEDLESS VARIANT.

communitize, communitization. A. And *unitize, unitization.* These two sets of terms, from the American law of oil and gas, are sometimes used interchangeably but are usefully distinguished. The following definitions are based on those contained in Williams & Meyers, *Oil and Gas Terms* 652, 938 (6th ed. 1984). *Unitization* = the joint operation of all or some portion of a producing reservoir. E.g., "[S]uch leases contain no words of pooling or *unitization.*" R.M. Myers, *The Law of Pooling and Unitization* 46 (1957). The verb *unitize* has been traced back to the mid-19th century, though then in a different context.

Communitize and *communitization* are legal NEOLOGISMS dating from the mid-20th century and recorded in no standard nonlegal dictionary. *Communitization* (known also as *pooling*) = the bringing together of small tracts sufficient for the granting of a well permit under applicable rules for the spacing of wells. E.g., "The Carter Oil Company's answer also alleged that there was an agreement between appellees and certain persons to *communitize* a certain other oil lease with that of plaintiff Rhodes." *Rhodes v. Davis,* 28 N.E.2d 113, 115 (Ill. 1940)./ "[T]here was no *communitization* as a matter of law because all of the royalty owners had not executed or ratified the lease." *May v. Cities Serv. Oil Co.,* 444 S.W.2d 822, 827 n.4 (Tex. Civ. App.—Beaumont 1969).

B. And *communize, communization.* Interestingly, the earliest appearance of *communitize* (c. 1939) was preceded by a variant form—*commu-*

nize (= to make classifiable as community property)—which was used during the 1920s through the 1950s. Professor Patrick H. Martin of Louisiana State University, in a letter of September 1989, observed that *communitize* displaced the shorter form because American farmers, especially in Oklahoma, probably did not want their activities in the 1940s through the 1960s being described as "communizing." Imagine the discomfort that the following sentences might have caused during the McCarthy era: "It is clear, then, that had the legislature attempted by the Community Property Law to transform property then owned by either spouse from separate into community property, such a provision could not have stood the test of constitutionality. But how is the situation different merely because, instead of a provision of that nature, the act *communizes* the future income from such property?" *Willcox v. Penn Mut. Life Ins. Co.,* 55 A.2d 521, 526 (Pa. 1947)./ "The 1939 Community Property Act, discussed by the administratrix, is only of historical significance, and compliance therewith evidenced an intent by husband and wife to *communize* their property." *Davis' Estate v. Oklahoma Tax Comm'n,* 246 P.2d 318, 319 (Okla. 1952).

community charge (BrE) = *poll tax* (BrE), i.e., Prime Minister Margaret Thatcher's controversial (and doomed) measure aimed at increasing government revenue. E.g., "The arguments in favour of a *community charge* are as strong as ever. The domestic rate which it replaces was an inequity founded on a fiction." Bruce Anderson, *The Poll Tax Finds a Worthy Champion,* Sunday Telegraph, 21 Jan. 1990, at 19./ "It must have seemed like a good idea when the Conservative Party proposed it in 1987: a *'community charge,'* the same for every citizen, to cover part of the cost of local government services and replace most real estate taxes. Now, with what has since become known pejoratively as the 'poll tax' and is about to go into effect in England and Wales on April 1, even many of Prime Minister Margaret Thatcher's Conservative Party supporters wish that they had never heard of it." Craig R. Whitney, *Violent Anger Rises in Britain as Date for 'Poll Tax' Nears,* N.Y. Times, 10 March 1990, at 2.

community property; separate property. *Community property* = (1) a system of marital-property rights derived from the Spanish law and now existing in eight American states: Arizona, California, Idaho, Louisiana, Nevada, New Mexico, Texas, and Washington; under this system, spouses are co-owners of all real and personal property that either acquires during the marriage—apart from acquisitions by gift, by will, or by inheritance; (2) property held under this system.

When used attributively as a phrasal adjective, the phrase should be hyphenated thus: *community-property state, community-property rules,* etc. See **ganancial.**

Separate property = property that a married person can sell, give away, or leave to somebody by will without the spouse's consent, and that remains that person's undivided property upon divorce. In specific ways, the phrase carries different meanings in community-property jurisdictions and in common-law (or equitable-distribution) jurisdictions. In community-property jurisdictions, *separate property* refers to a married person's property that is (a) acquired before marriage; (b) acquired during the marriage by gift, by will, or with premarital holdings; or (c) acquired after permanent separation. For the other meanings of *separate property,* see **separate property.**

community service is an increasingly common penal sentence for those whose crimes have injured the community in some way, but who (it is thought) deserve only light punishment. E.g., "Before his brief declaration, his lawyer, Stephen E. Kaufman, asked Judge Lowe to impose a sentence of *community service,* saying that a jail term would serve no purpose." Stephen Labaton, *GAF Fined; Executive Sentenced,* N.Y. Times, 31 March 1990, at 17.

communize. See **communitize (B).**

commute. A. And *commutate.* The latter is a technical term relating to electricity. *Commute* is the legal term meaning (1) "to exchange (a punishment or penalty) for one of less severity"; or (2) "to change (one kind of payment) into or for another; esp. to substitute a single payment for a number of payments, a fixed payment for an irregular or uncertain one, or a payment in money for one in kind (e.g., a tithe)" (*OED*). Today sense (1) of *commute* is more common <the governor commuted his prison sentence to sixty days of community service>.

B. And *pardon.* To *commute* a punishment or penalty is to reduce it, or to substitute in its place a milder punishment or penalty. To *pardon* one who has been convicted or punished is to excuse that person without exacting any penalty.

comp is AmE slang for *compensation*—used most often in the phrase *workers' comp.* E.g., "The House proposal . . . stands a better chance of controlling the *worker comp* drain than the Senate proposal ramrodded by trial lawyer and labor proponents." *Comp Showdown,* Dallas Morning News, 1 Dec. 1989, at 30A.

compact, n., adj. & v.t. The noun is accented on the first syllable, the verb on the second. The adjective is rendered both ways, preferably */kəm-**pakt**/* except in reference to small cars.

compactible; compactable. The former is preferred. See -ABLE (A).

company; corporation. At common law, the technical legal term for an entity having a legal personality was *corporation.* The word *company* could refer to a partnership or other unincorporated association of persons. In current usage, however, *company* almost always refers to an incorporated company—i.e., a corporation. See **corporation.**

company law is the British equivalent of the American phrase *corporate law*—e.g.: "My Lords, this appeal raises a question of some importance to those concerned with the niceties of *company law.*" (Eng.)/ "The bill [the 1856 Joint Stock Companies Bill] was passed, and as consolidated in the giant Companies Act of 1862 is the basis of modern company law." Alan Harding, *A Social History of English Law* 376 (1966). See **corporate law.**

COMPANY NAMES are commonly given abbreviated forms in legal prose. Often writers go to absurd lengths to specify what the short form of the company name is in parentheses, e.g., *Morgan Data Processing and Filming Co., Inc. (hereinafter "Morgan").* This habit becomes ridiculous after we have seen three or four parties with distinctive names treated in this way. The better practice in most legal writing is to give the full name when the party is first identified, and then to use the short form thereafter without parenthetical explanation. When companies named, in short form, *Morgan* and *Stevens* and *Broadmoor* and *Datapoint* are involved in litigation or are parties to a contract, nobody will confuse one with another if only these abbreviated names are used. Omitting the cumbersome *hereinafter* phrases also minimizes the somnifacient effects of LEGALESE.

The exception to this advice, of course, occurs when a man named *Morgan* is sued in conjunction with his company *Morgan, Inc.* When names are confusingly similar, it is best to spell out exactly which abbreviation is used with which name, and then to use those forms consistently. This practice does not require *hereinafter.* E.g., "Plaintiff has sued both John Morgan ('Morgan') and Morgan Inc. ('the Company')."

On the issue of creating acronyms and initialisms from company names—such as "MURB" from Morgan Utility Regulatory Board—see INITIALESE.

comparable; comparative. The former is stressed on the first syllable, the latter on the second. *Comparable* = capable of being compared; worthy of comparison <comparable salaries>. *Comparative* = (1) of or pertaining to comparison <a comparative discourse of the laws>; (2) involving comparison <the field of comparative law>; or (3) estimated by comparison <comparative distances>.

Occasionally *comparative* is used where *comparable* is called for: "A new system permits women members of staff to complain if they feel they are being paid less than men of *comparative* [read *comparable*] skill." Simon Hoggart, *Observer,* 22 Sept. 1991, at 22. Though the *OED* documents this use of *comparative* with four examples ranging from the early 17th to the early 19th century, it labels the usage obsolete.

comparative law. See **jurisprudence (D).**

comparative negligence; contributory negligence. In the U.S., a plaintiff's *contributory negligence* (= his own carelessness for his own safety or interests, which contributes materially to damage suffered by him as a result partly of his own fault and partly of the fault of another person or persons [*CDL*]) has traditionally, in accordance with the common-law rule, acted as a complete bar to recovery. But most states have now adopted statutes providing for *comparative negligence,* which acts to reduce the plaintiff's recovery proportionally to his fault in the damage rather than to bar recovery completely. The terms *contributory negligence* and *comparative negligence* have remained quite distinct.

In G.B., however, the separate term *comparative negligence* is not used. The common-law rule of contributory negligence was altered by the Law Reform (Contributory Negligence) Act of 1945, which provides that "if the plaintiff is partly in fault, his claim is not defeated, but the damages recoverable are to be reduced to such extent as the court or jury thinks just and equitable having regard to the claimant's share in the responsibility for the damage" (*OCL*). Thus *contributory negligence* in G.B. means roughly what *comparative negligence* means in the U.S.; rather than devising a new term, the English have continued using the old term, but with a new meaning. See **assumption of the risk.**

Comparatives and Superlatives. A. Choice Between Comparative and Superlative. When two items are being compared, a comparative adjective should be used <the greater of the two>; when more than two are being compared, the superlative should be used <the greatest of the three>. The blunder of using the superlative adjective when only two items are compared is not at all uncommon: "That is only half the story, and not the *most* [read *more*] important half."/ "The table reveals that, as between closely held and public corporations, the closely held corporation is by far the *most* [read *more*] numerous."

B. Which to Use—Suffixes, or *more* and *most*? Apart from anomalies like *good > better > best,* comparatives and superlatives are formed either internally by the addition of the suffixes *-er* and *-est* (e.g., *broader, broadest*) or externally with the words *more* and *most* (e.g., *more critical, most critical*). A number of words have a choice of forms (e.g., *commoner, -est* or *more, most common; tranquil(l)er, -est* or *more, most tranquil; stupider, -est* or *more, most stupid; naiver, -est* or *more, most naive*). The terminational forms are usually older, and some of them are obsolescent; the choice of form in any given context will depend on which form sounds better. The variation in forms here is not to be stifled by absolute rules.

Still, if a word ordinarily takes either the *-er* or the *-est* suffix—and that formation sounds most natural—it is poor style to use *more* or *most* instead. E.g., "It was easy to generalize this as a contest between the individual and society, and it became *more easy* [read *easier*] to do so . . . ." Roscoe Pound, *An Introduction to Philosophy* 21 (1922; repr. 1975)./ "The witness offer is an even *more simple* [read *simpler*] procedure than the tangible offer." John Kaplan & Jon R. Waltz, *Cases and Materials on Evidence* 56 (5th ed. 1984).

C. Swapping Horses. The form of a comparison cannot change once the construction has begun. One writes *more . . . than,* or *as . . . as;* but the two do not mix: "Nowhere else is there a *greater* need to substitute a panel of three experienced judges for a jury *as* [read *than*] in medical malpractice." See SWAPPING HORSES.

D. *Be*-Verbs Repeated After Comparatives. It is almost always unnecessary to repeat the verb *to be* before the second element of the comparison. The prolix and infelicitous construction seems to thrive more in legal than in other writing. E.g., "Such a law *is less likely than is* [omit the second *is*] the Texas education statute to qualify as the least onerous alternative."

comparator (= something with which something else is compared) "is a new bit of legalese. The word does exist, but is usually used in the scientific context [to denote] an instrument used for making comparisons." *Hein v. Oregon College of Educ.,* 718 F.2d 910, 912–13 n.2 (9th Cir. 1983). But in legal contexts, it frequently appears in discussions of the Equal Pay Act, under which, for example, female plaintiffs contrast their remuneration with that of male *comparators.* See *id.* at 912. E.g., "At trial, the EEOC sought to prove that it was entitled to recover the pay of a *comparator* male employed by Smith Pontiac for the period commencing in December 1983 . . . ." *EEOC v. Mike Smith Pontiac GMC, Inc.,* 896 F.2d 524, 527 (11th Cir. 1990). As the Ninth Circuit observed, "The use of '*comparator*' in the context of the Equal Pay Act has convenience, if not elegance, to commend it." *Hein,* 718 F.2d at 913 n.2.

compare (with) (to). The usual phrase is *compare with;* this phrase means "to place side by side, noting differences and similarities between" <let us compare his goals with his actual accomplishments>. *Compare to* = to observe or point only to likenesses between <the psychologist compared this action to Hinckley's assassination attempt>.

Compare and contrast is an English teacher's tautology, for in comparing two things (one thing *with* another) one notes both similarities and differences.

Comparisons, False. See ILLOGIC (A).

compartment(al)ize. The longer form is standard in both AmE and BrE. E.g., "Assuming that it makes sense to *compartmentalize* in this manner the diagnosis of such a formless 'disease,' tremendous gaps in our knowledge remain, which the record in this case does nothing to fill." *Powell v. Texas,* 392 U.S. 514, 524 (1968). See -IZE.

compel; impel. *Compel* is the stronger word, connoting force or coercion, with little or no volition on the part of the one compelled. *Impel* connotes persuasive urging, with some degree of volition on the part of the one impelled. *Compel* is properly used when the legal process is brought to bear on people's actions: "The pleas are no more improperly *compelled* than is the decision by a defendant at the close of the state's evidence at trial that he must take the stand or face certain conviction."/ "He has not yet reached the age of 25 years, and he brings this bill to *compel* the trustees to pay to him the remainder of the trust fund."

In the following sentences *impel* is properly used, in the first two the object (*court*) being an UNDERSTOOD WORD: "Applying these notions to the present case *impels* [the court to] the conclusion that appellant's motion at the close of all the evidence should be read as a motion for a directed verdict."/ "Does a procedural merger of law and equity automatically *impel* [the court to] a modification of principles of equitable jurisdiction?"/ "With these principles in mind, we [the justices of the court of appeals] are *impelled* to agree with the probate court's decision that appellants violated the in terrorem clause of decedent's will."

But the courts have been less than punctilious about the distinction between *compel* and *impel.* Sentences like the following are common: "Our analysis *compels* the conclusion that FERC lacks the authority to suspend initial rate filings." Perhaps this use of *compel* stems from a desire for the court (again, the understood object) to suggest that it simply had no choice in its holding. The device is largely rhetorical and is so clichéd as to be ineffective. Lon Fuller—through the voice of a fictitious judge—subtly mocked the device in a famous article: "For us to assert that the law we uphold and expound *compels* us to a conclusion we are ashamed of . . . seems to me to amount to an admission that the law of this Commonwealth no longer pretends to incorporate justice." *The Case of the Speluncean Explorers,* 62 Harv. L. Rev. 616, 620 (1949). See **impel.**

compellable, primarily a legal term, has traditionally been used in the broad sense "that may be compelled (to do something)." E.g., "Both Plato and Aristotle approved abortion for this purpose, the latter suggesting that a mother should be *compellable* to commit abortion after she had borne an allotted number of children." Glanville Williams, *The Sanctity of Life and the Criminal Law* 148 (1957; repr. 1972).

Today the word is more widely used in the sense "subject to being compelled (to testify)." The term is far more common in BrE than in AmE. E.g., "[I]t is only within certain limits that husband and wife are competent, and within narrower limits that they are *compellable,* to give evidence against one another, in criminal proceedings." William Geldart, *Introduction to English Law* 49 (D.C.M. Yardley ed., 9th ed. 1984)./ "[N]ot until 1898 were accused persons made competent (but not *compellable*) witnesses at their trial." Theodore F.T. Plucknett, *A Concise History of the Common Law* 437 (5th ed. 1956).

compendious means "abridged, succinct," not "voluminous," as several federal judges mistakenly believe—e.g.: "Of course, Richmond could have built an even more *compendious* record of past discrimination, one including additional stark statistics and additional individual accounts of past discrimination." *City of Richmond v. J.A. Croson Co.,* 488 U.S. 469, 547–48 (1989) (Marshall, J., dissenting)./ "We need go no further. Having attentively reviewed the *compendious* record in this long-running suit, we discern no reversible error." *HMG Property Investors, Inc. v. Parque Indus. Rio Canas, Inc.,* 847 F.2d 908, 919–20 (1st Cir. 1988) (referring elsewhere to "the hoariness of the controversy and the girth of the record" [at 919]).

Perhaps the error stems from the idea that a compendium is, at best, a fairly comprehensive abridgment. But, properly speaking, the emphasis falls on *abridgment,* not on *comprehensive.* And some would say that the word does not at all suggest comprehensiveness: "But as a *compendium* of feminist art history . . . and a catalogue—commodious though not, of course, comprehensive—of women artists, this will be an enormously useful work." L. Hughes-Hallet, Book Rev., Sunday Times, 10 June 1990, at 8-10.

compendium. Pl. *-ia.* See PLURALS (A). For the sense of the word, see **compendious.**

compensable. A. And *compensatory.* A nuance exists between these terms. *Compensable damages* = those damages capable of being recovered; damages for which compensation is available. *Compensatory damages* = those damages intended to make the plaintiff whole again; actual damages. *Compensable damages* are hypothetical; *compensatory damages* are those actually awarded or to be awarded to a party.

The form *compensatable* is an error for *compensable:* "[The] loss [is] *compensatable* [read *compensable*] by interest of not more than $405." *Metz v. Tusico, Inc.,* 167 F. Supp. 393, 398 (E.D. Va. 1958). See -ATABLE.

B. Spelling. *Compensable*—not *compensible*—is the preferred form. The *-ible* spelling is incorrect; the frequency of its use is explained perhaps by a mistaken analogy to *comprehensible.* See -ABLE (A).

compensatable. See **compensable.**

compensate. A. Transitive or Intransitive. *Compensate* may or may not take *for,* and either way means "to make up for, to counterbalance." E.g., "When it is conceded that mental suffering may be *compensated (for)* in actions of tort, the right of the plaintiff to recover in this case is established." The modern tendency is to omit *for,* but the sound of a sentence may outweigh the interests of concision.

B. And *recompense.* These verbs are almost precisely synonymous <to recompense the victim

for his injuries>, but *recompense,* q.v., is a FORMAL WORD less commonly used.

compensation = (1) remuneration; that which is given in recompense; (2) (in AmE) salary or wages; (3) (in BrE) consideration paid for expropriated land. For an early treatise devoted to compensation in sense (3), see Henry C. Richards & J.P.H. Soper, *The Law and Practice of Compensation* (n.d. [1898]); though nearly unknown in AmE, this BrE sense is not confined to lawyers, as witness the lyrics of Jethro Tull's popular song about compulsory purchase, "Farm on the Freeway" ("They say they paid me compensation/ That's not what I'm chasing, I was a rich man before yesterday.").

In sense (1), the phrase *money compensation* might at first appear to be a REDUNDANCY. But *compensation* can take forms other than money, as John Austin's quotation in the *OED* makes clear by referring to *compensation in money or in kind.* Here Geldart is contrasting *money compensation* with other kinds, such as strict performance in equity: "With few exceptions the only thing that Common Law can do is to give him *money compensation.*" William Geldart, *Introduction to English Law* 29 (D.C.M. Yardley ed., 9th ed. 1984).

compensatory; compensative. The latter is a NEEDLESS VARIANT. Cf. **recompensive.**

competence; competency. A. Of Persons. Though Fowler considered *competency* a NEEDLESS VARIANT, these terms have come to exhibit some DIFFERENTIATION, which should be further encouraged. *Competence* usually has the lay sense "a basic or minimal ability to do something." E.g., "An exhaustive study of the deficiencies of applying a mechanism originally developed to decide who owns title to Blackacre to the management of general disasters is beyond the *competence* and available time of its writer."/ "*Incompetence* of counsel is not necessarily established by omission of a claim."

Today *competency* is a NEEDLESS VARIANT in all but one sense. It is increasingly confined to the legal sense of "the ability to understand problems and make decisions; ability to stand trial." A severely mentally retarded person, an incompetent, is said to suffer from legal *incompetency. Competency to stand trial* is the usual phrase.

In referring to qualifications in general, as to witness a will or to testify in court, *-ce* is the usual form. E.g., "The common-law rules concerning the *competence* [i.e., the qualification to testify in court] of attesters were derived from the rules concerning the *competence* of witnesses in litigation."/ "Statutes in the United States tend to correlate the standard of *competence* to attest a will with the ability of the witness to comprehend and relate the facts." Only when the reference is clearly and solely to mental disability is *-cy* the preferred form.

Sometimes *competency* is confused with *competence:* "Where the station agent incidentally acts as the telegraph agent in many sparsely settled communities where the business will not permit the employment of a full-time telegraph agent, it is apparent that such *competency* [read *competence*] cannot be secured." And vice versa: "Appellants contend that their son lacks the mental *competence* [read *competency*] to waive his legal rights, and they maintain that he lacks the *competence* [read *competency*] to decide whether to pursue or to waive the benefits of 28 U.S.C. § 2254."

Writers should avoid the INELEGANT VARIATION of alternating between the two terms in a single writing: "Enriquez's *competency* challenge is twofold. First, he contends that he was denied due process because the state trial court did not . . . hold a hearing to determine his *competence* [read *competency*] to stand trial. . . . [T]he Supreme Court [has] held that a defendant has a procedural due process right to a *competency* hearing." *Enriquez v. Procunier,* 752 F.2d 111, 113 (5th Cir. 1984).

B. Used of Adjudicative or Rule-Making Bodies. *Competence* is frequently used for qualification or capacity of an official body to do something. E.g., "Before any court can enter a valid judgment or decree, it must have *competence* to do so."/ "Hardly anyone has ever doubted the *competence* of a legislature to enact a comparative negligence statute."/ "With respect to most crimes, the credibility of a witness is peculiarly within the *competence* of the jury, whose common experience affords sufficient basis for the assessment of credibility."

C. Of Evidence. In older legal writing, *competence* = admissibility. Thus references to the *competence of evidence* were once fairly common. Again, *-cy* is a NEEDLESS VARIANT in this context. Following is an example in the adjectival form: "Evidence of a conviction is only prima facie, and may be rebutted by *competent* evidence that impeaches the validity of the judgment." See **incompetence & competent.**

competent is used in archaic senses in the law. Generally the word is used only of persons, whereas in law it is used of courts, of evidence, and of cases. It is even used indefinitely: "It seems *competent,* if war exists, for the military authorities to use special military court machinery, and to impose any sentence, even death, without being disabled, in another case, from applying procedure of a more limited character." (Eng.) This use of the word, in the sense "proper, appropriate," was labeled obsolete by the *OED*. Yet it still appears in legal writing, albeit less and less frequently. E.g., "The general rule is that recital of a written instrument as to consideration is not conclusive, and it is *competent* to inquire into consideration and to show by parol evidence the real nature of the consideration."/ "In the present case it was *competent* for the plaintiff to recover for the intestate's pain, suffering, and disability during his period of life following the assault."

More frequently, *competent* = (1) (of a judge or court) having jurisdiction or authority to act <When a court of competent jurisdiction has obtained control of property, that control may not be disturbed by any other court>; (2) (of witnesses) having capacity; qualified to testify in court concerning the material facts <A will is void unless attested by the number of competent witnesses required by statute>; (3) (of a case) within the jurisdiction of the court; or (4) (of evidence) admissible. See **competence** & **incompetent.**

This word is still further complicated in legal contexts by its frequent appearance in its lay sense (= professionally adequate; properly qualified): "Omission of the testimony may have been so material as to deprive the proceeding of fundamental fairness, despite appellant's otherwise *competent* representation."/ "A jury could conclude that appellee failed to fulfill its dual obligation to provide a *competent* service engineer to supervise installation of the purchased equipment."

complacency; complacence. The latter is a NEEDLESS VARIANT.

complacent; complaisant. The former means "self-satisfied; smug." The latter means "obliging; tending to go along with others."

complainant; complainer. *Complainant* is, both in AmE and in BrE (except Scotland), the technical term for one who enters a legal complaint against another. It is traditionally the term used in courts of equity, but by the early 20th century the equity courts had already adopted the term used in courts of law—*plaintiff.* See Walter C. Clephane, *Equity Pleading* vi (1926).

Some writers prefer *complainant* over *prosecutrix,* q.v., in the context of sexual offenses—e.g.: "In *State v. Connelly,* a turn-of-the-century Minnesota case, the *complainant* was a seventeen-year-old girl who testified that she had been raped by the priest who moved in with his family next door." Susan Estrich, *Real Rape* 44 (1987).

Complainer is the Scottish equivalent of *complainant.* E.g., "Seven months later there were served upon the *complainer,* not one, but five separate complaints." (Scot.)/ "In the heart of the Island of Lewis near the head of Loch Erisort there is a clachan called Balallan, in which the *complainer* keeps the local store, selling articles of clothing, provisions, and general merchandise." (Scot.) In the U.S., *complainer* is generally understood as meaning "one who habitually complains." Cf. **pursuer.** See **plaintiff.**

complainee has appeared as a correlative of *complainer*—e.g.: "The action is one seeking to recover concealed assets of the estate of Isabel S. Jones, deceased, which the complainant alleges to be in the possession of *complainee.*" *In re Jones' Estate,* 122 N.E.2d 111, 111–12 (Ohio App. 1952). Perhaps it has something to commend it, but that something is hard to imagine. Proper names would surely be preferable. See -EE & PARTY APPELLATIONS.

complainer. See **complainant.**

complaint, well-pleaded. See **well-pleaded complaint.**

complaisant. See **complacent.**

compleat is an archaic variant of *complete* with no place in modern contexts, unless facetiousness is intended. Even so, it is a one-word CLICHÉ.

complement. See **compliment.**

complete diversity. See **diversity.**

compliance. See **suggestibility.**

complicitous; complicit, adj. The former is the standard term; the latter, in fact, is not recorded in the *OED* or *W3.* "Far from attacking racism at its root, Mr. [Monroe] Freedman charges, Finch was *complicit* [read *complicitous*] in it." David Margolick, *Chipping at Atticus Finch's Pedestal,* N.Y. Times, 28 Feb. 1992, at B1.

complicity, which derives from the idea of being an accomplice, has been extended "to include guilt based upon induced conduct of an *innocent* person." Rollin M. Perkins & Ronald N. Boyce, *Criminal Law* 767 (3d ed. 1982). That broadening of sense is probably a desirable one because the conceptual subtlety involved is unlikely to give rise to a widely adopted verbal subtlety.

compliment; complement. These words are often confounded. The first means "to praise," the second "to supplement appropriately or adequately."

comply takes *with,* not *to.* E.g., "You have also asked whether the budget for Cameron County *complies* in form *to* [read *with*] the requirements of the county budget statutes."

compose; comprise. Correct use of these words is simple, but increasingly rare. The parts *compose* the whole; the whole *comprises* the parts; the whole is *composed* of the parts; the parts are *comprised* in the whole. *Comprise,* the more troublesome word in this pair, means "to contain; to consist of." E.g., "The evidence clearly showed that the committee *comprised* members from inside as well as outside the Bank."/ "Every act causing an obstruction to another in the exercise of the right *comprised* within this description would, if damage should be caused thereby to the party obstructed, be a violation of this prohibition." (Eng.) A number of mistakes occur with *comprise:*

A. Erroneous Use of *is comprised of.* The phrase *is comprised of* is always wrong and should be replaced by either *is composed of* or *comprises.* E.g., "We also judicially notice that the 123d Judicial District Court of Shelby County *is comprised of* [read *comprises*] two counties, Panola and Shelby."/ "The law of the professional lawyer *was comprised of* [read *comprised*] rules derived from judges' *dicta* . . . ." Alan Harding, *A Social History of English Law* 134 (1966).

Sometimes the simplest of verb phrases is what is needed: "In the course of the search, the agents noticed that the ceiling of the barracks was *comprised* [read *made up*] of removable acoustical tiles." Following is the correct use of *is composed of* where the careless writer would put *is comprised of:* "The organization *is composed of* certain employees of the Chicago Railway Co."

B. *Comprise* for *are comprised in.* "Discriminatory tests are impermissible unless shown by professionally acceptable methods to be predictive or significantly correlated with important elements of work behavior that *comprise* [read *are comprised in*] the job for which the candidates are being evaluated."

C. *Comprise* for *constitute.* *Comprise* is more and more commonly used in a sense opposite its true meaning ("to contain, include, embrace"). It should not be used for *compose* or *constitute.* E.g., "To the extent that pension rights derive from employment during coverture, they *comprise* [read *constitute*] a community asset subject to division in a dissolution proceeding."/ "Cotenants *comprise* [read *constitute*] not a number of individuals, each owning an undivided interest, but a corporate entity."/ "With a joint tenancy, cotenants *comprise* [read *constitute*] a corporate unity."/ "The front and back of this Order *comprise* [read *constitute*] the entire agreement affecting this purchase."

D. *Comprise* for *are.* This is an odd error based on a misunderstanding of the meaning of *comprise.* E.g., "The appellants *comprise* [read *are*] nine of sixteen defendants convicted in the federal district court on one or more counts of an eleven-count indictment."

E. Correct use of *comprise.* E.g., "The advisory group, which *comprises* attorneys and representatives of major categories of litigants, will analyze the trends in case filings, the demands on the court's resources, and the principal causes of cost and delay in civil litigation." Theodore R. Tetzlaff, *Federal Courts, Their Rules, and Their Roles,* Litigation 1, 1 (Spring 1992)./ "Together, the first two volumes of 'The Years of Lyndon Johnson' *comprise,* with notes, 1,387 pages." Frank J. Prial, *Author's Kind Word for Johnson,* N.Y. Times, 31 March 1990, at 13.

F. *Compose* in the sense of *compound.* See **composition.**

composition means, at common law, (1) the act of adjusting a debt, or avoiding a liability, by compensation agreed to by the parties; or (2) the compensation paid as part of such an agreement. This noun corresponds to the verb *to compound,* q.v., and often means merely "a compounding." E.g., "This being by act of the creditor, since without his participation the *composition* would be ineffective to affect the debt, the surety is discharged." Laurence P. Simpson, *Handbook on the Law of Suretyship* 312 (1950) (corresponding to sense (2) of *compound*)./ "If a slave killed a freeman, he was to be surrendered for one half of the *composition* to the relatives of the slain man, and the master was to pay the other half." Oliver W. Holmes, *The Common Law* 17 (1881; repr. 1946) (corresponding to sense (3) of *compound*).

Similarly, *compose* is sometimes used as a synonym for *compound* (in the legal sense): "It was . . . an attempt [by the defendant] to *compose* a dispute, . . . to find a mutually satisfactory middle ground between the two divergent conceptions of the original offer to sell." *Frese v. Gaston,* 161 F.2d 890, 891 (D.C. Cir. 1947) (per curiam).

compos mentis. See ***non compos mentis.***

compound, v.t., has been the victim of a SLIPSHOD EXTENSION arising from its primarily legal sense. The word has three basic meanings: (1) "to put together, combine, construct, compose" <to compound sand and gravel>; (2) "to settle (any matter) by a money payment, in lieu of other liability" <to compound a debt>; and (3) "to forbear from prosecuting for consideration, or to cause (a prosecutor) so to forbear" <to compound a felony>. For senses (2) and (3)—the legal senses—the noun corresponding to this verb is *composition,* q.v.

Sense (3) has historically been the more common one—e.g.: "Among certain grizzled sea gossips . . . went a rumor perdue that the master-at-arms was a *chevalier* who had volunteered into the king's navy by way of *compounding* for some mysterious swindle whereof he had been arraigned at the King's Bench." Herman Melville, *Billy Budd* 28 (1891; repr. 1979).

The word has been sloppily extended because "nonlawyers have misapprehended the meaning of *to compound a felony* . . . . [The word] is now widely abused to mean: to make worse, aggravate, multiply, increase." Philip Howard, *New Words for Old* 19 (1977). Examples of this looseness of diction abound now even in legal writing. E.g., "This deliberate perpetuation of the unconstitutional dual system can only have *compounded* the harm of such a system." *Green v. County School Bd.,* 391 U.S. 430, 438 (1968)./ "The elective share is further reduced in jurisdictions that compute the share on the basis of the net estate after taxes, thus *compounding* the loss of protection for the spouse."/ "With the expansion of equity jurisdiction, such problems have been enormously *compounded.*"/ "The situation for the prosecution was *compounded* by the star witness's evasion of subpoenas by hiding in Ireland."

It is not quite true, then, at least in the U.S., that "to write 'he *compounded* the offence' (when what is meant is that he did something to aggravate the offence) is to vex every lawyer who reads the sentence, and to provoke numbers of them to litigious correspondence in defence of their jargon." Philip Howard, *New Words for Old* 20 (1977). Nevertheless, we may justifiably lament the fact that generations of young lawyers will not understand the phrase *to compound a felony* when they see it in the older lawbooks.

Notably, *compound* has also been used in civil cases to refer to a settlement (sense 2): "The parties *compounded* the case after completing discovery."/ "He *compounded* the case with the defendant for a cash payment." Whereas *compounding a felony* is a criminal offense, *compounding a civil case* is perfectly proper. In civil contexts, however, *settle* is by far the more common term.

compounder = (1) one who compounds for a liability, debt, or charge; (2) one who compounds a felony or offense; (3) one who pays a lump sum in discharge of a liability requiring recurrent payments; (4) one who, as a stranger to a dispute, tries to help parties settle their differences (an arbitrator with extensive equitable powers was formerly known as an *amicable compounder*); (5) one who knows of another's crime and agrees, for some reward received or promised, not to inform or prosecute.

compounding a crime = accepting something of value under an unlawful agreement not to prosecute a known criminal offender or to handicap the prosecution. Thus, the sense differs from that which many readers would intuitively (and mistakenly) attribute to the phrase (something like "adding to a crime"). See **compound.**

compound larceny. See **larceny (B).**

comprehend. In lay contexts, this word means, almost exclusively, "to grasp mentally"; in legal contexts, it frequently means "to include, encompass." E.g., "These instructions would *comprehend* damages for any disfigurement of the plaintiff's nose."/ "No judicial opinion can *comprehend* the protean variety of the street encounter, and we can only judge the facts of the case before us."/ "By confining herself to the use of the generic term, the present testatrix *comprehended* all the various religious, educational, benevolent, and humanitarian objects that the single word 'charity' connotes." See **apprehend.** Cf. **embrace.**

comprehensible; comprehendible. The latter is a NEEDLESS VARIANT.

comprise. See **compose.**

compromise = (1) to agree to settle a matter <the parties compromised and dropped their claims against each other>; or (2) to endanger <the disclosure of the information might compromise intelligence sources>. See **accord and satisfaction.**

compromise; settlement. See **accord and satisfaction.**

compromise and settlement agreement. This is the more usual (and the better) wording—not *compromise settlement agreement.*

compromise settlement agreement. See **compromise and settlement agreement.**

comptroller is pronounced identically with *controller.* To pronounce the *-p-* has traditionally been considered semiliterate. *Comptroller* is used especially of public offices; *controller,* however, means the same thing and is not deceptively spelled. *Comptroller* is more common in AmE than in BrE, where it is archaic.

The strange spelling of *comptroller* originated in the zeal of 15th-century Latinists who sought to respell medieval French loanwords on the "purer" Latin model. Thus *account* became *accompt,* and *count* became *compt. Comptroller* is one of the few survivals among such respellings, and it is also one of the bungles perpetrated by those ardent Latinists: the *con-* in *controller* was mistakenly associated with the word *count,* when in fact it is merely the Latin prefix (the true derivation being fr. L. *contrā-rotulātor*). Thus the respelling should never have been. But we are several centuries too late in correcting it.

compulsive; compulsory. Today, *compulsive* primarily means "of, pertaining to, resulting from, or suggesting psychological obsession." Although it was once commonly used in the sense "mandatory, coercive," that meaning is best denoted today by the word *compulsory.* In short, the two words have undergone DIFFERENTIATION. Therefore, in the following passage, *compulsory* is the better choice—if only to prevent a MISCUE: "Perhaps the most natural usage would take 'damages caused by a public vessel' to mean physical damages arising out of her operation. But there is nothing *compulsive* [read *compulsory*] about such an understanding." Grant Gilmore & Charles L. Black, Jr., *The Law of Admiralty* 984 (2d ed. 1974).

compulsory counterclaim. See **counterclaim.**

compulsory purchase is the BrE term for *expropriation* or the exercise of *eminent domain.* Here the phrase appears in verb form: "Tophams also contended that, since the racecourse would in any event be closed down and left derelict, when it would be *compulsorily purchased* by the local authority for housing purposes, an injunction would be of no benefit to Lord Sefton." (Eng.) See **eminent domain, condemn & compensation.**

compurgator is stuffy for *character witness,* unless (as in the first two examples) the context is historical: "Although the historical origins of the 'voucher' rule are uncertain, it appears to be a remnant of primitive English trial practice in which 'oath-takers' or '*compurgators*' were called to stand behind a particular party's position in any controversy." *Chambers v. Mississippi,* 410 U.S. 284, 296 (1973)./ "The old '*compurgators*' have come to life in our present day 'character witnesses.'" Ephraim Tutt, *Yankee Lawyer* 73 n.* (1943)./ "The *Partin* inquiries test the witnesses' capacity and competence; the instant ones place the psychiatrist in the posture of a *compurgator* [read *character witness*] . . . ." *U.S. v. Wertis,* 505 F.2d 683, 685 (5th Cir. 1974)./ "[A]ll but one witness, including one of appellant's two *compurgators* [read *character witnesses*], testified that appellant could receive a fair trial." *James v. State,* 772 S.W.2d 84, 93 (Tex. Crim. App. 1989) (en banc).

COMPUTERESE, the jargon of computer wizards, is making inroads into standard English. Thus *access* and *format* and *sequence* and *interface* have become verbs, *input* has enjoyed widespread use as both noun and verb, and *on-line* and *user-friendly* have begun to be used as a model for NEOLOGISMS (e.g., *on-stream* used of an oil well, *reader-friendly* used of well-written documents). No one can rightly object, of course, to the use of computerese in computing contexts, where it is undeniably useful. But many computer terms have come to have figurative senses, thereby invading the general language rather than remaining denizens of a restricted jargon. Careful users of language are wary of adopting any of these trendy locutions. Though some of them may remain and become standard, just as many may well become defunct as the technology of communication changes. And others may never lose the jargonistic stigma attaching to them.

computerize. See -IZE.

comstockery (often capitalized) refers to prudish censorship, or attempted censorship, of supposed immorality in art or literature. In 1873, the American Congress passed the so-called Comstock Law, a federal act to control obscenity, pushed through by one Anthony Comstock (1844–1915), who was a leader of the New York Society for the Suppression of Vice. George Bernard Shaw invented the word *comstockery,* pejorative from the first, when he wrote in the *New York Times* in 1905: "*Comstockery* is the world's standing joke at the expense of the United States."

conceal = (1) to keep from the knowledge of others; refrain from disclosing; or (2) to remove or keep out of sight or notice; to hide. In a statute defining the crime of an accessory after the fact, sense (2) obtains—the word *conceal* implies an act or refusal to act by which the person intends to prevent or hinder a crime's discovery—a mere failure to give information is not enough. See

Rollin M. Perkins & Ronald N. Boyce, *Criminal Law* 750 (3d ed. 1982).

concede. See **cede.**

concededly. See **reportedly, confessedly** & -EDLY.

concensus. See **consensus.**

concept; conception. Both *concept* and *conception* may mean "an abstract idea." *Conception* also means "the act of forming abstract ideas." Fowler wrote that *conception* is the ordinary term, *concept* the philosophical term. (*MEU1* at 88.) Often the latter is used as a high-flown equivalent of simpler words such as *design, program, thought,* or *idea.* When not used pretentiously for one of those simpler words, *concept* is likely to have negative connotations, as here: "Yet no *concept,* or combination of *concepts,* or rule built out of *concepts*—as all legal rules are built—can of itself provide an automatic solution to the simplest conceivable human problem." Fred Rodell, *Woe Unto You, Lawyers!* 37 (1939; repr. 1980).

Wesley Newman Hohfeld used the more appropriate word in titling his *Fundamental Legal Conceptions* (1919). Similarly, the better ordinary use is illustrated here: "Such a holding would directly contradict fair-market-value standards and our *conceptions* of justice."

conceptual(istic); conceptive; conceptional. These words are very close. *Conceptual* and *conceptional* both mean "of or pertaining to a conception or idea"—*conceptual* being the usual term. *Conceptive* = of or relating to the process of mental conception (i.e., conceiving).

When not being used as a NEEDLESS VARIANT of *conceptual,* the word *conceptional* serves as the adjective corresponding to a different kind of conception (= the fertilization of an egg): "It is not easy to reconcile this attitude with the papal concession of some kinds of *anti-conceptional* measures." Glanville Williams, *The Sanctity of Life and the Criminal Law* 69 (1957; repr. 1972).

Conceptualistic = (1) of or relating to the philosophical or psychological doctrine of conceptualism (a nonlegal technical sense); or (2) employing or based on conceptions. In sense (2), *conceptualistic* is more than slightly pejorative: "Appellants put forth the *conceptualistic* argument that the promoter cannot be the corporation's agent when the corporation has not yet been formed."

conceptualize is often a bloated word that can be advantageously replaced by *conceive* or *visualize.*

concerned with, be. This verb phrase is weak; usually *concern* can be put into the active voice with a gain in directness. E.g., "The *Green* case *was concerned with* [read *concerned*] whether a violation that continued after a freedom-of-choice plan was initiated required affirmative action."/ "This appeal *is primarily concerned with* [read *concerns primarily*] orders of the district court directing that two public institutions of higher education be merged into a single institution." Cf. **deal with.**

concert = agreement of two or more persons or parties in a plan, design, or enterprise. E.g., "The Third Circuit reversed, finding direct and circumstantial evidence of *concert* of action tending to show that injurious *concert* also occurred." Steven A. Childress, *A New Era for Summary Judgments,* 116 F.R.D. 183, 185 (1987). This sense thrives in legal language but is all but defunct in lay language, apart from the adjective *concerted,* q.v., and the phrase *in concert.*

In concert = working collectively toward the same end. It does not mean merely "together," as here: "Individual symptoms of intoxication, when manifesting themselves alone *instead of in concert* [read *instead of simultaneously* or *together*], bear little relation to ascertainable criminal conduct." Here the phrase is correctly used: "The amended complaint alleges that defendant worked *in concert* with Cooke in illegally breaching the franchise agreement."

concerted means "unified, accomplished with the aid of others," not "strong" or "strenuous." Thus "He did not make a *concerted* effort to get to work on time" is an anacoluthon, inasmuch as one person cannot make a concerted effort. See **concert.**

concessionaire; concessioner. The former is standard, the latter a NEEDLESS VARIANT.

concessive; concessionary; concessional. *Concessive* = of or tending to concession <a concessive stance in negotiating>. *Concessionary* = of or relating to concession or a concession <the concessionary company—i.e., the one with a concession>. *Concessional* is a NEEDLESS VARIANT of either of the previous two; here it appears where *concessive* would serve better: "Generous *concessional* [read *concessive*] treatment of debt-burdened African economies is essential if the continent's development crisis is to end." *Aid and Reform in Nigeria,* Fin. Times, 6 Jan. 1992, at 10.

conciliation. See **mediation** (B).

conciliatory; conciliative. *Conciliatory* = (1) tending to conciliate; or (2) of or relating to conciliation or mediation. *Conciliative* is a NEEDLESS VARIANT: "Both agencies have incentives to compromise . . . . This *conciliative* [read *conciliatory*] process could be initiated effectively by recognizing areas of common interest . . . ." Jerry W. Markham & Rita M. Stephanz, *The Stock Market Crash of 1987,* 76 Geo. L.J. 1993, 2030–31 (1988)./ "After *conciliative* [read *conciliatory*] efforts failed, plaintiff filed this action." *Barnes v. Lerner Shops of Texas, Inc.,* 323 F. Supp. 617, 619 (S.D. Tex. 1971).

conciliatrix; conciliatress. See SEXISM (C).

concision; conciseness. Drawing a fine distinction, Fowler wrote that "*concision* means the process of cutting down, and *conciseness* the cut-down state" (*MEU2* 304).

conclude, in law, has these special senses:

1. (of a treaty, convention, or contract) to ratify or formalize. E.g., "The comparative study of judicial intervention to change or modify a validly *concluded* contract is difficult." Jean-Louis Baudouin, "Theory of Imprevision and Judicial Intervention to Change a Contract," in *Essays on the Civil Law of Obligations* 151 (Joseph Dainow ed. 1969).
2. to bind. E.g., "The inconsistent statements may be evidentiary as admissions—convincing, persuasive or of little weight, . . . but in and of themselves, they will not *conclude* a party as a matter of law." *Parkinson v. California Co.,* 233 F.2d 432, 438 (10th Cir. 1956).
3. to estop. This sense is archaic—Lord Coke once wrote that to *conclude* is "to determine, to finish, to shut up, to estoppe or barre a man to plead or claime any other thing." Sir Edward Coke, *Institutes of the Laws of England* 36b (1628; repr. 1823).

conclusion = (1a) the last part or section of a speech or writing, such as the summation to the jury or court; (1b) the final clause or section of a pleading; (1c) the concluding part of a deed or conveyance; (2a) a judgment or statement arrived at by reasoning; (2b) an inferential statement—often an allegation that is insufficiently supported by the underlying facts giving rise to the inference; (3) the concluding, settling, or final arranging (as of a treaty); or (4) an act by which one estops oneself from doing anything inconsistent with it.

conclusionary; conclusional. See **conclusive.**

conclusion of fact; conclusion of law. A *conclusion of fact* is an evidentiary inference—a factual deduction drawn from observed or proven facts. A *conclusion of law* is a legal inference—a judicial deduction made upon a showing of certain facts, no further evidence being required.

conclusive; conclusory; conclusionary; conclusional. *Conclusive* is the common word, meaning "authoritative; decisive." E.g., "The statements of individual legislators, even sponsors, are much less *conclusive* on the issue of congressional intent than are official committee reports."/ "Admissions are rarely *conclusive* of the facts stated."

Most general English dictionaries fail to list *conclusory* as a main entry; the few that do misdefine it. The *OED,* labeling it a variant of *conclusive,* calls it "rare." Yet the word is now quite common in American legal writing—and increasingly in British legal writing—and it does not coincide in meaning with *conclusive.* The DIFFERENTIATION is worth encouraging. *Conclusory* = expressing a factual inference without expressing the fundamental facts on which the inference is based. The word often describes evidence that is not specific enough to be competent to prove what it addresses. For example, the statement "She is an illegal alien" is conclusory, whereas "She told me that she is an illegal alien" is not.

Born in New York, the term has gained widespread currency since it first appeared in the 1920s. E.g.:

- "[T]he motion [is] granted, to the extent of directing the service of an amended complaint, omitting paragraphs 16, 17, and 30, and all *conclusory* matter of the nature pointed out herein." *Ringler v. Jetter,* 201 N.Y.S. 525, 525 (App. Div. 1923).
- "Facts in detail supporting *conclusory* statements herein are available in the record." *People v. Hines,* 29 N.E.2d 483, 487 (N.Y. 1940).
- "So accustomed are we to concentrating on reasons of policy and on the *conclusory* nature of legal categories that we tend to forget how channeled we are by nothing more than a conceptual structure." Joseph Vining, *Legal Identity: The Coming of Age of Public Law* 24 (1978).
- "Ultimately, this [plain-meaning approach to 19th-century boilerplate] produces a largely insensitive and *conclusory* historical inquiry . . . ." *Oregon Dep't of Fish and Wildlife v. Klamath Indian Tribe,* 473 U.S. 753, 787 (1985) (Marshall, J., dissenting).

Still, despite its currency—its appearance in tens of thousands of published sources—its absence from dictionaries gives some legal writers pause. The Wyoming Supreme Court in 1987 used the phrase *conclusory affidavits,* and stated in a footnote: "After painstaking deliberation, we have decided that we like the word *conclusory,* and we are distressed by its omission from the English language. We now proclaim that henceforth *conclusory* is appropriately used in the opinions of this court. Furthermore, its usage is welcomed in briefs submitted for this court's review. Webster's, take heed." *Greenwood v. Wierdsma,* 741 P.2d 1079, 1086 n.3 (Wyo. 1987).

Take heed, indeed. Gary W. Saltzgiver, a Michigan lawyer, has sent me a letter from the G.&C. Merriam Company dated 24 November 1976, in which the great dictionary company did not take heed; the letter says that *conclusory* was dropped from Merriam-Webster dictionaries because (1) it is extremely rare, and (2) it is a close synonym of *conclusive.*

Both of those conclusions—or "conclusory statements," we might say—are and were wrong. "A computer search of American judicial opinions, conducted in April 1988, revealed more than 21,000 cases in which *conclusory* appears. It has been used for more than sixty years in state and federal courts, including the United States Supreme Court." Bryan A. Garner, "The Missing Common-Law Words," in *The State of the Language* 235, 239–40 (Christopher Ricks & Leonard Michaels eds., 1990).

Some legal writers, apparently loath to use *conclusory,* have resorted to *conclusional* in the sense previously given: "[T]he allegations are vague, *conclusional* [read *conclusory*], or inartistically expressed." *Sanders v. U.S.,* 373 U.S. 1, 22 (1963)./ "[T]he stricken portions of [the] affidavits contained *conclusional* [read *conclusory*] statements which neither the trial court nor this court may consider in passing upon motions for summary judgment." *Public Utility Dist. v. Washington Pub. Supply Sys.*, 705 P.2d 1195, 1202 (Wash. 1985) (en banc)./ "While the moving papers contend [that] the employment of new counsel will entail additional expense, the application on this point is *conclusional* [read *conclusory*] and does not establish [that] the hiring would work a substantial hardship." *In re Adler,* 494 N.Y.S.2d 828, 830 (N.Y. Surr. Ct. 1985). The *OED* defines *conclusional* as "of or pertaining to the conclusion; final," and calls it not only "rare" but "obsolete" as well. *W3* lists *conclusional,* however, and attributes to it the sense "constituting a conclusion," very nearly the sense here given to *conclusory.* Yet, in American law at least, *conclusory* has become so widespread that *conclusional* should be considered a mere NEEDLESS VARIANT.

Still another such variant is *conclusionary,* which was experimented with for a time and still occasionally appears—but it has lost the battle for supremacy and should be rejected: "[W]e are moreover impelled to adhere to the opinion, derived from our experience . . . , that *conclusionary* [read *conclusory*] evidence of this nature is immaterial to the issues." *NLRB v. Donnelly Garment Co.,* 330 U.S. 219, 230 (1947)./ "The defendant's second numbered contention makes a broad *conclusionary* [read *conclusory*] statement . . . ." *U.S. v. Boykin,* 275 F. Supp. 16, 17 (M.D. Pa. 1967)./ "Frequently information is sought by way of discovery . . . which is susceptible of objective ascertainment and *conclusionary* [read *conclusory*] summarization without its usefulness being impaired." 2 R.M. Milgrim, *Milgrim on Trade Secrets* § 7.06[1], at 7-95 (1988).

Occasionally, *conclusionary* is used as a synonym for *concluding* or *final,* as in this vague passage, which ends with a confused parenthetical: "[T]he decision or disposition is the *conclusionary* [read *final*] action of a competent tribunal (the verdict)." John Murray, *The Media Law Dictionary* 29 (1978).

conclusive evidence; conclusive proof. These synonymous phrases have two very different senses. On the one hand, most writers use either phrase to refer to evidence so strong as to overbear any other evidence to the contrary—i.e., evidence that must, as a matter of law, be taken to establish some fact in issue and that cannot be disputed. An example is a certificate of corporation offered as evidence of a company's incorporation. E.g., "I have no doubt that the words *'conclusive evidence'* mean what they say; that they are to be a bar to any evidence being tendered to show that the statements in the minutes are not correct." *Kerr v. John Mottram Ltd.,* [1940] Ch. 657, 660.

On the other hand, some writers mean something less by these phrases: evidence that, though not irrebuttable, so preponderates as to oblige a jury to come to a certain conclusion. E.g., "The term *'conclusive proof'* requires a claimant to sustain his burden merely by proof [that] is clear and convincing." *Bun v. Central Pa. Quarry, Shipping & Constr. Co.,* 169 A.2d 804, 807 (Pa. Super. Ct. 1961). See **preponderance of the evidence.**

conclusory. See **conclusive.**

concord. A. And *concordat*. *Concord* is the FORMAL WORD generally meaning "an amicable arrangement between parties, esp. between peoples or nations; compact; treaty." In law the word has sometimes been used as a NEEDLESS VARIANT of *accord* or *compromise* in the senses outlined under **accord and satisfaction.**

The word *concord* also has two archaic legal senses: (1) an in-court agreement in which a *deforciant* (q.v.) acknowledges that the lands in question belong to the complainant; and (2) an agreement to compromise and settle a case in trespass.

Concordat = an agreement between church and state. E.g., "For decades, under a system affirmed by a 1929 *Concordat* between the Government and the Vatican, Italy's 40,000 priests have been paid in large part out of state funds." Clyde Haberman, *Church Shares Pie with Caesar: How Big a Piece?* N.Y. Times, 8 Dec. 1989, at 4. Usually, as in the preceding quotation, *concordats* involve agreements with the Catholic Church; one authority defines them as "agreements between the Roman Pontiff and the civil ruler concerning matters of mutual interest to both high contracting parties." Matthew Ramstein, *Manual of Canon Law* 42 (1948).

The word has been the subject of SLIPSHOD EXTENSION, perhaps as writers have been seduced by inflated diction—that is, the possibility of calling a contract between important entities a *concordat.* E.g., "The case is far stronger for the reason that the purposes for which Temple is operated pursuant to the *concordat* between the University and the Commonwealth, which matured in the legislation of 1965, are public purposes." *Schier v. Temple Univ.,* 576 F. Supp. 1569, 1577 (E.D. Pa. 1984).

The word *concordat* has also been used as a variant of *concord,* but is to be avoided in that sense as a NEEDLESS VARIANT.

B. And *accord,* n. See **accord.**

CONCORD = grammatical agreement of one word with another to which it relates. Concord embraces number, person, case, and gender. It applies most often to (1) a subject and its verb; (2) a noun and its pronoun; (3) a noun and its appositive; and (4) a relative and its antecedent. Errors in concord are not at all uncommon.

A. Subject-Verb Disagreement. Errors in SUBJECT-VERB AGREEMENT are, unfortunately, legion in legal writing—e.g.: "Contracts for the sale of land have been enforced specifically in equity since the fifteenth century because damages *is* [read *are*] not an adequate substitute for the specific land to which the plaintiff is entitled under his contract." William F. Walsh, *A Treatise on Equity* 300 (1930)./ "The largest group of such cases *arise* [read *arises*] on motions for temporary restraining orders or preliminary injunctions." Douglas Laycock, *The Death of the Irreparable Injury Rule* 5 (1991)./ "As usual there *seems* [read *seem*] to be a million things happening around the Texas Law Center." Karen Johnson, *What's Happening at the Texas Law Center?* Tex. B.J., May 1992, at 514. See SYNESIS.

Are these merely symptoms of the decay of 20th-century English? Consider: "[T]he adequate narration may take up a term less brief, especially if explanation or comment here and there *seem* [read *seems*] requisite to the better understanding of such incidents." Herman Melville, *Billy Budd* 73 (1891; repr. Signet ed. 1979).

Quoting Melville is not to excuse lapses of this kind: every generation might be more vigilant than it is about its subjects and verbs. But we should not think of these problems as having been unthinkable two or three generations ago.

B. Noun-Pronoun Disagreement. Depending on how you look at it, this is either one of the most frequent blunders in modern writing or a godsend that allows us to avoid SEXISM. Where disagreement can be avoided, I recommend avoiding it; where it cannot be avoided, I recommend resorting to it cautiously because some readers (esp. speakers of AmE) may doubt your literacy. E.g., "Yet one can only teach a person something if that person can comprehend and use what is being taught *to them* [delete *to them*]." J.M. Balkin, *Turandot's Victory,* 2 Yale J. Law & Humanities 299, 302 (1990)./ "The *prosecution* contends that *it* has a right pursuant to Federal Rule of Evidence 607 to impeach its own witnesses; in addition, *they assert* [read *it asserts*] that a prior inconsistent statement of the witness may be admitted to attack his credibility." (Or use *prosecutors . . . they.*)/ "Neither party has waived *their* [read *his or her* or *its*] right to a jury trial."/ "The issue on this appeal is whether the district court abused its discretion in ordering *each party* to bear *their* [read *his or her,* or *its*] own costs and expenses in this litigation." See **each (A)** & **every (A).**

In BrE—to a surprising degree, and even when the purpose cannot be to avoid sexist usage—this type of disagreement in number is common. For example, Glanville Williams here makes a *firm* become *they,* not *it:* "[A]n all-round practice gives better training than a specialised one—but it may be well worth taking articles in a specialised *firm* if you are assured that *they are* [read *it is*] looking out for a bright young man/woman like you to be a partner." *Learning the Law* 209 (11th ed. 1982).

Even more startling examples abound in BrE—e.g.: "[I]t would indeed be rather surprising if it were the same crime to strike a blow at *a person* and then to lock *them* up and keep *them* in custody for six months." K.A. Aickin, *Kidnapping at Common Law,* 1 Res Judicatae 130, 130 (1935–1938)./ "Neither father nor mother can deprive *themselves* of *their* rights, except in the case of a separation agreement between husband and wife

. . . ." William Geldart, *Introduction to English Law* 46 (D.C.M. Yardley 9th ed. 1984)./ "*Anyone* can set *themselves* up as an acupuncturist . . . ." Sarah Lonsdale, *Sharp Practice Pricks Reputation of Acupuncture,* Observer Sunday, 15 Dec. 1991, at 4./ "A starting point could be to give more support to the company *secretary. They are,* or should be, privy to the confidential deliberations and secrets of the board and the company." Ronald Severn, *Protecting the Secretary Bird,* Fin. Times, 6 Jan. 1992, at 8. And most startling of all: "Under new rules to be announced tomorrow, it will be illegal for *anyone* to donate an organ to *their wife* [read *his wife* or *a spouse*] . . . ." Ballantyne, *Transplant Jury to Vet Live Donors,* Sunday Times, 25 March 1990, at A3.

As this seeming sloppiness mounts—and bids fair to invade edited American English—the complaints mount as well. For example: "Columnist James Brady . . . noted on Page 38 that Richard F. Shepard was grammatically incorrect when he wrote, 'Nobody remembers a journalist for their writing.' Perhaps it was Mr. Shepard who wrote the headline for the AT&T ad that appeared on page 37 of the same issue: 'This florist wilted because of *their* 800 service.'" Letter of Jerry Galvin, Advertising Age, 4 Nov. 1991, at 26.

Why is this usage becoming so common? It is the most likely solution to the problems brought on by sexist language—the generic masculine pronoun. Advertisements now say, "*Every student* can own *their* own computer," so as to avoid saying *his computer*—a phrasing that would likely alienate some consumers. The *Macmillan Dictionary of Business and Management* (1988) defines *cognitive dissonance* as "a concept in psychology [that] describes the condition in which *a person's* attitudes conflict with *their* behavior" (p. 38). And the President of the United States, in his 1991 State of the Union address, said: "If *anyone* tells you that America's best days are behind her, then *they're* looking the wrong way." And one of the best-edited American papers allows this: "If the newspaper can't fire him for an ethical breach surely *they* [read *it?*] can fire him for being stupid." Michael Gartner, *U.S. Law Says We Have to Kill Saddam Hussein the Hard Way,* Wall St. J., 31 Jan. 1991, at A15.

C. One Result Wrongly Attributed to Two or More Subjects. Another common mistake—in AmE and BrE alike—is to attribute one result to two separate subjects, when logically a separate result necessarily occurred with each subject. E.g., "Barry Kendall Hogan and Mark Bradford Hogan appeal their *conviction* [read *convictions*] of importing marijuana and conspiracy to import and possession with the intent to distribute the drug."/ "Undocumented creditors who fail to prove *their claim* [read *their claims*] at the meeting on the 6th February, or such later date as is provided in the Scheme of Arrangement . . . ." Notice to Creditors (from Bank of Credit & Commerce (Botswana) Limited), Fin. Times, 6 Jan. 1992, at 10./ "In school, seats are not assigned, yet students tend to sit in the same seats or nearly the same each time, and sometimes feel vaguely resentful if someone else gets there first and takes 'their' *seat* [read *seats*]." Robin T. Lakoff, *Talking Power* 121 (1990).

The following sentence presents a close call: "The government argues that the *stop of appellees' cars* need be justified only by reasonable suspicion." Or should it be *stops of appellees' cars?* Not if government officers stopped several cars with one action.

concubine = (1) a woman who cohabits with a man without being his wife; or (2) a mistress or prostitute. Sense (2) is a loose usage—an example of SLIPSHOD EXTENSION.

concur, to a nonlawyer, means "to agree." To American judges it has two senses: (1) "to join in a judicial decision, adopting the reasoning and result as one's own"; (2) "to join in a judicial decision while not agreeing with the grounds expressed in the majority opinion supporting the decision." *Concur* takes *in* <concur in the opinion> or *with* <I concur with you>. See **agree (A).**

Sense (2) is really a form of *to concur specially* (= *to write specially,* q.v.), that is, to express one's concurrence in a separate opinion. E.g., "Lenroot, Associate Judge, *specially concurs.*" *In re Schnell,* 46 F.2d 203, 211 (Ct. Cust. & Pat. App. 1931)./ "Two of the judges *specially concur* upon the ground that the starting of the car . . . was not improper." *Ranous v. Seattle Elect. Co.,* 92 P. 382, 384 (Wash. 1907).

concurrence; concurrency. *Concurrence* = (1) accordance, agreement, assent; (2) a vote cast by a judge in favor of the judgment reached, often on grounds differing from those expressed in the majority opinion explaining the judgment; or (3) a separate written opinion explaining such a vote. Sense (1) is the general one, not peculiarly legal—e.g.: "[A]ll true legal rights are concurrent in equity, wherever such *concurrence* is material . . . ." William F. Walsh, *A Treatise on Equity* 94 (1930). Senses (2) and (3) are omitted from most general English-language dictionaries. But they are common in law—e.g.: (Sense 2) "Another variant is the *concurrence* dictated by a desire to produce a badly needed majority opinion instead of a plurality opinion." Bernard E. Witkin, *Appel-*

late Court Opinions 224 (1977)./ (Sense 3) "There remain, however, two other types of opinion, the *concurrence* and the dissent, which any Justice is free to use at any time he desires." John P. Frank, *Marble Palace* 123 (1958).

Concurrency = (of a criminal sentence) the quality or fact of being concurrent in duration. E.g., "It is settled in this state that where no words of *concurrency* of sentences appear in the judgment entry, the sentences are deemed to be consecutive." *Lee v. State,* 349 So. 2d 138, 140 (Ala. Crim. App. 1977)./ "[H]e would then be returned to serve his California sentences, less time gained by *concurrency.*" *In re Cain,* 52 Cal. Rptr. 860, 861–62 (Cal. App. 1966).

concurrent; consecutive; cumulative. See **concurrent sentences.**

concurrent interests; co-ownership; estates in community; interests in community. Each of these phrases may be used for the four types of co-ownership recognized by Anglo-American law: joint tenancy, tenancy in common, coparcenary, and tenancy by the entireties. See **coparcenary, joint tenancy** (distinguishing that term from *tenancy in common*), and **tenancy by the entireties.**

concurrent jurisdiction; pendent jurisdiction. These terms may confuse even experienced lawyers. *Concurrent jurisdiction* = overlapping jurisdiction; jurisdiction exercised by more than one court at the same time over the same subject matter and within the same territory, the litigant having the initial discretion of choosing the court that will adjudicate the matter. E.g., "[E]xceptional but important cases exist . . . which raise questions of conflict of laws, particularly in respect of the *concurrent jurisdiction* of two countries with regard to the same crime . . . ." R.H. Graveson, *Conflict of Laws* 5 (7th ed. 1974).

That much is well known about *concurrent jurisdiction.* But American caselaw has given the phrase an additional sense, having to do with physical boundaries—esp. rivers and other bodies of water. E.g., "It has been decided in many jurisdictions . . . that '*concurrent jurisdiction* on the river' extends only to the water and floatable objects therein, not to bridges, dams or any other objects of a permanent nature." *Roberts v. Fullerton,* 93 N.W. 1111, 1112 (Wis. 1903)./ "The right to exercise *concurrent jurisdiction* over rivers forming state boundaries will be found discussed by Mr. Rorer in his work on Interstate Law." *State v. Nielsen,* 95 P. 720, 721 (Or. 1908).

Pendent jurisdiction = (in U.S.) exercise by federal courts of jurisdiction over matters falling under the purview of state law, on grounds that the state-law claims are so intertwined with the federal claims that they are best adjudicated in tandem. See **jurisdiction.**

concurrent negligence is an infrequent synonym of *contributory negligence.* For more on that term, see **comparative negligence.**

concurrent resolution = a legislative resolution that does not require the executive's signature and that does not ordinarily have the force of law, such as a measure to regulate Congress's internal affairs. E.g., "The Act was adopted as a temporary wartime measure, and provides . . . for its termination on June 30, 1943, unless sooner terminated by Presidential proclamation or *concurrent resolution* of Congress." *Yakus v. U.S.,* 321 U.S. 414, 419–20 (1944). The phrase applies to many state legislatures as well—e.g.: "In March, 1873, the General Assembly of Missouri adopted a *concurrent resolution* reciting that grave doubts had arisen as to the constitutionality of the act of March 31st, 1868, just quoted." *Woodson v. Murdock,* 89 U.S. 351, 357 (1874).

concurrent sentences; consecutive sentences; cumulative sentences. These phrases are used in reference to more than one penal sentence assessed against a person. *Concurrent sentences* run simultaneously—i.e., the time served in prison is credited against two or more sentences. *Consecutive sentences* (known also as *cumulative sentences*) run one after the other—i.e., the prisoner begins serving the second sentence only after completely serving the first. E.g., "[L]egal usage shows that the phrase [*cumulative sentences*] denotes consecutive sentences, whether imposed under counts of the same indictment or under different indictments, as distinguished from concurrent sentences." *Brosius v. Botkin,* 114 F.2d 22, 23 n.2 (D.C. Cir. 1940). (For the sense of *cumulative* in corporate contexts, see the entry under that word.)

concurring opinion = *concurrence,* q.v., in sense (3).

concussion; contusion. *Concussion* = (1) violent shaking; shock; or (2) injury to the head caused by a heavy blow. *Contusion* = a bruise; an injury resulting from a blow that does not break the skin.

condemn; contemn. To *condemn,* in one sense, is to render judgment against a person or thing <the court condemned the prisoner to life in prison>. E.g., "A criminal could not be *condemned* in his absence . . . ." Alan Harding, *A Social History of English Law* 121 (1966).

The word has mostly passed from legal usage into general usage in figurative senses <his looks condemn him>. E.g., "We would have serious doubts about this case if the encouragement of guilty pleas by offers of leniency substantially increased the likelihood that defendants, advised by competent counsel, would falsely *condemn* themselves."

In the U.S., *condemn* has the additional legal sense "to pronounce judicially (land, etc.) as converted or convertible to public use, subject to reasonable compensation. E.g., "To *condemn* land is to set it apart or expropriate it for public use." *San Joaquin Land & Water Co. v. Belding,* 35 P. 353, 356 (Cal. 1894)./ "A leasehold interest, of course, is a property interest and consequently may not be *condemned* for a public use without just compensation." *In re Commonwealth,* 447 A.2d 342, 344 (Pa. Commw. 1982).

To *contemn* is to hold in contempt, to despise. By far the rarer word, *contemn* is occasionally used in contexts of the legal sanction of *contempt,* q.v. More commonly, however, *contemn* is a literary word. In legal contexts, the related agent noun *contemnor,* q.v., is common. See **contemn.**

condemnation. See **eminent domain & compulsory purchase.**

condemnation money is not a familiar term to most modern lawyers, who would probably suppose it to mean "damages paid by an expropriator of land to the landowner for taking the property." In fact, at least one court has used the term in this way: "The heart of the controversy in this litigation is what disposition should be made of the *condemnation moneys* paid into the District Court by the United States as estimated just compensation for the taking of the Hotel Buckminster, the property of the debtor." *John Hancock Mutual Life Ins. Co. v. Casey,* 141 F.2d 104, 107 (1st Cir. 1944).

But the phrase traditionally refers to something quite different: "damages that a losing party in a lawsuit is condemned to pay." E.g., "Since there was no judgment for plaintiff there was no '*condemnation money.*'" *Allen v. Hartford Accident & Indem. Co.,* 123 P.2d 252, 253 (Okla. 1942)./ "[T]he appellant will pay all *condemnation money* and costs [that] may be found against him." *Maloney v. Johnson-McLean,* 100 N.W. 423, 424 (Neb. 1904).

condemned, n., becomes awkward when used in the possessive. "I also believe that a ruling on a *condemned's* competency to waive federal collateral relief should not be cloaked by the hands-off deference of Fed. R. Civ. P. 52(a)." The periphrastic possessive (*of the condemned*) is to be preferred where it is possible. Cf. **accused, deceased & insured.** See PLURALS (D) & POSSESSIVES (F).

condemnee, omitted from most English dictionaries, is an American legal NEOLOGISM meaning "one whose property is expropriated for public use or damaged by a public-works project." It dates from the late 19th century—e.g.: "Cases between a railroad company and a grantor or *condemnee* fall in the same class." *Illinois Cent. R.R. v. Anderson,* 73 Ill. App. 621, 627 (1898)./ "[T]he *condemnee* whose lands were flooded by the works was permitted to abandon in the appellate court the charge of negligence." *State v. Dart,* 202 P. 237, 239 (Ariz. 1921)./ "A tenant, therefore, is a *condemnee* . . . when its leasehold interest is taken, injured or destroyed." *In re Commonwealth,* 447 A.2d 342, 344 (Pa. Commw. 1982). See -EE.

condemner; condemnor. The *-er* spelling is preferred in the general sense of "one that disapproves." But in the U.S., *-or* predominates in the sense "a public or semipublic entity that expropriates private property for public use." E.g., "[T]he *condemnor* (i.e., the party condemning) need not wait for possession until the trial has been held." Robert Kratovil, *Real Estate Law* 321 (1946; repr. 1950). See -ER (A).

condensable; condensible. The former spelling is preferred. See -ABLE (A).

condign = well-deserved. Today the word is generally restricted to forms of punishment, not of praise. To write of *condign awards* or *laurels* is to betray a deafness to modern idiom.

condition. A. And *covenant*. The distinction between these terms is especially important in the law of leases. A broken *condition,* which is a fundamental term of a lease, can be enforced by voiding the contract; a broken *covenant,* by contrast, merely entitles the wronged party to sue for relief, but the wronged party must continue to perform under the contract. See **covenant & warranty (B).**

Holmes defined *condition* as "an event, the happening of which authorizes the person in whose favor the condition is reserved to treat the contract as if it had not been made,—to avoid it, as is commonly said,—that is, to insist on both parties being restored to the position in which they stood before the contract was made." Oliver W. Holmes, *The Common Law* 249 (1881; repr. 1963).

B. And *limitation.* A *limitation* specifies the time when an interest (such as a remainder, q.v.) vests—and how long it will last—whereas a *condition* cuts short the precedent estate and allows an entry for condition broken. See A.W.B. Simpson, *An Introduction to the History of the Land Law* 199 n.2 (1961; repr. 1964). A condition benefits only the grantor, whereas a limitation may benefit a stranger.

conditional limitation is an ambiguous term in American property law, carrying either of two very different senses: (1) an executory interest such as an executory devise, springing use, or shifting use; or (2) a special limitation, i.e., conveyancing language that creates a determinable estate. See Cornelius J. Moynihan, *Introduction to the Law of Real Property* 190 (2d ed. 1988). See **condition (B), special limitation & springing use.**

conditional sales contract. See **chattel mortgage.**

conditioned that for *on condition that* is a loose usage that almost invariably leads to a MISPLACED MODIFIER (i.e., *conditioned*): "Defendant A.B. Co., Inc., as principal, and Big Insurance Co., as surety, obligate themselves to pay to Goode Bond, District Clerk, the sum of $1,000, *conditioned that* [*on condition that*] A.B. shall prosecute its appeal with effect and shall pay all costs." The phrase is analogous to *provided that,* q.v.

condition of repair is wordy for *condition.* E.g., "When the Texas Flag is in such a *condition of repair* [read *condition*] that it is no longer a suitable Emblem for display, it should be totally destroyed, preferably by burning, and that privately."

condition precedent; condition subsequent. A *condition precedent* is something that must occur before something else can occur. "The creditor's nonperformance of a *condition precedent* to the principal's duty discharges the surety." Laurence P. Simpson, *Handbook on the Law of Suretyship* 292 (1950).

A *condition subsequent* is something that, if it occurs, will bring something else to an end. See **subsequent** & POSTPOSITIVE ADJECTIVES.

condole, v.i.; **console,** v.t. To *condole* is to express sympathy; one *condoles with* another *on* a loss. To *console* is to comfort (another), esp. in grief or depression.

condominium. Pl. *-iums.* A judge who used the correct plural once needlessly apologized: "To the purist who winces when Latin is misused, the plural of *condominium* is *condominia.*" *Hornstein v. Barry,* 560 A.2d 530, 533 n.4 (D.C. App. 1989). But a stylist winces at *condominia.* See PLURALS (A).

For the international-law sense of the word, see **confederation.**

condonation; condonement; condonance. *Condonation* = the complete forgiveness and blotting out of a conjugal offense (even to the extent of surrendering all claim for damages against the adulterer), followed by cohabitation (*Stroud's Judicial Dictionary,* 4th ed.). E.g., "On any view, if the wife be right in her evidence, the intercourse which she had with her husband in the van in February 1966 amounted to *condonation* of the cruelty which she alleged." (Eng.) To a nonlawyer, the quoted sentence sounds bizarre (as if one *condones* cruelty by later giving in to sexual advances).

The original sense of the word was much broader: "the pardoning or remission of an offense or fault; action toward the offender that implies his offense is passed over" (*OED*). E.g., "Every denunciation of existing law tends in some measure to increase the probability that there will be violation of it. *Condonation* of a breach enhances the probability." *Whitney v. California,* 274 U.S. 357, 376 (1927) (Brandeis, J., concurring). Today, in both AmE and BrE, the word is fairly rare—smacking of sesquipedality—and in law is usually confined to discussions of matrimonial offenses.

Condonance is a NEEDLESS VARIANT. *Condonement* is a technical term in certain card games.

conduce is often a better and shorter way of saying *be conducive:* "The people have an original right to establish such principles as shall most *conduce to* their own happiness."/ "Nothing *conduces to* brevity like the caving in of the knees" (Holmes, J., explaining his habit of writing opinions while standing). See BE-VERBS (B).

conduit, a favorite legal metaphor, is pronounced /***kon**-doo-it*/ in AmE, /***kon**-dit*/ or /***kən**-dit*/ in BrE.

confect = to prepare (something), usually from varied materials. It is a FORMAL WORD, unbefitting a mundane context in which it means merely "to draft": "The issue is whether summary judgment was appropriate where the language of the release in question was arguably ambiguous and there had been no discovery as to the intent of the parties in *confecting* [read *drafting*] the release."

confederacy. See **combination.**

confederate; conspirator. Whereas *conspirator* (= one engaged in a conspiracy) always carries negative connotations, *confederate* may be connotatively neutral. Its primary sense is "a person or state in league with another or others for mutual support or joint action; an ally" (*OED*). (See **confederation.**) But *confederate* also—primarily in legal contexts—has what the *OED* calls a "bad sense": "a person in league with another or others for an unlawful or evil purpose; an accomplice."

Sometimes the words are used interchangeably, as here, in an example of INELEGANT VARIATION: "A *conspirator* who had entered a plea of guilty and appeared as a witness against his two *confederates,* was convicted although a nolle prosequi was entered as to the others after two trials failed to reach a verdict." Rollin M. Perkins & Ronald N. Boyce, *Criminal Law* 694 n.94 (3d ed. 1982) (using *confederate* for *coconspirator*).

confederation; federation; condominium; consociation; confiliation. These terms denote various constitutional arrangements for the distribution of political power within the borders of a nation-state. Each term denotes a different allocation or division of governmental functions between a central national government and regional governments or groups.

A *confederation* is a league or union of states, groups, or peoples—each of which retains some degree of sovereignty. The states, groups, or peoples may delegate their rights and powers to a central authority, but they do not delegate their sovereignty.

A *federation* is a similarly arranged system with a strong central authority and no regional sovereignties, though the individual states, groups, or peoples may retain rights of varying degrees.

The distinction between these two words is crucial but subtle. William Safire observes that, in 1789, the United States changed, in Northerners' minds, from a *confederation* to a *federation.* But to Southerners, the nation retained the characteristics of a confederation. Later, of course, in 1860, Southerners thought that the union could be dissolved. When the Southern states seceded, they chose the word *confederation* to describe their own grouping—though they did not put a right to secede in their own constitution, an ambiguity noted in the North. See William Safire, *Confederacy Rises Again,* N.Y. Times, 29 Sept. 1991, § 6, at 18.

A *condominium* is a joint sovereignty or joint rule by two or more states over a single territorial entity (e.g., the Anglo-Egyptian government of the Sudan, 1899–1955, or the New Hebrides, an Anglo-French colony until 1980).

A *consociation* is a political regime for power-sharing among competing groups within a given geographic area; it involves a coalition of political leaders from all segments of a pluralistic society. (The term *consociation* was coined by Arend Lijphart, the political scientist. See his two books, *Power-Sharing in South Africa* (1985) and *Democracy in Plural Societies* (1977).)

A *confiliation* preserves group rights within a nonfederal centralized state, members of each separate ethnic, religious, or linguistic group being afforded autonomy wherever they may be located within the state. For example, their laws of inheritance and marriage, as well as their school systems, are preserved against the operation of majority rule. See Albert P. Blaustein & Jay A. Sigler, "Confederation, Condominium, Consociation, Confiliation," in 3 *The Guide to American Law* 138–40 (1983) (these two authors having coined the term *confiliation*).

confer. In Latin, *confer* meant "to compare," whence the present meaning of the abbreviated form of *compare,* namely *cf.* The unabbreviated form *confer* no longer has this meaning; today it means (intransitively) "to come together to take counsel and exchange views" or (transitively) "to bestow, usually from a position of authority." In this latter sense, one *confers* something *on,* not *in,* another. E.g., "We cannot accept the proposition that appellant's acquiescence to Ilsa's desire to live with her mother *conferred* jurisdiction over appellant *in* [read *on*] the California courts in this action." See **convey (B).**

conferencee (= a conference participant) is a needless NEOLOGISM, a word that does further violence both to -EE and to *conference,* and an ugly bit of conference-goers' jargon. E.g., *Conferencees* [read *Conferees*] *Strive to Define Goals of Professionalism,* Dallas Bar Ass'n Headnotes, 15 Aug. 1991, at 4./ "Magnan obviously provided McClaskey and the rest of the *conferencees* [read *conference-goers*] with champagne service." Richard Rambeck, *Larry Magnan: Staying at the Westin,* Seattle Business, July 1989, at 1-8.

As the interpolations just above illustrate, either *conference-goer* or *conferee,* an Americanism dating from the late 18th century, suffices in place of *conferencee.*

conferencing. The *OED* records *conference* as a (rare) verb from 1846. The *OED* and *W3* omit it.

Though increasingly common among American lawyers, *conferencing* is a bloated NEEDLESS VARIANT of *conferring.* The word has also become rather widespread in the U.S. in the form *teleconferencing,* a favorite activity of some lawyers; it may survive in that MORPHOLOGICAL DEFORMITY. See NOUNS AS VERBS.

conferment; conferral. Dictionaries suggest that the latter is a NEEDLESS VARIANT, and it ought to be treated as such. But caselaw suggests otherwise: in denoting the act of conferring, *conferral* appears in hundreds of federal cases—more than 20 times as often as *conferment*—and in hundreds of state cases—almost six times as often. Judicial usage, then, inclines dramatically toward *conferral.* E.g., "[A] distinct feature of our Nation's system of governance has been the *conferral* of political power upon public and municipal corporations for the management of matters of local concern." *Owen v. City of Independence,* 445 U.S. 622, 638 (1980).

Conferment, on the other hand, appears almost twice as frequently in the popular press as *conferral.* E.g., "Over the years, Congress has tried to use the denial of MFN—or what might more accurately be called the *conferment* of LFN (least-favored-nation)—status as a stick to make countries behave." Strobe Talbott, *America Abroad,* Time, 3 Aug. 1992, at 53. And respected legal commentators use it—e.g.: "[T]he Acts prohibit the conferment on English courts of appellate jurisdiction over Scottish courts." P.S. Atiyah, *Law and Modern Society* 60 (1983).

The question is a straightforward one: are we to model the noun after *referral* or *deferment?* Most linguistic questions like this one were settled hundreds of years ago, but *confer* is one of those verbs for which English speakers have less frequently needed a corresponding noun. Having both forms is wasteful and mildly confusing.

So the question ought to be settled—indeed, it is more important to settle the question than to settle it "correctly." I vote for the traditional form, here used by the U.S. Supreme Court: "The plaintiff here would force the Congress to choose between unconditional *conferment* of United States citizenship at birth and deferment of citizenship until a condition precedent is fulfilled." *Rogers v. Bellei,* 401 U.S. 815, 835 (1971).

confer(r)able. This word is spelled *-rr-* and is stressed on the second syllable.

conferral. See **conferment.**

confess (to). Generally, confessors *confess* crimes, charges, weaknesses, faults, and the like. Less commonly—though at least since the 18th century—confessors have *confessed to* these things. Euphony should govern the phrasing. In the following three examples, *confess to* sounds better than *confess* alone would have: "[D]id ever anybody seriously *confess to* envy?" Herman Melville, *Billy Budd* 39 (1891; repr. Signet ed. 1979)./ "I *confess to* never having attended a tractor pull . . . ." William Safire, *Virile Women Target Tobacco Men,* N.Y. Times, 11 March 1990, § 6, at 18./ "But worse, he was convicted even after the lead witness against him, Ivan F. Boesky, *confessed to* keeping millions of dollars in ill-gotten profits . . . ." *Adding Insult to Injury,* N.Y. Times, 15 July 1990, at 2F. Cf. *admit to,* for which see **admit (A).**

confessedly = (1) by general admission or acknowledgment; (2) by personal confession (*OED*). Follett too narrowly ruled that "the test of legitimacy for an adverb made from an adjective is that it fit the formula *in* [*x*] *manner*" (*Modern American Usage* 279 [1966]), a formula that *confessedly* does not fit. Follett's primary objection was to *reportedly,* q.v., the earliest recorded use of which was 1901. *Confessedly* has been used since at least 1640, however, and undeniably (or perhaps confessedly) is useful, especially in legal writing. Still, adverbs ending in -EDLY can be easily overworked.

Following are two typical—and unobjectionable—uses of *confessedly:* "As far as equitable rules differ from those of the law, they are *confessedly* more just and righteous, and their disappearance would be a long step backward in the progress of civilization."/ "No poll, no majority vote of the affected, no rule of expediency, and certainly no *confessedly* subjective or idiosyncratic view justifies a judicial determination." See -EDLY, **allegedly** & **reportedly.**

confession and avoidance = a pleading admitting the facts stated by the plaintiff but alleging other facts that destroy their legal effect, in whole or in part. Glanville Williams calls this the *retort courteous* and gives this example: "True, I negligently ran you down, but you were guilty of contributory negligence." *Learning the Law* 21 (11th ed. 1982).

confidant(e); confident, n. The forms *confidant* and *confidante* have an interesting history. Up to 1700 or so, the English word was *confident* (= a trusty friend or adherent), the correct French forms being *confident* and *confidente.* But early in the 18th century, English writers began substituting an *-a-* for the *-e-* in the final syllable, perhaps because of the French nasal pronunciation of *-ent* and *-ente.* Today the forms *confidant* and *confidante* predominate in both AmE and BrE, though *confidante* is falling into disuse because of what is increasingly thought to be a needless distinction between males and females. Despite the poor etymology, I confidently recommend using *confidant* for both sexes, as it is predominantly used in American caselaw. E.g., "[S]he testified . . . that she was a *confidant* of his." *Spears v. State,* 568 S.W.2d 492, 497 (Ark. 1978). See SEXISM (C).

confide in; confide to. The former phrase (= to trust or have faith in) is more common in general usage <to confide in one's friends>. *Confide to* (= to entrust [an object of care or a task], to communicate [something] in confidence) still commonly appears in legal prose. E.g., "Discretion was *confided to* the governing board."/ "The courts will not interfere with the exercise of discretion by school directors in matters *confided* by laws *to* their judgment."

confidence = (1) assured expectation; firm trust; (2) the entrusting of private matters; or (3) (under the Model Rules of Professional Conduct) information protected by the attorney-client privilege under local law.

Sense (2) has limited currency in general usage, as in the phrase *to take another into one's confidence* (i.e., to tell another private matters in trust). It is more generally used in law, as in this sentence from the Statute of Frauds, 29 Chas. II, c. 3 (1677), which illustrates a use of the word not uncommon today in legal prose: "And . . . from and after the said four and twentieth day of June all declarations or creations of trusts or *confidences* of any lands, tenements, or hereditaments shall be manifested and proved by some writing signed by the party."

Sense (3) is almost unknown to nonlawyers, apart from the legally sophisticated. Even so, it occasionally appears in the press: "If Parliament does not legislate, judges will keep expanding the law of '*confidence*' to stop embarrassing facts being disclosed." Economist, 28 Jan.–3 Feb. 1989, at 18.

confident, n. See **confidant(e).**

confide to. See **confide in.**

configuration. See **constellation.**

confiliation. See **confederation.**

confinee (= a person held in confinement), though it appears in *RH2,* is missing from most major English dictionaries, such as the *OED* and *W3.* Sometimes it looks suspiciously like a mere EUPHEMISM for *prisoner*—e.g.: "There's also plenty of recreational opportunities and commonly a rather sizable contingent of well-educated and formerly prominent *confinees.*" Paul Galloway, *Celebrity Cons Put Prisons on Guard,* Chicago Tribune, 29 Oct. 1989, at 1C.

At other times, though, it performs the useful function of distinguishing between those confined for criminal offenses and those confined (perhaps temporarily) for other reasons—e.g.: "*Thompson* rejected a claim that Treatment Center patients were entitled to an annual review similar to the one afforded *confinees* under Chapter 123." *Pearson v. Fair,* 935 F.2d 401, 413 (1st Cir. 1991). See NEOLOGISMS.

confine(s). Modern usage mandates the plural when referring to boundaries or limits: "In the dark *confine* [read *confines*] of the cave there was just no method for saving lives."

confirmatory; confirmative. The latter is a NEEDLESS VARIANT. In the law of evidence, *confirmatory* is sometimes used as an equivalent of *corroborative,* q.v.

confirmer; confirmor. The general word for "one who confirms" is *confirmer.* The obsolescent legal term (meaning "one who confirms a voidable estate; the grantor in a deed of confirmation") is spelled *-or.* See -ER (A).

confiscable; confiscatable. The latter is a malformed NEEDLESS VARIANT. E.g., "Money is defined as *confiscatable* [read *confiscable*] contraband in the Inmate Handbook . . . ." *Lowery v. Cuyler,* 521 F. Supp. 430, 431 (E.D. Pa. 1981). See -ATABLE.

confiscatory is the adjectival form corresponding to the verb *confiscate.* It means "of the nature of, or tending to, confiscation" (*OED*). E.g., "The rate of return prescribed by the commission would have to be clearly *confiscatory* or outside the purview of the statute to permit judicial interference with the determination." Colloquially, it has been used in the sense "robbing under legal authority" <confiscatory landlords> (*OED*).

conflict, n., (= a lawyer's duty to a client whose interests prevent the lawyer from representing another client) is a slightly transmuted shortening of the phrase *conflict of interest,* q.v.

conflicted, adj., (= full of conflicting emotions) is psychological cant contributed to the English language by the 1980s. E.g., "Look who's '*conflicted*' now: the psychiatrists." Pamela Sebastian, *Psychiatrists Hold Mass Meeting as Oedipus Wrecks Mother's Day,* Wall St. J., 11 May 1990, at B1./ "Much as seems to be the case in the Soviet Union now, the mid-1920's was a period of true flux, of mixed emotions, *conflicted* loyalties, wild uncertainties." Frank Rich, *Life in Moscow After the Revolution,* N.Y. Times, 11 May 1990, at B3./ "William Beard, . . . an adviser to the board of the Other Bar, admits he feels *conflicted* about not reporting illegal drug use by an attorney." Caroline V. Clarke, *Management,* Am. Law., March 1990, at 45.

conflict of interest. Today the phrase "ranges from being a euphemism for the result of outright bribery to describing a situation in which one subject to a duty takes a position inconsistent with that duty." John T. Noonan, Jr., *Bribes* 446 (1984).

conflict (out) = (v.i.) (of a lawyer) to be disqualified by virtue of a conflict between clients' interests; (v.t.) to disqualify (a lawyer) by virtue of a conflict among clients' interests. E.g., "His usual outside counsel . . . was *conflicted out.*" William Horne, *Inside Moves,* Am. Lawyer, March 1990, at 37. See PHRASAL VERBS.

conflict of laws; choice of law. Graveson defines *conflict of laws,* sometimes more narrowly referred to as *private international law,* as "that branch of law [that] deals with cases in which some relevant fact has a connection with another system of law on either territorial or personal grounds, and may, on that account, raise a question as to the application of one's own or the appropriate alternative (usually foreign) law to the determination of the issue, or as to the exercise of jurisdiction by one's own or foreign courts." R.H. Graveson, *Conflict of Laws* 3 (7th ed. 1974).

Choice of law, a subset of *conflict of laws,* concerns the necessity that courts choose between differing substantive laws of interested states. See Robert A. Leflar, *The Nature of Conflicts Law,* 81 Colum. L. Rev. 1080 (1981).

conflicts (referring to the law of choice of law) is often used as a shortened form of *conflict of laws.* E.g., "The late Brainerd Currie spearheaded the drive to focus attention on the often overlooked key to intelligent *conflicts* analysis—the policies underlying the laws of different states in putative conflict."

conflictual (= of, relating to, or characterized by conflict) is documented in the *OED* from 1961. E.g., "As to the *conflictual* state of Alabama law arising out of *Lee v. State, Brasher v. State,* and *Durham v. State,* I consider that *Brasher* is the paramount authority on the narrow point therein decided . . . ." *Kilpatrick v. State,* 285 So. 2d 516, 524–25 (Ala. Crim. App. 1973) (Cates, P.J., concurring).

A California court has ill-advisedly flagged with a "[*sic*]" a psychiatrist's use of the word. See *Shapira v. Superior Court,* 224 Cal. App. 3d 1249, 1252 (1990): "[T]he diagnosis of organic encephalopathy is . . . inherently *conflictual* [*sic*] with numerous other aspects of this patient's situation."

Scholars writing in the field of conflict of laws have adopted the word in a more limited sense—e.g.: "The *conflictual* aspects of flight obviously arise only in those situations in which some relevant fact has a geographical connection with a foreign country." R.H. Graveson, *Conflict of Laws* 585 (7th ed. 1974).

confluence; conflux. The latter is a NEEDLESS VARIANT.

conform takes the preposition *to* or *with.* Fowler objected to *conform with,* but most authorities find it quite acceptable. E.g., "Libya said the investigations *conformed with* international law and did not violate its sovereignty." Paul Lewis, *Libya Offers Some Cooperation in Plane Bombings,* N.Y. Times, 15 Feb. 1992, at A5.

conformable; conformably. These terms are today used almost exclusively in legal contexts. *Conformable* = according in form or character to. E.g., "The Court of Appeal altered its own order as not being *conformable* to the order pronounced." (Eng.)

Conformably to = in conformity with; in a manner conformable to. E.g., "*Conformably* to what has been said above, we are of opinion that the testatrix did not contemplate that the words 'contracts or debts' should apply to those natural obligations which a husband owes to his wife."/ "[I]f both the law and the constitution apply to a particular case, so that the court must either decide that case *conformably* to the law, disregarding the constitution; or *conformably* to the constitution, disregarding the law; the court must determine which of these conflicting rules governs the case." *Marbury v. Madison,* 5 U.S. (1 Cranch) 137, 178 (1803) (per Marshall, C.J.). The rarer phrase *conformably with* = in accordance with.

conformity; conformance. *Conformity* is the standard term, *conformance* being a NEEDLESS VARIANT that is not uncommon in legal prose. E.g.,

"I consider the disclosure not to be in *conformance* [read *conformity*] with section 171."/ "This holding is in *conformance* [read *conformity*] with the statute as well as with the federal regulations."

Like its corresponding verb, *conformity* takes either *to* or *with:* "*Conformity to* state procedure in actions at law . . . was reaffirmed in a permanent statute adopted in 1792." Charles A. Wright, *The Law of Federal Courts* 400 (4th ed. 1983)./ "The judge's discretion is not unbridled but is . . . to be exercised in *conformity with* the standards governing the judicial office." *Id.* at 629.

confront for *present* is now almost a VOGUE WORD among American judges. It is essentially hyperbolic, suggesting that the court comes "face to face with" the issues it decides. E.g., "This case *confronts us with the question whether* [read *presents the question whether*] a nonresident plaintiff asserting a cause of action based on a tort that occurred outside the state is exempt from these qualification requirements."/ "The court here *confronts* [read *addresses* or *decides*] issues no less difficult than those discussed in the court's recent opinion concerning the layoffs of firefighters."/ "When *confronted* [read *presented*] with a statute that is plain and unambiguous on its face, we ordinarily do not look to the legislative history as a guide to its meaning." In this last example *confront* is especially inappropriate because it connotes grappling or resistance, and an unambiguous statute gives no trouble to the interpreter.

confuror. See **conjuror.**

confusable; confusible. The former spelling is preferred. See -ABLE (A).

congeries is a singular noun. *Congery* and *congerie* are false singular nouns formed on the mistaken assumption that *congeries* (Fr. "a collection, aggregation") is the plural of such a noun. All forms but *congeries,* sing. & pl., should be avoided. E.g., "The analytic bent of most of those now so engaged leads them to reduce 'person' to a *congerie* [read *congeries*] of 'rights' . . . ." John T. Noonan, Jr., *Persons and Masks of the Law* xi–xii (1976).

The word is pronounced /***kon***-*jə-reez*/ in AmE, and /*kən*-***jeer***-*eez*/ or /*kən*-***jeer***-*y-eez*/ in BrE.

congratulatory; congratulative; congratulant. *Congratulatory* is the usual word. The other forms are NEEDLESS VARIANTS.

Congress does not require an article. "*The Congress* [read *Congress*] has said that interest 'shall be calculated from the date of the entry of the judgment.'" *Affiliated Capital Corp. v. City of Houston,* 793 F.2d 706, 713 (5th Cir. 1986) (Higginbotham, J., concurring). *The Congress* is a quirk to be avoided.

The possessive form is *Congress's.*

congressional, like *constitutional* and *federal,* should be written with the lowercase *-c-,* even though the noun corresponding to the adjective is capitalized. See **constitutional.**

Congressperson is unnecessary for *representative, congressional representative, Congressman,* or *Congresswoman.* See SEXISM (B).

congruent; congruous. These words are largely synonymous in meaning "in agreement or harmony; appropriate." Distinctions in use are possible, however. *Congruous* is the more widely used term, meaning "appropriate, fitting; marked by harmonious agreement." The negative form *incongruous* appears even more frequently than the positive form.

Congruent has legitimate uses in math and physics, and is also prevalent in the sense "coincident throughout; in accordance with." E.g., "The court has established procedures and standards for the admissibility of co-conspirator statements *congruent* with the Federal Rules of Evidence."

The corresponding nouns are *congruence* and *congruity. Congruency* is a NEEDLESS VARIANT.

conjoin generally provides no nuance not included in *join* or *combine.* E.g., "The lower court rejected appellant's contention that the terms of the will and the circumstances surrounding testatrix when it was executed *conjoined* [read *joined* or *combined*] to reflect an intention to exercise the power of appointment."

W10 defines *conjoin* as "to join together for a common purpose." *Join together* is, of course, a venial REDUNDANCY, just as *conjoin* is something of a one-word redundancy. But these phrases do slightly shade *join.* Perhaps on rare occasions when the precise nuance suggested by the *W10* definition is desired, *conjoin* is the proper word.

conjurator. See **conjurer.**

conjure. In the sense "to supplicate, beseech," this verb is accented on the second syllable /*kən*-***joor***/; in the sense "to play the sorcerer," the first syllable is stressed /***kon***-*jər*/.

conjurer; conjuror; conjurator. *Conjurator* is an obsolete LEGALISM meaning "one joined with others by an oath; a co-conspirator." *Conjurer* is the preferred spelling for the word meaning "a magician; juggler."

connectible; connectable. The former is preferred. See -ABLE (A).

connection; connexion; connexity. The spelling *-tion* is preferred in AmE; *-xion* is an almost obsolete spelling formerly preferred in BrE. The word means basically (1) "the act of connecting" <the connection of these loose ends>; (2) "the state of being connected" <the connection of these events>; or (3) "a connecting part" <the bridge's connection with the land>.

Lawyers use *connexity* in a distinct way, synonymously with *connectedness* (= the quality of being connected). E.g., "The more likely the public is to make an assumption of *connexity* between the providers of related services, the less similarity in the trademarks is needed for a finding that confusion is likely."

At times, though, it acts as a NEEDLESS VARIANT of *connection:* "As with the antitrust claims, RICO must relate to interstate commerce. But the *connexity* [read *connection*] required is minimal." *Cowan v. Corley,* 814 F.2d 223, 227 (5th Cir. 1987). Cf. **nexus.**

connection with, in. See **in connection with.**

connect together is a common REDUNDANCY. If the intended sense is "to connect with one another," *interconnect* is the appropriate word: E.g.,"A transaction is a group of facts so *connected together* [read *interconnected*] as to be referred to as a legal name, as a crime, as a contract, a wrong, or any other subject of inquiry that may be in issue." (Eng.) See **together.**

connexity. See **connection.**

connivance [fr. L. *connīvēre* to blink, wink at] is not, as popularly supposed, "conspiracy to act together for an illegal end," although it is a form of collusion. *Connivance* is passively allowing another to act illegally or immorally—silence and neglect when one should be vocal and monitory.

In England, *connivance* is usually confined to marital settings; the *CDL* defines it as "behaviour of a person designed to cause his or her spouse to commit a matrimonial offence." Cf. *Stroud's Judicial Dictionary* (4th ed.) ("the willing consent to a conjugal offence [in the sense of being an accessory before the fact], or a culpable acquiescence in a course of conduct reasonably likely to lead to the offence being committed").

connive = (1) to avoid noticing something that one should oppose or condemn; (2) to conspire or cooperate secretly. Sense (2) is loose, sense (1) being the original and the better one, as here illustrated: "An instance occurred in England during the last war, when a woman killed her newly born child and her own mother *connived* at the act." Glanville Williams, *The Sanctity of Life and the Criminal Law* 29 (1957; repr. 1972)./ "It is often the same citizen who originally supports the passage of such laws who later *connives* at their violation." Lon L. Fuller, *The Anatomy of the Law* 41 (1968).

connotate. See **connote.**

connotation does not mean "ramification" or "suggestion," as in these two statements by President Carter: "The political *connotations* [of the release of the American hostages in Iran] do not concern me."/ "Secretary of State Vance did not want any action with any *connotation* of military action." In the latter sentence, the word is used in the sense of "suggestion," which is close to a correct usage. But words connote; actions do not.

Connotations are the emotive nuances of words, including tone, flavor, and associational senses. Here the term is correctly used: "If, therefore, the title of this article suggests a merely philosophical inquiry into the nature of law and legal relations, the writer may be pardoned for repudiating such a *connotation* in advance."/ "Some authorities suggest that 'issue,' unlike 'children,' has a biological *connotation.*"

Sometimes *connotation* has been confused with *denotation* (= the literal meaning of a term). E.g., "'Contest of a will' is a term of art, the *connotation* [read *meaning*] of which is made clear in the context of the appropriate Probate Code sections." See the two entries following.

CONNOTATION AND DENOTATION. Those sensitive to language understand not just the dictionary definitions of words and sentences (*denotation*), but the undercurrent of suggestions and implications that inheres in all language (*connotation*). This sensitivity is no less important to the judge interpreting a statute than it is to the literary critic. In a will, for example, connotations may be the real clues to the testator's intent where the literal meanings of words provide no clues.

But connotative sensitivity is also what informs great writing. When complimenting Lord Esher's style, Cardozo appreciated the effect of connotation: "What a cobweb of fine-spun casuistry is dissipated in a breath by the simple statement of Lord Esher in *Ex parte Simonds,* that the court will not suffer its own officer 'to do a shabby thing.' If the word *shabby* had been left out, and *unworthy* or *dishonorable* substituted, I suppose the sense would have been much the same. But what a drop in emotional value would have followed. As it is, we feel the tingle of the hot blood of resentment mounting to our cheeks." Benjamin N. Cardozo, *Law and Literature,* 52 Harv. L. Rev. 471, 480 (1939).

connote; denote. *Connote* = to imply in addition to the literal meaning; *denote* = to signify the literal meaning, to indicate. *Denote* is rarely if ever misused; *connote,* however, is becoming rarer by the day in its correct senses, here illustrated: "The essential characteristics of an estate, then, are three in number: first, an estate is always an interest in land; second, an estate is always an interest that is, will, or may become possessory; and third, the term always *connotes* ownership measured in terms of duration."

How is *connote* misused? It is frequently confused with *denote,* just as *literally* is often misused for *figuratively.* E.g., "The tendency of judges to adhere to concepts and doctrines familiar to past ages is hardly anywhere more evident than it is in the law relating to the relationships *connoted* [read *denoted*] by such terms as 'leasehold,' 'landlord,' and 'tenant.'"/ "'Cannot' *connotes* [read *denotes*], not unwillingness, but inability."/ "A plea is invalid if the defendant has not a full understanding of what the plea *connotes* [read *means*]."

Moreover, words connote, not acts: "The mere act of sending a child to California to live with her mother is not a commercial act and *connotes* [read *suggests*] no intent to obtain a corresponding benefit in the State." Nor do readers connote: "While we are accustomed to *connote* [read *think of*] the same ideas in morals and ethics, and while to a considerable extent the two words involve the same general notion, yet they are distinct in that morality represents existing facts, while ethics is the scientific hypothesis for the explanation of existing facts." See **connotation.**

In the following sentence, *connote* is used in the sense "to suggest; to lead to the conclusion of." With this example one can see just how mushy this word has become: "If such testimony must necessarily *connote* [read *lead to the conclusion of*] adultery on her part, then it cannot be said that the common law has otherwise closed its eyes to this fact of life." (The ANTHROPOMORPHISM in this sentence is unobtrusive and even effective.)

Connotate is a NEEDLESS VARIANT of *connote.*

consanguineous; consanguineal; consanguinean; consanguine. The preferred legal adjective corresponding to *consanguinity* is *consanguineous* (= descended from the same parent or ancestor). E.g., "English judges . . . interpreted it as a general prohibition against the succession of the half-blood, and extended it to *consanguineous* brothers, that is to sons of the same father by different wives." Henry S. Maine, *Ancient Law* 125–26 (17th ed. 1901; repr. [New Universal Lib.] 1905, 1910). *Consanguineous* is opposed to *affinal.* See **affinity.**

Consanguinean is the Roman law term meaning "having the same father." It is opposed to *uterine* (= having the same mother).

Consanguine and *consanguineal* have been taken up by anthropologists and linguists and given DIFFERENTIATION. Thus *consanguine* = based on an extended group of blood relations esp. of unilinear descent and constituting the functional familial unit in a society (*W3*). *Consanguineal,* which shares this sense, is a NEEDLESS VARIANT of *consanguine.*

consanguinity (= relationship by blood) is a lay as well as a legal term. Here is a classical legal use: "Neither of these two women was related to the testator either by marriage [i.e., by affinity] or by *consanguinity,* while the contestant was his nephew and his only heir at law." Degrees of consanguinity are determined differently by the various legal systems of the world.

Often *consanguinity* is used figuratively: "There is apparently no intimate *consanguinity* between the case sub judice and the proceeding that pends in an alien jurisdiction." *Relation* might be better than such bombastic uses of *consanguinity,* however. See **affinity** & **kindred.** See also **degree.**

conscience, v.t., has not been recorded in most dictionaries, but legal writers occasionally use it as if it were equivalent to *contemplate:* "The rule does not *conscience* [read *contemplate*] joinder."/ "The Fourteenth Amendment does not *conscience* [read *allow* or *contemplate*] discretion in such matters." *Workman v. Cardwell,* 338 F. Supp. 893, 901 (N.D. Ohio 1972). The only related use recorded in the *OED* is *conscienced* (= having a conscience) <a loose-conscienced person>. For another use of *conscience,* see **Keeper of the King's Conscience.**

conscionable is not a mere NEEDLESS VARIANT of *conscientious,* though some dictionaries suggest it. As a positive correlative of *unconscionable,* it means "conforming with good conscience; just and reasonable" and is used of things as opposed to persons <a conscionable bargain>. E.g., "[I]mplied warranties may be limited in duration . . . if such limitation is *conscionable.*" 15 U.S.C. § 2308(b) (1988). See **unconscionable.**

consecutive sentences. See **concurrent sentences.**

consensual; consentaneous; consentient. *Consensual,* the most common of these terms, means "having or expressing or made with consent." *Consentaneous* and *consentient* are both used in that sense, as well as two others: (1) "unanimous," or (2) "agreeing." When used for *consensual,* either of the other two words is a NEEDLESS VARIANT; when used in the other two senses, each is easily simplified—as the defining words above suggest.

consensus = a widely held opinion or generally accepted view. Hence two common phrases, *consensus of opinion* and *general consensus,* are prolix. E.g., "There was a *general consensus* [omit *general*] that to drink whisky is wrong and that to be a nurse is discreditable." In the following sentence, we are accosted by a double REDUNDANCY: "The *general consensus of opinion* [omit *general* and *of opinion*] seems to be that the gist and foundation of the right in all cases is the wrongful act."

Because *consensus* refers to the collective unanimous opinion of several people, a consensus of two is impossible: "An acceptance of an offer made ought to be notified to the person who makes the offer, in order that the two minds may come together; unless this is done, the two minds may be apart, and there is not that consensus [read *agreement*] which is necessary to the English law to make a contract."

Consensus is unrelated to *census;* confusion between the two causes some writers to lapse into the misspelling *concensus*—a form that has appeared several hundred times in American law reports.

consensus *ad idem.* See **meeting of the minds** & ***ad idem.***

consent for *concede* is an odd error—e.g.: "He *consented* [read *conceded*] that he might also have had other reasons for buying the car." See **assent.**

consentaneous. See **consensual.**

consent decree (AmE) = *agreed verdict* (BrE).

consentient. See **consensual.**

consequent. A. And *consequential.* *Consequent* = following as a result. *Consequential,* a rarer and usually legal term, means "following as an indirect or secondary result" <consequential damages>. In its other proper sense, *consequential* may serve as an opposite of *inconsequential,* and hence mean "important," and occasionally "self-important." In the following sentence it means "important; of consequence," a sense prematurely labeled obsolete by the *OED*: "A few months' further delay pending determination on the governing issue in the District of Columbia litigation cannot be seriously *consequential.*"

In all other senses, *consequent* is the correct term where the choice is between the shorter and longer forms. E.g., "The evidence tended to show that the plaintiff was very much excited, and that the happening of the accident and the *consequent* injury to the casket and the body occasioned her serious mental pain and suffering."/ "The registrar transferred the application to the Divorce Registry so that it might be heard in London; *consequent upon* that direction, the application came before Mr. Registrar Kenworthy." (Eng.)

B. And *subsequent.* Frequently, *consequent* is misused for *subsequent* (= later), perhaps partly because of the logical fallacy *post hoc ergo propter hoc* (= after this, therefore because of this), which snares persons who equate sequence with causation, thinking that if one event occurred after another, the second event must have been caused by the first. See **subsequently (B).**

consequentials, n., = consequential damages. E.g., "Had the parties excluded *consequentials* by contract, the court would have had to identify the value differential [q.v.] component of the buyer's total loss." This lawyers' colloquialism should be discouraged in formal legal writing. Cf. **incidentals & exemplaries.**

consequently. See **consequent (A).**

conserva(n)cy. The preferred spelling of this essentially BrE word is *conservancy* (= a commission or court having jurisdiction over a port or river, to regulate the fisheries, navigation, etc. [*OED*]). In all other senses, *conservancy* is a NEEDLESS VARIANT of *conservation.*

conservational; conservative; conservatory. These words are to be distinguished. *Conservational* = of or pertaining to conservation. *Conservative* = characterized by a tendency to preserve or keep intact or unchanged; believing in the maintenance of existing political and social institutions. *Conservatory* = preservative.

conservator; curator. Both are general as well as specific legal terms. *Conservator* is often used in the sense "a court-appointed guardian of an incompetent" <the conservator shall have the charge of the incapable person>. Primarily a civil-law term (used, e.g., in Scotland), *curator* has an identical meaning; this term has been adopted in a number of common-law jurisdictions, however, as in several American states.

conservatory, adj. See **conservational.**

consider (as) (to be). When followed by a noun, a noun phrase, or an adjective, *consider as* is never justified stylistically; many authorities consider it an error. "Such conduct has long been *considered as solicitation* [read *considered solicitation*]." "Furthermore, the grand jury is *considered as* [read *considered*] unnecessary, particularly in England, where the preliminary examination is considered sufficient." C. Gordon Post, *An Introduction to the Law* 110 (1963).

Consider may, however, properly be followed by the infinitive *to be,* especially if the noun phrase after *consider* is at all long. "Ignoring our many precedents to the contrary, he *considers* the tax code, and especially that portion implementing the personal income tax, *to be* unconstitutional."/ "Prescott drove in his own car from Chelsea to Boston by way of the Mystic River Bridge, which he *considered was* [read *considered to be*; or delete *was* and omit *to be*] the most direct route."

The collocation of *consider* and *as* is acceptable when the phrase is followed by a participial phrase: "He is not *considered as* abandoning his objection because he does not submit to further proceedings without contest."

considerable used adverbially is a dialectal usage. "Bylaws usually may be amended with *considerable* [read *considerably*] more facility than the articles of incorporation."

consideration. **A. Legal Sense.** The law uses *consideration* in a technical sense generally unknown to nonlawyers: "the act, forbearance, or promise by which one party to a contract buys the promise of the other." Generally, a contractual promise is not binding unless it is supported by consideration (or made in a deed). This proposition has, since the 19th century, been known as the *doctrine of consideration.*

This word is one of the lawyer's basic TERMS OF ART, but even lawyers sometimes misconceive the word: "One must be careful not to think of *'consideration'* as if it was synonymous with 'recompense'; rather the word [at common law] connoted some *sound reason* for the conveyance, and the payment of money by the feoffee was only one possible reason." A.W.B. Simpson, *An Introduction to the History of the Land Law* 167 (1961; repr. 1964).

B. As a Count Noun. In law, by virtue of the technical meaning explained under (A), *consideration* may be a COUNT NOUN whereas in general English usage it is not so used. E.g., "A basic principle of contract law is that one *consideration* will support multiple promises by the other contracting party." Nevertheless, the phrase *other valuable consideration* is used rather than *other valuable considerations.*

C. Idiomatic Constructions. Legal idiom requires *in consideration of* but *as consideration for,* in the sense of the word given under (A).

D. *Valuable consideration* and *good consideration.* The former phrase refers to an act, forbearance, or promise having some economic value; the latter refers to natural love or affection, or moral duty. To create an enforceable contract, *valuable consideration* is required. *Good consideration* is no good.

Still, deeds customarily recite a consideration of $1 or $10, plus *other good and valuable consideration* so as to obscure the true price. The DOUBLET is unnecessary, however, as *other valuable consideration* suffices. See **and other good and valuable consideration.**

E. *Nominal consideration* and *inadequate consideration.* See **nominal consideration.**

F. *In consideration of the mutual covenants* . . . . See **in consideration of the mutual covenants herein contained.**

G. *In consideration of the premises.* See **in consideration of the premises.**

H. *Past consideration.* This phrase, meaning "an act done or a promise given by a promisee before the making of a promise sought to be enforced," is an OXYMORON of sorts. For *past consideration* is no consideration, since it has not been given in exchange for the promise sought to be enforced.

consignatary; consignatory. For this civil-law term equivalent to *consignee, Black's* gives *-tory,* and *W3* and *OED* give *-tary.* The *OED* lists *consignatory* only as a variant of *cosignatory* (= a joint signatory). Historical civilian usage seems to recommend *consignatary.*

consignation. See **consignment.**

consignee (= one to whom goods are consigned) is pronounced */kon-si-**nee**/* or */kon-sɪ-**nee**/*. Cf. **consignor.**

consigner. See **consignor.**

consignment; consignation. These words denote quite different things, though the root concept is the same. *Consignment* is the more usual term in common-law jurisdictions, meaning "the act of delivering goods to a carrier to be transmitted to a designated agent." *Consignation,* primarily a term from Scots and French law, means "the act of formally paying over money, as into a bank, or to a person legally appointed to receive it, often because it is the subject of a dispute."

consignor; consigner. *Consignor* is the technical correlative of *consignee,* q.v. A *consignor* dispatches goods to another in *consignment.* In Scots law, a *consigner* is one who makes a *consignation* of money in dispute. The two words are often pronounced differently: *consignor /kon-si-**nohr**/* or */kən-**sɪ**-nohr/; consigner /kən-**sɪ**-nər/.*

consistence is a NEEDLESS VARIANT for *consistency.* E.g., "[Two judges] voted to affirm the rule on institutional considerations, feeling that judicial *consistence* [read *consistency*] on these attachments was more important than the correctness of the attachment procedure itself." *Podolsky v. Devinney,* 281 F. Supp. 488, 492 n.7 (S.D.N.Y. 1968).

consistent with. A. Wrongly Made Adverbial. A common illiteracy in American law is to use this phrase adverbially rather than adjectivally. For adverbial uses, *consistently with* (= in a manner consistent with) is the correct phrase. In the following sentence, the first use is adverbial, whereas the second is (properly) adjectival: "Thereafter, all medical facilities will be equipped *consistent with* [read *consistently with*] these standards and all new construction of health care facilities will be *consistent with* the standards."

B. And *not inconsistent with.* When the U.S. Supreme Court reverses and remands a judgment of a federal court of appeals, it directs that the further proceedings be *consistent with* the Court's opinion. But when it reverses and remands a state-court judgment, it directs that the further proceedings be *not inconsistent with* the Court's opinion.

Why the difference? Because *consistent with* shows that the Court retains plenary power over the lower federal court. *Not inconsistent with,* by contrast, shows that the state court is much more independent to fashion its holdings on substantive law.

consist in; consist of. American writers too often ignore the distinction. *Consist of* is used in reference to materials; it precedes the physical elements that compose a tangible thing; cement, for example, *consists of* alumina, lime, silica, iron oxide, and magnesia. E.g., "The document admitted to probate *consists of* a single sheet of legal cap paper, folded in the middle in the usual way along the short dimension, making four pages of equal size."

Consist in (= has as its essence) precedes abstract elements or qualities, or intangible things; e.g., a good moral character *consists in* integrity, decency, fairness, and compassion. The proper use of *consist in* is illustrated in the following sentences: "And those who argue that the progress of civilization *consists in* raising our standards of conduct, even though that means increasing the number of criminals, are blandly begging the question." Morris R. Cohen, *Reason and Law* 45 (1961)./ "The cruelty that *consists in* beating is unmistakable." Max Radin, *The Law and You* 62 (1962).

In the sentences that follow, *consist of* is wrongly used for *consist in;* the mistake is especially common in AmE: "The alleged negligence *consisted of* [read *in*] the act of a hospital nurse in injecting a foreign substance into plaintiff's left arm, causing pain and permanent injury."/ "In understanding any major political move, it is a mistake to focus only on the move itself. Understanding depends upon seeing all of the interrelations; the art of politics *consists of* [read *in*] using those interrelations."/ "Where the plaintiff's contributory negligence *consists of* [read *in*] being inattentive, and not discovering a risk he should have discovered, he will not be barred from strict liability recovery."

The opposite mistake—using *consist in* for *consist of*—is rare but does occur: "Typically [the bill of complaint in equity] *consisted in* [read *consisted of*] three parts: the narrative, the charging, and the interrogative parts." Fleming James, *Civil Procedure* § 2.4, at 64 (1965).

consociation. See **confederation.**

console. See **condole.**

consolidating statute; codifying statute. A *consolidating statute* collects the legislative provisions on a particular topic and embodies them in a single statute, often with minor amendments and drafting improvements. A *codifying statute,* by contrast, purports to be exhaustive in restating the whole of the law on a particular topic, including prior caselaw as well as legislative provisions. Courts generally presume that a *consolidating statute* leaves prior caselaw intact, whereas a *codifying statute* generally supersedes prior caselaw.

consolidation. See **code, joinder (B) & merger (A).**

consols (= [BrE] funded government securities with no maturity date) is invariably in the plural form, because it originated as an abbreviation for *consolidated annuities.* E.g., "In *Standing v. Bouring, consols* were transferred from the plaintiff's name into the joint names of herself and her godson, a person to whom, it was held, she was not in loco parentis." (Eng.) See **consul.**

consortium; society. In the phrases *loss of consortium* and *loss of society,* the two words are synonymous in the context of husband and wife. *Society,* however, is a broader term, describing other than marital relationships, such as father-child and brother-sister. Thus generally only a spouse may sue for *loss of consortium* (L. "partnership"—related to *consort*), whereas any close relation may sue for *loss of society.* Both terms refer to the nonpecuniary interests a person may have in the company, cooperation, affection, and aid of another. See **society.**

In England, where only a husband could sue for loss of consortium, the cause of action was abolished as a cause of action by the Administration of Justice Act of 1982. *Consortium* is pronounced */kon-**sor**-shi-əm/* or, more usually, in BrE, */kon-**sor**-di-əm/.* The plural is *-tia.*

conspectus; prospectus. These terms are not synonymous. A *conspectus* is a comprehensive survey, summary, or synopsis. A *prospectus* is a document describing the chief features of something that is forthcoming.

conspiracy. See **combination.**

conspirative; conspirational. See **conspiratorial.**

conspirator (= one engaged in a conspiracy) finds a NEEDLESS VARIANT in *conspiratorialist*—e.g.: "He ordered Christic and its chief *conspiratorialist* [read *conspirator*], Daniel Sheehan, to pay $1 million toward the defendants' legal bills." L. Gordon Crovitz, *Lawyers Make Frivolous Arguments at Their Own Risk,* Wall St. J., 20 June 1990, at A17. Cf. **confederate.**

conspiratorial; conspirative; conspiratory; conspirational. The first is standard; the others are NEEDLESS VARIANTS.

conspire together is a common REDUNDANCY. "The defendants *conspired together* [omit *together*] with persons unknown to import cannabis resin." (Eng.)/ "The defendants have *conspired together* [omit *together*] to conceal their tortious and fraudulent conduct." See **together.**

constellation, like *configuration,* is often used figuratively to describe a specific group of facts in a case. E.g., "The contrary is likely to be true if both parties have moved for summary judgment on different legal theories dependent on different *constellations* of material facts."

constitute is often an overblown substitute for *make.* And it is an ARCHAISM to give *constitute,* like *make,* a direct object followed by an objective complement. E.g., "No particular words, technical or otherwise, or form of expression in an instrument are necessary to *constitute* [read *make*] it a lease."/ "I deem it unnecessary to consider whether such an interest would *constitute* [read *make*] her a legal representative of J.P. Robertson after his death, as I do not believe she ever acquired such an interest."

To use *constitute* in the sense "to make up, compose" is more in accord with modern usage. E.g., "This system of classification is employed for convenience in describing the effect upon the operation of provisions in the will caused by changes in property *constituting* the estate after the will is executed." See **compose (C).**

constitution. The sense referring to a selection or collection of fundamental principles was not usual until the time of the American and French Revolutions. Only since the Americans declared in 1787—"We the people of the United States . . . do ordain and establish this Constitution for the United States of America"—did the practice of having a written document containing the principles of governmental organization become established. At the same time, *constitution* took on what is now its most common meaning. See Kenneth C. Wheare, *Modern Constitutions* 3 (2d ed. 1966). Originally, the Latin word *consitutiones* referred to the law-making utterances of the Roman emperors, esp. as collected and abridged in the Theodosian and earlier codes.

When referring to the U.S. Constitution, writers customarily capitalize the word *Constitution* whether or not the word appears with the qualifying place name (*U.S.*).

constitutional should not generally be capitalized, though *Constitution* (in reference to the U.S. Constitution or any particular constitution) should be. Cf. **congressional & federal.**

The adjective has two meanings: (1) "of or relating to the Constitution" <constitutional rights>; and (2) "proper under the Constitution" <constitutional actions>. Thus sense (1): "The diversion of a job to a competitor is not an invasion of a *constitutional* right." And sense (2): "The Wisconsin statute, which is similar to the Norris-LaGuardia Act, has also been held *constitutional.*" The opposite of *constitutional* in sense (1) is *nonconstitutional,* and in sense (2) *unconstitutional.* See **nonconstitutional.**

constitutionalism = (1) a constitutional system of government; or (2) adherence to constitutional principles. Sense (2) is now more common—e.g.: "Whatever one may think of Robert Bork's brand of *constitutionalism,* his willingness to defend that vision openly and forthrightly was admirable." Stephen Macedo, *Stricter Senate Review,* N.Y. Times, 23 Oct. 1991, at A11.

constitution(al)ist. The standard form of the term is *constitutionalist* (= [1] one who studies or writes on the Constitution; or [2] a supporter of constitutional principles).

constitutionality (= the quality or state of being constitutional) was originally an Americanism (dating from 1801 in the *OED*), but it is now common in BrE as well.

constitutionalize = (1) to provide with a constitution <to constitutionalize the new government>; (2) to make constitutional; to bring into line with the Constitution <plans to constitutionalize the currently segregated school district>; or (3) to import the Constitution into <the dissenter accused the majority of unnecessarily constitutionalizing its decision>. Senses (2) and (3) are relatively new and are unrecorded in the *OED* and *W3.* Here is an example of sense (3): "*New York Times v. Sullivan* was the first major step in what proved to be a seemingly irreversible process of *constitutionalizing* the entire law of libel and slander."

The (ungainly) noun is *constitutionalization*—e.g.: "I want to . . . discuss the *constitutionalization* of common law since 1937." Erwin Chemerinsky, *The Constitution and the Common Law,* 73 Judicature 149, 150 (1989).

constitutional law = body of law spawned by *Marbury v. Madison,* which declared the judiciary's power to construe the Constitution. Rodell explained it as "the cumulative efforts of the Supreme Court to explain, justify, or excuse the restrictions it lays down." Fred Rodell, *Woe Unto You, Lawyers!* 48 (1939; repr. 1980). An infrequent synonym is *fundamental law.*

constitutionally has at least four senses in legal contexts: (1) "in a constitutional manner; in a way that comports with the Constitution" <constitutionally assembled> <constitutionally enacted>; (2) "under the provisions of the Constitution" <constitutionally deficient> <constitutionally impermissible>; (3) "so as to bear on the Constitution" <constitutionally speaking>; (4) "by the Constitution" <constitutionally prohibited>. Sense (1) is the only legal sense given by the *OED* and *W3.*

constrain = (1) to force; or (2) to confine forcibly. Sense (1) is the more common of the two. It is a favorite word of dissenting judges: "It is for such reasons that I am *constrained* to dissent."/ "I regret that I am *constrained* to dissent from the holding of the court in this case." Sense (2) is primarily literary.

construct for *construe* occurs frequently when nonlawyers write about legal subjects—e.g.: "In his historical interpretation of the Supreme Court's role in *constructing* [read *construing*] the United States Constitution, the late Robert G. McCloskey divided constitutional law into three periods . . . ." Barbara H. Craig, *Chadha: The Story of an Epic Constitutional Struggle* vii–viii (1988). See **construction.**

construction is the noun form of both *construct* and *construe,* in law usually the latter. A nonlawyer might think that *construction of statutes* is the business of legislatures, since they *construct* (i.e., build) statutes; but *construction* in that phrase means "the process of construing," which is the business of the courts. See **interpretation.**

The phrase *construction of law* means something slightly different—the "construing" of a statute to cover what it does not explicitly mention.

construction lien. See **mechanic's lien.**

constructive; constructional. These terms are not to be confused. *Constructive* is given a meaning in law that is unknown elsewhere; it "denotes that an act, statement, or other fact has an effect in law though it may not have had that effect in fact" (*OCL*). Thus we have the phrases *constructive fraud* and *constructive trust* (qq.v.) and other phrases describing legal FICTIONS. See **actual.**

Constructional = of or pertaining to the act or process of construing. E.g., "When the taker of a prior interest is one of several heirs of the designated ancestor at the ancestor's death, no *constructional* tendency is sufficiently definite to be capable of statement."/ "The *constructional* problem is complicated by a so-called rule of repugnancy." Cornelius J. Moynihan, *Introduction to the Law of Real Property* 31 (2d ed. 1988).

constructive fraud; legal fraud. The former is the more common phrase denoting forms of unintentional deception or misrepresentation that are held to be fraudulent. It is also clearer: *legal fraud* might suggest to the unwary that the fraud is, e.g., presumed or sanctioned by law, rather than that it is considered in law to be fraud. For the difference between *fraud in law* and *legal fraud,* see **fraud** (C).

constructive seisin. See **seisin** (A).

constructive trust. A. Synonyms. The phrase *constructive trust* (= a trust that the law creates against one who has obtained property by wrongdoing) has various equivalents—*trust de son tort, trust ex maleficio, involuntary trust, trust ex delicto*—none of which is as common. Though the other phrases may have some advantages over the confusing phrase *constructive trustee* (see (B)), that term is so common that the others merit being labeled NEEDLESS VARIANTS.

B. And *express trust*. Properly speaking, *constructive trust* and *express trust* are not really antonyms because they exist on different verbal planes. As the *Restatement of Restitution* § 160, comment a at 641 (1937), explains: "The term *constructive trust* is not altogether a felicitous one. It might be thought to suggest the idea that it is a fiduciary relation similar to an express trust, whereas it is in fact something quite different . . . . A constructive trust does not, like an express trust, arise because of a manifestation of an intention to create it, but it is imposed as a remedy to prevent unjust enrichment. A constructive trust, unlike an express trust, is not a fiduciary relation, although the circumstances [that] give rise to a constructive trust may or may not involve a fiduciary relation."

C. And *resulting trust*. The phrase *constructive trust* is likewise distinguishable from a *resulting trust* (= a trust imposed by law when someone transfers property under circumstances suggesting that he or she did not intend the transferee to have the beneficial interest in the property). A *resulting trust,* then, arises because of the transferor's intention, while the law imposes a *constructive trust* to prevent the wrongful holder of property from being unjustly enriched. The *resulting trustee* is a genuine trustee—in a fiduciary relation to the beneficiary—while the *constructive trustee* has no such fiduciary relation.

construe (= to explain or interpret for legal purposes) applies happily to statutes, rules, and the like—but not to doctrines, as here: "Because it impedes full and free discovery of the truth, the attorney–client privilege is strictly *construed* [read *applied*]." *Weil v. Investment / Indicators Research & Management, Inc.,* 647 F.2d 18, 24 (9th Cir. 1981).

For another mistaken usage, see **construct.**

construe, strictly. See **strict construction.**

consul; counsel; council. *Consul* = a governmental representative living in a foreign country to oversee commercial matters. *Counsel* = a legal adviser or legal advisers. (See **counsel & attorney** (A).) *Council* = a body of representatives. See **council.**

consulate; consulship. *Consulate* = the office, term of office, jurisdiction, or residence of a consul. *Consulship* = the office or term of office of a consul. *Consulate* is the more common and (therefore) the broader term. *Consulship* may be useful in conveying precisely one's meaning.

consult takes the prepositions *with* (documents or other persons), *on* or *upon,* or *about* (a matter). The verb may be used transitively <to consult the will itself> as well as intransitively, in combination with any of the prepositions previously named.

consultation. The English writer Philip Howard has stated that *consultation*

> can mean a conference at which the parties, for example, lawyers or doctors, *consult* or deliberate. Modern legal usage confines this sense to meetings with more than one counsel present. You can have a *consultation* with your doctor on your own. But you must be able to afford the fees of at least two lawyers simultaneously before you can properly describe your meeting with them as a *consultation.*
> Philip Howard, *Weasel Words* 57 (1979).

The *OCL* defines *consultation* as "a meeting of two or more counsel and the solicitor instructing them for discussion and advice."

No such restrictive meaning is given the term in AmE. If you consult with your lawyer on a certain matter, then that act is *consultation.*

consult(at)ive; consult(at)ory. The forms ending in *-ory* are NEEDLESS VARIANTS. Both *consultative* and *consultive* are old, the former recorded from 1583, the latter from 1616. Because the adjectival form of Latinate words in *-tion* follows from the nominal form, *consultative* is the preferable form: "Purely *consultive* [read *consultative*] experts are those not relied upon in whole or in part by testifying experts." See **consultation.**

consummate has two pronunciations as an adjective (either /kən-**səm**-it/ or /**kon**-sə-mət/), and still another as a verb /**kon**-sə-mayt/. For its sense, see **inchoate.**

contact, v.t. Though vehemently objected to in the 1950s, *contact* is now firmly ensconced as a verb. Brevity recommends it over "to get in touch with" or "communicate with"; it should not be considered stylistically infelicitous even in formal contexts. E.g., "These witnesses were recently *contacted* by petitioner's counsel and agreed to make new affidavits."

If, however, the writer means either *call* or *write*—as opposed to *call or write*—the specific verb is preferable.

contagious; infectious. These words are misused even by educated writers and speakers. A *contagious* disease is communicable by contact with those suffering from it. An *infectious* disease spreads by contact with the germs, e.g., in the air or in water. Some *contagious* diseases are not *infectious,* and vice versa.

contemn = to treat (as laws or court orders) with contemptuous disregard. E.g., "We find that jurisdiction exists based on both the inherent power of a court to reach those who knowingly *contemn* its orders and the minimum contacts analysis set out below." The *OED* notes that this word is "chiefly a literary word," but it is used just as frequently in legal as in literary contexts. See **condemn.**

contemner; contemnor. Most dictionaries list the spelling in *-er* as the predominant one; 19th-century BrE and AmE overwhelmingly preferred that spelling, which is still the better one. The *-or* spelling, now common in the U.S., remains inferior. See -ER (A).

contemplative is accented on the second syllable /*kən-***tem***-plə-tiv*/.

contemporary; contemporaneous. Both refer to simultaneity. *Contemporaneous* usually refers to either actions or things, *contemporary* to persons. *Contemporary* has the additional informal meaning "modern," but this sense should be avoided in contexts referring to past times, as in this example: "An anti-Jeffersonian charge by Justice Chase in 1803, reprinted in this collection, was one count in his impeachment by a Jeffersonian Congress; more *contemporary* items in the collection include papers by Justices Hugo Black and Robert H. Jackson." When no other time frame is mentioned, then we may infer "contemporary with us" (= modern), but not in historical contexts. *Cotemporaneous* is a NEEDLESS VARIANT of *contemporaneous;* likewise, *cotemporary* is a NEEDLESS VARIANT of *contemporary.*

Here *contemporary* is misused for *contemporaneous,* unless the writer meant to personify the statute mentioned (an unlikely intention): "As the court acknowledges, the 1924 statute must be examined in light of its *contemporary* [read *contemporaneous*] legal context."

Contemporaneous does not precisely mean "simultaneous"; rather, it means "belonging to the same time or period; occurring at about the same time." Thus the following sentences are correct, although *simultaneous* does not properly fit in each slot filled by *contemporaneous:* "Courts regard with particular respect the *contemporaneous* construction of a statute by those initially charged with its enforcement."/ "Where a conveyance in trust is made voluntarily, without solicitation or undue influence, and no fraud is shown prior to, or *contemporaneous* with, the execution of the deed, but consists in repudiating the agreement to reconvey, the case is not removed from the operation of the Statute of Frauds."/ "These uncertainties in proof by parol evidence are at least partially eliminated in the Uniform Probate Code by the requirement that the advancement be 'declared in a *contemporaneous* writing by the decedent or acknowledged in writing by the heir.'"

contempt; contemptibility; contemptuousness. These words are quite distinct. *Contempt* = (1) (generally) the act or state of despising; the condition of being despised; (2) (in law) action interfering with the administration of justice. *Contemptibility* = the quality or fact of being worthy of scorn. *Contemptuousness* = the quality of being scornful or disdainful. See **contumac(it)y.**

contempt of court = action that interferes with the administration of justice by the various courts of law. There are several different types. *Direct contempt* is that which occurs in open court (e.g., foul language spoken to a judge). For example, in the 19th century, a drunken lawyer in Tombstone, Arizona, Allen English, upon being fined $25 for contempt of court, said to the judge, "Your honor, $25 wouldn't pay for half the contempt I have for this court." That statement was a direct contempt. By contrast, *constructive contempt* (sometimes called *indirect* or *consequential contempt*) results from actions outside court, such as failing to comply with orders.

Another dichotomy is that between *civil* and *criminal contempt*; the former consists in failing to do something ordered by the court for another litigant's benefit, whereas the latter consists in acts that obstruct justice.

contemptuous. A. And *contemptible.* The former means "expressing contempt," the latter "worthy of contempt or scorn." Both terms are disparaging, *contemptible* being the stronger of the two. See **contempt.**

B. And *contumacious*. See **contumacious.**

contemptuousness. See **contempt.**

contend. See **allege** & **contest,** v.t.

content(s). When referring to written matter or oral presentation, *content* = the ideas or thoughts contained in the words as opposed to the method of presentation. Follett disapproved the modern tendency to use *content* as well as *contents* for "what is contained," but the usage is old and is now common. E.g., "Since Justice Black did not define the *content* and scope of this exception, that critical task has fallen to the lower courts."

Contents refers to material and nonmaterial ingredients alike. E.g., "The bottles were securely and completely wrapped in paper and tied with a string so that the *contents* of the package could not be seen or observed."/ "The declarations of a deceased testator as to his testamentary intentions, and as to the *contents* of his will, are deemed to be relevant when his will has been lost, and when there is a question about what were its *contents.*" (Eng.)/ "The testator who has revoked a previous will should not be fettered by the *contents* of that previous will when he sets about his new testamentary work." Still, *content* is now more common for the nonmaterial things contained in something (as in documents).

The word *contents* should never refer to human beings, as the callous sentence that follows demonstrates: "The impact and disintegration of the aircraft extended over several seconds *before the aircraft and its human contents came to rest* [read *before the aircraft and those aboard came to rest*]."

conterminous. See **coterminous.**

contest, n.; **contestation; litiscontestation.** These terms are to be differentiated. *Contest* = (1) debate; controversy; dispute <without contest> <will contest>; or (2) a friendly competition. *Contestation* = disputation or controversy, as between parties at law; verbal contention; keen argument (*OED*); (2) the contesting or disputing (of a point or claim) <assertions not open to contestation>; or (3) an assertion contended for <the appellant's contestation is untenable>. *Litiscontestation,* a legal term used primarily in Scots and civil law, means (1) "the formal entry of a suit in a court of law" (*OED*); or (2) "a legal process by which controverted issues are established and a joinder of issues arrived at" (*W3*).

contest, v.t.; **contend.** In the sense "to fight (for)," *contest* is almost always transitive <to contest a will> <to contest an election>, and *contend* is intransitive <to contend against an opponent>. *Contend* may be transitive when it means "to maintain, assert," and is followed by *that* <appellants contend that the notice was not timely filed>.

contestant; contestor. *Contestant* = (1) one who contests a will (*caveator,* q.v., being a synonym); (2) a participant in a sporting event. The word has been common only since the mid-19th century. *Contestor* is a NEEDLESS VARIANT for sense (1)—e.g.: "Appellant argues that the will *contestors* [read *contestants*] failed to introduce evidence to establish they were interested parties." *Keener v. Archibald,* 533 N.E.2d 1268, 1269 (Ind. Ct. App. 1989). See **contestee.**

contestation. See **contest,** n.

contested election, in AmE, means either (1) "an election the validity of whose results has been challenged," or (2) "a political race with more than one candidate." Sense (2) is the sole meaning in BrE. See **candidacy.**

contestee is a 19th-century Americanism listed in the *OED* as meaning "a candidate for election who is in the position of having his seat contested by another"—a sense recorded from 1870. Even earlier, though, lawyers had begun to use *contestee* in a sense corresponding to *contestant* or *contestor,* as here: "[T]he witness . . . proceeded to state what he had heard the *contestee,* Anthony Banning, Jr., say a few days after his father's death, in respect to his father's will . . . ." *Banning v. Banning,* 12 Ohio St. 437, 444 (1861)./ "[T]he secretary of the interior found from the evidence that the *contestee* was not a *bona fide* homestead claimant." *Carr v. Fife,* 44 F. 713, 713 syl. 3 (C.C.D. Wash. 1891).

Today the word appears fairly frequently in American legal writing, usu. paired against *contestant*—e.g.: "The *contestants* sought to raise various alleged violations of the Kentucky Corrupt Practices Act, the legality of support alleged to have been given the *contestees* by the school superintendent . . . ." *Stearns v. Davis,* 707 S.W.2d 787, 787–88 (Ky. Ct. App. 1985). See -EE & **contestant.**

contestor. See **contestant.**

context of, in the; in a . . . context. This phrase is often used superfluously. E.g., "The Commission's rationale for the mosaic that finally emerges [see METAPHORS (A)] with respect to principal transactions not only is interesting, *but also may be helpful in the context of understanding* [read *but also may be helpful in understanding*] the related issue of a dealer's obligation in principal transactions to charge prices reasonably related to the market price."/ "During the seventh century B.C., Egypt was repeatedly though always briefly occupied by Assyrian armies and later *infiltrated by Greek and other Aegean elements in a military and subsequently a commercial context* [read *infiltrated militarily and later commercially by Greek and other Aegean elements*]."

contiguous means, not merely "close to" or "near," but "adjacent." It is commonly misused in the phrase *the forty-eight contiguous states,* which is illogical: only a few states can be *contiguous* to one another. *Contiguous to* for *next to* is sometimes a pomposity. (See **adjacent.** Cf. **adjoin.**) This adjective should always be construed with *to.* E.g., "In this appeal, Mirador argues that it has a valid easement over Booker's lot, which is *contiguous* on the southern side *to* Mirador's landlocked parcel."

contingency; contingence. The latter is a NEEDLESS VARIANT. *Contingency* is sometimes used elliptically for *contingent fee,* q.v., as here: "Loftin, . . . who was working on a 40 percent *contingency,* played the role of the homespun Fort Worth boy: His shirttail hanging out, he sniffled from a head cold." Dana Rubin, *Courting Costs,* Texas Monthly, May 1992, at 52, 58.

contingent fee; contingency fee. The former is the preferred term. It denotes an agreement that no fee will be charged for the lawyer's services unless the lawsuit is successful or is settled out of court. Usually, a contingent fee calls for larger compensation to be paid than the lawyer would normally charge, often a percentage of the money recovered or the money saved, to compensate for the risk involved. See **champerty (A) & no-win-no-fee system.**

contingent-fee lawyer is a journalistic variation of *plaintiff's lawyer*—and a more specific one, since the two phrases are not always interchangeable. Note that *contingent-fee* is hyphenated when preceding *lawyer* as a PHRASAL ADJECTIVE: "There was nothing new about *contingent-fee lawyers'* moving in when they smelled the kill, but here was an instance when the public at large might benefit from the economic self-aggrandizement of the trial lawyers." John A. Jenkins, *The Litigators* 120 (1989; repr. 1991).

contingent remainder; contingent interest. Each phrase is used on both sides of the Atlantic, but the former is more common in both AmE and BrE.

The phrase *contingent remainder* has led to confusion between the interest subject to a condition precedent and a vested defeasible interest subject to a condition subsequent. Unlike a *vested remainder,* q.v., a *contingent remainder* is not an estate at all—it is a limitation whereby an estate will vest in interest when a contingent event happens, and then vest in possession when a prior estate ends.

To remedy this confusion, the *Restatement of Property* discarded the term and substituted in its place a more descriptive phrase *remainder subject to a condition precedent.* Even so, courts continue to use the older term. See **remainder.**

continual; continuous. *Continual* = frequently recurring. E.g., "The agents are *continually* acting in reliance upon the effectiveness of the survivorship provisions." *Continuous* = occurring without interruption. E.g., "*Continuously* since prior to May 28, 1906, Mrs. M.E. Skeen and J.C. Skeen have been . . . husband and wife . . . ." *McClintic v. Midland Grocery & Dry Goods Co.,* 154 S.W. 1157, 1157 (Tex. 1913).

The two words are frequently confused, most frequently with *continuous* horning in where *continual* belongs—e.g.: "Luckily Mandy liked dogs, for the C.J., in spite of his intelligence, loyalty and other endearing qualities, involved us in *continuous* [read *continual*] excitement." Ephraim Tutt, *Yankee Lawyer* 197 (1943)./ "Bar associations have *continuously* [read *continually*] tried to define the professional responsibilities of attorneys inside and outside the courtroom." Norman Dorsen & Leon Friedman, *Disorder in the Court* 136 (1973)./ "Minutes after the arrest, Wayne Forrest, a Deputy Attorney General helping prosecute the case, told the presiding judge, Charles R. DiGisi, that the sheriff's office had been engaged in a '*continuous* [read *continual*] course of misconduct' in the Spath case." Robert Hanley, *Courthouse Arrest Roils Trial of Officer in Teaneck Killing,* N.Y. Times, 18 Jan. 1992, at A9.

continuance; continuation; continuity. *Continuance* has virtually opposite senses in lay and legal usage. Generally, it means (1) "keeping up, going on with, maintaining, or prolonging"; or (2) "duration; time of continuing." E.g., "Plaintiff is entitled to this higher salary during his *continuance* in defendant's employ."/ "The fact that any person was born during the *continuance* of a valid marriage between his mother and any man is generally conclusive proof that he is the legitimate child of his mother's husband." (Eng.)

But in American law, it means "postponement; the adjournment or deferring of a trial or other proceeding until a future date" <motion for continuance>. E.g., "There is no support in the record for the complaint that the district court failed to grant a *continuance* to the defense." See **continue.**

Continuation = continued maintenance; carrying on or resumption of (an action, etc.); that by which a thing is continued (*COD*). E.g., "The question whether a corporation is a *continuation* of a predecessor has been fermenting in the past decade."/ "During the *continuation* of the relation, the attorney, for most purposes, stands in the place of the client, who will be bound by whatever the attorney may do or say, in the regular course of practice, in the conduct of the cause."/ "*Continuation* of the use of the property as a municipal park carries out a larger share of Bacon's purpose than the complete destruction of such use by the decree we today affirm."

Continuity = connectedness; unbrokenness; uninterruptedness <the continuity of the litigation process was broken up by a number of continuances>.

continuation in part. See **c.i.p.**

continue; stay, v.t. "We are accustomed to *continue* an action in the sense of plodding on. But it was possible in Scotland and was once possible in England (and still is in legal language) to *continue* in the sense of knocking off or adjourning." Ivor Brown, *I Give You My Word* 112 (1964). It is this transitive use of *continue* (= to postpone) in legal contexts that yields the legal use of *continuance,* q.v.

Only in legal parlance is *stay* current as a transitive verb. Stronger than *continue, stay* means "to stop, arrest, delay, prevent (an action or proceeding)" <to stay the proceedings>. E.g., "I do order that until such indemnity be given all further proceedings be *stayed.*" (Eng.) See **stay.**

continue liable is an old legal idiom—shorthand for *continue to be liable.* E.g., "[T]here are a number of Tennessee cases [holding] that the father *continues liable* for the support of his minor children even though there has been a divorce and award of custody to the mother." *Livingston v. Livingston,* 429 S.W.2d 452, 458 (Tenn. Ct. App. 1967)./ "[The] policy . . . must be regarded as subsisting in contemplation of law, and the insurer continues liable to a third-party claimant until relieved from its obligation . . . ." *State Ins. Fund v. Brooks,* 755 P.2d 653, 656 (Okla. 1988).

continue on is a minor but bothersome prolixity. E.g., "The pleader's standoffish 'one' *continued on* [read *persisted*] as meaningless rote."/ "The shift to a new continent cut off Americans from much of the change that *continued on* [read *continued*] in England."

continuity. See **continuance.**

continuous. See **continual.**

continuum. Pl. *continuums* or *continua.* The foreign plural should be avoided. See PLURALS (A).

contorts, n., (= the overlapping domain of contract law and tort law; a specific wrong that falls within that domain) is Professor Grant Gilmore's NEOLOGISM—a PORTMANTEAU WORD (*contract* + *tort*) dating from the 1970s: "I have occasionally suggested to my students that a desirable reform in legal education would be to merge the first-year courses in Contracts and Torts into a single course [that] we would call *Contorts.*" Grant Gilmore, *The Death of Contract* 90 (1974)./ "Interestingly, Dean Prosser seems also to recognize this peculiar possibility and to identify it as an issue existing on the fringes of contract and tort law, the so-called '*contort*' of recent renown." *Schlange-Schoeningen v. Parrish,* 767 F.2d 788, 793 n.3 (11th Cir. 1985).

contours is such a popular metaphor that it has become a VOGUE WORD among lawyers and judges. E.g., "The EEOC administrative regulations provide some basis for outlining the *contours* of the accommodation duty."

contra, n., adj., adv., & prep., is a LEGALISM for *against, contrary,* etc. Except as a signal in citations, it should be avoided in favor of its more common equivalents. E.g., "Partitions in kind as well as partitions by sale and division of the proceeds were sustained, although there was some *contra* [read *contrary*] authority invalidating a partition in kind."/ "These provisions of the Code are, of course, *contra* [read *contrary*] to the common-law rules that have discouraged use of powers of attorney."/ "That case is, on its surface, *contra* [read *to the contrary*], but the use of a questionnaire and its relationship to Rule 4(a) were not considered by the court."

contracept, v.i., is a BACK-FORMATION that is not included in the dictionaries. It is a jargonistic word popular among social workers. E.g., "Rather than become pregnant, our adolescents should learn about sex and, if they are to be active, *contracept* [read *use contraception*]."

contraceptionist. See **contraceptor.**

contraceptivism. In the days when contraceptives were illegal, this term referred to unlawful trafficking in contraceptives. See Rollin M. Perkins, *Criminal Law* 108 (1957).

contraceptor; contraceptionist. What is the agent-noun corresponding to *contraception?* William Safire prefers *contraceptionist.* See *On Language,* N.Y. Times, 30 Dec. 1990, § 6, at 6. But *contraceptor* is five times as common, and usage suggests a worthwhile distinction: a *contraceptor* is one who uses contraception, while a *contraceptionist* is one who advocates its use.

contract, n. & v. **A. Noun Senses.** The word has many more senses than most dictionaries—even the *OED* and *W3*—acknowledge. In tackling the problem of defining this word, Patrick Atiyah acutely observes: "A definition of a contract presupposes that the law recognizes a single concept of contract. In fact it is doubtful if this is really the case. Certainly there is one very central and powerful concept in the middle of contract law . . . . But contractual obligations arise in such a very wide variety of circumstances, and are based on such a wide variety of grounds, that there is little relationship between cases on the outer extremities of contract law." P.S. Atiyah, *An Introduction to the Law of Contract* 30 (3d ed. 1981). Following are the six primary senses, with subsenses noted:

1. An agreement between two or more parties to do or not to do a thing or set of things; a compact—e.g.: "A *contract* in the popular sense of the word is an agreement between two or more parties." Lawrence Friedman, *Contract Law in America* 15 (1965).
2. **a.** An agreement between two or more parties creating obligations that are enforceable or otherwise recognizable at law—e.g.: "A *contract* is valid if valid under the law of the settled place of business or residence of the party wishing to enforce the contract." Russell Weintraub, *A Defense of Interest Analysis in the Conflict of Laws* [*etc.*], 46 Ohio St. L.J. 493, 498 (1985). **b.** A writing executed by the parties to evidence the terms of such an agreement—e.g.: "[T]he execution of the *contracts* was not a condition of employment." *J.I. Case Co. v. NLRB,* 321 U.S. 332, 333 (1944). **c.** Arising out of or operating under such an agreement <contract rights> <contract work>. **d.** The legal relation resulting from such an agreement—e.g.: "[T]he *contract* is a subsisting relation, of value to the plaintiff, and presumably to continue in effect." *Landess v. Borden, Inc.,* 667 F.2d 628, 631 (7th Cir. 1981) (quoting William Prosser, *Torts* 726 (2d ed. 1955). **e.** The task or assignment for which such an agreement has been entered into—e.g.: "The six *contracts* of the defendants, were assigned to, and completed in the name of the New Jersey Wood Paving Company." *American Nicholson Pavement Co. v. City of Elizabeth,* 1 F. Cas. 691, 699 (C.C.N.J. 1874) (No. 309). **f.** In futures markets, the smallest amount of a given commodity that can be exchanged by agreement of traders, i.e., the standard unit of sale—e.g.: "The normal trading unit is one *contract* consisting of 5000 bushels." *Cargill, Inc. v. Hardin,* 452 F.2d 1154, 1156 (8th Cir. 1971).
3. More broadly, any legal duty or set of duties not imposed by the law of tort; esp., a duty created by a decree or declaration of a court in the phrase *contract of record,* q.v.—e.g.: "An obligation of record, as a judgment, recognizance, or the like, is included within the term "*contract.*" A bequest falls under the term "*contract,*" and when the will is admitted to probate it is to be regarded as a contract of record." *Quinn v. Shields,* 17 N.W. 437, 442 (Iowa 1883). Cf. **quasi-contract.**
4. **a.** A promise or set of promises, by a party to a transaction, enforceable or otherwise recognizable at law—e.g.: "[T]he defendant agreed to let rooms to the plaintiff; and then, finding that the rooms were to be used for the delivery of blasphemous lectures, declined to carry out his *contract.*" William R. Anson, *Some Notes on Terminology in Contract,* 7 Law Q. Rev. 337, 339 (1891). **b.** A writing that expresses such a promise—e.g.: "Alternative promises in bonds giving bondholders option to elect payment in dollars, guilders, pounds, marks or francs were not separate and independent *contracts* or obligations . . . ." *Guaranty Trust Co. v. Henwood,* 59 S. Ct. 847, 848 syl. 2 (1939).
5. The division or body of law dealing with contracts. *Often cap.*E.g.: "A general theory of *contract* asserts that there is at least a substantial body of rules which applies to all contracts in common." G.H. Treitel, *An Outline of the Law of Contract* 2 (5th ed. 1979).
6. The terms of a contract, or any particular term—e.g.: "[I]t does not appear whether there was any express *contract* as to when the money was payable." *Civil Serv. Coop. v. Gen. Steam Navigation Co.,* 2 K.B. 756, 762 n.1 (1903)./ "A similar usage allows *contract* to be applied to . . . the terms or a particular term of a *contract.*" R.M. Jackson, *The Scope of the Term "Contract,"* 53 Law Q. Rev. 525, 536 (1937).

B. General Slipperiness. "One moment the word [*contract*] may be *the agreement* of the parties; and then, with a rapid and unexpected shift, the writer or speaker may use the term to indicate the *contractual obligation* created by law as a result of the agreement." Wesley N. Hohfeld, *Fundamental Legal Conceptions* 31 (1919; repr. 1946). Legal writers should be sensitive to any such semantic change within a given context.

C. And *promise*. The distinction between these words (despite sense 4 above) has long been urged, and perhaps ought to be observed for conceptual clarity. An influential English writer felt the slippage even in 1845, the words *in strictness* signaling a losing battle: "There is in strictness a distinction between a promise and a contract; for the latter involves the idea of mutuality, which the former does not." 2 Henry J. Stephen, *New Commentaries on the Laws of England* 59 (1886).

D. And *covenant*. *Contract* is the general term. *Covenant* now applies (1) to agreements under seal, and (2) to undertakings contained in deeds or implied by law in deeds, as in the phrase *covenant running with the land.*

E. And *agreement, bargain*. See **agreement & bargain.**

F. *Contract*, v.i.; ***enter into a contract with.*** The tighter wording, *to contract,* is almost always preferable to the longer, *to enter into a contract with.*

G. *Verbal contract*. See **verbal contract.**

H. *Illegal contract*. See **illegal contract.**

I. Pronunciation. As a noun, *contract* is accented on the first syllable /***kon***-*trakt*/; as a verb, on the second /*kən*-***trakt***/. Cf. **contrast & compact.**

contract breach is inferior to *breach of contract.* E.g., "It is true, as plaintiffs contend, that the victim of the *contract breach* [read *breach of contract*] may recover damages that would place him in the same position he would have occupied if the defaulting party had performed." (Using *victim* in reference to one disadvantaged by breach of contract borders on OVERSTATEMENT.)

contract-breaker = breacher. E.g., "A *contract-breaker* can be charged with the amount of an expected gain that his breach has prevented, if, when the contract was made, he had reason to foresee that his breach would prevent it from occurring."/ "[T]he wicked *contract-breaker* should pay no more in damage than the innocent and the pure in heart." Grant Gilmore, *The Death of Contract* 14–15 (1974). See **breacher.**

contractee (= a person with whom a contract is made) is attested in but one source (dated 1875) in the *OED;* it appears in neither *W3* nor *Black's.* The word was infrequently used in the 19th century—as early as 1815—but fell into disuse in the 20th century, probably for two reasons. First, its meaning duplicates that of *contractor,* so that using the two as correlatives makes little sense. Second, the terminology *offeror* and *offeree* more sharply defines the relationships to be denoted.

Still, a few notable writers have fallen for this word—e.g.: "If a man is induced to contract with another by a fraudulent representation of the latter that he is a great-grandson of Thomas Jefferson, I do not suppose that the contract would be voidable unless the *contractee* [read *contractor* or maybe *offeror*] knew that, for special reasons, his lie would tend to bring the contract about." Oliver Wendell Holmes, *The Common Law* 255 (1881; repr. 1963). See -EE.

contract for sale; contract of sale; contract to sell; executory sale. A. Senses. These various phrases have traditionally been used in the law of sales. The newest of them is *contract for sale,* used in the Uniform Commercial Code to include both "a present sale of goods and a contract to sell goods at a future time." U.C.D. § 2-106(1). In G.B., *contract of sale* bears this meaning in the Sale of Goods Act 1893.

The other phrases are narrower because they relate to a future transfer. *Contract to sell* denotes "a contract whereby the seller agrees to transfer the property in goods to the buyer for a consideration called the price." 1 Samuel Williston, *The Law Governing Sales of Goods* § 1, at 2 (1948). Williston notes that this idea is also "not very happily called an *executory sale.*" *Id.* at 3. The problem with *executory sale* is that it suggests that a sale has occurred when in fact it has yet to occur.

B. Criticism of *contract for sale* and *contract of sale;* Answer. The broadest of these phrases (*contract for sale* and *contract of sale*) have come under criticism because they include two types of transfers: present sales and future sales. Williston complained—unavailingly, in retrospect—that "it is unfortunate . . . to use the same term for two transactions, differing so vitally in their legal effect." 1 Samuel Williston, *The Law Governing Sales of Goods* § 1, at 4 (1948). His recommendation was that "[t]he unambiguous terms, *'contract to sell'* and *'sale'* should be used . . . to express the respective meanings." *Id.*

The consensus of modern scholarly opinion resists this criticism: "The distinction between exchanges that involve promises and those that involve only present transfers is not as sharp as might at first appear, since the law often attaches implied obligations of a promissory character to exchanges involving only present transfers (e.g., the seller usually makes implied warranties in the case of a present sale of goods). The Uniform Commercial Code avoids the distinction [by using the phrase] *contract for sale* . . . ." E. Allan Farnsworth, *Contracts* § 1.1, at 4 n.6 (1982).

contract implied in law. See **quasi-contract & implied contract.**

CONTRACTIONS are generally avoided in formal writing. Legal writers tend to feel uncomfortable with them—judges, say, in their judicial opinions; appellate lawyers in their briefs; business lawyers in their contracts; academic lawyers in their law-review articles; and all lawyers, even in the less formal context of their business correspondence. Perhaps contractions don't generally belong in appellate opinions, briefs, contracts, and law review articles.

But why shouldn't we use them in writing to clients or colleagues? Because we've become inured to stuffiness. It has become a natural tone for much of the legal profession. And many of us carry over our tone from one type of discourse (an appellate brief, say) to other types of discourse (chiding a five-year-old child: "Now comes your mother . . . .").

Some excellent legal writers use contractions to good effect, especially when driving home a powerful point in the modern idiom. E.g.:

- "What our forefathers said, they said. What they *didn't* say, they meant to leave to us . . . ." Charles P. Curtis, Jr., *Lions Under the Throne* 7–8 (1947).
- "Of course the bailee would have the action against the thief, if he could be found. But probably that *wasn't* worth very much." Edward Jenks, *The Book of English Law* 272 (P.B. Fairest ed., 6th ed. 1967).
- "You *won't* drive the nail properly if you *don't* hold it straight and so also you *won't* achieve an effective system of law unless you give some heed to what I have called principles of legality." Lon L. Fuller, *The Morality of Law* 200 (rev. ed. 1969).
- "Each of these three solutions is old-fashioned. But many lawyers use them and many lawyers who *don't* use them *don't* understand why they *don't*." Thomas L. Shaffer, *The Planning and Drafting of Wills and Trusts* 202 (2d ed. 1979).
- "This may seem rather curious today: why should a person be unwilling to answer questions properly put to him by duly authorized courts or officials? And if he is unwilling, *isn't* it likely that this is because he has something to hide?" P.S. Atiyah, *Law and Modern Society* 45 (1983).
- Of course, we do have our property taxes and our inheritance taxes. If we *don't* pay them, we can lose our land." Thomas F. Bergin & Paul G. Haskell, *Preface to Estates in Land and Future Interests* 18 (2d ed. 1984).
- "The only thing left to do is for the jury to engage in a densely textured judgment upon the defendant's conduct—either it was deviant or it *wasn't*." Bruce A. Ackerman, *Reconstructing American Law* 28 (1984).

Using contractions at every turn, of course, can make the writing seem breezy; for most of us, though, that risk is nil: a gentle breeze might refresh our readers. See **cannot** & SUPERSTITIONS (J).

contract of deed. See **chattel mortgage.**

contract of lease. The courts sometimes use this phrase rather than *lease* alone, as if ignoring the fact that a lease is primarily a contract—not a conveyance. "[If] used at all," states one commentator, the phrase *contract of lease* "should be applied merely to the aggregate of the covenants into which the parties may have entered in connection with the making of the conveyance by way of lease." 1 Herbert T. Tiffany, *The Law of Real Property* § 74, at 111 (3d ed., B. Jones ed., 1939).

contract of record. This phrase, ironically, denotes "no contract at all, and has nothing whatever to do with the law of contracts." P.S. Atiyah, *An Introduction to the Law of Contract* 31 (3d ed. 1981). A *contract of record* is an obligation imposed by a judgment or recognizance of a court of record; the phrase came about merely because such a judgment or recognizance was enforceable in common-law procedure by the same type of action as was used for contractual cases. For other phrases using *contract* but not truly involving a contract, see **void contract** & **unenforceable contract.**

contractor. See **independent contractor** & **contractee.**

contract quasi. See **implied contract** & **quasi-contract.**

contracts—like its singular—denotes an entire legal field, as do other plurals such as torts and conflicts, qq.v. E.g., "The field of Law known as *Contracts* is one of the most settled, most venerable, and least politically complicated fields of Law." Fred Rodell, *Woe Unto You, Lawyers!* 28 (1939; repr. 1980). Cf. sense (5) listed at **contract.**

contractual is sometimes erroneously written (or pronounced) *contractural,* with an intrusive *-r-*. The *OED* illustrates the blunder with quotations from such reputable publications as *The New York Times* and *The Washington Post.*

Alas, the word has invaded even higher ground: "There is no essential difference between *contractural* [read *contractual*] and statutory limitations." *Kornberg v. Carnival Cruise Lines, Inc.,* 741 F.2d 1332, 1337 (11th Cir. 1984). The U.S. Supreme Court has sic'd this solecism on more than one occasion. See *O'Connor v. Ortega,* 480 U.S. 709, 727 (1987) (quoting a deposition); *Shaffer v. Heitner,* 433 U.S. 186, 191 (1977) (quoting a party's affidavit).

contract under seal. See **seal** (B).

contractural. See **contractual.**

contradict. See **gainsay.**

contradictory; contradictive; contradictional; contradictious. *Contradictory* = opposite, contrary. *Contradictious* = inclined to contradict or quarrel; the word is applied to persons. *Contradictive* and *contradictional* are NEEDLESS VARIANTS of *contradictory.*

contradistinction; contrast. These words may be distinguished, if not contradistinguished. *Contradistinction* = distinction by opposition; *contrast* = dissimilarity (but not necessarily opposition). E.g., "The Seventh Amendment preserves the right to a jury trial not only for suits in which the right existed at common law, but also for suits in which legal rights were to be ascertained and determined, in *contradistinction* to those in which equitable rights alone were recognized, and equitable remedies were administered."/ "The word 'children' in its primary and natural sense is always a word of purchase and not of limitation; it is employed in *contradistinction* to the term 'issue.' "/ "[T]hese differences in phraseology . . . must not be too literally *contradistinguished* [i.e., be too literally made to seem opposites]." *Brush v. I.R.C.,* 300 U.S. 352, 362 (1937).

Contradistinction should not be used where *contrast* suffices. E.g., "The term 'constitution' is ordinarily employed to designate organic law in *contradistinction* [read *contrast*] to the term 'laws,' which is generally used to designate statutes or legislative acts."

contraindicate began as a medical term meaning "to make (as a treatment) inadvisable." It has made its way into legal parlance, despite the contraindication of using such jargon. E.g., "The plan shall include provision for a system to ensure that no prisoner is assigned to do work that is *contraindicated* [read *inadvisable*] given his medical condition."

contra proferentem. **A. Sense.** This TERM OF ART names the doctrine that, in interpreting documents, ambiguities are to be construed unfavorably to the drafter. E.g., "Faced with this ambiguity, the district court adopted the state law rule of contract interpretation *contra proferentem* in fashioning the federal common law . . . ." *Phillips v. Lincoln Nat'l Life Ins. Co.,* 978 F.2d 302, 306 (7th Cir. 1992).

B. Spelled *contra proferentes.* The phrase is sometimes rendered *contra proferentes,* an alternative Latin form that is no longer current—e.g.: "The fact that the company appears and interposes a claim to the steamer does not change the legal nature of the proceeding from one in rem to one in personam, so as to bring it within the terms of the special contract on the back of the bill of lading, which are to be *contra proferentes.*" *Pacific Coast S.S. Co. v. Bancroft-Whitney Co.,* 94 F. 180, 186 (9th Cir. 1899)./ "I cannot adopt the suggestion that there is in this policy any ambiguous language to be construed *contra proferentes.*" *Re Stooley Hill Rubber & Chem. Co. v. Royal Ins. Co.,* [1920] 1 K.B. 257, 274.

contrary. A. *Contrary to* or *contrary from.* *Contrary* takes the preposition *to; from* is no longer standard.

B. *On the contrary; to the contrary.* *On the contrary* marks a contrast with an entire argument or position just mentioned <The respondent argues that we must dismiss the petition. On the contrary, we consider it well taken>. *To the contrary* marks a contrast with a specific noun just mentioned <Reynolds sought relief; Griffin, to the contrary, decided not to litigate>.

contrast. A. Prepositions with. One *contrasts* something *with* something else, not *to;* but it is permissible to write either *in contrast to* or *in contrast with.*

B. *Compare and contrast.* This is an English teacher's REDUNDANCY. See **compare (with) (to).**

C. Pronunciation. As a noun, *contrast* is accented on the first syllable /***kon**-trast*/; as a verb, on the second /*kən-**trast***/.

contravene. A. And *controvert.* These words, occasionally confused, should be distinguished. *Contravene* = (1) (of persons) to transgress, infringe (as a law); to defy; (2) (of things) to be contrary to, come in conflict with. E.g., "It is argued that the regulation, in limiting the amount of money any single household may receive, *contravenes* a basic purpose of federal law."/ "The court ruled that the statutory provision was a penalty and that allowing a wrongdoer to insure himself against it would *contravene* public policy."

Controvert = to dispute or contest; to debate; to contend against or oppose in argument. E.g., "Under the pleadings, when the issues were joined in fraud, undue influence, failure of consideration, and mistake, the court had jurisdiction to hear and determine the *controverted* facts."/ "The appellant's counsel does not very seriously *controvert* the correctness of the answer finding the minor guilty of contributory negligence."

B. And "*controvene.*" The form *controvene* is a misrendering caused by confusion between the two words discussed in (A). E.g., "The State's use of a jailhouse informant to elicit inculpatory information from Wilson *controvened* [read *contravened*] his right to counsel . . . ." *Wilson v. Henderson,* 742 F.2d 741, 748 (2d Cir. 1984). The same problem occurs in the noun form: "In fact, the Appellees argue that Appellant acted in direct *controvention* [read *contravention*] of their interests." *Winfree v. Philadelphia Elec. Co.,* 554 A.2d 485, 488 (Pa. 1989).

C. And *contravent.* The form *contravent* is a misbegotten BACK-FORMATION innovated by writers who, reaching for the verb corresponding to *contravention,* forgot that *contravene* is the correct form. E.g., "[D]ecision appears to *contravent* [read *contravene*] clear legislative intent of IEEPA." Jules Lobel, *Emergency Power and the Decline of Liberalism,* 98 Yale L.J. 1385, 1417 n.175 (1989).

contravent. See **contravene (C).**

contravert. See **controvert & contravene (A).**

contributary. See **contributory,** n.

contribute for *attribute* is nothing less than a MALAPROPISM. But it is surprisingly common in the U.S.: "The great majority of these deaths can be *contributed* [read *attributed*] to misuse of smoking materials."/ "To what may we *contribute* [read *attribute*] the company's success on appeal?"

contribution; indemnity. These words frequently appear in tandem in the legal phrase *contribution and indemnity,* but many users of the phrase forget the individual significations of the words. *Contribution* is (1) the right to demand that another who is jointly responsible for injury to another contribute to the one required to compensate the victim, or (2) the actual payment by a joint tortfeasor of his share of what is due. It may entail an equal sharing of the loss, but in some jurisdictions entails a payment proportional to one's fault. *Indemnity* is (1) a duty to make good any loss, damage, or liability another has incurred, or (2) the right of an injured person to claim reimbursement for his loss. Whereas *contribution* involves a partial shifting of the economic loss, *indemnity* involves a complete shifting of the economic loss. See **indemnity.**

Rather than use the phrase *contribution and indemnity* imprecisely and indiscriminately, the party seeking recompense should decide whether he is entitled only to one or the other, and then use that term only.

contributory; contributive; contributorial; contributional. Each of these word forms has a different meaning. *Contributory* = (1) making contribution; that contributes to a common fund; or (2) bearing a share toward a purpose or result <contributory negligence>. *Contributive* = having the power of contributing; conducive <exercise is contributive to health>. *Contributorial* = of or relating to a contributor. *Contributional* = of or relating to (a) contribution. *Contributary* is a NEEDLESS VARIANT of *contributory.*

contributory, n.; **contributary,** n. In the sense "one who, or that which, contributes," *contributory* is now standard—e.g.: "The company cannot put the beneficiary on the list of *contributories* . . . ." J. Charlesworth, *The Principles of Company Law* 70 (4th ed. 1945)./ "The question was whether a person who was a member of the provisional committee on the formation of a joint stock company, and had accepted shares in the company, thereby became liable as a *contributory* when the second company failed." R.E. Megarry, *A Second Miscellany-at-Law* 143 (1973).

As in its adjectival use, *contributary* is a NEEDLESS VARIANT.

contributory negligence. See **comparative negligence & assumption of the risk.**

controller. See **comptroller.**

controvene. See **contravene (B) & controvert.**

controversion, a fairly uncommon word, is the noun corresponding to *controvert*—e.g.: "The fact that Austin's workers' compensation carrier filed a statement of *controversion* is also irrelevant." *Archem Co. v. Austin Indus., Inc.,* 804 S.W.2d 268, 270 (Tex. App.—Houston [1st Dist.] 1991)./ "The record establishes, without *controversion,* that the defendant was twice advised of his constitutional rights . . . ." *People v. Kelland,* 567 N.Y.S.2d 810, 812 (App. Div. 1991).

controversy. A. Misspelling. *Controversy* appears surprisingly often in the mangled form *controversary*—e.g.: "We feel that this long-standing *controversary* [read *controversy*] can be significantly reduced and perhaps eliminated . . . ." *Evans v. Yankeetown Dock Corp.,* 491 N.E.2d 969, 974 (Ind. 1986).

B. *Case or controversy.* See **case or controversy.**

controvert. So spelled—not *contravert,* a misspelling that litters more than 150 pages of American caselaw: "To adopt this analysis would be to directly *contravert* [read *controvert*] an express holding of the Court of Appeals." *Harper v. Harper,* 472 A.2d 1018, 1021 (Md. Ct. App. 1984). See **contravene (A)** & **(C).**

controvertible. So spelled. See -ABLE (A).

contumacious; contemptuous. Both terms mean roughly "scornful," but the former is more frequently used as a legal term meaning "willfully disobedient of a court order." E.g., "Although certain money decrees are enforceable by contempt because they are not debts, imprisonment is nevertheless permissible only for *contumacious* behavior."/ "Finding that the record does not support a finding of *contumacious* conduct or a clear record of unexplained delay, we reverse the dismissal for plaintiff's failure to prosecute."

Here *contumacious* is used in the lay sense ("recalcitrant"), in which it is chiefly a literary word: "We should not encourage litigants to act *contumaciously* out of fear that otherwise their constitutional rights will evaporate."/ "Despite respondent's adamant—even *contumacious*—refusal to cooperate with Hotchkiss or to take the stand as Hotchkiss advised, Hotchkiss succeeded in getting a 'hung jury' [q.v.] on the two most serious charges at the first trial."

Contemptuous is the more usual term among nonlawyers as the adjective for *contempt,* but it is used also in legal contexts, which usually favor *contumacious:* "Ordinarily purpose or intent is irrelevant in determining whether an offensive act is *contemptuous*; the nature of the act itself is determinative." *Ex parte Krupps,* 712 S.W.2d 144, 154 (Tex. Crim. App. 1986)./ "The NLRB petitioned this court for an adjudication of civil contempt against the company for violating an order of this court; the company's allegedly *contemptuous* conduct consists in maintaining an overbroad rule prohibiting employee solicitation and distribution of materials, including union campaign materials." See **contemptuous (A).**

contumac(it)y; contumely. *Contumacity* is a long NEEDLESS VARIANT for *contumacy* (= willful contempt of court). *Contumacy,* then, is a particular kind of *contempt of court,* q.v. E.g., "In case of *contumacy,* the Chancellor would order the arrest of the defendant, and his imprisonment for contempt." (Eng.) The adjectival form is *contumacious,* q.v.

Contumaciousness should be reserved for the sense "the quality of being contumacious," and should not be used as a longer variant of the preferred noun: "While we do not wish to understate the significance of this omission, we find it to be more a matter of negligence than of purposeful delay or *contumaciousness* [read *contumacy*]."

Contumely, easily confused with *contumacy,* is a literary word meaning "rude and haughty language." Thus Shakespeare wrote, in *Hamlet,* of "the proud man's *contumely.*"

contusion. See **concussion.**

conundrum. Pl. *conundrums.* E.g., "Not surprisingly, the drafting of the earliest statutes gave rise to a host of judicial *conundrums.*" Alan Harding, *A Social History of English Law* 230 (1966)./ "In order to avoid *conundra* [read *conundrums*] of this sort it is necessary to abandon the simple dichotomy of 'proprietary' and 'possessory' . . . ." A.W.B. Simpson, *An Introduction to the History of the Land Law* 35 (1961; repr. 1964). See PLURALS (A).

conusance —in the *OED*'s words, "an early form of *cognizance,* retained to recent times in legal use"—is a NEEDLESS VARIANT.

convener; convenor. The first is the preferred form. See -ER (A)

convention. See **treaty.**

conventione(e)r. Today the usual term for one attending a convention is *conventioneer.*

conversable. See **conversible.**

conversation(al)ist. The standard term is *conversationalist.* Older authorities preferred *conversationist,* but the word is little used.

conversation, criminal. See **criminal conversation** & EUPHEMISMS.

converse; reverse; obverse; inverse. These words denote various types of opposition. *Converse* = a statement derived from another statement by transposing important antithetical members (e.g., equitable support without legal foundation, legal foundation without equitable support). *Obverse* = the inference of another proposition with a contradictory predicate by changing the quality of the original proposition (e.g., no men are immortal, all men are mortal) (*COD*). *Inverse* = the inference of another proposition in which the subject term is the negative of the subject of the original proposition and the predicate is unchanged (e.g., no colorable challenge of this trial could be entirely frivolous, some noncolorable challenge of this appeal could be frivolous). *Reverse,* the broadest of these terms, means simply "the contrary."

Conversely = in the converse manner or order; by conversion. E.g., "Words that are libelous per se do not need an innuendo, and, *conversely,* words that need an innuendo are not libelous per se." Here the word is nonsensically used: "Subadditivity means that it is always cheaper to have a single firm produce whatever combination of outputs is supplied to the market, *and conversely* [read *and it is more expensive to have several firms produce whatever output is supplied to the market*]."

conversible; conversable; convertible. *Conversible* is a NEEDLESS VARIANT of *convertible* (= capable of being exchanged or otherwise converted). *Conversable* = oral. See -ABLE (A).

conversion means, in tort law, "the wrongful disposition of another's tangible property (other than land) as if it were one's own." It does not include mere acts of damage or even a taking that does not equate with denying the owner's right of property—it does include, however, acts such as taking possession, refusing to give up the goods on demand, giving them to a third person, or destroying them. This legal sense is virtually unknown to nonlawyers. The adjectival form of the word is *conversionary.*

convertible. See **conversible.**

convey. A. And *conveyance,* v.t. The latter, hypothetically "to accomplish the conveyance of," does not exist except as implied in the form of the agent noun *conveyancer* and the gerund *conveyancing,* q.v. This verb denotes what the lawyer does. *Convey* denotes what the seller does (usu. through a lawyer). See **conveyor (B).**

In the phrase *convey away, away* is unnecessary. See PARTICLES, UNNECESSARY.

B. For *confer.* This is an inexplicable lapse. E.g., "Appellee's and appellant's respective citizenships of France and Georgia therefore *conveyed* [read *conferred*] diversity jurisdiction on the federal courts." See **confer.**

conveyance, n. **A. Legal Senses.** In law, the noun *conveyance* refers not only to the actual transfer of an interest in land, but also to the document (usually a deed) by which the transfer occurs.

B. For *car* or *automobile.* *Conveyance* is sometimes used as a FORMAL WORD for *car.* It should be avoided when possible. E.g., "The negligence of a driver of a private *conveyance* [read *car*] was not imputed to the guest." The only context in which it might be justified is that in which the writer intends to be so broad as to cover any vehicle, vessel, or aircraft.

C. And *conveyal.* *Conveyance* is the better noun corresponding to the verb *to convey; conveyal* is a NEEDLESS VARIANT.

conveyance, v.t. See **convey (A).**

conveyancer. See **conveyor (B).**

conveyancing, a term more common in BrE than in AmE, is often understood in a sense analogous to that of *conveyance* (= the document by which land is purchased). E.g., "Lawyers have been doing basically the same things—*conveyancing* property, drawing up wills, and so on—for a long time." (Eng.) Actually, however, it can have a wider import; *conveyancing* comprises the drafting and completion of all kinds of legal instruments, not just those having to do with the transfer of land. E.g., "Even in those statutes, the same objectives in administering trusts can be obtained by proper *conveyancing* techniques."

Still, in modern usage, *conveyancing* more and more commonly takes on a more restricted sense: "The law of *conveyancing* is essentially the law relating to the creation and transfer of estates and interests in land." I.R. Storey, *Conveyancing* 3 (2d ed. 1987).

conveyee (= one to whom property is conveyed) is a legal NEOLOGISM not recorded in dictionaries. E.g., "Since seisin passed to the feoffee at the time of feoffment, or not at all, there could be no springing freehold estate to arise in the *conveyee* out of the estate of the conveyor at a future time." Cornelius J. Moynihan, *Introduction to the Law of Real Property* 163–64 (2d ed. 1988)./ "[S]ometimes the conveyor produced a knife, which he used to dig a clod of earth from the land or to cut a twig from a tree on the land, and the clod or twig was then handed to the *conveyee* together with the knife." Peter Butt, *Land Law* 455 (2d ed. 1988). See -EE.

conveyor. A. And *conveyer*. In legal contexts, the *-or* form predominates. Outside law, *conveyer* is the general spelling for "one that conveys." In mechanical uses, however, as in *conveyor belt,* the *-or* spelling is standard.

B. And *conveyancer*. These two terms are distinct. A *conveyor* is the person who transfers or delivers title to another. E.g., "The conveyance shall be given effect according to the intention of the *conveyor*."/ "After the English Chancellor began to enforce uses it was contended that a use for the *conveyor* or the person furnishing the consideration for the conveyance was presumed if no consideration was furnished by the conveyee and no use was expressed for the conveyee." See -ER (A) & **convey.**

A *conveyor* must usually have a *conveyancer,* that is, a lawyer specializing in real-estate transactions. E.g., "The practice of *conveyancers*—lawyers whose business it is to draw up conveyances, wills, and other legal documents—is sometimes valuable evidence of what the law is." William Geldart, *Introduction to English Law* 15 (D.C.M. Yardley ed., 9th ed. 1984). See the English law journal entitled *The Conveyancer*. See **conveyancing.**

convict, n. For a NEEDLESS VARIANT, see **convictee.**

convict, v.t. In the legal idiom, one is convicted *of* crimes but *on* counts. See **conviction.**

convictable; convictible. The former is preferred. See -ABLE (A).

convictability, a late-20th-century American NEOLOGISM, refers to the likelihood that a prosecution will result in conviction. Lawyers refer to the *convictability* of cases as well as defendants—e.g.: "The reform effort did not lead more women to report rapes, nor did it change the way prosecutors assessed the '*convictability*' of cases." Susan Estrich, *Real Rape* 88 (1987).

convicted. A. Meaning. A person pleads guilty to a felony and receives probation. Has that person been *convicted?* The question matters because, in some states, being convicted means that you lose your voting rights. A California court has held that a man who had pleaded guilty, served 90 days in jail, and then withdrawn his guilty plea—whereupon the case was dismissed—had not been "convicted." See *Truchon v. Toomey,* 254 P.2d 638, 644 (Cal. App. 1953).

B. Prepositions with. A person is *convicted of* a crime or *convicted for* the act of committing a crime, but is not *convicted in* a crime: "A Palestinian suspected in the bombing of Pan Am Flight 103 was convicted today along with three codefendants *in* [read *for*] a series of attacks in northern Europe four years ago." *Pan Am Bombing Suspect Convicted in Other Attacks,* N.Y. Times, 22 Dec. 1989, at A3.

convictee. Omitted from most dictionaries, *convictee* is a legal NEOLOGISM and, what is worse, a NEEDLESS VARIANT of the noun *convict.* E.g., "We respectfully suggest that the legislature give consideration to amending the probation statute to eliminate optional rejection of probation by a *convictee* [read *convict*]." *State v. Migliorino,* 442 N.W.2d 36, 48 (Wis. 1989)./ "[The] view that inmate violence is to be expected in a maximum security prison that houses violent *convictees* [read *convicts*] has little if any relevance to the instant case." *Madison County Jail Inmates v. Thompson,* 773 F.2d 834, 849 (7th Cir. 1985) (Flaum, J., concurring in part & dissenting in part). Cf. **acquittee.** See -EE.

convictible. See **convictable.**

conviction, it may surprise some readers to know, is used in reference to misdemeanors as well as to felonies. See **convict,** v.t.

conviction-prone. See **guilt-prone.**

convince; persuade. Generally, the word *convince* is properly followed by an *of*-phrase or a *that*-clause <he convinced the jury of his client's innocence> <he convinced the jury that his client was innocent>. *Persuade* is usually followed by an infinitive. It is a fall from stylistic grace to write "He *convinced her to go through with the crime* [read *persuaded her to go through with the crime*; or better: *persuaded her to commit the crime*]." See **persuade.**

co-opt = (1) to select as a member; or (2) to assimilate; absorb. The preferred noun form is *co-optation,* not *co-option;* the preferred adjectival form is *co-optative,* not *co-optive.* See CO- (A).

co-ownership (= title giving two or more persons concurrent possession and enjoyment of property) is hyphenated thus. (See CO- (A).) Traditionally, *co-ownership* has taken three forms: coparcenary, tenancy in common, or joint tenancy.

The first of these is now a defunct tenancy. On the others, see **joint tenancy.**

copacetic; copesetic. The former spelling is preferred for this tongue-in-cheek term meaning "okay; satisfactory." The word is informal and jocular.

coparcenary, though looking like an adjective, is usu. a noun, meaning "an estate in land descended from an ancestor to two or more persons who possess equal title to it"—as when a tenant in *tail* (q.v.) died intestate and left two female heirs. The *OED* notes that a rarer form, ending *-ery,* is "more etymological"; it is also more recognizable as a noun. But this form, like two others—*coparceny* and *parcenary*—is now classifiable only as a NEEDLESS VARIANT.

The estate was abolished in England in 1925. In the U.S., *coparcenary* came into use in the mid-19th century, mostly in the Northeast and the Midwest. E.g., "It is contended, that the distinction is merely technical, and does not affect the enjoyment of the estate, whether held in *coparcenary* or in common, as in Maryland there is very little, if any difference . . . ." *Gilpin v. Hollingsworth,* 3 Md. 190, 196 (1852). Surprisingly, the estate remains current in some jurisdictions, such as Ohio, which declares by statute: "When a person dies intestate having title or right to any personal property, or to any real estate or inheritance, in this state, the personal property shall be distributed, and the real estate or inheritance shall descend and pass in *parcenary* . . . ." Ohio Rev. Code § 2105.06 (1988).

coparcener. A. And *parcener.* Dating from the 13th century, *parcener* has become a NEEDLESS VARIANT of *coparcener,* which did not appear until the 15th century. The prefix *co-* emphasizes the jointness in the term's meaning "a joint heir." Cf. **copartner.** See CO- (A).

B. And *copartner.* According to one etymological theory, *coparcener* and *copartner* were originally the same word, *partner* having been a corrupt spelling of—a scribal error for—*parcener* in the 13th century. That is unlikely, however, since many 14th-century manuscripts spelled the word *parsener,* thus belying the idea that medieval scribes merely confused the *-c-* for a *-t-,* without any sense-association. In any event, DIFFERENTIATION between the words is so complete that few would now associate the two words. See the following entry.

copartner need not exist alongside *partner.* The joint relationship (i.e., that the existence of one partner implies the existence of one or more other partners) is clear to all native speakers of English. (That jointness is not clear in *parcener*—see **coparcener.**) Because *copartner* adds nothing to the language of the law, it should be avoided. E.g., "The same form of relief was given at law in cases of contribution between cosureties and *copartners* [read *partners*]." William F. Walsh, *A Treatise on Equity* 90 (1930). See NEEDLESS VARIANTS.

copartnership is a NEEDLESS VARIANT of *partnership*—e.g.: "Although, in a strict sense, not a *copartnership* [read *partnership*], a joint venture generally is governed by rules and principles applicable to partnership relationships." *Austin P. Keller Constr. Co. v. Commercial Union Ins. Co.,* 379 N.W.2d 533, 535 (Minn. 1986).

copending is an adj. used to describe two or more applications that are simultaneously on file and active in the Patent Office. See Louis B. Applebaum et al., *Glossary of United States Patent Practice* 26 (1969). E.g., "Peerless' argument that the application recited the existence of the *copending* application is misplaced." *Gardco Mfg., Inc. v. Herst Lighting Co.,* 820 F.2d 1209, 1215 (Fed. Cir. 1987).

copesetic. See **copacetic.**

coplaintiff, though infrequent, is not the nonce word that the *OED* suggests it is. E.g., "[The] stockholder['s] application was one for intervention as *coplaintiff.*" *Auerbach v. Bennett,* 393 N.E.2d 994, 995 syl. 5 (N.Y. App. 1979). The word should not be hyphenated after the first syllable—e.g.: "Daughter to Sir Edward Poole and afterwards wife to and *co-plaintiff* [read *coplaintiff*] with Sir Ralph Dutton." C.H.S. Fifoot, *History and Sources of the Common Law* 425 n.9 (1949). See CO- (A). For the corresponding term, see **codefendant.**

copulable derives from *couple,* v.t., not from *copulate.*

COPULAS, ADVERBS OR ADJECTIVES AFTER. See ADVERBS, PROBLEMS WITH (C).

copulate. See **fornicate.**

copy, v.t., in the sense "to send a copy to" <He copied me with the letter>, is a voguish casualism to be avoided. It is fast becoming standard American lawyer's JARGON. E.g., "It is therefore legitimate to *copy* [read *send a copy to*] the recipient's boss." Mark H. McCormack, *What They Don't*

Teach You at Harvard Business School 138 (1984).

copyeditor. One word.

copyleft is a NEOLOGISM jocularly formed as a counteragent to *copyright.* The brainchild of Richard Stallman, a computer hacker, *copyleft* is a form of copyright that obliges software users to distribute source code for no more than the cost of reproducing it. E.g., "Stallman's main worry was that some company would take the operating system he wrote, make some changes, and then say that their 'improved' programs were separate inventions and proprietary. To prevent that, he invented a new kind of licensing agreement, the 'Copyleft,' which lets people do anything they want with the software except restrict others' right to copy it." Simson L. Garfinkel, *Programs to the People: Computer Whiz Richard Stallman Is Determined to Make Software Free,* Tech. Rev., Feb.–Mar. 1991, at 52.

copyright. See **intellectual property.**

copyright, v.t. This verb has existed since the early 19th century. Hence the adjective *copyrightable.* For a mistaken form, see **copywrite.**

copyright(ed), adj. For the sense "secured or protected by copyright," *copyrighted* is the better and by far the more usual form. As an adjective, the form *copyright* is uncommon enough that it does not sufficiently announce what part of speech it is playing—e.g.: "Thanks and appreciation for the use of *copyright* [read *copyrighted*] material." Jefferson D. Bates, *Writing with Precision* xviii (rev. ed. 1985; repr. 1988).

copywrite is a not infrequent mistake for *copyright,* v.t. E.g., "[O]wnership of a copyright is something distinct from ownership of a physical object in which the *copywritten* [read *copyrighted*] work is embodied." *Nika Corp. v. City of Kansas City,* 582 F. Supp. 343, 367 (W.D. Mo. 1984). A similar mistake is seen in *playwriting* for *playwrighting.*

coram (lit., "in the presence of") begins many of the LATINISMS known to the law. *Coram nobis* (= before us; the court of King's Bench, originally) was the name of a writ of error directed to a court for review of its own judgments and predicated on alleged errors of fact. E.g., "This is an appeal from a judgment denying this appellant's petition for writ of error *coram nobis.*" *Coram vobis* (= before you) gave its name to the writ of error by an appellate court to a trial court for correction of the latter's error of fact. These phrases are obsolescent if not obsolete in most jurisdictions.

Two other phrases in which *coram* appears are *coram judice* (= in the presence of a judge) and *coram populo* (= in public). Both are unjustifiable LATINISMS. See ***coram non judice.***

coram non judice = (1) outside the presence of a judge; or (2) before a judge but not the proper one, or one who cannot take legal cognizance of the matter. This is the one LATINISM beginning with *coram* that is still fairly frequently used. E.g., "When a judge acts in the clear absence of all jurisdiction, the proceeding is *coram non judice.*"/ "If a judge issues a pretended process, one unknown to the law, the proceeding is *coram non judice* and the judge is liable in trespass to the party injured." See LATINISMS & ***coram.***

corespondent; correspondent. There is an important difference between these terms. In jurisdictions in which appellees are called *respondents, corespondent* = co-appellee. This word has a more specific legal meaning, however; in divorce suits, when adultery was commonly a ground for divorce, the *corespondent* was the man charged with the adultery and sued together with the wife, or *respondent.* E.g., "The judge clearly disbelieved the *corespondent,* who was the key witness on the issue of adultery." (Eng.)/ "The *corespondent* cited in the supplemental petition was called and gave evidence of adultery which was completely denied by the wife." (Eng.)

A *correspondent,* of course, is a letter-writer, an on-location news-gatherer, or a business representative.

corollarily, having appeared in a dozen reported American decisions, may (one hopes) never live more than a shadow of an existence. The *OED* notes that the adjectival use of *corollary* is "rare"; the adverbial use is not mentioned, but here it is: "Tenneco *corollarily* [read *also*] contends that the trial court erred when it struck affidavits filed by it opposing the motion for summary judgment." *Hanover Petroleum Corp. v. Tenneco, Inc.,* 521 So. 2d 1234, 1236 (La. Ct. App. 1988)./ "*Corollarily* [read *As a corollary*], it would follow that such an extent of actual application may occur as to provide substantial probativeness of the reasonableness of the understanding and belief engaged in . . . ." *United Medical Labs., Inc. v. Columbia Broadcasting Sys., Inc.,* 404 F.2d 706, 708 (9th Cir. 1968). See SENTENCE ADVERBS.

coroner; coronator. The latter is a NEEDLESS VARIANT.

corpora. See **corpus.**

corporal; corporeal. These terms have undergone DIFFERENTIATION. *Corporal* = of or affecting the body <corporal punishment>. The meaning is unclear here: "He participated in four *corporal* lineups."

Corporeal = having a physical material body, substantial <corporeal beings, as opposed to spiritual ones>. E.g., "Ancient German law, like ancient Roman law, sees great difficulties in the way of an assignment of a debt or other benefit of a contract; men do not see how there can be a transfer of a right unless that right is embodied in some *corporeal* thing."

In the following sentence, *corporeal* is used for *corporal:* "The court may punish *corporeally* [read *corporally*] by imprisonment." The *OED* calls this usage obsolete, but it persists in odd places—e.g.: "it involves idea [*sic*] of punishment, *corporeal* [read *corporal*] or pecuniary . . . ." *Black's Law Dictionary* 1133 (6th ed. 1990). See **corporeal.**

corporate law; corporation law; company law. The usual term in the U.S. for the law of corporations is *corporate law.* The equivalent in G.B. is *company law,* q.v. *Corporation law* is a variant phrase occasionally used. See **corporate lawyer.**

corporate lawyer; corporation lawyer. There is a subtle distinction. A *corporate lawyer* is either (1) an office practitioner specializing in corporate law (q.v.), or (2) in-house counsel to a corporation. The phrase is colorless. *Corporation lawyer,* by contrast, is usu. connotatively charged, referring to a lawyer, usu. a litigator, who represents major corporations and who makes a name as a "mouthpiece" for profitable ventures that may harm the environment, society, or individuals. In other words, those who use the phrase are not, generally speaking, well disposed to the person referred to—e.g.: "[N]o more than any other President did Lincoln look to merit alone; indeed, his first appointment was one of the worst ever made to the Court, for Noah Swayne of Ohio—named as a barefaced sop to certain business interests who were supporting the war for less than idealistic reasons—was a *corporation lawyer,* as successful as he was callously unethical, who was not to change his spots or his spottiness throughout his long judicial career." Fred Rodell, *Nine Men* 137 (1955).

corporateness now has only the sense "the quality of being a body corporate [i.e., a corporation]." E.g., "The name of a corporation must contain a word indicating *corporateness.*" Formerly it meant "corpulence" and "bodiliness" as well.

corporation, in the U.S., refers to "an entity (usu. a business) with authority under law to act as a single person, with rights to issue stock and exist indefinitely." In England, *corporation* (or *body corporate,* q.v.) is defined more broadly as "an entity that has legal personality, i.e., that is capable of enjoying and being subject to legal rights and duties" (*CDL*). Often, in G.B., where *company* is the more usual term, *corporation* is used elliptically to mean a *municipal corporation* (= the authorities of a municipality that carry on civic business). See **company, corporation sole & juristic person.** See also **firm.**

corporation aggregate. See **corporation sole.**

corporational is a NEEDLESS VARIANT of *corporate.* E.g., "A judgment adverse to the plaintiffs on count 2, involving charges that excessive compensation had been paid to the individual defendant as a *corporational* [read *corporate*] officer, was affirmed . . . ." *Saigh v. Bush,* 403 S.W.2d 559, 561 (Mo. 1966).

corporation law. See **corporate law.**

corporation sole; corporation aggregate. A *corporation sole* is "an individual, being a member of a series of individuals, who is invested by a fiction with the qualities of a [c]orporation." Henry S. Maine, *Ancient Law* 155 (17th ed. 1901; repr. [New Universal Lib.] 1905, 1910). By a "series of individuals," Maine meant that a continuous legal personality is attributed to successive holders of certain monarchical or ecclesiastical positions, such as kings, bishops, rectors, vicars, and the like.

A *corporation aggregate* is merely the full name for what we generally know as a *corporation*; the full phrase generally appears only when a writer contrasts it with a *corporation sole.*

corporatization. See -IZE.

corporeal; incorporeal. The early common law adopted the Roman distinction between *corporeal* (= tangible) and *incorporeal* (= intangible) property, reasoning that land—a material "thing"—has physical substance, whereas a right of way—which is not material—does not. Peter Butt comments that "[m]odern jurisprudence, more familiar with the nature of rights, regards this distinction as unsatisfactory, for incorporeal 'things' are simply rights. A right of way, for example, is simply a right over land, and becomes a 'thing' only by a more or less convenient figure of speech. But the medieval lawyers of England preferred to deal with 'things' and so accepted the Roman classification." Peter Butt, *Land Law* 302 (2d ed. 1988). See **corporal & hereditament(s).**

corporeal hereditaments = land and fixtures. The defining words are preferable to this highfalutin LEGALISM, the precise meaning of which is unclear even to some seasoned lawyers. See **hereditament(s).**

corpus; principal; res; trust property; trust estate; subject matter of the trust. These are the various terms used in reference to the property held by a trustee. *Principal,* q.v., *trust property,* and *subject matter of the trust* are perhaps most comprehensible to nonlawyers and might be preferred on that account. The five terms are widely used in legal writing, however, and it is unlikely that any of them will disappear completely in the next few decades.

Still, the more widely accessible terms may be on the rise. The influential *Restatement of Trusts* uses *trust property* in preference to *res* because the drafters "felt it unnecessary to drag in a Latin word when English words are available and quite sufficient." 1 A.W. Scott & W.F. Fratcher, *The Law of Trusts* § 3.1, at 52 (4th ed. 1987). See **res.**

Corpus is the Latin word meaning "body." It usually denotes an abstract collection or body <a substantial corpus of legal commentary in this field>. In the following sentences, *corpus* is used in its most usual legal context, involving trusts: "The *corpus* of the trust was composed of securities."/ "The trustee was authorized to distribute trust income or *corpus* to the beneficiaries."/ "The power to pay out trust *corpus* necessarily involves a power to terminate the trust in whole or in part."

The plural form is *corpora.* E.g., "[T]he *corpora* of the trusts were [held] not . . . taxable to the settlor's estate . . . ." *State St. Trust Co. v. United States,* 263 F.2d 635, 637 (1st Cir. 1959).

Occasionally it is misrendered *corpuses*—e.g.: "She will have at least $1,500,000 in assets left after the property distribution orders, and current assets and trust *corpuses* [read *corpora*]." *Weinstein v. Weinstein,* 561 A.2d 443, 450 n.4 (Conn. Ct. App. 1989)./ "[D]ifferent aspects of an article may be protected by different *corpuses* [read *corpora*] of law." David Bender, *Protection of Computer Programs,* 47 U. Pitt. L. Rev. 907, 914–15 (1986). The plural is *corpora* even in the phrase *habeas corpus,* q.v. See PLURALS (A).

corpus delicti —meaning "the body of a crime" and emphatically not "dead body"—is generally outmoded as a variant of *actus reus,* q.v. The general sense of *corpus delicti* is "the nature of the transgression." E.g., "The confession in evidence was an extrajudicial confession—voluntary and without pressure, after caution and after the *corpus delicti* had been established." *McDaniel v. Commonwealth,* 32 S.E.2d 667, 670 (Va. 1945).

In cases of felonious homicide, the *corpus delicti* is usu. evidence of a death and of a criminal agency as its cause. Thus, *corpus delicti* "has traditionally been established by proof of the dead body and evidence of an unnatural cause of death." *State v. Allen,* 197 N.W.2d 874, 876 (Mich. App. 1972). But the dead body is not necessary to establish a *corpus delicti.* "Despite clarification of the early confusion about the meaning of the Latin idiom . . . as used in homicide cases, there remains, among many laymen at least, some lingering misunderstanding that the *corpus delicti* in such cases refers to the body of the deceased. It does not, of course, and refers instead to the body (*corpus*) of the wrong (*delicti*), 'the loss sustained.'" *People v. Williams,* 373 N.W.2d 567, 571 (Mich. 1985). See **overt act.**

The phrase is sometimes misspelled *corpus delecti,* a sort of macabre etymological double entendre. See ***delecti.***

corpus juris (= the body of law; the law as the sum of laws) is a generic term derived ultimately from the *Corpus Juris Civilis*; the original name of Justinian's code (534 A.D.). E.g., "The maritime law is not a *corpus juris*—it is a very limited body of customs and ordinances of the sea." *Southern Pacific Co. v. Jensen,* 244 U.S. 205, 220 (1917) (Holmes, J., dissenting).

The term remains well known to American lawyers because of the treatise entitled *Corpus Juris Secundum*; in general contexts, however, it is best to write *body of law.* See LATINISMS.

correctable; correctible. The former is preferred. See -ABLE (A).

correctional; corrective. *Correctional* = of or pertaining to correction, usu. penal correction <correctional institution>. E.g., "He demonstrated by his plea that he is ready and willing to admit his crime and to enter the *correctional* system in a frame of mind that affords hope for success in rehabilitation." *Corrective* = tending to correct <corrective measures>.

correctitude; correctness. *Correctitude* is a PORTMANTEAU WORD or blend of *correct* and *rectitude.* It refers to what is proper in conduct or behavior, and has moralistic overtones. E.g., "[T]he local political allies of the west tend to be unrepresentative, dissolute or repressive rulers

. . . . Against them Islam seems to provide certainty of belief and *correctitude* of behaviour." Godfrey Jansen, *The Soldiers of Allah,* Economist, 27 Jan. 1979, at 45.

Correctness serves as the noun of *correct,* adj., in all its other senses. E.g., "The *correctness* of the decision is maintained, with an able and elaborate discussion of reasons and authorities, in *Langdell on Contracts."*

correctness. See **correctitude.**

CORRELATIVE CONJUNCTIONS, or conjunctions used in pairs, should frame structurally identical sentence-parts, sometimes called "matching parts." Simple nouns never cause problems: *both lions and wolves.* When we use constructions with noun phrases and even clauses, however, PARALLELISM may become a problem. Following are examples with some of the more common correlative conjunctions.

A. *Neither . . . nor.* "The jury may have concluded that the entrance was neither negligently constructed *nor maintained* [read *nor negligently maintained*] by the Investment Company."/ "Finding *neither error of law or fact* [read *neither error of law nor error of fact,* or *error neither of fact nor of law*], we affirm."

B. *Either . . . or.* "Easements *can be of either an affirmative or negative nature* [read *can be either affirmative or negative in nature*]." See **either** (A).

C. *Both . . . and.* "*Both* teachers *and* students have pressed their first amendment rights of free speech to *both* assign and read materials *and* to discuss topics of their choice." Using *both . . . and* twice in one sentence should be avoided. In this sentence note also that students have not *pressed to assign materials*—only *teachers* have. One must be certain that all that follows modifies both subjects, not just one. Further, the splitting of the infinitive here adds to the reader's burden; "to both assign" should read "both to assign . . . and to discuss topics of their choice."

D. *Although . . . yet.* "*Although* the rule is apparently otherwise in a majority of the other American jurisdictions, *yet* we hold that statutes of limitation run as well between spouses as between strangers." This construction, like the one illustrated in (E), occurs in formal prose; it has become less and less common to use both *although* and *yet.*

E. *Notwithstanding . . . yet.* "*Notwithstanding* that the interests may be adverse, *yet* if they are to be amicably adjusted there may be no impropriety in having each side represented by the same counsel." See (D).

F. Other Correlatives. Some of the other correlatives in English are:

- *although . . . nevertheless;*
- *as . . . as;*
- *if . . . then;*
- *just as . . . so;*
- *not only . . . but also;*
- *since . . . therefore;*
- *when . . . then;*
- *where . . . there;*
- *whether . . . or.*

correspondent. See **corespondent.**

corrigendum; erratum. These words are used synonymously to note errors made in printing discovered only after the work has been printed. *Corrigendum* (lit., "correction") is perhaps technically more accurate (inasmuch as a correction is being made). But *erratum* (lit., "error") is older in English and more common. The plurals are *corrigenda* and *errata.*

corroborate. A. Senses and Uses. *Corroborate* = (1) to support (a statement, argument, etc.) with agreeing statements; to provide or be additional evidence for; to confirm; or (2) to confirm formally (a law, etc.). Sense (1) is more usual: "[T]he evidence of an accomplice must be corroborated." Glanville Williams, *The Sanctity of Life and the Criminal Law* 157 (1957; repr. 1972).

In either sense, this verb should be transitive <the last witness corroborated the testimony of other witnesses>. The intransitive use ("to give confirmation," in contrast with "to give confirmation *to*") should be avoided. Thus one writes, "The circumstances *corroborate* his presence in the city when the crime was committed," not, "The circumstances *corroborate* with his presence in the city when the crime was committed." In other words, *corroborate with* is inferior to *corroborate.*

B. Pronunciation. In October 1991, during Justice Clarence Thomas's confirmation hearings, Senator Biden and other members of the Senate Judiciary Committee consistently pronounced this word as if it were *cooberate*—in other words, *cooperate* with a *-b-* instead of a *-p-*. The correct pronunciation is */kə-**rob**-ə-rayt/.*

C. And *collaborate.* The word *corroborate* is occasionally used where *collaborate* (= to work jointly with [another] in producing) belongs, as here: "The two scholars *corroborated* [read *collaborated*] for more than three years in writing the book."

corroboration = (1) the confirmation of (a statement) by additional evidence; or (2) the formal confirmation of (a law, etc.). Sense (1) is much more common—e.g.: "Because the testimony of a settlor seeking to revoke a trust is likely to be unreliable, and because solemn written instruments are not to be lightly overturned, strong *corroboration* of the settlor's testimony is required in order to warrant the granting of relief."

corroborative; corroboratory. The former is standard, *-tory* being a NEEDLESS VARIANT.

corrodible; corrosible. The former is preferable because with it the underlying verb, *corrode,* is more readily apparent. See -ABLE (A).

corrupter; corruptor. The *-er* spelling is preferred. See -ER (A).

corruptible. See -ABLE (A).

cost-effective and *cost-efficient* are the current jargonistic adjectival phrases for *economical. Cost-effective* is more than three times as common as *cost-efficient.* See VOGUE WORDS.

cost, insurance, and freight is commonly abbreviated *C.I.F.* For the distinction between it and *F.O.B.,* see **F.O.B.**

costomal. See **custumal.**

costs, in the sense of "charges, expenses," is obsolete except in law—the specific definitions of the word being either (1) the charges or fees "taxed" by the court, such as filing fees, jury fees, courthouse fees, and reporter fees; or (2) the expenses of litigation, prosecution, or other legal transaction, especially those allowed in favor of one party against the other. In England—under the *English Rule,* q.v.—sense (2) applies: *costs* include not only court charges but also a litigant's attorney's fees. American lawyers sometimes call these *litigation costs,* as opposed to *court costs* (or *costs of court*), which is a more explicit way of using *costs* in sense (1).

cosurety. So spelled—without a hyphen. See CO- (A).

cotemporaneous; cotemporary. See **contemporary.**

cotenancy; cotenant. The words are so spelled—without a hyphen. (See CO- (A).) The most common types of *cotenancies* are *joint tenancy,* q.v., *tenancy by the entireties,* q.v., and *tenancy in common* (explained under *joint tenancy*).

coterminous; coterminant; coterminate; coterminal; conterminous. *Conterminous* is the oldest and the basic term meaning "having or enclosed within a common boundary." *Coterminous,* an altered form of the original term, shares the meaning of *conterminous* but also means "coextensive in extent or duration." For the sake of DIFFERENTIATION, *coterminous* should be confined to this figurative or metaphorical sense, and *conterminous* reserved for physical and tangible senses. E.g., "A proprietor whose full rights of ownership extend up to a common terminal with those of the petitioner is an immediately *conterminous* [read *coterminous*] proprietor." (Eng.)/ "It cannot be seriously argued as a general matter that the constitutional limits of congressional power are *coterminous* with the extent of its exercise in the late eighteenth and early nineteenth centuries."

Coterminant, coterminate, and *coterminal* are NEEDLESS VARIANTS.

cotortfeasor is inferior to *co-tortfeasor,* because the length of the word deceives the eye; in addition, *cotort* (suggesting *cohort*) wrongly seems at first to be the primary word rather than *tortfeasor.* See CO- (A).

couch fee (= sexual favors taken by a lawyer instead of a monetary fee) is a flippant term to denote a serious ethical breach. E.g., "I had heard sotto voce comments about '*couch fees*' from other lawyers (and not all of them divorce specialists, either), but this Chicagoan was the first to boast about taking sex from a client in lieu of money." Joseph Goulden, *The Million Dollar Lawyers* 31 (1978).

could. See **should.**

could not help but. See **cannot help but.**

council; counsel. *Council* (= a deliberative assembly) is primarily a noun. *Counsel* (= to advise) is primarily a verb, but in legal writing it is used commonly as a noun in the sense "a legal adviser or legal advisers." See **counsel & consul.**

councillor; counselor. The former is a member of a council, the latter one who gives advice (usu. legal advice). See **attorney (A).**

councilmanic is an unfortunate adjectival form of *councilman,* which itself is objectionable to writers who try to avoid SEXISM. The nonsexist *council member* can substitute for *councilman*—in which case the manic adjective need not intrude.

counsel. A. Scope of Term. In BrE, *counsel* is used only of barristers (litigators), whereas in AmE it is frequently used of office practitioners (e.g., *general counsel*) as well as of litigators. See **attorney** (A), **consul, council** & **of counsel.**

B. Number. *Counsel* may be either singular or plural; in practice it is usually plural. But examples of the singular use are common enough: "[T]here is no excuse for a *counsel* who has obtained a thorough understanding of the case at bar . . . presenting to the court a statement [that] has no definite plan, which mingles material and immaterial facts, and which is verbose and discursive." William M. Lile et al., *Brief Making and the Use of Law Books* 370 (3d ed. 1914)./ "*Counsel* arguing a case is permitted to assert that a precedent has had unhappy consequences . . . ." Michael Zander, *The Law-Making Process* 239 (2d ed. 1985).

More typically, *counsel* is used as a plural. In 1819, for example, the court reporter in *McCulloch v. Maryland* wrote: "The Court dispensed with its general rule, permitting only *two counsel* to argue for each party."

Counsels is sometimes mistakenly used as a plural of *counsel*—esp. when nonlawyers are writing about the law: "[T]his might seem a strange approach for *counsels* [read *counsel*] responsible for representing not just Valeo and Henshaw but the interests of their employers, the U.S. House and Senate as well." Barbara H. Craig, *Chadha: The Story of an Epic Constitutional Struggle* 73 (1988)./ "[F]our lawyers were named Nov. 25 to *serve* as legal *counsels* [read *counsel*] for the transition." *Clinton's Justice Review Team Named,* Nat'l L.J., 7 Dec. 1992, at 2.

C. For *of counsel*. See **of counsel.**

counsel fees. See **attorney's fees.**

counselless. So spelled in both AmE and BrE. In the wake of *Gideon v. Wainwright,* 372 U.S. 335 (1963) (holding that an indigent criminal defendant must be provided counsel even in a noncapital case), the word is often used in a phrase illustrating HYPALLAGE: *counselless convictions.* See, e.g., *U.S. v. Coyer,* 732 F.2d 196, 200–01 (D.C. Cir. 1984) ("the sentencing court had relied upon *counselless convictions* rendered nugatory by *Gideon v. Wainwright*"). It is not the *convictions* that are counselless, of course, but the *convicts.*

counsel(l)or; counsel(l)ing; counsel(l)able. The preferred spellings are *counselor, counseling,* and *counselable* in AmE, and *counsellor, counselling,* and *counsellable* in BrE. See DOUBLING OF FINAL CONSONANTS & **attorney** (A).

counselor. See **councillor.**

count, n. In addition to its use in criminal indictments and informations—in which it means "a part that details or charges a distinct grievance or offense"—this word is used in patent practice to mean "a claim made by the parties to an interference [q.v.]." See Louis B. Applebaum et al., *Glossary of United States Patent Practice* 28 (1969).

countenance, give . . . to is usually an unnecessary PERIPHRASIS for *countenance,* v.t. E.g., "Courts have indeed used language that *seems to give countenance to* [read *seems to countenance*] the notion that, if a plot is worked out, it cannot be copyrighted."

COUNTER- (= done, directed, or acting against, in opposition to, as a rejoinder or reply to another thing of the same kind already made or in existence [*OED*]) is a common prefix in law because of our adversary system. About half the modern examples in the *OED* are unhyphenated; the better practice nowadays is not to hyphenate such a prefix. Among the law words, both nouns and verbs, beginning with this prefix are these:

counteraccusation	counternotice
counteraffidavit	counteroffer
counteraffirmation	counterperformance
counterappeal	counterpetition
countercondemnation	counterplea
counterdeclaration	counterpromise
counterestoppel	counterproof
counterexplanation	countersign
counterfactual	counterstatement
countergift	countersue
counterinterpretation	countertitle
counterlaw	countersuggestion
counterlegislation	countervindication

Sometimes the prefix is doubled up: "And if, by any chance, the boss had come back at Tony with 'How about fifty-five?', *that* would have been a *counter-counter-offer* involving an Implied, etc." Fred Rodell, *Woe Unto You, Lawyers!* 30 (1939; repr. 1980).

counterclaim is one word, unhyphenated. See COUNTER-. For the meaning of *counterclaim,* see **cross-claim.**

counterfactual, n., is, like its better-known synonym *hypothetical,* an attributive noun. E.g., "The 'but for' standard requires the factfinder to address a *counterfactual:* whether a prosecutor would have struck the challenged Afro-American jurors if his decisions had not been clouded by impermissible racial considerations." *Wilkerson v. Texas,* 493 U.S. 924, 926 (1989) (Marshall, J., dissenting)./ "The last *counterfactual* is the easiest." *Shelton v. Office of Workers' Compensation Programs,* 899 F.2d 690, 692 (7th Cir. 1990).

The word sometimes remains an adjective—e.g.: "This type of statement is a *counterfactual* conditional statement, i.e., it is conditional in form and runs counter to fact." *Maddocks v. Bennett,* 456 P.2d 453, 460 n.11 (Alaska 1969).

Whether as a noun or as an adjective, though, *counterfactual* is unusual enough to be slightly pompous in place of *hypothetical.* See COUNTER-.

counterfeiting; forgery. These words overlap to some degree. To *counterfeit* (lit., to imitate) means to unlawfully make false money that passes for the genuine. Before the advent of paper money, the distinction between *counterfeiting* and *forgery* was clear because it referred only to the making of false metallic coins. To *forge* (lit., to falsify or fabricate) is to fraudulently make or alter a document in a way that harms another's rights. In reference to paper money, then, the two words are virtually interchangeable. See **forgery.**

countermand, n. & v.t. This word is most commonly a verb meaning (1) "to annul (an earlier command or action) by a contrary command" <the partner countermanded the previous assignment>; or (2) "to recall by a contrary order" <countermanding that shipment>. Sense (1) is most usual—e.g.:

- "The day before the Indianapolis hearing, the judge called Mr. Atanga and, *countermanding* his earlier entry, ordered Mr. Atanga to be in Lafayette the next day." *In re Atanga,* 636 N.E.2d 1253, 1258 (Ind. 1994) Sullivan, Jr., dissenting).
- "In fact, Brown's employees testified that they had the authority to *countermand* Fontenot's orders to perform personal work if Freeman was needed at the store." *Hebert v. Gigna,* 637 So. 2d 1221, 1225 (La. Ct. App. 1994).
- "In May 1989, Brownlow *countermanded* an order for a piece of equipment that Jones had placed with a dealer on behalf of the Corporation." *Cecil Sand & Gravel, Inc. v. Jones,* 644 A.2d 529, 532 (Md. Ct. App. 1994).
- "The order must be signed by a party, received by the financial institution prior to death, and not *countermanded* by other written order of the same party prior to death." *Jordan v. Burgbacher,* 883 P.2d 458, 463 (Ariz. Ct. App. 1994) (synopsizing a statute).

But sense (2) also occurs in legal contexts—e.g.: "The court distinguished *Chan Siew Lai* on the basis that when a bank issues a cashier's check the check becomes the primary obligation of the bank and the purchaser has no authority to *countermand* a cashier's check because of fraud allegedly practiced on the purchaser by the payee." *Godat v. Mercantile Bank of Northwest County,* 884 S.W.2d 1, 4 (Mo. Ct. App. 1994) (en banc).

As a noun, *countermand* refers to either (1) a contrary command or order that revokes or annuls an earlier one; or (2) an action that nullifies something previously executed. Sense (2) is the more specific legal one, but sense (1) predominates in both legal and nonlegal contexts—e.g.: "So far as the record shows, there was no *countermand* of the direction in the telegram and no effort on the part of Dyches or his attorney to have the appeal brought before the appellate court . . . ." *Dyches v. Ellis,* 199 S.W.2d 694, 697 (Tex. Civ. App.—Austin 1947).

Countermandment, labeled "obsolete" in the *OED,* really ought to be so. But because it still lives, it could be more aptly described as a NEEDLESS VARIANT—e.g.: "The Bank contends, however, that in some circumstances a cashier's check should be subject to *countermandment* [read *countermand*], like a certified check, where the issuance is a result of error or fraud and the rights of no other party have intervened." *Foreman v. Martin,* 286 N.E.2d 80, 82 (Ill. App. Ct. 1972).

counteroffer; cross-offer. In the law of contract, a *counteroffer* is an offeree's new offer that varies the terms of the original offer and that therefore constitutes a rejection of the original offer. (See COUNTER-.) A *cross-offer,* by contrast, is an offer made to another in ignorance that the offeree has made the same offer.

counterproof, n. The *OED* prematurely calls this word, meaning "evidence in opposition to other evidence," obsolete. American lawyers continue to find it useful—e.g.: "If the proof and *counterproof* on the issue depend upon the credibility factors or inferences to be drawn from conflicting evidence, the question is one of fact for the jury." *U.S. v. Martinez,* 429 F.2d 971, 976 (9th Cir. 1970)./ "A fair rule either would afford this chance or would restrict the prosecution's *counterproof* in the same way his own is limited." *Michelson v. U.S.,* 335 U.S. 469, 493 (1948) (Rutledge, J., dissenting). See COUNTER-.

countersignature = a second signature attesting to the authenticity of the instrument on which it appears. The *OED* traces this word back to 1842, but in fact it appeared some 35 years earlier in AmE: "The act, as to the *countersignature* by the secretary and recording the same, is directory . . . ." *Philips v. Erwin,* 19 F. Cas. 500, 500 (C.C.D.N.C. 1807) (No. 11,093). *Countersign* is the verb. See COUNTER-.

countersue is a nontechnical way of saying *counterclaim,* v.t. E.g., "Mr. Aboud *countersued,* claiming he had losses of $200,000 because casino employees had given him free drinks." R.B. Smith, *Casinos May Be Held Liable for Drunken Patrons* [*sic*] *Losses,* Wall St. J., 23 June 1989, at B1. See COUNTER-.

countervail = to counterbalance; to compensate for. This word is probably used 100 times in legal writing for every time it appears in nonlegal writing. E.g., "The interests of nonminorities in not taking another test do not sufficiently *countervail* these needs."

The word most often appears as a participial adjective. E.g., "Vidrine filed no *countervailing* affidavits."/ "Nevertheless, *countervailing* policy considerations have been evident ever since the Statutes of Mortmain, restricting the amounts of wealth that may be transferred out of the normal channels of social organization." There is nothing inherently wrong with the word, but *countervailing considerations* is on the verge of becoming a legal CLICHÉ.

countez was, at common law, the Law French term that the court crier used in numbering the jury, but it was soon corrupted into *count these,* as Blackstone explained: "Of this ignorance [of Law Latin and Law French] we may see daily instances in the abuse of two legal terms of ancient French; one, the prologue to all proclamations, '*oyez,* or hear ye,' which is generally pronounced most unmeaningly, 'O yes'; the other, a more pardonable mistake, *viz.* when the jury are all sworn, the officer bids the crier number them, for which the word in law-french is '*countez*'; but we hear it pronounced in very good English, 'count these.'" 4 William Blackstone, *Commentaries* 334 n. (1769). See ***oyez.***

countless applies only to COUNT NOUNS. E.g., "Porters recently have been carrying *countless* baggage to and from passengers' cars." One may have *countless bags* but not *countless baggage.* See COUNT NOUNS AND MASS NOUNS.

COUNT NOUNS AND MASS NOUNS. Count nouns are those that denote enumerable things, and that are capable of forming plurals (e.g., *cases, parties, settlements, offers*); mass (noncount) nouns are often abstract nouns—they cannot be enumerated (e.g., *mitigation, courage, mud*). Many nouns can be both count ("He gave several *talks*") and mass ("*Talk* is cheap"), depending on the sense. These are few, however, in comparison to the nouns that are exclusively either count or mass. Use of these two types of nouns may implicate problems with NUMBER, especially when the use of count nouns strays into a use of mass nouns or vice versa. See PLURALS (B).

A. *Fewer* and *less*. A good rule of thumb is to use *fewer* to modify plural nouns (*calories, soldiers*) and *less* to modify singular nouns (*unemployment, discrimination*). A beer may have fewer, but not less, calories. See **less** (A).

B. Treating a Mass Noun as a Count Noun. One may have a "congeries of negligent acts," but not a "congeries of negligence." Some writers mistakenly treat mass nouns as if they were countable—e.g.: "For *every violence* [read *every act of violence*], there is a victim."/ "*A compliance with* [read *Compliance with*] the demand would have exposed defendant to danger of bodily harm." For a similar example, see **miscellaneous.** See also PLURALS (B). On a related point, see COLLECTIVE NOUNS.

country. In the 12th through the 14th centuries, a jury was a body of neighborhood witnesses summoned to decide by their sworn verdict (q.v.) a dispute between litigants. The controverted facts were said to be tried by the *country* (L. *patria,* Fr. *pays*), which came to be the equivalent in law to "jury." To this day—though somewhat archaically—a litigant demanding a jury sometimes *puts himself (or herself) upon the country* (L. *ponit se super patriam*). So it was in medieval times: "The normal administration of justice was restored in 1218, and the justices found the gaols full of criminals whom they could not try—unless they allowed the accused to 'put themselves upon their country' (a jury of neighbours), on the general question of guilt or innocence; and that was the solution adopted." Alan Harding, *A Social History of English Law* 61 (1966).

country lawyer (= a rural lawyer, usu. a general practitioner, who knows the ways of the people). Unlike *city lawyer,* the term *country lawyer* carries a connotation that is sometimes neutral, sometimes positive, sometimes negative. E.g., (Neutral) "The testator was a *country lawyer* who had acquired a large estate, both real and personal." *McClellan v. MacKenzie,* 126 F. 701, 702 (6th Cir. 1903)./ (Positive) "The Judge having been a *country lawyer* himself took a fatherly interest in my career . . . ." Ephraim Tutt, *Yankee Lawyer* 52 (1943)./ (Negative) "The rule of reason . . . should now allow one to put an antitrust theory of liability or justification into terms that a *country lawyer* can understand." Lawrence A. Sullivan, *The Viability of the Current Law on Horizontal Restraints,* 75 Calif. L. Rev. 835, 847 (1987). Cf. **city lawyer.**

county, n., in 20th-century American lawyers' slang, is a shortening of *county detective.* E.g., "Directly opposite on the same corridor was a large room given over to process servers known as 'county detectives' or '*counties.*'" Ephraim Tutt, *Yankee Lawyer* 87 (1943).

coup de grace. This GALLICISM is sometimes mispronounced /*koo-də-**grah***/, as if the last word were spelled *gras* (as in *pâté de foie gras*). The correct pronunciation is /*koo-də-**grahs***/.

COUPLED SYNONYMS. See DOUBLETS, TRIPLETS, AND SYNONYM STRINGS.

coupled with, like *together with,* q.v., results in a singular and not a plural verb when it couples two singular nouns—e.g.: "The absence of crude petroleum and iron ore, *coupled with* limited indigenous supplies of coal and natural gas, *ensures* [not *ensure*] that Japanese industry must import to survive." Roger Buckley, *Japan Today* 67 (2d ed. 1990).

couple (of) dozen, hundred, etc. It is slipshod to omit the *of* in such a construction as this: "Is a used toilet seat worth $1 million? Or even a *couple* [read *couple of*] hundred thousand dollars?" Lindsey Gruson, *Is It Art or Just a Toilet Seat? Bidders Will Have to Decide,* N.Y. Times, 15 Jan. 1992, at B1.

coupon should be pronounced /***koo**-pon*/. The first syllable is distressingly often sounded as /***kyu***/. This pronunciation betrays an ignorance of French and of the finer points of English.

course, as (a matter) of. See **as of course** & **of course.**

court. A. Metonymy. *Court* is frequently used as a metonymic substitute for *judge.* E.g., "The *court himself,* possessed of a countenance and bearing elsewhere commanding, appeared little more than a pygmy here, in spite of *his* elevation on the bench." (Ex. fr. H.W. Horwill, *Modern American Usage* 88 (1935).)/ "The district *court* again stated the opinion that *he* disagreed with the circuit court and its conclusion bearing on the sufficiency of evidence."/ "In our opinion, it would seriously restrict the trial *court's* ability to partition the community estate fairly if *he* had no power to direct the named insured of title to life insurance policies that are an integral part of the community estate." This usage has sometimes bemused nonlawyers: "In the sometimes-strange jargon of jurists, the words *court* and *judge* were often synonymous." John A. Jenkins, *The Litigators* 155 (1989; repr. 1991).

B. As a Collective Noun. Today *court* is used in AmE as a COLLECTIVE NOUN taking a singular verb. In BrE, the plural verb usually appears with this noun when more than one judge sits on the court: "The *court* of appeal *have* concurred." (Eng.) Long ago, this construction was common even in the U.S.: "The *Court were* unanimously of opinion, that writs of error to remove causes to this court from inferior courts, can regularly issue only from the clerk's office of this court." *West v. Barnes,* 2 U.S. (2 Dall.) 401, 401 (1791) (mem.).

C. *Open court, in.* See **open court, in.**

court costs. See **costs.**

court crier. See **crier.**

court, go to; come to court. The former is the usu. AmE phrase, the latter the usu. BrE phrase. See **come to court.**

courthouse. One word.

court-made is frequently used as an equivalent of *judge-made*—e.g.: "Although it is commonly said that when the United States sues, it comes into court on an equality with private litigants, in fact it enjoys a number of advantages, both statutory and *court-made* . . . ." Charles A. Wright, *The Law of Federal Courts* 114–15 (4th ed. 1983). See **judge-made.**

court-martial is hyphenated both as noun and as verb. The *OED* lists the verb as colloquial, an observation now antiquated. As to spelling, in AmE, the final *-l* is not doubled in *court-martialed* and *court-martialing,* although in BrE it is. See DOUBLING OF FINAL CONSONANTS. The plural of the noun is *courts-martial.*

In older texts, the term is sometimes rendered *martial court*—e.g.: "[A] *martial court* must needs in the present case confine its attention to the blow's consequence . . . ." Herman Melville, *Billy Budd* 66 (1891; repr. [Signet ed.] 1979). See POSTPOSITIVE ADJECTIVES.

court of appeal(s). Both forms appear, but *appeals* is more common in AmE, whereas *appeal* is the only form in BrE. The correct form is the statutorily prescribed or the customary form of a given jurisdiction. Following is an example of the less usual American form: "In 93 Cal. App. 2d 43, the Court of *Appeal* affirmed the judgment."

For the proper possessive form with *court of appeals,* see POSSESSIVES (A).

Court of Customs and Patent Appeals. This American court, created in 1909, no longer exists, having been merged in 1982 into the Court of Appeals for the Federal Circuit.

court of first instance = (1) a court in which any proceedings are initiated; or (2) the trial court as opposed to an appellate court. The *CDL* marks sense (2) as a loose usage, but the great historian Theodore F.T. Plucknett appears to have used it in this sense: "There was thus one court of appeal and one *court of first instance.*" *A Concise History of the Common Law* 211 (5th ed. 1956). See **first instance.**

Court of International Trade. Originally this court, created in 1909, was known as the Board of General Appraisers, then as the Customs Court, and, since 1980, as the Court of International Trade. It hears cases involving customs and duties.

court of justice is a solemn and slightly antique equivalent of *court of law.* E.g., "Men go from a court of justice, after witnessing a severe contest, and in reporting their opinion of the arguments, they will say that one of the advocates had no fault that they can precisely define, and yet there was a prevailing heaviness or a want of impressiveness." Edward T. Channing, "Judicial Eloquence," in *Lectures Read to the Seniors in Harvard College* 98, 103 (1856; repr. [Dorothy I. Anderson & Waldo W. Braden eds.] 1968).

court of law, formerly used in contrast with *court of equity,* is now a formal phrase for *court,* which suffices in ordinary legal contexts. E.g., "The word 'say' is important in this context, because when a document is under scrutiny in a *court of law,* attention will be paid only to what, as a piece of natural language, it appears actually to declare." (Eng.) Today *court of law* often merely emphasizes the dignity of the judicial institution referred to; but in a few jurisdictions, and certainly in historical contexts, it may usefully distinguish a lawcourt from a court of equity or from some other type of court. Cf. **court of justice.** See **lawcourt.**

court, open. See **open court.**

Court-packing plan. This phrase refers to President Franklin D. Roosevelt's plan, presented to Congress on February 5, 1937, to appoint six new justices to the U.S. Supreme Court. It would have enabled him to appoint a new judge to supplement any judge who, upon reaching 70, did not retire. With more than six sitting judges over that age, the plan would have ensured that Roosevelt could win judicial approval of the New Deal program. "The bitter fight that led to the defeat of this *'court-packing' plan,*" writes the leading scholar on federal courts, "has given the notion of a nine-man Court such sanctity that it is unlikely that the size will again be changed." Charles A. Wright, *The Law of Federal Courts* 13 (4th ed. 1983).

court papers = all papers that a party files with the court, including pleadings. Technically, *pleadings* has a restricted sense—referring to complaints, answers, counterclaims, cross-claims, and the like, but not to motions, notices, petitions for leave, and other court papers. American lawyers frequently use *pleadings* loosely as if it were synonymous with *court papers* (known also as *suit papers*)—e.g.: "That record . . . is made up of all the *'suit papers,'* the pleadings in the case . . . ." John Kaplan & Jon R. Waltz, *Cases and Materials on Evidence* 1 (5th ed. 1984). See **pleadings (B).**

The phrase *court papers* is often shortened to *papers*—e.g.: "The *papers* filed today by the prosecuting team . . . were in response to the motion of Mr. Barry's lawyers." B. Drummond Ayres, *Capital Mayor Used Drugs Many Times, Court Is Told,* N.Y. Times, 21 April 1990, at 8.

court reporter. Before 1900, this phrase usually denoted a set of books, as in *Superior Court Reporter.* By the late 19th century, however, it had taken on a new sense: "one, usu. a stenographer, who records and transcribes court proceedings, depositions, and the like." E.g., "A *court reporter,* though a sworn public officer, receiving a fixed salary for his labors, is not, in the absence of a statute, deprived of any privilege of taking out a copyright, which he would otherwise have." *Callaghan v. Myers,* 128 U.S. 617, 617 (1888). For more on the term *reporter,* see **report (A).**

In journalism, the phrase *court reporter* commonly refers to a journalist whose beat is a royal court—e.g.: "The book by Mr Whitaker, the *Daily Mirror's court reporter,* is the most gripping. Charles, he reveals, slept with his mistress, Camilla, two nights before he married Di." *Westenders,* Economist, 19 June 1993, at 94.

courtroom. So spelled—without a hyphen.

Court Street lawyer = a disreputable, wheeling-and-dealing New York lawyer practicing in

Brooklyn near Court Street, where many state and federal courts are located. E.g., "Newfield countered the report by writing that the author of the report was a *'Court Street' lawyer* 'with ties to the Brooklyn clubhouses' and had interviewed only the plaintiff in preparing the report." *Rinaldi v. Holt, Rinehart & Winston,* 366 N.E.2d 1299, 1304 (N.Y. 1977)./ "[I]f Mr. Halpern was not a Wall Street lawyer, nor was he a *Court Street lawyer,* at least not as that term is usually used—a synonym for ambulance chaser, fast talker, exploiter of the miserable." David Margolick, *At the Bar,* N.Y. Times, 9 Feb. 1990, at B11. See LAWYERS, DEROGATORY NAMES FOR (A).

court suit (BrE) = lawsuit. E.g., "The legal challenges, involving more than 40 *court suits,* are still far from over." *Towering Troubles,* Economist, 30 Sept.–6 Oct. 1989, at 26.

cousinhood; cousinage. *Cousinage* has the disadvantage of possible confusion with *cozenage* (= fraud); thus *cousinhood* might be considered preferable.

couth, a BACK-FORMATION from *uncouth,* has never been accepted by authorities as a proper word.

covenant, n., = (1) a promise made in a deed; or (2) an obligation burdening or favoring a landowner. Sense (1) is the strict one, sense (2) being less fastidious but probably more common. For example, in referring to the various covenants that are implied by law into a lease in the absence of an agreement—such as the *covenant for quiet enjoyment* and the *covenant against encumbrances* – the word *covenant* is synonymous with *term,* q.v. See **condition (A), restrictive covenant & warranty (A), (B).**

Commentators frequently remark how much *covenant* has slipped from its traditional moorings—e.g.: "In equity, . . . an equitable right *in rem* arises in favor of the covenantee, his heirs and assigns, when the parties intended that the restriction should bind the estate of the covenantor or promisor for the benefit of the land of the covenantee or promisee. The use of the term '*covenant*' in these cases is hardly justified, because the promise may be without seal or by parol." William F. Walsh, *A Treatise on Equity* 456 (1930).

covenant, v.i. & v.t. To *covenant* is to enter into a covenant or formal agreement, to agree or subscribe to by promise under seal. E.g., "A father *covenants* to transfer an estate to his daughter and her husband-to-be."/ "Other claims made by the appellant in respect of dispositions made by himself were allowed but the claim to deduct Mrs. Reynolds's *covenanted* payments was disallowed." (Eng.) Nonlawyers are unaccustomed to the legal uses of the word; ordinarily, in modern contexts, the better practice is to write *agree.* See **contract (D).**

covenant and agree is a needless doublet common in DRAFTING. *Agree* suffices in virtually every context in which the phrase appears. See DOUBLETS, TRIPLETS, AND SYNONYM-STRINGS.

covenantee = the person to whom a promise by covenant is made. E.g., "And the use thus raised would be executed by the Statute of Uses, thereby transferring the legal estate to the *covenantee.*" Cornelius J. Moynihan, *Introduction to the Law of Real Property* 186 (2d ed. 1988)./ "A restraint is only valid if it goes no further than is reasonably necessary for the protection of the *covenantee*'s interest." G.H. Treitel, *The Law of Contract* 406 (8th ed. 1991). (On the position of *only* in the last-quoted sentence, see **only.**) See -EE.

covenant not to compete. See **noncompetition covenant.**

covenant of seisin; covenant of good right to convey. These phrases are synonymous. In a deed, either phrase assures the grantee that the grantor is, at the time of the conveyance, the lawful owner with power to convey the land.

covenantor; covenanter. This agent noun, meaning "the person who makes a promise by covenant," is preferably spelled *-or.* See -ER (A).

coverages. This plural of what has traditionally been a mass noun is now common—e.g.: "Mr. P. is being paid a salary of approximately $61,000 per year including certain insurance *coverages.*" See PLURALS (B) & COUNT NOUNS AND MASS NOUNS.

covert; overt. *Covert* is best pronounced like *covered,* except with a *-t-* at the end /**kəv**-ərt/. Still, /**koh**-vərt/, nearly rhyming with *overt* (but for the accented syllable), is the more common pronunciation in AmE nowadays. See **discovert.**

coverture = the condition or position of a woman during her married life, when she is by law under the authority and protection of her husband (*OED*). The word reeks of SEXISM, although it is unobjectionable in historical contexts. Traditionally used only in reference to wives, this word has recently been applied to husbands as well: "In community-property jurisdictions, with some exceptions, the spouse has an interest during *coverture* in the community fund."/ "At common law, dower attached only to an estate of inheritance of which the husband was seised at some time during *coverture.*"

Usually, in contemporary contexts, some phrase such as *during marriage* will suffice in place of the legalistic *during coverture.* E.g., "Community property is a system of regulating rights and obligations of husband and wife *during coverture* [read *during marriage*]."

coworker. So spelled—without a hyphen. See CO- (A) & **co-employee.**

cozen is a literary and archaic word meaning "to cheat." The word has never been used as a specific legal term, and is generally to be avoided in legal writing. See **cousinhood.**

cozenage. See **cousinhood.**

-CRACY. See GOVERNMENTAL FORMS.

cramdown, a late 20th-century term now common in bankruptcy law, refers to a reorganization plan that creditors are required to accept as long as the plan attains minimum standards established by the Bankruptcy Code. E.g., "Section 1129(b)(1) of the bankruptcy code [11 U.S.C.] provides that a debtor may 'cram down' its plan over the objection of a creditor 'if the plan does not discriminate unfairly, and is fair and equitable with respect to each class . . . .'" *In re D & F Constr., Inc.,* 865 F.2d 673, 675 (5th Cir. 1989).

creator is a somewhat exalted name for one who establishes a trust. E.g., "The second type of statute provides that where the *creator* of such trust reserves to himself for his own benefit a power of revocation, a court, at the suit of any creditor of the *creator,* may compel the exercise of such power of revocation so reserved, to the same extent and under the same conditions that such *creator* could have exercised them." See **settlor.**

creature. Legal idiom has developed a peculiar kind of taxonomy, in which legal doctrines or principles are described as *creatures.* E.g., "Adoption, in this country, is entirely a *creature of statute* and is unknown at common law."/ "The cause of action is wholly a *creature of equity.*" The *OED* quotes the following English example from 1855: "The railway and the rights of the railway are the *creatures* of the Act of Parliament." A useful phrase, *creature of* etc. should not be so overworked as to become another tiresome legal CLICHÉ.

credal. See **cre(e)dal.**

credible; credulous; creditable. *Credible* = believable; *credulous* = gullible, tending to believe; and *creditable* = worthy of credit, laudable. See **incredible.**

credit (= to give credence to) for *believe,* now almost peculiar to legal writing, is an acceptable though slightly pretentious legal idiom: "Black and Danley contradicted each other in their testimony, and the court *credited* Danley."/ "It may be that the court below did not consider such evidence substantial or did not *credit* its validity, but we are unable to determine from a silent record the thought processes of the court below."/ "The trial judge was entitled to *credit* her testimony."

creditable; credulous. See **credible.**

credulity (= gullibility) should not be confused with *credibility* (= believability), as it is in the phrase *it strains credulity*—e.g.: "It simply strains *credulity* [read *credibility*] for the Court to assert that 'propaganda' is a neutral classification." *Meese v. Keene,* 481 U.S. 465, 490 (1987) (Blackmun, J., dissenting)./ "[I]t strains *credulity* [read *credibility*] to argue that Congress simply assumed that one view rather than the other would govern." *Smith v. Wade,* 461 U.S. 30, 93 (1983) (O'Connor, J., dissenting).

cre(e)dal. The preferred spelling is *creedal;* the spelling *credal* is a nonstandard variant.

crevice; crevasse. These two words are often confused. A *crevice* is a narrow crack or break, as in a sidewalk or a wall. A *crevasse* is a large split or rupture, as in a levee, glacier, or embankment. E.g., "It is a fundamental principle that no damages lie against federal or state government, or local agencies, on account of an accidental *crevasse* in the levees."

Crevice is pronounced /***krev**-is*/, and *crevasse* /*krə-**vas***/.

crier (= a court officer who calls the court to order) has the variant spelling *cryer,* which is to be eschewed. Today the bailiff usually acts as crier; hence *bailiff* has almost supplanted the term *crier,* which sometimes appears in the phrase *court crier:* "Adam Johnson testified that he was a deputy marshal, and was *court crier* on April 17, 1902, and was in court when the order was made for the open venire . . . ." *Richards v. U.S.,* 126 F. 105, 107 (9th Cir. 1903). See **hear ye, *oyez* & *countez.***

crim. con. See **criminal conversation.**

crime = any social harm that the law defines and makes punishable. Broadly speaking, this term is to be distinguished from *civil wrong* or *tort.* An important point for the novice is to avoid trying to distinguish the two on the basis of the act giving rise to the crime or civil wrong, because the same act may be both a crime and a civil wrong. For example, a murder may be both criminal and tortious—including such torts as assault, battery, and wrongful death. The act may give rise both to a criminal prosecution (seeking punishment) and to a civil suit for damages (seeking redress).

Interestingly, this distinction is a modern one. In the early days of the common law, criminal law was also the law of torts, so that, as Plucknett put it, "the modern distinction between crime and tort is . . . one of those classifications [that] it is futile to press upon mediaeval law." Theodore F.T. Plucknett, *A Concise History of the Common Law* 422 (5th ed. 1956). See **criminal offense.**

crime against nature. See EUPHEMISMS.

crime, infamous. See **infamous crime.**

crimen falsi (lit., "the crime of falsifying") has gradually grown from describing crimes such as perjury and forgery to include any crime involving dishonesty, fraud, or corruption. It is a handy phrase—not a pointless LATINISM—because a paraphrase uses up many more words and is more cumbersome to repeat again and again. E.g., "This case presents the question whether a district court has the discretion . . . to prohibit the impeachment of a witness with a conviction for a crime involving dishonesty or false statement (a *crimen falsi*)." *U.S. v. Toney,* 615 F.2d 277, 278 (5th Cir. 1980).

The plural form is *crimina falsi,* which is the form that should have appeared here: "[T]he House Committee on the Judiciary amended the bill to permit admission only of prior convictions of *crimen falsi* [read *crimina falsi*]." James McMahon, Note, *Prior Convictions Offered for Impeachment in Civil Trials,* 54 Fordham L. Rev. 1063, 1071 (1986).

The phrase is commonly written with the words reversed (*falsi crimen*). Either version is good Latin—and *falsi crimen* better approximates English word-order—but *crimen falsi* is slightly more common.

crime of passion. See ***crime passionnel.***

crime passionnel; crime passionel. The English phrase *crime of passion* is perfectly serviceable. If the GALLICISM must appear, however, the better form is with two ens (*-nn-*) in the second word.

criminal = (1) of or relating to crime <criminal justice>; or (2) constituting a crime <criminal activities>. The adjective is analogous, then, to *grammatical,* which of course is proper in the phrase *grammatical error* (*grammatical* here meaning not "complying with grammar" but "relating to grammar"). It is quite proper—and hardly risible—to speak of a *criminal judge,* a *criminal lawyer,* or the *criminal bar,* just as it is to speak of the *criminal law.*

criminal abortion. See **abortion.**

criminal action—as opposed to *criminal prosecution*—is, strictly speaking, considered a solecism in BrE, in which *action* is reserved for civil lawsuits. See Glanville Williams, *Learning the Law* 4 (11th ed. 1982) ("'Criminal action' . . . is a misnomer"). In AmE, though, the phrase is quite common and quite unobjectionable.

criminal attempt. See **attempt** (A).

criminal conversation = (1) unlawful sexual intercourse with a married person; or (2) a tort action based on such unlawful intercourse. The idea of using *conversation* in this way is not merely modern euphemizing. In the Renaissance, *conversation* fairly routinely referred to sexual intercourse or intimacy. In modern law, then, this phrase—commonly abbreviated *crim. con.*—is an ARCHAISM more than a EUPHEMISM.

At common law, the tort action could be maintained by a husband but not by a wife. In the several American jurisdictions in which it remains a cause of action today, that double-standard has been erased, so that wives as well as husbands may sue. *Criminal conversation* was abolished in England in 1857.

To the extent that it can be differentiated from *alienation of affections,* the distinction is this: *criminal conversation* might result, for example, from a one-time act of adultery that does not affect the wayward spouse's affections, whereas an *alienation of affections* occurs when the wayward spouse's emotions are affected in such a way as to deprive the other of consortium.

criminal damage. See **malicious damage.**

criminal intent is used in a variety of ways: (1) to refer to the intent to do wrong; (2) to refer to the intent to break a specific law; (3) to serve as the equivalent of *mens rea,* q.v., being the mental element requisite for guilt of the offense charged; (4) to serve as a synonym for criminal negligence. Surveying the semantic confusion, Rollin Perkins has suggested a tidy distinction: "Some other term such as mens rea or guilty mind should be employed for more general purposes, and 'criminal intent' be restricted to those situations in which there is (1) an intent to do the *actus reus* [q.v.], and (2) no circumstance of exculpation." Rollin M. Perkins & Ronald N. Boyce, *Criminal Law* 834 (3d ed. 1982).

criminality = the quality or fact of being criminal. E.g., "But the use, until 1963, of the M'Naghten Rules to excuse insane cruelty and refuse divorce on that ground shows that unfortunate hints of *criminality* still attach to a divorce suit (there is generally too much talk of the 'innocent' and the 'guilty' party)." Alan Harding, *A Social History of English Law* 403 (1966). This term has the NEEDLESS VARIANTS *criminalness* and *criminalty,* neither of which should appear in modern legal writing.

criminalize, an Americanism coined in the 1950s, means "to make illegal; to outlaw." E.g., "Relying on . . . Iowa Code § 721.2 . . . , which *criminalizes* subornation of perjury, the Iowa court concluded that . . . Robinson's actions . . . were required." *Nix v. Whiteside,* 475 U.S. 157, 162 (1986)./ "Many experts believe that restricting abortion would prove about as successful as Prohibition, when a small but vocal minority managed to *criminalize* liquor." *The Battle Over Abortion,* Newsweek, 1 May 1989, at 30. See -IZE.

criminal law, a phrase that often includes the entirety of what we know as the administration of criminal justice, can encompass several legal fields: substantive criminal law, criminal procedure, law enforcement, and penology. Generally, however, a lawyer who speaks of *criminal law* means the substantive criminal law. See **civil law (A).**

criminal lawyer. See **grammatical error.**

criminally = (1) in a criminal manner <he acted criminally>; or (2) under criminal law <criminally liable>. Sense (2) is largely confined to lawyers' writing—e.g.: "[T]he wrongdoer may be prosecuted criminally." J.N. Pomeroy, *Equity Jurisprudence* § 1051, at 114–15 (Symons ed., 5th ed. 1941).

criminal mischief. See **malicious mischief.**

criminalness; criminalty. See **criminality.**

criminal offense; crime. In distinguishing between these expressions, the U.S. Supreme Court has suggested that the former is broader because it includes petty offenses: "[W]hen the change [in Article III of the Constitution] was made from 'criminal offenses' to 'crimes,' and made in the light of the popular understanding of the meaning of the word 'crimes,' . . . it is obvious that the intent was to exclude from the constitutional requirement of a jury the trial of petty criminal offenses." *Schick v. U.S.,* 195 U.S. 65, 70 (1904). Whether this distinction would hold today is doubtful—*criminal offense* seeming to be nothing more than a verbose synonym of *crime.*

criminal protector. See **perpetrator.**

criminate; incriminate. *Incriminate* is now the more usual form in both AmE and BrE, although 100 years ago *criminate* was the more common of the two. Today it is a NEEDLESS VARIANT. E.g., "The constable told the prisoner that he need not say anything to *criminate* [read *incriminate*] himself, but that what he did say would be taken down and used as evidence against him." (Eng.)/ "This Act qualifies the rule that a witness is not bound to answer questions that *criminate* [read *incriminate*] himself by declaring that he is not excused from answering questions that fix him with a civil liability." (Eng.)/ "In the law of evidence, the privilege against *self-crimination* [read (today) *self-incrimination*] signifies the mere negation of a duty to testify." (Hohfeld)/ "In trials of contested elections, . . . no person shall be permitted to withhold his testimony on the ground that it may *criminate* [read *incriminate*] himself . . . ." Colo. Const. art. 7, § 9. See **incriminate.**

criminative; criminatory. These are NEEDLESS VARIANTS of *incriminatory,* q.v. See **criminate.**

criminous = (1) of the nature of a crime; (2) accusing of a crime; or (3) (of a person) guilty of a crime. Although the historical term *criminous clerks* is quite proper in reference to those who at common law availed themselves of the *benefit of clergy,* q.v., the word *criminous* is a pompous ARCHAISM when used as a NEEDLESS VARIANT of *criminal*—e.g.: "Mr. Fischl's intentions were quite sufficient, in our view, to make his conduct *criminous* [read *criminal*]." *U.S. v. Fischl,* 797 F.2d 306, 311 (6th Cir. 1986)./ "This belief goes beyond the assumption that many suspects are *criminous* [read *criminal*] by nature or profession." Marc

Miller, *Pretrial Detention and Punishment,* 75 Minn. L. Rev. 335, 374 (1990).

crisis forms the plural *crises,* not *crisises.*

crit; critter. These are slang words referring to an adherent of Critical Legal Studies. E.g., "Harvard may no longer be 'the Beirut of legal education,' as one *Crit* denied tenure charged, but it's still full of land mines." Ken Emerson, *When Legal Titans Clash,* N.Y. Times, 22 April 1990, § 6 at 26, 28./ "This is a piece about the *crits* for people who do not like them." John D. Ayer, *Not So Fast on the Crits,* 1 Scribes J. Legal Writing 45 (1990). See **Critical Legal Studies.**

criterion is the (orig. Gk.) singular, *criteria* the plural. Oddly, a number of writers somehow believe the word ends in *-ium* and therefore use the mistaken form *criterium*—e.g.:

- "The record, at present, does not indicate which, if any, of the individuals named as defendants may meet this *criterium* [read *criterion*]." *Heller v. Bushey,* 759 F.2d 1371, 1375–76 (9th Cir. 1985).
- "But no matter how much people made it, it was still subjective, and made on a subjective *criterium* [read *criterion*]." *Wallace v. Department of the Air Force,* 879 F.2d 829, 837 (Fed. Cir. 1989) (Skelton, J., dissenting).
- "So far as the fourth service plan *criterium* [read *criterion*], the court found a hint of change, where cleanliness around the home seemed to pick up . . . ." *In re J.M.,* 858 P.2d 118, 122 (Okla. Ct. App. 1993).
- "Finally, Montgomery's fourth *criterium* [read *criterion*] is difficult to apply to the instant case because the State was not requested to explain *it's* [read *its*] proffer of the injured patrons [*sic*] evidence." *Duncantelle v. State,* 877 S.W.2d 859, 862 (Tex. App.—Beaumont 1994).

This word is troublesome in various other ways. For example, one infrequently sees—though not infrequently enough—the double-plural form *criterias.* And the plural *criterions* was tried for a time but failed to become standard.

Writers often want to make *criteria* a singular—e.g.: "The determining *criteria* [read *criterion*] is the function of the attorneys' fees in the litigation process."/ "Appellant contends that the trial court used an improper *criteria* [read *criterion*] and denied appellant due process by basing its decision on its prior belief." Cf. **phenomena.**

Criterion has even been mistaken as a plural, perhaps because *criteria* is so frequently misused as a singular: "In *Johnson,* a panel of this court noted that it was appropriate to carefully review the basis upon which the district court made its award, upon finding that improper *criterion* [read *criteria*] were utilized." See PLURALS (A).

critter. See **crit.**

Critical Legal Studies describes a vaguely defined movement involving lawyer-intellectuals—mostly with leftist leanings—who have tried to posit a new method of discussing law by borrowing from deconstructionist philosophy and Marxist rhetoric, among other disparate sources. Adherents generally call themselves *crits* (q.v.), *critters,* or *CLSers.* For the most part, their writings are characterized by a newfangled vocabulary and ABSTRACTITIS. See Mark Kelman, *A Guide to Critical Legal Studies* (1987); Roberto Unger, *The Critical Legal Studies Movement* (1983); Louis B. Schwartz, *With Gun and Camera Through Darkest CLS-Land,* 36 Stan. L. Rev. 413 (1984). See **crit.**

cross, in lawyers' verbal shorthand, refers to *cross-examination,* q.v. E.g., "There's no way you can do a first-rate *cross* if you don't speak the other guy's language." Joseph Goulden, *The Million Dollar Lawyers* 287 (1978) (quoting an anonymous N.Y. lawyer). Cf. **direct.**

cross-claim; counterclaim. In most American jurisdictions, *counterclaim,* q.v., refers to a claim by a defendant against the plaintiff used as an offset against the original claim; and a *cross-claim* is a claim by one coparty against another, as by one defendant against a codefendant. Each word has been used for the other, but this DIFFERENTIATION should be encouraged and fastidiously followed in practice. See Fed. R. Civ. P. 13. *Cross-claim* is now often spelled in the U.S. as one unhyphenated word.

In BrE, *counterclaim* is defined as "a cross-claim brought by a defendant in civil proceedings that asserts an independent cause of action but is not also a defense to the claim made in the action by the plaintiff" (*CDL*). *Cross-action* is frequently used in BrE for *cross-claim.* These terms are somewhat less restricted in BrE than in AmE, for *cross-claim* may refer either to (1) an action brought by the defendant against the plaintiff, or (2) an action brought by a defendant against a codefendant in the same suit.

cross-complain, v.i., is a variant of *cross-claim*—e.g.: "The defendant *cross-complained* under the same contract."

cross-examination is hyphenated; *direct examination,* q.v., is not. See **cross.**

cross-national should always be hyphenated, just as *cross-cultural* should be. Many social scientists drop the hyphens to form single words. Cf. **transnational.**

cross-offer. See **counteroffer.**

cross-question = a question on cross-examination. The hyphen is important because the best *cross-questions* are not cross questions. E.g., "Certainly it would ordinarily be unfair for a trial court to require an offer of proof during cross-examination. [But] enough must be done to show that the sustaining of an objection to a *cross-question* was error. The *cross-question* must on its face be proper." John Kaplan & Jon R. Waltz, *Cases and Materials on Evidence* 52 (5th ed. 1984).

cruel and unusual punishment. The Eighth Amendment states: "Excessive bail shall not be required, nor excessive fines imposed, nor cruel and unusual punishments inflicted." U.S. Const. amend. VIII. The U.S. Supreme Court has construed the phrase *cruel and unusual punishment* to include not just barbarities such as torture but also punishment that is excessive for the crime committed. See *Coker v. Georgia,* 433 U.S. 584, 598 (1977) (stating that a death sentence was a disproportionate punishment for rape because "rape . . . in terms of moral depravity and of the injury to the person and to the public . . . does not compare with murder, which does involve the unjustified taking of human life").

crystallize. See DOUBLING OF FINAL CONSONANTS.

c.t.a. See **administrator.**

cubiclize. See -IZE.

culpa is a civil-law term meaning "actionable negligence." The English words *fault* and *negligence* are far preferable in English contexts. Pl. *-ae.*

culpability. See **guilt.**

culpable; inculpable; culpatory; culpose. *Culpable* = guilty, blameworthy. (See **blameworthy (A).**) *Inculpable* is a troublesome word to be avoided, for it may be interpreted as meaning either "able to be inculpated [i.e., guilty]," or "not culpable [i.e., innocent]." The latter sense has historically been attributed to the word.

Culpatory and *culpose* are rare terms, the former meaning "expressing blame," the latter "characterized by criminal negligence." Neither has anything to recommend it; one who uses either term in discussing Anglo-American law, or *inculpable* for that matter, is culpable of a stylistic infelicity.

culprit has one of the most interesting of all legal etymologies. "According to the legal tradition, found in print shortly after 1700," explains the *OED,* "*culprit* was not originally a word, but a fortuitous or ignorant running together of two words (the fusion being made possible by the abbreviated writing of legal records), viz. Anglo-Fr. *culpable* or L. *culpabilis* 'guilty', abbreviated *cul.,* and *prit* or *prist* = OF. *prest* 'ready'. It is supposed that when the prisoner had pleaded 'Not guilty', the Clerk of the Crown replied with '*Culpable: prest d'averrer nostre bille,*' i.e., 'Guilty: [and I am] *ready* to aver our indictment'; that this reply was noted on the roll in the form *cul. prist,* etc.; and that, at a later time, after the disuse of Law French, this formula was mistaken for an appellation addressed to the accused." In short, *culprit* is quintessentially a POPULARIZED LEGAL TECHNICALITY.

Nevertheless, the word still appears in legal contexts to denote a wrongdoer—e.g.: "Some Forces exclude the question of punishment altogether, the Chief Constable refraining from prosecution if the *culprit* has parents or friends or even the Salvation Army to go to and is willing to be looked after; on the other hand there will be prosecution if the *culprit* declares that he is going to do it again." Glanville Williams, *The Sanctity of Life and the Criminal Law* 278–79 (1957; repr. 1972).

cultiv(at)able. The shorter form is preferred. E.g., "[T]he remaining 200 acres is *cultivatable* [read *cultivable*] land." *Sell v. Cohen,* 293 F. Supp. 684, 685 (E.D. Ky. 1968). See -ATABLE.

cultured; cultivated. Correctly, the former is used of the person, the latter of the mind. A *cultured* person has refined tastes; a *cultivated* mind is well trained and highly developed.

cumbrance is a NEEDLESS VARIANT of *encumbrance,* q.v.

cum testamento annexo. See **administrator.**

cumulate. See **accumulate.**

cumulative, in its general lay sense, means "composed of successively added parts; acquiring or increasing in force or cogency in successive additions" <cumulative effect or argument>. The term has various specific legal senses. The most complex of these, used now chiefly in the corporate field, relates to a system of voting developed originally in 19th-century British school-board elections. *Cumulative voting* = a system of voting, still in use, by which each voter has a number of votes equal to the number of representatives (usu. corporate officers) to be elected, and may either concentrate all his or her votes on one person or distribute them among the candidates.

Cumulative is used of evidence in the sense "tending to prove the same point that other evidence has already been offered to prove." In the context of wills, *cumulative* is sometimes used of legacies in the sense "given by the same testator to the same legatee."

In criminal law *cumulative sentences* are the same as *consecutive sentences.* See **concurrent sentences.**

CUPOS is an ACRONYM of recent vintage meaning "a cohabiting unmarried person of the opposite sex." E.g., "Her reason for leaving home is that she prefers her own life style of living with this young boy as a CUPOS (cohabiting unmarried person of opposite sex)." *Jackman v. State Dep't of Social & Health Serv.,* 643 P.2d 889, 890 (Wash. Ct. App. 1982). See **cohabitant.** See also NEOLOGISMS.

curable. In general English usage this word is used only of diseases; in legal usage, it is used in reference to any defects or deficiencies. Here *curable* = remediable, correctable: "We are confident that the deficiencies in the affidavits are readily *curable.*"/ "Whatever harmful inferences might have been drawn from these questions were of the *curable* type and were removed by the court's instructions." See **cure.**

cur. adv. vult is the abbreviation of *Curia advisari vult* (= the court wishes to consider the matter). It appears at the end of the written arguments reproduced in British law reports and indicates that the judgment of the court was delivered (as Americans might always expect) on a date later than the hearing, rather than extemporaneously at the conclusion of the hearing, as is common in England. Such a "reserved" judgment carries additional weight as an authority.

An alternative abbreviation is *C.A.V.* or (less commonly) *c.a.v.* And an alternative (and now defunct) spelling is *curia advisare vult*—given by several old law dictionaries such as John Bouvier, *Bouvier's Law Dictionary* (Francis Rawles ed., 3d ed. 1914) and Thomas Tayler, *The Law Glossary* (1877).

curative; curatory; curatorial. For the meaning "of or relating to the cure of diseases," *curative* is preferred. *Curative* is also used in the legal sense "corrective" <curative instructions to the jury>. (See **cure & curable.**) *Curatory* is a NEEDLESS VARIANT. *Curatorial* = of or relating to a curator.

curator. See **conservator.**

curatory; curatorial. See **curative.**

cure = to correct. In general usage, *cure* is used only in reference to diseases, literal or metaphorical; but in law it is used, as legal JARGON, in reference to any defect or deficiency. Thus *incurable error* means "error at trial that cannot be corrected by the judge." E.g., "The plan proposed to *cure* a prepetition default and acceleration on a debt on Grubb's principal residence." See **curable.**

curfew began as an Anglo-Saxon custom and only in the 1800s came to refer to an official order or regulation to keep off the streets at certain hours. In the 14th century, *corfu* referred to the ringing of a bell every evening at a fixed hour as a signal to cover the fires [OF. *couvre feu* "cover the fire"]. Even after the ritual of putting out the fires discontinued, the bell-ringing continued as a signal to clear the streets after dark.

curia advisari vult. See ***cur. adv. vult.***

currently. See **presently.**

curriculum. Pl. *-a* or *-ums.* The Latin plural is slightly more common, but the Englished version may be gaining ground. E.g., "Universities multiplied rapidly, first in Italy and then elsewhere, many of them starting as law schools and later broadening their *curriculums* . . . ." René A. Wormser, *The Story of the Law* 195 (1962). See PLURALS (A).

cursory; cursorial. *Cursory* = perfunctory; superficial. *Cursorial* = of or pertaining to running.

curtail means "to cut back," not "to stop completely." Therefore, it is difficult to ascertain what distinction the writer of this sentence intended: "Irrigation has cut down on, if not *curtailed,* water production of springs that once fed it."

Here *curtail* is correctly used: "Although a testator has broad power to dispose of his property by will, his power is *curtailed* to a limited degree by the operation of certain statutes and collateral common-law rules."

CURTAILED WORDS. See BACK-FORMATIONS.

curtesy; dower. These medieval common-law terms, which are defunct in England (the rights they represent having been abolished in 1925), live on in several American jurisdictions. The words denote correlative rights. At common law, *curtesy* = the right of a husband, on his wife's death, to a life estate in the land that his deceased wife owned during their marriage. The husband has this right only if a child was born alive to the couple. The word began as a variant spelling of *courtesy* (tenancy by the courtesy of England). Several jurisdictions that retain the terms have abolished the requirement of a child born alive and have reduced the amount from all land to half the land. *Dower* = the right of a wife, on her husband's death, to a life estate in a third of the land that he owned, of which, with few exceptions, she cannot be deprived by any alienation made by him. "Today in most states an elective share, supplanting or supplementing *dower* and *curtesy,* has evolved." See **dower.**

Inchoate dower and *curtesy initiate* are the terms denoting the spouse's interest in the other spouse's estate while both are living and after the birth of issue capable of inheriting. "*Inchoate dower* once prevented the husband from transferring realty during his life to defeat his wife's *dower;* the common-law marital right together with his *curtesy initiate* ensured his interest in the wife's realty."/ "Such a scheme to defraud the spouse was impossible when wealth consisted of realty, and either *inchoate dower* or *curtesy initiate* operated to bar conveyance without consent." See **initiate tenant by curtesy.**

curtilage (= the land around a house and within an enclosure) is sometimes misspelled *curtilege,* perhaps on the mistaken analogy of *privilege.*

The term is used in the U.S. and in England but not in Scotland. For police searches under the Fourth Amendment, the *curtilage* is the area within which police may not, in most cases, search without a warrant: "[C]ourts have extended Fourth Amendment protection to the *curtilage;* and they have defined the *curtilage,* as did the common law, by reference to the factors that determine whether an individual reasonably may expect that an area immediately adjacent to the home will remain private." *Oliver v. U.S.,* 466 U.S. 170, 180 (1984).

cushion, v.t., = to condition (jury interrogatories) by placing an instruction between two in order to prevent the second from appearing to presume a given answer to the first.

custodial interrogation = police questioning begun after a person has been taken into custody or had his or her freedom otherwise curtailed. See *Miranda v. Arizona,* 384 U.S. 436, 444 (1966) ("By *custodial interrogation,* we mean questioning initiated by law enforcement officers after a person has been taken into custody or otherwise deprived of his freedom of action in any significant way").

custodian. In the legal sense, this word means "guardian" or "protector." It is used euphemistically in lay contexts to mean "janitor."

custody; possession. Whereas one may have *custody* of both persons and things, one may have *possession* of things only. But a further distinction is possible in criminal law: "The distinction between *possession* and *custody* . . . was gradually developed in a long line of decided cases . . . . In general it is important to distinguish between servants and others, because usually a servant who has control of a chattel belonging to his master has custody only (and not possession), whereas the actual control of a chattel by one not a servant is usually possession." Rollin M. Perkins, *Criminal Law* 196 (1957). See **possession (C).**

customer. See **client.**

custumal; costomal. The former is the usual spelling for "a written collection of a city's customs."

customary law = practices and beliefs that are so vital and intrinsic a part of a social and economic system that they are treated as if they were laws. *Customary law* is handed down for many generations as unwritten law, though it is usu. collected finally in a written code. See **unwritten law.**

Customs Court. See **Court of International Trade.**

cut against; cut in favor of. These idioms are favorites of the legal profession; they should be used sparingly lest they become full-fledged CLICHÉS. "Although we do not find *Murdoch* particularly relevant here, it *cuts,* if at all, *against* RSR's position."/ "In any event, we find that the first factor *cuts in favor of* the mother and against the father." *In re Marriage of Haslett,* 629 N.E.2d 182, 188 (Ill. App. Ct. 1994).

cut-and-dried case is a CLICHÉ that, when used, needs to be hyphenated thus. E.g., "Take one of the coldest, *cut-and-dried cases* imaginable, a sane man deliberately kills another man in the sight of several reliable witnesses." Fred Rodell, *Woe Unto You, Lawyers!* 105 (1939; repr. 1980).

cut in favor of. See **cut against.**

cutting edge is a legal CLICHÉ and a VOGUE WORD. E.g., "By and large, the gains made in the safe and efficient administration of our prisons may be attributed to the anonymous professionals who daily toil at the *cutting edge* of our efforts to improve, while at the same time securing, our penal institutions." In the cant of our day, every law review seeks to be *on the cutting edge* of the law.

CUTTING OUT THE CHAFF refers to eliminating excess words. It is not an easy task; indeed, verbosity and obscurity are usually the result of facile and slapdash writing. Judges occasionally confess as much about their own writing. For example: "This opinion is too long. I apologize for its length but I simply didn't have time to write a shorter one." *U.S. v. Price,* 448 F. Supp. 503, 503 (D. Colo. 1978).

Many recurrent phrases are mere deadwood. For example, *Speaking for myself, I think . . . ,* aside from being redundant, adds nothing to the sentence when we know who is speaking and have intelligence enough to deduce that the speaker is stating an opinion. Some courts have written of *reasonable-minded defendants,* as if there might be *reasonable-footed* or *reasonable-chested* defendants; reason is only in the mind.

The following are wordy sentences with more concise alternatives supplied: "*In a large part* [*in large part* is idiomatic], it was our anticipation of this type of claim *which* [read *that*] cautioned us for so long against abrogation of the immunity rule." [Better: *Our foresight of such claims long cautioned us against abrogating the immunity rule.*]/ "*It was a package of small size . . .* [read *It was a small package . . .*]."/ "The economist's goal in formulating normative rules is *that of* [delete *that of*] 'efficiency' [note that *efficiency* needs no quotation marks]."/ "A will is ambulatory in character and subject to change at any time." [Read *A will is ambulatory* or *A will is always subject to change (while the testator lives).*]

The unfortunate legal predilection for nouns over verbs, for gerunds over verbal participles, is the cause of much deadweight. E.g., "The defendants had the duty to take reasonable care to protect her, *including probably the giving of a warning to her or to the plaintiff* [read *including, probably, warning her or the plaintiff*]." See VERBOSITY, REDUNDANCY (A), FLOTSAM PHRASES & SUPERFLUITIES.

cy(-)pres. This LAW FRENCH term, denoting the doctrine that written instruments should be construed as near to the parties' intention as possible, is predominantly spelled as two words. The British hyphenate the phrase and use an accent grave thus: *cy-près.* Meaning "as near as" and pronounced /sɪ-***pray***/, *cy pres* (originally *sì près, ici-près* or *aussi-près*) is used in the context of charitable gifts.

This phrase carries different senses modernly and at common law.

> At common law . . . , the Crown exercised its prerogative power to apply funds given for a charitable, but illegal, purpose to some valid charitable purpose without regard for the settlor's intention. Property otherwise given for a particular charitable purpose which became incapable of fulfillment was directed by the chancellor under the doctrine of *cy pres* to another charitable purpose which fell within the general charitable intention of the settlor.
>
> The prerogative power, of course, does not exist in this country. The *cy pres* doctrine applied in the United States is a rule of judicial construction designed to approximate as closely as possible the desires of the settlor.
>
> *La Fond v. City of Detroit,* 98 N.W.2d 530, 534 n.1 (Mich. 1959).

Today, however, the sense is the same in G.B. as in the U.S., the court being bound by this doctrine to make a scheme for the funds to be applied to a charitable purpose as close as possible to the original one.

The state of Georgia has a statute with the following explanation: "When a valid charitable bequest is incapable for some reason of execution in the exact manner provided by the testator, donor, or founder, a court of equity will carry it into effect in such a way as will [as] nearly as possible effectuate his intention." Ga. Code Ann. § 108-202 (1959).

D

damage, adj., corresponds to *damages,* n.; that is, *damage claim = claim for damages.* This use of *damage,* dating from the late 19th century, is omitted from most general English-language dictionaries but is common in law. E.g., "If a *damage claim* is within the scope of the arbitration, the arbitrators at common law . . . may depart from the rules of law." Charles T. McCormick, *Handbook on the Law of Damages* § 4, at 19–20 (1935)./ "[A]lternative safeguards . . . reduce the need for a private *damage action* [= *action for damages*]." *Forrester v. White,* 792 F.2d 647, 658 (7th Cir. 1986)./ "Nader's *damage action* for fraudulent misrepresentation had exposed the industry's deliberate practice of over-booking to maximize profits." Barbara H. Craig, *Chadha: The Story of an Epic Constitutional Struggle* 62 (1988).

Sometimes, however—esp. in BrE—the plural form *damages* is used adjectivally. E.g., "[T]he *Sun* paid £1m in an out-of-court *damages settlement* to the singer Elton John." The Independent, 13 Dec. 1988, at 4./ "A permanent injunction . . . can translate into more real financial benefit than a *damages judgment* [read, in AmE, *damage judgment*]." Michael Tigar, Book Review, 17 Litigation 49, 49 (Winter 1991).

damage, n.; **injury.** There is a modern tendency to refer to *damage to property,* but *injury to the person.* It is not an established distinction. Blackstone did not observe it, having titled one section of his great treatise *Injury to Property,* and neither the English nor the American courts have consistently observed it. One could not be faulted for restricting one's usage in this way, but neither could one be faulted for writing *damage to persons* or *injury to property.*

damage feasant. See **feasant.**

damage(s), n. **A. Generally.** "[T]he word *damage,* meaning 'Loss, injury, or deterioration,' is 'to be distinguished from its plural,—*damages*—which means a compensation in money for a loss or *damage.*'" *American Stevedores, Inc. v. Porello,* 330 U.S. 446, 450 n.6 (1947) (quoting *Black's*). In the following sentence, the two terms are correctly used: "After actual *damage* is shown it is unnecessary to show its money extent to sustain a judgment for exemplary *damages.*"

Often, however, the words are misused: "In Massachusetts exemplary *damages* are not recoverable in an action for libel; only actual *damage* [read *damages*] may be recovered."/ "The tornado caused an estimated $20,000,000 in *damages* [read *damage*]."/ "Where the chattel is unique, . . . money *damage* [read *damages*] will be inadequate . . . ." William F. Walsh, *A Treatise on Equity* 307 (1930). See **money damages.**

In the following sentence, two senses are incorrectly conflated; one recovers *damages* but suffers *damage:* "Ferranti International Signal plans imminent legal action to recover as much as possible of the *damages* it has suffered as a result of an alleged £215m fraud." Hugo Dixon & Charles Leadbeater, *Ferranti Plans Legal Action,* Fin. Times, 18–19 Nov. 1989, at 1. This error bears the technical name ZEUGMA.

An English writer assesses this linguistic situation pessimistically: "It is a melancholy example of the poverty of the language of English Law that it can find no better word than 'damages' for the compensation [that] it awards in civil cases . . . ." Edward Jenks, *The Book of English Law* 207 (P.B. Fairest ed., 6th ed. 1967). But, in the upshot, he is correct: "[T]he confusion between 'damage,' i.e. the loss [that] is the cause of the award of 'damages,' and 'damages' themselves, is an endless source of perplexity to students of . . . law. But it would be hopeless now to try to alter the practice." *Id.*

B. *Damages* in the Context of Restitution. A leading English authority on the law of contract holds that "[a] claim for restitution may not, strictly speaking, be one for *'damages'*; its purpose is not to compensate the plaintiff for a loss, but to deprive the defendant of a benefit." G.H. Treitel, *The Law of Contract* 832 (8th ed. 1991). Although this limit on the use of the word *damages* might promote analytical rigor, American lawyers routinely refer to any money acquired by way of judgment—in any type of action—as *damages.*

C. Other Terms. For the distinction between *general damages* and *special damages,* see **general damages.** For other types, see **hedonic damages, liquidated damages** & **punitive damages,** as well as **consequentials** & **incidentals.**

damages, punitive (or exemplary). See **punitive damages, punitives, punies** & **exemplaries.**

Dame Grand Cross (or Dame Commander) of the Order of the British Empire (O.B.E.). Men who are appointed to the High Court and higher courts are invariably knighted, whereas women are made Dames Commander of the Order of the British Empire. Abbreviation: D.B.E. The mode of salutation is *my lady.* See **my lord.**

damn, adj. & adv., for *damned*—as in *that damn case*—though attested from the 18th century, remains a casualism. E.g., "An attentive study of the four illustrations will lead any analyst to the despairing conclusion, which is of course reinforced by the mysterious text of § 90 itself, that no one had any idea what the *damn* [or, less casually, *damned*] thing meant." Grant Gilmore, *The Death of Contract* 64–65 (1974).

damnatory. Though this word might appear to be related to *damnum* and *damnify,* qq.v., the relation is etymological only. This is not a legal term per se, but a general word equivalent to *condemnatory,* which is more comprehensible. E.g., "If the person sued is proved to have allowed his view to be distorted by malice, it is quite immaterial that somebody else might without malice have written an equally *damnatory* criticism." (Eng.)

damned, adj. See **damn.**

damnify (= to inflict injury upon) is generally an unnecessary LEGALISM for *injure.* The *OED* notes that this word was common in the 17th century but is now rare. One might excuse the word's use in the second example below, but not in the first: "I am satisfied that the injured person is *damnified* by having cut short the period during which he had a normal expectation of enjoying life." (Eng.) (The writer did not want to repeat *injure*—this use smacks of INELEGANT VARIATION.)/ "Where the principle of *damnum sine injuria* applies, the person *damnified* has no right of action against the person responsible for causing the loss because the latter has not, in causing or allowing the harm to befall, been in breach of legal duty to him." (Eng.) (It would make no sense to say the person had been *injured* when we have just stated that that same person was *sine injuria* [= without wrongful act].) See ***damnum.***

The antonym is much better known: *indemnify.* Though it has the same etymology as *damnify* with a negative prefix (*in-* "not" + *damnum* "loss, damage"), the vowel shifts to *-e-* in the negative form. See **indemnify.**

damnosa h(a)ereditas = an inheritance more onerous (e.g., because burdened with debts) than profitable. Generally the term is spelled *haereditas.* Originally a Roman-law term, *damnosa haereditas* has been extended by modern legal writers to refer to anything one acquires that turns out to be disadvantageous.

damnous = of, relating to, or causing a *damnum* (q.v.). Usually, the term means "causing loss or damage." The word is obsolescent legal JARGON, not a TERM OF ART. "They have injuriously, as distinguished from *damnously,* affected the plaintiff's rights." See ***damnum absque injuria.***

damnum = damage suffered. E.g., "The loss, *damnum,* is capable of being estimated in terms of money." (Eng.) This term is hardly justified in any context not involving the doctrine of *damnum absque injuria* (q.v.). In the sentence quoted it adds nothing. See ***damnum infectum.***

damnum absque injuria; damnum sine injuria. These synonymous LATINISMS may both be translated *damage without wrongful act.* They denote damage for which there is no legal remedy. A 19th-century commentator stated that *damnum sine injuria,* "standing alone as a sort of compound noun, seems hardly good Latin. English lawyers, however, have so used it since the fifteenth century at the latest." Note, 2 Law Q. Rev. 117, 117 (1886).

Still used with some frequency in British legal writing, the phrases are comparatively rare in American legal prose. E.g., "If disturbances or loss come as a result of competition or the exercise of like results by others, it is *damnum absque injuria* unless some superior right by contract or otherwise is interfered with." (Eng.)/ "He says that it is *damnum absque injuria,* intimating that the acts of the defendant, who justifies a libelous publication, do not constitute a wrong in its legal sense, and then proceeds to observe that this is agreeable to the reasoning of the civil law." Cf. ***injuria absque damno.***

damnum infectum = loss not yet suffered but only apprehended. This LATINISM is more a hindrance than an aid to analysis, for most readers must look it up.

damnum sine injuria. See ***damnum absque injuria.***

DANGLERS are ordinarily unattached participles, either present participles (ending in *-ing*) or past participles (ending usu. in *-ed*), that do not relate syntactically to the nouns they are supposed to modify. In effect, the participle tries to sever its relationship with its noun or pronoun. Gerunds may also dangle precariously (see (C)). Usually, recasting the sentence will remedy the incoherence, AMBIGUITY, or ILLOGIC.

Danglers are of two types, the majority being unacceptable and a few being acceptable because of long-standing usage. In the normal word order, a participial phrase beginning a sentence *(Running by the lake,)* should be followed directly by the noun acting as subject in the main clause *(I saw the two defendants).* When that word order is changed, as by changing the verb in the main clause to the passive voice, the sentence becomes illogical or misleading: *Running by the lake, the two defendants were seen.* It was not the two defendants who were running, but the witness. This is the unacceptable type of dangling modifier.

Examples of acceptable danglers are easy to come by. We all know that there is nothing wrong with *Considering the current atmosphere in the legislature, it is unlikely that the legislation will pass.* Several other examples are discussed in (D) below.

A. Danglers Ending in *-ing*. In the sentences that follow, mispositioned words have caused grammatical blunders. Perhaps the most common legal sentence containing a dangling participle is this: "Finding no error, the judgment of the district court is affirmed." Literally, this sentence says that the judgment found no error; the proper subject, namely *the court,* remains unmentioned. [A possible revision: *Finding no error, we affirm the judgment of the district court.*] This is the type of problematic dangler cited at the outset: an active participle is followed by a main clause in the passive voice.

The classic example occurs when the wrong noun begins the main clause, that is, a noun other than the one expected by the reader who has digested the introductory participial phrase. E.g., "*Accepting* for present purposes the showing made, *the facts* of the claim *were* as follows." [A possible revision: *We accept* for present purposes the showing [*that was*] made *and find the facts to be* as follows." (It is not the facts that *accept:* it is the writer who *accepts* (and *finds*). The error seems to have resulted from the writer's fear of FIRST PERSON.)]/ "*Having reached* that conclusion [read, e.g., *Since we have reached* that conclusion], all that remains is to choose an appropriate remedy and to frame the appropriate relief."/ "*Viewing the record* [read *If we view the record*] in the light most favorable to appellants, the most that can be said is that Yellow Cab secured from the city an exclusive concession whose anticompetitive effects stem primarily from a valid municipal policy."

The error occurs also when the main clause begins with an EXPLETIVE (e.g., *it* or *there*) after an introductory participial phrase:

- "Applying those principles to the facts in the case at bar, *it* is clear that plaintiffs cannot recover." [A possible revision: *If we apply these principles to the case at bar, it becomes clear that . . . .*]
- "Reviewing the theories of judicial decision current in the last century, *it* will be seen that we began with a creative theory [that] was used to make an American common law . . . ." Roscoe Pound, *The Formative Era of American Law* 116–17 (1938). [A possible revision: *Reviewing the theories of judicial decision current in the last century shows that . . . .*]
- "*Being* in derogation of the common law, *it* is often said that the statute of frauds should be strictly construed." Laurence P. Simpson, *Handbook on the Law of Suretyship* 117 (1950). [A possible revision: *Being in derogation of the common law, the statute of frauds is often said to require strict construction.*]
- "*Turning* to England, *it* ought to be noted first that that country, though late in doing so, participated fully in the medieval development sketched above." Grant Gilmore & Charles L. Black, Jr., *The Law of Admiralty* 8 (2d ed. 1975). [A possible revision: *Though England was late to do so, it participated fully in the medieval development sketched above.*]
- "*Looking* at the passage as a whole, *it* is by no means clear that Lord Atkin meant to confine manslaughter to cases of recklessness in the subjective sense." J.H. Baker, *An Introduction to English Legal History* 226 (3d ed. 1990). [A possible revision: *The passage as a whole does not make clear whether Lord Atkin meant . . . .*]

Midsentence danglers are just as bad but are harder for the untrained eye to spot. E.g., "It is the purpose of this note to re-examine the existing law, *placing emphasis upon* [read *to emphasize*] the interests to be protected, and to draw some conclusions as to its adequacy in protecting them." (This is poor writing because it could be included as boilerplate in almost any lawnote imaginable; the writer should craft the language specifically for the case at hand, generalizing, to be sure, but not making it so general that it is well-nigh universal. Further, the writer should have been aware of the natural triad lurking in the sentence, i.e., the infinitive phrases: *to re-examine; to place* [*to emphasize*]; *to draw.*)

B. Past-Participial Danglers. These are especially common when the main clause begins with a possessive—e.g.: "Born on March 12, 1944, in Dalton, Georgia, Larry Lee Simms's qualifications . . . ." Barbara H. Craig, *Chadha: The Story of an Epic Constitutional Struggle* 79 (1988). (Simms's qualifications were not born on March 12—*he* was.) [A possible revision: *Born on March 12, 1944, in Dalton, Georgia, Larry Lee Simms had qualifications that . . . .*]

But the problem also sometimes appears when a run-of-the-mill noun begins the main clause—e.g.: "*Applied* to the situation at bar, *the likelihood* that a barge will break from her fasts, and the damage she will do, vary with the place and time . . . ." *U.S. v. Carroll Towing Co.,* 159 F.2d 169, 173 (2d Cir. 1947) (per L. Hand, J.). [A possible revision: *When those principles are applied to the situation at bar . . . .*]

C. Dangling Gerunds. These are close allies to

dangling participles, but here the participle acts as a noun rather than as an adjective:

- *"In handling* this problem *the satellite concept* of illicit commodities developed." Edward H. Levi, *An Introduction to Legal Reasoning* 62 (1949). [A possible revision: *In handling this problem, the courts developed the satellite concept of illicit commodities.*]
- *"In considering* whether conduct is intentional, *it* is unnecessary to ascertain whether the party knew of the rule of law . . . ." Glanville Williams, *Criminal Law* 44 (2d ed. 1961). [A possible revision: *In considering whether conduct is intentional, the court need not ascertain whether* . . . .]
- "[*I*]*n construing* a criminal statute, *the prisoner* must be given the benefit of the doubt . . . ." Edward Jenks, *The Book of English Law* 40 (P.B. Fairest ed., 6th ed. 1967). [A possible revision: *In construing a criminal statute, the court must give the prisoner the benefit of the doubt* . . . .]
- *"In gauging* the force of this argument *it* should be recalled that in many contexts punishments and reward will appear as opposite sides of the same coin." Lon L. Fuller, *Anatomy of the Law* 51 (1968). [A possible revision: *In gauging the force of this argument, one should recall that* . . . .]
- *"In discussing* the definition of contract given in the American Restatement *it* was pointed out that . . . ." P.S. Atiyah, *An Introduction to the Law of Contract* 42 (3d ed. 1981). [A possible revision: *In discussing* . . . *, one commentator pointed out* . . . .]

D. Acceptable Danglers or Disguised Conjunctions. Any number of present participles have been used as conjunctions or prepositions for so long that they have lost the participial duty to modify specific nouns. In effect, the clauses they introduce are adverbial; they stand apart from and comment on the content of the sentence. Among the commonest of these are *according, assuming, barring, concerning, considering, judging, owing, regarding, respecting, speaking, taking* (usu. *account of, into account*). E.g., *"Speaking* geographically, the Atlantic seaboard with a few gaps allows these unions, which become more and more wicked as we cross the Appalachians." Max Radin, *The Law and You* 42 (1948)./ *"Assuming* its maritime nature, almost any type of service claim will today be held within the Lien Act . . . ." Grant Gilmore & Charles L. Black, Jr., *The Law of Admiralty* 659 (2d ed. 1975).

E. Ending Sentences with. Traditionally, grammarians frowned on *all* danglers, but during the 20th century they generally loosened the strictures for participial constructions at the end of a sentence. Early-20th-century grammarians might have disapproved the following sentences, but they have long been considered acceptable—e.g.: "Robert stepped to the door, seeking his companion."/ "Tom's arm hung useless, broken by the blow."

Usually, as in the first of the two examples just quoted, the end-of-the-sentence dangler is introduced by a so-called coordinating participle: *seeking* is equivalent to *and sought.* Similarly:

- "Vexed by these frequent demands upon her time, she finally called upon her friend, *imploring* him to come to her aid." *(Imploring = and implored.)*
- "The New Orleans-bound steamer rammed and sank the freighter ten miles from its destination, *sending* her to the bottom in 10 minutes." *(Sending = and sent.)*
- "She predeceased him *leaving* a husband and two children." Anthony R. Mellows, *The Law of Succession* 515 (3d ed. 1977). *(Leaving = and left.)*

A few editors would consider each of those participles misattached, but in fact they are acceptable as coordinating participles. As for the few who object, one wonders what they would do with the following sentence: "The boy ran out of the house *crying.*"

daresay. So spelled, generally, as one word.

DASHES. See PUNCTUATION (D).

data, technically the plural of *datum,* has, since the 1940s, been increasingly often thought of as a mass noun taking a singular verb. But in formal contexts it is preferably treated as a plural—e.g.: "If new *data do* not fit, either the system must be modified to accommodate *them,* or *they* must be modified to fit the system." John H. Merryman, *The Civil Law Tradition* 67 (1969).

Many writers lapse, however:

- *"There is no data* [read *There are no data*] available on the number of pesticide containers recycled in the state."
- "No finger was lifted to ascertain whether some of the *data was* [read *data were*] available . . . ." *Boreri v. Fiat S.P.A.,* 663 F.2d 17, 23 (1st Cir. 1985).
- "I believe plaintiff's *data raises* [read *data raise*] a rational basis for evaluating the response of the prison."
- "It was equally apparent that the *data* gathered on Law and Psychology *was* [read *data* . . .

were] not amenable to such categorization." Elizabeth V. Gemmette, *Law and Literature,* 23 Valparaiso U.L. Rev. 267, 268 (1989).

The *Oxford Guide* allows the singular use of *data* in computing and allied disciplines (see COMPUTERESE); whether lawyers own computers or not, they should use *data* as a plural.

In one particular context, though, *data* is invariably treated as a plural: when it begins a clause and is not preceded by the definite article. E.g., "*Data* over the last two years *suggest* that the rate at which gay men get AIDS has finally begun to flatten out." Lawrence K. Altman, *Who's Stricken and How: AIDS Pattern Is Shifting,* N.Y. Times, 5 Feb. 1989, at 1.

Datum, the "true" singular, is still used when a single piece of information is referred to: "The latter statement merely states that a certain *datum* has not been located in records regularly made and preserved." *U.S. v. Yakobov,* 712 F.2d 20, 26 (2d Cir. 1983)./ "This was not a case [in which] some 'presumptively prejudicial' *datum,* like an attempted bribe, had come to light." *Neron v. Tierney,* 841 F.2d 1197, 1203 (1st Cir. 1988).

Because *data* is a count noun, *many data* is correct—e.g.: "Numerous expert and representative interests are consulted, and *many data* assembled, often over a long period . . . ." Carleton K. Allen, *Law in the Making* 433 (7th ed. 1964)./ "But *much* [read *many*] of the *data* in present personnel files *is* [read *are*] highly subjective." William O. Douglas, *Points of Rebellion* 21 (1970). (In that book, Justice Douglas twice used *data* as a plural on page 19.) See COUNT NOUNS AND MASS NOUNS.

As a historian of the English language once put it, "A student with one year of Latin [knows] that *data* and *phenomena* are plural." Albert C. Baugh, *The Gift of Style,* 34 Pa. B. Ass'n, 101, 105–06 (1962).

database. One word.

DATES. A. Order. One may unimpeachably write either *May 26, 1984,* or *26 May 1984.* The latter—the primarily BrE method—is often better in prose, for it takes no commas.

Of the American method—*May 26, 1984*—the first editor of the *OED* said: "This is not logical: 19 May 1862 is. *Begin* at day, *ascend* to month, *ascend* to year; not *begin* at month, *descend* to day, then *ascend* to year." Sir James A.H. Murray, as quoted in *Hart's Rules for Compositors and Readers at the OUP* 18 n.1 (39th ed. 1983).

B. Month and Year. *February 1985* is better than *February of 1985.* There is no need for a comma between the month and the year.

C. As Adjectives. Our generation has taken to making adjectives out of dates, just as it has out of PLACE-NAMES. E.g., "This matter arises out of a *September 1980* divorce decree." Today this occurs even in formal legal prose. The more traditional rendering of the sentence just quoted would be, "This matter arises out of a divorce decree of September 1980." Although occasionally using dates adjectivally is a space-saver, the device should not be overworked: it gives prose a breezy, journalistic look.

And it is particularly clumsy when the day as well as the month is given—e.g.: "The court reconsidered the July 12, 1994 privilege order." Stylists who use this phrasing typically omit the comma after the year—and rightly so: in the midst of an adjective phrase (i.e., the date), it impedes the flow of the writing too much.

D. Written Out. Although the validity of a legal document almost never depends on its being dated, lawyers often go to extreme lengths to express the date in words; *1 January 1988* becomes *the first day of January, One thousand nine hundred and eighty-eight.*" A waste.

E. In Contracts. To avoid litigation on the question whether *until December 31, 1986* includes all of that day, the drafter should state explicitly that an option, e.g., will expire at noon Central Standard Time on a certain day.

For another common problem relating to dates in contracts, see **later of [date] or [date].**

datum. See **data.**

day. Three legal conventions relate to this word. First, when given as the period of a notice, and prescribed as a necessary interval between two acts or events, *day* excludes the day of the notice and the act to be performed. Hence the full number of days prescribed intervenes, unless the law provides otherwise.

Second, when used as a period of time, *day* means the period of 24 hours, beginning at the stroke of midnight.

Third, when used in contrast to *night,* the word ordinarily denotes the period beginning at half an hour before sunrise and ending half an hour after sunset.

day in court is a LOAN TRANSLATION of the Law French *jour en banc,* which, by the 17th century, had been translated (partly) to *jour in court.* Whereas the plaintiff ordinarily wants a day in court, the defendant ordinarily wants—in legal parlance—to "go hence without day." (See **go hence without day** & ***sine die.***) E.g., "[T]he principal [suggestion] is that the plaintiff was not made a party to the proceeding, and has not had his *day in court,* in opposition to the final decision [that] ordered the sale." *Howard v. Railway Co.,* 101 U.S. 837, 847 (1879)./ "[I]f a party fails to ask for and to secure all relief, both legal and equitable, to which he is entitled in the action, he cannot, after final disposition of the case, bring another action on the same facts for further relief. He has had his *day in court.*" William F. Walsh, *A Treatise on Equity* 38 (1930)./ "Many attorneys said one big effect of the two decisions may be to deprive middle-income and lower-income employees of their *days in court* because attorneys will be less inclined to bring cases where compensatory damages are relatively small." Richard B. Schmitt, *California Court Further Restricts Right of Fired Workers to Sue Ex-Employers,* Wall St. J., 26 May 1989, at A3. Cf. **one bite at the apple.**

d.b.n. See **administrator.**

deadbeat (= a person who evades debts), a 19th-century coinage, is a favorite word of American lawyers trying to collect on judgments. Some use it tendentiously for any judgment debtor, and often the epithet is apt. Even courts use the word in published opinions—e.g.: "The Court's decision is indefensible. It permits a *deadbeat* husband to use the Bankruptcy Code's grace for honest debtors as a slick scheme for euchring his former wife out of her 'sole and separate property' in one-half of the benefits he receives under a pension plan." *Bush v. Taylor,* 893 F.2d 962, 967 (8th Cir. 1990) (Bowman, J., dissenting).

dead capital. See **mortgage.**

deadhand. See **mortmain.**

dead investment. See **mortgage.**

deadline is one word; formerly it was hyphenated.

deadlocked jury. See **hung jury.**

deadly; deathly. The former means "able to cause death." (See **lethal.**) The latter means "like death." The CLICHÉ is properly rendered *deathly dull,* not *deadly dull.*

dead man's statute; dead-man statute. The usual form is the possessive *dead man's statute.* When the phrase first appeared, in the late 19th century, it referred to a statutory requirement that all claims against a decedent must be brought within a fixed time (such as two and a half years) from the date when the executor is officially qualified. By the early 20th century, however, the phrase had taken on its modern sense: "a law that makes a decedent's declarations inadmissible as evidence in certain circumstances, as when the witness seeks to support a claim against the estate." E.g., "The first section of the Act forbade the exclusion of witnesses, 'by reason of incapacity from crime or interest'; it also contained a *'dead man's statute'* proviso." *Ferguson v. Georgia,* 365 U.S. 570, 576 n.5 (1961).

Of course, the phrase *dead man* has yielded a variety of terms in the English language, including plant names such as *dead man's fingers* (a type of orchid) and *dead man's hand* (variously an orchid, a fern, or a type of seaweed), as well as *dead man's switch* or *handle* (an automatic shut-off device installed on machinery to protect an operator who releases the controls).

Still, since the early 1980s, some writers have rejected *dead man's statute* on grounds of SEXISM, preferring instead *dead person's statute:* "She argued the *'dead person's statute'* bars Mr. Crowley's testimony because that testimony would be unfair to her." *Ellis v. William Penn Life Ins. Co.,* 873 P.2d 1185, 1187 (Wash. 1994) (en banc). See *Viscito v. Fred S. Carbon Co.,* 636 So. 2d 194, 195 n.1 (Fla. Dist. Ct. App. 1994) (exhorting the legislature to amend the statute by changing *man* to *person*). The use of *person* in this context is certainly less vivid than *man,* but the phrase *dead person's statute* may soon seem as natural as *reasonable person* (in place of *reasonable man*). See SEXISM (B) & **reasonable person.**

dead pledge. See **mortgage.**

deal with; deal in. People in business *deal in* what they buy and sell <she deals in stocks and bonds>, but they *deal with* other persons. *Deal* should not be used transitively where *deal in* is intended. Although one *deals* cards, one does not (except in street slang) *deal drugs;* one *deals in drugs* (if one is utterly reprobate). "The principal witness for the government was S., an undercover detective who had been assigned to investigate allegations that C. was *dealing* [read *dealing in*] drugs."

Deal with is a vague PHRASAL VERB for which there is almost always a better, more specific substitute. E.g., "This commentary will *deal with* [read *discuss*] a variety of matters, including problems of judicial jurisdiction and constitutional limitations on choice of law."/ "We do not *deal with* [read *discuss*] various objections to the plan of merger filed after this appeal was taken." (Cf. **concerned with, be.**) Where, however, *deal with* is roughly equivalent to *handle,* it is unobjectionable: "The court held that state courts dividing community property in divorce proceedings could not *deal with* nondisability military retirement benefits."

dearth = scarcity. It is commonly misunderstood, however, as meaning "lack." E.g., "There is a complete *dearth of* [read *lack of,* or *There is no*] authority on the application of the words 'cause or permit' consequent upon the absolute conveyance of the freehold." (Eng.)

death; demise; decease, n.**; surcease.** *Death* is the common word, the other three being FORMAL WORDS (in order of increasing formality) that act almost as EUPHEMISMS. There is nothing wrong with the word *death,* although it has inherently unpleasant connotations. But that is the nature of the subject, and writing *decease* or *surcease* in legal contexts is only a little less ridiculous than writing *going to meet his Maker.* See **demise, deceased** & **surcease.**

death case (sometimes *death action*), as used by the federal courts, commonly means "a criminal case in which the death sentence has been imposed." In criminal cases, then, the phrase has nothing to do with *wrongful death*—e.g.: "The measure of an individual's competency under *Rees* to waive federal habeas review in a *death case* is informed by considerations very different from those underlying the standard for competency to stand trial."/ Peter Applebome, *Death Cases: The Law Is Reluctant to Start Over,* N.Y. Times, 28 Aug. 1988, at E6 ("But beneath that immediate dilemma is a question at the heart of a number of *death-row cases.*").

But in tort contexts, lawyers frequently say and write *death case* as a shorthand form of *wrongful-death case.* E.g., "In *death cases,* the law should allow juries to award money as compensation only for what can reasonably be compensated for by money." Randal R. Craft, Jr., *Put Limits on Death Compensation,* N.Y. Times, 8 Oct. 1989, at 2F.

deathly. See **deadly.**

death penalty; death sentence. A phrase dating from the late 19th century, *death penalty* is a plain-speaking alternative to the euphemism *capital punishment,* q.v. *Death sentence*—as opposed to *death penalty*—usually refers to a particular convict's punishment. "The prisoner was convicted, but the *death sentence* (still the penalty for treason) was commuted, and he was released later." William Geldart, *Introduction to English Law* 153 (D.C.M. Yardley ed., 9th ed. 1984).

death-qualified jurors are jurors who cannot be disqualified for serving on a jury under the test set forth in *Witherspoon v. Illinois,* 391 U.S. 510 (1968); in other words, *death-qualified jurors* have been selected because they have no absolute ideological bias against the death penalty. A *death-qualified jury,* then, is held fit to decide cases involving the death penalty. E.g., "Appellant argues that more recent studies provide stronger empirical evidence that *death-qualified jurors* are biased in favor of conviction and tend to belong to certain discrete groups."

death row is an Americanism dating from the early 1940s (though *W10* dates it only from 1950). E.g., "A. I was put in *death row.* That's in a line of cells running crossways, east and west, on the *death row.* Q. How far was that, approximately, from the electric chair?" *Daugherty v. State,* 17 So. 2d 290, 294 (Fla. 1944) (en banc) (Chapman, J., dissenting) (quoting testimony). Though the phrases in that quotation are *in death row* and *on the death row,* the usual phrase today is *on death row.*

To most speakers of AmE, the term still refers concretely to the area of a prison where those who have been sentenced to death are confined. But there is a tendency to use the term more abstractly in reference to anyone who has been senteced to death—regardless of the location in a prison.

death sentence. See **death penalty.**

death statute; survival statute. In the context of wrongful-death cases, these phrases must be distinguished. A *death statute* protects the interests of the decedent's family and other dependents, who may recover in damages what they would have received from the decedent if the death had not occurred. A *survival statute,* by contrast, protects the decedent's own interest: the estate recovers for the decedent's pain and suffering before death, medical expenses, lost wages, and (sometimes, oddly) funeral expenses.

The ideas represented by these phrases are a popular subject of law reform: "Historically *death statutes* came first in most jurisdictions and were later supplemented by *survival statutes.* The end result of this secular legislative process will no doubt be that both interests will be protected in all jurisdictions; while the process continues each state must be looked on as a law to itself." Grant Gilmore & Charles L. Black, Jr., *The Law of Admiralty* 360 (2d ed. 1975).

debar. See **bar.**

debark. See **disembark.**

debarkation; debarcation. The former is the preferred spelling.

debate, v.t. & n. In BrE, the verb *debate* equates to AmE *argue,* and the noun *debate* to AmE *argument.* Thus British lawyers typically use *debate* when American lawyers would write *oral argument* or *argue.* E.g., "Since the matter has been *debated,* it may be desirable for me to say that I accept counsel's view that the test of practicability is that of workability." (Eng.)/ "I would refer first to contracts for the sale of goods which were touched on in the course of the *debate.*" (Eng.) See **oral argument.**

debauch; debouch. These words are liable to confusion. The former means "to defile; to seduce away from virtue; to corrupt"; the latter means "to emerge or cause to emerge; to come out into open ground." The nouns are *debauchery* and *debouchment. Debauch* is pronounced /*di-**bawch***/, and *debouch* /*di-**boosh***/.

de bene esse /*də-**ben**-ay-**es**-ay*/ (lit. "of well-being") denotes a course of action that is the best that can be done under the circumstances, or in anticipation of the future. Though this LAW LATIN phrase is of unknown origin and does not appear in Classical Latin, it serves as useful JARGON in the age-old phrase *deposition de bene esse* (sometimes written *de bene esse deposition*). Such a deposition is taken when the witness will likely be unable to attend a scheduled court hearing. Unlike most depositions, a *deposition de bene esse* is not a so-called "discovery deposition" but a deposition to preserve testimony.

Formerly, the phrase *appearance de bene esse* was used as a variant of *special appearance.* Today, this substitution is not recommended. One court has even ridiculed it: "[The defendant] is no longer required at the door of the federal courthouse to intone that ancient abracadabra of the law, *de bene esse,* in order by its magic power to enable himself to remain outside even while he steps within." *Orange Theatre Corp. v. Rayherstz Amusement Corp.,* 139 F.2d 871, 874 (3d Cir. 1944). Cf. **esse** & ***in esse.***

During the 20th century, the phrase took on another sense in American and British legal writing, namely, "for what it is worth." This use seems pretentious.

debenture; bond. *Debenture* = (1) a writing that acknowledges a debt; (2) a bond secured by nothing more than the credit and financial reputation of the issuer, as opposed to a lien on property; or (3) a customhouse certificate providing for a refund of money paid on duties for imported goods when the importer reexports the goods rather than selling them in the country in which they were imported.

In BrE, *debenture* denotes any security issued by a company other than its shares, including what in AmE are commonly called *bonds.* In AmE, *debenture* generally denotes an instrument secured by a floating charge junior to other charges secured by fixed mortgages; more specifically, it means a series of securities secured by a group of securities held in trust for the benefit of the debenture holders. Sometimes a debenture is no more than a corporation's unsecured promissory note bearing a fixed rate of interest.

debility; debilitation. *Debility* = weakness; feebleness. *Debilitation* = the action of making weak or feeble.

debitum, an ARCHAISM and a NEEDLESS VARIANT of *debt,* is still sometimes used by Scottish lawyers in traditional phrases such as *debitum fundi* (= a debt of the estate).

de bonis asportatis. See **trespass.**

de bonis non. See **administrator.**

debouch. See **debauch.**

debrief, used chiefly in military or espionage operations, means (1) "to interrogate (e.g., a spy) to obtain valuable information"; (2) "to instruct someone not to reveal any classified information after that person leaves a sensitive position"; or (3) "(colloquially) to obtain information from (a person) on the completion of a mission or after a journey" (*OED*). Here sense (1) applies: "Driver asserts that the government knew from its '*debriefing*' of the coconspirators pursuant to their plea agreements which of the hundreds of calls were made by Benton to other drug sources." *U.S. v. Driver,* 798 F.2d 248, 251 (7th Cir. 1986).

Some law firms apparently fancy themselves involved in the espionage business. One, in its firm résumé, states: "Feedback is an important part of a summer associate's experience at the firm; in addition to regular informal contact, we have periodic *debriefings* for each summer associate throughout the summer, and one at the conclusion of the summer associate's stay." Even in a figurative sense, this use of *debrief* fails, for the associate no doubt is primarily the recipient, not the source, of the transfer of information; hence, *brief* (= to give important information to) is the correct verb.

debt = (1) a specified sum of money due under a contract or otherwise; (2) a nonmonetary thing that one person owes another, such as goods or services; or (3) at common law, a writ that lay for the recovery of a liquidated sum. See **indebtedness & indebtment.**

debut. This word, when used as a verb, is disapproved by 97 percent of the usage panel for the *AHD,* for what that is worth. The forms *debuted* and *debuting* are certainly ugly to the philologist. The *OED,* surprisingly, records examples as far back as 1830. For the moment, however, the verb *debut* has taken on the character of a VOGUE WORD and should be avoided on that account.

decarceration, a word included in none of the major English-language dictionaries, refers to the state-sponsored shutting down of all substandard asylums, prisons, and reformatories, so that those who would ordinarily occupy such institutions are either discharged or denied admission. E.g., "Those who espoused rehabilitation as the primary purpose of imprisonment included both those who enthusiastically approved of imprisonment and those who favored *decarceration.*" Franklin E. Zimring & Gordon Hawkins, *Dangerousness and Criminal Justice,* 85 Mich. L. Rev. 481, 485 (1986).

decease, n. See **death.**

decease, v.i. = to die. "He *deceased* without issue." This verbal use of *decease* is even more pompous than the nominal use. The straightforward *die* is almost always better. Cf. **death.**

deceased, n.; **decedent.** When these terms are used in the possessive case, no one would argue that *deceased's* is more euphonious than *decedent's.* Yet the term *deceased's* appears frequently in legal prose, esp. in BrE, in which *decedent* is obsolete. The awkwardness of *-ed's* can be overcome either by resort to *decedent's* or by writing *of the deceased* (which is, unfortunately, not possible in all contexts). Cf. **accused & insured.** See PLURALS (D) & POSSESSIVES (F).

We may find no solace in our unhappy dilemma between these words, for even *decedent* sounds especially legalistic; it is common, however, in American legal writing. E.g., "Appellant was under no duty to speak or inquire concerning detail of *decedent's* wealth."

deceit = (1) the act of giving a false impression; or (2) a tort arising from a false statement of fact made knowingly or recklessly with the intent that another person should act on it, with the result that the person who acts on it suffers damage. Within this broad definition, *deceit* is capable of sharing in the first four senses of *fraud,* q.v.

deceive; defraud. To *deceive* is to induce someone to believe in a falsehood. The deceiver may know the statement to be false or may make it recklessly. To *defraud* is to cause some kind of injury or loss by deceit. *Defrauding* leads a person to take action, whereas *deceiving* merely leads a person into a state of mind. But see sense (2) of *deceit.*

deceptive; deceptious. The latter is a NEEDLESS VARIANT.

decide on is usually prolix for *decide.* E.g., "The meaning of 'defect' is for the courts to *decide on* [read *decide*]." See PARTICLES, UNNECESSARY.

decimate. Originally this word meant "to kill one in every ten," but this etymological sense, because so uncommon, has been abandoned except in historical contexts. Now *decimate* generally means "to cause great loss of life; to destroy a large part of." Preferably, the word should not be used of a complete obliteration or defeat. Nor should it be used lightly of just any defeat.

decision; opinion; judgment. Technically, in the U.S., judges are said to write *opinions* to justify their *decisions* or *judgments;* they do not write *decisions* or *judgments.* E.g., "Last July, Judge Scalia wrote a majority *decision* [read *opinion*] that subjects defendants who claim insanity to examination, without requiring that their lawyers be present, by government psychiatrists, who may testify against them." See JUDGMENTS, APPELLATE-COURT & **opinion.** Cf. **speech.**

decisional. See **decisive.**

decision(al) law. The preferred form of this American equivalent of *case law* is *decisional law.* E.g., "The rule of our *decision law* [read *decisional law*] puts upon the bailee the burden of proving that the loss did not result from his negligence."/ "Present *decisional law* would seemingly entitle plaintiff to relief under section 1983."/ "The weight of *decisional law* is now to the effect that when a married man makes provision in his will for his wife, and is thereafter divorced, with a property settlement between them, such change in condition and circumstances of the parties impliedly [q.v.] revokes the previously executed will in favor of the wife."/ "The statutes have produced a respectable body of *decisional* law."/ "Apart from the statute, the plaintiff is entitled to interest as a matter of *decisional law.*" Cf. **organic law.** See **case(-)law & jurisprudence** (B). See also **decisive.**

decisioning for *deciding* or *decision-making* is an example of abhorrent social-science cant.

decision-making, n., is a generic term for *deciding* and, though useful in some contexts, is much overworked in current legal writing. The word smacks of sociological cant, and is often merely a grandiloquent way of saying *deciding:* after all, when one makes decisions, one decides.

It is now frequently spelled as one word, even by the U.S. Supreme Court. And the word is so spelled in Paul Brest's book *Processes of Constitutional Decisionmaking* (1975). One sees the same one-wordism tendency at work in the term *budget-making,* q.v. These compounds are too bulky to look like anything but jargonistic English; a simple hyphen does a lot.

decisive; decisional. *Decisive,* frequently used in the sense "determinative" in legal writing, refers to things as opposed to persons. In lay contexts, of course, *decisive* almost always refers to persons and means "resolute." Following are examples of the legal usage. "It is this last-mentioned omission in our statute that is *decisive* against the contention of the defendants that the law of this Commonwealth has been changed in their favor."/ "The determinative facts presented in the case at bar are, however, few, and the *decisive* principles are established."/ "The fact that the contractors are forced to do what they do not want to do is not *decisive* of the legality of the labor union's acts."/ "Although the facts in that case are wholly dissimilar from the facts in the case at bar, the principle thus broadly and tersely stated is one that should be *decisive* of this case."

Decisional = of, or of the nature of, deciding or a decision. The *OED* notes that *decisional* is "rare." It may have been rare in the 19th century, but today it is common in American legal writing. E.g., "This court's *decisional* process would not be significantly aided by oral argument."/ "Moreover, the employees had, as part of their *decisional* process, examined copies of the work-rules agreement in effect in Texaco's Louisiana plant." See **decisional law.**

declaim; disclaim. The former is what lawyers do in court, the latter what manufacturers do in warranties. To *declaim* is to speak formally in public (whence the adjective *declamatory*); this word is frequently misused for *disclaim,* meaning "to make a disclaimer, disavow, repudiate."

declamatory. See **declarative.**

declarant, esp. in the context of hearsay evidence, has long been the law's agent noun corresponding to the verb *to state* or *to say.* A *declarant* does not "state vehemently," as the association with *declare* might suggest. E.g., "Alaska Rule of Evidence 803(3) carves out an exception to the hearsay rule when a statement is not offered to prove the truth of the matter asserted but is offered to prove the *declarant's* state of mind." *State v. McDonald,* 872 P.2d 627, 642 (Alaska Ct. App. 1994).

declaration = (1) at common law, the pleading by which a plaintiff formally presents a claim for relief in a civil action; (2) in the law of evidence, an unsworn statement made by someone having knowledge of facts relating to an event in dispute; (3) in a few American jurisdictions (such as California), a formal written statement resembling an affidavit and attesting, under penalty of perjury, to facts known by the declarant; (4) a U.S. Customs form on which anyone entering the U.S. must record the value of the goods and cash that he or she is bringing into the country; or (5) a document that governs legal rights to certain types of realty, such as a condominium or a residential subdivision.

Sense (3) remains unrecorded in most legal and nonlegal dictionaries. For more on sense (1), see **statement of claim, treaty** & COMMON-LAW PLEADINGS.

declaration of trust; trust deed; trust agreement. These terms are variously used to name the instrument creating a trust.

declarative; declaratory; declamatory. In grammar we have *declarative* sentences, but in law we have *declaratory* judgments, statutes, and acts. Both words mean "having the function of declaring, setting forth, or explaining"; their DIFFERENTIATION lies in established uses, not in meaning. For virtually all legal contexts, *declaratory* is the word. E.g., "In the seventeenth and eighteenth centuries, Roman law was taken to be *declaratory* of the law of nature." (Roscoe Pound)

Declamatory, which is sometimes confused with *declaratory,* means "haranguing; of or pertaining to declaiming oratorically."

declarator is not an agent noun, but an old-fashioned equivalent of *declaratory-judgment action* (= a lawsuit in which a legal right or status is declared without the plaintiff's seeking further relief). The form *declarator* remains common in Scots law. See -ER (B).

declaratory. See **declarative.**

declaratory-judgment action. Because the first two words form a PHRASAL ADJECTIVE, they are hyphenated thus.

declaratory precedent. See **precedent (D).**

declare. In the context of Anglo-American caselaw, this verb often fosters the legal FICTION "that courts do not 'make' law but only 'discover' or *'declare'* it . . . ." Lon L. Fuller, *Legal Fictions* 88 (1967). As Fuller suggests, *discover* is equally misleading when used in reference to a court's pronouncements on the law.

declination; declinature; declension. All three words are used in denoting the act of courteously refusing, but *declination* now far outstrips the other two in frequency of use. In referring to the act of declining, *declinature* and *declension* ought to be considered NEEDLESS VARIANTS of *declination.*

decline, v.i. & v.t. This verb, which has two distinct senses, yields two noun forms. *Declination* derives from *decline* in the sense "to refuse," and *decline,* n., derives from *decline* in the sense "to go downhill." See **declination.**

deconstruction (= a method of reading by which one finds the subtext beneath the text and inverts their relative importance) for *destruction* is an odd error that might be considered a telling slip of the tongue—e.g.: "Fire is an extremely fast and effective means of *deconstruction.* All urban fires are in some sense man-made . . . ." Thomas Hine, *Don't Blame Mrs. O'Leary,* N.Y. Times, 15 July 1990, § 7, at 13.

decorous is pronounced with the primary accent on the first syllable: /***dek***-ə-rəs/.

decree; judgment. Traditionally, judicial decisions are termed *decrees* in courts of equity, admiralty, divorce, and probate; they are termed *judgments* in courts of law. E.g., "Such a testamentary trust may be terminated only by a *decree of a court of equity,* regardless of any stipulation by all parties in interest."

Nevertheless, in modern usage *decree* is broad enough to refer to any court order, whether or not the relief granted or denied is equitable in nature. E.g., "[T]he [Supreme] Court's *decrees* are backed only by its own prestige and ultimately by the willingness of the President to help enforce them." Robert G. McCloskey, *The American Supreme Court* 57 (1960). See **judgment (C).**

decree, v.t. = (1) to command by decree; or (2) to award judicially; to assign authoritatively. Here sense (2), undifferentiated in most dictionaries, applies because it is construed with a direct object and a *to*-phrase: "But the probate court did not *decree* the estate to the widow, and then make her a constructive trustee of such estate for the benefit of the parents."

decree absolute; decree nisi. These phrases, more usual in G.B. than in the U.S., are very similar. *Decree nisi* = a conditional court decree that will become absolute unless the adversely affected party shows the court, within a specified time, why it should be set aside. In England, a *decree nisi* ordinarily relates to divorce, annulling a marriage, or decreeing that a missing spouse is presumed dead. E.g., "In March she commenced proceedings for restitution of conjugal rights, and on July 30 she obtained a *decree nisi.*" (Eng.)/ "A child had been born to the wife petitioner between petition and the *decree nisi* and the court was not informed of its birth." (Eng.)

Decree absolute = a ripened decree nisi, that is, one whose time limit has passed, so that the court's decree has become unconditional. In England, a *decree absolute* is ordinarily a decree of divorce, nullity, or presumption of death that ends a legal marriage and enables the parties to remarry. The (conditional) *decree nisi* becomes a (final) *decree absolute* after a time (usu. six weeks) if there is no contrary reason.

Rule absolute and *rule nisi* are often used as equivalents of *decree absolute* and *decree nisi.* See **nisi.**

decretal = of or relating to a decree. E.g., "The decree is modified on the law by striking from the first *decretal* paragraph the following words . . . ." *Decretorial, decretory,* and *decretive* are NEEDLESS VARIANTS.

Decretal may also be a noun—e.g.: "The precedents of compulsion to accomplish governmental *decretals* are found rather in the Court of the Star Chamber, of unhappy memory." *Decrees* would actually be the better word in that sentence, for *decretals* specifically are "letters containing a papal ruling, particularly one relating to matters of canonical discipline, and most precisely a papal rescript in response to an appeal" (*OCL*).

decriminalize (= to reclassify [an activity] so that it is no longer considered a crime) is a NEOLOGISM dating only from 1969. Today it is commonplace—e.g.: "As a legislator in Arizona, O'Connor once voted to *decriminalize* abortion." *All Eyes on Justice O'Connor,* Newsweek, 1 May 1989, at 34.

decry; descry. *Decry* = to disapprove of; to disparage. E.g., "In 1908 Roscoe Pound *decried* decision-making from first principles—a process described in Germany as *Begriffsjurisprudenz*—and warned against the law becoming too scientific."

Descry /di-**skrı**/ = to see in the distance, to discern with the eye. Here it is used figuratively: "In the foregoing paragraphs we have endeavored, by the relations and facts that may be gathered and by the words used by the testator, to *descry* the testator's intention."

de cursu. See **of course.**

dedicatory; dedicative; dedicatorial. The first form is preferred; the other two are NEEDLESS VARIANTS.

deduce; deduct. The former means "to infer"; the latter "to subtract." *Deduct* is sometimes misused in place of *deduce.* Here *deduce* is wrongly used: "We *deduce* [read *glean?*] from approved authorities the following principles as pertinent to this case." See **adduce & deducible.**

deducible; deductible. The former means "inferable." E.g., "The government agents relied on evidence not otherwise known or *deducible* by them."/ "I believe the governing principles to be *deducible* from the terms of the pertinent statutes."

Deductible, a favorite word of tax specialists, means "capable of being (usu. lawfully) subtracted." It is sometimes misspelled *deductable.* See **deduce.**

deduct. See **deduce.**

deductible. See **deducible.**

deed. A. As Noun Referring to an Instrument. At common law, *deed* referred to any written instrument that was signed, sealed, and delivered. In BrE, this broad sense still applies. In AmE, however, the narrower sense of a writing by which land is conveyed is almost uniformly applicable. See **signed, sealed, and delivered.**

B. As Verb. *Deed,* v.t., is an Americanism dating from the early 19th century. Now commonplace in AmE, this verb seems never to be used in BrE, in which solicitors are said to *convey* or *transfer by deed.* The verb *deed* is considerably more economical—e.g.: "On December 23, 1952, he *deeded* to Geneva that half of the homestead upon which the improvements had been made." *Green v. Green,* 113 F. Supp. 697, 697 (D. Alaska 1953)./ "[Several factors] sufficiently explain the decedent's motives in *deeding* the property back to her grantor." *Daniels v. Cummins,* 321 N.Y.S.2d 1009, 1013 (Sup. Ct. 1971).

deed of crime. See ***mens rea.***

deed of trust; trust deed. The classical form of this term is *deed of trust,* meaning "a deed conveying property in trust, and usu. evidencing a mortgage." But either form suffices, and the latter has the advantage of using one-third fewer words. See **of (A).**

de-emphasize. This word should always be hyphenated, for the reader may at first see *deem.* See PUNCTUATION (F).

deem = to treat [a thing] as being something that it is not, or as possessing certain qualities that it does not possess. It is a FORMAL WORD often used in legislation to create legal FICTIONS; that is, a statute may provide that something is or is not to be *deemed* something else, or, with a significant difference, that this something is to be *deemed* not something else.

But in general usage, *deem* is archaic for *consider, think, judge,* or *esteem*—e.g.: "I *deemed it expedient* [read *thought it best*] to conduct a number of stress tests at various loads to prove the different effects of the bolting." (Can.)/ "Questions regarding the way Yudof handles the preliminary stages of the lawsuit should therefore not be *deemed as* [read *considered* or *seen as*] irrelevant in determining his fitness for office." *New President Must Not Let Discrimination Hurt UT,* Daily Texan, 5 Oct. 1992, at 4.

deemster. See **dempster.**

deep-seeded is a misbegotten metaphor—a MALAPROPISM—for *deep-seated.*

de facto. A. And *de jure.* The use of either phrase implies the question whether something exists merely in fact *(de facto)* or by right or according to law *(de jure).*

De facto /di-***fak***-*toh*/ sometimes signals that there is some formal defect that makes the thing described voidable, as in the phrases *de facto contract* and *de facto marriage.* At other times it denotes pure illegitimacy, as in *de facto government* (i.e., one that has displaced the rightful legal government).

De jure /*di-**joor**-ay*/ may be opposed not only to *de facto,* but also to *de gratia* (= by grace or favor), in opposition to which *de jure* means "as a matter of right."

Both phrases were traditionally POSTPOSITIVE

ADJECTIVES, but they now commonly precede the nouns they modify <de facto segregation> <de jure corporation>.

B. And *in fact*. Although the terms convey the same notion, their uses are well distinguished. *De facto* is used prepositively, whereas *in fact* is used after the noun it modifies <de facto segregation, attorney in fact>.

C. Two Words, Not One. Some writers have tried to solidify the phrase, but it remains two words—e.g.: "The uniform equality of all as subjects of the state was, for Kant, consistent with *defacto* [read *de facto*] inequalities of a physical, mental, or material nature." Cornelius F. Murphy, *Jurisprudence and the Social Contract,* 33 Am. J. Juris. 207, 218 (1988).

de facto segregation. See **segregation, de facto.**

defalcate. A. And *peculate; embezzle*. These three words are broadly synonymous, all three meaning "to misappropriate money in one's charge." *Defalcate* and *peculate,* the latter being slightly more common and referring to public moneys, are FORMAL WORDS that are neutral in color. *Embezzle* is the popular word that is more highly charged with negative CONNOTATIONS. See **defalcation, defalcator, embezzle & peculation.**

B. Pronunciation. Several pronounciation guides suggest that it is acceptable to stress this word on the first syllable: /***def***-*al-kayt*/ or /***def***-*əl-kayt*/. See, e.g., John B. Opdycke, *Don't Say It: A Cyclopedia of English Use and Abuse* 236 (1939). Others suggest that the corresponding noun may be pronounced /*def-al-**kay**-shən*/. See, e.g., William H. Phyfe, *20,000 Words Often Mispronounced* 244 (1937).

But these pronounciations have a problem. Anyone who hears them is likely to think of *defecate* and *defecation*. Therefore, if one must utter these words at all, the safest course is to use the following pronunciations, which all pronunciation guides accept as standard: *defalcate* /*dee-**fal**-kayt*/ or /*di-**fal**-kayt*/; *defalcation* /*dee-fal-**kay**-shən*/.

defalcation may refer either to the act of embezzling or to the money embezzled. E.g., "No one would venture to expose corporate *defalcation* [i.e., the act] if every word and sentence, and every fact and every inference, had to be justified by unquestionable legal evidence."/ "Evidence was adduced tending to show that the *defalcation* [i.e., the money embezzled] was wasted on horse racing and other forms of gambling." See **defalcate & peculation.**

By SLIPSHOD EXTENSION, some writers have misused *defalcation* when referring merely to a nonfraudulent default or to any failure to meet a duty. To be a *defalcation,* a deficiency in money matters must be fraudulent, and it must be by someone put in trust of the money.

For the pronunciation of *defalcation,* see **defalcate (B).**

defalcator is the agent noun corresponding to *defalcate*—e.g.: "[O]ne will not on this basis soothsay that . . . if the *defalcator* be only 'agent' for A but happens to be 'trustee' for B, there will be a difference in result . . . ." Karl Llewellyn, *The Common Law Tradition: Deciding Appeals* 442 (1960). See **defalcate.**

defamacast (= a defamatory broadcast) is a PORTMANTEAU WORD and a recent NEOLOGISM that has enjoyed a limited success within law—e.g.: "In this category, defamation by broadcast or *'defamacast'* is actionable per se." *American Broadcasting–Paramount Theatres, Inc. v. Simpson,* 126 S.E.2d 873, 879 (Ga. Ct. App. 1962)./ "Judge Homer C. Eberhardt of the Georgia Court of Appeals coined a new word, now in general use, which is quite descriptive of being defamed by television, to wit *'defamacast.'" Montgomery v. Pacific & Southern Co.,* 206 S.E.2d 631, 634 (Ga. Ct. App. 1974)./ "Since a *'defamacast'* . . . is not considered 'slander,' the usual rules of respondeat superior are applicable, as with libel." *Williamson v. Lucas,* 304 S.E.2d 412, 415 (Ga. Ct. App. 1983).

The leading American book on tort law suggests that *defamacast,* a "barbarism," was born of a desire to avoid calling defamation by radio or television either *slander* or *libel.* See William L. Prosser & W. Page Keeton, *Prosser & Keeton on Torts* § 112, at 787 (5th ed. 1984).

defamation; libel; slander. These three terms are distinguished in English and American law. *Defamation* = an attack upon the reputation of another. It encompasses both *libel* (in permanent form, esp. writing) and *slander* (in transitory form, esp. spoken words). See **libel.**

In Scots law, however, *libel* and *slander* are equivalent to (and therefore interchangeable with) *defamation.*

defamatory; defamative. *Defamatory* is the usual word; *defamative* is a NEEDLESS VARIANT.

default, n. & vb. A *default* is a failure to act when an action is required, esp. the failure to pay a debt—either interest or principal—as it becomes due.

As a verb, *default* may be either transitive or

intransitive. Usually it is the latter <she defaulted on the loan>, but the transitive uses are not unusual in legal writing <she defaulted the loan>—e.g.: "Further, if the mortgage is later *defaulted* [many would write *defaulted on*], the mortgagee may find that he is not insured if he cannot deliver clear title to the FHA." Robert Kratovil, *Real Estate Law* 191 (1946)./ "The Government advocates untenably that plaintiff should have accepted this offer in order not to *default* the contract, regardless of disproportionate cost." *Aerodex, Inc. v. U.S.,* 417 F.2d 1361, 1364 n.3 (Ct. Cl. 1969).

The agent noun is *defaulter.*

default judgment; judgment by default. The latter is somewhat wordy.

defeasance = (1) the rendering null and void (of a previous condition); (2) a condition upon the performance of which a deed or other instrument is defeated or made void, or a contractual provision containing such a condition.

Sense (1) is more usual—e.g.: "The provision in the will that the interest was to be divided among 'them' every year necessitates the construction that the testatrix intended the gift of income also to be subject to *defeasance* by not surviving until the respective dates of distribution."

But sense (2) is not uncommon—e.g.: "In absence of a clause of *defeasance,* or one providing for a change of beneficiaries, the beneficiary in an ordinary policy of life insurance has a vested interest, which the insured cannot divest at his mere volition."

defeasible. The antonym to this word (*indefeasible*) is known to learned nonlawyers, but *defeasible* itself is almost exclusively a legal term, meaning "capable of being made void." E.g., "The law enforced the mortgage deed literally as a *defeasible* conveyance to the mortgagee." William F. Walsh, *A Treatise on Equity* 88 (1930). For the phrase *fee simple defeasible,* see **fee simple (E).**

defective; defectible; deficient. The primary difference to be noted is between the words *defective* (= faulty; imperfect; subnormal) and *deficient* (= insufficient; lacking in quantity). *Defectible,* the least common of the three terms, means "likely to fail or become defective."

The same basic distinction holds for the nouns *defect* and *deficiency.* In the following sentence, *deficiency* is misused for *defect:* "The trial court failed to submit to the jury an issue inquiring whether the multipiece wheel *was defective due to a design deficiency* [read *had a design defect*] that would cause the wheel to separate explosively during foreseeable uses." The blunder may have been caused by an attempt at INELEGANT VARIATION.

defence. See **defense.**

defendant. A. Pronunciation. *Defendant* is sometimes pronounced, esp. it seems by law school professors, with a strong accent on the last syllable, rhyming with *ant.* Presumably, this pronunciation helps legal neophytes remember how to spell the word. Apart from this pedagogically affected pronunciation, the correct way to pronounce the word is */di-**fen**-dənt/.*

B. As a Postpositive Adjective. The adjective *defendant* is commonly placed after the noun it modifies when that noun is *party.* E.g., "The plaintiff chose both the forum and the *parties defendant* . . . ." (Harlan, J.). Some writers use this construction with other nouns, the result being an example of ARCHAISM: "Chief Judge William H. Becker . . . dryly noted that auto companies *defendant* in such situations 'have been unusually evasive and loath to make discovery.'" Joseph Goulden, *The Million Dollar Lawyers* 287 (1978). See POSTPOSITIVE ADJECTIVES.

C. And *prisoner*. In criminal-law contexts, *defendant* is regarded as less prejudicial—and therefore as generally more appropriate—than either *the accused* or *the prisoner.* But *accused* is said to be the norm in Scots law. See John A. Beaton, *Scots Law Terms and Expressions* 30 (1982). See **prisoner & accused.**

defendant in error = respondent, appellee. See **error (A) & plaintiff in error.**

defendant in person. See **pro se.**

defender is used in Scotland for *defendant,* as the name of the party opposite a *pursuer,* q.v., in civil actions.

Elsewhere, the word takes on other senses. Sometimes it appears in reference to one who uses self-defense—e.g.: "Such a *defender,* not being entirely free from fault, must not resort to deadly force if there is any other reasonable method of saving himself." Rollin M. Perkins & Ronald N. Boyce, *Criminal Law* 1121 (3d ed. 1982). At other times it refers to defense counsel in a criminal case—e.g.: "In many other respects the basic duties of professionalism of prosecutor and *defender* are the same." David Mellinkoff, *Lawyers and the System of Justice* 543 (1976). In still other contexts, it refers more broadly to anyone who defends an ideal: "Any such power as that authorizing the federal judiciary to entertain suits by individuals against the states had been expressly disclaimed, and even resented, by the great *defenders* of the Constitution whilst it was on its trial before the American people." *Hans v. Louisiana,* 134 U.S. 1, 12 (1890).

defense; defence. **A. Spelling.** *Defence* is the BrE, *defense* the AmE spelling. Yet the British spelling was used by American courts through the early 20th century; Judge Learned Hand, for example, used the *-ce* spelling in *Sinram v. Pennsylvania R.R.,* 61 F.2d 767, 769 (2d Cir. 1932). Today, however, the British spelling is best avoided in the U.S., lest one's writing seem affected.

B. In Criminal Law. Some writers worry that this word can lead to misunderstandings because it is used in different ways. Ordinarily, a *defense* is something that the defendant has the burden of proving. But that is not true of the doctrines of justifiable force, alibi, mistake, and self-defense: "If there is evidence, usually raised by the defendant, that the conduct may have been justifiable, the prosecution bears the burden of proving beyond reasonable doubt that the conduct was *not* justifiable or lawful. Thus, justifiable force is a *defence,* in the sense that it may lead to an acquittal, but the defendant does not have to establish its elements—the prosecution has to negative them." Andrew Ashworth, *Principles of Criminal Law* 110–11 (1991).

Glanville Williams, though, considers these worries pedantic: "A *'defence'* is any matter that the defendant will in practice raise, whether he is legally obliged to do so or not. If the word were confined to matter the burden of proof of which rests on the defendant, there would be virtually no *'defences'* at common law." *Textbook of Criminal Law* 114 n.3 (1978).

defer; defer to. *Defer,* meaning "to postpone," yields the nouns *deferment,* q.v., and its NEEDLESS VARIANT *deferral. Defer* to, meaning "to give way to," yields the noun *deference.*

deferential. See **differential (C).**

deferment; deferral. *Deferral* is less good than *deferment* as the noun corresponding to the verb *to defer.* "The filing of the state action mandates *deferral* [read *deferment*] of our decision." See **defer.**

defer(r)able. The preferred form is *deferrable.* See DOUBLING OF FINAL CONSONANTS.

deferral. See **deferment.**

deficiency. See **defective.**

deficient. See **defective.**

definite; definitive. These words are increasingly confused. *Definite* = fixed, exact, explicit. *Definitive* = authoritative; conclusive; exhaustive; providing a final solution. E.g., "Usually the standard of 'certainty' is applied *definitively* by the trial judge in passing upon the admissibility of evidence and in deciding whether the case is to be submitted to the jury at all."/ "The trial court raised, but did not rule *definitively* on, the timeliness question."

The most frequent error is misuse of *definitive* for *definite.* E.g., "The ALJ erred in not setting forth, in *definitive* [read *definite*] language, his assessment of the relative credibility of the evidence."

DEFINITIONS. The best advice is to be a minimalist, for "a definition . . . often creates more problems than it solves." *Brutus v. Cozens,* [1972] 3 W.L.R. 521, 525 (per Lord Reid). Yet legal writers—especially drafters of documents—use definitions abundantly, so some guidance is in order.

A. When to Use. The best legal writers and drafters use definitions only when they are necessary—i.e., where there is a gain in clarity and precision. Poor writers and drafters frequently define terms that they either never use again or use perhaps once or twice after the definition. See PLAIN LANGUAGE (D).

If a commonsense shortened name presents itself, use that shortened form. For example, if there is a law firm called Brown, Underwood, Smith, Tennison & Osgood, call it *the Brown firm* or *Brown, Underwood.* But don't invent the acronym *BUSTO* for this purpose. That approach will mire your writing in INITIALESE.

B. Lexical and Stipulative Definitions. Lexical definitions are like dictionary definitions; they purport to give the entire meaning of a word ("'Litigation' means . . ."). Stipulative definitions, by contrast, rely on the ordinary meaning of the word and merely expand a word's meaning ("'Litigation' includes mediation") or contract a word's meaning ("'Litigation' does not include prefiling investigations"). As an English writer put it in the context of statutes, "when an interpretation clause states that a word or phrase 'means . . . ,' any other meaning is excluded, whereas the word 'includes' indicates an extension of the ordinary meaning [that] continues to apply in appropriate cases." Rupert Cross, *Statutory Interpretation* 103 (1976).

When using stipulative definitions—which can be extremely helpful to the drafter—one must be careful not to use counterintuitive definitions, as by saying that the word *dog* is deemed to include all horses. Reed Dickerson made this point authoritatively: "it is important for the legal draftsman not to define a word in a sense significantly different from the way it is normally understood by the persons to whom it is primarily addressed. This is a fundamental principle of communication, and it is one of the shames of the legal profession that draftsmen so flagrantly violate it." *Fundamentals of Legal Drafting* § 7.3, at 144 (2d ed. 1986).

The reason for this admonition, of course, is plain: "whenever we define a word . . . in a manner that departs from current customary usage, we sooner or later unwittingly fall back on the common use and thus confuse the meanings of our terms." Morris R. Cohen, *Reason and Law* 77 (1961). This confusion may occur either in the writer or in the reader. Either way, the result can be dangerous.

Still, some specialists engage in this type of overstipulation. For example, the Longshoremen's and Harbor Workers' Compensation Act defines *vessel* not only as any vessel "upon which or in connection with which" an injury or death may have occurred, but also as "said vessel's owner, owner pro hac vice, agent, operator, charter [sic], or a bareboat charterer, master, officer, or crew member." 33 U.S.C. § 902 (21) (1988).

C. Inept Definitional Terms. The best practice is to use *means* for a complete definition, *includes* for a stipulated expansion in meaning, and *does not include* for a stipulated contraction of meaning.

Yet many drafters fall into unfortunate forms, such as the following:

1. *Bears the meaning.* Use the tighter *means* instead.
2. *Means and includes.* Use *means* if that is what you mean. The expressions *means and includes* "should not be used because complete and incomplete meaning cannot be stipulated at one and the same time." G.C. Thornton, *Legislative Drafting* 166 (2d ed. 1979).
3. *Includes only.* Use *means* instead.
4. *Shall mean.* "[D]o not say that the defined words 'shall mean' something or other, as though you were ordering them to do so, or as though you were directing the definitions to go into effect at some later time." Barbara Child, *Drafting Legal Documents* 116 n. (2d ed. 1992). Also in this category are the wordy phrases *shall have the meaning* and *shall mean and refer to.*
5. *Is where; is when.* Reword the definition entirely. These phrases are inappropriate ways to introduce definitions. See **is when.**

D. "Stuffed" Definitions. Readers are entitled to assume that definitions—and definitional sections of documents—contain nothing more than definitions. Yet many contractual definitions, such as those in badly drafted insurance policies, contain substantive provisions. Such definitions are called "stuffed" definitions.

E. Placement. When more than a few definitions appear, the drafter is faced with choosing an appropriate place for them within the document. Some drafters place them in a schedule at the end; others collect them at the beginning; still others define them as they appear; and some use a combination of these methods.

It is impossible to frame an absolute recommendation, but a caution is in order against one common practice: putting page after page of definitions at the beginning of a document. If you need more than, say, 10 definitions, a schedule at the end is probably a better solution than using the opening pages in this way.

F. Signaling Defined Terms in Text. Drafters' habits vary. The most common way to tell the reader that a term is defined is by using initial capitals—a practice that is not so bad if you keep definitions to a minimum. Others have experimented with boldfacing or italicizing defined terms whenever they appear in text, but this practice can lead to unsightly text. Still others don't signal in any way that a particular word is a defined term, but most legal readers find this practice unacceptable. Drafters who typeset their materials sometimes use running footers to tell the readers which words on a given page are defined in the schedule at the end—a time-consuming and costly practice.

G. When to Compose. There are two advantages to defining terms late in the drafting process. First, you'll be less likely to have a defined term with more than one meaning, because you'll be familiar with the entire document. Second, you won't define terms that aren't used much—or never appear at all.

definitive. See **definite.**

deforce = (1) to keep (lands) from the true owner by means of force; (2) to oust another from possession by force; or (3) to detain (a creditor's money) unjustly and forcibly. Here, the writer apparently mistook *deforce* as a correlative of *enforce:* "One may maintain an action to enforce a lien against another who has *deforced* it."

deforciant; deforcer. In all but Scots law, *deforcer* is a NEEDLESS VARIANT of *deforciant* (= one who deforces). That is unfortunate, since *deforcer* might be more readily understood to anyone who began to learn what the verb *deforce* means. See **deforce.**

defraud. See **deceive.**

defraudation; defraudment. Lawyers seldom have occasion to use a noun formed from the verb *defraud,* perhaps because the noun *fraud* itself usually suffices. When they find the occasion, however, the word is *defraudation*—e.g.: "[B]enefits obtained by a contracting party subsequent to his *defraudation* are not admissible on the issue of damages . . . ." *Philip Chang & Sons Assocs. v. La Casa Novato,* 222 Cal. Rptr. 800, 803 (Cal. Ct. App. 1986)./ "It was a matter of legal interpretation whether Dauphin County had jurisdiction to try a case involving *defraudation* of a Commonwealth agency." *Commonwealth v. Keenan,* 530 A.2d 90, 94 (Pa. Super. 1987). *Defraudment* is a NEEDLESS VARIANT.

defraudulent is a NEEDLESS VARIANT of *fraudulent.*

degenerative; degeneratory. The latter is a NEEDLESS VARIANT.

degradation (= a lowering in dignity, character, or quality) is a MALAPROPISM when used for *derogation* (= an abrogation or violation), as here: "Immunity from suit is in *degradation* [read *derogation*] of this common-law principle and must therefore be strictly construed." *Bush v. Bush,* 231 A.2d 245, 249 (N.J. Super. Ct. Law Div. 1967)./ "The court concluded . . . that the rebate and veto provisions of the settlement agreement . . . deprived [the third parties], in *degradation* [read *derogation*] of the strong policy favoring settlements, of a chance themselves to compromise Bass' claims against them." *Bass v. Phoenix Seadrill / 78, Ltd.,* 749 F.2d 1154, 1158 (5th Cir. 1985). But the words *degradation* and *derogation* do share one sense: "detraction from the honor or reputation of; lowering or lessening in value or estimation" (*OED*). See **derogation of, in.**

de gratia. See **de facto (A).**

degree is the word used in law for various classifications and specifications, as for steps in *consanguinity,* q.v., and grades based on the seriousness of crimes. Today most American jurisdictions differentiate first-degree from second-degree murder on the basis of the gravity of the offense (gauged, e.g., by premeditation and purpose), whereas at common law first- and second-degree felons were principals and accessories, respectively. See **murder (A).**

dehors is a pompous little LAW FRENCH word (meaning "outside of; beyond the scope of") that should generally be avoided. The plethora of examples, selected from writings of the 1980s, indicates the prevalence of this nasty-sounding term /*di-**hohr***/. It serves absolutely no purpose but to sound legalistic—e.g.:

- "For present purposes, . . . statutory words [that] are 'ambiguous' are not 'unequivocal,' and judicial ingenuity to resolve the ambiguity, *dehors* [read *outside* or *beyond*] the statute, is inappropriately exercised." *U.S. v. John C. Grimberg Co.,* 702 F.2d 1362, 1378 (Fed. Cir. 1983) (Nichols, J., concurring).
- "Adopting the controlling state-law rule in this diversity case, we find that the court erred in excluding all evidence *dehors* [read *outside*] the contract . . . ." *Haeberle v. Texas Int'l Airlines,* 738 F.2d 1434, 1436 (5th Cir. 1984).
- "Appellants argue that the circuit court erred in reversing HPERB's decision because the court improperly considered evidence adduced in the Ryan case which is *dehors* [read *outside*] the record in this case." *Ariyoshi v. Hawaii Pub. Employment Relations Bd.,* 704 P.2d 917, 924 n.10 (Haw. Ct. App. 1985).
- "[T]his document, assuming it exists, is *dehors* [read *outside*] the record and the Gordons' reliance on such information is improper." *Gordon v. Wisconsin Health Org. Ins. Corp.,* 510 N.W.2d 832, 834 (Wis. Ct. App. 1993).

The term was formerly spelled as two words—e.g.: "These bills are open to the same defenses as other bills; . . . by answer if the objection is for matter *de hors* the record." Eugene A. Jones, *Manual of Equity Pleading and Practice* 64 (1916)./ "A misdescription cannot be rectified by affidavit or evidence *de hors* (from outside the document) . . . ." 2 E.W. Chance, *Principles of Mercantile Law* 40 (P.W. French ed., 10th ed. 1951).

DEICTIC TERMS (e.g., *this, that, it, the*) are "pointing words," that is, words that try to point directly at an antecedent. Etymologically, *deictic* means "capable of proof," and conjures up the notion of pointing to conclusive evidence.

A pointing word such as *this* or *these* should always have an identifiable referent. But in the sentence that follows—an all too typical example—the word *these* does not point to one: "Officials at checkpoints that are judicially deemed the functional equivalent of a border have been granted increasingly intrusive power in connection with the search of vehicles at these checkpoints, without any requirement of probable cause or reasonable suspicion. *These* include the power to stop and question occupants about aliens and to search in automobile cavities that could conceal aliens." *U.S. v. Oyarzun,* 760 F.2d 570, 577 (5th Cir. 1985) (Hill, J., concurring). We can deduce, of course, that the writer meant *powers,* though the singular noun *power* is used in the first sentence.

Some writers believe that, in the rule stated at the outset of the preceding paragraph, the phrase "an identifiable referent" means a specific noun. They say that you should never use *this* or *these* without a noun following it. But most grammarians take a more relaxed position: "The antecedent of *this* and *that* may be any single noun . . . . *This* and *that* may also refer to a phrase, clause, or sentence, or even to an implied thought. Reference of this kind must, however, be immediately clear and apparent; otherwise the thought will be obscure." James G. Fernald, *English Grammar Simplified* 40 (Cedric Gale ed., rev. ed. 1979). Fernald is not alone: "*This,* like *that,* is regularly used to refer to the idea of a preceding clause or sentence: 'He had always had his own way at home, and this made him a poor roommate.'/ 'The company train their salesmen in their own school. This [More formally: This practice] assures them a group of men with the same sales methods.'" Porter G. Perrin, *Writer's Guide and Index to English* 794 (rev. ed. 1950) (bracketed language in orig.). Perrin's notation in his second example accurately describes the difference between *this* and *this practice:* it is a question of formality, not of correctness.

Actually, the grammarians' rule against vague reference is just that: a rule that forbids ambiguities of the kind listed here: "The most important activity is the editing of a college newspaper. *This* has grown with the college." (Ex. drawn fr. Richard Summers & David L. Patrick, *College Composition* 129 (1946).) What has grown with the college? Editing? The newspaper? The importance of editing the college newspaper? You simply cannot tell what the writer intended—if indeed the writer knew.

All one needs in good writing, then, is a sensitivity to antecedents, whether explicit or implicit. Good writers routinely use pointing words to refer to something that, although clear, is less specific than a particular noun—e.g.:

- "In civilized society men must be able to assume that they may control, for purposes beneficial to themselves, what they have discovered and appropriated to their own use, what they have created by their own labor, and what they have acquired under the existing social and economic order. *This* is a jural postulate of civilized society as we know it." Roscoe Pound, *An Introduction to the Philosophy of Law* 108 (1922; repr. 1975).
- "Courts of Quarter Sessions also have the power to make an order that barristers shall have exclusive audience; *this* is usually done in those Sessions where a sufficient number of barristers practice regularly." Pendleton Howard, *Criminal Justice in England* 364 (1931).
- "The inference is that if a given law aims at the common good, it is law, but if it does not achieve its aim there is no moral obligation to obey it. If, however, it does not even aim at the common good, it is not law at all; it is not even legally binding. No lawyer would accept *this.*" W.W. Buckland, *Some Reflections on Jurisprudence* 12 (1945).
- "It is said that one cannot delve into the mind but must judge a man on his outward acts. *This* is a half-truth." Glanville Williams, *Criminal Law* 91 (2d ed. 1961).
- "If the trial were nothing but the battle [that] in some respects it resembles, each party would want to leave his opponent guessing about the shape of his array. To some extent *this* is permitted, but not to the point where the opponent would be taken by surprise." Patrick Devlin, *The Judge* 56 (1979).
- "Normally, the corporation is accountable for a person only if he was an officer, director, or managing agent at the time the deposition was taken. *This* is to protect the party from the admissions of disgruntled former officers or agents . . . ." Charles A. Wright, *The Law of Federal Courts* 568 (4th ed. 1983).
- "[T]he rule is simply that courts do not use the contempt power to coerce the payment of money. *This* is an important rule for choosing among remedies, but it has nothing to do with irreparable injury." Douglas Laycock, *The Death of the Irreparable Injury Rule* 17 (1991).

The test for knowing when the word *this* is acceptable in such a context is this: ask yourself, This what? If an answer immediately comes to mind, the word *this* is probably fine. If none comes immediately to mind, you may need to add a noun.

But a word of warning: in each of the examples in the bulleted list above, a noun would have marred the style. One way to spoil such sentences is to insert, after *this,* an abstract noun or noun phrase such as *fact, idea, practice,* or *state of affairs.*

For a related problem with the relative pronoun *which,* also a deictic term, see REMOTE RELATIVES.

de jure has three senses: (1) "of right; lawful"; (2) "as a matter of right"; and (3) "by law." In sense (1) it is contrasted with *de facto* (= in fact, but usually unlawfully so) <de facto as opposed to de jure segregation>. In sense (2), it is contrasted with *de gratia* (= as a favor gratuitously bestowed). And in sense (3) it is opposed to *de aequitate* (= by equity).

Sense (1), illustrated in the following sentence, is the most usual: "That issue will have to be determined in light of the fact that the United States recognizes the West German Government as the *de jure* government over the territory it controls but does not recognize the East German Government." See **de facto (A).**

de jure segregation. See **segregation, de facto.**

delapidation. See **dilapidation.**

***del credere* agent** (= an agent who guarantees the solvency of the third party with whom the agent makes a contract for the principal) is one of the few Italianisms to have earned a place in Anglo-American law. *Del credere* (It. "of belief or trust") began as an Italian mercantile phrase that English writers borrowed in the 18th century.

delecti for *delicti* is a misuse that occurs in several LATINISMS, such as *corpus delicti* and *lex loci delicti.* For an example of the latter, see the following sentence: "Most of the numerous inadequacies inherent in *lex loci delecti* [read *lex loci delicti*] also exist in the other traditional *lex loci* rules." *Duncan v. Cessna Aircraft Co.,* 665 S.W.2d 414, 421 (Tex. 1984). See ***corpus delicti*** & ***lex loci delicti.***

delegable is the word, not *delegatable.* Many writers mistakenly use the latter form—e.g.: "[H]e . . . had a wide range of responsibilities not *delegatable* [read *delegable*] to his subordinates." *Holt v. Gamewell Corp.,* 797 F.2d 36, 38 (1st Cir. 1986). See -ATABLE.

delegate. See **relegate.**

delegatee (= one to whom a debtor's matter is delegated) is not, despite its appearances to the contrary, a NEEDLESS VARIANT of *delegate* (= one who represents or acts for another or a group of others). See -EE.

delegatus non potest delegare. See MAXIMS.

deliberate; deliberative. These words have clear DIFFERENTIATION. *Deliberate* = (1) intentional, fully considered; or (2) unimpulsive, slow in deciding. *Deliberative* = of, or appointed for the purpose of, deliberation or debate (*COD*).

Deliberative is misused for *deliberate* in both sense (1) and sense (2). Here is an example of the former: "The express revocation of a will is a *deliberative* [read *deliberate*] act and operates as an immediate revocation of the will to which it refers."

deliberate speed. See **with all deliberate speed.**

deliberative. See **deliberate.**

delict; delictum; deliction. The preferred term is *tort. Delict* (= an offense against the law) is the more common of the two variants here to be discussed, but both are inferior in Anglo-American contexts to the usual word *(tort).* E.g., "*A child of tender years* [read *a young child*] may be incapable of committing a *legal delict* [read *tort*] because of his lack of capacity to discern the consequences of his act."/ "Thus recovery of a sum of money by way of penalty for a *delict* [read *tort*] is the historical starting point of liability." Roscoe Pound, *An Introduction to the Philosophy of Law* 75 (1922; repr. 1975)./ "The simple fact that one *delict* [read *tort*] has already occurred is in no way indicative of the likely merits of subsequent claims." *Procup v. Strickland,* 792 F.2d 1069, 1081 (11th Cir. 1986) (Johnson, J., dissenting).

Delictum is a Latinate variant used primarily in discussions of Roman law—e.g.: "There was another class of obligations, to be looked at presently, which had their origin in a *delictum* (a delict or delinquency), a wrong, unlawful act done by one party to the other." James Hadley, *Introduction to Roman Law* 237 (N.Y., D. Appleton & Co. 1881)./ "Bateman Eichler contends that the respondents' *delictum* [read *delict* or *tort*] was substantially par to that of Lazzaro and Neadeau for two reasons." *Bateman Eichler, Hill Richards Inc. v. Berner,* 472 U.S. 299, 312 (1985).

Additionally, *deliction,* a NEEDLESS VARIANT of *delict,* is not recorded in the dictionaries—e.g.: "[The] common-law status of the plaintiff's case is accentuated by the statutory element of *deliction* [read *delict*]." *Schnackenberg v. Delaware, L. & W. Ry.,* 98 A. 266, 266 (N.J. 1916)./ "The individuals whose alleged *deliction* [read *delict*] caused the death were not sued . . . ." *Garber v. Prudential Ins. Co.,* 22 Cal. Rptr. 123, 131 (1962) (Files, J., dissenting)./ "A suit for damages instituted as a result of a proprietor's violation of the obligation . . . is not a tort action in the sense that *deliction* [read *delict*] in its usual connotation is a necessary element." *Hero Lands Co. v. Texaco, Inc.,* 310 So. 2d 93, 97 (La. 1975).

delictal; delictive. See **delictual.**

delictu for *delicto,* a mistake unknown in English law, has occurred in many dozens of American cases. See ***in flagrante delicto, ex delicto*** & ***in pari delicto.***

delictum. See **delict.**

delictual; delictal; delictive. The preferred form is *delictual,* assuming this word is to be used advisedly in place of its near-equivalent, *tortious.* In civil-law contexts, of course, it is the normal word—e.g.: "The Louisiana Supreme Court held that Article 2971 limited only the innkeeper's contractual, not his *delictual,* responsibility."/ "I would like to raise the question whether we are justified to speak of a general law of obligations including the categories of contractual, *delictual,* quasi-contractual, and quasi-*delictual* obligations, or should we, perhaps, approach each category of obligations separately?" A.N. Yiannopoulos, "Comments and Questions," in *Essays on the Civil Law of Obligations* 45 (Joseph Dainow ed. 1969).

Delictual may be more useful than its sibling *delict,* for it signifies "of or relating to a tort," whereas *tortious* signifies either "relating to a tort" or "constituting a tort" <tortious conduct>. See **tortious (A).**

Delictal, recorded in the *OED* as appearing in only one source (in 1913), is a NEEDLESS VARIANT of *delictual.* E.g., "An obscure text suggests that where the *delictal* [read *delictual*] action aimed merely at compensation . . . , they were quite distinct." W.W. Buckland, *A Text-Book of Roman Law* 711 (1921)./ "Such a postulate is the basis of *delictal* [read *delictual*] *culpa,* using *culpa* in the narrower sense, and of our doctrine of negligence." Roscoe Pound, *An Introduction to the Philosophy of Law* 86 (1922; repr. 1975)./ "[W]e think the rules heretofore set out relating to the right to legal subrogation in conventional debts apply also to *delictal* [read *delictual*] obligations." *A.O. Smith-Inland, Inc. v. Union Carbide Corp.,* 547 F. Supp. 344, 347 (M.D. La. 1982).

Still another NEEDLESS VARIANT is *delictive*—e.g.: "Fault (culpa) involves *delictive* [read *delictual*] conduct of an affirmative or voluntary nature." *Colmenares Vivas v. San Alliance Ins. Co.,* 807 F.2d 1102, 1109 (1st Cir. 1986).

delictum. See **delict.**

delimit(ate). *Delimit,* the preferred form, is not merely a fancy variation of *limit* (= to restrict the bounds of), as many seem to believe. E.g., "The manufacturer may possibly *delimit* [read *limit*] the scope of his potential liability by use of a disclaimer in compliance with the statute."/ "The court held on several occasions that certain congressional attempts to *delimit* [read *limit*] its jurisdiction were unconstitutional attempts to invade the judicial province."

Properly, *delimit* means "to define; delineate," as here: "If the challenged conduct of respondents constitutes state action as *delimited* by our prior decisions, then that conduct was also action under color of state law and will support a suit under § 1983."

delineate, (lit. "to draw or sketch") means figuratively "to represent in words; to describe." It is sometimes misused for *differentiate.* E.g., "A corporate seal is probably desirable since it helps to *delineate* [read *differentiate*] corporate transactions from individual transactions."

delinquent, in AmE, can apply to either things or people <delinquent taxes> <juvenile delinquents>. In BrE, it applies only to people.

delirium tremens. This word denotes a mental disease characterized by violent mania, with tremors and hallucinations, induced by a sudden abstinence from alcohol or another drug after one has used it excessively over a prolonged period. The phrase should not be used, as it sometimes is, to describe mere frenzied drunkenness, which is something else entirely.

deliverance, when used for *opinion,* is somewhat grandiose; it is an extension of the Scots law sense "a judicial or administrative order." E.g., "In days not far remote, judges were not unwilling to embellish their *deliverances* with quotations from the poets." Benjamin N. Cardozo, *Law and Literature,* 52 Harv. L. Rev. 471, 484 (1939)./ "Fully aware of Mississippi's imprimatur on § 6 we might—by piecing together some of our own *deliverances* and the District Court opinions dutifully following them—come up with a fair prediction of what Mississippi would hold in this case, but we do not think this would be a wise course." See **delivery (A)** & **opinion.**

delivery. A. And *deliverance.* *Delivery* is the more usual word to describe a transfer or conveyance (of something), an utterance <a stammering delivery of the speech>, or giving birth. In the law relating to deeds, *delivery* "does not mean transfer of possession, but conduct indicating that the person who has executed the deed intends to be bound by it." G.H. Treitel, *The Law of Contract* 145 (8th ed. 1991). Thus "it is perfectly possible for the grantor to 'deliver' the deed and yet keep possession of it." *Id.* Such a delivery is termed *constructive delivery.*

Deliverance is a legal and religious term usu. meaning "rescue, release," although at one time it overlapped with *delivery* in almost every sense. In law, *deliverance* can mean (1) "a jury's verdict"; (2) "in an action of replevin, the delivery of goods unlawfully taken"; or (3) "a judicial opinion or a judgment that a judge delivers." See **deliverance.**

B. And *livery*. The word *livery* has a number of obsolete and archaic senses, but in law has been used in the sense "the legal delivery of property into a person's possession," as in the phrases *livery of seisin* and *to take (or have) livery of.* The student can better understand *livery* by reading it mentally as "delivery." See **livery of seisin.**

C. Cant Uses. It has become voguish in some circles to use *delivery of* where *providing* or *provision for* would normally appear, esp. in reference to services. Like any other trendy expression, it ought to be avoided. E.g., "It is irrational to equate the cost of total confinement with the alleged harm resulting from a change in method of *the delivery of* [read *providing*] dental services." See VOGUE WORDS.

delusion. See **hallucination & illusion.**

delusive; delusory; delusional. *Delusive* = (1) tending to delude, deceptive; or (2) of the nature of a delusion. Usually sense (1) applies. *Delusional* is the more usual term for sense (2). E.g., "Defendant acted under a completely *delusional* perception of reality." *Delusory* is a NEEDLESS VARIANT.

demagoguery; demagogy. *Demagoguery* (= the practices of a political agitator who appeals to mob instincts) is the usual word, *demagogy* being a NEEDLESS VARIANT.

demandant. Formerly, in real actions (i.e., lawsuits over land), the plaintiff was called the *demandant* and the defendant the *tenant.* See **real action.**

demarcation; demarkation. The former is the preferred spelling.

demean; bemean. Formerly, authorities on usage disapproved of *demean* in the sense "to lower, degrade," holding that instead it properly should be used reflexively in the sense "to conduct (oneself)." For example, an early usage critic wrote that "*demean* signifies 'to behave' and does not mean *debase* or *degrade.*" Frank H. Vizitelly, *A Desk-Book of Errors in English* 62 (1909). The meaning "to behave," now somewhat archaic, is used infrequently in legal contexts—e.g.: "The oath of office now generally administered in all the states requires the lawyer to uphold the law; to *demean* himself, as an officer of the court, uprightly; to be faithful to his trust." See Fed. R. App. P. 46(a) ("I . . . do solemnly swear . . . that I will *demean* myself as an attorney and counselor of this court . . . .").

Yet the more common lay sense is now widespread even in legal prose, and has been with us since at least 1601. E.g., "Nowhere in the common-law world—indeed in any modern society—is a woman regarded as a chattel or *demeaned* by denial of a separate legal identity and the dignity associated with recognition as a whole human being."/ "This illogical result *demeans* the values protected by the Confrontation Clause." *Richardson v. Marsh,* 481 U.S. 200, 212 (1987) (Stevens, J., dissenting).

Meanwhile, the word with which *demean* was confused in arriving at its popular meaning, *bemean* (= to debase), has become virtually obsolete.

demesne (= at common law, a lord's land held as his absolute property and not as feudal property through a superior) is pronounced either /*di-****meen***/ or /*di-****mayn***/. Today, unless the word appears in a historical context, it is ordinarily figurative—e.g.: "Collins, without authorization from the directors, ruled the corporation as a personal *demesne* for the benefit of himself and his son." *Jackson v. Nicolai-Neppach Co.,* 348 P.2d 9, 20 (Or. 1959).

de minimis. **A. The Maxim.** *De minimis* is a shortened form of the Latin maxim *de minimis non curat lex* (= the law does not concern itself with trifles). E.g., "Perhaps this is still true today, but if so this area of procedure has become so shrunken as to fall within the maxim *de minimis.*" Charles A. Wright, *The Law of Federal Courts* 272 (4th ed. 1983). Though most legal writers find it legitimate and useful, in practice there is something to Ephraim Tutt's quip that "[n]o one knows exactly what it means." *Yankee Lawyer* 356 (1943).

De minimis non curat lex is a sentence in itself. When invoking the maxim by declaring something to be a mere trifle, one writes that it is *de minimis.* The entire maxim should not be inserted when only the "trifling" portion is called for: "The testimony regarding the landscaping in the common areas was unsatisfactory, but this insufficiency is considered to be *de minimis non curat lex.*" The sentence is grammatically nonsensical. If an entire maxim is used, it should fit into the sentence syntactically. But here we have, in translation, "this insufficiency is considered to be [*the law does not concern itself with trifles*].” The writer should have ended the sentence with *de minimis*. See MAXIMS.

B. The Phrase. Lawyers often use the phrase not as a shortened version of the maxim, but in the sense “so insignificant that a court may overlook (it or them) in deciding the issue or case.” E.g., “Winter maintains that his unauthorized sales of non-Carvel products were *de minimis* and cannot possibly be deemed to have a sufficient effect on interstate commerce.” *Franchised Stores of N.Y., Inc. v. Winter,* 394 F.2d 664, 670 (2d Cir. 1968)./ “[T]he dictum that plaintiff's injury must pass some threshold of seriousness, more than *de minimis,* makes no sense at all.” Douglas Laycock, *The Death of the Irreparable Injury Rule* 74 (1991).

The phrase sometimes appears, as in the following sentences, to act merely as a fancy substitute for *minimal:* “The amount of advertising by plaintiff was *de minimis* [read *minimal*], as it had been in business only a matter of months.”/ “To require TWA to bear more than a *de minimis* cost in order to give Hardison Saturdays off is an undue hardship.” *Trans World Airlines, Inc. v. Hardison,* 432 U.S. 63, 84 (1977).

Sometimes the phrase is used as an attributive noun (meaning “something that is de minimis”): “CPI may be barred from asserting its trademark rights nationwide because of its failure to challenge what it may have considered a *de minimis.*”

demise, vb. & n. The meanings of the verb *demise* are (1) “to convey by will or lease”; (2) “to pass by descent or bequest”; or (3) “to die.”

The corresponding definitions of *demise* as a noun are (1) “the conveyance of an estate by will or lease, or the lease itself”; (2) “the passing of property by descent or bequest”; and (3) “death.”

The popular sense of *demise,* of course, is as a noun: “death.” Because most nonlawyers understand the word in this sense, the legal senses are likely to bewilder them. The popular meaning is an extension of the legal meanings, for historically the transference of property usually resulted from a sovereign's death. Hence the change of focus from conveyance to death. Sometimes even in legal contexts *demise* carries its nominal lay meaning: “Equating isolated instances of lawyer misconduct with the *demise* of legal ethics would be as foolhardy as ignoring the problem.”/ “Mrs. Byrd's will was drawn by a Virginia practitioner two months after her husband's *demise.*” See **death.**

Sense (1) of the verb and noun is illustrated in the following sentences. Because even sense (1) contains two quite distinct meanings, a more specific word might be better: “If land is *demised* [read *leased*] for the term of 100 years or more, the term shall, as long as 50 years thereof remain unexpired, be regarded as an estate in fee simple.”/ “A chargee by way of legal mortgage is to be deemed to have a charge by way of *subdemise* [read *sublease*], and therefore a legal estate in the property charged.” (Eng.)

The adjective is *demisable:* “Because this tenure derived its whole force from custom, the lands must have been *demisable* by copy of court roll from time immemorial . . . .” W.A. Jowitt, *The Dictionary of English Law* 491 (1959) (s.v. *copyhold*).

democracy. This term, meaning literally “government by the people,” is often employed loosely, often tendentiously, often vaguely, and sometimes disingenuously (as when the post–World War II U.S.S.R. was referred to as a “democracy”). Originally a Greek term, *democracy* was understood by the Greeks in a very different sense from the current understanding: Greek democracy was a limited institution—limited to clan members, who were citizens; a huge population of slaves and other subordinated classes were disfranchised. The same, of course, might be said of the U.S. before the abolition of slavery and before women gained the right to vote. Notions of democracy change over time, mostly as notions of who are “the people” change. Throughout history, the term has come gradually to be more and more inclusive.

demonstrable /*di-**mon**-strə-bəl*/ is the word, not *demonstratable,* a NEEDLESS VARIANT. E.g., “Such an inference clearly cannot be supported absent a *demonstratable* [read *demonstrable*] nexus between the defendant and the act sought to be introduced against him.” *State v. English,* 383 S.E.2d 436, 438 (N.C. Ct. App. 1989).

demonstrative legacy. See **legacy.**

dempster; deemster. These are variant forms of the same word, which for most purposes has only historical significance. Both mean basically “a judge.” *Dempster* was formerly used in Scotland, and *deemster* is still used on the Isle of Man. The *OED* notes that *deemster* “has been used in the general sense as a historical ARCHAISM by some modern writers”; the temptation to do so should be resisted.

demur, n. See **demurrer.**

demur, vb.; **demure.** *Demur,* v.i., = to file a demurrer, which effectively admits the truth of a fact stated but denies that the complainant is legally entitled to relief. E.g., "Defendant *demurred* to each count."

Demure is the adjective meaning (1) "sober, grave, serious"; or (2) "coy in an affected way."

demurrable = that may be demurred to. Lawyers have traditionally spoken of *demurrable allegations, demurrable indictments,* and the like—e.g.: "There is authority for the position that the indictment must be specific in charging the burglarious intent, and is *demurrable* if it merely alleges an intent to commit 'a felony.'" Rollin M. Perkins & Ronald N. Boyce, *Criminal Law* 266 (3d ed. 1982).

demurrer; demurral; demur, n.; **demurrage.** A *demurrer* was a common-law pleading that stated that even if the other party's allegations were proved, the other party would not be entitled to succeed, and therefore that the demurring party was entitled in law to succeed on the facts alleged and admitted by the other. E.g., "The court was right in sustaining the *demurrer.*" Today, *demurrers* are obsolete in England (since 1883) and in most if not all American jurisdictions. But they are still used in states such as California, Connecticut, Nebraska, Oregon, and Pennsylvania, among others. See -ER (B).

Idiomatically speaking, *demurrers* were said to be *interposed:* "The circuit court of Cook County sustained a *demurrer interposed* by appellants to a bill for injunction filed by appellees and entered a decree dismissing the bill for want of equity."/ "A *demurrer* can be *interposed* only to a bill." Walter C. Clephane, *Equity Pleading and Practice* 191 (1926).

Demur, n., is the archaic nonlegal word for "the act of demurring; an objection raised or exception taken to a proposed course of action" (*OED*). The word is now chiefly literary. *Demurral* is a NEEDLESS VARIANT of *demur.*

Demurrage is a maritime-law word meaning "a [liquidated] penalty imposed on a charterer of a vessel, or in some instances the consignee of the vessel's goods, for delays in loading or unloading the ship's cargo." *Trans-Asiatic Oil, Ltd. v. Apex Oil Co.,* 804 F.2d 773, 774 n.1 (1st Cir. 1986). It is usually used in the plural, *demurrages.*

denial of justice, an important phrase in international law, has been the object of SLIPSHOD EXTENSION: "The term . . . is sometimes loosely used to denote *any* international delinquency towards an alien for which a state is liable to make reparation. In this sense it is an unnecessary and confusing term. Its more proper sense is an injury involving the responsibility of the state committed by a court of justice . . . ." J.L. Brierly, *The Law of Nations* 226–27 (5th ed. 1955).

denization (= the action of making a person a denizen, i.e., a resident alien), a legal term dating from 1601, is sometimes incorrectly rendered *denizenation.*

denote (= to mean; stand for) for *denominate* (= to give a name to; call) is a not uncommon error—e.g.: "The issue can reasonably be *denoted as* [read *denominated,* or better, *called*] one of procedure."/ "M.Y.J. promised to pay $5,000 to Allegheny College by a writing *denoted* [read *denominated*] an Estate Pledge." See **connote.**

denouncement. See **denunciation.**

de novo, adv. & adj. This LATINISM, usually an adjective <de novo review>, as an adverb means "anew." E.g., "We review a summary judgment *de novo.*"

denunciation; denouncement. The latter is a NEEDLESS VARIANT.

deny (= to declare untrue; repudiate; to refuse to recognize or acknowledge) is frequently misused for other words.

A. For *refuse.* These words are synonymous in certain constructions <He was denied (or refused) this>. But in modern usage *refuse* properly precedes an infinitive, whereas with *deny* this construction is an ARCHAISM: "The Federal Judge ordered the Governor to testify, but he *denied* [read *refused*] to do so."

B. For *deprive:* "The cumulative effect of the errors *denied them of a fair trial* [read either *denied them a fair trial* or *deprived them of a fair trial*]."

depart, a FORMAL WORD meaning "to go" or "to leave," may be a transitive verb, and often is in legal prose, although in lay usage it is almost always intransitive. Hence legal writers state that someone *departed the premises,* whereas the nonlawyer would probably say that someone *departed from the premises.* The better phrasing—in either a legal or a nonlegal context—would be to say that the person *left.*

depart from, in the context of discussing precedents, is sometimes a euphemism for *overturn* or *overrule.* When a court says that it *departs from* a precedent, it in effect overturns the precedent, usu. without expressly so stating. The expression is more appropriate in referring to mere persuasive authority, as opposed to what would ordinarily be considered binding authority.

dépeçage, n. /*dep-ə-***sahj**/, is a mid-20th-century borrowing from French law. It derives from the French verb *dépecer* (= to cut up, dismember), and it means "choice of law issue by issue; the practice of applying rules of different jurisdictions to different issues in a legal dispute"—e.g.: "For a long time, courts and writers agreed that a choice-of-law involved a choice of a 'governing' legal system rather than of an individual rule. Much of this ideology remains intact in the language of the courts. But it is increasingly recognized that it is always a rule rather than a legal system to which we are referred . . . . [T]he implementation of this finding has been called *depecage* or *scission.*" Albert Ehrenzweig, *Conflicts in a Nutshell* 219 (2d ed. 1970)./ "*Depecage* occurs where the rules of one legal system are applied to regulate certain issues arising from a given transaction or occurrence, while those of another system regulate the other issues. The technique permits a more nuanced handling of certain multistate situations and thus forwards the policy of aptness." Arthur T. von Mehren, *Special Substantive Rules for Multi-State Problems,* 88 Harv. L. Rev. 347, 356 n.24 (1974).

dependence; dependency. These variants have undergone DIFFERENTIATION. *Dependence* is the general word meaning (1) "the quality or state of being dependent"; or (2) "reliance." *Dependency* is a geopolitical term meaning "a territory under the jurisdiction of, but not formally annexed by, a nation." (See **territory.**) These words are commonly misspelled *-ance, -ancy.*

dependent, n.**; dependant,** n. The older spelling is *-ant.* The *OED* notes: "from the 18th c. often (like the adj.) spelt *dependent,* after L.; but the spelling *-ant* still predominates in the [noun]." *W10* countenances *-ent* over *-ant.* The *COD* continues the Oxonian preference for *-ant,* noting that *-ent* is chiefly American. Certainly the British DIFFERENTIATION in spelling between the adjective (*dependent*) and the noun (*dependant*) is a useful one; but American writers cannot be faulted for using the *-ent* spelling for the noun.

dependent relative revocation. "The doctrine of *dependent relative revocation* is basically an application of the rule that a testator's intention governs; it is not a doctrine of defeating that intent." This phrase, common in the American and British law of wills, confuses all but specialists in wills and estates. It has nothing to do with revoking one's dependent relatives; rather, it means "revocation of a will by a testator who intends to replace it by another, effective will" (*CDL*). The law regards as mutually dependent the acts of destroying one will and of substituting another in its place, when both acts are parts of one plan. The two acts are thus "related," or *relative.*

We might wish for a less monstrous phrase, such as *conditional revocation:* "The name of this doctrine [*dependent relative revocation*] seems to me to be somewhat overloaded with unnecessary polysyllables. The resounding adjectives add very little, it seems to me, to any clear idea of what is meant. The whole matter can be quite simply expressed by the word 'conditional.'" *In re Hope Brown,* [1942] P. 136, 138 (per Langton, J.).

deplane. This word, like *inplane* and *reinplane,* is characteristic of airlinese, a relatively new brand of JARGON. Careful writers and speakers stick to time-honored expressions like *get off, get on,* and *get on again.* See **inplane.**

depone. See **depose.**

deponee. See **deponent.**

deponent (= one who testifies by deposition) is sometimes incorrectly rendered *deponee, deposee,* and even *deposer*—e.g.: "It is ordered that each *deponee* [read *deponent*] produce at his deposition only those items in his custody and described in the subpoena duces tecum."/ "The Superior Court's decision was silent as to plaintiff's questions to both *deposees* [read *deponents*] . . . ." *Matheson v. Bangor Publishing Co.,* 414 A.2d 1203, 1205 (Me. 1980)./ "We find no error in the trial judge's ruling that excluded from being read to the jury . . . his own introductory comments during the deposition proceeding. In fact, their inclusion would have, it seems to us, given inordinate weight and buttressed the *deposer's* [read *deponent's*] testimony . . . ." *State v. Harriston,* 253 S.E.2d 685, 688 (W.V. 1979). See **affirmant.**

deport; disport. The latter word is sometimes confused with the former, which means (1) "to behave (oneself)"; or (2) "to banish, remove." The latter is a reflexive verb meaning "to display oneself sportively."

deportation; deportment. Both derive ultimately from L. *deportare* (= to carry off, convey away), but to say that these words have undergone DIFFERENTIATION is a great understatement. *Deportation* = the act of removing (a person) to another country; the expulsion of an alien from a country. *Deportment* = the bearing, demeanor, or manners of a person.

deportee. See -EE.

deportment. See **deportation.**

depose; depone. In legal contexts, to *depose* (v.i.) is to bear witness or testify, or (v.t.) to take a deposition of someone. *Depose* also has the historical meaning "to dethrone or kill (a king)." *Depone,* a relatively rare word meaning "to testify," ought to be considered a NEEDLESS VARIANT.

Krapp recorded *depose* as being used in legal contexts for "to state"—e.g.: "The witness *deposes* that he has seen . . . ." George P. Krapp, *A Comprehensive Guide to Good English* 188 (1927). Actually, today that sense survives in AmE only in the doublet *deposes and states* or *deposes and says,* a common phrase in affidavits. But in BrE it has more currency—e.g.: "[T]he manufacturer's secretary was called and *deposed* that in the previous six years the manufacturer had treated by a similar process 4,737,600 of these garments . . . ." *Grant v. Australian Knitting Mills Ltd.,* [1936] A.C. 85, 95 (per Lord Wright).

But the more common use today is the transitive one—e.g.: "The defendant's attorney then *deposed* the plaintiff." As that example illustrates, American lawyers today almost invariably say that the lawyer deposes the witness, not that the deponent deposes. In the following sentence, then, a lawyer would have put the verb into PASSIVE VOICE: "If [the witness] has not *deposed* [read *been deposed*], the other lawyer won't be able to emphasize his pain and suffering by reading the questions and answers to the jury." Joseph C. Goulden, *The Million Dollar Lawyers* 107 (1978).

For lawyers, the nonlegal sense ("to dethrone") occasionally causes MISCUES—e.g.: "President George Bush . . . again urged that President Saddam Hussein be *deposed,* saying 'It's only terror that's keeping him in power.'" *Marines Replace Iraqis in North,* Int'l Herald Tribune, 27–28 April 1991, at 1. That is so especially in contexts involving trial preparation—e.g.: "The judge in the drug and racketeering trial of Gen. Manuel Antonio Noriega privately questioned an important prosecution witness this afternoon to determine whether the witness lied when he testified against the *deposed* Panamanian leader last fall." Larry Rohter, *Judge Examines Truthfulness of Noriega Witness,* N.Y. Times, 26 March 1992, at A8.

deposee. See **deponent.**

deposer. See **deponent.**

deposeth. See -ETH.

depositary; depository; depositee. Most authorities on usage have agreed through the years that *depositary* is the better term in reference to persons with whom one leaves valuables or money for safekeeping, and that *depository* is preferred in reference to places. The Uniform Commercial Code, however, contains the term *depositary bank,* and this phrase has therefore become common. E.g., "*Depositary banks* rely on a strict set of rules to know when a check has been accepted or dishonored." Following is an example of the traditional use of *depositary:* "The *depositary* in escrow . . . has the absolute duty to carry out the terms of the agreement." *In re Missionary Baptist Found.,* 792 F.2d 502, 504 (5th Cir. 1986).

Depository has continued to be used consistently of places. E.g., "The Nuclear Waste Policy Act of 1982 . . . is a comprehensive statute providing for the establishment by the Department of Energy of a geologic *depository* for the disposal of high-level radioactive waste."

Depositee is a NEEDLESS VARIANT of *depositary*—e.g.: "A *depositee* [read *depositary*] who made away with the thing was liable *ex deposito* . . . ." W.W. Buckland, *A Text-Book of Roman Law* 709 (1921).

deposition. **A. As Verb.** *Deposition* should not be used as a verb in place of *depose.* E.g.,"After they were *depositioned* [read *deposed*], they were asked to come forward with the relevant discoverable documents." See **depose.**

B. As Noun. In its legal senses, as the noun corresponding to *depose,* the word *deposition* = (1) a witness's out-of-court testimony that is recorded by a court reporter and reduced to writing for later use in court; (2) the session at which such out-of-court testimony is recorded; or (3) in ecclesiastical law, a penalty by which a member of the clergy may be divested of a patronage or other dignity. *Deposition* serves as the noun for both *depose* and *deposit.* "The landfill sites were physically unsuitable for hazardous-waste *deposition* [= the act of depositing]."

C. *Oral deposition.* This phrase is not a REDUNDANCY because, under most court rules, it is possible to take a *deposition upon written interrogatories* (sometimes called a *deposition on written questions*).

depository. See **depositary.**

depravity; depravation. The former is the condition of being depraved or corrupt; the latter is the act or process of depraving or corrupting. Cf. **deprivation.**

deprecate; depreciate. The former is increasingly misused for the figurative senses of the latter, whereas the latter is too often confined to its literal meaning. *Deprecate* = to disapprove regretfully. E.g., "[O]ne of the earliest and most uncompromising advocates of unlimited sovereignty, Bodin, *deprecated* any attempt to make laws unrepealable." Carleton K. Allen, *Law in the Making* 469 (7th ed. 1964).

The phrase *self-deprecating* is, literally speaking, an unlikely description except perhaps for those suffering from extreme neuroses. *Depreciate,* transitively, means "to belittle, disparage"; and intransitively, "to fall in value" (used of securities or investments). Thus *self-depreciating,* with *depreciate* in its transitive sense, is the correct phrase—e.g.: "But in him modesty is not an expression of shyness or *self-depreciation* or self-distrust." Felix Frankfurter, "Calvert Magruder," in *Of Law and Life and Other Things* 136, 138 (Philip B. Kurland ed., 1967).

In the following sentence, the U.S. Supreme Court nodded: "We do not *deprecate* [read *depreciate*] Fourth Amendment rights. The security of persons and property remains a fundamental value which law enforcement officers must respect." *Alderman v. U.S.,* 394 U.S. 165, 175 (1969).

The intransitive use of *depreciate* (= to decline in value), primarily financial and legal, has evolved into the transitive sense "to claim tax deductions (for) on the basis of depreciation" <he depreciated his house>. This use of the word is colloquial, and should be avoided in formal legal contexts.

depreciatory; depreciative. Both mean "disparaging." In BrE, *depreciatory* is the predominant term; in AmE, the two forms are used almost equally often. Still, *depreciative* might reasonably be labeled a NEEDLESS VARIANT.

deprivation; privation. Both mean "the action of depriving or taking away." The words share that general sense as well as specific senses relating to the depriving of an office, position, or benefice. *Deprivation* is the ordinary word; *privation* is more literary. Cf. **depravity.**

depute, v.t.; **deputize.** To *depute* is to delegate <these responsibilities she deputed to her attorney-in-fact>, and to *deputize* is to make (another) one's deputy or to act as deputy <the sheriff then deputized four people who had offered to help in the search>.

deraign, v.t., a legal ARCHAISM still often referred to, means "to settle (a dispute or claim) by combat or wager." A right-minded folk etymologist might conclude that the word was arrived at by metathesis of *derange.*

dereliction = abandonment, esp. through neglect or moral wrong, as in *dereliction of duty.* E.g., "By hypothesis he has committed the gravest *dereliction* possible—a complete repudiation of the trust he expressly assumed." The *OED* notes that in legal prose *dereliction* is still used in the neutral sense of physical abandonment; if this sense persists at all in current legal usage, it is obsolescent.

derisive; derisory; derisible. *Derisive* = scoffing; expressing derision <a derisive sneer>. *Derisory* = worthy of derision or of being scoffed at <that argument is so bad that judges would consider it derisory>. Though *derisive* and *derisory* at one time overlapped and were frequently synonymous, the DIFFERENTIATION is now complete, and using the two as synonyms is erroneous. *Derisible* is a NEEDLESS VARIANT of *derisory.*

derivative action = "a suit by a beneficiary of a fiduciary to enforce a right running to the fiduciary as such." *Goldstein v. Groesbeck,* 142 F.2d 422, 425 (2d Cir. 1944). Synonymous phrases include *derivative suit* and (somewhat more narrowly) *shareholder derivative suit.*

derogate is regularly used in two quite distinct senses in legal prose: (1) transitively, it means "to disparage" <we do not derogate these values, however, if we are unable to find them to be protected by the Constitution>; and (2) intransitively, it is used with the prep. *from* and means "to detract" <the court's position derogates from the highly sensitive discretion that is inherent in the parole function>.

derogation of, in. This phrase is used 99 times in legal contexts for every one use in nonlegal contexts. It means "in abrogation or repeal of (a law, contract, or right)." Hence the maxim: *Statutes in derogation of the common law are to be strictly construed.* In a sense, that maxim is senseless, for, as Grant Gilmore once quipped, "what statute is not?" *The Ages of American Law* 62 (1977). E.g., "The district court found that the intervenor's position would effectively give the employer control of the settlement process *in derogation of* the policy that settlements are favored in the law."

Derogation from is another idiom, meaning "prejudice, destruction (e.g., of a right or grant)." E.g., "It is an established rule that a grantor cannot be permitted to *derogate from* his grant."/

"If the perpetrator of this fraud is the counsel in the case, then, as an officer of the court he has offended and may be punished for a *derogation from* professional integrity." See **degradation.**

descend, v.i.; **distribute.** In the legal idiom relating to intestacy, real property is said upon death to *descend* (= to pass) to the heirs. E.g., "If it is a remainder in fee simple it will *descend* on the death of the remainderman intestate to his heirs." Cornelius J. Moynihan, *Introduction to the Law of Real Property* 139 (2d ed. 1988). Personal property, by contrast, is *distributed* to the intestate's next-of-kin. Hence the phrase *statute of descent and distribution* contains no REDUNDANCY. See **descent (B).** For more on *heirs, next-of-kin,* and *distributees,* see **heir (C).**

descendant. In proper usage, only a decedent is said to have *descendants*—a live parent does not. See **ascendant.**

descender. See -ER (B).

descendible, not *descendable,* is the preferred form. See -ABLE (A).

descent. A. And *purchase.* These words are distinguished in the law of property. *Descent* refers to the acquisition of property by act of law (as by inheritance), whereas *purchase* is acquisition of property by the act of oneself or another (as by will or gift). In legal contexts, then, *purchase* is much broader than the general lay sense of "buying." E.g., "These incidents did not accrue if the property was acquired through *purchase,* and, in order to obviate this means of curtailing the payment of incidents, title by *descent* was declared to be more worthy than title by *purchase;* if a gift over might pass to an heir by *descent* rather than by *gift* [i.e., *purchase*], he took his title through inheritance." See **purchase, buy & words of purchase.**

B. And *distribution; inheritance.* At common law, intestate real property passes by *descent* and intestate personal property passes by *distribution.* Both *heirs* (who take by descent) and *distributees* (who take by distribution) may properly be said to *inherit* or *take by inheritance.* In the U.S., the Uniform Probate Code has simplified the historical terminology, supplanting all these specific terms with the general phrase *intestate succession.* See **descend & succession.**

descry. See **decry.**

desegregation; integration. No distinction between a legal requirement of *integration* and a legal requirement of *desegregation* is ordinarily observed in legal usage, but the distinction may be important in understanding the constitutional law of race and the schools. Certainly it would be useful, in reference to schools in the U.S., if we distinguished between court-ordered *desegregation* (= the abrogation of policies that segregate races into different institutions and facilities) and court-ordered *integration* (= the incorporation of different races into existing institutions for the purpose of achieving a racial balance).

deserts. See **just deserts.**

deshabille. See **dishabille.**

desiderata (= things wanted or needed) is the plural form of *desideratum.* Although the plural is more common, the singular has many appropriate uses—e.g.: "The first *desideratum* of a system for subjecting human conduct to governance of rules is an obvious one: there must be rules." Lon L. Fuller, *The Morality of Law* 46 (rev. ed. 1969).

designatee. See **designee.**

designedly, in criminal law, is sometimes used synonymously with—but is not as good as—*intentionally.*

designee; designatee. *Designee* (= a person designated), a word dating from 1925 and commonly used by lawyers, is sometimes displaced by *designatee,* a NEEDLESS VARIANT. E.g., "[T]he commissioner, or a competent *designatee* [read *designee*], is required to inspect and approve all construction work." *Ross v. Consumers Power Co.,* 363 N.W.2d 641, 669 (Mich. 1984). See -EE.

desirable; desirous. *Desirable* is used in reference to things (or members of the opposite sex), *desirous* in reference to people's emotions. What is *desirable* is attractive and worth seeking; the word applies to anything that arouses a desire. *Desirous* = impelled by desire.

The phrase *be desirous of* is usually a circumlocution for the verb *desire* or *want.* E.g., "The appellant *was desirous of securing* [read *desired (or wanted) to secure*] the property immediately."/ "Plaintiff's brother and sister, his cobeneficiaries under the trust, *were not desirous of terminating it* [read *did not want to terminate it*]."/ "In these cases, the plaintiffs ask equity to enjoin white property owners *who are desirous of selling* [read *who want to sell*] their houses to Negro buyers simply because the houses were subject to an original agreement not to have them pass to Negro ownership." See BE-VERBS (B).

desist is a FORMAL WORD for *stop* or *leave off.* E.g., "If he *desists* from the act of signing because of weakness or for some other reason, the partial signature may not be the signature that the statute requires." See **cease-and-desist order.** Cf. **cease.**

de son tort, JARGON from LAW FRENCH (lit. "by his own wrongdoing"), means "wrongful." It is typically used in the two phrases *executor de son tort* (= wrongful executor) and *trustee de son tort* (= wrongful trustee). The phrase denotes the breach of a fiduciary duty.

An *executor de son tort* is a person who, without legal authority, takes it on himself to act as executor or administrator as by acting or dealing with any of the decedent's property, apart from acts necessitated by humanity or necessity (*OCL*). Usually an *executor de son tort* acts to the detriment of beneficiaries or creditors of the estate.

A *trustee de son tort* acts similarly in respect of a living person's property. E.g., "Plaintiff contended that when the first trust was consolidated with the Union Trust Co., the office of trustee, under the terms of the will, thereby automatically became vacant and that the successor, from that time on, acted as trustee *de son tort.*" See ***ex maleficio.***

despatch. See **dispatch.**

despite; in spite of. The two are interchangeable. The compactness of *despite* recommends it.

despiteous; dispiteous. *Despiteous* = with despite; despiteful; scornful. *Dispiteous* = pitiless.

despoilation for *despoliation* (= pillaging, plundering) is a not uncommon blunder that surprises primarily because it occurs in otherwise highly literate writing. The word is also a NEEDLESS VARIANT of *spoliation,* q.v.

destination. See **ultimate destination.**

destructible; destroyable. The latter is a NEEDLESS VARIANT. *Destructible,* as well as its corresponding noun *destructibility,* is frequently used in the law: "There is ample justification for a search of the arrestee's person and the area within his immediate control—construing that phrase to mean the area from within which he might gain possession of a weapon or *destructible* evidence."/ "The *destructibility* of contingent remainders posed a threat to the stability of English family settlements of land and the conveyancing bar set to work to circumvent the *destructibility* rule." Cornelius J. Moynihan, *Introduction to the Law of Real Property* 137 (2d ed. 1988).

desuetude /***de***-*swə-tyood*/ (= disuse) has, in law, become the name of a doctrine whereby if a statute is left unenforced long enough, it will no longer be regarded by the courts as having any legal effect even though not repealed. It has a limited application in American law, and little if any application in English law: "English law, unlike Roman and Scots law, has never admitted that an Act of Parliament may be repealed or cease to have effect by obsolescence." O. Hood Phillips, *A First Book of English Law* 105 (3d ed. 1955). E.g., "There is no doctrine of *desuetude* in English law, so a statute never ceases to be in force merely because it is obsolete." Rupert Cross, *Statutory Interpretation* 3 (1976).

detainal. See **detention.**

detainee (= a person held in custody) is a 20th-century NEOLOGISM that has proved useful in legal contexts. E.g., "The *detainee* must be promptly brought before a magistrate for a probable cause determination." See -EE.

detainer. See **detention** & -ER (B).

detainment; detainer. See **detention.**

detectable; detectible. The former spelling is preferred. See -ABLE (A).

detector; detecter. The former spelling is preferred. See -ER (A).

detention; detainment; detainal; detainer. *Detention* = holding in custody; confinement; compulsory delay. *Detainment* and *detainal* are NEEDLESS VARIANTS. *Detainer* is a specialized legal term meaning (1) "the action of detaining, withholding, or keeping in one's possession"; (2) "the confinement of a person in custody"; or (3) "a writ authorizing prison officials to continue holding a prisoner in custody." See -ER (B).

determent. See **deterrent.**

determinable = (1) terminable; or (2) able to be determined or ascertained. Sense (1) is common in the law <determinable fee>, but it generally ought to be avoided in deference to the more universally understandable *terminable.* In a few SET PHRASES, it should be allowed to remain. E.g., "A possibility of reverter is the future interest left in one who creates a fee simple conditional or a *fee simple determinable.*" (See **fee simple (F).**)

But in other contexts, it ought to be simplified, for it is merely an unnecessary LEGALISM: "The award constituted the employment as one that was *determinable* [read *terminable*] on a day's notice." (Aus.)

The following sentences illustrate sense (2): "The applicant has a *determinable* physical impairment that can be expected to result in death."/ "To have standing under the Clayton Act, an antitrust plaintiff must demonstrate that the extent of his injury is *determinable* and not speculative."/ "This court affirmed the dismissal of the federal claims, but held that the validity of the state-law claims was a matter of state law best *determinable* by the state courts."

determinacy, the correct form, is sometimes incorrectly rendered *determinancy.* E.g., "A number of jurisdictions have increased markedly the *determinancy* [read *determinacy*] with which sentences are set."

determinant. See **determiner.**

determinate, adj., = having defined limits; definite; conclusive. *Determinate sentencing* came in response to the phrase *indeterminate sentencing,* which denotes a practice that was common in the U.S. up until the early 1970s (no specific time being set for prison sentences, e.g., "10 to 20 years"). E.g., "A *determinate* jail sentence for disobedience of a negative injunction is usually considered to be improper in civil contempt actions." The adverb *determinately* is sometimes confused with *determinedly* (= with determination).

determination of whether. The preposition *of* is unnecessary. See **whether.**

determine. A. Archaic Sense. Used without a direct object, *determine* in legal prose is an ARCHAISM in the sense "to terminate; bring or come to an end." E.g., "He had a determinable [q.v.] estate; it was never *determined;* he died owning it, and now after the *determination* of the trust it is part of the intestate estate, to be distributed as such."/ "If no issue of her body then survive, then all the principal of said estate then remaining shall be divided among my heirs-at-law in proportion to their heirship and upon the principal of said fund being distributed in accordance with the directions of this clause, then said trust shall cease and *determine.*" Nonlawyers are likely to be confused by this legalistic usage; hence a simpler wording might often be called for—e.g.: "The trust shall *terminate* [or *end*]."

On the use of the verbose phrase *cease and determine,* see DOUBLETS, TRIPLETS, AND SYNONYM-STRINGS.

B. *Determine (whether) (if).* *Determine if* is now regarded as inferior to *determine whether* in formal writing. The latter phrase is five times more common in American judicial opinions.

determiner; determinant. Both mean "that which determines." Preference might be given to the Anglo-Saxon suffix *-er,* but one could not be faulted for using either term: euphony should be the determiner. E.g., "Much has been written about the *determinants* of foreign policy in the new states of Africa." Only *determiner* suffices when the word is an agent noun meaning "a person who determines."

deterrent, n.; **deterrence; determent.** A *deterrent* is that which deters, that is, inhibits or discourages. *Deterrence* is preventing by fear. *Determent* is the act or fact of deterring.

dethrone; disenthrone. The latter is a NEEDLESS VARIANT.

detinet. See **detinuit.**

detinue; replevin; trover. *Detinue* and *replevin* are common-law remedies for the specific recovery of personal property. *Detinue* developed from the writ of debt to provide for the return of wrongfully detained goods (even if not wrongfully taken). The losing defendant had the option, at common law, of returning the property or paying the plaintiff an amount equal to its value, as determined at trial. *Detinue* still exists in many American jurisdictions but was statutorily abolished in England in 1977 (and replaced by the tort of *wrongful interference with goods*).

Replevin originated as an action to test the legality of another's seizure of goods (*distraint,* q.v.). In England, it has been restricted to this particular situation, whereas in the U.S. *replevin* has become an available remedy for any case of wrongful taking of chattels.

Trover is a common-law remedy for compensatory damages for conversion of personal property. See **conversion.**

detinuit; detinet. These common-law actions have deceptively similar names. *Detinuit* (lit., "he has detained") = an action of replevin in which the plaintiff already possesses the goods sued upon. *Detinet* (lit., "he detains") = an action alleging simply that the defendant is wrongfully withholding money or chattels.

detoxicate; detoxify. *Detoxify* is prevalent in AmE, *detoxicate* in BrE.

detractive; detractory. The latter is a NEEDLESS VARIANT of *detractive* (= tending to detract; defamatory).

detrimental reliance = reliance [usu. on another's promise or representation] that turns out to be disadvantageous or to cause a loss. Though it is now a fundamental term in contract law, it did not begin appearing in legal discourse until the mid-20th century. Today, of course, it is commonplace—e.g.: "For *detrimental reliance* seems to be the key to promissory estoppel, and it is also, of course, one of the twin legs of the doctrine of consideration." P.S. Atiyah, *An Introduction to the Law of Contract* 125 (3d ed. 1981)./ "*Detrimental reliance* by the promisee can therefore give rise to a proprietary estoppel even though no benefit is conferred on the promisor." G.H. Treitel, *The Law of Contract* 126 (8th ed. 1991).

deuterogamy. See **bigamy.**

devastavit; devisavit. These terms are easily confusable; they call for explanation in modern contexts. *Devastavit* (L. "he has wasted") = the failure of a personal representative to administer a decedent's estate promptly and properly. E.g., "The writ may be used to enforce the personal liability of an executor or administrator, where a *devastavit* has been committed." See **waste.**

Devisavit is invariably used in the phrase *devisavit vel non* (L. "he devises or not"), which in former practice was an issue sent from an equity or probate court to a court of law to determine the validity of a purported will. E.g., "One may, upon an issue of *devisavit vel non,* prove that a part of the executed instrument was not the testator's will." See **vel non.**

deviance; deviancy; deviation. The general term for "an act or instance of deviating" is *deviation* <a ship's deviation from its voyage route> <deviation from orthodox religion>. E.g., "Pioneer contends that, in proceedings under section 10207, a charitable corporation must be given an opportunity to correct its *deviation* from its articles, as it would if the proceedings were quo warranto." *Deviation* is more neutral in connotation than *deviance,* which means "the quality or state of deviating from established norms, esp. in social customs." *Deviancy* is a NEEDLESS VARIANT.

deviant; deviate. **A. As Adjectives.** *Deviant* is normal. The first edition of the *OED* (1928) labeled both of these adjectives "obsolete" and "rare." The *OED Supp.* (1972) deleted the tag on *deviant* and cited many examples in the sense "deviating from normal social standards or behavior." The word is common in legal writing: "The government failed to present the expert testimony necessary to establish that the photographs would appeal to the prurient interest of a clearly defined *deviant* group."

W3 records *deviate* as an adjective, and it is, unfortunately, common in American legal prose: "The hospital and morgue staff all testified that no *deviate* sexual intercourse was performed on complainant while she was under their care and control." Even so, *deviate* (adj.) is a NEEDLESS VARIANT of *deviant,* the preferred adjective.

Deviant is often used in figurative senses; for example: "*Deviant* rulings by circuit courts of appeals, particularly in apparent dicta, cannot generally provide the justified reliance necessary to warrant withholding retroactive application of a decision construing a statute as Congress intended it."

B. As Nouns. Both *deviate* and *deviant* are used as (generally pejorative) nouns meaning "a person who, or thing which, deviates, esp. from normal social standards or behavior; spec., a sexual pervert" (*OED*). Deviate, which is slightly more common, ought to be accepted as standard. A few writers use *deviationist,* but that word is uncommon enough to be labeled a NEEDLESS VARIANT.

deviation. See **deviance.**

devil, in BrE usage, has an interesting sense: "a junior legal counsel working for a principal" (*SOED*). E.g., "The term *'devil'* is a regular and serious name [in England] for a young barrister who, in wig and gown, serves without compensation and without fame, often for from five to seven years, supplying a junior with ammunition." Henry S. Drinker, *Legal Ethics* 18 (1953).

The term is also used as a verb, usu. in the phrase *to devil for (a principal).* E.g., "He *devilled* for his uncle, was made counsel to the Commissioners of Customs in 1840, and soon got a good practice on circuit and at Westminster." 16 William Holdswerth, *A History of English Law* 155 (1966)./ "Judges and advocates who were trained in those days . . . had to spend four years gaining an honours degree, followed by two years unpaid work apprenticed to a solicitor and *'devilling'* for an advocate." Robert Porter, *Fraud Case Fuels Rumour in Gay Scandal,* Sunday Telegraph, 21 Jan. 1990, at 2.

devisability; divisibility. The former means "the capability of being devised or bequeathed"; the latter means "the capability of being divided."

devisavit. See **devastavit.**

devise, n.; **bequest; legacy.** These words denote types of clauses in wills, each having acquired through DIFFERENTIATION a more or less generally accepted sense among lawyers. A *devise* traditionally disposes of real property (only in legal usage is this word a noun). In the U.S. this tradition has been changed by statutes (see the next entry), but the traditional wording is strongly rooted, and most legal writers confine *devise* to contexts involving real property: "The court, to conform to the testator's true intent, included part of lot 16 in this *devise*."/ "In *Matter of Champion,* the testator executed a will containing a *devise* of land 'now in my occupation.'"

A *bequest* disposes of personal property other than money, although the modern tendency is to include testamentary gifts of money as well as gifts of other personalty. *Legacy* is the more proper term for a clause disposing of money. Each of the terms may refer not only to the clause in the will, but to the gift itself. See **will & bequest.**

devise, v.t.; **bequeath.** In the traditional legal idiom, one *bequeaths* personal property and *devises* real property. E.g., "Apple's intention to *devise* him a mere life estate in the property would have severely hindered his real estate development scheme." The restriction to real property has not always obtained, however; the *OED* quotes an Englishman who in 1347 *devised* his gold ring to a lady companion. Similar usages appeared up to the 18th century.

Under both the Restatement of Property and the Uniform Probate Code (in the U.S.), neither of which distinguishes in terminology between real and personal property, to dispose of any property by will is to *devise* it, the recipients being *devisees* even if the subject of the disposition is personal property. In England, however, *devise* is said to refer properly only to dispositions of real property (*OCL & CDL*).

It should not escape our attention that the simple verb *give* almost always suffices as well as, and with less confusion than, *bequeath* or *devise.* See **give, devise, and bequeath.**

The general nonlegal sense of *devise* (= to plan or invent) is also used in legal contexts: "The Rule in Shelley's Case was *devised* in feudal times."/ "The old real actions such as writs of right and writs of entry, dating back to the Norman Conquest, were *devised* to provide for the specific recovery of real property." See **bequeath.**

devisee; legatee; heir. These words have traditionally been distinguished, although in practice *devisee* and *legatee* are often used interchangeably. A *devisee* is the recipient of a *devise,* q.v. *Devisee of land* would once have been considered redundant, but arguably is not redundant in light of the extended meaning in the U.S. of *devise.* E.g., "A *devisee of land* is usually regarded as receiving his title at the instant of the testator's death."/ "We are of the opinion that this case falls within the general rule, and that the property in question passes to the residuary *devisees.*"

A *legatee* is one who receives a legacy. It is sometimes opposed to *devisee.* E.g., "Where partial revocation by physical act is permitted, there can be no partial revocation of the words of a will if the effect is to change the construction of the remainder clause or to increase a provision made for someone other than the residuary *legatee* or *devisee.*"/ "Neither a *legatee* nor, in most states, a *devisee,* can establish his rights against third parties until the will under which he takes is probated."

An *heir* takes by inheritance (or *descent,* q.v.) rather than through a will or gift (by purchase); thus *heir* is not properly used of a *devisee* or *legatee.*

deviser; devisor; divisor. A *deviser* is one who invents or contrives. A *devisor* is one who disposes of property by will (usu. real property). E.g., "The will must be subscribed and attested in the presence of the *devisor* by three or four credible witnesses, or else it will be utterly void and of no effect." *Divisor* is a mathematical term referring to the number by which another number is divided. See **testator (B).**

devoid, a variant of *void,* adj., is current only in the idiom *devoid of:* "The case was totally *devoid of* evidence that any such crime had been committed." This phrase, a favorite of hyperbolists, should be used cautiously.

devoir /*di-vwahr*/ is a far-fetched, fanciful term when used in place of *duty, responsibility,* or *burden.* E.g., "The ALJ's findings were reasonable, responsive to the proof (or the lack thereof) as adduced at the hearing, and consistent with the allocation of the *devoir* [read *burden*] of persuasion." *Migneault v. Heckler,* 632 F. Supp. 153, 159 (D.R.I. 1985)./ "The objectors . . . must carry the *devoir* [read *burden*] of persuasion." *F.T.C. v. Standard Fin. Management Corp.,* 830 F.2d 404, 411 (1st Cir. 1987).

devolution; devolvement. The latter is a NEEDLESS VARIANT. In the first two specimens that follow, *devolution* means "the passing of the power or authority of one person or body to another" (*OED*); in the third, it means "the causing of anything to descend or fall upon (anyone)" (*id.*). "It may be convenient to deal first with the *devolution* of that appointive power."/ "The circumstance that the settlor specifically reserved a power to appoint a taker means, if it means anything, that she wanted to affirm and emphasize that she desired to retain control of her property up to the time of her death and to direct its *devolution* thereafter."/ "The reasoning for so deciding is that *devolution* of property of a decedent is controlled entirely by the statutes of descent and distribution."

devolutive; devolutionary. The former is the preferred adjective corresponding to the noun *devolution,* q.v. "The Viators took a *devolutive* appeal from the judgments against them in the trial court." (La.) *Devolutionary* is a NEEDLESS VARIANT.

devolve = (1) v.t., to pass on (duties, rights, or powers) to another; or (2) v.i., to pass to another by transmission or succession. In sense (2), the verb takes the preposition *on, upon,* or *to.* E.g., "Where a person has been held to answer a criminal charge it *devolves upon* [or *on* or *to*] the state's attorney to duly prosecute the charge regardless of his personal views." See **bequeath (A).**

devolvement. See **devolution.**

devotee. See -EE.

dext(e)rous; dextral. *Dexterous* (the preferred spelling in AmE is with the *-e-*) means "clever, adept, skillful, artful." In BrE the term is spelled *dextrous. Dextral* = on the right; right-handed.

diagnose. See BACK-FORMATIONS.

diagnosis; prognosis. Courts recognize the important distinction between these words. A *diagnosis* is an analysis of one's present bodily condition with reference to disease or disorder. A *prognosis* is the projected future course of a present disease or disorder. E.g., "As to the *diagnoses* and *prognoses* of the physicians, they are not so clear and consistent as to validate removing the issue of arbitrary and capricious denial of the maintenance and cure from the jury." See **prognosis.**

diagram(m)ing. See **program(m)er** & DOUBLING OF FINAL CONSONANTS.

dialectal; dialectic(al). These words are frequently confused. The adjective for *dialect* (= a regional variety of language) is *dialectal.* The wrong word appears in the following sentence: "The court stated that the word 'opry' is a *dialectical* [read *dialectal*] variation of 'opera,' which has been in common use from the eighteenth century to the present, and that 'opry' has been and is now used to describe a show consisting of country music, dancing, and comedy routines."

Dialectical = of or relating to logical argument, historical development, or the resolution of contradictory ideas. The term is usually confined to philosophical contexts. As an adjective, *dialectic* is a NEEDLESS VARIANT of *dialectical.*

Of course, *dialectic* is useful as a noun in several senses related to the following core meaning: "a technique of reasoning or arguing by juxtaposing and then resolving contradictory ideas or positions."

dialog(ue); duologue. *Dialogue* = (1) a conversation between two or more persons; or (2) the exchange of ideas. The longer spelling is preferred. (Cf. **catalog(ue).**) *Duologue,* a rather uncommon term, means "a conversation between two persons only."

dicta. See **dictum.**

dictatrix. See SEXISM (C).

diction = (1) enunciation, distinctness of pronunciation; or (2) word-choice. Often sense (2) is overlooked. This book addresses in large measure problems of legal diction.

dictum. A. Full Phrase. *Dictum* is a shortened form of *obiter dictum* (= a nonbinding, incidental opinion on a point of law given by a judge in the course of a written opinion delivered in support of a judgment). The full phrase still occasionally appears: "The principle of stare decisis impliedly imposes upon the writer of the opinion the obligation to refrain from *obiter dicta* and to confine himself to the precise questions involved." Judge Posner has aptly defined *dictum* as "a statement in a judicial opinion that could have been deleted without seriously impairing the analytical foundations of the holding—that, being peripheral, may not have received the full and careful consideration of the court that uttered it." *Sarnoff v. American Home Prods. Corp.,* 798 F.2d 1075, 1084 (7th Cir. 1986).

British legal texts use *dictum* as well as *obiter* as the shortened form of *obiter dictum.* E.g., "In considering the *dicta* cited to us from the cases to which we referred[,] we bore in mind the importance of interpreting judicial pronouncements in the context of the questions which the court had to decide." (Eng.)/ "The view of Lord Tenterden C.J. in *Collier v. Hicks,* although *obiter,* has always been accepted as authoritative on this aspect of the law." (Eng.) See **obiter dictum.**

B. Types Other Than *obiter dictum.* *Obiter dictum* is not the only type of dictum. *Black's* notes also *simplex dictum* (= *ipse dixit,* q.v.) and *gratis dictum* (= a statement made by a party, but not obligatorily). One can safely assert that *dictum* as used in modern legal writing almost never stands for either of these highly specialized terms.

Still another type—an important one—is *judicial dictum,* which refers to an opinion by a court on a question that is directly involved, briefed, and argued by counsel, and even passed on by the court, but that is not essential to the decision. See *Cerro Metal Prods. v. Marshall,* 620 F.2d 964, 978 n.39 (3d Cir. 1980). Thus *judicial dictum* differs from *obiter dictum* because it results from considered controversy, whereas *obiter dictum* is more in the nature of a peripheral, off-the-cuff judicial remark. See Peter J. Bonani, Note, *Judicial Dictum Versus Obiter Dictum,* 16 Temple U.L.Q. 427, 431 (1942). And *judicial dictum* carries more weight: "*Judicial dictum* has been held binding precedent even by modern day 'liberal courts.' *Obiter dicta* [read *Obiter dictum*] on the other hand . . . *is* not binding authority though *it* may be persuasive." *Wolf v. Meister-Neiberg, Inc.* 551 N.E.2d 353, 355 (Ill. App. Ct. 1990).

C. Number. *Dictum* is the singular form of *dicta,* which in law are "remarks made in a judicial opinion that are not binding law." The plural form *dicta* is frequently misused as a singular noun—e.g.: "[T]his was *dicta* [read *dictum*]." William F. Walsh, *A Treatise on Equity* 446 n.78 (1930)./ "The above-quoted *dicta* [read *dictum*] in *Stack v. Boyle* is far too slender a reed on which to rest this argument." *U.S. v. Salerno,* 481 U.S. 739, 753 (1987).

Able writers generally have no difficulty getting the number correct—e.g.:

- "[T]he numerous *dicta* in this case *were* repeated some years later and gained force in the repetition." Theodore F.T. Plucknett, *A Concise History of the Common Law* 467 (5th ed. 1956).
- "Pioneer contends that the Constitution of the United States compels us to follow here the *dictum* in the College of California case; it is settled, however, that judicial decisions may be overruled and *dicta* disapproved without violating either the due process clause or the contract clause of the Constitution." *In re Los Angeles County Pioneer Society,* 257 P.2d 1, 9 (Cal. 1953) (per Traynor, J.)
- "Fully considered *dicta* in the House of Lords *are* usually treated as more weighty than the *ratio* of a judge at first instance in the High Court." P.S. Atiyah, *Law and Modern Society* 135 (1983).
- "Later *dicta,* as well as a decision at first instance, *support* Romer L.J.'s view . . . ." G.H. Treitel, *The Law of Contract* 893 (8th ed. 1991).

D. Articles with. In the legal idiom, *dictum* generally does not take an article unless the article is acting as a DEICTIC TERM. E.g., "The *dictum* in the principal case is derived from the treatment of mistakes in revocation." Usually, however, the article is unnecessary: "The court of appeals correctly identified *a dictum* [read *dictum*] in *Brown v. United States* as the source of what has become known as the 'substitute facilities doctrine.'" / "Counsel inform us that this court has never answered the question, and that they are confident in asserting that the point has not been directly passed upon in the United States and that any reference to this question of law in any case is pure *dictum.*" In short, the word is sometimes a COUNT NOUN but is usually not.

E. Lay Sense. In general nonlegal contexts, *dictum* often means (1) "a statement of opinion or belief held to be authoritative because of the dignity of the person making it"; or (2) "a familiar rule." In these lay senses, *dictum* takes an article. E.g., in sense (2): "It is a familiar *dictum* that the law will scrutinize with jealous care all transactions between parties who stand in confidential relations."

dictum page. See **pinpoint citation.**

dietitian; dietician. The former spelling is preferred.

die without issue. This phrase is ambiguous: does it mean to die without ever having had issue, or to die without having surviving issue? Further, of course, the word *issue* is itself the source of much AMBIGUITY. See **issue (E).**

differ (from) (with). To *differ from* is to be unlike, whereas to *differ with* is to express a divergent opinion. E.g., "With respect to legacies out of the personal estate, the civil law, which in this respect has been adopted by courts of equity, *differs* in some respects *from* the common law in its treatment of conditions precedent."

difference. See **differential (A).**

different (from) (than). *Different than* is often considered inferior to *different from.* The problem is that *than* should follow a comparative adjective (e.g., *larger than, sooner than,* etc.), and *different* is not comparative—though, to be sure, it is a word of contrast. Writers should generally prefer *different from. Than* implies a comparison, i.e., a matter of degree; but *differences* are ordinarily qualitative, not quantitative, and the adj. *different* is not strictly comparative. E.g., "Minors are treated differently *than* [read *from*] adults in the criminal justice system."

Still, it is indisputable that *different than* is sometimes idiomatic, and even useful insofar as *different from* frequently is not interchangeable with it, as here: "Corporate residency is *different* for venue *than* for diversity purposes." Also, *different than* may properly begin clauses, where attempting to use *different from* would be so awkward as to require another construction: "The record establishes that Wakefield is a *different* person mentally and emotionally *than* he was before his loss of hearing."

Where, however, *from* nicely fills the slot of *than,* it is to be preferred: "The fact that the injury occurred in a *different* manner *than* [read *from*] that which might have been expected does not prevent the chauffeur's negligence from being in law the cause of the injury." *Palsgraf v. Long Island R.R.,* 162 N.E. 99, 104 (N.Y. 1928) (Andrews, J., dissenting)./ "If the testator makes a gift of property that is of a different nature *than* [read *from*] that of the property bequeathed, an application of the doctrine of ejusdem generis gives rise to a presumption that he did not intend to adeem." The *Oxford Guide* (p. 102) notes that when the adverb *differently* is used, *than* is "especially common . . . and has been employed by good writers since the seventeenth century." E.g., "A civil-rights suit is to be treated no differently *than* any other civil action."

Different to is a common British construction, unobjectionable when used by British writers: "He may say that the other has wholly failed in performance and given him a thing *different* in kind *to* that which was bargained for, or of no substantial value." (Eng.)

Not infrequently, writers will use *different* superfluously with *other than:* "The right of the district court to require the commissioners' court, by mandamus, to place a *different* [delete] valuation on the property of the railway company *other than* the value theretofore placed on said property by the commissioners' court is discussed in the case of *Dillon v. Bave.*"

differentia (= a distinguishing mark or characteristic) is a technical biological term that was long ago appropriated by legal writers, although often it is used merely to mean "a distinction." The term is more common in BrE than in AmE. E.g., "The only *differentia* that can exist must arise, if at all, out of the fact that the acts done are the joint acts of several capitalists, and not of one capitalist only." (Eng.)/ "The question in every case is whether the tribunal in question has similar attributes to a court of justice or acts in a manner similar to that in which such courts act. This is of necessity a *differentia* that is not capable of precise limitation." (Eng.) The plural is *differentiae.* Cf. **distinguish.**

differentiable. See -ATABLE.

differential. A. For *difference.* The *OED* records the noun *differential* only in specialized mathematical and biological senses. As a popularized technicality, it was extended to mean "a difference in wage or salary." E.g., "[P]ayment [may be] made pursuant to . . . a *differential* based on any other factor other [*sic*] than sex." Equal Pay Act, 29 U.S.C. § 206(d) (1) (1988) (emphasis added).

The intrusion of this word into the domain of *difference* should stop there, however. The following use of *differential* was ill advised: "Most of the foreign news reaches this country at the City of New York, and because of this, and of time *differentials* [read *differences*] due to the earth's rotation, the distribution of news matter throughout the country is principally from east to west."

B. As Adjective. *Differential,* adj. = (1) of, exhibiting, depending on, a difference; or (2) constituting a specific difference. The adjective is not nearly as often misused as the noun (see (A) above): "*Differential* treatment of parties who are similarly situated raises questions about whether the agency is administering its program in a fair, impartial, and competent manner."/ "I am unhappily aware that this ruling will create anomalies through *differential* recognition of the acts of judges appointed respectively before and after U.D.I." (Eng.)/ "This tactic enables the court to characterize state goals that have been legitimated by Congress itself as improper solely because it disagrees with the concededly rational means of *differential* taxation selected by the legislature."

C. And *deferential.* These near-homophones sometimes trip up semiconscious writers and speakers. *Deferential* = showing deference; respectful.

differentiate. See **delineate.**

DIFFERENTIATION is the linguistic process by which words of common etymology gradually diverge in meaning, each taking on a distinct sense. An appreciation of this linguistic virtue is essential to the true stylist. Meanwhile, that appreciation can lead to a continual disenchantment with the forces that are exerted on language.

Richard Grant White, a 19th-century usage critic, extolled the virtue of differentiation while condemning the vice of SLIPSHOD EXTENSION: "The desynonymizing tendency of language enriches it by producing words adapted to the expression of various delicate shades of meaning. But the promiscuous use of two words each of which has a meaning peculiar to itself, by confounding distinctions impoverishes language, and deprives it at once of range and of power." Richard G. White, *Words and Their Uses, Past and Present* 161 (2d ed. 1872).

Legal scholars, too, have warned of what happens when writers lose any sense of differentiation: "If two words have each a precise sense the one including the other, as sanctions are a class of motives, to confuse them is to impoverish the language." W.W. Buckland, *Some Reflections on Jurisprudence* 89 (1945).

differently than. See **different (from) (than).**

different than. See **different (from) (than).**

difficult of, an archaic construction, is common still in legal prose. E.g., "The complications that can arise when divorces are invalid are *difficult of* solution." Formerly this phrasing was seen in literary as well as in legal writing. See **of (C).**

digamy. See **bigamy.**

digital is commonly used as the adjective corresponding to *finger* in contexts such as the following: "[T]he issue of *digital* rape was raised at trial." *State v. Roden,* 380 N.W.2d 669, 670 (S.D. 1986)./ "William Caldwell [argues] . . . that . . . officials subjected him to a *digital* rectal search that violated his fourth, fifth, and eighth amendment rights." *U.S. v. Caldwell,* 750 F.2d 341, 342 (5th Cir. 1984).

dignitas is a preposterous LATINISM in place of the ordinary word *dignity.* E.g., "I accept the fact, therefore, that the applicant has suffered an injury to his *dignitas* [read *dignity*] by the respondent's actions." (Rhod.)

dignity exists in law in a sense obsolete in nonlegal contexts. It is used to mean "rank; magnitude," esp. in the phrase *of constitutional dignity.* E.g., "A statute and a constitution, although of unequal *dignity,* are both laws, and rest on the will of the people."/ "The constitutional requirement of substantial equality and fair process can be attained only where counsel acts in the role of an active advocate in behalf of his client, as opposed to that of amicus curiae; the no-merit letter and the procedure it triggers do not reach that *dignity.*"/ "The duty that Botkin owed defendant, in making those payments, was of a *dignity* with, if not superior to, any that he owed to plaintiff."

dijudicate. See **adjudge.**

dilapidation. So spelled; *delapidation* is a common misspelling.

dilat(at)ion. The better noun form of the verb *to dilate,* from an etymological point of view, is *dilatation.* But *dilation* is common in AmE medical contexts. In other senses, *dilatation* (= [1] speaking or writing at length; or [2] expansion) is better—but it is a bookish term.

As for the medical term, there is a misconception afoot that *dilation of the eyes* means "constriction or narrowing of the pupils," when in fact just the opposite is meant. To *dilate* on a subject is to expand on it, and for one's pupils to *dilate* (e.g., from being in the dark or from the use of certain drugs) is likewise for them to enlarge.

dilatory (= tending to cause delay) is commonly used by lawyers <dilatory pleas or exceptions>, but is little known to nonlawyers.

dilemma = a choice between two unpleasant or difficult alternatives. This word should not be used by SLIPSHOD EXTENSION for *plight* or *predicament.* Originally a Greek word meaning "two horns," the word often appears in the CLICHÉ *horns of a dilemma,* but at least the cliché shows ETYMOLOGICAL AWARENESS—e.g.: "I think that Judge Hand would agree that often—though not always—both branches of the antinomy can be served and the *horns of the dilemma* avoided by eschewing a woodenly logical reading of the written law . . . ." Archibald Cox, *The Role of the Supreme Court: Judicial Activism or Self-Restraint?* 47 Md. L. Rev. 118, 124 (1987). Cf. **Hobson's choice.**

The adjective is *dilemmatic.*

dilutee = an unskilled worker added to a staff of skilled workers. See -EE.

diminished, n., in BrE, means "a criminal defense—recognized at common law in Scotland from 1867 and introduced into English law in 1957—that allows one who is on the borderline of insanity to receive a comparatively light sentence." The word is short for *diminished responsibility*—e.g.: "The defence of '*diminished*' (as it is sometimes abbreviated in informal speech) has the superficial attraction of offering an escape from the mad–bad dichotomy." Glanville Williams, *Textbook of Criminal Law* 624 (1978).

diminution; diminishment. The latter is a NEEDLESS VARIANT. "Another consequence of the slide of our adversary system into the police inquisition has been the *diminishment* [read *diminution*] of defence activity." Patrick Devlin, *The Judge* 74 (1979). *Diminution* /*dim-i-**nyoo**-shən*/ or /***noo**-shən*/ is often mispronounced /*dim-yoo-**nish**-ən*/, by metathesis, and sometimes is erroneously spelled *dimunition.*

diminutive, meaning "small" is not pronounced /*di-**min**-ə-tiv*/, but rather /*di-**min**-yə-tiv*/, with a liquid *-u-*.

diplomat; diplomatist. The latter is a NEEDLESS VARIANT sometimes (but less and less often) used in BrE.

direct is often used as an ellipsis for *direct examination.* E.g., "His testimony on *direct* did not relate to any inculpatory or exculpatory comments by Mr. P." Cf. **cross** & **redirect.**

direct cause. See CAUSATION (A).

directed verdict; instructed verdict. The phrases are synonymous. The Federal Rules of Civil Procedure use *directed verdict.* Both phrases exemplify HYPALLAGE, inasmuch as the jury, and not the verdict, is what is directed or instructed.

direct estoppel. See **collateral estopped (B).**

direct evidence; original evidence. Both of these phrases are used as antonyms of *hearsay evidence* and *circumstantial evidence* (or *indirect evidence*). *Direct evidence* is more common. As an opposite of *hearsay,* it means "a witness's statement that he or she perceived a fact in issue by one of the five senses or that he or she was in a particular physical or mental state." As an antonym of *circumstantial evidence,* the phrase *direct evidence* means "evidence that proves a fact without any inference or presumption."

It would be helpful by way of DIFFERENTIATION to use *original evidence* as an antonym of *hearsay evidence,* and *direct evidence* as an antonym of *circumstantial evidence.*

direct examination; examination-in-chief. The latter is a variant, chiefly BrE, of the former. Though *cross-examination* is hyphenated thus, *direct examination,* by convention, is not hyphenated. See **direct & cross-examination.**

direction. See **jury instruction.**

directional. See **directory.**

DIRECTIONAL WORDS. A. Ending in *-ward(s).* BrE has an affinity for *-wards* words—e.g.: "There was a taxicab proceeding *westwards* whose driver was called as a witness." (Eng.) In AmE *-ward* is the preferred form across the board. Hence *toward* is preferred in the U.S., *towards* in G.B.

B. Verbose Constructions. Use of such words as *easterly* and *northerly* in phrases like *in an easterly direction* is prolix. In fact, the simple word for the direction (*east*) usually suffices in place of the words ending in either *-erly* or *-wardly.* "The appellee was riding his bicycle *northwardly* [read *north*] on 29th Street just before the accident; appellant was driving his car *in a southerly direction* [read *south*] on Jackson Street." The one useful distinctive sense that *southwardly* and *southerly* convey is "in a direction more or less south."

C. Capitalization. The words *north, south, east,* and *west* should not be capitalized when used to express directions; they are properly capitalized when they denote regions of the world or of a country (e.g., Midwest, Far East, the South).

directorial, not *directoral,* is the adjective corresponding to *director*—e.g.: "[T]he rule's detractors recognize that it is not a complete bar to judicial review of *directoral* [read *directorial*] decision-making." Julia V. Parry, *Special Litigation Committees and the Business Judgment Rule,* 14 Conn. L. Rev. 193, 198 (1981).

directors' and officers' insurance. So written, with the possessives. The phrase is often, in speech and writing, shortened to *D & O insurance.*

directory; imperative. These words are distinguished for purposes of statutory interpretation: "Mandatory provisions [in a statute] have . . . frequently been classified as either *imperative* (when failure to comply renders all subsequent proceedings void) or *directory* (when the subsequent proceedings are valid, though the persons failing to carry out the action enjoined [i.e., mandated] by Parliament may sometimes be punishable) . . . ." *F. v. F.,* [1971] P. 1, 11. E.g., "It has been held that a violation is a substantial and not a mere technical error, since such a statute is *imperative* and not *directory.*"

In the U.S., frequently, the distinction is rather

different: *directory* is opposed to *mandatory* and is only a little stronger than *precatory,* q.v.: "Statutes that regulate and prescribe the time in which public officers shall perform specified duties are generally regarded as *directory* only."

In the following sentence, *directional* (= of or relating to, or indicating, spatial direction) is wrongly used for *directory:* "The sentence is a *directional* [read *directory*] provision indicating when and how she is to receive the payments." *Coker v. Coker,* 650 S.W.2d 391, 395 (Tex. 1983) (Spears, J., dissenting).

directress; directrix. See SEXISM (C).

dirt lawyer is a jocular, self-effacing dysphemism in AmE for a real-estate lawyer.

disability. A. And *liability; inability.* These words, which overlap only slightly but are sometimes confounded, are best sharply distinguished. *Disability* = (1) the lack of ability to perform some function; or (2) incapacity in the eyes of the law. *Liability* = (1) probability; (2) a pecuniary obligation; (3) a drawback; or (4) a duty or burden <liability for military service>. *Inability* = the lack of power or means.

B. And *disablement.* *Disablement* = (1) the action of crippling or incapacitating; or (2) the imposition of a legal disability. Here sense (1) applies: "Under a credit insurance policy the beneficiary is the creditor and, upon the death or *disablement* of the insured, the benefits or proceeds of the policy automatically accrue to the creditor for the purpose of discharging the debtor's financial obligations."

disabling statute (= a statute that curbs or limits certain rights) is an antonym of *enabling statute* only in the older sense of the latter phrase—i.e., a statute that grants certain rights. See **enabling statute.**

disadvantage, v.t., appears regularly in legal writing, but generally only the past participial form *disadvantaged* appears in lay writing, usu. functioning as an adjective <disadvantaged student>. Following are examples of typical legal usage: "The statute *disadvantages* those who would benefit from laws barring racial, religious, or ancestral discrimination."/ "The state may no more *disadvantage* any particular group by making it more difficult to enact legislation in its behalf than it may dilute a person's vote."

disaffirmation; disaffirmance. For the word meaning "repudiation," the distinction drawn at *affirmance* (q.v.) would recommend the form *disaffirmation.* The *COD* recommends *-tion,* but *W10* records only *-ance,* a common form in AmE. Try as we might for consistency, we are unlikely to achieve it here: *disaffirmation* is better, but *disaffirmance* cannot be strongly criticized. E.g., "[A] guarantor for a minor remains bound although the minor principal may be discharged by *disaffirmance.*" *Gervis v. Knapp,* 43 N.Y.S.2d 849, 850 (N.Y. Sup. Ct. 1943)./ "[T]he defense of fraud at law was ineffective in cases where there was nothing to return unless a rescission or *disaffirmance* of the contract was established." William F. Walsh, *A Treatise on Equity* 497–98 (1930).

disappoint (of) (in). *Disappoint* is used in legal contexts in a sense rare in lay contexts, namely, "to deprive; to frustrate in one's expectations." E.g., "A court of equity will then sequester the benefits intended for the electing beneficiary, to secure compensation to those persons whom his election *disappoints.*"/ "The courts will not *disappoint* the interest of those for whose benefit the party is called upon to exercise the power."

Usually the term *disappointed* refers to heirs who take neither an intestate share of an estate nor a share by will. E.g., "Under such circumstances, the gift to the class is implied, and the testator could not have intended the objects of the power to be *disappointed* of his bounty by the failure of the donee to exercise such power in their favor." To be *disappointed in* a thing, as opposed to *of* it, is to have received or attained it but to consider it as not measuring up to one's expectations.

Often *disappointed* is used as a past-participial adjective: "He is known in the law as a *disappointed* legatee, and the doctrine of acceleration of remainders should be adopted at the expense of *disappointed* legatees."

disapprobation is an especially FORMAL WORD meaning "disapproval." It is perhaps allowable in weighty contexts: "On the opening of the cause, Lord Kenyon expressed his *disapprobation* of the action; but his lordship permitted the cause to proceed." (Eng.) But in ordinary prose, this noun—like so many other BURIED VERBS ending in *-tion*—leads to topheaviness: "Employees may feel the need to sign the petition in order to curry favor with or avoid *disapprobation* [read *disapproval*] by company officials." See **approbation.**

disapprove, like *approve,* q.v., may be transitive as well as intransitive—and is used transitively far more often in legal than in nonlegal writing—e.g.: "We *disapprove* the dicta in that case."/ "Congress not only retained the legislative veto but expanded it to allow either house to *disapprove* any portion of a rule the body concluded was a 'single separate rule of law.'" Barbara H. Craig, *Chadha: The Story of an Epic Constitutional Struggle* 69 (1988).

disassemble. See **dissemble.**

disassociate; dissociate. Though common, *disassociate* is inferior to *dissociate,* of which it is a NEEDLESS VARIANT. E.g., "This gives the law a twist [that] *disassociates* [read *dissociates*] it from morality and, I think, to some extent from sound sense." Patrick Devlin, *The Enforcement of Morals* 24 (1968). Eleven years after writing that sentence, Lord Devlin did better: "In the course of their work judges quite often *dissociate* themselves from the law." Patrick Devlin, *The Judge* 4 (1979). See **dissociate.**

disastrous is so spelled—not *disasterous,* a fairly common misspelling.

disbar. See **bar.**

disbark. See **disembark.**

disbarment; disbarring. Both mean "the action of expelling a lawyer from the bar." *Disbarment* is the more common noun in AmE. E.g., "The effect of a *disbarment* is the utter extinction of professional character."/ "But it would stretch fairness to impose a prison term when the usual penalty, according to experts in legal ethics, is *disbarment.*" Dorothy J. Samuels, *Behind Mel Miller's Downfall,* N.Y. Times, 21 Dec. 1991, at 14.

In BrE, the gerund in *-ing* is common: "*Disbarring* may be imposed by the benchers as the ultimate punishment on a barrister guilty of conduct unbecoming the profession." (Eng.) See **bar.**

disbelief; unbelief; nonbelief; misbelief. *Disbelief* is the mental rejection of something after considering its plausibility; it results from active, conscious decision. *Unbelief* denotes the state of doubt, but of not having made up one's mind. *Nonbelief* is a NEEDLESS VARIANT of *unbelief.* "*Nonbelief* [read *Unbelief*] of the prosecutor in the guilt of the person charged with crime is evidence of want of probable cause for the prosecution." A *misbelief* is an erroneous or false belief.

disburse; disperse. *Disburse* is used only in reference to distribution of money <the directors disbursed dividends to the stockholders>. *Disperse* is used in reference to distribution of all other things, such as crowds or diseases.

disc. See **disk.**

discernible; discernable. The former spelling is preferred. See -ABLE (B).

discharge = (1) to pay a debt or satisfy some other obligation <Jones discharged all the debts>; (2) to release (a bankrupt) from monetary obligations, upon adjudication of bankruptcy <Jones was discharged from those debts>; (3) to dismiss (a case) <case discharged>; (4) to cancel the original provisional force of an injunction or other court order <the T.R.O. was then discharged>; (5) to free (a prisoner) from confinement <the offender was granted a conditional discharge>; (6) to relieve (a jury) of further responsibilities in considering a case <at 6:00 p.m. that Friday, the jury was discharged>; or (7) to fire (an employee) <employers may hire and discharge when they please>. In sum, *discharge* is a CHAMELEON-HUED WORD.

disciplinary; disciplinatory. *Disciplinary* = (1) related to discipline; or (2) carrying out punishment. In the following sentence, sense (2) applies: "The special master considered the company's disparate enforcement of its no-solicitation policy to be mitigated by the legality of the warning, apology, mistake, or failure to result in *disciplinary* action." *Disciplinatory* is a NEEDLESS VARIANT.

disclaim. See **declaim.**

disclaimer. See -ER (B).

disclose; expose. There are important differences. *Disclose* = to reveal (any factual matter). *Expose* = (1) to lay bare or unmask (something bad); or (2) to place in a perilous condition.

disclosee (= one to whom information is disclosed) is a NEOLOGISM unrecorded in most English-language dictionaries—e.g.: "Being duly sworn [*disclosee*] pursuant to interposition states . . . ." 2 Roger M. Milgrim, *Milgrim on Trade Secrets* § 7.06[1], at 7-105 (1988) (bracketed interpolation in original). See -EE.

disclosural, a newly formed adjective corresponding to the noun *disclosure,* is a potentially useful NEOLOGISM—e.g.: Bridget Mast, *Disclosural Privacy in Florida—Drawing the Line After* Doe v. State, 22 Stetson L. Rev. 283 (1992).

discomfit(ure). *Discomfit* (= to frustrate, disconcert) is best used only as a verb. The preferred noun is *discomfiture.* Ill-trained writers use phrases such as *much to his discomfit,* in which either *discomfort* or *discomfiture* is intended.

Discomforture is incorrect for either *discomfort* or *discomfiture*—e.g.: "How does a court determine whether a defendant is in fact maintaining a nuisance on his property to the *discomforture* [read *discomfort* or, more likely, *discomfiture*] of his neighbors?" C. Gordon Post, *An Introduction to the Law* 105 (1963).

discomfort. See **discomfit(ure).**

discommend is the opposite of *recommend,* not of *commend.*

disconcertion; disconcertment. The preferred noun corresponding to the verb *to disconcert* is *disconcertion.*

discontinuation; discontinuance; discontinuity. See **continuance.**

discover, v.t., is generally obsolete in the sense "to uncover, reveal," except in legal JARGON—e.g.: "This rule does not protect a defendant from *discovering* facts indicating moral turpitude on his part unless they amount to a punishable offense . . . ." Eugene A. Jones, *Manual of Equity Pleading and Practice* 23 (1916). The verb now generally means "to find, detect." See **discovery.**

For the use in which judges are said to "discover" the common law, see **declare.**

discoverable, in American law, means "subject to pretrial discovery" <discoverable documents of the corporation>. This sense goes beyond the general meaning of "ascertainable."

discovert is not an opposite of *covert* as ordinarily used—*overt* is. *Discovert* means "unmarried, whether widowed, divorced, or never having married," or, more technically, "not subject to the disabilities of coverture." Acceptable in historical contexts, the word is now obsolete because there are no "disabilities of coverture" (i.e., legal disabilities resulting from a woman's being married). See **covert.**

discovery, as a term of legal JARGON, means "disclosure by a party to an action, at the other party's instance, of facts or documents relevant to the lawsuit." E.g., "The English invented *discovery* while casting about for a substitute for torture for parties unwilling to reveal facts at issue in a lawsuit. Their idea was a good one; but the way it is carried out causes the litigants less torment only in the sense that their agony is mental, not physical." William B. Spawn (ABA president), in a speech before the North Carolina State Bar in 1977 (as quoted in Joseph C. Goulden, *The Million Dollar Lawyers* 286 n. (1978)). See **discover.**

discovery abuse is a broad term that covers many disparate things: "Thus it is useful to subdivide 'abuse' into 'misuse' and 'overuse.' What is referred to as 'misuse' would include not only direct violation of the rules, as by failing to respond to a discovery request within the stated time limit, but also more subtle attempts to harass or obstruct an opponent as by giving obviously inadequate answers or by requesting information that clearly is outside the scope of discovery." Charles A. Wright, *The Law of Federal Courts* 542 (4th ed. 1983).

"Discovery overuse," by contrast, refers to "asking for more discovery than is necessary or appropriate to the particular case." *Id.* And the term *overuse* "can be subdivided into problems of 'depth' and of 'breadth,' with 'depth' referring to discovery that may be relevant but is simply excessive and 'breadth' referring to discovery requests that go into matters too far removed from the case." *Id.*

discrete; discreet. The former means "separate, distinct," the latter "cautious, judicious." *Discreet* is most commonly used in reference to speaking or writing. The usual error is to misuse *discreet,* the more common term in nonlegal language, for *discrete*—e.g.: "Although Texas has moved away from a system of submitting *discreet* [read *discrete*] fact questions on each element of a claim or defense, Texas still employs broad form issues in virtually every case and does not allow the jury to be informed of the effect of its answers . . . ." Frank Cicero, Jr. & Roger L. Taylor, *Verdict Strategy,* 17 Litigation 41, 42 (Summer 1991).

In the following quotations, though, the opposite blunder is committed: "Consider again Pound, ante, p. 64, Hierarchy of Sources and Forms in Law. *Compare* Keeton's discussion of overruling precedents—rules vis-à-vis principles—ante, pp. 839–40, *with* Pound. Is the average opinion writer this *discrete* [read *discreet*]?"/ "Mr. Bradshaw said almost everything the group did locally was *discrete* [read *discreet*]." Peter Applebome, *Bloody Sunday's Roots in Deep Religious Soil,* N.Y. Times, 2 March 1993, at A8.

Discrete is sometimes used meaninglessly: "The prosecution apparently made the strikes simply in an effort to procure, from among those summoned and not disqualified, a jury that, under the *discrete* [read *peculiar?*] facts of this particular case, would be least likely to be partial to

Leslie." In the following sentence, it is correctly used: "The petitioner made no suggestion below that any *discrete* portion of the work product from the administrative proceedings was work that was both useful and of a type ordinarily necessary to advance the civil-rights litigation to the stage it reached before settlement."

discretion is traditionally a mass noun, not a COUNT NOUN. Thus references to "the exercise of *a* sound discretion" and to a court's having "*a* large discretion" are unidiomatic. See 6 James W. Moore et al., *Moore's Federal Practice* ¶ 54.70[5], at 54-344, 54-348 (2d ed. 1988) (using the phrases quoted).

discriminant. See **discriminatory.**

discriminate, v.i., cannot properly be used transitively, as here: "Blacks are *discriminated* [read *discriminated against*] in that city." The same problem crops up in the past-participial adjective—e.g.: "[T]he Secretary's action bars a private suit by the *discriminated employee* [read *employee who has been discriminated against*]." *Marshall v. Sun Oil Co.,* 605 F.2d 1331, 1338 n.8 (5th Cir. 1979).

discriminated, adj. See **discriminate.**

discriminatee = a person unlawfully discriminated against. None of the dictionaries record this term, but it is increasingly common in American legal writing. E.g., "[I]t appears advisable to make disposition of that portion of the Board's order which directs the company and the Unions 'jointly and severally to make the *discriminatees* whole for any loss of pay they may have suffered by reason of the discrimination against them . . . .'" *Progressive Mine Workers v. N.L.R.B.,* 187 F.2d 298, 306 (7th Cir. 1951)./ "In the instant case, back seniority . . . is just as necessary to make *discriminatees* 'whole' under Title VI." *Guardians Ass'n v. Civil Serv. Comm'n,* 466 F. Supp. 1273, 1287 (S.D.N.Y. 1979)./ "The NLRB routinely awards backpay to restore *discriminatees* to the economic position they would have enjoyed absent the unfair labor practice." *Warehouse & Office Workers' Union v. N.L.R.B.,* 795 F.2d 705, 718 (9th Cir. 1986). See -EE.

discriminating. See **discriminatory.**

discrimination has not traditionally been considered a COUNT NOUN. Thus one should not write *discriminations* for *discriminatory practices* or *instances of discrimination.* See PLURALS (B).

discriminatory; discriminative; discriminating; discriminant. Of these, only *discriminative* is ambiguous, it being a NEEDLESS VARIANT of both *discriminatory* (= applying discrimination in treatment, esp. on racial or ethnic grounds) and *discriminating* (= keen, discerning, judicious). *Discriminant* is a NEEDLESS VARIANT of *discriminating.*

Because *discriminatory* has extremely negative connotations, and *discriminating* quite positive connotations, the noun *discrimination* suffers from a split personality, sometimes brought to the surface in judicial writing: "The majority's fallacy lies in using the word *discrimination* as a synonym for *discrimination on the basis of race.* Such usage may suffice in common parlance, but for purposes of analyzing the proof in a [42 U.S.C.] § 1981 suit it is, if I may not be misunderstood in so expressing it, too *undiscriminating.*" *Carter v. Duncan-Huggins, Ltd.,* 727 F.2d 1225, 1247 (D.C. Cir. 1984) (Scalia, J., dissenting).

discussible is poor when used as a pseudo-softener for *debatable,* as here: "It is *discussible* [read *debatable*] whether such a policy was wise."

disease of the mind. See **mental illness.**

disembark is generally considered preferable to *debark* or *disbark.*

disenable is a NEEDLESS VARIANT of *disable.* See **disabling statute.**

disenact, which the *OED* notes as being "rare," is an unnecessary word, inasmuch as we have *repeal, revoke, set aside, abolish,* and various other more specific words.

disenfranchise. See **disfranchise.**

disentail = to bar the entail (on an estate) and convert (the estate) into a fee simple. See **entail.**

disenthrone. See **dethrone.**

disentitle takes the preposition *to,* not *from.* E.g., "At this third intermediate stage, the delay will not be a repudiation but will *disentitle* the responsible person *from* [read *to*] specific performance." (Eng.)/ "Although the husband and the wife agreed that their financial position was such that only a nominal order could be made against the husband, they wished to have determined the issue whether the wife's conduct *disentitled* her *to* an order for maintenance." (Eng.)

disfranchise; disenfranchise. Though the latter is increasingly common, the former remains the preferred form of this word, meaning "to deprive of the right to exercise a franchise or privilege, esp. to vote." E.g., "In a memorandum opinion, the district court found that . . . there had not been a showing that provisions *disenfranchising* [read *disfranchising*] those convicted of crimes were based upon the racism present at the constitutional convention."/ "In *Toney,* the registrar of the same parish misapplied Louisiana election statutes in purging voter lists, resulting in the *disenfranchisement* [read *disfranchisement*] of many more blacks than whites."/ "A pathbreaking extension of effective legal personhood into the ranks of hitherto *disfranchised* minors?" Neil MacCormick, *With Due Respect,* TLS, 22 Jan. 1993, at 3.

disfunctional. See **dysfunctional.**

dishabille /*dis-ə-**beel***/ is so spelled.

disherison; disinherison. *Disherison* (= [1] the act of disinheriting, [2] the state of being disinherited), labeled obsolete in *Black's,* still enjoys limited currency. It ought to be treated as a NEEDLESS VARIANT of *disinheritance,* which is a simpler word that far more readers and listeners will understand—e.g.: *"Disherison* [read *Disinheritance*] of a child invites contest of the will. When a child is disinherited a trial judge is likely to submit the will to a jury on an issue of mental capacity, fraud, or undue influence." John Ritchie et al., *Decedents' Estates and Trusts* 142 (1971)./ "Posthumous avarice leading to *disherison* [read *disinheritance*] is bad; living greediness is bad too."

Disinherison, a term generally used in civil law, is likewise a NEEDLESS VARIANT in common-law contexts—e.g.: "The power of *disinherison* [read *disinheritance*] he [Bracton] explains here in the same way as in the case of the fee simple . . . ." A.W.B. Simpson, *An Introduction to the History of the Land Law* 62 (1961).

disherit; disheritance; disheritor. These are NEEDLESS VARIANTS of *disinherit, disinheritance,* and *disinheritor.* E.g., "She was the sister who had been *disherited* [read *disinherited*] by her mother." *Stonesifer v. Swanson,* 146 F.2d 671, 673 (7th Cir. 1945)./ "[T]here is also an almost equally strong presumption against virtual *disheritance* [read *disinheritance*] of testatrix'[s] sole distributee . . . ." *In re Vetroock's Will,* 230 N.Y.S.2d 485, 500 (N.Y. Surr. Ct. 1962).

disincentive; nonincentive. The former provides an incentive not to do something; the latter is no incentive at all.

disinformation; misinformation. These words are not synonyms. *Disinformation* = false information deliberately created and spread <Soviet disinformation of the 1960s>. *Misinformation* = incorrect information.

disinherison. See **disherison.**

disinherit. See **disherit.**

disinheritance. See **disherison** & **disherit.**

disintegrative; disintegratory. The latter is a NEEDLESS VARIANT.

disinterest(ed); uninterest(ed). *Disinterest* is impartiality or freedom from bias or chance of financial benefit—e.g.: "An inherent qualification for a quasi-judicial decision-maker is *disinterest* in the result." *Central Life Ins. Co. v. Aetna Casualty & Sur. Co.,* 466 N.W. 2d 257, 261 (Iowa 1991). Thus, *disinterested* means "impartial."

Uninterest (recorded fr. 1952) means "lack of concern or attention" and *uninterested* "having no concern or care (about something)." E.g., "If Orenstein believed that Erb knew or would surely find out about paragraph 34, it was not dishonest or opportunistic to fail to flag that paragraph, . . . especially given the *uninterest* . . . that Erb fairly radiated." *Market Street Assocs. Ltd. v. Frey,* 941 F.2d 588, 598 (7th Cir. 1991).

Traditionally, though, the DIFFERENTIATION between these words was not as marked as it might have been: *disinterest* has, in addition to its primary meaning of impartiality, denoted "lack of concern or attention" (i.e., as a synonym of *uninterest*). Given the overlapping nouns, writers have found it difficult to keep the past participial adjectives entirely separate, and many have given up the fight to preserve the distinction between them.

Nevertheless, the distinction is still best recognized and followed, especially in the law, where the sense of *interest* that gives rise to *disinterested* (as in "interested party") still commonly appears. E.g., "Any other rule would make important questions of the title to real estate largely dependent upon the uncertain recollection and testimony of *interested* parties."/ "In each case 'due process of law' requires an evaluation based on a *disinterested* inquiry pursued in the spirit of science." (Frankfurter, J.) Because it is a virtue for judges to remain *disinterested,* we had better not forget what that word means: "The district court thus rejected the not totally *disinterested* testimony of the family members on the issue of fraudulent transfer."/ "No *disinterested* person reading the article can come to the conclusion that it was printed in a spirit of fair criticism or designed for the public good."

Disinterested is frequently misused for *uninterested*—e.g.: "Many people are *disinterested* [read *uninterested*] in politics and do not vote." Charles A. Wright et al., *Federal Practice and Procedure* § 3611, at 511 (1984)./ "The son of a lawyer who practiced here, he grew up removed from politics, and today he remains totally *disinterested* [read *uninterested*] in politics—to the point of never voting."

disinvestment; divestment. Defined as "consumption of capital," in *W9, disinvestment* has come to mean "the withdrawal of investments, esp. for political reasons" (as acknowledged in *W10*). E.g., "The arguments opposing *disinvestment* [from South Africa] fall into two categories."/ "About half of the 200 American companies in Kenya have *disinvested* and unemployment is growing." Andrew Hogg, *Frightened Moi Vows He Will Cull Democratic "Rats,"* Sunday Times, 8 July 1990, at 1-20. *Divestment* is also used in this sense. See **divest(it)ure.**

disjoinder (= the undoing of the joinder of [parties, actions, etc.]) is a useful NEOLOGISM omitted from most legal and nonlegal dictionaries. E.g., "[T]he question of *disjoinder* is not embraced in the present procedure." *People v. Nickel,* 69 N.Y.S.2d 791, 794 (King's County Ct. 1947)./ "Authority for this *disjoinder* of the 'force, violence, or fear' and the 'color of official right' phrases of § 1951(b)(2) was said to be found in [several cases cited]." *U.S. v. Cerilli,* 603 F.2d 415, 428 (3d Cir. 1979) (Aldisert, J., dissenting). See **joinder.** Cf. **misjoinder.**

disk; disc. *Disk* is the more usual spelling in all but three specific meanings. *Disc* is the spelling used for the senses (1) "a phonograph record"; (2) "a videodisc"; and (3) "a tool making up part of a plow." Otherwise, *disk* is the preferred spelling for general reference to thin circular objects, intervertebral disks, celestial bodies, and computer disks.

dismissal; dismission. The much older word *dismission* (1547) has given way almost completely to the upstart *dismissal* (1806), considered a mere variant less than a century ago. Today, *dismission* is, except in some highly specialized contexts, an obsolete and NEEDLESS VARIANT.

dismissible. So spelled. See -ABLE (A).

dismission. See **dismissal.**

disorderly conduct is a vague term embracing an array of petty violations of public decency and order—from the paid-for conduct at a disorderly house (a EUPHEMISM for *brothel*) to fomenting political division—e.g.: "If opposition to the national government should arise from the *disorderly conduct* of refractory or seditious individuals." *The Federalist* No. 16, at 117 (Alexander Hamilton) (Clinton Rossiter ed., 1961).

The Constitution contains a variant phrase, *disorderly behavior:* "Each House may determine the Rules of its Proceedings, punish its Members for *disorderly Behavior,* and with the Concurrence of two thirds, expel a Member." U.S. Const. art. I, § 5.

disorderly house. See **bawdy house.**

disorganized; unorganized. The former means "in confusion or disarray; broken up"; the latter means "not having been organized" merely in the negative, but not in the pejorative, sense.

disorient(ate). The longer form is a NEEDLESS VARIANT of the shorter—e.g.: "But people elect not to answer questions for many reasons, starting with the possibility that they are *disorientated* [read *disoriented*] by the experience of being arrested and accused of serious crime of which they are innocent, and simply do not know how to respond." David Rose, *To Be Silent Will Imply Guilt,* Observer Sunday, 15 Dec. 1991, at 16. See **orient.**

disparaging (= slighting, insulting) for *disconcerting* or *discouraging* is a MALAPROPISM. E.g., "The plight of the Mexican national in the United States has been *disparaging* [read *discouraging*]." See MALAPROPISMS.

dispatch; despatch. The former spelling is preferred in both AmE and BrE.

dispatent. King's Counsel or Queen's Counsel are appointed to that rank by a so-called *patent.* To be stripped of that rank is, in BrE, to be *dispatented*—e.g.: "He practised for a while in London, but in 1929 he had himself disbarred in England and Ireland, and *dispatented.*" R.E. Megarry, *Miscellany-at-Law* 14 (1955). In a footnote, Megarry adds: "The term 'desilked' has mercifully yet to be used . . . ." *Id.* See **silk.**

dispel. So spelled—not *dispell.*

disperse. See **disburse.**

dispiteous. See **despiteous.**

dispone is a term from Scots law meaning "to convey formally or in legal form." From the verb are derived the terms *disponer* (= grantor), *disponee* (= grantee), and *disponible* (= capable of being assigned). E.g., "Such *disponer* shall, nevertheless, during the period of the minority of such minor, be liable to be taxed in respect of the sums so payable as if such disposition had not been made." (Scot.)/ "It is implicit in the ordinance that the husband and no one else may dispose of the wife's income; the husband therefore is the only possible *disponer.*" (Scot.)

disport. See **deport.**

disposal; disposition. Both mean generally "a getting rid of," but *disposal* has more often to do with trash or inconsequential items, whereas *disposition* is used of assets given to relatives and friends by will. *Disposition* connotes a preconceived plan and an orderly arrangement. *Disposal,* by contrast, bears derogatory connotations—more so in AmE than in BrE.

dispose for *dispose of.* "In the past, pesticide wastes *disposed* [read *disposed of*] in the ground have contaminated groundwater used for drinking and irrigation."

disposition. See **disposal.**

dispositive; dispository. In BrE and AmE alike, *dispositive* may mean "conclusive, determinative." In this sense, the word is extremely useful to lawyers—e.g.: "The court's resolution of this case would be greatly simplified if it ruled only on either of these *dispositive* issues." *Dispository* is a NEEDLESS VARIANT—e.g.: "This negative type of evidence is not *dispository* [read *dispositive*] of the guilt issue . . . ." *Riley v. Sigler,* 437 F.2d 258, 260 (8th Cir. 1971).

In AmE and Scots law, *dispositive* is the usual word used in reference to testamentary plans, *dispository* again being a NEEDLESS VARIANT—e.g.: "The relevant *dispository* [read *dispositive*] provisions of the decedent's will gave two million dollars in real estate, securities or other property to the Hofheinz Family Trust No. 2 . . . ." *Hofheinz v. U.S.,* 511 F.2d 661, 662 (5th Cir. 1975). In England, neither word is used in this way.

dispository. See **dispositive.**

disproportionate; disproportional. See **proportionate.**

dispunishable (= not punishable) was a common legal term through the mid-19th century. Today, however, it is uncommon enough that most readers would consider it needlessly obscure.

dispute; disputation. These words should be differentiated. *Dispute* = controversy <goods in dispute>, whereas *disputation* = formal argument or debate.

disqualified; unqualified. These words have quite different senses. *Unqualified* = not meeting the requirements. *Disqualified* = disabled; debarred. An *unqualified* judge should not be a judge. A *disqualified* judge must withdraw from hearing a case when one of the parties is, for example, a close relative.

disqualify. See **recuse.**

disquiet is used in law in the sense of disturbing a person's possession of property. E.g., "If the buyer is *disquieted* in his possession, he may suspend the payment of his price until the seller has restored him to quiet possession." See **quiet.**

disrobe, which ordinarily means "to undress," should not be used in the sense "to remove a judge from the bench"—unless jocularity is clearly intended. In the following example, one cannot say with confidence that humor is intended: "But as of July 1968, no attorneys have been disbarred, no judges *disrobed* and none of the 'excessive' fees dislodged." Murray T. Bloom, *The Trouble with Lawyers* 323 (1970).

dissatisfied; unsatisfied. Some DIFFERENTIATION exists between these words. To be *unsatisfied* is to be less than completely satisfied, whereas to be *dissatisfied* is to be positively bothered by the lack of satisfaction. In law, when one is in arrears, one's debts remain *unsatisfied.*

disseise; disseize. The preferred form of this legal word, meaning "to dispossess wrongfully," is *disseise.* See **seise.**

disseisor; disseisee. These are the correlative terms for the parties involved in disseisin (= dispossession of a person of estates). E.g., "The *disseisee* of goods, as well as the *disseisee* of land, has a right in rem."/ "The dispossessed owner of land, as we have seen, could always recover possession by an action; though deprived of the res, he still had a right in rem. The *disseisor* acquired only a defeasible estate."/ "The equitable beneficiary of a restrictive covenant has rights even against wrongful possessors, or *disseisors,* of the servient land that they shall not act contrary to the terms of the restrictive agreement." See **seisin.**

disseize. See **disseise.**

dissemble; disassemble. The former means "to present a false appearance," the latter "to take apart."

dissent, n.**; dissension; dissention.** *Dissent* refers to a difference of opinion, whether among judges or others. *A dissent,* as opposed to *dissent* as an uncountable noun, refers to a dissenting judicial opinion—e.g.: "Justices Frankfurter and Roberts concurred in this *dissent.*" Samuel Bader, *Coerced Confessions and the Due Process Clause,* 15 Brook. L. Rev. 51, 62 (1948)./ "The *dissent* regards the interest in maintaining our nation's adherence to long-standing principles of international law as not compelling." *Finzer v. Barry,* 798 F.2d 1450, 1464 (D.C. Cir. 1986).

Dissension (the *-sion* spelling is preferred) refers to contentious or partisan arguing. E.g., "The contract terms had already been substantially executed when the *dissension* arose among those jointly interested in the venture."

Dissention is a mistaken form of *dissension*—e.g.: "A sudden *dissention* [read *dissension*] among those who have gathered lawfully may proceed to violence without amounting to more than an affray . . . ." Rollin M. Perkins & Ronald N. Boyce, *Criminal Law* 484 (3d ed. 1982).

dissent, v.i., takes *from* or *against,* not *to* or *with.* E.g., "I must dissent *to* [read *from*] the majority's holding that appellant's detention and ensuing search and seizure were lawful."/ "Because of the waste of time, resources, and effort of the criminal justice system that will ensue, I must dissent *to* [read *from*] what the majority does in this cause."/ "Scalia . . . dissented *with* [read *from*] the court when it ruled that judges must instruct the jury to consider evidence favorable to the defendant when deciding whether to impose the death sentence." Kobayashi, *Mercy Is Not Always Dispensed Justly, Scalia Says,* Honolulu Advertiser, 8 Aug. 1989, at A-3.

The preposition *against* is idiomatic but relatively uncommon. E.g., "But three of Taney's Democratic colleagues violently dissented *against* their Chief's apparently aberrational veto of a state law in order to protect vested rights of a non-agrarian kind . . . ." Fred Rodell, *Nine Men* 126 (1955).

dissenter; dissentient, n. *Dissenter* is the standard term in AmE for "one who withholds assent, or does not approve or agree"; *dissentient* is the more usual form in BrE, because the term *dissenter* (usu. with an initial cap.) has a special religious and social meaning in British history ("i.e., one who dissents or refuses to conform—specif., from the 17th c. on—to the tenets and practices of the Church of England"). E.g., "Lewis J., one of the former *dissentients,* had become C.J." R.E. Megarry, *A Second Miscellany-at-Law* 140 (1973)./ "The real difference between the majority and the *dissentients* in *Maunsell v. Olins* was over the question whether there was an ambiguity." Rupert Cross, *Statutory Interpretation* 145 (1976).

dissenting; dissentient, adj.**; dissentious.** *Dissentient* is sometimes used in BrE where *dissenting* would ordinarily appear in AmE. E.g., "The agent was appointed to execute an instrument of transfer on a *dissentient* shareholder's behalf." (Eng.)/ "In the court of appeals the judge delivered a *dissentient* judgment in favor of the appellants." (Eng.) The word is not unknown in American legal writing: "Without retracting or in any way departing from our former *dissentient* views, I concur in the action taken by the majority on the instant appeal. . . ." *In re King's Estate,* 66 A.2d 68, 72 (Pa. 1949) (Jones, J., concurring). One ambiguity that may be caused by use of *dissentient* is that readers might interpret it as a derogatory word opposite to *sentient;* the true opposite of *sentient* (= feeling), however, is *insentient. Dissentious* = given to dissension; quarrelsome.

dissimilar takes the preposition *to* rather than *from.* E.g., "The facts in that case are wholly dissimilar *from* [read *to*] the facts in the case at bar." Here the preferable collocation is illustrated: "Those cases were decided under facts *dissimilar to* those existing in the present case." Cf. **disentitle.**

dissiminate is a fairly common misspelling of *disseminate.*

dissociate; disassociate. *Dissociate* is the preferred term; *disassociate* is a NEEDLESS VARIANT. *Dissociate* takes the preposition *from.* E.g., "*Disassociated with* [read *Dissociated from*] the subject thereof, whatever it may be, a title or a name composed of ordinary words cannot acquire the status of property, as all who speak or write have the inherent right to use any and all words in the English language."/ "Austin . . . answers that this is to *dissociate* sanction *from* command altogether, confusing sanction and motive." W.W.

Buckland, *Some Reflections on Jurisprudence* 89 (1945). See **disassociate.**

dissolution. See **marriage dissolution & divorce (B).**

distil(l). The spelling *distill* is preferred in AmE, *distil* in BrE.

distinct; distinctive. The first means "well defined, discernibly separate" <distinct speech>, and the second means "serving to distinguish, set off by appearance" <a distinctive red bow tie>. *Distinct* speech is well enunciated, whereas *distinctive* speech is idiosyncratically accented, different from that of surrounding speakers. *Distinctive* is sometimes misused for *distinguished* (= notable; famous).

distinguish can be used either transitively, in the sense "to note a difference" <that fact distinguished the first case from the second>, or intransitively, in the sense "to make a distinction" <the court distinguished between premeditated and spontaneous acts>.

In legal contexts, the transitive use appears frequently in the phrase *to distinguish a case,* meaning to provide reasons for deciding a case under consideration differently from a similar case cited as a possible precedent. E.g., "[A]n apparent precedent may be evaded by '*distinguishing*' the facts, which are never identical in any two cases. Distinguishing may either be genuine or strained." O. Hood Phillips, *A First Book of English Law* 124 (3d ed. 1955). Cf. **differentia.**

distrain, vb., = (1) to seize goods by a legal remedy known as "distress," which entitles a rightful possessor to recover personal property wrongfully taken; or (2) to force (a person, often a tenant), by the seizure and detention of personal property, to perform some duty (such as paying overdue rent). Today sense (2) is the more common one—e.g.: "In most states the landlord has the right . . . to seize and sell certain of the tenant's personal property in order to satisfy unpaid rent. This right exists either by virtue of the landlord's right to *distrain* for rent due or by virtue of the landlord's lien . . . ." Robert Kratovil, *Real Estate Law* 306 (1946)./ "Three days later he seized the furniture because he had heard that the plaintiff's landlord intended to *distrain* it for arrears of rent." G.H. Treitel, *The Law of Contract* 106 (8th ed. 1991). See **distraint.**

distrainor; distrainer. The *OED* states that *-or* is "a more technical form than *distrainer,* and correlative to *distrainee.*" Of course, *distrain* itself is a technical word; it may as well have a technical Latinate agent-noun suffix *(-or).* See -ER (A).

distraint; distress. In legal contexts, both mean either "the seizure of goods as security for the performance of a duty" or "the legal remedy authorizing such a seizure." *Distraint* would seem to be the better term, for it looks like the verb from which it derives (Fr. *distraindre,* fr. L. *distringere*) and does not, like *distress,* have an ordinary English meaning. But *distress* is the prevalent term for this sense. See **distrain.**

Though not widely accepted, a possible DIFFERENTIATION appears in one historian's use of *distress* for the legal remedy and *distraint* for the exercise of that remedy: "In practice the remedy of *distress* might not be so effective, for the tenants of the land might be poor men, unable to perform the service, and *distraint* to compel them to do so would be a waste of effort." A.W.B. Simpson, *An Introduction to the History of the Land Law* 50 (1961).

distress. See **distraint.**

distribute. See **descend.**

distributee. See **heir (C).**

distribute out is prolix for *distribute*—e.g.: "No income is *distributed out* [omit *out*] (or is deemed to be *distributed out* [omit *out*] under the DNI rules) to the residuary beneficiaries." See **out** & PARTICLES, UNNECESSARY.

For the difference between property *descending* and *being distributed,* see **descend.**

distribution. See **descent (B).**

divergence; divergency. The form *divergency* is a NEEDLESS VARIANT of *divergence.*

divers; diverse. These words have distinct meanings. Very simply, *divers* implies severalty, and *diverse* implies difference. *Divers* (= various, sundry) remains a part of the language in the U.S. only as a curiosity. Formerly it meant not only "various," but "several" as well: "[T]he rent was behind for *divers* years . . . ." *Sir Anthony Sturlyn v. Albany,* Cro. Eliz. 67, 78 Eng. Repr. 327 (Q.B. 1587). Today it is an ARCHAISM, and its only accepted meaning is "various," as in Frankfurter's phrase "divers judicially inappropriate and elusive determinants." *Baker v. Carr,* 369 U.S. 186, 268 (1962) (Frankfurter, J., dissenting). Other modern examples follow: "Defendant is possessed of large means and is engaged in the business of a banker in said village of Howard Lake, at Dassel, Minnesota, and at *divers* other places."/ "Defendants inserted the said notice as an advertisement in *divers* local and other newspapers." (Eng.)/ "Two months later he was indicted in Florida for conspiring there and in *divers* other districts."

Diverse means "markedly different; unlike." It takes the preposition *from.* E.g., "Each case incorporated state-law tort claims against manufacturers of protective respiratory equipment, all of whose citizenship was *diverse* from that of the plaintiff."

Frequently it is used in AmE, without a preposition, to denote a difference in citizenship that gives rise to federal jurisdiction: "We granted the motion because the record otherwise evidences a substantial likelihood of *diverse* citizenship." See **diversity.**

diversity. As a noun in American legal writing, *diversity* often appears as a shorthand form of the phrase *diversity of citizenship*—e.g.: "Gearench . . . had no burden to prove *diversity* between the original parties or between it and its third-party defendants . . . ." *Molett v. Penrod Drilling Co.,* 872 F.2d 1221, 1228 (5th Cir. 1989).

As an adjective in American legal writing, *diversity* is frequently used as a shortened form of the PHRASAL ADJECTIVE *diversity-jurisdiction*—e.g.: "In a *diversity* case in this circuit, federal courts apply a federal rather than a state standard."

divest(it)ure; divestment. The standard noun corresponding to the verb *to divest* is *divestiture.* E.g., "It is agreed that the history and language of the laws for control of monopolization properly permit the application by the courts of orders requiring *divestiture* of properties of an existing monopolist in order to prevent the continuance of the evil." *Divesture* is an obsolete variant.

The other variant, *divestment,* not at all uncommon, might seem to be a NEEDLESS VARIANT; yet it appears in a number of SET PHRASES in property law, such as *vested interest subject to divestment.* E.g., "Many courts hold that the beneficiary takes a vested interest subject to *divestment* upon change of beneficiary in accordance with the provisions of the policy."/ "The registration of stock ownership on the books of the corporation in appropriate statutory language is sufficient to vest legal title, subject to *divestment* if the circumstances surrounding the transaction warrant it." See **disinvestment.**

dividable. See **divisible.**

dividend; interest. In corporate law, these terms signal an important distinction. *Interest* (= a charge one pays for getting a loan, usu. measured as a percentage of principal) is payable out of the company's assets generally. But a *dividend* (= a share of profits distributed to a shareholder) is a voluntary distribution by the company and does not become a debt until after the company has declared it. Dividends can be declared only out of the assets legally available—especially the company's earnings or profits, but not its general assets.

divide up. See PARTICLES, UNNECESSARY.

divisibility. See **devisability.**

divisible; dividable. The latter is a NEEDLESS VARIANT.

divisional court. For an explanation of the divisional courts of the (English) High Court, see **high court.**

divisor. See **deviser.**

divorce. A. And *annulment.* A *divorce* recognizes the existence of a valid marriage, whereas an *annulment* treats the marriage as if it had never existed. Even so, in most jurisdictions the "nonexistence" of the marriage is not considered absolute: any children produced by such a void or voidable marriage are traditionally considered legitimate.

B. And *dissolution of marriage.* In the 1970s, the word *divorce* was struck from many statutes and replaced by the EUPHEMISM *dissolution of marriage* or *marriage dissolution.* See **marriage dissolution.**

C. Idiom. One gets a divorce from a *spouse,* not from a *marriage*—e.g.: "Another suit . . . commenced . . . by the defendant for a *divorce from a marriage with the plaintiff* [read *divorce from the plaintiff*] . . . was . . . removed to this court." *Sharon v. Hill,* 26 F. 337, 338 (C.C.D. Cal. 1885).

D. *No-fault divorce.* See **no-fault divorce.**

E. *Divorce a mensa et thoro.* See ***a mensa et thoro.***

divorcement is now obsolete for *divorce* in the sense "the dissolution of the marriage tie," although it persisted in this sense through the early 20th century. E.g., "[I]n the event of the death or *divorcement* of the wife before the decease of the husband, he shall have the right to designate another beneficiary." Mo. Rev. St. § 7895 (1906). David O. Selznick directed Katharine Hepburn in the 1932 film "A Bill of Divorcement."

Divorcement survives in the general figurative

sense "the severance or complete separation of any close relation" <the divorcement of church and state in the U.S.>.

divulgence; divulgation; divulgement. Even though the latter two date from the early 17th century, *divulgence,* which dates from the mid-19th century, is now the preferred noun corresponding to the verb *to divulge.*

do. See **as (B)** & ANTICIPATORY REFERENCE (A).

dock, in British legal writing, means "the enclosure in a criminal court in which the prisoner is placed during trial"—e.g.: "Before he died, the little doctor at least had the comfort of knowing that Ethel Le Neve had left the dock a free woman." Stanley Jackson, *The Life and Cases of Mr. Justice Humphreys* 85 (n.d. [1951])./ "Even where the old rule that a man is to be presumed innocent till proved guilty has not been abrogated by statutes placing on the defence the burden of proving innocence, it may be subtly undermined by the terms used to refer to the man in the *dock*—not 'Mr Smith,' but 'Smith' or 'the accused.'" Alan Harding, *A Social History of English Law* 419 (1966). See **dock brief.**

American writers sometimes mangle the set phrase *in the dock*—in the following example with a MALAPROPISM: "For the judiciary, then, to say to the sovereign that only judges know what the law is, is one thing. . . . For the judiciary to say this to a man *in the docket* [read *in the dock*] or to a woman sued in tort is quite another." Mary J. Morrison, *Excursions into the Nature of Legal Language,* 37 Clev. State L. Rev. 271, 285–86 (1989).

dock brief; docker. A *dock brief,* in former English practice, was a brief handed in court directly to a barrister selected from among those present by an indigent criminal defendant in the dock (instead of through the agency of a solicitor), the effect of which was that the barrister then represented the defendant, who was known as a *docker.* See **dock.**

docket, in AmE, means "a schedule of cases pending." In BrE, it means "a register of judgments issued by the court."

Docket may be used as a verb in both BrE and AmE. E.g., "The case was *docketed* and tried shortly thereafter."/ "Thereafter he has either 60 or 90 days in which to *docket* the case with the Supreme Court . . . ." Charles A. Wright, *The Law of Federal Courts* 755 (4th ed. 1983). See **calendar & cause-list.**

dockominium, a PORTMANTEAU WORD made from combining *boat dock* with *condominium,* refers to an idea originated in the early 1980s of selling boat slips, as opposed to renting them. E.g., "Such projects, known informally as '*dockominiums,*' have become very popular in many waterfront communities throughout the metropolitan area, and the developers of many projects are finding more than they expected are being lived in year-round." Anthony DePalma, *Styling Vacation Homes for All Seasons,* N.Y. Times, § 8, at 1./ "The recreational boating system may well be headed toward a system of individual ownership of slip spaces. Just as rental apartments can be converted for sale as condominiums, rental slip spaces can be converted for sale as *dockominiums.*" Mark Cheung, *Dockominiums: An Expansion of Riparian Rights That Violates the Public Trust Doctrine,* 16 B.C. Envtl. Aff. L. Rev. 821, 821 (1989).

doctrinal; doctrinaire; doctrinary. The first is the neutral term, meaning "of or relating to a doctrine." E.g., "The *doctrinal* commentary upon *Taddeo* thus far has been unanimously favorable." *Doctrinaire* = dogmatic; slavishly, impractically adhering to dogma. *Doctrinary* is a NEEDLESS VARIANT of *doctrinaire.*

Doctrinaire is sometimes misspelled *doctrinnaire,* on the apparent analogy of *questionnaire*—e.g.: "[T]he Black–Douglas position was too *doctrinnaire* [read *doctrinaire*] . . . ." Maurice Kelman, *The Forked Path of Dissent,* 1985 Sup. Ct. Rev. 227, 257.

doctrine of original intent. See **original intent, doctrine of.**

document; instrument. These terms are similar in meaning, but *document* is slightly broader. *Document* refers to anything written, whereas *instrument* (q.v.) usually refers to a legal document with a specific legal import.

documentary; documental. The latter is a NEEDLESS VARIANT.

DOCUMENT DESIGN. Traditionally, lawyers have been relatively unconcerned with the look of their documents—even the lawyers who consider themselves stylists. This failing (and it is a serious one) did not have such horrible consequences in the days of typewriters, when the primary design choices were the width of the margins and the amount of underlining and capitals.

With the advent of word processing, document design has become much more important as writers are presented with all kinds of new printing options. Failing to use these options knowledgeably puts the writer at a disadvantage because most readers have become accustomed to well-designed documents. In short, it has become highly desirable to know something about typography and design.

In this space, of course, it is impossible to offer even the simplest primer on the subject. But a few points deserve mention:

A. A Readable Typeface. For text, a readable typeface probably means a serifed typeface, such as the one used throughout this text (New Century Schoolbook), as opposed to a sans-serif (*/san-**ser**-if/*) typeface made up of only straight lines. A serif is a short stroke that projects from the ends of the main strokes that make up a character.

> This is a serifed typeface: Trump Medieval.
> This is a sans-serif typeface: Optima.

Although sans-serif typefaces often work well in headings and the like, they can be difficult to read in text. Among the better serifed typefaces are Bookman, Caslon, Garamond, Palatino, and Times Roman. The one typeface to avoid at all costs still predominated in American legal writing in the mid-1990s: Courier. It is an eyesore.

B. White Space. Ample white space makes a page more inviting. The primary ways to create white space on the page are to use generous margins (for letters and briefs, for example, margins greater than one inch), to use headings and subheadings, and to enumerate items in separate paragraphs, subparagraphs, or bulleted lists.

C. Headings and Subheadings. Artfully employed, headings and subheadings make a document much easier to follow. Not only do they serve as navigational aids for readers; they also help writers organize thoughts more logically than they might otherwise. See PLAIN LANGUAGE (D).

D. Avoiding All Caps. See CAPITALIZATION (A).

E. Avoiding Underlines. Generally, italicizing is preferable to underlining, which was traditionally nothing more than a (poor) substitute for italics. The effect of underlining is to take up white space between lines and therefore to make the lines harder for readers to discern.

F. Listing. Enumerate items by breaking down lists into paragraphs and subparagraphs. Using a tabulated list allows the writer not only to display the points better, but also to improve the sentence structure. Ensure that the list falls at the end of the sentence—not at the beginning or in the middle. See ENUMERATIONS & PLAIN LANGUAGE (D).

G. Bullets. When you don't mean to imply that one thing in a list is any more important than another—that is, when you're not signaling that there is a rank order—and there is little likelihood that the list will need to be cited, you might use bullet dots. They draw the eye immediately to the salient points and thereby enhance readability. Examples appear throughout this book.

There is a notable difference, however, between how the bullets appear in this book and how they ought to appear in most documents. Although here the bullets fall at the left margin, they should generally be indented further than a paragraph indent. They are not indented here because a double-column format does not allow it.

H. Hanging Indents. In most texts, when you indent an item to be listed—whether it's a bulleted item or an entire paragraph—ensure that the second line of the item does not begin at the left margin. The second line of text should begin just below the first one, as here:

- The managing general partner must send notice to the bankrupt partner before the 180th day after receiving notice of the event that causes the bankruptcy.
- The bankrupt partner and the managing partner must agree on a fair market value for the sale of the interest.

I. A Ragged-Right Margin. Many readability specialists insist that unjustified right margins are more readable than justified ones. In letters, contracts, briefs, and the like, an unjustified right margin is often desirable.

J. Citations in Footnotes. Citations tend to clutter the text; you can easily minimize this cluttering by moving citations to footnotes (and avoiding footnotes for other purposes). See CITATION OF CASES (D).

K. Characters Per Line. Ideally, a line of type should accommodate 45 to 70 characters, but the "fine print" that characterizes so many legal documents often spans 150 characters to the line. In text of that kind, the reader's eye tends to get lost in mid-line or in moving from the end of one line to the beginning of the next. One way to improve a document with a large block of text—and, typically, small margins on each side—is to use a double-column format. That design can be extremely helpful, for example, in consumer contracts such as residential leases.

Doe, John; Richard Roe. The fictitious names *John Doe* and *Richard Roe* regularly appeared in actions of ejectment, q.v., at common law. *Doe* was the nominal plaintiff, who, by a FICTION was said to have entered land under a valid lease; *Roe* was said to have ejected *Doe,* and the lawsuit took the title *Doe v. Roe.* These fictional allegations disappeared upon the enactment of the Common

Law Procedure Act of 1852. Meanwhile, though, *John Doe*—which began as a LEGALISM—had become a POPULARIZED LEGAL TECHNICALITY.

Beyond actions of ejectment, and esp. in the U.S., *John Doe, Jane Doe, Richard Roe, Jane Roe,* and *Peter Poe* have come to identify a party to a lawsuit whose true name is either unknown or purposely shielded.

DOG FRENCH. See LAW FRENCH.

DOG LATIN. See LAW LATIN.

dogma. Pl. *dogmas, -mata.* The English plural is preferred—e.g.: "[A] number of scholastic and, as it seems to me, unprofitable *dogmas* have grown up [that] tend to obscure the real function of precedent in our legal reasoning." Carleton K. Allen, *Law in the Making* 268 (7th ed. 1964).

dolus (= fraud, deceit, or intentional aggression) is a civil-law term that appears frequently in discussions of general legal principles. E.g., "The typical delict required *dolus*—intentional aggression upon the personality or the substance of another." Roscoe Pound, *An Introduction to the Philosophy of Law* 78 (1922)./ "Liability for damage caused by intention *(dolus)* or negligence *(culpa)* was a general principle in Roman law, as it is in Scots law, Roman-Dutch law and French law." O. Hood Phillips, *A First Book of English Law* 226 (3d ed. 1955).

Domesday Book; Doomsday Book. The former is the accepted spelling in modern texts of the name for the great census or survey of England's landholdings, buildings, people, and livestock that was ordered by William the Conqueror and completed (except for several districts in the North) in 1086.

domesticate; domesticize. See **domiciliate.**

domicil(e). A. Spelling. *Domicile* is spelled both with and without the final *-e,* but the better and more common spelling is with it.

B. And *residence*. The two words are often "confused as synonymous." *In re Lemen,* 208 F. 80, 82 (N.D. Ohio 1912). They are not: "*Residence* comprehends no more than a fixed abode where one actually lives for the time being. It is distinguished from *domicile* in that *domicile* is the place where a person intends eventually to return and remain." *Catalanotto v. Palazzolo,* 259 N.Y.S.2d 473, 475 (1965).

More specifically, *domicile* means "the place with which a person has a settled connection for certain legal purposes, either because his home is there, or because that place is assigned to him by the law." *Restatement (First) of Conflict of Laws* § 9, at 17 (1934).

In England, *domicile* means "the country that a person treats as a permanent home and to which he or she has the closest legal attachment." See **citizenship.**

C. *Domicile of origin; domicile of choice; commercial domicile.* *Domicile of origin* = the domicile that is imposed by operation of law on every person at birth. *Domicile of choice* = a domicile chosen by a person having full age and capacity.

Commercial domicile, known also as *quasi-domicile,* "is in no sense true domicile. It is a legal concept used merely as a test of enemy character in time of war. It attaches to any person or firm voluntarily resident or carrying on business in enemy territory or even in enemy-occupied territory. . . . It has chiefly been used to determine the liability of property to seizure, and in a number of cases property itself has been said to possess a commercial domicile." R.H. Graveson, *Conflict of Laws* 221 (7th ed. 1974).

domiciliary is both adjective ("of or pertaining to domicile") and noun ("one belonging to a domicile").

domiciliate; domesticate; domesticize. *Domiciliate* = to establish a domicile or home. *Domesticate* = (1) to tame; or (2) to make a member of the household. Sense (1) here applies: "Before the jury retired, Colonial intimated that it intended to request the court to take judicial notice of the *domesticated* Oregon judgment." *Domesticize* is a NEEDLESS VARIANT of *domesticate.*

dominance; domination. *Dominance* = the fact or position of being dominant. *Domination* = the act of dominating; the exercise of ruling power.

dominant; servient. These terms are usually used in reference to *estates* or *tenements* in the law of easements. A *dominant* estate has the benefit of a servitude or easement over the *servient* estate.

domination. See **dominance.**

dominion is a FORMAL WORD used in legal contexts, esp. in AmE, to mean "control, possession." E.g., "Alford argues that the evidence presented as to that count failed to demonstrate that she had any *dominion* over any marijuana in the Western District of Texas."

dominium is the Roman-law term for absolute ownership. In some contexts it can be "particularly confusing, since in medieval times it is also the word for lordship." J.H. Baker, *An Introduction to English Legal History* 255 (3d ed. 1990).

donate, a BACK-FORMATION from *donation,* was formerly considered a vulgar equivalent of *give.* Today, however, it is a more FORMAL WORD than *give* that is frequently used of charitable bequests.

donatio mortis causa is an unjustified LATINISM for the slightly less Latinate *gift causa mortis.* Pl. *donationes mortis causa.* See ***causa mortis.***

donative; donatory. As an adjective, the latter is a NEEDLESS VARIANT. "This evidence is far short of the clear and convincing proof necessary to rebut the presumption of *donative* intent." For the nominal sense of *donatory,* see **donee.**

donator. See **donor.**

donee; donatory, n. *Donee* (= one to whom something is given) is the usual term. E.g., "Where the inconsistency lies in a gift of the same thing to two persons both *donees* will take some interest in that thing." Anthony R. Mellows, *The Law of Succession* 161 (3d ed. 1977). *Donatory* is a little-used equivalent. See **donor** & -EE.

donor; donator. The latter is a problematic word, meaning either (1) "donor" or (2) "donee." It should be avoided in favor of *donor* or *donee,* q.v. See **settlor.**

Doomsday Book. See **Domesday Book.**

doomster; doomsman. These are both variants of *deemster* or *dempster,* q.v.

dotal, adj., = (1) at common law, relating to a dower, q.v.; or (2) in civil law, relating to a dowry.

doth for *does,* though archaic and obsolete, still occasionally appears in judicial pronouncements, such as this, by the Mississippi Supreme Court in 1981: "[T]his Court having sufficiently examined and considered the same and being of the opinion that the same should be denied *doth* order that said motion be and the same is hereby denied." Order quoted in *Jones v. Thigpen,* 741 F.2d 805, 809 (5th Cir. 1984). Methinks, forsooth, that we should throw over this term, as well as the rest of the LEGALESE verily immortalized in that sentence.

The word is also used in orders of the English courts. E.g., "This court *doth* declare that there was a valid and binding contract." (Eng.) See -ETH.

double entendre originally referred to any verbal expression giving rise to more than one meaning. Now, however, it also connotes that one of those meanings is indecent or risqué.

double jeopardy; former jeopardy. These terms are not precisely the same. *Double jeopardy* is the fact of being prosecuted twice for substantially the same offense. A plea of *former jeopardy* informs the court that one has previously been prosecuted for the same offense. E.g., "This precise point was addressed in a case in which, the defendant having been indicted for perjury and having filed a plea of *former jeopardy,* it was held that subsequent falsehoods on the same trial under the same oath did not make new perjuries, but only exhibited additional ways in which the perjury was committed."/ "Conditioning an appeal of one offense on a coerced surrender of a valid plea of *former jeopardy* for another offense exacts a forfeiture in plain conflict with the constitutional bar against *double jeopardy.*"

DOUBLE NEGATIVES. See NEGATIVES (B).

DOUBLETS, TRIPLETS, AND SYNONYM-STRINGS. Amplification by synonym has long been a part of the English language, and especially a part of the language of the law. In the English Renaissance, this habit was a common figure of speech called *synonymia.* It is often supposed that the purpose of these paired or strung-along synonyms was etymological, that is, that writers in the Middle Ages and Renaissance would pair a French or Latinate term with an Anglo-Saxon approximation as a gloss on the foreign word. Thus we have, as survivals in legal language, *acknowledge and confess* (Old English and Old French), *act and deed* (Latin and Old English), and *goods and chattels* (Old English and Old French).

The philologist George Philip Krapp argued against this explanation. He saw the purpose of this mannerism as "rhetorical or oratorical rather than etymological." George P. Krapp, *Modern English: Its Growth and Present Use* 251 (1909). He pointed out that such doubling occurred abundantly in Old English, when no substantial foreign element existed in the language, and that it often occurs in later writings without regard for etymology. Although Krapp was undoubtedly correct to emphasize the rhetorical importance of doubling, he was wrong to assume that the figure did not take on a utilitarian significance as well in Middle and early Modern English. The purpose of doubling was dual: to give rhetorical weight and balance to the phrase, and to maximize the understanding of readers or listeners.

Still another explanation has emerged for the

particular fondness that lawyers have for this stylistic quirk. It is a cynical one: "This multiplication of useless expressions probably owed its origin to the want of knowledge of the true meaning and due application of each word, and a consequent apprehension, that if one word alone were used, a wrong one might be adopted and the right one omitted; and to this something must be added for carelessness and the general disposition of the profession to seek safety in verbosity rather than in discrimination of language." 1 Charles Davidson, *Precedents and Forms in Conveyancing* 67 (3d ed. 1860).

The phrases most obviously inspired by rhetorical concerns are alliterative. Rhetoricians call them reduplicative phrases—e.g.: *aid and abet; have and hold; part and parcel; trials and tribulations; rest, residue, and remainder; laid and levied; mind and memory*. Many others, in addition to conveying no nuance in meaning, have no aesthetically redeeming qualities, but even informed opinions on a point of this kind are likely to diverge. Following are two lists, the first containing common doublets in legal writing, the second containing some of the common triplets. Any number of variations, as by inversion (or, with triplets, by reordering), are possible.

Doublets
able and willing
act and deed
agree and covenant
agreed and declared
aid and abet (q.v.)
aid and comfort
all and singular (q.v.)
all and sundry
amount or quantum
annoy or molest
annulled and set aside (see **annul**)
answerable and accountable
any and all (q.v.)
appropriate and proper
attached and annexed
authorize and direct
authorize and empower
betting or wagering
bills and notes
bind and obligate
by and between (q.v.)
by and through (q.v.)
by and under
by and with
canceled and set aside
cease and come to an end
cease and determine (see **determine (A)**)
chargeable and accountable
covenant and agree (q.v.)
custom and usage
deed and assurance
deem and consider
definite and certain
demises and leases
deposes and says
desire and require
do and perform
dominion and authority
due and owing
due and payable (see **due**)
each and all (q.v.)
each and every (q.v.)
ends and objects
escape and evade
exact and specific
execute and perform
false and untrue
final and conclusive
finish and complete
fit and proper (q.v.)
for and in behalf of
force and effect (q.v.)
fraud and deceit
free and clear
from and after
full and complete
full faith and credit
good and effectual
good and tenantable
goods and chattels
have and hold
keep and maintain
kind and character
kind and nature
known and described as
laid and levied
leave and license
legal and valid
liens and encumbrances (q.v.)
made and signed
maintenance and upkeep
make and enter into (a contract)
make and execute
means and includes
messuage and dwelling-house
mind and memory (q.v.)
name and style
new and novel
nominate and appoint
null and of no effect
null and void (q.v.)
object and purpose
order and direct
other and further (relief)
over and above
pains and penalties
pardon and forgive

part and parcel (q.v.)
peace and quiet
perform and discharge
power and authority
premeditation and malice aforethought
repair and make good
restrain and enjoin
reverts to and falls back upon
save and except
seised and possessed (of)
separate and apart (q.v.)
separate and distinct
set aside and vacate
shall and will
shun and avoid
similar and like
sole and exclusive
son and heir
successors and assigns
supersede and displace
surmise and conjecture
terms and conditions
then and in that event
title and interest
total and entire
touch and concern
true and correct
truth and veracity
type and kind
uncontroverted and uncontradicted
understood and agreed
unless and until
uphold and support
used and applied
various and sundry
will and testament

Triplets and Longer Strings
cancel, annul, and set aside
form, manner, and method
general, vague, and indefinite
give, devise, and bequeath (q.v.)
grant, bargain, sell and convey (q.v.)
grants, demises, and lets
hold, possess, and enjoy
lands, tenements, and hereditaments (q.v.)
make, publish, and declare
name, constitute, and appoint
ordered, adjudged, and decreed (q.v.)
pay, satisfy, and discharge
possession, custody, and control (q.v.)
promise, agree, and covenant
ready, willing, and able (q.v.)
remise, release, and forever discharge
remise, release, and forever quitclaim
repair, uphold, and maintain
rest, residue, and remainder (q.v.)
right, title, and interest (q.v.)
signed, sealed, and delivered (q.v.)
situate, lying, and being in
vague, nonspecific, and indefinite
way, shape, or form

One commentator recommends avoiding virtually all coupled synonyms. See David Mellinkoff, *Legal Writing: Sense and Nonsense* 189–90 (1982); *The Language of the Law* 349–62 (1963). At least one writer has taken issue with this recommendation on grounds that doublets are a prosodic feature of English and many other languages. He argues: "Since coupled synonyms are by definition redundant, they do not increase the density of ideas contained within a sentence; therefore, they rarely endanger its clarity. Since coupled synonyms add beauty to writing without sacrificing clarity, I see nothing sinful in their moderate use." Robert P. Charrow, Book Review, 30 U.C.L.A. L. Rev. 1094, 1102 (1983).

The primary problem with such arguments, on either side of the issue, is that they fail to identify the types of writing in which doublets may appear or should not appear. In DRAFTING documents to be interpreted, for example, the legal effects of this stylistic mannerism must be considered. *Stroud's Judicial Dictionary* (4th ed. 1971), under *contiguous,* q.v., states that *contiguous* is "as nearly as possible" synonymous with *adjoining,* but points to a case in which the phrase *adjoining or contiguous* was read by the court as if it were *adjoining or near to,* "so as to give *contiguous* a cognate, but not identical, meaning with *adjoining.*" If the drafter of that phrase meant contiguous when writing *contiguous,* then coupling it with *adjoining* caused trouble. (Cf. **adjacent.**) The problem stems, of course, from the fundamental canon of construing legal documents that states that every word is to be given meaning and nothing is to be read as mere surplusage. In drafting, then, doublets may be given unforeseen meanings by clever interpreters. This danger, however, is more likely to appear with less common doublets and triplets: no judge would interpret *rest, residue, and remainder* as referring to three discrete things.

A second context to be considered is ritual language, as in *the truth, the whole truth, and nothing but the truth,* a resounding phrase that conveys the gravity and majesty of the oath being taken. *Last will and testament,* q.v., may also properly be placed under the heading of ritual language, which is always directed to a lay rather than to a legal audience, the purpose being as much emotive as it is informational.

A third context in which doubling occurs is that of legal commentary and judicial opinions. Here the coupling of synonyms can rarely be said to "add beauty," as the writer quoted above suggested; rather, it is almost always a blemish. For in this context, legal style most nearly approximates literary style, and amplification by synonym has been out of rhetorical fashion for hundreds of years. Although one might well title a client's will *Last Will and Testament,* if one were to write an opinion construing that document, it would be better to begin, "In this appeal we are called upon to construe the disposition of realty in *John Doe's will*" rather than *John Doe's last will and testament.*

Yet one might well write *vague and indefinite* in patent practice, in which that doublet is generally considered a TERM OF ART describing a patent application that lacks particularity and distinctness. See Louis B. Applebaum et al., *Glossary of United States Patent Practice* 126 (1969). The inclusion of both words is widely thought to add a nuance. That is the test in ordinary legal prose: Is a shade of meaning supplied by the second or third synonym, or is it just so much deadwood?

DOUBLING OF FINAL CONSONANTS. Unaccented syllables in inflected words are sometimes spelled differently in AmE and in BrE. Americans generally do not double a final *-l-* before the inflectional suffix, whereas the British generally do. Thus:

AmE	*BrE*
canceled, canceling	cancelled, cancelling
dueled, dueling	duelled, duelling
funneled, funneling	funnelled, funnelling
initialed, initialing	initialled, initialling
labeled, labeling	labelled, labelling
marshaled, marshaling	marshalled, marshalling
parceled, parceling	parcelled, parcelling
signaled, signaling	signalled, signalling
totaled, totaling	totalled, totalling
traveled, traveling	travelled, travelling
unraveled, unraveling	unravelled, unravelling

The split between AmE and BrE is seen also in words like *jewel(l)er, pupil(l)age,* and *travel(l)er,* the British preferring two *-l-*s rather than the one used by Americans. But there are exceptions: British writers use the forms *paralleled* and *paralleling*—just as Americans do—presumably to avoid the ungainly appearance of four *-l-*s in quick succession.

The British always double the final consonant after a full vowel in words such as *kidnapped, -ing* and *worshipped, -ing.* In AmE, *kidnapping* is preferred over *kidnaping* (see **kidnapping (A)**) as an exceptional form (cf. *formatted, formatting*), though *worshiped, -ing* follows the general American rule. *Programmed* and *programming* are the preferred spellings on both sides of the Atlantic, the single *-m-* spellings being secondary variants in AmE; for the probable reason underlying this American inconsistency, see **program(m)er.**

Writers and editors should make themselves aware of these minor transatlantic differences in spelling and avoid inserting *sic* (q.v.) when quoting a foreign text.

Apart from words ending in *-l-* and exceptions noted (*kidnapping, programming,* and *worship(p)ed*), all English-speaking countries follow the same rules on doubling. When a suffix beginning with a vowel is added, the final consonant of the word is repeated only if (1) the vowel sound preceding the consonant is represented by a single letter (hence *bed, bedding* but *head, heading*); or (2) the final syllable bears the main stress (hence *oc-'cur, oc-'curred* but *'of-fer, 'of-fered*).

Among the more commonly misspelled words not already mentioned are these: *biased, busing* (see **bus**), *combated, focused, benefited,* and *transferred.*

doubt. A. *Doubt that; doubt whether.* The former is used primarily in negative sentences and in questions. E.g., "We do not *doubt that,* had the time spent in federal prison not been credited to any sentence, appellant would be entitled to have that prison time credited against his state sentence." *Doubt whether* is used in positive assertions. E.g., "We *doubt whether* such conduct falls within the ambit of appellant's duties as supervisor."

B. Followed by a Negative. *Doubt* can be a confusing word when followed by a negative, as in: "I *doubt* whether the court will not take the further step when necessary." This sentence merely states that the writer thinks courts *will* take the further step referred to.

C. And *misdoubt.* See **misdoubt.**

doubtful torts; doubtful wrongs. These phrases express a useful nuance in the law of torts. *Doubtful torts* are injuries that are no doubt unlawful wrongs of some sort, but of which we cannot say with certainty that they are torts. *Doubtful wrongs,* by contrast, are injuries that, if they are unlawful, are torts, but are probably not unlawful. See T.E. Lewis, *Winfield on Tort* (6th ed. 1954).

doubtless(ly). *Doubtlessly* is incorrect for *doubtless* (a mild expression of certainty), *no doubt* (a stronger expression of certainty), or *undoubtedly* (the strongest of these three expressions of certainty). The word *doubtless* is itself an adverb <the Framers doubtless feared the executive's as-

sertion of an independent military authority unchecked by the people>; therefore, *doubtlessly* is unnecessary. E.g., "Had Zellars been driving in the wrong lane he would *doubtlessly* [read *doubtless*] have had a little more time and a better chance to avoid striking the child."/ "While it is not impossible to say precisely when men first arrived in North America, *doubtlessly* [read *doubtless*] the original Americans emigrated from Asia at least fifteen thousand years ago and entered the continent during the Pleistocene epoch, or Ice Age, by way of the Bering Land Bridge." See ADVERBS, PROBLEMS WITH (D), HYPERCORRECTION (D), **clearly & obviously.**

doubt of is unidiomatic for *doubt about.* E.g., "The language of the statute leaves no doubt *of* [read *about*] its intent." On the other usage question raised by that example—that of a statute having intent—see HYPALLAGE.

doubt that; doubt whether. (See **doubt (A).**

dowable = (of a widow) entitled to dower. (See **dower.**) E.g., "A wife is *dowable* in equity of all lands in which her husband possessed a beneficial interest at the time of his death."/ "According to the early English common law, the widow of a trust beneficiary was not *dowable* in the trust property . . . ."

dowager; doweress. *Dowager* (= a landowner's widow who possesses her dower interest in her deceased husband's land) is now slightly derogatory in nonlegal usage, in the sense "an elderly woman with social standing."

Doweress, according to the *OED,* has long been considered a NEEDLESS VARIANT. Nevertheless, it has occurred in good legal writing: "And consequently, a *doweress* [read *dowager*] could not demand dower unless she handed over her late husband's charters . . . ." Theodore F.T. Plucknett, *A Concise History of the Common Law* 365 (5th ed. 1956).

dower; dowry. These waning terms are related etymologically (fr. L. *dot-*, *dos* "gift, marriage portion"), but they are best kept distinct in modern usage. *Dower* = the widow's legal share during her lifetime of the real estate owned by her deceased husband—at common law dower was only a life estate, but in many American jurisdictions dower (or the elective share) has been expanded into a fee. E.g., "In a few states the widow has *dower* only when the husband was trust beneficiary at his death." See **curtesy.**

Dowry is occasionally used as a synonym of *dower,* but doing so muddles the DIFFERENTIATION between the words. In the best usage, *dowry* means "the money, goods, or real estate that a woman brings to her husband in marriage."

doweress. See **dowager.**

down payment. Two words.

downplay, v.t., is not the best usage, *play down* being preferred. E.g., "[E]ach side also tends to discuss only that role occupied by Wynn favorable to its position and *downplays* [read *plays down*] the other." *Mills Land & Water Co. v. Golden West Ref. Co.,* 230 Cal. Rptr. 461, 466 (Cal. Ct. App. 1986). Both expressions are colloquial.

dowry. See **dower.**

draconian; draconic. *Draconian* (the usual form) is derived from the name *Draco,* a Greek legislator of the 7th century B.C. who drafted a code of severe laws that included the death penalty for anyone caught stealing a cabbage. Today, *Draconian* (usually capitalized) refers to any harsh aspect of law, not necessarily just legislation.

And sometimes the word is the victim of SLIPSHOD EXTENSION; that is, it is used in reference to what, in comparison to the cabbage example, can only be considered mild impositions—e.g.: "Phil Seelig, president of the Correction Officers Benevolent Association, said his organization would appeal the decision to the State Court of Appeals on the ground that random drug testing was unnecessarily *draconian* [better: *Draconian*] and violated constitutional protection against unlawful searches." *Court Upholds Drug Testing of Correction Officers,* N.Y. Times, 13 Oct. 1989, at 10.

Draconic is a NEEDLESS VARIANT—e.g.: "A general 'control' of the Common Law over statute . . . does not amount to a right to resist even the most *Draconic* [read *Draconian*] statute . . . ." Carleton K. Allen, *Law in the Making* 456 (7th ed. 1964).

For a judicial analogue, see **rhadamanthine.**

draft. See **note.**

draft; draught. See **drafter.**

drafter; draftsman; draughtsman. *Drafter* is a neutral, nonsexist equivalent preferred by those wary of terms ending in *-man. Draftsperson* is a wholly unnecessary NEOLOGISM. See SEXISM (B).

Draughtsman is the older BrE spelling of *draftsman.* E.g., "The ingenuity of equity *draughtsmen* was under that system greatly exercised in drawing answers in such a form that it was impossible to read part of them without reading the whole." (Eng.) In American writing, that spelling smacks of pedantry—e.g.: "He [Samuel Tutt] was thoroughly read in the law, an expert pleader and *draughtsman* [read *draftsman* or, if the book were being written today, *drafter*], reveled in technicalities and, in preparing a case for trial, left no point uncovered." Ephraim Tutt, *Yankee Lawyer* 313 (1943).

DRAFTING is a specific type of legal writing dealing with legislation, instruments, or other legal documents that are to be construed by others. Statutes, rules, regulations, contracts, and wills are examples of legal drafting. The style is considerably different from that of other legal writing, such as in judicial opinions and legal commentary. Many of the worst mannerisms of LEGALESE pervade legal drafting, for the MYTH OF PRECISION has traditionally been one of the drafter's tenets.

A 19th-century English practitioner delineated the specific characteristics of drafting. The style of good drafting, he wrote,

> is free from all colour, from all emotion, from all rhetoric. It is impersonal, as if the voice, not of any man, but of the law, dealing with the necessary facts. It disdains emphasis and all other artifices. It uses no metaphors or figures of speech. It is always consistent and never contradicts itself. It never hesitates or doubts. It says in the plainest language, with the simplest, fewest, and fittest words, precisely what it means. These are qualities which might be used to advantage more frequently than is common in literature, and unfortunately they are not to be found in many legal compositions, but they are essential to good legal composition, and are not essential to literary composition.
>
> J.G. Mackay, *Introduction to an Essay on the Art of Legal Composition Commonly Called Drafting,* 3 Law Q. Rev. 326, 326 (1887).

For suggested guides on drafting, see LEGAL WRITING STYLE (C). See also PLAIN LANGUAGE.

draftsman. See **drafter.**

draftsmanship; draughtsmanship. The only nonsexist equivalent of these terms is *drafting,* which (unfortunately) refers not only to the art but also to the product.

It is a mistake for American writers to use *draughtsmanship,* the BrE spelling, which appears in Kenneth H. York & John A. Bauman, *Remedies* 182 (1973).

drag > dragged > dragged. See **drug.**

dragnet clause. See **Mother Hubbard clause.**

dramshop = a business selling alcoholic drinks; a bar. Of 18th-century origin, the term appears today only in the phrases *dramshop suits, dramshop claims,* and *dramshop statutes. Dramshop claims* involve allegations that liquor establishments serving underage or obviously intoxicated patrons should be held liable for consequent drunk-driving accidents.

draughtsman. See **drafter.**

draw. Only in the legal idiom does *draw* retain the sense "to frame (a writing or document) in due form" (*OED*), as a synonym of *draft* <to draw a will>. E.g., "While the petition has been *drawn,* with obvious meticulous care, to avoid the semblance of seeking mandatory relief, in essence and effect it presents no other objective." *American Nat'l Bank v. Sheppard,* 175 S.W.2d 626, 628 (Tex. Civ. App.—Austin 1943)./ "[I]t takes time and knowledge to *draw* a statute carefully." Robert G. McCloskey, *The American Supreme Court* 203 (1960).

More casually—and in nonlegal as well as legal writing—*draw* is coupled with the particle *up,* for a PHRASAL VERB. E.g., "[O]f all the many business contracts and legal agreements of every sort that are *drawn up* and signed every day, only a very small fraction are eventually carried to court." Fred Rodell, *Woe Unto You, Lawyers!* 115 (1939).

drawee = payor <drawee bank>. Because lawyers understand *drawee* and *payor* to be synonymous, the coupling of the two in the phrase *drawee/payor* makes little sense—e.g.: "A payee or other true owner of an instrument that is cashed under a forged endorsement may sue directly *the drawee/payer* [read either *the drawee* or *the payor*] bank."

drink-driving. See **drunk driving.**

droitural; droiturel. *Droitural* [fr. F. *droit* "a legal right"]—the more common spelling of this uncommon word—means "relating to an ownership right in property, as distinguished from mere possession." E.g., "The law may . . . bar the owner from asserting his rights by a *droitural* action and thus leave these rights suspended in a state of unenforceability . . . ." Marian P. Opala, *Praescriptio Temporis and Its Relation to Prescriptive Easements in the Anglo-American Law,* 7 Tulsa L.J. 107, 107 (1971)./ "As a result of these changes, the assize became a '*droitural*' action—that is, it tried right rather than recent possession—and by 1400 the writs of right and entry had been largely driven out of use . . . ." J.H. Baker, *An Introduction to English Legal History* 270 (3d ed. 1990).

Maitland's habitual spelling, *droiturel,* is a variant that is all but obsolete.

drought; drouth. The latter is archaic in BrE, but still frequently appears in AmE texts. Still, *drought* is the preferred form in both linguistic communities.

drug for *dragged* is a nonstandard dialectal form common in the southern U.S.: "He then *drug* [read *dragged*] the body into the house."

drumhead court. The original phrase, *drumhead court-martial,* was an early 19th-century term denoting a military tribunal held around an up-turned drum to deal summarily with offenses during military operations. The phrase quickly took on figurative senses, first in reference to any summary court-martial—e.g.: "In the face of the enemy, it is permitted to try an alleged spy summarily before a *drumhead court-martial,* and execute him if found guilty . . . ." *Filbin Corp. v. U.S.,* 266 F. 911, 917 (E.D.S.C. 1920).

The phrase was later extended to refer to any tribunal with loose procedures that result in questionable justice. In this extended sense, the phrase is sometimes *drumhead court,* sometimes *drumhead court-martial*—e.g.: "It is the protection from arbitrary punishments through the right to a judicial trial with all these safeguards which over the years has distinguished America from lands where *drumhead courts* and other similar 'tribunals' deprive the weak and the unorthodox of life, liberty and property without due process of law." *Barenblatt v. U.S.,* 360 U.S. 109, 162 (1959) (Black, J., dissenting)./ "One of the attorneys in *United States v. Hoffa* was convicted of contempt for saying that the court was conducting a *'drum head court martial'* [read *'drumhead court-martial'*] and 'a star chamber proceeding.'" Norman Dorsen & Leon Friedman, *Disorder in the Court* 150 (1973).

drunk; drunken. "In older and literary usage," the *Oxford Guide* notes, *drunk* and *drunken* were "the predicative and attributive forms respectively; now usually allocated to distinct senses, namely 'intoxicated' and 'given to drink.'"

We do, however, have the idiom *drunken driving,* defined by the *CDL* as "driving while affected by alcohol." *Drunken* here means "exhibiting or evidencing intoxication." E.g., "England in the mid-1980s still regulates licensing hours (though not perhaps for much longer) and the age at which people can lawfully buy alcohol, while *drunken driving* is a criminal offence." Simon Lee, *Law and Morals* 1–2 (1986). Because *drunken* implies a habitual state, the phrase *drunk driving* is preferable. See **drunk driving.**

drunk driving (AmE) = *drink-driving* (BrE). The American form—*drunk driving*—exemplifies HYPALLAGE because it is the driver, not the driving, that is drunk. On the less acceptable form—*drunken driving*—see **drunk.**

To American eyes, though, the BrE form looks extremely odd—e.g.: "A *drink-driving* offender will probably be charged with one of the specialised offences . . . rather than with careless driving, since the penalty for the former is higher (and can be imprisonment)." Glanville Williams, *Textbook of Criminal Law* 271 (1978)./ "In the West Midlands, 30 officers have been convicted of *drink-driving* in the last two years." Mazher Mahmood, *Drink-Driving Immunity—The Police Force "Perk,"* Sunday Times, 11 Dec. 1988, at A3.

drunken. See **drunk.**

drunkometer. See **breathalyzer.**

dual is sometimes misspelled *duel*—e.g.: "The trial court erred in holding that a cause filed against an individual, who occupies a *duel* [read *dual*] status . . . , is a matter incident to an estate." *Speer v. Stover,* 711 S.W.2d 730, 735 (Tex. App.—San Antonio 1986).

dualism. See **monism.**

dubious distinction has the dubious distinction of being one of our most overworked CLICHÉS.

dubitante = doubting. The term is used in law reports of a judge who is doubtful about a legal proposition but is loath to declare it wrong. E.g., "Mr Justice Rutledge acquiesces in the Court's opinion and judgment *dubitante* on the question of equal protection of the laws."

This term is sometimes used after a judge's name, as an analogue to *concurring* or *dissenting.* It signals that the judge had grave doubts about the soundness of the majority opinion, but not so grave as to spark a dissent. E.g., "The Court decided to do so, Baggallay L.J. *dubitante* but not *dissentiente* [i.e., doubting but not dissenting]." Carleton K. Allen, *Law in the Making* 493 (7th ed. 1964). See OPINIONS, JUDICIAL (C).

duces tecum. See **subpoena (C).**

due. Traditionally, this word has contained an ambiguity, since it could mean either (1) "payable; owing; constituting a debt"; or (2) "immediately enforceable." Sense (1) relates to fact of indebtedness, sense (2) to the time of payment. Today, sense (2) is almost invariably the applicable one, as illustrated in an early-20th-century edition of Bouvier: "[*Due*] differs from *owing* in this, that sometimes what is owing is not due: a note payable thirty days after date is owing immediately after it is delivered to the payee, but it is not *due* until the thirty days have elapsed." 1 John Bouvier, *Bouvier's Law Dictionary* 946 (Francis Rawle ed., 3d ed. 1914).

Because a debt cannot be *due* without also being *payable,* the doublet *due and payable* is unnecessary in place of *due.* See DOUBLETS, TRIPLETS, AND SYNONYM-STRINGS.

due and payable. See **due.**

duel. See **dual.**

due process of law. When applied to judicial proceedings, this phrase—often shortened to *due process*—traditionally "mean[s] a course of legal proceedings according to those rules and principles which have been established in our system of jurisprudence for the protection and enforcement of private rights." *Pennoyer v. Neff,* 95 U.S. 714, 733 (1877).

By the late 19th century, the U.S. Supreme Court had built general substantive principles around the phrase, which scholars came to call *substantive due process.* Rather than forbidding only unfair procedures, the due-process clause was held to forbid certain actions no matter how they might be carried out. Substantive due process is today a limited doctrine that, for example, bars most curtailments of free speech (by state governments) and such encroachments into the right of privacy as statutes prohibiting abortions.

Fred Rodell once called the phrase *due process* "that lovely limpid LEGALISM." Fred Rodell, *Woe Unto You, Lawyers!* 51 (1939). It may be lovely, but it is not "limpid" (i.e., clear or transparent). More accurately, Atiyah says: "The fact is that this concept is probably the greatest contribution ever made to modern civilization by lawyers or perhaps any other professional group." P.S. Atiyah, *Law and Modern Society* 42 (1983).

As a PHRASAL ADJECTIVE, it is hyphenated—e.g.: "They came close in a couple of cases challenging the *due-process* propriety of laws passed by two Western states . . . ." Fred Rodell, *Nine Men* 201 (1955)./ "The early *due-process* legislation was chiefly aimed against irregular or inferior jurisdictions." J.H. Baker, *An Introduction to English Legal History* 538 (3d ed. 1990).

due to should be used to mean "attributable to," and often follows the verb *to be* (sometimes understood in context). But the stylist may wish to avoid even correct uses of the phrase, which one writer calls a "graceless phrase, even when used correctly," adding: "Avoid it altogether." Lucile V. Payne, *The Lively Art of Writing* 148 (1965).

The phrase is commonly misused as a conjunctive adverb for *because of, owing to, caused by,* or *on grounds of*—e.g.:

- "The trial was lost *due to* [read *because of*] his damaging admissions."
- "*Due to* [read *Because of*] the close interrelation between these two rights, we believe that Wiggins's petition fairly raised the issue of his right to counsel."
- "Because the state court did not specify whether it denied habeas relief on the merits or *due to* [read *on grounds of*] procedural default, we must interpret the state court's silence."
- "*Due in part to* [read *In part because of*] the widespread enactment of pretermitted heir statutes, the majority of the courts have been unwilling to hold that birth of issue alone revokes a will."

In the following examples, the phrase *due to* is used correctly; but, as Payne notes, the sentences might be improved by eliminating it. E.g., "We conclude that the *failure of the government due to* clerical error or oversight does not violate the statute." [A possible revision: "We conclude that the *government's failure from* clerical error or oversight does not violate the statute."]/ "A distinction must be drawn between cases in which the difficulties *are due to* uncertainty as to the causation in which questions of remoteness arise, and those which are *due to* the assessment of damages that cannot be made with any mathematical accuracy." (Eng.) [A possible revision: "A distinction must be drawn between cases in which the difficulties *arise from* uncertainty *about what caused* the damage and those in which difficulties *arise from* the impossibility of assessing damages accurately."]

Due followed by an infinitive is not a form of the phrase *due to,* although it looks deceptively similar. E.g., "Because 'security center' is a generic term not entitled to service mark protection, the district court decision is *due to be* reversed."

due to the fact that can often be boiled down to *because.*

dul(l)ness. *Dullness* is correct.

duly authorized. Because *authorize* denotes the giving of actual or official power, *duly* (i.e., "properly") is usually unnecessary.

dump truck. See LAWYERS, DEROGATORY NAMES FOR (A).

duologue. See **dialogue.**

duplicate, n., = (1) a reproduction of an original document having the same substance and often the same validity as the original; or (2) a new original of a document, often made to replace one that is lost or destroyed. Because sense (2) is slightly misleading, the fuller phrase *duplicate original* is more accurate.

duplicitous; duplicative; duplicatory. *Duplicitous* is a late-19th-century coinage generally understood to mean "deceitful." American and British legal writers have latched onto the word in the sense of doubleness, from the old legal meaning of *duplicity* (= double pleading). A nonlawyer would likely be confused by the following uses of the word:

- "An information charging a conspiracy to commit burglary is not *duplicitous* because it alleges that the conspiracy was to commit two or more different burglaries." *Hamilton v. People,* 51 P. 425, 425 syl. 4 (Colo. 1897). (The specimen just quoted antedates the earliest known use [1928] given in *W10.*)
- "The allegation in a single count of a conspiracy to commit several crimes is not *duplicitous.*" *Braverman v. U.S.,* 317 U.S. 49, 54 (1942).
- "If an offence can be committed intentionally or recklessly, the information or indictment may charge it in those terms. The fact that the mental element is stated in the alternative does not make the charge '*duplicitous.*'" Glanville Williams, *Textbook of Criminal Law* 80 (1978).
- "A *duplicitous* indictment is one charging two separate crimes in the same count." *U.S. v. Ellis,* 595 F.2d 154, 163 (3d Cir. 1979).
- "Acosta argues further that the indictment was *duplicitous* because it joined separate conspiracies into one count." *U.S. v. Acosta,* 763 F.2d 671, 696 (5th Cir. 1985).

Duplicitous should not be extended beyond its sense of doubleness in pleading, indictments, etc., as it is here: "There is a suggestion that some of the work performed by counsel for Baxter was *duplicitous* [read *duplicative*] because of a change in counsel during the preparation stages of the litigation." *Baxter v. Savannah Sugar Ref. Corp.,* 495 F.2d 437, 447 (5th Cir. 1974).

Duplicative, which one might have preferred in the sense given to *duplicitous,* has been adopted for other uses in the law. "[A]s between federal district courts, . . . the general principle is to avoid *duplicative* litigation." *Colorado River Water Conserv. Dist. v. U.S.,* 424 U.S. 800, 817 (1976)./ "Recent Supreme Court decisions have emphasized the risk of *duplicative* recoveries and other factors without mentioning antitrust standing as a distinct inquiry."/ "The policy of minimization of *duplicative* enforcement might well prevail over concerns of centralization."/ "We realized at the time of the decision that unifying school systems often would cause elimination of *duplicative* jobs." *Duplicatory* is a NEEDLESS VARIANT. See **multiplici(t)ous (B).**

duplicity is frequently used in law for *duplication.* E.g., "The defendant suggested that the 340 billable hours resulted from a *duplicity* of time spent by the plaintiff's attorney and his five associates."/ "The county prosecutor was even heard boasting to a member of the press that he had a '*duplicity*' of evidence!" Mark McKinnon, "South Toward Home," in *Texas, Our Texas: Remembrances of The University* 145, 146 (Bryan A. Garner ed. 1984).

Those uses of the word are poor. They derive from the true legal meaning "the pleading of two (or more) matters in one plea; double pleading" (*OED*), properly illustrated here: "Pleading had long since ceased to convey any true information, though the rules against '*duplicity*' might require a party to admit all but one of his opponent's falsehoods." Alan Harding, *A Social History of English Law* 332 (1966). The word should not, by SLIPSHOD EXTENSION, be used of other types of doubleness. See **duplicitous.**

The nonlegal sense of *duplicity* (= deceitfulness, double-dealing) is also quite common in legal contexts: "When a lawyer's falsehood and *duplicity* is established he becomes a professional outcast."/ "The trial judge stated that he doubted the plaintiff's veracity; but the right of a party to have his own statement is not diminished when the district court suspects *duplicity.*"

duress; durance. *Duress* = (1) the infliction of hardship; (2) forcible restraint; illegal imprisonment; or (3) compulsion illegally exercised to force a person to perform some act. *Durance* is an archaic LEGALISM sharing sense (2) of *duress,* for which it is a NEEDLESS VARIANT.

duress of circumstances. See **necessity.**

during such time as is verbose for *while.*

during the course of is almost always verbose for *during.*

duteous. See **dutiful.**

dutiable = subject to the levy of a duty, i.e., a tax on goods. E.g., "The dual purpose of the search is to ascertain whether an illegal alien is seeking to cross the border and whether contraband or *dutiable* property is being smuggled."

dutiful; duteous. The usual term is *dutiful.* Although formerly in good use, *duteous* is an archaic NEEDLESS VARIANT.

duty = (1) that which one is required to do or refrain from doing, esp. as occupant of some position, role, or office; or (2) a complex of rights and standards of care imposed by a legal relationship. Sense (2) appears primarily in tort law, in which writers use *duty* only to mean that there could be liability. See **obligation.**

duty(-)bound. This term from legal JARGON, a PHRASAL ADJECTIVE corresponding to the age-old phrase *bounden duty,* is written sometimes as two words and sometimes as one. The best practice is to hyphenate it <those are rights that federal courts are duty-bound to protect>.

duty, nondelegable. See **nondelegable duty.**

dwelling-house; dwelling; usual place of abode. Legal writers have traditionally used the quaint terms *dwelling* and *dwelling-house* to denote "a structure in which human beings sleep." These terms named the subject of common-law burglary, which could take place only in a dwelling-house and not in a business building. Burglary statutes have, of course, broadened the scope of buildings included within the definition of burglary.

As between *dwelling* and *dwelling-house,* the former is more current in the general language; but the latter predominates in legal writing, perhaps because lawyers may fear creating a MISCUE (i.e., if *dwelling* were read as a participial verb and not as a gerund).

The phrase *usual place of abode* often appears in the alternative alongside *dwelling-house* in rules about serving legal papers. The DOUBLET is doubtless justified, since some homeless people cannot be said to live in a *dwelling-house* but can certainly be said to have a *usual place of abode.*

dynamic, n., is a VOGUE WORD generally best avoided. E.g., "In the first case, a negotiation is stipulated. In the second, *the dynamic leads almost inevitably in that direction* [read *a negotiation is almost inevitable*]."

dynamite charge; shotgun instruction; nitroglycerine charge; *Allen* charge; Chip Smith charge. Each of these phrases refers to a supplemental jury instruction given by the court to encourage a deadlocked jury, after prolonged deliberations, to reach a unanimous verdict. The legality of such a jury instruction was upheld in *Allen v. U.S.,* 164 U.S. 492 (1896)—hence the phrase *Allen charge.* See CASE REFERENCES (C).

What is perhaps the most widely used phrase today, *dynamite charge,* originated in the mid-20th century. It contains a clever pun—as PUNS go in legal terminology—and has appeared in a wide range of legal writings—e.g.: "The jurors were then excused until Monday morning, September 10, 1973. At 11:15 that morning, the judge gave the jury the *Allen* or *'dynamite' charge* without any admonition that the majority re-examine its position." *Gray v. Martindale Lumber Co.,* 515 F.2d 1218, 1219–20 (5th Cir. 1975).

Chip Smith charge is the Connecticut version, deriving from *State v. James ("Chip") Smith,* 49 Conn. 376 (1881). E.g., "It is settled that a *'Chip Smith' charge* is an acceptable method of assisting the jury to achieve unanimity." *State v. Wooten,* 631 A.2d 271, 286 (Conn. 1993). The other forms are likewise regional variants; they are exquisite enough that it would be a grave mistake to brand them NEEDLESS VARIANTS.

dysfunctional (= functioning abnormally) is frequently misspelled *disfunctional.*

E

each. A. Number. *Each* takes a singular verb, and pronouns having *each* as an antecedent must be in the singular. E.g., "*Each is* entitled to benefits under this program."/ "Persuasive arguments exist that *each* of the first two criteria *is* satisfied."/ "[This balancing of rights] is done by recognizing that *each have* [read *each has*] rights over the whole . . . ." Patrick Devlin, *The Enforcement of Morals* 16 (1968).

Sometimes *each* is mistaken as the subject in a sentence in which it acts in apposition, as here: "The mortgagor and mortgagee *each has* [read *each have*] an insurable interest." Robert Kratovil, *Real Estate Law* 138 (1946)./ "JR's four Tokyo commuter lines each *has* [read *have*] *its* [read *their*] own color." Peter McGill, *The American Express Pocket Guide to Tokyo* 13 (1988). See APPOSITIVES (A).

Still another problem occurs with phrases such as *each of us who.* The word *who* is in apposition to *us* and therefore takes a plural verb, but many writers want to make it singular because they mistakenly think that *each* is the subject of the verb—e.g.: "Neither is the practice of law fully intelligible without reference to the inner mind of each of us who *engages* [read *engage*] in law practice." Geoffrey C. Hazard, Jr. & Susan P. Koniak, *The Law and Ethics of Lawyering* xxi (1990). For a similar error, see **one of those ——s who (*or* that).**

B. Delimiting the Application of *each.* Especially in contexts in which *all* appears before *each,* it may be important to use defining words after *each.* E.g., "[S]uppose a statute required *all directors* to take an oath of secrecy, and imposed a penalty on *each director* in the event of a violation. If half the directors took the oath and half failed, could they all be prosecuted or only those who failed?" Elmer A. Driedger, *The Composition of Legislation* 78 (1957). The remedy lies, of course, in writing that the penalty is imposed on *each director who fails to take the oath,* assuming that is the intended meaning.

each and all. This LEGALISM is no more helpful or necessary than *each and every,* q.v. See DOUBLETS, TRIPLETS, AND SYNONYM-STRINGS.

each and every. This trite phrase should generally be eschewed, but especially it should not be plugged in where only one of the adjectives properly modifies what follows. E.g., "Plaintiff has performed *each and every* of his obligations under the contract." *Each* works fine here, but not *every,* for one cannot say, "He has performed *every* of his obligations." One who insists on being bromidic should write: "Plaintiff has performed *each and every one* of his obligations under the contract." Cf. **and/or** & **if and when.** See DOUBLETS, TRIPLETS, AND SYNONYM-STRINGS.

each other; one another. The former phrase is used of two persons or entities; the latter is best confined to contexts involving more than two. E.g., "One of us would turn to the foregoing comment and find that the two terms cancel *one another* [read *each other*]."/ "Horrible noise on the one hand; money on the other. How do you relate them to *one another* [read *each other*]?" Richard A. Lanham, *Revising Prose* 109 (1979).

In using these phrases, one must know precisely what is being compared. In the following sentence, *elements constituting the basis of damages* are being compared, although the writer mistook *causes of action* as the units of comparison: "Having examined the jury instructions and the special verdict in this case, we find that the elements constituting the basis of damages of *each* of the two causes of action were not sufficiently distinguished *from one another* [read *from those of the other*] to ensure that there was no double compensation." The use of *each* before *one another* is what caused the problem; the writer was guilty of SWAPPING HORSES from *each other* to *one another.*

early on is not the odious locution that some people think. Slightly informal, it is perfectly idiomatic in both AmE and BrE. E.g., "My pupil master told me *early on* of the client's complaint: 'I want your opinion and not your doubts' . . . ." Lord Denning, *The Discipline of Law* 7 (1979).

earnest (= something given or done beforehand as a pledge or a sign of good faith, esp. a partial payment of the purchase price of goods sold or a delivery of some of the goods themselves, for the purpose of concluding an agreement) generally appears in the phrase *earnest money.* But in Scotland the word is commonly used alone—e.g.: "[*E*]*arnest* is to be held merely as evidence of the completion of the bargain . . . . *Earnest* is in no case essential to the completion of the bargain." R. Bell, *Dictionary and Digest of the Law of Scotland* (7th ed. 1890) (s.v. *earnest*).

earwitness (= a witness who testifies about something that he or she heard) is formed on the analogy of *eyewitness,* q.v. Both words date from the 16th century.

easement. A. *Positive* and *Negative Easements.* An easement is a legal or equitable right acquired by the owner of one piece of land to use another's land for a special purpose. *Positive easements* give rights of entry upon another's land, as to cross through to reach one's own land or to discharge water. *Negative easements* consist in the right to prevent the landowner from doing something such as blocking sunlight or erecting buildings that would prevent the use of a runway on nearby land. For *avigational easement,* see **aviate.**

B. Types. An *easement by prescription* arises by adverse use over some specified period, such as 20 years. An *easement in gross* (a rarity) is a personal right benefiting someone who need not—and usu. does not—own any land adjoining the servient tenement (q.v.). An *easement of necessity* arises by reservation (either express or implied) when a landowner sells part of his or her land and leaves no outlet to a highway. An *easement appurtenant* is one created for the benefit of another tract of land.

C. And *right of way.* The terms are not synonymous; *right of way* (= the right to pass over another's land) is often a type of *positive easement.* But not always: a *right of way* may be granted by license (to the person) as well as by easement (inuring to the land)—see (D). See **right of way.**

D. And *license.* An easement is a property right; a license is a revocable permission to commit some act that would otherwise be unlawful. An easement is usu. created by written instrument; a license is often created orally. An easement is a more or less permanent right; a license is temporary. An easement usu. changes ownership as the ownership of the land to which it belongs changes; a license is a purely personal right that cannot be sold. See **licence (B).**

eastwardly; easterly. See DIRECTIONAL WORDS.

easy judge (= a judge who sentences criminal defendants leniently) is an AmE antonym of *hanging judge*—e.g.: "[T]he judges develop and decide cases in very different ways . . . . Some have become known as *'easy' judges,* others as 'hanging' judges. There *seems* [read *seem*] to be more *'easy' judges* than 'hanging' judges, however." *Stieberger v. Heckler,* 615 F. Supp. 1315, 1388 (S.D.N.Y. 1985) (quoting Senator Bellmon)./ "The Court: Has anybody told you that you don't have to worry, that this is an *easy judge?* The Defendant: No, sir." *Stokes v. U.S.,* 366 F. Supp. 879, 886 n.3 (D. Md. 1973) (quoting testimony).

ebullit. See BACK-FORMATIONS.

ecclesiastical law; canon law. Although these generic terms overlap a great deal, *ecclesiastical law* broadly covers all laws relating to a church, whether from state law, divine law, natural law, or societal rules; *canon law* is more restricted, referring only to the body of law constituted by ecclesiastical authority for the organization and governance of a Christian church. See **canon law.**

economic; economical. *Economical* means "thrifty," or, in the current jargon, "cost-effective." *Economic* should be used for every other meaning possible for the words, almost always in reference to the study of economics. Hence we have *economic studies* and *economic interest* but *economical shopping.* See **uneconomic(al).**

edict = (1) in Roman law, an intimation by a magistrate (urban or peregrine praetor) stating what actions and defenses would be allowed, and, in the course of time, a settled body of such rules (esp. the Praeterian Edict); (2) a law promulgated by the sovereign and applying either to the entire state or some of its divisions, but usu. relating to affairs of state; (3) in Scottish ecclesiastical law, an official notice from the pulpit to the congregation; or (4) any formal decree, command, or proclamation. When modern courts refer to their "edicts" (sense 3), they do so usu. with a subtle self-mockery, the word *edict* connoting that the issuer is all-powerful.

Though the noun *edict* dates from the 13th century in English, the corresponding adjective, *edictal,* dates only from the early 19th century. It corresponds to sense (1) of *edict*—e.g.: "The *Edictal law* would therefore enforce the dispositions of a Testator, when, instead of being symbolised through the forms of mancipation, they were simply evidenced by the seals of seven witnesses." Henry S. Maine, *Ancient Law* 175 (17th ed. 1901; repr. [New Universal Lib.] 1905, 1910).

EDITORIAL "WE." See FIRST PERSON (B).

-EDLY. Words ending in this way are more pervasive in law than elsewhere. For example, Blackstone wrote that "if one intends to do another a felony, and *undesignedly* kills a man, this is also murder." 4 William Blackstone, *Commentaries* *200–01. Lawyers write of *premeditatedly* committed crimes, of *mitigatedly* committed crimes, and of the Warren Court's "*unwarrantedly* sweeping readings of constitutional guarantees . . . ." Jan Deutsch, *Chiarella v. United States: A Study in Legal Style,* 58 Tex. L. Rev. 1291, 1300 (1980).

With words formed in this way, the classic adverbial formula *in a . . . manner* does not work with these words; thus *allegedly* does not mean "in an alleged manner," *purportedly* does not mean "in a purported manner," and *admittedly* does not mean "in an admitted manner." Rather, the unorthodox formula for these words is *it is . . . -ed that,* i.e., *allegedly* (= it is alleged that) and so on. Instead of bewailing the unorthodoxy of these words in *-edly,* we should welcome the conciseness they promote and continue to use them (if only sparingly). We have many of them, such as *admittedly, allegedly, assertedly, concededly, confessedly, reportedly,* and *supposedly.* See **allegedly, confessedly & reportedly.**

Nonetheless, forms in *-edly* ought to be avoided if a ready substitute exists: "[A] bank may indeed be *liable for unauthorizedly revealing* [read *liable for revealing without authorization*] the state of a depositor's accounts to his creditors." *Schuster v. Banco de Iberoamerica, S.A.,* 476 So. 2d 253, 255 (Fla. Dist. Ct. App. 1985) (Schwartz, J., dissenting). See **qualifiedly.**

educ(at)able. The shorter form is correct. See -ATABLE & **educible.**

education(al)ist; educator. *Educationist* (the preferred form) = an educational theorist. In the U.S., the term has acquired negative connotations. In G.B., it has come to be used in the sense of *educator,* which in the U.S. means "a teacher; one engaged in educational work."

educational; educative; educatory; educable. *Educational* = (1) having to do with education <educational issues>; or (2) serving to further education <educational films>. *Educative* = tending to educate; instructive <educative lectures>. *Educatory* is a NEEDLESS VARIANT of *educative.* *Educable* = capable of being educated <educable pupils>.

educator. See **education(al)ist.**

educe, vb., (= to elicit; evoke) should be distinguished from the verb *adduce* (= to bring forward for analysis) and from *educt,* n. (= something educed). E.g., "In the present case, the factual showing thus *educed* [i.e., *developed, brought out*] does not so unequivocally point to a borrowed employee relationship as to permit a summary judgment." Here the sense is correct, but the word is matched with the wrong subject: "We need not reach this issue, because *no factual showing was educed* [read either *no showing was made* or *no facts were educed*] by the defendant to negate the allegations of her complaint that the failure to reemploy her resulted from gender-based discrimination." See **adduce.**

educible; educable. The former means "capable of being educed, or drawn out." The latter means "capable of being educated." See **educational.**

-EE. A. General Principles. This suffix (fr. French past participial *-é*) originally denoted "one who is acted upon"; the sense is inherently passive. Thus:

acquittee = one who is acquitted
arrestee = one who is arrested
conscriptee = one who is conscripted
detainee = one who is detained
educatee = one who is educated (by an educator)
ejectee = one who is ejected
enrollee = one who is enrolled
expellee = one who is expelled
inauguree = one who is inaugurated
indictee = one who is indicted
invitee = one who is invited
liberee = one who is liberated
permittee = one who is permitted
returnee = one who is returned
selectee = one who is selected
separatee = one who is separated
shelteree = one who is sheltered
smugglee = one who is smuggled
telephonee = one who is telephoned

The suffix has also a dative sense, in which it acts as the passive agent noun for the indirect object. This is the sense in which the suffix is most commonly used in peculiarly legal terminology:

abandonee = one to whom property rights are relinquished
advancee = one to whom money is advanced
allocatee = one to whom something is allocated
allottee = one to whom something is allotted
consignee = a person to whom something is consigned
covenantee = one to whom something is covenanted
deliveree = one to whom something is delivered
disclosee = one to whom something is disclosed
grantee = one to whom property is granted
indorsee = one to whom a negotiable instrument is indorsed
lessee = one to whom property is leased
patentee = one to whom a patent has been issued
pledgee = one to whom something is pledged
referee = one to whom something is referred
remittee = one to whom something is remitted
trustee = one to whom something is entrusted
vendee = one to whom something is sold

At least one word in *-ee* has both a normal passive sense and a dative sense. *Appointee* = (1) one who is appointed; or (2) one to whom an estate is appointed. Sense (2), of course, is primarily legal.

The suffix *-ee,* then, is correlative in sense to *-or,* the active agent-noun suffix: some words in *-ee* are formed as passive analogues to *-or* agent nouns, and not from any verb stem. Examples are *indemnitee* (= one who is indemnified; analogue to *indemnitor*) and *preceptee* (= student; analogue to *preceptor*).

These are the traditional uses of the suffix; there is a tendency today, however, to make *-ee* a general agent-noun suffix without regard to its passive sense or the limitations within which it may take on passive senses. Hence the suffix has been extended to PHRASAL VERBS, even though only the first word in the phrase appears in the *-ee* word. Thus *discriminatee* (= one who is discriminated against) and *tippee* (= one who is tipped off). Then other prepositional phrases have gradually come into the wide embrace of *-ee: abortee* (= a woman upon whom an abortion is performed); *confiscatee* (= one from whom goods have been confiscated); *depositee* (= one with whom goods are deposited); *optionee* (= one against whose interests another has an option). Some *-ee* words contain implicit possessives: *amputee* (= one whose limb has been removed); *breachee* (= one whose contract is breached); *condemnee* (= one whose property has been condemned). In still other words, *-ee* does not even have its primary passive sense:

arrivee	=	one who arrives
asylee	=	one who seeks asylum
benefitee	=	one who benefits (or, possibly, "is benefited")
escapee	=	one who escapes
standee	=	one who stands

Adjudicatee, oddly, has no direct relation to its verb; in civil law, it means "a purchaser at a judicial sale." Finally, the suffix is sometimes used to coin jocular words such as *cheatee* (= one who is cheated).

The upshot of this discussion is that *-ee* has been much abused and that writers must be careful of the forms they use. For active senses we have *-er, -or,* and *-ist* at our service; we should be wary of adopting any new active forms in *-ee,* and do our best to see that *standee, escapee,* and similar forms wither and die, or else remain odd exceptions. Otherwise we risk wasting any sense to be found in this suffix. It was with justifiable concern for the language and logic that Fowler noted: "the unskilled workers used to 'dilute' skilled workers in time of war should have been called *diluters* instead of *dilutees;* the skilled were the *dilutees" (MEU2* 146). See -ER (A).

B. Word Formation. The principles applying to words in -ATABLE apply also to agent nouns in *-ee.* Thus we have *inauguree,* not *inauguratee; subrogee,* not *subrogatee* (though the latter is sometimes used mistakenly for the former). See **subrogee.**

C. Stylistic Use of. Stylists know that *-ee* agent nouns are often inferior to more descriptive terms. They sometimes objectify the persons they describe, though the writer may intend no callousness—e.g.: "On October 19, 1966, a jury convicted Enriquez of capital murder of Kay Foss, the *abductee* [read *the woman he abducted*], and imposed the death penalty."

Furthermore, the endings *-or* and *-ee* can be easily transposed by mistake. As a general matter, therefore, good drafters prefer *buyer* and *seller* over *vendee* and *vendor; buyer* and *seller* over *bargainee* and *bargainor;* and, in appropriate circumstances, *borrower* and *lender* over *mortgagor* and *mortgagee.* The stakes are often so high that it makes little sense to use forms that increase the possibility of error. See **vendee & vendor.**

effect, v.t. **A. Generally.** This verb—meaning "to bring about" or "to make happen"—though increasingly rare in English generally, abounds in legal writing. E.g., "This classification process *effected* by the maximum grant regulation produces a basic denial of equal treatment."

One writer calls it a "little word whose uses are insufficiently praised." Richard Wincor, *Contracts in Plain English* 33 (1976). True, it can be an effective way of avoiding the awkward contract-drafter's ritual, *remove or cause to be removed* or *produce or cause to be produced,* so as to include agents. (See **cause to be.**) One merely requires the party to *effect removal* or to *effect production,* so that the party may arrange with third parties to do whatever is required. This can undoubtedly aid anyone engaged in DRAFTING.

Often, however, using *effect* as the verb merely spawns wordiness. The verb tends to occur alongside BURIED VERBS, such as *settlement* and *improvement.* E.g., "Appellant petitioned to *effect a final settlement of the estate* [read *settle the estate*]."/ "The Act, which has been adopted in some other parts of the Commonwealth, has undoubtedly *effected a great improvement in practice* [read *improved practice*]." (Omitting *great* or *greatly* does the sentence no damage, as *undoubtedly* adequately conveys the intended sense.)

B. And *affect.* *Effect* (= to bring about) is often misused for *affect* (= to influence, have an effect on): "The fact that findings and conclusions under Rule 296 are not titled separately from the judgment does not *effect* [read *affect*] their validity."/ "[E]ven a revocatory clause [that] is immaterial because testator had disposed of all his property in the will, [does] not *effect* [read *affect*] the will." Thomas E. Atkinson, *Handbook of the Law of Wills* 306 (2d ed. 1953). See **affect.**

C. And *effectuate.* Most dictionaries define these words identically, but their DIFFERENTIATION should be encouraged. Although both mean "to accomplish, bring about, or cause to happen," stylists have generally considered *effect* the preferable word, *effectuate* a NEEDLESS VARIANT. No longer need this be so.

The growing distinction—common esp. in law—is that *effect* means "to cause to happen, to bring about" <effect a coup>, whereas *effectuate* means "to give effect to, to bring into effect" <effectuate the testator's intentions>. E.g., "[P]erhaps nothing more discreditable is involved than an unwillingness to acknowledge in the words of the statute itself the element of discretion that must be exercised in *effectuating* its purposes." Lon L. Fuller, *Anatomy of the Law* 42 (1968).

Of the three confusable terms—*affect, effect,* and *effectuate*—the last is the least common. Ordinarily in legal contexts, *effectuate* means "to give effect to" and not "to bring about." Thus it is *not,* despite what some think, synonymous with *effect:* "The board also ordered the following affirmative action which it was found would *effectuate* [i.e., 'give effect to,' not 'bring about'] the policies of the administration."/ "The rule has been read by courts in a manner that *effectuates* its function of timely notice without creating technical traps for the unwary."/ "A court of equity will *effectuate* the gift by declaring his heir to be a constructive trustee."

Effect is sometimes misused for *effectuate*—e.g.: "We properly must inquire beyond those minimal historical safeguards for securing trial by reason to ensure that the commands of justice are *effected* [read *effectuated* (i.e., 'given effect')]." The opposite error occurs here: "In this case, nurses from around the country have earned law degrees to *effectuate* [read *effect*] changes in the health care system." John Katzman, *Heal the System,* Tex. B.J., May 1992, at 474.

In practice, *effectuate* is not trouble-free. Some writers use it fuzzily—e.g.: "If the statutory authority is nothing more than a pretext for *effectuating* personal hostility, an award of monetary damages will be upheld." Mark M. Grossman, *The Question of Arbitrability* 109 (1984). Erroneous forms, too, such as *affectuate,* have popped up (and need to be stamped on): "Notice of release by appellant in and of itself certainly is sufficient notice to *affectuate* [read *effectuate*] a valid release." See **affect.**

effective. See **effectual.**

effective cause. See CAUSATION (B).

effectively = (1) in an effective manner; well <to speak effectively>; (2) in effect, actually <the plaintiff is effectively barred from exercising the powers of her office>; or (3) completely <he repudiated the contract just as effectively as if he had explicitly stated his intention>. Sense (2) is common in legal writing—e.g.: "The United States Courts of Appeals are *effectively* [i.e., *in effect*] courts of last resort."

Effectually is incorrect for sense (3) of *effectively:* "Such property is withdrawn from the jurisdiction of the courts of the other authority as *effectually* [read *effectively*] as if the property had been entirely removed to the territory of another sovereignty."/ "He was damaged by appellant's willful trespass just as *effectually* [read *effectively*] as if he were the real owner of the bridge." The same is true of sense (2): "*Effectually* [read *Effectively*], since this carpet measures only 54 inches in width, there are many more seams than would be necessary in a standard 12-foot carpet." See **effectual.**

effectual; effective; efficacious; efficient. All these words mean generally "having effect," but they have distinctive applications. *Effective* = (1) having a high degree of effect (used of a thing done or of the doer) <the court's power to fashion an *effective* equitable remedy>; or (2) coming into effect <effective June 3, 1994>. *Efficacious* = certain to have the desired effect (used of things) <efficacious drugs>. *Efficient* = competent to perform a task; capable of bringing about a desired effect (used of agents or their actions or instruments) <an efficient organization>. *Efficient* increasingly has economic connotations in law that are evident, e.g., in the phrase *cost-efficient,* q.v.

Effectual, perhaps the most troublesome of these words in practice, means "achieving the complete effect aimed at"; it is used apart from the agent. E.g., "I think that unity of organization is necessary to make the contest of labor *effectual.*" (Holmes)/ "If that were so, every imperfect security, however invalid as a real right, would be *effectual* as a trust." (Eng.) On the use of *effectually* for *effectively, see* **effectively.**

effectuate. See **effect** (C).

effete does not mean "effeminate" or "sophisticated and snobbish." Rather, it means "worn out, barren, exhausted."

efficacious; efficient. See **effectual.**

effrontery (= shameless insolence) for *affront* (= an open insult) is a MALAPROPISM. E.g., "To overturn the judge's denial of the motion to recuse would be an *effrontery* [read *affront*] to his character."

effulge. See BACK-FORMATIONS.

e.g., the abbreviation for the Latin phrase *exempli gratia* (= for example), introduces representative examples. In AmE, it is preferably followed by a comma (or, depending on the construction, a colon) and unitalicized. In their fine book on admiralty, Grant Gilmore and Charles L. Black (or their publishers) pedantically put a space between the two letters (*e. g.*), sometimes without a comma following. See *The Law of Admiralty* 10 (2d ed. 1975). In BrE, the periods as well as the comma are sometimes omitted—e.g.: "The problem with seeking a legislative cure for the ethical disease is that most of the perceived outrages are either already illegal (*eg,* Pentagon officials taking bribes) or beyond the reach of the law (politicians' sexual adventures)." *Washington on an Ethics Kick,* Economist, 28 Jan.–3 Feb. 1989, at 19. To American eyes, *eg* looks like *egg* misspelled.

Using the abbreviation *etc.* after an enumeration following *e.g.* creates a superfluity, since one expects nothing more than a representative sample of possibilities. But *etc.* might be required after *i.e.* (L. *id est* "that is") to show the incompleteness of the list.

In two editions, *Black's* (5th & 6th) misused *i.e.* for *e.g.* in its entry for *layman:* "One who is not of a particular profession (i.e. non-lawyer)." The abbreviation should be *e.g.,* not *i.e.,* because under the definition a nondoctor as well as a nonlawyer would be a *layman;* the parenthetical *nonlawyer* is intended only to provide an example.

One should be certain that it is clear what the signal refers to: "Out-of-pocket losses include medical expenses, lost earnings, and the cost of any labor required to do things that the plaintiff can no longer do himself (*e.g.,* a housekeeper)." But "things the plaintiff can no longer do himself" are not exemplified by *a housekeeper.* (Or does the writer mean *be a housekeeper?*) In any event, wherever readers encounter an *e.g.* they rightly expect a sampling of appropriate items—not an ambiguous or an all-inclusive listing. Here it might be, *e.g., keep house, drive a car, tend the garden.* See **i.e.**

egality is the anglicized form of the French *égalité* (= equality). The *OED* pronounces it obsolete, and so it should be, in deference to *equality.* E.g., "Is this a sign of greater *egality* [read *equality*], inverted snobbery, or simple confusion?" Robert Harris, *The Way We Were,* Sunday Times (Books), 22 July 1990, at 8-1.

egoism; egotism; egocentrism; egocentricity; egomania. *Egoism* is a legitimate philosophical term meaning "a doctrine that self-betterment is the guiding method of existence, or that self-interest is the primary motive in all one's actions." The use of *egoism* in the sense "selfishness" is a SLIPSHOD EXTENSION. *Egotism* = arrogance; an exaggerated sense of self-importance; self-praise. *Egocentrism* and *egocentricity* are synonymous, with perhaps a slight nuance. *Egocentrism* = the quality of being self-centered and selfish; looking only to one's own feelings and needs. *Egocentricity* = the quality of being egocentric, individualistic, or self-centered. *Egomania* is extreme *egocentrism.*

egregious /*i-**gree**-jəs*/ formerly meant merely "outstanding," but has been specialized in a pejorative sense so that it now means "outstandingly bad."

egress; ingress. *Egress* = the right or liberty of going out. *Ingress* = the right or liberty of going in. The correct prepositions are illustrated here: "The company breached its duty to furnish Rivers with a safe means of *ingress* to and *egress* from the vessel."

The legal phrase *ingress, egress, and regress* = the right to enter, leave, and reenter. Courts and lawyers have sometimes mistaken the import of these terms. *Black's* (1st–6th eds.) erroneously defines *ingress, egress, and regress* as "the right (as of a lessee) to enter, *go upon* [read *leave*], and *return from* [read *return to*] the lands in question." The same dictionary states that *egress* is "often used interchangeably with the word *access,*" apparently confusing *egress* with *ingress.*

eight corners. See **four corners of the instrument.**

either. A. Number of Elements. Most properly, *either . . . or* can frame only two alternatives, and no more: "He testified that in the last few years terrazzo had been used more extensively in entranceways than *either* marble, tile, cement, *or* asphalt [omit *either*]." See CORRELATIVE CONJUNCTIONS (B).

B. Singular or Plural. Nouns framed by *either . . . or* take a singular verb when they are both singular, or where only the latter is singular. E.g., "There was no evidence that either DeGraft or his corporation *were* [read *was*] under the control of defendants."

The same principle applies to nouns that should agree in number with the subject: "The situation should not be viewed in terms of whether the Constitution somehow makes a teacher or librarian the proper *selectors* [read *selector*] of a curriculum or books."/ "If *either* had been a male *they* [read *the couple,* or, depending on the sense, *he*] would have been prohibited from intermarrying." See CONCORD & SUBJECT-VERB AGREEMENT (E).

C. *Not . . . either.* These should be made into *neither . . . nor* constructions. E.g., "Other states *do not require either a notice or registration* [read *require neither notice nor registration*], although they may require filing of a report of sale."

D. *Either or both.* This phrase denotes the meaning generally assigned to *and/or,* q.v., but neither phrase finds a place in good legal writing. E.g., "One must plead *either or both that* [read *either that*] the state has established a procedure that itself is constitutionally deficient *or that* it has provided no adequate remedy for aberrational [q.v.] departures by the servants from proper procedures [add a comma, and then: *or both*]."/ "Judicial sanctions in civil contempt proceedings may, in a proper case, be employed *for either or both of two purposes* [read *for either of two purposes*]." (If *both* rationales exist, then no one would seriously argue that the sanctions are unavailable.)

E. *Either . . . and/or.* This construction is illogical: "Plaintiff states that she has no responsive documents that she is withholding from Defendant *under any claim of either the attorney-client and/or the work-product privileges* [read *under the attorney-client or work-product privilege*]." See **and/or.**

ejaculate can no longer be used in sober writing as a synonym for "exclaim."

ejectee. See -EE.

ejectment; ejection; ouster. These terms are deceptively similar but have important differences. *Ejectment* and *ejection* are names of actions at law, whereas *ouster* is a legal wrong. *Ejectment* = (1) ejection of a tenant or occupier from property; or (2) trespass to try title—a legal action in which a person ejected from property seeks to recover possession and damages. This action was abolished in England in 1852 but persists in some American jurisdictions. E.g., "We think it is clear in this case that the complainants in this bill might have brought *ejectment* for the land against the tenants in possession." *Ejection* is the term for a similar action in Scots law.

Ouster is something different: "the act of wrongfully dispossessing someone of any kind of hereditament, such as freehold property" (*CDL*).

ejusdem generis is a canon of construction providing that when general words follow the enumeration of persons or things of a specific meaning, the general words will be construed as applying only to persons or things of the same general class as those enumerated. For example, in the Sunday Observance Act 1677, the language *no tradesman, artificer, workman, labourer or other person whatever* was held not to include a coach proprietor, a farmer, a barber, or a real-estate agent; the general words *or other person whatever* were held confined to persons with similar occupations to those specifically listed—despite the breadth of *whatever.* Similarly, if a lease forbade the tenant to keep *kerosene, camphene, burning fluid, or any other illuminating material,* the general language at the end would not include a light bulb, though it is indisputably an "illuminating material" if the language is taken literally.

The phrase is often used adjectivally—e.g.: "The assembly of machinery is not *ejusdem generis* with 'cleaning, lubricating, and painting.'" Sometimes it functions as an adverb—e.g.: "The general words at the end of the perils clause have been construed *ejusdem generis* with the preceding enumerated perils." Grant Gilmore & Charles L. Black, Jr., *The Law of Admiralty* 74 (2d ed. 1975).

The term is pronounced /*ee-**joos**-dəm-**jen**-ə-ris*/, /*ee-**yoos**-dəm*/, or (BrE) /*ee-**jəs**-dəm*/, and is occasionally spelled *eiusdem generis* (the classical way, which is Latin but not English).

eke out. Journalists often misuse this PHRASAL VERB by writing, for example, that Smith *eked out* a victory over Jones in the election (as if the phrase meant, in colloquial terms, "squeaked by Jones"). *Eke out* properly means "to supplement, add to, or make go farther or last longer." Here the phrase is correctly used: "There have been many cases in which there was nothing in the way of context or other laws *in pari materia* by which to *eke out* a statute where the provisions were so obscure that a court, with best of intention, could not ascertain and declare its proper meaning." Roscoe Pound, *The Formative Era of American Law* 68 (1938)./ "It was considered possible to solve all legal problems by deduction from the actual rules of English law, *eked out* [i.e., supplemented] perhaps by careful borrowing from the Roman jurists."

One may *eke out* one's income by working nights as well as days. But one does not, properly, *eke out* an existence: "Appellant claimed to have brought more than $70,000 with him from Vermont, when his testimony showed that during his period there he was *barely able to eke out an existence* [read *barely able to make ends meet,* or some other CLICHÉ]." Nor does the phrase mean "to acquire by difficulty or drudgery."

elaborate, v.i. & v.t., is commonly intransitive in nonlegal contexts <to elaborate on a point>, and transitive in legal contexts <to elaborate a point>. E.g., "A well-known passage in Blackstone's Commentaries *elaborates* the so-called fourfold unity of a joint tenancy." Although both *to elaborate* and *to elaborate on* may mean "to work out in detail," the former suggests "to produce by labor," and the latter suggests "to explain at greater length." Awareness of this nuance allows one to choose the apter phrasing.

elder; eldest. These are variants of *older* and *oldest,* with restricted uses: one refers to an *elder* brother or sister, or to the *eldest* son or daughter, but elsewhere the form is out of place. *Older* and *oldest* may always substitute for *elder* and *eldest.*

elect is a LEGALISM meaning "to choose deliberately." A FORMAL WORD generally followed by an infinitive in legal prose, *elect* should not be used where a simple *choose* will suffice. E.g., "The petitioner *elected* [read *chose*] to declare the entire indebtedness to be immediately due and payable."/ "It is suggested that he does not have the mental capability to *elect* [read *choose*] to continue further judicial examination of his conviction."/ "With the consent of the trustees, he may *elect* [read *choose*] to take his benefits in a lump sum, or part lump sum and part annuity." The changes here suggested are stylistic merely; *elect* cannot be said to be wrong—it is merely symptomatic of LEGALESE.

electee (= [1] one chosen or elected; or [2] one to whom the law gives a choice about status) is recorded in the *OED* and supported by a single quotation, from 1593. One might suppose that, because *electee* is omitted from most unabridged dictionaries, it was a 16th-century nonce word that is long since defunct. So prudent writers would suppose; yet the word has been successfully revived. E.g., sense (1): "Petitioners would enjoin the *electees* from acting." *Littig v. Democratic County Comm.* 38 N.Y.S.2d 214, 216 (Sup. Ct. 1942). Whether this word will gain currency as a correlative of *elector* it is too early to say.

Sense (2) is an illogical use of the -EE suffix, since the *electee* is the person put to the election—the *elector,* in effect: "A section 411 *electee* . . . is qualified to make an election to have his retired pay computed under section 402(d)." *Aflague v. U.S.,* 298 F.2d 446, 449 (Ct. Cl. 1962).

elective. This term is used primarily in relation to political elections. *Elective* = appointed by election; subject to election. In legal writing, however, *elective* is used more broadly of legal choices: "The widow took her *elective share* of the estate."

elector = (1) esp. in BrE, a legally qualified voter; or (2) in AmE, a member of the electoral college chosen by the states to elect the president and vice president. Sense (1) appears occasionally in AmE, esp. in older works—e.g.: "The first view to be taken of this part of the government relates to the qualifications of the *electors* and the elected." *The Federalist* No. 52, at 325 (James Madison) (Clinton Rossiter ed., 1961). Sense (2) is more usual in modern AmE—e.g.: "[T]he President held office for four years and then had to be given—or denied—a second term by *electors* picked by the people." Fred Rodell, *Nine Men* 44 (1955).

electorial is a common error for *electoral* (= of or relating to electors). E.g., "The new district would be divided into *electorial* [read *electoral*] subdistricts utilizing the current community college district boundaries." *Liddell v. Board of Educ.,* 733 F. Supp. 1324, 1327 (E.D. Mo. 1990).

eleemosynary */el-ə-**mos**-ə-ner-ee/*, related etymologically to the word *alms,* is a FORMAL WORD for *charitable.* It is more common in legal than in nonlegal prose. E.g., "The church seeks and obtains the *eleemosynary* contributions of the laity, not for private gain, but for the aid of pious institutions and objects of every nature."/ "The court held the cy-pres statutes inapplicable because the trust was not for a charitable, benevolent, or *eleemosynary* purpose."

ELEGANT VARIATION. See INELEGANT VARIATION.

elemental; elementary. *Elemental* is the more specific term, meaning "of or relating to the elements of something; essential." E.g., "We do what *elemental* justice and fundamental fairness demand under the necessitous circumstances." *Elementary* means "introductory; simple; fundamental." E.g., "It is *elementary* that an executory contract, in order to be enforceable, must be based upon a valuable consideration."

eligible may equally well be construed with either *for* or *to* (an office). *Eligible for* is more common today than *eligible to,* but the latter has unimpeachable credentials: "No person except a natural born citizen . . . shall be *eligible to* the office of president." U.S. Const. art. II, § 1./ "No judge of any court . . . shall during the term for which he is elected or appointed, be *eligible to* the legislature." Tex. Const. art. III, § 19.

elisor */ə-**lı**-zər/*, omitted from *W3* but generally included in unabridged dictionaries, means "a person appointed by a court to return a jury, serve a writ, or perform other duties of the sheriff or a coroner in case of his disqualification" *(W2).* Though comparatively rare, the term is still used in some American jurisdictions. E.g., "In view of our holding that the *elisor* was an interested person, we do not reach a determination as to the validity of the service of process under Bahamian law." *Wakeman v. Farish,* 356 So. 2d 1323, 1325 (Fla. Dist. Ct. App. 1978). The form *eslisor* is a NEEDLESS VARIANT.

ELLIPSES. See QUOTATIONS (E).

elocution; locution; allocution. *Elocution* = style in speaking; the art of speaking persuasively. *Locution* = a word or phrase. For *allocution,* see the entry under that word.

eloi(g)n is an archaic legal term meaning "to convey or remove out of the jurisdiction of the court or of the sheriff" *(OED).* Generally the word is spelled *eloign* rather than *eloin.*

elope. The *OED* and many other dictionaries define this term as if it had historically been a "sexist" one in law: "**a.** *Law.* Of a wife: To run away from her husband in the company of a paramour. **b.** In popular language also (and more frequently) said of a woman running away from home with a lover for the purpose of being married" (*OED*). These definitions suggest that only women can elope, but legal contexts have long made men as well as women elopers—e.g.: "[I]f evidence was admitted to show that House had armed himself, and was hunting for Steadman under the impression that the latter had *eloped* with his wife, and was secreting himself in that vicinity, it is difficult to see upon what principle his threats in that connection were excluded." *Alexander v. U.S.,* 138 U.S. 353, 356 (1891)./ "James Campbell had *eloped* with the wife of one Ludlow . . . ." *Adger v. Ackerman,* 115 F. 124, 130 (8th Cir. 1902).

else's. Such possessive constructions as *anyone else's* and *everybody else's* are preferred to the obsolete constructions *anyone's else* and *everybody's else. See* POSSESSIVES (G).

elude. See **allude.**

elusive; elusory; illusive; illusory. *Elusive* (rather than *elusory*) is the usual adjective related to *elude*; *illusory* (rather than *illusive*) is the usual adjective related to *illusion.* Here *illusive* has almost certainly been misused for *elusive:* "The discussion almost inevitably returns to the *illusive* [read *elusive*] subject of what the Supreme Court really held. . . ." *B-U Acquisition Group, Inc. v. Utica Mut. Ins. Co.,* 52 B.R. 541, 544 (Bankr. S.D. Ohio 1985). See **illusory.**

EM-, IM-. See EN-.

emanate = (1) to flow forth, issue, originate from a person or thing as a source; or (2) to proceed from a material source (*OED*). Sense (2) applies to physical senses. E.g., "The use of a human investigator was a factor involved in *State v. Groves,* where an airplane pilot's detection of an odor *emanating* from luggage he was unloading led to a sniff of that luggage by a trained police dog."

The word is coming to be overworked in sense (1), rising almost to the level of a VOGUE WORD. Its use in the law is old: "In discussing this question, the counsel for the State of Maryland have deemed it of some importance, in the construction of the constitution, to consider that instrument not as *emanating* from the people, but as the act of sovereign and independent States." *McCulloch v. Maryland,* 17 U.S. (4 Wheat.) 316, 402 (1819) (per Marshall, C.J.).

Judges today seemed enamored of the word, which is fast becoming another legal CLICHÉ: "Moreover, there are other suggestions such as that *emanating* from Dean Wigmore at a time when the question whether the parol evidence rule was proper subject-matter for evidence or contracts had not been decided."/ "It appears that the first advancement statute was based on the custom of London and York, and that the custom must have *emanated* from the Roman (or civil) law principle of collatio bonorum, requiring a bringing into hotchpot [q.v.]."/ "Defendant pleaded guilty to two counts of bank robbery charged in an indictment *emanating* from the District of Minnesota."

emancipate = to set free (as a minor or a slave) from legal, social, or political restraint. In modern legal contexts, one most frequently encounters this term in reference to minors—e.g.: "Plaintiff Adele Gelbman was the passenger in an automobile owned by her and operated by her *unemancipated* 16-year-old son." *Gelbman v. Gelbman,* 245 N.E.2d 192, 192 (N.Y. Ct. App. 1969).

emancipation; mancipation. The former means "the act of freeing from slavery," the latter "the act of enslaving."

emasculate means literally "to castrate," but has come figuratively to mean "to deprive of strength and vigor, to weaken." The word is a favorite of judges in dissent. E.g., "More important in the long run than this misreading of the federal statute, however, is the court's *emasculation* of the equal protection clause as a constitutional principle applicable to the area of social welfare administration."/ "Under the majority's *emasculation* of the Act, no determination need be made whether the substantial question is likely to be determined favorably on appeal." Cf. **eviscerate.**

embarrass. Only in legal contexts is this word today used in the sense "to encumber, hamper, impede." E.g., "Even in Tucker Act cases the problem of joinder should not be *embarrassed* by any doctrine of sovereign immunity." (The Tucker Act allows certain persons to sue the government.)/ "We think that the arguments of the parties are considerably *embarrassed* by factors not touched upon by the parties." Most nonlawyers would find puzzling these uses of *embarrass.* See EUPHEMISMS.

embassador. See **ambassador.**

embassy; legation. Often assumed to be synonymous, these words should be distinguished. An *embassy* is under an ambassador, and a *legation* is under a minister, envoy, chargé d'affaires, or some other diplomatic agent.

embezzle; misappropriate; steal. *Embezzle* (= to fraudulently convert personal property that one has been entrusted with) is now always used in reference to fiduciaries. *Misappropriate* means "to take for oneself wrongfully" and may or may not be used of a fiduciary. *Steal,* like *misappropriate,* is generally a broader term than *embezzle*; it has the same meaning as *misappropriate,* but much stronger negative connotations. See **defalcate, misappropriate, peculation** & **steal.**

emblements (= [1] crop production, or profits from crops produced by the cultivator's labor, or [2] a common-law doctrine giving the planter of crops ownership rights in those crops after the planter has unexpectedly lost possession of the land before harvest) is a Law French term [fr. OF. *emblaer* "to sow with wheat or oats"] that persists in modern legal writing—but it is surely preferable to its Latin alternative, *fructus industriales.* E.g., "The duration of a life estate being uncertain, the law encourages the life tenant to cultivate the land by giving him the right to '*emblements.*' This is the right of the legal personal representatives of a deceased life tenant . . . to enter the land after the life estate has come to an end and reap the crops which the life tenant has sown." Peter Butt, *Land Law* 111 (2d ed. 1988). The word is anglicized in pronunciation: /***em**-bli-mənts*/.

embrace, in figurative senses, may mean either (1) "to include" or (2) "to adopt." Here sense (1), largely a legal sense, applies: "Personal liberty or the right of property *embraces* the right to make contracts for the sale of one's own labor and the employment of one's individual and industrial sources."/ "There is no support in the record for the proposition that Bombay's business and goodwill could be protected only by a restrictive covenant *embracing* almost all of the North American continent."/ "The general article was interpreted to *embrace* only crimes the commission of which had some direct impact on military discipline."

Sense (2), used in legal and nonlegal contexts alike, is exemplified in this sentence: "While appellants try to argue that dilution cases involve a mixed question of law and fact not governed by the clearly erroneous standard, we cannot *embrace* this argument."

embracee. See **embrace(o)r.**

embrace(o)r. This term, meaning "one guilty of embracery [= the offense of influencing a jury illegally and corruptly]," is best spelled *embracer,* preferred by the *OED* and the *AHD. W3* and *Webster's New World Dictionary* include their main entries under *embraceor,* with the ill-formed suffix.

Some writers use the NEOLOGISM *embracee* as the correlative of *embracer*—e.g.: "If it takes the form of a bribe and is accepted, both the *embracer* (giver) and *embracee* (taker) are guilty of bribery." Rollin M. Perkins & Ronald N. Boyce, *Criminal Law* 551 (3d ed. 1982).

embracery; imbracery; bracery. The first form is standard for this word, which denotes the offense of attempting to corrupt or instruct a jury to reach a particular conclusion by means other than evidence or argument in court, as by bribing or threatening jurors. The popular term for this offense is *jury-tampering.* See **jury-packing.**

Imbracery and *bracery* are NEEDLESS VARIANTS.

emend. See **amend.**

emigrant; émigré. There is a latent DIFFERENTIATION between these words. An *emigrant* is one who leaves a country to settle in another. *Émigré* has the same sense, but applies especially to one in political exile. The first acute accent is often omitted (*emigré*) in AmE.

emigrate. See **immigrate.**

émigré. See **emigrant.**

eminence (= loftiness, prominence) is misused in the following sentence, but whether the desired word is *imminence* (= the quality or state of being ready to take place) or *immanence* (= inherence) is unclear: "The phrase 'imminent danger,' for example, suggested immediacy, inherence, and *eminence* [read *imminence* or *immanence,* either one of which would create a REDUNDANCY]." Edward H. Levi, *An Introduction to Legal Reasoning* 27 (1949; repr. 1972).

eminent. See **imminent.**

eminent domain; condemnation; expropriation. The 17th-century civilian Grotius coined the term *eminens dominium,* from which our phrase derives. In BrE, *eminent domain* is primarily a term of international law. In AmE, it refers to the power of federal and local governments to pronounce judicially (land, etc.) as converted to public use. The usual BrE term for this sense is *expropriation. Condemnation,* an Americanism, has virtually the same sense: "judicial assignation (of property) to public purposes, subject to reasonable compensation." E.g., "This is a *condemnation* proceeding brought by the County of Matagorda to condemn four parcels of land." See **compulsory purchase.**

emote. See BACK-FORMATIONS.

empanel; impanel. *Empanel* (= to swear a jury to try an issue [*CDL*]) is now the preferred spelling in both AmE and BrE. E.g., "The cause came on for trial with a jury duly *empaneled." Impanel* was formerly a common spelling, used, e.g., in *Franklin v. South Carolina,* 218 U.S. 161, 166 (1910).

empathy; sympathy. *Empathy* is the ability to imagine oneself in another person's position and to experience all the sensations connected with it. *Sympathy* is compassion for or commiseration with another.

emphasis added; emphasis supplied. These citation signals are both used to indicate that, in quoting another's words, the writer has italicized some of them. There is no distinction in meaning between the phrases, as some writers occasionally assume. *Emphasis in original* is used to indicate that the italics appear in the original material as here quoted.

emphyteusis (= the right of a person who is not the owner of a piece of land to use it as his or her own in perpetuity, subject to forfeiture for nonpayment of a fixed rent) is a civil-law term that appears sometimes in Anglo-American legal writing. E.g., "This is the *Emphyteusis,* upon which the Fief of the middle ages has often been fathered, though without much knowledge of the exact share which it had in bringing feudal ownership into the world." Henry S. Maine, *Ancient Law* 248 (17th ed. 1901; repr. [New Universal Lib.] 1905, 1910)./ "[A]lthough the Romans used the term 'dominium,' the holder of land by *emphyteusis* was also treated in many ways as an owner." *Butler v. Baber,* 529 So. 2d 374, 381 (La. 1988). The corresponding adjective is *emphyteutic.*

empiricize, not in the dictionaries, has made an appearance in an American law report: "Just as experienced physicians render diagnoses on the basis of symptoms they sense, but often cannot *empiricize* [= confirm or verify by testing] or articulate, so too, we are told, can those who work among prisoners develop 'senses' concerning the potential for impending disobedience or unrest." *Abdul Wali v. Coughlin,* 754 F.2d 1015, 1018 (2d Cir. 1985).

empirics is not in good use for *empiricism.* Cf. **esoterics.**

emplead. See **implead.**

employe(e). Although *employé,* the French form, might logically be thought to be better as a generic term, *employée* (which in French denotes the feminine gender) is so widespread (without the accent mark) that it is not likely to be uprooted. *The Wall Street Journal* and a few other publications remain staunch adherents to the form *employe* (minus the acute accent on the final *-e*); but *employee* is standard.

It did not always have such a stronghold, however. *Employe* was once common in English. E.g., "We need hardly repeat the statement . . . that in the Employers' Liability Act Congress used the words 'employé' and 'employed' in their natural sense, and intended to describe the conventional relation of employer and *employé.*" *Hull v. Philadelphia & R.R.,* 40 S. Ct. 358, 359 (1920) (spelled *employee* at 252 U.S. 475, 479). See **independent contractor.**

employer and employee; master and servant. The former phrase seems to be supplanting the latter, which at best sounds antiquarian and, to many, derogatory. Also, *employee* is more transparently distinguishable from *agent* than *servant* is. See **agent.**

empty-chair defense is an Americanism referring to a common tactic of defendants: when one defendant has settled before trial, the remaining defendant can try to put all fault on the absent one (i.e., the one not occupying a chair at trial).

emulate; immolate. The former is to strive to equal or rival, to copy or imitate with the object of equaling. The latter is to kill as a sacrifice.

Emulate is frequently misused, as, e.g., here for *adopt:* "I cannot believe that a company trying to estimate the effect of a marketing tool would *emulate* [read *adopt*] the methods that lawyers use in taking depositions."

EN-, IN-. No consistent rules exist for determining which form of the prefix to use before a given word. In AmE at present, the spellings *entrust, enclose, inquire* (= to ask), and *increase* are standard. The BrE spellings are *entrust, enclose, enquire* (= to ask), and *increase,* but the variants *intrust* and *inclose* still appear with some frequency. Especially troublesome to writers are word-pairs with varying prefixes according to inflection: *encrust* but *incrustation*; *engrain* (= to dye in the raw state) but *ingrained* (= deeply rooted). For a discussion of *in-* as both privative and intensive, see NEGATIVES (B).

enabling statute. This phrase was perhaps first used specifically in reference to the act (32 Hen. VIII. c. 28) by which tenants-in-fee and certain others were "enabled" to make leases (*OED*). Now the phrase is used in reference to any statute conferring powers, and in the U.S. usually to a congressional statute conferring powers on executive agencies to carry out various tasks delegated to them. E.g., "Procedural uniformity seems to be weakening, as the Congress has become increasingly willing to prescribe detailed codes of procedure in *enabling* legislation." See **disabling statute & disenable.**

enact. The platitude is that courts adjudicate, rather than legislate. Some judicial decisions seem to belie this principle; still, it is unidiomatic to refer to a court as enacting doctrines: "The Supreme Court has *enacted* [read *enunciated* or some other word] a 'public safety' exception to *Miranda.*"

enactment = (1) the action or process of making (a legislative bill) into law <enactment of the bill>; or (2) a statute <a recent enactment>. The word is best not used by legal writers in sense (2), although it has been so used almost from its beginning in the early 19th century. Still, to use *enactment* in sense (2) is to add an unneeded synonym and to muddle a useful distinction. The plural almost always manifests this stylistically poor use: "*Congressional enactments* [read *Congressional acts* or *Federal statutes*] come to this court with an extremely heavy presumption of validity." See **act (C).**

Nevertheless, sense (2) is so pervasive that we can do little else but avoid it in our own writing; criticism of its users (as opposed to its use) is unfair, given its pervasiveness. The *OCL* and *CDL* define *enactment* only in sense (2): "a statute or Act of Parliament, statutory instrument, by-law or other statement of law made by a person or body with legislative powers" (*OCL*). Likewise, it is used in sense (2) in the Assimilative Crimes Act, 18 U.S.C. § 13 (1982), which states that certain acts or omissions are "not made punishable by any enactment of Congress." Perhaps the use of the term in the last-quoted example arose from the mistaken notion that *act* in *acts and omissions* might be confused with *act of Congress.* Even were that true, *federal statute* would suffice in place of *act of Congress.*

en banc; in banc; in banco; in bank. A. Spelling and Pronunciation. *W3* lists only *en banc* (= in full court; F. lit. "on the bench"), the predominant form in English-speaking countries. *In banc* and *in bank* also appear in a few jurisdictions, but these are not widespread. The Arizona courts use *in banc*—as in *Spur Industries, Inc. v. Del E. Webb Development Co.,* 494 P.2d 700 (Ariz. 1972) (*in banc*)—and so do the Maryland courts, though the commentators wonder why: "There is no justification for the spelling *in banc* other than the fact that it was used by the drafters of the Maryland Constitution." Paul V. Niemeyer & Linda M. Richards, *Maryland Rules Commentary* 339 (1984).

Unfortunately, the Federal Rules of Appellate Procedure, as well as statutes addressing appellate procedure, use the spelling *in banc.* Judge Jon O. Newman, of the Second Circuit, reluctantly acquiesced to *in banc* in an article discussing *en banc* proceedings: "Grudgingly, I accept the spelling of '*in banc*' adopted by the pertinent statute, 28 U.S.C. § 46(c) (1982), and the federal rule, Fed. R. App. P. 35. Use of the term as it appeared in Old French, '*en banc,*' seems preferable." *In Banc Practice in the Second Circuit,* 50 Brooklyn L. Rev. 365, 365 n.1 (1984).

The Supreme Court of California, meanwhile, uses *in bank.* See, e.g., *In re Los Angeles County Pioneer Society,* 257 P.2d 1 (Cal. 1953) *(in bank).* *In banco* is listed in *Black's* (6th ed.) but is rarely if ever used.

En banc being now the usual spelling, the burden falls on English-speaking lawyers to pronounce the word correctly. Certainly the anglicized pronunciation /*in-**bank***/ is unexceptionable; the French approximation /*on-**bonk***/ is also common, though some may consider it precious. And reporters are likely to misspell the phrase—e.g.: "'In fact there had been a fair degree of unanimity on this until last September, when the Fifth Circuit sitting *en banque* [read *en banc*] took their renegade path,' said Mr. McDuff." Ronald Smothers, *Challenges to Judicial Elections Revive,* N.Y. Times, 22 June 1991, at 9.

B. Adjective or Adverb. The phrase *en banc* may be either adjectival <en banc proceedings> or adverbial <the court heard the case en banc>. Chief Justice Rehnquist has even used the phrase as a SENTENCE ADVERB: "*En banc,* the Court of Appeals for the Fifth Circuit reversed." *Crawford Fitting Co. v. J.T. Gibbons, Inc.,* 482 U.S. 437, 439 (1987) (per Rehnquist, C.J.).

enbancworthy (= worthy of being considered en banc) is a term concocted by, and still generally confined to, the judges of the United States Court of Appeals for the Fifth Circuit. As legal JARGON formed on the model of words like *seaworthy* and *airworthy,* it is useful shorthand, though odd-sounding. E.g., "This opens up a whole array of influences which for nearly all cases [affect] . . . whether the case is *enbancworthy.*" *Allen v. Johnson,* 391 F.2d 527, 532 (5th Cir. 1968) (per Brown, C.J)./ "As one who shares his misgivings, I feel obligated to state concisely my reasons for believing that the present case is *enbancworthy.*" *Becker v. Thompson,* 463 F.2d 1338, 1339 (5th Cir. 1972) (Brown, C.J., dissenting)./ "Briefs and oral arguments on rehearing en banc lead the Court to conclude that this case is not *enbancworthy.*" *McLaurin v. Columbia Mun. Separate Sch. Dist.,* 486 F.2d 1049, 1050 (5th Cir. 1973)./ "Although standing alone, this problem would hardly be *enbancworthy,* we conclude that action by us is appropriate rather than letting stand the panel's analysis of third-party beneficiary." *Hercules, Inc. v. Stevens Shipping Co.,* 698 F.2d 726, 736 (5th Cir. 1983). Cf. **certworthy.**

The corresponding noun is *enbancworthiness,* and the antonym is *unenbancworthy*—e.g.: "I would agree that this case would be *unenbancworthy* if the panel had avoided the Chambers question on any one of the several grounds suggested . . . ." *Maness v. Wainwright,* 528 F.2d 1381, 1381 (5th Cir. 1976) (Goldberg, J., dissenting).Cf. **unenbanc.**

enclose; inclose. The former spelling is now preferred in all senses. E.g., "The complaint alleged that certain statements in the publication (those *inclosed* [read *enclosed*] in brackets) were false." See EN-.

enclosed herewith and *enclosed herein* are unnecessary for *enclosed;* in both phrases, the first word conveys the idea redundantly expressed by the second. See **enclosed please find.**

enclosed please find is archaic deadwood in lawyers' correspondence for *enclosed is* or *I have enclosed.* Whether the phrase was originally commercialese or LEGALESE, it has been cant since its creation.

In referring to a variant form of this phrase—*please find enclosed*—a 19th-century commentator aptly remarked: "A more ridiculous use of words, it seems to me, there could not be." Richard G. White, *Every-Day English* 492 (1880).

enclosure; inclosure. The former spelling is preferred in all senses. See EN-.

encomium. Pl. *-iums, -ia.* The English plural is preferred—e.g.: "In truth, the book is in no sense a law book, and some of the most enthusiastic *encomiums* of it that I have heard have come from gentlemen who have never opened a law book." C.C. Langdell, *Dominant Opinions in England During the Nineteenth Century,* 19 Harv. L. Rev. 151, 153 (1906). See PLURALS (A).

encrease is an obsolete spelling of *increase* used, e.g., in the U.S. Const., art. I, § 6. See EN-.

encrust; incrust. See EN-.

encumber. See **incumber.**

encumbrance; incumbrance; cumbrance. The preferred spelling of this word, meaning "a claim or liability that is attached to property and that may lessen its value," is *encumbrance* in both AmE and BrE. E.g., "The court erred in holding that the shares of stock to Lillian Conway Fine are free and clear of liens and *encumbrances.*" Yet *incumbrance* is the spelling used in the British Finance Act of 1975. *Cumbrance* is a NEEDLESS VARIANT. See **liens and encumbrances.**

encumbrancer (= a person who holds an encumbrance) is a slightly archaic word that can often be replaced by *lienholder.* (See **lienor.**) A variant spelling to be avoided is *incumbrancer.*

endeavor is a FORMAL WORD for *attempt* or *try.* E.g., "No such clemency can be extended to an attorney who deliberately and persistently *endeavors* to submit evidence that is clearly incompetent and that, as a lawyer, he is presumed to know is incompetent."

The same is true of *endeavor* as a noun: "To attempt to limit English competition in this way would be as hopeless an *endeavour* as the experiment of King Canute." (Eng.)

On the difference between the AmE and the BrE spelling, see -OR.

endemic. See **epidemic.**

end(ing). *End,* not *ending,* is the proper correlative of *beginning.* E.g., "The turnover of the Sinai is a beginning, not an *ending* [read *end*]." Obviously, the writer was trying for parallel *-ings.*

endnote. See **footnote.**

endorse; indorse. The usual spelling in nonlegal contexts is *endorse;* that is the only acceptable spelling of the word when used figuratively to mean "to express approval of." In legal senses relating to negotiable instruments, *indorse* predominates in the U.S., and the word is so spelled throughout the Uniform Commercial Code. This latent DIFFERENTIATION ought to be encouraged. In Great Britain, however, *endorse* is the more frequent spelling even in the context of commercial paper.

Indorse on the back is a REDUNDANCY; the root *dors-* means "back."

endorsee. See -EE.

endowment has two quite different senses: (1) "the assignment of a wife's dower"; or (2) "the bestowal of money, income, or property to some person or institution."

end product is usually a REDUNDANCY for *product.* Cf. **end result.**

end result is a REDUNDANCY for *result.* Safire calls it "redundant, tautological and unnecessarily repetitive, not to mention prolix and wordy." William Safire, *Peace-ese,* N.Y. Times, 17 Nov. 1991, § 6, at 22. E.g., "The *end result* [read *result*] of the Supreme Court's labors was that many maritime workers . . . could recover full damages in the unseaworthiness action . . . ." Grant Gilmore & Charles L. Black, Jr., *The Law of Admiralty* 411 (2d ed. 1975). Cf. **final result** & **final destination.**

endue. See **indue.**

ends and objects. See DOUBLETS, TRIPLETS, AND SYNONYM-STRINGS.

enervate; innervate. The former means "to drain the vigor out of," the latter "to supply with energy."

enfeoff; infeoff. See **feoff.**

enforce; inforce. **A. Spelling.** The latter is an archaic spelling whose only vestige appears in *reinforce.* See EN-.

B. "Enforcing" a Contract. Lawyers continually speak of *enforcing* contracts, though this term is not apt unless one is seeking specific performance. Usually, the law merely specifies a remedy for breach of contract—damages—and does not compel performance.

enforceable; enforcible. *Enforceable* is the preferred, standard spelling in both AmE and BrE. E.g., "A contract is *enforcible* [read *enforceable*] even though it does not specify the type of deed to be given." Robert Kratovil, *Real Estate Law* 83 (1946).

enfranchise. See **franchise.**

English rule, the. American lawyers speak of *the English rule* in many contexts in which English law differs from American law. But throughout the 1980s, the phrase increasingly denoted only one rule: that the losing party in litigation must pay the winner's costs and attorney's fees. E.g., "Most American lawyers abhor *the English rule.* It requires the losing side in a civil suit to pay the winning side's attorneys' costs. This approach would discourage weak or frivolous suits, while encouraging defendants to settle strong suits against them. More generally, it would promote new and less costly ways of resolving conflicts aside from litigation." Robert J. Samuelson, *I Am a Big Lawyer Basher,* Newsweek, 27 April 1992, at 62./ "I would think real, real seriously about adopting *the English Rule.* You lose, you pay." Michele Galen, *Guilty! Too Many Lawyers and Too Much Litigation,* BusinessWeek, 13 April 1992, at 60, 65 (quoting Scott Turow). A synonymous phrase—and a sharper one—is *the loser-pays rule.*

engraft; ingraft. The word is best spelled *engraft.* See EN-.

engrandize. See **aggrandize.**

engross, ingross; enrol(l), inrol(l). The preferred spellings are *engross* and *enroll* (AmE), *enrol* (BrE). Both words have to do with the preparation of legal documents. To *engross* a legal document (as a deed) is to prepare a fair copy ready for execution. To *enroll* it is to enter it into an official record upon execution. See **enrol(l)ment.**

enjeopard. See **jeopardize.**

enjoin (from) (upon). *Enjoin* has two basic meanings, each the exact opposite of the other. In sense (1), which is positive in intent, *enjoin* means to prescribe, to mandate, or to order that something be done. This sense, used most frequently in BrE (though not wholly unknown in AmE), occurs with either of two prepositions: *upon* or *to.* E.g., "In France and Germany, for example, equity has been a clearly recognized element in the administration of justice, and *enjoined upon* the judge, but assigned to no special jurisdiction." Carleton K. Allen, *Law in the Making* 414 (7th ed. 1964)./ "Courts are ill-suited to resolve hypothetical issues and are constitutionally *enjoined to* decide only concrete cases." (Eng.)

In sense (2), which is negative in intent, *enjoin* means to prohibit, to forbid, or to restrain someone by court order from doing a specific act or behaving in a certain way. In this second meaning, the verb takes the preposition *from*—not *to* or *upon.* E.g., "The court *enjoined* the company *from* selling any further cargoes of Nigerian oil to buyers other than the plaintiff."

In the sense "to prohibit by injunction," *enjoin* is preferable to the BACK-FORMATION *injunct,* dated in the *OED* from 1872. See **enjoinder & injunction enjoining.**

enjoinable (= capable of being prohibited by injunction), dating from the late 19th century, is contained in no major English dictionary but has proved useful to American judges—e.g.:

- "[A]ll such activity would be properly *enjoinable* insofar as it advocated a strike by public employees." *In re Berry,* 436 P.2d 273, 285 (Cal. 1968) (en banc).
- "Spur's operation was an *enjoinable* public nuisance." *Spur Indus., Inc. v. Del E. Webb Dev. Co.,* 494 P.2d 700, 706 (Ariz. 1972) (en banc).
- "[W]e find that appellees' use of the house and adjoining premises as a church constitutes a clear and *enjoinable* violation of the restriction in issue here." *Kessler v. Stough,* 361 So. 2d 1048, 1050 (Ala. 1978).
- "That secondary picketing is unlawful and *enjoinable* today in almost every other industry is none of our business." *Burlington N. R.R. v. Brotherhood of Maintenance of Way Employees,* 793 F.2d 795, 802 (7th Cir. 1986).

enjoinder; enjoinment; injunction. The words of the Fowler brothers are as apt today as they were at the turn of the 20th century:

> As *rejoin rejoinder,* so *enjoin enjoinder.* The word is not given in the [*OED*], from which it seems likely that Dickens ["Merely nodding his head as an *enjoinder* to be careful."] invented it, consciously or unconsciously. The only objection to such a word is that its having had to wait so long, in spite of its obviousness, before being made is a strong argument against the necessity of it. We may regret that *injunction* holds the field, having a much less English appearance; but it does; and in language the old-established that can still do the work is not to be turned out for the new-fangled that might do it a shade better, but must first get itself known and accepted.
>
> H.W. Fowler & F.G. Fowler, *The King's English* 53 (3d ed. 1931; repr. 1978).

The *OED* contains two illustrative examples of *enjoinder,* but *injunction* still generally "holds the field" in both positive and negative senses of *enjoin,* q.v.

Yet *enjoinder* has become more common than it was in Fowler's day in the sense of "a command, esp. one that prohibits." E.g., "But the constitutional *enjoinder* against waste does not mean that the riparian owner must . . . clear all water-consuming native growth . . . ." *Allen v. California Water & Tel. Co.,* 176 P.2d 8, 18 (Cal. 1946) (en banc). Through SLIPSHOD EXTENSION it has been used as an equivalent of *admonition,* as here: "[Bishop] is also reputed to have written that classical *enjoinder,* 'Hard cases make bad law.'" *Horsley v. State,* 374 So. 2d 375, 377 (Ala. 1979) (Beatty, J., dissenting).

Enjoinment, labeled archaic in *W3* and missing from *W2,* is recorded in the *OED* from the 17th century in the sense "the action of enjoining." Today this word might almost be considered common in law; certainly, in denoting the action itself rather than the result of the action (an *injunction*), it is useful. E.g., "[I]t in and of itself constitutes a sufficient basis for the *enjoinment* of defendant's continued picketing." *Baldwin v. Arizona Flame Restaurant,* 313 P.2d 759, 765 (Ariz. 1957).

In the following sentence, *enjoinder* is used where *enjoinment* would be more apt: "The trial court's restraint and *enjoinder* [read *enjoinment*] of defendants from interfering in the liquidation is mooted and reversed by virtue of our ruling." *Heard v. Carter,* 285 S.E.2d 246, 249 (Ga. Ct. App. 1981).

enjoy is frequently used in legal writing in the sense "to have, possess." E.g., "This covenant ensures that the tenant shall *enjoy* the possession of the premises in peace and without disturbance by hostile claimants." The word fails, however, in reference to having or possessing something undesirable, as in "He *enjoys* failing health," labeled a catachrestic use by the *OED.* (That sentence actually looks more jocular than catachrestic.) Occasionally a clever writer recognizes the ironic possibilities of the word: "With a couple of rare exceptions, required by the Constitution, the Justices for the past thirty years have *enjoyed*—and the verb is accurate—the power to refuse to hear any case that anybody, railroaded convict or President of the United States, tries to bring before them." Fred Rodell, *Nine Men* 14 (1955).

enjoyment (= the exercise of a right) occurs now only in legal contexts. E.g., "The right of *enjoyment* implies rights of user, and of acquiring the fruits or increase of the thing, as timber, the young of cattle, or soil added to an estate by alluvion." Thomas E. Holland, *The Elements of Jurisprudence* 210 (13th ed. 1924; repr. 1937)./ "[A] man has no right of light for his windows unless such a right has been acquired by grant or by long *enjoyment* . . . ." William Geldart, *Introduction to English Law* 144 (D.C.M. Yardley 9th ed., 1984).

enlarge has figurative senses (*extend* or *broaden*) in legal writing that it lacks in other contexts. Thus it is used of abstractions like powers and even time. In references to powers, rights, and the like, the metaphor conveyed by *enlarge* is entirely natural—e.g.: "The *enlarged* property right that the legislature intended to confer is only an expectant interest dependent upon the contingency that the property to which the interest attaches becomes part of a decedent's estate."/ "An agent cannot *enlarge* or qualify the testator's express instructions even when acting bona fide." (Eng.)

But in references to time, *extend* is preferable to *enlarge,* which strikes most nonlawyers as unidiomatic—e.g.: "We hold that the *enlarged* [read *extended*] visitation time would be in the best interest of the child."

enlargement, in the legal idiom, often means "extension." E.g., "The company had filed a request with this Court for a thirty-day *enlargement* of time in which to file an appellate brief." See **enlarge.**

Enoc(h) Arden law. This phrase contains one of the few LITERARY ALLUSIONS that have given names to legal doctrines. "Enoch Arden," a poem by Tennyson, tells the story of a man who, lost at sea for many years, returns home to find his wife married happily to his former rival for her affections; broken-hearted, he resolves that they shall not know of his return until after his death. Thus *Enoch Arden law* = a statute providing for divorce or exempting from liability a person who remarries when his or her spouse has been absent without explanation for a specified number of years, usu. seven. The term first appeared in American caselaw in the 1920s—e.g.: "The '*Enoch Arden law,*' so-called . . . , is an anomaly in the legislative history of the State, and a strict compliance with its terms is required before such extraordinary relief may be granted." *Frankish v. Frankish,* 200 N.Y.S. 667, 668 (App. Div. 1923) (quoting the uncited opinion of *Schubert v. Schubert*).

enormity; enormousness. The historical DIFFERENTIATION between these words should not be muddled. *Enormousness* = hugeness, vastness. *Enormity* = outrageousness, ghastliness, hideousness. For example, Alan Dershowitz once said that Noam Chomsky "trivializes the *enormity* of the Chinese massacre [at Tiananmen Square in 1990]." Letter of Alan Dershowitz, *Left's Response to Beijing Massacre,* L.A. Times, 13 July 1989, at 2-6. But President Bush was less fastidious: on 10 July 1989, he was buoyed and cheered by what he called "the enormity of this moment," which he said presented a historic challenge to reform the Polish economy.

Plucknett typifies the careful writer's usage: "The plaintiff has been beaten, wounded, chained, imprisoned, starved, carried away to a foreign country, and has suffered many '*enormities.*' " Theodore F.T. Plucknett, *A Concise History of the Common Law* 465 (5th ed. 1956).

But misuse of *enormity* is all too frequent: "Third, if by chance the jury had discovered the penalty sections of appellant's pleadings, these too were relevant to offset appellant's argument about the *enormity* of the excess charge." (In this sentence the writer no doubt intended to refer to the magnitude [*enormousness*] of the excess, not its wickedness [*enormity*].)/ "The *enormity* [read *enormousness*] of the problem was indicated by Congress's extended hearings." (The correction assumes that the writer intended to refer to the *extent* of the problem, rather than to its moral implications, an assumption borne out by the context from which the quotation was pulled.)

enounce. See **announce.**

enquire. See **inquire.**

enquiry is the regular British form for the word equivalent to *question*; *inquiry,* in BrE, means "an official investigation." In AmE, *inquiry* serves in both senses. See EN-.

en re is downright wrong for *in re,* but it has occurred in otherwise good prose. See **in re.**

enrichment. See **impoverishment** & **unjust enrichment.**

enroll. See **engross.**

enrollee. See -EE.

enrol(l)ment (= the official registration of a document) is spelled *-ll-* in AmE and *-l-* in BrE. See **engross.**

en route. Two words. The *en* is best pronounced like "on," an approximation of the French pronunciation; /en/ is acceptable, but /in/ should be avoided.

This term is now voguish in figurative senses: "*En route* to its conclusion, the court rejected the defendant's argument that under the now-repealed Youth Corrections Act, any probation imposed upon a defendant eligible for YCA treatment had to be imposed under the Act rather than under the adult probation provision."

In route is a solecism: "Since the truck was departing from Florida *in route* [read *en route*] to New Orleans on November 12, appellant required that appellee's products be in Miami in time to be loaded on appellant's truck."

ensample is an ARCHAISM for *example.*

ensue; insue. The former spelling is standard. E.g., "This was an assault, although no harm *ensued* to the plaintiff."/ "If the persuasion be used for the indirect purpose of injuring the plaintiff or of benefiting the defendant at the expense of the plaintiff, it is a malicious act that is actionable if injury *ensues* from it."

ensurance. See **assurance.**

ensure. See **assure.**

entail, n. & v.t. The transitive verb *entail* = (1) (in general usage) to make necessary, to involve; or (2) (in legal usage) to provide that an estate may pass only to the grantee and the heirs of his body, so that none of the heirs can give it away or sell it. Specifically, an *entailed* interest is an equitable interest in land under which ownership is limited to a person and the heirs of his body (either generally or those of a specified class) (*CDL*). E.g., "A devise followed by a direction that the property should be 'closely *entailed*' was cut down to a tenancy for life, remainder to the issue." (Eng.) See **disentail.**

In addition to sense (2) of the verb, the general nonlegal sense often appears in legal writing: "An unprivileged falsehood need not *entail* universal hatred to constitute a cause of action."/ "The district court's analysis did not *entail* sufficient scrutiny of the particular negligent acts that were found to have been committed."

There are two noun forms. The noun *entail* (= a fee limited to the grantee's issue or a class of his issue) corresponds only to sense (2) of the verb. E.g., "Johnson spoke well of *entails,* to preserve lines of men whom mankind are accustomed to reverence." (Eng.) (See **fee tail (A).**) The noun *entailment* corresponds to sense (1) of the verb.

enter for *enter into.* Idiomatically speaking, one *enters into* a contract with another; one does not merely *enter* a contract. E.g., "It was the intent of appellant and appellee at the time the contract was *entered* [read *entered into*] that appellant was obligated to provide insurance necessary to cover its indemnity obligations."/ "At the time the contract is *entered* [read *entered into*], the agreed-upon payment must be a reasonable forecast of just compensation for the harm that would be caused by a breach." Even so, *to enter into a contract with* is usually prolix for *to contract with.* See **enter in.**

enter in is a REDUNDANCY for *enter.* E.g., "With his presently appealed claims to tens of millions of dollars in punitive damages against defendants enjoying immunity to all such claims, to attorneys' fees when he at all times acted *pro se,* and the like, we stand at the gate of the realms of fantasy; we decline to *enter in* [read *enter*]."/ "Defendant's agents *entered into Texas* [read *entered Texas*] on several occasions for the purpose of financing the constitution." On an idiomatic use of *enter into* in law, see **enter.**

entering judgment. See **rendition of judgment.**

enter into. See **enter** & **enter in.**

entertain = to give judicial consideration to. E.g., "Under *Pennhurst II,* the court below had no power to *entertain* Kitchens's contract claim regardless of the existence or fate of her other causes of action."/ "The court held that since Hanzl's payments were voluntary and received innocently by the defendants, there was no jurisdiction to *entertain* the suit."

enthral(l); inthral(l). The spelling *enthrall* is standard in the U.S., *enthral* in G.B. The *in-* spellings are to be avoided.

enthuse is a widely criticized BACK-FORMATION avoided by writers and speakers who care about their language. E.g., "He *enthused* [read *stated enthusiastically,* or perhaps *gushed*] that she was remarkable shortly after meeting her." *Enthused,* adj., is always inferior to *enthusiastic.*

entitled to, is. See WORDS OF AUTHORITY (G).

entirety; entireties. See **tenancy by the entireties.**

entrance; entry. Both *entrance* and *entry* may refer to the act of entering. In reference to structures, *entrance* connotes a single opening, such as a door, whereas *entranceway* and *entry* suggest a longer means of access, as a corridor or vestibule.

entrapment. As several writers on criminal law acknowledge, this term is an inaccurate one—but it is so well established that it is unlikely to be changed. The problem is that *entrap* connotes merely setting a trap, and doing so is not just legal but desirable in bringing to justice those bent on crime, as long as the trap-setter does not instigate the crime. But, confusingly, the legal term *entrapment* denotes what occurs when officers themselves instigate the crime.

entrust, not *intrust,* is now the usual and preferred spelling. The latter is often seen in legal opinions of the late 19th and early 20th centuries. See EN-.

entry. See **entrance.**

entry of judgment. See **rendition of judgment.**

enumerable; innumerable. Though close in pronunciation, these words have opposite meanings. *Innumerable* = unable to be counted. *Enumerable* = countable. The words should be pronounced distinctly, lest those listening misunderstand.

ENUMERATIONS. A. *First(ly), second(ly), third(ly); one, two, three.* The best method of enumerating items is the straightforward *first, second,* and *third.* The forms *firstly, secondly,* and *thirdly* have an unnecessary syllable, and *one, two,* and *three* seem especially informal. E.g, "This leaves but two possible effects of the service mark's continued use: *One* [read *First*], no one will know what CONAN means. *Two* [read *Second*], those who are familiar with the plaintiff's property will continue to associate CONAN with THE BARBARIAN." See **firstly.**

B. Comma Before the Last Member. "How to punctuate . . . enumerations," wrote Follett, "is argued with more heat than is called forth by any other rhetorical problem except the split infinitive." Wilson Follett, *Modern American Usage* 397–98 (1966). Fashions in public-school textbooks and journalists' manuals come and go, but only one method is ironclad in avoiding unnecessary ambiguities: inserting a comma before the final member. Thus *a, b, and c* rather than *a, b and c.* The problems arise with members containing two or more items, as *a and b, c and d, e and f, and g and h.* The last two members are muddled if the comma is omitted. See PUNCTUATION (C)(2).

C. Bullets. See DOCUMENT DESIGN (G).

D. As a Method for Enhancing Readability. See PLAIN LANGUAGE (D).

enunciate (= to state publicly) is often used of judicial pronouncements, especially where legal doctrines are concerned. E.g., "The validity of petitioner's larceny conviction must be judged not by the watered-down standard *enunciated* in *Palko,* but under this court's interpretations of the Fifth Amendment double-jeopardy provision."/ "We approve of the majority rule as *enunciated* in the cases appearing in the note quoted above." See **announce.**

enure. See **inure.**

envelop is the verb ("to wrap or cover"), *envelope* the noun ("wrapper, covering").

en ventre sa mere (= *in utero*) is an unnecessary LEGALISM. Instead of *child en ventre sa mere,* write *fetus, unborn child,* or *child in the mother's womb.* E.g., "[A] life in being includes a *person en ventre sa mere* [read *child in the mother's womb*] at the time when the will or settlement takes effect." William Geldart, *Introduction to English Law* 41 (D.C.M. Yardley ed., 9th ed. 1984). Cf. **venter.**

enviable; envious. That which is *enviable* is worthy of envy or arouses envy. A person who is *envious* suffers from envy. *Envious* usually takes the preposition *of* <she was envious of her sister's success>, but may take also *against* or *at.* See **jealousy.**

Some writers confuse the two words—e.g.: "Mr. Strauss's financial disclosure statement . . . details what is already widely known: the 72-year-old lawyer is a power broker of abundant wealth and *envious* [read *enviable*] political and corporate connections." Stephen Labaton, *Strauss to Forgo $4 Million in Pay to Take Moscow Post,* N.Y. Times, 13 July 1991, at 3.

envisage; envision. The former has been used since the early 19th century, whereas the latter was born in the early 20th century. Today *envision* is more common in the U.S., *envisage* being somewhat literary. Both mean "to visualize," but there is perhaps an incipient DIFFERENTIATION under way. As suggested by *W10, envision* means "to picture to oneself," whereas *envisage* means "to contemplate or view in a certain way." Thus: "We conclude that orders denying appointment of counsel to litigants who cannot afford counsel fall into the class of order *envisaged* by *Cohen.*"/ "Who is it that is *envisaged* by the instrument as an object of the possible bounty of the bank?" (Eng.)/ "The constructive trust as *envisaged* by the court in *Elliott* is a hybrid remedy."/ "In some of the older authorities it seems to have been *envisaged* that there were only two possible outcomes—either the transaction was void or it was valid." (Eng.)

Envisage seems more appropriate when inanimate objects are the subject; hence *envision,* which denotes a more human process, seems inapposite in this sentence: "The UCC clearly *envisions* [read *envisages*] that a contract came into being under the facts of this case." Yet it seems quite defensible here: "But there is no doubt that the Senate *envisioned* no role for the states on Indian lands."

envy. See **jealousy & enviable.**

eo instante; eo instanti. The dilemma in spelling is best resolved by writing *at the very instant, instantly,* or *immediately.* E.g., "To avoid the rule that a dead man could not be a felon, a suicide was to be counted a felon *eo instante* [read *at the instant*] he killed himself."/ "When the contract is made, the existing, binding law, whatever it may be, being the obligation on promisor to perform his undertaking, *eo instanti, attaches* [read *attaches immediately*]."/ "The judgment of the appellee attached *eo instante* [read *instantly*] on the intestate's death."

epic. See **epochal.**

epidemic; endemic. A disease is *epidemic* that breaks out and rages in a community, only to subside some time afterward. A disease is *endemic* that is constantly with a certain population or region.

epilog(ue). The longer spelling is customary and preferred. Cf. **prolog(ue).**

epithet; expletive. *Epithet* = (1) an especially apt adjective, whether the quality described is favorable or unfavorable; or (2) an abusive term. Sense (2) is slowly driving out sense (1), a trend to be fought against. *Expletive* = (1) an interjectory word or expression (esp. a profane one); (2) in grammar, a dummy word that fills the syntactic position of another (most commonly *it* or *there*), as in *It is difficult to describe how . . .* or *There are three . . . .* See EXPLETIVES.

epoch = (1) a date of an occurrence that starts things going under new conditions; or (2) "a period of history." Some stylists object to sense (2) as an example of SLIPSHOD EXTENSION, but that extension occurred in the 17th century, and the best writers today use the word in that sense: "Some historians have said that a meaningful history of humankind could be written around *epochs,* with each *epoch* having its own pervasive characteristics, and that the pervasive characteristic of the age in which we live is technological change." (Page Keeton)

epochal; epic(al). The former means "marking an epoch, or a new period in chronology." The word should not be used lightly. "Five devastating *epochal* floods have visited the valley since the establishment of the commission." (Only if the writer intended to convey that five epochs had passed since the establishment of the commission—an unlikely meaning—would *epochal* have been correct.)

Epical is a NEEDLESS VARIANT of the adjective *epic,* meaning (1) "of or relating to an epic [= a long heroic narrative]," or (2) "surpassing what is ordinary or usual."

equable. See **equitable.**

equally. This word should not be used with *both,* as it is here: *"Both magistracies* [read *"The two magistrates*] are *equally* independent in the sphere of action assigned to handing down sentences of fine and imprisonment." *Both . . . equally* is redundant. See **equally as (C).**

equally as is almost always incorrect. The exceptions are noted under (E).

A. ***Equally as . . . as.*** This phrasing is incorrect for *as much . . . as* or *as . . . as.* E.g., "The evidence is insufficient where it merely establishes that it is *equally as* [omit *equally*] probable that the requisite connection between the injury and the employment exists *as* that such connection does not exist."

B. ***As equally as.*** This is a variant of the usual blunder illustrated under (A). "To hold otherwise would be to succumb to a nominalism and a rigid trial scenario *as equally* [omit *equally*] at variance *as* ambush with the spirit of our rules."

C. ***Both . . . equally as.*** This is a double REDUNDANCY. *"Both* appeals are *equally as* frivolous."

[Read *The appeals are equally frivolous.*] See **equally.**

D. Inversion. The phrase is sometimes inverted and rendered *as equally* after NEGATIVES; still it is wrong. "No valid reason is apparent why the aforesaid categories are *not as equally* [read *not equally*] applicable to convictions for crimes in other states." See INVERSIONS, GRAMMATICAL.

E. Permissible Uses. If the words *equally as* simply appear together, but are really parts of other constructions, all is well—e.g.: "I love you equally as a nephew and as a friend."/ "If the deceased, in his lifetime, has done anything that would operate as a bar to recovery by him of damages for the personal injury, this will operate *equally as* a bar in an action by his personal representatives after his death."

equate takes the preposition *with,* not *to.*

equitable; equable. *Equable* = even; tranquil; level. *Equitable* derives from *equity,* q.v., and has associations of justice and fairness, or of that which can be sustained in a court of equity. To nonlawyers it generally means "fair," whereas to lawyers it may mean "fair" but just as often means "in equity" <equitable jurisdiction> <equitable remedies>.

Even though law and equity have been merged into unified courts in most American jurisdictions, we continue to speak of *equitable* rights, titles, and remedies, because they had their origins in equity. Such distinctions are useful, and they give parity to legal and equitable rights: after all, "[n]o one suggests that legal rights be called *'equitable'* merely because they have been merged with equity." William F. Walsh, *A Treatise on Equity* 98 (1930).

equitable estoppel. See **estoppel (B).**

equity is a CHAMELEON-HUED WORD whose senses have never before been adequately broken down. The primary dichotomy is between sense (1), the popular sense, and sense (4), the lawyer's usual sense. When, under sense (4), lawyers contrast *law* with *equity,* they are contrasting the common law with equity; the reader or listener must remember that equity is law. The word has more than a dozen senses, including subsenses:

1. **a.** In ordinary language, the quality of being equal or fair; fairness, impartiality; evenhanded dealing—e.g.: "In ordinary parlance *equity* is an abstract term, connoting natural justice." Wilbur Larremore, *Continental Regulation of Contempt of Court,* 13 Harv. L. Rev. 615, 621 (1900). **b.** What is fair and right in a given instance; something that is fair and right—e.g.: "The essence of *equity* is the power to do equity. It is a blend of what is fair and what is just." *In re Gloria Mfg. Corp.,* 65 B.R. 341, 347 (Bankr. E.D. Va. 1985). **c.** Equal or impartial treatment of parties with conflicting claims—e.g.: "[*Equity* de]notes equal and impartial justice as between two persons whose rights or claims are in conflict." *Demers v. Gerety,* 595 P.2d 387, 395–96 (N.M. Ct. App. 1978).
2. The body of principles constituting what is fair and right; natural law—e.g.: "The term *equity* may also be used in a wider sense to cover the whole of the field of natural justice, i.e., good conscience." Cenydd I. Howells, *Equity in a Nutshell* 1 (1966).
3. **a.** The recourse to principles of justice to correct or supplement the law as applied to particular circumstances—e.g.: "The qualities of mercy and practicality have made *equity* the instrument for nice adjustment and reconciliation between the public interest and private needs as well as between competing private claims." *Hecht Co. v. Bowles,* 321 U.S. 321, 329–30 (1944). **b.** The construing of a law according to its reason and spirit—e.g.: "*'Equitie'* is a construction made by the judges that cases out of the letter of a statute, yet being within the same mischief or cause of the making of the same, shall be within the same remedy that the statute provideth." Coke, *Institutes,* Bk. 1, 24b (1628).
4. **a.** The system of law or body of principles originating in the English Court of Chancery and superseding the common and statute law (together called "law" in the narrower sense) when the two conflict—e.g.: "[*E*]*quity* [is] in essence, a system of doctrines and procedures which developed side by side with the common law and statute law." L.B. Curzon, *Equity* 4 (1967). **b.** Any system of law or body of principles analogous to Anglo-American equity, such as the praetorian law of the Romans—e.g.: "*Equity,* meaning any body of rules existing by the side of the original civil law, founded on distinct principles and claiming incidentally to supersede the civil law in virtue of a superior sanctity inherent in those principles." Henry S. Maine, *Ancient Law* ii (1861; repr. 1870).
5. **a.** An equitable right or interest, i.e., one recognizable by a court of equity. Often *pl.* E.g., "Often, however, the term 'balance of *equities*' is used to denote only a balancing of private and public interests." Zygmunt J.B. Plater, *Statutory Violations and Equitable Discretion,* 70 Cal. L. Rev. 524, 535 (1982). **b.** The owner-

ship interest of shareholders in a corporation—e.g.: "She now has *equity* in the professional corporation." **c.** A speculative right or interest in property—e.g.: "[P]rofits realized from the purchase and sale . . . of an *equity* security within a period of less than 6 months are recoverable by the corporation." *Chenery Corp. v. SEC,* 128 F.2d 303, 308 (D.C. Cir. 1942).

6. The right to relief in a court of equity, or the reasons for deserving such relief; equitable merit—e.g.: "Where there is equal *equity* in two contending parties, it is always an unpleasant task to decide between them." *Graff v. Smith's Adm'rs,* 1 U.S. (1 Dall.) 481, 484 (Pa. Common Pleas 1789).

7. A matter that can or must be decided in a court of equity. Usu. in phr. *equity reserved*—e.g.: "[U]pon the *equity* reserved under and by the said interlocutory order, it is further ordered, decreed and adjudged, that the injunction heretofore granted in this cause be . . . perpetuated." *U.S. v. Nourse,* 31 U.S. (6 Pet.) 470, 484 (1832).

8. The meaning, intent, or general purpose (of a statute)—e.g.: "These cases thus out of the letter, are said to be within the *Equity* of an Act of Parliament." 3 William Blackstone, *Commentaries* *431 (1765)./ "'[W]ithin the *equity,*' means the same thing as 'within the mischief' of the statute." *Shuttleworth v. Le Fleming,* 19 C.B.N.S. 703 (1865). Today, this sense is said to "have disappeared as a term of art or as an element of our [modern] jurisprudence." Carleton K. Allen, *Law in the Making* 456 (7th ed. 1964).

9. An equitable remedy—e.g.: "Nor is there any equity against the Plaintiff in error." *Clarke v. Russel,* 3 U.S. (3 Dall.) 415, 421 (1799)./ "A remedy in a court of equity is frequently called an equity." *Harrison v. Craddock,* 178 S.W.2d 296, 301 (Tex. Civ. App.—Galveston 1944).

10. *Civ. law.* Where positive law is absent or ambiguous, the method of deciding cases by natural law or the inferred intent of the legislature—e.g.: "[E]quity in the sense that writers in Continental Europe and Latin and Scandinavian countries use it in observing that ideas of equity are the basis of law and are consequently supplementary law." Vilhelm Lundstedt, 25 Tul. L. Rev. 59, 59 (1950)./ "[T]he *equity* of the statute . . . seems to be a continental notion . . . . When the courts spoke of the *equity* of a statute they meant only that adjustment of detail which is necessary when applying a general rule to a specific case." Theodore F.T. Plucknett, *A Concise History of the Common Law* 334–35 (5th ed. 1956).

11. The right to decide matters in equity; equity jurisdiction; equitable power—e.g.: "[*Equity*] describes the power belonging to the judge—a power which must . . . be exercised according to his own standard of right." John N. Pomeroy, *Equity Jurisprudence* § 45, at 46 (1881; repr. 1892).

12. a. The amount by which the value of a property or an interest in property exceeds secured claims or liens—e.g.: "'[*E*]*quity*' . . . is the value, above all secured claims against the property, that can be realized from the sale of the property for the benefit of the unsecured creditors." *In re Mellor,* 734 F.2d 1396, 1400 n.2 (9th Cir. 1984). **b.** In accounting, the paid-in capital plus retained earnings.

13. A share in a public company quoted on the stock exhange. E.g., "On the other hand, investment in shares of public companies quoted on the Stock Exchange *('equities')* introduced the risk of dependence upon the fortunes of the company selected . . . . Investment in *equities* involved risk." William Geldart, *Introduction to English Law* 86 (D.C.M. Yardley 9th ed. 1984).

The term is used in several phrases. A *countervailing equity* is an equitable right or interest that clashes with another. A *latent equity* is an equitable claim that has been concealed from one or more interested parties. (The phrase *secret equity* is synonymous with *latent equity.*) A *natural equity* is that which a conscientious person would consider fair or just in the absence of legal guidance. A *perfect equity* is the interest that a buyer of real estate has after fulfilling all obligations in the purchase, but before receiving the deed. See **chancery.**

equity abhors a forfeiture; the law abhors a forfeiture. The first is the traditional (and correct) maxim. The second has arisen only since the merger of law and equity—e.g.: "The law abhors forfeiture unless it is plainly intended by the legislature." *E.H. Crump Co. v. Millar,* 391 S.E.2d 775, 778–79 (Ga. Ct. App. 1990).

equity of redemption. See **cloud on title.**

Equity Pleadings. There were seven distinct forms of pleadings in equity:

- The *bill* (or *information*).
- The *demurrer.*
- The *plea.*
- The *answer.*

- The *cross-bill.*
- The *disclaimer.*
- The *replication.*

See COMMON-LAW PLEADINGS & WORLD COURT PLEADINGS.

-ER. A. And *-or*. These agent-noun suffixes can be especially vexatious to the legal writer. The historical tendency in the law has been to make the Latinate *-or* the correlative of *-ee* (q.v.), hence *indemnitee / indemnitor, obligee / obligor, transferee / transferor, offeree / offeror, donee / donor.* Often, however, the choice of suffix seems based on caprice. In the famous contracts case *Household Fire & Carriage Accident Ins. Co. v. Grant,* [1879] 4 Ex.D. 216 (C.A.), Lord Justice Thesiger used the spellings *acceptor* and *offerer,* whereas the modern trend is to write *accepter* and *offeror* in legal contexts.

Attempts to confine *-er* to words of Anglo-Saxon origin and *-or* to those of Latin origin are fruitless because so many exceptions exist on both sides of the aisle. Nevertheless, it may fairly be said that Latinate words usually take *-or,* though there are many exceptions—a few of which appear below in the *-er* column:

-er	*-or*
adapter	abductor
conjurer	abettor
corrupter	collector
digester	corrector
dispenser	distributor
eraser	ejector
idolater	impostor
indorser	purveyor
promoter	surveyor

Sometimes there is a distinction in meaning between variant forms of the same word with these two suffixes, as with *bargainer* and *bargainor,* q.v., or latent distinctions, as with *bailer* and *bailor,* q.v.

B. Suffix *-er* Misleadingly Suggesting Agent Noun in Law Words. In many legal words, the suffix *-er* might seem to signal an agent noun when actually it denotes some nonhuman object or abstract idea. The result, for the less-than-alert legal reader, is a MISCUE. Most such words are LAW FRENCH infinitives that came into use as English nouns invested with technical legal meanings. Among the most common examples are these:

cesser = (1) the neglect to do something; or (2) the premature ending of a term (as of an estate). See **cesser.**

demurrer = a defending party's pleading alleging that, even if the complaining party's allegations are true, there is no reason why the case should proceed further. See **demurrer.**

descender = hereditary succession.

detainer = detention; the action of keeping a person against his or her will, or of keeping property from its owner.

disclaimer = a disavowal or renunciation.

impleader = a procedure by which a litigant brings a new party into the litigation because that party may be liable on a pending claim. See **impleader.**

interpleader = an equitable proceeding in which the court determines which of two or more rival claimants owns property in dispute—the property often being held by a neutral third party called a "stakeholder." See **interpleader.**

nonuser = neglect to use a right. Cf. **user.**

rebutter = in COMMON-LAW PLEADING, the defendant's answer to the plaintiff's surrejoinder. See **rebutter.**

rejoinder = in COMMON-LAW PLEADING, the defendant's answer to the plaintiff's reply or replication. See **rejoinder.**

repleader = a court's allowance of a party to plead anew when the original pleading failed to raise a material issue.

reverter = a reversionary interest that arises when a grant is limited so that it may come to an end. See **reversion.**

surrebutter = in COMMON-LAW PLEADING, the plaintiff's answer to the defendant's rebutter.

surrejoinder = a pleading by which a plaintiff answers to a defendant's rejoinder. See **rejoinder.**

user = the continued use, exercise, or enjoyment of a right. See **user.**

C. And *-re*. Words borrowed from French generally arrived in English with the *-re* spelling. Most such words have gradually made the transition to *-er.* A few words may be spelled only *-re,* such as *acre, chancre, massacre,* and *mediocre,* because of the preceding *-c-*. Still others—the great majority—have variant spellings, the *-er* ending usually being more common in AmE and the *-re* ending normal in BrE. The following words have variants subject to this distinction: *accouter, -re; caliber, -re; center, -re; goiter, -re; liter, -re; louver, -re; luster, -re; maneuver, -re; meager, -re; meter, -re* (in BrE, *meter* = the measuring device as well as the measure); *miter, -re; niter, -re; reconnoiter, -re; scepter, -re; sepulcher, -re; somber, -re; specter, -re; theater, -re.*

ergo, a slightly archaic equivalent of *therefore,* is occasionally useful for its succinctness. E.g., "The United States Supreme Court does not recognize the vicarious exclusionary rule; *ergo,* Daan cannot assert the illegality of Bryan's intention and the seizure of the marijuana cigarettes." But, because *ergo* is no longer a part of everyday language, its effective use depends almost entirely on the audience to whom it is directed.

***Erie*-bound** = (of a federal court in the U.S.) required to apply the holding in *Erie R. Co. v. Tompkins,* 304 U.S. 64 (1938). This term is frequently used by American federal courts, which must follow the teachings of *Erie v. Tompkins:* where federal laws are not involved, a federal court exercising diversity jurisdiction (and therefore applying state law) must follow the common law of the state in which it sits. *Erie-bound* is fast becoming a CLICHÉ, because the proposition is so well established that ordinarily there need be no invocation of *Erie v. Tompkins* every time a federal court applies state law. Following are two typical examples of use of the phrase: "In this diversity case, we are *Erie-bound* to follow the substantive law of Mississippi."/ "The result we think a Louisiana court would reach, and the one we are *Erie-bound* to follow in this diversity case, was reached by the district court." See CASE REFERENCES (C).

The *Erie* case has spawned some less-well-accepted NEOLOGISMS too, including a whimsical nonce-word originating in the Second Circuit: "My senior colleague Judge Learned Hand has a way of startling counsel in these *'erieantompkinated'* days by saying, as they approach that inevitable citation: 'I don't suppose a civil appeal can now be argued to us without counsel sooner or later quoting large portions of Erie Railroad v. Tompkins.'" Charles E. Clark, *State Law in the Federal Courts: The Brooding Omnipresence of Erie v. Tompkins,* 55 Yale L.J. 267, 269 (1946).

eristic(al), meaning "of or pertaining to controversy or disputation," is best spelled *eristic.*

ermine (the fur of a weasel-like animal) has come to be used figuratively with reference to the ermine in the official robes of judges in England. The word evokes rather grand notions of a judgeship. This use of the word occurs even in the U.S., where ermine is not used in judges' robes. E.g., "A judge loses none of his social instincts by assuming the *ermine,* and while his position is changed he is still a lawyer."/ "From such liability, the justice cannot hide behind his judicial *ermine.*" Cf. **woolsack.**

erodible; erodable; erosible. The best form is *erodible.* See -ABLE (A).

err, one of the most commonly mispronounced words in legal contexts, should properly rhyme with *purr.* It is incorrect, from a strict point of view, to mouth it like *air.* See **error (C).**

errant = (1) traveling <knight errant>; (2) fallible, straying from what is proper. Sense (2) overwhelmingly predominates: "The February 14 order neither granted nor denied an order of any such character or effect; at best the court *errantly* issued an 'advisory opinion' over which it retained the power of revision."/ "Instead, the Supreme Court instructs, the proper recourse is an objection to the trial judge and prompt action from the bench in the form of corrective instructions to the jury, and when necessary, an admonition to the *errant* advocate."

Errant is properly used of persons or their actions; it is not synonymous with *erroneous,* as one writer apparently thought: "Appellant argues that the district court failed to consider the evidence urged as being 'newly discovered'; this *errant* [read *erroneous*] conclusion is based on a misinterpretation of the district court's opinion." See **arrant.**

errata. Like *addenda* and *corrigenda,* the plural form *errata* should be used only when one is listing more than one item. If there is only one, the heading should be *erratum.* The English plural *erratums* is not used. See **corrigendum.**

erroneous mistake is a REDUNDANCY. E.g., "the Magistrate further found that Plaintiff adequately pled the third element by alleging that it operated under *an erroneous mistake* [read *a mistake*] of fact . . . ." *Captial Factors, Inc. v. Heller Fin., Inc.,* 712 F. Supp. 908, 915 (S.D. Fla. 1989).

erronious is an erroneous spelling of *erroneous.*

error, n. **A. General Senses.** *Error* = (1) a mistake of law in a court's judgment, opinion, or order; (2) an appeal; or (3) *in Scots law,* a mistaken belief by one or both parties about some matter of fact or law material to their bargain—i.e., as an equivalent of the Anglo-American legal term *mistake.* See **mistake (B) & mutual mistake.**

To illustrate sense (2), *proceedings in error* are not the same as *erroneous proceedings,* as a nonlawyer might think. In fact, the official name of the highest court in Connecticut is the Supreme Court of Errors. The report in *McCulloch v. Maryland,* 17 U.S. (4 Wheat.) 316, 317 (1819), contains the heading "*Error* to the Court of Appeals of the state of Maryland." This sense developed as an elliptical form of *writ of error*—e.g.: "There was a judgment of the Court of Civil Appeals affirming a judgment for plaintiff, and defendant brings *error.*" See **plaintiff in error & defendant in error.**

B. For *in error* or *erroneous.* This use, though fairly old and increasingly common in AmE, should be avoided, for it wrongly makes *error* adjectival. E.g., "[I]t was *error* [read *erroneous*] to direct a verdict." *Soule v. Bon Ami Co.,* 195 N.Y.S. 574, 577 (N.Y. Sup. 1922) (Rich & Kelly, JJ., dissenting)./ "Defendants argue that this instruction was *error* [read *erroneous*] because it allowed the jury to determine the admissibility of the hearsay statements of co-conspirators."/ "Hauser contends that this holding *is error* [read *is in error*], asserting that the defendant was not entitled to a reasonable time in which to place flares when the emergency was created by the defendant's negligence."

C. For *err,* v.i. This mistake commonly appears in appellate briefs. If we were inclined to be generous to the lawyers who err in this way, we might attribute the mistake to secretaries who misunderstand dictation. Yet the fault cannot rightly be laid on the secretaries. The court in *Stolte v. Mack Fin. Corp.,* 457 S.W.2d 172, 174 (Tex. Civ. App.—Texarkana 1970), subtly highlighted this error in an advocate's brief in three successive points of error. Here is a typical misuse: "Justice Stevens . . . held that the district court *errored* [read *erred*] in granting retroactive relief in Manhart." Pamela S. Anderson, *Gender-Based Determination of Retirement Benefits,* 19 Tulsa L.J. 755, 762 (1984). Correctly pronouncing *err,* q.v., would reduce the frequency of this blunder.

error, writ of. See **writ of error.**

erstwhile; quondam; sometime; whilom. Each of these terms means "one-time, former, at a former time." By far the most common in AmE and BrE is *erstwhile* (called "literary" in the *OED*). The least common are *quondam* and (even rarer) *whilom*—e.g.: "Gerald Asher, the *whilom* wine merchant and distinguished wine writer, was in town recently to talk about . . . Chardonnay clones." Frank J. Prial, *Wine Talk,* N.Y. Times, 25 April 1990, at C11. The word *sometime* (q.v.), an invitation to a MISCUE, is often misused as if it meant "occasional, from time to time."

We need one of these words in English—probably *erstwhile*—because *former* and *one-time* do not always suffice. Our embarrassment of riches, with four synonyms for one sense, is exceeded only by most writers' embarrassment at having to use any one of them in addressing a less-than-learned audience.

escalate, in the sense "to increase in seriousness or intensity," is voguish. E.g., "The encounter with the suspect did not *escalate* into an arrest." See VOGUE WORDS.

escape. A. Legal Senses. In law, the word refers to an unlawful departure from legal custody without the use of force; it does not properly refer to a suspect's avoidance of capture.

In older writings, *escape* was the name of the offense committed by a law-enforcement officer (esp. a jailer) who somehow allowed a suspected criminal to escape, either through inadvertence or because he or she had been bribed. So a jailer convicted of *escape* was one who had been at fault in a prisoner's successful departure from custody. Two modern commentators note that this usage "seems inappropriate." Rollin M. Perkins & Ronald N. Boyce, *Criminal Law* 560 (3d ed. 1982). To be sure, if one asked a group of lawyers (much less nonlawyers) just who had been guilty of escape, almost none today would point to the jailer.

B. *Escape (from).* As an intransitive verb construed with *from* or *out of, escape* means "to gain one's liberty by fleeing, to get free from detention or control" <he escaped from prison>. As a transitive verb taking a direct object, the verb means either (1) "to succeed in avoiding (something unwelcome)" <they escaped suspicion>, or (2) "to elude (observation, search, etc.)" <its significance had previously escaped me>.

escapee (= one who escapes) should more logically be *escaper* or *escapist.* (See -EE (A).) The *OED* suggests that *escapee* is waning in use and that *escapist* is emerging as the standard BrE agent noun. American writers seem to prefer *escaper.* As long as *escapee* is displaced, it might seem to matter little which alternative prevails. But *escaper* might be better for two reasons. First, *escapist* suggests Houdini, i.e., one who makes a living putting on "escapes" from difficult predicaments (also known as an *escapologist*); second, it has irrelevant figurative uses, as in *escapist fiction* (i.e., as the adjective corresponding to *escapism*).

One writer defines *escapee* as "one who has been caught after escaping, or while preparing to escape." Paul Tempest, *Lag's Lexicon* 75 (1950). Perhaps that is how a *lag* (= a convict sentenced to penal servitude) understands the term, but being caught is not really necessary to the definition. Most writers and speakers of English would find nothing wrong with saying, "The *escapees* were never caught"—they would merely find something wrong with the fact of their not being caught.

escheat may be both noun and verb. As the former, it means "the lapsing of land to the state (in G.B., to the Crown) upon the death of the intestate owner without heirs." A Law French word originally meaning "inheritance," it came to apply at common law to the lord's succession to a tenant's fief when the tenant died seised without heir. From the perceived unfairness of the system—once the lords had begun to abuse it—evolved the aphaeretic form *cheat,* q.v.

Escheat is used more commonly as a verb than as a noun in legal writing, as here: "The lands of a person convicted of petty treason . . . or felony *escheated* (i.e. reverted) to his lord." L.B. Curzon, *English Legal History* 233 (2d ed. 1979). But the noun use is hardly uncommon—e.g.: "The court would be less concerned with the influencer's motive in a contest between him and the state claiming an *escheat* than it would be in a contest between him and the donor's surviving spouse." *Escheatment* and *escheatage* are NEEDLESS VARIANTS.

Originally applied in feudal land law to instances of "failure of title" (when there was no titleholder), *escheat* has been extended—grossly some would say—in AmE. Since World War II, with the enactment of the Uniform Disposition of Unclaimed Property Act in various states—the act itself not using *escheat*—the word is now popularly used by nonlawyers as a verb referring to what happens to abandoned and unclaimed personal property. To the real-property purist, this usage, resulting from both SLIPSHOD EXTENSION and POPULARIZED LEGAL TECHNICALITY, is irksome. Cf. ***bona vacantia.***

eschew; eschewal, n. The second syllable of both words is pronounced just as the word *chew* is pronounced, /*es*-***choo***/. For some reason, many seem to believe that the *esch-* sequence in this term is pronounced *esh-*. It is not. The pronunciation with an *esh-* sound sounds like a sneeze.

escrow has three noun senses: (1) "a deed delivered but not to become operative until a future date or until some condition has been fulfilled"; (2) "a deposit held in trust or as security" <in escrow>; or (3) "an escrow holder." Sense (1) is the traditional one. Sense (2), labeled "a perversion" by *Black's* (4th ed.), was a 19th-century American coinage that is now current in both AmE and BrE. Sense (3), a result of HYPALLAGE, has brevity on its side but little else: it is likely to cause MISCUES.

The verb uses of *escrow,* recorded from 1916, are now common in American legal writing. As a verb, *escrow* means "to put into *escrow* [sense (2)]." E.g., "The cognizant officials of FDIC consented to the sale and to the *escrowing* of proceeds of sale with the rights of all claimants to follow those proceeds." *In re Jeter,* 48 B.R. 404, 409 (Bankr. N.D. Tex. 1985)./ "By *escrowing* the funds for the purpose of improving municipal services in the black community, the court took the first step toward ensuring that the unconstitutional disparities would be corrected rather than perpetuated." Today it is common in American real-estate law to speak of *escrowing* all types of documents—that is, holding them with the understanding that they will not be released until some condition is met. This use corresponds to sense (1) of the noun.

escrowee (= the depositary of an escrow) is a curious term, there being no correlative agent noun in *-er* or *-or*. Recorded in *W3* but ignored in the *OED,* the term is not uncommon in modern AmE. E.g., "[T]he assignment from Avon to the *escrowees* was recorded in the Patent and Trademark Office." *Haymaker Sports, Inc. v. Turian,* 581 F.2d 257, 262 (C.C.P.A. 1978) (Baldwin, J., dissenting). Even so, the phrases *escrow holder* or *escrow agent*—both being precise equivalents—are more widely understandable.

eslisor. See **elisor.**

esoterics is, strictly speaking, incorrect for *esoterica.* But it is almost as common in AmE, and, in some plain-spoken contexts, *esoterics* sounds natural where *esoterica* would seem precious—e.g.: "The same easy strength is there, and the same earthy approach to the *esoterics* of law." Fred Rodell, *Nine Men* 331 (1955). Cf. **empirics.**

especial; special. Traditionally speaking, *especial* (= distinctive, significant, peculiar) is the opposite of *ordinary*. E.g., "The public press is entitled to peculiar indulgence and has *especial* rights and privileges." *Special* (= specific, particular) is the opposite of *general* <the jury answered special issues>, though increasingly it has ousted *especial* from its rightful territory.

Especial is so rarely used in AmE today—even in learned and legal prose—that some might term it obsolescent. But it does occasionally appear, most often modifying a noun made from an adjective; that is, a writer who might otherwise refer to something that is *especially harsh* would refer to its *especial harshness,* as in this BrE example: "Conduct of the type last named with regard to goods constitutes the tort of conversion, which bears with *especial* harshness on one who has, in all good faith, bought goods from one who had no title to them." William Geldart, *Introduction to English Law* 132 (D.C.M. Yardley ed., 9th ed. 1984).

In the following sentence, *especial* is wrongly used for *special,* used in contrast to *general:* "Positive laws either contain general principles embodied in the rules of law or for *especial* [read *special*] reasons they establish something that differs from those general principles."

espouse = (1) to marry or give in marriage; or (2) to adopt or support (as a doctrine or cause). Sense (1), the literal sense, is rarely seen today even in legal writing, but it does occur: "She was accused afterward of being depressed because she had discovered that there were thirty other persons whom she could not legally *espouse* even if they did ask her."

Espouse in sense (2) is often misused. In the following sentence, it is used as if it were synonymous with *endorse* (applied to persons as well as things): "In defeating plaintiff, we do not decry him, nor do we *espouse* [read *endorse*] his adversary." And here it is incorrectly used for *expound* or *set forth:* "Having *espoused* [read *expounded*] our view of the intent of Congress, we are nonetheless bound by the prior decisions of this circuit." (The court obviously did not *espouse* a view if it could not follow it.)

The proper use of the word in sense (2) appears here: "Some people see in the conduct of lawsuits something more than mere forensic battles waged by paid champions ready to *espouse* either side of an argument."

Esq., in AmE, "is often used as a title signifying that the holder is a lawyer . . . ." R.D. Rotunda, *Professional Responsibility* 396 (2d ed. 1988). The mild honorific is used nowadays with the names of men and women alike; it is incorrect, however, to use this title with any other title, such as *Mr.* or *Ms.* In BrE, of course, *esquire* is used of any man thought to have the social status of a gentleman.

One law review has devoted several pages to an article on whether women attorneys should use *esquire.* See Richard B. Eaton, *An Historical View of the Term Esquire as Used by Modern Women Attorneys,* 80 W. Va. L. Rev. 209 (1978). As to the title and purpose of that article, however, it is worth noting that "*Esq.* is . . . not used on oneself, e.g. neither on a card (which bears *Mr.*) nor on a stamped-and-addressed envelope enclosed for a reply (which has merely A-B.X—or A.B.X.—without prefix)." Alan S.C. Ross, "U and Non-U: An Essay in Sociological Linguistics," in *Noblesse Oblige* (Nancy Mitford ed., 1956). But somehow, the idea has gotten out that *Esq.* is something you put after your own name—e.g.: "[T]hese [lawyers] assembled here are not ordinary litigators. Instead of appending a mere 'Esq.' after their names, they are 'Factl'—Fellows of the American College of Trial Lawyers." David Margolick, *At the Bar,* N.Y. Times, 10 March 1989, at 23.

The real question in AmE is not whether women should append *Esq.* to their own names, but whether others should append it to women attorneys' names. The answer: this practice is perfectly acceptable and extremely common. Anyone who is bothered by this practice should pretend that *Esq.,* when used after a woman's name, stands for *esquiress* (recorded in the *OED* from 1596). See SEXISM (C).

essay, v.t. See **assay.**

-ESS. See SEXISM (C).

esse (= essence, essential nature) is a pedantic LATINISM. E.g., "This appeal forces us to acknowledge a lumbering, antediluvian concept that remains embedded in the judicial *esse.*" *Coastal (Bermuda) Ltd. v. E.W. Saybolt & Co.,* 761 F.2d 198, 200 (5th Cir. 1985). Cf. ***in esse*** & ***de bene esse.***

essence, time is of the. See **time is of the essence.**

essoi(g)n, n. & v. *Essoin* /e-***soin***/ is the preferred spelling for both noun and verb; *essoign* is a variant spelling of the noun only. The word (meaning "an excuse for not appearing in court at the appointed time") is used only in BrE. E.g., "But one cannot wait for ever; that would be unfair to the other party; so a great deal of law is evolved as to the excuses for non-appearance, in technical language the *essoins,* that a man may proffer." F.W. Maitland, *The Forms of Action at Common Law* 20 (1909; A.H. Chaytor & W.J. Whittaker eds. 1971).

estate = (1) all that a person owns, including both heritable and movable property <she has a modest estate, even if one includes her stock>; (2) the degree, quantity, or nature of a person's rights in land <leasehold estate>; or (3) the land itself <the Biltmore estate>.

estate for years. See **term of years.**

estate planning, though now a commonplace phrase in American law, is an odd EUPHEMISM that may help lawyers avoid confronting their clients too starkly with the dread subject of dying. At least one writer has set his face against the phrase: "An occasional client . . . is probably justified when he calls his personal aggregation of material things an 'estate,' if he wants to call it that. But it is wildly inaccurate to represent that he or anyone else planned it, or that a mere lawyer is going to 'plan' it for him—whatever that means—now that he has it. What is being planned for is death and the fact that one's things go the way of one's mortal coil. 'Estate planning' is an evasive, fawning, pretentious phrase, and I propose to begin by refusing to be associated with it." Thomas L. Shaffer, *The Planning and Drafting of Wills and Trusts* 1 (2d ed. 1979). Shaffer and several other writers use *property settlement* instead of *estate planning.* Shaffer adds: "I regret . . . the connotation the phrase [*property settlement*] has taken from divorce practice." *Id.* at 2 n.1.

estates in community. See **concurrent interests.**

estate tail. See **tail & entail.**

estimate, n.; **estimation.** A distinction should be observed. *Estimate* = an approximate calculation or judgment. *Estimation* = the process of approximately calculating or judging.

estop (= to stop, bar, hinder, or preclude) is now a legal term only. It may be construed either with an infinitive or with *from* [verb + *-ing*]. Thus: "The licensee of a trademark is *estopped* to deny the mark's validity."/ "The trust company is *estopped* from disputing the effect of the decree."

This verb may also be reflexive, in the sense "to be precluded by one's own previous act or declaration from doing or alleging something" (*OED*). E.g., "While the case ostensibly presents the question whether a common carrier by water may ever *estop itself* by inequitable conduct from exacting the full measure of the shipper's obligation to pay tariff charges, the true nature shows it to be something quite different." Here, again, the construction with *from* [verb + *-ing*] occurs.

estoppel. A. Spelling. The word *estoppel* /es-**top**-əl/ is so spelled. The word is sometimes misspelled *estoppal,* as in Arthur A. Leff, *The Leff Dictionary of Law,* 94 Yale L.J. 1855, 1974, 2104 (1985), under *agency by estoppal* and *authority by estoppal.* For the difference between *estoppel* and *waiver,* see **waiver (C).**

B. Estoppel; estoppel by representation; estoppel in pais; equitable estoppel; promissory estoppel. Most broadly, *estoppel* denotes a bar that precludes a person from denying or contradicting something that he or she has said before or that has been legally established as true. Traditionally, the only real distinction between any of the terms listed above turns on whether the party's statement relates to a present fact or to future conduct.

Estoppel, estoppel by representation, and *estoppel in pais* all relate to a party's saying something about an existing matter of fact. The most usual term today is *estoppel* alone—a shorthand form of *estoppel by representation.*

Promissory estoppel and *equitable estoppel* both relate to a party's saying something about his or her intentions to do something in the future. The phrase *promissory estoppel* has "gradually won out over the term *'equitable estoppel,'* which had been used with some frequency in the earlier cases." Grant Gilmore, *The Death of Contract* 129 n.145 (1974).

Indeed, the term *equitable estoppel* is extraordinarily fuzzy and ought therefore to be avoided. G.H. Treitel criticizes an English decision that "somewhat puzzlingly seems to distinguish between *'promissory'* and *'equitable' estoppel.* Terminological difficulty is compounded by the occasional use of the phrase *'equitable estoppel'* to refer to true *estoppel* by representation . . . ." *The Law of Contract* 109 (8th ed. 1991). See **promissory estoppel.**

estray is an ARCHAISM used in law for "stray animal." See **waifs and (e)strays.**

estrep(e)ment. The longer spelling of this word, which means "waste of land caused by a tenant," is more usual—e.g.: "[A] touchstone . . . is afforded by supposing an attempt at removal by the tenant and a writ of *estrepement* issued or bill in equity filed by the landlord to restrain the removal as the commitment of waste." *In re Ameri-*

can Pile Fabrics Co., 12 F. Supp. 86, 88 (E.D. Pa. 1935).

et al. is most commonly the abbreviated form of the Latin phrase *et alii* (= and others), though it may also be the masculine singular (*et alius*), the feminine singular (*et alia*), or the feminine plural (*et aliae*). It is used only of persons, whereas *etc.* is used of things. American lawyers commonly write *et al, et. al.,* or *et. al*—all of which are wrong.

The abbreviation does not fit comfortably alongside possessives: "Clifford T. Honicker's chilling account of Louis Slotin's, S. Allan Kline's *et al.* encounter [read *and others' encounters*] with the Nuclear Age is as horrific as it is emblematic . . . ." Letter of Glenn Alcalay, N.Y. Times, 10 Dec. 1989, § 6, at 14. Cf. **etc.**

etc. A French proverb states, "God save us from a lawyer's *et cetera.*" The point is well taken. More than 400 years ago, John Florio wrote: "The heaviest thing that is, is one *Etcetera.*" It is heaviest because it implies a quantity of things too numerous to mention. These are some of the most sensible words ever written on *etc.*:

> Every writer should be on his guard against the excessive use of *etc.* Instead of finishing a thought completely, it is easy to end with an *etc.,* throwing the burden of finishing the thought upon the reader. If the thought is adequately expressed, *etc.* is not needed. If the thought is not adequately expressed, *etc.* will not take the place of that which has not been said. The use of *etc.* tends to become a slovenly habit, the corrective for which is to refrain from using *etc.* except in the dryest [read *driest*] and most documentary kind of writing.
>
> George P. Krapp, *A Comprehensive Guide to Good English* 229 (1927).

Lawyers should generally—in pleadings, for example—attempt to be as specific as possible rather than make use of this term. Still, it would be foolish to lay down an absolute proscription against using *etc.*, for often one simply *cannot* practicably list all that should be listed in a given context. Hence, rather than convey to the reader that a list is seemingly complete when it is not, the writer might justifiably use *etc.* (always the abbreviation).

And etc. is an ignorant error, *et* being the Latin *and. Etc.* differs from *et al.* in that it refers to things and not to people. (See **et al.**) The *-t-* in the first syllable of *etc.* should never be pronounced as a *-k-*. On the use of *etc.* with *e.g.* and *i.e.,* see **e.g.**

etched in stone. See **stone, etched in.**

-ETH. At its fringes, legal language retains a few words ending this way—e.g., *deposeth, sayeth,* and *witnesseth.* None is a TERM OF ART. None is even useful. Up to the 17th century, the *-eth* suffix was merely an alternate third-person singular inflection for an English verb; used primarily in southern England, it had, by the end of that century, become obsolete. *She calls* and *he answers* took the place of *she calleth* and *he answereth.*

Perversely, these obsolete forms continue to haunt legal contexts, never with happy results. When using words with this ending, lawyers have long been inconsistent in their approach; for example, a late 19th-century verification stated, "W.J. Bound . . . *deposeth and says* . . . ." *Dorman v. Crozier,* 14 Kan. 177, 177–78 (1875) (quoting a verification). Why not *deposeth and sayeth?*

More to the point, modern lawyers commonly mangle tenses when *-eth* crops up, often by thinking that *-eth* signifies a past tense: "E.W. Kelley, being first duly cautioned and sworn, *deposeth* and said that one Paul De Golyer . . . ." *City of Cincinnati v. De Golyer,* 270 N.E.2d 663, 664 (Ohio Ct. App. 1969). Modern lawyers also misuse *witnesseth* at the outset of a contract as if it were imperative instead of present-tense indicative. The careful legal writer junketh the ending. See **doth, saith & witnesseth.** See also **hath & further affiant (A).**

ethicist; ethician. *Ethician* is more than two centuries older—dating from the early 17th century—and is therefore given precedence in most English-language dictionaries. Even so, *ethicist* so overwhelmingly predominates in modern usage that *ethician* ought to be labeled a NEEDLESS VARIANT. E.g., "*Ethicists* and moral theologians offer a variety of explanations for the duty to keep promises . . . ." Douglas Laycock, *The Death of the Irreparable Injury Rule* 255 (1991).

ethics; ethos. The distinction escapes many writers, but it is plain. *Ethics* = the field of moral science. Bentham defined *ethics* as "the art of directing men's actions to the production of the greatest possible quantity of happiness, on the part of those whose interest is in view." Jeremy Bentham, *An Introduction to the Principles of Morals and Legislation* 310 (1823; repr. 1948). The singular form *ethic* means "a set of moral principles."

Ethos = the characteristic spirit and beliefs of a community, people, system, or person. Here the nicety keenly appears: "We introduce here no new or radical *ethic* since our *ethos* has never given moral sanction to piracy." *E.I. duPont deNemours & Co. v. Christopher,* 431 F.2d 1012, 1016–17 (5th Cir. 1970).

etiology for *cause* is unnecessary and pompous. "What was the *etiology* [read *cause*] for his withdrawal from the position?" This use apparently stems from the medical use: "There are several diagnostic tests a physician may perform to determine the *etiology* of a painful back condition." *Aetiology* is the BrE spelling whereas *aitiology* is a secondary spelling to be avoided.

ETIOLOGY. See CAUSATION.

et seq. When citing a statute, it is better to give the reader an end point as well as a beginning one. Otherwise, the reader is left to conjecture just how many sections are encompassed in 29 U.S.C. §§ 621 *et seq.* Hence the phrase *et seq.* (short for *et sequentes* = the following ones) should be used sparingly if at all. The problem is exacerbated by the fact that *et seq.* serves also as the abbreviation for the singular *et sequens* (= and the following one), though presumably few users of the phrase know that.

-ETTE. See SEXISM (C).

et ux. See **ux.**

ETYMOLOGICAL AWARENESS is developed only by increased reading and a conscious sensitivity to words and their origins. Ignorance of etymologies can easily lead writers astray, as when a journalist gave the label *holocaust* (Gk. "burnt whole") to a flood. Following are sentences in which writers wandered into etymological bogs:

- "The right to exclude or to expel aliens in war or in peace is an inherent and *inalienable* right of every independent nation." (Here the root *alien-* causes problems, when we say a country has an *inalienable* right to exclude *aliens.*)
- "What we are concerned with here is the automobile and its *peripatetic* [= able to walk up and down, not just *itinerant*] character." (Automobiles can hardly be said to walk.)
- "This is a result which, if at all possible *consonant* [lit., "sounding together"] with *sound* judicial policy, should be avoided."

In the first and third specimens, a senseless repetition of the root sense occurs; in the second, the writer has insensitively abstracted and broadened a word still ineluctably tied to its root sense. Cf. VERBAL AWARENESS.

Euclidean; Euclidian. The *-ean* spelling is standard.

EUPHEMISMS are supposedly soft or unobjectionable terms substituted in place of harsh or objectionable ones. The purpose is to soften; the means is usually indirection. To discerning readers, of course, some euphemisms are objectionable because unnecessarily mealy-mouthed.

We euphemize if we say, not that someone is drunk, but *inebriated* or *intoxicated;* not that someone is a *drug addict,* but (much more vaguely) that the person is *impaired;* not that someone has *died,* but *passed away;* not that someone is *mentally retarded,* but *exceptional* or *special.*

In some contexts, to be sure, you might prefer a euphemism. If plain talk is going to provoke unnecessary controversy—if talk about *illegitimate children* or *sodomy* will divert attention from your point by offending people—then use an established euphemism.

Indeed, the phrase *illegitimate children* exemplifies the need sometimes to throw over old forms of expression. West Publishing Company's key-note system of indexing legal topics has gone from *Bastards* in the Eighth Decennial Digest (1966–76) to *Illegitimate Children* in the Ninth Decennial Digest (1976–81) to *Children Out-of-Wedlock* in the Federal Digest 3d (1985). Some legal writers use *nonmarital children* to convey the idea. The point, of course, is that we shouldn't scar innocent children with ugly epithets.

Other euphemisms, however, are roundabout and clumsy. Some writers use *rodent operative* or *extermination engineer* in place of *ratcatcher.* We see *pregnancy termination* rather than *abortion; sexually ambidextrous* rather than *bisexual; armed reconnaissance* rather than *bombing; permanent layoff* rather than firing. Whatever the unpleasant or socially awkward subject, there are several euphemisms available. In law, *unnatural offense* (or *crime) against nature* is not uncommon in place of *homosexuality.* Indeed, Arthur Leff gives *abominable and detestable crime against nature* as a "rather enthusiastic euphemism . . . found in many 19th-century (and some current) statutes, referring to a not fully specified range of sexual crimes." Arthur A. Leff, *The Leff Dictionary of Law,* 94 Yale L.J. 1855, 1866 (1985). The problem that courts encounter—now more than in yesteryear—is deciding what constitutes a *crime against nature* and the like, and whether any criminal statute using such a phrase is so vague as to be unconstitutional. See David Abbott, *Crimes Against Language and Nature,* 3 Scribes J. Legal Writing 149 (1992).

Euphemisms are often subtle. Thus *incident* appears in place of *accident* in a U.S. statute limiting total liability to $200 million for a single "nuclear incident," presumably because *incident* sounds vaguer and less alarmist. Today *revenue enhancement* (= tax increase) and *investment* (=

increased government spending) are commonly used by American politicians who are reluctant to call things by their more understandable names.

In the mock-heroic style that was popular in the 19th century—and even up to a few decades ago—euphemisms were quite common. In the following sentence, for example, a judge uses an elaborate euphemism for the hymen: "[The statute] further says to the libertine, who would rob a virtuous maiden, under the age of 18 years, of *the priceless and crowning jewel of maidenhood,* that he does so at his peril." *Bishop v. Liston,* 199 N.W. 825, 827 (Neb. 1924).

Some subjects call out for euphemisms or circumlocutions. Explicitness or directness would be undesirable to almost everyone here: "Due process concerns were not offended when a prison inmate was subjected to an attempted *digital* rectal search, based upon a reliable informer's tip." (Advocate's description of *U.S. v. Caldwell,* 750 F.2d 341 (5th Cir. 1984)). Still, the final phrase might advantageously be changed, because *tip* verges on losing its metaphorical quality in that particular context. See **digital.**

In a sense, euphemisms are at war against logical accuracy and clarity. Indeed, they reflect basic human impulses that oppose logical accuracy and clarity: "There are . . . unpleasant truths from which we turn away our minds almost as instinctively as we cover our eyes or turn away our heads from too strong a light or from a horrible sight. And when we cannot but admit such truths, we do not like to speak of them except through euphemisms." Morris R. Cohen, *Reason and Law* 14 (1961). Cohen calls this tendency "a fruitful source of legal fictions." *Id.* See FICTIONS.

EUPHONY. See SOUND OF PROSE, THE.

EUPHUISM. See PURPLE PROSE.

euthanasia; mercy killing. These synonyms are widespread, the former perhaps being more connotatively neutral.

euthan(at)ize = to subject to euthanasia. If we must have such a word, the longer version might seem the better candidate because it is properly formed, strictly speaking, and is older, dating in the *OED* from 1873. But in modern legal writing, *euthanize* predominates to such an extent that it ought to be accepted as standard—e.g.: "[T]he Circuit Court of Monongalia County . . . reinstated the magistrate's order to *euthanize* appellant's dog." *State v. Molisee,* 378 S.E.2d 100, 100 (W. Va. 1989) (per curiam)./ "Dr. Ennulat told Ms. Lambiotte that the horse needed to be *euthanized,* and Ms. Lambiotte called her director . . . ." *State v. Talley,* 429 S.E.2d 604, 606 (N.C. Ct. App. 1993). See -IZE (A).

evacuee. See -EE (A).

evanescence is sometimes used incorrectly to mean "departure" or "disappearance." E.g., "Upon his aunt's *evanescence* [read *departure*], he continued to drive the mower, still in first gear."

Here the adjective *evanescent* is correctly used in the sense "tending to vanish away": "The evidence in *Cupp,* to be sure, was highly *evanescent;* but no less so is any evidence that an alerted suspect can dispose of if the police should wait to act until they have obtained a warrant."/ "Interests of beneficiaries of private express trusts run the gamut from valuable substantialities to *evanescent* hopes."

evangelical; evangelistic. Today the older term *evangelical* (fr. ca. 1531) is so closely tied with fundamentalist, proselytizing Christians that it should not be applied more generally. *Evangelistic* (fr. ca. 1845), though also redolent with Christian associations, may be used more broadly to mean "militantly zealous."

even date for *the same date* originated in commercialese but has infected lawyers' writing as well. The best practice is to name the date a second time or to write *the same date.* E.g., "The court did not rule on either the request for preliminary injunction or the motion to dismiss until January 30, 1984, *at which time* [read *when*] the court dismissed the case with prejudice for the reasons set forth in the court's memorandum and order *of even date* [read *of the same date*]."

event, in the. The AmE phrase is invariably *in the event that* [+ clause]—an equivalent of *if.* BrE generally favors *in the event of* [+ noun phrase] (usu. a BURIED VERB)—a locution that appears also in AmE, sometimes without the *of.* Either phrase is inferior to *if.* See **in the event of** & **in the event that.**

In BrE, *in the event* also means "in (the) result," a usage likely to result in a MISCUE for American readers—e.g.: "Allowing the appeal, the Court of Appeal stated that although the Swiss were sensitive about their banking secrecy laws by court order from other countries, that by itself would not be a ground for interfering with the order. However, *in the event,* although the documents might prove relevant at a later stage of the proceedings, that was an insufficient ground for upholding the judge's order . . . ." *Bank of Crete v. Koskotas,* Fin. Times, 31 May 1991, at 8.

The phrase *in the eventuality* is especially pretentious. E.g., "The statutes provide that, *in that eventuality* [read *in that event*], the named person shall be deemed to have died immediately after the testator."

eventuality is a needless pomposity for *event.* E.g., "Bobbitt would be amply protected from this *eventuality* [read *event*]." *Hospital Consultants, Inc. v. Potyka,* 531 S.W.2d 657, 665 (Tex. Civ. App.—San Antonio 1975). See **event, in the.**

eventuate is "an elaborate journalistic word that can usually be replaced by a simpler word to advantage." George P. Krapp, *A Comprehensive Guide to Good English* 231 (1927). E.g., "It is quite plain that the Fourth Amendment governs 'seizures' of the person that do not *eventuate* [read *result*] in a trip to the station house and prosecution for the crime."/ "Their final argument is that their Fifth Amendment rights were not adequately protected by the grant of use immunity by the state court, since it would not protect them from use of their compelled testimony in a federal prosecution, should one *eventuate* [read *ensue* or *occur*]."/ "As a general proposition, one who executes a will believes that the testament covers all contingencies that might *eventuate* [read *occur* or *happen*]." (Note the INELEGANT VARIATION of *will* and *testament* in the final specimen.)

every. A. *Every-*: Singular or Plural? Today it is standard BrE to write, "Almost *everybody* now seems to be a 'victim' of something—of society or *their* own weaknesses." Susan Crosland, *The Aftershock of Anger,* Sunday Times, 22 Oct. 1989, at B2./ "[T]he compilation of the *OED* made it possible for *everyone* to have before *them* the historical shape and configuration of the language . . . ." Robert W. Burchfield, *Unlocking the English Language* 169 (1989).

But most Americans continue to think of this usage as slipshod, *everybody* requiring a singular; after all, they reason, nobody would say *everybody think* instead of *everybody thinks.* An early usage critic remarked insightfully (while disapproving): "[T]he use of this word is made difficult by the lack of a singular pronoun of dual sex . . . . Nevertheless, this is no warrant for the conjunction of *every* and *them.*" Richard G. White, *Every-Day English* 420–21 (1884). Many Americans now take the same stand, thereby making a happy solution elusive. See CONCORD (B) & SEXISM (A).

B. *Each and every.* See **each and every.**

C. *Every . . . not.* This construction often results in an error in logic. Literally, *every one is not* means "none is." But rarely is that what the writer means—e.g.: "[*E*]*very important case is not reported* [Read *Not every important case is reported* . . . .], or at all events not reported in those places where we might reasonably expect to find it . . . ." Carleton K. Allen, *Law in the Making* 374 (7th ed. 1964). Cf. **all (B)** & **everyone . . . not.**

everybody. See **every (A)** & CONCORD (B).

everybody else's. See **else's** & POSSESSIVES (G).

every day, adv.; **everyday,** adj. One tries to accomplish something *every day;* but an *everyday* feat would hardly be worth accomplishing. The two are occasionally confused—e.g.: "But what of the phrase 'per stirpes,' symbolic here of the hundreds of Latin and law French words still used *everyday* [read *every day*] by fully modernized American lawyers whose penchant for foreign languages probably extends no further?" Richard Weisberg, *When Lawyers Write* 99 (1987).

every man's house is his castle. See **castle doctrine.**

everyone; everybody. See **every (A),** CONCORD (B) & SEXISM (A).

everyone else's. See **else's** & POSSESSIVES (G).

everyone . . . not, in place of *not everyone,* is just as illogical as *all . . . not,* q.v. "But if richness needs gifts with which *everyone is not endowed* [read *not everyone is endowed*], simplicity by no means comes by nature." W. Somerset Maugham, "Lucidity, Simplicity, Euphony," in *The Summing Up* 321, 322 (1938). Cf. **all (B)** & **every (C).**

everyone . . . them. See **every (A),** CONCORD & SEXISM (A).

everyplace should be avoided as a vulgarism; *everywhere* is the proper word.

evict. Whether to lawyers or nonlawyers, this word generally means "to expel (a person, esp. a tenant) from land or a building, usu. by legal process." But in law it also means "to recover (property or title to property) *from* a person by legal process."

evidence, n. **A. And *testimony.*** These words overlap but are not always interchangeable. *Testimony* is a species of *evidence*; it refers only to evidence received through the medium of witnesses. *Evidence,* on the contrary, includes all means by which a fact in issue is established or disproved; thus, *evidence* may include documents and tangible objects. The word *evidence* has also long been used in the sense "the law of evidence." See James B. Thayer, *Presumptions and the Law of Evidence,* 3 Harv. L. Rev. 141, 142 (1889).

B. And *proof.* Strictly speaking, the two words are not synonymous. Unlike *evidence,* the word *proof* should be applied "to the *effect* of the evidence, and not to the *medium* by which truth is established." 1 Simon Greenleaf, *A Treatise on the Law of Evidence* 3 (I.F. Redfield ed., 12th ed. 1866). See **proof.**

C. As a Count Noun. *Evidence* is not generally taken to be a count noun; hence the plural form is unusual at best. E.g., "Yet in spite of all these *evidences* of judicial humility in these areas, it would be an error to assume that the judiciary had lost self-confidence altogether as a result of its chastening experience in the 1930's." Robert G. McCloskey, *The American Supreme Court* 190 (1960). See COUNT NOUNS AND MASS NOUNS (B).

D. Other Phrases. See **forensic** (last par.), **give evidence** & **put on.**

evidence, v.t.; **evince.** These words, which are lawyers' favorites, are often inferior to *show* or *express* or *indicate.* Properly, to *evidence* something is to be the proof, or to serve as evidence, of its existence or happening or truth. Here it is correctly used: "If the owner of an interest in land declares himself trustee of the interest for the benefit of another, the writing *evidencing* the trust may be signed by the declarant before, at the time of, or after the declaration."/ "Admittedly the distinction between acts *evidencing* a continuing conspiracy and acts constituting further agreements or fresh conspiracies is a fine one." (Eng.)

More often than not, however, it is used loosely for *show, demonstrate,* or *express:* "Texas asserts, without support, that the Bus Act *evidences* [read *shows*] an intent not to grant the ICC jurisdiction over intrastate charter operations and charges that the legislative history of the statute further *evidences* [read *demonstrates*] Congress's intent to provide for the preemption of intrastate regular-route transportation and not of intrastate charter transportation."/ "Even the majority opinion *evidenced* [read *showed*] a subtle but potentially powerful shift in the law."

Evince properly means "to show, exhibit, make manifest," but has been objected to as "a bad word and unnecessary . . . a favourite with callow journalists." Eric Partridge, *Usage and Abusage* 113 (rev. ed. 1973). It is greatly overworked in legal writing, as the cornucopia of specimens evinces: "The court in that opinion *evinced* even more reluctance to compare the worth of unequal jobs."/ "Although the testator may not have intended that Charles share as legatee or devisee under his will, he *evinced* no intention that he was to be excluded as next of kin, through operation of the laws of intestacy."/ "Had the petitioners challenged the underlying convictions and requested an opportunity to replead, the court stated, the cases would not have been moot; the court thus *evinced* a tendency to favor specific requests for relief in habeas petitions."/ "As in the 93d and 94th Congresses, at no time did the 95th Congress *evince* an intent to afford states reclamation authority on non-reservation Indian lands."

evidenciary is wrong for *evidentiary.* See **evidentiary.**

evidential. See **evidentiary.**

evidentiarily is the adverb corresponding to *evidentiary,* adj. It is often used—somewhat clumsily—as a SENTENCE ADVERB in the sense "in terms of evidence." E.g., "It turns out, however, that *evidentiarily* we do not now have such a case before us." *McLaurin v. Columbia Mun. Separate Sch. Dist.,* 486 F.2d 1049, 1050 (5th Cir. 1973) (Coleman, J., concurring). See ADVERBS (B).

evidentiary; evidential. It would be convenient to pronounce *evidential* a NEEDLESS VARIANT and be done with it, but that (older) form seems to predominate in BrE (see *OED* & *COD*). Even so, the *-ary* form—a NEOLOGISM innovated by Jeremy Bentham—also appears in BrE. We might, however, brand *evidential* a NEEDLESS VARIANT in AmE, in which *evidentiary* far outstrips *evidential* in frequency of use. E.g., "There is a kind of *evidential* [read *evidentiary*] estoppel." *Holly Hill Citrus Growers' Ass'n v. Holly Hill Fruit Prods., Inc.,* 75 F.2d 13, 17 (5th Cir. 1935)./ "If, therefore, the unaltered document is produced for inspection, the facts thus ascertained must, as regards the alleged contractual agreement, be purely *evidential* [read *evidentiary*] in character."

Still, *evidential* has been useful to some legal theorists, like Hohfeld, in meaning "furnishing evidence" as opposed to "of or relating to evidence" (the sense in which *evidentiary* predominates). If we could enhance this latent DIFFERENTIATION, the language of the law of evidence would be richer for it. Following are two examples from Wesley N. Hohfeld, *Fundamental Legal Conceptions* (1919): "An *evidential* fact is one which, on being ascertained, affords some logical basis—not conclusive—for inferring some other fact."/ "The facts important in relation to a given jural transaction may be either operative facts or *evidential* facts."

evince. See **evidence,** v.t.

eviscerate (= to disembowel) has become a VOGUE WORD among legal writers in its metaphorical applications. Because of its strong meaning, it is not to be used lightly. "Clearly *eviscerating* the Tenth Amendment's restrictions on the accretion of power by the United States Government, *Garcia* offered the conservative wing of the court an opportunity to express its displeasure at the majority's rejection of 'almost 200 years of the understanding of the constitutional status of federalism.'"

Here *eviscerate* approaches meaninglessness: "To permit any complainant to restart the limitations period by petitioning for review of a rule would *eviscerate* the congressional concern for finality embodied in time limitations on review." The metaphor of *eviscerating* does not work with a gossamer object like *concern,* even if it is said to be "embodied." Cf. **emasculate.**

evoke (= [1] to call forth; or [2] to bring to mind) is a near-MALAPROPISM when misused for *invoke* (= [1] to call upon; or [2] to cause). E.g., "If Rumbaugh is incompetent to waive his right to federal habeas review, his parents have standing to *evoke* [read *invoke*] a next-friend proceeding."

ex-, when meaning "former," should be hyphenated: "A bitter *exemployee* [read *ex-employee*] can do great harm . . . . [W]hen people feel they have been fired 'fairly' . . . they will be reluctant to bad-mouth their *excompany* [read *ex-company*]." Mark H. McCormack, *What They Don't Teach You at Harvard Business School* 199 (1984).

exact from sometimes signals a wordy construction—e.g.: "In the present case, however, *the compelled production of the journal was exacted from defendant's attorneys* [read *the defendant's attorneys were compelled to produce the journal*]." *State v. Barrett,* 401 N.W.2d 184, 191 (Iowa 1987). For the reasons why *production* should be made into the present infinitive of the verb *produce,* see BURIED VERBS.

exalt; exult. To *exalt* is to raise in rank, place in a high position, or extol. To *exult* is to rejoice exceedingly.

Exalt is rather frequently misspelled *exhalt* or *exhault*—e.g.: "The serjeant might perform military duties rather less *exhalted* [read *exalted*] than those of a knight . . . ." Alan Harding, *A Social History of English Law* 32 (1966)./ "It would be *exhalting* [read *exalting*] form over substance to require the Committee . . . to amend its complaint. . . ." *Committee on Professional Ethics & Conduct v. Munger,* 375 N.W.2d 248, 251 (Iowa 1985). For a similar misspelling, see **exorbitant.**

examination-in-chief. See **direct examination.**

example; exemplar; exemplum; exemplification. *Example* is the general term. *Exemplar* = an ideal or typical example. E.g., "The Court of Appeals found critical significance in the fact that the grand jury had summoned approximately 20 witnesses to furnish voice *exemplars* [i.e., typical specimens]." *U.S. v. Dionisio,* 410 U.S. 1, 12 (1973) (per Stewart, J.)./ "A testator of sound mind may prefer a prodigal son or even an unrepentant sinner to a son who has been an *exemplar* [i.e. an *ideal example*] and pattern of virtue." *Exemplum,* except in specialized literary senses, is a NEEDLESS VARIANT of *example. Exemplification* = (1) (in law) an attested copy of a document <an exemplification is a copy of a record set out either under the Great Seal or under the Seal of the Court>; (2) the act or process of serving as an example <by way of exemplification>; or (3) a case in point.

example where is always inferior to *example in which.* See **where (B).** Cf. **case where.**

ex ante; ex post. These LATINISMS, which may act either as adverbs or as adjectives, are likely to confuse most readers. *Ex ante* = based on assumption and prediction; subjective; prospective. *Ex post* = based on knowledge and facts; objective; retrospective. In the following sentences, *prospectively* and *retrospectively* would lead to greater comprehensibility with no loss in the sense: "Judges should be aware that their decisions create incentives influencing conduct *ex ante* [read *prospectively*] and that attempts to divide the stakes fairly *ex post* [read *retrospectively*] will alter or reverse the signals that are desirable from *an ex ante* [read *a prospective*] point of view."/ "Attorneys general were generally effective *in determining ex ante* [read *in predicting*] the policy orientation of future judges." See **ex post facto.**

ex cathedra; ex officio. *Ex cathedra* = (1) (adv.) from the chair; with authority; (2) (adj.) authoritative. Following is a literal adverbial use: "In expressing this view, both in legal literature and *ex cathedra,* he was, in effect, reverting to the standpoint of Lord Mansfield, who regarded quasi-contract as being essentially an equitable institution." (Eng.) Increasingly today, *ex cathedra* has connotations of a peremptory attitude—e.g.: "The Attorney General's letter asserts *ex ca-*

thedra and without citation of a single authority that. . . ." Peter Shane & Harold Bruff, *The Law of Presidential Power* 205 (1988).

Ex officio (= by virtue of one's office) may likewise be both adj. and adv. <the chair is an ex officio member of all standing committees> <the chair became a member ex officio>. *Ex officiis* is a NEEDLESS VARIANT. *Ex officio* should be neither hyphenated nor spelled as one word.

exceed. See **accede.**

exceedingly is hyperbolic when used for *quite* or *very*. E.g., "Newspaper prices seldom change; the prices of chewing gum, flashlight batteries, and chloroform are *exceedingly* [read *quite*] stable."

excel. So spelled; *excell* is an infrequent misspelling.

except. A. As Verb. *Except* = (1) to exclude, omit <present company excepted>; (2) = to object, take exception <I except to that statement>. The latter is the more frequent legal meaning: "The court overruled the objection, and the defendants *excepted.*" Sense (2) has given rise to the special legal sense of the word, "to appeal." E.g., "Verdict was for plaintiff in each action, and defendant *excepts.*"

B. As Preposition and Conjunction. When *except* begins a noun phrase rather than a clause (i.e., a phrase with a verb), it is a simple preposition not followed by the relative pronoun *that* <all persons except farmers owning fewer than 500 acres>. But when, as a conjunction, *except* introduces a clause, it should be followed by *that,* which is here incorrectly omitted: "The corporate existence shall be deemed to have continued without interruption from the date of dissolution, *except* [read *except that*] the reinstatement shall have no effect upon any issue of personal liability of the directors."

C. As Conjunction. *Except* for *unless* is an ARCHAISM that persists only as a vulgarism. Here is the archaic use: "I devise this land to A and her heirs forever, *except* she should die without heir born of her own body." Will quoted in *Roach v. Martin's Lessee,* 1 Har. 548, 28 Am. Dec. 746 (1835). And here is the modern vulgarism: "Wheat produced on excess acreage may be neither disposed of nor used except upon payment of the penalty, or *except* [read *unless*] it is stored as required by the Act or delivered to the Secretary of Agriculture." See (E), (G), (H).

D. *Excepting.* This word should not be used as a substitute for *except,* except in the phrase *not excepting.* E.g., "The majority of the cases dealing with the problem, *excepting* [read *except*] two, have applied the ruling to the case which resulted in the abolition of the doctrine of sovereign immunity."/ "He further provided that the property should under no circumstances be sold or alienated or at any time devoted to any other purpose or use *excepting as far as herein specifically authorized* [read other purpose or use *than is herein authorized*]."

E. *Except as.* In DRAFTING, *unless* is preferable to *except as* when referring to a future action—e.g.: "*Except as* [read *Unless*] otherwise stipulated or directed by the court . . . ." Fed. R. Civ. P. 26(a)(2)(B).

Except as may be appropriate when referring to something that an existing rule or statue does—e.g.: "*Except as* otherwise provided in Rule 26(b) . . . ."

F. *Except that.* This phrase is generally inferior to *but* or some other, more pointed term—e.g.: "[T]he parties may by written stipulation . . . modify other procedures . . . , *except that* [read *but*] stipulations extending the time provided in Rules 33, 34, and 36 for responses to discovery may . . . be made only with the approval of the court." Fed. R. Civ. P. 29.

G. *Except when.* The word *unless* is usually much preferable—e.g.: "*Except when* [read *Unless*] a federal statute or these rules provide otherwise, ..." (Cf. **except as.**) Even with the slightly improved wording, however, this type of wide-open exception makes DRAFTING less easily comprehensible: the reader must research all of federal law to find out whether the exception applies. Such a provision is therefore antithetical to principles of PLAIN LANGUAGE.

H. *Except with.* This phrase, usually followed by a noun phrase, is ordinarily inferior to *unless* (usually followed by a subject and verb)—e.g.: "*Except with the written consent of the defendant,* [read *Unless the defendant consents in writing,*] the report [must] not be submitted to the court . . . ." Fed. R. Crim. App. 32(b)(1).

except as. See **except (E).**

except as otherwise provided. See **notwithstanding anything to the contrary contained herein.**

exception takes the preposition *to,* not *from.* E.g., "Application of foreign law must be analytically understood as an exception *from* [read *to*] the basic rule calling for the application of the lex fori."

exceptionable; exceptional. The first is sometimes misused for the second. *Exceptionable* = open to exception; objectionable <she was admonished for her exceptionable behavior>. *Excep-*

tional = out of the ordinary; uncommon; rare; superior <an exceptional achievement>.

exception proves the rule, the. This phrase is the popular rendering of what was originally a legal maxim, "The exception proves (or confirms) the rule in the cases not excepted" *(exceptio probat regulam in casibus non exceptis).* Originally *exception* in this maxim meant "the action of excepting"—not, as is commonly supposed, "that which is excepted"—so that the true sense of the maxim was that by specifying the cases excepted, one strengthens the hold of the rule over all cases not excepted.

At least two spurious explanations of *the exception proves the rule* exist. One is that because a rule does not hold in all instances (i.e., has exceptions), the rule must be valid. This misunderstanding of the phrase commonly manifests itself in the discourse of those who wish to argue that every rule must have exceptions. A more sophisticated, but equally false, explanation of the phrase is that *prove* here retains its Elizabethan sense (derived from the Latin) "to test," so that the sense of the phrase is that an exception to a rule "tests" the validity of the rule. This erroneous explanation appears, of all places, in Tom Burnam, *A Dictionary of Misinformation* 79 (1975).

exceptor (= one who excepts or objects) was formerly used in some jurisdictions as an equivalent of *appellant.* E.g., "*Exceptors* place considerable stress on the case of *Marshall v. Frazier.*" See **plaintiff** & **except** (A).

except that. See **except** (F).

except when. See **except** (G).

except with. See **except** (H).

excess of, in (= beyond the confines of) is a LEGALISM used in the context of actions *ultra vires,* q.v. The phrase is unobjectionable per se. E.g., "The district court ruled that the regulations had been promulgated *in excess of* the EPA's authority under the Clean Air Act."/ "It is contended that the minister acted *in excess of* his jurisdiction." (Eng.)

Exchequer is so spelled. Some writers have tried to make it *Exchequor*—e.g.: "This work required a law court in the modern sense made up of a small number of judges of education and ability skilled in the law which sat regularly term after term, generally at Westminster, often at the *Exchequor* [read *Exchequer*]." William F. Walsh, *A Treatise on Equity* 3 (1930).

excise. There are two unrelated verbs *excise:* (1) "to remove"; and (2) "to impose an excise tax [q.v.] on." Here sense (1) applies: "The jury had been selected at the time the sealing was entered; therefore, *excising* the documents and releasing them to the public was an alternative to sealing that should have been considered." To illustrate sense (2), the *OED* quotes Blackstone as follows: "Brandies and other spirits are now *excised* at the distillery." The *OED* labels this sense obsolete, but *W3* and *W10* suggest that it lives on.

excise tax has two quite distinct meanings: (1) "a tax imposed on specific commodities that are produced, sold, or transported within a country—for example, liquor and tobacco"; or (2) "a tax imposed on a license to pursue a specified trade or occupation."

exciseman; excisor. In view of the modern trend of avoiding needless SEXISM in language, *excisor* is to be preferred.

excludable; excludible; exclusible. The preferred form is *excludable.* See -ABLE (A).

exclusionary = tending to exclude, or characterized by exclusion <exclusionary rule>. This word, recorded first (fr. 1817) in the works of Jeremy Bentham (1748–1832), began as a peculiarly legal word and has remained so.

exclusive means "with no exceptions" and should be used carefully. An ill-advised use appears in 28 U.S.C. § 1346: "The district courts . . . shall have *exclusive* jurisdiction of civil actions on claims against the United States." This is not so, since circuit courts and the Supreme Court may also properly have jurisdiction on appeal. What was meant is "exclusive original jurisdiction." See OVERSTATEMENT.

exclusive federal jurisdiction. See **preemption, federal.**

ex contractu; ex delicto. The phrases *in contract* and *in tort* are much preferable to these LATINISMS. E.g., "Doubtless this is the rule of law today in all ordinary actions, either *ex contractu or ex delicto* [read *in contract or in tort*]."/ "Appellee maintains that it is entitled to attorneys' fees and costs incurred in the successful defense against appellant's *ex delicto claim* [read *tort claim*]."/ "Precise classification of rights *as ex contractu or ex delicto* [read *as being in contract or in tort*] was no more characteristic of 15th-century English legal thought than it is today."/ "Any one of various possible groups of specific operative facts would suffice, as far as the defendant's obligation *ex delicto* [read *in tort*] is concerned." See **delictual.**

exculpate; exonerate. Whereas the former has the primary sense "to free from blame or accusation," the latter means literally "to free from a burden," and only by extension is synonymous with the former. See **exonerate** & **inculpate.**

exculpatee (= one who has been exculpated) is an AmE NEOLOGISM—e.g.: "An exculpatory clause covers the risk of harm sustained by the exculpator that might be caused by the *exculpatee.*" *Weaver v. American Oil Co.,* 261 N.E.2d 99, 102 (Ind. Ct. App. 1970). Though rarely heard, the word should—if it must be pronounced at all—be pronounced /*ek-skəl-pə-****tee***/. See -EE.

exculpatory; exculpative. The latter is a NEEDLESS VARIANT.

excusal; excusation. In reference to prospective jurors, the correct phraseology is, e.g., *excusal for cause from the venire panel. Excusation* is an obsolete word meaning "the action of offering an excuse" *(OED).*

excuse; justification. In many areas of the law, these terms are used interchangeably. But they have undergone DIFFERENTIATION in criminal law.

An *excuse* is a defense that arises because the defendant is not blameworthy for having acted in a way that would otherwise be criminal. Traditionally, the following defenses were excuses: duress, entrapment, infancy, insanity, and involuntary intoxication.

A *justification,* by contrast, is a defense that arises when the defendant has acted in a way that the criminal law does not seek to prevent. Traditionally, the following defenses were justifications: the defendant's choice of a lesser harm or evil, consent, defense of others, defense of property, self-defense, the use of force to make an arrest, and the use of force by public authority.

ex delictu is a mistaken form of *ex delicto* caused by confusion with the ending of *ex contractu*—e.g.: "An examination of her pleadings only reinforces the *ex delictu* [read *ex delicto*] nature of Ms. Williams' claim." *Page v. U.S. Indus., Inc.,* 556 F.2d 346, 352 (5th Cir. 1977). The reason for the difference is that *delictum* is a second-declension Latin noun whose ablative singular is *delicto,* not *delictu,* whereas *contractus* is a fourth-declension noun whose ablative singular is *contractu.* See ***ex contractu.***

execute. A. Senses. *Execute* (= to sign and deliver; to make valid by observing certain required formalities) is lawyers' JARGON used in reference to completing legal documents <she executed her will>. In this sense the word means "to go through the formalities necessary to the validity of (a legal act)—hence, to complete and give validity to (the instrument by which such an act is effected) by performing what the law requires to be done" (adapted fr. *OED*). But the word *sign* is often preferable, especially in communicating with nonlawyers.

Execute also has several other senses in law: (1) "to carry into effect ministerially (a law, a judicial sentence, etc.)"; (2) "to perform or carry out the provisions of a will" (i.e., what the executor does—this use of the term is now somewhat rare) see (c); (3) "to perform acts of (justice, e.g.) or give effect to a court's judgment"; or (4) "to levy execution *on* (property of a judgment debtor)" <when the judgment became final, the prevailing plaintiff's attorney had the marshal execute on defendant's nonexempt property>. Sense (4) appears to be peculiar to AmE, and is given in none of the standard unabridged dictionaries. But it falls logically under the second broad sense listed in the *OED:* "to do execution upon."

B. For issue. Though legal instruments and the like are *executed,* writs, warrants, and the like are said to *issue from* (or *be issued by*) courts or other official bodies—e.g.: "The bureau [the Federal Bureau of Investigation] said search warrants were *executed* [read *issued*] Thursday on five locations in the Washington area and suburban Atlanta to look for evidence of a wide-ranging criminal conspiracy." Steve McGonigle, *U.S. Treasurer's Home Searched in FBI Influence-Peddling Probe,* Dallas Morning News, 31 Oct. 1992, at 1A./ "If the trial court's action is abusive, mandamus will *execute* [read *issue*] to cure it." See **issue.**

C. Used in Reference to Wills. Although the testator *executes* (i.e., performs an action necessary to validate) a will by signing it, the (aptly named) executor is also said to *execute* it when carrying out the will's provisions. This latter use occurs infrequently—e.g.: "Name an executor who is both able and willing to do the job. *Executing* a will can be time-consuming and labor-intensive." G.W. Weinstein, *Planning Your Estate,* Investment Vision, July/Aug. 1990, at 50.

executed contract. See **executory contract.**

executer. See **executor.**

execution-proof, adj. See **judgment-proof,** adj.

executive agreement. See **treaty.**

executor; executer. The *-er* spelling is obsolete. An *executor* is (1) "one who does or performs some act"; (2) "one who, appointed in a testator's will, administers the estate"; or (3) *in American patent practice,* one who represents a legally incapacitated inventor. In senses (2) and (3), the accent falls (familiarly) on the second syllable */ig-**zek**-yə-tər/*; in sense (1), the accent is on the first syllable */**ek**-sə-kyoot-ər/*. See **administrator.**

executory; executorial. *Executory* = taking full effect at a future time <an executory judgment> <executory contract>. *Executorial* = of or pertaining to an executor.

executory contract; executed contract. An *executory contract* is one that remains wholly unperformed or for which there remains something still to be done on both sides. An *executed contract* is one that has been entirely performed on one side.

executory limitation. See **special limitation.**

executory sale. See **contract for sale.**

executrix; executress. *Executrix* (pl. *-trices*) is the usual feminine form of *executor,* which may itself serve as a neuter form covering both sexes. Though legal writers have traditionally distinguished between the sexes by suffix, *executor* is now the preferable term for men and women alike. See SEXISM (C).

exegesis; epexegesis; eisegesis. Knowledge of these terms is useful to anyone having to interpret writings. *Exegesis* = explanation or exposition (as of a word or sentence). E.g., "[I]n interpretation of federal statutes and Congressional intent . . . semantic *exegesis* is not conclusive." *International Union v. Marshall,* 584 F.2d 390, 397 (D.C. Cir. 1978). *Epexegesis* = the addition of a word or words to convey more clearly the meaning implied, or the specific sense intended, in a preceding word or sentence (*OED*). *Eisegesis* = the interpretation of a word or passage by reading into it one's own ideas (*OED*).

exemplar. See **example.**

exemplary has two almost contradictory connotations: *exemplary damages* make an example out of a wrongdoer, whereas *exemplary behavior* is model behavior. *Exemplary* is sometimes misunderstood as meaning "severe" in phrases such as *exemplary punishment.*

exemplaries (= exemplary damages) is an attributive noun in AmE—a common part of trial lawyers' JARGON. Cf. **punitives & punies.** See **punitive damages.**

exemplary damages. See **punitive damages.**

exemplification. See **example.**

exemplum. See **example.**

exempt appears commonly in the U.S. as an ellipsis for *tax-exempt.* Usually this usage occurs in contexts in which the reader has already learned that the subject at hand is tax exemptions, and not other types of exemptions. Following is a typical specimen: "An *exempt* organization has the privilege of preferred second- or third-class mailing rates." Craig Weinlein, *Federal Taxation of Not-for-Profit Arts Organizations,* 12 J. Arts, Mgmt., & Law 33, 33–34 (Summer 1982).

exequatur [fr. L. *exsequor* "let him perform"] = (1) originally, a temporal sovereign's *act* in authorizing a bishop to perform—under authority of the Pope—the clerical and administrative duties of a diocese; later, a sovereign's *right* either to so empower a bishop or to permit the publication of a papal bull; (2) in international law, a receiving state's authorization by which the head of a consular post is admitted to the exercise of his or her functions; or (3) in international law, the executive judgment or order by which a foreign judgment or an arbitral award is made locally enforceable. See Clive Parry & J.P. Grant, *Encyclopedic Dictionary of International Law* 123 (1986).

exercise for *existence* is a puzzling error. E.g., "A presumption of undue influence arises from proof of the *exercise* [read *existence?*] of a confidential relation between the testator and such a beneficiary, coupled with activity on the part of the latter in the preparation of the will." (A *confidential relation* is not *exercised.*)

exertive; exertional. *Exertive* = tending to exert or rouse to action *(OED)* <resolve is an exertive emotion>. *Exertional,* though recorded in none of the Oxford or Merriam-Webster dictionaries, has appeared (usu. in the negative form) in American law cases in the field of social-security disabilities. *Exertional* = of or pertaining to physical effort. E.g., "[H]e is unable to return to his past relevant work and suffers from a *nonexertional* impairment." *Warmoth v. Bowen,* 798 F.2d 1109, 1110 (7th Cir. 1986)./ "[W]henever a *nonexertional* impairment is presented the Secretary must introduce a vocational expert to testify that jobs in the workplace exist for a person with that particular disability." *Bapp v. Bowen,* 802 F.2d 601, 604 (2d Cir. 1986).

ex facie (= in view of what is apparent, lit., "from the face") is not justified as a legal LATINISM, inasmuch as so many ordinary English words, such as *evidently, apparently,* or *on its face,* suffice in its stead. "*Ex facie* [read *Patently*] those transfers would be the same in form and in effect precisely as the instrument of transfer now before us." (Eng.) Here the phrase is wrongly made adjectival: "The Companies Act of 1948 brought into being that which was *ex facie* [read *evident*] in all its essential characteristics." (Eng.) See **face, on its.**

ex gratia; a gratia. *Ex gratia* means "as a favor, not by legal necessity" <*ex gratia* payment>. E.g., "[T]his punishment is not directly or mainly beneficial to the person injured, though a scheme whereby the State pays compensation *ex gratia* to victims of violence was started in 1964." William Geldart, *Introduction to English Law* 146 (D.C.M. Yardley ed., 9th ed. 1984). *A gratia* is a NEEDLESS VARIANT.

exha(u)lt is a misspelling of *exalt,* q.v.

exhorbitant is a misspelling of *exorbitant,* q.v.

ex hypothesi is a needless LATINISM meaning *hypothetically* or *hypothetical.* E.g., "[H]ow can there be a price for what is, *ex hypothesi* [read *hypothetically*], a gratuitous transaction?" P.S. Atiyah, *An Introduction to the Law of Contract* 121 (3d ed. 1981).

exigency; exigence. The form in *-cy* is standard; the other is a NEEDLESS VARIANT.

exige(a)nt. *Exigeant* is a NEEDLESS VARIANT of the standard form, *exigent* (= requiring immediate action).

existing. Legal drafters should use this ambiguous word cautiously. It may mean "existing at the time of the writing" or "existing at some time after the writing," if not specifically put within a time frame.

exit has been an acceptable verb since the early 17th century. Those who object to it on grounds that one does not "entrance" a building have a misplaced prejudice.

exlex; *ex lege.* Good legal writers have little or no use for these terms. Still, it is well to know their meanings: *exlex* is an adjective meaning "outside the law, without legal authority" <an exlex government>, whereas *ex lege* is an adverb meaning "by virtue of law; as a matter of law" <property forfeited *ex lege*>.

ex maleficio = (adv.) by malfeasance; (adj.) tortious. There is no reason why this phrase should not be Englished. E.g., "We do not find these allegations sufficient, either on authority or on principle, to establish a constructive trust *ex maleficio* [read *resulting from malfeasance*]."/ "In the character of a trustee *ex maleficio* [read *by virtue of malfeasance*], he shall be held to make good the things to the person who would have the property." See ***de son tort.***

ex necessitate (= of necessity) is a Latinistic pollutant. E.g., "They argue that adoption of the doctrine would be a nullification of the rule that executory limitations are void unless they take effect *ex necessitate* [read *of necessity*] and in all possible contingencies within the prescribed period." See LATINISMS.

exodus, a much abused word, refers to the simultaneous departure of many people. It is not the term to describe one lawyer's leaving a firm: "Likewise, negotiations failed on whether Poindexter's ex-firm was entitled to reimbursement of several thousand dollars in costs expended on the Nicol case upon Poindexter's *exodus* [read *exit*] or upon the conclusion of the case." Occasionally *exodus* is mistakenly thought to be the equivalent of *influx,* which is actually an antonym.

Exodus should be avoided as a verb: "Poor people have no ability to *exodus from* [read *leave en masse*] an impoverished state for richer ones."

ex officio. See **ex cathedra.**

exonerate, in the sense "to free from responsibility," should be used only in reference to people. E.g., "Contracts to *exonerate* the plaintiff from the payment of debts or demands assumed by the defendant are enforced for a like reason expressed in a different form." William F. Walsh, *A Treatise on Equity* 317 (1930).

Hence the following use, which refers to a rocket booster as opposed to a person, is erroneous: "Held, affirmed for DuPont since there was no evidence that the booster [a component in an explosive device] was responsible for the explosion, and the evidence offered by plaintiff tended to *exonerate* [read *rule out*] the booster." Cf. **exculpate.**

In its sense "to free from encumbrances," of course, *exonerate* is used in reference to burdened property. E.g., "We find that the decedent did not expressly signify any intention not to *exonerate* the property here from the mortgage lien." Whereas *acquit* takes *of, exonerate* takes the preposition *from:* "We affirm the lower court's holding that it was the intention of the testator that this legacy be *exonerated from* all liens." See **subrogation (C).**

ex'or is an archaic abbreviation of *executor,* q.v.

exorbitant (lit., "having departed or deviated from one's track [*orbita*] or rut") is sometimes mistakenly spelled *exhorbitant*—perhaps because it is confused with *exhort.* E.g., "Daon's own appraiser agreed that this price was *exhorbitant* [read *exorbitant*]." *Foster v. Daon Corp.*, 713 F.2d 148, 149 (5th Cir. 1983). Cf. the misspellings *exhalt* and *exhault:* see **exalt.**

exordium. See **introductory clause.**

expandable; expandible; expansible. The first is the preferred form. See -ABLE (A).

ex parte. A. And *inter partes.* These correlative terms—legal JARGON, both—are familiar enough to all lawyers to be useful; they should be simplified for the lay audience, however.

An *ex parte* proceeding involves only one party since the basic meaning of this Latin phrase is "from or on behalf of only one side to a lawsuit." E.g., "Because appellee declined to participate in the proceeding, the arbitration was conducted *ex parte.*"/ "Petitioner maintains that the judge was unduly and falsely influenced during an allegedly *ex parte* conversation with the prosecution."

In an *inter partes* proceeding, more than one party is involved, since *inter partes* means "between (and among) parties; involving all sides to a lawsuit." This term is used less frequently than *ex parte.* E.g., "In other states these courts may conduct *inter partes* proceedings if the contestant files a caveat after the *ex parte* proceeding has begun." See ***inter partes.***

B. Misused for *sua sponte.* *Ex parte* is sometimes ignorantly misused for *sua sponte,* a term meaning "spontaneously; on one's own motion or initiative without prompting from others." E.g., "The court was not free to deny plaintiff's motion to vacate judgment under Rule 60(b)(2) based upon its *ex parte* [read *sua sponte*] determination that to do otherwise would be somehow contrary to the public policy of bringing disputes to a conclusion." See ***sua sponte.***

expatiate; expatriate. *Expatiate* means (1) "to wander"; or (2) "to discourse on (a subject) at length." *Expatriate* means (1) "to leave one's home country to live elsewhere"; or (2) "to banish; exile."

expect is informal or colloquial for *think* or *suppose,* as here: "I *expect* that it will take three weeks," instead of, "I think it will take three weeks." Most properly, *expect* means "to look forward to and rely on." See **anticipate.**

expectancy. A. And *expectant estate.* *Expectancy* = (1) the possibility that an heir apparent or presumptive or a presumptive next-of-kin will acquire property by succession on intestacy; or (2) the possibility that a presumptive legatee or devisee will acquire property by will. *Expectant estate* = a reversion, a remainder either vested or contingent, or an executory interest. See Lewis M. Simes & A.F. Smith, *The Law of Future Interests* § 2, at 5–6 (2d ed. 1956).

B. And *expectation.* We have the idioms *life expectancy* and *meet one's expectations,* but aside from distinguishing uses in these phrases, most lawyers would be hard put to set out the distinction. Despite an overlap in actual use, there is a clear-cut DIFFERENTIATION that ought to be observed with care. For *expectancy,* see (A). *Expectation* = the action of mentally looking for someone to come, forecasting something to happen, or anticipating something to be received (*OED*). E.g., "The statute creates a presumption that parole release will be granted, which in turn creates a legitimate *expectation* of release absent the requisite finding that one of the justifications for deferral exists."/ "Perhaps the most common recovery sought in contract cases is a reimbursement for damage to what is known as the plaintiff's *expectation* interest."

Here idiom is violated by *life expectation:* "By the wrongful injury his normal life *expectation* [read *expectancy*] had been shortened." The opposite error here occurs, *expectancy* for *expectation:* "Punishment of the contract-breaker is so subordinated to the main goal of fulfilling the injured party's *expectancy* [read *expectation*] of gain that it has received practically no recognition as a remedial consideration."

Writers who misguidedly favor INELEGANT VARIATION are especially drawn to these terms. E.g., "The district court considered the balance due on Todd's repair contract in computing Auto's damages solely in order to ensure that Auto received no more than its *expectation.* Because the repairers were obligated in solido to *pay this expectancy* [read *pay the amount of this expectation*], the district court correctly subtracted the balance due under the contract from the amount of their total liability."

expectant heir. See **heir** (B).

expectation. See **expectancy.**

expediency; expedience. The former is usual; the latter is a NEEDLESS VARIANT.

expeditious; expedient; expediential. *Expeditious* = quickly accomplished, prompt <an expeditious decision>. *Expedient* = (1) desirable, advantageous <a surprisingly expedient device for controlling a difficult problem>; or (2) based on self-interest <a purely expedient decision>. *Expediential* is a NEEDLESS VARIANT.

The word *expedient* was once synonymous with *expeditious,* but this use of the word has long been considered obsolete. Oddly, however, it persists in legal contexts in which *expeditious* would be the better word—e.g.: "In addition, the intent of the Declaratory Judgment Act is to promote the simple, *expedient* [read *expeditious*] trial of cases where the nature of the questions involved lend themselves readily to trial without the usual formalities to the end that resolution may be speedily achieved." *Gulotta v. Cutshaw,* 258 So. 2d 555, 559 (La. Ct. App. 1972)./ "The Court notes plaintiff's motion of August 9, 1982, for *expedient* [read *expeditious*] trial, and has kept in mind 5 U.S.C. § 552(a)(4)(D) . . . ." *Fiumara v. Higgins,* 572 F. Supp. 1093, 1098 (D.N.H. 1983)./ "Similarly, a defendant should not be permitted to frustrate the trial court's efforts to conduct an orderly, fair and *expedient* [read *expeditious*] trial, and then benefit from an alleged error by the court which he invited through his own conduct." *People v. Johnson,* 518 N.E.2d 100, 108 (Ill. 1988). (For a discussion of the problem that the word *which* caused in this last example, see REMOTE RELATIVES.)

expend is a FORMAL WORD for *spend;* it is not always appropriate in ordinary contexts. E.g., "Generally speaking, students have no constitutional right to *expend* [read *spend*] classroom time on a subject unrelated to what they are supposed to be learning."

expense, v.t., = (in bookkeeping) to charge or record as an expense. E.g., "The telephone system will last for quite some time; it is appropriate, therefore, to *expense* the $300 over the period of time the telephone system will last."

experimentalize is a NEEDLESS VARIANT of *experiment.*

expiration; expiry. The word *end* is best where it will suffice. *Expiry* is the usual word for "termination" in BrE, whereas in AmE *expiration* is far more common. Thus: "There could be no difficulty here about the date of performance; it was on the *expiry* of the two years." (Eng.)/ "The district court denied reinstatement to Marchelos, reasoning that Marchelos had no security interest in his job because he had no reasonable expectation of continued employment beyond the *expiration* of his contract on August 31, 1979."

expire. See **run** (A).

expiry. See **expiration.**

explain. See **explicate.**

explanatorily. See SENTENCE ADVERBS.

EXPLETIVES. In general usage, *expletives* are understood to be curse words or exclamations. This sense was fortified in AmE during the Watergate hearings, when coarse language was omitted from the White House tapes with the phrase *expletive deleted.* In grammar, however, expletives are words that have no special meaning, but stand (usu. at the beginning of a clause) for a delayed subject. (See **epithet.**) The two most common expletives are *it* and *there* when beginning clauses or sentences.

A. With Passives. When used after verbs in the passive voice, expletives often give the misimpression that they have antecedents. E.g., "The burial was to take place at Highgate, and *it* was intended to take the body by train from Winooski to Cambridge Junction over the defendant's road and thence over the connecting road to Highgate." (The full passive is *it was intended (by someone) to take the body;* yet, on first reading, *it* appears to refer to *burial.*)/ "Despite her prediction that the economic recovery will be slow, it is expected that the company will flourish during the next few quarters." (*It* seems at first to refer to *economic recovery* when in fact it is merely an expletive.) See MISCUES.

B. Number. The INVERSION occasioned by expletives sometimes confuses writers about the number of the subject. "*There remains* for trial *these issues* [read *There remain . . . these issues*] raised in respondent's counterclaim." See SUBJECT-VERB AGREEMENT (J).

C. Expletive *it* Alongside Pronoun *it*. The expletive *it* should not be used in the same immediate context as the pronoun *it.* "*It* is concluded that *it* [i.e., the plaintiff corporation] is entitled to interest." [Read *We conclude that it is entitled to interest.*] See **it.**

explicate; explain. The terms are synonymous, but are used in different contexts. *Explain* is the ordinary term. *Explicate* (lit., "to open up pleats; to unfold") is more learned and connotes formal, orderly presentation or justification. Oddly, the adjectives *explicable* and *inexplicable* are more frequently used than the verb *to explicate.*

explodable; explosible. The former is preferred.

exploitative; exploitatory; exploitive. The second and third forms are NEEDLESS VARIANTS.

explosible. See **explodable.**

exportize is an abomination for *export,* v.t. See -IZE.

expose. See **disclose.**

exposé should have the acute accent on the final letter (*-é*) to prevent confusion with the verb *to expose.* E.g., "Investigative reports, following in the tradition of the muckrakers, are always looking for an *expose* [read *exposé*]."

ex post. See ***ex ante.***

ex post facto is slightly pompous but fairly common when used for *after the fact.* The phrase does have legitimate uses in the sense "retroactive," as in *ex post facto laws.* E.g., "Application of the newly enacted burden to this defendant runs afoul of the *ex post facto* prohibition [i.e., the prohibition against enacting laws that punish retroactively]." An English writer once called this use, which appears in the U.S. Constitution and in Blackstone, "a grotesque misuse of the expression." Note, 34 Law Q. Rev. 8, 9 (1918). His was the grotesque error.

Ex post for *ex post facto* is an odd ellipsis without literary legitimacy. "As a rule, therefore, courts will not engage in *ex post inquiries* [read *ex post facto inquiries*] regarding the substantive fairness of contract terms." Maureen B. Callahan, Note, *Post-Employment Restraint Agreements,* 52 U. Chi. L. Rev. 703, 704 (1985). (On the technically correct sense of *ex post,* see ***ex ante.***) Yet another strange shortening is *post facto:* "[C]hanges may not be instituted now in the expectation of *post facto* [read *ex post facto*] ratification at some indeterminate future time." *Henderson v. Graddick,* 641 F. Supp. 1192, 1202 (M.D. Ala. 1986).

The phrase was formerly spelled *ex postfacto* on occasion, but this spelling is archaic. Some writers hyphenate the phrase when it functions as a PHRASAL ADJECTIVE <ex-post-facto reasoning>, but the hyphens are unnecessary in this SET PHRASE.

expound; propound. The former means "to explain," the latter "to set forth; put forward for consideration." *Expound* is often misused. E.g., "Perhaps a sixteen-year-old boy would choose to refrain from sex in fear of the druggist's calling his father; then males as well as females would be virgins when they are married, as traditional views would *expound* [read *encourage* or *favor*]."/ "The board considered the wearing of the black arm band in class a political act *expounding* [read *conveying?*] to the students only one side of a controversial issue and, as such, constituting an unethical practice by a member of the teaching profession."

Expound is best used transitively: one *expounds* an idea or doctrine; one does not need to expound *on* it. Likewise, one *propounds* evidence. See **propound & proponent.**

express(ed). Sometimes within the same writing will be found references to "*express* and implied contracts" and to "*expressed* and implied contracts." The preferred adjective in the sense "specific, definite, clear" is *express.* E.g., "The decision depends in no way on an agreement, *expressed* [read *express*] or implied." (Eng.) See **implied.**

Occasionally, the transitive verb *express* functions as a correlative of *imply*—e.g.: "There are multifarious occasions on which persons who act or speak in the name of a state do acts or make declarations which either express or imply some view on a matter of international law." J.L. Brierly, *The Law of Nations* 61 (5th ed. 1955).

expressible; expressable. The former is preferred. See -ABLE (A).

expressio unius est exclusio alterius. See ***inclusio unius est exclusio alterius.***

express trust. See **constructive trust (B).**

expropriate. See **appropriate.**

expropriation. See **eminent domain.**

expunction; expungement. The latter, which is recorded in neither the *OED* nor *W3,* is a NEEDLESS VARIANT that surfaces from time to time—e.g.: "He sought declaratory and injunctive relief, damages, and the *expungement* [read *expunction*] of his prison disciplinary record." *Hewitt v. Helms,* 482 U.S. 755, 764 (1987) (Marshall, J., dissenting).

exquisite is best pronounced with the first syllable accented /***eks**-kwiz-it*/; it is acceptable in AmE, however, to stress the second /*ek-**skwiz**-it*/.

Although there is historical justification for using *exquisite* (= acute) in reference to pain, modern readers are likely to find this use macabre at best, for they generally understand the word as meaning "keenly discriminating" <exquisite taste> or "especially beautiful" <an exquisite vase>. For many readers, the obsolescent sense is merely a MISCUE: "From this we cannot say that it was unreasonable for the jury to infer that the decedent was conscious after impact and[,] before her death, suffering [read *suffered*] during that period from both impact injuries and the *exquisite* [read *excruciating*] pain of massive burns."

And when the word is used figuratively in the sense "acute, intense," the MISCUE is aggravated—e.g.: "Claimant's counsel might be faced with the *exquisite* [omit *exquisite*] dilemma of whether to forgo any fee application and thereby preserve his client's meager judgment, or jeopardize the client's judgment by applying for fees and thereby giving the government an incentive to appeal."

ex rel., the abbreviation for L. *ex relatione* (= upon the relation or information of), is now used almost exclusively in styles of cases brought by the government on the application of a *relator,* q.v., who is a private party that is somehow interested in the matter (as in an action to abate a public nuisance). A typical case style is as follows: *U.S. ex rel. Carter v. Jennings,* 333 F. Supp. 1392 (E.D. Pa. 1971). See **qui tam.**

In pre-20th-century lawbooks, *ex rel.* ordinarily denotes that the reporter did not personally witness the proceedings but got an account secondhand.

extemporaneous; extempore, adj.; **extemporary; extemporal.** In AmE, the first is the usual form. The others might be considered NEEDLESS VARIANTS, but *extempore* is most common in BrE.

extemporaneously; ex tempore, adv. In AmE, the latter is the Latin-lover's (or Anglophile's) NEEDLESS VARIANT of the former. *Ex tempore,* like the adjective *extempore,* is the usual form in BrE.

extend. See **enlarge.**

extendable; extendible; extensible. The preferred form is *extendable.* See -ABLE (A).

extended opinion = a separate opinion. E.g., "Mr. Justice Brennan, concurring in part and dissenting in part, filed an *extended opinion.*" See **write specially.**

extension; renewal. Both of these words are used in referring to the continuation of a legal contract, such as a lease. But the two have undergone a subtle DIFFERENTIATION with sometimes important ramifications: an *extension* continues the same contract for a specified period, whereas a *renewal* institutes a new contract that replaces the old one. Unfortunately, some courts muddle the two words, using them interchangeably or using both but not defining the difference.

extenuate (= to lessen the seriousness of [a fault or a crime] by partial excuse) should be used only of the fault that is minimized, not of the person. The *OED* cites improper uses (so labeled) such as, "The pursuer's steward . . . *extenuated* himself calmly enough," in which the word is used as if it meant "to extenuate the guilt of; to plead partial excuses for" (*OED*).

extern. See **clerk.**

extinguishment; extinction. Both words are nouns corresponding to the verb *to extinguish.* If there is a DIFFERENTIATION, it is that *extinguishment* refers to the process, and *extinction* to the resultant state. *Extinguishment* means in law "the cessation or cancellation of some right or interest" (*CDL*). E.g., "Both the Senate Bill and the House amendments provided for recordation of mining claims and for *extinguishment* of abandoned claims."

extortion; bribery. For public officials, the line of demarcation is unclear. *Extortion* = the corrupt obtaining of property by an officer under color of office. *Bribery* = something of value given or promised to an officer in return for corrupt behavior. If the briber takes the initiative, it is bribery; if the bribee takes the initiative, it is extortion. See **briber & bribery.**

extortionate; extortionary; extortive; extorsive. *Extortionate* (= [1] given to or characterized by extortion; [2] [of prices] exorbitant) is the standard term, the others being NEEDLESS VARIANTS. E.g., "The vice arises only when he employs *extortive* [read *extortionate*] measures, or when, lacking good faith, he makes improper demands." *State Nat'l Bank v. Farah Mfg. Co.,* 678 S.W.2d 661, 684 (Tex. App.—El Paso 1984)./ "Wright and Armstrong urge, among other things, that the court erred in finding a nexus between the *extortionate* conduct and interstate commerce." *U.S. v. Wright,* 804 F.2d 843, 844 (5th Cir. 1986).

extortioner; extortionist; extorter. The first is most usual, the others being NEEDLESS VARIANTS.

extortive. See **extortionate.**

EXTRA- (= lying outside the province or scope of) is a prefix that in modern English has formed hundreds of new adjectives, mostly for learned or literary purposes. The prefix has been adopted by many legal writers to form NEOLOGISMS not yet found in unabridged dictionaries. These writers usually do no harm, and in fact occasionally coin useful words. *Extralegal* and *extrajudicial* both date from the early 17th century; *extraconstitutional* dates from the early 19th century. Following are four representative examples of 20th-century legal neologisms using this prefix:

- "[T]he business judgment rule would shield the directors' decision to terminate a derivative suit against an *extracorporate* party." Mark P. Krysinski, Note, *Derivative Suits and the Special Litigation Committee,* 29 Wayne L. Rev. 149, 167 (1982).
- Laurie R. Wallach, Note, *Intercircuit Conflicts and the Enforcement of Extracircuit Judgments,* 95 Yale L.J. 1500 (1986).
- "The decision to withhold enforcement of the immigration laws is *extrastatutory*; it constitutes one of the Executive's inherent prerogatives." *Hotel & Restaurant Employees Union v. Attorney General,* 804 F.2d 1256, 1279 (D.C. Cir. 1986) (Silberman, J., concurring in part and dissenting in part).
- "Even if the goods themselves were destroyed by a defect giving rise to a tort action based on strict liability, the interest protected is basically an *extra-contractual* [read *extracontractual*] one." Peter Schlechtriem, *The Borderland of Tort and Contract—Opening a New Frontier?* 21 Cornell Int'l L.J. 467, 474 (1988).

extracurial; extracuriam. The first is the better form because it is a properly formed adjective—e.g.: "The decision in *Baker v. Carr* represents a gamble that *extracurial* processes of political adjustment and compromise will produce an issue digestible, as it were, by the Court." Lon Fuller, *The Morality of Law* 178 (1964)./ "Much of the *extra-curiam* [read *extracurial*] activity in which the Supreme Court justices have engaged has not been sufficiently consequential to matter . . . ." Robert Scigliano, *The Supreme Court and the Presidency* 81 (1971).

extrajudicial. A. And *out-of-court*. These terms are generally equivalent (see (B)). The latter is more readily comprehensible to readers and listeners, but it can be awkward. Euphony should govern the word choice—e.g.: "The constitutional privilege has no application to an *extrajudicial* confession, whether or not it is under oath."/ "The mere fact that sworn testimony may differ from *extrajudicial* statements does not constitute perjury, particularly where the discrepancy is extremely slight."/ "The due process clause should not be treated as a uniform command that courts throughout the nation abandon their age-old practice of seeking information from *out-of-court* sources to guide their judgment toward a more enlightened and just sentence."

B. Special Sense. Occasionally, this term means "outside the judicial process" as opposed to "out of court"—e.g.: "Saying there had been 'a cascade of *extrajudicial* executions, arbitrary arrests, disappearances and torture,' the [Americas Watch] organization commented that the attitude of the Government of President Alan Garcia 'might best be described as one of resignation.'" Alan Riding, *Human Rights Group Criticizes Peru,* N.Y. Times, 3 Nov. 1988, at 4.

extralegal (= beyond the province of law), dating from the mid-17th century and now in fairly frequent use, is omitted from most legal and nonlegal (extralegal?) dictionaries. E.g., "To a great extent they are *extra-legal,* existing under the sanctions of religion and morality, but not of human law." James Hadley, *Introduction to Roman Law* 248 (N.Y., D. Appleton & Co. 1881)./ "[T]hey often develop a tendency to pursue their purposes *extralegally,* or even illegally . . . ." J.L. Brierly, *The Law of Nations* 49 (5th ed. 1955)./ "[W]here law is largely a reflection of *extralegal* morality, what appears in form as retrospective legislation may in substance represent merely the confirmation of views already held . . . ." Lon Fuller, *The Morality of Law* 92 (1964). Today the word is written as a solid, without the hyphen. Cf. **alegal & nonlegal.**

extraordinary writs. See **prerogative writs.**

extrastatutory. See EXTRA-.

ex turpi causa non oritur actio. See MAXIMS.

exult. See **exalt.**

ex vi termini = by the force of the term; by the very meaning of the expression used. This LATINISM has no place in modern legal writing. "It is said that words not actionable *ex vi termini* [read *in themselves*] cannot be made so by innuendo."/ "In the second will there are no words that *ex vi termini* [omit *ex vi termini*] import a disposition of real property."

eyeing. So spelled; *eying* is a blunder.

eye of the law. See ANTHROPOMORPHISM.

eyewitness is spelled as one word, not two. Avoid *eyeball witness.* Cf. **earwitness.**

F

face of, in the = in front of; directly opposite; when confronted with. This idiomatic expression has become a part of legal JARGON. E.g., "Commenting upon the recent disarmament of the Highlanders, which had been so drastic that they were defenseless *in the face of* a gang of robbers or pirates, he remarked that 'Laws that place the subjects in such a state of insecurity contravene the first principles of the compact of authority: they exact obedience, and yield not protection.'" (Eng.)/ "Nor will equity engraft the doctrine of subrogation on a transaction *in the face of* an agreement that negates the idea of subrogation." See **fly in the face of.**

face, on its. In this age-old legal expression, *face* refers to the inscribed side of a document. The full phrase means "in the words of, in the plain sense of" <the document on its face indicates testamentary intent>. The phrase is sometimes used with a possessive noun in place of *its*—e.g.: "The difference between this law and the law in the *McCray* case is that the purpose to control child labor is evident *on the law's face* . . . ." Robert G. McCloskey, *The American Supreme Court* 143 (1960). And it is sometimes used figuratively of things other than documents—e.g.: "A libel is harmful *on its face*."

One must be careful of context with this shopworn phrase. When the subject is plural, and the phrase becomes *on their face,* there is a technical failure of CONCORD that can sometimes be risible: "Most laws, however, discriminate or mete out different treatment *on their face.*" (No one wants to see treatment meted out on anyone's face; though the sentence refers to the face of the statute, nonetheless the imagery suggests something different.)/ "*On their face,* the municipal historic preservation ordinances satisfy requisite due process criteria."/ "Some of these statutes were held to be unconstitutional *on their face* or as applied." (Note that in these last two sentences the plural form *on their faces* would be even worse.) See METAPHORS, ***ex facie*** & **facial.**

facial = complete; on its face; as a whole. E.g., "The cases before us are governed by the normal rule that partial, rather than *facial,* invalidation is the required course for such statutes."/ "The doctrine asserts that the constitutionality of an overbroad law should be judged on its face. The result is that the statute is upheld or invalidated in toto and not as it applies in a particular case. This approach is called '*facial*' review." Peter W. Low et al., *Criminal Law: Cases and Materials* 77 (1982).

The adverb *facially* is almost as common as the adjective *facial.* Though it might appear to mean "in a facial manner," *facially* means "on its face": "The court of appeals erred by *facially invalidating the statute in its entirety* [i.e., *invalidating the statute on its face*]."/ "We hold that the plaintiff has standing to challenge the constitutionality of the ordinance, and that the section in its present form is *facially overbroad and unconstitutional* [i.e., *overbroad and unconstitutional on its face*]."

facilitate (= to aid, help) is a FORMAL WORD to be used sparingly, for it often is jargonistic, as is the agent noun *facilitator* (= helper). E.g., "The commission's improved decision undoubtedly *facilitates* this court's review by clarifying the issues involved." As Fowler and others have noted, it is better to write that an *action* (e.g., the *court's review,* in the sentence just quoted) is facilitated rather than that the *actor* (e.g., *the court*) is facilitated.

facility. This word is surplusage in phrases such as *jail facility* and *museum facility.*

facsimile transmission. See **fax.**

fact, adj.; **factual.** In phrases such as *fact(ual) question,* the longer form is preferable. Notwithstanding that *fact question* is jarring, it is potentially misleading to the reader. In the following sentence, for instance, the use of *factual* would have circumvented the reader's thinking that *existence of fact* is an unhyphenated phrasal adjective: "If the proceedings are characterized as a trial on a stipulated record, the existence of *fact questions* [read *factual questions*] will not undermine the result." The sentences that follow illustrate the better usage: "We are directed by statute and Supreme Court precedent to accord a presumption of correctness to such state court *factual findings.*"/ "Petitioners contend that the ICC impermissibly substituted its judgment for the *factual findings* of the state commission."

Notably, *factual* has two meanings: (1) "of or involving facts" <factual issue>; (2) "true" <a factual depiction>. Here sense (2) is illustrated in a sentence in which *fact* would be not just inferior, but wrong: "If this were a *factual* account of what happened, the plaintiff would not have a cause of action." See **fact-finding & fact situation.**

Sense (1) of *factual,* the more usual meaning, appears in the following sentences: "The ICC's section 11501(c) jurisdiction is not of a limited nature, but in a proper case is plenary, and may allow the ICC to delve into the *factual* record before the state agency."/ "The rule contemplates that only *factual* questions will be submitted to the jury to which the judge will apply the law, supplementing, if necessary, any *factual* determinations not submitted to the jury."

fact, n.; **factum.** *Fact* (lit., "a thing done") means "an action performed, an event, an occurrence, or a circumstance." In legal writing, *fact* has the additional particularized sense "an evil deed; a crime." Thus we have the expressions *before the fact, after the fact,* and *confess the fact.*

Factum, the Latinate form of the word, has several meanings: (1) [regarding change in domicile] "a person's physical presence in a new domicile"; (2) "due execution of a will"; (3) "a fact or statement of facts"; and (4) "an act or deed." In senses (3) and (4), the only ones contained in the *OED,* the word has no merit in modern contexts (except in the phrase *fraud in the factum* [senses 2 & 4], for which see **fraud (B)**); few lawyers would understand *factum* when so used. In sense (1), *factum* is perhaps a TERM OF ART; nevertheless, the term calls for elucidation.

Sense (2) occurs frequently in the context of wills, where it is generally no more useful or specific than *execution:* "It might be argued that logically the only question upon the probate was the *factum* [read *execution*] of the instrument." In the SET PHRASE *fraud* or *mistake in the factum,* however, the use of *factum* is well ensconced: "There is a close analogy, however, to the situation in which a provision in a will by mistake in the *factum* is denied effect."/ "When there has been a fraudulent representation concerning the nature of the instrument or its contents, usually described as a fraud in the *factum,* it is well settled that the will or a fraudulently induced part of a will should be denied probate."

Although *RH2* lists *facta* as the plural of *factum,* the form most common in published sources is *factums.* See PLURALS (A).

fact, actual. See **actual fact & facts.**

fact(-)bound. Sometimes written as a single word, it is usually hyphenated as a PHRASAL ADJECTIVE—e.g.: "The three [Justices O'Connor, Kennedy, and Souter] tend to be cautious, *fact-bound* judges who decide cases based on their practical effects rather than some lofty, dispassionate doctrine." David A. Kaplan & Bob Cohn, *"Nine Scorpions in a Bottle,"* Newsweek, 13 July 1992, at 20.

fact(-)finder should be hyphenated, not spelled as two words. Likewise, *fact-finding* is best hyphenated. The trend is to make both terms solid, but that trend is at best incipient.

fact-finding = the finding of facts; *factual finding* = a finding of fact. E.g., "The agency's decision that an impact statement was not required pretermitted the *fact-finding* process designed by Congress."/ "The court's *factual finding* on that issue precluded recovery by the plaintiff."

Fact-finding is often mistakenly used not in reference to the process, but to mean "a finding of fact"—e.g.: "The earlier ruling was a *fact-finding* [read *factual finding*]."/ "On the basis of the above *fact-findings* [read *factual findings*], plaintiff has failed to make out a prima facie case."/ "The magistrate declined to enter any meaningful *fact-findings* [read *factual findings*] on the incidents surrounding the workover crew's hotel room arrangement, which appellant contended had precipitated the discharge." See **finding.**

factional; factious; fractious. These words are confusingly similar. *Factional* = of or relating to a faction. *Factious* = given to faction; acting for partisan purposes. *Fractious* = refractory, unruly, fretful, peevish.

factitious; fictitious. Both have the basic sense "artificial." *Factitious* = (1) man-made and not natural; (2) sham; produced by contrivance. *Fictitious* = imaginary, not real. This latter term is often used of testimony, accounts of facts, or stories. See **fictional.**

fact of the matter, the. This phrase is trite FUSTIAN that may serve as a filler in speech, but that generally has no justification in writing. Infrequently it gives the needed rhythm.

factor properly means "an agent or cause that contributes to a particular result." It should not be used, by SLIPSHOD EXTENSION, in the sense "a thing to be considered; event; occurrence." In law *factor* is used also—chiefly in BrE—in the sense "consignee" or "commission agent." E.g., "Among the more important classes recognised by English law are *'factors,'* who are employed to sell goods for their principal." Thomas E. Holland, *The Elements of Jurisprudence* 303 (13th ed. 1924).

In Scotland, *factor* usually refers to "a manager acting on behalf of an owner of heritable property." Andrew D. Gibb, *Glossary of Scottish Law Terms* 37 (A.G.M. Duncan ed., 2d ed. 1982).

In some American states, meanwhile, *factor* may refer to a garnishee: "In Vermont and Connecticut, he [the garnishee] is also sometimes called *factor,* and the process [of garnishing], *factorizing process.*" Charles D. Drake, *A Treatise on the Law of Suits by Attachment in the United States* § 451, at 386 (7th ed. 1891). This use of *factor* and *factorize* is now infrequent, but it does occur—e.g.: "[D]ebtor became insolvent and plaintiff, a creditor of the debtor, *'factorized'* the $169.88 garnishee owed debtor . . . ." *Dick Warner Cargo Handling Corp. v. Aetna Business Credit, Inc.,* 538 F. Supp. 1049, 1054 (D. Conn. 1982).

factorize. See **factor** (3d par.).

factotum = a general servant with myriad duties. The correct plural is *-tums,* not *-ta.* E.g., "The agents suspected that the appellees were driving stolen vehicles, not that they served as *factota* [read *factotums*] of illegal aliens." *U.S. v. Miranda-Perez,* 764 F.2d 285, 289 (5th Cir. 1985). See PLURALS (A).

fact pleading. See **code pleading.**

fact question. See **fact,** adj.

facts cannot literally be false; if something is a fact, then it is by its very nature true. Yet in law one often reads and hears of the "truth" or "falsity" of certain facts. E.g., "Presumably there were good reasons in the interest of justice nearly 100 years ago which impelled the court to fetter its own power to get at the *true facts.*" (Eng.)/ "No order shall recite *untrue facts.*" In such a context, *facts* is really an elliptical form of *alleged facts.* Hence: "Subject to later case development, the Texas measure of probative value, 'tending to establish the presence or absence, *truth or falsity of a fact,*' does not seem functionally distinct from the federal definition, 'to make the existence of the *fact* more probable or less probable.'" But the best practice is to speak of *false* or *untrue allegations,* not *false* or *untrue facts.* See **true facts.**

fact-sensitive; fact-specific. Both are hyphenated thus.

fact situation; factual situation. *Fact situation* = a situation with a given set of facts (hypothetical or actual). *Factual situation* = a situation that exists or existed in fact. When coupled with the noun *situation, factual* tends to take on sense (2) listed in the entry under **fact,** adj.

facts, judicial. See **judicial notice.**

facts, under the, is an acceptable legal idiom. E.g., "*Under the facts* of the case at bar, we cannot say that the district court erred in allowing the inclusion of this testimony." Cf. **circumstances.**

fact that, the. It is imprudent to say, as some have, that this phrase ought never to be used. At times it cannot reasonably be avoided. One writer has suggested that *because* will usually suffice for *the fact that.* See "Vigilans" [Eric Partridge], *Chamber of Horrors* 63 (1952). Yet rarely, if ever, is *because* a good substitute.

Where *the fact that* can be easily avoided, however, it should be. E.g., "*The fact that* [read *That*] the police officer was engaged in the performance of his duties did not relieve him of the duty of care at intersections." See **that (D).**

The common phrase *notwithstanding the fact that* can almost always be replaced by *although* or *even if*—e.g.: "The creditor's release of the principal debtor discharges the surety, *notwithstanding the fact that* [read *even if*] the creditor was induced to execute the release by the principal's fraud." Laurence P. Simpson, *Handbook on the Law of Suretyship* 307 (1950). See **notwithstanding the fact that.**

The pluralized form, as in "*The facts that . . . ,*" is usually unnecessary and awkward for the singular, where the discrete facts discussed are easily considered part of an overall structure or pattern. "*The facts that* [read *The fact that* or *That*] the records in this case were made by the proprietor and were in his possession *were* [read *was*] irrelevant to the determination whether their creation was compelled, the majority said." See FLOTSAM PHRASES.

fact-trier. See **trier of fact.**

factual. See **fact,** adj.

factual finding. See **fact-finding.**

factum. See **fact,** n. & ***non est factum.***

fail; failure. These are charged words. The late Judge Thomas Gibbs Gee, of the U.S. Court of Appeals for the Fifth Circuit, used to admonish his clerks: "Be gentle with district judges. Never, for example, use *failure* in referring to an action of a district judge." *A Few of Wisdom's Idiosyncrasies and a Few of Ignorance's,* 1 Scribes J. Legal Writing 55, 58 (1990). Likewise, a modern commentator should not say that Cardozo, in *Palsgraf,* "failed" to mention the plaintiff's occupation and precise injury; not mentioning these things was no doubt a conscious stylistic choice—not a "failure" at all.

fair, properly an adjective, is sometimes misused for the verb *fare* (= [1] to experience good or bad fortune or treatment; or [2] to happen or turn out)—e.g.: "While the proofs on retrial, as at the prior trial, obviously indicate guilt, defendant *faired* [read *fared*] better with this jury and was found guilty of manslaughter." *People v. Ansley,* 192 N.W.2d 41, 41 (Mich. Ct. App. 1971)./ "From all outward appearances the business was *fairing* [read *faring*] well until Abbott purchased a jet airplane for approximately one million dollars in December of 1974 . . . ." *Abbott v. Southern Subaru Star, Inc.,* 574 S.W.2d 684, 685 (Ky. Ct. App. 1978)./ "McAfee reiterated his view that the diagnosis of gout was incorrect in this case, and he stated that plaintiff would have *faired* [read *fared*] better had he been operated on sooner." *Nastasi v. United Mine Workers of Am. Union Hosp.,* 567 N.E.2d 1358, 1362-63 (Ill. App. Ct. 1991).

fair comment denotes a defense in libel actions. The substance of it is that the words complained of were honestly made on a matter of public interest. *Fair* does not here mean "balanced; restrained; moderate"; rather, it means "honest; not malicious." The defense is rebutted by proof that the words were uttered maliciously.

fair dealing. See **fair use.**

fair play. In legal usage, this phrase, dating from the 18th century at the latest, is the quintessential expression for equitable and impartial treatment. It is often seen in procedural or due-process contexts.

fair use; fair dealing. The defense of *fair use,* in actions for copyright infringement, is known also as *fair dealing* in BrE. The term *fair use* (not *fair usage*) is the one applied in 17 U.S.C. § 107 to describe the kinds of limitations the law places on the exclusive rights of copyright.

fair wear and tear. See **wear and tear.**

falderol. See **folderol.**

fall = to be struck down, often on grounds of unconstitutionality. E.g., "But since the evil aimed at here, child labor, occurs *before* interstate commerce begins, and since the product transported (for example, a can of shrimp) is in itself harmless, the law must *fall.*" Robert G. McCloskey, *The American Supreme Court* 145–46 (1960)./ "On the other hand, although initially it was merely the 'hot oil' provisions of the National Recovery Act of 1933 . . . that *fell* as an unconstitutional delegation of legislative power in January 1935, four months later the codes, too, and with them the entire structure of the act, *fell* on similar grounds." Henry J. Abraham, *The Judicial Process* 374 (2d ed. 1968).

fall due is the legal idiom meaning "to become due." It is used in reference to negotiable instruments—e.g.: "He paid the notes as they *fell due.*"

false, in a phrase such as *false statement,* is potentially ambiguous, since the word may mean either "erroneous, incorrect" or "purposely deceptive."

false arrest. See **false imprisonment.**

false check. See **check, worthless.**

false imprisonment; false arrest. Both are ARCHAISMS, the former being more common and a little less quaint. Both denote the act of detaining a person unlawfully—a common-law misdemeanor and tort.

false misrepresentation. See **misrepresentation.**

false oath. See **perjury.**

false plea; sham plea. Both terms mean "an obviously frivolous or absurd pleading that is made only for purposes of vexation or delay." *Sham plea* (or *pleading*) has been the more common of the two in the U.S.; the *CDL* (British) contains the main entry under *false plea.*

false pretenses, an elliptical form of *obtaining property by false pretenses,* means "knowingly obtaining another's property by means of a misrepresentation of fact with intent to defraud." Though still in use in most American jurisdictions, *false pretences* (as spelled in BrE) has been largely replaced in England by a clearer name: *obtaining by deception.* See **cheat** & **common law** (B).

Some have complained that the phrase *false pretenses* is a REDUNDANCY because *pretense* suggests falsity. That is certainly the connotation today, but formerly *pretense* was a more neutral word denoting "the putting forth of a claim." That it now seems redundant is not a good cause for tampering with the name, unless lawmakers wished to make a wholesale clarification such as *obtaining by deception.*

false representation. See **misrepresentation.**

false swearing. See **perjury.**

falsi crimen. See ***crimen falsi.***

family of nations. Writers formerly took a more restrictive view about what this phrase means than most would today: "'The *family of nations'* is an aggregate of States which, as the result of their historical antecedents, have inherited a common civilisation, and are at a similar level of moral and political opinion." Thomas E. Holland, *The Elements of Jurisprudence* 396 (13th ed. 1924). Today, by contrast, virtually any member-state of the United Nations is considered a part of the family of nations. Perhaps the only nations to be excluded are those that regularly engage in state-sponsored terrorism.

fantasy; phantasy. The former is now the preferred spelling in both AmE and BrE.

far-reaching is one of our most overburdened adjectival phrases. This otiose metaphor should be used cautiously; the phrase should always be hyphenated. E.g., "This argument, which is of *far-reaching* significance, was designed to show that the union was not in breach of the court's orders." (Eng.)/ "They had no notification that any complaint was being made under section 6(k), which is a different and, in this case, more *far-reaching* matter." (Eng.)

fare, n. Because this word, in one of its senses, means "food," the phrase *food fare* is a REDUNDANCY—e.g.: "Purchased sandwiches constituted the solid *food fare* [read *food* or *fare*] given the prisoners." *Davis v. North Carolina,* 310 F.2d 904, 910 (4th Cir. 1962)./ "Out-of-town colleagues in town for the American Bar Association annual meeting this month may want to sample Chicago's *food fare* [read *food,* or, perhaps, *cuisine*]." Jerold Jacover, *Lawyers Wax Caloric Over Favorite Chicago Restaurants,* Chicago Law., Aug. 1990, at 53.

fare, vb. See **fair.**

farmoutee; farmoutor; farm(in)ee; farm(in)or. Readers first encountering these terms may suspect a joke. Who, after all, would use *farmoutor* for someone who farms out work, or *farmoutee* for the person to whom the work is farmed out?

The answer is American oil-and-gas lawyers and business people. The odd thing, though, is that *farmor* = *farminor* = *farmoutor.* Usage varies, obviously—but that is so even within a given jurisdiction. Many published sources contain *farmor* and *farmee* as correlatives—e.g.: "Generally speaking, a farm-out involves an assignment of, or agreement to assign, leasehold acreage (by the *farmor*) in exchange for an obligation to drill (by the *farmee*). *Burke v. Blumenthal,* 504 F. Supp. 35, 36 (N.D. Tex. 1980)./ "He claimed that their relationship with Cambridge was transformed from a relationship of lessor-lessee, *farmor-farmee,* to a particular fiduciary relationship because Cambridge had promised in writing to handle future royalty payments with more propriety than it had in the past." *Cambridge Oil Co. v. Huggins,* 765 S.W.2d 540, 542 (Tex. App.—Corpus Christi 1989).

In other sources, the correlative terms are *farmoutor* and *farmoutee*—e.g.: "Pan American paid royalties on the same rate to the oil and gas lease royalty owners and transmitted payments at the same rate to its *farmoutees* mentioned in finding No. 13 below, for the period from January 1, 1954, through December 22, 1957." *Waechter v. Amoco Prod. Co.,* 537 P.2d 228, 232 (Kan. 1975)./ "It is first necessary to determine the meaning of the parties in the farmout agreement with respect to 'all costs and expenses incurred in drilling, testing, completing, equipping . . . any test well drilled hereunder . . .' which were the sole responsibility of the *farmoutee,* for which *farmouters* would never be liable, according to the contract." *Continental Oil Co. v. American Quasar Petroleum Co.,* 438 F. Supp. 909, 912 (D. Wyo. 1977)./ "In July 1982, Manges, on behalf of himself, DCRC (Manges) and as agent for the State under the Relinquishment Act, brought suit against Mobil, Exxon, the royalty owners under the lease, and some of the *farmoutees* under the lease." *Scott v. Exxon Corp.,* 763 S.W.2d 764, 765 (Tex. 1988).

Despite the second example above, the spelling *farmoutor* is more common than *-er*—e.g.: "*Farmoutor* should pay rentals and be reimbursed by the farmoutee without liability for improper payment." R.L. Harkinson & R.L. Harkinson, Jr., *Landman's Encyclopedia* 188 (2d ed. 1981).

farther; further. Both are comparative degrees of *far,* but they have undergone DIFFERENTIATION. In the best usage, the former refers to physical distances, the latter to figurative distances. E.g.,

"The Supreme Court looks no *farther* [read *further*] than whether the distinctions have some 'rational basis.'"/ "But the immunity goes *farther* [read *further*]."

In BrE, *further* is used both physically and figuratively, whereas *farther* is physical only. But there are exceptions, which some would call peccadilloes: "It cannot now be seriously contended that the so-called restrictive force of International Law goes *farther* [read *further*] than this . . . ." Carleton K. Allen, *Law in the Making* 461 (7th ed. 1964) (an English work).

The superlatives—*farthest* and *furthest*—follow the same patterns. E.g., "With intense questioning, the Justices pushed the lawyers into the *farthest* [read *furthest*] rhetorical corners of their arguments . . . ." Linda Greenhouse, *Right-to-Die Case Gets First Hearing in Supreme Court,* N.Y. Times, 7 Dec. 1989, at 1. *Furthermost* is rare for *farthest* (not *furthest*).

F.A.S. See **F.O.B.**

fastly is an obsolete form that now exists only as a barbarism, inasmuch as *fast* is an adverb as well as an adjective. Even so, American courts have recently published opinions using the following phrases: *the standard is fastly placed, the fastly held rule,* and *fastly becoming so.* In the first two phrases, *firmly,* and in the last, *fast,* would serve better.

fatal. A. In Legal Jargon. In law, this word commonly means "providing grounds for legal invalidity"—e.g.: "The court pointed out that uncertainty as to the fact of damage is *fatal.*"/ "While the parties have extensively argued and briefed a number of questions, one basic proposition is dispositive of, and *fatal* to, the position taken by the plaintiffs."/ "The fundamental, and in the end *fatal,* deficiency in Montana's reading of the statute is its failure to acknowledge, much less account for, language that equally plainly compels the conclusion that Congress did not intend that funds derived from Indian lands be distributed to the states."

B. And *fateful*. Though both are tied etymologically to the noun *fate,* they have undergone DIFFERENTIATION. *Fatal* means "of or relating to death," while *fateful* means "producing grave consequences." The most common mistake is to use *fatal* when *fateful* would be more appropriate, but sometimes one would be presumptuous to suggest any change, so close is the call: "Like Henry Kissinger and other modern scholars, Mr. Gelb considers the *fatal* turning point not Munich in 1938, but the failure by France and Britain to oppose German reoccupation of the Rhineland in 1936." John Lehman, *The "Heroic" Retreat Was Really a Rout,* Wall St. J., 9 Oct. 1989, at A6.

father-in-law. Pl. *fathers-in-law.*

fault, at or *in.* See **at fault & in fault.**

favorite of the law. This phrase, referring to any person or status entitled to extremely generous treatment in legal doctrine, exemplifies the PERSONIFICATION of law in which lawyers habitually engage—e.g.: "It has long been said that the surety is a *favorite of the law* and his contract strictissimi-juris." Laurence P. Simpson, *Handbook on the Law of Suretyship* 94 (1950).

fax. This term is now all but universal, in the face of which *facsimile transmission* became an instant ARCHAISM—and a trifle pompous at that. *Fax* is perfectly appropriate in formal contexts—e.g.: "*Fax* messages seem to occupy an intermediate position." G.H. Treitel, *The Law of Contract* 25 (8th ed. 1991). Pl. *faxes.*

faze. See **phase.**

fealty, a feudal term, formerly meant "the fidelity owed by a feudal tenant or vassal to a lord"—a fidelity implying duties not to do the lord harm or to blacken the lord's reputation, but to facilitate his prosperity. Today it is used figuratively as an ARCHAISM for *fidelity:* "If I begin to quote from the opinions of Mr. Justice Holmes, I hardly know where I shall end, yet *fealty* to a master makes me reluctant to hold back." Benjamin N. Cardozo, *Law and Literature,* 52 Harv. L. Rev. 472, 480 (1939).

feasance (= the doing or execution of a condition or obligation), though branded "obsolete" in the *OED,* is current in legal usage. Even so, the term is not nearly as common as the negatives *malfeasance* and *misfeasance.* See **malfeasance.**

feasant. Though not listed in the *OED* or in *W3,* this term has been used consistently in American law since the 19th century. The word means merely "doing" and is used primarily in the phrase *damage feasant,* which could almost always be improved by changing the phrase to refer to something "doing" or "causing" damage—e.g.: "In *Sackrider v. McDonald,* . . . it was held to be such an abuse of the power of distraining animals *damage feasant* [read *that cause damage*], to impound them before the damages were assessed, as to render the original seizure a trespass." *Webber v. Hartman,* 1 P. 230, 234 (Colo. 1883)./ "It belongs to that small category of personal rights, the assertion of which has always been independent of legal procedure, of which the right to abate a nuisance, under certain circumstances, and the right to distrain cattle *damage feasant* [read *doing damage* or *causing damage*], are examples." *Jones v. Ford,* 254 F. 645, 649 (8th Cir. 1918)./ "When the shipowner's liability presupposes no preceding consensual relation with the injured party, but arises from a base invasion of his interests, it can be safely asserted that the surrender of only the *damage feasant* [read *damage-causing*] vessel is necessary in order to secure limitation." *In re U.S. Dredging Corp.,* 264 F.2d 339, 340 (2d Cir. 1959).

feasible = practicable—i.e., capable of being done or carried out. It does not mean "possible" or "probable," though "[u]nfortunately, most courts . . . have used *'feasible'* and 'probable' interchangeably." *In re Rape,* 104 B.R. 741, 748 n.9 (W.D.N.C. 1989).

feasor. Most commonly appearing in the compound *tortfeasor* (q.v.), the word *feasor* often appears on its own or in some other combination. Ordinarily it can be simplified—e.g.: "The referee in the court below decided the case upon the theory that one joint *feasor* [read *tortfeasor* or *actor*] could not recover from another." *Johnson v. Matson,* 45 F.2d 550, 551 (9th Cir. 1930)./ "On February 17, 1960, counsel for Mahlum having further mulled over the quizzical prospect of paying Carlson, the alleged *non-feasor* [read *non-actor*], the proceeds of the sale of his boat, filed a motion to withhold paying Carlson because the money ought to go to Mahlum when he got his decree." *Mahlum v. Carlson,* 304 F.2d 285, 287 (9th Cir. 1962)./ "Evidence which shows that, following the crime charged, defendant and his *joint crime-feasor* [read *accomplice* or *partner in crime*] possessed weapons with which the crime was committed is relevant . . . ." *Ross v. State,* 601 S.W.2d 672, 675 (Mo. Ct. App. 1980).

federal. This word should be lowercased unless it is part of a title or of an organization's name. See **national.**

federal common law; federal general common law. In *Erie R.R. v. Tompkins,* 304 U.S. 64, 78 (1938), Justice Brandeis declared: "There is no federal general common law." Apart from a so-called *general* common law, however, there is a very substantial *federal common law,* "involving matters in which the federal interest is so strong that the federal courts are free to develop substantive rules to protect that interest." Charles A. Wright, *The Law of Federal Courts* 273 (4th ed. 1983). The federal common law applies, for example, in disputes between two states.

federal jurisdiction, exclusive. See **preemption, federal.**

federalism, in AmE, has traditionally referred to the "coordinate relationship and distribution of power between the individual states and the national government." Cathleen C. Herasimchuk, *The New Federalism,* 68 Tex. L. Rev. 1481, 1485 (1990). Cf. **our federalism.**

federally, for *in federal court* or *by federal court(s),* is unidiomatic among those working with federal courts. E.g., "The appellant argues that the waiver provision as spelled out *federally* [read *in federal court*] by *Johnson v. Zerbst* and locally by Maryland Rule 719c had not been complied with." *Howell v. State,* 425 A.2d 1361, 1371 (Md. Ct. App. 1981).

federation. See **confederation.**

fee = an inheritable interest in land, constituting the maximum of legal ownership <fee simple> <fee tail>. Plurals formed from phrases containing this word can be problematic. One textbook, for example, has *fee tails* but *fees simple.* The better practice is to make *fees* plural, whether the phrase is *fees simple absolute, fees simple determinable,* or *fees tail.* See POSTPOSITIVE ADJECTIVES.

Fee often acts as an elliptical form of *fee simple absolute:* "Although it is probably good practice to use the word 'absolute' whenever one is referring to an estate in fee simple that is free of special limitation, condition subsequent, or executory limitation, lawyers frequently refer to such an estate as a 'fee simple' or even as a 'fee.' We may find ourselves slipping into that usage as we go along." Thomas F. Bergin & Paul G. Haskell, *Preface to Estates in Land and Future Interests* 24 (2d ed. 1984). See **fee simple.**

feebleness literally denotes a debilitated physical state; *feeblemindedness* denotes the mental state. In the following sentence, the two are confused: "Traditionally, in cases of incapacity, incompetency, or simply *feebleness* [read *feeblemindedness*], a court-supervised guardianship was the only remedy."

feel. A. For *think*. *Feel* is a weak and informal substitute for *think* or *believe* or *maintain* or *submit.* E.g., "In order for this opinion to have any real meaning, we *feel* [read *believe*] the stipulation of facts should be summarized in considerable detail." When an idea is phrased on an emotional rather than a cognitive level, the resulting sentence seems to minimize the thoughts being reported—e.g.: "She *feels* [read *thinks* or *believes*] that crime prevention must start with helping small children find their way out of poverty and neglect, and that society's resources should go toward better education and housing, not more jails." Bob Cohn & Eleanor Clift, *The Contrary Voice of Janet Reno,* Newsweek, 11 Oct. 1993, at 30.

B. *Feel bad(ly).* When someone is sick or unhappy, that person feels *bad*—not *badly.* See ADVERBS (C).

C. *Feel like.* To avoid using *like* as a conjunction, writers usually need to change this phrase to *feel as if.* E.g., "But on a combined income of $60,000, McDonald and his wife Cindy, who have five children, *feel like* [read *feel as if*] they're just scraping by." Marc Levinson, *Living on the Edge,* Newsweek, 4 Nov. 1991, at 23. See **like (A).**

fee simple. **A. Generally.** *Fee simple,* the name of the most comprehensive estate in land, "is a term not likely to be found in modern conversation between laymen, who would in all probability find it quite unintelligible. Yet to a layman of the 14th century the term would have been perfectly intelligible, for it refers to the elementary social relationship of feudalism with which he was fully familiar: the words 'fee' and 'feudal' are closely related." Peter Butt, *Land Law* 35 (2d ed. 1988). A *fee simple* was originally an estate that existed only as long as its original owner or any of that owner's heirs were living; since the Middle Ages, the estate has continued indefinitely even when the original owner and all heirs have died.

The phrase *in fee simple* is a LOAN TRANSLATION of the LAW LATIN *in feodo simpliciter,* which appears in the statute *Quia Emptores* (1289).

The common-law fee-simple estates are: (1) fee simple absolute; (2) fee simple conditional; (3) fee simple determinable; and (4) fee simple subject to a condition subsequent. The different estates, which have confusingly similar names—as well as the different names for the same estates—are discussed in the sections that follow. See **fee.**

B. *Fee simple* with No Other Words. When *fee simple* is used alone, *fee simple absolute* is almost invariably the intended meaning: "Their contention is that the will vested a life estate only in Fred Sybert, while respondent contends that the Rule in Shelley's Case operated to vest a *fee simple* estate in him." *Sybert v. Sybert,* 254 S.W.2d 999, 1000 (Tex. 1953). The plural is *fees simple.* See **fee.**

C. *Fee simple absolute; fee simple absolute in possession.* Since the Law of Property Act was enacted in 1925, England has had only two legal estates: the *fee simple absolute in possession* and the *term of years absolute.* Thus, "[i]f one retains the old concepts in all strictness the fee simple has been abolished [in England]." A.W.B. Simpson, *An Introduction to the History of the Land Law* 64 n.1 (1961). In AmE, by contrast, *fee simple absolute* is the usual form—not *fee simple absolute in possession.*

In the phrase *fee simple absolute,* the word *absolute* takes on a special meaning: "perpetual."

D. *Fee simple conditional.* A mostly obsolete estate—lingering only in Iowa, Oregon, and South Carolina—the *fee simple conditional* is an estate restricted to some specified heirs, exclusive of others. This term should not be confused with the similarly named *fee simple subject to a condition subsequent* (see G).

E. *Fee simple defeasible; qualified fee.* These synonyms refer to an estate that ends either because there are no more heirs of the body of the person to whom it is granted, or because a special limitation, condition subsequent, or executory limitation takes effect before the line of heirs runs out. See (F)–(I). See **defeasible.**

F. *Fee simple determinable; fee simple subject to special limitation; fee simple subject to common-law limitation.* These synonyms refer to an estate that will automatically end if some specified event ever occurs. If the event is sure to occur (e.g., someone's death), then these terms are inappropriate. The usual phrase is *fee simple determinable.* (See **determinable.**) The future interest retained by the grantor is called a *possibility of reverter.* For more on that phrase, see **reversion.**

G. *Fee simple subject to a condition subsequent; fee simple on a condition subsequent; fee simple upon condition; fee simple subject to a power of termination.* These terms denote an estate subject to the grantor's power to end the estate if some specified event happens. American lawyers tend to use the phrase *fee simple subject to a condition subsequent,* whereas English lawyers tend to use *fee simple upon condition.* The future interest retained by the grantor is called a *power of termination* or a *right of entry for condition broken,* q.v.

H. *Fee simple subject to an executory limitation.* This phrase denotes a type of fee simple defeasible (see (E)) subject to divestment in favor of someone other than the grantor if a specified event happens.

I. *Fee simple subject to special limitation.* See (F).

fee-splitting is, in the view of some lawyers, a EUPHEMISM for a certain type of kickback that lawyers on a contingent fee use to reward other lawyers who send them cases: "One rotten aspect worth mentioning is *fee splitting,* a kind name for kickbacks from personal injury specialists to other lawyers who refer them cases." Letter of John M. Beal, N.Y. Times, 1 Dec. 1989, at 30. In some American states, the practice is considered unethical, but in others it is tolerated.

When used as a PHRASAL ADJECTIVE, naturally, the expression needs a hyphen—e.g.: "If he wasn't aware of Chesley's *fee-splitting* arrangement with Coale, apparently no one was going to enlighten him." John A. Jenkins, *The Litigators* 86 (1989).

fee tail. A. Generally. A LOAN TRANSLATION of the LAW LATIN *feodum talliatum* (lit., "a cut-down fee"), the phrase *fee tail* means "an estate that is inheritable only by specified descendants of the original grantee." The TERM OF ART formerly used to create a *fee tail* was the phrase *and the heirs of his* (or *her*) *body.* By special wording, the fee tail might be restricted to male or female descendants: a *tail male* was formerly common, a *tail female* rare. The estate is defunct in most American jurisdictions—the exceptions being Delaware, Maine, Massachusetts, and Rhode Island—and was generally abolished in England in 1925 (though it survives there as an equitable interest). See **entail, fee & tail.**

The expressions *estate tail, estate in fee tail, entailed estate, tenancy in tail,* and *entail* (n.) are sometimes used as synonyms.

B. *Fee tail general* and *fee tail special.* A *fee tail special* arose if the grant was to a donee and the heirs of his body by a particular spouse. A *fee tail general* arose if no spouse was named.

feign; feint. These words, though they derive from the same French verb (*feindre* "to touch or shape"), have undergone DIFFERENTIATION in English. To *feign* is either to make up or fabricate <she feigned an excuse> or to make a false show of <he feigned illness>. To *feint* is to deliver a pretended blow or attack designed to confuse an opponent momentarily. The word is also, in its older (but still current) sense, used as a noun meaning either a sham or a pretended blow or attack (i.e., the act of *feinting*).

fellow-servant rule (= the common-law doctrine, now generally defunct, holding that an employer could avoid liability to an employee by showing that an injury to the latter was caused by another employee's negligence) should be hyphenated thus. See PHRASAL ADJECTIVES.

felo-de-se (lit., "felon with respect to oneself") is a synonym and perhaps a EUPHEMISM for *suicide* (in both senses—i.e., both for the act and for the actor). In modern writing, this GALLICISM seems to appear primarily when the writer wishes to avoid repeating the word *suicide*—e.g.: "English law stigmatised suicide as a felony; the *felo-de-se*'s property was forfeited, leaving his family impoverished . . . ." Glanville Williams, *Textbook of Criminal Law* 530 (1978). See **suicide.**

felonious = (1) of, relating to, or involving a felony <felonious intent>; or (2) constituting or having the character of a felony <felonious assault>. In whichever sense, the word is used rarely of persons, almost always of acts. E.g., "Over the last twenty-five years five judges have been disciplined for associating with criminals; in most of the cases, the judges performed specific favors for their *felonious friends* [better: *felon-friends*]." The *OED* cites but one (19th-century) sentence in which *felonious* is used of a person in the sense of someone who "has committed felony."

felony (originally a LAW FRENCH word meaning "wicked" or "treacherous") was recognized, as early as the 18th century, to be "a term of loose signification even in the common law of England; and of various import in the statute law of that kingdom." *The Federalist* No. 42, at 266 (James Madison) (Clinton Rossiter ed., 1961). Generally, *felony* denotes one of the two classes of crimes at common law, *felonies* being serious crimes and *misdemeanors* being minor crimes. A felony was any offense that involved either the death penalty or a forfeiture of the felon's land and goods.

As that suggests, the difference between a *felony* and a *misdemeanor* is determined solely by the possible punishments: in most American states today, a *felony* is any crime punishable by death or by imprisonment for a year or more, while a *misdemeanor* is any crime with a lesser punishment.

Before the felony-misdemeanor distinction was abolished in England in 1967, it was widely condemned—e.g.: "[I]n form [the criminal law] remains a sprawling and unwieldy mass, and it still contains a number of anachronisms and anomalies—such as the now valueless and inconvenient distinction between felonies and misdemeanours—which hardly a lawyer in the land would be prepared to defend." Carleton K. Allen, *Law in the Making* 353–54 (7th ed. 1964). Odd though it seems, most American lawyers would likely resist any move to abolish the distinction. See **misdemeano(u)r (B).**

felony murder = a death occurring as a result of the commission of a dangerous felony. E.g., "One day in 1931 while waiting to argue a motion in Part One [a New York court], I was for a time an involuntary spectator at the trial of Eric Martin, a youth, hardly more than a boy, charged with a murder committed during a burglary, that is to say *'felony murder.'* " Ephraim Tutt, *Yankee Lawyer* 324 (1943).

The so-called *felony-murder rule* (hyphenated thus) refers to the oft-cited doctrine that any homicide resulting from a felony or attempted felony is murder. The frequent formulation, "Homicide committed while perpetrating or attempting a felony is murder," is too broad because it suggests that mere coincidence is sufficient, as opposed to causation. See Rollin M. Perkins, *Criminal Law* 35 (1957). The best formulation today, then, explicitly excepts all felonies that carry no appreciable risk to human safety. Hence, any homicide is considered murder if the death results from a person's committing (or trying to commit) an inherently dangerous felony. Abolished in England in 1957, the *felony-murder rule* remains current in most American jurisdictions.

feme covert. See ***fem(m)e co(u)vert(e).***

feme sole = (1) an unmarried woman; (2) a married woman handling the affairs of her separate estate. This LAW FRENCH term is now obsolescent since the distinctions that it denotes are falling into disuse. Following are typical traditional uses: "During their natural lives, they were to use and enjoy the house, subject to their own control, and to be managed by them as *femes sole*."/ "The court relied upon the analogy of a *feme sole* who makes a bequest to her surviving husband, saying that the subsequent exercise of volition could not be deemed testamentary in a legal sense."

Historically, *feme* referred primarily to a married woman: hence a *feme sole* was ordinarily a woman who had been divorced or widowed, as opposed to just any unmarried woman. For a discussion of other sex-specific forms, see SEXISM (C).

FEMININE ENDINGS. See SEXISM (C).

FEMININE PRONOUNS USED GENERICALLY. See SEXISM (A).

fem(m)e co(u)vert(e) /fem-***kəv***-ərt/, literally "protected woman" or "sheltered woman," is the traditional term for a married woman. Though it would be spelled differently in modern French, this LAW FRENCH term, in Anglo-American law, is generally spelled *feme covert* (omitting all the optional letters)—a spelling preferred since Blackstone's time. The plural is *femes covert.* Today, of course, this term (meaning "a married woman") is entirely unnecessary. See **coverture &** LAW FRENCH. For a discussion of other sex-specific forms, see SEXISM (C).

femme sole. See ***feme sole.***

fence = (1) a receiver of stolen goods; or (2) a place where stolen goods are sold. Though this use of the word began as underworld slang, it has become standard in criminal law—e.g.: "The receivers of stolen goods almost never 'know' that they have been stolen, in the sense that they could testify to it in a courtroom. The business could not be so conducted, for those who sell the goods—the *'fences'*—must keep up a more respectable front than is generally possible for the thieves." *U.S. v. Werner,* 160 F.2d 438, 441 (2d Cir. 1947)./ "[T]here are professional *'fences'* who act as outlets for stolen goods, and goods are sometimes stolen 'to order' . . . ." Andrew Ashworth, *Principles of Criminal Law* 347 (1991).

feodum talliatum. See **fee tail.**

feoff, v.t.; **enfeoff; infeoff.** The usual form of the verb meaning "to put in legal possession (of a freehold interest)" is *enfeoff. Feoff* and *infeoff* are NEEDLESS VARIANTS.

feoff. A. And *enfeoff.* Although most of the derivatives are based on *feoff*—e.g., *feoffment, feoffor, feoffee*—the usual verb is *enfeoff* (= to put in legal possession). E.g., "O *enfeoffed* T and his (or her) heirs to the use of A and his (of her) heirs." A. James Casner & W. Barton Leach, *Cases and Text on Property* 320 (1984). The verb *feoff* is properly classifiable as a NEEDLESS VARIANT.

B. And *fief.* Both *fief* and *feoff* are pronounced /feef/. Whereas *feoff* is the variant verb, *fief* is a noun denoting a fee, or an estate in land held on condition of homage and service to a superior lord, by whom it is granted and in whom the ownership remains. See **fee.**

C. For *feoffee.* Occasionally, *feoff* is misused for *feoffee*—e.g.: "The Rule [in Shelley's Case] was devised in feudal times to insure feudal landlords the receipt of their rents from their *feoffs* [read *feoffees*], or tenants." *Sybert v. Sybert,* 254 S.W.2d 999, 1001 (Tex. 1953) (Griffin, J., concurring).

feoffee = the transferee of an estate in fee simple; the person to whom a freehold estate in land is conveyed by feoffment, or a trustee invested with a freehold estate in land. E.g., "A collateral relation who inherited had to be of the blood of the first purchaser (or *feoffee*) of the land."/ "Each *feoffee* (recipient of a fief), having received the seisin from his feoffor, would be said to be seised, or possessed of an interest in the land." Thomas F. Bergin & Paul G. Haskell, *Preface to Estates in Land and Future Interests* 11 (2d ed. 1984). See -EE & **feoff (C).**

feoffer. See **feoffor.**

feoffment */fef-mənt/* (fr. L. *feoffare* "to give one a fief") is an ancient form of conveyance usually involving livery of seisin. (See **livery of seisin.**) At common law, it is the transaction by which a fee is granted. Blackstone defines it as "the gift of any corporeal hereditament to another." 2 William Blackstone, *Commentaries on the Laws of England* 310 (1766). E.g., "The English common law, influenced by the notion that a life tenant could make a tortious *feoffment* that barred subsequent exercise of the power, permitted release of all except a power simply collateral."/ "No collateral of the half-blood inherited in any event; when collaterals did inherit, the land remained within the family into which it had been brought by *feoffment.*"

feoffor; feoffer. This word, meaning "the transferor of a fee simple," is generally spelled *-or.* E.g., "On the creation of any estate of freehold, whether in possession or remainder, the seisin must pass out of the transferor (the *feoffor*), i.e., there must be a livery of seisin."/ "Since the value of the use depended upon the ability of the cestui que use to enforce his claim, the transfer of freeholds to the use of the *feoffor* or a third-party became common when the Chancellor enforced the feoffee's duties as a routine matter."

The *OED* notes that, in old lawbooks (from the 15th to the 17th centuries), *feoffor* was "often misused for *feoffee.*"

ferae naturae (L. "of a wild nature") is the law's rather pretentious way, in referring to animals, of saying "wild." The best modern practice, of course, is simply to use the phrase *wild animals.* See Robert Megarry & H.W.R. Wade, *The Law of Real Property* 65 (5th ed. 1984) (consistently using *wild animals*).

But traditionally, legal writers have not been so straightforward. They formerly used the phrase *ferae naturae* adjectivally, in phrases such as *beasts ferae naturae* or *animals ferae naturae*—e.g.: "Any one who stores up a great bulk of water in a reservoir, or keeps a caravan of beasts *ferae naturae,* is said, by English law, to do so 'at his peril' . . . ." Thomas E. Holland, *The Elements of Jurisprudence* 173 (13th ed. 1924).

By extension, this Latin genitive has come to take on a noun sense in legal writing, so that it means "wild animals" <a caravan of *ferae naturae*>. Though Latin purists would probably consider this use a SLIPSHOD EXTENSION, it is now established in American legal writing. Perhaps the solution is to write *wild animals* instead.

The Latin purists are quite right, however, to lament another development: some writers mistakenly write *fera* rather than *ferae*—e.g.: "Ideas have been compared to *fera naturae* [read *ferae naturae*], property rights . . . which are dependent on possession and are lost by escape of a wild animal and likewise by disclosure of an idea." *Schonwald v. F. Burkart Mfg. Co.,* 202 S.W.2d 7, 12 (Mo. 1947). The best solution is to dispense with the Latin altogether.

Festschrift (= a collection of writings forming a volume presented by the authors as a tribute to a [usu. senior] scholar), a German loanword, forms the plurals *Festschriften* and *Festschrifts.* For reasons given at PLURALS (A), the better plural in an English-language context is *Festschrifts.*

feticide. See **abortion.**

fetus is the clinical term denoting, most broadly, "the product of pregnancy up to the time of birth." Glanville Williams, *Textbook of Criminal Law* 250 (1978). More narrowly, it has been defined as "a viable unborn child." *People v. Smith,* 129 Cal. Rptr. 498, 504 (Cal. Ct. App. 1976).

The plural form is *fetuses.* The old BrE spelling—*fœtus*—is now disappearing in favor of *fetus.*

A more connotatively charged term, which partisans sometimes find more suitable to their purposes, is *unborn child.*

feu (= a feudal holding) is today obsolete everywhere but in Scotland, where it is used not only as a noun—the counterpart of *fief*—but also as a verb meaning "to give out land upon a feudal arrangement whereby the vassal (buyer) holds land of a superior (the landowner) usually upon the terms that he builds on the land and pays a perpetual rent, or feuduty." Andrew D. Gibb, *Students' Glossary of Scottish Legal Terms* 38 (A.G.M. Duncan ed., 2d ed. 1982). The verb is inflected *feued, feuing.*

feudal; feudatory; feudatary; feudatorial. The only important words are *feudal* and *feudatory,* the others being NEEDLESS VARIANTS. *Feudal* = of or relating to a feud or *fief,* q.v.

Feudatory, as an adjective, means "owing feudal allegiance *to;* under the overlordship *of*"; and, as a noun, "one who holds lands by feudal tenure; a feudal vassal." E.g., "In France, every *feudatory* legislated for his own demesne, but as a necessary result, it followed that an overlord, and even the King, could not legislate for the demesnes of his under-tenants for they were under the jurisdiction of their immediate lord." Theodore F.T. Plucknett, *A Concise History of the Common Law* 317 (5th ed. 1956).

In the following sentence, *feudatory* appears where *feudal* belongs: "The exclusive right of the first-born to the succession and the rules for entailment of estates were originally promulgated in the 'house laws' of the great *feudatory* [read *feudal*] chiefs, who compelled weak sovereigns to incorporate them in their land grants . . . ." Stephen Pfeil, "Law," in 17 *Encyclopedia Americana* 86, 89 (1953).

feudalism. This word, a vague word of modern origin, "was completely unknown in the ages to which we apply it, [being] nothing more than a rough generalisation upon the character of mediaeval society." Theodore F.T. Plucknett, *A Concise History of the Common Law* 507 (5th ed. 1956). Still, the word *feudalism* is "a convenient way of referring to certain fundamental similarities [that], in spite of large local variations, can be discerned in the social development of all the peoples of western Europe from about the ninth to the thirteenth centuries." J.L. Brierly, *The Law of Nations* 2 (5th ed. 1955).

What are those similarities? They involved dependent land holding in return for the rendition of services—typically military service. Society was organized largely through a tenurial system, in which everyone—from king to the lowest landowner—was bound by obligation of service and defense. In the later, more sophisticated forms of feudalism, the rights of defense and service are supplemented by the right of jurisdiction. See **feu.**

feudal system. See **feudalism.**

feudatary; feudatory; feudatorial. See **feudal.**

feuduty. See **feu.**

fewer; less. *Fewer* emphasizes number, and *less* emphasizes degree or quantity. *Fewer number* and *fewest number* are illogical tautologies, inasmuch as *fewer* means "of smaller number." E.g., "The *fewest number* [read *smallest number*] of people use the library between 4:30 and 7:00 p.m." [Or, better, read *The fewest people use the library between 4:30 and 7:00 p.m.*] See **less (A)** & COUNT NOUNS AND MASS NOUNS.

few in number is a common REDUNDANCY.

fiasco (= a complete failure) forms the plural *fiascoes.* See PLURALS (C).

fiat (= a judge's decree) means "let it be done" in Latin. The word in its broad, popular sense has come to connote arbitrariness: "I cannot pretend to the power by judicial *fiat* to affect property located in the Bahamas."/ "We agree with the Seventh Circuit that a ruling that the marketing of handguns constitutes an ultrahazardous activity would in practice drive manufacturers out of the business and would produce a handgun ban by judicial *fiat.*"

More technically, *fiat* also denotes in many Anglo-American jurisdictions any one of a number of decrees rendered by a court in pursuance of its jurisdiction. For example, in Texas practice, most motions must contain a *fiat* (to be filled in by the court) fixing the time for a hearing on the motion.

fiber is the AmE, *fibre* the BrE spelling. Frequently in asbestosis cases in the U.S., *fibre* appears instead of *fiber.* But the latter spelling is preferred in any context in the U.S.

fictional; fictitious; fictive. These forms are distinguishable. *Fictional* = of, pertaining to, or having the characteristics of "an intentional fabrication" of the mind, i.e., of "a convenient assumption that overlooks known facts in order to achieve an immediate goal" (*W3*). This is the adjective to be used of legal FICTIONS. E.g., "There are many instances in which equity has protected purely personal rights, though in some instances the courts have reached that result by finding *fictional* property rights—declaring things property rights that were in truth not of that character."/ "The use of these words in connection with legal relations is, strictly speaking, figurative or *fictional.*"

Fictitious = (1) sham; or (2) imaginary. Here sense (1) is illustrated: "Government officials should be free to make decisions without fear or threat of vexatious or *fictitious* suits and alleged personal liability."/ "The question is whether A, the acceptor of a bill of exchange, knew that the name of the payee was *fictitious.*" (Eng.)/ "The aspect of the Abscam investigation leading to this bribe began in 1979 when an FBI agent took on the undercover role of one Tony DeVito, president of the *fictitious* Abdul Enterprises."

Sense (2) here obtains: "After describing a *fictitious* vehicle on each certificate, he then obtained titles and registrations from the state."/ "The ejectment action involved a *fictitious* party plaintiff."

In the following sentences, *fictitious* is used where *fictional* would be better: "That some rule of evidence or law could have been evolved by the court to require the court to hold by some *fictitious* [read *fictional*] or artificial reasoning that the testatrix did not know the contents of the will is repugnant, to say the least." (Eng.)/ "The decision of Sachs J. in the *Crerar* case will help the probate court to give effect to the wishes of other testators, and to avoid imputing to them a *fictitious* [read *fictional*] knowledge and approval of testamentary documents whose meaning they did not know and would not have approved." (Eng.)

Fictive = having the capacity of imaginative creation <fictive talent>. Apart from this narrow sense, rarely of use in legal writing, *fictive* is used as a NEEDLESS VARIANT of both *fictional* and *fictitious.* E.g., "There has been some *fictive* [read *fictional*] talk to the effect that the reason why a nonresident can be subjected to a state's jurisdiction is that the nonresident has impliedly consented to be sued there." (Beginning and ending a sentence with the word *there* is to be avoided.)

FICTIONS. To lawyers, fictions are assumptions that conceal, or presume to conceal, the fact that a rule of law has undergone alteration, its letter remaining unchanged, its operation being modified. See Henry S. Maine, *Ancient Law* 21–22 (17th ed. 1901; repr. [New Universal Lib.] 1905, 1910). To nonlawyers, of course, the phrase *legal fiction* means "a surreal untruth."

> In jurisprudence a legal fiction denotes an uncontrovertible averment in an action. In the history of English law legal fictions have had three main functions. The first was to extend the jurisdiction of a court: such was the averment, used to give the Court of Exchequer jurisdiction, that the plaintiff was indebted to the Crown but was the less capable of discharging his debt by reason of the defendant's default to him (which was the true cause of action); or the averment that a contract in fact made abroad was made at the Royal Exchange in Cheapside—a decisive step towards the embodiment into the common law of the whole body of the law merchant. Secondly, legal fictions were designed to avoid cumbersome and archaic forms of action: thus, the fictitious lease, entry and ouster made the action of ejectment applicable to freeholds to the exclusion of the old real actions. Thirdly, fictions were used to extend the scope of a remedy: for example, the allegation that the defendant had found the plaintiff's chattel but refused to deliver it up made the superior remedy in trover not only supersede the action of detinue [q.v.] but also available for most claims in relation to chattels.
>
> Jocelyn Simon, *English Idioms from the Law,* 76 Law Q. Rev. 283, 304 (1960).

To understand legal fictions we must understand the difference between what is said and what is actually meant: "The best way to talk clearly and precisely and to talk sense is to understand as fully as possible the relation between predication and suggestion, between 'saying' and 'meaning.'" Owen Barfield, "Poetic Diction and Legal Fictions," in *The Importance of Language* 51, 71 (Max Black ed. 1962). A legal fiction is intended not to deceive, but to mask a change in the law; hence it is appropriately termed a "growing pain" in the language of the law. See Lon L. Fuller, *Legal Fictions* 21–22 (1967).

Lord Devlin's caution is an apt one: "Legal fictions are dangerous because they have a tendency to spread." Patrick Devlin, *The Judge* 162 (1979).

fictitious; fictive. See **fictional.**

fides. See ***bona fides & mala fide(s).***

fiduciary; fiducial. *Fiduciary,* as both adjective and noun, is the unvarying legal form of the word <fiduciary relationship> <bound as a fiduciary>. *Fiducial,* used by historians and philosophers in certain contexts, has not found a home in the law.

fief. See **feoff.**

fiefdom is a NEEDLESS VARIANT of *fief.*

fieri facias (lit. "that you cause to be done") is a LATINISM that has given its name to a writ of execution for the collection of a money judgment; it directs the marshal or sheriff to seize and sell enough of the defendant's property to satisfy the judgment. It is commonly abbreviated *fi. fa.* or *Fi. Fa.* and pronounced */**fi**-fay/*, not */**fee**-fah/*—e.g.: "*Fi. Fa.* and writs of possession are still in common use, and (retaining their common-law form) have turned out to be the principal survivors of the medieval writ system." J.H. Baker, *An Introduction to English Legal History* 79 (3d ed. 1990).

Fifth Amendment. The idiom is *to take the Fifth Amendment* (= to remain silent in order to avoid incriminating oneself), not *to plead the Fifth Amendment*—e.g.: "The possibility that the money possessed by Ms. Perez was generated by another illegal activity, prostitution, was presented when Ms. Perez *pleaded* [read *took*] the *Fifth Amendment* when the state asked her if she earned any of her money from prostitution." *State v. Seventy-Seven Thousand Fourteen & No/100 ($77,014.00) Dollars,* 607 So. 2d 576, 585 (La. Ct. App. 1992)./ "They denied beating the defendant, seeing him beaten or that the defendant ever asked for an attorney or *pleaded the Fifth Amendment* [read *invoked the Fifth Amendment*]." *People v. Hendrix,* 620 N.E.2d 1176, 1185 (Ill. App. Ct. 1993).

Fifteen, the. This phrase formerly referred to the old Court of Session, in Scotland. E.g., "'The

Fifteen' decided against the minister and awarded damages against him." Arnold D. McNair, *Dr Johnson and the Law* 54 (1948). Today the Court of Session has 25 (or more) judges.

filt(e)rable. The preferred spelling is *filterable.*

file is often used as an ellipsis for *file suit* <file against the company>.

final. In reference to judgments, Justice Hugo Black exaggerated only slightly in commenting that "there is no more ambiguous word [than *final*] in all the legal lexicon." *F.T.C. v. Minneapolis-Honeywell Regulator Co.,* 344 U.S. 206, 215 (1952) (Black, J., dissenting). The reason is that the U.S. Supreme Court's holdings on what constitutes a final judgment are inconsistent. But the problem is one of vagueness, properly speaking, not AMBIGUITY, as Black termed it. And, though a verbal formula for finality has proved elusive, "in almost all situations it is entirely clear, either from the nature of the order or from a crystallized body of decisions, that a particular order is or is not final." Charles A. Wright, *Law of Federal Courts* 740 (5th ed. 1994).

final analysis, in the. See **in the final analysis.**

final destination. See **ultimate destination.**

finalize = (1) (v.t.) to complete; bring to an end; put in final form; or (2) (v.i.) to conclude. Originally an Australianism, *finalize* is a favorite word of jargonmongers. For that reason alone, and also because it is a NEOLOGISM that does not fill a gap in the language, it is to be avoided. E.g., "No decision of this court has squarely held that we have a capricious residual power to *finalize* [read *make final* or *bring to an end*] otherwise nonfinal appeals."/ "Westinghouse responded to the solicitation with a series of bids that were *finalized* [read *made final*] in a full proposal to Reynolds offering to manufacture the desired equipment for about $250,000." See -IZE.

final outcome; final result. These are common REDUNDANCIES, inasmuch as an *outcome* or *result,* as generally understood, is final. E.g., "We do not intimate what the *final result* [better: omit *final*] should be, but as for an alleged violation of the Voting Rights Act, we should not write until the court below shows that it considered all the evidence." Cf. **end result** & **ultimate destination.**

FINAL PREPOSITION. See PREPOSITIONS (A).

final result. See **final outcome.**

financeable. So spelled.

financ(i)er. *Financer* = one who finances a particular undertaking or on a particular occasion. E.g., "Prior to 1972, commentators debated inconclusively over whether a 'true' consigner was required to notify a secured *financer* of the consignee's inventory whose agreement included an after-acquired property clause." *Financier* = one whose business it is to lend money.

finders, keepers. See MAXIMS.

finding; holding. A court properly makes *findings of fact* and *holdings* or *conclusions of law.* The writer of the following sentence observed the distinction meticulously: "Because we *find* that the jury's finding of concurrent fault is amply supported by the evidence, we *hold* that appellee is entitled to full indemnity."

In appellate courts, properly, only *holdings* are affirmed, whereas *factual findings* are disturbed only when clearly erroneous, against the great weight of the evidence, etc., depending on the standard of review. Generally, it is not correct for an appellate court to say that it *affirms* a finding of fact.

Nor should the verb *find* be used when the court rules on a point of law. E.g., "We *find* [read *hold*] that the trial court properly instructed the jury on the Louisiana law of strict liability of the custodian of a defective thing under La. Civil Code art. 2317." See JUDGMENTS, APPELLATE-COURT & **fact-finding.**

fin(e)able. See MUTE E.

finicky is the preferred spelling—not *finnicky. Finical* is a pedantic variant.

finis = end; conclusion. This term should be used just as if one of the defining words were in its place: "But sometimes it denotes the judgment that writes *finis* [read *a finis*] to the entire litigation, after all appellate remedies have been either exhausted or, as here, abandoned." Sometimes *finis* is used to signal the end of a book; using it in this way has the sanction of long tradition.

In BrE, the word sometimes denotes a compromise and settlement—e.g.: "The parties then applied to the court to compromise the action; by the terms of the compromise (*finis*) the intending vendor admitted that the land belonged to the intending purchaser because he had given it to him, and the terms of the compromise were recorded in the court records." Peter Butt, *Land Law* 102 (2d ed. 1988).

finnicky. See **finicky.**

firing the client. When deciding that they will no longer represent a given client, lawyers (like literary agents and accountants) sometimes say that they are "firing" the client—e.g.:

- "In sum, it seems fair to say that the courts look the least favorably on conflicts created by a lawyer filing suit against a current client, and then *'firing' the client* who refuses to consent to conflict." Samuel R. Miller et al., *Conflicts of Interest in Corporate Litigation,* Bus. Lawyer, Nov. 1992, at 141, 195.
- "Has the client hired and fired other lawyers? Has another lawyer *fired the client?*" Carole C. Jordan, *Hungry Lawyers Need to Choose Work Carefully,* Nat'l L.J., 12 April 1993, at S16.
- "When one client insisted that he answer his telephone calls, Natsis took an unusual step. 'I *fired the client,*' he says. 'I'm not just a lawyer.' " *Commercial Real Estate Who's Who Towers of Influence: Rising Stars,* L.A. Bus. J., 20 March 1994, § 2, at 11.

This phrasing makes perfect sense when read in light of the relevant *OED* definition of *fire,* which is labeled American slang dating from the late 19th century: "to turn (any one) out of a place; to eject or expel forcibly; to dismiss or discharge peremptorily."

But it is an odd usage, since generally in AmE only the party who hires can be said to *fire. W10* perhaps more accurately defines this sense—"to dismiss from a position"—for only the employer can be said to *fire* the employee, not vice versa. One can understand, however, how the usage emerged among lawyers: they retain the upper hand in their client relations if they can be said to *fire* clients, even though they could never go out and "hire" clients.

The age-old struggle to establish just who rejected whom is typified by the following exchange between two friends: "I quit because the boss used repulsive language." "What did he say?" "He said, 'You're fired!' " Anon., as quoted in *The Penguin Dictionary of Modern Humorous Quotations* 258 (Fred Metcalf ed., 1987).

firm. This term is the title under which one or more persons carry on business jointly, or the partnership itself by which they are united for business purposes. A *firm* is not a corporation but an association. Cf. **organization.**

firm offer = one that includes a promise not to revoke it for a specified period.

first and foremost is a CLICHÉ that should not be used merely for *first.* The *OED* describes it as a "strengthened" phrase and dates it from the 16th century.

first blush, at. See **at first blush** & **face, on its.**

first-come-first-served is correct; *first-come-first-serve* is the mistaken rendition that is commonly encountered.

first degree; second degree. See **degree** & **murder** (A).

First Dissenter. See **Great Dissenter.**

first impression, case (or question) of. This phrase is an English equivalent of the LATINISMS *res nova* and *res integra.* E.g., "With that principle in mind, we shall proceed to consider the appropriate scope of Section 501, a *question of first impression* in this circuit." See **res integra.**

first instance. The phrase *in the first instance,* a chameleon-hued and often a FLOTSAM PHRASE, is "now used alternatively to *first, at first,* or *in the first place.* It comes from the sense of *instance* as a suit or process in a court of justice. . . . We still speak of a *court of first instance* [i.e., a trial court]." Jocelyn Simon, *English Idioms from the Law,* 76 Law Q. Rev. 429, 433 (1960). E.g., "It seemed to him undesirable that there should be conflicting decisions by judges of *first instance* [i.e., trial judges] on such a point."/ "At *first instance* Uthwatt, J. thought that the annuitants had a right to the capital sum, the rule being a rule of law." Anthony R. Mellows, *The Law of Succession* 569 (3d ed. 1977). See CHAMELEON-HUED WORDS & **court of first instance.**

Here the phrase is used for *in the first place:* "The purpose of that legal maxim *in the first instance* is the protection of minor children." We might classify *in the first instance* as a SET PHRASE, ruling out the variation here in evidence: "The trial court should have considered this overlooked but timely factual opposition in the *original instance* [read *first instance*]." See **instance.**

firstly, secondly, thirdly, etc. are today considered inferior to *first, second, third,* etc. Many stylists prefer using *first* over *firstly* even where the remaining signposts are *secondly* and *thirdly.* See ENUMERATIONS (A).

first option to buy. See **option.**

first part, party of the; first party. See **party of the first part.**

FIRST PERSON. As a general matter, it has been said that "the first person (*I, we, us*) is not usually used in legal writing because in an analysis of fact and law it seems best to have the emphasis on the facts and the law, and not on the analyzer." Norman Brand & John O. White, *Legal Writing: The Strategy of Persuasion* 123 (1976). This statement is true of DRAFTING and of BRIEF WRITING, but not of other types of legal writing, such as business letters, judicial opinions, and scholarly commentary. It is difficult if not impossible to state a sweeping rule applicable to all legal writing, diverse as it is. Instead, a few specific topics are here addressed in turn.

A. Awkward Avoidance of First Person. Such artifices as *this writer, the present writer,* and other graceless circumlocutions serve no real stylistic purpose and are inferior to the straightforward pronouns *I* and *me.* Late in his career as a legal writer, Jerome Frank confessed that he had long shunned the first-person pronoun, preferring *the writer* to *I* on the assumption that the indirect phrasing signified modesty. With age he became wiser and concluded: "To say *I* removes a false impression of a Jovian aloofness." *Courts on Trial* vii–viii (1950).

Of one common set of self-obscuring devices—*it is suggested that, it is proposed that,* and *it is submitted that*—Fred Rodell observed, "whether the writers really suppose that such constructions clothe them in anonymity so that people cannot guess who is suggesting and who is proposing, I do not know." *Goodbye to Law Reviews—Revisited,* 48 Va. L. Rev. 279, 280 (1962). We do know, however, that these phrases often make sentences read as if they had been "translated from the German by someone with a rather meager knowledge of English." *Id.* See **it is submitted that** & **undersigned.**

None of this should suggest, however, that every personal opinion should include the word *I.* Most opinions are transparently opinions, and they therefore need no direct mention of the writer—e.g.: "Though Holmes is routinely lionized as a great writer, Justice Jackson was the finest writer ever to sit on the high court." No moderately sophisticated reader would assume that this statement is anything more than an opinion. Even so, it is *much* more forceful and convincing when stated without the first person.

B. The Collegial *we* of Judges. The collegial *we* in which judges write their opinions is a useful stylistic device; but it sometimes traverses time with mind-boggling ease: "The court of appeals holding conflicts with *our* holdings in *Hendon v. Pugh,* 46 Tex. 211, 212 (1876) and *Faver v. Robinson,* 46 Tex. 204 (1876). In *Hendon, we* remanded a default judgment." *Uvalde Country Club v. Martin Linen Supply Co.,* 690 S.W.2d 884, 884 (Tex. 1985). It is questionable whether *we* really works when used by a modern court to overleap such a stretch of time; some less strained expression like *this court* might have been better in that sentence.

C. Approaching Autobiography. For a highly autobiographical and first-personish judicial opinion, see *Paine & Williams v. Baldwin Rubber Co.,* 23 F. Supp. 485 (E.D. Mich. 1938) (per Tuttle, J.). This opinion on a patent question is larded with language such as, "I hold that . . . ." "I take the case as I would an ordinary patent case," and "It seems to me that . . . ." The capstone, however, is the following passage, which I quote at length to convey the full flavor of the autobiographical style at its most personal and anecdotal:

> My experience began in the country and on the farm. I never laid the carpet directly in contact with the floor. The floor was a pretty rough one. Our loosely compacted base was straw or the old weekly newspapers. The usual thing was to put straw or paper under that carpet to protect it. The purposes were just the same as the purposes that this patent had in mind. It was yielding and would come back with a certain degree of resilience, it made it warmer when the wind got under the house, it protected against the cold, made the temperature more uniform, was nicer to walk over, didn't wear out so quickly. I can't think of any of the things that would be in the Turner patent that were not right in that old carpet with the papers under it, unless it be the fabric, and I say that is no[t] a material part of the claim. That, however, was in a way present. It was not uncommon to cover the floor with straw, place papers over the straw, and then stretch the carpet over the paper. The paper served as a fabric to hold the loose straw in place.
>
> The carpets of our boyhood were not only flexible but they extended out beyond the margin of the fibrous substance which was underneath the carpet. No one ever carried the straw out to the edge of the carpet. We always kept it back. We didn't want it sticking out with the whiskery effect described. No woman would want straw sticking out around her carpet.
>
> *Id.* at 486–87.

fisc [fr. L. *fiscus* "the imperial treasury"] = the public treasury. The *OED* notes that the word is "now rare," but it is not uncommon in American legal writing. E.g., "[C]ases like this . . . cumulatively pose a negligible threat to the *national fisc.*" *Swietlik v. U.S.,* 779 F.2d 1306, 1313 (7th Cir. 1985) (Cudahy, J., dissenting)./ "But protection of the *fisc* does not motivate all 'impoundments'; the executive can also use that power to obstruct programs and policies with which he disagrees."/ "Any profits obtained by Ginnie Mae inure solely to the benefit of the federal *fisc.*" (N.B.: *Public fisc,* unlike *federal fisc,* is a REDUNDANCY.)

In Scots law, the word was formerly spelled *fisk,* and it means specifically "the public treasury or 'Crown,' to which estates lapse by escheat" (*OED*).

fishing expedition is a CLICHÉ used to describe (contemptuously) an opponent's attempt, through discovery, to elicit information that might help that opponent. The phrase ought to be given a rest, as the Supreme Court urged long ago: "No longer can the time-honored cry of '*fishing expedition*' serve to preclude a party from inquiring into the facts underlying his opponent's case." *Hickman v. Taylor,* 329 U.S. 495, 507 (1947).

fit > fitted > fitted; fit > fit > fit. Historically, the verb *fit* became *fitted* in both the past tense and the past participle. Since the mid-20th century, however, AmE has witnessed a shift from *fitted* to *fit*.

Traditionally, *fit* would have been considered incorrect as a past-tense verb. But it began appearing in journalism and even scholarly writing as early as the 1950s. See David S. Berkeley, *The Past Tense of "Fit,"* 30 Am. Speech 311 (1955). This casualism appears even in what is generally considered well-edited journalism: "Gordon Getty had never quite *fit* in at his father's oil company." Wall St. J., 20 Dec. 1985, at 1./ "Judge Ciparick was overruled by an appeals court, which said that even a lopsided race *fit* the precise wording of the America's Cup deed." L. Gordon Crovitz, *Even Gentlemanly Yachtsmen Go to Court, But Why Let Them?* Wall St. J., 16 May 1990, at A17. And it has surfaced in fine scholarly writing—e.g.: "English land tenure, and the English way of life among landed gentry, *fit* [read *fitted*] this social order more than was true in the North." Lawrence M. Friedman, *A History of American Law* 66 (2d ed. 1985).

The traditionally correct past tense still surfaces—esp. in BrE—but in AmE it is becoming rarer (and stuffier) year by year: "We may leave to others the question whether the conception can be *fitted* to our old and modern systems of pleading." W.W. Buckland, *Some Reflections on Jurisprudence* 100 (1945)./ "[I]t is wise before deciding to use it to have regard to the tools with which it can be *fitted* and to the machinery [that] operates it." Patrick Devlin, *The Enforcement of Morals* 20 (1968)./ "Absolute liability also *fitted* into an aspect of the objective theory of contract . . . ." Grant Gilmore, *The Death of Contract* 48 (1974). Cf. **retrofit.**

fit and proper is a tiresome legalistic doublet with no claim to being either a TERM OF ART or a melodious phrase. One should write either *fit* or *proper,* without yoking them together so predictably. See DOUBLETS, TRIPLETS, AND SYNONYM-STRINGS.

fitted. See **fit.**

fixture = an article that has been attached to land in such a way that, in law, it forms part of the land. The term denotes a special type of property that is a hybrid between real property and personal property: a *fixture,* though considered real property, was once personal property and may be again someday (if removed).

flack. See **flak.**

flagrancy; flagrance. The latter is a NEEDLESS VARIANT.

flagrant. See **blatant.**

flagrante delicto. See ***in flagrante delicto.***

flagrant necessity. See **blatant.**

flair. See **flare.**

flak (= criticism) is sometimes misspelled *flack,* which is the proper spelling of the term meaning "a press agent."

flammable; inflammable. The former is now accepted as standard in BrE and AmE alike. Though examples of its use date back to 1813, in recent years it has become widespread as a substitute for *inflammable,* in which some persons mistook the prefix *in-* to be negative rather than intensive. Traditionally, the forms were *inflammable* and *noninflammable;* today they are *flammable* and *nonflammable.* Purists have lost the fight to retain the older forms. See NEGATIVES (B) & NON-.

flare; flair. *Flare,* n., = a sudden outburst of flame; an unsteady light. *Flair,* n., = (1) outstanding skill or ability in some field; or (2) originality, stylishness. The most common confusion occurs when *flare* displaces *flair*—e.g.: "District Attorney Jerome, who was an intimate friend of Hapgood, turned the actual trial of the case over to Keyran O'Conner, a capable assistant with a *flare* [read *flair*] for picturesque diction." Ephraim Tutt, *Yankee Lawyer* 168 (1943)./ "It is a chance to show we have the imagination and the *flare* [read *flair*] and the vision." Geordie Grieg, *£1 Billion Plan to Restore Britain's Heritage by AD 2000,* Sunday Times, 1 July 1990, at 1-1.

Although *flair* is exclusively a noun, *flare* can function as a verb in several senses: (1) to burst into flame; (2) to erupt suddenly; (3) to become suddenly angry; (4) to expand outward in shape; or (5) to signal with a flash of light. Occasionally, *flair* is misused for *flare* in its verb senses, here in sense (2): "The controversy surrounding frozen embryos *flaired* [read *flared*] recently with the death of a wealthy Los Angeles couple and the discovery of two 'orphaned' embryos which the couple had frozen and stored in Australia." Marcia J. Wurmbrand, Note, *Frozen Embryos: Moral, Social, and Legal Implications,* 59 S. Cal. L. Rev. 1079, 1100 n.18 (1986).

flaunt; flout. Confusion of these terms is distressingly common. *Flout* means "to contravene or disregard; to treat with contempt." *Flaunt* means "to show off or parade (something) in an ostentatious manner," but is often incorrectly used for *flout,* perhaps because it is misunderstood as a telescoped version of *flout* and *taunt.* E.g., "Despite the fact that both parties *flaunt* [read *flout*] local rules regarding the length of supporting memoranda, neither really addresses the 'successor in interest' notice question in any meaningful way." *Hemstreet v. Banctec, Inc.,* 748 F. Supp. 667, 669 n.2 (N.D. Ill. 1990)./ "CSW *flaunted* [read *flouted*] the rules and failed to properly credit and calculate student refunds." *Jackson v. Culinary Sch. of Washington,* 788 F. Supp. 1233, 1243 (D.D.C. 1992).

Of course, *flaunt* is most often used correctly—e.g.: "In February 1978, Bryant urged the Oklahoma legislature to pass the anti-advocacy statute to stop 'the *flaunting* of homosexuality' and to protect schoolchildren."/ "Words like 'reasonable,' 'substantial,' and 'satisfactory' *flaunt* their lack of precision."

Flout, meanwhile, never seems to cause a problem—e.g.: "The offenses did not involve any question of the *flouting* of military authority, the security of a military post, or the integrity of military property."/ "A man may not *flout* with impunity his obligation to provide necessaries to his dependent children."

One federal appellate judge who misused *flaunt* for *flout* in a published opinion, only to be *sic*'d and corrected by judges who later quoted him, appealed to *W3* and its editors, who, of course, accept as standard any usage that can be documented with any frequency at all. The judge then attempted to justify his error and pledged to persist in it. See William Safire, *I Stand Corrected* 158–59 (1984). Seeking refuge in a nonprescriptive dictionary, however, merely ignores the all-important distinction between formal contexts, on the one hand, in which the strictest standards of usage must apply, and informal contexts, on the other, in which venial faults of grammar or usage may, if we are lucky, go unnoticed (or unmentioned). Judges' written opinions fall into the former category.

floes (= sheets of ice [fr. Norweg. *flo,* meaning "flat layer"]) should not be confused with *flows:* "Hovering over the ice *flows* [read *floes*], they looked for survivors amid the wreckage and debris."

flood of, a. See SYNESIS.

flotsam; jetsam; lagan. Blackstone called these "the barbarous and uncouth appellations" for goods abandoned at sea. 2 William Blackstone, *Commentaries* 292–93 (Tucker ed. 1803). *Flotsam* is goods that are cast into the sea and float on the surface of the water. *Jetsam* is goods thrown overboard that sink in the sea and remain under water. *Lagan* is goods sunk in the sea but attached to a buoy so that they may be found again. *Flotsan* and *ligan* are obsolete spellings of *flotsam* and *lagan.*

These terms have largely outlived their usefulness, except in metaphorical senses. *Flotsam and jetsam* is the CLICHÉ used figuratively to mean "miscellaneous unimportant materials; dispensable articles."

FLOTSAM PHRASES just take up space without adding to the meaning of a sentence. Thus there is usually no reason, where it is clear whose opinion is being expressed, to write *In my opinion* or *It seems to me that.* Other examples are *hereby, in terms of, on a . . . basis, my sense is that, in the first instance,* and *the fact that.* (Admittedly, some of these phrases may be useful in speech.) A favorite flotsam phrase of lawyers in their pleadings is *at all relevant times:* "*At all relevant times,* Burndy and Teledyne were competitors in the manufacture and sale of split bolt connectors." We have enough written words without these mere space-fillers.

flounder; founder. Both verbs signal failure, but the literal senses, and therefore the images conveyed metaphorically, differ. To *flounder* is to struggle and plunge as if in mud. To *founder* is (of a ship) to fill with water and sink, (of a building) to fall down or give way, (of a horseback rider) to fall to the ground.

flout. See **flaunt.**

flowchart, v.t. The verbal use of this word is not recorded in the dictionaries, although it was perhaps inevitable, what with the verbal use of *chart. W10* records the gerund *flowcharting* but not the verb *to flowchart,* here illustrated: "To the extent that actual, historical vacancies in the employer's workforce can be *flowcharted* with reasonable accuracy, the court should award back pay to the minority employees who . . . would have occupied those vacancies but for discrimination." *U.S. v. U.S. Steel Corp.,* 520 F.2d 1043, 1055 (5th Cir. 1975).

flowed; flown. These words, surprisingly, are frequently confused. *Flowed* is the past tense and past participle of *flow. Flown* is the past participle of *fly.* See **overfly.**

flow from. In legal writing, few things *derive from, result from,* or are *caused by* other things; effects always seem to *flow from* causes. This is one of our most overworked legal CLICHÉS. E.g., "Our analysis necessarily *flows from Strickland v. Washington.*"/ "To show antitrust injury, the plaintiff must establish that the injury to his business *flowed from* defendant's alleged monopolization of the retail truck market."/ "There is no injury in law resulting in damages except that which *flows from* an unlawful act."/ "We conclude that any fraud conferred on Borg-Warner no rights in addition to those *flowing from* its status as a holder of an unperfected security interest."

A related locution is *follow from:* "The complaint also states that Swift was substantially certain the Trupiano's injuries would *follow from* its intentional acts."/ "The trust doctrine purportedly *follows from* normative principles."

flown. See **flowed.**

fly in the face of is a legal CLICHÉ. E.g., "[I]f we said that . . . , we should be *flying in the face of* a rule that is based on a very wide induction." (Maitland)/ "In the present case it *flies in the face of* common sense to say that there was a true consent to the marriage when the parties knew each other by sight for no more than minutes and when they have not even spent one whole day together as man and wife." (Eng.)

Fly in the teeth of is an inexcusable rending of the cliché. "[N]either court is required to accept, as credible, unsupported self-serving testimony that *flies in the teeth of* unimpeachable contradictory evidence and universal experience." *New England Merchants Nat'l Bank v. Rosenfield,* 679 F.2d 467, 473 (5th Cir. 1982). Cf. **face of, in the.**

F.O.B.; F.A.S.; C.I.F. These mercantile abbreviations—short for *free on board, free alongside,* and *cost, insurance, and freight*—denote types of contracts for the international sale of goods, and now also sales involving domestic transportation. With an *F.O.B.* contract, the seller's duty is fulfilled by placing the goods aboard the carrier. (Though some writers make the letters lowercase (*f.o.b.*), the capitalized form predominates.) Domestically, the use of *F.O.B.* [*destination*] indicates that freight charges have been paid to transport the goods as far as the named destination, whatever it may be (e.g., seller's plant or buyer's dock).

The term *F.A.S.* is nearly synonymous with *F.O.B.* in the context of contracts of water carriage. The phrasing is commonly *F.A.S. vessel* at a named port. But *F.A.S. vessel* differs from *F.O.B. vessel* in a significant way: "In the former case seller delivers at the wharf but is under no duty to see the loading: a 'received for shipment' bill of lading would be an appropriate document for him to tender. *F.O.B. vessel,* however, requires seller to bear the risk until the loading has been completed; only an 'on board' bill of lading would evidence the completion of his duties." Grant Gilmore & Charles L. Black, Jr., *The Law of Admiralty* 106 (2d ed. 1975).

With a *C.I.F.* contract, the seller agrees not only to supply the goods but also to make a contract of carriage with a sea carrier (under which the goods will be delivered at the contract port of destination), to pay the freight, and to insure the goods while they are in transit.

focus, n. Pl. *foci* /**foh**-sɪ/ or *focuses.* The plural *foci* may strike readers as pretentious in ordinary prose—e.g.: "One of the *foci* [read, perhaps, *focuses*] of recent discussions of tort reform has been the suggestion that a prevailing defendant be allowed to resolve its attorney's fees."

foia, v.t.; **foiable.** In the slang of administrative lawyers, *foiable* documents are subject to disclosure under the Freedom of Information Act (FOIA), and citizens may *foia* (= seek to obtain) them under that Act. Common in oral use, there is little written evidence of these terms.

foist (= to falsely present [something] as genuine or superior) takes the preposition *on.* E.g., "It does not in fact impute moral turpitude to plaintiff in *foisting* an article of the characteristics described by defendant *upon* [read *on*] the public." When the phrase is as unidiomatic as *foist with,* a different verb is in order: "An employer *is foisted with* [read *bears the*] responsibility to a third party if his employee commits a tort in the course of his employment." Stanley Berwin, *Pocket Lawyer* 231 (1986).

Foist off on is awkward and prolix: "Defendant has been shown to have *foisted* bogus companies *off on* [read *on*] the public." The *OED* quotes

Charlotte Brontë as having written *foist off on* but calls the phrase "rare."

folderol; falderol. The former is the preferred spelling for this word, which means either "nonsense" or "a useless trifle."

follow; apply. In the best usage, these terms are distinguishable in describing a court's actions. A court is said to *follow* a precedent when it rules that the precedent bears on and affects the decision on an important point in a pending dispute. Typically, this verb suggests that the court has discretion to choose between two or more lines of authority, or holds the precedent to be persuasive rather than binding. *Apply,* by contrast, usually suggests that a precedent unambiguously binds the decision-maker, so that the decision is more mechanical and less discretionary. Loosely, however, the two verbs are used interchangeably.

follow from. See **flow from.**

following (= after), when used to begin a sentence or clause, often results in a MISPLACED MODIFIER and a MISCUE—e.g.: "*Following* [read *After*] a bench trial, the district court voided portions of the plaintiff's settlement agreement."/ "*Following* [read *After*] a bench trial on the issue of liability, the district court held that the lessees and operators of the Galveston Bridge were 80% at fault." The problem, of course, is that the reader might expect *following* to function as a participle, as here: "Following these precedents, we affirm."

foment is incorrect as a noun for *fomentation.* "There is a lot of *foment* [read *fomentation*] going on around the Israeli border." It seems likely, however, that the writer confused *ferment* (= agitation) with *foment* (= to incite or rouse).

food fare. See **fare.**

fool for a client. From the early 19th century, it has been commonly said: "A man who is his own lawyer has a fool for a client." The earliest recorded variant dates from 1809: "He who is always his own counsellor will often have a fool for his client." *Port Folio* (Philadelphia), Aug. 1809, at 132.

Many occurrences are allusive only. For example, in 1887, when the Alabama Bar Association considered a code of conduct for its members, one suggested provision would have prevented lawyers from conducting their own cases. But that was deleted on constitutional grounds, the proponent of the change saying, "It is one of the American privileges to make a fool of yourself, and it is guaranteed by the Constitution, and I do not see anything wrong with it." Quoted in Walter P. Armstrong, Jr., *A Century of Legal Ethics,* 64 A.B.A. J. 1063, 1064 (1978).

Today, the quip is common in AmE and BrE alike—common enough, perhaps, to be a CLICHÉ that fresh writers would prefer to frame anew: "[A] lawyer never appears to worse advantage than when pleading his own cause." Lon L. Fuller, *The Morality of Law* 188 (1969).

Like many other quotations and SET PHRASES, this one sometimes gets mangled, usually when the writer substitutes *attorney* for *client* as the final word: "[Y]ou know, the old expression, someone who represents himself has a *fool for an attorney.*" *U.S. v. Hoffer,* 423 F. Supp. 811, 814 (S.D.N.Y. 1976)./ "The old saying that the person who fights his own case has a *fool for an attorney* may have been invented by lawyers, but there is a lot of truth in it." *Be Careful How You Say "I Quit,"* Sunday Times, 26 Nov. 1989, at E20. Although, logically speaking, the two formulations add up to the same thing, the original formulation is far wittier because of the ironic turn at the end (shifting from lawyer to client as if they were two persons).

footnote; endnote. Technically, *footnotes* appear at the foot of the page, and *endnotes* at the end of an article or chapter or at the end of a book. But *endnotes* are often called *footnotes.*

FOOTNOTES. A. Textual Footnotes. In modern legal writing, textual footnotes are mostly a scourge. As a writer, you might advantageously learn to detest them.

The thoroughly sensible policy of *The Scribes Journal of Legal Writing,* as stated inside the front cover, merits wide adherence: "We discourage footnotes that contain substantive discussion; footnotes used to cite pertinent materials are fully acceptable."

B. For Citations. In most types of legal writing, footnotes are a splendid place for citations, especially if the citations are followed by brief explanatory parentheticals. See CITATIONS OF CASES (D).

FOR-, FORE-. These prefixes, it will be observed in many of the entries following, have caused a great deal of confusion. One can usually arrive at the correct prefix for any given word by remembering that *for-* means either "completely" or "against," and that *fore-* means "before." See **forbear** & **forego**.

The two are confused here: "The traditional English approach rests on three doctrines—*unforseen* [read *unforeseen*] mode, mistaken object, and transferred fault." Andrew Ashworth, *Principles of Criminal Law* 174 (1991).

for. See **as (A).**

fora. See **forum.**

for all intents and purposes; to all intents and purposes. These synonymous phrases both mean "for practical purposes." They are about equally common—e.g.: "The legacy should pass to the heirs, devisees, distributees, etc. of such devisee or legatee, in like manner, *to all intents and purposes,* in law and in equity, as if such devisee or legatee had survived the testator and had then died intestate."/ "On these facts the Seventh Circuit held that the district court erred in referring the case to a magistrate without the consent of the parties because the hearing before the magistrate was, *for all intents and purposes,* a civil trial." Often this collocation qualifies as a FLOTSAM PHRASE.

Because some people mishear the phrase, the erroneous form *all intensive purposes* has arisen—e.g.: "[T]heir fellow officer . . . was *for all intensive purposes* [read *for all intents and purposes*] an eye witness to the commission of this offense." *State v. Bland,* 255 So. 2d 723, 725 (La. 1971)./ "When the charge, *for all intensive purposes* [read *for all intents and purposes*], is that the jury will be sequestered, then there is actual prejudice to the defendant." *Underwood v. Kelly,* 692 F. Supp. 146, 152 (E.D.N.Y. 1988)./ "In *American Computer Communication Corp., Inc. (American),* a Delaware corporation, which, *for all intensive purposes* [read *for all intents and purposes*], had all of its operations in Ohio, proposed to make an offering to Ohio residents under the Rule." Kevin C. Dicken, *Rule 147: Those Hard to Find No-Action Letters,* 17 Cap. U.L. Rev. 17, 33 (1987).

forbade. See **forbid.**

forbear, v.t.; **forebear,** n. These words are not cognate, though they are confused in every conceivable way. *Forbear* is the verb meaning "to refrain from objecting to; to tolerate." The verb is inflected *forbear > forbore > forborne.* E.g., "The plaintiff alleged that she *forbore* to sing for him, though engaged, whereby she lost great profits." (Eng.)

Forebear, the noun, means "ancestor" (usually used in the plural). *Forebearer* is an incorrect form of this noun. *Forbear* is occasionally misused for *forebear:* "We approach the study of history not merely in a spirit of piety to our *forbears* [read *forebears*] but our purpose will be to scan the panorama with a certain discernment."/ "D refused to vacate rooms belonging to the Government which he and his *forbears* [read *forebears*] had occupied for seventy years . . . ." Glanville Williams, *Criminal Law* 42 (2d ed. 1961).

The opposite error, though less common, also occurs (quite ironically, in the second sentence): "A promise to *forebear* [read *forbear*], even where a promise is implicit, may be sufficient consideration." L.B. Curzon, *English Legal History* 295 (2d ed. 1979)./ "It is tempting, but I *forebear* [read *forbear*] to comment on Vickers' own English lest someone else go on to find the faults in mine . . . ." Letter from H. Young, City Voice [Wellington, N.Z.], 23 Sept. 1993, at 18.

Forebearance is not a word; the term is *forbearance:* "It appears to be settled law that the *forebearance* [read *forbearance*] of some of the salvors to press their claims, whatever the reason for their *forebearance* [read *forbearance*], does not result in a windfall recovery for those who do claim." Grant Gilmore & Charles L. Black, Jr., *The Law of Admiralty* 570 (2d ed. 1975).

For the difference between *forbearance* and *omission,* see **omission.**

forbid > forbade > forbidden. *Forbid* generally takes the preposition *to* or, less formally, *from.* Fowler stated that *forbid from doing* is unidiomatic, but it is increasingly common in AmE—e.g.: "[Locke] sharply distinguished the respective spheres of Church and State and *forbade* each *from meddling* in the other." Clifford Orwin, *Civility,* 60 Am. Scholar 553, 557 (1991).

Even so, *forbid to* remains preferable in formal contexts—e.g.: "Quia Emptores . . . did not *forbid* a tenant in fee simple *to* grant estates smaller than the fee simple absolute." Thomas F. Bergin & Paul G. Haskell, *Preface to Estates in Land and Future Interests* 27 (2d ed. 1984).

The past tense is *forbade* (rhyming with *glad*)—e.g.: "The plaintiff neither *forbade* nor encouraged its employees to join the union." *Forbid* is sometimes wrongly used as a past-tense form: "Paul testified she did not think the order *forbid* [read *forbade*] her from trying to make such contacts with her children." *Paul v. Johnson,* 604 So. 2d 883, 884 (Fla. Dist. Ct. App. 1992).

Some writers—no doubt those who pronounce *forbade* correctly—mistakenly spell the word *forbad.* E.g., "Prouty had been found guilty of contempt for violating a decree of divorce against him which *forbad* [read *forbade*] either party to marry again within the time prohibited by the Illinois statute." William F. Walsh, *A Treatise on Equity* 201 (1930).

forbidden parts is a EUPHEMISM that is generally too vague to be helpful. But some criminal-law writers have found justifiable uses for the phrase when referring to various jurisdictions in which different bodily parts might be forbidden—e.g.: "[T]he general holding is that the crime [i.e., sodomy] is completed by any penetration into *forbidden parts.*" Rollin M. Perkins & Ronald N. Boyce, *Criminal Law* 466–67 (3d ed. 1982).

FORBIDDEN WORDS AND PHRASES. Blanket prohibitions are rarely valid, but they are useful in establishing rules to be flouted only in the rarest instances. It would hardly be an exaggeration to say that no sentence, and no document, would suffer from the absence of the following terms. As one court said, in a different context: "They spell wasted time, trouble for everyone and the delay of justice. Do not use them." *People v. Wright,* 289 N.W.2d 1, 20 (Mich. 1980).

A. Generally Useless Words and Phrases. Each of the following terms is discussed in a separate entry:

ad idem
aforementioned
and/or
anent
comes now
herein
hereinabove
hereinafter
hopefully
instanter
interface
inter se
irregardless
know all men by these presents
now comes
ore tenus
parameters
provided that
pursuant to
quoad
said (for *the,* etc.)
same, n. (for *it,* etc.)
simpliciter
ss.
such (for *the, that,* etc.)
to wit
understood and agreed
vel non
wheresoever
whosoever
-wise (*taxwise,* etc.)
witnesseth

B. Ignorant Malformations. Some terms have misbegotten by-forms—e.g.:

corpus delecti for *corpus delicti*
idealogy *for* ideology
miniscule *for* minuscule

forbore. See **forbear.**

forborne. See **forbear.**

forceable. See **forcible.**

force and arms, with, is a LOAN TRANSLATION of *vi et armis.* See **trespass** & ***vi et armis.***

force and effect is a doublet that has become part of the legal idiom in the phrases *in full force and effect* and *of no force or effect,* neither of which is a TERM OF ART. Either synonym would suffice just as well as the doublet; but the emphasis gained by *force and effect* may justify use of the phrase, more likely in DRAFTING (contracts and statutes) than in judicial opinions. See DOUBLETS, TRIPLETS, AND SYNONYM-STRINGS & OPINIONS, JUDICIAL.

force majeure; force majesture. Literally "a superior force," *force majeure* is the usual form of this LEGALISM denoting an event or effect that can be neither anticipated nor controlled. It is the LAW FRENCH equivalent of the LAW LATIN *vis major. Force majesture* is a NEEDLESS VARIANT.

Both *force majeure* and *vis major* are broader terms than *act of God* (q.v.) because they include acts not only of nature but also of people (e.g., riots, strikes, governmental interventions, acts of war). See ***vis major.***

forcible; forceable; forceful. Oddly, we have *forcible* but *enforceable,* q.v. *Forcible,* the usual and preferred term, means "obtaining something by physical strength or a display of violence." E.g., "Piracy is defined as robbery or *forcible* depredation on the high seas."/ "In an action for *forcible* abduction of children, the father is entitled to damages for the injury done to his feelings."

Properly referring only to physical force, *forcible* has frequently been misused for *forceful,* which may be used figuratively as well as literally: "The intention of the parties is *forcibly* [read *forcefully*] expressed in the agreement."/ "Counsel may state the facts as *forcibly* [read *forcefully*] as possible, but he must not enlarge them."/ "This case *forcibly* [read *forcefully*] points out the anomaly brought about by the Rule in Shelley's Case."

The spelling *forceable* at one point seemed entrenched in the phrase *forceable entry and detainer* in Texas, although the Texas Rules have now changed to the spelling *forcible. Forceable* frequently appears where *forcible* should: "The jury found that Flynn *forceably* [read *forcibly*] dispossessed plaintiff of his dinner plate."/ "The condemned are not [unduly] rushed and are not *forceably* [read *forcibly*] thrust into the chair, except as a last means." Aubrey Holmes, *The Wake of a Lawyer* 54 (1960). See -ABLE (A).

FORE-. See FOR-.

forebear. See **forbear.**

forebearance. See **forbear.**

forecast forms the past tense *forecast,* not *forecasted*—e.g.: "It can be shaped to meet real problems that have arisen and not possible problems *forecasted* [read *forecast*]." Patrick Devlin, *The Judge* 182 (1979). See **broadcast.**

foreclose (a person) *from* (an action) is an archaic construction still used in the law: "The rule against double recovery *forecloses* the wife *from* recovering for the loss of her husband's financial support." Today *foreclose* most commonly takes as an object one or more possibilities or choices <his failure of the exam forecloses the possibility of a promotion>.

Forclose is an erroneous form of *foreclose.* "If there is only one beneficiary, against whom there is a defense, this [*sic*] obviously *forcloses* [read *forecloses*] the action."

In the context of a real-estate foreclosure, the verb *foreclose* is generally intransitive: one *forecloses on* property or a mortgage. Formerly, however, the verb was transitive even in this context—e.g.: "[H]e proposes to *foreclose* the second mortgage . . . ." *Swain v. Seamens,* 76 U.S. (9 Wall.) 254, 273 (1869). This usage still occurs from time to time—e.g.: "He alleged that . . . appellees . . . failed to make installment payments on existing mortgages and allowed the mortgages to be *foreclosed.*" *Roberts v. Mullen,* 446 S.W.2d 86, 88 (Tex. Civ. App.—Dallas 1969)./ "On the following April 10 the Bank instituted an action to *foreclose* its mortgage." Grant Gilmore & Charles L. Black, Jr., *The Law of Admiralty* 953 (2d ed. 1975).

foregather. See **forgather.**

forego; forgo. The former, as suggested by the prefix, means "to go before." The latter is the term meaning "to do without; to pass up voluntarily; waive; renounce." One of the most persistent errors in legal and other writing is the use of *forego* where *forgo* is intended. One court has actually construed *forego* as meaning "voluntarily relinquishing," misspelling the very word it was interpreting. See *O'Neill v. Keegan,* 103 A.2d 909, 911 (Pa. 1954).

Examples of the misuse are legion—e.g.: "The public finds it hard to *forego* [read *forgo*] its belief that the law should be so certain that an unequivocal answer could be given in every case . . . ." Max Radin, *The Law and You* 13 (1948)./ "The promise of one creditor is regarded as sufficient consideration for the promise of another creditor to *forego* [read *forgo*] part of his claim." James A. MacLachlan, *Handbook of the Law of Bankruptcy* 4 (1956)./ "Must such a one *forego* [read *forgo*] the profit of this transaction at the risk of being held a party to the crime if the surmise proves correct?" Rollin M. Perkins & Ronald N. Boyce, *Criminal Law* 745–46 (3d ed. 1982).

The opposite mistake—misusing *forgo* for *forego*—is less common: "Based on the *forgoing* [read *foregoing*] authorities, we hold that the allegations . . . state a cause of action." *Garrido v. Burger King Corp.,* 558 So. 2d 79, 83 (Fla. Dist. Ct. App. 1990).

Forwent and *forewent* are the past-tense forms, and *forgone* and *foregone* the past-participial forms. The past participle *forgone* is more frequent in practice than *forwent;* yet, because legal writing is usually formal in tone, *forwent* is not as uncommon as in general practice. E.g., "Defendants admitted at trial that vestiges of de jure segregation still exist; hence the trial court *forwent* development of liability at trial, and concentrated solely on remedies."/ "If . . . a professor who relied on that promise *forwent* the first opportunity to raise his challenge, the university could not deprive him of the second opportunity without violating due process." See **foregone.**

foregoing is occasionally mistaken for *following.* "Although the *foregoing quote* [read *following quotation*] is a long one, it succinctly states the entire problem with this regulation: [a long quotation follows, and none precedes this statement]." (Note also the unconscious irony in a *long* quotation that *succinctly* states a proposition!)

foregone is correct in *foregone conclusion,* but not here: "He based that part of his holding on the thought that the Aldecoa had '*foregone* [read *forgone*] an opportunity' to engage in the profitable work of property salvage." Grant Gilmore & Charles L. Black, Jr., *The Law of Admiralty* 573 (2d ed. 1975). See **forego.**

forehead. The preferable pronunciation of this word rhymes with *horrid.*

foreign. In law, this word means "of another jurisdiction," not necessarily "of another country."

Thus it is not uncommon for a court in Florida, say, to refer to a judgment of a New Mexico court as a *foreign judgment.* Exceptions occur, however, so one must read carefully. Here *foreign* occurs in the nonlawyer's sense: "Courts of equity have, as between the parties, reviewed the judgments of *foreign* courts; a specific performance of a contract of sale of land situated in a *foreign* country will be decreed in equity."

forejudge is an archaic equivalent of *prejudge* for which the *OED* includes only one citation more recent than the 18th century, and that from 1860. Perhaps the most notable use of the term was in the Mutiny Act of 1689, 1 Wm. & Mary, ch. 5: "[N]o man may be *forejudged* of Life or Limb, or subjected to any kind of Punishment by Martial Law, or in any other manner than by the Judgment of his Peers, and according to the known and established Laws of this Realm." In modern contexts, however, the word is a fusty ARCHAISM—e.g.: "[W]e do not mean to *forejudge* [read *prejudge*] the substantial and novel question involving disputed evidence of motivation and causation . . . ." *Automatic Radio Mfg. Co. v. Ford Motor Co.,* 390 F.2d 113, 117 (1st Cir. 1968).

foreman; foreperson; presiding juror. The best nonsexist choice is *presiding juror.* Unfortunately, *foreperson* has crept into official court rules. See Fed. R. Crim. P. 6(c). See SEXISM (B).

It is mildly surprising to see *foreman* and *foreperson* used for purposes of INELEGANT VARIATION: "And since the *foreperson* is the single most influential person on a jury, lawyers will do anything to keep good *foreman* material off." Robin T. Lakoff, *Talking Power: The Politics of Language in Our Lives* 114–15 (1990).

forensic = used in or suitable to courts of law or public debate. E.g., "It is the duty of the king, as parens patriae, to protect property devoted to charitable uses; and that duty is executed by the officer who represents the crown for all *forensic* purposes." (Eng.)/ "Where Parliament has used in nontechnical legislation words that, in their ordinary meaning, cover the situation before the court, it is a reasonable presumption that Parliament or its draftsmen envisaged the actual *forensic* situation." (Eng.)

Other senses have grown out of the primary one. For example, the adj. *forensic* has come to mean "rhetorical" or "argumentative" in certain contexts, the language or manner to which it refers being analogized to courtroom talk. Traditionally *forensics* = the art of argumentative discourse.

Today *forensics,* as a shortening of *forensic ballistics,* is used by police officers to refer to the section of law enforcement dealing with legal evidence relating to firearms. Thus the phrase *forensic evidence* has cropped up—a phrase understandably deplored by traditionalists but likely to become permanently ensconced in the language. It is especially common in BrE—e.g.: "*Forensic evidence* also showed Scottish detectives the bomb was in a brown Samsonite suitcase, similar to one belonging to Khreesat." David Black & Harvey Morris, *Investigators Followed False Trail to Palestinian Cell,* The Independent, 14 Dec. 1990, at 3./ "Defence lawyers are seeking more details of *forensic evidence* that has lain hidden from them for 16 years." Stewart Tendler, *Six Decide Against Bail Plea,* The Times (London), 19 Dec. 1990, at 3.

foreperson. See **foreman** & SEXISM (B).

foresaid. See **aforesaid.**

foresake. See **forsake.**

foresee. See FOR- & **anticipate.**

foreseeable is occasionally misspelled *forseeable.* See FOR-.

foreword; preface. The word *foreword* denotes a book preface written by someone other than the author. It is often mistaken with its homophone, *forward*—e.g.: "Nathan S. Hefferman, Chief Justice of the Wisconsin Supreme Court, embellishes this concept in his *forward* [read *foreword*] to the book by reducing the title *Modern Appellate Practice* to an acronym . . . ." Robert L. Black, Jr., Book Review, 53 U. Cin. L. Rev. 171, 173 (1984).

The word *preface,* by contrast, usually refers to an introductory essay written by the author.

forfeit > forfeited > forfeited. Using *forfeit* as a past participle is an ARCHAISM in AmE and, as the *OED* suggests, in BrE as well—e.g.: "The Cinque Ports alone at this time had a general rule that bailed goods are not *forfeit* [read *forfeited*] by the felony of the bailee." Theodore F.T. Plucknett, *A Concise History of the Common Law* 474 (5th ed. 1956).

The adjectival use—which in some sentences is hardly distinguishable from the past-participial use—is still current in literary BrE. E.g., "[I]f a man were killed by an animal or thing, it was *forfeit* to the king, who usually sold it and paid the proceeds to the next-of-kin." Glanville Williams, *Textbook of Criminal Law* 29 n.2 (1978).

forfeiture is naturally pronounced /*for*-*fi*-*chər*/; pompous speakers are fond of pronouncing the final syllable /*tyoor*/.

forfend, in all but the literary (and precious) exclamation *Heaven forfend!,* is an ARCHAISM better replaced by *prevent*—e.g.: "To that end it imposes on the homeowner a liability to respond in damages for any injury received because his sidewalks are left in an icy condition—a liability [that] he can, of course, *forfend* [read *prevent*] by scraping the ice off or sprinkling it with sand or ashes." Lon L. Fuller, *Anatomy of the Law* 64 (1968).

forgather; foregather. The former is preferable, inasmuch as either might be said to be "preferable." *Gather* usually suffices.

forgery = (1) a false document, or false part of a document, that someone has tried to make look genuine; or (2) the act of making a false document so that it may be used as if it were genuine. In sense (1), the thing forged must be a document: imitating a sculpture, even with fraudulent intent, is not forgery. And in both senses, the phrase *false document* does not mean a document that tells a lie; it means a document that *is* a lie. See **counterfeiting.**

forgo. See **forego.**

formal contract; informal contract. Virtually every legal system has two ways in which promises may become binding as contracts. One is by giving the transaction a certain form in writing (i.e., making a *formal contract*); the other is by complying with the requisites of the transaction in some way other than satisfying requisites of form (i.e., making an *informal contract*). *Formal contracts* were traditionally made under seal; the only test for an *informal contract* is whether it contains the element of "valuable consideration." See **informal contract.**

formalism; formality. These words are quite distinct. *Formality* denotes conformity to rules, propriety, or precision of manners. *Formalism,* by contrast, is invariably a pejorative term, meaning "excessive adherence to prescribed forms; use of forms without regard to substantive import." Examples of the rigid, inflexible *formalism* that once characterized English law are legion: "[T]he omission of a single downstroke or contraction sign, or an error of Latin accidence, were fatal mistakes in a writ." J.H. Baker, *An Introduction to English Legal History* 103 (3d ed. 1990).

The corresponding adjective—*formalistic*—is perhaps even more pejorative than *formalism*—e.g.: "The distinction between aggravating and mitigating facts has been criticized as *formalistic.*" *McMillan v. Pennsylvania,* 477 U.S. 79, 100 (1986) (Stevens, J., dissenting)./ "The dissenting judge rejected the majority's '*formalistic,* technical and unrealistic application of *Miranda'* . . . ." *Duckworth v. Eagan,* 492 U.S. 195, 200 (1989). Cf. **legalistic.** See **formulaic.**

FORMAL WORDS are those occupying an elevated level of diction. The English language has a number of levels of diction, and even synonyms that exist on different levels. Thus *his honor* is formal, *the judge* is the ordinary phrase, and *the beak* (BrE slang) is vulgar.

The language of the law is perhaps top-heavy with formal words, as the courts are one of the institutions in Western societies that are most fully bedecked with pomp and regalia. Legal language reflects that formality, often quite appropriately. But many lawyers (and especially nonlawyers talking to lawyers, it seems) go overboard, resorting to unnatural pomposities (e.g., *this honorable court* used repeatedly) where ordinary words are called for (e.g., *the court*).

Early in the 19th century, the novelist James Fenimore Cooper worried that "[t]he love of turgid expressions is gaining ground, and ought to be corrected." "On Language," in *The American Democrat* 117 (Cooperstown, H.E. Phinney, 1838) (repr. in *A Language for Writers* 110, 113 (James R. Gaskin & Jack Suberman eds., 1966). For stylists, that worry is perpetual, as each generation becomes enamored of its own brands of linguistic inflation: doublespeak, gobbledegook, legaldegook, officialese, and the like. The phrase *formal words* is virtually a EUPHEMISM for those stylistic disturbances. In the left-hand column are some of the chief symptoms:

Formal Word	*Ordinary Word*
annex	attach
announce	give out
append	attach
approximately	about
assign	give
cease	stop
commence	begin
complete	finish
conceal	hide
deem	consider
demise	death
desist	stop, leave off
detain	hold
determine	end
donate	give
effectuate	carry out

emoluments	pay
employ	use
endeavor	try
evince	show
expedite	hasten
expend	spend
expiration, expiry	end
extend	give
forthwith	immediately, soon
imbibe	drink
inaugurate	begin
indicate	state, show, say
initiate	begin
inquire	ask
institute	begin
interrogate	question
intimate	suggest
necessitate	require
occasion, v.t.	cause
peruse	read
portion	part
possess	have
present	give
preserve	keep
prior	earlier
proceed	go (ahead)
purchase	buy
remainder	rest
request	ask
retain	keep
remove	take away
suborn	bribe (a juror or witness)
summon	send for, call
terminate	end
utilize	use

forma pauperis. See ***in forma pauperis.***

format, v.t., makes *formatted, formatting.* See DOUBLING OF FINAL CONSONANTS.

formation. See **formulation.**

formbook. One word.

former and *latter* can apply only to a series of two. The *former* is the first of two, the *latter* the second of two. In contexts in which more than two elements occur, *first* should be used rather than *former, last* or *last-mentioned* rather than *latter.* E.g., "Cities Service sued Lee-Vac and American Hoist. The *latter* [read *last two*] cross-claimed against each other."

These latter is not an impossibility if the second of the two elements is plural—e.g.: "This case was brought at the instance of the F.D.A. in the name of the United States against the individuals named as defendants, praying that *these latter* be restrained from introducing into interstate commerce certain misbranded drugs."

Former and *latter* can bewilder the reader when the elements referred to are numbers. E.g., "The second rationale is distinguished from the first because with the *latter,* both parties are aware of the special circumstances under which the contract was made." The latter here syntactically is "the first," but the context in which this sentence appeared made it clear that the writer meant to say the second rationale; that is, he used *latter* in a temporal rather than in a syntactic sense.

May one have a *latter* without a *former?* Strictly speaking, not any more than one can have an *other hand* without a *one hand,* even if only implicitly. Formerly, it was not uncommon to use *latter* without a correlative. E.g., "In view of what has already been said, very little may suffice concerning a liability as such. The *latter* [i.e., liability], as we have seen, is the correlative of power, and the opposite of immunity (or exemption)." (Hohfeld) Latterly, however, this use of the term is uncommon.

former jeopardy. See **double jeopardy.**

form of action. Although it has virtually no current significance in modern law practice, this phrase is basic to an understanding of Anglo-American legal history. True, the forms of action have been buried, but "they still rule us from their graves." F.W. Maitland, *The Forms of Action at Common Law* 1 (1936; repr. 1971).

A *form of action* was a compartment of law and practice associated with a particular writ, each of which had specific forms of process and specific modes of pleading, of trial, of judgment, and of executing the judgment. Some forms of action had exotic names, such as *mort d'ancestor, writ of entry in the per and cui, writ of besaiel,* and *quare impedit.* In 1830, some 72 forms existed; in 1874, the number had dwindled to 12; and in 1875, they were abolished in England. About the same time, or shortly afterwards, they were abolished in most American jurisdictions.

FORMS OF ADDRESS. To avoid professional blunders in correspondence and other writings, the legal writer must know how to refer to judges and other dignitaries. The American rules are much simpler than the British ones. Only a few of the most basic questions are treated here. For a fuller discussion, consult one of the several modern books on forms of address, or a good book of etiquette.

A. Addressing Federal Judges. In addressing judges, err on the side of formality, but not to the point of archaism or pedantry. Thus, in court papers, instead of *To the Honorable Judge of Said Court,* write either *To the Honorable Court* or *To the Honorable Alicemarie H. Stotler, U.S. District Judge.*

In corresponding with the federal judiciary in the U.S., follow these forms:

Chief Justice

Very formal:

The Chief Justice of the United States
(address)

Dear Mr. Chief Justice:

Less formal:

The Honorable William H. Rehnquist
The Chief Justice of the United States
(address)

Dear Chief Justice Rehnquist:

Associate Justice

The Honorable Ruth Bader Ginsburg
The Supreme Court of the United States
(address)

Dear Justice Ginsburg:

Other federal judge

The Honorable William R. Wilson, Jr.
United States District Court, W.D. Arkansas
(address)

Dear Judge Wilson:

B. Addressing State-Court Judges. In corresponding with state judges, follow these forms (applicable in most states):

Chief Justice of the highest appellate tribunal

The Honorable (full name)
Chief Justice, (name of court)
(address)

Dear Chief Justice (surname):

Other state judge

The Honorable (full name)
(name of court)
(address)

Dear Judge (surname):

C. Four Rules in Using *The Honorable.* First, *Honorable* should be capitalized whenever coupled with a person's name. Second, never write *The Honorable O'Connor* or *Hon. O'Connor; Honorable* always takes a full name:

The Honorable Sandra Day O'Connor

Third, abbreviate *Honorable* only in addresses, and omit *The* when abbreviating:

Hon. Sandra Day O'Connor

Fourth, when writing a British, Canadian, or Australian correspondent and spelling out the word, use the BrE spelling:

The Right Honourable the Lord Goff of Chieveley

D. *Mr. Justice; Mrs. Justice; Madam Justice.* Many readers, especially in the U.S., find these labels gratuitously sexist. *Justice* alone suffices.

In the U.S. Supreme Court, the *Mr.* disappeared before *Justice* shortly after Justice Sandra Day O'Connor ascended to the bench. See SEXISM.

E. Third-Person References. Whereas British legal writers tend to refer in discourse to *Denning M.R.* and *Woolf J.*—without even a comma after the name—Americans generally refer to *Justice Scalia* (not *Scalia J.*) or *Judge Robert E. Keeton* (on first mention, and later *Judge Keeton.* In third-person contexts, avoid honorifics such as *The Honorable.*

F. Lawyer-to-Lawyer References. The American practice of appending *Esq.* to other lawyers' names is entirely acceptable, but no other titles—not even *Mr.*—may be used in conjunction with it. See **Esq.**

If you prefer not to use *Esq.* (some consider it clubby), a mere *Mr.* or *Ms.* or *Mrs.* (or even *Miss,* if that is the addressee's known preference) will always suffice.

British lawyers often have titles or affiliations that a correspondent is obliged to include after the addressee's name, such as *Q.C.* (Queen's Counsel) and *F.B.A.* (Fellow of the British Academy).

G. Signing Off. When ending a letter, dispense with the archaic flourishes: instead of *I am, my dear sir, Sincerely yours,* write *Sincerely yours.*

In business and personal letters, you may show some individuality in the complimentary close by adopting any of the several standard forms:

Very formal and deferential

Respectfully (yours),
Very respectfully yours,

Less formal, without deference (as in demand letters)

Very truly yours,
Yours very truly,
Yours truly,

General

Sincerely yours,
Yours sincerely,
Sincerely, (see H)

Informal

With best wishes,
Best wishes,
With best regards,
Best regards,
Kindest personal regards,
Best,

Intimate

As ever,

Fondly,
Yours,
Yours ever,
Yours always,

H. The Lone *Sincerely.* A foul canard is afoot in the American legal profession: some believe that it is an error to close with *Sincerely, Respectfully, Fondly,* or any other adverb without adding *yours.* Do not believe it: every modern complimentary close contains UNDERSTOOD WORDS. Respected writers from Supreme Court justices to eminent law professors, even great poets, use *Sincerely* without saying whose. See *An Epistolary Essay: The Wright-Garner-Maugans Correspondence on Complimentary Closes,* 2 Scribes J. Legal Writing 83 (1991); *A Sequel to "An Epistolary Essay,"* 3 Scribes J. Legal Writing 95 (1992).

formula. Pl. *-as, -ae.* The English plural, ending in *-s,* is preferred in all but scientific writing. Legal writers are somehow fond of the Latinate ending. See PLURALS (A).

formulaic; formulistic; formalistic. *Formulaic* = of, relating to, or constituting a formula. *Formulistic* = fond of formulas. *Formalistic* = adhering unduly to a set way of saying and doing something without regard to its substance or inner meaning.

formulation (= a setting forth systematically) for *formation* (= the act of forming, or the thing formed) is an odd error. In 1993, a newly formed (formulated?) law firm sent out tens of thousands of announcements that read, "X and Y are pleased to announce the *formulation* [*sic*] of their professional corporation for the practice of personal injury law under the name X & Y, P.C."

fornicate; copulate. *Copulate* is a neutral verb referring to the sexual act without regard to legality or the legal status of the parties. *Fornicate* is not neutral: it describes a criminal offense in some American jurisdictions; for example, Virginia Code § 18.2–344 provides that "[a]ny person, not being married, who voluntarily shall have sexual intercourse with any other person, shall be guilty of *fornication,* punishable as a Class 4 misdemeanor."

fornication. See **adultery.**

forsake > forsook > forsaken. *Forsake* (= to desert or renounce) is sometimes corrupted into *foresake.*

forseeable. See **foreseeable.**

for sure is colloquial for *certain* or *certainly.*

forswear; foreswear. The latter does not properly exist. If it did, it might mean "to swear before," since the prefix *fore-* denotes a previous time. *Forswear* is the proper synonym of *renounce* or *abrogate.* Cf. **forego.**

forswearing. See **perjury.**

forte (= a person's strong point) is preferably pronounced with one syllable, like *fort.* But many English-speaking people persist in the two-syllable version, /***for**-tay*/, which can hardly be strongly condemned.

for the duration of is verbose for *during.*

for the reason that is prolix for *because*—e.g.: "It is still thought that magistrates are too disinclined to reject police evidence, however implausible, perhaps *for the reason that* [read *because*] they feel the police should always be supported as a matter of principle." P.S. Atiyah, *Law and Modern Society* 26 (1983).

for the sake of (the) argument is a perfectly good phrase that is universally understandable to those who speak English—and therefore much preferable to *arguendo* (q.v.). Legal stylists frequently use it—e.g.: "But even if, *for the sake of the argument,* we concede the identity of the two Romes, we may go on to observe that the style and trappings of Catholic Rome were quite different from the style and trappings of Imperial Rome." Grant Gilmore, *The Ages of American Law* 68 (1977). The phrase is most commonly rendered without a definite article before *argument:* hence *for the sake of argument.*

forthwith, adv., is a usefully vague term, although it may strike some readers as antiquarian. The writer who intends a precise meaning must be wary: the word has been attributed every shade of meaning from "instantly" to "within 24 hours" to "within a reasonable or convenient time." It is a fuzzy word with no pretense of precision.

Forthwith makes no sense as an adjective, as in the phrase *a forthwith subpoena.*

fortuitous (= occurring by chance) is commonly misused for *fortunate.* Here the correct use of the term is illustrated: "Contrary to defendants' argument, the occasional *fortuitous* inclusion of a tenant in the resolution of a claim between the housing authority and the landlord affords no protection to a tenant."/ "Whether that result would follow in any other case is entirely *fortuitous,* and it may be that such a result was not intended." See **aleatory & gratuitous.**

In phrase *fortuitous accident,* the word *fortuitous* is correctly used but it results in a REDUNDANCY: every accident is fortuitous. E.g., "[T]he owners of other non-stationary property such as farm animals or trains [that] may sustain damage in a motor vehicle accident on a public highway are usually not at fault and thus should not be required to maintain their own insurance to cover *fortuitous accidents* [read *accidents*] [that] might occur." *Pioneer State Mut. Ins. Co. v. Allstate Ins. Co.,* 339 N.W.2d 470, 475 (Mich. 1985).

Fortuity is the seldom-seen noun corresponding to *fortuitous.* E.g., "[The rule] tolerates opposite results depending upon the pure *fortuity* of the outcome of the race to the courthouse." *Chapman v. International Ladies' Garment Workers' Union,* 401 F.2d 626, 628 (4th Cir. 1968). *Fortuitousness,* which emphasizes the *quality* as opposed to the *state* of being fortuitous, is also used.

forum. The preferred plural is *forums,* not *fora.* E.g., "Public *fora* [read *forums*] generally are those places which by long tradition or by government fiat have been devoted to assembly and debate." *ACORN v. City of Phoenix,* 798 F.2d 1260, 1264 (9th Cir. 1986)./ "Her scepticism is grounded in her suspicion that the legal techniques of interpretation and the *forums* in which interpretation proceeds are biased by the conscious and even more the unconscious mind-sets of bench and bar." Neil MacCormick, *With Due Respect,* TLS, 22 Jan. 1993, at 3. See PLURALS (A).

forum non conveniens = the doctrine that an inappropriate forum, even though competent under the law, may be divested of jurisdiction if, for the convenience of the litigants and the witnesses, it appears that the action should be instituted in another forum in which the action might originally have been brought. This LATINISM has become a TERM OF ART. E.g., "The common-law *forum non conveniens,* with its stress on contacts and fairness, unhampered by a mythology of power and sovereignty, may yet create a new American law of jurisdiction based on the *forum conveniens.*"

forum-shopping, n., an Americanism dating from the early 1950s, should be hyphenated thus. The phrase refers to the practice of choosing the most favorable jurisdiction or court in which a claim might be heard. Cf. **panel-shopping.**

forward(s). See -WARD(S).

forwent. See **forego.**

founder. See **flounder.**

fountain of justice is a SET PHRASE, of which *fountainhead of justice* is a mangling: "The king was the *fountainhead* [read *fountain*] of justice . . . ." C. Gordon Post, *An Introduction to the Law* 41 (1963).

four corners of the instrument (= the face of a legal document) derives from the age-old view that every deed was supposed to have been written on one skin of parchment having only four corners. The phrase is common in legal JARGON, esp. when it is argued that the court should not consider evidence extraneous to the legal document in question. E.g., "If the *four corners of the deed* provide a coherent expression of the parties' intent, we need search no further, but if an ambiguity or a reasonable doubt appears from a perusal of the particular symbols of expression our horizons must be broadened to encompass the circumstances surrounding the transaction." *Oldfield v. Stoeco Homes, Inc.,* 139 A.2d 291, 297 (N.J. 1958).

Sometimes the phrase is used figuratively of things other than single documents: "In the resulting amalgam it is not possible to distinguish which notes and coins belong to the trust fund and which do not; all that can be said is that the trust fund is somewhere within the *four corners* of the account." (Eng.) (An *account* does not have four corners, although perhaps *account records* was intended.)

There is also a doctrine called the *eight-corners rule*—e.g.: "Texas courts follow the *'eight corners'* rule when determining an insurer's duty to defend the insured. Under this rule, a court looks only to the pleadings and the insurance policy to determine whether the duty to defend exists . . . ." *Cluett v. Medical Protective Co.,* 829 S.W.2d 822, 829 (Tex. App.—Dallas 1992).

Four Horsemen. In allusion to the Four Horsemen of the Apocalypse—allegorical figures in the Bible (Rev. 6:1–8)—this phrase formerly referred to four U.S. Supreme Court Justices who consistently opposed New Deal legislation: George Sutherland, Pierce Butler, Willis Van Devanter, and James McReynolds. For an example of a legal writer's use of the phrase, see **bad.**

fours, on all. See **on all fours.**

four, rule of. See **rule of four.**

four unities. In his "Poetics," Aristotle devised "three unities" for dramatic composition, namely that a play should consist of one main action, should occur at one time (or within 24 hours), and should occur in one place. In allusion to these dramatic principles, real-estate lawyers devised four unities for the creation of a joint tenancy: time, title, interest, and possession. The joint tenants must have the same interest beginning at the same time, deriving from the same title, and consisting of the same undivided possession.

fractious. See **factional.**

FRAGMENTS, SENTENCE. See INCOMPLETE SENTENCES.

fram(e)able. The *-e-* is best omitted. See MUTE E.

framers in AmE is capitalized only in reference to the drafters of the U.S. Constitution. In all other contexts in which this word refers to legislative drafters, the word is lowercased.

franchise, n., has two quite distinct senses: (1) "the right to vote"; (2) "the sole right of engaging in a certain business or in a business with a particular trademark in a certain area." Sense (1) is the less common one today, but it remains in use—e.g.: "In earlier times this led to obvious legal changes such as the gradual emancipation of married women, and the spread of the *franchise.*" P.S. Atiyah, *Law and Modern Society* 117 (1983).

In English and Scottish legal history, *franchise* also denoted an area enjoying exemption from royal justice. In a franchise, justice was administered by a noble or other person who had a grant of the power to do justice—hence the term *franchise courts.*

franchise, v.t.; **enfranchise; affranchise.** *Enfranchise* = (1) to set free, release from bondage; (2) to give to a person or class of persons the right to vote; (3) to give to an area or class of persons the right to be represented in an elected body (*CDL*); or (4) to endow with a franchise. *Affranchise* is a NEEDLESS VARIANT. See **disfranchise.**

Franchise = to grant (to another) the sole right of engaging in a certain business or in a business with a particular trademark in a certain area. See **franchise,** n.

franchiser; franchisor. *Franchiser* is preferred. *W3* contains only the *-er* form; the *OED* lists *-or* as a variant.

frankalmoi(g)n(e); almoi(g)n. This obsolete form of English land tenure—a holding in free alms, in return for prayers—is generally spelled *frankalmoin* in modern texts. *Almoign* and *almoin* are historical variants.

fraud. A. Defining Generally. "Courts refrain from defining fraud," it was once said, "lest they be confronted by their own definition and it be found too broad or too narrow to cover cases that may subsequently arise." Eugene A. Jones, *Manual of Equity Pleading and Practice* 43–44 (1916). *Fraud,* in other words, is a CHAMELEON-HUED WORD. It may mean: (1) a tort consisting in a knowing misrepresentation made with the intention that the person receiving that misrepresentation should act on it; (2) the misrepresentation resulting in that tort; (3) a tort consisting in a representation made recklessly without any belief in its truth, but made with the intention that the person receiving that misrepresentation should act on it; (4) a misrepresentation made recklessly without any belief in its truth; (5) unconscionable dealing short of actionable deceit at common law; (6) in the context of conspiracy to defraud, a surreptitious taking of property without deception; or (7) in the law of contract, an unconscientious use of the power arising out of the relative positions of the parties and resulting in an unconscionable bargain. Because *fraud* occupies shifting ground, it is best braced with a modifier (see below). See **deceit.**

B. *Fraud in fact; fraud in the factum.* These terms refer to two very different principles. *Fraud in fact* is what is also known as *actual* or *positive fraud,* that is, a concealment or false representation by means of a statement or conduct that causes injury to another. Scienter (q.v.) is usu. required. *Fraud in the factum* occurs when a legal instrument (a "factum" at common law) as actually executed differs from the one intended for execution by the person who executes it, or when the instrument may have had no legal existence (as, e.g., because the substance of the document was misrepresented to a blind signatory). See **fact,** n.

C. *Fraud in law; legal fraud.* These phrases are deceptively similar. *Fraud in law* is fraud that is presumed under the circumstances, as, for example, when a debtor transfers assets and thereby impairs the efforts of creditors to collect sums due. *Legal fraud* is another term for *constructive fraud* or unintentional deception that causes injury to another. (To complicate matters, it is occasionally also called *fraud in contemplation of law.*) Because *legal fraud* is potentially ambiguous, *constructive fraud* is the better phrase. See **constructive fraud.**

fraudfeasor (= one who has committed fraud) is a legal NEOLOGISM not listed in most English-language dictionaries or law dictionaries. The word should be solid, not hyphenated. E.g., "[H]e may elect to disaffirm the fraudulent transaction and to make claim, or sue in equity, for rescission—to follow his property into the hands of the *fraudfeasors* or those who took with knowledge of the fraud, and to get it back . . . ." *Western Newspaper Union v. Woodward,* 133 F. Supp. 17, 25 (W.D. Mo. 1955)./ "In seeking to choose between a *fraudfeasor* and a negligent party, the Georgia law unfortunately goes with the alleged crook." *Lariscy v. Hill,* 159 S.E.2d 443, 444 (Ga. Ct. App. 1968)./ "Failure to correct another's delusion is obviously fraudulent if the circumstances are such that the *fraud-feasor's* [read *fraudfeasor's*] very silence reasonably causes the misapprehension . . . ." *Estate of Jones v. Kvamme,* 430 N.W.2d 188, 193 (Minn. Ct. App. 1988). See **feasor.**

fraud in contemplation of law. See **fraud (C).**

fraudulent; fraudful. The latter is a NEEDLESS VARIANT.

fraudulent representation; fraudulent misrepresentation. Although the latter phrase cannot be called a REDUNDANCY—since not every misrepresentation is fraudulent—it is nevertheless inferior to the former phrase. Oliver Wendell Holmes, among others, used *fraudulent representation.* See *The Common Law* 255 (1881; repr. 1963).

fray. See **affray.**

freedom. See **liberty.**

freedom of contract, a fuzzy phrase often used in 19th-century and early 20th-century judicial opinions, embraced two connected but distinct ideas: "In the first place it indicated that contracts were based on mutual agreement, while in the second place it emphasized that the creation of a contract was the result of a free choice unhampered by external control such as government or legislative interference." P.S. Atiyah, *An Introduction to the Law of Contract* 5 (3d ed. 1981).

free from; free of. Both are correct, the former being preferred by most writers on style. Note the shift in nominal forms: *freedom of speech* but *freedom from oppression, pestilence, coercion,* etc.

free gift is a common REDUNDANCY.

freehold has been defined in two quite different ways. Most recently, the *CDL* has defined it as "the most complete form of ownership in land: a legal estate held in fee simple absolute in possession." The *OED* and other modern authorities more accurately define *freehold* as "a tenure by which an estate is held in fee simple, fee-tail, or for term of life." The *CDL*'s definition is unduly restrictive, for a life estate is held in freehold. See **fee, fee simple & fee tail.**

freeholder technically means "one who holds an estate in fee simple, an estate in fee tail, or a life estate." In fact, though, most uses of *freeholder* refer to an owner in fee simple absolute. Still, it is incorrect to define freeholder, as one book does, as "[o]ne who owns land that he or she can transfer without anyone's permission." John W. Reilly, *The Language of Real Estate* 206 (2d ed. 1982). See **freehold, fee simple & fee tail.**

free reign is an incorrect rendering of *free rein*—e.g.: "Considering Mrs. Waldman had *free reign* [read *free rein*] in spending $52,500, we affirm that part of the order allowing the set off for the suit money and costs she claims she is still due." *Waldman v. Waldman,* 612 So. 2d 703, 705 (Fla. Dist. Ct. App. 1993). Cf. **rein in.**

freight = (1) goods transported by water as well as by land (though until recently in BrE it referred only to goods shipped by water); or (2) in a contract for water carriage, the payment made by the sender of goods to the shipowner.

frequently. This adverb can be ambiguous when used with a plural subject and verb. Do individuals do something frequently, or is the characteristic true of a group that may do something only once? Note the MISCUE here: "A study last year by Jack Hadley of the Georgetown University School of Medicine showed that uninsured patients arrived at the hospital sicker than those with health insurance, and *died in the hospital more frequently* [read *more frequently died in the hospital*]." Jane Bryant Quinn, *Woe to the Reformers,* Newsweek, 19 Oct. 1992, at 55. If the phrase *more frequently* is moved after the conjunction *and,* the miscue disappears. See MISPLACED MODIFIERS.

fresh pursuit; hot pursuit. The former is the traditional legal phrase, dating from 1626 in the *OED* and denoting close and continuous chasing of a criminal suspect by police, often across jurisdictional boundaries. The phrase is often used, however, in extended senses: "There is no doubt that during continuance of war a rebel guilty of treason may be slain in actual conflict or *fresh pursuit.*" (Ir.)

Hot pursuit, first used in the 1920s, is an equivalent term that is better known among nonlawyers.

friend. Advocates with a sense of tradition and civility typically, during any argument before the bench, refer to an adversary as *my learned friend* or *my friend*—never *my opponent* or *my adversary.* Unfortunately, though, this custom is fading as fast as the Bar's other traditions of civility.

friendly suit; amicable action. These synonymous phrases refer to a lawsuit in which all the parties have agreed beforehand to allow a court to resolve the issues involved. *Friendly suit* is more common today. "It never was the thought that, by means of a *friendly suit,* a party beaten in the legislature could transfer to the courts an inquiry as to the constitutionality of the legislative act." *Chicago & Grand Trunk Ry. v. Wellman,* 143 U.S. 339, 345 (1892)./ "If full-fledged litigation were needed to get the right decision, the Justices would have to throw out of Court, as they do not, the many *'friendly suits,'* dressed up to resemble the genuine article, that are staged to get important problems decided less slowly." Fred Rodell, *Nine Men* 57 (1955).

friend of the court. See **amicus curiae.**

from hence; from thence. The words *hence* and *thence* (as well as *whence*) are sufficient without the preposition *from* and are therefore preferred singly; yet grammarians have not considered *from hence,* etc., incorrect. *Hence* includes the idea of "from," inasmuch as it means "from this time, from this place." Boswell, not best known for his achievements in law, used *from thence:* "Mr. Scott of University College, Oxford . . . accompanied [Johnson] *from thence* to Edinburgh." 5 *Life of Johnson* 16 (1791). See **thence & whence.**

from henceforth is redundant for *henceforth,* as in: "The will of the giver, according to the form in the deed of gift manifestly expressed, shall be *from henceforth observed* [read *observed henceforth*]."

from whence. See **from hence, thence & whence.**

frontal attack. This late 19th-century expression has become common in legal JARGON to denote a direct attack on a judgment, statute, etc. "This appeal makes the *frontal attack* that the court erred in not instructing a verdict in the bailor's favor for the total loss of the airplane."/ "Our statute does not make a *frontal attack* on the pre-existing law."

fructus industriales; fructus naturales. Lawyers might use terms such as *crops* and *perennials,* but instead they have used these LATINISMS. *Fructus industriales* are annual crops produced by labor (e.g., wheat, corn, potatoes, beets); *fructus naturales* are perennial plants (e.g., trees, grasses, perennial bushes). The latter are considered part of the real property, whereas the former usually are not.

fruit(s). Idiomatically speaking, one refers to the *fruits of one's labor* and *fruits of a crime,* but to the *fruit of the poisonous tree* (= in a criminal investigation, any tip or lead that results from an illegal search or seizure of evidence). E.g., "Because the illegally seized evidence provided the sole basis for the homicide arrest warrant and led directly to incriminating statements on that day, the warrant and statements are also inadmissible as *fruit of the poisonous tree.*" A leading criminal-law text credits Justice Felix Frankfurter with having coined the phrase in *Nardone v. U.S.,* 308 U.S. 338, 341 (1939). See Wayne R. LaFave & Jerold H. Israel, *Criminal Procedure* § 9.3, at 471 (1992).

Often, however, the idiom is paraphrased or foreshortened, and *fruit* is made plural: "The district court committed no error when it refused to suppress the *fruits* of the recorded conversations."/ "Because the amendment now affords protection against the uninvited ear, oral statements, if illegally overheard, and their *fruits* are also subject to suppression."

frustration = the doctrine that, if the entire performance of a contract becomes fundamentally changed without any fault on either side, the contract is considered dissolved. Theoretically—though rarely, it might be said, in pragmatic terms—frustration is imposed automatically by law and does not require either party to do anything. See **impossibility & mistake (B).**

FUDGE WORDS are common in mediocre and poor legal writing; they occur seldom in clean, precise prose. The typical phrases are *it would seem to appear that, it is suggested that,* and *it is submitted that.* E.g., "*It would appear to be clear that the Pioneer Society was* [read either *The Pioneer Society was* or *It is clear that the Pioneer Society was*] organized by a group of people who were brought together by their common interest in the history and historical relics of Los Angeles County and the State." Cf. WEASEL WORDS.

fugitive. Only in formal writing does this word mean, in its adjectival sense, "evanescent, fleeting." E.g., "It is no answer to say that complainant spends its money for that which is too *fugitive* or evanescent to be the subject of property."/ "It is further argued that that for which the Associated Press spends its money is too *fugitive* to be recognized as property." An even more learned equivalent is *fugacious.*

fulfil(l)ment is spelled *-ll-* in AmE, *-l-* in BrE.

full-blown is often unnecessary, as in the following example: "The collective knowledge of the investigating officers amounted to probable cause for a *full-blown* arrest of appellant." An officer can either arrest or not arrest someone: *full-blown* adds nothing.

The phrase is fast becoming a CLICHÉ in legal writing. E.g., "All final orders in *full-blown* commission licensing proceedings would be reviewed initially by the court of appeals."/ "The officers stopped short of a technical arrest or a *full-blown* search."

full-faith-and-credit clause. As a PHRASAL ADJECTIVE, *full-faith-and-credit* should be hyphenated.

full-fledged is the phrase, not *fully fledged.*

full force and effect. See **force and effect.**

full power is a common REDUNDANCY. E.g., "The corporation shall have *full power* to . . . ." The corporation would have just as much power if *full* were deleted.

full-scale, a PHRASAL ADJECTIVE, should be hyphenated—e.g.: "A *full scale* [read *full-scale*] criminal investigation was initiated in September 1970 and indictments against eight alleged coconspirators were returned in January 1971."

fully and finally. This DOUBLET is justified in some contexts, as in the phrase *fully and finally discharged: fully* refers to the extent of the discharge (as opposed to a partial discharge), and *finally* refers to the time of the discharge (the order is not an interlocutory one). On the other hand, to say that one is *discharged* probably implies that the discharge is both full and final.

fully fledged. See **full-fledged.**

fulsome (= abundant to excess; offensive to normal tastes or sensibilities) is often incorrectly taken to mean "very full." Here, for example, *fulsomely* is used for *fully:* "The expectation that one who enters the 'public, political arena' must be prepared to take a certain amount of 'political bumping' is already *fulsomely* [read *fully*] assured by the *New York Times Co. v. Sullivan* requirement of actual malice in the defamation of public figures." *Ollman v. Evans,* 750 F.2d 970, 1036 (D.C. Cir. 1984) (Scalia, J., dissenting) (citations omitted). Surely the writer of that sentence did not mean to impugn the U.S. Supreme Court.

functus officio is a LATINISM that literally means "having performed his or her office." In practice, the phrase denotes the idea that the specific duties and functions that an officer was legally empowered and charged to perform have now been wholly accomplished, and thus that the officer has no further authority or legal competence based on the original commission.

This term serves the purposes of conciseness but not of lucidity. E.g., "[A trustee's removal may be effected by] his becoming *functus officio,* that is, completing his duties as Trustee, by reason of the estate having been wound up or of some scheme of arrangement having been accepted by his creditors." 2 E.W. Chance, *Principles of Mercantile Law* 253 (P.W. French ed., 10th ed. 1951)./ "It is only when the tribunal is closed, when the jury that decided the case is *functus officio,* and there is no way of getting another one, that the judges are forced themselves to determine what a jury might think." Patrick Devlin, *The Judge* 142 (1979).

Pl. *functi officio.*

fundament = (1) basis; or (2) anus or buttocks. This word can hardly be used without creating a double-entendre. "That policy has remained the *fundament* [read *foundation*] of federal appellate jurisdiction."

fundamental law. See **constitutional law.**

fundamental term = a contractual provision that specifies an essential purpose of the contract, so that a breach of that provision through inadequate performance makes the performance not only defective but essentially different from what had been promised. For example, a caterer might have contracted to deliver crepes but instead delivered burritos. The doctrine supplying the innocent party with an excuse if the other party breaches a fundamental term has often been used—since the 1950s—to overcome an exemption clause protecting the culpable party from liability. See **term.**

funds, when used as a COUNT NOUN, can confuse readers who usually encounter the plural form *funds* as an aggregate <the funds were [= money was] promptly deposited>. The following usage is odd enough to be considered unidiomatic: "*Hundreds of funds* are held for the benefit of students enrolled at the university. *Each of these funds,* which includes funds for endowments, scholarships, and student loans, has a designated fund manager." *Report Accompanies Indictments,* Amarillo Globe-Times, 11 Dec. 1991, at 8C.

funeral; funereal; funerary; funebrial. *Funeral,* commonly a noun, serves as its own adjective <funeral expenses>. *Funereal,* which is frequently confused with *funeral,* adj., means "solemn, mournful, somber." *Funerary* = of, used for, or connected with burial. *Funebrial* is a NEEDLESS VARIANT of *funereal.* Of *funerary* and *funebrial,* Fowler wrote that "no one uses [them] if he can help it" (*MEU1* 205).

fungible (= regarded as exchangeable with other property of the same kind) is most commonly an adjective <fungible goods>—as just defined—but it may also serve as a noun <a fungible is any property regarded as exchangeable with other property of the same kind>.

funnily. See ADVERBS, PROBLEMS WITH (B).

furnish is a useful word in the drafting of contracts because its alternatives—*deliver, give, assign, transmit,* and the like—are often too specific about the means of supplying a thing. *Furnish* can be usefully vague.

further. See **farther.**

further affiant . . . . American lawyers frequently end affidavits with some variation of this sentence: "Further affiant [= the person giving the affidavit] sayeth not." This sentence gives rise to three stylistic dilemmas: first, is it *sayeth* or *saith;* second, is it *not* or *naught;* and third, is the sentence necessary at all?

A. *Sayeth* or *saith.* It is surprising how often American lawyers stop to puzzle over this choice in spelling. (English lawyers use neither spelling because they do not use the phrase.) Both forms are good Elizabethan usage. Among American lawyers who use the phrase, *sayeth* predominates; among American lawyers who rightly pride themselves on their style, the phrase does not appear at all. See -ETH.

B. *Not* or *naught.* The predominant form is *Further affiant sayeth not.* But this is nonsense, because it is literally translatable as, "The affiant says not further," or "The affiant does not say further." Does not say what? The form with *naught,* by contrast, makes literal sense: "The affiant says nothing further." E.g., "Further your affiant sayeth *naught.*" *State v. Malkin,* 722 P.2d 943, 944 n.3 (Alaska 1986) (quoting an affidavit).

The best choice, stylistically speaking, is to use these phrases not. See **naught.**

FUSED PARTICIPLES. A. The General Rule. Fowler gave the name "fused participle" to a participle used as a noun (i.e., a gerund) that is preceded by a noun or pronoun not in the possessive case. Thus *Me going home made her sad* rather than the preferred *My going home made her sad.* The fused participle is said to lack a proper grammatical relationship to the preceding noun or pronoun. No one today doubts that Fowler overstated his case in calling fused participles "grammatically indefensible" and in never admitting an exception. The grammarians Jespersen and Curme have cited any number of historical examples and have illustrated the absolute necessity of the fused participle in some sentences, barring some recasting of the sentence. E.g., *The chance of that ever happening is slight.* (One would not want to write, *The chance of that's ever happening is slight.*)

But Fowler had a stylistic if not a grammatical point. Especially in formal prose, the possessive ought to be used whenever it is not unidiomatic or unnatural. In the following sentences, then, possessives would have been better used than the nouns in the objective case:

- "Abolition of the distinction would result in *manufacturers being* [read *manufacturers' being*] liable for damages of unknown and unlimited scope."
- "In the second place, the danger of the *courts reaching* [read *courts' reaching*] an inequitable conclusion by refusing to modify the results of applying the legal incidents of joint tenancy to the partnership relation is done away with."
- "This is a divorce case in which the only remaining question concerns the propriety of the *trial court granting* [read *trial court's granting*] the wife a fractional interest in future military retirement benefits if and when received by the husband."
- "He told the jury that the really important issue was whether the plaintiff had consented to the *journalist publishing* [read *journalist's publishing*] the information about her and her former husband."
- "The plaintiffs are the freeholders of the locus in quo, and as such they have the right to forbid *anybody coming* [read *anybody's coming*] on

their land or in any way interfering with it."

- "Arrest in retaliation to civil proceedings is privileged only by *one having* [read *one's having*] a warrant."
- "The extensive civil-service structure Congress had constructed militated against the *court extending* [read *court's extending*] constitutional tort liability to federal employees."
- "A question arose as to *appellant being* [read *appellant's being*] entitled to a longer notice of discontinuance." (Eng.)
- "The district court accepted the prosecutor's representation that it did not believe the additional charge would result in *Krezdorn receiving* [read *Krezdorn's receiving*] a sentence greater than the one initially imposed."
- "When an uncopyrighted combination of words is published, there is no general right to forbid other *people repeating* [read *people's repeating*] them." (Eng.)
- "There is a difference in probability between *one* [read *one's*] intentionally depositing and unintentionally forgetting and the hole-in-the-pocket man."
- "The problem of *lawyers saying* [read *lawyers' saying*] too much is discussed in Chapter XIV."
- "In consideration of *appellant having* [read *appellant's having*] prevented him from sustaining death, McGowin agreed with him to care for and maintain him."
- "It is elementary that the propriety of a *court instructing* [read *court's instructing*] a verdict in favor of a party must depend on the evidence introduced before the jury."
- "The jury could find that through constant wear the terrazzo slab had over a period of time become smooth, resulting in *it being* [read *its being*] very slippery when wet."

There are many exceptions to this rule of style, however. The *Oxford Guide* states: "When using most non-personal nouns (e.g. *luggage, meaning, permission*), groups of nouns (e.g. *father and mother, surface area*), non-personal pronouns (e.g. *anything, something*), and groups of pronouns (e.g. *some of them*), there is no choice of construction: the possessive would not sound idiomatic at all." *Oxford Guide* 156 (1983). Examples follow:

- "An attempt to create a passive trust in this country usually results in the legal *title passing* to the trust beneficiary."
- "The judgment does not result in the *property being* attached to the locus."
- "Upon the proper *facts being shown,* the attachment may be sued out against lands, tenements, goods, and credits of the debtor."
- "There can therefore be no question about the claim here *being ripe* for presentation to the United States Courts."
- "The remainder is subject to being divested on the contingency of *one of the children of Ross Kost dying* before the life tenant and leaving lawful children."
- "In 1908 Roscoe Pound decried decision-making from first principles and warned against the *law becoming* too scientific."
- "The ability to watch a *decision being* made on the most elemental level is of some significance."
- "The undisputed evidence precludes the possibility of *speed being* a proximate cause of this collision."

B. Unnecessary Participles. Even when there is no choice in the idiom, there is the choice of reconstructing the sentence to avoid the questionable usage. Sometimes it is even possible merely to omit the participle, as here: "Often such an accident results from something *being* [delete *being*] in the road ahead of the preceding car."

C. No Fused Participle. Adjectival participles sometimes appear on first sight to be fused participles, but they are not. E.g., "A donee beneficiary's rights vest automatically upon the working of the contract, *knowledge* of the beneficiary *being* unnecessary."/ "This appeal arises from an *order* of the Santa Fe County District Court *granting* the motion of defendant State of New Mexico to dismiss on the ground that the action was barred by the doctrine of sovereign immunity."

FUSTIAN (lit. a kind of cotton cloth) has given its name to pompous, empty speech and writing, or highfalutin words for ordinary ideas. The following sentence, for example, might be placed in virtually any judicial opinion on any subject: "The case presents questions of far-reaching importance which demand and have received mature and deliberate consideration by the court." We should take all that for granted. See FLOTSAM PHRASES.

futilely, adv., is sometimes misspelled *futiley*—e.g.: "The school *futiley* [read *futilely*] offered him assistance to prepare for the Boards, but he rejected any such help." *DeMarco v. University of Health Sciences,* 352 N.E.2d 356, 368 (Ill. App. Ct. 1976) (Burman, J., dissenting).

future interest is a phrase that dates from the mid-19th century. See 1 Charles Fearne, *Contingent Remainders* 381 (10th ed. 1844). The phrase denotes an interest in property in which the privilege of possession or of enjoyment is future and not present. A noted treatise states that "the interest is an existing interest from the time of its creation, and is looked upon as a part of the total ownership of the land or other thing [that] is its subject matter. In that sense, *future interest* is somewhat misleading, and it is applied only to indicate that the possession or enjoyment of the subject matter is to take place in the future." Lewis M. Simes & Allan F. Smith, *The Law of Future Interests* § 1, at 2–3 (2d ed. 1956).

The future interests commonly recognized are the reversion, the possibility of reverter, the power of termination (known also as the right of entry for condition broken), and the remainder. Some have suggested that this list might be supplemented with the rights of escheat, inchoate dower, and curtesy initiate, but "these interests . . . are not commonly classified as future interests." Cornelius J. Moynihan, *Introduction to the Law of Real Property* 103–04 (2d ed. 1988). See **remainder, reversion & right of entry for condition broken.**

future, in (the). See **in future.**

G

GAAP. See **generally accepted accounting principles.**

gainsay; contradict. Originally *gainsay* was the popular word, and *contradict* the learned one; today just the opposite is true. *Gainsay* may now appropriately be labeled a FORMAL WORD. E.g., "Judge Cire was in the unique position of being able to judge the credibility of what he saw and heard firsthand, and he should not be *gainsaid* [i.e., contradicted]."/ "The eminent position of the familial right to privacy in our jurisprudence cannot now be *gainsaid* [i.e., denied]."

Gaius, as a classical name, makes the possessive form *Gaius',* not *Gaius's:* "It consists of excerpts from the Theodosian Code and from *Paulus's* [read *Paulus'*] *Sentences,* of post-Theodosian *Novellae,* of an abridgment of *Gaius's* [read *Gaius'*] *Institutes* . . . ." Hans J. Wolff, *Roman Law* 175 (1951; repr. 1982). See POSSESSIVES (A).

GALLICISMS appear frequently in English prose, and no less frequently in legal than in nonlegal writing. By Gallicisms is not generally meant the LAW FRENCH terminology that is so prevalent in law (e.g., *voir dire, de son tort*), but French terms and phrases of a nonlegal character, such as *coup de grace, coup d'état, tour de force, succès d'estime, cul-de-sac, blasé, tête-à-tête,* and *joie de vivre.* None of these is unduly recherché, to use yet another. But foreignisms of any kind become affectations when used in place of a perfectly good English term, e.g., *peu à peu* for *little by little,* or *en passant* for *in passing,* or *sans* for *without.*

One stylist of high repute cautions sternly against all but thoroughly anglicized Gallicisms: "Of *Gallicisms* . . . it is perhaps not necessary to say much: they are universally recognized as a sign of bad taste, especially if they presuppose the knowledge of a foreign language. A few foreign words, such as *cliché,* have no English equivalent and are in current use; and there may be others [that] are desirable. But except in technical works it will generally be found possible to avoid them." Herbert Read, *English Prose Style* 10 (1952). Cf. LATINISMS.

gaming; gambling. The former is the law's EUPHEMISM for the latter. "[S]tate officialdom, when hoping to sound professional and clinical, uses the term *gaming* as having an ameliorative sense. By contrast, . . . *gambling* has a pejorative connotation." Thomas L. Clark, *Gaming and/or Gambling: You Pays Your Money,* 10 Verbatim 20 (Spring 1984). In traditional legal idiom, a wager or a bet is known as a *gaming contract.* And in the U.K., the Gaming Act 1968 set up the Gaming Board, which regulates gaming.

ganancial (= of, relating to, or consisting of community property) originated as a Spanish-law term, from the Spanish *ganancias* (= earnings, winnings); the Spanish equivalent of *community property* is *gananciales.* The only form of the word to have entered English is the adjective *ganancial,* which unfortunately is omitted from the *OED, RH2, W3,* and most other general English-language dictionaries. E.g., "The husband has the active control and administration of the *ganancial* property during the matrimony." *Stramler v. Coe,* 15 Tex. 211, 215 (1855)./ "Because the legal concept of the community property or *ganancial* system is so foreign to that of the common law, it is frequently very difficult for the judge or lawyer, trained or versed in the common law, to grasp and understand its principles." 1 William Q. deFuniak, *Principles of Community Property* § 3, at 7–8 (1943)./ "The community or *'ganancial'* system was introduced by the Visigothic invaders of the Roman Empire in the early part of the fifth century into what is now Spain and portions of

France . . . ." *Willcox v. Penn. Mut. Life Ins. Co.,* 55 A.2d 521, 524 (Pa. 1947). See **community property.**

gantlet; gauntlet. Although the latter is more common in most senses, the former is still preferred in one of them. One runs the *gantlet* (= a kind of ordeal or punishment) but throws down the *gauntlet* (= a glove). The trend, however, is to use *gauntlet* for *gantlet.* Like many trends, it is worth resisting—e.g.: "Even if he is initially successful in convincing his client and executing a thoroughly professional draft, it will still have to run the *gauntlet* [read *gantlet*] of many minds." Reed Dickerson, *The Fundamentals of Legal Drafting* § 4.15, at 77 (2d ed. 1986)./ "[T]he Code did not require the taxpayers to run the administrative *gantlet* in 1985 to obtain a judicial determination of the 1985 value." *Estepp v. Miller,* 731 S.W.2d 677, 682 (Tex. App.—Austin 1987) (Shannon, C.J., concurring).

Gauntlet is correctly used in the following sentences: "In substance, the plaintiffs argue, the Department should have ignored the federal administrator's warnings, thrown down the *gauntlet,* litigated the matter and taken its chances on losing federal funds." *Hightower v. Duffy,* 548 N.E.2d 495, 505 (Ill. App. Ct. 1989)./ "At some point, we must throw down the *gauntlet* against the evil of racism." Anthony E. Cook, *The Death of God in American Pragmatism and Realism,* 82 Geo. L.J. 1431, 1504 (1994).

gaol; gaoler. These are variant BrE spellings of *jail* and *jailer.* The terms are pronounced the same regardless of spelling. See **jail delivery.**

garden-variety, adj., (= of the ordinary or familiar kind) is becoming a garden-variety CLICHÉ in legal prose. E.g., "Because *Eichelberger* was nothing more, nor less, than a *garden-variety* divorce case, one would normally have thought that the litigation had ended when the court of civil appeals overruled Mr. Eichelberger's motion for rehearing."

garnish; garnishee, v.t. In AmE, the usual verb form is *garnish* (= to take property, usu. a portion of someone's salary, by legal authority). *Garnishee* is usually reserved for the nominal sense ("a person or institution, such as a bank, that is indebted to or is bailee for another whose property has been subjected to garnishment"). The noun corresponding to *garnish* is *garnishment.*

In BrE, however, and in a few American jurisdictions, *garnishee* as well as *garnish* is used as a verb: "As it was composed entirely of money that did not belong to Smith, it could not be *garnisheed* by his creditor and this was sufficient to dispose of the case." (Eng.)

The *OED* gives passing notice to *garnishee* as a verb and its corresponding noun *garnisheement;* the main entries are under *garnish* and *garnishment.*

garnishable (= subject to garnishment), a 20th-century NEOLOGISM omitted from most general English-language dictionaries, is a useful term—e.g.: "[T]he Court of Appeals added a qualification to whether a check is a *garnishable* asset . . . ." *Water Processing Co. v. Southern Golf Builders, Inc.,* 285 S.E.2d 21, 22 (Ga. 1981).

garnisher; garnishor. *Garnisher* is preferred; it is the only spelling listed in *W3* and the prevalent spelling in legal texts.

garnishment. See **sequestration.**

garnishment order (AmE) = *garnishee order* (BrE).

gases, not *gasses,* is the plural form of the noun *gas;* nevertheless, for the verb *to gas, gassed* is the accepted past tense and *gasses* is the third-person singular form. Cf. **bus.**

gauntlet. See **gantlet.**

gavel. Though everyone knows what a judge's gavel is, few seem to know the name of the piece of wood that is struck by a gavel. The term is *sound block.*

gazump (BrE) = (1) *v.i.,* to act improperly in the sale of houses, as by raising the price after accepting an offer; (2) *v.t.,* (of a seller) to treat a buyer of a house unfairly by raising the price after accepting the buyer's offer; or (3) *v.t.,* (of a competing house buyer) to place a higher bid for a house than the one that the seller has already accepted, thereby encouraging the seller to back out of a contract. This early 20th-century BrE NEOLOGISM, labeled "slang" in the *OED* and in the *COD,* is a word of unknown origin.

The past tense is *gazumped,* not *gazumpted*—e.g.: (sense 3) "During the go-go Thatcher years, it was not uncommon for apartments under contracts 'duly signed by both party's [*sic*] solicitors' to be *'gazumpted'* [read *'gazumped'*] by a higher bidder the day before closing." Paul Schneider, *A Flat in London,* Esquire, Dec. 1991, at 72.

g.b.h.; G.B.H.; GBH. Some English criminal-law writers use this initialism for *grievous bodily harm*—e.g.: "[C]ausing grievous bodily harm with intent is an alternative. The abbreviation *'g.b.h.'* is frequently used in conversation, though not in court." Glanville Williams, *Textbook of Criminal Law* 151–52 (1978)./ "[T]he House of Lords has now decided that there can be an 'infliction' of *GBH* without proof of an assault." Andrew Ashworth, *Principles of Criminal Law* 279 (1991). Though such an initialism may speed communication among specialists, nonspecialists are likely to consider it obscure and off-putting. If it must be used, the best form, for the sake of readability, is *g.b.h.* See ACRONYMS AND INITIALISMS.

gender has long been used as a grammatical distinction of a word according to the sex referred to. It has newly been established in the language of the law in phrases such as *gender-based discrimination,* a use disapproved as jargonistic by some authorities. What this adds to *sex discrimination,* aside from eight letters and one hyphen, one can only guess.

Here, the better usage is illustrated: "In the court's view, the ordinance creates a conflict between first-amendment free speech guaranties and the fourteenth-amendment right to be free from *sex-based* discrimination." See **sex.**

gendered is a NEOLOGISM meaning "biased in favor of one sex." Built on the trendy use of *gender* (q.v.), this adjective dates from the early 1970s. E.g., "Yet the *gendered* structure of wage labor is not being challenged." Joan C. Williams, *Deconstructing Gender,* 87 Mich. L. Rev. 797, 801 (1989)./ "This Article and its analysis is 'feminist' in the sense that it seeks to uncover and examine the *gendered* nature of discourse—in this case, an opera by Giacomo Puccini." J.M. Balkin, *Turandot's Victory,* 2 Yale J. Law & Humanities 299, 300 n.1 (1990). See NOUNS AS VERBS.

general common law, federal. See **federal common law.**

general consensus. See **consensus.**

general court, in some New England states, refers to the legislature, which historically convened itself as the highest judicial tribunal: "In 1639, Massachusetts Bay had a full system of courts, organized in a way that would not strike a modern lawyer as unduly exotic. The *general court,* acting both as legislature and as the highest court, stood at the crown of the system. As a court, it confined itself mostly to appeals, though its exact jurisdiction was a bit vague." Lawrence M. Friedman, *A History of American Law* 39–40 (2d ed. 1985). See **judicial court.**

general damages; special damages. *General damages* are "those elements of loss or damage [that] need not be claimed or mentioned in the complaint in order to be the subject of proof and recovery at the trial"; and *special damages* are "those which must be specifically claimed and described if recovery for them is to be allowed." Charles T. McCormick, *Handbook of the Law of Damages* § 8, at 32–33 (1935). Another way of expressing the distinction is this: *general damages* are those that the law presumes follow from the type of wrong complained of; *special damages* are those that are alleged to have been sustained in the particular circumstances of the particular wrong, and they must be specifically claimed and proved to have been sustained. The terms, when "used in relation to the problem of pleading, relate to the question, Could the adversary foresee, at the time he reads the complaint, a claim of harm asserted at the trial?" *Id.* n.3. See **damages.**

general denial. See **demurrer.**

general intent, in criminal law, is problematic: "Most courts use the term without explanation as though everyone understood it. When an explanation is offered, it is frequently in terms that one suspects the court does not really mean or at least is not willing to generalize across offenses." Peter W. Low et al., *Criminal Law: Cases and Materials* 231–32 (1982). The phrase *general intent* has two senses: (1) negligence involving blameworthy inadvertence; and (2) recklessness involving actual awareness of a risk and the culpable taking of that risk. See **intent(ion).**

general intention. See **intent(ion)** (F).

general issue; special issue. At common law, a *general issue* arose in litigation—still arises in some jurisdictions—upon the defendant's filing a general denial, which questioned the truth of every material allegation in the plaintiff's pleading. In a suit based on a contract under seal, the general issue was *non est factum* (q.v.); in detinue it was *non detinet* ("he does not detain"); in trespass it was "not guilty."

A *special issue,* by contrast, arose from pleading by specific as opposed to general allegations. For the most part, *special issues*—long the delight of acutely technical lawyers—have fallen into disuse.

A *general issue* results in *general verdict*—e.g.: "In most federal cases, the traditional *general verdict* is used, by which the jury merely finds for one or the other of the parties." Charles A. Wright, *The Law of Federal Courts* 630 (4th ed. 1983). See **special verdict.**

generalized (= made general) sometimes wrongly displaces *general.* E.g., "Some courts, refusing to find in the rather *generalized* [read *general*] language of the usual statute a legislative intent to abolish the concept of marital unity, have sought to adapt the incidents of ownership by the entirety to the principle that neither spouse has rights or powers superior to those of the other." The sentence does not intend to convey that the language was *made general* (by the legislature, presumably), but that it *is general.* Cf. **particularized.**

general jurisprudence. See **jurisprudence (D).**

general legacy. See **legacy.**

generally has three basic meanings: (1) "disregarding insignificant exceptions" <the level of advocacy in this court is generally very high>; (2) "in many ways" <he was the most generally qualified applicant>; (3) "usually; most of the time" <he generally left the office at five o'clock>. Sense (3) is least good in formal writing, although at times it merges with sense (1).

generally accepted accounting principles; generally accepted accountancy principles. The former is the usual phrase in AmE, the latter in BrE. *Accountancy* is, however, used in the U.S. in other phrases and contexts.

The phrases are often abbreviated *GAAP* */gap/*—e.g.: "The court gave great deference to generally accepted accounting principles—GAAP—that would have guided the parties at the time of the acquisition." Stewart M. Landefeld, *A Guide for the Fraudulent Transfer Law Maze,* Nat'l L.J., 6 Nov. 1989, at 57. Because *GAAP* is an acronym, it should not have periods after each letter. See ACRONYMS AND INITIALISMS.

general pleading. See **code pleading.**

general property; special property. Some legal theorists refer to ownership as *general property* and rightful possession as *special property.* See **possession (B)** & **property (A).**

general verdict; general interrogatory; general issue. See **special verdict** & **general issue.**

generative; generational. The distinction is clear: *generative* = procreative; *generational* = pertaining to generations. "The degree of kinship between a decedent and a claimant was reckoned by taking the number of *generative* [read *generational*] steps between them or by adding the numbers of such steps between both of them and their nearest common ancestor."

generic. See **genus (A).**

generic(al)ness; genericism. Although it is odd-looking, *genericness* is now the most widely used noun corresponding to *generic,* adj. It is recorded from 1939 in the *OED* and appears most commonly in reference to trademarks. E.g., "As I view the cases, a defendant alleging invalidity of a trademark for *genericness* must show that to the consuming public as a whole the word has lost all its trademark significance." *Marks v. Polaroid Corp.,* 129 F. Supp. 243, 270 (D. Mass. 1955)./ "Rovira's affirmative defense of *genericness* was not barred by the federal rules." *Keebler Co. v. Rovira Biscuit Corp.,* 624 F.2d 366, 374 n.7 (1st Cir. 1980)./ "Indeed, BVA's own witnesses and exhibits effectively demonstrated the *genericness* of 'blinded veterans,' for they employed the term repeatedly to denote formerly sighted former warriors." *Blinded Veterans Ass'n v. Blinded Am. Veterans Found.,* 872 F.2d 1035, 1041 (D.C. Cir. 1989). Despite its specialized currency, *genericness* retains an un-English appearance. Cf. **prolificness.**

Genericalness is listed in the *OED* and *W2;* it does not, like *genericness,* flout principles of English word formation and might be preferred on that ground. It is omitted from *W3,* which labels the adj. *generical* archaic.

Genericism has also appeared—e.g.: "There remain two defenses that licensees might make: descriptiveness and *genericism.*" James M. Treece, *Licensee Estoppel in Trademark Cases,* 58 Trademark Rep. 728, 738 (1968). Labeled rare in the *OED, genericism* is perhaps the most realistic alternative to oust *genericness.*

genericide, a late-20th-century NEOLOGISM in the law of trademarks, means "the loss of a trademark that no longer distinguishes one owner's goods from others' goods." It makes little literal sense, as *-cide* (lit. "killer, slayer" or "killing, slaying") is made to refer merely to the death of a trademark—not its killing. One court calls the term a MALAPROPISM, stating: "It refers to the death of the trademark, not to the death of the generic name for the product. A more accurate term might be *trademarkicide,* or perhaps even *generization,* either of which seems to better capture the idea that the trademark dies by becoming a generic name." *Plasticolor Molded Prods. v. Ford Motor Co.,* 713 F. Supp. 1329, 1344 n.22 (C.D. Cal. 1989). Nevertheless, the word *genericide* is "firmly ensconced in the literature." *Id.*

E.g., Jacqueline Stern, *Genericide: Cancellation of a Registered Trademark,* 51 Fordham L. Rev. 666 (1983)./ "In the usual *'genericide'* case a venerable mark has come under attack because, over the course of years, consumers have come to regard it as a name for the genus of a product rather than as a brand name of a particular product from a single source." *G. Heileman Brewing Co. v. Anheuser-Busch, Inc.,* 676 F. Supp. 1436, 1488 (E.D. Wis. 1987).

GENITIVES. See POSSESSIVES (G).

genius (= the prevailing character or spirit; characteristic method or procedure) is often used in reference to law. E.g., "A federal cause of action 'brought at any distance of time' would be 'utterly repugnant to the *genius* of our laws.'" *Wilson v. Garcia,* 471 U.S. 261, 271 (1985) (quoting *Adams v. Woods,* 6 U.S. (2 Cranch) 336, 342 (1805)).

The plural *geniuses* is preferred over *genii* except in the sense of demons or spirits. See PLURALS (A).

gentleman should not be used indiscriminately as a genteelism for *man,* the generic term. *Gentleman* should be reserved for reference to a cultured, refined man. It is a sign of the times that "[n]o word could be, it seems, more thoroughly out of style than *gentleman.*" John Mortimer, *Wooster Sauce,* Sunday Times, 29 Sept. 1991, at 7-6 (reviewing Hugh David, *Heroes, Mavericks and Bounders* (1991)).

In BrE, the word formerly referred to a man of independent means and not working gainfully.

gentlemen's agreement; gentleman's agreement. The former is better, since at least two must agree. One writer defines the phrase as an agreement that "is not an agreement, made between two persons, neither of whom is a gentleman, whereby each expects the other to be strictly bound without himself being bound at all." R.E. Megarry, *A Second Miscellany-at-Law* 326 (1973). A *gentlemen's agreement* differs from a contract because it is unenforceable.

The phrase runs afoul of the drive to eliminate SEXISM but is nevertheless widely used. Several alternative phrases are offered in Rosalie Maggio's *Bias-Free Word Finder* (1992)—among them *honorable agreement, informal agreement,* and *your word.* But these phrases are patently inadequate. The upshot is that the phrase *gentlemen's agreement* will probably stump many writers who want to be nonsexist.

gentlepersons; gentlepeople. These are occasionally used as neutral terms in salutations, but they have never lost their look of jocularity. *The Second Barnhart Dictionary of New English* (1980) says of *gentleperson,* "often used humorously or ironically." The lawyers who write "Dear Gentlepeople" (they do exist) apparently do so with a straight face, but their readers probably cannot keep one. Better choices are available for salutations: *Ladies and Gentlemen,* for example, or *Dear Counsel* (if all the recipients are lawyers).

genus. A. And *species*. Analytical jurists borrowed these terms from logic and biology. A *genus* is a major class or kind of things, which includes several subclasses usually called *species.* The corresponding adjectives are *generic* and *specific.* Thus, trademark is a species within the genus of intellectual property; murder is a species of the genus of crime, i.e., it is a particular crime.

B. Plural. The only plural form included in *W10* is *genera,* but both the *OED* and *RH2* include the variant *genuses,* which has appeared repeatedly in legal writing—e.g.: "There are other contentions, or, at least, other species of the above *genuses.*" *In re Missouri Pac. R. Co.,* 13 F. Supp. 888, 891 (E.D. Mo. 1935)./ "Scholars sought to classify and categorize legal doctrines and cases much as biologists would *genuses* and species . . . ." Peter R. Teachout, Book Review, 67 Va. L. Rev. 815, 825 (1981)./ "Rather, 'tasty' is 'merely descriptive' and describes a quality found in many *genuses* [read, perhaps, *types*] of salad dressing." *Henri's Food Prods. Co. v. Tasty Snacks, Inc.,* 817 F.2d 1303, 1306 (7th Cir. 1987). Though purists decry this form, it is undeniably more comprehensible to more people. See PLURALS (A).

gerrymander, an early-19th-century satirical PORTMANTEAU WORD, combines the name of Elbridge Gerry (the governor of Massachusetts) with the ending of *salamander.* When Gerry's party redistricted Massachusetts in 1812 to favor the antifederalists, Essex County was divided in a way that made one voting district look something like a salamander. Hence *gerrymandering* came to refer to the practice of arranging electoral divisions in a way that gives one political party an unfair advantage.

Though the original sense is still the primary one, this word has had its meaning extended. Some legal writers, for example, refer to *jurisdictional gerrymandering,* in which *jurisdiction* may carry either a geographical sense (as in *E.E.O.C. v. Int'l Union of Operating Eng'rs,* 553 F.2d 251, 254 (2d Cir. 1977)) or a sense conveying the idea of legal power (as in Laurence H. Tribe, *Jurisdictional Gerrymandering: Zoning Disfavored Rights*

Out of the Federal Courts, 16 Harv. Civ. Rights & Civ. Liberties Rev. 129 (1981)).

Those extensions in meaning seem reasonable, but the word has also been subjected to what could only be described as SLIPSHOD EXTENSION: "In the last few years, the 30-second 'attack ad' and the 10-second television news 'sound bite' have become such prominent . . . features of political campaigns that members of Congress have introduced more than two dozen bills in an attempt to *gerrymander* them out of existence." Randall Rothenberg, *Politics on TV: Too Fast, Too Loose?* N.Y. Times, 15 July 1990, at E1. How the metaphor of gerrymandering fits that sentence is anyone's guess.

GERUNDS. The legal writer's prejudice against nouns ending in *-ing* is unfounded. When it comes to CUTTING OUT THE CHAFF, one effective way of reducing prolixity is to use gerunds directly; thus *adjudicating that case was difficult* rather than *the adjudication of that case was difficult; presenting the arguments* rather than *the presentation of the arguments,* etc. See BURIED VERBS, FUSED PARTICIPLES (A) & DANGLERS (C).

Gestalt (= a shape, configuration, or structure that, as an object of perception, forms a specific whole or unity incapable of expression simply in terms of its parts), a VOGUE WORD, is usually capitalized and italicized. Why? Because it is still treated as a German noun (hence italics), and in German all nouns are capitalized. E.g., "Virtually all fact-finding was subjectively based, depending ultimately on intuition and emotion, 'hunching' in *Gestalt*-like response to the situation."

get > got > gotten, got. The past participle *gotten* predominates in AmE, *got* in BrE.

get is good English. Yet many lawyers want to avoid it because they consider it too informal; they prefer *obtain* or *procure,* two FORMAL WORDS. The same tendency is at work here that leads lawyers to shun *before* in favor of *prior to* or *antecedent to, later* in favor of *subsequent to,* and the like. Yet confident, relaxed legal writers use the word *get* quite naturally—e.g.: "It was until recently a civil offense, called 'alienation of affections,' for which either spouse could *get* damages." Max Radin, *The Law and You* 54 (1948)./ "And if he goes there and *gets* divorced there is no reason why the divorce should not be valid." *Id.* at 65. (On other stylistic points in the second sentence quoted, see **and (A)** & **reason why.**) See COLLOQUIALITY.

gibe; jibe. *Gibe* is both noun and verb. As a noun, it means "a caustic remark or taunt." E.g., "The *gibes* hurled at Chancery . . . had led to a determination on the part of some Chancellors that their decisions would be impeccable and would be rooted firmly in precedent." L.B. Curzon, *English Legal History* 129 (2d ed. 1979).

Jibe is generally considered a verb only, meaning "to make things fit, uniform, or consistent." E.g., "These laws *jibe* well enough with his notions of right and wrong; the trouble is they do not *jibe* with his capacity to act on his own professed convictions." Lon L. Fuller, *Anatomy of the Law* 41 (1968). But Fuller, who was fond of the word, used it also as a noun meaning "agreement; consistency"—e.g.: "What we have here is a lack of *jibe* between words and actions at a level below that of the courts." *Id.* at 24.

gift, it may be surprising to learn, has acted as a verb since the 16th century. E.g., "All the property was *gifted* property [i.e., it took the form of gifts]." Though this usage is old, it is not now standard. English has the uncanny ability, however, to transform nouns into verbs, and to revive moribund usages. Twenty years ago *contact* was objected to as a verb, though it had been used that way since the early 19th century; few writers now feel uncomfortable using the word as a verb. See NOUNS AS VERBS.

Gift may soon be in the same class—still, cautious writers may prefer to use it only as a noun if the verb causes discomfort, as it well may: "The stock may not be *gifted,* pledged, or hypothecated without the board's approval." One is accustomed to thinking of *gifted children,* but not of *gifted stock.*

gift over. See **over (A).**

gin up (= [1] to rev up (as an engine); or [2] to concoct) is a late-19th-century AmE NEOLOGISM that is barely mentioned in the *OED* and appears to have been missed by most American lexicographers (being omitted from *W10, RH2, W3, AHD,* and the like). The PHRASAL VERB is a common one in discussions of law—e.g.: "The Government has taken tax charges, *ginned* them *up* into mail-fraud charges, *ginned* that *up* into a RICO case, and obtained an indictment of an ongoing business of this size." Oral argument in *U.S. v. Regan,* 2d Cir., Docket #88-1344, 17 Aug. 1988./ "So they *ginned up* a 'law and order' message suggesting that Democrats were soft on crime . . . ." David S. Broder, *Mudball Politics,* Wash. Post, 4 Nov. 1990, at C7./ "This is a law enacted by Congress. This is not something we just *ginned up* out of whole cloth." Carl Ingram, *Debt-Reduction Bill*

Could Cost Community Colleges, L.A. Times, 21 Dec. 1990, at A3 (quoting Bill Moran of the U.S. Department of Education).

gipsy. See **gypsy.**

girl. This word is widely (and understandably) regarded as an affront when used in reference to an adult, just as *boy* would be. But for a female minor, *girl* is the appropriate word; for an odd avoidance of the word in its proper context, see **minor woman.**

gist /*jist*/ began as a legal term meaning "the real ground or point (of an action, indictment, etc.)" (*OED*) and has since passed into nonlegal parlance. Yet it is still (perhaps unwittingly) used in the legal sense: "The *gist* of the libel is that certain articles called lubricators are not good articles." See POPULARIZED LEGAL TECHNICALITIES. Cf. **gravamen.**

give, devise, and bequeath. The leading American scholars on the law of wills and trusts should resolve any doubt: "In drafting wills, 'I give' is an excellent substitute for 'I devise,' 'I bequeath,' and 'I give, devise, and bequeath.' 'I give' will effectively transfer any kind of property, and no fly-specking lawyer can ever fault you for using the wrong verb." Jesse Dukeminier, Jr. & Stanley M. Johanson, *Family Wealth Transactions* 11 (1972). They are not alone: "'I give' is better than 'I give, devise, and bequeath.'" Thomas L. Shaffer, *The Planning and Drafting of Wills and Trusts* 170 (2d ed. 1979). See **bequeath, devise** & DOUBLETS, TRIPLETS, AND SYNONYM-STRINGS.

give evidence is more vague and more verbose than *testify.* E.g., "The defendant *gave evidence* [read *testified*] that he was elsewhere at the time of the alleged sale and did not make it." *Dunn v. U.S.,* 284 U.S. 390, 392 (1932)./ "She looked strained and ill, but *gave her evidence* [read *testified* or, perhaps, *gave her testimony*] in a quiet, subdued fashion that was most impressive." Stanley Jackson, *The Life and Cases of Mr. Justice Humphreys* 200 (n.d. [1951]).

Even if people generally understood *give evidence* as an equivalent of *testify,* the phrase would still be plagued with an AMBIGUITY: *give evidence* sometimes has nothing to do with testimony. E.g., "The American Bar Association is of the opinion that every candidate for admission to the bar should *give evidence* of graduation from a law school . . . ." "Law, American Schools of," in 17 *Encyclopedia Americana* 93, 96 (1953).

give judgment for = to rule in favor of. E.g., "The court finds that Paul's patent is valid and that it is being infringed, and *gives judgment for* Paul." Charles A. Wright, *The Law of Federal Courts* 682 (4th ed. 1983).

Glanvil(l)(e). The purported author of the treatise that was truly the first book on English law (*Tractatus de Legibus et Consuetudinibus Angliae*)—and the justiciar of England from 1180 to 1189—was named Sir Ranulf de Glanvill. Though a few writers spell the name *Glanvil* (and even *Glanville* or *de Glanville*), most modern legal historians make it *Glanvill.*

global (= embracing a number of items or categories) is used commonly in American and British legal writing. E.g., "The wife's net income has to be calculated so as to ascertain the sum that is deemed to be the husband's by section 18 and must be added to his income similarly quantified; from this *global* sum must be deducted all that is allowable as allowances personal to him." (Eng.)/ "Plaintiff made *global* objections to the jury charge."

gloss, originally "a word inserted between the lines or in the margin as an explanatory equivalent of a foreign or otherwise difficult word in the text" (*OED*), is used in extended senses in legal contexts. E.g., "The function of chancery was to supply the deficiencies of the common law; thus equity was, in the words of Maitland, 'a *gloss* on the common law.'" (Eng.)

In its most extended sense, *gloss* is used as a COLLECTIVE NOUN equivalent to "pronouncements (usu. by a court)." E.g., "The act and its judicial *gloss* also provide the manner for distributing the recovery, if any, obtained from a third party [several cases interpreting the act are mentioned]." This sense is analogous to the nonlegal sense "a collection of explanations, glossary," and is not really exceptionable.

glossator. The *Glossators* were scholars principally in Bologna who, in the Middle Ages, annotated Justinian's legislation with marginal or interliner glosses, passage by passage. By convention, the name of this school of annotators is capitalized.

That practice is convenient, for purposes of DIFFERENTIATION, because the word *glossator* (always lowercase) also commonly denotes any modern scholar or court who provides glosses—e.g.: "Sometimes a *glossator* has relied on supposed purposes of the legislators, or on their debates at the time of enactment, or on their recitals of evils sought to be remedied, or on their putative responses to circumstances strictly contemporary with the enactments." *Richards v. Thurston,* 304 F. Supp. 449, 455 (D. Mass. 1969)./ "Most jurors encounter the arcane language of instructions infrequently—maybe only once in a lifetime—and it is therefore important to give them instructions that do not require scholastic *glossators* to impart meaning." *U.S. v. Ramsey,* 785 F.2d 184, 190 (7th Cir. 1986).

glue, v.t., preferably makes *gluing,* not *glueing:* "The systems have come unstuck and we see, presently, no way of *glueing* [read *gluing*] them back together again." Grant Gilmore, *The Death of Contract* 102 (1974).

go. See **go to.**

GOBBLEDYGOOK is the obscure language characteristic of jargon-mongering bureaucrats. Thus *iterative naturalistic inquiry methodology* supposedly refers to a series of interviews. Much legal writing is open to the criticism of being gobbledygook. One of the purposes of this book is to wage a battle against it. See JARGON, LATINISMS, LEGALESE & OBSCURITY.

"The besetting sin of jurists," writes a well-known Australian authority, "is to conceal threadbare thoughts in elaborate and difficult language. In spite of the difficulties inherent in the subject, the problems of jurisprudence can be expressed in fairly simple language." G.W. Paton, *A Textbook of Jurisprudence* 1–2 (4th ed. 1972).

goes to. See **go to.**

goes without saying, it, is not generally suitable for formal contexts, although it may be appropriate in speech or in informal prose. If it goes without saying, then it need not be said.

go hence without day. This phrase, an old standard in defensive pleadings, is routinely used by lawyers who have absolutely no idea what they mean by it. Perhaps they reason just as Chief Justice Fortescue did in the 15th century: "Sir, the law is as I say it is, and so it has been laid down ever since the law began; and we have several set forms which are held as law, and so held and used for good reason, though we cannot at present remember that reason." Y.B. 36 Hen. VI, ff. 25b–26 (1458) (as translated in 3 William S. Holdsworth, *A History of English Law* 626 (3d ed. 1923)).

In fact, the phrase originated in what Sir Matthew Hale, the 17th-century chief justice of the King's Bench, called "the golden age of pleading" before 1500. See Margaret Hastings, *The Court of Common Pleas in Fifteenth Century England* 186 (1947). It is but a LOAN TRANSLATION of the LAW FRENCH phrase *aller sans jour* (lit., "to go without day"), used in medieval times. The phrase meant merely that the defendant would like to leave court without any further settings on the court's docket.

At common law, some time after Law French fell into disuse, a longer Latin phrase appeared in orders of dismissal: *eat inde sine die,* that is, "that he may go hence without day." The defendant was free to go; he would not have what he did not want—his day in court. This form of order was still used in England until 1733, when use of the English language became compulsory. See W.A. Jowitt, *The Dictionary of English Law* 679 (1959). See ***sine die*** & **day in court.**

Yet the English translation of the phrase, *without day,* cropped up well before 1733, In the 1701 edition of John's Cowel's *Interpreter,* we learn that "[t]o be dismissed without *Day,* is to be finally discharged [by] the Court." Dismissed cases were said to be *put without day.*

American lawyers mindlessly parrot the phrase: in Texas, for example, where most defensive pleadings contain the phrase, not one lawyer in fifty can explain what the phrase means. Though *go hence without day* is not current everywhere, it ought to be current nowhere.

golden rule. In the realm of morality, everyone knows about the do-unto-others Golden Rule. In law, the phrase *golden rule* takes on other meanings: (1) the principle that, in construing all written instruments, a court should adhere to the grammatical and ordinary sense of the words unless that adherence would lead to some manifest absurdity; (2) the principle, in legal drafting, that one should be consistent in terminology by employing one invariable term for one idea. For a discussion of the latter principle, see INELEGANT VARIATION.

good, n. See **goods.**

good and valuable consideration. See **consideration (D)** & **and other good and valuable consideration.**

good behavior is a well-known standard by which judges are considered fit to continue their tenure: "The Judges, both of the supreme and inferior Courts, shall hold their Offices during good Behavior . . . ." U.S. Const. art. III, § 1. But the phrase was not original with the constitutional Framers: in 1700, the Act of Settlement provided that judges' commissions would be *quamdiu se bene gesserint,* i.e., "during good behavior." Our phrase began as a LOAN TRANSLATION. See ***quamdiu se bene gesserint.***

good cause shown is one of the few standard legal expressions that are neither prolix nor inaccessible to nonlawyers. E.g., "A writ of sequestration may be quashed or dissolved for *good cause shown.*" In statutes and rules, the participle *shown* is advisable because it places a burden on the party to demonstrate whatever must be demonstrated. But in advocates' arguments about whether the standard has been met—esp. in the argument of the advocate who is doing the showing—the word *shown* is often inadvisable because it emphasizes the wrong idea: *shown* rather than *good cause.* See SENTENCE ENDINGS. Cf. **show cause & probable cause.**

good consideration. See **consideration (D).**

good(-)faith. *Good faith* is the noun phrase <in good faith>, *good-faith* the adjectival phrase <good-faith efforts>. See **bona fide(s).**

good law. See **not law.**

good men and true. See **twelve free and lawful men.**

good right to convey. See **covenant of seisin.**

goods has a variety of senses, two of which are here relevant. In the legal sense, *goods* refers to chattels or personalty. In the economic sense, however, it often refers to things that have value, whether tangible or not. For example: "The meaning and value of all *goods* (money, power, love, and so forth) are socially created and vary from one society to the next. Social *goods* do not include privately valued goods, such as sunsets or mountain air." (From a review of M. Walzer's *Spheres of Justice* (1983).)

In the sense "tangible or movable pieces of property," *goods* has traditionally appeared only in the plural form. In recent years, however, *good* has developed the sense "a tangible or movable piece of property other than money." Though still considered unidiomatic by those with sensitive ears, this usage has made such inroads that it is unlikely to be stopped: "The buyer-seller relationship between the shipowner and *the supplier of a good* [better usage requires *a supplier of goods,* even if there is only one kind of goods] simply does not give rise to a duty on the shipowner's part not to act in such a manner as to cause an injured third party to sue the supplier as a possible defendant liable for the injuries."

goods and chattels. See ***bona et catalla*** & DOUBLETS, TRIPLETS, AND SYNONYM-STRINGS.

goodwill. Formerly two words, then hyphenated, the term has now become one word.

goose case is legal slang for what in legal JARGON is termed *a case on all fours.* E.g., "While there is no *'goose' case* in this circuit, Instruction 31 of the Fifth Circuit Pattern Jury Instructions (Criminal Cases) (1979), informs our judgment." *U.S. v. Gaber,* 745 F.2d 952, 954 (5th Cir. 1984)./ "One need not find a *'goose case'* to imbue a warden at a jail with a constitutional duty to protect a prisoner prone to suicide from self-destruction." *Lewis v. Parish of Terrebone,* 894 F.2d 142, 145 (5th Cir. 1990). See **whitehorse case & on all fours.**

gorilla. For the misuse of this word for *guerrilla,* see **guerrilla.**

got, p.pl. See **get.**

go to, in the sense "to bear on the issue of," is a distinctive legal usage that is current in both AmE and BrE. Oddly, though, it seems to have escaped the attention of American and British lexicographers to date.

Law students frequently say that it puzzles them at first, but soon they begin using it unconsciously. It is a commonplace in good legal writing: "Mistake *going to* the interpretation of the rule of law is not generally a defence." Glanville Williams, *Criminal Law* 183 (2d ed. 1961)./ "Questions of substantive validity *go to* the consistency of the substance of the statute with constitutional provisions . . . ." John H. Merryman, *The Civil Law Tradition* 145 (1969)./ "The discretion of the court does not *go* merely *to* terms and conditions, but extends to whether to permit a nonsuit at all." Charles A. Wright, *The Law of Federal Courts* 654 (4th ed. 1983).

go to court. See **court, go to.**

go to law = to sue. E.g., "If, for instance, a milk company *goes to law* to protest against a state statute setting the price of milk, the past profits—or lack of profits—of the milk distributors, the medical need of milk for slum children, the present financial shape of dairy farmers, the personnel and ability of the government agency doing the price-setting, all may be treated as just as important as the 'due process clause' . . . ." Fred Rodell, *Woe Unto You, Lawyers!* 142 (1939)./ "In such circumstances it may be unreal to suggest that the buyer should resist the demand and *go to law* to enforce his right to the ship without extra payment." P.S. Atiyah, *An Introduction to the Law of Contract* 230 (3d ed. 1981).

go to the jury. See **jury, go to the.**

go to trial (AmE & BrE) = *come to court* (BrE). See **come to court.**

gotten. See **get.**

governance. Fowler pronounced *governance* an ARCHAISM for which either *government* or *control* suffices, allowing it only in "rhetorical or solemn contexts." Yet this noun is frequently used in law to refer to running or governing a corporation. E.g., "The court emphasized that a proceeding in bankruptcy court does not address the same issues of corporate *governance* that the Delaware statute was intended to cover."

Governance does not mean "the quality of a jurisdiction's law that governs in a particular case." E.g., "While California has a significant interest *in the governance of* [read *in having its law govern*] these relationships, Texas has few, if any."

governmental; government, adj. When we have an adjective (*governmental*) to do the job, we need not resort to a noun (*government*) to do the work of the adjective. Though the trend today is to write *government agency,* the stylist writes *governmental agency.* These are the niceties of writing that make the reader's task a little easier and that distinguish between formal and ordinary prose. Following are a few examples of the better usage: "If a *governmental* institution is to be fair, one group cannot always be expected to win."/ "The City of Akron has not attempted to allocate *governmental* power on the basis of any general principle."/ "The decision whether a public facility shall be operated in compliance with the Constitution is an essential *governmental* decision."

GOVERNMENTAL FORMS. The English language abounds in words to denote almost every conceivable form of government, usually ending in either of the suffixes *-cracy* and *-archy.* Following is a sampling of the hundreds of familiar and arcane terms in the English language, too numerous for inclusion here:

clerisocracy	=	government by priests or scholars
democracy	=	government by the people
dyarchy	=	government by two rulers
gerontocracy	=	government by the elderly
gynecocracy	=	government by women
jurocracy (q.v.)	=	government by the courts
monocracy	=	government by a single person
polyarchy	=	government by many persons
plutocracy	=	government by the wealthy
technocracy	=	government by technicians

gownsman (= one who wears a gown as an indication of his office or profession) was formerly used in G.B. of judges and barristers, but is now more likely to be used in reference to academics. See **silk** & SEXISM (B).

grab law refers not to law but to a kind of lawlessness: it means "aggressive collection practices." The phrase frequently appears in discussions of bankruptcy—e.g.: "Such an unfair result is contrary to the policy of the Bankruptcy Act. Its policy is not to subject creditors to the haphazard chance of '*grab law.*' Its chief purpose is to afford all creditors an equal opportunity to realize on their indebtedness." *England v. Sanderson,* 236 F.2d 641, 643–44 (9th Cir. 1956)./ "[The automatic stay provisions of the Bankruptcy Act were designed for] protection of the estate of the bankrupt against the ravages that would be inflicted on the estate if *grab law* were allowed to govern." Frank R. Kennedy, *The Automatic Stay in Bankruptcy,* 11 U. Mich. J.L. Reform 175, 187 (1978).

Sometimes the phrase is used attributively as a PHRASAL ADJECTIVE—e.g.: "By such *grab-law* tactics Armstrong claims possession of the entire building, which contained the property of six tenants . . . ." *In re Process-Manz Press, Inc.,* 369 F.2d 513, 524 (7th Cir. 1966).

GRAMMAR. The very word is considered anathema by many persons, even those with an advanced education, not so much because it is boring (which it can be) as because it seems intimidating. Often this intimidation causes scoffers to dismiss grammar as an unimportant, trifling pursuit. To be sure, there are more important things in life, but the significance of good grammar should not be underestimated, especially by those engaged in a learned profession.

The courts have frequently addressed the subject with good sense. For example, the Supreme Court of Florida has stated: "The legislature is presumed to know the meaning of words and the rules of grammar, and the only way that a court is advised of what the legislature intends is by giving the generally accepted construction, not only to the phraseology of an act but to the manner in which it is punctuated." *Florida State Rac-*

ing Comm'n v. Bourquardez, 42 So. 2d 87, 88 (Fla. 1949) (en banc).

Courts give more leeway to nonlawyers but still take a commonsense approach. In examining wills, e.g., courts will forgive every error this book is designed to prevent: "When it becomes necessary to do so in order to effectuate the testator's intention as ascertained from the context of the will, the court may disregard clerical mistakes in writing, improper use of capital letters, paragraphing, abbreviation of words, punctuation, misspelling and grammatical inaccuracies, especially where the will is written by a layman who is unlearned, illiterate, or unskilled. In order to ascertain and give effect to the testator's intent, the court may disregard rules of grammar and verbal niceties, but unless a different construction is required, the ordinary rules of punctuation, capitalization, and grammar should be adhered to in construing a will." 95 C.J.S. *Wills* § 612 (1957).

Likewise with contracts: "[T]he use of inapt words or bad English . . . will not affect the validity of the agreement, although it may affect its construction." 17 C.J.S. *Contracts* § 57 (1963). And affidavits: "Where the meaning substantially appears, ordinarily errors or mistakes on the part of the draftsman in the body of [an] affidavit will be overlooked, and mere grammatical errors . . . will not vitiate the effectiveness of the instrument." 2A C.J.S. *Affidavits* § 43 (1972).

The same is true even in pleading: "Bad grammar does not vitiate a declaration, nor do other faults of style have that effect, unless they produce such a degree of obscurity as to give rise to the belief that the tribunal before whom the cause is heard might be misled as to the true issue." 41 Am. Jur. *Pleading* § 28 (1942).

Nevertheless, this book seeks to guide legal writers around these pitfalls in the belief that, even if a document's enforceability will not be marred by such lapses, the court's confidence in its reliability may well be adversely affected. Grammar is not, however, to be followed slavishly without regard for what is effective and what is idiomatic. "Wherever by small grammatical negligences the energy of an idea can be condensed, or a word stands for a sentence, I hold grammatical rigor in contempt." Thomas Jefferson, Letter to Madison, 12 Nov. 1801, in 8 *Writings of Thomas Jefferson* 108–09 (1897).

GRAMMATICAL AMBIGUITY. See AMBIGUITY.

grammatical error. Because *grammatical* may mean either (1) "relating to grammar" <grammatical subject> or (2) "consistent with grammar" <a grammatical sentence>, there is nothing wrong with the age-old phrase *grammatical error* (sense 1). Cf. the phrases *criminal lawyer* and *logical fallacy.* See ILLOGIC.

grammaticality is to *grammar* as *constitutionality* is to *constitution.*

grandfather clause = a clause in the constitutions of some southern American states that exempted from suffrage restrictions the descendants of men who voted before the Civil War. The *OED* misleadingly labels this phrase colloquial; it is the only available name for these statutes, and it appears in formal writing. E.g., "A state law directly denying Negroes the right would be overthrown as a matter of course, and in 1915 the Court had invalidated a so-called *'grandfather clause'* [that] required literacy tests of those who were *not* descendants of those who could vote in 1867." Robert G. McCloskey, *The American Supreme Court* 212 (1960). Moreover, it has extended senses, referring to any statutory or regulatory clause exempting a class of persons or transactions because of circumstances existing before the clause takes effect.

This phrase has given rise to the verb *to grandfather,* meaning "to cover (a person) with the benefits of a grandfather clause." E.g., "Beginning in 1972, several States passed statutes permitting such acquisitions in limited circumstances or for specialized purposes. For example, Iowa passed a *grandfathering* statute which had the effect of permitting the only out-of-state bank holding company owning an Iowa bank to maintain and expand its in-state banking activities. . . ." *Northeast Bancorp, Inc. v. Federal Reserve Sys.,* 472 U.S. 159, 163 (1985). To be *grandfathered* is to have the advantage of a grandfather clause <get yourself grandfathered by establishing priority in an interest>.

A few writers and speakers—sometimes in jest—have resorted to *grandparent clause* to avoid what might be perceived as SEXISM. But that neutering skews the historical sense and is likely to strike most readers and listeners as jocular.

grand jury. A. Generally. In most American states, a prosecutor cannot proceed in a case involving a felony or serious misdemeanor without first coming before a body of (often 23) people who are chosen to sit permanently for at least a month—and sometimes a year—and who, in *ex parte* proceedings, decide whether an indictment should be issued. This body is known as a *grand jury.* If the grand jury decides that the evidence is strong enough to hold the suspect for trial, it returns a *true bill* (q.v.), i.e., a bill of indictment, charging the suspect with a specific crime.

The grand jury was abolished in England—with insignificant exceptions in London and Middlesex—in 1933. Even these exceptions were wiped away by the Criminal Justice Act 1948.

Historical variants of the phrase *grand jury* include *presenting jury, accusing jury,* and *jury of indictment.*

B. And *petit jury*. Whereas a *grand jury* determines whether sufficient evidence exists to accuse a person of a crime and to bring a criminal prosecution, a *petit jury* ultimately determines the guilt or innocence of the accused and may convict only when the government has proved guilt beyond a reasonable doubt. See **petit jury.**

grand larceny. See **larceny (B).**

grant = (1) the formal transfer of real property; (2) the document by which such a transfer is effected; or (3) the property transferred. Sense (1) contains a historical AMBIGUITY. Originally, the verb *grant* was used only when the grantor conveyed a nonfreehold interest—that is, carved out a smaller interest—such as an easement or a lease. But today the verb is commonly used when the grantor's full interest, such as a fee simple absolute, is being conveyed.

grant, bargain, sell, and convey. The word *grant* or *convey* alone suffices: the rest is deadwood. See DOUBLETS, TRIPLETS, AND SYNONYM-STRINGS.

gratify has been used in legal writing synonymously with *satisfy* in reference to rules or requirements. Neither the *OED* nor *W3* records this use. E.g., "This averment does not *gratify* the rule requiring certainty in pleading."/ "Not only the language of the statute but also the fundamental purposes can be *gratified* only by a definite decree of the court that adjudicates the illegality of the practice in the past and enjoins the defendant from repetition thereof in the future."

gratis dictum. See **dictum (B).**

gratuitous; fortuitous. These two words are occasionally confounded. *Gratuitous* = (1) done or performed without obligation to do so; given without consideration <gratuitous promises>; or (2) done unnecessarily <gratuitous criticisms>. *Fortuitous* = occurring by chance <fortuitous circumstances>. See **fortuitous.**

gravamen /*grə-vay-mən*/ = the point of a complaint or grievance. E.g., "Under the fourth and fifth complaints, the *gravamen* of the charge was that he had failed to preserve for a period of twelve months from the date of delivery the invoices relating to those and certain other goods." (Eng.)/ "The *gravamen* of plaintiffs' claim is that Apopka has intentionally maintained a racially and geographically segregated system of municipal services."/ "The *gravamen* of the complaint in this case, to quote exactly, is as follows."/ "Here, of course, there is no final order—indeed, the lack of a final order is the very *gravamen* of the petitioner's complaint."

Gravamen is used also of criminal accusations <gravamen of the charge>, but not, properly, of crimes: "*The gravamen of the crime* [read *The gist of the crime*] is that the accused has used a fictitious credit card." See **gist.**

Today, nine out of ten times when this word appears, it is in the phrase *gravamen of the complaint;* inasmuch as *gravamen* in itself means "the material part of a complaint," the phrase seems redundant. The *OED* quotes no sentences containing *the gravamen of the complaint,* although it quotes several containing *the gravamen of the charge.* Perhaps it is felt in modern prose that the phrase *of the complaint* elucidates the meaning of *gravamen;* if so, the word is recondite on its own and infelicitously redundant in the common phrase.

Gravamen is frequently misused for *crux* or *gist,* both of which are broader—e.g.: "The *gravamen* [read *crux*] of appellant's argument is that he is entitled to have this 'dead time' credited against his federal sentence."/ "The *gravamen* [read *gist*] of the relief sought is the reformation or cancellation of records."/ "The *gravamen* [read *gist*] of the medical opinion in support of petitioners' position is that Rumbaugh is not able to countenance the delay inherent in the continuation of legal proceedings and the possible conversion of his death sentence to life imprisonment."

Gravaman is a common misspelling—e.g.: "The *gravaman* [read *gravamen*] of the tort action of alienation of affections was a spouse's loss of the love, society, companionship, and comfort of the other spouse." *Koestler v. Pollard,* 471 N.W.2d 7, 12 (Wis. 1991) (Abrahamson, J., dissenting).

The plural forms are *gravamens* and *gravamina,* the former being preferred.

gray; grey. The former spelling is more common in AmE, the latter in BrE; both are old, and neither is incorrect.

graymail originated in the late 1970s as a C.I.A. EUPHEMISM for *blackmail.* It refers to the "practice whereby a criminal defendant threatens to reveal classified information during the course of his trial in the hope of forcing the government to drop the criminal charge against him." *U.S. v.*

Smith, 780 F.2d 1102, 1105 (4th Cir. 1985). The Classified Information Procedure Act (1980), often shortened to the acronym *CIPA,* is informally called the *Graymail Act.*

gray mule case. See **whitehorse case.**

Great Britain consists of England, Scotland, and Wales. It differs from *United Kingdom,* which includes Northern Ireland.

Great Charter, the. This phrase is a slightly affected synonym of *Magna Carta*—e.g.: "The ground plan to which the common-law polity has built ever since was given by *the Great Charter.*" Roscoe Pound, *The Development of Constitutional Guarantees of Liberty* 18 (1957).

Great Dissenter; First Dissenter. The *Great Dissenter*—no other judge has even approached his greatness as an author of dissenting opinions—was Justice Oliver Wendell Holmes. The nickname has become standard in American legal parlance—e.g.: "Even Justice Holmes, the *Great Dissenter* himself, remarked in his first dissent that dissents are generally 'useless' and 'undesirable.'" William J. Brennan, Jr., *In Defense of Dissents,* 37 Hastings L.J. 427, 429 (1986)./ "Antiformalism in modern habeas interpretation was first heralded by Justice Holmes in his frequently cited dissent in *Frank v. Mangum* . . . . There, the *Great Dissenter* observed . . . ." *Chatman-Bey v. Thornburgh,* 864 F.2d 804, 807 (D.C. Cir. 1988). In this phrase, the more important word is *great,* not *dissenter,* for Holmes "in fact dissented less often than most of his colleagues." Ruth Bader Ginsburg, *Remarks on Writing Separately,* 65 Wash. L. Rev. 133, 142 (1990).

Interestingly, though, Holmes was not the first to bear this nickname: the phrase was applied originally to the first Justice Harlan. See T.J. Knight, *The Dissenting Opinions of Justice Harlan,* 51 Am. L. Rev. 481, 484 (1917). A 1970 Harlan biography by Frank Latham bore the title *The Great Dissenter.*

The so-called *First Dissenter* was Justice William Johnson, who was urged by the president who appointed him, Thomas Jefferson, to write a separate opinion in each case so as to check Chief Justice John Marshall's dominance on the Court. Johnson did so only sporadically, but he disagreed with the majority enough to earn this moniker.

great seal, to take the. This phrase, in BrE, means "to attain the office of Lord Chancellor." E.g., "The law itself had been changed to permit a Catholic (Lord Rawlinson) to *take the great seal,* but after the fanfare came the silence." *Maths Genius Does His Homework on the Law's Reform,* Sunday Times, 11 Dec. 1988, at A13. The phrase originated in the Lord Chancellor's acting as Keeper of the Great Seal. The Lord Chancellor, who is appointed by being handed the Great Seal, carries it in a bag as the badge of office.

Great Writ has long been used as an exalted synonym for *habeas corpus*—e.g.: "There has been a halo about the *'Great Writ'* that no one would wish to dim." *Schneckloth v. Bustamonte,* 412 U.S. 218, 275 (1973) (Powell, J., concurring)./ "The *'Great Writ,'* as it has been called by the Supreme Court from John Marshall's day to this, is available by statute in four different situations." Charles A. Wright, *The Law of Federal Courts* 331 (4th ed. 1983).

greenmail, a PORTMANTEAU WORD made from *greenbacks* plus *blackmail,* was coined in the early 1980s. It carries two senses: (1) the act of buying enough stock in a company to threaten a hostile takeover, and of then agreeing to sell the stock back to the corporation at an inflated price; or (2) the money paid for stock in the corporation's buy-back. E.g., "There is no dispute that in the instant case, the common law claims and the federal Securities Exchange Act claims arise from the same transaction, i.e., the alleged misrepresentation by the Basses of their motives for acquiring the Texaco stock and the ensuing alleged *'greenmail'* between the Bass defendants and Texaco." *Seagoing Uniform Corp. v. Texaco, Inc.,* 705 F. Supp. 918, 921 (S.D.N.Y. 1989)./ "They are particularly infuriated at a suggestion to offer Goldsmith *'greenmail,'* a controversial American takeover practice whereby a company under siege buys off a predator by giving it a large profit on its shares." Ivan Fallon & Tony Lorenz, *Revealed: Secret Plot to Thwart Goldsmith BAT Bid,* Sunday Times, 26 Nov. 1989, at A1.

The word has also been used as a verb, *to greenmail,* on the analogy of *to blackmail.*

Green Paper. See **White Paper.**

grey. See **gray.**

grievable, adj., = of, constituting, or giving rise to a valid grievance. This word is almost certainly an unconscious revival of an old word that the *OED* records as having died off about 1500 (when it meant merely "causing distress"). It suddenly emerged in the mid-20th century—e.g.: "While not all *'grievable'* disputes are arbitrable under the contract, this one is . . . ." *Engineers Ass'n v. Sperry Gyroscope Co.,* 148 F. Supp. 521, 526 (S.D.N.Y. 1957)./ "The collective-bargaining agreement involved here prohibited without qualification all manner of invidious discrimination and made any claimed violation a *grievable* issue." *Emporium Capwell Co. v. Western Addition Community Org.,* 420 U.S. 50, 66 (1975)./ "The Village refused to consider the grievance, declaring it *non-grievable* and stating that Fletcher's only appeal was pursuant to the Fire and Police Commission Act." *Village of Creve Coeur v. Fletcher,* 543 N.E.2d 323, 323 (Ill. App. Ct. 1989).

grievance; aggrievance. The latter is a NEEDLESS VARIANT.

grievant; grievancer; aggrievant. The first term is commonly used in AmE in the context of arbitration. *W3* defines *grievant* as "one who submits a grievance for arbitration." E.g., "[An arbitrator's] job is to define the relief that will compensate the *grievant* if his claim is upheld." *Hotel & Restaurant Employees & Bartenders Int'l Union v. Michelson's Food Servs., Inc.,* 545 F.2d 1248, 1254 (9th Cir. 1976).

In practice, *grievant* often refers more narrowly to an employee who registers a complaint with an employer. Katharine Seide, *A Dictionary of Arbitration* 106 (1970). E.g., "Thomas Rogers and Robert Wilson, Jr. (*grievants*), were employed by General Services Administration . . . ." *Cornelius v. Nutt,* 472 U.S. 648, 653 (1985).

The *OED* lists *grievancer* (= one who occasions a grievance or gives ground for complaint) but not *grievant,* a NEOLOGISM dating back only to 1956: "[T]he *grievant* [was entitled] to have such question submitted to final and binding arbitration . . . ." *Wisconsin Motor Corp. v. Wisconsin Employment Relations Bd.,* 79 N.W.2d 119, 122 (Wis. 1956). Thus far, *grievant* has not yet spread beyond American legal writing. It is indisputably a useful term even if one might originally have objected to its formation.

Aggrievant is a NEEDLESS VARIANT.

grieve is most often an intransitive verb meaning "to feel grief." It could also, traditionally, be a transitive verb meaning "to cause distress to"—e.g.: "The murders that Gary Tison and Randy Greenawalt committed revolt and *grieve* all who learn of them." *Tison v. Arizona,* 481 U.S. 137, 159 (1987) (Brennan, J., dissenting).

But recently the verb has taken on a new meaning: "to bring a grievance for the purpose of protesting." The emergence of this sense is not entirely surprising because it is implied by the words *grievable* and *grievant.* Stylists are not likely to use the verb, but neither are they likely to succeed in expunging it. E.g., "Again, the Union was *grieving* G.E.'s subcontracting . . . ." *General Elec. Co. v. N.L.R.B.,* 916 F.2d 1163, 1165 (7th Cir. 1990)./ "[E]mployees could *grieve* any discharge, suspension, or general dispute." *Johnson v. Beatrice Foods Co.,* 921 F.2d 1015, 1016 (10th Cir. 1990)./ "After the 1987 ratification, the Union *grieved* AP's right to add the new inspection without modifying the standard hours figure." *AP Parts Co. v. Int'l Union, United Auto Aerospace & Agric. Implement Workers,* 923 F.2d 488, 490 (6th Cir. 1991).

grievous is frequently misspelled *grievious,* just as *mischievous* is frequently misspelled *mischievious.* These are grievous and mischievous malformations.

grievous bodily harm, a term commonly used in criminal law and in tort law, is a purposely vague term meaning physical harm that is truly serious; it is purposely vague because, ordinarily, the finder of fact must decide in any given case whether the injury meets this general standard. The term "has no specifically legal meaning." Glanville Williams, *Textbook of Criminal Law* 127–28 (1978). See **g.b.h.**

gross. See **in gross.**

gross negligence. See **negligence** (A).

Grotian is the adjective corresponding to the name *Grotius* (1587–1645), the famous 17th-century Dutch jurist. E.g., "[T]he doctrines of the *Grotian* school had prevailed." Henry S. Maine, *Ancient Law* 83 (17th ed. 1901; repr. [New Universal Lib.] 1905, 1910).

ground. See **ground(s).**

ground of action. See **cause of action.**

ground(s). Although one does not count as one ground or two grounds every argument one can muster, it is acceptable to speak of a party's relying on a certain *ground* (= reason). Yet even the writer who has only one reason for a position can take that position *on grounds of* whatever that reason is.

In the speech and writing of American lawyers, the singular *ground* is loosely equivalent to sense (1) of *ratio decidendi* (q.v.)—that is, meaning the court's basis for a decision.

grounds for appeal; grounds of appeal. Either is correct, but *grounds for appeal* is perhaps more common.

ground(s) that, on (the). See **ground(s).**

groundwater. One word.

group of, a. See SYNESIS.

guarantee. **A. And *warranty*.** Originally the same word, *warranty* and *guarantee* (or *-ty*) arrived in the language through different medieval French dialects. Both terms denote undertakings by one party to another to indemnify an assured party against some possible default or defect. But there are important differences.

Guarantee relates to the future, in meaning either (1) the act of giving a security; the undertaking with respect to (a contract, performance of a legal act, etc.) that it will be duly carried out, or (2) something given or existing as security, e.g., to fulfill a future engagement or a condition subsequent.

Warranty relates to the present or past and has somewhat more specific and elaborate senses: (1) a covenant (either express or implied) annexed to a conveyance of realty by which the seller warrants the security of the title conveyed; (2) an assurance, express or implied, given by the seller of goods, that he will be answerable for their possession of some quality attributed to them <the seller hereby disclaims all warranties>; or (3) in an insurance contract, an insured's engagement that certain statements are true or that certain conditions will be fulfilled. See **warranty.**

B. And *guaranty*. The distinction in BrE once was that the former is the verb, the latter the noun. Yet *guarantee* is now commonly used as both n. & v.t. in both AmE and BrE. Following are examples of the nominal use: "Negro citizens, North and South, who saw in the Thirteenth Amendment a promise of freedom would be left with a mere paper *guarantee* if Congress were powerless to ensure that a dollar in the hands of a Negro will purchase the same thing as a dollar in the hands of a white man."/ "Without the exclusionary rule the constitutional *guarantee* against unreasonable searches and seizures would be a mere 'form of words.'"

In practice, *guarantee,* n., is the usual term, seen often, for example, in the context of consumer warranties or other assurances of quality or performance. *Guaranty,* in contrast, is now used primarily in financial and banking contexts in the sense "a promise to answer for the debt of another." *Guaranty* is now rarely seen in nonlegal writing, whether in G.B. or in the U.S. Some legal writers prefer *guaranty* in all nominal senses.

Guaranty was formerly used as a verb but is now obsolete as a variant of *guarantee,* v.t. In the following sentence, it appears in its more modern legal use as a noun: "Footnote 10 indicates that Congress is without power to undercut the equal-protection *guaranty* of racial equality in the guise of implementing the Fourteenth Amendment."

C. And *guarantor*. Both *guarantee* (fr. 1679) and *guarantor* (fr. 1853) have filled the role of agent noun for the verb *to guarantee.* These words have shared the sense "one who makes a guaranty or gives a security," but today *guarantor* has taken the field, rendering *guarantee* in this sense but a NEEDLESS VARIANT. Oddly, *guarantee* has been used not only as an equivalent of *guarantor,* but also as a passive correlative of it consistently with other forms in -EE. Thus the *OED* quotes the following specimen of *guarantee* (= a person to whom a guarantee is given): "Guarantors are relieved by the *guarantee* being compelled, if one is ready to pay the whole, to sell him the debt of the others." This use of *guarantee* may be useful in tandem with *-or,* but the actual occurrences of it in legal prose are rare.

guarantor. See **guarantee** (C) & **surety.**

guardhouse lawyer. See LAWYERS, DEROGATORY NAMES FOR (B).

guardian *ad litem*; special guardian. These synonymous phrases denote a court-appointed guardian who acts in litigation on behalf of someone under a disability, such as a minor or a mentally defective person. E.g., "Since then the Appellate Division has ruled that no *special guardians,* or *guardians ad litem,* as they've been renamed, are needed in VA estates of less than $2,500." Murray T. Bloom, *The Trouble with Lawyers* 309 (1970). See ***ad litem,*** **next friend** & ***prochein ami.***

guerrilla [Sp. "raiding party"] = a member of a small band of military fighters who, mostly through surprise raids, try to harass and undermine occupying forces. The word is preferably so spelled—not *guerilla.*

And misusing *gorilla* for this word is a laughable MALAPROPISM—e.g.: "Alien . . . did not show that her alleged persecutors had attributed political opinions to her as result of any deliberate action on her part, such as refusal to join *gorilla* [read *guerrilla*] forces . . . ." *Estrada-Posada v. INS,* 924 F.2d 916, 916 syl. 5 (9th Cir. 1991).

guilt; culpability. The latter is a matter of fact regardless of whether it ever becomes known; the former what is determined by a trier of fact. Judge Learned Hand is said to have remarked that anyone can be a killer, but only a jury can make a murderer. See **guilty.**

guilt-prone (opposed to *acquittal-prone*) is coming to be used of juries in the sense "likely to convict." E.g., "Appellant contends that the process of excluding from the guilt phase of the trial prospective jurors who are unwilling to consider imposing capital punishment resulted in a jury that was impermissibly *guilt-prone* and unrepresentative of the community."

A variant is *conviction-prone:* "The argument assumes that if the prosecution strikes minority-group members on the basis of their group affiliation, then majority-group members inevitably must be likely to be as *conviction-prone* as the minority-group members are *acquittal-prone.*" Cf. **death-qualified jurors.**

guilty. Lawyers and nonlawyers alike generally associate this word with criminal contexts. But some lawyers, esp. in BrE, use it in civil contexts as well—e.g.: "The better opinion is that co-tenants in fee are not *guilty* of waste in using and enjoying the property in any way [that] is in accord with the reasonable exercise of prudent ownership by the average man." William F. Walsh, *A Treatise on Equity* 146 (1930)./ "A person is *guilty* of misrepresentation, though all the facts stated by him are true, if his statement is misleading as a whole because it does not refer to other facts affecting the weight of those stated." G.H. Treitel, *The Law of Contract* 353 (8th ed. 1991).

Sometimes the idea of guilt can be eliminated through deft editing—e.g.: "The plaintiff was *guilty of contributory negligence* [better: *contributorily negligent*]." See **blameworthy.**

guilty mind. See ***mens rea.***

gunslinger. See LAWYERS, DEROGATORY NAMES FOR (A).

gypsy; gipsy. The former spelling is preferred in AmE, the latter in BrE.

H

habeas is often used in AmE as an abbreviated form of *habeas corpus,* as in the common phrase *habeas relief.* E.g., "This pro se appeal concerns Timothy Rudolph's second federal *habeas* petition."/ "In 1982, we affirmed the dismissal of a prior petition for federal *habeas* relief." See **habeas corpus.**

habeas corpus (lit., "that you may have the body") is the quintessential justified LATINISM that has taken on a peculiar meaning that no homegrown English term could now supply. Though it has become one of the basic devices to protect civil liberties, it was originally used in *capias* writs not to release people from prison but to secure their presence in custody. In the 16th century, the King's Bench began issuing the writ called *habeas corpus ad subjiciendum,* primarily so that subjects could challenge the constitutionality of imprisonment. In 1679, the writ was legislatively enshrined in the Habeas Corpus Act. Nearly a century later, in the famous *Somersett's Case* (1772), Lord Mansfield held that slavery had no standing in England, so that the writ was sufficient to release a black slave from a ship on the Thames. Today it is considered "perhaps the most important writ known to the constitutional law of England . . . ." *Secretary of State for Home Affairs v. O'Brien,* [1923] A.C. 603, 609. See **prerogative writs.**

When used as a PHRASAL ADJECTIVE, the term is best hyphenated: "The Senate is scheduled to consider crime legislation, including *habeas-corpus* proposals, possibly as soon as next week." Wall St. J., 16 May 1990, at B6.

The plural (rarely used) is *habeas corpora.* See **corpus.**

habendum (L. "to be possessed") denotes the part of a deed that defines the estate or interest being transferred. The clause beginning "to have and to hold" is the habendum and tenendum combined, though it is traditionally called the *habendum*—e.g.: "The *habendum* clause is as follows: 'To have and to hold, all and singular, the premises above mentioned, unto the said C.M. Dubois, bishop of Galveston.'" *Gabert v. Olcott,* 23 S.W. 985, 986 (Tex. 1893).

The best plural form is not *habenda,* but *habendums*—e.g.: "There were other words in both deeds between the granting clauses and the *habendums* signifying the intention of the grantor . . . ." *U.S. v. 31,600 Acres of Land,* 47 F. Supp. 21, 24 (E.D.S.C. 1942).

habitability; inhabitability. Because of confusion over the prefix *in-,* which is intensive and not negative in *inhabitability* (as in *inflammable*), today the positive form is *habitability,* the negative form *uninhabitability. Inhabitable* is little used today, and it is unfortunately ambiguous now when it *is* used.

habitation is an abstract word best replaced by *house* or *dwelling.*

had and received. This DOUBLET has historically been a TERM OF ART in the phrase *money had and received;* in pleading in assumpsit, the plaintiff declares that the defendant *had and received* certain money. In most Anglo-American jurisdictions the phrase is no longer required in pleadings. See **money had and received, action for.**

had ought is a substandard usage in place of *ought*—e.g.: "[I]f his services are as valuable as he contended at the trial, he *had ought* [read *ought*] to be able to find substantial employment here or elsewhere . . . ." *Roberts v. I-T-E Circuit Breaker Co.,* 316 F. Supp. 133, 134 (D. Minn. 1970).

haec verba, in. See ***in haec verba.***

haeres, the medieval Latin spelling of the Latin word *heres* (= heir), still sometimes appears: "[H]is interest passes to the state as *ultima haeres.*" *Spiegel's Estate v. C.I.R.,* 335 U.S. 701, 723 n.9 (1949) (Burton, J., dissenting). Justice Burton erred slightly in his Latin, as the correct form is *ultimus,* not *ultima,* before *haeres.*

Hague, The. The definite article in this place-name should be capitalized.

hairbrained. See **harebrained.**

hairlip. See **harelip.**

hale. A. *Hale into court; haul into court.* These phrases are equally common. In *hale into court,* the verb *hale* means "to compel to go; pull"—e.g.: "Taney ordered that the general himself be *haled* into court . . . ." Robert G. McCloskey, *The American Supreme Court* 98 (1960)./ "*Hans* was not expressing some narrow objection to the particular federal power by which Louisiana had been *haled into court,* but was rather enunciating a fundamental principle of federalism . . . ." *Pennsylvania v. Union Gas Co.,* 491 U.S. 1, 37 (1989) (Scalia, J., concurring in part & dissenting in part).

Haul into court has the advantage of being at once more picturesque, because the verb *haul* conjures up a distinct image, and immune from the error discussed in (B)—e.g.: "There is even authority that anyone who takes steps deliberately to thwart the enforcement of a judicial decree can be *hauled into court* and dealt with summarily . . . ." *U.S. v. Board of Educ.,* 11 F.3d 668, 673 (7th Cir. 1993)./ "Airlines have begun changing their policies even before being *hauled into court.*" Reena N. Glazer, Note, *Women's Body Image and the Law,* 43 Duke L.J. 113, 144 (1993).

B. The Solecism *hail into court.* Properly, the verb *hail*—apart from meteorological senses—means (1) "to greet or salute" <they hailed her warmly>; (2) "to praise enthusiastically" <hailed as a great innovator>; or (3) "to call out to" <hail a cab>. Sense (2) is most common in legal writing—e.g.: "[M]ost of the feminist scholars who have treated the battered woman syndrome defense have explicitly endorsed the defense, *hailing* the court's acceptance of the theory as an important first step . . . ." Anne M. Coughlin, *Excusing Women,* 82 Cal. L. Rev. 1, 27 (1994).

The blunder *hail into court* is surprisingly common—e.g.:

- "When corporations are *hailed* [read *haled*] into court, they are well aware that many corporate secrets may be revealed as a result of discovery." Jacqueline S. Guenego, *Trends in Protective Orders Under Federal Rule of Civil Procedure 26(c),* 60 Fordham L. Rev. 541, 543 (1991).
- "The defendant took no actions purposefully directed at Illinois residents such that he would have fair warning that he would be *hailed* [read *haled*] into court in Illinois." *Excel Energy Co. v. Pittman,* 606 N.E.2d 637, 640 (Ill. App. Ct. 1992).
- "It is the defendant who, involuntarily *hailed* [read *haled*] into court, needs the protection of Rule 19." Susan S. Grover, *The Silenced Majority:* Martin v. Wilks *and the Legislative Response,* 1992 U. Ill. L. Rev. 43, 103 n.174 (1992).
- "When the commission was *hailed* [read *haled*] into court for failing to act, it claimed its process had not yet been appropriately exhausted by the plaintiffs." *Klein v. Sullivan,* 978 F.2d 520, 523 (9th Cir. 1992).

half (of). The preposition *of* is usu. unnecessary—e.g.: "[T]he insured may claim for a constructive total where the cost of repair, reconditioning, refloating, or the like would exceed *half* the value." Grant Gilmore & Charles L. Black, Jr., *The Law of Admiralty* 84 (2d ed. 1975)./ "*Half* the intentional killings of adult males are in a rage or a quarrel . . . ." Glanville Williams, *Textbook of Criminal Law* 477 (1978).

half-yearly. See **biannual.**

hallucination; delusion. A *hallucination* results from disturbed perceptions, as when a person "hears voices" or "sees ghosts." A *delusion* is a belief that results from disturbed thinking, as when a person incorrectly imagines that he or she is being persecuted. For the difference between *delusion* and *illusion,* see **illusion.** See also **allusion.**

halting (= limping) sometimes causes a MISCUE—e.g.: "Progress is slow and halting." The writer of that sentence probably meant "limping along," but the sentence gives the impression of "coming to a halt."

halve (= to separate into two equal portions) is pronounced like *have.*

hand down a decision; hand out a decision. The former is the American, the latter said to be the traditional British legal idiom, as H.L. Mencken observed in *The American Language* 246 (4th ed. 1960). Following is an example of the American phrase: "It is not extravagant to argue that *Ex parte Young* is one of the three most important decisions the Supreme Court of the United States has ever *handed down.*" The BrE idiom *hand out* is seldom if ever used today.

The traditional idiom has been stretched by journalists, who occasionally use it to refer not to what a judge does, but to what a jury does: "The verdict is noteworthy, lawyers say, because it is believed to be one of the largest sums ever *handed down* in an invasion of privacy case." Paul M. Barrett, Wall St. J., 16 Feb. 1990, at B6. Cf. **hand up.**

handful. Pl. *handfuls.* On the question whether *handful,* as a subject, takes a singular or a plural verb, see SYNESIS.

hand up. This idiom traditionally referred to a grand jury's passing a matter on to a criminal court—e.g.: "At the time the grand jury reported, five indictments were *handed up,* three of which were sealed and two open." *People v. Bailey,* 149 N.Y.S. 823, 824 (App. Div. 1914)./ "Had these indictments been *handed up* on the 21st, when the district attorney offered to have them prepared, the case . . . would be free from any doubt." *U.S. v. Garsson,* 291 F. 646, 648 (S.D.N.Y. 1923) (per L. Hand, J.).

Sometimes writers choose the wrong idiom, namely *hand down*—e.g.: "The indictment, *handed down* [read *handed up*] after a 2½-year investigation, cites 11 instances of racketeering . . . ." Ann Bancroft, *Coastal Official Indicted,* San Francisco Chronicle, 8 May 1992, at A1. See **hand down a decision.**

hang, v.i., = (of a jury) to be unable to reach a verdict. This Americanism dates from the mid-19th century and is still common—e.g.: "Prosecutor Murphy's own rhetoric in the second Hiss trial (after the first jury *hung*) was even more powerful." Daniel Levitt, *Rhetoric in Closing Argument,* 17 Litigation 17, 18 (Winter 1991).

Less commonly, *hang* is used as a transitive verb in the sense "to cause (a jury) to be unable to reach a verdict," as here: "One way to *hang* a jury is to have at least one person on it who is likely to raise the hackles of at least one of the others." Robin T. Lakoff, *Talking Power: The Politics of Language in Our Lives* 116 (1990).

hanged; hung. Coats and pictures are *hung,* and sometimes even juries. But criminals found guilty of capital offenses are *hanged*—at least in some jurisdictions. See **hung jury.**

hanging judge (= a judge who is esp. harsh with defendants accused of capital crimes, and sometimes corruptly so) dates at least from the mid-19th century. Some modern references, though, suggest that the phrase might be older—e.g.: "Too often their attitude appears to be that of the *'hanging judges'* of the seventeenth century." *Ex parte Mouratis,* 21 F.2d 694, 695 (N.D. Cal. 1927). See **maximum [+ name].**

Hansard = the official reports of the proceedings of the British Parliament. They take their name from Luke Hansard, printer of the *Journal of the House of Commons* from 1774 to 1828, and his son, Thomas Curson Hansard, printer of the *Parliamentary Debates* during the early 19th century.

happily means "fortunately," not "in a happy manner," when used as in the following examples: "The seventeenth- and eighteenth-century jurists were chiefly teachers and philosophers. *Happily* they had been trained to accept the Roman law as something of paramount authority." Roscoe Pound, *An Introduction to the Philosophy of Law* 16 (1922; repr. 1975)./ "*Happily,* the Criminal Law Act sweeps aside these anomalies . . . ." Glanville Williams, *Textbook of Criminal Law* 349 (1978). See SENTENCE ADVERBS. Cf. **hopefully.**

harass may be pronounced in either of two ways: /***har***-iss/ or /hə-***ras***/. The former is often thought to be preferable, but the latter prevails in AmE. The verb is often misspelled *harrass.* See, e.g., *Suss v. Schammel,* 375 N.W.2d 252, 256 (Iowa 1985).

harassment. During the Senate's confirmation hearings on the appointment of Justice Clarence Thomas in October 1991, senators divided over whether to say /***har**-is-mənt*/ or /*hə-**ras**-mənt*/ (and over other issues as well). Because the proceedings were closely watched throughout the U.S., the correct pronunciation became a popular subject of discussion. Although in BrE /***har**-is-mənt*/ predominates—and many Americans (therefore?) consider it preferable—in AmE /*hə-**ras**-mənt*/ is standard.

hard and fast rule. This CLICHÉ is common, and sometimes useful, in legal prose. E.g., "There is no *hard and fast rule* by which it can be determined when the court will interfere by injunction to prevent what is practically a fraud upon a person engaged in business by the unfair methods of competition."/ "We have expressly rejected the suggestion that we adopt a *hard and fast* time limit for a permissible *Terry* stop." Cf. the cousin of this phrase, **bright-line rule.**

hard cases make bad law. This catchphrase refers to the danger that a decision operating harshly on the defendant may lead a court to make an unwarranted exception or otherwise alter the law. Glanville Williams wrote wishfully when pronouncing this byword passé: "It used to be said that *hard cases make bad law*—a proposition that our less pedantic age regards as doubtful. What is certain is that cases in which the moral indignation of the judge is aroused frequently make bad law." *The Sanctity of Life and the Criminal Law* 105 (1957). In fact, this CLICHÉ is probably used as frequently today as it ever was—and sometimes unmeaningfully.

hard law. See **soft law.**

hardly. The word may mean "vigorously, harshly" <he was beaten hardly>, but this sense is confusing because the word's primary meaning today is "only just, barely"—e.g.: "The judge said *hardly* anything." The difference in placement between *he was beaten hardly* and *he was hardly beaten* is not enough to eliminate doubts about what the writer intends. Still, *hardly* in its primary sense is hardly ever ambiguous.

hard sell; hard sale. *Hard sell* = pressure tactics used in selling. E.g., "While at the funeral home, she was given the *hard sell:* the director implied that the cost of the casket should be proportional to the degree of love she felt for her deceased husband."

Hard sale = a difficult selling job, usu. on an unlikely buyer. Sometimes *hard sell* is used where *sale* belongs—e.g.: "The movie is going to be a *hard sell* [read *hard sale*] for most of today's audiences." Vincent Canby, *"Stanley and Iris": A World Not Seen,* N.Y. Times, 9 Feb. 1990, at B4.

harebrained is the correct form; *hairbrained* is the common blunder. The misspelling falls just short of being what it attempts to denote. A prosecutor is quoted in *People v. Jolly,* 214 N.W.2d 849, 851 (Mich. App. 1974), as having stated to the jury: "This was no *hair-brained* young kid." The court reporter should have written *harebrained.*

harelip. So spelled. This congenital condition got its name from the resemblance it bears to the cleft lip of a hare. Yet *hairlip* is a common error—e.g.: "If a suspect is described to the police as having one eye, a *hairlip* [read *harelip*], and a four-inch scar on his cheek, a line-up or a confrontation serves no purpose beyond cumulation." *McRae v. U.S.,* 420 F.2d 1283, 1292 (D.C. Cir. 1969)./ "[S]ome reasonable persons might conclude that a slight genetic *hairlip* [read *harelip*] should qualify before the diabetes defect because they prefer a shorter life with a pretty face to a longer life without one." Edward J. Larson, *Human Gene Therapy and the Law,* 39 Emory L.J. 855, 861 (1990).

hark back is now preferred over *harken back* or *hearken back.* E.g., "We are not *harking back* to Latin bywords without sanction of our highest Court . . . ." *In re City of Houston,* 745 F.2d 925, 928 (5th Cir. 1984).

harmless (= not capable of being harmed)—as in the phrase *indemnify and hold harmless*—differs significantly from the lay sense ("not capable of harming"). E.g., "Lone Star forever releases, quitclaims, discharges, and *holds harmless* Harris Hospital from any and all claims and causes of action."

The phrase is sometimes written *save harmless*—e.g.: "Amoco would not be fully indemnified and *saved harmless* from any loss." *Patch v. Amoco Oil Co.,* 845 F.2d 571, 572 (5th Cir. 1988).

hath. See -ETH.

haul. See **hale.**

have and hold. See **habendum** & DOUBLETS, TRIPLETS, AND SYNONYM-STRINGS.

havoc, v.i., forms *havocking* and *havocked.*

havoc, to wreak. Although the phrases *create havoc, make havoc, play havoc,* and *work havoc* were once common, the usu. phrase today is *wreak havoc.* The past tense is *wreaked havoc,* not *wrought havoc* (as many writers mistakenly think)—e.g.: "[T]here are abundant examples of linguistic havoc *wrought* [read *wreaked*] by lawyers and legal scholars as well." Robert C. Cumbow, *The Subverting of the Goeduck: Sex and Gender, Which and That, and Other Adventures in the Language of the Law,* 14 Univ. Puget Sound L. Rev. 755, 777 (1991).

H.D.C.; H.I.D.C. Both abbreviations denote a "holder in due course," the former being more common. Because they are initialisms and not acronyms, they should take periods (as opposed to being written *HDC* and *HDIC*), though this battle for reason may already be lost. See ACRONYMS AND INITIALISMS.

Whether one uses *H.D.C.* or *H.I.D.C.,* the indefinite article preceding the initialism should be *an,* not *a:* "In order to be *a HIDC* [read *an H.D.C.*], one must first be a "holder" which means that the party must be in possession of the documents of title or an instrument." *In re Singer Prods. Co.,* 102 B.R. 912, 931 (Bankr. E.D.N.Y. 1989).

he/she. See **he or she** & SEXISM (A).

head has special meanings in legal documents: (1) "a heading in legislation" <the 282-paragraph code was regularly arranged under heads and subheads>; (2) "in an abstract of title, the description of the land covered by the abstract (sometimes also called the *caption*)" <the head misdefined the realty>. These uses of *head* may be slowly disappearing, however; for sense (1), *heading* is now becoming the more usu. word, and for sense (2), either *caption* or *property description* is more common.

headlease. In BrE legal writing, this term denotes a primary lease under which subleases are in effect—e.g.: "The former sublease has been destroyed by the forfeiture of the *headlease,* and the court order does not and cannot revive that sublease." Peter Butt, *Land Law* 293 (2d ed. 1988). Thus, *headlessor* is the BrE correlative of *sublessor,* and *headlessee* of *sublessee.* In AmE, the words *lease, lessor,* and *lessee* generally refer to the primary lease.

headnote, in AmE and BrE alike, refers to the reporter's summary of a judicial opinion; usu. placed at the beginning of the reported case, the headnote states each rule of law that the case supposedly involves. A synonym of *headnote* is *syllabus,* q.v.

healthful; healthy. *Healthy* is used of a person in good health, *healthful* of whatever promotes good health.

hearing officer. See **administrative-law judge.**

hearken back. See **hark back.**

hearsay evidence; secondhand evidence. The former is the preferred, universally understood term for evidence of the oral statements of someone other than the witness testifying and statements in documents offered to prove the truth of the matter asserted.

Hearsay is sometimes made *heresay,* an appalling error committed infrequently by legal secretaries. Heaven forbid that lawyers should perpetrate it. To do so would be heresy. See **direct evidence.**

heart-rending is sometimes malapropistically rendered *heart-rendering.* E.g., "The true ground of action is the outrage and deprivation; the injury the father sustains in the loss of his child; the *heart-rendering* [read *heart-rending*] agony he must suffer in the destruction of his dearest hopes." The verb *rend* (= to split, tear) has nothing to do with the verb *render.* See MALAPROPISMS.

hear ye, hear ye, hear ye; oyez, oyez, oyez. Both forms of the cry are used today in American courts. The first is archaic English, the second vestigial LAW FRENCH with the same meaning. See **oyez, oyez, oyez** & ***countez.***

hedonic damages measure the taking away of the pleasure of being alive; such damages are not allowed in most jurisdictions. The phrase was innovated in the 1980s: "An Illinois jury has awarded *hedonic damages.*" Nat'l L.J., Nov. 26, 1984, at 3./ "The amount of so-called *hedonic damages* was decided following an economist's evaluation of what the youth's enjoyment of life would have been worth had he not been killed." *Court and Government Decisions with Impact on Business, Employees, Consumers,* U.S. News & World Rep., 17 Dec. 1984, at 80./ "Pushed by a handful of imaginative plaintiff lawyers and expert witnesses-for-hire, *hedonic damages* are sought in personal-injury cases as compensation for the loss of the pleasure of living." Paul M. Barrett, *Accept Hedonic Damages, Study Urges, but Fight for Proper Use,* Wall St. J., 21 Aug. 1989, at 3B. See **damages.**

hegemony /*hi-**jem**-ə-nee*/ is a fundamentally political term ("political dominance; the leadership or predominant authority of one state of a confederacy or union over the others") that has been imported into nonpolitical contexts. E.g., "The court's duty is to protect the public from the activities of those who, because of the lack of professional skills, may cause injury; this does not mean, however, that attorneys' *hegemony* over the practice of law must be absolute."/ "With the passing of the *hegemony* of historical jurisprudence at the close of the last century there came a revival of comparative law." (Roscoe Pound)

height has a distinct *-t-* sound at the end; to pronounce this word as if it were *heighth* is semiliterate.

heinous */hay-nəs/*—rhyming with "pain us"—is one of the most commonly mispronounced words in legal contexts. It is also frequently misspelled *heinious.*

heir. **A. *Heir (at law); (in)heritor.*** These terms denote "the person entitled by statute to the land of an intestate." *Heir,* the most common term, is commonly misunderstood: "Laymen—and sometimes first-year law students taking exams—wrongly assume that one who receives real property by will is an heir. Technically, the word *'heir'* is reserved for one who receives real property by action of the laws of intestacy, which operate today only in the absence of a valid will." Thomas F. Bergin & Paul G. Haskell, *Preface to Estates in Land and Future Interests* 14 n.32 (2d ed. 1984).

Strictly speaking, *heirs* cannot be determined until the ancestor dies, though we commonly speak of *heirs apparent* and *heirs presumptive* (see B). *Heir* ordinarily differs from the term *children,* for brothers and sisters can be heirs.

Legal heir (= the heir of an intestate by operation of law) is another way of rendering *heir at law:* "There is nothing in the will or in the record that sustains a conclusion that she made the bequest because she wanted to make certain her *legal heirs* would not share in the estate." Still another variant synonymous with *heir at law* is *heir general.* Usually, though, *heir* alone is sufficient.

Inheritor, often used in extended senses <inheritors of the Western tradition>, predominates over *heritor.*

B. Types of Heirs: *expectant heir; prospective heir; heir apparent; heir presumptive.* A living person has no heirs, but various terms have been devised to describe potential heirs. An *expectant heir* is one who has a reversionary or remainder interest in property, or a chance of succeeding to it. E.g., "Even the *expectant heir,* who has no interest at all, may make a valid and specifically enforceable contract to convey for an adequate consideration."

A *prospective heir* is one who may inherit but may be excluded; this term embraces the two other types of heirs, *presumptive* and *apparent.* An *heir presumptive* is a person who will inherit if the potential intestate dies immediately, but who may be excluded if another more closely related heir is born. An *heir apparent* is certain to inherit unless he or she dies first or is excluded by a valid will.

On the placement of the adjectives in these phrases, see POSTPOSITIVE ADJECTIVES. Sometimes the adjectives are used prepositively: "With the exception of the trustee, all the parties as thus represented—including contingent remaindermen and the *presumptive heirs*—joined in a petition to the court to consider and approve the proposed compromise of the litigation."

C. *Heir; distributee; next of kin.* Technically, *heir* should refer only to the person entitled to the land of an intestate; either *distributee* or *next of kin* should be used of one entitled to an intestate's personal property. But the technically correct forms are rarely followed even in the ordinary speech of lawyers: "[T]oday the word *'heirs'* usually means those persons designated by the applicable statute to take a decedent's intestate property, real and personal." Jesse Dukeminier & Stanley M. Johanson, *Family Wealth Transactions* 11–12 (1972). See **devisee.**

heirs of the body. See **bodily heirs.**

helix yields either of the plurals *helixes* or *helices.* The unpretentious plural ending in *-xes* is better. Cf. **appendixes** & **indexes.** See PLURALS (A).

help but. See **cannot help but.**

helpmate; helpmeet. *Helpmeet,* now archaic, was the original form, yet folk etymology changed the spelling to *-mate,* which is now the prevalent form. Though *helpmate* means "a companion or helper," it is generally restricted in use to one's spouse.

help (to). Where the *to* can be idiomatically omitted, it ought to be—e.g.: "All this may *help to* [read *help*] explain, though perhaps *not to justify,* [read *not justify*], the bias in the legal profession and the courts towards traditional goals and values." P.S. Atiyah, *Law and Modern Society* 87 (1983).

hence. See **thence.**

henceforth; henceforward. The latter is a NEEDLESS VARIANT. See **from henceforth.**

he or she. The traditional view was that the masculine pronouns are generic, comprehending both male and female. But this view is now widely assailed as embodying SEXISM. One way to avoid the generic masculine *he, his* and *him* is to use—not at every turn, but sparingly—*he or she,* and *his or her,* and *him or her.* E.g., "If a juror could be challenged for cause merely because *he or she* was against the death penalty in the circumstances at issue, a prosecutor could describe the particular facts of the case and demand to know how each veniremember would vote at the penalty phase."

Another way to avoid the problem—not possible in all contexts—is to make the antecedent of the pronoun plural if possible. E.g., "If *jurors* could be challenged for cause merely because *they* were against the death penalty in the circumstances at issue, a prosecutor could describe the particular facts of the case and demand to know how each venireman would vote at the penalty phase." The disadvantage of such a wording is that it often too strongly suggests a singleness of mind in the group, as opposed to the uniqueness of an individual mind.

Interestingly, the forms *he or she* and *his or her* have long found acceptance in our typically verbose legal writing. Weseen wrote, "Outside of legal writing, it is not considered good form to use double pronouns, as *he or she, his or her.*" Maurice H. Weseen, *Crowell's Dictionary of English Grammar* 198 (1928). The phrase is by no means a newfangled concession to feminism. In 1837, the English Wills Act stated: "And be it further enacted, That every Will made by a Man or Woman shall be revoked by *his or her* Marriage (except a Will made in exercise of Appointment . . .)." 7 Wm. IV & 1 Vict., c. 26 (1837). See SEXISM (A).

HERE- AND THERE- WORDS. These abound in legal writing (unfortunately they do *not* occur just here and there), usually thrown in gratuitously to give legal documents that musty legal smell. Following are typical examples:

- "Each capitalized term used *herein* which is defined in the loan and security agreement as *hereby* amended is used *herein* as defined *therein* unless otherwise defined *herein* or unless the context requires otherwise." (From a loan and security agreement.)
- "The exclusive right to enter upon the land, to drill wells *thereon,* to remove *therefrom* the oil to exhaustion, and to pay *therefor* a portion of the oil extracted or the equivalent of such portion, is a property right that the law protects." (From an oil-and-gas treatise.) See **therefore.**
- " . . . all as fully appears from the affidavit of the publisher *thereof heretofore herein* filed." (From a court paper quoted in *Penn v. Pensacola–Escambia Gov'tal Ctr. Auth.,* 311 So. 2d 97, 102 (Fla. 1975)).
- "[I]t is not necessary for us to take up each assignment seriatim and reply *thereto,* because from what we have *heretofore* said and what we will *hereinafter* say we have concluded this is a complete answer . . . ." *Saunders v. State,* 345 S.W.2d 899, 904–05 (Tenn. 1961).

These words are generally to be used only as a last resort to avoid awkward phrasing. They are certainly not to be used one after another in a passage that is already stylistically abhorrent.

hereabout(s). This term, meaning "in this vicinity," is preferably spelled with the final *-s.*

hereafter; hereinafter. Perhaps because *hereinafter* sounds especially legalistic, some plain-language advocates have misguidedly recommended *hereafter* in its place. The two words have distinct meanings, however; and in any event, *hereafter* could hardly be cheered as a plain-language triumph over *hereinafter.*

Hereafter = (1) henceforth; (2) at some future time. The existence of these two meanings may make the word ambiguous, for example in legislation that is said to be *effective hereafter.* A more precise rendering of the intended meaning is *effective with the passage of this Act* or *after the day this Act takes effect.* Sense (1) is the more usual meaning of *hereafter.* A similar ambiguity plagues *heretofore.* See **hitherto.**

Hereinafter = in a part of this document that follows. E.g., "The parties have stipulated that an exchange of telegrams *hereinafter* referred to constitutes the contract." Often, as in that sentence, the *hereinafter*-phrase ought to be omitted because it does not enhance clarity. Sometimes this compound word may even cloud the thought, as when drafters misuse it for *hereinbefore* and thus prompt courts to declare that it really does mean "hereinbefore" in such contexts.

As with *herein,* the legal writer is best advised to make the reference exact, by stating, e.g., *later in this will* or *later in this paragraph* rather than *hereinafter.* Moreover, in introducing abbreviated names, *hereinafter* is redundant: rather than *Mobil Oil Corporation (hereinafter "Mobil"),* one should write *Mobil Oil Corporation ("Mobil").* See HERE- AND THERE- WORDS & **hereinabove.**

hereby is often a FLOTSAM PHRASE that can be excised with no loss of meaning: *I hereby declare* has no advantages over *I declare.* Sometimes the word is (correctly) omitted where you might expect to find it—e.g.: "The writs of scire facias and mandamus are abolished." Fed. R. Civ. P. 81(b). The less-polished drafter would have written *are hereby abolished.* See HERE- AND THERE- WORDS.

hereditable /hə-**red**-i-tə-bəl/ = subject to inheritance. "'Children' is not a word of limitation; it does not point to *hereditable* succession." Apart from its use in the standard phrase *hereditable succession, hereditable* is a NEEDLESS VARIANT of *inheritable.* See **inheritable.**

hereditament(s). This term, which is best accented on the second rather than the third syllable /hə-**red**-i-tə-mənt/, suggests a relation in meaning to *inheritance.* This is misleading, even though the term originally did mean "things capable of being inherited." Today it means merely "land, real property" and should be avoided as an obscure LEGALISM. It is often redundant—e.g.: "No tenant and no person claiming through any tenant of any land or *hereditament* of which he has been let into possession is, till he has given up possession, permitted to deny that the landlord had, at the time when the tenant was let into possession, a title to such land or *hereditament.*" (Eng.)

Traditionally, the law distinguished between *corporeal hereditaments* (= tangible items of property, such as land or buildings) and *incorporeal hereditaments* (= intangible rights in land, such as easements). See **corporeal hereditaments & lands.**

In England, *hereditament* has the additional sense "a unit of land that has been separately assessed for rating purposes" (*CDL*).

hereditary. See **inheritable.**

heredity for *inheritance* or *inheritability,* though once possible, is today confusingly legalistic. *Heredity* has now been confined largely to biological senses in nonlegal writing; hence legal writing need not perpetuate an archaic sense of the word. "The decedent's many prolonged affairs make the problems of *heredity* [read *inheritability*] quite complex." The nonlegal reader would interpret the quoted sentence as addressing bastardy rather than inheritance.

herein (= in this) is a vague word in legal documents, for the reader can rarely be certain whether it means *in this subsection, in this section* (or *paragraph*), *in this document,* or *in this transaction.* A more precise phrase, such as any of the three just listed, is preferable. See HERE- AND THERE- WORDS & **herewith.**

hereinabove is almost always unnecessary for *above.* E.g., "I am of the opinion that defendant is liable by virtue of the express provisions of Act 34 of 1926, as I have related elsewhere *hereinabove* [read *above*]."/ "For lack of the essential findings *hereinabove discussed* [read *discussed above*], the judgment is reversed." See **above (B), hereafter & hereinbefore.** See also HERE- AND THERE- WORDS.

hereinafter. See **hereafter & hereinbefore.**

hereinafter referred to as; hereinafter called. These stilted LEGALISMS are easily avoided. Ordinarily, a parenthetical short form ought to appear without a lead-in—e.g.: "Acme Fire & Casualty Company (*hereinafter called "Acme"*) [read (*"Acme"*)] moves that the court dismiss the action."

hereinbefore; hereinafter. In legislative DRAFTING, these words should be avoided, because amendments and repeals may effect a reordering of the statute, and make either of these words inaccurate or misleading. The better practice is to be specific and write *in this act* or *in this section.* See **hereafter & hereinabove.** See also HERE- AND THERE- WORDS.

herein fail not (= please adhere closely to your instructions) is legalistic deadwood often found in writs directed to process-servers. E.g., "*Herein fail not,* and have you the said money, together with this writ, before this court within 60 days from the date of this writ." See **herein.**

heres is the L. equivalent of the singular word *heir*—not of the plural *heirs.* The plural of *heres* is *heredes.*

hereto (= to this) is sometimes misused for *heretofore* (= up to this time). E.g., "Hedonic damages have not *hereto* [read *heretofore*] been recoverable in this state." In any event, the word is best eliminated—e.g.: "This agreement shall be binding upon the parties *hereto* and their respective heirs, successors, and assigns." [Read *This Agreement binds the parties as well as their heirs, successors, and assigns.*] See HERE- AND THERE-WORDS & **hereafter.**

heretofore. See **hitherto & up to now.**

hereunder. This word can almost always be deleted unmisgivingly—e.g.: "If the Employee fails to use full vacation privileges *hereunder* [delete *hereunder*], the Employee is not entitled to additional compensation for the additional time worked." See HERE- AND THERE- WORDS.

herewith. See HERE- AND THERE- WORDS & **enclosed herewith.**

heritable. See **inheritable.**

heritor. See **heir (A).**

heritrix; heritress. See SEXISM (C).

he/she. See SEXISM (A) & **he or she.**

hesitancy; hesitance; hesitation. *Hesitancy* is a quality ("the state of being hesitant; reluctance"), whereas *hesitation* is an act ("the act of hesitating"). Thus: "The courts had no *hesitancy* in holding the defamatory matter libelous."/ "We have no *hesitation* [read *hesitancy,* i.e., reluctance] in declaring that public policy requires that the interest of the beneficiary of a trust should be subject to the claims for support of his children." *Hesitance* is a NEEDLESS VARIANT.

hew = (1) to chop, cut; or (2) to adhere or conform (to). Thus sense (1): "The appellants contend that the wife took title to the estate of her husband in fee simple absolute, which is not *hewed* down to a lesser estate by words of weaker import." And sense (2), which is more common in modern legal prose: "In any event, we *hew* to the Supreme Court's broad language; if that is to be trimmed, it is for the court to do, not for us."

The preferred past participle is *hewn* in BrE and *hewed* in AmE. E.g., "The substantive distinction between admonitions and instructions is not always clear or closely *hewn to* [read, in AmE, *hewed to*]." (Eng.)

hiatus. Pl. *hiatuses.* See HYPERCORRECTION (A).

H.I.D.C. See **H.D.C.**

high court; High Court. In AmE, *high court* or *high bench* usu. refers to the U.S. Supreme Court—e.g.: "Four protesters, objecting to the Supreme Court's ruling last spring allowing states to further restrict abortions, disrupted the *high court's* session yesterday." *Disorder in the Court,* Wall St. J., 8 Nov. 1989, at B8.

In England and Northern Ireland, by contrast, the *High Court* is a trial and (for some purposes) appellate court having mainly civil jurisdiction and divided into three divisions: the Queen's Bench Division, the Chancery Division, and the Family Division. One judge sits at a trial. Two or three judges usu. sit in these divisional courts to review certain proceedings of a lower tribunal or to hear appeals from magistrates' decisions in summary criminal trials. Appeal lies in the Court of Appeal, Civil Division.

In Scotland, the High Court (of Justiciary) is the superior criminal court with trial and appellate jurisdiction.

higher court; upper court. Both phrases are used to denote an appellate court that reviews the judgment of a *lower court,* q.v. *Higher court* is more common in AmE and BrE; *upper court* appears occasionally in BrE. Cf. **inferior (B).**

highest law of the land. See **law of the land.**

highfalutin. So spelled—not *highfaluting, highfalutin',* or *hifalutin.*

high seas; open seas. Of these synonyms—meaning "the seas or oceans apart from territorial waters"—the former is now more common.

hijack. Vehicles and planes are *hijacked,* but not people. E.g., "Lipsig spent two years trying to get political asylum for Tshombe, who was mysteriously *hijacked* [read *abducted?*] to Algiers in the mid-sixties and detained in prison." See **skyjack.**

hindering impediment. See **impedient impediment.**

hired gun. See LAWYERS, DEROGATORY NAMES FOR (A).

hire purchase, n., is a late-19th-century BrE neologism equivalent to the AmE phrases *lease-purchase contract* (or *agreement*), *rent-to-own contract* (or *agreement*), or *lease-to-own contract* (or *agreement*). *Hire purchase,* which began as the longer phrase *hire and purchase,* is now usu. two words as a noun phrase and hyphenated as a PHRASAL ADJECTIVE <the hire-purchase system>.

It is also sometimes used as a verb phrase (hyphenated): "[W]here a person examines goods and subsequently makes an offer to buy or *hire-purchase* them, it may be an implied term of the offer that the goods should remain in substantially the same state in which they were when the offer was made." G.H. Treitel, *The Law of Contract* 43–44 (8th ed. 1991).

hirer (BrE) = *lessee* (AmE).

his or her. See **he or she** & SEXISM (A).

historical; historic. The former, meaning "of or relating to or occurring in history," is called upon for use far more frequently. The latter means "historically significant" <the Alamo is a historic building>. An event that makes history is *historic;* an event of no great importance that occurred in history is *historical.* Momentous happenings or developments are *historic;* merely documented happenings or developments are *historical.*

In the following sentences, *historic* is correctly used: "Chief Justice Cardozo's *historic* and oft-quoted dissent in *Graf v. Hope Bldg. Corp.* has become equity's modern fount in cases in which the tyrant demands his dollars and cents on legal time whatever the impact of sickening hardship his victim suffers."/ "In *Brown II* the Court referred to its *historic* opinion in *Brown I* as declaring the fundamental principle that racial discrimination in public education is unconstitutional."

Examples of *historic* used incorrectly for *historical* could easily run for several pages, so common is this error—e.g.: "The *historic* [read *historical*] option of a maritime suitor pursuing a common-law remedy to select his forum, state or federal, would be taken away by an expanded view of section 1331." *Romero v. International Terminal Operating Co.,* 358 U.S. 354, 371 (1959) (per Frankfurter, J.)./ "Conceivably *historic* [read *historical*] skepticism about the propriety of nonpossessory security in personal property also stems from this mentality." R.E. Speidel et al., *Commercial Law Teaching Materials* 28 (4th ed. 1987).

On the question whether to write *a* or *an historic(al),* see **a** (A).

HISTORICAL PRESENT TENSE IN JUDICIAL OPINIONS. See OPINIONS, JUDICIAL (A).

hitherto; thitherto. *Hitherto* = up to now, i.e., heretofore. *Thitherto* = up to some specified or implied time in the past, i.e., theretofore. Obviously these ARCHAISMS are hardly worth using since the terms just used in defining them—*heretofore* (or *up to now*) and *theretofore*—are perfectly equivalent and much more common. In the following example, a legal writer mistook the import of *hitherto,* which does not properly appear with the past-perfect tense: "The Superior Court, conceding that it *hitherto* [read *thitherto* or, better, *theretofore*] had refused to enjoin such conduct, recognized the growing tendency in courts to grant equitable relief under such circumstances." See **up to now.**

Hobbesian choice. See **Hobson's choice** (C).

Hobson's choice. A. Generally. This ever-growing CLICHÉ has loosened its etymological tether. Tradition has it that Thomas Hobson (1549–1631), a hostler in Cambridge, England, always gave his customers only one choice among his horses: whichever one was closest to the door. Hence, in literary usage, a *Hobson's choice* came to denote no choice at all—either taking what is offered or taking nothing at all.

BrE writers tend to stick to that sense, as here: "The tribunal . . . concluded that the employees were faced with *Hobson's choice*[,] that they had no real option but to accept the move . . . ." *Sheet Metal Components Ltd. v. Plumridge,* [1974] I.C.R. 373, 377 (Nat'l Indus. Relations Ct.).

Though purists resist the change, the prevailing sense in AmE—in legal and nonlegal writing alike—is not that of having no choice at all, but of having two bad choices. E.g., "Ithaca faced a *Hobson's choice* when confronted with Dean's uncompromising and adamant refusal to work on Sunday. Ithaca could either totally capitulate to Dean's demands and require other employees to perform his work or replace Dean with an employee willing to make reciprocal accommodations." *E.E.O.C. v. Ithaca Indus., Inc.,* 829 F.2d 519, 521 (4th Cir. 1987)./ "This important public policy will not be advanced by presenting a party with the *Hobson's choice* of either dropping its claim or revealing all confidential communications related to a criminal defense." *Greater Newburyport Clamshell Alliance v. Public Serv. Co.,* 838 F.2d 13, 22 (1st Cir. 1988). Cf. **dilemma.**

B. Article with. Traditionally—and still in BrE—the phrase takes no article; that is, you are faced not with *a Hobson's choice* but with *Hobson's choice.* In modern AmE, the phrase usu. takes either *a* or *the.*

C. "Hobbesian choice." Amazingly, some writers have confused the obscure Thomas Hobson with his famous contemporary, the philosopher Thomas Hobbes (1588–1679). The resulting MALAPROPISM is beautifully grotesque:

- "A mere request for administrative relief, however, does not bind the property owner to the *Hobbesian choice* [read *Hobson's choice*] of countenancing all the delays a vast federal bureaucracy can produce." *White v. Acree,* 594 F.2d 1385, 1390 (10th Cir. 1979).
- "The court need not slap an innocent client with a judgment regardless of the merits, leaving the client with a *Hobbesian choice* [read *Hobson's choice*] of suffering in silence or of making a distasteful claim against his own lawyer." *Fisher v. Crest Corp.,* 735 P.2d 1052, 1058 (Idaho Ct. App. 1987) (Burnett, J., dissenting).
- "Were the law otherwise, the officers' invitation

to depart would present the subject of interrogation with a *Hobbesian choice* [read *Hobson's choice*]. To stay could lead to inculpation; to depart surely would." *U.S. v. Sterling,* 909 F.2d 1078, 1082 (7th Cir. 1990).

hodgepodge. See **hotchpot.**

hoi polloi (= the common people, the masses). Inasmuch as *hoi* in Greek means "the (plural)," *the hoi polloi* is a technical REDUNDANCY. Nevertheless, *the hoi polloi* overwhelmingly predominates in modern usage.

hold, vb. **A. As Transitive Verb.** When used properly in the legal sense (signifying "to decide," probably from "hold the opinion that"), this verb describes *what* judges do and is thus transitive. It should not be used intransitively to describe *how* judges do. In the following two sentences, the intransitive use is wrong: "Without the scarcity rationale, it seems unlikely that the *Red Lion* Court would have *held as it did,* even more unlikely that the present Court would do so."/ "This court's task, then, is to decide *how* [read *what*] the Oregon courts would hold when faced with the issue." (Courts hold *something;* they do not hold *in a certain manner.* Thus, in the second example, the noun *what,* not the adverb *how,* is the proper word.) In general English usage, of course, the intransitive use of *hold* is quite acceptable in such clauses as *The argument does not hold.*

B. *Hold (to be).* *Hold* need not be followed by *to be* or *as,* although *to be* may sometimes add clarity. E.g., "We *hold permissible* [better: *hold to be permissible*] an award of extraordinary damages for frivolous appeal."/ "In *Bryan v. Bigelow,* the unincorporated letter was *held testamentary* [better: *held to be testamentary*] and not admissible in evidence to rebut a resulting trust in favor of the residuary estate." But here the shorter form works better. "The defendant was *held to be liable* [read *held liable*] for breach of contract and conversion." *Held as* <the award was held as permissible> is idiomatically inferior.

C. *It was held that.* This phrase has traditionally been used in the sense "the law as repeatedly stated by the courts was that"—e.g.: "Previous to the case of Ackroyd v. Smithson, *it was held that* an unqualified direction by a testator in his will to sell land, or to buy land with his money, created a complete conversion in equity of the land into money." C.C. Langdell, *Equitable Conversion,* 19 Harv. L. Rev. 1, 1 (1905).

hold a brief for is a lawyers' idiom that has passed into general usage in a broadened sense. Originally, it meant "to be retained as counsel for," but now it generally means merely "to defend or support." E.g., "In setting forth the claims of the revived natural law of today, I am not *holding a brief* for the old natural law." Roscoe Pound, *The Formative Era of American Law* 29 (1938).

holden is an archaic past participle of *hold,* used as recently as 1850 in *Brown v. Kendall,* 60 Mass. (6 Cush.) 292, 295 (1850): "There certainly are cases in the books, where, the injury being direct and immediate, trespass has been *holden* to lie, though the injury was not intentional." This ARCHAISM has even found its way into 20th-century texts: "The rule has been adopted out of regard to the interests of justice, which cannot be *upholden* . . . ." Eugene A. Jones, *Manual of Equity Pleading and Practice* 25 (1916).

holder in due course = a person who in good faith has given value for a negotiable instrument that is complete and regular on its face, is not overdue, and, to the possessor's knowledge, has not been dishonored.

holding. As a noun, *holding* involves a determination of a matter of law that is pivotal to a judicial decision. Here it is loosely used in a lay sense: "Justice Jacobs quoted an 1859 New Jersey *holding* that '[f]ew statutes would stand if tried by standards of logic, grammar, or rhetoric.'" The opinion may have made this *statement;* but, inasmuch as it is not a statement of law, it cannot be a *holding.* See JUDGMENTS, APPELLATE-COURT & **finding.**

holding over is legal JARGON denoting a tenant's action in continuing to occupy the leased premises after the lease term has expired. E.g., "The tenant, *holding over* despite efforts to evict him, planted a crop that eventually the landlord harvested."

The tenant is often referred to as a *holdover tenant*—e.g.: "In Montana a *holdover tenant* is charged treble rent." Robert Kratovil, *Real Estate Law* 297 (1946)./ "In addition to delineating prohibited conduct, the legislature provided a remedy for landlords with *holdover tenants* and others guilty of forcible entry and detainer and unlawful detainer." *Gorman v. Ratliff,* 712 S.W.2d 888, 890 (Ark. 1986).

holiday (fr. *holy day*) = (AmE) a day on which one is exempt from one's usual work; or (BrE) a vacation. This term has long plagued American courts interpreting time computations in statutes and rules. In 1992, for example, the Supreme Court of Texas decided that *holiday* includes both a day that the commissioners' court in the county where the case is pending has determined to be a holiday, and a day on which the clerk's office for the court in which the case is pending is officially closed. See *In re V.C.,* 829 S.W.2d 772 (Tex. 1992).

Holmesian; Holmesean. The former is the better and more common spelling.

holocaust (lit., "burnt whole," fr. Gk.) is one of our most hyperbolic words, beloved of jargonmongers and second-rate journalists. The historical meaning that the term acquired after World War II, of course, is beyond question. Figurative applications of the word, however, are often questionable. Here it is used to no avail in reference to a scandal: "C.R. would soon be engulfed in a *holocaust of controversy and pain* [read *painful controversy*] that would maim several lives, including his own, wound hundreds of other people, and jostle the foundations of the world's most glamorous industry." Inherent in the sense of the word, whether literal or figurative, is the idea of a complete burning; thus, it may be used appropriately of fires, but not, for example, of floods. See ETYMOLOGICAL AWARENESS & OVERSTATEMENT.

holograph, n.; **olograph.** In the law of wills, a *holograph* is a will that is entirely written, dated, and signed in the hand of the testator; in many American states, such a will is valid even if it is not witnessed. E.g., "Unfortunately, much litigation is stimulated by other requirements for the execution of *holographs,* and the difficulty in integrating *holographs* at probate is particularly acute." The spelling *olograph* is a NEEDLESS VARIANT that has appeared in a few hundred cases—but many hundreds fewer than the etymologically preferable *holograph.* Even so, the spelling *olograph* is prevalent in Louisiana.

The word *holograph* is not to be confused with *hologram* (= a three-dimensional picture).

holographic; holograph, adj. The word *holographic* is the better adjective, not *holograph:* "[T]he district court found that it was a *holograph* [read *holographic*] will." *In re Estate of Buckley,* 536 F.2d 580, 581 (3d Cir. 1976).

The form *olographic* is common in Louisiana but not elsewhere.

homage (orig., the ceremony by which the tenant became the lord's "man") is best pronounced /***hom***-*ij*/. It is a pretension to omit the *-h-* sound. See **humble.**

home in, not *hone in,* is the correct phrase. In the 19th century, the metaphor referred to what homing pigeons do; by the middle of the 20th century, it referred also to what aircraft and missiles do.

And by the late 20th century, some writers had begun mistaking the phrase by using the wrong verb, *hone* instead of *home*—e.g.: "True, the challenge was launched in general terms and did not *hone in* [read *home in*] on the determinative element . . . ." *In re Allison H.,* 281 Cal. Rptr. 178, 180 (App. Ct. 1991)./ *Prosecutors Hone* [read *Home*] *in on Gilley,* Amarillo Sunday News-Globe, 10 Nov. 1991, at 1.

homeowner. One word.

homered, to be; hometowned, to be. In AmE legal slang, *to be homered* or *to be hometowned* is to be bested in a rural courthouse by a local lawyer, usu. because of a judge's provincial biases. E.g., "Though city judges are accused of bias as often or more so than country judges, the distressing fact is that outsiders who lose their cases in rural courthouses may charge they've been '*homered.*' " Allen G. Minker, *Justice Out Here,* 17 Litigation 3, 3 (Spring 1991).

Though in both phrases the primary reference is to hometown favoritism, the idiom *to be homered* was no doubt influenced by the baseball term *homer* (= a home run), which is used also as a verb, as in *he homered* (i.e., hit a home run).

homestead, n. In most American states, the land owned and occupied by a husband and wife as their home is known as their *homestead,* as long as the land does not exceed in area or value the limits fixed by law. *Homestead laws* or *homestead rights* exempt a homestead from execution or judicial sale for debt, unless both the husband and the wife have jointly mortgaged the property or otherwise subjected it to creditors' claims.

homestead, v.t. The past tense of this verb is *homesteaded.* E.g., "The Chancellor adjudged the subject property *to be homestead* [read *to be homesteaded* or *to be a homestead*] under Article X of the Florida Constitution." One who homesteads is a *homesteader.* Congress enacted the Homestead Act in 1862.

hometowned, to be. See **homered, to be.**

homicide refers not to a crime (as is commonly thought), but to the lawful or unlawful killing of a person. The word is frequently misspelled *homocide.* See **murder** & -CIDE.

homogen(e)ous. *Homogeneous* (five syllables) is the usual and the etymologically preferable form.

Homogeneal, homogenetic, homogenetical are rare forms to be avoided; they have failed to become standard and should be laid to rest.

hone in. See **home in.**

Honorable, in AmE, is a title of respect given to judges, members of the U.S. Congress, ambassadors, and the like. It should be used not with surnames only, but with complete names (e.g., *The Honorable Antonin Scalia*) or with a title of courtesy (e.g., *The Honorable Mr. Scalia*). The abbreviation *Hon.* should be used only in mailing addresses.

In the U.K., the title *Honourable* (so spelled) is given to judges of the High Court and equivalents, and to children of viscounts and barons. Members of the Privy Council (which includes ministers of the Crown, Lords Justices of Appeal, and certain others) are styled *Right Honourable.* Judges at circuit courts in England are styled *His Honour Judge So-and-So* and addressed "Your Honour." Cf. **my lord** & **your Honor.**

honorable court, this. Commonly sprinkled throughout briefs, this phrase should be sparingly used, for it tends to nauseate even those judges most susceptible to flattery. E.g., "Review by *this Honorable Court* of the granting by the district court of the motion for preliminary injunction is a routine matter in which *this Honorable Court* need determine only whether the district court abused its broad discretion in granting the preliminary injunction." The references should be to *the Court* or *this Court,* apart from the first reference in, e.g., the commencement of a pleading. The capitalization of *court* is compliment enough.

honorarium. Pl. *-ia, -iums.* Though *honorariums* has much to commend itself as a homegrown plural—and is the form used by *The New York Times*—*honoraria* generally prevails in AmE and BrE alike. See PLURALS (A).

Honor, your. See **your Honor.**

honoree; honorand. In the early 1950s, these two forms sprang up, both denoting a person who receives an honor. Both words are acceptably formed. The *OED* records only *honorand,* which has probably predominated in BrE. In AmE, however, *honoree* has taken the field—e.g.: "We know of no reason . . . why the name of the donor [cannot appear] under the name of the *honoree* thereon." *State v. Morrison,* 57 So. 2d 238, 247 (La. Ct. App. 1952)./ "Neither the hostess nor the *honoree* testified." *State v. Brown,* 160 S.E.2d 508, 511 (N.C. Ct. App. 1968./ "Of the approximately ninety inquiries from judges to the committee in the past ten years, most have concerned three areas: thirty-five (about 40 percent) have sought guidance on the appropriateness of the inquiring judge's attending events as a guest or an *honoree* . . . ." *In re Access to Certain Records of Rhode Island Advisory Committee on the Code of Judicial Conduct,* 637 A.2d 1063, 1069 (R.I. 1994) (Lederberg, J., concurring). See -EE.

hopefully. So much has been written of this word that little can be added here except to suggest striking this word from your vocabulary. (See FORBIDDEN WORDS.) Briefly, the objections are that (1) *hopefully* properly means "in a hopeful manner" and should not be used merely to mean *I hope* or *it is to be hoped;* (2) in constructions such as, "Hopefully, it will rain today," the writer illogically attributes an emotion (*hopefulness*) to an inanimate object (*it*).

The first objection is to SLIPSHOD EXTENSION and is defensible. The second objection is unsound because it ignores similar SENTENCE ADVERBS such as *sadly* and *happily,* qq.v.

In 1932—the year in which the extended sense was first recorded—*hopefully* still generally meant "in a hopeful manner." E.g., "[D]efendant would be placed in a state of servitude, for which she might *hopefully* expect to realize only her room and board in return for carrying a full share of her load." *Botkin v. Pyle,* 14 P.2d 187, 192 (Colo. 1932). By 1949, the SLIPSHOD EXTENSION of *hopefully* was well on its way: "This is the third, *hopefully* the last, stage in the adjudication of the rights of the parties in this controversy." *In re King's Estate,* 66 A.2d 68, 69 (Pa. 1949).

Today, the word is all but ubiquitous—even in legal print. E.g., "[T]he protection of the American investing public against depredations by foreign nationals must be implemented by whatever tools are available, *hopefully* with more rather than less effectiveness." *S.E.C. v. Myers,* 285 F. Supp. 743, 750 (D. Md. 1968)./ "*Hopefully,* everyone ought to share the view that we are our 'brother's keeper' . . . ." *Ross v. Ross,* 200 N.W.2d 149, 154 (Minn. 1972) (Rogosheske, J., concurring)./ "[T]he trial court, *hopefully* imbued with a fair amount of common sense as well as an understanding of the applicable law, views the questioning as a whole." *Wainwright v. Witt,* 469 U.S. 412, 435 (1985)./ "[T]his is a decision which will need to be taken by the parents (*hopefully* without the intervention of the court) in the future." *Evans v. Evans,* [1990] 2 All E.R. 147, 153.

Even so, the word received so much negative attention in the 1970s and 1980s that many writers have blacklisted it, so using it at all today is a precarious venture. Indeed, careful writers and speakers avoid the word even in its traditional sense, for they are likely to be misunderstood if they use it in the old sense.

horizontal restraints; vertical restraints. In the terminology of antitrust law, restraints imposed by agreement between competitors are called *horizontal restraints;* those imposed by agreement between firms at different levels of distribution are called *vertical restraints.* See *Business Elecs. Corp. v. Sharp Elecs. Corp.,* 485 U.S. 717, 730 (1988).

hornbook law = *black-letter law,* q.v. *Hornbooks* were originally leaves of paper with the alphabet depicted on them; these were covered by a thin plate of translucent horn and mounted on a tablet of wood for use by schoolchildren. By extension, *hornbook* came to be applied to lawbooks containing the rudiments of law. E.g., "It is *hornbook* tort *law* that one who undertakes to warn the public of danger and thereby induces reliance must perform his 'good samaritan' task in a careful manner."/ "It is *hornbook law* everywhere that silence of itself does not constitute assent."

hornbook method. See **casebook method.**

horse case. See **whitehorse case.**

horseshed, v.t., = to prepare (a witness favorable to one's cause, often a client) to testify, esp. with instructions about the proper method of responding to questions while testifying. E.g., "[E]very trial lawyer knows that the 'preparing' of witnesses may embrace a multitude of other measures, including some ethical lapses believed to be more common than we would wish. The process is labeled archly in lawyer's slang as *'horseshedding'* the witness . . . . [T]he process often extends beyond organizing what the witness knows, and moves in the direction of helping the witness to know new things." Marvin Frankel, *Partisan Justice* 15 (1980)./ "Equally revealing is the slang used to describe the preparation of ordinary witnesses: 'sandpapering' and *'horseshedding.'* " John H. Langbein, *The German Advantage in Civil Procedure,* 52 U. Chi. L. Rev. 823, 835 n.36 (1985).

This old Americanism has evolved since the novelist James Fenimore Cooper used it in a related sense ("to wheedle, cajole"): "Your regular *'horse shedder'* is employed to frequent taverns where jurors stay, and drop hints before them touching the merits of causes known to be on the calendars." James F. Cooper, *The Redskins* 240 (1846).

host of, a. See SYNESIS.

hotchpot; hotchpotch; hodgepodge. The original form (a LAW FRENCH term referring to a dish mixed by shaking it up), still the preferred legal term, is *hotchpot. Hotchpot* was originally the blending of properties to secure equality of division, esp. as practiced in cases in which an intestate's property is to be distributed. E.g., "Ademption by satisfaction is related to the doctrine of advancements in intestacy, except that there is no opportunity on the part of the testamentary donee to come into *hotchpot.*" Blackstone called it a "housewifely metaphor" and explained it in Littleton's words: "it seemeth that this word, *hotchpot,* is in English a pudding; for in a pudding is not commonly put one thing alone, but one thing with other things together." 2 William Blackstone, *Commentaries* 190 (1766) (quoting Co. Litt. 164).

This word was corrupted into *hotchpotch* (used by some courts), then into *hodgepodge,* which is now the usual nonlegal term meaning "an unorganized mixture." E.g., "The Bankruptcy Act of 1898 proved deficient because of its erratic and uncertain application resulting from a *hodgepodge* of state and federal statutory provisions."

In community-property states in the U.S., the term is also used in reference to the property that falls within the community estate.

hot pursuit. See **fresh pursuit.**

housebreaking is a little-used variant of *burglary* in its modern statutory sense (as opposed to the common-law sense). Though the word suggests that it relates only to dwellings, its meaning is broader: "unlawfully breaking into any building, public or private, at any hour, and committing a felony [inside], or, having committed a felony [inside], breaking out." Edward Jenks, *The Book of English Law* 175 (P.B. Fairest ed., 6th ed. 1967). E.g., "Petitioner was charged with attempted *housebreaking,* and assault with attempt to rape in violation of articles 80, 130, and 134 of the Uniform Code of Military Justice." *Breaking and entering* is a frequently used DOUBLET in that sense. See **burglary (B).**

In Scotland, there is no crime of burglary—only housebreaking—and in that context *house* refers to any secured building.

houseburning. See **arson.**

house counsel; in-house counsel. These variant terms refer to one or more lawyers employed full-time by a company. The shorter phrase, *house* *counsel,* is stylistically preferable, though both phrases are common.

house of ill fame. See **bawdy house.**

House of Lords. Ever since 1876, this phrase has contained an ambiguity. In most people's minds, the House of Lords is most commonly known as the upper chamber of the British Parliament. But in 1876, the judicial House of Lords—a subset of the upper chamber—was created. It is a court composed of 11 professionally qualified judges who, together with peers who have had high judicial experience, sit independently of the parliamentary sittings of the House. It usually sits in panels of five, or occasionally seven. In civil matters, it is the court of final appeal for England, Wales, Scotland, and Northern Ireland; in criminal matters, it is the court of final appeal for England, Wales, and Northern Ireland. See **Law Lord & Lord of Appeal in Ordinary.**

howbeit. See **albeit.**

how come is very informal, almost slang, for *why.* It should be avoided in writing.

however. Most writers have heard that sentences should not begin with this word. But doing so is not a grammatical error; it is merely a stylistic lapse, the word *but* ordinarily being much preferable. (See **but (A).**) E.g., "*However,* [read *But*] we regard the statutory history of section 702c as being less than univocal on this point, so we cannot assent to appellants' view." See Bryan A. Garner, *On Beginning Sentences with "But,"* 3 Scribes J. Legal Writing 87 (1992).

Yet, used in the sense "in whatever way" or "to whatever extent," *however* is unimpeachable at the beginning of a sentence. E.g., "*However* extraordinary this new doctrine may appear, it nevertheless has its advocates . . . ." *The Federalist* No. 2, at 37–38 (John Jay) (Clinton Rossiter ed., 1961). See RUN-ON SENTENCES.

howsoever is always inferior to *however.*

hue and cry is an archaic LEGALISM that has passed into the vernacular. At common law it referred either to the public uproar that a citizen was expected to initiate after discovering a crime, or the chase after a felon accompanying such an uproar. The words in this DOUBLET may originally have been distinct, some scholars believing that *hue* may have referred to inarticulate sounds, such as horns or indistinct yells, while *cry* may have referred to distinctly audible words. See POPULARIZED LEGAL TECHNICALITIES.

human, n., for *human being* was long held objectionable by a few purists, but it is so pervasive today even in formal writing that it should be accepted as standard.

humankind; mankind. The former, a 17th-century creation, is unexceptionable, while the latter is, to many people, a sexist word. The prudent writer will therefore resort to *humankind.* E.g., "Native Americans fulfill this duty through ceremonies and rituals designed to preserve and stabilize the earth and to protect *humankind* from disease and other catastrophes." *Lyng v. Northwest Indian Cemetery Protective Ass'n,* 485 U.S. 439, 460 (1988) (Brennan, J., dissenting). See SEXISM (B).

humble is preferably pronounced with the *-h-* sounded /***hum***-*bəl*/. (Cf. **homage.**) Inexplicably, the precious pronunciation without sounding the initial *-h-* is common in AmE. One judge went so far as to use *an* before the Humble Oil trademark: "To the contrary, purchasers were informed that the selected shipments would bear the HUMBLE name or be accompanied *by an* HUMBLE *invoice* [read *by a* HUMBLE *invoice*] but were the desired Exxon products." *Exxon Corp. v. Humble Exploration Co.,* 695 F.2d 96, 100 (5th Cir. 1983).

hung. See **hanged.**

hung jury (= a jury whose members cannot arrive at a verdict) does not require apologetic quotation marks, as if signaling that it is slang. It is not; it is a useful legal term (finding a synonymous phrase in *deadlocked jury*). See the quotation in par. 2 under **contumacious.**

hurt (= a legal injury) surprises the nonlegal reader, for whom *hurt* connotes physical or emotional pain only. E.g., "The *hurts* to relations fall in numerous patterns, some simple and some complex."

husband and wife. See **man and wife.**

HYBRIDS, or words made up of morphemes from different languages, have become even more common in the last 50 years than they were in Fowler's day. Perhaps it is our increasing ignorance of Classical tongues, or our disregard for the morphological integrity of the words we coin, that causes the problem. As an American lexicographer once observed, "Not many people care whether a word has Greek and Latin elements mixed in it." M.M. Mathews, *American Words* 93 (1959).

Virtually all the hybrids condemned by Fowler (e.g., *amoral, bureaucracy, cablegram, climactic, coastal, coloration, gullible, pacifist, racial, speedometer*) are now passed over without mention even by those who consider themselves purists. Others that Fowler did not mention also fall into this class, such as *antedate, likable, lumpectomy, merriment, postwar, retrofit, riddance, telegenic,* and *transship*. We also have our own fringe hybrids, however: *botheration, raticide,* and *scatteration,* and *monokini* (the last being a MORPHOLOGICAL DEFORMITY as well).

In law, one rarely hears complaints about hybrids, though Mario Pei once called *venireman* a product of "the worst kind of hybridization (. . . half Latin, half Anglo-Saxon)." Mario Pei, *Words in Sheep's Clothing* 83 (1969). The nonsexist *veniremember,* of course, solves that problem. See **venireman.**

Other law-related hybrids are widely accepted. *Breathalyzer* (formerly *drunkometer*) has become standard, although in 1965 Gowers wrote that this term was "stillborn, it may be hoped" (*MEU2* 253). *Creedal,* q.v., is a near-commonplace. *Quo warranto,* q.v., is an example dating back to the 13th century. *Automendacity,* a word expressing the idea that a forgery tells not just a lie but a lie about itself—about what the very document is—has proved convenient for writers on criminal law. And Fowler may not be resting in peace.

hygiene used to have something to do with cleanliness and healthfulness, esp. with regard to the body. Then the bureaucrats and psychologists sullied this word with figurative senses, giving us, for example, the phrase *mental hygiene* (see *State of California Dept. of Mental Hygiene v. Bank of Southwest,* 354 S.W.2d 576 (Tex. 1962)). And this: "What she offers in the place of a system of punishment is in fact a system of purely forward-looking *social hygiene* in which our only concern when we have an offender to deal with is with the future and the rational aim of prevention of future crime." Careful writers shun this, as they shun all bureaucratic JARGON.

HYPALLAGE, known also as the transferred epithet, is a figure of speech in which the proper subject is displaced by what rightfully would be the object. Usually hypallage is a mere idiomatic curiosity. It has a distinguished lineage—a famous example being Shakespeare's line from *Julius Caesar:* "This was the most unkindest cut of all." It was not the *cut* that was unkind, but rather the *cutter*. Hence the object has become the subject.

An example from legal language is the phrase "negligent tort." It is the tortfeasor, not the tort, that is negligent. Likewise in these phrases:

abutting owner
angry confirmation fight
arrestable offense
bigamous cohabitation
convictable case
culpable silence
disgruntled complaints
drunk-driving cases
English-speaking countries
extraditable violations
humble opinion
immunized testimony
imprisonable crime
in-custody statements
indictable offense
intestate share
reversible error
uncounseled confession
well-educated home

But this figure of speech can sometimes be used inartfully, or cause problems if the writer is not himself aware of the true subject. E.g., "The final *subclass* of originalism, what Brest calls 'moderate originalism,' *views* the text of the Constitution as. . . ." [A subclass does not view.]/ "State *courts* generally *mirrored* this theistic viewpoint." [State courts did not mirror the point of view discussed; rather, their *decisions* or *opinions* did.]/ "The authorities sustain the validity of the direction of the testator, and equity will afford protection to the donor to a charitable corporation in that the attorney general may maintain a suit to *compel the property to be held* for the charitable purpose for which it was given to the corporation." [The *property* is not being *compelled to be held;* someone is *being compelled to hold the property.*]/ "*The arguments* of the parties have *addressed themselves* in considerable part to the propriety of the district court's exercising its equitable jurisdiction to enjoin the strike in question once the findings set forth above have been made." [*The arguments themselves* haven't done the *addressing;* rather, in their arguments, *the parties have addressed themselves.*]

Hypallage can also lead to faulty metaphors: "The defendants in this case have reduced the husband to a physical wreck. The *wife is the victim of that wreck.*" [The writer does not mean to say that the *wife is a victim of her husband,* a paraplegic. Rather, she is *a victim of the defendants' actions.*]

HYPERCORRECTION. Sometimes people strive to abide by the strictest etiquette, but in the process they behave inappropriately. The same human motivations that result in this irony can play havoc with the langauge: a person will strive for a correct linguistic form but instead fall into error. Linguists call this phenomenon "hypercorrection"—a shortcoming to which legal writers are particularly susceptible.

This foible can have several causes. Often, it results from an attempt to avoid what is incorrectly thought to be a grammatical error. (See SUPERSTITIONS.) At other times, it results when the writer has an imcomplete grasp of a foreign language's grammar—but insists on trying to conform to that grammar. And, yet again, it sometimes results when the writer allows a misplaced sense of logic to override a well-established idiom. A few of the most common manifestations are enumerated below.

A. False Latin Plurals. One with a smattering of Latin learns that, in that language, most nouns ending in *-us* have a plural ending in *-i: genius* forms *genii, nimbus* forms *nimbi, syllabus* forms *syllabi, terminus* forms *termini,* and so on. The trouble is that not all of them do end in *-i,* so traps abound for those who wish to show off their sketchy knowledge of Latin:

Hypercorrect Form	*Latin Form*	*English Form*
apparati	apparatus	apparatuses
cestuis que trustent	[none]	cestuis que trust
cestuis que usent	[none]	cestuis que use
fori	fora	forums
hiati	hiatus	hiatuses
ignorami	[vb. in L.]	ignoramuses
mandami	[vb. in L.]	mandamuses
mittimi	[vb. in L.]	mittimuses
nexi	nexus	nexuses
octopi	octopodes (Gk.)	octopuses
prospecti	prospectus	prospectuses
stati	status	statuses

B. *Between you and I.* Some users of the English language learn a thing or two about pronoun cases, but little more. They learn, for example, that it is incorrect to say "It is me" or "Me and Jane are going to school now." (See **it is I.**) But this knowledge puts them on tenterhooks: through the logical fallacy known as "hasty generalization," they come to fear that there is something wrong with the word *me*—that perhaps it's safer to stick with *I.*

They therefore begin to use *I* even when the objective case is called for: "She had the biggest surprise for Blair and *I* [read *me*]." "Please won't you keep this between you and *I* [read *me*]." These are gross linguistic gaffes, but it is perennially surprising how many otherwise educated speakers commit them. See **between (C)** & NOMINATIVE AND OBJECTIVE CASES.

Many writers and speakers try to avoid the problem by resorting to *myself,* but that is hardly an improvement. See **myself.**

C. Number Problems. Sometimes, in the quest for correctness, writers let their sense of grammar override long-established idioms. They may write, for example, "A number of people was there," when the correct form is "A number of people were there." Or they will write, "A handful of problems arises from that approach," instead of "A handful of problems arise from that approach." For more on these correct but "antigrammatical" constructions, see SYNESIS & **number of, a.**

D. Redundantly Formed Adverbs. The forms *doubtless, much,* and *thus* are adverbs, yet some writers overcompensate by adding *-ly* and thereby forming barbarisms: *doubtlessly, muchly,* and *thusly.* See ADVERBS, PROBLEMS WITH (D), **doubtless(ly), illy, muchly, & thus (B).**

E. *As* for *like.* When writers fear using *like* as a conjunction, they sometimes fail to use it when it would function appropriately as a preposition or adverb. Thus, "She writes like a lawyer" becomes "She writes as a lawyer." But the latter sentence sounds as if it is explaining the capacity in which she writes. The hypercorrection, then, results in a MISCUE. See **like (A).**

F. *Whom* for *who.* Perhaps writers should get points for trying, but those who do not know how to use *whom* should abstain in questionable contexts. That is, *against whom, for whom,* and the like may generally be instances in which the writer knows to choose *whom.* But things can get moderately tricky—e.g.: "[W]hat someone who intends to mug an approaching stranger *whom* [read *who*] he realizes is grey-haired and sunburnt intends is to mug a grey-haired and sunburnt stranger, though it was no part of his aim that the intended victim should be grey-haired and sunburnt." Alan R. White, *Misleading Cases* 60 (1991). Although, in that sentence, *whom* may seem to be the object of *realizes,* in fact it is the subject of the verb *is.* See **who (A)** & NOMINATIVE AND OBJECTIVE CASES.

G. Unsplit Infinitives Causing Miscues. Writers who have given in to the most widespread of superstitions—or who believe that most of the readers have done so—avoid all split infinitives. They should at least avoid introducing squinting modifiers into their prose. But many writers do introduce them, and the result is often a MISCUE or AMBIGUITY—e.g.: "Each is *trying subtly to exert* his or her influence over the other." Mark H. McCormack, *What They Don't Teach You at Harvard Business School* 26 (1984). In that sentence, does *subtly* modify the participle *trying* or the infinitive *to exert?* Because we cannot tell, the sentence needs to be revised in any of the following ways: (1) *Each is subtly trying to exert his or her influence over the other,* (2) *Each is trying to exert his or her influence subtly over the other,* or (3) *Each is trying to subtly exert his or her influence over the other.* See SPLIT INFINITIVES (C), SUPERSTITIONS (B) & MISCUES.

H. Unsplit Verb Phrases. A surprising number of writers believe that it's a mistake to put an adverb in the midst of a verb phrase. The surprise is for them: every language authority who addresses the question holds just the opposite view—that the adverb generally *belongs* in the midst of a verb phrase. (See ADVERBS, PROBLEMS WITH (A).) The canard to the contrary frequently causes awkwardness and artificiality—e.g.: "I *soon will be calling* you." [Read *I will soon be calling you.*] See SUPERSTITIONS (C).

I. Prepositions Moved from the End of the Sentence. "That is the type of arrant pedantry up with which I shall not put," said Winston Churchill, mocking the pedantry that causes some writers and speakers to avoid ending with a preposition. See PREPOSITIONS (A) & SUPERSTITIONS (A).

J. Borrowed Articles for Borrowed Nouns. When a naturalized or quasi-naturalized foreignism appears in an English-language context, the surrounding words—with a few exceptions, such as *hoi polloi* (q.v.)—should be English. Thus, one refers to *finding the mot juste,* not *finding le mot juste* (a common error among the would-be literati).

K. Overrefined Pronunciation. Some foreignisms acquire English and American pronunciations. For example, *lingerie* is pronounced in a way that the French would consider utterly barbarous: */lon-zhə-**ray**/*, as opposed to */lan-**zhree**/*. But for a native speaker of AmE to use the latter pronunciation would be foolish-sounding.

Similarly, American and English printers refer to the more modern typefaces—the ones without small projections coming off the straight lines—as *sans serif /sanz-**ser**-if/*, not */sahnz-sə-**reef**/*. The latter pronunciation may show a familiarity with the French language, but it belies an unfamiliarity both with publishing and with the English language.

Even native-English words can cause problems. The word *often,* for example, preferably has a silent *-t-,* yet some speakers (unnaturally) pronounce it because of the spelling. The next logical step would be to pronounce *administration /ad-min-i-**stray**-tee-on/*, and all other words with the *-tion* suffix similarly. See PRONUNCIATION (A).

HYPHENS. See PUNCTUATION (D) & PHRASAL ADJECTIVES.

hypnotism and *hypnosis* are not interchangeable. One might use either term to name the art of mesmerism, but one would never say, "He is under *hypnotism.*" *Hypnotism* names only the practice or art; *hypnosis* refers either to the practice or to the state of consciousness itself.

The two words are susceptible to INELEGANT VARIATION, as Chief Justice Rehnquist has demonstrated. See *Rock v. Arkansas,* 483 U.S. 44 (1987) (in which Rehnquist referred to "increased confidence in both true and false memories following *hypnosis*" (p. 62) and then to "increased confidence inspired by *hypnotism*" (at 63)).

hypo. See **hypo(thet).**

hypostatize; hypostasize. The standard form is *hypostatize* (= to make an idea into, or to regard it, as a self-existent substance or person).

hypothecate is not, as some writers believe, a synonym of *hypothesize.* Properly, *hypothecate* is an admiralty and civil-law term meaning "to pledge without delivery of title or possession." *Hypothesize* means "to make a hypothesis," which is a proposition put forward as a basis for argument. President George Bush, for example, fell into error on 8 August 1990, when, after sending armed forces to Saudi Arabia in the wake of Saddam Hussein's invasion of Kuwait, he said he would not "hypothecate" about this or that scenario. But the confusion is nothing new: "Was the district court, then, bound, in opposition to these facts, to instruct the jury . . . hypothetically, that . . . . [A]ny instruction . . . *hypothecated* [read *hypothesized*] on the absence of such calls, could only tend to confuse or mislead the jury." *Boardman v. Lessees of Reed,* 31 U.S. (6 Pet.) 328, 344 (1832). *Hypotheticate* is a mistaken form of *hypothecate.*

Hypothecation is best preceded by *a* rather than by *an.* E.g., "In my opinion, the definition given by Pothier of *an hypothecation* [read *a hypothecation*] is an accurate description of a maritime lien under our law." See **a (A).**

hypo(thet). *Hypothetical* was originally used adjectivally, but has come to be an attributive noun as well. *Hypothet* is an old-fashioned American shortening of *hypothetical* in legal contexts. *Hypo* is now the more widespread legal colloquialism, and it undoubtedly sounds better. E.g., "[I]n fact, fictional stories (*'hypos'* in the jargon of the law schools) will serve just as well . . . ." A.W.B. Simpson, *Trouble with the Case,* TLS, 14–20 Dec. 1990, at 1344.

hypothetic(al), adj. The longer form is now usual. E.g., "In the supplemental charge, the court expressly indicated that its prior remarks had been made in *hypothetic* [read *hypothetical*] form for illustrative purposes." See **hypo(thet).**

I

I; me. See NOMINATIVE AND OBJECTIVE CASES. For the error *between you and I,* see **between** (C) & HYPERCORRECTION (B).

ibid. Short for *ibidem* (= in the same place), this abbreviation is rarely used in legal citations. *Id.,* the abbreviation for *idem* (= the same person or thing), does the same job for a lawyer.

id. See ***idem.***

idea or concept. Many writers seem unable to say *idea* without adding *or concept.* The habit is a bad one, the two words being virtually interchangeable—e.g.: "[T]hey are all appealing to the same fundamental *idea or concept,* though it is extraordinarily difficult to define exactly the nature of that *idea or concept.*" Edward Jenks, *The Book of English Law* 2 (P.B. Fairest ed., 6th ed. 1967). In that sentence, *idea* alone would suffice in both places.

idealogical. See **ideological.**

idem (= the same), in its abbreviated form *id.,* is used in citations to refer to the cited authority immediately preceding. For example, if footnote 2 reads, "Mauet, *Fundamentals of Trial Techniques* 380 (1980)," footnote 3 might read, "*Id.* at 381."

The full word appears in the LATINISM *idem sonans* (lit., "having the same sound"), a rule of law that a variant spelling of a name in a document will not render the document void if the misspelling is pronounced in the same way as the true spelling (as *Growgan* for *Grogan* on a traffic ticket). E.g., "[U]nder our random system it sometimes happens that your name is *idem sonans* with mine, and it may be the same even in spelling." Oliver W. Holmes, *The Theory of Legal Interpretation,* 12 Harv. L. Rev. 417, 418 (1899).

identical preferably takes *with,* not *to.* One has *identity with* something or someone, not *to* it. *Identical to* was not widely used until the mid-20th century. The *OED,* in fact, quotes illustrative examples only with the phrase *identical with.* Here the better phrasing is used: "Under a constitutional provision *identical with* our own, the Missouri courts have held consistently that the question of libel or no libel is for the jury."/ "The evidence is that the two prior wills contained residuary devises *identical with* those in the latest will."

Just as frequently, however, and esp. in AmE, *to* appears. It has come to be the predominant nonliterary idiom—e.g.: "The code may then provide a term substantially *identical to* [read *with*] one of those rejected."/ "Section 35031 is virtually *identical to* [read *with*] section 72411."/ "Petitioner then filed his first federal habeas petition, raising issues *identical to* [read *with*] those raised and ruled on in his state appeal."

identify with. This phrase—used without a direct object following *identify*—has recently become a cant phrase, associated especially with slang of the 1960s and 1970s. Here it is inappropriately used in reference to a 19th-century historical figure. "Randolph *identified with* the books he read, and took upon himself the roles suggested by his favorite authors."

ideological. So spelled, though many misapprehend its etymology, believing the word is somehow derived from our modern word *idea,* and thus misspell it *idealogical.* The blunder has become common enough that it appears in *W3* (cf. **miniscule**), but inclusion in that dictionary is not a persuasive defense of its use. Like several other, more learned words beginning with *ideo-* (e.g., *ideograph*), *ideology* passed into English through French (F. *idéologie*) and has been spelled *ideo-* in English since the 18th century.

id est. See **i.e.**

idiosyncrasy. So spelled, though often erroneously rendered *-cracy* (as if the word denoted a form of government)—e.g.: "Their *idiosyncracies* [read *idiosyncrasies*] are patrician." David Margolick, *Similar Histories, and Views, for 2 Court Finalists,* N.Y. Times, 30 May 1993, at 9.

idyllic (= of, belonging to, or of the nature of an idyll [a short picturesque poem usu. describing rustic life]; full of charm or picturesqueness) is often misused as if it meant *ideal* (= perfect). E.g., "If unprofessional conduct . . . , deliberately employed as a means of thwarting the prosecution, *was* [read *were*] to be deemed per se ineffective assistance, then the accused would be placed in an *idyllic* [read *ideal*] situation." *Chappee v. Vose,* 843 F.2d 25, 33 (1st Cir. 1988). (On the change of *was* to *were* in that sentence, see SUBJUNCTIVES.)

i.e., the abbreviation for *id est* (L. "that is"), introduces explanatory phrases or clauses. The abbreviation is perfectly appropriate in legal writing. Formerly it was said that, in speaking or reading, the abbreviation should be rendered *id est.* But this is never heard today, whereas the abbreviated letters *i.e.* are frequently heard in lawyers' speech. (See **e.g.**) Generally, a comma follows *i.e.* in AmE (though not in BrE).

if. A. And *whether.* It is best to distinguish between the ways in which these words are used. *Whether* is generally preferable where one intends to express not a conditional idea, but an alternative or possibility. *If* is often used where, in formal writing at least, *whether* is the better word. E.g., "One person inquired *if* [read *whether*] the money was lost."

In some contexts, however, use of the different words may actually shade the meaning. E.g., "Please let me know *if* you need any advice" means to get in touch only if you need advice. "Please let me know *whether* you need any advice" means to advise in any event, whether the answer is yes or no.

B. *If, and only if.* This is inferior and adds nothing but unnecessary emphasis to *only if.* E.g., "Money is an adequate remedy *if, and only if,* [read *only if*] it can be used to replace the specific thing that was lost." Douglas Laycock, *The Death of the Irreparable Injury Rule* 246 (1991). The variation *if, but only if,* which sometimes occurs in legal writing, is unnecessary and even nonsensical for *only if.*

C. And *in the event that.* See **in the event that.**

if and when is a legalistic phrase of questionable validity—e.g.: "*If and when* the Patent and Trademark Office decides the trademark is registrable, it will be published in a weekly bulletin called the *Official Gazette.*" What is the antecedent of *it?* Will the *trademark* be published, or the *decision* of registrability?

Fowler enumerated a number of suspicions that keen readers are likely to have about users of this phrase: "There is the suspicion that he is a mere parrot, who cannot say part of what he has often heard without saying the rest also; there is the suspicion that he likes verbiage for its own sake; there is the suspicion that he is a timid swordsman who thinks he will be safer with a second sword in his left hand; there is the suspicion that he has merely been too lazy to make up his mind between *if* and *when*" (*MEU1* 254). In short, one is ill advised to use the phrase, which almost invariably is improved when simplified: "Appellant has not specifically requested backpay; *if and when* [read *if*] he does, that issue might be judged by a different standard."

An even worse manifestation of the phrase is *if, as, and when:* "Decisions in other community property states have disagreed on whether future contingent payments may be apportioned *if, as, and when* [read *as* or *when*] they mature and are received by the retired spouse."/ "We shall offer these bonds at this price, *if, as, and when* [read *if* or *when*] they are issued by the trust company." One of the three words is suitable virtually wherever this phrase appears. Cf. **unless and until.**

if any. Instead of putting *if any* after the noun, try putting *any* before it—e.g.: "[T]he complaint must further show . . . *what voyages or trips, if any* [read *any voyages or trips*], *she* [read *the ship*] has made since the voyage or trip on which the claims sought to be limited arose." Supp. R. Adm. & Mar. Claims F(2).

iffy for *uncertain* is a casualism unfit for formal legal prose. E.g., "We conclude that this court should not undertake the *iffy* [read *uncertain*] task of determining whether each appellant is entitled to immunity."

if it ain't broke, don't fix it. This is a favorite CLICHÉ of American lawyers seeking to preserve the status quo—and often merely to entrench mediocrity.

if it be. See SUBJUNCTIVES.

if not is an ambiguous phrase best avoided. It may mean either (1) lit., "(even) if it is, (we are, etc.) not; though not," or (2) "maybe even." Sense (2) is exemplified in the following sentences: "Justices of the peace who handle petty criminal cases and small claims are close to the general public and are an important, *if not* [i.e., and even an] essential, element in any state's system of justice."/ "Many, *if not* [i.e., even] most, courts are now willing to allow a substantial award for loss of the 'companionship' of the child."

Sense (1) is confusing if, as is quite likely, the reader first thinks of the phrase in terms of the more common sense (2): "We are apt *if not* vigilant to overlook the true status of the defendant husband and the defendant wife when they undertook acquisition by the entirety of the home lot." The sentence means: We are apt, *if we are not vigilant,* to overlook . . . ." But the reader more familiar with sense (2) will misperceive the sentence as meaning: We are apt, *and even vigilant,* to overlook . . . ." See AMBIGUITY.

if you will. This phrase typifies the language of those who engage in WORD-PATRONAGE—e.g.: "[W]ith regard to a large area of the legal field the experiments of the law, if they can be so called—the engineering appliances, *if you will*—are brought to bear *ex post facto.*" Carleton K. Allen, *Law in the Making* 36 (7th ed. 1964). This phrase, meaning in full *if you will allow me to use the phrase,* is almost always (as in the example quoted) best deleted.

ignis fatuus (= will o' the wisp; a delusive hope or desire) forms the plural *ignes fatui.*

ignitable. So spelled. See -ABLE (A).

ignominy is accented on the first, not the second, syllable /***ig**-nə-min-ee*/.

ignoramus. Until 1934 in England, if a grand jury considered the evidence of an alleged crime insufficient, it would endorse the bill *ignoramus,* meaning literally "we do not know" or "we know nothing of this." This use of the term was a survival of the medieval practice of having juries act on personal knowledge. Today, the phrases *No bill, No true bill,* and *Not a true bill* have replaced *ignoramus.*

By the early 17th century, though, the word *ignoramus* had come to mean, by extension, "an ignorant person." (See POPULARIZED LEGAL TECHNICALITIES.) In 1615, George Ruggle wrote a play called *Ignoramus,* about a lawyer who knew nothing about the law; and this fictional lawyer soon gave his name to all manner of know-nothings, whether lawyers or nonlawyers.

The modern nonlegal meaning appears more frequently in modern legal writing than the historical legal meaning: "Thus, to accuse a lawyer of being an *ignoramus,* when spoken of him in his calling, is actionable per se, without proof of special damages." Pl. *ignoramuses;* the form *ignorami* is a pseudo-learned blunder (*ignoramus* is a verb and not one of the Latin nouns in *-us*). See PLURALS (A).

ignorance. See **mistake** (A).

ignorance of the law is no excuse. See ***ignorantia juris.***

ignorant; stupid. Fastidious users of language distinguish between these terms. *Stupid* refers to innate ability, whereas *ignorant* refers merely to the state of one's knowledge on a particular subject. Geniuses are *ignorant* of certain facts; *stupid* people are *ignorant* of most facts.

ignorantia facti excusat. See MAXIMS.

ignorantia juris is a moderately useful LATINISM denoting the legal doctrine that ignorance of the law is no excuse (rendered in Latin *ignorantia juris neminem excusat* [lit., "ignorance of law excuses no one"]). E.g., "The effect of this provision is to continue the *ignorantia juris* principle as part of the Model Code culpability structure." The full maxim itself, however, is best rendered in English. See MAXIMS.

Some writers use the phrase *ignorantia legis* rather than *ignorantia juris.* Strictly speaking, *jus* (and its genitive *juris*) means the science of law or the whole body of the law, whereas *lex* (genitive *legis*) means a legislative act or pronouncement, or sometimes the body of enacted law as distinct from principles of common law (or judge-made law). Hence, strictly, *ignorantia juris* means ignorance of the law and *ignorantia legis* ignorance of a specific statute or ordinance. But no such DIFFERENTIATION seems to exist in practice. Ironically, the issue in most cases is ignorance of a specific provision, not of the law in general; but *ignorantia juris* remains the more common form.

ignore, when used in reference to a grand jury, means "to sign a bill with *ignoramus* [q.v.]"—e.g.: "[T]he grand jury may *ignore* the bill, and decline to find any indictment . . . ." *Post v. U.S.,* 161 U.S. 583, 587 (1896)./ "Russo's testimony before the grand jury as to Foster, Baker and Weller, contradicted his testimony before the committing magistrate and in effect made it necessary for the grand jury to *ignore* all three bills." *Commonwealth v. Russo,* 111 A.2d 359, 364 (Pa. Super. Ct. 1955)./ "The grand jury takes it [the case] up anew, and may present or *ignore* the bill, without any reference whatever to the fact that one indictment has been presented and set aside." *State v. Silver,* 398 P.2d 178, 180 (Or. 1965) (en banc).

ilk correctly means "the same"; hence *of that ilk* means "of that same kind." E.g., "The evidence in this case was of the *ilk* that would tax the patience and wisdom of Solomon." *Mink v. Mink,* 395 S.E.2d 237, 239 (Ga. Ct. App. 1990). Yet the word is commonly misapprehended as relating to race or family—it is not that specific.

ill. The comparative form of this adjective is *worse,* the superlative *worst.* The adverb is *ill,* *illy* being an illiterate form. Yet illiteracies have been known to creep into legal writing and even into judicial opinions: see **illy.**

illation (= the act of inferring or something inferred) is a learned term little used today, though a few modern judges are quite fond of it. *Inference* serves just as well, and more understandably.

illegal; illicit; unlawful. These three terms are fundamentally synonymous, although *illicit* <illicit love affairs> carries moral overtones in addition to the basic sense "not in accordance with or sanctioned by law."

Illegal is not synonymous with *criminal,* though some writers mistakenly assume that it is. (See **undocumented alien.**) Anything against the law—even the civil law—is, technically speaking, "illegal." See **illegal contract, nonlegal & unlawful.**

illegal alien. See **undocumented alien.**

illegal contract. This phrase is "exceptionally difficult to define." P.A. Atiyah, *An Introduction to the Law of Contract* 38 (3d ed. 1981). The phrase does not denote merely "a contract contrary to the criminal law, although such a contract would indubitably be illegal. But a contract can well be illegal without contravening the criminal law, because there are certain activities [that] the law does not actually prohibit, but at the same time regards as contrary to the public interest and definitely to be discouraged, for instance, prostitution." *Id.*

illegal entrant. See **undocumented alien.**

illegal entry. This phrase, in some jurisdictions, denotes a lesser-included offense of *burglary* (q.v.)—e.g.: "A murderer, who might get the chair, would be offered a plea to 'manslaughter,' or a burglar, liable for twenty years, one to *'illegal entry,'* depending on how strong the evidence in either case might be." Ephraim Tutt, *Yankee Lawyer* 88 (1943).

illegible; unreadable. *Illegible* = not plain or clear enough to be read (used of handwriting or defaced printing). *Unreadable* = too dull or obfuscatory to be read (used of bad writing).

illegitimate child. Though the phrase is still often used, it is undeniably insensitive. As a far-sighted judge once observed, "[T]here are no *illegitimate children,* only illegitimate parents." *In re Estate of Woodward,* 40 Cal. Rptr. 781, 784 (1964) (per Yankwich, J.). A New York judge contends that "[t]he preferable modern term is *nonmarital child.*" Letter of Arthur E. Blyn, *Nonmarital Children,* N.Y. Times, 10 March 1991, at 14. See EUPHEMISMS, **bastard & natural child.**

illicit (= illegal), when used for *elicit* (= to bring out), is a mistake. One might have thought this error impossible, but it does occur—e.g.: "[T]he trial court's subsequent inquiries could not have *illicited* [read *elicited*] honest responses." *U.S. v. Washita Constr. Co.,* 789 F.2d 809, 818 (10th Cir. 1986)./ "[P]laintiff's attorney *illicited* [read *elicited*] from Loftsgard the amount of expenses and also the amount covered by insurance." *Loftsgard v. Dorrian,* 476 N.W.2d 730, 733 (Iowa Ct. App. 1991)./ "The record reveals defendant did not attempt to develop this version of the accident by *illiciting* [read *eliciting*] trial testimony or submitting expert opinion." *Bordelon v. South Cent. Bell Tel. Co.,* 617 So. 2d 1337, 1340 (La. Ct. App. 1993).

For the proper use of *illicit,* see **illegal.**

illiterate = (1) unable to read or write; or (2) unlettered. Justice Holmes was wont to use this word in sense (2), the heightened sense of the word: "In the case at bar we have an *illiterate* woman writing her own will. Obviously the first sentence, 'I am going on a journey and may not ever return,' expresses the fact that was on her mind as the occasion and inducement for writing it." *Eaton v. Brown,* 193 U.S. 411, 414 (1904) (per Holmes, J.).

ILLOGIC. The writer on language who would dare drag logic into the discussion must do so warily. For centuries, grammarians labored under the mistaken belief that grammar is but applied logic and therefore tried to rid language of everything illogical.

But, to paraphrase Oliver Wendell Holmes, Jr., the life of the language has not been logic: it has been experience. No serious student believes anymore that grammatical distinctions necessarily reflect logical ones. Our language is full of idioms that defy logic, many of them literary and many colloquial. We should not, for example, fret over the synonymy of *fat chance* and *slim chance.* Applying "linguistic logic" to established ways of saying things is a misconceived effort.

We see that misconceived effort today when armchair grammarians insist that *grammatical error* is an Irish bull; that *I don't think so* is wrong in place of *I think not;* that *the reason why* is wrong (no more so, certainly, than *place where* or *time when*); that *a number of people* must take a singular not a plural verb (see SYNESIS); or that, in *Don't spend any more time than you can help,* the final words should be *can't help.* When logic is used for such purposes, it is worse than idle: it is harmful.

That does not mean, of course, that logic is of no concern to the writer. For rhetorical purposes, logic is essential. A few readers will look for holes in the wording. In evaluating our own writing, therefore, we should strictly follow idiom and usage, but otherwise apply logic.

The exercise will tighten your prose. Since idiom does not yet prefer *could care less,* much less require it, write *couldn't care less.* (Logically speaking, if you say you *could care less,* then you are admitting that you care to some extent.) No longer might you say, *I was scared literally to death,* because you recognize the literal meaning of *literally* and you are still alive to report how scared you were. Likewise, logic would have you banish such thoughtless words as *preplanned* and use words such as *reiterate* (q.v.) more carefully, so as to distinguish it from *iterate.*

Logic also rids prose of the various errors in thinking that workaday writers commonly commit. To avoid the ills catalogued below, consider closely how your words and sentences relate to one another.

A. Illogical Comparison. This lapse occurs commonly in locutions like *as large if not larger than,* which, when telescoped, becomes *as large . . . than*; properly, one writes *as large as if not larger than.* Similar problems occur with classes. For example, when members of classes are being compared, a word such as *other* must be used to restrict the class: "Our system of justice is better than any [other] in the world."

Another problem of comparison occurs when the writer forgets the point of reference in the comparison:

- "Like the hard-hitting Dianne Feinstein, a candidate for California's governorship, Silber's views are striking a chord among many Democrats tired of losing." Graham, *Democrats' New Breed Upsets the Party Old Guard,* Sunday Times, 15 April 1990, at A23. (The sentence compares a person to someone's views.)
- "I cannot ignore our culpability in this situation and, like parricide in the Athenian law, pass it over in silence." *Brown v. United States,* 454 F.2d 999, 1016 (D.C. Cir. 1971) (Tamm, J., dissenting). (*Parricide* didn't pass over anything in silence; rather, the Athenian law passed over *parricide* in silence, the writer means to say.)
- "Like the young Bentham, an ardent crusader, he [Rodell] lacks Bentham's patience [read *he lacks patience*]." Jerome Frank, Introduction, *Woe Unto You, Lawyers!* xii (1980 ed). (As a comparison of young Jeremy Bentham with old Jeremy Bentham, the sentence does not work, because the source of the comparison is also the source of difference.)
- "This case involves facts virtually identical with *the previous case* [read *those in the previous case*]."
- "May a defendant who has settled with the plaintiff recover contribution from other potential defendants?" (The phrase *other potential defendants* is wrong because anyone who has settled is no longer a *potential* defendant.)

For related problems, see **as much as or more, as well as or better than** & OVERSTATEMENT.

B. Danglers and Misplaced Modifiers. Every dangler or misplaced modifier, in some degree, perverts logic, sometimes humorously—e.g.: "I saw the Statue of Liberty flying into Newark." To avoid these disruptions of thought, remember that participles should relate to nouns that are truly capable of performing the action of the participle. Here, for example, note that neither a definition nor a belief construes: "Any definition is likely to distinguish between religion and mere conscientious belief, *construing* the first amendment to govern the former but not the latter." For a fuller discussion of these matters, see DANGLERS & MISPLACED MODIFIERS.

C. Disjointed Appositives. Phrases intended to be in apposition should not be separated. (See APPOSITIVES.) E.g., "A respected English legal authority on the common law, the view of William Blackstone permeated much of the early thinking on freedom of expression." John Murray, *The Media Law Dictionary* 11 (1978). (Blackstone himself, not Blackstone's *view,* is the respected authority.)

D. Mistaken Subject of a Prepositional Phrase. This problem crops up usually when a word or phrase intervenes between the noun and the prepositional phrase referring to that noun. Often, as in the first example below, the noun (*school bus*) functions as an adjective: "*Wallin was the school bus driver in which* [read *Wallin was driving the school bus in which*] Hillman and Ellington and Kleven were passengers."/ "Of the three persons involved, the entire loss fell upon the only one who was himself free from all negligence." (What is the relationship between *the three persons involved,* the *loss* incurred, and the degree of *negligence?* Read *Of the three persons involved, the only one to incur a loss was the one free from all negligence.*)

E. Insensitivity to Metaphor. Illogical metaphors abound in American writing. The scholar's *virgin field pregnant with possibilities* is among the more risible examples. Others less humorous are only a little less difficult to spot:

- "In my opinion that foundation is not weakened by the fact that it is buttressed by other provisions that are also designed to avoid the insidious evils of government propaganda favoring particular points of view." (Buttresses serve only to strengthen, not to weaken.)
- "That doctrine was bastardized by its progeny." (Parents, not children, create bastards.)
- "The nineteenth century has provided new impetus to literary studies, putting them on untraveled roads." (Travel creates roads; they do not exist in a vacuum.)

See METAPHORS (A).

F. Poor Exposition of Sequence. Do not ask your readers to assume what is not logically possible by your very assumptions—e.g.: "Indeed, the condition of the plane after the crash *eliminated an air collision* [read *was such as to eliminate further speculation about an air collision* or *ruled out an air collision as the cause of the crash*]."/ "The obligation of the deceased to transfer certain property, as a minimum, during his life does not negate a desire to leave the other property after death . . . ." (A deceased person cannot have obligations of any kind, much less obligations to transfer property during his life. This is an example of the rhetorical figure called "prolepsis.")

G. Vexatious Little Words with Plain Meanings. Writers often confound their meaning by misusing simple words—e.g.: "Acceptances must be communicated to the offeror *after* [read *in*] a reasonable amount of time." (If *after* a reasonable amount of time, then the period has become *unreasonable!*)

H. Complete Obliviousness in the Task of Writing. We all take leave of our senses, from time to time, especially while composing. We save ourselves, however, by applying our critical faculties while revising. Most of us do, anyway. But some writers don't—e.g.: "The courts are more reluctant in considering extrinsic evidence to construe a will than to construe an inter vivos transfer." [Read *Courts are more reluctant to consider extrinsic evidence in construing a will than in construing an inter vivos transfer.*] (The original sentence suggests that courts have a choice of what to construe, as if a judge might say, "Well, here I am considering some extrinsic evidence. Why, I think I'll construe an inter vivos transfer—that would be more fun than a will!")

I. Progression of Tenses. See TENSES.

illude. See **allude (B).**

illusion; delusion. These words are used differently despite their similar meanings. An *illusion* exists in one's fancy or imagination. A *delusion* is an idea or thing that deceives or misleads a person about some aspect of the real world.

For the difference between *illusion* and *allusion,* see **allusion.** For the difference between *delusion* and *hallucination,* see **hallucination.**

illusory; illusive. The former is preferred. See **elusive.**

illustrate, in modern usage, means "to provide a good example of (something); to exemplify." In the following sentence it is used ambiguously: *"Hohfeld's analysis illustrates* [read *In his analysis, Hohfeld examines*] the fallacy of accepting too literally the 'artificial entity' theory." The writer here is not claiming—as the sentence seems to do—that Hohfeld's analysis is itself a good example of "the fallacy of accepting too literally the 'artificial entity' theory." Rather, the sentence is intended to point to Hohfeld's analysis as one that elucidates well the nature of this fallacy.

Illustrate is usually accented on the first syllable: /***il***-*ə-strayt*/.

illustrative. The second syllable is accented: /*i-**lus**-trə-tiv*/.

illy is not an acceptable adverb in formal writing, perhaps not even in nondialectal informal writing. *Ill* itself acts as an adverb. E.g., "It is freely conceded that there are many decisions contrary to this view; but, when carried to the extent contended for by the appellant, we think they are unsafe, unsound, and *illy* [read *ill*] adapted to modern conditions." See **ill** & HYPERCORRECTION (D).

imbibe is a FORMAL WORD meaning "to drink." It occurs more frequently in legal than in nonlegal contexts. E.g., "In *Kelly v. Gwinnell,* the New Jersey Supreme Court took a major step in holding social hosts liable for the torts of their guests whom they have allowed to over*imbibe.*"

imbracery. See **embracery.**

immanent. See **imminent.**

immaterial; nonmaterial. The former term is called for in most legal contexts. "Should even a *nonmaterial* [read *immaterial*] error, if made with the intent to deceive the magistrate, invalidate a warrant?"/ "A testator is not induced by the misrepresentation if he knows the facts, or if the facts misrepresented are *immaterial.*" Although both may mean "not consisting of a material substance," *immaterial* tends to mean "of no substantial importance; inconsequential"; *nonmaterial,* in contrast, generally means "cultural, aesthetic" <the nonmaterial rewards of a career in law are sometimes debated>. See **material.**

immediate cause. See CAUSATION (B).

immemorial. See **time immemorial** & **memory of man runneth not to the contrary.**

immigrate; emigrate. *Immigrate* [*im* (into) + *migrate* (to move from one place to another)] = to enter a country with the intention of settling there permanently. *Emigrate* [*e* (from) + *migrate* (to move from one place to another)] = to depart or exit from one country in the hope of settling in another. Some countries are plagued by illegal *immigration* (e.g., the United States); others have been plagued by attempts at illegal *emigration* (e.g., the former Soviet Union).

Both verbs are intransitive and hence do not take objects. In the following sentence, *immigrate* is wrongly made transitive: "*Because you cannot immigrate your grandmother* [Read *Because your grandmother cannot immigrate*], she and her husband and her six children will remain undocumented."

The agent nouns are *immigrant* and *emigrant* (the GALLICISM *émigré* being a NEEDLESS VARIANT of the latter).

imminent; eminent; immanent. *Imminent* means "certain and very near, impending," as in the legal phrases *imminent bodily harm, imminent danger,* and *imminent death.* E.g., "Obviously there should be some bar to letting the owner transfer solely for the purpose of cutting down his estate tax at a time when that tax becomes *imminent.*"

Imminent does not mean merely "probable," as here incorrectly used: "We cannot assume reasonably that the Legislature intended that a statute enacted for the preservation of life and limb of pedestrians must be observed when observance would subject them to more *imminent* [read *probable*] danger."

Eminent = distinguished, of excellent repute <Judge Friendly of the Second Circuit was long considered an eminent jurist>. The adverb *eminently* is frequently used to mean "very," as in "He is *eminently* deserving of this award," or, "The court's decision was *eminently* fair." See **eminence.**

Immanent, primarily a theological term, means "inherent; pervading the material world" <the immanent goodness of the divine will>.

immolate. See **emulate.**

immoral; unmoral; amoral. These three words have distinct meanings. *Immoral,* the opposite of *moral,* means "evil, depraved." The word is highly judgmental. *Unmoral* means merely "without moral sense, not moral," and is used, for example, of animals and inanimate objects. *Amoral,* perhaps the most commonly misused of these terms, means "not moral, outside the sphere of morality; being neither moral nor immoral." It is loosely applied to people in the sense "not having morals or scruples."

immovable, in its fullest sense, is land, but, by extension, the word applies also to buildings and other permanent structures. In law, *immovable* has become a noun as well as an adjective, and is used almost always in the plural form. E.g., "All the cases before *Langlois* that imposed absolute liability involved dangerous activities relating to land or other *immovables* that were within the terms of those articles." (See ADJECTIVES (C).) The term *immovables* encompasses all immovable property, such as land, trees, buildings, and servitudes.

immune best takes *from,* not *to.* E.g., "The fact that Hale viewed husbands as *immune from* rape prosecution is not surprising." Susan Estrich, *Real Rape* 73 (1987)./ "Executive officers and other fellow employees of the injured employee are similarly *immune to* [read *from*] third-party demands." Still, *to* is acceptable, and so is *against.*

immunity; impunity. In legal contexts, *immunity* is the broader term because it relates to any type of exemption from a liability, service, or duty. *Impunity,* by contrast, refers merely to an exemption from punishment. E.g., "[I]f the pendency of an administrative petition conferred *immunity* from both civil forfeiture and criminal liability, a handler could violate the Act with *impunity* . . . ." *U.S. v. Riverbend Farms, Inc.,* 847 F.2d 553, 557 (9th Cir. 1988).

immunize = to render immune from or insusceptible to poison or infection (*OED*). By extension it means "to protect (from something bad)." The sense of some contagion or danger is an important element of the word in figurative as well as literal senses: "The Court concluded that the proprietary position of the state did not *immunize* it from the Fourteenth Amendment." (The Fourteenth Amendment to the U.S. Constitution is generally seen as a good thing, not a bad one.)

Through HYPALLAGE, it is often said not that the *witness* is immunized against the effects of his or her testimony, but that the *testimony* is immunized—e.g.: "Yesterday, the high court refused to hear arguments that Mrs. Helmsley is entitled to a pre-trial hearing to determine if her indictment is based on *immunized testimony* from an earlier grand jury." Wall St. J., 16 May 1989, at B7.

impact, n., is not generally understood to be a count noun. "It is apparent that the ICC found Steere's 'melodramatic' list of *adverse impacts upon* [better: *adverse effects on*] the motor carrier industry unpersuasive." This use of the noun *impact* is an extension of the verbal use disapproved at **impact,** v.i. & v.t. See COUNT NOUNS AND MASS NOUNS.

impact, v.i. & v.t. *Impact* has traditionally been only a noun. In recent years, however, it has undergone a semantic shift that has allowed it to act as a verb. Thus uses such as, "Five states have adopted plain English laws, but only New Jersey's law severely *impacts upon* lawyers in their private practice," have become widespread (and also widely condemned by stylists). E.g., "The termination of a tenured public schoolteacher adversely *impacts on* the teacher's personal and professional standing in both the educational community and the greater societal community."/ "The recently filed pro se application of Rumbaugh dramatically *impacts on* the issue before us."/ "The city argues that any step in the process that *impacts* adversely *on* black applicants is job-related and essential to the operation of the police department."

These uses of the word would be applauded if *impact* were performing any function not as ably performed by *affect* or *influence.* If *affect* as a verb is not sufficiently straightforward in context, then the careful writer might have recourse to *have an impact on,* which, though longer, to many is unquestionably preferable to the jarring impact of *impacts upon. Impact* is best reserved as a noun form.

Impact has also been used as a transitive verb, but the direct object does not make the verb any more acceptable. E.g., "Petitioner maintains that the commission must adhere to the rulemaking requirements of the APA when it conclusively affects and substantially *impacts* [better: *redefines*] pre-existing rights with a retroactive rule that has the force of law." Nor should the verb appear as a transitive verb in the passive voice—e.g.: "There was no evidence that, had he joined the medical staff, patient care would have been negatively *impacted* [better: *affected*]." See NOUNS AS VERBS.

impanel. See **empanel.**

imparl, v.i.; **imparlance,** n. In England, the practice of *imparling* (= obtaining leave of court to adjourn proceedings so that the parties can try to settle the case) was abolished in 1853. Historians occasionally discuss the practice—e.g.: "Instead of putting up a defence Brown asks for 'leave to *imparl*'—that is, he asks the court for an adjournment whilst he talks the matter over with Jones in the hope of reaching a settlement, and he and Jones leave court to have their imparlance." A.W.B. Simpson, *An Introduction to the History of the Land Law* 122 (1961).

The terms *imparl* and its corresponding noun, *imparlance,* now appear more frequently in AmE than in BrE. But even in AmE, the terms are rare enough to be properly classifiable as ARCHAISMS—e.g.: "Whereupon Judge Blount held his decision in abeyance for three hours and directed parties and counsel to *imparl* [read *discuss settlement*] during the interim and attempt 'to clear the matter up.'" *Sutton v. Figgatt,* 185 S.E.2d 97, 98 (N.C. 1971)./ "*An imparlance* [read *A settlement conference*] followed and has been held under my supervision, in accordance with the usual regular procedure applicable to pre-trials." *Martinez v. 348 East 104 Street Corp.,* 300 N.Y.S.2d 992, 993 (Sup. Ct. 1969).

impartable; impartible. These are two different words. *Impartable* = capable of being made known or granted (i.e., of being "imparted"). *Impartible* = indivisible. The latter word is chiefly legal, used primarily in describing estates <the question is whether the estate is partible or impartible>. See -ABLE (A).

impassible; impassable. *Impassible* = incapable of feeling or suffering. *Impassable* = not capable of being passed. See -ABLE (A). Cf. **passable.**

impeach = (1) to charge a public official with a crime in office and to constitute a legal tribunal to adjudge whether the official should be removed; esp., in the U.K., to try before the House of Lords at the instance of the House of Commons, and, in the U.S., to try before the Senate at the instance of the House of Representatives <Richard Nixon resigned to avoid being impeached>; (2) to discredit the veracity of (a witness) <counsel thoroughly impeached the witness on cross-examination>; (3) to challenge the authenticity or accuracy of (a document); or (4) in Scotland, to set up the defense, in a criminal case, that another named person committed the crime charged. In sense (1), *impeach* means, not "to remove from office," but "to bring a charge or accusation against." *Impeachment* may, of course, result in removal from office.

impecunious (= poor; penniless) is sometimes misused as if it meant "hapless," as when someone refers to an *impecunious associate* who is forced by a partner to sign pleadings.

impedient impediment; hindering impediment. *Impedient* = that impedes; obstructive. Thus *impedient impediment* is the most elementary type of REDUNDANCY. Yet it has acquired a specific legal meaning: "some fact that bars a marriage if known but that does not void the marriage after the ceremony." It is also called *hindering impediment,* which is just as redundant, albeit in a less obtrusive way.

impediment. See **impedient impediment.**

impel. For the difference between this word and *compel,* see the entry under that word. *Impel to* [+ noun phrase] is a construction not available with *compel.* E.g., "In the interest of the public good this is a hardness to be endured courageously if not cheerfully by the man whose ideals *impel* him *to* such a course."

impeller; impellor. The former spelling is preferred.

imperative. See **directory.**

imperfect, adj. In Roman law and in some modern writings, this word is given a curious sense. An *imperfect* statute is one that prohibits, but does not render void, an objectionable transaction; it provides a penalty for disobedience without depriving a violative transaction of its legal effect.

imperial; imperious. Deriving from the same root (L. *imper-* "power over a family, region, or state"), these words have been differentiated by their suffixes. *Imperial* = of or belonging to an emperor or empire. *Imperious* = overbearing, supercilious, tyrannical.

Additionally, *imperious* = urgent, absolute, imperative. E.g., "Can we adopt that construction, unless the words *imperiously* require it, which would impute to the framers of that instrument . . . the intention of impeding their exercise by withholding a choice of means?" *McCulloch v. Maryland,* 17 U.S. (4 Wheat.) 316, 408 (1819) (per Marshall, C. J.)./ "Because taxes are the life-blood of government, and their prompt and certain availability an *imperious* need, Congress has created a formidable arsenal of collection tools."

imperium (= supreme authority) forms the pl. *imperia.* The word appears frequently in discussions of Roman law, but also in modern contexts—e.g.: "The function was so well performed that not even the monumental indiscretion of the *Dred Scott* decision could quite destroy the judicial *imperium.*" Robert G. McCloskey, *The American Supreme Court* 85 (1960).

impermissible. So spelled. See -ABLE.

IMPERSONAL "IT." See EXPLETIVES.

impersonation; personation. The latter is a NEEDLESS VARIANT.

impersuadable; impersuasible. See **persuadable.**

impertinence in nonlegal contexts is taken to mean "presumptuous or forward rudeness of behavior or speech, esp. to a superior; insolence" (*OED*). This sense originated as a colloquialism. In legal contexts, the original sense of the term is retained: "the fact or character of not pertaining to the matter at hand; lack of pertinence; irrelevance." See **impertinent & pertinence.**

impertinent does not, in most legal contexts, have its ordinary meaning, "saucy, impudent." Rather, it means "not pertinent or relevant." E.g., "[T]he court may order stricken from any pleading any insufficient defense or any redundant, immaterial, *impertinent,* or scandalous matter." Fed. R. Civ. P. 12(f). Lawyers should beware in their pleadings of making impertinent statements of either kind. See **impertinence.**

impervious; imperviable. *Impervious* = not allowing something to pass through; not open to <some people are impervious to reason>. The word should be avoided in the sense "not affected by" <he was impervious to her screams for help> <expert-witnesses impervious to harsh cross-examination>. *Imperviable* is a NEEDLESS VARIANT.

impetration, in the sense "the obtaining (of a writ)," is an obsolescent LEGALISM—e.g.: "The jury allowed interest only from date of demand, which they fixed as the *impetration* [read *issuance*] of the writ, August 21, 1957, at the figure of $350." *Peyton v. Margiotti,* 156 A.2d 865, 869 (Pa. 1959)./ "Thus, the rule developed that a plaintiff could re-issue the writ (i.e., file the alias) within the statutory period beginning from the *impetration* (issuance) of the unserved writ." *Anderson v.*

Bernhard Realty Sales Co., 329 A.2d 852, 858 (Pa. Super. Ct. 1974).

In its literary sense, *impetration* (= an urgent entreaty) is a FORMAL WORD—e.g.: "Though plaintiff's *impetration* regarding its support of the war effort reflects a commendable attitude, the plaintiff in *Teutsch* was no less well motivated." *Kraemer Mills, Inc. v. U.S.,* 319 F.2d 535, 539 (Ct. Cl. 1963).

impetus. See **impotence.**

impignorate = to mortgage, pledge, or pawn. Any of these more specific, simpler terms should be used rather than this rare, pedantic LATINISM. *Pignorate* is another form of the same word.

impinge; infringe. *Impinge* is used intransitively only; it is followed by *on* or *upon* <they impinged on the voter's rights>. *Infringe,* by contrast, may be either transitive or intransitive <to infringe someone's rights> <to infringe on someone's rights>.

Though *impinge* and *infringe* are often used as if they were interchangeable, we might keep in mind the following connotations: *impinge* = (lit.) to strike or dash *upon* something else, whereas *infringe* = to break in (damage, violate, or weaken).

Impinge should not be used without an object to impinge *upon,* as here: "These policies also *impinge* [on what or whom?] when we consider the potential for their abuse." The writer of that sentence should have supplied the object. See **infringe.**

implead; emplead. The former spelling is standard. See **plead** & EN-.

impleader is recorded in the *OED* only as an agent noun (meaning "one who impleads"), but the word has not been used in that way since the early 18th century. Today it means "a procedure by which a third party is brought into a lawsuit, usu. through a defendant's third-party action." See -ER (B).

implement, v.t., is a VOGUE WORD beloved by jargonmongers, in whose language *policies are implemented. Carry out* is usually better, and certainly less vague.

implementer; implementor. The former spelling is preferred.

implicate = (1) to bring into play; to involve in its nature or meaning, or as a consequence <forcible searching implicates a constitutionally protected interest>; (2) to involve (a person) *in* a charge or crime <each party, striving to implicate the other in this heinous deed>.

implication is the noun corresponding to both *implicate* and *imply.* Thus it means (1) "the action of implicating, or involving, entangling, or entwining" <Smith's implication of Jones in the crime>; (2) "the action of implying; the fact of being implied or involved" <by necessary implication>; or (3) "that which is implied or involved" <implications of wrongdoing>.

Legal *implication*—an extension of sense (2)—occurs when one statement is treated under the law as including another (regardless of what the speaker or writer intended). Contracts, for example, often contain terms implied by law, though the parties never contemplated them.

implication of law. See **imply.**

implicit, meaning "implied," has come to be misused in the sense "complete, unmitigated" <I have implicit trust in her> <I trust her implicitly>. The *OED* labels this usage both erroneous and obsolete; with its resurgence in recent years, one can no longer call it obsolete but can confidently call it erroneous. E.g., "[D]efendant testified that he was plaintiff's employee and friend and had *implicit* [read *complete* or *unqualified*] trust in and loyalty to plaintiff." *Scafidi v. Johnson,* 409 So. 2d 316, 317 (La. Ct. App. 1981)./ "Solicitors take counsel's opinion on difficult questions, and usually rely upon the resulting opinion *implicitly* [read *completely* or *without qualification* or *unquestioningly*] . . . ." P.S. Atiyah, *Law and Modern Society* 29 (1983). See **impliedly.**

implied; express. These adjectives are correlative. *Expressed* is sometimes incorrectly contrasted with *implied.* See **express(ed).**

implied contract; quasi-contract. "[I]f a lawyer writes: 'The proper meaning of *implied contract* is contract implied in fact, not *quasi-contract,*' he does not express what is now the invariable usage of lawyers . . . ." Glanville Williams, *Language and the Law,* 61 Law Q. Rev. 384, 385 (1945). The terms *implied contract* and *quasi-contract* are now generally considered synonymous in denoting a contract not created by express words but inferred by a court from the conduct of the parties, from some special relationship between them, or because one of them has been unjustly enriched.

Formerly, *implied contract* was limited in use to a contract inferred by the courts by reason of the conduct of the parties or of a special relationship between them (implied in fact), and *quasi-contract* was used of an equitable remedy (also termed *indebitatis assumpsit*) imposed by courts when one party was unjustly enriched to the detriment of the other (implied in law). Some writers—including Scottish lawyers—continue to observe this distinction.

Implied contract is a phrase that is best avoided, however, because it "has given rise to great confusion in the law." 1 Samuel Williston & W.H.E. Jaeger, *A Treatise on the Law of Contracts* § 3, at 9 (3d ed. 1957). The confusion arises precisely because *implied contract* carries the two senses noted above, namely, both *quasi-contract* and *implied-in-fact contract* (= a mutual agreement and intent to promise without any expression in words). See **implied in fact** & **quasi-contract.**

implied in fact; implied in law. The DIFFERENTIATION between these terms is sometimes muddled. *Implied in fact* = inferable from the facts of a case. *Implied in law* = imposed by operation of law, and not because of any inferences that can be drawn about the facts of a case. E.g., "Numerous decisions have held that this waiver of sovereign immunity is limited to express contracts and contracts *implied in fact* and does not extend to contracts *implied in law* or founded upon equitable principles." See **implied contract.**

impliedly; implicitly. Though neither form is strictly incorrect, *impliedly* is awkward and characteristic of LEGALESE. Fowler wrote merely that "*impliedly* is a bad form" (*MEU1* 260). Though almost unknown to nonlawyers, it is a favorite of lawyers. *Impliedly* is old, dating in the *OED* from ca. 1400. Nevertheless, *implicitly* is almost always an improvement: "Because the quantity of court work influences quality, judicial administrators have at least *impliedly* [read *implicitly*] focused on the quality of judicial output."/ "When a person adopts the profession of law, and assumes to exercise its duties in behalf of another, for hire and reward, he *impliedly* [read *implicitly*] represents that he possesses the requisite knowledge and skill to properly conduct the matter for which he is engaged."/ "An effective argument might be made that the federal government *impliedly* [read *implicitly*] licenses an enemy alien to succeed to land by intestate succession or by will."/ "These decisions *impliedly* [read *implicitly*] hold that searches for contraband at checkpoints that are the functional equivalent of a border need not be preceded by any form of cause or suspicion."

Used on both sides of the Atlantic, *impliedly* is a graceless LEGALISM with virtually no advantages over *implicitly,* which is much to be preferred. Still, *implied* might be thought to be more concise and direct than *implicit.* Some authorities strain to differentiate the two, but such attempts are futile. See **implicit.**

implied warranty of merchantability; implied warranty of fitness for a particular purpose. Legal systems commonly insert a provision into some contracts—particularly those for the sale or supply of consumer goods—warranting that goods supplied under the contract will measure up to a prescribed standard. An *implied warranty of merchantability,* in most jurisdictions, means that the goods (a) pass as described without objection in the trade; (b) are fit for the ordinary uses to which the goods are put; (c) are adequately packaged and labeled; and (d) conform to the factual statements made on the packaging.

An *implied warranty of fitness for a particular purpose* is more specific: if the manufacturer, distributor, or retailer has reason to know a particular use to which the goods are to be put, and the buyer relies on the skill and judgment of the seller in selecting the goods, then the seller implicitly warrants that the goods are fit for that purpose.

imply. A. Uses and Misuses of Legal Senses. Anglo-American judges, who continually evaluate facts, often use the phrase *by implication* (= by what is implied, though not formally expressed, by natural inference), along with its various cognates. Judges (by implication) draw "natural inferences" and thereby decide that something or other was, in the circumstances, "implied." Through the process of HYPALLAGE—a semantic shift by which the attributes of the true subject are transferred to another subject—the word *imply* has come to be used in reference to what the judges do, as opposed to the circumstances. This specialized use of *imply* runs counter to popular lay use and is not adequately treated in English-language dictionaries.

Specifically, the word *imply* often means "(of a court) to impute or impose on equitable or legal grounds." An *implied* contract is not always one implied from the facts of the case, but may be one implied by the court, i.e., imposed by the judge or judges as a result of their inferences.

In using *imply* in this way, courts are said to find a doctrinally posited fact (a condition, restriction, remedy, right of action, or the like) that controls a judicial decision. Thus:

- "[I]t would be more literally accurate to acknowledge that . . . the court *implies* the conditions from reasons of equity." *Susswein v. Penn-*

sylvania Steel Co., 184 F. 102, 106 (C.C.D.N.Y. 1910).

- "This court cannot, upon some supposed hardship, defeat an estate by *implying* a condition which the grantor has not expressed, nor in the least intimated by the language of his conveyance." *Brown v. State,* 5 Colo. 496, 504 (1881).
- "The difficulty with the arguments seeking to *imply* Mary Silva's survival of Joseph as a condition is that they would result in holding that because it is express that Joseph must survive until the period of distribution to take an inheritable interest, a similar contingency should be *implied* as to Mary." *In re Estate of Ferry,* 361 P.2d 900, 904 (Cal. 1961) (en banc).
- "Judicial willingness to *imply* new remedies in areas governed by federal law has been expressed in a number of ways." *S.E.C. v. Texas Gulf Sulphur Co.,* 312 F. Supp. 77, 91 (S.D.N.Y. 1970).
- "[I]n my view, the Members of Congress merely assumed that the federal courts would follow the ancient maxim *'ubi jus, ibi remedium'* and *imply* a private right of action." *California v. Sierra Club,* 451 U.S. 287, 300 (1981) (Stevens, J., concurring). See MAXIMS.

When put in the passive voice, *imply* may be especially confusing, because the person who does the implying is left unclear. The user of any unabridged English-language dictionary would either find it hard to divine precisely what *imply* means, or deduce an incorrect meaning: "[T]he remaining provisions of the Insurance Law would lack substance if no private right of action were *implied.*" *Corcoran v. Frank B. Hall & Co.,* 545 N.Y.S.2d 278, 284 (App. Div. 1989). In that sentence, the passive voice masks the subject. The writer apparently means to say that a court would allow such a cause of action: thus the court would *imply* a right of action, i.e., impose it on equitable or legal grounds.

This special legal sense is most keenly demonstrated when *imply* is coupled with *impute,* as here: "When deciding the shares, we look to their [the husband's and the wife's] respective contributions and we see what trust is to be *implied* or *imputed* to them." *Cracknell v. Cracknell,* [1971] 3 All E.R. 552, 554.

Often one could actually read *impute* in place of *imply* and have the same sense (read *impute to* for *imply on*): "Under special circumstances the Court may *imply* knowledge *on* the speaker, such as the inventor of a machine, 'who must be fully informed as to [the machine's] good and bad qualities.'" *Brickell v. Collins,* 262 S.E.2d 387, 390 (N.C. Ct. App. 1980).

In some contexts, *imply* seems to take on a slightly different sense, "to read into (a document)," as here: "[O]ne has to look merely at what is clearly said. There is no room for any intendment . . . . Nothing is to be read in, nothing is to be *implied.* One can only look fairly at the language used." *Cape Brandy Syndicate v. I.R.C.,* [1921] 1 K.B. 64, 71. But such uses comport with the general sense here outlined, since "reading in" provisions has the same effect as "imputing" them.

The lawyer's *imply* has directly encroached on the word *infer.* Whereas nonlawyers frequently use *infer* for *imply,* lawyers and judges conflate the two in the opposite direction, by using *imply* for *infer.* In analyzing the facts of a case, judges will *imply* one fact from certain others. (*From* is a telling preposition.) Nonlawyers believe they must be *inferring* an additional fact from those already known; if contractual terms are *implied,* they must surely be implied by the words or circumstances of the contract and not by the judges.

Perhaps using this reasoning, some legal writers have recoiled from *imply* and have resorted instead to *infer.* E.g., "Apart from the difficulty of *inferring* a contract where none has been made, no agreement between husband and wife for future separation can be recognized." *Pettitt v. Pettitt,* [1970] A.C. 777, 811 (H.L.)./ "When a party voluntarily accepts a valuable service or benefit, having option to accept or reject it, the Court may *infer* a promise to pay." *Lewis v. Holy Spirit Ass'n,* 589 F. Supp. 10, 13 (D. Mass. 1983). In the following sentence, in which the court writes *imply or infer from,* the word *imply* adds nothing, unless *by the circumstances* (i.e., *implicit in the circumstances*) is to be understood, and *or* is to be read as *and:* "Rather, the crucial question is when can a waiver of rights be *implied or inferred from* the actions and words of the person interrogated." *McDonald v. Lucas,* 677 F.2d 518, 520 (5th Cir. 1982).

In the following sentences, *infer* might have served better than *imply.* One would be tempted to call these misuses, were some specimens not so ancient: "[T]here is nothing averred from which the court can *imply* that those conditions were performed." *Cutting v. Myers,* 6 F. Cas. 1081, 1082 (C.C.D. Pa. 1818) (No. 3,520)./ "The requirements of the rule are met if such an intention may be clearly *implied* from the language, the purposes of the agreement, and all the surrounding facts and circumstances." *Salamy v. New York Cent. Sys.,* 146 N.Y.S.2d 814, 817 (App. Div. 1955). Note that the facts here posited (performance of a condition, intention) are of a lower level of abstraction than those in the examples given at the outset of this paper. Using *imply* with low-level abstractions, as opposed to doctrinally posited facts, is comparatively uncommon in modern legal usage.

Adding still more color to this CHAMELEON-HUED WORD in legal contexts is the ordinary nonlegal sense: "We do not mean to *imply* that where joint ownership is set up in conformity with the statutory provisions, a court of equity is thereby foreclosed from looking behind the form of the transaction and determining questions of real and beneficial interest as between the parties." *Frey v. Wubbena,* 185 N.E.2d 850, 855 (Ill. 1962)./ "There is nothing in the former decision [that] would *imply* that the 'sole discretion' vested in and exercised by the trustees in this case is beyond court review." *In re Ferrall's Estate,* 258 P.2d 1009, 1013 (Cal. 1953) (en banc).

It is not wholly surprising that the legal uses of *imply* have not found a place in English-language dictionaries. Common in American and British law alike, the uses here outlined have not yet spread from legal to nonlegal contexts—and may never do so. Moreover, because lexicographic reading programs seldom glean citations from legal texts, lexicographers often overlook linguistic innovation in law. See Bryan A. Garner, "The Missing Common Law Words," in *The State of the Language* 234–45 (Christopher Ricks & Leonard Michaels eds. 1990).

B. The Nonlegal Blunder. Courts are not immune from the general misusage of *infer* for *imply:* "The mere fact that Avondale's activities and conduct may have occurred ashore does not *infer* [read *imply,* or *suggest*] that Louisiana law would automatically apply."/ "The circuit court's remanding the case *inferred* [read *implied*], in the district court's view, that plaintiff's motion for new trial should be favorably considered."/ "We find no order, ruling, or stipulation stating or *inferring* [read *implying*] that the magistrate was bound by any prior evidentiary rulings of the district judge." See **infer.**

importunacy. See **importunity.**

importune is a verb meaning "to beg or beseech; entreat." It is also a NEEDLESS VARIANT for the adjective *importunate* (= troublesomely urgent), and an obsolete variant of inopportune (= inconvenient, untimely). The intended meaning in the following sentence is not clear, but perhaps *inopportune* would have been the right word: "Although sanctions against judges may be leveled *importunely* [read *inopportunely? inappropriately?*], the interests of the administration of justice demand that the error be on that side rather than on the side of retaining without forfeiture a judge whose effectiveness is damaged in the public view."

importunity; importunacy. The latter is a NEEDLESS VARIANT of the former, meaning "bothersome pertinacity in soliciting something."

impossibility; frustration. In AmE, writers on the law of contract began using *frustration* instead of *impossibility* shortly after the turn of the 20th century. But as a would-be TERM OF ART, "*frustration* never acquired much precision or clarity of meaning; most of the time it was used as a sort of loose synonym for . . . *impossibility.*" Grant Gilmore, *The Death of Contract* 80–81 (1974). Some writers take the view that this change in terminology heralded a change in meaning: that it was "intended to widen the scope of the doctrine of discharge by supervening events." G.H. Treitel, *The Law of Contract* 779–80 (8th ed. 1991). English writers such as Treitel resist the terminological and the corresponding doctrinal change.

Some writers distinguish between *legal impossibility* (e.g., having two spouses simultaneously) and *physical impossibility* (e.g., a person's leaping unaided across the Grand Canyon). See **mistake (B).**

impostor; imposter. In most states this word, as it appears in the heading of § 3-405 of the Uniform Commercial Code, is spelled *impostor.* In other states, it is spelled *imposter.* The *-or* spelling is preferred. See -ER (A).

impotence; impotency. The latter is a NEEDLESS VARIANT. *Impotence* in the modern literal sense should be used only in reference to men, a fact not recognized by the writer of this sentence: "The statute authorizes suit to annul a marriage if, at the time of the marriage, either party was permanently *impotent* for physical or mental reasons." *Black's* notes that *impotence* is "properly used of the male; but it has also been used synonymously with *sterility.*" Any such use in modern contexts is an abuse of the term. The corresponding affliction for women, sometimes alleged to be spurious, is *frigidity.* See **potence.**

Impotence for *impetus* is a MALAPROPISM worthy of Mrs. Malaprop, Mistress Quickly, or Archie Bunker. E.g., "The main *impotence* [read *impetus*] for recruiting someone who has published is to ensure that he is used to long hours." *Impetus* means "force, impulse."

impoverishment. Only theoretically—not idiomatically—is *impoverishment* an antonym of *enrichment.* Whereas *enrich* means "to make rich *or* *richer,*" *impoverish* means "to make poor; to reduce to indigency." E.g., "Like many a testator, who with specific devise and bequest has unwittingly *impoverished* the members of his family after his death, the settlor *impoverished* himself when he conveyed all his property in trust, and divested himself of the only means of livelihood he had." Finding a ten-dollar bill *enriches* one to some extent; but, for most, losing a ten-dollar bill would not constitute *impoverishment.*

In the following sentence, *impoverishment* is incorrectly made the correlative of the legal phrase *unjust enrichment:* "Under Louisiana law, recovery may be had for unjust enrichment only if the plaintiff proves the amount of his *impoverishment* [read *damages?*] and that the defendant was *enriched* to that extent." See **unjust enrichment.**

impower is an obsolete spelling of *empower.*

impracticability (= practical impossibility) is sometimes wrongly spelled *impractibility.*

impractical; unpractical. Fowler had a point in believing that "the constant confusion between *practicable* and *practical* is a special reason for making use of *im-* and *un-* to add to the difference in the negatives" (*MEU1* 260), but *unpractical* has not been idiomatically accepted in the U.S. It is not included in *W10,* and even in the (British) *COD* the entry under *impractical* is longer than under *unpractical.* To a few British stalwarts, it may be worth keeping up the fight.

For the distinction between *practical* and *practicable,* see **practical.**

imprescriptible; imprescribable. The former is the preferred form for this word, meaning "not subject to being extinguished by lapse of time under the rules of prescription; that cannot in any circumstances be legally taken away or abandoned" (*OED*). E.g., "[O]ne of the most sacred *imprescriptible* rights of man, is violated." *The Slaughter-House Cases,* 83 U.S. (16 Wall.) 36, 110 (1872) (Field, J., dissenting). It is worth warning that "*imprescriptible* is one of the words that are often used without a clear conception of their meaning" (*MEU1* 261). It may be overstating the case, however, to say that the word is *often* used.

impress, n.; **impressment; impression; impressure.** In the legal idiom, constructive trusts are *impressed* by courts upon property obtained by fraud, or the obtaining of which results in unjust enrichment. (See **impress,** v.t.) The question remains what to call the act of impressing a constructive trust. The answer is *impressment:* "In this instance it is doubtful that any property would have become available for trust *impressment.*"

Impress, n., = a characteristic mark or quality. E.g., "A fixed contract right acquired before marriage was property the character of which takes its *impress* from the date of the contract." *Impression* = (1) the impressing (of a mark); (2) the mark impressed; (3) an effect produced on the mind or feelings; (4) a notion (*COD*). Impressure is an archaic NEEDLESS VARIANT of *impression.*

impress, v.t. This verb is used of a court's imposition of a constructive trust on equitable grounds. For an explanation of characteristic phraseology, see **impress,** n. Following are examples of each of the two legal idioms with this verb: "In many cases equity *impresses* a trust upon money or property secured by fraud." William F. Walsh, *A Treatise on Equity* 494 (1930)./ "To determine whether its assets were *impressed* with a trust, Pioneer filed an action for declaratory relief against a member of the society." See OBJECT-SHUFFLING.

impressible; impressable. The former spelling is preferred. See -ABLE (A).

impression; impressment; impressure. See **impress,** n.

imprimatur(a). The preferred form for ordinary purposes is *imprimatur* (/im-**prim**-ə-tər/ or /im-pri-**mah**-tər/), meaning literally "let it be printed, from the formula used in the Roman Catholic Church by an official licenser, approving a work to be printed." This term (now meaning "commendatory license or sanction") is construed with the preposition *on.* E.g., "The trial judge placed his *imprimatur on* a defendant's theory."/ "It is the cause element that confers the *imprimatur* of constitutionality *on* the right."/ "A ruling admitting evidence in a criminal trial has the necessary effect of legitimizing the conduct that produced the evidence, while an application of the exclusionary rule withholds the constitutional *imprimatur.*"

imprisonable crime is a typical example of HYPALLAGE, the perpetrator and not the crime being what is truly imprisonable. Glanville Williams calls *imprisonable* "[p]olice jargon, but a convenient word." *Textbook of Criminal Law* 20 n.17 (1978).

improve (= to develop, as land) is a LEGALISM that is generally understandable to most nonlawyers. E.g., "The appellant negotiated for the purchase of an *improved* parcel of land in Baltimore." If confusion occurs, it is likely to result from the odd fact that, in lawyers' parlance, an *improvement* to land—say, a ramshackle house—may actually lessen the land's value.

improvident is a FORMAL WORD meaning "heedless, unwary, not circumspect." Judges use the word far more than other writers. E.g., "The chancellor ruled that Gilden's contract was a mere offer until approved by him, and that the trustee acted hastily, with inexperience, and *improvidently*."/ "It is not unreasonable to expect a state's highest legal officer to know the state's law and to bring to this Court's attention the rules of state law that might demonstrate that we granted the writ of certiorari *improvidently*."

improviser; improvisor; improvisator(e). The usual term for "one who improvises" is *improviser*. The *-or* spelling is not preferred. *Improvisator* is a formal equivalent, and *improvisatore* is an Italianate literary word meaning "one who composes verse or drama extemporaneously."

imprudent; impudent. *Imprudent* = rash, indiscreet. *Impudent* = insolently disrespectful; shamelessly presumptuous.

impugn; oppugn; repugn. *Impugn* = to challenge, call into question. E.g., "A most unfortunate result is that, to support its holding, the court, despite its disclaimers, *impugns* the integrity of public school teachers."/ "The ethical standards of the wife's solicitors have never been *impugned*." (Eng.) The noun is *impugnment*, q.v.

Impugn does not mean merely "to affect adversely." E.g., "The agreement's economic realignment of the parties did not *impugn* [read *impair*] the fact-finding process." In a footnote to this sentence, the court stated that the agreement "did not *affect* the ability of the court to make accurate findings of fact."

Oppugn and *repugn* are less frequently encountered than *impugn*. *Oppugn* = to controvert or call into question; to fight against. *Repugn* is an ARCHAISM meaning "to offer opposition or strive against; to affect disagreeably or be repugnant to."

impugnment; impugnation. The latter is an obsolete variant. Here is an example of the standard term: "Appellant contends that the district judge made many errors in his rulings concerning the conduct of the trial and the admissibility of evidence; the *impugnment* is more than a challenge to specific rulings, however."

impunity. See **immunity.**

impute (= to ascribe; to regard [usu. something undesirable] as being done, caused, or possessed by [*COD*]) takes *to*. E.g., "We are reluctant to *impute* a different meaning *to* the term where it has been used without modification, absent a compelling and certain impetus."/ "Appellee also failed to establish at trial that Agnes assigned the claim against Aetna to it, and indeed no attempt to show an assignment was made at trial; accordingly, we will not *impute* [to Agnes] such an assignment."

We see over and over again the growing idiomatic bias in favor of *imputing* undesirable things or qualities: "If the malice essential to support an action for libel can be found under such circumstances, it must be *imputed*. Malice in law is such as the law infers to exist without just or lawful excuse. The law will *impute* malice where a defamatory publication is made without sufficient cause or excuse." (See **imply.**)/ "We ought not to *impute to* others instincts contrary to our own."/ "Lafourche would be negligent only by virtue of an *imputation* of the negligence of another, in this case of its employee Savoie."

IN-. See EN- & NEGATIVES (C).

in; into. This mistake can cause a MISCUE—e.g.: "But to conclude that the motorist has actually agreed to be sued and has thus waived his federal venue rights is surely to move *in* [read *into*] the world of Alice in Wonderland." (Frankfurter, J.)

inability. See **disability (A).**

in accord; in accordance. See **accord.**

in actual fact. See **actual fact.**

inadequate consideration. See **nominal consideration & consideration.**

inadmissible; inadmissable. The former spelling is correct. See -ABLE (A). See **admissible.**

inadvertence; inadvertency. The DIFFERENTIATION between these terms should be carefully observed. *Inadvertence* = a fault resulting from not paying attention; a mistake caused by an oversight. E.g., "We cannot conclude that the district court abused its discretion in taking into account the lulling of Judge Bagley even though there is no suggestion that it was other than the product of oversight or *inadvertence*." *Carbalan v. Vaughn*, 760 F.2d 662, 665 (5th Cir. 1985). *Inadvertency* = the quality or state of being inadvertent <the inadvertency of the act is not disputed>.

Inadvertancy and *inadvertance* are common misspellings.

inalienable; unalienable. The former, used by Jefferson in the Declaration of Independence, is slightly better formed (with a Latinate prefix as well as suffix). E.g., "The New York statutes make the interest of the beneficiary of a trust to receive the income from realty or personalty *inalienable;* most trusts thus become indestructible." Some writers have recently revived *unalienable.* See NEGATIVES (B).

in all things. This phrase is LEGALESE commonly found in court papers addressing motions—e.g.: "Defendant's motion should be *in all things* denied." Generally it adds nothing.

in any event. See **at all events.**

inapt. Though many English-language dictionaries would suggest that *inapt* is a NEEDLESS VARIANT of *unapt* (and perhaps also of *inept*), it occurs far more frequently in legal writing than *unapt,* which itself ought to be branded as unnecessary.

inasmuch as, in as much as; insofar as, in so far as. In modern AmE usage, the standard spelling of each group is *inasmuch as* and *insofar as,* both single words except for the final element. In modern BrE, usage is split: *inasmuch as* is standard and the expression *in so far as* is preferred as four separate words.

However the phrase is spelled, though, *inasmuch as* is almost always inferior to *because* or *since.* See **insofar as.**

inaugural, n.; **inauguration.** The ceremony for a president entering office is an *inauguration;* the speech that the new president makes on this occasion is the *inaugural address,* sometimes shortened to *inaugural.*

inaugurate is a FORMAL WORD, some might say pompous, for *begin* or *start,* being more formal even than *commence,* q.v. Sometimes another term, such as *open* or *establish,* is the desired substitute. E.g., "Thirteen years after *Brown II,* the only step that the Tennessee defendants had taken toward dismantling the dual system of public higher education was *inauguration of* [read *setting up* or *starting*] an open admissions policy." Little has changed since Richard Grant White wrote that *inaugurate* "is a word [that] might better be eschewed by all those who do not wish to talk high-flying nonsense . . . ." *Words and Their Uses, Past and Present* 128 (2d ed. 1872).

in back of. See **back of.**

in banc(o); in bank. See **en banc.**

in behalf of; on behalf of. See **behalf.**

in being; *in esse.* John Chipman Gray's classic formulation of the Rule Against Perpetuities states: "No interest is good unless it must vest, if at all, not later than 21 years after some life *in being* at the creation of the trust." Through this formulation, *in being* has become a TERM OF ART used commonly in discussions of wills and trusts. "On the date of Tilley's death, Lathan and Barrett and one great-grandchild were *in being.*"/ "At the time of executing the will, the testator had several grandchildren *in being.*"

In esse is a LATINISM equivalent to *in being.* Except as a correlative of *in posse* (= in possibility, but not in actual existence), *in esse* has no justification in place of the Anglo-Saxon phrase: "These words were not used in reference to children who possibly may—but possibly may not—ever be *in esse* [read *in being*], and certainly not to those of whose existence, of course, the testator would have no knowledge." See **esse** & ***in esse.***

in between. Omit *in* when the phrase is followed by one or more objects—e.g.: "Ms. Smithweck sat *in between* [read *between*] Ms. Esquenazi and Mr. Sostek."

in brief is understood by most readers as meaning "briefly." In American legal writing, however, it sometimes means "in a brief addressed to a court," as here: "[Justice Jackson] meant that an oral argument requires an intense rethinking of your whole case, not in your terms already used *in brief,* but in terms of the questions likely to occur to the judges." George D. Gibson, *Elements of Legal Style,* 22 Bus. Law. 547, 555 (1967).

Inc. Unless otherwise required by syntax, a comma need not follow this abbreviation—e.g.: "Pedernales, *Inc.* was founded in 1994."

in camera = in the chamber; privately. Though this phrase usually refers to a judge's chambers, it may also refer to a courtroom from which all spectators are excluded. Thus, one cannot be sure where the examination took place in a sentence such as the following: "The documents were examined by the judge in camera." The phrase should not be used in reference to lawyers' offices—e.g.: "Usually, neither side needs to depose its own witnesses because its witnesses' information is generally obtained cooperatively *in camera* [read *in private*]." Peter M. Panken, *The Art of Deposing in Employment Litigation,* 36 Pract. Law. 23, 24 (June 1990).

The phrase may be an adverb that follows the verb it modifies—e.g.: "This court has reviewed *in camera* the portions of the memorandum that the IRS seeks to withhold." The phrase may also serve as an adjective that precedes the noun it modifies—e.g.: "The government invoked a 'deliberative processes' privilege for documents that it had turned over to the district court for *in camera* review."/ "Defense counsel conceded that he would be bound by the judge's decision after an *in camera* examination of the prosecution's reasons for refusal of the charge." Some writers would hyphenate the PHRASAL ADJECTIVE in the two immediately preceding examples.

The phrase should be used of inspections, but not, through HYPALLAGE, of documents inspected. E.g., "Plaintiff then filed a motion seeking the right to inspection *of the in camera documents* [read *of the documents that the court had examined in camera*]."

In chambers is sometimes used rather than *in camera* in citing an opinion by a single judge. For example, *Lenhard v. Wolff,* 444 U.S. 1301 (1979) (*in-chambers* opinion of Rehnquist, J.). Cf. **open court, in.**

incapable is usu. applied to persons in modern nonlegal contexts, in the sense "unable, unfit." In law it retains its broader use in reference to things as well as to persons. E.g., "In certain cases, no doubt, perhaps many cases, a rule [that] a statute attempts to lay down may be *incapable of* practical application till it has been explained by a judge or judges . . . ." Edward Jenks, *The Book of English Law* 23 (P.B. Fairest ed., 6th ed. 1967). In such a context, *incapable* means "not allowing or admitting of." See **capable of.**

incapacitate = to deprive of legal capacity. E.g., "The Uniform Probate Code is applied to all subject matter relating to the estates of decedents, including protection of minors and *incapacitated* persons." *Incapacify* is a NEEDLESS VARIANT. See **capacitate.**

incapacitation; incapacity. These words should be distinguished as follows: *incapacitation* = the action of incapacitating or rendering incapable; *incapacity* = lack of ability in some legal respect. See **capacity.**

in case is generally much inferior to *if.* See **case (A).**

in cases in which is usually verbose for *when* or *whenever.* See **case (A).**

inception; incipiency. Both words mean "beginning, commencement, initiation." The difference is that *inception* refers to the action or process of beginning, whereas *incipiency* refers to the fact or state of having begun. Here the two words are used merely in an attempt at INELEGANT VARIATION: "That pattern fixes the character of title at the time of its *inception* or acquisition. It depends on the existence or nonexistence of the marriage at the time of the *incipiency* [read *inception*] of the right in virtue of which the title is finally extended." *Inception* is far more commonly the appropriate word.

incest, denoting a statutory as opposed to a common-law crime, has been criticized for having an unduly restricted sense. In most English-speaking jurisdictions, a man commits incest by having sexual intercourse with a female he knows to be his granddaughter, daughter, sister, or mother; a woman (over the age of 16) commits incest by having sexual intercourse with her grandfather, father, brother, or son. The definitions are limited to sexual intercourse; i.e., oral and anal sex are excluded. A prominent English writer suggests reforming the law: "Surely the offence of *incest* should cover all cases of vaginal or anal penetration or penetration involving the penis." Andrew Ashworth, *Principles of Criminal Law* 316 (1991).

incestuous is sometimes mistakenly written *incestious.*

in chambers. See **in camera.**

in chief (= principal, as opposed to collateral or incidental) is legal JARGON denoting the part of a trial, or of a witness's testimony, in which the main body of evidence is presented. "Witnesses examined in open court must be first examined *in chief,* then cross-examined, and then re-examined." Cf. **case-in-chief** & **tenant-in-chief.**

inchoate, pronounced /*in-**koh**-ət*/ in AmE and /***in**-koh-ət*/ in BrE, means "just begun, not yet fully developed." The prefix is an intensive *in-*, not a negative or privative *in-*. (See **choate.**) The law has found many uses for this word. In criminal law, for example, there are three *inchoate offenses:* attempt, conspiracy, and incitement. The word also appears in other legal contexts—e.g.: "Nor would common-law dower, giving her an *inchoate* right during the husband's lifetime, help her, for dower applies only to real estate."/ "In determining whether the officer acted reasonably in such circumstances, we must give due weight not to his *inchoate* suspicion or 'hunch,' but to the specific reasonable inferences that he is entitled to draw from the facts in light of his experience."

The antonym to *inchoate* is ordinarily either *consummate* <her dower becomes consummate> or *consummated* <they were consummated crimes>.

The word is sometimes a pomposity that usurps the place of an ordinary word. E.g., "Given the summary disposition of these issues, we cannot say at this *inchoate* [read *early*] stage that a fact-finder would be precluded from reasonably inferring the existence of a relevant submarket of third-party firms."

inchoate dower. See **curtesy.**

incidence = occurrence or rate of occurrence <the incidence of syphilis continues to decline>. Using this word as a variant for *instance* (= case or example) is a mistake: "As subsequent cases will establish, the rationale herein *has been rejected in most incidences* [read *has been rejected in most instances,* or better yet, *has usually* (or *almost always*) *been rejected*]." See **incidents & instance.**

incident, n. **A. And *instance.*** An *incident* is an occurrence or happening; an *instance* is an example. See **instance.** Cf. **incidence.**

B. Meaning "a concomitant." This sense, which originated in the feudal law of England, denotes the idea that a thing may be naturally and inseparably connected with something else that is more important. The usage has remained common in legal contexts, esp. in the context of either property law or judicial power. E.g., "The decedent had the *incidents* of ownership to the life insurance."/ "Courts of justice as an *incident* of their jurisdiction have inherent power to appoint guardians ad litem."

For the adjectival use, see **incident to.**

C. And *accident.* See **accident** & EUPHEMISMS.

incidentally; incidently. The former means "loosely, casually" or "by the way," and the latter means "so as to be incident; so as to depend on or appertain to something else." The most common mistake with these words is to misuse *incidently* for *incidentally*—e.g.: "Section 474, to the extent it prohibits expression at all, does so only inadvertently and *incidently* [read *incidentally*]." *Regan v. Time, Inc.,* 468 U.S. 641, 695 (1984) (Stevens, J., concurring in part & dissenting in part). See **incident to.**

incidentals is elliptical for *incidental damages.* Cf. **consequentials, exemplaries & punitives.** See **damages.**

incidently. See **incidentally.**

incidents and *incidence,* q.v., are homophones that may give listeners trouble. See **incident.**

incident to; incidental to. Though to some extent interchangeable historically, these phrases have undergone a plain DIFFERENTIATION that has gained acceptance among stylists. The former means "closely related to; naturally appearing with"; the latter, "happening by chance and subordinate to some other thing; peripheral." In the following sentence, *incident* is properly used: "In an action for fraud, exemplary damages are *incident to* and dependent on the recovery of actual damages." Here *incidental* is correctly used: "It is clear that testator's plan of accumulation was merely *incidental to* his primary charitable intention to create a source that would provide continuing income over the 400-year term for the maintenance of Masonic homes."

In the following quotations, *incidental* is misused for *incident,* a common blunder: "A half century ago, in that case, we denied damages for wrongful libel of a vessel save when the seizure resulted from bad faith, malice, or gross negligence. *Incidental thereto, on the same grounds we denied* [read *Incident to that denial, we denied on the same grounds*] recovery for attorney's fees incurred in obtaining the release of the vessel seized, without differentiating between attorney's fees and other damages."/ "The court held that the search was not *incidental to* [read *incident to*] the arrest because it was conducted six hours after the arrest and at a place other than the arrest scene." *Incidental to* has even had to be construed as meaning *incident to,* primarily because of slipshod drafting of statutes. See, e.g., *U.S. v. Shursen,* 649 F.2d 1250, 1257 (8th Cir. 1981).

Sometimes courts are inconsistent in their use of these terms in a single opinion: "Closer in point . . . are cases holding that . . . [a club's] outside profits must be . . . strictly *incidental to* [read *incident to*] club activities. . . . Here the rental income was not *incident to* the operation of the club." *U.S. v. Fort Worth Club,* 345 F.2d 52, 57 (5th Cir. 1965). See INELEGANT VARIATION.

Incidental is sometimes wrongly used for *incident,* adj., when the word precedes the noun it modifies: "Their primary objective is not to require the defendant to perform a contract, to carry out a trust, or to undo the effects of a fraud, but to determine the title and *incidental* [read *incident*] right to possession of the land."

incipiency. See **inception.**

incipient; insipient. The former means "beginning, in an initial stage"; the latter is an obsolete word meaning "unwise, foolish." Chapter C of J. Gillis Wetler's *Style of Judicial Opinions* (1960) is entitled "Arkansas: American Style, and *Insipient* Transformation." A reading of the first paragraph of that chapter shows that *incipient,* not *insipient,* was the intended word. The misuse, especially for its being in such a prominent place, might be characterized as insipient.

inciteful; incitive; incitative; incitatory. What is the adjective meaning "tending to incite"? Most American dictionaries do not list one, and the *OED* merely records sparse and ancient examples of *incitive, incitative,* and *incitatory*—all of which today might be considered NEEDLESS VARIANTS of *inciteful.* This word is the legal NEOLOGISM that first appeared in mid-20th-century AmE. Today it is fairly common—e.g.:

- "Wall relied upon Enlow's alleged *inciteful* speech to create probable cause for the arrest." *Enlow v. Tishomingo County,* 962 F.2d 501, 505 (5th Cir. 1992).
- "Many courts have adopted a rule that 'mere words cannot be sufficient provocation to reduce a murder charge to voluntary manslaughter, no matter how insulting or *inciteful.*'" *State v. Shane,* 590 N.E.2d 272, 277 (Ohio 1992).
- "The derogatory and *inciteful* language in the newsletter used by Union members in reference to the Employees' activities further supports this Court's finding that violence may occur at the 'mass trials.'" *Kinney v. International Union of Operating Eng'rs.,* 786 F. Supp. 1431, 1441 (N.D. Ind. 1992).
- "As the State presumably recognizes, were it to cast the cross burning law as an attempt to regulate only the most *inciteful* of constitutionally proscribable fighting words, it would commit the same mistake as Minnesota in selecting only certain socially charged words for prosecution." *State v. Sheldon,* 629 A.2d 753, 761 (Md. Ct. App. 1993).
- "[T]he statute is the product of a legislative intent to cover intentional *inciteful* acts or conduct aimed at one's opponents as well as one's supporters." *Land v. State,* 426 S.E.2d 370, 372 (Ga. 1993).
- "Defendant contends . . . that a cross which is functionally and symbolically equivalent to a cross used by the Ku Klux Klan at a private rally is, as a matter of law, sufficiently injurious and *inciteful* when left unattended as public property as to constitutionally permit a government to prohibit its display." *Knight Riders of the Ku Klux Klan v. City of Cincinnati,* 863 F. Supp. 587, 589 (S.D. Ohio 1994).

Unfortunately, the word can be confused with its homophone, *insightful.* See **insightful.**

incitement; incitation. The latter is a NEEDLESS VARIANT.

inciter (= one who incites) is so spelled. See **perpetrator.**

inclement. See **inclimate.**

inclimate is a spreading MALAPROPISM for *inclement* (= unmerciful; stormy). Because *inclement weather* has become such a common phrase—either a SET PHRASE or a CLICHÉ, depending on whom one asks—many have come to hear the phrase as a redundant comment on the *climate* as well as the *weather:* hence the erroneous *inclimate weather.* E.g., "According to Glascock, the test is used to determine the maximum safe speed at which a vehicle can traverse a curve under the most *inclimate* [read *inclement*] highway conditions, that is, with the highway surface being wet." *Vervik v. State,* 278 So. 2d 530, 535 (La. Ct. App. 1973)./ "He also contends that the Secretary's decision to not postpone the February 28th election date due to *inclimate* [read *inclement*] weather was arbitrary and capricious." *Donovan v. Westside Local 174, AFL-CIO,* 783 F.2d 616, 623 (6th Cir. 1986).

inclose. See **enclose.**

inclosure is an archaic form of *enclosure,* q.v.

included. See **including.**

includable; includible; inclusible. *Includible* is usual in estate-planning texts, and is a main entry in the *OED; includable,* however, is given primary sanction in *W3* and *W10* and is now the more prevalent of the two in more general legal contexts. *Inclusible* is a NEEDLESS VARIANT. See -ABLE (A).

including is sometimes misused for *namely.* But it should not be used to introduce an exhaustive list, for it implies that the list is only partial. In the words of one federal court, "It is hornbook law that the use of the word *including* indicates that the specified list . . . is illustrative, not exclusive." *Puerto Rico Maritime Shipping Auth. v. I.C.C.,* 645 F.2d 1102, 1112 n.26 (D.C. Cir. 1981). E.g., "Several business-law courses will be offered next year, *including* [read *namely*] one this summer and four next year."

Included for *including* must be a rare error: "The agreement provides that it is an Arizona agreement and that it shall be governed by the laws of the State of Arizona in all matters, *included* [read *including*] but not limited to validity, obligation, interpretation, construction, and termination." See **including but not limited to.**

including but not limited to; including without limitation. In DRAFTING, these cautious phrases are often essential to defeat three canons of construction: *inclusio unius est exclusio alterius* ("to express one thing is to exclude the other"), *noscitur a sociis* ("it is known by its associates"), and *ejusdem generis* ("of the same class or nature"). See ***inclusio unius est exclusio alterius*** & ***ejusdem generis.***

Even though the word *including* itself means that the list is merely exemplary and not exhaustive, the courts have not invariably so held. So the longer, more explicit variations may be considered necessary by some drafters. Of course, drafters do not help matters when they use these phrases to introduce what is actually intended to be a comprehensive list.

inclusible. See **includable.**

inclusio unius est exclusio alterius; expressio unius est exclusio alterius. These interchangeable maxims of interpretation hold that to include or express one thing implies the exclusion of the other, or of the alternative (L. *alterius* meaning "of the other two"). For example, a rule that "each citizen is entitled . . . " implies that noncitizens do not share in the entitlement.

inclusive. This word is often helpful in expressing lengths of time. For example, the phrase *from November 1 to December 15 inclusive* makes clear that both the starting date and the ending date are included; without the word *inclusive,* the meaning is debatable.

incommensurate; incommensurable. See **commensurate.**

incomparable. The primary accent falls on the second syllable—hence */in-**kom**-pə-rə-bəl/*, not */in-kəm-**par**-ə-bəl /*. See **comparable.**

incompetence; incompetency. Some lay authorities have stated that *incompetence* is the preferred form, but in legal writing a growing distinction exists between the forms. The best advice is to reserve the *-cy* form to contexts involving sanity or ability to stand trial or to testify, and to use *-ce* form when referring to less than acceptable levels of ability. E.g., "The various newspaper stories commenting on both appellant's alleged *incompetence* [read *incompetency*] to stand trial and a grand jury investigation of the district's operations also fall short of the requirements set forth in *Bollow.*" These two word-forms are favorites of writers who engage in INELEGANT VARIATION; one must be consistent when the sense does not vary. See **competence (A).**

incompetent is the adjective serving both *incompetence* and *incompetency,* q.v. Here it is the adjective for *incompetency:* "Their testimony, if accepted, clearly shows that Mary was not totally *incompetent* and at times she was normal and in possession of her mental and physical faculties." And here for *incompetence:* "The evidence shows that her discharge stemmed from her being generally *incompetent* at her job: she was unable to type satisfactorily, to add and subtract, and to file in alphabetical order." See **competent.**

INCOMPLETE SENTENCES. A. Fragments. Grammarians typically define *fragment* as a part of a sentence punctuated as if it were complete. Usually denoting an error—as opposed to literary license—the term *fragment* (or *frag.*) appears frequently in the marginal jottings of high-school and college English teachers. That is to say, some high-school and college students don't know how to write complete sentences. Thus, elementary grammars warn against constructions such as the following one, in which a main clause and a subordinate clause are each written as complete sentences:

> "We usually go to the fair in the evening. Because everything is more glamorous under the lights."
>
> Ex. fr. Philip Gucker, *Essential English Grammar* 133 (1966).

The fragment might be corrected in any of several ways:

> "We usually go to the fair in the evening because everything is more glamorous under the lights."

> "We usually go to the fair in the evening; everything is more glamorous under the lights."

> "We usually go to the fair in the evening. Everything is more glamorous under the lights."

This type of elementary problem rarely occurs in the writing of lawyers, who generally know enough about writing to be able to construct complete sentences. (The more frequent problem is RUN-ON SENTENCES, which occur when writers punctuate two sentences as if they were one.) Therefore, basic advice on avoiding fragments—"don't write a phrase or dependent clause as if it were a complete sentence"—is of limited utility to legal writers. Further, for reasons discussed in (B), that advice might be misleading.

B. Incomplete Sentences in Informal Writing. Grammarians' definitions of the word *sentence* range widely. Here is a sampling:

- "A sentence is a group of words containing a subject and a predicate and expressing a complete thought." C. Rexford Davis, *Toward Correct English* 1 (1936).
- "A complete sentence says something about something." Robert M. Gorrell & Charlton Laird, *Modern English Handbook* 195 (2d ed. 1956).
- "Sentence . . . [means] a group of words consisting of a finite verb and its subject as well as any complement that may be present and any modifiers that belong to the verb, to the subject, to the complement, or the entire statement, the whole group of words constituting a grammatically complete statement, i.e., a statement that is clearly not part of a larger structure." Ralph M. Albaugh, *English: A Dictionary of Grammar and Structure* 170 (1964).
- "A sentence is a combination of words so connected as to express a complete thought: Man is mortal. Is man mortal? How mortal man is!" James G. Fernald, *English Grammar Simplified* 161 (Cedric Gale ed., 2d ed. 1979).

Given that the word *complete* appears in each of those definitions, one might surmise—as many writers believe—that it is impossible to write an *incomplete* sentence and still be within the bounds of good usage.

Yet the more sophisticated grammarians have long qualified the notion of "completeness." The great linguist Otto Jespersen defined *sentence* as "a (relatively) complete and independent unit of communication . . .—the completeness and independence being shown by its standing alone or its capability of standing alone, i.e. of being uttered by itself." *Essentials of English Grammar* 106 (1933; repr. 1964). Similarly but more specifically, C.T. Onions defined *sentence* as a group of words—or sometimes a single word—that makes a statement <I'm a lawyer>, a command <Open the window>, an expression of a wish <Let's go>, a question <How are you?>, or an exclamation <What a verdict!>. *Modern English Syntax* 1 (B.D.H. Miller, ed., 1971). More recently still, a grammatical dictionary states that a sentence "usually" has a subject and a predicate. Sylvia Chalker & Edmund Weiner, *The Oxford Dictionary of English Grammar* 358 (1994).

It appears possible, then, to have an "incomplete" sentence—i.e., one in which the subject or the verb is at best implicit. Jespersen called one type "amorphous sentences," noting both that they are "more suitable for the emotional side of human nature" and that it would be impossible to say precisely what is "left out." *Essentials* at 105, 106. Examples are *Yes!* / *Goodbye!* / *Thanks!* / *Nonsense!* / *Of course!* / *Why all this fuss?* / *Hence his financial difficulties! Id.* at 105–06.

Sir Ernest Gowers, in fact, classified six common types of "verbless sentences": transitional, afterthought, dramatic climax, comment, pictorial, and aggressive. *MEU2* at 674–75. The types that appear in modern legal writing might be classified somewhat differently. As the examples below illustrate, the important quality in each type is that the sentence be short enough that the reader will recognize it as purposely incomplete:

- Transitional: "One other thing. If they're not needed for a month or two, they never complain." James W. McElhaney, *How I Write,* 4 Scribes J. Legal Writing 39, 41 (1993).
- Afterthought: "It is tempting to set Cardozo and Corbin over against them as the engineers of its destruction. Tempting and by no means untrue." Grant Gilmore, *The Death of Contract* 57 (1974).
- Emphatic: "For Mansfield this was intolerable; for Willes it was in the last resort right. In the last resort." Patrick Devlin, *The Judge* 129 (1979).
- Negating: "Several past efforts at translating Kelsen have been sad, broken-backed affairs. Not Hartney's." Neil MacCormick, *Doing and Discussing,* TLS, 19 July 1991, at 22.
- Responding: "Do we say, then, that history is everything and comparison nothing, or that comparative enquiry is merely an application of the historical method? By no means." Frederick Pollock, "The History of Comparative Jurisprudence," in *Essays in the Law* 1, 7 (1922; repr. 1969).
- Explanatory: "For the compromise theory the question of justice is a question of balance, and the balance is both impersonal and intuitive. Impersonal because individuals become the instruments of achieving aggregate quantities—of equality as much as of utility. Intuitive because the correct balance must be a matter of inarticulate 'feel.'" Ronald Dworkin, *A Matter of Principle* 272 (1985).
- Qualifying or Recanting: "The Age of Aquarius has finally dawned in Presidential politics. Sort

of." Maureen Dowd, *2 Baby Boomers on 1 Ticket: A First, But Will It Work?* N.Y. Times, 13 July 1992, at 1A.

- Summing up: "How different is this Treaty! It lays down general principles. It expresses its aims and purposes. All in sentences of moderate length and commendable style." *H.P. Bulmer Ltd. v. J. Bollinger S.A.,* [1974] 1 Ch. 401, 425 (C.A.) (per Lord Denning, M.R.).
- Lively, staccato effect: "Men rather than women, black men if possible. Older people rather than younger. Discerning rather than deferential. Shepherds rather than sheep, football buffs rather than football widows, fans of 'L.A. Law' rather than 'NYPD Blue.' And though there are no longer any blank slates when it comes to O.J. Simpson . . . it's better that they get their news from 'MacNeil/Lehrer' or Newsweek than 'Geraldo!' or The Star. [¶] Among lawyers and jury consultants that is the consensus prescription for Mr. Simpson's ideal juror . . . ." David Margolick, *Ideal Juror for O.J. Simpson: Football Fan Who Can Listen,* N.Y. Times, 23 Sept. 1994, at A1.

Whatever the purpose, though, the incomplete or verbless sentence carries some degree of risk. You risk your not being expert enough to carry it off adroitly. You risk your readers' being suspicious about whether you have carried it off. You should therefore be wary: "Most writers . . . use the incomplete sentence sparingly, except in reports of conversation. It is a special device, to be used for special effects. In the hands of anyone but an expert, it is usually unsuccessful because the basic patterns have not been established, and missing ideas cannot be supplied." Robert M. Gorrell & Charlton Laird, *Modern English Handbook* 202 (2d ed. 1956).

Generally, incomplete or verbless sentences of the acceptable type are not classified as "fragments," but technically they are precisely that. Thus, it is possible, in good usage, to write fragments. Possible but difficult.

in concert. See **concert.**

incongruent; incongruous. Both are preferably accented on the second rather than the third syllable. For the distinction, see **congruent.**

in connection with is always a vague, loose connective. Occasionally—very occasionally—it is the only connective that will do: it should always be used as a last resort. E.g., "Plaintiff sued defendant *in connection with* [read *on?*] an irrigation-system lease." (For breach of the lease? Who was the lessee, who the lessor?)/ "One of the most difficult problems *in connection with* [read *with*] the duty to take care is the problem of the unforeseeable plaintiff." C. Gordon Post, *An Introduction to the Law* 74 (1963).

in consideration of the mutual covenants herein contained. In contract DRAFTING, this hoary phrase supposedly makes clear that the contract cannot fail for lack of consideration. In fact, though, the phrase is deadwood: courts look to the mutual promises to ascertain whether consideration exists, and if one side has promised nothing, vague recitals of consideration will not suffice to save the contract.

in consideration of the premises. Use *therefore* instead.

inconsistency; inconsistence. Writers on usage formerly tried to distinguish between the forms, reserving *inconsistency* for the sense "the general quality of being inconsistent," and making *inconsistence* mean "an act of an inconsistent nature or an instance of being inconsistent." Today, however, *inconsistency* has ousted *-ce* in all senses. *Inconsistence* should be eschewed as a NEEDLESS VARIANT.

inconsistent pleading. See **Codd's Puzzle.**

in contrast with; in contrast to. These are equally good. See **contrast (A).**

incontrovertible. So spelled.

incorporeal; incorporal. See **corporal & corporeal.**

incorporeal hereditament. See **corporeal hereditaments & hereditament(s).**

increasingly less. See **increasingly more.**

increasingly more is increasingly—or, rather, more and more—common as a REDUNDANCY. E.g., "As the business becomes *increasingly more* [read *increasingly* or *more*] competitive, do publishers care which books they publish or what shape the manuscripts are in when they hit the press?" Roger Cohen, *When a Best Seller Is at Stake, Publishers Can Lose Control,* N.Y. Times, 12 May 1991, at 4E.

The phrase *increasingly less* [read *less and less* or *decreasing*] is equally bad: an OXYMORON. E.g., "They have *increasingly less* time for thorough first-hand work upon the vast mass of available material." Roscoe Pound, *The Formative Era of American Law* 164 (1938).

incredible; incredulous. *Incredible* = not believable. E.g., "We find *incredible* the testimony that the lawn mower slid laterally five to six feet across the grass on flat ground."/ "Sources of information are sometimes given because naming the source gives authority to an otherwise *incredible* statement." *Noncredible* is a NEEDLESS VARIANT.

Incredulous (= skeptical) is sometimes misused for *incredible*—e.g.: "The statute of limitations runs against the predecessors of the plaintiffs and in favor of the defendants; to argue otherwise is to border on being *incredulous* [read *incredible*]."/ "No court is required to believe, or should be bound by improbable, *incredulous* [read *incredible*], or unreasonable evidence supporting a verdict. . . ." *Baker Serv. Tools, Inc. v. Buckley,* 500 So. 2d 970, 971 (Miss. 1986). See **credible.**

increscitur is a NEEDLESS VARIANT of *additur*—e.g.: F.E. Mathews, *Increscitur* [read *Additur*] *in Personal Injury Cases,* 15 St. Louis L. Rev. 169 (1930). See **additur.**

incriminate has two important senses: (1) "to charge with a crime"; (2) "to indicate involvement in the commission of a crime." The latter sense is more frequent; it applies in the phrase *self-incrimination,* and, e.g., here: "When he presents his witnesses, he must reveal their identity and submit them to cross-examination, which in itself may prove *incriminating,* or which may furnish the state with leads to *incriminating* rebuttal evidence."/ "The fingerprints were not the only evidence linking Walborn to the *incriminating* documents."

The equivalent verb *criminate,* q.v., was formerly common in AmE and BrE but seldom appears in modern prose. E.g., "It has also been held that the fact that a witness voluntarily testifies to matters concerning which he might refuse to answer on the ground that the answer might tend to *criminate* him does not constitute any defense to a charge of perjury." *Criminate* is now but a NEEDLESS VARIANT of *incriminate.*

incriminatory; criminatory. The former is more common, just as *incriminate* is now more common than *criminate,* q.v. "[H]e must prove the *criminatory* [read *incriminatory*] character of what it is his privilege to suppress just because it is *criminatory* [read *incriminatory*]." *U.S. v. Weisman,* 111 F.2d 260, 262 (2d Cir. 1940).

incrust. See EN-.

inculcatable. So spelled. See -ATABLE.

inculcate (into) for *indoctrinate.* Although these are both transitive verbs (i.e., they take direct objects), the nature of the objects is different. One *inculcates* values into people; and one *indoctrinates* people with certain values. One does not *inculcate* people, but rather values or beliefs or ideas. The title of a law review article contains this infelicity: Tyll van Geel, *The Search for Constitutional Limits on Governmental Authority to Inculcate Youth,* 62 Tex. L. Rev. 197 (1983). Fowler noted this aberration and called it "a curious mistake" (*MEU1* 266); no longer is it curious, but it is still a mistake. See OBJECT-SHUFFLING.

inculpatable, not *inculpable,* is the correct form of the word meaning "capable of being inculpated." (See -ATABLE.) *Inculpable* is, however, a negative form that generally means "not culpable; blameless; free from guilt." Use of the term may cause ambiguities. See **culpable & nonculpable.**

inculpate = to accuse or incriminate. Although its antonym (*exculpate,* q.v.) can be found in nonlegal writing, *inculpate* rarely appears in nonlegal prose. But it is common in contexts involving criminal law and torts—e.g.: "The prosecution asserts that a prior inconsistent statement of the witness may be admitted to attack his credibility even if the statement tends to directly *inculpate* the defendant."/ "The right to confront a witness arises only when that witness *inculpates* a defendant."

The adjective is *inculpatory:* "Defense counsel heard this testimony of Masorlian, which was exculpatory with respect to her and Brissa and *inculpatory* with respect to petitioner." *U.S. ex rel. Tonaldi v. Elrod,* 782 F.2d 665, 666 (7th Cir. 1986). See -ATABLE.

incumbent upon or *on* has become a CLICHÉ as a way of expressing a duty or obligation. E.g., "If, however, a valid reason exists for the retention of a fund by the executor, it is *incumbent upon* him not to permit such fund to remain idle, but to invest it."

incumber; encumber. The latter is the preferred spelling. See EN-.

incumbrance. See **encumbrance.**

incumbrancer. See **encumbrancer.**

incuria. British legal writers use *incuria* (lit., "carelessness") to denote the idea that a case was decided *per incuriam,* that is, in ignorance of the relevant law. E.g., "Viscount Simon L.C. had erroneously assumed, with the concurrence of the other (including Scottish) peers, that the law of the two countries was the same. *Quaere,* whether this was *incuria;* or is *incuria* unthinkable in the House of Lords?" Carleton K. Allen, *Law in the Making* 257 (7th ed. 1964). See ***per incuriam.***

incurrence; incurment. The latter is a NEEDLESS VARIANT of the noun corresponding to the verb *to incur* (= [1] to run into (some undesirable consequence), or [2] to bring upon oneself). E.g., "The fault in the *incurrence* of the danger does not free the defendant from liability."/ "When a 'loss contingency' exists, the likelihood that the future event will confirm the loss or impairment of an asset or the *incurrence* of a liability can range from probable to remote." *Incurrence* is sometimes misspelled *incurrance.*

indebitatus assumpsit. See **assumpsit, implied contract & quasi-contract.**

indebtedness = the state or fact of being indebted. E.g., "For purposes of 12 U.S.C. § 82, a national bank's *indebtedness* or liability does not include Federal Funds Purchased or obligations to repurchase securities sold."

Indebtedness is frequently used where the simpler word *debt* would be preferable: "The petitioner elected to declare the entire *indebtedness* [better: *debt*] to be immediately due and payable."/ "The *indebtedness* [better: *debt*] has not been paid." In this sense, *indebtedness* is a NEEDLESS VARIANT of *debt,* although in some contexts one can hardly discern what is being referred to: the state of being indebted or the actual debt. See **debt & indebtment.**

indebtment, a NEEDLESS VARIANT of *indebtedness* or *debt,* was much more common up to the mid-20th century than it is today. E.g., "The transfer from Godfrey was a simple collateral security, taken as additional security for the old *indebtment* [read *debt*] . . . ." *People's Sav. Bank v. Bates,* 120 U.S. 556, 565 (1887). A few latter-day examples persist: "[T]he . . . amount due under an absolute *indebtment* [read *debt* or *indebtedness*] may be unascertained . . . ." *Loyal Erectors Inc. v. Hamilton & Son, Inc.,* 312 A.2d 748, 752 (Me. 1973). See **indebtedness & debt.**

indecency. See **obscenity (B).**

indecent assault is the BrE phrase denoting a statutory crime that includes all forms of sexual assault other than rape, buggery (q.v.), and attempts to commit either of those crimes. The nearest AmE equivalent is *sexual assault.* See **rape (C).**

INDEFINITE ANTECEDENT. See ANTECEDENTS, FALSE.

indemnifiable; indemnitable. The former is better.

indemnificate, a BACK-FORMATION from **indemnification,** is a NEEDLESS VARIANT of **indemnify,** q.v.

indemnification. See **indemnity.**

indemnificatory; indemnitory. Both mean "of, relating to, or constituting an indemnity." The standard term is *indemnificatory.* The other term, *indemnitory,* is a NEEDLESS VARIANT not recorded in the major unabridged dictionaries, but it occurs occasionally in American legal writing. "Among these problems are those arising from the possibility of multiple subrogation claims [and from] determining what types or lines of insurance are *indemnitory* [read *indemnificatory*]." *Shelby Mut. Ins. Co. v. Birch,* 196 So. 2d 482, 485 (Fla. Dist. Ct. App. 1967) (Andrews, J., dissenting)./ "[N]o decision is necessary at this time on whether the *indemnitory* [read *indemnificatory*] theory should be limited only to owners of premises." *Waller v. J.E. Brenneman Co.,* 307 A.2d 550, 553 (Del. Super. Ct. 1973).

indemnifier. See **indemnitor.**

indemnify. A. And *hold harmless.* *Indemnify* = (1) to make good a loss that someone has suffered because of another's act or default; (2) to promise to make good such a loss; or (3) to give security against such a loss.

Etymologically, the word derives from *indemnis* (= harmless) combined with *facere* (= to make). Thus, *indemnify* has long been held to be perfectly synonymous with *hold harmless* and *save harmless.* See *Brentnal v. Holmes,* 1 Root (Conn.) 291, 1 Am. Dec. 44 (1791).

That being so, the common DOUBLET *indemnify and hold harmless* (sometimes written *indemnify and save harmless*) is stylistically and substantively indefensible. But it is so common today that lawyers routinely use it without asking themselves what distinction, if any, exists between the two parts of the doublet. See DOUBLETS, TRIPLETS, AND SYNONYM-STRINGS.

B. Intransitive and Transitive Uses. *Indemnify* takes the preposition *from, against,* or *for.* E.g., "Based on this finding, the district court ordered Lee-Vac to pay Cities Service's damages and to *indemnify* American Hoist *for* the expenses of its successful defense."

Usually one *indemnifies from* or *against* losses; the *OED* records the transitive sense "to compensate, make up for" <indemnify this defect>, and calls this sense "Obs. rare," but it has been revived: "The agreement did not require Atlas to *indemnify* losses caused by its own negligence." This sense arose apparently through HYPALLAGE, by transference of object from the person compensated to the thing for which that person is compensated.

indemnitable. See **indemnifiable.**

indemnitee and *indemnitor* (q.v.) are MORPHOLOGICAL DEFORMITIES, since personal suffixes such as *-or* and *-ee* should be applied to verbs, and not to nouns. Yet the words are established beyond question in AmE, where they originated in the 19th century. E.g., "An *indemnitee* owes no obligation whatever to the creditor apart from his promise . . . ." Laurence P. Simpson, *Handbook on the Law of Suretyship* 130 (1950)./ "In a contract of indemnity the *indemnitor* agrees to make the *indemnitee* whole for losses incurred when the *indemnitee* is sued." *Sekeres v. Arbaugh,* 508 N.E.2d 941, 946 (Ohio 1987). See -EE.

indemnitor; indemnifier; indemnor. The first two words are absolutely synonymous, the former being the usual form in American legal writing. E.g., "[T]hat court granted a summary judgment in favor of the *indemnitor* . . . ." *Patch v. Amoco Oil Co.,* 845 F.2d 571, 573 (5th Cir. 1988). *Indemnifier* would probably be slightly more comprehensible to educated nonlawyers. *Indemnor,* which appears in some 19th-century lawbooks, is a NEEDLESS VARIANT.

indemnitory. See **indemnificatory.**

indemnity; indemnification. There is a distinction. *Indemnity* = (1) security or protection against contingent hurt, damage, or loss; or (2) a legal exemption from the penalties or liabilities incurred by any course of action (*OED*). *Indemnification* = the action of compensating for actual loss or damage sustained; the payment made with this object (*OED*). In the following example, *indemnity* appears where *indemnification* was the intended word: "If an injury is caused by defendant's tort, a sum of money may be awarded as compensation or *indemnity* [read *indemnification*] for the loss."

For the distinction between *indemnity* and *contribution,* see **contribution.**

indemnor. See **indemnitor.**

indenture (= [1] a deed made by more than one party; or [2] a contract) is so called because, formerly, each party's copy was cut or indented like the teeth of a saw, so that they all corresponded; the zig-zagging edges reduced the possibility of forgeries. Today, *indenture* almost always bears sense (2), as in the phrases *trust indenture* and *corporate indenture.* And indentures rarely, if ever, have serrated edges.

But, as late as the mid-19th century, it was said that "[c]areful conveyancers . . . even in the United States, continue to notch or scallop the edge of the paper at the top of deeds, which, however unimportant in its legal significance, is not without significance, as an expression of the real character of the instrument." 2 Alexander M. Burrill, *A Law Dictionary and Glossary* 69 (N.Y., John S. Voorhies 1860).

independent contractor; employee. Unlike an *employee,* an *independent contractor* is left free to do the assigned work and to choose the method for accomplishing it. And unlike an *employee,* an *independent contractor* does not, upon committing a wrong while carrying out the work, create liability for an employer who did not authorize the wrongful acts. For example, a taxi driver is an independent contractor, while a private chauffeur is an employee. See **employee.**

independent(ly). A. Preposition with. *Independent* should take the preposition *of,* not *from.*

B. Adverb or Adjective. The proper adverbial phrase is *independently of.* E.g., "The respondent may be liable, *independently of* his tort against the owner."/ "The former class of rights exists *independently of* contract; the latter frequently arises out of contract." The phrase *independent of* is sometimes wrongly made to act as an adverbial phrase. E.g., "When a new remedy is given by statute for a right of action existing *independent of* [read *independently of*] it, without excluding other remedies already known to the law, the statutory remedy is a cumulative remedy."/ "That it differs from what is called by the same name in the common law is clear; for it exists *independent of* [read *independently of*] possession."

INDETERMINATE SUBJECTS. See EXPLETIVES.

indexes; indices. For ordinary purposes, *indexes* is the preferable plural. E.g., "With all our carefully compiled statute books and elaborate *indexes,* modern legislators often fail to foresee points of rub between their innovations and the body of law against which they are projected."

Lon L. Fuller, *Anatomy of the Law* 84 (1968)./ "Case-name and subject *indexes* are maintained on a cumulative basis." Michael Zander, *The Law-Making Process* 211 (2d ed. 1985).

Indices, though less pretentious than *fora* or *dogmata,* is pretentious nevertheless. Some writers prefer it in technical contexts, as in mathematics and the sciences. Though not the best plural for *index, indices* is permissible in the sense "indicators"—e.g.: "The existence of one or more of these *indices* does not necessarily preclude a summary determination that certain products or services either are reasonably interchangeable or demonstrate a high cross-elasticity of demand." Cf. **appendixes.** See PLURALS (A).

Writers who use the highfalutin form, of course, should spell it correctly. Some misspell it with a mediate *-e-* on the influence of *index.* See, e.g., 10 Cardozo L. Rev., Table of Contents ([Aug.] 1989) (*"indeces"*).

indicable. See -ATABLE.

indicant. See **indicative.**

indicate should not appear where *say, state,* or *show* will suffice.

indicative; indicatory; indicant; indicial. *Indicative* is the usual adjective corresponding to the noun *indication* and meaning "that indicates." *Indicant* and *indicatory* are NEEDLESS VARIANTS except in archaic medical contexts. *Indicial*—the adjective corresponding to both *indicia,* q.v., and *index*—means (1) "of the nature of an indicia, indicative"; or (2) "of the nature or form of an index."

indices. See **indexes.**

indicia, the plural of *indicium* (= an indication, sign, token), is treated as a singular noun forming the plurals *indicia* and *indicias,* the former being preferred: "In *Evans v. Newton,* we held that the park had acquired such unalterable *indicia* of a public facility that for the purposes of the equal protection clause it remained public even after the city officials were replaced as trustees by a board of private citizens."

The singular *indicium* is still sometimes used: "The most reliable *indicium* of common interests among employees is similarity of their work, skills, qualifications, duties and working conditions." *N.L.R.B. v. DMR Corp.,* 795 F.2d 472, 475 (5th Cir. 1986)./ "The challenged information is 'false' or 'unreliable' if it lacks some minimal *indicium* of reliability beyond mere allegation."/ "The word 'trademark' B used here in its broadest sense to include any *indicium* that indicates origin." (Compare *data* and *datum:* see **data.**) In the civil law, *indicium* is a species of proof similar to common-law circumstantial evidence.

indicial. See **indicative.**

indicium. See **indicia.**

indict; indite. Both words are pronounced /in-***dɪt***/. The former means "to charge formally with a crime"; the latter, "to write, compose, dictate." A literary term, *indite* is rarely used today.

indictable offence. See **summary offence.**

indictable offense. See HYPALLAGE.

indictee (= a person charged with a crime) is not a newfangled passive noun in *-ee;* it has been used in English since the 16th century. See -EE.

indicter. See **indictor.**

indictment; information; presentment. In the federal courts of the U.S., a distinction exists between these charging instruments. Any offense punishable by death, or for imprisonment for more than one year or by hard labor, must be prosecuted by *indictment;* any other offense may be prosecuted by either an *indictment* or an *information.* Fed. R. Crim. P. 7(a). An *information* may be filed without leave of court by a prosecutor, who need not obtain the approval of a grand jury. An *indictment,* by contrast, is issuable only by a grand jury. E.g., "In some states, while the grand jury still functions, it has lost a great deal of its importance, since the district attorney can begin the case with a simple *'information,'* which does as well as the *indictment.*" Max Radin, *The Law and You* 110 (1948).

Presentments are not used in American federal procedure; formerly, a *presentment* was "the notice taken, or statement made, by a grand jury of any offense or unlawful state of affairs from their own knowledge or observation, without any bill of indictment laid before them" (*W2*).

Through a historical transference of meaning, *indictment,* which originally referred to the accusation of the grand jury, came to signify in the 16th century the document containing the accusation. (See HYPALLAGE.) In both AmE and BrE, *indictment* may refer to the proceeding or to the charging instrument known more particularly as a *bill of indictment.* See **arraignment.**

To a nonlawyer it may seem strange to see *information* (the charging instrument) used as a count noun: "Appellant was prosecuted under two *informations,* in two courts, which charged that he personally sold a sixteen-year-old boy two 'girlie' magazines on each of two dates in October 1965."

indictor; indicter. The *-or* spelling is preferred.

indifference; indifferency. The latter is archaic.

indigency; indigence. *Indigency,* once the less common form, is now four times as common as *indigence* in AmE. *Indigence* ought therefore to be regarded as a NEEDLESS VARIANT.

indirect evidence. See **circumstantial evidence** & **direct evidence.**

indiscernible; indiscernable. The former spelling is preferred. See -ABLE (A).

indiscrete; indiscreet. See **discrete.**

indispensable; necessary; proper. Justice Harlan wrote, in *Provident Tradesmens Bank & Trust Co. v. Patterson,* 390 U.S. 102, 118 (1968): "To use the familiar but confusing terminology, the decision to proceed is a decision that the absent person is merely *necessary,* while the decision to dismiss is a decision that he is *indispensable.*" With regard to possible parties to a lawsuit, *necessary* refers to those who should be included but need not be, *indispensable* to those without whom the action must be dismissed. In other words, in American legal English *indispensable* means "more necessary than *necessary.*" The label *proper* "is used if the party is one who can be joined or not at plaintiff's option." Charles A. Wright, *The Law of Federal Courts* 457 (4th ed. 1983).

The words *indispensable* and *necessary* are opposed in other legal contexts—e.g.: "This does not mean that the transcript must have been *'indispensable'* to the litigation to satisfy this test; it simply must have been *'necessary'* to counsel's effective performance or the court's handling of the case." 10 Charles A. Wright et al., *Federal Practice and Procedure* § 2677, at 350–51 (1983).

The two words should not be redundantly coupled when no nuance is intended: "The rule has no doubt been considerably relaxed since *Peirce* [*sic*] *v. Corf* was decided in 1874, but I think it is still *indispensably necessary* [read either *indispensable* or *necessary*] that there should be a document signed by the party to be charged." (Eng.) Similarly, the REDUNDANCY *indispensable necessity* occurs at least twice in *The Federalist.*

indisputable should receive its primary accent on the second, not the third, syllable /*in-**dis**-pyoot-ə-bəl*/. A common and acceptable pronunciation on both sides of the Atlantic is /*in-di-**spyoo**-tə-bəl*/.

indisputedly, misused for *indisputably* or *undisputedly,* is an odd error—e.g.: "Civil commitment *indisputedly* [read *indisputably*] entails a substantial curtailment of liberty." *Project Release v. Prevost,* 551 F. Supp. 1298, 1308 (E.D.N.Y. 1982)./ "She is the mother of three sons, which *indisputedly* [read *indisputably*] makes her the only justice to have experienced pregnancy." *All Eyes on Justice O'Connor,* Newsweek, 1 May 1989, at 34.

indite. See **indict.**

individual was formerly thought to be a newfangled barbarism as a noun substituting for *man, woman,* or *person.* Certainly, those more specific terms are generally to be preferred over *individual,* but this word should no longer be stigmatized. Still, *individual* is best confined to contexts in which the writer intends to distinguish the single (noncorporate) person from the group or crowd.

individualize; individuate. Both are commonly used, and they have basically the same sense ("to make individual in character, to give individuality to"); both are also so common that it would be inappropriate to call either a NEEDLESS VARIANT, and subtle writers may in fact intend nuances. *Individualize* is much more common in legal writing. E.g., "This approach injects hypothetical extraneous considerations into the sentencing process and contradicts the judicially approved policy of *individualizing* sentences that are tailored to fit the offender." Indeed, in AmE, *individualize* has become a VOGUE WORD meaning "to humanize; to portray as an individual human being." Hence: "Even if the jury had been presented *individualized* evidence that he was a human being and that he had no extended record of violent crime, we cannot say that counsel was ineffective unless it is shown affirmatively that the death penalty would not have been imposed had the sentencing jury been afforded this testimony."

Individuate is often used in scientific contexts and in Jungian psychology in highly technical senses, and ought generally to be confined to these uses.

individual proprietor. See **sole proprietor.**

indorse. See **endorse.**

indorsee. See -EE.

indorser. So spelled, even though its correlative is -EE. See -ER (A).

indubitably See **clearly & obviously.**

inducement; inductance; induction. *Inducement* ordinarily means "that which influences or persuades." E.g., "The interests of representative and represented must, however, be so identical that the motive and *inducement* to protect and preserve may be assumed in each." In pleading, it has an additional sense in BrE: "Matters of *inducement* are introductory averments stating who the parties are, how connected and other surrounding circumstances leading up to the matter in dispute, but not stating such matter" (quoted in *OED*). Thus: "The first count of the declaration, after the usual *inducement* of the plaintiff's good conduct, stated that, before the [defendant's] speaking and publishing [various] defamatory words . . . the plaintiff was . . . [a] clerk . . . ." *Lumby v. Allday,* (1831) 1 Cr. & J. 301, 148 Eng. Rep. 1434 (Ex.).

Induction, in the context of reasoning, means "the establishment of a general proposition from a number of particular instances." *Inductance* is a technical electrical term.

inductee. See -EE.

induction. See **inducement.**

indue; endue. The preferred spelling is *endue* (= to put on or clothe) <endued with the mantle of apparent authority>.

ineffective; ineffectual; inefficacious; inefficient. See **effectual.**

INELEGANT VARIATION. "A draftsman should never be afraid of repeating a word as often as may be necessary in order to avoid ambiguity." Alison Russell, *Legislative Drafting and Forms* 103 (1938). Fowler referred to as "elegant variation" the ludicrous practice of never using the same word twice in the same sentence. When Fowler named this vice of language in the 1920s, *elegant* was almost a pejorative word, commonly associated with precious overrefinement. Today, however, the word has positive connotations. E.g., "The book is exceedingly well edited, and several essays are *elegantly* written."

Lest the reader misapprehend that the subject of this article is a virtue rather than a vice in writing, I have renamed it unambiguously: *in*elegant variation. The rule of thumb with regard to undue repetition is that one should not repeat a word in the same sentence if it can be felicitously avoided; this is hardly an absolute proscription, however.

The problem is that if one uses terms that vary slightly in form, the reader is likely to deduce that some differentiation is intended. Thus one does not write *punitive damages, punitory damages,* and *punishment damages* all in the same opinion or brief, lest the reader infer that one intends to convey a distinction. Yet one judge did just that in a single dissent. See *Jones v. Fisher,* 166 N.W.2d 175 (Wis. 1969) (Hansen, J., dissenting) (using *punitive damages* and *punitory damages*). Other judges have used both forms in a single sentence: "There is an argument for regarding the *punitory* theory of *punitive* damages as anachronistic." See **punitive.**

One frequently encounters writing on criminal law in which *informer* and *informant* (q.v.) are used alternatively, but with no purpose. "Can the *informant's* general reliability be established by an officer's interview with the *informer?*" The second use could have been easily avoided by using *him* or *her.* The following example of inelegant variation occurred within the space of two paragraphs: "A counter-letter such as we have now before us does not affect *marketability.* . . . The lots were not rendered *unmerchantable.*" See **marketable.**

The basic type of variation found objectionable by Fowler is the simple change from the straightforward term to some slightly more fanciful synonym, as here:

- "Several Southwestern states have established elaborate procedures for allocation of *water* and adjudication of conflicting claims to *that resource* [read *water*]."
- "Such a judgment of probate cannot be collaterally *attacked and can be assailed only in the manner provided by statute* [read *attacked; it can be attacked only in the statutory manner*]."
- "The court held merely that a *protestant* who could have sought, but did not seek, review may not now do so by unilaterally petitioning for a repeal or an amendment; to permit any *complainant* [read here *protestant;* or read *complainant* in each slot] to restart the limitations period . . . ."
- "*Lawyers* generally have a bad reputation; today the American public holds a grudge against the half-million *counselors* [read *lawyers*] who handle its legal affairs."
- "State law makes no provisions for mandatory *autopsies,* which means that justices of the peace follow different policies for seeking *postmortems* [read *autopsies* or *them*]."
- "One who executes a *will* believes that *the testament* [read *it*] covers all contingencies."

Equally common in modern legal writing is the switch from one form of a word to another. For example, Justice White alternated *contributory neglect* with *contributory negligence* throughout his opinion in *Mosheuvel v. District of Columbia,* 191 U.S. 247, 252 (1903). Similar examples of the distemper are legion:

- "Some courts have held that the gift passes by intestacy on the theory that there can be no *residue* of a *residuum* [read *residue*]."
- "The *in rem theory* would permit enforcement of the injunction by the contempt power even against persons who had no notice of the decree, since the *res theory* [read *in rem theory*] is that the whole world is bound by the court's control of the property."
- "And unlike Blackstone's blurred account, Coke made clear that his *fictional death* would not create new property rights or destroy old ones. . . . Without resort to *fictitious death* [read *fictional death*] the law stripped the felon of his property as a part of his punishment."
- "[H]is counsel, with *commendable* candor, includes in his brief a statement to the effect he concedes that if this court is satisfied [that] the judgment of the trial court is supported by evidence[,] such judgment will not be disturbed on appeal . . . . [E]ven in the absence of this *commendatory* [read *commendable*] concession . . . ." *Redman v. Mutual Benefit Health & Accident Ass'n,* 327 P.2d 854, 860 (Kan. 1958).

Certain pairs may lend themselves to this snare: *arbiter* and *arbitrator, adjudicative* and *adjudicatory, investigative* and *investigatory, exigency* and *exigence.* In fact, it sometimes seems that amateurish writers believe that NEEDLESS VARIANTS were made for this specific stylistic purpose.

Particularly confusing are pointless switches from a phrase such as *admiralty law* to *maritime law*—e.g.: "Finally, the court held that traditional concepts of the role of *admiralty law* did not require the finding of a substantial maritime relationship because allowing the parties to pursue state law remedies would not disturb the federal interest of maintaining the uniformity of *maritime law.*" Jeanmarie B. Tade, *The Texas and Louisiana Anti-Indemnity Statutes as Applied to Oil and Gas Industry Offshore Contracts,* 24 Hous. L. Rev. 665, 692 (1987).

"The point to be observed," wrote Fowler, "is that, even if the words meant exactly the same, it would be better to keep the first selected on duty than to change guard" (*MEU2* 150).

inept. See **inapt.**

inequity; iniquity. The first means "unfairness"; the second, "evil."

in error. See **error** (B).

in esse; in posse. *In esse* = in actual existence; in being. *In posse* = potential; not realized. E.g., "There is no legal objection to constituting such a trustee in favor of one who was not *in esse* when the fraud was perpetrated."/ "A court would not intervene to deprive the children—*in esse* or *in posse*—of their property rights under such a provision." There is no good reason why the phrases *in being* and *potential* should not be substituted in place of these LATINISMS. See **in being, esse** & ***de bene esse.***

inexpense is not, by the normal measures, a legitimate English word; it is listed in no major unabridged dictionary and does not fill a need in the language. E.g., "[E]ven an absentee landlord could *with relative inexpense* [read *rather inexpensively*] employ someone regularly present to remove these hazards." *Liability for Failure to Remove or Render Safe Ice and Snow on Common Passageways and Approaches,* 41 Colum. L. Rev. 349, 352 (1941)./ "We have yet to figure out how the relative *inexpense* [read *inexpensiveness*] of attending this university relates in any way to the fact that the administration is illegitimately spending interest generated from student money." See NEOLOGISMS & BACK-FORMATIONS.

inexpert, adj.; **nonexpert,** adj. An important distinction exists. *Inexpert* = unskilled <the novice's inexpert cross-examination>. *Nonexpert* = not of or by an expert, but not necessarily unskilled <a rule permitting proof by nonexpert testimony>.

inexplicable (= unexplainable) is accented on the second syllable /*in-**ek**-spli-kə-bəl*/ or the third /*in-ek-**splik**-ə-bəl*/.

inexpressible; inexpressable. The former spelling is correct. See -ABLE (A).

in extenso (= unabridged) is a pompous LEGALISM for the simple English phrase *in full.* E.g., "Convinced beyond peradventure that *Oliver* has no impact on those parts of our opinion, we reinstate those paragraphs as if set forth here *in extenso* [read *in full*] and verbatim."/ "I asked for a full transcript of the judgment in that case and I shall read *in extenso* [read *in full*] the passage of general importance in case the instant case is reported." (Eng.) See LATINISMS.

in extremis (= at the point of death; at the last gasp) is better known than most LATINISMS and may be used purposefully as a EUPHEMISM. E.g., "The test for imminence of death, which is required for an effective gift causa mortis, is equally indefinite: the donor must anticipate more than the general mortality of man, yet he need not be *in extremis.*"

infamous crime. Originally, an *infamous crime* was one for which part of the penalty was infamy, i.e., being declared ineligible to serve on a jury, hold public office, or testify. These consequences were abolished in the 19th century. In England, the Larceny Act 1861 (repealed) defined *infamous crime* as "the abominable crime of buggery, committed with mankind or with beast . . . ." That statutory meaning is long since defunct. More commonly, legal writers equate the phrase with felony.

But it is simplistic to say, as writers occasionally do, that "an 'infamous crime' is a felony . . . ." C. Gordon Post, *An Introduction to the Law* 108 (1963). In fact, *infamous crime* is something of a chameleon-hued phrase that takes its meaning from the context. The California Supreme Court has held that, although for some purposes any felony is an infamous crime, in the context of disfranchisement the phrase is limited to crimes involving moral corruption and dishonesty. See *Otsuka v. Hite,* 414 P.2d 412 (Cal. 1966) (en banc).

For purposes of the Fifth Amendment to the U.S. Constitution, which requires an indictment or presentment for "a capital or otherwise infamous crime," the canon of construction termed *ejusdem generis* (q.v.) suggests that we should look to the potential penalty to decide whether a crime is infamous. "The potential penalty is bound to control," says one authority, "because the determination must be made in the early stages of the prosecution." Rollin M. Perkins, *Criminal Law* 19 (1957). If we translate *capital or otherwise infamous* to "involving capital punishment or similarly grave penalties," it remains problematical to determine what penalty is grave enough to be considered similar to capital punishment.

In sum, *infamous crime* is a vague term in modern usage. See CHAMELEON-HUED WORDS.

infancy = the state or condition of being a minor. E.g., "At birth a child enters the condition of infancy—a condition [that] ceases at the age of eighteen years, or, rather, at the first moment of the day preceding the eighteenth birthday." William Geldart, *Introduction to English Law* 41 (D.C.M. Yardley ed., 9th ed. 1984). Cf. **nonage.** See **minority (A).**

infant (= a minor) is peculiar to legal language; in nonlegal contexts, *infant* means "a small child, a baby." But in law it is quite possible to write of, say, a *17-year-old infant.* E.g., "An exception was made for the time of filing for *infants,* incompetents, and nonresidents." The more usual—and less confusing—term is *minor.* Cf. **infanticide.** See **minority (A) & age of capacity.**

infanticide = (1) the killing of a baby by a parent or with a parent's consent; or (2) a parent who kills a baby, or one who kills a baby with a parent's consent. Sense (2) invariably takes an article <a merciless infanticide>, whereas sense (1) only sometimes takes an article <the infanticide committed by a deranged father> <infanticide committed by a mother with postpartum depression>.

According to the definitions just given, not every killer of a baby has committed infanticide. The killing of another person's child is simple murder or manslaughter. Infanticide, by definition, must be by or on behalf of a parent. See Glanville Williams, *The Sanctity of Life and the Criminal Law* 13 (1957).

Despite the legal meaning of *infant* (q.v.), the word *infanticide* is restricted to baby-killing. A parent who kills a 17-year-old child would not be called an "infanticide" (sense 2). (In England, the Infanticide Act applies to the killing of a child up to one year old.) The slightly broader term *child-slaying,* however, might cover situations in which children who are old enough to walk—and up to the age of 18—are killed. By contrast, the most restrictive term is *neonaticide,* which refers to the killing of a newborn. Among the three terms—*infanticide, child-slaying,* and *neonaticide*—the first two are the most emotive terms because they are widely known, and the third is a clinical, abstract description that many would read or hear without understanding.

in fault. See **at fault.**

infeasible; unfeasible. The former is better.

infect = (1) to taint with crime; or (2) to involve (a ship or cargo) in the seizure to which contraband is liable. This verb is among the more vivid METAPHORS in traditional legal terminology.

infectious is sometimes erroneously rendered *infectuous.* See **contagious.**

infeft is a Scottish variant of *enfeoffed.* See **feoff.**

in feodo simpliciter. See **fee simple (A).**

infeoff. See **feoff.**

infer is generally correctly used in legal writing. Properly, it means "to deduce; to reason from premises to a conclusion." E.g., "The court *inferred* that Congress must have intended to extend the suspension power to embrace initial as well as changed rates, and it relied on this *inference* to buttress its reading of the statute's literal language."

A common mistake among nonlawyers is to use *infer* when *imply* (= to hint at; suggest) is the correct word. Yet this nonlawyer's blunder has occasionally insinuated itself into legal writing. E.g., "Exclusion from venires focuses on the inherent attributes of the excluded group and *infers* [read *implies*] its inferiority. . . ." *U.S. v. Leslie,* 759 F.2d 381, 392 (5th Cir. 1985). See **imply (B).**

In Scots law, *infer* is used in a special sense: "to involve as a consequence"—e.g.: "In lay usage only a person infers, but in legal usage such and such a course of conduct, for example, infers a penalty." Andrew D. Gibb, *Students' Glossary of Scottish Legal Terms* 45 (A.G.M. Duncan ed., 2d ed. 1982).

inferable. See **infer(r)able.**

inference. One *draws,* not *makes,* inferences. If one says "to make an inference" (like "to make a deduction"), then many listeners will confuse *inference* with *implication.* The verb *to draw* is therefore clearer. See **infer.**

inferentially for *we can infer that.* The *OED* states that *inferentially* = in an inferential manner, but allows that it is used "sometimes qualifying the whole clause or statement: = as an inference, as may be inferred." This use defies explication but is common in legal writing—e.g.: "Judge Lumbard pointed out that even though defendant destroyed its records, the evidence *inferentially* established profits of over $1000."/ "*Inferentially,* at least, the accused is entitled to counsel and to compulsory process for bringing in his witnesses."/ "The second paragraph of the statute, by providing that an adopted child may not take by representation property coming from collateral kindred of the adopting parent, *inferentially* contemplates the child may so take from lineal kin." See SENTENCE ADVERBS. Cf. **hopefully & thankfully.**

inferior; superior. A. Generally. These comparative adjectives cannot act as adverbs. E.g., "The statute is unconstitutional not only because it *treats* former mental patients differently from *and inferior to* [read *and as inferior to*] convicts, but also because it presumptively denies former mental patients the opportunity to establish that they no longer present the danger against which the statute was intended to guard."

Only etymologically are these words comparatives; they take *to,* not *than.* They are qualified by *much* or *far,* not by *more,* which is a fairly common error.

B. In Classifying Courts. Traditionally, the hierarchical system of courts within a given jurisdiction is broken down into *inferior courts* and *superior courts.* Many American judges feel uncomfortable with these terms, preferring to speak of *trial courts* and *appellate courts. Inferior* suggests, to many readers and listeners, a lower level of competence.

British legal writers, however, use the classification regularly, not least because many courts have both trial and appellate jurisdiction. In England and Wales, the superior courts include the House of Lords, the Court of Appeal, and the High Court; inferior courts include circuit courts and magistrates' courts.

inferior court. See **inferior (B) & higher court.**

infer(r)able; infer(r)ible. The preferred form is *inferable,* accented on the second syllable /*in-**fur**-ə-bəl*/. Fifty years ago *inferrible* was considered the best spelling, because of the rule that a consonant should be doubled after a stressed syllable. *Inferable,* which has now ousted the other spelling, is anomalous. See DOUBLING OF FINAL CONSONANTS.

infeudation (= the granting of an estate in fee; enfeoffment) is rarer than both its equivalent, *enfeoffment,* and its derivative, *subinfeudation.* E.g., "The tenures created during this era of universal *infeudation* were as various as the conditions [that] the tenants made with their new chiefs or were forced to accept from them." Henry S. Maine, *Ancient Law* 192 (17th ed. 1901; repr. [New Universal Lib.] 1905, 1910). See **subinfeudation.**

in fine, a turgid, legalistic phrase for *in conclusion* or *finally.* E.g., "*In fine,* [read *In conclusion,* or *Finally,*] we reject the appellant's claim that the district court's treatment of the summaries unduly prejudiced his trial."/ "*In fine,* [read *In conclusion,* or *Finally,*] the jury would be warranted in finding that the defendant's conduct was a high-handed and unlawful means of collecting a debt."

infinitely (= endlessly, limitlessly) for *eminently* (= to a high degree) is either gross OVERSTATEMENT or a MALAPROPISM—e.g.: "You want to persuade the appellate court that the jury was *infinitely* [read *eminently*] reasonable."

infirm is frequently used in reference to fatal weaknesses, whether constitutional or statutory. In fact, *constitutionally infirm* might accurately be labeled a legal CLICHÉ. E.g., "The state argues further that the statute is not constitutionally *infirm* simply because the legislature could have achieved the same result by other means."/ "Our review of the record indicates no *infirmities* in the jury's findings." See **fatal (A).**

in flagrante delicto (= red-handed; in the act of committing an offense) is a term now more commonly used for polysyllabic humor in nonlegal contexts than as a serious word in law. See LATINISMS.

Some writers mistake the spelling—e.g.: "We do not doubt that NASA blushes whenever one of its own is caught *in flagrante delictu* [read *in flagrante delicto* or *red-handed*] . . . ." *Norton v. Macy,* 417 F.2d 1161, 1167 (D.C. Cir. 1969)./ "Two wrongs, usually of very unequal weight, should never equal a right to escape when caught *in flagrante delictu* [read *in flagrante delicto* or *red-handed*]." *Commonwealth v. Weisenthal,* 535 A.2d 600, 601 (Pa. 1988). See ITALICS (C).

inflammable. See **flammable.**

inflatus. See **afflatus.**

inflict; afflict. These terms are infrequently confused. *Afflict* takes *with; inflict* takes *on.* Living things, esp. humans, are *afflicted with* diseases; inanimate objects, esp. scourges or punishments, are *inflicted on* people. But misusing *inflict* for *afflict* is increasingly common—e.g.: "[A]s the evidence indicates, the severed muscles in the plaintiff's face have *inflicted* [read *afflicted*] him with a tic." *Rogers v. Moody,* 242 A.2d 276, 279 (Pa. 1968)./ "The problems *inflicting* [read *afflicting*] this case and ultimately causing a remand have their genesis in the indictment . . . ." *Honc v. State,* 698 S.W.2d 218, 220 (Tex. App.—Corpus Christi 1985).

inflicter; inflictor. The former spelling is better.

influence. The first syllable, not the second, receives the primary accent /***in***-*floo-əns*/, whether the part of speech is noun or verb.

inforce is an obsolete spelling of *enforce,* except in the prefixed *reinforce.* See EN- & **enforce.**

inform, in the sense "to determine, give form to, permeate" is somewhat archaic, but it is common in scholarly legal writing. E.g., "Whether vocational education produces salutary outcomes is *informed* in part by the nature of the dependent variable under consideration."/ "To the extent that economic analysis *informs* our decision here, we think that it favors retention of the present rule."

informal contract; simple contract; parol contract. These phrases each denote the same idea: a contract that derives its efficacy not from the form of the transaction but from its substance. Williston preferred the term *informal contract* because *simple contract* is misleading. See 1 Samuel Williston & W.H.E. Jaeger, *A Treatise on the Law of Contract* § 12, at 22 (3d ed. 1957). The phrase *parol contract* is even more likely to mislead, because, though it suggests an oral contract, it (surprisingly) can be in writing. See **formal contract.**

informant; informer. Both terms are used in reference to those who confidentially supply police with information about crimes. *Informant* is twice as common in American legal contexts, *informer* slightly more common in British ones. The Evanses write that *informant* is neutral, whereas *informer,* which acquired strong connotations of detestation in the 17th and 18th centuries, remains a connotatively charged term. Bergen Evans & Cornelia Evans, *A Dictionary of Contemporary American Usage* 245 (1957). If that is true in lay contexts, it certainly is not true in legal writing. See INELEGANT VARIATION.

in forma pauperis (= in the form of a poor person; not liable for costs of court) is a TERM OF ART in AmE (but is no longer used in BrE). E.g., "Under well-settled principles, a timely motion to proceed *in forma pauperis* on appeal is the substantial equivalent of a notice of appeal and is effective to invoke appellate jurisdiction." Judges frequently use the abbreviation *IFP* <an IFP motion>.

Where the entire phrase is not used, *pauper* should appear rather than *forma pauperis.* E.g., "This packet includes four copies of a complaint form and two copies of *a forma pauperis* [read *a pauper*] petition."/ "In sum, assuming *forma pauperis status* [read *pauper status*], the prisoner complaints must be filed."/ "We grant the motion for *pauper* status but deny the application for stay of execution." See **pauper.**

Additionally, in the full phrase one should italicize the *in,* not just *forma pauperis:* "Late in the trial, Wellington, proceeding in *forma pauperis,* [read *in forma pauperis*], unsuccessfully submitted an ex parte application." *U.S. v. Nivica,* 887 F.2d 1110, 1117 (1st Cir. 1989). See ITALICS (C).

information. See **indictment.**

information and belief. In traditional pleading, an allegation made only on information—unaccompanied by the pleader's asserting that he or she believes the allegation to be true—is insufficient. It has therefore become standard practice for pleaders to make allegations *on information and belief.*

Among those not used to the practice, it can be confusing. Take a count that reads: "On information and belief, a vice-president of the Bank then recorded the incorrect account number on the deposit slip." Grammatically speaking, *on information and belief* refers to the vice-president's state of mind. Actually, though, the allegation is shorthand for this: *On information and belief, the plaintiff alleges that the vice-president of the Bank then* . . . . The judges and lawyers who read such sentences are never misled because they understand the JARGON, which saves several words. If such a pleading comes before a jury, however, it will likely cause confusion.

informative; informatory. The latter is a NEEDLESS VARIANT, except in bridge, the card game.

informer. See **informant.**

in foro conscientiae (lit., "in the forum of conscience") is used in the sense "privately or morally rather than legally" (*W3*). E.g., "The moral obligation exerts just as much force the day after the limit expired as it did the day before, and, *in foro conscientiae,* the debtor should discharge the debt." See LATINISMS.

infra; supra. These ubiquitous signals could advantageously be banished from all legal writing. One writer calls them "disconsolate inadequacies," explaining: "They border on the discourteous unless the point referred to is but a few lines away, and in that even they are not needed." Raymond S. Wilkins, "The Argument of an Appeal," in *Advocacy and the King's English* 277, 281 (George Rossman ed. 1960). See ***ante.***

infract (= to break in; violate; infringe) is chiefly an Americanism. Even so, it is little used outside legal writing. E.g., "We find that article 6 was *infracted* because no treaty provision justifies the second boarding or the ultimate seizure of the La Rosa." *U.S. v. Postal,* 589 F.2d 862, 872 (5th Cir. 1979)./ "The court's determination that chapter 93A was *infracted* appears sustainable . . . ." *Peckham v. Continental Cas. Ins. Co.,* 895 F.2d 830, 842 (1st Cir. 1990). See **infringe.**

infraction (= violation, infringement) is used in legal and in sports JARGON. E.g., "Appellants urge several other evidentiary *infractions.*"

infrequent; unfrequent. The latter is a NEEDLESS VARIANT.

infringe, v.t. & v.i. Fowler held (just as a highest court *holds*) that *infringe* is best used transitively, as here: "The association *infringed* no legal right of the appellant by its nondisclosure of this fact." The transitive is especially useful where the passive voice is called for: "An association of college faculty members and five individual educators seek vindication of their First Amendment rights, which they contend *were infringed* by the action of a state college in attempting to destroy the association, in discharging one faculty member, and in discriminating against others."

Rather than *infringe upon* or *on,* some other verb such as *impinge, encroach,* or *trespass* is better when an intransitive verb is desired: "The plaintiff was free to make any legal contract with defendant that did not wrongfully *infringe upon* [read *impinge on*] the legal rights of others or offend against public rights." (Eng.)/ "The production of evidence demanded here does not *infringe on* [read *encroach* or *impinge on*] British sovereignty, as it calls merely for documents and not for personal appearance." See **infract** & **impinge.**

infringer. So spelled.

in future. This phrase is BrE, perhaps a direct translation of the Latin phrase *in futuro,* q.v. AmE uses the definite article: *in the future.*

in futuro is a legalistic LATINISM conveying (or failing to convey) an elementary notion for which the English language has adequate words. E.g., "It is an elementary rule that such a gift cannot be made to take effect in possession *in futuro* [read *in the future*]."/ "The point of distinction between a vested gift to be paid *in futuro* [read *in the future*] and a contingent gift to be paid to a person only upon reaching a certain age is made by Chief Justice Booth in *Carey v. Pettyjohn.*" See **in future** & ***in praesenti.***

ingenious; ingenuous. These words, virtual antonyms, are frequently confused. *Ingenious,* means "crafty, skillful, inventive." *Ingenuous* means "artless, innocent, simple."

ingenuity was once the nominal form of *ingenuous,* and *ingeniosity* (last used in 1608) the noun for *ingenious.* Through a curious historical reversal of the role of *ingenuity,* it came to mean "ingeniousness." *Ingenuousness* was the only term left to do the work of the noun corresponding to the adjective *ingenuous.* Thus, although *ingenuity* appears to be the correlative of *ingenuous,* it no longer is.

ingenuous. See **ingenious.**

ingraft. See **engraft.**

ingress. See **egress.**

ingross. See **engross.**

in gross, when used of servitudes, means "personal as distinguished from appurtenant to land." The phrase may be placed either before or after the noun it modifies. E.g., "A *servitude in gross* threatens the servient owner's autonomy, and thus deserves scrutiny."/ "This reasoning does not adequately address whether the burden should run if, as in the case of *in gross* conservation *servitudes,* there is never a benefited parcel." Cf. **run (B).**

inhabitability. See **habitability.**

in haec verba (= in these words) is the worst sort of puffed-up LATINISM for an ordinary idea—*verbatim* invariably being a good substitute. Often the term is used as an unhyphenated PHRASAL ADJECTIVE. E.g., "Nevertheless, the use of *in haec verba* pleadings on defamation charges is favored." *Asay v. Hallmark Cards, Inc.,* 594 F.2d 692, 699 (8th Cir. 1979). The sentence would be far more comprehensible without the LATINISM, and with a few more words: *The use of pleadings that give the defamatory words verbatim is favored.* See **verbatim.** Cf. ***ipsissima verba.***

in hand. See **at hand.**

inhere. A. Preposition with. *Inhere* takes the preposition *in;* it will not tolerate *within.* "Since a number of violations inhered *within* [read *in*] the same transaction, the defendant was not prosecuted more than once for the same statutory offense."

B. For *inure.* This MALAPROPISM is a stunning one—e.g.: "[T]he benefit of the enhancement *inhered* [read *inured*] to all users and all listeners, no matter what apparatus was employed for playback purposes." *U.S. v. Chaudhry,* 850 F.2d 851, 855 (1st Cir. 1988). See **inure.**

inherent takes *in,* not *to.* "We are dealing with a complexity *inherent to* [read *inherent in*] dual organizations."

The use of *inherent* in the following sentence resulted from ignorance of the word's meaning (as if it were equivalent to *prejudicial* or *inflammatory*): "Nothing in the letters is of such an *inherent* [read *prejudicial* or *inflammatory*] nature as to inflame the passions of the jury or invoke its sympathies." *Jackson v. Johns-Manville Sales Corp.,* 750 F.2d 1314, 1319 (5th Cir. 1985). See **inhere.**

inheritability; inheritableness. The former being standard, the latter is a NEEDLESS VARIANT: "The *inheritableness* [read *inheritability*] of a knight's fee was accompanied by the rule of primogeniture . . . ." Alan Harding, *A Social History of English Law* 34 (1966).

inheritable; heritable; hereditary. As between the first two, the first is the more common; it means "capable of being inherited": "[L]ands held in feudal knight service immediately after the Conquest were not freely *inheritable.*" Thomas F. Bergin & Paul G. Haskell, *Preface to Estates in Land and Future Interests* 7 (2d ed. 1984)./ "In the twelfth century the term *fee* came to be used to designate an *inheritable* interest in land rather than a mere life interest." Roger A. Cunningham et al., *The Law of Property* 15 n.6 (2d ed. 1993).

Heritable is infrequent enough today to be classed a NEEDLESS VARIANT for most purposes, although it persists in Scotland and in civil-law jurisdictions.

The negative form of the adjective has been rendered both *uninheritable* (*OED*) and *nonheritable* (*W3*). The latter is more common in AmE—e.g.: "[I]t would create an estate in fee simple which . . . would be *nonheritable.*" William F. Fratcher, *Bequests of Orts,* 48 Mo. L. Rev. 476, 478 (1983).

Hereditary has a more restricted sense: "descending by inheritance from generation to generation" (*OED*): "In the American States it is a fundamental principle that no man can be a magistrate, a legislator, or a judge by *hereditary* right." (Eng.) See **hereditable & heredity.**

inheritableness. See **inheritability.**

inheritance. See **descent (B).**

inheritor; heritor. See **heir (A).**

inheritrix; inheritress. See SEXISM (C).

inhibitory; inhibitive. The latter is a NEEDLESS VARIANT.

in his own right; in her own right. See **right, in one's own.**

in-house counsel. See **house counsel.**

inimical (= hostile, injurious, adverse), a common word in legal writing, is almost a CLICHÉ in place of *adverse,* esp. in collocation with the word *interests.* "A settlor cannot force the courts to sanction his scheme of disposition if it is *inimical* to the interests of the state."

Inimicable for *inimical* is a fairly common error. The *OED* records *inimicable* as a "rare" adjective: it is not rare enough in AmE. E.g., "For anything believed to be *inimicable* [read *inimical*] to his best interests can be thwarted or prevented by simply revoking the trust or amending it in such a way as to conform to his wishes." *Farkas v. Williams,* 125 N.E.2d 600, 607 (Ill. 1955)./ "They argue that Tullos was on board the rig for purposes *inimicable* [read *inimical*] to the legitimate interests of the rig owner."

in initio. See ***ab initio.***

in invitum is unnecessary JARGON meaning "against an unwilling person." E.g., "[A constructive trust is] entirely *in invitum* [read *nonconsensual*] and forced upon the conscience of the trustee for the purpose of working out right and justice or frustrating fraud." *Motley's Admin'rs v. Tabor,* 271 S.W. 1064, 1065 (Ky. 1925)./ "Finally, in *West,* a nonparty was allowed to appeal after having been compelled to participate in the district court proceedings *'in invitum'* [read *unwillingly*]." *In re Grand Jury Proceedings,* 643 F.2d 641, 643 n.2 (9th Cir. 1981). See LATINISMS.

iniquity. See **inequity**.

in issue. See **issue (A).**

INITIALESE. Justice Rehnquist (as he then was) once wrote, after stating the facts of a case in which seven different groups of initials were used for identification: "The terminology required to describe the present controversy suggests that the 'alphabet soup' of the New Deal era was, by comparison, a clear broth." *Chrysler Corp. v. Brown,* 441 U.S. 281, 287 n.4 (1979). He was alluding, of course, to one of the most irritating types of pedantry that have gained a foothold in legal writing: the overuse of acronyms and abbreviations. Originally, to be sure, abbreviations were intended to serve the convenience of the reader by shortening names; with their use, cumbersome phrases would not have to be repeated in their entirety. The purported simplifications actually simplified. E.g., "For the sake of brevity and to avoid confusion, since all persons involved in this litigation, except Mrs. Robinson, have the same surname, we will refer to Mrs. Annie S. Harlan as Annie; to Mrs. Sue Robinson as Sue; to Messrs. Jay W. Harlan and George L. Harlan as Jay and George." *Harlan v. Citizens Nat'l Bank,* 251 S.W.2d 284, 284 (Ky. 1952).

Now, however, many writers seem to have lost sight of this goal: they allow abbreviated names to proliferate in their writing, which quickly becomes a system of hieroglyphs requiring the reader constantly to refer to the original use of the term so that he will understand the significance of the hieroglyphs. It may be thought that this kind of writing is more scholarly than ordinary, straightforward prose. It is not. Rather, it is tiresome and inconsiderate writing; it betrays the writer's thoughtlessness toward the reader and a fascination with the insubstantial trappings of scholarship.

A typical, and by no means exaggerated, example of this vice recently appeared in *Ryder Energy Distrib. Corp. v. Merrill Lynch Commodities, Inc.,* 748 F.2d 774 (2d Cir. 1984). In this opinion seven hieroglyphs appear, often clumped together. We learn throughout the first few pages of the opinion that REDCO = Ryder Energy Distribution Corporation (why not call it Ryder?); NYME = New York Mercantile Exchange; FCM = futures commission merchant; CFTC = Commodity Futures Trading Commission; EFP = exchange of futures for physical; and TOI = Two Oil, Inc. Braced with this knowledge, if we can hold it, we encounter the following:

> [U]nlike Hutton's, Merrill's duty sprang from two sources. Like Hutton, Merrill had the duty of an FCM representing the buyer—REDCO. In addition, however, Merrill had the duty of an FCM representing the seller—TOI. It was in its capacity as TOI's FCM that Merrill was required, under Form EFP-1, to certify that TOI owned and had possession of enough oil to cover its EFP obligations.

And this:

> The following facts cannot be found in the complaint: REDCO's previous dealings with TOI, REDCO's reasons for conducting an EFP, Merrill's inability to find REDCO an EFP partner, REDCO's introduction of TOI to Merrill, Hutton and NYME's lack of knowledge of TOI's default until June 11, and NYME's instigation of a rules compliance investigation after June 11.

And so it goes throughout the opinion, which would have reached the summit of initialese if only Merrill Lynch Commodities, Inc. had been termed MLCI, and E.F. Hutton & Co. Inc. termed EFHCO.

Almost as bad is *Kierstead v. City of San Antonio,* 643 S.W.2d 118, 120 (Tex. 1982), in which *EMT* = emergency medical technician, *FY* = fiscal year, and *FPERA* = Fire and Police Employee Relations Act: "Both parties presented their interpretations of the application of Art. 1269p, § 6 vis-à-vis the override provision of FPERA, § 20 during the bench trial of the EMTs' claim in November 1979. The trial court awarded the EMTs overtime on the early contracts but denied awards for the FY 1978 and FY 1979 agreements that had specifically mentioned a 56-hour work week obligation for the EMTs." Why not *technician,* a statement that all references to years mean fiscal years, and *the Act?*

The simple solution, of course, is to adopt simplified names for parties and frequently repeated phrases, rather than initials in all capitals that depersonalize and obscure. Instead of referring to "TDMHMR" (Texas Department of Mental Health and Mental Retardation) again and again, one should refer to "the Department" when only one is involved.

In naming something new, one's task is sometimes hopeless: the choice is clear between *ALI–ABA CLE Review* and *American Law Institute–American Bar Association Continuing Legal Education Review,* but one cannot choose either enthusiastically. Both entities must have their due (in part so that they can have their dues), and the acronyms gradually become familiar. But they are not ideal because they are sure to turn off readers initially.

The legal writer should never forget that effective communication takes *two*—the writer and the reader. In the words of Quiller-Couch,

> the obligation of courtesy rests first with the author, who invites the seance, and commonly charges for it. What follows, but that in speaking or writing we have an obligation to put ourselves into the hearer's or reader's place? It is *his* comfort, *his* convenience, we have to consult. To *express* ourselves is a very small part of the business: very small and unimportant as compares with *impressing* ourselves: the aim of the whole process being to persuade.
> Arthur Quiller-Couch, *The Art of Writing* 291–92 (1916; repr. ed. 1961).

See ACRONYMS AND INITIALISMS & OBSCURITY (B).

initial(l)ing. *Initialing* is AmE, *initialling* BrE. See DOUBLING OF FINAL CONSONANTS.

initiate is a FORMAL WORD for *begin, open,* or *introduce.*

initiate tenant by curtesy; tenant by the curtesy initiate. These phrases are both used, but are falling into disuse. See **curtesy.**

initio. See ***ab initio.***

injoin is an obsolete spelling of *enjoin,* q.v. See EN-.

injudicious; injudicial. The latter is a NEEDLESS VARIANT. The antonym of *judicial* is *nonjudicial.* See **judicial.**

injunct is at best colloquial, and at worst downright wrong, for *enjoin.* E.g., "'There are no more copies left to be *injuncted,*' said the editor after the ruling." The word generally, and quite appropriately, does not appear in legal prose. See **enjoin.**

injunction. *Temporary injunction* (AmE) = *interlocutory injunction* (BrE). *Permanent injunction* (AmE) = *perpetual injunction* (BrE). See **enjoinder.** For the Scots-law equivalent of *injunction,* see **interdict.**

injunctional. See **injunctive.**

injunction enjoining is a common REDUNDANCY. E.g., "On the basis of these allegations, plaintiff moved for a temporary *injunction enjoining* [better: *injunction prohibiting*] the enforcement of the Michigan order." See **enjoin.**

injunctive; injunctional; injunctory. *Injunctive* is the standard word. E.g., "Monetary awards, like *injunctive* decrees, should be measured by the trade secrets' probable life." *Injunctional,* a NEEDLESS VARIANT not recorded in the major English-language dictionaries, has now been almost wholly displaced by *injunctive*—e.g.: "[T]here is a noticeable absence of judicial attempt so to enumerate the subjects of the remedy or delimit its field as to hamper the power of equity to grant *injunctional* [read *injunctive*] relief . . . ." *Funk Jewelry Co. v. State ex rel. La Prade,* 50 P.2d 945, 947 (Ariz. 1935)./ "[T]he *injunctional* [read *injunctive*] prohibition against picketing was supported by evidence of the unlawful purpose." *International Bhd. of Carpenters & Joiners v. Todd L. Storms Constr. Co.,* 324 P.2d 1002, 1004 (Ariz. 1958).

The other NEEDLESS VARIANT, *injunctory,* is also uncommon—e.g.: "[S]he demands *injunctory* [read *injunctive*] relief." *O'Hair v. Paine,* 432 F.2d 66, 67 n.1 (5th Cir. 1970)./ "[T]he issue presented was whether plaintiff had standing . . . to bring this cause of action seeking *injunctory* [read *injunctive*] relief." *Helbig v. Murray,* 558 S.W.2d 772, 774 (Mo. Ct. App. 1977).

injuria. See **injury.**

injuria absque damno; injuria sine damno. The English equivalent of each phrase is *injury without damage,* which denotes a legal wrong that causes no actual damage. E.g., "It is a well-established principle that an *injury without damage* creates no right to compensation." (Cf. ***damnum absque injuria.***) In this context, *injuria* and *injury* mean "a legal wrong," not "hurt." See LATINISMS.

injury; *injuria.* The latter, a LATINISM, is a NEEDLESS VARIANT in common-law contexts. See **damage.**

Inland Revenue Service. See **Internal Revenue Service.**

in-law, n., is generally hyphenated or spelled as one word.

in law. See **under law.**

in lieu of. A. Generally. The phrase *in lieu of* is now English, and *instead of* will not always suffice in its stead—e.g.: "The defendant was released *in lieu of* $10,000 bond."/ "It has been held that a testamentary gift *in lieu of* dower has priority over all other testamentary gifts."

B. *In lieu* without *of.* Omitting *of* from the phrase is a sure sign that *instead* would be an improvement over *in lieu*—e.g.: "[T]he Court is now empowered to refuse to permit rescission and to award damages *in lieu* [read *instead*]." P.S. Atiyah, *An Introduction to the Law of Contract* 309 (3d ed. 1981)./ "[A]n injunction is sometimes available against a refusal to contract; and it may be that damages can be awarded *in lieu* [read *instead*] even though the refusal gives rise to no cause of action at common law." G.H. Treitel, *The Law of Contract* 925 (8th ed. 1991).

C. For *in view of.* The day after President Clinton announced his health-care plan in the fall of 1993, a radio host, broadcasting from the lawn of the White House, said to his listeners: "This morning we're going to discuss what state health care means *in lieu of* the President's new federal plan." This mistake—which is spreading—results from a confusion of *in view of* and *in light of,* either of which would have sufficed in that sentence. As it is, *in lieu of* is a MALAPROPISM when used for either of the other phrases.

in limine (= at the threshold or outset; preliminarily) is a LATINISM not likely to be displaced in lawyers' JARGON, esp. in the phrase *motion in limine.* But apart from that phrase, *in limine* is easily and advantageously Englished—e.g.: "[W]e are faced *in limine* [read *initially*] with a jurisdictional question." *Haynes v. Felder,* 239 F.2d 868, 869 (5th Cir. 1957)./ "If the courts continue to insist on a fiduciary relationship, a restitutionary proprietary claim against a tortfeasor may be defeated *in limine* [read *at the outset*]." Lord Goff of Chieveley & Gareth Jones, *The Law of Restitution* 622 (3d ed. 1986).

in loco parentis (= in the place of a parent) is perhaps a justified LATINISM. Generally, the term applies to guardians and not to trustees, but much depends upon context: "The trustee is requested to remember that, the child's guardians having gone away, he is expected to act *in loco parentis.*" (Eng.)/ "In a majority of states, if the testator stands *in loco parentis* to the donee, the *inter vivos* gift is presumed to be intended in satisfaction of the testamentary provision." The *in* is a part of the Latin phrase and should be italicized if the rest of the phrase is in italics. See ITALICS (C).

A clever or not-so-clever law student—it is impossible to know which—once asked whether *in loco parentis* is synonymous with *en ventre sa mère.*

in memoriam is sometimes misspelled *in memorium*—e.g.: "A few days before May 13, 1970, in *memorium* [read *memoriam*] to the dead students at Kent State, white and black students at SFA conducted a large so-called 'candlelight march' . . . ." *McGuire v. Roebuck,* 347 F. Supp. 1111, 1115 (E.D. Tex. 1972).

inner bar = silks (taken collectively). See **silk.** Cf. **outer bar.**

innervate. See **enervate.**

innocence; innocency. The latter is an obsolete variant.

innocent. See **plead innocent.**

innocent until proven guilty. This, the usual rendering of the phrase, is perhaps tendentious because it suggests that guilt will ultimately be proved. Some criminal-law specialists therefore resort to the longer *innocent unless and until proven guilty,* which violates the SET PHRASE but is more legally accurate—e.g.: "The principle that a person should be presumed innocent *unless and* *until proven guilty* is a fundamental principle of fairness, although its relation to the law of evidence means that it is not always included in discussions of the criminal law." Andrew Ashworth, *Principles of Criminal Law* 74 (1991).

innoculation. See **inoculation.**

innovative; innovatory; innovational. The second and third are NEEDLESS VARIANTS of the first: "Considerations of this sort did not . . . commend themselves to the judges of 1907 or their immediate successors. It was another unfortunate provision, they doubtless felt, in this *innovatory* [read *innovative*] Act." Patrick Devlin, *The Judge* 113 (1979)./ "Differences in the way firms explore these combinations lead to different *innovational* [read *innovative*] approaches and, ultimately, different degrees of success." Robert P. Merges, *Commercial Success and Patent Standards,* 76 Calif. L. Rev. 803, 853 (1988).

in no wise. See **nowise.**

Inns of Court. This phrase, a proper noun, refers to four autonomous institutions in which English barristers receive their training: the Honourable Societies of Lincoln's Inn, the Middle Temple, the Inner Temple, and Gray's Inn. These powerful bodies examine candidates for the Bar, "call" them to the Bar, and award the degree of barrister. Every bar student must join one of them, and every barrister remains a member for life unless he or she resigns or is disbarred. These bodies have been known as *Inns of Court* since the 1420s, though for centuries the phrase denoted primarily the buildings in which the four legal societies were housed.

innuendo. Early in its life as an English word, *innuendo* was a POPULARIZED LEGAL TECHNICALITY. In medieval Latin, *innuendo* (lit. "by nodding; meaning; to wit; that is to say") was used in legal documents to introduce a parenthetical explanation of precisely what a preceding noun or pronoun referred to. Thus Thomas Blount, in his early law dictionary entitled *Glossographia* (1656), wrote that *innuendo* "is a Law term, most used in Declarations and other pleadings . . . to declare and design the person or thing which was named incertain before; as to say, he (*innuendo* the Plaintiff) is a Theef."

By the 17th century, the word had taken on its current meaning, "an oblique remark or indirect suggestion, usu. of a derogatory nature." Because, by its nature, an *innuendo* must be in words, the phrase *verbal innuendo* is a REDUNDANCY—e.g.: "Yes of course sexual harassment by *verbal innuendo* [read *innuendo*] is vulgar . . . ." Russell Baker, *Potomac Breakdown,* N.Y. Times, 12 Oct. 1991, at 19. See **verbal.**

Pl. *innuendos.*

innumerable. See **enumerable.**

innundate. See **inundate.**

inoculation. So spelled. This word is often misspelled *innoculation* or *inocculation.*

inoperative is a LEGALISM usu. meaning "invalid." E.g., "I do not find that part of the will would be *inoperative* unless applied to the power." In recent years it has become a VOGUE WORD among government bureaucrats.

In the law of contract, legal writers have given it a special and useful nuance. If a condition precedent fails, it is more precise to say that the contract is *inoperative* rather than *void*—i.e., the validity of the contract itself does not depend on the fulfillment of the condition precedent. See P.S. Atiyah, *An Introduction to the Law of Contract* 146–47 (3d ed. 1981).

inopposite is a surprising, and happily infrequent, solecism for *inapposite.*

in order (to) (for) (that). The phrase *in order to* is often wordy for the simple infinitive: "We granted the writ of error *in order to resolve* [read *to resolve*] the conflicting decisions among courts of appeals."/ "*In order to* [read *To*] avoid probate and administration, it is often urged that a joint estate in the account has been created." Thomas E. Atkinson, *Handbook of the Law of Wills* 168 (2d ed. 1953).

In order for, which takes a noun, is often wordy for *for:* "The transformers had been *energized in order for use by Jones* [read *energized for use by Jones*] in the building operations."

Finally, *in order that,* which needs no reduction, begins a noun phrase expressing purpose: "We remand on the sentencing issue *in order that* the district court might conduct an evidentiary hearing on that issue." See LEGALISMS AND LAWYERISMS.

in pais (= outside court or legal proceedings) is legal JARGON deriving from LAW FRENCH, meaning literally "in the country (as opposed to in court)." *Matter in pais,* for example, means "a matter of fact that is not in writing." E.g., "[T]he facts from which equitable estoppels arise are all matters *in pais* as distinguished from records and deeds." 3 John N. Pomeroy & Spencer W. Symons, *Equity Jurisprudence* § 802, at 180 (5th ed. 1941).

Estoppel in pais = an estoppel not arising from a deed or contract, but, for example, from an express statement implied by conduct or negligence. E.g., "These articles embody the principal cases of *estoppels in pais,* as distinguished from estoppels by deed or by record." (Eng.) See **estop & estoppel (B).**

in pari delicto is legal JARGON meaning "in equal fault; equally culpable." E.g., "Plaintiffs who are truly *in pari delicto* are those who have themselves violated the law in cooperation with the defendant."/ "The district court dismissed the complaint, concluding that the investors were *in pari delicto* with the defendants and thus barred from recovery."

Some writers mistakenly write *delictu*—e.g.: "The court rejected the plaintiff's reliance on Buttrey to defeat the defense of *in pari delictu* [read *in pari delicto*] . . . ." *Lank v. New York Stock Exch.,* 405 F. Supp. 1031, 1038 (S.D.N.Y. 1975). Cf. ***in flagrante delicto.*** See LATINISMS.

in pari materia (= upon the same matter or subject) is legal JARGON used in the context of interpreting statutes. The common maxim is that statutes *in pari materia* are to be construed together. Usually the phrase functions as an adjective—e.g.: "Sometimes there is, by statute, an appeal from them to the High Court, in which case it may be presumed that the High Court will consider itself bound by its previous decisions *in pari materia.*" Carleton K. Allen, *Law in the Making* 237 (7th Cir. 1964)./ "[I]t seems that the present position is that, when an earlier statute is *in pari materia* with a later one, it is simply part of its context to be considered by the judge in deciding whether the meaning of a provision in the later statute is plain." Rupert Cross, *Statutory Interpretation* 128 (1976).

At times the phrase denotes the doctrine and is therefore used as a noun—e.g.: "*In pari materia* finds its greatest force when the statutes are enacted by the same legislative body at the same time."

At other times the phrase is used adverbially—e.g.: "The federal estate tax and the federal gift tax . . . are construed *in pari materia* . . . ." *Harris v. I.R.C.,* 340 U.S. 106, 107 (1950)./ "[T]he Maryland constitutional provision is construed *in pari materia* with the Fourth Amendment." *Maryland v. Garrison,* 55 U.S.L.W. 4190, 4192 (1987). See ITALICS (C) & LATINISMS.

in part. See **in whole & in pertinent part.**

in-patient should be hyphenated. Otherwise it is easily mistaken for *impatient.* E.g., "A limitation on *in-patient* hospital service to twenty-one days does not violate federal regulations." See PHRASAL ADJECTIVES (A).

in pectore. See LOAN TRANSLATIONS.

in personam. A. And *personal.* In personam is inferior to *personal* when used in the phrase *in personam jurisdiction* (= jurisdiction over a legal person). In many contexts, however, *personal* cannot substitute for *in personam:* "Plaintiff asserted an *in personam* admiralty claim against defendant for breach of the charter agreement." A claim *in personam* is one that is vested in a person and that imposes a liability against another person (such as a claim for repayment of a debt).

In personam occurs sometimes after, sometimes before the noun it qualifies. Traditionally it follows—e.g.: "The vast majority of federal cases are actions *in personam.*" Likewise one refers to a *judgment in personam* (= a judgment rendered against a legal person) and to a *right in personam* (= a right availing against a specific legal person for liability). See POSTPOSITIVE ADJECTIVES.

B. And *in rem.* An action is *in personam* when its purpose is to determine the rights and interests of the parties themselves in the subject matter of the action; an action is *in rem* when the court's judgment determines the title to property and the rights of the parties, not merely among themselves, but also against all persons at any time claiming an interest in the property at issue. *In rem,* then, means "availing against other persons generally and imposing on everyone a legal liability to respect the claimant's right."

Walter Wheeler Cook classified several very different ways in which these phrases are used:

> There seem to be at least four different uses which need to be distinguished: 1. These phrases are used in the classification of the so-called 'primary' rights which legal and equitable actions are supposed to protect and enforce. The classification here is, of course, the well-known one of *rights in rem* and *rights in personam.* 2. The next use has to do with the equally well-known classification of actions as *actions in rem* and *actions in personam.* 3. A third use is in the classification of judgments and decrees as *in rem* or *in personam.* 4. The fourth use refers to the procedure used by a court in the enforcement of its judgment or decree. Here the court is said to *act in rem* or *act in personam,* as the case may be, the usual statement being that the law does the former and equity the latter.
>
> Walter W. Cook, *The Powers of Courts of Equity,* 15 Colum. L. Rev. 37, 39 (1915).

C. Misspelled *in personum.* This fairly common mistake drew a "[*sic*]" from one court: "On March 31, 1976, attorneys for the other defendant in the case filed an amended motion to dismiss, alleging for the first time as grounds therein that '[t]his court lacks *in personum* [*sic*] jurisdiction over this defendant.'" *Rauch v. Day & Night Mfg. Corp.,* 576 F.2d 697, 699 (6th Cir. 1978).

in pertinent part; in relevant part; in part. The last is best; the second, a variant of the first, is as verbose and jejune as the first. See QUOTATIONS (B).

inplane. See **deplane.**

in point; on point. Both terms, applied to prior judicial decisions, mean "apposite; discussing the precise issue now at hand." *On point* is now the more common phrase, but both are well established in the legal idiom. E.g., "Those cases fall into two classes, only one of which, in fact, is *on point.*"/ "These cases are not *in point* as authority in our case."/ "More *in point,* the duties owed by a landowner depend on the role of the person injured on his premises."

Case in point is a popular idiom that originated in the law. See **off point** & POPULARIZED LEGAL TECHNICALITIES.

in point of fact is verbose for *in fact* or *actually.* E.g., "It was early held that 'parents' and 'children' were words used to show an intention of indicating *a family relation in point of fact* [*in fact a family relation*] as the foundation of the right of action."

in posse. See ***in esse.***

in praesenti, which means merely "in the present," is a LATINISM wholly without merit. E.g., "The question here determined is whether there was a valid declaration of trust operating *in praesenti* [omit *in praesenti*] between January 28 and May 3, 1929."/ "An irrevocable *gift in praesenti* [read *present gift*] of money or property, real or personal, to a child by a parent to enable the donee to anticipate his inheritance to the extent of the gift is known as an advancement." See ***in futuro.***

in propria persona = pro se (q.v.). E.g., "Edward W. Bergquist appeared *in propria persona.*" *In re Victoria Co.,* 42 B.R. 533, 534 (Bankr. D. Minn. 1984)./ "He filed a claim of appeal and a brief *in propria persona* in the Court of Appeals." *In re Sanchez,* 375 N.W.2d 353, 355 (Mich. 1985). See ***pro persona.***

input, n. & v.t. This jargonmonger's word is generally eschewed by careful writers. "Each decision-maker [q.v.] has a different optimal point of *informational input* [read *advice* or *comment*]."/ "Analysis is not restricted to studying *the influence of precareer inputs* [read *the effect of precareer influences*]." The English have the phrase *input tax,* statutorily defined in the Finance Act of 1977.

inquire; enquire. *Inquire* is a FORMAL WORD for *ask.* In AmE, *in-* is the preferred spelling. See EN- & **enquiry.**

inquirer; inquisitor. *Inquirer* is the more general of the two terms, meaning "one who asks questions or investigates." *Inquisitor,* not to be used where *inquirer* is called for, means "one who examines others to obtain information," and carries with it historical connotations of the Spanish Inquisition or trial by inquisition.

inquiry. See **enquiry** & EN-.

inquisitive; inquisitorial; inquisitional. *Inquisitive* = given to inquiry or questioning <a highly inquisitive mind>.

Inquisitorial has quite different connotations: "of the character of an inquisitor; offensively or impertinently inquiring, prying" (*OED*). E.g., "In an *inquisitorial* system of trial, the accused would himself be questioned by or before a judge, and the truth might then emerge." To contrast *inquisitorial* with *accusatorial,* see **accusatorial.**

Inquisitional is a NEEDLESS VARIANT of *inquisitorial*—e.g.: "A defendant may assert her own Fifth Amendment right to a fair trial as a valid objection to the introduction of statements extracted from a nondefendant by coercion or other *inquisitional* [read *inquisitorial*] tactics."

inquisitor. See **inquirer.**

in re; en re; re. The correct spelling of the two-word version is *in re* (= regarding, in the matter of). Known to nonlawyers as a legalistic term, *in re* was once commonly used at the outset of legal documents, and now is often used before case names (particularly in uncontested proceedings)—e.g., *In re Wolfson's Estate,* which is frequently Englished *In the Matter of Wolfson's Estate. The Bluebook* (15th ed.) recommends (p. 57) changing citations that begin *In the Matter of* to *In re.*

Sometimes, in the driest of commercial correspondence, *in re* is shortened to *re,* the ablative inflection of the noun *res;* the ellipsis carries the same meaning as *in re.* Although some authorities object to this use of the term, its conciseness makes it well-nigh irreplaceable. The best practice is to restrict it to use as a signal or introductory title announcing the subject of correspondence, and to avoid using it in sentences as part of one's syntax.

in rebus. See **in rem.**

in regards to is semiliterate. The idiomatic phrases are *in regard to, in respect to* (or *of*), and *with respect to.* E.g., "This phone call to Howard on behalf of Servotech was *in regards to* [read *in regard to*] purchasing weapons in the United States for delivery in the Republic of South Africa." See **as regards.**

in relevant part. See **in pertinent part.**

in rem; *in rebus.* The former is accusative singular ("in or against the thing"), the latter ablative plural ("in things"). Both are common parts of lengthier LATINISMS. See **in personam.**

in respect of can usually be replaced by a simpler substitute, as the New Zealand Court of Appeal has recognized: "*In respect of* is a phrase used more by lawyers and in official and business documents than in other writing or ordinary speech. Yet it cannot be said to have a precise legal meaning. Fowler's *Modern English Usage* does it justice by recommending that it be used as seldom as possible." *Phonographic Performances (NZ) Ltd v. Lion Breweries Ltd,* [1980] F.S.R. 383, (1979).

inroll. See **engross.**

in route. See **en route.**

insanity. Although this word has a strong hold in criminal law, leading criminal-law writers have tried their best to uproot it. The primary objections are that the word *insanity* (1) is not as clear as *mental disorder,* which more obviously includes disease of the mind, congenital problems, and damage resulting from traumatic injury; (2) suggests misleadingly that it refers to a specific mental condition when in fact it refers to a broad array of conditions; (3) is mere legal JARGON, not a medical term at all. As to the third point, one writer states: "[*Insanity*] is a legal term only, and one that is not used by the psychiatrist; the latter prefers to speak of mental disorder, mental illness, or of psychosis or neurosis." Winfred Overholser, *Psychiatry and the Law,* 38 Mental Hygiene 243, 244 (1954).

inside of. Omit the *of.* See **of (C).**

insider is sometimes used as a shorthand for *inside trader* or *trader in inside information.* E.g., Kurt Eichenwald, *Two Firms Are Charged as Insiders,* N.Y. Times, 3 Nov. 1988, at 29.

insider trading; insider dealing. The former phrase predominates in AmE. E.g., "Only after being arraigned and fingerprinted did Mr. Wigton learn that he was being charged with *insider trading* . . . ." Steve Swartz & James B. Stewart, *Kidder's Mr. Wigton, Charged as "Insider," Ends His Long Ordeal,* Wall St. J., 21 Aug. 1989, at A10.

The phrase *insider dealing* is a primarily BrE term that denotes dealing on the stock exchange by a person who was, within the previous six months, knowingly connected with the company whose stock is dealt in. Such conduct is penalized by the U.K. Company Securities (Insider Dealing) Act 1985.

insidious; invidious. A distinction exists between these words. *Insidious* = (of persons and things) lying in wait or seeking to entrap or ensnare; operating subtly or secretly so as not to excite suspicion. E.g., "The officers of a trust company owe allegiance to the shareholders as well as to the beneficiaries, and the temptation to favor the shareholders may well be more *insidious* than the temptation of an individual trustee to favor himself."

Invidious = offensive; entailing odium or ill will upon the person performing, discharging, or discussing; giving offense to others (*OED*). This term is often used of discrimination, and has been for more than two centuries. E.g., "He failed to allege motivations of class-based *invidious* discrimination." The two words ought not to be used in the same sentence, as here: "Ugly in its practice and *insidious* in its effects, *invidious* racial discrimination deserves protection in no area of society, least of all in the administration of justice in federal courts." A workable revision might be to drop *insidious* altogether and write "*invidious* in its effects, racial discrimination . . . ."

insightful. This vague one-word CLICHÉ is sometimes misspelled *inciteful*—e.g.: "In assessing *Morales'* impact on the common law claims of plaintiffs, the court is fortunate to have available the *inciteful* [read *insightful*] opinion in *Vail v. Pan Am Corp.* . . ." *El-Menshawy v. Egypt Air,* 647 A.2d 491, 492 (N.J. Super. Ct. Law Div. 1994). See **inciteful.**

insignia; insigne. Today *insignia* (technically plural) is regarded as the singular, *insignias* as its plural. E.g., "This *insignia* is two feet three inches in length and one foot four inches in height." *Chicago Park Dist. v. Canfield,* 19 N.E.2d 376, 377 (Ill. 1939). Cf. **indicia.**

The Latin singular *insigne* is rarely used, and when it does occasionally appear, it would be better as *insignia*—e.g.: "It was undisputed that he had never made use of the Indian *insigne* [read *insignia*] and had never attempted to imitate or copy the script of printing of the words, White Kitchen, as used by the plaintiff." *Faciane v. Starner,* 230 F.2d 732, 735 (5th Cir. 1956).

insipient. See **incipient.**

insist takes the preposition *on,* not *in.* E.g., "In a society that *persists and insists in* [read *persists in and insists on,* if the ALLITERATION is really necessary] permitting its citizens to own and possess weapons, it becomes necessary to determine who may and who may not acquire them."

insistence. So spelled—often misspelled *-ance.* See **instance.**

insistment, a NEEDLESS VARIANT of *insistence,* appears occasionally in legal writing, though it is not recorded in most English-language dictionaries. E.g., "The *insistment* [read *insistence*] of the plaintiff is twofold." *Jelinek v. Sotak,* 86 A.2d 684, 687 (N.J. 1952)./ "The wife objected, asserting that she would live in one room if need be rather than reside with her mother-in-law, but her spouse remained 'obdurate in his *insistment* [read *insistence*].'" *Koch v. Koch,* 232 A.2d 157, 160 (N.J. Super. Ct. 1967).

in situ (= in its original place; back in place) is a LATINISM used in property law. It is almost always unnecessary.

insofar as (= in such degree as), spelled thus in AmE and *in so far as* in BrE, is sometimes misused because its meaning is misunderstood. One does not know exactly what this writer, for instance, had in mind: "*Insofar as* important to this appeal, Greyhound defended this suit on the grounds that, when plaintiff's cause of action arose, O was not its employee, but was B's employee or an independent contractor." A better—and grammatical—way of beginning this sentence would be, *What is important in this appeal is that Greyhound defended . . . .* See **inasmuch as.**

insoluble; insolvable; unsolvable. *Insoluble* is used both of substances that will not dissolve in liquids and of problems that cannot be solved. E.g., "The powder, which is *insoluble,* sits at the bottom of the vial."/ "It relieves the legislature of a problem *insoluble* in bulk."

Insolvable is used only of problems that cannot be solved; some stylists prefer it to *insoluble.* Judge Henry Friendly, for example, referred to *an essentially insolvable problem. Schine v. Schine,* 367 F.2d 685, 688 (2d Cir. 1966) (Friendly, J., concurring).

Unsolvable should be avoided as a NEEDLESS VARIANT.

insolvency = (1) generally, the inability to pay debts as they mature; (2) under the (U.S.) Bankruptcy Act of 1898, the insufficiency of assets at a fair valuation to pay debts; or (3) under other laws, the insufficiency of assets at a fair salable valuation to pay debts. See James A. MacLachlan, *Handbook of the Law of Bankruptcy* 10–13 (1956). Sense (2), sometimes called the *balance-sheet insolvency test,* is the predominant sense in civil-law jurisdictions. See **bankruptcy.**

insolvent. Nonlawyers are accustomed to using this word as an adjective <an insolvent debtor>, but lawyers sometimes used it attributively as a noun <an insolvent>—e.g.: "An *insolvent* can obey an order not to commit a threatened tort . . . ." Douglas Laycock, *The Death of the Irreparable Injury Rule* 76 (1991).

in specie. See **specie.**

in spite of. See **despite.**

inst. = short for *instant.* Wood writes that this was "once a quite respectable legal term, now a piece of commercial jargon for 'the present month' (e.g., 'We beg to recognise the receipt of your letter of the 25th *inst.*'). Use the name of the month instead." F.T. Wood, *Current English Usage* 123 (1962). The advice is well taken. Cf. **ult.**

instal(l)ment. *Instalment* is the BrE spelling, *installment* the spelling preferred in AmE.

instance; instancy. *Instance* "in the sense of urgent solicitation or insistence [always in the phrase *at the instance of*] is a useful word; in any other sense it is useless." Percy Marks, *The Craft of Writing* 53 (1932). Another legitimate meaning of the word is "an illustrative example." Here the word is useless: "It seems plain that *in at least the vast majority of instances* [delete the italicized words] such a purported conveyance of lifetime services would usually (or almost always) be unenforceable and essentially nugatory under applicable state law."

Following are examples of the use, largely legal, that has substantive value: "Thousands of government employees would object to being forced to take polygraph tests at the *instance* of their supervisors."/ "In 1804, the Court of Session of Scotland interdicted, at the *instance* of the children, the publication of the manuscript letters of the poet Burns."/ "Apart from a limited class of expectations, a minor's contracts are not void but only voidable at his *instance.*"

Instancy, a rare term, means "urgency; pressing nature; imminence" <the instancy of the danger was apparent to all>.

For the misuse of *incidence* for *instance,* see **incidence.**

instance, v.t., = to cite as an instance, to adduce as an example in illustration or proof (*OED*). E.g., "Nowhere in the record is to be found any remark by the trial judge smacking of impropriety in the faintest degree, let alone any such as those *instanced* above."/ "'Uno' is better analogized to a term such as 'Del Monte,' *instanced* in *Pick 'N' Fly, Inc. v. Park & Fly, Inc.*"

instance court is an old-fashioned expression for a court of first instance or trial court.

instantaneously; instantly. "*Instantly* is virtually a synonym of at once, directly, and immediately, though perhaps the strongest of the four. *Instantaneously* is applied to something that takes an inappreciable time to occur, like the taking of an instantaneous photograph, especially to two events that occur so nearly simultaneously that the difference is imperceptible" (*MEU2* 288). E.g., "He was killed *instantaneously* [read *instantly*] in the collision of that car with the truck driven by the defendant." Cf. **instanter.**

instant case; instant cause; present case; case at bar. These equivalent phrases, though sometimes useful, can often be avoided by *here,* if not used vaguely. Some variation of all these terms may be desirable to avoid verbal tedium, but one should not be so obvious as to lapse into INELEGANT VARIATION.

Instant case is sometimes used where *this case* would be preferable. E.g., "Appellant and her husband brought *the instant* [read *this*] products liability *case* against the manufacturer of the chair."

Instant (= now under consideration), labeled an ARCHAISM by the *OED,* is alive in the law, and has been extended beyond the basic phrase *instant case:* "Since the *instant* will has been previously construed as permitting newborn grandnieces and grandnephews to enter the class, the composition of the class has not yet been determined."/ "According to the parties' stipulation in this case, it is expected with respect to the *instant* bonds that more than half of the debt service requirements will be satisfied not from real property taxes but from revenues from other local taxes."/ "The district court dismissed the *instant* petition for abuse of the writ." This bit of legal JARGON ought to be used sparingly if at all. See **case at bar.**

instanter, a silly LATINISM to find in an English-language context, easily makes our list of FORBIDDEN WORDS. Apart from facetiousness, there is no good reason for preferring *instanter* to *instantly* or *at once.* There are several reasons, however, for preferring *instantly.* First, it is universally comprehensible among speakers of English. Second, it conveys the nuances available to either term. Third, it is not, like its cousin the Latinism, pompous (e.g., "Study of, and, if study warrants, changes in land use control cannot be completed *instanter* [read *instantly*]."). And fourth, it is not susceptible to the ambiguity of *instanter,* which a few courts have held to mean "within 24 hours."

Adding to the utter dispensability of *instanter,* some legal writers have failed to understand that the term is an adverb and have misused it as if it were an adjective: "It was an excessive statement made in the heat of the closing argument of a hard-fought case, one which was objected to and subjected to [see ALLITERATION] an *instanter* cautionary instruction." The writer should have used *immediate.*

All that being said, the jocular contexts do exist in which *instanter* is just the word—e.g.: "The worst woman I ever knew . . . had a face [that] for purity and innocence I can only compare with Raphael's 'Madonna,' and some of the best men and women who have crossed my path would have been convicted *instanter* under any laws founded on Cesare Lombroso's theories." F.W. Ashley, *My Sixty Years in the Law* 163 (1936).

instantiate (= to represent by an instance), a vintage World War II NEOLOGISM of questionable value. E.g., "The reference to defendant's silence constitutes harmless error; Chapman's fate is to *instantiate* [read *exemplify*] this third rule."

instantly. See **instantaneously.**

in statu quo is a LATINISM properly equivalent to *in statu quo ante* (= in the same condition as previously). Some writers have quite understandably assumed that there was a distinction between *in statu quo* and *in statu quo ante,* and have used the former merely to mean "in the status quo; in the same condition as now exists." In the two examples that follow, the phrase is correctly used: "The fact that the parties cannot be put *in statu quo* precisely as to the subject-matter of the contract will not preclude a decree for rescission."/ "Depriving one of the benefit of a contract that he supposes he has made leaves everything *in statu quo,* rather than imposing a liability to which no limit can be placed." See ITALICS (C).

The foregoing discussion is largely beside the point, however, since the English renditions of the phrase are preferable to the Latinate. One should write *in the status quo* (present condition) or *in the status quo ante* (previous condition). See **status quo.**

instil(l). The preferred spelling in AmE is *instill. Instil* is preferred in BrE. This word takes the preposition *(in)to,* not *with* <he instilled character as well as knowledge into his students>. Use of the latter preposition occurs as a result of confusion of *inspire* with *instill.* See OBJECT-SHUFFLING.

In the following sentence, *instill in* is misused for *confer on:* "Presence within a state, even temporary or transitory presence, is still a common-law basis *instilling competence in* [read *conferring competence on*] the courts of that state to adjudicate claims against a person."

instillation; instillment. The latter is a NEEDLESS VARIANT.

instinct (= imbued or charged *with*) is a recherché usage that has given the law a memorable idiom: "The whole contract is *instinct* with such an obligation."/ "There are times when reciprocal engagements do not fit each other like the parts of an indented deed, and yet the whole contract . . . may be '*instinct* with an obligation,' imperfectly expressed." (Cardozo, J.)/ "The personal atmosphere of the Court of Appeal today is *instinct* with comity and friendliness." Asquith, L.J., [1950] J.S.P.T.L. 353.

instinctive; instinctual. The latter is a NEEDLESS VARIANT.

institute is a FORMAL WORD for *begin* or *start.* Cf. **commence.** See **begin (B).**

institute proceedings is a highfalutin way of saying *file suit.*

instruct = to give information as a client to (as a solicitor) or as a solicitor to (a counsel); or (2) to authorize (a solicitor or barrister) to act for one. E.g., "This cause has been carefully *instructed* with evidence by the practisers, who have had the conduct of it." (Eng.) See **advise (C).**

instructed verdict. See **directed verdict.**

instrument = a formal legal document that entails rights, duties, and liabilities, such as a contract, will, note, bill of exchange, money order, share certificate, and the like. E.g., "A will and codicil are separate *instruments* for the purpose of execution; it would seem better to require separate physical acts of revocation." Often the word can be supplanted to advantage by *writing* or *document,* terms understandable to nonlawyers.

The word *instrument* strongly suggests a document that is the result of DRAFTING—i.e., a document that sets forth the rights, duties, and liabilities of parties or beneficiaries. To call a piece of written advocacy an *instrument* is to mangle the legal idiom: "No *instrument* [read *document*] of this character [i.e., a brief] is in use in England." William M. Lile et al. *Brief Making and the Use of Law Books* 366 (3d ed. 1914). [Or: *No such document is in use in England.*]

In any event, the phrase *written instrument* and *instrument in writing* are redundancies when a legal instrument is clearly contemplated, inasmuch as there is no such thing as an *oral instrument.* See **document.** Cf. **statutory instrument.**

insubstantial; unsubstantial. The latter is a NEEDLESS VARIANT.

insue is an archaic spelling of *ensue,* q.v.

in suit = in dispute, or (engaged) in a lawsuit. E.g., "No further incentive is needed to produce the information *in suit.*" The notation in the *OED* that this phrase from legal JARGON is obsolete proved to be premature. Yet the phrase is hardly common.

insurable. So spelled.

insurance. A. Pronunciation. This word is pronounced with the primary accent on the second syllable /*in-**shoor**-əns*/.

B. Two Species. Insurance is of two kinds. One is insurance against accidents: buildings burning, ships sinking, cars colliding, being injured, and the like. The other—in BrE frequently called *assurance*—is provision for designated persons on the occurrence of death (*life insurance* [AmE] or *life assurance* [BrE]). See **assurance.**

insurance adjuster (AmE) = *insurance assessor* (BrE).

insure. See **assure.**

insured, n., like *deceased* and *accused,* forms an awkward plural and possessive. E.g., "This type of policy is often used to provide for the education of children or for the *insured's* retirement." An equivalent term, *insurant,* solves this infelicity but is little known. See PLURALS (D) & POSSESSIVES (F).

insurer; insuror. The *-or* form should be avoided. See **underwriter.**

insurgence; insurgency. These two words have undergone DIFFERENTIATION. *Insurgence* = a revolt; the action of rising against authority. *Insurgency* = the quality or state of being in revolt; the tendency to rise in revolt (*OED*).

insurrection. See **sedition.**

insurrectionary; insurrectional. The latter is a NEEDLESS VARIANT.

in tail. See **tail.**

integral; integrant. The latter is a NEEDLESS VARIANT as an adjective; but it exists legitimately as a noun (meaning "component"): "A res is a necessary *integrant* of the concept of 'constructive trust.'"

Integral is often misspelled *intergral.*

integr(at)able. The correct form is *integrable.* See -ATABLE.

integrated bar. This is an odd name for a bar in which membership is compulsory for anyone wishing to practice law. To the nonlawyer, the phrase is likely to give rise to a MISCUE, as one writer recognized with his parenthetical: "Twenty-seven states have *integrated bars.* (Nothing to do with racial relations. All lawyers in these integrated-bar states have to be members of the bar association in order to practice.)" Murray T. Bloom, *The Trouble with Lawyers* 161 (1970). See **bar.**

integration. See **desegregation.**

integration clause; merger clause. These synonymous terms refer to a contractual provision stating that the contract represents the parties' complete and final agreement and supersedes all informal understandings and oral agreements relating to the subject matter of the contract.

intellectual property comprises two subdivisions: industrial property and copyright. *Industrial property* includes patents, inventions, trademarks, and industrial designs. *Copyrights* are property rights in literary, musical, artistic, photographic, and film works, as well as in maps and technical drawings. See R.P. Benko, *Protecting Intellectual Property Rights* 2–3 (1987).

intelligent. In lay usage this word is usually confined to descriptions of persons; in legal writing it is used just as frequently of acts as it is of persons. An *intelligent* act is one that is carried out comprehendingly. E.g., "When a defendant admits his guilt in open court, he may attack only the voluntary and *intelligent* character of the act." See HYPALLAGE.

intelligent; intelligible. The former means (of persons) "having mental power or grasp," the latter (of statements) "understandable."

intend = (1) in ordinary language, to desire that a consequence will follow from one's conduct; or (2) in legal language, to contemplate that consequences of one's act will necessarily or probably follow from the act, whether or not those consequences are desired for their own sake.

intendment = (1) the sense in which the law understands something; or (2) a decision-maker's inference about the true meaning or intention of (a legal instrument). E.g. (Sense 1): "The evidence produced upon the trial, with all its legal *intendments,* failed to fairly tend to prove that plaintiff's discharge was accomplished by the illegal acts of defendant."/ (Sense 2): "We must take the language of the section as we find it; there is no reason for any *intendment.*"

Lon Fuller explained the term somewhat differently: "Our institutions and our formalized interactions with one another are accompanied by certain interlocking expectations that may be called *intendments,* even though there is seldom occasion to bring these underlying expectations across the threshold of consciousness. In a very real sense when I cast my vote in an election my conduct is directed and conditioned on the anticipation that my ballot will be counted in favor of the candidate I actually vote for. . . . [T]he institution of elections may be said to contain an intendment that the votes cast will be faithfully tallied . . . ." Lon L. Fuller, *The Morality of Law* 217 (rev. ed. 1976).

This specialized legal term should never be used as a fancy variant of *intention* or *intent* (both of which mean "purpose, aim, design, meaning). (See **intent.**) *Common intendment* = the natural meaning in legal construction. *Intendiment* is an obsolete form of *intendment.*

intense; intensive. The best advice, which is conventional, is to shun *intensive* wherever *intense* will fit the context. *Intensive* is really a philosophical and scientific term best left to philosophers and scientists; we lawyers can make do rather nicely with *intense:* "A firsthand familiarity with the type of participation required of a defendant would not be meaningfully supplemented by *intensive* [read *intense*] scrutiny on appeal."/ "The striking divergence of opinion conspicuously exemplifies the need for dealing somewhat more *intensively* [read *intensely*] and systematically than is usual with the nature and analysis of all types of jural interests."

intent(ion). A. Defining *intention*. "The general legal opinion," writes Glanville Williams, "is that *intention* cannot be satisfactorily defined and does not need a definition, since everyone knows what it means. This is largely true. Trouble has been caused in the past because when judges have offered to give definitions or tests of intention for the benefit of the jury they have used wide language going beyond the ordinary meaning of the word." *Textbook of Criminal Law* 51 (1978). The same must be said of *intent,* though the two words have subtle connotative differences. See (B).

B. *Intent* and *intention*. If any distinction may be drawn between *intent* and *intention,* it must be connotative: one has evil intent, but good intentions; one has the intent to murder, and the intention to do something either morally neutral or laudable. This distinction has not been fossilized in the language, however; often *intent* is used of neutral and even good motives, and arguably one may have bad as well as good *intentions.* Euphony usually governs the choice of word.

The usual phrase is *testamentary intent,* although *testamentary intention* has appeared. Following are sentences in which *intent* appears in reference to gifts or transfers of property: "We discovered the *intent* of the grantor from other factors, as shown by the instrument, to give full effect to the words of limitation."/ "The charity has no large discretionary power in carrying out the general *intent* of the donor."/ "The analogy of the 'fraudulent conveyance' from the creditors'-rights field has appealed to some courts, but others consider the issue of *intent* too difficult to administer."

Intention is also sometimes used: "The next question is whether it is a valid defence to an action for passing off that the defendant had no *intention* to deceive." (Eng.)/ "As long as the purposes to which the property is to be applied are limited to charitable purposes, there is no reason why the trust should not be carried out in accordance with the *intention* of the testator." *Intention* takes the infinitive form of the verb, not the present participle. E.g., "He then announced his *intention of running* [read *intention to run*] for governor."

Intent and *intention* are liable to INELEGANT VARIATION. E.g., "Such a construction results in a rule that the grantor must expressly indicate his *intention* [read *intent,* for the sake of consistency] to create a remainder in his heirs, or a presumption in favor of reversions that may be rebutted by indication of the grantor's contrary *intent.*"/ "Her *intent* in executing the paper, at least as far as such *intent* is now before us, must be determined by the court as a matter of law. The paper writing does not declare an *intention* [read *intent*] to revoke the will except through its destruction, either wholly or as far as Hart is concerned by O'Kennedy."

C. And *motive*. The *motive* is the inducement for doing an act; the *intent* is the resolve to commit an act. Stated differently, *motive* relates to the end; *intent* relates to the means. One court has said of these two words (and two others, *deliberation* and *purpose*): "One reason [that these words] are often confused is that they are used synonymously in ordinary speech." *Snakenberg v. Hartford Casualty Ins. Co.,* 383 S.E.2d 2, 7 n.7 (S.C. Ct. App. 1989). See **motive.**

D. And *purpose*. For the erroneous use of *purpose* for *intention,* see **purpose (B).**

E. *Specific intent* in Criminal Law. *Specific intent* = any intention involved in the definition of a crime. Williams considers the phrase unhelpful: "The adjective 'specific' seems to be somewhat pointless, for the intent is no more specific than any other intent required in criminal law. The most it can mean is that the intent is specifically referred to in the indictment. There is no substantive difference between an intent specifically mentioned and one implied in the name of the crime." Glanville Williams, *Criminal Law* 49 (2d ed. 1961).

Other writers point out, however, that because the test for *specific intent* is subjective rather than objective—and therefore more particularized to a defendant's actual state of mind—it conveys a useful sense: "There is no question . . . that [*specific intent*] refers to a subjective inquiry into the defendant's actual state of mind. For this reason, in a prosecution for a specific-intent crime many courts do not permit an instruction that a person is presumed to intend the natural and probable consequences of his acts. Intent to kill, intent to steal, and intent to rape would all be *'specific intents'* . . . . The phrase thus refers to some particular state of mind required by the definition of the offense." Peter W. Low et al., *Criminal*

Law: Cases and Materials 230–31 (1982). See **general intent.**

F. ***Particular intention; general intention; transferred intention.*** These are the three types of criminal intention (or *malice,* q.v.) from the victim's point of view. *Particular intention* involves a particular victim as its target. *General intention* (sometimes called *general malice*) involves no particular victim (as when someone explodes a bomb to destroy a building), but the intention to harm anyone who ends up being harmed is generally ascribed to the perpetrator. *Transferred intention* (or *transferred malice*) occurs when harm intended for one person befalls another by accident.

intentional. For the distinction between *unintentional* and *involuntary,* see **unintentional.**

intentional murder. See **murder (A).**

intents and purposes, for all. See **for all intents and purposes.**

INTER-, INTRA-. These prefixes have quite different meanings. *Inter-* means "between, among." *Intra-* means "within, in." Thus *interstate* means "between states" and *intrastate* means "within a state." Lawyers have recently created any number of NEOLOGISMS with these prefixes, primarily with *inter-: interagency, interbranch, intercircuit, intercorporate, intermunicipal,* and the like.

inter alia; inter alios. The best course, undoubtedly, is to use *among others,* a phrase that can refer to people or things. The Latin is not so simple. Whereas *inter alia* (= among other things) refers to anything that is not human, *inter alios* (= among other persons) refers to people. (The unanglicized form *inter alias* means "among other female persons.")

Both anglicized phrases are used more in legal writing than elsewhere. *Inter alia* is the much more common phrase—e.g.: "When the balance of the purchase price was not paid on the due date, the vendor resold the house and brought this action for damages for, *inter alia,* the deficiency on the resale." (Aus.) Though not common, *inter alios* occurs far more frequently in legal than in nonlegal writing: "The Senate report stated that the residual section was intended to reach, *inter alios,* 'a person who induces another to remain silent or to give misleading information to a federal law enforcement officer.'"

The misuse of *inter alia* for *inter alios* is on the rise—e.g.: "It makes no sense to create a system in which the inferior officers of the Environmental Protection Agency, for example—which may include, *inter alia* [read *inter alios*] bureau chiefs, the general counsel and administrative law judges—must be appointed by the President, the Courts of Law, or the Secretary of Something Else." *Freytag v. I.R.C.,* 501 U.S. 868, 919–20 (1991) (Scalia, J., concurring).

In the following sentence, the phrase is not only wrong but also misplaced: "A contract *between, inter alia, the manufacturer and one of its former employees,* [read *between the manufacturer and, inter alios, one of its former employees,*] wherein the former employee expressly agreed not to disclose any of the processes and methods of the manufacturer, was an admission of a positive character that such processes and methods were secret."

interceptor; intercepter. The former spelling is preferred. See -ER (A).

intercourse. In modern usage, even *lawful intercourse* has sexual overtones that are not to be ignored. The term is best avoided in its traditional sense "mutual dealings and communication." E.g., "Notwithstanding that lawyers are often arrayed against each other as champions of opposing forces, their *intercourse* [read *dealings with one another*] should be friendly."/ "The means commonly used is the inducing of others to withdraw from such companies their patronage and business *intercourse* by threats."/ "The libel in this case deprived plaintiff of the benefits of public confidence and social *intercourse.*" To most modern readers this use of the term is an ARCHAISM.

Commerce was formerly used in virtually all senses of *intercourse,* including in the phrase *sexual commerce* (= sexual intercourse): "*Sexual commerce* or *intercourse* and *carnal knowledge* are synonymous terms." 44 Am. Jur. *Rape* § 2 (1942). See **commerce.**

interdict (= to forbid, restrain) is a FORMAL WORD often occurring in legal writing. E.g., "A supersedeas bond is a privilege extended to the judgment debtor as a price of *interdicting* the validity of an order to pay money."/ "Both cases followed and applied the due process test set out in *Ferguson* and construed its bias prohibition to *interdict* only actual bias, not the mere appearance of bias."/ "The defendants argue that all the interests in Bernard's estate will necessarily vest before the expiration of the period *interdicted* by the Rule against Perpetuities." The noun is *interdiction.* E.g., "In November 1981, the United States entered into an arrangement with Great Britain respecting the *interdiction* of vessels suspected of carrying illicit drugs."/ "On May 27, after a three-day hearing, the court granted a preliminary injunction that continued the *interdictions* of the restraining order."

Interdict is also a civil-law term used as a noun in a sense close to "injunction." E.g., "This is an application on notice of motion in which the applicant asks for a declaration of rights and for an *interdict.*" (Rhod.) It also serves as a verb: in Scotland, for example, one petitions the court to *interdict* trespass.

interest. For its most general sense, see **right, title, and interest.** For the distinction between *interest* and *dividend* in corporate law, see **dividend.**

interest, legal rate of. The phrase refers to the rate of interest imposed as a matter of law where none is provided for contractually. But it suggests, perhaps misleadingly, a legal ceiling.

interests in community. See **concurrent interests.**

interface, v.i., is jargonmongers' talk. E.g., "This man possesses the ability to *interface* and relate with people from all social and economic levels." *Interface* should be left to COMPUTERESE.

interferee, for *person interfered with,* is legal JARGON without much to be said in its defense—e.g.: "The court is not aware of any decisions in which the relationship between the interferer and the *interferee* [read *person interfered with*] was that of coventures or prospective coventures." *United Euram Corp. v. Occidental Petroleum Corp.,* 474 N.Y.S.2d 372, 375 (Sup. Ct. 1984)./ "[T]ortious interference with a business relationship . . . has four requirements: . . . (2) knowledge of the relationship or expectancy on the part of the *interferee* [read *party interfered with*] . . . ." *Upjohn Co. v. Riahom Corp.,* 650 F. Supp. 485, 488 n.4 (D. Del. 1986). See -EE.

interference, in the JARGON of American patent lawyers, has a special legal meaning: "a proceeding to decide which of two patent applicants is the first inventor." The interference may involve an application and a patent, as long as the claim is made in the application before one year from the date on which the patent was issued. See Louis B. Applebaum et al., *Glossary of United States Patent Practice* 63 (1969).

interfering with contractual relations. See **tortious interference with contractual relations.**

interim relief. See **interlocutory relief.**

interlocutor = (1) a person who takes part in a dialogue (U.S. and G.B.); or (2) a judicial pronouncement or court order (Scots law).

interlocutory injunction. See **injunction.**

interlocutory relief; interim relief. *Interlocutory relief* is the phrase used in AmE and BrE to mean "a temporary judicial remedy, such as a preliminary injunction." *Interim relief* is an equivalent term sometimes used in BrE.

intermarriage. One word, but usu. a NEEDLESS VARIANT of *marriage*—e.g.: "Some statutes provide that *intermarriage* [read *marriage*] of the parties subsequent to the offense [of seduction] is a bar to prosecution therefor . . . ." Rollin M. Perkins & Ronald N. Boyce, *Criminal Law* 464 (3d ed. 1982).

intermarry should not be used for *marry,* which itself necessarily implies mutuality. This old-fashioned LEGALISM suggests to the modern reader a hint that the writer is concerned about miscegenation—e.g.: "Before that time, his daughter, Martha Florence, *had intermarried with* [read *had married*] R.P. Watson, and five children were born unto them." *Intermarry* should be laid to rest, except when one conveys the nuance of marrying only within a specified group.

intermeddle is always spelled with two *d*'s. One might not have thought *intermedling* to be anything but a typographical error, but it appears that way consistently in a popular primer on torts.

intermeddler, officious. See **officious.**

interment; internment. *Interment* = burial. *Internment* = detention, esp. of aliens in wartime.

In burial contexts, the word *internment* frequently ousts the proper word—e.g.: "[T]he *internment* [read *interment*] or other disposition of the deceased's body is an extremely important emotional catharsis for the family and friends of the deceased." *Bock v. Los Angeles County,* 197 Cal. Rptr. 470, 474 (Ct. App. 1983)./ "These cases make clear that the common law rule applies only to individual purchasers of burial spaces for direct *internment* [read *interment*] purposes." *In re Memorial Estates, Inc.,* 90 B.R. 886, 901 (N.D. Ill. 1988).

in terms. See **terms, in.**

in terms of is often nothing more than a FLOTSAM PHRASE—e.g.: "The development in the application of a constitutional provision may be shown *in terms of* [read *through*] the power of the federal government to prohibit commerce." Edward H. Levi, *An Introduction to Legal Reasoning* 62 (1949; repr. 1972). See VERBOSITY.

Internal Revenue Service (U.S.) = Inland Revenue Service (U.K.). Each is referred to informally as *the IRS.*

international. To the international lawyer, the word *international* (= of or relating to the legal relations among states or nations) is an antonym of *municipal* (= of or relating to the internal government of a state or nation). See **municipal.**

International Court of Justice in The Hague. See **World Court.**

international law; *jus gentium;* law of nations. These phrases are generally synonymous in meaning "the system of law regulating the interrelationship of sovereign states and their rights and duties vis-à-vis one another." *International law*—the newest of these phrases, a Bentham NEOLOGISM dating from 1789—is the predominant term nowadays. See ***jus gentium.***

The phrase *international law,* however, also has a broader sense, in which it covers not just the law of nations (as defined above) but also *private international law,* or the conflict of laws. In this broader sense, *international law* is concerned with "the rights of persons within the territory and dominion of one nation, by reason of acts, private or public, done within the dominions of another nation . . . ." *Hilton v. Guyot,* 159 U.S. 113, 163 (1895).

internecine = mutually deadly; destructive of both parties. The word is often misused in hyperbolic ways—e.g.: "[T]he judiciary, in fact and of necessity, has absolutely no interest in *internecine* [read *rancorous*] battles over social etiquette or the unprofessional personality clashes [that] frequently occur among opposing counsel these days." *Amax Coal Co. v. Adams,* 597 N.E.2d 350, 352 (Ind. Ct. App. 1992)./ "A private association of volunteer fire fighters chose to remove four individuals from its membership after *an internecine* [read *a bitter*?] struggle." *Yeager v. City of McGregor,* 980 F.2d 337, 344 (5th Cir. 1993)./ "During the Carter administration, the biggest *internecine* [delete *internecine*] schism within the Democratic Party involved disagreements over health care reform." James F. Blumstein, *Health Care Reform: The Policy Context,* 29 Wake Forest L. Rev. 15, 15 (1994).

internment. See **interment.**

interoffice. One word.

inter partes, the antonym of *ex parte* (q.v.), means "between parties; involving all parties to a lawsuit." This LATINISM—hardly a TERM OF ART—seems to be of little use. It is rare in American but common in British legal writing. E.g., "On its face it is an instrument *inter partes* [read *between parties*]." (Eng.)/ "In *an inter partes proceeding* [read *a proceeding between two or more parties* or *an adversary proceeding,*] notice on the petition is given to all interested persons by publication."/ "In the *inter-partes* [read *adversary*] proceeding, based upon the English 'solemn' form, notice to interested parties is required and the contestant submits evidence against the will."

If the phrase were to be Englished, *interparty,* which already has limited currency, would serve well—but only preceding the noun it modifies.

interpellate. See **interpolate.**

interplead, v.t. **A. Who Interpleads.** In an *interpleader,* it is traditionally the adverse parties claiming a right to the property held by the stakeholder that are said to *interplead* their claims. Jowitt, for example, states: "When a person is in possession of property in which he claims no interest, but to which two or more other persons lay claim, and he, not knowing to whom he may safely give it up, is sued by one or both, he can compel them to *interplead* . . . ." W.A. Jowitt, *The Dictionary of English Law* 997 (Clifford Walsh ed., 1959).

From the late 19th century, however, it has become common to say that the stakeholder *interpleads* the two contending parties. E.g., "The insurance company, not knowing where the payment should *go between the three, interpleaded the claimants* [read *go, initiated an interpleader among the three claimants*]."/ "The insurance company *interpleaded* the parties . . . ." William F. Walsh, *A Treatise on Equity* 59 (1930). See **interpleader (A).**

B. Past Tense and Past Participle. The past-tense and past-participle forms are *interpleaded,* not *interpled.* E.g., "The adverse claims of the *interpled parties* [read *interpleaded parties* or, better, *interpleading parties*] must, of course, concern the same property or the same debt." See **plead.**

interpleader. A. General Sense and Uses. *Interpleader* = a suit pleaded between two parties to determine a matter of claim or right to property held by a usu. disinterested third party (called a *stakeholder,* q.v.) who is in doubt about which claimant should have the property, the purpose of the suit being to determine to which claimant delivery or payment ought to be made. Despite its appearance, then, *interpleader* generally denotes a type of lawsuit and not a person; that is, the word is not ordinarily an agent noun. See -ER (B).

The equivalent term in Scots law is *multiplepoinding.*

B. As an Agent Noun. The *OED* lists, as one sense of *interpleader,* "one who interpleads," but notes: "it is doubtful whether the word is more than a dictionary assumption due to a misunderstanding . . . ." The sole support for the definition and note is a quotation from Worcester's 1846 dictionary. Today the word is not a "dictionary assumption"; it is a bona fide blunder. E.g., "[A]n interpleader action cannot be maintained if the *interpleader* [read *stakeholder*] asserts any right or interest against interpleaded claimants." *State Compensation Fund v. Superior Court,* 466 P.2d 802, 806 (Ariz. Ct. App. 1970)./ "Affirmed order to allow *interpleaders* [read *interpleading parties*] access to discovery." Stan Soocher, *Court Decisions—U.S. Circuit Courts of Appeals,* Nat'l L.J., 6 Aug. 1990, at 46. See -ER (B).

interpolate; interpellate. The former means "to insert into a text or writing"; the latter, used in legislative reports, means "to question formally; to seek information."

interpose for *submit* <to interpose a demurrer> is the term traditionally used for pleadings and motions made by the defense. E.g., "The counterclaimant has failed to advance a justifiable reason for its failure to timely *interpose* a claim."/ "The defense of forum non conveniens could be *interposed,* and, if meritorious, the Illinois court would dismiss the case."

interpretate, an obsolete BACK-FORMATION, is a NEEDLESS VARIANT of *interpret.* "The legislative history of section 5851 strongly supports *interpretating* [read *interpreting*] an 'action' as similar to formal proceedings under the Act."

interpretation; construction. There are two schools of thought with regard to how these terms apply to statutes and other types of DRAFTING. One has it that, although "*interpretation* and *construction* are generally regarded as synonymous and used interchangeably, it is not only possible, but desirable as well, to draw a distinction. The word *interpretation* is used with respect to language itself; it is the process of applying the legal standard to expressions found in the agreement in order to determine their meaning. *Construction,* on the other hand, is used to determine, not the sense of the words or symbols, but the legal meaning of the entire contract; the word is rightly used wherever the import of the writing is made to depend upon a special sense imposed by law." 4 Samuel Williston, *Treatise on the Law of Contracts* § 602, at 320 (3d ed. 1961). See Frederick Bowers, *Linguistic Aspects of Legislative Expression* 166 (1989) (calling the distinction "in keeping with general hermeneutic terminology"). See **construction.**

The other school of thought—perhaps more consistent with actual usage—utterly rejects Williston's view: "Some authors have attempted to introduce a distinction between *interpretation* and *construction.* Etymologically there is, perhaps, a distinction; but it has not been accepted by the profession. For practical purposes any such distinction may be ignored, in view of the real object of both interpretation and construction, which is merely to ascertain the meaning and will of the lawmaking body, in order that it may be enforced." William M. Lile et al., *Brief Making and the Use of Law Books* 337 (3d ed. 1914).

interpretative; interpretive; interpretational. Generally, one forms the adjective on the model of the nominal form of a word. Hence *prevention* yields *preventive,* not *preventative.* But with *interpretation,* the correct adjectival form is *interpretative* (= having the character or function of interpreting; explanatory), which should be used consistently. E.g., "[T]he common law, or even statute law, once encrusted with *interpretative* case-law, is not the work of a single mind, or even of a small number of minds." P.S. Atiyah, *Law and Modern Society* 73 (1983).

Interpretive, although it has gained ground in the last 50 years, should be laid to rest. E.g., "Appellant filed for rehearing of the new *interpretive* [read *interpretative*] rule under the FPA."/ "The question here is whether due process authorizes the Court to resort to *noninterpretive* [read *noninterpretative*] modes of constitutional adjudication."

Given, though, the fact that *interpretivism* (q.v.) is a linguistic fait accompli, one would be hard put to argue very strenuously against *interpretive.* Though it may not be condemned, it should be avoided by those who know better.

Interpretational is a NEEDLESS VARIANT—e.g.: "The courts do not all follow a single basic *interpretational* [read *interpretative*] technique . . . ." James J. White & Robert S. Summers, *Uniform Commercial Code* § 4, at 18 (3d ed. 1988).

interpretivism; noninterpretivism. Among American constitutional lawyers, the terms *interpretivism* and *noninterpretivism* have become standard words for certain doctrines of constitutional interpretation. Although they have been called "misleading labels," they are unlikely to disappear. Though one might have preferred that the words be *interpretationism* and *noninterpretationism,* the ill-formed versions are probably too well entrenched to be easily uprooted. Cf. **interpretative.**

The so-called *interpretivists* "believe that the Court must confine itself to norms clearly stated or implied in the language of the Constitution," while the *noninterpretivists* "believe that the Court may protect norms not mentioned in the Constitution's text or in its preratification history." Erwin Chemerinsky, *The Price of Asking the Wrong Question,* 62 Tex. L. Rev. 1207, 1208–09 (1984). Cf. **strict construction.**

interregnum. Pl. *-nums, -na.* The English plural (*-ums*) is preferred. See PLURALS (A).

interrogate is a FORMAL WORD for *question;* it suggests formal or rigorous questioning.

interrogatee; interrogee. *W3* lists *interrogee* (= someone interrogated), not *interrogatee,* but the *OED* lists *interrogatee,* not *interrogee.* Since the agent noun is *interrogator,* it makes more sense to prefer the corresponding passive form, *interrogatee.*

interrogation. See **custodial interrogation.**

interrogative; interrogatory, adj.; **interrogational.** *Interrogative* (= of, pertaining to, or of the nature of, questioning; having the form or force of a question [*OED*]). The other forms are NEEDLESS VARIANTS.

interrogatory, n.; **interrogation.** *Interrogatory* = a legal questionnaire submitted to an opposing party as part of pretrial discovery. *Interrogation* = (1) the act or process of questioning in depth; or (2) questioning as a form of discourse.

interrogee. See **interrogatee.**

in terrorem (= as a warning; intimidating) is used in legal JARGON primarily of clauses in wills that threaten to dispossess any beneficiaries who challenge the terms of the will. E.g., "The *in terrorem* clause provides the penalty of forfeiture against anyone who shall contest in any court any of the provisions of this instrument."/ "Whatever else may be said, it is clear that when equity contempt decrees rely upon *in terrorem* fines, or the prospect of compensatory damages for effectiveness, the contention that equity acts in personam is further modified." Justice Frankfurter made literary use of the LATINISM: "[T]here is nothing judicially more unseemly nor more self-defeating than for this Court to make *in terrorem* pronouncements. . . ." *Baker v. Carr,* 369 U.S. 186, 270 (1962) (Frankfurter, J., dissenting). See ITALICS (C).

No-contest clause is often used as an anglicized equivalent of *in terrorem clause* in the context of wills. E.g., "While we find that the appellant cannot take under the provisions of the will by virtue of the *no-contest clause,* the testator cannot rewrite sections 41 and 43 of the Probate Code to prevent appellant from exercising her right to take as an heir."

interrupter; interruptor. The former spelling is preferred. See -ER (A).

inter se (= between or among themselves) is an unjustified LATINISM. "The parties are supposed to have agreed *inter se* [read *among themselves*] that the deed shall not be given in evidence without the attesting witness's being called to depose to the circumstances attending its execution."/ "'Consortium' has come to mean the reciprocal rights and duties of both husband and wife *inter se* [omit *inter se:* it is redundant after *reciprocal* and *both*] resulting from marriage."/ "The Uniform Commercial Code reaffirms from the first the general freedom of the parties to determine their obligations *inter se* [read *between themselves*]." See FORBIDDEN WORDS (A) & LATINISMS.

Inter sese is a variant form of the phrase without any difference in meaning—e.g.: "Many arrangements for economy of expense and for convenience of administration may be made between carriers without subjecting them to liability as partners or as coadventurers either *inter sese* or as to third parties." *Berkey v. Third Ave. Ry. Co.,* 155 N.E. 58, 60 (N.Y. 1926) (per Cardozo, J.)./ "The rights of the co-owners *inter sese* are not determined by the . . . Arkansas statutes . . . ." *U.S. v. National Bank of Commerce,* 726 F.2d 1292, 1295 (8th Cir. 1984).

interspousal (= between spouses) is a relatively recent legal NEOLOGISM, included in neither the *OED* nor *W3.* It probably originated in and is largely confined to AmE—e.g.: "The *interspousal* communication sought to be disclosed appears from the record to have been confidential . . . ." *C.M.D. v. J.R.D.,* 710 S.W.2d 474, 478 (Mo. Ct. App. 1986)./ "She argues that the 'something more' test should be applied only to complaints seeking to modify *interspousal* support provisions in independent separation agreements . . . ." *Ames v. Perry,* 547 N.E.2d 309, 311 (Mass. 1989). See **spousal.**

interstate; intrastate. These adjectives should not be used adverbially, as here: "Organized crime operates *interstate* [read *in interstate commerce* or *across state lines* or *throughout the states*]." See INTER-.

interstitial; intersticial. The former spelling is preferred.

intervener. See **intervenor.**

intervenience. See **intervention.**

intervening cause. See CAUSATION (D).

intervenor; intervener. Although most English-language dictionaries prefer *intervener,* the U.S. Supreme Court (predominantly) and the leading American treatise on federal courts (uniformly) prefer *intervenor.* See Charles A. Wright et al., *Federal Practice and Procedure* § 1902, at 231 n.3 (1986).

English writers—perhaps finding the *SOED* more persuasive authority than the U.S. Supreme Court—tend to use *intervener.* E.g.: "We have suggested that an *intervener* should be required to show that there was an emergency and that he did not act officiously but in the defendant's best interests." Robert Goff & Gareth Jones, *The Law of Restitution* 350 (3d ed. 1986).

intervention; intervenience. The latter is a NEEDLESS VARIANT.

inter vivos, meaning "between living persons," should be spelled as two words. The phrase may either precede or follow the noun it modifies. Traditionally it functions as an adjective following the noun: "The rule of law is well settled that in transactions *inter vivos,* where a party stands in confidential relations to another, if the dominant party receives the benefit during the existence of such relation, the party reposing the confidence may obtain relief."/ "A gift *inter vivos* may be made of land or personal property." See POSTPOSITIVE ADJECTIVES.

In the following specimens, *inter vivos* appears as an adjective preceding the noun: "Employment contracts and employment retirement programs have proved popular for *inter vivos* dispositions."/ "It does not relate to the *inter vivos* gifts to the children, of which Ruth received the greater share; consequently the truth or falsity of the statement stands independently of the history of *inter vivos* donations." Some writers hyphenate this PHRASAL ADJECTIVE—e.g.: "In most states these statutes can be evaded by *inter-vivos* transfers, even deathbed transfers." Thomas L. Shaffer, *The Planning and Drafting of Wills and Trusts* 184 (2d ed. 1979).

Occasionally the phrase is used adverbially—e.g.: "Moreover it could be argued that the control of an owner, in order to be complete, must include not only the power to give *inter vivos* but also the power to provide for devolution after death as a sort of postponed gift." Roscoe Pound, *An Introduction to the Philosophy of Law* 115 (1922; repr. 1975).

***inter vivos* trust; living trust.** These are the terms used to describe trusts created by the settlor during his or her lifetime. *Inter vivos,* though a LATINISM, has been so commonly used as a general adjective (see the preceding entry) as to be unobjectionable in legal writing. Even so, *inter vivos trust,* though once more common than *living trust,* seems to be fading.

intestacy. See **testacy.**

intestate (= a person who dies without a will) is an attributive noun, the adjective *intestate* having appeared several centuries before the noun. *Intestate,* n., frequently follows a possessive proper noun, although literally the usage curiously suggests that the decedent somehow "belonged" to the heir: "David Kling, the present *plaintiff's intestate,* brought this action in his lifetime, claiming damages for an alleged malicious and willful assault."/ "*Plaintiff's intestate* made with the government two contracts in relation to the monitor." See **testate.**

Intestate, adj., is usually used of persons, but sometimes, through HYPALLAGE, of property: "The court's conclusion that under the Hubinger case the surplus income is *intestate* is correct."

in that is commonly used for *because* or *since* in legal prose, often with considerable awkwardness—e.g.: "*In that* [read *Because*] we have overruled appellant's fourth ground of error, we also overrule ground of error number five."/ "A pledge differs from a chattel mortgage *in that* [read *because*] in the pledge the general ownership of the goods remains in the pledgor . . . ." R.A. Brown, *The Law of Personal Property* 622 (1936; repr. 1955).

in the circumstances. See **circumstances.**

in the event of. This phrase, which usually precedes a BURIED VERB, can often be changed to *if*—e.g.: *"In the event of the termination of the Employee's employment* [read *If the Employee's employment terminates*] for any reason, ..." See **event, in the & of** (A).

in the event that is unnecessarily prolix for *if.* And it is poor form in DRAFTING—e.g.: *"In the event that* [read *If*] any patent or patent claim included within the Licensor's patent rights is held invalid in a final decision by a court of competent jurisdiction and last resort, all obligation to pay royalties based on the patent or claim ceases as of the date of the final decision." See **event, in the.**

in the final analysis; in the last analysis. Both are CLICHÉS: *"In the last analysis,* the testator had an absolute right to divert his property from this contestant; he was under no obligation to assign any reason for so doing." These trite expressions only detract from one's prose. One might better simply state the proposition without this tepid lead-in.

in the first instance. See **first instance.**

in the future. See ***in futuro.***

in the midst of. See **amid(st).**

in the last analysis. See **in the final analysis.**

inthral(l). See **enthral(l).**

in the light of is inferior to *in light of,* itself a CLICHÉ.

in the offing. See **offing.**

into. See **in.**

in toto (= completely, entirely, wholly) is a LATINISM expressing such a fundamental notion, and having so many ready English synonyms, that it is seldom if ever justified. E.g., "That material omission *negates the authorization in toto* [read *completely negates the authorization*]."/ "Neither do all the plaintiff's policies, taken *in toto* [read *as a whole*], allow, in this court's opinion, the application of that doctrine to the use of the National YWCA."

intoxilyzer. See **breathalyzer.**

INTRA-. See INTER-.

in transitu is an unjustified LATINISM; the English phrase *in transit* suffices. E.g., "The right of stoppage *in transitu* [read *in transit*] was first recognized and enforced in England in the year 1690."/ "The creditors are entitled to share ratably in the assets of the defendant (except in the coke stopped *in transitu* [read *in transit*])." But many statutes, such as the U.K. Sale of Goods Act, 1979, still bear the phrase.

intrastate. See **interstate.**

intraversion. See **introversion.**

intra vires (= within the powers [of]) is the antonym of, but is not nearly as familiar as, *ultra vires* (q.v.). E.g., "Courts interfere seldom to control such discretion *intra vires* the corporation." *United Copper Sec. Co. v. Amalgamated Copper Co.,* 244 U.S. 261, 263–64 (1917)./ "What we have said, however, only applies when the tort committed is a wrongful way of doing what the corporation has power to do ('*intra vires* tort,' as it is paradoxically called)." O. Hood Phillips, *A First Book of English Law* 281–82 (3d ed. 1955)./ "[T]he sum it spent on *intra vires* functions would fully absorb the sum paid by the banks together with accrued interest." Aviva Golden, *Digest of Trinity Term* (reporting *In re a Company No. 0013734 of 1991*), Fin. Times, 5 Aug. 1992, at 8. See LATINISMS.

intrigue, v.i., = to carry on a plot or secret love affair. It should not be used in formal prose for *interest* or *fascinate,* although this sense has long been usual in informal speech. E.g., "The question presented in appellant's first point of error is an *intriguing* [read *interesting* or *fascinating*] one."

introduce in(to) evidence. Although both forms commonly appear, one is demonstrably superior: because the phrase suggests movement (physical or metaphorical), *into* is the better preposition. E.g., "As the use of the deposition becomes further removed from its introduction *in* [read *into*] evidence, it is more difficult to predict whether a court will tax the expenses associated with a particular deposition."

introductory should never be used in the phrase *be introductory of* (something); one should instead write *introduce.* E.g., "This first section *is introductory of* [read *introduces*] some of the constitutional provisions that constitute part of that framework." See BE-VERBS (B).

As a noun, *introductory* sometimes serves as a chapter title, but it is inferior to *introduction.*

introductory clause; commencement; exordium. In DRAFTING, these are the three names given to the paragraph, placed at the outset of a contract, that gives introductory material. The best of the three phrases is *introductory clause,* and the worst *exordium.* The phrase *introductory clause* applies aptly even if there is more than one sentence. See **clause.**

INTRODUCTORY "IT" AND "THERE." See EXPLETIVES, **it & there is.**

introversion; intraversion. The former is the preferred spelling.

intrust is an obsolete form of *entrust,* q.v.

inundate. So spelled, though it is often misspelled *inn-,* as here: "Lawyers and judges are among those who are *innundated* [read *inundated*] with these media images." Letter of David A. Sharp, 18 Barrister 6 (Winter 1991–1992).

inure; enure. The former is the standard spelling in both legal and nonlegal texts. *Inure* = (1) to take effect, come into use; or (2) to make accustomed to something unpleasant; habituate. Sense (1) is the sense that usually appears in legal contexts: "The rule is well established that whenever a contract between attorney and client *inures* to the benefit or advantage of the attorney the court will not only closely scrutinize but will actually change the ordinary rules of evidence to arrive at a determination."/ "The damages must *inure* to the exclusive benefit of the widow and children." The noun is *inurement.*

Although in sense (2) persons are *inured* to unpleasant things <many battered women, tragically, become inured to violence>, in sense (1) *inure* is used only of positive effects: *inure to the detriment of* is an idiomatic impossibility. The author of the following sentence lacked idiomatic sensibility: "No prejudice has *inured* [read resulted] to the defendant because of any procedural default leading to the suspensions." Sense (2) occasionally appears in legal writing: "The steady parade of human savagery that is presented to us has an *inuring* effect."

Sometimes *inhere* is misused for *inure.* See **inhere (B).**

in utero. See ***en ventre sa mere.***

invade is the metaphor used in the law of trusts to denote withdrawals from an initial or principal investment. E.g., "She had unlimited power to *invade* the corpus of the trust if she so desired."/ "The settlor can authorize the trustee to *invade* the principal or corpus of the trust for the benefit of the wife." See **corpus.**

invalidate; invalid, v.t. In the sense "to nullify," the latter is a NEEDLESS VARIANT seen only in legal writing. E.g., "[W]e turn to the question whether such a meritorious patent is to be *invalided* [read *invalidated*] as held by the court below . . . ." *Seiberling v. John E. Thropp's Sons Co.,* 284 F. 746, 756 (3d Cir. 1922).

inventable; inventible. The former spelling is preferred. See -ABLE (A).

inventory is commonly a verb as well as a noun in legal and business contexts. This use of the word, dating back to the 16th century, is perfectly acceptable—e.g.: "The officer *inventories* the contents of the car."/ "Local police departments generally follow a routine practice of securing and *inventorying* the automobile's contents."/ "While the husband was creating joint tenancies for the benefit of his daughters, he was building up the value of the farm chattels, which were *inventoried* at $22,850.29."

inverse. See **converse.**

INVERSIONS, GRAMMATICAL. Awkward are most, though not all, inversions. They commonly appear in legalistic phrasing—e.g.: "Personally appeared before the undersigned notary public, John Ivan Simon, who . . . ."/ "Came on for consideration the above-referenced civil action." Other standard inversions include *Comes now the plaintiff* and the variant *Now comes the plaintiff,* both of which have recently fallen into disrepute as unnecessary LEGALESE. See **come(s) now.**

The inversions especially to be avoided are those whose existence is attributable to amateurish literary striving. The problem with these is that, "like the atmospheric inversion that is blamed for smog, the inversion of sentences creates a kind of linguistic smog that puts the reader to work sorting out the disarranged elements, causes his eyes to smart, and perhaps makes him wish he were reading something else." Roy H. Copperud, *American Usage and Style* 210 (1980).

What prompts writers to use inversion? Most commonly, they are quite commendably striving to vary the structure of their sentences. But this method often results in sentences that sound insincere and contrived—e.g.: "*Unaffected would be the current status of the defense,* in which the risk is expressly assumed." [Better: "*The current status of the defense,* in which the risk is expressly assumed, *would be unaffected.*"]/ "*Therefore, concludes defendant,* there being no privity of relationship between her and plaintiff, and no fraud or deceit alleged, she has the right to the property." [Better: "There being no privity of relationship between defendant and plaintiff, and no fraud or deceit alleged, *the defendant therefore concludes* that she has the right to the property."]

Some legislative drafters are addicted to minor inversions, such as *notwithstanding anything in this Act contained.* They may be minor inversions, but they cloy immediately, even on the first reading of the first one. In this example, because the word *contained* is superfluous, an acceptable phrasing is *notwithstanding anything in this Act.* See **notwithstanding & notwithstanding anything to the contrary contained herein.**

Often those who use inversion are no better at grammar than they are at style; thus they have problems with number, being unable to distinguish the inverted predicate from the subject: "To judicial bravery and congressional impetus *belong* the credit for large-scale rectification of racial injustices." (Here the verb should be singular—*belongs*—because, without the inversion, the clause reads: The credit for large-scale rectification of racial injustices *belongs* to judicial bravery and congressional impetus.")/ "By the term literature *is* [read *are*] meant those written or printed compositions that preserve the thought and experience of a race recorded in artistic form."

Occasionally inversion is called for idiomatically but is wrongly omitted: "It is much easier to answer this at the end rather than at the beginning, for only after prolonged study *one may* [read *may one*] look back and appreciate the significance of the hornbook definition of equitable jurisprudence."

invest; vest. These words are synonymous in meaning "to establish (a person) in the possession of any office, position, or property; to endow or furnish (a person or institution) with power, authority, or privilege." *Vest* is more usual in general English usage; the use of *invest* in this sense is chiefly confined to legal writing and evangelical preaching <By the power invested in me by the Holy Spirit, I declare that you shall be instantly healed!>.

Not surprisingly, the legal examples have a different tone from the evangelical ones: "By the Constitution of the United States, the President is *invested* with certain important political powers . . . ." *Marbury v. Madison,* 5 U.S. (1 Cranch) 137, 165 (1803)./ "In a proper legal sense, the holder of the legal title is not seised until he is fully *invested* with the possession, actual or constructive."/ "His status as a cabinet officer is not itself sufficient to *invest* him with absolute immunity."/ "Article V, section 5 of the Texas Constitution has *invested* the court of criminal appeals with a mandamus power comparable to that granted the supreme court." See **vest.**

investigable is the proper form—not *investigatable.* See -ATABLE.

investigative; investigatory. *W3* calls *investigatory* "chiefly British," but it occurs almost as commonly as *investigative* does in American legal contexts. E.g., "It is not unreasonably intrusive, courts have often held, for a police officer to aid his own *investigatory* senses with devices that serve only to enhance those senses, such as flashlights and binoculars."/ "These statements involved alleged incompetence and *investigatory* grand jury proceedings."/ "The frisk, it was held, was essential to the proper performance of the officer's *investigatory* duties."

The *COD* lists *investigative* before *-tory,* and it does appear more frequently—e.g.: "The particular interests involved here were the neutralization of danger to the policeman in the *investigative* circumstance and the sanctity of the individual."/ "It was this legitimate *investigative* function that Officer McFadden was discharging when he decided to approach petitioner and his companions."

There is certainly no need for the two variants to coexist. We might be well advised to throw over *investigatory* and stick with *investigative,* or to develop some heretofore unhinted-at DIFFERENTIATION. In any event, the two terms should not be used interchangeably in a single piece of writing, as they are in *Terry v. Ohio,* 392 U.S. 1 (1968). See INELEGANT VARIATION.

invidious. See **insidious.**

in view of. See **in lieu of.**

in view of the fact that is a weak equivalent of *because.*

inviolate; inviolable. The latter suggests that something is incapable of being violated, whereas the former suggests merely that the thing has not been violated. In practice, however, the words are often used interchangeably. *Inviolate* sometimes appears as a POSTPOSITIVE ADJECTIVE. E.g., "The Court weakens, if indeed it does not in fact submerge, this basic principle by finding, in effect, a grant of substantive legislative power in the constitutional provision for a federal court system, and through it, setting up the Federal Rules as a body of law *inviolate.*"

invitation to treat. See **offer** (B).

invite is a verb; it should be avoided as a noun displacing *invitation.*

invitee. Although nonlawyers might assume that an *invitee* is someone expressly invited onto property, lawyers use the term to include those who have implied permission to enter the premises, such as postal and delivery workers.

inviter; invitor. The former is preferred. See -ER (A).

invoke. See **evoke.**

involuntary. An *involuntary* act, as Jeremy Bentham phrased it, is an act "in the performance of which the will has no sort of share: such as the contraction of the heart and arteries." *An Introduction to the Principles of Morals and Legislation* 83–84 n.1 (1823 ed.; repr. 1948). For the unusual meaning attributed to the word in the phrase *involuntary manslaughter,* see **manslaughter (A).** For the distinction between *involuntary* and *unintentional,* see **unintentional.**

in whole; in part. Follett wrote that *in whole* is unidiomatic for *as a whole,* the former phrase having been created as a needed parallel of *in part.* He was wrong, unless we want to trace what is idiomatic back before the sixteenth century and ignore steady uses up till the present time. Both *in whole* and *as a whole* are acceptable idioms; indeed, they are not even used in quite the same way. Both mean "as a complete thing," but, whereas *as a whole* is the general phrase, *in whole* is always used as a correlative of *in part.* E.g., "In one form a statute may create a new right, while neglecting *in whole* or *in part* the matter of the remedy."

in witness whereof (= signed), one of the quintessential LEGALISMS, is the phrase that introduces the testimonium clause in a legal document. E.g., "An appropriate testimonium or concluding clause is '*In witness whereof* I have subscribed my name this —— day of 19—,' although 'Witness my signature this —— day of 19—' will do just as well." Thomas E. Atkinson, *Handbook of the Law of Wills* 820 (2d ed. 1953). See **testimonium clause & attestation clause.**

I personally is prolix for a simple *I.* Occasionally it is legitimately used to contrast one's personal opinions with an official stance that one takes for reasons of a position one holds. See FIRST PERSON.

ipse dixit (lit., "he himself said it") = something said but not proved; a dogmatic statement. E.g., "The realm of procedure is after all the judge's special domain; the construction of statutes is a peculiarly judicial art; and the Court's *ipse dixit* seems more authoritative in these areas than it might if substantive issues of policy were being decided." Robert G. McCloskey, *The American Supreme Court* 204 (1960). Cf. ***probatum.*** See **dictum (B).**

ipsissima verba = the very (same) words. E.g., "So far as possible, I have tried to preserve the *ipsissima verba* of the original author . . . ." P.B. Fairest, Foreword to Edward Jenks, *The Book of English Law* xiv (P.B. Fairest ed., 6th ed. 1967).

Another form of the phrase, *ipsissimis verbis,* means "*in* the very (same) words." In the following example, though, the Supreme Court mangled its Latin with a meaningless phrase, *ipsissima verbis:* "The record does not purport to give *ipsissima verbis* [read *ipsissimis verbis* or *verbatim*] the form of the oath administered to the jurors." *Baldwin v. Kansas,* 129 U.S. 52, 55 (1889).

The phrases are easily simplified—e.g.: "Now Texas has hastened to fall into line, and has enacted this North Dakota resolve *ipsissimis verbis* [read *in the very same words* or *verbatim*]" (ex. fr. G. Krapp, *A Comprehensive Guide to Good English* 334 (1927)). Cf. ***in haec verba.*** See **verbatim** & LATINISMS.

ipso facto (= by the fact or act itself; by its very nature) is sometimes replaceable by the phrase *in itself*—e.g.: "Lunacy does not *ipso facto* [read *in itself*] dissolve a partnership unless the articles so provide . . . ." 2 E.W. Chance, *Principles of Mercantile Law* 9 (1951). But the LATINISM sometimes seems useful—e.g.: "The court said that the statute was against common right and Magna Carta and *ipso facto* void." Roscoe Pound, *The Development of Constitutional Guarantees of Liberty* 101 (1957). The phrase need not be italicized.

I respectfully submit. It is as easy for an advocate to hedge too much as it is to pound too hard. Some lawyers, arguing a position, use *I respectfully submit* as a verbal tic—even when the statement that follows is quite uncontroversial. The result is an undesirable, namby-pamby tone. See **respectfully.**

ironic(al). *Ironic* is standard, *ironical* being a NEEDLESS VARIANT.

IRONY is the use of words whose literal and figurative senses are opposites—that is, it is the difference between what seems to be said and what is meant. The chief weapon of satirists, irony subverts the reader's expectations.

A word of warning: "[M]ost attempts by legal writers to employ irony . . . range from ill-advised to pathetic." Jordan H. Leibman & James P. White, *How the Student-Edited Law Journals Make Their Publication Decisions,* 39 J. Legal Educ. 387, 423 (1989). But the warning should not deter unduly. As the following examples illustrate, irony can be an effective rhetorical tool:

- "[T]he only thing about the appeals [that] we can commend is the hardihood in supposing that they could possibly succeed." *U.S. v. Minneci,* 142 F.2d 428, 429 (2d Cir. 1944) (per L. Hand, J.).
- "Ownership meant no more to [the Shoshone Indians] than to roam the land as a great common, and to possess and enjoy it in the same way that they possessed and enjoyed sunlight and the west wind and the feel of spring in the air. Acquisitiveness, which develops a law of real property, is an accomplishment only of the 'civilized.'" *Northwestern Bands of Shoshone Indians v. U.S.,* 324 U.S. 335, 357 (1945) (Jackson, J., concurring).
- "I cannot say that I know much about the law, having been far more interested in justice." William Temple, the former Archbishop of Canterbury, as quoted in Lord Denning, *The Road to Justice* 1 (1955).
- "[W]e hold that the first amendment does not clothe these plaintiffs with a constitutional right to sunbathe in the nude . . . . They remain able to advocate the benefits of nude sunbathing, albeit while fully dressed." *South Florida Free Beaches, Inc. v. Miami,* 734 F.2d 608, 610 (11th Cir. 1984) (per Henderson, J.).

One of the most common types of irony is the Swiftian modest proposal, here carried out with some success: "Of course, a simple mechanism for deterring violations such as [police brutality] would be to amend section 1983 to provide that violators will be drawn and quartered. This seems like a very powerful deterrent and might substantially reduce violations of federal rights under color of state law. Aside from problems relating to fairness, however, this solution also poses problems in the deterrence framework. A powerful deterrent such as drawing and quartering offenders might also deter worthwhile conduct [by the police]. . . . So, the deterrence rationale calls for neither too much nor too little deterrence; we need to find the right amount." *Dobson v. Camden,* 705 F.2d 759, 765 (5th Cir. 1983) (per Goldberg, J.).

irrebuttable; irrefutable. See **rebut.**

irrefragable (= unanswerable; not to be controverted), a useful term in the law, is underused today—so much so that its pronunciation has caused problems even in the Old Country: "In 1955 leading counsel pronounced it [*/ir-i-**frag**-ə-bəl/*], but Harman J. asserted that it was [*/ir-i-**fray**-gə-bəl/*]; and thus it was for the rest of the case. However, on appeal (on another point) one of the juniors invoked the *Oxford English Dictionary,* and his leader persuaded a reluctant and suspicious Court of Appeal to shift the accent from the third syllable to the second, and pronounce the word [*/i-**ref**-rə-gə-bəl/*]." R.E. Megarry, *A Second Miscellany-at-Law* 164 (1973). Only Harman J. got it entirely wrong, both of the other pronunciations being acceptable (and the last one given being preferred).

irrefutable. See **rebut.**

irregardless, a semiliterate PORTMANTEAU WORD from *irrespective* and *regardless,* should long ago have been stamped out. *Irregardless* is common enough in speech in the U.S. that it has found its way into judicial opinions. See, e.g., *State ex rel. Fisher v. McKinney,* 85 N.E.2d 562, 563 (Ohio Ct. App. 1949).

On the second day of the U.S. Supreme Court's 1986–1987 term, Chief Justice Rehnquist upbraided a lawyer who used *irregardless,* saying: "I feel bound to inform you there is no word *irregardless* in the English language. The word is *regardless.*" Linguistic fastidiousness is no less important in oral than in written argument.

In American legal writing, most of the published examples of *irregardless* appear in quoted testimony, in which the word is followed by "[*sic*]" in three of every four instances. Of the handful of published examples that originated in a federal judge's writing—as opposed to originating as oral statements that are later quoted—a third appear in a single Illinois judge's opinions.

Although this widely scorned word seems unlikely to spread and flourish, careful users of language must continually stamp on it when they encounter it.

irrelevance; irrelevancy. The former is generally preferred. The only plural form, however, is *irrelevancies.* See **relevance.**

irreparable is pronounced */i-**rep**-ə-rə-bəl/.*

irreparable injury is a phrase that "generally produces more dust than light." *Studebaker Corp. v. Gittlin,* 360 F.2d 692, 698 (2d Cir. 1966). Often misunderstood, *irreparable injury* means merely that the injury cannot be remedied through an award of damages. As Douglas Laycock has convincingly shown, "That an injury has little monetary value is often a cause of irreparability, not an antidote." *The Death of the Irreparable Injury Rule* 74 (1991).

irreplevi(s)able. See **repleviable.**

irrespective of = regardless of. E.g., "It is true that the author is the owner of the composition as property *irrespective of* its value." William F. Walsh, *A Treatise on Equity* 217 (1930).

Confusion of the words *irrespective* and *regardless* has given rise to the mistaken form *irregardless,* q.v.

irresponsive. See **unresponsive.**

irrevocable; unrevokable. The former is preferred. It is pronounced */i-**rev**-ə-kə-bəl/.*

is comprised of. See **compose (A).**

-ISE. See -IZE.

is entitled to. See WORDS OF AUTHORITY (G).

isle (= island) for *aisle* (= a passage for foot traffic) results from mistaking homophones—e.g.: "[A]s she was walking down one of the *isles* [read *aisles*] in the store she slipped on a potato sprout near the potato bin and fell . . . ." *Houtchens v. Kyle's Grocery Corp.,* 390 S.W.2d 325, 326 (Tex. Civ. App.—Eastland 1965).

isolable, not *isolatable,* is the correct form. E.g., "We do not believe the events are so easily *isolable.*" *U.S. v. Jeffers,* 342 U.S. 48, 52 (1951)./ "The State . . . bas[es] its position on the fact that the petitioner has established no *isolatable* [read *isolable*] prejudice . . . ." *Estes v. Texas,* 381 U.S. 532, 542 (1965). See -ATABLE.

The word is pronounced */**ɪ**-sə-lə-bəl/.*

issuable. In nonlegal contexts this word means "capable of being issued"—and sometimes in legal writing as well. E.g., "It is fair to say that though the writ of habeas corpus was *issuable* at common law its present form in England has had its origin in the Act of 1679." C. Gordon Post, *An Introduction to the Law* 60 (1963).

The word carries a special legal sense, however: "that admits of an issue being taken; in regard to which or during which issue may be joined" (*OED*). E.g., "No *issuable* fact or condition existed that would authorize the governing board to exercise the discretion confided to it in the passage of that part of the zoning ordinance under attack."

issuance. See **issue (C).**

issue. A. *At issue; in issue.* *At issue* is the common idiomatic phrase, whereas *in issue* is purely a specialized legal phrase. *At issue* = (1) (of people) in controversy; taking opposite sides of a case or contrary views of a matter; at variance <his views are at issue with mine>; (2) (of matters or questions) in dispute; under discussion; in question <the allegations at issue> (*OED*). The *OED* notes that *in issue* shares sense (2) of *at issue,* but calls it rare.

Having originated in mid-19th-century legal contexts, *in issue* is not at all rare today—e.g.: "In the law of evidence, facts *in issue* are either: (1) facts that, in the pleadings, are affirmed on one side and denied on the other; or (2) in actions without pleadings, all facts from the establishment of which would follow the existence, nonexistence, nature, or extent of any right, liability, disability, or immunity asserted or denied in the case." (Eng.)/ "Roman law confined to the judge, when questions of law were *in issue,* the purely mechanical task of counting and of determining the numerical preponderance of authority."/ "The test to be applied in passing on the validity of a gift such as the one *in issue* is that of reasonableness."

B. *Issue as to whether; issue of whether.* These phrases are prolix for *issue whether.* Cf. **question (as to) whether.** See **as to (A).**

C. *Issue* and *issuance.* *Issuance* was not used until the mid-nineteenth century, up until which time *issue* was the noun corresponding to the verb *to issue.* E.g., "These lawyers reported that not only was there a strong current of precedent during the last century for the *issue* of such injunctions, but the common-law judges had themselves advised parties to apply to the Chancery." (Eng.) A nonlawyer in the U.S. today would think *issuance* to have been an apter term in the sentence quoted.

D. *Join issue.* This phrase may mean: (1) "to submit an issue jointly for decision"; (2) "to accept or adopt a disputed point as the basis of argument in a controversy"; or (3) "to take up the opposite side of a case, or a contrary view *on* a question" (*OED*). The idiom is more common in BrE than in AmE.

The nominal phrase is *joinder of issue.* E.g., "After *joinder of issue,* defendant moved for summary judgment." *Bradley v. Burroughs Wellcome Co.,* 497 N.Y.S.2d 401, 402 (N.Y. App. Div. 1986).

E. In the Sense of "Offspring" or "Descendants." In the drafting of wills and trusts, the word *issue* invites litigation. English courts—as well as courts in New York and New Jersey—have held that it means all lineal descendants, however remote. Other courts have held that the word refers only to children and not to descendants more remote. And whether it covers adopted children is a question that courts will answer differently. See *In re Upjohn's Will,* 107 N.E.2d 492, 495 (N.Y. 1952). In sum, the word is best avoided altogether.

But if it is not to be avoided, it ought to be used grammatically. The question sometimes arises whether the word should be treated as a singular or as a plural noun. The answer is either—e.g.: "Any *issue who is a minor* [or *issue who are minors*] will be treated as if. . . ." See **die without issue.**

F. *General issue; special issue.* See **general issue.**

issue estoppel. See **issue preclusion** & **collateral estoppel** (A).

ISSUE-FRAMING. **A. Generally.** There is no more important point in persuasive and analytical writings—and certainly no point that is more commonly bungled—than framing the issue. If you have clearly in mind what question you're addressing, the writing will inevitably be much clearer than it otherwise would be.

That may sound obvious, but in fact very few legal writers frame their issues well. As a result, legal memos and briefs are often diffuse, repetitive, and poorly organized. Sometimes—even to the reader who works hard to find out—memos and briefs do not reveal precisely what question they purport to answer. When confronting such writing, the reader works impatiently to find the point—the gist—the upshot.

Any piece of persuasive or analytical writing must deliver three things: the question, the answer, and the reasons for that answer. The better the writing, the more clearly and quickly those things are delivered. The legal stylist should probably insist that the writing lead the reader to have those things well in mind within 60 seconds of picking up the document, whether it is a brief, an analytical memo, or a judicial opinion.

To do this consistently, open the discussion with a factually specific issue that captures the essence of the problem. The issue should be brief—no more than 75 words—and should be phrased in separate sentences. The format is generally as follows: statement, statement, question. Or, phrased differently: premise, premise, conclusion (followed by a question mark).

Although few legal writers have mastered this technique, it is old. Consider the following issue, framed in 1835:

> A Turk, having three wives, to whom he was lawfully married, according to the laws of his own country, and three sons, one by each wife, comes to Philadelphia with his family, and dies, leaving his three wives and three sons alive, and also real property in this State to a large amount. Will it go to the three children equally, under the intestate law of Pennsylvania? [67 words]
>
> *Conflict of Laws,* 14 Am. Jurist 275, 275 (1835).

Anyone of moderate legal sophistication can understand that question. And most readers, having seen the question, would probably like to know the answer.

But six American lawyers in ten would probably build up to the question with at least two pages of facts explaining how the Turk came to the U.S., when and where the marriages were solemnized, what the names and birthdates of each of the sons are, and so on. In other words, those six writers would engage in a badly overparticularized statement of facts—a statement that would leave many readers bewildered about the upshot of it all. See OVERPARTICULARIZATION.

Three more of the ten would probably assume that the intended reader knows the facts and therefore dispense with them altogether. The so-called "issue" in an analytical memo would read something like this: "Is our client entitled to take one-third under Pennsylvania law?" Then the writing would launch into a legal discussion of the intestacy laws. Never mind that the intended reader and the writer do not have an identical understanding of the facts—a point that will likely never emerge if the memo is written in this way. Further, any other reader will remain none the wiser even after reading the entire memo, which as a result can never be useful in future research.

Perhaps the one remaining lawyer of the ten would write an issue more nearly resembling the 1835 version than either the overparticularized or the overvague approach, but perhaps not one in a hundred would frame it with equal brevity and clarity.

B. Deep vs. Surface Issues. A "deep" issue is concrete: it sums up the case in a nutshell—and is therefore difficult to frame but easy to understand. A "surface" issue is abstract: it requires the reader to know everything about the case before it can be truly comprehended—and is therefore easy to frame but hard to understand.

Assume that a defendant is moving for summary judgment. Which of the following statements is more helpful?

1. Can Jones maintain an action for fraud?
2. To maintain a cause of action for fraud under California law, a plaintiff must show that the defendant made a false representation. In his deposition, Jones concedes that neither Continental nor its agents or employees made a false representation. Is Continental entitled to

summary judgment on Jones's fraud claim? [49 words]

The longer version asks the reader to do considerably less work. The shorter version sends the reader elsewhere to learn what, precisely, the issue is. Whereas the surface issue says next to nothing about what the court is being asked to decide, the deep issue explains precisely what that something is. To put it differently, the surface issue does not disclose the decisional premises; the deep issue makes them explicit.

The goal is ease of understanding. One way to analyze the difference between a deep issue and a surface issue is to focus on the level of abstraction. Generally speaking, the more abstract an issue is, the more superficial it is: the reader must learn that much more to make any sense of it. The more concrete the issue is, the deeper it is: the reader need hardly exercise the brain to understand.

C. Persuasive vs. Analytical Issues. Unlike the deep-vs.-surface dichotomy, this split is not a matter of good and bad: writing that aims to persuade must have persuasive issues, whereas writing that seeks to analyze in an objective way must have analytical issues. Persuasive issues answer themselves; analytical issues are open-ended.

Karl Llewellyn, one of the great legal thinkers and writers of the 20th century, well understood the importance of a persuasive issue in effective advocacy: "The first art is framing the issue so that if your framing is accepted the case comes out your way. Got that? Second, you have to capture the issue, because your opponent will be framing an issue very differently . . . . And third, you have to build a technique of phrasing your issue which not only will help you capture the Court but which will stick your capture into the Court's head so that it can't forget it." *A Lecture on Appellate Advocacy,* 29 U. Chi. L. Rev. 627, 630 (1962).

Llewellyn's initial point is the most powerful: the *first* art is framing the issue so that, if your framing is accepted, you win. The persuasive issue, then, can have only one answer. Still, it is far more persuasive than a mere statement of the conclusion. The advocate comes forward simply asking the court to address a straightforward question—e.g.:

- "Texas law provides that a lease predating a lien is not affected in foreclosure. Nelson's lease predates Marshall's lien, on which Marshall judicially foreclosed last month. Was Nelson's lease affected by the foreclosure?" [33 words]
- "Liability-insurance coverage for directors and officers of financial institutions is universally required to recruit well-qualified directors and officers. When the Trew Group acquired First Eastern from the FDIC in 1987, the FDIC agree to pay the 'reasonable and necessary' operating costs of First Eastern. Is the FDIC obligated to pay the cost of directors' and officers' liability insurance for First Eastern?" [62 words]
- "On dozens of occasions over the course of a decade, United Peoria hired and paid a waste-hauler to haul its hazardous liquid waste to a landfill. In accordance with United Peoria's instructions, the hauler discharged thousands of gallons of United Peoria's waste into the landfill. Were these discharges an 'accident' from United Peoria's point of view?" [57 words]
- "Boskey Insurance issued an excess-insurance policy to BEC for liability exceeding $100,000. BEC represented to Boskey that it had purchased primary coverage for the first $100,000 of liability from Cooper Insurance. If Cooper becomes insolvent, should Boskey be required to step down and provide primary coverage when it never bargained for a role as—or contracted to be—a primary insurer, and when its premium reflected only the risk taken as an excess insurer?" [75 words]

As in the first two examples, an issue often proceeds from the law to the facts. Yet, as in the third and fourth examples, it may nearly as often proceed from the facts to the law. The only key to organizing the statements is to allow the whole to be readily absorbed—and this usually means putting the most easily comprehensible part in the middle of the issue.

These same characteristics hold true with analytical issues, but unlike persuasive ones, they are open-ended. The reader doesn't know the answer upon reading the question, but probably yearns to—e.g.:

- "Section 273 of the Immigration Act makes it a crime to bring an undocumented alien to the U.S. Meanwhile, section 2304 of the Maritime Act makes it a crime for the master of a vessel to fail to rescue persons aboard a vessel in distress. Does a master commit a crime under the Immigration Act when he rescues illegal aliens aboard a ship in distress and brings them to the U.S.? If so, what are his defenses?" [75 words]
- "Mr. and Mrs. Zephyr were killed in the crash of an airplane negligently piloted by Mr. Zephyr. Their daughter, Kate, has sued the estate of her deceased father for the wrongful death of her mother. Does the doctrine of interspousal immunity bar Kate's recovery when there is no marital harmony to preserve?" [52 words]
- "A six-year-old plaintiff rode his bicycle in front of our client's truck before being struck by the

truck. Is the six-year-old capable of contributory negligence?" [29 words]

- "In Massachusetts, a dead body is the property of the decedent's family members. As a result, the authority to order an autopsy generally rests with the relatives. In what circumstances is that authority transferred from the family to the medical examiner?" [41 words]

In an analytical memo, such an issue should be followed immediately by a brief answer (with reasons embedded in the answer), so that the question and the answer amount to something resembling an executive summary: the reader understands the gist of the memo merely by reading the first few lines.

D. Readers' Reactions. The purpose of using separate sentences and of limiting the issue to 75 words is to help the reader. A one-sentence issue of 75 or so words is difficult to follow, especially when the interrogative word begins the sentence and the end is merely a succession of *when*-clauses—e.g.:

> Can Barndt Insurance deny insurance coverage on grounds of late notice when Fiver's insurance policy required Fiver to give Barndt notice of a claim "immediately," and when in May 1994, one of Fiver's offices was damaged by smoke from a fire in another tenant's space, and when 10 months later, Fiver gave notice, and when Barndt investigated the claim for 6 months before denying coverage and did not raise a late-notice defense until 18 months after the claim was filed? [81 words]

That is a muddle. Readers forget the question by the time they reach the question mark. Part of the reason is that the time is out of joint: we begin with a present question, then back up to what happened, and then, with the question mark, jump back to the present.

The better strategy is to follow a more or less chronological order, telling a story in miniature. Then, the pointed question—which emerges inevitably from the story—comes at the end:

> Fiver's insurance policy required it to give Barndt Insurance notice of a claim "immediately." In May 1994, one of Fiver's offices was damaged by smoke from a fire in another tenant's space. Ten months later, Fiver gave notice. Barndt investigated the claim for 6 months before denying coverage and did not raise a late-notice claim until 18 months after the claim was filed. Can Barndt now deny coverage because of late notice? [73 words]

Instead of one 81-word-long sentence, we have five sentences with an average length of 15 words. (See SENTENCE LENGTH.) And the information is presented in a way that readers can easily understand.

Because seasoned legal readers are always impatient to reach the issue, the practice of opening a memo, brief, or judicial opinion with the deep issue always satisfies a need that readers feel.

But is the 75-word limit a fair one? Where does it come from? It is the rare case indeed—in fact, I have yet to encounter it—in which issues cannot be framed in 75 words. The 75-word limit is the result of experimentation and informal testing: once an issue goes beyond that length, it is likely to be rambling. You lose the rigor of a concentrated statement. And you probably lose some readers.

It is no accident that the most readable judicial opinions invariably begin with a brief statement of the overarching issue in the case. Among the ablest practitioners of this art was Judge Thomas Gibbs Gee, of the Fifth Circuit, who enshrined it as the first principle in his style sheet for opinions: "Try to state the principal question in the first sentence." *A Few of Wisdom's Idiosyncrasies and a Few of Ignorance's: A Judicial Style Sheet,* 1 Scribes J. Legal Writing 55, 56 (1990).

E. The Importance of It All. These principles of issue-framing may seem elementary at first glance. Yet, judging from most legal writing, they are not at all obvious. And, in any event, stylists who cultivate the ability to frame good issues know just how difficult it is: it requires a great deal of mental energy.

It is therefore easy to forgo the effort, and many writers do. Legal writers everywhere seem preoccupied with answers—with conclusions—and rarely with the questions they are answering, or the premises from which their conclusions might follow. As a result, much of the "analysis" and advocacy that goes on is sloppy, or worse.

Even the greatest legal intellects must remain vigilant about these points. One of the most important 20th-century legal philosophers warned about how easy it is to stumble over fundamentals: "One principal source of trouble is obvious: it is always necessary to bear in mind, and fatally easy to forget, the number of different questions about punishment which theories of punishment ambitiously seek to answer." H.L.A. Hart, "Postscript: Responsibility and Retribution," in *Punishment and Responsibility: Essays in the Philosophy of Law* 210, 231 (1968).

issue preclusion (AmE) = *issue estoppel* (BrE). See **collateral estoppel** (A) & **claim preclusion.**

is when; is where. These locutions are improper means of introducing a definition. Instead of writing, "'Livery of seisin' *is where* the grantor delivers possession," one should write, "'Livery of seisin' *is* the grantor's delivery of possession." Examples of ill-phrased definitions abound in legal writing: "*A bill of exchange is when a person takes money* in one country or city upon exchange, and draws a bill whereby he directs another person in another country or city to pay so much to A on order for value received of B and subscribes it." (Eng.) The idea of defining is here misplaced. [Read *"With a bill of exchange, one takes money . . . ."*] See **where (C)** & DEFINITIONS (C).

it. A. Overuse. This expletive and pronoun often appears too many times in one sentence. Careful writers restrict it (*it,* that is) to one meaning in a given sentence—no more. And still one must be vigilant about whether the antecedent is the closest noun—e.g.:

- "Within such a unitary jurisdictional framework, the appellate court will, of course, require the trial court to conform to constitutional mandates, but *it* [read *the appellate court*] may likewise require *it* [read *the trial court*] to follow procedures deemed desirable from the viewpoint of sound judicial practice."
- "Applying the test of an apportionable or apportioned consideration to the contract in question, *it will be seen* [read *one will see*] at once that *it* [read *such consideration*] is severable."
- "*It is here that* [Read *Here*] the advantage of an absolute sovereign is most apparent, for *it* [read *the sovereign*] makes it possible for immediate effect to be given to the will of the people." H.G. Hanbury, *English Courts of Law* 20 (2d ed. 1953).
- "For *it* is often this sovereign power which gives to the jury *its* place in the constitution. Bereft of *it* [read *the power*], *it* [read *the criminal jury*] will become an expensive and unwieldy fact-finding tribunal which sooner or later will go the way of the civil jury." Patrick Devlin, *The Judge* 145 (1979).

Sometimes a single *it* may be problematic in having no identifiable antecedent: "Paraphrasing the opinion of Judge Vann in *Tabor v. Hoffman,* because an inspection of plaintiff's models may be by fair means, *it* [?] does not justify obtaining the same by unfair means." See ANTECEDENTS, FALSE (A), EXPLETIVES (A) & DANGLERS.

B. Referring to a Person. Although a young baby is often referred to as an *it,* other persons should not be, and especially not judges—e.g.: "In this case an experienced and careful district judge heard and reviewed the quantitative apportionment testimony and exhibits in this case, and *it* [read *he*—i.e., Lucius D. Bunton III] possessed opportunities to assess their convincingness far superior to those of this (appellate) court." *In re Bell Petroleum Servs., Inc.,* 3 F.3d 889, 911 (5th Cir. 1993).

Even in reference to an older child, the word *it* seems inappropriately dehumanizing: "To begin with it was held that a child could not be guilty of crime unless *it* [read *he or she*] had reached the age of twelve." J.W. Cecil Turner, *Kenny's Outlines of Criminal Law* 66 (1952). Perhaps a preferable edit—to avoid *he or she*—would be simply to write *could not be guilty of crime before the age of twelve.* See **he or she.**

ITALICS. A. Generally. Fowler's shot across the bow is worth heeding: "To those who, however competent on their special subject, have not had enough experience of writing to have learnt [the] rudiments, it comes as natural to italicize every tenth sentence or so as it comes to the letter-writing schoolgirl to underline whatever she enjoys recording" (*MEU1* 304).

How does one avoid overitalicizing? First, if the italicized words appear in quotations, try making the quoted passage shorter. Second, if the italicized words are one's own, try rearranging the sentence so that the italicized words appear at the end. Third, try the deliberate repetition characterizing any one of several rhetorical devices. (See *The Elements of Legal Style* 165–72 (1991).)

Ralph Waldo Emerson overstated the case: "'Tis a good rule of rhetoric [that] Schlegel gives—'In good prose, every word is underscored,' which, I suppose, means, Never italicize." "Lectures and Biographical Sketches," in 10 *Complete Works of Emerson* 169 (1904). By parity of reasoning, of course, one might say we should abolish question marks, exclamation points, and even commas. The point is to italicize only when one *must.*

B. Foreign Phrases. Anglicized terms of foreign origin appear in roman—i.e., nonitalic—type (e.g., bonus). Unnaturalized terms are italicized. Throughout this dictionary, the fuzzy line between naturalized and unnaturalized foreignisms is drawn through the headwords, which appear in either italic or nonitalic boldface type. See GALLICISMS & LATINISMS.

C. Latin Phrases Beginning with *in*. Some writers italicize only *flagrante delicto, forma pauperis, loco parentis, pari materia, statu quo,* and *terrorem.* But the word *in,* which is a part of each of these Latin phrases, ought to be italicized as well.

itemization is often unnecessary for *list,* q.v.

iterate. See **reiterate.**

it is I; it is me. In formal English, *it is I* is the preferred expression, *it is me* being passable in the speech of most persons (less commonly in writing).

E.B. White told an amusing story about the fear that so many writers have of making a mistake:

"One time a newspaper sent us to a morgue to get a story on a woman whose body was being held for identification. A man believed to be her husband was brought in. Somebody pulled the sheet back; the man took one agonizing look, and cried, 'My God, it's her!' When we reported this grim incident, the editor diligently changed it to 'My God, it's she!'" E.B. White, "English Usage," in *The Second Tree from the Corner* 150, 150–51 (1954). See NOMINATIVE AND OBJECTIVE CASES.

it is important to note that; it is interesting to note that. These sentence-nonstarters merely gather lint. They should be abolished.

it is me. See **it is I.**

it is plain that. See **clearly & obviously.**

it is submitted that. This phrase is an especially weak sentence-opener, usually a face-saving mannerism to avoid saying *I think.*

its; it's. The possessive form of *it* is *its;* the contraction for *it is* is *it's.*

it's me. See **it is I.**

it was held that. See **hold (C).**

iudex. See **judex.**

ius. See ***jus.***

-IZE, -ISE. **A. Verbs Ending in *-ize.*** Adding the suffix *-ize* to an adjective or noun is one of the most frequently used means of forming new verbs. Many verbs so formed are objectionable. In AmE, *-ize* is more usual than in BrE, in which *-ise* is more common. But even in BrE, *-ize* is preferred to *-ise* in words in which either form of the suffix may appear. The possibility of choice between *-ise* and *-ize* arises only with words ending with the pronounciation *"eyes,"* not with that of *"ice," "iss,"* or *"eez."* For example, in *precise,* the suffix is pronounced *"ice,"* not *"eyes"*; in *promise* it is pronounced *"iss,"* not *"eyes"*; and in *expertise* it is pronounced *"eez."*

Generally, *-ize* verbs are formed on familiar English words or stems—e.g.: *authorize, familiarize, symbolize;* or with a slight alteration to the stem—e.g.: *agonize, dogmatize, sterilize.* A few words have no such immediate stem: *aggrandize* (cf. *aggrandizement*), *appetize* (cf. *appetite*), *baptize* (cf. *baptism*), *catechize* (cf. *catechism*), *recognize* (cf. *recognition*), and *capsize.*

NEOLOGISMS in *-ize* are generally to be discouraged, for they are invariably ungainly and often superfluous. Thus we have no use for *accessorize, artificialize, cubiclize, fenderize* (= to fix a dented fender), *funeralize, ghettoize, Mirandize* (q.v.), *nakedize,* and so on. The law has many of its own curiosities in *-ize* (e.g., *privatize, collateralize, communitize, Lochnerize*), and probably needs no more. Careful writers are wary of new words formed with this suffix.

B. Verbs Ending in *-ise.* Verbs that correspond to nouns having *-is-* as a part of the stem (e.g., in the syllables *-vis-, -cis-, -mis-*), or that are identical with a noun in *-ise,* similarly take *-ise* rather than *-ize* (from which they are precluded). Some of the common verbs in *-ise* are:

advertise	despise	merchandise
advise	disfranchise	premise
apprise	disguise	prise (open)
arise	enfranchise	revise
chastise	enterprise	supervise
circumcise	excise	surmise
comprise	exercise	surprise
compromise	improvise	televise
demise	incise	

J

J. is the abbreviation for *Judge* or *Justice.* In American legal writing, one commonly sees references such as *Scalia, J., dissenting.* In British legal writing, no comma is used, even in midtext: "The policy reason advanced by La Forest J. seems to me to be quite inadequate to support his rule of irrecoverability. As Wilson J. pointed out, the idea of fiscal disruption hardly seems sufficient to cast the burden of governmental error on the innocent taxpayer." Peter W. Hogg, *Liability of the Crown* 184 (2d ed. 1989). The plural is *JJ.*

jackleg lawyer. See LAWYERS, DEROGATORY NAMES FOR (A).

jactation; jactitation. *Jactation,* lit. "a tossing or swinging of the body to and fro" (*OED*), came figuratively to mean (in both Latin and English) "boasting, bragging, ostentatious display" (*OED*). It is a learned word.

Its sibling *jactitation* derives from the same Latin verb and also has the sense "a boastful declaration." In law the term has been applied specifically to boasts of marriage. Today *jactitation of marriage* = a false assertion that one is married to someone to whom one is not in fact married (*CDL*). E.g., "A decree in a suit of *jactitation* of marriage, forbidding C to claim to be the husband of A, on the ground that he was not her husband, is deemed to be irrelevant." (Eng.)/ "This is an action in *jactitation* instituted by the eleven named plaintiffs who prayed that defendant be ordered to disclaim title to the property described in plaintiffs' petition . . . ." *Holmes v. Wyatt Lumber Co.,* 104 So. 2d 293, 293 (La. Ct. App. 1958).

jail delivery, in AmE, means "an escape by several prisoners from a jail"; in BrE, the phrase (spelled *gaol delivery*) means "the bringing of prisoners to trial."

jailhouse lawyer. See LAWYERS, DEROGATORY NAMES FOR (B).

Jane Doe. See **Doe, John.**

JANUS-FACED TERMS. Janus is an ancient Italian deity, the god of thresholds such as doorways, gates, and even (by figurative extension) the month of January. He is depicted with two faces—one on each side of the head. Hence "Janus-faced terms" are, because of syntactic construction, overburdened in being asked to look backward and forward simultaneously. (They sometimes look forward at two different objects, or backward.) As here defined, a word so called upon can properly look one way, but not both.

Commonly known as ZEUGMA, this fault of writing occurs when a verb is incorrectly associated with two subjects or objects, an adjective with two nouns, or a noun with an antecedent and a consequent that are different. Some specimens follow, with short explanations of the problems.

A. Simultaneously Referring to the Case Name and the Name of the Person. "It is now doubtful whether McCardle (the defendant) would now be sustained," in which the writer means the opinion with the short-title form *McCardle,* though the parenthesis refers to the person. Another such example would be: "Shakespeare's powers were perhaps greatest in *Hamlet,* the most famous of tragedic protagonists," in which the writer is unconsciously referring to the character and the play at the same time. Following is a sentence that avoids the problem just illustrated: "The *Roskos* court found that the plaintiff, Roskos, was coerced into resignation."

B. Pronoun Used Also as an Expletive. "When Mr. Crick writes about the nature and origin of life, it is always prudent and often a delight to pay attention." *Is There Life Elsewhere, and Did It Come Here?* N.Y. Times, 29 Nov. 1981, at 7-1. In this sentence, *it* first appears to refer to Crick's writing (though it has no clear antecedent) and then is used as an introductory filler or expletive. [Read *It is always prudent and often delightful to pay attention to Mr. Crick's writing about the nature and origin of life.*]

C. Two Different Senses of the Same Word. "Why ought Louisiana [the state government] to have power over one who has had an auto accident there [the place]?"

D. Word Referred to as a Word, While Purporting to Have Substantive Meaning as Well. "Derived from *Slav,* of which people many were enslaved by the conquering Romans, the word [*slave*] has acquired connotations of servility, timidity, and cowardice." (Bergen Evans) The reference to *Slav* is to the word, not the people; hence the phrase that follows is illogical.

E. Preposition Given Two Meanings. "The shareholders will transact such other business as may properly come before the meeting or any adjournment thereof." Here *before* is asked to mean both "in front of" (before the convocation or meeting) and "prior to" (before adjournment). See ZEUGMA AND SYLLEPSIS (A).

JARGON. **A. Definition.** Jargon refers to the language, spoken and written, that members of any social, occupational, or professional group use to communicate with one another. As used in this book, the term refers to the full range of specialized vocabulary, devised by lawyers to save themselves time and space in communicating with each other, and sometimes even to conceal meaning from those uninitiated into the law.

Jargon covers a broad range of legal vocabulary from the almost slangy (*horse case*) to the almost technically precise (*res ipsa loquitur*). And although an expression that is labeled "jargon" fails to rise to the level of a TERM OF ART, it remains a useful bit of shorthand for presenting ideas that would ordinarily need explaining in other, more circumlocutory terms if persons who lack experience in the law are to understand them.

Thus, a strong in-group property characterizes jargon, which may be acceptable—even desirable—when one lawyer talks with another or addresses a judge. But jargon is unacceptable when the purpose of using it is to demonstrate how much more the speaker or writer knows as a specialist than ordinary listeners or readers do. The intended audience, then, should be the primary concern of a lawyer in deciding which words to use to communicate intelligibly. In a bench trial a lawyer may be justified in referring to the *corpus delicti* (not truly a TERM OF ART), but in a jury trial, a lawyer who uses this term is likely to lead the jury into confusion, puzzlement, and even misjudgment.

As an archetypal example of jargon, the phrase *case on all fours* denotes "a reported case in which the facts and law are so closely similar to the one at hand as to be indistinguishable from it." This phrase, containing only four short words, is much more economical than the definition. But the shorthand phrase, useful as it is to lawyers, remains inscrutable, unless explained, to virtually all nonlawyers. Such jargonistic phrases collectively fall under the rubric of this entry. See **on all fours.**

The following are typical jargonistic words and phrases, all of which are treated in other entries: *adhesion contract* (see **adherence (A)**), *alter ego, Blackacre, case at bar, case-in-chief, clean hands, clog on the equity, cloud on title, conclusory, four corners of the instrument, in personam, instant case, on all fours, pierce the corporate veil, reasonable person, res integra* (or *res nova*), *res ipsa loquitur, sidebar, Whiteacre.* For a related phenomenon, see ABSTRACTITIS. For the opposite tendency, see PLAIN LANGUAGE.

B. Jargonmongering. Some would say that to be a lawyer (or at least a good one) is necessarily to be a jargonmonger, that word-shuffling is the nature of the business. That pessimistic view is not borne out by the evidence of the many successful straight-talking and straight-writing practitioners. If such a jaded view has any validity, the best one can do is to prove its falsity by one's own example.

It is difficult to improve on Sir Arthur Quiller-Couch's seminal analysis of jargon in his *Art of Writing* (1916; repr. 1961). He sets out its two primary vices: "The first is that it uses circumlocution rather than short straight speech. It says: '*In the case of* John Jenkins deceased, the coffin' when it means 'John Jenkins's coffin'; and its yea is not yea, neither is its nay nay; but its answer is *in the affirmative* or *in the negative,* as the foolish and superfluous *case* may be. The second vice is that it habitually chooses vague wooly abstract nouns rather than concrete ones" (*id.* at 105). "To write jargon is to be perpetually shuffling around in a fog and cotton-wool of abstract terms" (*id.* at 117). See ABSTRACTITIS.

Nothing nauseates like the real thing: "A supplement to the draft or final EIS on file will be prepared whenever significant impacts resulting from changes in the proposed plan or new significant impact information, criteria or circumstances relevant to environmental considerations impact on the recommended plan or proposed action." 33 C.F.R. § 2502.9(c)(1) (1988). See INITIALESE.

jaywalker (= a pedestrian who crosses a street without heeding traffic regulations) began as an early-20th-century Americanism but is now used also in BrE. In the 1910s, *jay* was a slang term meaning "a stupid, silly person; a simpleton," and at about that time *jaywalker* and its BACK-FORMATION *jaywalk* came to refer to someone stupid enough to cross streets unsafely.

J.D. is now the predominantly awarded law degree in the U.S.—*LL.B.* (q.v.) formerly having this distinction. The abbreviation *J.D.* generally stands for *Juris Doctor* (= doctor of law).

jealousy; envy. The careful writer distinguishes between these terms. *Jealousy* is properly restricted to contexts involving love and affairs of the heart, whereas *envy* is used more broadly of resentful contemplation of a more fortunate person.

Jeddart justice; Jedburgh justice; Jedwood justice. The first is now the usual form of this term, meaning "execution first, trial afterwards." The name derives from Jedburgh in Roxburghshire, Scotland, a town near the English border where bands of raiders frequently skirmished on both sides. (*Jeddart* is probably a corrupted form of "Jedworth," the old name of the place.) Apparently of 16th-century origin, *Jeddart justice* "differs from *lynch law* in that it was done by a kind of summary court, not by persons wholly unauthorized" (*OCL*).

jemmy. See **jimmy.**

jeofails (= mistakes or oversights in pleading), for the most part an obsolete term, is pronounced /jə-***faylz***/. Formerly thought to be the LAW FRENCH form of *j'ai faillé,* meaning "I have made an error," the term is now generally thought to derive from *jocus,* as in *jeopardy* (= *jocus partitus*). See John H. Baker & M.S. Arnold, *Origin of "Jeofail,"* 87 Law Q. Rev. 166 (1971).

jeopardize; (en)jeopard. Horwill wrote that in AmE "*jeopard* is preferred to *jeopardize,* the common term in England." *Modern American Usage* 178 (2d ed. 1944). This was not true in 1935, and it is not true today. E.g., "Fanciful rights of accused persons cannot be allowed to prevent the functioning of the police and so to *jeopardize* the safety of the public." *Enjeopard* and *jeopard* are NEEDLESS VARIANTS.

jeopardy. See **double jeopardy.**

jetsam. See **flotsam.**

jibe. See **gibe.**

Jim Crow laws (= laws enacted or purposely interpreted to discriminate against blacks) is an early-19th-century American coinage deriving from *Jim Crow* (1838), a derogatory name for a black man. The institution of American segregation came to be called *Jim Crowism* at about the same time.

jimmy; jemmy. A burglar's crowbar is spelled *jimmy* in AmE, *jemmy* in BrE.

JJ. (invariably capitalized) is the abbreviation for *judges* or *justices.*

j.n.o.v. (= judgment *non obstante veredicto*) is usually abbreviated thus in lower case. Some courts write *JNOV,* but the capital letters and dropping of periods are distracting. The abbreviation is sometimes shortened to *n.o.v.:* "Appellee may bring his grounds for new trial to the trial court's attention when defendant first makes *an n.o.v.* [better: *a j.n.o.v.*] motion." See **judgment *non obstante veredicto.***

job site should be spelled as two words. Cf. **worksite.**

John a Nokes; John a Stiles. These fictitious names of parties in a lawsuit, dating from the 15th and used well into the 19th century, derive from *John atten Oke* (= John who dwells at the oak) and *John atte Stile* (= John who dwells at the stile). They were frequently abbreviated *J.N.* and *J.S.* See Oliver W. Holmes, *The Common Law* 25 (1881) (referring to John at Stile).

Occasionally these names are not fictitious. For example, *Stiles v. Blunt,* 912 F.2d 260 (8th Cir. 1990), involves John A. Stiles's candidacy for the Missouri House of Representatives. Cf. **Doe, John.**

John Doe. See **Doe, John.**

join = (1) to unite (several causes of action) in a lawsuit; or (2) to unite (several parties) in a lawsuit.

joinder. A. And *jointure.* These are different words. *Joinder,* the noun corresponding to the verb *to join,* q.v., is the usual term in law for the uniting of several causes of action or of parties in a single suit. E.g., "The proceeding was one that by statute binds such future interest without either *joinder* or representation of the person in favor of whom it was limited." See **issue (D).**

Jointure, a much less common term, means "a widow's freehold life estate in land, made in lieu of dower." E.g., "A *jointure* or any pecuniary provision that is made for the benefit of the intended wife, and in lieu of her dower, shall bar her right to dower provided she assents to the *jointure.*" John W. Reilly, *The Language of Real Estate* 261 (2d ed. 1982)./ "It became usual instead to provide in a marriage settlement for some land to be settled on the husband and wife jointly for the life of the survivor, so that a widow would have the land until her death in lieu of a dower. Such a provision was called a *'jointure.'*" J.H. Baker, *An Introduction to English Legal History* 309 (3d ed. 1990).

B. And *consolidation.* Whereas *joinder* has come to be used usually in the sense of uniting parties in a suit, *consolidation* has become in AmE the more usual word for uniting two or more lawsuits into a single suit. See **disjoinder & misjoinder.**

C. *Compulsory joinder; permissive joinder.* The Federal Rules of Civil Procedure, which have served as the model for many other sets of court rules, distinguish between *compulsory joinder* and *permissive joinder.* Under Rule 19(a), a party whose presence will not deprive the court of subject-matter jurisdiction must be joined if either of the following is true: (1) in that party's absence, those already involved in the lawsuit cannot receive complete relief; or (2) the absence of such a party, claiming an interest in the subject of the action, might either impair the protection of that interest or leave some other party subject to multiple or inconsistent obligations. These provisions equate with *compulsory joinder,* although the word *compulsory* appears nowhere in the rule. Commentators arrived at the name *compulsory joinder* because the rule uses the mandatory *shall.* (If a party who falls under this rule cannot be joined for some reason, the court must then decide whether the party is *indispensable* or merely *necessary.* See **indispensable.**)

Permissive joinder, meanwhile, falls under Rule 20, which is given that very heading. Under this rule, persons may be joined as plaintiffs if they assert a right to relief jointly, severally, or in the alternative in respect of the same transaction or occurrence, and if any legal or factual question common to all plaintiffs will arise. Persons may be joined as defendants if any right to relief is asserted against them jointly, severally, or in respect of the same transaction or occurrence, and if any legal or factual question common to all defendants will arise.

D. *Joinder of issue.* See **issue (D).**

join issue. See **issue (D).**

joint adventure. See **joint venture.**

joint and several = together and in separation. When two or more persons bind themselves to do something for another person, their liability on the contract is *joint and several* if both or all first bind themselves by one promise, and then each of them makes a separate promise to the same effect. E.g., "Appellants *jointly and severally* covenanted and agreed that they would pay the principal sum of $280,000 on February 1."/ "When a partner dies, his private estate is *jointly and severally* liable . . . for debts and obligations of the firm incurred while he was a partner." 2 E.W. Chance, *Principles of Mercantile Law* 14 (1951).

With *joint and several liability,* the liability of two or more obligors may be enforced against them all by a joint action or against any of them by an individual action. *Solidary liability* is used in this sense in Louisiana, Puerto Rico, and civil-law countries. In addition to *joint and several* obligations, Scottish lawyers refer to *conjunct and several* obligations. See **several.**

joint cooperation is a REDUNDANCY.

joint enterprise. Unlike *joint venture,* q.v., the phrase *joint enterprise* occurs primarily in criminal law. It is apt when two or more persons set out to commit an offense they have conspired to commit; it should not apply when two or more persons are involved in an unplanned and unforeseen incident that has arisen unexpectedly.

jointly and severally. See **joint and several.**

joint-stock company. Hyphenated thus. See PHRASAL ADJECTIVES (A).

joint tenancy; tenancy in common. The distinction between these two terms is basic to the law of property. *Joint tenancy* = ownership of property by two or more persons who have identical interests in the whole of the property, with a right of survivorship. *Tenancy in common* = equitable ownership of property by two or more persons in equal or unequal undivided shares, with no right of survivorship. The property for each of these tenancies may be either real (land) or personal (e.g., a bank account), although the *CDL,* which reflects British legal practices, confines its definitions to real property.

join together is a REDUNDANCY that should be allowed to survive only in the marriage service, and there only because it is a bona fide remnant of Elizabethan English.

jointure. See **joinder** (A).

joint venture; joint adventure. The latter, an ARCHAISM, still occasionally appears, but *joint venture*—a clearer phrase—ought to displace it. E.g., "[I]n each case the parties were *joint adventurers* [read *joint venturers*] and were unquestionably in a confidential relationship . . . ." *Dairy Queen of Duncanville, Inc. v. O'Quinn,* 502 S.W.2d 889, 892 (Tex. Civ. App.—Dallas 1973). Cf. **joint enterprise.**

joint wills. See **mutual wills.**

joker = an ambiguous clause in a legislative bill inserted to render it inoperative or uncertain in some respect without arousing opposition at time of passage. See *Bennet v. Commercial Advertiser Ass'n,* 129 N.E. 343, 345 (N.Y. 1920). More broadly—and less malignantly—the term may also refer to a rider or amendment that is extraneous to the subject of the bill. E.g., "Such a holding seems to me to throw both general and special revenue acts wide open as convenient vehicles for the enactment, under the concealment of their titles, of *'joker'* legislation . . . ." *Macke v. Commonwealth,* 159 S.E. 148, 151 (Va. 1931) (Espes, J., dissenting).

journal, v.t.; **journalize.** Both terms are used in the sense "to record in a journal." *Journalize* is more usual in legal contexts—e.g.: "He filed an appeal after the district judge officially *journalized* the judgment." The verb *to journal* has additional, nonlegal senses.

JOURNALESE. See TITULAR TOMFOOLERY.

joyrider; joyriding. These early-20th-century American coinages remain colloquialisms—yet criminal-law texts use them because they are the only available terms. *Joyrider* = one who drives someone else's car without permission. The verb, a BACK-FORMATION, is hyphenated: *to joy-ride.*

J.P. = Justice of the Peace. Conventionally, if the abbreviation is used, the plural would be *J.P.'s,* because the abbreviation contains periods—e.g.: "From the *J.P.s* [read *J.P.'s*] odium and contempt spread to the higher justices, usually *J.P.s* [read *J.P.'s*] in their own localities . . . ." Alan Harding, *A Social History of English Law* 71 (1966). In the sentence quoted, however, one can understand the author's desire to avoid a MISCUE caused by the apostrophe's seeming to make *J.P.* a possessive. Oddly, however, the same writer used the pl. *Q.C.'s* (see quot. at **junior**).

judex, except in historical contexts—e.g.: "English Chancery Courts, heavy borrowers from the civil law, may have derived the system of special masters from the civilian *judex* of the Roman Republic and Early Empire"—is an unnecessary equivalent of *judge.* Pl. *judices.*

judge; justice. A. An Array of Distinctions. In the U.S., as a general rule, judges sitting on the highest appellate level of a jurisdiction are known as *justices.* Trial judges and appellate judges on intermediate levels are generally called *judges,* not *justices.* (New York, Texas, and a few other jurisdictions depart from these general rules. In New York, *justices* sit on the trial court of general jurisdiction [the Supreme Court, oddly], whereas *judges* sit on the appellate courts. In Texas, *justices* sit on the courts of appeals [between the trial court and the Supreme Court—the latter being the highest court of civil appeal—which is also composed of *justices*]; *judges* sit on the Texas Court of Criminal Appeals, the highest criminal court, and on trial courts.)

In England and Northern Ireland, similarly, judges of the Supreme Court at trial level are *justices* and at the appellate level *lords justices. Judges* sit on circuit courts and *justices* in magistrates' courts.

Horwill wrote that "*judge* carries with it in America by no means such dignified associations as it possesses in Eng. It may mean [in AmE] no more than a *magistrate* of a police court." H.W. Horwill, *Modern American Usage* 180 (2d ed. 1944). *Justice* may also denote, in AmE and BrE alike, a low-ranking judge or inferior magistrate, as in the phrases *justice of the peace* and *police justice.* When, however, the word refers to the highest American judges—the Justices of the Supreme Court of the United States—the word *Justice* is ordinarily capitalized, even if no particular Justice is named.

Judges often look unkindly on mistakes in their titles, as by inserting "[*sic*]" after mistakes—e.g.: "By two identical motions filed January 3, 1985 in these related actions, defendant moves for an order 'disqualifying the Honorable Mr. Justice [*sic*] Charles L. Brieant from hearing this matter on the ground that said Honorable Charles L. Brieant was the presiding justice [*sic*] in the trial of *Lamy Optic Industries, Inc. v. Passport International Ltd . . . .*'" *Tenzer v. Lewitinn,* 599 F. Supp. 973, 974 (S.D.N.Y. 1985) (per Brieant, J.). Similarly, Chief Justice Rehnquist, during oral argument, has corrected counsel who have addressed him as "Judge." See David Margolick, *At the Bar,* N.Y. Times, 26 April 1991, at B9.

B. In Informal Contexts. In AmE, lawyers conventionally call all but U.S. Supreme Court Justices "judge" in informal settings. *Judge Phillips* is permissible in talking with the Chief Justice of the Texas Supreme Court, though in referring to him in a conversation with someone else, one would say either *the Chief Justice* or *Chief Justice Phillips,* or perhaps *Justice Phillips* (less proper).

In BrE, the conventions are quite different: "Never say 'Justice Smith' or (except for a circuit or county court judge) 'Judge Smith'; these are Americanisms, to be shunned and avoided on this side of the Atlantic." Glanville Williams, *Learning the Law* 64 (11th ed. 1982). Williams is emphatic about this point: do not just shun them—avoid them as well. What are the proper forms? Williams recommends "'Mr. Justice Smith' (or Mrs. Justice Smith, as the case may be) . . . when speaking of him in public." *Id.* He does not mention *Ms. Justice Smith,* the title *Ms.* not having caught on in BrE to the extent it has in AmE. See **my lord** & FORMS OF ADDRESS (D).

judgeable. So spelled.

judge advocate. Pl. *judge advocates.*

judge, v.t. See **adjudge.**

judgeless is a legal NEOLOGISM denoting an unhappy state of affairs—e.g.: "To so require would leave a number of rural Texas counties *judgeless* in some criminal cases." *Joshua v. State,* 696 S.W.2d 451, 456 (Tex. App.—Houston [14th Dist.] 1985)./ "Eventually, the jury might be on its own, without even a judge. [¶] The last move—from lawless to *judgeless* juries—suggests another process change." Leonard R. Jaffee, *Empathetic Adjustment—An Alternative to Rules, Policies, and Politics,* 58 U. Cin. L. Rev. 1161, 1225 (1990).

judge-made, adj., is used generally as an antonym of *statutory.* E.g., "No system of law—whether it be *judge-made* or legislatively enacted—can be so perfectly drafted as to leave no room for dispute." Lon L. Fuller, *The Morality of Law* 56 (rev. ed. 1969)./ "Such *judge-made* law would be disastrous for press freedom." Economist, 28 Jan.–3 Feb. 1989, at 18.

The exceptions are many, but a latent DIFFERENTIATION appears to be emerging between *judge-made law* and *common law:* though the common law is literally *judge-made* law, modern writers tend to use *judge-made law* in reference to recent developments and *common law* in reference to the remote past.

The phrase *bench-made* is a less frequent variant. See Henry J. Abraham, *The Judicial Process* 9 (2d ed. 1968) (*bench-made law*).

judgement. See **judgment.**

judge-shopping = using any of various means to bring a case before a judge who might be more favorably inclined to a litigant than some other judge might be. Though the following examples do not contain hyphens, the phrase is best hyphenated: "[W]e emphasize that the requirement of showing the unavailability of the trial judge must be strictly met in order to avoid the obvious possibilities of conflict or *'judge shopping'* for a favorable ruling." *Shafer v. Northside Inn, Inc.,* 184 N.E.2d 756, 758–59 (Ill. App. Ct. 1962)./ "*'Judge shopping'* in this overloaded court is rarely tolerated." Barbara H. Craig, *Chadha: The Story of an Epic Constitutional Struggle* 112 (1988)./ "Payments previously varied from judge to judge, a situation that sometimes led to *'judge shopping.'*" Michael deC. Hinds, *Better Traps Being Built for Delinquent Parents,* N.Y. Times, 9 Dec. 1989, at 10.

judgey (= characteristic of or like a judge) is a NEOLOGISM carrying negative connotations—e.g.: "Edwards is less *'judgey'* than most judges. He is not modest, but neither is he pompous." Donald D. Jackson, *Judges* 324 (1974).

judgment. **A. Spelling.** *Judgment* is the preferred form in AmE and seems to be preferred in British legal texts, even as far back as the 19th century. *Judgement* is prevalent in British nonlegal texts, and was thought by Fowler to be the better form; Glanville Williams states that, in BrE, "*judgement* should really be the preferred spelling." *Learning the Law* 153 (11th ed. 1982).

B. AmE & BrE Senses. In AmE, a *judgment* is the final decisive act of a court in defining the rights of the parties. It "includes a decree and any order from which an appeal lies." Fed. R. Civ. P. 54(a).

In BrE, *judgment* is commonly used in the sense in which *judicial opinion* is used in AmE: "The facts of this case, which are fully stated in the *judgment* of Lord Hanworth M.R., were briefly as follows." (Eng.) Continental legal systems likewise use *judgment* in this way. See JUDGMENTS, APPELLATE-COURT, **decision & opinion.**

C. And *decree.* Though *decree* is traditionally the term for a final disposition in equity, the term *judgment* applies, in most American states, to the final disposition made by a court in an equitable as well as in a legal proceeding. See *Restatement of Judgments,* Intro. at 3 (1942). See **decree.**

D. *Court judgment.* This phrase is a REDUNDANCY, though perhaps an understandable one when the likely readers are nonlawyers. For example, the title of the following book might have miscued general readers if the word *court* had been removed: Gini G. Scott et al., *Collect Your Court Judgment* (1991).

E. And *verdict.* See **verdict (D).**

judgment as a matter of law. See **judgment *non obstante veredicto* (A).**

judgment by default. See **default judgment.**

judgmental; judgmatic. *Judgmental* = (1) of or relating to judgment; or (2) judging when uncalled for. Sense (2) is now more common <a judgmental critic>, but sense (1) still appears. E.g., "The qualification is generally undertaken only in an effort to make meaningful a whole host of *judgmental* factors applicable at a particular time." *Judgmatic,* called by Fowler a "facetious formation" because of its irregular formation on the analogy of *dogmatic,* is a NEEDLESS VARIANT of *judicious.* See **judicial.**

judgment-book; judgment-roll. In most jurisdictions, these terms refer synonymously to the book kept by the clerk of court for the entry or recordation of judgments. (See **rendition of judgment.**) But some American jurisdictions call for *entry* of judgments in the *judgment-roll* and mere *recordation* of judgments in the *judgment-book.* The usual term in BrE is *judgment-roll.*

judgment *non obstante veredicto.* **A. And *judgment notwithstanding the verdict; j.n.o.v.; judgment n.o.v.*** In AmE, the tendency is to substitute all these phrases with *judgment as a matter of law,* q.v. But, of the headwords listed, perhaps the best unabbreviated one is *judgment notwithstanding the verdict.* We must not forget the Latin phrase, however, lest new generations of lawyers come to miss the import of *j.n.o.v.*—an abbreviation that litters many legal texts. See **j.n.o.v.**

B. Shortened form of *non obstante veredicto.* The phrase *non obstante veredicto* is sometimes used in the shortened form *non obstante*—e.g.: "This appeal requires us to determine whether the trial judge's action in granting judgment *non obstante* for the defendant was correct."

C. A Common Misspelling. A surprisingly high percentage of the time, American lawyers mangle the Latin and write *verdicto*—e.g.: "[I]f the jury's verdict is clearly arbitrary, the court may enter judgment *non obstante verdicto* [read *veredicto*]." Constance S. Huttner, Note, *Unfit for Jury Determination,* 20 B.C. L. Rev. 511, 534 (1979). All the more reason to stick to *judgment as a matter* *of law, judgment notwithstanding the verdict,* or *j.n.o.v.*

judgment-proof; execution-proof. Both of these phrases, in reference to a judgment-debtor, mean "having insufficient assets to satisfy a money judgment." Although *judgment-proof* is much more common, *execution-proof* is more accurate: the judgment-creditor may have had little difficulty obtaining the judgment (i.e., winning the lawsuit), but collecting on the judgment through execution may be another matter entirely. Thus, the penniless loser is insulated not from judgment but from execution.

judgment-roll. See **judgment-book.**

JUDGMENTS, APPELLATE-COURT. *Judgment* in this article means the final decree of an appellate court that acts upon a lower-court judgment, whether affirming, reversing, vacating, or whatever. British lawyers ordinarily use *judgment* synonymously with *opinion,* whereas Americans distinguish between the *opinion* (which sets out the reasons for the disposition) and the judgment (the pronouncement of the disposition itself). This article, then, reflects primarily American practices.

A cardinal principle of judgment-drafting is that appellate opinions should make explicit how the court is disposing of the judgment or order below. Appellate courts have sometimes left the parties and the trial court uncertain about the status of a case by using vague terms such as *so ordered* and *ordered accordingly,* unaccompanied by a clear statement of the disposition preceding these phrases. This practice is, happily, obsolescent. Of course, if the judgment is particularly complex—as when an appellate court affirms certain parts of the trial court's judgment, vacates another part, and orders the trial court to dismiss what remains as moot—the *so ordered* might be just the phrase for concluding such an admirably precise judgment.

A second important point is that judges should almost make a fetish of the following distinctions: an appeals court affirms, reverses, or modifies *judgments* or *orders;* it agrees with, approves, or disapproves *opinions* or *decisions;* and it remands *cases* (or *causes*) and *actions.* When the lower court lacked jurisdiction, the proper disposition by the appellate court is to *vacate* the judgment of the trial court and *dismiss* the case from the docket of the trial court (or *order* the trial court *to dismiss*). If the trial court had jurisdiction over the case, but entered an order beyond its jurisdiction, the proper disposition is to *vacate* the order and remand the case. In each of these circumstances, the appellate court had jurisdiction over the appeal for the limited purpose of making the disposition described. If the appeal raised other issues about the judgment (or order) of the trial court, the proper disposition might add: in other respects the appeal is *dismissed.*

When the appellate court lacks jurisdiction to hear any aspect of the appeal, the proper disposition is usually *appeal dismissed.* Although an appellate court in its opinions may approve or disapprove the trial court's statement or use of legal propositions, the judgment proper operates only on the judgment or order appealed from—that is, appellate courts do not affirm or reverse opinions, only orders or judgments. (The appellate court may, for example, affirm the judgment below but substitute a rationale leading to that judgment.)

The terms *vacate* and *reverse* can be problematic. Practices vary: some courts *reverse* the judgment below when the trial court should have disposed of the case differently, and *vacate* when the trial court may not have been incorrect, but needs to be unconstrained by its former judgment as it carries out the further directions of the appellate court. E.g., "We *vacate* the judgment of the district court and remand the case for proceedings consistent with this opinion." Still other courts *vacate* only injunctions or administrative orders, or judgments or orders made without jurisdiction, *reversing* all other erroneous dispositions below. Courts ought to encourage consistency among their particular judges in these matters of usage.

With these guidelines in mind, we may usefully consider a number of appellate-court judgments, as well as statements about judgments, that are illustrative of the pitfalls awaiting the unwary. The first seven examples of poor drafting that follow have been adapted, with some additions, from the excellent discussion of the former Chief Justice of the Supreme Court of Texas, Robert W. Calvert, in his *Appellate Court Judgments,* 6 Tex. Tech L. Rev. 915, 923–24 (1975).

1. Mistaking the Lower Court for Its Judgment. "We deny the petitions and *affirm* [read *affirm the order of*] the Interstate Commerce Commission."/ "In an opinion by Justice Brennan, the Supreme Court *affirmed* [read *affirmed the judgment of*] the Fourth Circuit."/ "For these reasons, I am of the opinion that the evidence was sufficient to warrant revocation in this case and would *affirm* [read *affirm the judgment of*] the lower court." The tribunal appealed from is not before the higher court for approval or disapproval, affirmance or reversal; rather, its *judgment* or *order* is.

2. Mistaking the Case for the Judgment Below.

"*The case* (or *cause*) [read *The judgment*] is affirmed." The case or cause remains the same; an appellate-court judgment acts directly upon a previous judgment in the case, but not upon the case itself.

3. Mistaking the Lower Court's Opinion for Its Judgment. "The *opinion* [read *judgment*] of the trial court is affirmed."/ "The *decision* [read *judgment*] of the district court is reversed."/ "For reasons stated below, we affirm the *decision* [read *judgment*] of the trial court." The appellate court may agree or disagree with the trial court's opinion or decision; again, however, it affirms or reverses the *judgment.*

4. Mistaking the Appellate Court's Judgment for the Trial Court's. "The *judgment* of the trial court is reversed and rendered." Appellate courts ordinarily have no power or jurisdiction to render a trial court's judgment; yet appellate courts are often authorized to render judgments that should have been rendered by the trial court. [Read *The judgment of the trial court is reversed;* [*on appeal,*] *we render judgment for* . . . .]

5. Purporting to Render a Judgment That the Court Simultaneously Reverses. "We *reverse* and *render* that judgment." Similar to #4. [Read *We reverse, and instead render judgment as follows:* . . . .]

6. Mistaking the Judgment for the Case. "The judgment of the trial court is reversed *and remanded* [read *and the case is remanded*]." (The judgment of the trial court may be reversed, but only the *case* may be remanded.)/ "We *vacate and remand* the case for consideration of whether these errors were harmless." (Understood, perhaps, are the words *the judgment of the trial court* after the word *vacate;* it is generally best not to rely on UNDERSTOOD WORDS in drafting judgments, however; yet see the next-to-last paragraph of this article.)/ "The trial court's judgment is *affirmed in part, and reversed and remanded in part* [read *affirmed in part, reversed in part, and the case is remanded*]." Though it is possible, cases are not ordinarily remanded in part. If the judgment is not stated in sentence form, it is quite proper to write *Affirmed in part, reversed in part, and remanded.*

7. Superfluously Granting Judgment After Reversal of a Plaintiff's Judgment. "The judgment for the plaintiff is reversed *and the judgment is here rendered for the defendant* [omit the italicized words]." If the defendant has not filed a counterclaim, the judgment should end after the word *reversed;* the judgment is favorable to the defendant merely in denying the plaintiff recovery.

8. Wrongly Omitting a Remand. "The judgment that the plaintiff take nothing is reversed and is here rendered for the plaintiff." The judgment is incomplete, unless there is only one possible form and measure of relief; if the plaintiff sought damages, the case would have to be remanded to the trial court to determine damages. [Read *We reverse the judgment and remand for a determination of damages.*]

9. Mistaking the Judgment for the Court Below or Its Judgment. "The district court's *judgment held* [read *opinion held,* or, better, *The district court held*] that the oral contract was dissolved by virtue of appellee's breach for failure to provide or secure the promised financing."

Finally, it is worth noting that the terms *affirm, reverse, remand,* etc. may have "understood" objects, as here: "We *affirm* on all issues with regard to Jack Ballard, but *reverse* insofar as the court held Mary Ballard liable for the 1969 and 1970 deficiencies."/ "We hold that Ohio's law of trade secrets is not preempted by the patent laws of the United States, and, accordingly, we *reverse*."/ "We *reverse* and *remand.*" These elliptical phrases are unexceptionable.

Lawyers as well as judges must be sensitive to these niceties if they are to draft meaningful prayers in their appellate briefs—and write more precise articles on appellate advocacy: "The appellee's brief should *tell* [read *say*] why *the trial court* [read *the trial court's judgment*] should be affirmed, not why appellant's brief is all wrong." James L. Robertson, *Reality on Appeal,* Litig., Fall 1990, at 3, 6.

judicable; justiciable. The former is a NEEDLESS VARIANT of the latter.

judicative; judicatorial; judicatory. *Judicative* is a NEEDLESS VARIANT of *adjudicative,* q.v., while *judicatorial* is a NEEDLESS VARIANT of *judicial,* q.v. *Judicatory,* adj., = (1) of or relating to judgment; (2) by which a judgment may be made; giving a decisive indication; critical. For the noun senses of *judicatory,* see **judicature.**

judicator. See **adjudicator.**

judicature; judicatory. *Judicature* = (1) a judge's office, function, or authority; (2) a body of judges; or (3) the action of judging or of administering justice through duly constituted courts. It is sometimes used in BrE where *judiciary,* q.v., usu. appears in AmE; hence the U.S. statute is the Judiciary Act of 1789, whereas Britain had the Judicature Acts 1873–75 and the Supreme Court of Judicature (Consolidation) Act 1925, now consolidated in the Supreme Court Act 1981. (That Act omits *judicature,* which may be obsolescent in BrE.) *Judicature* is used in a few American names such as the American Judicature Society, which publishes the journal *Judicature,* by its own terms "a forum for fact and opinion relating to all aspects of the administration of justice and its improvement."

On the whole, however, *judicature* has generally been far more common in BrE than in AmE. E.g., "The chancery division placed stress upon certain provisions of the *judicature* act." (Eng.)/ "It is a basic rule of English *judicature* that our courts do justice in public." (Eng.)/ "What in later times were seen as two distinct branches of the constitution—the legislature and the *judicature*—had their origins in a less sophisticated notion of kingship in which legislation and adjudication were not distinguishable." J.H. Baker, *An Introduction to English Legal History* 234 (3d ed. 1990).

Judicatory = judiciary; judicature. E.g., "[C]onfusion . . . would unavoidably result from the contradictory decisions of a number of independent *judicatories* . . . ." *The Federalist* No. 22, at 150 (Alexander Hamilton) (Clinton Rossiter ed., 1961). Today, except in specialized senses in Scotland and in the Presbyterian Church, this term should be avoided as a NEEDLESS VARIANT. For its adjectival sense, see **judicative & adjudicative.**

judicial; judicious. *Judicial* = (1) of, relating to, or by the court <judicial officers>; (2) in court <judicial admissions>; (3) legal <the Attorney General took no judicial action>; or (4) of or relating to a judgment <judicial interest at the rate of four percent per annum>. Following are illustrations of the four senses of this complex word.

Sense (1)—the usual sense: "The requirements of this section had been *judicially* interpreted [i.e., interpreted by the court] well before defendants' actions."/ "Far more imposing is the edifice of private remedies *judicially* extracted from the Securities and Exchange Act of 1934."

Sense (2)—closely related to sense (1) but distinct: "The record further revealed that the trial court erroneously apprised the defendant of the effect of his plea (i.e., by failing to inform him that his *judicial* stipulation had foreclosed a merit consideration of his appeal from the adverse ruling on the motion to suppress)."/ "Appellant then took the witness stand and *judicially* confessed that she had committed the offense alleged against her in the indictment."

Sense (3)—in which the court is quite remote: "Mr. Rogerson . . . was arrested that evening and charged with manslaughter, but in the first week of December last year a grand jury declined to indict him. In the months afterward, . . . Mrs. Wood's husband, Kevin, and other residents who were upset at the lack of *judicial* action have written letters to newspapers and government officials in an attempt to pressure the Attorney General's office to seek an indictment again." Lyn Riddle, *Deer Hunter Is Indicted in Accidental Killing of Woman in Maine,* N.Y. Times, 9 Dec. 1989, at 10.

Sense (4)—a sense not recorded in unabridged or legal dictionaries, but not uncommon in legal contexts, especially in AmE: "Todd's liability for Auto's attorney's fees, therefore, is fundamentally different from, for example, liability for interest on a judgment. . . . Whereas an award of *judicial* interest is collateral to and independent of the action itself, attorney's fees awarded as a result of breach of an implied warranty of workmanlike performance are an integral part of the merits of the case and the scope of relief." *Todd Shipyards Corp. v. Auto Transp., S.A.,* 763 F.2d 745, 756 (5th Cir. 1985). Though hardly unusual, this use of the word is certainly suspect.

Judicious is a much simpler word, meaning "well considered, discreet, wisely circumspect." E.g., "The court *judiciously* exercised its inherent equitable power to fashion a remedy appropriate to the wrongs committed."/ "By *judicious* application of Rule 403, a trial judge can afford the defendant in an obscenity case a fair opportunity to prove that the community displays a reasonable degree of acceptance of comparable material."/ "My theory was expressed too widely in certain parts, and not widely enough in others; and Mr. Whitworth's pamphlet appeared to me to have corrected and completed it in a *judicious* manner." (Eng.) *Judgmatic* is a NEEDLESS VARIANT of *judicious.* See **judgmental.**

judicial cognizance. See **judicial notice.**

judicial court. In Massachusetts and Maine (and, formerly, New Hampshire), this phrase is not a redundancy: the legislature was originally called the *general court,* and therefore by distinction *judicial court* emerged in the 17th century and has persisted. See **general court.**

judicial dictum. See **dictum (B).**

judicialize = to treat judicially, arrive at a judgment or decision upon (*OED*). More modernly it has evolved to mean "to take into the province of the courts" and appears usu. in a lament—e.g.: "A legal process designed to make the law judge-proof has become steadily more *judicialized,* and today the rate of *judicialization* is accelerating throughout the civil law world." J.H. Merryman, *The Civil Law Tradition* 155 (1969)./ "As lawyers we have a natural inclination to '*judicialize*' every function of government." Lon L. Fuller, *The Mo-*

rality of Law 176 (rev. ed. 1969; repr. 1976). See -IZE.

The noun *judicialization* (used above in the Merryman quotation) is fairly common—e.g.: "He [Richard A. Epstein] talks, for example, of putting an end to government intervention in the area of labor relations, which he says has led to '*judicialization*' of labor contracts." Deborah Graham, *Conservative Academics: Rising Stars,* Legal Times, 18 March 1985, at 1. Cf. **juridification.**

judicial notice; judicial cognizance. The former phrase (referring to the means by which a court may take as proved certain facts without hearing evidence) is now the more common of the two in both AmE and BrE. A court takes *judicial notice* of a fact for one of two reasons: either it relates to a general legal question (such as statutory construction or constitutionality) that can better be explored by the judge free of evidentiary limitations, or it is so indisputably settled that, although normally within the fact-finder's purview, it can be resolved by the judge without hearing evidence.

The verb phrase is either *notice judicially* or *judicially notice:* "While there are few absolutes in this area, we can *notice judicially,* if we need, that contemporary wills more often than not use the residuary clause to carry out the most important provisions."/ "According to professional etiquette, which is *judicially noticed,* a barrister may take instructions only from solicitors and not directly from lay clients . . . ." O. Hood Phillips, *A First Book of English Law* 22 (3d ed. 1955).

judicial opinion. See **judgment** (B), JUDGMENTS, APPELLATE-COURT & OPINIONS, JUDICIAL.

judicial review. A. In AmE. *Judicial review* has specialized senses that are not at all apparent in the phrase itself. It means either (1) "the court's power to refuse to enforce an unconstitutional act of either the state or the national government"; or (2) "the court's exercise of that power." E.g., "This right of *judicial review* is indeed the most potent and pregnant fact of Supreme Court power; and its most dramatic and controversial manifestation is in the vetoing by the justices of things done by the other two supposedly equal branches of the national government, the Congress and the President." Fred Rodell, *Nine Men* 36 (1955)./ "Does the Constitution make it clear that the Court has this final authority of '*judicial review*' over national legislative enactments?" Robert G. McCloskey, *The American Supreme Court* 7–8 (1960).

Occasionally—and esp. in journalistic writing—*judicial review* is used as a synonym of *appellate review.* This usage, however, is not strictly proper.

B. In BrE. The BrE uses are quite different because G.B. does not have judicial review in the American sense: courts cannot invalidate primary legislation (though they review the decisions of lower courts). British writers use *judicial review* to refer to a relatively new procedure in England and Scotland, a procedure that enables a litigant to challenge an administrative action by a public body—and, in England, to secure a declaration; an order for mandamus, certiorari, or prohibition; or an award of damages. E.g., "The Labour-controlled authority is also among 21 councils contesting a *judicial review* in the High Court next week, in the hope of overturning proposals to cap their poll tax charges." Peter Davenport, *Council Introduces "Austerity Cuts" Because of Poll Tax,* Times (London), 2 June 1990, at 2.

judicial separation. See **separation.**

JUDICIAL WRITING. See OPINIONS, JUDICIAL (B).

judiciary, adj. Ordinarily a noun, *judiciary* is used in *W3* adjectivally in the phrase *with full judiciary authority* (in definition of *en banc*). *W3* records *judiciary* as an adjective equivalent to *judicial.* Today, though, it is rarely so used in legal contexts and should be avoided in that sense as a NEEDLESS VARIANT: "This procedure agrees with the *judiciary* [read *judicial*] practice in the United States." J.D. Hannan, *The Canon Law of Wills,* Catholic Univ. Am. Canon Law Studies, No. 86, at 135 (1934)./ "This system of checks and balances was not the result, as in the American Constitution, of a division of power between the legislative, executive, and *judiciary* [read *judicial*] branches of the government." Hans J. Wolff, *Roman Law* 27 (1951). See **judicative.**

But in the sense "of or relating to the judiciary," which means something different from *judicial* (= of or relating to a court or courts), the adjective *judiciary* is useful. E.g., "If the history of the interpretation of *judiciary* legislation teaches anything, it teaches the duty to reject treating such statutes as a wooden set of self-sufficient words . . . ." *Romero v. International Terminal Operating Co.,* 358 U.S. 354, 379 (1959). In that sentence, *judicial legislation* would have created a miscue, suggesting judicial activism rather than statutes affecting the judiciary. See **judicial.**

judiciary, n., (= the judicial branch of government) is used in both AmE and BrE. (See **judicature.**) E.g., "In *Crouch v. Crouch,* we gave reasons for the federal *judiciary's* traditional refusal to exercise diversity jurisdiction in domestic relations cases."/ "I believe we should have rights of audience but this is only on condition that we satisfy the *judiciary* and the public that those rights will be exercised completely and fully." Valerie Elliott, *Prosecutors Seek Senior Lawyers,* Sunday Telegraph, 11 Feb. 1990, at 5 (quoting Allan Green, Q.C.).

judicious. See **judicial.**

judiocracy. See **jurocracy.**

jump bail (= to leave [a place] illegally while free on bail) began as slang, but has now become a respectable expression used even by judges in written opinions. E.g., "If the principal *jumps bail* and is not re-arrested, complete and permanent forfeiture of bail seems to be universal." *U.S. v. Ciena,* 195 F. Supp. 511, 511 (S.D.N.Y. 1961)./ "The defendant *jumped bail* before trial." *Supreme Court Ponders Sanction for Violation of Speedy Trial Act,* 56 U.S.L.W. 1176, 1176 (17 May 1988). See **bail jump.**

jump citation. See **pinpoint citation.**

juncture. The phrase *at this juncture* should be used in reference to a crisis or a critically important time; it is not equivalent merely to "at this time" or "now." When used with these latter meanings, it is a pomposity. Here it is appropriate: "There can be no question that respondent was 'in custody' at least as of the moment he was placed under arrest; because he was not informed of his constitutional rights at this *juncture,* respondent's subsequent admissions should not have been used against him." And here it is inappropriate: "The controversy *at this juncture merely points up* [read *at this point merely illustrates*] the indefiniteness and uncertainty of the controversial portion of the decree."/ "Texas argues that delay of review is not all that it seeks to avoid by petitioning *at this juncture* [read *at this point* or *now*]."

jungle fighter. See LAWYERS, DEROGATORY NAMES FOR (A).

junior (BrE) = a barrister who has not taken silk, regardless of age. E.g., "To the *juniors*—those who are not Q.C.'s—is reserved the work of drafting pleadings, so that the man who 'takes silk' must start all over again, with as much chance of failing as he ever had." Alan Harding, *A Social History of English Law* 390 (1966). See **silk & devil.**

junior party; senior party. In American patent-law practice, *junior party* refers to the applicant involved in an interference (q.v.) who filed later; *senior party* refers to the applicant who filed earlier.

junk bond = a security issued by a company that is too young or has too much debt to earn an investment-grade rating from an agency such as Moody's Investor's Service Inc. or Standard & Poor's Corporation. Such a bond pays a higher return and is considered riskier than an investment-grade bond.

junta; junto. Of Spanish origin, *junta* (= a political or military group in power, esp. after a coup d'état) is pronounced either /***hoon***-*tə*/ or /***jən***-*tə*/. It is much more common in AmE than its altered form, *junto* /***jən***-*toh*/, which has undergone slight DIFFERENTIATION to mean "a self-appointed committee having political aims." Gowers wrote that *junto* "is an erroneous form" (*MEU2* at 319), but it appears frequently in BrE where an American would write *junta*—e.g.: "Even so, a compliant civilian government may not be easy for the deeply unpopular *junto* to achieve." *Myanmar: Deja Vu,* Economist, 16 Jan. 1993, at 34 (Am. ed.).

jura. See ***jus.***

jural; juristic; juridic; juridical; juratory; juratorial. *Jural* = (1) of or relating to law or its administration; legal; or (2) of or pertaining to rights and obligations <jural relations>. Today, *jural* is more common in sense (2)—e.g.: "The rule was cast in terms of *jural* relations, with a particular suit falling into one class or another according to the character of the right sought to be enforced . . . ." Charles A. Wright, *The Law of Federal Courts* 476 (4th ed. 1983)./ "The same points and the same examples seem valid in relation to all possible kinds of *jural* interests, legal as well as equitable."

In sense (1), *jural* appears to be only a NEEDLESS VARIANT of simpler terms, such as *legal.* But some legal theorists make a case for it, arguing that, whereas *legal* can be ambiguous as between "pertaining to law" and "conforming to the law," *jural* (in sense 1) unambiguously carries the former meaning. Also, *jural* is ordinarily confined to contexts involving legal theory. "Witnesses are often required to describe in meticulous detail a happening that occurred months and years before the *jural* [delete *jural,* or read *juridical*] finding of facts."/ "One legacy of the Enlightenment is the belief that law is something separate from the state, a set of longstanding *jural* [read *legal*] rules or immutable principles resting on God or 'nature' that the state supposedly enforces."

Juristic = (1) of or relating to a jurist, or jurists generally; or (2) of or relating to law or the study of law. Sense (1), though not common, is surely the more useful meaning of this term—e.g.: "A few words now as to the authority attached to this *juristic* literature [the Digest]." James Hadley, *Introduction to Roman Law* 65 (N.Y., D. Appleton & Co., 1881)./ "The goal of modern Romanistics is to obtain as complete a picture as possible of the evolution of Roman legal institutions and of the forms of *juristic* thinking revealed by them from the earliest stages discernible down to Justinian and beyond . . . ." Hans J. Wolff, *Roman Law* 224 (1951). In sense (2), the word is merely a fuzzy equivalent of *legal:* "The transition from unwritten to written code marks a stage in the history of almost every *juristic* [read *legal*] system." Stephen Pfeil, "Law," in 17 *Encyclopedia Americana* 86, 87 (1953). See **juristic person.**

Juridical = (1) relating to judicial proceedings or to the law; or (2) of or relating to law. The form in *-idical* is standard. Sense (1) is perhaps justifiable—e.g.: "I cannot believe that the court ever meant, in listing the criteria that usually attend the creation of a remainder, to express an inflexible rule or an inexorable *juridical* formula by the use of which we would be able to derive an automatic answer in all cases." But in sense (2), the word is merely a puffed-up equivalent of *legal*—e.g.: "The line of departure will be set by that unfinished classic of *juridical* [read *legal*] righteousness, the statement that for every wrong there is a remedy."/ "The intent that must be manifested by the settlor is an intent to create the *juridical* [read *legal*] relationship known to the law as a trust." *Juridical* is sometimes mispronounced as if it were spelled *juridicial,* with a soft *-c-*.

Juratory, a rare term today, means "of or pertaining to an oath or oaths; expressed or contained in an oath" (*OED*). *Juratorial,* also rare, means "of or belonging to a jury" (*OED*).

jurat; jurant. Both mean "one who has taken an oath"; *jurant* is a NEEDLESS VARIANT that is little used. *Jurat* usually refers to a public official as, in Jersey, to a bailiff's assistant. But historically *jurat* could refer to a juror: "On his left was a group of twelve sworn *jurats,* selected not for their ignorance of or impartiality for the matters at hand, but precisely because they were more likely to know the truth in advance." (Eng.)

Jurat has an additional, and perhaps more common, sense: "a clause placed at the end of an affidavit stating the time, place, and officer before whom the affidavit was made." E.g., "It further appears that the *jurat* to the loyalty affidavit has been properly executed."

jurator = (1) one who swears; or (2) a juror. In sense (2), of course, the word is a NEEDLESS VARIANT. See **juror.**

juratory; juratorial. See **jural.**

jure gentium. See ***jus gentium.***

juridic; juridical. See **jural.**

JURIDICO-, a combining form common in Spanish and French legal writing, has come to be used with some frequency in English as well—e.g.: "They were the first to work out methods for the discovery of interpolations in the Digest and to realize that much *juridico*-historical information is found in sources outside of Justinian's *Corpus Iuris.*" Hans J. Wolff, *Roman Law* 211 (1951)./ "[T]hese relations of production are defined as entailing *juridico*-political (even ideological) conditions as well as economic ones." Catherine Colliot-Thelene, "Afterword" to I. Rubin, *A History of Economic Thought: Part 5* 426–29 (D. Filtzer, trans., 1979) (as quoted in Duncan Kennedy, *The Role of Law in Economic Thought,* 34 Am. U.L. Rev. 939, 1000 n.64 (1985)).

The prefix owes its existence to the perceived ineptitude of any derivative from *legal* as the first part of a compound. Writers who use *sociological* and *historico-legal* often feel uncomfortable with the newfangled and ill-formed *lego-* (q.v.), so they resort instead to *juridico-*.

juridification, a NEOLOGISM dating from the mid-1980s, is a LOAN TRANSLATION of the German word *Verrechtlichung,* which denotes the process of transforming social relations into legal relations—and social conflicts into legal conflicts—primarily through legislation and judicial decisions. Though probably destined never to move beyond the realm of theoretical JARGON, the word usefully describes modern society's increasing reliance on courts to adjudicate questions that were formerly dealt with by other, less formal means (for example, within the family or neighborhood). E.g., "[A] case exists for lesser *juridification* of labour relations, and for greater reliance on other political and social factors that have generated the transformations the country is now undergoing . . . ." Waclaw Szubert, *New Trends in Polish Labour Relations,* 12 Comp. Lab. L.J. 62, 72 (1990)./ "Some observers note the increasing encroachment of law on daily life—the *'juridification'* of the social sphere—with trepidation." Robert Anderson et al., *The Impact of Information*

Technology on Judicial Administration, 66 S. Cal. L. Rev. 1761, 1799 (1993).

The verb *juridify,* seemingly a BACK-FORMATION, is somewhat less common—e.g.: "[J]ust as dismissal procedures in Great Britain were increasingly *juridified,* despite the apparent predominance of an entirely different tradition, so attempts to limit the debate on dismissals in the United States to reflections exclusively addressing collective agreements and their implications failed." Spiros Simitis, *Denationalizing Labour Law: The Case Against Age Discrimination,* 15 Comp. Lab. L.J. 321, 324 (1994). Cf. **judicialize.**

jurimetrics, n., = the social science that attempts to "measure" those aspects of justice that are of an empirical nature. The term originated in the early 1960s in Lee Loevinger's article entitled *Jurimetrics: The Methodology of Legal Inquiry,* 28 Law & Contemp. Probs. 5 (1963). E.g., "Those who search for a technological and practical aspect of the law include writers espousing *jurimetrics.*" Forte, *Natural Law and Natural Laws,* 26 Univ. Bookman 75, 75 (1986)./ "Glendon Schubert, the leader of a school known as Behavioral Jurisprudence and called by some *'Jurimetrics,'* built on the work of Underhill Moore. He sought to develop a systematic, behavioral method for predicting judgments." W.M. Reisman & A.M. Schreiber, *Jurisprudence* 458–59 (1987). Today a journal called *Jurimetrics Journal* publishes papers within the field.

Jurimetrician refers to a lawyer, esp. an academic lawyer, who tries to solve legal problems scientifically.

jurisconsult (= one learned in law, esp. in civil or international law; jurist; a master of jurisprudence [*OED*]) is a well-known word from Roman law but is little used today. Perhaps it merits wider service—e.g.: "The judges [of the International Court of Justice] . . . must be qualified in their own country for the highest judicial office or be *juris-consults* of recognized capacity in international law . . . ." J.L. Brierly, *The Law of Nations* 279 (5th ed. 1955). Despite Brierly's spelling, the term should be solid, not hyphenated.

jurisdiction. A. Senses. As Alexander Hamilton observed, the word is "composed of *jus* and *dicto, juris, dictio,* or a speaking or pronouncing of the law." *The Federalist* No. 81, at 489 n.* (Clinton Rossiter ed., 1961). It may mean (1) "the power of a nation to speak with binding effect concerning legal relations" <Iraq's jurisdiction>; (2) within a nation, the power of a smaller governmental unit (such as an American state) to create interests that, under the principles of the common law, will be recognized as valid in other states" <Arizona's jurisdiction>; (3) "the power of a court to decide a case or enter a decree" <the constitutional grant of jurisdiction>; (4) "the territory within which an authority may exercise its power" <the accused fled the jurisdiction>; or (5) "a political or judicial entity within such a territory" <other jurisdictions make a similar distinction>. Senses (1) and (2) are most commonly used within the field of conflict of laws; sense (3) is the ordinary legal sense; sense (4) is the most prevalent outside law, but lawyers use the word in this sense as well; sense (5) is common but rarely mentioned by those who catalogue the meanings of the word. See **concurrent jurisdiction.**

B. And *venue.* *Venue* refers to the possible or proper *places* for the trial of a lawsuit, as distinguished from the proper *forums* in which *jurisdiction* (the *power* to hear the case) might be established. *Jurisdiction* over a suit may exist in a particular district, though its venue there would be improper; conversely, the *venue* of a suit may be appropriate in a particular district, though it must be dismissed there for lack of jurisdiction. The most important difference between the two is that a party may consent to be sued in an improper venue, waiving any objection to venue. But a party cannot consent to subject-matter jurisdiction, which the parties cannot confer on a court.

C. Prepositions With. *Jurisdiction* takes *of* or *over.* "This court does not have *jurisdiction over* the appeal."/ "How such a magistrate can be said to have had no *jurisdiction over* the charge at all, it is hard to see." (Eng.)/ "This court has *jurisdiction of* the subject matter of the claims asserted in plaintiff's first amended complaint."

jurisdictional; jurisdictive. *Jurisdictional,* the ordinary word, means "of or relating to jurisdiction." E.g., "The time limit fixed by Rule 59(e) is *jurisdictional:* it may not be extended by waiver of the parties or by rule of the district court."

Jurisdictive, a much rarer term, means "having jurisdiction." E.g., "Turning to the central issue presented in this case, we must decide what court is *jurisdictive* of this suit." *Owner-Operators Indep. Drivers Ass'n v. State,* 541 A.2d 69, 71 (R.I. 1988). The DIFFERENTIATION between the two headwords has only recently emerged, *jurisdictive* being, in its other senses, a NEEDLESS VARIANT of *jurisdictional.*

jurisdictionless (= not having jurisdiction) is a late-20th-century NEOLOGISM. E.g., "This after-the-event resuscitation will encourage plaintiffs to try, and District Judges to tolerate, impleaders in the certain knowledge that all will be purified by the Court of Appeals whose wand of dismissal disinfects the infected *jurisdictionless* Court." *Burleson v. Coastal Recreation, Inc.*, 595 F.2d 332, 339 (5th Cir. 1978) (Brown, C.J., dissenting)./ "In addition, the court held that the *Goldlawr* case only provided for *jurisdictionless* transfer in cases under § 1406(a)." *Reed v. Brown,* 623 F. Supp. 342, 346 (D. Nev. 1985).

jurisdiction over (of) the subject matter. See **subject-matter jurisdiction.**

jurisdictive. See **jurisdictional.**

juris gentium. See ***jus gentium.***

jurisprude, not recorded in the *OED,* is listed in *W3* as a BACK-FORMATION from *jurisprudence* with the meaning "a person who makes ostentatious show of learning in jurisprudence and the philosophy of law or who regards legal doctrine with undue solemnity or veneration."

The word deserves wider currency, but not without recognition of its pejorative connotations. (For the neutral personal noun corresponding to *jurisprudence,* see **jurisprudent.**) Occasionally, *jurisprude* is misapplied as if it were a neutral noun: "Our point of view has been expressed aptly by one of your most influential *jurisprudes* [i.e., Karl Llewellyn—hence, read *jurisprudents*] . . . ." Glenn W. Ferguson, *Vocabulary, Veil, and Vested Interest,* 10 J. Legal Educ. 87, 88 (1957)./ "Yet all these scientific theories of law still leave contemporary *jurisprudes* [read *jurisprudents*] unsatisfied, and for good reason." Forte, *Natural Law and Natural Laws,* 26 Univ. Bookman 75, 75–76 (1986).

jurisprudence. A. Practical and Theoretical Senses. This uncertain term has evolved curiously. The *OED* assigns to it three senses: (1) "knowledge of or skill in law"; (2) "the science that treats of human laws (written or unwritten) in general"; and (3) "a system or body of law." Sense (1), denoting practical skill in the law—the original sense—shifted to create the meanings (2 & 3) that emphasize the body of knowledge with which skilled practitioners work.

Though derivatives of *jurisprudence* exist in a number of Western languages, this shift in meaning from the practical to the theoretical has apparently occurred only in English. Although both senses remain alive, the theoretical one, equivalent now roughly to "philosophy of the law," or "general theory of law," now predominates. The result, one writer has argued, is that "a word of distinguished pedigree and a well-established English meaning not essentially different from that which it bears in other languages has been made to colour like a chameleon and finally emerge as a self-contradictory chimera." A.H. Campbell, *A Note on the Word Jurisprudence,* 58 Law Q. Rev. 334, 339 (1942).

Well, not exactly. We might wish for less confusion, but it looks today as if the theoretical *jurisprudence* (senses 2 & 3) will oust its practical competitor (sense 1), which is labeled archaic by *W3,* and at this point there is little we can do but take note.

But Holland's lament—that many writers use *jurisprudence* as a highfalutin equivalent of *law*—remains a valid caution in many contexts: "The imposing quadrisyllable is constantly introduced into a phrase on grounds of euphony alone. Thus we have books upon 'Equity Jurisprudence' [as by Story and Pomeroy], which are nothing more nor less than treatises upon the law administered by Courts of Equity . . . . This sacrifice of sense to sound might more readily be pardoned, had it not misled serious and accurate thinkers." Thomas E. Holland, *The Elements of Jurisprudence* 4–5 (13th ed. 1924; repr. 1937). In defense of Story and Pomeroy, though, *Equity Law* would certainly have been a confusing title.

B. For *caselaw.* In AmE *jurisprudence* has been extended further than elsewhere in the English-speaking world, from "body of law" to "caselaw; court decisions." E.g., "The seaman's cause of action against a shipowner for unseaworthiness of the vessel is largely a child of twentieth-century federal *jurisprudence.*" Note, *The Doctrine of Unseaworthiness in the Lower Federal Courts,* 76 Harv. L. Rev. 819, 819 (1963)./ "This holding recognized and applied as part of the general maritime law a principle previously applied by either statute or *jurisprudence* in other contexts." The French term *la jurisprudence* has precisely this sense, as does the German *die Jurisprudenz. Case-law* and *decisional law* are less grandiose terms in English. See **case(-)law** & **decision(al) law.**

C. As a Count Noun. *Jurisprudence* is not properly a COUNT NOUN. E.g., "The courts for many years refused to acknowledge the existence of 'administrative law' as *a jurisprudence* [read *a branch of jurisprudence*]."

D. General, Particular, and Comparative Jurisprudence. The phrase *general jurisprudence* refers to legal theory applied to law and legal systems generally. *Particular jurisprudence* is the scholarly study of the legal system within a particular jurisdiction. *Comparative jurisprudence,* a term in growing use, is preferred by some scholars to *comparative law.*

jurisprudent; jurisprudential. *Jurisprudent,* though appearing to be an adjective, is a noun meaning "a jurist, or learned lawyer." E.g., "We have no difficulty with the theoretical concept, expressed in various ways by modern *jurisprudents,* that intentional, willful, or malicious harms of any kind are actionable unless justified." *Trautwein v. Harbourt,* 123 A.2d 30, 40 (N.J. Super. Ct. App. Div. 1956)./ "When there is no rule to follow the court must make one, or, as some *jurisprudents* prefer, 'discover' one." *Britt v. Sears,* 277 N.E.2d 20, 21 (Ind. App. 1971). Cf. **jurisprude.**

Jurisprudential = of or relating to jurisprudence. E.g., "In a real and practical sense, when such an opportunity arises, the remedial considerations (not theoretical or *jurisprudential* concepts) totally dictate the course of action the plaintiff should pursue."

jurist. In BrE, this word is reserved for those having made outstanding contributions to legal thought and legal literature. In AmE, it is rather loosely applied to every judge of whatever level, and sometimes even to nonscholarly practitioners who are well respected.

Here the term is used correctly: "These topics would lead us into a very enlarged inquiry, incompatible with the object of this summary sketch; but they deserve the attention of all students of the law of prize, and it is to be hoped that some eminent *jurist* will, hereafter, examine them . . . ." Appendix on Prize Causes, 15 U.S. (2 Wheat.) 37 (1817)./ "I cannot doubt that Livingston will be held the great jurist of nineteenth-century America and one to rank with Bentham among English-speaking *jurists.*" Roscoe Pound, *The Formative Era of American Law* 167 (1938)./ "The great German *jurist* Savigny described law as the product of the common consciousness of the people." H.G. Hanbury, *English Courts of Law* 15 (2d ed. 1953).

The most common error in AmE is to suppose that *jurist* is merely an equivalent of *judge:* "We find no constitutional question concerning the validity of Charles Milton's conviction and sentence of death about which reasonable *jurists* [read *judges*] could differ."

The word has also been appropriated by those who work in legal philosophy—but *jurisprudent* is the more accurate term in this sense. Sometimes, of course, the senses overlap: "The legal scholar (whom we may, perhaps, here term a *'jurist'* or *'jurisprudent'*) is finally limited only by the communication value of his creations and the usefulness of the resulting concepts . . . ." Julius Stone, *Legal System and Lawyers' Reasoning* 205 (1968).

juristic; juristical. The latter is a NEEDLESS VARIANT. See **jural.**

juristic person; artificial person. These phrases, which are esp. common in BrE, are ordinarily defined as "a corporate entity." Holland's definitions are more precise: (1) "a mass of property or a group of human beings that, in the eye of the law, is capable of rights and liabilities"; or (2) "such a mass of property or group of humans to which the law gives a status." See Thomas E. Holland, *The Elements of Jurisprudence* 97–98 (13th ed. 1924; repr. 1937).

Juristic person is the usual phrase. E.g., "Countries ordinarily accept the existence of *juristic persons* brought into being in their country of origin." (Eng.)/ "The phrase includes damages arising from those acts for which a private ship is held legally responsible as a *juristic person* under the customary legal terminology of the admiralty law." Grant Gilmore & Charles L. Black, Jr., *The Law of Admiralty* 984 (2d ed. 1975).

Other names for *juristic person* are *conventional person, fictitious person,* and *juridical person,* all of which should be avoided as NEEDLESS VARIANTS.

jurocracy = government by the courts. See, e.g., D.L. Horowitz, *The Jurocracy: Government Lawyers, Agency Programs, and Judicial Decisions* (1977). The term is recorded in none of the major dictionaries, although certainly it is a useful addition to the language. See GOVERNMENTAL FORMS.

A less-well-formed equivalent is *judiocracy,* coined by a noted conservative writer: "As our judges have become the makers of law, our Congress has become a colony of actors. In an era of judicial restraint, they are going to have to take responsibility for their acts and answer to the electorate. Times change. We move from *judiocracy* [read *jurocracy*] back to old-fashioned democracy." R. Emmett Tyrrell, *Bork, Now More Than Ever,* Am. Spectator, Nov. 1987, at 10.

juror; juryman; jurywoman; jurator. *Juror* is the modern word. *Juryman* and *jurywoman* should be avoided on grounds of SEXISM, although they still occasionally appear. E.g., "A petty juror may not, and it is doubtful whether a grand juror may, give evidence as to what passed between the *jurymen* [read *jurors*] in the discharge of their duties." (Eng.) *Jurator* is an obsolete equivalent.

Juror ought to be distinguished from *potential juror* or *veniremember*—e.g.: "When the court was cleared of unchosen *jurors* [read *veniremembers*], the spectators waiting in the corridor were allowed inside." John Bryson, *Evil Angels* 346 (1985). See **venireman.**

jury is a COLLECTIVE NOUN in AmE; hence, in most contexts, it takes a singular verb. To emphasize the individual members of the jury, we have the word *jurors.* In AmE, *jury* is almost always treated as a singular noun—e.g.: "A *jury* of twelve *was* chosen." *Thiel v. Southern Pac. Co.,* 328 U.S. 217, 219 (1946)./ "Judges do not decide questions of fact; the *jury do* [read *does*] not decide questions of law."/ "The *jury have* [read *has*] little use for a smart-aleck cross-examiner."

In BrE, however, where using plural verbs with collective nouns is common, *jury* usually takes a plural verb—e.g.: "As a result of Shaw's case, virtually any cooperative conduct is criminal if a *jury consider* it *ex post facto* to have been immoral." H.L.A. Hart, *Law Liberty, and Morality* 12 (1963; repr. 1969). But exceptions do occur in BrE—e.g.: "[I]t is only when this *jury has* determined the facts that the judge is empowered to impose sentence . . . ." 1 Winston Churchill, *A History of the English Speaking Peoples* 222 (1956; repr. 1983).

Jury is both adjective and noun. Here it acts as an adjective: "*Dunn* still has a sound rationale, Justice Rehnquist declares: the possibility that the inconsistency was a product of *jury* lenity." The legal writer should be aware that, as a general English adjective, *jury* has, in addition to the ordinary legal meaning "of or relating to a jury," the maritime meaning "makeshift" <a jury rig>.

jurybox; jury-stand. *Jurybox* is the standard term in AmE and BrE alike, though it is often spelled as two words (*jury box*) on both sides of the Atlantic. *Jury-stand* is a NEEDLESS VARIANT.

jury-fixing. See **jury-packing.**

jury, go to the. When a case *goes to the jury,* the jury begins its deliberations. E.g., Wade Lambert & Paul M. Barrett, *Haas Stock-Fraud Trial to Go to Jury,* Wall St. J., 4 Dec. 1989, at B4./ "Cynthia Dowaliby was acquitted by the judge before the case *went to the jury.*" Janita Poe & Terry Wilson, *Dowaliby Case Status Unaltered by Reports,* Chicago Tribune, 6 Jan. 1993, at 3.

jury instruction (AmE) = *jury direction* (BrE).

juryless (= without a jury) is one of Jeremy Bentham's modest successes as a word-coiner. In the early 19th century, he wrote of "a wicked and *jury-less* Court of Conscience act." Jeremy Bentham, *Scottish Reform Considered* 29 (1808). The word has occurred in many modern contexts—e.g.: "[T]he Board differs from a trial judge (in a *juryless* case) who hears and sees the witnesses . . . ." *NLRB v. Universal Camera Corp.,* 190 F.2d 429, 432 (2d Cir. 1951) (Frank, J., concurring)./ "The strategy of the English government was to remove litigation to the *juryless* forum of the vice-admiralty courts . . . ." Grant Gilmore, *The Ages of American Law* 9 (1977).

jury lottery. Those who are not fond of the jury system use this phrase to describe the unpredictability of juries, esp. those that award high amounts of punitive damages. E.g., "But awards far larger than necessary to achieve deterrence are naked and economically counterproductive transfers of wealth through a capricious *jury lottery.*" Stuart Taylor, Jr., *High Court Should Set Limits in Punitive Damages Sweepstakes,* Manhattan Law., 25 April 1989, at 10./ "Last week's was a typically absurd case of law by *jury lottery* . . . ." L. Gordon Crovitz, *A Legal Rule for the Justices: Never Forget the Consumer,* Wall St. J., 13 March 1991, at A13.

juryman. See **juror** & SEXISM (B).

jury of indictment. See **grand jury** (A).

jury-packing; jury-tampering; jury-fixing. *Jury-packing* = contriving to have the jury peopled with those who are predisposed toward one side or the other. *Jury-tampering* = engaging in any activity that might improperly influence one or more jurors. (Another term for jury-tampering is *embracery,* q.v.) *Jury-fixing* = corruptly procuring the cooperation of jurors who actually influence the outcome of a trial.

jury-stand. See **jurybox.**

juryroom. One word, increasingly, though the *OED* lists it in hyphenated form and *W3* lists it as two words.

jury-tampering. See **jury-packing.**

jury trial. Two words, no hyphen.

jury venire. See **venire.**

jury wheel = (traditionally) a contraption, usu. a circular box revolving on a crank, that aids officials in randomly choosing those who will be called in for jury duty. In several jurisdictions today, *jury wheel* has come to apply to the computer methods that have displaced the old-fashioned crank-up devices. E.g., "Richard J. Masotta, associate director of the Yale University Computer Center, which has a contract with the federal government to compile the master list and the so-called *jury wheel,* also had no answer to the mystery." William Cockerham, *Federal Jury Picks Questioned,* Hartford Courant, 29 July 1992, at A1.

jurywoman. See **juror** & SEXISM (B).

jus (= law in the most abstract and general sense; a legal right, rule, or principle of law) forms the plural *jura.* E.g., "Such a lien secures the creditor neither *jus in rem* nor *jus ad rem.*"/ "Rights to things, *jura in rem,* have for their subject some material thing, as land or goods, which the owner may use or dispose of in any manner he pleases within the limits prescribed by the terms of his right." The term is spelled also *ius.* See ***jus in re(m).***

Inexplicably, one learned writer fell into error by pluralizing the word as if it were a masculine Latin noun rather than a neuter: "The question can be approached from another angle, that of the clarity of the rules about particular aspects of the law, the content of the *iures* [read *iura*], so to speak. . . ." E.Z. Tabuteau, *Transfers of Property in Eleventh-Century Norman Law* 225 (1988). For Latinists—and there are still a few in the law—*so to speak* is an abomination.

jus ad bellum. See ***jus in bello.***

jus ad rem. See ***jus in re(m).***

jus civile; jus gentium. *Jus civile* denoted the legal rules and principles applicable to citizens only—the common law of ancient Rome. *Jus gentium* denoted the legal rules and principles derived from customs of various peoples and nations or from fundamental ideas of right and wrong applicable to foreigners litigating in Rome and later supposed by some to be universal in the human mind. See ***jus gentium,* civil law (A)** & **international law.**

jus cogens = the peremptory norms of international law. E.g., "Such [peremptory] norms, often referred to as *jus cogens* (or 'compelling law'), enjoy the highest status in international law . . . ." *Committee of U.S. Citizens Living in Nicaragua v. Reagan,* 859 F.2d 929, 935 (D.C. Cir. 1988).

jus disponendi (= the right to dispose of property) is an unnecessary LATINISM that masks as a TERM OF ART. E.g., "He has the entire *jus disponendi* [read *right to dispose of the property*], which imports that he may give it absolutely, or may impose any restriction or fetters not repugnant to the nature of the estate that he gives."/ "Here, undoubtedly, the devisee is given an estate in fee simple by clear, unambiguous, and explicit words; this carries the *jus disponendi* [read *right of disposition*]."

jus gentium; juris gentium; jure gentium. The *jus gentium,* literally, is the law of nations. More specifically, it means either (1) "the body of law governing the status of foreigners in ancient Rome and their relations with foreign citizens (*jus civile* [q.v.], by contrast, applying to Roman citizens only); or (2) ever since the time of Grotius (1583–1645), the customary law of nations. See **international law.**

Juris gentium is the genitive form meaning "of the law of nations"—e.g.: "Tradition . . . was set down as an institution *Juris Gentium,* or rule of the Law common to all Nations." Henry S. Maine, *Ancient Law* 41 (17th ed. 1901; repr. [New Universal Lib.] 1905, 1910). *Jure gentium* is the ablative form meaning "by the law of nations" among other things—e.g.: "[S]imilar instances may be found . . . in common law offences regarded as crimes *jure gentium,* such as piracy on the high seas." R.H. Graveson, *Conflict of Laws* 181 (7th ed. 1974).

jus in bello; jus ad bellum. The first means "the corpus of the laws and customs of war." The second means "the right of making war."

jus in re(m); jus ad rem. The distinction is a simple one, although of decreasing importance: "A *jus in re* is a right, or property in a thing, valid as against all mankind. A *jus ad rem* is a valid claim on one or more persons to do something, by force of which a *jus in re* will be acquired." *The Young Mechanic,* 30 F. Cas. 873, 876 (C.C.D. Me. 1855) (No. 18,180). The usual phrase in Anglo-American law is *jus in rem* (lit., "right against a thing"), not *jus in re* (lit., "right in or over a thing"). For the distinction between *in rem* and *in personam,* see **in personam (B).**

jus naturale. See **natural law (A).**

jus sanguinis = a legal rule whereby a child's citizenship is that of his parents. We have no other name for it.

just deserts (= a reward or punishment that is deserved) is occasionally misrendered *just desserts,* as here: "Nor can Horizon avoid its just *desserts* [read *deserts*] by its pleonastic harping on the fact that its conduct . . . has been impeccable since at least mid-June of 1983." *NLRB v. Horizon Air Servs., Inc.,* 761 F.2d 22, 32 (1st Cir. 1985).

jus tertii (= the right of a third party) generally is not a useful enough LATINISM to justify its presence in legal prose. E.g., "Recovery in trover by a mere possessor against the defense of title in a third party (*jus tertii*) [omit parenthetical phrase] is apparently allowed in most states in which the question has been raised."/ "Respondents may be correct that petitioner does not possess standing *jus tertii* [read *as a third party*], but that is not the issue."/ "But in the third case, *i.e.,* where the plaintiff was not in possession, the defendant may *set up a jus tertii, i.e.,* [delete the italicized language immediately preceding] prove that some other person has a better title . . . ." O. Hood Phillips, *A First Book of English Law* 230 (3d ed. 1955).

justice. See **judge.**

justice of the peace. See **J.P.**

justiceship; justicedom; justicehood. The first is the usual term; the others are NEEDLESS VARIANTS.

justiciability, in the federal law of the U.S., is a TERM OF ART employed to give expression to the limitation placed upon federal courts by the case-or-controversy doctrine. A matter that is a case or controversy is susceptible of a judicial determination—is justiciable. See **case or controversy & justiciable.**

justiciable; judicable. The former is preferred in the sense "susceptible of judicial decision; triable" <justiciable cases and controversies>. In the following quotation, however, the word is used nonsensically; Justice Thurgood Marshall, in quoting this sentence, appropriately *sic*'d it: "[T]here has not been enough time in which *justiciably* [*sic*] to decide the case." As quoted in *Dobbert v. Wainwright,* 468 U.S. 1231, 1242 (1984) (Marshall, J., dissenting). *Judicable* is a NEEDLESS VARIANT, and *justiceable* is a fairly common misspelling.

justicial. The *OED* defines this term as "of or pertaining to justice or its administration"—a use last recorded in 1826. Some writers, such as Fred Rodell, use it as the adjective corresponding to the title *justice,* as in *Supreme Court Justice:* "A month after Grant took office, and while the first of the Legal Tender cases was still on its way up to the Court, Congress, perhaps foreseeing trouble, had increased the number of Justices to nine (at which figure, despite Franklin Roosevelt's bid to raise the *Justicial* ante, it has remained ever since)." Fred Rodell, *Nine Men* 158 (1955).

justiciar, n.; **justiciary.** The former is obsolete in all but historical senses relating to medieval England and Scotland. The latter survives in the names *Clerk of Justiciary* and *High Court of Justiciary,* both relating to the supreme criminal courts of Scotland, and as an adjective in related contexts, e.g., *justiciary gowns, justiciary cases,* and *Lords Commissions of Justiciary.*

justification. See **excuse.**

justificatory; justificative. The latter is a NEEDLESS VARIANT of the former. But *justificatory* itself is often part of a longer phrase that can be tightened: "The plaintiff should have *marshaled justificatory reasons for* [better: *justified*] allowance of the amount sought."

justify, like *warrant,* q.v., generally takes as its object an action or belief, not a person. E.g., "The instant cases furnish sufficient additional indications of the settlor's intent to *justify* our giving effect to the language of the instrument limiting an estate to the grantor's heirs."

In legal prose, however, this verb frequently takes personal objects. E.g., "M. told the officer nothing that would *justify the officer* in concluding that T. was about to escape."/ "The decision relied upon as *justifying the sheriff* in the levy of execution and sale of the property is *James v. Western North Carolina Ry. Co.*"

This usage is old, and perhaps only today could be considered a LEGALISM: "If, therefore, the process could be commenced in rem, the authority of *Bynkershoek* would *justify* us . . . ." *Chisholm v. Georgia,* 2 U.S. (2 Dall.) 419, 425–26 (1793). Nevertheless, it strikes the modern ear as unidiomatic and illogical.

Justinian is a proper noun, the name of the Roman emperor (483–565 A.D.) who was perhaps the greatest legal codifier ever, responsible for promulgating the *Corpus Juris Civilis.*

For the adjective corresponding to his name, some books use *Justinianean* /*jəs-tin-ee-**an**-ee-ən*/, a clumsy word whose only advantage is that it is distinct from the name itself. Other books use *Justinian* as the adjective as well as the noun (see, e.g., the Hadley quotation under **reception**). The former spelling seems stilted; the latter is quite acceptable.

juvenile. See **child.**

juvenile offender. This phrase, like *juvenile delinquent,* is a technical term deriving from 20th-century legislation. It generally refers to a minor who commits a criminal offense. Just why it offends some—in a juvenile way, one might say—is hard to fathom: "Among all legal expressions that lend themselves to weasely interpretations, there is one that deserves nomination for the Weasel Award. 'Juvenile (or Child) Offender' is a jewel of understatement created by welfare workers and a judiciary subject to political pressures." Mario Pei, *Words in Sheep's Clothing* 87 (1969). What would Mr. Pei have us call such offenders? *Hooligans?*

juxtaposition cannot be a verb; although one may *position* a thing, one may not *juxtaposition* two things. *Juxtapose* is the correct verb form.

K

kangaroo court (= a court, often illegitimately held, in which the principles of law and justice are disregarded and perverted) originated in the mid-19th century as American slang but is now an acceptable phrase, if responsibly applied, even in formal writing. *W2* records three particular types of kangaroo courts: (1) "a mock court held by vagabonds or by prisoners in a jail"; (2) "an irregularly conducted minor court in a frontier or unsettled district"; and (3) "formerly, one of a number of courts in Ohio with county-wide jurisdiction, whose judge was paid by fines imposed by him upon conviction of accused persons."

K.B. = King's Bench.

K.C. = King's Counsel.

Keeper of the King's Conscience = (historically) the Lord Chancellor, who had the royal power of deciding equitable petitions to the King—a power that gave rise to the system of *equity,* q.v. E.g., "In his character of 'Keeper of the King's Conscience,' [the Chancellor] was held justified in thus exerting the undefined residuary authority which in early times was attributed to an English king." Thomas E. Holland, *The Elements of Jurisprudence* 73 (13th ed. 1924; repr. 1937). See **chancellor.**

keeper of the peace is a LOAN TRANSLATION of the Latin phrase *custos pacis,* a phrase sometimes Englished as *guardian of the peace.* Our phrase *to keep the peace* derives from the agent-noun phrase.

key number. This phrase refers to the elaborate indexing system developed by West Publishing Co. for cataloguing the whole of American caselaw with brief (or not-so-brief) headnotes. The phrase is older than many lawyers suspect—e.g.: "The section number . . . affixed to the first catchword of the headnote paragraph is a *'key-number,'* unlocking the door to all future and past decisions involving a similar principle." William M. Lile et al., *Brief Making and the Use of Law Books* 41 (3d ed. 1914)./ "The West *Key Number* system gives a crude sense of the numerical dominance of opinions on preliminary relief." Douglas Laycock, *The Death of the Irreparable Injury Rule* 110 (1991).

kidnapping. A. Spelling. The spellings in *-pp-* are, by convention, preferred. The inferior spelling *kidnaping* occasionally appears, however, as in *People v. Norris,* 706 P.2d 1141 (Cal. 1985) (en banc).

That spelling has its defenders, among them Rollin Perkins: "The form with a single 'p' is to be preferred because it is a general rule of spelling that the accent determines whether or not to double the letter when the suffix is to be added to a word ending in a *single consonant* preceded by a *single vowel* . . . . [T]he final consonant is *not* doubled if the word has more than one syllable and the accent is not on the last." Rollin M. Perkins, *Criminal Law* 134 n.1 (1957) (citing the examples of *develop, offer,* and *suffer*).

Perkins's final statement, explaining the general rule, is sound. But it overlooks the exceptional nature of *kidnapping.* First, the word is formed on the model of the shorter verb: *nap, napping.* Second, up to the 19th century, *kidnap* was generally accented on the second syllable. Third, *kidnapping* is between five and ten times as common as *kidnaping* in printed sources. See DOUBLING OF FINAL CONSONANTS.

B. Sense. *Kidnapping* = the act or an instance of taking or carrying away a person without his or her consent, by force or fraud, and without lawful excuse. Glanville Williams addresses the question whether *kidnapping* refers, as its etymology suggests, to the napping of kids:

> Well, apparently not: not in the modern sense. It seems that when the term originated the "kids" who were napped were not the young of the human species but labourers (called "kids") who were recruited by force or guile for agricultural service in the American colonies. And the crime has always been as much concerned with the taking of adults as with the taking of children. Indeed, the

> original kidnap is the taking of adults: infants were not of much use in the plantations.
>
> Glanville Williams, *Can Babies Be Kidnapped?* 1989 Crim. L. Rev. 473, 473.

Williams notes that the generally accepted definition of *kidnap*—given just above—is actually a definition of the term *adult-kidnap. Id.* With *child-kidnap* (popularly termed *child-stealing* or *baby-snatching*), the element of force or fraud is often missing, as when someone makes off with a baby-stroller. *Id.* See **abduction.**

kill . . . dead is a REDUNDANCY popularly promoted (alas) in television commercials touting insecticides that, it is said, will "kill bugs dead."

kind of is a poor substitute for *somewhat, rather, somehow,* and other adverbs. It properly functions as a noun, however, signifying category or class in phrases such as *this kind of writ.* See **these kind of.**

kindred, n., = relationship by consanguinity. E.g., "The policy of our laws is that heirs or next of kin who are in equal degree of *kindred* to the intestate, inherit per capita in equal shares, while those in a more remote degree, take per stirpes, or such portion as their immediate ancestor would inherit if living." See **consanguinity & affinity.**

King; Queen. In English legal decisions, if the monarch is a party, he or she is, in civil cases, sometimes called "The King" or "The Queen" in the style of the case. The abbreviated form *R.* (for *Rex* or *Regina*) is also commonly used, esp. in criminal cases. Even so, the case name *R. v. Baker* is pronounced "The Queen against Baker." See CASE REFERENCES & **R.**

king's conscience. See **Keeper of the King's Conscience.**

King's Court is a LOAN TRANSLATION of the phrase *Curia Regis,* q.v. Most historians refer to the *Curia Regis,* but others, such as Plucknett, use *King's Court* as well. See Theodore F.T. Plucknett, *A Concise History of the Common Law* 142 (5th ed. 1956).

King's evidence, to turn. See **turn state's evidence.**

king's foot. See **chancellor's foot.**

king's peace. See **against the peace.**

kinsman (= a relative) is less and less used, perhaps because of the desire to avoid sexism. See SEXISM (B).

KITCHEN FRENCH. See LAW FRENCH.

kleptomania; cleptomania. The former spelling is now standard.

knit has the past-tense forms *knit* and *knitted,* the former being preferred. Cf. **fit.**

knitpick. See **nitpick.**

knock-for-knock agreement (= an arrangement between insurers that each will pay the claim of its insured without claiming against the other party's insurer) should be hyphenated thus. See PHRASAL ADJECTIVES.

know all men by these presents (= take notice) is a FLOTSAM PHRASE—as sexist as it is inscrutable to most readers—that needlessly begins many legal documents. Following is a typical beginning of a bond: "*Know all men by these presents,* that we, X Corp., as principal, and Y Insurance Co., as surety, are held and firmly bound unto the Clerk of the United States District Court for the Eastern District of Texas, in the sum of $100." The phrase originated as a LOAN TRANSLATION of the LATINISM *noverint universi* (= know all persons).

know-how = the information, practical knowledge, techniques, and skill required to achieve some practical end, particularly in industry or technology. *Know-how* is considered incorporeal property, in which rights may be bought and sold. E.g., "Gates seeks to recover the damages that it allegedly incurred as a result of defendant Yuasa's alleged breach of an agreement with Gates regarding the nondisclosure of trade-secret technical *know-how.*" The phrase is best hyphenated.

knowledge; notice. As a general matter, *knowledge* requires awareness of a fact or condition, while *notice* requires merely a reason to know of a fact or condition. *Knowledge* is subsumed within *notice* because actual awareness is well above the threshold requirement of a reason to be aware. See *Restatement (Second) of Agency* § 9 (1958). E.g., "*'Notice'* and *'knowledge'* are not synonyms; when one says of a person that he was 'on notice' of a fact, one may mean just that he should have known, not that he did know." *Shacket v. Philko Aviation, Inc.,* 841 F.2d 166, 170 (7th Cir. 1988).

The phrase *constructive knowledge* is equivalent to—and inferior to—*notice.*

kudos (fr. Gk. *kydos* "glory") is a singular noun meaning "praise, glory." It is sometimes erroneously thought to be a plural. So *kudo,* a false singular—and therefore *kudoes,* a mistaken plural—have come to plague many texts. E.g., "I appreciate profoundly the *kudo* [read *kudos*—and read on] for loquacity bestowed upon me by my learned colleague of the majority . . . . I return it to him for placement wherever he is wont to place *kudoes* [read *kudos*]." *Nelson v. Miller,* 480 P.2d 467, 480 (Utah 1971) (Henriod, J., dissenting). Other writers mistakenly use a plural verb with *kudos,* as here: "Kudos *are* [read *is*] not awarded for these skills . . . ." Gertrude Block, *Effective Legal Writing* 1 (2d ed. 1983). Cf. HYPERCORRECTION (A).

L

label makes *labeled, labeling* (AmE), or *labelled, labelling* (BrE). See DOUBLING OF FINAL CONSONANTS.

labor, v.t. See **belabor.**

Labo(u)r Party. In Great Britain, the spelling is *Labour Party;* in Australia, the spelling is *Labor Party.* How should Americans spell the name of the British party? Most newspapers Americanize the spelling, making it *Labor,* but the better practice is to spell this proper name, like any other, just as it is spelled in BrE.

laches. **A. Sense.** *Laches* (LAW FRENCH meaning "remissness, slackness") = unreasonable delay or negligence in pursuing a right or claim, esp. an equitable one, that may disentitle a claimant to relief. The doctrine exemplifies the reserved power of equity to withhold relief otherwise regularly granted when the relief would be unfair or unjust.

The *OED* records a transferred sense—"culpable negligence in general"—which modern lawyers would find difficult to accept. E.g., "[I]n his heart he felt rather ashamed that his conduct had shown *laches* which others who did not get benefices were free from." George Eliot, *Middlemarch* 375 (1873; repr. 1956).

B. Pronunciation. The word is pronounced /***lach***-*əz*/ (AmE) or /***lay***-*chəz*/ (BrE).

C. Singular Noun. Though plural in appearance, *laches* is a singular noun that is sometimes incorrectly coupled with a plural verb. E.g., "Laches *are* [read *is*] pleaded as a defense, but the claim here is essentially at law, not in equity."

D. And *limitation.* The guiding principle in distinguishing these two is that "*laches* is not, like *limitation,* a mere matter of time; but principally a question of the inequity of permitting the claim to be enforced . . . ." *Galliher v. Cadwell,* 145 U.S. 368, 373 (1892). An old legal saw states that laches is a penalty for sleeping on one's rights. See **limitation.**

E. *Run* Idiom Inappropriate. Although we say, idiomatically, that the statute of limitations has *run,* it is not proper to use that verb with *laches. Run,* in this context, means "(of a period of time) to come to an end, be complete, expire." Because *laches* does not refer to any specific period of time but is determined after the fact by courts, it cannot be said to have *run,* but merely to *apply* in a given case. E.g., "Because the indemnity action had not yet vested, *laches on the action had not begun to run* [read *the period to which laches might later apply had not begun*]."

lacuna is a FORMAL WORD for *gap:* "If there is such a *lacuna* in the legislative scheme, the proper remedy is not for the courts to distort the plain language of section 1512, but for Congress to enact legislation to close the gap." (Note the INELEGANT VARIATION, which is remedied by changing *lacuna* to *gap.*) The plural *lacunae* is preferable to *lacunas.* See PLURALS (A).

lade (= to load) is an ARCHAISM in all senses, although it frequently appears in shipping contexts. See **laden (A) & lading, bill of.**

laden. **A. As a Past Participle Equivalent to *loaded.*** To the extent that *laden* lives, it lives primarily as a participial adjective <a laden barge> and not as a past participle. To use *laden* as a part of the verb phrase is to be guilty of ARCHAISM, although it is still used in shipping contexts. E.g., "The holder of the bill of lading had actual notice at the time of receiving the bill of lading that the goods had not in fact been *laden* on board." (Eng.) See **lade.**

B. For *ridden.* *Ridden* is the more general term, meaning "infested with" or "full of." *Laden* has not shed its strong connotation of "loaded down." Hence a place might be *laden* with things if they had been stacked there; or, more plausibly, a truck or barge might be *laden* with goods. But figuratively, *laden* fails as an effective adjective if the original suggestion of loading is ignored. E.g., "A seaman who removed his life jacket before diving into the *eddy-laden* [read *eddy-ridden*]

Mississippi River to rescue another seaman was held to be contributorily negligent."

lading, bill of. *Lading* is the Old English equivalent of *loading.* Dating from the 16th century, *bill of lading* = a document acknowledging the shipment of a consignor's goods for carriage by sea (*CDL*). See **laden (A).**

lady lawyer is an objectionable phrase to a great many lawyers (many but not all of them women). (See SEXISM.) The phrase sometimes merely supplements the already evident bias that some of its users harbor—e.g.: "At the trial, the relator was assigned two attorneys, Mr. Sheridan and Mr. Gellman. A *lady lawyer,* Katherine Bitses, . . . later became imbued with the cause of Kling after the trial." *U.S. ex rel. Kling v. La Vallee,* 188 F. Supp. 470, 472 (N.D.N.Y. 1960).

laesae majestatis; laesae majestas. See **lese majesty.**

lagan. See **flotsam.**

laic; lay. Whereas *laic* = nonclerical, nonecclesiastical, *lay,* which shares this sense, is broader, and encompasses the sense "nonprofessional, not expert, esp. with reference to law and medicine" (*OED*). Lawyers referred to jurors as *lay* ("unlearned, illiterate") in the LAW FRENCH of the Middle Ages. See **laity & layman.**

lain. See **lie & lay.**

laissez-faire; laisser-faire. The former spelling has long been standard. Some British publications, however, continue to use the outmoded spelling—e.g.: "Should Hongkong's *laisser-faire* [read *laissez-faire*] government do an about-face to build Hongkong Inc?" *Farewell to Adam Smith,* Economist, 30 Sept.–6 Oct. 1989, at 71.

laity is the noun corresponding to the adjective *lay.* But while *lay* is used about as commonly in legal as in church matters, *laity* appears far more commonly in religious than in legal contexts. Still, the *OED* includes the sense "unprofessional people, as opposed to those who follow some learned profession." E.g., "Fortunately for the bar and for the public, there are no rules of morality for the lawyers which do not apply with equal force to the *laity,* and it is well that there should not be." See **laic & layman.**

lament, v.t., should not be made intransitive by the addition of a preposition. E.g., "In this space we have often *lamented over* [omit *over*] the recent rise of ultraconservatism."

lamentable is preferably accented on the first, not the second, syllable /***lam***-ən-tə-bəl/.

land. When thinking of land, most speakers of English visualize the earth's surface. But in law, the word includes everything above and below the surface—even gases, liquids, and buildings. As a legal concept, then, *land* is an area of three-dimensional space, an inverted pyramid with its tip at the center of the earth and extending outward through the surface of the earth—where natural or imaginary points locate it by reference—and continuing upward to the sky. Land is both immovable and indestructible.

land charge; land law; land tax. Two words in each phrase.

landlocked (= shut in or enclosed by land; almost entirely surrounded by land) is usually used in literal senses in the law. But it has its figurative uses as well: "The Chancellor is no longer fixed to the woolsack: he may stride the quarter-deck of maritime jurisprudence and, in the role of admiralty judge, dispense as would his *landlocked* brother, that which equity and good conscience impel."

landlord = (1) at common law, the lord who, under the feudal system, retained the fee of the land; or (2) one who owns or holds real property and lets it out to others.

Some writers have begun to use *landlord* as a verb—e.g.: "Learning *landlording* from a book can be difficult . . . ." Edwards, *Renting Tips for Landlords,* Chicago Tribune, 15 Feb. 1991, at C17./ Leigh Robinson, *Landlording* (5th ed. 1988). The usage seems unlikely to spread, but see NOUNS AS VERBS.

landman. A. Generally. In the law of oil and gas, *landman* refers to a person who, usu. on behalf of an oil company, contracts with landowners for the mineral rights to their land. In this field (as in the oil fields), women as well as men refer to themselves as *landmen.* (A less common variant is *leaseman.*) Many female landmen say they are reluctant to adopt a nonsexist alternative that would apply only to them, because their male counterparts are unlikely to abandon the term. Still, various nonsexist equivalents—such as *exploration manager, land manager,* and *land agent*—have achieved limited currency.

A less likely candidate for eventual success is *landwoman:* "Betsy Spomer, a *landwoman* [read *land manager* or *land agent*] for Gulf in Casper, said the company plans to assign a full-time person to resolve differences . . . ." *Gulf Temporarily Shelves Little Knife Unit Plan,* Oil & Gas J., 9 Jan. 1984, at 47, 47. See SEXISM (B).

B. Meaning *"terre-tenant."* *Landman* was formerly used as a LOAN TRANSLATION equivalent to *terre-tenant,* q.v. Because this usage is likely to confuse readers, it is best avoided. If an English phrase is needed, *land-tenant* is a better substitute.

C. And *landsman.* Unlike *landman,* the word *landsman* usu. refers to someone who lives and works on land. But it may also refer to an inexperienced sailor—e.g.: "The seaman, while on his vessel, is subject to the rigorous discipline of the sea and has little opportunity to appeal to the protection from abuse of power which the law makes readily available to the *landsman.*" *Socony–Vacuum Oil Co. v. Smith,* 305 U.S. 424, 430 (1939)./ "This limitation serves much the same purpose for maritime ventures that the corporate fiction serves for the *landsman's* enterprises." *Black Diamond S.S. v. Robert Stewart & Sons,* 336 U.S. 386, 399 (1949) (Jackson, J., dissenting). See SEXISM (B).

landmark of the law is, as the following quotation suggests, a CLICHÉ to be sparingly bestowed on cases. E.g., "The critical decision is that of Lord Mansfield in *Moses v. MacFerlan* that truly merits the cliché, a *landmark of the law.*" See WORD-PATRONAGE.

landowner is written as one word in AmE and BrE. So is *landownership.*

lands, tenements, and hereditaments. This triplet is the traditional means of referring to real property. Though now frequently used as mere legalistic deadwood, the phrase may be parsed without REDUNDANCY.

Land, of course, denotes the terrestrial earth and what is above and below it, including water. See **land.**

Tenement = anything that might be the subject of common-law tenure. "The word . . . is of a more extensive signification than *land,* which it includes, in addition to most . . . incorporeal things real." 1 Herbert T. Tiffany, *The Law of Real Property* § 10, at 13 (3d ed. rev. Basil Jones 1939).

Hereditament traditionally includes whatever, upon the owner's death, passes by intestacy. "The term is more extensive in its signification than the word *tenement,* which it generally, though not always, includes, and it may, in England at least, include things of a personal character." *Id.* at 13–14. See **hereditament(s)** & DOUBLETS, TRIPLETS, AND SYNONYM-STRINGS.

land scrip is an Americanism meaning "a negotiable instrument entitling the holder, usu. an individual or company engaged in public service, to possess specified areas of public land." E.g., "[T]he United States issued *land scrip* to Mann for location on 'unoccupied and unappropriated public lands' and the holder made location on tidelands and received the register's certificate therefor." *Hynes v. Grimes Packing Co.,* 337 U.S. 86, 115 (1949)./ "'Color of title' [includes] a consecutive chain of transfers to the person in possession that . . . is based on a certificate of headright, land warrant, or *land scrip.*" Tex. Civ. Pract. & Rem. Code § 16.021 (West 1990).

landsman. See **landman** (C).

land tax. See **land charge.**

land-tenant. See **terre-tenant.**

language in the sense "wording (of a document)" is peculiar to the law. E.g., "Defendant points out that both sections 2223 and 2224 employ the *language* 'one who gains a thing,' and argues that the sense of the word 'gain' as thus used is to acquire a tangible benefit or an unconscionable thing." For an example illustrating the improper pluralizing of this MASS NOUN, see PLURALS (B).

lappage = (1) an overlapping of two claims to land; or (2) the portion of land over which rival claimants have overlapping claims. In AmE, almost every reported example originates in North Carolina—e.g.: "The rules of *lappage* [sense (1)] direct that when the title deeds of two rival claimants to land lap upon each other, and neither claimant is in actual possession of any of the land covered by the deeds, the claimant with the better title is deemed in possession of the *lappage* [sense (2)]." *Willis v. Mann,* 386 S.E.2d 68, 72 (N.C. Ct. App. 1989).

lapse, v.i., = (1) (of an estate or right) to pass away, revert (*to* someone) because conditions have not been fulfilled or because a person entitled to possession has failed in some duty; or (2) (of a devise or grant) to become void. Sense (2) is now much more usual—e.g.: "Suppose a man makes a will leaving all his property to his friend, *A. A* dies before the testator does. The gift to *A* is said to *lapse.* It becomes void, and the property goes to the testator's heirs." Robert Kratovil, *Real Estate Law* 247 (1946; repr. 1950). Cf. **ademption.**

lapse statute; antilapse statute; nonlapse statute. All three phrases denote (in AmE) the same type of statute, the meaning of which is illuminated in the quotations: "Nearly all states have enacted *lapse statutes* designed to provide a substitute beneficiary for the deceased legatee in certain situations."/ "A majority of the states have held that a *nonlapse statute* does not apply to a member of a class who was dead at the time of the execution of the will."/ "If an *antilapse statute* applies to save gifts of persons living when the will is executed but not the gifts of persons who die before the will is executed, republication of the will by codicil after the death of a legatee should not prevent an application of the statute to save the gift."

Today *lapse statute* is the most common phrase, even though it is the least logical (since the effect of the statute is to *prevent* the lapse of testamentary gifts). The most lucid phrase is *antilapse statute.* There are judicial opinions in which both *nonlapse* and *antilapse* appear in reference to the selfsame statute; yet the terms should not be varied in a single writing. See INELEGANT VARIATION.

lapsus linguae; lapsus calami. These LATINISMS are fancy ways of referring to slips of the tongue (*linguae*) or of the pen (*calami*). The phrase *lapsus linguae* is the more common one. For example, in a case in which the trial court incorrectly referred to a witness as "Mrs. Argentine," the appellate court wrote: "This obvious *lapsus linguae* was plainly meant to refer to Mrs. Larsen . . . ." *U.S. v. Argentine,* 814 F.2d 783, 787 n.5 (1st Cir. 1987).

As for *lapsus calami* (= a slip of the pen), a good example—though it may merely be a misprint—occurs in a judicial opinion that looks as if it represents a backslide in First Amendment rights. A judge writes: "The First Amendment is not a fetish. *Reversed* it must be, but this *reverence* must be tempered with a realistic approach to such problems as that now at bar." Without *reverence* to prompt the reader to understand that the judge means *Revered* and not *Reversed,* we might be quite confused about his purpose.

larcenable (= subject to larceny) is listed in neither the *OED* nor most other dictionaries, but legal writers occasionally find it useful—e.g.: "The common law judges strained the law so as to discover reasons which would place the stealing of certain types of article outside the scope of larceny, *e.g.* some domestic animals, growing crops, were held not *larcenable* at common law." L.B. Curzon, *English Legal History* 243–44 (1968; 2d ed. 1979)./ "For example, the realty and things which 'savour of the realty' were not *larcenable* at common law." Eli Lederman, *Criminal Liability for Breach of Confidential Commercial Information,* 38 Emory L.J. 921, 941 n.81 (1989).

larcenist; larcener. *Larcenist* (= one who commits larceny) is the ordinary term; *larcener* is a primarily BrE variant.

larcenous = of, relating to, or tainted with larceny; thievish. E.g., "The Court . . . concluded that 'stolen' does not refer exclusively to *larcenously* taken automobiles . . . ." *U.S. v. McClain,* 545 F.2d 988, 994–95 (5th Cir. 1977)./ "[I]n *C. Doris H. Pepper* . . . , a lawyer was allowed to deduct business expense amounts to recompense clients to whom he had recommended a promoter who turned out to be *larcenous.*" Erwin Griswold, *Cases and Materials on Federal Taxation* 347 (6th ed. 1966).

larceny. A. Sense. *Larceny* = the unlawful taking and carrying away of someone else's goods with the intent to appropriate them. With the Theft Act 1968, English law replaced larceny with the statutory crime of theft. Many American states retain the old scheme of *grand larceny* and *petty larceny,* which was first set forth in the Statute of Westminster I, c. 15 (1275). The LAW FRENCH term was *larcyn,* from the LAW LATIN *latrocinium* (fr. *latro* "robber"). See **asportation.**

Classically, *larceny* has differed from *embezzlement,* in that the latter involves an employee or bailee already in lawful possession. But modern statutes in many jurisdictions have widened the sense of *larceny* to include common-law embezzlement. See **embezzle.**

B. *Grand* and *petty larceny; simple* and *aggravated larceny.* Two dichotomies exist in the legal analysis of larceny—at least, in the English-speaking jurisdictions that retain *larceny* as a crime. *Petty larceny* (or *petit larceny*) was at common law, and is today in many U.S. states, contrasted with *grand larceny,* the difference lying in the value of the goods stolen. *Simple larceny* is distinguished from *aggravated larceny,* the difference lying in the presence or absence of aggravating circumstances.

C. Spelling of *petty (petit) larceny.* *Petit larceny* is the older spelling of the term (which is still properly pronounced *petty*). The anglicized *petty larceny* is slightly more common, having been adopted for use in the Model Penal Code § 223.1(2)(b). The advantage of *petty larceny* is that the correct pronunciation is immediately apparent; the disadvantage is that it suggests a triviality. Merely for the sake of consistency, it would be convenient for writers to follow the

Model Penal Code by writing *petty* instead of *petit.* See **petit larceny.**

D. *Larceny by trick (and device).* The elongation of this phrase—denoting a larceny in which the taker intended to keep the goods even as the rightful possessor, being misled, consensually handed them over—is optional. That being so, the shorter phrase, *larceny by trick,* is recommended.

E. *Larceny from the person.* This statutory offense is slightly different from *robbery* because it need not involve violence or intimidation—the victim usu. being taken unawares. For example, if a thief cuts a necklace and removes it from the owner's neck without her being aware, the thief commits *larceny from the person.* A thief who uses threats or force, on the other hand, commits *robbery.* For more on these distinctions, see **burglary (A).**

largess(e). The Englished spelling *largess* is preferred, but the Frenchified pronunciation */lahr-**zhes**/* is standard.

Las (Siete) Partidas (lit., "the seven parts") refers to the Spanish code compiled in 1250 by Alphonso X and based on the civil law, Spanish customary law, and canon law. First enacted in 1348, it still influences the law of Florida, Louisiana, and Texas. It is referred to either as *Las Partidas* or *Las Siete Partidas,* the latter being slightly more common.

last analysis, in the. See **in the final analysis.**

last but not least is a CLICHÉ to be avoided.

last rites is occasionally misrendered *last rights*—e.g.: "[I]ncident to the administration of the *last rights* [read *last rites*] to deceased by a priest who asked deceased if he was married the reply was 'Yes' . . . ." *Flores v. Nicholson Terminal & Dock Co.,* 299 N.W. 786, 786–87 (Mich. 1941). Actually, that entire sentence is maladroit and mystifying. The awkwardness might be improved as follows, but the mystery is heightened: "While administering *last rites,* the priest asked the deceased whether he was married. The reply was 'yes.' "

last will and testament is a phrase with ancient resonances. Lord Coke, for example, referred to an *ultima voluntas in scriptis* (= last will in writing). Much ink has been spilled by at least one well-known writer in opposition to this phrase. See David Mellinkoff, *The Language of the Law* 77–79, 331–33 (1963). The argument against it is that coupling *testament* with *will* is redundant, and that *last* is usually inaccurate. "When a testator has been made will-conscious, and likes the habit, *last will* adds spice to a will contest. For example [an actual case]: will No. 1 revoked by will No. 2; a later 'codicil to my last will' held to refer to No. 1, reviving it and revoking No. 2. The testator was talking about his first, not his second, when he said his *last will*" (*id.* at 333).

A curious case, to be sure, and one that might lead some to conclude that *last will and testament* "is redundant, confusing, and usually inaccurate" (*id.*). Yet nonlawyers know the phrase well and understand it as a ceremonious equivalent of *will.* The DOUBLET *will and testament* is no more disturbing than many others that exist undisturbed in our language, and that even enrich it. See DOUBLETS, TRIPLETS, AND SYNONYM-STRINGS, **testament & will.**

The only recommendation to be made here is that the phrase be confined to use as a title to the document it refers to, and that general references to the document be couched in the single word *will.* If our goal is to clean up legal writing, there are worthier objects of our reforms than *last will and testament.*

latecoming. Although *latecomer,* the agent noun, dates from the late 19th century and is recorded in most English dictionaries, the adjective *latecoming* is unrecorded in most modern dictionaries. The word—a useful one, surely—appears in several reported American opinions. E.g., "But the rules vest the trial court, not this court, with the discretionary authority to pass upon *latecoming* motions to amend the pleadings." *Janikowski v. Bendix Corp.,* 823 F.2d 945, 954 (6th Cir. 1987) (Ryan, J., dissenting in part)./ "Plaintiffs fear price was the problem here and believe they were simply outbid by a *latecoming* buyer." *Trenta v. Gay,* 468 A.2d 737, 739 (N.J. Super. Ch. Div. 1983).

latent ambiguity. See AMBIGUITY.

later. A. Without Temporal Context. *Later* should not be used unless a proper temporal context has first been established. E.g., "As Charles Evans Hughes, *later a chief justice of the Supreme Court,* [read *who was to become a chief justice,*] stated in 1907, ..." Cf. **then (A).**

B. *Later on.* This collocation is venially verbose for *later.* E.g., "That deed and the description therein contained will be considered more particularly *later on* [read *later*] in this opinion."

later of [date] or [date]; later of [date] and [date]. Drafters frequently debate whether the proper conjunction in this phrase is *or* or *and*. The better idiomatic choice is *or*—nine of every ten lawyers believing it is the proper choice.

True, *and* has logic on its side. If we paraphrase by saying *the later of two dates,* it becomes clear that the sense must be plural (conjunctive *and*), not singular (disjunctive *or*). But the wording with *and* sounds as pedantic—and as wrong—as *a number of people was there.* See SYNESIS.

For a brief treatment of this issue, see Richard H. Miller, *A Drafting Dilemma,* 4 Scribes J. Legal Writing 127 (1993).

LATINATE PLURALS. See PLURALS (A).

LATINISMS. Can there be any doubt that modern judges and scholars have grown impatient with Anglo-American lawyers' fondness for Latin terminology?

- "On the whole the lesson of this part of our legal history should be that it is dangerous to play with foreign terms unless we know very well what we are about." F.W. Maitland, *The Forms of Action at Common Law* 63 (1909; A.H. Chaytor & W.J. Whittaker eds. 1971).
- "The marvelous capacity of a Latin phrase to serve as a substitute for reasoning, and the confusion of thought inevitably accompanying the use of inaccurate terminology, are nowhere better illustrated than in the decisions dealing with the admissibility of evidence as *res gestae.*" Edmund M. Morgan, *A Suggested Classification of Utterances Admissible as Res Gestae,* 31 Yale L.J. 229, 229 (1922).
- "I cannot help deprecating the use of Latin . . . phrases in this way. They only distract the mind from the true problem which is to apply the principles of English law to the realities of the case." *Smith, Hogg & Co. v. Black Sea and Baltic Gen. Ins. Co.,* [1940] A.C. 997, 1003 (per Lord Wright).
- "I think the cases are comparatively few in which much light is obtained by a liberal use of Latin phrases. . . . Nobody can derive any assistance from the phrase *novus actus interveniens* until it is translated into English . . . ." *Ingram v. United Auto. Servs., Ltd.,* [1943] 2 All E.R. 71, 73 (per du Parcq, L.J.).
- "Pruitt's letter to the Clerk of the Virginia Supreme Court of Appeals, his correspondence with his attorney, and his petition in the district court spoke of his 'being met with a plea of res judicata' in the state court. It is difficult to follow his line of reasoning or indeed to make any sense out of his prolix and confused arguments. One thing, however, is clear—he, not unlike some lawyers, thought he had discovered magic in a Latin phrase." *Pruitt v. Peyton,* 338 F.2d 859, 861 (4th Cir. 1964).

A century ago, scholars recognized that Latin MAXIMS had rapidly, for the most part, become obsolete: "The Latin maxims have largely disappeared from arguments and opinions. In their original phraseology they convey no idea that cannot be well expressed in modern English." William C. Anderson, *Law Dictionaries,* 28 Am. L. Rev. 531, 532 (1894). Still, several Latinisms have proved themselves useful—often in shortened forms, that is, as phrases and not so much as maxims—such as *de minimis, contra proferentem, ejusdem generis,* and *noscitur a sociis.*

Despite the overwhelming obsolescence of Latin—more overwhelming in AmE than in BrE—nonlawyers still generally misunderstand the nature of legal language. The linguist Mario Pei, for example, estimated that "[h]alf of our specifically legal terminology is Latin." Mario Pei, *Words in Sheep's Clothing* 83 (1969). That statement, of course, is nonsense. Probably more than 90 percent of our legal terminology is of Latin origin—English words and phrases such as *contract, declaratory judgment, issue preclusion, realty, subordinated debt*—but these phrases are English, not Latin.

Nevertheless, legal readers often encounter Latin in modern texts—some of it necessary and some of it not. In legal writing we must distinguish between TERMS OF ART, for which there are no ordinary English equivalents, and those terms that are merely vestigial Latinisms with simple English substitutes. The former category comprises useful Latinisms such as *prima facie, ex parte, de minimis, habeas corpus, alibi,* and *quorum.* Some words that do have ordinary English equivalents have nevertheless become such standard terms that they are unobjectionable, e.g., *bona fide* (= good faith), *amicus curiae* (= friend of the court), and *versus* (= against). These words have become a part of the English language, or at least necessary parts of the language of the law, and one would be misdirected to rail against them.

The rightful objects of our condemnation are the bombastic, vestigial Latinisms that serve no purpose but to give the writer a false sense of erudition. These terms convey no special legal meanings, no delicate nuances apprehended only by lawyers. They are pompous, turgid deadwood. Just as a mathematician would seem ludicrous to write 386/1544 rather than 1/4 merely in an attempt to sound more scholarly, so the lawyer who writes *sub suo periculo* instead of *at his own risk,* strikes the reader as a laughable, if vexatious, figure.

Other phrases in this category are illustrated in the following sentences, in which the simple English equivalents are bracketed:

- "But a legacy to one, to be paid when he attains the age of twenty one years, is a vested legacy; an interest which commences *in praesenti* [read *in the present*], although it be *solvendum in futuro* [read *paid in the future*]: and, if the legatee dies before that age, his representatives shall receive it out of the testator's personal estate . . . ." 2 William Blackstone, *Commentaries* 513 (1766).
- "There is a *contradictio in adjecto* [read *contradiction in terms*] when we speak of the general damages appropriate to an indeterminate transaction." *Kerr S.S. v. Radio Corp. of Am.,* 157 N.E. 140, 142 (N.Y. 1927) (per Cardozo, C.J.).
- "Ancillary administration in this state, without assets presently here for administration, would be *mere brutum fulmen* [read *mere empty noise* (lit.), or *ineffective*]." *In re Rogers' Will,* 232 N.Y.S. 609, 613 (App. Div. 1929).
- "A father is directly responsible for the existence of his offspring and it would accordingly be *contra bonos mores* [read *immoral*] to allow a father to bring children into the world and avoid responsibility for them by himself departing the world." *Lloyd v. Menzies,* 1956 (2) S.A.L.R. 97, 102 (quoting curator ad litem's report).
- "The author did not look upon section 44 as a section inserted *ex abundanti cautela* [read *out of abundant caution*] but as a very important protection." (Eng.)

Reasonableness dictates that legal writers simplify where possible, allowing the more complicated locutions to stand only if they are legally or linguistically irreducible. Otherwise, our language is easily beclouded (the Latinist would say *obnubilated*) and becomes, before we know it, a fog of words in which our readers or listeners become hopelessly lost. This is no less true in STATUTE DRAFTING than in expository writing: "In the selection of words, Latin words and, where possible without a sacrifice of accuracy, technical phraseology should be avoided; the word best adapted to express a thought in ordinary composition will generally be found to be the best that can be used." Henry Thring, *Practical Legislation* 81 (1902).

Words are the primary tools of lawyers. Can we afford, then, to be undiscriminating in our use of those tools? Can we engage in unchecked ABSTRACTITIS with impunity? As Justice Holmes, who was doubtless aware of his oversimplification, wrote toward the end of the 19th century, "We must think things not words, or at least we must constantly translate our words into the facts for which they stand, if we are to keep to the real and the true." Oliver W. Holmes, *Law in Science and Science in Law,* 12 Harv. L. Rev. 443, 460 (1899). Such internal translation is most easily achieved if we use ordinary language when possible. Lawyers must learn the language of the law but wield it carefully, never losing the idiomatic flavor of the vernacular.

Particular Latinisms, their utility or their turgidity, are discussed throughout this work under particular entries. For examples of needless Latinity, see ***capacitas rationalis*** & **res gestae.** See also LAW LATIN, MINGLE-MANGLE & PLAIN LANGUAGE. Cf. GALLICISMS. On questions of pronouncing Latin terms, see PRONUNCIATION (C).

latrine lawyer. See LAWYERS, DEROGATORY NAMES FOR (A).

latter. See **former.**

latterly is an ARCHAISM for *later* or *lately.* E.g., "But there is a notion that *latterly* [read *lately*] has been insisted on a good deal, that a combination of persons to do what any one of them might lawfully do by himself will make the otherwise lawful conduct unlawful."

laudatory; laudative; laudable. The adjectives *laudatory* and *laudative* both mean "expressing praise." But *laudative* is a NEEDLESS VARIANT, *laudatory* being the common word. *Laudable,* in contrast, means "deserving praise." The distinction is the same as that between *praiseworthy* (= *laudable*) and the active *praiseful* (= *laudatory*).

The misuse of *laudatory* for *laudable* is lamentably common: "That the decision may achieve a *laudatory* [read *laudable*] result is not a valid consideration."/ "The more stringent provisions of the new act, while *laudatory* [read *laudable*] in purpose, cannot be used to enhance the punishment of individuals who committed crimes in possible reliance on the previous standards."/ "A subsequently adopted program, no matter how *laudatory* [read *laudable*], is wholly irrelevant to the issue of racial discrimination at an earlier date."

laughing heir, a LOAN TRANSLATION of the German phrase *der lachende Erbe,* refers to an heir who, being so remotely linked to a deceased relative as to suffer no sense of bereavement, receives a windfall from the estate. E.g., "A court-appointed guardian, Jonathan G. Blattmacher, a partner with Milbank, Tweed, Hadley & McCloy, said recently that rummaging through an old shoe box containing dog-eared letters led to a distant relative living in a trailer park in Terre Haute, Ind. The relative eventually became a *'laughing heir,'* inheriting several hundred thousand dollars." Jay G. Baris, *Personal Finance,* N.Y. Times, 15 Feb. 1987, at C11./ "To decree . . . defeasance results in unnecessary loss to the beneficiaries of the inter vivos transfer and a possible gain for the *'laughing heirs.'*" Macdonald, *Fraud on the Widow's Share* 130–31 (as quoted in *In re Estate of Curtis,* 663 S.W.2d 420, 425 (Mo. Ct. App. 1983)).

laundry list, in use only since 1958, is the slang phrase American lawyers commonly use to denote a statutory enumeration of items.

law, n. **A. General Senses.** This word, by Jerome Frank's sobering assessment, "drips with ambiguity. But it has a traditionally emotive quality which makes it highly serviceable to the legal magicians. There are dozens of discrepant definitions of that word." Jerome Frank, *Courts on Trial* 66 (1950). Those who have tried to define *law* agree only that no definition is fully satisfactory. Still, it is worthwhile to try to sort out the senses.

Roscoe Pound catalogued four meanings for the word *law.* They are:

1. the legal order, that is, the regime that orders human activities and relations through systematic application of the force of politically organized society, or through social pressure, backed by force, in such a society <respect for law>;
2. the aggregate of legislation and accepted legal precepts; the body of authoritative grounds of judicial and administrative action established in an organized society <justice according to law> <systems of law>;
3. the judicial and administrative process, i.e., the process of determining controversies, whether as it actually takes place, or as the public, the jurists, and the practitioners in the courts hold it ought to take place <law is whatever is officially done>;
4. some combination of the previous three definitions <law and morals>.

See Roscoe Pound, *What Constitutes a Good Legal Education,* 7 Am. L. Sch. Rev. 887, 891 (1933).

The word has at least three more senses for lawyers, though:

5. a statute <There should be a law!>;
6. the common law (q.v.) <law but not equity>;
7. the legal profession <one may live greatly in the law as elsewhere>.

The word also has senses in other realms of human activity—senses that lawyers sometimes decry:

8. in science and philosophy, a general formula expressing a de facto uniformity in nature as we find it <law of gravitation>;
9. in science and philosophy, a general formula expressing a necessary property of all conceivable worlds <the law of contradiction, which says that no proposition can at once be both true and false>.

Of the legal senses, (4) and (5) present the most interesting idiomatic distinction. Lawyers distinguish between *a law* (sense 5) and *the law* (sense 4). The former refers to a particular and concrete instance of a legal precept. Thus statutes such as the Sherman Antitrust Act (U.S.) and the Theft Act (Eng.)—or parts of them—can each be called *a law.*

The law, by contrast, is used for something much broader and more general, sometimes together with words describing a recognized branch of legal science, e.g., the law of torts, or with words descriptive of a particular system of law, e.g., the law of the United States.

Most Indo-European languages have different words for the concrete and abstract senses of *law.* For example, in Latin, there is *lex* for the concrete sense, *jus* for the abstract; in Italian, *legge* and *diritto;* in French, *loi* and *droit;* in Spanish, *ley* and *derecho;* in German, *Gesetz* and *Recht.* The English word *right* has long sense lost its sense corresponding to the German *Recht*—so English speakers have had to press *law* into double service. See ***lex*** **(A).**

As a result of our doing so, we have had to confront practical problems that might otherwise have been avoided. In *Swift v. Tyson,* a famous American constitutional-law case, the Supreme Court based its decision in part on the distinction between *law* and *a law* (or *laws,* in the plural): "In the ordinary use of language it will hardly be contended that the decisions of Courts constitute *laws.* They are, at most, only evidence of what the *laws* are; and are not of themselves *laws.*" 41 U.S. (16 Pet.) 1, 18 (1842). Accord, 2 Alexander M. Burrill, *A Law Dictionary and Glossary* 132 (2d ed. 1860) ("*A law* . . . undoubtedly imports an act of the legislature; and the term is quite inapplicable to a decision of a court of justice . . . .").

The decision in *Swift v. Tyson* might have been decided differently, of course, if the statute at issue—the Rules of Decision Act—had declared that state *law,* as opposed to state *laws,* controlled questions of common law as applied by federal courts. Thus a drafter's lapse—using *laws* where *law* was probably intended—may have resulted in 96 years of bad law (not *laws*), until *Swift v. Tyson* was overturned in *Erie R.R. v. Tompkins,* 304 U.S. 64 (1938).

law, adj. *Law,* like *legal,* acts as an adjective for *law,* n. No strict DIFFERENTIATION is possible, for we have *law studies* beside *legal studies* and *lawbooks* beside *legal books;* but *legal firm* is an un-English phrase for *law firm,* just as *law doctrine* is not used for *legal doctrine.* The *OED* contains hundreds of examples of the attributive adjective *law,* such as *lawcourt* and *Law Lords.*

Law shares with *legal* the sense "pertaining to the law as a body of rules, or as a field of study." E.g., "The principal *law* question on the cross-appeals is whether the Supreme Court committed reversible error in awarding exemplary damages as incidental to injunctive relief." *Legal* has the additional sense "permitted under law; not forbidden" <legal acts>, as the antonym of *illegal.*

law abhors a forfeiture, the. See **equity abhors a forfeiture.**

law-abiding (= abiding by, maintaining, or submitting to the law) is a PHRASAL ADJECTIVE dating from the early 19th century. E.g., "Courts do not depart from the rule that equity may not interfere, except to protect property rights of a pecuniary nature, in enjoining criminal acts exercised by one dealer to enhance his sales to the calculated pecuniary injury of a *law-abiding* competitor." See **abide.**

The corresponding noun—an awkward-looking form that does not exactly abide by the laws of English word-formation—is *law-abidingness.* E.g., "*State v. Baird* . . . expressly decides proof of reputation for *'law-abidingness'* has no place in the case." *State v. Shepard,* 67 S.W.2d 91, 94 (Mo. 1933)./ "[T]he defendant's character witnesses . . . testified as to his reputation for honesty and *law-abidingness* . . . ." *U.S. v. Londono-Villa,* 898 F.2d 328, 329 (2d Cir. 1990).

law and order. The phrase—originating not in AmE but in 19th-century BrE—is hyphenated only when it functions as an adjective—e.g.: "Had Ervin been extra careful about appearing tough on *law-and-order* issues, he probably never would have done these things." Paul R. Clancy, *Just a Country Lawyer* 202 (1974). As a noun phrase, it should remain unhyphenated: "[T]hen all respect for *law-and-order* [read *law and order*] would vanish . . . ." Fred Rodell, *Woe Unto You, Lawyers!* 179 (1939; repr. 1980).

lawbook. One word.

lawbreaker; lawbreaking. Each of these is one word.

law clerk. See **clerk.**

lawcourt, one word, is another form of *court of law,* q.v. In most modern contexts—wherever the distinction between *courts of equity* and *courts of law* is not an issue—*lawcourt* is a one-word redundancy—e.g.: "To do so was its province as fact-finder as well as the *lawcourt* [read *court*]." *City of Saginaw v. Garvey Elevators, Inc.,* 431 S.W.2d 575, 579 (Tex. Civ. App.—Fort Worth 1968).

In other contexts, however—esp. historical contexts—it provides a concise contrast to courts of equity, as here: "In England the *law courts* [read *lawcourts*] at first refused to recognize a decree for money in equity as creating a debt on which an action at law could be maintained." William F. Walsh, *A Treatise on Equity* 67 (1930). See **law,** adj.

law day. This phrase has undergone quite a metamorphosis in recent years. Originally, *law day* was the yearly or twice-yearly meeting of one of the early common-law courts. By the 15th century and for a long time after, it came to denote the day appointed for the debtor to discharge a mortgage or else forfeit the property to the mortgagee.

Since 1958, the American Bar Association has sponsored *Law Day* on May 1 of each year—a day in which American schools, public assemblies, and courts draw attention to the importance of law in modern society.

law factory, a derogatory term for a major law firm, dates from the mid-20th century—e.g.: "That is why the center of the nation's law business is in New York City and why the bulk of the nation's influential and profitable law practice is carried on in the Wall Street *law factories.*" Fred Rodell, *Woe Unto You, Lawyers!* 155 (1939; repr. 1980)./ "Hotchkiss, Levy & Hogan was a typical Wall Street *law factory,* occupying two entire stories in a white-stone office building within spitting distance of J.P. Morgan & Co." Ephraim Tutt, *Yankee Lawyer* 142 (1943).

law firm. See **firm.**

LAW FRENCH refers to the Anglo-Norman patois used in legal documents and all judicial proceedings from the 1260s to the reign of Edward III (1327–1377), and used with frequency in legal literature up to the early 18th century. When first introduced into England, this brand of French was the standard language used in Normandy; by the 1300s, through linguistic isolation, it became a corrupted language—by French standards, at any rate. In the 17th century, Sir Edward Coke wrote that Law French could not be either "pure or well pronounced," and that one could find within it "a whole army of words, which cannot defend themselves *in bello grammaticali,* in the grammatical war, and yet are most significant, compendious, and effectual to express the true sense of the matter." Edward Coke, *Commentary on Littleton* xxxix–xl (Butler ed. 1832).

English law cases were reported in Law French until the end of the 17th century. Even as late as the early 18th century, surprisingly, Law French had its apologists: "Really the Law is scarcely expressible properly in English." Roger North, *A Discourse on the Study of the Laws* 13 (c. 1710; repr. London: C. Baldwyn ed., 1824). Perhaps the best book written in Law French was Sir John Comyn's *Digest of the Laws of England* (1762-1767).

Though Law French may be obscure to the English-speaking lawyer, its remnants abound in the language of the law, in common words such as *appeal, assault, arrest, attainder, counsel, defer, defy, demand, demise, disclaimer, escheat, escrow, heir, indictment, interpleader, joinder, laches, larceny, lay, lien, merger, mortgage, negligence, nuisance, ouster, party, process, proof, remainder, reverter, suit, tender, tort, trespass, verdict,* and *voir dire.* There are also remnants somewhat more arcane, such as *cestui que trust,* and *en ventre sa mere.*

Law French was always a highly technical language that preserved many old Anglo-Normanisms, but English forms, inflections, word order, and construction finally took it over. A notorious example: in the Salisbury assizes of 1631, a prisoner condemned by the Chief Justice of Common Pleas was said to have *"ject un brickbat a le dit Justice que narrowly mist";* for that outburst, *"son dexter manus* [was] *ampute"* and the man himself *"immediatment hange in presence de Court."* One noted writer has referred to Law French as "something very like a Sid Caesar version of a foreign language." Charles Rembar, *The Law of the Land* 178 n.* (1980). Though we have retained much of the vocabulary, Anglo-American lawyers no longer try to communicate with each other in this cabalistic dialect.

For what remains, though, of Law French, a word about pronunciation is in order. English and, to a lesser extent, American lawyers have generally preserved the medieval pronunciations given to Law French terms—pronunciations that resemble modern English much more than they do modern French. Thus the "correct" pronunciation of *oyez* is /oh-**yez**/ or /oh-**yes**/, not /oh-**yay**/, and of *autrefois acquit* /**oh**-tər-foyz/ not /oh-tər-**fwah**/. See J.H. Baker, *Manual of Law French* (2d ed. 1990); J.H. Baker, "Law French," in 7 *Guide to American Law* 80–81 (1984). Cf. LAW LATIN. See MINGLE-MANGLE.

lawful. See **legal.**

lawful cause (= good cause; legal justification) is not to be confused with *legal cause* (= proximate cause). See CAUSATION (A).

lawgiver; lawmaker. Both are equivalent to *legislator,* but *lawgiver* suggests one who promulgates an entire code of laws, and is therefore more magisterial in tone: "To the Middle Ages the academic ideal of all Europe as the empire for which Justinian had been the *law-giver* made Roman law a universal law." (R. Pound)/ "Alfred [was] two hundred years later than the first English *lawgivers* quoted." (Holmes) Both *lawgiver* and *lawmaker* are now preferably written as single, unhyphenated words.

law is no respecter of persons, the. See **no respecter of persons, the law is.**

LAW LATIN, sometimes formerly called "dog Latin," is the bastardized or debased Latin formerly used in law and legal documents. For the most part, we have escaped from its clutches. In 1730, Parliament abolished Law Latin in legal proceedings, but two years later found it necessary to allow Latin phrases that had previously been in common use, such as *fieri facias, habeas corpus, ne exeat,* and *nisi prius.* As Blackstone would later say, some Latinisms were "not . . . capable of an English dress with any degree of seriousness." 3 William Blackstone, *Commentaries* 323 (1768).

Brewer's *Dictionary of Phrase and Fable* quotes the following jocular example: "As the law classically expresses it, a kitchen is 'camera necessaria pro usus cookare; cum sauce-pannis, stewpannis, scullero, dressero, coalholo, stovis, smoak-jacko; pro roastandum, boilandum, fryandum, et plum-pudding-mixandum.'" Stevens, *A Law Report* (Daniel v. Dishclout) (quoted in Brewer, *Dictionary of Phrase and Fable* (1894), s.v. "Dog-Latin"). See E.H. Jackson, *Law Latin* (1897); E. Hilton Jackson, *Latin for Lawyers* (1915); John Trayner, *Latin Phrases and Maxims* (4th ed. 1894); Herbert Broom, *Legal Maxims* (10th ed. 1939). Cf. LAW FRENCH. See MINGLE-MANGLE & LATINISMS.

lawlike (one word meaning "resembling or characteristic of law") is labeled "rare" in the *OED.*

The word *is* rare in the law reports, but not in legal commentary—e.g.: "[N]orms are more or less *lawlike* depending upon how formal they are . . . ." Larry A. Alexander, *Painting Without the Numbers,* 8 U. Dayton L. Rev. 447, 460 (1983)./ "The essence of a causal generalization is the belief that we attach to the generalization: the belief in its causal or *lawlike* character." Richard W. Wright, *Causation in Tort Law,* 73 Cal. L. Rev. 1735, 1823 (1985)./ "Gordon's basic strategy is to deconstruct the '*lawlike*' qualities of the law by descending into ever finer levels of microstructural analysis." Steve Fuller, *Playing Without a Full Deck,* 97 Yale L.J. 549, 570–71 (1988).

Law Lord. This title refers to any member of the Appellate Committee of the House of Lords—the Lord Chancellor, the salaried Lords of Appeal in Ordinary, and any peer who holds or has held high judicial office. The Law Lords (usu. capitalized thus) form the highest court of appeal in the United Kingdom—roughly equivalent to the Supreme Court of the United States. E.g., "And this was the view of a majority of the *law lords* on that occasion, Lords Brougham and Campbell agreeing with Lord Lyndhurst." *In re Broderick's Will,* 88 U.S. 503, 512 (1874)./ "The *Law Lords* reached this view by analysing the meaning of the words without regard to their context or legislative intent." Michael Zander, *The Law-Making Process* 95 (2d ed. 1985). See **House of Lords, Lords & Lord of Appeal in Ordinary.**

lawmaker. One word. Although historically this term was thought to be equivalent to *legislator,* the advent of legal realism made it apply just as fully to a judge as to a legislator. Thus, Pound's use of the phrase *legislative lawmaker* is not a careless redundancy: "But they make the path of the legislative *lawmaker* a rough one." Roscoe Pound, *The Formative Era of American Law* 48 (1938). See **lawgiver.**

lawman = (1) historically, an official whose duty it was to declare the law; (2) a man of law, or lawyer; or (3) a law-enforcement officer. Sense (3) is the only sense recently in general use.

Sense (2) is labeled "obsolete except as a nonce-word" in the *OED,* and it probably *ought* to be obsolete. Yet: "Mispronunciations aside, do the modern *lawmen* [read *lawyers*] who use [legal terms] know something about their origin?" Mario Pei, *Words in Sheep's Clothing* 83 (1969). And, in the same year, Glendon Schubert wrote of Justice Robert H. Jackson, "For over forty years, from late adolescence until the very day of his death, his was the life of a *law-man,*" adding—"The idiom is that of Karl Llewellyn rather than of Matt Dillon." *Dispassionate Justice* 285 & n.3 (1969). Schubert's use of the term—referring as it does to a particular man—seems more justifiable than Pei's, but either is likely to strike some readers as sexist. See SEXISM (B).

law merchant = a system of customary law that grew up in Europe during the Middle Ages and regulated the dealings of mariners and merchants in all the commercial countries of the world. Many of its principles came to be incorporated into the common law. The plural form is *laws merchant,* the second word (as in the singular) being a POSTPOSITIVE ADJECTIVE. This phrase is a LOAN TRANSLATION of *lex mercatoria.* See **commercial law** & ***lex mercatoria.***

lawmonger. See LAWYERS, DEROGATORY NAMES FOR (A).

lawnote. See **annotation, note & casenote.**

law of nations = (1) *jus gentium* (q.v.); or (2) international law. The phrase *law of nations* began as a LOAN TRANSLATION of *jus gentium* (the common law of peoples) but eventually took on a more restrictive sense, as a synonym of *international law* (= the body of rules and principles that bind civilized states in their relations with one another). As between these synonyms, "[m]ost writers and practitioners have for the past century preferred the term *international law.*" Clive Parry & John P. Grant, *Encyclopedic Dictionary of International Law* 210 (1986). A notable exception is J.L. Brierly, *The Law of Nations* (5th ed. 1955). See **international law.**

law of nature. See **natural law.**

law of the case = (1) the decision rendered in a former appeal of a case, which by legal doctrine is held to be binding; or (2) the doctrine so holding. Thus, if a case is appealed a second time to a panel of a U.S. Court of Appeals, and a panel with a different makeup from the first panel hears the case the second time, the second panel will generally hold itself bound by the writings of the first panel whether or not its members agree with those earlier writings. This phrase, in Holmes's words, "merely expresses the practice of courts generally to refuse to reopen what has been decided, not a limit to their power." *Messenger v. Anderson,* 225 U.S. 436, 444 (1912). *Law of the case* is to be distinguished from *res judicata* and *stare decisis,* qq.v.

law of the land is a LOAN TRANSLATION of the phrase *lex terrae* (LAW LATIN) or *ley de terre* (LAW

FRENCH). First used in Magna Carta (in the phrase *per legem terrae*), the phrase generally means "the law in effect in a country and applicable to all members of the community, whether resulting from the highest court's pronouncements or from legislative enactment." E.g., "*Gertz* is now the *law of the land,* and until it is overruled, it must, under the principle of stare decisis, be applied by this court." In AmE, this phrase also sometimes signifies "due process of law."

law of the sea. See **admiralty.**

law proper = positive law. Pl. *laws proper.*

law report. See **report.**

LAW REVIEWESE is the stilted, often jargonistic writing style characteristically found in law reviews. Judge Posner, an accomplished stylist who has written in many law reviews, bemoans "the drab, Latinate, plethoric, euphemistic style of law reviews." Richard A. Posner, *Goodbye to the Bluebook,* 53 U. Chi. L. Rev. 1343, 1349 (1986). Unless the author is a famous one whose prose the editors dare not tamper with, the edited and published writing usually takes on an "official" law-review style that is lacking in personality or individual idiom, overburdened with abstract phraseology, bottom-heavy with footnotes, humorless, and generally unobservant of good grammar and diction. This last fault is perhaps ineradicable, at least in the U.S., inasmuch as legally trained young men and women are called upon to be professional editors when not one in fifty has a background suitable to the task. Nevertheless, the industry and thought that go into publishing a law review are good training, however inconsequential the product often is.

"The ideal law review," writes James C. Raymond in an iconoclastic essay,

> is one that is designed not only to be referred to, but actually (and here comes the revolutionary proposal) to be read. Its articles are selected not on the basis of the number of footnotes they contain, but on the basis of the timeliness of the topic and the soundness of the scholarship. They may have no footnotes or dozens of them—all that are necessary to satisfy the curiosity of intelligent readers who are particularly interested in the topic, but no more.
>
> In the ideal review, articles are also selected, or even solicited, at least partly on the basis of how well their authors can write. Ideal editors are prepared to instruct their assistants and even their contributors on the elements of good writing. They refuse to publish anything that they consider dull, and they have the courage to demand a revision of anything they cannot understand. They know from their own reading that the best legal writers are always more than crabbed logicians of the law. They are capable of clarity without any compromise in precision, and, when the occasion warrants, of eloquence no less memorable than Cicero's.
>
> James C. Raymond, *Editing Law Reviews,* 12 Pepp. L. Rev. 371, 378–79 (1985).

No such law review yet exists, or is likely to. Still, there is a move afoot to establish faculty-edited law reviews; let us hope that these bring much-needed reform. If they do, then Karl Llewellyn's words would lose their sting: "There is not, as far as I know, in the world an academic faculty which pins its reputation before the public on the work of undergraduate students—there is none, that is, except in the American law reviews." *The Bramble Bush* 107 (1930).

law's delay. The possessive is necessary in this phrase, which derives from Shakespeare: "For who would bear . . . the *law's delay* . . . when he might his quietus make with a bare bodkin [i.e., dagger]." *Hamlet* 3.1.69–75. The allusion is sometimes mistakenly rendered in the more emphatic plural, as *the law's delays.*

Law Society = a professional association originally formed in 1825 to prevent abuses among and (later) to regulate solicitors in England and Wales. Separate societies now exist in Australia, Northern Ireland, and Scotland—as well as other jurisdictions in which the dual system of solicitors and barristers exists.

lawsuit is best written as one word in AmE and BrE.

laws. See **law,** n.

lawyer, n. See **attorney (A).**

lawyer, v.i. & v.t.; **lawyering.** The *OED* lists *lawyering* ("colloquial") but not the verb *lawyer. W2* contains the verb *lawyer,* defining it as (1) "to conduct a lawsuit against" and (2) "to practice as a lawyer," noting that the term is "rare" in both senses. *W3* omits *lawyer* as a verb and appends the note "often used disparagingly" to *lawyering.*

None of these treatments adequately describes these Americanisms. *Lawyer* is no longer rare as a verb—e.g.: "Of course, ever since lawyers began to *lawyer,* there have been losing counsel aplenty who have so believed in their causes that they have bitterly blamed the court." Karl Llewellyn, *The Common Law Tradition* 3 (1960).

And it has taken on another sense: "to supply with lawyers"—e.g.: "China has never been a *lawyered* country and it is only beginning to understand and accept that for a foreign investor to come with an attorney for negotiation is not an unduly aggressive or untrusting act."

Finally, although *lawyering* may be used disparagingly in some quarters, many lawyers use it as a neutral term to describe what they do, and even as a laudatory term. E.g., "The real skill in judging, as it is in *lawyering,* is in being able properly to find and articulate the issues." *Varol v. Blue Cross & Blue Shield,* 708 F. Supp. 826, 827 (E.D. Mich. 1989)./ "This was a prodigious feat of *lawyering* on the part of defense counsel." *People v. Gragg,* 264 Cal. Rptr. 765, 773 (Ct. App. 1989) (referring to defense counsel's obtaining an acquittal for a defendant portrayed as a "brutish" person)./ "If *lawyering* is truly a public profession, it is no more seemly for the members of the bar to live lives of luxury than it was for the clergy of old." Jethro K. Lieberman, *Crisis at the Bar* 227 (1978). See **attorney (C).**

lawyer-basher, lawyer-bashing. Hyphenated thus.

lawyerdom (= the world of lawyers) is more than just a nonce-word, though most dictionaries do not record it. E.g., "[Cardozo's] style received wide acclaim in *lawyerdom.*" Jerome N. Frank, *Some Reflections on Judge Learned Hand,* 24 U. Chi. L. Rev. 666, 672 (1957)./ "Seliger cannot fairly be placed in a limbo unoccupied by the rest of *lawyerdom.*" *Strama v. Peterson,* 561 F. Supp. 997, 999 (N.D. Ill. 1983)./ "Is there any road through the labyrinth of *lawyerdom?*" Glenna Whitley, *Why We Love to Hate Lawyers,* D Mag., May 1991, at 47, 51.

Attorneydom is an occasional variant. E.g., "They also seem less prone to the sort of loophole chicanery and fine-print-chasing endemic to Washington *attorneydom.*" Ken Ringle, *The Soviets' Cram Course in Freedom,* Washington Post, 11 Oct. 1989, at B1./ "They were, it seems, not the green cloth bags which afterwards became a synonym for *attorneydom,* but of black buckram." E.B.V. Christian, *A Short History of Solicitors* 56 (1896; repr. 1983).

lawyeress [according to the *OED*] = (1) the wife of a lawyer; or (2) a female lawyer. Neither sense (1), a surprising one, nor sense (2) has much of a place in modern legal writing. See SEXISM (C).

lawyering. See **lawyer,** v.i. & v.t.

lawyerish is the disparaging counterpart to *lawyerlike.* E.g., "The constitutional amendment . . . is advocated by the people who have lost patience with *lawyerish* logic and want to settle the question once and for all." *The Flag Burners,* Washington Post, 20 July 1989, at A22./ "He has nicked his own name down to Dick Thornburgh, from more *lawyerish* Richard L. Thornburgh." J. Randolph Murray, *Chicago Tribune,* 26 March 1989, at 4C./ "It is a lengthy, involved, and complicated document 13 typewritten pages in length . . . . Its language is *'lawyerish,'* full of technical terms . . . ." *Mercantile-Commerce Bank & Trust Co. v. Binowitz,* 238 S.W.2d 893, 897 (Mo. Ct. App. 1951). See **lawyerly.**

lawyerism = (1) a mannerism, esp. of speech or writing, characteristic of lawyers; or (2) the influence, principles, or practices of lawyers. Examples of sense (1) are legion—e.g.: "The use of *'lawyerisms'* that becloud clarity of expression is to be avoided." Edward Re, *Brief Writing and Oral Argument* 7 (6th ed. 1987).

Sense (2), however, is less common—e.g.: "Trial-*lawyerism* 'is the only salient issue of the campaign since there's no judicial record for either candidate,' Ross added." Walter Borges, *In Judge Race, GOP Hits Kidd with TTLA Label,* Texas Law., 20 Aug. 1990, at 6./ "OAG . . . concluded that control over environmental problems from oil and gas operations on state land lay in not leasing in the first place, the kind of *lawyerism* which drives most clients to ignore the answer they didn't want in the second place." *Michigan Oil Co. v. Natural Resources Comm'n,* 249 N.W.2d 135, 149 n.7 (Mich. Ct. App. 1976).

LAWYERISMS. See LEGALISMS AND LAWYERISMS.

lawyerize, lawyerization. Many question the need for such terms, esp. since so many NEOLOGISMS formed with the *-ize* suffix are needless and ephemeral. But these words have appeared again and again in legal and nonlegal publications. Sometimes the meaning can be gleaned from the passage—e.g.: "The *lawyerization* of America has not reached that point." *Sally Beauty Co. v. Nexxus Prods. Co.,* 801 F.2d 1001, 1010 (7th Cir. 1986) (Posner, J., dissenting)./ "[W]e ought to consider the potential impact on the dockets of our busy district courts, and ultimately on our crowded docket, of *'lawyerizing'* prisoner civil litigation." *Merritt v. Faulkner,* 697 F.2d 761, 771 (7th Cir. 1983) (Posner, J., dissenting in part). By *lawyerize,* Posner probably means "to put (a thing) under the control of lawyers, the implication being that the adversary system is the only appropriate or effective way to proceed."

In other contexts, the sense is not so easily ascertained—e.g.: "Gilmore minimizes the importance of *lawyerizing* and laws through skepticism—how can one make rules in an existence that is fundamentally unknowable and perpetually in flux?" James G. Wilson, *The Morality of Formalism,* 33 UCLA L. Rev. 431, 437 (1985)./

"*Lawyerization* outside urban enclaves has been most dramatic in the state's north-central valley . . . ." Gail D. Cox, *100,000 Practitioners*, Nat'l L.J., 21 Nov. 1988, at 1. In the latter sentence, *lawyerization* seems to mean "populating (an area) with lawyers."

lawyerly; lawyerlike. Most American and English dictionaries record *lawyerlike* but not *lawyerly*—this despite the greater currency of the latter word. *Lawyerly* first appeared in Milton's *Eikonoklastes* (1650), but then it fell into a long period of disuse. See 3 *Complete Works of John Milton* 403 (1962) ("the more Lawyerlie mooting on this point"). The first dictionary to record *lawyerly* was, appropriately, written by a lawyer: Noah Webster, *Dictionary of the English Language* (1828). Until recently, however, most other dictionary-makers, being unlawyerly, have ignored the word.

Whether *lawyerly* is a term of praise or of abuse depends on one's general disposition toward lawyers. Sometimes it is used admiringly: "What Marshall did was a stroke of political genius, salted with *lawyerly* adroitness." Fred Rodell, *Nine Men* 87 (1955). Sometimes not: "With every half line of testimony interrupted by half a page of *lawyerly* harangue, it was exceedingly difficult for the witness to develop his thesis and the search for the truth was well nigh lost in the process." *Watson v. State,* 306 A.2d 599, 608 (Md. Ct. Spec. App. 1973)./ "But the judges, with *lawyerly* indirection, have not avowed the interest of the judiciary in orderly resort to the courts as a basis for their decision . . . ." *Miles v. Illinois Central R.R.,* 315 U.S. 698, 706 (1942) (Jackson, J., concurring).

Lawyerlike, on the other hand, is almost invariably a term of praise—e.g.: "This is not very *lawyerlike,* nor very respectful to the Court." *Rhode Island v. Massachusetts,* 37 U.S. (12 Pet.) 657, 699 (1838) (argument of counsel)./ "Counsel for both sides tried this case on a very high plane and in a very objective, *lawyerlike* fashion." *Reed v. Gulf Oil Corp.,* 217 F. Supp. 370, 373 (D.D.C. 1963)./ "Without exception, despite the emotional overtones of the proceeding, the briefs and oral arguments were temperate, *lawyerlike* and constructive." *South Carolina v. Katzenbach,* 383 U.S. 301, 308 (1966).

LAWYERS, DEROGATORY NAMES FOR. The chief irony of lawyerdom is that poll after poll shows that (1) the public holds lawyers in low esteem, but (2) of all the possible careers that are available, parents would prefer to have their children become lawyers. Whole books could be written about that inconsistency. This is not the place, however, for a discussion of why people disparage lawyers; it is, however, the place to examine the vocabulary with which people do it.

The English language has a formidable stock of disparaging names for lawyers. Of course, every language has its proverbs that reflect poorly in one way or another on lawyers (maybe uncomprehendingly), but probably no other has the range in depreciative vocabulary—from the mild to the harsh. Of course, much depends on who is mouthing the word; some people use *lawyer* itself in derogatory ways—hence the unfortunate tendency for lawyers to call themselves *attorneys* (q.v.) instead of *lawyers.*

A. Names Actually Given to Lawyers. The following 33 terms have been used at various times and in various places to refer to lawyers in ways that are less than flattering:

- *ack-ack* = (20th-c. AmE criminal cant) a court-appointed lawyer. One writer says that the expression "is both a pun on the World War II antiaircraft gun and also a partial acronym for 'ambulance chaser.'" Joel Homer, *Jargon* 76 (1979).
- *ambidexter* = (16th–19th-c. BrE) an unscrupulous lawyer who takes fees (or sometimes bribes) "with both hands," that is, from both sides of a controversy.
- *ambulance chaser* = (19th–20th c.) a lawyer who solicits business from accident victims at the scene of an accident or shortly thereafter; by extension, an unscrupulous plaintiffs' lawyer. E.g., "[I]rresponsible reporters and editors . . . might, for example, describe the lawyer as a 'mob mouthpiece' for representing a client with a serious prior criminal record, or as an '*ambulance chaser*' for representing a claimant in a personal injury action." *Gertz v. Robert Welch, Inc.,* 418 U.S. 323, 355 (1974) (Burger, C.J., dissenting). See **ambulance chaser.**
- *Blackstone lawyer* = (19th–20th-c. AmE) a self-educated antebellum lawyer whose legal training consisted primarily in reading Blackstone's *Commentaries.* Thomas Jefferson complained that "a student finds there a smattering of everything, and his indolence easily persuades him that if he understands that book, he is a master of the whole body of law." The "unlettered common people" applied "the appellation of *Blackstone lawyers* to these ephemeral insects of the law." Letter from Thomas Jefferson to Judge John Tyler, 17 June 1812, in 13 *The Writings of Thomas Jefferson* 166–67 (Andrew Lipscomb ed. 1905).
- *chaser* = (20th-c. AmE) an ambulance chaser. E.g., "Practicing attorneys often tell us [i.e., the disciplinary authorities]: why don't you go get

so-and-so, the big guys, the publicity seekers, the big *chasers* . . . ." Murray T. Bloom, *The Trouble With Lawyers* 156 (1970) (quoting Vincent Cullinan, president of the San Francisco Bar, 1967–1968). The term also refers to a "runner" employed by the lawyer for purposes of soliciting business from accident victims.

- *city lawyer.* This term (19th–20th c.) is self-explanatory, except that the people who use the term are usually from rural areas. E.g., "They talked about the avaricious *city lawyers* who soon would be descending upon the company and demanding private documents." Joseph C. Goulden, *The Million Dollar Lawyers* 283 (1978). See **city lawyer.**
- *country lawyer* = (19th–20th-c. AmE) a rural lawyer. This term can carry positive connotations, but it sometimes suggests modest intellectual abilities—e.g.: "The rule of reason . . . should now allow one to put an antitrust theory of liability or justification into terms that a *country lawyer* can understand." Lawrence A. Sullivan, *The Viability of the Current Law on Horizontal Restraints,* 75 Calif. L. Rev. 835, 847 (1987). See **country lawyer.**
- *Court Street lawyer* = (20th-c. AmE) a (sometimes disreputable) lawyer with a practice—usu. a trial practice—centered in the borough hall area of Brooklyn. E.g., "Before the Depression, real estate lawyers were typically wheeler-dealers, called *'Court Street lawyers'* after the Brooklyn street where many of them set up practice." Rachelle DePalma, *The Role of the Pro in Real Estate Deals,* Crain's N.Y. Bus., 28 April 1986, at 30. Today the term is also used loosely to distinguish lawyers who practice in the outer boroughs (principally Brooklyn) from those, usu. white-shoe lawyers, who practice in the federal courts and the state courts of the borough of Manhattan, which is co-extensive with New York County.
- *dump truck* = (20th-c. AmE) a public defender. E.g., "Clients often refer to their public defenders as *'dump trucks,'* a term that apparently derives from the defendant's belief that defenders are not interested in giving a vigorous defense, but rather seek only to 'dump' them as quickly as possible." Suzanne E. Mounts, *Public Defender Programs, Professional Responsibility, and Competent Representation,* 1982 Wis. L. Rev. 473, 474.
- *green bag* = (17th–19th c.) a lawyer—through the process of metonymy: for their papers, lawyers formerly carried bags made of green canvas or cloth.
- *gunslinger* = (20th-c. AmE) a hired gun. E.g., "Some lawyers were disturbed when I wrote that lawyers should be 'healers not *gunslingers*' but I have not hesitated to restate it." Warren E. Burger, *Foreward* [*sic*]: *American Law Institute Study on Paths to a "Better Way,"* 1989 Duke L.J. 808, 809.
- *hired gun* = (20th-c. AmE) a lawyer who acts like an aggressive gunfighter in the Old West, and who will do anything for a fee. E.g., "Kevin Mulligan, president of the union, said an agreement was reached in only three months because the *'hired guns'* were not present during negotiations. He said that when the lawyers for both sides were involved in the last contract,the process took 18 months." Carol Stream, *Firefighters Sign 3-Year Contract,* Chicago Tribune, 15 May 1992, at 3D.
- *horse lawyer* = (19th–20th-c. AmE) a lawyer of little ability. See 3 Richard H. Thornton, *An American Glossary* 196 (Louise Hanley ed. 1962).
- *jackleg lawyer* = (20th-c. AmE) an amateurish and dishonest lawyer. E.g., "She did have a chat with a couple of lawyers. The lawyers couldn't do a thing. *'Jackleg lawyers,'* she says, and flicks ashes." Wil Haygood, *A Time Revisited,* Boston Globe, 16 March 1989, at 85.
- *jungle fighter* = (20th-c. AmE) a lawyer who practices in the lower criminal courts. E.g., "It may well be that the standard of decorum usually prevailing in the sedate precincts of chancery should also be observed by the *jungle-fighters* in the pit of police and criminal courts, but it would be somewhat less than realistic . . . ." *Kentucky State Bar Ass'n v. Taylor,* 482 S.W.2d 574, 583 (Ky. Ct. App. 1972).
- *latrine lawyer* = (20th-c. AmE) a lawyer who gets business from the rumors spread in the latrine.
- *lawmonger* = (17th-c. BrE) a low practitioner of law; a pettifogger. E.g., "[T]hough this catering *Law-monger* be bold to call it wicked." John Milton, "Colasterion" (1645), in *The Works of John Milton* 233, 259 (Frank A. Patterson et al. eds. 1931).
- *legal beagle* = (20th c.) a lawyer. Like *legal eagle,* this term is generally found in the speech and writing of nonlawyers, sometimes with positive and sometimes with negative connotations. Sometimes it occurs with dog metaphors—e.g.: "Even if council's *legal beagles* sniff out a loophole to invalidate the petition, the mayor's suggestion to put voter-rejected water metering back on the ballot morally compels the council to repeat the fluoridation vote." Don Martin, *Fluoride Forces Better Brush Up for Battle,* Calgary Herald, 11 Oct. 1991, at B1. See **legal eagle.**
- *legal eagle* = (20th-c. AmE) a lawyer. Like *legal beagle,* this term is almost invariably used by

those outside the legal profession, usu. with positive connotations. But not always—e.g.: "The *legal eagles* snookered a federal judge into swallowing their sophistry . . . ." Samuel Francis, *The Long Count on Executions,* Washington Times, 1 May 1992, at F3. See **legal eagle.**

- *leguleian* = (17th–19th-c. BrE) a pettifogger—as the *OED* puts it, "a contemptuous term for a lawyer." E.g., "You do but that . . . which some silly *Leguleians* now and then do, to argue unawares against their own clients." John Milton, "A Defence of the People of England," in *The Prose Works of John Milton* 1, 179 (J.A. St. John ed. 1910 [Joseph Washington trans. 1692]).
- *lip* = (20th-c. AmE) a criminal lawyer (viewed cynically).
- *mob mouthpiece* = (20th-c. AmE) a defense lawyer for mobsters. E.g., "Oscar Goodman has defended a federal judge and the mayor of San Diego, derailed a U.S. attorney general's effort and proudly wears the title *'mob mouthpiece,'* having represented a who's who of alleged crime figures." Robert Macy, *Money's Source "Irrelevant": "Mob Mouthpiece" Fights U.S. Attempt to Seize Fees,* L.A. Times, 6 April 1986, at 2-8.
- *mouthpiece* = (19th–20th-c. AmE & BrE) defense counsel hired to speak at the client's bidding. E.g., "[A]n attorney is not merely the client's 'alter ego' functioning only as the client's *'mouthpiece.'*" *Morrison v. State,* 373 S.E.2d 506, 509 (Ga. 1988).
- *pettifogger* = (16th–20th-c. BrE & AmE) a petty and disreputable lawyer who niggles over inconsequential details; a "rascally attorney" (*OED*). E.g., "Quite the contrary, counsel in that case were not *pettifoggers* . . . ." *Nebeker v. Piper Aircraft Corp.*, 747 P.2d 18, 38 (Idaho 1987). See **pettifogger.**
- *Philadelphia lawyer* = (18th–20th-c. AmE) an ultracompetent lawyer who knows the ins and outs of legal technicalities; also, a shrewdly unscrupulous lawyer. (This term has long been known in AmE and BrE alike. Similar geographic terms are used as regionalisms. For example, *Dallas lawyer* is often snidely used in Fort Worth; *Houston lawyer* is often snidely used in Dallas; and *New York lawyer* is snidely used by lawyers almost everywhere else.) See **Philadelphia lawyer.**
- *shady lawyer* (self-explanatory): "A *shady lawyer* named Kantor, who had been assigned as counsel to the defendant, managed by terrifying the mother as to the possible outcome of the case, to extort from her her entire savings amounting to four hundred and thirty-five dollars." Ephraim Tutt, *Yankee Lawyer* 106 (1943).
- *ship's lawyer* = (19th–20th-c. AmE) an unskillful lawyer. See 3 Richard H. Thornton, *An American Glossary* 348 (Louise Hanley ed. 1962).
- *shyster* = (19th–20th-c. AmE) a professionally unscrupulous lawyer. For the fascinating etymology of this word, see **shyster.** For the distinction between a *pettifogger* and a *shyster,* see **pettifogger.**
- *shyster lawyer* (redundant and self-explanatory): "[T]he *shyster lawyer* assigned by the court wanted to squeeze all the money he could out of the boy's family . . . ." Ephraim Tutt, *Yankee Lawyer* 106 (1943). For the etymology, see **shyster.**
- *silk-stocking lawyer* = (19th–20th-c. AmE) a patrician lawyer. E.g., "'Do you want ivory tower, *silk stocking lawyers* defending these people?' the house speaker shouted at him. Mr. [Gary] Parker replied, 'That's better than no lawyer at all.'" Marianne Lavelle, *Piercing Racism's Heart,* Nat'l L.J., 24 Dec. 1990, at 1.
- *sore-back lawyer* = (20th-c. AmE) a personal-injury lawyer. E.g., "[My father] really didn't like this bleep I was doing, you know, suing businesses, being a *sore-back lawyer* (legalslang for a personal injury lawyer), and he was oriented the other way." Joe Jamail (as quoted in Steve Coll, *Down Home with Texas' $10.5 Billion Barrister Pennzoil Attorney Joe Jamail,* Wash. Post, 31 July 1986, at B1).
- *Tombs lawyer* = (19th–20th-c. AmE) an unscrupulous New York practitioner. Thornton defines the term *Tombs lawyers* as "a class of men in New York, resembling the 'Old Bailey practitioners,' but, if possible, more unscrupulous," with this illustration: "A man as corrupt as sin, as venal as a *Tombs lawyer* . . . ." 3 Richard H. Thornton, *An American Glossary* 196 (Louise Hanley ed. 1962).
- *white-shoe lawyer* = (20th-c. AmE) an establishment lawyer. E.g., "Lifland rejected Gold's suggestion, appointing *white-shoe lawyer* Leon Silverman of New York's Fried, Frank, Harris, Shriver & Jacobson instead of someone from the ranks of organized labor." Caroline V. Clarke, *Labor's Turn to Take on Manville,* American Law., Jan.–Feb. 1991, at 44, 44. See **white-shoe lawyer.**

B. Prejudicial Names for Other Forms of Life. Sometimes, people and things are referred to as lawyers, usually for the purpose of making the reference derogatory—e.g.:

- *barrack lawyer* = (20th-c. BrE criminal cant) a prisoner who thinks he knows all there is to know regarding prison rules. One text defines the phrase as follows: "Generally a solicitor's ex-clerk posing as a lawyer and always ready to give 'expert' advice on 'how to get on special release.'" Paul Tempest, *Lag's Lexicon* 11 (1950).

- *bush lawyer* = (19th–20th-c. Australianism) one who parades a merely fancied knowledge of the law. E.g., "Well, in the old days in the bush, there were no registered lawyers, so some half-shrewd mug, usually a barber, would set himself up to adivse all and sundry. So now anyone who throws around a lot of free advice is called a *bush lawyer*." F. Hardy, *Billy Borker Yarns Again* 135 (1967).
- *guardhouse lawyer* = (20th-c. AmE) a jailhouse lawyer. E.g., "If we are going to administer criminal justice properly to those whose cases call for our attention, if we are going to devote our attention to matters meriting attention and not submerge ourselves in a great bog of rhetorical trivia, mostly dreamed up by *guardhouse lawyers,* we must exercise some degree of rational selection." *Surratt v. U.S.,* 262 F.2d 691, 694 (D.C. Cir. 1958) (Prettyman, C.J., dissenting).
- *high lawyer* = (16th–18th-c. BrE) a mounted highway robber. E.g., "The legerdemaine [*sic*] of . . . *high Lawyers.*" Robert Greene, *Groats-Worth of Wit* XXIX (Dyce ed. 1617). See Eric Partridge, *A Dictionary of of the Underworld* 331 (1950).
- *jailhouse lawyer* = (20rh-c. AmE) an inmate who acquires some legal learning and counsels fellow inmates on drafting complaints and briefs.
- *lake lawyer* = (19th-c. AmE) either of two different fishes, the bow-fin and the burbot—named because of their "ferocious looks and voracious habits." John R. Bartlett, *The Dictionary of Americanisms* 198 (1849).
- *lawyer* = (19th-c. AmE) the black-necked stilt—so named because of its "long bill" (*OED*).
- *lynch lawyer* = (19th-c. AmE) a practitioner of lynch law. E.g., "In the middle [of the plaza] is planted a tall liberty pole, near which is erected a rude rostrum for *lynch-lawyers* and noisy politicians." Hinton R. Helper, *The Land of Gold* 74 (1855). See **lynch law.**
- *pelican* = (20th-c. AmE) a jailhouse lawyer specializing in appeals. See Joel Homer, *Jargon* 78 (1979).
- *sea lawyer* = (19th–20th-c. BrE & AmE) a captious or carping sailor—or, by extension, other person. E.g., "So long as the teacher acts reasonably the Constitution does not require him to work in an atmosphere of litigious contest with any juvenile *sea-lawyer* who may appear in his class." *Meyers v. Arcata High Sch. Dist.,* 75 Cal. Rptr. 68, 78 (Ct. App. 1969) (Christian, J., dissenting). Originally, in the early 19th c., *sea lawyer* was a name given to the tiger shark.

lawyer's lawyer. This CLICHÉ is among highest compliments that one lawyer can pay another. E.g., "Robert Houghwout Jackson was an eloquent spokesman for the pattern of beliefs and feelings characteristic of the political ideology of the American lawyer. More than any other Supreme Court justice of the twentieth century, Jackson was a *lawyer's lawyer.*" Glendon Schubert, *Dispassionate Justice* 1 (1969). For the definitive treatment of all that this phrase embodies, see William H. Harbaugh, *Lawyer's Lawyer: The Life of John W. Davis* (1973). Unfortunately, however, the phrase is coming to be used with little discrimination.

lay, adj. See **laic, laity & layman.**

lay; lie. These verbs are commonly misused—even by members of our learned profession. Witness these specimens: "He said he played with guns all the time, and that he picked up a pistol *laying* [read *lying*] on the bedside table and began *waiving* [read *waving*] it around . . . ." *Still v. State,* 709 S.W.2d 672, 674 (Tex. App.—Tyler 1983)./ "Mr. Armstrong [debating against Alan Dershowitz] was not to be outdone . . . . But Mr. Dershowitz did not *lay* [read *lie*] down." William Glaberson, *Face to Face, 2 Lawyers Feud Away, Slap for Slap,* N.Y. Times, 19 Jan. 1991, at 15./ "Susman started looking around for a lucrative niche in the Houston legal market, and he thought the big money might *lay* [read *lie*] in plaintiffs' antitrust class action work." John A. Jenkins, *The Litigators* 259–60 (1989; repr. 1991).

Very simply, *lie* (= to recline, be situated) is intransitive <he lies on his bed>, whereas *lay* (= to put down, arrange) is transitive only <she laid her hand on his shoulder> <they laid the body in its grave>. The verbs are declined *lie* > *lay* > *lain* and *lay* > *laid* > *laid.* To use *lay* intransitively to mean "lie" <I want to lay down> is nonstandard, even though (alas) fairly common in speech. See **lie.**

lay low. See **lie low.**

layman; layperson; lay person; nonlawyer. *Layman* is the most common among these terms and has traditionally been regarded as unexceptionable—in reference to members of both sexes, of course. E.g., "[A] *layman* was needed to evaluate the success or failure of my effort to translate rules of law into understandable English prose. Therefore, with infinite patience, my wife read and reread every section of this text . . . ." Robert

Kratovil, *Real Estate Law* iv (1946; repr. 1950). Still, modern writers increasingly avoid *layman* on grounds of SEXISM. For those seeking a nonsexist substitute, *nonlawyer* is the best choice.

W10 records *layperson* from 1972; the one-word form appears to be an Americanism. E.g., "The average *layperson* would no doubt disagree with A if he said, 'I didn't intend to injure C.'" Here it appears in plural form *lay people,* an alternative to *laypersons:* "If they continue in their druidic isolation, the only course *lay people* might have is what Dick the butcher, in *Henry IV, Part Two,* suggested: 'The first thing we do, let's kill all the lawyers.'" For the reason to avoid *layperson,* like all other words ending with the *-person* suffix, see SEXISM (B). See also **laity, nonlawyer, people (A)** & BIBLICAL AFFECTATION.

leach, vb.; **leech,** vb. To *leach* is to pass through by percolation, or to separate a solid from a solution by percolation. To *leech* is to apply bloodsuckers to the skin in order to cause bleeding (no longer a favored medical technique); metaphorically, *leeching* occurs when a person acts like a blood-sucker.

Surprisingly often, *leech* is misused for *leach*—e.g.:

- "The advent of agriculture in the Imperial Valley and the Coachella Valley, with its attendant irrigation, *leeching* [read *leaching*], and drainage significantly changed the inflow into the Sea." *U.S. v. Imperial Irrigation Dist.,* 799 F. Supp. 1052, 1058 (S.D. Cal. 1992).
- "Testimony was elicited regarding a condition known as 'new building syndrome,' indicating that new buildings have a greater accumulation of allergens and *leeching* [read *leaching*] of noxious vapors [that] subside with the passage of time." *Champion v. Beale,* 833 S.W.2d 799, 800 (Ky. 1992).
- "Plaintiffs in California, Illinois, and New York are alleging that children whose mothers had implants prior to their conception may have been injured from silicone *leeching* [read *leaching*] through their mothers' bloodstream and breast milk." Todd P. Myers, Casenote, *Ohio Rejects Preconception Cause of Action for DES Grandchildren,* 62 U. Cin. L. Rev. 283, 320 n.267 (1993).

lead is sometimes wrongly used for *led,* perhaps on the mistaken analogy of *read/read,* and perhaps also because of confusion with the metal. E.g., "Claimant has failed to prove that her work injury has *lead* [read *led*] employers to refuse her employment . . . ." *Perman v. North Dakota Workers Compensation Bureau,* 458 N.W.2d 484, 486 (N.D. 1990).

leader (at the bar) is a Britishism meaning "the senior barrister for a party in a case." In the U.S., *lead counsel* is the usual phrase.

leading case = (1) most strictly, a judicial precedent that first definitely settled an important rule or principle of law and that has since been often and consistently followed; (2) less strictly, an important, often the most important, judicial precedent on a particular legal issue; or (3) loosely, a reported case that determines an issue being litigated; a *ruling case,* q.v. Sense (1) is the classic one, referring to cases such as these:

- *McNaghten's Case,* 8 Eng. Rep. 718, 10 Cl. & Fin. 200 (1843) (first setting forth the grounds of the insanity defense). See **McNaghten.**
- *Palsgraf v. Long Island R.R.,* 162 N.E. 99 (N.Y. 1928) (establishing the doctrine that a defendant's duty in a negligence action is limited to plaintiffs within the zone of apparent danger—to whom damage could be reasonably foreseen).
- *Erie R.R. v. Tompkins,* 304 U.S. 64 (1938) (holding that on questions of state law, a federal court sitting in diversity is bound by the law as declared by the highest state court).
- *Miranda v. Arizona,* 384 U.S. 436 (1966) (creating the exclusionary rule for evidence obtained improperly from a suspect being interrogated while in police custody).

leading question; categorical question. Nonlawyers frequently misapprehend *leading question* as referring to a question showing hostility or posed just to embarrass or take unfair advantage. Actually, as litigators well know, a *leading question* is one that suggests the answer to the person being interrogated. In Anglo-American law such questions are generally permissible only on cross-examination. *Categorical question,* another name for the same practice, is today little used.

leaflet(t)ing. This word arises in First Amendment cases, such as *Jews for Jesus, Inc. v. Board of Airport Comm'rs,* 661 F. Supp. 1223, 1224, 1225 (C.D. Cal. 1985), in which the word is spelling *leafletting* on one page and *leafleting* on the next. The better spelling in AmE is *leafleting;* in BrE, *leafletting.* See DOUBLING OF FINAL CONSONANTS.

leapt is the correct past-tense form of *leap.* See **lept.**

learned; learnt. As an adjective, *learned* has two syllables, and as a past tense one. *Learnt* is a BrE variant of the past tense *learned.*

learned counsel; learned friend; learned court. These are tiresome legal CLICHÉS; examples like the following one show just how debased such phrases have become: "*Learned counsel* . . . contend . . . . This contention is unsound, and . . . is bottomed wholly on a false premise . . . ." *Ford v. Moody,* 276 S.W. 595, 597 (Ark. 1925). *Learned friend* is a common variation, as in, "It may be helpful to your Lordship and my *learned friend* if I . . . ," meaning, as David Pannick points out, "it will certainly be helpful to me." Pannick adds that to say, "In all fairness to my *learned friend,*" means that one is about to "put the legal boot in." David Pannick, *Judges* 153 (1987).

Even *learned court* is likely to sound patronizing, esp. when used by an appellate court in reference to a lower court—e.g.: "The *learned court* at special term has found that, although the instrument relied upon by the defendant was testamentary in character, it did not comply with the statutory requirements of a will and is therefore void."

learnt. See **learned.**

leasable. So spelled.

lease, n., = (1) a conveyance of real property, usu. in return for rent, made for life, for a fixed period, or at will—but always for less time than the lessor has a right to; (2) both such a conveyance and all other covenants attached to the conveyance; (3) the written instrument in which such a conveyance, together with the covenants, is incorporated; (4) in North America and Australia, a piece of real property that is held on lease; or (5) a temporary conveyance of personal property in return for consideration.

When sense (5) arose in the 19th century, it was considered a loose usage. Today, however, leases of cars and office equipment, for example, are common.

lease, v.t.**; let.** *Let* (10th c.) is 300 years older than *lease* (13th c.) in the sense "to grant the temporary possession and use of (land, buildings, rooms, movable property) to another in return for rent or other consideration." But both are well established, and they are equally good. As used by (real) estate agents in BrE, the term "To Let" is more common than the phrase "For Rent," the usual term in AmE.

To say that one *leases* property nowadays does not tell the reader or listener whether one is lessor or lessee. From its first verbal use in the 13th century, *lease* meant "to grant the possession of," but in the mid-19th century it took on the additional sense "to take a lease of; to hold by a lease." This ambiguity has made the preposition used important to clarity: the lessor *leases to* and the lessee *leases from.*

leaseback (= the sale of property on the understanding, or with the express option, that the seller may lease the property immediately upon the sale) dates from the mid-20th century. Though technically a REDUNDANCY, the common phrase *sale and leaseback* helps clarify the meaning.

leasee. See **leasor.**

lease for years. See **term of years.**

lease from. See **lease,** v.t.

leaseholder (BrE) = *lessee* (AmE). Both terms are used in both speech communities—for example, *leaseholder* is fairly common in American oil-and-gas cases—but *leaseholder* is the more general term in BrE, *lessee* the more general term in AmE.

lease-lend. See **lend-lease.**

leaseman. See **landman.**

lease-purchase agreement; hire-purchase agreement. The first is standard AmE; the second is the BrE equivalent. The AmE phrase is sometimes written *lease-to-purchase agreement.* See **hire purchase.**

lease to. See **lease,** v.t.

leasor; leasee. These are blunders for *lessor* and *lessee.* E.g., "[T]he legal status of a third person coming upon a *leasor's* [read *lessor's*] property at the invitation of a *leasee* [read *lessee*] is immaterial." *Flott v. Cates,* 528 N.E.2d 847, 849 (Ind. Ct. App. 1988)./ "[T]he city would require the *leasee* [read *lessee*] to construct at least 55,000 square feet of maintenance hangar space . . . ." *Government Actions,* Wash. Post, 12 April 1990, at V5. See **lessor.**

leave of court = judicial permission to follow a nonroutine procedure. In the sense of permission, *leave* had become archaic by the 19th century in every field but law. Rather than just leaving it alone, sometimes lawyers use the word *leave* alone—e.g.: "Your honor, we seek *leave* to amend our complaint under these extraordinary circumstances."

lecture method. See **casebook method.**

leech, vb. See **leach.**

legacy = a gift by will, esp. of personal property and often of money. Several types of legacies are distinguishable. A *specific legacy* or *bequest* is a testamentary gift of property that can be distinguished with reasonable accuracy from the other property forming the testator's estate. A *demonstrative legacy* is paid from a particular source; but if the source is insufficient to satisfy the legacy, then the legacy is paid from the general assets of the estate to the extent that the specific source is lacking. A *general legacy* or *bequest* is a gift of personal property that the testator intends to come from the general assets of the estate.

A *residuary legacy* or *bequest* is a gift of the estate remaining after all claims against the estate have been satisfied, and all specific, demonstrative, and general legacies have been paid out. Cf. **bequest (A).** See **devise.**

legacy, v.t. See **legate.**

legal, adj.; **lawful; licit.** *Legal* is the broadest term, meaning either (1) "of or pertaining to law, falling within the province of law," or (2) "established, permitted, or not forbidden by law." These two senses are used with about equal frequency.

Lawful and *licit* share with *legal* sense (2), "according or not contrary to law, permitted by law." *Lawful* is quite common—e.g.: "In March 1977, the company posted a notice on the bulletin board that contained a *lawful* statement on the solicitation and distribution of materials." The least frequently used of these terms is *licit* <licit acts> <the licit use of force>, which usu. occurs in direct contrast to *illicit.*

Lawful should not be used in sense (1) of *legal,* as it sometimes is—e.g.: "The judgment must be affirmed if there is sufficient evidence to support it on any *lawful* [read *legal*] theory, and every fact issue sufficiently raised by the evidence must be resolved in support of the judgment." See **illegal.**

legal, as an attributive noun, means "the legal description of real property" <I have enclosed the legal on the parcel you asked about>. This usage began as surveyors' cant but has gradually infected lawyers' language. See ADJECTIVES (B).

legal assistant. See **paralegal (B).**

legal beagle. See **legal eagle.**

legal cause. See CAUSATION (A).

legal centr(al)ism = a doctrine holding that the legal entities erected by the state occupy the center of legal life and stand in a relation of hierarchic control over other, lesser norms that define appropriate behavior and social relationships, such as the family, the corporation, or business networks. The form *legal centralism* is more usual—e.g.: "This is the defining belief of *'Legal Centralism,'* the almost-universally accepted dogma of legal professionals." David Luban, *Difference Made Legal: The Court and Dr. King,* 87 Mich. L. Rev. 2152, 2184 n.100 (1989)./ "Recently, legal scholars have begun to challenge the fundamental assumption of *'legal centrism'* [read *'legal centralism'*], which emphasizes the importance of the promulgated law as a behavior-guiding force in society." Lynn A. Baker, *Promulgating the Marriage Contract,* 23 U. Mich. J.L. Ref. 217, 220 n.20 (1990). As for the variant form *legocentrism,* see **lego-.**

legaldegook = legal gobbledygook; the worst manifestations of LEGALESE. Each year beginning in the early 1990s, the Plain-Language Committee of the State Bar of Texas has bestowed its "Legaldegook Awards" to bring attention to what it calls "delightfully atrocious" examples of legal writing.

The adjective *legaldegooky* originated in the writings of Fred Rodell, who, in his famous essay, wrote: "Else why—once they have won their full professorships, at any rate—do they keep submitting that turgid, *legaldegooky* garbage to law reviews—for free?" *Goodbye to Law Reviews—Revisited,* 48 Va. L. Rev. 279, 288 (1962). See GOBBLEDYGOOK.

legal eagle; legal beagle. Linguists call phrases like these "reduplicative"—other more or less common ones being *fuddy-duddy, hoity-toity, namby-pamby, nolens volens,* and *wishy-washy.* Both *legal beagle* and *legal eagle* are journalists' favorites, and they both seem to be used sometimes with positive connotations, sometimes neutrally, and sometimes with negative connotations. If there is a difference, *legal beagle* seems more frequently to convey the idea (vaguely) of lawyer-as-lapdog—e.g.: "Fuller, meanwhile, has come off to many as the stereotypical high-paid *legal beagle* defending a rich celebrity." Jon Saraceno, *Attorneys Present Dueling Images,* USA Today, 4 Feb. 1992, at 2C.

Legal eagle, an Americanism that is more than twice as common as *legal beagle* in journalistic AmE, provides writers with a little trick for "enlivening" their prose by avoiding the word *lawyer.* E.g., "Hillary Clinton, feminist, children's rights activist, *legal eagle* and betrayed wife, has won

The Family Circle chocolate chip cookie recipe contest." Sandra Gotlieb, *Hillary Bakes Up a Winning Image,* Financial Post, 16 Oct. 1992, at 9. See LAWYERS, DEROGATORY NAMES FOR (A).

LEGALESE. Ironically, many dictionaries label *legalese* a "colloquialism." It denotes what is perhaps the least colloquial of all forms of English writing: the complicated language of legal documents. The *OED* traces *legalese*—the word, not the thing—back to the second decade of the 20th century, with this example: "He signed his name at the foot of a bald formal agreement, written in the most incomprehensible *legalese.*" C.J.C. Hyne, *Firemen Hot* 189 (1914).

Though the name for it is fairly new, legalese itself has, throughout the history of Anglo-American law, been a scourge of the profession. Thomas Jefferson railed against statutes "which, from their verbosity, their endless tautologies, their involutions of case within case, and parenthesis within parenthesis, and their multiplied efforts at certainty, by *saids* and *aforesaids*, by *ors* and *ands*, to make them more plain, are really rendered more perplexed and incomprehensible, not only to common readers, but to the lawyers themselves." 1 *The Writings of Thomas Jefferson* 65 (Lipscomb ed. 1903).

The same is true, of course, of all types of legal writing, not just statutes or even just DRAFTING. For a humorous epitome of legalese, the following 19th-century example, describing a collision, is without equal:

> The declaration stated, that the plaintiff theretofore, and at the time of the committing of the grievance thereinafter mentioned, to wit, on, etc., was lawfully possessed of a certain donkey, which said donkey of the plaintiff was then lawfully in a certain highway, and the defendant was then possessed of a certain waggon and certain horses drawing the same, which said waggon and horses of the defendant were then under the care, government, and direction of a certain then servant of the defendant, in and along the said highway; nevertheless the defendant, by his said servant, so carelessly, negligently, unskilfully, and improperly governed and directed his said waggon and horses, that by and through the carelessness, negligence, unskilfulness, and improper conduct of the defendant, by his said servant, the said waggon and horses of the defendant then ran and struck with great violence against the said donkey of the plaintiff, and thereby then wounded, crushed, and killed the same, etc.
>
> *Davies v. Mann,* (1842) 10 M. & W. 546, 152 Eng. Rep. 588.

Even in the 20th century, collisions have sounded much the same in legalese—e.g.: "On information and belief, Defendants Newton and Kautz, immediately prior to operating their vehicles on the aforesaid Route 315, had attended a party sponsored by defendant Roach Incorporated on Powell Road in Powell, Ohio; said Defendants left the party at approximately the same time; said Defendants Newton and Kautz were racing their automobiles pursuant to an agreement reached at said party shortly prior to the aforesaid collision . . . ." Pleading quoted in *Baird v. Roach, Inc.,* 462 N.E.2d 1229, 1231 (Ohio Ct. App. 1983).

Legalese is often highly compressed—e.g.: "The question here is whether service of citation was proper in the face of a writ of error attack on a default judgment." And it flaunts legal ceremony, which arguably has a place in some documents: "In testimony whereof, I have hereunto subscribed my name and affixed my seal, this 24th day of June, in the year of our Lord, one thousand nine hundred and eighty five."

We have enough examples, however, of what not to do. The nauseous (q.v.) effect of the passage from *Davies v. Mann,* and other passages throughout this work, should purge readers of any attraction to legalese. See DOUBLETS, TRIPLETS, AND SYNONYM-STRINGS, LEGALISMS AND LAWYERISMS & PLAIN LANGUAGE.

LEGAL FICTIONS. See FICTIONS.

legal fraternity is a traditional phrase that, unfortunately, carries strong associations of maleness—and is therefore unlikely to survive the spreading intolerance toward sexist language. Nonsexist substitutes include *legal community, the bar* (in AmE)*, bench and bar, the legal world,* and the like. On the unflattering side, Fred Rodell referred to the *legal tribe:* "Those amendments begin to look more important than the whole original Constitution; and to any of the *legal tribe,* they are." Fred Rodell, *Woe Unto You, Lawyers!* 56 (1939; repr. 1980). See SEXISM.

legal fraud. See **constructive fraud** & **fraud (C).**

legalism; legality. *Legality* = strict adherence to law, prescription, or doctrine; the quality of being legal. E.g., "A genuine dispute exists as to the *legality* of any ownership claim made by the codepositors." *Legalism* = (1) formalism carried almost to the point of meaninglessness; a disposition to exalt the importance of law or formulated rule in any department of action, (2) a mode of expression characteristic of lawyers. See **legalist & legalistic.**

LEGALISMS AND LAWYERISMS are the circumlocutions, FORMAL WORDS, and ARCHAISMS that characterize lawyers' speech and writing, esp. in DRAFT-

ING. Little can be said by way of advice except that generally lawyers and legislators should try hard to avoid them.

Legalistic	*Ordinary*
abutting	next to
adequate number of	enough
adjacent to	next to
anterior to	before
at the time when	when
be able to	can
be authorized	may
be binding upon	bind
be empowered to	may
be unable to	cannot
by means of	by
cause to be done	effect (vb.) *or* have (a thing) done
contiguous to	next to
during such time as	while, during
enter into an agreement with	agree with, contract with
enter into a contract with	contract with
excessive number of	too many
for the duration of	while, during
for the reason that	because
in case	if
in order to	to
in the event that	if
in the interest of	for
it is directed	must
it is the duty	must
it shall be lawful	may
it shall be legal	may
it shall be the duty of	must
it shall not be lawful to	may not, must not
on or about	on, about
or in the alternative	or
per annum	a year, annual
per diem	a day
period of time	period, time
point in time	point, time
previous to	before
prior to	before
prosecute (a business)	carry on
pursuant to	under, in accordance with
subsequent to	after
sufficient number of	enough
the reason being that	because
under the provisions of	under
until such time as	until

See LATINISMS & PLAIN LANGUAGE.

legalist = one who adheres to legalistic thinking. E.g., "Some *legalists* suggest the literal translation of this statute to mean marital assets may be sold only upon entry of a judgment of divorce." *Glatthorn v. Wisniewski,* 566 A.2d 242, 244 (N.J. Super. Ct. Ch. Div. 1989).

legalistic is a rather contemptuous term meaning "formalistic; exalting the importance of formulated rules in any department of action." E.g., "In the course of time the inevitable happened, and *legalistic* elaboration of this form of action pursued its stultifying course, so that a mass of complex law grew up around the writ." A.W.B. Simpson, *An Introduction to the History of the Land Law* 29 (1961).

The word has taken on such negative connotations that it has been perverted by at least one writer to mean "without any imaginable legal support": "The Trout of the title is a psychopathic storekeeper who guns down a twelve-year-old girl on the strictly *legalistic* grounds that her foster-brother owes him instalments on a car loan." John Sutherland, *Tangling with the Mob,* TLS, 21 Feb. 1992, at 32. See **legalism.**

legalitarian, adj.; **legalitarianism,** n. The *SOED* records *legalitarianism* as having two senses: (1) "advocacy of conformity with the law"; and (2) "legal egalitarianism." Only sense (2)—in which the term is a PORTMANTEAU WORD combining *legal* and *egalitarianism*—is really sensible. E.g., "Such a result may be acceptable to a *legalitarian* . . . ." *Travelers Indem. Co. v. Peacock Constr. Co.,* 423 F.2d 1153, 1160 (5th Cir. 1970) (per Brown, C.J.).

legalize = (1) to make legal; to justify by legal sanction; to authorize; (2) to imbue with the spirit of the law, often making (a thing) legalistic; or (3) to practice as a lawyer. Sense (1) is the common one—e.g.: "[Lithuania's] parliament voted overwhelmingly today to *legalize* rival political parties." Esther B. Fein, *Lithuania Legalizes Rival Parties, Removing Communists' Monopoly,* N.Y. Times, 8 Dec. 1989, at 1.

Sense (2) is not so common but still appears—e.g.: "But it is difficult or perhaps impossible for him to avoid a certain distortion of the way in which *legalized* conceptions and legal institutions operate to distribute power in society . . . ." A.W.B. Simpson, *Trouble with the Case,* TLS, 14–20 Dec. 1990, at 1344.

Sense (3) is a nonce-use illustrated by a single quotation in the *OED:* "Jobson still *legalizes* in Gray's Inn." John R. Leifchild, *Cornwall: Its Mines and Miners* 244 (1855).

legally sometimes functions as a SENTENCE ADVERB in the sense "from a legal point of view." E.g., "*Legally,* however, it seems impossible to differentiate between the sexes, except possibly by confining the theory of maim to the fighting sex." Glanville Williams, *The Sanctity of Life and the Criminal Law* 107 (1957; repr. 1972)./ "*Legally* he knows that of which he has notice." William F. Walsh, *A Treatise on Equity* 509 (1930).

LEGAL MAXIMS. See MAXIMS.

legal memory. See **memory of man runneth not to the contrary & time immemorial.**

legalness is a NEEDLESS VARIANT of *legality.*

legal portion. See ***legitim(e).***

legal positivism. See **positivism.**

legal science. "The terms *legal science* and *jurisprudence,*" writes David M. Walker, "are themselves . . . of very indefinite connotation. The main meanings are probably: all knowledge of and about law; the knowledge of the more theoretical problems of law, as contrasted with knowledge of principles in force; and the systematic analysis and exposition of knowledge of and about law." David M. Walker, *The Scottish Jurists* 6 n.1 (1985).

The term *legal science* is rarely encountered in contemporary writing, perhaps because lawyers know that they are not scientists—perhaps not even to the extent that social scientists might be called "scientists." There are "hard sciences"—such as chemistry, physics, biology—and there are "soft sciences"—such as sociology, psychology, and political science. Law is a soft science at best; the better view, though, is that it has little enough in common with any science as to make it illegitimate to call it a "science."

legalspeak is another term for *legalese,* with connotations perhaps even more negative. It is formed from the fairly new suffix *-speak,* which came into vogue after George Orwell coined *Newspeak* and *Oldspeak* in his apocalyptic book *1984* (1949). Like its forerunners, *legalspeak* vaguely suggests a conspiracy. E.g., "[T]o use the appropriate *legalspeak,* there was no 'privity'—no direct contact between Becker and Klein." Geoffrey Smith, *Revenge of the Nerds,* Forbes, 22 Oct. 1984, at 102./ "In China, *legalspeak* makes an unflattering distinction between barristers and lawyers by terming barristers 'big lawyers' and solicitors simply 'lawyers.'" *Point of Order,* Daily Telegraph, 8 Sept. 1990, at 15. See LEGALESE.

legal tender = (1) the money—bills or coins—approved by a state; or (2) a tender (of something) that is legally sufficient.

legal title. See **title.**

LEGAL WRITING STYLE. A sound legal style is not so very different from a sound style in any other realm of writing—except perhaps that it is rarer. As legal writers, we begin with several disadvantages:

- We continually resort to lawbooks that overflow with writing contaminated by stylistic infections—but few readers effectively inoculate themselves.
- Built as it is on precedent, Anglo-American law discourages lawyers from writing differently from their predecessors.
- Our law schools generally shunt legal writing off to the periphery of the curriculum, thereby signaling in effect that attainments in writing are of minimal importance.
- The modern practice of law does not tolerate the type of revisory process necessary to produce a polished product—the "well-managed" law firm has more work to do than it can complete in a given span of time.
- As a whole, the profession disdains literary accomplishment within law—it believes in a sharp (and illusory) split between style and substance.
- Even those lawyers who care about writing style are often inured to—and therefore help perpetuate—the worst conventions of legal writing.

How often do legal writers overcome these obstacles? Not often.

Why? Perhaps because mistaken notions of "style" mislead so many talented lawyers. They imitate law reviews. (See LAW REVIEWESE.) For continuing-legal-education programs, they try to write "scholarly" papers jam-packed with discursive footnotes. In client letters, they try to sound "professional" but instead come across as pompous. They learn LEGALESE and forget idiomatic English. They become habituated to their *prior tos*, their *pursuant tos*, their *hereinafters*, their *incident theretos*, and all their other ballyhoos—and they forget what it is to speak or write directly and simply. They try to be showy instead of being lucid and brief.

Few have written as lucidly and briefly about stylistic excellence in law as Walker Gibson, who delineated the literary contours of legal prose:

> There is no reason why almost any piece of legal writing—and certainly judicial writing—may not move us with its sensitive and wise and gracious handling of language. It is true that the legal writer operates within limiting situations, and he must attend painstakingly to the minutiae of facts that confront him. Yet it is also true that he is engaged in expressing in words the chaos of

life, and no poet can say more. Judicial opinions and poetry are obviously not identical forms of expression; yet, in Frost's memorable phrase about poets, the legal writer too is attempting "a momentary stay against confusion." It is hard to think of a finer thing for a man to do.

A curious humility, or an equally curious arrogance, is apparent in the attitude that legal writers sometimes express toward their performances in language. One hears a lawyer or a judge remark, "Oh, I'm no stylist—I just write down the facts in plain words." This is both humble and arrogant—humble in surrendering elegance to the "creative artists," arrogant in suggesting that only "the facts" really matter. But the situation is surely quite otherwise. The poet or novelist, the historian, the physicist, the appellate judge are all deeply involved in one essential responsibility: the expression of life's complexities in mere man-made words. Wherever he starts, whatever trivial item of human experience he initially confronts, the legal writer can make his stab at eloquence. If Holmes was right, that "a man may live greatly in the law as well as elsewhere," then the consequence is that he must *write* greatly, for in law as well as in literature there is no other meaning of greatness.

Walker Gibson, *Literary Minds and Judicial Style,* 36 N.Y.U. L. Rev. 915, 930 (1961).

Following are works that merit the legal writer's study. These represent the most helpful references available in the specific niches of legal writing.

A. General Legal Writing. Bryan A. Garner, *The Elements of Legal Style* (1991); Mark Adler, *Clarity* (1990); Tom Goldstein & Jethro K. Lieberman, *The Lawyer's Guide to Writing Well* (1989); C. Edward Good, *Mightier Than the Sword* (1989); Ronald Goldfarb & James C. Raymond, *Clear Understandings* (1982); Christopher T. Lutz, "Why Can't Lawyers Write?" in *Appellate Practice Manual* 167 (Priscilla A. Schwab ed. 1992).

B. Brief-Writing. "It should never be forgotten that in a law office you will find three English styles: (1) the style of a contract, a mortgage, a conveyance, etc. [see (C) below]; (2) the style of a pleading; and (3) the style which should characterize briefs. A brief written in the other two styles is a monstrosity." Paxton Blair, "Appellate Briefs and Advocacy," in *Advocacy and the King's English* 788, 791 (1960). For recommended works to forestall all such monstrosities, see BRIEF-WRITING.

C. Drafting. The style of contracts, rules, and statutes differs dramatically from the style of briefs, judicial opinions, legal memos, and other types of legal writing. The paramount aim of the drafter is to be unmistakable, not interesting.

Some say that "it is even more difficult to write intelligibly about drafting than to draft intelligibly . . . ." Noel Hutton, *Mechanics of Law Reform,* 24 Mod. L. Rev. 18, 21 (1961). A few writers, however, have succeeded. The following works are useful for the legislative or legal drafter: Barbara Child, *Drafting Legal Documents* (2d ed. 1992); Reed Dickerson, *The Fundamentals of Legal Drafting* (2d ed. 1985); Elmer Driedger, *The Composition of Legislation* (1957). See DRAFTING & STATUTE DRAFTING.

D. Judicial Opinions. Unfortunately, there is a dearth of good writing on this difficult subject. Ruggero Aldisert's *Opinion Writing* (1990) and B.E. Witkin's *Manual on Appellate Court Opinions* (1977) both contain much useful information, but they are not widely available. Four articles worth consulting are Walker Gibson, *Literary Minds and Judicial Style,* 36 N.Y.U. L. Rev. 915 (1961); Glen Leggett, *Judicial Writing: An Observation by a Teacher of Writing,* 58 Law Lib. J. 114 (1965); George R. Smith, *A Primer of Opinion Writing, for Four New Judges,* 21 Ark. L. Rev. 197 (1967); and Irving Younger, *On Judicial Opinions Considered as One of the Fine Arts,* 51 U. Colo. L. Rev. 341 (1980). See OPINIONS, JUDICIAL.

legatary, n. See **legatee.**

legate, v.t.; **legacy,** v.t. Both may mean "to give or leave as a legacy; to bequeath a legacy to." *Legacy* is an ARCHAISM in this verbal sense, and *legate* is rather rare. *Bequeath,* q.v., is the usual word.

legatee = one who is named in a will to take personal property; one who has received a legacy or bequest. In strict common-law terminology, a distinction was drawn between a *legatee* and a *devisee,* the former receiving personal property and the latter real property. E.g., "A devise or bequest to a child does not lapse by death, but the property so devised or bequeathed shall vest in the surviving child or other descendant of the *legatee* or devisee, as if such *legatee* or devisee had survived the testator and had died intestate." But *legatee* is often loosely used for one to whom a devise is given. See **devisee.**

Legatary, n., is a NEEDLESS VARIANT.

legation. See **embassy.**

legator, a NEEDLESS VARIANT of *testator,* is infrequently used. It may occasionally be in meaning "one who bequeaths a legacy," as opposed to one devising real property—but some readers will likely be puzzled. See **devise** & **bequeath.**

legible. See **illegible.**

legislate = (1) (v.i.) to make laws; (2) (v.t.) to bring (something) into or out of existence by making laws; to (attempt to) bring about or control by legislation. Sense (1) is the more common one—e.g.: "Montana is free to *legislate* with respect to the liability incurred." *Miller v. Fallon County,* 721 P.2d 342, 347 (Mont. 1986). Sense (2), though, is common enough to be a part of the general language—e.g.: "The critics contend the court far exceeded its authority to interpret the law and instead used *Roe* to *legislate* social policy from the bench." *The Battle Over Abortion,* Newsweek, 1 May 1989, at 29.

A BACK-FORMATION from *legislation,* the verb *to legislate* was rarely used before the 19th century. Before that time, laws were said to be not *legislated,* but *enacted* or *ordained.*

legislation = (1) the action of making or giving a positive law in written form, according to some type of formal procedure, by a branch of government constituted to perform this action <legislation is an arduous process>; or (2) what a legislature has enacted; the whole body of enacted laws <the legislation threatens the university's independence>. On the question whether *legislation* includes things that are not statutes, see **statutory legislation.**

legislational is a NEEDLESS VARIANT of *legislative.* E.g., Arthur Lenhoff, *Extra-Legislational* [read *Extra-Legislative*] *Process of Law,* 28 Neb. L. Rev. 542 (1949). See **legislative.**

legislative; legislatorial. The first corresponds to *legislation,* the second (in good usage) to *legislator,* q.v. See **legislatorial.**

legislative facts; adjudicative facts. The difference between these phrases is "the cardinal distinction [that], more than any other, governs the use of extra-record facts by courts and agencies." Kenneth C. Davis, *Administrative Law Text* § 15.03, at 296 (3d ed. 1972). *Legislative facts,* which are ordinarily general and do not concern the immediate parties, are facts that "help the tribunal to exercise its judgment or discretion in determining what course of action to take"; they are implicated "whenever a tribunal engages in the creation of law or of policy." *Id.* They are, for example, the kinds of facts that are used in a *Brandeis brief,* q.v.

Adjudicative facts are those found by a court or agency "concerning the immediate parties—who did what, where, when, how, and with what motive or intent." *Id.* In finding adjudicative facts, then, the court or agency performs an adjudicative function.

legislative veto (AmE) = a practice that, originating in the 1930s and valid until held unconstitutional in 1983, allowed Congress to block a federal executive or agency action within a specified time (usu. 60 or 90 working days) without presidential approval. E.g., "Short, dark-haired, and tending toward stockiness, this pipe-puffing, feisty constitutional expert [Antonin Scalia] had no doubts in his mind about the *legislative veto*'s unconstitutionality, and no hesitancy in speaking his mind to anyone who would listen." Barbara H. Craig, *Chadha: The Story of an Epic Constitutional Struggle* 53 (1988) (which tells the story behind *INS v. Chadha,* 462 U.S. 919 (1983), the case holding the legislative veto unconstitutional).

legislatorial = (1) of or pertaining to a legislator; or (2) of or pertaining to legislation. In sense (2), the word is a NEEDLESS VARIANT of *legislative.* In sense (1), however, the term is useful—e.g.: "An examination of the act impresses that there was *legislatorial* doubt in its enactment." *Hume-Sinclair Coal Mining Co. v. Nee,* 12 F. Supp. 801, 805 (W.D. Mo. 1935). See **legislative.**

legist = one learned or skilled in the law; a lawyer; a jurist. This word is underused—it appears in only a few modern cases. E.g., "[N]o *legist* meriting deference has noticeably recorded the opinion that a witness could be adjudged in contempt of court for the failure to comply with the terms of a mere summons in such circumstances." *In re Roberts,* 30 A.2d 900, 902 (N.J. Ch. 1943)./ "[C]ertain 'proceedings' were had out of the hearing of the jury panel, in the course of which the Cooperative's *legists* reverted in this wise to the above-quoted statement by opposing counsel . . . ." *M & A Elec. Power Coop. v. True,* 480 S.W.2d 310, 313 (Mo. Ct. App. 1972).

legitim. See ***legitim(e).***

legitimacy; legitimation; legitimization; legitimatization. *Legitimacy* = the fact of being legitimate. *Legitimation* is the best word for the sense (1) "the action or process of rendering or authoritatively declaring (a person) legitimate" (*OED*); or (2) "the action of making lawful; authorization" (*id.*). E.g., "An illegitimate child may be *legitimated* by the marriage of his parents, although several states require, in addition, an acknowledgment by the father. A few states have judicial procedures for *legitimation.*" *Legitimization* and *legitimatization* are NEEDLESS VARIANTS.

legitimate, v.t.; **legitimize; legitimatize.** The first is preferred in all senses and is by far the most common of the three forms. E.g., "[T]his end is undoubtedly better answered by *legitimating* all issue born after wedlock, than by *legitimating* issue of the same parties, even born before wedlock, so as wedlock afterwards ensues . . . ." 1

William Blackstone, *Commentaries on the Laws of England* 443 (1765)./ "This fact suggests implicit recognition of the value of the larger body as a means of *legitimating* society's decision to impose the death penalty."

Legitimize and *legitimatize* are both NEEDLESS VARIANTS. Though formed incorrectly, the former is much more common than the latter. See -IZE.

legitimation; legitimization. See **legitimacy.**

legitim(e). This civil-law term, meaning "the part of a decedent's estate to which his or her issue are entitled as a legal right," is usu. spelled *legitim* in Scotland and *legitime* in Louisiana. E.g., "There is no case for imputation of advances where only one of several children claims *legitim.*" 4 David M. Walker, *Principles of Scottish Private Law* 127 (3d ed. 1983)./ "[A] testator may not by testamentary dispositions infringe on the *legitime* of his forced heirs." A.N. Yiannopoulos, *Of Legal Usufruct, the Surviving Spouse, and Article 890 of the Louisiana Civil Code,* 49 La. L. Rev. 803, 803 (1989). Other terms for *legitime* are *legal portion* and *forced portion.*

LEGO-, as a prefix meaning "legal," has no etymological warrant. It occurs most frequently (and perhaps occurred originally) in *legocentrism*—a word coined on the analogy of *ethnocentrism.* The following quotation makes its sense apparent: "Lawyers and judges tend to develop a form of tunnel vision which causes them to view the litigation process as if it were the most vital part of our society. We must avoid such *'legocentrism.'*" Gregory Gelfand, *"Taking" Informational Property Through Discovery,* 66 Wash. U.L.Q. 703, 727 (1988). The corresponding adjective, also a NEOLOGISM, is *legocentric*—e.g.: "Gold has a 'legocentric' view of people." J. Alexander Tanford & Sarah Tanford, *Better Trials Through Science,* 66 N.C. L. Rev. 741, 746 (1988). See **legal centr(al)ism.**

legulian. See LAWYERS, DEROGATORY NAMES FOR.

lemon law. The word *lemon,* in the sense "something bad or undesirable," originated as an Americanism in the early 20th century. In AmE, the word has increasingly been specialized to refer to cars with persistent problems. Hence, a *lemon law* is a statute designed to protect consumers who buy substandard cars. In 1992, 45 of the 50 U.S. states had lemon laws in effect.

BrE was quick to adopt *lemon* but has not narrowed the term, as AmE has. So *lemon law* has a broader sense, referring to faulty consumer goods of any kind—e.g.: "The attempt by Mr Martyn Jones, Labour MP for Clwyd South-West, to introduce a *'lemon law'* to protect consumers buying faulty items has all-party support at Westminster . . . ." Julia Langdon, *Consumers' Minister May Try to Squash Lemon Bill,* Sunday Telegraph, 21 Jan. 1990, at 4.

lend. See **loan.**

lend-lease; lease-lend. Both phrases refer to either (1) "an arrangement made in 1941, under the Lend-Lease Act, whereby sites in British overseas possessions were leased to the United States as bases in exchange for the loan of U.S. destroyers"; or, by extension, (2) "a cooperative arrangement made between friendly entities." The phrase *lend-lease,* which comes directly from the statute, is more common—so it would not be amiss to label *lease-lend* a NEEDLESS VARIANT.

leniency; lenience. The first form is preferred.

leonine contract is another term for *adhesion contract.* In Roman law, a *leonina societas* was a partnership in which one party took all the profits and the other all the losses. Cf. the Spanish term *contrato leonino.*

lept for *leapt* or *leaped* is a mistaken past-tense form. E.g., "John J. Sirica *lept* [read *leapt*] to his feet, shouting, 'It ain't fair. It ain't fair!'" *Sirica, 88, Dies; Persistent Judge in Fall of Nixon,* N.Y. Times, 15 Aug. 1992, at 1, 11./ "McGensey who by then had reached the top of the wall *lept* [read *leapt*] down on Rivera." *Gates v. Rivera,* 993 F.2d 697, 698 (9th Cir. 1993).

lese majesty; lèse majesty; leze majesty; *lèse-majesté; laesae majestas; laesae majestatis.* The preferred form of this originally civil-law term—meaning "a crime against the state, esp. against the ruler" or "an attack on a custom or traditional belief"—is the anglicized *lese majesty.* The variant spellings should be avoided. In BrE, the phrase tends to be hyphenated; in AmE it usually is not.

In spelling the full LATINISM naming the crime, however, the phrase is spelled *crimen laesae majestatis*—e.g.: "Counterfeiting has usually been classified as an offense affecting the administration of governmental functions, which unquestionably it is, having been considered *crimen laesae majestatis* and punished as treason at one time in England." Rollin M. Perkins & Ronald N. Boyce, *Criminal Law* 432 (3d ed. 1982). *Laesae majestas* is a hybrid: half LAW LATIN and half LAW FRENCH.

less. **A. And *fewer.*** *Less* applies to mass nouns <less tonic water, please> or units of measure <less than six ounces of epoxy>. The latter applies to COUNT NOUNS <fewer than ten guests arrived> or numbers of things <fewer than six limes are left>.

The only exception in using *fewer* occurs when count nouns are so great as to render the idea of individual increments meaningless. E.g., "A District Court has concurrent jurisdiction under the Tucker Act over suits for *fewer* [read *less*] than $10,000." Here, because the dollars are taken not individually but collectively as an amount, *less* is appropriate. Hence we say *less discovery* but *fewer depositions; less testimony* but *fewer witnesses; less documentation* but *fewer documents; less argumentation* but *fewer arguments; less whispering* but *fewer sidebars* (q.v.); *less ambiguity* but *fewer ambiguities; less of a burden* but *fewer burdens; less material* but *fewer items; less fattening* but *fewer calories.*

Less is used correctly with time—e.g.: "More than three but *less* than six years after the completion of the cleanup operations, the United States instituted civil actions to recover its cleanup costs."/ "The Supreme Court denied certiorari, and Milton's execution was scheduled again, for June 25, 1985, *fewer* [read *less*] than two hours from this writing." In the sentence just quoted, not only is *fewer* used incorrectly with a period of time but also with the number two, which is illogical. (One hesitates to fault the style of a judge who works under such exigencies.) But if the units of time are countable as whole and rather fractional units, then *fewer* is called for—e.g.: "The time must be not *less* [read *fewer*] than fourteen nor more than twenty-one days after the receipt of the warrant . . . ." H.C. Richards & J.P.H. Soper, *The Law and Practice of Compensation* 143 (n.d. [1898]).

Less for *fewer* is an all-too-frequent error: "From 1970 to 1975, the number of pending criminal cases increased from 20,910 to 22,411, a caseload difference of *less* [read *fewer*] than four cases per authorized judgeship."/ "Further, this rule also provides that if three or *less* [read *fewer*] jurors become disabled or otherwise unable to serve, the remaining jurors may render a verdict."/ "The principal felt that this particular pupil might create *less* [read *fewer*] problems if he remained in the main school building."/ "What the juvenile court system needs is not more but *less* [read *fewer*] of the trappings of legal procedure and formalism."/ "Over the years, membership in the organization decreased until in 1941 there were *less* [read *fewer*] than 100 members; at the time of this action there were approximately 58 members still living."

Less power but *fewer powers:* hence the adjective should be *fewer* here: "The move from the Articles of Confederation to the Constitution was a shift from a central government with *less* [read *fewer*] powers to one with more powers." See **fewer.**

B. And *lesser.* *Lesser* is an exact synonym of *less,* but is confined to use as an adjective before a noun and following an article <the lesser crime>, thus performing a function no longer idiomatically possible with *less.* Dating from the 13th century, this formal usage allows *lesser* to act as an antonym of *greater,* as here: "The *lesser* punishments are just as fit for the *lesser* crimes as the greater for the greater." Oliver W. Holmes, *The Common Law* 46 (1881; repr. 1916)./ "His thought and his memories pervade the whole with greater or *lesser* distinction."

Perhaps because of its decreasing use, *lesser* was, esp. in the early and mid-20th century, mistakenly supplanted by *less,* which is awkward when used attributively: "Riot, rout, and unlawful assembly are kindred offenses and greater includes the *less* [read *lesser*]." *Commonwealth v. Duitch,* 67 A.2d 821, 822 (Pa. Super. Ct. 1949) (quoting 54 C.J., *Riot,* at 829)./ "The effect of the creation of a *less* [read *lesser*] estate is to deprive the owner of the fee simple estate of the right of immediate possession . . . ." 1 Herbert T. Tiffany, *The Law of Real Property* § 23, at 31 (3d ed., B. Jones ed., 1939).

The opposite offense against idiom also occurs: "The constitutional rights of minors do not receive *lesser* [read *less*] protection than the rights of adults." The *OED* states that the construction *lesser than* is obsolete.

Should *lesser* (when properly used) seem stilted, one might use *smaller* or, depending on the context, *lower.* Often *smaller* seems more natural. E.g., "The defendant in such a case would have to pay a much *lesser* [read *smaller*] amount."/ "A lease is a conveyance, usually in consideration of rent or other recompense, for life, years, or at will, but always for a *less* [read *lesser,* or—because *lessor* appears later in the sentence—*shorter*] time than lessor has in the premises."

Less is sometimes used in the sense "of lesser seriousness." E.g., "He was convicted of three felonies *less* than capital." *Lesser* is commonly used in the phrase from American criminal law, *lesser included offense:* "We also have serious doubts about whether the offense to which Garrett pleaded guilty in Washington was a *lesser included offense* within the continuing criminal enterprise charge."

lesseeship = the condition or position of a lessee (tenant). E.g., "The defendants argue in the alternative to their theory of *co-lesseeship* that they may assert a violation of their Fourth Amendment rights . . . ." *U.S. v. Potter,* 419 F. Supp. 1151, 1154 (N.D. Ill. 1976)./ "[T]here must be an ownership or a *lesseeship* in mail stages . . . ." *Great Lakes Stages, Inc. v. Laing,* 174 N.E. 784, 786 (Ohio Ct. App. 1930).

lesser included offense = a less serious crime than the one charged, but one that an accused necessarily committed in carrying out the more serious crime. E.g., "Joyriding is a *lesser-included offense* of theft of a motor vehicle." Rollin M. Perkins & Ronald N. Boyce, *Criminal Law* 334 n.97 (3d ed. 1982). As in the preceding quotation, the phrase is often rendered *lesser-included offense,* but it is best not hyphenated because it is not, strictly speaking, a PHRASAL ADJECTIVE.

lessor; lessee. *Landlord* and *tenant* are simpler equivalents that are more comprehensible to most nonlawyers. And they do not run the risk of typographical errors reversing the suffixes.

lest is best followed by a SUBJUNCTIVE. E.g., "[S]trict scrutiny of the classification which a State makes in a sterilization law is essential, *lest* unwittingly, or otherwise, invidious discriminations *are* [read *be*] made against groups or types of individuals in violation of the constitutional guaranty of just and equal laws." *Skinner v. Oklahoma,* 316 U.S. 535, 541 (1942) (per Douglas, J.)./ "The court should not instruct the jury to weigh carefully the evidence of insanity, *lest* an ingenious counterfeit of the disease *furnish* protection to guilt."

let (= hindrance or obstacle) is used in the legal doublet *without let or hindrance.* This meaning of *let* is archaic except in law, poetry, and tennis (*let ball* = net ball). The word differs in origin from the verb *let* (= to permit, allow, rent), though both terms appeared in Old English. See DOUBLETS, TRIPLETS, AND SYNONYM-STRINGS.

Nonlawyers have sometimes misunderstood the meaning of *let* in the phrase *without let or hindrance,* as if *let* were an antonym rather than a synonym of *hindrance.* Thus Theodore Dreiser wrote of something descending on somebody "without his let or hindrance," confusing the lay with the legal meaning of *let.*

let, v.t. See **lease.**

lethal (= deadly, mortal) is generally used of poisons and medicines in nonlegal usage, but in legal usage still appears in the older sense relating to weapons and wounds as well: "We cannot condone *lethal* use of force as a first measure taken by police." Unlike *fatal,* q.v., which can be both literal and figurative, *lethal* is ordinarily confined to literal senses.

letter de cachet. See ***lettre de cachet.***

letter of attorney. See **power of attorney.**

letter of the law, the. This metaphor, referring to the strict literal meaning of the law, is opposed to the *spirit of the law.* E.g., "Equity was based upon the idea of natural justice, as opposed to the strict *letter of the law.*" 1 E.W. Chance, *Principles of Mercantile Law* 2 (13th ed. rev. P.W. French 1950). See **spirit.**

letters of credence = the papers appointing a foreign diplomatic agent, who presents them to the head of government to which he or she is accredited. E.g., "[T]he United States Government is prepared to proceed with the issuance of appropriate *letters of credence* accrediting the United States Ambassador in Belgrade to the new Yugoslav regime." *Artukovic v. Boyle,* 107 F. Supp. 11, 34 n.5 (S.D. Cal. 1952) (quoting an official letter).

letters of marque = licenses to engage in reprisal against citizens or vessels of another nation. E.g., "[F]ormerly it was not uncommon for a state to issue *'letters of marque'* to one of its own subjects, who had met with a denial of justice in another state, authorizing him to redress the wrong for himself by forcible action, such as the seizure of the property of subjects of the delinquent state." J.L. Brierly, *The Law of Nations* 321 (5th ed. 1955)./ "Private maritime wars were legalized by *letters of marque,* allowing a merchant whose ship had been plundered to become a *privateer* and take revenge and compensation from other ships of the offender's nation." Alan Harding, *A Social History of English Law* 306 (1966). The wordy phrase *letters of marque and reprisal,* is traditional and appears, for example, in the U.S. Constitution; nevertheless, it should be avoided.

letters of request. See **letters rogatory.**

letters patent. Historically, this phrase, plural in form but singular in sense, denoted an open letter, under governmental seal, granting some right or privilege. E.g., "In the middle ages all local government was carried on by authority of the king's writs of commission (*letters-patent*)." Alan Harding, *A Social History of English Law* 72 (1966). The phrase was used in opposition to *letters secret* (= governmental documents closed and sealed, and hence not available for general perusal).

In modern law, the phrase *letters patent* has taken on a specialized sense, referring to a governmental grant of the exclusive right to use an invention or design. See **patent.**

letters rogatory; letter(s) of request. Both terms are used in the sense "a request issued to a foreign court requesting a judge to take evidence from a specific person within that court's jurisdiction." *Letters rogatory* has traditionally been the usual term, but it is slowly disappearing: in 1993, the Federal Rules of Civil Procedure were amended to replace the phrase with *letter of request.* Either *letter of request* or *rogatory letter* is used in G.B. Americans use the plural *letters* for the single request, whereas the British use the singular *letter.*

Historically, *letters of request* had a completely different meaning: "a documentary request sent by the judge of one ecclesiastical court to another, esp. to desire that a case may be withdrawn from his own jurisdiction to that of a superior court" (*OED*).

letters secret. See **letters patent.**

letters testamentary = the instrument by which a probate court approves the appointment of an executor under a will and authorizes that executor to administer the estate. In this phrase, *testamentary* acts as a POSTPOSITIVE ADJECTIVE.

***lettre de cachet;* letter de cachet.** The partial anglicization (*-er*) serves no purpose; for this French borrowing, *lettre de cachet* is the preferred spelling. The phrase denotes a warrant issued for the imprisonment of a person without trial. E.g., "The main thrust [of the Fourth Amendment] was directed at the invasion of privacy through general warrants of assistance and *lettres de cachet.*" *Ford v. U.S.,* 352 F.2d 927, 932 (D.C. Cir. 1965)./ "The tendency of fourth amendment orthodoxy to focus on citizen autonomy can undoubtedly be attributed to the Framers' fear of arbitrary and unrestrained state incursions on individuals' liberty and property interests. This fear was rooted in early experiences with England's infamous general warrants and writs of assistance and France's *lettres de cachet,* all of which permitted assertions of police power that were unaccountable to magistrate or judge." *Developments in the Law—Race and the Criminal Process,* 101 Harv. L. Rev. 1472, 1500 n.26 (1988).

levee. See **levy.**

leverage, v.t. = (1) to provide (a borower or investor) with credit or funds to improve the ability to speculate and to achieve a high rate of return; or (2) to supplement (available capital) with credit or outside funds. This verb is a mid-20th-century Americanism <a leveraged portfolio is one with a high amount of debt>. The term has definite meaning, but nevertheless may be characterized as a term used primarily by financial jargonmongers. See JARGON (B).

leviable = (1) that may be levied <leviable tax>; or (2) that may be levied upon; capable of being seized in execution. <The sheriff found no leviable assets>. Sense (2) is an AmE legalism.

levy; levee. *Levy* is usually a verb meaning (1) "to impose (as a fine or a tax) by legal sanction" <the court levied a fine of $500>; (2) "to conscript for service in the military" <the troops were soon levied>; (3) "to wage (a war)" <the rebels then levied war against the government>; or (4) to take or seize (property) in execution of a judgment—usually with the preposition *on* <the judgment creditor may levy on the debtor's assets>.

Levy may act also as a noun, however, in two senses: (1) "the imposition of a fine or tax, or the fine or tax so imposed"; and (2) "the conscription of men for military service, or the troops so conscripted."

Levee, meanwhile, is the noun meaning "a river embankment; dike; pier." In G.B. primarily, it also has the sense "a formal reception." Occasionally *levee* is used as a verb, meaning "to provide with a levee (dike)."

lex. **A. Senses.** *Lex* = (1) in Roman law, a legislative bill; (2) a collection of uncodified laws within a jurisdiction; (3) a system or body of laws, written or unwritten, that are peculiar to a jurisdiction or to a field of human activity; or (4) positive law, as opposed to natural law. Some scholars argue that senses (1) and (4) are the correct ones—e.g.: "The positive law formulated and fixed by a legislative body is called *lex, loi, Gesetz;* the general unwritten law is called *ius, droit, Recht.*" 1 Joseph H. Beale, *A Treatise on the Conflict of Laws* 23 (1935).

The plural form of *lex* is *leges.*

B. Anglicizing Phrases Beginning with *lex.* The field known as *conflict of laws* (q.v.) was once rife with phrases—and a few maxims—beginning with the word *lex.* Several of them are discussed in the entries that follow; many are unnecessary LATINISMS that some scholars manage to avoid. For example, Ehrenzweig prefers to anglicize the phrases—e.g.: "Once both the *place-of-contracting* [i.e., *lex loci contractus*] and the *place-of-performance* [i.e., *lex loci solutionis*] rules had been found unsatisfactory, some courts returned to the law expressly or impliedly intended by the parties, as an alternative or even as an exclusive solution." Albert A. Ehrenzweig, *A Treatise on the Conflict of Laws* 462 (1962). More American scholars than British scholars now make the phrases English; more on both sides of the Atlantic ought to try.

C. A Redundancy: *law of the lex.* To write *the law of the lex* . . . is redundant and nonsensical—e.g.: "[T]he Court of Appeals has differed in determining whether the right to bring an action is of a substantive nature requiring the application of the *law of the lex loci* [read *lex loci*] or a remedy requiring the application of the law of the forum." *Reale v. Herco, Inc.,* as reported in the New York L.J., 13 Sept. 1990, at 21.

lex actus; lex loci actus. The phrase, which means "the law of the place where a document is executed," seems to be a NEEDLESS VARIANT of *lex loci contractus* or *lex loci celebrationis.* The phrase is most often written *lex actus* /leks-**ak**-təs/—which is merely a shortened LAW LATIN form of the full phrase *lex loci actus* /leks-**loh**-sɪ-**ak**-təs/. Graveson has it both ways: "The strength of this presumption in favour of the *lex actus* was affirmed by the Court of Appeal in *Jacobs v. Crédit Lyonnais.*" R.H. Graveson, *Conflict of Laws* 414 (7th ed. 1974)./ "[C]apacity is governed by the *lex loci actus.*" *Id.* at 402.

lex domicilii /**leks**-dah-mə-**sil**-ee-ɪ/ = (1) the law of the country in which a person is domiciled; or (2) the determination of a person's rights by establishing where, in law, he or she is domiciled. E.g., "It is . . . in all cases the *lex domicilii* which should determine the right of succession." John Anderson Foote, *Private International Jurisprudence* 253 (Coleman Phillipson ed., 4th ed. 1914).

lex fori /leks-**fohr**-ɪ/ = the law of the forum. E.g., "[T]he *lex fori* (the law of the court) governs the procedure and remedies to be applied . . . ." René A. Wormser, *The Story of the Law* 493 (1962)./ "The requirement of writing is classified as a rule of evidence and must therefore traditionally be governed by the *lex fori* of any proceedings." R.H. Graveson, *Conflict of Laws* 533 (7th ed. 1974).

Lex fori is sometimes Englished *forum law:* "In conflicts cases concerning the validity of contracts, Professor Ehrenzweig would displace the basic rule pointing to *forum law* [i.e., the law of a particular forum] with the *lex validitatis.*"

lex loci /leks-**loh**-sɪ/ = (1) the law of the place; local law; or (2) the law of the place where a contract was executed (as a shorthand form of *lex loci contractus*). Sense (2) is increasingly conventional but potentially confusing to nonspecialists because any number of phrases—many more than the six listed here—begin with the words *lex loci.* See ***lex loci contractus.***

lex loci actus. See ***lex actus.***

lex loci celebrationis /leks-**loh**-sɪ-sel-ə-bray-shee-**oh**-nəs/ = the law of the place where a legal ceremony, such as a marriage or execution of a contract, was performed. E.g., "Thus parental consent is classified as a formality, not because it is a formality or bears any resemblance to part of the ceremony of marriage, but because the courts have decided that it should be governed by the *lex loci celebrationis.*" R.H. Graveson, *Conflict of Laws* 251 (7th ed. 1974). See ***lex loci contractus.***

lex loci contractus /leks-**loh**-sɪ-kən-**trak**-təs/ = the law of the place where the contract was executed—often the proper law by which to decide contractual disputes. E.g., "[T]he *lex loci contractus* (the law of the place where the contract was made) governs the interpretation of a contract." René A. Wormser, *The Story of the Law* 493 (1962)./ "The stipulations were valid by the *lex loci contractus,* but invalid by the law of the forum." Herbert F. Goodrich, *Handbook of the Conflict of Laws* § 110, at 215 (Eugene F. Scoles ed., 4th ed. 1964). Though it is confusing, given the number of phrases that begin with *lex loci,* this phrase is often shortened just to those two words. See ***lex loci.***

Literally, the phrase means "the law of the place of the contract"—as opposed to "where the contract was made"—and this literal meaning can give rise to an ambiguity: "The *lex loci contractus* has always been an ambiguous term, which jurists have interpreted either as the *lex loci celebrationis* or *solutionis,* the law of the place where the contract was entered into, or of that where it was to be performed, according to the tendency of their peculiar views." John A. Foote, *Private International Jurisprudence* 337 (Coleman Phillipson ed., 4th ed. 1914). In practice, however, modern courts and scholars invariably use the term to refer to the law of the place where the contract is executed, not performed.

lex (loci) delicti; lex loci delictus. **A. Latin vs. English Form.** The best Latin form, *lex loci delicti* (= the law of the place where the tort was committed) is shortened from *lex loci delicti commissi.* The form *delicti* is ten times more common than *delictus* in modern American caselaw. E.g., "The traditional rule of *lex loci delicti* requires the application of the tort law of the jurisdiction where the injury occurred." *International Paper Co. v. Ouellette,* 479 U.S. 481, 502 n.1 (1987)./ "A number of American states still follow *lex loci delicti* in their most recent decisions, though the number of such states decreases every year." Robert A. Leflar, *American Conflicts Law* § 132, at 267 (1977).

But the best Latin form is the second-best form: Ehrenzweig's anglicized phrase, *place-of-wrong rule* or *place-of-wrong law,* seems the most sensible of the available options.

B. Pronunciation. The phrase *lex loci delicti* is pronounced /*leks-**loh**-sɪ-dee-**lik**-tɪ*/. See PRONUNCIATION (C).

C. Mistaken Forms. Perhaps the best argument against the Latin is that English-speaking lawyers—and Americans especially—cannot seem to get the Latin right. The form *lex loci delictus,* for example, mangles the Latin on the mistaken analogy of *lex loci contractus*—but the noun *delictus* forms its genitive differently from *contractus:* Being a masculine noun of the fourth declension, *contractus* stays the same in the genitive (*contractus*); *delictus,* meanwhile, is a neuter noun of the second declension, forming *delicti* in the genitive. But legal writers occasionally fall into error. E.g., "We note that Utah also followed the rule of *lex loci delictus* [read *lex loci delicti*] regarding torts." *Mountain Fuel Supply v. Reliance Ins. Co.,* 933 F.2d 882, 888 (10th Cir. 1991).

The phrase is also sometimes mistakenly rendered *lex loci delecti*—e.g.: "At one time Arkansas courts followed the traditional approach of the First Restatement, termed *lex loci delecti* [read *delicti*] (law of the place of injury)." Carmen L. Arick, Note, *Conflict of Laws—Multistate Torts,* 10 U. Ark. Little Rock L.J. 511, 516 (1987–1988) (repeatedly using the wrong spelling). Cf. **corpus delicti.** See ***delecti.***

Another occasional mistake is to write *lex loci delictu*—e.g.: "[T]he cases have read in the forum or *lex loci delictu* [read *lex loci delicti*] limitation provisions." *Amdur v. Lizars,* 39 F.R.D. 29, 36 n.12 (D. Md. 1965).

lex loci rei sitae /*leks-**loh**-sɪ-**ree-ɪ-sɪ**-dɪ*/ = the law of the place where a thing is situated. This phrase is a NEEDLESS VARIANT of *lex situs.* E.g., "[H]e is before the Court as a party to the suit not warranting any interference as to the foreign real estate, with the *lex loci rei sitæ* [read *lex situs*]." John A. Foote, *Private International Jurisprudence* 208 (Coleman Phillipson ed., 4th ed. 1914). See ***lex situs.***

lex loci solutionis /*leks-**loh**-sɪ-sə-loo-shee-**oh**-nəs*/ = the law of the place where a contract is performed. E.g., "[I]f a contract made in one country is to be wholly or partly performed in another, it is presumed that the parties intended the mode of performance to be governed by the law of the country of performance (*lex loci solutionis*)." 1 E.W. Chance, *Principles of Mercantile Law* 87 (P.W. French ed., 13th ed. 1950)./ "The courts will give effect to the exchange control regulations of the proper law of the contract and of the *lex loci solutionis.*" R.H. Graveson, *Conflict of Laws* 179 (7th ed. 1974).

lex mercatoria; lex mercatorum. The first phrase means "the law merchant"—and the phrase *law merchant* (q.v.), a TERM OF ART, ought to replace it in modern writing. The second phrase means "the law of merchants," which means something slightly different from *law merchant.* Both phrases ought to be anglicized.

lex monetae = the law of the country whose money is at issue. E.g., "In such cases the meaning of units of that currency, *e.g.* pounds or francs, is determined by reference to the law of the country whose money is in question, sometimes called the *lex monetae.*" R.H. Graveson, *Conflict of Laws* 433 (7th ed. 1974).

lex naturae. See **natural law.**

lex patriae. See **personal law.**

lex situs /*leks-**sɪ**-dəs*/ = the law of the place where property is located. The phrase is modern LAW LATIN, not classical Latin. E.g., "[W]ith regard to contracts concerning land it is governed by the proper law of the contract, usually the law of the country in which the land is situated (*lex situs*)." 1 E.W. Chance, *Principles of Mercantile Law* 87 (P.W. French ed., 13th ed. 1950)./ "The essential validity is governed by the proper law of the transaction, subject in the case of immovables to any overriding provision of the *lex situs.*" R.H. Graveson, *Conflict of Laws* 356 (7th ed. 1974).

lex talionis /*leks-tal-ee-**oh**-nəs*/ = the law of retaliation—the retributive theory of punishment—based on the Mosaic principle of "an eye for an eye, a tooth for a tooth." E.g., "We are content to stand upon ground higher than the common urge of outraged reprisal which revives the *lex talionis,* demanding a life for a life." *Musselwhite v. State,* 60 So. 2d 807, 811 (Miss. 1952)./ "The '*lex talionis* of Moses' was literally an 'eye for eye, a leg for a leg.'" *Armstrong v. State,* 444 A.2d 1049, 1052 n.8 (Md. Ct. Spec. App. 1982) (citation omitted).

lex terrae. See **law of the land.**

leze majesty. See **lese majesty.**

liability. See **disability (A).**

liability without fault. See **strict liability.**

liable (= subject to or exposed to) should not be used merely for *likely* (= expected; probably) or *apt* (= inclined toward; fit). *Liable* best refers to something the occurrence of which risks being permanent or recurrent. E.g., "If the act is one that the party ought, in the exercise of ordinary care, to have *anticipated* [read *foreseen*] was *liable* [read *likely*] to result in injury to others, then he is liable for any injury proximately resulting from it."/ "The parties are competitors in this field; and when the rights or privileges of the one are *liable* to conflict with those of the other, each party is under a duty so to conduct its own business as not unnecessarily or unfairly to injure that of the other." The idea of recurrence is far more salient in the second than in the first sentence just quoted. Cf. **apt.**

Liable may also mean "responsible; subject to liability." In this sense, the word is usually confined to civil contexts in AmE, but in BrE it is used in criminal as well as civil contexts—e.g.: "She does not become *liable* merely by assisting her husband to escape punishment for a crime which she knows him to have committed . . . ." William Geldart, *Introduction to English Law* 49 (D.C.M. Yardley ed., 9th ed. 1984)./ "The trial court concluded that the appellant's conduct made him a socius criminis in the crime and, as such, that he was *liable* as a principal." (Eng.)

Liable has three syllables, not two, and is thus pronounced differently from *libel,* q.v.

liable, continue. See **continue liable.**

liaise, v.i., is a BACK-FORMATION from *liaison,* meaning "to establish liaison" or "to act as a liaison officer" <diplomats who liaise with Japanese officials>. First used in the 1920s, this word is still stigmatized as being cant or jargon. It is pronounced */lee-**ayz**/.*

liaison is pronounced either */**lee**-uh-zən/* or */lee-**ay**-zən/,* the latter being more common in both AmE and BrE. The nontechnical senses of the word are (1) (n.) "an illicit love affair"; (2) (n.) "communication established for the promotion of mutual understanding; one who establishes such communication"; and (3) (adj.) "acting as an intermediary" <liaison officer>.

The word is commonly misspelled *laison* and esp. *liason.*

libel; slander. The former is written defamation, the latter oral defamation. In English, the distinction emerged in the 1600s, before which time both words applied to what was either written or spoken. Perhaps the 17th-century legists were following the distinction observed in Roman law between *famosus libellus* (libel) and *injuria verbalis* (slander). As Gowers points out, the modern distinction is not well fixed in lay minds.

> In popular usage [the terms] are synonymous, meaning a deliberate, untrue, derogatory statement, usually about a person, whether made in writing or orally. In legal usage there are important differences. Each is an untrue and defamatory imputation made by one person about another which, if 'published' (i.e. communicated to a third person), can be a ground for a civil action in damages. Such an imputation is a *libel* if made in permanent form (writing, pictures, etc.) or by broadcasting. It is a *slander* if made in fugitive form (e.g. by speaking or gestures). A further distinction is that an action for *slander* cannot ordinarily succeed without proof that actual damage has been caused; in an action for *libel* this is unnecessary. In both cases proof that the allegation was true is a good defence.
>
> *MEU2* at 333.

Here *libel* is misused for *slander:* "According to the complaint, the *libel* [read *slander*] was uttered in the presence of only one person." (See **defamation.**) *Verbal slander* is a common REDUNDANCY. See **verbal.**

Libel has the additional sense in admiralty "the complaint or initial pleading in an admiralty or ecclesiastical case." The word is used also as a verb in this context—e.g.: "And so, in our own admiralty law, if a ship does you any injury, you *'libel'* or attach, and actually sue, the ship." René A. Wormser, *The Story of the Law* 16 (1962). Hence *libelant,* for which see **libel(l)ant.**

libel(l)ant = an injured sailor. E.g., "The *libelants* recovered in both Courts below." *Robins Dry Rock & Repair Co. v. Flint,* 275 U.S. 303, 307 (1927). One *-l-* is preferred in AmE, two in BrE. (See DOUBLING OF FINAL CONSONANTS.) The accent of *libelant* is on the first syllable.

Historically *libelant* has been an admiralty term as just defined, but the word has come to mean additionally "one who publishes a defamatory statement; a libeler." *Libeler* (in BrE *libeller*) is the older and better term for this sense, for it forestalls confusion about what the cause of action is.

libel(l)ee (= one against whom a libel has been filed) is correlative not with *libeler,* but with *libelant.* The word is spelled *libelee* in AmE, *libellee* in BrE. See -EE.

libel(l)er. See **libel(l)ant.**

libel(l)ous (= defamatory, constituting libel) is spelled *-l-* in AmE, *-ll-* in BrE. E.g., "The question is whether a writing published by A of B is *libellous* or not." (Eng.) See DOUBLING OF FINAL CONSONANTS.

liberty; freedom. These synonyms have connotative distinctions. *Freedom* is the broader, all-encompassing term that carries strong positive connotations. *Liberty,* slightly less emotive, generally suggests the past removal of restraints on specific freedoms.

Pound explained the distinction between Kantian liberty and constitutional liberty as guaranteed in the Bill of Rights:

> Kant's idea of the liberty of each—the free self-assertion of each—limited only by the like liberty of all, was generally accepted. Liberty was a condition in which free exercise of the will was restrained only so far as necessary to secure a harmonious coexistence of the free will of each and the free will of all others. But I am not speaking of the Kantian idea of liberty, in which my generation was brought up. Whatever "liberty" may mean today, the liberty guaranteed by our bills of rights is a reservation to the individual of certain fundamental reasonable expectations involved in life in civilized society and a freedom from arbitrary and unreasonable exercise of the power and authority of those who are designated or chosen in a politically organized society to adjust relations and order conduct, and so are able to apply the force of that society to individuals.
>
> Roscoe Pound, *The Development of Constitutional Guarantees of Liberty* 1 (1957; repr. 1975).

license. A. And *licence.* The AmE spelling of the noun and the verb is *license;* that is the BrE spelling of the verb, but *licence* is the BrE spelling of the noun.

B. And *easement.* An *easement* (q.v.) is a right of property; a license is a revocable permission to commit some act that would otherwise be unlawful. An *easement* is usu. created by a written document; a *license* is often created orally. An *easement* is more or less permanent; a *license* is temporary. An *easement* cannot be revoked; a *license* is revocable.

licensee = (1) one to whom a license is granted; or (2) one who enters an occupier's property not for business purposes but with the occupier's permission.

licenser; licensor. The former spelling is preferred.

licentiate (= one who has obtained a license or authoritative permission to exercise some function) is sometimes used of lawyers. E.g., "In the U.S. a *licentiate* in law is admitted to practice as an 'attorney and counselor,' a combination of names and functions unknown to the English law." (Eng.)/ "When the conduct of the *licentiate* clearly shows, either that the court was deceived at the time of his admission, or that there has been a moral degeneracy since that time, a proper case for discipline may be presented."

licit. See **legal,** adj.

lie (= to have foundation in the law; to be legally supportable, sustainable, or proper) is a peculiar legal idiom. E.g., "A writ of certiorari does not *lie* to review the proceedings of a board the function of which is to ascertain the competency of militia officers."/ "An action will *lie* for interference with enforceable contractual rights if there is no sufficient justification for the interference."/ "If review is available by appeal, mandamus will not *lie.*"/ "As a general rule, replevin will not *lie* for an undivided share in a larger mass."

Lie is used additionally in law in the figurative sense "to reside, exist." E.g., "Final appeal *lay* to the House of Lords." (Eng.) Cf. **sound.**

For the difference between *lie* and *lay,* see **lay.**

lie low; lay low. The latter phrase is incorrect. E.g., "Another reason I *laid low* [read *lay low*] was to be in a position to help a friend back out of what he now must know to be a dead end." William Safire, *Buchanan's Campaign,* N.Y. Times, 16 Dec. 1991, at A15. See **lay.**

lien, n., (= a legal right or interest that a creditor has in another's property, lasting usu. until a debt that it secures is satisfied) is pronounced, most properly, */**lee**-ən/* or */lin/*; and commonly, but less properly, */leen/*. In G.B., it is customary for the lienholder to retain possession of the property on which the lien has been obtained, whereas in the U.S. it is more usual that a lien does not involve retention by the lienholder. In the U.S., when the creditor possesses the collateral, *pledge* is the more usual term. See **liens and encumbrances.**

lien, v.t., a 19th-century innovation, is increasingly common, though it is not yet listed in most dictionaries. E.g., "In addition, the Northcutts allege that the Hancocks wrongfully *liened* the property." *Hancock v. Northcutt,* 808 P.2d 251, 253 (Alaska 1991).

Liened = burdened with a lien. E.g., "The proceeds of the water power are *liened* for the discharge of the canal debt by the act of 1825." *McArthur v. Kelly,* 5 Ohio 140, 152 (1831)./ "[S]ome courts have held *liened* penalty claims allowable . . . ." *Simonson v. Granquist,* 369 U.S. 38, 42 (1962).

lienable = capable of being subjected to a lien. E.g., "Certain kinds of labor and materials are not *lienable.*" Robert Kratovil, *Real Estate Law* 203 (1946; repr. 1950). This 20th-century Americanism is not listed in the *OED;* it appears in *W3,* but not in its predecessor, *W2.*

liened, adj. See **lien,** v.t.

lienee means, in AmE, "one whose property is subject to a lien," but in Australia it is synonymous with *lienholder.* The Australian usage mangles any sense left in the suffix -EE, q.v.

lienor; lienholder. The former, an Americanism, is best left unused; it is hardly known in BrE. *Lienholder* is also more likely to be understood by nonlawyers—and is more common in published materials. E.g., "The debtor listed the purported *lienholder's* claim as unsecured and the *lienholder* did not object to confirmation of the plan."/ "It is also clear that the *lienor* [read *lienholder*] has, by virtue of his possession per se, rights in rem against all others that they shall not disturb that possession or harm the object possessed." See **encumbrancer.**

liens and encumbrances. Though common, this phrase is redundant and illogical because a lien is one type of encumbrance. The better phrasing, then, would be *liens and other encumbrances,* or perhaps just *encumbrances* alone. See DOUBLETS, TRIPLETS, AND SYNONYM-STRINGS. See also **encumbrance.**

lieu of, in. See **in lieu of.**

life-and-death; life-or-death. Though the sense is "relating to a matter of life *or* death," idiom has sanctioned *and* in this PHRASAL ADJECTIVE, not *or*—e.g.: "An individual justice has no power to dispose of cases on the merits, but may make a variety of interim orders, sometimes of literally *life-and-death* significance." Charles A. Wright, *The Law of Federal Courts* 763 (4th ed. 1983)./ "'It's good enough for a *life-and-death* decision,' says one of the judges." James W. McElhaney, *The Law of Experts,* Litigation, Summer 1991, at 47, 50.

life assurance. See **life insurance.**

life estate = an estate that the grantee holds for life—resulting, for example, from a grant "to X during his life," by will, deed, or trust. Today, most life estates are beneficial interests under trusts, the corpus being personal property, not real property.

life insurance; life assurance. The former is usual in AmE, the latter in BrE.

life-or-death. See **life-and-death.**

lifting the corporate veil. See **piercing the corporate veil.**

ligan. See **flotsam.**

light of, in (the). See **in the light of.**

lighted; lit. Both are standard past-tense forms.

like; as. A. *Like* as a Conjunction. In standard usage, *like* is a preposition that governs nouns and noun phrases, not a conjunction that governs verbs or clauses. Its function is adjectival, not adverbial. Hence one does not write, properly, "He argued this case *like* he argued the previous one," but, "He argued this case *as* he argued the previous one." If we change *argue* to *argument, like* is possible: "His argument in this case was *like* his argument in the previous one."/ "In fact, the term 'legal writing' has become synonymous with poor writing: specifically, verbose and inflated prose that reads *like* [*as if*]—well, *like* [*as if*] it was written by a lawyer." Steven Stark, *Why Lawyers Can't Write,* 97 Harv. L. Rev. 1389, 1389 (1984) (though the change does change the tone).

This relatively simple precept is generally observed in writing but has been increasingly flouted in American speech. Examples of *like* used conjunctively can be found throughout the Middle English period; but the usage has been considered nonstandard at least since the 17th century. For the opposite error (*as* for *like*), see **as (B).**

B. Faulty Comparison: *like* for *as in.* "*Like Bush* [read *As in Bush*], administrative procedures are available to plaintiff to redress her grievance."/ "The State may, *like in* [read *as in*] cases where the offense charged includes lesser offenses, reduce the offense charged to the lesser included offense." See ILLOGIC (A).

In the following sentence, *like* appears erroneously in place of *as with.* "*Like other* [read *As with other*] judicial rules, however, exceptions to the warrantless search-and-seizure rule have been recognized by the courts."

likely has different shades of meaning. Most often it indicates a degree of probability greater than five on a scale of one to ten. The probability is, of course, greater when the word is preceded by a qualifier such as *quite, very,* or *extremely.* But it may also refer to a degree of possibility that is less than five on that same scale. See **probable.**

limine. See **in limine.**

limitation; repose. A *limitation* period bars a lawsuit if the plaintiff does not sue within a set time from the date when the cause of action accrued. A period of *repose,* meanwhile, bars a lawsuit for a fixed number of years after an action by the defendant (such as manufacturing a product), even if this period ends before the plaintiff suffers any injury. *Beard v. J.I. Case Co.,* 823 F.2d 1095, 1097 n.1 (7th Cir. 1987). Cf. **laches (D).**

limitation over. See **over (A).**

limitation(s) period. See **statute(s) of limitation(s).**

linchpin; lynchpin. The first spelling is standard.

lineal kinship. See **collateral kinship.**

lines and corners. See **metes and bounds.**

liquefy. So spelled. *Liquify* is a common misspelling.

liquidated damages, originally a EUPHEMISM for *forfeiture* or *penalty,* has, in many jurisdictions, become a TERM OF ART distinguishable from those other terms. *Liquidated damages* applies when the parties to a contract have agreed in advance on the measure of damages to be assessed in the event of default. It should be distinguished from *forfeiture* or *penalty,* which involves a provision imposed as a threat of punishment rather than as a genuine estimate of damages upon default.

Of course, the line between a *penalty* and *liquidated damages* is not always easy to draw. Regardless of what the sum might be called, the courts decide the true nature of the agreed-upon sum. Three conditions commonly lead a court to decide that a sum called "liquidated damages" is really a penalty: (1) if the sum grossly exceeds the probable damages on breach; (2) if the same sum is made payable for any variety of different breaches (some major, some minor); and (3) if a mere delay in payment has been listed among the events of default. See **damages (A).**

liquify. See **liquefy.**

lis (= a piece of litigation; a controversy) is brief but, probably to many readers, obscure. E.g., "The courts are concerned with the practical business of deciding a *lis* . . . ." *Attorney-General v. Prince Ernest Augustus of Hanover,* [1957] A.C. 436, 467 (per Lord Normand).

lis pendens; *lis alibi pendens; lite pendente; pendente lite.* *Lis pendens* (L. "a pending lawsuit"), pronounced /*lis-**pen**-dənz*/, is a useful LATINISM that has given its name to a notice required in some jurisdictions to warn all persons that certain property is the subject matter of litigation, and that any interests acquired during the pendency of the suit must be subject to the outcome of the litigation. Traditionally this notice was called the *notice of lis pendens,* but 20th-century American lawyers have shortened the phrase to merely *lis pendens.* E.g., "The defendant says that the plaintiff's harsh conduct in holding up a whole subdivision by the *lis pendens* in this action disentitles him to such relief."

Lis alibi pendens = a lawsuit pending elsewhere. E.g., "Where actions *in personam* are started in two courts of concurrent authority of the same country, the plea *lis alibi pendens* is a good defence to the second action." R.H. Graveson, *Conflict of Laws* 144 (7th ed. 1974).

Pendente lite /*pen-**den**-tee-**lI**-tee*/, less usually written *lite pendente,* is the same phrase in the present participial form, meaning "pending the lawsuit; during litigation." In G.B., administrators *pendente lite* are appointed to handle estates in dispute; in the U.S., matters are said to be *pendente lite* when they are contingent on the outcome of litigation.

Sometimes the phrase unnecessarily displaces an English phrase—e.g.: "The funds were deposited with the clerk of court, *pendente lite* [read *pending the outcome of the suit*]." The extra words provide extra comprehensibility.

list. There cannot be a list of one. E.g., "The name of the winner is *listed* below." [Read *The winner is named below.*]

literal canon; literal rule. These are both alternate names for strict constructionism, i.e., the doctrinal view of judicial construction holding that judges should apply the literal words of a statute or document without looking to the purpose behind them. E.g., "Then, should the *literal canon* be dislodged from, or relegated to the position of a presumption in a modern theory of interpretation? . . . [I]t is submitted that the formal approach is within its province most consonant with the judicial function." E. Russell Hopkins, *The Literal Canon and the Golden Rule,* 15 Can. B. Rev. 689, 695–96 (1937)./ "The *literal rule* is a rule against using intelligence in understanding language. Anyone who in ordinary life interpreted words literally, being indifferent to what the speaker or writer meant, would be regarded as a pedant, a mischief-maker or an idiot." Glanville Williams, *Learning the Law* 105 (11th ed. 1982).

literal construction. See **original intent** & **strict construction.**

literally = (1) with truth to the letter; or (2) exactly; according to the strict sense of the word or words. The use of this word in the sense "truly, completely," is an example of SLIPSHOD EXTENSION. E.g., "Behavioralists and postbehavioralists alike, literally or figuratively, learn what they know of science from the natural sciences, from the outside." [Read *Behavioralists and postbehavioralists alike learn what they know of science from the natural sciences, from the outside.*]

When used for *figuratively,* where *figuratively* would not ordinarily be used, *literally* is distorted beyond recognition: "Mr. Gladstone had sat *literally* glued to the Treasury Bench." Because we know it is a metaphor, simply say: "Mr. Gladstone had sat glued to the Treasury Bench."

LITERARY ALLUSION, if not too arcane, can add substantially to the subtlety and effectiveness of writing. Allusiveness assumes a common body of literature with which all cultured persons are familiar. The effective writer is wary on the one hand of allusions that are hackneyed, and on the other hand of allusions so learned that they are inaccessible to the average educated reader. It is perhaps easier for judges than for practicing lawyers to use literary allusions, for judges have a guaranteed readership and do not suffer directly if anyone (or everyone) fails to appreciate their allusions. A lawyer submitting a brief to a judge, on the contrary, is likely to be less adventurous in literary flights of fancy. A few specimens follow, with short explanations.

A. Effective Use of Allusion. The following quotations illustrate some of the most common types of allusion used to good effect.

1. Proverbial. A good example of effective allusiveness appears in the dissent of Justice Robert W. Hansen of the Wisconsin Supreme Court, in *Jones v. Fisher,* 166 N.W.2d 175 (Wis. 1969). He plays with an old proverb: "The *road* that has brought us to the present state of affairs in regard to punitive damages in Wisconsin courts *is* a long one, *paved with good intentions.*" *Id.* at 182. Justice Hansen here subtly suggests that this is the road to hell, conjuring up the saying that "the road to hell is paved with good intentions." He might have ruined the effect by quoting the aphorism directly.

2. Biblical. "One of the prime concerns addressed in the [Magnuson-Moss Warranty] Act was the warranty wherein the large print *giveth* but the small print *taketh away.*" *Gorman v. Saf-T-Mate, Inc.,* 513 F. Supp. 1028, 1035 (N.D. Ind. 1981). This alludes to Job 1:21: "Naked came I out of my mother's womb, and naked shall I return thither: the Lord gave, and the Lord hath taken away." See BIBLICAL AFFECTATION.

3. Shakespearean. "La. Rev. Stat. 14:27(A) . . . requires specific intent to commit a crime, and in Stewart's eyes *there is the rub.*" *Stewart v. Blackburn,* 746 F.2d 262, 264 (5th Cir. 1984). This allusion may confuse the reader because of the proximity of *rub* and *eyes;* the phrase *there's the rub* (orig. fr. *Hamlet* 3.1.64) has passed into common parlance.

4. Mythological and Classical. "This appeal requires this Court to make another trek through that *Serbonian bog* of damages in maritime cases." *Delta S.S. Lines v. Avondale Shipyards, Inc.,* 747 F.2d 995, 997 (5th Cir. 1984). *Serbonian bog* (= a quagmire or predicament from which there is no way of extricating oneself) has become a judges' CLICHÉ, though it may have been fresh when Cardozo wrote: "The attempted distinction between accidental results and accidental means will plunge this branch of law into a *Serbonian Bog.*" *Landress v. Phoenix Mut. Life Ins. Co.,* 291 U.S. 491, 499 (1934) (Cardozo, J., dissenting). The Serbonian bog is said to have been between Egypt and Palestine. Milton wrote: "A gulf profound as that *Serbonian Bog,*/ Betwixt Damiata and Mount Casius old,/ Where armies whole have sunk." *Paradise Lost* 2.592.

Here is another typical allusion to ancient history: "Most of the arguments and points made by the en banc opinion have been addressed by our panel opinion, and I will let the matter rest upon what has been said; for me to write more on the subject, which now appears settled by virtue of the majority here and the Second Circuit in *In re Taddeo,* would be largely repetitious and amount to no more than a *Parthian shot.*" *Grubbs v. Houston First Am. Savs. Ass'n,* 730 F.2d 236, 247–48 (5th Cir. 1984) (en banc) (Jolly, J., dissenting). A *Parthian shot* is a parting shot, an allusion to the people of ancient Parthia, noted for their method of fighting on horseback with the bow as their only weapon; after each discharge of an arrow the horse turned as if in flight—hence the modern meaning.

5. Other Literary. "We will not oblige the state to *joust windmills* by requiring that it prove what is not wrong with that which is not there to be seen." (In Cervantes' *Don Quixote,* the protagonist Don Quixote tilts at windmills under the delusion that they are giants.)/ "This old but little used section is *a kind of legal Lohengrin;* although it has been with us since the first Judiciary Act, . . . no one seems to know whence it came." *IIT v. Vencap, Ltd.,* 519 F.2d 1001, 1015 (2d Cir. 1975). (Lohengrin, hero of R. Wagner's opera of the same name and a knight of the Holy Grail, refuses to reveal, even to his wife, the mystery of his origins.)/ "There are village tyrants as well as village Hampdens, but none who acts under color of law is beyond reach of the Constitution." *West Virginia State Bd. of Educ. v. Barnette,* 319 U.S. 624, 638 (1943) (referring to Gray's "Elegy Written in a Country Churchyard"). See Charles A. Wright, *Literary Allusion in Legal Writing,* 1 Scribes J. Legal Writing 1, 3–4 (1990).

B. Poor Use of Allusion. Not always does allusion work, however. Following are some examples with brief explanations of pitfalls.

1. Hackneyed Allusions. "What *is and what is not* a sham is the Hamlet-like question that has perplexed the lower courts in the two decades since the Supreme Court, in a 'new and unusual application of the Sherman Act,' enunciated the *Noerr* doctrine." *To be or not to be* (to live or not to live) is rather a different kind of question from what is and is not a sham. Moreover, *To be or not to be* (*Hamlet* 3.1.55) is a greatly overworked phrase.

Hyperbolic allusion, especially if it smacks of BIBLICAL AFFECTATION, is also ineffective. E.g., "The words, both singly and conjunctively, have been in common use and generally understood since Moses delivered the commandments and the law to his people, and up to the present time." The judge who wrote that, in the process of construing a legal document written in English, merely detracted from his persuasiveness. See OVERSTATEMENT.

2. Contrived Literariness. Some judges and advocates, in their quest for originality, go off the deep end. Perhaps the worst manifestation of this phenomenon is what we might term "literary foppery," consisting in the legal writer's going to absurd lengths to display the breadth of his literary knowledge. For example, Sterne's *Tristram Shandy* is quite irrelevantly dragged into *Farr v. Nordman,* 78 N.W.2d 186, 193 (Mich. 1956) (Black, J., dissenting). Contrived allusions and references invariably detract from the message to be conveyed.

In a striking example of artificially engrafted literariness, an American judge recently peppered one of his opinions with wholly impertinent allusions and references to William Faulkner. The opinion itself discusses the constitutionality under the Fourth Amendment of a lessor's inspection of his land to determine whether the lessee has wrongfully diverted oil production. The first sentence of the statement of facts reads: "The events underlying Auster's claims could have arisen in Yoknapatawpha County, Mississippi, but most of them happened in Calcasieu Parish, Louisiana, where Stream owned the surface and mineral rights in oil-producing property." A footnote, of course, explains that Yoknapatawpha County is the fictional setting of many of Faulkner's novels (and cites works on Faulkner by the renowned critics Cleanth Brooks and Irving Howe). The contrivance has neither purpose nor subtlety.

Worse yet, however, are the headings and subheadings throughout the opinion. We begin with "The Sound and the Fury," which is followed by "Lease in August" *(Light in August),* "The Reivers," "Intruders in the Dust" *(Intruder in the Dust),* "Auster's Gambit" *(Knight's Gambit),* "Go Down, Auster" *(Go Down, Moses),* "Requiem for a Plaintiff" *(Requiem for a Nun),* "Sanctuary," "Microchip! Microchip!" *(Absolom! Absolom!?),* "Trooper's Pay" *(Soldiers' Pay),* "As the Wells Lay Pumping" *(As I Lay Dying),* and "The Unvanquished." In short, the references and allusions to Faulkner are entirely factitious. See *Auster Oil & Gas, Inc. v. Stream,* 764 F.2d 381 (5th Cir. 1985).

To those with an undiscerning literary sensibility, such contrivances may be appealing.

literatim. See **verbatim.**

litigant has denoted "a party to a lawsuit" since the mid-17th century. Originally, in the early 17th century, *litigant* was always an adjective, as in the phrase *party litigant.* Soon, however, the word came to act as a noun, without the necessity of pairing it always with *party.* Rarely nowadays does one encounter the adjectival use of *litigant;* instead, examples like the following abound: "It is quite possible that a *litigant* will find that his case will fit some two or three of these pigeonholes." F.W. Maitland, *The Forms of Action at Common Law* 3 (1909; A.H. Chaytor & W.J. Whittaker eds., 1971)./ "A bait was needed with which to draw *litigants* to the royal courts; the King must offer them better justice than they could have at the hands of their lords." 1 Winston

Churchill, *A History of the English Speaking Peoples* 217 (1956; repr. 1983). Cf. **litigator.**

litig(at)able. The correct form is *litigable:* "[N]one of the summoned witnesses . . . raised any *litigatable* [read *litigable*] objections . . . ." *U.S. v. Newman,* 441 F.2d 165, 173 (5th Cir. 1971). See -ATABLE.

litigate = (1) to be a party to, or carry on, a lawsuit; (2) to make the subject of a lawsuit, to contest at law; (3) to dispute, contest (e.g., a point). Thus in sense (1), one *litigates* cases and causes, but in sense (2) one may *litigate* property or consequences, etc. E.g., "Qualified immunity is in part an entitlement not to be forced to *litigate* the consequences of official conduct." Cf. **adjudicate (A).**

The phrase *litigate against* (a certain type of opponent) has become common in late 20th-century legal writing—e.g.: "New York's highest court ruled that lawyers *litigating against* a corporation can informally interview certain employees without the consent of the corporation's lawyers." Wall St. J., 6 July 1990, at B5.

litigated judgment is often a REDUNDANCY—e.g.: "The decision will result in the dismissal of key claims in literally thousands of pending lawsuits—and some *litigated judgments* [read *judgments* or *final judgments*]—and is bound to further depress the number of such suits filed in the future." Schmitt, *California Court Further Restricts Right of Fired Workers to Sue Ex-Employers,* Wall St. J., 26 May 1989, at A3. When used in contrast to *consent judgment,* however, *litigated judgment* makes perfect sense: "The distinction between a consent judgment and a *litigated judgment* has not been widely addressed by Michigan courts." *Trendell v. Solomon,* 443 N.W.2d 509, 510 (Mich. Ct. App. 1989).

litigation, n. Ordinarily, *litigation* refers to the process of carrying on lawsuits or a specific lawsuit. Hence the plural *litigations* might seem to make little sense. But *litigation* occasionally serves as a synonym for *lawsuit.* Though it may seem unidiomatic to make *litigation* a COUNT NOUN in this way, the usage is old and is today common. E.g., "In numberless *litigations* the description of the landscape must be studied to see whether vision has been obstructed . . . ." Benjamin N. Cardozo, *The Nature of the Judicial Process* 165 (1921)./ "[The] first and second parties now have certain *litigations* pending in the Mercer Circuit Court . . . ." *Reed v. Carter,* 103 S.W.2d 663, 664 (Ky. Ct. App. 1937)./ "And unexpected things did happen in *litigations* in which they were retained." Ephraim Tutt, *Yankee Lawyer* 176 (1943). See PLURALS (B).

litigation, adj.; **litigational; litigative.** See **litigatory.**

litigator. When it originated—in the late 19th century—*litigator* was a NEEDLESS VARIANT of *litigant,* as here: "When a succession is in progress of litigation, the interest of the *litigators* is *de ducto aeri aliendo* . . . ." *Irwin v. Flynn,* 34 So. 794, 794 syl. 2 (La. 1903). This sense persisted into the mid-20th century—e.g.: "Government agencies are the heaviest *litigators* in the United States courts . . . ." *Lane v. Fitzsimmons Stores, Ltd.,* 62 F. Supp. 89, 91 n.7 (S.D. Cal. 1945). (Cf. **litigant.**) At the same time, the word was coming to refer to a lawyer who specializes in litigation, as an alternate term for *trial lawyer,* q.v.

But now those two terms have been sharply differentiated. With the advent, in the U.S., of seemingly endless discovery before trial—which never seems to come—*litigator* has come to connote a lawyer who works in litigation but never sets foot in a courtroom. Trial lawyers try cases; litigators, it is sometimes said, merely prepare discovery requests.

litigatory; litigative; litigational. There is no single widely accepted neutral adjective corresponding to *litigation* and meaning "of, pertaining to, or involving litigation." *Litigious,* q.v., is close structurally, but its strong associations with disputatiousness and contentiousness impair its candidacy—in AmE, at any rate. (BrE continues to use *litigious* in neutral contexts.) *Litigable* <litigable claims> and *litigant* <parties litigant> have other specific senses. *Litigation* sometimes functions as an adjective, as in the title of Leon Green's collection of essays *The Litigation Process in Tort Law* (1965). It works in some phrases, such as *litigation battles* or *litigation crisis,* but not in others.

Litigatory, litigational, and *litigative* have been pressed into service in the desired neutral sense. *Litigatory* is listed in *W2,* but is omitted from *W3* and has appeared in neither the *OED* nor its *Supplement.* Yet it is no stranger to American legal prose—e.g.:

- "The controlling declaration . . . is that equity can and should intervene whenever it is made to appear that one party, public or private, seeks unjustly to enrich himself at the expense of another on account of his own mistake and the other's want of immediate vigilance—*litigatory* or otherwise." *Spoon-Shacket Co. v. County of Oakland,* 97 N.W.2d 25, 28 (Mich. 1959).

- "Certain Florida cases, though having *litigatory* objectives different from the one at bar, employ the principle . . . ." *Brown v. Hutch,* 156 So. 2d 683, 686 (Fla. Dist. Ct. App. 1963).
- "Considering the overall strength of the factual and legal bases of the surety's rejection of the claim and the *litigatory* posture of the surety . . . , we believe that its rejection . . . was not preponderately [q.v.] reasonable . . . ." *U.S. Fidelity & Guar. Co. v. Clover Creek Cattle Co.,* 452 P.2d 993, 1005 (Idaho 1969).
- "Not only do the decided cases lead us to this decision but such ruling accords with modern jurisprudence which seeks to eliminate the hidden *litigatory* pitfall." *Federal Ins. Co. v. Oakwood Steel Co.,* 191 S.E.2d 298, 300 (Ga. Ct. App. 1972).
- "[O]ur affirmance in the present case is predicated upon the purposes and objectives underlying declaratory judgment actions and the *litigatory* posture of the dispute involving the parties herein." *Volkswagenwerk, A.G. v. Watson,* 390 N.E.2d 1082, 1084 (Ind. Ct. App. 1979).

Litigational, a NEEDLESS VARIANT of *litigatory,* has been similarly neglected in general English-language dictionaries, though it is not uncommon. E.g., "*Litigational background of both appeals was* [read *In the litigatory background of both appeals was*] a suit instituted by plaintiff . . . ." *Morton v. Indemnity Ins. Co.,* 137 So. 2d 618, 619 (Fla. Dist. Ct. App. 1962)./ "[W]e now consider briefly a second form of specific jurisdiction . . . relating not only to the plaintiff but also to the taking of evidence and other *litigational* [read *litigatory*] considerations." Arthur T. von Mehren & Donald T. Trautman, *Jurisdiction to Adjudicate,* 79 Harv. L. Rev. 1121, 1173 (1966)./ "[T]he *Finney* court recognize[d] that the binding nature of a stipulation of dispositiveness supported the parties in their exercise of *litigational* [read *litigatory*] strategy . . . ." *Zeigler v. State,* 471 So. 2d 172, 176 (Fla. Dist. Ct. App. 1985).

Litigative is likewise a NEEDLESS VARIANT—e.g.: "The transfer of the stock was not actually made until April 1944 because of an unsuccessful *litigative* [read *litigatory*] attempt to prevent the same." *Western Pac. R. R. Corp. v. Western Pac. R. R. Co.,* 85 F. Supp. 868, 870 (N.D. Cal. 1949)./ "For these reasons, I simply cannot accept the shift in the *litigative* [read *litigatory*] burden of proof adopted by the Court." *Columbus Bd. of Educ. v. Penick,* 443 U.S. 449, 473 (1979) (Stewart, J., dissenting).

litigiosity; litigiousness. If there is a nuance between these words, it is that *litigiosity* denotes the *fact* or *state* of being litigious, whereas *litigiousness* denotes the *quality* of being litigious. The fussiness of this distinction suggests that euphony is a better ground for choice between the two.

In Scots law, however, *litigiosity* has a special sense: "a legal prohibition on a debtor's alienating heritable property to the effect of defeating an action . . . commenced or inchoate" (*OCL*).

litigious = (1) fond of legal disputes, contentious <our litigious society>; (2) that is the subject of a lawsuit <the litigious property>; or (3) of or pertaining to lawsuits or litigation <dragged into a litigious dispute>. In AmE, the word has been narrowed to sense (1) exclusively. In BrE, however, the word is capable of taking on the neutral senses of (2) and (3)—e.g.: "The Statute codified procedure for a new jurisdiction, and may therefore have been more precise than current *litigious* practice." C.H.S. Fifoot, *History and Sources of the Common Law* 27 n.18 (1949)./ "[A] good deal of *litigious* work is disposed of not in open court but before a judge or master in chambers." Glanville Williams, *Learning the Law* 190 (11th ed. 1982). See **litigatory.**

litiscontestation, a Scots law term, means "joinder of issue, arising after the defense in a lawsuit has been lodged." The word derives from the Roman term *litis contestatio,* the process by which a legal issue emerges from the oppposing statements of the parties, which still occasionally appears in English and American lawbooks: "A discussion of the influence on modern German procedure of the notion involved in the Roman *litis contestatio* (as a pretended contract of submission) will be found in Bülow . . . ." Lon L. Fuller, *Legal Fictions* 89 n.74 (1967; repr. 1977). See **contest,** n.

liv(e)able. The spelling *livable* is preferred in AmE, *liveable* in BrE. See MUTE E.

livery of seisin (= the ceremonial procedure at common law by which a grantor conveyed land to a grantee) is LAW FRENCH (orig. *bail de la seisine*) for *delivery of seisin.* It is sanctioned by centuries of legal usage, and today ordinarily appears only in historical contexts. The ceremony involved going on the land and having the grantor symbolically deliver possession of the land to the grantee by handing over a twig, a clod, or a piece of turf. Alternatively, *livery of seisin* could be accomplished by the grantor's telling the grantee, in view of the land, that possession was given to the grantee, followed by the grantee's entering the land. E.g., "A transferor, A, having an estate in fee simple, could provide, upon making *livery of* *seisin* to B, that he should have occupancy of the land for his lifetime."

The *OED* notes that *livery and seisin* is a common error for *livery of seisin.* See **delivery (B)** & **seisin.**

living trust. See ***inter vivos* trust.**

living will; advance directive. *Living will,* a phrase that dates from the early 1970s, is not a statutory term—in fact, it is really misnamed, because the document to which it refers is not a will at all. It refers to a legal document instructing doctors, relatives, and others when to refrain from using life-support measures to prolong one's life during a catastrophic illness. E.g., "*Living wills* are useful for people who would rather bow out quickly and gracefully than fight for their lives as long as possible." Letter of F. Ackerman, N.Y. Times, 13 Oct. 1989, at 22./ "Under common law these situations can also be addressed in a *living will,* but the patient would never know it from the materials distributed . . . . There is no reason these *advance directives* should not be physician managed, just as surgical consent forms, anatomical gift forms and do-not-resuscitate orders are." Letter of Alan D. Lieberson, *Law on "Living Wills" Doesn't Go Far Enough,* N.Y. Times, 21 Dec. 1991, at 14.

A less commonly known term, *advance directive,* refers to a document much like a *living will,* but broader in scope and more detailed. An advance directive is a durable power of attorney designating a surrogate decision-maker for health-care matters. An advance directive takes effect upon incompetency—and is "durable" because, unlike most powers of attorney, it remains in effect during the maker's incompetency. E.g., "The federal Patient Self-Determination Act now requires hospitals to inform patients of their rights under state law to create '*advance directives*' relating to their medical care and to find out whether patients have such *advance directives.*" Tom Mayo, *Patients' Rights,* Dallas Morning News, 15 Dec. 1991, at 4J.

L.J., an abbreviation for "Lord Justice," is pluralized *LL.J.*

loadstar. See **lodestar.**

loadstone; lodestone. This term, meaning "something that strongly attracts," is spelled *loadstone* in BrE and *lodestone* in AmE. E.g., "The intention of the testator is the guide, or in the phrase of Lord Coke, the *lodestone* of the court." Cf. **lodestar.**

loan; lend. In formal usage, it is best to use *lend* as the verb and *loan* as the noun. *Loan* is considered permissible, however, when used as a verb denoting the lending of money (as distinguished from the lending of articles).

LOAN TRANSLATIONS are English terms arrived at by translating foreign terms into English equivalents. Thus we arrive at the un-English-sounding *next friend* as a loan translation (or calque) of *prochein ami.* The language of the law has many such terms, usually translated from Latin or French. (See LAW FRENCH & LAW LATIN.) Among the most common loan translations in legal writing are these:

English Term	*Foreign Term*
action on the case	*action sur le case* (L.F.)
against the form of the statute	*contra formam statuti* (L.)
against the peace	*contra pacem* (L.)
a year and a day	*ann et jour* (L.F.)
as of right	*de jure* (L.)
burden of proof	*onus probandi* (L.)
civil death	*mors civilis* (L.)
damage without injury	*damnum absque injuria* (L.)
dead-hand	*mortmain* (L.F.)
defender of the faith	*fidei defensor* (L.)
friend of the court	*amicus curiae* (L.)
go hence without day	*aller sans jour* (L.F.)
goods and chattels	*bona et catalla* (L.F.)
half-blood	*demy-sangue* (L.F.)
have and hold	*habendum et tenendum* (L.) *aver et tener* (L.F.)
injury without damage	*injuria absque damno* (L.)
in the breast	*in pectore* (L.)
juridification	*Verrechtlichung* (Ger.)
keeper of the peace	*custos pacis* (L.)
King's Court	*Curia Regis* (L.)
know all persons	*noverint universi* (L.)
last will	*ultima voluntas* (L.)
law merchant	*lex mercatoria* (L.)
malice aforethought	*malitia praecogitata* (L.)
mere right	*jus merum* (L.) *meer dreit* (L.F.)
naked contract	*nudum pactum* (L.)
next friend	*prochein ami* (L.F.)
notwithstanding the verdict	*non obstante veredicto* (L.)
on pain of	*sur peine de* (L.F.)
on the high sea	*super altum mare* (L.)

plead not guilty	*plaider de rien culpable* (L.F.)
these presents	*hac praesentes litterae* (L.)
true bill	*billa vera* (L.)
under pain of	*sous pein de* (L.F.) *sub poena* (L.)
unwritten law	*lex non scripta* (L.)
with force and arms	*vi et armis* (L.)

Sometimes the Englished versions require skillful inference to arrive at the meaning. E.g., "An acceptance that remains *in the breast* of the accepter without being actually and by legal implication communicated to the offeror is not a binding acceptance." (Eng.) Others have no literal significance, but have been adopted as legal names (as TERMS OF ART or legal JARGON) for doctrines and causes of action, such as *trespass with force and arms:* "This is an action in trespass that the defendant, *with force and arms,* wilfully and maliciously assaulted, debauched, and carnally knew the daughter and servant of the plaintiff." (Eng.)

The tendency toward translating unassimilated foreign terms that are used in law into English is salutary on the whole. *Dead-hand* may never displace *mortmain,* and *friend of the court* may never displace *amicus curiae,* but most of the foreign language law terms have fallen into disuse. And most of the loan translations listed above have become familiar. Now there is little call for more loan translations, because legal English increasingly approximates general-purpose English.

loathe; lo(a)th. *Loathe* is the verb meaning "to abhor, detest." *Loath,* with its NEEDLESS VARIANT *loth,* is an adjective meaning "reluctant." Here the verb spelling is used wrongly for the adjective, a frequent error: "[J]udges and crown prosecutors were not *loathe* [read *loath*] to intimidate a jury and even to punish the jurymen if they returned a verdict deemed improper by the judge." C. Gordon Post, *An Introduction to the Law* 53 (1963)./ "Courts have generally been *loathe* [read *loath*] to refuse the offer of an aid to difficult problems of interpretation."/ "Yellow Cab has proved *loathe* [read *loath*] to loosen its grip on the airport market."

lobby. The legislative senses derive ultimately from the architectural sense of the word. In 19th-century AmE, *lobby* came to denote, through METONYMY, the persons who habitually occupy the lobby in a legislative chamber for the purpose of carrying on business with legislators, esp. influencing their votes.

As a verb, *lobby* has come to mean: (1) to frequent legislative chambers for the purpose of influencing the members' official actions <the group lobbied against the proposed reforms>; or (2) to promote or oppose (a measure) by soliciting legislative votes <the organization lobbied a measure through the House>.

The agent-noun *lobbyist,* meaning "one who lobbies," originated during the American Civil War.

lobbyist; lobbyer; lobbier. The second and third forms are NEEDLESS VARIANTS. See **lobby.**

locale; locality. Both terms are frequently used; for the most part they are equivalent, but only *locale* has the sense "the setting or scene of action or of a story."

locate for *set up shop* or *establish residence* is an Americanism that, despite its having been criticized by several grammarians, has become standard <after several years in the Plaza, the firm located in the Crescent>. *Locate* is transitive in BrE and means "to place" or "to ascertain the whereabouts of." In AmE, the word is used in these senses, but also in the colloquial intransitive sense of "to settle, begin residing." The sense "to fix or establish in a place" is also distinctively AmE: "Subsection (b) of the statute would seem generally to *locate* review of licensing proceedings in the courts of appeals." This usage is by no means new: "[The 1869 law] is aptly framed to remove from the more densely populated part of the city, the noxious slaughter-houses, and large and offensive collections of animals necessarily incident to [them], and to *locate* them where the convenience, health, and comfort of the people require they shall be located." *The Slaughter-House Cases,* 83 U.S. (16 Wall.) 36, 64 (1872) (per Miller, J.).

LOCATIVES. See CASE REFERENCES (B).

Lochnerize, vb.; **Lochnerization,** n. These terms derive from the case name *Lochner v. New York,* 198 U.S. 45 (1905). *Lochnerize* = to scrutinize and invalidate economic regulations under the guise of enforcing the due-process clause. The term carries no small degree of opprobrium. "*Lochnerizing* has become so much an epithet that the very use of the label may obscure attempts at understanding." Laurence Tribe, *American Constitutional Law* 435 (1978). E.g., "*Lochner v. New York* . . . (invalidating New York's maximum hours law for bakers) has come to typify the period of 'substantive due process' review, during which the Supreme Court over a strong dissent invalidated state economic and social legislation for interfering with the liberty of contract." *Town of Ball v. Rapides Parish Police Jury,* 746 F.2d 1049, 1056 n.21 (5th Cir. 1984)./ "[E]qual protection was so disfavored that, during the heyday of *'Lochnerizing,'* it was called 'the usual last resort of constitutional arguments.'" (*Id.*)/ "Of course we are *Lochnerizing* and intruding into the affairs of a state." *Dunagin v. City of Oxford,* 718 F.2d 738, 755 (5th Cir. 1983) (Higginbotham, J., dissenting).

lockout, n., = (1) an employer's closing of a business or across-the-board dismissal of employees due to disagreement over the terms of employment; or (2) employees' refusal to work because the employer unreasonably refuses to abide by an expired employment contract while a new one is being negotiated.

loco parentis. See ***in loco parentis.***

locus; situs. Both terms are used in law to mean "a place in which something is situated or is done." *Locus* is the more concrete, specific term: "We hold that at the death of John Girdler's widow, his three daughters and granddaughter held undivided equal estates tail in the *locus.*" *Situs,* to the contrary, is more abstract, with a usu. broader, territorial sense of "place": "Such a decree ought to be entitled to full faith and credit at the *situs* of the land."/ "Holding that Mexico rather than Texas was the *situs* of the bank deposits furthers the general policies of the act of state doctrine." See **situs.**

locus in quo (= the place where something is alleged to have been done) is common in property law, but is often unnecessary in place of *locus* or *location.* Here it is perhaps justifiable, because its use implicitly incorporates the notion of allegations in a lawsuit: "It is proper to admit photographs of a *locus in quo* even though taken 15½ months after the accident . . . ." *Hamilton v. Fean,* 221 A.2d 309, 315 (Pa. 1966).

locus poenitentiae /***loh**-kəs-pen-i-**ten**-shee-ɪ*/ = a point at which it is not too late for a person to change his or her legal position; the possibility of withdrawing from a contemplated course of action, esp. a wrong, before being committed to it. E.g., "He would have us hold that so long as the cause or proceeding in which false testimony is given is not closed there remains a *locus poenitentiae* of which he was entitled to and did avail himself. The implications and results of such a doctrine prove its unsoundness." *U.S. v. Norris,* 300 U.S. 564, 573–74 (1937)./ "Mrs. Rosenblum enjoyed a *locus poenitentiae,* of which she could take advantage until Jacks or Better somehow changed its position; and she acted promptly in recalling the words of rescission." *Rosenblum v. Jacks or Better of Am. West, Inc.,* 745 S.W.2d 754, 759 (Mo. Ct. App. 1988).

locus standi (= the right to bring an action or to be heard in a given forum) seems to be an unnecessary LATINISM, in view of the more common American legal term *standing. Locus standi* is common in G.B., however. E.g., "First, it may be asked what, if any, *locus standi* the Law Society has in a matter of this kind." (Eng.)/ "In my view, it would be most unfortunate if the intervenor did not have a *locus standi* in appropriate cases." (Eng.)/ "The Italian standpoint is that at the present juncture the League has no *locus standi* in the dispute." (Eng.) Formerly it was used in the sense "credentials, established position of high standing." (See **standing.**) The phrase is medieval in origin—it does not appear in classical Roman sources.

locution. See **elocution.**

lodestar; loadstar. The former spelling is preferred in both AmE and BrE for this term meaning "a guiding star." (The word derives fr. O.E. *lād* [= way, course] + *star.*) The term has jargonistic uses in setting fees and damages, and these lead to mixed metaphors: "In awarding attorneys' fees, the district court *increased* the *lodestar*—the product of the number of hours reasonably expended multiplied by a reasonable hourly rate—to compensate counsel for the delay in actual payment for the legal services rendered." (The figurative does not impinge on the literal sense if we write of *raising* a lodestar, but it does so impinge if we write of *increasing* a lodestar.) See METAPHORS (A).

lodestone. See **loadstone.**

LOGIC. See ILLOGIC.

logical fallacy. See **grammatical error.**

logomachy = a contention about words. E.g., "The student of jurisprudence is at times troubled by the thought that he is dealing not with things, but with words, that he is busy with the shape and size of counters in a game of *logomachy* . . . ." John C. Gray, *Nature and Sources of the Law* viii (1909)./ "I know for myself that for the past thirty years and more a great part of my daily business has been to give opinions, to argue or to decide as to the meaning of words. These disputes are by no means always barren *logoma-*

chies." Lord Macmillan, *Law and Other Things* 154 (1937).

logorrhea (= diarrhea of the mouth) is an affliction of which lawyers must beware.

long, adv., can stand alone, without *for* preceding it. E.g., "[W]e have *now for long* [read *now long*] been accustomed, with some archaic survivals, to the doctrine that imposed liability depends in part upon the conscious attitude which a supposititious normal person would take towards the damage resulting from his acts." *Sinram v. Pennsylvania R. Co.,* 61 F.2d 767, 770 (2d Cir. 1932) (per L. Hand, J.).

long-arm statute (= a statute providing for the maintenance of jurisdiction over nonresident defendants) derives from the catchphrase *the (long) arm of the law.*

longer than. See **above (A).**

longshoreman. See SEXISM (B).

long-standing, adj. So spelled.

look over. See **overlook.**

loom large. See **bulk large.**

loophole. This term, dating from 1591 (*OED*), originally referred to a narrow vertical opening, widening inward, cut in a wall or door to allow through the passage either cannon fire and other missiles, or light and air. The word *loop* in this compound does not bear its modern sense, but instead derives from the medieval Dutch verb *lupen,* meaning "to lie in wait, watch, or peer."

By the late 1600s, the word had taken on its figurative sense in reference to an ambiguity, omission, or exception in a statute or other legal document. Today this figurative sense prevails—e.g.: "The court was also out to close all *loopholes,* such as the possibility of the brokers and title companies getting legislation giving them the right to do what they had been doing all along . . . ." Murray T. Bloom, *The Trouble With Lawyers* 103 (1970).

loose, v.t.; **loosen.** Both words mean "to unbind; release." The DIFFERENTIATION between the two is that *loose* generally refers to a complete release <loosing criminals on the community>, *loosen* generally to a partial release <loosening one's belt>. Additionally, *loosen* is figurative more often than *loose.* See **lose.**

Lord Chancellor. The plural is sometimes made *Lords Chancellor,* sometimes *Lord Chancellors,* and sometimes *Lords Chancellors.* The prevailing, and the best, form is *Lord Chancellors.* But cf. **lord justice.** See **Chancellor & Keeper of the King's Conscience.**

Lord High Chancellor. See **chancellor.**

lord justice, the title of a judge on the (English) Court of Appeal, is generally pluralized *lords justices.* But *lord justices* might be an improvement. See **Lord Chancellor.**

Lord of Appeal in Ordinary; Lord Ordinary. Terms such as these often baffle those unacquainted with the British legal system. The *Lords of Appeal in Ordinary,* known also as *Law Lords,* sit in the House of Lords as the highest appellate court in the U.K. The *Lords Ordinary* sit in Scotland as the trial judges in the Court of Session. See **Law Lord.**

Lords is sometimes used as an elliptical term for *House of Lords*—e.g.: "Decision-making in the *Lords* does not take place in a vacuum." Alan Paterson, *The Law Lords* 9 (1982)./ "Oliver Cromwell later explained that the *Lords* was 'very forward to give up the people's rights . . . .'" *Peering Ahead,* Economist, 9–15 June 1990, at 68. See **House of Lords.**

lose; loose. *Lose,* v.t., = to suffer the deprivation of; to part with. *Loose* is both adj. & v.t., meaning in the latter use "to release; unfasten." Writers sometimes misuse *loose* for *lose*—e.g.: "Plaintiff and the other man ran and the police pursued, *loosing* [read *losing*] sight of the two for approximately 30 to 60 seconds." *Stratton v. City of Albany,* 612 N.Y.S.2d 286, 288 (App. Div. 1994)./ "Martini chased defendant, never *loosing* [read losing] eye contact with him." *People v. Pulliam,* 626 N.E.2d 356, 357 (Ill. App. Ct. 1994). (In the latter example, notice also the misuse of *eye contact* for *sight.*) See **loose.**

loser; winner. Courts sometimes use *loser* and *winner* as substitutes for *appellant* and *appellee,* respectively. E.g., "We may affirm a summary judgment only if the record, read in the light most favorable to the *loser* [i.e., appellant] reveals no genuine issues of material fact and shows that the *winners* [i.e., appellees] were entitled to judgment as a matter of law."

loser-pays rule. See **English Rule.**

loss-of-bargain damages; lost-expectation damages. These phrases, which should be hyphenated thus, both refer to breach-of-contract damages that would place the injured party in the position he or she would have been in had the contract been performed. E.g., "Another major shift in the law appears to lie in an increased reluctance to award pure 'lost expectation' damages, except perhaps in straightforward commercial cases." P.S. Atiyah, *An Introduction to the Law of Contract* 21–22 (3d ed. 1981; repr. 1986).

lost earnings; lost earning capacity. In personal-injury cases, the distinction is an important one. To determine *lost earnings,* the court looks to what a plaintiff actually earned before the injury. To determine *lost earning capacity,* the court looks (more expansively) to the plaintiff's diminished earning power resulting from the injury.

lost property; mislaid property; abandoned property. At common law, these descriptions governed the disposition of property found by someone other than its original owner. The distinctions are still valid in many English-speaking jurisdictions. Property is said to be *lost* when the owner has involuntarily relinquished possession of it, usually by accident or forgetfulness, and cannot or is highly unlikely to recover it by diligent search. Property is *mislaid* when the owner has intentionally put it in a place and then forgotten it, but may find it by diligent searching. It is *abandoned* if the owner has knowingly forsaken interest in the property.

loth. See **loathe.**

lower court. See **higher court** & **inferior (B).**

L.S. (= *locus sigilli,* meaning "place of the seal") is occasionally used on contracts and deeds in place of an actual seal. As contracts under seal have fallen into disuse, so has the need for this abbreviation. See **seal.** Cf. **ss.**

lucri causa /loo-kree-**kaw**-zə/ (= for the sake of gain) was once considered a necessary element of larceny: the thief must have been motivated by some purpose of gain or advantage. Today, in jurisdictions that retain larceny as a crime, *lucri causa* is generally considered an inessential element, the intent to deprive the owner of his or her property being sufficient.

lunatic, once a clinical medical description, was formerly used frequently in legal writing. E.g., "A *lunatic* has the capacity to take and hold title to property and therefore may become a trustee." Today, however, the term is one of opprobrium because of its figurative abuses; it should be used cautiously if at all.

luxuriant; luxurious. *Luxuriant,* a favorite word of metaphrasts, means "growing abundantly, lush." E.g., "The states have decided that it is better to leave a few of its noxious branches to their *luxuriant* growth, than by pruning them away to injure the vigor of those yielding the proper fruits."

Luxurious = characteristic of luxury. Sometimes the word is confused with *luxuriant*—e.g.: "With his *luxuriously* [read *luxuriantly*] curly white hair, dark bushy eyebrows, olive skin and direct gaze, Judge Botein reminds one lawyer I know of 'an implacable Old Testament Judge.'" Murray T. Bloom, *The Trouble With Lawyers* 168 (1970).

lynch law = the administration of summary punishment, esp. death, for an alleged crime, without legal authority. The phrase connotes mob lawlessness brought about by a perception that justice will be either denied or grossly delayed.

The phrase has an interesting etymology. Originally *Lynch's law,* it took its name from William Lynch (1742–1820) of Virginia, who in 1780 organized his neighbors to maintain order and punish lawlessness in their community. At first the phrase referred to punishments milder than death—whipping, tarring and feathering, burning houses, and the like—but since the late 19th century, the term has been increasingly confined to sentences of death by hanging. The verb *to lynch,* for example, carries that meaning exclusively: "to hang (a person) by lynch law."

lynchpin. See **linchpin.**

M

MACARONISM. See MINGLE-MANGLE.

McCulloch v. Maryland. This is the conventional spelling of the ground-breaking case in which the U.S. Supreme Court first used federal constitutional analysis to invalidate a state law. See 17 U.S. (4 Wheat.) 316 (1819). But the bank cashier involved in that case actually spelled his name *McCulloh.* See Charles A. Wright, *The Law of Federal Courts* 370 n.5 (5th ed. 1994).

McKenzie; McKenzie man. In *McKenzie v. McKenzie,* [1970] 3 W.L.R. 472 (C.A.), the Court of Appeal ruled that any litigant is entitled to nonprofessional assistance in court. Hence in BrE, *McKenzie* or *McKenzie man* has come to denote a nonprofessional who attends trial as a party's helper or adviser.

McNaghten; M'Naghten; McNaughton; Macnaghten; MacNaughton; M'Naughten. In 1843, the House of Lords answered a series of questions about what a criminal defendant must show to succeed on the defense of insanity. (For the citation, see **leading case.**) These answers are generally known as the *McNaghten rules* (so spelled). Glanville Williams remarks: "The spelling of the defendant's name in this famous case varies; for simplicity, I have adopted one of the two versions [*McNaghten*] used in the Law Reports, though it is probably [historically] wrong." *Textbook of Criminal Law* 98 n.6 (1978). Historically wrong, perhaps, but so prevalent today that writers everywhere ought to settle on it as the standard spelling.

Justice Felix Frankfurter felt certain that *M'Naghten* was the correct spelling and, in 1952, wrote the editor of *The Times* (London) to reform the spelling used by that newspaper: "It is M'Naghten, not M'Naughten or any of the variants of its misspelling." Felix Frankfurter, "Postscript to M'Naghten's Case," in *Of Law and Life and Other Things That Matter* 1, 1 (Philip B. Kurland ed., 1967). The learned editor of *The Times*—Sir William Haley—produced historical evidence of ten variations, including the prisoner's own version during trial: *M'Naughten.* See *id.*

mad is a casualism when used as a synonym for *angry.*

madding crowd; maddening crowd. By historical convention, *madding crowd* is the idiom, dating from the late 16th century. Unlike *maddening,* which describes the observer, *madding* (= frenzied) describes the crowd itself. Thomas Gray's "Elegy in a Country Churchyard" (1749) and Thomas Hardy's novel *Far From the Madding Crowd* (1874) helped establish this idiom, especially Gray's "far from the *madding crowd*'s ignoble strife." In modern published writings, *madding crowd* remains about seven times as common as its corrupted form.

maelstrom, originally a Dutch word referring to a grinding or turning stream, is frequently misspelled *maelstorm*—e.g.: "The application of any other Rule [than res judicata], in our judgment, would result in a *maelstorm* [read *maelstrom*] of uncertainty, lack of judicial finality and ultimate chaos." *In re Van Deusen's Will,* 196 N.Y.S.2d 737, 743 (Sur. Ct. 1960).

magisterial; magistral. Although *magisterial* carries connotations of nobility, command, and even dictatorialness, it is also the preferred adjective corresponding to the noun *magistrate.* E.g., "While we may review *magistral* [read *magisterial*] findings of fact subject only to the 'clearly erroneous' standard, we may overturn any conclusions of law that contradict or ignore applicable precepts of law as found in the Constitution, statutes, or case precedent." *Magistratic* and *magistratical* are NEEDLESS VARIANTS. *Magistral* = (1) of a master or masters <an absolutely magistral work>; or (2) formulated by a physician <a magistral ointment>.

magistracy; magistrature; magistrateship. The first of these is the standard term for the office, district, or power of a magistrate, or body of magistrates. *Magistrature* and *magistrateship* are NEEDLESS VARIANTS.

magistral. See **magisterial.**

magistrate, in both AmE and BrE, is now generally understood as referring to a judicial officer with strictly limited jurisdiction and authority, often on the local level. In G.B., for example, *magistrate* is synonymous with *justice of the peace* and frequently appears in the phrases *police magistrate, metropolitan magistrate, stipendiary magistrate,* and *magistrates' courts.* (See **stipe.**) In Ireland the phrase is *resident magistrate.* The common characteristic is that *magistrate* "generally means a judge of inferior rank." Max Radin, *The Law and You* 110 (1948).

Formerly, however, the word retained a meaning closer to its etymological sense. Derived from L. *magistratus* or *magister* (= master), it once referred to the official first in rank in a branch of government. Hence an emperor, or a monarch, or a president might have been termed a *magistrate.* E.g., "*Edicta,* laws which the emperor himself put forth, in his character as highest magistrate . . . ." James Hadley, *Introduction to Roman Law* 6–7 (N.Y., D. Appleton & Co. 1881). Thus it is that Cardozo referred to Chief Justice Marshall, with the greatest respect, as the *magistrate* who wrote *Marbury v. Madison.* See *Law and Literature,* 52 Harv. L. Rev. 471, 476 (1939).

But because the connotations of *magistrate* had fallen so, United States Magistrates—i.e., those at the federal level—lobbied in the late 1980s for a name change. In 1990 they got it, in the Judicial Improvements Act, and they are now called *United States Magistrate Judges.* See **magisterial.**

magistrates' courts. In England—as a result of the Magistrates' Courts Act 1952—this term refers to what were formerly known as *Courts of Summary Jurisdiction,* i.e., the Justices in Petty Sessions and special sessions called Juvenile Courts and Matrimonial Courts.

magistrateship; magistrature. See **magistracy.**

Magna C(h)arta. The usual—and the better—form is *Magna Carta. Time* magazine used the secondary spelling and found itself on the defensive: "[W]e were unfairly reproved for our spelling of the document Magna Charta . . . . Although many publications use the more familiar Magna Carta, most dictionaries prefer the word we used, *charta,* from the Latin word for paper." *Going by the Rules,* Time, 16 Dec. 1991, at 9. Which dictionaries? Not *W3, RH2, W10,* or the *OED*—the last of which shows that the great document was known exclusively as *Magna Carta* from the 13th to the 17th centuries. And the leading British textbooks, by W.H. McKechnie and J.C. Holt, use *Carta.*

And what about the *Time* editors' argument that *charta* is the Latin word for paper? That argument is empty: *charta* and *carta* are variant forms bearing the same meaning in Latin.

Magna Carta does not take a definite article: one says *Magna Carta,* not *the Magna Carta.* E.g., "Habeas corpus is shown by ample evidence to have been in use before the memorable occasion when royal recognition was given it in the great document of *Magna Carta.*"

magnanimous (= big-spirited, high-minded, and generous) has come to be misused as an ironic equivalent of *magnificent,* especially in reference to sums of money. But this usage is at best a MALAPROPISM—e.g.: "The sum in the general account is not a particularly handsome one in view of the trustees' unpaid obligations, but it is a *magnanimous* [read *magnificent*] amount compared to the balance in the general account on March 19, 1971, which was $11.70." *In re Flying W Airways, Inc.,* 341 F. Supp. 26, 84 (E.D. Pa. 1972)./ "The judgment herein awarded the wife the *magnanimous* [read *magnificent*] sum of $250 per month for a period of three years as maintenance . . . ." *Combs v. Combs,* 622 S.W.2d 679, 680 (Ky. Ct. App. 1981)./ "Ex-husband was given 'for spending money' the *magnanimous* [read *magnificent*] amount of $45 per week for working in the grocery store. This does not approach the salary of carryout boys in grocery stores." *Tuttle v. Tuttle,* 399 N.W.2d 876, 880 n.* (S.D. 1986).

maihem. See **mayhem (C).**

maim. See **mayhem (B).**

main opinion (AmE) = *majority opinion,* q.v.

mainour. This word is a historical curiosity in modern opinions—e.g.: "[W]e are convinced that there was no proof that appellant was 'taken with the *mainour*' . . . ." *King v. State,* 645 S.W.2d 782, 785 (Tex. Crim. App. 1981) (explaining, in note 2: "A thief caught with the stolen goods in his possession was said to be taken 'with the mainour,' i.e., with the goods in manu, in his hands."). Thus *with the mainour* is synonymous with *in flagrante delicto,* q.v.

mainprise; mainprize. This word, referring to an old procedure for compelling a sheriff to take sureties for a prisoner's appearance, is generally spelled *mainprise.* The etymological meaning is taking by the hand (fr. Fr. *main* & *pris.*).

mainstream, v.t., is a jargonistic VOGUE WORD to be avoided—e.g.: "'It means Hispanics are *mainstreaming themselves* [read *moving into the mainstream*],' said Robin Rorapaugh, Texas director for the Clinton campaign." Sam Attlesey, *Texas Politics,* Dallas Morning News, 22 March 1992, at 46A. See NOUNS AS VERBS.

maintain <to maintain a lawsuit> is not synonymous with *begin* or *institute;* it embraces the idea of *continuing* or *upholding.* See *George Moore Ice Cream Co. v. Rose,* 289 U.S. 373, 377 (1933).

maintenance. A. Legal Senses. *Maintenance* = (1) the care and work put into a building to keep it operating and productive; general repair and upkeep; (2) help in a lawsuit given by a stranger to it who has no lawful cause; meddling in somebody else's litigation; or (3) court-ordered support for an estranged spouse or for children.

B. For *maintain.* Using *maintenance* as a verb in place of *maintain,* v.t. <to maintenance a certain line of inquiry>, is poor. See NOUNS AS VERBS.

C. And *champerty.* See **champerty (A).**

maintenance and cure (= compensation afforded by maritime law to a sailor who gets sick or is injured while working on a vessel) is a TERM OF ART in admiralty contexts: "The seaman's right to *maintenance and cure* for illness or injury occurring while he is in the service of the ship is often analogized to workmen's compensation. While the origins of the right are customarily traced back to the mediæval sea codes, it appears to have been first recognized in this country by Justice Story in two cases [that] he decided on circuit." Grant Gilmore & Charles L. Black, Jr., *The Law of Admiralty* 281 (2d ed. 1975).

maintainer; maintainor. The *-er* spelling is preferred in all senses.

majorat (= [1] the right of primogeniture in Spain, Italy, and other countries; or [2] an estate attached to the right of primogeniture) is pronounced /mə-**zhor**-əl/. In the plural form (*majorats*), the pronunciation remains the same. See **primogeniture.**

majority. A. And *plurality.* These terms are frequently used in reference to judicial opinions, as well as elections. *Majority* = a group of more than 50 percent (e.g., five of nine judges). *Plurality* = the group with the largest percentage where none of the percentages is 50 percent or more (e.g., four of nine judges, when three have adopted a different position, and two others still another position). See **majority opinion** & **plurality opinion.**

B. Number. *Majority,* like *minority,* is generally used in AmE as a COLLECTIVE NOUN, so that it takes a singular verb. E.g., "The majority *deem* [read *deems*] negotiations leading to execution of contracts admissible."/ "The majority *reach* [read *reaches*] *their* [read *its*] conclusion regarding the 50% stock dividend and the proceeds of sale by expressly overruling *Crawford Estate.*"

But in the phrase *a majority of (people or things),* the word *majority* is generally treated as a plural in both AmE and BrE—e.g.: "[T]he great *majority* of prosecutions *are* in theory private." Patrick Devlin, *The Criminal Prosecution in England* 16 (1960)./ "A *minority* of the chairmen and deputy chairmen . . . of the county Quarter Sessions *are* also practising barristers." *Id.* at 24. See SYNESIS.

C. References in Dissenting Opinions. In some courts, such as the U.S. Court of Appeals for the First Circuit, it has generally been considered bad form to refer in a dissent to what the "majority" says. The thought was that, because the majority speaks for the court as a whole, a temperate dissenter should use the term *court* instead of *majority.* See OPINIONS, JUDICIAL.

D. For *full age.* This LEGALISM <age of majority> is common in both the U.S. and G.B. E.g., "In the law of contract, persons below the age of *majority* were formerly called infants . . . ." G.H. Treitel, *The Law of Contract* 481 (8th ed. 1991). Cf. **minority (A).**

majority opinion (AmE) = the chief opinion of an appellate court when more than one opinion is filed. See **opinion of the court.**

make (= to draw up [a legal document]) is an old legal idiom, dating from the 14th century <they made their wills>. In several phrases, such as *make answer,* it contributes to wordiness—e.g.: "Within twenty days, if the case is to come before the New York Supreme Court, the defendant must *make his answer* [read *answer*] unless he secures an extension of time from the court." C. Gordon Post, *An Introduction to the Law* 134 (1963).

make a mockery of is a CLICHÉ to be avoided.

make due is blunder for *make do,* the 20th-century idiom meaning "to manage with what happens to be available, however inadequate it may be." The error has become distressingly common—e.g.: "Respondent's own testimony showed just the slight difference of $80 per month, despite her claim that the children had to *make due* [read *make do*] with considerably less expensive clothes . . . ." *Esposito v. Esposito,* 371 N.W.2d 608, 610 (Minn. Ct. App. 1985)./ "When individuals or organizations satisfice, they *make due* [read *make do*] with means and ends they deem 'good enough' rather than try in vain to optimize." David M. Frankford, *The Medicare DRGs: Efficiency and Organizational Rationality,* 10 Yale J. Reg. 273, 346 n.87 (1993).

make efforts is verbose for *try*—e.g.: "Thus a contract by which a marriage bureau simply undertakes to *make efforts* [read *try*] to find a spouse for a client has been held invalid." G.H. Treitel, *The Law of Contract* 390 (8th ed. 1991).

make good (= to compensate for, restore, or effect) is a legal as well as a lay idiom. Its primary use in law is in the field of contracts—e.g.: "The person who had brought about the mixing was entitled to claim his proper quantity, but subject to the other proprietor's being first *made good* out of the whole mass."/ "[U]nless the articles so require a company is not legally bound to *make good* losses of fixed capital before distributing current profits." 2 E.W. Chance, *Principles of Mercantile Law* 207 (P.W. French ed., 10th ed. 1951).

Occasionally, when this PHRASAL VERB has a direct object, it creates a MISCUE—e.g.: "There is, however, nothing objectionable about a promise to *make good defalcations* for which the promisor is personally responsible . . . ." P.S. Atiyah, *An Introduction to the Law of Contract* 231 (3d ed. 1981). The reader may wonder for an instant whether there has been a problem with *bad defalcations?* What is a *good defalcation,* and how does one make it? Of course, the miscue vanishes after a moment's reflection, but the problem with miscues is precisely that they demand a moment's reflection.

make law. When applied to a legislature, this phrase means one thing. When applied to a court, it means another: "In applying the expression to the judge, we use it only in a derivative or secondary sense. Otherwise we are in danger of obscuring his essentially interpretative function. In this secondary sense, but only so, the judge does undoubtedly *'make' law.* It is not an original act of creation. Every act of interpretation shapes something new, in a secondary sense." Carleton K. Allen, *Law in the Making* 309 (7th ed. 1964).

make oath and say. This DOUBLET is an archaic equivalent of *testify*—e.g.: "I, Xavier Y. Clarke, Barrister and Solicitor, of 5678 Unknown Road, Vancouver, British Columbia, *make oath and say* [read *testify*] as follows . . . ." (Can.)

make provision for is wordy in place of *provide for.* Further, *provision* is a BURIED VERB.

make return of (e.g., a warrant) is wordy for *return.*

make-whole, adj. To be *made whole* is to be returned to the *status quo ante* (q.v.); the verb phrase *to make whole* has been transformed into the adjectival phrase *make-whole*—e.g.: "The market value of the property deviated significantly from the *make-whole* remedy intended by the just compensation clause."

mala fide(s). *Mala fide* (= in bad faith) is the adverb or adjective. *Mala fides /mal-ə-**fɪ**-deez/* (= bad faith) is the noun. Unlike *bona fide,* neither *mala fide* nor *mala fides* is understandable to most nonlawyers, and only infrequently is either phrase encountered in modern legal texts. The best advice is to avoid it and use the well-known Anglo-Saxon equivalent. See **bad(-)faith, *bona fides*** & **good(-)faith.**

The two specimens following date from the late 19th century: "If advice given *mala fide,* and loss sustained, entitle me to damages, why, though the advice be given honestly [i.e., *bona fide*], but under wrong information, with a loss sustained, am I not entitled to them [i.e., damages]?"/ "Therefore, we are all of opinion that the defendant ought in justice to refund this money thus *mala fide* recovered."

mala in se; mala prohibita. See ***malum in se.***

MALAPROPISMS are words used incorrectly that produce a humorous effect. The term derives from the character Mrs. Malaprop in Sheridan's play *The Rivals;* Mrs. Malaprop loves big words but uses them ignorantly to create hilarious solecisms and occasionally embarrassing double entendres. One of Mrs. Malaprop's famous similes is *as headstrong as an allegory on the banks of the Nile.*

Legal malapropisms are more common than one might expect. One lawyer apparently mistook *meretricious* (= marked by falsity; superficially attractive but fake nevertheless) for *meritorious* with embarrassing consequences: a plaintiff's lawyer, he asked a judge to rule favorably on his client's "meretricious claim." Similarly, Senator Sam Ervin recalled a lawyer who, in arguing that his client had been provoked by name-calling (*epithets*), said: "I hope that in passing sentence on my client upon his conviction for assault and battery, your honor will bear in mind that he was provoked to do so by the *epitaphs* hurled at him by the witness." Quoted in Paul R. Clancy, *Just a Country Lawyer* 121 (1974).

Other illustrations are *nefarious* (= evil) for *multifarious* ("Ties, shirts, shoes, belts, socks, and all the other *nefarious* parts of one's wardrobe") and *voracity* (= greediness with food) for *veracity* ("There would have been nothing to be gained by trying to impeach the truthfulness or *voracity* of those witnesses."). For other examples, see **avert, contribute, degradation, disparaging, effrontery, evoke, Hobson's choice (C), illicit, impotence, panacea, prodigious, prospectus (B), solicit (A) & surcease.**

malefaction. See **malfeasance.**

malefactor ***/mal**-ə-fak-tər/* = criminal; felon. Although the term is now primarily literary, the *OED* contains the following quotation of Herbert Spencer from 1862: "By a *malefactor,* we now understand a convicted criminal, which is far from being the acceptation of 'evil-doer'."

malefeasance. See **malfeasance.**

malevolent; maleficent. Whereas the former means "desirous of evil to others," the latter means positively "hurtful or criminal to others." Hence *malevolent* has to do with malicious desires, and *maleficent* with malicious actions. See **malice** (final par.).

malfeasance; malfeazance; malefeasance; misfeasance; malefaction. Because the words *malfeasance* and *misfeasance* are imprecise in AmE, we begin with the clear-cut BrE distinctions. In BrE, *malfeasance* refers to an unlawful act, whereas *misfeasance* refers to an otherwise lawful act performed in a wrongful manner. *Malefeasance* and *malfeazance* are obsolete spellings of *malfeasance.*

In AmE, *malfeasance* is often confined to the sense "misprision; misconduct or wrongdoing by a public official." *Misfeasance* is a more general word meaning "transgression, trespass."

In AmE, the notion in the word *malfeasance* of public office is sometimes important; but the word is often used of corporate as well as of public officials, and sometimes of other persons—e.g.: "Defendants have not cited any persuasive authorities to support their view that Washington, the successor, is tainted in equity by the *malfeasance* of Oaks, its predecessor."/ "The contract shall not cover any loss of production due to the neglect or *malfeasance* of the insured."

The legislative drafter of the following statutory provision was not unorthodox in using both *malfeasance* and *misfeasance:* "Respondents were classified civil service employees, entitled under Ohio Rev. Code Ann. § 124.34 (1984) to retain their positions 'during good behavior and efficient service,' who could not be dismissed 'except for *misfeasance, malfeasance,* or *nonfeasance* in office.'" See **feasance & nonfeasance.**

Malefaction (= crime, offense) is a FORMAL WORD that has become an ARCHAISM.

malfeasant, adj., corresponds to the noun *malfeasance,* q.v. See **feasant.**

malfeazance. See **malfeasance.**

MALFORMATIONS. See MORPHOLOGICAL DEFORMITIES.

malice is often ambiguous because it has been diluted in legal writing. Early in the 20th century the dilution was noted and objected to: "[W]hen all that is meant by *malice* is an intention to commit an unlawful act without reference to spite or ill-feeling, it is better to drop the word *malice* and so avoid all misunderstanding." *South Wales Miners Fed'n v. Glamorgan Coal Co.,* [1905] A.C. 239, 255. Even in the 19th century, however, the attenuated legal meaning had taken hold: "*Malice,* in the definition of murder, has not the same meaning as in common speech ["strong ill will"], and . . . has been thought to mean criminal intention." Oliver W. Holmes, *The Common Law* 53 (1881; repr. 1946).

The legal and nonlegal senses can be pointedly in contrast: "Although when used in its non-legal sense the word clearly denotes an evil or wicked state of mind, at law it does not necessarily have such a connotation; at law it simply means that the actor intentionally did something unlawful. Thus, the legal meaning of *'malice'* is confusing to a non-lawyer because an individual may act with good reason or from humanitarian motives but, as a matter of legal terminology, he has acted with *'malice'* if his act is against the law." Jonathan M. Purver, *The Language of Murder,* 14 U.C.L.A. L. Rev. 1306, 1306 (1967). As a noncriminal example, the *malice* requirement in proving libel of a public figure does not involve spite or ill will, only knowing falsity or a reckless disregard for the truth.

Lord Wright suggested that lawyers should use *malevolence* instead of *malice* whenever the idea of ill will is involved. See *Crofter Hand Woven Tweed Co. v. Veitch,* [1942] A.C. 435, 463. Others have suggested avoiding *malice* in the legal sense because "the criminal law ought not to need translation." Glanville Williams, *Criminal Law* 75 (2d ed. 1961). In its place, the phrase *intention or recklessness* could be substituted.

malice aforethought "is a TERM OF ART, if not a term of deception." Glanville Williams, *Textbook of Criminal Law* 208 (1978). In this phrase, in fact, *malice,* q.v., does not even bear its usual legal meaning. The phrase *malice aforethought* does not "mean a state of the defendant's mind, as is often thought, except in the sense that he knew circumstances which did in fact make his conduct dangerous. It is, in truth, an allegation like that of negligence, which asserts that the party did not come up to the legal standard of action under the circumstances in which he found himself, and also that there was no exceptional fact or excuse present which took the case out of the general rule." Oliver W. Holmes, *The Common Law* 62–63 (1881; repr. 1946). This phrase, in other words, is neither self-explanatory nor descriptive of a single and invariable frame of mind: it expresses the idea merely that an accused killed the victim intentionally, or under such circumstances that the accused will be treated as severely as if the killing had been intentional. See **aforethought & wil(l)fulness.**

The word *aforethought*—a 16th-century LOAN TRANSLATION of *prepense,* q.v., or *praecogitata*—should not obscure the sense, as it is liable to. The word was long ago added to *malice* to indicate a design conceived well before the fatal act, but the cases that arose at common law involved such a variety of killings that the courts placed little emphasis on the idea of a well-laid plan. Today, the only requirement is that the intention not be an *after*thought.

Perkins contends that, because "the whole development of the mental requirement of the crime of murder has centered [on] the words *malice aforethought,* it will probably be wise to retain this phrase to express the concept." Rollin M. Perkins, *Criminal Law* 30 (1957). Even so, Perkins suggests *person-endangering state of mind* as a clearer substitute. *Id.* at 38. But even that phrase fails to account for circumstances that justify, excuse, or mitigate.

malicious (= intentional or reckless) bears a legal sense corresponding to the noun *malice,* q.v. Glanville Williams recommends substituting the phrase *intentional or reckless* in place of *malicious.* See *Criminal Law* 76 (2d ed. 1961). Likewise, the phrase *intentionally or recklessly* might replace the adverb *maliciously.*

malicious damage is the former name in BrE for what is now called *criminal damage.* The name change resulted from the Criminal Damage Act 1971.

maliciously. See **malicious.**

malicious mischief; criminal mischief. The traditional phrase, *malicious mischief,* refers to the common-law misdemeanor of intentionally destroying or damaging another's property. Variant phrases include *malicious mischief and trespass, malicious injury, malicious trespass,* and *maliciously damaging the property of another.* To avoid the problematic word *malice,* the drafters of the Model Penal Code invented the term *criminal mischief,* a term now used in several American jurisdictions.

malicious prosecution; abuse of process. Charles McCormick suggested a demarcation between cases in which "process rightfully issued is wrongfully used, which should be termed *abuse of process,* and cases of malicious procurement of the issuance of process, which should be termed *malicious prosecution.*" Charles T. McCormick, *Handbook of the Law of Damages* § 109, at 385 (1935). That distinction is as often blurred today as it was in McCormick's time, but it would still promote clear thinking if lawyers observed it.

malignancy; malignity. *Malignancy* should be confined to denoting any cancerous disease. *Malignity* = wicked or deep-rooted ill will or hatred; malignant feelings or actions.

malodorous. See **odorous.**

malpractice is confined in AmE to negligence or incompetence on the part of professionals (e.g., lawyers and doctors); in BrE, however, it has this meaning as well as a sense similar to *misfeasance:* "The mortgagees are not parties to the *malpractices* of the Waites, and the tenants, who were the victims of those *malpractices.*" (Eng.) The *OED* records two senses not current in the U.S.: (1) "illegal action by which a person in a position of trust seeks a personal benefit at the cost of others"; and (2) "a criminal or overtly mischievous action; wrongdoing; misconduct." Cf. **malfeasance.**

maltreat. See **mistreat.**

malum in se; malum prohibitum. Pl. *mala in se* and *mala prohibita.* These LATINISMS are frequently used by common-law writers, and knowing the distinction between them helps one understand the relation between morality and law. *Malum in se* = evil in itself; something inherently and universally considered evil. *Malum prohibitum* = wrong merely because it is proscribed; made unlawful by statute. Thus murder is the usual example of a crime *malum in se,* but running a traffic light is said to be *malum prohibitum.* E.g., "A *malum prohibitum* is just as much a crime as a *malum in se.*" Oliver W. Holmes, *The Common Law* 46 (1881; repr. 1946).

The phrases are sometimes used not as nouns, but as POSTPOSITIVE ADJECTIVES—e.g.: "Acts *mala in se* include, in addition to felonies, all breaches of public order, injuries to person and property, outrages upon public decency or good morals, and breaches of official duty, when done wilfully or corruptly. Acts *mala prohibita* include any matter forbidden or commanded by statute, but not otherwise wrong." *Commonwealth v. Adams,* 114 Mass. 323, 324 (1873).

malversation. This arcane term, meaning "official corruption," has on occasion been misrendered *malversion*—e.g.: "Although the defendants' expert interpreted the phrase in question to connote more of an 'abuse,' 'misuse' or *'malversion'* [read *'malversation'*] of Post 12's $7,000, we find . . . that the issue was not whether the term used meant 'embezzlement,' but whether or not it was libelous." *Laniecki v. Polish Army Veterans Ass'n,* 480 A.2d 1101, 1107 (Pa. Super. Ct. 1984)./ "[D]efalcations under the Act of 1898 were not limited to deliberate *malversions* [read *malversations*]." *In re Johnson,* 691 F.2d 249, 254 (6th Cir. 1982). Cf. **misconduct in office.**

The agent noun, which seems never before to have been recorded in a dictionary, is *malversator:* "That case has at times been thought to lay down a different rule, treating the infringer in all cases as a trustee *ex maleficio,* and therefore subject to the severe standard imposed upon *malversators.*" *Cincinnati Car Co. v. New York Rapid Transit Corp.,* 66 F.2d 592, 593 (2d Cir. 1933).

-MAN; -PERSON. See SEXISM (B).

man. See SEXISM (B).

man and wife. Since the 1960s, this phrase has been steadily decreasing in frequency of use in American judicial opinions. The reason is that it does not accord the female an equal status—i.e., she is referred to only by reference to her marital status. A more balanced phrasing—though less idiomatic—is *husband and wife.* See SEXISM (D).

mancipation. See **emancipation.**

M & A, in late 20th-century legal slang, is the abbreviated form of *mergers and acquisitions.*

mandamus, n., was originally a prerogative writ that, up to the 19th century, was used as a writ of restitution for those wrongfully deprived of public offices, as in *Marbury v. Madison,* 5 U.S. (1 Cranch) 137 (1803). Thus, it was instrumental in securing democratic principles in the common law. Since the late 19th century, the writ has grown in use: a superior court issues it to compel a lower court or a government officer to perform mandatory or purely ministerial duties correctly. In England, *mandamus* has, since 1938, been an *order,* as opposed to a writ. See **prerogative writs.**

Pl. *mandamuses.* See HYPERCORRECTION (A).

mandamus, v.t., = to order (a lower court or a government official) to perform a specified act. This verb began as a colloquialism in the early 19th century. It is labeled colloquial in *W2* (1934) but has no such notation in *W3* (1961). It has come to appear even in published opinions—e.g.: "The prayer was that the county treasurer be *mandamused* to pay . . . the sum of $1,565 . . . ." *Farson, Son & Co. v. Bird,* 248 U.S. 268, 270 (1919)./ "Walker urges this Court to issue a Writ of Mandamus to the Court of Appeals ordering that court to *mandamus* Johnson to produce the statement of facts . . . ." *Pat Walker & Co. v. Johnson,* 623 S.W.2d 306, 308 (Tex. 1981).

Actually, the use of *mandamus* as a verb is closer to the etymological sense (L. "we charge or command") than the nominal use. The brevity of *to mandamus* recommends its more widespread adoption; no valid reasons exist to oppose it.

mandatary. See **mandatory.**

mandate = (1) an order from an appellate court directing a lower court to take a specified action; (2) a judicial command directed to an officer of the court to enforce a court order; (3) in civil law, a written command given by a principal to an agent; (4) in Roman law, a commission by which one person (the mandator) requests someone (the mandatary) to perform some service gratuitously, the commission becoming effective when the mandatary agrees—a synonym in this sense is *mandatum;* (5) in international law, an authority given by the League of Nations to certain governments to take over the administration and development of certain territories (replaced after 1945 by *trusteeship*); or (6) in politics, the electorate's overwhelming show of approval for a given political platform. See CHAMELEON-HUED WORDS.

mandate, v.t., for *prescribe* is merely verbal sloppiness. "The Federal Rules of Appellate Procedure *mandate* [read *prescribe*] the time for filing a notice of appeal."

mandator. See **mandate** (sense 4).

mandatory; mandatary. Horwill wrote in the 1930s that *mandatory*—frequently used in AmE—is uncommon in England, and that *obligatory* and *compulsory* are more common. The latter two terms may still be predominant, but *mandatory injunction* is now a common phrase in English law reports. The three words—*mandatory, obligatory,* and *compulsory*—are close synonyms. See **directory.**

Mandatary, n. & adj., is a civil-law term. As a noun, it is a close equivalent to what in common-law jurisdictions is called an *agent,* though a mandatary usually (as in Scotland) acts gratuitously—e.g.: "[A]s respects liability for misconduct and limitation of action therefor they are more exactly agents or *mandataries.*" *Anderson v. Gailey,* 33 F.2d 589, 592 (N.D. Ga. 1929)./ "[T]he fraud committed by a *mandatary* in exercise of the mandate is regarded as fraud committed by the principal by virtue of the rules governing representation." Saul Litvinoff, *Vices of Consent, Error, Fraud, Duress and an Epilogue on Lesion,* 50 La. L. Rev. 1, 71 (1989). As an adjective, the word means "of or relating to an agency relationship"—e.g.: "[T]his contract is also a contract of a certain kind; it is a *mandatary* contract, establishing an agency relationship . . . ." *Commonwealth Capital Corp. v. Enterprise Fed. Sav. & Loan Ass'n,* 630 F. Supp. 1199, 1201 (E.D. La. 1986).

For the Roman-law sense of *mandatary,* see **mandate** (sense 4).

mandatory injunction; prohibitory injunction. The former court order requires a positive action; the latter requires restraint from action. See **injunction.**

manifest, adj., often functions in suspect ways in legal writing: "Someone has observed that whenever a lawyer says that something or other was the manifest intention of a man, *'manifest'* means that the man never really had such an intention." Jerome Frank, *Law and the Modern Mind* 30 (1930; repr. 1963). This word is one of those vague terms by which lawyers "create an appearance of continuity, uniformity and definiteness [that does] not in fact exist." *Id.*

manifesto. Pl. *-os.* See PLURALS (C).

man-killing is still occasionally used in law to refer to the action of one person against another, but rarely in nonlegal writing. "Homicidal mania is the morbid and uncontrollable appetite for *man-killing.*" See **murder (A)** & SEXISM (B).

mankind. See **humankind** & SEXISM (B).

manner, in a ——. This phrase typifies the style of a writer whose prose reads slowly. *In a professional manner* should be *professionally; in a rigid manner* should be *rigidly; in a childish manner* should be *childishly.* Good editors do not leave such phrases untouched.

Still, some phrases cannot be made into *-ly* adverbs: *in a Rambo-like manner; in a determined manner* (few editors would choose *determinedly*—see -EDLY); *in a catch-as-catch-can manner.* In many such contexts, though, the word *way* would be an improvement over *manner.*

manner in which is almost always unnecessarily verbose for *how.*

man-of-law (= a man skilled in law; a lawyer), a word with decidedly positive connotations, is little used today, probably because it is considered sexist. (See SEXISM (B).) Some writers omit the hyphens—e.g.: "Never before had any society taken a professional *man of law*—Holmes, about whom I shall have more to say presently—as the embodiment of its dream." Grant Gilmore, *The Ages of American Law* 42 (1977).

manpower. See SEXISM (B).

manservant. The plural form, oddly, makes both words in the compound plural: *menservants.*

manslaughter, n. **A. *Voluntary manslaughter* and *involuntary manslaughter.*** Because the term *manslaughter* (= unlawful homicide committed without malice aforethought) extends from the verge of murder to the verge of excusable homicide, it became necessary to divide the term into categories. *Voluntary manslaughter* means "an act of murder reduced to manslaughter because of extenuating circumstances such as provocation or diminished responsibility." In some jurisdictions, this crime is known as *intentional manslaughter.*

The other category, by natural contrast, is called *involuntary manslaughter,* but in this phrase the word *involuntary* is used quite unnaturally as a catch-all: the phrase means "homicide in which there is no intention to kill or do grievous bodily harm."

In England, *involuntary manslaughter* is subdivided still further into what one writer calls *straightforward manslaughter* and *constructive manslaughter.* The "straightforward" type "requires the prosecution to prove that the defendant *caused* the death in question by an act or omission, amounting in either case to gross negligence or recklessness (which one is not finally settled) in breach of a duty of care." Glanville Williams, *Textbook of Criminal Law* 224 (1978). *Constructive manslaughter,* in contrast, consists in "a killing in the course of certain kinds of unlawful acts, and then only when the defendant is negligent as to causing bodily injury." *Id.* at 238. See **murder (B).**

B. And *causing death by reckless or dangerous driving.* In 1956, this EUPHEMISM became established in English statutory law "owing to the notorious reluctance of juries to convict of 'motor manslaughter.'" William Geldart, *Introduction to English Law* 158 (D.C.M. Yardley ed., 9th ed. 1984).

manslaughter, v.t. (= to kill [a person] unlawfully but without malice aforethought) is rightly listed as a colloquialism in the *SOED.* Though not common, it has appeared in reported opinions—e.g.: "In *Burney,* . . . the defendant assaulted victim Williams with a deadly weapon and *manslaughtered* victim Grant during a crowded bar room quarrel culminating in a shooting." *People v. Masters,* 241 Cal. Rptr. 511, 517 (Ct. App. 1988).

manslaughterer (= one who commits manslaughter) is infrequent but arguably useful—e.g.: "It was thought that actors whose emotions were stirred by other forms of outrageous conduct . . . also should be punished as *manslaughterers* rather than murderers." *Patterson v. New York,*

432 U.S. 197, 218 (1977)./ "Defendant's planning activity rendered him more culpable than other *manslaughterers* . . . ." *People v. Levitt,* 203 Cal. Rptr. 276, 287 (Ct. App. 1984).

mantle; mantel. *Mantle* means, among other things, "a loose robe," and is frequently used by legal writers in figurative senses—e.g.: "The *mantle* of immunity should be withdrawn."/ "The court has not felt constrained by stare decisis in its expansion of the protective *mantle* of sovereign immunity." See **clothe.**

Mantel is a different and more common word in everyday speech. It means "a structure of wood or marble above or around a fireplace; a shelf." In legal writing, the spelling *mantel* is frequently used where *mantle* belongs.

manufacturer. So spelled. Some legal writers mistakenly write *-or.* See -ER (A).

many. **A. And *much.*** *Many* is used with count nouns (i.e., those that comprise a number of discrete or separable entities). *Much* is used with mass nouns (i.e., those that refer to amounts as distinguished from numbers). Hence, *many persons* but *much salt.* Here *much* is used incorrectly: "We do not have *much* [read *many*] facts here." Cf. *less* for *fewer,* and note that *less* is the correlative of *much,* whereas *fewer* is the correlative of *many.* See **less (A)** & COUNT NOUNS AND MASS NOUNS (A).

Sometimes the writer must decide whether a word such as *data,* q.v., is a count noun (as it traditionally has been) or a mass noun (as it has recently come to be). E.g., "But *much* [read *many?*] of the data in present personnel files is highly subjective." William O. Douglas, *Points of Rebellion* 21 (1970). Of course, the choice of the singular verb *is* shows that Justice Douglas considered *data* a mass noun—so *much* was the appropriate word.

B. *Many . . . abound.* This phrasing commonly creates a REDUNDANCY—e.g.: "Certainly it must be conceded *that many valid reasons abound* [read *that valid reasons abound*] for choosing private over public education . . . ." *Cook v. Hudson,* 511 F.2d 744, 752 (5th Cir. 1975) (Clark, J., dissenting)./ "*Many other examples abound* [read *Other examples abound*] in the general statutes of local application passed by the Alabama legislature prior to the adoption of Amendments 375 and 397." *Phalen v. Birmingham Racing Comm'n,* 481 So. 2d 1108, 1122 (Ala. 1985).

margin (= footnotes) occurs today primarily in legal writing, although scholars in all disciplines once commonly used it. "The order and decree dismissing the bill is set out in the *margin.*" This usage harks back to a bygone era when notes were set out in the outer margins rather than at the foot of the page.

marginal notes, in British STATUTE DRAFTING, are brief notes indicating the scope or subject matter of an Act of Parliament. Generally, they enhance readability, but they are not authoritative as a guide to interpretation because they are not debated as part of the bill and may be misleading.

mariage de convenance. See **marriage of convenience.**

marijuana; marihuana. The former now predominates in judicial opinions and should be preferred. Justice Lewis F. Powell, speaking in 1986 at a luncheon, stated: "The big problem we had in the Court this past Term was how to spell *marijuana.* We were about equally divided between a 'j' and an 'h' and since I was supposed to be the swing vote on the court, and just to show my impartiality, I added a footnote in a case . . . in which I spelled *marijuana* with a 'j' once and an 'h' in the same sentence." Quoted in *News,* A.B.A. J., 1 Oct. 1986, at 17, 34.

mariner is a serviceable replacement for *seaman,* which not only is sexist but also has an awkward homophone. See **able-bodied seaman, seaman** & SEXISM (B).

mariner's will. See **oral will.**

marital. See **matrimonial law** & **marriage,** adj.

marital rape was a type of OXYMORON at common law, since a husband was held to be exempt from rape charges if he had nonconsensual sexual intercourse with his wife. The so-called *marital-rape exemption,* though, is gradually disappearing as Anglo-American jurisdictions have generally abolished it. As one writer puts it, abolition "is surely important as a statement of the married woman's autonomy and freedom of choice in sexual matters." Andrew Ashworth, *Principles of Criminal Law* 303 (1991). See **rape (A).**

marital relation is often wordy for *marriage*—e.g.: "A valid divorce terminates the *marital relation* [read *marriage*] and with it the duty of the husband to support his wife and vice versa . . . ." Rollin M. Perkins & Ronald N. Boyce, *Criminal Law* 676 (3d ed. 1982). In the plural form, *marital* *relations* is sometimes used as a EUPHEMISM for sexual relations between husband and wife.

maritime. See **admiralty (A).**

marked is pronounced /*markt*/, as one syllable. The pronunciation /***mar**-kəd*/, in two syllables, is a vestige of the correct adverbial pronunciation /***mar**-kəd-lee*/.

marketable; merchantable. The latter might well be termed a legal ARCHAISM, for it has no nuance not conveyed by the former. E.g., "Delivery was made subject to the condition that appellant furnish *merchantable* [read *marketable*] title." (*Marketable title* = a seller's nondefective title to property.) But *merchantable* appears in many statutes—such as the U.K. Sale of Goods Act—and is therefore unlikely to disappear anytime soon.

market overt usu. means something more specific than *open market. Market overt* = an open, legally regulated public market where buyers, with some exceptions, acquire good title to products regardless of any defects in the seller's title. *Open market,* though it sometimes shares that sense, generally means "a market with no competitive restrictions on price or availability of products."

Market overt is the less common term: "Conceivably the common-law judges might have refused to allow the bailor to recover in detinue against a bona fide purchaser, as they did refuse it against a purchaser in *market overt;* but this would have involved a weighing of ethical considerations altogether foreign to the medieval mode of thought."

marque, letters of. See **letters of marque.**

marriable. See **marriageable.**

marriage, adj. The word *marital* is better than *marriage* in adjectival senses. E.g., "An aggrieved spouse is not compelled to seek the courts of another state for the protection of her *marriage* [read *marital*] status." See NOUNS AS ADJECTIVES.

marriage, n. See **common-law marriage.**

marriageable; marriable. The latter is an ARCHAISM to be avoided.

marriage dissolution is a EUPHEMISM for *divorce* or *annulment.* E.g., "The Family Law Act, a response to general dissatisfaction with the social and legal procedures affecting divorce actions in California, effected substantial changes in the substantive law and procedure in proceedings for *dissolution of marriage.*" Note the INELEGANT VARIATION in that sentence (*divorce . . . dissolution of marriage*)./ "The State Bar of Texas sponsored the *Marriage Dissolution* Institute in Fort Worth in February 1985." That *marriage dissolution* may technically encompass annulments as well as divorces does not redeem it. See **divorce (B).**

marriage of convenience; *mariage de convenance.* The anglicized version is to be preferred over the GALLICISM. But it should be understood rightly: *marriage of convenience* is not "an ill-considered marriage that happens to be convenient to the parties involved," but "a marriage contracted for social or financial advantages rather than out of mutual love."

married. See **wed (B).**

marshal, n., = (1) a law-enforcement officer with duties similar to those of a sheriff; (2) a judicial officer who provides court security, executes process, and performs other tasks for a court; or (3) in England, a recently called barrister who acts as personal officer of and secretary to a High Court judge on circuit. The word is preferably so spelled—not *marshall.*

marshal, v.t. (= to arrange in order), in its past-tense and participial forms, is frequently misspelled in AmE with a doubled *-l-*. E.g., "The strongest support *marshalled* [read, in AmE, *marshaled*] by the majority opinion is the statement by Dean Page Keeton." See DOUBLING OF FINAL CONSONANTS.

In BrE, the inflected form is *marshalled,* but the uninflected form is still *marshal,* as in AmE: "If one side can *marshall* [read *marshal*] a precedent that is binding and in point, that will conclude the debate." Michael Zander, *The Law-Making Process* 234 (2d ed. 1985).

martial law; military law. The two are distinct, as Holland suggests: "'Martial' as opposed to 'military law' is not recognised by the law of England [or of the U.S.]." Thomas E. Holland, *The Elements of Jurisprudence* 377 n.2 (13th ed. 1924). *Martial law* is the body of rules applied on grounds of necessity by a country's rulers when the civil government has failed or looks as if it might fail to function, the armed forces assuming control purportedly until civil processes and courts can be restored to their lawful places. Martial law applies only within a given country—not within occupied enemy territory. *Military law,* on the other hand, refers to the special branch of law that governs military discipline and other rules regarding service in the armed forces. Thus *martial law* usu. applies to civilians as well as soldiers, whereas *military law* almost never applies to civilians.

Mary Carter agreement, which owes its name to *Booth v. Mary Carter Paint Co.,* 202 So. 2d 8 (Fla. Dist. Ct. App. 1967), refers to a contract by which a codefendant settles with the plaintiff and obtains a release, with the further agreement that the codefendant will receive a portion of any amount that the plaintiff may recover from one or more other defendants. In short, the codefendant settles and then joins forces with the plaintiff against the remaining codefendants. See CASE REFERENCES (C).

Some lawyers shorten the phrase to *Mary Carter* <Sinergy then entered into a Mary Carter with the plaintiff>. Much more slangily, lawyers sometimes use the phrase as a verb <Sinergy was Mary Cartered out of the case>.

MASCULINE AND FEMININE PRONOUNS. See SEXISM (A).

mass of, a. See SYNESIS.

mass tort = a large number of tort claims with a common cause—such as a single-accident disaster, a defective product that injures many people, or environmental contamination at a single site—that has injured many victims. This term has, by extension, given rise to some odd JARGON such as *mass litigation* and even *mass defendant.* To avoid giving *mass* these contorted senses, the better practice is to write *mass-tort litigation* and *mass-tort defendant.*

master. A. Meaning "employer." The word *master* was once regularly used to mean "employer" in legal language, and *servant* to mean "employee." But this terminology has long been obsolescent: "Even the legal vocabulary changes; younger lawyers in the spirit of modern labor relations scorn to speak of the law of *master* and servant, under which rubric we used to find the little law that was especially directed to employment." Robert H. Jackson, Foreword to *Jurisprudence in Action* iii (1953). See **employer and employee & servant.**

B. Referring to a Parajudicial Officer. During the Middle Ages, the Court of Chancery began appointing officers to assist in various equitable proceedings. These officers were known as *masters.* Though the British Parliament abolished the office in the late 19th century, many American jurisdictions have continued using officers bearing the title *master,* without regard to the equitable or legal nature of the proceedings. Among the functions they may perform are taking testimony, computing interest, valuing annuities, investigating encumbrances on land titles, and the like—virtually always with a written report to the court.

master and servant. See **employer and employee & master** (A).

masterful; masterly. *Masterful* describes a powerful, even bullying, superior as opposed to *servant* or *slave. Masterly* indicates the skill of a master of a profession or trade as opposed to *an unskilled worker.* A master craftsman is *masterly;* a boorish tyrant is *masterful.* Which is the correct term in the following sentence, from a nonlegal text? "Though Britain's Derek Jacobi looks about as much like Adolph Hitler as Archie Bunker, he evokes the Fuhrer with *masterful* verve." (The actor is *masterly;* Hitler was *masterful.*)

Perhaps one reason the two words are so frequently confounded is that when an adverb for *masterly* is needed, *masterfully* seems more natural than *masterlily.* (See ADVERBS (B).) Indeed, "He writes *masterfully*" strikes one as much less stilted than "He writes *masterlily.*" This problem with the adverbial form threatens to destroy a useful distinction between the two adjectival forms. Perhaps *masterlily* would seem less pedantic if we were to use it more often. Barring that, *in a masterly way* is always available.

master of the bench. See **bencher.**

Master of the Rolls = president of the Court of Appeal (Civil Division) in England.

MATCHING PARTS. See PARALLELISM.

material, adj.; **relevant.** The distinction between these terms—traditionally fundamental to the law of evidence—is counterintuitive and therefore sometimes confusing. *Relevant* = tending to prove or disprove a matter in issue. *Material* = having some logical connection with the consequential facts.

Why counterintuitive? Because the definition of *material* is the one that most educated people would match with *relevant.* The result of this confusion, among lawyers and nonlawyers alike, is that the drafters of the Federal Rules of Evidence felt compelled to "avoid 'the loosely used and ambiguous word *material,*' using instead the phrase 'of consequence in determination of the action' in defining relevance." *Huff v. White Motor Corp.,* 609 F.2d 286, 294 n.13 (7th Cir. 1979) (quoting advisory comm. note to Fed. R. Evid. 401).

Material, the victim of lawyers' SLIPSHOD EXTENSION, is frequently used in the sense "significant." E.g., "An immediate appeal would *materially* [i.e., significantly] advance the ultimate termination of the litigation." This sense is now commonplace in American securities law, where it is too pervasive to be considered exceptionable. It is also common in other legal contexts.

materialman. See **mechanic's lien** & SEXISM (B).

matrimonial law. We might question why *matrimonial* rather than *marital* came to be used in this and related phrases. *Matrimonial* is a FORMAL WORD rarely used outside the law except in reference to wedding services. Yet the law on both sides of the Atlantic has embraced this word in phrases such as *matrimonial home, matrimonial offense,* and *matrimonial cohabitation.* E.g., "Strangely, however, the changes in the method of quantifying rights in the *matrimonial* home have gone unnoticed." (Eng.)/ "In *matrimonial* causes because the state has an interest, special duties are laid on solicitors and the bar." (Eng.) The American Academy of Matrimonial Lawyers is unlikely to approve of a change in terminology.

Still, in some contexts *matrimonial* is inarguably turgid in place of *marital:* "This language frequently has been applied as a general rule and the federal courts consistently have refused to entertain actions involving *matrimonial* [read *marital*] status." See **marriage,** adj.

matter is sometimes viewed as the lawyer's puffed-up equivalent of *case.* It commonly occurs in contexts such as these: "I handled a fascinating *matter* [read *case*] the other day."/ "How many *matters* [read *cases*] are there on the docket?" And it appears in BrE as well as AmE—e.g.: "It should be noted that section 76(i) extends not only to *matters* arising under the Constitution but also to *matters* involving its interpretation." James Crawford, *Australian Courts of Law* 146 (1982).

Actually, the term derives from the language of equity: "for the Queen's Bench Division we usually talk about 'actions,' denoting the idea of litigants who have a dispute to be determined, whilst in the Chancery Division we are more apt to speak of 'actions and *matters.*' Some of the causes in the Chancery Division are normal litigation between contesting parties, but *'matters'* do not necessarily mean that there is a dispute." R.M. Jackson, *The Machinery of Justice in England* 50–51 (5th ed. 1967).

That quotation suggests a workable distinction for AmE and BrE alike: *case* or *action* refers to a pending lawsuit in which there is a genuine dispute; *matter* refers to any other affair in which a lawyer becomes professionally involved. It therefore makes good sense for law firms to keep records, as they ordinarily do, of "client-matter" numbers. A *matter* might involve legal advice where litigation is never contemplated.

maugre */maw-gər/* = despite. Listed as obsolete or archaic in virtually every English-language dictionary, this word is just one more ARCHAISM in which legal inkhornists can indulge. E.g., "*Maugre* this: shall we repudiate such 'excellent method of decision,' as violative of the common law of England in 1791?" *Sunray Oil Corp. v. Allbritton,* 187 F.2d 475, 480–81 (5th Cir. 1951)./ "Complaint is next made that the court erred in permitting the prosecutor to state in his final argument[,] *maugre* timely objection by counsel for the defendant, the following: . . . ." *Shadle v. State,* 194 So. 2d 538, 542–43 (Ala. 1967).

maximal. See **maximum.**

MAXIMS. A maxim is a traditional legal principle that has been frozen into a concise expression. There are a few legal and quasi-legal maxims that everyone knows, such as these:

- A man's home is his castle. See **castle doctrine.**
- *Caveat emptor.* See **caveat.**
- Ignorance of the law is no excuse. This phrase is a close LOAN TRANSLATION of *ignorantia juris neminem excusat* (= ignorance of the law excuses nobody). See ***ignorantia juris.***
- Possession is nine-tenths of the law. See **possession is nine-tenths of the law.**

Then there are the thousands of maxims dressed up in Latin, few of which most lawyers seem nowadays to know. Among the more common ones are these:

- *Actus non facit reum nisi mens sit rea* (= an act does not make the doer guilty unless his or her mind is guilty). See ***actus non facit reum nisi mens sit rea.***
- *Delegatus non potest delegare* (= a person to whom work is delegated cannot himself [or herself] delegate it).
- *De minimis non curat lex* (= the law does not concern itself with trifles). "No one knows exactly what it means." Ephraim Tutt, *Yankee Lawyer* 356 (1943). See ***de minimis* (A).**
- *Ex turpi causa non oritur actio* (= from an illegal transaction no action arises).
- *Ignorantia facti excusat* (= ignorance of fact excuses, i.e., is a ground for relief).

- *Nulla poena sine lege* (= no punishment except in accordance with the law). See ***nulla poena sine lege.***
- *Qui facit per alium facit per se* (= he who acts through another acts himself; she who acts through another acts herself).
- *Sic utere tuo, ut alienum non laedas* (= one should use one's own property in a manner that does not injure that of another). See ***sic utere.***
- *Transit in rem iudicatam* (= it passes into a matter adjudged, i.e., becomes res judicata).
- *Ubi remedium, ibi ius* (= where there is a remedy, there is a right).
- *Volenti non fit injuria* (= that to which a person consents cannot be considered an injury). See ***volenti non fit injuria.***

Though these and other maxims dot the pages of lawbooks—especially older lawbooks—most legal thinkers consider them unnecessary to a mature legal system. Roscoe Pound, for example, suggested that they characterize a legal system still in its formative stages: "[A] body of primitive law . . . often contains a certain number of sententious legal proverbs, put in striking form so as to stick in the memory but vague in their content." *An Introduction to the Philosophy of Law* 48–49 (1922; repr. 1975). Lon Fuller echoed this view: "Undeveloped systems of law have a decided penchant for such brocards." *Legal Fictions* 33–34 (1967; repr. 1977).

Several writers have suggested that we are better off depositing maxims in the dustbin of history:

- "It seems to me that legal maxims in general are little more than pert headings of chapters. They are rather minims than maxims, for they give not a particularly great but a particularly small amount of information. As often as not, the exceptions and qualifications to them are more important than the so-called rules." 2 James F. Stephen, *History of the Criminal Law of England* 94 n.1 (1883).
- "[T]he fact that the great majority of legal maxims are clothed in the words of a dead language has had, in some instances, the effect of preventing proper inquiry into their meaning. A phrase couched in Latin seems to some persons invested with 'a kind of halo.'" Jeremiah Smith, *The Use of Maxims in Jurisprudence,* 9 Harv. L. Rev. 13, 25–26 (1895).
- "General propositions do not decide concrete cases." *Lochner v. New York,* 198 U.S. 45, 76 (1905) (Holmes, J., dissenting).
- "[N]o one who reflects on the subject can doubt that some useless Latin maxims, and some untrue Latin maxims, have continued current, and that other Latin maxims have been misapplied, when this would not have happened if those maxims had been expressed only in the vernacular." *Sperbeck v. A.L. Burbank Co.,* 190 F.2d 449, 455 n.8 (2d Cir. 1951).
- "Happily such 'short, dark maxims' are not so common as they once were. When they are used today, it is for the sake of their flavor of antiquity, rather than because of any notion that they are actually explanatory." Lon L. Fuller, *Legal Fictions* 33–34 (1967; repr. 1977).

For the most nearly definitive work on maxims in Anglo-American law, see Herbert Broom, *A Selection of Legal Maxims* (10th ed. 1939). For a collection of more than a thousand maxims, see E. Hilton Jackson, *Latin for Lawyers* (1937; repr. 1992). See LATINISMS.

maximum, n. & adj.; **maximal,** adj. More and more frequently, *maximum* (like *minimum*) has come to act as its own adjective. E.g., "In bidding, the contractor shall expose to the bidders the *maximum* quantities required by the work."

Maximal usually means "the greatest possible," rather than merely "of, relating to, or constituting a maximum." E.g., "The state's interest in swift and efficient punishment need not eviscerate its interest in *maximal* certainty of application." See **minimal.**

The plural of the noun *maximum* is *maxima*—e.g.: "Moreover, a majority of the states pay less than their determined standard of need, and twenty of these states impose *maximums* [read *maxima*] on family grants of the kind here in issue."/ "To appreciate the truth of this assertion it is only necessary to think of the imposition of prison sentences within the *maxima* allowed by the various statutes . . . ." Rupert Cross, *Statutory Interpretation* 41 (1976). See PLURALS (A).

maximum [+ name] is another way of describing a "hanging judge" (q.v.). The phrase suggests that the judge routinely imposes the maximum sentence—e.g.: "But he had been at least as stern in earlier criminal cases, sentencing convicted defendants to long terms, thus earning the nickname *'maximum John.'" Sirica, 88, Dies; Persistent Judge in Fall of Nixon,* N.Y. Times, 15 Aug. 1992, at 1, 11.

may = (1) has discretion to; is permitted to <suit may be brought in any district court>; (2) possibly will <the court may apply this doctrine>; or (3) shall. Sense (3), though a lexical perversion, has come about because "courts not infrequently construe *may* as *shall* or *must* to the end that justice may not be the slave of grammar" (*Black's* 6th ed.).

But no drafter who means *must* should consciously use *may;* the liberties taken by the courts in construing drafters' oversights should not be allowed to change the essential meanings of basic words like *may.* See **can** & WORDS OF AUTHORITY (E).

mayhem. A. Senses. *Mayhem* = (1) malicious injury to or maiming of a person, orig. so as to impair or destroy the victim's capacity for self-defense; (2) violent and damaging action; violent destruction; or (3) rowdy confusion, disruption, chaos. Sense (3) is inappropriately attenuated.

B. And *maim,* n. Though etymologically identical, *mayhem* and *maim* have undergone DIFFERENTIATION. In the best usage, *mayhem* refers to the crime (sense 1) and *maim* to the type of injury required for the crime.

C. And *maihem.* This spelling amounts to nothing more than a NEEDLESS VARIANT.

may it please the court is the standard introductory phrase that lawyers use when speaking to an appellate court. Some people call it LEGALESE, but it is not really in that category. The phrase helps establish a tone of civility and respect in an oral argument.

may not is sometimes the source of AMBIGUITY: it may mean either "is disallowed from" or "might or might not." For example, if an application contained a notice that read, "Applications received after September 30 may not be considered by this office," the question arises whether the office is prohibited from considering it or the decision about considering it depends on how the office exercises its discretion (or whim).

In stating a prohibition, some writers would solve the problem by resorting to *cannot,* but doing so blurs the widely recognized distinction between *can* and *may.* See **can.**

A better way to solve the problem in many contexts is to use the phrase *must not.* Thus, instead of saying that a brief *may not* contain addenda, one might say that a brief *must not* (preferably not *shall not*) contain addenda. (See WORDS OF AUTHORITY (A).) The phrasing with *must* is certainly unambiguous.

In drafted documents, however, the basic phrase at issue—*may not*—is conventionally viewed as unambiguous. Why? Because in DRAFTING, in which one sets forth rights, duties, and liabilities, one never has occasion to speculate in the sense of "might or might not." So, generally speaking, *may not* does not cause interpretative difficulties in statutes, rules, contracts, bylaws, and the like. But those who want to forestall even a minute possibility of a problem use *must not.* See WORDS OF AUTHORITY (F).

me; I. See NOMINATIVE AND OBJECTIVE CASES. For the error *between you and I,* see **between (C).**

mean, adj., = (1) small; (2) obstreperous; or (3) median, average. Readers today often misunderstand sense (1). A *mean-spirited* person is not malevolent or evil; rather, the person has a small spirit, a petty mind.

mean, n.; **median.** Writers should distinguish between these two words. The *mean* is the average. The *median* is the point in a series of numbers above which is half the series and below which is the other half.

meaningful (= full of meaning or expression) has, with some irony, rightly been criticized as a meaningless buzzword, esp. when used for *reasonable.* Here its meaning is stretched to the breaking point: "Options should be used carefully and sparingly; any options issued must expire a *meaningful* [read *reasonable*] time before the earliest possible conversion date."/ "Due process requires an opportunity for a hearing to be granted at a *meaningful* [read *reasonable*] time and in a *meaningful* [read *reasonable*] manner." *Meaningful* has also been used to mean "significant, important," as here: "We find no *meaningful* constitutional infraction." These uses have made *meaningful* a VOGUE WORD that careful writers avoid.

means and includes. See DEFINITIONS (B) & (C).

meantime; meanwhile. *In the meantime* is idiomatic; *in the meanwhile* is not. Both *meanwhile* and *meantime* can be used alone, though the former more naturally so.

meat out. See **mete out.**

mechanic's lien; mechanic's and materialman's lien. A *mechanic* furnishes labor to the construction of improvements on land; a *materialman* furnishes materials. Because the mechanic and the materialman are usually one and the same, and because the legal distinction between the two is outmoded in most jurisdictions, it has become customary to refer to both in one breath, in the general phrase *mechanic's lien* or *construction lien.*

Such a lien secures payment for labor or materials supplied in improving, repairing, or maintaining real property. In many jurisdictions, the rules for perfecting such a lien are highly technical and rigid.

The word *materialman* is, from the viewpoint of eradicating sexist language, a particularly difficult one to replace. The word *supplier* is a possible candidate, but the word may not need a replacement at all if we merely refer to a *mechanic's lien* or *construction lien.* See SEXISM (B).

media; medium. *Media,* the plural of *medium,* cannot properly be used as a singular. And *medias,* which has recently raised its ugly head, can only be described as illiterate.

Mediums is the correct plural when the sense of *medium* is "a clairvoyant; spiritualist"—e.g.: "A similar state of dissociation seems to account for the manifestations of some 'psychic *mediums.*'" Glanville Williams, *Criminal Law* 37 (2d ed. 1961). Otherwise, the form should be avoided: "It is true that one of the *mediums* [read *media*] of the lawyer's art is rules, and the lawyer must know rules . . . ." James B. White, *The Legal Imagination* xxxv (1973)./ "Reporters for printed *mediums* [read *media*] also focus criticism on television for using all-purpose experts to express an opinion on a wide variety of subjects." Charles Rothfeld, *On Legal Pundits and How They Got That Way,* N.Y. Times, 4 May 1990, at B10.

Media is often used as a shortened form of *communications media.* E.g., "If one viewpoint monopolizes the *media,* however, the discussion that flows from it will not be full and unrestricted."

median. See **mean.**

mediate, adj., = occupying a middle position; acting through an intermediate person or thing. It is frequently used in contrast with *immediate.* The Rule in Shelley's Case is often stated thus: "[W]here the ancestor takes an estate of freehold, and in the same gift or conveyance, an estate is limited either *mediately* or immediately to his heirs, either in fee or in tail, 'the heirs' are words of limitation of the estate, and not words of purchase." *Baker v. Scott,* 62 Ill. 86, 90 (1871).

mediation. A. Generally. *Mediation* "has long been a relatively complex word in English." Raymond Williams, *Keywords: A Vocabulary of Culture and Society* 170 (1976). The most common, but conflicting, senses are the following, for which Williams suggests alternatives (in parentheses): (1) "intermediary action designed to bring about reconciliation or agreement" (*conciliation*); (2) "an activity that indirectly or deviously expresses a relationship between otherwise separated facts, actions, and experiences" (*ideology* or *rationalization*); and (3) "an activity that directly expresses otherwise unexpressed relations" (*form*).

B. And *conciliation*. The distinction between *mediation* and *conciliation* is widely debated among those interested in ADR (q.v.), arbitration, and international diplomacy. Some suggest that *conciliation* is "a nonbinding arbitration," whereas *mediation* is merely "assisted negotiation." Others put it this way: *conciliation* involves a third party's trying to bring together disputing parties to help them reconcile their differences, whereas *mediation* goes further by allowing the third party to suggest terms on which the dispute might be resolved. Still others reject these attempts at DIFFERENTIATION and contend that there is no consensus about what the two words mean—that they are generally interchangeable. Though a distinction would be convenient, those who argue that usage indicates a broad synonymy are most accurate.

mediatory; mediative; mediatorial. The second is a NEEDLESS VARIANT of the first. *Mediatorial,* however, corresponds not to *mediation* but to *mediator*—e.g.: "It is the high province of this Court to interpose its benign and *mediatorial* influence." *Gibbons v. Ogden,* 22 U.S. (9 Wheat.) 1, 184 (1824) (argument of counsel).

medical; medicinal. The former applies to all aspects of a physician's practice, the latter only to what is associated with medicines.

medication; medicament. See **medicine.**

medicinal. See **medical.**

medicine; medication; medicament. *Medication* has traditionally meant "the action of treating medically," but, through SLIPSHOD EXTENSION, has recently come to mean "a medicinal substance, medicament"—a sense that careful writers avoid. *Medicament* (= a substance taken internally or used externally in curative treatment) and *medicine* (= a substance taken internally in curative treatment) are synonymous with the loose meaning of *medication.*

medicolegal (= involving the application of medical science to law), though perhaps seeming to be a NEOLOGISM, was first used in the early 19th century. It has proved useful enough to be used frequently—e.g.: L. Thoinot & A.W. Weysse, *Medico-Legal Moral Offenses* (1911)./ "That these tests are very far from reality cannot, we think, be successfully disputed. Certainly, many competent *medicolegal* writers have so indicated and in our opinion they have proved their case." *U.S. ex rel.*

Smith v. Baldi, 192 F.2d 540, 566 (3d Cir. 1951)./ "M-LCS described itself as 'the only full-time consulting firm dedicated to assisting attorneys in all jurisdictions with screening and preparing *medico-legal* cases . . . .'" Joseph Goulden, *The Million Dollar Lawyers* 122 (1978) (quoting advertisement). The best modern spelling is *medicolegal*—with no hyphen. Cf. **psycholegal.**

medium. See **media.**

meeting of the minds. Grant Gilmore called this phrase "quaintly archaic." *The Death of Contract* 43 (1974). It is not quite a LOAN TRANSLATION, but perhaps a loan paraphrase, for the Roman-law phrase *consensus ad idem.* Holmes, Williston, and others treated *meeting of the minds* with contempt because it denotes a subjective rather than an objective theory of contracts. Thus, it is more than quaintly archaic; as a matter of substantive law, it is long since outmoded. Cf. **mutuality of obligation.**

meld together is a common REDUNDANCY.

meliorate. See **ameliorate.**

member of the bar. While in the U.S. any licensed lawyer is a member of the bar, in G.B. only barristers (and advocates in Scotland) can claim this membership, solicitors being members of the Law Society or the Law Society of Scotland.

member of the legal profession. This phrase is a needless circumlocution for *lawyer.*

memento. So spelled.

memoranda; memorandums. *Memorandum* is always the singular noun. Either *-dums* or *-da* is correct as a plural. No less a writer than Shakespeare used *memorandums* (*Henry IV, Part 1,* 3.3.157–63), but *memoranda* now predominates. See PLURALS (A).

Occasionally the Latinate plural is misused as a singular: "Once a valid agreement is evidenced by such a *memoranda* [read *memorandum*], the statute comes into play to prevent contradiction of the terms included in the *memoranda* [read *memorandum*] by evidence of any prior agreement."

memorandize (= to put into a memo), an -IZE neologism with little merit, appears to be a NEEDLESS VARIANT of *memorialize,* q.v. E.g., "[T]he two-year leaseback . . . was oral, and is not *'memorandized'* [read *memorialized*] by any writing as required by the statute of frauds." *Truslow v. Woodruff,* 60 Cal. Rptr. 304, 308 n.1 (Ct. App. 1967).

memorandums. See **memoranda.**

memorialize (= to preserve the memory of; to supply the memorial of) is a word of great seriousness in lay contexts <to memorialize the plight of European Jews in World War II>. In legal writing, by contrast, it is used in far more mundane contexts: "A plea agreement letter *memorialized* the respective promises of the witness and the government."/ "According to the district court, the parties intended the paragraph *memorializing* their agreed right to cease option payments only to establish a right of succession to partnership interests."

memory of man runneth not to the contrary. This immemorial phrase expresses immemoriality—or the point before which *legal memory* began (fixed as the year 1189), also known as *time immemorial,* q.v. By the early 16th century, English courts were coming to use legal memory to restrict the growth of custom, which could be established only if it predated 1189.

The phrase is frequently used in extended senses in American judicial opinions as well as in legal commentary. E.g., "[W]e are not dealing with a traditional common law crime such as assault and battery, a crime in existence since the *memory of man runneth not to the contrary.*" *Prinz v. Great Bay Casino Corp.* 705 F.2d 692, 701 (3d Cir. 1983) (A. Leon Higginbotham, J., dissenting).

Though the phrase dates from the 13th century at the latest, some have mistakenly thought it to have less antiquity. The phrase is often attributed to Blackstone, who himself hinted at its antiquity: "Whence it is that in our law the goodness of a custom depends upon it's [*sic*] having been used time out of mind; or, in the solemnity of our legal phrase, time whereof the *memory of man runneth not to the contrary.*" 1 William Blackstone, *Commentaries* 67 (1769). The phrase (somewhat mangled) has also been attributed to the King James Version of the Bible (1611): "Myles Ambrose has been around this town . . . since as the Bible says, the *mind of man runneth not to the contrary . . . .*" *Fourth Annual Judicial Conference of the United States Court of Appeals for the Federal Circuit,* 112 F.R.D. 439, 550 (1986) (Dave Busby introducing Myles Ambrose).

As in that last example, the phrase is sometimes misrendered *mind of man* (suggesting that no one could *think* otherwise) instead of *memory of man* (suggesting that no one could *remember* otherwise)—e.g.: "We have been operating on this premise for so long that the *mind* [read *memory*] *of a man runneth not to the contrary.*" *Okaw Drainage Dist. v. National Distillers & Chem. Corp.,* 882 F.2d 1241, 1245 (7th Cir. 1989) (quoting Mills, J., the trial judge). Note also that the phrase is *memory of man* (i.e., mankind or humankind), not *memory of a man,* as in the preceding example. See SEXISM (B).

memory, sound mind and. See **mind and memory.**

mendacity; mendicity. The former is deceptiveness, the latter beggarliness.

mens rea; actus reus. *Actus reus* = a wrongful act; the element of conduct, as opposed to the mental state, that must be proved to convict a criminal defendant. *Mens rea* = the state of mind that the prosecution, to secure a conviction, must prove that a defendant had when committing a crime. Although these dovetailing TERMS OF ART—both deriving from LAW LATIN—have traditionally been basic to criminal law, one writer cautions against slavish adherence: "This way of dividing up the general elements in crimes is rather 'rough and ready,' and is certainly a better servant than master." Andrew Ashworth, *Principles of Criminal Law* 78 (1991).

Mens rea does not bear a literal meaning (i.e., "bad mind" or "guilty mind"), because one who breaks the law even with the best of motives still commits a crime: "The language is no longer meant to convey the idea of general malevolence characteristic of early common-law usage." Peter W. Low et al., *Criminal Law: Cases and Materials* 627 (1982). The true translation is criminal intention or recklessness. Words typically imposing a *mens-rea* requirement include *willfully, maliciously, fraudulently, recklessly, negligently, scienter, corruptly, feloniously,* and *wantonly.* See **mental element.**

Some writers wisely hyphenate the phrase when it appears as a phrasal adjective—e.g.: "Such an offense does not have the normal *mens-rea* requirement . . . ." Rollin M. Perkins & Ronald N. Boyce, *Criminal Law* 716–17 (3d ed. 1982)./ "[I]t is important to treat common-law *mens-rea* terms, and indeed much of the language of the law, as words that must be translated into ordinary language before one can learn what they mean and how to use them." Peter W. Low et al., *Criminal Law: Cases and Materials* 204–05 (1982). See PHRASAL ADJECTIVES (B).

mental attitude is a common REDUNDANCY—e.g.: "What lifts ordinary negligence into gross negligence is the *mental attitude* [read *mental state*] of the defendant."

mental illness; mental disorder; disease of the mind. The McNaghten rules (q.v.) refer to a "defect of reason, from disease of the mind," a phrase that doctors no longer use. Instead, doctors tend to speak nowadays of *mental illness* or *mental disorder,* the latter being the broader of the two, encompassing any disorder of mind. But neither *mental illness* nor *mental disorder* is precisely synonymous with *disease of the mind,* which includes physically based pathologies such as cerebral arteriosclerosis (diminishing the flow of blood to the brain).

Thus, when it comes to applying the McNaghten rules, and getting expert witnesses to have a common understanding of what they are talking about, "the practical legal position is very confused." Glanville Williams, *Textbook of Criminal Law* 593 (1978). Cf. **insanity.**

mental element is a phrase that criminal-law writers often use synonymously with *mens rea,* q.v.

mentee. See -EE.

mercantile is a FORMAL WORD that is equivalent to *commercial.*

merchantable. See **marketable.**

merciament. See **amercement.**

mercilessly. See **unmercilessly.**

mercy killing. See **euthanasia.**

mere right (= a right without possession) is a LOAN TRANSLATION of the LAW LATIN *jus merum,* which appeared in LAW FRENCH as *meer dreit.*

meretricious (= alluring by false show) has not lost its strong etymological connection with the Latin word for "prostitute" (*meretrix*). A *meretricious marriage* is one that involves either two people of the same sex or lack of capacity on the part of one party. E.g., "If he is right in his contention that the respondent is a man, the ceremony of marriage in this case was in fact, if not in intention, a mere sham and the resulting 'marriage' not merely a void but a *meretricious* marriage, which could not in any circumstances give rise to anything remotely matrimonial in character." (Eng.) For a humorous misuse of the word, see MALAPROPISMS.

mergee is a mid-20th-century NEOLOGISM denoting a participant in a merger. E.g., "[I]n the event of a true statutory merger, the *mergee* corporation was entitled to the deductions of the other corporation." *E. & J. Gallo Winery v. Commissioner,* 227 F.2d 699, 703 (9th Cir. 1955)./ "Downs continued to solicit each of the *mergees* and made written reports more than five years after the first contact . . . ." *Cherry, Bekaert & Holland v. Downs,* 640 F. Supp. 1096, 1099 (W.D. N.C. 1986). See -EE.

merger. A. And *consolidation; amalgamation.* These terms are distinct in denoting types of corporate restructuring. In a *merger,* one company is absorbed by another, the latter retaining its own name, identity, articles of incorporation, and bylaws, and acquiring all the assets, liabilities, and powers of the absorbed company, which ceases its separate existence. In a *consolidation,* the corporations that are absorbed into a new entity lose their previous identities to form a new corporation.

In English law, the different forms of corporate union are referred to as *amalgamation.* As one writer states in recommending this word, "It is convenient to have some such inclusive term for corporate unions, as they have many elements in common." H.W. Ballantine, *Ballantine on Corporations* § 288, at 680–81 (rev. ed. 1946).

B. And *bar.* In the law of procedure, *merger* describes the effect of a judgment for the plaintiff. Such a judgment extinguishes any claim that was the subject of an earlier lawsuit and merges it into the judgment, so that the plaintiff's rights are confined to enforcing the judgment. *Bar,* on the other hand, describes the effect of a judgment on the merits for a defendant. Such a judgment extinguishes any claim that was the subject of a lawsuit in which judgment was rendered, including parts of that claim that were not raised in the earlier lawsuit.

C. Of Law and Equity. In traditional legal idiom, the joining of the procedural aspects of law and equity is termed "merger"—e.g.: "The history of the *merger* of law and equity, first in New York under the Old Code, and later in twenty-nine other states and territories in which codes similar to the New York Code were adopted, and in England by the Judicature Acts, which took effect in 1875, has been covered in Chapter II." William F. Walsh, *A Treatise on Equity* 96 (1930). Actually, despite Walsh's suggestion that merger did not occur in England until 1875, the fusion of law and equity began in that country with the Common Law Procedure Act 1854.

D. *Doctrine of merger.* This phrase means that something of greater importance subsumes something of lesser importance, but the context determines the precise signification. In the law of contract, for example, *merger* refers to the substitution of a superior form of contract for an inferior form, as when a written contract supersedes all oral agreements and prior understandings. Hence, a *merger clause* (also known as an *integration clause*) states expressly that the contract has this effect.

In criminal law, under the *doctrine of merger*—abolished in some jurisdictions, as in England—a charge of attempt would be defeated if the evidence showed that the defendant had actually committed a felony.

In the property lawyer's vocabulary, the word *merger* denotes the doctrine that, if a greater estate and a lesser estate in the same land become one person's property, the lesser estate is destroyed or "merged" into the greater.

merger clause. See **integration clause.**

merge together is a REDUNDANCY. See **together.**

merit takes the preposition *in* or *to,* not *of.* "There is no *merit of* [read *merit to*] this contention."

meritless. See **unmeritorious.**

meritorious usu. refers to parties' claims in AmE, and not to the parties themselves. This restriction does not hold in BrE: "There are no doubt a considerable number of cases in which an *unmeritorious* defendant escapes and a *meritorious* plaintiff suffers hardship because of his actions being statute-barred owing to bad advice on the law from his trade union or solicitor." (Eng.)

merits is often used as an ellipsis for *merits of the case* (= the substantive considerations to be taken into account in making a decision, in contrast to extraneous or technical points, esp. of procedure), as in the phrase *trial on the merits.*

mesalliance; misalliance. *Mesalliance,* a GALLICISM, means "a marriage with a social inferior; a morganatic marriage." *Misalliance* is best kept distinct in the senses (1) "an improper alliance"; or (2) "a marriage in which the partners are ill-suited for each other." A *mesalliance /may-zahl-**yahns**/* may be a happy marriage, but a *misalliance /mis-ə-**lɪ**-əns/* never is.

mesne */meen/* denotes the idea of occupying a middle position, and has two important senses in the law. Usually the word is used in historical contexts. In feudal contexts, a *mesne lord* is one who holds an estate of a superior lord while being a lord over tenants. The estate of a mesne lord was termed the *mesnalty.* The *OED* notes that *mesne tenant* is "inaccurately used to denote one who holds of a mesne lord."

Mesne may also signify "occurring or performed at a time intermediate between two dates" (*OED*). Thus *mesne profits* are the profits of an estate received by a tenant in wrongful possession between two dates. E.g., "The court has the power of allowing the verdict to be given for *mesne profits.*" *Mesne process* = all process issued between the commencement of a lawsuit by the initial writ or pleading and the termination of the suit. E.g., "The writ upon which the plaintiff was arrested on *mesne process* was of no effect."

mesonomic. See **zygnomic.**

Messrs. is the abbreviation for *Messieurs,* the plural of the French *Monsieur.* In English it acts as the plural of *Mr.* The feminine equivalents are *Mesdames* (*Mmes.*) for married women and *Mademoiselles* (*Mlles.*) for unmarried women. Fortunately, the feminine French forms are not a regular part of the English language. See SEXISM (D).

messuage /*mes*-*wij*/ "is usually understood to mean 'a house,' but it includes more than the actual buildings." Henry C. Richards & John P.H. Soper, *The Law and Practice of Compensation* 17 (n.d. [1898]). What else does it include? Generally any garden or orchard associated with the house and any outbuildings. If the term is used with the degree of particularity specified in its definition, then it may be justified in legal contexts. Often, however, one senses that it is a highfalutin LEGALISM for *house.* E.g., "The curtilage is a garden, yard, field, or piece of void ground lying near and belonging to the *messuage.*" (Eng.) See also **tenement.**

metalaw is a 20th-century NEOLOGISM meaning "a hypothetical legal code based on the principles underlying existing legal codes and designed to provide a framework of agreement between diverse legal systems (orig. conceived as between terrestrial and possible extraterrestrial beings)" (*OED*). The word, then, has a specific sense; it should not be used in vague, half-sensical ways.

METAPHORS. *A metaphor* is a figure of speech in which one thing is called by the name of something else, or is said to be that other thing. Unlike *similes,* which use *like* or *as,* metaphorical comparisons are implicit rather than explicit. (See SIMILES.) Skillful use of metaphor is one of the highest attainments of writing; graceless and even aesthetically offensive use of metaphors is one of the most common scourges of writing, and especially of legal writing characterized by PURPLE PROSE. Those who use metaphors unrestrainedly and ineffectively almost always fancy themselves supreme stylists; hence the problem of educating readers on the uses and abuses of metaphor is a delicate one, for the worst offenders are likely to consider themselves masterly artists.

A. Mixed and Mangled Metaphors. Lord Keith of Avonholm has shrewdly addressed the use of metaphors in legal writing: "A graphic phrase, or expression, has its uses even in a law report and can give force to a legal principle, but it must be related to the circumstances in which it is used." *White & Carter Councils, Ltd. v. McGregor,* [1962] A.C. 413, 438 (H.L.). The Law Lord displayed a great deal of insight in that passage, for the *vehicle* of the metaphor (i.e., the literal sense of the metaphorical language) must be consonant with the *tenor* of the metaphor (i.e., the ultimate, metaphorical sense), which is to say the means must fit the end. In the statement, *That lawyer's brief is a patchwork quilt without discernible design,* the composition of the brief is the tenor, and the quilt is the vehicle. It is the comparison of the tenor with the vehicle that makes or breaks a metaphor.

A writer would be ill advised, for example, to use rustic metaphors in a discussion of the problems of air pollution, which is essentially a problem of the bigger cities and outlying areas. Following are two characteristic specimens in which the vehicle of the metaphor is mismatched with the tenor: "By their very nature, the assumptions on which we proceed today cannot be cast in stone." (Things can be *cast* in iron or clay, but not in stone, though one may cast [i.e., throw] stones and things may be etched in stone.) / "If money drives the program, paperwork provides the tinder." (*Tinder* must start something, inflame it—paperwork is an ongoing and usu. a dull process.)

Yet the greater problem in using metaphors is that one metaphor should not crowd another. The purpose of an image is to fix the idea in the reader's or listener's mind; if disparate images appear in abundance, the audience is left confused or sometimes, at the writer's expense, kneeslapping. E.g., "*On the one hand,* the contract between the two is a *bipartite umbilical cord fed* by Medicare and Medicaid funds such that Lifetron can be properly termed a recipient of federal financial assistance . . . . *On the other hand,* the *parameters limned* by the Supreme Court . . . *constrain* us to hold that the actions of this private defendant cannot be fairly attributed to the state . . . ." *Frazier v. Board of Trustees,* 765 F.2d 1278, 1295 (5th Cir. 1985). This cascade of metaphors bothers the intelligent reader far more than it helps. In fact, the metaphors make no sense: umbilical cords feed, they are not fed; and exactly what shape a bipartite umbilical cord would assume we have no idea, esp. if it is (rather grotesquely) resting on a hand.

Badly used metaphors are more forgivable in oratory than in writing, for with the latter the perpetrator can be charged with malice aforethought. Oratorical falls from grace are legion. Some time ago a newspaper article collected some of the oratorical gems of Michigan legislators. E.g., "This bill goes to the very heart of the moral fiber of the human anatomy."/ "From now on, I am watching everything you do with a fine-toothed comb." The following classic illustration comes from a speech by Boyle Roche in the Irish Parliament, delivered in about 1790: "Mr. Speaker, I smell a rat. I see him floating in the air. But mark me, sir, I will nip him in the bud." (Quoted by Jocelyn Simon, *English Idioms from the Law,* 76 Law Q. Rev. 283, 287 (1960).) Perhaps the supreme example of the comic misuse of metaphor occurred in the speech of a scientist who referred to "a virgin field pregnant with possibilities."

Legal writers must not play fast and loose with their images; they are not, like their speaking counterparts, to be forgiven so easily. To use metaphors badly in prose is amateurish and ultimately embarrassing. Writers should use metaphors sparingly, should wait for the aptest moments, elsewhere using a more straightforward style. The disadvantages in not doing so are easily enough demonstrated. Anyone who reads the following examples, and occasionally rereads them, is likely never to acquire the bad habit:

- "There are but two *conduits* or *cables,* the statutes of wills, and of descents and distributions, by which the *Grim Reaper* may at the moment of and *by the stroke of his scythe flash* the transfer and transmission of property and estate to the quick from the dead." (The Grim Reaper flashes a scythe by means of a conduit or cable?)
- "Although Sutter has *clothed* her complaint in the *garb* of a civil-rights action, we agree with the district court that her claim *boils down* to a demand for custody of the child." (A complaint clothed in a certain garb is boiled down?)
- "We need not explore the *full depths* of those issues, however. Our case may be resolved on two *narrower grounds.*" (One might, presumably, avoid full depths by standing on narrow grounds, but not on narrower grounds. Narrower than what?)
- "The court has a *voracious appetite* for judicial activism in its Fourth Amendment jurisprudence, at least when it comes to restricting the constitutional rights of citizens." (Do judges who restrict constitutional rights of citizens feed on judicial activism? The metaphor makes no sense.)
- "Equal protection has become a *stout shield* to protect against the discriminatory *bite* of governmental classification." (What does a stout shield look like? Short and fat? And are shields ordinarily, or ever, used against biting attackers?)
- "To assume competency is to let the *enigmas* of psychology *breathe* our *miasmic* decree." (How do enigmas breathe miasmas?)
- "The rules of offer and acceptance have a *grip on the vision* and indeed on the affections held by no other rules of law, real or pseudo." (One cannot grip a vision.)
- "There is a long leap between a public right under the First Amendment to attend trials and a public right under the First Amendment to see a given trial televised. It is a leap that is not supported by history." (What leaps are supported by history?)
- "The legal foundation upon which *Schneckloth* rides is fiction." (A case does not "ride upon" a foundation, esp. a fictional one.)

Yet another pitfall for the unwary is the cliché-metaphor that the writer renders incorrectly. E.g., things may be *stretched to the breaking point,* but not: "Cases that take years to prepare, involve reams of documents and hundreds of hours of depositions, and require weeks or months to try have *taxed* the resources of our judicial system to the *breaking point.*" See SET PHRASES & ILLOGIC (E).

B. Legal Metaphors. The legal idiom abounds in special metaphors not used elsewhere. For example, statutes of limitation are said to *run,* plaintiffs *shoulder* the burden of proof, plaintiffs have *clean* or *unclean hands,* defendants are sometimes *insulated* from liability, agents may be *clothed* with the *mantle* of apparent authority, we have suits to *quiet* title, government action may have a *chilling effect* on First Amendment rights, and we may sue to remove a *cloud* on title. (See CLICHÉS.) These are dormant rather than active metaphors; originally they were creatively expressive, whereas now they are merely expressive. When used with other metaphors, however, they may clash; hence writers must try to be sensitive to the compatibility of dormant with active metaphors.

C. The Overwrought Metaphor. Extended metaphors have been out of fashion for more than a century. The most we can tolerate nowadays is the two-part metaphor: "We are faced with the further problem of *fitting the foot* of modern-day usage and understanding of gifts of intangible personal property through survivorship arrangements *into the rigid shoe* of common-law principles." Even that type of sustained metaphor strikes most readers as facile. Here are more examples of metaphorical surfeit: "Notwithstanding Golemis's alarming *diagnosis* of the *maladies* . . . the ordinance has caused, he has come to the wrong place for an immediate *antidote.* The plaintiff's present effort to use a federal venue as an *emetic* against the municipal action which (in his view) has tainted the *eupepsia* of his property rights cannot be *swallowed* . . . . [H]e must look to the Rhode Island courts for a *cure.*" *Golemis v. Kirby,* 632 F. Supp. 159, 164–65 (D.R.I. 1985)./ "Summary judgment is a *potent weapon,* and courts must be mindful of its *aims* and *targets* and beware of *overkill* in its use."/ "We find no such *hybrid* instrument, with its *dual personality,* self-executing and shifting gears, *chameleon characteristics* and *Phoenix-like qualities* as yet unknown to the law."/ "It is an error in one of these findings that *tars* the finding of likelihood of confusion with the *brush* of clear error."

mete out, v.t. (from an old word for "measure") is the correct phrase, not *meet out* or *meat out.* E.g., "Washington's penalty . . . marks the first time the maximum fine of $10,000 has been *meeted out* [read *meted out*] since O'Brien asked the NBA board of governors to expand his disciplinary powers." Nancy Scannell, *Violence in the NBA: Getting Worse?* Wash. Post, 16 Dec. 1977, at E1./ "For Europeans, the death sentences *meeted out* [read *meted out*] to 'rioters' . . . [have] an all too familiar ring." Robert Mauthner, *Salvage from the Wreckage,* Fin. Times, 20 June 1989, at I23.

metes and bounds; butts and bounds; lines and corners. All three phrases are used in deeds and surveys to describe the territorial limits of property; the surveyor measures distances and angles from designated landmarks and in relation to adjoining properties.

The most familiar phrase is *metes and bounds,* in which *mete* derives from the Latin term *meta* (= a mark or object around which chariots turned in a Roman race-course). At common law, *mete* denoted a visible object in line with a boundary, such as a stone or tree, showing where a line ended.

The term *butts* "is very obscurely defined in the old books." 1 Alexander M. Burrill, *A Law Dictionary and Glossary* 235 (2d ed. 1859). Today that could be held to include the *OED,* over which Burrill's treatment is an improvement: "In lands of ordinary rectangular shape, *butts* are the lines at the *ends* (Fr. *bouts*), and bounds are those on the *sides,* or *sidings,* as they were formerly termed. . . . But in lands of irregular shape, *butts* are the angular points, or corners, where the boundary lines stop and turn in a new direction." *Id.*

methinks is a creaky ARCHAISM used primarily by the lone judge in dissent—e.g.: "*Methinks* his silence indicates that Baskin had no non-gender-based reason for his action and his superiors well knew it." *Smith v. Texas Dep't of Water Resources,* 818 F.2d 363, 368 (5th Cir. 1987) (Politz, J., dissenting).

Only in allusions to *Hamlet* is the word perhaps appropriate—e.g.: "[*M*]*ethinks* my brothers and sisters protest too much about their general discussion of the writ." *Kuhlmann v. Wilson,* 477 U.S. 436, 463 n.2 (1986) (Brennan, J., dissenting).

methodology is frequently misused for *method.* Correctly used, *methodology* means "the science or study of method." Here are examples of the misuse: "Because this case involves the role of depreciation rates and *methodologies* [read *methods*] in determining the revenue requirements of a regulated utility, we begin by briefly reviewing certain basic principles of regulatory ratemaking."/ "The recent decision in *Chevron* elaborates on these principles and sets out the appropriate *methodology* [read *method*] for ascertaining whether to afford deference to an agency's construction of its governing statute."/ "The passage enumerating the factors was meant to be an expression of the *methodology* [read *method*] to be used in deciding whether an activity should be held to be within the reach of that statute's imposition of liability."

Methodology is correctly used in the following example; the sentence was hard to come by: "Writing in a time in which *methodology in the social sciences* [i.e., the study of method in the social sciences] has become the prevailing approach, Professor von Mehren speaks of comparative study of law rather than of comparative law." (R. Pound)

mid; midst. See **amidst.**

midwife, v.t.; **midwive.** The first is the preferred form. E.g., "This may happen when a writing judge believes with heart and soul that his position is right, but he knows that his majority is shaky; here persuasiveness must *midwive* [read *midwife*] the opinion if it is to come into existence at all."

mien (= demeanor, appearance, bearing) often carries connotations of formidableness <his imposing mien>. The word is pronounced */meen/*.

migratory worker. See **undocumented alien.**

milieu is sometimes misspelled *mileau*. See, e.g., *New Eng. Patriots Football Club, Inc. v. University of Colo.*, 592 F.2d 1196, 1198 (1st Cir. 1979).

The plural *milieus* is preferable to *milieux*—e.g.: "But marriages between first cousins are so usual that in many *milieus* they are almost normal." Max Radin, *The Law and You* 42 (1948). See PLURALS (A).

military law. See **martial law.**

military testament. See **oral will.**

militate. See **mitigate.**

millennium [L. *mille* "thousand" + *annus* "year"] forms two plurals: *-ia* and *-iums*. The preferred plural is *-ia* in the AmE, and *-iums* in BrE; but either is acceptable on both sides of the Atlantic. See PLURALS (A).

The word is often deprived of one *-n-* and misspelled *millenium*—e.g.: "The irreparable injury rule has been a fixture of Anglo-American law for half a *millenium* [read *millennium*]." Douglas Laycock, *The Death of the Irreparable Injury Rule* vii (1991). In fact, this misspelling has even found its way into a proper name: the hotel across from the World Trade Center in New York City is called *The Millenium*. Perhaps that should be called not a proper name but an improper name.

millionaire is so spelled—not, like *questionnaire*, with *-nn-*. E.g., "[A] *millionnaire* [read *millionaire*] with a small pension could qualify for an adjustment under the ordinance." *Halstead v. City of Flint*, 338 N.W.2d 903, 905 (Mich. Ct. App. 1983). For another word susceptible to this problem—*doctrinaire*—see **doctrinal.**

mimic, v.t., makes *mimicking* and *mimicked*.

mind and memory is a common DOUBLET <of sound mind and memory> in the context of establishing testamentary capacity. Mellinkoff calls it "a snatch of confusing nonsense . . . . As in England, American lawyers have long recognized that they were using *memory* here in a special way, in the sense of understanding or mind, and that *mind and memory* did no more for testamentary capacity than *mind* alone." David Mellinkoff, *The Language of the Law* 333, 335 (1963).

The snare lies in failing to recognize the phrase as an archaic doublet, and in misunderstanding it as setting forth independent criteria for judging testamentary capacity, since historically *mind* = *memory*. Especially in writing to be read by nonlawyers (as in jury instructions), the second half of this doublet should be avoided. As the law is currently understood, one may be very forgetful and still be "of sound mind and memory." *Sound mind* is sufficient and far less confusing.

In wills, the recitation that the testator is of *sound mind and memory* is falling into disuse for an additional reason: it not only does no good, it may even raise suspicions about mental capacity. See Thomas E. Atkinson, *Handbook of the Law of Wills* 819 (2d ed. 1953). See DOUBLETS, TRIPLETS, AND SYNONYM-STRINGS.

MINGLE-MANGLE, known in erudite circles as *macaronism, soraismus,* or *cacozelia,* was a common vice of language in early English opinions. It consists in English larded with Latin or French, as in the following example from *Weaver v. Ward,* decided by the King's Bench in 1616:

> The defendant pleaded . . . that he was . . . a trained soldier in London, of the band of one Andrews captain; and so was plaintiff, and that they were skirmishing with their musquets charged with powder for their exercise in re militari, against another captain and his band; and as they were so skirmishing, the defendant casualiter et per infortunium et contra voluntatem suam, in discharging his piece, did hurt and wound the plaintiff, which is the same, etc. absque hoc, that he was guilty aliter sive alio modo.
>
> Hob. 134, 80 Eng. Rep. 284.

For modern legal readers, mingle-mangle makes for fascinating, if not entirely comprehensible, reading. Following is another Latin-English example, this also from a well-known torts case: "Trespass quare vi & armis clausum fregit, & herbam suam pedibus conculcando consumpsit in six acres. The defendant pleads, that he hath an acre lying next the said six acres, and upon it a hedge of thorns, and he cut the thorns, and they ipso invito fell upon the plaintiff's land." *The Case of the Thorns,* 6 Ed. 4, Mich. 7a, pl. 18 (1466) (summarized thus in *Bessey v. Olliot & Lambert,* T. Raym. 467 (1681)).

English-French was another mongrel dialect of the law: one early report referred to a prisoner being sentenced who "ject un Brickbat a le dit Justice que narrowly mist, & pur ceo immediately fuit Indictment drawn per Noy envers le prisoner, & son dexter manus ampute & fix al Gibbet sur que luy mesme immediatement hange in presence de Court." (Quoted fr. Dyer's Reports 188b

(1688) in Frederick Pollock, *A First Book of Jurisprudence* 301 (4th ed. 1918).)

The 17th-century English reporters most inclined to engage in mingle-mangle were Rolle and Latch. See LAW LATIN & LAW FRENCH.

minify. See **minimize.**

minim (= something minute) is sometimes used in the context of the maxim *de minimis non curat lex.* E.g., "The *minim* of the injury here obscures and tempts neglect of the importance of the issue." See ***de minimis.***

minima. See **minimum.**

minimal; minimum, adj. Both words are used adjectivally, *minimum* as an attributive adjective in phrases such as *minimum wage.* If there is a valid nuance distinguishing these two adjectival forms, it is that *minimal* = few, little, smallest <with minimal disturbance> <minimal support> <minimal objections>, whereas *minimum,* adj., = consisting in the fewest necessary things, or the least acceptable or lawful amount <minimum contacts as a basis for jurisdiction> <minimum wage>. E.g., "Most statutes set up *minimum* requirements with respect to the corporate name."/ "Congress accommodated state fears by allowing the states to retain *minimal* residency requirements." See **maximum.**

minimalize. See **minimize.**

minimize; minify. These words have distinct meanings, and the latter is too much neglected. Properly, *minimize* = to keep to a minimum, and *minify* = to belittle, degrade; to represent something as smaller than it really is. *Minimalize* is not a word.

minimum, n. Pl. *minima.* E.g., "In so ruling, however, the Court did not dispense with the Sixth Amendment's substantive *minima* of effectiveness . . . ." *U.S. v. Owens,* 484 U.S. 554, 568 n.1 (1988) (Brennan, J., dissenting)./ "The deprivation of his protected property interest was accomplished without adherence to due process *minimums* [read *minima*]." See **maximum.**

minions of the law is a CLICHÉ referring to police officers or other law-enforcement officers.

miniscule is one of the commonest misspellings in legal texts, the correct spelling being *minuscule.* E.g., "There has recently come into the possession of Lincoln's Inn, as the gift of the author's granddaughter, his working copy of the first edition covered and interleaved with *miniscule* [read *minuscule*] writing." P.V. Baker, Book Review, 103 Law Q. Rev. 650, 651 (1987). The word derives from the word *minus,* and has nothing to do with the prefix *mini-*. The counterpart—a rarity—is *majuscule.*

minister. See **administer.**

minor. See **child.**

minority. A. And *infancy; nonage.* These synonyms denote the period during which a person is underage—that is, when a person has not yet reached full age and therefore cannot vote, buy alcoholic beverages, and the like. Notably, a person may be underage for some purposes (such as buying liquor) but not for others (such as voting).

Minority, which is more generally used than either of the others, is the preferable term. It encompasses the full range of persons who fall into underage categories: children, infants, juveniles, young persons, and (in Scotland) pupils. (See **child & infant.**) *Minority* is much more common in general usage than its antonym, *majority* (= full age), which is largely confined to legal contexts. See **age of capacity & majority (D).**

Infancy is likely to mislead many readers, and nonage is obscure to many lawyers as well as nonlawyers. See **infancy, infant & nonage.**

B. Singular or Plural? See **majority (B)** & SYNESIS.

minor woman is an odd combination of EUPHEMISM, MISCUE, and near-OXYMORON that displaces a more natural wording such as *girl, female minor,* or, if the sex of the person is obvious, *minor.* E.g., "[H]is reference to a 'mature' woman means he does not favor the right of a *minor woman* [read *minor*] to choose to have an abortion without parental or judicial consent." Susan Yoachum, *Wilson Campaign Sticks to Familiar Topics,* S.F. Chronicle, 2 Nov. 1990, at A21.

minuscule. So spelled. See **miniscule.**

minutia (= a trivial detail; a trifling matter) is the singular of the plural *minutiae.* Though much less common than the plural form, *minutia* is hardly unknown. Unfortunately, almost every time it appears it is a misuse for the plural—e.g.: "Once one wades through the unhelpful *minutia* [read *minutiae*] three legal arguments remain . . . ." *Lentomyynti Oy v. Medivac, Inc.,* 997 F.2d 364, 370 (7th Cir. 1993).

Then again, the plural form of the noun is sometimes mistakenly coupled with a singular verb—e.g.: "[W]e conclude . . . that such *minutiae is* [read *are*] without consequence in determining priority of jurisdiction." *A.E. Staley Mfg. Co. v. Swift & Co.,* 399 N.E.2d 339, 341 (Ill. App. Ct. 1980)./ "We hardly believe such *minutiae is* [read *are*] cause for finding that a wrong principle of law was employed." *Jackson County Bd. of Comm'rs v. State Tax Comm'n,* 343 N.W.2d 255, 260 (Mich. Ct. App. 1983).

Mirandize (= to read an arrestee rights under *Miranda v. Arizona,* 384 U.S. 436 (1966)) has become common as police-officer slang in the U.S.; it is therefore coming to be adopted by some criminal lawyers and even judges—e.g.: "First, defendant claims that the trial court erred in ruling inadmissible his exculpatory statements made to the officer after defendant was arrested and *Mirandized.*" *People v. Barrick,* 654 P.2d 1243, 1253 (Cal. 1982) (en banc)./ "So, too, inculpatory words from the suspect, though duly *Mirandized,* might be suppressed as 'fruit' of the unlawful arrest." H. Richard Uviller, *Seizure by Gunshot,* 14 N.Y.U. Rev. L. & Soc. Change 705, 708 (1986)./ "They are read their rights (*'mirandized'*) and interrogated . . . ." Robin T. Lakoff, *Talking Power: The Politics of Language in Our Lives* 87 (1990).

Surely, though, this -IZE neologism is a blemish in place of some acceptable periphrasis, such as *to read* (arrestees) *their Miranda rights.* Surprisingly, 23 percent of the usage panelists for the *Harper Book of Contemporary Usage* (2d ed. 1985) consider the word "a useful addition to the language." A more circumspect 77 percent disapprove.

misadventure = (1) a mishap or misfortune; or (2) homicide committed accidentally by a person doing a lawful act and having no intention to injure. The word now appears most frequently in the phrases *death by misadventure* and *homicide by misadventure.*

misalliance. See **mesalliance.**

misappropriate; appropriate, v.t. The former means "to apply (as another's money) dishonestly to one's own use." E.g., "It was held to be gross negligence for an administratrix to permit an attorney in fact to handle an estate for nine years without an accounting and settlement, during which time he *misappropriated* funds."/ "If he took title in his own name in bad faith, intending to *misappropriate* the property, he is liable for the full amount of the mortgage and interest thereon."

Appropriate has a more neutral, nonaccusatory connotation. Still, in meaning "to take from a particular person or organization for a particular purpose," it is tinged with some of the negative connotations made explicit in *misappropriate.* See **appropriate & embezzle.**

misbelief. See **disbelief.**

miscarriage. See **abortion.**

miscellaneous must be followed by a plural COUNT NOUN <miscellaneous charges>; it does not work with an abstract mass noun <miscellaneous legislation>. Though one might refer to *miscellaneous languages* (and thereby include Chinese, English, French, Thai, and Vietnamese), it makes no sense to write *miscellaneous contract language,* as in Mark M. Grossman, *The Question of Arbitrability* 57 (1984) (section title).

mischief is a slight ARCHAISM as lawyers commonly use it, that is, to denote "a condition in which a person suffers a wrong or is under some hardship, esp. one that a statute seeks to remove or for which equity provides a remedy." E.g., "It was permissible to consider what the law was before the statute, what *'mischief'* the statute was meant to remedy, and what the statute actually said . . . ." Theodore F.T. Plucknett, *A Concise History of the Common Law* 335 (5th ed. 1956).

From this use of *mischief*—common esp. in the context of statutory construction—has arisen the phrase *mischief rule,* known also as the *rule in Heydon's case* ([1584] 3 Co. Rep. 7a). That rule encourages judges construing an ambiguous statute to consider to what "mischief" the statute was addressed and then to adopt an interpretation that will curtail the mischief and advance the remedy. The *mischief rule* is often contrasted with two other approaches to statutory construction: the *golden rule* (q.v.) and the *plain-meaning rule* (or, as it is termed in BrE, *literal interpretation*).

mischievious is a common misspelling and mispronunciation of *mischievous.* Cf. **grievous.**

misconcept should not displace *misconception,* the ordinary word that is (unlike the shorter form) recognized as a living word in English-language dictionaries—e.g.: "The 'impeach' *misconcept* [read *misconception*] was the judge's, not counsel's." *In re Jose S.,* 144 Cal. Rptr. 309, 313 (Ct. App. 1978)./ "Another *misconcept* [read *misconception*] is that it is necessary for the airplane to have a relatively-high pitch altitude in order for it to stall." *New Hampshire Ins. Co. v. U.S.,* 641 F. Supp. 642, 646 (D.P.R. 1986).

misconduct in office; official misconduct. These synonymous phrases refer to the common-law misdemeanor consisting in a public officer's corrupt violation of his or her duties by malfeasance (q.v.), misfeasance, or nonfeasance (q.v.). Other synonymous expressions include *misbehavior in office, malconduct in office, malpractice in office, misdemeanor in office, corruption in office,* and *official corruption.* Cf. **malversation.**

MISCUES. A miscue is an inadvertent misdirection that causes the reader to proceed momentarily with an incorrect assumption about how—in mechanics or in sense—a sentence or passage will end. The misdirection is not serious enough to cause a true AMBIGUITY because, on reflection, the reader can figure out the meaning. Thus:

> The court decided the question did not need to be addressed.

The mere omission of *that* after the verb *decided* induces the reader to believe that *the question* is the direct object—that is, to believe (if only for an immeasurably short moment) that the court decided the question. In fact, of course, the court decided not to decide the question.

Miscues are of innumerable varieties; the only consistent cure is for the editor or self-editor to develop a keen empathy for the reader. Part of what the editor or self-editor must do, then, is to approach the text as a stranger might. Further, though, a good edit must involve the kind of skeptical reading in which one imagines how one reader in ten might misread the sentence.

Following are discussions of six of the most common causes of miscues.

A. Unintended Word Association. Sometimes a word appearing late in a passage seems to echo an earlier word to which it really has no relation. In the following example, *barred,* in the final clause, suggests some relation to *disbarred* in the opening sentence: "[I]n 1948 he was found guilty of unprofessional conduct and *disbarred* for three years by a federal judge. The decision was appealed and reversed three years later. In 1958 Fisher, a thin-faced, thinning-haired socialite, was censured by the Illinois Supreme Court for actions against clients—but the Chicago Bar Association had asked that he be *barred* from practice for five years." Murray T. Bloom, *The Trouble with Lawyers* 158 (1970) (quoting an Illinois bar official).

Then again, sometimes the word association is extratextual. In the following examples, the following things occur on first reading: litigators try cases, clothes are laid down, flattery induces a woman to engage in sex, and somebody engages in murder attacks:

- "All litigators have had the experience of trying to settle cases before trial, starting trial, and then settling during trial." (What litigators do is *try cases.* So when the writer says, *All litigators have had the experience of trying . . . ,* the legal reader expects to read about some type of case that litigators try. In this particular sentence, *attempting* would probably be a better choice than *trying.*)
- "The Tudor justices enforced laws against Roman Catholic recusants, regulations *laying down the clothes* people might wear and the price they should pay for them . . . ." Alan Harding, *A Social History of English Law* 72 (1966). (Did 16th-century judges mandate nudity for Roman Catholics?)
- "Flattery induced a woman to submit to intercourse by pretending to perform a surgical operation. He was convicted of rape." Glanville Williams, *Textbook of Criminal Law* 514 (1978). (A man named Flattery committed a crime, but his name suggests the wile he might have used in committing it. The miscue might be removed by referring to *Mr. Flattery* instead of *Flattery.*)
- "Small-minded, episodic murder attacks the basis of our taken-for-granted values so fundamentally that it generates anxiety." David Canter, *Anxious, Appalled . . . But Still Drawn to Horror,* Sunday Times, 13 March 1994, at 4-6. (It looks on first reading as if the noun phrase *murder attacks* is the subject, but *murder* is the subject and *attacks* is the verb.)

B. Misplaced Modifiers. When modifying words are separated from the words they modify, readers have a hard time processing the information. Indeed, they are likely to attach the modifying language first to a nearby word or phrase—e.g.: "Ms. Connally knew Denotte before she had her surgical procedure on a casual basis." (The phrase *on a casual basis,* or perhaps *casually,* belongs after *Denotte;* otherwise, it sounds as if the surgical procedure was a casual one.)/ "The right to redeem collateral after default is available to the debtor unless otherwise agreed in writing after default." (In that sentence, the reader momentarily believes that the time when default becomes available is important; in fact, though, it is the right that is available. That is, we're not talking about the right to redeem *after default is available.* [Read: *After default, the right to redeem collateral is available to the debtor unless . . . .* Or: *After default, the debtor may redeem collateral unless . . . .*]) See MISPLACED MODIFIERS.

C. Remote Antecedents. "There are various reasons that juries hang, some better than others . . . ." Robin T. Lakoff, *Talking Power: The Politics of Language in Our Lives* 126 (1990). (The writer means *some reasons,* not *some juries,* but some readers will not see this immediately.)/ "Until recently, the inns showed themselves particularly ill-equipped to handle the overseas students, including many Africans and such future statesmen as Mr Nehru, who by 1960 made up two thirds of all those called to the English bar." Alan Harding, *A Social History of English Law* 389 (1966). (This sentence involves a REMOTE RELATIVE that makes Mr. Nehru sound like a very big man indeed.) See ANTECEDENTS, FALSE (B).

D. Failure to Hyphenate Phrasal Adjectives. The reason for hyphenating phrasal adjectives is precisely to avoid miscues: think of the difference between a *small-claims court* and a *(very) small claims court.* Other, less striking instances abound—e.g.: "The uncontroverted evidence establishes that Super Ships, Inc., never manufactured, sold, or distributed any asbestos containing products to Cereola." Unless the phrase *asbestos-containing products* is hyphenated thus, readers are likely to think at first that the company never manufactured or sold asbestos, as opposed to products containing asbestos. See PHRASAL ADJECTIVES.

E. Misleading Phraseology. In the following example, the phrase *make good*—in the sense "to indemnify"—is paired with *defalcations* (= failures to meet expectations or honor promises) in an odd way. The reader may think at first that the promisor is making defalcations that are good: "There is, however, nothing objectionable about a promise to *make good defalcations* for which the promisor is personally responsible . . . ." P.S. Atiyah, *An Introduction to the Law of Contract* 231 (3d ed. 1981).

Sometimes, as in the following example, the confusing syntax results from a preposition (*for*) that appears to have a single-word object (*which*), as opposed to a phrasal object (*which of several payment plans*): "Here there is no problem in using blanks for which of several payment plans the borrower wants to use." Barbara Child, *Drafting Legal Documents* 138 (2d ed. 1992).

Yet again, the first word in a participial phrase (*up the coast of New England*) sometimes seems to be a particle, i.e., a part of a verb (*blew up*): "The storm also blew up the coast of New England." John J. Goldman, *Northeast Slammed by Storm; 7 Killed,* Austin American-Statesman, 12 Dec. 1992, at A1.

F. Ill-Advisedly Deleted *that*. The widespread but largely unfounded prejudice against *that* leads many writers to omit it when it is necessary—e.g.:

- "In *Phillips,* the Illinois Supreme Court held hotels and hospitals were not in the business of transmitting messages under either the State or City messages tax." (Add *that* after *held.*)
- "In *Cox,* the court held a contract indemnifying a casualty company for all liability under the Structural Work Act was void as against public policy." (Add *that* after *held.*)
- "The court also pointed out an executor cannot appeal for the protection of the interests of a particular devisee or legatee who is able to take an appeal." (Add *that* after *pointed out.*)

See **that** (A).

G. Omitted Commas. See PUNCTUATION (C) (last par.).

H. Unsplit Infinitives. See HYPERCORRECTION (G).

misdemeanant (= one who has committed a misdemeanor) is the analogue of a *felon.* E.g., "It is immaterial, for technical purposes, whether a *misdemeanant* was principal at the fact or before the fact." J.W. Cecil Turner, *Kenny's Outlines of Criminal Law* 89 (16th ed. 1952)./ "Some statutes have provided a penalty for the criminal protector of a *misdemeanant.*" Rollin M. Perkins & Ronald N. Boyce, *Criminal Law* 726 n.34 (3d ed. 1982). Unlike *felon,* however, *misdemeanant* is little known outside the law.

Whether *convicted misdemeanant* is a REDUNDANCY is a close question; surely most legal readers would not think that it is: "A prosecutor clearly has a considerable stake in discouraging convicted *misdemeanants* from appealing and thus obtaining a trial de novo in the Superior Court."

Like *felon, misdemeanant* should not refer merely to one suspected or charged, as opposed to one who has been convicted: "The better rule seems to be that an officer is not justified in killing a mere *misdemeanant* [read *suspected misdemeanant*] to effectuate his arrests."

The *OED* includes also the lay sense "a person guilty of misconduct," but legal writers should avoid using this technical term in this overbroad sense.

misdemeano(u)r. **A. Spelling.** The *-our* is the British spelling, *-or* the American. (See -OR.) The word is archaically spelled *misdemesnors,* as in Blackstone: "[S]maller faults, and omissions of less consequence, are comprized under the gentler name of *'misdemesnors'* only." 4 William Blackstone, *Commentaries* 5 (1769).

B. Modern Uses. Before the distinction between felonies and misdemeanors was abolished by the Criminal Law Act 1967, English lawyers used *misdemeanour* (as they spelled it) to refer to any criminal offense that was neither a felony nor treason. In BrE, the word is primarily of historical interest. But most American jurisdictions retain the felony-misdemeanor distinction. See **felony.**

misdoubt, equivalent to *doubt,* is an unnecessary and confusing ARCHAISM. See **doubt.**

misfeasance. See **malfeasance.**

misfeasor (= one who commits a misfeasance) is the correct agent noun, but it is little used.

misinformation. See **disinformation.**

misjoinder = (1) in civil actions, the improper joinder of parties in an action; or (2) in criminal actions, the improper joinder of distinct offenses in a criminal prosecution. See **joinder.** Cf. **disjoinder.**

mislaid property. See **lost property.**

mislead. See **lead.**

misnomer (= the use of a wrong name) in law may mean "a mistake in naming a person or place," whereas in nonlegal contexts it usually refers to a misdescription of a thing. E.g., "A *misnomer* of the plaintiff in the petition does not ordinarily affect the rule that the running of the statute of limitations is interrupted by the filing of a suit."

MISPLACED MODIFIERS. When using participial forms (and especially when beginning a sentence with an *-ing* phrase), one must be sure that the noun introducing the clause that follows is what the participle modifies. Hence the preceding sentence would be incorrect if it read: "When using participial forms . . . , the noun in the main clause must be modified by the participle"—because this construction suggests that a *noun* (as opposed to a writer) can "use" a *participle.* Here is another example: "*After reading* that case, *the initial impulse* of the reader might well be to nominate it for the most arbitrary equal protection decision in recent times." Note the problem that remains here if we change the main clause to "the reader's initial impulse," where *impulse,* not *reader,* is still improperly the subject of the clause. Some of the pitfalls in this area are treated under DANGLERS and MISCUES (B).

The problem often crops up where the writer inserts a passive verb phrase after an introductory participial phrase. E.g., "In applying the intermediate standard of review, *the challenged statute must be analyzed* [read *the court must analyze the challenged statute*] to determine whether it furthers a substantial state interest."/ "In determining whether a foreign corporation should be required to defend itself in a suit in Texas arising out of a contract between it and a Texas corporation, *each case must be decided* [read *the courts must decide each case*] on its own facts." The problem is easily remedied by making certain that an *actor* or *agent* appears in the main clause, and that this actor or agent is the one *doing* something in the participial phrase.

Following is a spate of examples of some misuses to which English sentences are susceptible. Brief comments (in parentheses) are appended before each sentence is recast in an improved form:

- "Without alleging fraud, accident, or mistake, the writing must be the entire contract and parol evidence must be excluded." (It is not the *writing* that alleges, but the person who seeks to have parol evidence admitted.) [Read *Unless one alleges fraud, accident, or mistake, the writing must be the entire contract and parol evidence must be excluded.*]
- "Awaiting the uncertainties as to quantum of damages, the delay in recovery may increase them." (The *delay* awaits *uncertainties?*) [Read *By awaiting (the resolution of all?) uncertainties as to quantum of damages, one may increase, by the delay, the damages incurred.*]
- "No discussion of the subject would be complete without an analysis of *Dalcan v. Dalcan;* read literally, the Texas Supreme Court addresses only two issues in that case." (What is read *literally? Dalcan v. Dalcan,* or *the Texas Supreme Court?*) [Read *No discussion of the subject would be complete without an analysis of* Dalcan v. Dalcan; *read literally, that Texas Supreme Court case addresses only two issues.*]
- "Having determined that none of the appellants' complaints presents any reversible error, the judgment of the district court is affirmed." (The *judgment* has determined that there is no *reversible error?*) [Read *Having determined that none of the appellants' complaints presents any reversible error, we affirm the judgment of the district court.*]
- "Kast argues that, having found CPL 2.25B to be a procedural rule, we should nevertheless not give effect to the APA's procedural-rules exception from the informal rulemaking requirements." (*Having* can here look either way: to *Kast* or to *we.* See JANUS-FACED TERMS (B).) [Read *Kast argues that, even though we have found CPL 2.25B to be a procedural rule, we should not give effect to the APA's procedural-rules exception to the informal rulemaking requirements.*]

- "Treating the papers whereon the appeal was taken as a petition for writ of certiorari, certiorari is denied." (Is it the *certiorari* that does the *treating?*) [Read *Treating the papers whereon the appeal was taken as a petition for writ of certiorari, we deny certiorari.*]
- "Having held that the commission had the power and authority to pass the order, and that such action was not arbitrary or an abuse of discretion, it must follow that this is a suit against the state that should be dismissed." (What *it* was it that *held?*) [Read *Having held that the commission had the power and authority to pass the order, and that such action was not arbitrary or an abuse of discretion, the court must dismiss this suit against the state.*]
- "Applying the rule to this case, plaintiff was arrested on a facially valid warrant and she has therefore alleged no deprivation of a right secured by the Constitution and laws of the United States." (The court, not the *plaintiff,* applies *the rule to this case.*) [Read *In applying the rule to this case, we hold that the plaintiff was arrested on a facially valid warrant and therefore had no ground to allege deprivation of a right secured by the Constitution and laws of the United States.*]
- "The record contains ample evidence to support the jury's verdict; synopsizing, plaintiffs offered evidence that attributed price increases to price-fixing." (The court does the *synopsizing,* not the *plaintiffs.*) Actually, this sentence needs no participle—see the rewrite. [Read *The record contains ample evidence to support the jury's verdict. In short, the plaintiffs offered evidence that attributed price increases to price-fixing.*]
- "Paraphrasing the opinion of Judge Vann in *Tabor v. Hoffman,* the fact that an inspection of plaintiff's models may be by fair means does not justify obtaining the same by unfair means." (The *fact* does not do the *paraphrasing.*) [Read *To paraphrase the opinion of Judge Vann in* Tabor v. Hoffman, *the fact that an inspection of the plaintiff's models may be by fair means does not justify obtaining the same information by unfair means.*]
- "Reasoning that 4,000 acres were, as both parties agreed, cleared by July 1970 as required, and that the lease also required a minimum of 700 acres to be cleared 'each year thereafter,' the contractual obligation mathematically had to be completely performed by July 1975." (The *contractual obligation* does not engage in *reasoning.*) [Read *Reasoning that 4,000 acres were, as both parties agreed, cleared by July 1970 as required, and that the lease also required a minimum of 700 acres to be cleared 'each year thereafter,' we have calculated that the contractual obligation had to be completely performed by July 1975.*]

misprision. In legal usage, this word usually means "concealment of treason or of felony by one not participating in the treason or felony." The phrase most commonly occurs in the phrases *misprision of felony* and *misprision of treason.* The word may also refer, however, to seditious conduct itself or to an official's failure to perform duties of public office. More popularly, *misprision* means "misunderstanding, mistake."

Some writers misspell the word *misprison,* perhaps because they mistakenly associate *felony* with *prison* in the phrase *misprision of felony.* E.g., "A person commits *misprison* [read *misprision*] of felony when he witnesses or has knowledge of a felony being committed or about to be committed, and conceals or fails to give information as to such crime. *Misprison* [read *Misprision*] of felony cannot be committed if the crime is a misdemeanor . . . ." Garn H. Webb, *Plain Language Law: Criminal Wrongs (Crimes)* 122 (1981) (consistently misspelling the word thus).

misprisor, a NEOLOGISM not to be found in the *OED* or *W3,* is confined to senses derived from the phrase *misprision of felony*—e.g.: "A *'misprisor'* is said to be one who knows of the commission of a felony and does not report it to the proper authorities." Rollin M. Perkins & Ronald N. Boyce, *Criminal Law* 728–29 (3d ed. 1982).

misremember means "to remember incorrectly," not "to forget."

misrepresent = (1) to make an untrue statement of fact, usu. with knowledge of its falsity, without belief in its truth, or recklessly; or (2) to conduct malpractice while representing; (of a lawyer) to represent (a client) inadequately. Sense (2) is an odd, unidiomatic use: "Mrs. Johnson has sued Shearman & Sterling, contending she was *misrepresented* by the firm and demanding that it return the nearly $3 million she has already paid." Ronald Sullivan, *Firms Still Jarred by Fallout Over Johnson Will,* N.Y. Times, 31 March 1989, at 22.

misrepresentation. This word is broad enough to describe a fraudulent as well as a negligent or innocent statement. Some readers may be surprised to learn that, in the law of contracts, the word can also describe a factually accurate statement: "A person is guilty of *misrepresentation* though all the facts stated by him are true, if his statement is misleading as a whole because it does not refer to other facts affecting the weight of those stated." G.H. Treitel, *The Law of Contract* 353 (8th ed. 1991). See ***suggestio falsi*** & **representation.**

The phrase *false misrepresentation* is a fairly common REDUNDANCY—e.g.: "MOT alleged (in its complaint) that the Coffeys made several *false misrepresentations* [read *misrepresentations* or *false representations*] . . . ." *Moore, Owen, Thomas & Co. v. Coffey,* 992 F.2d 1439, 1445 (6th Cir. 1993).

misrepresentee is an -EE neologism that serves as a correlative to *misrepresentor* (as it is sometimes, alas, spelled)—e.g.: "The *misrepresentee* can, however, still rescind . . . ." G.H. Treitel, *The Law of Contract* 321 (8th ed. 1991). Cf. **representee.**

misrepresenter; misrepresentor. The *-er* spelling is better.

mistake. A. And *ignorance.* These words, some authorities have said, "do not import the same significance and should not be confounded. Ignorance implies a total want of knowledge in reference to the subject matter. Mistake admits a knowledge, but implies a wrong conclusion." *Hutton v. Edgerton,* 6 S.C. 485, 489 (1875). But other authorities say that "[a] mistake, in its legal sense, is 'that result of ignorance of law or of fact which has misled a person to commit that which, if he had not been in error, he would not have done.'" 3 G.W. Field, *Field's Lawyers' Briefs* 109 (1885) (quoting an old equity treatise). The latter authorities, in other words, reject the distinction as being "a refinement too subtle to be applied to the every-day business of life." *Schlesinger v. U.S.,* 1 Ct. Cl. 16, 25 (1863). And they are in the majority.

In fact, *ignorance* is the broader term—it includes *mistake:* "Every mistake involves ignorance but not *vice versa.* Ignorance is lack of true knowledge, either (1) because the mind is a complete blank or (2) because it is filled with untrue (mistaken) knowledge on a particular subject. The first variety, lack of knowledge without mistaken knowledge, may be called simple ignorance. The second variety, lack of true knowledge coupled with mistaken knowledge, is mistake. Ignorance is the genus of which simple ignorance and mistake are the species." Glanville Williams, *Criminal Law* 151–52 (2d ed. 1961).

B. And *frustration.* In the law of contract, *mistake* and *frustration* are "merely different ways of talking about the same thing—that is, the real world has in some way failed to correspond with the imaginary world hypothesized by the parties to the contract." Grant Gilmore, *The Death of Contract* 81 (1974). With either a mistake or frustration, consent may be nullified because of the extreme injustice of holding one of the parties to the contract. See **frustration & impossibility.**

C. *Mutual mistake.* See **mutual mistake.**

Mr. See **Messrs.**

mistreat; maltreat. Most writers on usage have held that there is a difference between these terms. "To *mistreat,*" write the Evanses, "is to treat badly or wrongly. The word suggests a deviation from some accepted norm of treatment and a deviation always towards the bad. To *maltreat,* to abuse, to handle roughly or cruelly, is to mistreat in a special way. The words are often used interchangeably (Horwill believes that Americans prefer *mistreat* and English *maltreat*), but *maltreat* is usu. restricted to the rougher forms of mistreating." Bergen Evans & Cornelia Evans, *A Dictionary of Contemporary American Usage* 302 (1957).

mistress. See **common-law wife.**

mistrial has two very distinct senses: (1) "a trial ending without a determination on the merits because of some procedural error or disruption during the proceedings"; or (2) "a trial that ends inconclusively because the jury cannot agree on a verdict." Sense (1) is common to AmE and BrE—e.g.: "When the judge discovered that Brumfield had hired a private detective to spy on the jurors and find out their opinions on smoking, he declared a *mistrial* and shoved Belli's case all the way to the bottom of his docket." Sense (2) occurs primarily in AmE—e.g.: "Bryant explained that the jury in a drug-possession case had been unable to agree, facing a *mistrial.*" Donald D. Jackson, *Judges* 92–93 (1974).

mistry, v.t., corresponds only to sense (1) of *mistrial,* q.v., but with an even stronger suggestion of fault—e.g.: "In the court below, the case was totally misconceived and *mistried.*" *Kramer v. Winslow,* 18 A. 923, 927 (Pa. 1890)./ "It is argued . . . that the case was *mistried* for this reason . . . ." *Van Riper v. U.S.,* 13 F.2d 961, 963 (2d Cir. 1926) (per L. Hand, J.)./ "The defendant then moved to dismiss the *mistried* RICO count . . . ." *U.S. v. Jenkins,* 902 F.2d 459, 462 (6th Cir. 1990).

misusage (= [1] mistreatment; or [2] the incorrect use of language) is increasingly misused for *misuse,* n. (= unauthorized use; misapplication)—e.g.: "[T]here has been no evidence presented as to actual confusion arising from the *misusage* [read *misuse*] of the APOLLO mark . . . ." *Apollo Distrib. Co. v. Jerry Kurtz Carpet Co.,* 696 F. Supp. 140, 142 (D.N.J. 1988).

mitigable is the correct form—not *mitigatable.* See -ATABLE.

mitigate; militate. *Mitigate* = to make less severe or intense; *militate* = to exert a strong influence. Here *mitigate* is correctly used: "In England, the power to *mitigate* the severity of the strict law was originally vested in the king."

Mitigate against is incorrect for *militate against;* Edmund Wilson called it "William Faulkner's favorite error." *The Bit Between My Teeth* 570 (1965). Faulkner's failings aside, the error is surprisingly common—e.g.: "[T]his factor *mitigates* [read *militates*] against immediate review." *Midway Mfg. Co. v. Omni Video Games, Inc.,* 668 F.2d 70, 72 (1st Cir. 1981)./ "Plaintiffs suggest there are two theories [that], if applied to this case, would *mitigate* [read *militate*] against the harsh application of the statute of limitations . . . ." *Cramsey v. Knoblock,* 547 N.E.2d 1358, 1364 (Ill. App. Ct. 1989).

Militate against, of course, is perfectly acceptable: "If the obvious facts *militate against* such an intention as expressed in the document, the court can act upon the real intention as found by the court." (Eng.)

In law, *militate* often takes *for* or *in favor of* as well as *against.* The *OED* calls this use "rare," but today it is common in legal writing: "He argues that the same values that do not require exhaustion of state remedies *militate in favor of* his contention that the Board's denial of his fitness be regarded as an administrative determination."/ "Factors are listed which *militate for* and *against* construing such a provision as creating a determinable fee."/ "These considerations *militate in favor of* academic freedom at colleges and universities."

Militate toward is unidiomatic: "Every incentive deriving from this decision would militate *toward* [read *in favor of*] the physicians' giving these tests."

mitigational. See **mitigatory.**

mitigation-of-damages doctrine, as a PHRASAL ADJECTIVE, should be hyphenated thus. A variant name for this doctrine—which requires a plaintiff, after an injury or breach of contract, to use ordinary care to alleviate its effects—is *avoidable-consequences doctrine.*

mitigatory; mitigative; mitigational. The first is the preferred form. *Mitigational,* a NEEDLESS VARIANT, sometimes appears where *mitigating* would be the natural word—e.g.: "The issue of ineffective assistance of counsel due to the absence of *mitigational* [read *mitigating*] evidence was first raised by the testimony of several witnesses during the November 16, 1984, evidentiary hearing . . . ." *Laws v. State,* 708 S.W.2d 182, 184 (Mo. Ct. App. 1986).

mittimus [L. "we send"] (= a warrant ordering a jailer to detain a person until ordered otherwise) is a Latin verb used in English as a noun. The plural is *mittimuses*—e.g.: "[T]hese items are for *mittimuses* issued after the examination is concluded . . . ." *U.S. v. Ewing,* 140 U.S. 142, 144 (1891). Through HYPERCORRECTION, some writers have mistakenly written *mittimi,* which is on the order of *ignorami* "In both of these *mittimi* [read *mittimuses*] the crime for which he was convicted was described as forgery . . . ." *Green v. State,* 113 F. Supp. 253, 256 (S.D. Me. 1953)./ "The jail *mittimi* [read *mittimuses*], the accuracy of which *are* [read *is*] not challenged, show that the defendant was represented by counsel and that he exercised his right of allocution." *People v. Montoya,* 640 P.2d 234, 237 (Colo. Ct. App. 1981). See HYPERCORRECTION (A). Cf. **ignoramus.**

mixed action. See **real action.**

M'Naghten. See **McNaghten.**

mob mouthpiece. See LAWYERS, DEROGATORY NAMES FOR (A).

mobocracy; ochlocracy. The latter is the better word in formal prose for "mob rule," the former being a MORPHOLOGICAL DEFORMITY. *Ochlocracy* has four centuries of use behind it, *mobocracy* but two. *Mobocracy* also retains a jocular overtone.

mockery. See **make a mockery of.**

modality (= a method or procedure) is a pretentious VOGUE WORD: "The mother's expert conceded a lack of awareness of any professional literature documenting the successful use of the *modalities* [read *methods*] he suggested in training the retarded to employ adequate parenting skills." *In re Karen "Y,"* 550 N.Y.S.2d 67, 69 (App. Div. 1989).

mode; module. There must be something in the root: these words, like *modality,* are inflated VOGUE WORDS.

In proper usage, *mode* means "manner," and *module* means "a unit of size." President George Bush often entered the "*mode* mode," as when he told a crowd in Los Angeles: "I am not here in the *mode* of politics, I am not here in the *mode* of partisanship, I am not here in the *mode* of blame. I am here to learn from the community." Robert B. Gunnison & Susan Yoachum, *Bush Visits Riot Zone,* San Francisco Chronicle, 8 May 1992, at A1. Such talk proved fruitful for Russell Baker's lively column in *The New York Times:* "President Bush says he is about to enter 'campaign mode.' Does this mean America will then have president *à la mode?* Absolutely not. Do you think the President is a slice of pie? This is the same answer I had from Mr. Bush's mode handler . . . . The mode Mr. Bush will enter is not a dessert, but a new technological product of the space program. Space-news fans will have noticed that multitudes of modes pour out of NASA press releases." Russell Baker, *In the Mode Mood,* N.Y. Times, 15 Aug. 1992, at 15.

modern-day is invariably inferior to *modern*—e.g.: "Punitive damages . . . are a *modern-day* [read *modern*] analog of 13th century amercements." *Browning-Ferris Indus. of Vt., Inc. v. Kelco Disposal, Inc.,* 492 U.S. 257, 268 (1989).

modernly (= in modern times) is accurately described by the *OED* as being "now rare"; more precisely, it might have stated "now rare, except in law." E.g., "*Modernly,* it is doubtful that *McCardle* would be sustained."/ "*Modernly,* the potential numerosity and severity of actions involving drinking drivers has become too serious to be ignored."/ "Chancery has ceased for long ages to issue new writs whereby supposed wrongs could be cured; such objectives are *modernly* to be accomplished by legislation."

Modifiers, Misplaced. See MISPLACED MODIFIERS.

module. See **mode.**

modus operandi (= a method of operating; a manner of procedure) is often a highfalutin substitute for *method.* Yet it is well established. Pl. *modi operandi.*

The phrase is sometimes misrendered *mode of operandi.* For humorous headnotes using *motor operandi,* see *U.S. v. Aguirre-Valenzuela,* 700 F.2d 161, 161 (Cir. 1983).

moiety. *Moiety,* a legal and literary ARCHAISM, does not, strictly speaking, mean "a small segment or portion," as some writers assume; rather, it means "half." This word should be part of the lawyer's recognition vocabulary, but not of one's working vocabulary, for *half* is the preferable and ordinary word, and the SLIPSHOD EXTENSION of *moiety* makes the word ambiguous. E.g., "We believe that in contributing the use of his *moiety* [read *half*] in the automobile, he was in fact furnishing the automobile to Clarice, a member of his family."/ "The testator devised lands to his wife for life, and at her death one to his heirs and the other *moiety* [read *half*] to his wife's heirs, as she might appoint."

But is *half* really the right word in the two examples just quoted? The *OED* notes that "loosely," the word *moiety* may denote "one of two (occasionally more) parts (not necessarily equal) into which something is divided." Max Radin's *Law Dictionary* defines the alternative meaning as "a fractional part less than half." Because legal writers use the word in this way almost as often as they do in the sense "half," the word really ought to be avoided altogether.

In American customs law, *moiety* has taken on still another meaning, illustrated in the following examples: "Under Customs Law, an informant is paid a *'moiety'* up to, but not exceeding, $50,000. *Moiety* is payment made to an informant who assisted in the seizure and ultimate forfeiture of an object." *U.S. v. Cresta,* 825 F.2d 538, 545 n.3 (1st Cir. 1987)./ "The plaintiff, Mr. Robert Rickard, seeks an award of compensation to informants (otherwise known as *moieties*), pursuant to statutory authority contained in 19 U.S.C. § 1619 (1976)." *Rickard v. U.S.,* 11 Ct. Cl. 874, 875 (1987). Although a better word might have been found for this type of reward, *moiety* appears to be established JARGON.

moment in time, at this, is a pomposity for *now,* or sometimes *today* and *nowadays.*

momentarily = for a moment. It does not, correctly, mean "in a moment." Cf. **presently.**

momento is a misspelling of *memento,* q.v.

monarchi(c)al. *Monarchial* is a NEEDLESS VARIANT of *monarchical,* the usual form.

monet(ar)ize. The longer form is incorrect for *monetize* (= [1] to put (coins or currency) into circulation as money; [2] to give fixed value as currency; or [3] to purchase debt and thereby free up moneys that would otherwise be used to service that debt). Sense (2): "[T]he benefits flowing from those services are, in theory, as difficult to *monetarize* [read *monetize*] as religious ones." *Neher v. Commissioner,* 852 F.2d 848, 855 (6th Cir. 1988).

monetary damages. See **money damages.**

money damages, like *monetary damages,* is a common REDUNDANCY—e.g.: "Where *money damages* [read *damages*] would not afford adequate compensation (as, for example, in the case of a breach of contract to convey land) equity would oblige a defendant to perform specifically his part of the agreement." L.B. Curzon, *English Legal History* 126 (2d ed. 1979). See **damage(s) (A).**

moneyed; monied. The former is preferred—e.g.: "Commerce might have been used to 'refer to the entire *moneyed* economy . . . .'" Edward H. Levi, *An Introduction to Legal Reasoning* 63 (1949) (quoting the Government's brief in *U.S. v. Darby,* 312 U.S. 100, 103 (1941)). See **monies.**

moneyed judgment seems like an odd mistake for *money judgment,* a common phrase today. Actually, however, *moneyed judgment* appeared in any number of 19th-century cases. Today it is an ARCHAISM that will strike many readers as an error.

money had and received, action for; money paid, action for. At common law, the *action for money had and received* was one by which the plaintiff could recover money that he or she had paid to the defendant, the money usually being recoverable for either of the following reasons: (a) the money had been paid under mistake or compulsion, or (b) the consideration had wholly failed. The *action for money paid,* by contrast, was one by which the plaintiff could recover money paid not to the defendant, but to a third party in circumstances in which the defendant had benefited.

monied. See **moneyed.**

monies is an illogical and misconceived plural. Because it is so common, however, it cannot be labeled a gross error. Still, *moneys* remains the preferred form, used, e.g., in the heading of 18 U.S.C. § 2314 (1988). *Monies* is only as logical as the obsolete plural *attornies.* Cf. **moneyed.**

monish. See **admonition.**

monism; dualism. In international law, *monism* denotes the doctrine that international and domestic law are but two manifestations of the same conception of law. *Dualism,* by contrast, holds that international law and domestic law of the several states are essentially different from each other in three ways: (1) in source; (2) in the relations they regulate; and (3) in substance. See 1 Lassa Oppenheim, *International Law* 37 (Hersch Lauterpacht ed., 8th ed. 1955).

monition. See **admonition.**

monopoly. A. In Antitrust Law. *Monopoly* is generally understood to mean "control by one supplier or producer over the commercial market within a given region." Nonlawyers often believe that this control must be complete, but the law in various jurisdictions now sets the level of control at a fraction of the overall market. In England, for example, under the Monopolies and Mergers Acts 1948 and 1965, a monopoly existed when the level of control reached one-third of a local or national market. That proportion was lessened by the Fair Trading Act 1973, under which companies can be prevented from controlling more than one-fourth of the supply of a product or service.

In the U.S., under the Sherman Antitrust Act, *monopoly* is an offense that can lead to criminal penalties and divestiture. The offense has two elements: (1) the possession of a "monopoly power" within the relevant market, i.e., the power to fix prices and exclude competitors; and (2) willfully acquiring or maintaining that power "as distinguished from growth or development as a consequence of a superior product, business acumen, or historical accident." *U.S. v. Grinnell Corp.,* 384 U.S. 563, 571 (1966).

B. In Patent Law. The word can be confusing in patent contexts, in which it bears no connotation of illegality. The solution may be to eliminate its patent-law uses: "Because of its antitrust connotations and association with illegality . . . , it often evokes negative reactions inappropriate to a dispassionate analysis of patent law problems." *In re Kaplan,* 789 F.2d 1574, 1578 n.3 (Fed. Cir. 1986). The modern tendency, therefore, is to speak of an *exclusive right* instead of a *monopoly*—that is, the exclusive right to make, use, and sell an invention.

C. And *monopolization.* Properly speaking, *monopoly* refers to the control or advantage itself, or the state of possessing that control or advantage; *monopolization* is the process or act of gaining that control or advantage.

D. And *monopsony.* Whereas *monopoly* (Gk. "sole seller") focuses on the source of goods and services, *monopsony* (Gk. "sole buyer") focuses on their immediate destination: *monopsony* "is the term used to describe a situation in which the relevant market for a factor of production is dominated by a single purchaser." *Permian Basin Area Rate Cases,* 390 U.S. 747, 794 n.64 (1968). E.g., "Once El Paso was certified, it held a virtual *monopsony* in the Basin since Southern Union Gas Company, the only other pipeline in the Basin, served only intrastate markets which were already fully utilized." *El Paso Natural Gas Co. v. Sun Oil Co.,* 426 F. Supp. 963, 965–66 n.5 (W.D. Tex. 1977). The word *monopsony* is far less common than *monopoly*—so much so that a few texts refer erroneously to "monopoly buyers."

monthlong is properly one word in AmE. E.g., "Onshore, an estimated 8,000 well-wishers braved the bad weather—the first encountered by the entourage since beginning the *monthlong* tour." The same is true of *yearlong, weeklong,* and *daylong.*

monument has two legal meanings: (1) "a written document or record" (a sense derived historically from confusion with *muniment,* q.v.); and (2) in AmE, "any natural or artificial object that is fixed permanently in the soil and referred to in the legal description of land."

moot. A. As Adjective. The *OED* lists only the sense "that can be argued; debatable; not decided, doubtful." Hence a *moot point* was classically seen as one that is arguable. A *moot case* was a hypothetical case proposed for discussion in a 'moot' of law students (see (C) below). In the U.S., law students practice arguing hypothetical cases before appellate courts in *moot court.*

From that sense of *moot* derived the extended sense "of no practical importance; hypothetical; academic." Hence, "There is no other question worthy of notice. We are asked to express an opinion as to the right of the appellants to give bail pending their appeal, but that is now a *moot* point." *Ah How v. U.S.,* 193 U.S. 65, 78 (1904) (per Holmes, J.)./ "There is thus presented the primary question as to whether there is anything for us to decide on this appeal or whether the question has become *moot* because defendant has surrendered possession to plaintiffs." *Price v. Wilson,* 32 A.2d 109, 109 (D.C. 1943).

Today, in AmE, the predominant sense of *moot* is "having no practical significance," in both legal and nonlegal writing. Bernstein and other writers have called this sense of the word incorrect, but it is now a *fait accompli.* To use *moot* in the sense "open to argument" in AmE today is to create an ambiguity, and to confuse most of one's readers. In BrE, the transformation in sense has been slower, and *moot* in its older sense retains vitality. Cf. **mootness.**

B. As Verb. Historically, *moot,* v.t., meant "to raise or bring forward (a point or question) for discussion." That sense is still current in BrE, and in older American usage. E.g., "*United States v. Rauscher* is noteworthy as involving the much-*mooted* question of the right to try a person for a crime other than that for which his extradition was secured . . . ." *Correspondence,* 1 Harv. L. Rev. 43, 43 (1887)./ "[A]lthough the Bar first *mooted* the idea, it was a joint enterprise." *Coming Together,* 130 Solic. J. 289, 289 (1986).

In American legal usage, however, a new sense has taken hold: "to render moot or of no practical significance." Thus, "The settlement did not *moot* the jurisdictional question."/ "These actions presented the *mooted* question of the coverage of the policy."

C. As Noun. In England, *moot* has the sense "a hypothetical legal problem discussed by students at the Inns of Court for practice" or "the discussion resulting from such a problem." E.g., "The maxim was never forgotten in the training of the English bar in the *moots* of the Inns of Court, nor in the long wrangling years of oral pleading." This use is unknown in the U.S., although its scent lingers in the phrase *moot court.*

mootness (= the fact or quality of having no practical importance) was an AmE NEOLOGISM when first used in the 1920s—e.g.: "The question of *mootness* is not discussed in the briefs of counsel for the government." *U.S. v. Northern Pac. Ry.,* 18 F.2d 299, 304 (E.D. Wash. 1927). As a noun corresponding to the modern AmE sense of *moot,* the word *mootness* has steadily become more frequent in American legal writing—e.g.:

- "The ruling excepted to, whether on the evidence or on the pleadings, in no wise affects the question of *mootness.*" *Brockett v. Maxwell,* 35 S.E.2d 906, 907 (Ga. 1945).
- "*Mootness* is a question of justiciability. If a case has become moot, . . . then there is no necessity for a judgment . . . ." *Ferguson v. Commercial Bank,* 578 So. 2d 1234, 1236 (Ala. 1991).
- "The issues in this mortgage foreclosure appeal concern the propriety of the dismissal of the appeal of the named defendant, Joseph Trantino, on the ground of *mootness.*" *Rothstein v. Trantino,* 635 A.2d 813, 813 (Conn. 1994).

Today, the phrase *mootness doctrine* or *mootness rule* denotes the principle that American courts will not decide moot cases—e.g.: "[T]he trial court issued another order on December 1 that found the *mootness doctrine* was inapplicable because petitioner was still in custody of the department . . . ." *Taylor v. Department of Corrections,* 556 So. 2d 494, 494 (Fla. Dist. Ct. App. 1990)./ "[T]here is a strong likelihood that application of the *mootness doctrine* may repeatedly frustrate review." *Peloza v. Freas,* 871 P.2d 687, 688 (Alaska 1994). See **moot (A).**

mooty, adj., is BrE legal slang meaning "debatable"—e.g.: "After discussing a *'mooty'* problem, try to avoid the weak conclusion that 'A is perhaps liable.'" Glanville Williams, *Learning the Law* 124 (11th ed. 1982)./ "*'Mooty'* as the case may be, it is unlikely that there are many *good* points to be made for your side." *Id.* at 164.

moral obligation, as used by legal theorists, usu. denotes a duty "semi-consciously followed and enforced rather by instinct and habit than by definite sanctions." Henry S. Maine, *Ancient Law* 121 (17th ed. 1901; repr. [New Universal Lib.] 1905, 1910). Thus, a *moral obligation* is not legally enforceable. Further, "its scope has been restricted and the label has become unfashionable." G.H. Treitel, *The Law of Contract* 76 (8th ed. 1991).

moratorium. Pl. *-ia.* E.g., "The Code of Justinian contains two provisions in regard to *moratoria.*" A.H. Feller, *Moratory Legislation: A Comparative Study,* 46 Harv. L. Rev. 1061, 1062 (1933).

more honored in the breach. See **breach, more honored in the.**

more important(ly). As an introductory phrase, *more important* has historically been considered an elliptical form of "What is more important . . . ," and hence the *-ly* form is thought to be the less desirable. E.g., "This provision, of course, directly conflicts with section 1235(k); *more importantly* [read *more important*], section 1273(a) defeats Montana's right to the funds collected on the ceded strip as much as it defeats that of the tribe."/ "Perhaps *most importantly* [read *most important*], the argument that *Gertz* should be limited to the media misapprehends our cases." Yet arguably, if we may begin a sentence, "*Importantly,* jurisdiction in the Supreme Court . . . ," we ought to be able to begin it, "*More importantly,* jurisdiction in the Supreme Court . . ." See SENTENCE ADVERBS.

The ellipsis does not work with less idiomatic phrases. E.g., one would not say: "*More notable,* Holmes wrote this opinion. . . ." *More notably* (as opposed to *More notable*) is called for in order that the sentence not sound alien, illogical, and even ungrammatical. The same is true of "*More interestingly,* . . . ." Furthermore, if the position of the phrase is changed from the beginning of the sentence in any significant way, the usual ellipsis becomes unidiomatic and *-ly* is quite acceptable: "But neither, and *more importantly* under the *Bradley* analysis, does the statute or the legislative history direct that the statute be applied prospectively only."/ "Second, and *more importantly,* this evidence improperly emphasized a 'reasonable man' standard of knowledge."

more interestingly; more interesting. See SENTENCE ADVERBS & **more important(ly).**

more or less (= somewhat) is often used imprecisely in the sense "some degree of," as here: "Keep in mind also that the phraseology used in an instrument quite commonly is not constructed by the grantor himself; the instrument is drafted by someone with *more or less* legal learning." Less legal learning than the grantor possessed?

more perfect. This phrase appears in the preamble to the U.S. Constitution: "We the People of the United States, in Order to form a more perfect Union . . . ." Some critics object that *perfect,* as an absolute quality, should not take a comparative adjective. The answer to those critics is an old one: "It is pedantic to object to the colloquial use of such expressions as 'more universal' [and] *'more perfect'* . . . . Of course, superficially viewed, these expressions are incorrect, as there cannot be degrees of universality or of perfection . . . ; yet what is really meant by 'more perfect' for example, is 'more *nearly* perfect' . . . ." Harry T. Peck, "What Is Good English?" in *What Is Good English? and Other Essays* 3, 16–17 (N.Y., Dodd, Mead & Co. 1899). See ADJECTIVES (B).

more preferable. See ADJECTIVES (B) & **preferable.**

more . . . than. **A. Parallel constructions.** To create parallel phrasing in the use of this construction, it is often important to repeat the preposition. E.g., "Most civil audits are *more* favorably settled by an open, honest discussion about what the agent wants *than having* [read *than by having*] the attorney treat the agent as the taxpayer's mortal enemy." See PARALLELISM & **above (A).**

B. More than one (is) (are). In the phrase *more than one court has held,* the phrase *more than* acts as a compound adverb modifying the adjective *one.* The subject of the clause is the singular noun *court*—hence the singular verb *has.* The same holds true if the singular noun is merely implied, i.e., is an UNDERSTOOD WORD: *more than one has,* not *more than one have.*

For many writers, this principle is counterintuitive because the sense denoted is a plural one. But this is one of the rare instances in English grammar in which the number of the verb is determined not by the meaning of the subject but by its grammatical form. See SYNESIS.

Mistakes, however, are common—e.g.: "If one [blood relative] is named, or if more than one *are* [read *is*] named, the court, aided by the curator, must make the further finding of whether there are any inheritance rights [that] presently exist." *Prentice v. Parker,* 376 So. 2d 568, 570 (La. Ct. App. 1979)./ "The use of a single culpability score . . . permits the impact of aggravating and mitigating sentencing factors to be considered along the same scale and, where more than one *are* [read *is*] present, to offset or accumulate culpability considerations to produce a final sentencing recommendation." Richard S. Gruner, *Towards an Organizational Jurisprudence: Transforming Corporate Criminal Law Through Federal Sentencing Reform,* 36 Ariz. L. Rev. 407, 445 (1994). See SUBJECT-VERB AGREEMENT (K).

C. ***More . . . than all; more . . . than any.*** See OVERSTATEMENT.

more unique. See ADJECTIVES (B).

moribund (= dying) does not mean "dead." Yet many lawyers misuse the word—e.g.: "[T]his matrimonial partnership is *completely moribund* [read, perhaps, *dead* or *over*], and cannot be revived . . . ." *Wang v. Wang,* 386 N.Y.S.2d 922, 925 (Sup. Ct. 1976)./ "That this rule saves the Clause from being completely *moribund* [read, perhaps, *lifeless*] does not . . . alter the reality that it is insufficient to ensure that federal law is paramount." *Green v. Mansour,* 474 U.S. 64, 77 (1985) (Brennan, J., dissenting).

MORPHOLOGICAL DEFORMITIES are words derived from other languages, usu. Latin or Greek, whose morphemes are so put together as to travesty the lending or borrowing language's principles of word formation. In some philologists' view, one does not combine the inseparable particle *dis-* with nouns to form English verbs (e.g., *dismember*) because it is impermissible by Latin morphology. In Latin, *dis-* was joined only with verbs to form privative verbs (e.g., *disentitle, disregard.*)

Any number of examples of ill-formed words made up of classical morphemes exist in modern English: *aborticide, abortuary* [a PORTMANTEAU WORD from *abortion mortuary*], *asylee, breathalyzer, deflation, drunkometer, homophobe, prosumerism* [a PORTMANTEAU WORD from *pro-consumerism*], *simulcast, slumpflation, stagflation, teletype, urinalysis, workaholic,* and on and on. The importance of knowing something about morphology, or how word elements properly compose whole words, is that we can then create and use NEOLOGISMS that are inoffensive to those who know the English language and other languages. And we can likewise avoid opposition to morphological deformities, which refined writers avoid as much as possible. Cf. HYBRIDS.

mors civilis. See **civil death.**

mortgage, n., = a property owner's promise that, if some obligation is not met, the creditor may take the property to satisfy that obligation. At common law, the word referred only to real property. But in mid-19th century AmE, the word *mortgage* was extended to apply to personalty as well as realty. Hence, the phrase *chattel mortgage* arose. Still, in actual usage *mortgage* much more frequently applies to real rather than personal property.

The word *mortgage* has two possible etymological meanings. One theory—the better one—holds that the word derives from OF. *mort gaige* "dead pledge," so called because the debt becomes void or "dead" when the mortgagor redeems the pledge. Another theory is that *dead pledge* means the same thing as the current phrases *dead capital* and *dead investment:* while land is in the possession of the lender, it is dead—it gives no return to the owner.

mortgageable. So spelled.

mortgage-holder is less clear than *mortgagee* because many readers might take it to mean "mortgagor"—e.g.: "Purchase money *mortgage holders* [read *mortgagees*] may improve their collateral positions by allowing the owner to improve the property at the expense of the mechanics' lienholders." *Shade v. Wheatcraft Indus., Inc.,* 809 P.2d 538, 542 (Kan. 1991).

mortgag(e)or; mortgager. Coke and Blackstone used the *-or* spelling; the lexicographers Johnson and Webster preferred *-er,* the latter terming *-or* "an orthography that should have no countenance." Noah Webster, *An American Dictionary of the English Language* (1828). The *Law Quarterly Review* and many other British publications use *-er;* the form *-or* predominates in AmE. The *-eor* spelling, which appeared in the Year Books, is nowhere used today.

mortis causa. See ***causa mortis.***

mortmain (lit., "deadhand") = the condition of lands or tenements held inalienably by an ecclesiastical or other corporation. The term suggests control from the grave, as here in a LOAN TRANSLATION: "The effect of the rule is to invalidate ab initio certain future interests that might otherwise remain in existence for a period of time considered inimical to society's interest in having reasonable limits to *deadhand* control and in facilitating the marketability of property."

The *OED* remarks: "It seems probable that

'dead hand' in English legal use is a metaphorical expression for impersonal ownership, and is unconnected with the older feudal use of *manus mortua* to denote the custom by which serfs (and other classes included under the term *homines manus mortuae*) had no power of testamentary disposition, their possessions, if they died without legitimate offspring, reverting to the lord."

most for *very* or *almost* is poor usage—e.g.: "The power of judicial review had a *most* inauspicious beginning." (The adjective *inauspicious* is actually stronger without a modifier; see WEASEL WORDS.)/ "*Most* [read *Almost*] everybody knows what a statute is, but what is a precedent?" C. Gordon Post, *An Introduction to the Law* 80 (1963). See **very (A).**

most-favored-nations clause. Commercial lawyers borrowed the diplomatic phrase *most favored nation* (a status that lowers import taxes) and used it to denote a contractual clause ensuring that a given buyer or royalty owner will be treated at least as favorably as any other buyer or royalty owner. The phrase *favored-nations clause* is a variant.

On the same principle, some commercial tenants negotiate a *most-favored-tenant clause,* which ensures that a tenant will be given any negotiating concessions given to other tenants.

most important(ly). See **more important(ly).**

Mother Hubbard clause; anaconda clause; dragnet clause. These synonymous phrases denote a clause stating that a mortgage (more specifically, an *anaconda mortgage*) secures all the debts that the mortgagor may at any time owe to the mortgagee. The metaphors underlying the terms are as follows: *Mother Hubbard* suggests that the mortgagor goes to great lengths to satisfy the mortgagee, just as Mother Hubbard (in the popular nursery rhyme) is absurdly solicitous toward her dog. E.g., "Amerada . . . invokes the 'coverall' (sometimes called the *'Mother Hubbard'*) clause in an oil and gas lease from Koch, dated January 19, 1945." *Gardner v. Amerada Petroleum Corp.,* 91 F. Supp. 134, 135 (S.D. Tex. 1950). *Anaconda* suggests that the unsuspecting debtor may get wrapped up in the serpentine clutches of indebtedness. The *dragnet* metaphor suggests a broadly cast net that sweeps in all past and future debts. Today, *Mother Hubbard clause* is the most usual phrase.

motion = an application requesting a court to make a specified order. Though it is properly classifiable as a court paper, a motion is not a pleading. See **court papers, application & pleading (B).**

motion, v.t., in the sense "to move (as a court)" is labeled obsolete in the *OED.* It ought to be obsolete, but strangely it persists in American legal writing—e.g.: "Warrington *motioned* [read *moved*] the court for summary judgment on both the conversion and securities fraud causes of action." *Levitz v. Warrington,* 877 P.2d 1245, 1246 (Utah Ct. App. 1994)./ "On March 24, 1993, Parson *motioned* [read *moved*] the court to increase child support . . . ." *Hernandez v. Hernandez,* 640 So. 2d 818, 819 (La. Ct. App. 1994). See **move (that) the court.**

motion for (a) new trial. This motion, which dates back to medieval times, is now generally called a *motion for new trial,* without the indefinite article. See ARTICLES (C).

motion in limine should not be hyphenated. See **in limine.**

motivate, -ation. See **actuate.**

motive is, as Wigmore has observed, a word with an unfortunate ambiguity: "That which has value to show the doing or not doing of the act is the inward emotion, passion, feeling, of the appropriate sort; but that which shows the probable existence of this emotion is termed—when it is . . . some outer fact—the *'motive.'* For example, the prior prosecution of A by B in a suit at law is said to have been a *'motive'* for A's subsequent burning of B's house. But in strictness the external fact of B's suit cannot be A's *'motive'*; for the motive is a state of mind of A; the external fact does tend to show the excitement of the hostile and vindictive emotion, but it is not identical with that emotion." J.H. Wigmore, *The Science of Judicial Proof* 117 (3d ed. 1937). Cf. **intent(ion).**

mouthpiece. See LAWYERS, DEROGATORY NAMES FOR (A).

movable, adj. & n., is the preferred spelling in both AmE and BrE. *Moveable,* chiefly a legal variant, should be avoided everywhere but in Scotland, where it is traditional. See **immovable,** -ABLE (A) & ADJECTIVES (C).

movant; mover. *Movant* (= one who makes a motion to the court) is a late-19th-century Americanism. Among the earliest recorded uses is this one: "The *movants* excepted to the rulings of the court . . . ." *Lanning v. Lockett,* 11 F. 814, 814 syl. (C.C.S.D. Ga. 1882).

In the U.S. today, *movant* is far more common than *mover.* It is the form used in most court rules and predominantly in reported cases. E.g., "While the *movant* need not always show a probability of success on the merits, he must present a substantial case on the merits." *Movent* is an incorrect variant spelling.

Mover, when used in the sense of *movant,* is a NEEDLESS VARIANT. E.g., "We must consider all the evidence—not just that evidence which supports the *nonmover's* [read *nonmovant's*] case—but in the light and with all reasonable inferences most favorable to the nonmoving party." Some people prefer *mover* over *movant* in parliamentary procedure.

moveable. See **movable.**

mover. See **movant.**

move (that) the court. "We *move the court* to grant a new trial." This construction appears from a logical point of view to be incorrect. Idiom would seem to require: "I *move that the court* grant a new trial." By analogy, one might say: "I hereby *move that we* adjourn," but not "I hereby *move us* to adjourn."

Yet the phrase *moving the court* is of long standing in legal language, including this from the syllabus in *Marbury v. Madison:* "At the last term, . . . William Marbury [et al.] severally *moved the court* for a rule to James Madison . . . ." *Marbury v. Madison,* 5 U.S. (1 Cranch) 137, 137 syl. (1803).

With either of those two constructions, *move* is transitive (*move the court* or *move that the court*), even when the object is understood: *move* [*the court*] *for relief* becomes *move for relief.*

much. See **many (A).**

muchly is nowadays considered a substandard form, though several centuries ago it was not so stigmatized. *Much* is the preferred form in all adverbial contexts. Surprisingly, *muchly* has appeared in reported American opinions. See ADVERBS, PROBLEMS WITH (D) & HYPERCORRECTION (D).

mulct /məlkt/ = to punish by a fine. The term is rarely encountered outside the law, and only infrequently within it—e.g.: "Let them then be *mulcted* to the uttermost in the penalty that Parliament has prescribed." Patrick Devlin, *The Enforcement of Morals* 60 (1968).

Mulct has the additional sense "to deprive or divest of," and carries pejorative connotations of mercilessness or deceit. E.g., "The panel opinion also permits a jury to *mulct* the defendant in a defamation action of more than compensatory damages."

multifarious = (1) improperly joining in one pleading distinct matters or causes of action, and thereby confounding them; (2) improperly joining parties in a lawsuit; or (3) diversified; many and various. Sense (3) is the common, nonlegal sense. In law, sense (1) predominates—e.g.: "The complaint as amended was dismissed . . . on the grounds of *multifarious* pleading and for failure to state a cause of action." *Bates & Rogers Constr. Corp. v. North Shore Sanitary Dist.,* 414 N.E.2d 1274, 1276 (Ill. App. Ct. 1980).

multiparty; multipartite. *Multiparty* is defined by the *OED* as a political term meaning "comprising several parties or members of parties; of an electoral or political system which results in the formation of three or more influential parties." Yet in law, the *party* in this word has come in the U.S. to refer to a party to a lawsuit. E.g., "When the intervention was allowed, the suit became a *multiparty* action within the meaning of Fed. R. Civ. P. 54(b)."

Multipartite = divided into many parts. In the following example, *multipartite* seems to be misused for *multiparty:* "*Multipartite* [read *multiparty?*] agreements between the debtor and his creditors, or several of them, may bind participating creditors. Non-consenting creditors will not be so bound." James A. MacLachlan, *Handbook of the Law of Bankruptcy* 4 (1956).

multiplici(t)ous. A. Form of the Word. Although both forms (*multiplicitous* and *multiplicious*) have existed in the English language, *W3* states (prematurely) that *multiplicious* is now obsolete. (It is the only form listed in the *OED.*) Certainly it is the rarer term, and it does not immediately reveal its relationship with the noun *multiplicity.* Nonetheless, *multiplicious* appears in the law reports. See, e.g., *U.S. v. Wesley,* 748 F.2d 962, 963 (5th Cir. 1984) ("Wesley argues that his convictions . . . are *multiplicious* and violative of the double jeopardy clause of the fifth amendment."); *U.S. v. Stanfa,* 685 F.2d 85, 88 (3d Cir. 1982) (*multiplicious* used four times in two paragraphs). But this word should not be resurrected: we should avoid multiplicitous forms of this word, and hold steady with *multiplicitous.* (When used—as in the previous sentence—for *multiple, multiplicitous* is a pomposity.)

The two forms of the word are susceptible to INELEGANT VARIATION. One judicial writer used both forms in consecutive paragraphs: "Even if a single fact pattern were present, the 'different evidence test' . . . would show that the counts in question were not *multiplicitous*. . . . The chief danger raised by a *multiplicious* [read *multiplicitous*] indictment is the possibility that the defendant will receive more than one sentence for a single offense." *U.S. v. Swaim,* 757 F.2d 1530, 1536–37 (5th Cir. 1985).

B. And *duplicitous*. The distinction is not what one might infer: "An indictment is *multiplicitous* when it charges one offense in several counts. An indictment is *duplicitous* when it charges numerous crimes in a single count." *U.S. v. Jones,* 648 F. Supp. 241, 242 (S.D.N.Y. 1986) (citations omitted). E.g., "If Lartey has any complaint, it is not that the indictment is *multiplicious* [read *multiplicitous*], but rather that it is *duplicitous,* charging numerous crimes in a single count." *U.S. v. Lartey,* 716 F.2d 955, 968 (2d Cir. 1983). See **duplicitous.**

multiply is an adverb as well as a verb: "Theresa is a *multiply* handicapped child with severe behavioral problems."

multistate. So spelled, without a hyphen.

multital. See **paucital.**

multitude of, a. See SYNESIS.

mumbo-jumbo. Many critics use this phrase to denote LEGALESE and JARGON—e.g.: "And only the solemn and mystifying *mumbo-jumbo* of legal language keeps the non-lawyers from catching on." Fred Rodell, *Woe Unto You, Lawyers!* 88 (1939; repr. 1980).

municipal = (1) of or relating to a town, city, or local governmental unit (as contrasted with *county, state,* or *national*); or (2) of or relating to the internal government of a state or nation (as contrasted with *international*). Sense (1) is ordinary. All but international lawyers are likely to find sense (2) odd—e.g.: "It is presumed that *municipal* law is to be interpreted to be in conformity with international law." Michael Zander, *The Law-Making Process* 128 (2d ed. 1985). See **international.**

muniment = a document (as a deed or charter) preserved as evidence in defense of rights or privileges belonging to a person, family, or corporation. Today this word is most commonly used in the phrase *muniment of title.* E.g., "A trust may not under those circumstances be engrafted upon a deed absolute in its terms because if that were the rule, deeds would no longer be valuable as *muniments of title.*" See **monument.**

murder. A. And *homicide; manslaughter; man-killing.* *Homicide* is the action of killing another human being; it is the general legal term. *Murder* is the unlawful killing of a human being with malice aforethought. It is the most heinous kind of criminal homicide. At common law, *murder* was not subdivided; but in most American jurisdictions statutes have created *first-degree murder, second-degree murder,* and *third-degree murder* (in descending order of reprehensibility). Indeed, *second-degree murder* is the same as common-law *murder,* as defined above. *First-degree murder,* a statutory crime, is the common-law crime of murder with an added element that aggravates the crime (e.g., arson, rape, robbery, burglary, larceny, kidnapping). See **degree.**

Manslaughter, which is a less serious crime than *murder,* is homicide committed without malice aforethought. The Scots-law equivalent is *culpable homicide.*

Man-killing, q.v., is a nonlegal synonym for *homicide,* used sometimes of nonhuman killers <a man-killing tiger>. But it is a sexist term: see SEXISM (B).

B. *Unintentional murder.* This phrase may strike some readers as an OXYMORON, but it is in widespread use—e.g.: "On Tuesday, the [California Supreme Court], in a major break with a 4-year-old precedent, ruled that a killer can be executed for an *unintentional murder.*" *Calif. Death Sentence Upheld,* L.A. Times, 15 Oct. 1987, at 1-1. And it is entirely proper to speak of an *unintentional murder,* as when a defendant, for no good reason, shoots a gun into an occupied room and kills somebody inside.

The distinction between *unintentional murder* and *manslaughter,* says one commentator, "has never been drawn with great clarity. What is clear is that murder requires a more culpable level of risk-taking than does manslaughter." Joshua Dressler, *Understanding Criminal Law* 462 (1987). The recklessness involved in unintentional murder is more extreme than that involved in manslaughter.

murder one; murder two; murder three. These are AmE colloquialisms for *first-degree murder, second-degree murder,* and *third-degree murder.*

must is used both factually and normatively. The factual use involves a judgment about something that has happened: "She *must* have known that he was there. Otherwise she never would have begun chanting the message." The normative *must* may be merely a strong *ought* ("You *must* always tell the truth.") or an absolute requirement ("To qualify, you *must* be at least 18 years of age.").

In DRAFTING, *must* is generally confined to the last of these senses. Many drafters, especially in Australia, Canada, and Great Britain, consider *must* a much better word than *shall* for stating requirements. And the trend seems to be for Americans to adopt this view. See WORDS OF AUTHORITY (A) & (C).

muster. The phrase *to pass muster* began as a military term meaning "to undergo review without censure." Lawyers have picked it up especially in the sense of constitutional review. E.g., "*To pass muster,* the classifications must serve important governmental objectives and be substantially related to the achievement of those objectives."/ "The admission of evidence in this case readily *passes muster.*"

This SET PHRASE is occasionally mangled: "Such political undertakings cannot *withstand constitutional muster* [read *pass constitutional muster*]." *Past muster* is an ignorant blunder for *pass muster:* "We assume that this explanation would *past muster* [read *pass muster*]."

must needs. See **needs must.**

must not. See WORDS OF AUTHORITY (F).

mutatis mutandis (= the necessary changes having been made; taking into consideration or allowing for the changes that must be made) is a useful LATINISM in learned writing, for the only English equivalents are far wordier. E.g., "What we have said in connection with the counterclaim applies *mutatis mutandis* to his defense to the complaint."/ "What has thus far been said concerning contracts completed by mail would seem to apply, *mutatis mutandis,* to every type of contract."/ "How far can the account given above of legal liability-responsibility be applied *mutatis mutandis* to moral responsibility?" H.L.A. Hart, "Postscript: Responsibility and Retribution," in *Punishment and Responsibility: Essays in the Philosophy of Law* 210, 225 (1968). Cf. ***ceteris paribus.***

mute. In nonlegal contexts this word has come to signify "dumb; destitute of the faculty of speech." In law, however, it retains its older use as a synonym of *silent.* E.g., "The petitioners' decision to remain *mute* during the deportability phase of the hearing was an appropriate exercise of their Fifth Amendment privilege."

MUTE E. In English, an unsounded final *-e-* is ordinarily dropped before the *-ing* and *-ed* inflections, e.g., *create, creating, created; rate, rating, rated; share, sharing, shared.* Exceptions to this rule are verbs with bases ending in *-ee, -ye,* and *-oe:* these do not drop the *-e-* before *-ing,* but they do drop it before *-ed: agree, agreeing, agreed; dye, dyeing, dyed; shoe, shoeing, shoed.*

The suffix *-able* often causes doubt when it is appended to a base ending in a mute *-e-*. Generally, the *-e-* is dropped when *-able* is added, but a number of exceptions exist in BrE (e.g., *hireable, liveable, nameable, rateable, ropeable, saleable, sizeable, unshakeable*). But in BrE, forms such as *blamable, exercisable,* and *finable,* which follow the American rule of dropping the *-e-*, are preferred.

The almost universal exception to the AmE rule of dropping the *-e-* before a vowel is that it should be kept if it is needed to indicate the soft sound of a preceding *-g-* or *-c-*, or to distinguish a word from another with a like spelling. E.g., *change, changeable; hinge, hingeing; singe, singeing; trace, traceable.* But even this exception to the rule is not uniform: *lunge* yields *lunging.* Because the given form of a word when inflected is easily forgotten and often the subject of disagreement even among lexicographers, the best course is to keep an up-to-date and reliable dictionary at one's side.

One other difference between AmE and BrE is of interest to legal writers: in AmE, the mute *-e-* is dropped after *-dg-* in words such as *acknowledgment, fledgling,* and *judgment,* whereas the *-e-* is retained in BrE (*acknowledgement, fledgeling,* and *judgement*). British legal writers, however, usu. prefer the spelling *judgment.* See **judgment & pledg(e)or.**

mutual; common. *Mutual* = reciprocal; directed by each toward the other(s). E.g., "This court has held that a contract made *by mutual letters* [read *by the mutual exchange of letters*] was not complete until the letter accepting the offer had been received by the person making the offer." *Common* = shared by two or more. *Friend in common* is preferable to *mutual friend,* although the latter has stuck because of Dickens's novel (the title to which, everyone forgets, comes from a sentence mouthed by an illiterate character). See **mutual mistake.**

Like *together,* q.v., *mutual* creates any number of redundant expressions. E.g., "We have repeatedly held that a party may not assume successive positions in the course of a suit, or series of suits, with reference to the same fact or state of facts, which are inconsistent with each other, or *mutually contradictory* [read merely *contradictory*]." Some of the more common prolixities with this word are *mutual agreement* and *mutual coopera-*

tion. Redundancies are especially common when *mutual* is used in conjunction with *both;* for instance, *mutually binding on both parties,* or: "An invitee has been described as one who enters on another's land with the owner's knowledge and *for the mutual benefit of both* [read either *for their mutual benefit* or *for the benefit of both*]."

mutuality of obligation (= the fact of both parties to a contract having agreed to be bound in some way) once allowed courts to decide that one party's promise was "illusory" and that the contract therefore failed for lack of consideration. Today, however, "the once powerful slogan of '*mutuality of obligation*' makes its rare appearance . . . as 'the now exploded theory of mutuality of obligation.'" Grant Gilmore, *The Death of Contract* 77 (1974). Cf. **meeting of the minds.**

mutually agree is a REDUNDANCY. See **mutual.**

mutually exclusive = each excluding the other. E.g., "It has always been hard to classify all government activity into three, and only three, neat and *mutually exclusive* categories." The phrase must be carefully used.

mutual mistake. Because this phrase, as it is ordinarily employed, involves a misuse of *mutual* for *common,* several writers on the law of contract—such as Cheshire, Fifoot, and Atiyah—have valiantly championed *common mistake* over *mutual mistake.* (See **mutual.**) Alas, the courts have not followed their grammatical lead and continue to refer overwhelmingly to *mutual mistake.*

It would be quite possible—and perhaps desirable—to distinguish between a *common mistake* and a *mutual mistake.* A *common mistake* occurs when both parties make the same mistake: when, for example, parties think that a painting is a genuine Van Gogh but in fact it is a fake. A *mutual mistake* occurs when each party is mistaken about the other's intent: when, for example, I think I am selling you my Honda Accord and you think you are buying my Acura. *Mutual* would be correct because I have mistaken your intent, and you have mistaken mine. But common-law judges typically lump both situations under the name *mutual mistake.*

mutual will; joint will. A *joint will* (sometimes wrongly called a *mutual will*) is one testamentary document executed by two persons. *Mutual wills* are separate documents in which two parties—usu. a husband and wife—establish identical testamentary provisions; such wills may contain or imply a contract not to revoke, so that the death of either party may bind the survivor to make no alteration.

my home is my castle. See **castle doctrine.**

my lady. See **my lord.**

my lord; your lordship. An English judge appointed to the High Court or some even higher court is invariably promoted within society: men are knighted and women are made Dames of the Order of the British Empire. Few become members of the House of Lords, but in court they are all nevertheless addressed *my lord* or *your lordship,* or *my lady* or *your ladyship.*

The *my* and *your* terms are not used interchangeably: *my lord* is used as a vocative in addressing a judge directly ("My lord, this case involves . . . "), whereas *your lordship* appears within a sentence as a polite alternative to *you* ("May it please your lordship, I am counsel for the plaintiff."). Cf. **Honorable** (2d par.).

In Scotland, judges of the Court of Session are, by courtesy, called *Lord X* and addressed in court as *my lord* or *your lordship,* even though they are rarely knighted or raised to the peerage. The origin of this practice was that superior-court judges were originally Lords of the King's Privy Council (i.e., "secret council"), from which the Court of Session evolved.

myriad is best used adjectivally, and not as a noun, for the adjectival use is more concise. E.g., "The Constitution does not empower this Court to second-guess state officials charged with the difficult responsibility of allocating limited public welfare funds *among the myriad of* [read *among the myriad*] potential recipients."

myself is best used either reflexively (e.g., "I have decided to recuse *myself.*") or intensively (e.g., "I *myself* will sue the corporation on behalf of the class of persons harmed.").

But *myself* should not appear as a substitute for *I* or *me.* Using it thus is thought somehow to be modest, as if the reference to oneself were less direct. But it is no less direct, and the writer may unconsciously cause the reader or listener to assume an intended jocularity, or that the writer is somewhat doltish. E.g., "After reconsideration, upon appellee's motion for rehearing, Mr. Justice B. and *myself* [read *I*] have reached the conclusion that this court has rendered an improper judgment, and that the motion for rehearing should be granted, and the judgment of the trial court affirmed." (Is it so difficult to say simply, "We have rendered an improper judgment"?)/ "Those ins and outs are largely a self-learning process, though knowing the experience of someone like *myself* [read *me*] might make the learning shorter, easier, and a lot less painful." Mark H. McCormack, *What They Don't Teach You at Harvard Business School* xii (1984). See FIRST PERSON.

MYTH OF PRECISION, THE. "Delusive exactness is a source of fallacy throughout the law." *Truax v. Corrigan,* 257 U.S. 312, 342 (1921) (Holmes, J., dissenting). When attacked for their inscrutable use of language, lawyers have traditionally sought refuge in precision, and often silenced their critics by the invocation of precision. Not everyone has been satisfied, however, by the explanation or excuse that legal language, despite its WOOLLINESS and frequent ugliness, is more precise than the general language. In words that still ring true, Jeremy Bentham wrote, in the early 19th century:

> For this redundancy, for the accumulation of excrementitious matter [i.e., legalese] in all its various shapes . . . [and] for all the pestilential effects that cannot be produced by this so enourmous a load of literary garbage,—the plea commonly pleaded . . . is, that it is necessary to *precision*—or, to use the word which on similar occasions they themselves are in the habit of using, certainty.
>
> But a more absolutely sham plea never was countenanced, or so much as pleaded, in either the King's Bench or Common Pleas.
>
> 3 Jeremy Bentham, *Works* 260 (J. Bowring ed. 1843).

A late 19th-century legist wrote, in words less vitriolic but even more telling:

> There is an abundance of affected accuracy in the addition of descriptions to distinguish persons and things needing no distinction, and in the expression of immaterial matters; but real accuracy and precision are attained quite as much by the omission of superfluous phrases, by the avoidance of tautology, by correct references and by a strict adherence to the rules of grammar, as by the use of apt words.
>
> 1 Charles Davidson, *Precedents and Forms in Conveyancing* 23 (4th ed. 1874).

The truth is that many people, lawyers included, buy into the fallacy that there must be a great deal of precision in LEGALESE. Why else—nonlawyers wonder—would lawyers *talk* so much about precision? Lon Fuller recognized the myth but not the extent of its currency: "For the time being it will be enough to put down one source of obfuscation. This is the notion current among laymen that lawyers, with all their forbidding jargon, have some uncanny ability to convey meaning to one another with great exactitude. Outside the area of a few TERMS OF ART, there is nothing to this belief." *The Anatomy of Law* 26 (1968). What Fuller did not realize is that the myth besots lawyers and nonlawyers alike. What everyone ought to recognize, though, is that, "[t]o fill in the spaces between their 'whereas's' and 'provided however's' lawyers have no resources except those available to any user of language." *Id.*

There is all too little precision in legal language, as many entries in this book should demonstrate. See PLAIN LANGUAGE.

N

naked is often used metaphorically in legal writing in the sense "having nothing that confirms or validates (a thing)." E.g., "The exceptions on this point present a *naked* proposition of law."/ "The plaintiff, having received only the *naked* ownership, never received any income from the property."

Naked trespasser describes not one who trespasses unclothed, but a trespasser with absolutely no claim to be present on the land: "Had A.S. entered upon this land as a *naked trespasser,* without any property right therein, he would have had no basis for a claim of title until the full period of limitation had run." In trademark law, a *naked* license is a license without provision for the licensor's exercise of quality control. And *naked contract*—a LOAN TRANSLATION of L. *nudum pactum*—denotes a contract not "clothed" with consideration. (See ***nudum pactum.***) For the correlative METAPHOR, see **clothe.**

nam(e)able. See MUTE E.

namely is generally preferable to *viz.* or *to wit,* qq.v.

Napoleonic Code. American lawyers esp. often refer to the "Napoleonic Code" as if it were the official name of a single code. Those who do so are wrong on two counts. First, although Napoleon commissioned the codification of French law, his name is only unofficially connected with the product. Second, it is more proper to refer to *Napoleonic codes,* in the plural and with a lowercase *-c-,* as David M. Walker does in the *OCL.*

The *Napoleonic codes* include the *Code civil* (1804), the *Code de procédure civil* (1806), the *Code de commerce* (1807), the *Code pénal* (1810), and the *Code d'instruction crimenelle* (1811). When American lawyers use the singular phrase, they seem to have in mind the *Code civil* (or *Civil Code,* as rendered in English).

narrative. In Scots law, the *narrative* in a deed is equivalent to the *recitals* in English and American deeds. The narrative sets forth the names of the grantor and the grantee, along with the reason for the conveyance.

nation; state. These two words have different meanings. A *nation* is a group of people inhabiting a defined territory, that group being distinct from other groups of people by the fact of its having allegiance to a single government exercising jurisdiction directly over each individual in the group. The *state,* by contrast, is the system of rules—or the machinery—by which jurisdiction is exercised over individuals within the group. It is therefore "illogical and confusing to use the terms *'State'* and *'Nation'* as though they were interchangeable, although this is frequently done. Thus we refer to the 'United Nations' although this is in fact an organization of States." Edward Jenks, *The Book of English Law* 5 (P.B. Fairest ed., 6th ed. 1967). See **state.**

national; federal. In a nation whose government has a federal system, these two terms might seem interchangeable. But the founders of the United States carefully distinguished them—particularly James Madison, who wrote:

> [T]he Constitution is to be founded on the assent and ratification of the people of America, given by deputies elected for the special purpose; but, on the other [hand], . . . this assent and ratification is to be given by the people, not as individuals composing one entire nation, but as composing the distinct and independent States to which they respectively belong. It is to be the assent and ratification of the several States, derived from the supreme authority in each State—the authority of the people themselves. The act, therefore, establishing the Constitution will not be a *national* but a *federal* act.
> *The Federalist* No. 39, at 243 (James Madison) (Clinton Rossiter ed., 1961).

Thus, as Madison explained, the foundation of the Constitution is *federal;* the operation of governmental powers under the Constitution is *national;* and the method of introducing amendments is *mixed. Id.* at 246.

National Reporter System. See **report (A).**

Native American. See **native-born citizen.**

native-born citizen. This phrase, though it has been fairly common since the 19th century, reeks of REDUNDANCY—e.g.: "The evidence in the record before us is not sufficiently compelling to require that we penalize a naturalized citizen for the expression of silly or even sinister-sounding views [that] *native-born citizens* [read *native citizens*] utter with impunity." *Baumgartner v. U.S.,* 322 U.S. 665, 677 (1944)./ "For the *native born citizen* [read *native citizen*] it is a right that is truly inalienable." *Kungys v. U.S.,* 485 U.S. 759, 784 (1988) (Stevens, J., concurring).

The modern temptation to brace the adjective *native* may come from two sources. First, in American law, the noun *native* has come to mean either (1) "a person born in the country"; or (2) "a person born outside the country of parents who are (at the time of the birth) citizens of that country and who are not permanently residing elsewhere." Sense (2) represents a slide in meaning, but the judicial writers quoted above could not possibly have wanted to protect against that extended meaning. Second, the phrase *Native American,* meaning *American Indian,* has recently popularized a secondary meaning of *native,* one having to do with heritage and not with birthplace: "one of the original or usual inhabitants of a country, as distinguished from strangers or foreigners; now *esp.* one belonging to a non-European race in a country in which Europeans hold political power" (*OED*).

natural. See **unnatural.**

natural child doubles as term equivalent to *biological child* and as a EUPHEMISM for *bastard, illegitimate child,* or *nonmarital child.* See **bastard & illegitimate child.**

natural justice is closely allied with *natural law,* q.v. A 19th-century court defined the phrase as "the natural sense of what is right and wrong." *Voinet v. Barrett* (1885) 55 L.J.Q.B. 39, 41. Although, on its face, the phrase is vague, its application tends to be specific: it usually turns up in discussions of whether a party has been afforded notice and a hearing. However desirable these procedural requirements may be, though, they are anything but "natural." So *natural justice* is really "a serious misnomer" by the use of which "lawyers may have underestimated their own contribution to one of the great principles of liberal societies." P.S. Atiyah, *Law and Modern Society* 41 (1983).

natural law. A. General Sense. Historically a number of senses have been attributed to this term; today the prevailing sense, esp. in legal contexts, is "law that determines what is right and wrong and that has power or is valid by nature, inherently, hence everywhere and always." L. Strauss, "Natural Law," 11 *Interna-*

tional Encyclopedia of the Social Sciences 80, 80 (1968). Because *natural law* and *positive law* (q.v.) are not mutually exclusive, a rule such as, "Thou shalt not kill," might be a rule equally in both systems.

Twentieth-century legal scholars have mostly rejected the notion of natural law on positivist grounds, because genuine scientific knowledge cannot validate value judgments, and natural law is composed fundamentally of value judgments. Stated differently, the problem with natural law is that, if it exists, there is no way to determine whose version of it is correct. The modern user of the term should be aware of the debate surrounding the concept and of the generally low regard in which the concept is now held.

Two synonymous phrases are *law of nature* and *jus naturale.*

B. Incorrect Sense. At least one writer has perversely used the phrase *natural law* as if it referred to the law (or lawlessness) of a state of nature: "Carr relished the good fight, and the opposition's propensity to settle contradicted his own *natural law.*" John A. Jenkins, *The Litigators* 350 (1989).

naturalist. To most people, Buffon and Darwin were naturalists, i.e., 19th-century biologists. Some lawyers use *naturalist,* however, to denote a natural-law adherent—e.g.: "Pufendorf, though differing in his concept of natural law, was also a *'naturalist.'*" René A. Wormser, *The Story of the Law* 513 (1962). The more usual (and comprehensible) phrase is *natural lawyer.*

natural lawyer. See **naturalist.**

natural life. The common conveyancing phrase *during his natural life* is better rendered *for life* or *as long as he lives.* See **civil death.**

natural person (= a human being) is unnecessary in place of either *person* or *human being,* except when contrast is made to *juristic person,* q.v.

natural right, like *natural law* and *natural justice,* is now generally considered a suspect phrase. Property lawyers have traditionally referred to the *natural right* of a landowner to have the land not be deprived of its support from adjacent tracts, to receive water from a stream, and the like. But "it is simpler and more intelligible to talk of the situations in which a landowner can sue in tort without proving the existence of a servitude, than to speak of *natural rights* and attempt to list these." A.W.B. Simpson, *An Introduction to the Land Law* 246 (1961).

naught; nought. These are different spellings of the same word, meaning "nothing." By convention *nought*—esp. in BrE—has come to signify the number zero (0). *Naught* is used in all nonmathematical contexts in which "nothing" is meant—e.g.: "The insurer may be put to the labor and expense of investigation that may, several years later, be found to have been for *naught.*"/ "The appointees in the case at bar have not appealed from the decree under consideration, and thus have evidenced their acceptance of what we have just said, although it sets at *naught* the intent of the donees." See **further affiant . . . .**

nausea, when used for *vomit,* n., is a badly employed EUPHEMISM.

nauseous (= inducing nausea) for *nauseated* is becoming so common that to call it an "error" is to exaggerate. Even so, careful writers follow the traditional distinction in formal writing: what is *nauseous* makes one feel *nauseated.* As of the early 1990s, the U.S. Supreme Court, in its seven uses of either word, had maintained a perfect record—e.g.: "It is made up entirely of repetitive descriptions of physical, sexual conduct, 'clinically' explicit and offensive to the point of being *nauseous;* there is only the most tenuous plot." *Kaplan v. California,* 413 U.S. 115, 116–17 (1973).

Lower courts, however, had helped spread the peccadillo—e.g.: "Once outside, however, Yunis felt *nauseous* [read *nauseated*]." *U.S. v. Yunis,* 859 F.2d 953, 956 (D.C. Cir. 1988)./ "He then became *nauseous* [read *nauseated*] and crawled into the bathroom and vomited." *State v. Thomas,* 407 S.E.2d 141, 145 (N.C. 1991).

nay. Except in the parliamentary procedure of taking votes either *yea* or *nay*—or *aye* and *nay*—the word *nay* smacks of pretentious posturing. E.g., "Moreover, parties must be encouraged, *nay required* [read *even required*], to raise their complaints about the arbitration during the arbitration process itself, when that is possible." *Marino v. Writers Guild of America, E., Inc.,* 992 F.2d 1480, 1483 (9th Cir. 1993)./ "The district court carefully juxtaposed selections from K-T's Licensed Materials with selections from the MPO program, thereby demonstrating a damning similarity—*nay identity* [read *even identity*]—of organization and language." *Kepner-Tregoe, Inc. v. Leadership Software, Inc.,* 12 F.3d 527, 534 (5th Cir. 1994)./ "I, for one, find it instructive—*nay, daunting* [read *no, daunting* or *even daunting*]—that no Supreme Court case utters so much as a whisper about the doctrine of implied authority that is the centerpiece of the majority's analysis."

Thomas v. INS, 35 F.3d 1332, 1344 (9th Cir. 1994) (Kozinski, J., dissenting). See ARCHAISM.

N.B. is the abbreviation for *nota bene* (= note well; take notice).

necessaries; necessities. In legal senses, *necessaries* is the usual term for "things that are indispensable (to life)." E.g., "Claims for *necessaries* furnished to the beneficiary of a spendthrift or support trust may be enforced against his trust interest." Though one might suppose that necessaries would be the same for everyone, the law does not so hold: "It might be held that ten suits of clothes are necessaries for one infant, whereas three suits might not be deemed necessary for another. The whole question turns upon the infant's status in life." 1 E.W. Chance, *Principles of Mercantile Law* 44–45 (P.W. French ed., 13th ed. 1950).

Necessities has the broader sense of "indispensable things," whatever the subject at hand may be.

necessary; necessitous. *Necessary,* the more common word, means "essential." (See **indispensable.**) Almost always used correctly, *necessary* is ill-used when it introduces an infinitive without a BE-VERB preceding it—e.g.: "The only Massachusetts case *necessary to analyze* [read *that it is necessary to analyze* or *that must be analyzed here*] is *Balch v. Stone, supra,* since all other cases from that state followed the *Balch* case without further discussion of the soundness of the rule." *Maud v. Catherwood,* 155 P.2d 111, 118 (Cal. Dist. Ct. App. 1945).

Necessitous = placed or living in a condition of necessity or poverty; hard-up. E.g., "It will be found that where a gift results in mere financial enrichment, a trust has been sustained only when the court found and concluded from the entire context of the will that the ultimate intended recipients were poor or in *necessitous* circumstances."

necessitate (= to make necessary) is often inferior to *require.* Yet *require* cannot always substitute for it: "The ALJ's failure to explain his reason for crediting certain testimony while ignoring more substantial evidence could normally *necessitate* a remand."/ "Appellant knew that his insistence on his right to represent himself would, perforce, *necessitate* his giving up his right to counsel."

necessities. See **necessaries.**

necessitous. See **necessary.**

necessity, in criminal law, denotes a utilitarian idea: that it is sometimes better to break the law than to follow it to the letter. It might lead an appellate court to overturn the murder convictions of four cave explorers who, having gone without food for 21 days and being on the verge of starvation, killed a companion and ate the flesh to survive. Then again, it might not. The doctrine of necessity might lead a court to approve a doctor's decision to perform an illegal, third-trimester abortion in order to save the mother's life. Some writers use *duress of circumstances* as an equivalent phrase.

neck verse. This phrase denotes the first verse of Psalm 51 (*Miserere mei, Deus* "Have mercy on me, O God"), which was traditionally used as a literacy test for an accused to claim *benefit of clergy.* Although judges might choose passages at random, they tended to stick to Psalm 51, with the result that, by the end of the 16th century, half of all convicted felons were able to save their necks by successfully claiming benefit of clergy. See J.H. Baker, *An Introduction to English Legal History* 587 (3d ed. 1990). The reading of the neck verse was abolished in 1707. See **benefit of clergy.**

NEEDLESS VARIANTS, two or more forms of the same word without nuance or DIFFERENTIATION, and seemingly without even hope for either, teem in the language of the law. They teem in the English language for that matter, especially in the outer reaches of the language—that is, in technical vocabulary. Unfortunately, the unnecessary coexistence of variant forms, adjectives in *-tive* and *-tory* for example, lead not to precision in technical writing but to uncertainties about authorial intention. (Trusting readers think to themselves, "The writer used *punitive* on the last page but now has pressed into service *punitory*—is a distinction intended?")

"It is a source not of strength," wrote Fowler, "but of weakness, that there should be two names for the same thing [by-forms differing merely in suffix or in some such minor point], because the reasonable assumption is that two words mean two things, and confusion results when they do not" (*MEU1* 373). The confusion is perhaps greatest when writers who are fond of INELEGANT VARIATION discover the boundless mutations of form that exist in law: they will write *res judicata* in one paragraph, *res adjudicata* in the next; *a quo* in one sentence, *a qua* in the next; *recusal, recusement,* then *recusation;* and so on.

"On the other hand," we are advised to take note, "it may be much too hastily assumed that two words do mean the same thing; they may, for instance, denote the same object without meaning the same thing if they imply that the aspect from which it is regarded is different, or are appropriate in different mouths, or differ in rhythmic value or in some other matter that may escape a cursory examination" (*MEU1* 373). Hence the nonlawyer should not jump to assume that *necessaries* is uncalled for in place of *necessities;* that *acquittance* has no place alongside *acquittal;* that *recusancy* is yet another needless variant of the three similar words cited above; that *burglarize* is as good for a British audience as it is for an American one; and so forth. For just such an incorrect assumption, see **wrong.**

Any number of entries throughout this work attempt to ferret out and discriminate between cognate words that have established or emerging distinctions and those that seem, at present, to have neither. To the extent possible, words and phrases rightly classifiable as needless variants ought to be dropped from the language.

need not necessarily is a REDUNDANCY. E.g., "One's misconduct *need not necessarily have* [read *need not have*] been of such a nature as to be punishable as a crime or as to justify legal proceedings of any character."/ "Those injured in accidents would come to understand that matters *need not necessarily* [read *need not*] end with a simple bow and a flourish of the checkbook."

needs must is an idiomatic phrase deriving from Elizabethan English. Its inverted sibling is *must needs,* which is slightly older. In both phrases, *needs* = necessarily. E.g., "White is not satisfied, as bolder activists are, to assert that Justices are not bound by the Constitution; he *needs must* attribute his 'eccentric' view to the Framers."

ne exeat is a LATINISM that has given its name to the writ, no longer widely used, ordering the person to whom it is addressed not to leave the country or the jurisdiction of the court. E.g., "The wife then prayed that a writ of *ne exeat* be issued forthwith to prevent the defendant from leaving the state until he had paid the support arrearages and attorneys' fees."

The name of the writ derives from the Roman-law writ of *ne exeat republica* (= let him not go out from the republic). See *Foote v. Foote,* 140 A. 312, 313 (N.J. 1928). The medieval writ was *ne exeat regno.*

negative, v.t. This verb—meaning "to deny, nullify, or render ineffective"—was one of the earliest Americanisms, having first appeared in the American colonies in the early 18th century. Today the usage is an ARCHAISM, *negate* having taken over the work formerly handled by the verb *to negative.*

Yet the verb *negative* persists in law, particularly (and oddly) in BrE—e.g.: "This contention is quite plainly *negatived* by the latter part of the provision." (Eng.)/ "Such an interference with a rival trader's right to a free course of trade leads to an almost irresistible inference of an indirect motive, and is therefore—unless the motive is *negatived*—a wrongful act as against his right." (Eng.) For more immediate comprehensibility to lawyers and nonlawyers alike, *negate* should be adopted as the preferred term.

negative, in the. See **affirmative, in the.**

negative pregnant; affirmative pregnant. *Negative pregnant* (= a negative implying or involving an affirmative) is an old POPULARIZED LEGAL TECHNICALITY. The idea usually involves a denial that implies (is pregnant with) its opposite. For example, if a suspected thief is asked, "Did you break into the house at #8 Country Club Drive on Tuesday?" and responds by saying, "No, I didn't do it on Tuesday," the implication is that only the day is wrong. The full phrase is *negative pregnant with an affirmative.*

The *affirmative pregnant* (= a nonresponsive positive statement implying or involving a negative) is not so well known. For example, if a suspected thief is asked, "Did you take the Geochron from the house?" and responds by saying, "I tried to return it the next day!" the implication is that the true answer was "yes."

NEGATIVES. A. Colliding Negatives. Lawyers have become notorious for their proclivity to pile negative upon negative. The result is sentences that most fellow lawyers have a hard time decoding:

- "The order *enjoined* required the five railroad companies to *abstain* from *refusing* to deliver interstate shipments of livestock." (Quoted in F.E. Cooper, *Effective Legal Writing* 29 (1954).)
- "The trial court temporarily *enjoined* defendant from *refusing* to supply water service to petitioners' house on account of their *not* having paid a deposit, *without* notice and *without* bond."
- "Notwithstanding anything in subsection (3) of section two of the principal Act, a disablement allowance need *not* be considered at intervals of *not* less than three years in any case where the Treasury so directs." (Eng.)
- "Courts should *not,* by self-imposed impotence, *not* required by the precedents, be less efficacious."

- "A plan shall *not* be treated as *not* satisfying the requirements of this section solely because the spouse of the participant is *not* entitled to receive a survivor annuity (whether or *not* an election has been made . . .), *unless* the participant and his spouse have been married throughout the 1-year period ending on the date of such participant's death." Employee Retirement Income Security Act of 1974, Pub. L. No. 93-406, § 205(d), 88 Stat. 829, 863 (1974).

See PLAIN LANGUAGE (D).

B. *Not un——; not in——.* Double negatives such as *not untimely* are often used quite needlessly in place of a more straightforward wording such as *timely.* Could an action be *not untimely* but somehow not be *timely?*

Sometimes however, the double-negative form conveys an important nuance. The difference often has to do not with logic but with the burden of proof. For example, many jurisdictions admit customs as law if they are *not unreasonable.* Thus, the party who proves the existence of a custom does not have the further burden of showing that it is *reasonable.* Rather, to defeat the custom, the disputing party must show that it is *unreasonable.* The rule, then, is that customs will be admitted *unless they are unreasonable,* not that they will be admitted *if they are reasonable.*

Such constructions may also have a wider embrace within gray areas. Consider, for example, a set of national rules that allow *local rules not inconsistent with these rules.* Would the same meaning be conveyed by *local rules consistent with these rules?* No: if, for example, the national rules were silent on a question such as the size of paper for filed materials, a local rule specifying such sizes might not be *consistent with* the local rules—but it would certainly be *not inconsistent with* them. *Not inconsistent* prevents clashes; *consistent with* ensures conformity.

Finally, the double-negative form, shorn of any greater context, often connotes something quite different from a positive rendering. E.g., "The doctrine of equitable conversion is *not unrestricted* in its application." 1 H.T. Tiffany, *The Law of Real Property* § 299, at 510 (B. Jones ed., 3d ed. 1939). The sense is changed by writing, *The doctrine . . . is restricted in its application.*

But when the negatives serve no such identifiable purpose, they ought to be avoided. To say, for example, that a point of law is *not uninteresting* or *not unintelligible* is to engage in a time-wasting rhetorical flourish.

C. Negative Prefixes. The primary negative prefixes in English are *un-*, *in-* (assimilated in many words to *il-*, *im-*, *ir-*), *non-*, and *anti-*. For purposes of simple negation, *in-* is the most particularized of these prefixes, since it generally goes only with certain Latin nouns, and *non-* is the broadest of them, for it may precede virtually any word. As a general rule, it is best to find the most suitable particularized prefix, and if none is really suitable, then to have recourse to *non-*. (*Anti-*, of course, has the special sense "against.") *Un-* usually precedes those Latin verbs ending in the Anglo-Saxon *-ed (unexhausted, undiluted, unsaturated).*

Consistency is often difficult to find with particular roots. For example, *unexhausted remedies* yields *nonexhaustion,* not *unexhaustion.* Likewise, we have *indubitable* but *undoubted, irresolute* but *unresolved, irrespective* but *unrespected.* From a typographical standpoint, negative prefixes cause trouble with phrasal adjectives, as in *uncross-examined civil deposition.* Roundabout wordings are usually preferable to such telescoping; hence, *a civil deposition in which the witness was not cross-examined.* See NON-.

D. Periphrastic Negatives. Generally, "We disagree" is preferable to "We do not agree," unless some emphatic form such as the latter is called for in context to rebut an assertion. Directness is better than indirectness; hence *violate* rather than *fail to comply with; violate* rather than *do not adhere to,* and the like.

E. *No* and *not*. Lawyers often seem to prefer quaint reversals of modern usage: they say *not* when most native speakers of English would say *no,* and vice-versa. This tendency is esp. common in the phrase *not more than* (for *no more than*), but it can be seen at work in other phrases as well. The better legal writers stick to the more natural, more modern idiom. E.g., "Congress has chosen, *wisely or no* [read *wisely or not*], to speak to the precise issue at hand through a Committee Report that was expressly adopted by both Houses." *ACLU v. FCC,* 823 F.2d 1554, 1583 (D.C. Cir. 1987) (Starr, J., dissenting in part). See **not** & ARCHAISMS.

F. Special Problems with *not*. See **not.**

neglect (= the act or condition of disregarding) does not necessarily involve *negligence.* For example, "neglect of a child" may be either negligent or willful. Then again, in some contexts neglect may even include inadvertent omission that does not rise to the level of negligence. Therefore *negligent neglect* is not necessarily a REDUNDANCY. Cf. **omission (B).**

A leading English treatise on criminal law distinguishes *neglect* from *negligence* in the following way. *Neglect* indicates, as a purely objective fact, that a person has not performed a duty, but it does not indicate the *reason* for the failure. *Negligence,* by contrast, denotes a subjective state of mind and indicates a particular reason why the person has failed to perform a duty—namely, because the person has not kept the duty in mind. See J.W. Cecil Turner, *Kenny's Outlines of Criminal Law* 108 n.1 (16th ed. 1952). See **negligence (A).**

neglectful; neglective. The latter is a NEEDLESS VARIANT that is rare or obsolete.

negligible; negligeable. The latter spelling should be avoided.

negligence. **A. Senses.** In general usage, *negligence* means "carelessness." But in legal usage, *negligence* = (1) the failure to exercise the standard of care that the doer as a reasonable person should have exercised in the circumstances; (2) undue indifference toward the consequences of one's act; or (3) a tort that includes the notions of duty, breach of that duty (unreasonable conduct), and resultant damage.

The term has various gradations: "Negligence in law ranges from inadvertence that is hardly more than accidental to sinful disregard of the safety of others." Patrick Devlin, *The Enforcement of Morals* 36 (1968). *Ordinary* or *simple negligence* is usu. sufficient to establish liability in a tort action. *Criminal* or *gross negligence* is usu. required before the court will impose a penalty. The phrase *gross negligence* has the disadvantage of applying both in civil actions (to increase damages) and in criminal actions (to establish criminal liability); many criminal lawyers therefore prefer *criminal negligence* in criminal-law contexts.

B. And *neglect*. See **neglect.**

C. And *negligency*. The word *negligency* is a NEEDLESS VARIANT of *negligence.*

negligent neglect. See **neglect.**

negotiability; assignability. These two terms are related but distinct. The two major ways in which *negotiability* differs from *assignability* are: (1) no notice need be given of the transfer of a negotiable instrument; and (2) the transfer of such an instrument is not subject to equitable remedies (i.e., from a claimant who might assert a right to or under the instrument). See **assignment & negotiable instrument.**

negotiable instrument; commercial paper. These terms are not interchangeable. *Commercial paper* is now the more widely used term in the U.S. because of its use in article three of the Uniform Commercial Code. As to the precise distinction, *commercial paper* is the broader term: it may include nonnegotiable as well as negotiable paper, whereas *negotiable instruments* are by definition negotiable ones only.

Generally, a writing is *negotiable* when it is signed by the maker or drawer; contains an unconditional promise or order to pay a sum certain in money, and no other promise, obligation, or power given by the maker or drawer; is payable on demand or at a definite time; and is payable to order or to bearer. The absence of any one of these elements makes commercial paper nonnegotiable.

negotiate = (1) to discuss or conduct a business transaction, such as a contract or sale; or (2) to transfer (a negotiable instrument [q.v.], such as a note or bond) in a way that makes the transferee the legal owner of the instrument. E.g., sense (2): "When a cheque is transferred, whether by delivery or endorsement, it is said to be negotiated, and negotiation is a kind of transfer [that] differs in important respects from the ordinary assignment of a contractual right." William Geldart, *Introduction to English Law* 124 (D.C.M. Yardley ed., 9th ed. 1984).

neither . . . nor. **A. Singular or Plural Verb.** When one of the two subjects is singular, and the other is plural, the verb takes its number from the closer subject. Thus, the verb is invariably singular if the second alternative is singular—e.g.: "*Neither the speed at which the car was traveling* [read *Neither the car's speed*] nor its operation through a red light *are* [read *is*] enough to make out a case against appellants provided there was no reckless disregard for the safety of others."/ "Neither of these views *are* [read *is*] acceptable." H.L.A. Hart, "Negligence, *Mens Rea,* and Criminal Responsibility," in *Punishment and Responsibility: Essays in the Philosophy of Law* 136, 150 (1968)./ "Neither hanging the governor in effigy nor hanging the governor *are* [read *is*] speech . . . ." Steven J. Burton, *An Introduction to Law and Legal Reasoning* 70 (1985). See SUBJECT-VERB AGREEMENT (E).

Moreover, the verb should match the nearest subject in number and person. Sometimes the correct form is admittedly awkward—e.g.: "Neither you nor I *is* [read *am*] likely to change the world . . . ." Jefferson D. Bates, *Writing with Precision* 82 (rev. ed. 1988).

B. Number of Elements. These CORRELATIVE CONJUNCTIONS should frame only two elements, not more; though it is possible to find modern and historical examples of *neither . . . nor* with more than two members, such constructions are, in Wilson Follett's words, "short of punctilious." E.g.,

"The October contract was *neither surrendered, abrogated, nor annulled* [read *was not surrendered, abrogated, or annulled*]."/ "We believe that the California Supreme Court's application of the minimum-contacts test in this case would, if sustained, sanction a result that is *neither fair, just, nor reasonable* [read *not fair, just, or reasonable* or *unfair, unjust, and unreasonable*]."/ "Finding the decision by the ICC to be supported by substantial evidence and *neither arbitrary, capricious, nor an abuse of discretion* [read *not arbitrary, capricious, or an abuse of discretion*], we deny the petitions./ "*Because Rummel neither signed, read, nor heard* [read *Because Rummel did not sign, read, or hear*] the entire document, these notes fail to qualify as a statement under this subsection."

It is permissible, however, to use a second *nor* emphatically in framing three elements: "*Neither* inadvertent failure to provide medical care, *nor* carelessness, *nor* even deliberate failure to conform to the standards suggested by the experts is cruel and unusual punishment." Cf. **either (E).**

C. Parallelism. Not only ought there to be no more than two elements, as explained in (B), but also the elements ought to match each other syntactically. (See PARALLELISM.) E.g., "P was held not liable for trespass to the person, the harm being accidental, and due *neither to negligence nor lack of caution* [read *neither to negligence nor to lack of caution*]." L.B. Curzon, *English Legal History* 256 (2d ed. 1979)./ "Ex parte New York No. 1 makes it clear that the State *can neither be proceeded against directly nor impleaded* [read: *can be neither proceeded against directly nor impleaded*] in an action brought against the private owners." Grant Gilmore & Charles L. Black, Jr., *The Law of Admiralty* 612 (2d ed. 1975).

D. *Neither . . . or.* This phraseology is a rank error—e.g.: "What if the intervention is *neither* foreseeable *or* [read *nor*] normal, but it leads to the same type of harm?"/"It appears that the admission was *neither* fraudulent *or* [read *nor*] willful and was due to oversight."/ "How is a 'male feminism' possible [that] assumes *neither* a false commonality of male and female experience *or* [read *nor*] a false essentialism?" J.M. Balkin, *Turandot's Victory,* 2 Yale J.L. & Human. 299, 302 (1990).

E. Beginning Sentences with. It is permissible, when introducing an additional point of contrast, to begin a sentence with *neither* or (more commonly) *nor*—e.g.: "[I]t is at least problematic whether the now official Catholic view, that a fetus has a full human soul at conception, is consistent with the Thomist tradition. *Nor* was that view thought necessary, in the past, to justify the strongest condemnation of even very early abortion." Ronald Dworkin, *Life's Dominion* 42–43 (1993). See **nor.**

nemine contradicente; nemine dissentiente. Both of these LATINISMS mean "without opposition or dissent." Either phrase may be more accurate than *unanimously* in a given context, for some of those entitled to vote may have abstained. In any event, the definition just given probably serves better than either of the recherché main entries.

NEOLOGISMS, or invented words, are to be used carefully and self-consciously. Usually they demand an explanation or justification, for the English language is quite well stocked as it is. The most obvious neologisms in -IZE, for example, are to be eschewed. New words must fill demonstrable voids, as *conclusory,* a 20th-century word, does. If a word is invented merely for the sake of novelty, then it is vexatious.

Some writers seem to relish neologisms, as if the new words alone could add freshness to writing. For most readers, they add merely irritation to writing—e.g.: "This would not be *contraventive* or *thwartive* of our mandate . . . ." *Buder v. Fiske,* 191 F.2d 321, 324 (8th Cir. 1951). (Why not *would not contravene or thwart our mandate?*)/ Lance S. Hamilton, *Ethnomiseducationalization: A Legal Challenge,* 100 Yale L.J. 1815 (1991). (Since the article is about ideas for which we already have words, why not *ethnocentric education, educational ethnocentrism, ethnocentric miseducation,* or some such phrase?)

Other writers self-consciously state that they have no adequate word. Their efforts are likely to fail (merely because the odds are stacked against neologists), but they have a utilitarian standard in mind—e.g.: "There is no accepted adjective from 'theft,' but the word *'theftous'* will here be used." Glanville Williams, *Textbook of Criminal Law* 645 n.2 (1978).

Legal language has been the source of many neologisms over the past century. In fact, lawyers have probably tended toward the latter of the two opposing disasters that Lon Fuller wrote of: "linguistic stagnation and grotesque fecundity." *Legal Fictions* 22 (1967). Thus Pollock and Maitland had it, rather uncharacteristically, all wrong: "The licence that the man of science can allow himself of coining new words is one which by the nature of the case is denied to lawyers." 2 Frederick Pollock & Frederic W. Maitland, *History of English Law* 31 (2d ed. 1905). Rather, "neologisms abound in modern legal writing, though both writer and reader are often unaware that certain commonplace law words have yet to find a home in English dictionaries." Bryan A. Garner, "The Missing Common-Law Words," in

The State of the Language 235, 237 (Christopher Ricks & Leonard Michaels eds., 1990). See LEGO-.

nephew; niece. Legally speaking, are the children of a spouse's siblings one's *nephews* and *nieces?* No: "It is only by courtesy that the children of a husband's or wife's brothers and sisters are called *'nephews'* and *'nieces'* . . . ." *Fedi v. Ryan,* 193 A. 801, 802 (N.J. 1937)./ "It is only 'loosely' that the son of a brother-in-law or sister-in-law is called a *nephew.*" *In re Estate of Terney,* 396 P.2d 557, 558 (Or. 1964).

nepotism is best reserved for the sense "bestowal of official favors upon members of one's family," and not attenuated to refer to any friends or political connections. The root sense of *nepot-* in Latin is "nephew, grandson."

NEUTER FORMS. See SEXISM.

new lease on life. See POPULARIZED LEGAL TECHNICALITIES.

news is a singular noun. "The *news* also *has* an exchange value to one who can misappropriate it."

newsagent. One word.

next friend; guardian *ad litem; prochein ami.* Technically, an incompetent or minor plaintiff sues by a *next friend,* whereas an incompetent or minor defendant is defended by a *guardian ad litem;* but the duties and powers of the representative are identical regardless of the title. *Dacanay v. Mendoza,* 573 F.2d 1075, 1076 n.1 (9th Cir. 1978).

Nonlawyers occasionally misunderstand *next friend* as if it were literal—e.g.: "We say that a minor brings a suit 'by his *next friend*'; that is, by his nearest friend." Richard Grant White, *Every-Day English* 415 (1880). "Nearest friend" is not a good translation: a *next friend* is usually a parent or general guardian.

The phrase *next friend* is to be preferred to the LAW FRENCH *prochein ami,* of which it is a LOAN TRANSLATION. E.g., "By this standard an individual is deemed competent or incompetent to assert his rights for purposes of conferring standing on *next-friend* petitioners."/ "The district court sought merely to clarify that the amount awarded to the minor children would be paid to their parents as their *next friends.*" See ***prochein ami.***

next of kin. See **heir (C).**

next preceding is an awkward phrase, arguably illogical, that commonly appears in DRAFTING. E.g., "All assurances mentioned herein must be satisfactorily tendered on the day *next preceding* [read *before*] the closing date."/ "Anything *in the next preceding paragraph of this contract* [read *in the paragraph immediately preceding this one*] notwithstanding . . . ."

nexus is the law's learned word for *connection* or *multiple connections.* Lawyers have long found it useful—e.g.: "The defendant's *nexus* with this country and with this district is not accidental."

The acceptable plural forms are either *nexuses* (English) or *nexus* (Latin)—e.g.: "When both *nexuses* are established, the litigant will have shown a taxpayer's stake in the outcome . . . ." *Flast v. Cohen,* 392 U.S. 83, 103 (1968). Some writers have betrayed their ignorance of Latin by writing *nexi,* as if it were a second-declension noun, whereas the word nexus is a fourth-declension noun—e.g.: "[T]he state's theory would broaden the *Skiriotes* concept of 'citizen' to encompass all American nationals, and hence most if not all of the Bering Sea crabbers, because of their numerous *nexi* [read *nexuses* or *nexus*] with Alaska." *State v. Bundrant,* 546 P.2d 530, 555 (Alaska 1976)./ "The Lees denied that the application and initial premium . . . had been delivered in the District and emphasized the various *nexi* [read *nexuses* or *nexus*] mentioned above with the State of Maryland." *Lee v. Wheeler,* 810 F.2d 303, 304 (D.C. Cir. 1987). (In Latin, *nexi* = persons who have been reduced to quasi-slavery for debt!) Cf. **apparatus & prospectus (A).** See PLURALS (A) & HYPERCORRECTION (A).

nice question = a subtle question. In this phrase, as in other similar ones, *nice* takes on the sense "not obvious or readily apprehended; difficult to decide or settle; demanding close consideration or thought" (*OED*). E.g., "*Nice questions* have arisen as to what constitutes a dedication to the public." William F. Walsh, *A Treatise on Equity* 218 (1930)./ "The cases are divided on this *nice question.*" Charles A. Wright, *The Law of Federal Courts* 245 (4th ed. 1983).

niece. See **nephew.**

niggardly (= grudging, stingy) derives from an Old Norse word (*hnøggr* "covetous, stingy"); it has nothing to do with the racial slur that is sounded similarly. E.g., "A tall, heavy-set, good-looking Irishman, he was never *niggardly* about attorney fees." Murray T. Bloom, *The Trouble with Lawyers* 272 (1970). Even so, some speakers and writers have come to shun it just to avoid MISCUES or even serious misunderstandings.

nihil ad rem (= irrelevant) serves no useful purpose in the language.

nil dicit; nihil dicit [L. "he (or she) says nothing."]. These Latin phrases are used adjectivally to mean "of or relating to a default judgment for the plaintiff entered after the defendant fails to file a timely answer." The form *nil dicit* slightly predominates. A contracted version of *nihil,* the form *nil* appeared even in classical Latin. E.g., "The court granted a *nil dicit* judgment for Nelson after First State failed to file an answer."

In Texas, a *nil dicit* default judgment is contrasted with a no-answer default judgment: with the latter, the defendant fails both to file an answer and to make an appearance, whereas with a *nil dicit* default judgment, the defendant appears, and may even file preliminary motions, but fails to file an answer.

Some writers wisely hyphenate the expression as a PHRASAL ADJECTIVE < a *nil-dicit* default judgment>.

nine (old) men. This phrase, denoting the U.S. Supreme Court, sprang up when, during the early 20th century, the Court blocked progressive legislation largely because of the majority's personal, political, and social views. In 1936, a book appeared in which the phrase was used as the title: Drew Pearson & Robert Allen, *Nine Old Men* (1936). Countless similar uses of the phrase soon began to appear—e.g.: "The *nine men* in black robes hold the entire structure of the nation in the hallowed hollows of their hands." Fred Rodell, *Woe Unto You, Lawyers!* 41 (1939; repr. 1980). (This use by Fred Rodell anticipates the title of his 1955 book, *Nine Men.*)/ "The *'nine old men'* of the United States Supreme Court are not so infirm that they cannot perform the most surprising handsprings." Ephraim Tutt, *Yankee Lawyer* 444 (1943)./ "[A]fter several setbacks Roosevelt vented his frustration with his 'court-packing' plan of 1937, railing at the *'nine old men'* (the youngest was sixty-two, their average age seventy-two) who blocked the path of progress." Donald D. Jackson, *Judges* 338 (1974). See **Court-packing plan.**

nisi /***nI***-sI, ***nI***-see, ***nee***-see, or ***nis***-ee/ [L. "unless"] = (of a court's ex parte ruling or grant of relief) having validity unless the adversely affected party appears and shows cause why it should be withdrawn. The word is commonly used in the phrase *rule nisi*—e.g.: "The motion to appoint counsel was filed and the *rule nisi* issued during pendency of James's notice of appeal. . . ." *State v. James,* 438 S.E.2d 399, 400 (Ga. Ct. App. 1993)./ "On October 13, 1992, the mother filed a petition for *rule nisi* requesting that the trial court hold the father in contempt for his failure to pay child support." *Leslie v. Beringer,* 636 So. 2d 441, 442 (Ala. Civ. App. 1994). See **decree absolute.**

nisi prius (lit., "unless before then") refers generally to a civil trial court in which issues are tried before the jury—as opposed to an appellate court. The curious reader may well wonder what the semantic path is from "unless before then" to "trial." The answer lies deep in the recesses of English legal history: the phrase *nisi prius* was a prominent one at the outset of the medieval writ directing the sheriff to summon a jury at Westminster, "unless before" the appointed date the judges of assize arrived in the county where the cause of action arose. If those itinerant justices did arrive, they would try the case locally instead of at Westminster. Because the writ concerned only trial by jury, it became associated with jury trials. In the U.S., the phrase has even been extended to refer to nonjury trials.

A little American law dictionary mangles this etymology, stating: "Literally translated [*nisi prius*] means 'unless the first,' i.e., unless it is the original or first forum it is not a *'nisi prius'* court." Stephen H. Gifis, *Law Dictionary* 320 (3d ed. 1991). The author's mistake lies in trying to find a modern meaning in the phrase *nisi prius,* which even 19th-century law reference works termed "unmeaning in its literal translation." 2 Alexander M. Burrill, *A Law Dictionary and Glossary* 233 (2d ed. 1867).

In England, the nisi prius system became defunct in 1971, when it was replaced by the system of Crown Courts. The phrase *nisi prius* is likewise obsolete in most parts of the U.S., but two American jurisdictions—New York and Oklahoma—continue to use the legal ARCHAISM. The phrase is almost always used attributively, that is, modifying a noun that follows—e.g.:

- "Recent jurisprudence, dispositive of all issues raised below, calls for reversal of the *nisi prius* postdecree order." *Evans v. Evans,* 852 P.2d 145, 147–48 (Okla. 1993).
- "The *nisi prius* court's position that any cause of action accrued in 1983 because plaintiff's assignor's right to future payments was rejected, is simply an assertion of an anticipatory breach by defendants." *Vigilant Ins. Co. v. Housing Auth.,* 614 N.Y.S.2d 533, 535 (App. Div. 1994).
- "Here the *nisi prius* judge's signature authenti-

cates the judgment on the face of the memorial." *Aven v. Reeh,* 878 P.2d 1069, 1074 (Okla. 1994).

In most American jurisdictions, the JARGON phrase *nisi prius* would be replaced with *trial court's* in the first example, and with *trial* in the second and third examples.

nitpick is so spelled—not *knitpick*—though pointing this out may seem nitpicky. E.g., "The *Hovanec* decision upon the facts there presented is hypertechnical, is an indulgence in *knitpicking* [read *nitpicking*], and is an obvious disregard of R.C. 4123.95 . . . ." *Wires v. Doehler-Jarvis Div. of NL Indus., Inc.,* 345 N.E.2d 629, 632 (Ohio Ct. App. 1974).

nitroglycerine charge. See **dynamite charge.**

no; not. See NEGATIVES (E).

no bill, v.t. See NOUNS AS VERBS.

nobody. See **no one.**

no case. In English criminal procedure, a submission of *no case* (or *no case to answer*) is the same as the American lawyer's motion for *judgment of acquittal* (in federal practice) or motion for *directed verdict* (abolished by the federal rules but still used in some states). In effect, the defense counsel, at the close of the prosecution's *case-in-chief* (q.v.), submits to the judge that there is no case that needs answering. British lawyers sometimes use the expression *directed verdict* as well.

nocent (= guilty) is obsolete. *Innocent,* the opposite form, is common.

no-compete covenant is an illogical form of *covenant* [or *agreement*] *not to compete* or *noncompetition covenant* [or *agreement*]. It should be avoided in favor of either of these longer phrases. E.g., "It seems reasonably clear that some allocation of the price to a covenant is necessary if a purchaser wants to deduct any amount for a *no-compete covenant* [read *covenant not to compete*]." See **noncompetition covenant.**

no contest; *nolo contendere.* The English phrase is no doubt preferable merely because it is more comprehensible to more people. Journalists rightly tend to use *no contest* even in jurisdictions in which the plea is called *nolo contendere.* E.g., "City Manager David Ivory pleaded *no contest* Thursday to two misdemeanor charges of improperly accepting cash from a company that was doing business with the city." Selwyn D. Crawford, *FW Official Pleads No Contest to Getting Cash,* Dallas Morning News, 8 Dec. 1989, at 33A. As a PHRASAL ADJECTIVE, it is hyphenated: *no-contest plea.*

With a plea of *no contest* or *nolo contendere* (lit., "I do not wish to contend"), the defendant does not admit guilt but nevertheless agrees not to offer a defense. The primary legal purpose of such a plea—whichever name is used—is that the defendant retains the right to deny the charge in any other judicial proceedings.

no doubt. See **doubtless(ly).**

no-fault divorce = divorce on either spouse's unilateral demand, without the necessity of proving elements that the law formerly required, such as adultery or cruelty. During the late 1960s and 1970s, the system of no-fault divorce was adopted throughout the U.S., as well as in England (1969) and Scotland (1977). The phrase is really a misnomer and an OXYMORON, for in divorce there is always enough fault to go around. What the courts and the parties (rightly) wanted to avoid was proving and apportioning fault in routine cases. See **divorce.**

noisome is sometimes misconstrued as meaning "noisy; loud; clamorous." In fact, it means "noxious; malodorous." (Cf. **fulsome.**) The word is related etymologically to *annoy.* Cardozo, naturally, used it correctly: "If the house is to be cleaned, it is for those who occupy and govern it, rather than for strangers, to do the *noisome* work." *People ex rel. Karlin v. Culkin,* 162 N.E. 487, 493 (N.Y. 1928).

no later than (= on or before) conveys an important nuance in the language of DRAFTING. It is not equivalent to *before,* which does not include the date specified.

Although *within 10 days after* might seem stylistically preferable to *no later than 10 days after,* the choice is not a stylistic one. The two phrases have different meanings, as the following examples illustrate: (a) a motion for relief filed *within* 10 days after entry of judgment; and (b) a motion for relief filed *no later than* 10 days after entry of judgment. In the first version, judgment must be entered for the provision to apply; in the second version, no entry of judgment need occur for the provision to apply. If an event triggers the clock, *within* requires one to wait for that triggering event, but *no later than* does not.

nolens volens (= willingly or unwillingly) would be considered a far-fetched LATINISM in most modern legal prose. E.g., "Correlative to all such legal powers are the legal liabilities in other persons—this meaning that the latter are subject *nolens volens* [read *willingly or unwillingly*] to the changes of jural relations involved in the exercise of A's powers." (Hohfeld) See **willy-nilly.**

no less. **A. And *no fewer*.** The phrase *no less,* just like *less,* q.v., best refers to amounts or to mass nouns, not countable numbers. *No fewer* is the better phrase when discussing numbers of things. But some excellent writers have nodded on this point:

- "America has already formed treaties with *no less* [read *no fewer*] than six foreign nations . . . ." *The Federalist* No. 3, at 42 (John Jay) (Clinton Rossiter ed., 1961).
- "[I]n *no less* [read *no fewer*] than twenty-four states, an acknowledgment by the father, orally or in writing, is sufficient." Max Radin, *The Law and You* 32 (1948).
- "[H]e had appointed *no less* [read *no fewer*] than forty-two new justices of the peace . . . ." Fred Rodell, *Nine Men* 86 (1955).
- "The settlor could employ *no less* [read *no fewer*] than three different types of future interest . . . ." A.W.B. Simpson, *An Introduction to the History of the Land Law* 217 (1961).
- "Beven identified *no less* [read *no fewer*] than fifty-seven varieties of duty." J.H. Baker, *An Introduction to English Legal History* 476–77 (3d ed. 1990).
- "The point of law involved was one of extreme complexity and it was considered by *no less* [read *no fewer*] than fourteen judges sitting in the Court for Crown Cases Reserved." Rupert Cross & J.W. Harris, *Precedent in English Law* 86 (4th ed. 1991).

B. And *not less*. In DRAFTING, the two phrases are indistinguishable, *no less* being the more natural and therefore the better form. E.g., "Each participating company must have *no less* than $10,000 in cash posted by May 31, 1994."

In other types of expository writing, however, *no less* connotes surprise: "He weighs *no less* than 300 pounds." That sentence expresses astonishment that he weighs so much. *Not less* is more clinical and dispassionate: "He weighs *not less* than 300 pounds." That sentence states matter-of-factly that he weighs at least that much and maybe more. See NEGATIVES (E).

nolle prosequi(tur); non prosequitur. **A. As Nouns.** The phrase *nolle prosequi* (lit., "not to wish to prosecute") denotes either (1) the legal notice of abandonment of suit, or (2) a docket entry showing that the plaintiff or the prosecution has relinquished the action. *Nolle* is frequently used as a shortened form—e.g.: "We conclude that the nine-month period between the *nolle* and the defendant's rearrest is not properly chargeable as a pretrial delay for purposes of speedy trial analysis." *State v. Gaston,* 503 A.2d 594, 597 (Conn. 1986).

Non prosequitur (lit., "he does not prosecute") is the judgment rendered against a plaintiff who has not pursued the case. *Non pros* is the shortened nominal form, here functioning adjectivally: "[A]ppellants contest on appeal the trial court's opening of a *non pros* judgment entered in their favor." *Geyer v. Steinbronn,* 506 A.2d 901, 905 (Pa. Super. Ct. 1986).

Nolle prosequitur is a hybrid form that is simply meaningless.

B. As Verbs. *Nolle prosequi* is only a noun in England, but has two verb forms in the U.S., *nol-pros* and *nolle pros.* The term means "to abandon a suit or have it dismissed by a nolle prosequi." E.g., "That plaintiff was arrested but never tried, and the charges against him were *nolle prossed.*" The earliest known use occurred in 1878.

Occasionally the phrase *nolle prosequi* is used as a verb in the U.S., although the shorter forms *nolle pros, nol-pros,* and *nol-pro* are more usual. E.g., "Gruskin's decision to permit defendant to admit responsibility for careless driving and to *nolle prosequi* the OUIL [operating a motor vehicle under the influence of intoxicating liquor] charge was an executive function . . . ." *People v. Stackpoole,* 375 N.W.2d 419, 424 (Mich. Ct. App. 1985).

Nonpros = to enter a *non prosequitur* against. The past tense form is *nonprossed.* Blackstone wrote *nonpros'd.* This word dates from about 1755.

nolo (L. "I do not wish") appears frequently as a shortened form of the full phrase, *nolo contendere.* E.g., "The reason the *nolo* plea makes a difference is that it protects defendants in subsequent criminal or civil litigation growing out of the act on which the criminal prosecution is based." Marcia Chambers, *'Nolo' Means You're Guilty Sort Of,* Nat'l L.J., 9 Nov. 1987, at 13./ "There are provisions for convictions based on *nolo* pleas and for verdicts of conviction that are not yet solidified in a judgment." Paul F. Rothstein, *Needed: A Rewrite,* Crim. Just. Summer 1989, at 20, 21.

nolo contendere (L. "I do not wish to contend") is so spelled. See **no contest.**

nominal = in name only, but not in reality. A *nominal party* is one who, having some interest in or title to the subject matter of the lawsuit, will not be affected by any judgment—an example being the disinterested stakeholder in a garnishment action. See **nominal consideration** & **nominal damages.**

nominal consideration; inadequate consideration. *Nominal consideration* is only of token value, whereas *inadequate consideration* has substantial value that is patently less than the value of the performance promised or rendered in return. Thus, to buy a $100,000 house, $10 might be termed *nominal consideration* while $30,000 might be termed *inadequate consideration.* The distinction matters in "exceptional cases in which the law treats promises or transfers supported only by nominal consideration differently from those supported by substantial or 'valuable' consideration (even though it may be inadequate)." G.H. Treitel, *The Law of Contract* 72 (8th ed. 1991).

nominal damages; substantial damages. The former are "awarded in a trivial amount merely as a recognition of some breach of a duty owed by a defendant to plaintiff and not as a measure of recompense for loss or detriment sustained"; the latter are "the result of an effort at measured compensation . . . ." Charles T. McCormick, *Handbook on the Law of Damages* § 20, at 85 (1935). *Nominal damages* are symbolic; *substantial damages* are compensatory.

NOMINALIZATIONS. See BURIED VERBS.

nominate, in the lawyer's vocabulary, is often just a highfalutin substitute for *name,* v.t. E.g., "In case the testator *nominates* [read *names*] no executor, or if for any reason the person *nominated* [read *named*] does not act, the court will appoint someone to perform the same functions . . . ." Thomas E. Atkinson, *Handbook of the Law of Wills* 5 (2d ed. 1953).

NOMINATIVE ABSOLUTES. See ABSOLUTE CONSTRUCTIONS.

NOMINATIVE AND OBJECTIVE CASES. One might think that a work of this kind, catering as it does to members of a learned profession, could pass over the differences between subjects and objects in pronouns. The two sentences that follow, however, belie that thought: the first was written by a lawyer, the second by a law professor. "We will need to confer with *whomever* works on this project and then have *he* or *she* draft a motion for summary judgment."/ "Third, the fault is said to lie in part with *we* 'eccentric professors.'" In the first example *whoever* should be the subject of *works* and the pronouns should be *him* and *her* as objects of *have;* in the second, *us* should be the object of the preposition *with.* See **who (A)** & HYPERCORRECTION (F).

Debilitated grammar seems ubiquitous—e.g.:

- "I would hold that Dr Rowland, when he made his will, intended by these words 'coinciding with' to cover *he* [read *him*] and his wife dying together in just such a calamity as in fact happened . . . ." *Re Rowland* [1963] 1 Ch. 1 (C.A.) (Lord Denning, M.R., dissenting).
- "Are we really that much smarter than *them* [read *they*]?" John B. Mitchell, *Current Theories on Expert and Novice Thinking,* 39 J. Legal Educ. 275, 275 (1989).
- "Winston [Churchill] was crouched like a great bird over the unusually small table, giving tea to his son Randolph, several years younger than *me* [read *I*]." Lord Hailsham, *Sad Memories of Dear Winston,* Sunday Times, 8 July 1990, at 3-16.
- "My mother was busy raising my brother and *I* [read *me*]."/ "Give Al Gore and *I* [read *me*] a chance to bring America back." Bill Clinton, accepting the Democratic nomination for President of the United States, 16 July 1992.

For *between you and I,* see **between (C)** & HYPERCORRECTION (B).

no more than. See **not more than.**

NON- (= not) is the general-purpose negative prefix that has gained a great deal of ground since the 19th century. *Non-* often contrasts with *in-* or *un-* in expressing a nongradable contrast, rather than the opposite end of a scale, e.g., *nonlegal* as compared to *illegal,* or *nonscientific* as compared to *unscientific.* (See **nonconstitutional.**) Ordinarily, esp. in AmE, the prefix is not hyphenated. A number of pitfalls lie in the way of its use, as categorized below. See generally NEGATIVES (B).

A. As a Separable Prefix. Except in a few historical phrases (e.g., the plea of *non assumpsit*), *non-* is properly used only as an inseparable or hyphenated prefix. Some legal writers, though, have tried to make it separable—e.g.: "But a trustee also has some *non statutory* [read *nonstatutory*] powers." R.T. Oerton, *Trustees and the Enduring Powers of Attorney Act 1985,* 130 Solic. J. 23, 23 (1986)./ "The Code seems to reflect a congressional perception that the taxation of the exercise of *non qualified* [read *nonqualified,* if not *unqualified*] stock options should be tightened up."/ "Rather, proof must be presented that the *non parties* [read *nonparties*] actively participated with the named party in violating the decree."

B. With Nouns. Before adding *non-* to a noun,

one should determine whether the noun being negated has an antonym that would suffice. For example, if *nonpretextual* means merely "valid" or "legitimate," it makes little sense to write: "The company showed that the reason for discharging the employee was *nonpretextual* [read, if appropriate, *legitimate*]." This infelicity may sometimes derive from tracking too closely statutory language, without searching for the most appropriate word. See SOUND OF PROSE, THE.

Another disadvantage in the use of *non-* is that it is beginning to displace the simplest negative, *not.* For example, "The cases relied upon in the opinion are *non-§ 1983 cases* [read *not § 1983 cases*] . . . ." *Grandstaff v. City of Borger,* 779 F.2d 1129, 1133 (5th Cir. 1986) (Hill, J., dissenting). As this example suggests, the use of this prefix to construct phrasal nouns can be especially awkward. "The critical issue before us concerns the order and allocation of proof in a *private, nonclass action* [read *private suit, not a class action,*] challenging employment discrimination."

C. With Adjectives. When adding *non-* to a compound adjective, the meaning can become especially murky: "noncivil rights suit"; "nonper stirpes distribution." E.g., "In *non-community property states* [read *common-law states*] the most troublesome issue confronting the courts and legislatures arises out of the rapid expansion of a variety of devices for bypassing probate." *Noncriminal* can usually be rendered more straightforwardly *civil;* hence *civil trial* rather than *noncriminal trial, private school* (in AmE) rather than *nonpublic school.*

But the purpose of some negatives with *non-* is to cover a range of antonyms. For example, *noncivil* might mean more than just "criminal"; it might mean "criminal or administrative." Without an explanation of course, this type of subtlety will be lost on many readers.

On the whole, *non-* adjectives should be avoided wherever possible, even if the avoidance means using more words. "In *nonautomobile cases* [read *cases not involving automobile accidents*] there may be a homeowner's policy that triggers the lawsuit and protects the parent in a direct suit or in an apportionment."/ "Chapman transferred *his only other non-cash asset,* [read *his only remaining asset other than cash*], a used car lot, to his two minor sons."/"A Tennessee statute that allows police officers to employ deadly force to prevent fleeing felons from escaping is unconstitutional insofar as it authorizes the use of such force to stop an apparently *unarmed and nondangerous suspect* [*unarmed* probably suffices; if not, then read *unarmed suspect who does not appear dangerous*]."/ "*A nonnegligent plaintiff* [read *A plaintiff who is not contributorily negligent*] may recover her total damages regardless of allocated damages."/ "We must therefore affirm the district court's declaratory judgment that the challenged provisions of the Arizona Constitution and statutes as *applied to exclude nonproperty owners from elections* [read *applied to exclude those who do not own property from elections*] for the approval of the issuance of general obligation bonds, violated the Equal Protection Clause of the U.S. Constitution."

As with noun phrases, using the prefix *non-* with PHRASAL ADJECTIVES produces awkward results, e.g., *nonfact-witness expert, nonincome-producing, noninterest-bearing, nonpar-value, nontaxpaid.* E.g., "It is undisputed that soybean production is a *non-water dependent activity* [read *is an activity not dependent on water*]."/ "A couple *in a non-community property jurisdiction* [read *living in a common-law jurisdiction*], one spouse being poorer than the other, will be subject to no gift taxation in interspousal transfers of property and will thus have the same tax advantages."

D. With Verbs. Although we have accepted verbal idioms such as *to nonplus a person* and *to nonsuit a case,* the prefix *non-* should not be used to create new verbs—e.g.: " '[The Board] erred by not finding that respondent violated the Texas Term Contract Nonrenewal Act when it *nonrenewed* [read *did not renew*] . . . the petitioner.' " *Burke v. Central Educ. Agency,* 725 S.W.2d 393, 398 (Tex. App.—Austin 1987) (quoting counsel).

nonact. See **nonfeasance.**

nonage /***non**-ij*/ = legal infancy; the condition of being under age. The term is rare today except in legal contexts. E.g., "The two major grounds for testamentary incapacity are *nonage* and mental disability." See **age of capacity** & **minority** (A).

nonbailable. See **bailable.**

nonbelief. See **disbelief.**

NONCE WORDS are terms coined for a particular occasion only. The inventor usu. has no hope that the term will become established in the language. Judge Charles E. Clark probably had no hope that his word *erieantompkinated* would catch on. (See ***Erie*-bound.**) The same must have been true of Frank Cooper's *res administrata,* q.v.

But that dictum is not absolute: the person who coined *lawyerphile* as an antonym of *lawyer-basher,* q.v., surely hoped that the word would suddenly spread throughout the land. It has not. As a failed NEOLOGISM, it became just another forgotten nonce word.

nonclergyable. See **clergyable.**

noncode state. See **code state.**

noncompetition covenant. The original phrase was *covenant not to compete* (= a provision in an employment agreement by which the employee agrees not to compete against the employer for some time after the employee leaves the job). In the late 20th century, this four-word phrase was reduced by half to form various phrases, including *noncompetition covenant* or *agreement,* which is preferable to *noncompete covenant* or *no-compete covenant.* The prefix *non-* may be joined to adjectives (as with *nonexistent, nonfatal, nonresponsive*), to nouns (as with *nonoccurrence, nonissue, nonacceptance*), or to present participles (as with *nonpaying, nonsmoking, nonvoting*). It is not at its best, however, when joined to a verb to make an adjective, as in *noncompete.* E.g., "The plaintiffs rely on four cases [that] they claim support their position that the amounts received pursuant to the *non-compete* [read *noncompetition*] agreements are 'personal service income.'" *Furman v. U.S.,* 602 F. Supp. 444, 451 (D.S.C. 1984). *Noncompete* is not listed in most dictionaries, and we may justifiably hope that it never gains widespread approval. See NON-, **no-compete covenant** & **anticompete.**

non compos mentis; compos mentis. These LATINISMS (meaning lit. "not master of one's mind" and "master of one's mind") are now little used. But as long as words such as *insane* and similar words are used figuratively as terms of disparagement, these learned terms may be pressed into service as EUPHEMISMS. *Incompetent,* however, usu. serves well in place of *non compos mentis.*

The *OED* contains no examples of *non compos mentis* used as an ATTRIBUTIVE NOUN, and it probably should not be so used: "When a minor, lunatic, idiot or a *non-compos mentis* [read *incompetent person*] may be a defendant to a suit and has no guardian . . . , the court shall appoint a guardian ad litem . . . ." Tex. R. Civ. P. 173 (West 1991). The strange hyphenation in that example suggests that the drafter somehow thought *non-compos* to be a PHRASAL ADJECTIVE and *mentis* a noun related to *men* or *man.* Of course, it really refers to the mind.

Although the plural form is *non compotes mentis,* that form is rarely if ever needed in English. When used as an English adjective, the phrase retains the singular form: "It may be said, therefore, that the equitable obligations resting upon . . . committees of persons *non compotes mentis* [read *non compos mentis*] . . . are analogous to those resting upon and given against actual trustees." 4 John N. Pomeroy & Spencer W. Symons, *Treatise on Equity Jurisprudence* § 1088, at 263–64 (5th ed. 1941). See PLURALS (A).

noncompliance is usu. inferior to *violation.*

nonconsent. In the context of rape accusations, courts have consistently interpreted this important word as requiring some type of physical resistance. At one time, the burden was rather high: the victim must have exhibited "utmost resistance." Susan Estrich, *Real Rape* 29 (1987). Today, the law having advanced, the meaning is not so rigid.

nonconstitutional; unconstitutional. As used by American practitioners, these terms have distinct meanings. *Nonconstitutional* = of or relating to some legal principle other than a principle found in the U.S. Constitution. E.g., "*Miranda* established a *nonconstitutional* prophylactic rule, the violation of which creates an irrebuttable presumption of coercion that is applicable in only a limited number of circumstances."/ "*Kent v. Dulles* did invalidate a burden on the right to travel; however, the restriction was voided on the *nonconstitutional* basis that Congress did not intend to give the Secretary of State power to create the restriction at issue."

Unconstitutional (the more familiar word) = in violation of, or not in accordance with, principles found in a constitution, esp. the U.S. Constitution. E.g., "The three-judge district court held that the Act and regulations in question were *unconstitutional* both under the equal protection clause of the Fourteenth Amendment and under the Constitution of Alaska."

nonculpable; inculpable. Because the latter is possibly ambiguous—meaning either "not culpable" or "able to be inculpated"—most criminal-law writers prefer *nonculpable.*

nondelegable duty. In tort law, this phrase does not mean what it literally says: a principal may indeed delegate a *nondelegable duty,* but upon doing so, the principal retains primary (as opposed to vicarious) responsibility if the duty is not properly performed. See *McDermid v. Nash Dredging & Reclamation Co.,* [1987] 3 W.L.R. 212, 215 (per Lord Hailsham). Cf. **duty.**

none. **A. Number.** *None* = (1) not one; or (2) not any. Hence it may correctly take either a singular or a plural verb. E.g., "*None* of these arguments *is* notably strong, let alone conclusive." Andrew Ashworth, *Principles of Criminal Law* 229 (1991)./ "[*N*]*one* of the promises *are* within the statute of frauds." Laurence P. Simpson, *Handbook on the Law of Suretyship* 132 (1950). Generally speaking, *none is* is the more emphatic way of expressing an idea.

B. *Of none effect.* This phrase is an ARCHAISM for *of no effect.*

noneconomic. See **uneconomic(al).**

nonenforceable. See **unenforceable.**

non est factum (lit., "it is not my deed") is LAW LATIN denoting the plea denying the execution of an instrument sued on. E.g., "The plea of *non est factum* was not available, but the case fell within the statute." (Eng.)/ "The exception is that if the defendant thought that the document he signed belonged to an entirely different legal category from that to which it in fact belonged, he can plead *non est factum* and escape liability although he did not trouble to read the document and although he misled the plaintiff into supposing that he was agreeing." (Eng.) Pl. *non est factums.* See **fact,** n. & **fraud (B).**

non est inventus. See **not found.**

nonetheless. One word in AmE, three (frequently) in BrE.

nonexpert. See **inexpert.**

nonfeasance; nonact. The two are distinguishable. Whereas *nonact* means merely the failure to act, *nonfeasance* implies the failure to act where a duty to act existed. E.g., "There is a presumption of adequate representation, which may be overcome by the intervenor only upon a showing of adversity of interest, the representative's collusion with the opposing party, or *nonfeasance* by the representative." See **feasance.** Cf. **malfeasance.**

nonforeseeable is a NEEDLESS VARIANT of *unforeseeable.*

nonheritable. See **inheritable.**

nonincentive. See **disincentive.**

noninterpretative. See **interpretative.**

nonjudicial. See **injudicious & judicial.**

nonjury, adj. Though the phrase *nonjury trial* is current in BrE as well as AmE, the more geographically limited phrase *bench trial* (a condensed version of *trial to the bench*) seems stylistically preferable: the better practice is to name something for what it is rather than for what it is not. Even so, some lawyers and judges, from New York to the State of Washington, find *bench trial* an alien phrase.

Several legal writers, unfortunately, have pressed the adjective *nonjury* into service as an adverb—e.g.: "[T]his case will proceed *nonjury* [read *without a jury*]." *Juckett v. Beecham Home Improvement Prods., Inc.,* 684 F. Supp. 448, 452 (N.D. Tex. 1988).

nonlapse statute. See **lapse statute.**

nonlawyer. It is a curious practice that lawyers (and others who write about law) divide the universe into *lawyers* and *nonlawyers.* But, of course, they do it of other professions and occupations as well—e.g.: "The Supreme Court later expressly limited the vessel owner's duty to *nonseamen* to situations where the workers were doing 'ship's work.'" Although the word *layman* is usually unambiguous, the masculine suffix is a major disadvantage. (See SEXISM (B).) And few would seriously argue that *laypersons* is a palatable alternative.

nonlegal = (1) not specifically related to law; or (2) not being a lawyer. Sense (1): "[D]espite what the lawyers say, it *is* possible to talk about legal principles and legal reasoning in everyday *nonlegal* language." Fred Rodell, *Woe Unto You, Lawyers!* 12 (1939; repr. 1980). Sense (2): "[The] Employment Appeal Tribunal . . . is presided over by a senior judge and behaves very much like an ordinary appeal court, though it also has *nonlegal* members." P.S. Atiyah, *Law and Modern Society* 27 (1983). Cf. **alegal & extralegal.**

nonliability is an unnecessary equivalent of *no liability* or *lack of liability.*

nonlitigious is the antonym of *litigious,* but not in the latter word's prevalent sense today (i.e., "fond of litigation"). Rather, *nonlitigious* corresponds to an older and today infrequent sense of *litigious* (i.e., "involving litigation"). Hence, *nonlitigious* means not "court-shy" but "not involving litigation"—e.g.: "The legal services considered were 'typical *nonlitigious* matters for which the amount and work requirements would be reasonably foreseeable.'" Murray T. Bloom, *The Trouble with Lawyers* 44 (1970).

nonmarital child. See **bastard, illegitimate child & natural child.**

nonmaterial. See **immaterial.**

nonmeritorious. See **unmeritorious.**

nonmovant (= a litigating party other than the one that has filed a motion currently under consideration) is omitted from most English-language dictionaries as well as most law dictionaries. But, in American courts, it occurs with great frequency—e.g.: "First National had to prove that a new trial would not prejudice the *nonmovant* . . . ." *First Nat'l Bank v. Peterson,* 709 S.W.2d 276, 279 (Tex. App.—Houston [14th Dist.] 1986).

nonnegotiable. See **negotiable instruments.**

nonobject. See **object.**

nonobjectionable is a NEEDLESS VARIANT of *unobjectionable.*

non obstante veredicto. See **judgment *non obstante veredicto.***

nonparticipating royalty, used often in oil-and-gas law, is a venial REDUNDANCY: all mineral royalties are nonparticipating.

nonplus(s)ed. The form *-ss-* is preferred.

nonpretextual = not founded on a pretext. E.g., "Appellant's lawful dismissal was found by the jury to be *nonpretextual.*" Actually, the jury found that the dismissal was not pretextual—thus the finding was a negative one. To say that it "found the dismissal to be nonpretextual" wrongly suggests that the jury answered a question asking whether the dismissal was *nonpretextual;* instead, the jury was asked whether the dismissal was *pretextual,* and it answered "no." See **pretextual** & NON- (B).

nonprobate = other than by will; of or relating to some method of disposition apart from wills. E.g., "Today the proportion of property passing under probate is decreasing and the proportion of property passing by *nonprobate* methods is increasing."

nonprofit; not-for-profit. The former is more common, but the latter is increasingly used in AmE for greater accuracy: *nonprofit corporation* misleadingly suggests that the corporation makes no profits; but such a corporation actually *does* earn profits and then applies them to charitable purposes. *Not-for-profit* is thought to reveal more accurately that the purpose is not for private gain, though indeed the organization may profit.

Whereas *nonprofit corporation* and *not-for-profit corporation* predominate in AmE, *nonprofit-making organization* is the usual BrE phrase.

nonpros. See ***nolle prosequi.***

nonrebuttable is a NEEDLESS VARIANT of *irrebuttable.* E.g., "In actual operation, therefore, the three statutes enact what in effect are *nonrebuttable* [read *irrebuttable*] presumptions that every applicant for assistance in his first year of residency came to the jurisdiction solely to obtain higher benefits."

nonrefoulement. See **refoulement.**

nonresponsive, rather than *unresponsive,* is the usual adjective to describe a witness's answer that is somehow off the point—e.g.: "Witnesses are warned to answer questions directly and to the point, and to add nothing superfluous, . . . because extra information may be objected to as *'unresponsive'* [read *'nonresponsive'*] by the cross-examining attorney . . . ." Robin T. Lakoff, *Talking Power: The Politics of Language in Our Lives* 90 (1990).

NONRESTRICTIVE CLAUSES. See RESTRICTIVE AND NONRESTRICTIVE CLAUSES.

non sequitur should be spelled as two words, not hyphenated or spelled as one word. The phrase is frequently misspelled *-tor* or *-tar.*

nonstatutory. This word is sometimes replaceable by *judicial, administrative,* or some other descriptive word, as in *judicial policy-making* rather than *nonstatutory policy-making.* If it fits, the more specific word should oust *nonstatutory.*

nonsuit, v.t., = (1) of a plaintiff, to seek a voluntary dismissal of (a case or a defendant); or (2) of a court, to dismiss (a case or a defendant) because the plaintiff has failed to make out a legal case or to proffer sufficient evidence. This verb has been part of lawyers' language since the 16th century. Sense (1): "The plaintiff then *nonsuited* the case." Sense (2): "The court *nonsuited* him and rendered judgment dismissing the action."

nonsuitability. The preferred antonyms of *suitable* and *suitability* are *unsuitable* and *unsuitableness. Nonsuitability,* a NEEDLESS VARIANT of *unsuitableness,* unsuitably suggests a relationship with *nonsuit,* q.v. Yet it is perversely used in AmE legal contexts. E.g., "The Secretary of Agriculture shall, within ten years after September 3, 1964, review, as to its suitability or *nonsuitability* [read *unsuitableness*] . . . for preservation as wilderness, each area." Wilderness Act, 16 U.S.C. § 1132(b) (1988).

nontaxpaid is an opaque, ugly word to avoid. E.g., "Defendant has had a reputation with me for over four years as being a trafficker of *nontaxpaid* distilled spirits." A less concise wording should be used, e.g., *trafficker of distilled spirits upon which no taxes had been paid.*

nontortious. Just as *tortuous* is sometimes misused for *tortious* (see **tortious (B)**), so *nontortuous* has been misused for *nontortious*—e.g.: "Plaintiffs insist that this is not a case involving conflicting claims to the ownership or *nontortuous* [read *nontortious*] use of water . . . ." *Friendswood Dev. Co. v. Smith-Southwest Indus., Inc.,* 576 S.W.2d 21, 24 (Tex. 1978).

nontriggerman = a murder defendant who did not actually kill the decedent, but who intended to do so. E.g., "The conduct of a *nontriggerman* during the planning and aftermath of a prison break, which eventually resulted in a quadruple murder, was sufficient for the imposition of a death penalty." The word is odd-looking but perhaps necessary; often *accomplice* suffices. See SEXISM (B).

nonuser. See **user** & -ER (B).

no one; nobody. These have traditionally been regarded as singular nouns that act as singular antecedents. E.g., "This means that *no one* should be punished for speaking unless *their* [read *his or her*] speech will immediately lead to a definite dangerous act." See **he or she.**

But the language is changing—BrE more rapidly than AmE—so that *no one . . . they* may soon be regarded as standard. Some consider this change a defilement, others a tremendous advance. However you characterize it, it seems inevitable. See SEXISM (A) & CONCORD (B). Cf. **none.**

noplace is a barbarism for *nowhere.*

no pun intended. See WORD-PATRONAGE & PUNS.

no question but that. The *but* in this phrase is unnecessary; the better phrase is *no question that.* E.g., "There can be *no question but that* [read *no question that*] jurisdiction to review and to affirm or set aside the Secretary's order became fully vested in the court upon the filing of the partnership's petition."

nor for *or.* Where the negative of a clause has already appeared and a disjunctive conjunction is needed, *or* is generally better than *nor.* The initial negative carries through to all the elements in an enumeration. E.g., "Religiosity insists that there is something called religion wholly apart from any specific religion, something that has no creed *nor* [read *or*] dogma, no theology or scriptures, something that may be felt and need not be understood."/ "Her symptoms were all subjective and not supported by any medical *nor* [read *or*] other corroborating evidence."/ "When on the witness stand at the trial of this case, however, he could not see the trial judge *nor* [read *or*] the examiner who was five feet away." See **not (C)** & **neither . . . nor (D).**

no respecter of persons, the law is. To many, this English-language legal MAXIM seems to say nearly the opposite of what it actually denotes. The point is not that the law disrespects persons, but that it pays no special regard to one's station in life: speaking ideally (if not idealistically), the law treats a homeless person with the same respect as it would a bishop. E.g.:

- "The law (as we are often told) is *no respecter of persons.* Without being universally true, this is a principle [that] has always applied with special force to the law of homicide. Thus, the villein could not be killed by his lord with impunity. Nor could the slave, even in Anglo-Saxon times, be killed by his master . . . ." J.W. Cecil Turner, *Kenny's Outlines of Criminal Law* 104 (16th ed. 1952).
- "The Criminal Court of Appeals in Oklahoma in 1913 spoke in the tradition of this country's dedication to due process and equal protection when it declared that the law is *no respecter of persons* . . . ." *Griffin v. Illinois,* 351 U.S. 12, 19 (1956).
- "The law is *no respecter of persons.* All persons including corporations stand equal before the law and are to be dealt with as equals in a Court of justice." *In re Bendectin Litig.,* 857 F.2d 290, 322 (6th Cir. 1988).

norm is generally considered a broad term, broader even than "legal rule." A *norm* establishes acceptable and unacceptable standards of behavior; these are addressed to nonlawyers as well as to judges. Norms include public-policy imperatives (e.g., Thou shalt not kill) but also rules for private transactions (e.g., if you offer to make a bargain and the other party accepts, you are contractually bound).

Roscoe Pound explained the so-called norm theory of law as viewing law as "a body of norms (models or patterns) of conduct or of decisions established or recognized by the state in the administration of justice." *Outlines of Lectures in Jurisprudence* 75 (5th ed. 1943). He conceived of a hierarchy of norms, presumably starting with "Thou shalt obey the Constitution," and descending through statutes, judicial decisions, regulations, and so on down to commercial customs that a court might recognize.

normalcy has traditionally been considered inferior to *normality.* Born in the mid-19th century and later used by President Harding, *normalcy* has never been accepted as standard by the best writing authorities. E.g., "The *normalcy* [read *normality*] of these operations changed when Press was told by his delegate that Montana-Austria requested a stop-off in Johannesburg."/ Daniel K. Tarullo, *Beyond* Normalcy [*read* Normality] *in the Regulation of International Trade,* 100 Harv. L. Rev. 547, 547 (1987).

normative = establishing or conforming to a norm or standard.

nostrum (= panacea) forms the plural *nostrums*—e.g.: "But advertisements of *nostrums* for restoration of 'lost manhood' have appeared in the daily newspapers for at least fifty years." See PLURALS (A).

not. A. Placement of. When used in constructions with *all* and *every, not* is usually best placed just before those words. E.g., "*Every disclosure of a trade secret does not result* [read *Not every disclosure of a trade secret results*] in an abandonment of its element of secrecy."/ "*Justice Holmes reminded us that every moral question could not* [read *Justice Holmes reminded us that not every moral question can*] be submitted to the law . . . ." Francis R. Kirkham, *Problems of Complex Civil Litigation,* 83 F.R.D. 497, 504 (1979). See **all (B).**

B. *Not* . . . *nor*. This construction should usu. (where short clauses are involved) be *not . . . or.* E.g., "Finding the lessee culpable is *not inherently inconsistent nor contrary to* [read *not inherently inconsistent with or contrary to*] the 'instructions.'" See **nor** & NEGATIVES.

C. In Typos. *Not* is a ready source of trouble. Sometimes it becomes *now,* and sometimes it drops completely from the sentence—e.g.: "The Legislature expressly refused to extend the concept of privilege when adopting the discovery procedures. Since privilege is created by statute it *should* [read *should not*] be extended by judicial fiat." John Kaplan & Jon R. Waltz, *Cases and Materials on Evidence* 506 (6th ed. 1988).

Problems of that kind have driven print journalists to "live in perpetual fear of the word *not* either being dropped by a printer or being changed from *not* to *now.* Therefore, wherever possible, they shy away from the word *not,* even at the expense of strict accuracy." Robert Sack, *Hearing Myself Think: Some Thoughts on Legal Prose,* 4 Scribes J. Legal Writing 93, 98 (1993). Notably, it is this very fear that leads newspaper writers to prefer *plead innocent* over the more accurate phrase, *plead not guilty.* See **plead innocent.**

D. And *naught*. See **further affiant . . . .**

E. *Not only* . . . *but also* . . . . See **not only . . . but also.**

notable; noteworthy; noticeable. *Noticeable* = easily seen or noticed (as, e.g., scars); it is generally confined to physical senses. *Notable* (having basically the same meaning) is applied to qualities as well as to material things. E.g., "The most *notable* thing about these observations is that quite obviously the word 'res', describing a thing, has a quite different connotation from 'subject matter'."/ "Some jurisdictions, *notably* New York, have attempted to solve this problem by applying more flexible and equitable standards."

Noteworthy, a near-synonym, means "worthy of notice or observation; remarkable." E.g., "It is *noteworthy* that the decree and codicil attached express conditions of survivorship to the interests of Joseph and to any wife or child of Joseph but do not add any words of that character to the limitation describing Mary Silva's interest."

not all. See **not (A) & all (B).**

notarial is the adjectival form of *notary.*

notarize, originally an Americanism dating from the 1930s, is now commonplace in AmE—e.g.: "In order to administer oaths to these workers and to *notarize* their statements for use in civil litigation, petitioner applied in 1978 to become a notary public." *Bernal v. Fainter,* 467 U.S. 216, 218 (1984). In BrE, the word is still, in some quarters, considered something of an atrocity; British lawyers tend to say *notarially validated* instead of *notarized.*

notary; notary public. *Notary* is a common ellipsis of *notary public* in both AmE and BrE. Pl. *notaries public.* In this phrase, *public* is a POSTPOSITIVE ADJECTIVE.

not . . . because. See **because (B).**

note; draft. A *note* is a simple promise by one party to pay money to another party or to bearer.

A *draft* is an order by one person (the drawer) to pay another person (the drawee), demanding that the drawee pay money to a third person (the payee) or to bearer.

note = lawnote. See **annotation.**

note up is the approximate British equivalent of the American term *shepardize,* q.v. The British call their citators *noter-ups,* or, in some Commonwealth countries, *noter-uppers.*

noteworthy. See **notable.**

not-for-profit. See **nonprofit.**

not found is the English-language equivalent of the LAW LATIN *non est inventus,* sometimes abbreviated *n.e.i.* One phrase or the other is commonly used on a sheriff's return of process, saying that the defendant is not to be found in the sheriff's jurisdiction. For obvious reasons, *not found* is preferable.

not guilty. If a jury finds that a criminal defendant is *not guilty,* that finding does not mean (as some mistakenly believe) that the defendant did not commit the act complained of. The defendant may not have had the requisite mental state or may have had some justification or excuse.

nothing less than. With this phrase, "the risks of ambiguity are very great" (*MEU2* at 398). The problem is that the word *less* may function either as an adjective or as an adverb, the resulting senses being contradictory.

When *less* functions as an adjective, the sense of the phrase *nothing less than* is "the same thing as; quite equal to." E.g., "In the context of insurance cases, so-called 'waiver' is *nothing less than* 'estoppel.'" That is, waiver and estoppel are the same in insurance cases.

But even in that sentence, *less* could be read as an adverb, so that the phrase *nothing less than* might mean "any thing other than; far from being." A reader who understands the phrase in that sense is in for a serious MISCUE. And the reader's misunderstanding is entirely understandable, as the following sentence illustrates: "It was a normal day to the thousands of workers who filed into the World Trade Center that morning; they expected *nothing less than* a terrorist bombing of their workplace."

notice, n., may refer to two quite different ideas: (1) legal notification required by law or imparted by operation of law as a result of some fact such as the recording of instruments; or (2) information that may be required under a contract. For the distinction between *notice* and *knowledge,* see **knowledge.** See also **judicial notice.**

notice, v.t. (= to give legal notice to or of) is a LEGALISM that is likely to strike nonlawyers as quite odd. E.g., "Under the present practice, however, the objecting party has no duty to *notice* a hearing, the initiative being shifted to the party seeking discovery."/ "We have not been *noticed* [i.e., received notice] to bring the records."/ "The magistrate heard the motions to set aside the default judgment apparently by virtue of the fact that they were *noticed* for a hearing before the magistrate rather than before the district court."/ "Unless you have already done so, *notice* the depositions of all expert witnesses being offered by your opponent."

Notice should be reserved for the giving of legal notice; legal writers should not use the word nonlegally, as here: "TACA International Airlines, in the midst of collective bargaining negotiations, *noticed* [read *let be known*] its intent to relocate its pilot base." (To the nonlawyer, this usage confusingly suggests *notice* in the sense "to observe.")/ "It has been *noticed* [read *noted,* i.e., previously in a book] that some lawyers and judges were of the opinion that . . . ."

notice, judicial. See **judicial notice.**

noticeable. See **notable.**

notice pleading. See **code pleading.**

notice to quit (BrE) = *notice to vacate* (AmE). See **quit.**

notifiable, in BrE phrases such as *notifiable disease* and *notifiable offence,* is built from an old sense of *notify* (not current in AmE): rather than bearing its common meaning ("to give notice of; inform"), *notify* here means "to make known; proclaim; announce." In G.B., some serious diseases (e.g., cholera, diphtheria, scarlet fever, and typhoid) are classed as *notifiable diseases*—that is, they require anyone with knowledge that someone has the disease to contact the authorities. A *notifiable offence* is a serious crime that can be tried in the Crown Court.

notify. See **notifiable.**

not law is a phrase that common-law lawyers use when arguing that an old court decision is wrong or obsolete—e.g.: "A decision, to be binding, must not only emanate from high authority, but must be 'good law': if it once earns the reputation of being 'not law,' it perishes, sometimes by express disapproval, more often by cold disregard. If all else fails, the blame for its defects may be laid at the door of the reporter—sometimes not without cause." Carleton K. Allen, *Law in the Making* 297 (7th ed. 1964).

not less. See **no less.**

not more than. The more natural idiom is *no more than.*

not only . . . but also. These CORRELATIVE CONJUNCTIONS must frame syntactic parts that match. E.g.,

- "The offer *had to not only be made in good faith but it had to also be* [read *had not only to be made in good faith but also to be*] in such a form that it could, by an acceptance of the offeree, ripen into a valid and binding contract that could be enforced by any party to it."
- "These disclosures *led not only to new calls for greater social responsibility of corporations but also focused on* [read *not only led to . . . but also focused on*] the role of the board of directors and the need for better control mechanisms to ensure that corporate management conform with legal and moral principles of conduct."
- "[E]ach of these policies designated *not only* Smith and his wife Sybil as insureds, *but also* a corporate name, Rolling Hills Golf and Racquet Club, Inc." *Smith v. Edward M. Thompson Agency, Inc.,* 430 So. 2d 859, 859 (Ala. 1983) (matching parts: noun [*Smith and his wife Sybil*], noun [*a corporate name*]).
- "The document that appears in the record of this case contains *not only* Smith's signature *but also* the signature of someone identified as his attorney at the place indicated on the document for his attorney to sign 'if represented.'" *Smith v. State,* 785 S.W.2d 465, 467 (Ark. 1990) (matching parts: noun [*Smith's signature*], noun [*signature of someone identified*]).

See PARALLELISM.

One common failing in the *not only* constructions is to omit the *also* after *but*—e.g.: "[N]o one has questioned the proposition that the holding covers *not only* such cross-claims *but* [add *also*] impleaders of third parties." Grant Gilmore & Charles L. Black, Jr., *The Law of Admiralty* 939 (2d ed. 1975)./ "A publication may be made *not only* intentionally *but* [*also*] negligently . . . ." William Geldart, *Introduction to English Law* 137 (D.C.M. Yardley ed., 9th ed. 1984). See **not (B).**

Another possible construction is *not only . . . but . . . as well.* But a writer who uses this phrasing should not add *also,* which is redundant with *as well*—e.g.: "[F]eminist methods and insights [must] be adopted *not only* by female scholars, *but also* by males *as well.*" J.M. Balkin, *Turandot's Victory,* 2 Yale J.L. & Human. 299, 302 (1990). In that sentence, *also* should have been omitted.

Not only . . . but also . . . as well is likewise redundant. E.g., "But we cannot quarrel with a conclusion of a school administrator that treating a particular student with such care might be to the advantage *not only* of the pupil *but also* [read *but*] of the other students in the school *as well.*"/

notorious may mean either "famous" or "infamous," though it usually carries connotations of the latter, i.e., unfavorably known. *Notoriety* is generally more neutral, although it is coming to be tinged with the connotations of its adjectival form.

not proven. See **proved.**

not unreasonable. See NEGATIVES (B).

notwithstanding. A. Grammatical Use. This preposition is an interesting word. In DRAFTING, it commonly means "despite," "in spite of," or "although" and appears in sentences such as this one: "Notwithstanding the limitations contained in § 3.5, Mondraff will be offered the first option to quote competitive terms and conditions to Nuboil."

The question that literalist drafters ask is, What doesn't withstand what else? Are the limitations of § 3.5 "not withstanding" (i.e., subordinated to) the present section, or is the present section "not withstanding" (subordinated to) § 3.5? Because the former is the correct reading, some believe that *notwithstanding* should be sent to the end of the phrase in which it appears: *The limitations contained in § 3.5 notwithstanding,* as opposed to *Notwithstanding the limitations contained in § 3.5.*

But that literalist argument is very much in vain, as the *OED* attests with a 14th-century example of *notwithstanding* as a prepositional sentence-starter. This usage has been constant from the 1300s to the present day. In fact, the construction with *notwithstanding* after the noun first appeared more than a century later, and has never been as frequent. The *Century Dictionary* explains: "As the noun usually follows [the word *notwithstanding*], the [word] came to be regarded as a prep. (as also with *during,* ppr.), and is now usually so construed." 3 *The Century Dictionary and Cyclopedia* 4029 (1914). The word is not a DANGLER because it does not function as a participle.

B. Followed by *that.* When introducing a verbless phrase, *notwithstanding* need not be followed by *that.* E.g., "Section 1322(b)(5) was amended to provide that its provisions were unchanged, *notwithstanding* section 1322 (b)(2)."

Otherwise, grammar demands that when the term introduces a clause, it should usually be followed by *that.* E.g., "The law is in accord in favoring free competition, since ordinarily it is essential to the general welfare of society, *notwithstanding* [insert *that*] competition is not altruistic but is fundamentally the play of interest against interest."/ "The instrument is likely to be upheld *notwithstanding* [insert *that*] it includes additionally the reservation of power to amend the trust in whole or in part." Even so, the phrase can be boiled down to a simpler wording: see **notwithstanding the fact that.**

notwithstanding anything to the contrary contained herein, an ungainly phrase often placed in complex contracts to introduce the most important provisions, can be fairly said to mean "the true agreement is as follows." It is best used when a lawyer wants one provision in a long, complex contract to override any arguably inconsistent provision.

The better phrasing avoids *herein,* q.v., by substituting *in this agreement* or *in this contract.* Better yet, the drafter should specify which provision might be read as contradictory.

The statutory equivalent is the phrase *notwithstanding any other provision of law,* as in Fed. R. Evid. 412(a) (1994).

The opposite effect—subordinating the current provision to all others—is achieved by the wording *except as otherwise provided.*

notwithstanding the fact that; notwithstanding that. These legalistic phrases are best replaced by either *although* or *even if*—e.g.: "The freedom that is worth having is freedom to do what you think to be good *notwithstanding that* [read *even if*] others think it to be bad." Patrick Devlin, *The Enforcement of Morals* 108 (1968). See **notwithstanding** & **fact that, the.**

nought. See **naught.**

NOUN PLAGUE is Wilson Follett's term for the piling up of nouns to modify other nouns. See Wilson Follett, *Modern American Usage* 229 (1966). When a sentence has more than three nouns in a row, it generally becomes much less readable. The following sentence is badly constructed because of the noun-upon-noun syndrome, which unfortunately is more common now than in Follett's day: "Consumers complained to their congressman about *the National Highway Traffic Safety Administration's automobile seat belt 'interlock' rule.*" One can hardly get to the end of the sentence to find out that we are talking about a rule. (Actually, many writers today would leave off the possessive after *Administration.*) In the interest of plague control, the following rewrite seems advisable: *the 'interlock' rule applied to automobile seat belts by the National Highway Traffic Safety Administration.*

Readability often drops when three words that are structurally nouns follow in succession, although exceptions such as *fidelity life insurance* certainly exist. Less readable examples such as the following are the rule rather than the exception, however: "Inasmuch as incentives are inevitably tied to immeasurable subjective evaluations, it is reassuring that the *information generation stimuli* of the adversary model rest in part on other foundations."/ "The *interpretation process* provides a reminder of the *federalism aspects* of *individual right concerns.*"

The plague is virtually never endurable when four nouns appear consecutively. E.g., "The direct *participation programs principal category* of registration is the minimum qualification requirement for persons whose supervisory functions are limited to direct participation programs."/ "The recent decisions compel little change in the current *state attorney solicitation rules.*" Similarly, what is a *retiree benefit litigation procedure?*

Frequently, noun plague is a cause of ambiguity. E.g., "My brother Harlan's objections to my *Adamson dissent history,* like that of most of the objectors, relies [*sic*] most heavily on a criticism written by Professor Charles Fairman . . . ." *Duncan v. Louisiana,* 391 U.S. 145, 165 (1968) (Black, J., concurring). Here Justice Black means "the history [of the incorporation doctrine] I recited in my dissent in *Adamson,*" but the reader could just as easily arrive at "my history of the *Adamson* dissent," or "the history of opinions that dissent from *Adamson.*" A couple of prepositions would have remedied the problem.

One aspect of noun plague in legal writing is the traditional—and misguided—preference for nouns over verbs. Jeremy Bentham's so-called substantive-preferring principle was developed as a result of his bias in favor of nouns, which could be modified and multiplied, whereas "[a] verb slips through your fingers like an eel . . . ." 10 Jeremy Bentham, *Works* 569 (J. Bowring ed. 1843). Thus Bentham, like his fellow lawyers, preferred *to give motion to* rather than *to move* and *to give extension to* rather than *to extend.* Even today, lawyers frequently use such circumlocutions.

Yet another root of the problem is the tendency

in modern writing to make adjectives out of nouns and noun phrases, often postponing the true subject until long after the reader has left off hoping for one: "This is a breach of contract/Deceptive Trade Practices Act, Tex. Bus. & Comm. Code Ann. (Vernon Supp. 1982–83) (hereinafter referred to as 'the Act') case." *Wolfe Masonry, Inc. v. Stewart,* 664 S.W.2d 102, 102–03 (Tex. App.—Corpus Christi 1983)./ "The Public Utilities Commission made a *question of law, not fact, determination* when it allowed the LCRA to intervene."

Finally, avoid loading a single statement with too many abstract nouns ending in *-tion.* The effect is not a pleasing one: "This case involves *protection* against a second *prosecution* for the *importation conviction.*"/ "The *regulation* of *solicitation* involves the *consideration* of whether there are 'ample alternative channels for *communication* of the *information.*'" See BE-VERBS (B), BURIED VERBS & SOUND OF PROSE (A).

NOUNS AS ADJECTIVES. English has long been noted for its ability to allow words to change parts of speech. The transmutation of nouns into adjectives is one of the most frequently seen shifts of this kind. Usually the change is unobjectionable, as in the first word in each of the following phrases: *lawbook, state action, telephone wires, home repairs, litigation problems.* A common example appears in this sentence: "In order to pose a *jury question* on the issue of *seaman status,* the plaintiff must present evidence of the following kind."

Occasionally, however, semantic shifts of this kind give rise to ambiguities or play tricks on the reader. For example, it would be unwise for one writing about a statute concerning invalids to call it an *invalid statute.* To make a somewhat different point, the reader's expectations are subverted when a noun is used adjectivally in place of the more usual adjectival form. E.g., "The subdivision was planned strictly for *residence* [read *residential*] purposes."

Often, of course, the sense conveyed is different when one uses the noun adjectivally as opposed to the adjectival form. For example, *negligence defendant* is something different from *negligent defendant,* the latter being judgmental; *negligence action* means something quite different from *negligent action; pornography litigation* seems to mean something different from *pornographic litigation* (which is somehow difficult to visualize).

Finally, relations often become vague when nouns that would normally follow prepositions are adjectives placed before nouns, and the relation-bearing prepositions are omitted. E.g., *victim awareness* is a vague phrase; does it mean *on the part of, of, by?* E.g., "*Victim awareness* gained momentum in the early 1980s, with the passage of the Victim and Witness Protection Act." We can deduce that the intended sense is *awareness (on the part of the public) of victims and their rights,* but perhaps we should not ask our readers to have to make such deductions. The same sort of uncertainty infects *victim restitution* (= full restitution to the victim of a crime).

NOUNS AS VERBS. A type of semantic shift less common than that of noun to adjective is for nouns to act as verbs. Often these usages are considered slangy—e.g.:

- "The movie would have *box-officed* $3 million."
- "She has been *mayoring* in Austin for six years."
- "Every youngster can *summer* in Europe."
- "If a man is not in the same city, his semen can be frozen and *air-expressed* to the doctor."
- "Though reported as a burglary, the incident was *'no-crimed'* by the policy: the property was called 'lost property' rather than 'stolen property.'"

Yet nouns used as verbs often make their way into legal parlance and finally into legal print: "The grand jury had not focused on specific individuals and was playing a broader investigative role than the typical grand jury asked simply to *true bill* or *no bill* a specific suspect." *Morrison v. City of Baton Rouge,* 761 F.2d 242, 247 (5th Cir. 1985). Though writers refer to *fast-tracking* budgets, *tasking* committees, and *mainstreaming* children, English is generally inhospitable to this sort of jargonistic innovation. Legal writers should be wary of adopting usages of this kind.

n.o.v. See **j.n.o.v.**

novate (= to replace by something new), a 17th-century BACK-FORMATION from *novation,* is labeled "rare" and as peculiar to Roman law in the *OED.* But the word sometimes appears in modern American legal writing—e.g.: "[H]e did not *novate* his indebtedness to the Johnstown bank." *Jones v. Costlow,* 36 A.2d 460, 462 (Pa. 1944)./ "[T]he original contract of sale between Rains County and McCallon was *novated* by the commissioners' court . . . ." *Simmons v. Ratliff,* 182 S.W.2d 827, 829 (Tex. Civ. App.—Amarillo 1944).

novation, originally a Roman-law term, denotes the act of substituting for an old contract a new one that either (a) replaces an existing obligation for a new obligation or (b) adds a party who was not a party to the old contract. The word also sometimes refers to the contract that brings about such a substitution. The effect of a novation, unlike that of *subrogation,* is not to transfer liability, but to replace an old liability with a new one. See **adoption & subrogation** (A).

novatory; novative; novational. None of these can be said to be common, but *novatory* is used more frequently than the others, which might therefore be labeled NEEDLESS VARIANTS.

novel and concrete. These words appear in virtually all cases involving the misappropriation of commercial ideas. Though they have assumed an "almost talismanic significance," the terms "have nonetheless gained little specific content. Presumably, *novel* means the opposite of *common* or, perhaps, *old. Concrete* is probably the antithesis of *abstract,* and also implies that, to be protectable, the ideas must be reduced to tangible form. Beyond this, the decisions offer nothing definitive." Paul Goldstein, *Copyright, Patent, Trademark and Related State Doctrines* 59 (2d ed. 1981).

novelty does not mean "an extreme rarity." Rather, it denotes something both rare *and new.* "Mother-son incest is so rare as to be regarded as a *novelty.*" The writer of this sentence could have better written, "Mother-son incest is an extreme rarity." *Oedipus Rex* belies any claim that incest might have to novelty.

novus actus interveniens is the primarily British legal phrase meaning literally "a new intervening act." (See CAUSATION (D) & LATINISMS.) *Novus actus* is sometimes used as an ellipsis for the full phrase. E.g., "On the assumed facts there would be in my view no *novus actus* when the trainees damaged the respondent's property." (Eng.)

now is sometimes mistakenly used for *present* or *current* as an opposite of *then,* as in *then-owner.* (See **then** (A).) "The defendants are purchasing two of the adjoining lots from the *now owners* [read *present owners*] thereof."

noway(s). See **nowise.**

now comes. See **come(s) now.**

nowhere near is colloquial for *not nearly.*

no-win–no-fee system is a phrase that some journalists use to describe contingent fees. E.g., "[E]ven the more modest *no-win–no-fee system* would in some cases create a dangerous pressure on lawyers to cheat in order to eat." Sedley, *Breaking the Law,* London Rev. Books, 18 May 1989, at 3. See **contingent fee.**

nowise (= in no way; not at all) is an adverb that should not be introduced by *in,* although legal writers seem to commit this error more often than not when using the word. *In no way* might even generally be preferable to *nowise.* E.g., "The statute *in no wise* [read *nowise* or *in no way*] indicates that the 602(2) definition is only transitory." *ACLU v. FCC,* 823 F.2d 1554, 1568 (D.C. Cir. 1987). Mistaken uses of the word, esp. in AmE, are legion.

Formerly spelled as two words, *nowise* should now be consistently treated as a single word. The following examples illustrate the traditionally correct use of the word: "The exemption of the Crown is *nowise* dependent upon the local or imperial character of the rate." (Eng.)/ "Defendant is a banker who is *nowise* in the occupation of a barber."

Noways, in legal writing at least, is a NEEDLESS VARIANT of *nowise,* although the Evanses state that it is more common in AmE than *nowise.* See Bergen Evans & Cornelia Evans, *A Dictionary of Contemporary American Usage* 326 (1957).

now pending is a commonplace REDUNDANCY, but no less sinful for that—e.g.: "[O]ur resolution of the dispute determines the course of proceedings if and when he is rearrested on the *charges now pending* [read *pending charges*]." *U.S. v. Montalvo-Murillo,* 495 U.S. 711, 713 (1990)./ "The Security Trust Company, N.A. attacks the validity of the deed of trust in a lawsuit *now pending* [read *pending*] in the United States District Court . . . ." *Democratic Nat'l Comm. v. Washington Metro. Area Transit Comm'n,* 21 F.3d 1145, 1147 n.2 (D.C. Cir. 1994).

noxal (= of or relating to a cause of action against an owner of an animal or slave for damage done by the animal or slave) is, though hardly on every lawyer's lips every day, common enough to merit inclusion in law dictionaries and in English-language dictionaries, from which it is regularly omitted. E.g., "The 1825 amendment created an exception to the ability of the owner to limit his liability by *noxal* surrender of the animal, a recognized Roman practice that foreshadowed limitation of liability in modern admiralty." William T. Tête, *In Defense of Fault in the Guard Under Article 2317,* 61 Tul. L. Rev. 759, 765 n.37 (1987). The phrase *noxal action* figures importantly in Oliver Wendell Holmes's book, *The Common Law* (1881).

NSF (= not sufficient funds) acts as an adjective where the full phrase is cumbersome and even ungrammatical <an NSF check>.

nuclear is pronounced /***noo**-klee-ər*/, though often it is mispronounced /***noo**-kyə-lər*/. Though presidents and other educated persons have had difficulty pronouncing the word correctly, you should if you can.

nudum pactum (= an unenforceable agreement) has taken on different particularized senses within different legal traditions. At common law, of course, a *nudum pactum* was an agreement that failed for lack of consideration. E.g., "An agreement made without consideration is a *nudum pactum;* i.e., it is an agreement [that] is destitute of legal effect." 1 E.W. Chance, *Principles of Mercantile Law* 9 (P.W. French ed., 13th ed. 1950)./ "An agreement [that] did not fall into any of the recognised classes was *nudum pactum;* there was no *causa* and therefore no legal obligation." O. Hood Phillips, *A First Book of English Law* 247 (3d ed. 1955).

In Roman law and civil law, in which consideration is not a necessary element of a contract, the term denoted unenforceability for some other reason, such as lack of a lawful "cause." The anglicized phrase *nude pact* has not been widely used, perhaps because each of those terms carries its own connotative baggage that may cause a MISCUE. See **naked.**

nugatory is not a legal word per se, but it is a learned word favored by lawyers. It means "of no force; useless; invalid." E.g., "These statutes were as effective when the Allen case was decided as now; they did not then serve to render the bequest involved *nugatory* under the circumstances."/ "But a person's liberty or right to deal with others is *nugatory* unless they are at liberty to deal with him if they choose to do so." (Eng.) Cf. **otiose.**

nuisance. Etymologically, *nuisance* derives from the Latin *nocere* "to hurt or harm," which has also given us the words *annoy, noise, noisome, noxious,* and *obnoxious.*

Some people, realizing that *nuisance* is a recognized legal wrong, therefore assume they might be able to sue people who annoy them. In fact, though, the legal requirement for nuisance is fairly specific: annoyance or disturbance in the enjoyment of property. Unlawful conduct of this kind is commonly put into two classes: (1) the acts of an owner or possessor of land who wrongfully uses that land in a way that unreasonably interferes with the rights of neighboring owners or possessors to enjoy their property; and (2) wrongful interference with easements and other incorporeal rights.

A *public nuisance* (also called a *common nuisance*) interferes with a communal right. Examples include obstructing a highway or allowing trash to accumulate in one's front yard to the annoyance of the neighborhood. A *private nuisance,* on the other hand, is an act that interferes with a person's enjoyment of his or her own land or premises. A common example occurs when someone living in an apartment plays music (or what passes for music) so loudly that the neighboring apartment dweller is unable to read or sleep. See **attractive nuisance.**

null (= void) is perfectly capable of standing alone. E.g., "The cancellation of the first will ought to be looked upon as *null* also, and therefore the first will is still subsisting and unrevoked."/ "Even in the compulsory areas, however, the effect of a transfer by unregistered deed is not entirely *null.*" Edward Jenks, *The Book of English Law* 298 (P.B. Fairest ed., 6th ed. 1967). See **null and void.**

nulla bona (= no goods) is a LATINISM that has given its name to the sheriff's return on a writ of execution when he has found no property of the defendant on which to levy. E.g., "The goods seized were then sold by the sheriff and the proceeds paid to Bird, a return of *nulla bona* being made to the plaintiff's writ." *Bankers Trust Co. v. Galadari,* [1987] 1 Q.B. 222, 227 [1986] 3 All E.R. 794, 798.

null and void. "If the powers of the legislature have not been exercised in conformity with the Constitution, the laws enacted are *null and void.*" This DOUBLET is old in the law, is readily understandable to nonlawyers, and is at worst a minor prolixity and a CLICHÉ. Though emphatic, *null and void* is susceptible to the frequent weakness of *void* alone, namely that of being interpreted to mean *voidable.* (See **void.**) *Null and void* is fundamentally innocuous, however; the fight for PLAIN LANGUAGE has far worse legalistic demons to eliminate. See **null** & DOUBLETS, TRIPLETS, AND SYNONYM-STRINGS.

nulla poena sine lege (= no punishment without a law authorizing it), one of the basic principles of civilized nations, is sometimes shortened to *nulla poena*—e.g.: "The doctrine of *nulla poena* would at first sight seem to require a very rigid criminal law and a severe pruning of the discretion allowed to the court in determining sentence." G.W. Paton, *A Textbook of Jurisprudence* 389 (4th ed. 1972).

A common variation on the phrase is *nullum crimen sine lege* (= no crime without a law authorizing it)—e.g.: "It is usual to begin a discussion of general principles of the criminal law by stating the maxim *nullum crimen sine lege,* sometimes known as the principle of legality." Andrew Ashworth, *Principles of Criminal Law* 59 (1991). See MAXIMS.

nullify. See **annul.**

nullip, a clipped form of the gynecological term *nullipara* (= a woman who has never borne children), has become common in litigation of mass-tort claims relating to female infertility. The appearance and sound of the word are startling at first, when one considers the context, which seems much more likely to give rise to soft-sounding EUPHEMISMS—e.g.: "A prime candidate is the young *nullip* who will settle for nothing less than the most modern, trouble-free method of birth control." *Hawkinson v. A.H. Robins Co.,* 595 F. Supp. 1290, 1305–06 (D. Colo. 1984) (quoting a corporate advertisement)./ "[T]he jury could consider defendant's statement that the Cu-7 was 'excellent for use' with *nullips* as a statement of fact, and not as an opinion." *Kociemba v. G.D. Searle & Co.,* 707 F. Supp. 1517, 1525 (D. Minn. 1989).

nullity = (1) the fact of being legally void <petition for nullity of marriage>; or (2) something that is legally void <the contract that is now regarded as a nullity>. Sense (2) is now more common—e.g.: "A forged transfer is a *nullity* . . . ." J. Charlesworth, *The Principles of Company Law* 89 (4th ed. 1945). But sense (1) also appears from time to time—e.g.: "In questions of *nullity* of marriage, English courts will generally recognise the validity of a foreign decree . . . ." R.H. Graveson, *Conflict of Laws* 332 (7th ed. 1974).

nullum crimen sine lege. See ***nulla poena sine lege.***

nul tiel is LAW LATIN meaning "no such," and it typically occurs in denials that something exists, as in the names of pleas called *nul tiel record, nul tiel corporation,* and *nul tiel debt.* E.g., "Appellant filed an answer containing an allegation that the debt was the debt of another, a plea of *'nul tiel debt,'* and a general denial." *Gregson v. Webb,* 239 S.E.2d 230, 231 (Ga. Ct. App. 1977)./ "The merits would be fully open to examination on a plea of the general issue, which would be nil nebet or non-assumpsit, and not *nul tiel record." De la Mata v. American Life Ins. Co.,* 771 F. Supp. 1375, 1381 n.13 (D. Del. 1991).

The phrase is less likely to be replaced than many other JARGON phrases because it is the *name* of a plea, and lawyers are unlikely to adopt a new name such as "the no-such-corporation plea." Even so, many American jurisdictions, including the federal courts, do quite well without the phrase.

NUMBER. See CONCORD, SEXISM (A) & SUBJECT-VERB AGREEMENT.

number of, a. This phrase is generally paired with a plural noun and a plural verb—i.e., *there are a number of reasons* instead of *there is a number of reasons.* The former is correct because of the linguistic principle known as SYNESIS—e.g.: *"There have been a number of cases* in which error or inadvertence has led to failure to comply with the provisions of section 33 or its forerunner."/ "[A] *number of* scholastic and, as it seems to me, unprofitable dogmas *have* grown up . . . ." Carleton K. Allen, *Law in the Making* 268 (7th ed. 1964)./ "There *is* [read *are*] a number of reasons for this." Patrick Devlin, *The Enforcement of Morals* vii (1968)./ "However, *there is* [read *there are*] *a number of* exceptions to this rule, whose importance appears to be increasing today." P.S. Atiyah, *An Introduction to the Law of Contract* 260 (3d ed. 1981) (Cf. p. 31: *"There are a number of* different ways of classifying contracts.").

But when *number* is modified with an adjective—that is, when the SET PHRASE that gives rise to the plural locution is changed—the focus shifts to the singular noun *number,* and the verb should become singular. E.g., "There *are* [read *is*] a considerable number of cases in the United States where courts have ordered the employer to pay the bonus notwithstanding language like that just quoted." Lon L. Fuller, *Anatomy of the Law* 128 (1968)./ *"There is a surprising number* of cases in the advance sheets [involving] joint and mutual wills . . . ." Thomas L. Shaffer, *The Planning and Drafting of Wills and Trusts* 184 (2d ed. 1979).

NUMERALS. A. General Guidance in Using. The best practice in legal writing is to spell out all numbers ten and below, and to use numerals for numbers 11 and above. This "rule" has five exceptions:

1. If numbers recur throughout the text or are being used for calculations—that is, if the context is quasi-mathematical—then use numerals.
2. Approximations are usually spelled out <about two hundred years ago>.
3. In units of measure, words substitute for rows of zeros where possible <$3 million, $3 billion>, and digits are used with words of measure <9 inches, 4 millimeters>.

4. Percentages may be spelled out <eight percent> or written as numbers <8 percent or 8%>.
5. Numbers that begin sentences must always be spelled out. (See C.)

B. Coupling Numerals with Words. In 1992, one lawyer wrote another, saying: "Dear Sally: I really enjoyed seeing you and your two (2) sons in the park last week." All that was missing was the clincher, "Please give my warm wishes to same."

The noxious habit of spelling words out and putting numerals in parentheses decreases the readability of much legal writing, especially DRAFTING. Following is a genuine example from a Canadian court order:

> That of the sum of twelve thousand five hundred dollars ($12,500) payable to the Infant, the sum of twelve thousand dollars ($12,000) be paid to the District Registrar of the Supreme Court of British Columbia, Vancouver, British Columbia, to the credit of the Infant to be held on behalf of the Infant until further order or until she shall attain the age of nineteen (19) years and that the remaining sum of five hundred dollars ($500) together with the sum of one thousand eight hundred and nineteen dollars and ninety-two cents ($1,819.92) be paid to X.Y. Clarke, Solicitor for the Petitioners and the Infant on account of legal fees and disbursements." (Can.)

This belt-and-suspenders practice seems to have originated in a fear of typographical errors: hence, words were used instead of numbers. (And we gained the canon of construction holding that, if ever a discrepancy emerges between spelled-out numbers and numerals, the words control.) But the words did not readily draw the eye to all the important numerical figures, so these were added in parentheses to alert readers. The result is often a bog.

Modern teachers of drafting tend to prefer using the numerals alone. They caution drafters about the urgent necessity of reviewing numerals carefully because, as they note, a misplaced decimal or an added zero (or three) can give rise to malpractice claims. But if clarity and readability are to be primary goals, the belt-and-suspenders approach must be rejected.

If, on the other hand, clarity and readability are not one's primary goal as a drafter—if one is more concerned with unmistakable meaning, however hard a reader might have to work to get at it—then the belt-and-suspenders approach makes perfect sense.

C. Not Beginning Sentences with Numerals. It is stylistically poor to begin a sentence—or, as in the following example, a paragraph—with numerals. E.g., "1984 saw the publication of three substantial books on the subject . . . ." George D. Gopen, *The State of Legal Writing: Res Ipsa Loquitur,* 86 Mich. L. Rev. 333, 364 (1987). Some journals, such as *The New Yorker,* would make that sentence begin, *Nineteen-eighty-four saw the publication* . . . . But most writers and editors would probably simply begin the sentence some other way, as by writing, *In 1984, three substantial books on the subject appeared.*

D. Round Numbers. Except when writing checks or other negotiable instruments, omit double zeros after a decimal: *$400* is better form than *$400.00.*

E. Decades. As late as the 1970s, editors regularly changed *1970s* to *1970's.* Today, however, the tendency is to omit the apostrophe.

F. Judicial Votes. The preferred method for recording an appellate court's votes in a particular case is to use numerals separated by an en-dash <a 5–4 decision> <voted 6–3 to reverse>. This method, which gives the reader more speed than spelling out the numbers <five-to-four decision>, is standard today—e.g.:

- "The majority was 6–3 and the opinion was by Chief Justice Warren—in itself significant, for the Chief Justice normally reserves for himself those onerous tasks likely to draw the most controversy." Robert A. Liston, *Tides of Justice: The Supreme Court and the Constitution in Our Time* 168 (1966).
- "In the 1974 Term, both Rehnquist and Powell wrote heavily in 6–3 and 5–4 cases, Powell writing in five 5–4 and three 6–3 rulings." Stephen L. Wasby, *The Supreme Court in the Federal Judicial System* 178 (1978).
- "Some would argue that one Justice or two would not make that much difference—and that even the many 5–4 splits would gradually disappear—if the Supreme Court were staffed, as they believe it should be, with men and women who understand that constitutional adjudication is simply the job of correctly reading the Constitution." Laurence H. Tribe, *God Save This Honorable Court* 49 (1985).

For more on the en-dash, see PUNCTUATION (D).

If one prefers to spell out *to* instead of using the en-dash, the phrase must be hyphenated if it functions as a PHRASAL ADJECTIVE—e.g.: "[M]ost of the dissenters in this *5 to 4* [read *5-to-4*] ruling feared that the majority had gone a long way in that direction." Gerald Gunther, *Constitutional Law* 1606 (11th ed. 1985). But if the numbers function adverbially in the sentence, there are no hyphens <voted 5 to 4 to affirm>.

numerous is often merely an inflated equivalent of *many*—e.g.: "*Numerous* [read *Many*] learned and brilliant men have believed in witchcraft."

Thomas E. Atkinson, *Handbook of the Law of Wills* 246 (2d ed. 1953).

nunc pro tunc (lit., "now for then") is used in reference to an act to show that it has retroactive legal effect. E.g., "The Commission of Appeals refused to treat the lower court decision as a judgment *nunc pro tunc.*" The LATINISM is useful legal JARGON, not a TERM OF ART, usu. appearing when a court has exercised its "inherent power . . . to make its records speak the truth by correcting the record at a later date to reflect what actually occurred [in earlier court proceedings]." *Ex parte Dickerson,* 702 S.W.2d 657, 658 (Tex. Crim. App. 1986).

nuncupative will. See **oral will.**

nuptial(s). Although *nuptial* is in good use as an adjective, the noun *nuptials* (= wedding) is generally a pomposity to be avoided. It should be left to its ineradicable place in newspaper reports of weddings, in which it allows ambitious young journalists to practice INELEGANT VARIATION.

nurturance looks like a NEEDLESS VARIANT of *nurture,* but the words have diverged in their connotations. Whereas *nurture* means either "upbringing" or "food," *nurturance*—a 20th-century NEOLOGISM dating from 1938—means "attentive care; emotional and physical nourishment." If this DIFFERENTIATION persists, then *nurturance* may earn a permanent position in the language. For now, it remains relatively uncommon—e.g.: "Albert was also depressed and needed environmental stimulation and *nurturance.*" *In re Albert B.,* 263 Cal. Rptr. 694, 696 (Ct. App. 1989)./ "He added that applicant's childhood of extreme emotional and economic deprivation and [of] growing up in a household where there was no *nurturance* was important." *Ex parte Lucas,* 877 S.W.2d 315, 321 (Tex. Crim. App. 1994) (Overstreet, J., dissenting).

O

oasis. Pl. *oases.*

oath. A. And *affirmation.* Apart from its nonlegal sense denoting a profane expression, *oath* has two different meanings: (1) a swearing to God that one's statement is true or that one will be bound to a promise; or (2) a statement or promise made when one so swears. An *affirmation* is a similar declaration without the religious invocation. See **affirmant.**

B. *Under oath* and *on oath.* The former is AmE as well as BrE; the latter is primarily BrE.

obiit sine prole. See **OSP.**

obiter dictum. A. Plural Form. The plural of *obiter dictum* (= a judge's passing remark) is *obiter dicta.* E.g., "Any comment in *Pegues I* regarding the merits of Pegues' *Singleton* claim was obiter *dicta* [read *dictum*]." A tangential comment is *dictum;* tangential comments are *dicta.* See **dictum** (C).

B. *Obiter* as a Shortened Form. *Obiter* is primarily a BrE shortening of the phrase *obiter dictum.* This elliptical form can be confusing when standing for the noun phrase, since *obiter* alone means "by the way"—e.g.: "In *The Christina* three out of five law lords expressed *obiter* doubts about the correctness of the previous English decisions . . . ." J.L. Brierly, *The Law of Nations* 193 (5th ed. 1955).

If the phrase must be shortened, *dictum* is the usual form in AmE and in BrE—e.g.: "The appellees and the trial court cite *Defreese v. Lake,* which, *by obiter* [read *in dictum*], quotes the passage above from *Washburn.*"/ "What Megaw, J. said in *Yeoman Credit Ltd. v. Gregory* was *obiter* [read *dictum*]." (Eng.)/ "This was certainly the intention in that case and therefore it is submitted that the statement within the parenthesis was *obiter* [read *dictum*]." See **dictum** (A).

C. In Dissenting Judicial Opinions. A British writer states that the phrase *obiter dicta* includes "the content of dissenting judgments made by a particular judge." Stephen Foster, *Business Law Terms* 73 (1988). That statement is itself misplaced *obiter dictum.* As generally used, *obiter dictum* relates to nondispositive remarks in a majority opinion.

object, n. Only in legal writing may persons be *objects*—e.g.: "If B is not a natural *object* of A's bounty, a presumption arises that A did not intend to make a gift of the property to B, but had some other reason for causing B to be named as grantee."/ "The rule that admits *objects* born after the testator's death and before the period of distribution, to share in the bequest, applies only where the total amount of the gift is independent of the number of *objects* among whom it is to be divided." (Eng.)

John W. Salmond, the influential legal philosopher, addressed this point head-on: "Certain writers . . . consider that the object of a right means some material thing to which it relates; . . . others admit that a person, as well as a material thing, may be the object of a right." *Salmond on Jurisprudence* 265 (Glanville Williams ed., 11th ed. 1957). To Salmond's way of thinking, the *subject* of a right is its content (e.g., an entitlement to claim damages), whereas the *object* of a right is the person or thing for whose benefit the right exists.

Moreover, in the legal idiom, some persons may be *objects* while others are *nonobjects:* "If a donee of a special power makes an appointment to an *object* of the power in consideration of a benefit conferred upon or promised to a *nonobject,* the appointment is ineffective to whatever extent it was motivated by the purpose to benefit the *nonobject.*"

objectant; objector. Both words mean "one who contests a will." For purposes of DIFFERENTIATION, *objectant* is perhaps preferable in this sense, inasmuch as *objector* has other uses in the language of the law, such as "one who objects to the admission of certain evidence at trial," or in the phrase *conscientious objector.*

In the context of wills, then, *objector* might be called a NEEDLESS VARIANT: "*Objectants,* who are the decedent's next of kin, appeal from a decree of the Surrogate's Court of King's County, which adjudged the bequest in that paragraph to be a valid charitable trust and directed that letters of trusteeship issue."/ "The language of the will and the actions of the *objectors* [read *objectants*] compel the conclusions that the *objectors* [read *objectants*] are entitled to $1.00 each and are not entitled to share in the residue of the estate because of the in terrorem clause." See **caveator & contestant.** Cf. **protestant.**

objectify; objectivize. *Objectify,* dating from the mid-19th century, means either (1) "to make into an object," or (2) "to render objective." *Objectivize,* dating from the late 19th century, means "to render objective." It would be convenient for the words to undergo DIFFERENTIATION, so that *objectify* would be confined to its sense (1), while *objectivize* would preempt *objectify* in the latter's sense (2). See **reify.**

objector. See **objectant.**

OBJECT-SHUFFLING. This term, in the words of its inventor, "describes what unwary writers are apt to do with some of the many verbs that require, besides a direct object, another noun bearing to them a somewhat similar relation, but attached to them by a preposition" (Fowler, *MEU1* 393). For example:

- "He continued the medicine a few days longer, and then *substituted the penicillin with tetracycline* [read *substituted tetracycline for the penicillin* or *replaced the penicillin with tetracycline*]." (This use of *substitute* for *replace,* resulting from a confusion over the type of object that each verb may take, is labeled "incorrect" in the *OED.*)
- "[T]he probability is that the judge himself will instruct a verdict of Not Guilty to be returned . . . ." P.S. Atiyah, *Law and Modern Society* 21 (1983). (The judge will instruct the jury, not the verdict. See HYPALLAGE.)
- "Counsel does not cite us a case that is any way analogous to the present case." (Counsel is citing not the court but a case.)

Unfortunately, there is no simple rule for determining which verbs are reversible and which are not; one must rely on a sensitivity to idiom and a knowledge of what type of subject acts upon what type of object with certain verbs. It is perfectly legitimate, for example, either to *inspire* a person *with* courage or to *inspire* courage *in* a person. *Impress,* likewise, is a reversible word. A court may *impress* a constructive trust *on* property, or *impress* property *with* a constructive trust. Cf. **oust & serve.**

But the switch does not work with similar words such as *instill* or *inculcate.* Good teachers *instill* or *inculcate values into* students but cannot properly be said to *instill* or *inculcate students with* values. See **inculcate.**

object to ——ing. The modern idiom uses a present participle, not an infinitive. E.g., "If any person called to give evidence *objects to take* [read *objects to taking*] an oath, such person must make the following promise and declaration."

obligable. So spelled. See -ATABLE.

obligant. See **obligee (D).**

obligate. See **oblige.**

obligatio. This Roman-law term carries no meaning that is not equally well conveyed by the ordinary English word *obligation.* "Being valid, the state law created an *obligatio,* a personal liability of the owner of the Hamilton, to the claimants." (Holmes, J.) Rarely did Justice Holmes so indulge himself in such unnecessarily recherché terms.

obligation, a basic word in the civil-law tradition, carries a double sense: (1) a duty to perform or to refrain from acting; or (2) a mutual legal relationship imposing a complex of rights and duties. Maine pointed out a "puzzling peculiarity" relating to sense (2)—a peculiarity because we are accustomed to acquainting *obligation* with *duty:* " *'Obligation'* [in Roman law] signified rights as well as duties, the right, for example, to have a debt paid as well as the duty of paying it." Henry S. Maine, *Ancient Law* 270 (17th ed. 1901; repr. [New Universal Lib.] 1905, 1910). In civil law, the term *obligation* embraces contracts, torts, and quasi-contracts. See **duty.**

obligative. See **obligatory.**

obligator. See **obligee (D).**

obligatory; obligative. The general term is *obligatory* (= required; mandatory). *Obligative* is a grammatical term for the mood of verbs expressing obligation or necessity.

oblige; obligate. The differences between these terms lie more in their uses than in their senses. Both words may mean "to bind by law or by moral duty." In legal contexts, the sense of both words is usually "to bind by law"—*obligate* occurring more frequently—whereas in lay contexts the sense of moral duty predominates.

Oblige is used in the sense "to bind by legal tie" only in legal writing. E.g., "While one, by making an entry to the other's debit, lays him under an obligation, it is only the latter that is *obliged.*" *Oblige* has the additional sense "to do a favor for; to bind (someone else) by doing a favor—a sense not shared by *obligate.*"

Obliged (= bound by law, duty, or moral tie) often functions adjectivally in a way that *obligated* ordinarily does not—e.g.: "The California Court of Appeals felt *obliged* to yield to the supremacy of a federal treaty over state law."

Oblige is a casualism in the sense "to favor, bestow, or entertain." E.g., "Appellant wrote the clerk of the court of appeals and requested that all motions filed by his counsel be withdrawn and that a mandate of affirmance issue forthwith; the court *obliged* and the mandate issued."/ "The court requested the government to summarize the evidence that would be offered at trial, and the government *obliged* with a description of the surveillance."

obligee; obligor. A. General Policy for Handling These Terms. The wisest policy is probably not to handle them at all: use *creditor* (= obligee) and *debtor* (= obligor) instead. A leading jurist explains why: "Etymologically, *'obligee'* suggests the idea of a person's being obliged, but in current usage this meaning is actually more commonly attached to the term *'obligor';* but where usage is neither logical nor securely established, one should avoid using potentially misleading expressions." D. Neil MacCormick, "General Legal Concepts," in 11 *The Laws of Scotland: Stair Memorial Encyclopaedia* 1029, at 371 n.3 (1990). For an example in which *obligee* and *obligor* are given senses opposite their ordinary current senses, see George J. Bell, *Principles of the Law of Scotland* § 26, at 14 (10th ed. 1899).

B. Pronunciation. *Obligee* has a soft *-g- /ob-li-**jee**/*, whereas *obligor* has a hard one */ob-li-**gohr**/*. Cf. **subrogee.**

C. Senses. Several dictionaries, such as *The Random House College Dictionary* (rev. ed. 1988) and *Webster's New World Dictionary* (1979), define *obligee* in its etymological sense, as if it were synonymous with *obligor. Random House,* for example, defines *obligee* as "a person who is under obligation," but that meaning ought to be reserved for *obligor.* An *obligee,* in modern usage, is one to whom an obligation is owed.

D. Variations on *obligor.* *Obliger* and *obligator* are NEEDLESS VARIANTS of *obligor,* the usual and therefore the preferable form in legal writing. *Obliger /ə-**blɪ**-jər/* is the nonlegal form. *Obligant* is also a NEEDLESS VARIANT, except in Scots law, in which it is the predominant form.

oblivious takes the preposition *of* in its strictest sense of "forgetful." (*Oblivion* = forgetfulness or forgottenness, not momentary distraction.) The more popular significance of *oblivious* today is "unmindful; unaware; unobservant." This semantic shift represents a grave attenuation in meaning. Today *to* is the more common mate of *oblivious,* though fastidious speakers and writers continue to use *of.*

Oblivious is here used correctly with regard to the preposition, and less correctly from an etymological point of view: "The law does not discriminate between the rescuer *oblivious of* peril and the one who counts the cost." (Cardozo)

obnoxious today generally means "offensive, objectionable." In legal writing, however, it often carries the sense "contrary," as here: "To give effect to the limitation in favor of C's heir, when he is ascertained, would be *obnoxious* to the cardinal principle that a man cannot create a springing interest."

An even rarer sense of the word, used only in legal and literary contexts, is "exposed to harm or liable to something undesirable." E.g., "This is a similar case, and it is *obnoxious* to similar criticism" (Eng.) (adapted from *OED* quotation).

obrogate. See **abrogate.**

obscenity. A. Sense. The multipronged tests for obscenity have evolved considerably since Justice Potter Stewart remarked, "[P]erhaps I could never succeed in intelligibly [defining *obscenity*], but I know it when I see it." *Jacobellis v. Ohio,* 378 U.S. 184, 197 (1964) (Stewart, J., concurring). In 1973, the U.S. Supreme Court spelled out a three-part test: if the average person applying contemporary community standards would find that, taken as a whole, the material appeals to the prurient interest in sex, portrays sexual conduct in a patently offensive way, and lacks serious literary, artistic, political, or scientific value. *Miller v. California,* 413 U.S. 15, 24 (1973).

Because that test involves a variable standard—"contemporary community standards"—the equation varies from locale to locale. In 1983, a judge on the U.S. Court of Appeals for the Second Circuit reluctantly concluded that "the community standards in New York are so low that nothing is obscene." *U.S. v. Various Articles of Obscene Merchandise,* 709 F.2d 132, 138 (2d Cir. 1983) (Meskill, J., concurring).

B. And *indecency*. Neither *obscenity* nor *indecency* named a common-law crime, but each described acts that were considered crimes. The two are sometimes considered interchangeable, although *indecency* is arguably broader because it may encompass anything that is outrageously disgusting.

The High Court of Justiciary, in Scotland, has held that *indecent* and *obscene* are not synonymous. See *McGowan v. Langmire,* 1931 J.C. 10, 13 (1930). *Indecency* was held to be the milder term: nudity, for example, is indecent but not necessarily obscene. As a matter of degree, therefore, *obscene* is the term to which stronger disapproval attaches.

C. And *obsceneness*. If there is a DIFFERENTIATION between the two, *obscenity* is more of a static fact and *obsceneness* more of a quality. The latter is more rare—e.g.: "[T]he search warrant (1) authorized seizure of all copies of the books in question and (2) was issued without an adversary hearing on the issue of their *obsceneness*." *A Quantity of Copies of Books v. Kansas,* 378 U.S. 205, 215 (1964) (Harlan, J., dissenting).

OBSCURITY, generally speaking, is a serious offense. Simple subjects are often made needlessly difficult, and difficult subjects are often made much more difficult than they need be.

Obscurity has myriad causes, most of them rooted in imprecise thought or lack of consideration for the reader. Following is an example of the kind of obscurity typically found in the worst of legal writing: "Upon the other hand, if the defendant in error could not possibly, by the use of reasonable means and due diligence, have procured the information necessary for her to have, in order to make due proof of the death of Archie Hicks, the law did not impose upon her, as a duty, the attempted doing of an impossible thing." This obtuseness is due perhaps partly to the metaphysical notion involved, but certainly also to the pompous phraseology. See WOOLLINESS & PLAIN LANGUAGE.

Indeed, the main root of the problem is purely psychological: "Most obscurity, I suspect, comes not so much from incompetence as from ambition—the ambition to be admired for depth of sense, or pomp of sound, or wealth of ornament." F.L. Lucas, *Style* 74 (1962). More bluntly still: "The truth is that many writers today of mediocre talent, or no talent at all, cultivate a studied obscurity that only too often deceives the critics, who tend to be afraid that behind the smoke-screen of words they are missing the effectual fire, and so for safety's sake give honour where no honour is due." G.H. Vallins, *The Best English* 106 (1960).

A. Overelaboration. One cannot improve upon what Cardozo wrote about the MYTH OF PRECISION: "There is an accuracy that defeats itself by the overemphasis of details. I often say that one must permit oneself, and that quite advisedly and deliberately, a certain margin of misstatement. . . . [T]he sentence may be so overloaded with all its possible qualifications that it will tumble down of its own weight." *Law and Literature,* 52 Harv. L. Rev. 471, 474 (1939). Edgar Allan Poe put the same point a little differently: "In one case out of a hundred a point is excessively discussed because it is obscure; in the ninety-nine remaining it is obscure because excessively discussed." (As quoted in Ashbel G. Gulliver, *Cases on Future Interests* 13 (1959).) See OVERPARTICULARIZATION.

B. Initialese. Another kind of obscurity results from the overuse of acronyms, with which the reader must repeatedly try to become familiar. E.g., "This memorandum examines the effect of a P.U.C. determination of L.C.R.A. standing to be an intervenor contestant as it affects plaintiff's claim that L.C.R.A. lacked sufficient interest to justify its opposition to the Texland application for C.C.N." One's writing should be more accessible to readers than that. If it is to contain acronyms, these should be few and should appear one at a time, not all together. See INITIALESE & ACRONYMS AND INITIALISMS.

C. Abstractness. See ABSTRACTITIS.

obsequies; obsequious. These words are unrelated in meaning. *Obsequies,* the noun, is a FORMAL WORD for *funeral. Obsequious,* the adjective, means "toadying, servilely attentive."

observance; observation. The DIFFERENTIATION between these two words is complete. *Observance* = heeding, obeying; the act of following a custom or rule—e.g.: "The defendant had a right to insist upon an *observance* of the terms of the contract." *Observation* = (1) scrutiny; study; or (2) a judgment or inference from what one has seen—e.g.: (Sense 2) "She made three original *observations* about the doctrine."

Observation is frequently misused for *observance*—e.g.: "[W]e would be fulfilling our obligation to locate the proper balance between competing demands for effective police protection and strict *observation* [read *observance*] of a suspect's fundamental constitutional rights." *People v. Knapp,* 441 N.E.2d 1057, 1064 (N.Y. Ct. App. 1982) (Jasen, J., dissenting)./ "If the testator's intent can be determined from the will itself, rigid *observation* [read *observance*] of precedent and other rules is not absolute and controlling." *Hudspeth v. Hudspeth,* 756 S.W.2d 29, 32 (Tex. App.—San Antonio 1988).

Less commonly, *observance* sometimes mistakenly displaces *observation*—e.g.: "This proceeding was heard ore tenus by the court, and its questions indicated its keen *observance* [read *observation*] of the demeanor of each and every witness who testified in the case." *Jenkins v. Jenkins,* 232 So. 2d 680, 681 (Ala. Ct. Civ. App. 1970).

obstetric(al). The common and preferred form is *obstetric.*

obstruction of justice (= interference with the orderly administration of law) is a broad phrase that captures every willful act of corruption, intimidation, or force that tends somehow to impair the machinery of the civil or criminal law.

obstructive; obstructional; obstructionary. The second and third forms are NEEDLESS VARIANTS.

obtain is a FORMAL WORD for *get.* For the corresponding noun, see **obtainment.**

obtainment; obtainance; obtainal; obtention. Though all four have appeared in legal writing, *obtainment* is the most natural and the most frequent. The others are NEEDLESS VARIANTS.

obverse. See **converse.**

obviate. Modern dictionaries that define *obviate* as meaning "to make unnecessary" are unduly restrictive (see, e.g., the *OAD*). The *OED* does not even list this sense. Although *obviate* may well carry this meaning, it means more usually "to meet and dispose of or do away with (a thing); to prevent by anticipatory measures" (*OED*). E.g., "The trial court can *obviate* the problem by approving appeals only regarding issues that have an adequate record."/ "The semblance of vindictiveness that arises from the imposition of a harsher sentence the second time around must be *obviated* so that the proceedings do not leave the impression of unfairness to the defendant."/ "Defendant cites the equitable maxim, 'equity acts in personam,' invoked since the days of Coke and Bacon to *obviate* open conflicts between law and equity courts."

In the sense "to make unnecessary," *obviate* often appears correctly in the phrase *obviate the necessity of* or *need for.* These phrases are not REDUNDANCIES, for the true sense of *obviate the necessity* is "to prevent the necessity (from arising)," hence to make unnecessary: "This posture of the case *obviates the necessity of* our attempting to articulate a generally applicable principle of 'finality' or 'ripeness' beyond what has already been said in the cited cases."/ "Professor Easterbrook would move us away from this core of first principles toward the periphery populated by managerial techniques—a realm in which the bureaucratic task of punching figures into a supposedly passive and neutral machine *obviates the need for* judges to make and defend hard choices."

Obviate is sometimes misunderstood as meaning "to make obvious" or "to remedy"; the latter error occurs here: "If the company realized that the slipperiness constituted an unreasonable risk to business visitors, it should have either taken steps to *obviate* [read *remedy*] the condition or given visitors warning thereof."

obviously, like other dogmatic words (*clearly, undoubtedly, undeniably*), is one that "lawyers tend to use when they are dealing with exceptionally obscure matters." Grant Gilmore, *The Death of Contract* 116 n.63 (1974). See **clearly** & **doubtless(ly).**

occupancy. Most speakers of English, when they hear this word, are likely to think about how full a building is, as in the "occupancy rate" of a hotel. But *occupancy* has a technical legal sense that nonlawyers are likely unaware of: "the taking possession of something having no owner, with a view to acquiring it as property." The term therefore appears often in the context of adverse possession—e.g.: "[W]e are of the view that the inquiry must focus on the events that led to defendant's exclusive *occupancy* of the property, which serves as the basis for his adverse possession claim." *Pitson v. Sellers,* 613 N.Y.S.2d 1005, 1006 (Sup. Ct. 1994)./ "Montana law requires *occupancy* and payment of taxes to prove adverse possession . . . ." *Lindey's, Inc. v. Goodover,* 872 P.2d 767, 771 (Mont. 1994).

occupant; occupier. These synonyms are both old, and both have historically been used in legal writing to denote "one who takes possession of property." If any distinction in use exists, it is that *occupier* is more common in BrE than in the AmE. E.g., "The scheme of the Act at least allows, if it does not encourage, agreement between the land *occupier* and the local planning authority." (Eng.) Nevertheless, *occupant* is also used with great frequency in BrE.

occurrence. So spelled; *occurence* and *occurance* are fairly common misspellings.

ochlocracy. See **mobocracy.**

-OCRACY. See GOVERNMENTAL FORMS.

octopus forms the plural *octopuses,* not *octopi*—e.g.: "This Court does not find the prosecutor's remark that defense counsel were 'trying to cloud the waters' as squid and *octopi* [read *octopuses*] are reputed to do . . . to be anything more than useless bloviation . . . ." *Snow v. Reid,* 619 F. Supp. 579, 585 (S.D.N.Y. 1985). See PLURALS (A) & HYPERCORRECTION (A).

ocular is turgid for *with one's eyes;* labeling it a FORMAL WORD is too tepid a description. E.g., "The testator must have the opportunity, through the evidence of *ocular* [read *visual*] observation, to see the attestation." The word is sometimes misspelled *occular.* Cf. **inoculation.**

odiferous. See **odorous.**

odious (= hateful) derives from *odium* (= hatred; the reproach that attaches to an act that people despise). E.g., "[D]iscrimination on the basis of race is *odious* and destructive . . . ." *Texas v. Johnson,* 491 U.S. 397, 418 (1989)./ "*Dred Scott* has the *odious* distinction of holding that slaves were still property, subject to return to their owners, even if they managed to find their way to non-slave states." *In re Marriage of Moschetta,* 30 Cal. Rptr. 893, 899 n.14 (Ct. App. 1994).

Though *odious* has nothing to do with *odor,* many writers mistakenly believe that it does. The result is nothing short of a MALAPROPISM—e.g.: "There is an *odious* [read *odorous* or *malodorous*] smell emanating from this case and one wonders for whose benefit the motion to dismiss Vaccaro was filed." *State Farm Mut. Auto. Ins. Co. v. Noble,* 430 S.E.2d 804, 808 (Ga. Ct. App. 1993) (Blackburn, J., dissenting)./ "O'Connell testified that her offices were not provided daily cleaning service, as required under her lease, and that *an odious stench* [read *stench*] had permeated the hallways as a result of the flooding in the restrooms." *Columbus Properties, Inc. v. O'Connell,* 644 A.2d 444, 446 (D.C. Ct. App. 1994). See **odorous.**

odorous; odoriferous; malodorous. *Odorous* = smelly. *Malodorous* carries even stronger negative connotations. *Odoriferous,* a frequently misused term, has historically almost always had positive connotations in the sense "fragrant." It should not be used in reference to foul odors. *Odiferous* is an inferior, shortened rendering of *odoriferous.* See **odious.**

-O(E)S. See PLURALS (C).

of. A. Signaling Verbosity. However innocuous it may appear, the word *of* is, in anything other than small doses, among the surest indications of flabby writing. Some fear that *of,* and the flabbiness it produces, are spreading: "Clearly, *of* is now something more than a mere preposition. It's a virus." *All About Of,* N.Y. Times, 8 March 1992, at 14. The only suitable vaccination is to cultivate a hardy skepticism about its utility in any given context. If it proves itself, fine. Often, though, it will fail to do so.

Some otherwise excellent writers have, on occasion, caught the virus:

- "The second clause *of* the second section *of* the second article empowers the President *of* the United States . . . ." *The Federalist* No. 67, at 409 (Alexander Hamilton) (Clinton Rossiter ed., 1961). [A possible revision: *The second clause of Article II, § 1 empowers . . . .* (From three *of*s to two.)]
- "On another occasion I have spoken more fully *of* the attempt *of* a leader among American teachers *of* law to give an economic interpretation *of* a well known English case . . . ." Roscoe Pound, *The Formative Era of American Law* 88 (1938). [A possible revision: *On another occasion I have discussed how American law teachers have tried to give an economic interpretation of a well known English case.* (From four *of*s to one.)]
- "Henry II had genius *of* a high order, which

never manifested itself more clearly than in his appreciation *of* the inevitability *of* the divergence *of* the paths *of* crime and *of* tort . . . ." H.G. Hanbury, *English Courts of Law* 43 (2d ed. 1953). [A possible revision: *Henry II had rare genius, which never manifested itself more clearly than in his appreciation that the paths of crime and of tort would inevitably diverge.* (From six *of*s to two.) The revision also fixes the REMOTE RELATIVE and uncovers a BURIED VERB (*divergence*).]

- "To one innocent *of* knowledge *of* the history *of* religions, the preoccupation *of* ecclesiastics, many *of* them celibate, with sexual matters may seem inexplicable." Glanville Williams, *The Sanctity of Life and the Criminal Law* 48 (1957). [A possible revision: *To one who knows nothing about the history of religions, the preoccupation of ecclesiastics—many of them celibate—with sexual matters may seem inexplicable.* (From five *of*s to two.)]
- "[I]n the judicial task *of* supervising the administration *of* estates *of* deceased persons, or *of* controlling the actions *of* trustees, judges are called upon to make simple orders [that] in practice will often be uncontested, and the task is then *of* an administrative character." P.S. Atiyah, *Law and Modern Society* 37 (1983). [A possible revision: *In the judicial task of supervising the administration of decedents' estates, or of controlling trustees' actions, judges are called upon to make simple orders that in practice will often be uncontested, and the task is then administrative.* (From six *of*s to three.)]

As the examples illustrate, reducing the *of*s by 50 percent or so can, even at the sentence level, greatly improve the briskness and readability of the prose.

B. Superfluous in Dates. *December of 1987* should be *December 1987.* See DATES (B).

C. *Difficult of*, etc. This construction, illustrated in the examples that follow, is now peculiar to the legal idiom. It is also easily improved by making the wording more direct: "We cannot say that this effort was so *improbable of success* [read *unlikely to succeed*] that all discovery ought to have been denied."/ "To attempt to catalogue the ways and means would be undesirable, and *impossible of attainment* [read *impossible to attain*]." (Eng.)/ "He has been guilty of inability to do that which in the case of such a store in such a place must be *far from easy of performance* [read *far from easy to perform*] in the absence of skilled clerical aid." (Eng.)/ "The question posed at first blush would appear to be *one easy of answer* [read *easy to answer*]."/ "The legislature does not intend a result that is absurd, *impossible of execution* [read *impossible to execute*], or unreasonable." Cf. NOUN PLAGUE. See **difficult of.**

D. *Of a . . . nature.* This phrasing is almost always unnecessary, for the adjective may always be used alone—and with greater force; e.g., *act of a tortious nature* reads better *tortious act.*

E. For *from.* This usage, an ARCHAISM, still appears with some frequency in legal writing—e.g.: "If I order mutton *of* [read *from*] X, and he supplies me with beef, or decomposed mutton, the failure of performance is as complete as if X had supplied nothing." It is commonly seen in the DOUBLET *to recover of and against.* See **purchase (C).**

of and from. This phrase is a hallmark of—not to say from—musty LEGALESE. The word *from* generally suffices as a replacement—e.g.: "Owner and Broker jointly covenant and agree to indemnify and hold such person harmless *of and from* [read *from*] any claim arising from the compliance with this authorization." That sentence could use a thorough overhaul, but the phrase *of and from* is as good a place to start as any.

of counsel. This anglicization of the LAW LATIN *a consiliis* is still sometimes applied to "the counsel employed by a party in a cause, and particularly to one employed to assist in the preparation or management of a cause, or in its presentation on appeal, but . . . not the principal attorney of record" (*Black's*).

But the term is more commonly used in the U.S. in reference to a lawyer (usu. semiretired) who is affiliated with a private law firm, though not as a member, partner, or associate. The phrase always indicates relationship, and often status as well. The phrase is often shortened to *counsel.* See **counsel.**

The phrase is becoming a title in the minds of American lawyers, many of whom therefore capitalize *Of Counsel* in midsentence. Otherwise, the phrase will create what for many readers is a MISCUE—e.g.: "As of 1991, Judge Gee became *Of Counsel* with Baker & Botts." Some writers delete the *of:* "As of 1991, Judge Gee became *Counsel* [or *counsel*] with Baker & Botts."

of course. This phrase, interestingly, seems to have originated as a POPULARIZED LEGAL TECHNICALITY. It appears to have been a LOAN TRANSLATION of the medieval phrase *writ de cursu* (= a writ issued as a matter of course), which in due time became *writ of course.* E.g., "The barons feared this growth of royal power and it was provided that, henceforth, the Chancellor would seal no writ, which was not an existing writ (known as writ *'of course'*), except with the sanction of the king and council." L.B. Curzon, *English Legal History* 28 (2d ed. 1979)./ "When trespass became a writ *of course,* about 1250, the recovery of unliquidated damages was a well-known practice . . . ." William F. Walsh, *A Treatise on Equity* 7 (1930). See **as of course.**

From the sense "as a matter of course," the phrase *of course* took on the sense "naturally; obviously; clearly." Like those defining words, it is sometimes used to fortify lame propositions. It therefore requires careful, responsible use. See **clearly.**

offence. See **offense.**

offendant is a NEEDLESS VARIANT of *offender*—e.g.: "But once again, many *offendants* [read *offenders*] do well in this category." George D. Gopen, *The State of Legal Writing: Res Ipsa Loquitur,* 86 Mich. L. Rev. 333, 348 (1987).

offense; offence. The first is the AmE spelling, the second the BrE spelling. In BrE and AmE alike, the word is preferably accented on the second syllable /ə-***fents***/. Unfortunately, because American sports-talk puts the accent on the first syllable (/***of***-*ents*/), many American police officers, criminal lawyers, and criminal-court judges have adopted this pronunciation even in the legal sense of the word. The sound of it puts the literate person's teeth on edge.

The word is sometimes used synonymously with *crime,* but at other times it is intended to have a broader meaning. Jeremy Bentham, for example, defined *offense* in two ways: (1) an act that "appear[s] . . . to have a tendency to produce mischief" (Jeremy Bentham, *The Principles of Morals and Legislation* 178 (1823 ed.; repr. 1948)); and (2) "an act prohibited, or, (what comes to the same thing) an act of which the contrary is commanded by the law" (*id.* at xix, § 1).

In BrE, and to a lesser extent in AmE, lawyers commonly distinguish *crimes* (at common law) from *offenses* (created by statute). It is common in both speech communities to use *offense* for the less serious infractions and *crime* for the more serious ones. Lawyers would not speak of the "offense" of murder. Nor would they refer to the "crime" of parking a car in the wrong place.

Even so, because *offense* is generally so closely associated with the idea of crime, the phrase *civil offense* is needlessly confusing. The phrase *civil wrong* (q.v.) is preferable. See **criminal offense.**

offer. A. And *promise.* "There is surely a difference," wrote a 19th-century English scholar, "a profound difference in legal significance, between an *offer* and a *promise.* An *offer* is an expression of willingness to be bound by contract to the person to whom the offer is made, if he accepts the offer unconditionally and within a reasonable time. The offer then becomes a *promise.* A contract is made up of one or more promises and when a contract is made, and not till then, the parties are bound. Therefore an *offer* is revocable, a *promise* is not." William R. Anson, *Some Notes on Terminology in Contract,* 7 Law Q. Rev. 337, 337 (1891). See **promise (A).**

B. And *invitation to treat.* "The distinction between an *offer* and an *invitation to treat* is often hard to draw as it depends on the elusive criterion of intention." G.H. Treitel, *The Law of Contract* 11 (8th ed. 1991). In BrE, the phrase *invitation to treat* denotes an invitation to make an offer, as opposed to an offer in itself; examples include a menu in a restaurant, wares displayed in a storefront window, and an auctioneer's request for bids. In AmE, the phrase is rarely if ever used: instead, writers on the law of contract generally use roundabout wordings such as *entertainment of bids, proposal made to the public,* and *invitation to make an offer.* The last of these has much to be said in its favor because it is immediately comprehensible to a broad spectrum of readers.

C. *Firm offer.* A "firm" offer contains a promise not to revoke it for a specified period.

D. *Offer* in Criminal Law. Criminal lawyers have given *offer* an odd meaning by making it synonymous with *attempt,* q.v. Thus an *offer to commit battery* is a threat that makes a person reasonably apprehend that he or she is about to be battered. One unfamiliar with this strange phraseology might mistakenly assume that the phrase *offer to commit battery* is contractual in nature and relates to sadomasochism.

offer of evidence; offer of proof. An *offer of evidence* is the last step in the introduction of evidence. The proponent of tangible evidence (writings, photographs, murder weapons, and the like), after evidence has been marked for identification, allows the judge and opposing counsel the courtesy of examining it before a witness authenticates it. Once the evidence has been authenticated, the proponent says, for example, "Your Honor, we now *offer into evidence* what has been marked Plaintiff's Exhibit No. 5." One "offers" testimonial evidence simply by engaging in direct examination or cross-examination.

An *offer of proof* is a means of preserving the record for appeal. It consists in a lawyer's adducing what that lawyer expects to be able to prove through a witness's testimony, and it usually occurs outside the jury's presence and only after a judge has sustained an objection to the introduction of the evidence. An offer may be made of tangible evidence, of testimony through questions and answers, or of testimony through the lawyer's own narrative description.

offeror; offerer. The former is now standard in legal texts, although the latter was much used in the 19th century. See -ER (A).

office, v.t., has become a commonplace expression among American lawyers in the southwestern U.S., but not among fastidious users of language. E.g., "*Although the defendant was officed there* [read *Although the defendant had an office there*] for a while, the business address of the company is the office on 51st Street." This is a classic example of the problem discussed under NOUNS AS VERBS.

officer of the court, in the sense "a lawyer," is an Americanism that evokes the close supervision and control that courts exercise over practicing lawyers, the considerable professional duties that lawyers owe to the judicial system, and the privileges that they receive. Although the courtroom lawyer is not an *officer* in the same sense as a bailiff, a marshal, or a police officer, he or she is nevertheless obligated to serve the disciplinary function of controlling the client in court.

The phrase most commonly crops up when one lawyer chides another for an alleged lapse in ethics or etiquette, or when a judge admonishes counsel to keep to a higher standard.

OFFICIALESE = the language of officialdom, characterized by bureaucratic turgidity and insubstantial fustian. The defining characteristic of officialese is the habitual use of inflated language that could be readily translated into simpler terms: "Let us now proceed to perambulate down the corridor to procure our midday comestibles." As translated: "Let's go down the hall for lunch."

Among the linguistically unsophisticated, puffed-up language seems more impressive. Thus, police officers never *get out of their cars;* instead, they *exit their vehicles.* They never *smell* anything; rather, they *detect it by olfaction.* They *proceed* to a *residence* and *observe* the suspect *partaking of food.* Rather than *sending* papers to each other, officials *transmit* them (by hand delivery, not by fax). And among lawyers, rather than *suing,* one *institutes legal proceedings against* or *brings an action against.* For sound guidance on how to avoid officialese, see Ernest Gowers, *The Complete Plain Words* (2d ed. 1973); and J.R. Masterson & W.B. Phillips, *Federal Prose: How to Write in and/or for Washington* (1948).

official misconduct. See **misconduct in office.**

officious. In Dr. Johnson's day, *officious* had positive connotations ("eager to please"). Today, however, it means "meddlesome; interfering with what is not one's concern." E.g., "When the necessary goods or services are furnished without the knowledge of the trustee, who is supporting the beneficiary, recovery should be denied on the ground that the person supplying the goods or services is acting *officiously.*" In legal contexts, the word frequently appears in the phrase *officious intermeddler:* "People who fertilize other people's land or play the good Samaritan are *'officious intermeddlers'*—volunteers whom even equity will not aid." Grant Gilmore, *The Death of Contract* 73 (1974).

In the context of diplomacy, the word has a strangely different sense: "having an extraneous relation to official matters or duties; having the character of a friendly communication, or informal action, on the part of a government or its official representatives" (*OED*) <an officious communication>.

The term is often misused, however. In the following sentence it is difficult to discern what meaning the writer intended it to have, but it is impossible for a policy to be *officiously applicable:* "It is upon this assumption, that the case will be tried in a convenient forum so that the forum's policies are properly and not *officiously applicable* [read *arbitrarily applied?*] to the case, that Professor Ehrenzweig advances his central suggestion for solution of choice-of-law problems."

Here the writer apparently mistook its meaning as being "official-looking": "He still lived in the same old dormitory, in a bigger and more *officious* room." The same error is plain in one court's reference to an *officious translation* of a Belgian statute; presumably *official translation* would have been the appropriate phrase.

offing. The traditional phrase is *in the offing* (= about to appear). *On the offing* is incorrect and unidiomatic.

offload, v.t., of South African origin, is a NEEDLESS VARIANT of *unload* or for *dump.* E.g., "The court finds that orders given to *offload* [read *dump*] garbage cannot possibly constitute unseaworthiness of the vessel."

off of is inferior to *off* without the preposition. E.g., "He jumped *off of* [read *off*] the bridge." The only exception occurs when *off* is part of a PHRASAL VERB, such as *write off*—e.g.: "This is a serious difficulty, but it need not lead to the *writing off* of the subjective definition of recklessness."

Glanville Williams, *Textbook of Criminal Law* 78 (1978). Cf. **outside of.**

off point has, in AmE, become the antonym of *on point*—e.g.: "The Ohio case is so far *off point* on its facts that one must stretch his imagination to compare that Court's holding and facts to the instant case." *Geurin Contractors, Inc. v. Bituminous Casualty Corp.,* 636 S.W.2d 638, 643 (Ark. Ct. App. 1982)./ "The dissent's cases are *off-point* [read *off point*]." *LeCroy v. Hanlon,* 713 S.W.2d 335, 342 n.10 (Tex. 1986)./ "The plaintiff's argument is *off point.*" *U.S. Leasing Corp. v. City of Chicopee,* 521 N.E.2d 741, 744 n.4 (Mass. 1988).

offrecord. See **off-the-record.**

offset, n., is perfectly acceptable in American legal writing. This usage is first recorded in the *OED* as an Americanism from 1769. Nearly fifty years later, John Pickering wrote: "This is much used by lawyers of America instead of the English term *set-off;* and it is also very common, in popular language, in the sense of equivalent. . . . It is not in the dictionaries." J. Pickering, *A Vocabulary* 142 (1816) (emphasis omitted).

Today the word is commonplace, in dictionaries and elsewhere—e.g.: "Allowable *offsets* are subtracted from the consumer's actual damages before trebling, necessarily reducing the amount of damages subject to trebling." Deborah J. Bullion, *An Understanding of Damages Recoverable Under the DTPA,* 20 St. Mary's L.J. 667, 685 (1989)./ "Finally, the Trustee argues that . . . we are, in effect, sanctioning an impermissible *offset* of a fraudulent conveyance against general unsecured claims." *United Energy Corp. v. Rider,* 944 F.2d 589, 597 (9th Cir. 1991)./ "[T]he only statutorily permissible *offset* to an approved progress payment is 'an amount necessary to satisfy any claims, liens or judgments' . . . ." *Christ Gatzonis Elec. Contractor, Inc. v. New York City Sch. Constr. Auth.,* 23 F.3d 636, 641 (2d Cir. 1994).

offset, v.t., is generally inferior to *set off,* although it cannot rightly be condemned as an error. E.g., "[T]he division of property was, or will be, approximately equal and the two amounts would *offset* each other." *Welsh v. Welsh,* 869 S.W.2d 802, 807 (Mo. Ct. App. 1994)./ "Specifically, Austin Mutual contends [that] the $100,000 collected from Leichtenberg's insurer should *offset* the $100,000 in total underinsured motorist limits under King's policy, leaving no remaining coverage due by Austin Mutual." *Austin Mut. Ins. Co. v. King,* 29 F.3d 385, 388 (8th Cir. 1994).

What can be condemned as an error—and a gross one—is using *offsetted* as a past tense or past participle. E.g., "NFO then refused to pay Smith, . . . contending that the amount NFO owed Smith was *offsetted* [read *offset*] by the damage caused by Smith's breach of his January 9, 1973 contract." *Nat'l Farmers Org. v. Smith,* 526 S.W.2d 759, 763 (Tex. Civ. App.—Corpus Christi 1975)./ "[T]he lower court . . . properly considered . . . the disparity between appellee's earning capacity and appellant's substantial income *offsetted* [read *offset*] by his reasonable expenses and direct support of Eric." *Steenland-Parker v. Parker,* 544 A.2d 1010, 1013 (Pa. Super. Ct. 1988). See **set-off.**

off-the-record, adj. This is the standard phrase for any comment explicitly not for recordation or attribution. As a PHRASAL ADJECTIVE preceding what it modifies, it should be hyphenated, but not when it follows what it modifies <an off-the-record statement> <a statement off the record>. Some writers have experimented with *offrecord;* that word is not yet standard.

of opinion. See **opinion, of (the).**

often, as an adverb, need not be hyphenated in phrases such as the one in the following sentence: "Occurring at the end of eight days of *often-starry* [read *often starry*] and emotional deliberation in State Supreme Court in Manhattan, the verdict ended a highly publicized and sensational murder trial in New York." Ronald Sullivan, *Steinberg Is Guilty of First-Degree Manslaughter,* N.Y. Times, 31 Jan. 1989, at A1.

oftentimes is, in all cases, unnecessary for *often.* E.g., "Both of these statutory schemes were in harmony with the common-law doctrine of sovereign immunity, but had the effect of lessening the *oftentimes* [read *often*] harsh results achieved in applying that doctrine."/ "The plaintiff gave no evidence of an intent that *oftentimes* [read *often*] appears to establish an enterprise independent of profits or losses." See REDUNDANCY.

of the essence. In the law of contract, this phrase makes certain stipulations more important than others; any failure to perform such a stipulation justifies a rescission. See **time is of the essence.**

of (the) opinion. See **opinion, of (the).**

olfaction, detect by is a laughable pomposity for *smell.* E.g., "The marijuana was discovered in plain view during the course of a subsequent maritime search of the vessel, and, in any event, the distinctive odor of the contraband weed apparently was ubiquitous and easily *detected by olfaction* on board and well beyond the Lady Mar." Here we also have INELEGANT VARIATION (*marijuana . . . the contraband weed*) and misuse of *ubiquitous* (= universal). Cf. **ocular.**

oligopoly; oligopsony. The former denotes control or domination of a market by a few large sellers; the latter, control or domination of a market by a few large customers. Cf. **monopoly (D).**

olograph. See **holograph.**

ombudsman; ombuds; ombudsperson. *Ombudsman* = (1) an official appointed to receive, investigate, and report on private citizens' complaints about the government; or (2) a similar appointee in a nongovernmental organization. Originally a Swedish word denoting a commissioner, *ombudsman* spread throughout the world during the mid-20th century as governments saw the wisdom of having such an official. Though the word entered the English language only as recently as 1959, it caught on remarkably well.

But, despite its prevalence throughout the English-speaking world, this word may prove to have a short life-span. Because of the *-man* suffix, many writers consider it sexist. Some have taken to lopping off the suffix, and, though the word *ombuds* looks distinctly un-English and remains unrecorded in most English dictionaries, it is surprisingly common—e.g.: "In Denmark, the Consumers' *Ombuds* has been given statutory responsibility for handling consumer complaints . . . ." *Evaluating Electronic Payment Systems in the UK,* American Banker, 28 Sept. 1987, at 25.

Several writers have tried *ombudsperson,* but that form should be allowed to wither. (See SEXISM (B).) Others have experimented with *ombuds officer,* which at least satisfies one's desire to have a word that looks as if it denotes a person—e.g.: "Columbia University last week named its first *'ombuds officer'* as a reference point on campus for people who have grievances within the university and are looking for options to deal with them." *Campus Life: Columbia,* N.Y. Times, 14 July 1991, § 1, pt. 2, at 31.

omissible; omittable. The latter is incorrect.

omission. A. Generally. Among nonlawyers, this word has a narrower sense than it does among lawyers. To the nonlawyer, an *omission* is either something left out (as of a brief or program) or the act of leaving something out. To the lawyer, this word, serving as a useful antonym of *commission,* ordinarily denotes the failure to do something. E.g., "Nor will the surety be discharged by the creditor's *omission* to inform him . . . ." Laurence P. Simpson, *Handbook on the Law of Suretyship* 406 (1950)./ "When we speak of an *omission* we mean something that the accused could have done if he had been minded to do so and had prepared himself in time, or at least something that another in his place could have done." Glanville Williams, *Criminal Law* 4 (2d ed. 1961). See **omit [+ infinitive].**

B. And *forbearance*. An *omission* is an unintentional negative act, whereas a *forbearance* is an intentional negative act. Unfortunately, some legal writers use *omission* when they mean *forbearance*—a habit contributing to sloppy analysis.

omit [+ infinitive]. This construction, in which *omit* means "to neglect," appears today primarily in legal prose. E.g., "A person who wrongfully *omits to perform* a particular act required of him is liable in damages for all the consequences that may ordinarily ensue therefrom." It is a lawyers' expression that is neither JARGON nor LEGALESE, but an obsolescent grammatical construction. See **omission (A).**

omittable. See **omissible.**

omnibus, adj. (= relating to or serving for numerous distinct objects at once; comprising a large number of items or particulars [*OED*]) is a LEGALISM most often used in the legislative phrase *omnibus bill.* But *omnibus* also has other uses in legal writing—e.g.: "The appeal brings up for review the denial, after a hearing, of . . . defendant's *omnibus* motion . . . ." *People v. Lopez,* 497 N.Y.S.2d 452, 452 (App. Div. 1986).

on; upon. These synonyms are used in virtually the same ways. The distinctions are primarily in tone and connotation. *On,* the more usual word, is generally preferable: it is better to write *service on a defendant* than *service upon a defendant.* E.g., "As this case centers *upon* [read *on*] the strength of local Mississippi policies, this course is mandated by the principles of federalism."/ "The burden is *upon* [read *on*] the petitioner to show that this is true."/ "Plaintiff alleged that in reliance *upon* [read *on*] an inaccurate FHA inspection made in approving FHA mortgage insurance, he was induced to buy a house for an excessive price."

But *upon* is the better word for introducing a condition or event—e.g.: "*Upon* being served with a request, a party must . . . ."

One should never alter an idiom in which *on* appears by making it *upon,* as here: "The plaintiff received an assignment of a mortgage which *upon its face* [read *on its face*] provided it was secured by a note described in the mortgage." See **face, on its, upon** (A) & SET PHRASES.

on a . . . basis. See **basis** (B).

on all fours (= squarely on point with regard to both facts and law) is useful legal JARGON that refers to highly pertinent legal precedents. The phrase began as a LOAN TRANSLATION of an old Latin maxim, *Nullum simile est idem nisi quatuor pedibus currit* ("No similar thing is the same, unless it runs on all four feet"). The metaphor, as the *OED* explains, is that of a quadruped running evenly—not limping like a lame dog. E.g., "Judges in this way are constantly reasoning not by explicit authority *'on all fours,'* but by analogy . . . ." Carleton K. Allen, *Law in the Making* 308 (7th ed. 1964)./ "Once you found cases *'on all fours'* you could sustain a good argument." Frank Maher, *Words, Words, Words,* 14 Melbourne U.L. Rev. 468, 469 (1984). Cf. **whitehorse case.**

Because of the special legal sense, lawyers may create a MISCUE if they suddenly use the phrase in reference to a person on hands and knees: "Coke made an ardent defense of the common-law courts that angered King James so violently that all the judges trembled and Coke himself 'fell flat *on all fours.*' " René A. Wormser, *The Story of the Law* 279 (1962).

on and after (a date) is usually unnecessary for *from, after,* or *since* (a date), unless it is important to convey explicitly the nuance that the date mentioned is included within the scope of applicability. See **on or about.**

on appeal; on the appeal. The former phrase is today considered more idiomatic in AmE. E.g., "*On the appeal* [read *On appeal*], the counterclaimants petitioned and were granted leave to intervene, argue, and file a brief." See **appeal** (A).

on behalf of. See **behalf.**

on circuit. See **circuit, to ride.**

one. A. The Overdone *one,* n. "[*O*]*ne* has an affirmative responsibility toward others when *one* has taken an active part in directing the manner in which these others perform their tasks or when *one* creates or is generally responsible for a dangerous situation that causes harm. . . . *One* is not liable, however, simply because *one* uses the services of an independent contractor. Nor is *one* liable because of the mere fact that the contractor performs his work on *one*'s land or, as in this case, on *one*'s ship." *Futo v. Lykes Bros. S.S. Co.,* 742 F.2d 209, 215 (5th Cir. 1984). Enough said.

B. *One . . . he.* This expression is inferior to *one . . . one,* partly because of the questionable grammar and partly because of the generic masculine pronoun. (See SEXISM (A).) But the infelicity is common—e.g.: "A constructive trust, on the other hand, arises when *one* obtains the legal title to property in violation of a duty *he* [better: *one*] owes to another."/ "If *one* were thoughtless, *he* [better: *one*] would be apt to say that this is a case in which part of the operative facts creating the original obligation are directly presented to the senses of the tribunal."

Even worse are constructions on the order of *one . . . such person,* as here: "The United States Supreme Court has held that *one* may be in custody for habeas corpus purposes despite the fact that *such person* [read *one*] has been released from jail or on personal bond." Cf. **one . . . you.**

C. *One* [+ *name*]. Using *one* as an adjective before a proper name, as in "*one* Howard James," is a pretentious LEGALISM with a valid pedigree in English, but generally without justification in modern prose. It might even hint at BIBLICAL AFFECTATION, for the *OED* quotes from the Bible: "and of *one* Jesus, which was dead, whom Paul affirmed to be alive." Today, however, the word *one* looks askance at any name following it.

one and the same is occasionally misrendered *one in the same.*

one another. See **each other.**

one bite at the apple; one bite at the cherry. The first is the usual AmE idiom today, the latter the invariably BrE idiom. Each one denotes the idea that a litigant gets but one chance to take advantage of certain opportunities or rights. American courts sometimes use *cherry* in place of *apple,* but the latter fruit vastly predominates. The American version is that rare SET PHRASE that is not so well set, variations on the phrase being more common than the main phrase itself—e.g.: "[U]nless a litigant gets a real *bite at the apple* of discord he should not be foreclosed from another attempt." *Angel v. Bullington,* 330 U.S. 183, 207 (1947) (Rutledge, J., dissenting)./ "Because 'one fair opportunity to litigate an issue is enough,' . . . we generally will not allow a *second bite at a single apple." A.J. Canfield Co. v. Vess Beverages, Inc.,* 859 F.2d 36, 37 (7th Cir. 1988) (citation omitted)./ "The interest of finality requires that parties generally get only *one bite at the Rule 59(e) apple* for the purpose of tolling the time for bringing an appeal." *Charles L.M. v. Northeast Indep. Sch. Dist.,* 884 F.2d 869, 871 (5th Cir. 1989).

Some British lawyers insist that their idiom—*one bite at the cherry*—makes more sense because the cherry is a fruit that, by its nature, is eaten in only one bite: it makes little sense to think of multiple bites at a cherry.

But it was not logic that seems to have led American lawyers to speak of apples. Up to the late 1940s, American lawyers, like their British counterparts, regularly said *one bite at the cherry:* dozens of examples appear in the law reports. But, from the 1920s on, *cherry* had assumed another sense in AmE, namely "hymen" or "virgin." The *OED* quotes an American book from the 1970s explaining that "'[t]o take or eat a cherry' means to deflower a virgin."

Thus, *one bite at the cherry* may well be the only legal idiom that has changed because its users felt embarrassment over a newfound double entendre.

one . . . his. See **one (B).**

one in the same. See **one and the same.**

one of those ——s who (*or* that). This construction requires a plural, not a singular, verb. Why? Because in this construction, *who* (or *that*) acts as the subject of the upcoming clause, and the relative pronoun takes its number from the plural noun immediately preceding—e.g.: "It is one of the few admiralty texts that *is* [read *are*] worth reading." The reason for this construction becomes apparent when we reword the sentence: "Of the few admiralty texts that *are* worth reading, it is one."

This point of usage trips up even the best writers. Thus, it is common—e.g.: "One of the few people who *continues* [read *continue*] to insist that he is a liberal in its original and true sense is Nobel laureate Friedrich Hayek." Thomas Sowell, *"Conservative" Means Even Less Than "Liberal,"* Dallas Morning News, 10 Feb. 1989, at 19A./ "One of the most important and difficult questions *which arises* [read *that arise*] in examining the extent of the parties' duties under a contract is to decide whether the parties are absolutely bound . . . ." P.S. Atiyah, *An Introduction to the Law of Contract* 184 (3d ed. 1981)./ "Martin Marietta, however, has not claimed that it was one distributor among many who *was* [read *were*] terminated for failing to price-fix . . . ." *O.K. Sand & Gravel, Inc. v. Martin Marietta Corp.,* 819 F. Supp. 771, 797 (S.D. Ind. 1992). For similar errors, see **crime** (last par.) & **each (A)** (last par.).

one's self is an ARCHAISM for *oneself.* "One should learn to pace *one's self* [read *oneself*]."

one . . . you. This shift from third person to second is even worse than *one . . . he.* (See **one (B).**) E.g., "*One* hears—and if *you* are like me, *you* acquiesce in—many complaints about the decline of civility in Western society." Clifford Orwin, *Civility,* 60 Am. Scholar 553, 553 (1991). [One possible revision: *You hear—and if you are like me, you acquiesce in—many . . . .*]

on his own application is LEGALESE for *at his request.*

on its face. See **face, on its.**

only is perhaps the most frequently misplaced of all English words. Its best placement is precisely before the words intended to be limited. The more words separating *only* from its correct position, the more awkward the sentence; and such a separation can lead to ambiguities. (Cf. **solely.**) E.g.:

- "A *pro se* complaint can *only* be dismissed for failure to state a claim if it appears beyond doubt that the plaintiff can prove no set of facts in support of his claim which would entitle him to relief." (Put *only* after the first *claim.*)
- "These public rights can *only* be destroyed by proper municipal action." (Put *only* after *destroyed.*)
- "*Erie* is *only* applicable where there is no controlling federal statute." (Put *only* after *applicable.*)
- If the intestate were a married woman and her husband became administrator, he succeeded to the *only* personalty that was not already his by the marital right." (Put *only* after *succeeded.*)
- "Suffice it to say that I am quite satisfied that the court in that case was saying that an interrogatory may *only* be administered as to the contents of a written document if secondary evidence of that document would be admissible at the trial or hearing." (Eng.) (Put *only* after the first occurrence of *document.*)
- "A conditional promise is one which the promisor need *only* perform if a specified condition occurs." (Put *only* after *perform.*)

on or about is the lawyer's hedge-phrase for dates, used esp. in pleadings. E.g., "*On or about* August 31, 1981, plaintiff and defendant entered into an assignment and assumption agreement." If the date is known with reasonable certainty, *on* is preferable. See FUDGE WORDS & **on and after.**

on pain of. See **pain of, on.**

on point. See **in point** & **off point.**

on the appeal. See **on appeal.**

on the offing. See **offing.**

on the other hand. It is pure pedantry to insist that this contrastive phrase must always be paired with *on the one hand.*

on the part of. This phrase is usually verbose—e.g.: "Remedies can be lost by delay, by the intervention of third-party interests, *or by a lack of complete probity on the part of the plaintiff.*" [Read *or by the plaintiff's not being completely honest.*]

onus, lit. "a burden" (L.), usually carries the extended meaning "a disagreeable responsibility; obligation." In law, it also acts as an elliptical form of *onus probandi,* meaning *burden of proof.* E.g., "The mode of suing for and recovering penalties and forfeitures does not necessarily include any rules . . . as to the *onus probandi.*" *The Abigail,* 1 F. Cas. 36, 37 (C.C.D. Mass. 1824) (No. 18).

Onus of proof is a BrE compromise between *onus probandi* and *burden of proof:* "The *onus of proof* should be put the other way round where a question of status of this nature arises." (Eng.) See **burden of proof (B)** & LOAN TRANSLATIONS.

op. cit. is the abbreviation for *opere citato* (= in the work cited). It is no longer used in legal citations and is obsolescent in other scholarly writing.

open court, in. This phrase, sometimes contrasted with *closed court* or *in camera,* means "during the public proceedings of a court." E.g., "Only once was Judge Taylor ever seen at a dead standstill *in open court,* and the Cunninghams stopped him." Harper Lee, *To Kill a Mockingbird* 167 (1960)./ "[I]t is difficult to imagine acceptance of a system under which, instead of trial *in open court,* a quiet and secluded inquiry by a committee of social scientists would determine whether an individual should be subjected to compulsory detention." Lon L. Fuller, *Anatomy of the Law* 55 (1968). Cf. **in camera.**

open-ended(ness) should be hyphenated, in order that it not look too monstrous.

open seas. See **high seas.**

open the door. This legal CLICHÉ generally denotes one of two ideas: (1) that one party makes it possible (i.e., "opens the door") for the other party to do something tending to be prejudicial; or (2) that a court or policy-maker is embarking on a *slippery slope,* q.v. Sense (1): "It would be ironic to hold that when a State embarks on such desirable experimentation it thereby *opens the door* to scrutiny by the federal courts, while States that choose not to adopt such procedural provisions entirely avoid the strictures of the Due Process Clause." *Hewitt v. Helms,* 459 U.S. 460, 471 (1983). Sense (2): "In adopting the rule it does, the Court *opens the door* to countless similarly situated prisoners to withdraw their guilty pleas many years after they were entered." *Henderson v. Morgan,* 426 U.S. 637, 659 (1976) (Rehnquist, J., dissenting).

operable; operative; operational. *Operable* is now commonly used in the sense "practicable; capable of being operated." *Operatable* for *operable* is an occasional error—e.g.: "The fact that [the machinery] was not *'operatable'* [read *operable*] after some repairs had been completed did not render it 'unrepairable.'" *Arizona Container Corp. v. Consolidated Freightways,* 522 P.2d 772, 774 (Ariz. Ct. App. 1974).

Operative = (1) having effect; in operation; efficacious <the statute is now operative>; or (2) having principal relevance <*may* is the operative word of the statute>.

Operational = engaged in operation; able to function; used in operation. E.g., "While a rate of slightly under ten violent incidents per month may seem shocking at first even for a large correctional institution, this figure must be evaluated in light of the fact that no *operational* definition of 'violence' has been established."

ophthalmology is sometimes misspelled *ophthamology* or *opthamology.*

ophthalmologist; oculist; optometrist; optician. The first two designate an M.D. whose specialty is the eye, although *ophthalmologist* is now more usual. An *optometrist* (with the degree of O.D.) is licensed to prescribe glasses and contact lenses. An *optician* makes the glasses in accordance with the prescription.

opine today usually connotes the forming of a judgment on insufficient grounds. It suggests the giving of an idle opinion, and thereby cheapens the opinion given. Formerly, however, the word was used in the sense "to express or pronounce a formal or authoritative opinion" (*OED*). The *OED* calls this sense rare; yet, in American law at least, this usage could hardly be accurately described as rare. Examples abound in which the verb is used of courts' pronouncements, without any suggestion of insufficiency of evidence. E.g., "None of the justices appear to have *opined* that the equal protection clause does not apply to illegal aliens."/ "The Supreme Court of New Jersey *opined,* in *Santor v. A. & M. Karaghensian,* that a cause of action under strict liability could be utilized to recover economic losses." We should not restrict *opine* because of its negative lay connotations; the term is a useful one in law.

It is unclear whether cheapening was here intended: "A plaintiff who does not have asbestos-related cancer may find a medical witness who will *opine* that there is a reasonable probability that he may later develop the disease." One cannot really *opine* about one's own thoughts: "I merely *opine* that I am hard-pressed to imagine a more appropriate case for the use of legislative history than the present one." [Read *I would be hard-pressed to imagine . . . .*] See **opinion,** v.t.

opinion is the AmE term for a judicial deliverance, i.e., the court's statement explaining its decision, including points of law, statements of fact, *rationes decidendi,* and dicta. The BrE equivalent is *judgment,* but the word *opinion* is also frequently used. (See **judgment (B).**) In BrE, *opinion* more commonly refers to advice given by counsel on facts set out in a case or in a memorandum submitted to counsel. See **decision & deliverance.**

opinion, v.t., is a NEEDLESS VARIANT of *opine,* q.v. "An F.B.I. document *opinioned* [read *opined*] that some of the writing on the government's exhibit was the same as handwriting exemplars taken from the defendant." (Note that to say a *document opines* is to engage in HYPALLAGE.)

opinion, of (the). Modern idiom requires *of the opinion;* to omit the definite article is to use an ARCHAISM that survives only in the law. In each of the following specimens, *the* should be inserted in the italicized phrase: "We are *of opinion* that the findings of fact by the district court entitled the appellee to the equitable relief sought."/ "If the court is *of opinion* that any evidence was improperly admitted or rejected, it must set aside the conviction." (Eng.)

Today, *of the opinion* seems to outnumber *of opinion* in legal opinions by three or four occurrences to one, in both BrE and AmE, despite what the examples just quoted might suggest. E.g., "We are *of the opinion* that plaintiff does not have a cause of action against this defendant."/ "For reasons to be stated, we are *of the opinion* that the judgment of the Supreme Court of Georgia should be affirmed."

opinion of the court. This phrase denotes the American-style judicial opinion that, though written usually by a single judge, speaks for the court as a whole. Within the common-law tradition, the alternative is *seriatim opinions,* in which each judge on the bench pronounces an individual opinion. For a brief history of how Chief Justice John Marshall established the opinion of the court in American law, see Bryan A. Garner, "Opinions, Style of," in *The Oxford Companion to the Supreme Court of the United States* 607, 608–09 (Kermit L. Hall ed. 1992).

opinions, rule against. This rule of evidence carries different senses in G.B. and in the U.S., primarily because of the different understandings of the word *opinion:*

> The opinion rule, though it developed from practices and expressions of the English courts, seems to be emphasized more generally and enforced more inflexibly here [in the U.S.] than in the mother country. In the first place a rule against 'opinions' may have had a different meaning for the English judge. We are told that in English usage of the 1700's and earlier *opinion* had the primary meaning of "notion" or "persuasion of the mind without proof or certain knowledge." It carried an implication of lack of grounds, which is absent from our present-day term *opinion* in this country. We use the word as denoting a belief, inference, or conclusion, without suggesting it is well- or ill-founded.
>
> Charles T. McCormick, *Handbook of the Law of Evidence* 22 (E. Cleary ed., 2d ed. 1972).

OPINIONS, JUDICIAL. Writing a judicial opinion is a peculiar task—quite different in many ways from writing other types of discursive or persuasive prose. The primary difficulty lies in giving either a "yes" or a "no" answer to what is often an extremely complicated problem. The decision generally must be consistent with previous judicial decisions, and must at the same time conform to the judge's notions of what justice dictates. Often, and especially in difficult cases, the doctrine of stare decisis plays tug-of-war with conscientious fairness. The dilemma is especially acute inasmuch as some of the most complex problems of society and of individual human lives must be reduced to the simplest of dichotomies: yea or nay. Not all the uncertainties can be plumbed by the judge writing an opinion; the task is to justify one's determination, crude as the framework may be for minimizing the possibly substantial merits of the losing side.

Wigmore identified six shortcomings of judicial opinions: (1) undiscriminating citation of authority; (2) unfamiliarity with controlling precedents;

(3) mechanical treatment of judicial questions; (4) misconception of the doctrine of precedents; (5) overconsideration of points of law; and (6) certain deficiencies peculiar to one-judge opinions. 1 Wigmore, *Evidence* § 8, at 615–18 (3d ed. 1940). There are so many aspects of writing effective judicial opinions that no short treatment could pretend to cover even the primary ones. A few short observations may be helpful, however. The reader who needs more detailed guidance may read any number of articles, or the one serviceable book on the subject. (See LEGAL WRITING STYLE (D).) But, all in all, we must await production of a first-rate treatise on this subject.

A. Tense. It is generally best in judicial opinions to write in the present tense when referring to the parties or facts before the court that have continuing validity, or seem to from all that appears in the record. Thus, if a judge writes, "The defendants *were* citizens of Clarksville, Tennessee," the reader must wonder whether they have moved or died. What the judge here doubtless meant is that these persons *were* defendants, but now that the trial is over they are no longer. Use of the past tense in this way needlessly puzzles the reader, even though the author knows that the past tense is technically correct because the opinion is being written some time after the trial or sitting.

Less troublesome, but also to be avoided, is the mannerism of using the future tense, as in "The judgment *will be* affirmed." Such statements often appear toward the beginning of an opinion, so that at the end, the court may conclude, "The judgment *will be, and hereby is,* affirmed." This messing about with tenses is unnecessary. The writing judge should be direct: "We affirm the judgment below."

B. Judicial Humor. Drollery and judicial opinions almost invariably make an unhappy combination. "[T]he form of opinion which aims at humor from beginning to end is a perilous adventure, which can be justified only by success, and even then is likely to find its critics almost as many as its eulogists." Benjamin N. Cardozo, *Law and Literature,* 52 Harv. L. Rev. 472, 483 (1939). One of those critics of judicial humor was Justice George Rose Smith, formerly of the Arkansas Supreme Court, who observed, "Judicial humor is neither judicial nor humorous. A lawsuit is a serious matter to those concerned in it. For a judge to take advantage of his criticism-insulated, retaliation-proof position to display his wit is contemptible, like hitting a man when he's down." George R. Smith, *A Primer of Opinion Writing, for Four New Judges,* 21 Ark. L. Rev. 197, 210 (1967). Justice Smith cited an egregious example of attempted stream-of-consciousness humor: *Hampton v. North Carolina Pulp Co.,* 49 F. Supp. 625 (E.D.N.C. 1943); it is one of the worst opinions that have come to my attention. For an example of failed poeticism and wasteful drivel, see *U.S. v. Sproed,* 628 F. Supp. 1234 (D. Or. 1986).

Lest we assume, however, that judicial writing should be cheerless and sober-sided, it is worth noting Cardozo's tempered judgment: "In all this I would not convey the thought that an opinion is the worse for being lightened by a smile. I am merely preaching caution." *Law and Literature,* 52 Harv. L. Rev. 472, 484 (1939).

C. Concurrences. Judges, and especially appellate judges, write not just for themselves, but for the entire court. In concurring opinions, of course, the writing usually becomes more individualistic:

> If a judge is occasionally possessed of an uncontrollable desire to express his personal views instead of having them continually absorbed in the compromise pronouncements of the court, he may gratify that urge by the writing of concurring or, if so disposed, even dissenting, opinions. But a concurring opinion must justify itself by furnishing a different reason for the court's decision, and even then should not be resorted to unless the writer of the majority opinion refuses to accept and incorporate the suggested additions or amendments. A concurring opinion which merely says the same thing in other language is not only valueless as a contribution to the science of the law but is somewhat of a reflection on the colleague to whom was assigned the duty of explaining the views . . . of the court.
>
> Horace Stern, *The Writing of Judicial Opinions,* 18 Pa. Bar Ass'n Q. 40, 44 (1946).

See ***dubitante*** & **write specially.**

D. Drafting Mandates. See JUDGMENTS, APPELLATE-COURT.

oppress; repress. *Oppress,* which has connotations that are more negative, means "to subject (a person or a people) to inhumane or other unfair treatment; to persecute." *Repress,* a closely related word, means either: (1) "to keep under control"; or (2) "to reduce (persons) to a subordinate position."

oppression = (1) in criminal law, any harm, other than extortion, that a public officer corruptly causes to a person; or (2) in the law of contract, coercion to enter into an illegal contract—used as a basis for allowing a person to recover money paid or property transferred under an illegal contract. In sense (2), as G.H. Treitel notes, *oppression* is "used in a somewhat broad sense." *The Law of Contract* 437–38 (8th ed. 1991).

oppugn. See **impugn.**

opt (in) (out) (for). *Opt* = to choose or decide. It is usually followed by *for* or *to*—e.g.: "Thiessen *opted to* receive the lump-sum payment." *Nebraska Equal Opportunity Comm'n v. State Employees Retirement Sys.,* 471 N.W.2d 398, 400 (Neb. 1991)./ "By *opting for* a *Pierringer*-type release, Unigard obviously was interested in more protection than the covenant not to sue or the general release would provide." *Unigard Ins. Co. v. Insurance Co. of N. Am.,* 516 N.W.2d 762, 765 (Wis. Ct. App. 1994).

In the language of class actions, however, plaintiffs are said to have the choice of *opting in* or *out* of the class. E.g., "Some states instead provide *opt-in* provisions for these rights; for example, a corporation's shareholders will not have preemptive rights unless the articles of incorporation specifically provide for them." In fact, the phrase has been extended to the persons who *opt in* or *out*; in modern American legal JARGON, they are known as *opt-ins* or *opt-outs.*

optimacy is not a variant of *optimality;* it means "aristocracy."

optimum is the noun, *optimal* the adjective. The adjective should be used in adjectival senses where it idiomatically fits. E.g., "The *optimum solution* [read *optimal solution*] is an adjudication of the permission question." Cf. **maximum.**

opt in. See **opt.**

option; right of preemption; first option to buy; right of first refusal. These terms are usefully distinguished in the law of contract. An *option* is an offer that, specifying the amount of consideration, becomes a contract when the offeree (or *optionee*) accepts it. For example, if Beverly has a three-year option to buy Charlie's house for $200,000, she may exercise that option, and make the sales contract binding, at any time within that period.

A *right of preemption* is a potential buyer's contractual right to have the first opportunity to buy, at a specified price, if the seller chooses to sell. For example, if Beverly has a right of preemption on Charlie's house for five years at $200,000, Charlie can keep the house for five years (in which case Beverly's right expires); but if he wishes to sell during those five years, he must offer the house to Beverly for $200,000. Beverly, in turn, can either buy or refuse to buy; if she refuses, Charlie can sell to somebody else. Nonlawyers often call Beverly's right an *option,* but lawyers ought to be more fastidious in their use of language. Of course, the synonymous phrase, *first option to buy,* is perfectly apt and perhaps even more descriptive than *right of preemption.*

A *right of first refusal* is a potential buyer's contractual right to meet the terms of a third party's offer if the seller intends to accept that offer. For example, if three conditions are met—Beverly has a right of first refusal on the purchase of Charlie's house, Ted offers to buy the house for $300,000, and Charlie intends to accept Ted's offer—then Beverly can match Ted's offer and thereby trump it.

option, v.t. (= to grant or take an option on), dates from ca. 1926, but remains a VOGUE WORD. E.g., "Her first screenplay was *optioned* for a mere $300,000." It may be useful legal slang or JARGON, but it is best restricted to speech.

optionee; optioner. See **optionor.**

option-giver; option-holder. These terms are more comprehensible than *optionor* and *optionee.* E.g., "In the present context, an option may be defined as a right possessed by one person (the *option-holder*) to insist that another person (the *option-giver*) grant or transfer a specified interest in land." Peter Butt, *Land Law* 171 (2d ed. 1988).

option-holder. See **option-giver.**

optionor; optioner. The *-or* form is now prevalent. It has the advantage of being more strictly accurate as a correlative of *optionee* (= the grantee in an option contract), although *option-giver,* q.v., is clearer.

optometrist. See **ophthalmologist.**

opt out. See **opt.**

-OR, -ER. See -ER (A).

-OR, -OUR. All agent nouns but *saviour* (BrE) take *-or* in both the AmE and BrE (e.g., *actor, relator*). The distinction between AmE (*-or*) and BrE (*-our*) usage occurs in abstract nouns. Hence the British write *behaviour, colour, flavour,* and *humour,* whereas Americans write *color, flavor,* and *humor.* The following words, however, end in *-or* on both sides of the Atlantic: *error, horror, languor, liquor, pallor, squalor, stupor, terror, torpor,* and *tremor. Glamour* is the primary exception to the rule of *-or* in the AmE.

In BrE, nouns ending in *-our* change to *-or* before the suffixes *-ation, -iferous, -ific, -ize,* and *-ous* (e.g., *coloration, honorific*). But *-our* keeps the *-u-* before *-able, -er, -ful, -ism, -ist, -ite,* and *-less* (e.g., *honourable, labourer, colourful*).

or. A. And *and*. "*Every* use of 'and' or 'or' as a conjunction involves *some* risk of ambiguity." Maurice B. Kirk, *Legal Drafting: The Ambiguity of "And" and "Or,"* 2 Texas Tech L. Rev. 235, 253 (1971) (emphasis in original). Thus, in the main text of *Words and Phrases* (1953)—excluding pocket parts—the word "and" takes up 61 pages of digested cases interpreting it in myriad ways, and the word "or" takes up another 84 pages of digested cases interpreting it in an equally broad array of senses. Virtually every book on drafting legal documents contains a section on the ambiguity of the two words.

Authorities agree that *and* has a several sense as well as a joint sense, and that *or* has an inclusive sense as well as an exclusive sense. Hence:

- The "several *and*": A and B, jointly or severally.
- The "joint *and*": A and B, jointly but not severally.
- The "inclusive *or*": A or B, or both.
- The "exclusive *or*": A or B, but not both.

See Scott J. Burnham, *The Contract Drafting Guidebook* 163 (1992). "The meaning of *and* is usually *several* . . . . The meaning of *or* is usually inclusive." *Id.* See **and (B).**

B. For *or else*. E.g., "[E]very clause in the contract is 'understood and agreed' *or* [read *or else*] it would not be written into it." Richard Wincor, *Contracts in Plain English* 29 (1976).

C. Beginning Sentences with. Like *and* and *but,* the word *or* is a perfectly appropriate word with which to begin a sentence—e.g.: "Thus a politically organized society may be under a patriarchal king, or, as so frequently in a Greek city-state, a tyrant, a more or less absolute ruler with no title to be king. *Or* it may be under an oligarchy, a caste derived from priestly heads of kin-groups." Roscoe Pound, *The Development of Constitutional Guarantees of Liberty* 4–5 (1957).

D. *Or/and*. See **and/or.**

oral. See **verbal** & **parol.**

oral argument (AmE & BrE) = *oral debate* (BrE). In AmE, the phrase is ordinarily *in* or *at oral argument,* but *on oral argument* also appears, esp. in New York. E.g., "The disclosure proposed and described by Wallenstein *on oral argument* would go only to particulars as to the results of the committee's investigation and work . . . ." *Auerbach v. Bennett,* 393 N.E.2d 994, 1004 (N.Y. 1979). See **debate.**

oral contract; verbal contract. The former—the correct phrase—outnumbers the latter by more than ten to one in American judicial opinions. See **verbal** & **parol (A).**

oral deposition. See **deposition (C).**

oral will; nuncupative will; sailor's will; soldier's will. The broadest term is *oral will,* of which there are two types, both obsolescent: *nuncupative wills* and *soldiers' and sailors' wills.*

Nuncupative will is an English adaptation of the LAW LATIN phrase *testamentum nuncupativum* (= an oral will). If *nuncupative wills* are valid in a given jurisdiction, the amount that may be conveyed in them is usually limited by statute. Customarily, the will must be made in the testator's last illness, and usually at home unless the testator falls ill elsewhere. Two competent witnesses are usually required.

Soldiers' and sailors' wills derive from ancient military and maritime custom; in England the privilege derives from statute. The soldier must be in military service, or the sailor at sea, and, in some jurisdictions, a single witness must be present. In Great Britain, the phrases *soldier's will, mariner's will,* and *military testament* are used.

Nuncupative is often used as broadly as *oral,* that is, to encompass soldiers' and sailors' wills—e.g.:

> A *nuncupative* will is not required to be in writing. It may be made by one who, at the time, is in actual military service in the field or doing duty on shipboard at sea, and in either case in actual contemplation, fear, or peril of death, or by one who, at the time, is in expectation of immediate death from an injury received the same day. It must be proved by two witnesses who were present at the making thereof, one of whom was asked by the testator, at the time, to bear witness that such was his will, or to that effect.
>
> Cal. Prob. Code § 54 (repealed).

The usual practice, however, is to use *nuncupative* only in reference to the second type of will mentioned in the statute just quoted—i.e., an oral will made in contemplation of imminent death from an injury recently incurred—to distinguish it from *soldiers' and sailors' wills. Oral* encompasses every one of these types.

orate. See **perorate** & BACK-FORMATIONS.

orchestrate, in nonmusical contexts, is a CLICHÉ and a VOGUE WORD. It is, however, arguably useful in indicating that an (apparently spontaneous) event was clandestinely arranged beforehand. Cf. **choreograph.**

ordain (= to establish by law; enact) has an archaic flavor in other than religious contexts <an

ordained minister>. The word does not mean "to provide," as the author of the following sentence mistakenly thought: "*Article 2106 ordains that* [read *Article 2106 provides that*], if the affair for which the debt has been contracted in solido concerns only one of the co-obligors in solido, that one is liable for the whole debt." (La.)

ordain and establish. This DOUBLET has a fine pedigree: "We the people of the United States, in order to form a more perfect Union, establish Justice, insure domestic Tranquility, provide for the common defence, promote the general Welfare, and secure the Blessings of Liberty to ourselves and our Posterity, do *ordain and establish* this Constitution for the United States of America." U.S. Const. pmbl. In most modern contexts, *establish* alone suffices, *ordain* being archaic in all but its religious senses.

ordeal. See POPULARIZED LEGAL TECHNICALITIES.

order = (1) a command or direction; (2) a judge's written direction; or (3) a written instrument (such as a check), made by one person and addressed to another, directing that other to pay money or deliver something to someone named in the instrument. In sense (2), a court's order may be either interlocutory (on some intermediate matter) or, more broadly, final (and thus dispositive of the entire case).

ordered, adjudged, and decreed. In many American jurisdictions, this wordy phrase routinely appears in court orders. The simple word *ordered* is generally much preferable—e.g.: "It is therefore *ordered, adjudged, and decreed* [read *ordered*] that the Plaintiff take nothing by her suit." See DOUBLETS, TRIPLETS, AND SYNONYM-STRINGS.

orderee is an unnecessary NEOLOGISM that surely will not survive with the fittest words in the language—e.g.: "The formal requirements of Rule 34 are . . . a safeguard by means of which the *orderees* are insured adequate apprisal of the terms of the court's mandate to them." *SEC v. Los Angeles Trust Deed & Mortgage Exch.,* 24 F.R.D. 460, 464 (S.D. Cal. 1959). [A possible revision: *Rule 34 ensures that the ordered persons will be adequately apprised of the court's mandate.*]/ "May [court orders] be ignored or disobeyed without sanction as here, creating a weakening of the court's authority through deliberate superimposition of the *orderee's* own judgment?" *Lamons v. State,* 335 S.E.2d 652, 656 (Ga. Ct. App. 1985) (Beasley, J., dissenting). [A possible revision: *May court orders be ignored and disobeyed with impunity? If so, a person under court order can weaken the court's authority merely by ignoring the order.*] See -EE (C).

order of licence. See **parole.**

Order of the Coif. This was the name, formerly, of the order of serjeants-at-law, the highest order of counsel at the English Bar. Through the mid-19th century, they had a monopoly over practice in the Court of Common Pleas. But when, by statute, that court was opened to the whole Bar in 1846, the Order began to wither. Nathaniel Lindley was the last serjeant to be appointed (1875) and to die (1921).

In the U.S. today, the origins of this order are not widely known among lawyers. But they all know that one must excel in law school to be elected to the Order of the Coif, an honorary legal fraternity composed of a select few law students with the highest grades. See **coif.**

ordinance; ordnance; ordonnance. *Ordinance* (= a municipal [i.e., city] law) is common in the AmE but rare in BrE, where *by-law* serves this purpose. In AmE, *bylaw* is generally used to mean "a corporate rule or regulation not included in the articles of incorporation." See **bylaw.**

Ordnance = military supplies; cannon; artillery. *Ordonnance* = the ordering of parts in a whole; arrangement.

ordinar(il)y prudent person. With compound modifiers, either two adjectives before a noun or an adverb and an adjective before a noun, one must look closely at the sense to determine whether the first word is properly an adjective or an adverb. One such problematic phrase in law is *ordinar(il)y prudent person,* familiar in discussions of torts. One sees both *ordinary* and *ordinarily* in the cases, but the latter is more logical, because *ordinary* modifies *person,* whereas *ordinarily* modifies the adjective *prudent.*

The intended meaning, of course, is *person of ordinary prudence.* We do not mean *an ordinary person;* we mean *a person who is prudent to an ordinary degree.* One problem is that *ordinarily* in one sense means "often, usually." And if we (incorrectly) give it that sense, we end up with a person who is *ordinarily* (but not always) prudent—i.e., one who sometimes may be given to imprudence. Because of that slight AMBIGUITY, one cannot be dogmatic in preferring *ordinarily prudent person* over *ordinary prudent person.* But it is preferable nevertheless—e.g.: "*Ordinarily prudent persons* . . . would not run at a rate of 20 to 25 miles per hour onto such a crossing

. . . ." *Veach's Adm'r v. Louisville & Interurban Ry.,* 228 S.W. 35, 36 (Ky. 1921).

On the variant phrase, *ordinarily prudent man,* see SEXISM (B).

ordinary law. In the U.S.—though not in England—this phrase is contrasted with *organic* or *constitutional law. Ordinary law* consists primarily of regular statutes, which may prove unconstitutional; *organic law,* or *constitutional law* (as it is more generally called), is superordinate and relatively fixed in its words, if not in its interpretation. Cf. **organic law.**

Ordinary, Lord of Appeal in. See **Lord of Appeal in Ordinary.**

ordnance; ordonnance. See **ordinance.**

ore tenus = by word of mouth. Either *oral* or *orally* is generally preferred to this term, which in most contexts ought to be considered a FORBIDDEN WORD. E.g., "Judge Wyzanski has referred to the 'enormous, nearly cancerous, growth of exhibits, depositions, and *ore tenus* [read *oral*] testimony' in antitrust cases . . . ." John R. Allison, *Arbitration Agreements and Antitrust Claims,* 64 N.C.L. Rev. 219, 247 (1986) (quoting *U.S. v. Grinnell Corp.,* 236 F. Supp. 244, 247 (D.R.I. 1964))./ "Following an *ore tenus* proceeding, the trial court determined that the employee's injury did not 'arise out of and in the course of his employment' . . . ." *Strickland v. Marshall Constr. & Repair, Inc.,* 553 So. 2d 591, 592 (Ala. Ct. Civ. App. 1988).

The phrase *ore tenus rule* now serves, in AmE, as the name for the presumption that a trial court's findings of fact are correct and should not be disturbed on appeal unless clearly wrong or unjust. The phrase seems to have come about through the realization that live witnesses, testifying orally, may make a very different impression from that which their words on paper make. E.g., "[A]s the evidence before the trial court was by stipulation of the parties and no testimony was taken orally, the *ore tenus rule* of review is not applicable to this appeal." *Kessler v. Stough,* 361 So. 2d 1048, 1049 (Ala. 1978). In this phrase alone is *ore tenus* arguably useful; even so, however, it is JARGON.

organic law = (in a civil-law jurisdiction such as Louisiana) decision(al) law. E.g., "Louisiana *organic law* allows an individual to contract concerning liability for negligence in all cases where such a contract is not contrary to public policy." See **decision(al) law.**

But the phrase has an entirely different sense in the common-law tradition: Bouvier defined *organic law* as "the fundamental law or constitution of a state or nation" and used the phrase in that sense. For example, in defining the "United States of America," Bouvier stated: "the republic whose *organic law* is the constitution adopted by the people of the thirteen states which declared their independence of the Government of Great Britain on the fourth day of July, 1776." The phrase is still used in this sense: "[A]t the time when our *organic laws* were adopted, criminal trials both here and in England had long been presumptively open." *Richmond Newspapers, Inc. v. Virginia,* 448 U.S. 555, 569 (1980). Cf. **ordinary law.**

Confusingly, the phrase *organic statute* is used of a legislative act establishing an administrative agency.

organization. Many legal writers use this as a general term that includes companies, partnerships, foundations, nationalized industries, government departments, and the like. Cf. **firm.**

orient; orientate. The latter is a NEEDLESS VARIANT of *orient,* which means "to get one's bearings or sense of direction." Sadly, the longer variant (a BACK-FORMATION from *orientation*) seems esp. common in BrE: "Not everyone, even in *market-orientated* [read *market-oriented*] America, is wholly happy with what is happening." Sunday Times, 11 Dec. 1988, at H1. Cf. **disorient(ate).**

original evidence. See **direct evidence.**

original instance. See **first instance.**

original intent, doctrine of; strict constructionism. These doctrines, which apply to constitutional and statutory constructions, differ significantly. The doctrine of *original intent* signifies that the interpreter tries to recapture the mental state of the enactors or drafters who were responsible for the Constitution, legislation, or other document. *Strict constructionism*—a more general term—signifies that one interprets the Constitution, legislation, or a document narrowly so as to make as little change in the law as possible. Both doctrines are founded on notions of judicial conservatism. *Original intent* is a controversial doctrine often founded also on conservative political notions. See **strict construction.**

original jurisdiction; primary jurisdiction. The first phrase, meaning "jurisdiction to take cognizance of a case at the outset, to try it, and to decide the issues," is usually contrasted with *appellate jurisdiction.* In the U.S., *primary jurisdiction* is original jurisdiction that lies in an administrative agency.

original precedent. See **precedent (D).**

orphan. Although, in the popular mind, *orphan* refers to a child whose mother and father are both dead, courts have sometimes interpreted the word differently. Depending on the facts at hand, *orphan* may be held to include a child who has lost only one parent. See *Jackman v. Nelson,* 17 N.E. 529, 530 (Mass. 1888). But the courts seem uniformly to have included in their definition of *orphan* the idea that the person so described be a minor.

orphanhood; orphancy; orphandom. The first is the usual word, the other two being NEEDLESS VARIANTS.

orphan's court. In some American states today—such as Delaware, Maryland, and Pennsylvania—this phrase denotes a probate court. (The orphan's courts originated in England but have long since become defunct there.) Generally speaking, the jurisdiction of an *orphan's court* is not limited to orphans or even to minors—a good reason, perhaps, to jettison the phrase in the few places where it still occurs.

Although the plural possessive form *orphans' court* might have made better sense, the singular possessive *orphan's* has long been standard. The form without an apostrophe is poor—e.g.: "At this point Judge Terzian had to point out rather sadly to Mrs. MacFarlane that even though she was chief judge of the probate court—called *orphans court* [read *orphan's court*] in Maryland—she couldn't do any more . . . ." Murray T. Bloom, *The Trouble with Lawyers* 215 (1970).

orse. is the abbreviated form of *otherwise,* q.v. "In his judgment, Sir Jocelyn Simon referred to some of the earlier decisions, including *H. v. H.* and the more recent decision of Scarman J. in *Buckland v. Buckland (orse. Camilleri).*" (Eng.)

OSP; *obiit sine prole.* The Latin phrase means "he died without issue"; the translation suffices if we are to write out a phrase. The abbreviation may sometimes be justified, if the targeted readers are certain to understand its import.

As with many other LATINISMS, American lawyers often get it wrong. *Black's* (5th ed.), for example, defines *obit sine prole* in the past tense, when in fact it is present tense. The past-tense form is *obiit.*

ostensible authority. See **apparent authority.**

ostensively for *ostensibly* (= from all that appears) is a solecism. E.g., "Although deposit insurance coverage is a function that *ostensively* [read *ostensibly*] could be handled by private enterprise, the United States also wanted to and did direct the FDIC to protect the public interest . . . ." *Rauscher Pierce Refsnes, Inc. v. FDIC,* 789 F.2d 313, 315 (5th Cir. 1986).

ostrich defense is a colloquialism that disparages a criminal defendant's claim not to have known of the criminal activities of his or her associates. E.g., "Whether or not Ramirez's implicit *ostrich defense* was credible is not for this court to determine . . . ." *State v. Amezola,* 741 P.2d 1024, 1033 (Wash. Ct. App. 1987) (Swanson, J., dissenting)./ "Instead, [the appellees] have simply ignored [the estoppel issue] and adopted the *ostrich defense* in addition to their attempted use of the Archimedean Lever." *Capitol Fish Co. v. Tanner,* 384 S.E.2d 394, 396 (Ga. Ct. App. 1989) (Deen, P.J., concurring).

other. See **otherwise (A).**

other good and valuable consideration. See **and other good and valuable consideration.**

otherwise. A. And *other*. Most properly, *other* is the adjective, *otherwise* the adverb—e.g.: "CPL 2.25B has no cognizable impact, substantial *or otherwise* [read *or other;* better: *or not*], on any right or interest of Kast."/ "An interested person may appear before an agency in a proceeding, whether interlocutory, summary, *or otherwise* [read *or other;* better: *or of some other kind*], or in connection with an agency function." Follett believed that "to pronounce this *otherwise* inadmissible would be to fly in the face of a strongly established usage. But usage, which can allow on sufferance, cannot prevent it from being rejected by more exact writers." Wilson Follett, *Modern American Usage* 242–43 (1966).

B. *Otherwise than.* This phrase is often misused for *other than.* Driedger is wrong to characterize *otherwise than* generally as "useful to specify one predicate modifier and expressly exclude all others." Elmer A. Driedger, *The Composition of Legislation* 86 (1957). Its legitimate uses are few.

In the sentences that follow, *other* is called for. "Transactions by dealers subject to Section 16 are exempted if the transactions are part of ordinary trading activities in the company's securities and incident to the dealer's establishment and maintenance of a primary or secondary market, *otherwise than* [read *other than*] on a national securities exchange or an exempt exchange."/ "What we must ensure in the welfare state, *otherwise than* [read *other than*] the welfare of almost half the nation, is the virtual certainty that only the members of the government, and those who implement their orders, shall be reputed intelligent." (Eng.)

C. *Other* . . . *other than.* A fairly common mistake is to repeat *other* in the phrase *other than.* E.g., "Payment may be made pursuant to a differential based on any *other* factor *other than* sex." Either one of the *others* should be dropped.

D. *Otherwise expressed.* This is cumbersome and jarring for "in other words." E.g., "*Otherwise expressed,* the law is that . . . ." See **to put it another way.**

E. As a Conjunction. This slipshod usage occurs primarily in BrE—e.g.: "If a promise is not made under seal, it must be supported by 'consideration' (that is, something given or undertaken in return for the promise), *otherwise* no contract will arise . . . ." 1 E.W. Chance, *Principles of Mercantile Law* 9 (P.W. French ed., 13th ed. 1950)./ "[I]t is essential that the promises themselves should be regarded as consideration for each other, *otherwise* there could be no such thing as a contract consisting of mutual promises at all." P.S. Atiyah, *An Introduction to the Law of Contract* 96 (3d ed. 1981). In each sentence, a semicolon should precede *otherwise.* For further elucidation of this common error, see RUN-ON SENTENCES.

otiose /*oh-shee-**ohs***/ = unneeded; not useful. The word is used more by lawyers than by other writers. E.g., "The question whether the assignees of the reversion were bound would have been wholly *otiose.*"/ "The words of the application for appointment are not to be struck out as being merely *otiose;* they are specific words." (Eng.)/ "If Mr Wiggins's argument is correct, the words 'as though the driver were in the hirer's direct employ' are *otiose,* since there is no need to import the notion of a vicarious responsibility in a matter in which the hirer has by his own direction caused the damage." (Eng.) Cf. **nugatory.**

-OUR. See -OR.

ought. A. Infinitive Following. *Ought* should always be followed by an infinitive, whether the phrase is *ought to* or *ought not to*—e.g.: "It was argued that theaters that patronized the union *ought not to be* patronized by the public."/ "Nor can I see how it can possibly be proved that we *ought not to feel* that way." Morris R. Cohen, *Reason and Law* 104 (1961)./ "*Ought* it *to be* made punishable when adultery is not?" Patrick Devlin, *The Enforcement of Morals* 1 (1968).

As some type of sham badge of scholasticism, American law professors tend to omit the particle *to* when the expression is in the negative or interrogative. But there is no warrant for this usage: "What *ought* the lawyers *do to* [read *to do to*] preclude litigation?"/ "A judge *ought not cease* [read *ought not to cease*] to be a citizen merely because he becomes a judge."/ "We *ought not* [read *ought not to*] impute to others instincts contrary to our own."

A few legal writers extend this precious oddity beyond negatives and interrogatives—e.g.: "We extend our efforts, as we *ought* [read *ought to*], toward effectuating the testator's intentions."/ "[N]either need the laws be interpreted so as to protect those who *ought* [read *ought to*] know better from their own indolence." *Hamel v. Prudential Ins. Co.,* 640 F. Supp. 103, 105 (D. Mass. 1986).

B. And *should.* *Ought* should be reserved for expressions of necessity, duty, or obligation; *should,* the weaker word, expresses mere appropriateness, suitability, or fittingness.

our federalism is an odd name for a legal doctrine, but in AmE this phrase denotes the controversial doctrine "that federal courts must refrain from hearing constitutional challenges to state action under certain circumstances in which federal action is regarded as an improper intrusion on the right of a state to enforce its laws in its own courts." Charles A. Wright, *The Law of Federal Courts* 320 (4th ed. 1983). The leading case on this point is *Younger v. Harris,* 401 U.S. 37 (1971). Perhaps because of its strange appearance—with the possessive first-person pronoun—the phrase is sometimes written *Our Federalism,* with initial capitals. See **federalism.**

ourself; theirself. *Ourself* is technically ill-formed, inasmuch as *our* is plural and *self* is singular. But it is established in the editorial or royal style. *Theirself* is indefensible, however.

oust = (1) to eject, dispossess, or disseise (construed with *of*); or (2) to exclude, bar, or take away (construed with *from* or *of*). Hence, idiomatically speaking, one may either *oust a court of jurisdiction* or *oust jurisdiction from a court.* Today the former expression is more common—e.g.: "A contract that makes a certain person a final arbiter of all disputes that may arise under it cannot *oust* the court *of* jurisdiction." But the alternative wording has persisted—e.g.: "The section obviously envisages action in a court on a cause of action and does not *oust* the court's jurisdiction of the action . . . ." *The Anaconda v. American Sugar Ref. Co.,* 322 U.S. 42, 44 (1944). See OBJECT-SHUFFLING.

In the language of nonlawyers, *oust* is generally confined to figurative uses. But lawyers continue to use the word in literal, concrete senses—e.g.: "[C]ourts have treated the tenant-shareholder as an owner or landlord, rather than a tenant, for the purpose of permitting him to *oust* a preceding tenant under provisions permitting such action by a landlord." 1 *American Law of Property* § 3.10, at 201 (A.J. Casner ed. 1952).

ouster. See **ejectment.**

out. A. As an Unnecessary Particle in Phrasal Verbs. *Out* commonly appears superfluously in phrases such as *distribute out, cancel out,* and *calculate out, segregate out,* and *separate out.* (Colloquially, it occurs in *lose out, test out,* and *try out.*) E.g., "Judge Critz with his energy to *study out* [read *study* or *study thoroughly*] a legal question did much to promote the orderly development of law in this state." See PHRASAL VERBS & PARTICLES, UNNECESSARY.

But sometimes *out* is necessary, as here: "Generally speaking, a manufacturer can *design out* danger only on the basis of the technology reasonably available to him at the time the design was made." The phrase *design out* (= to rid of [an undesirable characteristic]) is common in patent and products-liability contexts.

B. As a Noun. This usage <counsel was looking for an out> is a casualism.

outcomes, a formerly uncommon plural form, has all the flavor of voguish GOBBLEDYGOOK. E.g., "The central issue, which began in discipline research but has direct corollaries for policy research, concerns the effects of variations in school programs on schooling *outcomes.*" Cf. PLURALS (B).

outer bar; utter bar. The former is the more usual form of this English phrase meaning "junior barristers, collectively, who sit outside the bar of the court, as opposed to Queen's Counsel, who sit within it" (*CDL*). Though an American should perhaps hesitate to tell English lawyers which of the two terms to use, *outer bar* at least makes literal sense to any reader or listener. Cf. **inner bar.**

Utter bar, an older form, is still occasionally used. When students are "called to the Bar" they are called to the *degree of the Utter Bar* and become *Utter Barristers.*

outlawry = (1) the action of putting a person out of the protection of the law; or, more usually, (2) defiance of the law. It is not synonymous with *proscription*—i.e., as a noun corresponding to the verb *to outlaw*—though here it is erroneously used in that sense: "Wright came to believe that the proponents of the *outlawry* [read *proscription*] of war did not expect immediate effects from the Pact but rather were thinking in terms of generations." The context makes it clear that renunciation of war is the subject of discussion (hence *the outlawing of war*); *outlawry* does not work, although one might feebly argue that war here is being personified. See ANTHROPOMORPHISM.

out-of-court. See **extrajudicial** (A).

out of time. Generally, this phrase refers to persons and means "having no more time available" <you're out of time>. In law, however, the phrase sometimes refers to things other than persons and means "untimely" <the motion was ruled to be out of time>. E.g., "The question was whether s. 8(1) of the Foreign Judgements (Reciprocal Enforcement) Act 1933 applied in favour of the defendant to a claim for money due on bills of exchange bought in England against a German company in whose favour a judgment had been given by a German court on an identical claim because, by German, unlike English law, it was *out of time.*" Rupert Cross, *Statutory Interpretation* 137 (1976).

outside of is always inferior to *outside*—e.g.: "History of a system of law is largely a history of borrowings of legal materials from other legal systems and of assimilation of materials from *outside of* [read *outside*] the law." Roscoe Pound, *The Formative Era of American Law* 94 (1938). Cf. **off of.**

over. A. Special Legal Uses. In the law of property, particularly of vested and contingent interests, *over* when used after a noun denotes that the interest named, whether vested or contingent, is preceded by some other possessory interest. For example, a *limitation over* includes a second estate in the same property to be enjoyed after the first estate granted expires. E.g., "A conveyance by a grantor with a *limitation over* to his heirs was said to be governed by the doctrine of worthier title, under which a *limitation over* to a grantor's heirs resulted in an automatic reversion in the grantor and nullified the *limitation over.*"

A *gift over* is one that follows another's life estate or fee simple determinable. E.g., "A few courts have taken the position that a provision for the forfeiture of a bequest upon contest is in terrorem and will not be enforced unless there is a provision for a *gift over* in case forfeiture occurs."/ "Since the sisters all predeceased George, the defendants assert that the alternative *gifts over* failed."

Remainder over is one type of *gift over.* Although *remainder* itself connotes a preceding estate, the phrase *remainder over* is a common one. E.g., "When a life estate with the *remainder over* is created in property, especially personal property of the nature that may be transferred or appropriated, a risk exists that the remainderman might not receive the property the testator intended he should have."/ "The chancellor found the effect of the deed was to convey a life estate to the husband's daughter, with a *contingent remainder over* to the wife's children." The plural form is *remainders over:* "She gave her husband a life estate in the family plate belonging to her, with *remainders over* after his decease."

B. For *more than.* This casualism is to be avoided in formal writing. E.g., "In *Coburn,* a class action was certified on behalf of the *over* [read *more than*] 200 victims of the Beverly Hills Supper Club fire."/ "The burden of proof is on the party claiming trademark abandonment, but when a prima facie case of abandonment exists because of nonuse of the mark for *over* [read *more than*] two consecutive years, the owner of the mark has the burden to demonstrate that circumstances do not justify the inference of intent not to resume use."/ "The auditorium was filled to capacity with *over* [read *more than*] eight hundred persons present." Cf. **above (A)** & **more than.**

C. In *pay over.* See **pay over.**

D. *Over-* as a Combining Form. See **overly.**

E. *Over . . . under.* See VERBAL AWARENESS.

overall is invariably a VOGUE WORD, often a lame SENTENCE ADVERB. E.g., "*Overall,* the argument was quite compelling."/ "Conclusory findings as to each of the *Zimmer* criteria are no more helpful than an *overall* conclusory finding of dilution."/ "The *overall* effect of the *Gibbs* decision has been to broaden pendent jurisdiction." All three quoted sentences would read better without *overall.*

overarching. The *-ch-* is not pronounced like a *-k-*.

overbreadth; vagueness. In American law, these terms are usefully distinguished. The *vagueness* doctrine, based on due process, requires that a penal statute state explicitly and definitely what acts are prohibited, so as to preclude the lack of fair warning and arbitrary enforcement. *Overbreadth,* by contrast, concerns the first amendment and relates to civil as well as criminal law. A statute is *overbroad* if it seemingly prohibits not only acts that it may legitimately forbid but also acts protected by First Amendment freedoms.

overbroad. See **overbreadth** & **overly.**

overflown is the correct past participle for *overfly,* q.v., but not for *overflow,* which properly makes *overflowed.*

overfly (= to fly over in an airplane) is uncommon except in legal usage and pilots' jargon. Following are examples from legal writing: "No prescriptive easement to *overfly* plaintiff's land was acquired."/ "During these five years plaintiffs did not actually use the *overflown* land; thus the airplanes harmed no one." See **aviate.**

overlook; oversee. The first is sometimes misused for the second. To *overlook* is to neglect or disregard. To *oversee* is to supervise or superintend. *Look over* is also differentiated from *overlook;* it means "to examine."

overly. Although this word is old, dating from about the 12th century, it is best avoided. *Overly* is almost always unnecessary because *over-* may be prefixed at will: *overbroad, overrefined, overoptimistic, overripe,* etc.; when it is not unnecessary, it is merely ugly. Some usage authorities consider *overly* semiliterate, although the editors of the Merriam-Webster dictionaries have used it in a number of definitions. Certainly this adverb should be avoided whenever possible, though admittedly *over-* as a prefix is sometimes ill-sounding. Yet it usually serves well—e.g.: "It assists the legislature to avoid cumbersome and *overelaborate* wording." (Eng.) When *over-* is awkward or ugly-sounding, one might have recourse to *too.*

Another possible substitute is *unduly* <an unduly lax standard>. E.g., "In our own country, the grand jury system has been looked upon as inflexible and *overly* [read *unduly*] formal." C. Gordon Post, *An Introduction to the Law* 109–10 (1963)./ "We are not scientists—not even social scientists—nor were meant to be. Let us not be *overly* [read *unduly*] depressed at that not altogether depressing thought." Grant Gilmore, *The Death of Contract* 4 (1974).

In any event, one should always be consistent within a piece of writing: In one U.S. Supreme Court opinion, we find, in successive paragraphs: "The Supreme Court affirmed, rejecting the contention that the statute violated the First and Fourteenth Amendments as being vague and *overbroad.* . . . It was held that a person could attack a statute as being *overly broad.*" (*Overbroad* is always preferable to *overly broad.*)

Other specimens follow, with suggested improvements: "The old 'legal memorandum rule' is now generally regarded as an *overly technical doctrine* [read *as an overtechnical doctrine* or *as too technical a doctrine*]."/ "The loss must be foreseeable when the contract is entered into; it cannot be *overly* [read *unduly*] speculative."/ "Courts have been eager to prevent direct interference without forcing one tribunal to be *overly cautious* [read *overcautious*] about the possibility that a prior suit in another forum may involve the property." See ADVERBS, PROBLEMS WITH (D).

OVERPARTICULARIZATION. This word describes, better than any other, the besetting sin of practicing lawyers' prose. One judge, satirizing the overparticularized style, deduces that lawyers work on the following principles (among others): "[E]very sentence should begin with a date, or at least have a date somewhere in it. No attempt should be made to explain the facts in relative time, such as several months before or several days after. Dates are important, even if they have nothing to do with any issue in the case. . . . Please do not try to limit the factual summary to subjects material to the issues in the case, since the Court's curiosity about irrelevancies is unbounded." Nathan L. Hecht, *Extra-Special Secrets of Appellate Brief Writing,* 3 Scribes J. Legal Writing 27, 29 (1992).

Hence, the wise admonition of Judge Thomas Gibbs Gee, whose formulation gave this sin its name: "No overparticularization, which can throw your reader off by causing him to try to keep track of things that do not matter. For example—do not write 'On April 1, 1990' unless the day is significant. Instead, write 'Last spring.'" *A Few of Wisdom's Idiosyncrasies and a Few of Ignorance's: A Judicial Style Sheet,* 1 Scribes J. Legal Writing 55, 57 (1990).

To illustrate the contrast between an overparticularized style and a more pointed style, consider these alternative versions of the opening paragraph in an appellate brief:

1. This is an appeal by Plaintiff, Trenton Medical Center, under section 19 of the Administrative Procedure and Texas Register Act, Article 6252-13a, V.T.C.S., from an order of the Texas Health Facilities Commission granting a Certificate of Need to Charter Fenton, Inc., a wholly-owned subsidiary of Acland Medical Corporation for Fenton Hospital, Houston, Texas. On December 10, 1984, the Commission accepted and dated the application of Fenton for a Certificate of Need to construct, equip and operate an 80-bed psychiatric and addictive disease facility containing 43,410 square feet to be located in northwest Houston. Fenton originally proposed 60 psychiatric and 20 addictive disease beds but later amended its application to 64 psychiatric and 16 addictive disease beds. Plaintiff filed a Notice of Intent to become a party to the application of Fenton which request was accepted by the Commission on January 11, 1985. Defendants, Post and Hospital Group, also filed and were accepted as parties to the application of Fenton.
2. This case involves contradictory decisions by the Texas Health Facilities Commission concerning three applications to build new 80-bed psychiatric hospitals in Houston.

   The hearing officer who heard all the evidence found a "proven need for two of the three" new hospitals. The Commission voted 3–0 to adopt her report but voted 2–1 to deny as "unnecessary" one of the two hospitals she recommended.

   Neither the Commission majority's stated findings of fact nor substantial record evidence supports this illogical result. The real reason for the majority's action arbitrarily violated the Commission's own rules of procedure. The result, if not rejected, would prevent elderly psychiatric patients in a 21-county area from receiving care that neither the newly approved hospital nor any existing hospital will provide.

The second version contains none of the clutter that plagues the first. Instead of worrying about the number of beds and the number of square feet—not to mention Article 6252-13a—the writer of the second version focuses immediately on the true issues in the case and on the human drama that gave rise to the dispute.

The sad fact is that, although virtually every lawyer and judge who examines the two will pronounce the second version far superior, every one of them hailing from the U.S. will also confess that the first is conventional and the second unusual. See OBSCURITY (A).

overreach = (1) to circumvent, outwit, or get the better of by cunning or artifice; (2) to defeat one's object by going too far; or (3) in BrE, to replace (an interest in land) with a direct right to money. Sense (1) often applies in legal contexts—e.g.: "If, from a consideration of all the facts concerning the situation of the parties at the time the contract was made, the trial court concludes that the intended wife was not *overreached,* the contract should be sustained."

Most American lawyers would likely be puzzled by sense (3)—e.g.: "Any equitable interest . . . may be *'overreached';* that is, transferred from one form of capital to another as the trustees, having the legal estate, may decide." Alan Harding, *A Social History of English Law* 401 (1966).

overrule; overturn; reverse; set aside; vacate. *Overrule* is often employed in reference to procedural points throughout a trial, as in evidence <"Objection!" "Overruled.">. *Overrule* also denotes what a superior court does to a precedent that it expressly decides should no longer be controlling law, whether that precedent is a lower court's or its own.

Overturn is somewhat broader: it describes any judicial reasoning, including express overruling, by which a court partly or completely abolishes an earlier rule of law. Whereas *overruling* and *overturning* are both ordinarily abrupt, one-time acts, *overturning* may also (in its broadest use) indicate a long-term process by which courts gradually whittle away the authority of a precedent.

Reverse, by contrast, is much narrower than either *overrule* or *overturn*: it describes an appellate court's change to the opposite result from that by the lower court in a given case.

Set aside and *vacate* are synonymously used to denote an appellate court's wiping clean the judgment slate. The effect is to nullify the previous decision, usually of a lower court, but not necessarily to dictate a contrary result in further proceedings. See JUDGMENTS, APPELLATE-COURT & **set aside (B).**

overrulement, an unlikely and unsightly American NEOLOGISM, was coined apparently because of a perceived need for a noun corresponding to the verb *to overrule.* A better phrasing is invariably possible if one merely uncovers the BURIED VERB—e.g.: "[T]he statute in such a case expressly allows a discretionary appeal *on the overrulement of a demurrer* [read *when a demurrer is overruled*]." *State ex. rel. Southerland v. Town of Greeneville,* 297 S.W.2d 68, 71 (Tenn. 1956)./ "[T]here are at least two reasons why this Court should reverse the trial court's order for a new trial in this case, even without *overrulement of* [read *overruling*] *Javis.*" *Snow v. Freeman,* 315 N.W.2d 125, 126 (Mich. 1982) (Ryan, J., dissenting). Cf. **overthrowal.**

oversee. See **overlook.**

oversight = (1) an unintentional error; or (2) intentional and watchful supervision. For sense (2), *oversight* is an unfortunate choice of word: *supervision* is preferable. Indeed, *administrative oversight* sounds less like a responsibility than like a bureaucratic botch. See **overlook.**

OVERSTATEMENT. Such words as *clearly, patently, obviously,* and *indisputably* are generally rightly seen as weakening rather than strengthening the statements they preface. They have been debased. Some legal scholars have noted that when a writer begins a sentence with one of these words, he or she is likely to be leading up to something questionable. See **clearly.**

Unconscious overstatement is also a problem in legal discourse. It is never good to overstate one's case, even in minor unconscious ways, for the writing will thereby lose credibility. Good writers remain wary of injudicious exaggeration. Perhaps the most common pitfalls involve comparisons, relative evaluations, and missing qualifications:

- "More black students are presently enrolled at the University of Texas Law School *than have attended the school in all its history* [read *than have attended the school in previous years cumulatively,* or *than have, all told, been heretofore admitted,* or *in all its history up to three years ago*]."
- "The approach used *in the United States* [read *in the judicial system of the United States*] to achieve information input [q.v.] and accurate output is mainly adversarial in nature."
- "In 1971, Congress enacted two important statutes—the Federal Election Campaign Fund Act and the Federal Election Campaign Act—both designed to reduce the corrupting influence of money on the political process." (No doubt the writer intended to say that 1971 saw the enactment of two major statutes designed to reduce financial corruption in campaigns; what the writer has said, however, is that 1971 saw the enactment of two major statutes, which, incidentally, had to do with reducing . . . . The problem is most easily identifiable if one reads the sentence without the names of the statutes set off by long dashes. The root of the problem is *both,* which makes the clause it introduces nonrestrictive rather than restrictive. The unconscious misstatement is eliminated when we omit *both.*)

Shoddy overstatement occurs frequently in popular journalism: "Perhaps Senator Kennedy is at his best with those *who count most in the world*—his family." Though one might get the impression from various catchpenny tabloids that the Kennedy family *does* comprise "those who count most in the world," this is not what the writer intended to convey. [Read *who for him count most in the world* or *who count most in the world to him.*] See ILLOGIC (A).

overt. See **covert.**

overt act is sometimes used in criminal-law contexts, particulary in treason, as an equivalent of *actus reus* or *corpus delicti.* The phrase *overt act,* as opposed to the synonymous phrases, emphasizes the idea that the act is "open," and thus perceptible to anyone who is there to observe it. But no one need be there to perceive it: "For legal purposes an act done in complete secrecy is an overt act or *actus reus* if later it can be proved against the defendant (as if he confesses to it)." Glanville Williams, *Textbook of Criminal Law* 32 (1978).

Because *overt act* is more widely comprehensible than either of the LATINISMS just mentioned, writers on the criminal law might achieve greater clarity if they uniformly adopted it. See ***actus reus*** & ***corpus delicti.***

overthrow is a synonym of *overturn,* but it is more picturesque—e.g.: "Tax laws were queried and sometimes *overthrown* on the ground that the state had no 'jurisdiction to tax' the source in question . . . ." Robert G. McCloskey, *The American Supreme Court* 152–53 (1960).

overthrowal, like *overrulement* (q.v.), is a NEOLOGISM that is neither recorded in most English-language dictionaries nor needed as part of the legal vocabulary. The noun *overthrow* or the participle *overthrowing* will serve in virtually any context in which one might be tempted to use *overthrowal*—e.g.: "It is entirely clear that what was done herein . . . is not an *overthrowal* [read *overthrow* or *overthrowing*] of the state assessment and levy upon discernible grounds of illegality." *In re Gould Mfg. Co.,* 11 F. Supp. 644, 651 (E.D. Wis. 1935)./ "*Overthrowal of* [read *Overthrowing*] the verdict is unwarrantable." *Sears v. Mid-City Motors, Inc.,* 136 N.W.2d 428, 431 (Neb. 1965).

overturn. See **overrule.**

OVERWRITING. See PURPLE PROSE.

owing, adj.; **owed.** Although *owing* in the sense of *owed* is an old and established usage, the more logical course is simply to write *owed* where one means *owed.* The active participle may sometimes cause ambiguities or mislead the reader, if only for a second. E.g., "In the present case, we must consider whether to recognize a new liability *owing from* [read *owed by*] parents to their children for negligent supervision."/ "This was a claim for the sum of £1108 alleged to be *owing* [read *owed*] by the defendant to the plaintiff under a contract alleged to have been made between the plaintiff and the defendant for the construction of concrete foundation work." (Aus.)/ "No claim was filed in the estate by the mortgagee of the real property, although a balance of approximately $5,000 was still *owing* [read *owed*]."/ "A promise will normally be implied from an unqualified acknowledgment that the debt is *owing* [read *owed*], or from a part payment of the debt." See PASSIVE VOICE (B).

owing to is an acceptable dangling modifier now primarily confined to BrE—e.g.: "No doubt until the time of Lord Nottingham the application of precedents was uncertain, *owing largely to* the scarcity of reliable reports . . . ." Carleton K. Allen, *Law in the Making* 380 (7th ed. 1964). See DANGLERS (D). Cf. **due to.**

own, in the sense "to admit," is now chiefly confined, in AmE, to the PHRASAL VERB *own up to.* But Learned Hand and several other accomplished legal writers have showed fondness for the one-word verb—e.g.: "[I]t must be *owned* that the law upon the subject is not free from doubt." *Schmidt v. U.S.,* 177 F.2d 450, 451 (2d Cir. 1949) (per L. Hand, J.).

ownership (= title) implies the right of control over an object, quite apart from any actual or constructive control. The word has both a physical sense (e.g., ownership of a house) and a figurative sense (e.g., ownership of a copyright). See **possession (B).**

The word *ownership* is subject to nearly the same doubleness of meaning as *property* (q.v.): "While it is usual to speak of *ownership of land,* what one owns is properly not the land, but rather the rights of possession and approximately unlimited use, present or future. In other words, one owns not the land, but rather an estate in the land. This is, in some degree, true of any material thing. One owns not the thing, but the right of possession and enjoyment of the thing." 1 H.T. Tiffany, *The Law of Real Property* § 2, at 4 (B. Jones ed., 3d ed. 1939).

OXYMORONS are immediate contradictions in terms, as in the word *bittersweet.* Any number of relative oxymorons exist in legal parlance, such as *ordered liberty, equitable servitude* (servitude in equity), *all deliberate speed* (from the U.S. desegregation cases), *substantive due process* (substantive process?), *involuntary bailee* (not actually a bailee at all), *attractive nuisance, innocent fraud, intentional negligence, compelled consent,* and *premeditative afterthought.* One criminal-law writer tried to invent the phrase *partial absolute liability,* which (understandably) did not take root. See Gerhard O.W. Mueller, *On Common Law Mens Rea,* 42 Minn. L. Rev. 1043, 1068 (1958). Cf. **consideration (H), unearned income, contract of record, unenforceable contract, unknown suspect & void contract.**

Nonlegal examples are more ostensibly contradictory—e.g.: "The Government is *advancing backwards* toward the regulation of share dealing."/ "They have *increasingly less* time." See **suicide victim.**

oyer and terminer (lit., "to hear and determine") is a phrase still sometimes encountered in modern legal writing. At common law, the commissioners of *oyer and terminer* heard criminal cases. In some American states, the phrase *courts of oyer and terminer* formerly denoted the higher criminal courts. (Delaware, New Jersey, and Pennsylvania had such courts through the mid-20th century.) The pure LAW FRENCH form—*oyer et terminer*—is less frequently seen.

When Lord Eldon was Lord Chancellor, from 1801 to 1827, the Chancery was so hypertechnical and slow that it became known as a court of *"oyer sans terminer."* See J.H. Baker, *An Introduction to English Legal History* 130 (3d ed. 1990).

oyez, oyez, oyez. This is the cry heard in court to call the courtroom to order when a session begins. The word *oyez* was the LAW FRENCH equivalent of *hear ye,* q.v., in the Middle Ages. The pronunciation was first /*oh-**yets***/, later /*oh-**yes***/ or /*oh-**yez***/. Hence in Anglo-American courts the word has traditionally been pronounced "oh yes" (the pronunciation given in the *OED*). Sometimes today *oyez* is given the Frenchified pronunciation /*oh-**yay***/. For Blackstone's view on pronouncing this word, see ***countez.***

It was no doubt this triplet incantation to which Clarence Darrow alluded when he wrote, "When court opens, the bailiff intones some voodoo singsong words in an ominous voice that carries fear and respect at the opening of the rite." "Attorney for the Defense," in *Verdicts Out of Court* 313, 314 (1963). The incantation and surrounding pomp typical of many appellate courts is as follows: "At precisely 1:00 p.m. the marshal announced, 'The Honorable, the Chief Justice and the Associate Justices of the Supreme Court of the United States. *Oyez! Oyez! Oyez!* All persons having business before the Honorable, the Supreme Court of the United States, are admonished to draw near and give their attention, for the Court is now sitting. God save the United States and this Honorable Court.'" Barbara H. Craig, *Chadha: The Story of an Epic Constitutional Struggle* 202–03 (1988).

Oyes, a variant spelling, is not now widely current.

P

pace /***pay**-see*/ or /***pah**-chay*/ [L. "with peace to"] = with all due respect to. This term is used most often when the writer expresses a contrary position—e.g.: "It is true, *pace* Savigny, that the reason and utility on which such customs rest often arise from purely local conditions . . . ." Carleton K. Allen, *Law in the Making* 98 (7th ed. 1964).

pacifist; pacificist. *Pacifist* is the established form. Etymologists formerly argued that *pacificist* is the better-formed word, but it is almost never seen.

pact. See **treaty.**

paction = (1) the act of making a bargain or pact; or (2) the pact so made. In sense (2), the word is merely a NEEDLESS VARIANT of *pact* or *agreement* or *bargain.* In sense (1) the word is useful, but rare.

paid over. See **pay over.**

pain of, on. The phrase *on pain of death* was once common in law to express a prohibition the violation of which would result in punishment by execution. The phrase has passed into lay contexts, in which it is ordinarily facetious. But it remains as a shortened phrase *on pain of* in legal usage. In this phrase, *pain* means "suffering or loss inflicted for a crime or offense; a punishment ranging from death to a small fine." E.g., "Is it reasonable to require prison employees to have foreseen, *on pain of* section 1983 damage liability, the future of prisoners' rights to the degree evolved under *Ruiz?*"/ "According to the principles of scientific jurisprudence, a rule [that] people are called upon to obey, *on pain of* some disagreeable consequence if they fail, ought first to be clearly and plainly stated . . . ." Edward Jenks, *The Book of English Law* 23 (P.B. Fairest ed., 6th ed. 1967). See LOAN TRANSLATIONS.

pair is incorrect as a plural form in, "He bought two *pair* [read *pairs*] of shoes."

On the question whether a phrase such as *pair of shoes,* as a subject, takes a singular or a plural verb, see SYNESIS.

pais (lit., "country") = the district or vicinage where the accused lives or where a crime was committed. A remnant of LAW FRENCH (fr. *pays*), this word sometimes signifies, in a transferred sense, the jury drawn from the district. Hence a *conclusion to the country* (a LOAN TRANSLATION) is a jury request and a *trial per pais* is a jury trial. See ***in pais.***

pale, beyond the. This phrase, which has passed into lay parlance in the sense "bizarre; outside the bounds of civilized behavior," derives from the legal sense of *pale* from English history ("a district or territory within determined bounds, or subject to a particular jurisdiction"). In medieval Ireland, the district around Dublin, settled by the English and considered a law-abiding area, was known as the *Pale* or *within the Pale.* The land beyond that area was characterized as wild "bandit country."

In legal writing the phrase is often used figuratively but with ETYMOLOGICAL AWARENESS, as here: "The jurisdiction of the Court of Appeals below turned on its determination that an interpretation of Rule 68 to include attorneys' fees is *beyond the pale* of the judiciary's rulemaking authority." See POPULARIZED LEGAL TECHNICALITIES.

palimony (= a court-ordered allowance paid by one member to the other of a couple that, though unmarried, formerly cohabited) is a PORTMANTEAU WORD first recorded in 1979. Though it has become fairly common, it is jocular in most contexts. E.g., "*Trimmer v. Van Bomel* . . . [was] a *'palimony'* case concerning an alleged oral agreement by which a wealthy widow was to pay her former male companion 'costs and expenses for sumptuous living and maintenance for the remainder of his life.'" *Gregg v. U.S. Indus., Inc.*, 715 F.2d 1522, 1537 (11th Cir. 1983). *Galimony,* a similar form that is even more jocular, has been used in reference to *palimony* between lesbians.

palming off; passing off. The two terms are perfectly synonymous ("putting into circulation or dispersing of fraudulently" [*OED*]), both being used with almost equal frequency in AmE and BrE. *Passing off* is more peculiarly legal. E.g., "Unfair competition is almost universally regarded as a question of whether the defendant is *passing off* his goods or services as those of the plaintiff."/ "*Passing off* may be found only where the defendant subjectively and knowingly intended to confuse buyers." *Palming off* is used additionally in lay senses, and might be called a POPULARIZED LEGAL TECHNICALITY—e.g.: "Have you not tried to *palm off* yesterday's pun?"

palpable (lit., "touchable") = tangible; apparent. There is nothing wrong with using this word in figurative senses <palpable weaknesses in the argument>, as it has been used since at least the 15th century.

pamphlet. This word is pronounced with the *-ph-* as if it were an *-f-*. A great many people incorrectly say */**pam**-plət/*. Similar mispronunciations occur with *ophthalmology* and *amphitheater.*

panacea (= cure-all; nostrum) is sometimes confused with other words. E.g., "To allow the state to raise new matters not brought out in the original appeal or on rehearing would *open up a panacea* [read *bring on a plethora?* or *open up a pandora's box?*] of problems by way of precedent." This is a MALAPROPISM.

pandemic (= [of a disease] prevalent over the whole of a country or continent, or over the whole world). The word is usually adjectival, but may be used as a noun: "The strain was related to the one that was prevalent during the 1918–19 swine flu *pandemic* that was responsible for 20 million deaths worldwide, including the deaths of 500,000 Americans." See **epidemic.**

panel-shopping, analogous to *forum-shopping* (q.v.), refers to panels usually consisting of three members of a court. E.g., "[T]he 'law of the case doctrine' discourages *panel shopping* at the circuit level, for in today's climate it is most likely that a different panel will hear subsequent appeals." *Lehrman v. Gulf Oil Corp.*, 500 F.2d 659, 662 (5th Cir. 1974). The hyphenated form is preferable.

panic, v.i., makes *panicked* and *panicking.* Usually intransitive, *panic* has also appeared as a transitive verb, meaning "to affect with panic." E.g., "She did not want to *panic* the audience."

paper has a special legal sense in the phrase *commercial paper* (= negotiable documents and bills of exchange). The plural *papers* often refers to pleadings and other court documents <We filed all the necessary papers>. See **negotiable instrument** & **court papers.**

paperwork. One word.

parachronism. See **anachronism.**

paradigm. The preferred plural is *paradigms,* not *paradigmata.* See PLURALS (A).

paragraph. In DRAFTING, a *paragraph* is a subdivision usu. numbered for reference and sometimes, in citations, indicated by the character "¶." The term can be confusing, however, because a drafted *paragraph* often consists of many individual paragraphs in the conventional sense of the word. At other times, it may consist of a two- or three-word phrase. When using cross-references, then, it is often more helpful to give the full citation—as, for example, by referring to "Rule 4(A)(4)(b)(ii)." That way, the terminology for each subdivision does not impede clarity.

parajudge has been used to refer to U.S. Magistrate Judges, who have some adjudicative power, but not the extent of power vested in Article III judges: "Under the *'para-judge'* rationale, the Magistrates Act comports with Article III [of the U.S. Constitution] because it subjects magistrates' rulings to de novo determination by a federal district judge." *U.S. v. Saunders,* 641 F.2d 659, 663 (9th Cir. 1980). The unhyphenated one-word form is best in AmE.

paralegal. A. Senses and Usage. *Paralegal* = (1) (adj.) of, relating to, or associated with law in an ancillary way; or (2) (n.) a paralegal aide.

In BrE, the term is sometimes spelled as two words, as it was repeatedly in the following article: "Compare that with the UK's largest single law firm Clifford Chance with 985 fee earners comprising 195 partners, 577 assistant solicitors, 206 articled clerks and 7 *para legals.*" Robert Rice, *Profession Still Bashful About the Business of Making Money,* Fin. Times, 9 April 1990, at 12.

B. And *legal assistant.* In sense (2), paralegal is rivaled in AmE by the term *legal assistant.* Some prefer calling themselves *paralegals;* others prefer calling themselves *legal assistants.* The two terms are about equally common.

paralegaling is a colloquialism to name what it is that a paralegal (or *legal assistant*) does. The term is similar to *bailiffing* (see **bailiff**). See NOUNS AS VERBS.

One text uses the more formal term *paralegalism* (= the calling of a paralegal)—see William P. Statsky, *Introduction to Paralegalism* (3d ed. 1986).

paralegalism. See **paralegaling.**

PARALEIPSIS is a rhetorical tactic whereby a speaker or writer mentions something in disclaiming any mention of it. For example, a less than scrupulous cross-examiner would engage in paraleipsis if he stated, "Mr. Smith, I won't bring up your unsavory past as a drug-dealer, but I would like to ask you some questions about your prior business dealings with the plaintiff." To which the fitting response is "Objection!" preferably after *unsavory.* Among the most common phrases introducing a paraleipsis are *to say nothing of, not to mention,* and *needless to say.*

In the following example of judicial paraleipsis, the judge appears to be suggesting a tactic to one of the parties: "I purposely refrain from commenting on the possibility of any relief against Malcolm Devers' attorney, Dalonas, which may be available to the defendants, or any title company that may have insured a Radnor Heights fee for one of them." *Devers v. Chateau Corp.,* 792 F.2d 1278, 1299 (4th Cir. 1986) (Murnaghan, J., dissenting).

And in the following example, Morris Cohen may have had in mind the difference between *referring* and *alluding,* but the resulting paraleipsis is nevertheless damning: "We need not refer to the Texas governor who pardoned hundreds of criminals for his political advantage." Morris R. Cohen, *Reason and Law* 65 (1961). The unfortunate thing about this passage is that Cohen shifts the reader's negative impression away from the individual perpetrator and onto the state. For a brief account of Governor Pa Ferguson's malfeasances in granting pardons—and his subsequent impeachment—see T.R. Fehrenbach, *Lone Star: A History of Texas and the Texans* 638–39 (1968).

PARALLELISM refers to matching parts, i.e., analogous sentence-parts that must match if the sentence is to make strictly logical sense—and the best grammatical sense. The problem of unparallel sentence-parts usually crops up in the use of CORRELATIVE CONJUNCTIONS and in lists. Following are a number of examples, with corrections in brackets within quotations or in parentheses following the quotations:

- "For federal diversity purposes, a corporation is a 'citizen' *of not only* [read *not only of*] the state in which it is incorporated, *but also of* the state where it has its principal place of business."
- "[M]arketing quotas *not only embrace* [read *embrace not only*] all that may be sold without penalty *but also* what may be consumed on the premises." *Wickard v. Filburn,* 317 U.S. 111, 119 (1942).
- "No person in this country who is committed to prison on a charge of crime can be kept long in confinement because he can insist upon either being let out on bail *or else of being* [read *or else being*] brought to speedy trial." Alfred Denning, *Freedom Under the Law* 9 (1949).
- "Its continuance is contingent upon legally recognized rights of tenure, transfer, and of succession [delete second *of* or insert *of* before *transfer*] in use and occupancy."
- "Defendants object to the request for production of documents on the grounds of relevancy, over-

breadth, *burdensome* [read *burdensomeness*], oppression, and confidentiality." (This sentence contains ILLOGIC as well, because each item in the list spells out why the defendants object to it—hence *irrelevancy* should appear where *relevancy* does.)
- "The trial court was correct in excluding both the testimony of V.T.W. and *in excluding* [delete *in excluding* and insert *the*] defendant's exhibits 7 and 11."

Failures of parallelism are especially common in cumulative sentences, as here: "The defendants *admitted* that they published the article; *disavowed* any intention to defame and injure the plaintiff in his good name and reputation; *denied* that the article was maliciously composed, printed, or published; [read *and asserted*] *that* the article appeared simply as a news item and was brought in by one of their news-gatherers."/ "Cars may be seized if they constitute a traffic hazard, are evidence, *or if they are* [read *or are*] subject to forfeiture proceedings." A writer who wished to be more emphatic, whatever the cost of repetition, could write: "Cars may be seized if they constitute a traffic hazard, if they are evidence, or if they are subject to forfeiture proceedings."

Less troubling is a lack of parallelism where two or more sentence-parts are balanced by *and;* but even this should be avoided: "The boy's operation of the car was unlawful and *negligence* [read *negligent*] per se."/ "Johann was a tall, thin man, dark-haired, near-sighted, not bad-looking, and *a fop* [read *foppish*]." (Here we have a string of adjectives—all implicitly modifying *man*—but the writer changes the last in the string to a noun phrase.) See PLAIN LANGUAGE (D).

paralyze; paralyse. The former spelling is the only one used in AmE; the latter (as well as the former) is used in BrE.

parameters. Technical contexts aside, this jargonistic VOGUE WORD is not used by those with a heightened sensitivity to language. To begin with, no one who is not a specialist in mathematics or computing knows precisely what it means: it is a mush word. Second, when it does have a discernible meaning, it is usurping the place of a far simpler and more straightforward term. Though the word does not appear in the best legal writing, it does abound—e.g.:

- "Since the parties have become legally obligated through their expression of assent, the *parameters* [read *boundaries?*] of their assent must be established, at least primarily, by their expressions."
- "The terms of its consent to be sued define the *parameters* [read *limits*] of the court's jurisdiction to entertain suit."
- "Within broad *parameters* [read *guidelines*], families are free to choose their method of child-rearing and to pick the values and aspirations transmitted to their offspring."
- "The purpose of pleadings is to put one's opponent on notice as to the *parameters* [read *grounds*] of the forthcoming battle."
- "Although it would have been appropriate to outline the *parameters* [read *elements*] of agency for purposes of the entrapment charge, a reading of the court's instructions satisfies us that the jury was neither misled nor confused."

Rarely is the word used in the singular, but it does occur: "The dismissal in the instant case falls within the *parameter* of the present rule." *Clifford Ragsdale, Inc. v. Morganti, Inc.,* 356 So. 2d 1321, 1323 (Fla. Dist. Ct. App. 1978).

Sometimes writers use *perimeter,* whose meaning has influenced the senses of *parameter,* ostensibly to sidestep any criticisms for the use of *parameter.* E.g., "The plurality held that the immunity extended even to malicious acts that were within the outer *perimeter* of the federal employee's line of duty."/ "All that is left for the district court to decide on is whether specific acts and allegations fall within this *perimeter.*" Although this usage makes literal sense, *limit* or *boundary* or *border* would be a simpler term for the same notion.

paramount means "superior to all others" or "most important"—not merely "important."

paramountcy is the noun corresponding to the adjective *paramount.* It is not often seen but is quite proper—e.g.: "One of these principles is undoubtedly the *paramountcy* of EEC law over municipal or national law." P.S. Atiyah, *Law and Modern Society* 62 (1983). *Paramouncy* is a NEEDLESS VARIANT.

paraphrase is occasionally misrendered *paraphraze,* as in *Eades v. Drake,* 332 S.W.2d 553, 556 (Tex. 1960). See **rephrase.**

parasitic, in reference to damages, does not mean merely "additional." Rather, the term means, in the words of Lord Denning, M.R.,

> that there are some heads of damage which, if they stood alone, would not be recoverable: but, nevertheless, if they can be annexed to some other legitimate claim for damages, may yet be recoverable. They are said to be *parasitic* because, like a parasite, in biology, they cannot exist on their own, but depend on others for their life or nourishment . . . . I do not like the very word *parasite.* A *parasite* is one who is a useless hanger-on sucking out the sub-

> stance of others. *Parasitic* is the adjective derived from it. It is a term of abuse. It is an opprobrious epithet. The phrase *parasitic damages* conveys to my mind the idea of damages which ought not in justice to be awarded, but which somehow or other have been allowed to get through by hanging on to others. If such be the concept underlying the doctrine, then the sooner it is got rid of the better . . . . I hope it will disappear from [the textbooks] after this case.
>
> *Spartan Steel & Alloys Ltd. v. Martin & Co.,* [1973] Q.B. 27, 34–35.

Parasitic should not be used as a fancy variant of *dependent,* as here: "The legal characteristics of an individual's mental state under *Rees* are *parasitic* [read *dependent*] on the factual conclusions rendered by those testifying on the issue." The quotation from Lord Denning makes plain the metaphorical baggage that *parasitic* carries with it; and unless the metaphor is perfectly apt, the word should not be used.

parcel, n. (= a tract of land), is now primarily a LEGALISM. E.g., "This is a suit for a declaratory judgment to establish a trust in a two-fifths interest in five *parcels* of land devised absolutely to the respondent."

parcel out is a common PHRASAL VERB in the legal idiom. E.g., "It is not our job to decide whether the FSLIC could *parcel out* Old North's assets in this particular manner."

parcenary. See **coparcenary.**

parcener. See **coparcener (A).**

pardon, v.t. See **commute (B).**

parens patriae (= the father of a country) refers in Great Britain to the king or queen, particularly as the sovereign (historically speaking) was thought to have a kind of guardianship over the nation and persons in need of care. E.g., "At common law the king is *parens patriae,* father of his country, which is but the medieval mode of putting what we mean today when we say that the state is the guardian of social interests." Roscoe Pound, *The Spirit of the Common Law* 68 (1921; repr. 1963).

In the U.S., *parens patriae* refers to the state as a sovereign—e.g.: "The Attorney General of Georgia was made a party after remand from this court, and, acting as *parens patriae* in all legal matters pertaining to the administration and disposition of charitable trusts in the State of Georgia in which the rights of beneficiaries are involved, he opposed the reversion to the heirs . . . ."

parentelic method; parentelic system. These phrases denote one scheme of computation used to determine the paternal or maternal collaterals entitled to inherit. The name derives from the technical term *parentela* (= a person's issue). E.g., "Under the laws of succession and marriage there are three different methods for determining degrees of relationship. The most common is the civil law method, used in Virginia to determine relationships in succession law. The second is the *parentelic method,* used in succession law in other states. The third is the canon law method, developed to establish the limits of permissible marriages between relatives." William J. O'Shaughnessy, Jr., Note, *Proxy Decisionmaking for the Terminally Ill: The Virginia Approach,* 70 Va. L. Rev. 1269, 1292–93 (1984)./ "This pattern of intestate inheritance resembles the common law's *parentelic system* for the descent of land." Carolyn S. Bratt, *A Primer on Kentucky Intestacy Laws,* 82 Ky. L.J. 29, 49 (1993–1994).

parentelic system. See **parentelic method.**

PARENTHESES. **A. Syntactic Effect.** Words contained within parentheses do not affect the syntax of the rest of the sentence. E.g., "We must determine whether each (or both) appellants are entitled to immunity." The writer of that sentence could have avoided this error (*each appellants are*) by reading the sentence without the parenthetical phrase. See PUNCTUATION (G).

B. Overuse of. Virtually any punctuation mark is subject to an annoying overuse, but this is especially true of parentheses—and long dashes—which to be effective must be used sparingly. When they appear at all frequently in writing, they tire the reader's eye, add to the burden of decoding, and cloy the reader's interest. The sentence begins to sag with the qualifications here and there. The following is a two-sentence example from an opinion published in 1985:

> Marshall also relies upon his cross-examination of the government investigator (Ms. Sandlin) and of a government witness (Bitner; the Four Seasons manager and the custodian of its records—although he was not called upon by the government to authenticate the Four Seasons lawn-mower records) as showing the unreliability of Ms. Sandlin's opinion that three (or any) lawn mowers were actually missing, as she had testified on the basis of her deductions from the (incomplete) Four Seasons records . . . . However, in the first place, if the testimony of Marshall's witnesses was to be believed (which was for the jury to determine), Marshall could not have been at the Frederick Street residence at the time Lee (thus mistakenly) believed that he saw him there.
>
> *U.S. v. Marshall,* 762 F.2d 419, 422 (5th Cir. 1985).

None of these parenthetical interpolations is syntactically or stylistically justified.

C. With Appositives. See APPOSITIVES (B).

pari delicto, in. See ***in pari delicto.***

pari materia, in. See ***in pari materia.***

pari passu (= with equal pace; equally; at the same time) is an adverb as well as an adjective. The phrase is frequently used in contracts when several persons are paid at the same level or out of a common fund. E.g., "Hence when this £25 is withdrawn and mixed with £175 in the second account, the charges extend over the whole resulting £200, but only to the extent of £25, and this is divided up *pari passu* amongst the ten." (Eng.)

The phrase *in pari passu* is wrong, *in* being no part of the phrase. In the following example, the writer appears to have meant *in pari materia,* q.v.: "[T]he Supreme Court has indicated that fee statutes using the same language are to be interpreted *in pari passu* [read *in pari materia* or *pari passu*]." James Moore et al., *Moore's Federal Practice* ¶ 54.77[.5-3], at 54-499 (1988).

Parliament. The definite article (*the*) is unnecessary before this word when it is used as a proper noun (i.e., in reference to a particular parliament). E.g., "*Parliament* voted to make such behaviour illegal." (Eng.) Cf. **Congress.**

parliamentary need not be capitalized except when one is referring to the doings of a particular parliament. Unlike *congressional,* which should not be capitalized, *parliamentary* as a lowercase adjective has other senses, most commonly in denoting procedural rules for governing meetings. Thus there may be more justification for the uppercase *Parliamentary* than an uppercase *Congressional.*

parliamentary history (BrE) = *legislative history* (AmE).

parol. A. Senses. *Parol* is most commonly used as an adjective equivalent to *oral:* "When the mother placed the deed in her eldest daughter's name and that of her husband, she was relying on more than a bare *parol* promise made by a grantee to a grantor."/ "As a general rule, a cloud that may be removed by suit to quiet title is not created by a mere *parol* assertion of ownership of an interest in property."

In contract law, however, *parol* includes the written as well as the spoken word. Thus, a *parol contract* is any contract that is not under seal. See **informal contract.**

Parol may also act as a noun meaning "word of mouth." E.g., "To permit such subsequent declarations to have such effect would be to convey an estate in land *by parol,* which is expressly prohibited by statute." *By parol* (= by word of mouth) is the most common construction with the noun *parol,* but *in parol* (= in something said or spoken; in a statement or declaration) is also used: "Such agreements were often *in parol,* and where an unenforceable agreement *in parol* is attended by certain special circumstances, equity resorts to the remedial device of a constructive trust to accomplish justice."/ "Certainly it was not intended to enable anyone to make out of record a title resting solely *in parol.*"

B. Pronunciation. *Parol* is most properly pronounced /**par**-əl/. Yet, in AmE, it is frequently pronounced like *parole,* namely /pə-**rohl**/. That pronunciation is acceptable.

C. Spelled *parole.* This variant spelling is uncommon enough to make it undesirable—e.g.: "Again, at this date the law had barely begun to acquire experience in the handling of *parole evidence* [read *parol evidence*] . . . ." Theodore F.T. Plucknett, *A Concise History of the Common Law* 56 (5th ed. 1956). But it is the usual form in Scotland.

parol contract. See **simple contract** & **informal contract.**

parole (= the conditional release of a prisoner from prison) has long been the standard term in AmE; it existed in British military terminology in a related sense from the 17th century, and in this century has become standard in BrE in the American sense. *Ticket-of-leave* and *order of licence* were earlier BrE variants; *release on licence* is still a common equivalent in British legal contexts.

For *parole* as a variant spelling of *parol,* see **parol (C).**

parolee. See **probationer.**

parol-evidence rule (= the rule that evidence cannot be admitted—or if admitted, cannot be used—if it has the effect of adding to, varying, or contradicting a legal instrument) is commonly thought of as an evidentiary rule, but "it is probably best regarded as a rule of substantive law." P.S. Atiyah, *An Introduction to the Law of Contract* 161–62 (3d ed. 1981). The question of admissibility is really only secondary, the primary question being whether, if admitted, the evidence will have the legal effect of varying the instrument.

parricide; patricide. *Parricide* is the more usual word meaning (1) "the murder of one's own father"; or (2) "one who murders his own father." E.g. (Sense 2): "The contention that quadriplegia is 'punishment enough'—like the *parricide*'s claim that he deserves mercy as an orphan—is one addressed to the sentencing court's discretion alone." *U.S. ex rel. Villa v. Fairman,* 810 F.2d 715, 717–18 (7th Cir. 1987).

It is also used in extended senses, such as "the murder of the ruler of a country" and "the murder of a close relative." These are not examples of SLIPSHOD EXTENSION, however, for even the Latin etymon (*parricida*) was used in these senses.

part. See **portion** & **city part.**

part, in. See **in pertinent part.**

partake is construed with either *in* or *of* in the sense "to take part or share in some action or condition; to participate." *In* is the more common preposition in this sense: "As lawyers are *partakers in* a common enterprise, the honor and reputation of every member should be the cause of all."

Of is common when the sense is "to receive, get, or have a share or portion *of;* to have something *of,* possess a certain amount *of*": "The view that the defendant's fault *partakes of* wanton and intentional wrong was questioned."/ "The venture does not come within the purview of a special business arrangement *partaking of* some essentials of partnership."/ "The restrictive view is that the court's interpretation *partakes of* the same quality as the statutory text itself."

part and parcel is an idiomatic DOUBLET and CLICHÉ that emphasizes the sense of "an essential or integral portion; something essentially belonging to a larger whole." E.g., "We specifically held in *Barksdale* that a revoking clause in a will is *part and parcel* of the will itself, without independent and immediate life or power, and that it survives or perishes with the will." See DOUBLETS, TRIPLETS, AND SYNONYM-STRINGS.

partially; partly. Whenever either word could suffice in a given context, *partly* is the better choice. *Partially* occasionally causes AMBIGUITY because of its other sense "in a manner exhibiting favoritism." *AHD* notes that *partly,* which has wider application, "is the choice when stress is laid on the part (in contrast to the whole), when the reference is to physical things, and when the sense is equivalent to *in part, to some extent*" <partly to blame> <a partly finished building>. "*Partially* is especially applicable to conditions or states in the sense of *to a certain degree;* as the equivalent of *incomplete,* it indirectly stresses the whole" (*AHD*) <partially dependent> <partially contributory>.

partial payment; part payment. Although *part payment* is common in the lawbooks, *partial payment* is more idiomatic today.

partial performance; part performance. Although *part performance,* like *part payment,* can be found throughout many fine books, *partial performance* is the more natural-sounding phrase.

partible; partitionable. The latter is a NEEDLESS VARIANT not recorded in the dictionaries. *Partible* = subject to partition; separable <the concurrent estate is partible>.

particeps criminis is an unjustified LATINISM in view of our simpler equivalent *accessory.* E.g., "A *particeps criminis* [read *accessory*] in the fraud has been permitted to recover in his own name against one who was no more guilty than he, when the marriage had taken place by reasons of such fraud." (Eng.) The plural form is *participes criminis.*

PARTICIPLES, PROBLEMS WITH. See ADJECTIVES (H), DANGLERS (B), FUSED PARTICIPLES & MISPLACED MODIFIERS.

PARTICLES, UNNECESSARY. Any number of English verbs are regularly given particles in informal or colloquial contexts, and these particles often help to establish the informality or colloquiality of the writing. Thus a Good Samaritan *helps out* a person rather than merely *helping* that person, litigants *fight out* a dispute rather than merely *fighting* it.

Unnecessary particles seem to find a more hospitable climate in BrE than in AmE—e.g.: "By a strange coincidence, on the very same day, so-called animal rights activists *injured up* [read *injured*] a 13-month-old baby in Bristol . . . ." Richard Ingrams, Observer, 24 June 1990, at 18./ "Competition in high schools . . . has not *slackened off* [read *slackened*]." Roger Buckley, *Japan Today* 93 (2d ed. 1990).

The following examples are best avoided in legal prose: *award over (award), continue on (continue), convey away (convey),* and *proceed on (proceed).*

Slight DIFFERENTIATION is possible with a number of phrases, such as *die off (die), face up to (face), meet up with (meet), lose out (lose), pay off* or *pay out (pay)* (see **pay & pay over**); with these phrases, the particles arguably add a nuance to the verb. One must always be on guard to ask whether the particles in one's writing pull their weight or give, instead, a breezy, slangy quality to the prose.

PARTICLE VERBS. See PHRASAL VERBS.

particularized is sometimes misused for *particular*—e.g.: "Note that the doctrine of partial performance antedated the general concept of promissory estoppel and has its own *particularized* [read *particular*] rules." The sense there is not "made particular" but "particular"; hence *particularized* is the wrong word for the context. Cf. **generalized.**

parties hereto is, 99 times out of 100, a rank REDUNDANCY. The one other time, either *parties to this case* or *parties to this agreement* would be preferable.

partisan; partizan. The former is the preferred spelling in both AmE and BrE. Although the term denotes "one who takes part or sides with another," it has connotations of "a blind, prejudiced, unreasoning, or fanatical adherent" (*OED*).

partition. To a nonlawyer this is something that separates, esp. one part of a space from another; to a lawyer, *partition* = a division of real property into severalty.

The word is also commonly a verb in legal writing; it means "to divide (land) into severalty" <action for partitioning an inheritance>. E.g., "Any one of a number of co-owners was entitled to have the property '*partitioned*,' i.e. divided, or at any rate to have the property sold and his share paid out to him." William Geldart, *Introduction to English Law* 78 (D.C.M. Yardley ed., 9th ed. 1984). See **partible.**

Both as a noun and as a verb, the word *petition* is sometimes misused for *partition,* the result being a gross MALAPROPISM—e.g.: "Children over approximately age 9 sat in an 11 by 14 enclosure, partially *petitioned* [read *partitioned*] off from the main waiting room." *Doe v. New York City Dep't of Social Servs.,* 670 F.Supp. 1145, 1181 (S.D.N.Y. 1987)./ "Structural components include walls, *petitions* [read *partitions*], floors, ceilings, windows, doors, [etc.] . . . ." Jacob Mertens, *Mertens Law of Federal Income Taxation* § 45.51, at 120 (1990).

partitionable. See **partible.**

partizan. See **partisan.**

partly. See **partially.**

partner. See **copartner & coparcener (B).**

partnership = (1) a voluntary joining together for business purposes by two or more persons of money, goods, labor, and skill, upon an agreement that the gain or loss will be divided proportionally between them; or (2) the relation that exists between those who carry on a business in common for the purpose of profit.

part payment. See **partial payment.**

party is a LEGALISM that is unjustified when it merely replaces *person.* If used as an elliptical form of *party to the contract* or *party to the lawsuit, party* is quite acceptable as a TERM OF ART. E.g., "Either *party* may enforce the terms of this contract, and in the event that either *party* must use attorneys to effect such enforcements, then such expenses and other fees may be charged against the other *party.*" See **party of the first part.**

Fred Rodell's quip is worth remembering: "Only The Law insists on making a '*party*' out of a single person." Fred Rodell, *Woe Unto You, Lawyers!* 28 (1939; repr. 1980). See **third(-)party.**

PARTY APPELLATIONS. Generally, in briefs and opinions, it is best to humanize parties by calling them by their names—e.g.: "Jones" and "Smith." Otherwise, the reader is forced continually to rethink who is the petitioner and who the respondent; who the appellant and who the appellee; or, worse yet, who was plaintiff below, now appellee (or is it appellant?). It is easier to remember that Mr. Gulbenkian is the appellant than that the appellant is Gulbenkian, for every case has an appellant, but not every case has a Gulbenkian. See Fed. R. App. P. 28(d).

Problems arise, however, with matters of procedure. "Gulbenkian failed to preserve error" is an invidious legal fiction, since it was Gulbenkian's attorney, not Gulbenkian, who failed to preserve error. Judicial opinions should avoid obscuring the responsibility for procedural mistakes. In such contexts, *appellant, appellee, plaintiff,* and other such appellations are preferable, for they more nearly connote attorney and client jointly. Even phrasing the statement thus, "Counsel for appellant failed to preserve error," would be appropriate, although from the lawyer's perspective it is a harsher statement. See **plaintiff, defendant.**

party in interest = a natural or juristic person having a legal or economic interest in litigation or arbitration. E.g., "The trouble with appellant's position in this case is that no stipulation was presented to the court signed by all *parties in interest.*"

party litigant. See POSTPOSITIVE ADJECTIVES.

party of the first part; party of the second part. These phrases—which have traditionally appeared in many types of instruments—are the worst types of ARCHAISMS. Not only are they cumbersome and verbose; they also invite mistakes. A glance at volume 31 of *Words and Phrases* (1957) hints at the amount of litigation caused by drafters who have inadvertently transposed *first* and *second.*

The best modern practice, in contractual drafting, is to use either real names or functional labels such as *buyer* and *seller; licensor* and *licensee; publisher* and *author;* and the like.

The most that can be said for the old phrases is that they have a mildly interesting history. Parties entering into contracts were once divided into classes, or "parts," according to their property interests in the transaction. Generally, the owner or seller was the *party of the first part* and the buyer was the *party of the second part*—e.g.:

- "Know all men by these presents, that John Doe, of the county of Arapahoe, in the state of Colorado, *party of the first part,* for and in consideration of the sum of $5,000, to him in hand paid by Richard Roe, of the county of Arapahoe and state aforesaid, *party of the second part,* the receipt of which is hereby acknowledged, does hereby grant, bargain and sell unto the said *party of the second part,* his heirs and assigns, the following goods and chattels, viz. . . . ." W.S. Walker, *Sayler's American Form Book* 97 (4th ed. 1913) (from a form chattel mortgage).
- "[T]he said *party of the first part,* for and in consideration of the sum of $1,000, in hand paid, at and before the sealing of these presents, the receipt whereof is hereby acknowledged, has granted, bargained, sold, aliened, conveyed and confirmed, and by these presents does grant, bargain, sell, alien, convey and confirm, unto the said *party of the second part,* his heirs and assigns, all [describe property]." W.S. Walker, *Sayler's American Form Book* 132 (4th ed. 1913) (from a form warranty deed to secure a loan).
- "This agreement entered into between _____ *party of the first part,* and _____ *party of the second part.*" Samuel G. Kling, *The Legal Encyclopedia for Home and Business* 93 (1957; repr. 1959) (simple form contract so punctuated).

These are the once-common uses, but there are two historically unwarranted variations.

First, during the 20th century the historical divisions between buyers and sellers fell apart: contract drafters came to use *party of the first part* for whichever party was named first. Often, that party was the one with the greatest degree of bargaining power—e.g.:

> "The *party of the first part* covenants and agrees to drill for the *party of the second part* [i.e., the landowner], its successors or assigns, a well for petroleum or gas . . . . The *party of the second part* covenants and agrees to pay to the *party of the first part,* provided the *party of the first part* shall complete said well in the manner, to the depth, and of the dimensions hereinafter specified, and when the said well shall be so completed, at the rate of [$____]."
>
> Robert T. Donley, *Coal, Oil and Gas in West Virginia and Virginia* 360 (1951) (from a form contract for drilling an oil or gas well).

Second, the idea of a *party of the third part* gradually arose, though this would have traditionally been considered a solecism. In most contracts, there were but two sides (or "parts"), so that in multiparty contracts there would be *parties of the first part* and *parties of the second part.* The idea was that a *third party* was a stranger to the contract. Thus, a turn-of-the-century dictionary described *third parties* as a "term used to include all persons who are not parties to the contract, agreement, or instrument of writing by which their interest in the thing conveyed is sought to be affected." Walter A. Shumaker & George F. Longsdorf, *The Cyclopedic Dictionary of Law* 909 (1901). But by the mid-20th century, drafters were using *party of the third part* to describe not a stranger, but another party to the contract—e.g.:

> Whereas the *party of the first part* has made certain discoveries relating to the manufacture of synthetic rubber, apparently of material commercial value, and has associated the *party of the second part* with him to further the marketing thereof, and the *party of the third part* is willing to form and finance a company to manufacture and market the same, if he finds to his satisfaction, after investigation, that said discoveries are valuable commercially . . . .
>
> Samuel G. Kling, *The Legal Encyclopedia for Home and Business* 101 (1957; repr. 1959) (from a form agreement to organize a corporation).

Any question about whether *party of the third part* is proper usage is best answered by saying that all these ancient expressions are poor usage in modern DRAFTING. See **chirograph, party** & PERSON.

party-opponent is generally hyphenated, as in Fed. R. Evid. 613(b), though there is hardly a good rationale for writing it this way.

pass. **A. Judicial Senses.** The phrase *pass on* or *pass upon* has a peculiar meaning in legal writing, namely, "to decide." It is used primarily of questions of law: "When our courts first came to *pass upon* constitutional questions, what they read in Coke's Second Institute . . . appeared but a common-law version of what they read in French and Dutch publicists as to an eternal and immutable natural law . . . ." Roscoe Pound, *The Spirit of the Common Law* 75 (1921; repr. 1963)./ "The state courts have power to *pass on* both state and federal questions . . . ." Charles A. Wright, *The Law of Federal Courts* 752 (4th ed. 1983).

Yet the phrase has been used also in reference to juries, which of course decide questions of fact: "It is not the province of this court to *pass upon* the weight of the evidence; we think there was a fair question for the jury, and they must *pass upon* it uninfluenced by any intimation from us."/ "Some courts have nearly gone to the extent of holding that where the language is severe, the jury should *pass upon* the case under proper instructions."

B. Testamentary Senses. In the context of wills and estates, *pass* (= to transfer or be transferred) may be either transitive or intransitive. Ordinarily it is intransitive—e.g.: "The purpose of the makers was that the property of the one first to die *pass* at his or her death as he or she directed . . . ."/ "Intestate real property *passes* by descent and intestate personal property *passes* by distribution."

But it may also be transitive—e.g.: "The instrument is supposed to *pass* property only upon death."/ "The judgment of the county court construing the first paragraph of the will to *pass* all personal property possessed by the testator at his death to his widow is affirmed."

passable; passible. The former means "capable of being passed; open"; the latter means "feeling; susceptible to pain or suffering." Cf. **impassible.** See -ABLE (A).

passerby. Pl. *passersby.*

passim (= here and there) is used in citing an authority in a general way and indicates that the point at hand is treated throughout the work. Specific references are preferred in legal citations; when a general reference is called for, *see generally* is the signal most frequently used. *Passim* is especially useful in the index of authorities contained in the front matter of a brief.

passing off, as a noun phrase, should be two words. A few writers have hyphenated the phrase—e.g.: Suman Naresh, *Passing-Off, Goodwill, and False Advertising,* 45 Cambridge L.J. 97 (1986)—but this rendering of the phrase is recommended only when it acts as a PHRASAL ADJECTIVE. See **palming off.**

PASSIVE VOICE. "Avoid the passive," one often hears; yet many do not really understand what voice is in grammar, let alone what the passive voice is. "Voice" refers to the relationship between the subject of a clause and its verb: if the verb performs the action of the subject (as in "Jane hit the ball"), the verb is active, whereas if it is acted upon (as in "The ball was hit by Jane"), the verb is passive.

True, the two sentences say essentially the same thing, but the emphasis is changed. The passive results in a wordier sentence, disrupts the ordinary sequence of events in the reader's mind, often causes DANGLERS, and often obscures the actor. Consider: "The ball was hit." As in that sentence, passive voice may lead to vagueness, or lend itself to purposeful obfuscation (see (E) below). Small wonder that politicians find so many uses for the passive (e.g., "Mistakes were made"—President Reagan's response to intense questioning about the Iran-Contra debacle). See PLAIN LANGUAGE (D).

More to the point, although the passive voice has its occasional legitimate uses—usually, when the actor is either unimportant or unknown—its frequent use makes a piece of writing much less interesting and readable. Avoiding the passive is good general advice; but one should not make a fetish of it. Following are different types of passive voice with their own peculiar problems, along with suggested remedies.

A. The Otiose Passive. This is the type of passive that results from lazy thinking, as in "The ball was hit by Jane." This syntax subverts the English-speaking reader's reasonable expectation of a direct actor-action-consequence sequence, unless a departure from that sequence is somehow an improvement. E.g., "Common trust fund legislation *is addressed to* [read *addresses*] a problem appropriate for state action."/ "The fee simple interest could have been conveyed by her to the defendant." [Read *She could have conveyed the fee simple interest to the defendant.*]/ "*It is not found that* [read *The court does not find that*] defendant did so with the intent and purpose of destroying the value of plaintiff's interest in the promissory note, as the complaint alleges."/ "After both sides had rested, *a conference was had between the trial judge and counsel* [read *the trial judge and counsel conferred* (or *had a conference*)]."/ "*It is insisted by Sue* [read *Sue insists*] that the power of appointment given George in their mother's will was nonexclusive."

B. Confusion of Active and Passive Constructions. Consider the following sentences: "Assuming Hager drew up the contract, it becomes even more clear that *it was done so without* [read *he did so without*] any approval by us."/ "Either review can be summarized, *as did Judge Rubin,* with the following observations." If the first clause is to be passive in the latter specimen quoted, then the second must also be passive [read *as was done by Judge Rubin*] to make the clauses parallel. But the best version would be to write both clauses in the active voice: "*One can summarize* either review, *as Judge Rubin did,* with the following observations."

Here the combination of active and passive constructions leads to problems of syntax and logic: "In his affidavit in opposition to defendants' motion, plaintiff Nishimura acknowledges *that plaintiffs were never interested by, much less sought* [read *that plaintiffs never had an interest in, nor sought*], rights to produce and distribute the teams' games on an exclusive, metropolitan-wide basis."

C. The Ambiguous Passive. Here an AMBIGUITY is caused by the writer's failure to specify who is acting in each instance: "To avoid dermatitis, skin contact with the epoxy must be minimized, rigorous personal cleanliness encouraged [by the user?], and suitable protective equipment used by the operator." The operator, hardly the one to *encourage* personal cleanliness, must *practice* it. The manufacturer is encouraging cleanliness.

D. Active Wrongly Used for Passive. With a few verbs, it has become voguish to use the active construction where, according to sense, the passive should appear. Thus the following statement was made to a psychiatric patient: "At the time you *were counseling* [read *receiving counseling* or *being counseled*], were you contemplating suicide?" Cf. the colloquial British usage, "You need your head *examining* [read *examined*]."/ "The video deposition *is now filming* [read *being filmed*]."/ "The cases *divide* [read *can be divided*] into two categories, roughly paralleling the sometimes fuzzy distinction between legislative and interpretative rules."

For a discussion of the *amount owing* and *amount owed* as idiomatic alternatives, see **owing.**

E. The Dishonest Passive. Sometimes the passive is used (but not as there!) in a way that is of questionable honesty. In a negligence case in which plaintiffs—a minor and his mother—have accused the retailer defendant of negligence in selling lighter fluid to the minor, this sentence occurs: "The minor plaintiff attempted to fill said lighter and *was caused to* set himself on fire."—*Was caused to* is superfluous and misleading, for one immediately wonders, by whom?

F. The Double Passive. The problem here is using one passive immediately after another. E.g., "This article refers to the portion of the votes *entitled to be cast* by virtue of the articles of incorporation." (Votes are not *entitled to be cast;* rather, persons are *entitled to cast* votes.)/ "Had an absolute liability theory *been intended to have been injected* into the Act, much more suitable models could have been found." Fowler writes that "monstrosities of this kind . . . are as repulsive to the grammarian as to the stylist" (*MEU2* 138).

In legal writing, the problem is especially common where the verb *attempt* appears: "The possibility that such a pleading informality may occur in a proceeding of this nature *has been attempted to be prevented* by our Rule 27(a)." [A suggested revision: *Preventing such informality in pleading in a case like this one is precisely the purpose of our Rule 27(a).*/ "The second ground on which this action *is attempted to be supported* fails also." (Eng.) [A suggested revision: *The plaintiff's second ground fails also.*]/ "Explosions were not what *was attempted to be guarded against* by the statute." [A suggested revision: *The statute did not purport to guard against explosions.*]

This construction is likewise common with *seek:* "The defendant against whom the option *was sought to be exercised* was in fact the assignee of the reversion." (Eng.) [A suggested revision: *Williams sought to exercise the option against the defendant who was in fact the assignee of the reversion.*]/ "A distinction *is sought to be drawn* between this case and those cases in which the decedent was an infant and the negligent parent a beneficiary." [A suggested revision: *Bronson seeks to distinguish this case from those in which the decedent was an infant and the negligent parent a beneficiary.*]

Some double passives are defensible—e.g.: "Offerings made in compliance with Regulation D *are not required to be registered* with the SEC under the Securities Act." As Fowler notes, "In legal or quasi-legal language this construction may sometimes be useful and unexceptionable: *Diplomatic privilege applies only to such things as are done or omitted to be done in the course of a person's official duties. / Motion made: that the words proposed to be left out stand part of the Question*" (*MEU2* 139). But these are of a different kind from *are sought to be included* and *are attempted to be refuted,* which can be easily remedied by recasting. "The rule," states the *Oxford Guide* (p. 148), "is that if the subject and the first passive verb can be changed into the active, leaving the passive infinitive intact, the sentence is correctly formed." Here, for example, a recasting of the first passive verb form into the active voice results in a sentence that makes sense:

Passive/Passive: The prisoners were ordered to be shot.
Active/Passive: He ordered the prisoners to be shot.

But in the following example, a recasting of the first passive verb into the active voice does not make sense:

Passive/Passive: The contention has been attempted to be made.
Active/Passive: He attempted the contention to be made (un-English).
Sense can be restored to this sentence by casting both parts in the active voice:
Active/Active: He attempted to make the contention.

G. Special Active Use with *issue.* In contexts discussing mandamus and other writs, *issue* is used actively where most nonlawyers would make it passive: "At the last term, viz., December term, 1801, William Marbury [et al.] severally moved the court for a rule to James Madison, Secretary of State of the United States, to show cause why a mandamus should not issue [a nonlawyer would write *be issued*] commanding him to cause to be delivered [better: *commanding him to deliver*] to them respectively their several commissions as justices of the peace." *Marbury v. Madison,* 5 U.S. (1 Cranch) 137, 137–38 (1803) (per Marshall, C.J.)./ "Mandamus will not *issue* to compel performance of an act that involves exercise of discretion." See **issue.**

pass muster. See **muster.**

pass on; pass upon. See **pass (A).**

past. This word occurs in many redundant phrases, such as *past history, past track record, past record,* and *past experience.* All these are REDUNDANCIES because the noun denotes something that by its very nature is rooted in the past.

past consideration. See **consideration (H).**

past experience is a common REDUNDANCY. See **past.**

pastime is sometimes misspelled *pasttime.* The misspelling derives from a misunderstanding of the word's origin, *pass* (v.t.) + *time,* not *past* + *time.*

PAST-PARTICIPIAL ADJECTIVES. See ADJECTIVES (H).

patdown, n. (= frisk), is one word.

patent, n., v.t. & adj. In the adjectival sense of "obvious, apparent," the preferred pronunciation is */**payt**-ənt/.* In all other senses and uses the pronunciation is */**pat**-ənt/.*

patentable began as a 19th-century Americanism but is now widely used in BrE as well as AmE.

patent ambiguity. See AMBIGUITY.

patentee. See -EE.

paterfamilias. In the usual English-language sense ("the male head of the household"), the preferred plural is *paterfamiliases.* In the Roman-law senses ("the head of a Roman household" or "a free Roman citizen"), the plural is *patresfamilias.*

pathos. See **bathos.**

patricide. See **parricide.**

paucital; multital. *Paucital* = in personam; *multital* = in rem. These legal terms were used by Wesley N. Hohfeld and other legal philosophers but are not recorded in most dictionaries. Now generally disused, the terms appeared mostly in early 20th-century academic writing—e.g.: "If B owes A a thousand dollars, A has an affirmative right in personam, or *paucital* right, that B shall do what is necessary to transfer to A the legal ownership of that amount of money. If, to put a contrasting situation, A already has title to one thousand dollars, his rights against others in relation thereto are *multital* rights, or rights in rem." (Hohfeld)/ "Some of the overspreading classifications consist in the following: relations in personam (*paucital* relations) and relations in rem (*multital* relations)." (Hohfeld)/ "[W]e should not allow any fiction of unity or jointness to blind us to the fact that the legal relations between joint promises and a promise are *'paucital'.* . . ." *Editor's Note, William R. Anson, Principles of the Law of Contract* 388 n.1 (Arthur L. Corbin ed., 3d Am. ed. 1919). See **in rem & in personam.**

paucity means "dearth; fewness" <a paucity of cases deciding this issue>. The word indicates a small quantity, not a complete lack of something, as the following sentences erroneously suggest:

- "Since there is *a complete paucity of* [read *no*] decisional law on the issue involved here, it might be wise, at this juncture, to defer to certain language contained within the preface of the AMA Guides themselves . . . ." *Adams v. Industrial Comm'n,* 547 P.2d 1089, 1096 (Ariz. Ct. App. 1976) (Wren, J., dissenting).

- "In the court's view, it was not necessary to reach this issue, which is essentially a matter of affirmative defense, because of the *total paucity* [read *absence*] of evidence probative of the basic elements of the plaintiff's case." *Murphy v. Owens-Corning Fiberglass Corp.,* 447 F. Supp. 557, 572 (D. Kan. 1977).
- "We are therefore unwilling, based on the *complete paucity* [read *absence*] of the evidence in the record, to reach the question . . . ." *State v. Repp,* 362 N.W.2d 415, 421 (Wis. 1985).
- "[T]here was *a complete paucity of* [read *no*] proof relating to a proximate cause between Plaintiff's minority age and his injuries." *Tierney v. Black Bros. Co.,* 852 F. Supp. 994, 1001 (M.D. Fla. 1994).

pauper is no longer used in lay contexts except for historical or humorous purposes. It is still used, however, by straight-faced judges of impecunious parties in litigation. E.g., "I am of the opinion that the defendant should pay the costs of this House to a successful *pauper appellant.*" (Eng.) See ***in forma pauperis.***

pawnor; pawnee. The *pawnor* is the owner of an item of goods who transfers it to another (the *pawnee*) as security for a debt. E.g., "Chattels could pass on death in other ways than those here described: e.g., on the death of a *pawnor* before redemption, the property passed to the *pawnee.*" J.H. Baker, *An Introduction to English Legal History* 435 (3d ed. 1990). Nonlegal writers and dictionaries use the spelling *pawner.*

pay; pay up. The latter means "to discharge completely (a debt)." The former may refer to partial or total payments. Thus, because of this slight DIFFERENTIATION, *up* is not a needless particle. Cf. **pay over.** See PARTICLES, UNNECESSARY.

payor. Although the *OED* and *W3* have their main entries under *-er, -or* is more common in American legal writing. E.g., "If the *payor* raises a purchase money resulting trust, the oral agreement is regarded as confirming the presumption of surplusage." Ironically, the spellings are *payor* but *taxpayer.* In BrE the spelling *payer* is common.

pay over. Though appearing to be a REDUNDANCY, this common legal idiom is often justifiable. *Over* signifies in this phrase the perfective aspect of the verb (the payment is completed); *pay* alone is imperfective. This is not to say that *pay over* is justified in all the examples quoted below, but it might well be in the first and fourth: "When sovereigns or banknotes are *paid over* as currency, as far as the payer is concerned, they cease ipso facto to be the subjects of specific title as chattels." (Eng.)/ "During the first three quarters of 1978, appellee failed to *pay over* [read *pay*] to the United States certain withheld income taxes."/ "The fact that the money was *paid over* [read *paid*] to the wife, for her support and the support of the children, certainly does not conflict with the order of this court."/ "Upon her death, the principal was to be *paid over* by the trustees to such persons as the settlor might appoint by will, or, in default of such appointment, to the settlor's heirs at law and next of kin as in intestacy." See PARTICLES, UNNECESSARY.

peaceable; peaceful. Generally, *peaceful* refers to a state of affairs; *peaceable* refers to the disposition of a person or a nation state. The two words overlap some, but a strict DIFFERENTIATION is worth encouraging.

peace, against the. See **against the peace.**

peace of mind; piece of (one's) mind. Whereas *peace of mind* is calm assurance, *a piece of one's mind* is something a person says in a fit of pique. But the two are surprisingly often confused—e.g.:

- "The policyholder should recover for mental distress caused by the insurance company's bad faith conduct because insurance is purchased to provide *piece* [read *peace*] of mind." *D'Ambrosio v. Pennsylvania Nat'l Mut. Casualty Ins. Co.,* 431 A.2d 966, 972 (Pa. 1981).
- "[T]he weaker party does not enter into the contract primarily for profit, but to secure an essential service or product, financial security or *piece* [read *peace*] of mind . . . ." Henry H. Perritt, Jr., *Implied Covenant: Anachronism or Augur?* 20 Seton Hall L. Rev. 683, 710–11 (1990).
- "Kansas courts have allowed recovery under nuisance theory to include annoyance, discomfort, inconvenience, endangerment of health, and loss of *piece* [read *peace*] of mind." Charles C. Steincamp, Note, *Toeing the Line: Compliance with the National Contingency Plan for Private Party Cost Recovery Under CERCLA,* 32 Washburn L.J. 190, 233 (1993).
- "Restrictions on obnoxious noise and public indecency protect people's sensibilities and *piece* [read *peace*] of mind, not their liberty." Samuel Freeman, *Criminal Liability and the Duty to*

Aid the Distressed, 142 U. Pa. L. Rev. 1455, 1487 n.112 (1994).

peak; peek. The distinction is so elementary as not to call for explanation. But mistakes do occur—e.g.: "[The court held] that citizens must be notified of entries and seizures pursuant to 'sneak and *peak* [read *peek*]' warrants which authorize a surreptitious entry for purposes of looking around or taking photographs." Ronald J. Bacigal, *The Right of the People to Be Secure,* 82 Ky. L.J. 145, 186 n.272 (1993–1994).

On the misuse of *peak* for *pique,* see **pique.**

peccadillo. Pl. *-oes.* See PLURALS (C).

peccavi (lit., "I have sinned") = an acknowledgment or confession of sin. The word is pronounced /*pə-****kah****-vee*/.

pectore, in. See LOAN TRANSLATIONS.

peculate. See **defalcate.**

peculation is essentially a fancy equivalent of—perhaps even a polite EUPHEMISM for—*embezzlement.* But the *OED* suggests a narrower meaning for *peculation:* "the appropriation of public money or property by one in an official position." If that were correct, then a public official *peculates* whereas a corporate employee *embezzles.*

Indeed, *peculation* was once used in this narrower sense—e.g.: "The power to control and direct the appropriations, constitutes a most useful and salutary check upon profusion and extravagance, as well as upon corrupt influence and public *peculation* . . . ." 2 Joseph Story, *Commentaries on the Constitution of the United States* §1348, at 222 (5th ed. 1891).

Today, however, the word routinely refers to violations of private trusts—e.g.: "But to analogize petitioners' scheme to a conventional case of *peculation* by an employee, whether public or private, is to disregard the facts of this case." *Parr v. U.S.,* 363 U.S. 370, 398–99 (1960) (Frankfurter, J., dissenting). That being so, there is little to commend the word in comparison with the ordinary term *embezzlement.* See **defalcate** & **embezzle.**

pecuniary; pecunious. The suffixes distinguish these words. *Pecuniary* = relating to or consisting of money. *Pecunious* = moneyed; wealthy. (Its opposite is *impecunious,* meaning "destitute.")

The adverb corresponding to *pecuniary* is *pecuniarily:* "They were quite unaware of the fact that it was to the plaintiff's advantage, *pecuniarily* or otherwise, to deal with Watson's rather than with Ritchie's." (Eng.)

pedal. See **peddle.**

peddle (= to sell) is sometimes misused for the verb *pedal,* esp. in the phrase *soft-pedaling* (orig., the practice of using the muffling pedal on a piano while playing it). E.g., "[T]hey adopted a strategy of *soft-peddling* [read *soft-pedaling*] the issue during the submission of evidence all with a view to seeking a mistrial . . . ." *Ginns v. Towle,* 361 F.2d 798, 801 (2d Cir. 1966)./ "It seems clear that the Court was *soft-peddling* [read *soft-pedaling*] language in the EEOC guidelines . . . ." E. Clayton Hipp, Jr., *Now You See It, Now You Don't: The "Hostile Work Environment" After* Meritor, 26 Am. Bus. L.J. 339, 346 (1988)./ "Almost always a smarmy, *soft-peddling* [read *soft-pedaling*] overvoice purring something like: 'This magic moment has been brought to you by . . . .'" Patricia J. Williams, *Commercial Rights and Constitutional Wrongs,* 49 Md. L. Rev. 293, 307 (1990).

pederasty. So spelled. Cf. **buggery.**

pediatrician; pediatrist. The former is the common, preferred term, meaning "a physician who specializes in children's medicine." The latter, a NEEDLESS VARIANT, has the liability of causing confusion with *podiatrist* (= a foot doctor).

peek. See **peak.**

pejorative. So spelled, though sometimes mistakenly spelled *perjorative,* as in the following examples: "The majority resorts to *perjoratives* [read *pejoratives*] . . . ." *Compagnie des Bauxites de Guinea v. Insurance Co. of N. Am.,* 651 F.2d 877, 889 (3d Cir. 1981) (Gibbons, J., dissenting)./ "[T]he female-gendered term is slightly *perjorative* [read *pejorative*] of this species of prosecution." Helen Leskovac, *Legal Writing and Plain English,* 38 Syracuse L. Rev. 1193, 1202 (1987).

penal; punitive; penological. *Penal* = of or relating to punishment or retribution. *Punitive* = serving to punish; intended to inflict punishment. *Penological* = of or relating to the study of the philosophy and methods of punishment and treatment of persons found guilty of crime. The words thus have distinct senses.

Penological is often used inappropriately for *penal,* perhaps because the usual phrase is *the state's penological interest,* and the state's interest sounds more clinical and dispassionate if *penological* rather than *penal* is used. That is not, however, a justification for misusing the word. E.g., "The state by this statute imposing a fine has declared its *penological* [read *penal*] interest—deterrence, retribution, and rehabilitation—satisfied by a monetary payment, and disclaimed, as serving any *penological* [read *penal*] purpose in such cases, a term in jail." See EUPHEMISMS.

penal institution is a EUPHEMISM for *prison.*

pend, v.i., (= [of a lawsuit] to be awaiting decision or settlement; to be pending) is a sense unrecorded by the *OED* and *W3.* In this novel AmE legal sense *pend* is really a BACK-FORMATION from the present participial form *pending* <the case has been pending for three years>.

The word dates from the early 20th century—e.g.: "The matter is really not procedural or controlled by the rules of court in which the litigation *pends.*" *Oklahoma Natural Gas Co. v. Oklahoma,* 273 U.S. 257, 259–60 (1927)./ "[W]hile plaintiff's case *pended* [read *was pending*] in the trial court, . . . the defendant had presented itself as contestant of any right of the plaintiff to obtain valid judgment . . . ." *Car & Concepts, Inc. v. Funston,* 601 S.W. 2d 801, 803 (Tex. Civ. App.—Ft. Worth 1980). *Pending* sounds more natural in most contexts in which *pend* appears.

pendant. See **pendent.**

pendency (= the state or condition of being pending or continuing undecided) is largely a legal term. E.g., "The district court erred in awarding appellant interest during the *pendency* of the first appeal." *Pendence* is a NEEDLESS VARIANT. E.g., "A severance will not be granted for the purpose of making a judgment final which otherwise would be interlocutory because of the continued *pendence* [read *pendency*] of other claims in the case." Dallas Civ. Court Rules § 1.4(a) (1981).

pendens. See **lis pendens.**

pendent; pendant. The first is an adjective literally meaning "hanging; suspended"; the second is a noun meaning "something suspended, as a chain around one's neck."

Pendent, common in the legal phrase *pendent jurisdiction,* is occasionally misspelled *-ant.* E.g., "[T]he Court is not inclined to grant injunctive relief on plaintiff's *pendant* [read *pendent*] State anti-dilution claim." *Home Box Office v. Showtime,* 665 F. Supp. 1079, 1087 (S.D.N.Y. 1987).

pendent jurisdiction. See **concurrent jurisdiction.**

pendente lite (= while the action is pending) is sometimes misspelled *pendent lite.* See **lis pendens.**

penetrable is preferable to *penetratable.* See -ATABLE.

penitentiary (= a reformatory or correctional prison) originally referred to an ecclesiastical office (i.e., a person appointed to deal with penitents). The idea of reform is embedded in the root meaning. Although for some time rehabilitation was not a major objective of American prisons, today it is on the rise.

penological. See **penal.**

pensioner. See **annuitant.**

penultimate; antepenultimate. The former means "next to the last," the latter "second from the last." *Penultimate* is common among educated writers, both lawyers and nonlawyers. E.g., "The *penultimate* paragraph of this opinion is deleted and the following is substituted."

penumbra. Though most English-language dictionaries list only the plural *-ae,* one could hardly be faulted for anglicizing the term and using *-as.* (See PLURALS (A).) Justice Douglas did just that in the quotation immediately following: "The foregoing cases suggest that specific guarantees in the Bill of Rights have *penumbras,* formed by emanations that help give them life and substance." *Griswold v. Connecticut,* 381 U.S. 479, 483 (1965)./ "[W]e see no persuasive reason to extend the right of privacy, based as it is on '*penumbras* and emanations' of other more explicit constitutional rights, to evidentiary matters protecting marital relationships . . . ." *Port v. Heard,* 764 F.2d 423, 430 (5th Cir. 1985).

penumbral; penumbrous. The latter is a NEEDLESS VARIANT.

people. A. And *persons.* *People* is general, *persons* specific. One refers to *English-speaking people* (or *peoples*) but to *the twelve persons on the jury. Persons* should virtually always be used with small, specific numbers.

B. And *state.* A *people* (collectively) is a great many persons united by a common language and by similar customs—usu. the result of common ancestry, religion, and historical circumstances. A *state* is a great many persons, generally occupying a given territory, among whom the will of the majority—or of an ascertainable class of persons—prevails against anyone who opposes that will. A *state* may coincide exactly with one *people,* as in France, or may embrace several, as in the U.S.

peoplekind is an unnecessary formation for *mankind* or *humankind.* E.g., "While this solution would make everyone truly equal, it would be undesirable, because there would be no extraordinary individuals to lead *peoplekind* [read *humankind*] to new frontiers or new ideas." See **humankind.**

people's court. This phrase originated, oddly enough, as a propagandistic phrase for totalitarian regimes—e.g.: "The custom of prejudging guilt or innocence and of injecting evidence and opinions upon the trial by publicity can easily proceed to such a point that verdicts in highly publicized American cases will no more really represent the jurors' dispassionate personal judgment on the legal evidence than do those of '*People's Courts*' we so criticize abroad." Robert H. Jackson, *The Advocate: Guardian of Our Traditional Liberties,* 36 A.B.A. J. 607, 609 (1950).

In the 1980s, a television show named "The People's Court" (Wapner, J., presiding) became extremely popular. Since that time, the phrase has come to mean a court in which ordinary people can solve their petty and not-so-petty disputes.

PER-. This prefix may mean "through" (*perspicuous, impervious*), or it may act as an intensive (*perfervid, perforce, perchance*).

per. **A. In Citations.** *Per* is used to indicate the judge who has written a majority opinion. E.g., *In re City of Houston,* 745 F.2d 925 (5th Cir. 1984) (per Reavley, J.). *The Bluebook* now recommends omitting *per;* it is sometimes useful, however, when a writer cites a case and believes that the authorship of the opinion is in some way noteworthy.

Even so, *per* should be avoided in text when no citation is involved—e.g.: "The dissent, *per* [read *by*] Justice White, objected that the majority's discussion of summary judgment rules is confusing and inconsistent . . . ." Steven A. Childress, *A New Era for Summary Judgments,* 116 F.R.D. 183, 187 (1987).

B. For a. *Per* may become a necessary substitute for *a* when it is used as part of a PHRASAL ADJECTIVE—e.g.: "Entwistle calculated a *per-winch* profit figure of $3.20."/ "Defendants appeal, contending that the award of $150,000 *per* parent is excessive." See **a (B).**

peradventure is archaic in what used to be its primary sense, "perhaps." In the hackneyed phrase *beyond peradventure,* it means "doubt." E.g., "It is clear *beyond peradventure* that the income tax on wages is constitutional."/ "The meaning of the term in that subdivision is plain *beyond all peradventure.*"

Beyond peradventure of a doubt is a REDUNDANCY: "But it is clear *beyond peradventure of a doubt that* [read *beyond peradventure that*] appellant and Nelda considered these weekends as devoted to recreation and refreshment." Cf. **cavil, beyond.**

per annum is unnecessary for *a year, per year,* or *each year.* Cf. **per diem.**

per anum (= through the anus), a EUPHEMISM appearing in contexts relating to sex crimes, is so spelled—not *per annum* (= per year), as some writers mistakenly render it: "Buggery is copulation *per annum* [read *per anum*] by a man with either another man or with a woman." Rollin M. Perkins & Ronald N. Boyce, *Criminal Law* 465 (3d ed. 1982). A better, more straightforward phrase than *copulation per anum* would be *anal copulation* or *anal sex.*

per capita. **A. And *per caput.*** The first is the frequently used plural ("by heads"), the second the rare singular ("a head; by the head").

B. And *per stirpes.* Both phrases (meaning, respectively, "by heads" and "by stocks") are commonly used in the context of wills and estates. They denote different methods for calculating what the heirs or next-of-kin will receive. For example, in an intestate succession *per capita,* all claimants entitled to intestate shares take equally regardless of the share to which an ancestor through whom they claim would have been entitled. In succession *per stirpes,* the shares are determined usu. at the first generation of takers: thus, if one family stock has skipped a generation because a child has predeceased the decedent, the grandchildren of the decedent would divide among themselves an amount equal to what their deceased parent would have been entitled to.

Per stirpes (= by family stocks) is sometimes cited as a term of art that cannot be simplified. In fact, though, the phrase is ambiguous in ways explained in the entry TERMS OF ART. Leading writers on wills and estates generally recommend avoiding it. See, e.g., Stanley M. Johanson, *In Defense of Plain Language,* 3 Scribes J. Legal Writing 37, 37–38 (1992).

percent; per-cent; per cent; per cent.; per centum. This sequence illustrates in reverse the evolution of this word, earlier a phrase. Today it is best spelled as a single word. The plural of *percent* is *percent;* adding an *-s,* though not uncommon, is substandard.

In most writing, *75%* is easier to read than *75 percent* or (worse yet) *seventy-five percent.*

percentage of, a. One writes, "A high percentage of it *is* there," but "A percentage of them *are* there." Cf. **proportion.** See SYNESIS.

perceptible. See **perceptive.**

perceptive (= keenly intuitive) for *perceptible* (= appreciable, recognizable) is an infrequent error—e.g.: "Those professions that have tried that solution have paid handsomely without *perceptive* [read *perceptible*] improvement in their images." Bob Dunn, *Contemplating Our Future,* Tex. B.J., May 1992, at 448.

perchance is an ARCHAISM for *perhaps*—e.g.: "For if your system, *perchance,* lacks absolute utility, it is so much more efficient than that which we have had in our own country as to lead some to look to you for the solution of many of our common problems." (Eng.)

per contra (= on the other hand; to the contrary; by contrast) may seem to be a useful LATINISM because of its brevity, but the English words are much more widely understood. E.g., "That doctrine . . . had as its major premise the idea that the shipowner's liability for unseaworthiness is based on negligence. *Per contra* [read *By contrast*], both Mahnich and Sieracki had made clear that negligence had no part in the brave new world of unseaworthiness." Grant Gilmore & Charles L. Black, Jr., *The Law of Admiralty* 395 (2d ed. 1975).

per curiam (= by the court) is primarily an adjective <per curiam opinion>, but is sometimes used as an elliptical form of *per curiam opinion.* E.g., "In the *per curiam* denying rehearing in *Bennett,* the en banc court for this circuit unanimously agreed on the statement of governing criteria by which a municipality's section 1983 liability is to be determined."

In still other contexts, the phrase is used adverbially—e.g.: "Presumably no one would have quarreled with the Calbeck majority if it had . . . reversed the Fifth Circuit *per curiam* . . . ." Grant Gilmore & Charles L. Black, Jr., *The Law of Admiralty* 422 (2d ed. 1975). See **by the court** & ***per incuriam.***

per diem = for or by the day <per diem fee>. Generally, it makes more sense to write *a day* <$50 a day> or *daily* <daily fee>. (See **a (B).**) *Per diem,* a LATINISM, has been defended when it is positioned before the noun it modifies, but *daily* is undoubtedly an improvement. In no legal context, one can safely say, is *per diem* the best available phrase.

perempt, v.t., in legal slang, is sometimes used as a BACK-FORMATION from *peremptory challenge,* the sense being "to exercise a peremptory challenge against"—e.g.: "We feel that under *Batson,* to *perempt* all the blacks on the panel . . . ." *Barfield v. Orange County,* 911 F.2d 644, 646 (11th Cir. 1990) (quoting counsel at trial). For another sense of the word, see **preempt.**

peremption. See **preemption.**

peremptory, adj., = admitting no contradiction or denial; incontrovertible. "The trial court erred in refusing to give the *peremptory* instruction that asked it to return a verdict of not guilty." *Peremptory* was originally a term from Roman law, meaning "that destroys, puts an end to, or precludes all debate, question, or delay" (*OED*) <peremptory edict>.

Since the early 20th century, *peremptory* has often been used as an elliptical form of *peremptory challenge* or *strike,* which denotes the removal of a veniremember without a showing of cause—e.g.:

- "[T]he trial judge went upon the theory that . . . plaintiff should have exhausted his *peremptories* upon the other two [jurors]." *Martin v. Farmers' Mut. Fire Ins. Co.,* 102 N.W. 656, 658 (Mich. 1905).
- "After all *peremptories* have been taken, or the parties satisfied, the jury shall then be sworn as a body to try the cause." *Avila v. U.S.,* 76 F.2d 39, 41 (9th Cir. 1935).
- "'You had *peremptories* still left that you could have exercised, had you thought you were not getting a fair jury.'" *People v. Hancock,* 40 N.W.2d 689, 698 (Mich. 1950) (quoting the trial judge).
- "While the fact that the jury included members of a group allegedly discriminated against is not conclusive, it is an indication of good faith in exercising *peremptories,* and an appropriate factor for the trial judge to consider in ruling on a *Wheeler* objection." *People v. Turner,* 32 Cal. Rptr. 2d 762, 777 (Cal. 1994) (en banc).

Cf. **causal challenge.**

The word is sometimes mistakenly written *preemptory,* no doubt as a result of the writer's mistakenly associating the word with the verb *preempt*—e.g.: "On Friday, Judge John Ouderkirk of State Superior Court dismissed a black woman after a challenge for cause and a black man after a *pre-emptory* [read *peremptory*] challenge by the prosecutor. In making *pre-emptory* [read *peremptory*] challenges, lawyers do not have to give a reason for wanting a prospective juror dismissed." *Jury Queries Resume in Beating Case,* N.Y. Times, 8 Aug. 1993, at 17./ "The State may not exercise its *preemptory* [read *peremptory*] challenges for purely racial reasons." *Wilson v. State,* 884 S.W.2d 904, 907 (Tex. App.—San Antonio 1994). For the correct use of *preemptory,* see **preemptive.**

perfect /pər-*fekt*/, v.t., = to bring to completion; to complete, finish, consummate; to carry through, accomplish (*OED*). This sense, now mostly legal, usu. appears in reference to perfecting appeals and perfecting liens. E.g., "[A] cadre of lawyers in Albany specializes in the art of *perfecting* bar appeals." Stephen Labaton, *At the Bar,* N.Y. Times, 18 Aug. 1989, at 20.

perfectible. So spelled. See -ABLE (A).

perfect-tender rule = the less-than-robust rule that, in contracts between merchants, every aspect of the seller's performance is a condition of the buyer's liability, so that the buyer is privileged to reject the goods if the seller deviates even slightly from the contractual requirements. The phrase should be hyphenated thus. See PHRASAL ADJECTIVES.

perimeter. See **parameters.**

per incuriam is not the opposite of *per curiam* (= by the court); rather, it means "through inadvertence; in ignorance of the relevant law." Today it is used more commonly in BrE than in AmE. E.g., "As a general rule the only cases in which decisions should be held to have given *per incuriam* are those of decisions given in ignorance or forgetfulness of some inconsistent statutory provision or of some authority binding on the court concerned . . . ." *Morrelle Ltd. v. Wakeling,* [1955] 2 Q.B. 389, 406./ "When the essence of a pervious decision with which a judge disagrees cannot so easily be dismissed as *obiter dictum,* the judge may, as a desperate last resort, categorize the previous decision as *per incuriam* (an acceptable legal euphemism for a judgment [that] was obviously wrong)." David Pannick, *Judges* 159 (1987).

periodic tenancy; tenancy from month to month; tenancy from year to year. The phrase *periodic tenancy* is the genus of which both *tenancy from month to month* and *tenancy from year to year* are species. A *periodic tenancy* continues for a year—or any fraction of a year—and for successive equivalent periods until terminated by either party with proper notice. This type of tenancy most commonly arises when a lease term ends and is automatically (and repeatedly) renewed another month or year.

Within the Anglo-American classifications of property rights, the *periodic tenancy* has a dual nature: "[P]eriodic tenancies of all types are now considered to be non-freehold 'estates in land,' although they are also 'chattels real'—i.e., personal rather than real property." Roger A. Cunningham et al., *The Law of Property* 82 (2d ed. 1993). See **chattels & estate.**

Though *periodic* tenancy is a general term, it is often used interchangeably with the more specific phrases (*tenancy from month to month* and *tenancy from year to year*), as periods other than months or years are highly unusual. The more specific phrases are often preferable because they are more universally comprehensible.

The more specific terms are often written *month-to-month tenancy* and *year-to-year tenancy,* the hyphens being necessary in a PHRASAL ADJECTIVE that precedes the noun.

period of time is usually unnecessary in place of either *period* or *time.*

PERIPHRASIS = a roundabout way of writing or speaking. Many a legal writer uses "jargon to shirk prose, palming off *periphrasis* upon us when with a little trouble he could have gone straight to the point." Arthur Quiller-Couch, *On the Art of Writing* 108 (1916; repr. 1961). See JARGON, EUPHEMISMS & REDUNDANCY.

PERIPHRASTIC COMPARATIVES. See COMPARATIVES AND SUPERLATIVES (B).

perjorative is a misspelling of *pejorative.* See **pejorative.**

perjure is now used only as a reflexive verb—e.g.: "The petitioner maintains that he was unable to discover that these witnesses *perjured themselves.*" See **perjury.**

perjured; perjurious; perjurial. *Perjured* is now the usual adjective corresponding to *perjury*—e.g.: "The evidence must show beyond the existence of a reasonable doubt that the alleged *perjured* testimony of the person suborned was under oath duly and legally administered." The word *perjurious* is somewhat broader because it means "involving perjury" as opposed to the more specific sense of *perjured* (= characterized by perjury). Thus, it is possible to speak of a person's *perjurious* tendencies but not of *perjured* tendencies.

Perjurous is an obsolete spelling of *perjurious,* which is analogous in formation to *injurious.* E.g., "[A]n affidavit . . . was [allegedly] 'false and *perjurious* . . . .'" *Sprecher v. Graber,* 716 F.2d 968, 970 (2d Cir. 1983)./ "[T]he Supreme Court of Arizona has held that succumbing to a client's demand to elicit obvious *perjurious* testimony . . . amounts to ineffective assistance of counsel . . . ." *Sanborn v. State,* 474 So. 2d 309, 313 (Fla. Dist. Ct. App. 1985).

The form *perjurial,* a NEEDLESS VARIANT, has no warrant: "There is a sea of motions, demands, claims, counterclaims and plenty of innuendoes on each side as to the *perjurial* [read *perjurious*] aptitude of the other . . . ." *Rocket Mining Corp. v. Gill,* 417 P.2d 120, 120 (Utah 1966).

perjurer. So spelled—not *perjuror.*

perjurial; perjurious. See **perjured.**

perjury; false swearing; forswearing. The popular meaning of the first two terms is the same, namely, "swearing to what the witness knows to be untrue." *Forswearing* is a little-used equivalent of *false swearing; forswearing* also means, of course, "repudiating, renouncing." The technical DIFFERENTIATION at common law between *perjury* and *false swearing,* apart from their being separate indictable offenses, is that *perjury* connotes corruption and recalcitrance, whereas *false swearing* (or *false oath*) connotes mere falsehood without these additional moral judgments.

permanence; permanency. Both forms are used frequently. The two share the sense "the quality or state of being permanent." But while *permanence* emphasizes durability <the permanence of the snow>, *permanency* emphasizes duration <the permanency of fees tail>.

permission; acquiescence. *Permission* connotes an authorization to do something, whereas *acquiescence* connotes the passive failure to object to someone's doing something.

permissive; permissory. The latter is a NEEDLESS VARIANT.

permit. See **allow (B).**

permit of = to leave room for <the words permit of more than one interpretation>. This phrase is common in contexts involving the interpretation of drafted documents, or statutes.

permittee. See -EE.

permute; permutate. *Permute,* v.t., is—apart from specialized mathematical uses—merely a fancy equivalent of the verb *to change. Permutate* is a NEEDLESS VARIANT.

perorate; orate. The former means "to conclude a formal address," although it is infrequently misunderstood as meaning "to declaim rhetorically or emotionally." *Orate,* a BACK-FORMATION, was once widely considered objectionable or merely humorous; yet it is losing this stigma.

peroration refers, most strictly, to the concluding part of a speech. And the word ordinarily bears that sense—e.g.: "In an eloquent *peroration,* Brennan concluded by observing . . . ." Geoffrey R. Stone, *Justice Brennan and the Freedom of Speech: A First Amendment Odyssey,* 139 U. Pa. L. Rev. 1333, 1352 (1991)./ "At the time, I thought my *peroration* was brilliant. I concluded my argument by rising with oratorical fervor . . . ." Stanley Mosk, *Culpability, Restitution, and the Environment: The Vitality of Common Law Rules,* 21 Ecology L.Q. 551, 554 (1994).

But, through SLIPSHOD EXTENSION—primarily because the closing of a speech is typically the most impassioned and rhetorical part—some writers have used the word as if it referred to any rhetorically charged speech or writing. E.g.: "Professor Tribe's *perorations* [read *comments? rhetoric?*] about the not-so-absolute absolutes should seem a very sorry affair against at least the science of general relativity . . . ." Stanley L. Jaki, *Patterns over Principles: The Pseudoscientific Roots of Law's Debacle,* 38 Am. J. Juris. 135, 144 (1993).

In any event, the word is unacceptably strained when asked to refer to opening remarks—e.g.: "*After opening with a passionate peroration* [read *After opening passionately*], the dissent begins its technical-legal analysis by quoting a New Deal dissent in *United States v Butler,* one of the Old Court's last desperate struggles on behalf of a Madisonian understanding of limited national powers." Bruce Ackerman, *Liberating Abstraction,* 59 U. Chi. L. Rev. 317, 327 (1992). Was Ackerman perhaps straining for an alliteration that led him astray of the sense?

Some writers seem to use the word with little idea of its true meaning. One can only guess at the authors' intentions in the following passages: "Harvey cites one judge's *peroration* [read *praise?*] of the merits of the British law of evidence as evidence that the judge was 'certifiable,' and, in the style of Rumpole, alludes to the law in general as a sort of formality." Richard H. Underwood,

Logic and the Common Law Trial, 18 Am. J. Trial Advoc. 151, 199 n.12 (1994)./ "The *Cooney* court preceded its discussion of interest analysis with a similar *peroration* [read *allusion* or *reference?*] to the fact that the conflict did not involve conduct-regulating rules . . . ." Aaron D. Twerski, *A Sheep in Wolf's Clothing: Territorialism in the Guise of Interest Analysis* [etc.], 59 Brook. L. Rev. 1351, 1361 (1994).

perpetrate. See **perpetuate.**

perpetrator; abettor; inciter; criminal protector. These terms name the four different kinds of criminally culpable parties at common law. *Perpetrator* = one who, with mens rea (q.v.), has caused a socially harmful occurrence either personally or through some tool or innocent agent. *Abettor* = one who is present at the scene of a crime, either actually or constructively, and who, with mens rea, either helps the perpetrator commit the crime or stands by with intent—known to the perpetrator—to help if needed, or otherwise encourages the perpetrator. *Inciter* = one who, with mens rea, helps, commands, or encourages another to commit a crime without being either actually or constructively present when it is carried out. *Criminal protector* = one who is in no way tainted with guilt of a crime when perpetrated but who, with full knowledge of the facts, later conceals the offender or helps prevent detection, arrest, trial, or punishment. See Rollin M. Perkins & Ronald N. Boyce, *Criminal Law* 723–26 (3d ed. 1982).

In the crime of treason, all such parties are principals. In misdemeanors, the first three are principals, and *criminal protectors* are not punishable. In felonies:

- Perpetrators are principals in the first degree.
- Abettors are principals in the second degree.
- Inciters are accessories before the fact.
- Criminal protectors are accessories after the fact.

Cf. **accomplice.** See **principal (B).**

perpetuable. So spelled—not *perpetuatable.* See -ATABLE.

perpetuate (= to make last indefinitely; prolong) and *perpetrate* (= to commit or carry out) are surprisingly often confounded. E.g., "In 1988, Federal District Judge James L. Kinf dismissed the suit as baseless, accused Mr. Shean of knowingly *perpetuating* [read *perpetrating*] a fraud and fined the Christie Institute . . . ." Michael Kelly, *Perot Shows Penchant for Seeing Conspiracy,* N.Y. Times, 26 Oct. 1992, at A10./ "This allowed Ogle to use said document to *perpetuate* [read *perpetrate*] a fraud on a bank lending institution in connection with a $100,000 loan." *Taylor v. Sullivan,* 613 N.Y.S.2d 397, 398 (App. Div. 1994).

The word *perpetuate* is correctly used in the following sentence: "Amassing wealth over an extended period of time may have been attractive to some of the landed gentry of England who sought to *perpetuate* family fortunes in the feudal tradition, unhampered by income or estate taxes."

per procurationem = by proxy. The phrase is abbreviated *per pro., p. proc., p. pro.,* or *p.p.*

perquisite; prerequisite. *Perquisite,* often shortened to *perk,* means "a privilege or benefit given in addition to one's salary or regular wages." *Prerequisite* = a previous condition or requirement.

***per quod;* per se.** Literally, *per quod* = whereby. In all tort actions, *per quod* once introduced the allegations giving rise to special damages by a showing of consequences stemming from the defendant's acts. *Per se* violations required no such showing. The phrases survive in defamation cases. See, e.g., *Kurz v. The Evening News Ass'n,* 375 N.W.2d 391, 394 (Mich. Ct. App. 1985). E.g., "The law has always made a distinction between false imputations that may be actionable in themselves, *per se,* and those that may be actionable only on allegation and proof of special damage, or *per quod.*"

Unfortunately, though, the use of *per se* in defamation contexts is ambiguous because it invites confusion with another distinction in the law of defamation: that between words that are facially defamatory ("You're an embezzler") and words that amount to subtle, veiled defamations. Statements of the latter type require some pleading and proof of innuendo or explanation. But this distinction, valuable as it is, has nothing whatever to do with whether special damages must be proved. Even so, some American courts have been misled by the linguistic similarity between *actionable per se* and *defamatory per se.* See Charles T. McCormick, *Handbook of the Law of Damages* § 113, at 417–18 (1935).

per se (lit., "through [or *in, by, of*] itself") = (1) standing alone; in itself; or (2) as a matter of law. The phrase is both adverb and adjective. Formerly used almost always after the adjective or noun it modifies, today it is commonly used before: "The district court submitted the case to the jury on the theory that such a conspiracy, if proved, is *per se* illegal."/ "The case is being closely watched by antitrust specialists, because the decision may revise an old and important antitrust doctrine known as the *per se* rule."/ "Appellant asserts that his back ailment is *per se* disabling."/ "There is no longer a presumption of specific deadly intent when a *per se* deadly weapon is used by the defendant."

The phrase usually takes no punctuation, even though its English equivalent *in itself* or *of itself* is ordinarily set off by commas. When, however, *per se* is used as a direct functional equivalent of one of these phrases, it should be set off: "That the propriety, *per se,* of searches of law offices is an area of some controversy makes it more, not less, imperative that public officials not disregard the strictures of the fourth amendment."

When used before the noun it modifies, *per se* often means "absolute." E.g., "This inquiry calls for line-drawing, but no fixed *per se* rule can be expressed or applied in any particular case."/ "We are not disposed to fashion a *per se* rule requiring reversal of every conviction following tardy appointment of counsel."

Per se has become a TERM OF ART in antitrust law, referring to an outright violation of the antitrust statutes. The Supreme Court of the United States has defined *per se* antitrust violations as those "which because of their pernicious effect on competition and lack of any redeeming virtue are conclusively presumed to be unreasonable and therefore illegal without elaborate inquiry as to the precise harm they have caused or the business excuse for their use." *Northern Pac. Ry. v. U.S.,* 356 U.S. 1, 5 (1958). *Per se* is not absolute in American antitrust law: there may be behavior that is a *per se* violation of the statute, yet the violator may still raise defenses, such as impossibility due to market conditions.

The phrase has been extended in antitrust contexts well beyond its usual sense, from *per se illegality* to *per se rules* or *analysis* to *per se language*—e.g.: "*Per se* language expresses a mood of undoubted hostility to a practice." 7 Phillip Areeda, *Antitrust Law* § 1510, at 417 (1986). See ***per quod.***

persecute. See **prosecute.**

persevere. Because this word is frequently a victim of the intrusive *-r-*, it is often mispronounced (and misspelled) *perservere.*

-PERSON. For a discussion of this suffix, see SEXISM (B).

person. This word illustrates the tendency lawyers have to take an ordinary English word and give it an unnatural meaning: "So far as legal theory is concerned, a person is any being whom the law regards as capable of rights and duties. Any being that is so capable is a person, whether a human being or not, and no being that is not so capable is a person, even though he be a man." J.W. Salmond, *Jurisprudence* 299 (P.J. Fitzgerald ed., 12th ed. 1966). Lon Fuller, among others, has questioned whether *person* is the most desirable word for the concept. See Lon L. Fuller, *Legal Fictions* 12–14 (1967). What term might be better? Fuller suggests *legal subject* or *right-and-duty bearing unit. Id.* On second thought, perhaps *person* is not quite so bad.

PERSON. It is important in any piece of writing, and especially in DRAFTING, not to confuse one's references to persons, as by switching the voice through which the prose is set down. The writer should not change the person through whom the writing speaks, as by slipping in and out of third person, with first person interspersed.

Following is an example from a will quoted in an opinion:

> The party of the first part . . . does hereby remise, release, and forever quitclaim unto the said party of the second part, his heirs and assigns forever, all the real estate of the said Ella F. Sherwood [the party of the first part], wherever situate, to have and to hold the same unto the party of the second part, his heirs, executors, and administrators and assigns forever, and for the same considerations, *I do* hereby sell . . . unto the party of the second part all personal property.

Here is another specimen, in which *testator* = party of the first part. "This conveyance and transfer is made upon the condition that the party of the second part, *my husband,* survive *me,* and the same is intended to vest and take effect upon *my decease* and until said time the same shall be subject to revocation upon the part of the *party of the first part.*" In both of these examples, certainly, use of the first person would be preferable throughout. See FIRST PERSON & **party of the first part.**

persona is singular, not plural—*personae* being the plural. Hence: "*Jowitt's Dictionary of English Law* in two volumes is quite detailed and because of its articles on long forgotten legal *persona* [read *personae* or, better yet, *personages*], incidents and maxims is an amusing read in itself." P.H. Kenny, *Studying Law* 47 (1985).

persona grata. See **persona non grata.**

personal action. See **real action.**

personal injury. When used as a noun phrase, two words unhyphenated; when used as a PHRASAL ADJECTIVE, hyphenated—e.g.: "But over the past year, *personal-injury attorneys* have been successful in having a number of such laws overturned." *Court in Washington Voids a Law Limiting Some Jury Awards,* Wall St. J., 1 May 1989, at B5.

personal law = the law that governs a given person in family matters, usu. regardless of where the person goes. In common-law systems, *personal law* refers to the law of the individual's domicile. (See ***lex domicilii.***) In civil-law systems, it refers to the law of the individual's nationality (and is sometimes called *lex patriae*). E.g., "[S]uccession to immovables on the basis of the *personal law* of the decedent, as distinct from the law of the situs, has long been the rule in a substantial number of civilian jurisdictions." Alfred Hill, *The Judicial Function in Choice of Law,* 85 Colum. L. Rev. 1585, 1647 (1985). The effect of the differing systems is that, in civilian countries, personal law follows the person, whereas in common-law countries it does not.

Still other, religion-based systems establish a *personal law* for some aspects of life such as marriage, divorce, inheritance, legitimacy, adoption, and many types of capacity—e.g.:

- "While the Hindu Code retains *personal law* for Hindus, that *personal law* has almost entirely eliminated traditional caste distinctions." Jamie Cassels, *Bitter Knowledge, Vibrant Action: Reflections of Law and Society in Modern India,* 1991 Wis. L. Rev. 109, 137 (book review).
- "While article 44 of the constitution envisages the eventual adoption of a uniform civil code, Hindus, Muslims and other religious communities are still subject in many respects to their *personal law* . . . ." *Id.* n.9.
- "All members of a religious community, whether a majority or minority—Jews, Muslims, and members of different Christian communities in Israel; Muslims and Hindus in India—may be subject to a religion-based family law that is applied by religious courts. Like power sharing, a *personal law* can provide an important degree of autonomy and cohesion even for minorities that are territorially dispersed." Henry J. Steiner, *Ideals and Counter-Ideals in the Struggle over Autonomy Regimes for Minorities,* 66 Notre Dame L. Rev. 1539, 1542 (1991).

Though limited in Anglo-American law, the concept still applies to some degree: although American and English courts look chiefly to the law of the person's domicile, a person of full age and capacity may establish a desired personal law merely by choosing a given place—the place where that law is in effect—as a domicile.

personal property. For the historical basis for the distinction between *real property* and *personal property,* see **real.**

personal representative is a broad term for a person who, on another's death, collects the decedent's property, pays the debts, and distributes what is left among those entitled under a will or under the rules of succession on intestacy. The two types of personal representatives are *executors* and *administrators.* See **administrator.**

personalty (= personal property) is contrasted with *realty.* E.g., "*Personalty* is transferred, leased, hired, mortgaged, lent in very simple ways. As a rule it can be done by word of mouth. It is very different with *realty.*" Max Radin, *The Law and You* 124–25 (1948). The word should not be confused with *personality.*

personam, in. See **in personam.**

persona non grata; persona grata. The plural forms are *personae non gratae* and *personae gratae.* See PLURALS (A).

personation. See **impersonation.**

personnel may take either a singular or a plural verb, depending on whether it is intended as a COLLECTIVE NOUN.

persons. See **people.**

person . . . them; person . . . they. See CONCORD (B).

perspicuous; perspicacious. *Perspicuous* is to *perspicacious* as *intelligible* is to *intelligent. Perspicuous* may be defined etymologically as "see-through-it-ive-ness"; it means "clear; lucid; seen readily," and is applied to thought and expression. E.g., in the nominal form: "The former term indicates with tolerable *perspicuity* a right available in personam." *Perspicacious* = penetrating in thought; acutely discerning; keen; shrewd <a scholar as perspicacious as Charles Alan Wright>.

per stirpes. See **per capita (B) & stirpital.**

persuadable; persuadible; persuasible. The preferred form is *persuadable.* See -ABLE (A).

persuade; convince. One *persuades* another *to do* something, but one *convinces* or, archaically, *persuades* another *of* something. Either *persuade* or *convince* may be used with a *that*-phrase object, although *persuade that* occurs seldom outside law. American judges seem addicted to the expression. E.g., "If the statutory language were not enough to *persuade* us *that* the Secretary's interpretation is incorrect, these limitless consequences would certainly give us pause."/ "We are *persuaded that* the indemnity provision clearly encompasses negligence of the indemnitee and losses arising from strict liability." See **convince.**

persuadible; persuasible. See **persuadable.**

persuasive burden. See **burden of proof (A).**

persuasive precedent. See **precedent (B).**

pertain. See **appertain.**

pertinence; pertinency. The first is now the usual and preferred form—e.g.: "I concede that a testator cannot prescribe in his will that an act to be performed by him, indifferent in itself and having no *pertinency* [read *pertinence*] except its effect on his testamentary dispositions, shall change such dispositions."/ "To appreciate the *pertinency* [read *pertinence*] of these statements, we may ask ourselves what the duty of counsel would have been had they been true." See **impertinence.**

pertinent part, in. See **in pertinent part.**

peruse means "to read with great care"; thus it should not be used merely as a fancy substitute for *read.* It is pronounced /pə-**rooz**/, and the noun *perusal* /pə-**rooz**-əl/.

petitio principii. See **begging the question.**

petition. For the misuse of this word for a similar-sounding word, see **partition.**

petitioner. See PARTY APPELLATIONS & **plaintiff.**

petit jury. A. And *petty jury.* The former is now the accepted spelling in AmE; the development is perhaps a favorable one, for nonlawyers are likely to read *petty* in its modern sense even though they are familiar with the phrase. (See **petty offense.**) A *petit jury* (= a trial jury) is contrasted with a *grand jury* (= the jury that decides whether to hand down an indictment or information). E.g., "It would, of course, be impossible to obtain a *petit jury* that reflects all the distinctive groups in a community."/ "The Supreme Court has stated that the systematic exclusion of persons based upon race from the grand jury pool, the *petit jury* pool, or the *petit jury* through the prosecutor's use of peremptory challenges, violates a defendant's equal protection rights guaranteed by the fourteenth amendment." Cf. **grand jury.**

In BrE, *petty jury* seems to be the predominant spelling—e.g.: "A prisoner who is indicted is tried by a *petty jury.*" O. Hood Phillips, *A First Book of English Law* 25 (3d ed. 1955).

B. Pronunciation. *Petit jury* should be pronounced in the same way as *petty jury.* But in some American jurisdictions—such as Texas, alas—the pronunciation /**pet**-it/ has taken hold. See HYPERCORRECTION (K).

petit larceny; petty larceny. The former is now the predominant spelling. See **larceny (C).**

petitory is an adjective used in reference to suits seeking to try title to real property or to a vessel, independently of possession. E.g., "Former Admiralty Rule 19 dealt with possessory and *petitory* actions."/ "Real actions were brought to recover lands, tenements, or hereditaments. They were of two classes, *petitory* and *possessory.* In *petitory* actions the controversy was concerning the property and right. In *possessory* actions the dispute was in relation only to the possession." Edwin E. Bryant, *The Law of Pleading Under the Codes of Civil Procedure* 4 (1899).

pettifogger; shyster. Both are contemptuous words for *lawyer,* but there is a difference, as explained here, rather magniloquently:

> The *pettifogger,* as a lawyer, is an unlearned, little, mean character, lacking in ability, sound judgment or good common sense, while the *shyster* may be possessed of much learning, great ability or an abundance of shrewdness and cunning, but he is a trickster and a dishonest schemer; he is a fomenter of litigation, strife and discord in the community; he is a manufacturer of evidence, a fosterer of perjury and a promoter of bribery; he is a cunning thief, who conceals his perfidy and rascality under the cloak of the law; he cunningly abuses the noble profession to which he has been admitted as a weapon of offense in deeds of unjust oppression, scheming knavery and the procurement of confidence and the repose of trust, which he basely abuses, when there is opportunity to profit by so doing.
>
> R. L. Harmon, addressing Alabama Bar Ass'n in 1897 (quoted in George W. Warvelle, *Essays in Legal Ethics* 69 (1902)).

Modern lawyers and judges use the term *pettifogger* with some frequency—e.g.: "Quite the contrary, counsel in that case were not *pettifoggers* . . . ." *Nebeker v. Piper Aircraft Corp.,* 747 P.2d 18, 38 (Idaho 1987). See LAWYERS, DEROGATORY NAMES FOR.

pettifoggery (= legal chicanery) is the noun corresponding to the agent noun *pettifogger,* q.v. E.g., "The opposition of Goodman and Dorsey to the motion to compel discovery was specious, replete with linguistic legerdemain, half truths and *pettifoggery.*" *In re Marriage of Lemen,* 170 Cal. Rptr. 642, 649 (Ct. App. 1980).

petty jury. See **petit jury.**

petty larceny. See **petit larceny.**

petty offense. In G.B., this phrase (spelled *petty offence* in BrE) has dropped from the criminal law because it was thought to minimize unduly a serious infraction of the law. In the U.S., some have wondered whether a *petty offense* is actually a crime. It is, despite the misleading terminology: a repealed federal statute provided that any misdemeanor "the penalty for which . . . does not exceed imprisonment for a period of six months or a fine of not more than $5,000, or both, is a *petty offense.*" 18 U.S.C. § 1(3) (1988). See **petit jury** (A).

phantasy. See **fantasy.**

phase for *faze* (= to disconcert) is an increasingly common blunder—e.g.: "The fact that the *Ohio* Supreme Court had ignored this slip and treated the tax as what, practically speaking, it was, didn't *phase* [read *faze*] the U.S. Supreme Court." Fred Rodell, *Woe Unto You, Lawyers!* 81 (1939; repr. 1980). In Rodell's case, the mistake was probably an editor's error; on page 134 of the same book appears a correct use: "[T]hat will not *faze* the law schools."

The mistake often appears in the form *unphased* (for *unfazed*)—e.g.: "NYCERS, apparently *unphased* [read *unfazed*] by the absence of any express legislative authority, maintains that it is nevertheless empowered to carve out substantial exclusions from the statutorily constituted membership class." *Doctors Council v. New York City Employees' Retirement Sys.,* 514 N.Y.S.2d 922, 933 (App. Div. 1987)./ "The people who are not dissuaded, however, are strongly attracted to the absence of constraints, and relatively *unphased* [read *unfazed*] by the absence of support." James M. Doyle, *"It's The Third World Down There!": The Colonialist Vocation and American Criminal Justice,* 27 Harv. C.R.-C.L. L. Rev. 71, 105 (1992)./ "*Unphased* [read *Unfazed*] by the absence of those critical terms, the court simply decided to superimpose 18 U.S.C. § 2's broad accomplice liability onto 21 U.S.C. § 848(e)(1)(B)." Brian Serr, *Of Crime and Punishment, Kingpins and Footsoldiers, Life and Death,* 25 Ariz. St. L.J. 895, 910 (1993).

Ph.D. (= Philosophical Doctor, Doctor of Philosophy) requires the internal period.

phenomena is a plural noun, *phenomenon* being the singular—e.g.: "The Supreme Court recently explained this *phenomena* [read *phenomenon*] in *Powers v. Ohio . . . .*" *People v. Boston,* 586 N.E.2d 326, 332 (Ill. App. Ct. 1991) (Johnson, J., dissenting). "The terminology for *this phenomena* [read *this phenomenon* or *these phenomena*] is 'mandates without funding.'" Montie Hasie, *School Boards Bearing Brunt of Taxpayers' Anger,* Amarillo News-Globe, 11 Oct. 1992, at 29A.

Philadelphia lawyer. In colonial America, Philadelphia was the center of legal, literary, and scientific endeavors. During that period, the phrase *Philadelphia lawyer* took on the meaning "a shrewd and learned lawyer." Why? One explanation is that the phrase resulted from Alexander Hamilton's successful defense of the New York printer John Peter Zenger against libel charges in 1735—a case that helped establish freedom of the press in the U.S. Observers are said to have noted that a *Philadelphia lawyer* got Zenger off. But the *OED* records no uses of the term until 1788, so the origin remains obscure.

Even today, though, the term is used in much the same way as it was in the late 18th century—e.g.: "[E]mployers say the rules are hopelessly complex and costly. 'A *Philadelphia lawyer* can't even figure these out,' says Kenneth Morrissey, FMC Corp. employee benefits manager." *Labor Letter,* Wall St. J., 11 Feb. 1992, at 1A. In other contexts, predictably, the phrase merely denotes a lawyer who hails from Philadelphia. What is difficult to say is what the phrase *connotes* in such a context. See LAWYERS, DEROGATORY NAMES FOR (A).

philosophical; philosophic. The latter is a NEEDLESS VARIANT.

PHRASAL ADJECTIVES. A. General Rule. When a phrase functions as an adjective—an increasingly frequent phenomenon in late-20th-century English—the phrase should ordinarily be hyphenated. Seemingly everyone in the literary world knows this except lawyers. For some unfathomable reason—perhaps because they are accustomed to slow, dull, heavy reading—lawyers resist these hyphens.

But professional editors regularly supply them, and rightly so. The primary reason for them is that they prevent MISCUES and make reading easier and faster. Thus:

affirmative-action policy
agency-enabling statute
breach-of-contract claims
child-support payments
civil-rights case
conspiracy-law dispute
federal-question case
good-faith exception
grand-jury probe
health-care provider
health-care-related issues
horse-and-buggy days
in-court testimony
paid-in capital
personal-injury lawyer
purchase-money mortgage
real-estate practice
stop-and-frisk procedures
subject-matter jurisdiction
third-degree assault
two-party check

When the reader encounters such a phrasal adjective, he or she is not misled into thinking momentarily that the modifying phrase is really a noun itself. (See MISCUES (D).) The following examples demonstrate the hesitation caused by a missing hyphen:

- "The *benefit of insurance and waiver of subrogation clauses* [read *benefit-of-insurance and waiver-of-subrogation clauses*] in the affreightment contracts are invalid because they conflict with the plaintiff's marine cargo insurance policy."
- "Merely because a *court made rule* [read *court-made rule*] has been in effect for many years does not render it invulnerable to judicial attack once it becomes obsolescent."
- "The applicable *one year statute of limitations* [read *one-year statute of limitations*] started to run from December 13, 1959."
- "Perhaps . . . it would have been possible to harmonize the *presumption of authority provisions* [read *presumption-of-authority provisions*] with the *duty to inquire provision* [read *duty-to-inquire provision*]." Grant Gilmore & Charles L. Black, Jr., *The Law of Admiralty* 674 (2d ed. 1975). (Elsewhere in their book, Gilmore and Black show better stylistic judgment—see (C).)
- "As the legal community and press became more interested in *comparative law firm economics* [read *comparative law-firm economics*], *public service* [read *public-service*] and *pro bono* [read *pro-bono*] representation decreased in importance." Paul J. Bschorr, *Challenges for the Decade,* Litig., Summer 1991, at 1, 1.

Hyphenating these phrasal adjectives also minimizes NOUN PLAGUE. For instance, *common law* is the noun phrase and *common-law* the adjectival phrase; when the phrase has no hyphen, the reader does not expect a noun to follow it.

One sees the pronounced improvement in readability especially when two compound adjectives modify one noun:

- common-law mirror-image rule
- long-latency occupational-disease cases
- 13-year-old court-ordered busing plan.

Following are examples in which enlightened legal writers supplied the necessary hyphens:

- "To the *law-of-nature school,* lawmaking was but an absolute development of absolute principles." Roscoe Pound, *An Introduction to the Philosophy of Law* 44 (1922).
- "[T]he main plea was that the entire *separate-but-equal doctrine* be discarded . . . ." Fred Rodell, *Nine Men* 323 (1955).
- "*Rank-and-file lawyers* were too untrained for Chitty." Lawrence M. Friedman, *A History of American Law* 146 (2d ed. 1985).
- "The petition . . . argues that the ruling 'took a major step away from settled law' in the First Amendment's *free-exercise-of-religion clause.*" Wall St. J., 11 May 1990, at B2.

When a compound modifier begins with an adverb that ends in *-ly,* the hyphen is dropped—e.g.: "This is the *legally-relevant* [read *legally relevant*] feature . . . ." Glanville Williams, *Criminal Law* 20 (2d ed. 1961)./ "With the *hotly-contested* [read *hotly contested*] Second Congressional District primary six days away, supporters of Sen. Bob Smith gathered last night . . . ." M.L. Elrick, *Kemp Coy on Plans for 1996,* Concord Monitor (N.H.), 8 Sept. 1994, at B1.

B. Phrasal Adjectives of Foreign Origin. A few phrasal adjectives, such as *bona fide, ex officio, mens rea, pro rata,* and *res ipsa loquitur*—in which the words generally have no English meaning when taken alone—are usually treated as exceptions to the rule of hyphenation.

Still, some writers grant them no exemption from hyphens—e.g.: "An entirely different approach to the problem of distinguishing preparation from attempt is suggested by the *res-ipsa-loquitur test.*" Peter W. Low et al., *Criminal Law: Cases and Materials* 134 (1982)./ "The origins of the common-law *mens-rea* requirement are obscure." *Id.* at 200./ "On one view, there is a *prima-*

facie duty of care . . . ." Rupert Cross & J.W. Harris, *Precedent in English Law* 45 (4th ed. 1991).

C. Snakelike Compounds. Instead of toying with snakelike compounds, writers are usually well advised to rework the sentence: "Each contract included *a waiver-of-all-rights-to-subrogation clause* [read *a clause waiving all rights to subrogation*]."/ "We found no merit in any other issue raised, *including an ineffective-assistance-of-counsel claim* [read *including a claim of ineffective assistance of counsel*]." Here is a particularly ugly specimen: "We are *law-of-the-case-bound* in this matter and thus cannot reconsider this contention." [Read *We are bound by law of the case and thus cannot reconsider this contention.*]

Some writers do use them, usually to create a jocular or self-mocking tone—e.g.: "For the political law of Holmes's time was, with a few . . . lapses and interludes, merely a more concentrated continuation of the *let-business-alone-and-let-it-run-the-country jurisprudence* that had come to full flower late in the preceding century." Fred Rodell, *Nine Men* 185 (1955)./ "The *no-lien-for-partial-execution-of-affreightment-contracts rule* of the Pacific Export case does have the merit of running both ways, as the so-called 'dead freight' cases show." Grant Gilmore & Charles L. Black, Jr., *The Law of Admiralty* 639 (2d ed. 1975).

Sometimes phrasal adjectives incorporate so many disparate elements that, when combined with the noun that follows, they have an effect similar to NOUN PLAGUE—e.g.: "A *child-sex-abuse defendant's* Sixth Amendment right to confront witnesses against him was violated . . . ." *Screening Defendant from Accuser Violates Confrontation Clause,* 57 U.S.L.W. 1003, 1003 (5 July 1988).

D. Suspension Hyphens. When two phrasal adjectives have a common element at the end, and this ending portion (usu. the last word) appears only with the second phrase, insert a suspension hyphen after the unattached words to show their relationship with the common element. The hyphens become especially important when the phrases are compounded in this way—e.g.: "The government argues that this designation is ineffective because it reflects a *ten-* rather than a *two-year* federal sentence."/ "A court faced with enforcing a *general-* or *public-interest* law, however, should give vent to its imagination, since such a law is designed to vest discretion in the judicial branch."

Here the hyphens are not supplied, to the reader's puzzlement: "The situs of this case is the small city of Apopka, Florida, located *in the fern and foliage growing region* [read *in the fern- and foliage-growing region*] north of Orlando."

For more on the use of hyphens, see PUNCTUATION (F).

E. Amount or Period of Time. With compound adjectives denoting periods of time and amounts, plurals should be dropped in the adjectival phrase. Hence, "The record is silent as to whether Annie Bell was born after a normal *nine months pregnancy* [read *nine-month pregnancy*]." Likewise, one should write *three-week hiatus, fourteen-hour-a-day schedule,* and *four-year decline.* The exception is with fractions <a two-thirds vote>.

F. Proper Noun. When a name is used attributively as a phrasal adjective, it ordinarily remains unhyphenated. E.g., "The *Terry Maher strategy* put immediate pressure on rival bookshop chains . . . ." Raymond Snoddy, *Book Price War Looms in Britain,* Financial Times, 28–29 Sept. 1991, at 1.

G. Phrasal Adjectives Following the Noun. When predicative, phrasal adjectives are not usually hyphenated: "This rule is *well worn,*" but "This is a *well-worn* rule." An exception is *short-lived,* which is always hyphenated.

H. Phrases with Only One Element Joined. When the first or second element in a phrasal adjective is compound, it too needs to be hyphenated: *post-cold-war norms,* not *post-cold war norms.* Otherwise, as in the example just quoted, *post* appears more closely related to *cold* than *war* does. E.g., "Palumbo wants a *Domesday book-style appraisal* [read *Domesday-book-style appraisal*] of all cultural buildings with a cash breakdown of the needed repairs." Geordie Grieg, *£1 Billion to Restore Britain's Heritage by AD 2000,* Sunday Times, 1 July 1990, at 1-1.

PHRASAL VERBS are verbs that are made up of more than one word, often a verb and a preposition. When using a phrasal verb, one must be certain to include the entire phrase and not just the primary verb. Thus statutes are *struck down,* not just *struck.* Likewise, contracts are *entered into,* not just *entered. Sue out,* q.v., means something different from *sue.* We must respect, then, the latter part of phrasal verbs as much as the earlier. *Prove up, make whole, hold over, hand down* or *out* (an opinion), *make payment for,* and *work out* (a settlement) are a few of the phrasal verbs common in law. Generally, writers should not be timid in using phrasal verbs; they are usually not substandard or even colloquial, unless the particle is unnecessary. (See PARTICLES, UNNECESSARY.) For a full collection of verbs of this kind, see G.W. Davidson, *Chambers Pocket Guide to Phrasal Verbs* (1982).

When one phrasal verb is part of a DOUBLET,

an AMBIGUITY may arise if an adverb occurs in the midst of the phrasal verb—e.g.: "In no case may a corporation purchase or make payment, *directly or indirectly,* for its own share when there is reasonable ground for believing that the corporation is insolvent." Does the phrase *directly or indirectly* apply to *purchase?* If so, read *purchase or make payment for, directly or indirectly.*

In the following specimen, the writer left the phrasal verb incomplete, apparently out of fear of using an unnecessary particle: "*Drawing* [read *Drawing on*] the principle that the acquisition of monopoly power is illegal only if not accomplished by legitimate means such as business acumen or historical accident, appellee observes that appellant's sole theory of exclusionary conduct is unsupported by the record." Cf. **strike.**

PHRASING refers to syntactic structures, their graceful logic or maladroit clumsiness. The writer should have some sense of how best to order the parts of a sentence, so that it will be logically, and preferably even elegantly, constructed. Many of the specific maladies of construction are discussed throughout this work. Hence this entry can do little more than exemplify some of the general problems and offer remedies—e.g.:

- "The plaintiff having conveyed away by deed, purporting to grant a fee simple interest in the lands in question, and having had them conveyed back to her, is now seized of a fee simple interest." This sentence can be greatly improved by repositioning the subject directly before the verb and by making the participial phrase an introductory one that leads into the main clause. [Read *Having purported to convey* (less redundant than *having conveyed away*) *a fee simple interest in the lands in question, and having had them conveyed back to her, the plaintiff is now seised* (the better spelling) *of a fee simple interest.*] See ANFRACTUOSITY.
- "The jury made a special finding that the defendant, in firing the bomb, exercised reasonable care." This sounds as if the bomb was fired *in order to pursue such care!* [Read *The jury made a special finding that the defendant exercised reasonable care in firing the bomb.*]
- "Clearly, if the policy was to be preserved some means was needed adapted to the new types of interest made possible by new methods of transforming ownership." [Read *If the policy was to be preserved, what was needed was some means adapted to the types of interest made possible by novel methods of conveyancing.*]
- "In the case of a vested remainder, there is a person in being ascertained and ready to take, has a present right of future enjoyment." This is downright ungrammatical. [Read . . . *there is a person in being, ascertained and ready to take, who* . . . .]
- "The Erie had contended that application of the Pennsylvania rule was required, among other things, by section 34 of the Federal Judiciary Act of September 24, 1789 . . . ." *Erie R.R. v. Tompkins,* 304 U.S. 64, 71 (1938). This phrasing suggests that the Pennsylvania rule was not just required, but mandated, demanded, necessitated ("among other things"). [Read *The Erie had contended that application of the Pennsylvania rule was required by, among other things, section 34* . . . .]

P.I., in lawyers' slang, refers to "personal-injury law." E.g., "Tingey finally quit Galane's firm in frustration over his mentor's refusal to take the steady, well-paying personal injury (PI) cases that would have amply subsidized Galane's other legal work." John A. Jenkins, *The Litigators* 18 (1989). This initialism is best written with periods after each letter. See ACRONYMS AND INITIALISMS.

picaresque; picturesque. These words are quite different. *Picaresque* = roguish. *Picturesque* = fit to be the subject of a picture; strikingly graphic.

picnic, v.i., makes *picnicking* and *picnicked.* Cf. **panic & mimic.**

picturesque. See **picaresque.**

piece of (one's) mind. See **peace of mind.**

piercing the corporate veil; lifting the corporate veil. The former is the AmE phrase, the latter the BrE phrase, meaning "the act of disregarding the veil of incorporation that separates the property of a corporation from the property of its security holders."

Sometimes *pierce* is used in extended, elliptical senses, as here: "Were a corporation to attempt to perpetrate a fraud on the court by improperly creating or destroying diversity jurisdiction, we would not elevate form over substance but would accomplish whatever *piercing* and adjustments were considered necessary to protect the court's jurisdiction." (The *piercing* referred to apparently would entail judicial directives or sanctions against corporate officials—in effect, the court would disregard the veil of incorporation.)

pinpoint citation; jump citation; dictum page. The first is the most usual of these synonymous phrases, which denote the page on which a quotation or relevant passage appears, as opposed to the page on which a case or article begins. For example, in the following citation, the number 595 denotes the pinpoint citation: *Groh v. Brooks,* 421 F.2d 589, 595 (3d Cir. 1970). Sometimes, the pinpoint citation coincides with the first page of the case or article cited, as here: *Groh v. Brooks,* 421 F.2d 589, 589 syl. 1 (3d Cir. 1970).

Today, *jump citation* is nearly as common as *pinpoint citation.* But *dictum page* appears to be obsolescent; it was used in the *Bluebook* in the 1950s but has long since been abandoned, perhaps because it misleadingly suggests that the quoted matter is dictum as opposed to the holding of the court. See **dictum.**

pique ([1] to irritate; or [2] to excite or arouse) is sometimes confused with *peak.* The proper phrase is *to pique someone's interest*—e.g.: "This court has held that statements designed to gain the trust and assurance of co-conspirators, to provide incentives for negotiations and to *peak* [read *pique*] interest are also in furtherance of a conspiracy." *U.S. v. Blakeney,* 942 F.2d 1001, 1020–21 (6th Cir. 1991).

For still another misuse, see **peak.**

pitiable; pitiful; piteous; pitiless. *Pitiable* = calling for or arousing pity. E.g., "The vast majority of criminals who come into the dock at Assizes or Sessions are *pitiable* creatures, a nuisance rather than a danger to the state." Patrick Devlin, *The Criminal Prosecution in England* 112 (1960)./ "[T]he fiction always seems *pitiably* obvious and naïve—in retrospect." Lon L. Fuller, *Legal Fictions* 93 (1967).

Pitiful, strictly, means "feeling pity," but in modern speech and writing it is almost always used in the sense "contemptible." The word *piteous* "had become misused as a form of *pitiable* as early as Shakespeare's time: for him hearts could be *piteous* in the active sense and corpses in the passive." Ivor Brown, *I Give You My Word & Say the Word* 235 (1964). Today *piteous* is archaic and poetic—not a word for ordinary uses. *Pitiless* = showing no pity.

PLACE-NAMES AS ADJECTIVES. See ADJECTIVES (F).

place where. This phrase is perfectly idiomatic. There is no good reason to insist on *place that.* Cf. **time when & reason why.**

plagiarize is often misspelled *plagarize* or *plagerize.*

plain, it is. See **clearly.**

PLAIN LANGUAGE. A. Generally. Albert Einstein once said that his goal in stating an idea was to make it as simple as possible but no simpler. If lawyers everywhere adopted this goal, the world would probably change in dramatic ways.

But there is little reason for hope when so many legal writers seem to believe that to seem good or competent or smart, their ideas must be stated in the most complex manner possible. Of course, this problem plagues many fields of intellectual endeavor, as the philosopher Bertrand Russell noted:

> I am allowed to use plain English because everybody knows that I could use mathematical logic if I chose. Take the statement: 'Some people marry their deceased wives' sisters.' I can express this in language [that] only becomes intelligible after years of study, and this gives me freedom. I suggest to young professors that their first work should be written in a jargon only to be understood by the erudite few. With that behind them, they can ever after say what they have to say in a language 'understanded of the people.' In these days, when our very lives are at the mercy of the professors, I cannot but think that they would deserve our gratitude if they adopted my advice.
>
> Bertrand Russell, "How I Write," in *The Basic Writings of Bertrand Russell* 63, 65 (Robert E. Egner & Lester E. Denonn eds., 1961).

But the professors have not heeded Russell's advice. Since Russell wrote that essay in the mid-1950s, things have gotten much worse in fields such as biology, linguistics, literary criticism, political science, psychology, and sociology. And they have gotten worse in law.

Consider the following statutory provision, a 272-word tangle that is as difficult to fathom as any algebraic theorem:

> 57AF(11) Where, but for this sub-section, this section would, by virtue of the preceding provisions of this section, have in relation to a relevant year of income as if, for the reference in sub-section (3) to $18,000 there were substituted a reference to another amount, being an amount that consists of a number of whole dollars and a number of cents (in this sub-section referred to as the 'relevant number of cents')—
> (a) in the case where the relevant number of cents is less than 50—the other amount shall be reduced by the relevant number of cents:
> (b) in any case—the other amount shall be increased by the amount by which the relevant number of cents is less than $1.
>
> (12) where, but for sub-section (5), this section would, by virtue of the preceding provisions of this section, have effect in relation to a relevant year of income as if, for the reference in sub-section (3) to $18,000, there were substituted a reference to another amount, being an amount that consists of a number of whole dollars and a number of cents (in this sub-section referred to as the 'relevant number of cents') then, for the purposes of the application of paragraph 4(b)—
> (a) in a case where the relevant number of cents is less

> than 50—the other amount shall be reduced by the relevant number of cents; or
> (b) in any case—the other amount shall be increased by the amount by which the relevant number of cents is less than $1.
>
> Income Tax Assessment Act [Australia] § 57AF(11), (12) (as quoted in David St. L. Kelly, "Plain English in Legislation," in *Essays on Legislative Drafting* 57, 58 (David St. L. Kelly ed. 1988)).

That is the type of DRAFTING that prompts an oft-repeated criticism: "So unintelligible is the phraseology of some statutes that suggestions have been made that draftsmen, like the Delphic Oracle, sometimes aim deliberately at obscurity . . . ." Carleton K. Allen, *Law in the Making* 486 (7th ed. 1964).

With some hard work, the all-but-inscrutable passage above can be transformed into a straightforward version of only 65 words:

> If either of the following amounts is not in whole dollars, the amount must be rounded up or down to the nearest dollar (or rounded up if the amount ends with 50 cents):
> (a) the amount of the motor-vehicle-depreciation limit; or
> (b) the amount that would have been the motor-vehicle-depreciation limit if the amount had equaled or exceeded $18,000.
>
> Revision based on that of Gavin Peck (quoted in Kelly, *supra* at 59).

Few would doubt that the original statute is unplain and that the revision is comparatively plain. True, the revision requires the reader to understand what a "motor-vehicle-depreciation limit" is, but some things can be stated only so simply.

When it comes to the legislative jungle of the tax code, as Justice Robert H. Jackson once wrote, "It can never be made simple, but we can try to avoid making it needlessly complex." *Dobson v. C.I.R.,* 320 U.S. 489, 495 (1943).

Still, some might protest that, after all, the law is a learned profession. Some seem to find an insult in the suggestion that lawyers should avoid complex verbiage. They want to express themselves in more sophisticated ways than nonprofessionals do.

Their objection needs a serious answer because it presents the most serious impediment to the plain-language movement. There are essentially four answers.

First, those who write in a difficult, laborious style risk being unclear not only to other readers but also to themselves. When you write obscurely, you're less likely to be thinking clearly. And you're less likely to appreciate the problems that are buried under such involuted prose. For the private practitioner, this could increase the possibility of malpractice.

Second, obscure writing wastes readers' time—a great deal of it, when the sum is totaled. An Australian study conducted in the 1980s found that lawyers and judges take twice as long deciphering legalistically worded statutes as they do plain-language revisions. Law Reform Comm'n of Victoria, *Plain English & the Law* 61–62 (1987).

Third, simplifying is a higher intellectual attainment than complexifying. Writing simply and directly is hard work, but a learned profession ought not to shrink from the challenge. In fact, the hallmark of all the greatest legal stylists is precisely that they take difficult ideas and express them as simply as possible. No nonprofessional could do it, and most lawyers can't do it. Only extraordinary minds are capable of the task. Still, every lawyer—brilliant or not—can aim at the mark.

Fourth, the very idea of professionalism demands that we not conspire against nonlawyers by adopting a style that makes our writing seem like a suffocating fog. Unless lawyers do the right thing and reform from within, outside forces may well cause a revolution that will marginalize the legal profession. See LEGALESE, LEGALISMS AND LAWYERISMS & OBSCURITY.

B. Definitions. "Plain language," generally speaking, is "the idiomatic and grammatical use of language that most effectively presents ideas to the reader." Garner, *The Elements of Legal Style* 7 (1991). Some have tried to reduce "plain language" to a mathematical formula, but any such attempt is doomed to failure. And that is no indictment of the idea: "[I]t is no criticism that Plain English cannot be precisely, mathematically defined. Neither can 'reasonable doubt' or 'good cause.' Like so many legal terms, it is inherently and appropriately vague." Joseph Kimble, *Plain English: A Charter for Clear Writing,* 9 Thomas M. Cooley L. Rev. 1, 14 (1992).

The fundamental principle is that anything translatable into simpler words in the same language is bad style. That may sound like a facile oversimplification that fails when put into practice—but it isn't and it doesn't.

C. An Old Idea. Of course, legal discourse has long been ridiculed for its incomprehensibility. Jonathan Swift skewered LEGALESE when he wrote of a society of lawyers who spoke in "a peculiar cant and jargon of their own, that no other mortal can understand." *Gulliver's Travels* 154 (1726; repr. 1952).

What is less well known than the ridicule is that good legal writers have long advocated a plain-language style. In the mid-19th century, for example, the leading authority on legislative drafting said that most legal documents can be written in "the common popular structure of plain English." George Coode, *On Legislative Expres-*

sion XXX (1842). A generation later, an English lawyer explained that good drafting "says in the plainest language, with the simplest, fewest, and fittest words, precisely what it means." J.G. Mackay, *Introduction to an Essay on the Art of Legal Composition Commonly Called Drafting,* 3 Law Q. Rev. 326, 326 (1887). Other writers could be cited, decade by decade, up to the present day. In short, there is nothing new about the idea.

D. Plain-Language Principles. "No lawyer can now safely navigate," writes a well-known law professor, "without knowing the problems of legalese and the principles of plain English." Robert W. Benson, *The End of Legalese,* 13 N.Y.U. Rev. Law & Soc. Change 519, 573 (1984–1985). Experienced editors have arrived at these plain-language principles through induction—through carrying out the principles again and again. Once you have revised hundreds of legal documents for the purposes of clarifying and simplifying, you can fairly accurately predict what problems the next document might hold in store.

Of these principles, perhaps the most important is to reject the MYTH OF PRECISION. Traditionally, lawyers have aimed for a type of "precision" that results in cumbersome writing, with many long sentences collapsing under the weight of obscure qualifications. That "precision" is often illusory for two reasons: (a) ambiguity routinely lurks within traditional, legalistic language; and (b) when words proliferate, ambiguities tend to as well.

Of course, where clarity and precision are truly at loggerheads, precision must usually prevail. But the instances of actual conflict are much rarer than lawyers often suppose. Precision is not sacrificed when the drafter uses technical words where necessary and avoids JARGON that serves no substantive purpose. As one commentator puts it, "[W]hat is often called 'legal phraseology' is no more than inept writing or the unnecessary use of obscure or entangled phrases." Samuel A. Goldberg, "Hints on Draftsmanship," in *Drafting Contracts and Commercial Instruments* 7, 8 (Research and Documentation Corp. ed., 1971).

As a rule, whether one is drafting legislation, contracts, or other documents, clarity is just as important as precision. In fact, clarity helps ensure precision because the drafter with an obscure style finds it less easy to warrant what the draft itself says.

The main work of the legislative drafter is "to state the law in a form clearer and more convenient than that in which it has hitherto existed, and that is a task for experts . . . ." J.L. Brierly, *The Law of Nations* 80 (5th ed. 1955). Of course, some influences leading to complexity cannot be overcome; among these are the difficulty of the subject matter itself and the fact that a final draft may reflect a compromise between different points of view. But, with hard work, other obscurantist influences—the ones that are linguistically based—can be overcome: long-windedness, needless jargon, and inconsistent style resulting from collaborative efforts.

The chief guidelines are as follows:

1. Achieve a reasonable average sentence length. Strive for an average sentence length of 20 words—and, in any event, ensure that you are below 30 words. Doing this involves following a maxim that, unfortunately, makes some legal drafters unnecessarily nervous: "[I]f you want to make a statement with a great many qualifications, put some of the qualifications in separate sentences." Bertrand Russell, "How I Write," in *The Basic Writings of Bertrand Russell* 63, 65 (Robert E. Egner & Lester E. Denonn eds., 1961). See SENTENCE LENGTH.
2. Prefer short words to long ones, simple to fancy. Minimize jargon and technical terms so that you achieve a straightforward style that nonlawyers as well as lawyers can understand. This means rejecting LEGALISMS such as *pursuant to* (under, in accordance with), *prior to* (before), *subsequent to* (after), *vel non* (or not, or the lack of it).
3. Avoid double and triple negatives. No reader wants to wrestle with a sentence like this one: "The investments need not be revalued at intervals of not more than two years if the trustee and the beneficiaries do not disagree." [Read: *If the trustee and beneficiaries agree, the investments need not be revalued every two years.*] See NEGATIVES (A).
4. Prefer the active voice. *Notice must be given* compares poorly with *The tenant must give notice* because (a) the first version does not spell out who must give notice, and (b) readers take in a sentence more easily if it meets their expectation of a subject-verb-object structure. See PASSIVE VOICE.
5. Keep related words together. In well-constructed sentences, related words go together—especially subject and verb, verb and object. See PHRASING.
6. Break up the text with headings. Headings and subheadings make the structure of a document overt, allowing readers to find their way around the document quickly and easily. See DOCUMENT DESIGN (C).
7. Use parallel structures for enumerations. See PARALLELISM, ENUMERATIONS & DOCUMENT DESIGN (F), (G).
8. Avoid excessive cross-references. The writer

who becomes zealous about cross-referencing usually creates linguistic mazes. The problem is that readers are asked to hold in mind the contents of several different provisions simultaneously. For a choice example, see WOOLLINESS.

9. Avoid overdefining. Although definitions are sometimes helpful, legal drafters grossly overuse them. Whenever you send the reader elsewhere in a legal document to understand what you're saying in a given provision, you impede understanding. And many drafters "pass the buck" in this way repeatedly for a single term, by using cross-references in definitions. See—if you like, but this is not intended as a pass-the-buck cross-reference—DEFINITIONS (A).
10. Use recitals and purpose clauses. In contracts, recitals help the reader understand what the drafter hopes to accomplish; in legislation, purpose clauses serve this function. Except in the simplest drafting projects—such as straightforward buy-sell agreements—you should generally presume that these orienting devices are necessary. And even simple documents should have descriptive titles (not *Agreement,* but *Agreement Restricting Stock Transfers*).

Finally, to gauge how effectively the principles are carried out, plain-language advocates recommend that certain documents be tested on typical readers. For documents that go out by the thousands and hundreds of thousands (like government forms) and for major legislation, time spent in testing at the front end can save enormous amounts of time and money in the long run.

E. Efforts to Use Plain Language. Since the 1970s, most American states have passed some type of plain-language legislation, and several federal statutes exist as well. See Joseph Kimble, *Plain English: A Charter for Clear Writing,* 9 Thomas M. Cooley L. Rev. 1, 31–35 (1992). Statutes of this type have not caused the problems that skeptics once warned of—unworkable standards, fatal ambiguities, decline in the quality of drafting. In fact, an empirical study would probably confirm precisely the opposite effects.

In addition to plain-language legislation, lawyers in many English-speaking jurisdictions have formed commissions and committees to promote plain language. In the U.S., for example, the State Bar of Michigan formed such a committee in 1979 and the State Bar of Texas in 1990; other state bar associations have begun to follow suit. In Australia, the Centre for Plain Legal Language has done much to promote the movement. In British Columbia, the Plain Language Institute thrived for a time and produced much good literature before being disbanded in 1993 for lack of governmental funding; other Canadian groups soon took up the slack. In England, the Plain English Campaign—a grassroots consumer organization—has met with considerable success. England is also the home of Clarity, an international organization that studies and promotes plain language in law. All these efforts have depended primarily on the determination of specific individuals.

Their opponents—the naysayers—have an increasingly difficult time as more and more excellent work is published in the field of plain language. For example, in 1994 Martin Cutts, an English writing consultant, redesigned and rewrote an act of Parliament: the Timeshare Act 1992. In doing so, he convincingly showed what immense improvements are possible in legislative drafting if only the official drafters approached their task with a greater command of plain-language principles. See Martin Cutts, *Lucid Law* (1994). The enduring problem—here as elsewhere—is whether reform can take place while the old guard remains in place.

In some places, though, official and semi-official bodies are changing standard forms. For example, the English Law Society's 1990 and 1992 editions of the Standard Conditions of Sale use "language that is as direct as the subject-matter allows, sentences that are relatively short and jargon-free, and a layout that is clear." Peter Butt, *Plain Language and Conveyancing,* Conveyancer & Property Lawyer, July–August 1993, at 256, 258. Similarly, in 1992 the Law Society of New South Wales issued a "plainer" form of contract for the sale of land—"plainer" than its predecessor, though not yet quite "plain." *Id.* In the early 1990s, the Real Estate Forms Committee of the State Bar of Texas issued plain-language forms for deeds, deeds of trust, leases, and other forms. These are but a few examples.

For a challenging but partly tongue-in-cheek approach to a legislative mandate for plain language, see David C. Elliott, *A Model Plain-Language Act,* 3 Scribes J. Legal Writing 51 (1992).

F. The Trouble with the Word "Plain." It is unfortunate that the SET PHRASES *plain language* and *plain English* contain the word *plain.* For that word, to many speakers of English, suggests the idea of "drab and ugly." But plain language is not drab: it is powerful and often beautiful. It is the language of the King James Version of the Bible, and it has a long literary tradition in the so-called Attic style of writing. See Garner, *The Elements of Legal Style* 7–15 (1991).

Despite the unfortunate associations that the

word *plain* carries, it has become established and is without a serious competitor. As a result, plain-language advocates must continually explain what they mean by "plain" language—or else critics and doubters will misunderstand it.

G. Prospects. We can point to significant progress in this area, but it remains sporadic. In the end, E.B. White may have been prescient: "I honestly worry about lawyers. They never write plain English themselves, and when you give them a bit of plain English to read, they say, 'Don't worry, it doesn't mean anything.'" E.B. White (as quoted in Thomas L. Shaffer, *The Planning and Drafting of Wills and Trusts* 149 (2d ed. 1979)).

There are those who say that "lawyers spend half their time trying to understand what other lawyers wrote; and the other half of their days writing things that other lawyers spend half their time trying to understand." Samuel A. Goldberg, "Hints on Draftsmanship," in *Drafting Contracts and Commercial Instruments* 7, 10 (Research & Documentation Corp. ed., 1971). That cynical view holds true only when poor writing becomes pervasive; and, alas, there is some truth in it today.

Beyond the mere inconveniences of obscurity, however, people actually suffer from it. Not least among the sufferers are judges who must try to make sense out of nonsense. But the vexation that judges feel pales in comparison with the economic and emotional suffering that clients often experience.

It is hardly an overstatement to say that plain-language reform is among the most important issues confronting the legal profession. And until this reform occurs, the profession will continue to have a badly tarnished image—no matter how many other altruistic endeavors it carries out. If we want the respect of the public, we must learn to communicate simply and directly.

H. A Plain-Language Library. Those wishing to consult further sources in the field may find the following books helpful:

- Mark Adler, *Clarity for Lawyers: The Use of Plain English in Legal Writing* (1990).
- Robert D. Eagleson, *Writing in Plain English* (1990).
- Carl Felsenfeld & Alan Siegel, *Writing Contracts in Plain English* (1981).
- Rudolf Flesch, *The Art of Plain Talk* (1951; repr. 1978).
- Rudolf Flesch, *The Art of Readable Writing* (1949).
- Rudolf Flesch, *How to Write Plain English: A Book for Lawyers and Consumers* (1979).
- Ernest Gowers, *The Complete Plain Words* (Sidney Greenbaum & Janet Whitcut eds., 3d ed. 1986).
- Robert Gunning, *The Technique of Clear Writing* (rev. ed. 1968).
- *How Plain English Works for Business: Twelve Case Studies* (U.S. Dep't of Commerce, Office of Consumer Affairs, 1984).
- Richard Lauchman, *Plain Style: Techniques for Simple, Concise, Emphatic Business Writing* (1993).
- *Plain English and the Law* (Law Reform Commission of Australia, Report No. 9, 1990).
- *Plain Language: Principles and Practice* (Erwin R. Steinberg ed., 1991).
- *The Plain English Story* (Plain English Campaign, rev. ed. 1993).
- Richard Wincor, *Contracts in Plain English* (1976).
- Richard Wydick, *Plain English for Lawyers* (3d ed. 1994).

plainly. See **clearly & obviously.**

plaint = a written statement of a cause of action, used to bring suit in a county court in England. Following is a 19th-century example of this term as still used in England: "The defendant refused to deliver them up, and the plaintiff consequently brought a *plaint* . . . to recover the notes." *Bridges v. Hawkesworth,* (1851) 21 L.J.Q.B. 75, 76.

The term is used in AmE only in nonlegal senses—e.g.: "I already hear the querulous *plaint* that questions dealt with in this opinion have not been raised in the court below or in the briefs on appeal."

plaintiff; complainant; demandant; objectant; exceptor. *Plaintiff* = the party who brings suit in a court of law. This party may have other special names, depending on the jurisdiction and the cause of action asserted. (See, e.g., **pursuer.**) *Complainant* is used in even more general senses of any party who brings a complaint. *Demandant* = one who makes a demand or claim, usu. a creditor.

The remaining terms are quite distinct from the others. *Objectant* = one who objects. *Exceptor* = one who objects or takes exception. See **exceptor & objectant.**

plaintiff, defendant; petitioner, respondent; appellant, appellee. A. Capitalizing. The American lawyer's conventions are generally as follows. To refer to a party in the present case, write: "Wisely, *Plaintiff* has chosen . . . ." It is generally better, of course, to use the party's real name. (See PARTY APPELLATIONS.) To refer to a party in some other (usu. reported) case, write: "In *Jones v. Smith, the plaintiff* . . . ."

B. Articles before. It is often useful in legal writing to omit *the, a,* or *an* before *Plaintiff* and other designations of parties in the present dispute, for cutting even such slight words can lead to leaner, more readable sentences.

Still, omission of articles can cause problems where two party denominations are proximate: "The motion preserves no error because it fails to specify which plaintiff defendant contends failed to prove a prima facie case." Inserting *the* before *defendant* removes the impediment to reading. See ARTICLES (A).

C. Relative Pronouns with. Though personal relative pronouns (i.e., *who* and *whom*) are normally used with these denominations, when *plaintiff,* etc., is a company, corporation, or entity other than an individual or a set of easily identifiable individuals, then *which* is correct in nonrestrictive clauses. The restrictive relative pronoun *that,* of course, may be used with either persons or companies. See PARTY APPELLATIONS & RESTRICTIVE AND NONRESTRICTIVE CLAUSES (A).

plaintiff in error; defendant in error. In some jurisdictions, the first is an equivalent of *appellant* or *petitioner,* the latter an equivalent of *appellee* or *respondent,* when the appeal is by writ of error. E.g., "The railway company and Mercer each filed an application for a writ of error and each application was granted, from which it results that in this court each party is both *plaintiff in error* and *defendant in error.*" See **error (A).**

plaintiff's lawyer; plaintiffs' lawyer; plaintiff lawyer. For one who regularly represents plaintiffs—in the U.S., usu. on contingent fees—the predominant form is *plaintiff's lawyer.* But *plaintiffs' lawyer* might be better for this purpose, since the singular possessive (*plaintiff's lawyer*) is often used in reference merely to one who represents a plaintiff in a particular action.

Plaintiff lawyer misleadingly suggests one who is a party to a lawsuit, as opposed to the one handling the lawsuit. E.g., "[S]anctions were sought in some 700 federal cases and granted in just over half. It's usually the *plaintiff lawyer* [read *plaintiff's lawyer*] who's fined." L. Gordon Crovitz, *Lawyers Make Frivolous Arguments at Their Own Risk,* Wall St. J., 20 June 1990, at A17.

plaintive was for centuries used interchangeably with *plaintiff* in legal prose. But now the sense "being or pertaining to the plaintiff in a suit" (*OED*) is an ARCHAISM, probably obsolete. The sole current meaning of *plaintive* is as an adjective: "sorrowful; mournful."

playwrighting; playwriting. The second is a corrupt form of the first. E.g., "[P]oets and *playwrites* [read *playwrights*] often use different meter and rhyme schemes when dealing with different characters." Paul T. Wangerin, *Skills Training in "Legal Analysis,"* 40 U. Miami L. Rev. 409, 438 (1986). For a similar error, see **copywrite.**

plea; pleading, n. A *plea* is now given only in criminal cases, although at common law a defendant's answer to the plaintiff's complaint was termed a *plea.* In U.S. federal courts today, the only criminal pleas are *guilty, not guilty,* and *nolo contendere.* A *pleading* is the complaint or answer in a civil case, or the criminal indictment and the answer in a criminal case.

plea bargain, n.; **plea-bargain,** v.i. As a noun, the phrase means "an agreement between the prosecution and the defense in a criminal case to allow the defendant to plead guilty or testify against others in return for a reduced charge or some other prosecutorial concession." The phrase dates only from the 1960s—e.g.: "This is not the usual case of an asserted *plea bargain* . . . ." *People v. Bannan,* 110 N.W.2d 673, 675 (Mich. 1961). The noun phrase *plea bargaining* is slightly older, dating from the 1950s.

As an intransitive verb, *plea-bargain* (hyphenated) means "to make a plea bargain."

plead. A. Sense. *Plead* does not ordinarily mean, as some nonlawyers think, "to argue a case in court." Eric Partridge amended his note on *lawyer* in *Usage and Abusage* by quoting a British lawyer who corrected Partridge's "layman's misusages" as follows: "A barrister does not *'plead'* in Court. He argues a case in Court, or—colloquially—*does* a case in Court. Pleadings are the written documents preparatory to a case, e.g., Statement of Claim, Defence in a civil action, Petition or Answer in divorce." *Usage and Abusage* 379 (1973). See **pleaded.**

B. Loose Usage with Objective Complement. In AmE, criminal lawyers increasingly say that they will *plead a client guilty.* Hence: "I had made a deal with the District Attorney's office to *plead him guilty* for four years in the State penitentiary for all cases." Aubrey Holmes, *The Wake of a Lawyer* 43 (1960)./ "Defendant contends, therefore, that in so doing defense counsel effectively *pleaded defendant guilty* to first-degree murder." *People v. Clark,* 565 N.E.2d 1373, 1380 (Ill. App. Ct. 1991).

Instead of this slipshod use of *plead,* the better phrasing in the sentences above would have been *have my client plead guilty* and *pleaded guilty on defendant's behalf.*

pleaded; pled; plead. Traditionally speaking, *pleaded* is the best past-tense and past-participial form. Commentators on usage have long said so, pouring drops of vitriol onto *has pled* and *has plead:*

- "Say, 'He *pleaded* guilty' (not *'pled'* or *'plead'*)." Sherwin Cody, *Dictionary of Errors* 118 (1905).
- "Careful speakers use *pleaded.*" Frank H. Vizetelly, *A Desk-Book of Errors in English* 167 (1906).
- "The past tense is *pleaded.* The use of *pled* or *plead* is colloquial." C.O. Sylvester Mawson, *Style-Book for Writers and Editors* 178 (1926).
- "These past tense forms [*plead* and *pled*] are by some authorities condemned as entirely incorrect, and by others classified as colloquial. The correct past tense of *plead* is *pleaded,* as 'He pleaded illness as an excuse.'" Maurice H. Weseen, *Crowell's Dictionary of English Grammar and Handbook of American Usage* 470 (1928).
- "The surely correct forms of the verb *to plead* in the past tense and past participle are *pleaded, has pleaded.* Colloquially, *plead* and *pled* are used as the past tense." Clarence Stratton, *Handbook of English* 245 (1940).
- "*Pleaded* is the approved past tense of *plead.* THUS: *He pleaded* (not 'pled' or 'plead') *not guilty.*" Alexander M. Witherspoon, *Common Errors in English and How to Avoid Them* 135 (1943).

The problem with these strong pronouncements, of course, is that *pled* and *plead* have gained some standing in AmE, as the Evanses noted in mid-century: "In the United States *pleaded* and *pled* are both acceptable for the past tense and for the participle. In Great Britain only the form *pleaded* is used and *pled* is considered an Americanism." Bergen Evans & Cornelia Evans, *A Dictionary of Contemporary American Usage* 372 (1957). The variant forms might not be the best usage, but neither can they be condemned as horrible.

Nevertheless, *pleaded* is the predominant form in both AmE and BrE—e.g.:

- "Elsewhere, it is generally required that the mitigating circumstances be *pleaded.*" Edwin E. Bryant, *The Law of Pleading Under the Codes of Civil Procedure* 248 (1899).
- "Contentions of law do not have to be *pleaded.*" Patrick Devlin, *The Judge* 56 (1979).
- "No case was to be *pleaded* at Superior Court for less than a three pound fee . . . ." Lawrence M. Friedman, *A History of American Law* 100–01 (2d ed. 1985).
- "Harding *pleaded* guilty to a conspiracy charge in the attack on Olympic silver medalist Nancy Kerrigan and resigned from the U.S. Figure Skating Association." Bob Baum, *Harding Pleads Guilty,* San Diego Union-Tribune, 17 March 1994, at A1.

The spelling *plead* as a past tense (for *pled*) appeared in the 18th century, apparently on the analogy of *read* > *read.* (Cf. **lead.**) E.g., "The legal proposition *plead* [read *pleaded*] by plaintiff is unpersuasive." One problem with this form is that many readers will suffer a MISCUE by seeing *plead* at first as a present-tense verb.

The other variant form, *pled,* dates from the 16th century. It is nearly obsolete in BrE except as a dialectal word. Nor is it considered quite standard in AmE, although it is a common variant in legal usage—e.g.: "In the second count of their petition, they *pled* [read *pleaded*] their title specially." *Jensen v. Wilkinson,* 133 S.W.2d 982, 983 (Tex. Civ. App.—Galveston 1939)./ "Defendant *pled* [read *pleaded*] guilty to the lesser offense . . . ." *State v. Carlberg,* 375 N.W.2d 275, 277 (Iowa Ct. App. 1985).

pleader; pleador. Only the former is correct.

plead guilty to is sometimes misrendered *plead guilty of,* which is really just a confusion of two legal idioms: one pleads *to* a charge but is guilty *of* a crime. E.g., "Mr. Krikava's wife, Carol, and son, Kevin, pleaded guilty *of* [read *to*] perjury and received only probation, since the guidelines allow leniency for defendants who plead guilty." Dirk Johnson, *A Farmer, 70, Saw No Choice; Nor Did the Sentencing Judge,* N.Y. Times, 20 July 1994, at A1, A9.

pleading. A. Senses. *Pleading* = (1) the art of preparing formal written statements in lawsuits; (2) a document containing the written allegations of fact that each party is required to communicate to the opponent before trial, so that each will know what contentions must be met by the evidence; or (3) oral advocacy of a case in court. Sense (3) is found more frequently in nonlawyers' writing than in lawyers'—unless one goes back to the 14th century, when pleadings were oral.

B. And *court paper*. In sense (2), *pleading* should be distinguished from *court paper,* which is a broader term. Motions, briefs, and affidavits are *court papers,* not *pleadings.* Examples of pleadings are complaints, petitions, counterclaims, and answers. A late-19th-century writer's explanation shows that this usage is time-honored: "*Pleadings* are the formal allegations of the parties of their respective claims and defences." Edwin E. Bryant, *The Law of Pleading Under the Codes of Civil Procedure* 178 (1899).

C. And *prayer*. The *pleading* is the document in which a party in a legal action sets out the cause of action or defense. A *pleading* consists of (1) a commencement; (2) a body (or charging part); (3) a prayer, or demand for judgment; (4) a signature; and, when required, (5) a verification. The *prayer,* which usually appears at the end of the pleading, is the request for relief from the court. E.g., "The court merely held that if there is a requirement that the complainant specifically plead for prejudgment interest, a *prayer* for general relief will not satisfy the requirement if the *pleadings* also contain a specific *prayer* for a different kind of interest."

A typical *prayer* reads: "Wherefore, defendant prays that plaintiff take nothing in this action (etc.)." A plain-language equivalent might read: "For these reasons, defendant requests that the court enter judgment that the plaintiff take nothing (etc.)." See **prayer.**

D. And *plea*. See **plea.**

E. Pleadings in Various Forums. See COMMON-LAW PLEADINGS, EQUITY PLEADINGS & WORLD COURT PLEADINGS.

pleading, inconsistent. See **Codd's Puzzle.**

plead innocent. It used to be that only journalists made the mistake of writing *plead innocent* rather than *plead not guilty,* but now this phrase has made it even into judges' writing: lawyers should avoid the phrase, as there is no such thing as a plea of innocent. Journalists, on the other hand, avoid *not guilty* merely because the word *not* might get accidentally dropped or changed to *now.* See **not (C).**

pleador. See **pleader.**

plea in abatement; plea of abatement. In jurisdictions in which the plea is used, *plea in abatement* is the usual form.

please find enclosed, like its inverted sibling, *enclosed please find,* is an old-fashioned, stilted phrase that lawyers are fond of using in letters. Better, more modern substitutes include *I am sending with this letter, I have enclosed, I am enclosing,* and *Enclosed are (or is).* See **enclosed please find.**

pled. See **pleaded.**

pledge. See **lien.**

pledgeable. So spelled.

pledgee = (1) one with whom a pledge or pawn is deposited; or (2) a person who takes a pledge (esp. an American college student who undertakes to enroll in a fraternity or sorority). Sense (1) makes some sense, but sense (2) is apt to bother careful readers (the college student really being a *pledger,* not a *pledgee*). See -EE (A).

pledg(e)or; pledger. The most logical spelling is *pledger,* not *pledgor* or *pledgeor.* Even so, *pledgor* is more than 50 times as common as *pledger* in American judicial opinions, largely because it is the regular correlative of *pledgee.* See MUTE E.

plenary is a FORMAL WORD for *full, complete,* or *entire.* E.g., "A *plenary trial* is hardly necessary to apprise the court that what it saw really happened." Here *full trial* would be better.

plenitude. So spelled; a common misspelling is *plentitude*—e.g.: "The rule is a salutary one in view of the different jurisdictions of the state courts and of this court. It leaves in both the full *plentitude* [read *plenitude*] of their powers." *Adams v. Russell,* 229 U.S. 353, 361 (1913).

plentiful; plenteous. No distinction in meaning being possible, writers should prefer the prevalent modern form, *plentiful. Plenteous* is archaic and poetic—in modern prose, a NEEDLESS VARIANT.

plentitude. See **plenitude.**

PLEONASM. See VERBOSITY.

plurality opinion = an appellate opinion without enough judges' votes to constitute a majority, but having received the greatest number of votes of any of the opinions filed. E.g., "Three justices, in the *plurality opinion* of Justice Rehnquist, took the position that § 16 of the Clayton Act does not meet the second half of the Mitchum text . . . ." Charles A. Wright, *The Law of Federal Courts* 283 (4th ed. 1983). The term dates from about 1960, when Justice Whittaker used it in *U.S. v. Kaiser,* 363 U.S. 299, 328 (1960) (Whittaker, J., dissenting). See **majority (A).**

PLURALS. A. Borrowed Words. Words transported into the English language from other languages, especially Greek and Latin, present some of the most troublesome aspects of English plurals. At a certain point borrowed words become thoroughly anglicized and take English plurals. But while words of Latin and Greek origin are still new and only questionably naturalized, writers who see the words as primarily foreignisms use the native-language plurals. Then again, with certain words, the foreign plurals become so well established that anglicization never takes place.

So many variations on this theme have occurred that it is impossible to make valid generalizations. *Minimum* makes *minima* but *premium* makes *premiums; pudendum* makes *pudenda* but *memorandum* makes either *-dums* or *-da; colloquium* generally makes *-quia* in BrE, *-quiums* preferably in AmE. The only reliable guide is a certain knowledge of specific words, or habitual reference to a usage guide.

In words with a choice of endings, one English and the other foreign, we should generally prefer the English plural. It is an affectation for college professors to insist on using *syllabi* rather than *syllabuses.* The fear of being wrong or sounding unacademic even leads some of them to use forms like *auditoria* and *stadia.*

Fowler called the benighted stab at correctness "out of the frying pan into the fire." Many writers who try to be sophisticated in their use of language are susceptible to writing, e.g., *ignorami* and *octopi,* unaware that neither is a Latin noun that, when inflected as a plural, becomes *-i.* The proper plural of the Greek word *octopus* is *octopodes;* the proper English plural is *octopuses. Ignoramus* makes only *ignoramuses,* for in Latin the word is a verb, not a noun. For several similar examples, see HYPERCORRECTION (A).

French words also present problems. *Fait accompli* becomes *faits accomplis* and *force majeure* becomes *forces majeures.* But then we have the LAW FRENCH words such as *feme sole,* which becomes *femes sole,* and *feme covert* (or *femme couverte*), which as a plural becomes *femes covert* (or *femmes couvertes*). The best policy is to make a habit of consulting a good dictionary, and to use it discriminatingly.

B. Mass (Noncount) Nouns. A recent trend in the language is to make plurals for mass nouns—general and abstract nouns that cannot be broken down into discrete units, and that therefore should not have plural forms. One example of this phenomenon is the psychologists' and sociologists' term *behaviors,* as if the ways in which one behaves are readily categorizable and therefore countable. Granted, one can have good or bad behavior, but not, properly, *a* good behavior or *a* bad behavior. Following are examples of other words infected by the contagion.

1. *Coverages.* "The policy allowed for separate *coverages* of the three cars."
2. *Discriminations.* "The statute disadvantages those who would benefit from laws barring racial, religious, or ancestral *discriminations* as against those who would bar other *discriminations* or who would otherwise regulate the real estate market in their favor." See **discrimination.**
3. *Inactions.* "The findings of the district court on the actions and *inactions* by the defendants are supported by substantial evidence and are not clearly erroneous."
4. *Languages.* Referring to different passages in a statute, a writer states: "The statutory *languages* are not enough to persuade us that the Secretary's interpretation is incorrect." See **language.**
5. *Litigations* and *attentions.* "Indeed, just as antitrust actions occupied the *attentions* of the litigation bar in the 1960s and class-action *litigations* proliferated in the 1970s, insurance-coverage *litigations* are currently engaging the *attentions* of many of the nation's most prominent litigators."/ "Under the circumstances, there need not be two *litigations* when one will suffice." See **litigation.**
6. *Managements.* "If followed, these procedures would have a beneficial effect on the *managements* of brokerage firms and those charged with supervision." (Does *managements* refer to managerial departments, or to methods of management? The plural causes this ambiguity.)
7. *Outputs.* "Interpersonal relations of the justices have been shown to have measurable effects on the court's public *outputs.*"
8. *Participations.* Sometimes this phenomenon occurs through attributive uses, as where *participation* is substituted for *unit of participation:* "The D.C. Circuit has declared that the Glass-Steagall Act does not prohibit banks from marking *participations* in collective investment trusts for I.R.A. assets." The same principle is at work when *proofs* is substituted for *elements of proof.* See **proof (C).**

C. Words Ending in *-o*. Fowler laid down a number of guiding principles for words ending in *-o:* first, monosyllables and words used as freely in the plural as in the singular usually have *-oes* (*embargoes, heroes, noes, potatoes, vetoes*); second, alien-looking words, proper names, words that are seldom used as plurals, words in which *-o-* is preceded by a vowel, and shortened words (e.g., *photo*) do not take the *-e-* (*hippos, kilos, embryos, ratios*). Good dictionaries guide users to the preferred spellings.

D. Nouns Formed From Past-Participial Adjectives. These are usually awkward and alien-looking to nonlawyers. But they are commonplace in legal writing—e.g.: "The firm represented one of the company's *insureds* in an action that had been brought against the insured in county court." See **condemned, deceased & insured.** See also POSSESSIVES (F).

E. Compound Nouns. Plurals of compound nouns made up of a noun and a POSTPOSITIVE

ADJECTIVE are formed by adding *-s* to the noun: *courts martial, heirs presumptive.* The British and Americans differ on the method of pluralizing *attorney general,* q.v. Those words in which the noun is now disguised add *-s* at the end of the word, as with all compounds ending in *-ful: lungfuls, spoonfuls, handfuls.*

F. Proper Names. Although few books on grammar mention the point, proper names often cause problems when writers try to make them plural. The rule is simple: most take a simple *-s,* while those ending in *s, x,* or *z,* or in a sibilant *ch* or *sh,* take *-es.* Thus:

Singular Form	*Plural Form*
Adam	Adams
Adams	Adamses
Bush	Bushes
Church	Churches
Cox	Coxes
Flowers	Flowerses
Jones	Joneses
Levy	Levys
Lipschutz	Lipschutzes
Mary	Marys
Rabiej	Rabiejs
Shapiro	Shapiros
Sinz	Sinzes
Thomas	Thomases

Plurals like these are often erroneously formed by calling (say) Mr. and Mrs. Sinz either *the Sinz* or *the Sinz'.* The latter form, with the apostrophe, merely results from confusion with possessives—and even *the Sinz'* is not a good possessive (the correct forms being *Sinz's* in the singular and *Sinzes'* in the plural).

ply (= layer; fold) forms the plural *plies. Plys* is incorrect—e.g.: "These [characteristics] included the tire's size, its maximum inflation pressure, its maximum load, the number of *plys* [read *plies*] . . . ." Jerry L. Mashaw & David L. Harfst, *Regulation and Legal Culture: The Case of Motor Vehicle Safety,* 4 Yale J. on Reg. 257, 316 n.70 (1987).

p.m. See **a.m.**

poetic justice, nowadays a CLICHÉ, refers to the system exemplified in older fiction in which villains always receive condign punishments, and heroes their fitting rewards.

point, in. See **in point.**

point of fact. See **in point of fact.**

point of law. This phrase refers to a discrete proposition or issue of law arising from the facts established in a given case. It is often shortened to the one word *point.*

point of view. See **viewpoint.**

point, on. See **in point.**

point out; point to; point up. *Point out* = (1) to observe; or (2) to call to others' attention. *Point to* = to direct attention to (as an answer or solution). *Point up* = illustrate. *Point up* is perhaps comparatively more frequent in legal than in nonlegal writing. E.g., "For Mr. Lucas, the case *points up* a key pitfall of seeking capital punishment . . . ." Dan R. Barber, *Law Could Curb Texas Executions,* Dallas Morning News, 18 April 1993, at 35A.

police, though a collective noun, is generally construed as a plural both in AmE and in BrE.

policy; polity. *Policy,* by far the more common of these words, means "a concerted course of action followed to achieve certain ends; a plan." It is more restricted in sense than *polity,* which means (1) "the principle upon which a government is based"; or (2) "the total governmental organization as based on its goals and policies." Sense (2) is more usual—e.g.: "The ancient doctrine of the common law, founded on the principles of the feudal system, that a private wrong is merged in a felony, is not applicable to the civil *polity* of this country."/ "As to the practicing lawyer, in our *polity* he is potentially law-writer, law teacher, legislator, or judge." (Roscoe Pound)

policyholder; policyowner. *Policyholder* is preferably spelled as one word. *Policyowner* is a NEEDLESS VARIANT.

policy-making should be hyphenated. Cf. **decision-making.**

policyowner. See **policyholder.**

politic, adj.; **political.** The adverbial forms are *politicly* (= in a politic manner; shrewdly; prudently) and *politically* (= in a political or partisan way or manner).

politic(al)ize. See **politick** (2d par.).

political rights. See **civil rights.**

politick, v.i.; **politicize.** *Politick,* a BACK-FORMATION from *politics,* at one time was not recognized as an acceptable word. Today it is more common in AmE than in BrE, and means "to engage in partisan political activities."

Politicize has a similar sense "to act the politician," but also the broader sense "to render political" <politicizing judicial races>. *Politicalize* is a NEEDLESS VARIANT.

politics may be either singular or plural. Today it is more commonly singular than plural <politics is dirty business>, although formerly the opposite was true.

polity. See **policy.**

pollicitation is an antique civilian LEGALISM meaning "an offer not yet formally accepted, and therefore usually revocable." E.g., "By a *promise* we mean accepted offer as opposed to an offer of a promise, or, as Austin called it, a *pollicitation.*" William R. Anson, *Principles of the Law of Contract* 6 (Arthur L. Corbin ed., 3d Am. ed. 1919)./ "Conventional obligations were subdivided into promise, *pollicitation* or offer, paction and contract." William W. McBryde, *The Law of Contract in Scotland* 2 (1987).

polygamy; polyandry; polygyny. The first is the broadest term, referring to a person's being simultaneously married to more than one spouse. *Polyandry* is the practice of having more than one husband; *polygyny* is the practice of having more than one wife. See **bigamy.**

pompous ass is a hackneyed phrase that could use a rest among lawyers and, especially, law students (usu. applying it to law professors). We might be tempted to characterize many fellow practitioners and academics in this way, but we should perhaps show more originality than to mouth this shopworn epithet.

pony case. See **whitehorse case.**

Ponzi scheme = a fraudulent investment scheme in which money placed by later investors pays artificially high dividends to the original investors, thereby attracting even larger investments. The scheme takes its name from Charles Ponzi, who in the late 1920s was convicted and punished for fraudulent schemes he conducted in Boston. E.g., "This was a proposal to furnish services on a commercial basis, and since we have always refused to distinguish for First Amendment purposes on the basis of content, it is no different from an advertisement for a bucket shop operation or a *Ponzi scheme* which has its headquarters in New York." *Bigelow v. Virginia,* 421 U.S. 809, 831 (1975) (Rehnquist, J., dissenting)./ "[T]he scheme was kept afloat by paying interest on existing certificates with the proceeds of new certificate sales . . . . It was . . . a massive *Ponzi scheme.*" Tim O'Brien, *Some Firms Never Learn,* Am. Law., Oct. 1989, at 63, 64.

pooling; unitization. See **communitize (A).**

POPULARIZED LEGAL TECHNICALITIES. Fowler observed that when technical terms pass into everyday speech and writing, two things often occur. First, the popular use more often than not misrepresents the original meaning; second, free indulgence in terms of this sort results in a tawdry style. These observations are no less true with legal technicalities than with those of other kinds.

The prime example is *alibi,* which in law refers to the defense in a criminal case of proving that one was elsewhere when the crime was committed. Nonlawyers snatched up the term and, through misunderstanding perhaps coupled with SLIPSHOD EXTENSION, came to use it as a synonym for *excuse,* especially a lame excuse. Today even lawyers misuse the term in this way. See **alibi (A).**

As the *OED* will confirm, any number of common expressions have their origins in law, such as these:

accountant
benefit of clergy
beyond the pale
case in point
culprit
follow suit
forestall
gist
have no right to
hold in contempt
homage
in his (or her) own right
hue and cry
innuendo
in point
moot point
new lease on life
of course
on point
ordeal
palming off
posse
premises (a place)
read the Riot Act
self-defense
sidebar
signed, sealed, and delivered
special pleading
time is of the essence

vested interest
vouch for
wear and tear

For other, mostly historical examples from the legal lexicon, see the discussions under **alias, compound, gist, ignoramus, hue and cry** & **pale, beyond the.**

populous (= thickly populated) for *populist* (= of or relating to a movement claiming to represent the whole of the people) is a startling error. E.g., "The advent of the Jacksonian era and its emphasis on democratic *populous* [read *populist*] ideals . . . promoted . . . the notion that . . . judges should be popularly elected . . . ." Norman Krivosha, *Acquiring Judges by the Merit Selection Method,* 40 Sw. L.J. (Special Issue), May 1986, at 15, 15.

pore (= to read carefully) should not be confused with *pour,* as it frequently is—e.g.: "Appellants' representatives spent about two and one-half years *pouring* [read *poring*] over the books and records of the Cincinnati School System in an effort to find something that was wrong." *Deal v. Cincinnati Bd. of Educ,* 419 F.2d 1387, 1394 (6th Cir. 1969)./ "Ms. Besso . . . now spends her evenings *pouring* [read *poring*] over brochures from Boston, Boulder, Colo., and Nashville." Sara Rimer, *Fleeing Los Angeles: Quake Is the Last Straw,* N.Y. Times, 18 Feb. 1994, at A1, A10. This error may well occur because *poring* appears less often in print than in speech.

portend (= to foretell or foreshadow) should not be used as a substitute for *to mean.* "The term 'beneficial shareholders' *portends* [read *means*] something different from 'shareholders.'" The word *portend* necessarily has negative connotations.

portentous (=[1] prophetic; [2] wondrous; [3] solemn; or [4] pompous) is so spelled. But the word is sometimes incorrectly written *portentious* or *portentuous*—e.g.: "[T]he court made a significant observation *portentious* [read *portentous*] of things to come . . . ." *O'Brien v. Barnes Bldg. Co.,* 380 N.Y.S.2d 405, 420 (Sup. Ct. 1974)./ "Can anyone imagine . . . a responsible government administrator . . . issuing regulations with as *portentuous* [read *portentous*] [an] effect as here on the same factual certainties that EPA had?" *Ethyl Corp. v. Environmental Protection Agency,* 541 F.2d 1, 87 n.81 (D.C. Cir. 1976) (en banc) (Wilkey, J., dissenting).

portion; part. There are connotative differences. *Portion* = share (as of an estate or of food). It is an entity cut or as if cut away from the whole <his portion of the contract> <her portion of the grain>. *Part,* in contrast, merely connotes a constituent part of the whole <part of a house, a country, etc.>.

In a common-law "strict settlement," a *portion* is a lump sum paid in trust to a settlor's children and receivable by them once they reach the age of majority or marry.

Portmanteau Words. Lewis Carroll improvised this term to denote words formed by combining the first part of one word with the last part of another. (Linguists use the term *blend* to name an example of this phenomenon.) Thus *insinuendo* was arrived at by combining *insinuation* with *innuendo; quasar* is from *quasi* and *stellar; aerobicise* derives from *aerobic exercise.* Other recent innovations are *avigation,* from *aviation* and *navigation, pictionary* for *picture-filled dictionary,* and *videbut* for *video debut.* Most portmanteau words are nonce words that do not gain currency; others, like *brunch (breakfast + lunch),* become standard. Among 20th-century portmanteau coinages are these:

breathalyzer *(breath + analyzer),* q.v.
brotel *(brothel + hotel)*
defamacast *(defamatory + broadcast),* q.v.
galimony *(gal + alimony)*
gazwelcher *(gazump + welcher)*
litigotiation *(litigation + negotiation)*
palimony *(pal + alimony),* q.v.

posit (= [1] to set in place, fix; or [2] to postulate or lay down as the basis for argument) should not be used for *to present,* as here: "The purpose is not to study procedure for its own sake; the procedural issues are raised and considered primarily as indicia of the overall problems *posited* [read *presented*] by the unique nature of complex litigation."

positive (= having real existence) is a common meaning of the word in law, but little used in nonlegal writing today. E.g., "The wrong was actuated by a *positive* design to injure the third person to whom the duty was due."

positive law. This term is sometimes used with little idea of its precise sense. *Positive law,* referring primarily to statutes and regulations, might be defined as "coercively implemented law laid down within a particular political community by political superiors, to govern members of the community, as distinct from moral law or law existing in an ideal community or in some nonpolitical community."

Associated originally with John Austin's jurisprudence, *positive law* is frequently used by common-law writers. E.g., "*Positive law,* the law applied and enforced in the courts, is the means by which the state [secures people in their natural rights] and is morally binding only so far as it conforms to natural law." Roscoe Pound, *The Development of Constitutional Guarantees of Liberty* 74 (1957)./ "Something like efficient breach theory is part of our *positive law* to this limited extent, but we do not need the irreparable injury rule to implement it." Douglas Laycock, *The Death of the Irreparable Injury Rule* 248–49 (1991).

Unfortunately, as several writers have pointed out, Austin used *positive* differently in different phrases. In *positive law,* it means "set by a political superior"; in *positive morality* (also an Austinian phrase), it means "set by human authority." See W.W. Buckland, *Some Reflections on Jurisprudence* 84–85 (1945). Hence Buckland's barb: "One may use a term in any sense one will, provided one uses it always in the same sense. Austin makes considerable use of the right, but is not very careful of the proviso." *Id.* Cf. **natural law (A).**

positive mental attitude. See **mental attitude.**

positivism. H.L.A. Hart once bemoaned that issues can be "clouded by the use of grand but vague words like *'Positivism'* and 'Natural Law.' Banners have been waved and parties formed in a loud but often confused debate." H.L.A. Hart, *Law, Liberty, and Morality* 2 (1963). The confusion has not abated, and *positivism* has remained vague—if not downright ambiguous. Whereas general philosophers tend to use the word as shorthand for *logical positivism* (a system involving formal verification of empirical questions), legal philosophers use the word to denote the theory of *positive law* (which postulates that legal rules are valid only because they are enacted by an existing political authority). E.g., "In the literature of legal *positivism* it is of course standard practice to examine at length the relations of law and morals." Lon L. Fuller, *The Morality of Law* 204 (rev. ed. 1969)./ "What, then, is law? The basic answer, which is the essence of legislative *positivism,* is that only statutes enacted by the legislative power could be law." John H. Merryman, *The Civil Law Tradition* 24 (1969). Cf. **natural law (A).** See **positive law.**

posse, in. See ***in esse.***

posse comitatus (lit., "the power of the county") = a body of able-bodied citizens called together by the sheriff to suppress riots, pursue felons, or act in military defense of the country. E.g., "Horizontal and nationwide class divisions had by 1700 made the *posse comitatus* unusable as a police force, since it included the very classes [that] were prone to riot." Alan Harding, *A Social History of English Law* 270 (1966). The American frontier term *posse* originated as a shortened form of this early common-law term.

possess. The passive construction *to be possessed of* is a LEGALISM for the active verb *to possess.* E.g., "[I]f A *was possessed of land* [read *possessed land*] under a ten-year lease from B, the owner of the fee, B, and not A, was said to be seised." 1 *American Law of Property* 12–13 (A.J. Casner ed. 1952).

possession. A. Senses. Of this CHAMELEON-HUED WORD, a legal philosopher pessimistically states: "[T]he search for [its] 'proper' meaning . . . is likely to be a fruitless one." G.W. Paton, *A Textbook of Jurisprudence* 553 (4th ed. 1972). Generally speaking, it can have three senses: (1) "the fact of having or holding property in one's power"; (2) "the right under which one may exercise power over something at pleasure, to the exclusion of all others"; or (3) *esp. in pl.,* "something that a person owns or controls; property."

Sense (1) is the classic sense; sense (2) is commonly considered a corruption (see (B)); and sense (3) is a predictable extension of meaning similar to the extension that *property* has undergone. See **property (A).**

B. And *ownership.* In sense (2), *possession* becomes confused with *ownership*—and legal writers ought to distinguish the two rigorously. Technically, *ownership* is a legal status: the aggregate of rights that give a person the fullest power to enjoy, destroy, or dispose of a thing; one of these rights is to possess the thing. *Possession,* meanwhile, is purely a matter of fact: a thief may acquire possession of a billfold, but the owner retains the rights of ownership. *Ownership* is always rightful, whereas *possession* might not be so. See **ownership.**

C. And *custody.* *Possession* and *custody* are usefully differentiated in criminal law. A person who takes shoes to a shoe-repair shop may leave the shoes for a few days to have new soles put on; in that event, the shoe-repairer takes *possession.* A shoe-repairer who can fix the shoes on the spot, while the customer waits, takes *custody* only.

Why the distinction? At common law, the cobbler with *possession* of shoes would, upon proof of misappropriation, be guilty of embezzlement. But the cobbler with *custody* would, on the same proof, be guilty of the lesser crime of *larceny*. See **custody.**

For more on these words in a different context, see **possession, custody, or control.**

possession, custody, or control. This phrase commonly appears in discovery requests that require another party to produce documents: one party asks another to produce all documents or things in the other's *possession, custody, or control.* The broadest of the three is generally considered *control,* since a person could turn something over to a fiduciary, thereby relinquishing possession and custody, but retaining control. See **possession (C)** & DOUBLETS, TRIPLETS, AND SYNONYM-STRINGS.

possession is nine-tenths of the law. Originally, in the 17th century—and well into the 19th—the catchphrase was *possession is nine parts* (or *points*) *of the law,* there supposedly being ten parts or points of the law. The substance of the idea was that one's having possession threw onto any other claimant the burden of showing an even better claim to possess. Throughout the 20th century, the phrase has generally been *nine-tenths* (not *nine parts*) in AmE and BrE alike.

It is a popular phrase, not really a legal one, and legal writers often slight the idea behind it when using it: "This rule partakes of the old adage that so frequently guides laymen in practical action, that *possession is nine tenths of the law.*" *In re Estate of Barassi,* 71 Cal. Rptr. 249, 254 (Ct. App. 1968)./ "Although we are familiar with the maxim, '*possession is nine-tenths of the law,*' we prefer to apply the remaining one-tenth . . . ." *U.S. v. One 1985 Cadillac Seville,* 866 F.2d 1142, 1146 (9th Cir. 1989). See MAXIMS.

possessive; possessory; possessorial. The terms *possessive* and *possessory* have undergone DIFFERENTIATION. *Possessive* = (1) exhibiting possession or the desire to possess; (2) [in grammar] denoting possession. *Possessory* = (1) of or pertaining to a possessor <possessory rights>; (2) arising from possession <possessory interest>; or (3) that is a possessor <possessory conservator>.

On *possessory* as opposed to *petitory actions,* see **petitory.**

POSSESSIVES. A. Singular Possessives. The best practice, advocated by Strunk and White in *The Elements of Style* and by every other authority of superior standing, is to add *-'s* to all singular possessives, hence *witness's, Vitex's, Jones's, Congress's, testatrix's.* So misunderstood is the rule that *witness's* actually gets a "[*sic*]" in *Yeager v. Greene,* 502 A.2d 980, 982 (D.C. Cir. 1985).

Legal stylists generally follow the rule just stated—e.g.: "We may summarize the foregoing by considering *Holmes's* much-cited dictum . . . ." Morris R. Cohen, *Reason and Law* 13 (1961)./ "*Holmes's* thinking may have been influenced by his membership in a group of young men who, calling themselves the Metaphysical Club, met regularly in Boston and Cambridge from 1870 to 1872." Grant Gilmore, *The Ages of American Law* 50 (1977)./ "It is this recognition, I think, that accounts for the resonant chord struck by John *Rawls's Theory of Justice* in American law schools." Bruce A. Ackerman, *Reconstructing American Law* 94 (1984).

There are two exceptions to this rule. The first is that biblical and classical names ending in *-s* take only an apostrophe, hence *Jesus' suffering, Moses' discovery, Aristophanes' plays, Grotius' writings.* Some writers ill-advisedly ignore this exception—e.g.: "From its very beginning, the aim of Justinian's legislation was more ambitious than that of *Theodosius's* [read *Theodosius'*] codification had been." Hans J. Wolff, *Roman Law* 170–71 (1951). See **Gaius.**

The second exception is for singular terms formed from a plural. Thus *Scribes,* the name of the organization devoted to improving legal writing, makes *Scribes'* as a possessive (*Scribes' president*). The same holds true for *General Motors:* "A merger by General Motors will excite great interest in an enforcement agency simply because of *General Motors's* [read *General Motors'*] size." E.W. Kintner, *An Antitrust Primer* 95 (2d ed. 1973).

B. Plural Possessives. To form the plural possessive, an apostrophe is added to the *-s-* of the plural, e.g. *bosses', Joneses', Sinzes', octopuses'.* The one exception is for plurals not ending in *-s-*, for which *-'s* is added as in the singular possessive: *brethren's, children's, men's, women's.*

The apostrophe is surprisingly often misplaced or omitted—e.g.: "The so-called 'Married *Womens'* [read *Women's*] Acts' permit them to sue and be sued as if they were *femes sole.*" Eugene A. Jones, *Manual of Equity Pleading and Practice* 32 n.29 (1916).

C. Units of Time or Value and the Genitive Adjective. The idiomatic possessive should be used with periods of time and statements of worth. E.g., "The court said the holding was a tenancy from year to year ordinarily requiring *60 days*['] *notice* to terminate, but the special statute was held controlling." (The correct phraseology is *sixty* [or *60*] *days' notice,* just as it is *several years' experience* and *two months' time.*)/ "The initial *six months confinement* [read *six months' confinement*] was to be followed by *eighteen months probation* [read *eighteen months' probation*]."/ "This lawsuit arises out of the alleged misappropriation of a million dollars' worth of equipment." (If the number is given in Arabic numerals, a possessive apostrophe is not used.)

D. Of Inanimate Things. Possessives of nouns denoting inanimate objects are generally unobjectionable. Indeed, they allow writers to avoid awkward uses of *of*—e.g.: *the book's title, the article's main point, the system's hub, the envelope's contents,* and *the car's price tag. See* **of (A).**

The old line was that it is better to use an "*of* phrase rather than the *'s* to indicate possession when the possessor is an inanimate object. Write *foot of the bed,* not *the bed's foot.*" Robert C. Whitford & James R. Foster, *Concise Dictionary of American Grammar and Usage* 96 (1955). *The foot of the bed,* of course, is a SET PHRASE, so the example is not a fair one. Whenever it is not a violation of idiom, the possessive in *'s* is preferable—e.g.: "The constitutional claim is rooted in the Fifth Amendment's guarantee of due process."

But such possessives can be overdone: "Section 922(f)*'s* unambiguous language regarding the section*'s* applicability requires us to decline the invitation to extend 922(f)*'s* coverage; 922(f)*'s* first sentence defines the statute*'s* scope." In fact, it is often best to avoid use of possessives with statutes: "Relying on *section 1471(a)'s legislative history* [better: *the legislative history of section 1471(a)*], the court found that the regulation was not reasonably adopted."

The practice of using possessives with case names becomes preposterous when later courts interpolate full citations, as here: "'Consistent with *Milliken* [*v. Bradley,* 433 U.S. 267, 97 S. Ct. 2749, 53 L. Ed. 2d 745 (1977)]'s teachings, a remedial order must be carefully tailored to correct the constitutionally infirm condition. . . .'" *U.S. v. Crucial,* 722 F.2d 1182, 1189 (5th Cir. 1983) (quoting *Valley* v. *Rapides Parish Sch. Bd.,* 702 F.2d 1221, 1226 (5th Cir. 1983)).

E. Incorrect Omission of Apostrophe. It seems that possessive apostrophes are increasingly omitted nowadays. This sloppy habit is to be avoided. E.g., "Brown had hired Jack Rogers, a Lake Charles attorney, to procure *Governor Edwards* [read *Governor Edwards's*] signature." *Brown v. Maggio,* 730 F.2d 293, 294 (5th Cir. 1984). Where two possessives are proximate, writers will often inadvertently omit one: "We have considered the import and admissibility of the Alexanders' expert *witnesses testimony* [read *witnesses' testimony*] touching on the drilling of additional wells." See **attorney's fees.**

F. Past-Participial Adjectives as Attributive Nouns. These can become awkward. With such phrases as *the insured's death* or *the deceased's residence,* it is better to use an *of*-phrase; hence *the death of the insured* and *the residence of the deceased.* (Better yet, one might prefer *decedent* to *deceased.*) See **accused, condemned, insured & deceased.** See also PLURALS (D).

G. Phrasal Possessives. These are to be avoided when possible, so that one does not end up with sentences like this, "*That strange man who lives down the block's daughter* [read *The daughter of that strange man who lives down the street*] was arrested last week." Genitives with *of* are only slightly longer; more important, however, they are correct:

- "The *plaintiff in error's* mother [read *mother of the plaintiff in error*] died before the trial court's decision was appealed."
- "The *court below's error* [read *error of the court below* or *trial court's error*] was in granting summary judgment."
- "The *trier of fact's award* [read *fact-trier's award*] is not to be disturbed unless it is entirely disproportionate to the injury sustained." (See **trier of fact.**)
- "These statements do let women in on *the man in question's view of* [read *how the man in question views*] our half of humanity."
- "The three of us have, naturally, divided up our writing by subjects. But each of us read and commented freely upon the *other two's* [read *others'*] work." Roger A. Cunningham et al., *The Law of Property* iv (2d ed. 1993).

With a phrase such as *court of appeals,* the possessive is acceptable and widely used—e.g.: "The *court of civil appeals' opinion* uses substantially the same alter ego test that is stated in the briefs." The other established forms of phrasal possessives are variations on *anybody else's:* "The court's ruling disposed of *no one else's* claim." See **else's.**

H. Followed by Relative Pronouns. The relative pronoun *who* should not follow a possessive noun. E.g., "Or there may have been inimical voices raised among the committee, such as *Palffy's* or Nikilaus *Esterhazy's,* who just then had had an unpleasant brush with the composer." [Read *Or there may have been raised among the committee inimical voices, such as those of Palffy or Nikilaus Esterhazy, who just then had had an unpleasant brush with the composer.*] See ANTECEDENTS, FALSE (C).

I. Attributive Possessives. Businesses are often named with a proper single name in possessive form, as *McDonald's* or *Sambo's.* Although possessive in form, these are functionally nouns, as in *Sambo's brings this action,* etc. How, then, does one make a possessive of the noun *Sambo's?* One court did it this way: "On February 26, 1973, *Sambo's* Certificate of Authority to do business in this state was forfeited . . . ." *Farris v. Sambo's*

Restaurants, Inc., 498 F. Supp. 143, 147 (N.D. Tex. 1980). The judge should have written *Sambo's',* because *Sambo's certificate* = certificate of Sambo, whereas *Sambo's' certificate* = certificate of Sambo's, the latter being the desired sense. Likewise, when *Buddy's Food Store* is shortened to *Buddy's,* one writes of *Buddy's' manager.* But good PHRASING requires *the manager of Buddy's.*

J. With Appositives. See APPOSITIVES (A).

possessor (= one who possesses) has the special legal sense "one who takes, occupies, or holds something without ownership, or as distinguished from the owner" (*OED*). Hence the following specimen in reference to a life estate: "The materials that follow are not intended to cover either the substantive law of waste under which the *possessor* may be liable to the holder of the future interest or the substantive law relating to liability of a *nonpossessor.*"

possessory. See **possessive.**

possibility of reverter. See **reversion.**

possible; practicable. The author of the following advice was ill informed: "Do not use *possible* when you should use *practicable,* as it may make a world of difference whether an act is to be done if *possible* or only if *practicable.*" *Notes on the Art of Drafting Contracts* 11 (Cornell Law School 1934). Rather, *practicable* (= feasible) is virtually a synonym of *possible;* the words to be distinguished are *practical,* q.v., and *practicable.*

For distinctions involving *possible, likely,* and *probable,* see **probable.**

POSSLQ */**pos**-əl-kyoo/* is an ACRONYM standing for "person of the opposite sex sharing living quarters." Used in the 1980 U.S. census, *POSSLQ* has received criticism because, although it is intended to include only unmarried couples, it literally includes "married couples and communal livers, neither of which is a meretricious relationship." *In re Eggers,* 638 P.2d 1267, 1270 n.2 (Wash. Ct. App. 1982). In the early 1980s, the word tended to be in lower case (*posslq*), but in more recent writing it is usually set in all capitals.

POST-, when used for *since* or *after* to create a SENTENCE ADVERB, is a sloppy way of achieving brevity. "*Post-Flanagan* [read *Since Flanagan*], only two circuits have spoken to the precise question." See PRE-.

post. See ***ante.***

post facto. See **ex post facto.**

posthaste is archaic in all but its adverbial sense.

post hoc (= [of or relating to] the fallacy of assuming causality from temporal sequence) for *ex post facto* or *after the fact* is a common error. E.g., "Petitioners observe correctly that if the lawyer's brief for the ICC had simply announced its clarifying analysis in the form of allegations or new explanations, such would constitute pure *post hoc* [read *after-the-fact*] rationalization not entitled to any consideration by this court. The clarifying opinion of the Commission, however, differs sharply from *after-the-fact* rationalizations made by attorneys or by courts." *Public Serv. Co. of Indiana, Inc. v. ICC,* 749 F.2d 753, 759 (D.C. Cir. 1984)./ "In applying these criteria, it is important that the district court resist the understandable temptation to engage in *post hoc* [read *after-the-fact*] reasoning by concluding that, because a plaintiff did not ultimately prevail, his action must have been unreasonable or without foundation." See ***post hoc, ergo propter hoc.***

post hoc, ergo propter hoc denotes the fallacy of confusing sequence with consequence. Literally, the phrase means "after this, therefore because of this." Two common usages, *since* for *because* (acceptable) and *consequent* for *subsequent* (unacceptable), exemplify the fallacy: they originated when speakers and writers confused causality with temporality. The following specimen demonstrates a canny use of the maxim: "Here, as elsewhere in the law, *propter hoc* must be distinguished from *post hoc.*" *Hennigan v. Ouachita Parish Sch. Bd.,* 749 F.2d 1148, 1152 (5th Cir. 1985) (per Rubin, J.). See **post hoc.**

postjudgment. One word.

postman. At early common law, this word was equivalent to *lawyer;* more particularly, it referred to a barrister in the Court of Exchequer who had precedence in motions except in Crown business. The *OED* records that "the name was derived from the post, the measure of length in excise cases, beside which he took his stand." Surely this sense of the word was unrelated to another sense recorded by the *OED:* "a hireling writer of libels or scurrilous falsehoods." But see LAWYERS, DEROGATORY NAMES FOR. See also **attorney (A)** & SEXISM (B).

postmortem. See **autopsy.**

postnuptial (= made, occurring, or existing after marriage) refers to the time after the wedding, not after a divorce. E.g., "The trend is toward upholding *postnuptial* agreements, even where obsolete statutes codify the common-law rules on jointure." See **antenuptial.**

POSTPOSITIVE ADJECTIVES come after the nouns they modify, generally because they follow Romance rather than Germanic (or English) syntax. They exist in English largely as a remnant of the Norman French influence during the Middle Ages, and especially in the century following the Norman Conquest. The French influence was most pronounced in the language of law, politics, religion, and heraldry.

In law as in these other fields, French phrases were adopted wholesale—syntax and all—and soon passed into the English language unchanged, though in English, adjectives almost invariably precede the nouns they modify. Following is a list of frequently used law-related phrases with postpositive adjectives:

accounts payable
accounts receivable
act malum in se
annuity certain
appearance corporal
attorney general
body corporate
body politic
brief amicus curiae
chattels personal
chattels real
condition precedent
condition subsequent
corporation de facto
corporation de jure
court martial
date certain
decree absolute
easement appurtenant
fee simple
fee simple defeasible
fee simple determinable
fee tail
gap certain
heir apparent
law merchant
letters patent
letters rogatory (U.S.)
letters testamentary
notary public
offense mala prohibita
parties defendant
parties litigant
postmaster general
president-elect
queen regent (*or* regnant)
secretary general
sum certain
sum total
twelve men good and true

On the troublesome issue of pluralizing the nouns in phrases such as these, see PLURALS (E).

At least two common English nouns, *things* and *matters,* often take postpositive adjectives that are ordinarily prepositive. Thus we say that someone is interested in *things philosophical,* or *matters philological.* And the adjective *alive* is always postpositive <the cattle were still alive>.

Sometimes a writer will attempt to create a prepositive adjectival phrase where properly the phrase would normally and most idiomatically be postpositive. The result is ungainly indeed: "*The complained of summaries* [read *The summaries complained of*] in this case are contained in the government's exhibit."

There is, however, a tendency in modern writing to make prepositive adjectival phrases out of what formerly would have been postpositive. Thus, instead of having *payments past due,* we just as often see *past-due payments:* "The precise issue is whether a bankruptcy court may decline to approve a Chapter 13 plan solely because a debtor proposes to pay off in installments during the term of the plan *past-due payments* on a promissory note."

posttrial. One word.

post-sentencing should be hyphenated for visual reasons. See PUNCTUATION (F).

potence; potency. Oddly, *potency* is more common in the positive, and *impotence* in the negative. See **impotence.**

potentiality is jargonistic when used merely for *potential,* n.

potential juror; prospective juror. These phrases are equally good plain-language translations of *veniremember*—e.g.: "Although he did not mention the Federal sentencing, the judge instructed a group of more than 50 *prospective jurors* that a verdict in the Denny case would not be reached . . . ." *Jury Queries Resume in Beating Case,* N.Y. Times, 8 Aug. 1993, at 17./ "The decision by Judge Glenn Berman in New Brunswick forced attorneys to begin qualifying additional candidates for a pool of *potential jurors* to sit on the trial of Nathaniel Harvey, 44." Jim O'Neill, *12 Potential Jurors Get Boot at Murder Trial,* Star-Ledger (N.J.), 29 Oct. 1994, at 19. See **venireman.**

pour. See **pore.**

pouree trust. See **pourover.**

pourover, a term used in estate planning, refers to testamentary assets that are incorporated into a living trust. E.g., "The doctrines of incorporation by reference and nontestamentary acts, both potentially involved in *pourovers* from wills to living trusts, are considered here with modern statutes designed to permit *pourovers* without complications produced by the Wills Acts."

Sometimes, by transference, *pourover* is used as an adjective denoting a statute that allows this type of incorporation of testamentary assets into a living trust—e.g.: "The enactment of *pourover* statutes may result in decreased reliance on the doctrine of incorporation by reference; but at the same time *pourover* statutes may induce the courts to become more liberal in applying the doctrine . . . ."

At least one writer considers *pourover* a misnomer because, he says, "wills and insurance contracts do the pouring; the trust is pouree." Thomas L. Shaffer, *The Planning and Drafting of Wills and Trusts* 207 (2d ed. 1979). He therefore uses the phrase *pouree trust,* but this phrase seems unlikely to catch on. And, in any event, *pourover trust* is no less logical than *spillover pond,* in which the pond does no spilling but instead holds the water that is spilled.

power. For lawyers, the most important senses are these: (1) "the ability to do something, esp. to alter a legal relation by doing or not doing a given act"; (2) "legal authorization"; (3) "a document giving legal authorization"; and (4) "political ascendancy or influence."

When used in sense (2), the word is frequently coupled with *right.* But the coupling is often superfluous, as Jeremy Bentham explained:

> Powers, though not a species of rights . . . , are yet so far included under rights that wherever the word *power* may be employed, the word *right* may also be employed: The reason is, that wherever you may speak of a person as having a power, you may also speak of him as having a right to such power: but the converse of this proposition does not hold good: there are cases in which, though you may speak of a man as having a right, you cannot speak of him as having a power, or in any other way make any mention of that word. On various occasions you have a *right,* for instance, to the services of the magistrate: but if you are a private person, you have no *power* over him: all the power is on his side. This being the case, as the word *right* was employed, the word *power* might perhaps, without any deficiency in the sense, have been omitted."
>
> Jeremy Bentham, *An Introduction to the Principles of Morals and Legislation* 224 n.1 (1823; repr. 1948).

power of attorney; letter of attorney. The former is the usual phrase in both AmE and BrE. *Letter of attorney* is a BrE variant that refers more properly to the *document* giving one authority to act on another's behalf, rather than to the *authority* itself. *Power of attorney,* however, is used both for the document and for the authority given by the document. The plural is *powers of attorney.* See PLURALS (E).

power of termination. See **right of entry for condition broken** & **fee simple** (G).

p.p. is an ambiguous abbreviation, for it may be short for *propria persona* (= in one's proper or own person), or *per procurationem* (= by proxy). (The abbreviation for *pages* (*pp.* or *pp*), of course, has no internal period.) For other abbreviations of the second phrase, see ***per procurationem.***

practicable. See **possible** & **practical.**

practical; practicable. Though similar, these words should be distinguished in use; in both words, the first syllable is stressed. *Practical* = manifested in practice; capable of being put to good use. The word is most frequently contrasted with *theoretical.*

Practicable = capable of being accomplished; feasible; possible. E.g., "As a matter of construction, the court must, irrespective of what is *practicable* by way of financial provision, determine whether grave financial hardship will be caused to the respondent as a result of dissolution." (Eng.)

Occasionally the two words are confused—e.g.: "Not only might it be unfair to give general guidance without knowledge of the day-to-day *practicability* [read *practicality*] of such guidance, but also in depriving itself of such knowledge the court might well deprive itself of the opportunity of giving the best guidance." (Eng.) See **possible.**

practice; practise. In AmE, the former is both the noun and verb; in BrE the former is the noun, the latter the verb. Occasionally *practise* is used by American writers, but *practice,* n. & v.t., is the preferred spelling. One well-known exception to the general rule in the U.S. is the lawyers' organization called the Practising Law Institute.

practitioner; practiser. The former is the term primarily used in AmE and BrE for "one who exercises a profession or occupation." The latter is used almost exclusively in BrE, though not commonly. E.g., "This cause has been carefully instructed with evidence by the *practisers.*" (Eng.) The variant *practicer* sometimes occurs in AmE.

praecipe /***pre***-*sə-pee*/ (lit., "command") denoted, at common law, a writ ordering a defendant to do some act demanded by the plaintiff or demandant, or to explain why (*ostensurus quare*) he or she should not do it. A *praecipe* action aims not at compensation for misconduct but at restoration of a right. For example, *praecipe in capite* was, at common law, the principal writ for the recovery of land in the King's court. *Praecipe quod reddat* was used (1) to claim chattels or debts that the defendant held unjustly; (2) to make the defendant perform a covenant; or (3) to obtain an accounting of moneys received. *Praecipe quod permittat* was used to order the defendant to allow the plaintiff to have or do something.

A modern example occurs in a court paper filed in the Supreme Court of British Columbia: "*Praecipe.* Required: To search for an Appearance entered on behalf of the Defendant XYZ Corporation. DATED ______. [Signature] Solicitor for the Plaintiff." (Can.)

A Pennsylvania judge writes that "*praecipe* may be correctly used as a verb as well as a noun . . . ." T.J. Terputac, *A Handbook of English Usage* 250 (1989). Primarily in Michigan and Pennsylvania, the word is used as a verb in three senses: (1) "to move for entry of judgment"; (2) "*of a court,* to rule (a case) ready for trial"; or (3) "*of a lawyer,* to move for a trial setting on the court's docket."

The use as a verb seems to have originated in Michigan, in senses (2) and (3)—e.g.: (Sense 2) "The defendant Runnells filed a plea September 12, 1924, and the case was *praeciped* on that date as ready for trial." *Robinson v. Sample,* 219 N.W. 661, 661 (Mich. 1928)./ (Sense 3) "During this period of time petitioners could have *praeciped* the cause for trial." *Hailey v. Wolf,* 30 N.W.2d 437, 439 (Mich. 1948). Later, these senses appeared in Pennsylvania—e.g.: (Sense 2) "[A] notice of rehearing by the Board . . . [stated] that the case had not been *praeciped* for trial or otherwise disposed." *Cudo v. Hallstead Foundry, Inc.,* 539 A.2d 792, 797 (Pa. 1988) (Flaherty, J., dissenting).

Sense (1) however, is more common today in Pennsylvania—e.g.: "On May 23, 1979, Evans, as attorney for Fitelson *praeciped* the arbitration award for judgment, because the time period for entry of an appeal from the arbitration award had passed." *Becker v. Evans,* 496 F. Supp. 20, 20 (M.D. Pa. 1980)./ "The Stricklers . . . *praeciped* for entry of judgment and the instant timely appeal by Royal Insurance Company followed." *Strickler v. Huffine,* 618 A.2d 430, 432 (Pa. Super. Ct. 1992)./ "When no responsive pleading was received from DPW within thirty days, the claimant *praeciped* for entry of default judgment . . . ." *Pennsylvania Inst. Health Servs., Inc. v. Commonwealth,* 647 A.2d 692, 694 n.2 (Pa. Commw. Ct. 1994).

Most American lawyers would doubtless consider these uses of the word obscure, to say the least. In most parts of the U.S., lawyers don't *praecipe* a case for trial; they simply *ask for a trial setting.* Nor do they *praecipe* for entry of judgment; they *move* for entry of judgment.

pr(a)edial /***pree***-*dee-əl*/ (= consisting of or pertaining to or attached to the land), the rough equivalent of *real* in the phrase *real property,* is usu. spelled *predial* in Louisiana and *praedial* in Scotland.

The usual phrase in law is *predial servitude,* which means, in Scots and civil law, "a servitude affecting land, such as a right of way, of light, of support, and the like." E.g., "A *predial servitude* is a charge on a servient estate for the benefit of a dominant estate." La. Civ. Code Ann. art. 646 (West 1980). See **servitude** (A).

pray, in the legal sense "to request earnestly," is a survival from Elizabethan usage, as in Shakespeare's "a conqueror that will *pray* in aid for kindness, where he for grace is kneeled to." *Antony & Cleopatra,* 5.2.27–28. The religious sense of *pray* grew alongside the broader secular sense, and neither it nor *prayer,* q.v., should be viewed as symptomatic of BIBLICAL AFFECTATION. E.g., "Appellants *pray* for an injunction restraining defendant from making the patented device."/ "The wife by her answer cross-*prayed* for a divorce on the ground of desertion." (Eng.)

prayer = (1) a request addressed to the court that appears at the end of a pleading; or (2) in British parliamentary practice, a negative resolution that challenges a statutory instrument. E.g.: (Sense 1) "Taking up first the *prayer* for an injunction pendente lite, I cannot find that any case has been made out for enjoining action by the two corporate defendants."/ (Sense 2) "But even if a group of Members decide to challenge such an instrument (by what is called a '*prayer*')—there is no guarantee that the government will provide time for a debate or the opportunity of a vote." Michael Zander, *The Law-Making Process* 70 (2d ed. 1985). See **pray** & **pleading** (C).

PRE- [+ NOUN]. Such a construction may be used adjectivally, as in the following examples: "But the prosperous fur-trading days of Astor and Chouteau were, in a sense, *pre-law.*" Robert MacCrate, *The Making of the American Lawyer,* 34 S.D. L. Rev. 227, 227 (1989)./ "The neutral mechanism, far from being the discriminatory act, is merely the means by which the *pre-act* and *pre-*

limitations disparate treatment is carried forward into the actionable time frame." *Sobel v. Yeshiva Univ.,* 839 F.2d 18, 29 (2d Cir. 1988).

But making the *pre-* phrase into an adverb modifying a verb is a poor substitute for the idiomatic construction: *before* plus the noun. E.g., "Not so with respect to the harm that many States believed, *pre-Roe* [read *before Roe*], and many may continue to believe, is caused by largely unrestricted abortion." *Webster v. Reprod. Health Servs.,* 492 U.S. 490, 535 (1989) (Scalia, J., concurring in part)./ "[D]efendant could have responded that he did inform the police and this statement was made *prearrest and pre-Miranda* [read *before they arrested him and read him his rights*]." *People v. Sutton,* 464 N.W.2d 276, 277 n.3 (Mich. 1990)./ "Any number of specific programs effective now were not *pre-Ruiz established* [read *established before Ruiz*]." See POST-.

preachify is a derogatory word for *preach;* the *OED* defines it as "to preach in a factitious or a tedious way." See **argufy** & **speechify.**

preamble takes the preposition *to* or, less commonly, *of.* The corresponding adjective is *preambular.*

precatory (= of, relating to, or expressing entreaty or supplication) is a word not much used outside the law. *Precatory words* in a will, or in motions at shareholders' meetings, are words praying or expressing a desire that a thing be done; ordinarily, precatory words are not binding. The word is usu. opposed to or contrasted with *mandatory.* E.g., "Testators frequently annex *precatory* words to devises or bequests and thus create doubt whether an absolute gift or trust is intended."/ "I vote to reverse and to dismiss the complaint upon the ground that the words of the will on which plaintiff's cause of action is based are *precatory* but not mandatory."

precautionary; precautious. These terms have undergone DIFFERENTIATION since they were first used in the 18th century. *Precautionary* = (1) suggesting or advising provident caution; or (2) of, relating to, or of the nature of a precaution. *Precautious* = using precaution; displaying previous or provident caution or care (*OED*). See **cautionary.**

precede. A. And *proceed.* These words are sometimes confused even by otherwise literate professionals. Both may mean "to go ahead," but in different senses. *Precede* = to go ahead of; to come before. *Proceed* = to go ahead; to continue. For a common misspelling, see (B).

B. Misspelled *preceed.* This misspelling seems to result from confusion with *proceed.* It occurs in print surprisingly often: see, e.g., *Drennen Land & Timber Co. v. Angell,* 475 So. 2d 1166, 1172 (Ala. 1985).

C. For *preface.* This seems to be an anomalous error—e.g.: "The publisher *precedes* [read *prefaces*] its collection of documents with an essay about the entire editorial process."

precedence; precedency. Today the latter is a NEEDLESS VARIANT of the former; it was used through the beginning of the 19th century, but today *-ce* serves more ably for all purposes.

precedence; precedents. Pronunciation of these words is traditionally distinguished in AmE. The former is often thought to be best pronounced with the second syllable stressed, i.e., /prə-**seed**-əns/, whereas the latter has the primary accent on the first syllable, i.e., /**pres**-ə-dəns/. *Precedence* is nevertheless acceptably pronounced /**pres**-ə-dəns/ in AmE, as it is usually sounded in the common phrase *take precedence over.* In BrE, /**pres**-ə-dəns/ is the only known pronunciation.

precedency. See **precedence.**

precedent, adj., is inferior to *prior* or *previous,* except when used as a POSTPOSITIVE ADJECTIVE in a phrase such as *condition precedent.* E.g., "This rule in no respect impinges on the doctrine that one who makes only a loan on such paper, or takes it as collateral security for a *precedent* [read *prior*] debt, may be limited in his recovery to the amount advanced or secured." This adjective is best pronounced /pri-**seed**-ənt/, although /**pres**-ə-dənt/ is acceptable.

The adjective *precedent* (= preceding in time or order) should not be used for *precedential* (= of the nature of, constituting, or relating to a precedent): "Under the *precedent* [read *precedential*] theory of this court, one panel may not overrule the decision of another panel of this court squarely on point and in the absence of intervening and overruling Supreme Court decisions."

precedent, n. **A. And *stare decisis.*** A *precedent* is a decided case that furnishes a basis for determining an identical or similar case that may arise later, or a similar question of law. *Stare decisis,* by contrast, is the practice of applying precedents to later cases.

B. As a Shortened Form of *binding precedent.* The word *precedent* alone is ambiguous, since it is a CHAMELEON-HUED WORD. That is, we have both *binding precedents* and *persuasive precedents,* and they do not carry the same weight of authority: a binding precedent must be followed, whereas a persuasive precedent need not be. Usually, a lawyer who uses the word *precedent* means *binding precedent.*

Without the qualifying adjective, however, the term can be very broad indeed: "If the term *'precedent'* is construed sufficiently broadly, there are very few cases in which there is literally none to serve as an analogy, however remote." Rupert Cross & J.W. Harris, *Precedent in English Law* 204 (4th ed. 1991).

C. And *custom.* Plucknett, like other writers, has emphasized the distinction: one case constitutes a *precedent,* whereas several cases serve as evidence of a *custom.* Theodore F.T. Plucknett, *A Concise History of the Common Law* 347 (5th ed. 1956).

D. *Original precedent; declaratory precedent.* Some writers distinguish between judicial deliverances that merely declare existing law (*declaratory precedents*) and those that lay down new law (*original precedents*). In fact, though, the difference is one of degree and not of kind: "If we have a case [that] deals with certain facts by applying an acknowledged rule, we really have an addition to the rule, because we now know that a certain kind of fact falls within it, and in the nature of things we can never have two sets of facts [that] are precisely similar. No precedent is purely *'declaratory'* or purely *'original.'* " William Geldart, *Introduction to English Law* 11 (D.C.M. Yardley ed., 9th ed. 1984).

E. Meaning "a legal form." In England, Australia, and Canada, lawyers use *precedent* to refer to a legal form. American lawyers speak of a *form,* while Scots lawyers speak of a *style.* See **style.**

precedential ordinarily means "furnishing a guide or rule for subsequent cases." (See **precedent,** n.) E.g., "The conferees believe the case does not comport with the legislative intent of the statute or with its interpretation from 1927 through 1983; the case should not have any *precedential* effect."

precedents. See **precedence.**

preceding, when used simply for *before,* is best replaced by that word. E.g., "Appellants alleged in their complaint that *preceding* [read *before*] their arrests they were engaged only in peaceful and constitutionally protected protest activities." Cf. **next preceding.**

preceed. See **precede (B).**

precipitancy; precipitance; precipitation. *Precipitancy* = excessive or unwise haste in action; rashness. *Precipitance* is a NEEDLESS VARIANT. *Precipitation* = (1) haste, hurry; (2) the act of precipitating <the precipitation of the riot is still a mystery>; or (3) something precipitated (as rain or snow).

precipitate, adj.; **precipitous.** These words are quite different, though often confused. *Precipitate* = sudden; hasty; rash; showing violent or uncontrollable speed. This word is applied to actions, movements, or demands. E.g., "Henry ensured that the only effect of *precipitate* action by a claimant should be the delay of the fulfillment of his claim, and the increase of its cost . . . ." H.G. Hanbury, *English Courts of Law* 39 (2d ed. 1953).

Precipitous = like a precipice; steep. It is properly applied to physical things—rarely to actions, except when the metaphor of steepness is apt. But *precipitous* is frequently misused for *precipitate*—e.g.: "A federal court should await a definitive construction by a state court rather than *precipitously* [read *precipitately*] indulging a facial challenge to the constitutional validity of a state statute."/ "Within weeks the price of yarn began a *precipitous* decline." Perhaps this last usage is excusable, if we picture a graph with a sharp drop, or if we visualize a decline; but if "sudden" is meant, *precipitate* is the word.

Precipitant is a NEEDLESS VARIANT for *precipitate*—e.g.: "The stakeholder may have instituted interpleader proceedings *precipitantly* [read *precipitately*] and without any reasonable fear of adverse claims."

precipitation. See **precipitancy.**

precision; precisian; precisionist. *Precision* = accuracy; *precisian* = a person who adheres to rigidly high standards (often with regard to moral conduct); *precisionist* = a person who prizes absolute correctness of expression and performance, esp. in language and ritual.

preclusive; preclusory. The latter is a NEEDLESS VARIANT.

precondition is usu. unnecessary in place of *condition*—e.g.: "For months the Government tried in vain to persuade him that he and the ANC should abandon some of the cornerstones of their strategy as a *pre-condition* [read *condition*] for future negotiations." Fred Bridgland, *Freedom Brings Mandela His Greatest Challenge,* Sunday Telegraph, 11 Feb. 1990, at 3.

precontractual; precontract, adj. Contract scholars—not contractual scholars—disagree in their practice: Grant Gilmore refers to *precontrac-*

tual duties, whereas G.H. Treitel refers to *precontract negotiations.* Gilmore's practice is probably better for two reasons: first, *precontract* is also a noun meaning "an agreement to marry," and thus may give rise to ambiguities; and second, it is better to use a genuinely adjectival form when it is available.

predacious; predaceous; predative; predatory; predatorial. *Predatory* = preying on other animals. The word is applied figuratively in the phrase from antitrust law, *predatory pricing.* The forms *predaceous, predatorial,* and *predative* are NEEDLESS VARIANTS. The spelling *predacious* has undergone DIFFERENTIATION and means "devouring; rapacious."

predate. See **antedate.**

predative; predatory; predatorial. See **predacious.**

predecease (= to die before), a Shakespearean coinage, has become a legal genteelism: "She *predeceased* him leaving a husband and two children." Anthony R. Mellows, *The Law of Succession* 515 (3d ed. 1977). And it surely has a place: if one says, *She died before him . . . ,* the words *She died* resonate in the mind—the reader wonders how and why. But the legal writer usu. wants to focus on something else entirely: "Should she *predecease* her husband, even this incipient right is automatically extinguished." Robert Kratovil, *Real Estate Law* 226 (1946). The writer who used *die before* in that sentence would lose some readers. Lawyers, in short, sometimes need to talk about death without thinking about it.

predecisional (of, relating to, or occurring during the time before a decision) is a mid-20th-century legal NEOLOGISM. E.g., "Total *predecisional* acceptance of Dr. Williams' report and Dr. Peltier's testimony is revealed by the following . . . ." *Lee v. Gardner,* 267 F. Supp. 578, 583 (W.D. Mo. 1967)./ "[O]ccasionally, on particular facts, a *predecisional* release has been criticized for the outside appearances it created . . . ." *FTC v. Cinderella Career & Finishing Schs., Inc.,* 404 F.2d 1308, 1323 (D.C. Cir. 1968).

predial. See **pr(a)edial.**

predicable; predicative; predicatory. The first means "that may be predicated or affirmed." The second means "having the quality of predicating, affirming, or asserting." The third means "of or pertaining to a preacher."

predicate, v.t. (= [1] to affirm a statement or proposition; or [2] to found, base), is usu. construed with *on* in modern writing. E.g., "Even without *Leavell,* we would decline to *predicate* a broad immunity *on* the basis of the narrow holding of *Miller.*"

PREDICATE NOMINATIVES are nouns or pronouns in the nominative or subjective case that appear after linking verbs—usually *be*-verbs. "It is *I,*" one writes, for instance, or, in formal contexts: "It seems to be *she,*" "You appeared to be *I,*" and so on. When the situation is formal, these constructions are not affectations; they are obligatory. For example, the following error occurred merely because of an imperfect knowledge of grammar, together with aspirations to correctness: "The description 'plaintiff-appellee' or 'respondent below' forces us to keep looking at the title block on the opinion's first page to keep track of who is *whom* [read *who*]."

Nevertheless, in informal contexts and primarily in speech, it is quite acceptable today to say "It's me." On formal occasions, or if one is particularly fastidious in language, one should feel perfectly comfortable saying "It is I." See NOMINATIVE AND OBJECTIVE CASES.

predicative; predicatory. See **predicable.**

predominate, adj., is a NEEDLESS VARIANT for *predominant.* In good usage, *predominate* is the verb, *predominant* the adjective. Readers may be confused when *predominate* is used adjectivally: "These facts were *predominate* [read *predominant*] in the court's decision to pierce the corporate veil."/ "The *Roth* opinion referred to the Model Penal Code definition of obscenity—material whose *predominate* [read *predominant*] appeal is to 'a shameful or morbid interest in nudity, sex, or excretion.'" Cf. **preponderantly.**

preempt; perempt. These words should be distinguished. *Preempt* (now generally spelled as one word without a hyphen) is a BACK-FORMATION from its noun, *preemption.* To *preempt* is to acquire beforehand to the exclusion of others, or to take precedence over.

To *perempt,* by contrast, is to quash, do away with, or extinguish. The *OED* and *W3* record *perempt* as an obsolete or archaic term, but it is current at least in Louisiana in intransitive uses: "The privilege contained in article 3237 *perempts* or dies at the end of six months."

preemption; peremption. *Preemption,* by far the more common word, means: (1) "the right to buy before others"; (2) "the purchase of something under this right"; (3) "an earlier seizure or appropriation"; (4) "the occupation of (public land) so as to establish a preemptive title"; or (5) in AmE, Congress's legislatively taking over of an entire subject matter so as to make it inherently federal. See **preempt.** For more on sense (5), see **preemption, federal.** For *right of preemption,* see **option.**

Peremption is a rare legal term meaning "the act or process of quashing" (*W3*), "a nonsuit." It is rare everywhere, apparently, but in Louisiana. E.g., "[*P*]*eremption* is but a form of prescription, a species thereof, but with the characteristic that it does not admit of interruption or suspension . . . ." *Flowers, Inc. v. Rausch,* 364 So. 2d 928, 931 (La. 1978)./ "Actually, *peremption* is a common law term which has crept into our [civil] jurisprudence. Its counterpart in the civil law is really *forfeiture.*" *Id.* at 931 n.1. *Peremption* and its derivatives are used throughout *Equilease Corp. v. M/V Sampson,* 756 F.2d 357 (5th Cir. 1985). See N. Stephan Kinsella, *A Civil Law to Common Law Dictionary,* 54 La. L. Rev. 1265, 1285 (1994).

preemption, federal; exclusive federal jurisdiction. Though many American legal writers fail to distinguish between these phrases, and use *preemption* for both senses, one jurist insists that, properly speaking, *federal preemption* should be kept distinct from *exclusive federal jurisdiction:* "In the former, federal substantive law supplants state law, but, absent other provisions, both state and federal courts have concurrent jurisdiction of actions arising under that law; in the latter, only the specified federal instrumentalities have jurisdiction of the matter, irrespective of the law to be applied." 1A *Moore's Federal Practice* ¶ 0.160, at 189 (2d ed. 1981).

preemptioner; preemptor. These words should be differentiated. A *preemptioner* holds the right to purchase public land by preemption—e.g.: "A *preemptioner* acquires no present right to affect the property, but holds only a general contract right to acquire a later interest should the property owner decide to sell." *Old Nat'l Bank v. Arneson,* 776 P.2d 145, 148 (Wash. Ct. App. 1989).

A *preemptor* actually acquires land by using this right. Of course, *preemptor* serves also as the general agent noun corresponding to the verb *preempt.*

preemptive; preemptory; peremptive; peremptory. The adjectives most commonly used and distinguished are *preemptive* (= relating to or of the nature of preemption) and *peremptory,* q.v.

The two other forms have bona fide existences, however. *Preemptory* correctly means "of or relating to a preemptor" (but is sometimes misused for *preemptive*). (For the correct use, see **preemptioner;** for the incorrect use, see **preemptory.**) *Peremptive* = of or relating to peremption. E.g., "Authority exists in Louisiana cases to support the proposition that a prescriptive period defined in a statute conferring a right is actually a *peremptive* period." See **preemption.**

PREEMPTIVE PHRASES. See ANTICIPATORY REFERENCE.

preemptor. See **preemptioner.**

preemptory for *peremptory* is a fairly common mistake. Properly, the former means "of or relating to a preemptor." See **preemptioner** & **preemptive.**

preestablished. So spelled.

preexisting. So spelled.

preface. See **foreword.**

prefatory; prefatorial; prefatial. The last two terms are NEEDLESS VARIANTS of the first.

prefer, which generally means "to like better," survives in a number of older senses in legal writing. For example, the *OED* records the sense "to advance oneself or one's interests," exemplified in this quotation: "People can properly *prefer* their own self-interests." Additionally, *prefer* has the sense "to lay (a matter) before anyone formally for consideration, approval, or sanction; to bring forward (as an indictment)" <to prefer charges>. Hence: "A state's attorney is under a moral duty to enter a nolle prosequi whenever he is satisfied that a prisoner is innocent of the charge *preferred* against him."/ "Informations were also *preferred* against the first defendant that he did aid and abet each of the other defendants to engage in retail trading on Sunday by providing them with a stall and pitch for the sale of their goods." (Eng.)

preferable is inherently a comparative adjective; therefore it should not be used with *more.* E.g., "Unsatisfied with the steps toward first use protection that have thus far occurred under the Federal Trademark Act of 1946, he suggests a more flexible interpretative approach by the courts and administrative agencies *or, more preferably* [read *or, preferably*], congressional amendment." See COMPARATIVES AND SUPERLATIVES & ADJECTIVES (B).

Preferable is accented on the first, not on the second, syllable.

pregnancy termination. See **abortion.**

pregnant, negative. See **negative pregnant.**

prejudge. See **forejudge.**

prejudice, n. & v.t., is a LEGALISM for *harm,* n. & v.t. In ordinary discourse, it is a lawyer's pomposity—e.g.: "I doubt that he will *prejudice* [read *hurt* or *harm*] her chances of getting a job by advancing too quickly." In the following two specimens, the reference is to legal harm: "The critical inquiry is whether, for whatever reason, counsel's performance was deficient and whether that deficiency *prejudiced* the defendant."/ "A stay of the plaintiff's action here will not *prejudice* him." (Eng.)

Sometimes the past participle *prejudiced* almost gives rise to a MISCUE, as some readers might take it to mean "having a strong bias against (something)"—e.g.: "The Louisiana revocatory action is available to a creditor who is *prejudiced* [i.e., *harmed*] at the time by a fraudulent transfer made by his debtor." Albert Tate, Jr., "The Revocatory Action in Louisiana Law," in *Essays on the Civil Law of Obligations* 133, 133 (Joseph Dainow ed., 1969).

prejudice, with(out). These terms are used in reference to whether a future action is barred. For example, if a court dismisses a lawsuit *with prejudice,* the court has adjudicated the merits of the case, so the dismissal constitutes a bar to future action. A *dismissal without prejudice* is not an adjudication on the merits; hence no right or remedy is foreclosed to the parties.

Increasingly, writers are placing *with(out) prejudice* before the noun *dismissal*—but the resulting PHRASAL ADJECTIVE jars the reader familiar with the legal idiom: "Government counsel told the justices that the district judge erred by not performing the balancing test the act mandates for choosing between *with-* and *without-prejudice* dismissal." *Supreme Court Ponders Sanction for Violation of Speedy Trial Act,* 56 U.S.L.W. 1176, 1176 (17 May 1988).

prejudicial. A. And *prejudiced.* *Prejudicial* (= tending to injure; harmful) applies to things and events; *prejudiced* (= harboring prejudices) applies to people. The meaning of a sentence can frequently be made clearer by using *harmful* in place of *prejudicial.*

Occasionally, writers misuse *prejudicial* for *prejudiced*—e.g.: "Indeed the rule shields the deliberations and conclusions of the chosen representatives of the board only if they possess a disinterested independence and do not stand in a dual relation which prevents an *unprejudicial* [read *unprejudiced*] exercise of judgment." *Auerbach v. Bennett,* 393 N.E.2d 994, 1001 (N.Y. 1979).

B. And *pre-judicial.* The hyphen makes an important difference. *Pre-judicial* was used in Roman law in reference to a class of preliminary actions in which questions of right or fact, usually as relating to status, were determined. Today the hyphenated form is often used somewhat differently, in reference to a time before a given person became a judge—e.g.: "Professor Schwartz opens his book with a brief chapter on Warren's *pre-judicial* career." See PUNCTUATION (F).

The more usual term is *prejudicial,* discussed in (A). E.g., "The allegedly *prejudicial* remarks pointed to by appellee were clearly made in the context of a hypothetical involving a worker who becomes disabled after a second accident."/ "The trial judge should have made a determination of the relative probative value of the 23-year-old conviction as against the *prejudicial* effect on the jury."

preliminary injunction. See **temporary restraining order.**

preliminary to, when used merely as an equivalent of *before,* is a silly pomposity—e.g.: "*Preliminary to* [read *Before*] the date set for trial a pretrial hearing was held by the state court." Cf. **preparatory to, prior to & antecedent.**

premeditated (= consciously considered beforehand) appears mostly in criminal-law contexts <premeditated murder>. Because it invariably precedes a bad act of some kind, the word has taken on strongly negative connotations.

premeditatively, adv., is used much more often than the corresponding adjective, *premeditative.* The adverb provides an alternative to the awkward term *premeditatedly,* which is also common. E.g., "Defendant was charged with willfully, deliberately, and *premeditatively* murdering her with malice aforethought . . . ." *State v. Hansen,* 225 N.W.2d 343, 345 (Iowa 1975). See -EDLY.

premia. See **premium.**

premise; premiss. Both refer to "a previous statement or proposition from which another is inferred as a conclusion." The first is the AmE, the second the BrE spelling.

premises. A. As a Popularized Legal Technicality. *Premises* (= a house or building) has a curious history in legal usage. Originally, in the sense of things mentioned previously, it denoted the part of a deed that sets forth the names of the grantor and grantee, as well as the things granted and the consideration. Then, through HYPALLAGE in the early 18th century, it was extended to refer to the subject of a conveyance or bequest as specified in the premises of the deed. Finally, it was extended to refer to a house or building along with its grounds. In short, someone who says, "No alcohol is allowed on these premises," is engaging unconsciously in a POPULARIZED LEGAL TECHNICALITY.

The term always takes a plural verb—e.g.: "The *premises* were put under surveillance." And it is improper to shorten *premises*—in the sense of a building together with its grounds—to the singular *premise.* E.g., "[A no-knock provision allows] law-enforcement officers to enter *a premise* [read *premises*] forcibly, without announcing their presence before entering, under certain circumstances." Ralph De Sola, *Crime Dictionary* 103 (1982).

B. Other Senses in Drafting. The word *premises* is sometimes used in the sense of matters (usu. preliminary facts or statements) previously referred to in the same instrument. In practice, this usage is often inarticulate and confusing, since the subject matter constituting the *premises* is rarely specified in the instrument. For example, one who writes *wherefore, premises considered* in the prayer of a court paper would be hard pressed to say what the premises are, other than everything that has gone before.

Occasionally, too, lawyers use *premises* in the logical, syllogistic sense of the grounds or bases for a legal argument or legal reasoning. See ISSUE-FRAMING.

premiss. See **premise.**

premium. Pl. *-iums.* The form *premia* is hopelessly pedantic: "Tender offers entail substantial *premia* [read *premiums*] compared with the prices shares carry before the bids—and afterward, should the offers be defeated." *Flamm v. Eberstadt,* 814 F.2d 1169, 1174 (7th Cir. 1987). See PLURALS (A).

premortal; premortem. See **antemortem.**

premortgage. So spelled, without a hyphen.

prenuptial. See **antenuptial.**

pre-owned for *used.* See EUPHEMISMS.

preparatory; preparative. As an adjective, *preparative* is a NEEDLESS VARIANT of *preparatory.* It is a legitimate noun, however, meaning "something that prepares the way for something else."

preparatory to, used in the sense "in preparation for," is legalistic—e.g.: "The demolition of the two-story building and the four-story building constituted work *preparatory to* [read *in preparation for*] the construction of the building . . . ." *Waikiki Resort Hotel, Inc. v. City & County of Honolulu,* 624 P.2d 1353, 1360 (Haw. 1981)./ "An admission made in court or *preparatory to* [read *in preparation for*] trial by a party or his attorney . . . removes the fact from the field of disputed issues in the particular case in which it is made." *Rice v. State Farm Ins. Co.,* 885 S.W.2d 775, 779 (Mo. Ct. App. 1994)./ "On April 6, 1994 defendant mailed proxy materials to its shareholders *preparatory to* [read *in preparation for*] the annual meeting scheduled for May 11, 1994." *Smith v. Orange & Rockland Utils., Inc.,* 617 N.Y.S.2d 278, 279 (Sup. Ct. 1994).

The phrase is likewise pretentious in place of *before*—e.g.: "Upon the appellant's conviction and *preparatory to* [read *before*] sentencing, the trial court ordered a presentence report pursuant to Code § 19.2-299." *Robinson v. Commonwealth,* 413 S.E.2d 661, 661 (Va. Ct. App. 1992). Cf. **preliminary to, prior to & antecedent to.**

prepense. The phrase *malice prepense* is obsolete for *malice aforethought.* See **aforethought & malice aforethought.**

preplan is illogical for *plan* because one can plan something beforehand only. E.g., "Ninety percent of wasting time and standing in line can be eliminated with a little *preplanning* [read *planning*] and some common sense." Mark H. McCormack, *What They Don't Teach You at Harvard Business School* 212 (1984). See ILLOGIC & REDUNDANCY.

preponderance of the evidence; clear and convincing evidence. The former, denoting the greater weight of the evidence, is the "traditional measure of persuasion in civil cases." John W. Strong et al., *McCormick on Evidence* § 340, at 575 (4th ed. 1992). The phrase *clear and convincing evidence*—as well as half a dozen or so variations, such as *clear, convincing, and satisfactory evidence*—denotes a "more exacting measure." *Id.* But this heightened standard, however expressed, remains fuzzy: "It has been persuasively suggested that [the standard] could be more simply and intelligibly translated to the jury if they were instructed that they must be persuaded that the truth of the contention is 'highly probable.'" *Id.* at 575–76.

preponderantly; preponderately. The better form is *preponderantly,* though the NEEDLESS VARIANT *preponderately* is becoming commonplace—e.g.: "For an award of supplemental earnings benefits, the claimant must *preponderately* [read *preponderantly*] prove an inability to earn 90 percent of pre-injury wages." *Britton v. Morton Thiokol, Inc.,* 604 So. 2d 130, 134 (La. Ct. App. 1992).

Preponderate should be used only as a verb, not as an adjective—or, by derivation, as an adverb. Cf. **predominate.**

PREPOSITIONS. A. Ending Sentences with. The spurious rule about not ending sentences with prepositions is a remnant of Latin grammar, in which a preposition was the one word that a writer could not end a sentence with. But Latin grammar never should have been thought to straitjacket English grammar. If the SUPERSTITION is a "rule" at all, it is a rule of rhetoric and not of grammar, the idea being to end sentences with strong words that drive the point home. That principle is sound, of course, but not to the extent of meriting lockstep adherence.

Churchill's witticism about this preposterous bugaboo should have laid it to rest. When someone once upbraided him for ending a sentence with a preposition, he rejoined, "That is the type of arrant pedantry up with which I shall not put." Avoiding a preposition at the end of the sentence sometimes leads to just such a preposterous monstrosity.

Perfectly natural-sounding sentences end with prepositions, particularly when a verb compounded with a preposition appears at the end (as in *follow up* or *ask for*). E.g., "The act must have some causal connection with the injury complained *of.*" When one decides against such formal (sometimes downright stilted) constructions as *of which, on which,* and *for which*—and instead chooses the relative *that*—the preposition is necessarily sent to the end of the sentence: "I must respectfully dissent, for this is a point on which I must insist" becomes far more natural as, "I must respectfully dissent, for this is a point that I must insist on."

Moreover, good writers often end their sentences with prepositions—e.g.:

- "But the admission of consuls into the United States, where no previous treaty has stipulated it, seems to have been nowhere provided for." *The Federalist* No. 42, at 265 (James Madison) (Clinton Rossiter ed., 1961).
- "At first sight it is little to the credit of Montesquieu's and Vico's contemporaries that their work was not followed up." Frederick Pollock, "The History of Comparative Jurisprudence," in *Essays in the Law* 1, 22 (1922; repr. 1969).
- "Sound objectives became confused and were even lost sight of." Fleming James, *Civil Procedure* § 2.5, at 66 (1965).
- "There is always some unrepealed junk that nobody will make an effort to get rid of." Patrick Devlin, *The Enforcement of Morals* 126 (1968).
- "The trouble is that Holmes failed to keep in mind his own profound insight into the complex interplay between new materials drawn from life and old materials from the past which have not yet been sloughed off." Grant Gilmore, *The Ages of American Law* 53 (1977).
- "The involuntary bailee can be quickly disposed of. He is one who has been sent goods that he did not ask for." Glanville Williams, *Textbook of Criminal Law* 694 (1978).
- "Perhaps it is possible for a particular case to be either within or without the judicial power, depending on the court it is in." Charles A. Wright, *The Law of Federal Courts* 45 (4th ed. 1983).
- "The result of this was that agreements in restraint of trade were frequently made and frequently abided by." P.S. Atiyah, *An Introduction to the Law of Contract* 248 (3d ed. 1986).

See HYPERCORRECTION (I) & SUPERSTITIONS (A).

For an interesting—and incorrect—example involving *where it is at,* see **at.**

B. Redundancy of. Writers often repeat prepositions unnecessarily when there are intervening phrases or clauses. E.g., "The Massachusetts court argued that promoters stand *in* as much *in* [omit the first *in*] a fiduciary position to the corporation when uninformed shareholders are expected to be brought in after the wrong has been perpetrated as when there are current shareholders to whom no disclosure is made." Cf. **so as + [infinitive].**

C. Wrongly Elided. Just as often, however, necessary prepositions are wrongly omitted, usually because of the proximity of the same preposition performing a different function—e.g.: "An acceptance that requests a change [*of*] or addition to terms *of* the offer is not thereby invalidated unless the acceptance is made to depend on assent to the changed or added terms."/ "Maxi Corporation is a Texas corporation [*of*] which Smith owns sixty percent *of* the stock."

Occasionally prepositions are omitted for fear of ending a sentence with one: "There are no unasserted claims and assessments of any nature that we are aware [*of*]." (Or, one might say, *of which we are aware.)*/ "The courts recognize that the seller and buyer are not the only persons interested in this transaction and have imposed duties on the selling shareholder with respect to whom he sells [*to*]." The writers should not have feared writing *aware of* and *sells to.* See (A).

There is at least one other type of problem caused by prepositions wrongly omitted: an AMBIGUITY may result. For example, *Attorney Solicitation* is the title of a law review article; yet from the title, one does not know whether the article refers to the solicitation of, or solicitation by, attorneys. That anyone with legal knowledge would presume the latter does not vindicate the writer's vagueness. See NOUN PLAGUE. See also (E) below.

D. Correctly Matching with Verbs. A useful rule of thumb—by no means to be taken as an absolute rule—in determining what preposition to use with a given verb is to follow the prefix of that verb. Hence *inhere in, comport with* (L. *com-* "with"), *attribute to* (L. *ad-* "to"), and so on. There are many exceptions, however. *Impute* takes *on, oblivious* takes *of,* and *in respect* can take either *of* or *to,* though *with respect* takes only *to.*

The verbs used in criminal law are sometimes tricky. Following are the correct prepositions for some of the common verbs:

acquitted *of* burglary
acquitted *on* an indictment, count, or charge of burglary
charged *in* (AmE) or *on* (BrE) an indictment or count
charged *with* murder
convicted *of* burglary
convicted *on* an indictment, count, or charge of burglary
indicted *for* embezzlement
indicted *on* a charge of embezzlement
pleaded guilty *to* a charge or count of murder
pleaded guilty *to* murder
sentenced *on* an indictment, count, or charge
tried *on* an indictment, count, or charge

Many other verbs are treated throughout this work. Readers with an interest in a more detailed, comprehensive treatment of this subject may benefit from the following works: Morton Benson et al., *The BBI Combinatory Dictionary of English: A Guide to Word Combinations* (1986); Frederick T. Wood, *English Prepositional Idioms* (1967); and A.P. Cowie & R. Mackin, *The Oxford Dictionary of Current Idiomatic English* (1975).

E. Repetition of After Conjunctions. Often it is useful in avoiding AMBIGUITY to repeat the preposition governing the noun after *or* or *and.* E.g., "Is it a question *of* law or *of* fact?"

A statute drafter's failure to repeat such a preposition resulted in litigation that worked its way to the U.S. Supreme Court. The question arose whether an agency could remove a case under the following provision:

> (a) A civil action or criminal prosecution commenced in a State court against any of the following persons may be removed by them to the district court of the United States . . . :
> (1) Any officer of the United States or [of] any agency thereof . . . .

The Supreme Court used grammatical analysis in concluding that the removal by an agency was improper: "We find that . . . the first clause of § 1442(a)(1) grants removal power to only one grammatical subject, '[a]ny officer,' which is then modified by a compound prepositional phrase: 'of the United States or [of] any agency thereof.'" *International Primate Protection League v. Tulane Educ. Fund,* 500 U.S. 72, 79–80 (1991). See (C) above.

F. Getting It Wrong. Writers often use the incorrect preposition—e.g.: "To get upset about Begelman in Hollywood is to get upset *about* [read *at*] a cannibal for chewing his own cuticles."/ "In sum, the common-law widow's election has no tax consequences *to* [read *for*] the surviving spouse." See **as to (A).**

prerequisite; requisite. Rarely is *prerequisite* used with the degree of punctilio that Eric Partridge prescribed: "Properly, a *prerequisite* has to be obtained or fulfilled before a *requisite* can be attended to. In short, *prerequisite* is rarely permissible." Vigilans [Eric Partridge], *Chamber of Horrors* 114 (1952). Probably it is more accurate to say that *prerequisite* simply includes a time element, whereas *requisite* does not.

prerogative; prerogatory. *Prerogative* (= of, relating to, or exercising an exclusive right or privilege) is the standard term. *Prerogatory* is a NEEDLESS VARIANT—e.g.: "At this time, a *prerogatory* [read *prerogative*] writ is not before the court in this case." *Mott v. England,* 604 P.2d 560, 564 (Wyo. 1979).

prerogative writs. During the 16th century, this name was given to administrative writs such as mandamus, certiorari, habeas corpus, and prohibition—each of which was originally in the nature of an administrative order from a superior official commanding a subordinate to do something, give some information, or the like. As a major legal historian notes, however, the name *prerogative writs* "was not altogether apt, because in the early stages of their expansion these writs were mainly used to curb prerogative activity by councillors and conciliar courts." J.H. Baker, *An Introduction to English Legal History* 165–66 (3d ed. 1990).

The phrase *extraordinary writs,* which is perfectly equivalent, is more genuinely descriptive, and therefore preferable.

prerogatory. See **prerogative.**

prescribe, v.i. In lay writing, *prescribe* is transitive only: doctors prescribe drugs and moralists prescribe rules of conduct. In Louisiana and Scots law, *prescribe* has a special intransitive sense: "[of an action] to suffer prescription; to lapse, to become invalid or void by passage of time; to be no longer capable of prosecution" (*OED*). Hence: "We need not unravel this jurisprudence to determine whether any of his trespass claims for damages for the actual taking of his property have *prescribed* [i.e., *become void by passage of time*]."/ "Appellee's right to claim just compensation for this interest does not *prescribe* [i.e., *cease to be capable of prosecution*] until two years from the date of the judgment of the district court."/ "The district court correctly held, therefore, that appellee's claims for damages incident to the taking of his property for use as a gas storage reservoir had *prescribed* [i.e., *lapsed*]." Cf. **prescription.**

The civilian sense of *prescribe* has also been employed transitively—a sense not listed in the *OED:* "It was shown that the property involved was the same property as that in a suit brought in the Louisiana court a few years earlier where the same restrictive covenant was held *to have been prescribed* by two years['] continued violation." *Warner v. Walsdorf,* 277 F.2d 679, 680 (5th Cir. 1960). See **proscribe.**

prescription. In law, this term frequently refers to the legal effect that the passage of time has on a person's rights or obligations. That effect may be to establish those rights or obligations (positive prescription), fortify them (another type of positive prescription), or extinguish them (negative prescription). For example, under the (English) Prescription Act 1832, a right to an easement may be established through continual use over 20 years' time. In the U.S., periods for prescription vary from state to state: they are sometimes 10, 15, or 20 years. Cf. **proscription.**

present. Phrases such as *the present testator* and *the present trust* have become common spin-offs of *the present case* and *the present writer.* (See FIRST PERSON (A).) Rarely, however, does *present* serve any purpose. See **instant case.**

presentable has nearly opposite senses in nonlegal and legal contexts. Whereas fops go to great lengths to make themselves "presentable," criminals subject to presentment are also said to be "presentable"—e.g.: "By the laws of New Jersey the Court of Oyer and Terminer and general jail delivery has 'cognizance of all crimes and offences whatsoever which, by law, are or shall be of an indictable or *presentable* nature . . . .'" *Andrews v. Swartz,* 156 U.S. 272, 275 (1895) (quoting a New Jersey statute).

present case. See **instant case.**

presenter; presentor. The preferred spelling is *-er.* The two legal senses are (1) "a person who makes a presentment"; and (2) "a person who presents a petition, bill, etc. (i.e., makes a presentation)." For more detail on sense (1), see **presentment.**

presentiment. See **presentment.**

presenting jury. See **grand jury** (A).

presently contains an ambiguity. In the days of Shakespeare, it meant "immediately." Soon its meaning evolved into "after a short time" (perhaps because people exaggerated about their promptitude); this sense is still current. Then, chiefly in the AmE, it took on the additional sense "at present; currently." Some writers deprecate this sense, but the *Oxford Guide* states that it is "widely used and often sounds more natural than *at present.*" It certainly appears in formal legal prose in this sense, esp. in AmE: "Enough instances of self-enrichment *presently* occur, even in the case of managers of public corporations, to suggest that the market cannot fully control this phenomenon."/ "*Presently* pending before this court is an appeal from the decision of the district court that denied appellants' application to present a next-friend petition for a writ of habeas corpus on behalf of their son, a death-sentenced prisoner." Cf. **momentarily.**

presentment; presentiment. The first means "the act of presenting or laying before a court or other tribunal a formal statement about a matter to be dealt with legally." (For the special sense of *presentment* in criminal law, see **indictment.**) The second means "a vague mental impression or feeling of a future event."

presentor. See **presenter.**

presents, know all men by these. See **know all men by these presents.**

present time, at the. This phrase is wordy for *now.*

present writer is today generally considered inferior to *I* or *me*. See **present** & FIRST PERSON (A).

preservation; preserval. The latter is a NEEDLESS VARIANT.

presidence; presidency. The former means "the action or fact of presiding"; the latter means "the office or function of president."

president. In corporate law, the term is used differently in AmE and BrE. In AmE, *president* often denotes the chief executive director of a company; but in BrE, it is a title usu. given to a nonexecutive former head of a company.

presiding judge. See **chief judge.**

presiding juror. See **foreman** & SEXISM (B).

prestatutory. So spelled. See PUNCTUATION (F).

presumably. See **presumptively.**

presume. See **assume.**

presumption = a judicially applied prediction of factual or legal probability. E.g., "After adjudication of insanity, a *presumption* of insanity continues, but a subsequent adjudication of restoration to sanity by competent authority restores the previous *presumption* of sanity until the contrary is made to appear."/ "By the provisions of the Restatement of the Law of Contracts it is expressly provided that there is a *presumption* that the offer is to enter into a bilateral contract."

In American law, the most basic distinction is between a *presumption of law* and a *presumption of fact.* A *presumption of law* is a rule of law by which the finding of a basic fact gives rise to a presumed fact capable of being rebutted. A *presumption of fact* is simply an argument; it is an inference that may be drawn from the establishment of a basic fact, but need not be drawn as a matter of law—e.g., that the possessor of recently stolen goods is the thief. This distinction is increasingly rejected. See **rebuttable presumption.**

British lawyers distinguish between the following types: (1) presumptions *juris et de jure,* which are irrebuttable; (2) presumptions *juris,* which are rebuttable by evidence; and (3) presumptions of fact, which are merely inferences.

presumptive; presumptuous. *Presumptive* = (1) giving reasonable grounds for presumption or belief; warranting inferences; or (2) based on presumption or inference. E.g., in sense (2): "The interest limited in that case was a remainder and the settlor's intent to revoke the instrument was ineffective since *presumptive* remaindermen were not parties to the revocation." (For *heir presumptive,* see **heir** (B).) *Presumptuous* = arrogant, presuming, bold, forward, impudent.

presumptively; presumably. These words are often used synonymously in English prose, but in legal writing are commonly differentiated. *Presumptively* = by legal presumption. E.g., "The literal words of the statute are *presumptively* conclusive of legislative intent, but that presumption may be defeated by contrary indications of intent also evident on the face of the statute." *Presumably* = as one may presume or reasonably suppose; by presumption or supposition.

presumptuous. See **presumptive.**

pretence. See **pretense.**

pretend as though for *pretend that* (by analogy to *act as though*) is unidiomatic.

pretense; pretence. The AmE spelling is *-se,* the BrE spelling *-ce.* See **false pretenses.**

pretentious (= making claim to great merit or importance) for *pedantic* (= overrating or parading book-learning or technical knowledge) is an unthinking blunder: "The line between owner and repairman is dull and elusive at best; fortunately, Congress has for future cases ended this sometimes *pretentious* [read *pedantic*] distinction."

pretermit. **A. Connotation of Purposefulness.** *Pretermit* generally connotes "to overlook or ignore purposely," as here: "Our deliberate choice, however, is to dispose finally of the appeal on its merits and *pretermit* a difficult jurisdictional issue."/ "*Pretermitting* other problems with appellant's claim, we find based on these facts that appellant's failure to present evidence of the existence of the vodka bottles was due to his own lack of diligence and that of his counsel."

Yet in the legal phrase *pretermitted child statutes,* the word *pretermitted* means "neglected or overlooked accidentally." E.g., "*Pretermitted* heir statutes are designed to prevent inadvertent disinheritance of a child or other descendant by the testator; the statutes are not intended to prevent the testator from disinheriting a child if he desires to do so." This sense derives from Roman law, which had the special term *preterition* for the omission by a testator to mention in his will one of his children or natural heirs.

B. For *prevent*. *Pretermit* does not properly

mean "to prevent, preclude, or obviate"—though legal writers commonly seem to attribute those meanings to the word. E.g., "We do not read *Weeks* as mandating remand in all cases where a removal petition is untimely; we are unwilling to allow a model defect to *pretermit* [read *prevent*] our substantive inquiry."/ "It is incorrect to read the 'subject only to' language as *pretermitting* [read *precluding*] a reading of the contract as a whole to flesh out the extent of Global Marine's obligation under this provision."/ "The disposition [that] we have made . . . *pretermits* [read *obviates*] the necessity for discussion of the third point." *Gray County v. Warner & Finney,* 727 S.W.2d 633, 640 (Tex. App.—Amarillo 1987).

pretextual (= constituting a pretext), though not recognized in the *OED, W10,* or *W3,* is common in American legal writing. E.g., "Whether the purpose of the statute is to screen the courts against *pretextual* grievances or to protect the respondent . . . , we need not inquire." *Cameron v. Cameron,* 56 S.E.2d 384, 388 (N.C. 1949)./ "There is no evidence to support a contention that the arrest for the traffic violation was *pretextual.*" *State v. Moody,* 443 S.W.2d 802, 804 (Mo. 1969)./ "[The] employer's proffered reason for her discharge was merely *'pretextual.'*" *Chavis v. Whitehall Labs., Inc.,* 664 F. Supp. 413, 413 (N.D. Ind. 1986) (case summary). See **nonpretextual.**

pretrial should not be hyphenated. See PUNCTUATION (F).

pretty, used as an adverb, is still considered informal or colloquial. E.g., "Handicapped as counsel was by a defendant under present confinement and with a rich history of earlier state convictions, it was *pretty* clear that counsel could not run the risk of putting the defendant on the stand." *Pretty* adds nothing to the sentence, unless it conveys a shade of doubt—*pretty clear* being less certain in some readers' minds than *clear.* See WEASEL WORDS.

prevalent is accented on the first, not the second, syllable: /***prev***-ə-lənt/.

prevent now ordinarily takes *from,* although archaically it is used with a direct object and a participle. E.g., "There are various matters that interfere with this normal course and *prevent* the action proceeding to final judgment." In BrE this usage remains common.

Prevent there causes ugly and ungrammatical constructions—e.g.: "Their action *prevented there from being* a quorum." [Read *Their action prevented a quorum from being reached.*]

prevent(at)ive. The correct form is *preventive*—both as noun and adjective—although the corrupt, extra-syllabled form *preventative* is unfortunately common. E.g., "As for . . . misplaced words—possibly the best *preventative* [read *preventive*] is a secretary who majored in English composition . . . ." Mortimer Levitan, *Confidential Chat on the Craft of Briefing,* 1957 Wis. L. Rev. 59, 62./ "It is in no sense a *preventative* [read *preventive*] remedy, but is prospective merely . . . ." 52 Am. Jur. 2d *Mandamus* § 9, at 337 (1970)./ "[G]reater willingness to make doctors liable means that they are forced to practise what is called *'preventative* [read *preventive*] medicine' and order costly, complicated, and often unnecessary tests." R.W.M. Dias & B.S. Markesinis, *Tort Law* 3 (1984).

preverdict. So spelled—without a hyphen. See PUNCTUATION (F).

previous. See **prior.**

previously; before, adv. Although *previous to* is much inferior to *before* as a preposition, just the opposite holds true for the adverbs. *Previously* is better than *before,* at least when the adverb comes before the verb—e.g.: "M. S. was then operating the filling station on lot three as *before* [read *previously*] mentioned."

previous to for *before* is unnecessarily highfalutin—e.g.: "*Previous to* [read *Before*] her service on the Supreme Court, Ginsburg served on the U.S. Court of Appeals for the District of Columbia."

One sometimes even finds *previously to*—e.g.: "Judge Critz was a member of the three-judge court, as well as having been a commissioner *previously to* [read *before*] becoming a judge." (An overhaul would greatly improve this sentence: *After serving as a commissioner, Judge Critz became a member of a three-judge court.*)/ "Throughout 1938 and for many years *previously and subsequently* [read *before and after*], defendants carried on their business in Newark."/ "*Previously to* [read *Before*] December 1950, appellants carried on business at Liverpool." (Eng.) See **prior to.** Cf. **anterior to & antecedent.**

prevision = foresight. E.g., "Life will have to be made over, and human nature transformed before *prevision* so extravagant can be accepted as the norm of conduct, the customary standard to which behavior must conform." *Palsgraf v. Long Island Ry.,* 162 N.E. 99, 100 (N.Y. 1928) (per Cardozo, C.J.). The word is not to be confused with the ordinary term, *provision.*

prideful. See **proud.**

prima facie (= at first sight) may function as either an adjective or an adverb, here as an adverb: "Publication of this language *prima facie* constitutes a cause of action and *prima facie* constitutes a wrong without any allegation or evidence of damage other than what is implied or presumed from the fact of publication." Occasionally, the phrase even serves as a SENTENCE ADVERB—e.g.: "*Prima facie,* a crime will be tried in the county in which it was committed . . . ." Edward Jenks, *The Book of English Law* 50 (P.B. Fairest ed., 6th ed. 1967).

Adjectival uses are perhaps even more common today—e.g.: "The cases at most attributed but *prima-facie* meaning to such words, and a competent draftsman would not deliberately pick a word that instead of controlling the context is easily colored by it."/ "On one view, there is a *prima-facie* duty of care where damage is within reasonable contemplation . . . ." Rupert Cross & J.W. Harris, *Precedent in English Law* 45 (4th ed. 1991). On hyphenating this phrase when it functions as an adjective, see PHRASAL ADJECTIVES (B).

Sometimes the phrase appears to have been misused for *per se,* as here: "There are certain exceptional cases where a communication is privileged, though *prima facie libelous* [read *libelous per se?*]." See **at first blush.**

prima-facie case = (1) the establishment of a legally required presumption that may be rebutted; or (2) the plaintiff's burden of producing enough evidence to permit the fact-trier to infer the fact at issue. *Texas Dep't of Community Affairs v. Burdine,* 450 U.S. 248, 254 n.7 (1981). The *CDL* defines *prima-facie case* as "a case that has been supported by sufficient evidence for it to be taken as proved in the absence of adequate evidence to the contrary." E.g., "Until he has proved that the defendant will in that case profit at his expense, he has not made out a *prima-facie case* to be paid anything, and until he has proved how much that profit will be, his *prima facie case* is not complete."

primary, in the JARGON of insurers, is sometimes used as an attributive noun for *primary beneficiary.* Following is an example from a life-insurance policy: "When the insured dies, payment will be made in equal shares to the primary beneficiaries living when payment is made. If a *primary* dies after the first payment is made, that *primary*'s unpaid share will be paid in equal shares to other *primaries* living when payment is made."

primary jurisdiction. See **original jurisdiction.**

prime (= to take priority over) is a usage unknown to lay writing. E.g., "It is undisputed that the 1977 and 1979 mortgages were preferred mortgages that *primed* Belcher's lien."/ "The letter states only that the rights of Rivercity under the option agreement will *prime* the rights of Whitney under the Act of Collateral Mortgage."

primer, in the sense of "an introductory or refresher book," is always pronounced /**prim**-ər/. The undercoat to paint is pronounced /**prɪ**-mər/.

primogenital; primogenitary; primogenitive. For the adjective corresponding to *primogeniture,* the prevailing form—though it may breed MISCUES—is *primogenital.* The other choices are NEEDLESS VARIANTS. See **primogeniture.**

primogeniture; primogenitureship; primogenitor. *Primogeniture* means (1) "the fact or condition of being the first-born of the children of the same parents"; or (2) (at common law) "the right of succession or inheritance belonging to the first-born, often involving the exclusion of all other children." In many civil-law countries, the equivalent term for sense (2) is *majorat.*

Primogenitureship is a NEEDLESS VARIANT of *primogeniture*—e.g.: "Considering that the purpose of introducing the words 'heirs and assigns' into deeds and wills was to prevent the operation of the principle of *primogenitureship* [read *primogeniture*], . . . it becomes readily apparent that the words as used here are meaningless and inaptly used." *Whitehead v. McCoy,* 29 A.2d 729, 731 (N.J. Ch. 1943).

Primogenitor denotes "the first parent; earliest ancestor." (Loosely, it is used for *progenitor* [= forefather, ancestor].) See **progenitor.**

principal. See **corpus.**

principal, n. **A. And *principle,*** n. In lay usage, it is usually enough to remember that *principal* (= chief, primary, most important) is almost always an adjective, and *principle* (= a truth, law, doctrine, or course of action) is virtually always a noun. Although *principle* is not a verb, we have *principled* as an adjective. (See **principled.**)

In legal language, *principal* is often a noun, an elliptical form of *principal person* or *actor,* primarily in agency law and criminal law. *Principal* also acts as a shortened form of *principal investment* in the context of investments, banking, and trusts. See **corpus & res.**

Misusing *principal* for *principle* is fairly common—e.g.: "The *principals* [read *principles*] underlying the anti-trust laws are as old as the early English statutes against combinations in restraint of trade and price-fixing agreements." Stephen Pfeil, "Law," in 17 *Encyclopedia Americana* 86, 92 (1953).

Likewise, the opposite error sometimes occurs—e.g.: "My *principle* [read *principal*] disagreement is . . . ." Lloyd L. Weinreb, *Fair's Fair: A Comment on the Fair Use Doctrine,* 103 Harv. L. Rev. 1137, 1140 (1990)./ "[The] portfolio of currently available securities . . . will return *principle* [read *principal*] and interest in future years to replace the lost nominal earnings." George A. Schieren, *On Using Minimum-Cost Portfolios to Determine Present Value,* 4 J. Legal. Econ. 47, 51 (1994).

B. And *accessory* in Criminal Law. At common law, *principal in the first degree* = the perpetrator of a crime; *principal in the second degree* = one who helped at the time of the crime; *accessory before the fact* = one who successfully incited a felony; and *accessory after the fact* = one who, knowing a felony has been committed, tried to help the felon escape punishment.

American and English experts in criminal law have written how advantageous it would be to speak in terms other than *principals* and *accessories* to crimes. In the U.S., for example, it "is much less confusing . . . to speak of a perpetrator of second degree murder, or an abettor of first degree murder, than it is to refer to a principal in the first degree to murder in the second degree, or a principal in the second degree to murder in the first degree." Rollin M. Perkins & Ronald N. Boyce, *Criminal Law* 735 (3d ed. 1982). Thus the Model Penal Code is not worded in terms of *principals* and *accessories.*

In Great Britain, the Criminal Law Act 1967 abolished the distinction between felonies and misdemeanors, consequently abolishing accessories and making every participant a principal. The better English authorities recommend *perpetrator* (= the person who in law performs the offense). See Glanville Williams, *Textbook of Criminal Law* 285–86 (1978). See **perpetrator.**

principled, as often used of decisions and judgments, means "resting on reasons that in their generality and neutrality transcend the immediate result involved." See Herbert Wechsler, *Toward Neutral Principles of Constitutional Law,* 73 Harv. L. Rev. 1, 19 (1959). When used of persons, *principled* means "having principles or scruples."

prior; previous. The adjective *prior* or *previous* for *earlier* is within the stylist's license; *prior to* and *previous to* in place of *before* are not. See **antecedent, previous to & prior to.**

prioritize. Writers with sound stylistic priorities avoid this word. See -IZE.

prior restraint = censorship before publication. E.g., "The photo processor thus becomes the censor of the nation's photographers; worse yet, his actions become a particularly obnoxious form of *prior restraint:* he condemns the photo before anyone, including the photographer or a neutral magistrate, has had an opportunity to see the final print."

prior to is a terribly overworked lawyerism. Only in rare contexts is it not much inferior to *before.* Even the U.S. Supreme Court has suggested that the phrase is "clumsy," noting that "[l]egislative drafting books are filled with suggestions that . . . *prior to* be replaced with the word *before.*" *U.S. v. Locke,* 471 U.S. 84, 96 n.11 (1985). Nevertheless, examples abound in virtually any piece of legal writing: "*Prior to* [read *Before*] hearing in the Appellate Division, we certified the cause on our own motion."/ "*Up to December 24, 1936, and for many years prior thereto* [read *For many years up to December 24, 1936*], petitioner and his wife were domiciled in the State of Oklahoma."

As Bernstein has pointed out, you should feel free to use *prior to* instead of *before* only if you are accustomed to using *posterior to* for *after.* Theodore M. Bernstein, *The Careful Writer* 347 (1979). Cf. **antecedent, anterior to, preliminary to, previous to & subsequent to.**

prise. See **prize.**

prisoned is a NEEDLESS VARIANT of *imprisoned.*

prisoner. English and American judges formerly referred in open court to criminal defendants as *prisoners,* but in the 20th century this usage fell into disuse because it can be highly prejudicial to the accused (also a negatively emotive word). *Defendant,* q.v., is a more appropriately neutral term.

privacy, right of. See **right of privacy.**

private bill. See **public Act.**

private international law. See **conflict of laws & international law.**

private prosecutor. See **prosecutor.**

privation. See **deprivation.**

privilege is a slippery legal word most commonly denoting a person's legal freedom to do or not to do a given act.

The word is often misspelled *priviledge.* The pages of American reporters are riddled with examples followed by "[*sic*]." And it even appears in law reviews—e.g.: "The court accepted his argument that the disclosure would violate his *priviledge* [read *privilege*] against self-incrimination since he was charged with violating the plaintiff's trademark." Sue Holloway, *"Black Box" Agreements: The Marketing of U.S. Technical Know-How in the Pacific Rim,* 23 Cal. W. Int'l L.J. 199, 211 n.98 (1992)./ "The assignee argued that the *priviledge* [read *privilege*] only encompassed the specific machines manufactured prior to the application date." F. Andrew Ubel, *Who's on First?—The Trade Secret Prior User or a Subsequent Patentee,* 76 J. Pat. & Trademark Off. Soc'y 401, 410 (1994).

privileges and immunities; privileges or immunities. The former phrase appears in Article 4, Section 2 of the U.S. Constitution; the latter appears in the Fourteenth Amendment. The *privileges and immunities* clause is the important one: "The Citizens of each State shall be entitled to all Privileges and Immunities of Citizens in the several States." This seminal clause prohibits a state from favoring its own citizens by discriminating against nonresidents who come into the state. See *Toomer v. Witsell,* 334 U.S. 385, 396 (1948).

The *privileges or immunities* clause, by comparison, is obscure and unimportant: "No State shall make or enforce any law which shall abridge the privileges or immunities of citizens of the United States . . . ." Five years after the Fourteenth Amendment was ratified, the Supreme Court read this clause as being limited to privileges of national, as opposed to state, citizenship. See *The Slaughter House Cases,* 83 U.S. (16 Wall.) 36, 55 (1873). And these privileges, while not trivial, are extremely limited; they encompass such liberties as being able to cross state lines freely and being able to vote in national elections.

privity; privy. To nonlawyers, a *privity* is something that is kept secret. To a lawyer, it is a relationship between two parties that is recognized by law, usually a mutual interest in a transaction or thing <in privity of contract>.

Privy likewise has different associations for nonlawyers and lawyers. To nonlawyers it is an adjective meaning "secret; private," or a plural noun (*privies*) meaning "outhouse; toilet." Lawyers mean no harm in calling other people *privies;* a *privy* in law is one who is a partaker or has any part or interest in any action, matter, or thing. E.g., "Respondents cite the portion of *Stiller* in which the New York court (the new forum) acknowledged that the Ohio court (the original forum that issued the injunction) lacked jurisdiction over the New York respondents who were *privies* with the enjoined party."

The word is also used adjectivally in this legal sense—e.g.: "Admissions may be made on behalf of the real party to any proceeding by any party who is *privy* in law, in blood, or in estate to any party to the proceeding on behalf of that party." (Eng.) Still, *privy* is used in its lay senses in legal writing—most commonly "participating in the knowledge of something private"—and the legal reader must be adept at discerning which sense is intended: "The jury was not *privy* to the parties' settlement negotiations."

prize; prise. The second is the better spelling in the sense "to pry or force open," although in AmE *prize* often appears in this sense. The DIFFERENTIATION is worth promoting, however. *Prize* is the spelling for all other senses.

pro and con; pro et con. The latter phrase is the LATINISM for "for and against." The English rendering—*pro and con*—is preferred. The phrase may be used nominally: "We are satisfied that the Commission adequately considered the *pros and cons* of the new grants of authority with a view toward the industry's economic well-being." Or it may be adverbial: "A number of affidavits are filed *pro and con,* which it is not necessary to consider." Or, again, it may be adjectival: "A number of *pro and con* briefs have been filed." One should not depart from the SET PHRASE: "Now we are obliged to advert to those elements of proof and legal concepts *pro and contra* [read *pro and con*] bearing upon the validity of the instrument in question." *In re Estate of Powers,* 134 N.W.2d 148, 151 (Mich. 1965).

Pro and con has also been used as a verb phrase <to pro-and-con the issue>, and although today this use sounds somewhat odd, it has the sanction of long standing. The *OED* and *W3* record another use not here recommended: the phrase has been used prepositionally <arguments pro and con the proposal>, but in such a phrase *for and against* would be better.

probable; likely; possible. These words—in order of decreasing strength—express gradations of the relative chance that something might happen. With a coin toss, for example, you cannot say that it is *probable* that it will turn up heads, though you might say that it is *likely.* (Of course, it would be equally likely to turn up tails.) The word *likely,* then, as Glanville Williams puts it, is "a strong *'possible'* but a weak *'probable.'*" Glanville Williams, *Criminal Law* 59 (2d ed. 1961). And the word *possible,* of course, embraces a wide gamut: everything from the remotest chance to a 100% certainty.

probable cause. The Fourth Amendment to the U.S. Constitution states that neither arrest warrants nor search warrants may issue without a prior showing of "probable cause." The standard probably began as a looser one than *good cause*—looser because more guesswork is involved in deciding whether cause is "probable" (i.e., "provable," from the Latin *probabilis*—not merely "likely") than whether it is "good."

Today, however, *probable cause* is such an important constitutional standard that it is rarely thought of in conjunction with *good cause.* It now has an established place as a TERM OF ART, though its precise contours will probably always remain vague. Cf. **good cause shown.**

probate, n., = the act by which a testamentary document is judicially established as having been a testator's final will. But the word has been extended well beyond that traditional sense. Today it often includes everything that a personal representative does in handling a decedent's estate.

As an adjective, the word takes on still other shades of meaning. *Probate code* = the entire written law of decedents' estates, substantive as well as procedural. *Probate law* = the law of succession, including both statutes and caselaw. See ***probatum*** & **proof (B).**

probate, as a transitive verb, is an Americanism. The word means "to admit (a will) to proof" <the will was probated in 1992>. By extension, it is sometimes said that a lawyer *probates an estate.*

During the 20th century, *probate* has acquired an unrelated sense, as the BACK-FORMATION from *probation:* "to grant probation to (a criminal), to reduce (a sentence) by means of probation." E.g., "[A] suspended sentence shall have the effect of *probating* the defendant . . . ." *Wood v. State,* 21 S.E.2d 915, 918 (Ga. Ct. App. 1942)./ "[T]he conviction['s] . . . validity plays no necessary part in the consideration of whether a *probated* prison term should be continued . . . ." *U.S. v. Franciscchine,* 512 F.2d 827, 828 (5th Cir. 1975).

probatee is a NEEDLESS VARIANT of *probationer*—e.g.: "Oregon's statutes required that a *probatee* [read *probationer*] not be required to pay said fees unless he is or will be able to do so . . . [and] that the *probatee* [read *probationer*] may petition to have the unpaid portion 'forgiven' . . . ." *White Eagle v. State,* 280 N.W.2d 659, 661 (S.D. 1979).

probation = (1) a procedure by which a convicted offender is released, subject to court-imposed conditions, rather than being sent to prison; or (2) the act of proving judicially (a will, etc.).

Sense (2), recorded in Scottish law dictionaries but rarely elsewhere, is attested in the *OED* by two 16th-century citations and nothing more recent. Although it is still used in some stock phrases such as *admit to probation* (Scot.), it is otherwise fairly uncommon. But it has been revived in 20th-century AmE—e.g.: "[W]hen an estate is in process of *probation,* the authority to sue for its assets rests in the administrator or executor." *Demmer v. Stroude,* 40 F. Supp. 795, 796 (N.D. Tex. 1941)./ "[T]he district court . . . remanded the estate to the probate court for completion of administration thereof, which in effect ordered *probation* of the will without limitation as to the property to be administered." *In re Estate of Jones,* 366 P.2d 792, 793 (Kan. 1961)./ "The caveators further alleged that 'their rights will be affected to their prejudice by the *probation* of said instruments as the Last Will and Testament and First Codicil.'" *In re Will of Ashley,* 208 S.E.2d 398, 399 (N.C. Ct. App. 1974).

probationary; probational. The latter form is a NEEDLESS VARIANT, as is *probatory.* See **probative.**

probationer; parolee. *Probationer* = one on probation. (See **probation & probatee.**) *Parolee* = one released on parole. See **parole.**

probative; probatory. *Probative* = (1) tending or serving to prove; (2) exploratory; serving to test; or (3) in Scots law, self-proving <a probative deed>. In the law of evidence, sense (1) is invariably the one intended, though it is of more recent origin. E.g., "In this circuit, we have found *probative* the fact that a hospital district was financed through levies that were separate from other county or state taxes and through bonds sold upon the full faith and credit of the district." See **probity.**

Probatory is a NEEDLESS VARIANT of either *probative* (most commonly) or *probationary.*

probativeness. See **probity.**

probatum = something proved or conclusively established. (Cf. ***ipse dixit.***) It sometimes appears in its plural form (*probata*) and is usually nothing but a highfalutin equivalent of *proof*—

e.g.: "Defendant Griffin contends there is a fatal variance between the *allegata* [read *allegations*] and the *probata* [read *proof*], arguing that the State's proof that he struck Dexter Harper with his feet and fists is insufficient to support his conviction for aggravated assault by shooting Dexter Harper with a handgun . . . ." *Griffin v. State,* 449 S.E.2d 341, 343 (Ga. Ct. App. 1994). See LATINISMS.

probity means "honesty; integrity." E.g., "It is beyond either human capacity or the demands of justice that the trial judge decide correctly every issue arising in the trial. What is required is not a perfect score, but fairness, *probity,* and the avoidance of substantial prejudice." *Ruiz v. Estelle,* 679 F.2d 1115, 1132 (5th Cir. 1982).

Unfortunately, *probativeness,* which means "the quality of tending to prove something," and its adjective, *probative,* are frequently confused with *probity.* E.g., "The majority addresses the trial court's ruling admitting cancer evidence; relevance, *probity* [read *probativeness*], and prejudice are dealt with separately."/ "Proof that the inhalation of asbestos fibers can cause cancer is not the sine qua non of plaintiff's case; it has only incremental *probity* [read *probativeness*]."/ "The *probative* value of the extrinsic offense correlates positively with its likeness to the offense charged; we cannot say that the district court abused its discretion in determining that the *probity* [read *probativeness*] of this proof outweighed its prejudice."

Probity is also occasionally misused for *propriety*—e.g.: "Although the *probity* [read *propriety*] of using affidavits to resolve fact issues is perhaps open to question, reliance upon the prosecutor's affidavits in this case is appropriate."

problematic(al). Both forms appear in modern writing. Though *problematic* is now more usual, euphony may sometimes lead a writer to choose *problematical.*

problem-solving, a VOGUE WORD among lawyers and social scientists, is best avoided when possible. E.g., "The emphasis is on the method or technique of *problem-solving* [read *solving problems*]."

pro bono publico. A. Historical and Grammatical Development. The phrase *pro bono publico* is an old one in Anglo-American law. Originally, it was not restricted to a lawyer's duty, but instead referred to anything done for the public good. The phrase can be found in Coke's 17th-century commentary on Littleton's *Tenures:* "[I]t appeareth that owners are in that case bound *pro bono publico* to maintain houses and mills which are for habitation and use of men." Co. Litt. 200b (1628). As in that example, the early British and American uses of the phrase were adverbial, and they related to anything done for the public good—e.g.:

- "[I]n the case of charity, the King, *pro bono publico,* has an original right to superintend the case thereof, so that, abstracted from the statute of Eliz., relating to charitable uses, and antecedent to it, as well as since, it has been every day's practice to file informations in Chancery, in the Attorney-General's name, for the establishment of charities." *Eyre v. Countess of Shaftsbury,* 2 P. Wms. 103, 119, 24 Eng. Rep. 659, 664 (1722).
- "Indeed, I know of no case, where the doctrine of relation, which is a mere fiction of law, is allowed to prevail, unless it be in furtherance and protection of rights, *pro bono publico.*" *In re Richardson,* 20 F. Cas. 699, 702 (C.C.D. Mass. 1843) (No. 11,777).
- "[I]t is sought here to hold a municipal corporation, acting *pro bono publico,* responsible not only for its own neglect to repair, but also for that of its officer in failing to observe the ordinance for the inspection of the bridge." *Weightman v. Corporation of Washington,* 66 U.S. (1 Black) 39, 44–45 (1861).

Today, of course, the phrase refers primarily to a lawyer's services performed for the public good (see (B)), but this usage is comparatively recent. Few reported decisions predating the 1970s refer to this lawyerly duty. But there is a late-19th-century reference in an Illinois opinion to a lawyer's acting for a client *pro bono publico:* "McKenzie & Calkins, *pro bono publico.*" *Board of Educ. v. Arnold,* 1 N.E. 163, 163 (Ill. 1884).

The adverbial uses have persisted, but most often when the full phrase appears, as opposed to the shortened form *pro bono* (see below)—e.g.: "[I]n a time when the need for legal services among the poor is growing and public funding for such services has not kept pace, lawyers' ethical obligation to volunteer their time and skills *pro bono publico* is manifest." *Mallard v. U.S. Dist. Ct. for S. Dist. of Iowa,* 490 U.S. 296, 310 (1989).

The adjectival uses, however, are perhaps the most common today—e.g.:

- "Although one proposal requiring mandatory *pro bono publico* work by attorneys was recently voted down by the American Bar Association, the very proposal itself indicates the awareness of the bar of its obligation to protect the right of indigent litigants." *Caruth v. Pinkney,* 683 F.2d 1044, 1049 (7th Cir. 1982).

- "A lawyer should aspire to render at least (50) hours of *pro bono publico* legal services per year." Model Rules of Professional Conduct Rule 6.1 (1994).
- "The Commission sought to accentuate the duties of lawyers that transcended their responsibilities to clients—for example, by . . . requiring lawyers to devote a portion of their time to *pro bono publico* work." Marc Galanter, *Predators and Parasites: Lawyer-Bashing and Civil Justice,* 28 Ga. L. Rev. 633, 642 (1994).

To avoid the awkward three-word PHRASAL ADJECTIVE—typically, alas, unhyphenated, as in the three examples just quoted—lawyers have shortened the phrase to *pro bono*—e.g.:

- "It is reasoned that an attorney, as an officer of the court, has the duty to assist the court, without compensation, in the administration of justice and, similarly, that every attorney is deemed to have consented to *pro bono* appointments by virtue of having accepted his license to practice law." *State v. Oakley,* 227 S.E.2d 314, 318–19 (W. Va. 1976).
- "[A]t the time that the 1853 law was passed, there was no clear conception of '*pro bono* work.' Those who debated the bill appeared to contemplate that one might do some uncompensated service for a constituent, a friend or a relative, but not for a needy stranger." Lisa G. Lerman, *Public Service by Public Servants,* 19 Hofstra L. Rev. 1141, 1176 (1991).
- "[L]awyers tend not to find time to fulfill their *pro bono* obligations." Harry T. Edwards, *The Growing Disjunction Between Legal Education and the Legal Profession,* 91 Mich. L. Rev. 34, 68 (1992).
- "*Pro bono* work will, by definition, take some time away from ordinary law practice, but there is no reason to think that it will compromise the 'ethic of excellence' with regard either to free or paying clients." Steven Lubet, *Professionalism Revisited,* 42 Emory L.J. 197, 204 (1993).
- "I have never found a case of a lawyer disbarred for not performing *pro bono* service." Patrick L. Baude, *An Essay on the Regulation of the Legal Profession and the Future of Lawyers' Characters,* 68 Ind. L.J. 647, 658 (1993).
- "A lawyer has an obligation to render public interest and *pro bono* legal service." N.Y. Jud. Law app., Code of Professional Responsibility EC 2–25 (McKinney Supp. 1994).

At times, the phrase *pro bono* is even used as an attributive noun, that is, as a short form of *pro bono work* or *pro bono services,* as in the title to the following article: Lewis S. Calderon et al., *Mandatory Pro Bono for Law Students: Another Dimension in Legal Education,* 1 J.L. & Pol'y 95 (1993).

B. Arguments over Modern Meaning. For a phrase whose modern content was only fairly recently acquired, *pro bono* has generated many hot debates about meaning. Broadly speaking, there are two camps: those who support a wide definition and those who support a narrow one.

Broadly, *pro bono* legal services include any uncompensated work that a lawyer performs for the public good. Some guides adopt the broad definition. For example, a Georgia guide defines *pro bono service* as "any uncompensated services performed by attorneys for the public good . . . , [including] civic, charitable and public service activities, as well as activities that improve the law, the legal system, and the legal profession." *State Bar of Georgia Handbook* 10 (Supp. 1993).

The narrow definition, by contrast, limits the work specifically to services performed for indigents, as opposed to charitable organizations such as symphonies, museums, and the like. E.g., "The purpose of a narrow definition of *pro bono* is to ensure that legal aid is provided to those who need it most—the poor." Kim Schimenti, *Pro Choice for Lawyers in a Revised Pro Bono System,* 23 Seton Hall L. Rev. 641, 694 n.254 (1993)./ "At Tulane, *pro bono* work is synonymous with poverty law and hence *pro bono* projects may not encompass work for the government such as working for the offices of the Public Defender or the District Attorney." Lewis S. Calderon et al., *Mandatory Pro Bono for Law Students: Another Dimension in Legal Education,* 1 J.L. & Pol'y 95, 103–04 (1993).

One reason for preferring the broad over the narrow definition is that specialists—such as those lawyers who work exclusively in corporate mergers and acquisitions—may find it difficult to take up the cause of the indigent, especially if that work were to involve court appearances. The literature on pro bono work reflects this very problem: "The focus must be on the definition of '*pro bono* services.' Such a term should be broadly defined to provide ample opportunities for contributions by all types of lawyers engaged in different specialties." '. . . *In the Spirit of Public Service': A Blueprint for the Rekindling of Lawyer Professionalism,* 112 F.R.D. 243, 297 (1986). Also, though one can hardly imagine more important work than what is done on behalf of the poor, society inarguably benefits from many other public services that lawyers perform. It is therefore difficult, if not impossible, to justify a dogmatic insistence on the narrow definition on historical grounds or linguistic grounds—indeed, on any grounds other than one's modern view of sound public policy.

In any event, of course, it is quite misleading to define *pro bono* as meaning merely "unpaid," as here: "[H]e was a strong proponent of requiring lawyers to perform '*pro bono*'—unpaid—services." Glenn Fowler, *Robert McKay, 70, Legal Scholar and Head of 1971 Attica Panel,* N.Y. Times, 14 July 1990, at 11.

C. Roman or Italic? Most legal writers today treat the phrase *pro bono* as being fully anglicized; therefore, they do not italicize it. (It is italicized in the preceding sentence only because it is a phrase being referred to as a phrase.)

D. Hyphenating the Phrasal Adjective. Some writers sensibly hyphenate *pro bono* when it serves as an adjective—e.g.: "In Atlanta, for example, five local bar associations have recruited 1,025 attorneys to do *pro-bono* indigent defense as part of the 1,000 Lawyers for Justice, which has taken on 305 cases thus far this year." Peter Applebome, *Indigent Defendants, Overworked Lawyers,* N.Y. Times, 17 May 1992, at 18./ "[T]he U.S. legal profession, more than any other, has fostered the idea of countervailing legal power, supporting legal services for the poor, [and] imposing a generalized obligation of *pro-bono* service . . . ." David M. Trubek et al., *Global Restructuring and the Law,* 44 Case W. Res. L. Rev. 407, 426 (1994).

Others, however, see *pro bono* as a SET PHRASE that needs no hyphen. See PHRASAL ADJECTIVES (B).

E. Mandatory pro bono. Some writers have suggested that the phrase *mandatory pro bono* is an OXYMORON—e.g.: "Because pro bono publico service historically has referred to charitably donated assistance, the term '*mandatory pro bono*' is itself a problem—a classic oxymoron, not unlike *jumbo shrimp* and *military intelligence.*" Esther F. Lardent, *Mandatory Pro Bono in Civil Cases: The Wrong Answer to the Right Question,* 49 Md. L. Rev. 78, 79 (1990)./ "In a sense, the concept of *mandatory pro bono* is an oxymoron, like military music." Roger C. Cramton, *Mandatory Pro Bono,* 19 Hofstra L. Rev. 1113, 1132–33 (1991).

The reason, of course, for seeing the phrase as a contradiction in terms is that, in the modern American lawyer's mind, *pro bono* equates with "voluntary." It has always been hard to compel charity—and impossible to compel charitableness.

proceduralist (= a specialist in legal procedure) is a 20th-century legal NEOLOGISM. E.g., "So wrote one of America's greatest *proceduralists,* Judge Charles E. Clark, in a 1945 dissent." Charles A. Wright, *The Law of Federal Courts* 678 (4th ed. 1983)./ "My friend was shocked. 'He's against diversity!!??' 'Diversity jurisdiction,' I said, realizing she was not a *proceduralist.*" Ann Althouse, *Late Night Confessions in the Hart and Wechsler Hotel,* 47 Vand. L. Rev. 993, 994 (1994).

procedural law; substantive law. Separating these two phrases presents no small conundrum. The problem, as Justice Frankfurter once observed, is that "*substance* and *procedure* are the same keywords to very different problems. Neither *substance* nor *procedure* represents the same invariants. Each implies different variables depending upon the particular problem for which it is used." *Guaranty Trust Co. v. York,* 326 U.S. 99, 108 (1945). The decision whether a particular issue is "substantive" or "procedural" may vary depending on whether the context relates to a court's rulemaking power, to resolving a question concerning conflict of laws, or to applying state or federal law.

Traditionally, *substantive law* (one of Bentham's coinages) denotes the law that lays down people's rights, duties, liberties, and powers. Thus substantive law addresses such issues as what rights one has against trespassers. *Procedural law* (also called *adjective law*), by contrast, consists of the rules by which one establishes one's rights, duties, liberties, and powers—either by litigation or otherwise. How to start an arbitration or a lawsuit and proceed with it—or how to get a clerk to issue a writ—is a matter of procedural law. See **adjective law.**

In some contexts—usually involving the law of a single jurisdiction—the dichotomy seems admirably straightforward. In criminal law and procedure, *substantive law* declares what acts are crimes and imposes penalties, while *procedural law* sets the steps by which a violator is brought to punishment. Similarly, in civil law and procedure, *substantive law* defines the rights and duties of persons, while *procedural law* defines the steps in having a right or duty judicially defined or enforced.

proceed. See **precede (A).**

proceeding(s). In reference to the business done by tribunals of all kinds, *the proceeding* and *the proceedings* are interchangeable. And both are so common that it would be impossible to brand either one as inferior.

proceeds, n. (= the value of land, goods, or investments when converted into money) takes a plural verb. But some writers want to write *proceeds is* instead of the correct form, *proceeds are.*

Also, this noun is accented on the first syllable (/***proh***-*seeds*/), not the second.

process has the special legal senses (1) "the proceedings in any action or prosecution" <due process>, and (2) "the summons by which a person is cited to appear in court" <service of process>. Sense (2) is especially baffling to nonlawyers unfamiliar with legal procedures. E.g., "An execution is a *process* of the court issued to enforce the judgment of that court."

In sense (2), *process* may serve either as a count noun (as in the preceding example) or as a mass noun (as in *service of process*).

processual (= of or relating to a legal process) began as a 19th-century term used by legal historians writing about Roman law. In the latter half of the 20th century, though, American legal writers adopted it—e.g.: "That court would . . . promptly have reversed and remanded for due hearing and with firm suggestion that the board examine and then conform to the *processual* religion of the act of 1952." *Superx Drugs Corp. v. State Bd. of Pharmacy,* 125 N.W.2d 13, 18 (Mich. 1963)./ "The clear statement and the standardless delegation doctrines are *processual* in nature." Franklin E. Fink, Note, Abourezk v. Reagan: *Curbing Recent Abuses of the Executive Immigration Power,* 21 Cornell Int'l L.J. 147, 178 (1988).

prochein ami (= a "next friend" who represents an underage plaintiff's interests in litigation) is preferably so spelled. E.g., "Sugimoto also represents Kristy Lacaran-Chong, a minor, as *prochein ami* or next friend . . . ." *Wong-Leong v. Hawaiian Indep. Refinery, Inc.,* 879 P.2d 538, 541 n.2 (Haw. 1994). *Prochein amy* (used by Blackstone), *prochain ami,* and *prochain amy* are variant spellings to be avoided. See **next friend** & LOAN TRANSLATIONS.

prochronism. See **anachronism.**

proconsulate; proconsulship. The latter is a NEEDLESS VARIANT.

procreative; procreational. The former is standard, *procreational* being a NEEDLESS VARIANT.

procuration; procurement; procurance; procuracy. Traditionally, *procuration* has meant "the act of appointing another as one's attorney-in-fact or agent." By transference the term has referred also to the authority vested in a person so appointed. E.g., "If a bill be drawn by *procuration,* no acceptor of the bill is permitted to deny the authority of the agent, by whom it purports to be drawn, to draw in the name of the principal." (Eng.)

Finally, *procuration* has been used as the generic noun for *procure,* but this broad sense is best reserved for *procurement,* as in the following examples: "Jureczki argues that White's improprieties in the *procurement* of the arrest warrant . . . place the defendants outside the immunity of *Baker v. McCollan.*"/ "The evidence of contestant failed to show any activity on the part of Mrs. Logan in the *procurement* of the will of decedent."/ "Appellee filed the motion to remand the contractual indemnity claim to permit *procurement* of documentary evidence."

Procurement has had another, more restricted sense in legal contexts: "persuading or inviting a woman or child to have sexual intercourse." E.g., "Defendant, Linda Sue Esch, appeals the judgment of conviction entered on a jury verdict finding her guilty of . . . two counts of *procurement* of a child for sexual exploitation . . . ." *People v. Esch,* 786 P.2d 462, 464 (Colo. Ct. App. 1989). *Procurance* is a NEEDLESS VARIANT.

Procuracy = a letter of agency; the document empowering an attorney-in-fact to act.

procurator. See **attorney (A).**

procure is a FORMAL WORD for *get* (the ordinary word) or *obtain* (a semiformal word).

procurement. See **procuration.**

procuring breach of contract. See **tortious interference with contractual relations.**

procuring cause. See CAUSATION (C).

prodigality; profligacy. *Prodigality* means "lavishness; extravagance." *Profligacy* means primarily "salaciousness; licentiousness," but it also shares the sense of *prodigality.*

prodigious for *prestigious* is a MALAPROPISM—e.g.: "The American Law Institute is one of the most select and *prodigious* [read *prestigious*] legal organizations in this country."

producible. So spelled; *producable* is an infrequent misspelling.

producing cause. See CAUSATION (C).

production burden. See **burden of proof (A).**

productive of, be. See BE-VERBS (B).

product(s) liability. The general area of law is known as *products liability.* Occasionally one sees the singular form *product liability,* usually in reference to a particular product of a particular manufacturer. When the phrase is used adjectivally, it should be hyphenated <products-liability case>. See PHRASAL ADJECTIVES.

pro et con. See **pro and con.**

profane; profanatory. That which is *profane* is irreverent or blasphemous; that which is *profanatory* tends to make (something) profane.

proferens = the party that proposes or adduces a contract or a condition in a contract. E.g., "If the clause contains language which expressly exempts the person in whose favour it is made (hereinafter called 'the *proferens*') from the consequence of the negligence of his own servants, effect must be given to that provision . . . ." *Smith v. South Wales Switchgear Ltd.,* [1978] 1 All E.R. 18 (H.L.). The plural is *proferentes.* See ***contra proferentem*** **(A).**

profession. This word has been much debased of late, primarily at the hands of egalitarians who call any occupation a profession. In any American city today, a person seeking a job as a barber, manicurist, or manager of a fast-food store turns in the classified advertisements to the section "Professions." A lawyer looking for a change in jobs turns to "Advanced Degree Required," a section of its own rather than a subsection of "Professions."

Traditionally there have been but three professions: theology, law, and medicine. These were known either as *the three professions* or as *the learned professions.* The term was ultimately extended to mean "one's principal vocation," which embraces prostitution as well as medicine. (*The oldest profession* originally had an irony much stronger than it has today.)

The restricted sense of *profession* no doubt strikes many people as snobbish and anachronistic. What about university professors, atomic physicists, and engineers? Perhaps three professions are not enough, but we ought at least to use *some* discrimination, with emphasis on "prolonged specialized training in a body of abstract knowledge." William J. Goode, *Encroachment, Charlatanism, and the Emerging Profession,* 25 Am. Soc. Rev. 902, 903 (1960). Professional training "must lead to some order of mastery of a generalized cultural tradition, and do so in a manner giving prominence to an *intellectual* component." Talcott Parsons, "Professions," 12 *International Encyclopedia of Social Science* 536, 536 (1968).

Notably, the traditional, artificially restricted view of the term has long been considered archaic. Holmes wrote in 1896: "It is not likely . . . that anybody will be prejudiced against business or will take formal views of the dignity of callings such as a hundred years ago put the ministry first, law and medicine next, and below them all other pursuits." Oliver W. Holmes, "The Bar as a Profession," in *Collected Legal Papers* 153, 153 (1952).

On the other side of the Atlantic, hardly a generation later, Lord Justice Scrutton wrote that, although *profession* used to be confined to the three learned professions, by 1919 it had a broader meaning: "[A] '*profession*' in the present use of language involves the idea of an occupation requiring either purely intellectual skill, or of manual skill controlled, as in painting and sculpture, or surgery, by the intellectual skill of the operator, as distinguished from an occupation which is substantially the production or sale or arrangements for the production or sale of commodities." *Commissions v. Maxse,* [1919] 1 K.B. 647, 657 (C.A.).

proffer is chiefly a literary and legal term; it is equivalent to *offer,* and like that word, may be both noun and verb. Thus, as a noun: "Because of Delaware's absolute rule, its courts did not have occasion to consider the *proffer* put forward by petitioner Franks."/ "Because the expert testified during the *proffer* of proof that he was not aware of the agreement, the district court's exclusion of the evidence was not an abuse of discretion." And as a verb: "The daughter *proffered* her own testimony to show, among other things, that the parents intended the conveyance to be an absolute gift and not an advancement."/ "We reject the *proffered* [i.e., suggested] distinctions."

It is occasionally misspelled *profer*—e.g.: "But the very point of the article, of course, is based on the *proferred* [read *proffered*] fact that Rehnquist is rapidly becoming the chief declarer of what the Constitution requires . . . ." Sanford Levinson, *Law as Literature,* 60 Tex. L. Rev. 373, 398–99 (1982).

profferer. So spelled—not *-or.*

profits. In DRAFTING, this word is often vague, so it is generally best defined. *Gross profits,* for example, is usually different from *gross receipts,* and whatever is to be deducted ought to be mentioned explicitly in the definition. Even more obviously in need of definition is *net receipts,* which patently involves deductions of some kind.

profits à prendre, known also as *right of common,* denotes the right exercised by one person to enter another's land and take away some part of the soil, such as the profits from the soil. As its form suggests, *profits à prendre* is a LAW FRENCH survival; it remains fairly common. E.g., "For example, trust property may consist of a life estate in land, a *profit à prendre* to remove minerals, an undivided interest in land as a tenant in common, or an absolute interest in a specific bond or share of stock."

Profit à prendre has been rendered *profit a' prendre* by some for whom the grave accent apparently was not typographically possible. See, e.g., *McDonald v. Board of Miss. Levee Comm'rs,* 646 F. Supp. 449, 469 (N.D. Miss. 1986). Omitting the accent completely from this phrase is preferable, however, to using an apostrophe in its stead.

profligacy. See **prodigality.**

pro forma (= as a matter of form; for the sake of form) usu. has a slightly depreciative tone in modern usage. The term need not be hyphenated as an adjectival phrase. See ADJECTIVES (C).

progenitor. A *progenitor* is one that yields *progeny*—e.g.: "As March 1, 1913, receded in time, the 1913 basis became increasingly moot, and the other initial basis rules, the illegitimate progeny of 1913 basis, became far more important than the *progenitor* rule itself." Calvin H. Johnson, *The Legitimacy of Basis from a Corporation's Own Stock,* 9 Am. J. Tax Pol'y 155, 174 (1991). See **primogenitor.**

progeny. A. Plural in Sense. *Progeny* is usu. plural in sense and thus takes a plural verb. E.g., "The *progeny* of *Williamson v. U.S. indicates* [read *indicate*] that *Williamson* requires reversal only when the specific defendant was picked out for the informer's effort by a government agent." Another word is required when the sense is singular, as in the following sentence: "*In a Blanchard progeny* [read *In a case that follows the rule in Blanchard*], *Chavers v. Exxon Corp.,* we quoted from and explained *Blanchard*'s holding."

B. Insensitively Used. In the context of the famous abortion case, *Roe v. Wade,* this metaphor shows a lack of VERBAL AWARENESS: "Part I of this Note examines the doctrine set forth in *Roe v. Wade* and its *progeny* . . . ." Note, *Potential Fathers and Abortion,* 55 Brook. L. Rev. 1359, 1363 (1990).

prognosis; prognostication; prognostic, n. *Prognosis* is ordinarily used in medicine to mean "a forecast of the probable course and termination of an illness." (See **diagnosis.**) *Prognostication* is more general, denoting "a prediction or prophecy" or "a conjecture of some future event formed upon some supposed sign." E.g., "Some kinds of *prognostications* simply are not possible: it is foreseeable that a thirsty man will drink, but it may not be possible to foretell his choice of beverage."/ "A picture of the future size of this accumulation can be painted with gigantic lines; such a *prognostication* is not without precedent." *Prognostic* = an advance indication or omen.

program(m)atic. The word is spelled *-mm-* in both BrE and AmE.

program(me). *Program* is the AmE, *programme* the BrE spelling. The ending *-am* is used in BrE, however, in reference to computer programs.

program(m)er; program(m)ing. The best spellings are in *-mm-* whether in AmE or in BrE. The double *-m-* in AmE appears to be descended from *programme,* the BrE spelling. A few American dictionaries give priority to *programer* and *programing,* but these forms are rare in practice. See DOUBLING OF FINAL CONSONANTS.

pro hac vice. A. Meaning and Uses. This LATINISM, meaning "for this occasion or particular purpose," is not easily simplified in much legal writing. Often it is used adjectivally—e.g.: "The question narrows therefore to whether Litton was the owner *pro hac vice* of the vessel."/ "Plaintiff alleges that defendant was the *pro hac vice* owner of the barges involved." The phrase is also used adverbially when a lawyer who has not been admitted to practice in a particular jurisdiction is admitted for the purpose of conducting a particular case—e.g: "Butler entered an appearance *pro hac vice* for respondent on January 26, 1981; his partner Allis was admitted *pro hac vice* on October 19, 1982." Cf. **ad hoc.**

B. Pronunciation. The phrase is usually pronounced */proh-hak-***vɪs***/* or */***vɪ***-see/.*

C. Incorrect Form. The phrase is sometimes misspelled *pro haec vice*—e.g.: "Chappee also argued to the SJC that he was denied effective assistance of counsel because his local lawyer neglected to move Simon's admission *pro haec vice* [read *pro hac vice*] . . . ." *Chappee v. Vose,* 843 F.2d 25, 33 n.5 (1st Cir. 1988). The difference between *hac* and *haec* is that *haec* is nominative, while *hac* is ablative (the case governed by *pro*). Cf. ***in haec verba.***

prohibit takes the preposition *from.* Formerly, this verb could be construed with *to* <the law prohibits persons to litter>, but this construction is now an ARCHAISM.

prohibition. A. Writ of Prohibition. This writ was a prerogative order issued to prevent either a lower court from exceeding its jurisdiction or a tenant from committing waste. Unlike *certiorari,* q.v., *prohibition* is anticipatory and preventive rather than after-the-fact and remedial. See **prerogative writs.**

B. And *proscription.* *Proscription* implies a written prohibition, whereas *prohibition,* in its everyday sense, connotes nothing about whether it appears in writing. See **proscription.**

prohibitive; prohibitory. These terms have undergone a latent DIFFERENTIATION that needs to be further encouraged. *Prohibitive* may mean generally "having the quality of prohibiting," but more and more in modern prose it has the sense "tending to preclude consumption or purchase because of expense" <the costs are prohibitive>. Thus the phrase *prohibitively expensive* is a REDUNDANCY: "Today, the economics of law practice make it *prohibitively expensive* [read *prohibitive*] to litigate small claims." Roger J. Miner, *Confronting the Communication Crisis in the Legal Profession,* 34 N.Y.L. Sch. L. Rev. 1, 7 (1989).

Frequently used in the phrase *prohibitory injunction,* the word *prohibitory* has carved out a niche in the law in the sense "expressing a prohibition or restraint." E.g., "It is established in New York that violation of a *prohibitory* statute gives rise to tort liability."/ "Appellee seeks a *prohibitory* injunction restraining appellant from operating the sign and a mandatory injunction requiring appellant to remove the sign."/ "One of the tests for determining whether a statute is directory or mandatory is the presence of negative or *prohibitory* words plainly importing that the act should be done in a particular manner or at a particular time, and not otherwise."

prohibitory injunction. See **mandatory injunction.**

prolificacy; prolificness. The first is the better-formed and more usual word—e.g.: "Perfection over *prolificacy* is Def Leppard's mode: No whine before its time." Robert J. Hawkins, *Def Leppard Wants to Be Perfect, Not Prolific,* San Diego Union-Tribune, 17 Sept. 1992, at 12.

The NEEDLESS VARIANT *prolificness* is a poorly formed HYBRID (a Latin base with an Anglo-Saxon suffix)—e.g.: "[Judge Richard A. Posner's] *prolificness* [read *prolificacy*] is no surprise to anyone familiar with his academic output: 11 books and more than 100 articles." David Ranii, *The Next Nominee?* Nat'l L.J., 26 Nov. 1984, at 1./ "In *Irving,* there would have been no dispute because all Indians would have had equal claims in all land, irrespective of the *prolificness* [read *prolificacy*] of their ancestors." T. Nicolaus Tideman, *Takings, Moral Evolution, and Justice,* 88 Colum. L. Rev. 1714, 1729 (1988). Cf. **generic(al)ness.**

PROLIXITY. See VERBOSITY.

prolog(ue). The longer, more traditional form is preferred.

promise. A. Moral and Legal Senses. *Promise* is frequently used in two different senses in law. One is the lay sense, in which *promise* denotes a pledge to which the law attaches no obligation. In the other, the legal sense, *promise* is synonymous with *contract.* One commentator insists on the latter meaning as the only one appropriate to legal contexts: "It is not conceivable . . . that the term *promise* as a legal idea can mean anything except words of promise to which the law annexes an obligation." Clarence D. Ashley, *What Is a Promise in Law?* 16 Harv. L. Rev. 319, 319 (1903). Because those words frequently remain unheeded, the acute reader must carefully determine what the word means in a given context; the acute writer should take pains to make that meaning clear. For more on this distinction, see the Anson quotation under **pollicitation.** See also **offer & contract (C).**

B. Promises and Policies in Drafting. The drafter often has a choice between stating an obligation either as a promise or as a policy. For example, a credit-card agreement might say: "The cardholder must make at least the minimum payment by the fifth day of each month." In signing the agreement, the cardholder makes what is in the nature of a promise.

To phrase the same obligation as a policy, the agreement might say: "The minimum balance is due on the fifth day of each month."

The difference, of course, is that the promissory language puts the obligation more emphatically. The policy language is more polite and slightly more vague. The substantive content is likely the same, but the language of promise is more likely to result in a common understanding of who must do what. See DRAFTING.

promisee is the preferred spelling, not *promissee.*

promisor; promiser. The usual legal spelling is *-or* (as the correlative to *promisee*), but *-er* is equally good. E.g., "To allow him to keep such a payment or other consideration would be giving the *promisor* something for nothing." Cf. **purchaser.** See -ER (A).

The spelling *promissor* is an inferior ARCHAISM: "[T]he *promissor* [read *promisor*] denied he had ever made the contract under consideration . . . ." *Burford v. Pounders,* 199 S.W.2d 141, 144 (Tex. 1947).

promissee. See **promisee.**

promissory. So spelled.

promissory estoppel. A. And *quasi-contract.* These phrases are closely related but distinct. *Promissory estoppel* ordinarily refers to the situation in which a plaintiff seeks recovery for loss or damage suffered as a result of relying on the defendant's promises or representations. *Quasi-contract,* q.v., refers to the situation in which a plaintiff seeks reimbursement for some benefit that he or she has conferred on the defendant. One well-known writer believed that the law might have done well with one or the other but not both: "It would seem, as a matter of jurisprudential economy, that both situations could have been dealt with under either slogan but the legal mind has always preferred multiplication to division." Grant Gilmore, *The Death of Contract* 88–89 (1974).

B. And *equitable estoppel.* The phrase *equitable estoppel* is an outmoded equivalent of *promissory estoppel.* See **estoppel (B).**

promissory note (= an unconditional promise in writing to pay a person a sum of money) formerly had the synonym *writing obligatory,* but that phrase has long since become an ARCHAISM.

promoter. So spelled—not *promotor.*

promotive = tending to promote. E.g., "It is claimed that the two yearly payments to be made to the children just before Christmas and Easter produce a 'desirable social effect' and are *promotive* of public convenience and needs, and happiness and contentment." See BE-VERBS (B).

promulgate, a word perhaps too well liked by lawyers, means (1) "to make known by public declaration"; or (2) "to disseminate (some creed or belief), or to proclaim (some law, decree, or tidings)" (*OED*). E.g., (Sense 2) "It is my desire that any disbursements made under this paragraph shall be made to persons who believe in the fundamental principles of the Christian religion and in the Bible and who are endeavoring to *promulgate* the same."

For the mistaken use of *propagate* for *promulgate,* see **propagate.**

prong. Courts often use this word to describe one part of a multifaceted—and often formalistic—legal test. The METAPHOR effectively shows that each part of the test must be met for a particular doctrine to apply: just as prongs are necessary to hold a stone in a piece of jewelry, so each element of a test (i.e., each "prong") must be satisfied before the legal doctrine applies. Justice Wiley B. Rutledge was one of the earliest American users of this word in this figurative sense. See *Oklahoma Press Pub. Co. v. Walling,* 327 U.S. 186, 192 (1946).

Since the mid-20th century, the word has all but become a VOGUE WORD. From 1970 to 1975, it appeared in only 9 opinions of the U.S. Supreme Court; from 1985 to 1990, though, it appeared in some 55. Meanwhile, the other federal courts and state courts have come to use it with great frequency. For a discussion of the opinion-writing style typified by layered sets of "prongs" and "hurdles" and other tests, see Garner, "Opinions, Style of," in *The Oxford Companion to the Supreme Court of the United States* 607, 607–08 (1992).

PRONOUNS. A. Underused in Legal Writing. "It is not simply that referential pronouns are avoided only where their use could raise genuine confusion; [in legal writing] they seem to be eschewed as a species." David Crystal & Derek Davy, *Investigating English Style* 202 (1967). The result is often a sentence that no native speaker of English—other than a lawyer—would ever perpetrate, such as: "Then Tina became very lethargic, at which time Tina was taken to the emergency room."

Why the fear of pronouns? Because lawyers have overlearned the lesson that pronouns sometimes have ambiguous referents. That being so, they (the lawyers, not the referents) swear off using them (the pronouns, not the lawyers) altogether. The result, to paraphrase Fred Rodell, is that many legal sentences read as if they have been translated from the German by someone who barely knows English.

Clunkers can be avoided by judiciously using pronouns and by finding other ways to avoid repeating nouns—e.g.: "After the persons obligated under the loan failed to pay *the loan* [delete the previous two words] as required, the bank foreclosed on the collateral and caused *the collateral* [read *it*] to be sold."

B. Pronouns, Preemptive. See ANTICIPATORY REFERENCE (C).

C. Restrictive and Nonrestrictive Relative Pronouns. See RESTRICTIVE AND NONRESTRICTIVE CLAUSES.

PRONUNCIATION. A. General Principles. The best course is to follow the pronunciation current among educated speakers in one's region. The Texas pronunciation of *voir dire* /*vohr-***dɪr**/ differs markedly from the New York pronunciation /*vwah-***deer**/, and it would be inappropriate for a

Texas lawyer to affect the New York pronunciation. On this point, Fowler still speaks to us with clarion wisdom: "The ambition to do better than our neighbours is in many departments of life a virtue; in pronunciation it is a vice; there the only right ambition is to do as our neighbours" (*MEU1* 466). See HYPERCORRECTION (K).

A few words have universally accepted pronunciations and rejected mispronunciations; where prescriptions on pronunciation appear in this book, the preferred pronunciation is generally preferred, regardless of the jurisdiction.

When it comes to words that are seldom pronounced by English-speaking people—as with any learned word, such as those from the law—the advice to conform with our neighbors' pronunciation becomes problematic. For here we find diversity, not uniformity—the result of the infrequency with which the words are pronounced. "Where there is a diversity of opinion and practice among reasonable [and educated] people, there must be also an equally broad charity in judgment. Could anything be more absurd than to stigmatize as incorrect a pronunciation which is actually in general use . . . ?" George P. Krapp, *The Pronunciation of Standard English in America* iv (1919).

B. Commonly Mispronounced Lawyers' Words. Many words that prove troublesome to lawyers are listed throughout this work, with the correct pronunciation noted. Among the most frequently mispronounced words in the law are *err /ər/, substantive /***səb***-stən-tiv/*, and (formerly) *cestui /***set***-ee/*. See **pamphlet.**

C. Latin Terms. Pronunciation of Latin terms that survive in the language of the law is always troublesome for lawyers, since so few are trained in Latin and all are compelled to use such terms in the course of practice. The difficulty is—depending on one's point of view—exacerbated or ameliorated by the existence of three distinct methods of Latin pronunciation. As an example, *sub judice,* q.v., is pronounced in two quite different ways, with minor variations on each.

Of the three methods of Latin pronunciation—Anglo-Latin, classical Latin, and Italianate—only one has found a permanent home in law: Anglo-Latin. For those who have studied Latin in high school and college, this legal preference can be bothersome because the resulting pronunciations can sound uncouth—e.g.:

Law-Latin Term	***Anglo-Latin Pronunciation***	***Classical Pronunciation***
nisi prius	*/nɪ-sɪ-***prɪ***-əs/*	*/nee-see-***pree***-əs/*
ratio decidendi	*/***ray***-shee-oh-dees-i-***den***-dɪ/*	*/***rah***-tee-oh-day-see-***den***-dee/*
sine die	*/***sɪ***-nee-***dɪ***-ee/*	*/***see***-nay-***dee***-ay/*

Further, several of legal LATINISMS are primarily read and not spoken (e.g., *inclusio unius est exclusio alterius*). Most of the common Latinisms, such as *de minimis, de facto,* and *ipso facto,* have readily apparent pronunciations. One should attempt to cultivate a sensitivity to the way Latin terms are pronounced within the professional community of one's geographic area, and stay within the mainstream in that community. Of course, using dictionaries is always helpful. (See LAW LATIN.) For more on this interesting subject, see H.A. Kelly, *Lawyers' Latin: Loquenda ut Vulgus?* 38 J. Leg. Educ. 195 (1988).

D. Law French. Lawyers generally pronounce Law-French words just as they were pronounced in the Middle Ages. To give them a modern French pronunciation, as by mouthing *oyez* as if it were */oh-***yay***/* instead of */oh-***yes***/* or */oh-***yez***/*, is a type of vulgarism.

E. BrE Idiosyncrasies. Glanville Williams notes several instances in which "lawyers still jealously retain the archaic pronunciations of English words." *Learning the Law* 63–64 (11th ed. 1982). Among them are these:

assured, n.	*/ə-***shur***-əd/*
cognisance (BrE spelling)	No *-g-* pronounced.
recognisance (BrE spelling)	No *-g-* pronounced.
record, n.	*/ri-***kord***/*

proof. A. Evidence Carrying Conviction. Whereas *evidence* includes all the means by which any alleged matter of fact can be established or disproved, *proof* is the result of evidence: the evidence may or may not be sufficient to establish the alleged facts—that is, may or may not amount to *proof.* See **evidence (B).**

B. For *probate.* *Proof* has the general legal senses (1) "evidence that determines the judgment of a court," and more specifically, (2) "an attested written document that constitutes legal evidence." In practice, sense (2) translates into the idiomatic equivalent of *probate:* "Bearing these opposing considerations in mind, the court is of the opinion that the will should be admitted to *proof.*" *Eaton v. Brown,* 193 U.S. 411, 414 (1904) (per Holmes, J.). *Proving a will* = obtaining probate of a will. See **probate,** n.

C. For *element of proof.* Generally, of course, *proof* is a mass noun. But when *proof* is used as an ellipsis for *element of proof* (as a type or a piece of evidence), it often takes the plural form *proofs,* as here: "A case is made for the jury whenever the *proofs* justify with reason the inference desired."/ "It is also the product of a procedure in which the litigant is assured of an opportunity to present *proofs* and arguments for a decision in his favour." Lon L. Fuller, *Anatomy of the Law* 159 (1968). See COUNT NOUNS AND MASS NOUNS & PLURALS (B).

D. Meaning "hearing" in Scots Law. In Scotland, *proof* also means "a hearing at which evidence is heard," as when a judge rules by saying, "I will allow a *proof*."

E. Ambiguity of the Phrase *burden of proof*. See **burden of proof** (A).

F. *Proof beyond a reasonable doubt*. See **balance of probability.**

propaganda, a singular noun, makes the plural *-das*. It is sometimes mistakenly thought to be a plural in the class of *data* and *strata*.

propagate (= to reproduce or extend) is occasionally confused with *promulgate* (= to proclaim; put [a law] into action)—e.g.: "The Department determined that the F.L.S.A. governed the wage claims, but did not then look to the regulations *propagated* [read *promulgated*] under the Act." *Stewart v. Region II Child & Fam. Servs.*, 788 P.2d 913, 916–17 (Mont. 1990)./ "Commissioner Beman testified that the issuance of the preliminary injunction would have dire consequences for the PGA. He testified that the PGA would not be able to *propagate* [read *promulgate*] any rules for the professional tournaments that it oversees." *Gilder v. PGA Tour, Inc.*, 936 F.2d 417, 421 (9th Cir. 1991).

propelment. See **propulsion.**

pro per. See **pro persona.**

proper. See **indispensable.**

properly. Placement of this word in relation to a linking verb or copula may affect meaning in significant ways: *be properly* means something different from *properly be*. The latter phrase means that the thing in question (the subject) is proper, or that it is proper for the thing to be done <this question may properly be raised on appeal>, whereas the former means that the thing should be done in a proper way <briefs should be properly submitted>. See BE-VERBS.

pro persona (= for one's own person, on one's own behalf) is a LATINISM used in some jurisdictions as an equivalent of *pro se* and *in propria persona*. E.g., "Defendant has raised a number of other issues in a *pro persona* brief." *State v. Kreps*, 706 P.2d 1213, 1218 (Ariz. 1985). The phrase is sometimes shortened to *pro per* <a pro per litigant>. See **pro se** & ***in propria persona.***

property. A. Legal Meaning. Hohfeld elucidated uses that were conventionally viewed to be correct and incorrect. The traditional legal meaning of the term is "a right over a determinate thing, either a tract of land or a chattel." The transferred sense that nonlawyers commonly attach to the term is "any external thing over which the rights of possession, use, and enjoyment are exercised." See Wesley N. Hohfeld, *Fundamental Legal Conceptions* 28–29 (1919; repr. 1946). Thus the correct emphasis was seen as being on the rights over a thing, and not on the thing itself.

Today, however, even in legal writing, *property* generally carries the nontechnical sense Hohfeld disapproved of. Felix Cohen, for example, graphically defined the term as a thing that could be labeled: "That is *property* to which the following label can be attached. To the world: Keep off unless you have my permission, which I may grant or withhold. Signed: Private citizen. Endorsed: The state." *Dialogue on Private Property,* 9 Rutgers L. Rev. 357, 374 (1954).

B. As a Count Noun. Generally, *property* used as a count noun is realtors' cant in AmE. E.g., "It was the second marriage for the bridegroom, a real estate lawyer with *properties* [read *property*] in Mexico, Italy, and Palm Beach."/ "People won't realize the effect of this act until they try to buy *a property* [omit *a*]."/ "That word is exceedingly comprehensive and covers *every property* [read *all the property*] that the decedent might have had."/ "Because only *one adjacent property* [read *one adjacent piece of property*] was flooded, the court properly concluded that the damage resulted from a condition solely related to appellant's premises and within appellant's control." See COUNT NOUNS AND MASS NOUNS.

property-settlement. See **estate planning.**

prophesy; prophecy. *Prophesy* is the verb meaning "to predict or foretell," *prophecy* the noun meaning "a prediction or foretelling." Some writers mistake the noun and the verb—e.g.: "*Prophesy* [read *Prophecy*] as to whether there will be speedy and widespread adoption can not be safely indulged in at this early time." Joseph J. O'Connell, 1 Samuel Williston, *The Law Governing Sales of Goods* (1948) (1960 Supp. at 3)./ "Plaintiffs thus acknowledge that their *prophecied* [read *prophesied*] losses may readily be compensated by money damages." *Schmidt v. Enertec Corp.*, 598 F. Supp. 1528, 1544 (S.D.N.Y. 1984).

The words are pronounced differently. The last syllable in *prophesy* is pronounced "sigh," whereas the last syllable in *prophecy* is pronounced "see."

prophylactic, n. To an educated nonlawyer, this word is synonymous with *condom.* Doctors use the term for anything that prevents disease. To lawyers, it means "anything that is designed to prevent (something undesirable)." E.g., "The Court recognized that the predeprivation notice and hearing were necessary *prophylactics* against a wrongful discharge." *Findeisen v. North East Indep. Sch. Dist.,* 749 F.2d 234, 238 (5th Cir. 1984). The example quoted does not demonstrate the keenest linguistic sensitivity: in view of the nonlawyer's understanding, it is perhaps unwise to use *prophylactic* in the same sentence with *discharge.* See VERBAL AWARENESS.

Prophylactic is also frequently an adjective in legal writing <a prophylactic rule>.

proponent; propounder. Both mean "one seeking to have a will admitted to probate." The usual term is *proponent,* the form *propounder* being a NEEDLESS VARIANT.

proportion, n., should not be used when *part* or *portion* is intended. See **portion.**

One writes, "A high proportion of it *is,*" but "A high proportion of them *are.*" Cf. **percentage of, a.** See SYNESIS.

proportion, v.t.; **proportionalize; proportionate,** v.t. The second and third are NEEDLESS VARIANTS.

proportionate; proportional; proportionable. The distinction to be observed is between *proportional* and *proportionate;* admittedly, at times the distinction is foiled by the frequent interchangeability of the terms. Nevertheless, it is possible to formulate the nuance that *proportional* = (1) of or relating to proportion; (2) in due proportion; whereas *proportionate* = proportioned, adjusted in proportion. As a Latinate perfect passive participle, *proportionate* suggests the conscious proportioning of an agent.

This nice distinction aside, *proportionate* seems to be used more commonly in legal writing than *proportional.* E.g., "The court rejected appellant's contention that appellee's claim for compensation had also prescribed and awarded appellee his *proportionate* share of the value of the recoverable reserves."/ "Defense fees and costs incurred in defending personal injury actions are assessable as an element of damages in *proportionate*-fault collision cases." Especially is this so in the negative form of the word: "If the provision made for the prospective bride is unreasonably *disproportionate* to that which she would receive out of her husband's estate but for the agreement, it will be presumed that the prospective bride was not sufficiently informed about the extent, nature, and value of her husband's property."

Proportionable is an ARCHAISM that still sometimes occurs in legal writing—e.g.: "The note for additional interest shall be *proportionably* [read *proportionately*] reduced." Cf. **commensurate.**

propound (= [1] to put forward [a will] as authentic; [2] to put forth for consideration or discussion; or [3] to make a proposal, to propose) is easily used correctly, as the examples following demonstrate. E.g., "The jury initially gave inconsistent answers to special interrogatories *propounded* to it by the court."/ "Where one party opposes summary judgment by *propounding* a reasonable interpretation of a disputed matter, it may be sufficient to defeat the motion."/ "Petitioner married the decedent on February 10, 1951; the *propounded* instrument was executed on May 18, 1951 and the decedent died on July 1, 1951."/ "The privilege of cross-examination does not carry with it the right to indulge in irrelevant investigations of the private life of the witness, or to *propound* questions intended only to degrade and humiliate him before the jury."

For the misuse of this verb, see **expound.**

propounder. See **proponent.**

proprietary; proprietory. The latter is an erroneous form. The adjectival form corresponding to the noun *proprietor* is either *proprietary* or *proprietorial. Proprietary* also means "of, relating to, or holding as property."

In the following sentence, *proprietorial* is almost certainly misused for *proprietary:* "[T]he contracts were negotiated not with the band's company, The Beatles, Ltd., which held the rights, but with NEMS, which did not possess any *proprietorial* [read *proprietary*] rights whatsoever, being simply a management organization." Albert Goldman, *The Lives of John Lennon* 335 (1988).

propulsion; propelment. The former is the usual term, the latter a NEEDLESS VARIANT.

propulsive; propulsory. The latter is a NEEDLESS VARIANT.

pro rata, adv., should be spelled as two words. E.g., "Appellant argues that the will shows that the testator intended his debts and estate costs to be paid *pro rata.*" *Proportionately* will sometimes serve in place of *pro rata.*

On the question whether to hyphenate *pro rata* when it functions as a phrasal adjective—that is, *pro-rata distribution* as opposed to *pro rata distribution*—see PHRASAL ADJECTIVES (B).

prorate (= to divide or assess proportionately) is an Americanism, although the British have now adopted the noun form *proration.* Instead of the AmE *prorating,* common in the law of oil and gas, the British use *prorationing.*

prorogue; prorogate. *Prorogue* = (1) to postpone; (2) to discontinue the meetings of (a legislative assembly, usually Parliament) for a definite or indefinite time without dissolving it; or (3) to discontinue meeting until the next session. *Prorogate* is a NEEDLESS VARIANT except in Scots and civil law, in which the term means "to extend by consent (the jurisdiction of a judge or court) to a cause in which jurisdiction would otherwise be incompetent."

proscribe; prescribe. The former means to prohibit, the latter to impose authoritatively. Here both are correctly used: "[D]ue process of law requires that a penal statute or ordinance state with reasonable clarity the act it *proscribes* and must also *prescribe* fixed standards for adjudging guilt when that person stands accused." *State v. Bloss,* 637 P.2d 1117, 1128 (Haw. 1981). See **prescribe.**

proscription; prescription. Like the corresponding verbs, these nouns are sometimes confused. Sometimes it is difficult to determine whether the use is proper or improper, as here: "The thrust of her argument is that she could not have been constitutionally arrested under the disorderly conduct statute because her conduct did not fit the *proscriptions* [read *prescriptions?*] of that statute." If the writer meant to say her conduct did not match the types of conduct prohibited by the statute, *proscription* was the correct word; but if the writer meant to say that her conduct did not fall within the definitions of disorderly conduct laid down by the statute, *prescription* would have been the correct word.

Even more serious is the MISCUE caused by *medical proscription* in the following example: "Gill . . . alleges only that Rudnickey forced him to paint despite his complaints that paint fumes made him 'dizzy and nauseous.' In the absence of any medical *proscriptions* known to Rudnickey, his decision to ignore Gill's complaints amounted to nothing more than a mere negligent act . . . ." *Gill v. Mooney,* 824 F.2d 192, 195 (2d Cir. 1987). See **prohibition (B).**

pro se = on one's own behalf. The phrase is two words, and should not be hyphenated. Functionally, the phrase may be either adjectival or adverbial. Here it is the former: "In this *pro se* action, plaintiff contends that defendant absconded with personal property and household goods belonging to him, in violation of a temporary restraining order." Just as frequently it is adverbial, as here: "The taxpayer-petitioner appeals *pro se* from an order and decision of the United States Tax Court." See ***in propria persona*** & **pro persona.**

prosecutable. So spelled.

prosecute; persecute. Heaven forbid that one with legal training should confuse these terms. *Prosecute* = to begin a case at law for punishment of a crime or of a legal violation. *Persecute* = to oppress, coerce, or treat unfairly, often out of religious hatred.

Today *prosecute* is largely confined to criminal contexts (= to institute legal proceedings against [a person] for some offense), but the word survives as an ARCHAISM in civil contexts in the sense "to carry out or engage in a legal action; to follow up on a legal claim." E.g., "A statute of Illinois provided that no action should be brought or *prosecuted* in that State for damages occasioned by death occurring in another State in consequence of wrongful conduct." *Kenney v. Supreme Lodge of the World, Loyal Order of Moose,* 252 U.S. 411, 414 (1920) (per Holmes, J.)./ "Appellants have *prosecuted* an appeal to this court."/ "There was a jury trial, resulting in a verdict and judgment in behalf of appellee, from which this appeal is *prosecuted.*"/ "Plaintiff *prosecutes* this appeal from a judgment of dismissal entered after sustaining of defendants' general demurrer."

When used in reference to something other than law, *prosecute* generally means "to carry on." In this sense, the term is a LEGALISM and an ARCHAISM <he continued to prosecute his business>. E.g., "All unexpended balances of appropriations prior to May 15, 1928, made for *prosecuting* work of flood control on the Mississippi River, are made available under this title."

prosecution meant originally (fr. 16th c.) "the following up, continuing, or carrying out of any action, scheme, or purpose, with a view to its accomplishment or attainment." Then it came to be associated with criminal law in the 18th century and took on the meaning "a criminal proceeding in which an accused person is tried."

Today, both in AmE and in BrE, it is also used for *prosecutor* or *prosecutors,* the process of HYPALLAGE having done its usual work—e.g.: "The *prosecution* made improper arguments."/ "The *prosecution* marshaled evidence tending to link appellant with these practices." In BrE, the word often takes a plural verb: "It is not altogether clear from the authorities what is the degree of risk that the *prosecution have* to prove."

Glanville Williams, *Textbook of Criminal Law* 73 (1978).

prosecutional; prosecutive. See **prosecutorial.**

prosecutor = (1) a legal officer who represents the state in criminal proceedings; or (2) a private person who institutes and carries on a suit—esp. a criminal suit—in court. Sense (2), though increasingly rare, persists primarily in BrE—e.g.: "A private *prosecutor* may relieve the local authority of some expense, but here the private prosecutor may receive from the local authority part of the cost he incurs." R.M. Jackson, *The Machinery of Justice in England* 324 (5th ed. 1967)./ "In some types of criminal case the title of the case will not contain *Rex* or *Reg.* before the 'v.,' but will contain the name of a private person. This happens when the case is tried summarily before magistrates (*i.e.* justices of the peace); here the name of the actual *prosecutor* (*e.g.* a policeman) appears instead of the nominal prosecutor, the Queen." Glanville Williams, *Learning the Law* 17 (11th ed. 1982). See **prosecution.**

prosecutorial; prosecutory; prosecutive; prosecutional. The most common term in criminal-law texts is *prosecutorial;* but this variant is not included in *W3. Prosecutory* and its NEEDLESS VARIANT *prosecutive*—less common words in legal writing—are defined as "of or pertaining to prosecution." A distinction might obtain if we restricted *prosecutorial* to be the adjective for *prosecutor,* already its primary function. E.g., "The *prosecutorial* decision not to prosecute has a deterrent effect on police misconduct." See, e.g., Bennett L. Gershman, *Prosecutorial Misconduct* (1985); Joseph F. Lawless, *Prosecutorial Misconduct: Law, Procedure, Forms* (1985).

But sometimes *prosecutorial* appears where *prosecutory* might be more appropriate—e.g.: "*Miranda* does not interfere with the *prosecutorial* [read *prosecutory*] function."/ "The bar committees are composed of private 'competitors' and perform both *prosecutorial* [read *prosecutory*] and adjudicative functions in enforcing a self-regulatory disciplinary process."/ "Todaro contends that this case presents such circumstances and invites us to ignore the government's asserted *prosecutorial* [read *prosecutory*] interest in the witnesses."/ "This case concerns the doctrines of judicial and *prosecutorial* [read *prosecutory*] immunity."

Prosecutional is but a NEEDLESS VARIANT not countenanced by the dictionaries.

prosecutrix /*pro-sə-**kyoo**-triks*/, a word traditionally used in reference to a female who brings criminal charges against a sexual assailant, has been objected to on grounds that it is sexist and obscurantist. See *Allen v. State,* 700 S.W.2d 924, 935–36 (Tex. Crim. App. 1985) (Miller, J., concurring). Judge Miller offers *victim* as a clearer, more sympathetic term. But *victim* would surely be prejudicial and ineffective if, for example, it has not been established that a rape actually took place or who the rapist was. (Cf. **complainant.**) Judge Miller observes that "if *prosecutrix* is used to refer to the female victim of a sexual assault, would not the term *prosecutor* be appropriate for a male victim of a sexual assault?" *Id.* at 936 n.2.

Of course, *prosecutor* is not today much used in that sense (but see sense (2) under that headword). And it is that lack of equivalency that lends some credence to the charge that the word evinces a discriminatory bias in the language. (See SEXISM (C).) More likely, however, the language of the law has not needed a word for adult male victims of sex crimes.

One admirable device that judges have begun using when writing about rape cases—a device that doesn't attach an awkward, aggressive-sounding epithet to the victim—is to use a pseudonym, such as *Mary Doe,* when presenting a factual narrative.

proselytize; proselyte, v.t. The former is preferred, the latter being a NEEDLESS VARIANT.

prospective heir. See **heir (B).**

prospective juror. See **potential juror.**

prospectus. A. Plural Form. The correct English plural is *prospectuses*—and it is the only form listed in English dictionaries. The Latin plural is *prospectus* (a fourth-declension noun), not *prospecti,* the product of ignorant hypercorrection: "Bismarck Realty prepared *prospecti* [read *prospectuses*] on the property . . . ." *Bismarck Realty Co. v. Folden,* 354 N.W.2d 636, 638 (N.D. 1984)./ "Put and call option trading on an underlying security is directly affected by the *prospecti* [read *prospectuses*], representations and omissions of the issuer of the underlying security." *Tolan v. Computervision Corp.,* 696 F. Supp. 771, 775 (D. Mass. 1988). Cf. **apparatus.** See HYPERCORRECTION (A).

B. For *perspective.* This is a MALAPROPISM—e.g.: "The players were able to keep everything in *prospectus* [read *perspective*]." Properly, of course, *prospectus* = a printed document describing the chief features of a school, commercial enterprise, forthcoming book, or the like. See **conspectus.**

prostate. See **prostrate.**

prostitution, meaning in one sense "the act of debasing," is connotatively charged with its other sense of harlotry. E.g., "Solicitation of clients by following accidents and soliciting retainers from the injured is a vile *prostitution* of the advocate's calling." Where the tone is intentionally provocative or connotatively charged, it may be the right word. *Prostitution* should not be used, however, wherever *debasement* might adequately be used.

In criminal law, the word was once confined to a female's taking money in exchange for sexual intercourse with a man. Today, however, the law recognizes that males as well as females engage in prostitution.

prostrate, vb. & adj.; **prostate,** n. These are very different words, but they are sometimes confused. In its verb sense, to *prostrate* oneself is to kneel down in humility or adoration. As an adjective, *prostrate* means either "lying face down" or "emotionally overcome." The noun *prostate,* by contrast, refers to the gland found in male mammals, surrounding the urethra at the base of the bladder.

The most common mistake is to say *prostrate gland* when one means *prostate gland*—e.g.: "He described acid phosphatase as an enzyme from the *prostrate* [read *prostate*] gland of a male person." *State v. Williams,* 196 S.E.2d 248, 249 (N.C. 1973)./ "The *Connell* plaintiff alleged that defendant physician breached a 'continuing duty to disclose material facts' (the physical examination findings, specifically, enlargement of the *prostrate* [read *prostate*] gland) relevant to the decedent's condition (eventually diagnosed as cancer)." Jennifer S.R. Lynn, *Connecticut Medical Malpractice,* 12 Bridgeport L. Rev. 381, 440 (1992)./ "One strain of mice, whose males develop enlarged *prostrate* [read *prostate*] glands, will be used to test potential drug treatments for *prostrate* [read *prostate*] enlargement as well as suspected carcinogens." Michael E. Sellers, Note, *Patenting Non-naturally Occurring, Man-Made Life,* 47 Ark. L. Rev. 269, 271–72 (1994).

protagonist. Literally, *protagonist* = the chief character in a drama; by extension, it means "a champion of a cause." It should not be used loosely of any upholder or supporter of a cause; it should refer to a prominent and active supporter. E.g., "The complexity of the community property system is not offset by those values claimed for the system by its most ardent *protagonists* [read *supporters*]."

Protagonist is all too frequently confused with *antagonist.* E.g., "On this point there was an internecine struggle in the Second Circuit, with Judges Clark and Friendly as the *protagonists* [read *antagonists*]." (Note that *internecine* means "mutually deadly," and that is hardly the intended meaning here.)/ "On this promising note the two *protagonists* [i.e., now angry litigants] parted." (This sentence contains an example of the rhetorical figure prolepsis—the representation of a future fact as presently existing; that is, when the two persons parted on a promising note, they were not antagonists or opponents; only in retrospect or from a current perspective may they be seen as angry litigants.)

In the following sentence, the writer attempted to use *protagonist* figuratively in its dramatic sense but failed in the metaphor because a drama has only one protagonist: "Slugs, larvae, nematodes, and rodents form the supporting cast in this trademark drama; the *protagonists* [read *principal characters*] are the terms *Larvacide* and *larvicide.*" *Soweco, Inc. v. Shell Oil Co.,* 617 F.2d 1178, 1181 (5th Cir. 1980).

Perhaps the most objectionable watering-down of the meaning of *protagonist* occurs when it is used as an equivalent of *proponent: "Protagonists* [read *Proponents*] of a more active role and greater freedom of technique for courts in private law reform have sometimes failed to recognize the need to revise, too, prevailing attitudes about the role and technique of legislatures."

pro tanto (= to that extent; as far as it goes) is a defensible LATINISM commonly used in law. No other word quite works without substantial rewording. It may be used adjectivally: "There may be a *pro tanto* ademption by satisfaction if the evidence indicated that the testator so intended the inter vivos gift to work such an ademption."/ "It would be a matter of pure speculation whether—whatever the change of conditions since her death—she would not want part of the corpus of the trust turned over to the petitioner, involving, as it would, the *pro tanto* depletion of the fund from which the income was to be derived."/ "It was an offer capable of being accepted and turned into a contract *pro tanto* on the occasion of each discount." (Eng.)

The phrase may also be used adverbially: "The bequest would be deemed *pro tanto* void if the testator had deliberately used unmeaning words." (Eng.)/ "We deal of course with a later Congress and an Act that sets aside by section 208(b) *pro tanto* the earlier Act."/ "If defendant received less than the value of plaintiff's work, as defendant seems to contend, then plaintiff should recover *pro tanto.*"

protectible; protectable. The former is preferred. Inconsistencies often arise even within one piece of writing. See, e.g., headnotes 1 and 5 of

Velo-Bind, Inc. v. Scheck, 485 F. Supp. 102, 102 (S.D.N.Y. 1979). See -ABLE (A).

protective; protectory. The latter is a NEEDLESS VARIANT.

pro tem. is the abbreviation for *pro tempore* (= for the time being). This fairly common LATINISM is used as a POSTPOSITIVE ADJECTIVE in phrases such as *mayor pro tem.*

protest, n.; **protestation.** The difference is that *protest,* the ordinary word, usually refers to a formal statement or action of dissent or disapproval, whereas *protestation,* a learned word, generally denotes a solemn affirmation.

protest, vb., is transitive or intransitive in AmE but is solely intransitive in most BrE writing. In G.B., one writes, "They *protested* against discrimination," but not, "They *protested* discrimination." Partridge considered the latter, which is acceptable AmE usage, incorrect and quoted an American writer as an offender against idiom. See Eric Partridge, *Usage and Abusage* 248 (1973). The phrase *protest against* is common also in the U.S. E.g., "Appellants were *protesting against* American policy in Vietnam." In AmE, however, *against* is regularly omitted. An exception to the general British legal idiom is the phrase *protest a bill of exchange.*

protestant /***prot***-ə-stənt/ (= a protesting person) is often used in law to mean "one who protests an administrative decision." E.g., "In arguing that the ICC's method of evaluating any *protestant's* proof of inconsistency with public convenience and necessity violates the national transportation policy, Steere insists that under current Commission policy it is impossible for a *protestant* to demonstrate that inconsistency."/ "Once a petitioner makes out a prima facie case, a presumption is created that the new authority will be consistent with the public convenience and necessity, and the burden of proof is shifted to the *protestant* that it will not." Cf. **caveator, contestant** & **objectant.**

protocol. See **treaty.**

prot(h)onotary means generally "the chief clerk of a court of law." The word is pronounced /*proh-**thon**-ə-tar-ee*/ or /*proh-thə-**nod**-ə-ree*/.

The spelling with the *-h-* is prevalent in both AmE and BrE—to the extent that this obsolescent word can be called "prevalent" at all. The office was abolished in England in 1837, the last holder surviving until 1874. But the term lingers in some American jurisdictions. E.g., "The trustee may, on the other hand, obtain an adjudication of his management of the trust by filing his account in the office of the *prothonotary* of the court . . . ." *Princess Lida v. Thompson,* 305 U.S. 456, 463 (1939)./ "As in Florida, a private party may obtain a prejudgment writ of replevin through a summary process of ex parte application to a *prothonotary.*" *Fuentes v. Shevin,* 407 U.S. 67, 75–76 (1972).

prototype. See **archetype.**

prototyp(ic)al. The usual and preferred form is *prototypical,* not *prototypal.* Cf. **archetyp(ic)al.**

protuberate is frequently misspelled and mispronounced as if it were *protruberate,* perhaps out of confusion with *protrude.* The adjective, likewise, is *protuberant,* not *protruberant*—e.g.: "Physical examination revealed plaintiff to be a very healthy appearing person with a *protruberant* [read *protuberant* or *protruding*] abdomen." *Coleman v. Califano,* 462 F. Supp. 77, 79–80 (N.D.N.Y. 1978).

proud; prideful. The connotative distinction to bear in mind is that *prideful* suggests excessive pride, haughtiness, and disdain. A favorite word of charismatic and evangelical Christians, *prideful* is also moralistic in tone.

prove; prove up. Generally, it is sufficient to use *prove* transitively, and hence to write, "He attempted to *prove* his title to the land." A common Americanism in law, however, is the phrasal verb *prove up* (= to adduce or complete the proof of right to (something); to show that one has fulfilled the legal conditions). E.g., "He attempted to *prove up* his title to the land." The *OED* indicates that this usage has spread to Canada. See PHRASAL VERBS & PARTICLES, UNNECESSARY.

proved; proven. *Proved* is the universally preferred past participle of *prove.* Often, however, *proven* ill-advisedly appears—e.g.: "In *Beaumont v. Feld,* a bequest to 'Catharine Earnley' was *proven* [read *proved*] to have been intended for Gertrude Yardley, and was given to the latter."/ "Since the serious bodily injury suffered by complainant at the hands of appellant was *proven* [read *proved*] beyond a reasonable doubt, the error, if any, was harmless."

In AmE and BrE alike, the past participle *proved* is much more common than *proven*—e.g.: "Our system does not interfere till harm has been done and has been *proved* to have been done with appropriate mens rea." H.L.A. Hart, "Punishment and the Elimination of Responsibility," in *Punishment and Responsibility: Essays in the Philosophy of Law* 158, 182 (1968).

Like *stricken,* however, *proven* is properly used only as an adjective. E.g., "Evidence may be offered, not to show its already *proven* existence, but . . . ."/ "In judging human conduct, intent is an elusive subjective concept, and its existence usually can be inferred only from *proven* facts." See **stricken.**

Proven has survived as a past participle in legal usage in two phrases: first, in the phrase *innocent until proven guilty;* second, in the verdict *Not proven,* a jury answer no longer widely used except in Scots law. As for *Not proven,* one writer has defined this verdict as meaning, "Not guilty, but don't do it again." William Roughead, *The Art of Murder* 131 (1943).

provenance; provenience. Both are FORMAL WORDS for *origin* or *source. Provenience* is chiefly an Americanism, but *provenance* prevails throughout the English-speaking world—including AmE.

proves the rule, the exception. See **exception proves the rule, the.**

prove too much = to make an overbroad argument; (of an argument) to be overbroad. E.g., "A very common criticism of Vaihinger is to say that he *proves too much.* If everything is a 'fiction,' then the meaning of the word 'fiction' has been lost, and 'as if' has become simply 'is.'" Lon L. Fuller, *Legal Fictions* 123 (1967)./ "[T]he government's argument *proves too much.* If an 'acquisition' as that term is used in the acquisition clause is also required under the notice clause, then the notice alternative would be rendered surplusage." *Cole v. Harris,* 571 F.2d 590, 596 (D.C. Cir. 1977).

prove up. See **prove.**

provided that. A. Provisos Generally. Writers on drafting have long cautioned drafters not to use provisos. In fact, the words *provided that* are a reliable signal that the draft is not going well.

The problem—recognized five centuries ago by Coke—is that the phrase means too many different things: *provided that* may create an exception, a limitation, a condition, or a mere addition. Sometimes the phrase is the functional equivalent of an adjectival phrase—e.g.: "*Provided that* an order under this section is approved, it shall be binding upon all persons concerned." [Read *An order approved under this section binds all persons concerned.*]

The matter contained in the proviso is often preferably integrated into a subordinate clause introduced by *but*—e.g.: "No person who has not attained the age of twelve years shall be competent to testify, *provided that,* if the court finds that any such person understands the nature and obligation of the oath, such person shall be competent to testify." This statute is best rephrased: "Persons over the age of twelve years are competent to testify, but a person under that age is also competent if the court finds that the person understands the nature and obligation of the oath." (Ex. fr. Irving Younger, *Persuasive Writing* 6, 6–7 (1990).) See **proviso.**

B. And *providing that.* As between *provided that* and *providing that*—assuming one wants to create a proviso despite what is said under (A)—the former is the preferred phrasing.

province, the peculiar, is a legal CLICHÉ throughout common-law countries. E.g., "It is, of course, within *the peculiar province* of the Queen's Proctor to know all that bears on his office, and he does." (Eng.)

provincial, in a country without provinces, has been narrowed primarily to its extended meaning, "parochial, narrow." Yet it still carries its primary sense, "of or relating to a province." Hence, "As the preparations for the *provincial* tour progressed, William became morose."

proving a will. See **proof (B).**

provision. See **prevision** & **proviso.**

provision of law is usually unnecessary for *law* or *provision.*

proviso generally has a narrower sense than *provision* (= a contractual term). In DRAFTING, a *proviso* is either a clause that is inserted in a legal or formal document and that makes some condition, stipulation, exception, or limitation, or a clause upon whose observance the operation or validity of the instrument depends. E.g., "When there is no accuracy or promptitude, the company should answer for all injury resulting, subject to the *proviso* that the injury must be the natural and direct consequence of the negligent act." For the reasons to avoid provisos, see **provided that (A).**

The plural is *provisos,* not *provisoes.*

provocation; revenge. In criminal law, killing in *provocation* is one type of killing in *revenge,* but generally *provocation* is considered quite separate. It gives rise to action in the heat of the moment, whereas *revenge* refers to planned, cold-blooded killing.

provocative; provocatory. The latter is a NEEDLESS VARIANT.

prox. See **ult.**

proximate; proximal. Both mean "lying very near or close." Yet *proximal* is primarily a technical, scientific term, whereas *proximate* is the ordinary term with the additional senses (1) "soon forthcoming; imminent"; (2) "next preceding" <proximate cause>; and (3) "nearly accurate; approximate." See **approximate.**

proximate cause, an anglicization of the LATINISM *causa proxima,* is a TERM OF ART having little to do with physical causation, emphasizing instead the continuity of the sequence that produces an event. The meaning is elusive: "a cause of which the law will take notice." The phrase is basic to tort law in AmE and is also used, though much less frequently, in BrE. One commentator rather uncharitably terms *proximate cause* "concise gibberish." David Mellinkoff, *The Language of the Law* 401 (1963). See CAUSATION (A).

Synonymous phrases—now, for the most part, rejects—are *primary cause, efficient cause, efficient proximate cause, efficient adequate cause, legal cause,* and *jural cause.*

proxy, in corporate law, has three distinct senses: (1) "a person who is authorized to vote another's shares"; (2) "the grant of authority by which a person is so authorized"; or (3) "the document granting that authority."

prudent(ial). *Prudent* = exhibiting prudence. *Prudential* = pertaining to, considered from the point of view of, or dictated by prudence. E.g., "This limitation is not constitutionally mandated but a rule of self-restraint justified by a *prudential* concern that courts should not adjudicate constitutional rights unnecessarily."/ "*Prudential* guidelines govern the administration of this rule."

"To call an act *prudent,*" wrote Fowler, "is normally to commend it; to call it *-ial* is more often than not to disparage it. A prisoner's refusal to go into the witness-box is prudential but not prudent if he refuses for fear of giving himself away but actually creates prejudice against himself, prudent but not prudential if it deprives the prosecution of a necessary link in the evidence but is dictated merely by bravado, and both or neither in conditions as easy to invent" (*MEU1* 473).

prurience; pruriency. The latter is a NEEDLESS VARIANT.

pseudonym = a fictitious name. In law, common pseudonyms for persons involved in suits are *John Doe, Jane Doe,* and *Richard Roe.* Here the word is wrongly used for *euphemism:* "Graglia implies that affirmative action is a *pseudonym* [read *euphemism*] for preferring blacks and browns over whites." See EUPHEMISMS. See also **anonym(e).**

PSITTACISM is the parrotlike use of language. If there is a malady endemic in legal writing, it is the practice or habit of mechanically repeating previously received ideas or images that reflect neither true reasoning nor feeling. Many legal opinions and law-review articles seem little more than ready-made legal phrases strung end on end to justify a given proposition. The clichés give themselves away with the first couple of words in the line, so that the adept reader knows what the psittacistic writer will say before reading the end of the line. *In derogation of* is rarely followed by anything other than *the common law;* and so endemic are such phrases as *case of first impression, it is well established that,* and *notwithstanding anything herein to the contrary* that they finally numb the intellect of both reader and writer. For more examples, see CLICHÉS.

George Orwell's thinking was as penetrating here as elsewhere: "[M]odern writing at its worst does not consist in picking out words for the sake of their meaning and inventing images in order to make the meaning clearer. It consists in gumming together long strips of words [that] have already been set in order by someone else, and making the results presentable by sheer humbug." George Orwell, "Politics and the English Language," in *Shooting an Elephant and Other Essays* 77, 85 (1945).

The best legal writers attempt to formulate their thoughts anew. Their writing is fresh and original. And it is rare.

psychic; psychal; psychical; psychological. *Psychic* = (1) of or relating to the psyche; (2) spiritual; or (3) paranormal. *Psychical* (= of or relating to the mind) is contrasted with *physical. Psychal* is a NEEDLESS VARIANT. *Psychological* = (1) of, pertaining to, or of the nature of psychology; dealing with psychology; (2) of or pertaining to the objects of psychological study; of or pertaining to the mind, mental (*OED*). The *OED* states that sense (2) of *psychological* is a loose usage, but it is now firmly established.

psycholegal (= involving the psychological implications of the legal process) is a late-20th-century NEOLOGISM—e.g.: Wallace D. Loh, *Psycholegal Research: Past and Present,* 79 Mich. L. Rev. 659 (1981); Gary B. Melton & Ralph B. Pliner, "Adolescent Abortion: A *Psycholegal* Analysis," in *Adolescent Abortion, Psychological and Legal Issues* 1 (G.B. Melton ed. 1986); Richard L. Wiener, *A Psycholegal and Empirical Approach to the Medical Standard of Care,* 69 Neb. L. Rev. 112 (1990). Cf. **medicolegal.**

psychological. See **psych(ic).**

pubes, a term that occasionally arises in criminal cases, refers either to the area surrounding a person's external genitals or to pubic hair. It is sometimes mispronounced /*pyoobs*/, though properly it has two syllables /***pyoo**-beez*/.

public, a COLLECTIVE NOUN, usually takes a singular verb in AmE <public is> and a plural verb in BrE <public are>.

public Act; private Act; public bill; private bill. In British statutory law (or "statute law" as it is known in BrE), a *public Act* is one that a court may take judicial notice of, whereas a *private Act* is one whose terms must be proved in court. But every Act passed since 1850 is considered public in this sense unless the Act expressly provides otherwise (a rarity). (For the reason behind capitalizing *Act,* see **act (c).**)

A *public bill* is one brought by a government minister or by a private member who has won a place on the ballot allowing him or her a chance to bring in the bill. A *private bill* is one promoted by a person or body (such as a local authority) to regulate its own affairs. Public and private bills are subject to different parliamentary procedures.

publication = (1) (in the law of defamation) the communication of defamatory words to someone other than the person defamed; or (2) (in the law of wills) the formal declaration made by a testator at the time of signing the will that it is the testator's will. Following are examples of sense (2), in which the word is a TERM OF ART: "Some states require the testator to indicate to the attesting witnesses that the document executed or to be executed by him is a will; this action is called *publication.*"/ "There is no point in *'publishing'* the will at the beginning; the witnesses will not be likely to see the *publication* there. It should be at the end of the will. In any case, 'I delcare that this is my will' is a *publication.*" Thomas L. Shaffer, *The Planning and Drafting of Wills and Trusts* 171 (2d ed. 1979).

In sense (1) as in sense (2), the verb corresponding to *publication* is *to publish.* In the law of defamation, to *publish* is to make public. E.g., "The libel was *published* by the attorney to persons having no relationship to the pending judicial proceeding." Spoken as well as written defamation is said to be *published.*

publicist (= one who is learned in public or international law; a writer on the law of nations [*OED*]) ordinarily means "publicity agent" to nonlawyers. Hence the legal use of the term generally requires explanation if the audience is a broad one.

public law = (1) constitutional law, criminal law, and administrative law taken together; or (2) published law. Sense (2) is far less common—e.g.: "A case decided is called a 'precedent,' and becomes at once *public law,* which, under many circumstances, binds a court to make the same decision in any future case similar to it." William M. Lile et al., *Brief Making and the Use of Law Books* 26 (3d ed. 1914).

publicly, not *publically,* is the adverb: "Marlin Fitzwater, the President's spokesman, said Mr. Bush felt assured that Dr. Sullivan, whatever his private views might be, would *publically* [read *publicly*] support the President's policy of opposing abortion in almost all cases." Steven V. Roberts, *Bush Will Stand by Nominee to Health Post, Officials Say,* N.Y. Times, 25 Jan. 1989, at 1.

public person. To most speakers of English, this phrase suggests a celebrity. But legal theorists use it quite differently: "By a *'Public person'* we mean either the State, or the sovereign part of it, or a body or individual holding delegated authority under it." Thomas E. Holland, *The Elements of Jurisprudence* 127 (13th ed. 1924).

public policy. In the context of policy-making, this phrase connotes the art of ruling wisely <implementing sound public policy>. The phrase refers rather vaguely to matters regarded by the legislature or by the courts as being of fundamental concern to the state and the whole of society.

In the context of contract law, *public policy* connotes an overriding public interest that may justify a court's decision to declare a contract void. In this context, too, the phrase is vague: "*Public policy* is a variable notion, depending on changing manners, morals and economic conditions. In theory, this flexibility of the doctrine of *public policy* could provide a judge with an excuse for invalidating any contract which he violently disliked." G.H. Treitel, *The Law of Contract* 424 (8th ed. 1991).

Today this term, when used as a noun, is not preceded by an article: "Generally, the duty of a parent to support children is grounded *on the public policy* [read *on public policy*]."

publish. See **publication.**

pudendum (= a genital organ) forms the plural *pudenda* (= genitals). See PLURALS (A).

puffing (= the action of praising a thing excessively but in general terms, esp. to advertise it) is perfectly appropriate in formal contexts; it is not a casualism. E.g., "Ours may be, for *puffing* purposes, a 'government of checks and balances,' but there is no check at all on what the Supreme Court does . . . ." Fred Rodell, *Nine Men* 4 (1955)./ "General commendations, commonly known as dealer's talk, seller's statements, or *puffing,* do not amount to actionable misrepresentations where the parties deal at arm's length and have equal means of information and are equally well qualified to judge the facts." 41 Tex. Jur. 3d *Fraud & Deceit* § 28 (1985).

While American writers tend to stick to the gerund *puffing,* British writers frequently refer to particular statements as "mere *puffs.*"

puisne (= younger or of lower rank), sometimes used in reference to a superior court judge who is less than a chief judge, is pronounced like *puny.* Etymologically, the LAW FRENCH *puisne* is *puis-né* (=later-born). The term has been extended in English legal usage to apply to mortgagees and other incumbrancers; it is also used in England as an attributive adjective in the sense "a puisne judge" <five puisnes upheld the plea>. E.g., "Often the court consisted of the Lord Chief Justice and two *puisne* judges, with a second and third court consisting of three *puisnes* . . . ." R.M. Jackson, *The Machinery of Justice in England* 123 (5th ed. 1967)./ "The motions were heard by Lord Chief Justice Mansfield sitting with his *puisnes,* Willes and Ashurst." Patrick Devlin, *The Judge* 122 (1979).

PUNCTUATION. Judges and jurists have written more nonsense about punctuation than about any other facet of the language. The well-known dictum that "punctuation is not a part of the statute" has given rise to even more surreal pronouncements: "[P]unctuation at any rate is not a part of the English language." *Kansas City Life Ins. Co. v. Wells,* 133 F.2d 224, 227 (8th Cir. 1943). Just as surreally, courts have minimized the effect of punctuation with bizarre statements: "[P]unctuation or the absence of punctuation will not of itself create ambiguity." *Anderson & Kerr Drilling Co. v. Bruhlmeyer,* 136 S.W.2d 800, 803 (Tex. 1940).

Can that be so? The resolution of at least two capital cases has rested on no more than how the court interpreted a comma. See *U.S. v. Palmer,* 16 U.S. (3 Wheat.) 610, 636 (1818) (in which Johnson, J., dissenting, stated: "[M]en's lives may depend upon a comma"); *Rex v. Casement,* [1917] 1 K.B. 98 (1916).

And consider the following statement shorn of the punctuation marks: "Woman—without her, man would be a savage."

The fallacies underlying the statements quoted in the first paragraph are too obvious to require extensive explanation. And occasionally—though not often enough—the courts refute them: "Punctuation is a rational part of English composition, and it is sometimes quite significantly employed. I see no reason for depriving legal documents of such significance as attaches to punctuation in other writings." *Houston v. Burns,* [1918] A.C. 337, 348.

Lawyers and judges have long mistrusted punctuation as a guide to meaning. See Richard C. Wydick, *Should Lawyers Punctuate?* 1 Scribes J. Legal Writing 7 (1990). Historically speaking, there are three primary reasons for this mistrust: (1) the uncertain state of English punctuation during the 17th and 18th centuries, a formative period for modern law; (2) the fact that printers typically controlled punctuation more than drafters; and (3) the age-old canard that English statutes were traditionally unpunctuated. See *id.* at 16–19. Wydick persuasively concludes that judges "should create a rebuttable presumption that legal documents have been punctuated in accordance with ordinary English usage, and they should use the punctuation, along with all of the other guides to meaning, when they interpret legal documents." *Id.* at 24.

Following, then, are the basic principles for punctuating in accordance with ordinary English usage. These principles are adapted, with elaboration, from the *Oxford Guide* (pp. 193–97). First, though, a warning. Poor punctuation often signals writing problems that go deeper than one might think: "[M]ost errors of punctuation arise from ill-designed, badly shaped sentences, and from the attempt to make them work by means of violent tricks with commas and colons and such like." Hugh Sykes Davies, *Grammar Without Tears* 167 (1951).

A. The Apostrophe [']. This punctuation mark is used in English for either of two purposes: (1) to indicate the possessive case—e.g.: "Lord Mansfield[']s speech"; "Mother Jones[']s recipe"; and (2) to mark the omission of one or more elements and the contracting of the remaining elements into a meaningful expression—e.g.:

"ever" into "e[']er"; "we will" into "we[']ll"; "1969" into "[']69." See POSSESSIVES.

On the misuse of an apostrophe to denote a plural, see PLURALS (F).

B. The Colon [:]. This mark may link two grammatically complete clauses by indicating a step forward from the first to the second: the step may be from an introduction to a main theme, from a cause to an effect, from a general statement to a particular instance, or from a premise to a conclusion. E.g., "The remedy is simple[:] enact legislation that discourages American employers from hiring illegal aliens." The colon is also used, and perhaps more commonly, to introduce a list of items, often after expressions such as "for example"; "namely"; "the following"; "as follows"; and "including." E.g., "The *following* judges were present[:] Hickman, C.J., Griffin, J., Calvert, J., and Smedley, J."

C. The Comma [,]. This is the least emphatic mark of punctuation, and the one used in the greatest variety of circumstances:

1. To separate adjectives that each qualify a noun in the same way <a cautious[,] reserved person>. E.g., "Is there to be one standard for the old, repulsive laws that preferred whites over blacks, and a *different, more forgiving* standard for new laws that give blacks special benefits in the name of historical redress?" Linda Greenhouse, *Signal on Job Rights,* N.Y. Times, 25 Jan. 1989, at 1./ "It almost goes without saying that the job of the president of the L.I.R.R. is not a weekday warrior's position—it is not a *five-days-a-week, 9-to-5* job." Matthew L. Wald, *Senator Assails L.I.R.R. Chief as Out of Touch,* N.Y. Times, 21 April 1994, at B6.

   But when adjectives qualify the noun in different ways, or when one adjective qualifies a noun phrase containing another adjective, no comma is used—e.g.: "a distinguished [no comma] foreign journalist"; "a bright [no comma] red tie." E.g., "I could quote dozens of similar remarks by *eminent, legal scholars* [read *eminent legal scholars*] and lawyers." Jerome Frank, *Courts on Trial* 61 (1949).
2. To separate items (including the last from the penultimate) in a list of more than two—e.g.: "the defendants, the third-party defendants[,] and the counterdefendants." The question whether to include the serial comma has sparked many arguments in law offices and judges' chambers. It is easily answered in favor of including the final comma, for its omission may cause ambiguities, whereas its inclusion never will—e.g.: "A and B, C and D, E and F[,] and G and H." When the members are compound, calling for *and* within themselves, clarity demands the final comma. See ENUMERATIONS (B).
3. To separate coordinated main clauses—e.g.: "Cars will turn here[,] and coaches will go straight." There are two exceptions: first, when the main clauses are closely linked (e.g., "Do as I tell you [no comma] and you will not regret it."); and second, when the subject of the second independent clause, being the same as in the first, is not repeated (e.g., "Remedies that prevent harm altogether are often better for plaintiffs [no comma] and are always closer to the ideal of corrective justice.").
4. To mark the beginning and ending of a parenthetical word or phrase—e.g.: "I am sure[,] however[,] that it will not happen."/ "Fred[,] who is bald[,] complained of the cold."

   Some writers mistakenly omit the second comma—e.g.: "Scienter, or knowledge of the falsity of representation[,] is required . . . ." William F. Walsh, *A Treatise on Equity* 490 (1930). "Mr. Rifkin's lawyer, John Lawrence[,] insisted that Mr. Rifkin did not know what he was doing and often drove around in a haze after strangling victims . . . ." John T. McQuiston, *Rifkin Guilty of Murder as Long Island Jury Rejects Insanity Defense,* N.Y. Times, 10 May 1994, at A16.

   Still others leave out both commas, often creating a MISCUE: "[S]uch warrantor must as a minimum remedy such consumer product within a reasonable time and without charge . . . ." 15 U.S.C. § 2304(a)(1) (1988). (A comma is needed after *must* and after *minimum*; otherwise, one reads *as a minimum remedy* as a single phrase.)

   Note that with restrictive clauses—that is, those that are necessary to define the antecedent or to limit it—*no* commas are used. E.g., "Men [no comma] who are bald [no comma] should wear hats."/ "Facts [no comma] not unlike those found in this record [no comma] were considered in that case.") See RESTRICTIVE AND NONRESTRICTIVE CLAUSES.
5. To separate a participial or verbless clause, a salutation, or a vocative—e.g.: "Having had breakfast[,] I went for a walk."/ "The sermon *over* [or *being over*], the congregation filed out."/ "Fellow lawyers[,] the bar must unite in seeking reform of the system of electing judges." (N.B.: Not "The sermon[,] being over[,] . . ."; and no comma with restrictive expressions like "My friend Judge Smith" or "my son John.")
6. To separate a phrase or subordinate clause from the main clause so as to avoid misunderstanding. E.g., "In the valley below[,] the vil-

lages looked very small."/ "In 1982[,] 1918 seemed like the distant past." (N.B.: A comma should not be used to separate a phrasal subject from its predicate, or a verb from an object that is a clause. E.g., "A car with such a high-powered *engine, should* [read *engine should*] not fail on that hill."/ "They *believed, that* [read *believed that*] nothing could go wrong.")

7. To distinguish indirect from direct speech. E.g., "They answered[,] 'Here we are.'"
8. To mark the end of the salutation, e.g., "Dear Mr. Crosthwaite[,]"; "Dear Rebecca[,]", etc. and the complimentary close, e.g., "Very truly yours[,]"; "Yours sincerely[,]"; etc. In formal letters, the salutation is separated from the body by a colon "Dear Sir[:]"; "Dear Madam[:]"; etc.

Writers cause needless confusion or distraction for their readers when they insert commas erroneously:

- *The Archaic Comma Preceding a Verb.* Formerly, it was common for writers to insert a comma in the main clause before the verb, but this practice has been out of fashion since the early 20th century. Today it is considered incorrect. E.g., "Whether or not a contract has been modified, [omit the comma] is a question of fact for the jury."/ "Only if this were true, [omit the comma] could it be said that plaintiffs received their bargained-for equivalent of the $30,000 payments."

  Even those who understand this principle are tempted sometimes to place a comma after a compound subject. That temptation should be avoided—e.g.: "Co-owners who are not joint tenants, tenants by the entireties, or owners of community property, [omit the comma] are tenants in common." Robert Kratovil, *Real Estate Law* 222 (1946).
- *Misplaced Emphasis.* "I, *accordingly,* [read *accordingly* without the embracing commas] dissent."/ "We, *therefore,* [read *therefore* without the embracing commas] conclude that the ancient doctrine of sovereign immunity has lost its underpinnings." (N.B.: If the emphasis in the preceding sentence is to fall on *We*—as clearly separated from some other group and its thinking—the commas should stand; but if the emphasis is to fall on the *therefore* as a simple consequence of our reasoning from the evidence, then the commas should be omitted. See **therefore (D).**)
- *Compound Sentences.* As explained above (#3 in the preceding list), no comma appears before the conjunction in a compound sentence when the second clause has an understood subject—e.g.: "The problem has not yet arisen, [omit comma] and is of little practical importance." P.S. Atiyah, *An Introduction to the Law of Contract* 57 (3d ed. 1981)./ "These are cases in which plaintiff seeks some equitable remedy, [omit comma] and is remitted to a legal remedy instead . . . ." Douglas Laycock, *The Death of the Irreparable Injury Rule* 100 (1991).
- *Dates.* No comma is needed between the month and year in dates written "December 1984" or "18 December 1984"; a comma is required when the date is written "December 18, 1984." See DATES (B).
- *The Comma Splice.* See RUN-ON SENTENCES.

The omission of commas can often blur the sense of a sentence, as in the following examples: "Substantial performance cannot occur where the breach is intentional [insert a comma] as it is the antithesis of material breach."/ "Because, prior to their filing [insert a comma] consignor's claims will be subordinate to those of lien creditors, in practice the consignee's creditors will have effective claims to the consigned goods."/ "Something may be said for it, since it furnishes a simple, if arbitrary [insert comma] test."

D. The Dash [— ; –]. There are two kinds of dashes, which typesetters are able to distinguish by their length. First, the *em-dash,* which is as wide as the square of the type size, is used to mark an interruption in the structure of a sentence. In typewriting, it is commonly represented by two hyphens, often with a space at either end of the pair (- -). A pair of em-dashes can be used to enclose a parenthetical remark or to mark the ending and the resumption of a statement by an interlocutor. E.g., "He was not[—]you may disagree with me, Henry[—]much of an artist."/ "[T]he courts were endeavouring to find the compromise—always difficult—between substantial justice and a proper discipline of form." Carleton K. Allen, *Law in the Making* 401 (7th ed. 1964). The em-dash can also be used to replace the colon.

In legal writing, em-dashes are the second most underused mark of punctuation (*periods* being the most underused). Whether in DRAFTING or in persuasive writing, dashes can often clarify a sentence that is clogged up with commas. Imagine the following sentences if commas replaced the well-chosen em-dashes:

- "He may make no pretension—he generally makes no pretension—to be an expert in any of these fields, but he would be a little ashamed if he was crassly ignorant of them." Max Radin, *The Law and You* 11 (1948).
- "In some jurisdictions, the judge, when using a special verdict, need not—should not—give any charge about the substantive legal rules beyond what is reasonably necessary to enable the jury

to answer intelligently the questions put to them." Jerome Frank, *Courts on Trial* 141 (1949).

- "If this be the correct principle—and, so far as we are aware, it has never before been laid down in terms—there seems to be no reason why it should not apply equally to the Divisional Court of the Queen's Bench." Carleton K. Allen, *Law in the Making* 240 (7th ed. 1964).
- "Why should not all people—Blacks as well as Whites—be allowed to appear, by right, before a tribunal that is impartial and not a stooge for the powerful Highway Lobby, to air their complaints and state their views?" William O. Douglas, *Points of Rebellion* 86 (1970).
- "When the plaintiff's attorney files a certificate stating that he or she believes a defendant cannot be personally served, because after diligent inquiry within the state where the complaint is filed the defendant's place of residence cannot be ascertained—or, if ascertained, that it is beyond the territorial limits of personal service as provided in this rule—this defendant must be served by publication in a newspaper published in the county where the property is located." Fed. R. Civ. P. 71A (1992 draft of Style Subcommittee, Standing Committee on Federal Practice and Procedure).

Second, the *en-dash,* which is half as wide as an *em-dash,* is distinct (in print) from the *hyphen.* It is ordinarily equivalent to the word *to.* In typewriting, it is commonly represented by one hyphen, occasionally with a space at either end (–). E.g., "The 1914[–]1918 war"; "Dallas[–]Toronto[–]Quebec route"; "pages 68–70."

Sometimes, the en-dash suggests tension and carries the sense "versus." For example, in circumstances involving a disjunction, the en-dash is usu. preferable to the slash—e.g.: "If we manage to get that far, the absurdity of attempting to preserve the nineteenth-century contract–tort dichotomy [not *contract/tort dichotomy*] will have become apparent . . . ." Grant Gilmore, *The Death of Contract* 90 (1974).

E. The Exclamation Mark [!]. This mark is used after an exclamatory word, phrase, or sentence. It usually counts as the concluding full stop, but need not. E.g., "Hail, Source of Being! Universal Soul!" It may also be used within square brackets, after or in the midst of a quotation, to express the editor's amusement, dissent, or surprise. Rarely is the exclamation mark called for in legal writing.

F. The Hyphen [-]. In all but one context, AmE is much more inhospitable to hyphens than BrE. Words with prefixes are generally made solid: *nonstatutory* (not *non-statutory*), *pretrial* (not *pre-trial*), *posttrial* (not *post-trial*), *preemption* (not *pre-emption*). This no-hyphen style seems aesthetically superior, but reasonable people will differ on such a question. They can agree, however, that the hyphen must appear when an AMBIGUITY, MISCUE, or eyesore results without it—e.g., *pre-judicial* (career), *re-sign* (the petition), *post-sentencing.* See RE- PAIRS.

And what is that one context in which AmE is hospitable to the hyphen? See PHRASAL ADJECTIVES.

G. Parentheses [(. . .)]. These marks enclose words, phrases, and even whole sentences (but usually not more than a whole paragraph). If what is enclosed is a full sentence, the closing parenthesis includes the end punctuation; if not, the end punctuation is swept outside, as in the previous sentence here. More specifically, parentheses are used as follows:

1. To indicate interpolations and remarks by the writer of the text, e.g., "Mrs. X (*as I shall call her*) now spoke."
2. To specify, in one's own running text, an authority, definition, explanation, reference, or translation.
3. To indicate, in the report of a speech, interruptions by the audience.
4. To separate reference letters or figures that do not need a full stop, e.g., (1) (a).

H. The Period or Full Stop [.]. This mark is used in two ways. First, it ends all sentences that are not questions or exclamations. The next word should normally begin with a capital letter.

Second, it indicates abbreviations (see ACRONYMS and INITIALISMS). If a point marking an abbreviation comes at the end of a sentence, it also serves as the closing full stop. E.g., "She also kept dogs, cats, birds, etc[.]" But where a closing parenthesis or bracket intervenes, a period is required: "She also kept pets (dogs, cats, birds, etc[.).]" When a sentence concludes with a quotation that ends with a period (i.e., a full stop), question mark, or exclamation mark, no further period is needed. E.g., "He cried, 'Be off!' [no period] But the child would not move."

I. The Question Mark [?]. A question mark follows every question that expects a separate answer; the next word should begin with a capital letter. "He asked me, 'Why are you here?' A foolish question." (N.B.: A question mark is not used after indirect questions, e.g., "He asked me why I was there.") A question mark may be placed in brackets after a word, etc., whose accuracy is doubted, e.g., "Sangad Anurugsa[?]"

J. Quotation Marks [" "]. In using quotation marks (or "inverted commas" as the British call them), writers and editors of AmE and BrE have developed conventions that are markedly different.

1. In AmE, double quotation marks are used for a first quotation; single marks for a quotation within a quotation; double again for a further quotation inside that, etc. In BrE, the practice is exactly the reverse at each step.
2. With a closing quotation mark, practices vary. In AmE, it is usual to place a period or comma within the closing quotation mark, whether or not the punctuation so placed is actually a part of the quoted matter. E.g., "Joan pointedly said, 'We do not intend to see "Les Miserables." ' " In BrE, by contrast, the closing quotation mark comes before all punctuation marks, unless these marks form a part of the quotation itself (or what is quoted is *less* than a full sentence in its own right). E.g., 'Joan pointedly said, "We do not intend to see 'Les Miserables'." '/ 'She looked back on her school years as being "unredeemably miserable".' (N.B.: In both of these specimens the outermost quotation marks indicate that a printed source is being quoted directly.)

   When question and exclamation marks are involved, AmE and BrE practice is the same. E.g., (AmE) "Did Nelson really say 'Kiss me, Hardy'?"; (BrE) 'Did Nelson really say "Kiss me, Hardy"?' But, when the question or exclamation mark is an integral part of what is being quoted, it is swept inside of all quotation marks (i.e., inverted commas). E.g., (AmE) "Banging her fist on the table, she exclaimed, 'And that's *that*!' "; (BrE) 'Banging her fist on the table, she exclaimed, "And that's *that*!" ' (N.B.: When the ending of an interrogatory or an exclamatory sentence coincides with the ending of another sentence that embraces it, the stronger mark of punctuation is sufficient to terminate *both* sentences; i.e., a period [i.e., a full stop] need not also be included after the question mark or exclamation mark inside the final quotation mark.)

   As to quotations that are interrupted to indicate a speaker, AmE and BrE again show different preferences. In AmE, the first comma is swept within the quotation mark. E.g., "Sally," he said, "is looking radiant today." In BrE, the first comma (usually) remains outside the inverted comma, just as though the attribution could be lifted neatly out of the speaker's actual words. E.g., 'Sally', he said, 'is looking radiant today'. See QUOTATIONS (B).
3. In nonlegal citations, quotation marks (and roman type) are often used when citing titles of articles in magazines, chapters in books, poems not published separately, and songs. (Titles of books and magazines are usually printed in italics in nonlegal citations.) See CITATION OF CASES.

K. Semicolon [;]. This mark separates those parts of a sentence between which there is a more distinct break than a comma can signal, but which are too closely connected to be made into separate sentences. Typically these will be clauses of similar importance and grammatical construction. E.g., "To err is human; to forgive, divine." (N.B.: The comma here flags the dropping of a word: *is.*)

L. Square Brackets ([ ]). These enclose comments, corrections, explanations, interpolations, notes, or translations that were not in the original text but have been added by subsequent authors, editors, or others. E.g., "My right honorable friend [John Smith] is mistaken."

In legal writing, brackets are customarily used for adjustments in quoted matter, such as making lowercase a letter that was uppercase in the source of the quotation ("The court stated that '[a]nother problem in determining the existence of apparent authority relates to the extent of the knowledge of the person invoking the doctrine.' ") or signifying an omission of an inflection in a word ("If the trustees 'fail[ ] to re-elect or re-employ the superintendent' without giving notice, his contract is automatically reviewable.").

This last use—bracketing empty space—should not supplant the ellipsis, as here: "The *choice of* [ ] *forum* [read *choice of . . . forum*] was made in an arm's-length negotiation . . . ." *Snyder v. Smith,* 736 F.2d 409, 419 (7th Cir. 1984) (quoting *The Bremen v. Zapata Off-Shore Co.,* 407 U.S. 1, 12 (1972)).

For further inquiry, the following works are useful: Karen E. Gordon, *The Well-Tempered Sentence: A Punctuation Handbook for the Innocent, the Eager, and the Doomed* (1983); G.V. Carey, *Mind the Stop* (1977 ed.); Harry Shaw, *Punctuate It Right!* (1963); and Eric Partridge, *You Have a Point There: A Guide to Punctuation and Its Allies* (1953; repr. 1978).

punies. American trial lawyers use this shortened word as a slang for *punitive damages*—e.g.: "Klausner, who says he has at least six clients with whistleblower actions, says last week's ruling is terrific. 'It's great if you know you can get *punies* from a government agency.' " Henry Gottlieb, *Whistleblower Punitives Allowed in Public Sector,* N.J.L.J., 6 Dec. 1993, at 1 (quoting Stephen Klausner, a lawyer in Somerville, N.J.)./ "[A] San Francisco County Superior Court jury awarded secretary Rena Weeks $6.9 million in *punies* from Baker & McKenzie—with 1,642 attorneys, the world's largest law firm—and $225,000 from rainmaker Martin Greenstein, whom Ms. Weeks had accused of unwanted sexual attention." Thom Weidlich, *Baker Verdict Not Major Concern,* Nat'l L.J., 19 Sept. 1994, at A6. Cf. **punitives.**

punishable. When used in reference to a person, *punishable* means "liable to punishment" <she is not legally punishable>. When used in reference to a crime, it means "entailing punishment" <an offense punishable by a $500 fine>. The latter sense—a good illustration of how HYPALLAGE works—is now the more common one.

punitive; punitory. *Punitory* is a NEEDLESS VARIANT of *punitive,* a word much more common in legal than in nonlegal texts. These two forms are commonly used by those who practice INELEGANT VARIATION. E.g., "Florida cases follow the orthodox theory that *punitive damages* are *punitory* [read *punitive*] and deterrent." Even worse: "The law with respect to *punitive damages* is that in order to justify the *infliction* [read *imposition?*] of *punitory damages* [read *punitive damages*] for the commission of a tort, the act complained of must have been done wantonly or maliciously." *Stenson v. Laclede Gas Co.,* 553 S.W.2d 309, 315 (Mo. Ct. App. 1977).

punitive damages; exemplary damages; vindictive damages; aggravated damages; retributory damages. The first two terms are by far the most common in both AmE and BrE. Each one tells only half the story, for the two-pronged rationale for awarding such damages in civil cases is (1) to punish the defendant, and (2) to make an example of the defendant so as to deter others. *Exemplary damages* appears to be the more usual phrase in BrE (although the *CDL* and the *OCL* mention only punishment as the basis), whereas in AmE the term *punitive damages* is slightly more frequent. (Colloquially, the phrase is sometimes shortened in AmE to *punitives* and even *punies,* qq.v.)

The other forms, sometimes used in strings (as in the following example), should be avoided as NEEDLESS VARIANTS. "Much has been written by the courts and by text writers upon the question whether *punitive, vindictive, exemplary, aggravated,* or *retributory damages* should be allowed in any case without reaching a generally accepted conclusion."/ "The question distinctly arises whether the plaintiff is entitled to recover *punitive* or *vindictive damages* against the defendants." See **parasitic & smart money.**

punitives, a shortened form of *punitive damages,* is a casualism—e.g.: "Not only that, Corboy wanted juries to concentrate on the compensatory damages, because that money was *tax-free* to the client (unlike *punitives,* which were taxed just like one huge paycheck) . . . ." John A. Jenkins, *The Litigators* 369 (1989)./ "Richard B. Miller led the defense team that saw the jury award Pennzoil more than $7 billion in compensatory damages and another $3 billion in *punitives.*" *Pennzoil v. Texaco,* Litig., Winter 1991, at 14, 14. Cf. **punies & exemplaries.**

punitory. See **punitive.**

PUNS. Plays on words—known popularly as puns and professorially as paronomasia—can add zest to writing if artfully used. Fowler and Bernstein have dispelled the notion that puns are the lowest form of wit. Bad puns, of course, create a bad impression in either speech or writing. But the well-wrought pun often serves to reinforce the point one is making. The good pun gives the sentence added meaning in both (or all) its senses, and it is not too obvious.

Puns seem increasingly popular in American legal prose. Some are good and some are not. The title of a law-review article by Robert P. Mosteller, *Simplifying Subpoena Law: Taking the Fifth Amendment Seriously,* 73 Va. L. Rev. 1 (1987), plays effectively on two English idioms, *to take the Fifth Amendment* and *to take (something) seriously.* Both senses fit the purpose of the article, hence the aptness of the pun. A more strained but nevertheless clever pun occurred to the federal appellate judge who wrote: "*Ticonic*'s cloth cannot be cut to fit Interfirst's suit." *Interfirst Bank v. FDIC,* 777 F.2d 1092, 1097 (5th Cir. 1985) (discussing *Ticonic Nat'l Bank v. Sprague,* 303 U.S. 406 (1938)). Here *suit* carries the double sense, on the one hand, of completing the tailoring metaphor (cutting cloth for a suit) and, on the other hand, of denoting the lawsuit at issue. Yet another aesthetically pleasing pun is this subtle one from the pen of Justice Frankfurter: "The liability rests on the inroad [that] the automobile has made on the decision of *Pennoyer v. Neff,* . . . as it has on so many aspects of our social scene." *Olberding v. Illinois Cent. R.R.,* 346 U.S. 338, 341 (1953). Ordinarily, of course, *inroad* is an abstract word, but Justice Frankfurter's placement of *automobile* near it gives the word a new and unexpected concrete sense; again, the pun is felicitous.

Chief Justice Rehnquist has used puns that would probably delight some readers and perturb others—depending entirely on their views on issues other than linguistic matters. One case, for example, involved several Indiana nightclubs that wanted to feature totally nude dancers. When Indiana officials began enforcing an indecent-exposure statute requiring dancers to wear "pasties" and G-strings, several dancers sued to enjoin enforcement of the statute on First Amendment grounds. Chief Justice Rehnquist's opinion upholding the statute concluded in this way: "It is without cavil that the public indecency statute is '*narrowly tailored*'; Indiana's requirement that the dancers wear at least pasties and a G-string is *modest,* and the *bare* minimum necessary to achieve the state's purpose." *Barnes v. Glen Theatre, Inc.,* 501 U.S. 560, 572 (1991) (emphasis added).

Probably half the puns one sees in modern legal writing, though, are the empty kind of wordplay in which one of the senses is inapposite or, at worst, gibberish. Some ill-wrought specimens:

- "The bells do not toll the statute of limitations while one ferrets out the facts." (The pun here is *toll,* which on the obvious level [*bells . . . toll*] means, nonsensically, "to ring"; the legal sense of *toll,* the one that gives meaning to the sentence, is "to abate." The pun in no way contributes to the sense; in fact, it is more likely to confuse than to enlighten.)
- "The official cannot hide behind a claim that the particular factual predicate in question has never appeared *in haec verba* in a reported opinion; if the application of settled principles to this factual tableau would inexorably lead to a conclusion of unconstitutionality, a prison official may not take solace in ostrachism." (*Ostrachism* here apparently means "the practice of hiding one's head in the sand," foreshadowed earlier in the sentence in the phrase *hide behind a claim.* The pun is on *ostracism* [= exclusion from association with another or others], but this near-homophone has nothing to do with the meaning of the sentence. Hence the writer has been at pains to create a punning NEOLOGISM whose suggestiveness bewilders, rather than charms, the reader.)

As Charles Lamb once observed, "A pun is not bound by the laws which limit nicer wit. It is a pistol let off at the ear; not a feather to tickle the intellect." "Popular Fallacies—. . . That the Worst Puns Are the Best," in *Essays of Elia and Last Essays of Elia* 306, 306–07 (1906). Still, in punning one must not abandon the intellect, for then one becomes a nuisance to the reader. Lamb also cautioned that puns sometimes show "much less wit than rudeness," adding: "We must take in the totality of time, place, and person." *Id.* at 308.

pupil(l)age. The *-l-* spelling is AmE, the *-ll-* spelling BrE.

pur autre vie — a LAW FRENCH phrase meaning "for another's life"—is pronounced /pər-**oh**-tər-**vee**/. E.g., "The grantee of a life tenant generally took an estate *pur autre vie,* measured by the grantor's life, not the grantee's." 1 *American Law of Property* 124 (A.J. Casner ed., 1952). The phrase is sometimes spelled *per autre vie.*

purchase. A. Meaning Generally "to buy." In legal writing, the verb *purchase* commonly appears as an equivalent of *buy.* So used, *purchase* is a FORMAL WORD that most good editors would probably want to change to *buy.*

B. Special Legal Sense. *Purchase* = to acquire real property other than by descent. Thus, in very technical legal parlance, gifts are *purchased* by those who receive them. The following sentence conveys this special legal sense of the word (here as a noun): "Every legal mode of acquisition of real property except by descent is denominated in law a *purchase,* and the person who thus acquires it is a *purchaser.*" This legal technicality appears also in the phrases *words of purchase* and *take by purchase.*

C. Choice of Preposition. The verb *purchase* may take *from* or *of,* though the latter form is an ARCHAISM. E.g., "Bunguss *purchased of* Blades the tract of land in controversy." See **words of purchase, buy & descent (A).**

purchase money. Two words as a noun phrase <the return of the purchase money>; hyphenated as a PHRASAL ADJECTIVE <purchase-money resulting trust> <purchase-money mortgage>.

purchaser; purchasor. The former is the only correct spelling. Usually, *purchaser* can advantageously be made *buyer.* See **purchase (A).**

PURPLE PROSE, or ostentatious writing, has a certain fascination for some legal writers, as it does for any number of aspiring novelists. Good writing *uses* words; purple prose *parades* them. The danger is that, "unless the pen be guided by the hand of genius, there is apt to result a sacrifice of legal sense to purely artificial verbiage. . . . An ornate, pretentious, grandiose style, replete with superfluous frills and rhetorical extravagances, can act only as an undesirable distraction." Horace Stern, *The Writing of Judicial Opinions,* 18 Pa. B. Ass'n Q. 40, 42 (1947).

Similes are especially likely to turn purple. Whereas METAPHORS are quite acceptable in legal writing, SIMILES tend to signal overwriting: "Getting information on the judgment-debtor's assets was like working at a deep archeological dig."

Rarely can a short sentence turn purple, but this one comes as close as any: "A miniscule [*sic*] error must coalesce with gargantuan guilt, even where the accused displays an imagination of Pantagruelian dimensions." *Chapman v. U.S.*, 547 F.2d 1240, 1250 (5th Cir. 1977).

Purple prose is seductive: it may skew the literary sensibilities especially of those who purport to be stylists, and is most common among those who fancy themselves masterly writers. To name three guilty parties, Norman Brand and John O. White, in their otherwise solid book *Legal Writing: The Strategy of Persuasion* 111–12 (1976), offer up as an example of a "well-written decision" the following, by Justice Carlin of New York:

> This case presents the ordinary man—that problem child of the law—in a most bizarre setting. As a lowly chauffeur in defendant's employ he became in a trice the protagonist in a breath-bating drama with a denouement almost tragic. It appears that a man, whose identity it would be indelicate to divulge[,] was feloniously relieved of his portable goods by two nondescript highwaymen in an alley near 26th Street and Third Avenue, Manhattan; they induced him to relinquish his possessions by a strong argument *ad hominem* couched in the convincing cant of the criminal and pressed at the point of a most persuasive pistol. Laden with their loot, but not thereby impeded, they took an abrupt departure and he, shuffling off the coil of that discretion which enmeshed him in the alley, quickly gave chase through 26th Street toward 2d Avenue, whither they were resorting "with expedition swift as thought" for most obvious reasons. Somewhere on that thoroughfare of escape they indulged the stratagem of separation ostensibly to disconcert their pursuer and allay the ardor of his pursuit. He then centered on for capture the man with the pistol whom he saw board the defendant's taxicab, which quickly veered south toward 25th Street on 2d Avenue where he saw the chauffeur jump out while the cab, still in motion, continued toward 24th Street; after the chauffeur relieved himself of the cumbersome burden of his fare the latter also is said to have similarly departed from the cab before it reached 24th Street. . . . The chauffeur—the ordinary man in this case—acted in a split second in a most harrowing experience. To call him negligent would be to brand him coward; the court does not do so in spite of what those swaggering heroes, "whose valor plucks dead lions by the beard," may bluster to the contrary. The court is loathe [q.v.] to see the plaintiffs go without recovery even though their damages were slight, but cannot hold the defendant liable upon the facts adduced at the trial. Motions, upon which decision was reserved, to dismiss the complaint are granted with exceptions to plaintiffs. Judgment for defendant against plaintiffs dismissing their complaint upon the merits.
>
> *Cordas v. Peerless Transp. Co.*, 27 N.Y.S.2d 198, 199, 202 (N.Y. City Ct. 1941).

This very opinion has been justly criticized for its purplishness in Ronald L. Goldfarb & James C. Raymond, *Clear Understandings* 142–43 (1982).

purport, n., = that which is conveyed or expressed, esp. by a formal document. As a noun, this term is now primarily a legal word (the verb *to purport* being common). E.g., "The circumstances of the publication must be such that either from the plain *purport* of what is published, or from the circumstances of the publication itself, the presumption of malice and injury is raised."/ "Other early decisions . . . are difficult to reconcile with the clear *purport* of Rule 12."

The verb—meaning "to profess or claim falsely" or "to seem to be"—is much more common—e.g.: "Hobart L. Arnold died leaving what *purported* to be a holographic will."/ "The result in this case ought to be intolerable in any society that *purports* to call itself an organized society."

purported, adj. = reputed, rumored. It does not mean "alleged," as here erroneously used: "There were many *purported* [read *alleged*] violations of the defendant's rights."

purpose, n. **A. And *object*,** n. A British writer suggests that *purpose* is more restricted than *object*. J. Charlesworth, *The Principles of Company Law* 16–17 (4th ed. 1945). That may be because *object* is more of a CHAMELEON-HUED WORD capable of bearing many meanings. But the two words are close synonyms in denoting "something one sets before oneself as a thing to be done; the end one has in view." In fact, the *OED* uses each word in defining the other.

B. And *intention*. Statutory drafters sometimes use *purpose* as if it were synonymous with *intention*. But, as Glanville Williams has observed, *purpose* ought not to include recklessness or a mere knowledge of probability, as *intention* generally does. See *Textbook of Criminal Law* 93 (1978). See **intent(ion) (B).**

purpose, v.t., = to set as a goal for oneself; to intend; to resolve. This FORMAL WORD is little used now in nonlegal contexts. Even in law it has a musty smell—e.g.: "Cardozo, as indicated, sees the case as presenting the *purposed* use of the car." Karl Llewellyn, *The Common Law Tradition: Deciding Appeals* 434 (1960).

purposeful. See **purposive.**

purposely; purposefully. The former means "on purpose; intentionally"; the latter means "with a specific purpose in mind; with the idea of accomplishing a certain result."

Some writers fall into INELEGANT VARIATION with these words: "The State did not exceed its authority in defining the crime of murder as *purposely* causing the death of another with prior calculation or design. . . . [T]he jury's verdict reflects that none of her self-defense evidence raised a reasonable doubt about the State's proof that she *purposefully* [read *purposely*] killed with prior calculation and design." *Martin v. Ohio,* 480 U.S. 228, 233 (1987).

purposive; purposeful. Fowler and the *OED* editors objected to *purposive* as an ill-formed hybrid. Today, however, it is usefully distinguished in one sense from *purposeful* (= [1] having a purpose; or [2] full of determination). *W10* records under *purposive* the sense "serving or effecting a useful function though not as a result of planning or design."

But in other senses it is a NEEDLESS VARIANT of *purposeful,* as in the following examples: "References to 'the *purposive* [read *purposeful*] use of ambiguity' are usually directed to the *purposive* [read *purposeful*] use of vagueness or generality."/ "There is ample evidence in this case of the correlation between municipal service disparities and racially tainted *purposiveness* [read *purposefulness*] to mandate a finding of discriminatory intent."

pursuance of, in. See **pursuant to.**

pursuant to = (1) in accordance with; (2) under; (3) as authorized by; or (4) in carrying out. Because the phrase means so many things, it is rarely—if ever—useful. Lawyers are nearly the only ones who use the phrase, and they often use it imprecisely. Following are some well-taken edits:

- "Appellant is a state prisoner incarcerated in the Louisiana State Penitentiary in Angola, Louisiana, *pursuant to* [read *for*] a 1964 aggravated rape conviction."
- "*Pursuant to* [read *Under*] the mandate of the Supreme Court in *Escondido,* the decision of the Federal Energy Regulatory Commission to grant a license in these proceedings is reversed."
- "The petitioners bring this petition *pursuant to* [read *under*] the provisions of the *Infants Act,* R.S.B.C. 1979, c. 196." (Can.)
- "Prior to the execution of both the aforementioned letters, the County Court of Woodward County issued an order to disburse funds *pursuant to an application authorizing payment* [delete italicized language] of $33.00 per month . . . ." *Western State Hosp. v. Stoner,* 614 P.2d 59, 64 (Okla. 1980).

British legal writers often use *in pursuance of*—e.g.: "Notice was therefore given to the plaintiffs that after May 2, 1972, the council would, under and *in pursuance of* section 15 of the Act of 1936, by their contractor proceed to construct the sewer." (Eng.) /"[S]ervices [were] rendered *in pursuance of* that request . . . ." William R. Anson, *Principles of the Law of Contract* 152 (Arthur L. Corbin ed., 3d Am. ed. 1919). This usage was formerly common in the U.S.

Partridge was wrong to call this phrase "OFFICIALESE for *after.*" *Usage and Abusage* 257 (1973). It may be officialese, but it does not, ordinarily, mean "after." Still, at least one American lawyer has privately admitted making the mistake of treating the phrase as an antonym of *prior to.* See **under.**

pursuer; defender. These are the names equivalent to *plaintiff* and *defendant* in Scots and canon law. E.g., "My Lords, the *pursuers* supply to local authorities litter bins which are placed in the streets. The *defender* carried on a garage in Clydebank and in 1954 he made an agreement with the pursuers . . . ." (Scot.)

purview. In the context of STATUTE DRAFTING, this neglected word denotes the body of a statute following the preamble, traditionally beginning with the language, *Be it enacted that* . . . . It was therefore an easy extension in meaning that gave *purview* its most common sense today (i.e., "scope; area of application")—a sense that borders on CLICHÉ: "The Hughes Court held that the right to dissent, protest, and march for that purpose was within the *purview* of the First Amendment." William O. Douglas, *Points of Rebellion* 5 (1970).

put, n.; **call,** n. *Put* is often used as a noun in securities law in the sense "an option to sell securities." E.g., "'*Puts*' and automatic buybacks at the same price should be avoided."/ "Although the uncertainty in Murchison's engagement to develop a potentially more lucrative *put* option may evidence an intent not to contract, we cannot say that the agreement lacks sufficient definiteness on that ground alone." In such contexts, *put* is usually contrasted with *call* (= an option to buy securities).

put, v.t., often means either (1) "to hypothesize for purposes of illustration" <in the case put>; or (2) "to argue (a case)" <even bishops appeared in court personally to put their cases>.

put another way. See **to put it another way.**

putative = supposed, believed, reputed. E.g., "The facts of causation were in the control of the *putative* defendant but unavailable to the plaintiff or at least very difficult to obtain." *Putative marriage,* a term originally from canon law, denotes a marriage that, though legally invalid, was contracted in good faith by at least one of the parties. E.g., "The court of civil appeals held that the *putative* wife's knowledge of pending divorce involving the husband terminated the *putative* marriage."/ "A *putative* marriage is one into which one or both spouses enter in good faith but which is invalid because of an existing impediment."

put on = (1) to call (a person) as a witness; or (2) to adduce (evidence)—e.g.: (Sense 1) "If a man has a record, you just don't *put* him *on* the stand. *Put on* his wife, his brother, his father and mother, but don't let him take the stand." Aubrey Holmes, *The Wake of a Lawyer* 51 (1960)./ (Sense 2) "'We just *put on* the evidence and went ahead without him,' said Assistant District Attorney Tom D'Amore . . . ." Melvin Belli, *Courts Specialize in Drugs,* Dallas Morning News, 1 July 1990, at 33A.

put oneself upon the country (= to demand a jury trial) is an ARCHAISM that still occasionally appears in modern defense pleadings. For an explanation of its common-law origins, see **country.**

put option. See **put.**

put to one's law. At common law, this phrase meant "to compel a person to undergo a judicial test, such as compurgation, ordeal, or combat." Magna Carta (1215), for example, contains a provision that states: "Let no bailiff be able to put any one to his law by his own simple word without credible witnesses." More modernly, the phrase means "to put a person to trial."

putrefy; putrify. The latter is a misspelling.

pyramiding inferences, rule against. This rule, followed in some jurisdictions, prohibits a fact-finder from piling one inference on another to arrive at a conclusion. But it is a confusing and unhelpful metaphor, as Judge John Minor Wisdom has aptly observed: "The so-called *rule against pyramiding inferences,* if there really is such a 'rule' and if it is anything more than an empty pejorative, is simple legalese fustian to cover a clumsy exclusion of evidence having little or no probative value." *NLRB v. Camco, Inc.,* 340 F.2d 803, 811 (5th Cir. 1965). Other leading authorities likewise cast doubt on it: "Whatever the vitality of the supposed *rule against pyramiding inferences,* it ought not to be taken as forbidding the use of one presumption as the mechanism for establishing the basic fact of another." 21 Charles A. Wright & Kenneth W. Graham, Jr., *Federal Practice and Procedure* § 5125, at 603 (1977). See LEGALESE.

Q

Q.B.D. = Queen's Bench Division. See **Queen's Bench.**

Q.C. = Queen's Counsel. **A. Plural Form.** Though some writers make the plural form *Q.C.s,* the better form is *Q.C.'s.*

B. Punctuation with. When the title appears in midsentence, a comma goes before and after it: "I hereby authorize Donald W. Zee, Q.C., to enter an appearance on behalf of the infant defendant."

Some writers omit the periods in this abbreviation—e.g.: "If a client wants to employ a Queen's Counsel or senior barrister, he must also employ—at two-thirds the QC's fee—a junior barrister as well." Anthony Sampson, *Anatomy of Britain* 149 (1962). The prevailing style—in BrE and AmE alike—is to include the periods.

Q.E.D. is the abbreviation for *quod erat demonstrandum* (= which was to be proved or demonstrated).

Q.E.F. is the abbreviation for *quod erat faciendum* (= which was to be done).

qq.v. See ***quod vide.***

qua (= in the capacity of; as; in the role of) is often misused and is little needed in English. "The real occasion for the use of *qua,*" wrote Fowler, "occurs when a person or thing spoken of can be regarded from more than one point of view or as the holder of various coexistent functions, and a statement about him (or it) is to be limited to him in one of these aspects" (*MEU1* 477). Fowler's example of a justifiable use of the term is this: "*Qua* lover he must be condemned for doing what *qua* citizen he would be condemned for not doing." This proper use of the term is seldom seen today, esp. in AmE.

One is hard-pressed to divine any purpose but rhetorical emphasis in the examples following: "We seek simply to keep the government, *qua* government, neutral with respect to any religious controversy."/ "The question of res, *qua* res, causes us no difficulty."/ "The only immunities in an official-capacity action are forms of sovereign immunity that the entity, *qua* entity, may possess."

Nor do most unemphatic modern uses justify the choice of *qua* over *as*. Indeed, these are the very types of uses that Fowler rightly objected to: "Hudspeth can challenge the FSLIC's behavior *qua* [read *as*] receiver before the FHLBB and, if unsatisfied, can seek judicial review under the APA."/ "*Qua* [read *To test its claim as a*] patent, we should at least have to decide, as tabula rasa, whether the design or machine was a new and required invention."/ "The right of fair comment, though shared by the public, is the right of every individual who asserts it, and is, *qua* [read *as claimed by*] him, an individual right whatever name it be called by, and comment by him which is coloured by malice cannot from his standpoint be deemed fair." (Eng.)

quadrennial; quadriennial. The latter is a NEEDLESS VARIANT.

***quaere;* query.** *Quaere* is the Latin word meaning "question." The original form of *query, quaere* is now but a NEEDLESS VARIANT in any sense other than a technical one: it is sometimes appended or prefixed to doubtful statements. E.g., "Whether a plea in abatement is not the proper mode of defense when the facts relied on do not appear of record, *quaere*." *Engelke & Feiner Milling Co. v. Grunthal,* 35 So. 17, 18 (Fla. 1903).

The term is used occasionally in modern writing: "*Quaere,* whether the bank would have been allowed . . . to plead a Section 7426 counterclaim." *U.S. v. National Bank of Commerce,* 726 F.2d 1292, 1298 (8th Cir. 1984)./ "One can affix one's signature to a document by writing thereon, and one can affix one sheet of paper to another with a staple or sticky tape; but *quaere* as to a paper clip." Arthur A. Leff, *The Leff Dictionary of Law,* 94 Yale L.J. 1855, 1969 (1985).

Using *quaere* for *query* is precious—e.g.: "The decision on these two *quaeries* [read *queries*] . . . will render moot the necessity for a discussion of the Government's remaining contentions . . . ." *U.S. v. Certain Parcels of Land,* 67 F. Supp. 780, 789 (S.D. Cal. 1946). The form *quere* is a misspelling.

quai. See **quay.**

qualified fee = fee simple defeasible. See **fee simple (E).**

qualifiedly (= in a qualified fashion) is an adverb that often ought to be made back into an adjective—e.g.: "*Although the sheriff is not qualifiedly privileged,* [read *Although the sheriff has no qualified privilege*], the summary judgment was entered in favor of the parish and not the sheriff." Unfortunately, adverbs in *-edly* are unqualifiedly fashionable in modern legal writing. See -EDLY.

QUALIFIERS, PREEMPTIVE. See ANTICIPATORY REFERENCE.

qualit(at)ive. The longer form is preferred. The adjective corresponds to *quality* in the sense of character or nature, not in the sense of merit or excellence. See **quality.** Cf. **quanti(ta)tive.**

quality, adj., meaning "of high quality" is a VOGUE WORD and a casualism <a quality law firm>. One is better advised to use *good* or *fine* or some other mundane adjective that is not branded as a cant term.

quamdiu se bene gesserint (= for as long as they behave themselves) is so spelled. This LATINISM, apparently introduced in the Act of Settlement of 1700, has traditionally been used in the appointment of judges for life, but today we use the sensible English-language equivalent: *during good behavior.* See **good behavior.**

quandary—a word of unknown origin—refers to a mental state of perplexity or confusion. E.g., "[T]he juror was left in a *quandary* as to whether to follow that instruction or the immediately preceding one it contradicted." *Francis v. Franklin,* 471 U.S. 307, 324 (1985)./ "Meanwhile, the trial courts have rendered divergent judicial interpretations of the attorney-client privilege and thereby created a *quandary* for patent agents and their clients." James J. Merek & David A. Guth, *The Attorney-Client Privilege and U.S. Patent Agents: A Workable Rule for Protecting Communications,* 76 J. Pat. & Trademark Off. Soc'y 591, 594 (1994).

As a result of SLIPSHOD EXTENSION, however, the word is often misapplied as if it referred to a difficult problem, dilemma, or enigma detached from any state of mind—e.g.:

- "[W]hile Exxon's definition accords more readily with everyday notions of 'natural gas,' these notions do not, without more, resolve the definitional *quandary* [read *problem*]." *Exxon Corp. v. Lujan,* 970 F.2d 757, 760 (10th Cir. 1992).
- "The *quandary* [read *difficulty* or *problem*] in this case is that case law has combined and shuffled the definitions of domicile, bona fide residence, legal residence and residence into a mix that resulted in the declaration by the court in *In re Ozias' Estate* . . . that residence and domicile are interchangeable and synonymous." *Genrich v. Williams,* 869 S.W.2d 209, 210 (Mo. Ct. App. 1993).

• "Crucial medical facts . . . would be presented, the shape of the ethical *quandary* [read *problem* or *dilemma*] would be sketched, and the care provider's position clarified." John D. Arras, *Principles and Particularity: The Role of Cases in Bioethics,* 69 Ind. L.J. 983, 987 (1994).

quanta. See **quantum.**

quantificational. See **quanti(ta)tive.**

quantify; quantitate. The latter is a NEEDLESS VARIANT newly popular with social scientists, whose choice of terms has never been a strong recommendation for the use of those terms.

quanti(ta)tive. The preferred form is *quantitative,* not *quantitive.* Variants such as *quantificational* should be avoided. Cf. **qualit(at)ive.**

quantity (usu. "portion, amount") is used by legal theorists in a sense borrowed from logic: "the extent in which a term in a given logical proposition is to be taken" (*W3*). E.g., "While, no doubt, in the great majority of cases no harm results from the use of such expressions, yet these forms of statement seem to represent a blending of non-legal and legal *quantities* which, in any problem requiring careful reasoning, should preferably be kept distinct."/ "If, however, the problem is analyzed, it will be seen that as of primary importance, the grantor has two legal *quantities:* the privilege of entering and the power, by means of such entry, to divest the estate of the grantee."

The *OED* notes that *quantity* in the sense "length or duration of time" exists now only in the legal phrase *quantity of estate* <the quantity of estate is 99 years>.

quantum, a favorite word of lawyers and judges, means "amount; share, portion; the required, desired, or allowed amount." Ordinarily in legal writing it appears as an inflated synonym of *amount*—e.g.: "The agent had been given that *quantum* [read *amount*] of reliable information necessary to application of the collective knowledge doctrine."/ "Although incarceration immediately following conviction is disadvantageous, it does not change the *quantum* [read *amount*] of punishment attached to the offense."/ "The only question remaining, then, is the *quantum* [read *amount*] and value of the commercially recoverable reserves."/ "My Lords, it is well established that in considering questions as to the *quantum* [read *amount*] of damages that have been awarded, the approach of an appellate court must differ according to whether the assessment has been by a judge or by a jury." (Eng.)

Occasionally the word causes problems in sense. The term should not be used for *degree,* as here: "The injury suffered by Lyons was several *quanta* [read *degrees*] greater than Raley's." And the writer should beware of creating a MISCUE by pairing it with *amount*—e.g.: "The consequences of that failure will *amount to* [read *determine*] the *quantum* of the compensation he will have to pay." See VERBAL AWARENESS.

The only accepted plural of this word is *quanta.* The erroneous form *quantums* is occasionally seen. E.g., "Without regard to the number of rungs that appellant may climb on an appellate ladder, if minimum evidentiary *quantums* [read *quanta*] have been satisfied, the American tradition generally does not permit a reviewing court to disturb findings of facts." This foreign plural is one of the exceptions to the general rule enunciated in the entry PLURALS (A). Following are examples of the correct plural: "There is a difference in the *quanta* and modes of proof required to establish guilt and probable cause."/ "Absent hard data, I would rather err on the side of receiving little additional benefit from imposing additional *quanta* of liability than err by adhering to *Robins*'s inequitable rule."

quantum meruit; quantum valeba(n)t. These counts were used at common law by pleaders in suits in assumpsit, and they are still used today. *Quantum meruit* = the reasonable value of services; *quantum valebant* = the reasonable value of goods and materials. *Quantum meruit* means literally "as much as he or she had earned," and shows no signs of waning in legal use. The term, however, "is ambiguous; it may mean (1) that there is a contract 'implied in fact' to pay the reasonable value of the services, or (2) that, to prevent unjust enrichment, the claimant may recover on a quasi-contract (an 'as if' contract) for that reasonable value." *Martin v. Campanaro,* 156 F.2d 127, 130 n.5 (2d Cir. 1946).

The distinction between *quantum meruit* and *quantum valeba(n)t* is that the former (often termed *quasi-contract*) is used of an action to recover for services that the plaintiff has performed, and the latter is used to recover for the value of goods that the plaintiff has supplied without a price having been set. E.g., "Although such fees are recoverable in an action based on *quantum meruit* or *valebant,* no attorneys' fees are recoverable if the *quantum meruit* or *valebant* claim is an insignificant part of the relief sought by a party." See **quasi-contract.**

Quantum valebant and *quantum valebat* both appear in the cases; and both are correct Latin: *quantum valebant* means "as much as they were worth," whereas *quantum valebat* means "as much as it was worth." Hence the choice is between using the singular or plural Latin construction. As a matter of usage, *valebant* predominates among American legal writers who use the phrase, and *valebat* among British legal writers. (Scots lawyers tend to use *quantum valeat* [= as much as it may be worth].) But gradually the phrases are falling into disuse.

quare clausum fregit (= whereas he or she has broken the close) is often the short form for *trespass quare clausum fregit,* which is the technical term for unlawfully entering land that is visibly enclosed. See **trespass.**

quash = (1) to suppress or subdue; to crush out, beat into pieces; or (2) to annul; to make void (as a writ or indictment); to put an end to (as legal proceedings). Sense (2) is the more frequent legal meaning: "Their petition for writ of certiorari was granted on December 11, 1980, but was subsequently *quashed* for lack of prosecution."

In AmE, a *motion to quash* is usu. a motion to nullify a writ or subpoena. In BrE, by contrast, *quash* has broader uses. For example, an indictment or a conviction may be said to be quashed—e.g.: "[T]he indictment can and must be quashed." Patrick Devlin, *The Criminal Prosecution in England* 102 (1960)./ "[T]he Court of Appeal Criminal Division unanimously *quashed* a conviction where the jury foreman had announced that the conviction was agreed to by ten of the jury but failed to state that two had dissented!" Michael Zander, *The Law-Making Process* 95 (2d ed. 1985). Though convictions are *quashed* in BrE, lower-court decisions are said to be *reversed,* and jury verdicts are *set aside.* See **set aside** (A).

quashal, the American noun corresponding to the verb *to quash,* is recorded in no major English-language dictionary. Yet it is fairly common in legal writing in the U.S. <quashal of the writ>, and it is useful.

The word first appeared in the late 19th century—e.g.: "[Y]et the judgment might . . . have been put there nunc pro tunc, even during the pending of the motion, with the effect of removing the ground of *quashal* . . . ." *Adams v. Higgins,* 1 So. 321, 324 (Fla. 1887)./ "When the appellate proceeding is irregular, . . . the policy of our statutes as to a regular hearing on the merits in due course of procedure is not contravened by a *quashal* or summary disposition . . . ." *Holland v. Webster,* 29 So. 625, 630 (Fla. 1901) (Mabry, J., dissenting)./ "It is urged by relator as his grounds for *quashal,* that the opinion of the Court of Appeals is in conflict with [another] case . . . ." *Mergenthaler Linotype Co. v. Davis,* 251 U.S. 256, 258 (1920).

Since those early uses of the word, of course, it has come to be used occasionally in most American jurisdictions. E.g., "Like the *quashal* of the subpoena, this injunctive relief was related to the central purpose of a proceeding that is essentially criminal in nature." *Lee v. Johnson,* 799 F.2d 31, 42 (3d Cir. 1986) (Becker, J., dissenting). Fowler might find fault with its formation in *-al,* but the etymon is appropriately Latin and there appears to be no serviceable alternative. Even if there were, *quashal* has taken hold.

quasi—pronounced /***kwah***-*zee*/ or /***kway***-*zɪ*/—means "as if; seeming or seemingly; in the nature of; nearly." It has been called "senseless jargon" by an 18th-century judge and "that ancient question-beggar" by a 20th-century legal theorist (Lon Fuller). Corbin wrote sensibly (though not quite idiomatically) of *quasi:* "The term *quasi* is introduced as a weasel word that sucks all the meaning *of* [read *from*] the word that follows it; but this is a fact the reader seldom realizes." *Corbin on Contracts* 27 (1st ed. 1952). See WEASEL WORDS.

Maine, by contrast, wrote idiomatically but took a great many words to say merely that *quasi* signals a strained (though not *violently* strained) analogy:

> This word *'quasi,'* prefixed to a term of Roman law, implies that the conception to which it serves as an index is connected with the conception [being compared, and that] the comparison is instituted by a strong superficial analogy or resemblance. It does not denote that the two conceptions are the same or that they belong to the same genus. On the contrary, it negatives the notion of an identity between them; but it points out that they are sufficiently similar for one to be classed as the sequel to the other . . . .
>
> Henry S. Maine, *Ancient Law* 286 (17th ed. 1901; repr. [New Universal Lib.] 1905, 1910).

In legal writing, *quasi* should generally appear as a hyphenated prefix. E.g., "Damages being insufficient, *quasi*-specific performance should be awarded in order to remedy the wrong."/ "We can hardly fail to recognize that for this purpose, and as between them, the news must be regarded as *quasi*-property, irrespective of the rights of either as against the other."/ "In such cases the communication is classified as privileged or *quasi*-privileged in the law."

The term has been prefixed to any number of adjectives and nouns, such as the following:

quasi-compulsory
quasi-contract (q.v.)
quasi-contractual
quasi-corporation

quasi-criminal
quasi-delict
quasi-domicile
quasi-estoppel
quasi-heir
quasi-judge
quasi-judicial
quasi-larceny
quasi-legal
quasi-legislation
quasi-legislative
quasi-monopoly
quasi-negotiable
quasi-possession
quasi-proprietary
quasi-public
quasi-remainder
quasi-rent
quasi-right
quasi-rule
quasi-theft
quasi-tort
quasi-usufruct

quasi-contract; contract implied in law. The terms are now regarded as synonymous in referring not to a contract at all, but to the FICTION necessary to promote justice by preventing unjust enrichment. See *U.S. v. Neidorf,* 522 F.2d 916, 919 (9th Cir. 1975), *cert. denied,* 423 U.S. 1087 (1976). Some writers express a strong preference for the phrase *quasi-contract:* "What is best called *quasi-contract* our lawyers call *contract implied in law,* though there is no agreement." W.W. Buckland, *Some Reflections on Jurisprudence* 63 (1945). See **implied contract.**

The irony, of course, is that whichever name one chooses, the thing being described is not a contract at all: "*Quasi-contracts* are a heterogeneous collection of cases [that] themselves have little more in common than the fact that one person is held obliged to restore or pay for some benefit received from another in order that a just result should be reached in the circumstances of the case." P.S. Atiyah, *An Introduction to the Law of Contract* 35 (3d ed. 1981). See **promissory estoppel (A), assumpsit, quantum meruit** & **unjust enrichment.**

The phrase *quasi-contract* should be hyphenated.

quasi-domicile. See **domicil(e) (C).**

quasi *ex contractu* = (1) as if from a contract; (2) in the nature of quasi-contract. E.g., "Surely, if a man is bona fide obliged to refund whatever money he has unlawfully received, an implied question is thereby raised, *quasi ex contractu.*" See ***ex contractu*** & **quasi-contract.**

quaternary, adj. & n., is often misspelled *quartenary.* The adjective means "consisting of four parts," the noun "a set of four things."

quay; quai. the first spelling is preferred.

que, in the phrases *cestui que trust* and *cestui que use,* is pronounced */kee/* or */kə/*, not */kyoo/*.

Queen. See **King** & **R.**

queen regnant; queen regent; queen consort; queen dowager. *Queen regnant* denotes a queen who rules in her own right. *Queen regent* denotes a queen who rules on behalf of another, such as a child king. *Queen consort* denotes the wife of a reigning king. And *queen dowager* denotes the widow of a deceased king. The plural forms are *queens regnant, queens regent,* and *queens consort.*

Queen's Bench. At common law, the *Court of Queen's Bench* was one of three central courts that administered different branches of the law; it issued prerogative writs to inferior courts and public officers, heard trespass cases as well as some personal actions, and had appellate jurisdiction in civil and criminal cases by writ of error. In 1875, when the English court system was reorganized, the *Queen's Bench Division* became one of the five divisions composing the High Court of Justice. Then, in 1880, two other divisions—Common Pleas and Exchequer—were merged into the Queen's Bench Division, which today hears actions founded on contract or tort, applications for judicial review, and some appeals from magistrates' courts. For more on the High Court, see **high court.**

Queen's Counsel. See **Q.C.** & **silk.**

Queen's evidence, to turn. See **turn state's evidence.**

querist. See **questioner.**

querulous (= apt to complain; whining) is a MALAPROPISM when used for *query-like.* E.g., "His statement was *querulous;* that is, it was framed as a question." [Read *His statement was framed as a question.*]

quere; query. See ***quaere.***

questionary. See **questionnaire.**

question (as to) whether; question (of) whether. The best phrasing is *question whether*—e.g.:

- "[I]f a person is accused of murder the *question whether* he was or was not legally responsible for the death may be intended to raise the *issue whether* the death was too remote a consequence of his acts for them to count as its cause." H.L.A. Hart, "Postscript: Responsibility and Retribution," in *Punishment and Responsibility: Essays in the Philosophy of Law* 210, 220 (1968). On *issue whether,* see **issue (B).**
- "This leaves the *question whether* there are any impersonal or institutional measures available that may serve as a kind of prophylaxis against the introduction of distortions into the law at the level of enforcement." Lon L. Fuller, *Anatomy of the Law* 37 (1968).
- "The real difference between the majority and the dissentients in *Maunsell v. Olins* was over the *question whether* there was an ambiguity." Rupert Cross, *Statutory Interpretation* 145 (1976).

The phrases *question as to whether* and *question of whether* are common prolixities. Examples of *question as to whether* are legion in the prose of lawyers and judges—e.g.: "The question sometimes *arises as to whether* [read *arises whether*] today a man may by a conveyance to himself and his wife create a tenancy by the entirety."/ "The *question as to whether* [read *question whether*] the equitable defense of unclean hands applies as a defense to a legal action appears to be one of first impression."

Even where *question* means "doubt," the preferred form is *question whether:* "There is some *question as to whether* [read *question whether*] the defendant could be held personally liable."

The only context in which *question as to whether* might be justified is where an intervening phrase might cause an ambiguity or awkwardness: "There may be a *question* of statutory interpretation *as to whether* this 'consent' comprehends only those actions done within the state or is broad enough to cover all personal actions."

The other common prolixity is *question of whether*—e.g.: "The answer to the *question of whether* [read *question whether*] the state courts of Ohio are open to a proceeding in personam rests entirely upon the law of Ohio."/ "Without mentioning the *question of whether* [read *question whether*] an adequate remedy at law was available, we have held that rights similar to those of the plaintiff in this case may be enforced by actions in the nature of specific performance." Yet *question of whether* is preferred when one uses the idiom *it is a question of . . .* , as in "a question of ethics" or "a question of materiality"—e.g.: "It is a *question of whether* the defendant is passing off his goods as those of the plaintiff."

question-begging is the adjectival form of the phrase *begging the question.* The phrase is commonly found in the writing of dissenting judges—e.g.: "Until this case I would have agreed with the majority's repeated, but *question-begging* assertion that the contours of the Sixth Amendment Confrontation Clause are identical to those of Missouri's face-to-face guarantee, but only because I had not imagined, and this Court had not faced, a statutory procedure that so clearly abrogates a constitutional guarantee." *State v. Naucke,* 829 S.W.2d 445, 465 (Mo. 1992) (Robertson, C.J., dissenting)./ "Indeed, Justice Brickley's conclusion that, since there is no evidence that Juillet was a drug dealer, the only reason for his 'delivery of drugs' was Bleser's incessant requests, . . . is classical *question-begging.*" *People v. Juillet,* 475 N.W.2d 786, 817 (Mich. 1991) (Boyle, J., concurring in part & dissenting in part). See **begging the question.**

questioner; querist. The former is the ordinary, more natural term.

questionnaire; questionary. The latter is a NEEDLESS VARIANT.

question (of) whether. See **question (as to) whether.**

quia timet (lit., "because he or she fears") denotes a legal doctrine under which a party seeks equitable relief because of a concern over future probable injury to certain rights or interests. *Quia timet* often forms a PHRASAL ADJECTIVE; when it does, the words ought to be hyphenated <quia-timet injunction>.

quick originally meant "alive," as in the surviving phrase *the quick and the dead,* used by one judge to turn a nice phrase: "There are only two conduits, the statute of wills and intestate succession, by which the transmission of property and estate to the *quick* from the dead may be effected."

Up to the 19th century, *quick* was used as an equivalent of *live* or *alive* in general contexts, as in the "Apostles' Creed": "From thence he shall come to judge *the quick* and the dead." Here is a specimen from 1865: "The defendant then proved that Dygert was arrested January 2, 1862, and held to bail upon a criminal warrant charging him with the criminal offense of assisting in procuring an abortion of a *quick* child upon the person of the plaintiff, at Ilion, July 5, 1861." Today this usage would be an affected ARCHAISM.

The illogical phrase *quick with child*—referring to a pregnant woman—began in the 15th century as an inversion of the strictly logical phrase, *with quick child.* The *OED* labels the phrase "rare or obsolete," but naturally legal writers continue to use it: "A woman is '*quick with child*' . . . after she has felt the child alive within her." Rollin M. Perkins, *Criminal Law* 100 (1957).

quid pro quo (= this for that; tit for tat) is a useful LATINISM, for the only English equivalent of this LATINISM is *tit for tat,* which is unsuitable in formal contexts. "The settlor seeking to revoke or modify the trust may supplement his appeal to equity with a *quid pro quo* offered to the heirs for their consent."/ "Assumpsit would lie in any case in which there was a promise to pay a sum certain upon receipt of a benefit (the *quid pro quo*)." The word *exchange* does not quite capture the right sense.

Quid pro quo is wrongly used in the following example: "The employer's liability under the act is made exclusive to counterbalance the imposition of absolute liability; there is *no comparable quid pro quo* [read *no comparable balancing*] in the relationship between the employer and third persons."

The best plural is *quid pro quos; quids pro quos* is a pedantic alternative. *Quids pro quo* is incorrect—a good example of HYPERCORRECTION.

quiescence; quiescency. The *-ce* form is standard, *quiescency* being a NEEDLESS VARIANT. *Quiesence* is a fairly common misspelling. See, e.g., Alison A. Clarke, Note, *State Legislation Denying Subsistence Benefits to Undocumented Aliens,* 61 Tex. L. Rev. 859, 866 (1983).

quiet, adj. In the so-called *covenant for quiet enjoyment,* the word *quiet* means "free from disturbance" or "peaceful," not merely "free from noise." Plucknett equates *quiet enjoyment* with *seisin* (q.v.): "If A unjustly and without a judgement disseised B of his free tenement, then it seemed reasonable that B should be restored to the enjoyment of his property upon satisfactory proof, first, that he was in *quiet enjoyment* (that is to say, seised), and secondly, that A had turned him out." Theodore F.T. Plucknett, *A Concise History of the Common Law* 358 (5th ed. 1956).

quiet, v.t.; **quieten.** The preferred verb form is *quiet,* as in the phrase *to quiet title.* E.g., "The same issue may be presented in other types of litigation such as a suit to *quiet title.*"/ "The assignee of an automobile conditional sales contract sued to *quiet title.*"/ "That was an action to recover possession of land, and to *quiet title.*" Chiefly a Britishism, *quieten* was considered a superfluous word by the great British writer on usage, H.W. Fowler; it is to be avoided.

Adjectivally, the phrase *quiet title* is hyphenated: "In the earlier *quiet-title* case in which the government's conduct was found to be unreasonable, the 'innocent spouse' issue was raised." *Sliwa v. Commissioner,* 839 F.2d 602, 610 (9th Cir. 1988).

quietus /*kwɪ-ee-təs*/ forms the plural *quietuses.*

qui facit per alium facit per se. See MAXIMS.

quiritary; quiritarian. The latter is a NEEDLESS VARIANT of the former term, which means "in accordance with Roman civil law; legal, as opposed to equitable."

quit = (1) to stop; or (2) to leave. For sense (1), the past tense is *quit* <the defendant then quit making the harassing phone calls>. For sense (2), the past tense is *quitted.* E.g., "It must now be considered clear law that a person who wrongfully or maliciously interrupts the relation subsisting between master and servant by harbouring and keeping him as servant after he has *quitted* it and during the time stipulated for as the period of service, commits a wrongful act for which he is responsible at law." (Eng.)/ "These authorities and practices were to the effect that alimony decreed to a wife would be enforced by a writ of ne exeat, but only to the extent of arrears actually due, against a husband before he *quitted* the realm."

qui tam [L. "who as well"] = an action under a statute that allows a private person to sue for a penalty, part of which the government or some specified public institution will receive. Etymologically speaking, the plaintiff is a suitor "who as well" sues for the state. E.g., "The False Claims Act . . . includes provisions allowing private citizens to bring civil suits on behalf of the government. They're based on a principle called *qui tam* . . . ." Rick Wartzman & Paul Barrett, *For Whistle-Blowers, Tune May Change,* Wall St. J., 27 Sept. 1989, at B1./ "A statutory *qui tam* action is one brought against a public official to recover [441] a penalty (treble damages) for the commission of injurious acts or for a failure to act in obedience to some duty." *State v. Town of Canute,* 858 P.2d 436, 440–41 (Okla. 1993) (Opala, J., dissenting).

Qui tam lawsuits originated in the 13th century—when private persons would seek to protect the King's interest—and were embodied in statutes during the 15th century. In the U.S., *qui tam* lawsuits have "been in existence . . . ever since the foundation of our government." *Marvin v. Trout,* 199 U.S. 212, 225 (1905). They are usually reported as being in the name of the government *ex rel.* (= on the relation of) the private citizen. See ***ex rel.***

quitclaim, vb. & adj. [L.F. "to proclaim free"]. *Quitclaim,* v.t., = (1) to renounce or give up (a claim or right); or (2) to convey all one's interest in (property) to whatever extent one has an interest. These senses are closely related, sense (2) having grown out of sense (1). Today, sense (2) is the most usual one—e.g.:

- "[This] tract of land [was] *quitclaimed* by R.E. Janes to R.E. Janes Gravel Co . . . ." *Thompson v. Janes,* 245 S.W.2d 718, 723 (Tex. Civ. App.—Austin 1952).
- "The Objectors fail to recognize that those 200 landowners are not part of this class since USRV *quitclaimed* any interests to those rights-of-way prior to this action, and those landowners may pursue any possible claims independent from this action." *Hefty v. All Other Members of the Certified Settlement Class,* 638 N.E.2d 1284, 1292 (Ind. Ct. App. 1994).
- "The record reveals that Raymond *quitclaimed* the property to Esther on September 10, 1990." *Ross v. Ross,* 638 N.E.2d 1301, 1303 (Ind. Ct. App. 1994).
- "Hocherl subsequently *quitclaimed* her interest in the ranch to Pete Stampter." *Sandstrom v. Sandstrom,* 880 P.2d 103, 104 (Wyo. 1994).

Occasionally the verb is used intransitively—e.g.: "[T]he undersigned hereby remises, releases and forever *quitclaims* unto [plaintiff], all right, title and interest of the undersigned in and to the [adjoining] property." *Davis v. Nelson,* 880 S.W.2d 658, 663 (Mo. Ct. App. 1994) (quoting release).

The traditional way of quitclaiming property is to convey all of one's "right, title, and interest." See **right, title, and interest.**

The word *quitclaim*—formerly two words, then hyphenated, and now invariably one word—functions as an adjective as well, usually in the phrase *quitclaim deed.* E.g., "Northrup had previously conveyed all her right, title and interest in The Strip to the Wallaces by virtue of the 1962 *quitclaim deed* referenced above." *Cloer Land Co. v. Wright,* 858 P.2d 110, 112 (Okla. Ct. App. 1993)./ "Two years later, while the parties were still separated but not yet divorced, Mr. Clark prepared, executed and delivered to Mrs. Clark a *quitclaim deed* which said that he was conveying to Mrs. Clark 'all of [his] right, title, and interest' in the house they had purchased." *Clark v. Clark,* 644 A.2d 449, 450 (D.C. Ct. App. 1994).

Occasionally, it even functions as a noun, as a shortened form of *quitclaim deed*—e.g.: "[B]ecause Campbell's conveyance was only by *quitclaim* and transferred only whatever 'right, title, and interest' he had in 1960, Campbell's heirs have a claim to their proportionate share of the land in question." *Rogers v. Ricane Enterprises, Inc.,* 884 S.W.2d 763, 769 n.5 (Tex. 1994).

quite = (1) entirely, completely; (2) very; or (3) fairly, moderately. Sense (3) occurs in BrE only, in which the word has undergone pejoration. To say that something is *quite good* is a compliment in AmE but nearly the opposite in BrE: "Some years ago I was hired by an American bank. I received a letter from the head of human resources that started: 'Dear John, I am *quite* pleased that you have decided to join us.' That '*quite*' cast a cloud. Then I discovered that in American English 'quite' does not mean 'fairly' but 'very.'" John Mole, *Body Language of World Business,* Sunday Times, 8 July 1990, at 6-1.

quittance = (1) the discharge from a debt or obligation; or (2) the document serving as evidence of the discharge. For the related word *acquittance,* see **acquittal.**

quitter; quittor. For "one who quits," the former is preferred. *Quittor* = an inflammation of the feet, usu. in horses.

quoad (= as regards; with regard to) is a LATINISM that is easily Englished. E.g., "It seems to me that, if anything, this was a case of wilful refusal; invincible repugnance is a lack of capacity *quoad* [read *as regards* or *with regard to*] this man." (Eng.) The term often appears in the phrase *quoad hoc* (= with regard to this). E.g., "When a justice undertakes the issuing of a warrant of arrest which commands and secures the arrest, and possibly the imprisonment, of the person charged, he *quoad hoc* [omit *quoad hoc,* which is superfluous] acts ministerially."

quo animo (lit., "with what intention or motive"), an arcane LATINISM, is used by some legal writers as an equivalent of *animus,* q.v. "Such acts are against the express declarations of the *quo animo.*" Those legal writers are, happily, becoming rarer.

The correct use of the phrase is not as a noun, but as an adverb—e.g.: "Indeed, once it is established that a payment has been accepted as rent, which is a question of fact, waiver results as a matter of law, and the question of *quo animo* [i.e., with what intention] the payment was accepted is irrelevant." Peter Butt, *Land Law* 284 (2d ed. 1988). Even this use, though, is questionable in modern writing.

quod erat demonstrandum. See **Q.E.D.**

quod erat faciendum. See **Q.E.F.**

quod vide = which see. The abbreviation *q.v.* (pl. *qq.v.*) is used throughout this work.

quondam (= former) is an ARCHAISM. See **erstwhile.**

quorum. Pl. *quorums.* See PLURALS (A).

QUOTATIONS. A. Use of Quoted Material. The deft and incidental use of quotations is a rare art. Legal writers—especially the bad ones—are apt to quote paragraph after paragraph in block quotations (see B). Those who do this abrogate their duty, namely, to *write.* Readers tend to skip over single-spaced mountains of prose, knowing how unlikely it is that so much of a previous writer's material pertains directly to the matter at hand. Especially to be avoided is quoting another writer at the end of a paragraph or section, a habit infused with laziness. The skillful quoter subordinates the quoted material to his or her own prose and uses only the most clearly applicable parts of the previous writing. And even then, one must weave it into one's own narrative or analysis, not allowing the quoted to overpower the quoter.

B. Handling Block Quotations. The best way to handle them, of course, is not to handle them at all: quote smaller chunks. Assuming, though, that this goal is unattainable—as most legal writers seem to think—then the biggest challenge is handling the quotation so that it will actually get read. The secret is in the lead-in.

Before discussing how a good lead-in reads, let us look at how 98% of them read. They are dead:

- The court observed: . . . .
- The court held: . . . .
- The court further held: . . . .
- As stated by the court: . . . .
- Rule 54(d) states: . . . .
- As the court specifically stated: . . . .
- The statute reads in pertinent part: . . . .
- The *Miranda* court stated: . . . .
- According to the 5th Circuit: . . . .
- That opinion enunciated the definition of the term "fixture" as follows: . . . .

Anyone who wants to become a good legal stylist must vow to try *never* to introduce a quotation in this way. Readers are sure to skip the quotation.

The better practice is to state the upshot of the quotation in the lead-in. With this method, the lead-in becomes an assertion, and the quotation becomes the support. The reader feels as if the writer has asserted something concrete and often, out of curiosity, wants to verify that assertion.

Consider, for example, how differently the following passage would read if the colon introducing the quotation followed *observed* instead of *bystanders:*

> As one Texas court has observed, modern legal practice is designed to prevent the vexatious suing of innocent bystanders:
>
> > Our statutes of limitation afford ample time for investigation before the institution of suit. Before and after that point, our rules of practice afford many means of investigating the circumstances of the case and of ascertaining the proper identity of the parties sued. We are unable to find any legal excuse for appellant's having sued the wrong corporation or for his delay in ascertaining this fact.

When the writer gives the upshot in the introductory words, readers are not left hunting for the central idea of the quotation.

This method has the benefit not only of ensuring that the quotation is read, but also of enhancing the writer's credibility. For if the lead-in is pointed as well as accurate, the reader will agree that the quotation supports the writer's assertion.

C. Punctuating the Lead-In. Writers usu. have four choices: the colon, the comma, a period (i.e., no lead-in, really—only an independent sentence before the quotation), or no punctuation. A long quotation ordinarily requires a colon. Some writers, though, let the lead-in and the quotation stand as separate sentences, as in the following example:

> As part of the "balancing" of equities, the Act provides that the statutory remedies shall serve as the employee's *exclusive remedy* if that employee sustains an injury compensable under the Act.
>
> > No common law or statutory right to recover damages from the employer, his insurer . . . or the agents or employees of any of them for injury or death sustained by any employee while engaged in the line of his duty as such employee, other than the compensation herein provided, is available to any employee who is covered by the provisions of this Act, to anyone wholly or partially dependent on him . . . or anyone otherwise entitled to recover damages for such injury.
> >
> > Ill. Rev. Stat. ch. 48, ¶ 138.5(a) (1986).

The writer there crafted a good lead-in by summarizing the provision in plain English. Letting the lead-in stand as one sentence, though, can leave the quotation in a sort of syntactic limbo. A colon, by contrast, helps the reader see how the quotation fits into the text: the quotation simply amplifies the lead-in.

When is it best to use no punctuation at all?

Only when the introductory language moves seamlessly into the quoted material—e.g.:

> Professor Bobbitt thinks that the view that moral arguments should generally be excluded from constitutional discourse
>
> justifies, for example, the phenomenon of federal habeas corpus, for which it is otherwise difficult to give good grounds. Habeas corpus severs the constitutional decision from the moral question of guilt or innocence, so that the former can be dispassionately weighed as one suspects it seldom can be in the context of a trial. At the same time federal habeas corpus gives the matter to a group of deciders whose customary business is, by comparison to state courts, largely amoral.

The mere fact that what is being introduced is a block quotation does not mean that some additional punctuation is necessary.

D. American and British Systems. In AmE, quotations that are short enough to be run into the text (usu. fewer than 50 words) are set off by pairs of *double* quotation marks (". . ."). In BrE, quoted text that is not long enough to be a block quotation is set off by *single* quotation marks ('. . .'). See PUNCTUATION (J).

E. Ellipses. A good way to trim down a bloated quotation—and thus to increase the odds of having it read—is to cut irrelevant parts. When you omit one or more words, you show the omission by using ellipsis points (a series of three period-dots) with one space between each one:

> The court may require any attorney . . . who vexatiously multiplies the proceedings to personally satisfy the excess costs, expenses, and attorneys' fees reasonably incurred because of that conduct.

Use a fourth period-dot when the omission falls between sentences in the quoted material or when your ellipsis ends a sentence.

The spacing between the last word of the sentence and the first ellipsis point depends on whether the last word before the ellipsis ends a sentence. In the following example, *intent* is the last word of the first sentence, and it therefore ends with a period followed by three ellipsis points:

> A circuit court must initially determine, as a question of law, whether the language of a purported contract is ambiguous as to the parties' intent. . . . If the terms of an alleged contract are ambiguous or capable of more than one interpretation, however, parol evidence is admissible to ascertain the parties' intent.

But if *intent* were not the last word of the first sentence, then the three ellipsis points would come first, and the (typographically identical) period after. The only difference would be the space between *intent* and the first dot:

> A circuit court must initially determine, as a question of law, whether the language of a purported contract is ambiguous as to the parties' intent . . . . If the terms of an alleged contract are ambiguous or capable of more than one interpretation, however, parol evidence is admissible to ascertain the parties' intent.

That distinction—a hairsplitting distinction, in the minds of some—is one that careful legal writers adhere to. In nonlegal writing, though, the convention is to close up the space before the first of four ellipsis points: "Note that there is no space between the period or other terminal punctuation and the preceding word, even though that word does not end the original sentence." *The Chicago Manual of Style* § 10.55, at 373 (14th ed. 1993).

Finally, when you omit more than one paragraph in a block quotation, use a whole line for the three ellipsis points (centered), which should have five to seven spaces between them—e.g:

> Everyone is familiar with the general distinction between what people mean to say and what they expect or hope will happen as a result of their having said it. People often say "Don't bother" when they hope the person they are speaking to will ignore what they have said and will indeed bother. The distinction is especially important when people give orders to make requests in language that is normally understood as abstract or in some other way requiring judgment.
>
> .   .   .
>
> The late-eighteenth-century authors of the Eighth Amendment (as we have defined them) declared that "cruel and unusual punishments" are unconstitutional. What did they intend to say?
>
> Ronald Dworkin, *Life's Dominion: An Argument About Abortion, Euthanasia, and Individual Freedom* 134–35 (1993).

quote (properly a verb) for *quotation* is a casualism that sometimes appears in formal contexts—e.g.: "This *quote* . . . clearly draws a distinction . . . ." *U.S. v. Sells Eng'g, Inc.,* 463 U.S. 418, 463 (1983). The problem with *quotation* is that, to the writer who hopes to deliver goods quickly, the three syllables sound and read as if they are taking too much time. The single syllable of *quote,* meanwhile, sounds apt to such a writer. And it sounds more and more natural all the time, as it seems to predominate in spoken English.

The negative form, too, is a casualism—e.g.: "The good brief-writer does not belabor *misquotes* in an opponent's brief." See **cite (B).**

quo warranto (lit., "by what authority?") is the HYBRID name (L. *quo* + A.S. *warrant*) of the common-law writ enshrined in two statutes enacted in 1289, each known as *Statutum de Quo Warranto.* Through this writ, a relator sought to discover either the extent of royal manors or the warrants by which royal rights and royal estates had passed to corporations or private individuals. Today, the writ is obsolete in England but persists in the U.S., where it is generally used to inquire into the authority by which a public office is held or a franchise is claimed. See **prerogative writs.**

The hybrid nature of this LAW LATIN term is apt to throw the linguist into a fit: "The term . . . is to a linguist a horripilating hybrid, using an English term like 'warrant' with a Latin ablative ending and combining it with a Latin interrogative pronoun." Mario Pei, *Double-Speak in America* 73 (1973).

q.v. See ***quod vide.***

R

R., the abbreviation for either *Regina* (= Queen) or *Rex* (King), is often used in G.B. in place of *The Queen* or *The King* in criminal case names.

racial discrimination; race discrimination. The former phrase is slightly better, because, other things being equal, the functional adjective (*racial* or *race*) should have the form as well as the function of an adjective (hence *racial*). But, predictably, idiomatic English is not entirely consistent: we speak of *racial equality* but *race relations.* Cf. **sex.**

rack. See **wrack.**

racketeer, n. & v.i. The noun *racketeering* = the business of racketeers; a system of organized crime traditionally involving the extortion of money from business firms by intimidation, violence, or other illegal methods. Oddly, this noun, as well as the verb *racketeer,* is characterized by the *OED* as an Americanism, whereas the adjective *racketeering* is exemplified in that dictionary only by British quotations. If the verb and its derivative forms began as Americanisms, they will inevitably spread to BrE, given the inroads already made.

In 1970, the U.S. Congress passed the Racketeer Influenced and Corrupt Organizations Act (RICO), 18 U.S.C. §§ 1961–68 (1988), which led to a resurgence of the word in AmE. Today *racketeering* often has the broad sense "the practice of engaging in a fraudulent scheme or enterprise."

radiocast. See **broadcast.**

railroad; railway. As nouns these words are virtually equivalent. *W2* makes the following distinction: "*Railroad* . . . is usually limited to roads [with lines or rails fixed to ties] for heavy steam transportation and also to steam roads partially or wholly electrified or roads for heavy traffic designed originally for electric traction. The lighter electric street-car lines and the like are usually termed *railways.*" In G.B., however, streetcar lines are commonly called *trainlines* or *tramways,* and the vehicles *traincars, tramcars,* or *trams.*

The two words are abbreviated *R.R.* and *Ry. Railroad* is used universally as a verb <passenger railroading>, figuratively as well as literally—e.g.: "An attempt is being made, while wartime psychology for national security is high, to *railroad* through Congress a bill providing for compulsory military training for one year of all young men between the ages of 18 and 22." This sense is now used in BrE as well as AmE.

rainmaker, in AmE, refers to a lawyer who, generally through wide contacts within the business community, generates a great deal of business for a law firm. E.g., "Ms. Miller . . . said that more and more firms are capitulating as Wilmer Cutler did, and are courting *rainmakers* from other firms." Kathleen Sylvester, *D.C. Firms Sporting a New Look,* Nat'l L.J, 26 March 1984, at 1, 26./ "It is well known that law firms often have partners who are socially prominent due to their civic, charitable, or political activities. They may do little legal work; their job is to bring in new clients. They are the '*rainmakers*' . . . ." Frederick C. Moss, *The Ethics of Law Practice Marketing,* 61 Notre Dame L. Rev. 601, 670 (1986).

raise. A. And *rear.* The old rule, still to be observed in formal contexts, is that crops and livestock are *raised* and children are *reared.*

B. *"Raising"* a Use. In the traditional legal idiom, to create a use (in the sense of equitable ownership) was to *raise* a use—e.g.: "The rule requiring a consideration to *raise a use,* has become merely nominal . . . ." *Jackson ex. dem. Hudson v. Alexander,* 3 Johns. 484, 492 (N.Y. Sup. Ct. 1808)./ "At the beginning of the sixteenth century it was settled that a use could be *raised* without a transfer of the seisin by means of a bargain and sale." Cornelius J. Moynihan, *Introduction to the Law of Real Property* 176 (2d ed. 1988). See **use.**

Rambo. This is the name of the "hero" in David Morrell's novel *First Blood,* which was popularized in the film by that name and in *Rambo:*

First Blood Part II and *Rambo III.* The character Rambo is a Vietnam veteran who is madly bent on violent revenge.

By an almost natural extension, the term came in the 1980s to denote ultra-aggressive lawyers, especially litigators. The *SOED* defines *Rambo* (with the initial capital) as "a man given to displays of physical violence or aggression, a macho man." But among American lawyers, the term has lost its sex-specific character, so that it is perfectly natural to speak of a female litigator as being a *Rambo.*

Sometimes, as in the first example quoted below, *Rambo* appears alone, but more often it is used attributively in the phrases *Rambo litigator, Rambo lawyer,* or *Rambo tactics*—e.g.:

- "I do not say to trust the untrustworthy or to retreat before *Rambos.*" Thomas M. Reavley, *Response to "One Year After Dondi": Time to Get Back to Litigating?* 17 Pepperdine L. Rev. 851, 852 (1990).
- "*Rambo lawyers,* the critics say, are perhaps the most blatant example of a widespread deterioration of professional legal standards." Dona Rubin, *The Rambo Boys,* Dallas Life Mag., 25 Feb. 1990, at 7.
- "If no one hires *Rambo-lawyer,* maybe he'll drop his arsenal of bad ethics and sleaze." Bruce Vielmetti, *New Wave Hopes for Kinder, Gentler Litigants,* St. Petersburg Times, 20 Dec. 1993, at 9.
- "This is the last refuge of *Rambo litigators,* a group that didn't appreciate the irony when Ambrose Bierce described lawyers as those 'skilled in circumventing the law.'" Richard M. Hunt, *Goodbye to the Warrior,* Texas Law., 12 Dec. 1994, at 19.
- "In addition, a new book by Mary Ann Glendon of the Harvard Law School contends that lawyers are becoming *'Rambo litigators'* in an effort to maximize billable hours." Marcia M. McBrien, *Fax Poll: Unhappy Lawyers Cite Hard Work, Few Rewards,* Mich. Law. Weekly, 26 Dec. 1994, at 1.
- "'The fact that *'Rambo' lawyers* get results, no matter what the personal cost in lawyer relations, begets more 'Rambos' as client expectations and loyalties change,' according to the [Seventh Circuit's 1991] study which often is cited as the most thorough on the subject." Chris Conley, *Order in the Court,* Commercial Appeal (Memphis), 26 Jan. 1995, at 1B.

Cf. LAWYERS, DEROGATORY NAMES FOR.

rape. A. Defined. Some authorities, especially older ones, define *rape* as "carnal knowledge of a woman forcibly against her will." 4 Blackstone, *Commentaries* *210. But the better view is that force should not be an element of the definition because if it is, then one must resort to a fictional "constructive force," which includes the threat of force. See **constructive.**

A better traditional, common-law definition is as follows: "A man commits rape when he engages in intercourse (in the old statutes, carnal knowledge) with a woman not his wife; by force or threat of force; against her will and without her consent." Susan Estrich, *Real Rape* 8 (1987). Gradually, the definition has been simplified. One criminal-law text defines it simply as "sexual intercourse with a female person without her consent." Rollin M. Perkins & Ronald N. Boyce, *Criminal Law* 197 (3d ed. 1982). See **marital rape.**

This definitional change took place in many American states during the 1970s. The pre-1974 rape statute in Texas defined *rape* as "the carnal knowledge of a woman without her consent and obtained by force, threats or fraud . . . ." Tex. Penal Code Ann. § 1183 (Vernon 1961). A 1974 amendment changed the definition so that a person is guilty of rape "if he has sexual intercourse with a female not his wife and without the female's consent . . . ." *Id.* § 21.02 (Vernon 1974). For the more modern development, see (C).

B. And *seduction.* Traditionally, the law has distinguished between *rape* and seduction. If consent is altogether lacking, the offense is called *rape.* If the consent is unfairly obtained—as through phony tenderness or false promises of an enduring relationship—the act is called seduction.

Many modern writers reject this definitional dichotomy, even if they accept its consequences in the punishability of one versus the other—e.g.: "But where does rape begin and seduction end? Germaine Greer has argued that the commonest form of rape is 'rape by fraud—by phony tenderness or false promises of an enduring relationship, for example.' Dr. Greer, however, acknowledged that this was *non-criminal* rape and nobody has ever argued that an attempt to get sexual intercourse through sweet but insincere words should be made an indictable offence." Kathy Marks, *Rape,* Independent, 23 Feb. 1992, at 19.

C. And *sexual assault; indecent assault.* During the 1980s, many American jurisdictions have abolished rape as a separate offense. Statutes have created a new offense called *sexual assault,* defined in Texas as follows: "a person commits an offense if the person intentionally or knowingly caused the penetration of the anus or female sexual organ of another person who is not the spouse of the actor by any means, without that person's consent." Tex. Penal Code Ann. § 22.011(a) (Vernon 1983). The result is that the statute covers not just females, but also males who are homosexually assaulted.

There are several variations. In New Jersey, simple sexual assault is defined as an act of sexual penetration committed when the "actor uses physical force or coercion, but the victim does not sustain severe personal injury." N.J. Stat. Ann. § 2C:14-2(c)(1) (West 1982). The Model Penal Code, however, is drafted much more broadly:

> A person who has sexual contact with another not his spouse, or causes such other to have sexual contact with him, is guilty of sexual assault, a misdemeanor, if . . . he knows that the contact is offensive to the other person . . . . Sexual contact is any touching of the sexual or other intimate parts of the person for the purpose of arousing or gratifying sexual desire.
>
> Model Penal Code § 213.4 (1980).

One state—Pennsylvania—even uses the term *indecent assault* as opposed to *sexual assault.* Under the Pennsylvania statute, a person who has "indecent contact" with another not his or her spouse is guilty of indecent assault if:

- the other person does not consent;
- the actor knows that the other person has a mental defect that impairs consent;
- the actor knows that the other person is unaware of the act;
- the actor has drugged the person;
- the other person is in custody in a hospital or other institution where the actor has supervisory or disciplinary authority;
- the actor is more than 18 years old and the other person is under 14.

See 18 Pa. C.S.A. § 3126 (1994). Under that same Pennsylvania statute, *indecent contact* is defined as "any touching of the sexual or other intimate parts of the person for the purpose of arousing or gratifying sexual desire, in either person." *Id.* § 3101.

In G.B., *indecent assault* is the usual term for a lesser offense than rape: touching without consent. It is punishable by up to two years' imprisonment. See Tony Honoré, *Sex Law* 65–68 (1978).

rara avis [lit., "rare bird"] is, as Fowler once noted, "seldom an improvement on *rarity*" (*MEU1* at 483).

rarefy is often misspelled *-ify*—e.g.: "[T]he intricate arguments of counsel . . . have by now reached a *rarified* [read *rarefied*] plane." Anthony Sampson, *Anatomy of Britain* 156 (1962)./ "This was high ground indeed; the Supreme Court found the air too *rarified* [read *rarefied*] . . . ." Grant Gilmore & Charles L. Black, *The Law of Admiralty* 224 (2d ed. 1975). Cf. **stupefy.**

rarely ever is incorrect for *rarely* or *rarely if ever.*

ratable; rateable. In AmE, the spelling *ratable* is preferred, whereas in BrE *rateable* is more common.

The adverb *ratably* is frequently used in legal writing in the sense "pro rata, proportionately" <they will share ratably in the assets>. E.g., "Co-owners must, as a rule, contribute *ratably* toward payment of taxes, special assessments, mortgages and repairs of the property." Robert Kratovil, *Real Estate Law* 223 (1946; repr. 1950)./ "Those [withdrawals] . . . from the deposit accounts were . . . to be borne *rateably* . . . ." Lord Goff of Chieveley & Gareth Jones, *The Law of Restitution* 75 (3d ed. 1986). See MUTE E.

rate(-)making, n. & adj., is best hyphenated.

rather. See **but rather.**

rather unique. See ADJECTIVES (B).

ratification = (1) in contract law, a person's binding adoption of an act already completed, but either not done in a way that originally produced a legal obligation or done by a stranger having at the time no authority to act as the person's agent; (2) in domestic law, the process by which a state indicates acceptance of the obligations contained in a treaty; or (3) in international law, the final confirmation by the parties to an international treaty, usu. including the documents reflecting the confirmation. See **adoption.**

ratio frequently serves as a shorthand form of *ratio decidendi*—e.g.: "Fully considered *dicta* in the House of Lords are usually treated as more weighty than the *ratio* of a judge at first instance in the High Court." P.S. Atiyah, *Law and Modern Society* 135 (1983). "The *ratio* . . . of a case is its central core of meaning, its sharpest cutting edge." Michael Zander, *The Law-Making Process* 225 (2d ed. 1985). The plural is *rationes.* See ***ratio decidendi.***

ratiocination; rationalization. *Ratiocination* /*ray-shee-oh-sə-**nay**-shən*/ = the process or an act of reasoning. *Rationalization* = (1) an act or instance of explaining (away) by bringing into conformity with reason; or (2) (colloq.) the finding of "reasons" for irrational or unworthy behavior. Sense (2) is responsible for the negative connotations of *rationalization* among nonlawyers.

ratiocinative; ratiocinatory. The latter is a NEEDLESS VARIANT.

ratio decidendi /***ray***-*shee-oh-des-i-***den***-dee*/ (lit., "the reason for deciding") = (1) the rule of law on which a court says its decision is founded; or (2) the rule of law on which a later court thinks that a previous court founded its decision. So, even though this term is basic to the common-law system of precedents, it is more than a little ambiguous. Still, sense (2) is much less common in practice than sense (1). As the *OCL* notes, a literal translation of the phrase ("the reason for the decision") is unsatisfactory "because the reason may in fact be something other, such as the judge's dislike of the defendant. Nor is the *ratio* the decision itself, for this binds only the parties [by *res judicata,* q.v.] whereas the *ratio* is the principle which is of application to subsequent cases and states the law for all parties."

Judicial opinions often contain no clearly ascertainable *ratio decidendi,* and therefore finding it often demands creativity and independent judgment. But many writers use this term without concerning themselves with the ambiguity or the subtleties—e.g.: "Lower courts read the opinions of this Court with a not unnatural alertness to catch intimations beyond the precise *ratio decidendi.*" *Johnson v. U.S.,* 333 U.S. 46, 56 (1948) (Frankfurter, J., dissenting in part)./ "The words of an opinion are not scriptural admonitions or statutory mandates; we are bound by the rationale of a decision, its *ratio decidendi,* not its explanatory language."/ "The observations of Lindley L.J. are less to the purpose, but indicate no dissent from the views of his brethren, which as part of our *ratio decidendi* cannot in our opinion be dismissed as merely obiter." (Eng.)/ "The actual point in this case did not arise in *Ringrose v. Bramham,* but still the *ratio decidendi* clearly applies." (Eng.)

The plural form of *ratio* is *rationes:* "[T]he substitution of negligent non-military personnel in place of military personnel would have no effect on these *rationes decidendi.*" *Sheppard v. U.S.,* 294 F. Supp. 7, 9 (E.D. Pa. 1969). "[A] general rule of interpretation, unlike other common law rules, can never be rendered more specific by the *rationes decidendi* of later cases." Rupert Cross, *Statutory Interpretation* 168 (1976). See **stare decisis.** Cf. **dictum (A)** & **obiter dictum (B).**

rational. See **reasonable.**

rationale (= a reasoned exposition of principles; an explanation or statement of reasons) is not to be confused with *rationalization* (see **ratiocination**).

Rationale is regularly three syllables, although Fowler believed that it should be four syllables based on etymology (*-ale* being two syllables). Today, his preferred pronunciation would be considered terribly pedantic in most company. The final syllable is pronounced like that in *morale* or *chorale.* See ***ratio decidendi.***

rationalization. See **ratiocination.**

rationalize for *analogize* or *harmonize* is an unlikely error. E.g., "Since the argument in this case, appellants have called our attention to the recent Supreme Court case of *Indian Towing Co. v. United States,* but it is difficult to *rationalize that case with* [read, depending on the sense, *analogize that case to* or *harmonize that case with*] the one at bar."

ration allotment is a REDUNDANCY. E.g., "Many people came up at night and asked, even demanded, a drink of water beyond their *ration allotment.*" Either word would be sufficient.

ravish (= to rape) is now more literary or archaic than is appropriate for modern legal contexts. E.g., "When a man is presented for rape or an attempt to *ravish* [read *rape*], it may be shown that the woman against whom the offence was committed was of a generally immoral character, although she is not cross-examined on the subject." (Eng.)

One problem with *ravish* is that it has romantic connotations: it means not only "to commit rape," but also "to fill with ecstasy or delight." The latter sense renders the word unfit for acting as a technical or legal equivalent of *rape.* The term describing the act should evoke outrage; it should not be a romantic abstraction, as *ravish* is.

-RE, -ER. See -ER (C).

re. See **in re.**

rea. See ***reus.***

reaction. A. For *response.* Several usage critics have objected to this use of the term, as in "What was the judge's *reaction* to this argument?" on grounds that *reaction* is primarily a scientific term that in any event is not applicable to people. The objection is a pedantic one.

B. For *effect.* Justice Holmes once nodded and made this mistake: "The question then is narrowed to whether the exercise of its otherwise constitutional power by Congress can be pronounced unconstitutional because of its possible *reaction* [read *effect*] upon the conduct of the

States in a matter upon which I have admitted that they are free from direct control." *Hammer v. Dagenhart,* 247 U.S. 251, 278 (1918) (Holmes, J., dissenting).

reactionary; reactionist; reactionarist. The second and third are NEEDLESS VARIANTS.

reading the Riot Act. The English "Riot Act," 1 Geo. I, stat. 2, c. 5 (1714) (repealed 1973), made it a capital offense for 12 or more rioters to assemble for an hour after a magistrate proclaimed that the rioters must disperse. As a 19th-century commentator observed, the magistrate's proclamation "is commonly, but very inaccurately, called reading the Riot Act." 1 James F. Stephen, *A History of the Criminal Law of England* 203 n.1 (London, Macmillan & Co., 1883). Why inaccurately? Because the statute itself was not read. Instead, a proclamation was read, calling on rioters to disperse.

By the early 19th century, the phrase *read the riot act* (usu. with the last two words in lower case) had become a catchphrase meaning "to tell someone off." See POPULARIZED LEGAL TECHNICALITIES.

ready, willing, and able is a phrase that traditionally refers to a prospective buyer of property who can legally and financially consummate the deal. A less common variant is *ready, able, and willing.* See DOUBLETS, TRIPLETS, AND SYNONYM-STRINGS.

real is casualism when used for *very*—e.g.: "Competition in recent years hasn't been *real* [read *very*] friendly . . . ." L. Gordon Crovitz, *Even Gentlemanly Yachtsmen Go to Court, but Why Let Them?* Wall St. J., 16 May 1990, at A17.

real; personal. The distinction between *real property* (or *realty*) and *personal property* (or *personalty*) is as old as Roman law, but the curious terminology is much more recent. From the early 17th century on, land was commonly called *real property* and chattels were called *personal property* merely because land could be recovered specifically in a real action, but chattels could be made the subject only of a damage action. See **real action.**

real action; personal action; mixed action. The distinctions between these three were fundamental to the common law. *Real actions* involved a *res,* or land, and a plaintiff (or demandant) claiming some interest in the land. *Personal actions* involved debts, personal duties, or damages arising from any cause. *Mixed actions* partook of the nature of the other two, as when the plaintiff claimed both real property and damages. See **demandant & real.**

real contract. This phrase, common among civilians, is rarely used by common-law writers and judges. Still, it describes an obligation enforced at common law from the earliest times: "A *real contract* is an obligation arising from the possession or transfer of a res. The *real contracts* known to the common law were enforced by the actions of account, detinue, and debt." 1 Samuel Williston & Walter H.E. Jaeger, *A Treatise on the Law of Contracts* § 8, at 19 (3d ed. 1957). For the most part, these forms of action fell into disuse with the rise of assumpsit. See **assumpsit.**

real covenant = a covenant running with the land. See **covenant.**

real estate. Richard Grant White's (19th-century) view of this phrase—"a pretentious intruder from the technical province of law"—remains surprisingly apt:

> Law makes the distinction of real and personal estate; but a man does not, therefore, talk of drawing some personal estate from the bank, or going to Tiffany's to buy some personal estate for his wife; nor, when he has an interest in the national debt, does he ask how personal estate is selling. He draws money, buys jewels, asks the price of bonds. *Real estate,* as ordinarily used, is a mere big-sounding, vulgar phrase for houses and land, and, so used, is a marked and unjustifiable Americanism. Our papers have columns headed in large letters, 'Real Estate Transactions,' the heading of which should be Sales of Land.
>
> Richard Grant White, *Words and Their Uses, Past and Present* 150 (2d ed. 1872).

real-estate agent. See **realtor.**

real facts. See **fact & actual fact, in.**

real party in interest. So written, though a few judges have ill-advisedly made this noun phrase *real-party-in-interest* or *real party-in-interest.* Only as a PHRASAL ADJECTIVE—as in *real-party-in-interest provision*—does the phrase need hyphens.

real property. For the historical basis for the distinction between *real property* and *personal property,* see **real.**

realtor (= a real estate agent or broker) has two syllables, not three. This Americanism is a MORPHOLOGICAL DEFORMITY, inasmuch as the *-or* suffix in Latin is appended only to verb elements, and *realt-* is not a verb element, but the term is too well established in AmE to quibble with its makeup. The shortness of the word commends it.

Some authorities suggest that it should be capitalized and used only in its proprietary trademark sense, that is, "a member of the National Association of Realtors"; the organization invented and registered the trademark in 1916. Seemingly few people know about the trademark, and consequently in AmE the term is used indiscriminately of real-estate agents generally. In BrE, real-estate agents are known as *estate agents; realtor* is virtually unknown there, and *real estate* is only a little better known to British nonlawyers.

realty. **A. Sense.** The only current sense of this term is the legal one, "real property." Formerly, the term could denote both "royalty" and "a reality." See **real estate.**

B. Precise Difference Between *realty* and *personalty.* Anglo-American courts have disagreed about whether an estate in land less than a freehold is properly considered *realty* or *personalty.* (At common law, a tenant for years was not regarded as having an interest in realty.) Today, courts most often "use the expressions *real estate* and *real property* in a broad sense as applicable to any estates in land, whether freehold or less than freehold, as well as to land itself, regarded as the object of rights." 1 Herbert T. Tiffany, *The Law of Real Property* § 3, at 7–8 (B. Jones ed., 3d ed. 1939). The increasing use of *realty* and its cognates in the broader sense, to include nonfreehold as well as freehold estates, is attributable to "the fact that it corresponds to the ordinary use of the expression . . . among members of the community in general" (*id.* at 8), otherwise known as SLIPSHOD EXTENSION.

rear. See **raise (A).**

reasonability. See **reasonableness.**

reasonable; rational. Generally, *reasonable* = according to reason; *rational* = having reason. Yet *reasonable* is often used in reference to persons in the sense "having the faculty of reason" <reasonable person>. When applied to things, the two words are perhaps more clearly differentiated: "In application to things *reasonable* and *rational* both signify according to *reason;* but the former is used in reference to the business of life, as a *reasonable* proposal, wish, etc.; *rational* to abstract matters, as *rational* motives, grounds, questions, etc." George Crabb, *Crabb's English Synonymes* 589 (John H. Finley ed., 2d ed. 1917).

reasonable doubt, beyond a. See **balance of probability.**

reasonable man. See **reasonable person.**

reasonable-minded is prolix for *reasonable*—e.g.: "Second, the Court says that the intrusion was not a serious one because a *reasonable-minded* [read *reasonable*] citizen would in fact want to be present at a search of his house unless he was fleeing to avoid arrest." *Michigan v. Summers,* 452 U.S. 692, 711 n.4 (1981) (Stewart, J., dissenting)./ "The appropriate standard of review is whether the evidence, viewed in the light most favorable to the non-moving party, is such that *reasonable-minded* [read *reasonable*] jurors in the exercise of prudent judgment could not differ in their decision as to the facts." *Conam Alaska v. Bell Lavalin, Inc.,* 842 P.2d 148, 157 n.22 (Alaska 1992). See REDUNDANCY.

reasonableness; reasonability. The latter is a NEEDLESS VARIANT of the former.

reasonable person. Most modern American opinions refer to a *reasonable person* instead of a *reasonable man,* the age-old sexist standard, which Lord Radcliffe called "the anthropomorphic conception of justice." *Davis Contractors Ltd. v. Fareham U.D.C.,* [1956] A.C. 696, 728. (See SEXISM (B).) The reasonable person—a hypothetical legal standard—acts sensibly, takes proper but not excessive precautions, does things without serious delay, and weighs evidence carefully but not overskeptically. The reasonable person is neither perfect nor indifferent.

When the locution functions as a PHRASAL ADJECTIVE, it should be hyphenated—e.g.: "If Parliament had intended to require people to live up to the objective, *reasonable-man standard* it would surely have said so . . . ." Glanville Williams, *Criminal Law* 145 (2d ed. 1961).

reason . . . is because. This construction is loose, because *reason* implies *because* and vice-versa. After the noun *reason* plus a *be*-verb or other linking verb, a noun phrase, predicate adjective, or clause introduced by *that* should appear. E.g., "The *reason* that most of us chatter so much *is* not *because* [read *that*] we suppose ourselves more competent than counsel." Charles E. Wyzanski, Jr., "A Trial Judge," in *Whereas—A Judge's Premises* 3, 3 (1965)./ "The *reason* why words are so important *is because* [read *that*] words are the vehicle of thought." Lord Denning, *The Discipline of Law* 5 (1979).

Better yet, in the latter example, would be to delete *The reason why . . . is:* "Words are important because they are the vehicle of thought."

Variations on the phrase, such as *reason . . . is due to,* are no better—e.g.: "Two prosecutors stated in affidavits that the *reason* the state moved to dismiss the enhancement counts *was due to* [omit *due to*] difficulty of proof."

reason of for *rationale for* is an ARCHAISM. "Clearly, the *reason of* [read *rationale for*] section 2-202 is sensible and should be applied by analogy to article eight."

reason why; reason that. Both forms are correct—e.g.: "The district court found that there was no *reason that* [or *why*] Hauser could not have joined in her husband's earlier action."

It is an unfortunate SUPERSTITION that *reason why* is an objectionable REDUNDANCY. True, it is mildly redundant—in the same way as *time when* and *place where*—but it has long been idiomatic, and good writers regularly use the phrase:

- "The *reason why* a lawyer does not mention that his client wore a white hat when he made a contract . . . is that he foresees that the public force will act in the same way whatever his client had upon his head." Oliver W. Holmes, "The Path of the Law" (1897), in *Collected Legal Papers* 167, 168 (1952).
- "There is another *reason why* Austin's 'General Jurisprudence' cannot be called a philosophy." W.W. Buckland, *Some Reflections on Jurisprudence* 42 (1945).
- "And if he goes there and gets divorced there is no *reason why* the divorce should not be valid." Max Radin, *The Law and You* 65 (1948).
- "There are also various *reasons why* certain people may by rule be exempted from the normal workings of the criminal law." Morris R. Cohen, *Reason and Law* 51 (1961).
- "The other *reason why* we tend to relegate the fiction to the past lies in our failure to realize that the law will be faced, in the future, with essentially *new* situations." Lon L. Fuller, *Legal Fictions* 94 (1967).
- "Packer captured the *reason why* the humanitarian focus is erroneous . . . ." Peter W. Low et al., *Criminal Law: Cases and Materials* 26 (1982).
- "[T]he *reason why* the other is not liable is that he is an undisclosed principal . . . ." G.H. Treitel, *The Law of Contract* 634 (8th ed. 1991).

Moreover, *reason that* is often a poor substitute—as in any of the examples just quoted—just as *time that* and *place that* are poor substitutes when adverbials of time and place are called for. But cf. the indefensible REDUNDANCY in the phrase **reason . . . is because.**

rebellion. See **sedition.**

rebound; re-bound. See RE- PAIRS.

rebus, in. See **in rem.**

rebut; refute. *Rebut* means "to attempt to refute." *Refute* means "to defeat (countervailing arguments)." Thus one who *rebuts* certainly hopes to *refute;* it is immodest to assume, however, that one has *refuted* another's arguments. *Rebut* is sometimes wrongly written *rebutt.* See **refute.**

rebuttable presumption (= a legal presumption subject to valid rebuttal) becomes illogical when the phrase is turned into an adverb and a verb—e.g.: "Texas courts *rebuttably presume* such warnings will be read and heeded." This suggests that the courts *presume in a rebuttable manner,* which is not the sense; a better way of phrasing the thought is to write: "Texas courts *adopt the rebuttable presumption* that such warnings will be read and heeded." See **presumption.**

rebuttal; surrebuttal. *Rebuttal* (= the act of rebutting) is often used in legal writing, and with good reason: it is much broader than *rebutter,* q.v., which is the name of the pleading intended to rebut.

Surrebuttal is not an answer to a rebuttal; it is a NEEDLESS VARIANT of *surrebutter,* a common-law pleading. See COMMON-LAW PLEADINGS.

rebutter = (1) (formerly) a defendant's answer to a plaintiff's surrejoinder; the pleading that followed the rejoinder and surrejoinder, and that might in turn be answered by the surrebutter; or (2) one who rebuts. Sense (1) is the only strictly legal sense of the term. See -ER (B) & COMMON-LAW PLEADINGS.

receipt, as a verb, began as an Americanism in the 18th century and has now spread to BrE. It is commercialese, but there is no grammatical problem in writing, "The bill must be *receipted,*" or "The sale was *receipted.*" *Receipt* is ordinarily used in the PASSIVE VOICE: "The preceding sentence shall not be construed [see STATUTE DRAFTING (A)] to mean that new receipts are to be obtained each year from continuing employees who have previously been *receipted* for copies of identical provisions." Still, the PHRASAL VERB *to be receipted for* is a REDUNDANCY, as well as a graceless phrase. "Each certificate issued by the corporation shall *be receipted for* by the person receiving it or by his or her duly authorized agent." [Read *The person who receives a certificate issued by the organization, or his or her duly authorized agent, shall execute a receipt for it.*] Cf. **receiptor.**

receipt and sufficiency of which are hereby acknowledged. This recital, common in contractual language, is almost always unnecessary and unhelpful. And, when *is* appears instead of *are,* it is ungrammatical.

receipt of, be in. This insipid phrase, which usually occurs in letters, is to be avoided as OFFICIALESE or commercialese or LEGALESE.

receiptor (= a person who receipts property attached by a sheriff; a bailee) is noted as being an Americanism by the *OED.* It dates from the early 19th century. The *-or* spelling is preferred to *-er.* See **receipt.**

receivables (= debts owed to a business and regarded as assets) began in the mid-19th century as an Americanism but is now current in BrE as well. It is the antonym of *payables.* See ADJECTIVES (C).

receive. See **reception.**

receiver is used in both AmE and BrE in the specific legal sense of "a person appointed by a court, or by a corporation or other person, for the protection or collection of property." Usually the *receiver* administers the property of a bankrupt, or property that is the subject of litigation, pending the outcome of a lawsuit.

recense. See **revise.**

recension (= the revision of a text) is not to be confused with *rescission.* (See **rescission.**) E.g., "The *recension* of statute law is not only destructive but constructive when it takes the form of codifying and consolidating acts." Carleton K. Allen, *Law in the Making* 476 (7th ed. 1964).

reception is the term commonly used to denote the adoption of an existing legal system originally developed elsewhere. E.g., "It is more remarkable that this revived Justinian law should find a similar *reception* in Germany." James Hadley, *Introduction to Roman Law* 38 (N.Y., D. Appleton & Co. 1881)./ "Despite the efforts of early law reformers, all of the original states, and most of the later ones, adopted English common law insofar as it was deemed applicable to local conditions. This '*reception*' of the common law, as it came to be called, was accomplished either by express statutory or constitutional provision or by judicial decision." Peter W. Low et al., *Criminal Law: Cases and Materials* 40 (1982).

The corresponding verb, of course, is *receive*—e.g.: "[A]ccording to a theory [that] was popular half a century ago, the Canon Law of the Western Church was, even before the Reformation, not regarded as wholly binding on the ecclesiastical courts in England, but only to the extent to which it was '*received*' or acknowledged by courts in England." Edward Jenks, *The Book of English Law* 30 (P.B. Fairest ed., 6th ed. 1967)./ "To this day, an occasional case still turns on whether some statute or doctrine had been '*received*' as common law in this or that state." Lawrence M. Friedman, *A History of American Law* 111 (2d ed. 1985).

receptioning (= to do the job of a receptionist) is American law-firm cant that illustrates the same tendency in modern usage as *paralegaling* and *bailiffing,* qq.v. See NOUNS AS VERBS.

recidivate is a fancy word for *relapse, backslide, fall back into crime,* or *rape (etc.) again.* Invented in the early 1500s, it fell into disuse toward the end of the following century, but 20th-century legal writers have revived it—e.g.:

- "Dr. Bohn would not testify to a reasonable degree of medical or psychological certainty that there was a substantial likelihood Tweedy would *recidivate.*" *In re Tweedy,* 488 N.W.2d 528, 532 (Neb. 1992).
- "Because the issue under the Guidelines is whether the offender engaged in past criminal conduct and, thus, is likely to *recidivate,* such a challenge is relevant only if the offender did not engage in the underlying conduct." *U.S. v. Roman,* 989 F.2d 1117, 1124 (11th Cir. 1993) (Tjoflat, C.J., concurring).
- "[T]he trial court . . . should consider . . . the base rate statistics for violent behavior among individuals of this person's background (e.g., data showing the rate at which rapists *recidivate,* the correlation between age and criminal sexual activity, etc.) . . . ." *In re Linehan,* 518 N.W.2d 609, 614 (Minn. 1994).

recidivous; recidivist. The former is the preferred adjective. The latter is the noun meaning "one who habitually relapses into crime" (*OED*).

reciprocity; reciprocation. *Reciprocity* = (1) the state of being reciprocal; or (2) the mutual concession of advantages or privileges for purposes of commercial or diplomatic relations. *Reciprocation* = the action of doing something in return. Though *reciprocity* is by far the more common term, some legal writers seem to use *reciprocation* in its place, esp. in sense (2): "[N]either statute requires a *reciprocation* [read *reciprocity*] of the regional limitation." *Northeast Bancorp,*

Inc. v. Federal Reserve Sys., 472 U.S. 159, 175 (1985).

recision; recission. See **rescission.**

recital; recitation. These words overlap, but are distinguishable. The DRAFTING term is *recital,* referring to the preliminary statement in a deed or contract explaining the background of the transaction and showing the existence of facts, or, in pleading, introducing a positive allegation. E.g., "This version of the parties' proposed consent decree contains no *recital,* finding, or adjudication of any illegality."/ "*Recitations* [read *Recitals*] of consideration and use in a recorded deed are not binding upon a complainant who seeks a purchase money resulting trust." More generally, *recital* may mean "a rehearsal, account, or description of some thing, fact, or incident." E.g., "The facts are sordid, but a brief *recital* of them must be made."

Recitation often connotes an oral delivery before an audience, whether in the classroom or on stage. Yet it is more often the general noun meaning "the act of reciting": "The interrogator's *recitation* of the suspect's rights was sufficient."/ "The carnage caused by drunk driving is well documented and needs no detailed *recitation* here."

reckless. See **wanton.** For an interesting error, see **wreckless.**

recklessness. In legal contexts, this term is used with several gradations of meaning, but the primary emerging sense is that recklessness occurs when the actor does not desire the consequence but foresees the possibility and consciously takes the risk. Another term for *recklessness* is *advertent negligence.* Cf. **carelessness.**

reckon (= to count or compute) is probably an ARCHAISM. E.g., "The law *reckons* in days, not commonly in fractions of days, and an agreement made at six o'clock in the morning stands on the same footing with one made at eleven o'clock in the evening." The word is dialectal in the sense "to suppose, think" <I reckon the judges will affirm>.

reclaim; re-claim. See RE- PAIRS.

recognizance; reconnaissance; reconnoisance. *Recognizance* = a bond or obligation, made in court, by which a person (called the *recognizor*) promises to perform some act or observe some condition (as to appear when called on, to pay a debt, or to keep the peace). E.g., "The suspect was released on his own *recognizance.*"

In BrE, the *-g-* in *recognisance* (as it is usu. spelled in BrE) is silent, reflecting that the current spelling is really only a latter-day Latinization of the spelling of the LAW FRENCH term *conusance.* But in AmE, the *-g-* is regularly sounded.

Reconnaissance = a preliminary survey; a military or intelligence-gathering examination of a region. *Reconnoisance* is an older spelling of *reconnaissance;* it is also a NEEDLESS VARIANT of *recognizance* and of *recognition.* The verb corresponding to *reconnaissance* is *reconnoiter, -re,* q.v. See **cognizance (A).**

recollect. A. And *remember.* The distinction is a subtle one worth observing. To *remember* is to recall what is ready at hand in one's memory. To *recollect* is to find something stored further back in the mind.

B. And re-collect. See RE- PAIRS.

recommend against. *Recommend* is a word with positive connotations; in all the examples in the *OED,* it is construed with *to.* The antonym of *recommend* is *discommend,* which should appear in place of *recommend against* in the following sentence: "Shortly thereafter, 45 college hours were required for applicants, even though civil-service officials *recommended against* [read *discommended*] this increase in the number of required hours." See **discommend.**

recompensable is a NEEDLESS VARIANT of *compensable*—e.g.: "The determination of the *recompensable* [read *compensable*] cost of the cleanup remains to be determined at a hearing subsequent to the filing of this opinion and order." *State ex rel. Celebrezze v. Specialized Finishers, Inc.,* 604 N.E.2d 842, 852 (Ohio Ct. Common Pleas 1991). See **compensable (A).**

recompense. A. Generally. This word, both a transitive verb ("to repay, compensate") and a noun ("payment in return for something"), is a FORMAL WORD that is equivalent to but more learned than *compensate* or *compensation.* In BrE the noun is sometimes spelled *-ce.*

Recompense is used more frequently as a noun than as a verb—e.g.: "As recompense for the loss of the M(O)ther, the child is promised access to other women and entrance into the society of Fathers through exchange." Jeanne L. Schroeder, *Virgin Territory: Margaret Radin's Imagery of Personal Property as the Inviolate Feminine Body,* 79 Minn. L. Rev. 55, 160 (1994)./ "For students who are the victims of peer harassment, a variety of means (failing formal resolution), exist to ameliorate the abusive environment or to seek *recompense* for injuries." Gail Sorenson, *Peer Sexual Harassment: Remedies and Guidelines Under Federal Law,* 92 Ed. Law Rep. 1, 16 (1994).

Although *compensate* is a much more common verb than *recompense,* the latter does frequently appear—more commonly in law than elsewhere. E.g., "It is possible to find exceptions, to be sure: a famous author tells a dunce tale at the expense of an industrial worker who loses a finger by accident, is *recompensed,* and decides to lose another . . . ." Richard Delgado & Jean Stefancic, *Scorn,* 35 Wm. & Mary L. Rev. 1061, 1092 (1994)./ "Section 1983 damages have the dual advantages over Rule 11 sanctions of (1) providing a discrete harm to be *recompensed,* and (2) supporting an award that incorporates the significance of constitutional violations." James W. Harper, Note, *Attorneys as State Actors,* 21 Hastings Const. L.Q. 405, 436 (1994). See **compensate (B).**

B. And Its Needless Variants. Both as a noun and as a verb, *recompense* has its NEEDLESS VARIANTS. The variant noun is *recompensation*—e.g.: "[T]he trial court is not compelled to order total *recompensation* [read *recompense* or *compensation*], but may order a modification with respect to any period . . . ." *Reid v. Reid,* 409 S.E.2d 155, 169 (Va. Ct. App. 1991)./ "Also, the trial court awarded Travelers $70,330.78 in *recompensation* [read *compensation*]." *Scamardo v. New Orleans Stevedoring Co.,* 595 So. 2d 1242, 1245 (La. Ct. App. 1992).

The needless verb is *recompensate*—e.g.: "If the employee is then unable to utilize her partial earning capacity because of her disability, an award of temporary disability benefits does not *recompensate* [read *recompense* or *compensate*] her for her permanent disability and no double compensation takes place." *Ahoe v. Quality Park Prods.,* 258 N.W.2d 885, 890 (Minn. 1977).

recompensive (= compensatory) is a rare term whose use in modern prose strikes the reader as a straining for the recherché term.

reconnaissance; reconnoisance. See **recognizance.**

reconnoiter; reconnoitre. The verb form corresponding to the noun *reconnaissance* is preferably spelled *-er* in AmE and *-re* in BrE. See **recognizance.**

record. **A. Usage and Sense.** *Record* frequently occurs in law in the phrases *in the record* and *of record* <attorney of record>. Usually *record* refers to the official report of the proceedings in any case, and it has three parts: all the filed papers in the case; the verbatim transcript of hearings, conferences, and testimony; and the tangible exhibits that the parties put in evidence. The *record* is read on appeal by the judges who review it for reversible errors. In administrative law, *record* refers to all considerations actually taken into account in deciding an issue.

Record has come to be used adjectivally as shorthand for *in the record.* E.g., "We find no *record support* [i.e., support in the record] for this contention." It is preferable not to collapse the prepositional phrase into a nominal adjective in this way because some readers will likely have a MISCUE. See NOUN PLAGUE.

B. And *transcript; report of proceedings; statement of facts.* Generally, a *transcript* or *report of proceedings* is an official copy of the recorded proceedings in a trial or hearing. But in Texas, the phrase *statement of facts* carries that sense, whereas *transcript* refers to the following: "in civil cases, the live pleadings upon which the trial was held; in criminal cases, copies of the indictment or information, any special pleas and motions of the defendant which were presented to the court and overruled, and any written waivers; the court's docket sheet; the charge of the court and the verdict of the jury, or the court's findings of fact and conclusions of law; the court's judgment or other order appealed from; any motion for new trial [etc.] . . . ." Tex. R. App. P. 51(a). In other words, Texas lawyers use *transcript* when other lawyers would use *record.* See **report of proceedings.**

C. BrE Pronunciation. In British legal English, the noun *record* "is pronounced like the verb, with the stress on the second syllable." Glanville Williams, *Learning the Law* 63 (11th ed. 1982).

recordation; recordal. The latter is not a proper word, though it has erroneously appeared in such phrases as "*recordal* of a trademark with the Treasury Department." *Recordation* is the word. E.g., "The supplemental complaint requests that both the Customs Service and Art's Way remove the *recordal* [read *recordation*] of the DION registration to permit unimpeded entry of the machinery into the United States." *B. & R. Choiniere Ltd. v. Art's-Way Mfg. Co.,* 207 U.S.P.Q. (BNA) 969, 971 (N.D.N.Y. 1979).

recorder = (1) in BrE, a practicing barrister who acts as a usu. part-time judge, esp. in a crown court; or (2) in AmE, a person with whom a deed or mortgage to be recorded is deposited.

record reveals that, the. This phrase is responsible for more sprawling sentences than perhaps any other stock phrase in appellate judicial opinions. And it is redundant: any facts being related by an appellate court *must* (with a few exceptions) be revealed in the record.

recount; re-count. See RE- PAIRS.

recourse; resort. *Recourse* = (1) application to a person or entity for help; or (2) the right of a holder of a negotiable instrument to demand payment from the drawer and endorsers when the first liable party fails to pay. The term is used in the idiomatic phrases *have recourse to* and *without recourse.* The latter is the peculiarly legal phrase that, when added to the endorsement of commercial paper, protects the endorser from liability to the indorsee and later holders. *Resort* (= that which one turns to for refuge or aid) is closely related to sense (1) of *recourse.*

recover (= to secure by legal process) takes *from* or *against* in modern usage. The collocation *recover of* is an ARCHAISM for *recover from.* E.g., "It is equally well settled that the reasonable expenses incurred by an indemnitee in defending a claim against him may be *recovered of* [read *recovered from*] his indemnitor."/ "This is an action of tort to *recover of* [read *recover from*] the defendant damages for a malicious abuse of process." Cf. **of (E).**

recoverable = compensable, q.v. The term originally meant "capable of being recovered or regained," but was extended in legal usage, because of the nature of damages, to "capable of being legally obtained." E.g., "The rule is that special damages for breach of contract are not *recoverable* unless they can fairly and reasonably be considered as arising naturally from the breach." Strictly speaking, the special damages are not to be *recovered,* for they are being awarded for the first time to the complainant; but this usage is quite permissible in the legal idiom.

recover back might appear to be a legal REDUNDANCY. E.g., "Generally, a co-owner who pays a disproportionate share of the necessary expenses of the property may *recover back* the excess in an action for contribution, accounting, or partition."

But in common-law terminology a distinction exists between *to recover* (= to obtain, as in recovering damages) and *to recover back* (= to secure the return of, as in recovering back money paid incorrectly, as by mistake). E.g., "The general rule is that money paid or property transferred under an illegal contract cannot be *recovered back.*"

recover of. See **recover.**

recreate; re-create. The former means either "(of a pastime or relaxation) to refresh or agreeably occupy" or "to amuse oneself, indulge in recreation" (*COD*); the latter means "to create anew." The hyphen makes a great difference: "The words of the witness cannot 'give' or *recreate* [read *re-create*] the 'facts,' that is, the objective situations or happenings about which the witness is testifying."/ "The company's termination of the positions was a pretext for unfair labor practices, which demonstrates that these positions must now be *re-created* to provide an efficacious remedy." See RE- PAIRS.

recreational; recreative. The former is the preferred adjective corresponding to the noun *recreation.* E.g., "During this additional time the employees variously slept, ate, played cards or engaged in other *recreative* [read *recreational*] activities." *Madera Police Officers' Ass'n v. City of Madera,* 194 Cal. Rptr. 648, 651 (Ct. App. 1983).

recriminatory; recriminative. The latter is a NEEDLESS VARIANT.

rectification = a court's equitable correction of a contractual term that is misstated, as where the rent is wrongly recorded in a lease or the area of land is recited incorrectly in a deed. To a degree, this term applies also to statutory construction—e.g.: "[I]t would be a mistake to suppose that the Courts never indulge in milder acts of *rectification.* Something of the sort happens whenever 'and' is read as 'or' or vice versa; but these milder acts of *rectification* are most exceptional." Rupert Cross, *Statutory Interpretation* 25 (1976).

recur. See **reoccur.**

recurrence; recurrency; reoccurrence. *Recurrence* is the preferred form, *reoccurrence* being a secondary variant meriting only careful avoidance. *Recurrency* is a NEEDLESS VARIANT.

recusal; recusation; recusement; recusancy; recusance. The preferred nominal form of the verb *recuse* (= to remove [oneself] as a judge considering a case) is *recusal,* though its earliest known use is as recent as 1950: "On the 13th of April, Judge Longshore filed an order of *recusal* accompanied by an order vacating his former order . . . ." *Methvin v. Haynes,* 46 So. 2d 815, 817 (Ala. 1950).

Recusation and *recusement* (the latter not listed in the *OED*) are now NEEDLESS VARIANTS in common-law contexts. *Recusation* is not uncommon, esp. in civil-law writing. See, e.g., *State v. DeMaio,* 58 A. 173 (N.J. 1904); *Stewart v. Reid,* 38 So. 70 (La. 1905). Although *recusation* is understandably common in Louisiana, it persists, oddly, in other jurisdictions. E.g., "[T]he plaintiff asserts the 'essence' of his motion for *recusation* [read *recusal*] is what the trial justice 'himself said and how he has ruled.'" *Barber v. Town of Fairfield,* 486 A.2d 150, 152 (Me. 1985)./ "The trial judge admitted making these remarks upon defendant's motion for . . . continuance and *recusation* [read *recusal*]." *State v. Majors,* 325 S.E.2d 689, 690 (N.C. Ct. App. 1985)./ "[O]nce a prosecutor recuses himself, the *recusation* [read *recusal*] applies to all aspects of the case." *Daugherty v. State,* 466 N.E.2d 46, 49 (Ind. Ct. App. 1984)./ "Canon 3C(1)(a) is basically a broad standard by which a judge should sua sponte [q.v.] determine the matter of *self-recusation* [read *recusal*]." *State v. Smith,* 242 N.W.2d 320, 323 (Iowa 1976). For an example of INELEGANT VARIATION with *recusal* and *recusation,* see *Reilly v. Southeastern Pa. Transp. Auth.,* 489 A.2d 1291, 1297–98 (Pa. 1985).

Recusement appears far less commonly—e.g.: "[P]laintiff filed a challenge for Mr. Booker's *recusement* [read *recusal*] upon the ground that he had prejudged the case." *Cobble Close Farm v. Board of Adjustment,* 92 A.2d 4, 10 (N.J. 1952)./ "Following our opinion . . . , the Honorable Paul M. Marko . . . entered an order of *recusement* [read *recusal*] in the fall of 1982 . . . ." *Irwin v. Irwin,* 455 So. 2d 1118, 1119 (Fla. Dist. Ct. App. 1984).

Recusancy is a different word, meaning "obstinate refusal to comply." *Recusance* is a NEEDLESS VARIANT of *recusancy.*

recuse; disqualify. The two words are not quite interchangeable in modern legal usage. *Disqualify* might always be used in place of *recuse,* but the reverse does not hold true. *Disqualify,* the broader term, may be used of witnesses, for example, as well as of judges, whereas *recuse* is applied only to someone who sits in judgment (usu. judges or jurors).

Recuse is almost invariably reflexive; that is, judges are said to *recuse themselves. Disqualify* may also be used reflexively <under these circumstances, the judge should disqualify herself from sitting in the case>. Just as commonly, though, lawyers use this verb nonreflexively <his years began to disqualify him from more active work>.

Recuse is by far the more interesting word, primarily because of its inadequate treatment in English-language dictionaries. Both *recuse* and its legal cognates are missing from *AHD* and were not included in Merriam-Webster dictionaries until the publication of *W10* (1993). The word might seem to be moribund in BrE, for the *Chambers 20th Century Dictionary* says: "to reject, object to (e.g. a judge) (arch.)." The sense of objecting to is fairly rare—e.g.: "[One-half of the plantation] with lien privilege to contribute to or *recuse* the contribution of the sum of [$7,347.30] . . . ." *Grant v. Buckner* 172 U.S. 232, 237 (1898) (quoting trial-court decree).

How the word evolved from that sense of objecting, as reflected in the *OED,* to the modern sense is curious indeed. Today, when we say *recuse,* we almost always mean "to remove (oneself) as judge in a legal matter." The one exception appears to be the phrase *motion to recuse,* in which the meaning is "to seek to have (a judge) removed from participating in the adjudication of a legal matter." Thus we encounter specimens such as these:

- "This motion denied, the trustee moved to *recuse* the examiner for bias and prejudice." *N.L.R.B. v. Phelps,* 136 F.2d 562, 565 (5th Cir. 1943).
- "Motion to *recuse* THE CHIEF JUSTICE denied." *Kerpelman v. Attorney Grievance Comm'n,* 450 U.S. 970, 970 (Order of 2 March 1981).
- "Motion to *recuse* JUSTICE POWELL denied." *Ernest v. United States Attorney,* 474 U.S. 1016, 1016 (Order of 9 Dec. 1985).

These are the exceptions, however, in modern usage. Today, 99% of the occurrences of *recuse* are reflexive.

How, then, did we get from (1) "to object to (a judge) as prejudiced" (*OED*), to (2) "to remove (oneself) as an adjudicator"? Surprisingly, the Supreme Court appears to have deprecated the newer meaning just after the turn of the 20th century, by enclosing the word in telltale quotation marks: "The plaintiffs, when the case was called for trial, filed a written motion or petition, challenging the right of the presiding judge to hear the case, and praying that he '*recuse*' himself." *McGuire v. Blount,* 199 U.S. 142, 143 (1905).

Yet a reporter of the Court's opinions had used the word in this sense more than a half-century before, in what appears to be the earliest use of the reflexive: "The judge *recused* himself, and the suit, by consent of the parties, was transferred for trial to the District Court." *Fourniquet v. Perkins,* 48 U.S. (7 How.) 160, 165 (1849) (reporter's rendition of appellant's argument).

In the 19th and early 20th centuries, the word was not at all common. In fact, a computer search reveals only 38 cases in which the uninflected verb *recuse* appeared before 1950, and 3,219 cases between 1950 and 1989. The paucity of uses before 1950 may explain the notation in *W2* that *recuse* is "obs. exc. in Civil and Canon Law."

Because *recuse* is virtually always reflexive today, it cannot be used in the PASSIVE VOICE, unlike *disqualify.* To say that a judge is *disqualified* is perfectly idiomatic, but to say one is *recused* is not.

When used reflexively, both verbs sometimes

take an understood object. These are nothing more than lawyers' elliptical expressions: "Had Black *disqualified,* he would have departed from the traditions of 150 years." John P. Frank, *Disqualification of Judges,* 56 Yale L.J. 605, 636 (1947)./ "[R]elief . . . for failure to *recuse* on the merits." 13A Charles A. Wright et al., *Federal Practice and Procedure* § 3550, at 627 n.8 (1984).

recusement. See **recusal.**

redact. See **revise.**

redeemable; redemptible. Writers should eschew the latter; it is pedantic, unnecessary, and irredeemable.

redemption, equity of. See **cloud on title.**

redemptive; redemptory; redemptional. *Redemptive* = tending to redeem, redeeming. *Redemptory* is a NEEDLESS VARIANT. *Redemptional* = of or pertaining to redemption—e.g.: "Having been divested of ownership prior to the sale and having incurred penalties for delinquent nonpayments which it has paid, its personal obligation for the *redemptional* penalty became a myth." *Weston Inv. Co. v. State,* 180 P.2d 962, 965 (Cal. Ct. App. 1947).

redhibition. Louisiana is the only American jurisdiction in which this civil-law term is used. It denotes the voidance of a sale as the result of an action brought on account of some defect in something sold, on grounds that the defect renders the thing sold either useless or so imperfect that the buyer would not have purchased it if the buyer had known of the defect. *Redhibitory* is the usual adjectival form.

redintegration. See **reintegration.**

redirect is a common shorthand form of *redirect examination,* which in American usage follows cross-examination. E.g., "Often the attorney, in cross-examination of a witness, produces from him statements that create an impression favorable to his own client. If the impression is misleading, it may lodge in the minds of the jurors and become ineradicable unless corrected; to correct it, the opposing attorney may readdress additional questions to his own witness. This is called the *redirect.*" C. Gordon Post, *An Introduction to the Law* 121 (1963)./ "On *redirect,* the Government inquired whether Lowe had any reason to try to protect himself. . . ." *U.S. v. Edwards,* 716 F.2d 822, 825 (11th Cir. 1983). The equivalent BrE term is *re-examination,* q.v. Cf. **direct.**

redound, now used most commonly in the CLICHÉ *to redound to the benefit of* (which is verbose for *to benefit*), may be used also in negative senses <to redound against or to the shame of>.

redressable; redressible. The former spelling is standard.

red tape. Lawyers and government officials formerly used red ribbons (called "tapes") to tie together their papers. Gradually during the 19th century, these red ribbons came to symbolize rigid adherence to time-consuming rules and regulations. Writers such as Scott, Longfellow, and Dickens used the term *red tape,* and now it has become universal—but its origins widely forgotten.

reduce should not be used as a reflexive verb when the subject is inanimate—e.g.: "The question *reduces itself* [read *is reducible* or *may be reduced*] to one of statutory interpretation."/ "The government's case *reduces itself* [read *is reducible*] to this: the defendant was in a public restaurant at a time when someone said that a drug deal might be going on."

REDUNDANCY. Washington Irving wrote that "redundancy of language is never found with deep reflection. Verbiage may indicate observation, but not thinking. He who thinks much says but little in proportion to his thoughts." Lawyers should think much about those words, and begin to write less. (See CUTTING OUT THE CHAFF.) Following are some of the typical manifestations of redundancy in legal writing.

A. General Redundancy. This linguistic pitfall is best exemplified, rather than discoursed on:

- "No one need fight city hall unnecessarily." [Read *One need not fight city hall.* Or: *It is unnecessary to fight city hall.*]/ "This type of obligation imposes an undue restriction on alienation or an *onerous burden* in perpetuity." (*Onus = burden,* hence *onerous burden* is redundant.)
- "National is discharged from all its *obligations* as *obligor.*" [Read *National is discharged as obligor.* Or: *National is discharged from all its obligations.*]
- "By allowing representatives of the tenants, who obviously *shared a common interest* [read *shared an interest* or *had an interest in common*], to maintain a single action, the equity court eliminated the necessity of trying the common questions repetitively in separate actions."
- "These two paragraphs are the least legible and the most difficult to read [omit *and the most difficult to read*] in the instrument, but they are

most important in the evaluation of the rights of the contesting parties." (In context, the sentence related exclusively to *legibility* and had nothing to do with *readability.*)

- "The mere fact that the association acquired its knowledge *later in point of time* [omit *in point of time*] gave the appellant no superior legal position over the association."
- "The purpose of the statute is to ensure a high standard of education for Texas citizens *while at the same time* [omit *at the same time*] lessening the incentive for aliens to enter the United States illegally."

See **while at the same time** & **oftentimes.**

B. Awkward Repetitions. Samuel Johnson once advised his readers to "avoid ponderous ponderosity." The repetition of roots was purposeful, of course. Many legal writers, however, engage in such repetitions with no sense of irony, as in the phrases *build a building, refer to a reference, point out points, an individualistic individual.* As great a writer as he was, Chief Justice Marshall seems not to have had a stylistic design in the following repetition, though he may have been striving for a rhetorical effect: "The question is, *in truth, a question of supremacy* [read *is, in truth, one of supremacy*] . . . ." *McCulloch v. Maryland,* 17 U.S. (4 Wheat.) 316, 433 (1819). In the sentences that follow, however, the repetitions are mere thoughtless errors:

- "*Said use of the trademark* [read *The trademark*] has been *used* in foreign commerce and interstate commerce in the United States continuously since 1926." The *use* has not been used, but rather the *trademark.* This sentence exemplifies one strain of ILLOGIC.
- "The plaintiffs' number was number 37." [Read *The plaintiffs' number was 37.*]
- "*This judicially required warrant requirement* [read *This judicial requirement of a warrant*] has been described as a 'narrow one.'" / "Notice was mailed by registered mail." [Read *Notice was sent by registered mail.*]
- "*The basis of his liability here was based* [read *His liability was based*] on a legal relationship only, not his primary negligence."
- "The subdivided lots were sold as individual lots *with deed restrictions restricting development to single-family homes* [read *with deeds restricting development to single-family homes*]."
- "The resolution of the board of directors accepting property for shares must *specify the specific* [omit *specific*] property involved."
- "By cheating, he avoids pursuing *knowledge* that he, according to his transcript, should *know* [read *have*]." (One does not know knowledge; one has it.)

See **injunction enjoining.**

C. Common Redundancies. Many of these are treated in separate entries. It is useful to be aware that phrases such as the following are redundant: *named nominee, adult parent* (but maybe this is no longer redundant), *to plead a plea, cost-expensive, active agent, end result, erroneous mistake, integral part, past history* (arguably established), *connect up* or *together, future forecast, merge together, mingle together, join together* (arguably acceptable), *mix together.* For idiomatic redundancies in the form of coupled synonyms, see DOUBLETS, TRIPLETS, AND SYNONYM-STRINGS.

redundancy pay. See **severance pay.**

reek; wreak. These homophones are occasionally confused. *Reek* = to give off an odor or vapor. As a noun, *reek* = an odorous vapor. *Wreak* = to inflict <to wreak havoc>.

reenactment is now written as a solid—without a hyphen after *re.* See PUNCTUATION (F).

re-enforce. See **reinforce.**

re-enter; re-entry. Both terms are best hyphenated.

re-establish should be so hyphenated.

re-examination, primarily a BrE term, is equivalent to the AmE term *redirect examination.* Following are examples of the noun and verb forms: "In *re-examination,* as in examination in chief, leading questions are ordinarily not permitted, unless they concern some matter not in dispute, when they are allowed in order to save time." Pendleton Howard, *Criminal Justice in England* 367 (1931)./ "Witnesses examined in open court must be first examined in chief, then cross-examined, and then *re-examined.*" (Eng.) See **direct examination** & **redirect.**

referable; referrable; referible. The preferred form is *referable,* which is accented on the first syllable; otherwise the final *-r-* would be doubled. The sense is "capable of being referred to." E.g., "The maxim of clean hands will not be invoked unless the inequitable conduct sought to be attributed to plaintiff is *referable* to the very transaction that is the source of the instant controversy."

Referrable often mistakenly appears; the form is old, but has long been held inferior to *referable.* E.g., "The only other causes of action pleaded by plaintiff *referrable* [read *referable*] to reimbursement are those of constructive fraud arising out of Tony's alleged operation of the corporation as his alter ego."/ "After review of the procedure followed, the board decided that the dispute was not *referrable* [read *referable*] to a public law board for reconsideration on the merits."

refer back is a common REDUNDANCY, *refer* alone nearly always being sufficient. E.g., "As to the use of memoranda, *refer back to* [read *refer to*] *Ward v. Morr Transfer & Storage Co.,* at page 446 *supra.*"/ "Section 72411.5 simply *refers us back to* [read *refers us to*] the contract." Cf. **relate back.** See **return back** & **revert (B).**

Refer back may be justified in those rare instances in which it means "to send back to one who or that which has previously been involved," as here: "The case is simply *referred back* to the arbitrator for a rewording of his opinion."

reference, as a verb meaning "to provide with references," is defensible. E.g., "The cross-*referenced* statute contains two subsections." It should not, however, be used for *refer,* as here: "He stated that, without *referencing* [read *referring* to] that file, he could not answer the question." See NOUNS AS VERBS.

reference, n. See **allude (A)** & **referral.**

referendum. Pl. *-da, -dums.* The English plural *-dums* seems to be on the rise—e.g.: "The most recent innovation of holding consultative *referendums* may also have come to have some impact . . . ." P.S. Atiyah, *Law and Modern Society* 107 (1983)./ "The main novelty in the new agreement is that . . . *referendums* would be held . . . ." Alan Riding, *Muslims and Serbs in Bosnian Accord,* N.Y. Times, 17 Sept. 1993, at A1. See PLURALS (A).

referrable. See **referable.**

referral; reference. Both mean "the act of referring." *Reference* is the broader, general term. *Referral,* which began as an Americanism in the early 20th century but now is used commonly in BrE as well, means specifically "the referring to a third party of personal information concerning another" or "the referring of a person to an expert or specialist for advice."

reflection; reflexion. The former spelling is preferred in both AmE and BrE. *Reflexion* was formerly common in British writing. Fowler recommended *-ction* in all senses.

reform; re-form. See RE- PAIRS.

refoulement /ri-*fowl*-mənt/ is a French term meaning "expulsion or return of a refugee from one state to another where his or her life or liberty would be threatened." It originally appeared as a title for Article 33 of the 1951 Geneva Convention Relating to the Status of Refugees, which reads: "No contracting state shall expel or return ('*refouler*') a refugee in any manner whatsoever to the frontiers of territories where his life or freedom would be threatened." (See *Lin v. Rinaldi,* 361 F. Supp. 177, 183 (D.N.J. 1973).) The title of that article of the Convention, *Refoulement,* is enclosed in quotation marks, no doubt signifying that in 1951 it was taken as a foreign word.

Its earliest known use as an English term, in the negative form, appears in *Chun v. Sava,* 708 F.2d 869, 877 n.25 (2d Cir. 1983): "[T]he United States appears to recognize a liberty interest, the right of *nonrefoulement* for a refugee." See also *Ramirez-Osorio v. I.N.S.,* 745 F.2d 937, 944 (5th Cir. 1984) ("[T]here is a sufficiently secured right of *nonrefoulement* . . . to give rise to a protectible liberty interest"). The word is yet to be recorded in an English dictionary.

refractory; refractive. These terms have undergone DIFFERENTIATION. *Refractory* = stubborn, unmanageable, rebellious. E.g., "Under such circumstances the disappointed legatee may in a court of equity compel the sequestration of the legacy to the *refractory* legatee for the purpose of diminishing the amount of his disappointment." *Refractive* = that refracts light.

refrain; restrain. Both mean generally "to put restraints upon," but *refrain* is used of oneself in the sense "to abstain" <he refrained from exchanging scurrilities with his accuser>, whereas *restrain* is used of another <the police illegally restrained the complainant from going into the stadium>.

refutation; refutal. The latter is an ill-formed NEEDLESS VARIANT of *refutation.* It is hardly ubiquitous, but it has turned up in some unlikely places—e.g.:

- "The majority determined the second clause to be a direct *refutal* [read *refutation*] of the Court's holding in *General Electric Co. v. Gilbert.*" Cathy M. Sellers, Note, *State Laws Permitting Preferential Treatment of Pregnant Employees Are Valid Under the Pregnancy Discrimination Act,* 15 Fla. St. U.L. Rev. 549, 561 (1987).
- "An evaluation is not subject to complete objective confirmation or *refutal* [read *refutation*]." *U.S. v. Jones,* 856 F.2d 146, 151 (11th Cir. 1988).

- "[A given book discusses] criticisms of Savigny's ideals and present[s] selected *refutals* [read *refutations*] by Savigny." Stephen A. Siegel, *Lochner Era Jurisprudence and the American Constitutional Tradition,* 70 N.C. L. Rev. 1, 76 n.384 (1991).

refutative; refutatory. The latter is a NEEDLESS VARIANT.

refute is not synonymous with *rebut.* It does not mean merely "to counter an argument," but "to disprove beyond doubt; to prove a statement false." Yet the word is commonly misused for *rebut,* as here: "The findings of the Commissioner carry a presumption of correctness and the taxpayer has the burden of *refuting* [read *rebutting*] them."/ "Appellant was allowed to put on witnesses to *refute* [read *rebut*] the sexual harassment charges, and he or his lawyer, or both, were present to cross-examine all the university's witnesses." See **rebut.**

In other contexts, the word seems to be misused for *reject*—e.g.: "Two-thirds of people *refuted* [read *rejected*] [Nicholas Ridley's] belief that European Monetary Union is a 'German racket to take over the whole of Europe' . . . ." Toby Helm, *Majority Back Euro Ideals,* Sunday Telegraph, 15 July 1990, at 1.

regard. A. As a Noun in the Phrases *with regard to* and *in regard to.* These two phrases are correct, but the forms *with regards to* and *in regards to* are, to put it charitably, poor usages—e.g.: "*With regards to* [read *With regard to*] the 1962 adoption of the at-large election scheme, plaintiffs argue with some merit that more should have been said about this event." The acceptable forms are best used as introductory phrases. Usually, however, they may advantageously be replaced by some simpler phrase such as *concerning, regarding, considering,* or even the simple prepositions *in, about,* or *for.*

The plural form, *regards,* is acceptable only in the phrase *as regards.* In other words, *with regards to* is bad form—e.g.: "*With regards to* [read *With regard to*] the 1962 adoption of the at-large election scheme, plaintiffs argue with some merit that more should have been said about this event."/ "He became furious at the mere mention of George F. Will, the columnist who accused him recently of 'judicial exhibitionism' *with regards to* [read *with regard to*] his trade-agreement ruling." Ruth M. Bond, *At Center of Trade-Accord Storm, Judge Bristles but Watches Image,* N.Y. Times, 17 Sept. 1993, at B11. See **as regards, in regards to & respect.**

B. As a Verb in the Phrases *highly regarded* and *widely regarded.* The verb *regard* commonly appears in these two combinations. The one phrase, *highly regarded,* is a vague expression of praise; the other, *widely regarded as* ——, usu. ends (i.e., the blank is usu. filled) with words of praise—though it would certainly be possible to say that someone is *widely regarded as beneath contempt.* It is a mistake, however, to truncate the latter phrase—to say *widely regarded* in place of *highly regarded:* "Crotty has had four major jury trials since leaving the firm, and he's *widely regarded* [read *highly regarded*] in both the plaintiffs' bar and the defense bar."

regardless (= without regard to) should not be used for *despite* (= in spite of). E.g., "The appellants voted to reject the plan, reiterating the grounds for their suit against Martin; *regardless of* [read *despite*] the appellants' vote, the plan was approved with two-thirds of the creditors voting for the plan." See **irregardless.**

regardless whether is incorrect for *regardless of whether.* E.g., "*Regardless whether* [read *Regardless of whether*] COGSA or Texas state law controls, appellee is not liable for any damages caused by the delay." See **whether.**

regards. See **regard (A) & as regards.**

regard to, in; with regard to. See **in regards to & regard (A).**

regist(e)rable. See **registrable.**

register; registrar. Both forms are used in referring to the governmental officer who keeps official records. The *OED* notes that *register* was commonly used in this sense from 1580 to 1800 and that *registrar* is now the usual word. But in AmE *register* retains vitality: various levels of government have *registers of deeds, registers of wills, registers of copyrights, registers of patents,* and the like. As a matter of AmE usage, a *registrar* is usu. a school official, whereas a *register* is usu. one who records documents for state or local government.

Apart from the agent-noun sense, the general meaning of *register* today is "a book or other record in which entries are made during the course of business." E.g., "A *register* of the proprietors of patents is kept at the Patent Office, and all assignments, licences, amendments, and revocations must be entered therein." 2 E.W. Chance, *Principles of Mercantile Law* 160 (1951).

registrable, not *registerable,* is the preferred spelling—e.g.: "Since 1925 restrictive covenants have been *registerable* [read *registrable*] . . . ." P.S. Atiyah, *An Introduction to the Law of Contract* 284 (3d ed. 1981).

registrant */rej-i-strənt/* does not rhyme, in the final syllable, with *restaurant.*

registrar. See **register.**

registrate is an ill-conceived BACK-FORMATION from *registration,* the verb *register* being standard—e.g.: "[O]wners of realty interposed defense that broker had operated under an assumed name without filing or *registrating* [read *registering*] the name . . . ." *Rathbun v. Hagn,* 99 N.E.2d 567, 567 syl. 2 (Ill. App. Ct. 1951). It is true, however, that *registrate* is correctly used when denoting the setting of pipe-organ stops.

regress. See **egress.**

regretful; regrettable. Errors made are *regrettable;* the persons who have committed them, assuming a normal level of contrition, are *regretful.* But writers often misuse *regretful* for *regrettable*—e.g:

- "The psychiatrists all agreed that it was not likely that the appellant would have had a lucid moment on the date of this *regretful* [read *regrettable*] incident." *Harris v. State,* 648 S.W.2d 47, 50 (Ark. 1983) (Purtle, J., dissenting).
- "This is the fourth time the Court has sustained the imposition of the death penalty. *Regretfully* [read *Regrettably*], its decision does nothing to clarify the confusion or to harmonize the inconsistencies of the Court's capital-murder jurisprudence." *State v. DiFrisco,* 645 A.2d 734, 773 (N.J. 1994) (Handler, J., dissenting).
- "*Regretfully* [read *Regrettably*], a legislature is seldom called upon to decide between right and wrong . . . ." *State v. Gainer,* 447 S.E.2d 887, 897 (W. Va. 1994).

regulable = able to be regulated; susceptible to regulation. *Regulatable* is incorrect, but it does occur—e.g.: "'[C]ommercial speech' . . . was *regulatable* [read *regulable*] under the law at that time . . . ." *Insurance Adjustment Bureau v. Insurance Comm'r,* 542 A.2d 1317, 1319 n.2 (Pa. 1988). See -ATABLE.

regulatory; regulative. The two forms of the adjective are both common, but *regulatory* predominates. That form is accented in AmE on the first syllable */**reg**-yə-lə-tohr-ee/*, in BrE often on the third */reg-yə-**lay**-tə-ree/*.

reify (= to make material, or convert mentally into a thing) is transitive only. It is sometimes misused as an intransitive verb—e.g.: "As soon as Schultz's objective *reifies* [read *materializes*], critics will have a more solid basis on which to evaluate his policies."

reign. See **free reign & rein in.**

reimbursement. See **subrogation (C).**

reinforce (= to strengthen) is the preferred form, though the noun is *enforce,* not *inforce.* (Likewise with *reinstate.*) Rather than hyphenate or use a diaeresis and retain the *-e-* in such words (e.g., re-enforce, *reënforce*), the *-e-* in each word is changed to *-i-* when the prefix is added. *Re-enforce* (= to enforce again) is sometimes seen in AmE.

rein in, not *reign in,* is the correct form of the phrase meaning "to check, restrain." The metaphorical image is of the rider pulling on the reins of the horse to slow down (i.e., "hold your horses"). But many writers get it wrong—e.g.:

- "[A] scheme that mandates a death sentence either for a specific crime or when the sentencer finds the existence of specified aggravating factors and the absence of specified mitigating circumstances, while surely *reigning in* [read *reining in*] jury discretion, impermissibly limits the jury's ability to consider the moral culpability of the defendant . . . ." *Williams v. Chrans,* 742 F. Supp. 472, 498 (N.D. Ill. 1990) (citations omitted).
- "Regulatory schemes are necessary [for] . . . *reigning in* [read *reining in*] unbridled upset of the environment and its ecological systems by miners." *U.S. v. Doremus,* 658 F. Supp. 752, 755 (D. Idaho 1987). Notice the striking insensitivity to METAPHOR in this example: it is impossible to *rein in* (much less *reign in*) an *unbridled* horse—yet the writer has pushed the two images together. See VERBAL AWARENESS.
- "This statement was but an echo which *reigned in* [read *reined in*] the defense encampment by which it was environed." *Primeaux v. Leapley,* 502 N.W.2d 265, 275 (S.D. 1993) (Henderson, J., dissenting).

Cf. **free reign.**

reintegration; redintegration. *Reintegration* is the usual form of the word in the sense "the act of restoring to a state of wholeness; renewal; reconstruction." *Redintegration* was formerly more common in this sense; it is still used in scientific and other technical contexts.

reiterate; iterate. It is perhaps not too literalistic to use *iterate* in the sense "to repeat," and *reiterate* in the sense "to repeat a second time [i.e., to state a third time]." The distinction is observed only by the most punctilious writers, *reiterate* being the usual term in either sense.

reject. In contract law, this is the verb ordinarily used to describe what an offeree does in turning down an offer, or a buyer in refusing tendered goods.

rejoinder; surrejoinder. A *rejoinder,* in former practice, was the pleading served by a defendant in answer to the plaintiff's reply (the pleading in answer to the defense). A *surrejoinder* was a plaintiff's pleading in reply to a defendant's rejoinder. See -ER (B) & COMMON-LAW PLEADINGS.

reknowned. See **renowned.**

relate back is not a REDUNDANCY in law; rather, the phrase invokes the doctrine of *relation back,* q.v. "Whenever the claim or defense asserted in the amended pleading arose out of the conduct, transaction, or occurrence set forth or attempted to be set forth in the original pleading, the amendment *relates back* to the date of the original pleading." Fed. R. Civ. P. 15(c)./ "Because the 1982 mortgages are between different parties from the 1977 mortgages, their priority does not *relate back.*"

relatedly is an adverb inferior even to *reportedly*—e.g.: "*Relatedly,* Idaho also adheres to the tenets of concurrent causation." Some better connective such as *moreover* or *furthermore* should be used. See **reportedly.**

relate to <a jury can relate to that experience>, when used as in the example just given, is a voguish expression characteristic of popular American cant in the 1970s and 1980s. It is unlikely to lose that stigma.

relater; relator. The former is the preferred spelling in the sense "narrator, one who relates." *Relator* is the legal term meaning "one who applies for a writ of mandamus or quo warranto on grounds that a defendant has breached—or threatens to breach—a public duty." E.g., "Members of the charitable organization can bring suit as *relators* in the name of the attorney general, but this is not always a practical remedy; not only do the *relators* bear the cost of the suit, but also the conduct of the litigation is controlled by the attorney general." See ***ex rel.***

relation. A. And *relative.* These terms are interchangeable in the sense "a person who is kin," although currently *relative* is slightly more usual.

B. Legal Sense. Some legal scholars, most notably Professor Leon Green, have used *relation* as "the best term available to express the value of one human being to another. . . . Relations may be classified as family relations, trade relations, professional and political relations, labor relations, and general social relations." Leon Green, *Cases on Injuries to Relations* 1 (1940).

C. And *relationship.* *Relation* is the broader term in this pair, inasmuch as *relationship* refers either to kinship or to the fact of being related by some specific bond. The phrase *in relationship with* is almost always incorrect for *in relation to.* To be correct, the phrase would almost have to be *in his* (or *her* or *its*) *relationship with,* etc.

relation back, in legal JARGON, refers to the doctrine that an act done at a later time is considered in the eyes of the law to have occurred at an earlier time. E.g., "To the extent that a power of appointment has been thought of as a mere authority to act for the donor in the completion of a disposition initiated by the donor, the agency factor has dominated and the doctrine of *relation back* has been applied."/ "How a magistrate who has acted within his jurisdiction up to the point at which the missing evidence should have been, but was not, given, can thereafter be said, by a kind of *relation back,* to have had no jurisdiction over the charge at all, it is hard to see." (Eng.) See **relate back.**

One court has ill-advisedly hyphenated the phrase throughout, both when (as a PHRASAL ADJECTIVE) it needs the hyphen <the relation-back rule> and when (as a noun) it does not <the doctrine of relation back>. See *Lemelson v. Synergistics Research Corp.,* 669 F. Supp. 642, 647–48 (S.D.N.Y. 1987).

relational = of or relating to relations between persons. E.g., "Out of the mass of decisions and scholarly writings it is now possible to chart a course of study for the lawyer whose professional activities will more and more be concerned with the protection of the *relational* interests of his clients" (i.e., interests in other human beings). The term is thus distinct from the adjective *relative.* See **relation (C).**

relationship. See **relation (C).**

relative, n.**; relation.** See **relation (A).**

relative(ly) to. *Relative to* is a variant of *in relation to* or *in comparison with;* usually one of these longer phrases adds clarity. Partridge called *relative to* GOBBLEDYGOOK. In no event is *relatively to* proper. "*Relatively to* [read *In relation to*] her, his act was not negligent."

The phrase is also an awkward substitute for *concerning* or *regarding:* "The latter part of the paragraph contains language similar to that of paragraph (a) *relative to* [read *concerning*] the discharge of the corporation's liability if an agreement is signed by the parties."

relator. See **relater.**

relatrix. See SEXISM (C).

relay; re-lay. See RE- PAIRS.

release. A. Senses. *Release* = (1) liberation from an obligation, duty, or demand; (2) a written discharge, acquittance, or receipt; (3) a written authorization or permission for publication; (4) the act of conveying an estate or right to another, or of legally disposing of it; (5) a deed or document effecting a conveyance; (6) the action of freeing or fact of being freed from restraint or confinement; or (7) a document giving formal discharge from custody.

B. And *re-lease.* See RE- PAIRS.

releasee. The *OED* defines the word as "one to whom an estate is released," but the usual sense today—in AmE and BrE alike—is "one who is released," either physically or by contractual discharge. The following examples illustrate these two senses: "[A] hearing shall be held . . . within a reasonable time, unless a hearing is waived by the probationer, parolee or conditional *releasee.*" Wyo. Stat. 7-13-408 (1985) (as quoted in *Pisano v. Shillinger,* 814 P.2d 274, 280 (Wyo. 1991))./ "[W]hen the actions or representations of the *releasee* so impair the mind and judgment of the releasor that he fails to understand the nature or consequence of his release, there has been no meeting of the minds." *Haller v. Borror Corp.,* 552 N.E.2d 207, 210 (Ohio 1990).

The correlative word is usually *releasor* in legal usage, though most dictionaries record only *releaser.* The *-or* form follows the typical preference for such spellings in answer to an *-ee* form. See -EE.

releasement, once a fairly common word, is now merely a NEEDLESS VARIANT of *release*—e.g.: "Their dispute concerning the advisability of the *releasement* [read *release*] in lieu of calling the police continued throughout the remainder of the afternoon . . . ." *Chavkin v. Rotter,* 245 N.Y.S.2d 435, 436 (App. Div. 1963). See **release (A).**

release on licence. See **parole.**

releasor; releaser. See **releasee.**

relegate; delegate. To *relegate* is to consign to an inferior position or to transfer for decision or execution. E.g., "The administratrix of the prisoner's estate was not *relegated* exclusively to an FTCA remedy." To *delegate* is to commit (as powers) to an agent or representative.

relevance; relevancy. The former is preferred in both AmE and BrE. *Relevancy* was the predominant form in American and British writings on evidence of the 19th century, but now *relevance* is more common except in Scotland. See **irrelevance.**

relevant (= pertinent) is sometimes misused for *applicable* or *appropriate.* E.g., "The board of directors might then allocate such amounts among the several outstanding series of stock on the basis of any criteria it deems *relevant* [read *applicable* or *appropriate*]." See **material.**

relevant part, in. See **in pertinent part.**

relic; relict; relique. *Relic* = a surviving trace or memorial; something interesting because of its age. E.g., "The Rule in Shelley's Case is a *relic,* not of the horse-and-buggy days, but of the preceding stone-cart-and-oxen days."/ "Today, decisions such as *Mochan* and *Donoghue* are widely viewed as *relics.*" Peter W. Low et al., *Criminal Law* 41 (1982). *Relique* is an archaic spelling of the word.

Relict = widow; survivor. Because *relict* is used only in legal writing, is unknown to nonlawyers, is sometimes mistaken for *relic,* and invariably means merely "widow" or "widower," we might justifiably seek to conform to general English usage and write *widow(er).* Some legal writers have resorted to the tautologous DOUBLET *widow and relict:* "After the husband's death, the wife obtained probate of his will in common form in which she is described as '*widow and relict* of the deceased.'" (Eng.) Widows and widowers unfamiliar with the term will not take kindly to being called *relicts.*

relief. See **remedy.**

relief over. See **over (A).**

relique. See **relic.**

relitigate. *RH2* aside, *relitigate* (= to litigate again) is not recorded in most English-language dictionaries, but it has been widely used since the mid-19th century and is unquestionably useful. E.g., "[H]e would still be free to *relitigate* the issue whether the driver had had his permission and thus whether the insurance proceeds should not be credited against his personal liability . . . ." Charles A. Wright, *The Law of Federal Courts* 463 (4th ed. 1983). The corresponding noun, *relitigation,* is equally common.

rem. See ***in rem.***

remainder. See **rest, residue, and remainder** & DOUBLETS, TRIPLETS, AND SYNONYM-STRINGS.

remainder; reversion. These terms are distinguishable on two grounds. First, a *reversion* always arises in the creator of a particular estate or in the creator's heirs; a *remainder* can never arise in the creator of the estate or in the creator's heirs. Second, a *reversion* may arise without any intent, express or implied, that the reversioner take; a *remainder* arises only when the instrument creating the present estate shows an intent that the remainderman take. See **reversion.**

remainderman (= the person to whom a remainder is devised) was formerly two words but is now regularly spelled as a single word. E.g., "A court may find, for example, that the donees take the property as joint tenants, as tenants in common, or that one donee takes as life tenant and the others as *remaindermen.*"

A possible nonsexist equivalent is *remainderer,* but it is extremely rare—e.g.: "In the mean time the *remainderer* would have had a right to anticipate payment . . . ." *Mellon's Appeal,* 8 A. 183, 187 (Pa. 1887). See SEXISM (B).

remainder over. See **over (A).**

remainder subject to a condition precedent. See **contingent remainder.**

remand, n.; **remandment.** The latter is a NEEDLESS VARIANT, as is *remission.* See **remission.**

remand, v.t. **A. Objects.** People as well as cases may be *remanded* (or "sent back"): *remand* = (1) to send (a case) back to the court from which it came for some further action; or (2) to recommit (an accused) to custody after a preliminary examination. Sense (2) is more common in BrE than in AmE—e.g.: "Fagan, who pleaded not guilty to the charge, was *remanded* to Brixton Prison for psychiatric and medical reports." (Eng.)/ "If the accused is *remanded* in custody, the adjournment must not be for longer than eight days." Patrick Devlin, *The Criminal Prosecution in England* 78 (1960).

B. *Remand back* as a Redundancy. *Remand* alone is preferable to *remand back*—e.g.: "*Maine v. Thornton* has been *remanded back* [omit *back*] to the Maine Supreme Judicial Court for action not inconsistent with the Supreme Court's decision."/ "The court *remanded* the case *back* [omit *back*] to the circuit court for a new hearing." See **send back.**

C. Pronunciation. *Remand* is pronounced /rə-***mand***/ both as a noun and as a verb.

remandment. See **remand,** n.

remanent. See **remnant.**

remark; re-mark. See RE- PAIRS.

remedial; remediable. *Remedial* (= providing a remedy; corrective; curative) is frequently pejorative in general English-language contexts <remedial learning>. In law, however, it usually acts as the adjective for *legal remedy:* "The constructive trust is a *remedial* device imposed to prevent a person from retaining title to property if the retention would unjustly enrich him at the expense of another."

Remediable = capable of being remedied. E.g., "A refusal to enforce that stems from a conflict of interest, that is the result of a bribe, vindictiveness, or retaliation, or that traces to personal or other corrupt motives ought to be judicially *remediable.*"

remediate is a BACK-FORMATION from *remediation*—and a NEEDLESS VARIANT of *remedy:* "[The agency is charged with the] solemn responsibility for *remediating* [read *remedying*] discrimination . . . ." *Hinfey v. Matawan Regional Bd. of Educ.,* 391 A.2d 899, 907 (N.J. 1978)./ "In some legislative schemes designed to *remediate* [read *remedy*] or prevent harm to certain portions of the public, the doctrine of equitable tolling has been allowed . . . ." *Dawe v. Old Ben Coal Co.,* 754 F.2d 225, 228 (7th Cir. 1985).

remediless; remedyless. As *penny* makes *penniless,* so *remedy* should make *remediless* (= without remedy; lacking any remedies)—e.g.: "The risk selected by the plaintiffs to pursue their tort claim under a collective liability theory which ultimately failed, thus leaving them *remedyless* [read *remediless*], was willingly assumed . . . ." Nina H. Compton & J. Douglas Compton, *DPT Vaccine Manufacturer Liability,* 20 N.M. L. Rev. 531, 549 (1990)./ "There were all sorts of problems with this characterization of marriage, including the fact that husbands would frequently desert their wives, leaving them *remediless* and without any property or other means of support." Margaret F. Brinig & Steven M. Crafton, *Marriage and Opportunism,* 23 J. Legal Stud. 869, 881 (1994).

remedy; relief. The latter has historically been more commonly used in the context of courts of equity, and the former in the context of courts of law. Thus one generally speaks of *legal remedies* and of *equitable relief.* See C.C. Langdell, *A Brief Survey of Equity Jurisdiction* (pt. 2), 1 Harv. L. Rev. 111, 111 (1887).

remember. See **recollect (A).**

remise = to give up, surrender, make over to another, release (any right, property, etc.) (*OED*). Though traditionally used in quitclaim deeds, the term is fast becoming a legal ARCHAISM. Several words—such as those just used in defining *remise*—are more specific and more widely understood.

remissible. So spelled. See -ABLE (A).

remission. As a noun meaning "the act of remanding," *remission* is a NEEDLESS VARIANT of *remand,* n. Here is an example suggesting the writer's indulgence in INELEGANT VARIATION: "[A]n appellate court 'may *remand* the cause . . . .' The procedure for *remission* [read *remand*] of the cause to the lower court . . . is further regulated and controlled generally by the rules of the appellate courts." 14A Stephen M. Flanagan, *Cyclopedia of Federal Procedure* § 69.01, at 65 (1984). See **remand, remit, remittance & renvoi.**

In BrE, *remission* refers not only to the sending back of a case to a lower court, but also to the part of a prison sentence that a convict is allowed not to serve (e.g., *remission* for good conduct in prison).

remit = (1) to pardon; (2) to abate, slacken; mitigate; (3) to refer (a matter for decision) to some authority, send back (a case) to a lower court; (4) to send or put back; or (5) to transmit (as money). Senses (1) and (2) are uncommon today. Sense (4) is frequent in legal writing: "[T]he breach by the landlord of his covenant does not justify the refusal of the tenant to perform his covenant to pay rent. . . . The tenant is *remitted* to the right to recoup himself in the damages resulting from the landlord's breach of his covenant to repair." *Mitchell v. Weiss,* 26 S.W.2d 699, 700-01 (Tex. Civ. App.—El Paso 1930)./ "In *remitting* the members of this class to a solution at the ballot box, rather than dangling the carrot of reform by judicial injunction before them, the district court followed the course of wisdom and practicality."

Sense (5) is also quite common <upon receiving the demand letter, she promptly remitted the amount due>.

Sense (3) was formerly common in legal prose, *remit* here being a synonym of *remand:* "The order should be reversed, with costs to the appellant payable out of the estate, and the proceedings *remitted* to the surrogate for entry of a decree in accordance with this opinion."/ "Nolan, Presiding Justice, dissents and votes to reverse and to *remit* the proceeding to Surrogate's Court for the entry of a decree as prayed for in the objections interposed by appellants."/ "The case is *remitted* to the Superior Court for the entry of a judgment on the verdict as directed." See **remission.**

remittance; remittal; remission; remitment. *Remittance* corresponds to sense (5) of *remit,* and means "money sent to a person, or the sending of money to a person." E.g., "On the other hand is the innocent shipper who paid the full amount of the charges to such defaulting party for *remittance* to the agent." *Remitment* is a NEEDLESS VARIANT.

Remission is the noun corresponding to senses (1) through (4) of *remit,* q.v.; it means either "forgiveness" or "diminution of force, effect, degree, or violence." *Remittal* is a NEEDLESS VARIANT.

remitter; remittor; remittitur. *Remitter* = (1) one who sends a remittance; (2) a principle by which a person having two titles to an estate, and entering on it by the later or more defective of these titles, is held to hold it by the earlier or more valid one; or (3) the act of remitting a case to another court. (See **remit.**) The *-or* spelling is inferior.

Remittitur = (1) the process by which the court reduces the damages awarded in a jury verdict; or (2) the action of sending the transcript of a case back from an appellate to a trial court, or the notice for doing so. For sense (2), the usual phrase is *remittitur of record.*

remittitur; remittitur of record; remittor. See **remitter.**

remnant; remanent. The latter is an archaic spelling to be avoided.

remonstrate. The second syllable is accented /*ri-**mon**-strayt*/ in AmE, the first syllable /***rem**-ən-strayt*/ in BrE.

remote has a special legal meaning in contexts involving the rule against perpetuities: "beyond the 21 years after some life in being by which a devise must vest." E.g., "In *Leake v. Robinson,* there actually were afterborn children with respect to whom the remainder might have vested *remotely.*" See **in being** & ***in esse.***

REMOTE RELATIVES. Surprisingly few grammarians discuss what has become an increasingly common problem: the separation of the relative pronoun (*that, which, who*) from its antecedent. For example, in the sentence "The files sitting in the courtroom that I was talking about yesterday are in disarray," the word *that* strictly modifies *courtroom,* not *files.* But many writers today would intend to have it modify *files*—they would loosely employ a "remote relative."

The best practice is simply to ensure that, whatever the relative pronoun, it immediately follow the noun that it modifies. As the following examples illustrate, lapses involving *which* are extremely common:

- "This work required a law court in the modern sense made up of a small number of judges of education and ability skilled in the law *which* sat regularly term after term, generally at Westminster, often at the Exchequer." William F. Walsh, *A Treatise on Equity* 3 (1930). *Which* modifies *court* (21 words and 7 nouns before). [A possible revision: *This work required a law court in the modern sense: one that was made up of a small number of judges of legal education and ability and that sat regularly term after term, generally at Westminster, often at the Exchequer.*]
- "States, like individuals, often put forward contentions for the purpose of supporting a particular case *which* do not necessarily represent their settled or impartial opinion . . . ." J.L. Brierly, *The Law of Nations* 61 (5th ed. 1955). *Which* modifies *contentions* (9 words and 3 nouns before). [A possible revision: *States, like individuals, often put forward contentions that support a particular case but do not necessarily represent their settled opinion.*]
- "If a terrorist places a bomb by the front door of a Cabinet Minister, *which* does damage but fortunately does not kill anybody, could this be an attempt to murder?" Glanville Williams, *Textbook of Criminal Law* 371 (1978). *Which* modifies *bomb* (9 words and 3 nouns before). [A possible revision: *If a terrorist places a bomb by the front door of a Cabinet Minister and that bomb does damage but fortunately does not kill anybody, could this be an attempt to murder?*]
- "The convenience of the litigants is the next quality in the administration of justice *which* I shall consider." Patrick Devlin, *The Judge* 59 (1979). *Which* modifies *quality* (6 words and 3 nouns before). [A possible revision: *The convenience of the litigants is the next quality that I shall consider in the administration of justice.*]
- "[T]here are today a great many other bodies exercising quasi-judicial powers *which* are not regarded strictly speaking as courts, though many of them do perform functions very closely analogous to those of ordinary courts." P.S. Atiyah, *Law and Modern Society* 27 (1983). *Which* modifies *bodies* (4 words and 2 nouns before). [A possible revision: *There are today a great many other bodies exercising quasi-judicial powers; these bodies are not regarded strictly speaking as courts, though many of them do perform functions very closely analogous to those of ordinary courts.*]
- "People may have claims against each other and against the State *which* are of a moral or political character . . . ." *Id.* at 112. *Which* modifies *claims* (8 words and 3 nouns before). [A possible revision: *People may have moral and political claims against each other and against the State.*]
- "Legislators are constantly making decisions about law reform *which* depend on moral values." Simon Lee, *Law and Morals* 3 (1986). *Which* modifies *decisions* (4 words and 2 nouns before). [A possible revision: *Legislators are constantly making decisions about law reform, and many of these decisions depend on moral values.*]

But *that* is almost as troublesome, and when used remotely is even more likely to cause confusion—e.g.:

- "The law has a way of looking at family relationships *that* is different, or may be different, from the moral, the social, or the religious way." Max Radin, *The Law and You* 17 (1948). *That* modifies *way* (6 words and 2 nouns before). [A possible revision: *The law has a way of looking at family relationships—a way that is different, or may be different, from the moral, the social, or the religious way.*]
- "All groups seem to develop noticeable characteristics, so that some can recognize sailors, clergymen, actors and other occupational groups *that* are not at all hereditary and hardly attributable to any definite physical cause." Morris R. Cohen, *Reason and Law* 42 (1961). *That* modifies *characteristics* (13 words and 6 nouns before). [A possible revision: *All groups seem to develop noticeable characteristics that are not at all hereditary or attributable to any definite physical cause, but that allow some peo-*

ple to recognize sailors, clergy, actors, and other occupational groups.]

- "There is another important aspect of the case, and that is whether, in placing so heavy a burden on the jury, it has brought about a shift of responsibility for decisions in the moral field *that* affects the democratic process I have endeavoured to describe." Patrick Devlin, *The Enforcement of Morals* 98 (1968). What affects the democratic process? The *moral field?* The *responsibility* for decisions? The *shift* in that responsibility? The answer seems to be *shift* (9 words and 4 nouns before). [A possible revision: *There is another important aspect of the case, and that is whether the heavy burden placed on the jury has brought about a shift of responsibility for decisions in the moral field—a shift that affects the democratic process I have endeavoured to describe.*]
- "The plain fact is that in most cases where doubt can arise as to whether a particular situation is covered by a statute, no intellectual resources are available to the legislature in deciding the question *that* are not equally available to the judge . . . ." Lon L. Fuller, *Anatomy of the Law* 33 (1968). *That* modifies *resources* (10 words and 3 nouns before). [A possible revision: *In most cases in which doubt can arise about whether a particular situation is covered by a statute, the legislature has no intellectual resources that are not equally available to the judge.*]
- "The most important changes in the law of future interests *that* the Statute of Uses wrought may be summarized in one sentence." Thomas F. Bergin & Paul G. Haskell, *Preface to Estates in Land and Future Interests* 113 (2d ed. 1984). *That* modifies *changes* (7 words and 3 nouns before). [A possible revision: *The most important changes that the Statute of Uses wrought in the law of future interests can be summarized in one sentence.*]
- "Lee Feltman, Esq., . . . appeals from an order of the district court, Edelstein, J., *that* adopted the findings and recommendations of Magistrate Gershon . . . ." *Sassower v. Sheriff of Westchester County,* 824 F.2d 184, 185 (2d Cir. 1987). Does that sentence refer to *an order that adopted* or *the district court that adopted?* It looks as if the writer meant to refer to *order* (7 words and 3 nouns before), not *court.* [A possible revision: *Lee Feltman, Esq., . . . appeals from a district-court order that adopted the findings and recommendations of Magistrate Gershon . . . .*]

Even *who* is used remotely, but its meaning is much more frequently clear—e.g.:

- "Gibson was a Democrat of Jackson's type (Jackson wished to put him on the Supreme Court of the United States), the son of a prosperous and successful man of business in a frontier community, who was also a colonel in the Revolutionary army." Roscoe Pound, *The Formative Era of American Law* 85 (1938). *Who* may modify either *son* (13 words and 4 nouns before) or *man* (7 words and 3 nouns before). It seems to modify the more remote of the two—*son.* [A possible revision: *Gibson was a Democrat . . . , the son of a prosperous and successful man of business in a frontier community. Gibson was also a colonel in the Revolutionary army.*]
- "The question whether one of a gang *who* is arrested at the scene of the crime continues to be 'present' there is considered in § 134." Glanville Williams, *Criminal Law* 354 (2d ed. 1961). *Who* modifies *one* (4 words and 2 nouns before.) [A possible revision: *The question whether a gang member who is arrested at the scene of the crime continues to be 'present' there is considered in § 134.*]
- "Patricia Buthmann and Tim Tyroler on Tuesday lost their effort to block being evicted from the Casa Carranza apartments . . . because they allowed a woman to stay with them *who* possessed two syringes suspected to be drug paraphernalia." Kris Mayes, *Renters Run Afoul of Eviction Law,* Phoenix Gazette, 29 Sept. 1994, at B1. At first, the relative pronoun *who* may seem to modify *them* as part of an archaic construction; in fact, it modifies *woman* (5 words and 2 nouns before). [A possible revision: *. . . because a woman who stayed with them possessed two syringes thought to be drug paraphernalia.*]

At times, the remote relative may even appear in a phrase such as *in which*—e.g.: "The unexpected announcement renewed speculation about the 74-year-old Pope's broader state of health, particularly because he planned an important speech at the United Nations on the family *in which* he was expected to discuss the Vatican's views of the recent population conference in Cairo." Alan Crowell, *Pope, Citing His Health, Cancels His Planned Trip to New York,* N.Y. Times, 23 Sept. 1994, at A1. *In which* modifies *speech* (8 words and 3 nouns before). [A possible revision: *The unexpected announcement renewed speculation about the 74-year-old Pope's broader state of health, particularly because he planned an important speech at the United Nations on the family. In that speech, he was expected to discuss the Vatican's views of the recent population conference in Cairo.*]

As in the example just quoted, remote relatives often seem to result from the writer's ill-advised combining of two sentences into one. Among the advantages of avoiding remote relatives—avoiding MISCUES and even AMBIGUITY—is that you also improve your average SENTENCE LENGTH. For more on using *that* and *which* correctly, see RESTRICTIVE AND NONRESTRICTIVE CLAUSES.

removable. This is the preferred spelling in both AmE and BrE, not *removeable.* See MUTE E.

remove, re-move. See RE- PAIRS.

remove; removal. In law, these terms have procedural senses that are generally unknown to nonlawyers. *Removal* = the transfer of an action from a court on one jurisdictional level to a court on another level. Thus, in the U.S., some state-court actions may be *removed* to federal court if the proper statutory basis exists. (The correlative term for transferring the action back to state court is *remand,* q.v.) In England, *removal* is the transfer of a High Court action from a district registry to London (or vice versa) or of a county court action to the High Court (or vice versa) (*CDL*).

removeable. See **removable.**

remuneration. So spelled; *renumeration* is an all-too-common misspelling and mispronunciation.

renant; reniant. At early common law, *renant* (the more common spelling) meant "denying." *Reniant* is a variant form.

rencontre; rencounter. Very little is certain about these words. *W10* lists the main entry for this word under *rencontre;* the *COD* lists the main entry under *rencounter,* as does *W2.* Under *rencontre,* the *COD* labels both archaic, although the Merriam-Webster dictionaries list *rencontre* as a current word in the senses (1) "a hostile meeting or contest between forces or individuals; combat"; and (2) "a casual meeting." The *OED* adds the sense "an organized but informal meeting of scientists," dating from 1975 in BrE.

rend. See **heart-rending.**

render = (1) to make, cause to be; or (2) to give. *Render* is a FORMAL WORD worthy of describing judicial actions, although generally it is used in this context primarily in the U.S. For example, with regard to sense (2), judicial decisions are *rendered.* Nonjudicial responses are *given,* not *rendered:* "The majority seizes upon the petitioner's seven-word response, 'Uh, yeah, I'd like to do that,' *rendered* [read *uttered*] during a colloquy that could not have taken five minutes." Such an inarticulate statement from a habeas corpus petitioner should hardly be said to have been *rendered.* See **heart-rending.**

In AmE, the usual expression is that judgment is *rendered;* in BrE it is commonly written that judgment is *given.* E.g., "Judgment accordingly was *given* for the plaintiffs for the balance of the claim." (Aus.)

rendezvous. A. Plural Form. The singular noun *rendezvous* has an identical plural form—i.e., *rendezvous,* not *-vouses.*

B. Verb Inflections. As a verb, *rendezvous* makes *rendezvouses* in the third-person present tense, and *rendezvoused* in the past tense. (In both inflected forms, the root *-s-* is silent.) The present participle is *rendezvousing.*

rendition. The prevalent meaning today—"the action of rendering, giving out or forth" began as an Americanism but has now become universal. BrE retains an older, quasi-legal sense as well: "the surrender of a suspected or convicted person, usu. betw. two Commonwealth countries."

rendition of judgment; entry of judgment. Courts have traditionally distinguished between *rendition of judgment* (= the oral or written ruling containing the judgment entered) and *entry of judgment* (= the formal recordation of a judgment by the court). It has been said that *rendition* is the ultimate judicial act, whereas *entry* is merely ministerial in nature and evidentiary in purpose.

This distinction at one time posed problems in some cases in which no terminal judicial act was required, as with a jury's general verdict. In current American practice (Fed. R. Civ. P. 58), the verdict *rendered* by a jury or the decision *rendered* by the judge is converted into an 'inchoate' judgment, effective upon *entry.*

renege; renegue; renig. The first is the preferred form in AmE, the second the standard spelling in BrE, although the first is making inroads. *Renig* is a variant spelling in AmE—a NEEDLESS VARIANT.

renewal. See **extension.**

renewal of judgment; revival of judgment. "[G]enerally speaking there exists an important distinction between *revival* and *renewal* of judgments. *Revival,* by judicial decree on scire facias, removes dormancy and authorizes belated issuance of a writ of execution. Conversely, *renewal,* by civil action on the judgment, consists [in] a new money judgment endowed with its own actionability, executability, and creation of a lien." Stefan A. Riesenfeld, *Creditors' Remedies and Debtors' Protection* 101 (1979).

reniant. See **renant.**

renig. See **renege.**

renouncement. See **renunciation.**

renowned. So spelled; *reknowned* is wrong but fairly common for *renowned.* E.g., "Byatt is *reknowned* [read *renowned*] for her intelligence." Mira Stout, *What Possessed A.S. Byatt,* N.Y. Times, 26 May 1991, § 6 at 13, 14. The noun form is *renown;* there is no verb, though the past participle *renowned* exists as an adjective.

rent, n.; **rental,** n. Generally, one should not use *rental* where *rent* will suffice. *Rental* denotes the amount paid as rent, the income received from rent, or a record of rental payments received (e.g., the Grossvener Estate rental). *Rental* sometimes encroaches on *rent* itself: "The lessee agrees to pay the agreed-upon *rental.*" If the writer had merely meant that the lessee must pay the rent (as opposed to a specific sum due periodically, e.g., monthly), then *rent* would have been the better term.

rent, v.t., is ambiguous insofar as it may refer to the action taken by either the lessor or the lessee; the word has had this doubleness of sense from at least the 16th century. Both the lessee and the lessor are *renters,* so to speak, though usually this term is reserved for tenants. Cf. **lease,** v.t.

rental, n. See **rent,** n.

rent(-)charge = the right to receive an annual sum from the income of land, usu. in perpetuity, and to retake possession if the payments are in arrears. Hyphenated in the *OED,* this word is now one word in BrE (as in the Rentcharges Act of 1977) and two words in AmE.

renumeration. See **remuneration.**

renunciation; renouncement. The latter is a NEEDLESS VARIANT.

renvoi /*ren-voi*/ (F. "sending back") = the problem arising in private international law when one country's rule on conflict of laws refers a case to the law of a foreign country, and the law of that country refers the case either back to the law of the first country (*remission*) or to the law of a third country (*transmission*) (*CDL*). Within federal systems such as that of the U.S., *renvoi* applies when one state's conflicts rule refers the case to the law of another state. See **remission.**

reoccur is a NEEDLESS VARIANT of the much preferable *recur.* See **recurrence.**

reoccurrence. See **recurrence.**

repairable. See **reparable.**

RE- PAIRS. Many English words beginning with the prefix *re-* take on different meanings depending on whether the prefix is hyphenated or is closed up. Some of these words, whose two different senses with and without the hyphen should be self-explanatory, are as follows:

re(-)bound
re(-)claim
re(-)call
re(-)collect
re(-)count
re(-)cover
re(-)create
re(-)dress
re(-)form
re(-)lay
re(-)lease
re(-)mark
re(-)move
re(-)place
re(-)prove
re(-)search
re(-)sign
re(-)sound
re(-)store
re(-)treat

reparable; repairable. Of these two terms, the former term has acquired a broader meaning. Used of damages, losses, or injuries, *reparable* means "capable of being set right again." Used of things, *repairable* means "capable of being repaired." The antonyms of these words are *irreparable* and *unrepairable.*

reparative; reparatory. The latter is a NEEDLESS VARIANT.

repay. A. Sense. This word means "to pay back"—it should not refer to paying something for the first time, however long the sum has been due: "Earlier this year, Michael took out a $45,000 loan to *repay* [read *pay*] the back taxes and interest he owed." *For Special Cases, a "Tax Therapist,"* N.Y. Times, 8 Dec. 1989, at 27.

B. *Repay back.* This is a REDUNDANCY.

repealer = (1) one who repeals; or (2) a legislative act abrogating an earlier act. Sense (2), of recent origin, is the more common one—e.g.: "Another method of reviving the judgment lien was docketing and indexing a writ of execution, now subject to special *repealer.*" See -ER (B).

repeat again; repeat back. Both are REDUNDANCIES.

repel; repulse. *Repulse* (= to drive or beat back [an assailant]) denotes primarily a physical act of resistance, or a metaphor based on such resistance—e.g.: "The attack upon the representatives, indeed, had already been launched, and, after an initial victory, had been *repulsed.*" C.H.S. Fifoot, *History and Sources of the Common Law: Tort and Contract* 358 (1949). *Repel,* by contrast, is primarily figurative. Hence *repel* is the verb corresponding most closely in meaning to the adjective *repulsive,* and a person who experiences *repulsion* is *repelled.* In the following sentences, *repel* is acceptably used as a near-synonym of *rebut:* "In such cases the burden of proof rests upon the party claiming the benefit under the transaction to *repel* the presumption thus created by law by showing a severance of the relation."/ "The circumstances *repel* any thought of fraud and speak cogently of the integrity of the instrument under review."

repellent; repulsive. Both mean, lit., "causing to turn away." *Repulsive* is the stronger word; it applies to whatever disgusts or offends in the extreme. *Repellant,* a variant spelling of *repellent,* is to be eschewed. See **repel.**

repetitive; repetitious; repetitional; repetitionary. A certain DIFFERENTIATION is emerging between these terms. *Repetitive* generally means "repeating, containing repetition." It is a largely colorless term. *Repetitious,* which has taken on pejorative connotations, means "containing tedious repetitions." E.g., "The court's holding today has the effect of requiring precisely this kind of *repetitious* appellate review."/ "None of the discovery sought, which in some instances is *repetitious,* cumulative, and peripheral, is relevant."

Repetitional and *repetitionary* are NEEDLESS VARIANTS of *repetitive.*

rephrase for *paraphrase.* One cannot use these two words interchangeably. One may *paraphrase* either statements or persons, but one may *rephrase* only statements. The writer of this sentence incorrectly used *rephrase* for *paraphrase:* "To *rephrase* [read *paraphrase*] Justice Frankfurter, newspapers are inherently available to all as a mode of expression."

replace; re-place. Here *replace* is used for *re-place:* "Where land or chattels have been wrongfully taken from a person, he can be *replaced* [read *re-placed*] substantially in the position which he formerly occupied by restoring to him in specie that which was taken from him." See RE- PAIRS.

repleader. See -ER (B).

repleat. See **replete.**

replenish makes the noun *replenishment,* not *repletion* (= a surfeit, plethora).

replete means not "complete," but "abundantly supplied with; full to overflowing." *Repleat* is an infrequent misspelling committed, e.g., by the court in *Commonwealth v. Belmonte,* 502 A.2d 1241, 1252 (Pa. Super. Ct. 1985).

repletion. See **replenish.**

repleviable; replevisable. Blackstone was ahead of his time in using *repleviable* rather than *replevisable,* which is now rightly considered a NEEDLESS VARIANT. The antonym of *repleviable* is *irrepleviable.* See **replevy.**

replevin; replevy, n. *Replevin* is the name of both a writ and a cause of action.

Replevy is an archaic variant of *replevin* as a noun, although it still appears: "A plaintiff who sought to recover a firearm allegedly illegally seized by a treasury agent was precluded from *replevy* [read *replevin*] of the weapon by a statute providing that all property taken under any revenue law of the United States shall not be *repleviable.*"/ "The statute was designed to aid the collection of federal taxes by preventing a *replevy* [read *replevin*] under a state law of property seized by the collector." See **detinue.**

replevin, v.t., is an obsolete variant of the verb *replevy.* (See **replevy.**) When *replevin* is used as a verb in modern American legal writing, it is simply an error—e.g.: "[T]he manufacturer wrongfully *replevined* [read *replevied*] a printing press." *Cummins v. Brodie,* 667 S.W.2d 759, 766 (Tenn. Ct. App. 1983)./ "Purchase of *replevined* [read *replevied*] vehicle by judge and cover-up." *Mississippi Judicial Performance Comm'n v. Walker,* 565 So. 2d 1117, 1130 (Miss. 1990) (Appendix B).

replevisable. See **repleviable.**

replevy, vb., = (1) v.t., to regain possession of (personal property) under a provisional remedy that allows the plaintiff, upon giving security, to regain the disputed property from the defendant and to hold it until the court decides who owns it; (2) v.t., to regain possession of (personal property) by a successful action in replevin; or (3) v.i., to bring an action for replevin.

Though sense (3) is fairly infrequent, senses (1) and (2) are common. The distinction between them involves merely the stage that the litigation has reached: if the lawsuit is still pending, sense (1) applies—e.g.:

- "The cardinal question in every replevin action is whether the plaintiff was entitled to immediate possession of the property *replevied* at the commencement of the action." *International Harvester Credit Corp, v. Lech,* 438 N.W.2d 474, 477 (Neb. 1989).
- "The mortgagee-finance company *replevied* the automobile from the purchaser, who then settled with the finance company by agreeing to pay the balance due on the mortgage." *In re People,* 505 N.W.2d 228, 233 (Mich. 1993).
- "The failure of the court to order a bond that complies with the replevin statute threatens the security of the person whose property is *replevied.*" *Child's Play Ltd. v. A & A, Inc.,* 642 A.2d 170, 172 (Me. 1994).

If, by contrast, the litigation has concluded and the plaintiff has prevailed, sense (2) applies—e.g.: "Lienholder *replevied* the vehicle and recovered attorney fees and costs from the wrecker service." *Sharp v. State,* 877 P.2d 629, 630 (Okla. 1994).

Sometimes one cannot tell, without the fuller context, whether sense (1) or sense (2) applies—e.g: "Homeowners allege that SCOF did not properly credit the individual accounts for items it *replevied* from the corresponding lots." *Dave Kolb Grading, Inc. v. Lieberman Corp.,* 837 S.W.2d 924, 933 (Mo. Ct. App. 1992)./ "PCA 'picked up and sold' some cattle and defendant Hopkins *replevied* the 88 head and sold them." *Central Prod. Credit Ass'n v. Hopkins,* 810 S.W.2d 108, 110 (Mo. Ct. App. 1991).

Only personal property can be *replevied,* as the following statement acknowledges: "In any event, someone out there had better tell the creditors who repossessed and hauled away center pivot systems from debt-ridden irrigators that those creditors have *replevied* real estate—quite a legal phenomenon to say the least." *Mapco Ammonia Pipeline, Inc. v. State Bd. of Equalization & Assessment,* 471 N.W.2d 734, 749 (Neb. 1991). See **replevin.** Cf. **detinue.**

replicatable is incorrect for *replicable*—e.g.: "The feeders' argument assumes . . . the mechanical (and therefore *replicatable* [read *replicable*]) application of such fixed numbers . . . ." *In re Beef Indus. Antitrust Litig.,* 542 F. Supp. 1122, 1141 (N.D. Tex. 1982). See -ATABLE.

report. A. And *reporter*. Traditionally, a law *report* is a written account of a proceeding and judicial decision, and the *reporter* is the person responsible for making and publishing that account. (Cf. **court reporter.**) In AmE, however, *reporter* has been blurred into *report*—primarily because of West Publishing Company's "National Reporter" system (established in 1879), each *Reporter* being a set of books containing judicial opinions from a geographic area within the country. Formerly, fastidious writers tried to distinguish the senses by capitalizing one but not the other, as the following quotation suggests, but this practice is not widely followed. E.g., "It may not come amiss to remark that the National Reporter System is usually spoken of as the '*Reporters,*' and one of the component parts of that system is in like manner spoken of as a '*Reporter.*' Wherever, in this or the succeeding chapters of this work, the word is used with a capital, it refers to one or more of the parts of the National Reporter System. When the word '*reporter*' is used without capitalization, it refers to the person who reports or edits the cases in any series of reports to which reference is being made." William M. Lile et al., *Brief Making and the Use of Law Books* 37 (3d ed. 1914).

A similar extension of *reporter* occurred in 19th-century Scotland, where the *Scottish Law Reporter* appeared from 1865 to 1925.

B. The Reports. In BrE, "the Reports" are Coke's 13 volumes that began to appear in 1600. Coke tried to present every previous authority bearing on each case he reported, and thus his work has remained the historian's first entrance into the study of medieval caselaw.

reportedly. "Newspapermen and broadcasters live on a steady diet of this adverb," wrote Wilson Follett. "It is so lacking in the characteristics of a respectable adverb that one would like to see its use confined to cable messages, where it saves money and can await translation into English." *Modern American Usage* 279 (1966). E.g., "Such convictions are extremely rare, and *reportedly* *there had been only four previous ones* [read, according to Follett, *only four previous ones had been reported*] since the law was passed."

To be sure, adverbs in *-edly* are often cumbersome and opaque (at first). *Reportedly* is not nearly as common in legal writing as *allegedly, confessedly,* and *assertedly.* All such forms ought to be avoided unless there is virtually no other concise way of saying what needs to be said. If that test is met, as it often is, we should use *reportedly* or any of the other terms without apology. See -EDLY, **allegedly** & **confessedly.**

reporter. See **report (A).**

report of proceedings. This term is used in various American jurisdictions to refer to the verbatim transcript of any on-the-record proceedings before a judge. In Texas, the anomalous phrase *statement of facts* is used in this sense. See **record (B).**

repose is not "indefinite dormancy," but rather suggests temporary rest, after which there will again be activity. Hence, in the following pronouncement, the court was not aspersing the doctrine in question as strongly as it might have thought: "As to sovereign immunity, that doctrine, insofar as it has been created by courts, seems headed for a deserved *repose.*" This is slovenly writing that makes little sense—why "insofar as it has been created by the courts," which is ambiguous? The judge might better have written, "Sovereign immunity as created by the courts seems to be moribund." This says the same thing in almost half the words. See CUTTING OUT THE CHAFF.

Statute of repose is a curious AmE legal usage for a statute that sets up a legal defense, usu. by the passage of time. It differs from a period of *limitation,* q.v., because it bars a suit a fixed number of years after the defendant acts in some way (as by manufacturing a product), whereas *limitation* bars an action if the plaintiff does not file suit within a set period of time from the date when the cause of action accrues. E.g., "[Article 5536a is] the ultimate *statute of repose* for architects, engineers, and builders. . . . [It] provides an absolute defense to a registered or licensed architect or engineer once more than ten years have passed since the substantial completion of any allegedly defective improvement to real property." *Brown v. M.W. Kellogg Co.,* 743 F.2d 265, 267 (5th Cir. 1984)./ "[W]here injury or death is alleged to have resulted from disease, the six-year statute of *repose* is inapplicable." *Guy v. E.I. DuPont de Nemours & Co.,* 792 F.2d 457, 460 (4th Cir. 1986).

repository; repositary. The former spelling is standard. Cf. **depositary.**

represent; re-present. See RE- PAIRS.

representation; misrepresentation. These two words require care: if by *fraudulent representation* one really means *fraudulent misrepresentation,* then the latter phrase ought to be used. Cf. **false representation.**

representee (= one to whom a representation has been made), a word that originated in the 17th century and then was disused for nearly two centuries, reemerged in 20th-century discussions of contract law. It has become fairly common as a correlative of *representor*—e.g.: "It is presumed that the *representor* in pursuing his own economic interest will necessarily protect the rights of the *representees* who have the same economic interest." *In re Will of Levy,* 496 N.Y.S.2d 911, 912 (Sur. Ct. 1985)./ "Each [doctrine] is based on a representation followed by reliance on the part of the *representee* . . . ." G.H. Treitel, *The Law of Contract* 109 (8th ed. 1991). Cf. **misrepresentee.**

repress. See **oppress.**

reprise, n.; **reprisal.** *Reprise* = (1) an annual deduction, duty, or payment out of a manor or estate, as an annuity or the like; or (2) (in music) a repetition. *Reprisal* = an act of retaliation, usu. of one nation against another but short of war.

reprobate (= to reject [as an instrument or deed] as not binding on one) is, in Scots law, the antonym of *approbate.* See **approbate.**

republish; revive. In the law of wills, there is a distinction between these verbs. *Republishing* involves bringing forward in time a will that has remained continuously valid since its making. *Reviving* a will involves restoring to effectiveness a will or codicil that has been revoked.

repudiation; rescission. *Repudiation* = a contracting party's words or actions that indicate an intention not to perform the contract in the future. *Rescission* = a party's unilateral unmaking of a contract for a legally sufficient reason, such as the other party's material breach.

Though the definitions suggest precise meanings for these terms, they are frequently confused. The main problem is that *repudiation* is a common-law term, whereas *rescission* is an equitable one. Thus, as P.S. Atiyah points out, "most books on the law of Contract discuss the right to repudiate the contract for breach of condition in a section on Remedies, while they treat of the right to rescind a contract in the section on Misrepresentation. Indeed, so different are repudiation and rescission believed to be, that serious confusion is caused in the law of sale of goods by the fact that the Sale of Goods Act regulates the former but not the latter." P.S. Atiyah, *An Introduction to the Law of Contract* 294 (3d ed. 1981). To compound the trouble, lawyers indiscriminately use *repudiation* for both a rightful and a wrongful termination.

repudiatory; repudiative. Despite the *OED*'s suggestion to the contrary, *repudiatory* is the usu. term—*repudiative* being a NEEDLESS VARIANT.

repugn. See **impugn.**

repugnant. This word, in law, is frequently used in its oldest sense, "inconsistent with; contrary or contradictory to." Legal writers use the word most commonly when contrasting two things—e.g.: "The annexing of such incident to such contract would be *repugnant* to the express terms of the contract." (Eng.)/ "The idea of judicial application of constitutional provisions and of judicial refusal to give effect to legislation *repugnant* to the Constitution . . . goes back to refusal of the common-law courts to give effect to acts of Parliament 'impertinent to be observed' . . . ." Roscoe Pound, *The Development of Constitutional Guarantees of Liberty* 96–97 (1957). In nonlegal usage, *repugnant* today denotes "causing distaste or aversion."

repulse. See **repel.**

repulsive. See **repellent.**

reputation. See **character.**

reputational (= of or pertaining to reputation) is not recorded in *W3,* but dates from 1921 in the *OED.* The term is useful to legal writers—e.g.: "Nor is any liberty or *reputational* interest implicated." *Findeisen v. North E. Indep. Sch. Dist.,* 749 F.2d 234, 240 (5th Cir. 1984) (Garwood, J., concurring)./ "Management may well value more highly the time that would be expended in litigation and any *reputational* effects of a loss, whereas plaintiffs might well assign a high value to the potentially recoverable damages."

requestee. Though recorded in neither the *OED* nor other major English-language dictionaries, *requestee* has achieved limited currency in law as a correlative of *requester* (or, less good, *-or*). E.g., "The burden as to the first prong would be on the *requestee* as the movant, while the burden as to the second prong is on the requestor." *Cielock v. Munn,* 262 S.E.2d 114, 115 (Ga. 1979). See -EE.

requiescat in pace. See **R.I.P.**

require. See **necessitate.**

requisite. See **prerequisite.**

requisite requirement is a patent REDUNDANCY.

requisition = (1) an authoritative, formal demand; or (2) a governmental seizure of property.

requital; requitement. The latter is a NEEDLESS VARIANT.

res; re; rem. *Res* (= thing), pronounced like *race* in AmE but like *reese* or *rays* in BrE, is used in a number of different ways in legal contexts. Most often it is a synonym of *principal* or *corpus* in reference to funds. E.g., "When the *res* of a gratuitous private express trust is excessive for the purpose specified by the settlor, a resulting trust of the excess is presumed for the benefit of the settlor or his successors in interest."/ "The difficulties of applying the common-law concept of joint tenancy to a fluctuating *res* prevent the traditional joint tenancy estate from providing a logical solution." See **corpus.**

Yet it is often used in its literal sense "thing," in reference to a particular thing, known or unknown. E.g., "We found, as a matter of trademark law, that the *res* in the case, the registered trademark of the Cuban corporation, was located in the United States."/ "Defendants argue that the superior court is without jurisdiction of the cause of action pleaded because the court does not have jurisdiction of the *res*—the realty in Illinois."

In more prudish days, *res* was even used in legal writing as a EUPHEMISM for "sexual organ": "[T]he weight of authority, both English and American, is that although [for rape to be proved] some penetration must be shown beyond a reasonable doubt, it need not be full penetration; nothing more than *res in re* being requisite." 44 Am. Jur. *Rape* § 3, at 903 (1942). In Latin, *rem* is the accusative case of the singular noun, and *re* is the ablative case (as in *In re Snooks*).

Res is the plural as well as the singular form: "German law uses the word 'thing' only for *res* that are corporeal." G.W. Paton, *A Textbook of Jurisprudence* 508 (4th ed. 1972). See ***jus in re(m)*** **&** ***in personam*** **(B).**

res adjudicata. See **res judicata (A).**

res administrata is a NEOLOGISM meaning "res judicata as applied to administrative decisions." E.g., "Nor is there any agreement as to precisely what degree of similarity should exist between the received conventions of res judicata and what might be called the doctrine of *'res administrata.'*" Frank E. Cooper, *State Administrative Law* 503 (1965)./ "Principles of res judicata—perhaps better dubbed *'res administrata'*—can apply to successive proceedings before a single agency." 18 Charles A. Wright et al., *Federal Practice and Procedure* § 4475, at 762 (1981).

rescindable; rescissible. The first form is better because of its more recognizable relation to the verb. It is the only form listed in the *OED; W3* contains both forms. Cf. **rescissory.**

rescindment is a NEEDLESS VARIANT of *rescission.*

rescissible. See **rescindable.**

rescission; recision; recission; rescision. In the sense "an act of rescinding, annulling, vacating, or canceling," *rescission* is the standard and the etymologically preferable spelling.

But some writers have been misled by their smattering of Latin: perhaps they have realized that *recision* is from the Latin noun *recisio,* meaning "a cutting back, or lopping off." And, through the process known as folk etymology, these writers may have wrongly thought *recision* to be the correct form, *rescission* a corruption. Yet *rescission* is the true Latin form (fr. the accusative *rescissionem*) as well as the true English form. *Rescission* is preferable also because of the consistency of spelling between verb and noun *(rescind / rescission).*

Yet the inferior spelling remains annoyingly common—e.g.: "The facts in the record on administrative review relate to the *recision* [read *rescission*] of the permit and whether the Zoning Board acted within the confines of the zoning ordinance." *Warren v. Zoning Bd. of Appeals,* 625 N.E.2d 1213, 1218 (Ill. App. Ct. 1994)./ "We are not called upon to address whether in an action for fraud in the inducement of a contract, Jones must elect between the remedies of damages and *recision* [read *rescission*] of the contract . . . ." *DeCoatsworth v. Jones,* 639 A.2d 792, 797 n.3 (Pa. 1994).

Some courts even mistakenly combine the misspelling *recision* with the correct spelling to arrive at still other, less frequent misspellings: *recission* and *rescision.* The former appears, e.g., in *Malone v. Safety-Guard Mfg. Co.,* 748 F.2d 312, 314 (5th Cir. 1984).

The sound of the *-ss-* in *rescission* is like that in *precision,* not that in *permission.* This is one of very few words in the English language in which the *-ss-* has the sound */zh/* instead of */sh/.* Two others are *fission* (in AmE) and *abscission.* Cf. *-mission* (with */sh/*) in its many forms.

For the distinction between *rescission* and *repudiation,* see **repudiation.**

rescissory; rescissionary; rescissional. *Rescissory* is the standard adjective corresponding to the noun *rescission* and the verb *to rescind.* E.g., "Through its fraud action, Cinerama seeks . . . an award of *rescissory* damages . . . ." *Cede & Co. v. Technicolor, Inc.,* 542 A.2d 1182, 1186 (Del. 1988). *Rescissionary* and *rescissional* are NEEDLESS VARIANTS. Cf. **rescindable.**

research; re-search. See RE- PAIRS.

res gestae (lit., "things done") has, it seems, irrevocably ensconced itself in the terminology of the law of evidence. But Wigmore considered it "not only entirely useless, but even positively harmful." 6 J.H. Wigmore, *Evidence in Trials at Common Law* § 1767, at 255 (James H. Chadbourn ed., 4th ed. 1976). And recent writers have said that the "ancient phrase can well be jettisoned, with due acknowledgment that it served its era in the evolution of evidence law." E.W. Cleary, *McCormick on Evidence* § 288, at 836 (3d ed. 1984).

The phrase is generally defined as "the events at issue or others contemporaneous with them." In the law of evidence, *res gestae* may be either a rule of relevance that makes testimony about the events forming part of the *res gestae* admissible, or an exception to the hearsay rule allowing for the admissibility of *res gestae* (e.g., if they accompany or explain a declarant's contemporaneous state of mind or physical sensations). See TERMS OF ART.

Res gesta, the singular form, is also sometimes used, as in R.N. Gooderson, *"Res Gesta" in Criminal Cases* (pt. 2), 1957 Cambridge L.J. 55 (so spelled throughout).

residence; residency. Although both are used in the sense "domicile," only *residence* is used as a FORMAL WORD—some would say pomposity—for "house" <a three-story residence>.

It would be useful to restrict *residence* to that sense and to use *residency* in the sense "domicile," but there is little consistency in today's usage. Following are some typical uses, with suggested revisions in brackets for the first two specimens: "Both those favoring lengthy *residence* [read *residency*] requirements and those opposing all requirements pleaded their cases during the congressional hearings on the Social Security Act."/ "Thirty-three states required at least one year of *residence* [read *residency*] in a particular town or county."/ "Unlike those states which condition veterans' preferences on either *residency* at the time of service or length of *residency* in the state, New Mexico requires only that a veteran establish *residency* sometime before a cut-off date, and that he currently qualify as a state resident." See **citizenship & domicil(e).**

resident. See **citizen (A).**

residuary; residual; residuous. In the context of residues of estates and trusts, *residuary* is the preferred adjective. E.g., "The instrument is signed by the testator and properly attested; the *residuary* dispositions are therefore revoked."/ "The codicil contained a bequest of his *residuary* estate to charity, but the bequest was not effective because the testator died within thirty days after the codicil was executed."

Yet there are many examples of *residual* used in such contexts. E.g., "We have before us taxpayers who have inherited what is effectively a *residual* [read *residuary*] estate."/ "On May 5, 1949, decedent executed a codicil partially revamping his testamentary scheme by establishing, in lieu of the outright *residual* [read *residuary*] gift, a trust for the benefit of his son Joseph." *Residual* and *residuary* are susceptible to INELEGANT VARIATION: "In 1965 the testatrix executed a holographic instrument distributing all the assets she controlled, the *residual* [read *residuary*] disposition omitting Mariana Erback, who was one of the *residuary* distributees in the 1945 will."

When one writes of a person's capabilities and functions remaining after an injury, *residual* is the correct term: "She retained a *residual* function to perform her relevant past work as a nurse's aid."/ "Dr. Barrio's final report stated that claimant's *residual* functional disability will interfere with her normal activities at work, which require significant physical effort as a sewing machine operator." *Residuous* is a NEEDLESS VARIANT of the other two words.

residuary legacy. See **legacy.**

residue; residuum; residual, n.; **residuary,** n. Both *residue* and *residuum* (pl. *-dua*) mean "that which remains." *Residue* is the usual and preferred term for contexts involving decedents' estates. It means "the property comprising a decedent's estate after payment of the estate's debts, funeral expenses, costs of administration, and all specific and demonstrative bequests" (*CDL*). E.g., "I give, bequeath, and devise the rest, *residue,* and remainder of my estate of every description, of which I shall die seised and possessed, to my son X."/ "The unmistakable intention of the testatrix, apparent upon the face of the will, was that the *residue* of her estate should go to the person who should have given her the best care in her declining years." Although Blackstone wrote that "the surplus or *residuum* must be paid to the residuary legatee," *residuum* is now to be avoided in such contexts: "The court ordered the executor to divide the *residuum* [read *residue*] among the residuary legatees."

Residuum is a technical term used correctly in chemical contexts. E.g., "There is testimony that a blend of *residuum* and diesel fuel or kerosene would satisfy the definition of crude oil." The plural is *residua.*

Residue and *residuum* often tempt those who fancy INELEGANT VARIATION. In the phrase *residue of a residue,* there is nothing wrong with repeating the word *residue.* Varying the form of the word is an affectation: "Some courts have held that the gift passes by intestacy on the theory that there can be no *residue of a residuum* [read *residue of a residue*]."

Residual, n., = a remainder; an amount still remaining after the main part is subtracted or accounted for (*OED*). E.g., "Some *residual* of the old civic duty to 'cry out' remains."

Residuary, when used elliptically as a noun for such full phrases as *residuary estate* (= *residue*) is uncommon and possibly confusing. It should be avoided. E.g., "He received the *residuary* [read *residue*] of his parents' estate long after his mother's death."

The word sometimes even elliptically denotes *residuary beneficiary,* a usage that can cause confusion—e.g.: "It was this reversion which passed to the *residuaries* [read *residuary beneficiaries*]." *Reeves v. American Sec. & Trust Co.,* 115 F.2d 145, 148 (D.C. Cir. 1940)./ "[This] conduct denied the nieces their inheritance as *residuaries* [read *residuary beneficiaries*] of the estate . . . ." *Krevatas v. Wright,* 518 So. 2d 435, 438 (Fla. Dist. Ct. App. 1988).

residuous. See **residuary.**

residuum. See **residue.**

resign; re-sign. See RE- PAIRS.

resign is almost always intransitive in the U.S. <resign from office>, but is often transitive in England <resign the office>.

res integra; res nova. These terms are moderately common in legal writing. Both mean "an undecided question; a case of first impression"; *res nova* is used primarily in AmE and *res integra* in BrE. Following are examples of the latter: "If the matter were *res integra* in this jurisdiction I should, for my part, have felt very much tempted to follow the views expressed by the majority of the court in *Skelton v. Collins.*" (Eng.)/ "If the matter were *res integra* it might not, to my mind, be a hopeless argument, but in the light of the long-standing law it is today an argument that must be rejected." (Eng.)/ "The court added that if it were *res integra* it would hold that calling a man a rogue or a woman a whore in public company is actionable."

American legal writers use *res nova* far more often than *res integra.* E.g., "[R]equiring the matter to be considered *res nova* by every single trial judge in every single case might seem to some to pose serious administrative difficulties." *Rock v. Arkansas,* 483 U.S. 44, 65 (1987) (Rehnquist, C.J., dissenting)./ "The case involves many issues that are *res nova,* and appellant feels that oral argument would be of great benefit to the court and to both parties." See **first impression, case of.**

The plural forms are *res integrae* and *res novae.*

res ipsa loquitur (= the thing speaks for itself) is known in G.B. but is far more common in the U.S., where it has become familiar enough that *res ipsa case* and even *resipsy* (also spelled *resipsey*) have become lawyers' elliptical colloquialisms. *Res ipsa loquitur* is one of those LATINISMS that have become so common in lawyers' JARGON, or more specifically as TERMS OF ART, that their usefulness is unquestioned.

The phrase refers to the doctrine allowing that, in some circumstances, the mere fact of an accident's occurrence raises an inference of negligence so as to establish a prima facie case. "The rule bearing this name *warrants* the inference of negligence but does not *compel* such an inference." *Johnson v. U.S.,* 333 U.S. 46, 48 (1948) (quotations & brackets omitted).

Many writers tend toward the elliptical dropping of the final word in the phrase—e.g.: "Evatt J. held in *Davis v. Bunn* that *res ipsa* raises only a presumption of fact . . . ." G.W. Paton, *Tort: Negligence—Res Ipsa Loquitur,* 4 Res Judicatae 106, 106 (1948)./ "The doctrine of *res ipsa* does not relieve the plaintiff of the burden of proving negligence." Charles Kramer, *The Rules of Evidence in Negligence Cases* 35 (3d ed. 1963)./ "Criticism of the *res-ipsa* test may be directed to its feasibility." Peter W. Low et al., *Criminal Law: Cases and Materials* 135 (1982).

It may be just as well to leave the last word off, because it is commonly misspelled. American judicial opinions contain examples of *locquitur, locquitor, loquiter, loquitor,* and *loguitur,* among other variations.

The phrase is often used attributively, as in, "She sought to recover on a *res ipsa loquitur* theory." Generally, because it is a foreign phrase, it is not hyphenated when so used. See PHRASAL ADJECTIVES (B).

resister; resistor. The former is the term meaning "one who resists." The latter is a technical electrical term.

resistible; resistable. The former spelling is preferred. See -ABLE (A).

res judicata. A. And *res adjudicata.* The phrase meaning literally "a thing adjudicated" is now universally spelled *res judicata.* The other form, *res adjudicata,* ought to be rejected as a NEEDLESS VARIANT.

But the spelling *adjudicata* was formerly common—e.g.: "[T]he jury's verdict of not guilty necessarily confirmed Bruce's title and rendered the issue *res adjudicata.*" Ephraim Tutt, *Yankee Lawyer* 70 (1943)./ "[The] rule . . . involves a departure from the ordinary principles of *res adjudicata* . . . ." Lon L. Fuller, *Legal Fictions* 4 (1967). Though occasionally in use as late as the 1960s, *adjudicata* is almost never seen in contemporary legal writing.

B. And *collateral estoppel.* See **collateral estoppel** (A).

C. Preposition with. *Res judicata,* which needs no italics, takes *of* or *to.* E.g., "[A]n acquittal on one [indictment] could not be pleaded as *res judicata* of the other." *Dunn v. U.S.,* 284 U.S. 390, 393 (1932) (per Holmes, J.)./ "If Stewart had been separately indicted and tried for armed robbery and a hung jury resulted in a mistrial, that could not be pleaded as *res judicata* to a subsequent separate indictment for attempted second degree murder." *Stewart v. Blackburn,* 746 F.2d 262, 264 (5th Cir. 1984).

In American legal writing the phrase is frequently used as a kind of predicate adjective, as here: "A judgment is not *res judicata* as to, or legally enforceable against, a nonparty." See **res administrata** & ***chose jugée.***

D. Plural. The plural, rarely if ever used, is *res judicatae*—e.g.: "[I]t is therefore not surprising that Cicero's inclusion of *res judicatae* among the sources of law does not reappear in the later jurists." Carleton K. Allen, *Law in the Making* 173 (7th ed. 1964).

res nova. See **res integra.**

resolvable; resolvible; resoluble. The first is far more common than the others in meaning "able to be resolved." E.g., "We held that the pilot base dispute was a 'major' dispute subject to the court's jurisdiction and not a 'minor' dispute *resolvable* by the Railway Labor Act's adjustment mechanism." *Resoluble* has the liability of meaning also "capable of being dissolved again." The variant spelling *resolvible* is to be avoided.

resort. See **recourse.**

resound; re-sound. See RE- PAIRS.

respect. A. *In respect of* and *with respect to.* These phrases are usually best replaced by simpler expressions, such as single prepositions. See **regard & as regards.**

B. *With respect, with great respect,* etc. David Pannick sardonically remarks: "The barrister presents his arguments *with respect, with great respect,* or, on difficult occasions, *with the greatest of respect.* The degree of respect voiced is, of course, in inverse proportion to the willingness indicated by the judge to agree with the arguments being advanced." David Pannick, *Judges* 153 (1987).

respecter of persons. See **no respecter of persons, the law is.**

respectfully. The term is greatly overworked in lawyers' writing directed at judges. E.g., "If this court were to allow recovery based on such speculative evidence, then we would *respectfully* wonder where this might lead us." See **I respectfully submit & respective.**

respective; respectively. Legal writers tend to overuse these pedantic terms. Respectively ought to mean "each one in relation to that one's own situation." E.g., "Appellee's and appellant's *respective* citizenships of France and Georgia therefore supported diversity jurisdiction." It would be more natural, however, to write, "Appellee's citizenship of France and appellant's citizenship of Georgia therefore supported diversity jurisdiction."

Often, *respectively* is not needed at all—e.g.: "In fact their decisions are much more consistent and ours are much less consistent than they appear *respectively* [delete *respectively*] in theory." Roscoe Pound, *The Formative Era of American Law* 123–24 (1938). And the same criticism applies to the adjective *respective:* "The order in which contracting parties must perform their *respective* [delete *respective*] obligations depends on the distinction between conditions precedent, concurrent conditions, and independent promises." G.H. Treitel, *The Law of Contract* 662 (8th ed. 1991). As Fowler wrote, "Delight in these words is a widespread but depraved taste; like soldiers and policemen, they have work to do, but, when the work is not there, the less we see of them the better; of ten sentences in which they occur, nine would be improved by their removal" (*MEU1* 500).

A well-known formbook contains a petition for recovery of unpaid rent with the closing, just before the line for the lawyer's signature, "Respectively submitted." One might have thought that everyone knows the difference between *respective* and *respectful.* See **respectfully.**

respondeat superior [L. "let the principal answer"] is a maxim that embodies the rule of vicarious liability. The phrase is invariably used as a noun—e.g.: "Under the ordinary rules of *respondeat superior,* the shipowner is responsible for his actions . . . ." Grant Gilmore & Charles L. Black, Jr., *The Law of Admiralty* 520 (2d ed. 1975). The first word is sometimes misspelled *respondiat.*

respondent is the PARTY APPELLATION generally used opposite *petitioner,* whether the petitioner seeks a writ of error, a writ of mandamus, or some other type of relief. Both *respondent* and *petitioner* are used most often on appeal and not in the trial court. But that has not always been true of *respondent:* in equity cases, formerly, the *orator* was the complainant and the *respondent* was the defendant.

responsibility, when used in the sense "liability to be made to account or pay," is a LEGALISM not generally understood by nonlawyers, although its sense is sometimes deducible. Whereas nonlawyers use this term in moral senses, lawyers give it legal senses—e.g.: "The mayor's freedom from monetary *responsibility* stems from his sovereign immunity." See **vicarious liability.**

In criminal contexts, *responsibility* refers to either (1) guilt; or (2) a person's mental fitness to answer in court for his or her actions.

-RESS. See SEXISM (C).

rest, v.i., = (AmE) to voluntarily conclude presenting evidence in a trial <after that testimony, the defense rested>. The idiom that one or the other side to a lawsuit *rests* dates from the late 19th century.

restaters = authors of the *Restatements* of the American Law Institute. E.g., "Indeed, this very problem has been addressed by the learned *restaters* in Comment F to § 611, Restatement (Second) of Torts (1977) . . . ." *Hinerman v. Daily Gazette Co.,* 423 S.E.2d 560, 578 (W. Va. 1992).

As in the preceding quotation, the word often appears to be limited to the reporters on a particular Restatement, but sometimes the word appears to refer to the entire membership of the Institute, and sometimes with a sneering tone that says more about the writer than about the restaters—e.g.: "Just as legal realism undercut the symmetrical doctrines beloved of the *restaters* of the ALI, so law and economics and CLS, from different ends of the spectrum, have undercut much of the rationality that Hart and Sacks put into training the legal generation who were at law school in the fifties." Robert Stevens, Book Review, 44 J. Legal Educ. 152, 154 (1994) (reviewing Anthony T. Kronman, *The Lost Lawyer: Failing Ideals of the Legal Profession* (1993)).

restaurateur. So spelled; *restauranteur* is a common error—e.g.: "I would also have doubted seriously the advisability of excluding the ordinary *restauranteur* [read *restaurateur*] as an 'ultimate consumer' . . . ." Ray J. Aiken, *Let's Not Oversimplify Legal Language,* 32 Rocky Mtn. L. Rev. 358, 361 (1960).

rest in peace. See **R.I.P.**

restitution. According to the leading English authorities, "[t]he law of *restitution* is the law relating to all claims, quasi-contractual or otherwise, [that] are founded upon the principle of unjust enrichment." Robert Goff & Gareth Jones, *The Law of Restitution* 3 (3d ed. 1986). This modern use of the term *restitution,* derived from Roman law, began as an Americanism but is now established in BrE as well.

At common law, *restitution* was ordinarily used to denote the return or restoration of some specific thing or condition. But 20th-century usage has extended the sense of the word to include not only the restoration or giving back of something, but also compensation, reimbursement, indemnification, or reparation for benefits derived from—or loss caused to—another.

restitutional; restitutionary; restitutive; restitutory. Restitution being a common subject in law, we find any number of examples of *restitutionary* and *restitutional* in law reports, although our unabridged dictionaries record only *restitutive* and *restitutory.* These last two are little known to American and British lawyers.

The standard form is *restitutionary,* and all other forms can properly be regarded as NEEDLESS VARIANTS. E.g., "The earliest proceedings in common-law courts were *restitutionary* in nature." *Restatement of Restitution* 5 (1937)./ "From the time of Lord Mansfield *restitutionary* remedies were dependent on the dictates of 'natural justice and equity' on which he laid stress." Charles A. Wright, *Cases on Remedies* 59 (1955)./ "*Restitutionary* remedies are designed to restore to plaintiff all that defendant gained at plaintiff's expense." Douglas Laycock, *Modern American Remedies* 3 (1985)./ "*Restitutionary* claims are to be found in equity as well as at law." Robert Goff & Gareth Jones, *The Law of Restitution* 3 (3d ed. 1986).

restive, despite its misleading appearance, does not mean "restful." Formerly it meant "stubborn, refusing to budge," but now it has become synonymous with *restless,* a development that some language critics lament.

restoration; restoral. The latter is a NEEDLESS VARIANT.

restore; re-store. See RE- PAIRS.

restrain. See **refrain.**

rest, residue, and remainder is a collocation beloved by drafters of wills. Those who strive for simplicity and PLAIN LANGUAGE usually write *all other property* instead. See DOUBLETS, TRIPLETS, AND SYNONYM-STRINGS & **residue.**

RESTRICTIVE AND NONRESTRICTIVE CLAUSES. Legal writers who fail to distinguish restrictive from nonrestrictive clauses—and especially *that* from *which*—risk their credibility with careful readers. It's therefore worthwhile to learn the difference so well that, when writing, you use the correct form automatically.

Consider the following sentence: "All the cases that were decided before the 1995 legislation support this argument." It illustrates a *restrictive* clause. Such a clause gives essential information about the preceding noun (here, *cases*) so as to distinguish it from similar items (here, cases that were not decided until after the 1995 legislation) with which it might be confused. In effect, the clause restricts the field of reference to just this one particular case or class of cases—hence the term *restrictive.* Restrictive clauses take no commas (for commas would present the added information as an aside)—e.g.:

- "The power to zone is a state power *that* has been delegated to cities."
- "The Consumer Installment Loan Act is the only statute *that* applies to the subsidiary."

- "Cases *that* have found inadvertent errors to be sanctionable did not involve clerical errors of the type committed by Fleischer."

Now let's punctuate our sample sentence differently and change the relative pronoun from *that* to *which:* "All the cases, which were decided before the 1995 legislation, support this argument." This version illustrates a *nonrestrictive* clause. Such a clause typically gives supplemental, nondefining information. Here, we already know from the context which court we are talking about. The sentence informs us that the cases support this argument—oh, and by the way, they were all decided before the 1995 legislation. The incidental detail is introduced by *which* and set off by commas to signal its relative unimportance. E.g.:

- "The land is contained in Burnham's City Charter, *which* was approved by the legislature in 1891 and again in 1926."
- "The motion for summary judgment deals with the entire breach-of-contract claim, *which* is the only cause of action under this civil-action number."
- "A body of law now deals with this question, *which* is still scarcely understood by the bar."

Restrictive clauses are essential to the grammatical and logical completeness of a sentence. Nonrestrictive clauses, by contrast, are so loosely connected with the essential meaning of the sentence that they might be omitted without changing the essential meaning.

Hence, three guidelines. First, if you cannot omit the clause without changing the basic meaning, the clause is restrictive; use *that* without a comma. Second, if you can omit the clause without changing the basic meaning, the clause is nonrestrictive; use *which* after a comma. Third, if you ever find yourself using a *which* that doesn't follow a comma, it probably needs to be a *that.*

For a good general discussion of these two relative pronouns, see Douglas Laycock, *"That" and "Which,"* 2 Scribes J. Legal Writing 37 (1991).

The word *who* is likewise a relative pronoun. With it, we rely entirely on punctuation to denote whether it functions restrictively or nonrestrictively.

Some of the common errors that occur with the two types of relative clauses are discussed in the sections below.

A. *Which* for *that*. Using which for *that* is perhaps the most common blunder with these words. In none of the sentences that follow could the phrase introduced by *which* be omitted without a nonsensical result or one with a drastically different sense. The word *which* should therefore be *that*—e.g.:

- "Beaver came and made a dam *which* [read *that*] in time created a lovely pond . . . ." William O. Douglas, *Points of Rebellion* 83 (1970).
- "Star Chamber did not usually try felonies *which* [read *that*] involved capital punishment." L.B. Curzon, *English Legal History* 181 (2d ed. 1979).
- "For this reason, the [sentence] *which* [read *that*] follows this passage ought to be either much longer or very short." Richard A. Lanham, *Revising Prose* 15 (1979).
- "Liberty is another value *which* [read *that*] seems to lie at the heart of our concern." Simon Lee, *Law and Morals* 77 (1986).
- "Despite all the uncertainty *which* [read *that*] surrounded the 1994 season—and the doubts *which* [read *that*] still linger like a hangover that just won't quit—Paul O'Neill was sure of one thing." Don Burke, *Yank's Ink O'Neill: 4 Years, $19M,* Star-Ledger (N.J.), 29 Oct. 1994, at 29.
- "In a shareholder's derivative suit, the cause of action *which* [read *that*] such a plaintiff brings before the court is not his own but the corporation's."
- "It is precisely the significance or lack of significance of these contacts *which* [read *that*] troubles us."
- "The injunction runs against only one of the parties of the dispute, a dispute *which* [read *that*] is of the kind *which* [read *that*] led to the passage of PKPA."
- "In such a case he would not be exercising his legal right, or doing an act *which* [read *that*] can be judged separately from the motive *which* [read *that*] actuated him."
- "For us to allow the judgment to stand as it is would risk an affirmance of a decision *which* [read *that*] might have been decided differently had the court below felt unconstrained."
- "We understand that every right *which* [read *that*] beneficiaries would otherwise have against the trust company is sealed and wholly terminated by the decree."

In the last sentence quoted, the first *that* made the writers want to vary the word in the second phrase, but they should not have succumbed to this misplaced desire.

B. Restrictive Clause Wrongly Made Nontrestrictive. This error is fairly common. The relative clauses illogically set off by commas are necessary to the meaning of the sentence; one could not drop those phrases out of the sentences and retain the intended meaning—e.g.: "A state will not exercise judicial *jurisdiction, which* [read *jurisdiction that*] has been obtained by fraud or unlawful force, over a defendant or his property."/ "The jury could find that a *woman, who* [read *woman who*] believed she had a special relationship with God and was the chosen one to survive the end of the world could believe that God would take over the direction of her life to the extent of driving her car."

C. Series. Some writers want to substitute *and who* or *and which* in place of *and that* for the last in a series of relative clauses beginning with a *that*-phrase. This tendency may result from a fear that the relative *that* may be confused with the demonstrative *that; which* and *who,* by contrast, are consistently relatives. Despite that concern, which is usually overblown, parallel phrasing is better—e.g.: "A corporation *that* has failed to pay its franchise taxes, *that* has persisted in its delinquency for mroe than one year, and *which* [read *that*] has had its charter revoked can no longer operate as a business within the state."

D. Remote Relative Pronouns. See REMOTE RELATIVES.

restrictive covenant = a private agreement, usu. in a deed or lease, that restricts the use and occupancy of real property, most commonly by specifying lot size, building lines, architectural styles, and the uses to which the property may be put. Formerly, such covenants were used in the U.S. to racist ends: "Finally, *'restrictive covenants'*—whereby property-owners in 'white sections' of Northern cities contracted never to sell or rent to people 'not of the Caucasian race'—were dealt a long-range death-blow in a set of rulings which said that state courts could not enforce such contracts, even in private lawsuits, without violating the Fourteenth Amendment." Fred Rodell, *Nine Men* 295 (1955). See **covenant.**

resultant, n., for *result* is an ARCHAISM—e.g.: "For the legislative purpose is the *resultant* [read *result*] of the pressure of conflicting interests in the legislature." Jerome Frank, *Courts on Trial* 302 (1950)./ "Human preferences do not seem to be the *resultants* [read *result* or *results*] of a few simple causes, but rather of a large scale and measured under experimental conditions." Morris R. Cohen, *Reason and Law* 105 (1961).

resulting trust. See **constructive trust (C).**

resurface, like *surface,* is both v.i. & v.t. *Resurface* = (1) to come to the top again <he resurfaced in the middle of the pond>; or (2) to put a new surface on <the state resurfaced the road>.

retainage; retainer. *Retainage* (AmE) = a percentage of what a landowner sets aside for a contractor, withholding the sum until the construction has been satisfactorily completed and all mechanics' liens either released or expired. Though the word is fairly common in American property law, it is omitted from every major English-language dictionary and from most law dictionaries.

Retainer = (1) a client's authorization for a lawyer to act in a case; (2) a fee paid to a lawyer to secure legal representation. A *special retainer* results in employment for a specific project. A *general retainer* results in employment for a specific length of time instead of for a specific project.

retaliatory; retaliative. The two forms have undergone DIFFERENTIATION. The former means "of, relating to, or of the nature of retaliation" <retaliatory eviction>, whereas the latter means "vindictive, tending to retaliation" <a retaliative landlord>.

reticence; reticency. The latter is a NEEDLESS VARIANT.

reticent (= reserved, disinclined to speak freely; taciturn) is frequently misunderstood as being synonymous with *reluctant.* E.g., "Contemporary courts have been more *reticent* [read *reluctant*] to discard the privity requirement and to permit recovery in warranty by a remote consumer for purely economic losses." Occasionally, the line between taciturnity and reluctance is an extremely subtle one—e.g.: "[M]any cases go unreported because of a *reticence* on the part of the victims to publicly accuse close relatives, much like the silence that often cloaks child abuse . . . ." Jon Nordheimer, *A New Abuse of Elderly: Theft by Kin and Friends,* N.Y. Times, 16 Dec. 1991, at A1.

retire. In the legal idiom, a jury is customarily said to *retire* for deliberations—e.g.: "After the jury had *retired* to deliberate, the court informed counsel that some communication had been received from the jury . . . ." *People v. Allen,* 197 N.W.2d 874, 878 (Mich. Ct. App. 1972). The noun *retirement* is much less common in this sense, but it does appear from time to time, esp. in BrE: "The Judge's summing-up was brief but thorough, and after a short *retirement* the jury brought in a verdict of guilty." Stanley Jackson, *The Life and Cases of Mr. Justice Humphreys* 175 (n.d. [1951]).

retorsion; retortion. Both spellings are used in international law in referring to "retaliation in kind for discourteous, unkind, or unfair acts, such as high tariffs or discriminatory duties." The *OED* gives preference to *retortion,* but most international-law texts use *retorsion.* See 2 L. Lassa Oppenheim, *International Law* 134 (7th ed.

1952). Thus, *retortion* is now best considered a NEEDLESS VARIANT.

retract. See **revoke.**

retractable; retractible. The former spelling is correct. See -ABLE (A).

retract(at)ion. In the figurative sense "the act of recanting" or "a statement in recantation," *retraction* is usual in AmE, *retractation* in BrE. In BrE, *retraction* is the noun corresponding to *retract* in literal senses ("to draw back," etc.).

retractible. See **retractable.**

retreat; re-treat. See RE- PAIRS.

retreat rule = the criminal-law doctrine holding that even the innocent victim of a murderous assault must choose a safe retreat, if there is one, instead of resorting to deadly force, unless either of the following circumstances exists: (a) the victim is in his or her "castle" at the time (see **castle doctrine**); or (b) the assailant is a robber or one whom the victim is trying to arrest. E.g., "The *retreat rule* occasioned strong controversy in the United States, where it was of practical importance because of the prevalence of handguns." Glanville Williams, *Textbook of Criminal Law* 460 (1978).

retribute, v.t. (= to pay back, visit retribution upon) is labeled "rare" in the *OED,* but modern writers on criminal law are reviving it after centuries of disuse. E.g., "[T]he just deserts principle does not prescribe a scale of penalties . . . beyond suggesting that punishments must be felt to be deserved, that is, felt somehow to *retribute* (pay back) for the moral and material injuries crimes cause." Ernest van den Haag, *Punishment: Desert and Crime Control,* 85 Mich. L. Rev. 1250, 1256 (1987)./ "Robbins had only *retributed* [read *paid back*] the past humiliations of William Jessup and other American sailors." Ruth Wedgwood, *The Revolutionary Martyrdom of Jonathan Robbins,* 100 Yale L.J. 229, 316 (1990).

retributive; retributory; retributional. *Retributive* = characterized by, or of the nature of, retribution (*OED*). E.g., "The fact that it is natural to hate a criminal does not prove that *retributive* punishment is justified." Glanville Williams, *The Sanctity of Life and the Criminal Law* 60 (1957)./ "Yet it is certainly something [that] should prevent our dismissing all *retributive* theory out of hand." H.L.A. Hart, *Law, Liberty, and Morality* 60 (1963).

Retributory = involving, producing, or characterized by retribution or recompense (*OED*). The only sense that *-tory* has that is lacking in *-tive* is that of causing or producing retribution; but euphony often governs the choice of term.

Retributional and *retributionary* are NEEDLESS VARIANTS not contained in the major English-language dictionaries. But they appear fairly frequently—e.g.: "[T]he connection . . . turns upon the conspiracy between the Texas defendants and Moses to subject the plaintiffs to *retributional* [read *retributive*] abuse without regard to constitutional rights." *Williams v. Garcia,* 569 F. Supp. 1452, 1454 (E.D. Mich. 1983)./ "Arguments in favor of the death penalty stress its deterrent, economic and *retributionary* [read *retributive*] effects." Gregory S. Brown, Comment, *Constitutional Law,* 27 Washburn L.J. 194, 196–97 (1987).

retributory damages. See **punitive damages.**

retroactive; retrospective; retrogressive. In law, the first two terms are used synonymously in reference to statutes that extend in scope or effect to matters that have occurred in the past. E.g., "[T]he court refused to give effect to a *retroactive* statute creating a special tribunal to try certain suits by a bank against its officers." Roscoe Pound, *The Formative Era of American Law* 57 (1938)./ "It is presumed that a statute does not have *retrospective* effect." Michael Zander, *The Law-Making Process* 128 (2d ed. 1985). The one advantage of *retrospective* is that it corresponds etymologically to its antonym *prospective.*

Retrogressive = retrograde; tending to go back to an inferior state; returning to a worse condition. E.g., "The court nevertheless upheld the procedures because they were not *retrogressive*—they would not exacerbate vote dilution in Lockhart."

retrofit, n. & v.t. The noun *retrofit* is a HYBRID meaning "a modification of equipment or a building to include developments not available at the time of original manufacture or construction." The term has been extended to use as a verb in both literal and figurative senses—e.g.: "On appeal Ronald has sought to *retrofit* his case by downplaying the degree to which his recovery was based on Bonnette's false statements of love and sexual desire." *Askew v. Askew,* 28 Cal. Rptr. 2d 284, 289–90 (Ct. App. 1994)./ "Plaintiff's position was that the astragal should have been removed by Coke and the door *retrofitted* with some sort of synthetic rubber cushion." *Fontana v. Coca-Cola Enterprises, Inc.,* 632 So. 2d 811, 814 (La. Ct. App. 1994).

As in the immediately preceding example, the past-tense form should be *retrofitted,* not *retrofit*—

e.g.: "To do so, Westinghouse has invested in a series of advanced technologies [that] are standard to new plant designs and [that] can be *retrofit* [read *retrofitted*] into existing units . . . ." *Wholesale Power Contracts,* Pub. Util. Fortnight, 16 March 1989, at 67, 72./ "Existing cars should be *retrofit* [read *retrofitted*] with meters, for an installation fee." Steven N. Brautigam, Note, *Rethinking the Regulation of Car Horn and Car Alarm Noise,* 19 Colum. J. Envtl. L. 391, 438 (1994). Cf. **fit.**

retrogressive. See **retroactive.**

retrospective. See **retroactive.**

return, n., = (1) a court officer's bringing back of an instrument to the court that issued it—as when a sheriff returns a citation; (2) the officer's indorsement on such an instrument, reporting what the officer did or found—as in a return of *nulla bona,* q.v.; or (3) an income-tax filing.

return back is a fairly common REDUNDANCY. Cf. **refer back & revert (B).**

returnee. See -EE.

re-urge should be hyphenated.

reus; rea. These are the masculine and feminine forms of the term used in Roman, civil, and canon law to denote "a defendant." The plural forms are *rei* and *reae. Reus* is the more commonly encountered form.

re(-)use. Generally this word is not hyphenated: *reuse.*

revalidate; revive. These words, used in reference to reestablishing the validity of revoked wills, are distinguished in use. *Revalidation* consists in repetition of the formalities of execution of the will previously revoked. *Revival* consists in revocation of the superseding or revoking will (i.e., the will that displaced or invalidated the original will).

revenge. See **avenge.**

reverence, v.t.; **revere.** The former is a FORMAL WORD equivalent to the latter. E.g., "No person more than the present writer *reverences* this internal mentor we call conscience, but the experience of the ages teaches us that it is a most fallible guide." See ***lapsus linguae.***

reverie; revery. The former spelling is preferred.

reversal; reversion; reverter. The first is the noun corresponding to the verb *to reverse.* The second and third are nouns corresponding to the verb *to revert.* Fowler quotes the following misuse of *reversion* for *reversal:* "The *reversion* [read *reversal*] of our free trade policy would, we are convinced, be a great detriment to the working class." For the distinction between *reversion* and *reverter,* see **reversion.**

reverse, n. See **converse.**

reverse, v.t.; **overrule.** An appellate court *reverses* a decision when it overturns what the trial court did below in the same case; it *overrules* a decision when it disapproves of the holding in an earlier case. See JUDGMENTS, APPELLATE-COURT.

reverse discrimination. This term refers to treating minorities preferentially, usu. through affirmative-action programs, in a way that adversely affects members of a majority group. The term first became popular with the U.S. Supreme Court's decision in *Regents of University of California v. Bakke,* 438 U.S. 265 (1978).

But the word is older. The *Second Barnhart Dictionary of New English* (1980) traces it back to 1971, and neither John Algeo's dictionary of neologisms, *Fifty Years Among the New Words* (1991), nor Jonathon Green's *Tuttle Dictionary of New Words Since 1960* (1992) takes it back any further.

In fact, though, the term was coined in the early 1960s, apparently by a state-court judge: "These constitutional guarantees mean that a non-white pupil has just as much right to be educated in a public school as a white pupil, but it also means, and equally so, that a child should not be enrolled or transported to a certain schoolhouse because he is white or non-white. To apply such a test, overtly or covertly, is *reverse discrimination* making racial membership a qualification for such a move, when it really should be irrelevant and immaterial." *Strippoli v. Bickal,* 248 N.Y.S.2d 588, 599 (Sup. Ct. 1964) (per William G. Easton, J.).

The next use in American caselaw—the first federal example—occurred four years later: "The history leads the court to conclude that Congress did not intend to require *'reverse discrimination';* that is, the act does not require that Negroes be preferred over white employees who possess employment seniority." *Quarles v. Philip Morris, Inc.,* 279 F. Supp. 505, 516 (E.D. Va. 1968).

reversible. So spelled. See -ABLE (A).

reversible error has been wrongly criticized on grounds that "*error* cannot be *reversed* per se, although its results can be remedied." William F. Haggerty, *Of Bards, Beguilers, and Barristers,* 66 Mich. B.J. 784, 785 (1987). Yet this is an acceptable example of HYPALLAGE.

reversion; reverter. Both are reversionary interests in property having been conveyed. A *reversion* is an interest in land arising by operation of law whenever the owner of an estate grants to another a particular estate, e.g., a life estate or a term of years, but does not dispose of the owner's entire interest (*OCL*). A *reverter* is a lesser interest—a possibility that the land might revert—arising when a grant is limited so that it might terminate. A *reversion* occurs automatically upon termination of the prior estate (as when a life tenant dies), whereas a *reverter*—usually termed a *possibility of reverter*—under orthodox theory, does not occur automatically, but is subject to a return to the grantor when a condition is breached (as upon the lapse of a conditional fee).

Reverter and *reversion* are susceptible to INELEGANT VARIATION. Justice Brennan, in his dissent in *Evans v. Abney,* 396 U.S. 435, 450–59 (1970), switches back and forth between the terms in describing the single interest that heirs had in a fee simple subject to condition subsequent. The correct term to describe such an estate is *power of termination* or *right of entry for condition broken.* See **remainder, reversal** & -ER (B).

reversionary; reversional. The latter is a NEEDLESS VARIANT—not common but hardly unknown: "[T]hey do afford an inference of an intention to invest full power in his wife to effectuate a complete separation of the 'home place' by conveyance from any *reversional* [read *reversionary*] interest on behalf of his estate." *Geyer v. Bookwalter,* 193 F. Supp. 57, 61–62 (W.D. Mo. 1961).

reversioner = the grantor or heir in reversion; one who possesses the reversion to an estate. E.g., "Under the doctrine of destructibility the holder of the life estate could defeat the contingent remaindermen by a tortious feoffment or by effecting a merger with the *reversioner*."/ "A statement made by a declarant holding a limited interest in any property and opposed to such interest is deemed to be relevant only as against those who claim under him, and not as against the *reversioner*." See **reversion & remainder.**

revert = (1) (of property) to return by reversion; (2) to return to a former state; to go back to (as a former state or condition); or (3) to turn (eyes or steps) back.

A. *Revert* for *refer*. This is a curious mistake: "By *reverting* [read *adverting* or *referring*] to the language of the contestant's petition, we can see that the contestant admits that the document under consideration actually bears the testator's and attesters' signatures." Even if the writer intended in this sentence to say that we were "going back" to focus on particular words, the use of *revert* was ill-advised, for sense (3) subsumes the connotations of sense (2) of returning to a former state or condition.

B. *Revert back*. This REDUNDANCY is common in AmE, less so in BrE. E.g., "If Nathaniel T. Braswell should die leaving no lawful heir from his body, then the land herein conveyed shall *revert back to the said James J. Braswell* [read *revert to James J. Braswell*] or to his lawful heirs."/ "Medieval town centers, once built for people on foot and a few carts and carriages, have partly *reverted back* [read *reverted*] to strollers . . . ." Marlise Simons, *Amsterdam Plans Wide Limit on Cars,* N.Y. Times, 28 Jan. 1993, at A5. Cf. **return back & refer back.**

reverter. See **reversal & reversion.**

revery. See **reverie.**

revest = to vest a second time. E.g., "[B]y breaking bulk, the bailee determines the bailment, and . . . the goods at once *revest* in the possession of the bailor." Oliver W. Holmes, *The Common Law* 177 (1881; repr. 1963)./ "Once control had been *revested* in the Assembly, the people realized that they must be alert in order to keep their power in the state." René A. Wormser, *The Story of the Law* 52 (1962).

The corresponding noun is *revestment*—e.g.: "[I]n addition to the State's right of *revestment* under the condition . . . , the reservation reserved to the State the right of entry and use . . . ." *Turiano v. State,* 519 N.Y.S.2d 180, 185 (Ct. Cl. 1987).

review, n. **A. And *appeal; certiorari*.** The word *review* denotes a genus, of which *appeal* and *certiorari* are species. In reference, then, to all types of appellate scrutiny—however the cases may have arrived in the appellate court—*review* is the most accurate term. See **appeal (B).**

B. And *reviewal*. *Reviewal* is a NEEDLESS VARIANT.

revisal. See **revision.**

revise; recense; redact. The first is the ordinary word that serves in most senses. The second and third terms are used especially of revising texts with close scrutiny. *Redact* = (1) to make a draft of; or (2) to edit. In American legal writing it is often used in the sense "to edit out or mask the privileged, impertinent, or objectionable matter in a document." *Recense* is more of a literary term in modern usage; it relates to scholarly editing of ancient texts and the like.

reviser; revisor. Both forms appear in modern legal prose. The *-er* form is preferred. E.g., "The *revisors* [read *revisers*] of the Code of 1919 had adopted some of the suggestions contained in the address but recommended no time limitation on probate."/ "As to the content of what constitutes revocation by implication of law, the *Reviser's* Note makes plain that the revision was merely an acceptance of *Pascucci,* which in turn merely accepted revocation by implication from a subsequent marriage and children as a common-law rule that had emerged before our Revolution."

revision; revisal. The latter is a NEEDLESS VARIANT. E.g., "Before the general *revisal* [read *revision*] of laws in this state in 1849, it was generally held that the destruction of a will containing a revocatory clause revived a preserved uncanceled will with no proof to the contrary being allowed."

revisionary; revisional; revisory. *Revisionary* = of, pertaining to, or made up of revision <revisionary methods>. *Revisional* is a NEEDLESS VARIANT. *Revisory* = having power to revise; engaged in revision <a revisory board>.

revisor. See **reviser.**

revisory. See **revisionary.**

revitalize has become a VOGUE WORD among politicians and business people <to revitalize the inner city>.

revival of judgment. See **renewal of judgment.**

revive. See **revalidate & republish.**

reviver; revivor. The two forms mean different things. *Reviver* = one who or that which revives. *Revivor* is a primarily BrE legal term denoting a proceeding for the revival of a suit or action abated by the death of one of the parties, or by some other circumstance (*OED*). E.g., "A number of jurisdictions extend the process of *revivor* to judgment liens."

revocability is pronounced */rev-ə-kə-**bil**-i-tee/.*

revocable; revokable. The first form is preferred; the word is pronounced */**rev**-ə-kə-bəl/. Revokable* (as well as *revokeable*) is a NEEDLESS VARIANT. See **irrevocable.**

revocatory; revocative. The former is preferred, whether in common-law phrases such as *revocatory acts* or *revocatory powers,* or in the civil-law phrase *revocatory action* (see, e.g., Quebec Civ. Code art. 1032).

revokable. See **revocable.**

revoke; retract. These two words are nearly synonymous. *Revoke* = to annul by taking back; *retract* = to withdraw or disavow. In the idiom of contract law, an offer is *revoked,* while an anticipatory repudiation of a contract is *retracted.*

revolt; revolution. See **sedition.**

rewrite is both noun and verb, although *write* itself cannot be a noun. E.g., "The Reagan administration's Treasury Department says that its proposed *rewrite* of the Internal Revenue Code will make taxes simpler and fairer."

Rex; Regina. See **R.**

rhadamant(h)in(e) */rad-ə-**man**-thən/.* This exotic term, meaning "of or relating to a rigorous or inflexible judge," is best spelled *rhadamanthine.* The word is a type of LITERARY ALLUSION (see (D)), Rhadamanthus being, in Greek mythology, Zeus and Europa's son who served as one of the judges in the lower world. E.g., "I do not suggest that every such *rhadamanthine* ruling restricting access to the courts is motivated solely by a desire to reduce judicial workload." Bernard S. Meyer, *Justice, Bureaucracy, Structure, and Simplification,* 42 Md. L. Rev. 659, 685 (1983)./ "In a series of cases . . . , some courts have utilized a *rhadamanthine* construction of the procedural requirements of the Rule." David S. Day, *Discovery Standards for the Testimonial Expert Under Federal Rule of Civil Procedure 26(b)(4),* 133 F.R.D. 209, 217 (1990). See **draconian.**

RHETORICAL QUESTIONS (those posed without the hope or expectation of an answer, often because the answer is obvious), especially when not unusually long, should end with a question mark. E.g., "Who would deny that the victim of a nuisance may have it abated regardless of the intent of the offending party?" Rhetorical questions quickly become tiresome if overused.

rhodomontade. See **rodomontade.**

rhyme or reason is a CLICHÉ to be avoided. E.g., "Nor do we find that the jury's verdict was *without rhyme or reason* [read *without reason*]."

Richard Roe. See **Doe, John.**

RICO (an acronym for the Racketeer Influenced and Corrupt Organizations Act) should be written in all capitals—not written *Rico,* as it predominantly appears in *Chapman & Cole v. Itel Container Int'l B.V.,* 116 F.R.D. 550 (S.D. Tex. 1987) (using both forms).

Some writers, esp. journalists, have begun to use the acronym as a verb meaning "to sue under RICO"—e.g.: "The plaintiff can't sue under the substantive law—here, the securities law—but hopes to get into court anyway by *RICOing* someone." L. Gordon Crovitz, *While Senate Fiddles, the Supreme Court Has Real Work to Do,* Wall St. J., 9 Oct. 1991, at A15./ "In my view, reputable businesses would not be *RICOed* if injured plaintiffs had an across-the-board express federal commercial/consumer fraud damages remedy . . . ." Arthur F. Mathews, *Shifting the Burden of Losses in the Securities Markets,* 65 Notre Dame L. Rev. 896, 962–63 (1990). So used, the word is a casualism.

rid > rid > rid. The past-tense and past-participial form *ridded* is now obsolete.

ridden. See **laden (B).**

ridiculous has moved a long way from its etymological suggestion of "causing laughter," so that writers nowadays often term *ridiculous* what causes them anger, frustration, distress, or even sadness. In other words, by SLIPSHOD EXTENSION it is frequently used when people are far from laughing. Today it is unrealistic to insist on etymological rigor with this word.

right, adj.**; righteous; rightful.** *Right* = correct, proper, just. *Righteous* = morally upright, virtuous, or law-abiding. This term has strong religious connotations, often of unctuousness. *Rightful* = (1) (of an action) equitable, fair <a rightful dispossession>; (2) (of a person) legitimately entitled to a position <the rightful heir>; or (3) (of an office or piece of property) that one is entitled to <his rightful inheritance>.

These terms are sometimes confused. In the following specimen, *rightfully* is misused for *rightly:* "The jury *rightfully* [read *rightly*] could reason that Marvin knew the conditions through which he had to fly." For a similar distinction—that between *purposely* and *purposefully*—see **purposely.**

right, n., is "one of the most ambiguous words in the English language." W.W. Buckland, *Some Reflections on Jurisprudence* 32 (1945). The most widely used definition is "an interest or expectation guaranteed by law." The nature of the guarantee—esp. its enforcement—leads to endless gradations in meaning.

right, as of. See **as of right.**

right but not obligation. This phrase, common in contracts, makes explicit that a party has the right but not the legal duty to do something. Because the conferment of a right sometimes implies an obligation to exercise that right, the phrase is a useful one.

righteous; rightful. See **right,** adj.

right, in one's own. Originally, this phrase referred to a person's particular title or claim to something. The phrase still sometimes bears this literal sense—e.g.:

- "[A]n association's standing depends upon a showing that its members would have standing to sue *in their own right.*" *Randolph-Sheppard Vendors v. Weinberger,* 795 F.2d 90, 99 (D.C. Cir. 1986).
- "Mrs. Brayman lacks standing to assert this cause of action in *her own right* or on behalf of her daughter, and the appellees were entitled to summary judgment as a matter of law." *Brayman v. DeLoach,* 439 S.E.2d 709, 711 (Ga. Ct. App. 1993).
- "The possibility of collusive litigation can no longer justify a doctrine that in effect informs families that an injured child member thereof cannot obtain compensation *in his or her own right* for injuries which if caused by a nonparent would be so compensable . . . ." *Terror Mining Co. v. Roter,* 866 P.2d 929, 949 (Colo. 1994).

Today, however, the word has an extended sense referring to an individual characteristic or qualification that a person might otherwise be thought to hold in common with someone else—e.g.: "They had inherited considerable property from their father, an unsuccessful Congregational clergyman turned successful lawyer, and their mother, a wealthy woman *in her own right.*" Carolyn C. Jones, *Dollars and Selves: Women's Tax Criticism and Resistance in the 1870s,* 1994 U. Ill. L. Rev. 265, 276. That sentence conveys the idea that the mother did not owe her wealth to her successful husband.

But if such distinction is not intended, the phrase is often merely a superfluity, the victim of SLIPSHOD EXTENSION—e.g.: "If Edell's redirect examination was devastating *in its own right* [delete *in its own right*], it also had far exceeded the bounds of permissible questioning . . . ." John A. Jenkins, *The Litigators* 207 (1989)./ "At the Rule 29.15 hearing, trial counsel testified that McAffee had a criminal record *in her own right* [delete *in her own right*]." *State v. Harris,* 870 S.W.2d 798, 817 (Mo. 1994). See SUPERFLUITIES.

right of action. See **cause of action.**

right of common. See **profits à prendre.**

right of entry; right of re-entry. The former is the standard phrase, to which the latter adds nothing.

right of entry for condition broken; right of entry for breach of condition; power of termination. All three phrases refer to the rights of the grantor and the grantor's successors after conveyance of a fee simple conditional, which creates a possibility of reverter. Though the most common phrase is *right of entry (for condition broken),* the word *right* is something of a misnomer: "The *right of entry* is not, strictly speaking, a 'right' in the sense of being a present legally enforceable claim. It is rather a power to terminate the granted estate on breach of the specified condition." Cornelius J. Moynihan, *Introduction to the Law of Real Property* 112 (2d ed. 1988). Hence, the trend is to use *power of termination.* See *Restatement of Property* § 24, at 60, special note to cmt. b (1936). See **reversion** & **fee simple (G).**

Some authorities use the phrase *right of entry for breach of condition,* but the modern trend is to prefer *power of termination.* See Roger A. Cunningham et al., *The Law of Property* 44–45 (2d ed. 1993).

right of first refusal; right of preemption. See **option.**

right of privacy; right to privacy. Although the phrase commonly appears with either preposition, *right of privacy* predominates.

When functioning as a noun, the phrase remains unhyphenated. But when it is used as a PHRASAL ADJECTIVE, it is preferably hyphenated <right-of-privacy case>.

right of re-entry. See **right of entry.**

right of survivorship (= a joint tenant's right to succeed to the whole estate upon the death of the other joint tenant—in the case of only two such tenants, and analogously when more than two are involved) is a LOAN TRANSLATION of the Latin phrase *jus accrescendi.* Deeds often make the right explicit by stating that the grantees are to hold "as joint tenants with the right of survivorship."

right of way = (1) a person's legal right, established by usage or by contract, to pass through grounds or property owned by another, or the land so used; (2) in AmE, the right to build and operate a railway line or highway on land belonging to another, or the land so used; or (3) the right to take precedence in traffic. The plural is *rights of way.* See **easement (C).**

right reason. An American court writes: "We conclude that, although the award as remitted by the trial judge was generous, it was not so gross as to be contrary to *right reason.*" The *OED* states that the phrase *right reason* is now rare; yet it remains common in much legal writing. It ought to be rare, since *reason* alone suffices in most contexts—or so reason tells us.

As might be expected, the phrase has a history: it is a LOAN TRANSLATION of the Latin phrase *rectam rationem.* Borrowed by St. Thomas Aquinas directly from Aristotle, *right reason* was one method of discovering the essence of natural law. E.g., "Natural law, or *jus naturale,* as defined by Roman philosophers and jurists, is that law which is naturally discerned by *right reason,* as opposed to the law found necessary and made by man for the safe conduct of the state under localized conditions or by agreement for the preservation of international rights." "Law, Natural," in 17 *Encyclopedia Americana,* 104, 105 (1953)./ "[The] essence [of natural law] is that there is an abstract justice, either God-given or ascertainable by man's *'right reason,'* and that laws are just or unjust in so far as they conform to or violate the pure, abstract, ultimate rules of conduct." René A. Wormser, *The Story of the Law* 482 (1962).

Whether the phrase *right reason* is outmoded depends largely on one's view of natural law. (See **natural law.**) In any event, though, the phrase hardly belongs in a context in which a court finds an award of damages reasonable, as in the sentence quoted at the outset of this entry.

right, title, and interest. This phrase, one of the classic triplets of the legal idiom, is the traditional language for conveying a quitclaim interest. (See **quitclaim** & DOUBLETS, TRIPLETS, AND SYNONYM-STRINGS.) Technically, only one of the three words is necessary, as the broad meaning of *interest* includes the others: though you can have an *interest* without having *title* and perhaps without a given *right,* you cannot have *title* or a *right* without having an *interest.*

Therefore, the more modern DRAFTING style is to replace the triplet with the broadest of the three words—e.g.: "[W]hen a parcel of land is used or purchased in violation of federal narcotics laws, all of the offending owner's *right, title, and interest* [read *interest*] immediately *transfer* [read *transfers*] to the government, regardless of when the forfeiture action is instituted." Damon G. Saltzburg, Note, *Real Property Forfeitures as a Weapon in the Government's War on Drugs,* 72 B.U. L. Rev. 217, 221 (1992).

Still, some traditionalists prefer to keep from varying the age-old idiom, which uses only two additional words. Why, they reason, create a test case with their documents merely to find out whether *interest* is indeed broad enough to encapsulate *right* and *title?*

American lawyers, when given the choice in transactional drafting—the pros and cons on both sides of the argument—split about equally on the two sides.

right to die. As a noun phrase, *right to die* is three words <advocates of the right to die>; but as a PHRASAL ADJECTIVE, it should be hyphenated: "Both sides of a *right-to-die* case received a skeptical hearing today at the Supreme Court . . . ." Linda Greenhouse, *Right-to-Die Case Gets First Hearing in Supreme Court,* N.Y. Times, 7 Dec. 1989, at 1.

right-to-lifer (= an opponent of abortion rights) is JOURNALESE—and is generally pejorative—e.g.: "The cast of characters includes . . . Attorney General Dick Thornburgh, a strident *right-to-lifer* who took the questionable step of asking the court to reconsider *Roe* . . . ." *The Battle over Abortion,* Newsweek, 1 May 1989, at 28.

right to privacy. See **right of privacy.**

rigorous (= extremely strict, austere) should not be misused for *rigid,* as here: "The *rigorous* [read *rigid*], inflexible view of the majority rejects the improvements to be gained by changing the old rule."

riot; unlawful assembly. An *unlawful assembly* is a meeting of three or more persons who intend either to commit a violent crime or to carry out some act, lawful or unlawful, that will constitute a breach of the peace. A *riot* is an unlawful assembly that has begun to fulfill its common purpose of breaching the peace and terrorizing the public.

Riot Act, reading the. See **reading the Riot Act.**

R.I.P.; *requiescat in pace;* rest in peace. The phrase *requiescat in pace* means "may he (or she) rest in peace." The abbreviated form, though commonly taken to be a shortened form of the English phrase, stands for the Latin phrase.

rising of court. This increasingly rare term, generally used as an antonym of *sitting* or *session,* refers to the court's final adjournment of the term. Loosely, however, it is also used in reference to a recess or temporary break in the court's business, as at the end of the day. E.g., "[T]he court gave judgment to Fail and Otho L. Hays for the amounts due them respectively, and ordered, in default of payment of the judgments within ten days from the *rising of court,* a sale of the mortgaged property." *Hays v. Galion Gas Light & Coal Co.,* 29 Ohio St. 330, 332 (1876).

risk = (1) the hazard of property loss covered by an insurance contract, or the degree of such a hazard; (2) a person or thing that the insurer considers a hazard; or (3) a known danger to which a person assents, thus foreclosing recovery for injuries suffered <assumption of the risk>. For more on sense (3), see **assumption of the risk** & ***volenti non fit injuria.***

risk of nonpersuasion. See **burden of proof (A).**

rob; steal; burglarize. Persons are *robbed;* things are *stolen;* and places are *burglarized.* The words are occasionally confused—e.g.: "The prosecution claimed that he, with two others, had plotted to *rob* [read *burglarize*] the pawnshop of one Leo Goldstein on Doyers Street . . . ." Ephraim Tutt, *Yankee Lawyer* 324 (1943). See **burglary.**

robbery = aggravated larceny, i.e., larceny from the person by violence or intimidation. "The nonlawyer speaks of 'robbing a bank' by driving a tunnel into the strong-room; but this is not legal usage. In law, *robbery* implies force or the threat of it." Glanville Williams, *Textbook of Criminal Law* 791 (1978). See **burglary (A).**

rodomontade; rhodomontade. Pronounced */rod-ə-mən-**tayd**/*, the word, meaning "boastful talk," is preferably spelled *rodomontade.*

Roe, Richard. See **Doe, John.**

rogatory letter. See **letters rogatory.**

role; roll. These two words are sometimes confused. *Roll* has many senses, including breadroll, but the only sense that seems to cause problems is "a list or register" <the teacher took roll>. *Role,* by contrast, means "a function or part, as in a drama."

The most common error is the use of *roll* where *role* belongs—e.g.: "Perhaps it is time once again to call to the prosecutor's attention the particularly sensitive *roll* [read *role*] played by the government attorney . . . ." *U.S. v. Anchondo-Sandoval,* 910 F.2d 1234, 1238 (5th Cir. 1990)./ "The court obviously . . . believed [that] the reason given by the State's attorney for striking Venireperson Austin was the real reason, and that race did not play a *roll* [read *role*] in the State's decision." *State v. Davis,* 835 S.W.2d 525, 527 (Mo. Ct. App. 1992). (On the use of *Venireperson Austin* in the preceding example, see TITULAR TOMFOOLERY & **venireman.**)

But the opposite blunder also occurs—e.g.: "She has no children with names such as Johnny, John, Peter, Paul, Mary or Martha. Instead, a sampling of names on one of her *roles* [read *rolls*] includes Tiana, Victoria, Carmen, Melissa, Christopher, Phillip, Tyler and Allegra." Marlene Feduris, *What's in a Name?* Amarillo Globe News, 24 May 1992, at D1.

Romanist = one who is versed in or practices Roman law; a lawyer of the Roman school. The term, generally capitalized, has also been a pejorative epithet for Roman Catholics.

Roman law = (1) the law of the Roman people; or (2) civil law. Max Radin calls sense (2) "improper," saying, "It is extremely important . . . to separate the two terms." Max Radin, *Law Dictionary* 302 (2d ed. 1970). But not all writers do separate them—e.g.: "By civil law—or *Roman law,* or *Roman civil law*—is meant that system of law in operation in the Roman Empire and set forth particularly in the compilations of Roman jurists (Justinian and his successors) and comprising the Institutes, the Codex, the Digest and the Novels collectively called the *Corpus Juris Civilis.*" C. Gordon Post, *An Introduction to the Law* 34 (1963). See **civil law.**

round. See **around.**

routinize is an -IZE neologism best avoided as GOBBLEDYGOOK. E.g., "Administration is a means of *routinizing coercion* [read *making coercion routine*]."/ "[B]usiness men . . . want to settle and *routinize* [read *and to make routine*] both practice and expectation." Grant Gilmore & Charles L. Black, Jr., *The Law of Admiralty* 15 (2d ed. 1975).

royalty. See **nonparticipating royalty.**

ruin, n.; **ruination.** The former is the ordinary term; the latter is humorous and colloquial. E.g, "The failure of Congress to do so explicitly shows that such a suit may not be entertained merely because collection would cause an irreparable injury, such as the *ruination* [read *ruin*] of the taxpayer's enterprise."

rule, v.t. In AmE, it could not be said that a dissenting judge *rules,* because the dissenter sets forth no binding rule. In BrE, however, it is apparently permissible (though inaccurate) to say that a dissenter *rules* in a certain way—e.g.: "Indeed, Sir Laurence Street in dissent *ruled* in favor of no injunction but an accounting of profits." Letter of Malcolm Turnbull, TLS, 9–15 Dec. 1988, at 1371.

rule absolute. See **decree absolute.**

rule against opinions. See **opinions, rule against.**

Rule against Perpetuities; rule against Perpetuities; Rule Against Perpetuities. "In Gray's book [John Chipman Gray, *The Rule against Perpetuities* (1886)] the Rule is capitalized *Rule against Perpetuities,* a style followed by the Blue Book until 1955. In that year, for mysterious reasons—perhaps merely a new font fetish—the Blue Book decreed that the Rule should be capitalized *Rule Against Perpetuities.*" Jesse Dukeminier & Stanley M. Johanson, *Family Wealth Transactions* 970 n.1 (1978).

Dukeminier has identified three styles of capitalizing the phrase: the classic style (*Rule against Perpetuities*); the modern style (*rule against perpetuities*); and the *Bluebook* style (*Rule Against Perpetuities*), sanctioned by the *Bluebook* in the ninth edition of 1955. See Jesse Dukeminier, *Perpetuities: Contagious Capitalization,* 20 J. Legal Educ. 341 (1968). His research turned up no historical justification for the *Bluebook* style (no longer specifically included in the *Bluebook*), but long-sanctioned use of both the classic and modern styles (the only ones known in BrE). Dukeminier himself prefers the classic style, perhaps as a nod of respect to Gray. In fact, though, Gray's style merely reflects the predominant 19th-century method of initial capitalization, in which all prepositions (such as *against*), no matter how long, remained lowercase.

Today, though, prepositions of more than four letters are routinely capitalized, so *Rule Against Perpetuities* accords with the prevailing conventions for initial capitals. But why have the initial capitals at all? The lowercase version—*rule against perpetuities*—is now predominant in American legal writing. See CAPITALIZATION (A).

Rule in Shelley's Case; Rule in *Shelley's Case*. British writers tend to italicize the case name; American writers tend not to.

rulemaker. One word.

rulemaking serves best as an adjective <rulemaking authority>, or an abstract noun <rulemaking in administrative law>, but not as a concrete noun <three rulemakings today>. This concrete use—which makes the word a COUNT NOUN—derives from administrative law, in which it means "the act or an instance of administratively legislating, through promulgated rules." E.g.: "When the agency used statistics derived from this survey in a formal *rulemaking* to set minimum wages for government contractors, it made available for cross-examination the statistician who had tabulated the figures." The usage smacks of JARGON, but it may well become accepted as standard AmE legal terminology. See PLURALS (B).

rule nisi. See **nisi & decree absolute.**

rule of four. This phrase denotes, in AmE, the convention that for certiorari to be granted by the U.S. Supreme Court, four justices must vote in favor of the grant.

rule of law. A. Senses. *Rule of law* = (1) the supremacy of regular as opposed to arbitrary power; (2) the doctrine that every person is subject to the ordinary law of the realm enforced in the ordinary tribunals; (3) the doctrine that general constitutional principles are the result of judicial decisions determining the rights of private individuals in the courts; or (4) any substantive legal principle. See A.V. Dicey, *The Law of the Constitution* 110–16 (8th ed. 1915; repr. 1982).

Since the 1960s, and especially in popular contexts, sense (1) has taken on more and more concrete connotations. Thus the phrase often suggests, not the abstract principle of regular power, but the wielders of that power in a given society—the establishment and the police force. E.g., "Many jurists now complain that there has been a breakdown in respect for 'the *rule of law*.' Their failure to note that the inadequacy of the legal system caused the broad social protest has served only to widen the gulf. The call has gone out for new and stiffer criminal sanctions against civil disobedience." Stephen M. Nagler, "The Language of the Law," in *Language in America* 218, 227–28 (Neil Postman et al. eds., 1969).

B. And *rule of construction*. A *rule of law* is a rule that a court follows to determine the substantive position of the parties; a *rule of construction* is a guide to the court in interpreting a statute or legal instrument. E.g., "Before its abolition in England, the Rule in Shelley's Case seems to have been a *rule of law* rather than a *rule of construction.*"

rule of optional completeness. Under this rule, when a party in an American trial uses deposition testimony, the opposing party may require that more of the passage be read to establish the greater context. E.g., "The part bracketed by us was introduced by appellant under the *rule of optional completeness.*" *Hobson v. State,* 644 S.W.2d 473, 476 n.3 (Tex. Crim. App. 1983).

rule, the. When American lawyers in the South and Southwest refer to *the rule,* they invoke an evidentiary and procedural rule by which all witnesses are excluded from the courtroom while another witness is testifying. The purpose of *the rule* is to aid in ascertaining the truth from witnesses by preventing them from hearing what others say on the witness stand. The most frequent idioms containing the phrase are *invoking "the rule"* and *being placed under "the rule";* legal writers generally use the quotation marks as just shown.

ruling. A *ruling* is the outcome of a court's decision either on some point of law (such as the admissibility of evidence) or on the case as a whole. The word is not synonymous with *opinion,* q.v., as here wrongly suggested: "The action by Mesa Partners II 'strongly suggests a studied effort by Mesa to conceal its true intent,' the judge wrote in a 33-page *ruling* [read *opinion*]." See JUDGMENTS, APPELLATE-COURT.

ruling case = a reported case that determines an issue being litigated. The phrase appears more commonly in BrE than in AmE, in which the phrase *leading case,* q.v., is often used for this sense.

run. A. Statutes of Limitation. In AmE, a statute of limitation is said to have *run* when the time limit has passed. In BrE, the usual phraseology is that the period set by the statute of limitation has *expired*—e.g.: "[T]he writ had been issued before the six-year period of limitation in respect of a tort had *expired.*" (Eng.) *Run* is also used in BrE, but is considered a casualism. See **laches.**

It is unidiomatic to speak of a statute of limitations *running out,* as opposed to merely *running*—e.g.: "The District 4-E Grievance Committee found [that] the respondent delayed filing suit in a personal injury matter and allowed the statute of limitations to *run out* [read *run*].” *Disciplinary Actions,* 53 Tex. B.J. 1309, 1309 (1990). The period allowed may properly be said to have “run out.”

B. *Running with the land.* Covenants are said to *run with the land* when the duty to perform or the right to another's performance is assignable with the land. E.g., “In the case of sales of land the benefit of the vendor's covenants for title ‘*runs*’ with the land purchased.” William Geldart, *Introduction to English Law* 123 (D.C.M. Yardley ed., 9th ed. 1984). Cf. **in gross.**

C. Meaning “to apply.” This is an idiom properly classed as a LEGALISM: “The injunction *runs* only against one of the parties in the dispute.”

runnable, runnability. The words are so spelled—as opposed to the incorrect forms *runable* and *runability.*

RUN-ON SENTENCES do not stop where they should. Many readers will recognize the term from their schooldays, when schoolteachers would scrawl “run on” in the margins of student papers. The problem usually occurs when the writer is uncertain about how to handle marks of PUNCTUATION, and how to handle such adverbs as *however* and *otherwise,* which are often mistakenly treated as conjunctions.

Some grammarians distinguish between a “run-on sentence” (or “fused sentence”) and a “comma splice” (or “run-together sentence”). In a run-on sentence, two independent clauses are not joined by a conjunction such as *and, but, for, or,* and *nor* but are incorrectly written with no punctuation between them. In a comma splice, two such independent clauses have merely a comma between them. Thus a run-on sentence might read, “The decision was unprecedented the court had never heard such a case.” As a sentence containing a comma splice, it would read, “The decision was unprecedented, the court had never heard such a case.” And correctly, it might read, “The decision was unprecedented; the court had never heard such a case.”

The presence or absence of a comma may seem hardly noteworthy, but true run-on sentences symbolize the writer's failure to grasp even the most fundamental rules of writing. They are rare in published legal writing, though they occur distressingly often in the writing of law students.

Comma splices, on the other hand, generally signal a less serious failing because the writer at least understands that some type of stop is necessary. That stop usually needs to be a period or a semicolon instead of a comma. Following are some specimens with suggested remedies in brackets:

- “In the final analysis, it fastens liability on the master where his servant is *negligent, otherwise* [read *negligent; otherwise*] there is no liability.”
- “The competitors got together, that [read *as,* or drop comma and put an *em*-dash between *together* and *that*] happens in business, politics, and the theater.”
- “State sovereignty is not a proper basis on which to rest *jurisdiction, instead* [read *jurisdiction; instead*] the focus is on whether the defendant's due process rights are infringed by the court's assertion of jurisdiction.”
- “There are two levels of qualification prescribed by the *NASD, one* [read *NASD: one*] is for principals and the other is for registered representatives.”
- “We do not now decide whether the INS has complied fully with its own *regulations, rather* [read *regulations; rather*] we decide that it must in the first instance address petitioner's specific factual claims that it failed to do so.”
- “It is true that defendants' right to the insurance payment was a contract right embodied in the policies of *insurance, nevertheless* [read *insurance; nevertheless,*] the indemnity payment was based in part on a claim of loss that did not exist.”
- “But the court has no power to do by indirection what it is doing *directly, particularly* [read *directly; particularly*] is that true in an action for specific performance in which a decree is given as a matter of grace and discretion.”
- “The generator's analysis may be used to justify a less-than-complete waste analysis by the site *operator, thus* [read *operator; thus,*] incompatible wastes may be buried in the same subcells, or restricted wastes may be entering the landfill.”
- “The operation of hauling gasoline is an inherently dangerous *activity, therefore, the* [read *activity; therefore, the*] standard of strict liability must be imposed.”

Most usage authorities accept comma splices when (1) the clauses are short and closely related, (2) there is no danger of a MISCUE, and (3) the context is informal. Thus: “Jane likes him, I don't.” But even when all three criteria are met, some readers are likely to object. Cf. INCOMPLETE SENTENCES.

run the ga(u)ntlet. See **gantlet.**

run with the land. See **run** (B).

rush to judgment. Lord Erskine, among the greatest advocates ever to practice at the English Bar, was apparently the first to use this phrase, around 1800. He was defending a man accused of trying to assassinate George III: "An attack upon the King is considered to be parricide against the state, and the jury and the witnesses, and even the judges, are the children. It is fit, on that account, that there should be a solemn pause before we *rush to judgment* . . . ." Thomas Erskine, "Speech in Defence of James Hadfield," in 4 *Erskine's Speeches* 163, 167 (James L. High ed., 1876).

The term was popularized in 1966 when Mark Lane, a Washington lawyer, published *Rush to Judgment,* a book about the assassination of President John F. Kennedy. William Safire, the great linguistic detective, wrote Mr. Lane to inquire about the phrase, and Lane explained: "When I wrote the book back in '64, I was looking for a title that would have some historic resonance. I came upon the phrase I needed in a speech by Lord Chancellor Thomas Erskine . . . ." William Safire, *On Language,* N.Y. Times, 26 Feb. 1995, § 6, at 18.

Today, of course, the phrase is all but ubiquitous whenever an advocate wants to forestall rash judgments, or to keep minds open when public opinion takes an adverse turn.

S

sacrilegious. So spelled; *sacreligious* is a common misspelling. E.g., "Surely moral merit is at least as elusive as other terms the Court has declared infirm, such as 'gangsters,' '*sacreligious* [read *sacrilegious*],' 'humane,' and 'credible and reliable.'" Deborah L. Rhode, *Moral Character as a Professional Credential,* 94 Yale L.J. 491, 571 (1985). The correct spelling can be remembered easily if one recalls the noun: *sacrilege.*

sadly. See SENTENCE ADVERBS.

safe; safety. In BrE, these words, when referring to criminal convictions or penalties, denote legal sufficiency. *Safe* = not liable to be overturned on any ground. E.g., "It is the opinion of this House on the *safety* of the verdict that is in debate."/ "The judge who tried the PC Blakelock murder case wrote the Home Office four years ago, stating that the verdict against one of the men convicted of the killing was *unsafe,* a defence lawyer claimed last night." David Rose, *Blakelock Judge Told Hurd: Verdict Unsafe,* Observer, 29 Sept. 1991, at 1./ "Mr. Simpson believes the trial judge expressed 'serious doubts about the *safety* of the conviction' of Braithwaite." *Id.*

safe harbor, a picturesque legal metaphor, has a general sense—"a means or area of protection"—as well as a number of specific applications, as in the law of sanctions and in tax law. Usually, the *safe harbor* is a potential wrongdoer's opportunity to correct a wrong before a penalty comes into effect.

safety. See **safe.**

said. A. Generally. *Said* should be rigorously eschewed as a substitute for *the, that, this,* or any other deictic or "pointing" word. Used for such a word, *said* typifies LEGALESE and is often parodied by nonlawyers. And lawyers occasionally fall into self-parody:

> A considerable number of persons were attracted to *said* square by *said* meeting, and *said* bombs and other fireworks which were being exploded there. A portion of the center of the square about 40 to 60 feet was roped off by the police of *said* Chelsea, and *said* bombs or shells were fired off within the space so inclosed, and no spectators were allowed to be within *said* inclosure. The plaintiffs were lawfully in *said* highway at the time of the explosion of *said* mortar, and near *said* ropes, and were in the exercise of due care. (Eng.)

The weed tends to spread profusely in drafted documents such as wills—e.g.:

> If the *said* Grant R. Shelley shall die, and leave surviving him children, it is my desire that, if my wife be then dead, or upon the death of my wife if she should survive *said* son, my trustee shall continue *said* trust for the benefit of *said* children of my son, Grant R. Shelley, and shall make periodic payments for their benefit at intervals of not less than three (3) months apart, and shall hold *said* estate in trust to and until the youngest child of Grant R. Shelley shall attain the age of twenty-one (21) years; thereupon, *said* trust shall terminate, and *said* estate shall be distributed to the children of my son, share and share alike; if any of *said* children die before the youngest attains the age of twenty-one (21) years, *said* distributable estate shall be distributed to the surviving children, share and share alike.
>
> Quoted in *Shelley v. Shelley,* 354 P.2d 282, 284 (Or. 1960).

This usage had its origins in LOAN TRANSLATION, *said* being the English equivalent of the Latin *dicti,* as in the 17th-century general demurrer: *tam contra pacem dicti nuper Regis* (= against the peace of the said late King).

Among the misinformation recently disseminated about this term is that of Richard Weisberg, who says that *said* "is bizarre, but it is irreplaceable not only to the drafter of wills but to other technical lawyers as well." *When Lawyers Write*

99 (1987). That statement is balderdash. Skilled drafters—no matter how "technical" the subject—have not relied on *said* in more than a century. *Said* never lends greater precision than *the, this, that, these,* or *those*—in many contexts it even introduces imprecision.

B. *The said.* As used in legal writing, the word *said* is a Middle-English sibling of *aforesaid,* having the sense "above-stated." Originally legal writers would write *the said defendant*—and still do in BrE—just as they would write *the aforesaid defendant* or *the above-stated defendant.* In AmE, however, *the* was dropped before *said,* which has come to act almost as an article. Hence *the said* seems redundant to American ears, though it was well established at one time. It still occasionally appears in American cases, but more often in British ones: "J.W.T. had induced his wife to furnish him money with which to acquire *the said* [omit *said*] property."/ "The transaction resulted in an exorbitant profit to *the said* [omit *said*] defendant." (Eng.)

One writer has stated that "*the said person* is better than *said person.*" Elmer A. Driedger, *The Composition of Legislation* 87 (1957). Stylistically, however, both are so horrid that the question is better framed, "Which is less bad?"

C. *His said,* etc. This collocation is similar to *the said;* both *said*s are quite superfluous here: "He wrongfully, knowingly, intentionally, and maliciously induced *said* [omit *said*] McClure to violate, repudiate, and break *his said* [omit *said*] agreement with the plaintiff."

D. In Pleadings. *Said* appears at the beginning of legalistically worded pleadings in the SET PHRASE *To the Honorable Judge of Said Court,* the word *said* referring to the name of the court in the caption (usu. just above this phrase). Legal stylists generally discard this and similar jargonistic deadwood. Lawyers who want a simpler substitute—who are unwilling to abandon the phrase completely—often write *To the Honorable Court.*

E. As Referring to Preceding Matter. When *said* is used in the way here disapproved, as we must grudgingly accept that it will be, it should refer to something above ("already said"), not to what is about to be said: "Any person who does any of the acts hereinafter enumerated thereby submits himself to the jurisdiction of the courts of this State regarding any cause of action arising from any of *said acts* [read *these acts*]: [an enumeration follows]."

F. As a Noun. As suggested above, *said* is merely a pointing word. Thus it cannot stand on its own as a noun. In this sentence, the writer has misused *said* for *same:* "Defendants exercised control over Mobay's ownership interest in that property, and thereby converted *said* [read *same*]." See **same (A).**

G. Modifying Proper Names. *Said* is especially ludicrous when used to modify a proper name, where no confusion could result from the name alone: "The first count of the indictment alleged, in substance, that George Smith was an idiot, and under the care, custody, and control of the respondents; that the respondents assaulted *said George* [read *George*]. . . ." (Cf. *said Chelsea* in the first passage quoted in this entry.)

sailor's will. See **oral will.**

saith; sayeth. The phrase once common in affidavits and still sometimes used—*Further affiant sayeth* (or *saith*) *not*—is completely superfluous. If it is to be used, the next-to-last word may be spelled either *saith* or *sayeth.* (*Sayeth* is slightly more common in American caselaw.) These are alternative Elizabethan forms. But if we are to write contemporary modern English, and not early modern English, the *-th* forms should disappear altogether.

Why? The *-th* termination for the third person singular verb for the present tense (*he maketh*) originated in the Midland dialectal form of Middle English; the termination *-s* (*he makes*) originated in northern England and became the predominant form in Shakespeare's day. The *-eth* forms have long been obsolete in every field except religion and law—two fields in which they are obsolescent. See -ETH.

When the affiant hath nothing further to say, the affiant generally stoppeth testifying. On the question whether to say *naught* or *not* in this phrase, see **not & further affiant (B).**

sale. See **hard sell.**

sal(e)able; sellable. The preferred spellings are *salable* in AmE (*W10 & W3*), and *saleable* in BrE (*OED & COD*). *Sellable,* arguably a more logical form, was formerly used by some writers, but never gained widespread currency.

sale, contract for; contract of sale. See **contract for sale.**

sale and leaseback. See **leaseback.**

Salic law; Salique law. The body of law developed by the Salians (or Salian Franks), after they settled in Gaul under King Pharamond at the beginning of the 5th century, is generally referred to as *Salic law.* Holmes and Holland used this spelling, and so do most other legal writers. E.g., "Now a Salian, wherever he might be, in whatever part of France, was judged by the *Salic law* . . . ." James Hadley, *Introduction to Roman Law* 28 (N.Y., D. Appleton & Co. 1881).

salience; saliency. The latter is a NEEDLESS VARIANT.

Salique law. See **Salic law.**

salutary; salutiferous; salubrious. *Salutary* = beneficial; wholesome. *Salutory* is a common misspelling. E.g., "The court must be careful to implement this sanction in a way that advances its *salutory* [read *salutary*] purpose while avoiding its potential danger." William W. Kilgarlin & Don Jackson, *Sanctions for Discovery Abuse Under New Rule 215,* 15 St. Mary's L.J. 767, 791 (1984)./ "It is a corollary to the necessary and *salutory* [read *salutary*] presumption that a child born during the pendency of a legal marriage is the legitimate offspring of the husband and wife."/ "Legal realism has probably, on the whole, had a *salutary* effect on the system." *Salutiferous* is a NEEDLESS VARIANT of *salutary. Salubrious,* a near-synonym of *salutary,* means "healthful; promoting health or well-being."

SALUTATIONS. See FORMS OF ADDRESS.

salvable. See **savable.**

salvage, n.; **selvage.** *Salvage* = the rescue of property (as at sea or from fire). *Selvage* = the woven edging that prevents raveling along either side of a width of cloth.

salvageable. See **savable.**

salvor; salvager; salvagor. Most dictionaries give preference to *salvager,* but *salvor* has long been the common term in admiralty law. E.g., "The last bottomry bond will ride over all that precedes it; and an abandonment to a *salvor* will supersede every prior claim." *The St. Jago de Cuba,* 22 U.S. (9 Wheat.) 409, 416 (1824) (per Johnson, J.)./ "*Salvors* of human life . . . are entitled to a fair share of the remuneration awarded to the *salvors* of the vessel . . . ." 46 U.S.C. § 729 (1988).

salvo. See **saving(s) clause** (C).

same. A. As a Pronoun. This usage, commonly exemplified in the phrase *acknowledging same,* is a primary symptom of LEGALESE. Fowler wrote trenchantly that it "is avoided by all who have any skill in writing" and that those who use it seem bent on giving the worst possible impression of themselves. (*MEU1* at 511.) The words *it, them,* or the noun itself (that is, *the envelope,* say, and not *same*) are words that come naturally to us all; *same* or *the same* is an unnatural English expression:

- "A will may be revoked by burning, tearing, cancelling or obliterating *the same* [read *it*]." Robert Kratovil, *Real Estate Law* 246 (1946; repr. 1950).
- "[E]quity enabled them to hold any kind of property in trust for their own benefit, and to dispose of *the same* [read *it*] at pleasure." Stephen Pfeil, "Law," in 17 *Encyclopedia Americana* 86, 90 (1953).
- "Tucker received said envelope and its said contents in due course the following day and he opened *same* and has refused to file *same.*" [Read *Tucker received the envelope the following day. He opened it and refused to file its contents.*]
- "We should not write until the court below shows that it considered all the evidence by discussing *same* [read *it*] in full."

As these examples illustrate, the phrase is rendered sometimes (and preferably) with the definite article, sometimes without. See **said** (F).

B. *Same . . . as are.* *Are* often appears superfluously in statements that two or more things are identical: "The government here does not suggest that appellee is not entitled to the *same* Fourth Amendment protection as *are* [omit *are*] citizens."/ "Every member of the proposed class is in the *same* position with respect to that question *as are* [read *as the*] plaintiffs." See **as . . . as** (B).

C. *Same difference.* This phrase is an illogical AmE casualism that is to be avoided not only in writing but in speech as well. "It's all the *same,*" "It's the *same* thing," etc., are better.

sanative; sanatory. See **sanitary.**

sanction = (1) to approve; or (2) to penalize. Nonlawyers usually understand *sanction* in sense (1); thus lawyers, who use it primarily in sense (2), are liable to be misunderstood. Yet sense (1) also appears in legal writing, as here: "The courts will not *sanction* a trust disposition if it is inimical to public policy."

As a noun, *sanction* is burdened by the same ambiguity, meaning either (1) "approval" <governmental sanction to sell the goods>, or (2) "penalty" <the statute provides sanctions for violations of the act>. In phrases such as *give sanction to,* the word means "approval"—while to *issue sanctions against* is a way of showing disapproval.

sanctionable. This word, like *sanction,* carries a double sense of approval and disapproval. Most often, *sanctionable* means "deserving punishment"—e.g.: "Specifically, the court found *sanctionable:* defense counsel's failure to supplement Mignona's deposition testimony . . . ." *Perkinson v. Gilbert/Robinson, Inc.,* 821 F.2d 686, 688–89 (D.C. Cir. 1987).

But the word sometimes means "approvable," as here: "It was our visit to the Flower Children . . . that suggested to me the need for an alternative to the polar position—the need for a totally new and socially *sanctionable* drug." Matthew Huxley, *Criteria for a Socially Sanctionable Drug,* 1 Interdisciplinary Sci. Rev. 176, 182 (1976).

sandpapering, in American trial lawyers' JARGON, refers to the preparation of witnesses before trial. The metaphor, of course, suggests that counsel can help soften the rough edges of their witnesses—e.g.: "We are not unmindful of the trial court's observations regarding Ms. Haynie's candor, or lack of it, and we suppose that if Diogenes, searching for an honest man, had wandered into the courtroom during the trial of this case, he might not have considered his quest at an end on meeting the plaintiff—although the rough edges on the plaintiff's testimony may have stemmed more from a lack of pre-trial preparation (*'sandpapering,'* in the trial court's terminology) on the part of her badly overworked counsel than from any inherent defect in the plaintiff's character." *Haynie v. Ross Gear Division of TRW, Inc.,* 799 F.2d 237, 242 (6th Cir. 1986). Cf. **horseshed.**

sanitary; sanatory; sanative. *Sanitary* = of or relating to health or, more usu., cleanliness. *Sanative* = health-producing; healthful. *Sanatory* is a NEEDLESS VARIANT.

sank. See **sink.**

sans is an archaic literary GALLICISM to be avoided, unless a tongue-in-cheek or archaic effect is intended. *Without* should always be favored over *sans* (as long as one is using the English language). E.g., "Arrogation to an appointed official of the denial of the right to hear and see a controversial play cannot be accomplished *sans* [read *without*] standards."/ "Has Findeisen alleged a deprivation under color of state law of a federally protected property right, *sans* [read *without*] due process?"

sans recours. See **without recourse.**

sat, in legal slang, is short for *satisfaction of judgment.* E.g., "[When a] man finishes paying a judgment, the lawyer involved should send a *'sat'*—a satisfaction of judgment to the county records section." Murray T. Bloom, *The Trouble With Lawyers* 89 (1970) (quoting Robert E. Blackman). See sense (2) of **satisfaction.**

satellite litigation = (1) lawsuits related to a major piece of litigation being conducted in one court, while the others are conducted usu. in other courts and often with different parties; or (2) peripheral skirmishes involved in the prosecution of a lawsuit. The phrase is late-20th-century AmE—e.g.: (Sense 1) "To avoid *satellite litigation,* the statutory elements of the crime must necessarily involve untruthfulness or falsification." Paul F. Rothstein, *Needed: A Rewrite,* Crim. Just., Summer 1989, at 20, 21./ (Sense 2) "Mr. Bickel and Mr. Brewer call the sanctions *'satellite litigation,'* drummed up by the opposition to deflect attention from the meatier issues." Dona Rubin, *The Rambo Boys,* Dallas Life Mag., 25 Feb. 1990, at 9.

satisfaction, as a LEGALISM, has nothing to do with being satisfied in the usual sense. It means (1) "the fulfillment of an obligation or claim, esp. the payment in full of a debt"; or (2) a document showing that an obligation, such as a mortgage or a court's judgment, has been fully paid. See **accord and satisfaction** & **sat.**

savable; salvable; salvageable. *Savable* = capable of being saved. Originally this word was used in theological senses, and it still carries religious connotations. *Salvable,* too, has the theological sense ("admitting of salvation"), as well as the sense (used of ships) "that can be saved or salvaged." *Salvageable,* dated from 1976 in the *OED* but actually much older in AmE, has become common in the sense "that can be salvaged"—e.g.: "[H]is agreement to the foregoing measure of *salvageable* value was not to be construed as an admission of liability . . . ." *Wheeler v. Aetna Ins. Co.,* 4 F. Supp. 820, 823 (E.D.N.Y. 1933).

save, as an ARCHAISM equivalent to *except,* is best avoided, although, as the examples following illustrate, it is still common in legal prose: "The law-of-the-circuit rule forbids one panel to overrule another *save* [read *except*] when a later statute or Supreme Court decision has changed the applicable law."/ "The district court granted summary judgment in favor of the defendants on all of appellant's due process claims *save* [read *except for*] those alleging bias, which were tried to the court."/ "As long as the law requires disclosure, the scales come down decisively, in my opinion, in favour of a renewed inquiry on or very shortly before the day of the hearing, *save* [read *except*] in very exceptional circumstances." (Eng.)

save and except is a common but unjustifiable REDUNDANCY. See DOUBLETS, TRIPLETS, AND SYNONYM-STRINGS.

save harmless. See **indemnify (A).**

saving(s) clause; saving-to-suitors clause. **A. Generally.** *Saving clause* (= a statutory provision exempting from coverage something that would otherwise be included) is the preferred form of this phrase generally, and particularly in admiralty law. See *Territory of Alaska v. American Can Co.,* 246 F.2d 493, 494 (9th Cir. 1957) (insisting that the proper form is singular, not plural). *Savings clause* is not an uncommon variant, but it is not as good, for it (1) suggests financial savings, and (2) makes *savings* a nominal rather than a participial adjective when the latter is more specific. E.g., "The note also contained a *savings clause* [read *saving clause*] providing that any charge that caused or was interpreted to cause the interest to exceed the maximum lawful rate was to be reduced to the extent necessary to eliminate the usurious violation."

The U.S. Constitution grants federal courts jurisdiction over "all Cases of admiralty and maritime Jurisdiction." U.S. Const. art. III, § 2. The statutory grant of this admiralty jurisdiction negated exclusive jurisdiction by "*saving to suitors,* in all cases, the right of a common[-]law remedy where the common law is competent to give it." 28 U.S.C. § 1333 (1988). This language is known as the *saving clause,* or *saving-to-suitors clause,* which allows a plaintiff to bring an action in any forum that will exercise jurisdiction over the case.

Though known esp. to American lawyers as a term relating to admiralty jurisdiction, the phrase has long had broader applications—e.g.: "[W]e need only suppose for a moment that the supremacy of the State constitutions had been left complete by a *saving clause* in their favor." *The Federalist* No. 44, at 286 (James Madison) (Clinton Rossiter ed., 1961)./ "[I]f all the possible repercussions of the new statute were to be foreseen and provided for, the text necessarily became long, full of enumerations, exceptions, provisions, *saving clauses* and the like." Theodore F.T. Plucknett, *A Concise History of the Common Law* 324 (5th ed. 1956).

B. As a Synonym of *severability clause.* *Saving clause* is sometimes used as a synonym of *severability clause,* whether in a statute or in a contract. This usage is loose and confusing, however, because *saving clause* generally means something quite different, (see (A)) and *severability clause* prevails over *saving clause* in this secondary sense. See **severability clause.**

C. Other Terms. A saving clause is sometimes, esp. in older texts, called a *salvo* (common from the 17th to the 19th centuries). For a discussion of one category of saving clauses, see **grandfather clause.**

say. See **hold.**

sayeth. See **saith.**

sc., the abbreviation for *scilicet* (= that is to say; namely), is a pedantic abbreviation—*namely* or *i.e.* being preferable because they are more widely known. Even *viz.* is better known than *sc.* See **viz.**

scandalous. Court rules in the U.S. and G.B. have long forbidden advocates to put *scandalous matter* in their submissions. See, e.g., Fed. R. Civ. P. 12. The *OED* quotes a phrase from *Vesey's Chancery Cases* (1809)—"The introduction of irrelevant and *scandalous matter* upon affidavits"—defining *scandalous* here as meaning "irrelevant." In yet another sense, the *OED* defines *scandalous* as meaning "defamatory" <scandalous and seditious letters>. And, of course, it records the primary meaning: "grossly disgraceful; of the nature of a scandal."

But is the great dictionary correct in saying that *scandalous matter* refers merely to *irrelevant* matter? Some modern legal scholars have scoffed at the suggestion. And they are right: the *OED* definition is incomplete. The phrase *scandalous matter* refers to what is both grossly disgraceful (or defamatory) *and* irrelevant, as an early-20th-century scholar explained: "*Scandal* consists in the allegation of anything [that] is unbecoming the dignity of the court to hear, or is contrary to decency or good manners, or which charges some person with a crime not necessary to be shown in the cause, to which may be added that any unnecessary allegation, bearing cruelly upon the moral character of an individual, is also scandalous. The matter alleged, however, must be not only offensive, but also *irrelevant* to the cause, for however offensive it be, if it be pertinent and material to the cause the party has a right to plead it." Eugene A. Jones, *Manual of Equity Pleading* 50–51 (1916).

scarify; scorify. *Scarify* means (1) "to make superficial incisions in, cut off skin from"; (2) "to pain by severe criticism"; or (3) "to loosen soil by means of an agricultural machine [a scarifier] with prongs for spiked road-breaking." *Scorify* means "to reduce to dross or slag."

scarlet-letter, adj., = of or relating to a type of punishment, esp. a condition of probation, that results in infamy or public scorn. The phrase alludes to Nathaniel Hawthorne's novella, *The Scarlet Letter* (1850), in which Hester Prynne is forced to wear a scarlet A on her blouse to proclaim her crime: adultery. In the 1980s, *scarlet-letter punishments* became fashionable in some parts of the U.S.—e.g.: "Of particular concern is the growing use of '*scarlet letter*' probation conditions which require signs to be posted on the offender's property warning the public by announcing the crime committed." Leonore H. Tavill, Note, *Scarlet Letter Punishment: Yesterday's Outlawed Penalty Is Today's Probation Condition,* 36 Clevel. St. L. Rev. 613, 615 (1988)./ "[T]his Note argues that modern *scarlet-letter* probation conditions resembling the historical antecedents of punishment constitute punishment by humiliation." Jon A. Brilliant, Note, *The Modern Day Scarlet Letter,* 1989 Duke L.J. 1357, 1359. Recorded examples of *scarlet-letter* probation conditions include requiring child molesters to post warning signs on their cars and in their front yards; requiring drunk drivers to proclaim their crimes on T-shirts that they must wear or on bumper stickers; and requiring drunk drivers to place apologies, along with their photographs, in local newspapers.

scatter-gun. See **blunderbuss.**

sceptic(al). See **skeptic(al).**

schism (= division; separation) is best pronounced /***siz***-əm/, not /***skiz***-əm/. The term is now usually used figuratively—e.g.: "The dispute in this case grows out of the *schism* between 'professional' and 'commercial' optometrists in Texas."

science. See **legal science.**

scienter /sɪ-***en***-tər/ (= [1] the fact of an act's having been done knowingly, esp. as a ground for damages or criminal punishment; or [2] prior knowledge) is a noun in Anglo-American jurisprudence, although the Latin word *scienter* is an adverb meaning *knowingly.* The term has been common in legal writing since the 19th century.

The term is often stretched beyond its true sense to mean "guilty knowledge," esp. in contexts announcing the standard for intent in fraud contexts. E.g., "[T]he account executive's *scienter,* defined as intent to defraud or reckless disregard, must be established." *Shad v. Dean Witter Reynolds, Inc.,* 799 F.2d 525, 530 (9th Cir. 1986). Two influential commentators decry this usage, which equates *scienter* with *mens rea.* See Rollin M. Perkins & Ronald N. Boyce, *Criminal Law* 861 (3d ed. 1982).

sci. fa. See **scire facias.**

scilicet. See **sc.**

scintilla (= a spark or minute particle) is often applied to law in the phrase *scintilla of evidence.* Pl. *-las.* The redundant phrase *mere scintilla* has become a legal CLICHÉ.

scire facias, literally "that you cause to know," denotes the judicial writ (which contained these words) founded upon a matter of record requiring the person against whom it is issued to show cause either why the record should not be annulled or vacated, or why a dormant judgment against that person should not be revived. E.g., "*Scire facias* to revive a judgment being a continuation of the suit, jurisdiction thereon is in the court where the judgment was rendered, regardless of the residency of the parties." The phrase is abbreviated *sci. fa.*

scission. See ***dépeçage.***

scofflaw (= one who treats the law with contempt) is a 20th-century AMERICANISM. Oddly enough, the word was coined by two entrants in a competition held in 1924 to characterize the "lawless drinker" of liquor illegally made or obtained. *Scofflaw* was chosen from more than 25,000 words, and since that time, of course, it has been extended beyond its original meaning, which lost its pungency with the repeal of Prohibition. Now *scofflaw* refers esp. to a person who avoids various laws that are not easily enforced. E.g., "[S]ome *scofflaws* try to avoid detection by hauling make-believe passengers: mannequins, blow-up dolls and dummies." Cecile Sorra, *It Takes Special Training to Tell They Aren't Federal Bureaucrats,* Wall St. J., 19 July 1989, at B1.

score = twenty, though various other numbers are often mistakenly attached to the word. *Four score and seven* = 87.

scorify. See **scarify.**

Scotch law; Scottish law; Scots law. F.T. Wood, an Englishman, writes: "The Scots (or Scotch?) themselves are less particular than the English in the matter of these three words [*Scotch, Scottish,* and *Scots*]." *Current English Usage* 207 (1962). He recommends *Scots* for the noun denoting the people; and *Scottish* when referring to characteristics of the country.

Boswell, a Scottish lawyer, used *Scotch law* throughout his *Life of Johnson,* and occasionally *Scottish law* as well. Even modern British writers do not use the terms consistently. E.g., "It follows that, if the proper law of the arbitration is to be held to be *Scots* law, this conclusion must come about by some inference . . . from the contract. . . . There is absolutely nothing in this contract from which it could be said to be governed by *Scottish* law." *James Miller & Partners Ltd v. Whitworth Street Estates Ltd,* 1970 A.C. 583, 599 (H.L.).

One might defensibly say that the preferred forms are *Scots law,* but *Scottish procedure, Scottish arbitration, Scottish legal forms.* (*Black's* uses *Scotch law* in references throughout.) *Scotch,* recorded in the *OED* as a "contracted variant of *Scottish,*" is best avoided by those in doubt. E.g., "When I look at the report, I find that Lord Cottenham abstains from laying down a rule in that case, but expresses a hope that the *Scotch judges* [*Scottish judges* would now be better] would take care to exercise the jurisdiction of the court with discretion and consistency." (Eng.)/ "Crawford sought to depose two principals of Hydrasum (Aberdeen) Ltd., a *Scottish* corporation."

It is sometimes said that *Scotch* should be used of material objects, as *Scotch tartans, Scotch whisky,* and *Scotch thistle.*

scot-free is a predicative adjective meaning "exempt from injury or punishment." E.g., "It would be contrary to the decided weight of authority to hold that since plaintiff has a cause of action against the company for breach of contract, Sander should go *scot-free.*" (Eng.) The phrase derives from the early English "scot" or contribution or payment into a common fund.

It is a mistake to capitalize *scot* as if it referred to someone from Scotland—e.g.: "To allow people to get away with this sort of crime *Scot* [read *scot*] free is a very disturbing trend." James Langton, *The Jury That Saw Two Wrongs as a Right,* Sunday Telegraph, 24 May 1992, at 4 (quoting the Rev. Anthony Higton, rector of Hawkwell in Essex).

Scottish; Scots. See **Scotch law.**

scrivener; scrivenor; scribe. The spelling *scrivener* is preferred over *scrivenor.* E.g., "David Smith, an attorney, a witness and *scrivener* of the 1965 will, testified that the original will was executed near the vault in the Montellow State Bank."/ "The testator thought the attorney was trying to place him in a mental hospital and had another *scrivener* draft a will in which he left the attorney nothing."

Scrivener, as illustrated in the two sentences just quoted, and *scribe,* as evidenced in the name of the American lawyers' organization devoted to improved legal writing (*Scribes*), either are frequently taken by lawyers to be terms of praise for the person named, or are unusual lawyers' attempts at self-effacement. Technically, a *scrivener* is merely a copyist or amanuensis, not a legal drafter. In *Bartleby the Scrivener,* Herman Melville described a *scrivener* as "a mere copyist"—"[c]opying law papers being proverbially a dry, husky sort of business."

The same is true of *scribe* in all but historical senses; the *OED* notes that it is additionally "applied to a political pamphleteer or journalist; chiefly with contemptuous notion, a party hack."

scrutiny, strict. See **strict scrutiny.**

scul(l)duggery. See **skul(l)duggery.**

sculpture, v.t.; **sculpt.** The preferred verb is *sculpture* <to sculpture a bust>, although *sculpt,* a BACK-FORMATION from *sculptor,* is commonly seen in AmE. *Sculptor* is preferred over *sculpturer* as the agent noun.

Scylla and Charybdis, between. As described by Homer, *Scylla* was a sea monster who had six heads (each with a triple row of teeth) and twelve feet. Though primarily a fish-eater, she was capable of snatching and devouring (in one swoop) six sailors if their ship ventured too near her cave in the Straits of Messina. (In the accounts of later writers, she is depicted as a rocky promontory.) Toward the opposite shore, not far from Scylla's lair, was *Charybdis,* a whirlpool strong enough thrice daily to suck into its vortex whole ships if they came too close.

Thus, *between Scylla and Charybdis* is the literary CLICHÉ roughly equivalent to "between a rock and a hard place." E.g., "In my attempt to steer a safe course *between the Scylla and Charybdis* of opposing absolutisms, I am not likely to have escaped serious error and may not even have made my main points tolerably clear." Morris R. Cohen, *Reason and Law* 112 (1961)./ "[A] refusal on the part of the federal courts to intervene . . . may place the hapless plaintiff *between the Scylla* of intentionally flouting state law *and the Charybdis* of forgoing what he believes to be constitutionally protected activity to avoid becoming enmeshed in a criminal proceeding." *Steffel v. Thompson,* 415 U.S. 452, 462 (1974). See LITERARY ALLUSION (A)(4).

seal. A. Origin and Sense. At common law, the seal was an impression made upon wax, a wafer (i.e., gummed paper), or other adhesive substance; attached to a legal document as a formality; and having various types of legal significance, depending on the document. Today, a *seal* is generally an impression stamped or embossed on paper to authenticate a document or attest to a signature, such as a corporate or notary seal. Some jurisdictions—esp. U.S. states on the eastern seaboard—require deeds to be sealed. A few even require leases to be under seal. See **L.S., signed, sealed, and delivered** & **wafer.**

B. Contracts Under Seal. Generally, of course, valuable consideration is necessary to make an enforceable contract. But for a *contract under seal,* no consideration is necessary. Traditionally, such a contract carries with it an irrebuttable presumption of consideration: "The Law long ago decided that a *seal,* real or imitation, attached to a promise, amounted to good Consideration for that promise, despite the fact that the man who makes the promise puts the *seal* there." Fred Rodell, *Woe Unto You, Lawyers!* 35 (1939; repr. 1980). But statutes in some jurisdictions, such as New York, have made the presumption of consideration rebuttable. In so changing the common law, these jurisdictions have progressed beyond "one of the quaintest freaks of legal conservatism, that the presence or absence of a gummed wafer or engraved mark on a document should, in this rationalistic age, make any difference in its legal effect." Edward Jenks, *The Book of English Law* 291 (P.B. Fairest ed., 6th ed. 1967). See **L.S.**

C. The Idiom *the case is sealed.* This phrase is a figurative extension of the literal contractual sense, the idea being that some occurrence fastens the outcome. E.g., "The legal errors he made representing himself in the wrongful-death suit probably *sealed* the case against him." *Verdict Against White Supremacist,* A.B.A. J., Jan. 1991, at 22.

sea lawyer. See LAWYERS, DEROGATORY NAMES FOR (B).

seaman. The term is common in admiralty contexts, but *mariner* carries the same meaning without the *-man* suffix. (See SEXISM (B).) *Seaman* is so well entrenched, however, that many admiralty lawyers would not consider changing it. See **mariner.**

search and seizure. Enshrined in the Fourth Amendment to the U.S. Constitution, the individual's right to be free from unreasonable searches and seizures derives ultimately from the Magna Carta. Roscoe Pound and others have connected this important constitutional right with "the clause in Magna Carta that the king would not 'send upon' a free man . . . ." Roscoe Pound, *The Development of Constitutional Guarantees of Liberty* 49 (1957; repr. 1975).

Today, under the exclusionary rule (q.v.), evidence obtained in violation of the Fourth Amendment right is excluded from any prosecution. Of course, the purposely vague word *unreasonable* has been the source of steady litigation. Today, warrantless searches are generally considered "unreasonable," but there are several exceptions, involving consent, an otherwise lawful arrest, and exigency. See **stop-and-frisk rule** & ***Terry* stop.**

When used as a PHRASAL ADJECTIVE, *search and seizure* should be hyphenated: *search-and-seizure rules.*

search warrant. Preferably two words, though some writers have hyphenated the phrase.

seasonable. A. And *seasonal.* *Seasonable* = (1) occurring at the right season; opportune; or (2) (of weather) suitable to the time of year (*OED*). *Seasonal* = (1) pertaining to or characteristic of the seasons of the year, or some one of them; or (2) dependent on the seasons, as certain trades (*OED*). For the noun sense, see **seasonal,** n.

B. And *timely.* In legal contexts, *seasonable* is often used to mean "timely," whereas in lay contexts it ordinarily means "in season." One writer has insisted that "these terms [*seasonable* and *timely*] are not synonymous. That which is *seasonable* is in harmony or keeping with the season or occasion; that which is *timely* is in good time. A thing may be *timely* in appearance that is not *seasonable.*" Frank H. Vizetelly, *A Desk-Book of Errors in English* 194 (1907). Yet in American legal writing, the word is regularly used as a synonym of *timely,* whether advisedly or not. E.g., "If the dominant party receives the benefit or donation during the existence of the confidential relation, the party reposing the confidence, on *seasonable* application to a court of equity, may obtain relief from the burdens and duties imposed simply by showing the transaction and the confidential relation."

seasonal, n., is sometimes used in AmE as an elliptical form of *seasonal worker.* E.g., "The policy that Congress adopted the adverse action protection to serve thus does not favor application of those protections to *seasonals'* layoffs." See ADJECTIVES (C).

seaward(s). See -WARD(S).

seaworthy. One word—not hyphenated.

secede. See **cede.**

2d; 2nd. The former is preferred in legal citations.

second bite at the apple — a favorite expression of defense lawyers—is an especially tiresome CLICHÉ. E.g., "The plaintiffs should not be given a *second bite at the apple* because . . . ." See **one bite at the apple.**

second chair, n.; **second-chair,** v.t. In AmE, the *second chair* at trial is a lawyer who helps the lead counsel in court, often by examining some of the witnesses, arguing some of the points of law, and handling parts of the voir dire, opening statement, and summation. For *lead counsel,* see **leader (at the bar).**

Since the late 20th century, the phrase *second chair* has come to be used also as a verb, preferably hyphenated—e.g.: "I learned this lesson as a novice, *second chairing* [read *second-chairing*] an experienced trial lawyer." Denis McInerney, *Counterclaims as Self-Inflicted Wounds,* Litigation, Spring 1992, at 2, 2. See NOUNS AS VERBS.

second degree = the second most serious category of a crime, as in *second-degree murder.* See **degree** & **murder** (A).

second-guess, vb. Hyphenated thus.

secondhand(ed). The *-ed* suffix is not just unnecessary—it is wrong. E.g., "Harvey contributed a *secondhanded* [read *secondhand*] boiler and some machinery . . . ." *Harvey v. Gartner,* 67 So. 197, 201 (La. 1915).

secondhand evidence. See **hearsay evidence.**

secondment */sə-**kond**-mənt/*, primarily a BrE term, means "a person's reassignment from his or her regular employment to some temporary assignment elsewhere." E.g., "A former Assistant Director of Public Prosecutions, he had to initiate systems, recruit staff, many on *secondment* for set periods . . . before the SFO could get down to business." *The Fraud Buster with 66 Cases on His Hands,* Sunday Telegraph, 11 Feb. 1990, at 28./ "He was a consultant on *secondment* from Bain & Co." Paul Durman, *Jury Told to Imagine "Nasty Surprises,"* The Independent, 17 Aug. 1990, at 19.

secretary = a corporate officer who is concerned with the corporation's business management and administration. In corporate law, then, this term denotes an office considerably more elevated than those outside business and law might suspect.

secretaryship; secretariship. The former spelling is standard.

secrete = (1) to hide; or (2) to exude or ooze through pores or glands; to produce by secretion. *Secrete away* is redundant. Sense (1) is becoming increasingly learned or literary, but it is frequently used in legal writing—e.g.: "The plaintiffs also suffer a heavy burden in having to commence actions wherever the enjoined party and his agents choose to *secrete* the funds."

secretive; secretory. The first is the adjective ("inclined to secrecy, uncommunicative") corresponding to sense (1) of *secrete;* the second is the adjective ("having the function of secreting") corresponding to sense (2) of *secrete. Secretive* is best pronounced */si-**kree**-tiv/*, and *secretory /si-**kree**-tə-ree/*.

section. In DRAFTING, a *section*—often indicated by the character "§"—is either a subdivision of a document or a subdivision of an article in a document, statutory title, or code. The plural form of the abbreviation is §§.

In contracts, *section* is often used interchangeably with *article* or, more commonly (and unfortunately), *paragraph.* See **article** & **paragraph.**

sectionalize (= to divide into sections) has become commonplace in lawyers' cant. E.g., "The firm is *sectionalized,* so that each associate will know to whom he or she may turn for consultation and advice. *Sectionalization* facilitates orderly distribution of work and the opportunity for concentration." See -IZE.

secular, like *lay,* has been extended beyond the religious meaning, namely, "outside the ecclesiastical calling," and now can refer to persons and things outside a profession, most commonly the law. Cf. **temporal.**

securitize = (1) to package (a traditional loan, such as a mortgage) into bondlike securities for resale to investors; or (2) to secure (a debt) with assets. This commercial NEOLOGISM has not yet found its way into most dictionaries, such as the *OED* and *W3.* E.g., "Over the past few months, the casino and real estate mogul . . . has discussed selling, refinancing or *securitizing* virtually every major asset he holds." Neil Barsky, *Trump's Growing Appetite for Cash,* Wall St. J., 27 April 1990, at B1./ "[T]he rate cap legislation would make it unprofitable for card issuers to *securitize* their credit card receivables." *Congress Backs Away From Credit Card Rate Cap, After Markets React,* 57 BNA's Banking Rep. 840, 842 (1991).

security = (1) an instrument given to secure the performance of an act; (2) collateral used to guarantee repayment of a debt; (3) a surety, or person bound by some type of guaranty [though *surety* is the proper and the more usual term for this sense]; or (4) an instrument (such as a stock, a bond, or an option) indicating one of three things: (a) ownership in a firm, (b) a creditor relationship with a firm or with a national or local government, or (c) some other rights to ownership. Senses (1) and (2) are the traditional legal senses, but sense (4) is the most common modern sense—the investor's sense. Sense (3) ought to be avoided in modern writing.

secus (= not so; otherwise) is an ARCHAISM, a LATINISM, and a LEGALISM—e.g.: "If a person devises to trustees, and by express clause gives them the power to appoint agents to manage the land, and they appoint one then solvent and good, though afterwards he proves insolvent, they shall not answer for him; *secus* if he were not solvent when he was nominated."

sedition; treason; insurrection; revolt; rebellion; revolution. *Sedition* = an agreement or communication aimed at stirring up treason or some lesser commotion, or (in BrE) at defaming a member of the royal family or of the government. *Treason* = attempting, through an overt act, to overthrow one's government.

One authority incorrectly states that the distinction between *sedition* and *treason* is that, "though the ultimate object of sedition is a violation of the public peace, or at least such a course of measures as evidently engenders it, yet it does not aim at direct and open violence against the laws or the subversion of the constitution." *Black's Law Dictionary* 1523 (4th ed. 1968). But the distinction does not lie in the objective, even though the objective of sedition may be less serious than what is required for treason; rather, the true distinction is that *sedition* is committed by preliminary steps while *treason* requires some overt act directed toward execution. See Rollin M. Perkins & Ronald N. Boyce, *Criminal Law* 508 (3d ed. 1982). See **treason & libel.**

The term *insurrection,* denoting "an open uprising against the government," goes beyond *sedition. Revolt* is stronger still, being an attempt to overthrow the government, while an *insurrection* seeks only a change within the existing government. A large-scale *revolt* is called a *rebellion,* which, if successful, becomes a *revolution.*

seditious libel. See **libel.**

seduction; seducement. Although the latter is sometimes used for the former, the two are best kept separate. *Seduction* = the action or an act of seducing (a person, esp. a woman) to err in conduct or belief, esp. of enticing the person to engage in illicit sexual intercourse. It differs from *rape,* in which there is no consent; in *seduction,* the consent is unfairly obtained. English common law had no crime known as *seduction,* but many state statutes in the U.S. make it a misdemeanor (or, formerly, a felony).

Seducement = something that seduces or serves as a means of seduction; an insidious temptation (*OED*).

seem. A. As a Weasel Word. The verb *seems* can often destroy the power of a passage, as here: "Synanon makes the astonishing assertion that the alleged wrongdoing—perjured testimony, document destruction, and similar misconduct—constitutes mere discovery abuse for which Synanon has been adequately punished by dismissal of its two lawsuits. Such a characterization *seems* disingenuous . . . ." *In re Sealed Case,* 754 F.2d 395, 401 (D.C. Cir. 1985). Given the plaintiff's egregious conduct as catalogued by the judge, *astonishing* is appropriate but the later *seems* is inappropriately weak. See WEASEL WORDS.

B. *Seem (to be)* [+ noun phrase]. In formal writing it is best to include the infinitive *to be.* E.g., "There certainly *seemed no enlightening purpose* [read *seemed to be no enlightening purpose*] served by giving some slick operator from the K.K.K. a nationwide forum on which to spread his rancid twaddle."

see you in court. This phrase is a CLICHÉ to which litigious people are drawn. E.g., "To me . . . [the English system of 'loser pays'] discourages frivolous lawsuits and the knee-jerk business reaction of *'see you in court.'* " Mark H. McCormack, *What They Don't Teach You at Harvard Business School* 207 (1984; repr. 1988).

segment, v.t.; **segment(al)ize.** The latter forms are NEEDLESS VARIANTS. Cf. **sectionalize.** See -IZE.

segregate for *separate* is often a puffed-up LEGALISM. E.g., "He then *segregated* [read *separated*] the few jewels that he wished to purchase from the rest of the lot." See **separate.**

segregate out. See **out.**

segregation, de facto; de jure segregation. These phrases denote two types of racial segregation. *De facto segregation* exists in fact but is not required by law. *De jure segration,* on the other hand, is required by law, as under the long-defunct rule of *Plessy v. Ferguson,* 163 U.S. 537

(1896). (See **separate but equal.**) *De jure segregation* is the more invidious type. See **de facto (A).**

segregative = having the power or property of separating. In American legal writing, the term is used almost exclusively of racial segregation. E.g., "Confronted with *segregative* assignment of faculty and administrators, *segregative* bus transportation of students and other *segregative* post-*Brown* decisions of the Ector County I.S.D., the district court held that the Ector County School District not only continued to fail to meet its duty to dismantle its dual school system, but actually increased the segregation in its schools." See **separate.**

seignor(i)al; seigneurial. In referring to a feudal lord (a *seignor*) in early England, *seignorial* is the predominant adjective in texts dealing with English legal history. *Seigneurial* refers to a feudal lord in France, or to a member of the landed gentry in Canada.

seignory (= [1] feudal lordship; or [2] the relation of a lord to the tenants of a manor) is the usual spelling, *seigniory* being a secondary variant.

seise; seize. The two identically pronounced words are related, but they have undergone DIFFERENTIATION. In the legal sense "to put in possession, invest with the fee simple of," the spelling *seise* is preferred in both AmE and BrE—e.g.: "Each feoffee (recipient of a fief), having received the seisin from his feoffor, would be said to be *seised,* or possessed of an interest in the land." Thomas F. Bergin & Paul G. Haskell, *Preface to Estates in Land and Future Interests* 11 (2d ed. 1984). See **disseise.**

Seize is principally a nontechnical lay word meaning: (1) "to take hold of (a thing or person) forcibly or suddenly or eagerly"; (2) "to take possession of (a thing) by legal right" <to seize contraband>; or (3) "to have a sudden overwhelming effect on" <to be seized by fear> (*OAD*). *Seize* should be confined to these senses. Thus, in the following examples, *seise* would have been the better spelling:

- "In 1814 the New York courts decided that the mortgagor was *seized* [read *seised*] of the freehold . . . ." William F. Walsh, *A Treatise on Equity* 124–25 (1930).
- "Neither of them could have died intestate *seized* [read *seised*] and possessed of the property."
- "This is a suit to enjoin the sale of real estate at sheriff's sale under an execution issued on a judgment against an heir of an intestate who died *seized* [read *seised*] of the land, although the heir had filed a renunciation of all interest in the estate."

The spelling *seize* would make sense if the noun were predominantly spelled *seizin;* but it is not. See **seisin.**

Seize is not infrequently used in the lay sense (1) in legal writing, a fact that provides still greater impetus for strict differentiation between the spellings: "Equity *seizes* the property on its way from the donor to the appointee, and applies it to the satisfaction of the obligations of the appointor."

seised in law; seised in deed. At common law, when the person with *seisin* (q.v.) dies, the heir is said to be *seised in law*—and the heir is *seised in deed* only upon entering the land. Thus, during the interval, the heir has some—though by no means all—of the advantages of seisin.

seisin /***see***-*zən*/. **A. Sense.** This feudal word originally meant "possession," then grew into a TERM OF ART in 18th- and 19th-century land law, much of which is now defunct. The term *seisin* has persisted, however, the spoor of a complicated history. Today it generally denotes "possession of a freehold estate in land" and connotes peace and quiet. But the word is impossible to define in a way that adequately evokes its historical importance in English law while serving to guide modern lawyers, who speak of ownership as depending upon title (without any reference to physically entering the land). As the leading English textbook states, "*Seisin* is no longer of importance, for the distinctions [that] gave it its peculiar meaning no longer exist." Robert E. Megarry & H.W.R. Wade, *The Law of Real Property* 47 (5th ed. 1984).

The best advice is to study seisin as a historical concept and to use the word *seisin* in historical contexts in which the sense is well defined. If *possession, ownership,* or *title* is all that is meant by *seisin,* one of those other words usually serves better. In modern statutes that use *seisin* as a synonym of *ownership,* for example, the latter word is preferable. See **covenant of seisin, livery of seisin, disseise & seise.**

B. Alternative Spelling. The word is sometimes spelled *seizin,* as in *RH2* (surprisingly) and in 2 B.W. Pope, *Legal Definitions* 1453 (1920). The *-zin* form was once more common than it is today, but it still appears from time to time. E.g., "If the grantor owns only part of the title, or if the grantor has only a life estate, the covenant of *seizin* [read *seisin*] is violated." Robert Kratovil, *Real Estate Law* 45 (1946; repr. 1950).

C. Seisin of Personal Property. To speak of the *seisin* of chattels, or of a *lessee's seisin,* is a solecism. For centuries, *seisin* has been a term appropriate only to real property.

seisinee (= one to whom seisin is transferred), though omitted from the *OED, W3,* and other major dictionaries, has appeared in published legal writings—e.g.: "The Statute was considered to have application only where a *seisinee* held to the use of another person and not himself." L.B. Curzon, *English Legal History* 121 (2d ed. 1979). Seemingly a NONCE WORD—and not a very useful one, at that—it is perhaps best forgotten. See -EE.

seize. See **seise.**

seizin. See **seisin (B).**

select, adj.; **selected.** The former is the adjective meaning "choice; esp. excellent." Here the past-participial form of the verb (*selected*) is used inappropriately for the adjective: "These students are all educated young men, and—since the law school's standards are known to be high, and the work is notoriously difficult—it may reasonably be supposed that they are a *selected* [read *select*] group." (Prosser)

selectee. See -EE.

selectman is an Americanism dating from 1635 and meaning "one of a board of officers elected annually to manage various local concerns in a New England township." Today there is a tendency to change the word to *selectperson,* which is not necessarily a happy development. (See SEXISM (B).) The term *selectman* is a difficult one for which to find a nonsexist equivalent formed from the same root; hence one book recommends replacing it with *representative.* See Bobbye D. Sorrels, *The Nonsexist Communicator* 149 (1983). Yet some writers prefer to use *selectman* as if it were gender-neutral—e.g.: "*Selectman* Anita Davidson said last week that her telephone had been surprisingly quiet regarding the new assessments." Karen Corrente, *Property Assessments Prompt Tax Questions,* Derry (N.H.) News, 7 Sept. 1994, at 1, 11.

self-admitted, like *self-confessed* (q.v.), is a REDUNDANCY: "Rep. Gerry E. Studds, 53, and Rep. Barney Frank, 50 . . . are *self-admitted* [read *admitted*] homosexuals, but that is not automatically grounds for Congressional expulsion." *Walter Scott's Personality Parade,* Dallas Morning News (Parade Mag.), 22 July 1990, at 2.

self-complacent is redundant; *complacent* is sufficient.

self-confessed is a common REDUNDANCY—e.g.: "A court that frees a *self-confessed* [read *confessed*] murderer on a technicality would seem to bear responsibility for any harm that criminal may do in the future." Mario Pei, *Words in Sheep's Clothing* 86 (1969).

self-crimination. See **criminate & incriminate.**

self-dealing (= financial dealing that is not at arm's length; esp., borrowing from or lending to a company by a controlling individual primarily to that individual's own advantage [*W10*]) is an Americanism that originated in the mid-20th century. E.g., "The conferred right to exercise all these plenary powers of ownership necessarily modified or displaced the otherwise absolute limitation against *self-dealing.*"

self-defender = one who resorts to *self-defense,* q.v. E.g., "This testimony indicates that the victim was the only one in the position of a *self-defender.*" *Bedford v. State,* 222 N.W.2d 658, 661 (Wis. 1974)./ "The negligent *self-defender* is arguably less culpable than the negligent rapist . . . ." Arnold H. Loewy, *Culpability, Dangerousness, and Harm,* 66 N.C.L. Rev. 283, 301 (1988).

self-defense = (1) the right to defend oneself with reasonable force against an attack, real or threatened; or (2) the right of a state to defend itself against an attack, real or threatened. Sense (1): "Not even *self-defence* [so spelled in BrE] would justify a defender in shooting the aggressor's wife in order to persuade him to desist." Glanville Williams, *Textbook of Criminal Law* 449 (1978)./ Sense (2): "Is the power of raising armies and equipping fleets necessary? . . . It is involved in the power of *self-defense.*" *The Federalist* No. 41, at 256 (James Madison) (Clinton Rossiter ed., 1961).

self-deprec(i)ating. See **deprecate.**

self-executing = not requiring anything additional to make (a document) binding. E.g., "Despite his strong statement, Justice Story apparently believed that the Constitution, though mandatory, was not *self-executing.*" Charles A. Wright, *The Law of Federal Courts* 38 (4th ed. 1983).

self-help. In lay usage, this phrase usu. represents something good (the work ethic, providing for oneself without relying on others). But in legal usage, it usu. represents something bad (redress of perceived wrongs without recourse to law)—e.g.: "*Self-help* is indeed but an unsatisfactory means of redress." Thomas E. Holland, *The Elements of Jurisprudence* 323 (13th ed. 1924; repr. 1937)./ "Ideally, reform would come according to reason and justice without *self-help* and disturbing, almost violent, forms of protest." Archibald Cox, *Civil Rights, the Constitution, and the Courts,* 40 N.Y. State B.J. 161, 169 (1968).

Still, in the law of oil and gas, if the rule of capture applies, *self-help* is the only recourse available to prevent losing the rights to resources under one's land.

self-incrimination. See **criminate.**

self-inculpation is a NEEDLESS VARIANT of *self-incrimination.*

self-killing; self-murder. See **suicide (A).**

self-proving, not included in any of the major dictionaries, denotes a type of affidavit appended to modern wills. *Self-proving affidavits* are signed by the witnesses to the will, and state that the testator was under no compulsion and had a sound mind when signing the will. E.g., "A useful device for discouraging a will contest is the '*self-proving*' affidavit, which is the sworn statement of the testator and witnesses about the execution ceremony." Barbara Child, *Drafting Legal Documents* 268 (2d ed. 1992).

self-slaughter. See **suicide.**

self-stultification = testifying about one's own bad morals. Hence *rule against self-stultification.* See **stultify.**

sell; sale. See **hard sell.**

sellable. See **sal(e)able.**

sell, contract to. See **contract for sale.**

seller. See **vendor.**

selvage. See **salvage.**

SEMANTICS. For solid treatments of general semantics as applied to law, see Glanville Williams, *Language and the Law* (pt. 4), 61 Law Q. Rev. 384–406 (1945); F.A. Philbrick, *Language and the Law* (1949); and Walter Probert, *Law, Language and Communication* (1972).

semble /*sem*-bəl/ (= it seems), a LAW FRENCH term, is used in law reports as a technical expression of uncertainty, usu. in introducing either an obiter dictum or the writer's less-than-confident interpretation of how a court's holding might be applied or extended. Today the term appears more often in BrE than in AmE—e.g.:

- "This judgment is not conclusive in an action by the owner of ship A for the damage done to ship B. (*Semble,* it is deemed to be irrelevant.)" (Eng.)
- "On a charge of attempting to sell meat in excess of the permitted price, it is not enough to show that the butcher had tickets in his drawer showing an excessive price; but, *semble,* it is sufficiently proximate if the tickets are applied to the meat." Glanville Williams, *Criminal Law* 629 (2d ed 1961).
- "If statutory language makes no sense whatever, *semble* it can be treated as *pro non scripto* [= as not written]; but the Court cannot escape the duty of interpretation merely because the language is difficult or ambiguous." Carleton K. Allen, *Law in the Making* 488 (7th ed. 1964).

semi-. See BI-.

semiannual (AmE)**; half-yearly** (BrE). See **biannual.**

senatorial courtesy has traditionally had a restricted sense in AmE; it refers to the tradition that the president must take care in filling high-level federal posts, such as judgeships, with persons agreeable to the nominees' home-state senators, lest the senators defeat confirmation. E.g., "A nomination approved by them [i.e., by senators from the state in which the office lies] is practically certain of final confirmation by the Senate as a whole. The arrangement is a 'logrolling' one, which has been dignified by the name of '*Senatorial courtesy.*' " Herbert W. Horwill, *The Usages of the American Constitution* 128–29 (1925)./ "No possible appointment could more have enraged the conservatives, in and out of the Senate, who had done the Court plan to death; but the silly rule of '*Senatorial courtesy,*' whereby members of the club never question very deeply the qualifications of a fellow member named to a new post, made Black's confirmation—just as Roosevelt knew it would—almost automatic." Fred Rodell, *Nine Men* 252 (1955).

As popularized, however, the term refers to civility among senators. Some writers lament the "decline of *senatorial courtesy*" and cite either the defeat of John Tower as President Bush's nominee for secretary of defense, or the treatment of Anita

Hill in Clarence Thomas's confirmation for the U.S. Supreme Court. Such uses are loose at best.

send. For general purposes, this word is much preferable to *transmit,* q.v.

send back is occasionally used in place of *remand,* the more formal legal term—e.g.: "This was clearly error, and of such vital importance that the case must be reversed and *sent back* for a new trial." See **remand (A).** Cf. **return back.**

senior = a Queen's Counsel. See **Q.C.** & **silk.** Cf. **junior.**

sensitize; sensitivize. Although Fowler championed the latter, the former is now usual in AmE and BrE.

sensor. See **censor.**

sensory; sensatory; sensorial. *Sensory* = of sensation or the senses. *Sensatory* is a NEEDLESS VARIANT. *Sensorial* = primarily responsive to sensations. For a misuse involving *sensory,* see **sensuous** (last par.).

sensuous; sensual. These words derive from the same root, meaning "appeal to the senses," but the precise meanings have undergone DIFFERENTIATION. *Sensuous* = of or relating to the five senses; arousing any of the five senses. The word properly has no risqué connotations, though it is gravely distorted by hack novelists. Here it is correctly used: "Words thus strung together fall on the ear like music. The appeal is *sensuous* rather than intellectual . . . ." W. Somerset Maugham, "Lucidity, Simplicity, Euphony," in *The Summing Up* 321, 322 (1938).

Sensual = relating to gratification of the senses, esp. sexual; salacious; voluptuous <sensual desires>. This is the word intended by the hack novelists who erroneously believe that *sensuous* carries sexy overtones—e.g.:

- "The spray painted drawings of female genitalia at issue here simply are not erotic or *sensual.*" *City of St. George v. Turner,* 860 P.2d 929, 934 (Utah 1993).
- "Since the illustrations were selected by the female, feminist editors, this volume was designed to demonstrate that women and feminists may find *sensual* pleasure . . . in sexually explicit imagery . . . ." Nadine Strossen, *A Feminist Critique of "the" Feminist Critique of Pornography,* 79 Va. L. Rev. 1099, 1109 (1993).
- "The grounds for the motion were . . . [that] the facts alleged did not offer sufficient indicia of a 'wicked, lustful, unchaste, licentious or *sensual* design' on Mitchell's part . . . ." *State v. Mitchell,* 624 So. 2d 859, 859 (Fla. Dist. Ct. App. 1993).
- "In order to satisfy her hot-blooded, passionate partner [the stereotype goes] . . . , the Latina must also be *sensual* and sexually responsive." Jenny Rivera, *Domestic Violence Against Latinas by Latino Males,* 14 B.C. Third World L.J. 231, 241 (1994).

Still, some writers are oblivious of these associations. They misuse *sensual* for *sensory*—e.g.: "It would be stronger still if these witnesses could explain in detail the nature of the *sensual* [read *sensory*] perceptions on which they based their 'conclusion' that the person they had seen was the defendant and that he was responsible for the events they observed." *Spinelli v. U.S.,* 393 U.S. 410, 429 (1969) (Black, J., dissenting)./ "Its true 'converse' would seem to be 'involuntarily,' i.e., an unconscious bodily movement through convulsion, reflex or other *sensual* [read *sensory* or, perhaps, *sensorial*] phenomenon." *Alford v. State,* 866 S.W.2d 619, 625 (Tex. Crim. App. 1993) (en banc) (Clinton, J., concurring). See **sensory.**

sentence. In most jurisdictions, criminal *sentences* (as opposed to *verdicts*) are imposed by judges and not by juries. E.g., "The Supreme Court of Alabama agrees that 'the jury is not the sentencing authority in . . . Alabama,' and has described the sentencing judge not as a reviewer of the jury's *'sentence,'* but as *the* sentencer." *Baldwin v. Alabama,* 472 U.S. 372, 384 (1985) (citations omitted). The term derives ultimately from Roman law. Cf. **verdict.** For the DIFFERENTIATION of *concurrent, consecutive,* and *cumulative sentences,* see **concurrent sentences.**

SENTENCE ADVERBS are adverbs conveying the writer's comment on the statement being made rather than adverbs qualifying a single word in the sentence. A sentence adverb does not resolve itself into the form *in a —— manner,* as most adverbs do. Thus, in *Happily, the bill did not go beyond the committee,* the introductory adverb *happily* conveys the writer's opinion on the message being imparted. The following words are among the most frequent sentence adverbs ending in *-ly.*

accordingly
admittedly
arguably
concededly
consequently
curiously
fortunately

importantly
interestingly
ironically
legally
logically
mercifully
oddly
paradoxically
regrettably
sadly
strangely
theoretically

Improvising sentence adverbs from traditional adverbs like *hopefully* (= in a hopeful manner) and *thankfully* (= in a thankful manner), qq.v., is objectionable to many stylists but seems to be on the rise. E.g., "*Explanatorily* [read *By way of explanation*], these consolidated causes were positioned as the ordinary and uncomplicated condemnation case." *O'Neil Corp. v. Perry Gas Transmission, Inc.,* 648 S.W.2d 335, 341 (Tex. App.—Amarillo 1983). (For a similar example, see **corollarily.**) Newfangled sentence adverbs of this kind are to be discouraged. In formal prose, even those like *hopefully* and *thankfully* should be avoided: they are increasingly common, but they have a beleaguered history.

Because sentence adverbs reveal the writer's own thoughts and biases, lawyers often overuse them in argumentation—but danger lurks in words such as *clearly, undoubtedly,* and *indisputably.* See **clearly** & OVERSTATEMENT.

SENTENCE ENDINGS. It was Karl Llewellyn's understanding of rhythm and emphasis that led him to say that a "sentence must be so written that the punch word comes at the end." *A Lecture on Appellate Advocacy,* 29 U. Chi. L. Rev. 627, 628 (1962). He knew, as a rhetorical matter, that the end of a sentence is the position of primary emphasis.

Of course, one must first try to achieve a reasonable average SENTENCE LENGTH, or else there is likely to be no regular position of emphasis. Once the average sentence length hovers around 20 or fewer words, the artistry of stressing final words becomes possible.

But legal writers are often tone-deaf and arrhythmic, hence unemphatic—e.g.:

- "The association's attorney did everything she could under the circumstances to protect the association's interest in this matter." [A possible revision: *The association's attorney did everything she could in this matter to protect the association's interest.*]
- "As the Austin court observed, the gravamen of Plaintiffs' complaint is more properly directed to the legislature if they feel there is a deficiency in the statutory manner in which notice of such legislative proceedings is prescribed to be given." [A possible revision: *As the Austin court observed, if the Plaintiffs believe that there is a deficiency in the statutory notice provision, then their complaint should be directed to the legislature.*]
- "The application of the court's decision strongly dictates that ESCO cannot be properly sued in Nueces County under Texas Civil Practice and Remedies Code, § 15.037 for foreign corporations." [A possible revision: *Under the Texas venue scheme and caselaw interpreting it, suing ESCO in Nueces County is improper.*]
- "My advice to her would be that it is probably not worth the potential hassles involved in creating a two-tiered pricing system until Tex. Rev. Civ. Stat. Ann. art. 5060-1.12 is repealed or there are cases tried more adequately interpreting it." [A possible revision: *I would advise her that, until article 5060-1.12 is repealed or new cases interpret it better, creating a two-tiered pricing system probably isn't worth the potential hassles.*]
- "It is also the desire of Dr. Goodfellow to amicably resolve any questions or concerns that you may presently have with regard to the contract and your performance of obligations thereunder." [A possible revision: *Dr. Goodfellow wants to resolve any remaining questions amicably.*]

In choosing words that can bear emphasis and ending with them, writers can usually rule out ending sentences with the following: (a) dates; (b) citations; and (c) prepositional phrases.

SENTENCE FRAGMENTS. See INCOMPLETE SENTENCES.

SENTENCE LENGTH. Among the more supportable indictments of legal writing in general is that it reads too slowly. It is plodding. It wastes time.

Among the cures is to reduce the average sentence length in a given piece of writing. Whereas long sentences slow the reader down and create a solemn, portentous impression, short sentences speed the reading and the thought. It is therefore "a counsel of perfection never to write a sentence without asking 'Might it not be better shorter?' " F.L. Lucas, *Style* 103 (1962).

Many things converge to create overlong sentences in legal writing. One is OVERPARTICULARIZATION—the wretched habit of trying to say too many things at once, with too much detail and too little sense of relevance. Another is the fear of qualifying a proposition in a separate sentence, as if an entire idea and all its qualifications had to be fitted into a single sentence. A third is the ill-founded fear of being simple and, by implication, simple-minded—of perhaps seeming to be insufficiently sophisticated. Yet a fourth is the nonsense-baggage that so many writers lug around on their backs: the idea that it is poor grammar to begin a sentence with *and* or *but*. See **and** (A), **but** (A) & SUPERSTITIONS (D).

Of course, many lawyers suffer from these turns of mind. And those who do have much hard work ahead if they wish to pursue a readable or even a clear style. It is not just their sentence length that will suffer. Overlong sentences are merely symptomatic of other problems—chiefly clutter and VERBOSITY.

What should the goal be? Experts in readability commonly say that, in technical writing, you want an average sentence length of 20 words or fewer. Some sentences ought to be 40 or 50 words, and some ought to be 3 or 4. There needs to be variety, but the average should be 20 or below. The writer who achieves this goal will generally achieve greater speed, clarity, and impact than the writer with longer sentences.

Of course, E.B. White and others have written much longer sentences that were perfectly readable. But they were typically writing in a different genre—fiction—and they typically had far greater skill in constructing sentences than most legal writers. Exceptions such as White do not disprove the point that legal writers ought to strive for an average sentence length of fewer than 20 words.

Is that goal realistic? Many good writers meet it, even when discussing difficult subjects. Consider how Buckland—with an average sentence length of 13 words—here sums up part of John Austin's philosophy:

> Austin's propositions come to this. There is in every community (but he does not really look beyond our community) a person or body [that] can enact what it will and is under no superior in this matter. That person or body he calls the Sovereign. The general rules [that] the Sovereign lays down are the law. This, at first sight, looks like circular reasoning. Law is law since it is made by the Sovereign. The Sovereign is Sovereign because he makes the law. But this is not circular reasoning; it is not reasoning at all. It is definition. Sovereign and law have much the same relation as centre and circumference. Neither term means anything without the other. In general what Austin says is true for us to-day, though some hold that it might be better to substitute 'enforced' for 'commanded.' Austin is diffuse and repetitive and there is here and there, or seems to be, a certain, not very important, confusion of thought. But, with the limitation that it is not universally true, there is not much to quarrel with in Austin's doctrine. [Total words: 184; avg. words per sentence: 13.]
>
> W.W. Buckland, *Some Reflections on Jurisprudence* 48 (1945).

The style is bold, confident, and quick. More legal writers ought to attempt such a style.

Instead, though, legal readers are too often fed lumpy, indigestible portions of words. Following are some examples, followed by possible revisions:

- "Though a clear case of continuing trespass exists for which the only relief at law, if ejectment should be impracticable, would be successive suits for damages, and therefore equity would intervene normally to prevent a multiplicity of suits, nevertheless equitable relief compelling the removal of the encroachment is denied because of the disproportionate loss to the defendant which would result." William F. Walsh, *A Treatise on Equity* 284 (1930). [Total words: 60; avg. words per sentence: 60.] [A possible revision: *A clear case of continuing trespass exists for which the only relief at law—if ejectment is impracticable—would be successive suits for damages. Normally, therefore, equity would intervene to prevent a multiplicity of suits. Still, equitable relief compelling the removal of the encroachment is denied because it would result in a disproportionate loss to the defendant.* [Total words: 57; avg. words per sentence: 19.]
- "Rules of morality are necessarily unstable and nearly always lacking in precision, changing from age to age, since they reflect mankind's emotional reaction to external conditions, and it should not be expected that the legal decisions and writings which have survived from those periods when a transgression of the current code of ethics was a requisite in criminal guilt can yield any precise definitions and distinctions, especially since the more ancient rule of strict accountability had not then, and indeed has not even now, entirely lost its force." J.W. Cecil Turner, *Kenny's Outlines of Criminal Law* 21 (1952). [Total words: 88; avg. words per sentence: 88.] [A possible revision: *Rules of morality are necessarily unstable and nearly always lacking in precision. They change from age to age because they reflect humans' emotional reaction to external conditions. And we should not expect to yield any precise definitions and distinctions from legal decisions and writings that have survived from those periods when a transgression of the current code of ethics was a requisite in criminal guilt. For the more ancient rule of strict accountability had not then entirely lost its force. Indeed, it has not even lost it now.* [Total words: 88; avg. words per sentence: 18.]
- "In modern codifications, beginning with those of Germany and Switzerland, dating from the turn of the century, to those recent codes and

drafts of Czechoslovakia, Ethiopia, Hungary, Italy, the Netherlands, Poland or Portugal, not to speak of France itself, that a structure of the law of obligations which appeared in France's Napoleonic Code and, inspired by the latter, in the Civil Code of Louisiana, has been refashioned along lines of considerably different systematic structure and legislative technique." Max Rheinstein, "Problems and Challenges of Contemporary Civil Law of Obligations," in *Essays on the Civil Law of Obligations* 1, 8–9 (Joseph Dainow ed., 1969). [Total words: 77; avg. words per sentence: 77.] [A possible revision: *In modern codifications, the structure of the law of obligations—as it originally appeared in the Napoleonic Code and then in the Louisiana Civil Code—has been refashioned. In those codes, the law differs in structure and in legislative technique. The codifications began with Germany and Switzerland at the turn of the century. Among the more recent codes and drafts are those of Czechoslovakia, Ethiopia, Hungary, Italy, the Netherlands, Poland, and Portugal—not to speak of France itself.* [Total words: 78; avg. words per sentence: 20.]

- "Though one could logically hold that attempting the impossible is non-criminal even though such attempts are in themselves possible—as, indeed, is held by those who argue that to do the impossible cannot, since it is impossible to do the impossible, be a crime, and that it cannot be a crime to attempt what is not a crime—usually those who have held that attempting the impossible is non-criminal have done so because they held that such an attempt is in itself impossible, while those who have held that attempting the impossible can be a crime have done so because they denied that it is impossible to attempt the impossible." Alan R. White, *Misleading Cases* 13 (1991). [Total words: 112; avg. words per sentence: 112.] [A possible revision: *One could logically hold that attempting the impossible is noncriminal even though such attempts are in themselves possible. Indeed, some do hold this view. They argue that to do the impossible cannot be a crime, since it is impossible to do the impossible. Further, they say that it cannot be a crime to attempt what is not a crime. But others hold that attempting the impossible is noncriminal for a different reason. They believe that such an attempt is in itself impossible. Still a different group—those who hold that attempting the impossible can be a crime—have done so because they denied that it is impossible to attempt the impossible.*] [Total words: 111; avg. words per sentence: 16.]

See ANFRACTUOSITY & PLAIN LANGUAGE (D).

separate. In the legal phrase *to separate the jury,* the verb *separate* means "to segregate." The *OED* suggests that this use of the word is "chiefly in Biblical language" and does not mention the legal use. See BIBLICAL AFFECTATION & **segregate.**

separate and apart; separate and distinct. Both phrases are common redundancies—e.g.: "[O]il and gas are subject to sale *separate and apart from* [read *separate from* or *apart from*] the surface of the earth." Robert Kratovil, *Real Estate Law* 4 (1946; repr. 1950)./ "In all countries where constitutional law is a *separate and distinct* [read *separate*] body of jurisprudence its prescriptions take precedence over all statutory enactments in case of a conflict between the two." James W. Garner, "Law, Constitutional," in 17 *Encyclopedia Americana* 96, 101 (1953). See DOUBLETS, TRIPLETS, AND SYNONYM-STRINGS.

separate but equal = the now-defunct legal doctrine that blacks could be segregated if granted "equal" opportunities and facilities in education, public transportation, and jobs. Deriving from the infamous decision in *Plessy v. Ferguson,* the term was originally phrased in reverse fashion: *equal but separate.* See 163 U.S. 537, 540 (1896). Notably, if the idea is phrased *equal but separate,* the idea of separateness receives emphasis, whereas *separate but equal* stresses the (supposed) equality. It is quite conceivable that the phrasing *separate but equal* gained easier acceptance in the popular mind of the late 19th and early 20th centuries. (For the rhetorical rationale for this speculation, see SENTENCE ENDINGS.) The famous civil-rights decisions of the 1950s and 1960s—beginning with *Brown v. Board of Educ.,* 347 U.S. 483 (1954)—ended the de jure segregation that the separate-but-equal doctrine represented.

As in the previous sentence, when the words are used as a phrasal adjective, they should be hyphenated: "[I]n cases urging admission of Negroes to a white Texas law school, a white Oklahoma graduate course, and the white section of Southern dining-cars, the main plea was that the entire *separate-but-equal* doctrine be discarded . . . ." Fred Rodell, *Nine Men* 323 (1955).

separate out. See **out** (A).

separate property = property that a married person owns in his or her own right during marriage. In AmE, the precise meaning of this term varies. In so-called common-law states, this term is contrasted with *marital property;* in community-property states, it is contrasted with *community property.* See **community property.**

separation = (1) an arrangement whereby a married couple stops living together while remaining married, either by mutual consent or by a judicial decree (often called *legal separation* or *judicial separation*); or (2) the status of a husband and wife having begun such an arrangement, or the judgment or contract that brings it about. Because the word *separation* may refer to arrangements involving various degrees of legal formality, on its own it is unclear.

separation of powers. The phrase is usu. associated with the U.S. Constitution's demarcation of powers in the executive, legislative, and judicial branches of government. But the idea is much older. John Locke wrote about the separation of legislative and executive powers in his *Two Treatises of Government* (1690). The phrase itself is at least a generation older than the Constitution. In his *Spirit of the Laws* (1748; translated into English in 1750), Montesquieu refined the idea that the virtue of the English constitution was a system of checks and balances among executive, legislature, and judiciary—a *separation of powers.*

When used as a PHRASAL ADJECTIVE, the words need hyphens: "On all the great *separation-of-powers* questions of our time—executive privilege, legislative vetoes, presidential appointment and impoundment power, and so on—the OLC has provided legal and constitutional guidance for the executive." Barbara H. Craig, *Chadha: The Story of an Epic Constitutional Struggle* 52 (1988).

sepulcher; sepulchre; sepulture. The preferred spelling of the first term is *sepulcher* in AmE, *-re* in BrE. The word means "burial place; tomb," and is pronounced /***sep**-əl-kər*/. *Sepulture,* sometimes a NEEDLESS VARIANT of *sepulcher,* justifies its separate form in the sense "burial." These words are very formal, even literary. They should be used cautiously.

sequential; sequacious. *Sequential* means "forming a sequence or consequence." *Sequacious* means "intellectually servile."

sequential order is often a REDUNDANCY. E.g., "The computer placed the checks *in sequential order* [read *in order* or *in sequence*] by account number."

sequester, n., = (1) in legislative parlance, an across-the-board cut in domestic spending; or (2) a person with whom litigants deposit the property being contested until the case has concluded. Sense (1)—"Darman ordered an across-the-board cut in domestic spending—called a *sequester*—of $2.3 million . . . ." Stuart Auerbach, *Bill Gives Rostenkowski a Way to Settle Accounts,* Wash. Post, 9 Oct. 1991, at F1.

In sense (2), the word is really a NEEDLESS VARIANT of *sequestrator,* q.v.—e.g.: "[It] concerned a former husband's suit against a receiver and *sequester* [read *sequestrator*] appointed by a state court to consolidate all the former husband's property available for fulfilling support obligations . . . ." *Firestone v. Cleveland Trust Co.,* 654 F.2d 1212, 1216 (6th Cir. 1981).

sequester, v.t.; **sequestrate.** Generally, *sequestrate* means nothing that *sequester,* the more common term, does not also mean. Both terms are old: *sequester* dates from the 14th century, *sequestrate* from the early 16th century. In law, *sequester* = to remove (as property) from the possession of the owner temporarily; to seize and hold the effects of a debtor until the claims of creditors are satisfied (*OED*). The lay meaning of the term, of course, is "to set aside, separate," as *to sequester* (or *separate*) the jury. See **separate.**

Sequestrate is given two slightly different senses by the *OED,* in addition to the overlapping senses: (1) "to divert the income of an estate or benefice, temporarily or permanently, from its owner into other hands"; and (2) (in Scots law) "to place . . . lands belonging to a bankrupt, or [those] of disputed ownership, . . . in the hands of a judicial trustee, for the prevention of waste." These two senses are rare, however, and—except in Scotland—it is best to avoid *sequestrate* as a NEEDLESS VARIANT unless a nuance conveyed by one of these specialized senses is intended.

The sole weakness of this advice is that the agent noun is *sequestrator* and not, ordinarily, *sequesterer.* See **sequestrator.**

In the following examples, no such nuance was intended, and *sequester* would have been the better word: "[I]t is difficult to see why a plaintiff in any action for a personal judgment in tort or contract may not . . . apply to the chancellor for a so-called injunction *sequestrating* [read *sequestering*] his opponent's assets pending recovery and satisfaction of a judgment in such a law action." *De Beers Consol. Mines v. U.S.,* 325 U.S. 212, 222–23 (1945)./ "The practice of *sequestrating* [read *sequestering*] the property of the defendant to coerce his obedience to the decree was soon developed."

sequestration; attachment; garnishment. In the context of civil remedies, these terms are closely related. *Sequestration* = the removal, by judicial authority, of real or personal property from its possessor, usu. to preserve it until a court has determined who has a right to it. *Attachment* = the prejudgment seizure of property and placement of it under the court's control as security to satisfy a judgment that the plaintiff may recover. (*Attachment* may also refer to the arrest of a person: see **attachment.**) *Garnishment* = a judicial proceeding in which a judgment creditor, or a suitor who may become a judgment creditor, serves notice on a third party who may be indebted to, or on a bailee for, the judgment debtor, that any of the debtor's property held by the person served must be turned over to the judgment creditor.

Garnishment differs from the other two terms in two important ways: it refers to a judicial proceeding—not to a seizure or removal—and the property stays in the third party's hands until judgment is pronounced.

sequestrator; sequesterer. Though not as logically formed as its alternative, *sequestrator* is the standard term meaning "one who sequesters property." E.g., "[C]ompelling the personal appearance of a nonresident defendant . . . is accomplished by the appointment of a *sequestrator* to seize and hold the property of the nonresident located in Delaware . . . ." *Shaffer v. Heitner,* 433 U.S. 186, 186–87 (1977). Sometimes, however, *sequestrator* means not the person who seizes, but the party at whose instance the sequestration occurs. Cf. **sequester,** n.

Serbonian bog. See LITERARY ALLUSION (A)(4).

serendipity forms the adjective *serendipitous,* a useful term of recent vintage (ca. 1943).

sergeant; serjeant. In medieval times this word (ultimately deriving fr. L. *servient* "serving") came to mean someone performing a specific function in the household or jurisdiction of a king, lord, or deliberative assembly and reporting directly to the top authority under which that person served. From the 14th century until 1875, *serjeants-at-law* were appointed as a superior order of advocates. They wore silk gowns and coifs and (until 1846) had an exclusive right of audience in the Court of Common Pleas. See **silk & Order of the Coif.**

Of the more than 50 variant spellings of the term over the centuries, the preferred spelling in AmE today is *sergeant.* In BrE, there is some DIFFERENTIATION between the spelling: *sergeant* is largely military (*sergeant-major*) and *serjeant* largely legal (*serjeant of the coif, serjeant-at-law, serjeant-at-arms*).

Sargeant is a common misspelling stemming perhaps from the military casualism *sarge.*

SERIAL COMMA. See PUNCTUATION (C).

seriatim = in turn; serially; one after another; in sequence; successively. Though common in references to *seriatim opinions,* this LATINISM in other contexts is generally best replaced with either of its anglicized siblings, *serially* and *in series,* or of one of the phrases used just above in defining the term. E.g., "After presenting the factual and procedural setting, we dispose of the issues *seriatim* [read *serially*]."/ "One court refused to sever the civil-rights claims or to dismiss the state law ones, electing to submit all claims *serially* to the same jury."

series is ordinarily used in the singular, though it serves as a plural where more than one series is intended. Here the verb is incorrectly plural: "There *have* [read *has*] been a *series* of efforts made by the central P.L.O. but also splinter groups to move through Jordan into the West Bank."

Boswell quoted Samuel Johnson as using the now-obsolete plural *serieses* in a legal context: "Entails are good, because it is good to preserve in a country, *serieses* of men, to whom the people are accustomed to look up as their leaders." 2 James Boswell, *Life of Johnson* 428 (1791).

serjeant. See **sergeant.**

serjeanty (or *sergeanty*) is the term for a form of feudal tenure under which a specified personal service was rendered to the king.

The spelling *sergeantry* is obsolete. See **sergeant.**

servant. A. And *agent.* See **agent.**

B. And *employee.* See **master & employer and employee.**

serve (= to make legal delivery of [a process or a writ] in a legally required manner) as a legal term dates back to the 15th century. In the legal idiom, one who serves process may either *serve* a writ *on* or *upon* another, or *serve* another *with* a writ. See OBJECT-SHUFFLING.

service was once only a noun, but since the late 19th century it has been used as a transitive verb as well. It may mean "to provide service for" <the mechanic serviced the copying machine>, "to pay interest on" <to service a debt>, or generally "to perform services for" <servicing corporate clients>. Ordinarily, the verb *to serve* ought to be used in broad senses; *service,* v.t., should be used only where the writer believes that *serve* would not be suitable in idiom or sense.

service(-)mark = a name, phrase, or other device intended to identify the services of a certain supplier. This term is increasingly made one word—e.g.: "[T]rade names, trademarks, and *servicemarks* are often referred to interchangeably . . . ." *Frances Denney, Inc. v. New Process Co.,* 670 F. Supp. 661, 667 (W.D. Va. 1985). It is odd that the writer did not make *tradename* (q.v.) one word in that quotation. See **trade(-)mark.**

service of process. See **process.**

servient. See **dominant.**

servitude. A. And *easement.* *Servitude* is primarily a civil-law term, deriving from L. *servitus* (= subjection), and equivalent to the term *easement* in common law. But even in the common law, *servitude* has a restricted currency in referring to a servient tenement (i.e., land subject to an easement), and meaning "a charge on an estate for the use of another estate belonging to another owner." The DIFFERENTIATION usu. observed in common-law countries is that *easement* refers to the personal enjoyment of the burdened property, and *servitude* either to the burden or to the burdened property itself.

International lawyers use *servitude* in an extended sense: "an international agreement giving a territory some permanent status, such as a demilitarized or neutralized status, or creating rights over bodies of water."

B. And *slavery.* "The word *servitude* is of larger meaning than *slavery,* as the latter is popularly understood in this country, and the obvious purpose [of the Thirteenth Amendment] was to forbid all shades and conditions of African slavery." *Slaughter-House Cases,* 83 U.S. (16 Wall.) 36, 69 (1872). Both terms, in addition to denoting "the condition of being a slave or serf, or of being the property of another person," carry the notion of subjection to excessive labor.

session = (1) the time during which a court or other body meets <court is in session>; or (2) a term of court—that is, a period that constitutes *termtime* (q.v.) <the October session of the Supreme Court>.

By historical extension, *session* came to signify certain courts, the most famous and longest lasting being the Court of Session, the supreme civil court of Scotland, established in 1532 and still in session today. See **cession.**

sessional; sessionary. The latter is a NEEDLESS VARIANT of the adjective corresponding to the noun *session.*

session laws = the statutes enacted by a legislative body and published in a form identifying them with the term in which the legislative session took place <Session Laws of 1994>. E.g., "[W]e can scarcely credit, as we know state legislation today, what the *session laws* of an older time disclose . . . ." Roscoe Pound, *The Formative Era of American Law* 53 (1938).

set aside. A. In Legal Jargon. This phrase, meaning "to vacate," is sometimes misunderstood by nonlawyers. One lay writer on legal language misinterpreted the phrase as possibly meaning "to lay to the side temporarily, as for review" (as "to take under advisement"). See Terri LeClercq, *Jargon 2: Just When You Thought It Was Safe . . . ,* 48 Tex. B.J. 852, 852 (1985) ("So if you are describing the action of a court, you might qualify how the court *set aside* the ruling by adding, for example, that the court *set aside* the ruling for review.").

Such are the linguistic traps that lawyers have needlessly laid for those unfamiliar with legal jargon, in which this quite ordinary English phrase is given the extraordinary meaning "to annul, to make void." *Migdol v. U.S.,* 298 F.2d 513, 516 (9th Cir. 1961). E.g., "[*Nullity*] can be used, and most commonly is, to describe a marriage that exists until either party obtains a decree of the court *setting* it *aside,* e.g. on the ground of impotence . . . ." Patrick Devlin, *The Enforcement of Morals* 67 (1968). See **overrule.**

B. *Set aside* and *vacate.* See DOUBLETS, TRIPLETS, AND SYNONYM-STRINGS.

setback. To a nonlawyer, of course, this term means "an unexpected interruption of progress." To real-estate lawyers, however, it refers to the amount of space required between a lot line and the building line to ensure that enough light and ventilation reach the ground. In land law, ironically, increased setbacks represent human progress.

set-off, n., = (1) a counterdemand, generally of a liquidated debt growing out of an independent transaction for which a lawsuit might be maintained; or (2) the general right of a debtor to reduce the amount of a debt by any sum that the creditor owes the debtor. It is older than the term *offset* and is considered more correct by purists. E.g., "That payment had been made only in respect of the plaintiff's claim and not in respect of the claim less the equitable *set-off.*" (Aus.) The *OCL* includes *set-off,* which is usual in BrE, but not *offset.* See **offset.**

As a verb, the hyphen is unnecessary: "On the other hand, a *subsequent* agreement between the parties to *set-off* [read *set off*] a claim of the buyer in satisfaction of part of the purchase price may satisfy the statute . . . ." E.W. Chance, *Principles of Mercantile Law* 236 (P.W. French ed., 13th ed. 1950).

set of facts is more elegant, dignified, and descriptive than either *factual situation* or *fact situation.* See **fact situation.**

set over = to transfer, convey. E.g., "Vendor does by these presents grant, bargain, sell, assign, convey, transfer, *set over,* and deliver to the purchaser the following described property."

SET PHRASES. Fossilized language should not be consciously defossilized—which is to say that one should not try to vary what has been set in stone. Thus *set in stone* should never become *set in shale,* or whatever variation one might lamely invent. Nor, to cite another example, should one change *madding crowd* to *maddening crowd.* See **madding crowd.**

Set phrases are sometimes changed out of a sense of cleverness, sometimes out of ignorance. Thus, the lawyer who writes, "Time is the essence of this subcontract," simply betrays an ignorance of the idiom *Time is of the essence (of this subcontract).*

Many expressions are so well entrenched in the English language that the slightest change will make them un-English. For example, we have the phrase *out from under,* ruined by a metamorphosis in this sentence: "[Plaintiff] was injured when the back of the teller stool on which she was sitting fell off and the chair rolled *out from underneath her* [read *out from under her*]." *Syrie v. Knoll Int'l,* 748 F.2d 304, 305 (5th Cir. 1984).

Wilson Follett called set phrases "inviolable" (if not quite inviolate): "the attempt to liven up old clichés by inserting modifiers into the set phrase is a mistake: the distended phrase is neither original, nor unobtrusive, nor brief, and sometimes it has ceased to be immediately clear, as in *They have been reticent to a tactical fault.*" *Modern American Usage* 303 (1966).

In addition to the fault of inserting modifiers into set phrases, three other faults commonly occur. First, it is wrong to wrench a set phrase into ungrammatical contexts, as here: "This was reported to *we the people.*" The phrase *we the people,* of course, derives from the U.S. Constitution; but the sentence calls for the objective *us.*

Second, it is bad style to substitute an alien word for the familiar one in a well-known phrase. For example, changing *in large part* or *in large measure* to *in large degree* simply does not work: "The prejudice to appellant is attributable *in large degree* [read *in large part*] to appellant's own conduct."

Third, it is poor to aim at novelty by reversing the usual order of a phrase: "Many persons must rely upon Medicaid for their well-being and health." (The standard phrase is *health and well-being.*) Cf. INELEGANT VARIATION.

settle. Ordinarily, litigants who compromise in order to end the litigation are said to *settle* the lawsuit. By extension in AmE, a judge who pressures the parties to compromise is likewise said to *settle* the lawsuit—e.g.: "Frustrated by a huge backlog of asbestos liability cases, a federal judge and a New York state judge have combined forces to try to *settle* hundreds of the lawsuits." Wade Lambert & Jill Abramson, *Judges Join Forces on Asbestos Litigation,* Wall St. J., 31 Jan. 1990, at B2.

settled. See **well-settled.**

settlement. See **compromise** & **accord and satisfaction.** For the phrase *property settlement,* see **estate planning.**

settlement sheet. See **closing statement.**

settler; settlor. The two forms usually convey different senses. *Settler* = (1) one who settles; or (2) a homesteader. *Settlor* = the creator of a trust; a party to an instrument. *Settlor* has also been used—confusingly—in reference to one who settles a case: "The *settlors* [read *settlers*] have agreed between themselves that the worker shall retain the face value of the settlement and that the third party shall be responsible for satisfaction of the compensation lien."

settlor; trustor; donor; creator. These four terms are used to name the person who establishes a trust. The first is the most common. It should be spelled with the *-or* suffix to differentiate it from the quite different word *settler,* q.v. Of these four forms, *trustor* is the least usual and most awkward, although *trustee* is the common name for the holder of the property in trust. See **creator** & **donor.**

set up = to raise (as a defense). Both civil and criminal defendants are traditionally said to *set up* defenses—e.g.:

- "[T]he dishonest contractor [could not] *set up* his original dishonest intent as an excuse for non-performance . . . ." Thomas E. Holland, *The Elements of Jurisprudence* 262 (13th ed. 1924; repr. 1937).

- "Suppose that D breaks and enters a house, and on a charge of burglary *sets up* the defence of insanity." Glanville Williams, *Criminal Law* 523 (2d ed. 1961).
- "[T]he promisee can *set up* such a promise as a defence to an action but cannot himself sue upon it." P.S. Atiyah, *An Introduction to the Law of Contract* 126 (3d ed. 1981).

severability clause = a contractual or statutory provision—usu. boilerplate—preventing the complete loss of the contract or statute if a court were to hold a single provision invalid. Typically, a *severability clause* states, "If any part of this agreement is for any reason found to be unenforceable, all other parts nevertheless remain enforceable." A variant name for this provision is *saving clause.* See **saving(s) clause (B).**

several for *separate,* an archaic remnant of Middle English, has survived only in legal language. The usage survives primarily in the phrase *joint and several liability,* but thrives in other contexts as well: "The share of each tenant in common is, unlike that of a joint tenant, *several* and distinct from the shares of his cotenants."/ "The constitutional rule requiring bills to be read on three *several* days in each house is hereby suspended."/ "The dispute does not cease to be a priori because it is a matter of the cumulative effect of *severally* inconclusive premises." (Eng.) See **joint and several.**

severalty = the condition of being separate or distinct. The legal phrase *in severalty* is used in law in reference to land, and means "held by an individual absolutely, not jointly or in common with another." E.g., "The whole transaction required the cooperation of all for its success; the division of the shares among them was as much a part of it as any other; they selected each other as owners *in severalty;* and they should be held liable for any defaults of those whom they chose, although their liability is secondary."/ "Suppose that Twose had thought that the common was land belonging to her *in severalty.*" Glanville Williams, *Criminal Law* 309 (2d ed. 1961).

severance pay. This AmE phrase, dating from 1940–45, denotes money (apart from backpay and wages) paid to an employee who is dismissed, often for reasons outside the employer's control. E.g., "In a more complex form, a termination clause might combine several of these possibilities, and it might add such considerations as acts of third parties, or further conditions, or some kind of '*severance pay.*'" David Crump, *The Five Elements of a Contract,* 43 Tex. B.J. 370, 371 (1980). The BrE equivalent is *redundancy pay.*

sewage; sewerage. *Sewage* is the refuse conveyed through sewers; *sewerage* refers either to the removal of sewage or to the system of removal.

sex, adj.; **sexual.** Both *sex discrimination* and *sexual discrimination* appear in law reports. The former is perhaps better, inasmuch as *sexual* has come to refer more to sexual intercourse and things pertaining to it than to questions of maleness or femaleness. See **gender.**

SEXISM. Many who at first shrugged off feminists' claims that the English language can be detrimentally sexist have come to acknowledge that many of the contentions are undeniably valid. And with that acknowledgment come certain responsibilities—and difficulties—for the writer concerned with maintaining credibility.

How does one deal with linguistic forms that have traditionally been sexist? The best course today is to eliminate sexist language while not resorting to ugly or awkward linguistic artifices. The purpose, of course, is to avoid distracting any variety of readers, from traditional grammarians to feminists.

A. The Pronoun Problem. English has a number of common-sex general words, such as *person, anyone, everyone,* and *no one,* but it has no common-sex singular personal pronouns. Instead, we have *he, she,* and *it,* the first denoting a male; the second denoting a female; and the third denoting a nonhuman object or being (though occasionally a baby). In general literary and legal usage, the traditional approach has been to use the masculine pronouns *he* and *him* to cover all persons, male and female alike. That this practice has come under increasing attack has caused the single most difficult problem in the realm of sexist language. Other snarls are far more readily solvable.

The inadequacy of the English language in this respect becomes apparent when one reads, for example, the words from an appellate brief excerpted in an opinion addressing medical malpractice in the performance of a hysterectomy: "The objective of the doctrine [of informed consent], the plaintiff asserts, 'is to insure the patient's right to self-determination by requiring that *he* have access to all [the] knowledge necessary for him to give an intelligent and informed consent . . . .'" *Bly v. Rhoads,* 222 S.E.2d 783, 785 (Va. 1976).

Actually, the generic masculine pronoun also sits uneasily in a sentence containing a female to which it is meant to refer—e.g.:

- "When a person, whether male or female, dies without leaving a will, *he* is called an 'intestate.'" Thomas E. Atkinson, *Handbook of the Law of Wills* 4 (2d ed. 1953).
- "Anyone, including a married woman, who has attained the age of twenty-one, has sufficient sense to know what *he* is doing, and is not under the influence of terror or fraud, can make a valid will." Edward Jenks, *The Book of English Law* 299 (P.B. Fairest ed., 6th ed. 1967).
- "That is not to say that the accessory will necessarily be punished as severely as the principal. Yet sometimes *he* may be the guiltier, as Lady Macbeth was. The master mind and guiding spirit of a crime ring will probably receive a heavier sentence than *his* tools." Glanville Williams, *Criminal Law* 404 (2d ed. 1961).
- "If a testator fails to provide by will for *his* surviving spouse [a *she?*] who married the testator after the execution of the will, the omitted spouse shall receive the same share of the estate *he* [i.e., the spouse] would have received if the decedent left no will . . . ." Unif. Probate Code § 2-301(a) (1989).

Even when the context does not make the masculine pronoun somewhat ludicrous, one may feel bludgeoned by its use at every turn—e.g.: "[I]n the acquisition of background information a judge should be left to *his* own devices. If *he* is left to *himself* to find *his* own sources of background information where *he* thinks *he* needs it and if in the acquisition of it *he* behaves in a discreet way, *he* will not be criticized." Patrick Devlin, *The Judge* 52 (1979).

"There are," Fowler notes, with contributions from Gowers,

> three makeshifts: first, *as anybody can see for himself or herself;* second, *as anybody can see for themselves;* and third, *as anybody can see for himself.* No one who can help it chooses the first; it is correct, and is sometimes necessary, but it is so clumsy as to be ridiculous except when explicitness is urgent, and it usually sounds like a bit of pedantic humour. The second is the popular solution; it sets the literary man's teeth on edge, and he exerts himself to give the same meaning in some entirely different way if he is not prepared to risk the third, which is here recommended. It involves the convention (statutory in the interpretation of documents) that where the matter of sex is not conspicuous or important the masculine form shall be allowed to represent a person instead of a man, or say a man (*homo*) instead of a man (*vir*).
>
> *MEU2* 404 (1965).

At least two other makeshifts are now available. The first is commonly used by American academics: *as anybody can see for herself.* Such phrases are often alternated with those containing masculine pronouns, or, in some writing, appear uniformly. Whether this phraseology will cease to sound strange to most readers only time will tell. This is one possibility, however, of (1) maintaining a grammatical construction; and (2) avoiding the awkwardness of alternatives such as *himself or herself.*

But the method carries two risks. First, unintended connotations may invade the writing. A recent novel was published in two versions, one using generic masculine pronouns and the other using generic feminine pronouns; the effects on readers of the two versions were reported to have been startlingly different in ways far too complex for discussion here. Second, this makeshift is likely to do a disservice to women in the long run, for it would likely be adopted only by a small minority of writers: the rest would continue with the generic masculine pronoun.

A second new makeshift has entered Canadian legislation: *as anybody can see for themself; if a judge decides to recuse themself.* The word *themself,* q.v., fills the need for a gender-neutral reflexive pronoun, but many readers and writers—especially Americans—bristle at the sight or the sound of it. Thus, for the legal writer, this makeshift carries a considerable risk of distracting readers.

Typographical gimmickry may once have served a political purpose, but it should be avoided as an answer to the problem. It is trendy, ugly, distracting, and usually unpronounceable. E.g., "A district judge who, on reflection, concludes that *s/he* erred may rectify that error when ruling on post-trial motions." *U.S. v. Miller,* 753 F.2d 19, 23 (3d Cir. 1985)./ "*S/he* is required to hold an appropriate qualification specified in the Companies Act and *s/he* must be appointed to hold office . . . ." S.B. Marsh & J.B. Bailey, *Terminology of Business and Company Law* 9 (1987).

Variants are *he/she* and *she/he,* and even the gloriously misbegotten double-entendre, *s/he/it.* If we must have alternatives, *he or she* is the furthest we should go. See **he or she.**

For the persuasive writer—for whom credibility is all—the writer's point of view does not matter as much as the reader's. Thus, if one is writing for an unknown or a broad readership, the only course that does not risk damaging one's credibility is to write around the problem. For this purpose, every writer ought to have available a repertoire of methods to avoid the generic masculine pronoun. No single method is sufficient. Thus, in a given context, one might consider doing any of the following:

- Delete the pronoun reference altogether. E.g., "The judge should read the briefs as soon as they are submitted *to him* [delete *to him*] by the parties."

- Change the pronoun to an article, such as *a* or *the.* "A judgment-creditor may use legal means to enforce *his* [read *a*] judgment."
- Pluralize, so that *he* becomes *they.* E.g., "A judge should meet *his* responsibility to avoid even the appearance of impropriety." [Read *Judges should meet their responsibility . . . ,* or re-word: *A judge should avoid . . . .*]
- Use the relative pronoun *who,* especially when the generic *he* follows an *if.* E.g., "If a student cannot write competently, *he* cannot be expected to understand complex legal problems." [Read *A student who cannot write competently cannot be expected to understand complex legal problems.*]
- Repeat the noun instead of using a pronoun, especially when the two are separated by several words. E.g., "When considering a motion to remand, the judge should evaluate the suitability of the alternative forum. In particular, *he* [read *the judge*] . . . ."

For a sensible discussion of the generic masculine pronoun, see Beverly Ray Burlingame, *Reaction and Distraction: The Pronoun Problem in Legal Persuasion,* 1 Scribes J. Legal Writing 87 (1990).

Though the masculine singular personal pronoun may survive awhile longer as a generic term, it will probably be displaced ultimately by *they,* which is coming to be used alternatively as singular or plural. (See CONCORD (B).) This usage is becoming commonplace—e.g.:

- "*Anyone* who has subscribed to the Literary Review for more than one year may join, as long as *they* are proposed by a writer known to the committee." K. Saunders, *Literati, Glitterati, Choose Your Party,* Sunday Times, 10 Sept. 1989, at F1.
- "It is assumed that, if *someone* is put under enough pressure, *they* will tell the truth, or the truth will emerge despite the teller." Robin T. Lakoff, *Talking Power: The Politics of Language in Our Lives* 90 (1990).
- "How the Elizabethans reacted is, alas, unknown, since *nobody* thought Shakespeare's plays important enough to bother recording *their* impressions." John Carey, *Stages of Hatred,* Sunday Times (Books), 4 Oct. 1992, at § 6, p. 8.
- "*Anyone* planning a dissertation on Hollywood's fling with yuppie demonology will want to include 'The Temp' in *their* calculations." Janet Maslin, *A Perfect Secretary, Temporarily,* N.Y. Times, 13 Feb. 1993, at 8.

Speakers of AmE resist this development more than speakers of BrE, in which the indeterminate *they* is already more or less standard. That it sets many literate Americans' teeth on edge is an unfortunate setback to what promises to be the ultimate solution to the problem. For a similar etymological progression, see **none.**

B. Words in *man-* and *-man.* "For the lawyer more than for most men, it is true that he who knows but cannot express what he knows might as well be ignorant." That sentence opens chapter 1 of Henry Weihofen's *Legal Writing Style* (2d ed. 1980)—a sentence that, ironically, is flanked by warnings against sexist language (pp. vii, 19–20). If Weihofen were writing today, no doubt he would express himself in neutral language.

Throughout the English-speaking world, writers' awareness of sexism seems to have been heightened most markedly during the 1980s. In September 1984, the Commonwealth Attorney-General's Department in Canberra, Australia, issued a press release entitled "Moves to Modify Language Sex Bias in Legislation." The release states that "[t]he Government accepts that drafting in 'masculine' language may contribute to some extent to the perpetuation of a society in which men and women see women as lesser beings." The press release recommends, "[w]here possible and appropriate, avoidance of the use of words ending in *man,* such as *chairman, serviceman, seaman,* and so on." See Note, *The De-Masculinisation of Language in Federal Legislation,* 58 Aus. L.J. 685, 685–86 (1984).

Three years later, the U.S. Supreme Court announced its adoption of changes in the Federal Rules of Civil Procedure to weed out gender-specific references; thus Rule 4(b) was changed so that *him* and *his* became *the defendant* and *the defendant's.* See 55 U.S.L.W. 1138, 4265–90 (March 10, 1987).

The process is at work elsewhere. The *Longshoremen's* and Harbor Workers' Compensation Act, 33 U.S.C. § 901 (1927), was amended by the *Longshore* and Harbor Workers' Compensation Act (1984).

Similarly, American courts have begun to write opinions in more neutral language, sometimes obtrusively neutral—e.g.:

- "The affreightment contracts are commercial undertakings entered into by sophisticated *businesspersons* [read *business people*]."
- "This diversity case involves a breach of a personal service contract between Gaylord, the owner of a New Orleans television station, and Lynn Gansar, *one of Gaylord's former news anchorpersons* [read *a former news anchor for Gaylord*]." *Gaylord Broadcasting Co. v. Cosmos Broadcasting, Inc.,* 746 F.2d 251, 252 (5th Cir. 1984).
- "Edison argues that the district court should

> have construed the 'doubtful' language of the escalation clause against the appellee, as the *draftperson* [read *drafter*]." *RCI Northeast Servs. Division v. Boston Edison Co.,* 822 F.2d 199, 203 n.3 (lst Cir. 1987).

Some of the extremes to which the trend has been taken seem absurd—e.g.: "This case presents another example of the waste of time, energy, legal and judicial *personpower* and consequent waste of money occasioned by the existence of the Family Court as a separate court of limited jurisdiction." *In re Anthony T.,* 389 N.Y.S.2d 86, 87 (Fam. Ct. 1976).

As a nonsexist alternative, the suffix *-person* leaves much to be desired. For every *chairperson, anchorperson, draftsperson, ombudsperson,* and *tribesperson,* there is a superior substitute: *chair, anchor, drafter, ombuds,* and *tribe member.* Words ending in *-person* are at once wooden and pompous. See **chairman.**

The traditional language of the law, of course, abounds in *-man* words: *remainderman, venireman, warehouseman, materialman, foreman, landman, bondsman,* and *juryman.* The last of these is virtually obsolete alongside *juror;* it was in common use, however, through the mid-20th century. Courts have experimented with replacements for *foreman*—e.g.: "[W]e are unable to conclude that the state trial judge erred in deciding that the *foreperson's* statement that the jury was unable to agree was more than an expression of present inability to agree." *Fay v. McCotter,* 765 F.2d 475, 478 (5th Cir. 1985). Because the *-person* words are so ugly and ineffective, a better nonsexist expression is *presiding juror.*

Venireman is gradually undergoing transmutation, or, more accurately, emasculation: "It was not error for the court to refuse to ask *venirepersons* whether the testimony of the government investigator was entitled to more weight than the testimony of any other witness."/ "I respectfully dissent from the holding that this case should be remanded for inquiry into the prosecution's reasons for exercising its peremptory challenges against black *venirepersons.*" Justice Rehnquist used both *venireman* and *veniremember* in a single opinion. See *Wainwright v. Witt,* 469 U.S. 412, 418–19 (1985). (See INELEGANT VARIATION.) In that opinion, one use of *venireman* was specifically in reference to a woman, a Mrs. Colby. (See *id.*) Justice Rehnquist is right, however, to avoid the *-person* form. *Veniremember* is the better option.

Remainderman, warehouseman, and *longshoreman* are less easily neutralized. Legal writers have experimented with *remainderperson, remainderer, -or,* and *remainor.* None is quite satisfactory. The *-er* suffix does show promise, though: *warehouser* is listed in *W3;* it would certainly take some getting used to, like all linguistic changes. Yet *longshorer* and *remainderer* are more difficult to pronounce distinctly with the *-er.* Perhaps we can satisfy ourselves, however, that, in having reached these words in our analysis of sexist terminology, we have traveled to the furthest reaches of the language.

For other entries bearing on this issue, see **castle doctrine, chairman, drafter, foreman, mechanic's lien, reasonable person** & **venireman.**

C. Feminine Forms in *-ess* and *-trix*. Legal prose is perhaps the last bastion of these feminine forms. We have *prosecutrix; testatrix; tutrix; relatrix; conciliatrix, -tress; heritrix, -tress; inheritrix, -tress,* and even such rarely seen oddities as *dictatrix, -tress; victrix, -ess;* and *aviatrix, -ess.* Most of these moribund terms ought to be sped along to their graves.

For most legal writers, it is far less bothersome to read of a *woman testator* than it is to read of a *lady booksalesman.* The Latinate agent nouns in *-or* are almost universally perceived as being common-sex terms. We have never, for example, thought it odd that women may be termed *litigators;* we have gotten along fine without *litigatrix.* With the loss of terms in *-ess* and *-trix* we lose a nuance in the language, but the nuance is not worth preserving: the sex of a testator does not matter.

D. Equivalences. Among the subtler problems of nonsexist usage is to refer to men and women in equivalent terms: not *man and wife,* but *husband and wife;* not *chairmen* and *chairs* (the latter being female), but *chairs* (for all); not *men* and *girls* (a word that diminishes the status of an adult female), but *men* and *women.*

Even *Mr.,* on the one hand, as contrasted with *Miss* or *Mrs.,* on the other, causes problems on this score. Differentiating between one woman and another on the basis of her marital status is invidious, really, if we do not make the same distinction for men. The idea that it matters as an item of personal information whether a woman is married—but that it doesn't matter whether a man is married—is surely an outmoded one. Though many people once considered *Ms.* an abomination, it is today accepted as the standard way of addressing a married or unmarried woman. Unless the writer knows that a woman prefers to use *Mrs.,* the surest course today is to use *Ms.*

E. Statute of Limitations. Those committed to nonsexist usage ought to adopt a statute of limitations that goes something like this: in quoted matter dating from before 1980, passages containing bland sexism—such as the use of the generic *he* or of *chairman*—can be quoted in good conscience because in those days the notions of gender-inclusiveness were entirely different from today's notions. Although it is quite fair to discuss cultural changes over time, it is unfair to criticize our predecessors for not conforming to present-day standards. How could they have done so? Therefore, using "[*sic*]" at every turn to point out old sexist phrases is at best an otiose exercise, at worst a historically irresponsible example of mean-spiritedness. For a choice example of this, see James R. Nafziger, *A Sicness Unto Death,* 1 Scribes J. Legal Writing 149 (1990).

sexual. See **sex.**

sexual assault. See **rape.**

SFO, in England, refers to the Serious Fraud Office—e.g.: "Set up by the Criminal Justice Act of 1987, the *SFO* already has two major investment cases apart from Guinness in the courts . . . plus 63 other cases at different stages." *The Fraud Buster with 66 Cases on His Hands,* Sunday Telegraph, 11 Feb. 1990, at 28.

shadow jury (AmE) = a group of mock jurors who are culled from jury lists and paid to sit through a trial and report to a jury consultant hired by one of the litigants. The *shadow jury,* which is matched as closely as possible to the jury, regularly reports on their reactions to what is taking place in the courtroom and thereby provide counsel with information about the jurors' likely perceptions.

shadow of a doubt, beyond the. This phrase is a CLICHÉ to be avoided. E.g., "It is clear *beyond the shadow of a doubt* [read *beyond doubt*] that no TVA employee with proper authority had either ordered or accepted this microfilm."

shall. See WORDS OF AUTHORITY (A).

shall and will. See DOUBLETS, TRIPLETS, AND SYNONYM-STRINGS.

sham, adj., (= pretended, counterfeit) is frequently used in legal writing in phrases such as *sham corporation, sham marriage,* and *sham wedding.* E.g., "In that case 193 persons who had been individually induced, by means of a fraudulent prospectus, to invest their money in a *sham corporation* were permitted to join in one action for fraud against the promoters." Charles A. Wright, *The Law of Federal Courts* 467 (4th ed. 1983)./ "It is alleged that a 'bride' would enter into a *sham marriage* with one of the 'aliens' in order to enable the alien, a native of Portugal, to apply for and obtain a non-quota immigrant visa to which he would not otherwise be entitled." *U.S. v. Rodriguez,* 182 F. Supp. 479, 482 (S.D. Cal. 1960).

sham plea. See **false plea.**

shanghai, v.t., (= [1] to drug or otherwise make insensible and then abduct for service on a ship needing crew members; or [2] to influence by fraud or compulsion) makes *shanghaied* and *shanghaiing.* See VOWEL CLUSTERS.

shareholder; shareowner; stockholder. All three terms refer to one who owns shares in a corporation.

shareholder derivative suit. See **derivative action.**

shareowner. See **shareholder.**

shares. See **stock.**

shark repellent (= a device by which a company, in either its bylaws or its articles of incorporation, makes it more difficult for an outsider to mount a corporate takeover) is one of several colorful metaphors that emerged in corporate law during the 1970s and 1980s. E.g., "[S]ection 14(e) requires that there actually be a tender offer before anything can be considered manipulative, so '*shark repellent*' techniques like 'poison pills' might fall outside its grasp." Dennis S. Karjala, *Federalism, Full Disclosure, and the National Markets in the Interpretation of Federal Securities Law,* 80 Nw. U.L. Rev. 1473, 1505 (1986)./ "From a shareholder perspective the best justification for *shark repellents* . . . is that they provide a means of coordinating shareholder response to a takeover bid . . . ." Jeffrey N. Gordon, *Ties That Bond: Dual Class Common Stock and the Problem of Shareholder Choice,* 76 Calif. L. Rev. 3, 14 n.35 (1988).

sharp practice. This phrase originally, in the early 19th century, referred merely to hard bargaining in business. But by the mid-19th century, it came to be associated with lawyers as well as business people, and it took on more strongly negative connotations. Since then, *sharp practice* has referred to unethical practices and trickery—e.g.:

- "In the course of time the law has evolved a number of remedies which protect me against *sharp practice* in such situations when I bail a chattel, and these remedies are common remedies, though they have to some extent been supplemented by the intervention of Equity." A.W.B. Simpson, *An Introduction to the History of the Land Law* 163 (1961; repr. 1964).

- "What raised the court's ire was the plaintiff's '*sharp practice*' in moving to strike." Monroe Freedman, *In the Matter of Manners,* Legal Times, 11 March 1991, at 23, 25.
- "Michael Joseph, author of *Lawyers Can Seriously Damage Your Health,* which first exposed *sharp practice* by solicitors five years ago, said only an independent complaints system can salvage solicitors' reputations." John Rowland, *Lawyers Bar Door to Outside Policing,* Sunday Times, 24 March 1991, in Features section.

shave > shaved > shaved. *Shaven* exists only as a past-participial adjective <clean-shaven face>. Cf. **proved.**

s/he. See SEXISM (A) & **he or she.**

sheaves is the plural both of *sheaf* (= a bundle) and of *sheave* (= a pulley). *Sheaves* is also, as a verb, the third-person singular of the verb *to sheave* (= to bind into a sheaf).

Shelley's Case, the Rule in. See Rule in Shelley's Case & CAPITALIZATION (C).

shepardize is a mid-20th-century -IZE NEOLOGISM derived from *Shepard's Citators.* Originally, the word was capitalized as a tradename: "If you have before you a recent case in a nisi prius court or in an intermediate court of appeal, do not rest content with *Shepardizing* it." Paxton Blair, *Appellate Briefs and Advocacy,* 18 Fordham L. Rev. 30, 40 (1949). But today, the word is increasingly written without the initial capital, as the tradename threatens to lose its uniqueness and become generic. E.g., "Apparently failing to properly *shepardize* that case, neither plaintiff's nor defendant's counsel cited to this Court a Florida case . . . which specifically rejects Toussaint." *Caster v. Hennessey,* 727 F.2d 1075, 1077 (11th Cir. 1984)./ "[K]een legal minds at the Dickinson School of Law, having time to spare since computers freed them from the drudgery of *shepardizing,* found application of the chess clock first to the teaching, thence to the practice of law." Robert E. Rains, *Of Clocks and Things,* 39 J. Legal Educ. 259, 259 (1989).

The process of shepardizing cases—once extremely tedious—has been greatly simplified by computer-assisted research. Now, instead of laboriously checking several volumes, one merely punches a button. But the process retains the old name.

In G.B., the equivalent volumes are termed *Current Law Citations,* or *noter-ups,* and one *notes up* one's cases. See **note up.**

sheriff. In England, a sheriff is the Crown's chief executive officer in a shire or county, responsible (now nominally in most areas) for keeping the peace, overseeing elections, and administering justice generally. In the U.S., the sheriff, an officer elected within each county, has similar responsibilities, but they are real, not nominal. An American sheriff has substantial police powers. In Scotland, the *sheriff principal* and the *sheriffs* are the judges of the main local courts.

sheriffalty; shrievalty. Both terms date from the early 16th century and refer to a sheriff: to his jurisdiction, to his term of office, to his responsibilities in office, or to all three. In English antiquity, the sheriff represented the royal authority in a district (i.e., a shire) and presided at the shire-moot, the judicial assembly of the shire. Today the position of high sheriff of a county (i.e., of a shire, a term no longer used officially, though it continues to have historical and literary meaning) is an honorary one, largely nominal and ceremonial.

W3 and the *OED* suggest that *shrievalty* is the more widely used term and that *sheriffalty* is a NEEDLESS VARIANT, even though *shrieve* is an obsolete variant of *sheriff.* Actually, both are extremely rare, with one citation apiece in federal decisions in the U.S.—and they are both 19th-century citations. If such a noun is needed today, *sheriffalty*—the form used in the Constitution of West Virginia (art. 9, § 3)—is surely more widely comprehensible.

sheriffdom; sheriffwick. See **bailiwick.**

shew, an obsolete spelling of *show,* occurred in AmE and BrE writing—legal and nonlegal—up to the early 19th century.

shield law = a state law governing a journalist's right to refuse to testify about sources of information or information not used in the journalist's reporting, such as notes and outtakes. E.g., "The term '*shield law*' is commonly and widely applied to statutes granting newsmen and other media representatives the privilege of declining to reveal confidential sources of information." *In re Farber,* 394 A.2d 330, 335 n.2 (N.J. 1978).

shifting use. See **springing use.**

shined. See **shone.**

shingle, to hang out (or set up) one's. This AmE casualism, meaning "to begin to practice a profession such as law or medicine, esp. on one's own," originated in the 1840s and has always been closely associated with law. The metaphor is not, of course, to be taken literally.

ship-money (= [in English legal history] a tax on ports and localities for providing ships for the king's service) is hyphenated thus.

shipowner. One word.

ship's lawyer. See LAWYERS, DEROGATORY NAMES FOR.

shire. See **sheriffalty.**

shire court is sometimes hyphenated *shire-court,* but most legal historians write it as two words. E.g., "The old *shire court* had nothing in common with the modern county court established by an Act of 1846 . . . ." H.G. Hanbury, *English Courts of Law* 29 (2d ed. 1953).

shock the conscience. This phrase, a CLICHÉ, expresses judicial disapproval of some type of outrageous conduct or outcome. It originated in equity courts in the late 18th century; an 1825 decision by the Ohio Supreme Court quotes Lord Eldon as using the phrase in a legal standard: "In the case of *Coles v. Trecothick,* 9 Ves. 246, Lord Eldon declared, that unless the inadequacy of price was such as to *shock the conscience,* . . . it was not itself a sufficient ground for refusing a specific performance." *Wills v. Cowper,* 2 Ohio 124, 148 (1825).

Over the years, the phrase has appeared in various ways, not just as a verb phrase. Cardozo used it as a noun phrase (*a shock to conscience*): "Still more common are the cases where the evil is less obvious, where there is room for difference of opinion, where some of the judges believe that the existing rules are right, at all events where there is no such *shock to conscience* that precedents will be abandoned." Benjamin N. Cardozo, *A Ministry of Justice,* 35 Harv. L. Rev. 113, 119 (1921). The phrase now sometimes appears attributively, as a PHRASAL ADJECTIVE: "[A] study of the cases indicates that the courts in thus parroting the rule had no occasion to insert the *shock-the-conscience* clause in the particular cases under consideration . . . ." *Golden v. Tomiyasu,* 387 P.2d 989, 993 (Nev. 1963).

shoe-in is incorrect for *shoo-in,* q.v.

shone; shined. The former is the past tense of the intransitive shine <the sun shone>, the latter the past tense of the transitive shine <he shined his shoes>.

shoo-in (= a candidate or competitor who is sure to win), a colloquialism, is so spelled.

shopping. See **forum-shopping** & **judge-shopping.**

shotgun instruction. See **dynamite charge.**

should. Oddly, *should,* like *may,* q.v., is sometimes used to create mandatory standards, as in the ABA Code of Judicial Conduct. In that code, in which "[t]he canons . . . establish mandatory standards unless otherwise indicated," six of the seven canons begin, "A Judge *should* . . . ." See **ought (B)** & **shall.**

should/could is the type of monstrosity that would-be profound writers, or terminally wishy-washy ones, are fond of. E.g., "*Should/could* states impose additional requirements that must be met in order to obtain a hearing?" Typographical gimmickry of this sort ought to be avoided; surely the perpetrator does not actually believe he or she conveys otherwise overlooked nuances. See **and/or (A).**

show > showed > shown. *Showed* is less good than *shown* as the past participle.

show [+ (to be) (as)]. The infinitive *to be* is generally preferable to *as* after this verb. E.g., "It is incumbent upon the district court to weigh that claim in light of the facts at hand and in light of any alternatives that may be *shown as* [read *shown to be*] feasible and more promising in their effectiveness."

show cause (= to give a legally satisfactory reason) is common legal JARGON. E.g., "Judge Arnold issued an order . . . directing appellants to *show cause* why they should not be deemed in contempt of court." *In re Farber,* 394 A.2d 330, 332 (N.J. 1978)./ "When he was let go, he was informed that he would have to appear at a hearing to *show cause* why he should not be deported." Barbara H. Craig, *Chadha: The Story of an Epic Constitutional Struggle* 9 (1988).

This verb phrase has recently given rise to a corresponding PHRASAL ADJECTIVE: "The *Ruiz* court may issue a *show-cause* order for criminal or civil contempt."/ "At the *show-cause* hearing, appellant testified that because no one had called to schedule his testimony, he assumed that the case had been settled or continued." Cf. **good cause shown.**

show trial = a trial, usu. in a nondemocratic country, that is staged primarily for propagandistic purposes, with the outcome predetermined. E.g., "In a case described by critics as a *'show trial,'* five democracy campaigners were convicted on Friday, Mr. Maude's last day in Peking, for using loudhailers . . . ." Andrew Higgins, *China Gives Maude a Stinging Send-Off,* The Independent, 30 July 1990, at 9./ "[T]he Stalin period [was] a time of purges, *show trials,* fabricated plots, executions and mass exile." Genieve Abdo, *Spoon Tells Tale of Suffering in Stalinist Camp,* L.A. Times, 5 Aug. 1990, at A3.

shrievalty. See **sheriffalty.**

shrink > shrank > shrunk. Some writers mistakenly use *shrunk* as the past-tense form.

shudder; shutter. These words sound the same, but they are otherwise very different. To *shudder* is to tremble or quiver. A *shutter* is the device, such as a screen for a window, that limits the passage of light. Most literate people know this distinction, but some writers forget—e.g.: " 'I *shutter* [read *shudder*] to think of the impact downtown if 18-year-olds were not allowed some means of activity,' she said." John Riley, *Pearl Street Club Wins Right to Entertain Teens,* Daily Hampshire Gazette, 17 Nov. 1993, at 1-3 (misquoting Judith Fine, a city-councilor-elect for Northampton, Mass.)./ "I wouldn't want to hold my breath until Castro is deposed, and I *shutter* [read *shudder*] to think how much it will cost our country through the hemorrhaging of our tax dollars to support such a system." Marianne Sikler, *Send Cubans, Haitians Back to Their Homes,* Arizona Republic, 10 Sept. 1994, at B7.

shun and avoid. See DOUBLETS, TRIPLETS, AND SYNONYM-STRINGS.

shutter. See **shudder.**

shyster = a rascally lawyer; one that is shrewdly dishonest. The word has long been an enigma to English-language etymologists, who have posited a dozen possible derivations. In his 124-page monograph entitled *Origin of the Term "Shyster"* (1982), Gerald L. Cohen conclusively solves the enigma by citing previously overlooked material in a New York City newspaper (1843–1844).

Shyster arose as part of the editor's crusade against legal and political corruption in the city. The correct etymology is that which derives from the vulgar German word *Scheisse* (= excrement), hence *Scheisser* became *shyster.*

Among the mistaken hypotheses are that the word comes from the proper name *Scheuster,* supposedly the name of a corrupt practitioner; from the Gaelic *siostair* (= barrator); from an allusion to Shylock, Shakespeare's villain in *The Merchant of Venice* (c. 1596); and variously from words in Yiddish, Dutch, and Anglo-Saxon.

Shyster referred originally to an unscrupulous lawyer, but its meaning has now widened to include unscrupulous persons in other professions as well. E.g., "[H]e told the group of cutters that the union officials were a bunch of *shysters* . . . ." *N.L.R.B. v. Lettie Lee, Inc.,* 140 F.2d 243, 245 (9th Cir. 1944). Thus, although the phrase *shyster lawyer* would have seemed redundant in the late 19th century, it did not by the mid-20th century: "[T]he *shyster lawyer* assigned by the court wanted to squeeze all the money he could out of the boy's family." Ephraim Tutt, *Yankee Lawyer* 106 (1943). See **pettifogger** & LAWYERS, DEROGATORY NAMES FOR (A).

S.I., in British legal writing, is an abbreviation for *Statutory Instruments,* formerly known as *Statutory Rules and Orders* (or *S.R. & O.*).

sibling (= brother or sister) is sometimes mistakenly thought to mean "child"—e.g.: "I went to see Tate. He opened the door himself, his youngest *sibling* [read *child*] clutching with sticky hands at the legs of his corduroy trousers." Angus Ross, *The Leeds Fiasco* 109 (1975).

sic. **A. Generally.** *Sic* (= thus, so), invariably put in brackets, is used to indicate that a preceding word or phrase in a quoted passage is reproduced as it appeared in the original document. *Sic* at its best is intended to aid the reader (or a typesetter following copy), who may be confused by whether it was the quoter or the quoted writer who is responsible for the spelling or grammatical anomaly.

This interpolation has been much on the rise: In Westlaw's Allstates-Old database, which includes all state-court opinions from the 19th century up to 1944, the word appeared 1,239 times; from 1945 to 1990, the word appeared 69,168 times. A similarly spectacular rise can be seen in recent federal opinions (from 616 in Allfeds-Old to 26,210 in Allfeds). This increase may result from a number of factors, but one major factor is the benighted use of *sic,* discussed just below.

B. Benighted Uses. Some writers use *sic* meanly—with a false sense of superiority. Its use may frequently reveal more about the quoter than about the author of the quoted material. For example, a recent book review of an English legal text contained a *sic* in its first sentence after the verb *analyse,* which appeared thus on the book's dustjacket. In AmE, of course, the preferred spelling is *analyze;* in BrE, however, the spelling *analyse* is not uncommon and certainly does not deserve a *sic.* In fact, all the quoter (or overzealous editor) demonstrated was ignorance of British usage: "The dust jacket tells us: 'In this book, the author brings to bear empirical evidence and legal theory in a critical comparison of English and American discovery, and *analyses* [*sic*] and evaluates the differences between the two systems.'" See Book Review, 61 Tex. L. Rev. 929, 929 (1983). The same publication also *sic*'d Plucknett's spelling of *skilful* (BrE)—see Thomas Lund, *The Modern Mind of the Medieval Lawyer,* 64 Tex. L. Rev. 1267, 1270 n. 14 (1986).

Another irksome use occurs when writers insert *sic* in others' citations, as if to belittle the person quoted for ignorance of correct citation form. For example, a federal appeals court judge had the audacity to *sic* the Supreme Court's citation of one of its own cases: "'We strike the balance in favor of institutional security, which we have noted is 'central to all other corrections goals,' *Pell v. Procunier,* 417 U.S., [*sic*] at 823, 94 S. Ct., [*sic*] at 2804." *Thorne v. Jones,* 765 F.2d 1270, 1275 (5th Cir. 1985). The better course would be to leave the citations as they are without comment or to give one's own "correct" version in brackets without comment.

C. Ironic Uses. In the following example, the author inserted *sic* after his own word choice, as if to say, "I really do think this is the right word": "[I]n 1951, it was the blessing bestowed on Judge Harold Medina's *prosecution* [*sic*] of the eleven so-called 'top native Communists,' which blessing meant giving the Smith Act the judicial nod of constitutionality." Fred Rodell, *Nine Men* 302 (1955).

sic transit. A fairly common Latin maxim from Classical literature is *Sic transit gloria mundi:* "So passes away the glory of the world." Some legal writers have adapted the first two words of the phrase to denote the lamentable passing of a convention or doctrine, as here: "With our decision today, all I can say is *sic transit* United Beef Producers, Inc. and Rule 320, Tex. R. Civ. P."

sic utere. The *sic utere* doctrine embodies the Latin maxim *sic utere tuo, ut alienum non lædas,* which means "use your own property in such a manner as not to injure that of another." E.g., "These sections of the Louisiana Civil Code owe an expression of the *sic utere* doctrine that limits the rights of proprietors in the use of their property." Holmes called this Latin maxim an "empty general proposition" that leads to "hollow deductions." Oliver W. Holmes, "Privilege, Malice, and Intent," in *Collected Legal Papers* 120 (1920). See MAXIMS.

sidebar. A. Sense. Originally, *sidebar* referred to a small fencelike partition, either in the Outer Parliament House in Edinburgh or in Westminster Hall. Each morning in term, attorneys argued motions to the judges *ex parte* from within the sidebar. Today, most American lawyers think of the *sidebar,* in its literal sense, as the side of the judge's bench, where counsel can confer with the judge beyond the jury's earshot. See **at (the) bar, bar & outer bar.**

B. *Sidebar Conference.* The phrase *sidebar conference* now usu. refers to a discussion among the judge and counsel—usu. over an evidentiary objection—outside the jury's hearing. At times, however—esp. during voir dire—it has been used in reference to a discussion between the judge and a juror or veniremember. See **bar.**

C. *Sidebar* as an Ellipsis. The word *sidebar* is often used in AmE as a shortening of *sidebar conference.* E.g., "[A]ppellate specialist John Pollok stuck strictly to arguing questions of procedure and admissibility during *sidebars.*" Gregg Krupa, *Teamwork, Sidebars Tipped Gotti Case,* Manhattan Lawyer, March 1990, at 1.

D. As a Popularized Legal Technicality. By the mid-20th century, journalists had come to use *sidebar* to refer to a short, secondary article within or accompanying a main story in a publication. Also, we speak of *sidebar remarks* or *sidebar comments,* which are comments incidental to the main point. These extended senses almost certainly derived from the connotation that *sidebar* has long carried in legal contexts—i.e., that the discussion is peripheral to the main issues. See POPULARIZED LEGAL TECHNICALITIES.

sideswipe; sidewipe. *Sideswipe* (= to strike a glancing blow), dating from the early automotive age (1926), is the term to use. *Sidewipe,* an artificial form, has no valid standing.

Siete Partidas. See ***Las (Siete) Partidas.***

sight unseen. From a strictly logical point of view, the phrase makes little sense. In practice, however, it has an accepted and useful meaning: an item is bought *sight unseen* when it has not been inspected before the purchase.

signatary, adj. See **signatory,** adj.

signatary, n.; **signatory; signator.** Fowler and Krapp both recommended in the 1920s that *signatary* be adopted as the preferred noun. See Fowler, *MEU1* 534; George P. Krapp, *A Comprehensive Guide to Good English* 540 (1927). Today, however, *signatary* is virtually never used; the *COD* and *W10* contain *signatory* only. E.g., "International commercial litigation involving nationals of *signatories* to the Hague Convention is not at all infrequent."/ "The Court has no jurisdiction to rectify the articles, even if it is proved that they were not in accordance with the intention of the original *signatories.*" J. Charlesworth, *The Principles of Company Law* 25 (4th ed. 1945).

Signatory may be an adjective as well as a noun (Krapp considered it the only adjectival form), often a POSTPOSITIVE ADJECTIVE—e.g.: "It has been finally executed by the parties *signatory,* and is, in and of itself, supposed to pass property only upon death." See **signatory.**

Signator, modeled on Latinate agent nouns, is a NEEDLESS VARIANT of *signatory,* n. E.g., "Liability under section 11 is limited to *signators* [read *signatories*] of the registration statement, directors or partners of the issuer, experts named as preparing or certifying a portion of the registration statement, or underwriters with respect to the issue."

signator. See **signatary,** n.

signatory, adj.; **signatural.** *Signatory* = forming one of those (persons or governments) whose signatures are attached to a document (*OED*) <the convention gives the signatory states rights to search one another's fishing vessels>. (See **signatary.**) *Signatural* = of or pertaining to signatures.

signature. See **countersignature.**

signed, sealed, and delivered. This phrase traditionally appears in the attestation clause of a deed, a contract under seal, or a specialty contract. (See **deed** & **special(i)ty.**) The only requirements of such a contract are that it be intended as such and that it be signed, sealed, and delivered. But two of three past participles in the triplet *signed, sealed, and delivered* are now fictions. Today, the seal is largely symbolic—a sticky wafer simply being attached to the document instead of a genuine seal. (See **seal (A).**) Likewise, "delivery" is not literally necessary, as long as the parties clearly intended the deed to be operative. E.g., "*Specialty Contracts* . . . must be executed with certain formalities. There must be a document, in print or in writing, and it must be *signed, sealed and delivered.*" 1 E.W. Chance, *Principles of Mercantile Law* 10 (P.W. French ed., 13th ed. 1950). See **seal (B),** POPULARIZED LEGAL TECHNICALITIES & DOUBLETS, TRIPLETS, AND SYNONYM-STRINGS.

significance; signification. These should be distinguished. *Significance* = (1) a subtly or indirectly conveyed meaning; suggestiveness; the quality of implying; or (2) the quality of being important or significant.

Signification = (1) the act of signifying, as by symbols; or (2) the sense intended to be conveyed by a word or other symbol. Writers occasionally misuse *significance* for *signification* (sense 2)—e.g.: "There may be social observances existing before it or without it, but they are not law in any proper *significance* [read *signification* or, better, *sense*] of that term." Carleton K. Allen, *Law in the Making* 2 (7th ed. 1964).

silk; silk gown. These terms are metonymic for "King's or Queen's Counsel." In England, a Queen's Counsel wears a silk gown; hence to obtain, receive, or take silk, means to become a Queen's Counsel, and *silk* and *silk gown* have come to denote a person who has achieved this rank. E.g., "Yet when North J. was first appointed to the Bench on November 1, 1881, he was assigned to the Queen's Bench Division, although his practice both as a junior and as a *silk* had lain on the Chancery side." R.E. Megarry, *Miscellany-at-Law* 10 (1955)./ "[A]mong the members of the Bar, there is a comparatively small group of senior [barristers], enjoying certain privileges and subject to certain disabilities, known as Queen's Counsel, or (from the fact that they wear silk instead of 'stuff' gowns in court) *silks.*" Edward Jenks, *The Book of English Law* 67 (P.B. Fairest ed., 6th ed. 1967). See **dispatent** & **take silk.**

silk-stocking lawyer. See LAWYERS, DEROGATORY NAMES FOR.

similar and like. See DOUBLETS, TRIPLETS, AND SYNONYM-STRINGS.

SIMILES, very simply, are comparisons constructed with *like* or *as.* They differ from METAPHORS because, with similes, the comparisons are explicit (e.g., "trying this case is like wrestling a grizzly bear"), not implicit (e.g., "this case is a real bear").

E. B. White's insight is characteristically telling: "The simile is a common device and a useful one, but similes coming in rapid fire, one right on top of another, are more distracting than illuminating. The reader needs time to catch his breath;

he can't be expected to compare everything else, and no relief in sight." William Strunk & E.B. White, *The Elements of Style* 80 (3d ed. 1979). That similes are useful is not to be doubted—e.g.:

- "To waste time and argument in proving that, without [the authority to make necessary and proper laws,] Congress might carry its powers into execution, would be not much less idle than to hold a lighted taper to the sun." *McCulloch v. Maryland,* 17 U.S. (4 Wheat.) 316, 419 (1819) (per Marshall, C.J.).
- "Like a coral reef, the common law thus becomes a structure of fossils." Robert H. Jackson, *The Struggle for Judicial Supremacy* 295 (1941).
- "The position of a judge has been likened to that of an oyster—anchored in one place, unable to take the initiative, unable to go out after things, restricted to working on and digesting what the fortuitous eddies and currents of litigation may wash his way." Calvert Magruder, *Mr. Justice Brandeis,* 55 Harv. L. Rev. 193, 194 (1941).
- "Just as, perforce, the musical composer delegates some subordinate creative activity to musical performers, so, perforce, the legislature delegates some subordinate (judicial) legislation—i.e., creative activity—to the courts." Jerome Frank, *Courts on Trial* 308 (1949; repr. 1963).
- "The [European Community] Treaty is like an incoming tide. It flows into the estuaries and up the rivers. It cannot be held back." *Bulmer Ltd v. Bollinger S.A.,* [1974] 2 All E.R. 1226 (C.A.) (per Lord Denning).
- "As a moth is drawn to the light, so is a litigant drawn to the United States." *Smith Kline & French Labs. v. Bloch,* [1982] 1 W.L.R. 730, 733 (C.A.) (per Lord Denning).
- "[T]he common law came down through the centuries with some of its past sticking to it, like a skin it never quite succeeded in molting." Lawrence M. Friedman, *A History of American Law* 24 (2d ed. 1985).

But, as White noted, the enthusiastic users of similes can easily fall into OVERSTATEMENT, and sometimes into foolish-sounding PURPLE PROSE—e.g.: "Not reversing this case would be like the United States failing to challenge the pernicious crimes of Hitler in the Second World War; the United States did so, and this honorable Court should likewise reverse." (This comparison of the Holocaust to one litigant's case is, in a sense, offensive to humanity.)/ "To allow what was done in the instant case would be not only to expand Rule 35 to a point where it is no longer frozen like a mastodon in a glacier but also to allow resentencing under Rule 35 to become like molten lava cascading down a mountain and destroying the remainder of the double jeopardy protection afforded by the Constitution." (The cascading similes here are simply distracting.)

simony. See **barratry.**

simple. In a phrase such as *fee simple,* the word *simple* denotes that the estate is inheritable by the owner's heirs with no conditions concerning *tail* (q.v.); in the phrase *simple contract,* q.v., the word *simple* means that the contract was not made under seal.

simple contract = a contract not under seal, whether express or implied, and whether oral or in writing. Oddly enough, the term *parol contract* is synonymous, even when the contract is in writing. Williston preferred the term *informal contract,* believing that the phrase *simple contract* could mislead. See **informal contract.**

simpliciter (= simply; summarily; taken alone unconditionally; absolutely) can usually be said more simpliciter—e.g.:

- "Both the Georgia statute and the Georgia prosecutor thus completely fail to provide the Court with any support for the conclusion that homosexual sodomy, *simpliciter,* [read *unconditionally*] is considered unacceptable conduct in that State . . . ." *Bowers v. Hardwick,* 478 U.S. 186, 220 (1986) (Stevens, J., dissenting).
- "I concur heartily in the court's judgment that a grand jury subpoena *simpliciter* [read *simply* or, depending on the sense, *taken alone*] does not satisfy the more rigorous requirements . . . ." *Doe v. DiGenova,* 779 F.2d 74, 92 (D.C. Cir. 1985) (Starr, J., concurring).
- "If we think that discrimination *simpliciter is* [read *is absolutely*] wrong, then even reverse discrimination is wrong." Simon Lee, *Law and Morals* 74 (1986).

The LATINISM adds only obscurity. See FORBIDDEN WORDS (A).

simplistic is a pejorative adjective meaning "oversimple; facile." E.g., "I do not mean to endorse the *simplistic* view that the words printed in the United States Code can answer all questions regarding the meaning of statutes." It is not a synonym for simple, though apparently used thus in this sentence: "The *simplistic* [read *simple?*] notion that parties exercise their volition by committing themselves to future action (or inaction), and that the law provides their circle of assent with the status of private law, is fundamental to any discussion of contracts."

simultaneous death. In cases of intestacy, this phrase denotes the death of two or more persons in the same mishap in circumstances making it impossible to determine who was the first to die or the last to survive. It describes a presumption, not necessarily a reality. See ***commorientes.***

In the phrase *simultaneous-death statute,* the hyphen is necessary because *simultaneous-death* functions as a PHRASAL ADJECTIVE.

since. See **as** (A).

since . . . then mangles the syntax of a causal construction. E.g., "*Since* plaintiff purchased the pool after defendant had built it for the previous owner, *then* the express warranty is void according to the terms of the contract." The problem is remedied by omitting *then,* and this particular sentence could be clarified still further by changing *since* to *because.*

sine damno (= without damage) is an unnecessary LATINISM. E.g., "If the act be *sine damno* [read *without damage*], no action on the case will lie." (Eng.) See ***damnum.***

sine die (= without a day being fixed) is used to indicate that no date has been set for resumption. The phrase is Officialese for "indefinitely." E.g., "The court adjourned *sine die.*" 2 U.S. (2 Dall.) 400, 400 (1790) (term notation). *Sine die* is used exclusively in reference to adjournment taken with no date set for resumption of the proceedings or meeting. See **go hence without day** & **day in court.**

A linguist complains that the phrase is "horribly mispronounced to the point where the first part sounds like the trigonometric function and the second like a synonym for 'perish' . . . ." Mario Pei, *Words in Sheep's Clothing* 83 (1969). But /*sI-ni-**dI**-ee*/ has long been established as the usual English-language pronunciation.

sine qua non /*sI-nee-kwah-**non***/ (L. "without which not") = an indispensable condition or thing. This LATINISM is common in both lay and legal writing and should remain unmolested by plain-English reform. E.g., "[A]mbiguity of constitutional language and uncertainty about constitution-makers' intent is the very *sine qua non* of judicial review as it has operated in the United States." Robert G. McCloskey, *The American Supreme Court* 117–18 (1960)./ "Goldfarb is not properly read as making compulsion a *sine qua non* to state-action immunity."/ "We are mindful that *sine qua non* [read *the sine qua non*] in a prosecutorial vindictiveness claim is that the second charge is in fact harsher than the first." Cf. **but for.**

singlehanded(ly). The preferred adverb is *singlehanded,* but only when this word follows the verb <she did it singlehanded>. When the adverb precedes the verb, *singlehandedly* is called for <she singlehandedly brought the corporation to the brink of bankruptcy>.

sink > sank > sunk. In AmE, some writers misuse the past participle for the simple past—e.g.: "The original owner of the vessel had failed to remove it after it *sunk* [read *sank* or *had sunk*] . . . ." *Magno v. Corros,* 630 F.2d 224, 227 (4th Cir. 1980)./ "After he sold the house, it *sunk* [read *sank*] into underlying permafrost." *Alaska Pac. Assurance Co. v. Collins,* 794 P.2d 936, 937 (Alaska 1990).

sister, as an adj. <sister state>, is rather quaintly used in a number of expressions, perhaps more commonly today in legal than in lay contexts. Like *she* in reference to states or ships, *sister* may be obsolescent because of whatever latent SEXISM may appear to those who seek to eliminate every vestige of male-female differentiation in the language.

Sister has traditionally been used in a number of contexts—e.g.: "Our holding is therefore that, as a matter of comity, we will enforce the equitable decrees of a *sister* state affecting Texas land as long as such enforcement does not contravene an established public policy in this State."/ "It is a general rule that, upon a sufficient showing of facts, a court of equity in any state may enjoin a citizen of that state from prosecuting a suit against another citizen thereof, in the courts of a *sister* state."

Not only does a state have 49 *sister states* in the U.S., but also the federal judicial circuits, by analogy, have *sister circuits.* E.g., "Four of our *sister* circuits have held that the time expended by an attorney litigating the fee claim is justifiably included in the court's fee award."

sistren is the archaic and dialectal equivalent of *brethren.* Karl Llewellyn began his last speech with the jocular remark, "Well, Brethren and *Sistren,* I find myself in a completely impossible position . . . ." Karl Llewellyn, *A Lecture on Appellate Advocacy,* 29 U. Chi. L. Rev. 627, 627 (1962). See **brethren.**

sit = (1) of a judge, to occupy a judicial seat; or (2) of a court, to hold judicial proceedings. E.g.:

(Sense 1) "Yet President Washington had difficulty finding men of national stature willing to *sit* on so inconsequential a court." Robert G. McCloskey, *The American Supreme Court* v (1960)./ (Sense 2) "No court in Britain normally *sits* behind closed doors, so you can walk in boldly and listen to its proceedings." Glanville Williams, *Learning the Law* 17 (11th ed. 1982).

site, v.t., = to locate, place, or provide with a site. E.g., "In Texas, the state [nuclear] repository stalled in court, with a ruling that set back the *siting* process by about four years." Shawn Hubler, *Only California Is on Track for Nuclear Dump,* L.A. Times (Orange Co.), 20 May 1991, at A1./ "The state law of Texas defines whether the taxpayer has a property right in the Texas-*sited* realty; if he does, it is subject to the government tax lien."

site, n. See **situs.**

situate, p.pl.; **situated.** The language of the law abounds in needless ARCHAISMS, and *situate* used as a past participle is one of them. Historically, it is one of a great many English participial adjectives formed from Latin perfect passive participles—e.g., *corrupt* (from the Latin *corruptus,* "having been spoiled"), *select, compact, effeminate, legitimate,* and *adequate.* In the Renaissance, many more such participial adjectives existed than do today. Those that have not survived in the Latinate *t*-form (ending in *-t* or *-te*) have been thoroughly anglicized, taking on the English past-participial suffix *-ed.* The verb *to situate* is among these.

Many wills contain phrases such as the following: "All the rest, residue, and remainder of my estate, real as well as personal and wheresoever *situate* [read *situated*], of which I die seised and possessed, I direct my executor to distribute as he considers it will be most effective in the advancement of Christ's Kingdom on Earth."/ "I give, devise, and bequeath all my property and estate of whatsoever nature whether real, personal, or mixed, and wheresoever *situate* [read *situated*], unto my two beloved children."

The usage appears even in judicial opinions, commentary, and statutes—e.g.: "The land in question, *situate* [read *situated*] in Multnomah County, was bought by the defendant Pennoyer at a sale upon the judgment of such suit."/ "The celebration must take place . . . in a recognized place of worship or Registrar's office *situate* [read *situated*] in the district in which one at least of the parties resides." William Geldart, *Introduction to English Law* 52–53 (D.C.M. Yardley ed., 9th ed. 1984)./ "[T]he county court of the district in which the registered office of the company is *situate* [read *situated*] shall . . . have concurrent jurisdiction with the High Court. . . ." Companies Act 1948 § 218(3).

Shakespeare, in *Love's Labour's Lost* (c. 1588), had one of his comically pompous characters say, "I know where it is *situate.*" Some lawyers continue to use the word similarly, probably unaware of the comic pomposity of the word. It is time they came into the 20th century and wrote *situated.*

One other point about this word merits attention. *Situate* is often superfluous, as in "Appellee's car was *situated* about three feet from the south curb of Jackson Street." The word could be dropped from the sentence with no change in meaning, and with enhanced concision.

situate, lying, and being in. See DOUBLETS, TRIPLETS, AND SYNONYM-STRINGS.

situation has, in one of its senses, become a VOGUE WORD, and is often used superfluously, as here: "The instructor told his class that there had been many instances *of starvation situations, where* [read *of starvation, when*] people simply could not eat monkey, snake, horse, or rodent meat, and died because of it."

It is also often used illogically: "He might be significantly affected by the *situation* he seeks to litigate." One does not litigate a *situation. Dispute, issue,* and *claim* are all more specific examples of what can be litigated. See **litigate.**

situs (= the location or position of [something] for legal purposes) is a legal word not quite equivalent to *site.* E.g., "Historically, federal courts used a *situs* or locality test to determine whether a tort action was within admiralty jurisdiction."/ "The validity of a will of land is determined by the *situs* of the land." As a legal term, the word dates from the early 19th century: "Personal contracts have no *situs;* they are to be governed by the law of the place, where they are to be performed." *Maisonnaire v. Keeting,* 16 F. Cas. 513, 516 (C.C.D. Mass. 1815) (No. 8,978). Pl. *situs.*

Sometimes *situs* is misleading: "If the will contains a devise of land, the will must be probated at the *situs* of the land [read in the jurisdiction in which the land is located] in order to establish title." (It is not necessary that probate be obtained at the very site where the land is; rather, the will must be probated by a court having territorial jurisdiction over the land.) See ***lex situs*** & **locus.**

six of one, half a dozen of the other is one of our most shopworn CLICHÉS.

siz(e)able. The preferred spelling is *sizable* in AmE, *sizeable* in BrE. See MUTE E.

skeptic(al); sceptic(al). The former is the AmE, the latter the BrE spelling.

skid is incorrect in the past tense; *skidded* is the correct form. "He *skid* [read *skidded*] down the slope."

skil(l)ful. The AmE spelling is *skillful,* the BrE *skilful.* Cf. **wil(l)ful.**

skul(l)duggery; scul(l)duggery. *Skullduggery* is a misspelling of *skulduggery* (= trickery; unscrupulous behavior), the spelling preferred over the forms beginning *sc-*.

skyjack; hijack. Today airline hijackings are still sometimes termed *skyjackings.* But *hijacking* remains the more common word. See **hijack** & PORTMANTEAU WORDS.

skyrocket, v.i., is a favorite CLICHÉ of hyperbolists; in the following sentence, however, it may be accurate: "Most close corporations simply do not have the capital to afford the *skyrocketing* costs of products liability insurance."

slander. See **libel** & **defamation.**

slanderize is a NEEDLESS VARIANT of *slander,* v.t.

slander of title denotes the tort that a person commits who makes false statements, orally or in writing, that cast doubt on another person's ownership of real property. Despite the name, this tort has nothing to do with *slander* in the sense of oral defamation. E.g., "Not dissimilar to the acts just discussed are statements in disparagement of title to property, giving rise to the action for *'slander of title.'*" Thomas E. Holland, *The Elements of Jurisprudence* 189 (13th ed. 1924; repr. 1937)./ "A false denial of the plaintiff's title to his property, whereby he was hindered in selling it, was actually called *'slander of title'* . . . ." J.H. Baker, *An Introduction to English Legal History* 521 (3d ed. 1990).

SLAPP is an ACRONYM for "Strategic Lawsuit Against Public Participation," i.e., one brought usu. by a developer, corporate executive, or elected official to stifle those who protest against some type of high-dollar initiative (often involving the environment). The term *SLAPP* is ordinarily used as a noun—e.g.: "Some legal experts familiar with *SLAPP*s say they are more a political muzzle than a legal remedy." *SLAPPing the Opposition,* Newsweek, 5 March 1990, at 22./ "But Mr. Pring and Ms. Canan say *SLAPPS* are unconstitutional actions against non-governmental individuals or groups because of their communications to a government body, official or the electorate on an issue of public concern." Bruce Nichols, *Firms SLAPPing Down Critics,* Dallas Morning News, 5 May 1991, at 45A.

But it appears also as a verb, as in the title of the two articles just quoted, and as in this quotation from the first article: "Those doing the *SLAPPing* almost always lose; the First Amendment generally protects activists like Betty Blake, whose case is pending." *SLAPPing the Opposition,* Newsweek, 5 March 1990, at 22.

slink > slunk > slunk. The verb is so inflected.

slip-and-fall case = (1) a lawsuit brought by a plaintiff for injuries sustained in slipping and falling, usu. on the defendant's property; or, by extension, (2) any minor case in tort. Sense (2) arose because the *slip-and-fall case* is the archetypal minor tort case—e.g.: "Young, who mostly hears *'slip and fall' cases,* soon will tackle a custody battle between Blount County's Junior and Marry Sue Davis that could set a legal precedent in the USA." *Judge to Decide Embryo Custody,* USA Today, 17 May 1989, at 2A. Because the phrase contains a PHRASAL ADJECTIVE, it should be hyphenated as at the outset of this entry.

slip opinion; advance sheet. In the U.S., reported opinions are published first individually in *slip opinions,* and are then collected in soft-cover *advance sheets,* before appearing in the hardcover reporters.

In some courts, the phrase *slip opinion* formerly referred to a preliminary draft of an opinion not yet ready for publication: "On the margin of one *'slip opinion,'* the preliminary draft of an opinion [that] is circulated among the justices, McReynolds wrote, 'This statement makes me sick.'" Donald D. Jackson, *Judges* 336 (1974).

slippery slope. This once-clever METAPHOR—a way of saying that if we take the first step there will be no stopping—has been all but exhausted as a legal CLICHÉ. First used in the mid-1960s, it gained widespread currency in the 1980s. Here are the first examples recorded in federal and state caselaw, respectively: "If agency power to designate programming 'not in the public interest' is a *slippery slope,* the Commission and the courts started down it too long ago to go back to the top now unless Congress or the Constitution sends them." *Banzhaf v. F.C.C.,* 405 F.2d 1082, 1094 (D.C. Cir. 1968) (per Bazelon, C.J.)./ "It seems more likely that a future court, armed with today's decision, will take one more 'logical' step down the *slippery slope* to absolute liability." *Renslow v. Mennonite Hosp.,* 367 N.E.2d 1250, 1265 (Ill. 1977) (Ryan, J., dissenting).

Justice Harlan played cleverly with the metaphor: "I, for one, however, do not believe that a '*slippery slope*' is necessarily without a constitutional toehold." *Walz v. Tax Comm'n,* 397 U.S. 664, 699–700 (1970) (Harlan, J., dissenting).

When used attributively, the phrase needs a hyphen: *slippery-slope argument, slippery-slope reasoning.* See PHRASAL ADJECTIVES (A).

SLIPSHOD EXTENSION. Several individual entries in this dictionary refer to this heading. Slipshod extension denotes the mistaken stretching of a word beyond what it is generally accepted as denoting or connoting, the mistake lying in a misunderstanding of the true sense. It occurs most often, explained H.W. Fowler, "when some accident gives currency among the uneducated to words of learned origin, and the more if they are isolated or have few relatives in the vernacular" (*MEU1* 540).

Today one might rightly accuse not only the uneducated, but the educated as well, of the linguistic distortion of *a priori* and *protagonist,* qq.v., to name but two of any number of possible examples. For other examples, see **ad hoc, alias, alibi, calculus, compound, dilemma, duplicity, egoism, enjoinder, factor, hopefully, literally, material, medicine, veracity, verbal, viable, & vitiate.** See also POPULARIZED LEGAL TECHNICALITIES.

slow has long been treated as an immediate adverb, that is, one not requiring the *-ly* suffix. It is ill-informed pedantry to insist that *slow* can be only an adjective. Though *slowly* is the more common adverb, and is certainly correct, *slow* is often just as good in the adverbial sense. Euphony should govern the choice. For example, Coleridge wrote, in "The Complaint of a Forsaken Indian Woman": "I'll follow you across the snow, / You travel heavily and *slow.*" The usage is common in legal contexts: "One should go *slow* about relying on decisions of the Supreme Court of the United States in any but the federal field."

slunk. See **slink.**

slush fund. Originally, in the early 19th century, this phrase was a nautical term referring to money collected from the sale of fat or grease obtained from meat boiled on board ship; the money was used to buy luxuries for the crew. By the late 19th century, the phrase had come to denote money used to supplement the salaries of government employees, esp. through bribes. Today the phrase always carries connotations of moral impropriety, and sometimes of legal impropriety.

small-claims court = a local tribunal in which disputes involving small amounts can be adjudicated quickly and cheaply, usu. without legal representation; the model for *small-claims courts* arose in the late 17th- and 18th-century England, and they were revived in the late 20th century. *Small-claims* is a PHRASAL ADJECTIVE when it precedes a noun, and thus requires a hyphen.

smart money (= punitive damages, i.e., an award that smarts) arose in the 18th century and has been more or less steadily used ever since—e.g.: "There has been much discussion in the Courts, and among elementary writers upon the subject of vindictive damages, or '*smart money*' as they are sometimes called." *Malone v. Murphy,* 2 Kan. 245, 257 (1864)./ "The purpose of punitive damages, sometimes denominated as exemplary damages or *smart money,* is two-fold: to punish the wrongdoing of the defendant and to deter others from engaging in similar conduct." *Rogers v. T.J.X. Cos.,* 404 S.E.2d 664, 666 (N.C. 1991).

smellfungus (= a faultfinder, grumbler) is too valuable a word, especially for lawyers in ad hominem reference to other lawyers, to be as neglected as it is.

snuck is a nonstandard past tense of *sneak* common in American dialectal and informal English. The past tense to be used in formal writing is *sneaked*—e.g.: "A degree of federalization was, so to say, *sneaked* in the back door . . . ." Grant Gilmore, *The Death of Contract* 96 (1974).

Surprisingly, though, *snuck* appears half as often in American caselaw as *sneaked*—e.g.: "Trujillo *snuck* [read *sneaked*] up behind Rodriguez and squeezed him so tightly that Rodriguez could not breathe." *Stripco Sales, Inc. v. NLRB,* 934 F.2d 123, 128 (7th Cir. 1991)./ "[D]uring the month before the shooting, he had *snuck* [read *sneaked*] out through the window several times while his mother was asleep and his father was at work." *Barrett v. Pacheco,* 815 P.2d 834, 835 (Wash. Ct. App. 1991).

so. A. Omission of. This error is not uncommon. E.g., "The court of appeals concluded, although it was the first *court to* [read *court so to*] hold, that the 19th-century joinder cases in this court created a federal, common-law, substantive right in a certain class of persons to be joined in the corresponding lawsuits."

B. For *very*. The casualism of substituting *so* for *very* or *terribly* should be avoided in formal writing. E.g., "He cannot reason *so well* [read *very well*]."

so as [+ infinitive]. This construction is a common and a useful one in legal writing, but it often leads to problems. Most common among these is the unnecessary repetition of *so:* "Was the omission by Jacobs *so* trivial and innocent *so as* [read *as*] not to be a breach of the condition?"/ "A change will not be tolerated if it is *so* dominant and pervasive *so as* [read *as*] to frustrate the purpose of the contract."/ "If you define it *so* broadly *so as* [read *as*] to exclude nothing, then you have done nothing."/ "The issue is whether the company *so* clothed H. with the mantel of authority *so as* [read *as*] to cause X. to rely upon his words."

In the following sentences, *as* has been suppressed, leaving the syntax incomplete: "We do not believe that the acceptance in the case at bar diverged *so* radically from the terms of the offer *to warrant* [read *as to warrant*] this result."/ "If a defendant's activities are not *so pervasive to subject* [read *so pervasive as to subject*] it to general jurisdiction, this court makes an evaluation in determining whether there is limited jurisdiction."

Here, the phrase is simply misused for *to* or *in order to:* "Res ipsa loquitur is invoked *here so as to avoid* [read *here to avoid*] having to name a particular defendant out of several possible defendants." The meaning of this sentence calls for the sense "in order to," not "in such a way as to," so that *to* can stand alone. Note also the ugly use of the PASSIVE VOICE, which deprives the verb *avoid* of an acting subject. [A possible revision: *By invoking res ipsa loquitur here, counsel avoids having to name one particular defendant out of several possible defendants.*]

Not infrequently, and especially in long sentences, *so as to* and *such as to* are improperly mixed, as here: "The necessity that the plaintiffs should join this association is not *so great,* nor is the association's relation to the rights of the defendants, as compared with the right of the plaintiffs to be free from molestation, *such as to* [read *as to*] bring the acts of the defendants under the shelter of the principles of trade competition." See **such** (C) & **sufficiently . . . as to.**

social. A. And *societal; societary*. These words overlap to some degree, but may be validly distinguished. *Social* = (1) living in companies or organized communities <humans are social animals>; (2) concerned with the mutual relations of (classes of) human beings <the social compact>; or (3) of or in or toward society <social interactions> (*COD*). *Societal* has replaced *societary* (now merely a NEEDLESS VARIANT) in the sense "of, pertaining to, concerned or dealing with, society or social conditions" (*OED*). E.g., "Certainly the defendant will accept the *societal* postulate that parents have the obligation to support their children."

B. And *sociable*. *Sociable* = ready for companionship, quick to unite with others, gregarious. *Social* = relating to persons in society, communities, or commonwealths.

social harm = an invasion of any social interest that the criminal law protects. Every crime involves a social harm committed by some person.

social-legal. See **sociolegal.**

societal; societary. See **social** (A).

societas, the Roman-law term for "partnership," sometimes appears in Anglo-American legal texts—e.g.: "When several persons unite for the purpose of carrying on business in common, which is usually done upon the terms that each of them shall be an agent for all the rest, the contract is called partnership, *'societas,'* and takes various shapes, according to the business contemplated." Thomas E. Holland, *The Elements of Jurisprudence* 304 (13th ed. 1924; repr. 1937).

society, in torts and family law, often means "consortium; sexual and other intimate companionship." E.g., "The spouse of an injured crew member who survives his injury may recover her loss of *society* in an action for unseaworthiness."/ "The jury could take into consideration only the bruises that the plaintiff sustained, and the loss of his wife's *society*."/ "The right of consortium is a right growing out of the marital relation, which the husband and wife have, to enjoy the *society* and companionship and affection of each other in their life together." See **consortium.**

sociolegal; social-legal. *Sociolegal* = relating to the field of law and society. E.g., "Historically, *sociolegal* scholars have not been able to assume the perspective of social scientists—to seek to learn how law as a phenomenon affects behavior in society . . . —because our theory has been tied to a concept of law which was developed by and for the use of judges and lawyers." Paul Lermack, *What Does Law Do?* 12 Legal Stud. F. 401, 401 (1988).

Social-legal is a NEEDLESS VARIANT: "He had, in effect, created a *social-legal* [read *sociolegal*] counterpart of that mathematical curiosity, the

Klein bottle, whose spout curves back into its mouth, so that it became a one-sided surface which is closed and has no boundary." Murray T. Bloom, *The Trouble With Lawyers* 252 (1970).

sociological jurisprudence denotes a philosophical approach to law stressing the actual social effects of legal institutions, doctrines, and practices. E.g., "In 1906, . . . [Roscoe Pound] startled the entire bar with an original, highly critical, and constructive analysis of the American legal system. His address shattered the complacency of many leaders of the bar, jurists and professors of law, and started a movement in the United States toward what is called '*sociological jurisprudence,*' which . . . has made enormous headway and has radically affected, sometimes directly and sometimes indirectly, the thinking of American jurists, judges, and lawyers." René A. Wormser, *The Story of the Law* 484–85 (1962)./ "Both *sociological jurisprudence*—which is the opposite of abstraction, formalism, and purism—and legal realism—which rejects scientism and system-building—emphasize the difficulty and the importance of focusing on the judicial process." John H. Merryman, *The Civil Law Tradition* 71 (1969). Cf. **analytical jurisprudence.**

socius criminis = a partner in crime; an accessory. This LATINISM, which appears primarily in BrE, is invariably unnecessary for *accessory.* E.g., "In *Mapolisa v. The Queen,* the board held that the relevant provision in the Law and Order (Maintenance) Act of 1960 applied to *a socius criminis* [read *an accessory*] and that a participant in a crime under that section was subject to the same mandatory penalty as the principal offender." (Eng.)

Socius is sometimes used as an elliptical form of *socius criminis.* E.g., "To establish the degree of proximity of the appellant to the crime, the evidence must establish that he had exact knowledge of the crime and of the identity of the principal; the appellant can be *a socius* [read *an accessory*] only on establishing his own mens rea." (Eng.) Cf. ***particeps criminis.*** See **accessory.**

sodomist; sodomite. The latter is an example of BIBLICAL AFFECTATION.

sodomize is plagued by the same ambiguities as *sodomy,* q.v. Not everyone would agree on what the following sentence describes: "LePage put the body in the back of the pickup and drove to a remote location, where he *sodomized* the corpse before disposing of it." *LePage v. Idaho,* 851 F.2d 251, 252 (9th Cir. 1988).

sodomy. This ambiguous term can include almost any kind of "unnatural" sex, though it is most often confined to bestiality and buggery. *Sodomy* was not a common-law offense, though an early statute criminalizing it became a part of the common law of many American jurisdictions, most of which now have anti-sodomy statutes.

so far as. See **as . . . as** & **insofar as.**

soft law; hard law. In the JARGON of international lawyers, *soft law* contains general principles that are widely accepted as international norms of conduct, as well as declaratory statements of those principles without specific obligations. *Hard law,* by contrast, is binding and requires an active decision on the part of a state to accede to or ratify it. A convention is an example of *hard law;* an international declaration is an example of *soft law.* E.g., "Much of the original '*soft law,*' or nonbinding principles, has served as the basis for the *hard law* of international conventions and agreements." Allegra Helfenstein, Comment, *U.S. Controls on International Disposal of Hazardous Waste,* 22 Int'l Law. 775, 784 (1988).

soft-pedal. For a fairly common error involving this term, see **peddle.**

so help me God. This formula concludes the oath as traditionally administered to a Christian witness in an Anglo-American court. The person administering the oath traditionally said, "So help *you* God," and the oath-taker would then say *me.* See 2 Alexander M. Burrill, *A Law Dictionary and Glossary* 472 (1860). Presumably, alternative forms have varied for witnesses of other faiths. Some such witnesses, as well as unbelievers, make an *affirmation* rather than taking an oath. See **affirmance.**

soi disant = self-proclaimed. This French affectation is inferior both to the translation just given and to *self-styled.* See GALLICISMS.

solace (= alleviation of sorrow or trouble; relief from distress) should not be used merely as a synonym of *comfort,* without the circumstance of grief or distress being implied. E.g., "Companies with the greatest market share often have a tendency to 'sit on a lead.' They will take *solace* [read *undue pride?*] in their numbers, become complacent, and lose their competitive edge." Mark H. McCormack, *What They Don't Teach You at Harvard Business School* 205–06 (1984). For a related MALAPROPISM, see **surcease.**

The following misuse is even more puzzling:

"No clear legal framework has ever provided for federal jurisdiction over aviation torts. Instead, cases involving aviation torts *find solace* [read *end up* or *are heard*] in federal courts via diversity or admiralty jurisdiction." Albert Lin, Comment, *Jurisdictional Splashdown: Should Aviation Torts* Find Solace [*read* Be Heard] *in Admiralty?* 60 J. Air L. & Com. 409, 411 (1994).

sole (= the one and only, single) should not be used with a plural noun, as in *the sole criteria* [read *the only criteria*]. See **fem(m)e sole.**

sole and exclusive is a legalistic REDUNDANCY. See DOUBLETS, TRIPLETS, AND SYNONYM-STRINGS.

sole cause. See CAUSATION (E).

solecism. Generally, *solecism* means "a grammatical or syntactic error." Here it is close to the literal sense: "It is no more a *solecism* to say 'immovable personal property' than it is to say 'removable fixtures,' nor more contradicting than in the division of actions to use the term 'in rem,' when, under the particular state of facts, the action is primarily 'in personam.'"

The word has been extended to figurative senses, however: "The common law recognized no such *solecism* as a right in the wife to the estate, and a right in someone else to use it as he pleased, and to enjoy all the advantages of its use."/ "The plaintiff asks for protection only during the season, and needs no more, for the designs are all ephemeral; it seeks in this way to persuade us that, if we interfere only a little, the *solecism,* if there be one, may be pardonable."

solely. The placement of this word sometimes causes trouble. E.g., "The responding document states a condition *solely advantageous* [read *advantageous solely*] to the party proposing it." Cf. **only.**

sole practitioner; solo practitioner. In AmE generally, *sole practitioner* is much more common. But there are areas, such as Texas, where *solo* predominates.

sole proprietor; individual proprietor. These synonymous phrases denote an individual who owns a business and is responsible for all its debts.

solicit. A. For *elicit.* This is a MALAPROPISM. E.g., "As noted by the Texas Court of Criminal Appeals, the question that came closest to *soliciting* [read *eliciting*] the information in question was a two-part question asked by the prosecutor." (Note also the awkward repetition of *question.*)

B. For What a Solicitor Does. Although *solicitor* (q.v.) is the BrE term for a certain kind of lawyer, it is incorrect to say that what such a lawyer does is *solicit.* (This sense of the verb has long been obsolete.) The confusion appears in this passage in a reference book: "In America, lawyers can both *solicit* cases and plead them in court, but in England *solicitors* handle the preliminaries, while *barristers* alone are members of the bar and can take cases to court." Robert Hendrickson, *Business Talk* 34 (1984). The quoted statement is so phrased that some word such as *prepare* would be necessary to fit the context. Apart from chamber practice (conveyancing, wills, probate), a solicitor prepares cases and instructs counsel. See **instruct.**

solicitate, a NEEDLESS VARIANT of *solicit,* was coined as a BACK-FORMATION from *solicitation.* But it serves no purpose: "[A]n employer in good faith discharged two employees whom it believed had made violent threats against the company when the employees tried to *solicitate* [read *solicit*] union memberships." *M.B. Zaninovich, Inc. v. ALRB,* 171 Cal. Rptr. 55, 66 (Ct. App. 1981).

solicitation. In criminal law, this broad term covers any word or actions by which one requests, urges, advises, counsels, tempts, commands, or otherwise entices or incites someone to commit a crime.

solicitor. In G.B., and many of the former Commonwealth countries, this term refers to a member of one of the two branches into which the legal profession is divided, handling usu. general legal and business advice, conveyancing, and instruction of and preparation of cases for counsel (barristers). They may do some pleading, particularly in lower courts. See **attorney (A).**

In AmE, the term generally refers to an advertiser or to one who solicits business—and is frequently used disparagingly. E.g., "[A] vocational expert . . . opined that the claimant should be able to perform the work of a telephone *soliciter* [*sic*] . . . ." *Beavers v. H.E.W.,* 577 F.2d 383, 385 (6th Cir. 1978). Regardless of the sense, the word should be spelled *-or.*

solicitor-general. In BrE and AmE alike, this term denotes the second-highest ranking legal officer in government, but there the similarities end. In G.B., the *solicitor-general* (hyphenated) is a Crown-appointed law officer who advises the cabinet on legal matters and supervises the passage of bills through Parliament. Ironically, the *solicitor-general* in England is invariably a barrister—not a solicitor. In the U.S., the *solicitor general* (unhyphenated) is the chief courtroom lawyer for the executive branch, with chambers at the Supreme Court as well as at the Justice Department. In AmE, the title *solicitor general* is often, after the first mention of the full title, shortened to *solicitor.*

solicitude has two important senses that may render the word ambiguous: (1) "anxiety"; and (2) "protectiveness."

solidary liability. See **joint and several.**

solo practitioner. See **sole practitioner.**

solon, journalese for *legislator,* is derived from the name of Solon, an Athenian statesman, merchant, and poet (ca. 640–560 B.C.). In the early 6th century, Solon achieved important political, commercial, and judicial reforms that greatly improved life in the city-state of Athens. He reversed the trend to convert impoverished Athenians into serfs at home or to sell them abroad as slaves. He also standardized Athenian coinage and its system of weights and measures, granted citizenship to immigrant craftsmen, and enhanced the prosperity and independence of Athenian farmers.

In modern times, his name has been used to denote either a "sage" or a "wiseacre" (*OED*). Today, the term "may be inescapable, and thus grudgingly admissible, in headlines, where *legislator, senator,* or *representative* will not fit, but in text it is to be avoided." Roy Copperud, *Webster's Dictionary of Usage and Style* 368–69 (1964).

When used in reference to legislating judges, *solon* often carries a mocking tone: "At any rate, concluded the nine *solons,* the dodge works; the statute doesn't cover the case; no tax." Fred Rodell, *Woe Unto You, Lawyers!* 46 (1939; repr. 1980).

so long as. See **as long as** & **as . . . as** (A).

soluble; solvable. *Soluble* is usually applied to substances in solvents, whereas *solvable* is usually applied to problems. *Soluble* is often used in reference to problems, however; this usage is acceptable, though not preferred. Cf. **resolvable.**

solution may take either *to* or *of* as its preposition.

solvabilité, in French civil law, means "solvency," not "solvability" or "solubility."

solvable. See **soluble.**

solvent. See **insolvent.**

some . . . as for *such . . . as* or *some . . . that.* E.g., "The two-year statute of limitations applicable to an action based on fraudulent inducement to execute a contract begins to run when plaintiff learns of the alleged wrongdoing or knows of facts sufficient to excite *some inquiry as* [read *such inquiry as* or *some inquiry that*] would have been made in the exercise of reasonable diligence."

somebody; someone. The words are equally good; euphony should govern the choice of term. *Someone* is often better by that standard. Each is a singular noun and hence, for purposes of CONCORD, the antecedent of a singular pronoun. *Some one* as two words is an obsolete spelling, though Cardozo used this spelling as recently as 1928.

someplace is informal for *somewhere;* it is out of place in formal prose, although it is acceptable in speech.

sometime; some time. *Sometime* = at a time in the future; *some time* = quite a while. The difference may be illustrated by contrasting the following two sentences: "It was not until *sometime* later [i.e., an unknown date] that he quit."/ "It was not until *some time* [i.e., awhile] later that he quit."

Sometime, in a slightly archaic sense, means "former"—e.g.: "Let me also recall my indebtedness to my former tutor, the late Professor F. deZueta; the late Sir John Miles, *sometime* Warden of Merton College . . . ." Carleton K. Allen, *Law in the Making* vi (7th ed. 1964). In such phrases as *my sometime friend,* it does not properly signify "on-again-off-again" or "on occasion." See **erstwhile.**

somewhat should be avoided as a WEASEL WORD—e.g.: "In approaching solution to this problem we must look *somewhat* [omit *somewhat*] beyond the immediate consequences of the decision in this case." See FLOTSAM PHRASES & FUSTIAN.

Son-of-Sam law denotes a statute that prevents a criminal from profiting from selling the rights to his or her story to a publisher or moviemaker. New York was the first state to enact such a law, in 1977, when the serial murderer David R. Berkowitz (known as "Son of Sam") was offered large sums for his life story.

About 40 American states have enacted such statutes. Generally, these statutes, enacted mostly in the 1980s, authorize prosecutors to seize royalties from convicted criminals. During his prosecution, O.J. Simpson was able to skirt the issue by arranging for his lawyers to profit from books sales, as opposed to Simpson himself. Further, of course, he had only been accused—not convicted—when he wrote his book entitled *I Want to Tell You* (1995).

sonorous is accented on the second syllable /*sə-**nohr**-əs*/ in AmE, and on the first syllable /***sohn**-ər-əs*/ in BrE. The latter pronunciation is a secondary variant in AmE.

sophic(al). See **sophistic(al).**

sophist(er). *Sophister* is, except in historical contexts denoting a certain rank of student, a NEEDLESS VARIANT of *sophist,* which today has primarily negative connotations in the sense "one who makes use of fallacious arguments; a specious reasoner." Formerly it was a respectable word meaning "one who is distinguished for learning; a wise or learned man" (*OED*).

sophistic(al); sophic(al). These words have opposite connotations. The former (usu. *sophistical*) means "quibbling, specious, or captious in reasoning." The latter (usu. *sophic*) means "learned; intellectual."

The disparaging term is more common: "The hospital makes the *sophistic* [read *sophistical*] argument that its admission requirement does not turn on the physician's academic medical degree, but on the nature of the institution at which he received his post-doctoral training."/ "Thence 'special pleader' came in time to be used for any disingenuous or *sophistical* disputant." (Eng.)

sorb. See **absorb.**

sore-back lawyer. See LAWYERS, DEROGATORY NAMES FOR (A).

sort of, adv., is a dialectal casualism to be avoided in writing. E.g., "The prosecutor *sort of* agreed that . . . ." It is also a FUDGE WORD and a WEASEL WORD.

For the problem raised by the phrase *these sort of,* see **these kind of.**

so . . . so as. See **so . . . as [+ infinitive].**

sought for. The preposition is unnecessary. E.g., "As the relief *sought* is the appointment of a trustee, and the necessity for such appointment requires the construction of the will as an incident to the relief *sought for* [read merely *sought*], the complainant is properly here."

sound, v.i. This verb has a special legal sense, "to be actionable (in)." E.g., "As for the claims *sounding* in malicious prosecution, however, neither Smith nor any of the other authorities advanced by appellees controls them."/ "There is no doubt that an easement may be created by words *sounding* in covenant."/ "It is, of course, to the advantage of any lienor . . . to plead his claim as *sounding* not in contract but in tort." Grant Gilmore & Charles L. Black, Jr., *The Law of Admiralty* 753 (2d ed. 1975).

The *OED* refers to the expression *sound in damages* (= to be concerned only with damages)—e.g.: "This covenant did not create a specifically ascertained debt, but only a claim which *sounded* in damages" (quoted in *OED*). Today the sense has been carried beyond "to be concerned only with," to the meaning set forth at the outset of this entry.

sound bite. So spelled—not *sound byte.*

sound block. See **gavel.**

sound mind. See **mind and memory.**

SOUND OF PROSE, THE. We all are occasionally guilty of having a tin ear. The effective writer is self-trained to avoid writing in a way that distracts by undue alliteration, unconscious puns, or unseemly images, for these may irritate or distract the reader. The writers of the following sentences might have benefited from reading their own prose aloud.

A. Undue Alliteration or Rhyme. Cardozo, a masterly stylist, wrote in one of his classic opinions: "Nothing in this situation gave notice that the fallen *package* had in it the *potency* of *peril* to *persons* thus removed." *Palsgraf v. Long Island R.R. Co.,* 162 N.E. 99, 99 (N.Y. App. Div. 1928). This type of wordplay should be undertaken cautiously, for it declares that one's purpose is to be wry or coy.

Intentional but ineffective alliteration is one thing. Thoughtless alliteration is quite another:

- "The unauthorized *publication* of *personal* letters is a *piracy* of a *portion* of the sender's *personality.*"
- "Such a claim makes little *sense since* the plaintiff in no way relied on the fact that he was trading with an insider."
- "The change in the *complexion* of *complex* litigation necessitates a more concentrated and prolonged inquiry into this area."

- "Such taxes merely apportion the cost of state services among all beneficiaries, and imports must *bear their fair share.*"
- "She was, at the time of the ceremony of marriage, and has been ever *since,* incapable of consummating the marriage with her husband in that she *evinced* an *invincible* repugnance to him." (Eng.)

See ALLITERATION.

B. Unwieldy or Illogical Imagery. "That case held that quasi in rem jurisdiction over a defendant could not be exercised unless the defendant had such 'minimum contacts' with the forum state that in personam jurisdiction could be exercised over him under *International Shoe.*" (Prepositional clash: *over . . . under;* image: *under . . . shoe.*)/ "The accounting problem has already *come to a head at the SEC* in connection with initial public offerings." (Two idioms collide in the reader's mind: *come to a head* and *head of an organizaiton or department.*)

C. Unnecessary or Awkward Repetition. "The decision in *Klaxon v. Stentor* would have suggested that Illinois conflict of laws should be looked *to to* determine whether Illinois or Indiana law on physical examination orders is to be observed." (Substitute *followed* for *looked to;* or, if this seems to change the meaning, insert *in order* before the second *to.*) See REDUNDANCY (B).

Having words with the same root in close proximity can be especially jarring. Legal writers often use in succession two different forms of the same root, as an agent noun and a verb. E.g., "In *conference* the *conferees* largely acceded to the Senate's approach to Indian regulatory authority."/ "By the first clause the *covenantor covenanted* as follows." (Eng.) Thoughtful writers vary one of these words, usually the verb—e.g.: "While meeting, the *conferees* largely acceded . . . ."/ "By the first clause the covenantor agreed [or *bound himself*] as follows."

This type of variation is unobjectionable, its purpose being to avoid an obtrusive repetition. Hence it is distinct from INELEGANT VARIATION.

In the following sentence, the same root appears in two words that, in context, have remote senses (the verb *impress* and the noun *impression*): "From what has been said we are convinced that appellant's profits in question were not *impressed* with a trust when they first came into existence; the board *was obviously of the impression* [read *obviously thought*] that the trust first attached when appellant credited them to the beneficiaries on his books of account."

D. Arrhythmic Plodding. "Nevertheless, the lengthy process of securing a final state-court judgment that reviews the Board's denial—which envisions state district court trial, intermediate state court appeal, and state supreme court certiorari review—augurs much-belated and possibly ineffective relief to a recent law-school graduate ultimately held to have been improperly denied a certificate of fitness that would have made him eligible to take a bar examination soon after he had completed his legal studies and received his law degree." This sentence can hardly be meaningfully read aloud on first or second try; it should be split into smaller clauses in which the emphasis, the author's implied intonation, is clearer.

E. Jarring Contrasts. "That such tenancy found its existence in the lease of July 14 is admittedly true, for plaintiff contends that defendant is holding *over under* it, and defendant contends that he is holding *under* it." (Who has the upper hand?) [Read: . . . *for the plaintiff contends that defendant is a holdover tenant—in violation of the lease—whereas the defendant contends that he is holding in accordance with the lease.*]/ "*There* is *here* no claimed invasion of any substantive constitutional right." [Contextual rewrite: *Smith does not claim that the University has invaded any substantive constitutional right.*]

F. Misleading Parts of Speech. In the following sentence, *will* (futurity) sounds like *will* (testament): "Although the courts have been more liberal in admitting extrinsic evidence for the purpose of integrating holographs than they have for the purpose of integrating attested *wills,* it is likely that the proponent *will* have to rely upon evidence appearing in the various pages because sufficient extrinsic evidence may be impossible to obtain."

For related subjects, see ANFRACTUOSITY, INITIALESE, MINGLE-MANGLE, MISCUES & SENTENCE LENGTH.

soup, in England, is legal slang equivalent to *dock brief,* q.v., or to the fee involved in such a brief.

source, though it has a respectable history as a verb in certain contexts, has recently been adopted by jargonmongers as a VOGUE WORD. Like other such words, it should be avoided. Examples of its objectionable uses follow: "This information is not *sourced* [i.e., its sources are not cited (intelligence jargon)]."/ "In making concessions on such questions as *sourcing*—where parts should be made—GM tacitly conceded Toyota's superiority in small-car design and manufacture."

sources of law. As Holland pointed out, this phrase is ambiguous. It is commonly used in four senses, i.e., to refer to: (1) the place from which we obtain our knowledge of the law, e.g., whether from the statute-book, the reports, or treatises (literary source); (2) the ultimate authority that backs up the law, i.e., the state (formal source); (3) the causes that have, seemingly automatically, brought into existence rules that have subsequently acquired legal force, such as custom, religion, and scientific discussion (historical or material sources); or (4) the organs through which the state either grants legal recognition to rules previously unauthoritative, or itself creates new law, such as legislation and adjudication (legal source). See Thomas E. Holland, *The Elements of Jurisprudence* 55 (13th ed. 1924; repr. 1937).

sour grapes is one of the most commonly misused idiomatic metaphors. It is not a mere synonym of *envy* or *jealousy;* rather, as in Aesop's fable of the fox who wanted the grapes he could not reach, *sour grapes* denotes the human tendency to disparage as undesirable what one really wants but cannot get (or has not got). Following is a typical journalistic misuse: "Great Britain's reaction [in the Falklands war] was more a case of *sour grapes* and wounded pride than any genuine desire to right a terrible wrong." Letter of Philip Naff, *Falklands Furor,* Time, 10 May 1982, at 5.

sovereignty; sovranty. The former spelling is preferred. Brierly rightly calls *sovereignty* a "much abused word." J.L. Brierly, *The Law of Nations* 150 (5th ed. 1955). It has three primary senses: (1) "supreme dominion, authority, or rule"; (2) "the position, rank, or control of a supreme ruler, such as a monarch, or controlling power, such as a democratically formed government"; or (3) "a territory under the rule of a sovereign, or existing as an independent state." To the international lawyer, *sovereignty* "is not a metaphysical concept, nor is it part of the essence of statehood; it is merely a term which designates an aggregate of particular and very extensive claims that states habitually make for themselves in their relations with other states [sense (1)]. To the extent that *sovereignty* had come to imply that there is something inherent in the nature of states that makes it impossible for them to be subjected to law, it is a false doctrine which the facts of international relations do not support." *Id.* at 48–49.

spatial; spacial. The former spelling is preferred both in AmE and in BrE.

spawn litigation is a legal CLICHÉ.

speaking. A. *Speaking Motions* and the Like. Through HYPALLAGE, *speaking* has evolved in legal JARGON as an adjective denoting some type of impermissible or extraordinary communication. A *speaking motion,* for example, is one that requires consideration of facts outside the pleadings; a *speaking objection* is one laced with comments or arguments that reach beyond the legal grounds for the objection; a *speaking demurrer,* in former practice, was one that introduced a new fact or facts not contained in the original petition.

A related term without the connotation of impermissibility is the phrase *speaking order* (= an order that not only commands but also gives reasons for the court's action). E.g., "The decision in the *Northumberland Case* opened up new possibilities in certiorari when there was a *'speaking order'*—i.e. a record of judgement or decision giving reasons [that] could, if necessary, be assailed for error of law." Carleton K. Allen, *Law in the Making* 573–74 (7th ed. 1964).

B. As a Sentence Adverb. The word *speaking* is among the few "acceptable danglers" or "disguised conjunctions" when used as a sentence adverb. E.g., "*Speaking in general terms,* it is desirable to speed the growth of technical legal meanings." Lon L. Fuller, *Legal Fictions* 23 (1967)./ "*Speaking very generally,* the answer to this question is that contractual obligations are absolute, and that absence of fault is no defence." P.S. Atiyah, *An Introduction to the Law of Contract* 184 (3d ed. 1981). See DANGLERS (A) & SENTENCE ADVERBS.

special. See **especial** & **write specially.**

special appearance. See ***de bene esse.***

special damages. See **general damages** & **damages.**

special guardian. See **guardian *ad litem.***

special interrogatory. See **special verdict.**

special issue. See **general issue** & **special verdict.**

special(i)ty. The legal term for a contract under seal is spelled *specialty* in both AmE and BrE. In the general lay sense "a special thing," the word is *specialty* in AmE, *speciality* in BrE.

special limitation; executory limitation; condition subsequent. The ideas denoted by these terms are so intricate that it is difficult if not impossible to explain them without falling into JARGON. Here is an attempt at least to minimize the jargon. A *special limitation* is a restriction on the estate of a grantee who is a first taker, arising either when the grant creates a possibility of reverter or when a third party acquires a defeasing interest after the grant. An *executory limita-*

tion is a restriction on the estate of a grantee who is the first taker, arising when a defeasing interest in a third party is granted simultaneously with the grantee's present interest. A *condition subsequent* is an event that, when it occurs or fails to occur, gives the grantor or the grantor's successors the right to end an existing estate. See **condition (B) & condition precedent.**

special litigation committee = a committee of independent corporate directors assigned to investigate the merits of a derivative shareholder action and, if appropriate, to recommend maintaining or dismissing the suit. The phrase dates from the 1970s, when the device it denotes sprang into existence in response to shareholder litigation.

special pleading. See POPULARIZED LEGAL TECHNICALITIES.

specialty. See **special(i)ty.**

special verdict; special interrogatory; special issue. These synonymous phrases refer to a jury question that requires detailed, specific answers about each factual issue—as opposed to a *general verdict, general interrogatory,* or *general issue,* which asks merely who wins. See **general issue.**

specie; species. *Specie* means "coined money"; it has no plural, unless one means to refer to different types of coined money. *Species* is both singular and plural and means "a group of similar plants and animals that can breed with each other but not with others." From that sense have grown natural extensions of the meaning of the word. Sometimes *species* is correctly used as an equivalent of *type,* as here: "Loss of services was the gist of this *species* of action." The writer of the following sentence was erroneously attempting to make *specie* a singular of *species:* "Penalties are a *specie* [read *species*] of punishment for wrongdoing and are not looked upon with favor." The same blunder appears in the title of an article: Harold S. Bloomenthal, *Shareholder Derivative Actions under the Securities Laws—Phoenix or Endangered Specie* [read *Species*]*?* 26 Ariz. L. Rev. 767 (1984). For more on *species,* see **genus (A).**

In specie (= in kind; specifically; without any kind of substitution) is a LATINISM that is sometimes justified in providing a valuable nuance to legal writing. E.g., "Apparently the Stuarts sought only to compel forced loans of money and impose taxes and levies under claim of prerogative, but not to take property *in specie.*" Roscoe Pound, *The Development of Constitutional Guarantees of Liberty* 108 (1957; repr. 1975)./ "It is presumed that the testator intended the transferee for life to receive the income arising from investing the proceeds realized on selling the consumables, rather than to enjoy the consumables *in specie.*"

In specie has given rise to the elliptical adjectival form *specie:* "The executor will permit beneficiaries of any and all trusts hereunder to enjoy the *specie* use or benefit of any household goods, chattels, or other tangible personal property."

-specific. In legal writing, this word is increasingly used as a combining form, as in *fact-specific, city-specific,* and even *newsrack-specific*—e.g.: "[T]he City of Lakewood finds itself between a rock and a hard place: make the rules *newsrack-specific,* and be accused of drawing the noose too tightly around First Amendment protected activities; apply more general rules to newsracks, and be told that your regulators lack standards sufficiently specific to pass constitutional muster." *City of Lakewood v. Plain Dealer Publishing Co.,* 486 U.S. 750, 795 (1988) (White, J., dissenting).

specific implement. See **specific performance.**

specific intent. See **intent(ion) (E) & general intent.**

specific legacy. See **legacy.**

specific performance; specific relief; specific implement. In contract cases in which damages would not be an adequate remedy—as where the sale of rare or valuable articles, or of land, is concerned—the court may use its equitable powers to order *specific performance,* i.e., that the contract be performed. E.g., "What is commonly called the *specific performance* of contracts is the doing of what was agreed to be done, but not at the time when it was agreed to be done; i.e., not till after the time when it was agreed to be done is past, and hence not till the contract is broken." C.C. Langdell, *A Brief Survey of Equity Jurisdiction* (pt. 3), 1 Harv. L. Rev. 355, 355–56 (1888)./ "In American commentary it has become a truism to say that the once exceptional remedy of *specific performance* is rapidly becoming the order of the day." Grant Gilmore, *The Death of Contract* 83 (1974).

In both AmE and BrE, *specific relief* is a synonym—e.g.: "Chancery intervened by granting *specific relief,* such as the performance of an obligation, or the return of goods which had been lent to defendant." L.B. Curzon, *English Legal History* 108 (2d ed. 1979).

Specific implement is the equivalent phrase in Scots law.

specious. See **spurious.**

spectate. See BACK-FORMATIONS.

specter; spectre. This favorite word of legal writers is preferably spelled *-er* in AmE, *-re* in BrE. Curiously, however, many Americans cling to the British spelling. A California court writes: "We were not halted by the *spectre* [read *specter*] of an inability to prejudge every future case."/ "Neither one objected below or raised on appeal the *spectre* [read *specter*] of an inadequate hearing." In American writing, the usual spelling of many words such as *theater* is *-er*. See -ER (C).

spectrum. Pl. *spectra.* See PLURALS (A).

sped. See **speeded.**

speech, in BrE, can refer to a judgment (i.e., a judicial opinion) in the House of Lords. The term derives from the law lords' custom of delivering their pronouncements orally, as parliamentary "speeches." E.g., "It should, however, be said that not all the law lords agreed with Lord Radcliffe, and that in a number of *speeches* (including, indeed, that of Lord Radcliffe himself) there is evidence of support for a third 'theory.'" P.S. Atiyah, *An Introduction to the Law of Contract* 209–10 (3d ed. 1981)./ "Lord Simon of Glaisdale also canvassed the possibility of prospective overruling in a dissenting *speech* in an earlier case . . . ." Rupert Cross & J.W. Harris, *Precedent in English Law* 232 (4th ed. 1991). See **decision.**

speechify (= to deliver a speech) is typically used in a mocking or derogatory way. Cf. **argufy.**

speed, all deliberate. See **with all deliberate speed.**

speeded; sped. The best preterit and past-participial form of the verb *to speed* is *sped,* except in the PHRASAL VERB *to speed up* (= to accelerate) <she speeded up to 80 m.p.h.>.

speedy trial. The Sixth Amendment to the U.S. Constitution declares that "[i]n all criminal prosecutions, the accused shall enjoy the right to a *speedy . . . trial* . . . ." In 1974, Congress enacted the Speedy Trial Act (18 U.S.C. § 3161), which set time limits for indicting, arraigning, and prosecuting federal criminal defendants. *Speedy* refers to the point of beginning important events in the prosecution—not the speed with which they are carried out.

speluncean /*spə-***lən***-see-ən*/ is often mispronounced /*spə-***lən***-kee-ən*/, esp. in references to Lon Fuller's brilliant article, *The Case of the Speluncean Explorers,* 62 Harv. L. Rev. 616 (1949). Though the cognate words *spelunker* and *spelunking* do indeed have the hard *-k-* sound, the *-c-* in *speluncean* is soft.

spiel (= a set monologue or rehearsed oral presentation) is pronounced /*speel*/, not in the mock-Yiddish fashion that has become so common (/*shpeel*/).

spirit, in matters of interpretation, refers to a general purpose: hence, the *spirit of the law* is frequently contrasted with the *letter of the law.* E.g., "As in all interpretations, the *'spirit'* of constitutional texts or the *'spirit'* of constitutions began to be invoked and it became necessary to give a content to abstract constitutional formulas exactly as the civilian has had to give a content for modern purposes to abstract oracular texts of the Roman Books." Roscoe Pound, *The Formative Era of American Law* 97 (1938)./"[I]t is an almost inevitable feature of legal systems in their adolescence that the *spirit* of the law is overshadowed by the letter of procedure, . . . the demands of precision far outweigh[ing] those of abstract justice." H.G. Hanbury, *English Courts of Law* 34 (2d ed. 1953). See **letter of the law, the.**

spiritual(istic); spirituous; spiritous; spirituel(le); spirited. *Spiritual* is the broadest of these terms, meaning "of spirit as opposed to matter; of the soul; concerned with sacred or religious things." *Spiritualistic* = of or relating to spiritualism, i.e., the belief that departed spirits communicate with and show themselves to the living, esp. through mediums. *Spirituous* = alcoholic. E.g., "The indictment charges the unlawful sale of *spirituous* liquors within two miles of Bethel Methodist Church in Macon County." *Spiritous* is an ARCHAISM in the sense of "highly refined or dematerialized," and is also a NEEDLESS VARIANT of *spirituous. Spirituel* (masculine) or *spirituelle* (feminine) means "witty" or "of a highly refined character or nature, esp. in conjunction with liveliness or quickness of mind" (*OED*).

spit > spat > spat. Occasionally *spit* wrongly displaces *spat* as the past-tense or past-participial form—e.g.: "The portraits of downtown life are almost always moving—in spite of the grime and foul language *spit* [read *spat*] through rotten teeth . . . ." Soto, *New Poems, Stories on America's "Unwashed,"* Japan Times, 3 June 1990, at 14.

spite of, in. See **despite.**

splendiferous is a usually comic or colloquial word for *splendid.*

split between (or in) the circuits. This phrase is used in American legal writing to denote that U.S. Courts of Appeals have arrived at contrary holdings on the same point of law. E.g., "Recognizing that the *split in the circuits* exists, we find that *Bailey* and not *Collins* provides the appropriate analysis, which we now follow." The U.S. Supreme Court or Congress is capable of remedying a split between the circuits, by laying down an explicit rule of law that the courts of appeals must afterwards follow.

SPLIT INFINITIVES abound in legal writing, often needlessly—but they are not invariably wrong. The English language gives us "the inestimable advantage of being able to put adverbs where they will be most effective, coloring the verbs to which they apply and becoming practically part of them . . . . If you think a verb cannot be split in two, just call the adverb a part of the verb and the difficulty will be solved." Joseph Lee, *A Defense of the Split Infinitive,* 37 Mass. L.Q. 65, 66 (1952).

Fowler divided the English-speaking world into five classes: (1) those who neither know nor care what a split infinitive is; (2) those who do not know, but care very much; (3) those who know and condemn; (4) those who know and approve; and (5) those who know and distinguish. (*MEU2* at 579.) It is this last class to which, if we have a good ear, we should aspire. See SUPERSTITIONS (B).

An infinitive, of course, is the tenseless form of a verb preceded by *to,* such as *to reverse* or *to modify.* Splitting the infinitive is placing one or more words between *to* and the verb, such as *to summarily reverse* or *to unwisely modify.*

A. Splits to Be Avoided. If a split is easily fixed by putting the adverb at the end of the phrase, and the meaning remains the same, then avoiding the split is the best course:

Split: "It is not necessary *to here enlarge* upon them."
Unsplit: "It is not necessary *to enlarge* upon them *here.*"

This is an excellent example of the capricious split infinitive, which serves no purpose, unless that purpose is to jar the reader. Similar examples turn up frequently in legal writing:

- "This issue is confusing the court, and *we would like to all clear it up* [read *we would all like to clear it up*]."
- "The equal protection clause will continue *to almost automatically invalidate* [read *to invalidate almost automatically*] classifications that are unmistakably racial on their face . . . ."
- "This statement appears to be an objection to the trial court's failure *to more clearly explain* [read *to explain more clearly*] Harper's defensive theory."
- "*In order for someone to voluntarily take a risk* [read *For someone to take a risk voluntarily*], he must know the dangers involved, and decide to take the chance anyway."

Wide splits are to be avoided—e.g.: "We encourage counsel on both sides to utilize the best efforts *to understandingly, sympathetically, and professionally arrive at* [read *to arrive understandingly, sympathetically, and professionally at*] a settlement regarding attorneys' fees."

With CORRELATIVE CONJUNCTIONS, a split infinitive simply displays carelessness—e.g.: "White was *to either make or obtain* a loan." [Read *White was either to make or to obtain a loan.*] See PARALLELISM.

B. Justified Splits. A number of infinitives are best split. Perhaps the most famous is from the 1960s television series, *Star Trek,* in which the opening voice-over included this phrase: *to boldly go where no man*—or, in the revival of the 1980s and 1990s, *where no one—has gone before.* The phrase sounds inevitable partly because it is so familiar, but also because the adverb most naturally bears the emphasis, not the verb *go.*

And that example is not a rarity. Consider: *She expects to more than double her profits next year.* We cannot merely move the adverbial phrase in that sentence—to "fix" the split, we would have to eliminate the infinitive, as by writing, *She expects her profits to more than double next year,* thereby giving the sentence a different nuance. (The woman seems less responsible for the increase.)

Again, though, knowing when to split an infinitive requires a good ear and a keen eye. Otherwise, the ability to distinguish—the ability Fowler mentioned—is not attainable. *To flatly state,* for example, suggests something different from *to state flatly.* In the sentences that follow, unsplitting the infinitive would either create an awkwardness or change the sense:

- "The confidentiality of a marketing concept does not create a continuing competitive advantage because, once it is implemented, it is exposed for the world to see and for competitors *to legally imitate.*" (Changing placement of the adverb here would change the meaning.)

- "The statute denies to respondent the right *to reasonably manage* or control its own business."
- "The majority improperly places the burden of proof on the appellees *to affirmatively establish* the existence of a statutory exemption."
- "He asserted self-defense in order *to affirmatively avoid* appellant's cause of action."
- "The statute prohibits supplying others with the necessary information and documents *to falsely claim* their income as tax exempt."
- "Appellants failed *to timely file* their notice of appeal."
- "Inability *to directly attain* the remedial goal of prevention of harm in tort cases is a major deficiency of the common-law system of substitutional money damages."
- "The great progress of the art, which owed little to financiers and much to operating men, had reduced costs fast enough *to pretty well cover* the manipulations of the holding companies." Robert H. Jackson, *The Struggle for Judicial Supremacy* 142 (1941).
- "Imagine what the Court would have said if Congress had tried *to expressly delegate* the matter to the Court." Charles P. Curtis, Jr., *Lions Under the Throne* 242 (1947).

Distinguishing these examples from those under (A) may not be easy for all readers. Those who find it difficult might advantageously avoid all splits.

C. Awkwardness Caused by Avoiding Splits. Occasionally, though, sticking to the old "rule" about split infinitives leads to gross phrasing. The following sentences illustrate clumsy attempts to avoid splitting the infinitive. In the first two examples, the adverb may be placed more naturally than it is without splitting the infinitive; in the third and fourth examples, a split is called for:

- "Now to legitimize *L*'s breach of the contract by the retroactive application of the October 1982 amendments would be *unjustly to enrich L* [read *to enrich L unjustly*] while unjustly penalizing U."
- "We should not permit Congress *to continue inadequately to compensate judges* [read *to continue to compensate judges inadequately*]."
- "The court does not have the resources necessary *effectively to superintend* [read *to effectively superintend*] the day-to-day details of the execution of the program to be set out in the decree."
- "We are not impressed with the soundness of the doctrine, which, in the case at bar, would be an attempt *judicially to interpret* [read *to judicially interpret*] the language of the donor provisions contrary to his actual intent as expressed."

split sentence = a criminal penalty involving a short jail term—to expose the offender to the unpleasantness of prison—followed by a period of probation. Its use is described and defended in *ABA Standards for Criminal Justice* ch. 18, 100–07 (2d ed. 1980), though as an unnamed "intermediate sanction" rather than under the name *split sentence.*

splitting the baby has become a legal CLICHÉ to describe an adjudicated compromise imposed on two contending parties—usu. with the implication that such a resolution is unsatisfactory. Alluding to the biblical story of Solomon's ruse that revealed which of two contending women was truly the baby's mother, this phrase appears to have come into legal use in AmE first in the mid-1960s: "Without questioning the Solomonic simplicity of this resolution, it is no more permissible than *splitting the baby* would have been conscionable." *Conlon v. McCoy,* 278 N.Y.S.2d 449, 452 (App. Div. 1967).

spoilation. See **spoliation.**

spoil(s). Although the word is plural in the phrase *spoils of war,* it is traditionally singular in the sense "goods, esp. such as are valuable, seized by force or confiscated." E.g., "No right to the *spoil* is vested in the piratical captor."

spoliation, a learned word, is, in the hands and mouths of the less-than-learned, often misspelled and mispronounced *spoilation,* as in a 1992 legal seminar on the subject of "*Spoilation* [read *Spoliation*] of Evidence." The difference between the form of the verb and of the noun—though etymologically the words are identical—is understandably the source of confusion. That difference arises from different paths by which the words came into English: in the 14th century, *spoil* was borrowed from Old French (*espoille*), whereas in the 15th century *spoliation* was borrowed from Latin (*spoliātio*).

For the same error in a related term, see **despoilation.**

spoonfuls; spoonsful. The former is preferred. See PLURALS (E).

spotted pony case. See **whitehorse case.**

spousal, adj. The *OED* defines this term as (1) "of, pertaining or relating to, espousal or marriage; nuptial; matrimonial"; or (2) "(of a hymn, poem, etc.) celebrating or commemorating an espousal or marriage." *W3* contains like definitions. In modern American law, however, *spousal* means "of, relating to, or by a spouse or spouses." E.g., "Pragmatically, *spousal* support now serves to deliver economic justice based on the financial needs of the specific parties involved in a dissolution proceeding." See **interspousal.**

spouse is a word that lawyers use much more often than nonlawyers, who are accustomed to husbands and wives. Certainly in referring to a particular husband or wife, *spouse* is not the best word—e.g.: "We know that the design and text of the Code bears the inimitable imprint of its chief draftsman, Karl N. Llewellyn, and that his *spouse* [read *wife*], Soia Mentschikoff, had a major hand in the entire project." James J. White & Robert S. Summers, *Uniform Commercial Code* § 1, at 5 (3d ed. 1988).

spread, v.t. The figurative parliamentary idiom *to spread upon the minutes* has been extended in legal usage to other printed matter, and, as in the second example, even to unprinted matter. E.g., "The court's findings that lesser sanctions would be inadequate must be *spread upon the record.*"/ "Appellee has had this picture of its indifference, or at least ineptness, *spread before a jury* and now *upon the pages of this reporter.*"

springing use; shifting use. A *springing use* is one that arises on the occurrence of a future event, whereas a *shifting use* is one that operates to terminate a preceding use. A *springing use* arises, for example, when property is given to Johnson to the use of Gilbert when Gilbert marries; Gilbert has a springing use that vests in him when he marries. A *shifting use,* by contrast, might arise when property is given to Johnson to the use of Gilbert, but then to Bradley when Foster pays $1,000 to Burke; Bradley has a shifting use that arises when Foster makes the specified payment. In G.B., *secondary use* is a variant of *shifting use,* although all these terms are of historical interest only there. See **use.**

spurious; specious. *Spurious* is used in reference to things, and *specious* arguments or reasoning. *Spurious* = not genuine. *Specious* = having superficial appeal but false. E.g., "Many *specious* reasons for practices revolting to our ideas of justice may be found in old books."

ss. A. As Mysterious Legal Abbreviation. The sign *ss.* is an abbreviation that often appears on the top of the first page of an affidavit or acknowledgment—e.g.:

> District of Columbia, *ss.:*
> John Rand, being duly sworn, deposes and says that he has read the foregoing bill by him subscribed and knows the contents . . . .
>
> Eugene A. Jones, *Manual of Equity Pleading and Practice* 39 (1916).

Many possible etymologies have been suggested for this mysterious abbreviation. One is that it signifies *scilicet* (= namely, to wit), which is usually abbreviated *sc.* or *scil.* Another is that *ss.* represents "[t]he two gold letters at the ends of the chain of office or 'collar' worn by the Lord Chief Justice of the King's Bench . . . ." Max Radin, *Law Dictionary* 327 (1955). Mellinkoff suggests that the precise etymology is unknown: "Lawyers have been using *ss* for nine hundred years and still are not sure what it means." David Mellinkoff, *The Language of the Law* 296 (1963).

In fact, though, it is a flourish deriving from the Year Books—an equivalent of the paragraph mark: "¶." Hence Lord Hardwicke's statement that *ss.* is nothing more than a division mark. See *Jodderrell v. Cowell,* 95 Eng. Rep. 222, 222 (K.B. 1737) ("[T]he word ss. I verily believe, was not originally meant to the county, but only a denotation of each section or paragraph in the record"). An early formbook writer incorporated it into his forms, and ever since it has been mindlessly perpetuated by one generation after another.

American lawyers have puzzled over its meaning and have even wasted time litigating whether it is necessary in affidavits. See, e.g., *Sway v. Shrader,* 95 N.W. 690, 691 (Neb. 1903). There are no judicious uses of this LEGALISM.

B. As an Equivalent of "§§." In BrE, *ss.* frequently means "sections"—e.g.: "Forgery Act 1913 ss. 8(2)." Citation in Glanville Williams, *Textbook of Criminal Law* 389 n.4 (1978)./ "Under the *Statute of Frauds,* 1667, ss. 1, 2, it was enacted that leases . . . had to be in writing." L.B. Curzon, *English Legal History* 317 (2d ed. 1979).

stabilize; stabilify; stabilitate. The second and third are NEEDLESS VARIANTS.

stadium. Several dictionaries seem to prefer *stadia* as the plural form, but *stadiums* is the more natural and the more usual form, even in formal legal writing of several generations ago.

stagflation. See MORPHOLOGICAL DEFORMITIES.

stakeholder; stockholder. These terms are not to be confused. *Stakeholder,* missed by the *OED* but included in *W2* and *W3,* originally meant "the holder of a stake or wager," a meaning it still carries. But in modern American legal writing it usually denotes one who holds property, the right or possession of which is disputed between two other parties (as in an interpleader action).

Stockholder = (1) a shareholder in a corporation; or (2) one who is a proprietor of stock in the public funds or the funds of a joint-stock company (*OED*). Sense (1) is labeled an Americanism in the *OED,* although the *COD* definition suggests that this sense is now current in BrE. Sense (2) is largely confined to BrE. See **shareholder.**

stale, in law, means "(of a claim, demand, or offer) having lain dormant for too long to be enforceable." The term provides one of the law's more picturesque METAPHORS—e.g.: "[I]t [may be] clear to the offeree that there has been such a long delay in the transmission of the offer as to make it obvious to the offeree that the offer was *stale* when it reached him." G.H. Treitel, *The Law of Contract* 16 (8th ed. 1991).

stanch. See **staunch.**

stand, n., is an AmE shortening of *witness stand*—e.g.: "As to any differences among themselves these clerical proficients might develop on the *stand,* these could hardly be greater than the direct contradictions exchanged between the remunerated medical experts." Herman Melville, *Billy Budd* 38 (1891; repr. N.Y., Signet, 1979). In the common idiom, a witness *takes the stand* after being sworn. See **witness-box.**

stand, v.i., = to remain good law. E.g., "Amanda Acquisition Corp. . . . claimed that the statute was unconstitutional and that if it were allowed to *stand,* the company's offer would be doomed." Laurie P. Cohen, *Court Upholds State Anti-Takeover Law That Makes Raiders Get Board Approval,* Wall St. J., 26 May 1989, at B3.

standard-form contract (= a preprinted contract, often referred to as an *adhesion contract*) is hyphenated thus. E.g., "*Standard-form contracts* are also widely used in transactions between businessmen." P.S. Atiyah, *An Introduction to the Law of Contract* 15 (3d ed. 1981).

For more on *adhesion contract,* see **adherence (A).**

standards of the industry. See **state of the art.**

stand down, in BrE, means "to step down" either literally <she stood down from the witness box> or figuratively <Tory supporters asked Margaret Thatcher to stand down before the 1990 election>.

standee. See -EE.

standing; locus standi. These synonymous TERMS OF ART mean "a position from which one may validly make a legal claim or seek to enforce a right or duty." The first is primarily AmE, and the second (a LATINISM) is commonly used in BrE. One is said to have *standing* when one's arguments on the merits of a case can be considered by an adjudicator. E.g., "The corporate interests have been largely taken care of by highly qualified lawyers acting in individual cases and by Bar Associations proposing procedural reforms that define, for example, the 'aggrieved' persons who have *standing* to object to agency orders or decisions." William O. Douglas, *Points of Rebellion* 79–80 (1970)./ "They . . . argue that no individual blind vendor or state agency would have *standing* because none has alleged a 'concrete, perceptible harm of a real, nonspeculative nature.'" *Randolph-Sheppard Vendors v. Weinberger,* 795 F.2d 90, 99 (D.C. Cir. 1986).

Joseph Vining's comments on *standing* show that its history is strikingly similar to that of many other legal NEOLOGISMS:

> The word *standing* is rather recent in the basic judicial vocabulary and does not appear to have been commonly used until the middle of [the 20th] century. No authority that I have found introduces the term with proper explanations or apologies and announces that henceforth *standing* should be used to describe who may be heard by a judge. Nor was there any sudden adoption by tacit consent. The word appears here and there, spreading very gradually with no discernible pattern. Judges and lawyers found themselves using the term and did not ask why they did so or where it came from.
>
> Joseph Vining, *Legal Identity* 55 (1978).

One of the earliest uses of the term occurred in 1877: "The mortgage and bonds under and by virtue of which the appellant claims a *standing* in court were executed by the Alabama and Chattanooga Railroad Company as a corporation." *Wallace v. Loomis,* 97 U.S. 146, 154 (1877). See ***locus standi.***

standpoint. See **viewpoint.**

standstill agreement (= an agreement to preserve the status quo) has become a commonplace phrase in reference to actions by parties involved in a legal dispute. The original *standstill agreement,* according to the *OED,* was concluded in 1931 between German and what would become Allied banking and commercial institutions, allowing Germany to postpone short-term credit repayments because of the country's severe economic plight. Shortly afterwards, the word came to be used in other banking situations—e.g.: "At this juncture the creditor banks in Chicago agreed to enter into what they term a *'standstill'* *agreement,* by the terms of which they would refrain from foreclosing on their collateral and from pressing for payment on their loans . . . ." *Lincoln Printing Co. v. Middle W. Utils. Co.,* 6 F. Supp. 663, 667 (N.D. Ill. 1934). Within a couple of decades, however, the phrase had been extended considerably beyond economic and banking contexts—e.g.: "During the course of the September 14 hearing, the parties reached a *'standstill' agreement* which had the effect, in part, of amending the prayer for relief." *Ramsburg v. American Inv. Co.,* 231 F.2d 333, 335 (7th Cir. 1956).

Star Chamber. In 16th- and early-17th-century England, the *Star Chamber* was a special equity court charged with keeping the peace by punishing libels, perjury, jury-packing, contempt of court, and conspiracies to pervert justice in any of the king's courts; it acted on private petition. Unacceptable practices such as compulsory self-accusation, unconscionable searches and seizures, and inquisitorial investigations "were among those intolerable abuses of the *Star Chamber,* which [was] brought . . . to an end at the hands of the Long Parliament in 1640." *Jones v. S.E.C.,* 298 U.S. 1, 28 (1936).

The origin of the court's name is unclear. Two explanations are current: (1) that the room in which the court sat had a ceiling decorated with gilded stars (*camera stellata, chambre d'estoiles*)—Coke's view (see 4 Inst. 66); or (2) that Jewish merchants' contracts, known as *starra,* were kept in the chamber in which the court conducted its work. Formerly, some writers conjectured that the name derived from OE. *steoran* "to steer or govern"; or from its punishing of cozenage, known as *crimen stellionatus.*

Today, the phrase *Star Chamber proceeding* usu. refers to an unfair judicial proceeding in which the outcome is predetermined.

stare decisis (L. "to stand by things decided") = the doctrine of precedent, under which it is necessary to follow earlier judicial decisions when the same points arise again in litigation. The full phrase is *stare decisis et quieta non movere* (= to stand by things decided and not disturb settled points). See **precedent (A).**

Though a verb phrase in Latin, the phrase is used as a noun phrase in English—e.g.: "The courts are actually returning more and more to a *stare decisis* of principles [that] prevailed during the earlier centuries of the law's history, as distinguished from a narrow *stare decisis* based on mere decisions." William F. Walsh, *A Treatise on Equity* iii (1930)./ "Judicial precedent has some persuasive effect almost everywhere because *stare decisis* (keep to what has been decided previously) is a maxim of practically universal application." Rupert Cross & J.W. Harris, *Precedent in English Law* 3 (4th ed. 1991).

In AmE, the phrase has even come to be used commonly as an adjectival phrase—e.g.: "The *stare decisis effect* [read *precedential effect*] of the judgment obtained by the plaintiff established as a matter of law the right of a discernible class of persons to collect upon similar claims." On the question whether to hyphenate such an adjectival use, see PHRASAL ADJECTIVES (B).

The phrase is pronounced /***stahr**-ee*/ or /***stair**-ee-də-**sɪ**-sis*/. As one might expect, judges are better at pronouncing the phrase than senators are: "One unresolved issue appeared to be the pronunciation for *'stare decisis.'* Clarence Thomas pronounced 'stare' like the word for a clear night—'starry'—while Sen. Orrin Hatch said 'stairay' and Sen. Patrick Leahy, 'star-ay.'" *Legal Lexicon,* A.B.A. J., Aug. 1993, at 44.

start. See **begin (B)** & **commence.**

state, n., = (in international law) an institutional system of relations that people within a territory establish among themselves to secure order. Brierly warns that *state* "should not be confused with the whole community of persons living on its territory; it is only one among a multitude of other institutions, such as churches and corporations, [that] a community establishes for securing different objects, though obviously it is one of tremendous importance . . . ." J.L. Brierly, *The Law of Nations* 118 (5th ed. 1955).

Within a legal system, as in the U.S., *state* may denote an institution of self-government (e.g., Vermont) within a larger entity (the United States), which can also be called a *state.* Many countries such as Canada have other political subdivisions, such as provinces; others, like England, have counties. The name chosen generally reflects the extent of the smaller entity's powers—*states* having more power than *provinces,* and *provinces* more power than *counties;* but there are no invariable rules on this point.

state action (= governmental feasance) is a phrase used in international as well as in constitutional law. E.g., "What the Crown does to foreigners by its agents is *state action* . . . beyond the scope of domestic jurisdiction." *Johnstone v. Pedlar,* 2 A.C. 262, 290 (1921) (per Lord Sumner).

In constitutional law, *state action* often appears in the context of civil rights and denotes some type of illegal governmental intrusion into a person's life. E.g., "If the State requires a certain electoral procedure, prescribes a general election ballot made up of party nominees so chosen and limits the choice of the electorate in general elections for state offices, practically speaking, to those whose names appear on such a ballot, it endorses, adopts and enforces the discrimination against Negroes . . . . This is *state action* within the meaning of the Fifteenth Amendment." *Smith v. Allwright,* 321 U.S. 649, 664 (1944). In the wake of *Smith,* the U.S. Supreme Court broadened the concept of state action to strike down segregation laws under the Fourteenth and Fifteenth Amendments.

stated. In the phrase *account stated,* the word *stated* means "settled, closed, at an end." E.g., "Norell Forest Products (Norell) sued H & S Lumber Company (H & S) on an *account stated.*" *Norell Forest Prods. v. H & S Lumber Co.,* 417 S.E.2d 96, 98 (S.C. Ct. App. 1992). The phrase is sometimes written *stated account.*

stated otherwise is a pompous version of *in other words.* E.g., "*Stated otherwise* [read *In other words*], the deduction will invariably affect the taxpayer's liability." Cf. **to put it another way.**

statehouse (= a state capitol) is an Americanism dating from the 17th century.

statement. Though to a nonlawyer the usage is counterintuitive, the word *statement* in law commonly includes expressive nonverbal behavior as well as the spoken word. For example, Rule 801(a) of the Federal Rules of Evidence defines *statement* as either "(1) an oral or written assertion or (2) nonverbal conduct of a person, if it is intended by the person as an assertion."

statement of claim is the modern BrE phrase for the plaintiff's first pleading. Formerly, at common law, it was called a *declaration.* (See **declaration.**) In the U.S., it is usu. called either a *complaint* or a *petition,* and in Scotland a *summons* or *initial writ.*

statement of facts. See **record (B)** & **report of proceedings.**

state of the art, n.; **state-of-the-art,** adj. These VOGUE WORDS illustrate the interests of a fast-changing society with rapidly produced technological innovations <state-of-the-art products>. For the moment, they are tainted by association with the cant of salespeople.

Notably, *state of the art* is distinguishable from *standards of the industry* because the former refers to that which the most advanced technology allows, as opposed to that which is in common use within an industry. See *Cantu v. John Deere Co.,* 603 P.2d 839, 840 (Wash. Ct. App. 1979) (saying, "We believe the two phrases are not synonymous . . . .").

state's evidence, to turn. See **turn state's evidence.**

states' rights (= those rights and powers not delegated to the federal government by the U.S. Constitution nor prohibited by it for the states to exercise) is so punctuated, unless used as a PHRASAL ADJECTIVE calling for a hyphen <a states'-rights argument>.

The agent noun is *states'-righter*—e.g.: "In recent times the situation has been the precise reverse, so that solid citizens are not *states'-righters* and liberals put greater faith in the federal government, even under conservative auspices." Fred Rodell, *Nine Men* 77 (1955).

stati. See **status (B).**

stationary; stationery. The former is the adjective ("remaining in one place"), the latter the noun ("materials for writing on or with").

statistic (= a single term or datum in a statistical compilation) is a BACK-FORMATION from *statistics* dating from the late 19th century. Today its correctness is beyond challenge. E.g., "When this *statistic* is considered with the massive discovery involved, and with the fact that few of the large class-action cases are ever tried, the real impact of complex litigation is seen."

statu quo, in. See ***in statu quo.***

status. A. Legal Sense. *Status* = a summation of or basis for the legal grounds of various capacities or incapacities, for example, one's age, mental state, and the like. "*Status* is . . . belonging to a particular class of persons to all of whom the law assigns particular legal powers, capacities, liabilities or incapacities . . . ." 1 David M. Walker, *Principles of Scottish Private Law* 198 (3d ed. 1982). Generally speaking, as *statuses* have been assimilated in Anglo-American law, *status* has dwindled in interest and importance as a legal topic. See D. Neil MacCormick, "General Legal Concepts," in 11 *The Laws of Scotland: Stair Memorial Encyclopedia* ¶ 1070, at 389 (1990).

B. Plural. *Status* forms the plural *statuses* (or, in Latin, *status*), not *stati:* "But this does not militate against the defendants' essential argument that while the jurors come from all socioeconomic *stati* [read *statuses*], they represent, on the whole, the higher echelons of the community as opposed to the lower." *U.S. v. Duke,* 263 F.

Supp. 828, 833–34 (S.D. Ind. 1967). See HYPERCORRECTION (A).

status quo; *status quo ante; status in quo.* *Status quo* means "the state of affairs at present"; hence *current status quo* is a REDUNDANCY. (See ***in statu quo.***) *Status quo ante* (= the state of affairs at a previous time) is a common and useful LATINISM in contexts involving torts or contracts. E.g., "The first and most obvious result of rescinding a contract is that, so far as is possible, the *status quo ante* must be restored . . . ." P.S. Atiyah, *An Introduction to the Law of Contract* 299 (3d ed. 1981)./ "[A] plaintiff's right to be restored to the *status quo ante* has always to be weighed against the duty to do what is reasonable to mitigate the cost to the defendant." R.W.M. Dias & B.S. Markesinis, *Tort Law* 428 (1984).

Status quo in the sense "the original condition" (as opposed to "the present condition") is a LEGALISM to be avoided, for lawyers as well as nonlawyers are likely to misunderstand the import. *Status in quo* is an archaic variant of *status quo.*

statutable. See **statutory.**

statute, in AmE, refers to a legislative act that the state gives the force of law. E.g., "American courts interpret the usual wording of the abortion *statutes,* quite remarkably, to prohibit the removal of a dead fetus from the mother." Glanville Williams, *The Sanctity of Life and the Criminal Law* 191 (1957; repr. 1972).

In BrE, however, *statute* bears a broader meaning: "It is common in popular and even, to some extent, in legal language to treat '*statute*' and 'Act of Parliament' as equivalent terms. That is quite incorrect. All Acts of Parliament are statutes; but [not] all statutes are . . . Acts of Parliament . . . ." Edward Jenks, *The Book of English Law* 40 (P.B. Fairest ed., 6th ed. 1967). How can that be? In G.B., *statutory instruments*—government orders akin to what in the U.S. are called "administrative regulations" and "executive orders"—are considered statutes. See **statutory instrument.**

statute book is two words—unhyphenated.

STATUTE DRAFTING. **A. Generally.** Perhaps the most sensible approach to the broad principles of drafting statutes are those of Montesquieu, who discussed the subject in *L'Esprit des Lois* (39, ch. 16):

- The style should be both concise and simple: whatever is grandiose or rhetorical should be omitted as distracting surplusage. See PLAIN LANGUAGE.
- The words chosen should be, as nearly as possible, absolute—not relative—so as to minimize differences of opinion.
- Statutes should be confined to the real and the actual, avoiding the metaphorical or hypothetical.
- They should not be subtle, but instead comprehensible to the average person.
- They should not confuse the main issue with exceptions, limitations, and modifications, unless such devices are absolutely necessary.
- They should not be argumentative: they should not give detailed reasons for their bases. (This is not to criticize general-purpose clauses, which are quite valuable.)
- They should be maturely considered and practically useful and should not shock the public sense of reason and justice.

Those goals are extraordinarily difficult to attain, and few have succeeded in attaining them. Samuel Williston (1861–1963), the author of many Uniform Acts approved by the Commissioners of Uniform State Laws between 1905 and 1920, was among those few: "Williston was one of the best statutory draftsmen who has ever worked at that mysterious art; he was the most ingenious system-builder in the history of our jurisprudence; he wrote with lucidity and grace." Grant Gilmore, *The Ages of American Law* 134 n.12 (1977). But Williston was the rare exception.

In fact, complaints about mediocre to horrible statutory drafting have echoed through the decades and centuries—e.g.:

- In 1857, Lord Campbell criticized "an ill-penned enactment, like too many others, putting Judges in the embarrassing situation of being bound to make sense out of nonsense, and to reconcile what is irreconcilable." *Fell v. Burchett,* (1857) 7 E. & B. 537, 539.
- "So unintelligible is the phraseology of some statutes that suggestions have been made that draftsmen, like the Delphic Oracle, sometimes aim deliberately at obscurity, as a disingenuous means of passing a Bill quickly through Parliament." Carleton K. Allen, *Law in the Making* 486 (7th ed. 1964).
- "Parliament has been industrious in multiplying offences, very inartistically drawn, but it is slow to remedy clear absurdities and deficiencies in the law as they come to light . . . ." Glanville Williams, *Textbook of Criminal Law* 8 (1978).
- "For over a century and a half judges have railed against incomprehensible drafting, only to be met with the bland reply that the judges are themselves to blame. The existing draftsmen are not only established but entrenched.

No other word than pathetic can describe Lord Gardiner's hope in 1971 to 'encourage' them to be simpler . . . ." J.A. Clarence Smith, *Legislative Drafting: English and Continental,* 1980 Statute L. Rev. 14, 22.

- "[T]he ultimate style and shape of much legislation is today increasingly unsatisfactory. Many statutes emerge from the parliamentary process obscure, turgid, and quite literally unintelligible without a guide or commentary." P.S. Atiyah, *Law and Modern Society* 127–28 (1983).
- "The Statute Law Society criticized the language of the statutes as: 'legalistic, often obscure and circumlocutious, requiring a certain type of expertise in order to gauge its meaning. Sentences are long and involved, the grammar is obscure, and archaisms, legally meaningless words and phrases, tortuous language, the preference for the double negative over the single positive, abound.'" Michael Zander, *The Law-Making Process* 22 (2d ed. 1985) (quoting the Report of the Renton Committee entitled *Preparation of Legislation*).

Perhaps the current state of affairs results mostly from the fact that "statutory drafting . . . [is] an insufficiently appreciated art." Rupert Cross, *Statutory Interpretation* 12 (1976). That holds as true in the U.S. as it does in Great Britain. Only someone with experience and wisdom recognizes that "[t]here is no more important, exciting, and intellectually rewarding work for a lawyer than that of drafting legislation." Glanville Williams, *Learning the Law* 214 (11th ed. 1982). The accomplished writer who tries legislative drafting will find that it taxes one's literary abilities as much as any other type of writing.

B. Choice of Words. The simplest, most concise English is the best for legislation: "The draftsman should bear in mind that his Act is supposed to be read by the plain man. In any case he may be sure that if he finds he can express his meaning in simple words all is going well with his draft, while if he finds himself driven to complicated expressions composed of long words it is a sign that he is getting lost and he should reconsider the form of the section." Alison Russell, *Legislative Drafting and Forms* 12 (4th ed. 1938). See PLAIN LANGUAGE (C).

C. Tenses Generally. In an important early work on the writing of statutes, George Coode laid down for the first time some important rules of drafting that have formed the basis for modern principles of drafting—and have been routinely ignored in practice. See George Coode, *On Legislative Expression* (1842).

The fundamental mode of expression in statutes, as worked out by Coode, is to recite facts concurrent with the statute's operation as if they were present facts, and facts precedent to the statute's operation as if they were past facts.

In elaboration of that deceptively simple statement, what follows is a modernization of Coode's precepts on the use of tenses in statutes, and especially the use of *shall* and *may.* (This adaptation paraphrases Coode as quoted in E.A. Driedger's *The Composition of Legislation,* 225–28 [1957].)

Coode recognized that much of the trouble in statute drafting originates in the use of *shall.* Proscriptions that begin "No person *shall* . . ." are inferior to those that begin "No person *may* . . ." because *shall* can be understood in two senses: simple futurity (i.e., *will*) and obligation (i.e., *must*). See WORDS OF AUTHORITY (A).

The drafter should not attempt to render every action referred to in a statute in a future tense. Some drafters erroneously assume that the words *shall* and *shall not* put the enacting verb into a future tense. Yet, in commanding, as in a statute that mandates a certain action, *shall* is modal rather than temporal. Thus it denotes compulsion—the obligation to act—not a prophecy that the person will or will not at some future time perform some act. The commandment "Thou shalt not murder" is not a prediction; it is obligatory in the present tense, continuously through all the time of the law's operation.

Likewise, when the verb *may* is used, the expression is not of a future possibility; instead, it is of permission and authority. The statement, "The chair *may canvass* committee members," means that the chair *is authorized to canvass* the committee members.

Yet, because the legal action referred to in a statute is sometimes—when *shall* is used—supposed to be in the future tense, drafters often attempt (for the sake of consistency) to express the circumstances that are required to precede the operation of the statute (i.e., all conditions) in the future or future perfect tenses. Thus, in poor drafting language, one frequently finds the following expressions:

- If any person *shall give* [read *gives*] notice, he *may* appeal . . . .
- If the commissioners *shall instruct* [read *instruct*] by any order . . . .
- All elections *shall* [read *must*] hereafter, so far as the commissioners *shall direct* [read *direct*] . . . .
- In case any person *shall willfully neglect or disobey* [read *willfully neglects or disobeys*] . . . .
- When such notice *shall have been published* [read *is published*] . . . .

• If any balance *shall have been found* [read *is found*] to be due . . . .

The fear that gives rise to this use of *shall* is that, if the condition for operation of the statute were expressed in the present tense (i.e., when any person is aggrieved), the law would be contemporaneous and would operate *only* on conditions that are met at the moment when the statute is enacted. Likewise, some drafters wrongly assume that if a statute were expressed in the present-perfect tense (i.e., when any person has been convicted), the law would be retrospective and would apply *only* to convictions that took place before the act was passed.

These apprehensions are mistaken. An elementary rule of statutory construction is that past tenses never give retrospective effect to a statute unless the intention for retrospectivity is clearly and distinctly framed in words to that effect. Any number of statutes are written in the present or present-perfect tense but still are interpreted prospectively only.

If the law is regarded, while it remains in force, as *constantly speaking,* then a simple two-part rule will serve to guide those who draft statutes:

1. Use the *present tense* to express all facts and conditions required to be concurrent with the operation of the legal action. E.g., "If by reason of the largeness of parishes the inhabitants *cannot* reap the benefits of this Act, two or more overseers *must be chosen.*" (The first clause in this conditional sentence is in the present tense; the main clause that follows contains obligatory language still in the present tense.) See WORDS OF AUTHORITY (A) & (D).
2. Use the *present perfect tense* to express all facts and conditions required as precedents to the legal action. E.g., "When the justices of the peace of any county *assembled* at quarter sessions *have agreed* that the ordinary peace officers *are* not sufficient to preserve the peace, the justices *may* appoint a chief constable." (The left-branching dependent clauses contain verbs in the past perfect [*assembled, have agreed*] to indicate necessary precedent conditions that now exist [*are*] and thus make legal action possible; the main clause is in the present [permissive] tense to indicate the specific legal action that is open to the justices of the peace.)

D. *Each, any, all, no* (etc.). See ADJECTIVES (G).

statute law. See **statutory law.**

statute-making is hyphenated thus.

statute of frauds. A. Senses. In 1677, Lord Nottingham (1621–1682) drafted the original Statute of Frauds, the best known act prescribing written formalities for some contracts. (In references to that original act, the words should have initial capitals.) It declared that certain contracts would be judicially unenforceable (but not void) if not committed to writing. Most Anglo-American jurisdictions have statutes modeled in some way on the original.

In BrE, the phrase *statute of frauds* also sometimes refers to an act affording relief against debtors who transfer assets to defraud or foil creditors.

B. *Within* (or *without*) *the statute of frauds.* These idioms, though fairly common, confuse even veteran lawyers. *Within the statute of frauds* = violative of the statute of frauds, i.e., within its coverage. E.g., "Oral promises to a creditor to answer for the debt or default of another are not *within the statute of frauds* where the promisor is already otherwise obligated, irrespective of his promise, to perform such duty." Laurence P. Simpson, *Handbook on the Law of Suretyship* 128 (1950). *Without the statute of frauds* = not violative of the statute.

statute of limitation(s) = a statute that establishes a time limit for suing or for prosecuting a crime. Either *statute of limitations* or *statutes of limitation* is idiomatic and correct. *Statute of limitations* is often made into the elliptical form *limitations:* "The court ruled that *limitations* were tolled for all 809 workers during the time that elapsed between the date suit was filed and the date the trial court denied class certification." (Cf. the English quotation under **run.**) See **repose, laches** (C) & **limitation.** See also **time-bar** & **toll.**

statute of repose. See **repose.**

statutorial. See **statutory** (A).

statutorification (= the excessive reliance upon legislation to cure society's ills) is a NEOLOGISM invented by Guido Calabresi, the dean of Yale Law School in the 1980s and 1990s. It is an ugly word for an ugly process—e.g.: "The '*statutorification*' of American law is not the only reason for these varied proposals and events." Guido Calabresi, *A Common Law for the Age of Statutes* 1 (1982)./ "Guido Calabresi has written a provocative book about the '*statutorification*' of American law, a neologism intended to be as ugly as the condition it describes." Dan Rosen, *A Common Law for the Ages of Intellectual Property,* 38 U. Miami L. Rev. 769, 770 (1984).

statutorily, not *statutorally,* is the correct adverbial form: "Thereafter McGlothin continued to wear a headdress, but only when she felt like it, until her dismissal for insubordination *statutorally* [read *statutorily*] defined as 'misconduct.'" *Mississippi Employment Sec. Comm'n v. McGlothin,* 556 So. 2d 324, 332 (Miss. 1990).

statutory. A. And *statutorial.* *Statutory* = (1) of or relating to legislation <statutory construction>; (2) legislatively created <the law of patents is purely statutory>; or (3) conformable to a statute <a statutory course of conduct>.

Statutorial is a NEEDLESS VARIANT not recognized in the dictionaries. E.g., "The hardship driving *statutorial* [read *statutory*] procedure, as interpreted in *Munson,* leaves a hole literally [q.v.] wide enough to drive any motorized vehicle through, calling for swift action by the General Assembly." *Burns v. Director of Revenue,* 784 S.W.2d 918, 919 (Mo. Ct. App. 1990).

The adverb *statutorily* is not infrequently rendered, by mistake, *statutorially* or *statutorally.* See **statutorily.**

B. And *statutable.* *Statutable* = (1) prescribed, authorized, or permitted by statute; (2) conformed to statutory requirements for quality, size, or amount; or (3) (of an offense) legally punishable (*OED*). Thus, *statutable* overlaps to a significant degree with the more usual word, *statutory.* In the 19th-century specimen that follows, *statutable* is used in a context in which *statutory* would inevitably appear today: "But there are express *statuteable* provisions, which directly apply to the present case." *Gelston v. Hoyt,* 16 U.S. (3 Wheat.) 246, 311 (1818). As in the preceding quotation, the word has occasionally been spelled *statuteable,* but that spelling is inferior. See MUTE E.

statutory charge. Copperud has observed that in lay parlance *statutory rape,* a precise term, has been stretched into phrases such as *statutory charge* or *statutory offense.* See Roy Copperud, *American Usage and Style* 363 (1980). These phrases are sometimes considered illogical, inasmuch as criminal offenses or charges are invariably statutorily defined or codified. But in some jurisdictions, such as Scotland, major crimes such as murder and theft are still defined by the common law only. So the phrase *statutory charge* may be quite sound, if it is used to dispel the possibility that one is referring to a common-law crime.

statutory construction. See **interpretation.**

statutory enactment is a REDUNDANCY for *statute,* and the word *enactment* is used loosely in this phrase. E.g., "This article is designed to cover general principles relating to *statutory enactments* [read *statutes*]." See **enactment.** Cf. **statutory legislation.**

statutory instrument, in BrE, refers to a government order similar to an executive order or agency regulation in the U.S. E.g., "The most important kind of legislation is the Act of Parliament (otherwise called a statute), though nowadays what is called delegated legislation, like the many government orders generally known as *statutory instruments,* has come to be of great importance as well." Glanville Williams, *Learning the Law* 24 (11th ed. 1982). See **statute.** Cf. **instrument.**

statutory law; statute law. Both forms appear in AmE, but the former is the more common. In BrE, *statute law* (preferably unhyphenated except as a PHRASAL ADJECTIVE) is the predominant form.

In some contexts, the phrases are not entirely synonymous. *Statute law* has two meanings: (1) "a law contained in a statute"; or (2) "the system of law and body of principles laid down in statutes, as distinct from the common law." *Statutory law* shares sense (2) with *statute law* but not sense (1).

statutory legislation is a REDUNDANCY—e.g.: "The distinction between the content of constitutional law and that of ordinary *statutory legislation* [read *legislation*] is largely one of degree and in the States of the American Union this distinction is fast disappearing." James W. Garner, "Law, Constitutional," in 17 *Encyclopedia Americana* 96–100 [page so numbered], 101 (1953)./ "In my view, the plain meaning of 'manslaughter' as used in early *statutory legislation* [read *statutes* or *legislation*] did not contemplate the offense of 'involuntary manslaughter' . . . ." *Morris v. U.S.,* 648 A.2d 958, 964 (D.C. Ct. App. 1994) (Mack, J., dissenting). Cf. **statutory enactment.**

statutory rape (= sexual intercourse with a person below the age of consent, regardless of whether it occurs against his or her will) is an Americanism that originated in the 19th century. Originally, statutory-rape laws applied only to female victims, but today the great majority of American states have sex-neutral legislation dealing with this offense. The term is a popular one, not a statutory one. See **rape.**

staunch; stanch. *Staunch* is preferable as the adjective ("trustworthy, loyal"), *stanch* as the verb ("to restrain the flow of [usu. blood]").

stay, n. & v.t. In law, *stay* means either (1) "postponement" or (2) "the order suspending a judicial proceeding or the judgment resulting from that proceeding" <stay of the mandate> <the court's stay of execution>.

Although the verb *to stay* is usually intransitive in lay contexts <he stayed awhile>, it is transitive in its legal senses: (1) to postpone, usu. until the court determines a contested issue <to stay the mandate>; or (2) to halt <to stay waste>. E.g., (Sense 1) "Filing of the petition under Chapter 11 automatically *stayed* the proposed sale to enforce the maritime lien."/ (Sense 2) "An injunction to *stay* waste may be granted in favor of one who is entitled to a contingent or executory estate of inheritance." See **continue.**

stayable (= capable of being legally postponed or halted) is a legal NEOLOGISM not recorded in the *OED, W3,* or most other dictionaries. E.g., "[J]udgments in actions for injunctions . . . are not *stayable* as of right." 9 James Moore et al., *Moore's Federal Practice* par. 208.04, at 8-11 (1987).

stay law (= a statute that suspends execution or some other legal procedure) is a 19th-century Americanism. E.g., "No advantage to be taken of *stay laws* or injunctions, & c." *Coe v. Pennock,* 5 F. Cas. 1172, 1172 (C.C.N.D. Ohio 1857) (No. 2,942)./ "I believe it was once held that a *stay-law* passed after a note was given could not affect that debt . . . ; but where the law is passed before the debt is created, a *stay-law* is good in every State." 2 Cong. Rec. 1,226 (5 Feb. 1874) (statement of Sen. Oliver P. Morton).

stay of execution = the suspending of the operation of a court's judgment or order. In lay parlance, the phrase usu. appears in reference to a death sentence, but not in legal parlance.

In the following example, Judge Learned Hand employed a variation on the phrase: "[T]he judge sentenced him to not less than five years nor more than ten, *execution to be stayed,* and the defendant to be placed on probation . . . ." *Repouille v. U.S.,* 165 F.2d 152, 153 (2d Cir. 1947).

ste(a)dfast. The preferred spelling is *steadfast.*

steal has a narrow and a broad sense. It may mean (narrowly) "to obtain by larceny" or (broadly) "to obtain by any one of the three principal forms of theft—embezzlement, false pretenses, or larceny. See **rob & embezzle.**

steamroll(er), v.t. The longer form of this verb is the preferred, except (oddly) in the *-ing* participle. E.g., "Theoretically, the inquisition model will produce more information than one premised upon heavy incentives to advance one's position and can prevent a wealthier opponent from *steamrolling* his adversary."

stedfast. See **ste(a)dfast.**

stereotypic(al). The longer form is preferred in figurative senses. E.g., "In *City of Thomas,* the Ninth Circuit recognized that constitutional concerns are heightened by any classification scheme singling out former mental patients for differential treatment because of the possibility that the scheme will implement inaccurate *stereotypic* [read *stereotypical*] fears about former mental patients." *Stereotypic* is the better form for the narrow sense "of or produced by stereotypy (the process of printing from stereotype plates)."

sterility; impotence. The first refers to the inability to procreate, the second to the inability to copulate.

stigma. Pl. *-mas, -mata.* As with many other such words, the English plural (*-mas*) is preferable. See PLURALS (A).

stimulus. Pl. *-li.* Unlike *stigma,* this word does not make a native-English plural. See PLURALS (A).

stipe is English slang for a *stipendiary magistrate* (= a salaried magistrate who is a lawyer appointed by the Lord Chancellor to hear small claims and minor criminal cases such as those heard by [unsalaried] justices of the peace).

stipital. See **stirpital.**

stipulate = (1) (of an agreement) to specify (something) as an essential part of the contract; (2) (of a party to an agreement) to require or insist upon (something) as an essential condition; or (3) to make express demand *for* something as a condition of an agreement.

This verb belongs to the language of contracts, and is not felicitously transported into contexts involving statutes, where it becomes a substitute for *provide.* E.g., "The statute *stipulates* [read *provides*] that any cause of action under this subsection must be brought before the court within two years."/ "The original statute *stipulated* [read *provided*] that parents must leave a portion of their wealth to their progeny . . . ." Frances Marcus, *Does Napoleonic Law Have Future in Louisiana?* N.Y. Times, 1 Dec. 1989, at 27.

Nor has the verb traditionally meant "(of counsel) to reach an agreement about business before a court," although this extension of contractual sense is not uncommon in American trial practice: "The relevant facts *are stipulated.*" *U.S. v. National Bank of Commerce,* 472 U.S. 713, 715 (1985)./ "The district court adopted a plan, *stipulated to* by the Ector County school district and by the United States but forcefully objected to by the plaintiff-intervenors."/ "This organization appeals the district court's adoption of the *stipulated* plan."

stipulative; stipulatory; stipulational. The first two are distinct. *Stipulative* = that stipulates or specifies as an essential condition <a stipulative definition>. *Stipulatory* = of or relating to (a) stipulation <a stipulatory engagement for the debt>.

Stipulational is a late 20th-century AmE NEOLOGISM—and it is a NEEDLESS VARIANT of *stipulatory:* "The facts which were thus given *stipulational* [read *stipulatory*] establishment were that the injury to plaintiff had occurred at the Roberts Theater . . . ." *Chenette v. Trustees of Iowa College,* 431 F.2d 49, 51 (8th Cir. 1970).

stirpes. See **stirps.**

stirpital; stipital. The preferred adjectival form of *stirps* (= branch of a family), used in reference to a per stirpes distribution, is *stirpital. Black's* (4th & 5th eds.) listed only *stipital* as the correct form, but changed to *stirpital* in the 6th edition (1990). *W3* defines *stipital* as "of or relating to the stipes," *stipes* being a botanical or zoological term meaning "peduncle" or, less commonly, "stirps." *W3* does not, however, include *stirpital.* And *Words and Phrases* contains *stirpital* but not *stipital.* The *OED* records *stirpital,* noting that it is ill-formed and should be *stirpal* if properly Latinized, and dates it from 1886 with the following quotation: "A division of the proceeds of sale per stirpes is more in accordance than a division per capita with the original *stirpital* division of the income." The *OED* does not contain *stipital.*

Stirpital is by far the more prevalent word—e.g.: "Counsel for the defendant Nolan, as an alternative claim, suggest the application of the doctrine of *stirpital* survivorship . . . ." *State Bank & Trust Co. v. Nolan,* 130 A. 483, 489 (Conn. 1925)./ "Some courts, on the other hand, take a position contrary, or at least in opposition, to the foregoing . . . *stirpital* distribution." 57 Am. Jur. *Wills* § 1292 (1948)./ "This analysis does not result in a consistently *stirpital* distribution of the settled fund as one might have expected." *Re Drummond's Settlement,* [1988] 1 All E.R. 449, 453 (1987).

Though it has the approval of some dictionaries, *stipital* is rarely encountered—e.g.: "Considering the circumstances it may be inferred that it would have been impracticable for the testator to have designated his half brothers as *stipital* progenitors . . . ." *Theopold v. Sears,* 258 N.E.2d 559, 561 (Mass. 1970).

With all due respect to *Black's* and *W3, stirpital* must be deemed better than *stipital* as the adjective of *per stirpes.* Most lawyers know the term *per stirpes* and understand *stirpital* if they hear or read it; *stipital* is another matter. And if a legal term is obscure to lawyers, what hope is there for the nonlawyer?

Then again, in most contexts the phrase *per stirpes* might be used where an adjective is called for <per stirpes distribution>. The phrase *per stirpital,* however, is a needless hybrid: In *Mercantile Trust Co. v. Davis,* 522 S.W.2d 798 (Mo. 1975) (en banc), the court quotes a lower court as having used *per stirpital* and attaches *sic* to the phrase (at 803), and then uses the phrase itself (at 805): "[T]his court reversed and ordered a *per stirpital* [read *per stirpes*] distribution to be made . . . ."/ "The Uniform Probate Code § 2-106 requires per capita distribution among surviving heirs in the nearest degree with *per stirpital* [read *per stirpes*] distribution among those entitled to take but who are in a more remote degree."

stirps. Pl. *stirpes.*

stochastic. See **aleatory.**

stock; shares. *Stock* = (1) the capital or principal fund raised by a corporation through subscribers' contributions or the sale of shares; (2) the proportional part of this capital credited to an individual shareholder and represented by the number of units he or she owns; or (3) the goods that a merchant has on hand.

Whereas *stock* is a mass noun, *shares* is a count noun closely related to sense (2) of *stock. Shares* = the units of capital that represent an ownership interest in a corporation or in its equity. See COUNT NOUNS AND MASS NOUNS.

stockholder. See **shareholder** & **stakeholder.**

stole, took, and carried away. The traditional phrasing of a larceny charge, these words are "clearly an old form derived from the simplest type of stealing, and [were] made the basis of the theory that larceny is a violation of possession." Theodore F.T. Plucknett, *A Concise History of the Common Law* 448 (5th ed. 1956). The phrase *carried away* met the requirement of alleging that an asportation had taken place. See **asportation.**

stone, etched in. This is a SET PHRASE. Variants such as *carved in stone, cast in concrete, cast in cement,* and the illogical *cast in stone* ought to be avoided.

stop-and-frisk rule = the American constitutional doctrine (announced in *Terry v. Ohio,* 392 U.S. 1 (1968)) that a police officer may, with neither a warrant nor probable cause, stop and search a person for concealed weapons. The PHRASAL ADJECTIVE should be hyphenated whatever the noun may be: *stop-and-frisk law, stop-and-frisk doctrine,* etc.

straitjacket; straightjacket. *Straightjacket* is a common error for *straitjacket*—e.g.: "Therefore no one should be able to put him in a *straightjacket* [read *straitjacket*] as to his method . . . ." *Redevelopment Agency v. Mitsui Inv., Inc.,* 522 P.2d 1370, 1373 (Utah 1974)./ "[W]e do not wish to put a *straightjacket* [read *straitjacket*] on the creative development of new forms of alternative dispute resolution . . . ." *Annapolis Professional Firefighters v. City of Annapolis,* 642 A.2d 889, 895 n.6 (Md. Ct. Spec. App. 1994).

straitlaced (= prudish, rigidly narrow in moral matters) referred originally, in the 16th century, to a tightly laced corset—*strait* meaning "narrow" or "closely fitting." Over time, writers have forgotten the etymology and have confused *strait* with *straight.* Hence the erroneous form *straightlaced*—e.g.:

- "In former days, a bootlegger would much rather trust his fate to a *straightlaced* [read *straitlaced*] prohibitionist minister than to a former saloonkeeper." *Local 36, Int'l Fishermen & Allied Workers v. U.S.,* 177 F.2d 320, 341 (9th Cir. 1949).
- "The standards of 'the Block' (an area in Baltimore in which there are a number of shops [that] deal with pornographic materials) are not the standards to be applied in this case, any more than the standards of the most *straightlaced* [read *straitlaced*] persons." *U.S. v. Womack,* 509 F.2d 368, 380 (D.C. Cir. 1972).
- "The court finds that the plaintiff is *'straightlaced'* [read *straitlaced*] and professional in her work." *Fox v. Ravinia Club, Inc.,* 761 F. Supp. 797, 799 (N.D. Ga. 1991).
- "Frankfort told [the plaintiff] not to tell Howard Moore, the Executive Vice President . . . of Purchasing, as he was very *straight-laced* [read *straitlaced*] and a family man . . . ." *T.L v. Toys 'R' Us, Inc.,* 605 A.2d 1125, 1128 (N.J. Super. Ct. 1992).

stranger, in law, means (1) "one not a privy or party to an act" <a stranger to the contract>; or (2) "one not standing toward another in some relation implied in the context" <the trustee was dealing with a stranger>.

stratagem. So spelled—but *strategem,* on the analogy of *strategy,* is a common misspelling. Though etymologically related, the words *stratagem* and *strategy* came into English by different routes, and their spellings diverged merely as a matter of long-standing convention.

stratum. Although the Latin plural *strata* is thoroughly established, some writers ill-advisedly experiment with an anglicized plural—e.g.: "They say nothing concerning depths, levels or *stratums* [read *strata*]." *Rogers v. Westhoma Oil Co.,* 291 F.2d 726, 732 (10th Cir. 1961) (Bratton, J., dissenting). See PLURALS (A).

straw man, lit. "a scarecrow made of straw," has come to mean primarily a fictitious person—always conveniently weak or flawed—used as a seeming adversary in an argument. A *straw-man argument* is easily overcome by the advocate who invents it as a foil to his or her own argument. See SEXISM (B).

stray. See **estray** & **waifs and (e)strays.**

stricken, though common as a past participle in much legal writing, is considered by the better authorities to be inferior to *struck.* It is an ARCHAISM in all but the adjectival sense <a stricken community>. Most modern uses of *stricken* occur as the ill-advised past participle, though: "Had George been suddenly *stricken* [read *struck*] blind instead of having become afflicted with an abdominal illness, the circumstances determining whether the attestation took place in his presence would have been no different."/ "Appellant also argues that the special term of parole authorized by 21 U.S.C. § 841(b)(1)(a) is unconstitutional, and should be *stricken* [read *struck*] from his sentence."/ "The government had not produced the criminal record of this witness, and Jennings therefore moved that the witness's testimony be *stricken* [read *struck*] and the jury instructed to disregard the testimony of the witness for failure to comply with the court's order."

The participial usage has given rise to the mistaken use of *stricken* for *strike* as a present-tense verb. E.g., "The law does not provide a remedy for every ill that may *stricken* [read *strike*] a community."/ "When such a tragedy *strickens* [read *strikes*] a community, the people must rely upon each other to a degree otherwise never realized." *Stricken* is sometimes used as a preterit in the guise of an adjective. E.g., "He has not shown that the striking was in fact premised on a determination of the merits of the allegation [that was] *stricken* [read *struck*]." See **strike (A).**

strict construction; strict constructionism. *Strict construction* refers to the literal construction of constitutions, statutes, contracts, and the like. E.g., "*Strict construction* of a statute is that which refuses to expand the law by implications or equitable considerations, but confines its operation to cases which are clearly within the letter of the statute, as well as within its spirit or reason, not so as to defeat the manifest purpose of the Legislature, but so as to resolve all reasonable doubts against the applicability of the statute to the particular case." William M. Lile et al., *Brief Making and the Use of Law Books* 343 (3d ed. 1914)./ "And the Constitution alone could not serve to quiet these misgivings, for, as the warring camps soon discovered, it could be cited on either side, depending on whether a '*strict construction*' or a 'loose construction' were adopted." Robert G. McCloskey, *The American Court* 29 (1960).

Strict constructionism denotes the doctrine that courts should interpret statutory and constitutional words strictly according to the letter, without considering their "spirit" or "tenor," lest the judges begin unpredictably to imbue statutes and constitutions with their own biases. E.g., "A judge or scholar who embraces a literalist theory (which is also referred to as '*strict constructionism*') relies on an analysis of the words and phrases of the Constitution and an analysis of the overall structure of government as ordained by the concepts of separation of powers and checks and balances in determining what the Constitution sanctions and what it forbids." Barbara H. Craig, *Chadha: The Story of an Epic Constitutional Struggle* 93 (1988).

The phrase has, unfortunately, acquired connotations that may limit its utility in some contexts. As one commentator observes, *strict construction* has—at least since the 1960s—been used to signal "a proclivity to reach constitutional judgments that will please political conservatives." John H. Ely, *Democracy and Distrust* 1 n.* (1980). Cf. **interpretivism.**

One who adheres to the doctrine of *strict constructionism* is known, not surprisingly, as a *strict constructionist.* E.g., "It sounds to me like a voice from the past . . . . It is the voice of the *strict constructionist.*" *Nothman v. Barnet Council,* [1978] 1 W.L.R. 220, 228 (per Denning, M.R.). See **original intent.**

strictest sense of the word, in the. See WORD-PATRONAGE & ***stricto sensu.***

stricti juris; strictissimi juris. The first phrase means "strictly according to the law, esp. as opposed to equity." The second, a stronger phrase, means "most strictly according to the law." These LATINISMS, as infrequently used in modern contexts, are not easily simplified—e.g.: "But this privilege or lien . . . is a secret one; it may operate to the prejudice of general creditors and purchasers without notice; it is therefore '*stricti juris,*' and cannot be extended by construction, analogy, or inference." Grant Gilmore & Charles L. Black, Jr., *The Law of Admiralty* 633 (2d ed. 1975).

strict liability; absolute liability; liability without fault. Among these broadly synonymous phrases, meaning "liability that does not depend upon actual negligence or intent to harm," *strict liability* is the most common term in both AmE and BrE. The second and third phrases were formerly common, and are still occasionally used.

In some contexts, legal writers distinguish between *strict* and *absolute liability.* L.B. Curzon, for example, differentiates between the *absolute-liability school of thought,* which views intent as being irrelevant in tort—a school represented by Holdsworth—and the *strict-liability school of thought,* which views intent as being minimally relevant in tort—a school represented by Winfield. See L.B. Curzon, *English Legal History* 254 (2d ed. 1979). But Winfield himself seems to have made no such distinction in sense—only in the choice of words: "Liability, then, we suggest, was never absolute . . . . It remains to add that the description of the rule in *Rylands v. Fletcher* as an example of absolute liability in tort is unhappy in view of some half dozen exceptions . . . [that] are admitted as qualifications of it. 'Strict liability' seems to be a better term." Percy H. Winfield, *The Myth of Absolute Liability,* 42 Law Q. Rev. 37, 46, 51 (1926).

strictly construe. See **strict construction.**

stricto sensu (= in the strict sense) is an unjustifiable LATINISM. E.g., "The category of defendant is not limited to manufacturers *stricto sensu* [read *in the strict sense*] either." R.W.M. Dias & B.S. Markesinis, *Tort Law* 103 (1984). The phrase is often translated into English—a fine practice: "As long as the principles of equity were administered by separate courts, questions of equity jurisdiction were often considered, *in the strict sense,* jurisdictional."

strict scrutiny = the standard of review that federal courts apply in equal-protection cases involving the constitutionality of governmental classifications that either are based on race or infringe fundamental constitutional rights. To pass muster, a challenged governmental action must be "closely related to a compelling governmental interest." This standard is the toughest of the three levels of scrutiny applied by federal courts—*ordinary scrutiny* and *heightened scrutiny* being the least tough and the intermediate levels. Few statutes survive a constitutional challenge judged by the standard of strict scrutiny.

Though this phrase did not emerge as a legal standard of appellate constitutional review until the mid-20th century, in *Skinner v. Oklahoma,* 316 U.S. 535 (1942), it first appeared much earlier, in *The Federalist Papers:* "And who is there that will either take the trouble or incur the odium of a *strict scrutiny* into the secret springs of the transaction?" *The Federalist* No. 70, at 428 (Alexander Hamilton) (Clinton Rossiter ed., 1961).

stride > strode > stridden. The past participle *stridden* is rare; *strode* is a variant past-participial form.

strike, vb. **A. Senses.** This word has more than 100 senses, all told. Among the important law-related senses are these: (1) (v.i.) of an employee or employees, to refuse to continue to work (at a workplace) until certain demands have been met <the employees struck for three days before a settlement was reached>; (2) (v.t.) of an employee or employees, to engage in a strike against <the steelworkers struck the Indiana Harbor Works>; (3) (v.t.) to reject (a veniremember) by a peremptory challenge <the prosecution then struck several blacks, thereby raising a *Batson* issue>; or (4) (v.t.) to expunge, as from a record <motion to strike>.

B. *Strike* for *strike down*. When a court invalidates a statute, it is best to write that the court *strikes it down.* E.g., "While the Rule against Perpetuities normally operates to *strike down* only the remote contingent interest, this interest may be so integral a part of the plan of distribution that the settlor or testator would have preferred a complete failure of the entire transfer."

Strike as a lone verb has so many other meanings that making it more precise in this context is desirable. "The Court *strikes* [read *strikes down*] Alaska's distribution scheme, purporting to rely solely upon the Equal Protection Clause of the Fourteenth Amendment." *Strike* yields *struck* for both its past tense and its past participle. *Stricken* is archaic as a past participle, and should be reserved only for adjectival uses <a stricken man>; <stricken with polio>. See **stricken.**

strike suit, in colloquial legal parlance, refers to a suit filed not because the courts are likely to think it meritorious but because the defendant seems likely to settle favorably regardless of the weakness of the plaintiff's case. E.g., "Of course it is error to deny trial when there is a genuine dispute of facts; but it is just as much error—perhaps more in cases of hardship, or where impetus is given to *strike suits*—to deny or postpone judgment where the ultimate legal result is clearly indicated." *Arnstein v. Porter,* 154 F.2d 464, 480 (2d Cir. 1946) (Clark, J., dissenting). Most specifically, *strike suits* are generally shareholder derivative actions begun "with the hope of winning large attorney's fees or private settlements, and with no intention of benefiting the corporation on behalf of which suit is theoretically brought." Note, *Security for Expenses Litigation,* 52 Colum. L. Rev. 267, 267 (1952).

strive > strove > striven. The past tense seems to cause the most trouble—e.g.: "Negotiators *strived* [read *strove*] to get South African power-sharing talks back on track." Wall St. J., 20 May 1991, at A1.

struck. See **stricken.**

stultify (now "to make stupid or cause to appear foolish") formerly meant "to attempt to prove one's own mental incapacity." E.g., "Dr. Johnson seemed much surprized [*sic*] that such a suit was admitted by Scottish law, and observed that in England no man is allowed to *stultify* himself." (Eng.) The term is now used in British legal writing of a witness who, e.g., casts doubt on his own account of a remark alleged to have been overheard by him by admitting that he was too far away to hear it. See Sidney L. Phipson, *The Law of Evidence* 394 (8th ed. 1959). See **self-stultification.**

The word is sometimes misunderstood as being synonymous with the verb *to disgrace* or *dishonor.* Nor is it equivalent to *retard* or *emasculate*—e.g.: "To hold that the Commission had no alternative in this proceeding but to approve the proposed transaction would be to *stultify* [read *weaken* or *enfeeble?*] the administrative process."

stupefy. So spelled; *stupify* is a fairly common misspelling—e.g.: "If a man, in order to cause a woman to succumb to his wishes, *stupifies* [read *stupefies*] her by drugs . . . , then of course she does not consent . . . ." Glanville Williams, *Textbook of Criminal Law* 520 (1978). Cf. **rarefy.**

stupid. See **ignorant.**

style = (1) in AmE and BrE, a case name <the style of the case>; (2) in BrE, the name or title of a person <royal style and titles>; and (3) in Scots law, a model form or precedent of a deed or pleading (*OCL*). For non-Scottish equivalents of sense (3), see **precedent (E).**

STYLE. See LEGAL WRITING STYLE.

STYLE, WORDS OF. See TERMS OF ART.

stylish; stylistic. *Stylish* = in style, in vogue. *Stylistic* = having to do with style (of general application); in the appropriate style (of music).

stymie; stymy. This verb, originally a golf term meaning "to obstruct," is best spelled *stymie*—even in the inflected form *stymieing.* (See VOWEL CLUSTERS.) E.g., "Commentators had argued that greater attention should be paid to this potential solution to the *stymieing* of joinder."

suability. Though *suable* (q.v.) appeared in the 17th century, the noun *suability* began as an Americanism (first used, as far as documentation reveals, by Chief Justice John Jay in 1798) and has remained so. Jay's 18th-century assessment remains valid today: "*Suability* and *suable* are words not in common use, but they concisely and correctly convey the idea annexed to them" (quoted in *OED*). E.g., Mary Q. Kelly, *Workmen's Compensation and Employer Suability,* 5 St. Mary's L.J. 818 (1974).

suable. The adjective *suable* has existed from the early 17th century. At times it means "capable of being sued" <a suable party>, at other times "capable of being sued out [i.e., enforced]" <a suable writ>. E.g., (Sense 1) "The Supreme Court has held that unincorporated labor unions are *suable* in their own names in the Federal courts for violation of the Anti-Trust Act . . . ." Charles E. Hughes, *The Supreme Court* 234 (1928; repr. 1966)./ (Sense 2) "The principal contracts known to the common law and *suable* in the King's Courts, a century after the Conquest, were suretyship and debt." Oliver W. Holmes, *The Common Law* 289 (1881; repr. 1963).

sua sponte /***soo*-ə-*spon*-*tee***/ (= on its own motion; without prompting) is ordinarily used in reference to courts, esp. in AmE. Usually, the LATINISM is readily translatable—e.g.: "It is the duty of a court to take notice *sua sponte* [read *on its own motion*] when it lacks jurisdiction, even though the question is not raised by the contending parties."

In the sentence that follows, the phrase is used illogically: "The court, *sua sponte,* granted defendant's motion for summary judgment." If there was a motion by the defendant before the court, then the court could not have granted it *sua sponte.*

The Latin, it must be remembered, means literally "on his or its own motion." Thus it is probably wrong for the courts to use this phrase in reference to their own actions, as here: "*Sua sponte* we note that the same problem exists in this case as existed in *Reyes* . . . ." *State v. White,* 706 P.2d 1331, 1333 (Haw. Ct. App. 1985). The phrase should have been entirely omitted in that sentence. The phrase may acceptably be used with a plural noun—e.g.: "*Courts* should not, *sua sponte,* take up waivable rights not asserted by the parties." The phrase is sometimes misspelled *sua sponti.*

SUB-. Legal writers are fond of *sub-* words. This fondness often manifests itself in fussy distinctions drawn as analogues to *subcontract* and *subheading* (e.g., *subcategory, subissue, subaspect, subagent, subbuyer*). The only adequate description of such forms is substandard. E.g., "There are several distinct *subaspects* of the doctrine."/ "These cases on waiver present two distinct *subissues.*" Surely there is a better way of saying that there are two issues within a broad issue, or more than one aspect within a broad aspect; words like *issue* and *aspect* are abstract enough without allowing them to become more so with prefixed forms. See ABSTRACTITIS.

The height of the fetish for this prefix consists in *subsub-*, illustrated in the following examples: "[T]he charter party was executed in the United States between the *subsubcharterer,* American corporation, and subcharterer, Liberian corporation . . . ." *Cardinal Shipping Corp. v. M/S Seisho Maru,* 744 F.2d 461, 462 syl. 1 (5th Cir. 1984)./ "Nor is it sufficient that Lake City, a *subsubagent,* might ordinarily have relied upon a subagent . . . to collect and forward funds due . . . ." *Lake City Stevedores, Inc. v. East West Shipping Agencies, Inc.,* 474 F.2d 1060, 1064 (5th Cir. 1973)./ "In September 1985, Peoples Construction Company . . . , a subcontractor, for a construction project in Foster City, California, hired Matson as a plastering *subsubcontractor* for that project." *Matson Plastering Co. v. Plasterers & Shophands Local No. 66,* 852 F.2d 1200, 1201 (9th Cir. 1988). The device, though inelegant, saves a little space and lends greater precision to some contexts.

subaspect. See SUB-.

sub-bidder should be spelled thus, with the hyphen.

subcontract (= a contract made by a party to another contract [*main contract* or *head contract*] for carrying it out, or a part of it) is now in common usage, though some judges have objected to it—e.g.: "Being of the opinion that *subcontract* is a malapropism, we prefer to use the phrase *contracting out* or *contract out.*" *International Union v. Webster Elec. Co.,* 299 F.2d 195, 197 n.2 (7th Cir. 1962).

subcontractor is not hyphenated.

subcontractual is the adjective corresponding to *subcontract,* q.v. E.g., "[R]ecord evidence suggests that Local 829 had no way of knowing the existence of *subcontractual* arrangements on particular shows." *United Scenic Artists v. NLRB,* 655 F.2d 1267, 1270 (D.C. Cir. 1981)./ "An exculpatory clause . . . is not an uncommon occurrence in instances in which a prime contractor with the federal government establishes a *subcontractual* relationship with other companies." *Atlantic States Constr., Inc. v. Hand, Arendall, Bedsole, Greaves & Johnston,* 892 F.2d 1530, 1538 (11th Cir. 1990).

subfeudation. See **subinfeudation.**

subfeudatory. See **subinfeudatory.**

subhead(ing). Both *subheading* and *subhead* are used in reference to a textual subdivision under a heading. *Subheading* is much more common. *Subhead* is used esp. in reference to legislation—e.g.: "This legislation [Hammurabi's Babylonian code of 2350 B.C.] took the form of a code of 282 paragraphs, regularly arranged under heads and *subheads,* dealing with the rights of persons, property, the family, contracts, torts and procedure in a very adequate manner." Stephen Pfeil, "Law," in 17 *Encyclopedia Americana* 86, 87 (1953). See **head.**

subinfeud(ate). This term, a BACK-FORMATION meaning "(of a feudal tenant-in-chief) to grant a piece of land to a subtenant, who would hold the land by one of the medieval tenures such as knight service, serjeanty, frankalmoin, or socage," is ordinarily spelled *subinfeudate*—the shorter form being a NEEDLESS VARIANT. E.g., "The feudal lord who '*subinfeudates*' to a feudal tenant should not be equated with the modern landlord who 'lets' to a tenant under a lease." Peter Butt, *Land Law* 38 (2d ed. 1988)./ "William the Conqueror '*leased*' the land to his chief followers, who in turn '*subinfeudated*' the land to others." *Bellikka v. Green,* 762 P.2d 997, 1004 n.10 (Or. 1988) (en banc)./ "Soon after the Norman Conquest tenants in chief who held by knight service began to *subinfeudate*—i.e., to grant portions of their lands . . . ." Roger A. Cunningham et al., *The Law of Property* 15 (2d ed. 1993).

Some legal writers use the term figuratively, but few readers are likely to follow the metaphor: "Indeed, were that not true, the Commission, when dealing at the outset with a colony of intricately *subinfeudated* companies would be obliged to stop unravelling them as soon as it reached any holding company . . . ." *Protective Comm. for Class A Stockholders v. SEC,* 184 F.2d 646, 648 (2d Cir. 1950).

subinfeudation; subfeudation. The latter is a NEEDLESS VARIANT.

subinfeudatory, dating from the 19th century, can be either an adjective ("of or relating to subinfeudation") or a noun ("one who holds land by subinfeudation"). The noun use is rarer: "In France . . . the *sub-infeudatories* . . . were expected to support their *immediate* lord in war . . . ." C. Gordon Post, *An Introduction to the Law* 21 (1963). *Subfeudatory* is a NEEDLESS VARIANT.

subissue. See SUB-.

subject, n. See **citizen (B).**

subject, adj., in the sense "that is or are the subject of examination or consideration" <the subject property>, is LEGALESE without redeeming value. E.g., "The first [prerequisite] is a prior, unrelated history of close and trusted dealings of the same general nature or scope as *the subject transactions* [read *these transactions* or *the transactions at issue*]." *Harris v. Sentry Title Co.,* 715 F.2d 941, 948 (5th Cir. 1983)./ "The *subject* [delete *subject*] property comprises 17,191 square feet of land zoned 'Waterfront Business . . . .' " *Golemis v. Kirby,* 632 F. Supp. 159, 160 (D.R.I. 1985). For a different adjectival use of *subject,* see **subject to contract.**

subjectability = the ability of something to be subject to (a law, etc.). E.g., "It would appear that the manufacturer and the importer, whose *subjectability to Oklahoma [read Oklahoma's*] jurisdiction is not challenged before this Court, ought not to be judgment-proof." *World-wide Volkswagen Corp. v. Woodson,* 444 U.S. 286, 317–18 (1980) (Blackmun, J., dissenting). The word is listed in neither *W2* nor *W3,* and is included in *OED* merely with the notation "in recent dictionaries." The word is arguably useful, though somewhat inaesthetic.

subject-matter is best hyphenated as an adjectival phrase <subject-matter jurisdiction> in both AmE and BrE. Only in BrE is the phrase hyphenated as a noun.

subject-matter jurisdiction; jurisdiction of the subject matter. The phrase is rendered both ways in modern legal writing. E.g., "The district court dismissed petitioner's complaint for want of *jurisdiction of the subject matter.*" *Subject-matter jurisdiction* is more common and usually less cumbersome.

Subject-matter jurisdiction (= the extent to which a court can claim to affect the conduct of persons) is contrasted with *personal jurisdiction* (= a court's power to bring persons into its adjudicative process).

subject matter of the trust. See **corpus.**

subject to change by mutual agreement. This phrase, seen occasionally in contracts, is worthless: everything in the contract is subject to a change of this kind.

subject to contract is a formulaic expression that has the effect of making a preliminary contract for the sale of land and houses nonbinding—until a formal or final contract records the agreement. The phrase is somewhat more common in G.B. than in the U.S., but it is used on both sides of the Atlantic. E.g., "The Court of Appeal held that, as the preliminary agreement was *'subject to a proper contract,'* neither party had ever become bound . . . ." 1 E.W. Chance, *Principles of Mercantile Law* 30 (P.W. French ed., 13th ed. 1950)./ "[A]n acceptance *'subject to contract'* or 'subject to title' or any similar term is conditional, and amounts to a counter-offer which may be accepted or rejected by the original offeror as he desires." *Id.* at 38.

subject to the provisions of this Act. This REDUNDANCY appears frequently in common-law STATUTE-DRAFTING. A variation is *subject to any contrary provision in this Act.* As often as not, it signals poorly organized drafting; certainly it makes the interpreter's job no easier. Cf. **notwithstanding anything to the contrary contained herein.**

SUBJECT-VERB AGREEMENT. A. False Attraction to Noun Intervening Between Subject and Verb. The simple rule is that plural subjects take plural verbs, and singular subjects take singular verbs. This subheading denotes a mistake in number usually resulting when a plural noun intervenes between a singular subject and the verb. The writer's eye is thrown off course by the plural noun that appears nearest the verb—e.g.:

- "This problem is also declining in importance as the *language* of statutes *are* [read *is*] modernized."
- "Concededly, the *length* of opinions *vary* [read *varies*] from case to case and from writer to writer."
- "At first, the *difference* between McCormick and Wigmore—or between McCormick and any of the other writers mentioned here—*are* [read *is*] a bit startling."
- "[I]ndeed the success of these cooperative enterprises *turn* [read *turns*] on this right . . . ." William F. Walsh, *A Treatise on Equity* 354 (1930).
- "The *cost* of all prosecutions *are* [read *is*] met out of the fund provided by the locality in which the proceedings take place . . . ." Patrick Devlin, *The Criminal Prosecution in England* 14 (1960).
- "A *group* of cases *have* [read *has,* or *several cases have*] enacted broad cy pres, or reformation, statutes, of which the Vermont statute is an example . . . ." Thomas F. Bergin & Paul G. Haskell, *Preface to Estates in Land and Future Interests* 218 (2d ed. 1984).
- "A third *set* of cases where plaintiffs seek only money *are* [read *includes* or *comprises*] suits to collect debts." Douglas Laycock, *The Death of the Irreparable Injury Rule* 17 (1991).
- "[C]ompliance with the administrative complaint requirements of Title VII . . . *are* [read *is*] also *applicable* [read *mandatory*?]." Jack B. Moynihan, *After the Civil Rights Act of 1991,* Tex. B.J., May 1992, at 450, 454.
- "Unnecessary *enumeration* of particulars *are* [read *is*] not uncommon . . . ." Elmer Doonan, *Drafting* 38 (1995).

This error sometimes occurs when two or more nouns, seeming to create a plural, intervene between the subject and the verb—e.g.: "This amazing transformation has not been achieved solely by a concept of 'interference,' for the *provision* of 'works' (water, drainage, houses, transport, power, schools, hospitals and so on) and of 'facilities' (such as education, health services and social security) *do* [read *does,* because the subject is *provision*] not seem to be essentially interferences except to a one-track mind." R.M. Jackson, *The*

Machinery of Justice in England 354 (5th ed. 1967)./ "Barefaced *defiance* of morals and law *were* [read *was,* because the subject is *defiance*] illegal." Lawrence M. Friedman, *Crime and Punishment in American History* 131 (1993). See SYNESIS.

The reverse error, plural to singular, also occurs—e.g.: "The *interests* of the class representative, Mr. Sampson, *is* [read *are*] not the same as those of the absent parties."/ "Strict *interpretations* of statutory language *has* [read *have*] been used at one time to mitigate the severity of the law and (much more rarely) at another time to increase it." J.W. Cecil Turner, *Kenny's Outlines of Criminal Law* 38 (1952).

B. Reverse False Attraction. This occurs when the writer ignores the true and proximate subject by wrongly searching for a more remote subject earlier in the sentence. E.g., "The character of the punitive damages depends on the function such damages *serves* [read *serve*]." (The writer apparently thought *function* to be the subject.)

C. False Attraction to Predicate Noun. Occasionally a writer incorrectly looks to the predicate rather than to the subject for the noun that will govern the verb. The "correct" way of phrasing the sentence is often awkward, so the writer is well advised to find another way of stating the idea—e.g.:

- "The appellate judge's immediate audience *are* [read *is*] his colleagues who sat with him when an appeal was argued."
- "The second type of case on which I shall spend a little time *are* [read *is*] cases of negligence . . . ." H.L.A. Hart, "Intention and Punishment," in *Punishment and Responsibility: Essays in the Philosophy of Law* 113, 132 (1968). [A suggested edit to avoid awkwardness: *The second type of case on which I shall spend a little time is the case involving negligence* . . . .]
- "Another *class* of case in which juries are notoriously more willing to acquit than magistrates *are* [read *is*] cases in which everything hinges upon a conflict between the evidence of police witnesses and of the accused." P.S. Atiyah, *Law and Modern Society* 22 (1983). [A suggested edit to avoid awkwardness: *Another class of case in which juries are notoriously more willing to acquit than magistrates is the case in which everything hinges upon a conflict between the evidence of police witnesses and of the accused.*]

D. Compound Subjects Joined Conjunctively. "But recent research and commentary *has* [read *have*] suggested that the emphasis upon eyewitness identification may lead to questionable results." (*Research* and *commentary* are different things.)/ "At the same time, the democratic process and the personal participation of the citizen in his government *is* [read *are*] not all we want." Charles P. Curtis, Jr., *Lions Under the Throne* 49 (1947) (*The democratic process* and *personal participation* are different things).

Sometimes the two nouns joined by *and* arguably express a single idea, and hence should take a singular verb: "The confusion and uncertainty *is* [*confusion and uncertainty* really describing a single mental state] compounded by doubt regarding the question whether the complete liquidation and reorganization provisions can have concurrent application."/ "Published *criticism and vituperation is* not necessarily libelous."

One must be careful of the compound noun phrase followed by a singular noun that properly is the singular subject: "First, we must decide whether the claim presented and the relief sought are of the type that *admit* [read *admits,* for the subject of the verb is *type*] of judicial resolution."

E. Alternatives. The last element in a disjunctive series determines the number of the verb. Thus:

- "Consent to contract may be vitiated if fraud, error, violence, or threats *induce* the consent."
- "But the jury or the court *are* [read *is*] not bound to accept the statement of a witness as true because it is not directly or expressly contradicted or impeached by other witnesses."
- "The decree undoubtedly contemplates that the government would be able to object where, as here, the process of combatting discrimination depends not merely on the development of particular lists, but on *which* of two alternative lists *are* [read *is*] used."
- "It can hardly be otherwise so long as justices or a court *have* [read *has*] to deal with applications, because they must act on insufficient information." R.M. Jackson, *The Machinery of Justice in England* 156 (5th ed. 1967).
- "Written defamation (libel) was, nevertheless, treated in a special way by the criminal law, where neither publication nor untruth *were* [read *was*] required to be shown." J.H. Baker, *An Introduction to English Legal History* 506–07 (3d ed. 1990). See **neither . . . nor (A).**
- "[W]henever the president or the governor *issue* [read *issues*] an executive order . . . ." Bob Dunn, *Contemplating Our Future,* Tex. B.J., May 1992, at 448.

See **either (B).**

F. Plural Words Referred to as Words. These take a singular verb. "Neither 'per stirpes' nor 'descendants' *were* [read *was*] used in reference to the part of the estate Sue would get had George died intestate."/ "But 'per stirpes' *were* [read *was*] not used in the phrase granting power of appointment; *they were used* [read *it* (i.e., the phrase) *was used*] only in disposing of the property if George died intestate."

G. Misleading Connectives. The phrases *as well as, added to, coupled with,* and *together with* do not affect the grammatical number of the nouns preceding or following them. When such a phrase joins two singular nouns, the singular verb is called for—e.g.:

- "The provision for the payment of interest on the fund held by appellee, *together with* the fact that there was no designation or segregation of any particular fund from which payment was to be made, *are* [read *is*] of interest in determining the settlor's intent."
- "Logic, *as well as* equity, *dictate* [read *dictates*] this result." *Affiliated Capital Corp. v. City of Houston,* 793 F.2d 706, 709 (5th Cir. 1986) (en banc).
- "[F]or example, he says, America's declining ability to compete in the global sale of automobiles and other manufactured products, as well as its status as the world's leading debtor nation, *are* [read *is*] partly the result of the declining cognitive abilities of workers and administrators." Malcolm W. Browne, *What Is Intelligence, and Who Has It?* N.Y. Times, 16 Oct. 1994, § 7, at 3, 41.

See **together with.**

H. Plural Units Denoting Amounts. In AmE, a plural noun denoting a small unit by which a larger amount is measured generally takes a singular verb—e.g.: "Five hours *are* [read *is*] enough time."/ "Fifteen minutes *pass* [read *passes*] more quickly than you might think."/ "Before the leak was detected and the flow of oil shut down, a period of about two weeks, approximately 2,400 barrels of crude oil *were* [read *was*] discharged into the creek." See COLLECTIVE NOUNS & SYNESIS.

I. The False Singular. "The situation of the employer and the employee in today's society is equivalent." [Read *The situation of the employer and that of the employee in today's society are equivalent.*] It is the situations of the employer and the employee, not the persons themselves, that are being compared. See ILLOGIC (A).

J. Inversion. In the sentence that follows, the two *that*-clauses, dual subjects, demand a plural verb, although the writer was misled by the INVERSION into thinking a singular was needed: "*That this court has jurisdiction* to enforce a covenant between the owner of the land and his neighbor purchasing a part of it, *and that the latter shall either use or abstain* from using the land purchased in a particular way, *is* [read *are*] what I never knew to be disputed."

The error is less understandable in a simpler sentence: "As usual there *seems* [read *seem*] to be a million things happening around the Texas Law Center." Karen Johnson, *What's Happening at the Texas Law Center?* Tex. B.J., May 1992, at 514. See **there is** (B).

As in the preceding example, sentences that begin with the expletive *there* invert the order of the subject and the verb, thereby frequently causing confusion in number—even where, as here, the subject being discussed is grammatical number: "The result of this evolution is that there *is* [read *are*] now both a plural *media* and a singular *media,* and each means something different." Robertson Cochrane, *Verbum Sap,* 21 Verbatim 11, 11 (1994).

K. *Thing after thing (is) (are).* E.g., "Exception after exception *have* [read *has*] whittled away the rule."/ "Assault after assault on the M'Naghten Rules *were* [read *was*] beaten off until 1957." H.L.A. Hart, "Changing Conceptions of Responsibility," in *Punishment and Responsibility: Essays in the Philosophy of Law* 186, 191 (1968). Cf. **more . . . than** (B). See CONCORD (A) & **media.**

L. Subject Area Implied. Some writers fall into the habit of implicitly prefacing plural nouns with UNDERSTOOD WORDS such as *the idea of* or *the law of.* To be sure, some of these wordings are, among lawyers, perfectly idiomatic—e.g.: "Torts is my favorite area of the law."

But the habit should not extend beyond the reach of idiomatic comfort—e.g.: "Estates and future interests *is* [read *make up*] a complex, highly technical body of material, foreign to most students' experience, and difficult to grasp." Thomas F. Bergin & Paul G. Haskell, *Preface to Estates in Land and Future Interests* v (2d ed. 1984)./ "Lives in being plus 21 years *has* no purpose in the commercial field." *Id.* at 208. [Read *The concept of lives in being plus 21 years has no purpose in the commercial field.*]

M. *One in five; one of every five.* This construction takes a singular: *one in three is not admitted, one of every five achieves a perfect score.* E.g., "The truth is that in the period 1805–10, one in five of reported crimes *were* [read *was*] not prosecuted . . . ." Alan Harding, *A Social History of English Law* 276 (1966).

N. *A number of people (is) (are).* See SYNESIS.

O. *One of those who (is) (are).* See **one of those ——s who (*or* that).**

P. *Each* as Subject. See **each** (A).

Q. *What* as Subject. See **what.**

subjoin (= to annex, append) was formerly extremely common in LEGALESE. E.g., "Other statements of the rule will be found in the *subjoined* footnote." Today the term is rarely used, *subjoined footnote* conveying nothing that *footnote* does not equally clearly convey. Where the word is not, as above, completely superfluous, *join* or *attach* will often suffice in place of this pomposity: "The next verbal repetition, 'consigned pianos,' is *subjoined* [read *attached*] to the stipulation for the dealer to make monthly stock reports."

sub judice (= before the court; awaiting judicial determination), though almost always an unnecessary phrase, rose tenfold in frequency of use between the 1940s and the 1980s in American judicial opinions. Structurally an adverbial of place, the phrase usu. functions as a POSTPOSITIVE ADJECTIVE <case *sub judice*>.

The phrase is easily translated. *Case sub judice* readily becomes *case at bar*. Better yet, one might write *this case* or *the present case*: "*In the case sub judice* [read *In this case*], extensive controversy was present in the medical opinions."/ "Appellees argue that *the case sub judice* [read *this case* or *the present case*] does not fall within any of the three categories enumerated in *Blagge*."/ "As in *Crouch, the case sub judice* [read *the present case*] involves none of the concerns upon which the domestic-relations exception exists."/ "*The case sub judice* [read *The present case*] is clearly distinguishable on its facts from those two cases." See **case at bar & instant case.** See also LATINISMS.

The phrase is best pronounced either /*sub-****joo****-di-see*/ or /*sub-****yoo****-di-kay*/—and it ought to be two words, not one.

subjugable. See -ATABLE.

subjugate (= [1] to conquer or bring under control; or [2] to subdue) should not be used for *subordinate*. E.g., "We decline to require them to name their remedy when to do so would be to *subjugate* [read *subordinate*] fairness and common sense to technical nicety."

SUBJUNCTIVES are concededly obsolete for the most part in English. They still survive in such constructions as "If I were," "If he were," etc. Legal writers frequently omit the subjunctive mood of the verb when they should use it, usually when the situation postulated is hypothetical or contrary to fact—e.g.:

- "Would your answer be different [hypothetical] if the basis of judicial jurisdiction *was* [read *were*] an attachment of real estate, the value of which would not be known until it was sold to satisfy judgment?"
- "Suppose now that the foreign corporation in question *was* [read *were* or *had been*] doing business within the state."
- "The claims of workmen who were employed in such a factory, and cannot continue to work there because of fire, represent only a small fraction of the claims which would arise if recovery *is* [read *were*, because the *if* is hypothetical] allowed in this class of cases."
- "If there were no state statutes, then of course the federal courts *did* [read *would*] not have to refer to state law at all, unless the action were local."
- "This section of the Act was designed to ensure *that the government was not prevented* [read *that the government not be prevented*] from exercising its leadership and planning functions."
- "Drafting is more than a mechanical process of recording the terms of a transaction in writing. If this *was* [read *were*] all that drafting involved, it would not be necessary to look to lawyers to do drafting." Elmer Doonan, *Drafting* 6–7 (1995).

It is ironic, in view of the sentences just quoted, that legal writers still often cling to basically outmoded subjunctives. Krapp labeled the usage *If I be* an "archaic survival" in 1927. See George P. Krapp, *A Comprehensive Guide to Good English* 651–52 (1927). But similar archaic examples abound in 20th-century legal prose:

- "If one partner *go* [read *goes* or *went*] to a third person to buy an article on time for the partnership, the other partner *cannot* [read as is if *goes* is in the first clause, or *could not* if *went* is in the first clause] prevent it by writing to the third person not to sell to him on time."
- "If the nonresident *have* [read *has*] no property in the state, there is nothing for the tribunals to adjudicate."
- "[I]f after conviction a prisoner *become* [read *becomes*] insane, he cannot be hanged until his recovery." J.W. Cecil Turner, *Kenny's Outlines of Criminal Law* 75 (1952).
- "The House of Lords does now enjoy—if that *be* [read *is*] the appropriate word—the freedom not to follow its own previous decisions—a freedom only very recently acquired, and not, it would seem, likely by over-use to degenerate into licence." Leslie Scarman, *English Law—The New Dimension* 5 (1974).

When one relates an indirect question asking about past condition, and no hypothetical or contrariety to truth is implied, the simple past should be employed, and not the subjunctive. Confusion on this point is the most common among those who profess to know how to handle subjunctives—e.g.:

- "One inquired whether the money *were* [read *was*] lost property, and the other inquired whether the money *was* [read *had been*] mislaid."

- "In *Wagner,* the court rejected the defendant's theory that it would be liable to a rescuer only if the rescue *were* [read *was*] 'instinctive'."
- "In the instant case, there was sufficient reason to allow the questioned demonstration; however, even if it *were* [read *was*] error, it was harmless error."
- "It was not that these scriveners did not know how to punctuate; they were simply operating under the old rules; if there *were* [read *was*] a compelling oral reason for punctuation, punctuation would be supplied."

The three following sentences contain constructions in which—even in the modern idiom—the subjunctive is needed. In the first two examples, a demand or intention is expressed (this is one of the few exceptions to the obsolescence of subjunctives); the third sentence describes a condition that is contrary to fact: "These prisoners demanded that they all *engaged* [read *engage*] in sex and, although the complainant was frightened, he refused and climbed back into bed."/ "Parties may intend that a certain document *is* [read *be*] the final expression of agreement as to matters dealt with in that writing."/ "Some courts have construed wills acts patterned upon the Statute of Frauds as if the signature rather than the will *was* [read *were*] the thing to be acknowledged by the testator."

But in the following group of sentences, the subjunctive is vestigial and moribund and should therefore be changed to the indicative: "What has been said, however, does not mean that the taxpayer had no right to carry out his declaration after the subject matter had come into existence, even though there *were* [read *was*] no consideration."/ "In Iowa, and generally elsewhere, the title to a decedent's real estate, whether he *die* [read *dies*] intestate or testate, including the right of dower, vests in the heir, devisee, or spouse instantly upon the death of the decedent, subject, of course, to the payment of his debts, and costs of administration."/ "In England, fair comment includes the inference of motives, if there *be* [read, in modern prose, *is*] foundation for the inference."

Having cited so many examples of misuse, this article might best end with a correct use of the subjunctive in its most common setting: "Where an attesting witness has denied all knowledge of the matter, the case stands *as if there were* no attesting witness." (Eng.)

On the consistent progression of mood within a sentence, see TENSES (B).

sublease, n.; **subtenancy; underlease.** The first is the usual term in AmE and BrE. The other two are primarily BrE variants.

Unlike an *assignment* of a lease, in which the lessee's entire interest is transferred to the assignee from the assignor, a *sublease* transfers only the unexpired portion of the lease (often less one day) to the sublessee from the sublessor, who retains a reversion in the lease.

sublease, v.t. See **let & underlease.**

sublessee; subtenant; undertenant. See **sublease,** n.

sublessor (AmE & BrE)**; underlessor** (BrE). See **sublease.**

sublet. See **let.**

submersible; submergible. Though the latter seems simpler (cf. *persuadable* and *persuasible*), the former is more common in both AmE and BrE. E.g., "That case involved claims for property damage arising from a blowout of a high-pressure gas well that occurred during workover operations on the well aboard a *submersible* drilling barge."

submissible; submissable; submittable. Even though it is labeled "rare" in the *OED, submissible* is frequently used in AmE. See, e.g., Charles A. Wright, *The Law of Federal Courts* 641 (4th ed. 1983) ("there is a *submissible* issue"). *Submissable* and *submittable* are NEEDLESS VARIANTS.

submission is used in several senses: (1) an argument by counsel in court <In his April 10 submission, Cochran argued to Judge Ito that the prosecution was trying to cause a mistrial>; (2) the agreement to abide by a decision or to obey an authority <our submission was limited to the 1992 dispute>; (3) the action of allowing, or agreement to allow, an authority to decide an issue <The voluntary submission of parties to the jurisdiction of courts>; or (4) the referring of a matter to arbitration <submission to arbitration by consent>.

submittal (= the act of submitting), though not uncommon in American legal writing, is a NEEDLESS VARIANT OF *submission.* E.g., "Counsel made his *submittal* [read *submission*] to the court *outside* [or *off*] the record."/ "[T]he public may obtain information, [or] make *submittals* [read *submissions*] or requests." Administrative Procedure Act, 5 U.S.C. § 552(a)(1)(a) (1982).

sub modo (= under a qualification; subject to a restriction or condition) is a recherché Latinism. "But whether a creditor or a grantee of the plaintiff in this case would be entitled to the immediate possession of the property, *or would only take the plaintiff's title sub modo* [read *or would take title subject to the restrictions on plaintiff's title*], need not be decided."

sub nom. (fr. L. *sub nomine*) = under the name. This abbreviation is commonly used, and justifiably so, in citations to note that a certain case may have involved different parties at an earlier or later procedural stage. E.g., "Again, in *In re Morgani,* [1942] Ch. 347, the Court of Appeal . . . was doubtless relieved when it was reversed by the House of Lords *sub nom. Perrin v. Morgan,* [1943] A.C. 399." Carleton K. Allen, *Law in the Making* 382 (7th ed. 1964).

suborn; subornate. *Suborn* = to get another to commit a crime, esp. perjury. E.g., "To bribe a trustee, as such, is in fact neither more nor less than to *suborn* him to be guilty of a breach or an abuse of trust." Jeremy Bentham, *An Introduction to the Principles of Morals and Legislation* 240 n.3 (Hafner Pub. Co. 1948) (1823).

Subornate, a BACK-FORMATION for *subornation,* is a NEEDLESS VARIANT of *suborn.* E.g., "The evidence . . . of the plaintiff's attempt to bribe the witness and *subornate* [read *suborn*] perjury was not being introduced to prove the plaintiff's character in order to show conformity as provided in Rule 404(b)." *Lay v. Mangum,* 360 S.E.2d 481, 483 (N.C. Ct. App. 1987).

subornation of perjury. Although *subornation* may mean in a general sense "the act of inducing or procuring a person to commit an evil action, by bribery, corruption, or the like" (*OED*), in practice today it almost invariably means "the act of procuring a person to commit perjury." Hence *subornation of perjury* is a virtual REDUNDANCY, though an established and therefore a pardonable one.

The verb corresponding to this noun is *suborn* (= to procure [another] to commit perjury) and the agent noun is *suborner.* See **suborn & suborner.**

subornee = one who is suborned. See -EE (A).

suborner is the only form of the word. E.g., "[T]he *suborner* was originally thought of as committing a separate crime because it was a more serious offense than perjury,—although it was not a felony except in very ancient times." Rollin M. Perkins & Ronald N. Boyce, *Criminal Law* 525 (3d ed. 1982). See -ER (A).

subpart. See SUB-.

subp(o)ena. A. Sense. *W3* lists *subpoena* as an adverb meaning "under penalty" (or "under pain"). This, of course, is its etymological sense. It virtually never appears in modern legal writing with this meaning, and should be considered obsolete in that use.

The modern use is as a noun. Even in medieval English practice, *subpoena* served as a noun denoting the writ that commenced civil proceedings by ordering the defendant to attend under pain of a monetary penalty. Today, its meaning is "a court order commanding the presence of a witness under a penalty of fine for failure."

B. Form and Pronunciation. *Subpena,* the spelling recommended by the *Government Printing Office Manual* up until the early 1980s, appears in any number of American federal statutes. *Subpoena* is, however, by far the more common spelling and for that reason alone is to be preferred. Moreover, the better view is reflected in the Government Printing Office's *Style Manual* as revised in 1984.

The form with the digraph *œ*—namely *subpœna*—is pedantic at best in modern writing.

The plural is *subpoenas,* not *subpoenae: In re Two Grand Jury Subpoenae* [read *Subpoenas*] *Duces Tecum,* 769 F.2d 52 (2d Cir. 1985). "The *subpoenae* [read *subpoenas*] specifically called for, once again, interview memoranda. On June 6, 1984, the Government filed a motion to quash the *subpoenae* [read *subpoenas*]." *U.S. v. Omni Int'l Corp.,* 634 F. Supp. 1414, 1427 (D.Md. 1986). The form *subpoenae* results from the mistaken view that *subpoena* is a Latin singular noun, whereas it is a Latin phrase used as an English noun. See HYPERCORRECTION (A).

The word is pronounced /*sə-***pee***-nə*/ as both noun and verb.

C. Types. A *subpoena ad testificandum* /*ad-tes-ti-fi-***kan***-dəm*/ is a subpoena to testify; usu., when *subpoena* is used alone, the word refers to this type. A *subpoena duces tecum* /*doo-səs-***tee***-kəm*/ commands the witness not only to appear but also to bring specified books, papers, or records.

subpoena, v.t. The inflected forms of this verb, which dates from the early 17th century, are *subpoenaed* and *subpoenaing.* The miscast forms *subpoened* and *subpoening* are fairly common—as is *subpoenaeing.*

Subpoena'd is an old BrE past-tense form. See, e.g., Sir John Hawles's *Remarks Upon Mr. Cor-*

nish's Trial, 11 How. St. Tr. 455, 460 (1685) ("any person may inform in point of fact, though not *subpoena'd* . . .").

subpoenable (= capable of being subpoenaed) is an ungainly NEOLOGISM of questionable utility—e.g.: "[T]he results could be *subpoenable* . . . ." *People v. Pezzette,* 444 N.E.2d 1386, 1387 (Ill. App. Ct. 1983)./ "That is what Bruce insisted he was entitled to from The Ohio State University, which is the formal and *subpoenable* name of his last employer." *Bruce Passes Up Shot at Last Laugh,* Chicago Tribune, 29 Nov. 1987, at C1.

subpoenal (= required or done under penalty) is listed in *W2,* but not in the *OED* or in *W3.* Still, it is occasionally useful as an adjective in the sense "required or done in compliance with a subpoena." E.g., "Additionally, the petitioners contend that their right to produce witnesses on their own behalf will be impinged upon and that their right against self-incrimination will be violated by requiring them to testify under *subpoenal* compulsion." *A v. Curran,* 306 N.Y.S.2d 753, 755–56 (Sup. Ct. 1969).

subrogate = to put (a person) in the place of, or substitute (a person) *for,* another in respect of a right or claim; to cause to succeed *to* the rights of another (*OED*). It was once a general English word, more literary than vernacular; today it is mostly confined to legal contexts.

subrogation. A. Senses. *Subrogation* = (1) generally, the substitution of one party for another as a creditor, with the transfer of rights and duties; *esp.,* an equitable assignment that substitutes a surety to the position of the creditor whom the surety has paid; (2) the principle under which an insurer that has paid the loss under an indemnity policy is entitled to take on all the rights and remedies belonging to the insured against a third party with respect to any injuries or breaches covered by the insurance policy; or (3) in civil law, the attribution of legal qualities usu. attached to one kind of property to another kind of property. Cf. **novation.**

B. *Legal* and *Conventional Subrogation.* *Legal subrogation* arises by operation of law or by implication in equity to prevent fraud or injustice. *Conventional subrogation* arises by contract.

C. And *reimbursement; contribution; exoneration.* All of these equitable doctrines serve to prevent the unearned enrichment of one party at the expense of another by creating a relation similar to a constructive trust in favor of the party making payment in the creditor's legal rights. See **constructive trust (B).**

subrogative; subrogatory; subrogational. Among these less-than-common adjectives, *subrogative* appears most frequently—twice as frequently as *subrogatory* and more than three times as frequently as *subrogational.* It would therefore be convenient if writers treated the *-tory* and *-tional* forms as NEEDLESS VARIANTS and avoided them.

subrogee; subrogatee. The usual form is *subrogee* (= a person put in the place or substituted for another in upholding a right or claim)—e.g.: "Subrogation is a legal fiction [that] results in the substitution of the *subrogee* to the position of the subrogor . . . ." John T. Hood, Jr., "Subrogation," in *Essays on the Civil Law of Obligations* 174 (Joseph Dainow ed., 1969). *Subrogatee* is an erroneous form—e.g.: "A drawee bank under current Texas law will not be deemed the equitable *subrogatee* [read *subrogee*] of the maker on the ground that the maker has a valid defense to the debt evidenced by the check."

Subrogee is pronounced /səb-rə-***jee***/. Cf. **obligee.** See -EE (B).

subrogor (= one who allows another to be substituted for oneself as creditor, with a transfer of rights and duties) is a 20th-century legal NEOLOGISM created to correspond to *subrogee,* q.v. It is listed in *W3* but not in the *OED* or in *W2.* As a term corresponding to *subrogee, subrogor* is quite acceptable. The word is pronounced /səb-rə-***gohr***/.

subscribe lit. means "to write (one's name or mark) on, orig. at the bottom of, a document, esp. as a witness or consenting party" (*OED*). In this sense the word is now purely a LEGALISM. Arguably it has its uses, although *sign* will almost always suffice more comprehensibly. E.g., "The summons is the mandate of the court and is *subscribed* [read *signed*] by an attorney who is an officer of the court."

For the misuse of *ascribe* for *subscribe,* see **ascribe.**

subsequently. A. For *later.* Using the four-syllable word in place of the two-syllable word is rarely, if ever, a good stylistic choice.

B. And *consequently.* Though both words contain the sense "following" or "occurring later," *consequently* has an added causal nuance: "occurring because of." See **consequent (B).**

subsequent to is a lawyer's pomposity for *after* or *later,* just as *prior to* is for *before.* E.g., "The controversy in *Kulko* involved an attempted modification of child custody and support several years *subsequent to* [read *after*] the divorce of the parents."/ "*Subsequent to* [read *After*] drawing the will in Detroit, the decedent became a resident of Webberville."/ "The petitioner may, of course, *subsequent to* [read *after*] the execution of the trust agreement, have issue, but until such issue come into being, they cannot be said to have the status of existing beneficiaries."

Used adjectivally (without *to*), *subsequent* is perfectly acceptable in phrases such as *condition subsequent* and *subsequent history* (of a case).

subserve is an ARCHAISM for *serve*. E.g., "In that way the ends of justice and the best interests of the public will be *subserved* [read *served*]."/ "The interests of the people are best *subserved* [read *served*] by sustaining the statute quoted as it is written."/ "The beneficial ends to be *subserved* [read *served*] by public discussion would in large measure be defeated if honesty must be handled with delicacy."

subsidence (= the act or process of settling or sinking) is pronounced /sub-**sɪd**-əns/ or /**səb**-sɪd-əns/. The word is sometimes misspelled *subsidance*—e.g.: "[A]ppellant asserts the trial court erred in . . . finding that the passage of a truck trailer over a three to five inch *subsidance* [read *subsidence*] in a road is a 'collision' within the meaning of the policy . . . ." *Nutchey v. Three R's Trucking Co.,* 674 S.W.2d 928, 929 (Tex. App.—Amarillo 1984).

subsidiarity = (1) the quality of being subsidiary; or (2) the principle that a central authority, such as the European Community, should have a subsidiary function, performing only tasks that cannot be performed effectively at a more immediate or local level. A NEOLOGISM dating from the 1930s, it arose as a paraphrase of a 1931 speech given by Pope Pius XI, in which he used the German word *subsidiarität* (in sense 1). In legal contexts, sense (1) has traditionally been most usual—e.g.: "The requirement of *subsidiarity,* that no other remedy be available at law, is met because no contract exists under which recovery could be had." *Howell v. Rhoades,* 547 So. 2d 1087, 1089 (La. Ct. App. 1989).

sub silentio, adj. & adv., is an often unnecessary LATINISM. In many contexts, *silent(ly), tacit(ly), under silence,* or *in silence* provides a good substitute. E.g., "The district court may have *accepted, sub silentio,* [read *tacitly accepted*] the appellees' contention that appellant waived all claims in his pleadings except the claim for denial of procedural due process."/ "It does not make sense that Congress intended *sub silentio* [read *silently*] to broaden the required exemption to preclude pro rata reductions."

subsist. This verb was formerly used regularly in the sense "to exist." This usage is now a legalistic ARCHAISM. E.g., "Such laws must be invariably obeyed, as long as the creature itself *subsists,* for its existence depends on that obedience." (Blackstone) The more common word *exist* should now be preferred, esp. since the usual meaning of *subsist* today is "to survive with a bare minimum of sustenance, to continue to exist; to keep oneself alive."

In the following sentences, *subsist* is used in its archaic sense: "Joint tenancy is a relationship *subsisting* [read *existing*] between two or more persons in respect to an interest in land."/ "The respondent by his amended answer has alleged that, at the time of the ceremony of marriage which he went through with the petitioner, there was already *a subsisting* [read *an existing*] marriage which had previously taken place between him and another lady in Pakistan." (Eng.)

The general lay sense also appears in legal writing, a fact that may lead to AMBIGUITY if the archaic sense is retained: "On the basis of this sole difference the first class is granted and the second class is denied welfare aid upon which may depend the ability of the families to obtain the very means to *subsist*—food, shelter, and other necessities of life."

subsistence is occasionally misspelled *subsistance.*

substantial damages. See **nominal damages.**

substantial performance = the equitable doctrine that, if a plaintiff fails to fulfill some of its detailed obligations under a contract, as by not performing quite on time, the plaintiff may nevertheless hold the defendant to his promise despite that failure if the substantial purpose of the contract is accomplished. E.g., "The rule that gives a remedy in cases of *substantial performance* with compensation for defects of trivial or inappreciable importance has been developed by the courts as an instrument of justice." *Jacob & Youngs, Inc. v. Kent,* 129 N.E. 889, 892 (N.Y. 1921)./ "Rules of '*substantial performance*' were developed to protect plaintiffs who had almost, but not quite, completed performance." Grant Gilmore, *The Death of Contract* 74 (1974).

substantive, one of the words most commonly mispronounced by lawyers, has three, not four syllables /**səb**-stən-tiv/. The common error in AmE is to insert what is known as an epenthetical

-e- after the second syllable /***səb**-stə-nə-tiv*/. Still another blunder is to accent the second syllable /*səb-**stan**-tiv*/.

substantive law. See **procedural law.**

substantuate is solecistic for *substantiate.*

substitute; replace. *Substitute* = to put a person or thing in place of another <she will substitute for him>. *Replace* = (1) to put something or someone back in the same place as before, restore to a former state; (2) to supply an equivalent of; (3) to return; (4) to repay; or (5) to put in a new place.

substituted service, a phrase contrasted with *personal service,* refers to any means of serving legal papers other than by delivering them directly to the person to be served. Examples of substituted service include service by publication in newspapers and service on the attorney instead of the party. The phrase *substituted service* is more common in AmE than its synonym, *constructive service.*

substitutional; substitutionary; substitutive. In law, *substitutional* is the preferred form, *substitutionary,* a late-19th-century coinage, being a NEEDLESS VARIANT. Even so, *substitutionary* appears almost as frequently as *-al* in the law of wills. It should, like all other such variants, be uprooted. E.g., "[A] remote power . . . will actually be exercised only by *substitutionary* [read *substitutional*] deed . . . ." *Comm'r v. Singer's Estate,* 161 F.2d 15, 18–19 (2d Cir. 1947). *Substitutive,* a learned word, almost never occurs in legal contexts.

SUBSUB-. See SUB-.

subsumed takes *under* or *in.*

sub suo periculo (= at his, her, or its peril) is a LATINISM with little to commend it. E.g., "[I]f the parent [who is] granted custody undertakes to foist restrictions [that] a court should not impose, he does so *sub suo periculo* [read *at his peril*]." *Asbell v. Asbell,* 430 S.W.2d 436, 439 (Mo. Ct. App. 1968)./ "When Patrolman Ward, relying on the statement of Regina Bailey, that he would not need his gun and unjudiciously holstered it, he did so '*sub suo periculo*' [read *at his peril*]." *Ward v. State,* 366 N.Y.S.2d 800, 808 (Ct. Cl. 1975).

subtenancy is a chiefly BrE variant of *sublease.* See **sublease.**

subterfuge is pronounced /***sub**-tər-fyooj*/, not /*fyoozh*/.

subtle; subtile. The latter is an archaic and NEEDLESS VARIANT. E.g., "It is enough for the present case that the law should at least be prompt to recognize the injuries that may arise from an unauthorized use in connection with other facts, even if more *subtilty* [read *subtlety*] is needed to state the wrong than is needed here."

subtraction, a common mathematical word, has a special meaning in law: "the withdrawal or withholding from a person of any right or privilege to which he or she is lawfully entitled." E.g., "Among rights 'in personam,' family rights, and their analogues, are infringed by '*subtraction,*' adultery, refusal of due aliment, ingratitude on the part of a freedman, or neglect by a vassal of his feudal duties . . . ." Thomas E. Holland, *The Elements of Jurisprudence* 334 (13th ed. 1924; repr. 1937).

subvention (= a grant of money—esp. a governmental grant—for the support of an object or institution), chiefly a BrE term, has no live verb corresponding to it: *subvene* and *subvent,* both illustrated with a single pre-1800 citation in the *OED,* are obsolete. But the noun is in fairly frequent use—e.g.: "On the Treasury accounts [legal aid] looks like a huge recurrent *subvention* to an indigent relative." Sedley, *Breaking the Law,* London Rev. Books, 18 May 1989, at 3.

succedent. See **successive.**

succeeding for *after* or *following* is unnecessarily stuffy in most contexts. E.g., "The year *succeeding* [read *after*] the sale the company sold its real-estate holdings."

succession, in law, has two primary senses: (1) the act or right of legally or officially coming into a predecessor's office, rank, or functions; (2) "the acquiring of an intestate share of an estate"; or (3) loosely, "the acquiring of property by will." E.g., "If a decedent died intestate, property passes by *intestate succession* to his heirs."/ "The daughter transferred the property to her mother upon an oral agreement to hold in trust for the daughter and to be returned to the daughter by *intestate succession.*" (See **descent (B).**) The adjectival form of *succession* in this sense is *successional.* (See **successive.**)

Like *success, succession* is pronounced with the first *-c-* as if it were a *-k-*. Otherwise it is easily confused with *secession.* Cf. **accession & accessory.**

successive; successional; succedent. *Successive* = consecutive; following one after another, in uninterrupted succession. *Successional* = proceeding or passing by succession or descent. (See **succession.**) *Succedent to* is a pompous phrase meaning "following, after, subsequent to."

successor in interest. The phrase need not be hyphenated.

successors and assigns. See DOUBLETS, TRIPLETS, AND SYNONYM-STRINGS.

succinct. The first *-c-* is hard in this word. Cf. **succession, accession & accessory.**

such. A. As a Demonstrative Adjective. *Such* is properly used as an adjective when reference has previously been made to a category of persons or things: thus *such* = of this kind, not *this, these,* or *those.* With this word two points should be kept in mind. First, when used as a demonstrative adjective to modify a singular noun, *such* typifies LEGALESE as much as *aforesaid* and *same,* n. Contrary to what some think, *such* is no more precise than *the, that,* or *those.* Second, *such* is a DEICTIC TERM that must refer to a clear antecedent. In the following sentence, *such* is used once vaguely (without an antecedent), once clearly: "The Association agreed to compile data on all conventions that will occur in cities where there are interested Gray Line members and to forward *such* report to *such* members." The first *such* would best have been omitted; no reports have been referred to—only the compilation of data, which is not necessarily the same as a report. The second *such,* less objectionable because the noun following it is plural, would read better as *those.*

Fowler calls the use of *such* in place of *the* or *that* "the illiterate *such.*" E.g., "We adopt the opinion of the Court of Appeal. *Such* [read *The*] opinion is as follows."/ "*Such* cause of action, if any *such* there was, survived her death." [Read *The cause of action, if there was any, survived her death.*]/ "The general rule is that objection to a juror because of his disqualification is waived by failure to object to *such* [read *that*] juror until after the verdict." Cf. **said & same.**

Like *said* and *same,* this word is much beloved of those who believe in the MYTH OF PRECISION. It therefore teems in the work of some drafters—e.g.:

> Notwithstanding section 502 of this title, there shall not be allowed in *such* partner's case a claim against *such* partner on which both *such* partner and *such* partnership are liable, except to any extent that *such* claim is secured only by property of *such* partner and not by property of *such* partnership. The claim of the trustee under this subsection is entitled to distribution in *such* partner's case under 726(a) of this title the same as any other claim of a kind specified in *such* section.
>
> 11 U.S.C. § 723 (1994).

In that passage, all but the last *such* could be advantageously replaced by *the;* the last should be *that.* But, from the viewpoint of good DRAFTING, the whole section needs rethinking.

B. As a Pronoun. Although the pronoun use of *such* has ancient history on its side—it dates from the 9th century—today it is best regarded as an ARCHAISM except in a few such phrases as *such is life.* In legal contexts, the word is barbarous-sounding—e.g.: "I must dissent from the majority's holding that appellant's detention and ensuing search and seizure were lawful; *such* [read *that holding*] is pure dictum." (Notice that the last clause is nonsensical—*holding* and *dictum* being antithetical.) Indeed, Krapp called it a "crude low colloquialism." George P. Krapp, *A Comprehensive Guide to Good English* 568 (1927).

C. *Such . . . as to.* This generally unobjectionable construction should not be split by more than a few words: "Nothing in the letters was *such* an outrage *as to* inflame the passions of the jury." See **so as [+ infinitive].**

D. Such [noun +s] *as are.* Rephrase to avoid this archaic construction—e.g.: "The terminating shareholder shall execute and deliver to the Corporation *such instruments as are* [read *all instruments*] necessary to transfer full and complete title.

sue, in the sense "to sue and win," is a common legal idiom in questions posed in law-school exams, as in, "Can Y sue X?" As fully expressed, this question means, "Can Y sue X *successfully?*" Glanville Williams laments the exam answer that states, "Y can sue X but he will fail": "This displays the writer's common sense but also his lack of knowledge of legal phraseology. It is true that there is virtually no restriction upon the bringing of actions: for instance, I can at this moment sue the Prime Minister for assault—though I shall fail in the action. But when a lawyer asserts that [Y] can sue [X], what he means is that [Y] can sue [X] successfully; if he meant his words to be taken literally, they would not have been worth the uttering." Glanville Williams, *Learning the Law* 131 (11th ed. 1982).

sue facts (= facts that bear on whether to bring suit, esp. whether to institute a shareholder derivative action alleging a state-law cause of action) is an ungainly phrase from corporate-law JARGON. The phrase turns the verb *sue* into an adjective. Scholars have found this phrase more useful than judges, who had not used it by 1990. E.g., "I will skip over Borden's intelligent analysis of the current state of the law in Delaware; interesting material on determining value and *'sue facts';* the line-by-line dissection of SEC Rule 13e-3 . . . ." James C. Freund, *Lawyer Confronts Peril in Going-Private Transactions,* Legal Times, 24 Jan. 1983, at 13./ *Rule 10b-5 and* Santa Fe—*Herein of* Sue Facts, *Shame Facts, and Other Matters,* 87 W. Va. L. Rev. 189 (1985)./ "It would be possible, of course, to interpret clause (b) as prohibiting only misrepresentations relating to investment decisions ('investment facts') rather than decisions to bring suit for an injunction or appraisal (*'sue facts'*), as several commentators have suggested." Dennis S. Karjala, *Federalism, Full Disclosure, and the National Market in the Interpretation of Federal Securities Law,* 80 Nw. U.L. Rev. 1473, 1545 (1986).

sue out. *Sue* is best known to lawyers and nonlawyers alike in the sense "to institute legal proceedings against." Historically it has also been used in the PHRASAL VERBS *sue out* and *sue forth,* more commonly the former, in the sense "to make application before a court for the grant of (a writ or other legal process), often with implication of further proceedings being taken upon the writ" (*OED*). E.g., "[The] certificate from the clerk of the Court . . . [must state] the cause . . . and certify[ ] that such writ of error or appeal had been duly *sued out* and allowed." Sup. Ct. R. 32, 19 U.S. (6 Wheat.) vii (1821)./ "Again the defendant *sued out* a writ of error . . . ." R.E. Megarry, *A Second Miscellany-at-Law* 140 (1973)./ "If no execution was *sued out* within a year and a day, the judgment became dormant."/ "'Defendant in error' is the distinctive term appropriate to the party against whom a writ of error is *sued out.*" The phrase *sue out,* then, is not one of the phrases in which a preposition (here *out*) is merely an unnecessary particle. See **out (A)** & PARTICLES, UNNECESSARY.

suffer (= to permit or acquiesce in) is legal JARGON—an archaic use of an ordinary English word.

sufferance. So spelled; *suffrance* is a common misspelling.

suffice it to say is the SUBJUNCTIVE form of *it suffices to say.* E.g., "*Suffice it to say* that those cases were decided under facts dissimilar to those existing in the present case." The phrase is sometimes wrongly transformed into either *suffice to say* or *sufficient to say*—e.g.: "*Suffice to say* [read *Suffice it to say*] that, as things stood in 1973, common-law rules of allowable pleading of matters in several counts of a single indictment, and the permissible consequences of so pleading, had been melded with predecessor articles before the 1965 changes in article 21.24."/ "Congress had no authority to ratify the sale of the lien lands; *sufficient to say* [read *suffice it to say*] that the law is complete on the subject."

sufficiency; sufficience. The latter is a NEEDLESS VARIANT.

sufficient. See **adequate.**

sufficiently . . . as to for *sufficiently . . . to* results from confusion with *so . . . as to.* E.g., "These anomalies appear *sufficiently* [read *so*] enmeshed in the current tangled web of the jurisprudence on this subject *as to* be beyond attempted amelioration by a panel of this circuit."/ "If the machine was in fact *sufficiently defective as to* [read *so defective as to*] create liability merely for marketing it, the failure to test adequately adds nothing." [Or read: *If the machine was in fact sufficiently defective to create liability . . . .*] See **so as [+ infinitive].**

sufficient number of is verbose for *enough*—e.g.: "It is obvious also that if *a sufficient number of* [read *enough*] individuals so weaken themselves, society will thereby be weakened." Patrick Devlin, *The Enforcement of Morals* 111 (1968).

suffrage (= [1] the right given to a member of a body, state, or society to vote in assent to a proposition or in favor of the election of a person; or [2] by extension, the right to vote for or against any controverted question or nomination) typically calls up notions of *women's suffrage* or *universal suffrage,* the most common phrases in which the word has appeared in the 20th century.

But the word has historically referred to the right of enfranchised citizens generally, without reference to disenfranchised groups—e.g.: "If we say that five or six hundred citizens are as many as can jointly exercise their right of *suffrage,* must we not deprive the people of the immediate choice of their public servants in every instance where the administration of the government does not require as many of them as will amount to one for that number of citizens?" *The Federalist* No. 57, at 354 (James Madison) (Clinton Rossiter ed., 1961).

suffrance. See **sufferance.**

suggestibility; compliance. These two terms have become key words in the law relating to false confessions. *Suggestibility* is the readiness with which a person accepts another's suggestion.

Generally speaking, people are more suggestible if they are unassertive, diffident, anxious, or unintelligent. Young people, too, are more suggestible than older people. *Compliance* is the extent to which a person will follow another's wishes to avoid confrontation or for some other short-term gain. A compliant person is usually eager to please and wants to avoid clashing with authority. *Compliance* can result from feelings of guilt. See Dorothy Wade, *Why Say "I Did It" If You Didn't?* The Independent, 23 Feb. 1992, at 22.

suggestible; suggestable. The former spelling is preferred. See -ABLE (A).

suggestio falsi; suppressio veri. *Suggestio falsi* (lit., "suggestion of an untruth") = misrepresentation without direct falsehood. *Suppressio veri* (lit., "suppression of the truth") = a tacit misrepresentation; a silent lie. These LATINISMS may be useful (probably with an accompanying explanation), for there are no comparably short English phrases that convey the same notions. Maitland cleverly used the phrases in figurative senses: "That is the worst of our mortgage deed—owing to the action of equity, it is one long *suppressio veri* and *suggestio falsi.* It does not in the least explain the rights of the parties; it suggests that they are other than they really are." F.W. Maitland, *Equity* 182 (J. Brunyate ed., 2d ed. 1936). See **misrepresentation.**

suicide. A. And *self-killing; self-murder; self-slaughter; felo-de-se.* The five terms are generally synonymous, though the phrases *self-murder* and *self-slaughter* are charged with extremely negative connotations. *Suicide* and *self-killing* are broad terms that include every instance in which a person causes his or her own death within the legal rules of causation. Not always, though, was *suicide* so broad; when first used in the 17th century, it referred only to "the self-killing of a criminal fearing a worse fate: its scope grew steadily, in step with the tendency, profitable to the crown, to declare forfeit the goods of anyone who died by violence." Alan Harding, *A Social History of English Law* 64 (1966).

Suicide used to be included within the definition of *homicide* (= the killing of a human being by a human being), but the modern trend has been to distinguish the one from the other by defining *homicide* as "the killing of a human being by *another* human being."

B. As an Agent Noun. In the early 18th century, *suicide* took on the secondary sense of "one who dies by his or her own hand," and the word has been steadily used with this meaning ever since—e.g.: "Both the elder of Anne's sisters, Jane, and an aunt, Frances, were *suicides.*" John Simon, *Connoisseur of Madness, Addict of Suicide,* New Criterion, Dec. 1991, at 58, 59. Earlier synonyms, now less frequently employed, include *self-destroyer, self-killer, self-murderer, self-slayer,* and *felo-de-se.*

C. As a Verb. The verb has been used intransitively <he suicided>, reflexively <he suicided himself>, and transitively <he suicided her>. In the intransitive and reflexive uses, the senses are self-evident; in the transitive use, the sense is "to drive to suicide." In legal writing, the most common use is the intransitive one—e.g.: "Three days later he *suicided* by drowning in Sanhican Creek." *Bullis v. Pitman,* 105 A. 589, 590 (N.J. Ch. 1918)./ "[W]hatever the diagnosis of Nott's case, the inescapable fact remains that he *suicided* within forty-eight hours after his discharge." *Nott v. State,* 75 N.Y.S.2d 737, 740 (Ct. Cl. 1947)./ "On November 14, 1963, his mother, Lorine Asher Toole, *suicided.*" *State v. Toole,* 173 So. 2d 872, 873 (La. Ct. App. 1965).

suicide victim, a seeming OXYMORON, is a phrase that suggests a dogmatic stand on the issue whether suicide is ever justifiable. The less doctrinaire equivalent, *suicide* (n.), probably better suits most legal contexts. E.g., "Typically, in his experience, the gun is found on the seat next to *suicide victims* [read *suicides*] or clutched in their hands." *State v. Barrett,* 445 N.W.2d 749, 756 (Iowa 1989) (Lavorato, J., dissenting).

sui juris; sui generis. *Sui juris* /soo-ee-**jur**-əs/ = (1) of full age and capacity; or (2) having full social and civil rights. Sense (1) is more usual—e.g.: "Since in the present case all the beneficiaries are not in being and *sui juris,* revocation by consent is impossible."/ "If the beneficiary is *sui juris,* the promisee, at his election, may maintain an action for breach of contract."/ "Resignation is effective only when approved by the proper court, unless the trust terms provide otherwise, or by consent of all the beneficiaries if they are *sui juris.*" Often this LATINISM is easily translated into ordinary English; when that is so, it should be.

Sui generis /soo-ee-**jen**-ə-rəs/ (= of its own kind; individual; like only to itself) is an acceptable LATINISM because of its familiarity. The phrase is singular only, and should not be used with plural nouns. E.g., "That case has always been considered *sui generis,* and inconsistent with the fundamental principle of the action."/ "Garnishment is an anomaly, a statutory invention *sui generis,* with no affinity to any action known to the common law."/ "The strictly fundamental legal relations are, after all, *sui generis;* and thus it is that attempts at formal definition are always unsatisfactory, if not altogether useless."

The terms are sometimes confused. In the following sentence, for example, *sui juris* is wrongly made *sui generis:* "The expression 'uninhabited dwelling' is *sui juris* [read *sui generis*] and should be given some meaning not covered by the term 'dwelling' itself." *Reeves v. State,* 16 So. 2d 699, 702 (Ala. 1943).

suit; bill; action. Anciently, a litigant brought a *suit* or *bill* in equity and an *action* at law. At an early date, however, *suit* was imported into common-law procedure—hence the development of *suit at law* and *lawsuit.* E.g., "In *suits* at common law, where the value in controversy shall exceed twenty dollars, the right of trial by jury shall be preserved . . . ." U.S. Const. amend. VII./ "[The] bill of peace originated as a means or remedy of seeking to enjoin repeated attempts to litigate the same right." William Q. deFuniak, *Handbook of Modern Equity* 241 (1956).

suit, v.t. (= to sue), is obsolete in legal English, although the negative form *nonsuit* is still used as a verb. See **action (A)** & **nonsuit.**

suitability, in the sense "liability to suit" <the suitability of the states of the union>, is recorded in none of the major dictionaries. This sense is obfuscatory at best for lawyer-readers as well as for nonlawyers; it should be avoided. See **nonsuitability.**

suit at law is an esp. formal way of saying *lawsuit,* the usual term today. Generally, the careful writer would prefer to use one word rather than three if no nuance is lost. But when law is contrasted with equity, as in the following example, using the phrase makes good sense: "Here, the Neuzils filed the *suit at law* [i.e., as opposed to an equitable action]." *Neuzil v. City of Iowa City,* 451 N.W.2d 159, 163 (Iowa 1990). See **suit.**

suit money. In some American jurisdictions, this phrase refers to the husband's payment of the wife's attorney's fees in a divorce action.

suitor has virtually opposite meanings in lay and legal language, though a 17th-century writer found common ground: "Amonge sutors in love and in lawe money is a comoun medler" (*OED* quot. fr. c. 1660). The lay *suitor* seeks matrimony; the legal *suitor* seeks legal redress.

Suitor is properly used only of a *complainant* or *plaintiff* in a suit, as opposed to a *defendant.* E.g., "[A] *suitor's* conduct in relation to the matter at hand may disentitle him to the relief he seeks." *Sanders v. U.S.,* 373 U.S. 1, 17 (1963)./ "Every *suitor* who resorts to chancery for any sort of relief by injunction may, on a mere statement of belief that the defendant can easily make away with or transport his money or goods, impose an injunction on him."/ "In an era when the greatest effort in history is being made to neutralize financial disparity in litigation, there is little reason why a *suitor* should have permitted his limited means to influence too late a start."

In the context of mergers and acquisitions, *suitor* retains its overtones of wooing: "The Delaware Supreme Court, in a ruling late yesterday afternoon, blocked a takeover of the publishing company by a rival *suitor,* Kohlberg, Davis, Roberts & Company, the leveraged-buyout firm." Jacob I. Fabrikant, *Maxwell Wins on Macmillan,* N.Y. Times, 3 Nov. 1988, at 29.

suit over. See **over (A).**

suit papers. See **court papers.**

suitwrong. This recent legal NEOLOGISM, unrecorded in the dictionaries, is hardly a model of lucidity. E.g., "The filing of the action against *a suitwrong* [read *an inappropriate*] corporate defendant did not toll the statute of limitations as to the correct defendant."

sum certain. See POSTPOSITIVE ADJECTIVES.

summarily = by summary legal procedure. E.g., "When you are prosecuted for dangerous driving you may, if you wish, refuse to have your case dealt with in the police court—i.e. *'summarily'*—and insist on being tried by a jury." Anon., *The Home Counsellor* 112 ([London: Odhams Press] c. 1940–45).

summary judgment = a judgment granted on a claim, about which there is no genuine issue of material fact and upon which the movant is entitled to prevail as a matter of law. See Fed. R. Civ. P. 56.

When used as a PHRASAL ADJECTIVE, *summary judgment* needs to be hyphenated: "And still more pressure was coming from Fish, who might well gut the Hunts' entire case by granting the banks' *summary judgment* [read *summary-judgment*] motion." John A. Jenkins, *The Litigators* 294 (1989).

summary offence; indictable offence. In England, crimes are divided into *summary offences,* which are triable in the lower courts (magistrates' courts) without a jury, and *indictable offences,* which are triable in the Crown Court by jury. A few indictable offences, sometimes known as *hybrid offences* or *dual offences,* are triable either on indictment or summarily. *Summary offences* were formerly known as *petty offences,* but the expression fell into disuse because it minimized the seriousness of the crimes it described.

As Glanville Williams notes, the phrase *summary offence* has two liabilities: it exemplifies HYPALLAGE and misleadingly suggests greater substantive differences than it denotes: "The term '*summary offence*' is now established, and is used in legislation; but it is somewhat inappropriate, since what is summary is not the offence itself but the mode of procedure. Even as applied to the mode of procedure 'summary' is an infelicitous adjective, because the procedure of magistrates' courts is supposed in general to be as careful and formal as trial by jury." Glanville Williams, *Textbook of Criminal Law* 10 (1978).

summation (AmE) = (1) the lawyer's closing argument at trial; or (2) formerly, a judge's closing speech to the jury summarizing the evidence (an equivalent of the BrE sense of *summing-up*)—e.g.: (Sense 2) "[T]he court in its *summation* of the evidence to the jury, referred to that fact . . . ." *Kelly v. Georgia,* 68 F. 652, 657 (S.D. Ga. 1895).

summing-up is the British phrase meaning "the judge's summary for the jury of the main points in evidence, together with his guidance on the form of the verdict to be given." E.g., "Their Lordships would repeat, it is the effect of the *summing-up* as a whole that matters and not any stated verbal formula used in the course of it." (Eng.)/ "The Judge's *summing-up* was brief but thorough, and after a short retirement the jury brought in a verdict of guilty." Stanley Jackson, *The Life and Cases of Mr. Justice Humphreys* 175 (n.d. [1951]). The AmE equivalent is *jury instructions* or *instructions to the jury.*

In AmE, *summing up* refers to the closing arguments of counsel: "The judge instructs the jury orally at the conclusion of the trial after the *summing up* arguments of counsel to the jury." Charles A. Wright, *The Law of Federal Courts* 672 (5th ed. 1994).

summer associate. See **clerk.**

summonee (= one who has been summoned) is omitted from the *OED, W3,* and most other dictionaries, but it has proved useful in legal writing. E.g., "The *summonees'* attempt to bring the *summoned* [read *summonsed* (q.v.)] documents within the work product doctrine is similarly meritless." *U.S. v. Davis,* 636 F.2d 1028, 1039 (5th Cir. 1981). See -EE (A).

summons, n., = (1) formerly, a writ directed to a sheriff and requiring him to summon a defendant to appear in court; or (2) a writ or process commencing the plaintiff's action and requiring a defendant to appear and answer.

summons, v.t., dates from the 17th century and is still in fairly common use in the sense (1) "to cite to appear before a court or a judge or magistrate"; or (2) "to request (information) by summons." The verb is properly inflected *summonsed* in the past tense, *summonses* in the third-person singular.

The term *summonsed* has some notable detractors, including U.S. District Judge Lynn N. Hughes, who has criticized the verb in private correspondence, and Glanville Williams: "The horrible expression '*summonsed* for an offence' (turning the noun 'summons' into a verb) has now become accepted usage, but 'summoned' remains not only allowable but preferable." Glanville Williams, *Learning the Law* 15 n.28 (11th ed. 1982).

When used in sense (1), as by saying that a *person* is *summonsed,* the verb appears to be a NEEDLESS VARIANT of *summon,* v.t.: "I came here because I had been *summonsed* [read *summoned*] by Medina council to pay £342 . . . ." David Sapsted, *Poll Tax Case Collapses in Confusion,* Times, 2 June 1990, at 1 (quoting David Icke).

In modern legal usage, however, a latent DIFFERENTIATION has emerged: by HYPALLAGE has arisen the idiom that *information* may be *summonsed,* as in sense (2). E.g.: "We view the requirement in this Circuit to be that the taxpayer must show that the Government actually possesses the information *summonsed,* such that enforcement of a summons is 'unnecessary.'" *U.S. v. Texas Heart Inst.,* 755 F.2d 469, 476 (5th Cir. 1985)./ "We conclude that the IRS is not already in possession of the *summonsed* information in the instant appeal."

summonses is the correct plural form of *summons,* n. E.g., "Mr. Winn does not ask us to send back the other *summonses* that are consequential *summonses.*" (Eng.)/ "Before us are two appeals from separate orders of the district court enforcing two sets of Internal Revenue Service *summonses.*"

sumptuous; sumptuary. These words have almost opposite senses. *Sumptuous* = excessively luxurious; made or produced at great cost. *Sump-*

tuary = relating to regulating expenditures by individuals on food, clothing, jewelry, and other personal items.

sundry (= various) is, in AmE, a quaint term with literary associations. The clichéd DOUBLET *various and sundry* ought to be avoided even in the most casual contexts, for it smacks of glibness.

sunk. See **sink.**

sunset law; sunshine law. Though superficially appearing as if they might be antonyms, these picturesque terms for administrative laws have little relation apart from their both arising in AmE during the 1970s.

Sunset law = a statute under which a governmental agency or program automatically terminates at the end of a fixed period unless it is formally renewed. By extension, the transitive verb *sunset* (= to subject to such a statute) likewise came into existence in the late 1970s. E.g., "[T]he legislature's failure to provide 'phase-out' deregulation resulted in the *sunsetting* of the entire state motor carrier regulatory scheme . . . ." *Alterman Transp. Liner, Inc. v. Department of Transp.,* 519 So. 2d 1005, 1008 (Fla. Dist. Ct. App. 1987). The past tense and past participle are awkwardly made *sunsetted*—e.g.: "We cannot decide to send this case first to the Collection Agency Board because it was *sunsetted* effective December 31, 1980 . . . ." *Wiginton v. Pacific Credit Corp.,* 634 P.2d 111, 117 (Haw. Ct. App. 1981).

Sunshine law = a statute requiring a governmental department or agency to open its meetings and its records to public access. E.g., "*Sunshine laws* are aimed chiefly at keeping administrative decisions above board. The underlying assumption of *sunshine laws* is that it is unwise to permit our administrators to make public policy decisions behind closed doors." Kenneth F. Warren, *Administrative Law in the American Political System* 187 (1982).

superadd (= to add over and above) is rarely used in lay, and infrequently in legal, contexts. It is usually pompous in place of *add*—e.g.: "In many legal systems, therefore, a discretionary or moderating influence has been *superadded* [read *added*] to the rigour of formulated law." Carleton K. Allen, *Law in the Making* 385 (7th ed. 1964).

supercede. See **supersede.**

supererogatory has two almost opposite sets of connotations, some positive and others negative. The core sense is "going beyond what is required." On the one hand, the word may connote "superfluous," and is often used in this way. On the other hand, it may mean "performing more than duty or circumstances require; doing more than is minimally needed."

superfirm = a large prestigious law firm. E.g., "Chris Harvey is from the Dallas *superfirm* of Strasburger, Price, Kelton, Martin and Unis, which has the reputation of being perhaps the best insurance defense office in Texas . . . ." Joseph C. Goulden, *The Million Dollar Lawyers* 72 (1978). Cf. **superlawyer.**

SUPERFLUITIES of various kinds may be found in most legal writing. This entry contains a few common examples of unnecessary words: "A foreign mining corporation may carry on such functional intrastate operations as *those of* [omit *those of*] mining or refining."

Verbs are often unnecessarily repeated in comparisons—e.g.: "Of the many possible forms of human capital, none has received more attention over the past two decades than *has* [omit *has*] the economics of education."

Superfluous commas abound in most older judicial opinions—e.g.: "The witness who proved this, [omit comma] said . . . ." (1809)/ "The declaration stated, [omit comma] that the plaintiff . . . ." (1842). Even today, sentences just like those two are commonplace.

The best contemporary writing is free from such minor refuse; the fewer impediments we put in the way, the more likely readers are to follow. See CUTTING OUT THE CHAFF & VERBOSITY.

superimpose; superpose. Both forms are used in legal writing, the older form, *superimpose* (1794), being more familiar to most readers. E.g., "*Superimposed* upon this uniform system is the maximum grant regulation, the operative effect of which is to create two classes of needy children and two classes of families." *Superpose,* today rightly counted among NEEDLESS VARIANTS, is recorded from 1823.

superior. See **inferior.**

superlawyer dates from the early 1960s but was not popularized until Joseph C. Goulden published his book *The Superlawyers* in 1971. The word, largely confined to journalism, is typical of the glitzy, hyperbolic labels characteristic of journalese—as the second and third examples illustrate: "The French *notaire* is a *superlawyer,* especially trained for his work, a combination of lawyer, court clerk, and petty judge." René A.

Wormser, *The Story of the Law* 213 n.† (1962)./ "[T]his man . . . makes probably as much money a year as . . . the fabled Washington *superlawyers* Clark Clifford and Lloyd Cutler . . . ." Joseph C. Goulden, *The Million Dollar Lawyers* 76 (1978)./ "The Harvard law professor and *superlawyer* has crowded his office in Cambridge, Mass., with enough paraphernalia to stock a Dershowitz museum." Steven Taylor, *Dershowitz on the Offensive,* National Jurist, April/May 1992, at 10.

The adjective *super-lawyerlike* may predate the noun: "In all likelihood, the general slant of the new Justice will be just about the opposite of Reed's—except for a similarly *super-lawyerlike* over-attention to detail." Fred Rodell, *Nine Men* 329 (1955). See **lawyerly.**

superlegislature. This tendentious term, dating from the 1920s, describes a court that usurps the power of the legislative branch of government. E.g., "To decide . . . [these matters] is, in my opinion, an exercise of the powers of a *superlegislature*—not the performance of the constitutional function of judicial review." *Jay Burns Baking Co. v. Bryan,* 264 U.S. 504, 534 (1924) (Brandeis, J., dissenting)./ "Our recent decisions make plain that we do not sit as a *superlegislature* to weigh the wisdom of legislation nor to decide whether the policy which it expresses offends the public welfare." *Day-Brite Lighting, Inc. v. Missouri,* 342 U.S. 421, 423 (1952)./ "Marshall made of the Court a sort of *superlegislature,* back in 1803 . . . ." Fred Rodell, *Nine Men* 25 (1955)./ "Rights such as these are in principle indistinguishable from those involved here, and to extend the 'compelling interest' rule to all cases in which such rights are affected would go far toward making this Court a '*superlegislature.*'" *Shapiro v. Thompson,* 394 U.S. 618, 661 (1969) (Harlan, J., dissenting).

superpose. See **superimpose.**

supersede. A. Spelling. This word—from the Latin root *-sed* "to sit," not *-ced* "to move"—is the proper spelling. But so many other English words end in *-cede* or *-ceed* that many writers unconsciously distort the spelling of *supersede.* Spelling it correctly is one of the hallmarks of a punctilious writer. The misspelling occurs in some surprising places, as in Arthur A. Leff, *The Leff Dictionary of Law,* 94 Yale L.J. 1855, 1867 (1985), under "Abortion Act," and in nearly a thousand federal judicial opinions in the U.S. It has even fouled a statute: "Any demand for a product of discovery *supercedes* [read *supersedes*] any inconsistent order . . . ." Tex. Bus. & Com. Code Ann. § 15.10(d)(2) (West 1987). And the title of a law-review article: Charles J. Yeager & Lee Hargrave, *The Power of the Attorney General to Supercede* [read *Supersede*] *a District Attorney,* 51 La. L. Rev. 733 (1991) (and passim in text).

B. Special Sense. In law, *supersede* sometimes carries the specialized sense "to invoke or make applicable the right of supersedeas against [an award of damages]," a sense unknown to nonlawyers, for whom the term means "to replace, supplant." Following are examples of the special legal use: "It is clear that, if the relator was entitled to *supersede* the judgment against him [i.e., post a supersedeas bond], the court of appeals has the power to enter any order necessary for that purpose."/ "In *Aetna Club v. Jackson,* the court of civil appeals had before it an original application for a writ of mandamus to require the trial judge to fix the amount of the bond necessary to *supersede* a final judgment granting an injunction."

C. Corresponding Noun. *Supersession* is the noun form, meaning either "the act of superseding" or "the state of being superseded." E.g., "[T]he writ of tolt died a natural death with the *supersession* of both forms of writ of right by the newer action of ejectment . . . ." H.G. Hanbury, *English Courts of Law* 46 (2d ed. 1953).

As with the verb, the internal *-s-* is sometimes incorrectly made *-c-:* "The Louisiana Supreme Court declared the statute authorizing *supercession* [read *supersession*] to be unconstitutional . . . ." Charles J. Yeager & Lee Hargrave, *The Power of the Attorney General to Supercede* [*sic*] *a District Attorney,* 51 La. L. Rev. 733, 734 (1991).

Supersedure is a NEEDLESS VARIANT in all but beekeeping contexts, but it still occasionally appears: "Despite the apparent *supersedure* [read *supersession*] of the act, however, some decisions continue to treat it as controlling in this area." E.W. Cleary, *McCormick on Evidence* § 97, at 24 (3d ed. Supp. 1987).

D. For *surpass.* This is a fairly unusual MALAPROPISM—e.g.: "Arguably, Russia *supersedes* [read *surpasses*] even England in the publication of Shakespeare's works and the staging of his plays." Melor Sturua, *O.J. Through Russian Eyes,* Wall St. J., 21 Sept. 1994, at A14.

supersede and displace. See DOUBLETS, TRIPLETS, AND SYNONYM-STRINGS.

supersedeas, when used elliptically as an attributive noun for *supersedeas bond* or *writ,* forms the plural in *-es.* E.g., "It also prescribed the conditions upon which such appeals or writs of error should operate as *supersedeases.*" *Holland v. Webster,* 29 So. 625, 630 (Fla. 1901) (Mabry, J., dissenting).

superseding cause. See CAUSATION (E).

supersedure; supersession. See **supersede (C).**

SUPERSTITIONS. In 1926, H.W. Fowler used the term "superstitions" in reference to what, in the field of writing, are merely "unintelligent applications of an unintelligent dogma" (*MEU1* at 586). Experts in usage have long railed against them as arrant nonsense, yet they retain a firm grip—if not a stranglehold—on the average person's mind when it comes to how best to put words on paper. Most of them are perpetuated in the classrooms in which children and adolescents learn to write.

Most of these superstitions are treated elsewhere in this book, in the entry to which the reader is referred at the end of each subentry. For additional perspectives on these points, below are briefly collected the views of respected authorities on style, grammar, and usage.

A. Never End a Sentence with a Preposition. "The origin of the misguided rule is not hard to ascertain. To begin with, there is the meaning of the word 'preposition' itself: stand before. The meaning derives from Latin, and in the Latin language prepositions do usually stand before the words they govern. But Latin is not English. In English prepositions have been used as terminal words in a sentence since the days of Chaucer, and in that position they are completely idiomatic." Theodore M. Bernstein, *Miss Thistlebottom's Hobgoblins: The Careful Writer's Guide to the Taboos, Bugbears, and Outmoded Rules of English Usage* 177 (1971). See PREPOSITIONS (A).

B. Never Split an Infinitive. "[T]he split infinitive is in full accord with the spirit of modern English and is now widely used by our best writers." George O. Curme, *English Grammar* 148 (1947; repr. 1955)./ "However offensive it may be to many persons, the split infinitive makes clear beyond all doubt what the adverb modifies." G.C. Thornton, *Legislative Drafting* 28 (2d ed. 1979). See SPLIT INFINITIVES.

C. Never Split a Verb Phrase. "When an adverb is to be used with [a compound verb], its normal place is between the auxiliary (or sometimes the first auxiliary if there are two or more) and the rest. Not only is there no objection to thus splitting a compound verb, but any other position for the adverb requires special justification: *I have never seen her,* not *I never have seen her,* is the ordinary idiom, though the rejected order becomes the right one if emphasis is to be put on *have* (*I may have had chances of seeing her but I never have*). But it is plain . . . that a prejudice has grown up against dividing compound verbs . . . . [I]t is entirely unfounded." H.W. Fowler, *A Dictionary of Modern English Usage* 464 (Ernest Gowers ed., 2d ed. 1965). See ADVERBS, PROBLEMS WITH (A).

D. Never Begin a Sentence with *and* or *but*. "Next to the groundless notion that it is incorrect to end an English sentence with a preposition, perhaps the most wide-spread of many false beliefs about the use of our language is the equally groundless notion that it is incorrect to begin one with 'but' or 'and.' As in the case of the superstition about the prepositional ending, no textbook supports it, but apparently about half of our teachers of English go out of their way to handicap their pupils by inculcating it. One cannot help wondering whether those who teach such a monstrous doctrine ever read any English themselves." Charles Allen Lloyd, *We Who Speak English* 19 (1938). See **and (A)** & **but (A).**

E. Never Write a One-sentence Paragraph. "[T]o interpose a one-sentence paragraph at intervals—at longish intervals—is prudent. Such a device helps the eye and enables the reader (especially if 'the going is heavy') to regain his breath between one impressive or weighty or abstruse paragraph and the next." Eric Partridge, *Usage and Abusage* 224–25 (5th ed. 1957; repr. 1963)./ "Basically, there are three situations . . . that can occasion a one-sentence paragraph: (a) when you wish to emphasize a crucial point that might otherwise be buried; (b) when you wish to dramatize a transition from one stage in your argument to the next; and (c) when instinct tells you that your reader is tiring and would appreciate a mental rest-station." John R. Trimble, *Writing with Style* 94 (1975).

F. Never Begin a Sentence with *because*. So novel and absurd is this superstition that seemingly no authority on writing has countered it in print. It appears to result from concern about fragments—e.g.: "Then the group broke for lunch. Because we were hungry." Of course, the second "sentence" is merely a fragment, not a complete sentence. (See INCOMPLETE SENTENCES (A).) But problems of that kind simply cannot give rise to a general prohibition against starting a sentence with *because.* Good writers do so frequently—e.g.: "*Because* of the war the situation in hospitals is, of course, serious." E.B. White, "A Weekend with the Angels," in *The Second Tree from the Corner* 3, 6 (1954)./ "*Because* the relationship between remarks is often vague in this passage, we could not rewrite it with certainty without knowing the facts . . . ." Donald Hall, *Writing Well* 104 (1973). See **because (D).**

G. Never Use *since* to Mean *because*. "It is a delusion that *since* may be used only as an adverb in a temporal sense ('We have been here since ten o'clock'). It is also a causal conjunction meaning *for* or *because:* 'Since it is raining, we had better take an umbrella.'" Roy H. Copperud, *American Usage and Style: The Consensus* 349 (1980). See **as** (A).

H. Never Use *between* with More Than Two Objects. "When Miss Thistlebottom taught you in grammar school that *between* applies only to two things and *among* to more than two, she was for the most part correct. *Between* essentially does apply to only two, but sometimes the 'two' relationship is present when more than two elements are involved. For example, it would be proper to say that 'The President was trying to start negotiations between Israel, Egypt, Syria and Jordan' if what was contemplated was not a round-table conference but separate talks involving Israel and each of the other three nations." Theodore M. Bernstein, *Dos, Don'ts & Maybes of English Usage* 29 (1977). See **between** (A).

I. Never Use the First-Person Pronouns *I* and *me*. "[I]f you want to write like a professional, just about the first thing you have to do is get used to the first person singular. Just plunge in and write 'I' whenever 'I' seems to be the word that is called for. Never mind the superstitious notion that it's immodest to do so. It just isn't so." Rudolf Flesch, *A New Way to Better English* 49 (1958). See FIRST PERSON (A).

J. Never Use Contractions. "Your style will obviously be warmer and truer to your personality if you use contractions like 'I'll' and 'won't' when they fit comfortably into what you're writing. 'I'll be glad to see them if they don't get mad' is less stiff than 'I will be glad to see them if they do not get mad.' There's no rule against such informality—trust your ear and your instincts." William Zinsser, *On Writing Well* 117 (3d ed. 1985). See CONTRACTIONS.

K. Never Use *you* in Referring to Your Reader. "Keep a running conversation with your reader. Use the second-person pronoun whenever you can. Translate everything into *you* language. *This applies to citizens over 65 = if you're over 65, this applies to you. It must be remembered that = you must remember. Many people don't realize = perhaps you don't realize.*

"Always write directly to *you,* the person you're trying to reach with your written message. Don't write in mental isolation; reach out to your reader." Rudolf Flesch, *How to Be Brief: An Index to Simple Writing* 114 (1962). See **you.**

supervene (= to come on or occur as something additional or extraneous; to come directly or shortly after something else, either as a consequence of it or in contrast with it) is rarely seen outside the law. E.g., "The attachment of a judgment lien will not sever the joint tenancy, thus leaving the judgment creditor exposed to the destruction of the lien by a *supervening* death of the judgment debtor."

supervening cause. See CAUSATION (D) & (E).

supervision. See **oversight.**

supervisory; supervisorial. *Supervisory* = of or relating to supervision. *Supervisorial* = of or relating to a supervisor. E.g., "There shall be in each county a board of supervisors, to consist of three members who shall be qualified electors of their *supervisorial* district . . . ." *McCarthy v. State,* 101 P.2d 449, 451 (Ariz. 1940) (quoting a statute).

supplemental pleading; amended pleading. American caselaw is rife with judicial statements that counsel mislabeled an *amended pleading* by calling it a *supplemental pleading,* or vice-versa. The important distinction concerns when the events pleaded occurred. A *supplemental pleading* puts into the record matter that is material to an issue that has arisen after the filing of a pleading. An *amended pleading,* by contrast, puts right a matter that might have been pleaded at the time the pleading being amended was filed, but that was erroneously or inadvertently omitted or misstated. See Fed. R. Civ. P. 15(a), 15(d).

supplementary; supplemental; suppletory; suppletive. *Supplementary* is the ordinary word. The other forms have the same meaning, namely, "of the nature of, forming, or serving as, a remedy to the deficiencies of something."

One might jump to brand the three other forms NEEDLESS VARIANTS, yet the law has found niches for two of them in special phrases. In the U.S., we refer usually to a *supplemental pleading* (q.v.), not *supplementary.* In older Anglo-American law, a *suppletory oath* was "an oath (given by a party in his own favor) admitted to supply a deficiency in legal evidence." These variant forms should be confined to these particular uses.

Suppletive is probably best considered a NEEDLESS VARIANT of *supplementary*—e.g.: "Here the legal need is for substantive *suppletive* [read *supplementary*] rules, rules which presuppose and supplement the incomplete private transaction with specific 'terms.'" R.E. Speidel et al., *Commercial Law Teaching Materials* 2 (4th ed. 1987)./"This framework consists mostly of *suppletive* [read *supplementary*] rules of law." A.N. Yiannopoulos, *Of Legal Usufruct, the Surviving Spouse, and Article 890 of the Louisiana Civil Code,* 49 La. L. Rev. 803, 803 (1989).

suppliant; supplicant. The latter is a NEEDLESS VARIANT of the former, an ARCHAISM referring to one who supplicates—i.e., who begs, prays, or humbly petitions or entreats. E.g., "Consequently, *suppliants* began to address their prayers to the Chancellor instead of to the King or Council."/ "In any petition the *suppliants* put forward an alternative ground for their claim." (Eng.)

supply an omission. In the modern idiom, we *make up for* or *remedy* or *compensate for* an omission rather than *supplying* it. E.g., "The class action rule does not suggest that the zeal or talent of the representative plaintiffs' attorney can *supply* [read *make up for*] the omission of the requirement that claims of the representative parties be typical of the class." Nothing can *supply* an omission. One can *supply* (= to make up a deficiency in [*OED*]) in an obsolete sense of the word. But today *supply* is so closely connected with the sense "to provide" that it seems almost contradictory to write of *supplying (providing) an omission.*

supposable; supposit(it)ious; suppositional; suppositive. *Supposable* = capable of being supposed; presumable. The words *suppositious* and *supposititious* sometimes cause confusion. Although some modern dictionaries list these as variants, some DIFFERENTIATION is both possible and desirable. *Suppositious* should be used to mean "hypothetical; theoretical; assumed." *Supposititious* should be confined to its usual sense, "illegitimate; spurious; counterfeit." E.g., "May there not be feigned legal relations, fictitious legal rights and duties, *supposititious* titles?" Lon L. Fuller, *Legal Fictions* 27 (1967). In legal contexts, *supposititious* when applied to a child means "falsely presented as a genuine heir" (*W10*). E.g., "The main question in dispute was whether one calling himself 'Archibald Douglas' was the legitimate child of Lady Jane Douglas or was *supposititious.*" (Eng.) The phrase *supposititious will* = a fake or falsified will.

Suppositional = conjectural, hypothetical. It has much the same sense as *suppositious,* and is perhaps generally the clearer word. *Suppositive* (= characterized by supposition; supposed) is a NEEDLESS VARIANT of *supposititious* and *suppositional.*

supposing is inferior to *suppose* in introducing a hypothetical. E.g., "*Supposing* [read *Suppose*] that car A collides with car B at this intersection."

supposition; supposal; suppose, n. In legal contexts, as in most contexts, *supposition* is the ordinary word, and the others are probably NEEDLESS VARIANTS. *Supposal* is sometimes used by logicians.

supposit(it)ious; suppositional; suppositive. See **supposable.**

suppressible; suppressable. The former spelling is standard. See -ABLE (A).

suppressio veri. See ***suggestio falsi.***

supra. This citational signal is disfavored in modern legal writing, inasmuch as short-form citations are more convenient for the reader. An archaic variant of *supra* is *ubi supra* (= as above). E.g., "In *Inches v. Hill, ubi supra* [read *698 F.2d at 344,* e.g., if the case has previously been cited in full], the same person had become owner of the equitable life estate and of the equitable remainder, and, no reason appearing to the contrary, the court decreed a conveyance by the trustees to the owner." See ***infra* (B)** & ***ante.***

supraconstitutional (= above the constitution) is a NEOLOGISM that might be apt in some circumstances but is ready-made for hyperbole. Following is the earliest known example: "Calling the court 'a *supraconstitutional* body that has made itself unaccountable to the people of Illinois,' [Professor Louisin] also took a swipe at the court's inability to 'root out corruption among judges.'" Paul Marcotte, *Auditing Dispute,* A.B.A. J., Aug. 1990, at 16, 16.

supralegal (= above the law) is a NEOLOGISM that has enjoyed moderate success in modern legal writing. E.g., "We might suppose from this phrase that Bodin intended his sovereign to be an irresponsible *supra-legal* power, and some of the language in the *Republic* does seem to support that interpretation." J.L. Brierly, *The Law of Nations* 9 (5th ed. 1955).

supranational is a term used of a body of law that is of higher authority and wider application than national law, but yet is not international or worldwide, such as European Community Law. E.g., "The decisions of the Community derive their binding force from the fact that they are taken by organs endowed with the appropriate power by the Treaties . . . . To describe this new type of political organism, the word '*supranational*' has been used." Trevor C. Hartley, *The Foundations of European Community Law* 6–7 (1981).

supra protest. The phrase can be translated *under protest,* and ought to be. Spelling the phrase with a circumflex (*suprâ protest*) is an error, perhaps the result of HYPERCORRECTION—e.g.: "Then any person, not being a party already liable thereon, may, with the consent of the holder, intervene and accept the bill *suprâ protest* [read *under protest* or *supra protest*] . . . ." 1 E.W. Chance, *Principles of Mercantile Law* 187 (P.W. French ed., 13th ed. 1950).

supreme court, in most American jurisdictions, denotes the highest court of appeal. New York, like South Africa, is an exception; *The New York Times* has editorialized about the names of the New York courts and their judges: "The trial court is misnamed the Supreme Court, which is what most people expect to find at the top. A system that uses the term Supreme Court justice for judges of original jurisdiction is a system that resists modernization and invites cynicism." N.Y. Times, 3 Jan. 1985, at Y18.

Supreme Court of Judicature, an English court, consists of the *High Court of Justice* (q.v.), the *Court of Appeal* (q.v.), and the *Crown Court.* The Supreme Court of Judicature Acts of 1873 and 1875 consolidated the following courts into the *Supreme Court of Judicature:* Queen's Bench, Common Pleas, Exchequer, Chancery, Probate, Divorce and Matrimonial Causes, Admiralty, and (from 1883) the London Court of Bankruptcy. The phrase is a misnomer, really, because the House of Lords is superior to all the courts just mentioned.

Supreme Court of the United States. See **United States Supreme Court.**

supreme law of the land. See **law of the land.**

sur appears in various LAW FRENCH phrases. It means merely "on"; the English word should supplant it wherever possible. E.g., "About 18 months thereafter the plaintiff caused to be issued an attachment *sur judgment* [read *on the judgment*] in which the City of Philadelphia Police Beneficiary Association was summoned as garnishee." *Mamlin v. Tener,* 23 A.2d 90, 91 (Pa. Super. Ct. 1941). For *action sur le case,* see **action on the case.**

surcease = a cessation; a temporary respite. To confuse this word with *solace* (= that which gives comfort when one has experienced disappointment, stress, or grief) is a MALAPROPISM. "Having failed to offer the challenged testimony in an acceptable manner, appellant may not draw *surcease* [read *solace*] from *Chambers,* which is inapplicable."/ "Knighton sought a stay of execution and other habeas *surcease* [read *solace*] in a petition filed in district court." See **death.**

surety, n., in law, usu. means either (1) "a formal engagement entered into, a pledge, bond, guarantee, or security given for the fulfillment of an undertaking," or (2) "one who undertakes some specific responsibility on behalf of another." Sense (1), illustrated in the following sentence, is slightly less usual: "One nominated as trustee is not required to take an oath that he will faithfully discharge his duties as trustee, or to execute a bond with satisfactory *sureties* conditioned upon the faithful performance of his duties." The archaic lay sense "certainty" is rarely encountered today.

In the broad sense, a *guarantor* is a type of surety (sense [2]). But some authorities distinguish between the two terms, giving *surety* a narrow sense: a *surety* joins in the same promise as the principal and becomes primarily liable, while a *guarantor* makes a separate promise and is only secondarily liable—i.e., liable only if the principal defaults.

The word *surety* has three syllables /***shoor**-ə-tee*/.

suretyship; suretiship. The former spelling is preferred.

surmisal is a NEEDLESS VARIANT of *surmise,* n.

surmise and conjecture. See DOUBLETS, TRIPLETS, AND SYNONYM-STRINGS.

surname; Christian name. The *surname* is the part of a name not given in baptism but acquired originally by accident or by custom and common to all the members of the family. In many cases it was derived from physical characteristics and later transmitted to descendants; in other cases it indicated paternity, e.g., Davidson. In Gaelic, *MacDonald* indicated the son of Donald. Such names came to be called surnames from the sire or father. A person can adopt any surname so long as he or she does not do so with fraudulent intent. In modern practice a woman, upon marrying, frequently adds (but need not) her husband's surname to her own, e.g., Hillary Rodham Clinton. And often, of course, she keeps her own without adding his.

The *Christian name* or *forename* is older; it was the baptismal name and in medieval England was the only name. Surnames were given later to differentiate, e.g., in a charter *Testibus Willelmo Cancellario et Roberto filio Haemonis.*

The first name of a person not of the Christian faith is better called a *forename.* E.g., "'Woranoj' is the *forename* and 'Anurugsa' is the *surname* of my friend in Bangkok."

surplus is the tendentiously humorous group term for lawyers—the invention of Eric Partridge. See *Usage and Abusage* 300 (5th ed. 1957). Hence we have a gaggle of geese, a bevy of quail, a flock of sheep, and a surplus of lawyers.

surplusage; surplus. The distinction is slight. *Surplus,* the fundamental term, means "what remains over, what is not required for the purpose at hand, esp. excess of public revenue over expenditure for the financial year" (*COD*). *Surplusage* is a NEEDLESS VARIANT in all senses but the primarily legal one: "an excess or superabundance of words; a word, clause, or statement in an indictment, plea, or legal instrument that is not necessary to its adequacy, or in a statute that is merely redundant and insignificant." Courts often recite the canon of construction that prevents them from reading statutory or contractual language in a way that renders part of it surplusage. *Surplusage,* like *surplus,* is stressed on the first syllable.

surrebutter; surrebuttal. See **rebuttal,** -ER (B) & COMMON-LAW PLEADINGS.

surrejoinder. See -ER (B) & COMMON-LAW PLEADINGS.

surrender, in the language of nonlawyers, is confined to contexts of battles, literal or metaphorical. In the language of the law, it continues in the archaic sense of yielding up something. For example, in the law of leaseholds, it is a TERM OF ART that denotes "the termination of a lease, which occurs when a tenant gives up his or her interest to the landlord, followed by delivery of possession of the premises"—e.g.: "A lease may be terminated by *surrender,* a 'yielding up' to the owner of the reversion or remainder." 1 *American Law of Property* 390 (A.J. Casner ed., 1952).

surrenderee (= one to whom property is surrendered) dates from the 17th century and is still occasionally used. E.g., "The estate surrendered would merge in the estate of the *surrenderee.*" Cornelius J. Moynihan, *Introduction to the Law of Real Property* 169 (2d ed. 1988). See -EE (A).

surrogacy; surrogateship. Both may mean "the position of a surrogate." (See **surrogate.**) *Surrogacy,* the more usual form, is the only one used in the sense "the fact or state of being a surrogate (as a surrogate mother)." E.g., "The British bill permits a surrogate mother to be paid for her services, which is reasonable, but then would throw the criminal law at any intermediary who might be involved, or at any service that advertises *surrogacy.*" (Eng.)/ "Proponents of *surrogacy* seek to distinguish *surrogacy* from babyselling and adoption . . . ." Irma S. Russell, *Within the Best Interests of the Child,* 27 J. Fam. L. 587, 596 (1989).

For the sense "the office of a [judicial] surrogate," it would be helpful to use *surrogateship* rather than *surrogacy* because of the specialized connotations becoming encrusted on the latter. The *Century Dictionary* supports this usage, which also appears in caselaw—e.g.: "[B]efore his *surrogateship,* [Surrogate David B. Ogden was] regarded by his contemporaries as not second to Webster at the federal bar . . . ." *In re de Saulles,* 167 N.Y.S. 445, 449 (Sur. Ct. 1917).

surrogate, n. = (1) something that is put in the place of another as a successor or substitute; (2) in some states of the U.S., a judge with probate jurisdiction; or (3) in G.B., the deputy of an ecclesiastical judge, of a bishop or bishop's chancellor, esp. one who grants licences to marry without banns (*OED*). Sense (1), the generic one, is by far the most widespread—e.g.:

- "To many observers, leading the Western World by standing up to the Soviets and their *surrogates* in this manner was the heart of the President's job." Jonathan A. Bush, Book Review, 80 Va. L. Rev. 1723, 1723 (1994) (reviewing John H. Ely, *War and Responsibility* (1993)).
- "Market share has long served as a *surrogate* for market power." Michael S. Jacobs, *The New Sophistication in Antitrust,* 79 Minn. L. Rev. 1, 53 n.44 (1994).
- "[W]hen a patient is incompetent and no *surrogate* is available, practitioners are forced either to use substituted judgment or to act in the best interest of the patient—in short, to adopt the family's viewpoint and bear their ethical burdens." Peter Cherbas, *Paradigms and Our Shrinking Bioethics,* 69 Ind. L.J. 1105, 1111 (1994).

Sense (2) appears mostly in New York and other jurisdictions in the eastern U.S. "[W]hile there undoubtedly is merit to that learned *Surrogate's* objection, it does not seem to this court that an objection of surmise is any more meritorious in the area of revocation of wills, than it is to other areas of probate law." *In re Will of Collins,* 458 N.Y.S.2d 987, 993 (Sur. Ct. 1982).

surveil is a relatively new, and decidedly useful, verb corresponding to the noun *surveillance.* It is, in fact, a BACK-FORMATION from the noun. The participial and past-tense forms are *surveilling* and *surveilled.* E.g., "The chief of police directed several police officers to *surveil* different locations in town."/ "The simple fact of a meeting at a restaurant takes on a much greater meaning based upon the information that the *surveilling* agents had obtained from the informants." The *OED* gives the year 1960 as the date of its first recorded use, by an American Court at that: "The plaintiff also stresses that the store as a whole, and the customer exits especially, were closely *surveilled.*" *Alexandre of London v. Indemnity Ins. Co.,* 182 F. Supp. 748, 750 (D.D.C. 1960).

William Safire spelled the verb *surveille* in his column dated 6 Oct. 1985, but this spelling is inferior. See *Invasion of the Verbs,* N.Y. Times, 6 Oct. 1985, at 6–12 ("Other Lexicographic Irregulars wince at such back-formations as to *surveille* [read *surveil*] . . .").

surveillance, place under, is an established phrase that was necessary before *surveil,* q.v., was developed as a verb. The metaphor of *placing under surveillance* does not work in all contexts, however. *Surveillance* can be had of both persons and places, but only persons can be "placed under surveillance," because the metaphor of "placing" will not work for real property (which, as an immovable, cannot conceivably be "placed"). E.g., "*The parking lot was placed under surveillance, and the watching officers* [read *The officers conducted surveillance of the parking lot and*] observed Miller drive up in a 1979 Lincoln Continental at 8:00 p.m."

survival statute. See **death statute.**

survivance is not a mere NEEDLESS VARIANT of *survival,* although it is increasingly rare. *Survivance* is used solely in G.B. and means "the succession to an estate, office, etc. of a survivor nominated before the death of the existing occupier or holder; the right of such succession in case of survival" (*OED*). E.g., "The right exists by virtue of *survivance* and cannot be excluded by will or otherwise, nor can it be apportioned unequally among the children." (Scot.)/ "He would have to exercise on *survivance* the rights, and come under the obligations, stipulated in regard to the surviving partner by the articles of association." (Eng.)

surviving widow(er). The gender-neutral equivalent, *surviving spouse* (= a spouse who outlives the other), is preferable in modern contexts. E.g., "[T]he proprietary interest of the estate of the appointor is one which arises only in default of appointment and in the event of there being no *surviving widow* [read *surviving spouse*]." *Baird v. Baird,* [1990] 2 All E.R. 300, 305 (P.C.).

survivorship = (1) the state or condition of being the one person out of two or more who remains alive after the others die; or (2) the right of a surviving party having a joint interest with others in an estate to take the whole. E.g., "Tenants in common are owners of undivided shares in the land. There is no *survivorship* between them, i.e., when one dies that person's share in the property passes to the decedent's heirs or devisees." A. James Casner & W. Barton Leach, *Cases and Text on Property* 255 (3d ed. 1984).

susceptible (of) (to) (for). The only prepositions with which this verb may properly be construed are *of* and *to.* Usage has differentiated *susceptible of* from *susceptible to,* the latter now being more common in ordinary lay contexts. *Susceptible to* = capable of receiving and being affected by (external impressions, influences, etc., esp. something injurious); sensitive to; liable or open to (attack, injury, etc.). E.g., "Some courts have not required that the contestant produce evidence to indicate that the testator is *susceptible to* undue influence."

Susceptible of was formerly used in this sense, but is now confined to the senses, common in law, of (1) "capable of undergoing, admitting of (some action or process such as interpretation)"; (2) "capable of taking or admitting (a form, meaning, or other attribute)"; or (3) "capable of receiving into the mind, conceiving, or being inwardly affected by (a thought, feeling, or emotion)." Sense (1) of *susceptible of* is perhaps most common—e.g.: "These damages are not *susceptible of* exact proof and the amount is left largely to the sound discretion and common sense of the jury."/ "The timberland was theoretically *susceptible of* such use."/ "Admittedly, this language is *susceptible of* the interpretation placed upon it by the district court." Sense (2) also frequently appears—e.g.: "A latent ambiguity exists where the language of the will, though clear on its face, is *susceptible of* more than one meaning, when applied to the extrinsic facts to which it refers."/ "News matter, however little *susceptible of* ownership or dominion in the absolute sense, is stock in trade to both parties alike."

In the following sentences, *to* wrongly displaces *of* in sense (2): "The phrase is *susceptible to* [read *of*] more than one interpretation."/ "The rule that statutes in derogation of the common law should be strictly construed does not mean that the statute should be given the narrowest meaning *to* [read *of*] which it is *susceptible.*"

Rarely is *susceptible of* misused for *susceptible to,* but the mistake does occur—e.g.: "The selection procedure is *susceptible of* [read *to*] abuse and is not racially neutral."/ "Appellant argues that that complaint, labeled conversion, does not state a cause of action because the subject matter is money, and mere money is not *susceptible of* [read *to*] conversion."

Susceptible for is quite wrong—e.g.: "We remanded for factual findings concerning whether the timberland at issue was *susceptible for* [read *of*] use to produce interest, dividends, rents, or royalties."

Susceptible is sometimes mispronounced, even by educated speakers, /*sək*-***sep***-*tə*-*bəl*/ rather than the correct /*sə*-***sep***-*tə*-*bəl*/.

suspect, adj.; **suspicious.** Generally, the former denotes a fully formulated impression, while the latter denotes only an incipient impression. *Suspect* = regarded with suspicion or distrust; suspected <suspect findings>. *Suspicious* = (1) open to, deserving of, or exciting suspicion <a suspicious character>; (2) full of, inclined to, or feeling suspicion <an unduly suspicious supervisor>.

suspect, n. See **unknown suspect.**

suspendible; suspendable; suspensible. The first is the standard term; the second and third are NEEDLESS VARIANTS. See -ABLE (A).

suspension of deportation; withholding of deportation. In American immigration law, these phrases denote distinctive procedures. A *suspension of deportation,* resulting in permanent residency, is granted when a potential deportee proves "extreme hardship"—an admittedly vague concept. A *withholding of deportation,* resulting only in temporary residency in the U.S., is granted when a potential deportee proves that he or she will suffer persecution (not just discrimination) because of race, religion, political opinion, or social position. See **deportee.**

suspensory; suspensive. *Suspensory conditions* are conditions precedent that suspend the operation of a contractual promise until those conditions are met. The phrase *suspensive conditions* is a NEEDLESS VARIANT—except in Scotland, where it is usual.

suspicious. See **suspect,** adj.

sustain is a CHAMELEON-HUED WORD if ever there was one. Idiomatically, we speak of *sustaining damage,* of *sustaining motions,* and of *sustaining a population.* Other variations with slight nuances are possible, and all are permissible because of historical usage. *Sustáin* may mean "to undergo, experience, have to submit to (evil, hardship or damage)" (*OED*). E.g., "The testatrix died from injuries she *sustained* in the automobile accident."/ "Various train cars *sustained* damage totaling over a million dollars." Or it may mean "to uphold the validity of." E.g., "The important question is whether the statute can be *sustained.*"

The sense "to nourish or support life in" is one of the general lay senses of the word. Additionally, *sustain* may mean "to keep up or keep going"—e.g.: "Green's medical records indicate that he has *sustained* [better *experienced*] remarkably good health during his confinement in the prison."

Given these multifarious senses, few uses of the word seem to be objectionable; in the following sentence, however, it appears to have been used as a turgid substitute for *have:* "Neither the defendant nor the man who made the patterns *sustained* [read *had*] any relation by contract with the plaintiff."

sustainment; sustentation. What is the noun corresponding to the verb *sustain,* as in "Objection sustained"? Up to 1940, the learned word *sustentation* was more common in legal texts, but since then *sustainment* has appeared nearly twice as often.

Even so, both forms are BURIED VERBS. Thus, one should try to use the verb instead of either of the nouns—e.g.: "The *sustentation* of the motion for sanctions was plain error only if a manifest injustice resulted therefrom." *State v. Williams,* 828 S.W.2d 894, 898 (Mo. Ct. App. 1992). [Read: *In sustaining the motion for sanctions, the court committed plain error only if a manifest injustice resulted.*]

SWAPPING HORSES while crossing the stream is H.W. Fowler's term for "changing a word's sense in the middle of a sentence, by vacillating between two constructions either of which might follow a word legitimately enough, by starting off with a subject that fits one verb but must have something tacitly substituted for it to fit another, and by other such performance." (*MEU1* 589.) E.g., "The subject of this paper, however, is the evidentiary rule and concerns those situations where evidence is sought from the lawyer through compulsion of law." The writer has switched gears mentally from "subject . . . is" to "paper . . . concerns." [Read *The subject of this paper, however, is the evidentiary rule and those situations in which . . . ,* or *This paper, however, concerns the evidentiary rule and those situations in which . . . .*]

For related discussions, see JANUS-FACED

TERMS & ZEUGMA AND SYLLEPSIS.

swear, v.t., in law often takes phrasal objects, whereas in nonlegal contexts its objects are almost uniformly clauses beginning with the relative pronoun *that.* Specimens of the legal usage follow: "I might add that the reference to *swearing* a petition and an affidavit in support is to a practice no longer in use." (Eng.)/ "In correct legal phraseology, the deponent *swears* an affidavit and the judge takes it."

Swear is also sometimes used as a shorthand form for *swear in*—e.g.: "*Swear* the witness."/ "One who calls a witness and has him *sworn,* vouches his credibility and is not permitted to discredit him unless taken by surprise." Eugene A. Jones, *Manual of Equity Pleading and Practice* 20 n.9 (1916)./ "When Stewart said that he preferred not to have the jury *sworn* until Monday, so that if a juror became ill over the week-end a replacement could be chosen on Monday morning, Darrow protested that the jury should be *sworn* at once . . . ." Ray Ginger, *Six Days or Forever?* 99 (1958).

swear out (= to obtain the issue of [a warrant for arrest] by making a charge upon oath) is an American legalism dating from the 19th century. E.g., "He walked into the trap, *swore out* a criminal warrant, and haled us before Judge Tompkins sitting as a magistrate." Ephraim Tutt, *Yankee Lawyer* 69 (1943). See **out (A)** & PARTICLES, UNNECESSARY.

sweat > sweat > sweat. So declined.

swing vote = an appellate judge's vote that determines an issue on which the other judges are evenly split. The agent noun is *swing voter*—e.g.: "Since President Reagan appointed O'Connor eight years ago, her role in many divisive issues—thanks in part to the arrival of two additional conservatives—has evolved from that of habitual dissenter to that of frequent *swing voter." All Eyes on Justice O'Connor,* Newsweek, 1 May 1989, at 34.

sworn affidavit is a common REDUNDANCY.

syllabus. Pl. *-buses, -bi.* American judges and college professors are fond, perhaps overfond, of the Latin plural. Though Gowers wrote (wishfully?) that "[t]he plural *-buses* is now more used than *-bi*" (*MEU2* at 610), in American judicial opinions *-bi* outstrips *-buses* by more than fifty to one. See PLURALS (A).

SYLLEPSIS. See ZEUGMA AND SYLLEPSIS.

sympathy. See **empathy.**

symposium. Pl. *-siums. Symposia* is a pedantry. See PLURALS (A).

synallagmatic contract (= [in civil law] a contract involving mutual obligations; a bilateral contract) dates back to the early 19th century. But in Anglo-American law, the sensible approach is to use the predominant Anglo-American term: *bilateral contract.* E.g., "Every *synallagmatic* [read *bilateral*] contract contains in it the seeds of the problem: in what event will a party be relieved of his undertaking to do that which he has agreed to do but has not yet done?" *Hong Kong Fir Shipping Co. v. Kawasaki Kisen Kaisha,* [1962] 2 Q.B. 26, 65 (per Diplock, L.J.)./ "[T]he judge referred to the well-known distinction discussed in the speeches between *synallagmatic* [read *bilateral*] contracts and unilateral or 'if' contracts, such as options . . . ." *Chiltern Court (Baker Street) Residents Ltd v. Wallabrook, Prop. Co.* [1988] 2 Est. Gaz. L. Rep. 253, 253.

sync, short for *synchronism* or *synchrony,* is preferred to *synch.* E.g., "Section 7 is simply out of *sync* with a changing jurisprudence."

synchronous; synchronic; synchronal. The second and third are NEEDLESS VARIANTS.

SYNESIS. In some contexts meaning, rather than the strict requirements of grammar or syntax, controls in the question of SUBJECT-VERB AGREEMENT. Henry Sweet, the 19th-century English grammarian, used the term "antigrammatical constructions" for these triumphs of logic over grammar. (Expressions in which grammar triumphs over logic are termed "antilogical.") Modern grammarians call the principle underlying these antigrammatical constructions "synesis."

The classic example of an antigrammatical construction is the phrase *a number of* (= several, many). It is routinely followed by a plural verb, even though technically the singular noun *number* is the subject: "[A] *number* of scholastic . . . dogmas *have* grown up which tend to obscure the real function of precedent in our legal reasoning." Carleton K. Allen, *Law in the Making* 268 (7th ed. 1964). (See **number of, a.**) But if the definite article *the* appears rather than the indefinite *a,* the verb is singular—e.g.: "She said that the number of participants was disappointing."

Of course, some writers use the construction *a number of things is,* but the resulting sentence invariably looks priggish—e.g.:

- "The Maccabaean Lecture aroused an interest greater than it deserved. There *is* [read *are*] *a*

number of reasons for this." Patrick Devlin, *The Enforcement of Morals* vii (1968).
- "However, there *is* [read *are*] *a number* of exceptions to this rule, whose importance appears to be increasing today." P.S. Atiyah, *An Introduction to the Law of Contract* 260 (3d ed. 1981).
- "*A number* of federal statutes which deal with the allowance of costs *has* [read *have*] been considered." 6 James W. Moore et al., *Moore's Federal Practice* par. 54.77[2], at 54-410 (1988).

Although writers are perfectly justified in writing *a number of people were there,* some avoid the construction merely to prevent raised eyebrows. Instead, they write *many people* or *several people.* This sound practice keeps readers from being distracted.

If *a number of people were* is grammatically safe, however, similar constructions involving collective nouns are somewhat more precarious. The rule consistently announced in 20th-century grammars is as follows: "Collective nouns take sometimes a singular and sometimes a plural verb. When the persons or things denoted are thought of as individuals, the plural should be used. When the collection is regarded as a unit, the singular should be used." George L. Kittredge & Frank E. Farley, *An Advanced English Grammar* 101 (1913). Generally, then, with nouns of multitude, one can justifiably use a plural verb.

Among the common nouns of multitude are *bulk, bunch, flood, handful, host, mass, majority, minority, percentage, proportion, variety.* Each of these is frequently followed by *of* + [plural noun] + [plural verb]—e.g.:

- "A great *variety* of techniques *were* employed." (*A variety of* = several.)
- "Few younger lawyers have escaped his influence, but only a *handful* of them *possesses* [read *possess*] his creative zest or renovating energy." (*A handful of* = several.)
- "A *flood* of questions *come* to mind as I consider the future application of such a theory."
- "In each of these instances, as so often in our history, a *majority* of the Justices *were* behind the political times." Fred Rodell, *Nine Men* 11 (1955).
- "A high *percentage* of cases *are* of a routine nature." Charles E. Wyzanski, Jr., "A Trial Judge," in *Whereas—A Judge's Premises* 3, 4 (1965).
- "Thus, in relation to the total number of prosecutions, only a small *proportion are* taken by the Director." R.M. Jackson, *The Machinery of Justice in England* 138 (5th ed. 1967).
- "A large *mass* of rules of evidence *restrict* the questions that might be asked . . . ." *Id.* at 142.
- "[T]he great *mass* of these social prohibitions *is* [read *are*] not directly against the making of contracts as such but against the doing of acts." Patrick Devlin, *The Enforcement of Morals* 55 (1968).
- "There *is* [read *are*] also a *host* of new difficulties that are even more salient in contract than they were in torts . . . ." Bruce A. Ackerman, *Reconstructing America* 61 (1984).
- "The vast *bulk* of recorded crimes *falls* [read *fall*] into the category of property offences." Andrew Ashworth, *Principles of Criminal Law* 39 (1991).

As shown in the last two examples, these nouns of multitude are not just acceptably treated as plural. One might go so far as to say that *host* and *mass* are preferably treated as plurals when they are followed by *of* and a plural noun.

Very occasionally, an AMBIGUITY arises: "*There is* now *a variety of* antidepressant drugs that can help lift these people out of their black moods." If the sense of *a variety of* is "several," then *are* is the appropriate verb; if the sense of the phrase is "a type of," then *is* is the appropriate verb.

But the nouns *amount, class, group,* and (ironically) *multitude* all typically call for singular verbs:

- "[S]pecific relief will be given if practicable where the *amount* of damages *are* [read *is*] so uncertain and speculative, for any reason, that the fixing of the amount . . . by the jury could not be guided by any definite standard . . . ." William F. Walsh, *A Treatise on Equity* 309 (1930).
- "Needless to say, there *are* [read *is*] a *multitude* of examples." Charles P. Curtis, Jr., *Lions Under the Throne* 220 (1947).
- "The most important *class* of chattels real *are* [read *is*] leasehold estates." William Geldart, *Introduction to English Law* 80 (D.C.M. Yardley ed., 9th ed. 1984). (The be-VERB follows the number of its subject, not of its predicate.)
- "A *group* of states *have* [read *has*] enacted broad cy pres, or reformation, statutes, of which the Vermont statute is an example . . . ." Thomas F. Bergin & Paul G. Haskell, *Preface to Estates in Land and Future Interests* 218 (2d ed. 1984).
- "But even if a *group* of members *decide* [read *decides*] to challenge such an agreement . . . there is no guarantee that the government will provide time for a debate or the opportunity of a vote." Michael Zander, *The Law-Making Process* 70 (2d ed. 1985). (In a BrE text, this usage is defensible; it would be less so in an AmE text. See COLLECTIVE NOUNS.)

There may be little or no logical consistency in the two sets of examples just given—justifiable plurals and less justifiable ones—but the problem lies just outside the realm of logic, in the genius of the language. It is no use trying to explain why we say, on the one hand, *that pair of shoes is getting old,* but on the other hand, *the pair were perfectly happy after their honeymoon.*

For more on grammatical agreement generally, see CONCORD & COLLECTIVE NOUNS.

synonym(it)y. *Synonymy* is the preferred form. See **synonymous.**

synonymous (in the sense "coextensive") is a LEGALISM not found in general lay writing. E.g., "Nor do we subscribe to the argument that Merrill's powers of control over partnership property as a general partner of a limited partnership are per se *synonymous* with the partnership's." The corresponding noun is used in an analogous sense—e.g.: "Given the *synonymy* between the limits of the Louisiana long-arm statute and those of due process, it becomes necessary to consider only whether the exercise of jurisdiction over a nonresident defendant comports with due process."

The word is frequently misspelled *synonomous,* as here: "'Special inquiry officer' is *synonomous* [read *synonymous*] with immigration judge." *Purba v. INS,* 884 F.2d 516, 517 (9th Cir. 1989).

SYNONYMY. The myth is that no two words in the language can have identical meanings, as stated here: "strictly speaking, no two words have the same meaning. There are connotations that attach to language and even two synonyms will suggest slightly different meanings to a reader." Norman Brand & J.O. White, *Legal Writing: The Strategy of Persuasion* 114 (1976). Adherents to this view must contend that *restitutional* and *restitutionary* are merely different forms of the same word—not different words—and must resort to etymology to distinguish *sedulous* from *assiduous.*

This belief may help explain the inclination of lawyers to use DOUBLETS, TRIPLETS, AND SYNONYM-STRINGS. E.g., "The indictment alleged that respondents unlawfully *kept, confined, and imprisoned* George in a *dark, cold,* and *unwholesome* room."/ "Vendor does *grant, bargain, sell, assign, convey, transfer, set over, and deliver* the land to the purchaser." Instead of using these verbal strings, the writer should determine which of the words can be subsumed under (and therefore omitted because of the presence of) broader terms. In the first sentence quoted above, *imprison* certainly encompasses *confine* and *keep;* in the second, *grant* or *convey* would easily suffice. Lawyers generally seek to cover every contingency, especially in DRAFTING; we should do so, however, discriminatingly rather than in blunderbuss fashion.

system(at)ize. *Systemize* is a NEEDLESS VARIANT of *systematize.*

systemic; systematic. *Systemic* should be *systematic* unless the reference is systems of the body, as in *systemic disorders.* E.g., "The plaintiffs alleged *systemic* [read *systematic*] disparate treatment of minority groups."/ "The complaint alleged across-the-board, *systemic* [read *systematic*] discrimination against black employees."

T

table, v.t., has nearly opposite senses in AmE and BrE. By *tabling* an item, Americans mean postponing discussion for a later time, while Britons mean putting forward for immediate discussion. Thus Americans might misunderstand a use like the following one: "MPs from both sides of the Commons will tomorrow *table* parliamentary questions demanding to know what official action has been taken to uncover the facts . . . ." John Furbisher & Richard Caseby, *"God's Policeman" Keeps Head Down as Bricks Fly,* Sunday Times, 10 June 1990, at 1-4.

taboo; tabu. The former spelling is standard. For the verb *to taboo* (= to exclude or prohibit by authority or social influence [*COD*]), the past tense is *tabooed* rather than *taboo'd.* E.g., "A copyrighted work is not *tabooed* to subsequent workers in the same field."

tabula rasa (= a blank tablet ready for writing; a clean slate) has been an esp. common metaphor in legal writing. It has grown into a CLICHÉ.

Pl. *tabulae rasae.*

tactile; tactual. The latter has become merely a NEEDLESS VARIANT. *Tactile* is the usual word meaning either "of or relating to touch" or "touchable; tangible."

tail, in the legal sense denoting a type of limited freehold estate, is a LAW FRENCH term, deriving ultimately from the Old French verb *taillier* "to cut, shape, hence to fix the precise form of, to limit." Formerly, the anglicized word was spelled *taille,* but today it is spelled *tail* as in *fee tail* and *in tail.* E.g., "It has been repeatedly determined that if there be tenant for life, remainder to his first son *in tail,* remainder over, and he is brought before the court before he has issue, the contingent remaindermen are barred." Sometimes the word is used also in the phrase *estate tail,* as here: "Under the first rule, if A devises his lands to B and to B's children or issue, and B has not any issue at the time of the devise, the same is an *estate tail.*" See **fee tail (A).**

Tail may be a noun taking POSTPOSITIVE ADJECTIVES (*tail female, tail special*) or may itself be a postpositive adjective (*fee tail*). Some writers hyphenate *tail-female, tail-male,* and even *estate-tail,* but the hyphens are better omitted. See **entail & disentail.**

taint. See **attaint.**

take. A. In Its Ordinary Sense. In its everyday uses, *take* "is an ambiguous word, particularly when one is speaking of an adult 'taking' a child somewhere, which could be construed as simply guiding or accompanying the child, or as a forcible taking." *U.S. v. Macklin,* 671 F.2d 60, 65 n.6 (2d Cir. 1982).

B. In the Context of Estates. *Take* (= to receive (property) by will or intestate succession) is peculiar to the legal idiom. E.g., "The will itself indicates the proportions according to which the beneficiaries shall *take.*" See **taker.** See also **bring.**

C. In the Phrase *stole, took, and carried away.* See **stole, took, and carried away.**

take articles. See **article,** v.t.

take exception. This phrase means "to object" in general lay contexts, but is used in legal writing in the sense "to posit an error on appeal." E.g., "The defendants *took* five *exceptions;* the questions raised by *exceptions* as we have shown are four."

take-it-or-leave-it contract. For this synonym of *adhesion contract* see **adherence (A).**

taken. Appeals to higher courts are said, in the legal idiom, to be *taken.* E.g., "We do not discuss various objections to the plan of merger filed after this *appeal* was *taken.*"

taken back, to be is an illiteracy when used for *take(n) aback.*

take-nothing judgment (= a judgment for the defendant providing that the plaintiff recover nothing) should be hyphenated thus. See PHRASAL ADJECTIVES.

take notice. This is a common substitute for—and a better phrase than—*know all men by these presents,* q.v. E.g., "*Take notice* that an application will be made by the Defendant to the presiding Judge or Master of the Courthouse at Law Courts, Begbie Square, New Westminster, at 9:45 o'clock in the forenoon, on the 10th day of October 1985, for an order under Rule 2(5) of the Rules of Court that the Plaintiffs' action be dismissed by reason of the failure of the Plaintiffs to make discovery of documents." (Can.) The phrase is often, alas, written entirely in capitals. See CAPITALIZATION (A).

take-or-pay; take or pay. When used as a PHRASAL ADJECTIVE, *take-or-pay* should be hyphenated, as in *take-or-pay obligations, take-or-pay clauses,* and *take-or-pay status.* Some writers use quotation marks with this phrase instead of hyphens (i.e., *"take or pay" contract*)—a usage to be avoided.

When, however, *take* and *pay* are used as alternative verbs, the phrase should not be hyphenated: "This right to restrict flow, however, did not operate to diminish Transmission's obligation to *take-or-pay* [read *take or pay*] for 75% of the wells' estimated yearly output." *Garshman v. Universal Resources Holding Inc.,* 824 F.2d 223, 226 (3d Cir. 1987).

takeover, n. One word.

take precedence. See **precedence.**

taker = one who receives property by will or intestate succession. E.g., "With respect to real estate, such a gift over, in the event of the indefinite failure of the issue of the *first taker,* was construed to cut down and limit the interest of the *first taker* to an estate tail."/ "The terms 'heirs,' 'issue,' and 'children' are commonly used in dispositive instruments to designate a class of *takers* . . . ." Thomas F. Bergin & Paul G. Haskell, *Preface to Estates in Land and Future Interests* 230 (2d ed. 1984). See **take (B).**

take silk is a BrE phrase meaning "to become a Queen's Counsel [Q.C.] or King's Counsel [K.C.]." See **silk.**

take the Fifth Amendment, to. See **Fifth Amendment.**

take under advisement. See **advisement.**

taking (= a taking of property by a governmental entity using eminent domain) is midway between JARGON and a TERM OF ART. Lawyers have long argued about just what constitutes a taking, but it is hard now to improve on a general statement of more than a century ago: "Anything may be said to amount to a *taking* [that] deprives the owner of the use, occupation, or enjoyment of his property." Alfred R. Haig, *The Law of Eminent Domain in Pennsylvania,* 39 Am. L. Reg. 449, 463 (1891).

tales; talesman; tales-juror. Originally, *tales* /***tay**-leez*/ (L. pl. meaning "such men") referred to persons selected from among those in court to serve on a jury in a case in which the original jury panel has become deficient in number by challenge or other cause. The *OED* notes that the word is "loosely applied in Eng. as a singular (*a tales*) to the supply of men (or even one man) so provided."

In AmE, this "loose" usage (as it is considered in BrE) was formerly common. That is, *tales* once referred to a supply of people available to replace jury panelists. But AmE, unlike BrE, does not use the term *tales* to refer to a *single* person who is available to serve as such a replacement. *Talesman* is used in this latter sense (though rarely) in both AmE and BrE. See SEXISM (B).

The word *tales* also refers in some contexts to the order or act of supplying such juror substitutes, as *to pray, grant, award a tales.* In England up to 1971, this usage was restricted to a summoning of common jurors to serve on a special jury.

In AmE, the term is becoming obsolete, though a few writers use it as a fancy substitute for *veniremember*—e.g.: "In strong terms, he repeatedly admonished the *talesmen* [read *veniremembers*] that they must 'not start out th[e] case with a predisposed state of mind because of something that happened in the past.'" *Neron v. Tierney,* 841 F.2d 1197, 1202 (1st Cir. 1988). See **venireman.**

Talesman has long been the usual form, *tales-juror* being a variant. Both terms are ARCHAISMS, as methods of selecting venires have become more sophisticated.

talisman (= a charm, amulet, or other thing supposed to be capable of working wonders), a favorite word of judges, is not to be confused with *talesman.* (See **talesman.**) E.g., "The law has outgrown its primitive stage of formation when the precise word was the sovereign *talisman,* and every slip was fatal." (Cardozo)/ "Freedom of choice is not a sacred *talisman;* it is only a means to a constitutionally required end—the abolition of the system of segregation and its effects." The plural form is *talismans,* not *talismen.*

The corresponding adjective is *talismanic*—e.g.: "There is nothing *talismanic* about neutral laws of general applicability . . . ." *Employment Div., Dep't of Human Resources v. Smith,* 494 U.S. 872, 901 (1990) (O' Connor, J., concurring)./ "Such a result could only be based on a *talismanic* reliance on mere words and labels that would be contrary to the spirit of the privilege." *Wiles v. Wiles,* 448 S.E.2d 681, 685 (Ga. 1994) (Sears-Collins, J., concurring)./ "Such a *talismanic* requirement would clearly place form over substance." *Commonwealth v. Blount,* 647 A.2d 199, 204 (Pa. 1994).

talk to; talk with. The former suggests a conversation in which the remarks strongly preponderate from one side, as between a superior and an inferior. The latter suggests a conversation between equals, with equal participation.

Taney, Roger Brooke. The last name of the Chief Justice of the United States from 1836 to 1854 is pronounced /***taw**-nee*/, not /***tay**-nee*/.

tantalize (= to torment or test [a person] by sight or promise of a desired thing withheld or kept just out of reach [*COD*]) is not infrequently confused with *titillate* (= to excite pleasantly or tickle).

The verb *tantalize* is derived from the Greek myth about Tantalus, king of Sipylos, born of the union of Zeus and the nymph Pluto. Tantalus offended the gods by stealing some of their food and giving it to mortals. Because the father of Tantalus was divine, Tantalus was himself immortal (though not a god) and thus could not be executed for his crime. Instead, as an eternal punishment, he was placed in a pool of fresh water up to his chin, while overhead boughs of edible fruit hung temptingly near. Whenever he dipped to drink, the water receded; whenever he stretched to eat, a wind blew the laden boughs out of reach.

tantamount is an adjective only, meaning "equivalent." Using it as a verb is incorrect: "The legal effect of the judgment in the class action . . . *tantamounts* [read *is tantamount*], we think, to removing [Humphrey] from the representative class . . . ." *Humphrey v. Knox,* 244 S.W.2d 309, 312 (Tex. Civ. App.—Dallas 1951).

tape-record, v.t. This verb is always hyphenated.

task, v.t. See VOGUE WORDS.

taskforce is increasingly made one word, esp. in BrE. That being so, it would be convenient for writers—in BrE and AmE alike—to make it one. E.g., "On June 11th he even got round to naming the members of the *taskforce* that will deal with it." *What the Centre Holds,* Economist, 19 June 1993, at 25.

tautologous; tautological. The latter, though older, has become a NEEDLESS VARIANT of the former. E.g., "The [lower] court's statement that the plaintiff must seek redress for an injury caused by conduct that RICO was designed to deter is unhelpfully *tautological* [read *tautologous*]." *Sedima, S.P.R.L. v. Imrex Co.,* 473 U.S. 479, 494 (1985).

TAUTOLOGY. "What's the first excellence in a lawyer? Tautology. What the second? Tautology. What the third? Tautology." Richard Steele, *The Funeral* (1701). It is worth pointing out, lest the irony escape those who have used this book at all and still are fond of LEGALESE, that the words quoted are derisive, not serious. Yet tautologies continue to proliferate: "Wide public participation in rulemaking *obviates* the problem of *singling out a single defendant* among a group of competitors for initial imposition of a new and inevitably costly legal obligation." See REDUNDANCY (B).

tax, n.; **assessment.** Some American writers distinguish these words usefully. A *tax* generally supports improvements for the entire community. An *assessment,* by contrast, is usu. levied only on property near some local municipal improvement—property that receives some special benefit different from that of the general public.

In BrE, by contrast, an *assessment* is a calculation of tax due and a *request* for payment. Tax inspectors issue assessments.

taxable = (1) subject to taxation <taxable income>; or (2) (of legal costs or fees) assessable <taxable expenses>. Sense (2): "Expert-witness fees are not *taxable* as costs of court."

taxation, in the sense "the taxing of costs," is an unusual idiom to many ears, whether law-trained or not—e.g.: "Petitioners argue that since § 1920 lists which expenses a court 'may' tax as costs, that section only authorizes *taxation* of certain items." *Crawford Fitting Co. v. J.T. Gibbons, Inc.,* 482 U.S. 437, 441 (1987).

tax avoidance; tax evasion. The difference between these phrases is the difference between what is legal (*avoidance*) and what is not (*evasion*).

taxpayer. See ARTICLES (B) & **payor.**

teachings = holdings and dicta in a judicial opinion. E.g., "The threshold question is whether appellant has stated a procedural due process claim under section 1983, particularly in light of the Supreme Court's *teachings* in *Parratt v. Taylor.*"/ "The failure of the interrogating officers to avoid asking more questions violated the *teachings* of *Miranda* and *Edwards v. Arizona,* thereby tainting his confession." See **hold & dictum.**

tear gas, n.; **teargas,** v.t. This term is spelled as two words for the noun, as one for the verb.

technic. See **technique.**

technical; technological. The distinction is sometimes a fine one. *Technical* = of or in a particular science, art, or handicraft; of or in vocational training. *Technological* = pertaining to the science of practical or industrial arts. *Technological* connotes recent experimental methods and development, whereas *technical* has no such connotation.

technique; technic. The latter, a variant spelling, is to be avoided.

technological. See **technical.**

telecast. See **broadcast.**

teleconferencing. See **conferencing.**

telephonee. See -EE (A).

telephonic is a highfalutin adjectival form of *telephone,* which ordinarily serves as its own adjective. E.g., "On request, the clerk will notify counsel who desire immediate collect *telephonic* notification when the decision is rendered." [Read *On request, the clerk will call counsel collect when the decision is rendered.*]/ "The residence was secured, and the officers obtained a *telephonic warrant* [read *telephone warrant*] and subsequently searched the apartment and seized the marijuana and related paraphernalia." *State v. Will,* 885 P.2d 715, 717–18 (Or. Ct. App. 1994)./ "The District Court, during a *telephonic pretrial conference* [read *pretrial telephone conference*], advised the parties that both pending motions were dismissed." *Roe v. Corbin Water Users' Ass'n,* 885 P.2d 419, 420 (Mont. 1994).

tell for *say. Tell* is a transitive verb that demands an indirect as well as a direct object. E.g., "One of the industry's major producers *told* [read *said*] recently that a large studio receives 20,000 stories or ideas per year, of which but twenty are made into motion pictures."

temperature is pronounced /***tem***-*pə-rə-chər*/, not /***tem***-*pə-rə-tyur*/, which is precious, or /***tem***-*pə-chər*/, which is slovenly. A combination of the precious and the slovenly, /***tem***-*pə-tyoor*/ is humorously affected.

temporal = (1) of or relating to time; (2) worldly; (3) nonecclesiastical; (4) transitory; (5) pertaining to the temple (part of one's head); or (6) pertaining to bones in the vertebrae. In other words, this is a classic CHAMELEON-HUED WORD. Usually, *temporal* refers to time (sense 1) in legal writing—e.g.: "Although not *temporally* clear from the record, it appears that while the attorneys and the trial judge were in chambers, the court coordinator and the bailiff conducted a shuffle of the panel." Sense (2) is also common: "The reason behind the exception is a simple one of human relationships, implicit in the principle that human laws, and other *temporal* things, are for the living."

Temporal was a favorite word of Justice Holmes, who used it in the special legal sense, a variation on sense (3) given above, namely "civil or common as opposed to criminal or ecclesiastical." E.g., "In numberless instances the law warrants the intentional infliction of *temporal* damage because it regards it as justified." (Holmes, J.)/ "Actions of tort are brought for *temporal* damage; the law recognizes *temporal* damage as an evil which its object is to prevent or to address." (Holmes, J.)

temporal limit is unidiomatic and stuffy in place of *time limit,* which is well established. E.g., "The Supreme Court has yet to decide how long an auto search may be delayed before a warrant must be obtained, or indeed whether there is a *temporal limit* [read *time limit*]."

TEMPORAL SEQUENCES. See TENSES (A).

temporary restraining order; preliminary injunction. A *temporary restraining order* (or *t.r.o.*) is an order provisionally granting injunctive relief in an emergency situation, but only for the short time (usu. a matter of days at most) until the court can hear evidence and consider longer-term injunctive relief.

A *preliminary injunction* is just such relief. It is an interlocutory injunction issued after notice and a hearing, and it restrains a party until a trial on the merits is concluded. See **interlocutory relief.**

temporize has three important senses: (1) "to act so as to gain time" <defendant temporized by filing dilatory pleas>; (2) "to comply with the requirements of the occasion" <politicians are adept at temporizing>; (3) "to negotiate or discuss terms of a compromise" <defendant attempted to temporize with plaintiff rather than go to trial>.

tenancy; tenantship; tenantry. The first is, of course, the usual term, meaning (1) "a holding or possession of lands or tenements, by any title of ownership"; (2) "occupancy of lands or tenements under a lease"; (3) "that which is held by a tenant"; or (4) "the period during which a tenant occupies land or a building."

To the extent that *tenantship* overlaps with any of those four meanings, it is a NEEDLESS VARIANT of *tenancy;* yet it does usefully mean "the state of being a tenant," as distinct from ownership. To the extent that *tenantry* overlaps with any of the senses outlined above, it too is a NEEDLESS VARIANT; yet *tenantry* may stand on its own in the sense "the body of tenants" <the tenantry is dissatisfied with the proposed improvements>.

tenancy by the entireties; tenancy by the entirety. The phrase refers to a joint tenancy between the husband and wife; it arises in some jurisdictions when a single instrument conveys realty to the husband and wife but nothing is said in the deed or will about the character of their ownership. Upon the death of either the husband or wife, the survivor automatically takes title to the deceased spouse's share.

The plural form *entireties* is slightly more common in both AmE and BrE, although *Black's* (6th ed.) contains its definition under *tenancy by the entirety,* which is also widespread.

tenancy in common. See **joint tenancy.**

tenancy from month to month. See **periodic tenancy.**

tenancy *per la verge;* tenancy by the verge; tenancy by the rod. These equivalent phrases denote a copyhold. The first is LAW FRENCH, the second somewhat anglicized version, and the third an anglicized LOAN TRANSLATION of the first phrase. The terms are little used but in historical contexts (the rod having been delivered for purposes of conveying *seisin,* q.v.). Each of these phrases ordinarily requires some explanation by the user.

tenant. A. Senses. *Tenant* = (1) the holder of land under a contract of tenancy; or (2) the defendant in a writ of right (the plaintiff being known as a *demandant,* q.v.).

B. And *tenanter*. The word *tenanter* is a NEEDLESS VARIANT.

tenant at sufferance; tenant by sufferance. The former is the traditional idiomatic phrase. See **sufferance.**

tenant at will. Although Henry S. Maine, among others, used hyphens (*tenant-at-will*), the noun phrase is best spelled without the hyphens. E.g., "In a law court, O is probably viewed simply as T's *tenant at will*—that is, as a tenant whose estate may be legally terminated at any time by T." Thomas F. Bergin & Paul G. Haskell, *Preface to Estates in Land and Future Interests* 84 (2d ed. 1984). See **at will.**

tenant by sufferance. See **tenant at sufferance.**

tenant by the curtesy initiate. See **curtesy & initiate tenant by curtesy.**

tenant by the entirety. See **tenancy by the entirety.**

tenanter. See **tenant (B).**

tenant-in-chief (= a person who holds land directly under the king) is most commonly written thus—with the hyphens—following the similar convention in the phrases *case-in-chief* (q.v.) and *editor-in-chief.*

In the Latin form of *tenant-in-chief,* namely *tenant-in-capite,* the last two words are best italicized. Cf. **in chief.**

tenantry; tenantship. See **tenancy.**

tendentious means "biased (usu. in favor of something); prejudiced." Its meaning is often misapprehended, as in this specimen, in which the writer apparently thought the word means "frivolous": "Even though Texas did not move to dismiss the appeal as frivolous, the fact is that it patently has no merit. The removal petition does not even colorably fall within the strict tests set out in *Johnson.* We believe the appellant had ample reason to know that his appeal lacked merit and that it was *merely tendentious.*" The phrase *merely tendentious* gives away the writer's ignorance of the meaning of the word *tendentious.*

Tendencious is a variant spelling to be eschewed.

tender, n. See **bid,** n.

tender, v.t., is a FORMAL WORD for *make* or *give.*

tendinitis; tendonitis. *Tendinitis* = inflammation of a tendon. *Tendonitis* is incorrectly arrived at by association with the spelling of the noun *tendon.*

tenement (= [in law] an estate in land) usu. denotes in lay contexts "a building or house." In lawbooks, *tenement* is often associated with the word *messuage* (q.v.). See **lands, tenements, and hereditaments.**

TENSES. **A. Sequence of.** The term *sequence of tenses* refers to the relationship of tenses in subordinate clauses to those in principal clauses. Generally, the former follow from the latter.

In careful writing, the tenses agree both logically and grammatically. The basic rules of tense-sequence are easily stated, although the plethora of examples that follow belie their ostensible simplicity in practice.

1. When the principal clause has a verb in the present (*he says*), present perfect (*he has said*), or future (*he will say*), the subordinate clause has a present-tense verb. Grammarians call this the primary sequence.
2. When the principal clause is in past tense (*he said, he was saying*) or past perfect (*he had said*), the subordinate clause has a past-tense verb. Grammarians call this the secondary sequence.

The primary sequence has proved to be a little less troublesome than the secondary sequence. Examples may be readily found, however, in which the primary sequence is mangled: "It *was* [read *is*] as a professor of law—teaching torts especially—that Leon Green *will be* remembered."

But it is the secondary sequence that most commonly trips up writers, as in the following examples:

- "The majority opinion *did not go* [read *does not go*] so far, Justice Marshall said, and he would have dissented if it did." [Or: "The majority opinion *did not go* so far, Justice Marshall said, and he would have dissented *if it did* [read *if it had*]."]
- "Unless there *was* a formed writ that exactly or nearly fitted the applicant's case, he generally *must* [read *had to*] take such inadequate relief as the inferior local courts offered."
- "It will be seen that Duguit set out to find a rational basis for law (though he cannot be said *to succeed* [read *to have succeeded*]) . . . ." W.W. Buckland, *Some Reflections on Jurisprudence* 11 (1945).
- "This power to imprison a man without trial,

not for what he had [read *has*] already done, but for what he might hereafter do, was entrusted by Parliament to the executive." Alfred Denning, *Freedom Under the Law* 11 (1949).

Continuous tenses cause problems when the action described in the subordinate clause is supposed to have preceded the action that is stated in the past tense in the governing clause—e.g.:

- "A jury being waived, the case was tried . . . ." [Read *A jury having been waived, the case was tried . . . .*"]
- "Fossils have been collected from the area on several occasions, the largest collection being [read *having been*] made by L. Kohl-Larsen in 1938–39."
- "Plaintiff sued in an Illinois District Court for damages he suffered in an accident occurring [read *that occurred* or *having occurred*] in Indiana." [Or, better still, end the sentence as follows: *suffered in an accident in Indiana,* but not *suffered in an Indiana accident.*]

A related problem occurs with (tenseless) infinitives, which, when put after a past-tense verb, are often wrongly made perfect infinitives, as here:

- "Accordingly, the trial judge was required *to have recused himself* [read *to recuse himself*] pursuant to the unambiguous dictates of the statute."
- "Although all but M. had served the number of years required for their pension benefits *to have accrued* [read *to accrue*], all were still on active duty when their marriages were dissolved."
- "Today we witness another startling valid legal reason why this court *should have aborted, rather than to have given birth to,* [read *should have aborted, rather than given birth to,*] the monster child now known in our legal circles as '*Almanza* the Terrible.'"
- "When this happened (and without any negligence on the part of the bus driver) there did not remain sufficient time and distance for the bus driver *to have done* [read *to do*] anything to avoid the collision."
- "To have been fortunate enough *to have grown up* [read *to grow up*] with this fascinating book at hand . . . we count among such blessings as to be healthy (which we are), wealthy (which we aren't), and wise (which we may yet become)."
- "Certainly, it *would have been* desirable for the court *to have instructed* [read *to instruct*] the jury as to the proper standard for judging unreasonableness."

Still another bugbear is the incomplete verb phrase by which the writer attempts to give two tenses, but only one tense is actually completed. The result is one type of zeugma—e.g.: "This mischaracterization of pension rights *has, and unless overturned, will continue to result* [read *has resulted and, unless overturned, will continue to result*] in inequitable division of community assets."/ "This diversity case is one of a multitude of asbestos cases, presently filed and reasonably anticipated, in which injured plaintiffs or their survivors *have or will seek damages* [read *have sought or will seek damages*] for injuries associated with exposure to asbestos." See ZEUGMA AND SYLLEPSIS.

B. Subjunctives. As Partridge has pointed out, not sequence but mood is involved in the correct use of SUBJUNCTIVES, but the mistakes are common enough and closely enough related to merit treatment here: "This would have been a funny story if the headhunter *were* [read *had been*] joking, but he wasn't."/ "William put his arm around Ann and she could not thrust him away for fear he *fell out of the door* [read *would fall out the door*]." (Eng.)/ "If the title *were acquired* [read *was acquired;* see SUBJUNCTIVES] by purchase, the disseisee's entry was not barred." See STATUTE DRAFTING (B).

C. The Historical Present. Some writers use the present tense to discuss what happened long ago. To many readers this mannerism is an affectation. E.g., "As regards the real estate of the deceased, it is settled by the end of the thirteenth century that he can make no will, except where there is a local custom to that effect." William Geldart, *Introduction to English Law* 36 (D.C.M. Yardley ed., 9th ed. 1984). Cf. FIRST PERSON (B).

D. Present Tense for Ongoing Truth. General and ongoing truths require the present tense, regardless of the tense of the principal verb—e.g.: "He observed that federal courts *had* [read *have*] a special place in our system of federalism."

E. Past-Perfect Tense. Many writers stumble on the correct use of this tense, formerly called the "pluperfect" tense. The past perfect (*had* [+ past participle]) represents a past action or state as having been completed before a more recent time in the past—e.g.: "In 1974, the court decided that the insurance-coverage team should not have communicated with the defense team. Two years earlier, in *Kelly,* it *had decided* that the defense lawyers owe an undivided loyalty to the insured." Because the second sentence takes us still further back in time, it is in the past perfect (*had decided*).

Increasingly—and especially in AmE—writers want to change the past perfect to the simple past. This trend, formerly characteristic only of colloquial speech, should be avoided—e.g.: "She began taping his conversations because she *heard* [read *had heard*] that he was intent upon firing all workers over the age of 45."

F. In Statute Drafting. See STATUTE DRAFTING (C).

tentative trust. See **Totten trust.**

tenurial, the adjective corresponding to *tenure,* is almost exclusively a legal term. E.g., "The basic idea of feudal land 'ownership,' then, was that it was *tenurial* in character—more a holding of land on good behavior than ownership as we think of it today." Thomas F. Bergin & Paul G. Haskell, *Preface to Estates in Land and Future Interests* 4 (2d ed. 1984).

term, n. (= a limit in space or duration), has the special legal senses "an estate or interest in land for a certain period" <term of years> and, as a plural (*terms*), "conditions or stipulations limiting what is proposed to be granted or done" (*OED*). See **fundamental term & terms.**

term for years. See **term of years & termor.**

terminus; terminal, n. *Terminus* = the city at the end of a railroad or bus line. Pl. *termini. Terminal* = the station of a transportation line.

terminus a quo; terminus ad quem. The former means "departure point"; the latter, "destination." Figuratively, the words are used of the beginning and ending points of an argument. Both figuratively and literally, the phrases are pomposities.

term loan; time loan. These phrases are interchangeable, *term loan* being slightly more common.

term of years; term for years; estate for years; lease for years. These synonymous phrases denote an estate whose duration is known—in years, weeks, and days—from the moment of its creation. As between *term of years* and *term for years,* the former is more common in BrE, whereas both forms are used in AmE.

termor = a person who holds lands or tenements for a term of years, or (rarely) for life. E.g., "[W]hen today we speak of someone taking on 'a new lease on life,' we do not think of him as a *termor.*"

terms has increasingly been used as an elliptical form of *terms of the contract* or *terms of payment.* See **term.**

terms and conditions. This phrase is among the most common redundancies in legal drafting. But, someone might ask, is *term* really broad enough to include *condition*—is not a *condition* something that must be satisfied before a contractual *term* applies? The *OED* defines *terms* as "conditions or stipulations limiting what is proposed to be granted or done," and that is its usual sense in law. Hence *terms* is sufficient.

terms and provisions is a REDUNDANCY.

terms, in. The phrase *in terms* means "expressly; in plain words." Though the *OED* labels the phrase "obsolete," it continues to thrive in legal contexts—e.g.: "The act *in terms* applies to all the courts of the United States . . . ." Eugene A. Jones, *Manual of Equity Pleading and Practice* 140 (1916).

TERMS OF ART are words having specific, precise meanings in a given specialty. Having its origins in Lord Coke's *vocabula artis,* the phrase *term of art* is common in law because the legal field has developed many technical words whose meanings are locked tight (e.g., *bailment, replevin*)—as well as JARGON, constituting would-be terms of art, whose meanings are often unhinged.

How can one say "unhinged"? Take *per stirpes,* a phrase that many lawyers cite as a quintessential term of art. Yet, as a leading expert in the field of wills and estates has remarked, "*per stirpes* is a textbook example of legalese that seductively suggests certainty but actually can produce ambiguity and litigation." Stanley M. Johanson, *In Defense of Plain Language,* 3 Scribes J. Legal Writing 37, 37 (1992). The phrase creates a problem in this scenario: Mary's will bequeaths property "to my descendants per stirpes." She has two children—John, who has two children, and Bob, who has four. The complication arises when both of Mary's children die before she does. Some courts would say that the shares are divided between John and Bob, others that the shares must be divided at the level of John's and Bob's children. And in many states, the issue has never been decided and would therefore have to be litigated. *Id.* at 38.

Jargon, then, creates more than just aesthetic problems, though some writers lament those most prominently: "the unnecessary or inartistic employment of more or less technical terms in the drafting of legal documents is by no means rare . . . ." *Lancaster Malleable Castings Co. v. Dunie,* 73 A.2d 417, 418 (Pa. 1950). Expert drafters, who know that clear, simple drafting is less subject to misinterpretation than legalistic drafting, recommend avoiding jargon precisely because it invites substantive problems.

On the other hand, "Not to use a technical word, even if it is a long one, in its proper place, would be an affectation as noticeable as the overfrequent use of such words where they are not needed." E.L. Piesse, *The Elements of Drafting* 46 (J.K. Aitken ed., 7th ed. 1987). Lawyers need not invent homegrown ways of saying *res ipsa loquitur.*

One secret of good legal writing is to distinguish rigorously between terms of art and mere jargon. It is elementary to know that *and his heirs* and *elegit* have historically been terms of art; yet only the first is a living term of art, the second having become archaic (and therefore useful primarily in historical contexts).

Is *res gestae* (q.v.) a term of art? Or *scire facias* and *fieri facias* (qq.v.)? Many such questions are debatable: but the debate is important, for we must attempt to winnow the useful law words from the verbal baggage amid which so many of them are buried. See JARGON & PLAIN LANGUAGE.

termtime (= the time of year during which a court is in session) is the antonym of *vacation,* q.v. E.g., "A judge of a district court may, either in *termtime* or [in] vacation, grant writs of mandamus . . . ." Tex. Govt. Code § 24.011 (West 1988).

British writers tend to use two words (*term time*)—e.g.: "At common law, serjeants had an exclusive right of audience in the Court of Common Pleas during *term time,* while sitting in banc." R.E. Megarry, *A Second Miscellany-at-Law* 23 (1973).

terre-tenant; tertenant; land-tenant. As between the first two, *terre-tenant* is the standard spelling of this LAW FRENCH term. *Tertenant,* a Middle English anglicized spelling, never gained widespread use. In the *OED*'s only listed sense of *terre-tenant*—"one who has the actual possession of land; the occupant of land"—the word hardly seems justified. But there is another definition, probably purely AmE: "a person, other than a judgment debtor, who has an interest in the debtor's land after the judgment creditor's lien attached to the land"—a sense that *Black's* (4th–6th eds.) limits to Pennsylvania.

No writer should use the phrase *terre-tenant* without both understanding and making clear the precise sense in which it is used, and without a sound reason for doing so. The thoroughly anglicized form, *land-tenant,* which is listed in some of the older law dictionaries, would be an improvement. See **landman (B).**

territory; dependency; commonwealth. The distinctions in AmE usage are as follows. A *territory* = a part of the United States not included within any state but organized with a separate legislature (*W10*). Guam and the U.S. Virgin Islands are *territories* of the United States; Alaska and Hawaii were formerly *territories. Dependency* = a land or territory geographically distinct from the country governing it, but belonging to it and governed by its laws. The Philippines was once a *dependency* of the United States. *Commonwealth* = a political unit having local autonomy but voluntarily united with the United States. Puerto Rico and the Northern Mariana Islands are *commonwealths.* Puerto Rico is sometimes referred to as a *dependency,* but its proper designation is *commonwealth.*

In BrE, *commonwealth* = a loose association of countries that recognize one sovereign as its head <the British Commonwealth>.

***Terry* stop** (= the act of a police officer's stopping a person whose behavior is reasonably considered suspicious and frisking that person for weapons) derives from *Terry v. Ohio,* 392 U.S. 1 (1968). E.g., "Upholding the legality of the *Terry* stop of a van that led to Jones' arrest, the D.C. Court of Appeals affirmed Jones' conviction . . . ." *D.C. Digests,* Legal Times, 4 Dec. 1989, at 37. See CASE REFERENCES (A).

tertenant. See **terre-tenant.**

tertius gaudens = a third party who profits when two others dispute. Literally, the term means "a rejoicing third." It is good to have a word for this concept, which is not uncommon in law, but it is unfortunate that the word is so abstruse.

testable = (1) that may be tested or tried; (2) legally qualified to bear witness; (3) legally qualified to make a will; or (4) willable; devisable by will. Only sense (1) can be said to be thriving; the other three are obsolescent if not obsolete.

testacy; intestacy. *Testacy* = the condition of leaving a valid will at death. *Intestacy* is its antonym. See **intestate.**

testament is not, as is sometimes supposed, obsolete outside the phrase *last will and testament,* q.v. In legal prose, it is still sometimes contrasted with *devise,* for in the legal idiom *testament* has come generally to signify a will disposing of personal property, whereas *devise* is traditionally the word for a will disposing of land. E.g., "The Wills Acts of 1837 eliminated substantive distinctions between devises and *testaments.*" Cf. **bequeath.**

Usually, however, the word is used not for reasons of fastidiousness, but for less good reasons. In the following sentences, for example, it is an archaic pomposity, to which *will* would have been preferable: "A valid *testament* [read *will*] includes two essential elements: there must be a sufficient designation of the beneficiary and of the property given to him."/ "In *In re Bluestein's Will,* both the language of the *testament* [read *will*] and the attendant circumstances were said to support the conclusion that, in context, the testator's 'request' bespoke a direction, imposing an obligation upon the legatee." See **will.**

In Scots law, the *testament* was formerly that part of a will in which the testator named an executor. Today, however, and elsewhere in the civil-law world, *testament* is used more broadly as a synonym of *will*—e.g.: "[T]he average citizen, relying on the existing legal framework governing intestate successions, will usually make no *testament.*" A.N. Yiannopolous, *Of Legal Usufruct, the Surviving Spouse, and Article 890 of the Louisiana Civil Code,* 49 La. L. Rev. 803, 803 (1989).

testamentary. A. Senses. *Testamentary* = (1) of or relating to a will or testament, as a document <testamentary papers>; (2) provided for or appointed by a will <testamentary guardian>; or (3) created by will <testamentary trust>. In sense (1), the word is not ordinarily confined to contexts involving testaments of personal property (as opposed to devises of real property)—e.g.: "It is everywhere recognized that the purpose of the law of wills is to give effect to the last valid *testamentary* act of the testator."

B. And *testamental.* The word is a NEEDLESS VARIANT that occurs mostly in lay writing.

C. For *testimonial.* Since the early 1960s, this error has become surprisingly common in reported American opinions. Usually, *testamentary* appears in tandem with *documentary*—hence the writer is misled by some kind of "false attraction" to the first suffix—e.g.: "[A] thorough review of the documentary and *testamentary* [read *testimonial*] evidence convinces us that the commissioner's findings on this point are amply supported by the record . . . ." *Lambert v. U.S.,* 153 Ct. Cl. 501, 510 (1961)./ "Bankrupts then offered documentary and *testamentary* [read *testimonial*] evidence to rebut the Government's proof." *Solari Furs v. U.S.,* 436 F.2d 683, 685 (8th Cir. 1971).

In the following sentence, the distinction is made clear: "Lay witnesses, before they may express a *testimonial* opinion as to *testamentary* capacity must testify first to facts inconsistent with sanity." *In re Estate of Powers,* 134 N.W.2d 148, 161 (Mich. 1965).

testate, n. (= a testate person), though corresponding in form to *intestate,* n., is generally a NEEDLESS VARIANT of *testator. Testatus* is the civil-law term. See **intestate.**

testate, v.i., = (1) to testify; or (2) to make one's will. In sense (1), the word is a NEEDLESS VARIANT of *testify.* In sense (2), the verb is so rare as to sound affected.

testation = the disposal of property by will <power of testation>. E.g., "But tenants soon acquired the right of alienation in their lifetime[s], though not, until much later, that of *testation.*" H.G. Hanbury, *English Courts of Law* 57 (2d ed. 1953)./ "Before 1600, the province of Canterbury (excepting Wales and London) came to permit complete freedom of *testation,* whereas the province of York adhered to the old system of parts until 1692." J.H. Baker, *An Introduction to English Legal History* 436 (3d ed. 1990).

testator. A. Senses. *Testator* = (1) a person who dies leaving a will; or (2) a person who makes or has made a will. Sense (1) is more usual, perhaps for two reasons: first, we have more occasion to refer to testators who have already died; and second, the living feel uncomfortable being called "testators."

B. And *devisor.* Because *testament* historically came to be more or less confined to dispositions of personal property, and *devise* to those of real property, it has been thought that *testator* was at one time confined to a person who left personal, as opposed to real, property. See, e.g., Morton S. Freeman, *A Treasury for Word Lovers* 173 (1983). No such crabbed meaning ever attached to the word, however; Blackstone wrote, as long ago as 1766, "that all devises of lands and tenements shall not only be in writing, but signed by the *testator*" (quoted in *OED*). See **testate & deviser.**

testatorial; testorial; testatory. The *OED* records only *testatory* as the adjective corresponding to *testator,* but this form is extremely rare. As between *testatorial* and *testorial,* the former is the more logical form—e.g.: "[A]n ademption may occur without *testatorial* intention." J.A. Ballentine, *Ballentine's Law Dictionary* 28 (3d ed. 1969).

But the most common form—which has no foundation in the *OED, W3,* or *Black's*—is *testorial:* "[I]t is enough if the circumstances, taken together, leave no doubt as to the *testorial* [read *testamentary*] intention, and in some cases it is said that the implication may be drawn from slight circumstances appearing from the will." 57 Am. Jur. *Wills* § 1192, at 783 (1948)./ "[T]he *testorial* intention will control . . . ." *Hixon v. Hixon,* 715 P.2d 1087, 1090 (Okl. 1985).

Often, *testamentary* will be the best option <testamentary intention>. It changes the meaning slightly, from "testator's intention" to "intention as expressed in the will," but ordinarily the latter is a more precise notion.

testatory. See **testatorial.**

testatrix. The word is useless, *testator* quite properly referring to men and women alike. See SEXISM (C).

testatus. See **testate.**

test case = a lawsuit brought to determine an unsettled legal point in some matter of broad application. E.g., "Should *test cases* be brought directly to the highest court and without the lower court procedure?" David Lawrence, *Nine Honest Men* 123 (1936)./ "The appeal is a *test case,* its purpose being to determine whether a juvenile or criminal court has the power to order compensation to be paid to the victim of crime by the local authority in whose care the child who committed the offence was at the time of the offence." *Leeds City Council v. West Yorkshire Metro. Police,* [1983] 1 A.C. 29, 37 (H.L.)./ "Constitutional lawyers say the large size of the punitive damages assessed against The Inquirer, if upheld on appeal, could become a *test case* for the United States Supreme Court, which is already considering the constitutionality of punitive awards." Michael deC. Hines, *Philadelphia Paper Assessed $34 Million for Libel,* N.Y. Times, 4 May 1990, at A1, A11.

teste is the name, in DRAFTING, of the clause that states the name of a witness and evidences the act of witnessing. E.g., "Judgments did not bind chattels, but at early common law a writ of fieri facias bound chattels from the date of the *teste,* i.e., the date of the issuance, thereby invalidating all subsequent alienations." In older instruments *teste* was used in much the same way as some legal writers use *witnesseth,* q.v., today. Cf. **testimonium clause.**

Like much legal terminology, this word is not in tune with the times. Several American judges have been known to joke that they would much prefer not to attach a *teste* to a document.

testification is an unnecessary word for *testimony* or *testifying.*

testifier. See **witness (C).**

testify. See **give evidence.**

testimonial, not *testamentary,* q.v., is the adjective corresponding to *testimony.* See **testamentary (C).**

testimonium clause, in a sworn legal document, is the attestation clause that traditionally begins with the phrase *In witness whereof,* which commonly concludes legal instruments and pleadings. Among the traditional forms are the following: "In witness whereof I have subscribed my name this ______ day of 19____."/ "Witness my signature this ______ day of 19____."/ "In witness whereof we hereto set our hands and seals."

The plural of *testimonium* is either *-iums* or *-ia,* the former being preferable. See **attestation clause & in witness whereof.** Cf. **teste.**

testimony is sometimes loosely used as a COUNT NOUN but the more natural-sounding usage is to treat it as a mass noun. E.g., "This court has no way of actually knowing *which testimonies or parts of testimonies* [read *which testimony*] the jury accepted as the most credible."/ "Even if the *testimonies* [read *testimony*] of the various witnesses *are* [read *is*] looked upon in the light most favorable to the appellees, the verdict returned by the jury is not supported by *those testimonies* [read *that testimony*]." See **evidence (A).**

testing-clause. See **attestation clause.**

testis [L.] = (1) a witness; or (2) a testicle. Modern witnesses are not likely to take kindly to being called *testes.* See **witness.** Cf. **teste.**

testorial. See **testamentary (A) & testatorial.**

text as an adjective is inferior to *textual:* "This is made clear by quotations from recognized *text* [read *textual*] authorities." See **textual.**

textual; textuary. As an adjective, the latter is a NEEDLESS VARIANT.

than. A. Verb Not Repeated After (*than is, than has*). Usually it is unnecessary to repeat *be*-verbs and *have*-verbs after *than.* E.g., "The controlling issue is whether the decision-makers who *are* in a better position *than is the judiciary* [read *than the judiciary*] to decide whether the public interest would be served have created a scheme with which the remedy would interfere." If you need to repeat the verb after *than* to avoid an AMBIGUITY, it should follow the *noun* after *than*—e.g.: "She is closer to her father *than her mother* [read, depending on the sense, *than her mother is* or *than to her mother*]."

B. *Than what.* This collocation usually signals a poor construction. E.g., "The jurisdictional reach of courts became substantially broader *than what* [omit *what*] it had been under the strict territorial guidelines of the *Pennoyer* case."

C. For *then.* This error is so elementary that

one might fairly wonder whether it is merely a lapse in proofreading; but it occurs with some frequency. E.g., "If Blom-Cooper's judgment is correct, *than* [read *then*] the failure is in Lord MacNaghten's style, not in his subject-matter." (Eng.)

D. Case of Pronoun After (*than me* or *than I*). Traditionally, grammarians have considered *than* a conjunction, not a preposition—hence *He is taller than I* [*am*]. That view has had its detractors, including Eric Partridge, who preferred the objective case: *You are a much greater loser than me.* See Eric Partridge, *Usage and Abusage* 332 (1947). But those siding with Partridge have been a small minority.

For formal contexts, I recommend the traditional usage. The prepositional use of *than* is acceptable only in the most relaxed, colloquial contexts. Here it seems ill-advised, even ironic: "[S]o many of our students seem to struggle . . . . (Are we really that much smarter than *them* [read *they*]?)" John B. Mitchell, *Current Theories on Expert and Novice Thinking,* 39 J. Legal Educ. 275, 275 (1989).

E. *Than whom.* This idiom, common since the latter part of the 16th century, originated perhaps as a LOAN TRANSLATION of the Latin comparative with *quam.* Strictly speaking, *than who* would have been preferable, since *than* is treated as a conjunction, not a preposition (see (D)). But the phrase *than whom*—as in, *Holmes was a judge than whom no other could be considered better*—is now established.

thankfully = gratefully; in a manner expressing thanks. The word should not be misused in the way that *hopefully,* q.v., is misused, namely, in the sense "thank goodness; I am (or we are) thankful that." Following are two examples of the all-too-common fall from stylistic grace: "Our country, *thankfully,* has never chosen that path." *Roberts v. U.S.,* 445 U.S. 552, 571 (1980) (Marshall, J., dissenting)./ "As Mustill L.J. has already remarked the many and complicated issues which were debated over many days before Mr. Justice Saville have now, *thankfully,* been considerably refined." *G & H Montage GmbH v. Irvani,* [1990] 1 W.L.R. 667, 687 (C.A.) (per Purchas, L.J.). See **hopefully** & SENTENCE ADVERBS.

that. A. Wrongly Suppressed *that* as Relative Pronoun. Although in any number of constructions it is perfectly permissible, and even preferred, to omit *that* by ellipsis (e.g., *The dog you gave me* rather than *The dog that you gave me*), in formal writing *that* is often ill-advisedly omitted where it creates an AMBIGUITY, even if only momentarily. E.g., "*I noticed those who left the city attorney's office* [read *I noticed that those who left the city attorney's office*] early in their careers were unhappy also in private practice." (The sentence at first leads the reader to believe that the writer refers to the persons who have left, not to their unhappiness.)/ "In *Eleason, we held the driver, an epileptic,* [read *we held that the driver, an epileptic,*] possessed knowledge that he was likely to have a seizure."/ "There are authorities *which* [read *that*] *generally hold insanity is not* [read *generally hold that insanity is not*] a defense in tort cases except for intentional torts."/ "She thought Batman was good [read *thought that Batman was good*] and was trying to help save the world and her husband [read *that her husband*] was possessed of the devil." (Without the relative pronoun, it sounds as if the writer is stating a fact—that her husband was possessed by the devil)./ "Carbide International *prays we reverse* [read *prays that we reverse*] an adverse trial court judgment." See MISCUES (F).

B. Unnecessarily Repeated *that* as Relative Pronoun. One must be careful not to repeat the relative pronoun after an intervening phrase; either suspend it till just before the verb, or use it early in the sentence and omit it before the verb. E.g., "The officers told Mr. P. *that,* if he would waive his right to receive any benefits from A.I. under the deferred compensation portion of his employment contract, *that* [omit *that*] they would take care of him."/ "Rule 10b-10(a) requires *that* prior to the completion of a transaction *that* [omit *that*] a written statement be sent or given to a customer setting forth prescribed information relating to the transaction."/ "Appellant argues *that* since Lent, Inc. was the principal in the indemnity agreement, *that* [omit *that*] it cannot also be an indemnitor in the same agreement."

C. The Biblical *that.* In lieu of *so that* or *in order that, that* often smacks of the biblical, as in: "A lawyer may never give unsolicited advice to a layman *that* [read *in order that*] he retain a client."/ "We must preserve the work of art *that* [read *so that*] it may continue to convey to the sympathetic spectator the creative ecstasy that went into its making." See BIBLICAL AFFECTATION.

D. As an Ellipsis for *the fact that.* This construction is often useful; here, however, the phrase is badly used, because the subject and verb are too far removed: "*That* the district court's order authorizing the sale of the Charles House property and judgment confirming the sale and passage of title to Southmark operated as a final judgment on the merits is evident." [Read *It is evident that* . . . .] See **fact that, the.**

E. Relative Adverb. E.g., "Many charities fail by change of circumstances and [by] the happening of contingencies that no human foresight can provide against." (See PREPOSITIONS (E).) Some lightweight authorities do not understand that the construction in the sentence just quoted is perfectly acceptable. One such manual for legal writers recommends, "The case *on which* the lawyer was working never went to trial," instead of, "The case *that* the lawyer *was* working *on* never went to trial," and labels the latter incorrect. See *Texas Law Review Manual on Style* 28–29 (4th ed. 1979). Actually, both constructions are correct—and the construction with *that* is far more natural-sounding.

F. For *so* or *very*: "This case is not *that* important." This usage is informal and colloquial and, though it hardly merits condemnation in speech, it should be avoided in writing: "This case is not *so* [or *very*] important."

G. *That of*. This phrase is often used unnecessarily. E.g., "In another comparative study, *that of* [omit *that of*] anthropology, they also find much to make them question current ethics."

H. And *which*. See RESTRICTIVE AND NONRESTRICTIVE CLAUSES & REMOTE RELATIVES.

I. And *who*. See **who.**

J. The Demonstrative *that*. See DEICTIC TERMS.

that is. The conventional wisdom is that, if this phrase is used to begin a sentence, the result is a fragment. (See INCOMPLETE SENTENCES (A).) But good writers regularly use it in this way, in place of *in other words*—e.g.: "A misrepresentation generally has no effect unless it is material. *That is,* it must be one [that] would affect the judgment of a reasonable person in deciding whether, or on what terms, to enter into the contract . . . ." G.H. Treitel, *The Law of Contract* 301 (8th ed. 1991)./ "They are punitive rather than remedial. *That is,* they do not attempt to restore any version of the status quo . . . ." Douglas Laycock, *The Death of the Irreparable Injury Rule* 199 (1991).

The longer phrase, *that is to say,* is usu. wordy in place of *that is*—e.g.: "[T]he statute does not speak with absolute crystalline clarity . . . . *That is to say* [read *That is*], Congress has chosen, wisely or no, to speak to the precise issue at hand through a Committee Report that was expressly adopted by both Houses." *ACLU v. FCC,* 823 F.2d 1554, 1583 (D.C. Cir. 1987) (Starr, J., dissenting in part). Cf. **viz.** & **namely.**

that is to say. See **that is.**

that which; those which; those that. When a noun introduced by *that,* as a DEICTIC TERM, is followed by defining matter, that matter is introduced by *which.* E.g.: "The commission merchant must exercise *that* degree of care *which* a prudent person would exercise in the conduct of his own affairs." Sometimes the construction is wrongly made *that . . . that,* as in: "We must distinguish between a belief in the literal truth and falsity of a statement and *that* type of belief in falsity *that* [read *which*] underlies the fraudulent misrepresentation." When *that* becomes, in plural, *those,* it is permissible for the second member of this construction to be either *which* or *that.* E.g.: "Deductible distributions are usually *those that* [or *those which*] are made to the residuary beneficiaries."/ "*Those issuers that* [or *Those issuers which* (or *who*)] have already issued stock under such plans will have to fight hard to obtain some sort of grandfathering relief."

the. See ARTICLES.

theater; theatre. See -ER (C).

the case of. This FLOTSAM PHRASE is almost always best omitted. See **case (A).**

the fact that. See **fact that, the.**

theft was not the name of a common-law crime. Rather, statutes such as England's Theft Act of 1968 have made theft a statutory crime. In ordinary usage, *theft* denotes the act of stealing. In legal usage, in some jurisdictions, it is used as a synonym of *larceny.*

In still others, such as England, *larceny* has been abolished and replaced by *theft*—which sometimes includes embezzlement and false pretenses. The Model Penal Code makes *theft* the name of all such acquisitive offenses. See **burglary (A).**

their; they're; there. A book like this one ought not to have to explain such distinctions. So it will not. But: "Liberals are again trying to explain why they lost their fifth presidential election in 20 years. They've been talking about what *they're* [read *their*] party should be for." *What's a Liberal For?* Wall St. J., 13 Jan. 1989, at A6./ "And that's where these radio stations are really missing the boat, because *there* [read *they're*] missing the folks who hold the purse strings to all the disposable income." Brad Tooley, *Canyon Views,* Canyon News, 13 Jan. 1994, at 1, 2.

theirself. See **ourself.**

the law abhors a forfeiture. See **equity abhors a forfeiture.**

themself is a part-plural, part-singular abomination. Sometimes it is intended as a gender-neutral equivalent of *himself or herself*—e.g.: "The successful applicant will identify *themself* through a proven record of generating respect . . . ." Various revisions suggest themselves: *The successful applicant must have a proven record . . . ; The successful applicant will have generated respect . . . ; The successful applicant will identify himself or herself through a proven record of generating respect . . . .*

In the early 1990s, Canadian statute drafters began using *themself* in legislation.

then. A. Adjective. *Then* should not be hyphenated when used in the sense "that existed or was so at that time." E.g., "In *Griggs* the Supreme Court noted that *the then-guidelines* [read *the then guidelines*] issued by the Equal Opportunity Commission were to be accorded 'great deference' by the courts."/ "The 1969 and 1962 convictions were proved for enhancement, and Carter received *the then-mandatory* [read *the then mandatory;* here the word is adverbial] life sentence."/ "At the time of the events critical to the determination of this case, three of the board members had been appointed by *the then* mayor."/ "In a trial presided over by *the then* magistrate, now district judge Marcel Livandais, the jury returned a verdict in favor of each parent." In most of those examples, however, the writer could have eliminated *then* altogether with no loss of meaning—a desirable result because of the awkward PHRASING that *then* creates.

B. For *than*. This is a distressingly common error, esp. in newsprint: "'I could not be any more excited *then* [read *than*] I am right now,' said C.B., a supporter of the measure."/ "Under section 183, if dependency is the basis of recovery, the measure of damages is very much greater *then* [read *than*] it would be under section 184." For the reverse error, see **than (C).**

thence; whence; hence. *Thence* = from that place or source; for that reason. *Whence* = from there. *Hence* = (1) from here; or (2) therefore. These are literaryisms as well as LEGALISMS, acceptable perhaps in the more literary style of legal prose, despite carping by those who advocate "consumer English."

thenceforth; thenceforward. The latter is a NEEDLESS VARIANT.

theoretic(al)(ly). The best, most usual form of the adjective is *theoretical,* not *theoretic.* Of a common use of *theoretical,* Walter Wheeler Cook aptly observed: "Theory which will not work in practice is not sound theory. 'It is *theoretically* correct but will not work in practice' is a common but erroneous statement. If a theory is '*theoretically* correct' it will work; if it will not work, it is '*theoretically* incorrect.'" Introduction to Wesley N. Hohfeld, *Fundamental Legal Conceptions* 21 (1919). Holmes likewise observed, "I know no reason why theory should disagree with the facts." Oliver W. Holmes, *The Theory of Legal Interpretation,* 12 Harv. L. Rev. 417, 417 (1899).

therap(eut)ist. The standard term is *therapist.*

there. See **their & there is.**

thereabout(s). The form *thereabout* is preferred.

there are. See **there is** & EXPLETIVES.

thereat (= there; at it). Even at the turn of the 20th century, when the *OED* was being compiled, this word was considered "formal [= pompous] and archaic." Today it is more so. E.g., "He was astonished *thereat* [read *at it*]."/ "The purpose of the bill as stated in the prayers for relief was to enjoin the defendants from combining and conspiring to interfere with the complainants in the practice of their trade and occupation, or to prevent them from obtaining further employment *thereat* [read *in their trade*]." The word is not a locative. Cf. **whereat.** See HERE- AND THERE-WORDS.

thereby cannot rightly be considered a FORBIDDEN WORD, but see HERE- AND THERE- WORDS.

therefore; therefor. The former (stress on first syllable) means "for that reason," "consequently," or "ergo"—this is the word known to nonlawyers; the latter (stress on last syllable) means "for that" or "for it." The proper use of *therefore,* which always states a conclusion, needs no illustration.

A. Proper Use of *therefor* Illustrated. In the following sentences, the musty word *therefor* is properly used—even so, though, it generally ought to be replaced for stylistic reasons: "The plaintiff discharged union cutters and shop foremen without just cause *therefor* [delete the word]."/ "We are not unmindful of the sound and salutary rule, and of the obvious *reasons therefor* [read *reasons for it*]."/ "Recovery should be limited, in any event, to the reasonable value of the necessaries furnished rather than *the contract price therefor* [read *their contract price*]."/ "Mrs. W. bought 275 acres of land soon after the death of her second husband, paying *therefor $2,000* [read *$2,000 for it*]." See HERE- AND THERE- WORDS.

***B. Therefore* for *therefor*.** In the sentences that follow, *therefore* is wrongly used for *therefor,* a surprising lapse: "This memorandum is solely for the use of the person named below and may not be reproduced or used for any other purpose; any action to the contrary may place the *persons responsible therefore* [read *persons responsible therefor,* or, better, *responsible persons*] in violation of state and federal securities laws."/ "Dividends on the stock may be declared and paid by the board of directors of the company only out of the funds legally available *therefore* [read *therefor,* or, better, *for that purpose*]."

C. *Therefor* for *therefore*. This is the slightly more usual error with these homophones. In the first example, the misuse occurs twice in two sentences: "The point is that the Delaware statute contains no such limiting language and *therefor* [read *therefore*] must be construed to authorize any reasonable corporate gift of a charitable or educational nature. Significantly, the corporation was incorporated in Delaware in 1958, before 8 Del. C. § 122(9) was cast in its present form; *therefor* [read *therefore*], no constitutional problem arises."/ "These were not the acts of a competent master; they *therefor* [read *therefore*] rendered the vessels unseaworthy to a gross degree."/ "The Supreme Court (per Vinson, C.J.) *therefor* [read *therefore*] shifted from constitutional to other grounds."

D. Punctuation Around *therefore*. One must take care in the punctuation of *therefore.* In short sentences it need not, indeed should not, be set off by commas. Punctuating around it in short sentences creates great awkwardness: "We, *therefore,* dismiss the appeal." (The commas destroy the rhythm and emphasize *we,* as opposed to *dismiss.*)/ "It, *therefore,* becomes our duty to review these findings and to determine for ourselves whether they are sustained by the weight of the evidence." (Again, omit the commas around *therefore.* Whenever a single word like *it* precedes *therefore,* the latter should not be enclosed in commas unless that initial word is to receive stress.)/ "The court, *therefore,* remanded the action to the Secretary with instructions that he furnish the court with the basis of his final determination." (Who else would remand the action? Omit the commas around *therefore.*)

E. Run-On Sentences with *therefore*. One should take care not to create run-on sentences in this common way: "These works might be of paramount public *interest, therefore* [read *interest; therefore*] the rights of their compilers are *accordingly* [omit *accordingly,* which is here redundant] in the public interest." See RUN-ON SENTENCES.

therefrom (= from that or it) for *therefor* (= for that or it) is an odd blunder. E.g., "Petitioner has not presented any valid reason for allowing costs in this particular case and, there being no indication that defendant's removal petition was not made in good faith, the court denies petitioner's request *therefrom* [read *therefor* or, better, *for costs*]."

Even in contexts in which *therefrom* is technically correct, it is stilted and often vague. Thus, an editor will usually improve on it—e.g.: "We note that the trial counsel referred to the testimony about the upcoming marriage of the prosecutrix and her decision to leave town in his argument and deduced *therefrom* [read *from those facts*] why she would not claim she did not consent."

therein. See HERE- AND THERE- WORDS.

there is; there are. A. As Signals of Clutter. These phrases are enemies of a lean writing style. Rarely do they add anything but clutter to a sentence—e.g.: "*In a few jurisdictions there are* [read *A few jurisdictions have*] special statutes of limitations prohibiting the initiation of administration proceedings after a designated number of years." Thomas E. Atkinson, *Handbook of the Law of Wills* 569 (2d ed. 1953)./ "*There is nothing in the record to indicate* [read *Nothing in the record indicates*] that Jones intentionally relinquished his right to have Acme procure insurance."

The exceptions to this dictum invariably occur when the writer is addressing the existence of something—e.g.: "In tribal times, *there were* the medicine men. In the Middle Ages, *there were* the priests. Today *there are* the lawyers." Fred Rodell, *Woe Unto You, Lawyers!* 1 (1939; repr. 1980).

B. Number with. The number of the verb is controlled by whether the subject that follows the inverted verb is singular or plural. Mistakes are common—e.g.: "[A] trial judge has an affirmative duty . . . to ascertain whether *there is* [read *there are*] irrelevant, immaterial, or privileged matters contained within the records or documents." *Peeples v. The Honorable Fourth Sup. J. Dist.,* 701 S.W.2d 635, 637 (Tex. 1985)./ "It has also been held (although dealing with exclusions from public places where *there are* [read *there is*] discrimination on the basis of race or color) that preventive relief is available where a public agency operates the public place." See EXPLETIVES & SUBJECT-VERB AGREEMENT (K).

C. Obliquely Phrased Duties in Drafting. In contractual and statutory DRAFTING, the phrase *there is* or, worse yet, *there shall be* displaces a more direct way of phrasing a duty—e.g.: "Because of the difficulty of ascertaining damages, *there shall be payable to* [read *Tenant must pay*] the Landlord $5,000 in liquidated damages for each such breach."

thereof. Avoid this legalistic word by rephrasing the thought—e.g.: "The Employee understands that this is a restrictive covenant and fully agrees *to the reasonability thereof* [read *that it is reasonable*]." See HERE- AND THERE- WORDS.

thereon. See HERE- AND THERE- WORDS.

thereout is an ARCHAISM for *therefrom*—e.g.: "[T]he Arbitration Act rendered a written provision in a contract by the parties to such a transaction, to arbitrate controversies arising *thereout* [read *therefrom,* or, better, *from the contract*], specifically enforceable." *The Anaconda v. American Sugar Ref. Co.,* 322 U.S. 42, 44 (1944)./ "But the gift is made subject to the payment *thereout* [read *from the fund*] of a rateable portion of capital transfer tax." (Eng.) See HERE- AND THERE- WORDS.

there shall be. See **there is (C).**

thereto. A. Superfluously Used. E.g., "Five of the children were born before the execution of the deed. The others were born *subsequently thereto* [read *later*]."/ "Probate of wills, and *litigation related thereto* [read *related litigation*], belonged to the Church courts until 1857." J.H. Baker, *An Introduction to English Legal History* 436 (3d ed. 1990). See HERE- AND THERE- WORDS & CUTTING OUT THE CHAFF.

B. For *thereon:* "It comes as a surprise that the 1972 Code amendments and official comments *thereto* [read *thereon*] refer to the 'requirement' of filing." (One *comments on,* not *to,* a statute.)

theretofore. See **hitherto.**

thereunto appertaining. Like diplomas, contracts often have catchall language referring to "every right and privilege [or appurtenance] *thereunto appertaining.*" Regardless of the context, though, this language is deadwood.

thereupon, adv., = at that instant. This word can usefully pinpoint the time of an action. The word should ordinarily not be used, however, to begin sentences. See **thereon,** HERE- AND THERE- WORDS & **whereupon.**

the said. See **said.**

thesaurus. Pl. *-ri.* See PLURALS (A).

these. See DEICTIC TERMS. For the phrase *both these,* see **both (D).**

these kind of; these type of; these sort of. These are illogical forms that, in a bolder day, would have been termed illiteracies because the demonstrative adjective *these* should modify a plural noun (e.g., *kinds*), not a singular one (e.g., *kind*). Today they merely brand the speaker or writer as being slovenly—e.g.: "The evidence shows that LTV's Board of Directors gave LTV's General Manager the requisite authority to enter into *these type* [read *these types*] of transactions." *LTV Fed. Credit Union v. UMIC Gov. Secs., Inc.,* 523 F. Supp. 819, 825 (N.D. Tex. 1981).

these sort of. See **these kind of.**

these type of. See **these kind of.**

they're. See **their.**

thieve, vb., may be either transitive (in the sense "to steal [a thing]") or intransitive (in the sense "to act as a thief"). In legal contexts today, the most common use is transitive—e.g.: "[D]efendant . . . told them he would melt down and dispose of any gold they could *thieve* . . . ." *State v. Lewis,* 293 S.E.2d 638, 641 (N.C. Ct. App. 1982)./ "A safe had been *thieved* and asported from the Canton Food Center." *State v. Gardner,* 429 N.W.2d 60, 62 n. (S.D. 1988) (Henderson, J., concurring).

thing. Users of this word are often chastised by ill-informed amateurs of usage. Though frequently derided, *thing* can be very useful in contexts in which no more specific or pseudospecific term is needed. Still, the word can easily be overused.

In law—which borrowed the term from philosophy—a *thing* is "the object of a right; i.e., is whatever is treated by the law as the object over which one person exercises a right, and with reference to which another person lies under a duty." Thomas E. Holland, *The Elements of Jurisprudence* 101 (13th ed. 1924).

thing in action. See **chose.**

things, in all. See **in all things.**

3d; 3rd. In legal writing, and esp. in citations, the first of these abbreviations is preferred. See **2d.**

third(-)party is spelled as two words as a noun <a third party> and is hyphenated as an adjective <a third-party action> and as a verb <they were third-partied>. For the origin of this phrase, see **party of the first part.**

third-party, v.t., = to bring into litigation as a third-party defendant. This phrase—a casualism—should be hyphenated. E.g., "The defendant hospital did not *third party* [read *third-party*] Travenol." *Richard v. Southwest La. Hosp. Ass'n,* 383 So. 2d 83, 90 (La. Ct. App. 1980). This usage is informal at best, although it is increasingly common in AmE. See NOUNS AS VERBS.

third-party plaintiff. Pl. *third-party plaintiffs.* E.g., "The settlement did not subrogate *third-parties plaintiff* [read *third-party plaintiffs*] to plaintiff's rights against Ford."

third person should be pluralized *third persons,* never *third people.*

this. See DEICTIC TERMS & ANTECEDENTS, FALSE.

thither = there; to that place. See **whither.**

thitherto. See **hitherto.**

thorough-going = thorough, but connotes zeal or ardor. It is not, therefore, merely a NEEDLESS VARIANT. E.g., "The conflicts on the applicable interest rates alone—which we do not think can be labeled 'false conflicts' without a more *thorough-going* treatment than was accorded them by the Supreme Court of Kansas—certainly amounted to millions of dollars in liability."

those. See DEICTIC TERMS.

those kind of; those sort. See **these kind of.**

though. See **although.**

those which; those that. See **that which.**

though . . . yet. See **although . . . yet** & CORRELATIVE CONJUNCTIONS.

threshold. So spelled; *threshhold* is a common misspelling (see, e.g., *Zweygardt v. Colorado Nat'l Bank,* 52 B.R. 229, 231 (Bankr. D. Colo. 1985)). The word is not a compound of the verb *hold,* but rather a modern form of OE *thaerscwold* (= doorsill). But cf. **withhold.**

thrice is a literary ARCHAISM, and sometimes a useful one, meaning "three times." E.g., "The words are *thrice* repeated in the statute." (A literalist would read this sentence as meaning that the words appear four times in the statute—once perhaps at the beginning and three times *repeated.*)/ "Before the instant conviction Avery, albeit a relatively young man, had at least *thrice* been convicted of felony charges."

thrift institution is the current jargon for *savings and loan association.*

thrive > thrived > thrived. *Thrived,* not *throve,* is the better past tense—e.g.: "Infantile sexuality lived and *throve* [read *thrived*]—in child and adult—before Freud brought it to scientific attention."

Likewise, *thrived,* not *thriven,* is the better past participle—e.g.: "[P]arody . . . has *thrived* from the time of Chaucer . . . ." *Berlin v. E.C. Publications, Inc.,* 329 F.2d 541, 545 (2d Cir. 1964).

throw out, as legal slang, means "to reverse, overturn, or hold unconstitutional." E.g., "A decision *throwing out* a newly written law may hint to the lawmakers how to get the same thing done in a different way which the Justices will then approve." Fred Rodell, *Nine Men* 12 (1955)./ "This was the second trial of Speller the court *threw out;* the first was overturned because he had been tried by an all-white jury." Paul R. Clancy, *Just a Country Lawyer: A Biography of Senator Sam Ervin* 150 (1974)./ "The Rhode Island attorney general . . . declined to prosecute for lack of corroborating evidence, and the charges were *thrown out* by a Rhode Island judge . . . ." *Hoffman v. Reali,* 973 F.2d 980, 983 (1st Cir. 1994).

thru, an aborted variant spelling of *through,* should be shunned. Oddly, it appears in parts of the Internal Revenue Code.

thus. A. General Senses. *Thus* has four meanings: (1) in this or that manner <One does it thus>; (2) so <thus far>; (3) hence, consequently <Thus, the doctrine does not apply>; and (4) as an example <There are several possible courses of action; thus, one might amend the pleadings, nonsuit the defendants, or move for dismissal>. In senses (3) and (4), *thus,* when it begins a clause, should usu. have a comma following.

Here *thus* is given none of these meanings: "The factors that determine whether Article 2 applies are thus: (i) the type of transaction (sale); and (ii) the subject matter of the transaction (goods)." The best approach to remedying the problem in that sentence would be to replace *thus* with *as follows.*

B. *Thusly.* *Thus* itself being an adverb, it needs no *-ly.* Formerly, one might have labeled the use of *thusly* illiterate. Still, though it has appeared in otherwise respectable writing, it remains a grave lapse: "Professor Choper summarized our school aid cases *thusly* [read *thus*]." *Edwards v.*

Aguillard, 482 U.S. 578, 639 n.7 (1987) (Scalia, J., dissenting)./ "*Grubbs* is hardly a surprising decision when it is *thusly interpreted* [read *interpreted thus*]." *Paxton v. Weaver,* 553 F.2d 936, 942 (5th Cir. 1977)./ "He illustrated his concern *thusly* [read *thus*] . . . ." Barbara H. Craig, *Chadha: The Story of an Epic Constitutional Struggle* 54 (1988). Cf. **overly & muchly.** See ADVERBS, PROBLEMS WITH (D).

ticket-of-leave. See **parole.**

tidings is an ARCHAISM in AmE, although it persists in BrE literary usage. "A sues B on a policy of insurance, and shows that the vessel insured went to sea, and that after a reasonable time no *tidings* of her have been received, but that her loss has been rumoured; the burden of proving that she has not foundered is on B." (Eng.)

tie makes *tying. Tieing* is incorrect. E.g., "The court's determination that the surplus income is intestate, effectively avoiding, as it does, *tieing up* [read *tying up*] and so depriving Olive and her children of the enjoyment of it for what might prove to be a long term of years, is a result that fortifies this conclusion."

till; until. *Till* is, like *until,* a bona fide preposition and conjunction. Though less formal than *until, till* is neither colloquial nor substandard—e.g.: "The present English doctrine was not thoroughly received *till* the nineteenth century." Roscoe Pound, *The Development of Constitutional Guarantees of Liberty* 54 (1957)./ "Our system does not interfere *till* harm has been done and has been proved to have been done with the appropriate *mens rea.*" H.L.A. Hart, "Punishment and the Elimination of Responsibility," in *Punishment and Responsibility: Essays in the Philosophy of Law* 158, 182 (1968).

The myth to the contrary persists, as some authors and editors mistakenly think that *till* deserves a bracketed *sic.* See, e.g., William Brewer & Francis B. Majorie, *One Year After* Dondi, 17 Pepperdine L. Rev. 833, 842 n.68 (1990).

If any form deserves a *sic,* it is *'til,* which is incorrect. E.g., R. Michael Otto, Comment, "*Wait* 'Til [*read* Till] *Your Mothers Get Home*": *Assessing the Rights of Polygamists as Custodial and Adoptive Parents,* 1991 Utah L. Rev. 881 (1991).

timbre; timber. These are different words in BrE and AmE. *Timbre* is primarily a musical term meaning "tone quality." *Timber* is the correct form in all other senses.

time-bar means "a bar to a legal claim arising from the lapse of a defined length of time, often contained in a statute of limitations." E.g., "The government bases its *time-bar* claim upon an earlier letter."

Hence *time-barred* = barred by the statute of limitations. The phrase is useful, though somewhat inelegant, shorthand—e.g.: "Kossick's action would have been *time-barred* under the federal maritime law." Grant Gilmore & Charles L. Black, Jr., *The Law of Admiralty* 466 (2d ed. 1975)./ "The result may indeed differ, depending upon what body of law governs the availability of a third-party claim in this case, when the cause of action accrues, and when it becomes *time-barred.*"

time immemorial. Popularly, this word means "a very long time." More technically, it means "a point in time so far back that no living person has knowledge or proof contradicting the right or custom alleged to have existed since then." See **memory of man runneth not to the contrary.**

time is of the essence. When a contractual stipulation relating to the time of performance is "of the essence" of a contract, a party's failure to meet that stipulation automatically justifies the other party's rescinding the contract—no matter how trivial the failure. If, on the other hand, time is not of the essence, then the failure to comply with a stipulation about time will justify rescission only if there is a substantial failure in performance. Gradually, the phrase *time is of the essence* has become so widespread that it is now classifiable as a POPULARIZED LEGAL TECHNICALITY.

timely, adj. & adv. Because *timely* may be an adverb as well as an adjective in AmE, phrases such as *in a timely fashion* and *in a timely manner* are wordy and should be shortened. E.g., "*Unless he renounces his power in timely fashion* [read *unless he timely renounces his power*], the trust corpus will be handled as part of his gross estate for tax purposes."/ "Here, Orpiano *filed his objections in a timely fashion* [read *timely filed his objections*], but the district court felt that a de novo determination of the portions Orpiano objected to was unnecessary." This adverbial use of *timely* is archaic in BrE. The rare adverbial form *timelily* is to be avoided.

In British law reports, *timeous* (= coming in due time) and *timeously* (= in a timely manner) are common. Though some Scots lawyers earnestly defend *timeous,* a Scottish glossary calls it "[a]n inelegant and unnecessary word." Andrew D. Gibb, *Students' Glossary of Scottish Legal Terms* 94 (A.G.M. Duncan ed., 2d ed. 1982). The word *timeous* is pronounced /*tɪ*-məs/, not /***tim***-ee-əs/. The word never occurs in AmE.

time when. See **reason why.**

time whereof the memory of man runneth not to the contrary. See **time immemorial** & **memory of man runneth not to the contrary.**

tippee = one who receives a tip (i.e., a critical bit of information); one who is illicitly tipped off. E.g., "Absent other culpable actions by a *tippee* that can fairly be said to outweigh these violations by insiders and broker-dealers, we do not believe that the *tippee* properly can be characterized as being of substantially equal culpability as his *tippers.*" *Bateman Eichler, Hill Richards, Inc. v. Berner,* 472 U.S. 299, 314 (1985)./ "The scope of that implied right of action for investors is yet again before the Supreme Court—this time in the context of several defrauded and defrauding *tippees* of inside information seeking to recover against their also defrauding *tipper.*"

The *OED* records the word from 1897 in a rather different sense: "the recipient of a 'tip' or gratuity." See -EE (A).

tipper; tipster. Both refer to a person who gives tips (i.e., critical pieces of information). *Tipster* often refers to one who gives tips to police in criminal investigations, or sells tips relating to speculative or gambling subjects. Here the former sense applies: "An anonymous *tipster,* whose information was relayed to police by a private investigator, implicated appellant."

Tipper shares the meaning with *tipster* of an informer who tips off police on illegal activities; more commonly in legal AmE, it signifies "one who gives or sells tips to securities and other investors." See **tippee.**

tipstaff (= a court crier) has two plural forms: *tipstaves* and *tipstaffs.* The former predominates in American law reports. See **crier.**

tipster. See **tipper.**

tiro. See **tyro.**

titillate. See **tantalize.**

title = (1) the legal link between a person and some object of property, e.g., ownership, possession, custody <What sort of title does she have?>; (2) legal ownership of property <No known person has title to the property>; (3) the grounds by which a landowner has rights of possession; or (4) the legal evidence of a person's ownership rights, or the means by which the owner comes to have those rights. Lon Fuller once remarked that *title* is an indispensable device of legal thought and expression, but that it has abuses when one speaks not of apportioning ownership rights between two or more persons: "[w]hen one's task necessitates breaking through the cover and apportioning the contents among different individuals, the cover [i.e., the word *title*] should be thrown away." Lon L. Fuller, *Legal Fictions* 121–22 (1967).

title-deed = a deed providing evidence of a person's legal ownership. In AmE, the term conveys nothing not included in the simple word *deed.* (See **deed (A).**) But in BrE, in which *deed* continues to refer to any sealed instrument, *title-deed* is a useful specification—e.g.: "No witness who is a party to a suit can be compelled to produce his *title-deeds* to any property." (Eng.)/ "Mortgages of shares are usually made by depositing the share certificate with the lender. This, like a deposit of *title-deeds* in the case of land . . . creates an equitable mortgage." William Geldart, *Introduction to English Law* 100 (D.C.M. Yardley ed., 9th ed. 1984). The plural form *title-deeds* is sometimes shortened to *titles.*

title member is synonymous in AmE with *name partner,* q.v.: "While the three *title members* of the firm were merely expert publicity men who devoted themselves to pulling in the business, the rest of the partners were capable, hard-working, high-minded attorneys who cringed at the antics of their masters, but who, for financial reasons, could not afford to sever their connection." Ephraim Tutt, *Yankee Lawyer* 147 (1943).

TITULAR TOMFOOLERY, primarily an outgrowth of weekly newspapers and news magazines in the U.S., consists in the creation of false titles for people. Instead of *Abraham Lincoln, the country lawyer*—or, for that matter, *the country lawyer Abraham Lincoln* (the prefixed *the* making a significant difference)—it is today commonplace to read of *country lawyer Abraham Lincoln,* or, worse yet, *Country Lawyer Abraham Lincoln. Officer,* granted, is a title to be prefixed to a person's name; *police officer* is not.

This informal verbal contagion originated in a misplaced desire for economy in both words and punctuation, since APPOSITIVES ordinarily require commas (see most of the revisions below).

- "*Venireman Hal Ray* [read *A venireman named Hal Ray*] was excluded properly because he was unable to follow the law."
- "Counsel asked *Juror Franklin* whether he had

any personal knowledge of the case." (In this sentence, if we already know Franklin is on the jury, omit *Juror;* if not, read *asked Franklin, one of the jurors, whether. . . .* Moreover, the term *juror* may be inappropriate here because, if the question was posed at voir dire, the proper term would be *veniremember.*)

- "The district judge then went into the chambers and called for *juror Graham* [read *the juror named Graham*]."
- "Early in 1979, Brown, with the help of *attorney Rogers* [read *his attorney, Rogers*], took steps to obtain credit for the time he served between arrest and conviction."
- "Marion Smith, *widow* [read *the widow*] of George P. Smith, and her six children appeal the dismissal of this diversity action under Fed. R. Civ. P. 12(b)(6)."
- "A few months ago, *second-year law student Jerry Coleman* [read *a second-year law student, Jerry Coleman,*] was unsure of whether to include on his résumé his membership in Columbia University's Gay and Lesbian Law Students' Association." *Job Opportunities Opening Up for Gays,* Nat'l Jurist, April/May 1992, at 6.
- "The district attorney also said he would request a new trial for one of the four policemen acquitted in the 1991 beating of *black motorist Rodney King* [read *Rodney King, a black motorist*]." Wall St. J., 14 May 1992, at A1.
- "*Lawyer Hamm* carried the case to the state's highest court, the Supreme Court of California." Murray T. Bloom, *The Trouble with Lawyers* 61 (1970). (Hamm has already been identified as a lawyer. This example—as one can tell from the fuller context—seems intended as a slight.)

TMESIS /*tə-**mee**-sis*/, the practice of separating parts of a compound word by inserting another word between those parts, occurs much more frequently in legal than in lay writing. A classic colloquial example—some would say dialectal example—is the phrase *a whole 'nother,* which, surprisingly, has actually appeared in legal contexts: "The plaintiff must have *a whole 'nother* trial." See SET PHRASES.

The traditional form of tmesis in legal prose, however, occurs with formal legal words ending in *-soever.* E.g., "Recusal is an act, of *what nature soever* it may be, by which a strange heir, by deeds or words, declares he will not be an heir."/ "A man is also prohibited on the ground of affinity from intermarrying with the wife of his father or father's father, *how high soever.*" The modern tendency, which we should heartily encourage, is to avoid such stuffiness by writing, e.g., *of whatever nature* and *however high.*

to for *until* or *up to* is a casualism—e.g.: "*To* [read *Up to*] September 1964, no Negro pupil had applied for admission to the New Kent school under this statute."

to all intents and purposes. See **for all intents and purposes.**

together appears in a number of REDUNDANCIES, such as *merge together, connect together, consolidate together, couple together,* and *join together,* q.v. These phrases should be avoided.

together with; coupled with; as well as; added to. These expressions do not affect the number of the terms that precede or follow them. E.g., "Johnson, *as well as* Tucker and Thurman, *was* [not *were*] present at the hearing." See SUBJECT-VERB AGREEMENT (H).

to go on circuit. See **circuit, to ride.**

tolerance; toleration. The former is the quality, the latter the act or practice.

toll. In the context of time limits—esp. statutes of limitation—*toll* means "to abate" or "to stop the running of (the statutory period)." E.g, "There are various ways in which the statute of limitations may be *tolled,* such as by the absence of the defendant from the state."/ "Plaintiff's delays after being required to perfect service could not *toll* the limitation period."

Toll in this special sense has been misunderstood as meaning "to set into motion"—that is, just the opposite of its true sense. See *Langford v. Shamburger,* 417 S.W.2d 438, 445 syls. 7 & 8 (Tex. Civ. App.—Fort Worth 1967). That blunder is an infrequent one.

tome refers not to any book, but to one that is imposingly or forbiddingly large.

too. A. Beginning Sentences with. When it means "also," *too* should not begin a sentence, although there is a tendency in facile journalism today to use the word in this position. E.g., "*Too* [read *Also*], existing laws are read into contracts in order to fix obligations between the parties." As in the preceding edit, *also* may unobjectionably appear at the beginning of a sentence. Also, words such as *moreover, further,* and *furthermore* serve ably in this position.

B. For *very*. This informal use of *too* occurs almost always in negative constructions, e.g., *not too common.* In such contexts, the word *very* is preferable to *too.*

C. *Too* [+ adj.] *a* [+ n.]. This idiom being perfectly acceptable, there is no reason to insist on the artificiality of *a too ——— ——*; that is, *too good a job* is better than *a too good job.* E.g., "[R]ights under a contract, in so far as they are not of *too personal a nature,* may form the subject of an assignment . . . ." William Geldart, *Introduction to English Law* 122 (D.C.M. Yardley ed., 9th ed. 1984).

toothless (= ineffectual; lacking the means of enforcement) is a snarl-word used, in legal discourse, to describe a statute or court decision that the writer or speaker considers too weak. E.g., "Even if something less than complete separability were required, the court's *toothless* standard disserves the important purposes underlying the separability requirement."

top court is a legal casualism referring to the court of last resort within a given jurisdiction. E.g., "The *top court,* in backing their convictions, rejected the defendants' reasoning." Sam H. Verhovek, *New York Court Says Defendants Can't Reject Jurors Based on Race,* N.Y. Times, 30 March 1990, at A1.

to put it another way; put another way. Either is acceptable, although the former is somewhat better from a literary point of view. Here the two idioms are confused: "*Or, put it another way* [read *Or, to put it another way*], they are estopped from denying that they were exercising the right they had under the original mortgage." Cf. **stated otherwise.**

to ride circuit. See **circuit, to ride.**

tornadic (= of or relating to a tornado or tornadoes) is almost always a pomposity—e.g.: "The Bossier Center, Inc. (Center) leased premises in its shopping center to Palais Royal (Palais) whose clothing store was heavily damaged by *the tornadic forces* [read *the tornado*]." *Bossier Ctr., Inc. v. Palais Royal, Inc.,* 385 So. 2d 886, 887 (La. Ct. App. 1980)./ "Specifically, plaintiff's allegations challeng[ed] the NWS' failure 'to detect, or to recognize, certain radar signatures' allegedly indicating severe *tornadic activity* [read *tornadoes*] . . . ." *Bergquist v. U.S.,* 849 F. Supp. 1221, 1230 (N.D. Ill. 1994).

torpid. See **turbid.**

Torrens system. In 1840, Robert Torrens moved from England to South Australia, where he assumed the post of Collector of Customs. While in that post, he developed a new system of conveyancing based on title certificates and enacted in the Real Property Act 1862.

In the U.S., the Torrens system is one of four types of evidence of title to real estate (the other three being *abstract and opinion, certificate of title,* and *title insurance*). A few counties with large metropolitan areas—e.g., Boston, Chicago, Minneapolis, and New York City—have adopted the Torrens system. Under this system, one who wants to establish title first acquires an abstract of title and then applies to a court for issuance of a certificate. This proceeding amounts to a lawsuit against all claimants to the land. Once the certificate is issued, it is conclusive evidence of ownership.

tort = a civil wrong; the breach of a duty that the law imposes on everyone. But those definitions are barely adequate, because "it is perhaps impossible to give an exact definition of 'a tort,' or 'the law of tort' or 'tortious liability,' and, as a corollary, it is certainly impossible to give a definition [that] will satisfy every theorist who has taken any interest in the topic." T.E. Lewis, *Winfield on Tort* 1 (6th ed. 1954). Why? Because there is no common set of traits that every tort possesses.

The word derives from LAW FRENCH, meaning lit. "wrong, injustice," and ultimately from L. *tortus* (= twisted, crooked). For the adjectival form, see **tortious.**

tortfeasor was once spelled as two words (as late as 1927 in the U.S. Supreme Court), then was hyphenated, and now has been fused into a single word. See **feasor.**

tortious. A. Two Senses. *Tortious* = (1) of or relating to tort <tortious causes of action>; or (2) constituting a tort <tortious acts that are also criminally punishable>. Sense (2) is now more common than sense (1), which is exemplified in this sentence: "In tort, the duty is imposed by law; the person under that *tortious* duty has no choice about whether he will shoulder it or not." See **delictual.**

B. And *tortuous; torturous.* Cardozo's famous opinion in *Palsgraf* demonstrated that a *tortious* act could result from a *tortuous* chain of events with *torturous* consequences. *Tortuous* = full of twists and turns <a tortuous path through the court system>. *Torturous* = of, characterized by, pertaining to torture <torturous abuse>. The word aptly appears in the phrase "the conscienceless or pitiless crime [that] is unnecessarily *torturous* to the victim." *State v. Dixon,* 283 So. 2d 1, 9 (Fla. 1973).

Tortuous is sometimes misused for *tortious*—e.g.: "Such duty falls into a very different category [from] the general duty to avoid *tortuous* [read *tortious*] conduct." *Walls v. Rees,* 569 A.2d 1161, 1167 (Del. 1990)./ "Petitioners urge that [defendants] . . . engaged in the intentional *tortuous* [read *tortious*] conduct specified below . . . ." *Korson v. Independence Mall I, Ltd.,* 595 So. 2d 1174, 1177 (La. Ct. App. 1992).

Similarly, *tortuous* is occasionally misused for *torturous:* "Eight-year-old Jenny, a second grader, left for school as usual at 7 a.m. on Dec. 10, 1991. It was still dark as she walked along the sidewalk. So she never saw the tall, thin stranger sneak up from behind and grab her by the back of the neck. She was forced into an alley and then put on the floorboard of the stranger's car and covered with a blanket. This young child was beginning a long, *tortuous* [read *torturous*] ordeal [involving repeated rapes]." Bill Walsh, *A Coordinated Approach to Crimes Against Children,* 55 Tex. B.J. 488, 488 (1992).

tortious interference with contractual relations; procuring (or inducing) breach of contract; interference with a subsisting contract. The first is the American phrase; the latter two are primarily British. Each one means "the tort of intentionally persuading or inducing someone to breach a contract made with a third party."

tortuous; torturous. See **tortious (B).**

totality of the circumstances is a common legal catchphrase, esp. in AmE. E.g., "Our recent cases have thoroughly rejected the *Palko* notion that basic constitutional rights can be denied by the states as long as the *totality of the circumstances* do not disclose a denial of fundamental fairness."

total(l)ed. See DOUBLING OF FINAL CONSONANTS.

to the effect that is often verbose for *that.*

Totten trust; tentative trust. These phrases, which are equivalent, denote "a revocable trust created by one's deposit of money in one's own name as a trustee for another." E.g., "It seems well settled that the creditor of one who deposits money in a savings account in the name of the depositor as trustee for another, in a jurisdiction in which this transaction creates a so-called *tentative* or *Totten trust,* can reach the deposit in satisfaction of his claims." The name *Totten trust,* which is perhaps slightly more common, derives from the case *In re Totten,* 71 N.E. 748 (N.Y. 1904). See CASE REFERENCES (C).

touch and concern. See DOUBLETS, TRIPLETS, AND SYNONYM-STRINGS.

touching (= concerning; about; bearing on) is today virtually peculiar to the legal idiom. E.g., "Such evidence as was adduced *touching* the affidavit for the search warrant showed that it was issued on information and belief without stating the grounds of belief." The *OED* labels this use of the word "somewhat archaic"; today it is rightly considered an ARCHAISM.

toward, which implies movement, is sometimes misused for *to*—e.g.: "One has an affirmative responsibility *toward* [read *to*] others when one has taken active part in directing the manner in which those others perform their work."/ "There is no legal objection *toward* [read *to*] constituting such a trustee in favor of one who was not in being when the fraud was perpetrated."

toward(s). In AmE, the preferred form is *toward; towards* is prevalent in BrE.

to(-)wit. The ordinary progression in such common phrases is from two words, to a hyphenated form, to a single word. Though Mellinkoff idiosyncratically spelled this as a single word throughout *The Language of the Law* (1963), and the hyphenated form was once common, today it seems that *to wit* is destined to remain two words, if indeed its destiny is not oblivion. *To wit* is a legal ARCHAISM in the place of which *namely* is almost always an improvement. Cf. **viz.**

toxic. When the context calls for a noun, the adjective *toxic* (= poisonous) should not displace the noun *toxin* (= poison). "Solvents can increase the mobility of certain *toxics* [read *toxins*] in the soil."

toxicology; toxology. *Toxicology* = the science of poisons; *toxology* = the branch of knowledge dealing with archery.

track is sometimes misused for *tract* (= a parcel of land) in the phrase *tract of land*—e.g.: "The defendant and two others cut down over two miles of continuous barbed wire fence on three adjacent *tracks* [read *tracts*] of land in one night." *State v. Lubrano,* 550 So. 2d 1283, 1286 (La. Ct. App. 1989).

Of course, the two words should be pronounced differently: *tract* /trakt/ and *track* /trak/.

trade(-)mark; trade(-)name. The unhyphenated, one-word spellings are preferred. Formerly, in AmE, these terms were distinguished: A *trademark* was an arbitrary, fanciful, or suggestive name of, or symbol for, a product or service that was protectible under trademark laws. A *tradename,* by contrast, was a descriptive, personal, or geographical name or symbol protectible under the law of unfair competition. With the enactment of the Lanham Act in 1946, this distinction became defunct.

Today in AmE, the term *trademark* embraces all the types of names or symbols just mentioned. Its two primary senses are: (1) "a word, phrase, logo, or other graphic symbol used by a manufacturer or seller to distinguish its products from those of others"; or (2) "the body of law dealing with how businesses distinguish their products and services from those of others." In sense (2), the word encompasses such narrower fields as service marks, tradenames, unfair competition, and palming off. See **service(-)mark.**

Tradename continues only in the sense "a symbol used to distinguish a company, partnership, or business (as opposed to a product or service)." See 1 J. Thomas McCarthy, *Trademarks and Unfair Competition* §§ 4.02–4.05 (3d ed. 1984); 3 Rudolf Callmann, *The Law of Unfair Competition, Trademarks, and Monopolies* § 17.05 (L. Altman ed., 4th ed. 1983).

In sum, *tradenames* identify businesses; *trademarks* identify goods produced by or services provided by businesses.

traduce is a literary word meaning "to slander; calumniate." It has never been a law word per se, although occasionally it is used in legal contexts. E.g., "Libelous statements tend to excite the wrath of the person so *traduced* or to deprive him of public confidence."

traffic, v.i., forms the participles *trafficking* and *trafficked,* but the adjective *trafficable* and the noun *trafficator.*

trammel is inflected *trammeled, trammeling* in AmE; and *trammelled, trammelling* in BrE. See DOUBLING OF FINAL CONSONANTS.

transcendent(al). *Transcendent* = surpassing or excelling others of its kind; preeminent. It is loosely used by some writers in the sense "excellent." *Transcendental* = supernatural; mystical; metaphysical; superhuman. The adverbial forms are *transcendently* and *transcendentally.*

transcript; transcription. The former is the written copy, the latter the process of producing it. See **record (B).**

transfer, v.t., is traditionally accented on the second syllable, hence the past-tense spelling *transferred,* not *transfered. Transferor* but *transferral; transferred, transferring,* but *transferable, transferability.* See DOUBLING OF FINAL CONSONANTS.

transfer, n.; **transference; transfer(r)al.** Of these three, *transfer* is the all-purpose noun. E.g., "As far as the question has been considered, this court is committed to the doctrine that a *transfer* of shares on the books of the corporation passes the legal title to the person named in the stock certificate." *Transfer* commonly appears in the legal phrase *transfer of venue. Transferral* (the spelling included in the *OED*) is a NEEDLESS VARIANT of *transfer.* The *W3* entry and the *W10* notation, strangely, appear under *transferal.*

Transference justifies its separate existence primarily in psychological contexts, in the sense "the redirection of feelings or desires." E.g., "Appellant also contends that the probability of *transference* of guilt was heightened because the two defendants were brothers."

transferable; transferrible. The former spelling is preferred. See -ABLE (A).

transference. See **transfer,** n.

transferor. So spelled in legal contexts—e.g.: "A transfer is effected by sending to the transferee a 'proper instrument of transfer' executed by the *transferor,* together with the share certificate relating to the shares comprised in the transfer." J. Charlesworth, *The Principles of Company Law* 89 (4th ed. 1945).

W3 lists *transferor* as a variant spelling of *transferrer,* but notes under the legal definition "usu. *transferor.*" For *transferee,* see -EE (A).

transferral. See **transfer,** n.

transferrible. See **transferable.**

transfusible; transfusable. The former spelling is preferred. See -ABLE (A).

transience; transiency. The latter is a NEEDLESS VARIANT.

transient; transitory; transitive. *Transient* = impermanent; quickly passing. The word is used in the phrase *transient jurisdiction. Transitory,* which has virtually the same meaning, is used in the legal phrase *transitory action* (= an action in which the venue might be proper in any county). *Transitive* is a grammatical term denoting a verb that takes a direct object.

transit in rem indicatam. See MAXIMS.

transitory. See **transient.**

transmissible; transmittable. The former is preferred; the latter is a NEEDLESS VARIANT. E.g., "This discussion leads to the principal question of the case: whether the testator intended that Mary Silva must survive the trust beneficiary before her interest could be *transmissible* to her heirs."

transmit is a minor pomposity—but a pomposity nevertheless—for *send.* E.g., "The clerk shall *transmit* [read *send*] the notice to the chief judge . . . ." Fed. R. Crim. App. 49(e).

transmittable. See **transmissible.**

transmittal; transmittance; transmission. *Transmittal* is more physical than *transmission,* just as *admittance* is more physical than *admission,* q.v. *Transmittal,* though labeled rare in the *OED,* is common in AmE legal writing, esp. in the phrase *transmittal letter* (= a cover letter accompanying documents or other things being conveyed to another). E.g., "The taxpayers contend that the corporation's *transmittal* of the loan proceeds to the partnership satisfies this criterion."/ "The company will send a check for the amount due directly to the beneficiary and will send the executor a copy of its letter of *transmittal* for his records."/ "Both the preparation of the report and its *transmittal* to Jaworski occurred several months before any negotiations for the sale of the subsidiary." *Transmittance* is a NEEDLESS VARIANT.

transmutation means "to change," not "to transfer," as used by some legal writers (as in the erroneous phrase used in some legal contexts for *transfer,* but conveys *transmutation of possession*).

transnational. So spelled.

transpire. The traditionally correct meaning of this word is "to pass through a surface; come to light; to become known by degrees"—e.g.: "[A]n indictment against a man as accessory before should be good even if it *transpires* [i.e., becomes known] that he is a principal in reality." Glanville Williams, *Criminal Law* 406 (2d ed. 1961). Because this usage grows rarer by the year, it is probably beyond redemption. Lawyers and judges should therefore be aware of the ambiguity created by the coexistence of the popular meaning: "to happen, occur."

When used in that sense, *transpire* is a mere pomposity displacing an everyday word (*happen*). The word is badly needed in its true sense, as it is used here: "[S]uppose that a person were to sell a second-hand car and were to state that the brakes were in good working order. If in fact it *transpired* that the brakes did not work at all the seller would find it difficult to convince a judge that he had merely been negligent rather than dishonest." P.S. Atiyah, *An Introduction to the Law of Contract* 228 (3d ed. 1981; repr. 1986).

The loose meaning, of course, is rampant—e.g.: "Many changes have *transpired* [read *occurred*] with regard to state-authorized administrative agencies."/ "A discussion then *transpired* [read *took place*] between the trial judge and counsel regarding the pleadings and damages, followed by the return of the jury and closing arguments."

Another loose usage occurs (not *transpires*) when *transpire* is used for *pass* or *elapse*—e.g.: "Only ten days *transpired* [read *passed*] between filing of the joint motion for entry of consent decrees and the time that plaintiffs first gave notice of appeal." The *OED* brands this usage "obsolete, rare, and erroneous"; only the last of these adjectives fits.

transportation; transportal; transportment. The second and third forms are NEEDLESS VARIANTS.

transship. So spelled—without a hyphen.

trauma, in pathology, means "a wound, or external bodily injury in general," although in popular contexts it has been largely confined to figurative (emotional) senses.

traverse, v.t. & n. This word is obsolescent in AmE, but it appears in many not-so-old cases. As a verb, *traverse* means "to deny a factual allegation made in the opposite party's pleading." E.g., "The declaration states that the ass was lawfully on the highway, and the defendant has not *traversed* that allegation."/ "[I]n reply to a claim, a defendant at common law may *traverse* the allegations of the plaintiff, i.e. deny the truth of his assertions." G.W. Paton, *A Textbook of Jurisprudence* 595 (4th ed. 1972).

As a noun, *traverse* means "a denial of a factual allegation made in the opposite party's pleading."

E.g., "Brown filed a *traverse* to the state's response, asserting that he failed to seek relief earlier because he was not aware of his right to file on his guilty plea."/ "At common law the respondent . . . was required to plead specially by distinct *traverse* of the allegations of the writ." *Sansom v. Mercer,* 5 S.W. 62, 65 (Tex. 1887). A denial of all the facts was, at common law, called a *general traverse;* a denial of one material fact was called a *special traverse.*

tread. See **trodden.**

treason. This word (fr. L. *tradere* "to give up or betray") originally meant treachery to one's lord rather than to the king. At common law, it was *petit treason* for a vassal to kill his lord, a wife her husband, a servant his master, or a clergyman his prelate; it was *high treason* to kill the king.

In the U.S. today, it is *treason* to levy war against the nation or to materially support its enemies.

treasonable; treasonous. The latter is a NEEDLESS VARIANT.

treasure trove, lit. "treasure found," is a remnant of LAW FRENCH. In Anglo-American law, it means "treasure (usu. gold or silver) found hidden in the ground or other place, the owner of which is unknown." E.g., "It is customary for the Treasury to recompense the owner of the land and the finder if it is declared *treasure trove,* as was the case with the collection of Roman silver plate found a few years ago at Mildenhall." O. Hood Phillips, *A First Book of English Law* 34 (3d ed. 1955).

treaty; convention; pact; act; declaration; protocol; executive agreement. Contracts between states are called by these various names, none of which has a single fixed meaning. The distinctions that follow are based on those contained in J.L. Brierly, *The Law of Nations* 243 (5th ed. 1955). A *treaty* is the most formal type of agreement between nations. A *convention* or *pact* is generally a less important and less formal agreement. An *act* generally results from a formal conference involving high officials. A *declaration* is ordinarily an agreement that declares the law or makes law (as in the *Declaration of Independence* or *Declaration of Paris*), though such an agreement is just as often called a convention (as in the *Hague Convention*). A *protocol* is usu. either the minutes of the proceedings at an international conference or an addendum to a treaty.

In the U.S., an *executive agreement* is an agreement between the U.S. and another nation. Unlike a *treaty,* which must have the advice and consent of the Senate, an *executive agreement* is made by the President but not ratified by the Senate. Some writers loosely refer to *executive agreements* as *treaties.*

treaty, v.i., (= to make a treaty *with*) is a NEOLOGISM that is not widespread—and is therefore subject to the objection that many readers will find it jarring. E.g., "Although the United States *treatied* [read *made treaties*] with tribes for the majority of the tribes' land claims, such negotiations did not always take place." James E. Torgerson, *Indians Against Immigrants—Old Rivals, New Rules,* 14 Am. Indian L. Rev. 57, 78 (1988).

treble; triple. These words are distinguishable though sometimes interchangeable. *Treble* is more usual as the verb, especially in legal contexts: "Before enactment in the 1979 amendments to the Deceptive Trade Practices Act, *trebling* of any damages was mandatory."

As an adjective, *treble* usually means "three times as much or as many" <treble damages>, whereas *triple* means "having three parts" <a triple bookshelf> <triple bypass surgery>.

trek (fr. Dutch *trekken* "to march or travel") is occasionally misspelled *treck*—e.g.: "[T]he campers would engage in such activities as water skiing, scuba diving, horseback *trecks* [read *treks*] into the Grand Canyon, mountain climbing, river trips on rubber rafts and fossil hunting." *Ferman v. Estwing Mfg. Co.,* 334 N.E.2d 171, 172 (Ill. App. Ct. 1975)./ "[T]he arrestees were allowed to retain control of [the potential weapons] during the long *treck* [read *trek*] back." *People v. Brisendine,* 531 P.2d 1099, 1102–03 (Cal. 1975) (en banc).

trespass. The LAW FRENCH word for transgression or wrongdoing, *trespass* began not as a term of art but as a word so broad as to encompass felony, misdemeanor, and disseisin.

In the later common law, the action of trespass took on a variety of forms, among which it is useful to distinguish. *Trespass vi et armis* = an action for intentional injuries to the person. *Trespass de bonis asportatis* (or *trespass de bonis*) = an action for the wrongful taking of chattels. *Trespass quare clausum fregit* (or *trespass q.c.f.*) = an action for invasion of possession of realty. *Trespass on the case* = an action for myriad other injuries, from negligence to nuisance to business torts. See **trespass on the case.**

trespasser; trespassor. The better spelling is *trespasser.*

trespassers will be prosecuted is, in itself, usually a lie. Trespass to land is a tort, not a crime. But trespassers who cause damage, as by damaging crops or breaking windows, can be prosecuted.

trespass on the case is a form of action that, at common law, provided compensation for a wide spectrum of injuries, from personal injuries caused by negligence to business torts and nuisances.

Case is often used as an elliptical form of the phrase *trespass on the case.* E.g., "While the actions of trespass and trover, and even *case,* are described above in the past tense, it is erroneous to assume that these legal labels have altogether dropped out of current usage."/ "The rule for ascertaining what damages a plaintiff could recover did not depend on whether his action was framed in *case* or assumpsit: the principles laid down in *Hadley v. Baxendale* applied in either case." (Eng.) See **action on the case.**

trespassor. See **trespasser.**

trespassorily. See **trespassory.**

trespassory, dating from 1888, is the adjective corresponding to the noun *trespass.* Included in *W2,* it is, oddly, missing from *W3.* Yet it is common—e.g.: "Before that time, South Carolina decisions had indicated a *trespassory* entry was necessary to conviction." *Sodergren v. State,* 715 P.2d 170, 175 (Wyo. 1986)./ "[A]n action on the case for nuisance gave him a remedy for *non-trepassory* interference with the use and enjoyment of his land." Roger A. Cunningham et al., *The Law of Property* 9 (2d ed. 1993).

The adverb is *trespassorily*—e.g.: "[A] defendant commits a robbery when, with the intent permanently to deprive, he *trespassorily* takes and carries away the personal property of another from the latter's person or presence by the use of force or threatened force." 4 *Wharton's Criminal Law* § 469, at 40 (14th ed. 1981).

-TRESS. SEE SEXISM (C).

triable = capable of being tried in a court of law; liable to judicial trial (*OED*). This term is used in reference to persons as well as issues and offenses, but primarily in reference to offenses—e.g.: "Whether a given offense is to be classed as a crime so as to require a jury trial or as a petty offense *triable* summarily without a jury depends primarily upon the nature of the offense."/ "[I]f there has been a demand but the case is not *triable* to a jury as of right, the case will be tried to the court." Charles A. Wright, *The Law of Federal Courts* 618 (4th ed. 1983).

trial, at; upon trial; on the trial. The usual idiom today is *at trial,* not *upon trial* or *on the trial.* E.g., "But if it develops *on the trial* [read *at trial*] that the plaintiff is not entitled to equitable relief in any form, equity will not retain the case to award damages." William F. Walsh, *A Treatise on Equity* 142 (1930)./ "To what extent, if any, equitable relief may ultimately be granted must rest with exigencies as they appear *upon trial* [read *at trial*] . . . ." *High v. Trade Union Courier Pub. Corp.,* 69 N.Y.S.2d 526, 529 (Sup. Ct. 1946). See **at (the) trial.**

trial, v.t. The *OED* records four instances of this verb, in the sense "to test (a thing, esp. a new product)," beginning in 1981 <several models are already being trialed>.

In Australia and the U.S., it is sometimes said that a defendant is "trialled" (or "trialed," as the word would be spelled in AmE). An Australian writer comments: "Apparently the *outré* misused word was supposed to mean that he or she had been brought to trial, or had been put to trial. What an unsavoury ill treatment of the English language." Theo Ruoff, *Murky Muddleheadedness or Magic?* 61 Law Inst. J. 734, 734 (1987). When this unsavory ill treatment occurs in AmE, it comes usu. from the mouth of a nonlawyer—e.g.: "I was *trialed* as a habitual offender."

trial lawyer, in AmE, has in two ways come to have connotations somewhat different from *litigator,* q.v. First, a *trial lawyer* is usu. one who actually feels comfortable going into court for trial, whereas a *litigator* is increasingly thought of as a pretrial paper-pusher.

Second, in journalism and even in some legal writing, *trial lawyer* often denotes one who represents primarily plaintiffs, esp. in tort actions. E.g., "Aside from the *trial lawyers* themselves, no group has lobbied as hard to expand the scope of liability as the consumer movement." Walter Olson, *A Naderite Backflip on Liability,* Wall St. J., March 11, 1986, at 30./ "Trial lawyers—used here, the term refers to the advocates for victims of what the law calls torts—are a virtually unknown class of the bar . . . ." John A. Jenkins, *The Litigators* xii (1989). The American Trial Lawyers' Association is composed primarily of the plaintiffs' bar, as opposed to defense counsel.

Just as often, however, *trial lawyer* is used in its broader sense, referring to defense counsel as well as plaintiffs' counsel—e.g.: "*Trial lawyers* view a disqualification motion as one of the most difficult maneuvers, because they recognize that they must appear before the judge for the rest of their careers." N.Y. Times, 3 Oct. 1988, at 26./ "It was thought that surprise, dearly cherished by an earlier generation of *trial lawyers,* would be minimized or ended altogether." Charles A. Wright, *The Law of Federal Courts* 540 (4th ed. 1983).

trial to the bench. See **bench trial.**

tribunal has two senses: (1) "a court or other adjudicatory body"; or (2) "the seat, bench, or place where judges sit." In its most usual application—sense (1)—*tribunal* is broader than *court* and generally refers to a body, other than a court, that exercises judicial functions <industrial tribunal> <social-security tribunal>.

trier of fact; fact-trier. These terms refer to the finder of fact in a judicial proceeding, i.e., the jury or, in a bench trial, the judge. *Trier of fact* is the older phrase, *fact-trier* a form that has recently come into use in AmE and that reduces the awkwardness of *trier of fact* when a possessive is called for <the fact-trier's impartiality>. See POSSESSIVES (G).

triggerman. See **nontriggerman** & SEXISM (B).

trillion, in the U.S. and France, means "a million millions," and traditionally in G.B., "a million million millions." The difference is more than substantial. Today many British writers follow the American usage, however. Cf. **billion.**

trip (= appeal) is judges' JARGON in AmE—e.g.: "In Milton's first habeas *trip,* we set out the procedural history of his case."

triple. See **treble.**

TRIPLETS. See DOUBLETS, TRIPLETS, AND SYNONYM-STRINGS.

triumphant; triumphal. Persons are *triumphant* (= celebrating a triumph), and things are *triumphal* (= of, pertaining to, or of the nature of a triumph).

-TRIX. See SEXISM (C).

T.R.O. = temporary restraining order. The letters in this abbreviation are usu. capitalized in AmE. Though the periods are often absent, the better practice is to use them, for *T.R.O.* is an initialism, not an acronym. See ACRONYMS AND INITIALISMS.

trodden is preferred to *trod* as the past participle of *tread.* Ironically, however, *untrod* is preferred to *untrodden* as the adjectival form.

troops. This plural form, which signifies *soldiers* <the troops were deployed along the crest of the ridge>, is usually modified by an adjective to indicate some special training the soldiers have completed or some special assignment <ski troops> <airborne troops> <desert troops>. An adjective may also designate the upper command level at which the soldiers are currently functioning <divisional troops> <corps troops> <army troops> <allied troops>. In the singular, a *troop* refers not to an individual soldier but to an assembled unit of soldiers of whatever special kind, mission, or affiliation <a troop of parachutists secured the airport> <a troop of cavalry passed in review> <a troop of divisional personnel set up the command post>. The plural term *troops* is meaningful when the soldiers referred to are five, six, or more in number <get these troops out of the sun>.

These military terms are not to be confused with the term *troupe* <a troupe of actors> <a troupe of circus performers> <a troupe of highwire acrobats>.

Both *troop* and *troupe* have their origin in the medieval French term *troupeau,* meaning a crowd or herd.

trove = accumulation, hoard. See **treasure trove.**

trover. See **detinue.**

true bill = the grand jury's notation that a criminal charge should go before a petty jury for trial. The phrase is an 18th-century LOAN TRANSLATION of the medieval LATINISM *billa vera.* E.g., "A second grand jury impaneled in Potter County returned a *true bill* indicting Miracle for aggravated robbery, a first-degree felony, with two felony convictions alleged for enhancement."/ "In theory anyone could put an accusation in a bill, lay it before the grand jury with supporting evidence, and invite them to call it a *true* bill." Patrick Devlin, *The Criminal Prosecution in England* 5 (1960). See **grand jury (A)** & LAW LATIN.

true-bill, v.t. = (1) to indict; or (2) to endorse (an indictment) in a way that shows that the grand jury finds the indictment to be sustained by the evidence. E.g., in sense 2: "It is formal notice at the time the indictment was *true-billed* . . . ." Clara Tuma, *Court Expands Weapon Notice Requirements,* Tex. Law., 14 May 1990, at 14.

(For another example, see the quotation under NOUNS AS VERBS.)

true facts. Although lawyers often use the word *facts* as shorthand for *alleged facts*—and can therefore make out a (weak) case for writing *true facts*—the latter phrase is usually nothing more than a commonplace REDUNDANCY. E.g., "Here, the *true facts are* [read *facts are*] that there is no coverage . . . ." *Ohio Casualty Ins. Co. v. Cooper Mach. Corp.,* 817 F. Supp. 45, 48 (N.D. Tex. 1993)./ "The status of 'insured' is to be determined by the *true facts* [read *facts*], not false, fraudulent, or otherwise incorrect *facts that might be alleged* [read *allegations*] . . . ." *Blue Ridge Ins. Co. v. Hanover Ins. Co.,* 748 F. Supp. 470, 473 (N.D. Tex. 1990). See **facts.** Cf. **actual fact, in.**

trump, n. & v.t. In cards, a *trump* is a card of a suit that, for the time being, ranks above the other three, so that any such card can 'take' any card of another suit. Thus, one says that this card *trumps* (i.e., overcomes) that one.

During the late 20th century, legal scholars began using this cardplaying metaphor in discussing legal doctrine. Though sometimes deplored as a casualism, the usage is now established—e.g.: "[I]t is hard to understand why . . . the same purpose should not also be sufficient to *trump* the per se rule in all other price-fixing cases that arguably permit cartel members to 'provide better services.'" *Business Elecs. Corp. v. Sharp Elecs. Corp.,* 485 U.S. 717, 756 (1988) (Stevens, J., dissenting)./ "[N]o Member of Congress came to the judgment that the District Court cases would *trump Johnson* on the point at issue here . . . ." *Blanchard v. Bergeron,* 489 U.S. 87, 98 (1989) (Scalia, J., concurring in part).

trust. A. Senses. *Trust* = (1) the confidence reposed in a person who looks after property for another's use or benefit; (2) an equitable estate committed to the charge of a fiduciary (trustee) for a beneficiary; (3) the relationship between the holder of the property and the property so held; or (4) a combination that aims at a monopoly <trustbuster>.

In sense (1), *trust* can apply to a variety of fiduciary relationships, including executorship, guardianship, and agency. The transference in meaning between (1) and (2) resulted from a type of HYPALLAGE; so successful was it that sense (2) is now the predominant one.

Sense (4) is an odd extension of meaning, but it is indeed an extension of sense (2): "The monopolistic *trusts* were originally so called because the stock of the combining corporations was transferred to technical trustees to accomplish a centralization of control." George T. Bogert, *Trusts* § 1, at 2 (6th ed. 1987).

B. *In trust* and *on trust*. In sense (1), the word commonly appears in two idioms. In a formal express trust, it is usual to designate the trustee as such and to state that the transfer is *in trust.* The phrase *on trust* is really just a variation of that idiom—e.g.: "A woman left her residuary estate *on trust* for her husband for life, remainder to trustees for her children." Erwin Griswold, *Cases and Materials on Taxation* 241 (6th ed. 1966).

C. *Trust* Without Qualifying Adjective. When *trust* appears without a qualifying adjective, the sense is almost always "express trust." When a *constructive trust* is intended, the entire phrase invariably appears. See *Restatement of Restitution* § 160 cmt. a, at 642 (1937).

D. Other Names for *constructive trust*. Though *constructive trust* is by far the most common phrase today for a trust imposed by a court on equitable grounds, legal writers formerly used in this sense the phrases *trust* de son tort, *implied trust, trust* ex delicto, *trust* ex maleficio, and *involuntary trust.*

trust agreement. See **declaration of trust.**

trust deed. See **deed of trust** & **declaration of trust.**

trust *de son tort*. See **trust** (D).

trustee, n. **A. And *trusty*.** *Trustee* = a person who, having a nominal title to property, holds it in trust for the benefit of one or more others, the beneficiaries. *Trusty,* n., is an Americanism meaning "a (trusted) convict or prisoner." E.g., "A *trusty* who had accompanied the officers crawled under the house and retrieved a lady's girdle from inside one of the vents underneath the house, along with several rectal syringes." *In re Wright,* 282 F. Supp. 999, 1005 (W.D. Ark. 1968).

B. And *executor*. In the context of wills, nonlawyers are frequently confused about the difference between an *executor* and a *trustee.* The *executor* collects the decedent's property, pays the debts, and hands over the remaining property to the persons who are entitled to it under the will. A *trustee* becomes necessary only when the property must be held for a time because it cannot, for some reason, be handed over at once to the persons entitled to it.

trustee, v.t., dates from the early 19th century, though it looks like a newfangled verbalization of a noun. The term has three senses: (1) "to place (a person or a person's property) in the hands of a trustee or trustees"; (2) (AmE) "to appoint (a person) trustee, often of a bankrupt's estate in order to restrain the creditor from collecting moneys due"; and (3) (AmE) "to attach (the effects of a debtor) in the hands of a third person." E.g., "He *trusteed* his publications." (Horwill)/ "The defendant in this case . . . is a jointly *trusteed* employee health and welfare benefit plan." *Powers v. South Cent. United Food & Commercial Workers Unions,* 719 F.2d 760, 761 (5th Cir. 1983). The first quotation illustrates sense (1), a use known in BrE; the second illustrates sense (2), which predominates in AmE.

trust estate. See **corpus.**

trustor. See **settlor.**

trust property. See **corpus.**

trusty. See **trustee (A).**

truth and veracity is an old but unjustified DOUBLET. To make any sense in modern English, the phrase should be *truthfulness and veracity.* In other words, *truth* in this phrase is shorthand for either *truthfulness* or *truth-telling,* but even most lawyers would be hard-pressed to explain why, since that meaning of *truth* passed into disuse in the 18th century. Today the phrase needs editing: "Parties in both civil and criminal actions are frequently assailed by the character witness who testifies that the reputation of one of the parties to the action is bad for *truth and veracity* [read *truthfulness*] . . . ." Asher L. Cornelius, *The Cross-Examination of Witnesses* 103 (1929).

truth, the whole truth, and nothing but the truth. This phrase is the quintessential example of ceremonial legal language—e.g.: "A young girl walked to the witness stand. As she raised her hand and swore that the evidence she gave would be *the truth, the whole truth, and nothing but the truth* so help her God, she seemed somehow fragile-looking, but when she sat facing us in the witness chair she became what she was, a thick-bodied girl accustomed to strenuous labor." Harper Lee, *To Kill a Mockingbird* 181 (1960).

try. In G.B., only judges and juries *try* cases; but in the U.S. lawyers, as well as judges and juries, are said to *try* cases. E.g., "The court would say unequivocally that this case has been well *tried* by excellent attorneys." See **litigate.**

try and is, in AmE, a casualism for *try to;* in BrE, however, it is a standard idiom.

tu quoque (lit. "you also") = a retort in kind; accusing an accuser of a similar offense.

turbid; turpid; torpid. *Turbid* = (of water) muddy, thick; (fig.) disordered. *Turpid* is a rare word meaning "filthy, worthless." *Torpid* = dormant, sluggish, apathetic.

turn state's evidence (AmE) = *turn King's* (or *Queen's*) *evidence* (BrE). This idiom dates from the early 18th century: an accomplice to a crime is said to *turn evidence* by cooperating with the prosecutors and testifying against other criminal defendants. E.g., "Matthews . . . had *turned Queen's evidence* in the hands of a police officer who was not above suspicion." Patrick Devlin, *The Judge* 170–71 (1979)./ "[A]nother legitimate use for pardons was found, as a means of persuading accomplices to *'turn king's evidence'* and testify against their fellows at their trial of indictment." J.H. Baker, *An Introduction to English Legal History* 589 (3d ed. 1990).

turpid. See **turbid.**

tutrix is a legal ARCHAISM meaning "a female guardian." The word *guardian* itself suffices. See SEXISM (C).

twelve free and lawful men; twelve good and lawful men; twelve men good and true; twelve good and true men. These hoary references to a 12-member jury are LOAN TRANSLATIONS of either of two Latin phrases: *duodecin liberos et legales homines* and *duodecin bonos et legales homines.* Variations on the phrase have appeared in a wide range of literature, though concerns about SEXISM will surely restrict their use to historical contexts, a tendency already evident—e.g.:

- "In the meantime make *twelve free and lawful men* of the neighbourhood view the land, and record their names." Alan Harding, *A Social History of English Law* 43 (1966) (translating an assize of novel disseisin from the time of Henry II).
- "[H]e uses every trick of oratory and acting to appeal to the crudest emotions of the *twelve good men and true.*" Jerome Frank, *Law and the Modern Mind* 197 (1930; repr. 1963).
- "Massachusetts, among other states, created a system of these courts in 1775—though, true to ideology, issues of fact were to be decided by *'twelve good and lawful men.'* " Lawrence M. Friedman, *A History of American Law* 53 (2d ed. 1985).
- "The *twelve free and lawful men* mentioned in

the writ were summoned to 'make recognition' of the facts, and were sometimes called recognitors." J.H. Baker, *An Introduction to English Legal History* 86 (3d ed. 1990).

With all the variations on this expression, it could hardly be termed a SET PHRASE. Thus, it is hardly surprising to see writers varying it still further—e.g.: "[I]n times of public excitement the participation of a *dozen or two 'good men and true'* may merely serve to lend a veneer of due process to expressions of mass hysteria." Lon L. Fuller, *Anatomy of the Law* 39 (1968).

twofold; threefold; fourfold. These and like terms should be spelled as one word.

two-witness rule = the rule that, to support a perjury conviction, two independent witnesses (or one witness together with corroborating evidence) must establish that the perjurer gave false evidence. In the context of treason, the *two-witness rule* appears in the Constitution: "No person shall be convicted of treason unless on the testimony of two witnesses to the same overt act, or on confession in open court." U.S. Const. art. IV, § 2, cl. 2.

type. For the problem raised by the phrase *these type of,* see **these kind of.**

type of is often used unnecessarily and inelegantly. E.g., "*In this type of case* [read *In a case of this kind*] it is not the function of the board to reconsider the evidence but only to consider whether there was evidence that, if reasonably considered by the trial court, would justify its view as to the appellant's guilt." (Eng.)

Of is dropped in the following examples, which are typical of the modern American colloquial trend. Again, however, the phrasing with *type* makes the sentence wordy: "Speedfast is not entitled to the rigid *type protection* [read *protection*] it seeks . . . ." *Julius M. Ames Co. v. Bostitch, Inc.,* 235 F. Supp. 856, 857 (S.D.N.Y. 1964)./ "[I]t was reasonably necessary to employ someone in this *type business* [read *business*] to keep the property rented . . . ." *Corpus Christi Bank & Trust v. Roberts,* 597 S.W.2d 752, 754 (Tex. 1980).

tyrannical; tyrannous. Though the senses often seem to merge, the former corresponds to *tyrant,* the latter to *tyranny.* In the following examples, a tyrant is being suggested: "[N]obody has yet been found to say a good word for King John. He was false, cowardly, and *tyrannical.*" H.G. Hanbury, *English Courts of Law* 49 (2d ed. 1953)./ "Even the most *tyrannical* despot, who may operate on the basis that his whim is law, soon discovers that his whims will be most effectively enforced if they are translated into 'real' law." P.S. Atiyah, *Law and Modern Society* 65 (1983).

But *tyrannous* is the appropriate word when referring to tyranny—e.g.: "[T]he representative character of the Commons forms one half of the safeguard against precipitate or *tyrannous* legislation . . . ." H.G. Hanbury, *English Courts of Law* 20 (2d ed. 1953).

Sometimes the two forms provoke suspicions of INELEGANT VARIATION—e.g.: "The colonists regarded the acts as *tyrannous* and oppressive . . . . American historians are generally in agreement that the Navigation Acts . . . , together with the ensuing *tyrannical* physical acts of forcible entry . . . [etc.] were the main causes of the American Revolution." *In re Site for Hunts Point Sewage Treatment Works,* 138 N.Y.S.2d 118, 121 (Sup. Ct. 1954). Perhaps, though, those uses are distinguishable, as *tyrannical* is inevitably more concrete than *tyrannous.*

tyro; tiro. This term, meaning "a novice," is spelled *tyro* in AmE, *tiro* in BrE.

U

uberrima fides; uberrimæ fidei. The first, a noun phrase meaning lit. "the utmost good faith," describes a class of contracts (such as insurance contracts) in which one party has a preliminary duty to disclose to the other material facts relevant to the subject matter. In American legal writing, the nominative form *uberrima fides* (as defined above) is more common <a contract requiring *uberrima fides*>; meanwhile, in British legal writing the genitive *uberrimæ fidei* (= of the utmost good faith) is prevalent <a contract *uberrimæ fidei*>.

When American lawyers use the genitive form, they sometimes mangle the second word, making it *fidae* (or *fidS*) instead of *fidei*—e.g.: "[W]e have considered the Underwriter's argument that East Coast owed them [*sic*] a duty *of uberrimae fidae* [read either *of ubberima fides* or *uberrimae fidei*], but we find it unpersuasive." *East Coast Tender Serv., Inc. v. Robert T. Winzinger, Inc.,* 759 F.2d 280, 284 n.3 (3d Cir. 1985)./ "Albany relied on the doctrine of utmost good faith or *uberrimae fidae* [read *uberrimae fidei*], seeking to void the policy from its inception based on the owner's representation as to value." Warren J. Marwedel, *Admiralty Jurisdiction and Recreational Craft Personal Injury Issues,* 68 Tul. L. Rev. 423, 469 (1994).

The phrases are pronounced in this way: *uberrima fides* /*yoo-bə-***ree***-mə-***fɪ***-deez*/ and *uberrimæ fidei* /*yoo-bə-***ree***-mɪ-***fɪ***-day-ee*/. See LATINISMS & PRONUNCIATION (C).

ubi remedium, ibi ius. See MAXIMS.

ubi supra. See ***ante*** & ***supra.***

ukase /*yoo-***kays**/, orig. a Russian term, meant lit. "a decree or edict, having the force of law, issued by the Russian emperor or government" (*OED*). By extension it has come to mean "any proclamation or decree, esp. of a final or arbitrary nature." E.g., "If the revolution in sexual mores that appellant proclaims is in fact ever to arrive, we think it must arrive through the moral choices of the people and their elected representatives, not through the *ukase* of this court."

Ulpian(us). Though the Roman form of the name is *Ulpianus,* Anglo-American writers usu. refer to this 3rd-century Roman treatise-writer as *Ulpian.*

ult. ([*ultimo*] = of last month); *prox.* ([*proximo*] = of next month); *inst.* ([*instant*] = of this month). These abbreviations, primarily from commercialese, are to be avoided in preference for straightforward terms such as *March 12,* or *next month,* or *last month.* See **inst.**

ultima ratio = the final argument; a last resort (often force). E.g., "[I]t seems to me clear that the *ultima ratio* . . . is force, and that at the bottom of all private relations, however tempered by sympathy and all the social feelings, is a justifiable self-preference." Oliver W. Holmes, *The Common Law* 38 (1881; repr. 1963).

ultimate destination is not necessarily a REDUNDANCY, as is often assumed. Where a shipment has a series of stops or transfers—i.e., a series of 'immediate destinations'—it may be appropriate to use the phrase *final* or *ultimate destination.* One may be on one's way to Bangkok, with a stopover in Tokyo. If, on that flight to Tokyo someone asks about one's destination, it would not be inappropriate to characterize Tokyo as the *immediate destination* (i.e., the destination of that particular flight) and Bangkok as the *ultimate destination* (the destination of the entire trip).

Yet the phrase *final destination* or *ultimate destination* should not be used (as it commonly is) in contexts in which such specificity is not called for. Cf. **final outcome** & **end result.**

ultimately = (1) in the end <she ultimately reached her destination>; or (2) at the beginning <the two doctrines are ultimately related>.

ultimatum. Pl. *-ums.* E.g., "It was only after these *ultimata* [read *ultimatums*] . . . that RFC reasonably concluded to cease making further loan advances." *Meriden Indus. Co. v. U.S.,* 386 F.2d 885, 895 (Ct. Cl. 1967). See PLURALS (A).

ultimo. See **ult.**

ultra (= [1] beyond due limit; extreme; or [2] extremist; fanatical), when used for *beyond,* is erroneous. E.g., "Exemplary damages are therefore damages *ultra* [read *beyond*] compensation."

ultra vires /*əl-trə-***vɪ***-reez*/ (= unauthorized; beyond one's power) is classically used as an adverb, as here: "Petitioner maintains that the commission acted *ultra vires* when it applied its new interpretation of its suspension powers to him." See ***intra vires.***

But this naturalized LATINISM is now perhaps more frequently used as an adjective—e.g.: "If a director parts with the company's money or property for an *ultra vires* purpose, he will be liable to the company for the loss it has sustained . . . ." J. Charlesworth, *The Principles of Company Law* 14 (4th ed. 1945)./ "If the contract is beyond the powers of the company, it is *ultra vires* . . . ." 2 E.W. Chance, *Principles of Mercantile Law* 214 (P.W. French ed., 10th ed. 1951).

The phrase has even come to be used as a noun—e.g.: "Under the doctrine of *ultra vires,* there is a limit in point of substance on the transactions into which a corporation may enter." William Geldart, *Introduction to English Law* 62 (D.C.M. Yardley ed., 9th ed. 1984).

UN-. See NEGATIVES.

unalienable. See **inalienable.**

unapt. See **inapt.**

unavailing = of no avail. E.g., "If Johnson lacks sufficient assets, reversing the district court on this issue as a part of this judgment would be *unavailing.*" See **avail.**

unbeknown(st). Krapp suggested that both forms are humorous, colloquial, and dialectal. George P. Krapp, *A Comprehensive Guide to Good English* 602 (1927). The *COD* likewise suggests that both are colloquial. Eric Partridge and John Simon have written, in conformity with the *OED,* that *unbeknown* is the preferred form in the phrase *unbeknown to,* and that *unbeknownst* is dialectal.

These inconsistent pronouncements serve as confusing guides. We can perhaps accept as British orthodoxy the pronouncement of the *COD* that in BrE the forms are colloquial (for *unknown*). In AmE, neither can really be called dialectal or colloquial, for the word is essentially literary. In current AmE usage, *unbeknownst* far outranges *unbeknown* in frequency of use, and it must therefore be considered at least acceptable. But a stylist might justifiably consider *unbeknown* preferable, since the *-st* forms (e.g., *whilst, amidst*) uniformly come less naturally to AmE.

Often, though, the ordinary word *unknown* would serve equally well if not better—e.g.: "The fact that, *unbeknownst* [read *unknown*] to Towers and Parks, undercover government involvement made any actual expert impossible does not alter the jury's finding."/ "The latter question has arisen where young girls have been invited to submit to acts in order to train their voice or to improve their breathing—*unbeknown* [read *unknown*] to them, the act [that] they were permitting was sexual intercourse." Andrew Ashworth, *Principles of Criminal Law* 306 (1991). See **unknown.**

unbelief. See **disbelief.**

unborn child. See **fetus.**

uncategorically is a silly but distressingly common mistake for *categorically* (= unconditionally; without qualification). And it has gotten wide exposure. In 1991, Judge Clarence Thomas, testifying before the Senate Judiciary Committee, "uncategorically" denied that he discussed pornographic materials with Anita Hill: "Senator, I would like to start by saying unequivocally, *uncategorically,* that I deny each and every single allegation against me today . . . ." *The Thomas Nomination,* N.Y. Times, 13 Oct. 1991, at 1-12.

Even by then, though, the illogically formed "nonword" had already made its way into American law reports: "[T]he statement . . . purports *uncategorically* [read *categorically*] to announce what a finite set of people—political scientists—think about a given subject—Ollman's scholarship." *Ollman v. Evans,* 750 F.2d 970, 1030 n.115 (D.C. Cir. 1984) (en banc) (Robinson, C.J., dissenting)./ "The affidavit of Hogan . . . and interrogatories of Butterworth . . . both state *uncategorically* [read *categorically*] that the religious or ethnic background of the sponsors was never considered or discussed." *Rogers v. Fair,* 902 F.2d 140, 143 (1st Cir. 1990).

unclean hands. See **clean hands.**

uncollectible. So spelled.

unconscionable = (1) (of persons) having no conscience; or (2) (of actions) showing no regard for conscience; not in accordance with what is right or reasonable. Lawyers use the word a great deal, often without fastidiously observing its meaning. For example, some writers and speakers use it hyperbolically in place of *inequitable,* which is a much softer word. See **conscionable & against conscience.**

unconstitutional. See **nonconstitutional.**

uncontrovertible should be *incontrovertible.*

uncounseled (= without the benefit or participation of legal counsel) is generally used today in constructions exhibiting HYPALLAGE; that is, the convict, not the conviction, is uncounseled, though we speak of *uncounseled convictions.* E.g., "In *Scott v. Illinois,* . . . this Court held that an *uncounseled* misdemeanor conviction is constitutionally valid if the offender is not incarcerated." *Moore v. Georgia,* 484 U.S. 904, 904 (1987) (White, J., dissenting).

UNCOUNTABLES. See COUNT NOUNS AND MASS NOUNS.

uncovered is inherently ambiguous; it may mean (1) "not covered," or (2) "having had the cover removed."

unctious is a not uncommon misspelling of *unctuous.*

undeniably. See **clearly, doubtless & obviously.**

under is preferable to *pursuant to* when the noun that follows refers to a rule, statute, contractual provision, or the like. It is better to say *service under Rule 4* than *service pursuant to Rule 4.* E.g., "*Under* Rule 32(a)(2), the deposition testimony may be used by an adverse party for any purpose at trial." Mark A. Cymrot, *The Forgotten Rule,* Litigation, Spring 1992, at 6, 6. In some contexts, though, *under* may be taken to have a spatial relation to the other words, and may therefore lead to MISCUES such as this one: "You cannot play hide the peanut *under* this rule." *Id.* at 8. See **pursuant to.**

under advisement. See **advisement.**

under appeal. See **appeal** (A).

underhand(ed). The shorter form is much older. E.g., "And what shall we say to the *underhand* manner in which the incompetence of the worker, and hence his lack of right to a share of the world's goods, are suggested in these verses?"/ "'Pettifogger' was also shortened as the 16th-century 'fogger,' applied mostly to lawyers, but also to others given to *underhand* practice for gain." *Underhanded* is also perfectly acceptable, however.

underinsurance refers not to a particular type of insurance one can purchase, but to the fact of being underinsured. In the following sentence, the word is used attributively: "Failure by Republic-Franklin Insurance Company to have responded within a reasonable time to notification of a settlement offer will void the subrogation clause in the *underinsurance* motorist provision of its policy, the Supreme Court of Ohio said." *Ohio Supreme Court Decision,* Daily Legal News, 17 Aug. 1989, at 1.

under law; in law; at law; by law. These idioms have long been common in Anglo-American legal writing. They are not interchangeable. *In law* most often means "in the eyes of the law"—e.g.: "Such invasions should be actionable *in law,* unless the newspaper can prove before a jury that its publication was in the public interest." Economist, 28 Jan.–3 Feb. 1989, at 18. *Under law* ordinarily means "in accordance with the law" or "in our system of law"—e.g.: "Every person has a right *under law* as between him and his fellow-subjects to full freedom in disposing of his own labour or his own capital according to his own will." (Eng.) The phrase *by law,* in contrast, usu. means "by statute"—e.g.: "*By law* all owners of firearms must have a permit." The idiom *at law* usu. signals a contrast with equity—that the *law* being referred to is the common law: "*At law,* laches was not a defense."

underlease is a BrE variant of *sublease,* q.v., the usual term in both AmE and BrE.

underlessee (BrE) = *sublessee* (AmE).

underlessor. See **sublessor.**

underlie. So spelled. *Underly* is an infrequent blunder—e.g.: "I have said that the morals [that] *underly* [read *underlie*] the law must be derived from the sense of right and wrong [that] resides in the community as a whole . . . ." Patrick Devlin, *The Enforcement of Morals* 22 (1968)./ "It is not enough that the same facts *underly* [read *underlie*] the claims." *Gagne v. Fair,* 835 F.2d 6, 7 (1st Cir. 1987). Writers fall into this error because they more commonly see the adjectival participle *underlying* than the uninflected verb.

under-mentioned. See **below-mentioned.**

undermine. See **circumvent.**

under my signature. This expression should not be taken too literally. It means "under my authorization," and has nothing necessarily to do with the physical placement of one's signature.

under seal. See **seal** (B).

undersigned, rarely used outside legal contexts, is a slightly preposterous way of avoiding the FIRST PERSON. Usually it is an attributive noun <the undersigned agrees to forbear from execution>.

A few lawyers, in writing their clients, actually conclude with, "If you have any questions, please do not hesitate to contact the *undersigned.*" That approach is hardly an endearing one.

understanding is a vague word sometimes used in DRAFTING as a weaker word than *agreement* or *contract.* If there is an agreement, then use the word *agreement;* if there is none, then *understanding* may suggest unsatisfactorily that there is. Phrases such as *It is the parties' understanding that* or *In accordance with the parties' understanding* are subject to a variety of interpretations—and ought therefore to be avoided.

understood and agreed. Some contracts teem with provisions that begin, *It is further understood and agreed that the Releasor hereby represents and declares that . . . .* For two reasons, the phrase *understood and agreed* ought to be struck everywhere it appears. First, the lead-in to the agreement already covers the point by saying something like, *The parties therefore agree as follows.* So the phrase *understood and agreed* later in a contract is mere surplusage. Second, if only some of the provisions are graced with the phrase, then the implication is that not every term is *understood and agreed.* The phrase could rightly be classed among FORBIDDEN WORDS. Understood? Agreed?

UNDERSTOOD WORDS are common in English and usually are not very troublesome if we are able to mentally supply them. Often they occur at the outset of sentences. *More important* is short for *What is more important; as pointed out earlier* is short for *as was pointed out earlier.*

Objects, too, are often elided with the understanding that the reader will know and mentally supply the missing term—e.g.: "Not mentioned was the fact that the standard auto liability policy also obligates the insurer to *defend.*" (After *defend,* the object *suit* is understood.)/ "A wrong was clearly committed. What circumstance will excuse?" (After *excuse,* an object such as *offender* or *wrongdoer* is understood.)

In a compound sentence, parts of a verb phrase can carry over from the first verb phrase to the second, in which they are understood: "Gorbachev has demanded that Lithuania suspend the declaration of independence before the blockade can be lifted and *talks begun.*" (That sentence is considerably more elegant than it would have been if the second verb phrase had appeared in full: *talks can be begun.*)

On verbs supposedly "understood" whose absence detracts from clarity, see BE-VERBS (A). See also JUDGMENTS, APPELLATE-COURT (next-to-last par.).

under submission = being considered by the court; under advisement. E.g., "*Norton v. National Bank of Commerce* remained *under submission* for nine months."

undertake, a word having both popular and legal senses, may mean (1) "to take upon oneself, try earnestly" <she has undertaken to help the unfortunate child>; (2) "to bind oneself contractually, to promise" <the builder impliedly undertook that the house would be safe>; or (3) "to become surety or security, to make oneself answer or responsible for a person, fact, or the like" <his friends undertook for his appearance in court>.

In historical contexts, *undertake* is common as a native-English-language equivalent of *assumpsit* (q.v.)—e.g.: "This position was turned by the development of *assumpsit;* the defendant will not be liable unless he *'undertook'* to produce a particular result." Theodore F.T. Plucknett, *A Concise History of the Common Law* 469 (5th ed. 1956).

undertaker. In AmE and BrE alike, this word predominantly refers to a person who is more euphemistically described as a *mortician* or *funeral director.* Using *undertaker* to refer colorlessly to somebody who undertakes to do something—more often today termed a *promisor*—is likely to result in a MISCUE, or at least a momentary distraction. E.g., "[W]e arrive at the classical form of the doctrine, that a valuable consideration is a benefit given or promised to the *undertaker* [read *promisor*], or some loss or liability incurred by the promisee, in return for the promise given by the *undertaker* [read *promisor*]." Edward Jenks, *The Book of English Law* 317 (P.B. Fairest ed., 6th ed. 1967).

undertaking (= a promise, pledge, or engagement) inhabits almost exclusively the domain of legal JARGON. It is perhaps more common today in BrE than in AmE dominions. E.g., "[T]here is another form of security, termed 'personal security,' which is an *undertaking* (e.g., a bond), unaccompanied by any charge on goods or property, to pay a debt." 2 E.W. Chance, *Principles of Mercantile Law* 30 (P.W. French ed., 10th ed. 1951).

undertenant (BrE) = *sublessee* (AmE & BrE).

under the circumstances. See **circumstances.**

under (the) law. See **under law.**

underway; under way. Some dictionaries record the term as two words when used adverbially, one word when used as an adjective preceding the noun <underway refueling>. In the phrases *get underway* (= to get into motion) and *be underway* (= to be in progress), the term is increasingly made one word, and it would be convenient to make that transformation, which is already underway, complete in all uses of the word.

Under weigh for *underway* is a MALAPROPISM.

underwrite. The literal sense, of course, is to write one's name at the bottom of a document. By extension, in everyday language, *underwrite* has come to mean "to support or reinforce." In law and business, however, the term has two specific senses: (1) "to assume a risk by insuring it; to insure life or property"; or (2) "to agree to buy unsold shares of a given number of securities to be offered for public sale."

underwriter; assurer; insurer; carrier. Each of these terms is commonly used in referring to one that insures a risk. In the context of marine insurance, *assurer* is the most frequently used term; elsewhere, the other three terms predominate.

Underwriter can also correspond to sense (2) of *underwrite,* q.v. In that sense, the agent-noun refers to a person or entity—usu. a bank or syndicate—that agrees to buy unsold shares of a given number of securities to be offered for public sale.

undocumented alien; undocumented (migratory) worker; illegal alien. The usual and preferable term in AmE is *illegal alien.* The other forms have arisen as needless EUPHEMISMS, and should be avoided as near-GOBBLEDYGOOK. The problem with *undocumented* is that it is intended to mean, by those who use it in this phrase, "not having the requisite documents to enter or stay in a country legally." But the word strongly suggests "unaccounted for" to those unfamiliar with this quasi-legal jargon, and it may therefore obscure the meaning.

More than one writer has argued in favor of *undocumented alien.* E.g., "An alien's unauthorized presence in the United States is not a crime under the Immigration and Naturalization Act of 1952 . . . . Thus many people find the term *undocumented alien* preferable to *illegal alien,* since the former avoids the implication that one's unauthorized presence in the United States is a crime." Elizabeth Hull, *Undocumented Aliens and the Equal Protection Clause,* 48 Brook. L. Rev. 43, 43 n.2 (1981).

That statement is only equivocally correct, however: although illegal aliens' presence in the country is no crime, their *entry* into the country is. As Justice Brennan wrote in *Plyler v. Doe,* 457 U.S. 202, 205 (1982): "Unsanctioned entry into the United States is a crime, 8 U.S.C. § 1325 . . . ." Moreover, it is wrong to equate illegality with criminality, inasmuch as many illegal acts are not criminal. *Illegal alien* is not an opprobrious epithet: it describes one present in a country in violation of the immigration laws (hence "illegal").

Those who enter the U.K. illegally are termed by statute *illegal entrants.*

undoubtably is an obsolete equivalent of *undoubtedly* and *indubitably.* Cf. **supposable.** See **doubtless.**

undoubtedly. See **clearly, doubtless & obviously.**

unearned income, to one unskilled in accountancy, may seem like an OXYMORON. The term refers to income derived from investments as opposed to personal labor.

uneconomic(al). The correct words are *uneconomical* (= not cost-effective) and *noneconomic* (= not relating to economics). The most common error is to use *uneconomic* for *uneconomical*—e.g.: "Manifestly *uneconomic* [read *uneconomical*] projects have been pursued . . . . Lavish spending on the new federal capital, Abuja, is at odds with economic [correct] realities." *Aid and Reform in Nigeria,* Fin. Times, 6 Jan. 1992, at 10. See **economic.**

unenbanc, v.t., (= to dismiss motion for hearing en banc after it has already been granted) is a NONCE WORD coined by a judge who enjoyed neologizing: "I dissent to the Court's *unenbancing* the case and refusing to reconsider the panel's opinion." *Burleson v. Coastal Recreation, Inc.,* 595 F.2d 332, 332 (5th Cir. 1978) (Brown, C.J., dissenting). The caselaw contains no examples of a positive form, *enbancing.* But cf. **enbancworthy.**

unenbancworthy. See **enbancworthy.**

unenforceable; nonenforceable. The former is preferable. See NON-.

unenforceable contract. The most important aspect of a valid contract is that it must be enforceable. So, in a sense, *unenforceable contract* denotes an OXYMORON. (For other phrases using *contract* but involving something other than a true contract, see **contract of record & void contract.**) Generally speaking, an *unenforceable contract* is invariably one that is not in writing despite a statute's requiring contracts of its type to be in writing (such as a guaranty or a contract for the sale of land).

unequivocal; unequivocable. The latter is erroneous, yet the error is surprisingly common. The dictionaries contain only the former, though undaunted lawyers and judges have written—e.g.: "The court *unequivocably* [read *unequivocally*] stated that it rejected its previous premise."/ "The court would say *unequivocably* [read *unequivocally*] that this case has been well tried by excellent attorneys." Even great writers err on this point: "Eastern systems (Hinduism and Buddhism) do not pronounce *unequivocably* [read *unequivocally*] and absolutely against suicide." Glanville Williams, *The Sanctity of Life and the Criminal Law* 249 (1957; repr. 1972).

unexceptionable; unexceptional. See **exceptionable.**

unfair competition. This is the name of a body of law that protects the first user of a name, brand, or other symbol in the sale of goods or services against a competitor whose use of the symbol confuses (or will likely confuse) consumers into believing that the first user, rather than the competitor, is the source of the goods or services. See Paul Goldstein, *Copyright, Patent, Trademark and Related State Doctrines* 88–89 (2d ed. 1981).

Of course, the phrase also denotes an instance of any practice to which that body of law applies

<the company had systematically engaged in unfair competition>.

unfair dismissal; wrongful dismissal. In English law, *unfair dismissal* is a breach of the Employment Protection (Consolidation) Act of 1978, which requires employers to conduct a dismissal fairly and reasonably. *Wrongful dismissal,* by contrast, is a cause of action arising at common law, e.g., when the dismissing employer either fails to give proper notice and to compensate the employee during the period of notice, or does not compensate the employee for the unexpired term of the contract.

In most American jurisdictions, the term equivalent to *wrongful dismissal* is *wrongful discharge* (or *wrongful termination*). For an inadvertently humorous use of *wrongful discharge,* see **prophylactic.**

unfeasible. See **infeasible.**

unfind (= to undo an earlier factual determination) is a NEOLOGISM dating from the 1950s; it is arguably quite useful, though it has yet to spread outside Texas. E.g., "A court of civil appeals has no power to 'find facts,' it may only *'unfind facts'* [that] a jury or trial judge has improperly found." *Alvey v. Goforth,* 263 S.W.2d 313, 319 (Tex. Civ. App.—Fort Worth 1953)./ "Other reasons and other names would require this Court to *'unfind'* the factual determination heretofore decided . . . ." *Longoria v. Robertson,* 669 S.W.2d 870, 872 (Tex. App.—Corpus Christi 1984) (Nye, C. J., concurring)./ "[A] court of appeals cannot make original findings of fact, it can only *'unfind'* facts." *Bellefonte Underwriters Ins. Co. v. Brown,* 704 S.W.2d 742, 745 (Tex. 1986).

unforeseen. So spelled. See FOR-.

unfrequent. See **infrequent.**

unhappily. See **happily.**

unidentified suspect. See **unknown suspect.**

uniformly is the adverb corresponding to the adjective *uniform.* But many writers get it wrong by writing *uniformally*—e.g.: "Those exceptions apply *uniformally* [read *uniformly*] to all persons 'chased' or arrested." Leonard Atkinson, Note, *The Origins of Wiretapping in Connecticut,* 12 U. Bridgeport L. Rev. 247, 292 n.111 (1991)./ "Judges McAuliffe and Eldridge . . . went so far as to urge trial judges to use *uniformally* [read *uniformly*] the pattern instruction on reasonable doubt." *Joyner-Pitts v. State,* 647 A.2d 116, 122 (Md. Ct. Spec. App. 1994)./ "In both state and federal courts nationwide, cocaine possession, manufacturing, and/or sale is *uniformally* [read *uniformly*] treated far more harshly than similar activity involving marijuana." *In re Doherty,* 650 A.2d 522, 523 (Vt. 1994).

unilateral contract. See **bilateral contract.**

uninheritable. See **inheritable.**

unintentional; involuntary. There is an important distinction between these two words, for one may commit a voluntary act that has unintentional consequences. An involuntary act is one outside the control of the will, such as a sneeze; an unintentional act is one not aimed at or desired, such as a person's death resulting from a misdirected shot. *Voluntariness* therefore generally refers to the cause, and *intentionality* to the effect. See **intent(ion).**

unintentional murder. See **murder (B).**

uninterest(ed). See **disinterest(ed).**

unique. A. Broad Definition in Contracts. In law, *unique* carries the sense "practically unique"; absolute uniqueness is usually too stringent a definition. E.g., "Is the new automobile *unique* or peculiar to the buyer, so as not to be measurable in money damages?"

B. For *unusual.* Strictly speaking, *unique* means "being one of a kind," not "unusual." Hence to write *very unique, quite unique, how unique,* and the like is slovenly. The *OED* notes that this tendency to hyperbole—to use *unique* when all that is meant is "uncommon, unusual, remarkable"—began in the 19th century. However old it is, the tendency is worth resisting.

But who can demand responsible use of the language from an ad-writer who is loose enough to say, in a national advertisement, that a certain luxury sedan is "so unique, it's capable of thought"? See ADJECTIVES (B).

United Kingdom. See **Great Britain.**

United States. A century ago, in AmE, this proper noun had "ceased to have any suggestion of plurality about it." Harry T. Peck, *What Is Good English?* 16 (1899). That represented a change, though, from just 50 years before, when particularism for states rights was rampant. Thus, much earlier even than 1850, it was usual to say *the United States have,* as Alexander Hamilton did in *The Federalist* No. 15, at 108 (Clinton Rossiter ed., 1961).

Today, however, it is quite unidiomatic to suggest plurality in referring to the U.S. But some BrE writers use the phrase in this way—e.g.: "It has been shown that under the law of *some* of the *United States* there is a legal advantage . . . ." Glanville Williams, *The Sanctity of Life and the Criminal Law* 183–84 (1957; repr. 1972).

United States Court of Appeals; United States Circuit Court of Appeals. The latter was the title from 1891 until 1948 but was changed in that year by the new § 43 of the Judicial Code.

United States Supreme Court. The more formal name is the *Supreme Court of the United States.* But if *United States* is used adjectivally—as it usually is—the name should be written as it is in the headword to this entry. Some British writers have made the mistake of putting a possessive apostrophe after *States*—e.g.: "One of the landmark cases in the United *States'* [read *States*] Supreme Court was *United States v. American Trucking Association* . . . ." Rupert Cross, *Statutory Interpretation* 132 (1976).

unitization (= the aggregation of two or more oil-producing properties, owned by different persons, to form a single property so that it can be operated as a single entity or unit under an arrangement for sharing costs and revenues) is a 20th-century NEOLOGISM dating from about 1930. See **communitize.**

unitize. See **communitize (A).**

unity. Four unities are traditionally required in creating a joint tenancy: of title, of time, of interest, and of possession. Without all four, a joint tenancy does not exist. *Unity of title* requires that all joint tenants acquire their interests under the same instrument. *Unity of title* requires that all joint tenants' interests vest at the same time. *Unity of interest* requires that the joint tenants' interests be identical in nature, extent, and duration. *Unity of possession* requires that each joint tenant be entitled to possession of the whole property (along with other joint tenants).

universal. On the phrase *more universal,* see ADJECTIVES (B).

unjust enrichment; unjust benefit; unjustified enrichment. *Unjust enrichment* = (1) a benefit obtained from another, not intended as a gift and not legally justifiable, for which the beneficiary must make restitution or recompense; or (2) the body of law governing claims for benefits of this kind. See **impoverishment.**

Unjust enrichment began its career as an AmE term but is now used on both sides of the Atlantic; *unjust benefit* is a primarily BrE variant, which some Britons stoutly prefer: "I can only surmise that while Lord Wright's position on quasi-contract or restitution was accepted, there was an objection to the expression *unjust enrichment,* perhaps because it was professorial or American." *Estok v. Heguy,* 43 W.W.R. 167, 173 (Br. Col. 1963). But the leading British treatise uses *unjust enrichment.* See Robert Goff & Gareth Jones, *The Law of Restitution* 13 (3d ed. 1986).

Unjustified enrichment is a NEEDLESS VARIANT.

unknown is perfectly acceptable where *unbeknown* might ordinarily appear—e.g.: "*Unknown* to the parties, there were two ships called 'Peerless,' each of which was carrying cotton from Bombay to Liverpool."/ "Bailhache J. based his judgement on a case [that], *unknown* to him and apparently to counsel, had been reversed by the Court of Appeal . . . ." Carleton K. Allen, *Law in the Making* 319 n.1 (7th ed. 1964). See **unbeknown(st).**

unknown suspect; unidentified suspect. The phrase *unknown suspect* is an OXYMORON; *unidentified suspect,* on the other hand, is not and is therefore preferable. To have a *suspect,* the authorities must have somebody in particular in mind. They may know a great deal about a suspect without having identified him or her—for example, they may have photographs or DNA samples—but to say *unknown* suggests that the authorities know nothing about the person. E.g., "[T]he officer became faced with the prospect of witnessing an *unknown* [read *unidentified*] suspect depart the area without taking any steps to satisfy himself that he could be found again." *Addison v. State,* 765 S.W.2d 566, 573 (Ark. 1989) (Perroni, S.J., concurring)./ "The books and pamphlet were found in the defendant's room in the house where he lived, along with components for making a bomb and clothing similar to that worn by an *unknown* [read *unidentified*] suspect in a previous bombing." *State v. Starkey,* 516 N.W.2d 918, 926 (Minn. 1994).

A similar—but worse—source of confusion appears in the following case name: *Bivens v. Six Unknown Named Agents of Federal Bureau of Narcotics,* 403 U.S. 388 (1971).

unlaw = (1) a violation of law; (2) lawlessness; or (3) a fine. The term is rare; Pollock and Maitland used it in sense (2): "Times of *unlaw* alternate with times of law" (quoted in *W2*).

unlawful = (1) unauthorized by law; (2) criminally punishable; or (3) involving moral turpitude. Sense (1) is most common, but senses (2) and (3) so complicate matters in using this term that they lessen its utility. See **illegal.**

unlawful assembly. See **riot.**

unlawfully. Though commonly included in criminal statutes, this word is best omitted: "If the courts made a habit of treating *'unlawfully'* as pleonastic, whenever a special meaning is not required, the beneficial result might be that this obscure word would be dropped from criminal statutes." Glanville Williams, *Criminal Law* 29 (2d ed. 1961). The primary problem with the word is that it typically prevents the reader from finding out precisely what conduct is prohibited. If the statute prohibits *unlawfully* engaging in some specified act, then it begs the question of precisely when that act is unlawful.

unless and until. In this doublet, of course, the two words are not synonymous—e.g.: "If the signature is obtained by fraud, . . . the innocent party may take steps to repudiate the contract, but *unless and until* he does so, the document will be binding . . . ." P.S. Atiyah, *An Introduction to the Law of Contract* 155–56 (3d ed. 1981). Even so, the meaning of *until* swallows that of *unless* in most contexts, so *until* is ordinarily sufficient. Cf. **if and when.** See DOUBLETS, TRIPLETS, AND SYNONYM-STRINGS.

unlike. A. For *despite what.* This is a solecism. E.g., "*Unlike some believe* [read *Despite what some believe*], that the name of 'Christ' came from 'Krishna,' which means 'the black one,' many scholars note that 'Christ' comes from the Greek 'Christos.' "

B. For *unlike in.* This misuse leads to faulty comparisons. E.g., "*Unlike* Bayou Bottling, *in which* [read *Unlike in* Bayou Bottling, *in which*], a full-line competitor would not have been unfairly threatened by the uniform decrease in price of a single product in its line, in this case appellant has produced evidence sufficient to support the possibility that appellee's product was predatory as to *appellant,* the sole victim of the lower prices."/ "Thus, *unlike the present case* [read *unlike in the present case*], allowing recovery in that suit would have been tantamount to having the court enforce the precise conduct that the antitrust laws forbid."/ "*Unlike the instant case* [read *Unlike in the instant case*], the original party that induced Hudson's breach of contract was a plaintiff in the action for an injunction, and thus sought to benefit from its own wrongdoing." (The original party is not being compared to the instant case, as the syntax suggests.) See ILLOGIC (A).

Though some usage critics have called the phrase a "gaucherie" and even worse things, *unlike in*—in which *unlike* takes on an adverbial sense—is now common usage in AmE and BrE alike. It occurs about 2 percent of the time in which the word *unlike* is used. (More than 4,000 instances of *unlike in* were recorded in the NEXIS/OMNI database in 1990.) E.g., "It seems unlikely that the deregulation of air traffic transport in Sweden next year—*unlike in* the U.S.—will produce genuine competition with more services and lower fares." Robert Taylor, *SAS to Cut Stake in Domestic Airline,* Fin. Times, 11 Sept. 1990, at 27./ "But *unlike in* the primary, Cropp won't be running with the support of John Ray's well-financed mayoral campaign." René Sanchez, *D.C. Council in the Throes of an Upheaval,* Wash. Post, 13 Sept. 1990, at C7.

unlimitedly, though an ugly word, has become common in the phrase *unlimitedly liable,* perhaps no longer an exaggeration given the proclivities of American juries. See -EDLY.

unliquidated damages are those that have not been previously specified or contractually provided for. These damages become liquidated only after a court or jury assesses them. Tort actions almost always involve unliquidated damages.

unmercilessly is a MALAPROPISM on the order of *uncategorically,* q.v. *Mercilessly,* of course, is the word: "He worked with top-flight professionals and drilled them *unmercilessly* [read *mercilessly*]." David Richards, *That Fosse Flair,* Wash. Post, 27 Sept. 1987, at F12./ "They were joined in their crime by the 'slashers' who cut away at the film gem *unmercilessly* [read *mercilessly*], undoubtedly to make room for all the commercials in its two-hour time slot." John A. Mason, *Television Desk,* L.A. Times, 24 Dec. 1989 (T.V. Times), at 2. *Unmercifully* might also suffice, though it adds another syllable.

unmeritorious is certainly preferable to *nonmeritorious,* which some writers use, but *meritless* is best when it suffices: of course, an *unmeritorious* applicant in a strong field is not quite the same as a *meritless* applicant.

unmoral. See **immoral.**

unnatural. "One of the surest ways of running off the rails," writes the estimable Glanville Williams,

> is to introduce the words 'natural' and 'unnatural.' . . . [T]he supposed connection between nature and morals . . . is completely mistaken. It is hardly necessary to point out that men do many things that are unnatural (in the sense of being a merely acquired skill or habit). Miscellaneous examples are washing, shaving, driving automobiles, building cathedrals, and giving blood transfusions, to which may be added all the rest of the intricate routine that has prolonged men's lives upon this planet. . . . The term 'unnatural' has been applied at different times to vaccination, anæsthetics, male gynæcologists, the emancipation of women, and the use of steam engines.
> Glanville Williams, *The Sanctity of Life and the Criminal Law* 59–60 (1957; repr. 1972).

In brief, this term frequently reflects both a fear of the unfamiliar and hidebound conformism.

unobjected to is a common idiom in the law of evidence. E.g., "The cross-examination complained to be prosecutorial misconduct was also *unobjected to.*" When the phrase is placed before the noun, it is hyphenated: "Clearly, the district court's *unobjected-to* comments, when reviewed in context, do not amount to fundamental error resulting in a miscarriage of justice." See PHRASAL ADJECTIVES (A).

unoccupied. See **vacant.**

unorganized. See **disorganized.**

unpaid, adj. One should not write "the unpaid automobile," because one does not pay an automobile—rather, one pays *for* it. (See HYPALLAGE.) Yet *unpaid-for automobile* is unpalatable because it is awkward. *Unpaid debt on the auto* is better; the loss in brevity is outweighed by the gain in clarity and euphony.

unpractical. See **impractical.**

unproportionate; unproportional. See **proportionate.**

unqualified. See **disqualified.**

unqualifiedly. See **qualifiedly.**

unreadable. See **illegible.**

unreason; unreasonableness; unreasonability. *Unreason* = absence of reason; indisposition or inability to act or think rationally or reasonably (*OED*). *Unreasonableness* = (1) an act not in accordance with reason or good sense; or (2) the fact of going beyond what is reasonable or equitable. *Unreasonability* is a NEEDLESS VARIANT of *unreasonableness.* Cf. **reasonableness.**

unreasonable. See **reasonable & arbitrary.**

unreasonableness. See **unreason.**

unresponsive; irresponsive. The former is more common, but *nonresponsive* (q.v.) is more common still.

unrevokable. See **irrevocable.**

unsafe. See **safe.**

unsatisfied. See **dissatisfied.**

unseen. See **sight unseen.**

unsolvable. See **insoluble.**

unsubstantial. See **insubstantial.**

unsuitable, unsuitableness. See **nonsuitability.**

untenable; untenantable. The former means "indefensible" (figuratively) as well as "unable to be occupied." The latter means "not capable of being occupied or lived in." In speech, many people seem to say *untenantable* when they mean *untenable.*

until. See **till.**

until such time as is verbose for *until.*

unto, an ARCHAISM for *to,* is common in legal prose and is easily overdone: "To have and to hold the same *unto* [read *to*] the said Martha Florence and *unto* [read *to*] her bodily heirs and assigns forever, with all *the appurtenances thereunto belonging* [read *its appurtenances*]."/ "Plaintiff assigned all claims arising out of the accident *unto* [read *to*] the intervenor-appellant."/ "Comes now the plaintiff . . . and will show *unto* [omit *unto*] the court the following: . . ." (See **comes now.**)/ "There were many alleged violations of *appellant's rights guaranteed unto him by the Constitution* [read *appellant's constitutional rights*]."/ "It seems *nigh unto* [read *almost*] superfluous to remind that § 1983 . . . provides a federal civil remedy in federal court for violations, under color of state law, of the rights, privileges and immunities secured by the Constitution and laws of the United States." *Findeisen v. North E. Indep. Sch. Dist.,* 749 F.2d 234, 236–37 (5th Cir. 1984).

Margaret M. Bryant prematurely pronounced this usage obsolete in 1930, stating: "Ordinarily [in general English contexts] *unto* denotes 'until.' If Mr. Brown says, '*Unto* this day, John has not taken a drink,' he means *until* this day. Its obsolete meaning is *to.* Many illustrations of this meaning are found in the Bible, such as 'Give *unto* the Lord,' signifying 'to the Lord.'" Margaret M. Bryant, *English in the Law Courts* 180 (1930).

untrod(den). See **trodden.**

untypical. See **atypical.**

unwieldy, an adj. meaning "difficult to handle," often seems to be mistaken for an adverb in *-ly.* E.g., "The FERC offered the carrot of blanket transportation certification . . . without the encumbrance of an *unwieldly* [read *unwieldy*] individual certification process." *Consolidated Edison Co. v. FERC,* 823 F.2d 630, 640 (D.C. Cir. 1987).

unwigged. See **wigged.**

unwisdom (= lack or absence of wisdom; ignorance; folly; stupidity) was common through the Middle Ages, fell into disuse in the 17th century, but was revived in the 19th century, much to the delight of common-law judges, who enjoy writing about it. E.g., "The conveyor indicated an intent to have the postponement operate solely as a protection of the taker against his possible intermediate *unwisdom,* rather than as a condition precedent of his interest."/ "His losses would not be attributable to the defendant's breach, but to the *unwisdom* of the bargain."

unwritten law is something of a misnomer. Though the phrase suggests that it relates to laws that are handed down orally from generation to generation, never being committed to paper, in fact it refers to the part of the law that has never been enacted in the form of a statute or ordinance. Of course, this law is "written," in the sense that it appears in thousands of judicial decisions, but it has not been the subject of legislation.

upholden. See **holden.**

upon is a FORMAL WORD that is usually unnecessary in place of *on,* especially when it seems habitual—e.g.: "The relief sought *upon* [read *on*] the second branch is *upon* [read *on*] a footing entirely apart from that prayed *upon* [read *for*] the first." *E. Edelmann & Co. v. Triple-A Specialty Co.,* 88 F.2d 852, 854 (7th Cir. 1937). As a general matter, then, it is better to write *service on a defendant* than to write *service upon a defendant.*

But *upon* is quite justifiable when it introduces a condition or event—e.g.: "*Upon* a proper showing, a permanent or temporary injunction, decree, or restraining order shall be granted without bond."/ "*Upon* plaintiff's refusal to amend, his action was dismissed and he appealed." The sense "with little or no interval after" is often an important nuance. E.g., "The order of the commission was made *upon* petition and *upon* hearing after due notice to plaintiff in error."

Upon is inferior, however, when a shorter, simpler, and more direct word will suffice.

A. For *on*. "My Lords, if these conclusions are applied to the present case, it is not difficult to arrive at a decision *upon* [read *on*] this appeal." (Eng.)/ "As the plaintiff had placed the perfected pump *upon* [read *on*] the market without obtaining the protection of the patent laws, he thereby published that invention to the world and no longer had any exclusive property therein." See **on.**

B. For *to*. "Threat *upon* [read *to*] the victim is an element of the crime of aggravated robbery."

C. For *in*. "At the time they were served, they were subject to a compulsory attendance *upon the* [read *in*] court." This is a legalistic ARCHAISM.

upon the trial. See **at (the) trial.**

upper court. See **higher court.**

upper house. The meaning depends on the country referred to. Rarely is this phrase used in reference to the U.S. Senate. It is the customary term for Great Britain's House of Lords, Germany's Bundesrat, and India's Rajya Sabha, as well as the upper chambers in the parliaments of Barbados, Japan, Nepal, and Poland, to name a few.

upset (= to set aside; overturn) is legal JARGON. E.g., "The court is loath to *upset* these restrictive covenants that have run with the land."/ "Any *mala fides* must be proved very clearly in order to *upset* the title . . . ." 1 E.W. Chance, *Principles of Mercantile Law* 98 (P.W. French ed., 13th ed. 1950)./ "The Appeal Court declined to *upset* the judgment of the lower court." Nigel Miller, *"Garden Leave" Enforceable Only in Cases of Real Risk to Employers,* Fin. Times, 22 Feb. 1990, at 18.

up-to-date should be hyphenated as an adjective, unhyphenated as an adverb. Hence, "Once the log is brought *up to date,* we will have an *up-to-date* log."

up to now is a comfortably idiomatic equivalent of *heretofore* and *hitherto*—e.g.: "It is unquestionably true that *up to now Erie* and the cases following it have not succeeded in articulating a workable doctrine governing choice of law in diversity actions." *Hanna v. Plumer,* 380 U.S. 460, 474 (1965) (Harlan, J., concurring). See **hither to.**

upward(s). See -WARD(S).

urge (in law) = (1) to argue in favor of; or (2) to argue. Sense (1): "Appellee *urges* affirmance of the order."/ "Appellant *urges* the first solution; appellee the second, adopted by the trial court, and by us."

When *urge* in sense (2) precedes a clause, it should be followed by *that:* "The plaintiff *urged payment* [read *urged that payment*] by the owner was a condition precedent to its duty to pay the subcontractors."/ "She *urges that* the district court abused its discretion by denying her request to amend her complaint." Sometimes, though, sense (2) is followed by a simple phrase: "Since the causes of action, as well as the facts and legal theories necessary to *urge* such causes of action, are very different in the two suits, a judgment on the merits in either one will not bar proceedings in the other."

usable. So spelled; *useable* is incorrect.

usage, in law, usu. means "a customary practice." E.g., "These fundamental principles are traceable to ancient customs and *usages* and are fixed by tradition and evidenced by the decisions of the courts."/ "While both the conception and the term 'privilege' find conspicuous exemplification under the law of libel and the law of evidence, they nevertheless have a much wider significance and utility as a matter of judicial *usage.*"/ "Both parties had adopted the practice in accordance with common business *usage.*" See **use.**

Usage also means "an idiom or form of speech," or forms of speech in general. E.g., "That the word has a wider signification even in ordinary nontechnical *usage* is sufficiently indicated, however, by the fact that the term 'special privileges' is so often used to indicate a contrast to ordinary or general privileges."

Here the *use* [not *usage*] of the word is poor: "But *bad language usage* [read *the bad use of language* or *bad usage*] can hurt good law; *good language usage* [read *the good use of language* or *good usage*] can promote respect for good law." Where *use* is possible, it should be used.

Usage for *use,* however, is not an uncommon error—e.g.: "Unless their impact on land *usage* [read *use*] denies the owner the 'justice and fairness' guaranteed by the Constitution, they should be upheld."/ "Holmes's position is an endorsement of the 'pretext' *usage* [read *use*] of the power."/ "I want to emphasize that this decision should not be read as an endorsement of a more generalized *usage* [read *use*] of the harmless error rule."/ "Defendant's expert testified that recent or excessive marijuana *usage* [read *use*] has a negative effect on police work."

The opposite error—*use* for *usage*—is quite uncommon but does occur: "This *Concise Dictionary* is primarily a manual for people who aspire to write a clear and forceful American in accord with current good *use* [read *usage*]." Robert C. Whitford & James R. Foster, *Concise Dictionary of American Grammar and Usage* v (1955). Given the title of the book, this sentence also illustrates INELEGANT VARIATION.

usance is unjustified in all senses but one: in mercantile law, the term refers to the customary time (varying in different countries) allowed for the payment of a bill of exchange or the like, esp. one drawn in a foreign country.

use, n. In phrases like *the Statute of Uses* and *cestui que use,* the word *use* means "benefit" and not "employment," as in everyday language. The etymology is completely separate from the ordinary word *use,* as Maitland explained: "It seems that at a very early period the French *oes, ues,* from the Latin *opus,* was confused in English with the French *us* from the Latin *usus,* and the *use* of our law is traceable directly to the former rather than to the latter." Note, 3 Law Q. Rev. 115, 116 (1887). E.g., "The will, therefore, creates a *use,* or, in more modern phraseology, a 'dry,' 'passive,' or 'naked' trust, and as such it is executed by force of the statute of uses." See **trust** & **springing use.**

use; utilization. *Use* is the general all-purpose noun and verb, ordinarily to be preferred over *utilize* and *utilization,* except in certain formal contexts in which the longer forms are more natural. *Utilize* is both more abstract and more favorable connotatively than *use. See* **utilize.**

Where the connotative nuance of using something to its best advantage is missing, *utilization* should not appear. Here it is defensible: "The section on efficient *utilization* of information concerns one of the most rapidly developing areas of law." (Still, it would no doubt improve the sentence to uncover the BURIED VERB: *The section on efficiently utilizing information . . . .*) Here it is not defensible: "Plaintiff's prompt *utilization* [read *use*] of the charge embraced in the criminal prosecution as the basis for a civil action was likewise voluntary."

useable. See **usable.**

used to could is semiliterate for *used to be able to* or *could formerly*—e.g.: "Juries *used to could not* [read *used not to be able to* or *formerly could not*] consider parole . . . ." *Onumonu v. State,* 787 S.W.2d 958, 960 (Tex. Crim. App. 1990) (en banc) (quoting a prosecutor's argument).

user (= continued use, exercise, or enjoyment of a right) almost always creates a MISCUE in the minds of most modern readers, who are likely to read *user* as an agent noun. E.g., "[T]he fullest enjoyment of land ownership demands the restraint of full freedom by forbidding unreasonable *user* interfering unreasonably with like rights of enjoyment of others . . . ." William F. Walsh, *A Treatise on Equity* 222 (1930)./ "Apart from express or implied grant, easements may arise by prescription, that is, by continual *user* over a period of at least 20 years." Peter Butt, *Land Law* 319 (2d ed. 1988). See -ER (B).

user-friendly. See COMPUTERESE.

U.S. Court of Appeals. See **United States Court of Appeals.**

usual place of abode. See **dwelling-house.**

usucaption; usucapion. Though neither can be said to be common, *usucaption* (= [in civil law] the prescriptive acquisition of ownership) is the more frequent form in American decisions. Academic writers tend to use either *usucapion* or the Latin form *usucapio.*

usufruct [L. *ususfructus,* Fr. *usufruit*], a civil-law term comparable to the common-law *life estate,* means "the lifelong right of possession, use, or enjoyment of another's property, as far as may be had without causing damage or prejudice to the owner." A common-law will might leave A a life estate with the remainder to B; a civilian will would ordinarily leave the property to B subject to a *usufruct* to A for life. E.g., "In 1961, Samuel Zemurray bequeathed the naked ownership of his one-half interest in the land to plaintiff and bequeathed to his wife Sarah the *usufruct.*" (La.)

Because *usufruct* is a COUNT NOUN, one refers to *a usufruct, the usufruct, this usufruct,* and so on.

usufructuary, n. & adj., = (adj.) of, relating to, or of the nature of, a usufruct; (n.) one having the usufruct of property. E.g., "The English lawyer treats the *usufructuary* as a limited owner—the nearest equivalent seems to be a life tenant." (Eng.)

usurious = of, relating to, or constituting excessive interest. E.g., "The finance company's motion for summary judgment might be defeated if the borrower had a lawyer who could show that the hidden charges, when cumulated, resulted in *usurious* charges." William O. Douglas, *Points of Rebellion* 61 (1970). See **usury.**

usurpation; usurpature. The latter is a NEEDLESS VARIANT.

usury is a word whose content has changed considerably over time. Originally, *usury* meant "compensation for the use of money; the lending of money for interest." By the 18th century, however, its meaning had been narrowed considerably to what it is today: "the lending of money at an excessive interest rate." The corresponding adjective is *usurious,* q.v.

As for the pronunciation of *usury* and *usurious,* the first syllable of these words is pronounced "you." Because the words begin with a consonant sound, *-y-*, they should be preceded by *a* and not *an* where an indefinite article is called for: "In its counterclaim, N.T. contended that M.'s prayer for interest amounted to *an usurious* [read *a usurious*] charge of interest in violation of the statute." See **a (A)** & **usurious.**

uterine. See **consanguineous.**

utilization. See **use.**

utilize = to apply profitably; put to good use. It is not an exact synonym of *use,* q.v.

ut infra = as below. See ***ante.***

ut supra = as above. See ***ante*** & ***supra.***

utter is a LEGALISM used in reference to written instruments to mean "to put or send (a document) into circulation." Hence, to *utter* a forged instrument is to present it to another with knowledge that it is a forgery. E.g., "On October 3, 1960, an indictment was filed in the U.S. District Court for the District of Columbia charging the applicant in four counts with forgery and four counts with *uttering* a fake check."

utter bar. See **outer bar.**

ux., an abbreviation of *uxor* (= wife), was once commonly used in the phrase *et ux.* to indicate that a wife is joined with her husband in a legal action. Today the wife is usually accorded the dignity of being named, or at least she should be. If her name does appear, there is certainly no reason for *et ux.,* as some real-estate brokers seem mistakenly to believe. See SEXISM (D).

In writing *ux.,* one should include the period to show that the word is an abbreviation (for *uxor*).

uxorial; uxorious. The first is neutral, the second pejorative. *Uxorial* = of or relating to a wife; *uxorious* = submissive to or excessively fond of one's wife.

V

v.; vs. A. Form of Abbreviation. Both are acceptable abbreviations of *versus,* but they differ in application: in case names, *v.* is the accepted abbreviation, while *vs.* is more common among nonlawyers.

B. Pronunciation. In pronouncing case names, one should be careful to say *versus* or *against* in AmE, not "vee." For some reason, people generally (not just lawyers) tend to say "Roe vee Wade," though few would say "Brown vee Board of Education." Perhaps "Roe vee Wade" became popular because the name consists of three one-syllable words.

In BrE, the abbreviation *v.* is pronounced "and" in the names of civil cases; thus, British lawyers write one thing but say something else. See **versus.**

C. Whether to Italicize. In American legal writing, it was formerly common to leave the *v.* in a case citation unitalicized <in *Hughes* v. *Rhodes,* the court declared . . . >. Today, however, the prevailing practice is to italicize the full case name, including *v.* <in *Hughes v. Rhodes,* the court declared . . . >. British legal writing has followed a similar evolution, though the unitalicized *v.* remains perhaps more common than in the U.S.

vacant; unoccupied. These words are often used in the context of insurance policies on buildings. They are not synonymous: *vacant* means without inanimate objects, while *unoccupied* means without human occupants.

vacate. See JUDGMENTS, APPELLATE-COURT, **overrule & set aside.**

vacation, n., in law may mean: (1) the period during which court is not in term; or (2) the act of vacating. Either sense is likely to amount to a MISCUE for the nonlawyer—e.g.: (Sense 1) "Under a statute authorizing a judge either before or during the term to order additional jurors, an order directing the additional jurors, made in *vacation,* is within the court's discretion."/ (Sense 2) "The remedy provided by the National Prohibition Act and the Espionage Act for *vacation* of a warrant improperly issued and for return of property was not applicable."

Justice Lewis F. Powell once complained of the popular misconception that justices enjoy a three- to four-month vacation (sense 1) each year. See Powell, *Myths and Misconceptions About the Supreme Court,* 61 A.B.A. J. 1344, 1344 (1975).

VAGUENESS. See AMBIGUITY. See also **void for vagueness.**

valeba(n)t. See **quantum meruit.**

valuable consideration. See **consideration (D) & and other good and valuable consideration.**

value received. This phrase is customarily inserted in bills of exchange, but it is invariably superfluous, as value is implied.

vara. This word denotes a measure used in some American states that were once under Spanish dominion. In California, the *vara* is equivalent to 33 inches, but in Texas it is 33⅓ inches.

variable; variant; variational; variative. *Variable* = subject to variation; characterized by variations. *Variant* = differing in form or in details from the one named or considered, differing thus among themselves (*COD*). *Variational* = of, pertaining to, or marked or characterized by variation. *Variative* shares the senses of *variational,* and, being the rarer word, might be considered a NEEDLESS VARIANT; but the courts have found uses for it—e.g.: "This *variative* approach to intrastate branching was nicely illustrated at the time by the structure in New York." *Northeast Bancorp, Inc. v. Federal Res. Sys.,* 472 U.S. 159, 172 (1985).

variance; at variance; variation; variant, n. *Variance* is common in legal writing in two widely divergent senses: (1) a difference or discrepancy between two statements or documents that ought to agree, such as allegations in the pleadings and the proof actually adduced on the record; or (2) a waiver of or exemption from a zoning law.

Sense (1) commonly appears in contexts referring to charging instruments—e.g.: "The second conviction was tainted by a *variance* between what was alleged in the indictment as the cause number and the proof."

At variance = (of persons) in a state of discord; (of things) conflicting; in a state of disagreement or difference. E.g., "In *Boxsius v. Goblet Frères,* Lord Esher expressed views quite *at variance* with his utterance in *Pullman v. Hill.*" (Eng.)/ "This exact question has not been decided by this court, and the decisions of the courts of other jurisdictions are somewhat *at variance.*"/ "Such a result is plainly *at variance* with the policy of the legislation as a whole."

Variation = (1) a departure from a former or normal condition or action or amount, or from a standard or type; or (2) the extent of this departure. The term is standard equipment in discussions of contract law—e.g.: "The rule . . . is always applied in cases in which there is a material *variation* between the actual principal contract and what the surety believes it to be." Laurence P. Simpson, *Handbook on the Law of Suretyship* 92 (1950)./ "[A] *variation* of a contract may amount to a rescission of the old contract followed by the making of a new one relating to the same subject-matter." G.H. Treitel, *The Law of Contract* 96 (8th ed. 1991).

The terms *variance* and *variation* are especially susceptible to INELEGANT VARIATION. E.g., "The plaintiffs as a matter of law do not have a cause of action for the allegedly arbitrary and discriminatory denial of their request for a zoning *variance* [sense 2]; in any event the denial of a zoning *variation* [read *variance*] is not a deprivation of property."

Variant = a form or modification differing in some respect from other forms of the same thing (*OED*). E.g., "Some jurisdictions having modern *variants* of the rule would approach the problem differently."

variant; variational; variative. See **variable.**

variety. When the phrase *a variety of* means "many," it is quite proper to use the plural form of the verb: "there *are* a *variety* of court-made rules by which particular orders are treated as 'final' and appealable as such." Charles A. Wright, *The Law of Federal Courts* 698 (4th ed. 1983). See SYNESIS.

For the problem raised by the phrase *these variety of,* see **these kind of.**

various different is a common REDUNDANCY—e.g.: "Pike then recounted that on *various different* [read *various*] occasions White had, in her presence, 'threatened to kill his wife.'" *White v. State,* 784 S.W.2d 453, 457 (Tex. App.—Tyler 1989). If, as one authority writes, *various different occasions* means "a number of different occasions," then the better wording would be *several different.*

vehement is pronounced /***vee***-ə-mənt/, not /və-***hee***-mənt/.

vehicle. The *-h-* is not pronounced; hence /***vee***-i-kəl/.

vehicular. A. *Vehicular homicide.* *Vehicular* /vee-***hik***-yə-lər/, an adjective dating from about 1900, is not objectionable per se. Several states in the U.S. have *Vehicular Homicide Statutes,* for which there is no ready substitute for *vehicular.* E.g., "A conviction of *vehicular homicide* requires, as a matter of law, a finding that the defendant has either driven recklessly or driven while under the influence of alcohol." But see (B).

B. *Vehicular accident.* The phrase is pompous LEGALESE and OFFICIALESE for *traffic accident, car accident,* or *motoring accident.*

C. *Vehicular unit.* The phrase is especially absurd for *car:* "The declaration sheet seeks to provide separate coverages for uninsured motorists on three *vehicular units.*" If *car* or *automobile* were too specific, then *vehicle* would suffice.

vel non (lit., "or not"), almost always superfluous, is *always* pompous. *W3* defines *vel non* as "whether or not," but that phrase could hardly be plugged into the following sentences: "We come finally to the merits *vel non* of this appeal."/ "We need address only the propriety of the ultimate finding of discrimination *vel non.*"/ "Yet another barometer of the descriptiveness *vel non* of a particular name is the extent to which it has been used in the tradenames of others offering a similar service or product." A more accurate definition of the phrase as frequently used in American legal writing is "or the lack of them (or of it)."

Usually the phrase is pretentious surplusage, as it can be either deleted or translated into simpler words—e.g.: "The ultimate issue, that of discrimination *vel non* [omit], is to be treated by the district and appellate courts in the same manner as any other issue of fact."/ "Clearly, the argument bears solely on the nature of the violation, not on the existence of a violation *vel non* [omit]."/ "The vice in the decree lies in the fact that it enjoins, not specific acts or omissions, but results, evidence of the existence *vel non* [omit] of which must be determined by the opinions of witnesses."

For the phrase *devisavit vel non,* see **devastavit.**

venal; venial. These words are frequently mistaken. *Venal* has two closely related senses: (1) "purchasable; for sale"; or (2) "highly mercenary;

amenable to bribes; corruptible." E.g., (Sense 2) "Child labor laws protect children against themselves, but also from the prospect of exploitation by *venal* parents."/ "Even though we admit that the advocate is ready to undertake either side of a cause for hire, it does not thereby follow that he is *venal* or that his attitude contravenes the principles of a sound morality."/ "That *venality* exists among certain members of the bar it would be idle to deny."

Venial = slight (used of sins); pardonable; excusable; trivial. E.g., "There will be no assumption of a purpose to visit *venial* faults with oppressive retribution." (Cardozo, J.)/ "[I]t is a habit . . . of counsel for the defence to make the most of minor uncertainties or discrepancies and to deal with a police officer in cross-examination as if any *venial* sin to which he might admit justified his professional damnation." Patrick Devlin, *The Criminal Prosecution in England* 40 (1960).

vend is now usu. commercialese for *sell,* though it has been established since the 17th century.

vendable. See **vendible.**

vendee, an unnecessary LEGALISM for *buyer* or *purchaser,* is most commonly used in real-estate transactions. Some might argue that it is useful in some contexts as a correlative of *vendor.* But using *vendee* and *vendor* invites serious typographical errors and, in any event, simpler words are available—e.g.: "A sale contract was then drawn, naming the Millers individually as *vendors* [read *sellers*], and the lessee's sister as *vendee* [read *buyer*]."/ "The rule of *Flureau v. Thornhill* restricted *vendee's* [read *the buyer's*] damages for seller's breach of a land contract by failure to make good title to what we would call the *vendee's* [read *buyer's*] reliance expenses—searching title and so on." Grant Gilmore, *The Death of Contract* 51–52 (1974). Cf. **breachee.** See -EE (A), (C) & **vendor.**

vendible; vendable. The *-ible* spelling is preferred (and more than five times as common), though the *-able* spelling appears fairly often—e.g.: "O.T. Hodge Chile Parlors only has the right to use 'Hodge's' as a trade name and not as a trademark to identify its *vendable* [read *vendible*] products." *Hodge Chile Co. v. KNA Food Distribs., Inc.,* 575 F. Supp. 210, 211 (E.D. Mo. 1983) (emphasis omitted). See -ABLE (A).

vendor. *Seller* is generally a better word, along with the corresponding *buyer* rather than *vendee.* (See **vendee.**) Using the better-known words increases readability and reduces the possibilities of typographical error. So real are those possibilities that they sometimes materialize: drafters have actually had to testify about their mistakenly using *vendor* in place of *vendee.* See *Prahmcoll Properties v. Sanford,* 474 N.W.2d 639, 643 (Minn. Ct. App. 1991).

In specific contexts, however, a DIFFERENTIATION is emerging: in computer contracting, the practice is to use *vendor* rather than *seller* almost exclusively. The term *vendor* is used in two senses: first, to refer to the entire class of business entities (often the manufacturers or producers) engaged in marketing the particular product that a prospective purchaser may be interested in acquiring; and second, to refer to the individual business entity that makes the ultimate sale (including a lease). In this context, *vending* and *selling* represent two distinct phases of commerce: *vending* emphasizes the process of engaging in marketing or offering a product for sale rather than the sale itself, while *selling* focuses on the final step in the process—the actual sale.

venerable is a CLICHÉ when used inaccurately for *old.* E.g., "This firmly rooted principle was first established *in the venerable case of* [read, e.g., *more than a century ago in*] *Strawbridge v. Curtiss.*" Properly, *venerable* = (of persons) worthy of being venerated, revered, or highly respected and esteemed, on account of character or position; commanding respect by reason of age combined with high personal character and dignity of appearance; (of things) worthy of veneration or deep respect.

venial. See **venal.**

venire, /və-*nɪ*-ree/ or /və-***neer***/, was originally an elliptical form of *venire facias* (lit., "that you cause to come"), the name of the writ directed to a sheriff requiring him to summon a jury to try a case or cases at issue between parties. Today *venire*—never italicized—is used in the sense "a panel of persons selected for jury duty and from which the jurors are to be chosen."

Jury venire is a fairly common REDUNDANCY—e.g.: "In *Witherspoon v. Illinois,* the Supreme Court held that those individuals *in the jury venire* [read *in the venire*] who indicate that they could never vote to impose the death penalty, or that they would refuse even to consider its imposition in the case before them, may be excluded from juries in the trial of the penalty phase in capital cases."

The phrase *venire panel* is also a redundancy—e.g.: "The *venire panel* [read *venire*] comprised 35 persons, 9 of whom were members of minority groups."

venireman; venireperson; veniremember. The terms all mean "a prospective juror." The best nonsexist form is *veniremember,* not *-person.* E.g., "[A] defense lawyer in a Mississippi capital case contacted thirty-one of the *veniremembers* in connection with a motion for a new trial." *King v. Lynaugh,* 850 F.2d 1055, 1062 (5th Cir. 1988) (Rubin, J., dissenting)./ "I dissent from the holding that this case should be remanded for inquiry into the prosecution's reasons for exercising its peremptory challenges against black *venirepersons* [read *veniremembers*]." Though today common in legal writing, both *venireperson* and *veniremember* are omitted from the standard English-language dictionaries. See SEXISM (B) & **potential juror.**

An additional advantage of *veniremember* over *venireman* is that the latter is a HYBRID. Thus a linguist refers to "[t]he ugly *venireman,* in use since 1444," noting that "its Latin part goes back to *venire facias* . . . ." Mario Pei, *Words in Sheep's Clothing* 84 (1969). See **venire.**

venire panel. See **venire.**

venireperson. See **venireman.**

venter [L. "womb"] (= one or the other of two or more women who are sources of the same man's offspring) is a term nowadays considered objectionable, as it refers to the woman merely as the possessor of a birth canal. E.g., "'That, whereas by the law as it now stands, the issue of an ancestor by one *venter* [read *mother*], cannot inherit to the issue of such ancestor by a different *venter* [read *mother*], whereby the real estate of an ancestor in some instances goes out of the family to the great injury of the remaining issue of such ancestor.'" *Ryder v. Myers,* 167 A. 22, 24 (N.J. Ch. 1933) (quoting *Pierson v. De Hart,* 3 N.J.L. 73, 78 (1809)). Cf. ***en ventre sa mere.***

venue = (1) originally, the neighborhood from which a jury had to be selected; (2) the county or other territorial unit over which a trial court has jurisdiction; or (3) the proper or a possible place for the trial of a lawsuit. One court has said that the exact etymology of the word is "obscured by a thick doubt," citing these possibilities: it could be derived "from the French as the anglicized spelling of the past participle of *venir,* to come, and thus it means '(those who) come,' or from the modern French substantive, meaning 'a coming,' or . . . from the Latin *vicinitatum,* meaning 'of the neighborhood,' shortened by usage to *visinetum,* and again in law Latin to *visnetum,* whence *visne,* which in early days was used and written interchangeably for *venue* . . . ." *Blair v. U.S.,* 32 F.2d 130, 132 (8th Cir. 1929) (citation omitted). Modern lexicographers have recorded the modern legal sense from 1531 and speculate on still a different etymology: that it derives immediately from the Middle English word *veneu* (= an assault or attack), which in turn derives from the French verb *venir,* the spelling *venue* being the feminine form of the past participle. See **jurisdiction (B).**

venued, adj. An odd usage has cropped up among some American legal writers, who prefer to say that a case *is venued* in a particular locale, rather than that a local court *has venue.* Most readers are likely to consider this newfangled phrasing unidiomatic—e.g.: "The FTC concedes that one of the original plaintiffs . . . was properly *venued* in Delaware . . . ." [Read *The FTC concedes that, for one of the original plaintiffs, venue was proper in Delaware.*] *Exxon Corp. v. F.T.C.,* 588 F.2d 895, 898 (3d Cir. 1978)./ "Where *a case is improperly venued it may* [read *venue is improper, the case may*], on agreement of counsel, be transferred to the county of proper venue." E.B. Gustafson, *Minnesota Tax Appeals* § 2.03, at 13 (1989).

The usage seems to have arisen in Minnesota at the turn of the 20th century: "The appellant made and served a reply *venued* in the county of Ramsey . . . ." *Clay County Land Co. v. Alcox,* 92 N.W. 464, 465 (Minn. 1902).

veracity = (1) truthfulness; observance of the truth; or (2) truth; accuracy. Sense (1), denoting a quality that persons have, is the traditionally correct use. Sense (2) began as a SLIPSHOD EXTENSION in the 18th century, and still might be so considered; it is not, however, uncommon in legal prose—e.g.: "The controversy over the *veracity* [read *accuracy*] of the search-warrant affidavit arose in connection with petitioner's state conviction for rape, kidnapping, and burglary."/ "The fact that there are clerks or carriers at the Greenville Post Office with seniority dates between September 1979 and April 1979 does nothing to call into question the *veracity* [read *accuracy*] of Smith's affidavit."/ "Control Data disputes the *veracity* [read *accuracy*] of each point, but the resolution of these factual issues is for another place and another time."

Veracity is not to be confused with *voracity* (= greediness in eating). See MALAPROPISMS.

verbage. See **verbiage.**

verbal is, unfortunately, "[a] term often used as meaning oral, parol, or unwritten." 92 C.J.S. at 995 (1955). But careful writers avoid this usage. *Verbal,* strictly speaking, means "of or relating to words" —e.g.: "The transposition of the words 'the court' and the addition of the word 'and' at the beginning of the first sentence [of the Rule] are merely *verbal* changes." Fed. R. Civ. P. 60(b) advisory committee's note. The movie producer Sam Goldwyn's supposedly ironic remark, "A *verbal* contract isn't worth the paper it's written on," was not ironic at all given the proper sense of the word *verbal,* because a written contract *is* verbal. The phrase requires *oral,* which is restricted to what is spoken. For those senses cited in *Corpus Juris Secundum* and quoted at the outset of this entry, *oral* or *unwritten* should be used. See **verbal contract.**

The error is especially acute when *verbal* is opposed to *written,* as in a statute quoted in *Franklin v. South Carolina,* 218 U.S. 161, 163 (1910): "Any laborer working on shares of crop or for wages in money or other valuable consideration under a *verbal* [read *oral*] or written contract to labor on farm lands, who shall receive advances . . . and thereafter wilfully . . . fail to perform the reasonable service required of him . . . shall be liable to prosecution for a misdemeanor . . . ."/ "A *verbal* [read *oral*] submission is not so advantageous as a written submission." 2 E.W. Chance, *Principles of Mercantile Law* 291 (P.W. French ed., 10th ed. 1951).

The misuse of *verbal* for *oral* has a long history and is still common. Nevertheless, the distinction is worth fighting for, especially in legal prose. Ironically, though, as one writer observes, lawyers "are among the chief offenders in the *oral-verbal* confusion . . . ." Robert C. Cumbow, *The Subverting of the Goeduck,* 14 U. Puget Sound L. Rev. 755, 778 (1991).

Because *verbal* is always used in reference to words, *verbal definition* is redundant, as there can be no definition without words: "Neither scientists nor philosophers have been more successful than judges in providing a *verbal definition* [omit *verbal*] for the concept of causality." Similarly, *verbal* is redundant in such phrases as *verbal promise, verbal denial, verbal affirmation,* and *verbal criticism,* as these activities usually cannot occur without words.

VERBAL AWARENESS. Lest writers commit unconscious gaffes or create MISCUES—as by referring to a "prophylactic against a wrongful discharge"—they must be aware of all the meanings of a given word, where one particular meaning is intended but other potential meanings may confuse or seem odd. And, of course, careful writers listen to what they say and read, so that they do not let a sign such as "Ears Pierced While You Wait" pass unnoticed. Nor do they overlook the humor in the church bulletin that reads, "All women wishing to become Young Mothers should visit the pastor in his office." Likewise, legal writers ought not to refer to "*Roe v. Wade* and its progeny"—though several prominent writers have done just that. Illustrations from law are legion—e.g.:

- "The language of the press may carry 'All the news that's fit to print'; the language of the law expresses the fit and the unfit, the *fleeting* and what *passes* for permanent." David Mellinkoff, *The Language of the Law* 33 (1963). (In that sentence, *passes* should not be used alongside *permanent*—esp. just after *fleeting*—because, in another sense, what passes is impermanent.)
- "At stake was no mere matter of taste; ammonium nitrate cakes when wet and is difficult to spread on fields as fertilizer." The proximity of *taste* and *cakes,* which may not at first be recognized as a verb, and the immediate proximity of *ammonium nitrate,* which must be torturous to the palate, do not make for pleasant reading. A less gustatory version would read: "At stake was no mere matter of personal preference; for ammonium nitrate, when wet, cakes and becomes difficult to spread on fields."
- " 'There is almost complete accord among many text writers that at common law commission of the crime [i.e. sodomy] required penetration *per anum* and that penetration *per os* did not constitute the offense.' This is the logical position . . . ." Rollin M. Perkins & Ronald N. Boyce, *Criminal Law* 466 (3d ed. 1982) (quoting a case). Once again, which position is more logical?

A heightening of verbal awareness would prevent writers from rending sentences with seeming contradictions: "After the *work stoppage started* [better: *workers walked off the job*], he was assigned to answer telephone complaints about company service." Cf. ETYMOLOGICAL AWARENESS & MISCUES.

And who knows exactly what kind of consciousness-raising a writer needs who entitles an article *Apprehending the Fetus En Ventre Sa Mere: A Study in Judicial Sleight of Hand?* See 53 Saskatchewan L. Rev. 113 (1989).

verbal contract should be *oral contract* or *unwritten contract*—e.g.: "[I]t is a safeguard against inadvertence and innocent mistake—e.g. in *verbal* [read *an oral*] contract or in the release of a debt." Carleton K. Allen, *Law in the Making* 395 (7th ed. 1964). See **verbal.** Cf. **informal contract** & **simple contract.**

verbals (BrE) = any remarks that an accused person has made in the presence of the police (*CDL*). The term appears to be an elliptical form of *verbal statements,* itself incorrect for *oral statements.* But *verbals* appears to be ensconced in BrE legal JARGON—e.g.: "'Verbals'—the oral comments made by defendants once arrested, or rather the comments policemen say they made—are often vital pieces of the prosecution's case. So, if his client denies having made them—and imaginative policemen are no more unusual than bent lawyers—a barrister has to pitch in to the police witness." *Yes You Did, No I Didn't,* Economist, 29 March 1972, at 27. See **verbal.**

verbatim; *ipsissima verba;* literatim. These near-synonyms carry slight nuances. *Verbatim* = word for word. *Literatim* = letter for letter. Sometimes the phrase *verbatim et literatim* is seen. *Ipsissima verba* (lit., "the selfsame words") = the exact language used by someone quoted (*W10*). E.g., "Had the application for costs against the solicitors personally been pursued in this case, it would have been a weighty factor in favor of the solicitors; moreover, the *ipsissima verba* of a judgment can be of help." (Eng.) See ***in haec verba*** & ***ipsissima verba.***

verbiage was formerly unerringly pejorative. It referred to prolix language and redundancies. More recently, it has come to signify, esp. to American lawyers, "wording, diction," in a neutral sense. Perhaps it is neutral because lawyers have become inured to their prolixities and inelegancies: "Mr. Smithson was preparing the *verbiage* for the agreement." Strictly, the word should maintain the negative connotations it has always had; *verbiage* describes a vice of language. In the sentence just quoted, the writer might have eliminated some clutter by writing, "Mr. Smithson was preparing the agreement." A somewhat different error is illustrated in this specimen: "It is well settled that the exact *verbiage* [read *wording*] of the statute need not be alleged in an indictment when there is no material difference between the language of the *statute* and the allegations employed."

Verbage for *verbiage* is a common error spawned perhaps by the analogy of *herbage*—e.g.: "Parker also forgoes equivocation and cuts through the *verbage* [read *verbiage*]." William Rice, *Clawing Their Way to the Top,* Chicago Tribune, 16 Oct. 1986, at 14C.

VERBOSITY. Samuel Johnson once said, "It is unjust, sir, to censure lawyers for multiplying words when they argue; it is often necessary for them to multiply words" (quoted in *Boswell's Life of Johnson* (1781)). Perhaps so. But lawyers must at least attempt to distinguish between those occasions when it is necessary and those when it is not. For verbosity is always an enemy of clarity.

As a result, verbosity is virtually never appropriate (much less necessary) in statutes. Yet it is especially common in STATUTE DRAFTING. The following statute says nothing more than that the industrial commission is to lay down rules to ensure safety in the handling of liquefied petroleum gases:

> The industrial commission shall ascertain, fix, and order such reasonable standards, rules, or regulations for the design, construction, location, installation, operation, repair, and maintenance of equipment for storage, handling, use, and transportation by tank truck or tank trailer, of liquefied petroleum gases for fuel purposes, and for the odorization of said gases used therewith, as shall render such equipment safe.
>
> Wis. Stat. § 101.105(2) (1963).

Certain BURIED VERBS and other verbose phrases recur in statutes—among the most common are these:

Verbose Expression	*Kernel Expression*
at the time of her death	when she dies (or died)
give consideration to	consider
give recognition to	recognize
have need of	need
have knowledge of	know
make application to	apply
make payment	pay
make provision for	provide for

Judicial writing is also a sanctuary for verbosity. Following are some typical specimens, with recommended ways of eliminating the clutter:

- "He contends that while assisting in hooking cables to the cover of said barge, while assisting in the offloading of it, he was injured when the cover of said barge was moved, causing him to sustain a downward fall." [This sentence appears to have been dictated and unedited. Read *He contends that, while offloading the barge and, in particular, assisting in hooking cables to its cover, he fell when the cover was moved.*]
- "Upon *the filing of the petition* [read *filing the petition*], appellant was appointed special guardian." See **of (A).**
- "The court should not attempt to enforce any variation of the relations between insured and insurer while the insurance contract is *in process of performance* [read *being performed, in effect,* or *under way*]."
- "With the benefit of *hindsight and its unerring superb visual acuity,* one might suggest that the trial strategy chosen by Austin's appointed counsel left much to be desired." (Omit that desultory amplification of hindsight, the qualities of which people know well enough.)

- "A *venture,* to constitute a joint *adventure,* must be for *profit in a financial or commercial sense* [read *financial profit*]." (On the variation of *venture/adventure,* see INELEGANT VARIATION.)
- "The existing partners and incoming partners desire by this amendatory agreement to admit the incoming partners as partners in the partnership." (This bit of verbosity needs no comment.)

Those are merely sentence-level examples of verbosity. When these sentences are aggregated, and the writings in which they appear are aggregated, obscurity proliferates. As Edgar Allan Poe is reputed to have said: "In one case out of a hundred a point is excessively discussed because it is obscure; in the ninety-nine remaining it is obscure because excessively discussed." See SUPERFLUITIES & FLOTSAM PHRASES. See also BE-VERBS (B), REDUNDANCY, DOUBLETS, TRIPLETS, AND SYNONYM-STRINGS & SYNONYMY.

VERB PHRASES. A. Incomplete. See ZEUGMA AND SYLLEPSIS.

B. Split. See ADVERBS, PROBLEMS WITH (A).

C. Phrasal Verbs. See PHRASAL VERBS.

verdict. A. Etymology. *Voir dire* (q.v.) is etymologically equivalent to *verdict,* having passed into English through French. *Verdict* came through Anglo-Norman (*verdit*) but was refashioned after the medieval Latin *vere dictum* or *verdictum,* itself based on the French *verdit.*

B. Who Hands Down. Juries, not judges, *hand down* verdicts (both civil and criminal). Strictly, verdicts are *returned by* juries, although we have the lay colloquialisms *to pass a verdict on* and *to give a verdict on.* Cf. **sentence.**

C. *Verdict* for *vote.* The jury collectively renders a *verdict;* individual jurors tender *votes,* not *verdicts.* E.g., "A prejudice against the defense of insanity will not disqualify one from sitting as juror where the nature of the prejudice is such that the court is satisfied that it will not influence the juror's *verdict* [read *vote*]."

D. *Verdict* for *judgment.* In journalistic references to appellate-court judgments, this error is frequent—e.g.:

- "I talked to John Baker a few months after the Supreme Court *verdict* [read *judgment*]." Murray T. Bloom, *The Trouble With Lawyers* 230 (1970) (referring to Wisconsin's highest appellate court).
- "At the time the Court of Appeal handed down its *verdict* [read *judgment*] on the Birmingham public house bombers in January[,] the Lord Chief Justice made it clear that the court would not welcome further referrals of such cases . . . ." *Final Decision,* Daily Telegraph, 19 Nov. 1988, at 12.
- "Associate Justice Sandra Day O'Connor jerked forward in her black leather chair, visibly astonished. . . . The *verdict* [read *decision*] is expected next year." Keith C. Epstein, *Ohio Free Speech Case Shocks Supreme Court,* Plain Dealer (Cleveland), 13 Oct. 1994, at 3A.

The mistake occurs also in reference to taking appeals—one appeals from a *judgment,* not a *verdict:* "A *verdict* [read *judgment*] for defendant was reversed by the Supreme Court and retrial ordered." Asher L. Cornelius, *The Cross-Examination of Witnesses* 116 (1929)./ "At a press conference, Mr. Lozano, 31, a Miami policeman for five years, said he would appeal the *verdict* [read *judgment*], and 'keep fighting for my job.'" José de Cordoba & Wade Lambert, *Miami Policeman Is Found Guilty in Deaths of Black Biker, Passenger,* Wall St. J., 8 Dec. 1989, at B5. See JUDGMENTS, APPELLATE-COURT.

veredicto. See **judgment *non obstante veredicto.***

verification. See **acknowledgment (B).**

verificational (= of or relating to a verification) is, in almost every conceivable context, a NEEDLESS VARIANT of *verified*—e.g.: ". . . a *verificational* [read *verified*] letter dated January 14, 1977, signed by the plaintiff . . . ." *Good v. Paine Furniture Co.,* 391 A.2d 741, 743 (Conn. Super. Ct. 1978)./ "[A]ny alleged problem raised by the lack of a jurat was cured by Mundinger's having filed his *verificational* [read *verified*] affidavits with jurats . . . ." *Lincoln Nat'l Bank v. Mundinger,* 528 N.E.2d 829, 836 (Ind. Ct. App. 1988).

verify = (1) to confirm by swearing <to verify her accounts by affidavit>; (2) to swear to (a statement) <he duly verified his affidavit at the end>; or (3) to check the accuracy of <to verify all the citations>.

verily (= in truth) is an affected ARCHAISM in modern contexts. It appears in old-style affidavits.

One usage critic, Margaret Nicholson, says that *I verily believe* means "it is almost incredible, yet facts surprise me into the belief." The phrase has never been used that way in American law, where the phrase is merely pretentious for *I believe*—e.g.: "*I verily believe* that Mr. White communicated these facts to the Richland County Attorneys [*sic*] office . . . ." *State v. Copeland,* 448 N.W.2d 611, 615 n.4 (N.D. 1989) (quoting an affidavit).

versus for *as against* (q.v.) is quite acceptable. E.g., "The FCC's decision is consistent with respect to the use of long- *versus* short-form procedures." This word need not be italicized as a foreign word. See **v.**

vertical restraints. See **horizontal restraints.**

very. A. As a Weasel Word. This intensifier, which functions as both an adjective and an adverb, surfaces repeatedly in flabby writing. In almost every context in which it appears, its omission would result in at most a negligible loss; in many contexts the idea would be more powerfully expressed without it. E.g., "We are *very* reluctant to substitute our views on damages for those of the jury." Here the word *very* weakens the adjective that follows; a simple statement would be more forceful: "We are reluctant to substitute our views . . . ." See **clearly, obviously** & WEASEL WORDS.

B. *Very disappointed*, etc. *Very* modifies adjectives (*sorry, sick,* etc.), and not, properly, past participles (*disappointed, uninterested,* etc.). Follett wrote that "finer ears are offended by past participles modified by *very* without the intervention of the quantitative *much,* which respects the verbal sense of an action undergone. Such writers require *very much disappointed, very much pleased, very much engrossed, very well satisfied,* etc. Only a few adjectives from verbs—*tired, drunk,* and possibly *depressed*—have shed enough of their verbal quality to stand an immediately preceding *very.*" Wilson Follett, *Modern American Usage* 343 (1966). *Very interested* is another acceptable idiom, although *very much interested* seems preferable in formal contexts. When a past participle has become thoroughly established as an adjective (e.g., *drunk*), it takes *very* rather than *very much.*

vest, v.t. & v.i., is used in a number of legal and lay idioms, particularly *to vest in* and *to vest with.* The primary senses are these: (1) "to confer ownership of (property) upon a person"; (2) "to invest (a person) with the full title to property"; or (3) to give (a person) an immediate, fixed right of present or future enjoyment." In all three senses, "the term has reference to the absence of a condition precedent to the future interest becoming possessory, other than the termination of the preceding estate or estates created by the same conveyance." Cornelius J. Moynihan, *Introduction to the Law of Real Property* 121 n.5 (2d ed. 1988).

At common law, in the ceremony known as investiture, the lord handed the vassal some object representing the land: "The vassal was thus *vested with* the fief and the fief was *vested in* him: from these terms developed the modern meanings of *to vest* as, first, to place or secure something in the possession of a person; secondly, to place or establish a person in possession or occupation of some thing; and, thirdly, to pass into possession—the senses, in other words, which are represented in the current idioms *vest in* or *be vested in* and *vest with* or *be vested with.*" J.E.S. Simon, *English Idioms from the Law* (pt. 3), 78 Law Q. Rev. 245, 249 (1962). See **invest.**

vested. A. And *contingent*. These terms are ordinarily opposed in reference to future interests. A *vested* interest is an estate that is invariably fixed in a determinate person, who will take upon the termination of a prior estate. A *contingent* interest, by contrast, involves uncertainty: there is some condition precedent to its taking effect in possession other than the mere termination of the preceding estate.

The word *vested* is occasionally, however, used in quite a different sense: in this sense, *vested* "is defined to mean that there is no condition precedent of survival. Or, as it has sometimes been said, the distinction is really whether or not the interest is 'transmissible' on the death of the owner before the time of distribution named in the creating instrument." 1 *American Law of Property* 460–61 (A. James Casner ed., 1952). This is the loose, confusing sense disapproved in the entry entitled **vested interest subject to a contingent remainder.**

B. *Vested interest* as a Popularized Legal Technicality. In the common idiom, any interest is known as a "vested interest." Whether the use is a SLIPSHOD EXTENSION or a useful metaphor is usually a matter of degree—e.g.: "The Pacific War is recalled for the public every year with massive media attention on the anniversary of the atomic bombing of Hiroshima, but no group in Japanese society has any *vested interest* in recalling the indignities and hardship of the first decade after surrender." Roger Buckley, *Japan Today* 53 (2d ed. 1990)./ "In the expense and delay the common run of lawyers had, of course, a *vested interest;* simple cheap conveyancing and certainty of titles do not increase the emoluments of attorneys." A.W.B. Simpson, *An Introduction to the History of the Land Law* 253 (1961). In the first sentence quoted, the phrase *vested interest* seems too attenuated from the literal sense; in the second, however, the metaphor seems quite natural and helpful to the passage. See POPULARIZED LEGAL TECHNICALITIES.

vested interest subject to a contingent remainder. This phrase is an ambiguous one referring apparently to a type of contingent remainder that is alienable or transmissible. "The phrase," according to leading commentators in property law, "is awkward and confusing . . . [and] its use is not desirable. If, by the use of the term, it is meant that the remainder in question is alienable or transmissible, then the remainder should simply be called alienable or transmissible and the reason given for attributing to it those legal characteristics." Lewis M. Simes & Allan F. Smith, *The Law of Future Interests* § 112, at 95 (2d ed. 1956).

vested interest subject to divestment; vested interest liable to be divested. The first is AmE, the second BrE.

vested remainder; contingent remainder. A *vested remainder* is a present estate of freehold in an existing and ascertained person who has the right to immediate possession whenever the preceding estate ends. A *contingent remainder* is not an estate at all; rather, it is a limitation by which an estate will arise when some contingent event occurs and then vest in possession when a preceding estate ends. See **contingent remainder.**

vestigial. So spelled; *vestigal* is a not uncommon misspelling.

via = (1) by way of (a place); passing through <they flew to Amarillo via Dallas>; or (2) by means of, through the agency of <we sent the letter via facsimile transmission>. Sense (2) is considered "certainly acceptable in informal use" by the *Oxford Guide,* though it remains questionable whenever a simple English preposition would suffice. Gowers called it a vulgarism in the revised edition of Fowler's *Modern English Usage,* and Follett (*Modern American Usage*) and Bernstein (*The Careful Writer*) concur.

The following sentences illustrate the objectionable sense, the result of SLIPSHOD EXTENSION: "Finally, she argues that the tax lien is subordinate to her interest in the property because it was not filed until she 'purchased' it *via* [read *through* or *in*] the divorce proceedings."/ "Once they arrived at the Army's criminal investigations headquarters, the FBI agents showed appellant their badges and gave him his *Miranda* warnings *via* [read *off* or *by reading aloud*] an advice-of-rights form."/ "When a party fails to secure a witness's voluntary cooperation by notice or commission procedure, it may seek discovery *via* [read *through*] a letter rogatory."

Here is an acceptable figurative use of sense (1): "Whereas the appellant in *Shelley v. Kramer* arrived *via* a state court, thereby permitting of disposition on Fourteenth Amendment grounds, the *Hurd* case arose in the District of Columbia."

viable originally meant "capable of living; fit to live," a sense that still applies in many phrases, such as *a viable fetus.* By acceptable extension it has come to refer figuratively to immaterial things or concepts, as here: "Ancillary jurisdiction presupposes the existence of an action that a federal court can adjudicate and should not be used to breathe life into a lawsuit that is not otherwise *viable.*"/ "We conclude that Powell's claim for back salary remains *viable* even though he has been seated in the 91st Congress and thus find it unnecessary to determine whether the other issues have become moot."

The word has lately been the victim of SLIPSHOD EXTENSION, when used in the sense "feasible, practicable" <a viable plan>. This sense is objectionable not alone in being slovenly, but also in its current status as a VOGUE WORD. One writer has noted that "dictionaries now give [as definitions for *viable*] *real, workable, vivid, practicable, important,* newer definitions that seem only to confirm the critics' complaints that the word has had the edge hopelessly ground off it." Roy Copperud, *American Usage and Style* 405 (1980). Thus such uses as the following are to be avoided; it is hard even to know what the writer of this sentence meant: "She intended to transport the aliens to the nearest *viable* [read *practical?*] Immigration and Naturalization Service office for the purpose of allowing them to file applications for asylum."

vicarious liability; vicarious responsibility. Both terms refer to indirect legal responsibility, such as an employer's liability for an employee's acts or a principal's liability for the agent's torts or contracts. *Vicarious liability* is the usual term in both AmE and BrE; *vicarious responsibility* is a primarily BrE variant.

The antonyms to these phrases are *primary liability* and *primary responsibility.* See **responsibility.**

vice versa (= the other way around; just the opposite) should have mirror-image referents, even if only implied. E.g., "It is unlikely that any of the participants in the debates about constitutional theory are going to have their minds changed by reading a polemic by a person of another sect, any more than Baptist theologians are likely to convert to Catholicism *or vice versa* [read *or Catholic theologians to Baptism*] when presented with a 'refutation' of [their] position." (The uncorrected sentence denotes, through *vice* *versa,* "or Catholicism is likely to convert to Baptist theologians.")

Vice versa does not work here: "A mother may inherit from an illegitimate child whom she has acknowledged and *vice versa.*" If we reverse the equation, we get this: "An illegitimate child may inherit from a mother whom she has acknowledged." An illegitimate child does not acknowledge her parent.

Nor does *vice versa* work with a verb like *distribute.* E.g., "The testatrix intended to give the trustees a broader and more discretionary power that would permit them, to some extent, to distribute as income what would otherwise go as principal and *vice versa.*" The writer did not intend to say, by *vice versa,* that the trustees had the power *to distribute as principal what would otherwise go as income.* The phraseology would work if the verb had been *to treat as.*

vicinity; vicinage. Though *vicinage* (= neighborhood; the relation of neighbors) is the older term in English, dating from the 14th century, it is (in AmE) a legalistic variant of *vicinity,* which dates from 1560. *Vicinity,* however, has far outranged *vicinage* in its usefulness.

The following example shows *vicinage* as a legalistic affectation for *venue:* "Changes of venue or continuances may subject the parties and courts to inconvenience and expense and may even violate the defendant's right to speedy trial in the *vicinage.*" Fowler aptly wrote that "*vicinage* is now, compared with *neighborhood,* a FORMAL WORD, and, compared with *vicinity,* a dying one" (*MEU1* 693).

victimless = (of a legal offense) having or involving no victims. This useful NEOLOGISM dates from the early 1970s, though the idea came earlier. See E.M. Schur, *Crimes Without Victims* (1965).

victor; victress; victrix. *Victor* applies to women as well as to men; the other forms are unnecessary. See SEXISM (C).

victory. The phrase *win a victory* is a common but venial REDUNDANCY.

victress; victrix. See **victor.**

victuals, spelled for colloquial uses *vittles,* is pronounced /***vit***-əlz/ with either spelling. It forms *victualer* (= one who provides food and drink for payment), *victualed,* and *victualing* in AmE; these three inflected forms double the *-l-* in BrE. See DOUBLING OF FINAL CONSONANTS.

videlicet. See **viz.**

vi et armis (= by or with force and arms) is a LEGALISM formerly common, but today moribund. It was a necessary part of the allegation, in medieval pleading, that a trespass had been committed with force and therefore was a matter for the King's Court because it involved a breach of the peace. In England, the term survived as a formal requirement of pleading until 1852 (*CDL*). See **trespass** & LOAN TRANSLATIONS.

viewpoint; point of view; standpoint. The first has been stigmatized by a few writers and grammarians who consider it "inferior to *point of view*" (*AHD*). Eric Partridge wrote that the term "has been deprecated by purists; not being a purist, I occasionally use it, although I perceive that it is unnecessary." *Usage and Abusage* 307 (1973). In fact, *viewpoint,* apart from being extremely common, conveniently says in one word what *point of view* says in three. No stigma should attach. E.g., "So far prosecutions have been considered from the *viewpoint* of the prosecutor." R.M. Jackson, *The Machinery of Justice in England* 145 (5th ed. 1967).

vilify is misspelled *villify* more than 10 percent of the time in American caselaw.

vindicable is the proper form—not *vindicatable,* which sometimes appears: "Only the named plaintiffs have any *vindicatable* [read *vindicable*] rights . . . ." *Schultz v. Owens-Illinois, Inc.,* 560 F.2d 849, 855 (7th Cir. 1977). See -ATABLE.

vindicate = (1) to clear from censure, criticism, suspicion, or doubt, by means of demonstration; or (2) to assert, maintain, make good, by means of action, esp. in one's own interest; to defend against encroachment or interference (*OED*). Sense (1) is the usual lay sense <I've been vindicated>.

Sense (2) is the legal sense—e.g.: "An arrest is the initial stage of a criminal prosecution; it is intended to *vindicate* society's interest in having its laws obeyed."/ "We do not pass upon other claims that may be available to him to *vindicate* his rights." The word implies success in justifying something. This sentence is therefore redundant: "Plaintiffs contend that a class action procedure is the only means of ensuring that the potential claimants will be able *to successfully vindicate* [read *to vindicate*] their rights."

vindicatory; vindicative; vindictive. *Vindicatory* = (1) providing vindication; or (2) punitive, retributive. *Vindicative* is a NEEDLESS VARIANT that, if ever used, would be liable to confusion with *vindictive,* a common word meaning "given to or characterized by revenge or retribution." E.g., "We note the interest of the public in shielding responsible federal government officials against the harassment and inevitable hazards of *vindictive* or ill-founded damage suits."

vindictive damages. See **punitive damages.**

violatable is incorrect for *violable*—e.g.: "The courts may then infer the receipt of confidences *violatable* [read *violable*] by the subsequent representation." *Brasseaux v. Girouard,* 214 So. 2d 401, 406 (La. Ct. App. 1968).

violate; contravene; abridge; breach; flout. These verbs are common in legal contexts, and in some contexts have virtually the same senses. *Violate* and *flout* commonly take *law* as an object <to flout the law>. (See **flaunt.**) *Contravene* is also common, but usu. refers to something less well defined, such as public policy <the rule contravenes public policy>. *Violate* and *abridge* are often used in reference to constitutional or statutory rights. (See **abridge.**) And *violate* and *breach* are often used of contractual provisions.

violative. The phrase *to be violative of* is verbose for *to violate.* E.g., "Even if residency requirements would be a permissible exercise of the commerce power, they are so unjustifiable as *to be violative of* [read *to violate*] due process." See BE-VERBS (B).

The *OED* records *violative* from 1856 at the earliest, but the word appeared more than half a century before, in *Marbury v. Madison:* "To withhold his commission, therefore, is an act deemed by the court not warranted by law, but *violative* of a vested legal right." 5 U.S. (1 Cranch) 137, 162 (1803).

vires is an unnecessary LATINISM for *power* or *authority.* E.g., "Right from the beginning he never had *vires* [read *the power*] to deal with the matters other than by reference to the Act." (Eng.) See **ultra vires** & ***intra vires.***

virile (lit. "masculine, manly") bears an odd sense in Louisiana civil law, namely "that can be rightly attributed to or assessed against (a person)." E.g., "The right to enforce contribution does not mature until there has been payment of the common obligation, or at least payment of more than the *virile* share."/ "Among solidary obligors, each is liable for his *virile* portion."

virtual, virtually. These are WEASEL WORDS: they weaken what they modify. E.g., "[R]igid trimester analysis . . . [has made] constitutional law in this area a *virtual* Procrustean bed." *Webster v. Reproductive Health Servs.,* 492 U.S. 490, 517 (1989) (per Rehnquist, C.J.).

virtue of, in & by. *By virtue of,* not *in virtue of,* is currently the idiomatic phrase; the latter is an ARCHAISM that remains fairly common in legal writing, however: "[*I*]*n virtue of* the State's jurisdiction over the property of the non-resident situated within its limits, [the state courts] can inquire into that non-resident's obligations to its own citizens . . . to the extent necessary to control the disposition of the property." *Pennoyer v. Neff,* 95 U.S. 714, 723 (1878)./ "The restricted range of international law is merely the counterpart of the wide freedom of independent action which states claim *in virtue of* their sovereignty . . . ." J.L. Brierly, *The Law of Nations* 74 (5th ed. 1955).

vis-à-vis is a CHAMELEON-HUED preposition and adverb in place of which it is usually desirable to use a more precise term. The traditional sense is adverbial, "in a position facing each other." The following sentences contain acceptable figurative uses: "The practical possibility is present in all intrafamilial legal relationships, particularly parent *vis-à-vis* child."/ "*Vis-à-vis* their lord they were unfree, though to some extent protected against ill usage, but *vis-à-vis* the rest of the world they were accorded the rights of free men." A.W.B. Simpson, *An Introduction to the History of the Land Law* 148 (1961).

As a preposition, *vis-à-vis* has been extended to the senses "opposite to; in relation to; as compared with." Usually simpler, more precise prepositions are better. E.g., "The advantage of equitable remedies for the misappropriation of money lies in establishing a preferred position *vis-à-vis* [read *over*] others having claims against the wrongdoer, by way of an equitable lien or through equitable subrogation."/ "It is harsh enough when, *vis-à-vis* [read *as between*] the carrier and the shipper, the law commands a shipper to pay the carrier twice the cargo if the latter has not in fact received the money."

viscera (= internal organs) is the plural of *viscus.* See PLURALS (A).

visit, n.; **visitation.** *Visit,* the ordinary word, means "a call on a person or at a place; temporary residence with a person or at a place" (*COD*). *Visitation* denotes a visit by an official, an unduly long visit, or the divine dispensation of punishment or reward. In family law, *visitation* is used in the phrases *visitation rights* (= provisions for spending time with one's children living with another, usu. the divorced spouse). E.g., "This case involves court orders regarding child-support obligations and *visitation* rights under a divorce decree."

visit upon = to inflict punishment for, to avenge. E.g., "The drastic remedy of an involuntary dismissal with prejudice may not under our jurisprudence be *visited upon* a client because of his attorney's deficiencies in professional courtesy."

***vis major;* force majeure; act of God.** The first is a LATINISM, the second a French equivalent, and the third a common English phrase. All are used in legal writing, and the first two appear almost exclusively in legal writing. All three phrases have undergone HYPALLAGE, so that the reference is now usually to the destruction caused by forces of nature, rather than to the forces of nature themselves. Also, the phrases refer to an "inevitable" accident that is not just caused by nature, but that occurs despite all reasonable precautions. The equivalent phrase in Scots law is *damnum fatale.*

The preferable phrase might seem to be *force majeure.* Though *act of God* is the most universal of these terms, it is the least desirable because it so easily misleads:

> As a technical term, *act of God* is untheological and infelicitous. It is an operation of 'natural forces' and this is apt to be confusing in that it might imply positive intervention of the Deity. This (at any rate a common understanding) is apparent in exceptionally severe snowfalls, thunderstorms and gales. But a layman would hardly describe the gnawing of a rat as an act of God, and yet the lawyer may, in some circumstances, style it such. The fact is that in law the essence of an act of God is not so much a positive intervention of the Deity as a process of nature not due to the act of man, and it is this negative side [that] needs emphasis.
>
> T.E. Lewis, *Winfield on Tort* 55–56 (6th ed. 1954).

See **act of God & force majeure.**

visualize does not mean "to see," but "to see in the mind's eye." The word is figurative, not literal. Here the word is wrongly used in a literal sense: "On May 10, 1973, the neurosurgeon performed the surgery. After opening her back, the defendant *visualized* [read *saw*] a slightly bulging annulus on the left at L5-S1."

vitiate = (1) to impair by the addition of (something); (2) to render corrupt in morals; (3) to corrupt or spoil in respect of substance; or (4) to render of no effect; to invalidate either completely or in part; to destroy or impair the legal effect or force of (a deed, etc.) (*OED*). Sense (1) is the most widely used. E.g., "The real complaint in this case, however, is that by treating reasonable retaliation as a separate and distinct element, the judge may have misled the jury and *vitiated* the effect of the proper direction which he had previously given."/ "Consent to contract may be *vitiated* if fraud, error, violence, or threats induce the consent [i.e., if one of these elements is added]."

Here *vitiate* is used in the sense "to impair by the subtraction or omission of something," an unexceptionable use: "Excising the racial indicia from Exhibit Z would have *vitiated* its relevance in rebutting the claim of discrimination."/ "The omission to refer to the lease did not *vitiate* the memorandum." (Eng.)

Sense (4) is the legal sense. E.g., "Where the object contemplated by one or both of the parties to a contract is unlawful or immoral, though it may not be directly punishable, the contract is *vitiated.*"/ "The fact that Hartford Insurance paid compensation to Blanks does not *vitiate* the statutory employment relationship between Blanks and ANR."/ "The Perrys assert that the merger doctrine is inoperative; to *vitiate* the merger doctrine on the basis of mutual mistake, the party seeking to avoid the doctrine must show that both parties had the same misunderstanding about the same material fact." It is perhaps a SLIPSHOD EXTENSION to stretch this sense into "to strike down": "The court *vitiated* [read *invalidated*] the statute on grounds that it conflicted with constitutional provisions."

A frequently misunderstood word, *vitiate* does not mean "to weaken or lessen," as used here: "It is conceded that anger can be *vitiated* [read *reduced*] by a change in physical surroundings." Nor does it mean "to belie": "Plaintiff's assertion is *vitiated* [read *belied*] by the plain language of the agreement." Nor "to correct": "[T]he court's later instruction . . . cannot be deemed to have *vitiated* [read *cured* or *corrected*] the prejudice caused by the court's earlier apparent indorsement of the improper questioning." *People v. Wood,* 488 N.E.2d 86, 90 (N.Y. 1985). The word is also sometimes misused for *obviate,* q.v.

vittles is not the literary spelling; *victuals,* q.v., is.

vituperative; vituperous. The former is the preferred adjectival form of *vituperation. Vituperous* is a NEEDLESS VARIANT.

viz. is an abbreviation of the Latin word *videlicet* (fr. *videbere* = to see; *licet* = it is permissible). The English-language equivalents are *namely* or *that is to say,* either of which is preferable to this LATINISM. Like its English counterparts, the term signifies that what follows particularizes a general statement, without contradicting what precedes, or that what follows explains certain obscurities that the writer acknowledges to be lurking in what has just been said. E.g., "[If a testator has] devised certain real estate to his widow, 'her heirs, *viz.,* her children and grandchildren and assigns,' the words following the *videlicet* have been held not to be repugnant to, but explanatory and restrictive of, the word 'heirs,' and to operate to limit the widow's estate to an estate for life." 57 Am. Jur. *Wills* § 1156, at 753 (1948)./ "In its second opinion, the district court certified the main issue, *viz.,* the executive officers' liability under section 23:1032."

The abbreviation is odd in two ways. First, how does one derive *viz.* for *videlicet?* The final *z* in the abbreviation represents the medieval Latin symbol of contraction for *et* or *-et* (*OED*). Second, how does one pronounce *viz.*? Preferably by saying "namely." As with *i.e.* and *e.g.* (qq.v.), the abbreviation is customarily set off from the rest of the sentence by a pair of commas. (Or, when given as the first word within a parenthetical expression, it is set off by one comma.)

vocation. See **avocation.**

vociferous; vociferant. The latter is a NEEDLESS VARIANT.

VOGUE WORDS are those faddish, trendy, ubiquitous words that have something new about them. They may be NEOLOGISMS or they may be old words in novel uses or senses. Often they quickly become CLICHÉS or standard idioms, and sometimes they pass into obscurity after a period of feverish popularity. For whatever reason, they have such a grip on the popular mind that they come to be used in contexts in which they serve no real purpose. As they become more popular and appear more frequently, says the *Oxford Guide,* "so their real denotative value drains away, a process that closely resembles monetary inflation. . . . One should carefully guard against using them either because they sound more learned and up to date than the more commonplace words in one's vocabulary, or as a short cut in communicating ideas that would be better set out in simple, clear, basic vocabulary" (1983).

The following list is a representative collection of modish diction:

constructive
cost-effective
cutting edge, on the
definitely
dialogue
downside (risks)
environment
escalate (= to intensify)
eventuate
exposure (= liability)
framework
identify with (as in "I can identify with you")
impact, v.i. & v.t. (except in reference to wisdom teeth)
interface
-IZE words
lifestyle
matrix
meaningful
need-to-know basis, on a
-oriented (e.g., law-oriented)
no-lose situation
no-win situation
overly
parameters
relate, v.i. (as in "I can relate to that")
scenario
state-of-the-art
upside
user-friendly (see COMPUTERESE)
viable
win-win situation
-WISE
worst-case scenario

void; voidable. "It is regrettable that the courts have used the term 'voidable' in the sense of both 'voidable' and 'void.'" Lewis A. Jeffrey, *Infants—Contract of Suretyship,* 3 Tex. L. Rev. 328, 329 (1925). The distinction should be evident. *Void* = absolutely null. *Voidable* = capable of being voided or confirmed. The practical effect is that a *void contract* (q.v.) gives no rights at all; a *voidable contract* gives certain rights, though one of the parties (such as a minor) may abruptly put an end to those rights.

Yet confusion seems to abound, as *Corpus Juris Secundum* points out: "There is great looseness and no little confusion in the books in the use of the words *void* and *voidable,* growing, perhaps, in some degree, out of the imperfection of the language, since there are several kinds of defects which are included under the expressions *void* and *voidable,* while there are but two terms to express them all." 92 C.J.S. at 1020–23 (1955).

The phrases *totally void* and *completely void* are REDUNDANCIES. (See ADJECTIVES (B).) *Null and void,* q.v., is questionable as a DOUBLET, *void* itself being perfectly strong: "The natural tendency of the condition contained in the will is to restrain all marriage and for that reason it is *void.*" See **null and void.**

voidance. See **avoid.**

void *ab initio* is an extremely common phrase, and some lawyers try to justify the LATINISM on grounds that it is not easily translated. But quite respectable writers have used *void from the beginning*—e.g.: "[T]he maxim is *'that which is void in the beginning cannot be cured by waiver, acquiescence or lapse of time.'*" Eugene A. Jones, *Manual of Equity Pleading and Practice* 12 n.24 (1916). See ***ab initio.***

void and of no(ne) effect. This DOUBLET is quite redundant. If the phrase must be used, modern idiom requires *void and of no effect.*

void and unenforceable is a common REDUNDANCY.

void contract. As Patrick Atiyah points out, *void contract* is "really a contradiction in terms inasmuch as a contract has already been defined in terms applicable only to a valid contract. However, the term is convenient and is universally used." P.S. Atiyah, *An Introduction to the Law of Contract* 36–37 (3d ed. 1981). Among typical *void contracts* are those in which:

- no consideration was given;
- the acceptance of an offer was not communicated;
- wagering is involved; or
- family relations are prejudiced.

In essence, a *void contract* is no contract at all—it is not necessarily unlawful, but it has no legal effect. For other phrases using *contract* but not truly involving a contract, see **contract of record & unenforceable contract.** See also OXYMORONS.

void for vagueness. This phrase was originally confined to the law of deeds and other instruments affecting real or personal property: if the property was not sufficiently identified—or some other critical provision was vaguely worded— the instrument would be declared *void for vagueness.* This usage first appeared in the mid-19th century and has persisted into the late 20th—e.g.:

- "[A]lthough our early decisions would hold them *void, for vagueness,* our decisons for the last ten and fifteen years, have gone further, and established the law to be liberal enough to sustain mortgages quite as indefinite and vague as the present." *Utley v. Smith,* 24 Conn. 290, 314 (1855).
- "Secondly, That said mortgage is void, for vagueness, and uncertainty in respect to the debts intended to be secured, and which were in existence at the time the mortgage was executed." *Gill v. Pinney's Adm'r,* 12 Ohio St. 38, 46 (Ohio 1861).
- "We are therefore of the opinion that the description is sufficient to cover and to convey this particular stock of goods, and that the mortgage is not *void for vagueness* or uncertainty." *Davis v. Turner,* 120 F. 605, 612 (4th Cir. 1903).
- "[T]he description [in the deed] is not *void for vagueness* and it may be aided by parol evidence." *Peel v. Calais,* 31 S.E.2d 440, 443 (N.C. 1944).
- "The *Hodges* court held that a devise of a specified number of acres out of a larger tract was *void for vagueness,* but relied on cases dealing with deeds, mortgages, and foreclosures rather than wills." Clayton W. Davidson III, Stephenson v. Rowe: *The Testator's Will Prevails,* 65 N.C. L. Rev. 1488, 1490 (1987).
- "She argues that . . . both the liquor license provision in the contract for deed and the default notice sent to her are *void for vagueness* . . . ." *Turbiville v. Hansen,* 761 P.2d 389, 391 (Mont. 1988).
- "We agree with appellees that this description was sufficient to constitute a key by which the property may be identified, and thus the contract was not void for vagueness due to any insufficiency of the description of the property." *Cole v. Shoffner,* 421 S.E.2d 322, 325 (Ga. Ct. App. 1992) (citation omitted).

Not until the early 20th century did the phrase come to bear what is today its most usual sense, in reference to statutes. If legislation establishes a requirement or a punishment without stating precisely what is required or what conduct is punishable, the courts generally hold that it is *void for vagueness* because it violates due process—e.g.:

- "Four reasons are assigned in the motion to quash, against the validity of the statute under the Constitution: . . . second, that it is *void for vagueness* and uncertainty . . . ." *U.S. v. U.S. Brewers' Ass'n,* 239 F. 163, 165 (W.D. Pa. 1916).
- "Exemption of vehicles operating within 'usual transfer delivery zone' from Motor Vehicle Transportation Tax Act [St. 1925, p. 833] § 9 held *void for vagueness.*" *Ex parte Schmolke,* 248 P. 244, 245 syl. 6 (Cal. 1926).
- "The word 'orchard' has always had a well-understood meaning, and the use of such a term in a statute could not possibly render the statute *void for vagueness.*" *Kelleher v. French,* 22 F.2d 341, 344 (W.D. Va. 1927).
- "[The defendant contends that] the statute under which defendant was prosecuted is *void for vagueness,* because it grants unlimited discretion to the state in deciding how many charges to bring for a course of criminal conduct . . . ." *State v. Altgilbers,* 786 P.2d 680, 691 (N.M. Ct. App. 1990).

When the expression is used as a PHRASAL ADJECTIVE, it should be hyphenated <void-for-vagueness doctrine>.

voidity. See **voidness.**

void marriage, like *void contract* (q.v.), is an OXYMORON: "The expression *'void marriage'* is but a convenient phrase. A void marriage is no marriage. Considered literally the expression is self-destructive and contradictory." *Ross Smith v. Ross Smith* [1963] A.C. 280, 314 (per Lord Morris of Borth-y-Gest).

voidness; voidity. The first is the usual noun. The second, a NEOLOGISM not recorded in most English-language dictionaries, is a NEEDLESS VARIANT—e.g.: "[*V*]*oidity* [read *Voidness*] of marriage requir[es] by the trend of the more modern cases an express statutory declaration . . . ." Karl Llewellyn, *The Common Law Tradition: Deciding Appeals* 488 (1960).

voir(e) dire, n., meaning literally "to speak the truth," is a LAW FRENCH equivalent of the Latinate *verdict* (*voir* having been the Norman-French word for the modern French *vrai*). But the two words have come to denote two distinct aspects of jury trials. The preferred spelling is *voir dire.* It is pronounced */vwah-**deer**/*, or, in the southern U.S., */vohr-**dɪr**/*. See **verdict (A)** & PRONUNCIATION (A).

voir dire, v.t., is a lawyer's colloquialism not listed in general English-language dictionaries. E.g., "When I *voir dired* the jury, I asked each prospective juror whether he could set his prejudices aside." John A. Jenkins, *The Litigators* 379 (1989) (quoting Rex Carr)./ "Some lawyers take voluminous notes as the panel is *voir dired* and pore over them intently as they strike their lists." Among the possible substitutes are the verbs *to examine* and *to question (on voir dire).* See NOUNS AS VERBS.

volenti non fit injuria (lit., "to a willing person a wrong is not done") denotes the tort defense that the plaintiff voluntarily accepted the risk with full knowledge. The LATINISM is gradually falling into disuse in AmE, though it is still used with great frequency in BrE, in which it is sometimes said that the injured person was *volens.*

The Fifth Circuit once wrote what amounts to a usage note on the phrase: "[T]he joint appellants claim that . . . Mobil was not liable to Gantt under the Texas doctrine of assumption of risk (usually referred to by Texas lawyers and courts in its Latin form, *'volenti non fit injuria,'* or *'volenti'* for short)." *Gantt v. Mobil Chem. Co.,* 463 F.2d 691, 699 (5th Cir. 1972). True, the clipped form *volenti* is fairly common, but in Texas judicial opinions, *assumption of the risk* (q.v.) is more than four times as common as the LATINISM in any form.

volitional; volitive. *Volitional* = of or belonging to volition (i.e., an act of willing or resolving); pertaining to the action of willing. E.g., "A change in a given relation may result from some superadded fact or group of facts not under the *volitional* control of a human being." *Volitive* is a NEEDLESS VARIANT.

voluntary. See **unintentional.**

voluntary manslaughter. See **manslaughter.**

voluntary waste. See **waste.**

voracious (= devouring large quantities of food) is sometimes misused for *vigorous.* Perhaps the confusion arose through the CLICHÉ *voracious reader,* in which many seem to have forgotten the metaphor of devouring. With reading (which involves mental ingestion), the metaphor works; with other activities in which the idea of consuming is absent, the metaphor flops—e.g.: "From the start, McCurley's team—which included his lawyer wife, Johanna, two associate attorneys, and a paralegal—attacked *voraciously* [read *vigorously*]. Dozens of depositions were taken, tens of thousands of documents assembled. Expert and character witnesses were flown in from around the country. At times McCurley and his crew worked in shifts, sixteen to twenty hours a day." Dana Rubin, *Courting Costs,* Tex. Monthly, May 1992, at 52, 58.

voracity. See MALAPROPISMS.

votary; votarist. The latter is a NEEDLESS VARIANT.

vote; ballot. These words "are sometimes confused, and, while they are sometimes used synonymously, the 'ballot' is, in fact, under our form of voting, the instrument by which the voter expresses his choice between candidates or in respect to propositions; and his *'vote'* is his choice or election, as expressed by his *ballot.*" *Clary v. Hurst,* 138 S.W. 566, 569 (Tex. 1911).

For the distinction between a juror's *vote* and a jury's verdict, see **verdict (C).**

vote damages, in AmE, is the lawyer's shorthand phrase for *vote to award damages*—e.g.: "An insurance functionary—a guy with a big title and a small salary—loves to go back to the office and write a memo telling his boss that he 'did the right thing' and refused [as a juror] to *vote damages.*" Joseph Goulden, *The Million Dollar Lawyers* 71 (1978) (quoting Franklin Jones, Jr.).

vouch, in modern lay contexts, almost invariably means "to answer *for,* be surety *for*" <she vouched for him> <vouched for his honesty>. Archaically, *vouch* = to call upon, rely on, or cite as authority; to confirm by evidence or assertion. E.g., "Jhering, emphasizing the effect of trade and commerce in liberalizing the strict law, *vouched* the introducing of Greek mercantile custom into the law of the old city of Rome." (Roscoe Pound) This sense appears to be an extension of the obsolete legal phrase *to vouch to warrant,* meaning "to cite, call, or summon (a person) into court to give warranty of title" (*OED*).

vouchsafe is not equivalent to *grant* or *provide,* as suggested here: "A person is entitled to the actual and continued enjoyment of his civil rights as *vouchsafed* by the statute, and these cannot be permanently thwarted by some other avenue of escape." Rather, today it ordinarily denotes "to grant something in a condescending way," or, more neutrally, "to grant something as a special favor." E.g., "[T]he Court does not *vouchsafe* the lower courts . . . guidelines for formulating specific, definite, wholly unprecedented remedies . . . ." *Baker v. Carr,* 369 U.S. 186, 267 (1962) (Frankfurter, J., dissenting).

VOWEL CLUSTERS are not indigenous to the English language, although one finds them in our imported vocabulary, in words such as *giaour* (= one outside the Muslim faith), *maieutic* (= Socratic), *moueing* (= making a pouting face), *onomatopoeia* (= the use of imitative or echoic words, such as *fizz* and *buzz*), *queuing* (AmE) or *queueing* (BrE). In forming NEOLOGISMS, esp. by agglutination, one should be wary of clumping vowels together in a way that would strike readers as un-English. Even three consecutive vowels may have this effect, as in *antiaircraft,* which is better hyphenated: *anti-aircraft.* For two more examples—*shanghaied* and *shanghaiing*—see **shanghai.**

vs. See **v.** & **versus.**

wafer, in law, is a small red piece of paper that is stuck on a document under seal—in place of a wax seal. Traditionally, the signer of the document, after signing, would touch the wafer with his or her finger. See **seal (A).**

waifs and (e)strays. This legal phrase has passed into common parlance in the sense "abandoned or neglected children," which is an extension of the original sense "unclaimed property; wandering animals." In lay usage, the second element is usually *strays.* Technically, *waifs* came to mean, at common law, things stolen and thrown away by the thief in flight, but not things left behind or hidden; they belonged to the Crown by prerogative right if they had been seized on its behalf (*OCL*). *Estrays,* q.v., = valuable tame animals, found wandering and ownerless; at common law, they belonged to the Crown or, by virtue of grant or prescriptive right, to the lord of the manor (*id.*).

wait. See **await.**

waivable, a word supported in the *OED* with but one citation from 1818, is common in modern legal contexts—e.g.: "The defects which were not *waivable* under either system were: want of jurisdiction over the subject matter, failure to state a cause of action, and lack of an indispensable party." Fleming James, *Civil Practice* §4.3, at 135 (1965)./ "The distinction between subject-matter jurisdiction and *waivable* defenses is not a mere nicety of legal metaphysics." *U.S. Catholic Conference v. Abortion Rights Mobilization, Inc.,* 487 U.S. 72, 77 (1988).

The noun *waivability* is likewise common, though it appears in none of the general English-language dictionaries. E.g., "Can finding of waiver of unionized employee's state civil rights and privacy law claims be predicated on federal court's mere assumption of *waivability?*" *Labor,* 57 U.S.L.W. 3727, 3727 (2 May 1989)./ "[T]he second [topic] involv[es] the nature and *waivability* of the Workers' Compensation defense." Robert A. Barker, *Collateral Estoppel,* N.Y.L.J., 23 April 1990, at 3.

waive. A. Narrowing of Sense. This word has undergone what linguists call "specialization," its primary sense having gotten narrower with time. Originally, *waive* was just as broad as *abandon.* In general usage today, *waive* means "to relinquish something that one has the right to expect"

<to waive the formalities>. And in legal usage, the word ordinarily means "to relinquish a legal right" <the company waived that defense>.

B. For *wave*. *Waive* (= to relinquish or abandon voluntarily) is sometimes used as a MALAPROPISM for *wave* (= to move to and fro with the hand)—e.g.: "But a new bidder—the Blockbuster Bowl, sponsored by the video store chain—threw the deal into doubt by *waiving* [read *waving*] a few extra dollars before the noses of our institutions of higher learning . . . ." Frederick C. Klein, *Who Cares Who's No. 1?* Wall St. J., 3 Jan. 1992, at A5. Cf. **waiver (D).**

waiver. A. Senses. *Waiver* = (1) the voluntary relinquishment or abandonment of a legal right or advantage <waiver of immunity>; or (2) the instrument by which a person relinquishes such a right or advantage <she signed the waiver>.

B. Imprecise Uses. *Waiver* is "an imprecise and generic term" when used, for example, to describe the action of a landlord who decides not to forfeit a lease that a tenant has breached, but the word is "used in many of the leading cases." Peter Butt, *Land Law* 284 (2d ed. 1988). Sometimes the word is used vaguely as a synonym for *laches,* esp. when a lien claimant has lost the lien by delay. As leading admiralty scholars put it, when "a lien has attached at the time . . . services were furnished, *waiver,* unless it refers to an express agreement by which the lienor releases his claim against the ship, seems to be merely a word [that] some judges like to use for stylistic effect, by itself or in double harness with its more industrious companion *laches.*" Grant Gilmore & Charles L. Black, Jr., *The Law of Admiralty* 786 (2d ed. 1975). Finally, *waiver* is sometimes confused with *estoppel,* q.v., but the words are quite "incorrectly regarded as synonymous." *Thomas N. Carlton Estate, Inc. v. Keller,* 52 So. 2d 131, 132–33 (Fla. 1951).

C. And *estoppel*. *Waiver* = the voluntary relinquishment of a known right. *Estoppel* = the legal abatement of somebody's rights and privileges when it would be inequitable to allow that person to assert them. Though the distinction is a fine one (and a frequently muddled one), it is worth carefully observing. In insurance law, for example, "[*w*]*aiver* arises by the act of one party; estoppel by operation of law. Waiver depends upon knowledge of the insurer; estoppel upon a prejudicial change of position by the insured. While they may coexist, they are not identical . . . . The term *estoppel* is broader than that of *waiver,* and may embrace it within its scope, in certain instances, since an insurer, after waiving certain rights, would be estopped thereafter to assert them. The converse is not true, as an estoppel need not be founded upon a waiver." 16B John A. Appleman & Jean Appleman, *Insurance Law and Practice* § 9081, at 497 (1981).

D. For *waver*. It is a MALAPROPISM to confuse *waiver* with *waver* (= to vacillate)—e.g.: "Mayor Koch . . . *waivered* [read *wavered*] between silence and support for months." *Bess Myerson Accused of Stealing $44 in Goods,* N.Y. Times, 28 May 1988, at 9./ "The Court has never *waivered* [read *wavered*] on this point." *U.S. v. Bates,* 917 F.2d 388, 395 n.10 (9th Cir. 1990)./ "[T]he firm—and Klein and Farr in particular—*waivered* [read *wavered*] over whether to embrace faster growth." Eleanor Kerlow, *Small Is No Longer Beautiful,* Legal Times, 27 May 1991, at 1.

E. For *waive*. When *waiver* is not misused for *waver,* it is often displacing the more straightforward verb *waive*—e.g.: "While none have been approved by EPA, the three 'tertiary' ethers are chemically similar to MTBE and would probably be *waivered* [read *waived*] by the EPA." George H. Unzelman, *U.S. Clean Air Act Expands Role for Oxygenates,* Oil & Gas J., 15 April 1991, at 44, 47–48.

waiver by estoppel. This phrase is a useless jumble: "[W]e feel that the term *waiver by estoppel* is confusing and tends to blur the useful distinction between *waiver* and *estoppel.* The *waiver by estoppel* term in our previous cases has always been applied in estoppel situations and should be understood to refer to estoppel and not waiver." *Reed v. Commercial Ins. Co.,* 432 P.2d 691, 692 (Or. 1967). For the distinction between *waiver* and *estoppel,* see **waiver (C).**

waive the tort. Many lawyers have heard this idiom but are unsure of its origin and meaning. In common-law pleading, a plaintiff often had the choice of framing a cause of action in contract or in tort. One who chose to sue in contract was said to *waive the tort.*

Actually, though, *waiver of tort* is a misnomer because a party "waives" the tort only in the sense of electing to sue in quasi-contract to recover the defendant's unjust benefit instead of suing in tort to recover damages. The remedies, in other words, are in the alternative. And, even when the plaintiff elects to sue in quasi-contract, "the tort is not extinguished. Indeed it is said that it is a *sine qua non* of both remedies that [the plaintiff] should establish that a tort has been committed." Lord Goff of Chieveley & Gareth Jones, *The Law of Restitution* 605 (3d ed. 1986).

waivor; waivee. These terms are surely needless, *waivor* being particularly susceptible of confusion with *waiver.* E.g., "[A] waiver of one misrepresentation does not constitute a waiver of another when the *'waivor'* [read *waiving party*] had no reason to believe the second representation was also false." *Housour v. Prudential Life Ins. Co.,* 136 N.W.2d 689, 691 (Mich. Ct. App. 1965)./ "[A] valid waiver requires a known legal right, relinquished for consideration, where such legal right is intended for the *waivor's* [read *waiving party's*] sole benefit and does not infringe on the rights of others." *Brannock v. Brannock,* 722 P.2d 636, 637 (N.M. 1986).

wake; awake; awaken; wake up; woke; waked; waked up; woke up; awakened; awaked; awoke. The past-tense and past-participial forms of *wake* and its various siblings are perhaps the most vexing in the language. Following are the preferred declensions:

wake > woke > waked (or woken)
awake > awoke > awaked (or awoken)
awaken > awakened > awakened
wake up > woke up > waked up

wane; wax. *Wane* = to decrease in strength or importance. E.g., "The aspect of *Lochner* that curtailed economic regulation has clearly *waned* since the 1930s."/ "The imperative of a predeprivation hearing *wanes* when impractical, as in a negligent tort situation." *Wax* (= [1] to increase in strength or importance, or [2] to become) is used primarily (in sense (2)) in clichés such as *to wax poetic, eloquent,* etc., or (in sense (1)) as a correlative of *wane* <the doctrine waxed and waned>.

wangle. See **wrangle.**

want, n., (= lack) is an especially formal word, sometimes used in literary contexts but frequently in legal writing <want of prosecution>. E.g., "The district court dismissed the action for *want* of jurisdiction, and this court reversed."/ "*Want* of probable cause and malice are seldom established by direct evidence of an ulterior motive." The participial *wanting* (= lacking) also appears often in legal prose: "We first consider the appellee's contention that federal jurisdiction is *wanting.*"/ "Authority on these points is *wanting.*" (Eng.)

wanton; reckless. The word *wanton* usu. denotes a greater degree of culpability than *reckless.* A *reckless* person is generally fully aware of the risks and may even be trying and hoping to avoid harm. A *wanton* person may be risking no more harm than the *reckless* person, but he or she is not trying to avoid the harm and is indifferent about whether it results. In criminal law, *wanton* usually connotes malice, but *reckless* does not. See **malice.**

ward has two primary legal senses today: (1) "a territorial division in a city, usu. defined for purposes of city government" <ward leader>; or (2) "a person—usu. a minor—who is under a guardian's charge or protection" <a ward of the state>. Though these meanings are seemingly unrelated, the term *ward* originally meant "guard"—hence sense (1) refers to a place to be guarded and sense (2) to a person to be guarded.

-WARD(S). In AmE, the preferred practice is to use the *-ward* form of directional words, as in *toward, forward, backward, westward.* Words in *-ward* may be either adjectives or adverbs, whereas words in *-wards,* common in BrE, may be adverbs only. See **toward(s).**

warehousemen. See SEXISM (B).

warning of caveat (= a notice given to a person who has entered a caveat warning him to appear and state what his interest is) is a curious but established REDUNDANCY. See **caveat.**

warrant, n., = (1) a writ directing or authorizing someone to do an act—esp. one directing a law enforcer to make an arrest, a search, or a seizure; or (2) a document conferring authority, esp. to pay or receive money. Sense (2) is often used figuratively—e.g.: "What warrant then had our four new judges for hoping that history would reject these rival claimants and confirm the Supreme Court's constitutional prerogative?" Robert G. McCloskey, *The American Supreme Court* 11 (1960).

warrant, v.t. **A. General Usage.** Today, *warrant* most commonly means "to justify." And in modern idiom, one naturally says that objects or actions are *warranted,* but not so naturally that people are *warranted.* Therefore, "Such a conclusion *warrants* federal judges in substituting their views for those of state legislators," reads better this way: *Such a conclusion warrants federal judges' substituting their views for those of state legislators.* To illustrate this point, we might say that acts or beliefs are *warranted* or *unwarranted,* but not that actors or believers are *warranted* or *unwarranted.*

Nevertheless, the *OED* contains examples of *warrant* used with personal objects from the 17th century, and the usage remains common in law, if not elsewhere. E.g., "The facts and circumstances must have been sufficient in themselves to *war-*

rant a man of reasonable caution in the belief that an offense has been or is being committed."

B. Legal Senses. In law, *warrant* may mean (1) "to guarantee the security of (realty or personalty, or even a person)" <the company will warrant him from any harm>; (2) "to give warranty of (title), to give warranty of title to (a person)" <the third party had warranted title>; or (3) "to authorize" <Who has warranted this search?>. In senses (1) and (2), the verb *to warrant* is closely connected with the noun *warranty.* Sometimes, however, lawyers use the word *warrant* loosely—esp. in contracts—by stating, for example, that a party *warrants* something when no warranty is intended; in modern usage, if a mere promise is intended, as opposed to a warranty, then *warrant* is the wrong word. See **justify.**

warranted (= authorized by a search warrant) is common in American legal writing. *Warranted* has had the sense "furnished with a legal or official warrant" (*OED*) since the mid-18th century. E.g., "[C]ourts have upheld the use of forceful breaking and entering where necessary to effect a *warranted search,* even though the warrant gave no indication that force had been contemplated." *Dalia v. U.S.,* 441 U.S. 238, 257 n.19 (1979)./ "The evidence found during the *warranted search* showed overwhelmingly that Lennick was growing marijuana in his home." *U.S. v. Lennick,* 18 F.3d 814, 818 (9th Cir. 1994).

The antonym of *warranted* in this sense is *warrantless,* not *unwarranted* (= unjustified). See **warrantless.**

warrantee—properly, the person to whom a warranty is given—is sometimes incorrectly used in place of *warranty.* The *OED* cites two examples of this misusage. See **guarantee (A).**

warranter. See **warrantor.**

warrantless = (1) without a warrant <a warrantless entry of police upon defendant's premises>; or (2) unjustified <completely warrantless accusations>.

warrantor, warranter. The former spelling is preferred.

warranty. A. General Senses. "The word *warranty* is multivocal throughout the law . . . ." Grant Gilmore & Charles L. Black, Jr., *The Law of Admiralty* 63 (2d ed. 1975). The word has three primary senses: (1) "[in property law] a covenant by which the grantor in a deed (a) binds himself or herself, as well as any heirs, to secure to the grantee the estate conveyed in the deed, and (b) pledges to compensate the grantee with other land of equivalent value if the grantee is evicted by someone possessing paramount title"; (2) "[in contract law] an express or implied undertaking by the seller of property that it is or will be as represented or promised to be"; or (3) "[in insurance law] a pledge or stipulation by the insured that the facts relating to the person insured, the thing insured, or the risk insured are as stated.

B. And *condition.* In modern usage, a contractual promise may be a *condition,* a *warranty,* or an intermediate term. The breach of a *condition* gives the innocent party the option of treating the entire contract as discharged, while a breach of a *warranty* (or *covenant*) merely entitles the innocent party to claim damages but does not discharge that party's remaining contractual duties. This distinction in terminology arose fairly recently: in older cases, *warranty* is often used to refer to any contractual term. Because the terms *condition* and *warranty* are often loosely used, courts often face difficult questions about whether the parties to a contract intended a term to be a condition or a warranty; such questions are answerable by resort either to express language or to inferences about the importance that the parties seem to have attached to a given term. See **condition (A).**

C. And *guarantee.* See **guarantee (A).**

wastage, as Gowers has noted, "is properly used of loss caused by wastefulness, decay, leakage, etc., or, in a staff, by death or resignation. It would be well if it were confined to this meaning instead of being used, as it habitually is, as a long variant of *waste*" (*MEU2* 688).

waste, as a legal term of art, carries the sense "permanent harm to real property committed by a tenant (for life or for years) to the prejudice of the heir, the reversioner, or the remainderman." E.g., "[I]t is the tenant's obligation to replace broken windows and to take other steps to preserve the premises from dilapidation. While a tenant may make repairs, he is not permitted to make any material change in the nature and character of the building leased. The making of such a material change is called *waste.*" Robert Kratovil, *Real Estate Law* 300 (1946; repr. 1950). The usual legal phrase is *to commit waste.* See **devastavit.**

Waste comes in a variety of types (listed here in order of commonness):

- *Commissive waste* (known also as *voluntary waste*) is caused by the affirmative acts of the tenant.
- *Permissive waste* is caused by the failure of the

tenant to make necessary repairs that would prevent deterioration and decay. (A life tenant, as opposed to a tenant for years, is not generally liable for permissive waste unless the instrument creating the tenancy imposes a duty to repair.)

- *Equitable waste* is caused by an exempt life tenant (see just above) who flagrantly destroys or damages the property.
- *Ameliorating waste* (BrE) occurs when a tenant improves the land, as by building a high rise on it. "Understandably," as the leading Australian authority puts it, "remaindermen and reversioners rarely complain about ameliorating waste." Peter Butt, *Land Law* 115 (2d ed. 1988). In the U.S., *ameliorating waste* is no waste at all.

wastewater. One word.

waver. See **waiver (D).**

wax. See **wane.**

way of necessity. See **easement (B).**

ways and means is—by virtue of the Ways and Means Committee in the U.S. House of Representatives and the House of Lords—a DOUBLET of unimpeachable credentials when used in reference to such a committee, which determines how money will be raised for various governmental projects. The phrase appears in some important 18th-century documents—e.g.: "[The States] have no right to question the propriety of the demand; no discretion beyond that of devising the *ways and means* of furnishing the sums demanded." *The Federalist* No. 30, at 189 (Alexander Hamilton) (Clinton Rossiter ed., 1961). Of course, in modern contexts divorced from historical discussions, *ways and means* is an inexcusable REDUNDANCY.

way which, unseparated by a comma, is erroneous for *way in which.* E.g., "One of the *ways which* [read *ways in which*] the consignor may protect his interests is by filing under Article 9 pursuant to section 2-326(3)(c)." But in sentences that, like that one, contain relative clauses, it is idiomatic to use *that* in place of *in which*—or even to omit the relative pronoun altogether. This usage is colloquial—e.g.: "One of the ways the consignor may protect the interest . . . ."

weald. See **wield.**

wear and tear. In the context of leases, the phrase *wear and tear*—a "reduplicative phrase," as linguists call it—includes not only the action of the weather but also the normal use of property. A tenant is not liable to replace a carpet that becomes dingy from normal use during the tenancy—but a spilled bottle of black ink is another matter. The phrase is usually preceded by a synonym, for good measure: *normal wear and tear, reasonable wear and tear,* and *fair wear and tear* are generally synonymous.

we are persuaded that is often just so much verbal baggage in judicial opinions. E.g., "*We are persuaded that* the principles announced in *Tabacalera* and *Maltina* are dispositive here." The sentence becomes much more forceful if the phrase is deleted: "The principles announced in *Tabacalera* and *Maltina* are dispositive here." See **persuade** & FLOTSAM PHRASES.

WEASEL WORDS. Theodore Roosevelt said, in a speech in St. Louis, May 31, 1916: "One of our defects as a nation is a tendency to use what have been called weasel words. When a weasel sucks eggs it sucks the meat out of the egg and leaves it an empty shell. If you use a weasel word after another there is nothing left of the other." Some writers have incorrectly assumed that the metaphor suggested itself because of the wriggling, evasive character of the weasel. In any event, sensitive writers are aware of how supposed intensives (for example *very,* q.v.) actually have the effect of weakening a statement. Many other words merely have the effect of rendering uncertain or toothless the statements in which they appear. Among these are *significantly, substantially, reasonable, meaningful, compelling, undue, clearly, obviously, manifestly, if practicable, with all deliberate speed* (orig. a weasel phrase, now with a history), *all reasonable means, or as soon thereafter as may be, rather, somewhat, duly, virtually,* and *quite.* See **clearly.** Cf. FUDGE WORDS.

wed. A. Past Tense and Past Participle. *Wedded* is the preferred past-participial form, but *wed* often edges it out—e.g.: "Last year, the singer [Dan Fogelberg] *wed* [read *wedded*] his longtime fiancée, Anastasia Savage, who shares his love of oil painting." Walter Scott, *Personality Parade,* Dallas Morning News (Parade Mag.), 3 Jan. 1993, at 4./ "In February 1951, we *wed* [read *wedded*] women we had met at college . . . ." Walter Goodman, *In Business for Profit; Imagine That!* N.Y. Times, 16 Oct. 1994, § 7, at 9. In the negative, the proper adjective is *unwed* <unwed mothers>.

B. Wrongly Referring to the State of Matrimony. The verb *wed* refers to an act, not to a state—to what happens during a wedding, not to what one is afterward: "[T]hat purchase occurred during the interval in which we were legally *wed* [read *married*] . . . ." Larry Wallberg, *"Marital Property": Divvying Up Those Intangibles,* Wall St. J., 23 Oct. 1990, at A16. *Married,* by contrast, contains just the ambiguity that the writer just quoted fell into; to say, "I was married last Saturday," may mean either that the wedding took place then or that a divorce has since occurred.

C. Figurative Uses. *Wed* is often used metaphorically in American legal prose for *adopt* or *endorse.* E.g., "But, though our Supreme Court has not yet *wedded* this new doctrine, it has certainly at least paid ardent courtship."

welcher. See **welsher.**

well, when forming an adjective with a past participial verb, is hyphenated when placed before the noun (e.g., *a well-known person, a well-written book*), but is not hyphenated when the phrase follows what it modifies (e.g., *a person who is well known, a book that is well written*). See ADJECTIVES (C).

well-being is hyphenated, not spelled as one word.

well-pleaded complaint; artful pleading. Although these terms may seem related, they are used very differently. A *well-pleaded complaint* is an original or initial claim that sufficiently sets forth a claim for relief, by including the grounds for the court's jurisdiction, the basis for the relief claimed, and a demand for judgment, so that a defendant may draft an answer that is truly responsive on the issues to be decided.

Artful pleading, by contrast, is a derogatory term referring to a plaintiff's disguising a federal claim as if it were solely a state claim in order to prevent a defendant from removing the case from state court to federal court.

well-settled, a CLICHÉ, is usually inferior to *settled* in reference to points of law, because, unfortunately, most legal writers use the one for the other undiscriminatingly. See WEASEL WORDS.

welsher; welcher. The former is usual; the term means "one who shirks his or her responsibility in a joint undertaking," and most commonly refers to one who does not pay gambling debts.

Many natives of Wales consider the word insulting, though there is no etymological evidence supporting a connection with *Welsh* (= of, relating to, or hailing from Wales). Even so, the popular mind makes this connection, and the careful writer must be heedful.

westerly. To denote something stationary, the term should be *west boundary;* to denote something moving, *westerly direction.* See DIRECTIONAL WORDS.

we the people. See SET PHRASES.

wharf. Pl. *wharves.*

what. Eric Partridge took the view that *what,* as the subject of a clause, takes a singular verb no matter what follows (not *what follow*). See *Usage and Abusage* 362 (5th ed. 1981). But good usage allows more variety than this straitjacketing advice: when used as a pronoun, *what* may be either singular or plural. The possibilities are several.

A. Singular *what* in the Noun Clause Followed by a Singular Predicate Noun. This construction is the easiest: *what* (= the thing that) takes a singular verb. E.g., "*What* the legal system needs *is* an apprentice system to ensure that every young lawyer has a mentor."

B. Singular *what* in the Noun Clause Followed by a Plural Predicate Noun. In this construction, as in (A), *what* = the thing that—but the main verb is (illogically) attracted to the plural noun that follows it. E.g., "But *what worries* restaurateurs more *are* customers like Eric Wyka." Molly O'Neill, *Recession and Guilt Pare Dining Trade and Menus,* N.Y. Times, 31 March 1991, at 1. Fowler would have recommended rewriting that sentence in this way: *What worries restaurateurs more is customers like Eric Wyka.* (See *MEU2* at 691–92.) Either sentence would be correct, but O'Neill's original sentence typifies modern usage more than the revision.

C. Plural *what* in the Noun Clause Followed by a Plural Predicate Noun. In this construction, *what* = the things that. E.g., "*What are* in issue *are* propositions, not facts." 3 Charles F. Chamberlayne, *The Modern Law of Evidence* § 1718a, at 2216 (1912)./ "*What* the judge principally wants to hear *are* the relevant cases . . . ." Glanville Williams, *Learning the Law* 163 (11th ed. 1982)./ "Ebullience and eccentricity are to be found on every page but *what are* harder to discover *are* the depths of the Hailsham character . . . ." John Mortimer, *High Court Jester,* Sunday Times, 8 July 1990, at 8-1.

D. Undetermined *what* Followed by a Plural Predicate Noun. In many contexts, *what* is the object in a noun clause; when that is so, the word is, in actual usage, plural three times as often as it is singular. The *what*s in this category are hard to resolve into a translated phrase, such as "things that" (a phrase that does not quite fit). E.g., "[T]he jury [will] award to the injured party *what are* called his damages." Edward T. Channing, *Judicial Eloquence,* in *Lectures Read to the Seniors in Harvard College* 98, 109 (1856; repr. [Dorothy I. Anderson & Waldo W. Braden eds.] 1968)./ "The Supreme Court case next discussed in the text is . . . the basic authority for turning *what are* essentially breach of contract claims into torts *pro hac vice.*" Grant Gilmore & Charles L. Black, Jr., *The Law of Admiralty* 740 (2d ed. 1975).

whatever; whatsoever. As an intensive meaning "at all," *whatsoever* is an established idiom in AmE <he had no reason whatsoever>, though it is obsolescent in BrE. Still, many American stylists prefer the shorter word, *whatever*—e.g.: "We now consider whether plaintiff was entitled to recover any damages *whatever* for the death of his wife."/ "In such cases there are no circumstances *whatever* that would give the court jurisdiction." On phrases such as *what nature soever,* see TMESIS.

what it is, is. Sentences such as the following are much on the rise: "*What* this case really *is, is* a contest of equities, not between the carrier and a shipper, but between a subrogee of a carrier and that shipper."/ "*What it is,* and as such acknowledged by fame, *is* one of humanity's stablest and strongest artistic treasures." This stylistically poor construction, common in sloppy speech, has thus made its way into sloppy writing. Instead of using a *what*-clause, one should state the sense more directly: *This case is really a contest of equities . . . ; it is, and is acknowledged to be, one of humanity's strongest artistic treasures.*

whatsoever. See **whatever.**

when. See **where (A).**

when and as. See **as and when & if and when.**

whence (= from where; from which; from what source) is an especially FORMAL WORD that some readers consider stilted. Flesch prematurely called it "obsolete," perhaps to reinforce his absolute recommendation to use *from where* instead. See Rudolf Flesch, *The ABC of Style: A Guide to Plain English* 294 (1964; repr. 1966). But *from where* would hardly work in every context, and *whence* retains some vigor—e.g.: "If his method is to work at all, it must at least work in the sorts of economic cases *whence* it sprang." True, the writer might have said *cases from which it sprang,* but surely not *cases from where it sprang.*

From whence is technically a REDUNDANCY—because *whence* implies *from*—but the locution has appeared continually in the great writing from the 16th century to the 20th; for example, Shakespeare, Dryden, and Dickens all used the phrase. And *from whence* is less stilted than *whence* alone, which requires a greater literary knowledge for it to be immediately understandable. E.g., "They cast the body into the *water from whence* it could not be reclaimed." Some people object to this usage, however well established; no one would object to *from which.* See **from hence & thence.**

whenever. In legal drafting, this term is inferior to *if* or *when*—e.g.: "*Whenever* [read *If* or *When*] a deposition is taken at the instance of the government, or *whenever* [read *if* or *when*] a deposition is taken at the instance of a defendant who is unable to bear the expenses of the taking of the deposition, the court may direct . . . ." Fed R. Crim. P. 15(b). See **where (A).**

where. A. And *when*. The best word in stating a circumstance to which a statement relates is either *if* or *when,* the word *where* being archaic and legalistic to nonlegal readers. Hence: "[*W*]*here* [read *When*] a person examines goods and subsequently makes an offer to buy or hire-purchase them, it may be an implied term of the offer that the goods should remain in substantially the same state in which they were when the offer was made." G.H. Treitel, *The Law of Contract* 43–44 (8th ed. 1991). But see **where, as here.**

One writer actually suggests a nuance between *when* and *where,* but actual usage has never reflected this distinction: "*Where* is used in cases where frequent occurrences of the event are contemplated. *When* is used when a single or rare occurrence of the event is contemplated." G.C. Thornton, *Legislative Drafting* 24–25 (2d ed. 1979). But the commentator's final words are sound: "*If* . . . is very often a better word because it is the word generally used to introduce a condition in ordinary everyday usage." *Id.* at 25.

B. For *in which*. In formal prose, *where* should not be used as a relative pronoun instead of as a locative. E.g., "Understanding the operation of equal protection in both of these situations, however, will facilitate an understanding of the equal protection clause in the very different situations *where* [read *in which*] it was meant to apply."/ "We agree that it is a situation *where* [read *in which*] the decedent's trustee would have an impossible burden of explaining how the accident happened if defendant himself could not explain it."/ "There are many cases *where* [read *in which*] as an incident to a judgment creditor's action the defendant has been required to convey to a representative of the court property outside the court's jurisdiction."

When a writer wants a relaxed tone, *where* may

be more suitable. In the following example, the contraction *I've* might not comfortably fit in the same sentence as *in which*—hence *where* is justifiable: "I've deliberately chosen an example *where* [read *in which*] this unspeakable cluster did *not* stand out . . . ." Richard A. Lanham, *Revising Prose* 29 (1979). See **case where** & CASE REFERENCES (B).

C. Wrongly Used in Defining. Those who are unfamiliar with the art of defining terms often use *where* (or *when*) to create maladroit and ambiguous definitions. E.g., "A breach is *where* one party does not fulfill his obligation." [Read *A breach is a party's failure to fulfill his obligation.*]/ "Substantial performance is defined as *where* the performance meets the essential purpose of the contract." [Read *Substantial performance is defined as performance that meets the essential purpose of the contract.*] See **is when.**

whereabout(s). *Whereabouts* is the preferred form. (See **thereabout(s).**) This word may take a singular or a plural verb. E.g., "The *whereabouts* of these persons *are* [or *is*] unknown."

whereas. In the sense "given the fact that," *whereas* is the archetypal LEGALISM—it was formerly every lawyer's idea of how to begin a recital in a contract. The more modern drafting style is to use a heading such as *Recitals* or *Background,* followed by short declarative sentences, as opposed to the sometimes unceasing stream of independent clauses linked by semicolons and *whereases.*

One significant feature of these *whereas* clauses is that they usually have no legal effect: they are merely preliminary statements providing introductory background information before the binding promissory language.

Whereas also has a cluster of literary senses, namely "although; while on the one hand; on the contrary; but by contrast." Whereas the contractual use is legalistic, these literary uses are a part of the general writer's idiom—e.g.: "*Whereas* both his parents have black hair, he has blond."

One usage critic has stated: "*Whereas* sounds stuffy. In spite of the objections of some grammarians, the common word is now *while.*" Rudolf Flesch, *The ABC of Style* 294 (1964). Yet *whereas* is better than *while* if the latter ambiguously suggests a time element—e.g.: "I developed the arguments and marshaled authorities, *while* [read *whereas* if the idea of simultaneity is absent] she wrote the brief itself." See **while.**

where, as here. This is a useful phrase—and one in which an editor would generally be ill-advised to change *where* to *when*—e.g.: "The general interpretive [read *interpretative*] principle . . . is of especial force *where, as here,* resort to legislative history is sought to support a result contrary to the statute's express terms." *ACLU v. FCC,* 823 F.2d 1554, 1568 (D.C. Cir. 1987) (emphasis omitted). But see **where** (A).

whereat is an old-fashioned word dating back to the 13th century. Still, it is best not used in modern writing, for *where,* a locative, includes the concept of "at." E.g., "The L.C.R.A. is correct in its brief at page 30, *whereat* [read *where*] it states that the quoted sections of *Galveston City Co.* are from appellants' brief." Cf. **thereat.**

whereby can be a useful word, though it is easily overworked. It means "by means of or by the agency of which; from which (as a source of information); according to which, in the matter of which" (*OED*). E.g., "There is a competing thought in the trust provision that permits the invasion of the trust corpus in case of an emergency *whereby* unusual and extraordinary expenditures are necessary for the support of the beneficiary's children."/ "The United States has brought suit for breach of a contract *whereby* defendants, it is said, agreed to buy from it 9599 twenty-five-pound boxes of raisins unfit for human consumption which could be converted to alcohol."

wherefor(e) = (1) for what? why? <Wherefore all this expense?>; (2) for which (preferably spelled *wherefor*) <he incurred the debt, the liability wherefor accrued more than two years ago>; (3) on account of which <the reason wherefore the accident occurred>; (4) therefore <Wherefore, premises considered, plaintiff prays . . . .>; or (5) the cause or reason <the whys and wherefores of the situation>. In all but sense (2), the word is preferably spelled *wherefore,* but in none of these senses is the word *wherefore* particularly useful in modern writing. There are almost always more straightforward equivalents—e.g.: "The children alleged that when the father changed his will he was incompetent, *wherefore* it was alleged that [read *and they therefore alleged that*] the change of beneficiaries was null and void."/ "Defendant breached the contract, *wherefore* plaintiff suffered severe damages." [Read *Defendant breached the contract; consequently, plaintiff suffered severe damages.* Or: *Because defendant breached the contract, plaintiff suffered severe damages.*] Cf. HERE- AND THERE- WORDS.

whereof (= of what; of which) is a FORMAL WORD, perhaps an ARCHAISM <he knows not whereof he speaks>. The word is best avoided, esp. if, as in the following example, the writer does not seem to know precisely how it is used: "Is this company one of the directors *whereof* have a controlling interest therein?" What does that mean?

wheresoever is an unnecessary and archaic legalism for *wherever.* See **whatever.**

whereupon (= upon [the occurrence or occasion of] which; immediately after and as a result of which) may, by convention, begin a sentence, though it technically creates a FRAGMENT. E.g., "Plaintiff demurred to those pleas, and the court of original jurisdiction gave judgment for the defendant. *Whereupon* the plaintiff brought error . . . ." *Christmas v. Russell,* 72 U.S. (5 Wall.) 290, 306 (1866)./ "Willis replied over the phone that he had not received the acceptance. *Whereupon* Morrow said he was very glad of it, and would then withdraw his acceptance, to which Willis assented."

But good legal writers just as often use this FORMAL WORD in midsentence—e.g.: "[T]he general, naturally obeying his commander-in-chief instead of Taney, paid no attention to the writ; *whereupon* Taney quixotically ordered the general arrested for contempt of court." Fred Rodell, *Nine Men* 136 (1955). Cf. **but & and.**

wherewithal = means, esp. pecuniary means. Hence *financial wherewithal* is redundant—e.g.: "[F]ew, if any, local authorities . . . have the *financial wherewithal* [read *wherewithal*] to provide necessary expert regulation . . . . " *Wisconsin Pub. Intervenor v. Mortier,* 501 U.S. 597, 618 (1991) (Scalia, J., concurring).

whether usually directly follows the noun whose dilemma it denotes: *decision whether, issue whether, question whether.* (See **question as to whether.**) E.g., "Under Kansas law, the liability of a principal for the negligent acts of his agent is controlled by a *determination as to whether* [read *determination whether*], at the time in question, the agent was engaged in the furtherance of the principal's business."/ "This test was not very helpful since the *determination of whether* [read *determination whether*] the agreement was 'collateral' was also the conclusion sought to be shown." *Regardless,* an adverb, makes *regardless of whether.* See **regardless whether.**

A. *As to whether.* This collocation, though rarely defensible (see **question (as to) whether**), is here justified: "We are of the opinion that reasonable men might well reach different conclusions *as to whether* [i.e., on the question whether] the servant was within the area of probable deviation, and therefore within his employment, when the accident occurred."

B. *Issue of whether.* Though this phrase is generally better without the *of* (i.e., as *issue whether*), it has certain uses in which *of* is obligatory, usu. when *issue* is modified by an adjective. E.g., "A host of public-policy considerations must be weighed in resolving the threshold *issue of whether* such a remedy should be an addition to or a substitute for the liability imposed by our civil damages suit." See **issue (B).**

C. *Whether or not.* Despite the SUPERSTITION to the contrary, the words *or not* are usu. superfluous, since *whether* implies *or not.* E.g., "It remains to be seen *whether or not* [read *whether*] the special litigation committee will determine that the derivative suit should have been brought." The only context in which *or not* necessarily appears occurs when *whether or not* means "regardless of whether" <the meeting will go on whether or not it rains>.

D. And *if.* See **if (A).**

which. A. *Which* [+ noun]. This construction is somewhat outmoded and stilted, though occasionally it is useful to avoid an ambiguity. In these examples it is unnecessary: "The resolution was to award the contract to Ivey subject to the approval of the Public Housing Administration, *which agency* [read *which*] subsequently approved the acceptance."/ "S.I. enclosed a $20,000 check along with its acceptance, which check was deposited." [Read *Along with its acceptance, S.I. enclosed a $20,000 check, which was deposited.*]/ "The facts showed unconscionable delays in the treatment of appellant for his gunshot wounds, *which delays* amounted to an unconscionable denial of medical treatment. [Better: *The facts showed that, when appellant was treated for gunshot wounds, there were unconscionable delays, which amounted to an unconscionable denial of medical treatment.*]

The *which* [+ noun] construction is defensible only if *which* is necessarily separated from its antecedent by a phrase—i.e., it overcomes the difficulty presented by the REMOTE RELATIVE. But *which* [+ noun] should never, as in the following sentence, directly follow its antecedent: "SEC sanctions can be imposed only after affording the respondent a notice of and an opportunity for a *hearing, which hearing* must comply with the hearing provisions of the Administrative Procedure Act." [Read *Only after the respondent is afforded a notice of and an opportunity for a hearing, which must comply with the hearing provisions of the Administrative Procedure Act, can SEC sanctions be imposed.*]

B. The Overeager *which.* One must be certain, before introducing a subordinate clause with *which,* that this word has a clear antecedent.

Often writers actually put the *which*-clause *before* the antecedent. E.g., "Once again, this Court is called upon to apply the law of New York to the issue of damages if it finds (*which appellant* vigorously urges would be an incorrect finding) that appellant is liable for breach of contract." [Read *Once again, this Court is called upon to apply New York law to the issue of damages if it finds that appellant is liable for breach of contract, a finding that appellant vigorously urges would be incorrect.*] See ANTICIPATORY REFERENCE.

C. *And which, or which,* and *but which.* These constructions often signal trouble, for there is only one quite limited context in which any of them can be proper. Each must follow a primary *which*-clause, with which it is parallel, not left floating at the end of a sentence without a shore in sight, as in the following sentence:

> The offer and sale of the certificates of deposit pursuant to the plan shall be conducted in such a manner as to be a separate, distinct offering not integrated with any related offer and sale of similar instruments pursuant to any subsequent pool or plan and the organizers shall not otherwise enter into subsequent transactions within a time period, *or which* otherwise satisfy the factual criteria set forth above, with the result that they might be integrated with offerings made pursuant to the plan.

To edit that sentence, one might break it into two sentences, neither having an overeager *which:*

> The offer and sale of the CD's under the plan must be conducted separately from any related offer and sale of similar instruments. In addition, the organizers may not, within a given period, either (a) engage in later transactions that satisfy the factual criteria set forth above, or (b) integrate the present offerings with later offerings under the same plan.

D. Without a Proper Antecedent. Grammarians have termed this mistake "broad reference": *which* refers to a general idea or an entire statement rather than to a specific antecedent. This fault should be carefully avoided. E.g., "Plaintiff is compelled to call the police department, after *which* the keys are returned." [Read *Plaintiff is compelled to call the police, and only then are the keys returned.*]/ "But the Saudi authorities refused to accept the animals, claiming they were diseased, *which* [read *a charge*] Australia denied." Richard Ellis, *Sheep Trapped on Death Trip,* Sunday Times, 15 Oct. 1989, at A2.

E. Wrongly Elided. E.g., "This is to advise you that as long as you continue to use the premises for the purposes [insert *for which*] you are now using them, namely, for sawmill and lumber yard purposes, and pay the rentals, your possession will not be disturbed."

F. In Rhetorical Disclaimers for *and*. E.g., "If surrogate motherhood is to be considered legally acceptable in this country (*which* [read *and*] I think it should not be), then state legislatures must act to legalize the contracts drawn up for these arrangements."/ "Even if it could be considered error, *which* [read *and*] this court does not consider it so, it would be harmless error."

G. And *that*. See RESTRICTIVE AND NONRESTRICTIVE CLAUSES.

H. The Remote *which*. See REMOTE RELATIVES.

while for *although* or *whereas* is permissible and often all but necessary, despite what purists say about the word's inherent temporality. Though *while* is a more relaxed and conversational term than *although* or *whereas,* it is usually quite at home in formal contexts. E.g., "*While* in form our law is chiefly the work of judges, in great part judges simply put the guinea stamp of the state's authority upon propositions [that] they found worked out for them in advance." Roscoe Pound, *The Formative Era of American Law* 138 (1938)./ "It is settled, too, that orders granting or denying a preliminary injunction are appealable, *while* similar orders involving a temporary restraining order are not." Charles A. Wright, *The Law of Federal Courts* 708 (4th ed. 1983). See **whereas.**

The writer who uses *while* in this way should be on guard for ambiguities. For instance, does it denote time or concession in the following sentences? "*While* [read *Although* or *During the time when?*] the police were waiting beside the house, they did not hear the burglars enter."/ "*While* [read *Although* or *During the time when?*] the mall was open to the public, its policy was not to permit any visitor to engage in publicly expressive activities."

While should not be used merely for *and.* "He is a lawyer *while* she is a doctor." [Read *He is a lawyer and she is a doctor.*] Sometimes this sloppy usage leads to preposterous statements—e.g.: "Len Hickman delivered the opening statement *while* Jim Bethell made the closing argument."

while at the same time is a common REDUNDANCY—e.g.: "*While* the husband was creating joint tenancies for the benefit of his daughters, he was *at the same time* [omit *at the same time*] building up the value of the farm chattels."/ "Motivate them to keep selling the company *while at the same time* [read *while*] taking credit for their particular accomplishment." Mark H. McCormack, *What They Don't Teach You at Harvard Business School* 194 (1984).

while away; wile away. The phrase *while away* (= to spend [time] idly) dates from the early 17th century and remains the predominant form. *Wile away,* a synonymous phrase dating from about

1800, began as a corrupt form but is included in modern dictionaries such as *W10* and *AHD* without any cautionary note. Most commonly, of course, *wile* is a noun meaning "a stratagem intended to deceive" or "trickery"; it may also function as a verb in the corresponding sense "to lure or intice." However old the mistaken form *wile away* is—and never mind that Charles Dickens used it—it is still inferior to *while away.* E.g., "Pizzas were ordered and the boys *wiled* [read *whiled*] away the time by examining defendant's unloaded guns." *Dino v. State,* 405 So. 2d 213, 214 (Fla. Dist. Ct. App. 1981)./ "Before Kim Peek saw *Rain Man,* the 1988 award-winning movie loosely based on his life, he stayed home and *wiled* [read *whiled*] away the time working and reading books." Rhonda Smith, *Into the World,* Austin American-Statesman, 28 April 1994, at D1.

whilom. See **erstwhile.**

whilst, though a correct form, is virtually obsolete in AmE and reeks of pretension in a modern American writer. *Whilst* is still common in BrE, however. E.g., "Defendant, knowing the premises, maliciously intended to injure plaintiff as lessee and manager of the theatre *whilst* the agreement with Wagner was in force." (Eng.)/ "The plaintiff's loss would have been only £5 plus a further £11 as his estimated loss through two months' deprivation of a vehicle *whilst* it was being repaired and a purchaser found." (Aus.)

Like its sibling *while,* it may be used for *although* or *whereas,* although this is not good usage in AmE. E.g., "The jurisprudence of this state is to the effect that *whilst* it is the rule that costs in a suit follow the judgment before execution, it is likewise the rule that after execution has taken place the question of costs comes before the appellate court as an independent issue."/ "*Whilst,* therefore, the end of the writing in point of space may be taken as the end of the disposition, it does not follow that in all cases the signature must, of necessity, be there written." For *amongst,* see **among (A).**

whistleblower (= an informant) is best written as one word, as the Whistleblower Protection Act of 1989 (U.S.).

Whiteacre is the mythical tract of land contrasted with *Blackacre* in hypothetical legal problems. E.g., "Let it be assumed, further, that, in consideration of $100 actually paid by A to B, the latter agrees with A never to enter on X's land, *Whiteacre.*" (Hohfeld) See **Blackacre.**

White Book = the two-volume compilation—published in white hardcover editions—of the procedural and administrative rules of the Supreme Court of England and Wales. Cf. **White Paper.**

whitehorse case; horse case; gray mule case; goose case; spotted pony case; pony case. These are terms meaning "a reported case with virtually identical facts, the disposition of which should determine the outcome of the instant case." The terms are now less commonly used in the law schools than formerly; but they are useful terms. E.g., "The decision mentioned is rather a *'white horse'* case . . . ." *Roosth & Genecov Prod. Co. v. White,* 262 S.W.2d 99, 101 (Tex. 1953).

Goose case is common in the southern U.S., esp. in Louisiana. Cf. **on all fours.**

White Paper; Green Paper. In British governmental affairs, a *White Paper* announces a firm government policy to be implemented (cf. **White Book**). A *Green Paper* announces a tentative proposal for discussion.

white-powder bar is a derogatory name for defense lawyers who represent cocaine dealers. E.g., "Neal R. Sonnett, the president of the National Association of Criminal Defense Lawyers, said such behavior was offensive to most trial lawyers, as was the term *'white-powder bar.'* 'There's no such thing as a *'white-powder bar,'* he said. 'It's a very pejorative term.'" Neil A. Lewis, *Drug Lawyers' Quandary: Lure of Money vs. Ethics,* N.Y. Times, 9 Feb. 1990, at A1, B11.

white-shoe lawyer. See LAWYERS, DEROGATORY NAMES FOR (A).

whither is an ARCHAISM meaning (1) "to what place or position" <Whither shall we go?>; or (2) "to which" <at Chelsea Square, whither we had gone>. It has virtually no place in modern writing. Cf. **thither.**

who. **A. *Who & whom.*** Edward Sapir, the philosopher of language, prophesied that "within a couple of hundred years from to-day not even the most learned jurist will be saying 'Whom did you see?' By that time the *whom* will be as delightfully archaic as the Elizabethan *his* for *its.* No logical or historical argument will avail to save this hapless *whom.*" Edward Sapir, *Language* 156–57 (1921; repr. 1949). A safer bet might have been that no one will be spelling *to-day* with a hyphen. In any event, writers in the late 20th and early 21st centuries ought to understand how the words *who* and *whom* are correctly used.

The distinction to keep in mind is that *who* acts as the subject of a verb, whereas *whom* acts as the object of a verb or preposition. Though not commonly observed in informal speech, the distinction is one to be strictly followed in formal legal prose.

Some lapses are so flagrant that one can hardly fathom how they could have been committed. E.g., "The three top finishers on the bar exam were Beverly Ray, Michelle Monse, and Kenneth Buck, *all of who* [read *all of whom*] took our bar review course!" Others are more forgivable because the correct use is less obvious:

- "Boyer said she knew the person *who* [read *whom*] she identified as Roy Summers as 'Tiny's' brother . . . ." *State v. Iwakiri,* 682 P.2d 571, 593 (Idaho 1984).
- "And he [Judge Stephen G. Breyer, as nominee to the Supreme Court] promised, following the admonition of the late Justice Arthur Goldberg, *who* [read *whom*] he served as a law clerk 30 years ago, to do his best to avoid footnotes." Ruth Marcus, *Judge Breyer Gets Day in Rose Garden,* Wash. Post, 17 May 1994, at A8.
- "At trial, Miller refused to testify unless the district court excluded four young African-American men *whom* [read *who*] she felt posed a threat to her personal safety." *Feazell v. State,* 906 P.2d 727, 728 (Nev. 1995).
- "Holeman stated to witnesses that the nolle prosequi left him open for a lawsuit, and he went directly to the district attorney, *whom* [read *who*] he said looks after policemen." *Smith v. Holeman,* 441 S.E.2d 487, 492 (Ga. Ct. App. 1994).

Although *whom* might seem to be the object of *reveal* in the sentence that follows, in fact the relative pronoun is the subject of an implied verb—*failed to reveal who* [*might have wanted to kill Robert Nachtsheim*]. Therefore, *who* is correct: "There are a number of people who might have wanted to kill Robert Nachtsheim in his Minneapolis flower shop early one morning in 1973, but the intervening two decades have failed to reveal *whom* [read *who*]." Kevin Diaz, *$4 Million Award's a Start Toward a Clean Slate,* Star Tribune (Minneapolis), 22 Oct. 1994, at 1A.

Many writers have announced the demise of *whom,* but it persists—especially in AmE. *Who* would be impossible, for example, in this sentence: "If the person on *whom* the duty of electing rests elects to take in conformity with the will or other instrument of donation, he thereby relinquishes his own property, and must release or convey it to the donee upon *whom* the instrument had assumed to confer it." And, in formal writing, the following instances of *whom* seem natural:

- "Proprietors of private enterprises, such as places of amusement and resort, were under no such obligation, enjoying an absolute power to serve *whomever* they pleased."
- "It will not restrain the person *whom* it purports to restrain, namely, the litigious troublemaker."
- "A fundamental principle of our representative democracy is, in Hamilton's words, 'that the people should choose *whom* they please to govern them.'"

The correct uses of *who* are sometimes tricky. But if the pronoun acts as the subject of a clause, it must be *who,* never *whom:*

- "If the servant, without authority, entrusts the instrumentality to one *who,* on account of his age, inexperience, or recklessness, he has reason to believe *is* likely to harm others, the master would be liable." (*Who* is the subject of *is.*)
- "It may, for instance, be negligent on the part of the employer to hire an employee *who* the employer should realize *is* unfit and poses a risk to others." (*Who* is the subject of *is.*)
- "An 'apparent agent' is one *who* the principal, either intentionally or else by lack of ordinary care, induces third persons to believe *is* his agent, even though no actual authority, either express or implied, has been granted to such agent." (Again, *who* is the subject of *is,* but the sentence, though correct in this respect, is badly phrased.)

Among the toughest contexts in which to get the pronouns right are those involving linking verbs. We say, for example, *who it is* for the same reason we say *It is I,* but some very good writers have nodded—e.g.: "The distinguished political and social philosopher Russell Kirk used the word 'energumen' to describe . . . *whom* [read *who*] it is I agitate against . . . ." William F. Buckley, *The Jeweler's Eye* 284 (1969)./ "Trials on indictment are in the name of the Queen . . . ; thus a criminal case is generally called *Reg. v. whomever* [read *whoever*] it is . . . ." Glanville Williams, *Learning the Law* 17 (11th ed. 1982). See HYPERCORRECTION (F).

William Safire takes an interesting approach for those caught between feeling pedantic (by using *whom*) or incorrect (by using *who* for *whom*): "When *whom* is correct, recast the sentence." *On Language,* N.Y. Times, 4 Oct. 1992, § 6, at 12. Thus *Whom do you trust?* becomes, in a political campaign, *Which candidate do you trust?* See PHRASING & NOMINATIVE AND OBJECTIVE CASES.

B. Placement of. In well-constructed sentences, *who* directly follows the name it refers to, or is interrupted at most by a parenthesis properly set off. Writers who violate this principle risk befuddling their readers—e.g.: "The largest collection of fossils was made by L. Kohl-Larson in 1938–1939, who also found a small fragment of hominid maxilla." [Read *The largest collection of fossils was made in 1938–1939 by L. Kohl-Larson, who also found a small fragment of hominid maxilla.*] See REMOTE RELATIVES.

C. Improper Use in Reference to Nonhuman Entities (*who* for *that* or *which*). *Who* and *that* are the relative pronouns for human beings; *that* and *which* are the relative pronouns for anything other than human beings. But writers sometimes forget this elementary point—e.g.: "In this diversity action, we are called upon to decide whether a drawee bank *who* [read *that*] has missed the midnight deadline is accountable to the payee under a special set of circumstances."/ "Many companies, I believe, *who* [read *that*] are busy buying new businesses and bringing in new management teams haven't even tested the outside edge of their profitability." Mark H. McCormack, *What They Don't Teach You at Harvard Business School* 203 (1984).

D. *Which* for *who* or *whom*. This misuse—the opposite of that illustrated in (C)—occurs when writers use *which* in referring to human beings—e.g.: "There are 21 shareholders in the corporation, two of *which* [read *whom*] are vying for the chairmanship." (The correction assumes, as the context bears out, that the shareholders referred to in the sentence are persons, as opposed to corporations.)/ "Exhibit 9 names the client *which* [read *whom* or *that*] Kroeneke served."

The word *that,* of course, is permissible when referring to humans: *the people that were present* or *the people who were present.* Editors tend, however, to prefer the latter phrasing.

whole. See **in whole.**

whoever. See **who(so)ever.**

wholistic is a mistaken form of *holistic.*

whom. See **who (A).**

whom(so)ever. See **who(so)ever.**

whoredom = (1) prostitution; or (2) idolatry.

who's; whose. The former is the contraction of *who is;* the latter is the possessive form of *who.* The two forms are occasionally confused, usually when *who's* erroneously displaces *whose*—e.g.: "At the very least, the burden of proof carried by one who would have rights cancelled should be greater than the burden of one *who's* [read *whose*] only purpose is to prevent a registration from issuing." *Food Specialty Co. v. Catz Am. Co.,* 433 F.2d 817, 819 (C.C.P.A. 1970) (Baldwin, J., dissenting)./ "Mr. Hahn also identified $628.00 as cashed checks, *who's* [read *whose*] purpose was unknown." *U.S. v. Curry,* 681 F.2d 406, 413 n.16 (5th Cir. 1982).

whose may usefully refer to nonpersons <an idea whose time has come>. This use of *whose,* formerly decried by some 19th-century grammarians and their predecessors, is often an inescapable way of avoiding clumsiness. *Which,* unfortunately, has no other possessive form, apart from *of which,* an inaesthetic phrase in many contexts: "What is commonly termed ownership is in fact tenancy, *the continuance of which* [read *whose continuance*] is contingent upon legally recognized rights of tenure, with corresponding duties."

But *whose* in place of *of which* can lead to such problems as these: "One of those dealers was J & S Government Securities, Inc., *whose* home office was in New York, but *who* also had offices in Houston." (See ANTHROPOMORPHISM.) The sentence could be recast in myriad ways—e.g.: "which had its home office in New York, but offices in Houston as well." (In the corrected sentence, *offices* is a plural noun, not a verb. See **office.**)

who(so)ever; whom(so)ever; whoso(ever); whomso(ever). A. Choice of Term. The forms *whoever* and *whomever* are preferred in modern writing. Users of *whosoever* and *whomsoever,* as well as *who(m)so,* are liable to criticism as LEGALESE, ARCHAISMS, and BIBLICAL AFFECTATION. Often these terms are completely superfluous, as here: "This is a right that avails against all persons *whomsoever* [omit *whomsoever*], and is distinguished from a right that avails against a particular individual or a determinate class of persons."

B. Case. The problem of proper case arises with these words, just as it does with *who* and *whom.* E.g., "*Whomever is* [read *Whoever is*] responsible for implementing the program is responsible for its faults." The *Oxford Guide* contains this rather poor advice: "Use *whoever* for the objective case as well as the subjective, rather than *whomever,* which is rather stilted" (135). Stilted, perhaps, but correct, and really not very stilted in formal prose. See NOMINATIVE AND OBJECTIVE CASES.

C. Possessives. *Whoever's* (colloquial) is incorrect (in formal prose) for *whosever.* "He denied telling appellant that she was going to jail, although he did admit saying that *whoever's* [read *whosever*] fingerprints were found in that vault could go to jail." *Williams v. State,* 441 So. 2d 653,

655 (Fla. Dist. Ct. App. 1983)./ "[T]he detective in charge of the interrogation testified that prior to the interrogation he had had a conversation with the fingerprint expert in which both agreed to almost a hundred per cent certainty that *whoever's* [read *whosever*] finger prints were on one side of the door panel which had been removed, the palm prints matched because they were in perfect configuration." *Commonwealth v. Haynes,* 577 A.2d 564, 572 n.2 (Pa. Super. Ct. 1990).

Justice Holmes sometimes used *whosesoever,* a correct form made unnecessary by the modern preference of *who(s)ever* over *who(se)soever.*

wide; broad. The former, when used in contexts in which idiomatic English would require the latter, is a LEGALISM. E.g., "A public body has *wide* discretion in soliciting and accepting bids for public improvements." *Baxter's Asphalt & Concrete, Inc. v. Department of Transp.,* 475 So. 2d 1284, 1287 (Fla. Dist. Ct. App. 1985)./ "The district court did not abuse its *wide* discretion." *Wide* is used more commonly in BrE in this sense—e.g.: "The terms of the order are too *wide.*" (Eng.)

widespread was, until the early 20th century, spelled as two words, but now it should always appear as one.

widespreadedly is a bastard formation. *W3* records no adverbial form of the adjective *widespread,* although if there were one it would be *widespreadly.* E.g., "[A]n adherent to current American doctrine in the negligence field would hardly reject a principle already so *widespreadly* accepted by judges and other scholars alike." *Hewitt v. Safeway Stores, Inc.,* 404 F.2d 1247, 1254 (D.C. Cir. 1968).

The form *widespreadedly,* malformed perhaps on the spurious analogy of *allegedly* and *reportedly,* wrongly assumes the existence of a past tense form *spreaded.* E.g., "[T]he area of public interest to which [the publications] relate—conditions allegedly capable of *wide-spreadedly* affecting public health—would seem . . . to be one of such inherent public concern and stake that there could be no possible question as to the applicability of the *New York Times* standard for any defeasance." *United Medical Labs., Inc. v. Columbia Broadcasting Sys., Inc.,* 404 F.2d 706, 711 (9th Cir. 1968). See -EDLY.

widow, n. The Supreme Court's phrase *surviving widows who administer estates* is a REDUNDANCY. See *Reed v. Reed,* 404 U.S. 71, 75 (1971) (paraphrased). A widow who administers her deceased husband's estate must—by the very nature of the situation—have survived him.

widow, v.t., may apply to a spouse of either sex. Thus *widowed man* is unobjectionable, although to many it may seem at first unnatural.

widow(er). Is one still a widow(er) when one remarries? No.

wield; weald. *Wield* is the verb meaning "to control; handle; hold and use" <he wields his power with good judgment>. Its rare homophone, *weald,* is the noun meaning "a forest" or "an uncultivated upland region."

wigged; unwigged. These attributive nouns denote barristers and solicitors, respectively—e.g.: "The two sides—the *wigged* and the *unwigged*—are kept severely apart: solicitors cannot have lunch in the barristers' Inns of Court, and barristers must never be seen at the solicitors' Law Society." Anthony Sampson, *Anatomy of Britain* 148 (1962).

wile away. See **while away.**

wilful. See **wil(l)ful.**

will. See WORDS OF AUTHORITY (D).

will; testament. A common belief among lawyers is that, at common law, a *will* disposed of real property and a *testament* of personal property. This belief is, strictly speaking, erroneous, although from the 18th century such a distinction in usage (unfounded in the substantive law) began to emerge. The distinction is now obsolete, however, so that in modern legal usage the words are interchangeable, although *will* remains the usual term.

The archaic distinction between the words is said to have grown out of the historical development of property dispositions. Ecclesiastical courts had jurisdiction of cases involving the distribution and use of personal property; appeals from these courts were to Rome, under the Catholic hierarchy, until 1533. The common-law courts of England, meanwhile, decided cases involving the use and disposition of real property. The two court systems developed distinct terms for decedents' estates. E.g., "The common-law courts took the position that a *will* was ambulatory in its revocatory effect; the ecclesiastical courts held that a *testament* was revoked at the time the revoking instrument was executed." As a result of the bifurcated judicial system, the myth goes, the terminology was Anglo-Saxon (*will*) for real property dispositions, and Latinate (*testament*) for personal property dispositions, the latter term having derived from Roman law.

History, especially linguistic history, never comes so neatly packaged, however. It is not surprising, then, to discover that medieval writers are recorded as having used *will* in reference to personal property, and *testament* in reference to land. Even so, the myth concerning these terms may be valid insofar as it explains the tendencies in usage that would later give rise to an idiomatic DIFFERENTIATION. It is at least possible that the DOUBLET *last will and testament,* q.v., had in its origins a purpose for the inclusion of both real and personal property. In any event, *will* now denotes the entire testamentary instrument, a place formerly said to be occupied by *devise,* q.v. See also **codicil** & **testament.**

will, as a verb meaning to dispose of by will, is always transitive. E.g., "In Louisiana a testator can *will* no more than one-tenth of his estate to a woman with whom he has lived in open concubinage."/ "Aliens could, at common law, *will* personalty and devise land, but the state could seize the land in the hands of his devisees."/ "I *will* and bequeath all my effects to my brothers and sisters, to be divided equally among them." See **devise,** v.t.

willable = transferable by will. E.g., "Land became *willable* with the Statute of Wills." The *OED* traces this sense back only to 1880.

wil(l)ful. *Wilful* is the preferred spelling in BrE, *willful* in AmE. *Willfull,* a misspelling, occasionally appears in the U.S.

"*Wilful* is not," commented Lord Justice Wright, "a term of art and is often used as meaning no more than a high degree of carelessness or recklessness. It is not necessarily limited in its use to intentional or deliberate wrong-doing." *Caswell v. Powell Duffryn Assoc. Collieries,* [1940] A.C. 152, 177 (H.L.). The same problem exists in AmE: "The word *wilful* or *wilfully* when used in the definition of a crime, it has been said time and again, means only intentionally or purposely as distinguished from accidentally or negligently and does not require any actual impropriety; while on the other hand it has been stated with equal repetition and insistence that the requirement added by such a word is not satisfied unless there is a bad purpose or evil intent." Rollin M. Perkins & Ronald N. Boyce, *Criminal Law* 875–76 (3d ed. 1982). One influential writer has therefore suggested that the word should not be used because of its AMBIGUITY. See G.W. Paton, *A Textbook of Jurisprudence* 313 n.2 (4th ed. 1972).

wil(l)fulness; malice aforethought. These terms are sometimes confused in criminal contexts. *Willfulness* is the broader term. "An act is done *willfully* if done voluntarily and intentionally, and with the specific intent to do something the law forbids." 1 Edward J. Devitt & Charles Blackmar, *Federal Jury Practice and Instructions* 384 (1977). But see **wil(l)ful.**

Malice aforethought, q.v., is used in the context of homicide: "*Malice aforethought* means an intent, at the time of a killing, wilfully to take the life of a human being, or an intent wilfully to act in callous or wanton disregard of the consequences to human life; but *malice aforethought* does not necessarily imply any ill will, spite, or hatred toward the individual killed." 2 Edward J. Devitt & Charles Blackmar, *Federal Jury Practice and Instructions* 215 (1977).

willy-nilly (= willingly or unwillingly; by compulsion) is an English equivalent of the LATINISM *nolens volens.* E.g., "If a federal court is to do it, it must act in its traditional manner, not as a military commander ordering people to work *willy-nilly,* nor as the President's Administrative Assistant." (Douglas, J.) It is sometimes, as the *OED* remarks, erroneously used for "undecided, shilly-shally" <a willy-nilly disposition>.

win a victory, to. See **victory.**

winner. See **loser.**

-WISE. Phrases arrived at with this combining form are generally to be discouraged, for they often displace a more direct wording, and they are invariably graceless and inelegant. E.g., "We must . . . respond to [the] claims . . . that even if acceptable *populationwise* [read *as applied to the population as a whole*], the . . . plan was invidiously discriminatory because a 'political fairness principle' was followed . . . ." *Gaffney v. Cummings,* 412 U.S. 735, 751–52 (1973)./ "Whether accumulation of earnings in the corporation is *cheaper tax-wise* [read *cheaper for tax purposes*] than accumulation in the partnership depends on a comparison of the corporate tax rate and the applicable rate to the individuals involved."/ "There are several other *advantages tax-wise* [read *tax advantages*] but these illustrate the tax inducements for making inter vivos transfers."/ "To continue this litigation, even though the parents should ultimately prevail, may well be, *at least money-wise* [read *at least financially*], like digging a hole to get the dirt to fill another hole."/ "A notice, signed by the commissioners, was file-stamped on the day of the hearing; *content-wise* [omit *content-wise* altogether] this notice met the statutory requirements."

wise (= manner, fashion, way) is an ARCHAISM that still appears infrequently in legal writing. E.g., "The testamentary revocation may be express, in order that the testator may do his new testamentary work without being *in any wise* [read *in any way*] fettered by the contents of his former will."/ "The judgment commands the defendant to refrain from *in any wise interfering* [read *interfering in any way*] with plaintiffs in the conduct of the business of their stable." See **nowise.**

wit, to. See **to-wit.**

withal is an ARCHAISM for *besides, nevertheless, with,* or *therewith.* E.g., "The documentation and literature of this case is of truly gargantuan proportions; yet *withal* [omit *withal*] there has been a strange dearth of real issues of fact or of law."

with all deliberate speed calls to mind the LATINISM *festina lente* (= make haste slowly). Made famous in *Brown v. Board of Educ.,* 349 U.S. 294, 301 (1955), the phrase is thought to have originated in English Chancery Courts: "[A] state cannot be expected to move with the celerity of a private business man; it is enough if it proceeds, in the language of the English Chancery, *with all deliberate speed." Virginia v. West Virginia,* 222 U.S. 17, 19–20 (1911) (per Holmes, J.). But the more frequent phrase in equity courts was *with all convenient speed.*

Deliberate speed, on the other hand, has literary as well as equitable origins. The English poets Lord Byron (1788–1824) and Francis Thompson (1859–1907) both used the phrase, as did Goethe (1749–1832), if one forces the translation a little.

The phrase "resembles poetry and resembles equity techniques of discretionary accommodation between principle and expediency, but [it] fits precisely one thing only, namely, the unique function of judicial review in the American system. . . . It means only that the Court, having announced its principle, and having required a measure of initial compliance, resumed its posture of passive receptiveness to the complaints of litigants." Alexander M. Bickel, *The Least Dangerous Branch* 253–54 (1962). However grandiose that may sound, the Court later said that the phrase "has turned out to be only a soft EUPHEMISM for delay." *Alexander v. Holmes County Bd. of Educ.,* 396 U.S. 1218, 1219 (1969). See OXYMORONS & WEASEL WORDS.

with force and arms. See ***vi et armis.***

withhold is sometimes used incorrectly for *deprive of* or *deny.* E.g., "Petitioner filed suit under 42 U.S.C. § 1983 seeking monetary damages and injunctive relief for being forced to work beyond his physical capabilities and for being *withheld* [read *denied* or *deprived of*] necessary medical treatment."

withholding of deportation. See **suspension of deportation.**

within, adj. "The legal tone is still too strong for common use in the *within* letter." Wilson Follett, *Modern American Usage* 45 (1966). Indeed, it is perhaps too strong even for use by legal writers, for *enclosed* is far more common and more natural. E.g., "The *within* property shall not be sold or encumbered without the express written consent of the *within* mortgagees." (This use is apparently elliptical for *within-named;* the writer should have omitted the word or phrase completely, for it adds nothing.)/ "Opposing counsel are being furnished with a copy of the *within* [read *enclosed*] response."

within-named. See **within.**

within the statute. See **statute of frauds (B).**

without is a FORMAL WORD when used as an equivalent of *outside.* Usually, *without* is contrasted to *with;* but in law it is frequently an opposite of *within.* Though somewhat archaic, in formal legal prose this usage should be considered unexceptionable. E.g., "Grants or devises are construed to bring them *within* or *without* the operation of the Rule in Shelley's Case."/ "The plaintiff put himself *without* the pale of the comparative negligence rule, since he was wholly at fault when he received his injury."

without day. See **go hence without day, *sine die*** & LOAN TRANSLATIONS.

without prejudice (= without loss of any rights) is peculiar to legal JARGON. The phrase describes a legal action—either judicial or among private parties—that in no way harms or cancels the legal rights or privileges of a party. The antonym is *with prejudice.*

without recourse; *sans recours.* The English phrase *without recourse* is preferred over the GALLICISM *sans recours* for the stipulation that the drawer or indorser of a bill of exchange may add to his signature, repudiating his liability to the holder.

with prejudice. See **without prejudice.**

with regards to. See **regard** (A).

with respect to. See **respect** (A).

with the object of ——ing is verbose for a simple infinitive, e.g., *with the object of preventing* in place of *to prevent.*

witness. **A. Senses.** *Witness* = (1) one who sees or knows something and testifies about it; or (2) one who gives evidence under oath or affirmation, either orally or by affidavit or deposition; or (3) one who, to vouch for the genuineness of a signature, affixes his or her name to an instrument that another has signed.

B. Possessive Form. The preferable possessive form is *witness's.*

C. And *testifier* or *testis*. *Testifier* is rarely if ever justified in practice; *testis* never is. They are both NEEDLESS VARIANTS. See **testis.**

witness, v.t. = to attest or act as a witness <to witness a will> is a LEGALISM that is fairly familiar in the lay idiom.

witness-box; witness stand. The former is primarily BrE, the latter primarily AmE—although there is some overlap on both sides of the Atlantic. Following are modern English and American examples of *witness box:* "Nor do I agree with the suggestion that the question be asked by the court when the client is in the *witness-box* or by requiring him to sign some pro forma document on the day of the hearing." (Eng.)/ "The court rearranged the *witness box* so that the jury would be unable to see the shackles." *State v. Calhoun,* 554 So. 2d 127, 132 (La. Ct. App. 1989). Cf. **jurybox.**

A British philologist writes that "in the middle 'fifties, a British judge vehemently rebuked the American defendant's use in 'his' court of the expression *witness-stand* and insisted with some heat on having *witness-box.*" Brian Foster, *The Changing English Language* 61–62 (1968). Before the end of the decade, however, *witness stand* had found its way onto B.B.C. airwaves. *Id.* at 62. See **stand.**

witnesseth is commonly used at the outset of contracts and affidavits. E.g., "*Witnesseth:* that whereas first and second parties have certain litigations pending in the Mercer Circuit Court . . . it is agreed between all of the parties that all said suits are to be dismissed." Says one writer: *Witnesseth that* is a phrase "admittedly archaic but so firmly entrenched in the draftsman's vocabulary as to allow of few, if any, substitutes." Sidney F. Parham, *The Fundamentals of Legal Writing* 23 (1976). Actually, the whole mess is easily dispensed with; drafters should get right to the point, without *whereas,* q.v., preceding the recital, and without *witnesseth* to introduce the *whereas*-clauses.

Actually, the modern use of *witnesseth* is premised on a mistake: that the word is a command in the imperative mood. Actually, it is the third-person singular verb—she *sings* = she *singeth;* he *says* = he *sayeth;* she *witnesses* = she *witnesseth.* The word at the outset of instruments is really just a remnant of a longer phrase, such as *This document witnesseth that . . . .* Hence to make WITNESSETH shout in all capitals from the top of a document makes no literal sense. It seems to have originated in an early formbook writer's mistake. See -ETH.

witness whereof, in. See **in witness whereof.**

woefully is a CLICHÉ, esp. when coupled with adjectives like *inadequate* or *insufficient.* E.g., "The meager record before us is lacking and *woefully insufficient* to establish that the covenant 'touches and concerns' the land."/ "As evidence of the proposition that the government pays a disproportionate share of the cost of hospital malpractice insurance, the Westat Study is *woefully inadequate.*"

woken. See **wake.**

womankind. See **humankind** & SEXISM (D).

woodshed, v.t. See **horseshed.**

WOOLLINESS is the quality in expression of being confused and hazy, indefinite and indistinct. Excessive use of cross-references in writing, as in the Internal Revenue Code, is perhaps the apotheosis of woolliness—e.g.: "For purposes of paragraph (3), an organization described in paragraph (2) shall be deemed to include an organization described in section 501(c)(4), (5), or (6) which would be described in paragraph (2) if it were an organization described in section 501(c)(3)." I.R.C. § 509(a) (1984). See OBSCURITY (A) & PLAIN LANGUAGE (D).

woolsack in G.B. refers to the sack of wool used as the Lord Chancellor's seat when he presides over the House of Lords. E.g., "I entirely agree with my right honorable and learned friend upon the *woolsack.*" (Eng.) By extension *woolsack* is sometimes used in the general sense "a seat of justice." Cf. **ermine.**

WORDINESS. See CUTTING OUT THE CHAFF, REDUNDANCY & VERBOSITY.

WORD-PATRONAGE is "the tendency to take out one's words and look at them, to apologize for expressions that either need no apology or should be quietly refrained from" (*MEU1* at 733). E.g., "Hopefully—to use an ugly word—the dilemma will be solved by the proposed legislation." In his preface to *MEU2,* Gowers indulged mildly in word-patronage when he wrote: "This was indeed an epoch-making book in the strict sense of that overworked phrase" (p. iii). The tendency is not at all uncommon:

- "He came to the conclusion then that the best way of exploiting this invention was to use the mills himself and to what has been described as 'trade grind'—*rather a lengthy split infinitive.*" *Young v. Wilson,* (1955) 72 R.P.C. 351, 353 (Ch.D.) (per Upjohn, J.). See SPLIT INFINITIVES.
- "You have got to so frame yours so that it 'sells the Court,' *to use the term of the marketplace, which I abhor* . . . ." Karl N. Llewellyn, *A Lecture on Appellate Advocacy,* 29 U. Chi. L. Rev. 627, 630 (1962). In that sentence, the *which*-clause is ambiguous: it may refer either to *marketplace* or (as Llewellyn intended) *term of the marketplace.* See REMOTE RELATIVES.
- "The language of this description is perhaps not very elegant, for it homologates (*if I may use that horrible word*) the noun 'dealer' with the participles which appear in the parenthesis." *Walter Chadburn and Son Ltd. v. Leeds Corp.,* (1969) 20 P.&C.R. 241, 241, 246 (C.A.).
- "The House of Lords does now enjoy—*if that be the word*—the freedom not to follow its own previous decisions . . . ." Leslie Scarman, *English Law—The New Dimension* 5 (1974).
- "*The last sentence is rather clumsy,* but what I mean is this." Glanville Williams, *Learning the Law* 75 (11th ed. 1982).
- "*Although it is a cliché to say so,* it is in every way encyclopedic: every form of every description in connection with any Queen's Bench action is here." Charles Joseph, Book Review, 83 Law Soc. Gazette 3667 (1986).

A variation of this mannerism occurs when one defends one's choice of words in anticipation of the reader's distaste: "The Maryland statute appears to be unique in the proper use of that much misused word." *Williams v. Patuxent Inst.,* 347 A.2d 179, 187 (Md. 1975)./ "The 'philosophy' of the Act (if I may be forgiven this neologistic use) was to allow a legally aided party to civil proceedings only one successful bite at the legal cherry . . . ." *Megarity v. Law Soc'y,* [1982] A.C. 81, 103 (per Lord Diplock)./ "[T]he bank may and should be held liable for gratuitously, officiously, and affirmatively—a surfeit of adverbs never hurt anyone—telling the government how to place its grasp upon its customer's funds." *Schuster v. Banco de Iberoamerica, S.A.,* 476 So. 2d 253, 255 (Fla. Dist. Ct. App. 1985) (Schwartz, J., dissenting)./ "Even a murderer can look forward to a parole after 17 years, in a manner best characterized by that much-misused word, '*hopefully.*' " *In re Clements,* 440 N.W.2d 133, 137 (Minn. Ct. App. 1989) (Irvine, J., dissenting). See **if you will.**

word processing, n. & adj., should be spelled as two words thus.

WORDS OF ART. See TERMS OF ART.

WORDS OF AUTHORITY. Few reforms would improve legal DRAFTING more than if drafters were to begin paying closer attention to the verbs by which they set forth duties, rights, prohibitions, and entitlements. In the current state of common-law drafting, these verbs are a horrific muddle—and, what is even more surprising, few drafters even recognize this fact. The primary problem is *shall,* to which we must immediately turn.

A. *Shall.* This word runs afoul of several basic principles of good drafting. The first is that a word used repeatedly in a given context is presumed to bear the same meaning throughout. (*Shall* commonly shifts its meaning even in midsentence.) The second principle is strongly allied with the first: when a word takes on too many senses and cannot be confined to one sense in a given document, it becomes useless to the drafter. (*Shall* has as many as eight senses in drafted documents.) The third principle has been recognized in the literature on legal drafting since the mid-19th century: good drafting generally ought to be in the present tense, not the future. (*Shall* is commonly used as a future-tense modal verb.) In fact, the selfsame quality in *shall*—the fact that it is a CHAMELEON-HUED WORD—causes it to violate each of those principles.

How can *shall* be so slippery, one may ask, when every lawyer knows that it denotes a mandatory action? Well, perhaps every lawyer has heard that it's mandatory, but very few consistently use it in that way. And, as a result, courts in virtually every English-speaking jurisdiction have held—by necessity—that *shall* means *may* in some contexts, and vice-versa. These holdings have been necessary primarily to give effect to slipshod drafting.

What, then, are the meanings of *shall?* The

shadings are sometimes subtle, but the following examples—all but the last two from a single set of court rules—illustrate the more common shades:

- "The court . . . *shall* enter an order for the relief prayed for . . . ." The word imposes a duty on the subject of the sentence.
- "Service *shall* be made on the parties . . . ." The word imposes a duty on an unnamed person, but not on the subject of the sentence ("service," an abstract thing).
- "The debtor *shall* be brought forthwith before the court that issued the order." The word seems at first to impose a duty on the debtor but actually imposes it on some unnamed actor.
- "Such time *shall* not be further extended except for cause shown." The word *shall* gives permission (as opposed to a duty), and *shall not* denies permission (i.e., it means "may not"). This problem—*shall* being equivalent to *may*—frequently appears also in the statutory phrase *No person shall.* Logically, the correct construction is *No person may,* because the provision negates permission, not a duty. See (E).
- "Objections to the proposed modification *shall* be filed and served on the debtor." The word purports to impose a duty on parties to object to proposed modifications, though the decision to object is discretionary. This amounts to a conditional duty: a party that wants to object must file and serve the objections.
- "The sender *shall* have fully complied with the requirement to send notice when the sender obtains electronic confirmation." The word acts as a future-tense modal verb (the full verb phrase being in the future perfect). Many readers of this sentence, however, encounter a MISCUE in reading the sentence, which confusingly suggests that the sender has a duty.
- "The secretary *shall* be reimbursed for all expenses." The word expresses an entitlement, not a duty.
- "Any person bringing a malpractice claim *shall,* within 15 days after the date of filing the action, file a request for mediation." Courts interpreting such a rule or statute often hold that *shall* is directory, not mandatory—that it equates with the softer word *should.*

So much for the "Golden Rule" of legal drafting, which Reed Dickerson put this way: "[T]he competent draftsman makes sure that each recurring word or term has been used consistently. He carefully avoids using the same word or term in more than one sense . . . . In brief, he always expresses the same idea in the same way and always expresses different ideas differently." *The Fundamentals of Legal Drafting* § 2.3.1, at 15-16 (2d ed. 1986).

One solution to the problem that *shall* poses is to restrict it to one sense. This solution—called the "American rule" because it is an approach followed by some careful American drafters—is to use *shall* only to mean "has a duty to." Under the American rule, only the first of the seven bulleted items above would be correct. The drafter might well say that a party *shall* send notice, but not that notice *shall* be sent by the party. (If this "has-a-duty-to" sense is the drafter's convention, *must* serves when the subject of the sentence is an inanimate object.) This solution leads to much greater consistency than is generally found in American drafting.

Another solution is the "ABC rule," so called because, in the late 1980s, it was most strongly advocated by certain Australian, British, and Canadian drafters. The ABC rule holds that legal drafters cannot be trusted to use the word *shall* under any circumstances. Under this view, lawyers are not educable on the subject of *shall,* so the only solution is complete abstinence. As a result, the drafter must always choose a more appropriate word: *must, may, will, is entitled to,* or some other expression.

This view has much to be said for it. American lawyers and judges who try to restrict *shall* to the sense "has a duty to" find it difficult to apply the convention consistently. Indeed, few lawyers have the semantic acuity to identify correct and incorrect *shalls* even after a few hours of study. That being so, there can hardly be much hope of the profession's using *shall* consistently.

Small wonder, then, that the ABC rule has fast been gaining ground in the U.S. For example, the federal government's Style Subcommittee—part of the Standing Committee on Rules of Practice and Procedure—a subcommittee that since 1991 has worked on all amendments to the various sets of federal court rules, adopted this approach, disallowing *shall,* in late 1992. (This came after a year of using *shall* only to impose a duty on the subject of the verb.) As a result, the rules have become sharper because the drafters are invariably forced into thinking more clearly and specifically about meaning.

There is, of course, a third approach: to allow *shall* its traditional promiscuity while pretending, as we have for centuries, that preserving its chastity is either hopeless or unimportant. Of course, that approach breeds litigation, as attested in 76 pages of small-type cases reported in *Words and Phrases,* all interpreting the word *shall.* As long as the mass of the profession remains unsensitized to the problems that *shall* causes, this appears to be the most likely course of inaction.

For more on the use of *must* as opposed to *shall* under the ABC rule, see (C). For further discussion of the general problem, see Robert Eagleson & Michele Asprey, *Must We Continue with "Shall"?* 63 Austl. L.J. 75 (1989); Robert Eagleson & Michele Asprey, *We Must Abandon "Shall,"* 63 Austl. L.J. 726 (1989); Jim Main, *"Must" Versus "Shall,"* 63 Austl. L.J. 860 (1989); Michele Asprey, *Plain Language for Lawyers* 149–52 (1991); Joseph Kimble, *The Many Misuses of "Shall,"* 3 Scribes J. Legal Writing 61 (1992); Michele Asprey, *"Shall" Must Go,* 3 Scribes J. Legal Writing 79 (1992). For a contrary (and unpersuasive) point of view, see J.M. Bennett, *In Defence of "Shall,"* 63 Austl. L.J. 522 (1989); J.M. Bennett, *Final Observations on the Use of "Shall,"* 64 Austl. L.J. 168 (1990).

A major cause of the litigation over *shall,* as Kimble observes in his thoughtful essay, is the relative strength of the word. That is, what are the consequences when somebody fails to honor a contractual or statutory duty? If it's a contractual duty, does a failure to honor a *shall*-provision always amount to a breach? Does it entitle the other party to rescind? If it's a statutory requirement, does a violation invalidate the proceedings? Or is it merely a directory provision? This unclarity about consequences is a continuing problem in any system that we adopt, however linguistically principled that system might be.

B. *Shall not.* Under the American rule (see A), this phrasing works as long as it means "has a duty not to." Thus, "Thou *shalt not* steal" works, but not "The money *shall not* remain in the court's registry for more than 30 days." In the latter example, the proper choice is either *must not* or *may not.* See (F).

C. *Must.* Under the American rule (see A), this word means "is required to" and is used primarily when an inanimate object appears as subject of the clause. Hence, "Notice *must* be sent within 30 days."

Under the ABC rule (see A), *must* denotes all required actions, whether or not the subject of the clause performs the action of the verb—e.g.: "The employee *must* send notice within 30 days."/ "Notice *must* be sent within 30 days."

The advantage of *must* over *shall* is that its meaning is fastened down more tightly in any given sentence. Take, for example, a sentence from a widely used commercial lease: "The premises *shall* be used by the tenant for general office purposes and for no other purposes." Once one decides to follow the ABC rule, the dilemma in meaning becomes clear: are we mandating something with that sentence (use of the premises), or are we merely limiting the tenant's freedom to use the premises for other purposes? One might revise the sentence—removing the PASSIVE VOICE—in either of two ways: (a) *The tenant must use the premises for general office purposes;* or (b) *The tenant may use the premises only for general office purposes.* Which meaning is correct? Perhaps somebody should litigate the question so that we might all find out.

In private drafting—contracts as opposed to statutes, rules, and regulations—some drafters consider *must* inappropriately bossy. The word may strike the wrong tone particularly when both parties to a contract are known quantities, such as two well-known corporations. It seems unlikely that, for example, an American car manufacturer and a Japanese car manufacturer engaging in a joint venture would want the word *must* to set forth their various responsibilities. Indeed, it seems odd to draft one's own contractual responsibilities with *must:* a lawyer for Ford Motor Company is unlikely to write *Ford must . . . Ford must . . . Ford must . . . .* The word *will* is probably the best solution here. See (D).

On the other hand, in a consumer contract or other adhesion contract, *must* is entirely appropriate for the party lacking the bargaining power. In the 1994 revision of its form residential lease—a document signed by a million Texas residents every year—the Texas Apartment Association changed the traditional *shall* to either *must* or *will.* The landlord became *we,* and the tenant became *you,* so that the form reads as follows: *You must . . . You must . . . You must . . . We will . . . We will . . . We will . . . .* Although one might think that the resulting tone would be irksome, none of the typical users on whom the form was tested expressed that thought. Indeed, the distinctive use of *must* for the tenant and *will* for the landlord is very much in keeping with the natural rhetoric of an adhesion contract. And it certainly informs the consumer precisely what his or her obligations are.

Must is a useful device to uncover client misunderstandings about obligations. Thus, some lawyers use it despite the danger of a bossy tone. And, because present-tense drafting reduces the incidence of *must,* the *musts* that remain in a given document will—in many contexts—offend no one.

D. *Will.* This word, like any other, ought to bear a consistent meaning within any drafted document. Two of its possible meanings are discussed in (C): it may express one's own client's obligations in an adhesion contract (as in a residential lease), or it may express both parties' obligations when the relationship is a delicate one (as in a corporate joint venture).

There is still a third possibility: if a future tense really is needed, as to express a future contingency, then *will* is the word. But this circumstance in not common, as the best drafting should generally be in the present, not the future, tense. See STATUTE DRAFTING (C).

E. *May.* This term, very simply, means "has discretion to; is permitted to." It should be the only term used to denote these senses. Thus, one would never write *the licensee is free to sell as many units as it desires,* as opposed to *the licensee may sell as many units as it desires.*

Sometimes, *may* should replace *shall*—e.g.: "No person *shall* [read *may*] set off fireworks without the prior authorization of the fire marshal." That sentence does not negate a duty; it negates permission. See (A) & STATUTE DRAFTING (C).

F. *Must not; may not.* These two are nearly synonymous. *Must not* = is required not to. *May not* = is not permitted to. For those following the ABC rule (see A), the phrase *must not* is usually the more appropriate wording.

Some drafters avoid *may not* because it is sometimes ambiguous—it can mean either "is not permitted to" or (esp. in AmE) "might not." For example, an application to a law school states: "This office *may not* consider applications received after April 30." Some readers would take that to mean that the office has discretion whether to consider applications received after April 30, whereas others would infer that some rule or regulation prohibits the office from doing so.

G. *Is entitled to.* This is the wording for expressing an entitlement. It means "has a right to." E.g., "The guardian ad litem *shall* [read *is entitled to*] be reimbursed for expenses reasonably incurred." See (A).

H. Using a Consistent Glossary. A disciplined drafter uses words of authority consistently. This involves, in part, restricting the vocabulary by which one sets forth duties, rights, prohibitions, and entitlements. The drafter who proliferates ways of wording duties, for example, flirts with the danger that somebody interpreting the document—most disastrously, in court—will presume that a difference in wording imports a difference in meaning.

Yet drafted documents are commonly riddled with inconsistencies. It is not uncommon, in American contracts, to find the following variations in paragraph after paragraph:

- "The employee *shall follow* . . . ."
- "The employee *agrees to follow* . . . ."
- "The employee *is to follow* . . . ."
- "The employee *must follow* . . . ."
- "The employee *understands her duty to follow* . . . ."
- "The employee *will follow* . . . ."
- "*It is the responsibility* of the employee *to follow* . . . ."

The better practice is this: after the lead-in (which states, "The parties therefore agree as follows: . . ."), use only words of authority. An adherent of the American rule would make each of the above items *the employee shall;* an adherent of the ABC rule would make each one *the employee must.*

The careful drafter might consider adopting either of the following glossaries, preferably the latter:

American Rule

shall	=	has a duty to
must	=	is required to [used for all requirements that are not duties imposed on the subject of the clause]
may not	=	is not permitted to; is disallowed from
must not	=	is required not to; is disallowed from; is not permitted to
may	=	has discretion to, is permitted to
is entitled to	=	has a right to
will	=	(expresses a future contingency)
should	=	(denotes a directory provision)

ABC Rule (Preferred)

must	=	is required to
must not	=	is required not to; is disallowed from; is not permitted to
may	=	has discretion to, is permitted to
may not	=	is not permitted to; is disallowed from
is entitled to	=	has a right to
will	=	[one of the following:] a. (expresses a future contingency) b. (in an adhesion contract, expresses one's own client's obligations) c. (where the relationship is a delicate one, expresses both parties' obligations)
should	=	(denotes a directory provision)

words of conveyance are the words—usu. DOUBLETS, TRIPLETS, AND SYNONYM-STRINGS—that effect a transfer of ownership in a deed. In a warranty deed, for example, the standard words of conveyance are *convey and warrant* or *grant, bargain, and sell;* in a quitclaim deed, the words are usu. *remise, release, and forever quitclaim* or *convey and quitclaim.*

words of purchase; words of limitation. In a grant or conveyance of a freehold estate, *words of purchase* designate the persons who are to receive the grant, and *words of limitation* describe the extent or quality of the estate. E.g., "In a transfer 'to A and his heirs,' the words 'and his heirs' are now *words of limitation* (words denoting the duration of the estate), not *words of purchase* (words denoting who is getting the estate). The name 'A' is the only *word of purchase;* A is the only person who is getting an estate." Thomas F. Bergin & Paul G. Haskell, *Preface to Estates in Land and Future Interests* 27 (2d ed. 1984).

wordy does not mean "sesquipedalian," as many seem to suppose; it means, rather, "verbose; prolix."

workaholic. See -AHOLIC & MORPHOLOGICAL DEFORMITIES.

work an ademption is a legal idiom akin to the lay idiom *work a hardship* (on someone). E.g., "A change in the form of a security bequeathed does not necessarily *work an ademption.*" See **adeem & ademption.**

worker's comp. See **comp.**

workers' compensation; workmen's compensation. These words contain a plural possessive, hence *workers'* and *workmen's,* not *worker's* and *workman's.* The former phrase is becoming more and more common, doubtless because of a sensitivity to the SEXISM of the other.

workforce; workload. Each is one word.

workman; workingman. Because of the growing awareness of sexism, it is better to use *worker* rather than either of these words. See SEXISM (B).

workplace. One word. See **worksite.**

workproduct is increasingly spelled as one word. The dictionaries still record the term as two words. But in legal contexts the trend, which is wholly salutary, is to hyphenate it or make it one word. E.g., "To what extent is the Court's equal protection *workproduct* based on a determinate political-moral principle?" Cf. **decision-making & policy-making.**

worksite. One word. Cf. **job site.**

World Court; International Court of Justice in The Hague. The latter is the official name, the former the popular name, for the tribunal that adjudicates international disputes between nations. The principal judicial organ of the U.N., it is the successor to the Permanent Court of International Justice, set up in 1920 under the League of Nations.

WORLD COURT PLEADINGS. The pleadings in an action before the World Court are as follows: (1) a *memorial* by the applicant state; (2) a *countermemorial* by the respondent state; (3) a *reply* by the applicant state; and (4) a *rejoinder* by the respondent state. Cf. COMMON-LAW PLEADINGS & EQUITY PLEADINGS.

worse comes to worst. See **worst comes to worst.**

worship(p)ed; worship(p)ing; worship(p)er. The *-p-* spellings are the preferred forms in AmE; the *-pp-* forms appear in BrE. See DOUBLING OF FINAL CONSONANTS.

worst comes to worst; worse comes to worst. The latter expression seems more logical, but the established idiom—as evidenced in the *OED* consistently from the 16th century—is *worst comes to (the) worst* (= if things fall out as badly as possible). E.g., "Such litigants are invariably solvent, and if *worse comes to worst* [read *worst comes to worst*], they have the authority to tax." *City of Mound Bayou v. Roy Collins Constr. Co.,* 457 So. 2d 337, 341 (Miss. 1984). See ILLOGIC.

worth. When this word is used with amounts, the preceding term denoting the amount should be possessive. E.g., "This claim is not for a few dollars' *worth* of hobby goods that were negligently lost." See POSSESSIVES (B).

worthless person. In this legal ARCHAISM, *worthless* means "without worldly goods." But the double sense of the word makes the phrase unworthy in modern writing.

worthwhile. One word.

wot (= to know) is an ARCHAISM that Fowler called a "Wardour Street" term, i.e., an "oddment" calculated to establish (in the eyes of some readers) the writer's claim to be someone of taste and the source of beautiful English. In modern writing, it is a gross affectation—e.g.: "[O]f the financial status of the other two [lawyers] we *wot* [read *know*] not." *Schine v. Schine,* 309 N.Y.S.2d 51, 52 (App. Div. 1970).

would is often used as a hedge-word, qualifying the absoluteness of the verb following it. For example, a federal court states: "*This court would* *agree* with the Texas Supreme Court's statement of the measure of damages." If the writer intended to question the applicability of the Texas Supreme Court's statement in certain circumstances, the sentence as written is perhaps right; but it would be better to say *This court agrees* if a direct statement is intended. See SUBJUNCTIVES & **appear.**

would have for *had.* This error is an example of a confused sequence of tenses. E.g., "[I]f the trial judge *would have* [read *had*] allowed impeachment with a limiting instruction . . . , Robinson would be before this court arguing that this alternative solution was error." *U.S. v. Robinson,* 783 F.2d 64, 68 (7th Cir. 1986).

would have liked. This phrase should invariably be followed by a present-tense infinitive—hence *would have liked to go, would have liked to read,* not *would have liked to have gone, would have liked to have read.* E.g., "Many Americans *would have liked to put* the administration of justice wholly on a non-technical basis of natural equity." Roscoe Pound, *The Formative Era of American Law* 107 (1938).

would seem is usu. inferior to *seems* or *seem.* E.g., "Mr. Kohl *would seem* [read *seems*] to have made another concession . . . ." Alan Riding, *European Leaders Give Their Backing to Monetary Plan,* N.Y. Times, 9 Dec. 1989, at 1.

wrack; rack. *Wrack* = to destroy utterly; to wreck. *Rack* = to torture or oppress.

Wrack is also, and primarily, a noun meaning (1) "wreckage"; or (2) "utter destruction." In sense (2), it most commonly appears in the phrase *wrack and ruin.* But *wrack* is sometimes confused with its homophone—e.g.: "[The plaintiff stated] . . . that the building was 'virtually a shell,' having been allowed to go to *rack* [read *wrack*] and ruin." *Hilton v. Federated Brokerage Group, Inc.,* 213 N.Y.S.2d 171, 177 (Sup. Ct. 1961)./ "Experience indicates that the state treasury would not fall to *rack* [read *wrack*] and ruin if the shield of immunity were lifted." *Brown v. Wichita State Univ.,* 547 P.2d 1015, 1037 (Kan. 1976) (Fatzer, C.J., concurring in part & dissenting in part).

wrangle; wangle. The two are occasionally confounded. *Wrangle* = to argue noisily or angrily; *wangle* = [v.t.] (1) to accomplish or obtain in a clever way; (2) to manage (a thing) despite difficulties; or [v.i.] (3) to use indirect methods to accomplish some end. E.g., "He has aptly demonstrated his advertising acumen by *wrangling* [read *wangling*] almost half a million dollars in free print media from *New York* Magazine." Letter of David Curry, N.Y. Mag., 23 Jan. 1989, at 9.

wraparound mortgage is current American legal JARGON meaning "a deed of trust whereby a purchaser incorporates into agreed payments to a grantor or third-party the grantor's obligation in the initial mortgage." A court recently defined it as "a junior mortgage that secures a promissory note with a face amount equal to the sum of the principal balance of an existing mortgage note plus any additional funds advanced by the second lender." *Mitchell v. Trustees of U.S. Real Estate Inv. Trust,* 375 N.W.2d 424, 428 (Mich. Ct. App. 1985) (with minor differences in wording).

wreak. The better past tense is *wreaked,* not *wrought.* See **reek.**

wreath(e). *Wreath* is the noun, *wreathe* the verb.

wreckless for *reckless* is a written MALAPROPISM that appears to denote precisely the opposite of what it is supposed to mean. As literacy in the higher sense has become ever shakier, it has become disturbingly common—e.g.:

- "The answer contains numerous allegations to the effect . . . that the trucks were being used by plaintiff on the highway in a careless and *wreckless* [read *reckless*] manner and greatly depreciating said trucks." *Place v. Parker,* 180 S.W.2d 538, 542 (Mo. Ct. App. 1944).
- "The trial judge also instructed the jury that if it found that the Union had acted with 'actual malice or *wreckless* [read *reckless*] or wanton indifference to the rights of the plaintiff' it might award punitive damages . . . ." *International Bhd. of Boilermakers v. Braswell,* 388 F.2d 193, 199 (5th Cir. 1968) (quoting trial court).
- "In their petition, plaintiffs allege that the sole cause of accident was the combined negligence, gross negligence, wanton, *wreckless* [read *reckless*] conduct and intentional *wrecklessness* [read *recklessness*] . . . of the executive officers and supervisors . . . ." *Benjamin v. First Horizon Ins. Co.,* 563 So. 2d 1337, 1339 (La. Ct. App. 1990).
- "Prior to 1969, a number of courts had concluded that the military employee is subject to military discipline pursuant to the UCMJ for *wreckless* [read *reckless*] or drunken operation of a vehicle . . . ." Michael P. Frederick, *Scope of Employment Under the Federal Tort Claims Act and Attempts to Expand the Limits,* 33 A.F. L. Rev. 69, 81 (1990).

One court even went so far as to "correct" the lawyers' use of *reckless*—the bracketed *-w-* being in the reported case: " 'Cross-defendants' failure to place and maintain plaintiffs' prior Group Health Policy was negligent, careless and [w]*reckless . . . .*'" *Kuperman v. Great Republic Life Ins. Co.,* 241 Cal. Rptr. 187, 188 (Ct. App. 1987) (quoting a pleading).

writ. A. As a Noun. At common law, a *writ* was any formal legal document in letter form, under seal, and in the king's name. Its meaning has evolved differently in AmE and BrE, though the following definition fits both: "a court's written command or order in the name of the sovereign, state, or other competent legal authority, directing or enjoining the addressee to do or refrain from doing some specified act." In AmE, *writ* generally applies to *judicial writs,* which are either extraordinary writs (e.g., mandamus, prohibition) or writs used in appellate procedure (e.g., writ of error, writ of certiorari).

In BrE, by contrast, *writ* is usu. synonymous with *original writ* (= one that begins an action), as an abbreviated form of *writ of summons.* E.g., "Claiming that the price of their homes had dropped because of the presence of their new neighbours, Tim and Sue Poeton, with nine other families, issued *writs* claiming that Heron Homes, the development company, had failed to tell them that part of the estate had been earmarked for council housing." Charles Oulton, *When Neighbours Become Good Enemies,* Sunday Times, 5 Nov. 1989, at A13./ "Lord Denning, 93, former Master of the Rolls, has had a High Court *writ* issued against him over his legal battle about the ownership of his old school at Whitchurch, Hants." Sunday Telegraph, 24 May 1992, at 2. As in the first of the two examples just quoted, it is good colloquial BrE to say that the plaintiff issues the writ, although in truth the court does the issuing at the plaintiff's request.

B. As a Verb. The *OED* records the verbal sense of *writ* "to serve (a person) with a writ or summons" <he was writted>, and notes that it is Anglo-Irish.

C. As a Past Participle. As a past participle, *writ* is an ARCHAISM for *written,* except in the CLICHÉ *writ large.* E.g., "If article 9 were *writ large,* it would set out that a director is not to be removed against his will." (Eng.)

write for *underwrite* is common in the insurance business. E.g., "St. Paul Fire & Marine *writes* about $2,500,000 worth of premiums in the lawyers' malpractice field and has become the largest in the field." Murray T. Bloom, *The Trouble With Lawyers* 57 (1970).

writ(e)able. The preferred spelling is *writable.* See MUTE E.

writer is an obsolescent Scottishism in the sense "an attorney or law-agent; an ordinary legal practitioner in country towns; a law-clerk" (*OED*).

writer, the present. See FIRST PERSON (A).

write specially = to concur in a separate opinion. E.g., "I fully concur in the opinion written by Judge Politz; however, I *write specially* to say that I believe the Secretary of Health and Human Services is right on track."/ "The three justices who voted for rehearing when the case was before them on appeal voted to deny the writ; these justices *specially* stated that, although each of them voted for a rehearing on the question of appellate review of the proportionality of the sentence, the issue was presented to the Court in a writ application and that application was denied."

writ of course. See **of course.**

writ of error. The preferred plural is *writs of error,* not *writs of errors* or *writ of errors.*

writ of right is a LOAN TRANSLATION of *breve de recto,* at common law "the highest and most solemn form of action." Cornelius J. Moynihan, *Introduction to the Law of Real Property* 100 (2d ed. 1988). Through the litigation initiated with this writ, the mesne lord would decide whether the demandant or the tenant—that is, the plaintiff or the defendant—had older and better seisin in the disputed property. See ***breve,* demandant & form of action.**

wrong, n. The word is not precisely equivalent to *tort:* legal writers who refer to *civil wrongs* usu. include not just torts but also breaches of contract and of trust, breaches of statutory duties, and defects in the performance of public duties. See **civil wrong & tort.**

wrong; wrongful. The distinction is an important one in law. *Wrong* = (1) out of order; (2) contrary to law or morality; wicked; or (3) other than the right or suitable or the more or most desirable (*COD*). *Wrongful* = characterized by unfairness or injustice; contrary to law; (of a person) not entitled to the position occupied <the wrongful possessor>. Occasionally the words happen to be coextensive—e.g.: "It is a malicious act, which is in law and in fact a *wrong* act, and therefore a *wrongful* act, and therefore an actionable act if injury ensues from it." (Eng.). Cf. **wrongous.**

One commentator takes a benighted view: "Does *wrongful* mean something different from *wrong? Wrong* alone implies a moral judgment. *Wrongful,* by adding a syllable, only makes the word more pompous and less clear." Robert C. Cumbow, *The Subverting of the Goeduck,* 14 U. Puget Sound L. Rev. 755, 779 (1991).

wrongdoer = one who violates the law. The term is used of tortfeasors as well as of criminals. E.g., "But the circumstance that the wife of one of the *wrongdoers* benefited by the imposition does not afford opportunity for relief of that character."/ "The policy of preventing the *wrongdoer* from escaping the penalties for his wrong, in this case punitive damages, is inapplicable."

wrongful. See **wrong.**

wrongful birth; wrongful life. These phrases refer to different causes of action. A *wrongful-birth* action is brought by parents usu. against a doctor for failing to advise them prospectively about their risks of having a child with birth defects. A *wrongful-life* action is brought by or on behalf of a child with birth defects, the allegations ordinarily being that, were it not for the doctor-defendant's negligent advice, the child's parents would not have conceived the child, or if they had conceived, would have aborted the fetus to avoid the pain and suffering resulting from the child's congenital defects.

wrongful death. See **death case** & **death statute.**

wrongful discharge (AmE) = *wrongful dismissal* (BrE). E.g., "The only other damages the plaintiff could claim if he had been *wrongfully dismissed* would have been purely nominal." (Aus.) *Wrongful termination* is sometimes used in the U.S. See **unfair dismissal.**

wrongful interference with goods. See **detinue.**

wrongful life. See **wrongful birth.**

wrong(ly). Both forms are proper adverbs; *wrongly,* which is less common, appears before the verb modified <the suspects were wrongly detained>, whereas *wrong* should be used if the adverb follows the noun <he answered the question wrong>.

wrongous, in Scots law, means "wrongful, illegal, unjust." It should be avoided by other than Scottish lawyers.

wroth (= angry) is an ARCHAISM—e.g.: "Petitti, 37, is so *wroth* [read *angry*] over what he sees in the videotape of his nuptial festivities that he has filed suit . . . ." Eric Zorn, *Taped Memories Are More Maddening Than Magical,* Chicago Trib., 20 March 1990, at 1C.

X

xerox is a registered trademark (Xerox) that is nevertheless used as a noun <he made a xerox of the document>, adjective <a xerox copy>, and verb <to xerox a will>. Sometimes the word is capitalized, but sometimes not—e.g.: "I had to get some letters from readers *xeroxed* last week." Godfrey Smith, Sunday Times, 22 Oct. 1989, at B3. Careful writers use *photocopy* or some other similar word. *Zerox* is a common misspelling.

x-ray; X-ray. Either form is correct, although the former is perhaps more common. *W10* suggests that the term is hyphenated as an adjective and verb (*x-ray*), and not hyphenated as a noun (*x ray*). The *COD* hyphenates the term in all parts of speech.

Y

y'all; ya'll. Perhaps the only time when the correct form of this Southernism arises is in transcriptions of testimony. For the record, *y'all* is the logically preferable and far more common form.

ye. See **hear ye** & **oyez.**

year and a day. The lapse of a year has many important effects in Anglo-American law. At common law, escheat was subject to the Crown's right to hold the land for *ann, jour et wast* (= one year, one day, including the right to commit waste). In English law today and in some American states, an act that causes death is not homicide if the death occurs more than a year and a day after the act was committed.

Why a year *and a day*—not just a year? Because several centuries ago, English lawyers computed times by including both the first and the last day, so that a year from January 1, 1500, was considered to be December 31, 1500. Hence the day was tacked on to make up a full year. Today, of course, times are generally computed by excluding the first day.

Year Book; Year-Book; year-book; yearbook. Each of these forms but the last has appeared in legal history books that discuss the unofficial English law reports dating from 1282 to 1537. The predominant form is *Year Book,* although the leading modern legal historian, J.H. Baker, refers to the *year-books.* See J.H. Baker, *An Introduction to English Legal History* 204–07 (3d ed. 1990). If that usage suggests a trend, then *yearbook* cannot be far away, since the manifest destiny of the hyphen is to disappear.

year of our Lord. See A.D.

yellow-dog contract (= an employment contract forbidding membership in a labor union) has become a part of American legal JARGON. The term dates from 1920. E.g., "The rapidly increasing use of the so-called *'yellow-dog contracts'* has grown into a serious threat to the very existence of labor unions. In view of the inequitable conditions that surround the formation of such agreements and the unfair division of their obligation, to appeal to equity for their enforcement is to disregard the fundamentally ethical foundations of courts of chancery." Felix Frankfurter & Nathan Greene, *Labor Injunctions and Federal Legislation,* 42 Harv. L. Rev. 766, 779 (1928).

Today such contracts are generally illegal, having been outlawed by the Wagner Act of 1935: "A chocolate manufacturing company proposed an unlawful *'yellow-dog contract'* when its president asked a job applicant if she would sign a statement pledging not to join a union or be affiliated in any way with unions . . . ." *Today's Summary and Analysis,* Daily Labor Rep., 3 April 1991, at A-A.

yet. See **as yet, but yet & although . . . yet.**

you, the second-person pronoun, is invaluable in drafting consumer contracts that are meant to be generally intelligible. Consider the difference between the following versions of a lease provision:

> Resident shall promptly reimburse owner for loss, damage, or cost of repairs or service caused in the apartment or community by improper use or negligence of resident or resident's guests or occupants.

vs.

> You must promptly reimburse us for loss, damage, or cost of repairs or service caused anywhere in the apartment community by your or any guest's or occupant's improper use.

Of course, the drafter must carefully define *you* and *us,* but doing so is usually a straightforward matter. See SUPERSTITIONS (K).

young person. See **child.**

your Honor. This is the accepted American way of addressing a judge in person, esp. in oral argument. Of British practice, an eminent barrister writes: "Judges prefer to be known as *my lord* or *your Honour* or *your Worship* (the last of these being an anachronistic but revealing indication of the vanity that can afflict adjudicators in minor courts and tribunals)." David Pannick, *Judges* 157 (1987).

your ladyship; your lordship. See **my lord.**

your petitioner, your defendant, your plaintiff, and like phrases are quaint ARCHAISMS to be avoided. E.g., "*Your petitioner* [read *The petitioner*] has reliable information and believes that the defendant intends to leave the jurisdiction before April 19, 1985."/ "*Your relator* [read *The relator*], George W. Strake, Jr., Chairman of the State Republican Executive Committee, requests temporary relief."

Z

zeitgeist should now be lowercase in both AmE and BrE.

zetetic(k). This adjective, meaning "proceeding by inquiry or investigation," is preferably spelled *zetetic* (*OED* & *W3*), though some law dictionaries anomalously spell it *zetetick.* The Center for Scientific Anomalies at Eastern Michigan University publishes a journal called *The Zetetic Scholar,* devoted to the skeptical analysis of paranormal claims.

ZEUGMA AND SYLLEPSIS. These are two closely related figures of speech. Zeugma is the better-known name, whereas syllepsis is the more common phenomenon. Our discussion might therefore usefully begin with the latter.

A. Syllepsis. Literally "a taking together, comprehension," *syllepsis* denotes the figure of speech in which a word—usually a verb or preposition—is applied to two other words or phrases in different senses (often literally in one sense and figuratively in the other). Unlike zeugma, syllepsis is not a grammatical error. It is usually both purposeful and humorous—e.g.:

- "Sir Charles Wilson, the newly elected member for Central Leeds, *took* the *oath* and his *seat.*" (*Take* has two objects, *oath* and *seat,* but applies to them in different senses.)
- "Noah Swayne of Ohio . . . was a corporation lawyer, as successful as he was callously unethical, who was not to *change his spots* or *his spottiness* throughout his long judicial career." Fred Rodell, *Nine Men* 137 (1955).
- "I just *blew my nose, a fuse,* and *three circuit breakers.*" (A character on "The Jim Henson Hour," 16 July 1989.)
- "We would venture out into the Gulf of Mexico off Port Aransas, where we *found king mackerel* and *serenity.*" Cactus Pryor, *He Called Me Puddin',* Tex. Monthly, Feb. 1992, at 101, 134.

B. Zeugma. Literally "a yoking or bonding," zeugma is a grammatical error. It occurs when a single word is applied to two or more words or phrases when it properly applies to only one of them. One species of zeugma (the nontransferable auxiliary) plagues legal writing because lawyers so frequently try to express themselves alternatively—e.g.:

- "But many of these holdings *have or will be overruled* [read *have been, or will be, overruled*]."
- "Plaintiff claims that he *has and will continue to receive* [read *has received and will continue to receive*] fewer benefits from the trust than he should."
- "[A] grand jury appearance by a defendant *may—as it often has—lead to* [read *may lead—as it often has led—to* his complete exoneration . . . ." *People v. Goldsborough,* 568 N.Y.S.2d 999, 1001 (Sup. Ct. 1991).
- "They were not liable at law for the continued suffering of the man who fell among thieves, which they *might, and morally ought to have, prevented* [read *might have, and morally ought to have, prevented*]."
- "If one party represents that he *has* (or *will*) *put* an oral agreement in writing, and the other party relies on this to his substantial detriment, the first party may be estopped to set up the Statute of Frauds as a defense." (*Put* is made to be both a past-tense and a future-tense verb.)

Cf. JANUS-FACED TERMS.

zonal; zonary. The adjective corresponding to *zone* is *zonal* in all but medical (obstetric) senses.

zonate(d). The term meaning "arranged in zones" is best made *zonate* rather than *zonated.*

zygnomic; mesonomic. These terms are the inventions of Albert Kocourek, the legal theorist and creative neologist. A *zygnomic* jural relation involves an act whose evolution directly abridges the freedom of the *servus* [= the legal person who bears a ligation (i.e., the generic term for the servient side of a jural relation—it includes duty, disability, liability, and inability)] in the enjoyment of a legal advantage. A *mesonomic* jural relation does not, legally speaking, directly affect a human being's natural physical freedom—yet it has legal consequences in its evolution. See Albert Kocourek, *Jural Relations* 69 (1927). Julius Stone summed up these NEOLOGISMS well: "Kocourek's mesonomic-zygnomic distinction is no doubt a valuable one, even if we shrink back at the neologisms." Julius Stone, *Legal System and Lawyers' Reasonings* 148 (1964). And who does not shrink back? It is all pure JARGON and GOBBLEDYGOOK. Still, for that very reason, it provides what some must consider a fitting conclusion to a law dictionary.

SELECT BIBLIOGRAPHY

English Dictionaries

The American Heritage Dictionary of the English Language. 3d ed. Boston: Houghton Mifflin, 1992.

Chambers Twentieth Century Dictionary. New ed. Cambridge: Cambridge University Press, 1983.

The Concise Oxford Dictionary of Current English. 8th ed. Oxford: Clarendon Press, 1990.

Merriam-Webster's Collegiate Dictionary. 10th ed. Springfield, Mass.: Merriam-Webster, 1993.

Oxford American Dictionary. Oxford and New York: Oxford University Press, 1980.

The Oxford English Dictionary. 20 vols. 2d ed. Oxford: Clarendon Press, 1989.

Webster's New International Dictionary of the English Language. 2d ed. Springfield, Mass.: Merriam, 1934.

Webster's Third International Dictionary of the English Language. Springfield, Mass.: Merriam, 1961.

Law Dictionaries and Legal Wordbooks

Ballentine, James A. *A Law Dictionary with Pronunciations.* Edited by William S. Anderson. 3d ed. New York: Lawyers Co-operative, 1969.

Black, Henry Campbell. *Black's Law Dictionary* (1891). 6th ed. St. Paul, Minn.: West, 1990.

Black's Law Dictionary. Pocket ed. Edited by Bryan A. Garner. St. Paul, Minn.: 1996.

Bouvier, John. *Bouvier's Law Dictionary* (1839). Revised and updated by William E. Baldwin. New York: Banks Law Publishing Co., 1926.

Burton, William C. *Legal Thesaurus.* New York: Macmillan, 1980.

A Concise Dictionary of Law. 2d ed. Oxford and New York: Oxford University Press, 1990.

Jowitt, Earl. *The Dictionary of English Law.* Edited by Clifford Walsh. London: Sweet & Maxwell, 1959.

Mozley, Herbert, and George Whiteley. *Law Dictionary.* 10th ed. Sydney: Butterworths, 1988.

Osborn's Concise Law Dictionary. Edited by Leslie Rutherford and Sheila Bone. 8th ed. London: Sweet & Maxwell, 1993.

Walker, David M. *The Oxford Campanion to Law.* Oxford: Oxford University Press, 1980.

Words & Phrases. 90 vols. and supps. St. Paul, Minn: West, 1940–1995.

Usage

Bernstein, Theodore M. *Miss Thistlebottom's Hobgoblins: The Careful Writer's Guide to the Taboos, Bugbears, and Outmoded Rules of English Usage.* New York: Farrar, Straus & Giroux, 1971.

Bernstein, Theodore M. *Dos, Don'ts, and Maybes of English Usage.* New York: Times Books, 1977.

Bernstein, Theodore M. *The Careful Writer* (1965). New York: Atheneum, 1979.

Copperud, Roy H. *American Usage and Style: The Consensus.* New York: Van Nostrand Reinhold, 1980.

Evans, Bergen. *Comfortable Words.* New York: Random House, 1962.

Evans, Bergen, and Cornelia Evans. *A Dictionary of Contemporary American Usage.* New York: Random House, 1957.

Ferguson, Don K. *Grammar Gremlins.* Lakewood, Colo.: Glenbridge Publishing Ltd., 1995.

Follett, Wilson. *Modern American Usage.* New York: Hill & Wang, 1966.

Fowler, H.W. *A Dictionary of Modern English Usage* (1926). 2d ed. Revised by Ernest Gowers. Oxford and New York: Oxford University Press, 1965.

Fowler, H.W., and F.G. Fowler. *The King's English* (1906). 3d ed. Oxford and New York: Oxford University Press, 1931.

Gowers, Ernest. *The Complete Plain Words* (1954). Harmondsworth: Penguin Books, 1980.

Hart's Rules for Compositors and Readers at the University Press, Oxford. 39th ed. Oxford and New York: Oxford University Press, 1983.

Janis, J. Harold. *Modern Business Language and Usage in Dictionary Form.* Garden City, N.Y.: Doubleday, 1984.

Krapp, George Philip. *A Comprehensive Guide to Good English* (1927). 2 vols. New York: Ungar, 1962.

Johnson, Edward D. *The Handbook of Good English.* Rev. ed. New York: Pocket Books, 1991.

Larsen, Karen. *The Miss Grammar Guidebook.* Lake Oswego, Ore.: Oregon State Bar, 1994.

Manser, Martin H., and Jeffrey McQuain, eds. *The World Almanac Guide to Good Word Usage.* New York: World Almanac, 1989.

Morris, William, and Mary Morris. *Harper Dictionary of Contemporary Usage.* 2d ed. New York: HarperPerennial, 1985.

Nicholson, Margaret. *A Dictionary of American-English Usage, Based on Fowler's Modern English Usage.* Oxford and New York: Oxford University Press, 1957.

Partridge, Eric. *Usage and Abusage* (1942). Edited by Janet Whitcut. London: Hamish Hamilton, 1994.

Safire, William. *On Language.* New York: Times Books, 1980.

Safire, William. *What's the Good Word?* New York: Times Books, 1982.

Safire, William. *I Stand Corrected.* New York: Times Books, 1984.

Safire, William. *Take My Word for It.* New York: Times Books, 1986.

Safire, William. *You Could Look It Up.* New York: Times Books, 1988.

Safire, William. *Language Maven Strikes Again.* New York: Doubleday, 1990.

Safire, William. *Coming to Terms.* New York: Doubleday, 1991.

Safire, William. *Quoth the Maven.* New York: Random House, 1993.

Weiner, E.S.C. *The Oxford Guide to English Usage* (1983). 2d ed. Oxford and New York: Oxford University Press, 1993.

Weseen, Maurice H. *Crowell's Dictionary of English Grammar and Handbook of American Usage.* New York: Crowell, 1928.

White, Richard Grant. *Words and Their Uses, Past and Present: A Study of the English Language.* 3d ed., rev. Boston: Houghton Mifflin, 1870.

White, Richard Grant. *Every-Day English.* Boston: Houghton Mifflin, 1880.

Wilson, Kenneth G. *The Columbia Guide to Standard American English.* New York: Columbia University Press, 1993.

Wood, Frederick T. *The Macmillan Dictionary of Current English Usage.* 2d ed. Revised by R.H. Flavell and L.M. Flavell. London: Macmillan, 1981.

Grammar

Chalker, Sylvia, and E.S.C. Weiner, eds. *The Oxford Dictionary of English Grammar.* Oxford and New York: Oxford University Press, 1994.

Curme, George O. *English Grammar.* New York: Barnes & Noble Books, 1947.

Jespersen, Otto. *Essentials of English Grammar* (1933). University: University of Alabama Press, 1964.

Kittredge, George Lyman, and Frank Edgar Farley. *An Advanced English Grammar.* Boston: Ginn, 1913.

Morsberger, Robert E. *Commonsense Grammar and Style.* 2d ed., rev. and exp. New York: Crowell, 1972.

Opdycke, John B. *Harper's English Grammar.* Revised by Stewart Benedict. New York: Popular Library, 1965.

Quirk, Randolph, et al. *A Grammar of Contemporary English.* London: Longmans, 1972.

Sledd, James H. *A Short Introduction to English Grammar.* Chicago: Scott Foresman, 1959.

Zandvoort, R.W. *A Handbook of English Grammar.* 3d ed. Englewood Cliffs, N.J.: Prentice-Hall, 1966.

Legal Language and Writing

Asprey, Michele M. *Plain Language for Lawyers.* Annandale, N.S.W.: Federation Press, 1991.

The Bluebook. 15th ed. Cambridge, Mass.: Harvard Law Review, 1991.

Dickerson, Reed. *The Fundamentals of Legal Drafting.* 2d ed. Boston: Little Brown, 1986.

Garner, Bryan A. *The Elements of Legal Style.* Oxford and New York: Oxford University Press, 1991.

Garner, Bryan A. *Guidelines for Drafting and Editing Court Rules.* Washington, D.C.: Administrative Office of the U.S. Courts, 1995.

Goldstein, Thomas, and Jethro K. Lieberman. *The Lawyer's Guide to Writing Well.* New York: McGraw-Hill, 1989.

Goldfarb, Ronald L., and James C. Raymond. *Clear Understandings: A Guide to Legal Writing.* New York: Random House, 1982.

Good, C. Edward. *Mightier Than the Sword: Powerful Writing in Class, on the Job.* Charlottesville, Va.: Blue Jeans Press, 1989.

Mellinkoff, David. *The Language of the Law.* Boston: Little Brown, 1963.

Perrin, Timothy. *Better Writing for Lawyers.* Toronto: Law Society of Upper Canada, 1990.

Piesse, E.L. *The Elements of Drafting.* 7th ed. Revised by J.K. Aitken. Sydney: Law Book Co., 1987.

Wydick, Richard C. *Plain English for Lawyers.* 3d ed. Durham, N.C.: Carolina Academic Press, 1994.

For additional references, see the dictionary entries BRIEF-WRITING, LEGAL WRITING STYLE, and PLAIN LANGUAGE.

Style

Baker, Sheridan. *The Practical Stylist.* 7th ed. New York: Harper & Row, 1990.

Barzun, Jacques. *Simple and Direct.* Rev. ed. New York: Harper & Row, 1984.

Graves, Robert, and Alan Hodge. *The Reader Over Your Shoulder: A Handbook for Writers of English Prose.* 2d ed., rev. and abr. New York: Random House, 1979.

Kilpatrick, James J. *The Writer's Art.* Kansas City: Andrews, McNeel & Parker, 1984.

Lanham, Richard A. *Revising Prose.* 3d ed. New York: Macmillan, 1987.

Payne, Lucile Vaughan. *The Lively Art of Writing* (1965). Chicago: Follett, 1982.

Quiller-Couch, Arthur. *On the Art of Writing* (1916). Folcroft, Pa.: Folcroft Library Editions, 1978.

Read, Herbert. *English Prose Style.* New ed. New York: Pantheon, 1952.

Simon, John. *Paradigms Lost: Reflections on Literacy and Its Decline.* New York: Potter, 1980.

Strunk, William, and E.B. White. *The Elements of Style.* 3d ed. New York: Macmillan, 1979.

Trimble, John R. *Writing with Style: Conversations on the Art of Writing.* Englewood Cliffs, N.J.: Prentice-Hall, 1975.

Zinsser, William. *On Writing Well: An Informal Guide to Writing Nonfiction.* 5th ed. New York: HarperPerennial, 1994.

Etymology

The Barnhart Dictionary of Etymology. Edited by Robert K. Barnhart. Bronx, N.Y.: H.W. Wilson, 1988.

The Concise Oxford Dictionary of English Etymology. Edited by T.F. Hoad. London: Oxford University Press, 1986.

Hendrickson, Robert. *The Facts on File Encyclopedia of Word and Phrase Origins.* New York: Facts on File, 1987.

The Oxford Dictionary of English Etymology. Edited by C.T. Onions et al. Oxford: Clarendon Press, 1966.

Partridge, Eric. *Origins: A Short Etymological Dictionary of Modern English.* 4th ed. London: Routledge & Kegan Paul, 1966.

Skeat, Walter W. *An Etymological Dictionary of the English Language.* 4th ed. Oxford: Clarendon Press, 1910.

Webster's Word Histories. Springfield, Mass.: Merriam-Webster, 1989.

Weekley, Ernest. *Etymological Dictionary of Modern English* (1921). 2 vols. New York: Dover, 1967.

Literary Terms

Abrams, M. H. *A Glossary of Literary Terms.* 6th ed. Fort Worth, Tex.: Holt, Rinehart & Winston, 1993.

Baldick, Chris. *The Concise Oxford Dictionary of Literary Terms.* Oxford and New York: Oxford University Press, 1990.

Barnet, Sylvan, et al. *A Dictionary of Literary Terms.* Boston: Little Brown, 1960.

Cuddon, J.A. *The Penguin Dictionary of Literary Terms and Literary Theory.* 3d ed. London: Penguin, 1992.

Lanham, Richard A. *A Handlist of Rhetorical Terms: A Guide for Students of English Literature.* 2d ed. Berkeley: University of California Press, 1991.

Liberman, M.M., and Edward E. Foster. *A Modern Lexicon of Literary Terms.* Glenview, Ill.: Scott Foresman, 1968.

Ruse, Christina, and Marilyn Hopton. *The Cassell Dictionary of Literary and Language Terms.* London: Cassell, 1992.

Scott, A.F. *Current Literary Terms: A Concise Dictionary of Their Origin and Use.* London: Macmillan, 1965.

Taaffe, James G. *A Student's Guide to Literary Terms.* Cleveland: World Pub. Co., 1967.

Pronunciation

Bender, James F. *NBC Handbook of Pronunciation.* 4th ed. Revised and updated by Eugene Ehrlich and Raymond Hand, Jr. New York: HarperPerennial, 1991.

Elster, Charles Harrington. *There Is No Zoo in Zoology, and Other Beastly Mispronunciations: An Opinionated Guide for the Well-Spoken.* New York: Collier, 1988.

Jones, Daniel. *An English Pronouncing Dictionary* (1921). 14th ed. Revised by A.C. Gimson. Cambridge: Cambridge University Press, 1991.

Kenyon, John S., and Thomas A. Knott. *A Pronouncing Dictionary of American English.* 2d ed. Springfield, Mass.: Merriam, 1953.

Lass, Abraham, and Betty Lass. *Dictionary of Pronunciation.* New York: New York Times Book Co., 1976.

Lewis, Norman. *Dictionary of Modern Pronunciation.* New York: Harper & Row, 1963.

Needleman, Morriss H. *A Manual of Pronunciation.* New York: Barnes & Noble, 1949.

Noory, Samuel. *Dictionary of Pronunciation.* 4th ed. New York: Cornwall, 1981.

Opdycke, John B. *Don't Say It: A Cyclopedia of English Use and Abuse.* 2d ed. New York: Funk & Wagnalls, 1943.

Phyfe, William Henry P. *20,000 Words Often Mispronounced.* New ed. Revised by Fred A. Sweet and Maud D. Williams. New York: Putnam's, 1937.

Princeton Language Institute. *21st Century Guide to Pronunciation.* New York: Bantam Doubleday Dell, 1994.

Punctuation

Brittain, Robert. *A Pocket Guide to Correct Punctuation.* 2d ed. New York: Barron's Educational Series, 1990.

Carey, G.V. *Mind the Stop: A Brief Guide to Punctuation with a Note on Proof-Correction.* Rev. ed. Harmondsworth: Penguin Books, 1971.

Gordon, Karen E. *The Well-Tempered Sentence: A Punctuation Handbook for the Innocent, the Eager, and the Doomed.* Rev. and exp. ed. New York: Ticknor & Fields, 1993.

Partridge, Eric. *You Have a Point There: A Guide to Punctuation and Its Allies.* London: Hamish Hamilton, 1953.

Paxson, William C. *The Mentor Guide to Punctuation.* New York: New American Library, 1986.

Shaw, Harry. *Punctuate It Right!* 2d ed. New York: HarperPerennial, 1993.

ACKNOWLEDGMENTS OF PERMISSION

Grateful acknowledgment is made to the following publishers and journals for their permission to quote from the works listed below.

Little, Brown & Co.
David Mellinkoff, *The Language of the Law* (1963).

New York University Law Review
Walker Gibson, *Literary Minds and Judicial Style,* 36 N.Y.U. L. Rev. 915, 930 (1961).

Oxford University Press
Concise Law Dictionary (1983).
H.W. Fowler, *A Dictionary of Modern English Usage* (1926 & 2d ed. 1965).
The Oxford English Dictionary (1933 & 2d ed. 1989).
David M. Walker, *The Oxford Companion to the Law* (1980).
E.S.C. Weiner, *The Oxford Guide to English Usage* (1983).

Pepperdine Law Review
James C. Raymond, *Editing Law Reviews: Some Practical Suggestions and a Moderately Revolutionary Proposal.* Reprinted from Pepperdine Law Review, Volume 12, Number 2, 1985, Copyright © 1985 by Pepperdine University School of Law.

Texas Tech Law Review
Roibert W. Calvert, *Appellate Court Judgments,* 6 Tex. Tech L. Rev. 915 (1975).

Yale Law Journal
Arthur A. Leff, *The Leff Dictionary of Law: A Fragment.* By permission of The Yale Law Journal Company and Fred B. Rothman & Company from *The Yale Law Journal,* Vol. 94, pp. 1855–2251.